FEB 0 4 2005

SHORT STORY INDEX

1999–2004

PERMANENT CUMULATIONS

1900–1949
1950–1954
1955–1958
1959–1963
1964–1968
1069–1973
1974–1978
1979–1983
1984–1988
1989–1993
1994–1998

SHORT STORY INDEX

1999-2004

AN INDEX TO STORIES IN COLLECTIONS AND PERIODICALS

Edited by

JOHN GREENFIELDT

NEW YORK • DUBLIN
THE H. W. WILSON COMPANY
2004

ISSN 0360-9774

Library of Congress Control Number 75-649762

Printed in the United States of America

Visit H.W. Wilson's Web site at: www://hwwilson.com

CONTENTS

Preface vii

Directions for Use viii

Part I. Author, Title, and Subject Index 1

Part II. List of Collections Indexed 889

Part III. Directory of Periodicals 961

PREFACE

This cumulative volume of *Short Story Index* covers short stories written in or translated into English that have appeared in collections and selected periodicals published from 1999-2004. The periodicals are those indexed in two other Wilson publications: *Readers' Guide to Periodical Literature* and *Humanities Index*.

Short Story Index is issued annually with a cumulation every five years. The dates of this volume comprise six calendar years rather than five, because the method of dating the index was changed in 2002 to reflect the date of indexing rather than the date the stories were published. It is nonetheless a cumulation of five years' indexing and is issued five years since the previous cumulation.

The continued appeal of the short story is reflected in the number contained in this cumulation, which indexes 21,591 stories. Of these, 19,900 stories appeared in 1,309 collections and 1,691 appeared in 86 periodicals.

As in previous volumes, the arrangement is by author, title, and subject in one alphabet. Stories in periodicals are indexed only by author and title. The author entry, which indicates the collection or periodical where the story can be found, is the fullest entry. A List of Collections Indexed and a Directory of Periodicals complete the volume. Further information about the content of entries is provided in the Directions for Use.

The H.W. Wilson Company is grateful to those publishers who provided copies of their books for indexing.

DIRECTIONS FOR USE

Part I of *Short Story Index*, the Author, Title, and Subject Index, is arranged in dictionary form with all entries in one alphabet. Part II is a List of Collections indexed. Part III is a Directory of Periodicals. The following directions apply to Part I.

Author entry

The author entry gives the name of the author and title of the story. For stories found in collections it also gives the title and editor of the collection. For stories found in periodicals it provides the periodical title, volume number, page numbers, and date.

Sample entry from a collection:

King, Stephen, 1947-
Children of the corn
The American fantasy tradition; ed. by B. M. Thomsen

The above example shows that the story by Stephen King entitled "Children of the corn" appeared in *The American fantasy tradition*, edited by B. M. Thomsen. Further information about the book is given in the List of Collections Indexed.

Sample entry from a periodical:

Lear, Patricia
The bridge playing ladies
The Antioch Review v61 no1 p5-26 Wint 2003

The above example indicates that the story by Patricia Lear entitled "The bridge playing ladies" appeared in *The Antioch Review*, volume 61, number 1, pages 5-26, in the Winter 2003 issue. For fuller information about the periodical consult the Directory of Periodicals.

Title entry

Title entries are used to identify the author under whose name the source of the story will be found. The first word (not an article) of each title is in boldface type.

Sample entries:

The **bridge** playing ladies. Lear, P.
Children of the corn. King, S.

Subject entry

Stories found in collections are listed under subjects with which they deal in whole or in part. Subject entries are printed in capital letters, in boldface type. Consult the author entry for the title of the story collection.

Sample entry:

CHRISTMAS STORIES
Bowles, P. The frozen fields

SHORT STORY INDEX, 1999-2004

PART I

Author, Title, and Subject Index

!. Dinh, L.
3 ½ x 5. Nissen, T.
3 women. Ortiz, S. J.
#4. Leave. Miller, E.
The **4-sided** triangle. Temple, W. F.
8 A.M. Jones, R.
10:07:24. Bisson, T.
10X50. Dinh, L.
10th grade. Weisberg, J.
The **12-inch** dog. Spencer, D.
13th parallel south. Santiesteban Prats, A.
20 burgers. O'Nan, S.
The **20ᵗʰ-Century** War Veteran Club. Bender, A.
The **24-hour** dog. Winterson, J.
29th Street Playground, September 1968. Nissen, T.
40, still at home. Jones, T.
'53 Buick. Phillips, G.
55 miles to the gas pump. Proulx, A.
The **#63** bus from the Gare de Lyon. Stern, D.
8-3-oh. Danger, N.
101. Searle, E.
140 Sunset. Burford, M.
193 Barker Street. Downs, M.
#361. Miller, B.
The **5:22.** Harrar, G.
555. Dinh, L.
819 Walnut. Nissen, T.
1016 to 1. Kelly, J. P.
1916 flood. Morgan, R.
1917. Swan, M.
1940: fall. Adams, A.
1944. Gilchrist, E.
1951. Bausch, R.
1967. Bottoms, G.
1984. Reilly, L.
10,000 Dildoes. Kuo, A.
31.12.99. Lupoff, R. A.
£250,000 electrical clearance. Dyson, J.
2BRO2B. Vonnegut, K.

A

A. Carter, E.
A. B. C. D. E. A. T. H. Lake, M. D.
A, B, C, D, E, F, G, H, I, J, K, L, M, N, O, P, Q, R, S, T, U, V, W, X, Y, Z. Bail, M.
A. wonderland. Wells, K.
Aadland, Dan
 East breeze
  Westward; a fictional history of the American West : 28 original stories celebrating the 50th anniversary of the Western Writers of America; edited by Dale L. Walker
Abandon in place. Oltion, J.

Abandoned child. Mo Yan
ABANDONED CHILDREN
 See also Orphans
 Bingham, S. The one true place
 DeMarinis, R. Your story
 Foster, K. Keep it from the flame
 Klass, P. City sidewalks
 Mo Yan. Abandoned child
 Sosin, D. What Mark couldn't see
 Tremain, R. John-Jin
 Vivante, A. The foundling
The **Abandoned** Factory. Hilbig, W.
ABANDONED TOWNS *See* Extinct cities
Abandoned writing projects. Berry, R. M.
The **Abandoner.** Ma Jian
ABANDONMENT OF FAMILY *See* Desertion and nonsupport
Abba's mark. Davenport, S.
Abbenyi, Juliana Makuchi Nfah- *See* Nfah-Abbenyi, Juliana Makuchi, 1958-
ABBESSES *See* Nuns
Abbey, Lynn
 The red lucky
  Thieve's world: turning points; edited by Lynn Abbey
The **Abbey** ghosts. Burke, J.
Abbey sinister. Tremayne, P.
ABBEYS
 See also Cathedrals; Churches; Convent life; Monasticism and religious orders
ABBOTT, GREGORY
 Flatland
 Rucker, R. v. B. Message found in a copy of Flatland
Abbott, Lee K.
 The heart never fits its wanting
  The Ohio Review no62/63 p14-22 2001
 Men of rough persuasion
  Daedalus v132 no3 p97-103 Summ 2003
 Once upon a time
  Fault lines; stories of divorce; collected and edited by Caitlin Shetterly
 One of Star wars, one of Doom
  The Georgia Review v55 no3 p565-84 Fall 2001
Abdoh, Salak
 (jt. auth) See Mortaz, Maryam
ABDUCTION *See* Kidnapping
Abejas Rubias. Carrillo, H. G.
Abel, Robert H.
 Soft Targets
  The Massachusetts Review v44 no3 p379-82 Fall 2003
Abiding by law. Meyers, K.
Able, Baker, Charlie, Dog. Vaughn, S.

ABNORMALITIES AND DEFORMITIES *See*
Deformities; Dwarfs; Face—Abnormalities
and deformities; Monsters
ABOLITIONISTS
See also Slavery
ABORIGINES, AUSTRALIAN *See* Australian
aborigines
ABORTION
Binchy, M. Shepherd's Bush
Boyle, T. C. Killing babies
Edwards, K. The story of my life
Estenssoro, M. V. The child that never was
Ferriss, L. Husband material
Friesner, E. M. A birthday
Gasco, E. The third person
Gilchrist, E. The abortion
Herling, G. Beata, Santa
Krouse, E. No universe
Lao She. Life choices
Lee, H. E. The serpent's gift [excerpt]
Lee, T. The abortionist's horse (a nightmare)
Masuri, N. Downfall
McBain, E. Terminal misunderstanding
Mogan, J. X and O
O'Connell, M. Saint Dymphna
Pak, W.-S. Three days in that autumn
Pronzini, B. Angel of mercy
Robotham, R. The cry
Sojourner, M. Monsters
Weldon, F. A libation of blood
Wesley, V. W. Afraid of the dark
The **abortion**. Gilchrist, E.
The **abortionist's** horse (a nightmare). Lee, T.
Aboulela, Leila
The museum
The Anchor book of modern African stories;
edited by Nadežda Obradovic ; with a fore-
word by Chinua Achebe
About fog and cappuccino. Lee, A.
About German mustaches and hair parts. Müller,
H.
About love. Chekhov, A. P.
About loving women. Douglas, E.
About Tere who was in Palomas. Gilb, D.
About the grass. Knoderer, T.
About the hooks. Berberova, N.
About the man who jumped from the bridge.
Moody, N. C.
Abouzeid, Chris
The Silence of the lambs
Agni no59 p193-203 2004
Aboveground. Betts, D.
Abraham, Daniel
An amicable divorce
Datlow, E. The dark; new ghost stories; ed-
ited by Ellen Datlow
Chimera 8
Vanishing acts; a science fiction anthology;
edited by Ellen Datlow
Abrams, Tom
The biggest rat in the world
Abrams, T. The drinking of spirits; stories
The book of thieves
Abrams, T. The drinking of spirits; stories
Changing horses
Abrams, T. The drinking of spirits; stories
Dream rider
Abrams, T. The drinking of spirits; stories

The drinking of spirits
Abrams, T. The drinking of spirits; stories
Fish tales
Abrams, T. The drinking of spirits; stories
Forgetting how to laugh
Abrams, T. The drinking of spirits; stories
The gaffer
Abrams, T. The drinking of spirits; stories
The good doctor
Abrams, T. The drinking of spirits; stories
I will hide in God
Abrams, T. The drinking of spirits; stories
In the gare at Bayonne
Abrams, T. The drinking of spirits; stories
Joe Grind
Abrams, T. The drinking of spirits; stories
The king of everything
Abrams, T. The drinking of spirits; stories
Monroe Puckett
Abrams, T. The drinking of spirits; stories
The parade
Abrams, T. The drinking of spirits; stories
Small arms fire
Abrams, T. The drinking of spirits; stories
A small thing that mattered greatly
Abrams, T. The drinking of spirits; stories
The star train
Abrams, T. The drinking of spirits; stories
A tale of two losers
Abrams, T. The drinking of spirits; stories
Top
Abrams, T. The drinking of spirits; stories
Abrupt extinctions at the end of the Triassic.
Glover, D. H.
The **absence** of Emily. Ritchie, J.
Absences. Bahr, A.
The **Absent** Painter. LaSalle, P.
The **absent** soldier. Sari, F.
Absolutely perfect. Mencken, S. H.
Absolution. Callaghan, M.
Absolution. Smolens, J.
The **absolution** of Hedda Borski. Bukoski, A.
Abu, Jaber, Diana
Sister
Ms. v13 no2 p82-5 Summ 2003
Abu al-Hassan ambushes an English car.
Kanafāni, G.
The **abuelita**. Troncoso, S.
ABUSE OF CHILDREN *See* Child abuse
ABUSED WIVES *See* Wife abuse
Abyss. Ford, R.
ABYSSINIA *See* Ethiopia
ACADIANS
Louisiana
See Cajuns
Acapulco gold. Lida, D.
Accame, Jorge
Diary of an explorer
Iowa Review v29 no1 p91-97 Spr 1999
Acceptance of responsibility. Huffman, B., Jr.
Accident. Anderson, D.
Accident. Christie, A.
The **Accident**. Gao Xingjian
The **accident**. Hall, D.
ACCIDENTAL DEATH *See* Accidents
Accidental death. Holt, T.
Accidental love. Nissen, T.

ACCIDENTS

See also Airplane accidents; Drowning; Fires; Hunting accidents; Mine accidents; Railroad accidents; Shipwrecks and castaways; Traffic accidents

Adam, C. Siren
Adams, A. Fog
Alcott, L. M. The lady and the woman
Armstrong, C. The second commandment
Banks, R. Success story
Bausch, R. Wise men at their end
Beattie, A. The big-breasted pilgrim
Blackwood, S. New years
Bocock, M. The tree
Bonnie, F. Roland Fogg
Bowles, P. Rumor and a ladder
Bradbury, R. The great collision of Monday last
Brkic, C. A. Afterdamp
Brownstein, G. Musée des Beaux Arts
Carter, E. New in north town
Chekhov, A. P. Rapture
Chopin, K. Ti Frère
Clarke, A. C. Technical error
Clyde, M. Jumping
Cunningham, M. White angel
Fairey, W. W. Over the hill
Fairman, P. W. The cosmic frame
Gay, W. Standing by peaceful waters
Gilchrist, E. The brown cape
Gilchrist, E. Miss Crystal's maid name Traceleen, she's talking, she's telling everything she knows
Greenberg, A. Closed Mondays
Gwyn, A. Of falling
Haake, K. All the water in the world
Hagy, A. C. Search bay
Haynes, M. Love like a bullet
Henley, P. Love you can't imagine
Houston, P. Cataract
Hribal, C. J. War babies
James, H. My friend Bingham
Jones, G. Veronica
Joseph, D. Bloodlines
Kohler, S. All the days of my life
Lavin, M. A gentle soul
Lavin, M. The girders
Le Clézio, J.-M. G. The round
López, L. To control a rabid rodent
Mazelis, J. The diving girls
Mazelis, J. On the edge
McNulty, J. The Slugger comes into his own
Means, D. What they did
Meloy, M. Accidents
Meloy, M. Four lean hounds, CA. 1976
Meyers, K. Wind rower
Parker, G. Well well well
Perabo, S. Gravity
Robison, M. May Queen
Shapiro, D. Plane crash theory
Thon, M. R. First, body
Troy, M. Turning colder
Vasseur, T. J. The life and death of stars
Wallace, D. F. Incarnations of burned children
Warren, D. Moving pictures

Accidents. Glave, T.
Accidents. Meloy, M.
Accidents are a sideshow. Nfah-Abbenyi, J. M.
Accidents happen. Hart, C. G.
Accommodations. Krawiec, R.

Accommodators. Pearlman, E.
Accomplice. Bynum, S. S.-L.
The **accomplice**. Vinge, V.
According to Poe. Škvorecký, J.
The **accordion**. Hemon, A.

ACCORDIONISTS

Bukoski, A. Closing time
The **account** of Mr. Ira Davidson. Davidson, A.

ACCOUNTANTS

Chekhov, A. P. Notes from the journal of a quick-tempered man
Eldridge, Courtney. Summer of mopeds
Lundquist, R. A stone house of many rooms
Roth, J. Career
Upadhyay, S. The good shopkeeper

ACCULTURATION

See also Race relations

Ace of hearts. Winegardner, M.
Acedia. Maleti, G.
Aces. Henley, P.
Ace's big entrance. Collins, S.
Achates McNeil. Boyle, T. C.

Achebe, Chinua

The Madman
    The Massachusetts Review v44 no1/2 p323-8 Spr/Summ 2003

Achilles' grave. Pastor, B.

Ackerman, Diane

Hummingbirds
    Ploughshares v27 no4 p23-32 Wint 2001/2002

Acorn pipes. Lincoln, C.

Acosta, Juvenal

Ginsberg's tie
    Points of departure; new stories from Mexico; edited by Mónica Lavín; translated by Gustavo Segade

Acquitted. Viganò, R.

ACROBATS

See also Stunt men

Day, C. Jennie Dixiana
Across from the Motoheads. Whisnant, L.
Across the darkness. Landis, G. A.
Across the smiling meadow. Aldrich, B. S.
Act Like a Man. Wildgen, M.
An **act** of vengeance. Allende, I.
An **act** of violence. Nolan, W. F.
Actaeon in the studio of Diana. Hanson, R.
Acting tips. Howe, M. J.
Activity in the flood plain. McBain, E.
The **actor**. Baker, P.
An **actor** prepares. Antrim, D.

ACTORS

See also Mimes; Motion picture actors and actresses; Theater life

Banville, J. Persona
Billman, J. Custer on Mondays
Brand, C. Clever and quick
Breen, J. L. The cat and the Kinetophone
Breen, J. L. It's hard to dance with the devil on your back (with Rita A. Breen)
Carlson, P. M. The world is mine; or, Deeds that make heaven weep
Chan, D. M. Goblin fruit
Chenoweth, A. Going back
Dodd, S. M. Song-and-dance man
Dybek, S. Qué quieres
Forsyth, F. The art of the matter
Foster, K. Another shoot

ACTORS—*Continued*

Foxwell, E. A Roman of no importance
Gifford, B. A fair price
Jacobs, M. The ballad of Tony Nail
Kawabata, Y. Nature
Kees, W. Do you like the mountains?
Kelley, D. A modern tragedy
Kureishi, H. Strangers when we meet
L'Amour, L. One night stand
Leavitt, D. Speonk
Mayo, W. B. Horror
McBrearty, R. G. Improvising
Mehra, D. The garden
Monteleone, T. F. Rehearsals
O'Farrell, J. Walking into the wind
Perabo, S. Thick as thieves
Reilly, G. Nixon under the bodhi tree
Rowell, J. Who lives you?
Royle, N. Empty stations
Saroyan, A. Love scenes
Shrake, E. Strange peaches [excerpt]
Singer, I. B. A friend of Kafka
Vukcevich, R. Season finale

The **actress**. Čeretková-Gállová, M.

ACTRESSES

    See also Mimes; Motion picture actors and actresses; Theater life

Adams, A. Raccoons
Adams, A. The visit
Alcott, L. M. Marion Earle; or, Only an actress!
Bradbury, R. One-woman show
Chekhov, A. P. A dreary story
Fairey, W. W. Family album
Greer, A. S. Titipu
Grut, V. Escape artist
Hendel, Y. Late revenge
Honig, L. Dispossessed
Howe, M. J. Acting tips
Krouse, E. What I wore
Malone, M. Red clay
Marías, J. Fewer scruples
Moody, R. On the carousel
Nolan, W. F. In real life
Onetti, J. C. Hell most feared
Poniatowska, E. Park Cinema
Searle, E. Celebrities in disgrace
Singer, I. B. The manuscript
Sojourner, M. Betabank
Trevanian. The engine of fate
Werve, S. If I were lemon pie
Wieland, L. Irradiation

Acts. Polansky, S.

Acts of memory, wisdom of man. Murray, J.

Actually. Blatnik, A.

ACUPUNCTURE

Austin, S. At Celilo

ADAM (BIBLICAL FIGURE)

               About

Connor, J. Adam and Eve at the automat

Adam, Christina

ASP
    Adam, C. Any small thing can save you; a bestiary

Bat
    Adam, C. Any small thing can save you; a bestiary

Cat
    Adam, C. Any small thing can save you; a bestiary

Dove
    Adam, C. Any small thing can save you; a bestiary

Emu and elephant
    Adam, C. Any small thing can save you; a bestiary

Fox
    Adam, C. Any small thing can save you; a bestiary

Goose
    Adam, C. Any small thing can save you; a bestiary

Hen
    Adam, C. Any small thing can save you; a bestiary

I is for impala
    Prairie Schooner v75 no3 p89-92 Fall 2001

Impala
    Adam, C. Any small thing can save you; a bestiary

Josie
    Adam, C. Any small thing can save you; a bestiary

Kestrel
    Adam, C. Any small thing can save you; a bestiary

Lark
    Adam, C. Any small thing can save you; a bestiary

Moose
    Adam, C. Any small thing can save you; a bestiary

Nightcrawler
    Adam, C. Any small thing can save you; a bestiary

O is for opossum
    Prairie Schooner v75 no3 p93-5 Fall 2001

Opossum
    Adam, C. Any small thing can save you; a bestiary

Porcupine
    Adam, C. Any small thing can save you; a bestiary

Quail
    Adam, C. Any small thing can save you; a bestiary

Red pony
    Adam, C. Any small thing can save you; a bestiary

Siren
    Adam, C. Any small thing can save you; a bestiary

Turtle
    Adam, C. Any small thing can save you; a bestiary

Ursus horribilis
    Adam, C. Any small thing can save you; a bestiary

Vulture
    Adam, C. Any small thing can save you; a bestiary

Watch dog
    Adam, C. Any small thing can save you; a bestiary

X: the unknown quantity
    Adam, C. Any small thing can save you; a bestiary

Adam, Christina—*Continued*
Yellow jacket
　Adam, C. Any small thing can save you; a
　　bestiary
Zoo
　Adam, C. Any small thing can save you; a
　　bestiary
Adams, Alice
1940: fall
　Adams, A. The stories of Alice Adams
Alaska
　Adams, A. The stories of Alice Adams
At the beach
　Adams, A. The stories of Alice Adams
Barcelona
　Adams, A. The stories of Alice Adams
Beautiful girl
　Adams, A. The stories of Alice Adams
Berkeley house
　Adams, A. The stories of Alice Adams
By the sea
　Adams, A. The stories of Alice Adams
The drinking club
　Adams, A. The last lovely city; stories
　Adams, A. The stories of Alice Adams
Earthquake damage
　Adams, A. The last lovely city; stories
　Adams, A. The stories of Alice Adams
Elizabeth
　Adams, A. The stories of Alice Adams
The end of the world
　Adams, A. The stories of Alice Adams
Favors
　Adams, A. The stories of Alice Adams
Flights
　Adams, A. The stories of Alice Adams
Fog
　Adams, A. The stories of Alice Adams
For good
　Adams, A. The stories of Alice Adams
The girl across the room
　Adams, A. The stories of Alice Adams
Great sex
　Adams, A. The last lovely city; stories
　Adams, A. The stories of Alice Adams
Greyhound people
　Adams, A. The stories of Alice Adams
The haunted beach
　Adams, A. The last lovely city; stories
　Adams, A. The stories of Alice Adams
Her unmentionables
　The Yale Review v87 no4 p44-51 O 1999
His women
　Adams, A. The last lovely city; stories
　Adams, A. The stories of Alice Adams
Home is where
　Adams, A. The stories of Alice Adams
The islands
　Adams, A. The last lovely city; stories
　Adams, A. The stories of Alice Adams
The last lovely city
　Adams, A. The last lovely city; stories
　Adams, A. The stories of Alice Adams
Legends
　Adams, A. The stories of Alice Adams
Lost luggage
　Adams, A. The stories of Alice Adams
Mexican dust
　Adams, A. The stories of Alice Adams

Molly's dog
　Adams, A. The stories of Alice Adams
New best friends
　Adams, A. The stories of Alice Adams
Ocracoke Island
　Adams, A. The stories of Alice Adams
Old love affairs
　Adams, A. The last lovely city; stories
　Adams, A. The stories of Alice Adams
A pale and perfectly oval moon
　Adams, A. The stories of Alice Adams
Patients
　Adams, A. The last lovely city; stories
A public pool
　Adams, A. The stories of Alice Adams
Raccoons
　Adams, A. The last lovely city; stories
　Adams, A. The stories of Alice Adams
Return trips
　Adams, A. The stories of Alice Adams
Roses, rhododendron
　Adams, A. The stories of Alice Adams
　The Best American short stories of the
　　century; John Updike, editor, Katrina
　　Kenison, coeditor; with an introduction by
　　John Updike
La Señora
　Adams, A. The stories of Alice Adams
Sintra
　Adams, A. The stories of Alice Adams
Snow
　Adams, A. The stories of Alice Adams
The swastika on our door
　Adams, A. The stories of Alice Adams
Tide pools
　Adams, A. The stories of Alice Adams
To see you again
　Adams, A. The stories of Alice Adams
Truth or consequences
　Adams, A. The stories of Alice Adams
An unscheduled stop
　Adams, A. The stories of Alice Adams
Verlie I say unto you
　Adams, A. The stories of Alice Adams
　Crossing the color line; readings in Black and
　　white; edited by Suzanne W. Jones
A very nice dog
　Adams, A. The last lovely city; stories
　Adams, A. The stories of Alice Adams
The visit
　Adams, A. The last lovely city; stories
　Adams, A. The stories of Alice Adams
Waiting for Stella
　Adams, A. The stories of Alice Adams
Winter rain
　Adams, A. The stories of Alice Adams
The wrong Mexico
　Adams, A. The last lovely city; stories
Your doctor loves you
　Adams, A. The stories of Alice Adams
Adams, Jane
Stealing the dark
　Murder most Celtic; tall tales of Irish may-
　　hem; edited by Martin H. Greenberg
Adams, Jessica
I do like to be beside the seaside
　Tart noir; edited by Stella Duffy & Lauren
　　Henderson

ADAMS, JOHN QUINCY, 1767-1848
About
Crider, B. Alligator tears
Adams. Saunders, G.
Adaptation. Willis, C.
The **adaptive** ultimate. Weinbaum, S. G.
Addenda. Wisniewski, M.
Addison, Linda
Twice, at once, separated
Dark matter; a century of speculative fiction from the African diaspora; edited by Sheree R. Thomas
Additional selected lives in brief. Cole, C. B.
Addonizio, Kim
Angels
Addonizio, K. In the box called pleasure; stories
Bedtime story
Addonizio, K. In the box called pleasure; stories
A brief history of condoms
Addonizio, K. In the box called pleasure; stories
Emergency room
Addonizio, K. In the box called pleasure; stories
The fall of Saigon
Addonizio, K. In the box called pleasure; stories
Gaps
Addonizio, K. In the box called pleasure; stories
Gas
Addonizio, K. In the box called pleasure; stories
The gift
Addonizio, K. In the box called pleasure; stories
Have you seen me?
Addonizio, K. In the box called pleasure; stories
In the box called pleasure
Addonizio, K. In the box called pleasure; stories
Inside out
Addonizio, K. In the box called pleasure; stories
Reading Sontag
Addonizio, K. In the box called pleasure; stories
Scores
Addonizio, K. In the box called pleasure; stories
Testimony
Addonizio, K. In the box called pleasure; stories
'Til there was you
Addonizio, K. In the box called pleasure; stories
Adele. Kaminsky, S. M.
The **Adeline** Shop. Pollack, H. A.
Adichie, Chimamanda Ngozi
The American embassy
The O. Henry Prize stories, 2003; edited and with an introduction by Laura Furman; jurers David Gutterson, Diane Johnson, Jennifer Egan
Light Skin
Calyx v21 no2 p49-63 Summ 2003

New Husband
Iowa Review v33 no1 p53-66 Spr 2003
A Private Experience
The Virginia Quarterly Review v80 no3 p170-9 Summ 2004
Adina. James, H.
ADIRONDACK MOUNTAINS (N.Y.)
Barrett, A. The cure
Doctorow, E. L. Loon lake
Adisa, Opal Palmer
Widows' walk
Whispers from the cotton tree root; Caribbean fabulist fiction; edited by Nalo Hopkinson
Adiyo, kerido. Brkic, C. A.
Adjusting the bite. Agee, J.
The **adjustment.** Stevenson, M. M.
Adler, Renata
Brownstone
Wonderful town; New York stories from The New Yorker; edited by David Remnick with Susan Choi
Admirable qualities. Seydel, M.
Admiral of the Swiss Navy. Lipsyte, S.
Admissions. Simpson, M.
The **admissions** officer. LaSalle, P.
The **admonitory** hippopotamus: or, Angelica and Sneezby. Gorey, E.
ADOBE WALLS, BATTLE OF, TEX., 1874
Braun, M. The stand
ADOLESCENCE
See also Boys; Girls; Youth
Alderete, P. Fire
Arnold, H. H. Bill's first airplane ride
Auchincloss, L. He knew he was right
Bail, M. The seduction of my sister
Banbury, J. Take, for example, meatpie
Barthelme, F. Grapette
Barthelme, F. Violet
Bauman, B. A. True
Beattie, A. See the pyramids
Bender, A. Jinx
Berry, W. Where did they go?
Bezmozgis, D. Natasha
Blair, J. Ghost river
Blaise, C. A North American education
Bocock, M. Play me "Stormy weather," please
Borges, J. L. The night of the gifts
Boswell, M. Born again
Boswell, M. New Wave
Brackenbury, R. The knowledge
Bradbury, R. The miracles of Jamie
Brown, J. She
Brown, J. The submariners
Brown, J. Thief
Budnitz, J. Chaperone
Campo, R. Like a banana
Canty, K. Flipper
Capote, T. A diamond guitar
Carlson, R. At Copper View
Carlson, R. Evil eye Allen
Carlson, R. Keith
Casares, O. Yolanda
Caspers, N. La maison de Madame Durard
Chabon, M. The Halloween party
Chan, D. M. Falling
Chekhov, A. P. After the theatre
Chekhov, A. P. Volodya
Clinton, M. T. Free your mind and your ass will follow

ADOLESCENCE—*Continued*

Clyde, M. Farming butterflies
Clyde, M. A good paved road
Clyde, M. Heartbreak house
Clyde, M. Krista had a treble clef rose
Clyde, M. Pruitt love
Cobb, T. Face the music
Cobb, W. J. Dark matter
Cohen, R. Theme from a summer place
Cohen, R. The boys at night
Collier, E. W. Marigolds
Connolly, C. Paradise Drive
Cooper, B. A man in the making
Daniels, J. Christmasmobile
Davenport, G. Gunnar and Nikolai
Davenport, G. The owl of Minerva
Davenport, G. The playing field
Davis, A. Faith; or, Tips for the successful young lady
Davis, C. A. Brand new boyfriend
DeLancey, K. A hole in the wall of noise
DeMarco, T. A boy's will is the winds's will
DeMarinis, R. Experience
DeMarinis, R. Hormone X
DeMarinis, R. Safe forever
DeMarinis, R. The Voice of America
Díaz, J. Nilda
Doble, J. Entries from Skipper Bitwell's journal
Doerr, A. For a long time this was Griselda's story
Doerr, A. So many chances
Drake, R. Every Friday afternoon
Dumas, H. Ark of bones
Dumas, H. A boll of roses
Dunmore, H. The clear and rolling water
Dybek, S. Blue boy
Dybek, S. We didn't
Ebershoff, D. The charm bracelet
Ebershoff, D. Regime
Ebershoff, D. Trespass
Edgerton, C. Debra's flap and snap
Eisenberg, D. What it was like, seeing Chris
Erian, A. On the occasion of my ruination
Evans, E. Suicide's girlfriend
Evans, E. Thieves
Evans, E. Voodoo girls on ice
Ferrell, C. Wonderful teen
Fischerová, D. Boarskin dances down the tables
Fulton, J. Outlaws
Fulton, J. Retribution
Galef, D. Portrait of a portrayal
Gartner, Z. Boys growing
Gay, W. The lightpainter
Gifford, B. The big love of Cherry Lane
Gilchrist, E. Music
Gilchrist, E. Some blue hills at sundown
Gingher, M. Teen angel
Glover, D. A piece of the True Cross
Goldstein, N. The Roberto touch
Gwyn, A. Against the pricks
Hagy, A. C. The snake hunters
Hall, D. The accident
Harfenist, J. Duck season
Harfenist, J. Pixie dust
Harfenist, J. The road out of Acorn Lake
Harfenist, J. Salad girls
Harfenist, J. Voluntary breathers
Henley, P. Labrador
Henley, P. Victory

Highsmith, P. In the plaza
Hirshberg, G. Struwwelpeter
Hoffman, A. Bake at 350°
Hoffman, A. Fate
Hoffman, A. True confession
Homes, A. M. The whiz kids
House, T. Scarecrow
Johnson, A. The eighth sea
Johnson, A. The history of cancer
Johnson, A. Teen sniper
Jones, T. I love you, Sophie Western
Jones, T. Thorazine Johnny Felsun loves me (from his permanent cage of lifelong confinement)
Kauffman, J. Patriotic
Kemper, M. God's goodness
LaValle, V. D. Class trip
LaValle, V. D. Getting paid
Le Clézio, J.-M. G. Ariadne
Le Clézio, J.-M. G. The round
Lipsyte, S. Torquemada
Lloyd, D. T. Boys only
López, L. Sophia
Lord, N. The baby who, according to his aunt, resembled his uncle
Lundquist, R. Into this house
Mann, W. J. Say goodbye to Middletown
Mazor, J. The lone star kid
McCourt, J. A plethora
McKillip, P. A. Oak Hill
McNally, J. The New Year
Meloy, M. Thirteen & a half
Meyers, K. Light in the crossing
Meyers, K. A strange brown fruit
Millhauser, S. Clair de lune
Mogan, J. X and O
Molyneux, J. Desire lines
Mueller, D. How animals mate
Mueller, D. P. M. R. C.
Mueller, D. Torturing creatures at night
Muñoz, M. The third myth
Muñoz, M. Zigzagger
Nailah, A. Alice & Jesse
Nailah, A. Four
Nair, M. The lodger in room 726
Nair, M. My grandfather dreams of fences
Nissen, T. Apple pie
Nissen, T. Way back when in the now before now
Oates, J. C. Cumberland breakdown
Oates, J. C. The high school sweetheart
Oates, J. C. Me & Wolfie, 1979
Oates, J. C. Tusk
Oates, J. C. Where are you going, where have you been?
Orner, P. At the Motel Rainbow
Orringer, J. The smoothest way is full of stones
Orringer, J. Stars of Motown shining bright
Orringer, J. Stations of the cross
Ortega, A. L. Naturalezas menores [excerpt]
Padilla, M. Carrying Sergei
Paschal, D. Moriya
Paz, S. Don't tell her you love her
Peterson, P. W. The as and is
Phillips, D. R. The woods at the back of our houses
Potok, C. Moon
Potvin, E. A. Invert and multiply
Pritchard, M. Salve Regina

ADOLESCENCE—*Continued*

Reifler, N. Julian
Reifler, N. Personal foundations of self-forming through auto-identification with otherness
Reifler, N. Rascal
Reifler, N. The river and Una
Reifler, N. Summer job
Richter, S. Prom night
Robison, M. Happy boy, Allen
Roorbach, B. Fog
Roth, J. Youth
Russo, R. The mysteries of Linwood Hart
Sandor, M. Capacity
Sanford, A. Nobody listens when I talk
Schoemperlen, D. Clues
Schoemperlen, D. Losing ground
Seiffert, R. Blue
Self, W. My idea of fun [excerpt]
Sellers, H. Fla. boys
Sellers, H. Florida law
Sellers, H. The Gulf of Mexico
Sellers, H. In the drink
Sellers, H. It's water, it's not going to kill you
Sellers, H. Myself as a delicious peach
Sellers, H. Sinking
Sellers, H. Sleep creep leap
Sellers, H. Spurt
Shade, E. Kaahumanu
Shade, E. The last night of the county fair
Shade, E. A rage forever
Shade, E. Superfly
Shepard, S. Berlin Wall piece
Shippen, J. R. I am not like Nuñez
Simpson, H. Golden apples
Škvorecký, J. Dr. Strass
Škvorecký, J. Eve was naked
Škvorecký, J. My teacher, Mr. Katz
Škvorecký, J. Why do people have soft noses?
Sosin, D. There are no green butterflies
Stolar, D. Crossing over
Stuckey-French, E. Famous poets
Taraqqi, G. My little friend
Taylor, P. H. Venus, cupid, folly and time
Tester, W. Wet
Tester, W. Whisperers
Thien, M. Alchemy
Thurm, M. Jumping ship
Touré. They're playing my song
Updike, J. Flight
Updike, J. A sense of shelter
Vanderhaeghe, G. The Jimi Hendrix experience
Vaswani, N. Bing-Chen
Vukcevich, R. Jumping
Wallace, D. F. Forever overhead
Watkins, S. Critterworld
Watson, B. The dead girl
Wells, K. Compression scars
Wexler, M. Save yourself
White, M. C. Voices
Williams, M. Cantaloupes
Williams, M. There aren't any foxes in that cave
Williams, M. Truth and goodness
Williams, M. The wall
Winegardner, M. Ace of hearts
Winegardner, M. How we came to Indiana
Winegardner, M. Janda's sister
Winegardner, M. Last love song at the Valentine
Winegardner, M. Song for a certain girl
Wuori, G. K. Murder
Yañez, R. Desert Vista
Yuknavitch, L. Cusp
Ziegler, I. Blue Springs
Ziegler, I. The stranger

ADOLESCENTS *See* Adolescence

Adolph, José B.
The falsifier
Cosmos latinos: an anthology of science fiction from Latin America and Spain; translated, edited, & with an introduction & notes by Andrea L. Bell & Yolanda Molina-Gavilán

ADOPTED CHILDREN *See* Adoption; Foster children

ADOPTION
See also Foster children
Adam, C. Hen
Alcott, L. M. Love and self-love
Brownstein, G. The inventor of love
Dobyns, S. Part of the story
Estep, M. One of us
Fromm, P. Cowbird
Gasco, E. Can you wave bye bye, baby?
Gasco, E. Elements
Gasco, E. Mother: not a true story
Gasco, E. The spider of Bumba
Gasco, E. The third person
Gasco, E. A well-imagined life
Gasco, E. You have the body
Gordimer, N. Karma
Hinger, C. Any old mother
Hood, A. Inside Gorbachev's head
Johnston, T. Irish girl
Krawiec, R. Saving Saul
Mencken, S. H. Grown-up
Nikas, E. Fatal tears
O'Neill, S. Butch
Rusch, K. K. Echea
Vasseur, T. J. The sins of Jesus

Adornato and Venus. Maleti, G.
The **adornment** of days. Stollman, A. L.

Adorno, Juan Nepomuceno
The distant future
Cosmos latinos: an anthology of science fiction from Latin America and Spain; translated, edited, & with an introduction & notes by Andrea L. Bell & Yolanda Molina-Gavilán

Adriázola, Claudia
Buttons
Death dines at 8:30; edited by Claudia Bishop and Nick DiChario

Adult education. Cohen, R.
Adult education. Dodd, S. M.
Adult Fiction: A Story. Clayton, J. J.
The **adult** holiday. Spencer, E.
Adult video. Boyd, W.
Adult world [I]. Wallace, D. F.
Adult world [II]. Wallace, D. F.
The **adulterous** woman. Kohler, S.

ADULTERY *See* Marriage problems

Advancing Luna—and Ida B. Wells. Walker, A.
Advenar. Schlein, K.

ADVENTURE

See also Buried treasure; Escapes; International intrigue; Manhunts; Pirates; Science fiction; Sea stories; Soldiers of fortune; Spies; Voyages and travels; Western stories

Beach, R. The weight of obligation
Brackenbury, R. Cuba run
Church, A. The Iliad for boys and girls [excerpt]
Dumas, A. The three musketeers [excerpt]
Ellison, H. Goodbye to all that
Forsyth, F. Whispering wind
Gorriti, J. M. The quena
Gorriti, J. M. The treasure of the Incas
Gorriti, J. M. A year in California
Haggard, H. R. Smith and the pharaohs
L'Amour, L. Coast patrol
L'Amour, L. The diamond of Jeru
L'Amour, L. May there be a road
L'Amour, L. Wings over Brazil
L'Amour, L. Wings over Khabarovsk
Shepard, J. Tedford and the megalodon
Verne, J. Five weeks in a balloon
Wägner, W. The Hegeling legend [excerpt]
Wägner, W. The legend of Beowulf
Wiggin, K. D. S. and Smith, N. A. The story of Ali Baba and the forty thieves
Yoshikawa, E. Musashi [excerpt]

The **Adventure**. McPhee, M.
An **adventure** in the Big Horn Mountains; or, The trials and tribulations of a recruit. Frierson, E. P.
Adventure of a lifetime. Winterson, J.
The **adventure** of Exham Priory. MacIntyre, F. G.
The **adventure** of Silver Blaze. Doyle, Sir A. C.
The **adventure** of the agitated actress. Stashower, D.
The **adventure** of the antiquarian's niece. Hambly, B.
The **adventure** of the Arab's manuscript. Reaves, M.
The **adventure** of the blind alley. Wellen, E.
The **adventure** of the Bruce-Partington plans. Doyle, Sir A. C.
The **adventure** of the celestial snows. Effinger, G. A.
The **adventure** of the curious canary. Day, B.
The **adventure** of the Dauphin doll. Queen, E.
The **adventure** of the dying doctor. Bruce, C.
The **adventure** of the Egyptian tomb. Christie, A.
The **adventure** of the forgotten umbrella. Gilden, M.
The **adventure** of the garter. Hodgson, W. H.
The **adventure** of the headland. Hodgson, W. H.
The **adventure** of the mooning sentry. Breen, J. L.
The **adventure** of the one-penny black. Queen, E.
The **adventure** of the Penny Magenta. Derleth, A. W.
The **adventure** of the President's half disme. Queen, E.
The **adventure** of the rara avis. Wheat, C.
The **adventure** of the Voorish Sign. Lupoff, R. A.
The **adventure** of the young British soldier. Crider, B.
The **adventure** with the claim jumpers. Hodgson, W. H.
Adventurer. Goran, L.
Adventures in babysitting. Rankin, I.

Adventures in further education. Atkins, P.
"The **adventures** of a tailor". Trueba, A. d.
The **adventures** of Mr. Tindle. Lupoff, R. A.
The **adventures** of the boulevard assassin. Lupoff, R. A.
The **adventures** of the Cheshire Cheese. Breen, J. L.

ADVERTISING

Arvin, N. Radio ads
Biggle, L. Tunesmith
Mickenberg, R. Direct male
Pohl, F. The tunnel under the world
Stern, D. Lunch with Gottlieb
Touré. The commercial channel: a unique business opportunity
Updike, J. Commercial
Wallace, D. F. Mister Squishy

Aeken, Hieronymus van See Bosch, Hieronymus, d. 1516
Aeon's child. Reed, R.

AERONAUTICS

See also Air pilots; Airships; Flight
Arvin, N. Aeronautics
Bradbury, R. Icarus Montgolfier Wright
Doyle, Sir A. C. The horror of the heights

Flights

See Air travel

AERONAUTICS, MILITARY See Military aeronautics

Aeronautics. Arvin, N.
The **aeroplanes** at Brescia. Davenport, G.
Aerosol halo. Lisick, B.

AESTHETICS

Chekhov, A. P. The beauties
Hawthorne, N. The artist of the beautiful
Henry, O. Art and the bronco

The **affair** with Rachel Ware. Stuart, J.
Affairs in order. Boylan, C.
The **affairs** of each beast. Benioff, D.
The **affirmation** [excerpt] Priest, C.

AFGHANISTAN

Russian Invasion, 1979

Turtledove, H. Black tulip

The **aficionados**. Carver, R.

Afolabi, S. A.

Now that I'm Back
    The Kenyon Review v24 no3/4 p17-24 Summ/Fall 2002

Afonka bida. Babel′, I.
Afraid of a gun. Hammett, D.
Afraid of the dark. Pickard, N.
Afraid of the dark. Wesley, V. W.

AFRICA

See also East Africa; North Africa; South Africa; West Africa

Ball, M. Shell game
Bhêly-Quénum, O. A child in the bush of ghosts
Deb, A. The three-piece suit
Enekwe, O. O. The last battle
Honwana, L. B. Papa, snake & I
Inyama, N. Hot days, long nights
Kohler, S. Ambush
Lopes, H. The advance
McDonald, I. Tendeléo's story
Murray, J. Watson and the shark
Ousmane, Sembène. Her three days
Saro-Wiwa, K. Africa kills her sun
Theroux, P. White lies

AFRICA—*Continued*
Native peoples
See also Kikuyu (African people); Masai
(African people); Zulus (African people)
Mungoshi, C. The brother
Race relations
Hunter, F. Madagascar
AFRICA, EAST *See* East Africa
AFRICA, GERMAN EAST *See* East Africa
AFRICA, NORTH *See* North Africa
AFRICA, SOUTH *See* South Africa
AFRICA, WEST *See* West Africa
Africa. Siler, J.
Africa, Africa!. Hunter, F.
Africa kills her sun. Saro-Wiwa, K.
AFRICAN AMERICAN CHILDREN
Bambara, T. C. Gorilla, my love
Coyne, T. Behind sharp branches
Grau, S. A. The beginning
Lincoln, C. All that's left
Lincoln, C. Wishes
McKnight, R. The kind of light that shines on
Texas
Posey, J. R. Ticket to freedom
AFRICAN AMERICAN SERVANTS
Adams, A. Verlie I say unto you
Bocock, M. The tree
Bradbury, R. We'll just act natural
Chesnutt, C. W. Her Virginia Mammy
Douglas, E. I just love Carrie Lee
Faulkner, W. That evening sun go down
MacDowell, K. S. B. Gran'mammy
MacDowell, K. S. B. Why Gran'mammy didn't
like pound-cake
McPherson, J. A. A solo song: for Doc
Williams, J. A. Son in the afternoon
AFRICAN AMERICAN SOLDIERS
Fleming, R. Arbeit Macht Frei
Irsfeld, J. H. Ambivalence Hardy Fire
Killens, J. O. God bless America
Yerby, F. Health card
AFRICAN AMERICAN WOMEN
Coleman, W. The Friday night shift at the Taco
House blues (wah-wah)
Collins, M. The walk
Cooper, J. C. The eagle flies
Cooper, J. C. A filet of soul
Cooper, J. C. The lost and the found
Cooper, J. C. A shooting star
Engel, M. P. Lowcountry cold
Lincoln, C. Like dove wings
Lincoln, C. Sap rising
McCorkle, J. Starlings
Mullen, H. R. Tenderhead
Naylor, G. Etta Mae Johnson
Walker, A. Advancing Luna—and Ida B. Wells
Walker, A. Kindred spirits
AFRICAN AMERICANS
See also African American children;
African American servants; African
American soldiers; African American wom-
en; Blacks; Mulattoes; Slavery
Allegra, D. Witness to the league of blond hip
hop dancers
Allen, S. Behind the black curtain
Allen, S. Carved in vinyl
Allen, S. Mud show
Allen, S. Souvenir
Allen, S. Yearbook

Aminoff, J. Fate
Anderson, B. Lark till dawn, princess
Bambara, T. C. Maggie of the green bottles
Barrett, N., Jr. Cush
Bocock, M. The funeral
Bocock, M. Heaven lies about
Bocock, M. Play me "Stormy weather," please
Boof, Kola. The one you meet everywhere
Bullins, E. Support your local police
Butler, R. O. Uncle Andrew
Capote, T. Preacher's legend
Chesnutt, C. W. The averted strike
Chesnutt, C. W. Cicely's dream
Chesnutt, C. W. Dave's neckliss
Chesnutt, C. W. The doll
Chesnutt, C. W. Hot-foot Hannibal
Chesnutt, C. W. Mars Jeems's nightmare
Chesnutt, C. W. The passing of Grandison
Chesnutt, C. W. Sis' Becky's pickaninny
Chesnutt, C. W. Uncle Wellington's wives
Chesnutt, C. W. The wife of his youth
Chopin, K. In Sabine
Clinton, M. T. Free your mind and your ass will
follow
Davis, M. M. A bamboula
Davis, W. The sharp light of trespassers
Day, C. The last member of the Boela tribe
Dickey, E. J. Café Piel
Dodd, S. M. Adult education
Dodd, S. M. Ethiopia
Dodd, S. M. In France they turn to stone when
they die
Dove, R. Damon and Vandalia
Dove, R. Second-hand man
Du Bois, W. E. B. Jesus Christ in Texas
Due, T. Trial day
Dumas, H. Ark of bones
Dumas, H. The bewitching bag; or, How the
man escaped from Hell
Dumas, H. A boll of roses
Dumas, H. Children of the sun
Dumas, H. The crossing
Dumas, H. Double nigger
Dumas, H. Echo tree
Dumas, H. Rain God
Dumas, H. Six days you shall labor
Dumas, H. Strike and fade
Dumas, H. Thrust counter thrust
Dumas, H. Will the circle be unbroken?
Dunbar, P. L. The ingrate
Dunbar, P. L. The lynching of Jube Benson
Duncan, A. Daddy Mention and the Monday
skull
Earle, S. Taneytown
Ellison, R. Mister Toussan
Engel, M. P. Dis aliter visum
Engel, M. P. Unnatural acts
Fleming, R. In my father's house
Fleming, R. A lizard's kiss
Fleming, R. Punish the young seed of Satan
Fleming, R. The ultimate bad luck
Gabriel, D. The reincarnation of Donaldo Fuer-
tes
Gifford, B. American Falls
Gilchrist, E. A tree to be desired
Glave, T. —and love them?
Gomez, J. Chicago 1927
Grau, S. A. The black prince
Groom, W. Just a little closer to the Lord

AFRICAN AMERICANS—*Continued*

Gurganus, A. Saint monster
Harris, E. L. Money can't buy me love
Harrison, H. American dead
Harrison, H. Mute Milton
Highsmith, P. The hollow oracle
Holman, J. Squabble
Hopkins, P. E. As the lord lives, he is one of our mother's children
Hughes, L. The gun
Johnson, C. R. The people speak
Johnson, C. R. The plague
Johnson, D. Bars
Johnson, D. Hot pepper
Johnson, D. Markers
Johnson, D. Melvin in the sixth grade
Johnson, D. Mouthful of sorrow
Johnson, D. Something to remember me by
Johnson, D. Three ladies sipping tea in a Persian garden
Kelley, W. M. Carlyle tries polygamy
Krawiec, R. Accommodations
Lansdale, J. R. Cowboy
Lee, A. Brothers and sisters around the world
Lee, A. The golden chariot
Lee, A. In France
Lee, H. E. The serpent's gift [excerpt]
Lewis, W. H. Germinating
Lewis, W. H. The trip back from Whidbey
Lincoln, C. Acorn pipes
Lincoln, C. At the water's end
Lincoln, C. Bug juice
Lincoln, C. A hook will sometimes keep you
Lincoln, C. Last will
Lincoln, C. A very close conspiracy
Lincoln, C. Winter's wheat
Little, B. The yellow sweater
Major, D. Shining through 24/7
McBain, E. The sharers
McKnight, R. Quitting smoking
Miller, A. L. Off-season travel
Mitchell, C. E. Black cowboy
Morrow, B. "Ciccone youths 1990"
Moses, J. Girls like you
Mosley, W. Pet fly
Nailah, A. Four
Nailah, A. Free
Nailah, A. French
Nailah, A. Inside out
Nailah, A. My side of the story
Nailah, A. Professor
Nash, S. Amen
Nesbitt, M. The children's book of victims
Nesbitt, M. Chimp shrink and backwards
Nesbitt, M. Gigantic
Nesbitt, M. Man in towel with gun
Nesbitt, M. The ones who may kill you in the morning
Nesbitt, M. Polly here somewhere
Nesbitt, M. Quality fuel for electric living
Nesbitt, M. Thursday the sixteenth
Nesbitt, M. What good is you anyway?
Packer, Z. The ant of the self
Packer, Z. Brownies
Packer, Z. Drinking coffee elsewhere
Packer, Z. Geese
Packer, Z. Our Lady of Peace
Packer, Z. Speaking in tongues
Patterson, A. Hussy Strutt

Peterson, P. W. Big brother
Peterson, P. W. Song of Camille
Pickens, W. Jim Crow in Texas
Reisman, N. Girl on a couch
Reynolds, A. Alcestis
Rhodes, J. P. Long distances
Salaam, K. I. Rosamojo
Sanford, A. In the Little Hunky River
Shange, N. Every time my lil' world seems blue
Shepherd, R. The black narcissus
Sherman, C. W. Emerald City: Third & Pike
Shockley, E. Separation anxiety
Smith, D. A. The pretended
Spencer, E. The little brown girl
Spencer, E. Sharon
Stolar, D. Crossing over
Thelwell, M. Community of victims
Thelwell, M. Direct action
Thomas, J. C. Young Reverend Zelma Lee Moses
Thompson, C. Judgment
Touré. The African-American aesthetics hall of fame; or, 101 elements of blackness (things that'll make you say: yes! that there's some really black
Touré. Afrolexicology today's biannual list of the top fifty words in African-American
Touré. Attack of the love dogma
Touré. Blackmanwalkin
Touré. The breakup ceremony
Touré. Falcon Malone can fly no mo
Touré. A hot time at the Church of Kentucky Fried Souls and the spectacular final Sunday sermon of the Right Revren Daddy Love
Touré. It's life and death at the Slush Puppie Open
Touré. My history
Touré. Once an oreo, always an oreo
Touré. The Sambomorphosis
Touré. Soul City Gazette profile: Crash Jinkin, last of the chronic crashees
Touré. The Steviewondermobile
Touré. They're playing my song
Touré. We words
Touré. You are who you kill
Touré. Young, black, and unstoppable; or, Death of a zeitgeist jockey
VanderMeer, J. Black Duke blues
Vega, A. L. Cloud cover Caribbean
Vega Yunqué, E. Eight morenos
Walker, A. Everyday use
Walker, D. L. York's story
Warren, R. P. Blackberry winter
Wideman, J. E. Doc's story
Wideman, J. E. Weight
Wier, A. Tehano [excerpt]
Wright, R. Bright and morning star
Yates, R. A really good jazz piano
Yerby, F. Health card

Civil rights

Dumas, H. The marchers
Grooms, A. Food that pleases, food to take home
McPherson, J. A. A loaf of bread
Packer, Z. Doris is coming
Updike, J. Marching through Boston

AFRICAN AMERICANS—*Continued*
Alabama
Brown, D. W. In the doorway of Rhee's Jazz Joint
Arkansas
Dumas, H. Goodbye, sweetwater
Baltimore (Md.)
Lincoln, C. More like us
California
Brown, C. Now is the time
Burris, J. Judah's a two-way street running out
Cleaver, E. The flashlight
Groves, J. W. Stop, thief!
Himes, C. Lunching at the Ritzmore
McPherson, J. A. Elbow room
Mosley, W. Blue lightning
Mosley, W. A day in the park
Mosley, W. Equal opportunity
Mosley, W. Mookie Kid
Mosley, W. Moving on
Mosley, W. The mugger
Mosley, W. Promise
Mosley, W. Rascals in the cane
Mosley, W. Rogue
Mosley, W. Shift, shift, shift
Mosley, W. That smell
Mosley, W. The thief
Mosley, W. Walkin' the dog
Mosley, W. What would you do?
Scott, J. The coming of the Hoodlum
Cuba
Cabrera Infante, G. The great ekbó
Florida
Butler, L. P. Booker T's coming home
Jones, M. Sim Denny
Georgia
Packer, Z. Brownies
Kansas
Clair, M. October Brown
Clair, M. Water seeks its own level
Kentucky
Jones, G. White rat
Louisiana
Bontemps, A. W. Why I returned
Chopin, K. A rude awakening
Maryland
Collier, E. W. Marigolds
Massachusetts
Thon, M. R. Little white sister
West, D. My baby . . .
Mississippi
Fleming, R. The astral visitor Delta blues
Walker, A. Roselily
Missouri
McElroy, C. J. A brief spell by the river
New Hampshire
Banks, R. Black man and white woman in dark green rowboat
New York (N.Y.)
Baida, P. No place to hide
Bambara, T. C. The hammer man
Du Bois, W. E. B. The comet
Dumas, H. Harlem
Dumas, H. A Harlem game
Dumas, H. Riot or revolt?
Dumas, H. Scout
Dumas, H. The voice
Ferrell, C. Proper library
Glave, T. The final inning

Updike, J. A gift from the city
Wilmot, J. Dirt angel
North Carolina
Chesnutt, C. W. Dave's neckliss
Chesnutt, C. W. A deep sleeper
Chesnutt, C. W. The dumb witness
Chesnutt, C. W. The goophered grapevine
Chesnutt, C. W. The gray wolf's ha'nt
Chesnutt, C. W. Lonesome Ben
Chesnutt, C. W. The march of progress
Chesnutt, C. W. Po' Sandy
Gurganus, A. Blessed assurance: a moral tale
Kenan, R. The foundations of the earth
Lee, A. Anthropology
Malone, M. The rising of the South and Flonnie Rogers
Philadelphia (Pa.)
Major, M. Kenya and Amir
Wideman, J. E. Fever
Southern States
Adams, A. Verlie I say unto you
Chesnutt, C. W. The bouquet
Chesnutt, C. W. The sheriff's children
Chesnutt, C. W. The web of circumstance
Dumas, H. Fon
Dumas, H. Rope of wind
Toomer, J. Blood-burning moon
Walker, A. Nineteen fifty-five
Texas
McKnight, R. The kind of light that shines on Texas
Sagstetter, K. The thing with Willie
Shange, N. Ridin' the moon in Texas
Wald, M. Keys to the city
Williams, M. Grazing in good pastures
Virginia
Hoffman, W. Stones
Page, T. N. Unc' Edinburg's drowndin'
Washington (D.C.)
Jones, E. P. A dark night
Jones, E. P. The first day
Jones, E. P. Marie
The **African** origins of UFOs [excerpt] Joseph, A.
AFRICAN TRIBES *See* Africa—Native peoples
AFRICANS
United States
Gabriel, D. The blind woman
Tangh, J. The Skinned
Africans. Kohler, S.
AFRIKANERS
Wellen, E. The plan of the snake
AFRO-AMERICANS *See* African Americans
Afrolexicology today's biannual list of the top fifty words in African-American. Touré
After. Honig, L.
After Caravaggio's Sacrifice of Isaac. Cusk, R.
After Chernobyl. Dwyer, M.
After Colette [excerpt] Lingard, J.
After Cowboy Chicken came to town. Ha Jin
After Dad shot Jesus. López, L.
After Dark. Harding, E.
After Holbein. Wharton, E.
After hours at Rick's. Trevanian
After I was thrown in the river and before I drowned. Eggers, D.
After Memphis. Lear, P.
After Rosa Parks. Desaulniers, J.
After the ball. Bradbury, R.
After the Ball. Tolstoy, L., graf

After the baptism. Bly, C.
After the battle. Babel′, I.
After the beep. Nixon, C.
After the divorce. Rifkin, A.
After the hurricane. Sanabria Santaliz, E.
After the Mailman. Maliszewski, P.
After the plague. Boyle, T. C.
After the rains. Galloway, J.
After the river. Parrish, T.
After the storm. Harrison, H.
After the theatre. Chekhov, A. P.
After the winter. Chopin, K.
After theatre. See Chekhov, A. P. After the theatre
After twenty-five years, at the Palais Royale. Nissen, T.
Afterbirth. Schwartz, S.
Afterdamp. Brkic, C. A.
Afterlife. Brown, J.
Afterlife. Cohen, G. K.
Afterlife. Lord, N.
The **afterlove**. Shrayer, M. D.
Aftermath. Gorman, E.
Aftermath. Waters, M. Y.
Afternoon at Schraffts. Dozois, G. R.
Afternoon of the Sassanoa. Brown, J.
Afternoon tea. Davies, R.
Afternoon with Antaeus. Bowles, P.
An **afternoon** with the old man. Dubus, A.
Aftershock. Wilson, F. P.
Afterward. Wharton, E.
Agabian, Nancy
  Ghosts and bags
    Hers 2: brilliant new fiction by lesbian writers; edited by Terry Wolverton with Robert Drake
Agafya. Chekhov, A. P.
Again—Part II. Dixon, S.
Against interpretation. Yuknavitch, L.
Against the odds. Trevor, W.
AGAMEMNON (GREEK MYTHOLOGY)
  Sheckley, R. Agamemnon's run
Agamemnon's run. Sheckley, R.
Agape among the robots. Steele, A. M.
Agatha's confession. Alcott, L. M.
The **age** of a wart. White, P.
Age of copper. Skinner, J.
The **age** of desire. Barker, C.
The **age** of discovery. Békés, P.
The **Age** of Enlightenment. Guian, S.
AGED *See* Elderly; Old age
Agee, Deedee
  Momentum
    Doubletake v8 no2 p90-3 Spr 2002
Agee, James
  Enter the Ford
    Doubletake v8 no2 p39 Spr 2002
Agee, Jonis
  Adjusting the bite
    Agee, J. Taking the wall; stories
  And blue
    Agee, J. Acts of love on Indigo Road; new & selected stories
  Aronson's Orchard
    Agee, J. Acts of love on Indigo Road; new & selected stories
  Asparagus
    Agee, J. Acts of love on Indigo Road; new & selected stories

At last
  Agee, J. Acts of love on Indigo Road; new & selected stories
Billy Kitchen
  Agee, J. Taking the wall; stories
Binding the devil
  Agee, J. Acts of love on Indigo Road; new & selected stories
  A different plain; contemporary Nebraska fiction writers; edited by Ladette Randolph ; introduction by Mary Pipher
Carl Millennium
  Agee, J. Acts of love on Indigo Road; new & selected stories
Caution
  Agee, J. Taking the wall; stories
Cleveland Pinkney
  Agee, J. Acts of love on Indigo Road; new & selected stories
The creek
  Agee, J. Acts of love on Indigo Road; new & selected stories
Cupid
  Agee, J. Acts of love on Indigo Road; new & selected stories
Dead space
  Agee, J. Acts of love on Indigo Road; new & selected stories
Dwight Tuggle
  Agee, J. Taking the wall; stories
Each time we meet
  Agee, J. Acts of love on Indigo Road; new & selected stories
Earl
  Agee, J. Acts of love on Indigo Road; new & selected stories
The first obligation
  Agee, J. Taking the wall; stories
Flat spotting
  Agee, J. Taking the wall; stories
Getting the heat up
  Agee, J. Taking the wall; stories
The god of gestures
  Agee, J. Acts of love on Indigo Road; new & selected stories
Good to go
  Agee, J. Acts of love on Indigo Road; new & selected stories
  Agee, J. Taking the wall; stories
The gun
  Agee, J. Acts of love on Indigo Road; new & selected stories
The house that Jane built
  Agee, J. Acts of love on Indigo Road; new & selected stories
How good I am to you
  Agee, J. Acts of love on Indigo Road; new & selected stories
I can't stop loving you
  Agee, J. Acts of love on Indigo Road; new & selected stories
Invisible
  Agee, J. Acts of love on Indigo Road; new & selected stories
The Jesus Barber Shop
  Agee, J. Acts of love on Indigo Road; new & selected stories

Agee, Jonis—*Continued*

The land you claim
> Agee, J. Acts of love on Indigo Road; new & selected stories

The level of my uncertainty
> Agee, J. Acts of love on Indigo Road; new & selected stories
> Agee, J. Taking the wall; stories

Losing downforce
> Agee, J. Acts of love on Indigo Road; new & selected stories
> Agee, J. Taking the wall; stories

The luck of Junior Strong
> Agee, J. Acts of love on Indigo Road; new & selected stories
> Agee, J. Taking the wall; stories

The man in the closet
> Agee, J. Acts of love on Indigo Road; new & selected stories

Mercury
> Agee, J. Acts of love on Indigo Road; new & selected stories

Mile a mud
> Agee, J. Taking the wall; stories

My last try
> Agee, J. Acts of love on Indigo Road; new & selected stories

My mother's hands
> Agee, J. Acts of love on Indigo Road; new & selected stories

Mystery of numbers
> Agee, J. Acts of love on Indigo Road; new & selected stories
> Agee, J. Taking the wall; stories

The October horse
> Agee, J. Acts of love on Indigo Road; new & selected stories

Omaha
> Agee, J. Acts of love on Indigo Road; new & selected stories
> Agee, J. Taking the wall; stories

Once the dogs are sleeping
> Agee, J. Acts of love on Indigo Road; new & selected stories

The only thing different
> Agee, J. Acts of love on Indigo Road; new & selected stories

Over the point of cohesion
> Agee, J. Acts of love on Indigo Road; new & selected stories
> Agee, J. Taking the wall; stories

A pleasant story
> Agee, J. Acts of love on Indigo Road; new & selected stories

The pop off valve
> Agee, J. Taking the wall; stories

The presence of absence
> Agee, J. Acts of love on Indigo Road; new & selected stories

The specific dreams of our republic
> Agee, J. Acts of love on Indigo Road; new & selected stories

Stiller's pond
> Agee, J. Acts of love on Indigo Road; new & selected stories

The suicide who came to visit
> Agee, J. Acts of love on Indigo Road; new & selected stories

The third gravitational pull
> Agee, J. Acts of love on Indigo Road; new & selected stories

This is for Chet
> Agee, J. Acts of love on Indigo Road; new & selected stories

Time only adds to the blame
> Agee, J. Acts of love on Indigo Road; new & selected stories

The tire man
> Agee, J. Acts of love on Indigo Road; new & selected stories

The trouble with the truth
> Agee, J. Acts of love on Indigo Road; new & selected stories
> Agee, J. Taking the wall; stories

The waiting
> Agee, J. Acts of love on Indigo Road; new & selected stories

Was
> Agee, J. Acts of love on Indigo Road; new & selected stories

What I'm doing in Missouri
> Agee, J. Taking the wall; stories

What the Fall brings
> Agee, J. Acts of love on Indigo Road; new & selected stories

What's it take?
> Agee, J. Taking the wall; stories

Winter dreaming
> Agee, J. Acts of love on Indigo Road; new & selected stories

The world. The text. The crime.
> Agee, J. Acts of love on Indigo Road; new & selected stories

You belong to me
> Agee, J. Acts of love on Indigo Road; new & selected stories

You know I am lying
> Agee, J. Acts of love on Indigo Road; new & selected stories
> Agee, J. Taking the wall; stories

Agénor, Monique

The tears of the solitaire
> *The Hudson Review* v54 no3 p371-84 Aut 2001

Agent of the Revolution. Spilman, R.

Agent provocateur. Irvine, A.

AGENTS, SECRET *See* Spies

Aggiornamento. Hochman, A.

Aggravation. Baron, D.

AGING

> *See also* Menopause

Beattie, A. The famous poet, amid Bougainvillea

DeMarinis, R. Borrowed hearts

Galef, D. Butch

Stern, R. G. The illegibility of this world

Updike, J. Killing

AGNES, SAINT, D. 304

> **About**

O'Connell, M. The patron saint of girls

Agnon, Shmuel Yosef

From foe to friend
> Sleepwalkers and other stories; the Arab in Hebrew fiction; edited by Ehud Ben-Ezer

Agnon, Shmuel Yosef—*Continued*
  The night
    When night fell; an anthology of Holocaust
      short stories; edited by Linda Schermer Ra-
      phael and Marc Lee Raphael
  Under the tree
    Sleepwalkers and other stories; the Arab in
      Hebrew fiction; edited by Ehud Ben-Ezer
Agognata. Maleti, G.
Agony column. Malzberg, B. N.
AGORAPHOBIA
  Eldridge, Courtney. Young professionals
  Nailah, A. Deena
AGRICULTURAL LABORERS *See* Farm work-
  ers
Aground and Aloft. Patterson, S.
Agustí, Miguel
  Rebirth [Cain and Abel]
    The World's finest mystery and crime stories,
      second annual collection; edited by Ed
      Gorman
Ahead!. Watson, I.
Ahmadi Khorasani, Nushin
  That day
    A Feast in the mirror; stories by contempo-
      rary Iranian women; translated and edited
      by Mohammad Mehdi Khorrami, Shouleh
      Vatanabadi
Ahuja, Akshay
  Tenanting
    Gettysburg Review v17 no2 p201-15 Summ
      2004
Ai witness. Thornton, K.
Aichinger, Ilse
  Ghosts on the lake
    Nightshade: 20th century ghost stories; edited
      by Robert Phillips
Aickman, Robert
  The cicerones
    Dark: stories of madness, murder, and the su-
      pernatural; edited by Clint Willis
Aida South, flower. Otis, M.
Aidoo, Ama Ata
  A gift from somewhere
    The Art of the story; an international antholo-
      gy of contemporary short stories; edited by
      Daniel Halpern
Aidoo, Christina Ama Ata *See* Aidoo, Ama Ata,
  1942-
AIDS (DISEASE)
  Alameddine, R. Duck
  Alvarez, A. Index card, index finger
  Bouldrey, B. The holy spirit bank
  Brownrigg, S. A gal of ambition
  Carson, M. Peter's buddies
  Carter, E. Ask Amelio
  Carter, E. Glory goes and gets some
  Cooper, B. Between the sheets
  Cooper, B. Exterior decoration
  Cooper, B. Hunters and gatherers
  Currier, J. Pasta night
  Dark, A. E. In the gloaming
  Davies, P. H. On the terraces
  Doenges, J. MIB
  Ebershoff, D. Chuck Paa
  Eldridge, Courtney. Young professionals
  Engel, M. P. Philosophy of education
  Ferriss, L. Rumpelstiltskin
  Fessel, K.-S. Lost faces

Glave, T. The final inning
Groff, D. The third person
Haslett, A. Reunion
Holleran, A. Amsterdam
Holleran, A. Sunday morning: Key West
Horton, H. The year draws in the day
Ingenito-DeSio, L. A really weird thing hap-
  pened recently
Kuhr, J. We're all chicken here
Kurlansky, M. Packets and paperscraps
Leavitt, D. The infection scene
Leegant, J. How to comfort the sick and dying
Marano, M. Burden
McCann, R. The universe, concealed
Morrow, B. "Ciccone youths 1990"
Mueller, D. Ice breaking
Mueller, D. Zero
Newman, D. A. Good news and bad news
Nfah-Abbenyi, J. M. Slow poison
O'Callaghan, M. Black is the color of my true
  love's heart
Ordoña, R. World without end
Peterson, P. W. Africa
Peterson, P. W. Alfie and Grace
Peterson, P. W. The as and is
Peterson, P. W. Big brother
Peterson, P. W. Cherry's ghost
Peterson, P. W. In the grove
Peterson, P. W. A miracle
Peterson, P. W. Song of Camille
Peterson, P. W. The woman in the long green
  coat
Pratt, D. Series
Price, R. An evening meal
Ryan, P. Second island
Sherman, C. W. Touch [excerpt]
Skillings, R. D. At least
Skillings, R. D. God knows
Skillings, R. D. The spiritus step
Skillings, R. D. The throes
Sojourner, M. Bear house
Sontag, S. The way we live now
Verghese, A. Lilacs
Vernon, D. Arrival
Wieland, L. You can sleep while I drive
Aiken, Joan
  Sonata for harp and bicycle
    Nightshade: 20th century ghost stories; edited
      by Robert Phillips
Aikman, Sandra
  Pia
    Dead on demand; the best of ghost story
      weekend; edited by Elizabeth Engstrom
Ailoura. Di Filippo, P.
Air and earth. Goliger, G.
An **air-conditioned** egg. Sammān, G.
AIR CRASHES *See* Airplane accidents
AIR PILOTS The white feather ace
  Arnold, H. H. Bill's first airplane ride
  Barrett, N., Jr. Sallie C.
  Berent, M. Raid on Thud Ridge
  Billman, J. Becky Weed
  Boyne, W. J. Cleveland airport August 1933
  Bradbury, R. Icarus Montgolfier Wright
  Brown, D. Powder River Moe
  Butler, R. O. This is Earl Sandt
  Clarke, A. C. Inheritance
  Coonts, S. Corey Ford buys the farm
  Deighton, L. Hell over Germany

AIR PILOTS—*Continued*

Del Giudice, D. All because of the mistake
Doyle, Sir A. C. The horror of the heights
Earle, S. Jaguar dance
Faulkner, W. All the dead pilots
Forsyth, F. Alone
Gann, E. K. An hour to San Francisco
Gartner, Z. How to survive in the bush
Grau, S. A. Sea change
Harrison, M. LZ ambush
Harrison, P. Zero-G dogfight
Heller, J. Chief White Halfoat
Hersey, J. The raid
Hunter, J. D. For want of a Fokker
Kittredge, W. Agriculture
Krouse, E. Too big to float
L'Amour, L. Coast patrol
L'Amour, L. Flight to the north
L'Amour, L. Wings over Brazil
L'Amour, L. Wings over Khabarovsk
LaSalle, P. A guide to some small border airports
Menendez, A. The last rescue
Michener, J. A. The milk run
Vasseur, T. J. Noonan
Yeates, V. M. Learning to fly

AIR RAID SHELTERS

Smolens, J. My one and only bomb shelter

AIR SHIPS *See* Airships

AIR TRAVEL

Gellhorn, M. Miami—New York
Nevins, F. M., Jr. Fair game

AIR WARFARE *See* Military aeronautics; World War, 1914-1918—Aerial operations; World War, 1939-1945—Aerial operations

AIRLINES

See also Airports
An **airman's** goodbye. DeMarinis, R.

AIRMEN *See* Air pilots

Airplane. Murakami, H.

AIRPLANE ACCIDENTS

Agee, J. The waiting
Butler, R. O. This is Earl Sandt
Engstrom, E. Riding the black horse
Grau, S. A. Hunter
Irsfeld, J. H. Finderkeepers
Leavitt, D. Black box
Morgan, R. The balm of Gilead tree
Schwartz, S. Afterbirth

AIRPLANES

Aylett, S. The passenger
Boyle, T. C. Friendly skies
Brockmeier, K. The passenger
Davenport, G. The aeroplanes at Brescia
Davis, L. J. Cowboys don't cry [excerpt]
Howard, C. Out of control
Irsfeld, J. H. The man who watched airplanes
Jong, E. En route to the congress of dreams; or, The zipless fuck
Keret, E. Jetlag
Klíma, I. Uranus in the house of death
Moline, K. No parachutes

Accidents

See Airplane accidents

Pilots

See Air pilots

AIRPORTS

Fawcett, B. Soul walker
Irsfeld, J. H. The man who watched airplanes

McBain, E. Terminal misunderstanding
Ponte, A. J. Because of men
Shaw, D. Holding pattern at D.C. National
Silvera, M. Caribbean chameleon

AIRSHIPS

Clarke, A. C. A meeting with Medusa

Aitken, Maureen

Bigfoot
Prairie Schooner v77 no2 p73-4 Summ 2003

Aiyejina, Funso

The one-handed hero
The Anchor book of modern African stories; edited by Nadežda Obradovic ; with a foreword by Chinua Achebe

Aizley, Harlyn

Harry at Crossroads
South Carolina Review v33 no2 p71-5 Spr 2001

Aizman, David

Countrymen: A Story
Commentary v115 no6 p30-40 Je 2003

Ajax Is All about Attack. Shepard, J.

Akens, Floyd *See* Baum, L. Frank (Lyman Frank), 1856-1919

AKHENATON, KING OF EGYPT, FL. CA. 1388-1358 B.C.

About

Horizon

Aki. Tomlinson, N. C.

Akins, Ellen

A matter of days before the collapse
The Georgia Review v53 no4 p757-74 Wint 1999

Akunin, Boris and others

The Man in the Back Row Has a Question: VIII
The Paris Review v44 p237-55 Wint 2002

Al-Shaykh, Hanan

The keeper of the virgins
The Art of the story; an international anthology of contemporary short stories; edited by Daniel Halpern

ALABAMA

Barthelme, F. Instructor
Bisson, T. The edge of the universe
Capote, T. A Christmas memory
Capote, T. My side of the matter
Capote, T. One Christmas
Capote, T. The Thanksgiving visitor
Erickson, Ben. Floundering
Fitzgerald, F. S. Two for a cent
Formichella, Joe. Lomax's trials
Franklin, T. Blue horses
Franklin, T. Dinosaurs
Franklin, T. Grit
Franklin, T. Poachers
Kiernan, C. R. In the water works (Birmingham, Alabama 1888)
Knight, M. A bad man, so pretty
Knight, M. Birdland
Knight, M. Gerald's monkey
Knight, M. The man who went out for cigarettes
Knight, M. Sleeping with my dog
Mencken, S. H. Alabama April

Farm life

See Farm life—Alabama

Mobile

Richmond, M. The last bad thing

ALABAMA—*Continued*
Montgomery
Mencken, S. H. Joe Moore and Callie Blasingame
Alabama April. Mencken, S. H.
Alameddine, Rabih
The changing room
  Alameddine, R. The perv; stories
Duck
  Alameddine, R. The perv; stories
A flight to Paris
  Alameddine, R. The perv; stories
Grace
  Alameddine, R. The perv; stories
My grandmother, the grandmaster
  Alameddine, R. The perv; stories
The perv
  Alameddine, R. The perv; stories
Remembering Nasser
  Alameddine, R. The perv; stories
Whore
  Alameddine, R. The perv; stories
ALAMO (SAN ANTONIO, TEX.)
Siege, 1836
Breen, J. V. A man alone
Gonzalez, R. The ghost of John Wayne
Alarcón, Daniel
City of Clowns
  The New Yorker v79 no16 p156-65, 167-9 Je 16-23 2003
Lima, Peru, July 28, 1979
  The Virginia Quarterly Review v80 no3 p4-13 Summ 2004
Alarcón, Pedro Antonio de
Captain Poison
  Alarcón, P. A. d. The nun and other stories; translated from the Spanish by Robert M. Fedorchek; introduction by Stephen Miller
"Death's friend"
  Fedorchek, R. M. Stories of enchantment from nineteenth-century Spain; translated from the Spanish by Robert M. Fredorchek; introduction by Alan E. Smith
Moors and Christians
  Alarcón, P. A. d. The nun and other stories; translated from the Spanish by Robert M. Fedorchek; introduction by Stephen Miller
The nun
  Alarcón, P. A. d. The nun and other stories; translated from the Spanish by Robert M. Fedorchek; introduction by Stephen Miller
The tall woman
  Alarcón, P. A. d. The nun and other stories; translated from the Spanish by Robert M. Fedorchek; introduction by Stephen Miller
Alarm. Polansky, S.
Alas, Leopoldo
The burial of the sardine
  Alas, L. Ten tales; translated from the Spanish by Robert M. Fedorchek; introduction by John W. Kronik
Change of light
  Alas, L. Ten tales; translated from the Spanish by Robert M. Fedorchek; introduction by John W. Kronik
A day laborer
  Alas, L. Ten tales; translated from the Spanish by Robert M. Fedorchek; introduction by John W. Kronik

Doña Berta
  Alas, L. Ten tales; translated from the Spanish by Robert M. Fedorchek; introduction by John W. Kronik
The golden rose
  Alas, L. Ten tales; translated from the Spanish by Robert M. Fedorchek; introduction by John W. Kronik
The lord
  Alas, L. Ten tales; translated from the Spanish by Robert M. Fedorchek; introduction by John W. Kronik
"My funeral"
  Fedorchek, R. M. Stories of enchantment from nineteenth-century Spain; translated from the Spanish by Robert M. Fredorchek; introduction by Alan E. Smith
Queen Margaret
  Alas, L. Ten tales; translated from the Spanish by Robert M. Fedorchek; introduction by John W. Kronik
"Socrates' rooster"
  Fedorchek, R. M. Stories of enchantment from nineteenth-century Spain; translated from the Spanish by Robert M. Fredorchek; introduction by Alan E. Smith
Torso
  Alas, L. Ten tales; translated from the Spanish by Robert M. Fedorchek; introduction by John W. Kronik
The two boxes
  Alas, L. Ten tales; translated from the Spanish by Robert M. Fedorchek; introduction by John W. Kronik
Two scholars
  Alas, L. Ten tales; translated from the Spanish by Robert M. Fedorchek; introduction by John W. Kronik
ALASKA
Beach, R. The weight of obligation
Boyle, T. C. Termination dust
Carlson, R. Blazo
Harrison, H. Rock diver
Kittredge, W. Do you hear your mother talking?
Lord, N. Afterlife
Lord, N. The census taker
Lord, N. The man who swam with beavers
Lord, N. Recall of the wild
Lord, N. The woman who would marry a bear
Mueller, D. The night my brother worked the header
Porter, J. A. Naufrage and diapason
Reid, E. Laura Borealis
Reid, E. What salmon know
Frontier and pioneer life
  See Frontier and pioneer life—Alaska
Anchorage
Doogan, M. War can be murder
Alaska. Adams, A.
Alaska. Franklin, T.
Alavi, Tahereh
Disappearance of an ordinary woman
  A Feast in the mirror; stories by contemporary Iranian women; translated and edited by Mohammad Mehdi Khorrami, Shouleh Vatanabadi
ALBANIANS
Italy
Maraini, D. Viollca, the child from Albania

ALBANY (N.Y.) *See* New York (State)—Albany
Albatross. Billman, J.
The **Alberscine's** vigil. Strauch, T. J.
Albert, Jack
  Byron
    Cat crimes through time; edited by Ed
    Gorman, Martin H. Greenberg, and Larry
    Segriff
Albert, Susan Wittig
  Bloom where you're planted
    Albert, S. W. An unthymely death and other
    garden mysteries
  A deadly chocolate valentine
    Albert, S. W. An unthymely death and other
    garden mysteries
  Death of a Rose Rustler
    Albert, S. W. An unthymely death and other
    garden mysteries
  Ivy's wild, wonderful weeds
    Albert, S. W. An unthymely death and other
    garden mysteries
  The knat who became a hero
    Albert, S. W. An unthymely death and other
    garden mysteries
  Mustard madness
    Albert, S. W. An unthymely death and other
    garden mysteries
  The pennyroyal plot
    Albert, S. W. An unthymely death and other
    garden mysteries
  The Rosemary caper
    Albert, S. W. An unthymely death and other
    garden mysteries
  An unthymely death
    Albert, S. W. An unthymely death and other
    garden mysteries
  A violet death
    Albert, S. W. An unthymely death and other
    garden mysteries
Albert Bert and Andy. Emin, T.
ALBERTA *See* Canada—Alberta
The **Albright** Kid. Lee, M.
Albritton, Laura
  At Least It's Free
    The Literary Review (Madison, N.J.) v46 no1
    p25-30 Fall 2002
ALBUQUERQUE (N.M.) *See* New Mexico—Albuquerque
Alcalá, Kathleen J.
  Altar
    Fantasmas; supernatural stories by Mexican
    American writers; edited by Rob Johnson;
    introduction by Kathleen J. Alcalá
Alcántara Almánzar, José
  He and she at the end of an afternoon
    Callaloo v24 no4 p955-9 Fall 2001
  My singular Irene
    Callaloo v24 no2 p384-8 Spr 2001
Alcatraz. Erian, A.
Alcestis. Reynolds, A.
Alchemy. Thien, M.
ALCIBIADES, CA. 450-404 B.C.
About
  Rucker, R. v. B. The square root of Pythagoras
ALCOHOLICS *See* Alcoholism; Drunkards
ALCOHOLISM
  See also Drunkards
  Adams, A. Beautiful girl
  Addonizio, K. Gaps

Addonizio, K. Testimony
Allen, D., Jr. End of the steam age
Baida, P. The rodent
Bausch, R. Luck
Bausch, R. Self knowledge
Bellow, S. Leaving the yellow house
Berry, W. Thicker than liquor
Braverman, K. Tall tales from the Mekong Delta
Braverman, K. Temporary light
Brown, J. Afterlife
Brown, J. Detox
Brown, J. Sadness of the body
Brownstein, G. The speedboat
Bukoski, A. Pesthouse
Calisher, H. In Greenwich, there are many gravelled walks
Callaghan, M. Absolution
Carter, E. A
Carver, R. Kindling
Carver, R. Where I'm calling from
Chaon, D. The bees
Chekhov, A. P. "Anna on the neck"
Cohen, S. Just another New York Christmas story
Connor, J. October
Crumley, J. Whores
Cummins, A. Bitterwater
Daniels, J. Sugar water
Davidson, R. Body work
Davidson, R. Maintenance
Davies, R. A human condition
Davies, Tristan. A night dive
Davis, L. Cat's out of the bag
DeMarco, T. Lieutenant America and Miss Apple Pie
DeMarinis, R. The Voice of America
Doenges, J. What she left me
Doolittle, S. Summa mathematica
Eldridge, Courtney. Unkempt
Estep, M. Animals
Franklin, T. The ballad of Duane Juarez
Gautreaux, T. Good for the soul
Gilchrist, E. The stucco house
Gilchrist, E. Traceleen at dawn
Gordon, C. The petrified woman
Gunn, K. Jesus, I know that guy
Hall, D. The accident
Hannah, B. Death and joy
Hood, A. Total cave darkness
Jakes, J. Tex
Kane, J. F. Evidence of old repairs
Kelman, J. The comfort
Kelman, J. Every fucking time
Koja, K. Road trip
Lankford, T. Detour Drive
Lida, D. Shuttered
López, L. Soy la Avon lady
Lustbader, E. V. An exaltation of termagants
Mazelis, J. Forbidden
McBrearty, R. G. The hellraiser
McCorkle, J. Intervention
McManus, J. Die like a lobster
McManus, J. The future is orange
McManus, J. Reaffirmation
Melville, P. Don't give me your sad stories
Meredith, D. Comic Valentine
Morrow, B. Lush
Nakagami, K. House on fire

ALCOHOLISM—*Continued*

Nesbitt, M. Man in towel with gun

Nesbitt, M. What good is you anyway?

Offutt, C. Barred owl

Padilla, M. Flora in shadows

Phillips, D. R. At the edge of the new world

Phillips, D. R. My people's waltz

Phillips, D. R. The woods at the back of our houses

Podolsky, R. Memory like ash borne on air

Reach, A. S. In the confessional

Reid, E. All that good stuff

Reid, E. Buffalo

Richter, S. The ocean

Rinehart, S. Kick in the head

Rodgers, S. J. The two husbands

Schmidt, H. J. Out of Purmort

Silva, D. B. Dry whiskey

Singleton, G. Dialectic, abrasions, the backs of heads again

Skillings, R. D. Job ops

Slavin, J. Rare is a cold red center

Sojourner, M. Huevos

Spencer, D. Please to forgive sloppiness

Stanton, M. How to converse in Italian

Stegner, L. Hired man

Thien, M. Four days from Oregon

Thien, M. House

Troy, M. Tulipville

Udall, B. Buckeye the elder

Vasseur, T. J. Noonan

Wellen, E. Hangover

Werve, S. If I were lemon pie

Wheat, C. Ghost Station

Williams, J. The farm

Wolven, S. The copper kings

Yoshimoto, B. Love songs

Alcott, Louisa May

Agatha's confession

    Alcott, L. M. The early stories of Louisa May Alcott, 1852-1860; with an introduction by Monika Elbert

Bertha

    Alcott, L. M. The early stories of Louisa May Alcott, 1852-1860; with an introduction by Monika Elbert

Bertie's box: a Christmas story

    Alcott, L. M. The uncollected works of Louisa May Alcott; v1 Short stories; with an introduction by Monika Elbert

Bonfires

    Alcott, L. M. The uncollected works of Louisa May Alcott; v1 Short stories; with an introduction by Monika Elbert

The cross on the church tower

    Alcott, L. M. The early stories of Louisa May Alcott, 1852-1860; with an introduction by Monika Elbert

The eaglet in the dove's nest

    Alcott, L. M. The uncollected works of Louisa May Alcott; v1 Short stories; with an introduction by Monika Elbert

A golden wedding: and what came of it

    Alcott, L. M. The uncollected works of Louisa May Alcott; v1 Short stories; with an introduction by Monika Elbert

Grandmama's pearls

    Alcott, L. M. The uncollected works of Louisa May Alcott; v1 Short stories; with an introduction by Monika Elbert

John Marlow's victory

    Alcott, L. M. The uncollected works of Louisa May Alcott; v1 Short stories; with an introduction by Monika Elbert

The lady and the woman

    Alcott, L. M. The early stories of Louisa May Alcott, 1852-1860; with an introduction by Monika Elbert

A little Cinderella

    Alcott, L. M. The uncollected works of Louisa May Alcott; v1 Short stories; with an introduction by Monika Elbert

Little Genevieve

    Alcott, L. M. The early stories of Louisa May Alcott, 1852-1860; with an introduction by Monika Elbert

Little Robin

    Alcott, L. M. The uncollected works of Louisa May Alcott; v1 Short stories; with an introduction by Monika Elbert

The little seed

    Alcott, L. M. The early stories of Louisa May Alcott, 1852-1860; with an introduction by Monika Elbert

Little sunbeam

    Alcott, L. M. The early stories of Louisa May Alcott, 1852-1860; with an introduction by Monika Elbert

Lost in a pyramid; or, The Mummy's Curse

    Alcott, L. M. The uncollected works of Louisa May Alcott; v1 Short stories; with an introduction by Monika Elbert

    Into the mummy's tomb; edited by John Richard Stephens

Love and self-love

    Alcott, L. M. The early stories of Louisa May Alcott, 1852-1860; with an introduction by Monika Elbert

Mabel's May day

    Alcott, L. M. The early stories of Louisa May Alcott, 1852-1860; with an introduction by Monika Elbert

Marion Earle; or, Only an actress!

    Alcott, L. M. The early stories of Louisa May Alcott, 1852-1860; with an introduction by Monika Elbert

Mark Field's mistake

    Alcott, L. M. The early stories of Louisa May Alcott, 1852-1860; with an introduction by Monika Elbert

Mark Field's success

    Alcott, L. M. The early stories of Louisa May Alcott, 1852-1860; with an introduction by Monika Elbert

The masked marriage

    Alcott, L. M. The early stories of Louisa May Alcott, 1852-1860; with an introduction by Monika Elbert

Milly's messenger

    Alcott, L. M. The uncollected works of Louisa May Alcott; v1 Short stories; with an introduction by Monika Elbert

Alcott, Louisa May—*Continued*

The monk's island: a legend of the Rhine
  Alcott, L. M. The early stories of Louisa May Alcott, 1852-1860; with an introduction by Monika Elbert

Mother's trial
  Alcott, L. M. The uncollected works of Louisa May Alcott; v1 Short stories; with an introduction by Monika Elbert

Mrs. Gay's hint, and how it was taken
  Alcott, L. M. The uncollected works of Louisa May Alcott; v1 Short stories; with an introduction by Monika Elbert

Mrs. Gay's prescription
  Alcott, L. M. The uncollected works of Louisa May Alcott; v1 Short stories; with an introduction by Monika Elbert

A New Year's blessing
  Alcott, L. M. The early stories of Louisa May Alcott, 1852-1860; with an introduction by Monika Elbert

Number eleven
  Alcott, L. M. The uncollected works of Louisa May Alcott; v1 Short stories; with an introduction by Monika Elbert

A pair of eyes; or, Modern magic
  Witches' brew; edited by Yvonne Jocks

The rival painters: a tale of Rome
  Alcott, L. M. The early stories of Louisa May Alcott, 1852-1860; with an introduction by Monika Elbert

The rival prima donnas
  Alcott, L. M. The early stories of Louisa May Alcott, 1852-1860; with an introduction by Monika Elbert

Rosy's journey
  The American fantasy tradition; edited by Brian M. Thomsen

Ruth's secret
  Alcott, L. M. The early stories of Louisa May Alcott, 1852-1860; with an introduction by Monika Elbert

Lu Sing
  Alcott, L. M. The uncollected works of Louisa May Alcott; v1 Short stories; with an introduction by Monika Elbert

The sisters' trial
  Alcott, L. M. The early stories of Louisa May Alcott, 1852-1860; with an introduction by Monika Elbert

Uncles Smiley's boys
  Alcott, L. M. The uncollected works of Louisa May Alcott; v1 Short stories; with an introduction by Monika Elbert

Victoria: a woman's statue
  Alcott, L. M. The uncollected works of Louisa May Alcott; v1 Short stories; with an introduction by Monika Elbert

Alderete, Pat

Fire
  Hers 3: brilliant new fiction by lesbian writers; edited by Terry Wolverton with Robert Drake

Victor the Bear
  Hers 2: brilliant new fiction by lesbian writers; edited by Terry Wolverton with Robert Drake

Aldiss, Brian Wilson

Apogee again
  Aldiss, B. W. Supertoys last all summer long; and other stories of future time

Becoming the full butterfly
  Aldiss, B. W. Supertoys last all summer long; and other stories of future time

Beef
  Aldiss, B. W. Supertoys last all summer long; and other stories of future time

Cognitive ability and the light bulb
  Aldiss, B. W. Supertoys last all summer long; and other stories of future time

Dark society
  Aldiss, B. W. Supertoys last all summer long; and other stories of future time

Galaxy Zee
  Aldiss, B. W. Supertoys last all summer long; and other stories of future time

Headless
  Aldiss, B. W. Supertoys last all summer long; and other stories of future time

III
  Aldiss, B. W. Supertoys last all summer long; and other stories of future time

Judas danced
  Nebula awards showcase 2001; the year's best SF and fantasy chosen by the science fiction and fantasy writers of America; edited by Robert Silverberg

A kind of artistry
  The Good old stuff; adventure SF in the grand tradition; edited by Gardner Dozois

Marvells of Utopia
  Aldiss, B. W. Supertoys last all summer long; and other stories of future time

A matter of mathematics
  Aldiss, B. W. Supertoys last all summer long; and other stories of future time

Near earth object
  Mars probes; edited by Peter Crowther

Nothing in life is ever enough
  Aldiss, B. W. Supertoys last all summer long; and other stories of future time

The old mythology
  Aldiss, B. W. Supertoys last all summer long; and other stories of future time

The pause button
  Aldiss, B. W. Supertoys last all summer long; and other stories of future time

Steppenpferd
  Aldiss, B. W. Supertoys last all summer long; and other stories of future time

Supertoys in other seasons
  Aldiss, B. W. Supertoys last all summer long; and other stories of future time

Supertoys last all summer long
  Aldiss, B. W. Supertoys last all summer long; and other stories of future time

Supertoys when winter comes
  Aldiss, B. W. Supertoys last all summer long; and other stories of future time

Three types of solitude
  Aldiss, B. W. Supertoys last all summer long; and other stories of future time

A whiter Mars
  Aldiss, B. W. Supertoys last all summer long; and other stories of future time

Aldiss, Brian Wilson—*Continued*
Who can replace a man?
  Masterpieces: the best science fiction of the century; edited by Orson Scott Card
Aldrich, Bess Streeter
Across the smiling meadow
  Aldrich, B. S. The collected short works, 1920-1954; edited and introduced by Carol Miles Petersen
Alma, meaning "To cherish"
  Aldrich, B. S. The collected short works, 1920-1954; edited and introduced by Carol Miles Petersen
The day of retaliation
  Aldrich, B. S. The collected short works, 1920-1954; edited and introduced by Carol Miles Petersen
Ginger cookies
  Aldrich, B. S. The collected short works, 1920-1954; edited and introduced by Carol Miles Petersen
The great wide world of men
  Aldrich, B. S. The collected short works, 1920-1954; edited and introduced by Carol Miles Petersen
He whom a dream hath possest
  Aldrich, B. S. The collected short works, 1920-1954; edited and introduced by Carol Miles Petersen
The heirs
  Aldrich, B. S. The collected short works, 1920-1954; edited and introduced by Carol Miles Petersen
How far is it to Hollywood?
  Aldrich, B. S. The collected short works, 1920-1954; edited and introduced by Carol Miles Petersen
It's never too late to live
  Aldrich, B. S. The collected short works, 1920-1954; edited and introduced by Carol Miles Petersen
Juno's swans
  Aldrich, B. S. The collected short works, 1920-1954; edited and introduced by Carol Miles Petersen
Last night when you kissed Blanche Thompson
  Aldrich, B. S. The collected short works, 1920-1954; edited and introduced by Carol Miles Petersen
The man who caught the weather
  Aldrich, B. S. The collected short works, 1920-1954; edited and introduced by Carol Miles Petersen
The man who dreaded to go home
  Aldrich, B. S. The collected short works, 1920-1954; edited and introduced by Carol Miles Petersen
The outsider
  Aldrich, B. S. The collected short works, 1920-1954; edited and introduced by Carol Miles Petersen
Pie
  Aldrich, B. S. The collected short works, 1920-1954; edited and introduced by Carol Miles Petersen
Romance in G minor
  Aldrich, B. S. The collected short works, 1920-1954; edited and introduced by Carol Miles Petersen

The runaway judge
  Aldrich, B. S. The collected short works, 1920-1954; edited and introduced by Carol Miles Petersen
Trust the Irish for that
  Aldrich, B. S. The collected short works, 1920-1954; edited and introduced by Carol Miles Petersen
The victory of Connie Lee
  Aldrich, B. S. The collected short works, 1920-1954; edited and introduced by Carol Miles Petersen
The weakling
  Aldrich, B. S. The collected short works, 1920-1954; edited and introduced by Carol Miles Petersen
Welcome home, Hal!
  Aldrich, B. S. The collected short works, 1920-1954; edited and introduced by Carol Miles Petersen
What God hath joined
  Aldrich, B. S. The collected short works, 1920-1954; edited and introduced by Carol Miles Petersen
Will the romance be the same?
  Aldrich, B. S. The collected short works, 1920-1954; edited and introduced by Carol Miles Petersen
The woman who was forgotten
  Aldrich, B. S. The collected short works, 1920-1954; edited and introduced by Carol Miles Petersen
Aldrich, Marcia
Life #5
  The North American Review v284 no5 p22 S/O 1999
Aleichem, Sholem *See* Sholem Aleichem, 1859-1916
The **aleph**. Borges, J. L.
Alessio, Carolyn
Casualidades
  TriQuarterly no110/111 p363-71 Fall 2001
Currency
  TriQuarterly no118 p27-40 Wint 2004
Alessio, Carolyn
Casualidades
  Pushcart prize XXVII; best of the small presses; edited by Bill Henderson with the Pushcart prize editors
ALEUTS
Mueller, D. The night my brother worked the header
Alexander, Andrew
Little bitty pretty one
  New stories from the South: the year's best, 1999; edited by Shannon Ravenel; with a preface by Tony Earley
Alexander, David
Conversations with the Doge of Venice
  The Literary Review (Madison, N.J.) v42 no3 p470-80 Spr 1999
Alexander, Eitan
Beneath the planet of the compulsives
  Circa 2000; gay fiction at the millennium; edited by Robert Drake & Terry Wolverton
Alexander the bait. Tenn, W.
Alexandre's wonderful experience. Chopin, K.

Alexie, Sherman
Assimilation
  Alexie, S. The toughest Indian in the world
Because my father always said he was the only
  Indian who saw Jimi Hendrix play "The
  Star-Spangled Banner" at Woodstock
  Fault lines; stories of divorce; collected and
  edited by Caitlin Shetterly
Can I get a witness?
  Alexie, S. Ten little Indians; stories
Class
  Alexie, S. The toughest Indian in the world
Dear John Wayne
  Alexie, S. The toughest Indian in the world
Do not go gentle
  Alexie, S. Ten little Indians; stories
Do you know where I am?
  Alexie, S. Ten little Indians; stories
Flight patterns
  Alexie, S. Ten little Indians; stories
Ghost dance
  McSweeney's mammoth treasury of thrilling
  tales; edited by Michael Chabon
Indian country
  Alexie, S. The toughest Indian in the world
Lawyer's League
  Alexie, S. Ten little Indians; stories
The life and times of Estelle Walks Above
  Alexie, S. Ten little Indians; stories
One good man
  Alexie, S. The toughest Indian in the world
Saint Junior
  Alexie, S. The toughest Indian in the world
The search engine
  Alexie, S. Ten little Indians; stories
The sin eaters
  Alexie, S. The toughest Indian in the world
South by Southwest
  Alexie, S. The toughest Indian in the world
This is what it means to say Phoenix, Arizona
  The Scribner anthology of contemporary short
  fiction; fifty North American stories since
  1970; Lex Williford and Michael Martone,
  editors
The toughest Indian in the world
  Alexie, S. The toughest Indian in the world
  The New Yorker v75 no16 p96+ Je 21-28
  1999
What ever happened to Frank Snake Church?
  Alexie, S. Ten little Indians; stories
What you pawn I will redeem
  Alexie, S. Ten little Indians; stories
  The New Yorker v79 no9 p168-77 Ap 21-28
  2003
Alexis, André
Despair: five stories of Ottawa
  Alexis, A. Despair and other stories
Horse
  Alexis, A. Despair and other stories
Kuala Lumpur
  Alexis, A. Despair and other stories
Metaphysics of morals
  Alexis, A. Despair and other stories
My Anabasis
  Alexis, A. Despair and other stories
The night piece
  Alexis, A. Despair and other stories
The road to Santiago de Compostela
  Alexis, A. Despair and other stories

The third terrace
  Alexis, A. Despair and other stories
Alger, Derek
Remembering the Rain
  The Literary Review (Madison, N.J.) v46 no1
  p59-68 Fall 2002
ALGERIA
  Bowles, P. He of the assembly
  Bowles, P. The time of friendship
Algren, Nelson
He swung and he missed
  Boxing's best short stories; edited by Paul D.
  Staudohar
Ali, Agha Shahid
  (jt. auth) See Heller, Yehudit Ben-Zvi
Ali, Monica
Dinner with Dr Azad
  Granta no81 p33-46 Spr 2003
Alias. Blackwood, S.
Alias Eleanor Roosevelt. Goran, L.
The **Alibi** Café. Troy, M.
ALIBIS
  Reiner, C. The people versus De Marco
Alice & Jesse. Nailah, A.
Alice and me. Bocock, M.
Alice opens the box. Mina, D.
Alice, rolling down the mountainside. Hurley, V.
Alice's ground. Cohen, M.
Alice's Soulbath. Butler, L. P.
Alicetta. Maraini, D.
Aliceville. Earley, T.
Alien love. Kilpatrick, N.
The **alien** machine. Jones, R. F.
ALIENATION (SOCIAL PSYCHOLOGY)
  See also Social isolation
  Arvin, N. Electric fence
  Reifler, N. Rascal
ALIENS, ILLEGAL *See* Undocumented aliens
ALIENS, UNDOCUMENTED *See* Undocument-
  ed aliens
Aliens. DeMarinis, R.
Aliens in the garden. Blake, J. C.
Alighieri, Dante *See* Dante Alighieri, 1265-1321
Alipio's kingdom. Arenas, R.
Alishan, Leonardo
The Belgian Governor and the Drunk
  Prairie Schooner v78 no1 p166-8 Spr 2004
The Black City
  Prairie Schooner v78 no1 p168-9 Spr 2004
Outside The Crowded Bus
  Prairie Schooner v78 no1 p164-6 Spr 2004
Alistair, James *See* Goligorsky, Eduardo, 1931-
Alive. Ha Jin
Alive, Alive-oh!. Athill, D.
All assassins. Malzberg, B. N.
All Aunt Hagar's Children. Jones, E. P.
All because of the mistake. Del Giudice, D.
All cats are gray. Norton, A.
All clear. Weihe, E.
All Cretans. Galef, D.
All day sun. Brandt, W.
All for sale. Campbell, R.
All God's children can dance. Murakami, H.
All Gold Cañon. See London, J. All Gold Canyon
All Gold Canyon. London, J.
All Her Dreams. Ellis, M. M.
All his sons. Raphael, F.
All in the telling. Dyson, J.
All Life's Grandeur. Kalotay, D.

All Saints Day. Pneuman, A.

All shall love me and despair. Thompson, J.

All Souls'. Wharton, E.

All summer in a day. Bradbury, R.

All Sweet Things Float. Mon Pere, C.

All that believe that, stand on their head!. Drake, R.

All that glitters. Hess, J.

All that good stuff. Reid, E.

All that may become a man. Auchincloss, L.

All that you love will be carried away. King, S.

All that's left. Lincoln, C.

All the birds of hell. Lee, T.

All the little loved ones. Rose, D.

All the men are called McCabe. Carter, E.

All the myriad ways. Niven, L.

All the nights of the world. Cavell, B.

All the rivers in the world. Murray, J.

All the time in the world. Clarke, A. C.

All the time in the world. Sneve, V. D. H.

All the Trimmings. Richard, M.

All the water in the world. Haake, K.

All the way. Miner, V.

All the years of her life. Callaghan, M.

All their secrets. Gilliland, G.

All these condemned. Gorman, E.

All this land. Haake, K.

All through the House. Coake, C.

All tomorrow's parties. McAuley, P. J.

All under one roof. Drake, R.

All-you-can-eat night. Bonnie, F.

"**All** you zombies—". Heinlein, R. A.

Allaback, Steven

Seal Territory

The North American Review v288 no5 p27-9 S/O 2003

Allal. Bowles, P.

Allan, John B.

For works written by this author under other names see Westlake, Donald E.

Allan, M. C.

Turtle

The Virginia Quarterly Review v78 no2 p256-66 Spr 2002

ALLEGORIES

See also Fables; Fantasies; Good and evil; Parables; Symbolism

Agnon, S. Y. From foe to friend

Alcott, L. M. The little seed

Alexie, S. The sin eaters

Allen, L. In the beginning

Anderson, P. Goat song

Appelfeld, A. In the isles of St. George

Biguenet, J. A plague of toads

Bocock, M. La humanidad

Bowles, P. The garden

Bradbury, R. Chrysalis

Bradbury, R. Death and the maiden

Buchan, J. Sleepwalkers

Chaudhuri, A. Confession of a sacrifice

Connor, J. Adam and Eve at the automat

Dumas, H. The eagle the dove and the blackbird

Englander, N. The tumblers

Galloway, J. Tourists from the south arrive in the independent state

Gordimer, N. Look-alikes

Hawthorne, N. The celestial railroad

Hawthorne, N. Egotism; or, The bosom serpent

Hawthorne, N. The great stone face

Hawthorne, N. The Maypole of Merry Mount

Hawthorne, N. The procession of life

Hejazi, K. Cling to life with your whole body

Hendel, Y. Small change

Kalfus, K. Salt

Lawrence, D. H. The man who loved islands

Le Guin, U. K. The ones who walk away from Omelas

McCann, C. Fishing the sloe-black river

Okri, B. What the tapster saw

Schulze, I. The ring

Shepley, J. A golem in Prague

Singer, I. B. Shiddah and Kuziba

Tran, V. The dragon hunt

Updike, J. The invention of the horse collar

Weldon, F. A hard time to be a father

Wolfe, G. The sailor who sailed after the sun

Allegra, Donna

The birthday presence

Allegra, D. Witness to the league of blond hip hop dancers; a novella and short stories

Bread from a stone

Allegra, D. Witness to the league of blond hip hop dancers; a novella and short stories

Dance of the cranes

Allegra, D. Witness to the league of blond hip hop dancers; a novella and short stories

Hers 2: brilliant new fiction by lesbian writers; edited by Terry Wolverton with Robert Drake

Einbahnstrasse

Allegra, D. Witness to the league of blond hip hop dancers; a novella and short stories

God lies in the details

Allegra, D. Witness to the league of blond hip hop dancers; a novella and short stories

In a pig's eye

Allegra, D. Witness to the league of blond hip hop dancers; a novella and short stories

Low-impact aerobics

Allegra, D. Witness to the league of blond hip hop dancers; a novella and short stories

Me and Mrs. Jones

Allegra, D. Witness to the league of blond hip hop dancers; a novella and short stories

The moon in cancer

Allegra, D. Witness to the league of blond hip hop dancers; a novella and short stories

Hers 3: brilliant new fiction by lesbian writers; edited by Terry Wolverton with Robert Drake

Navigating by stars

Allegra, D. Witness to the league of blond hip hop dancers; a novella and short stories

Sacrament in the wind and the storm

Allegra, D. Witness to the league of blond hip hop dancers; a novella and short stories

Snatched

Allegra, D. Witness to the league of blond hip hop dancers; a novella and short stories

Witness to the league of blond hip hop dancers

Allegra, D. Witness to the league of blond hip hop dancers; a novella and short stories

Allegro marcato. Malzberg, B. N.

Allen, Celeste

Last Chance Gravity Fill Station

Such a pretty face; edited by Lee Martindale

Allen, Dwight, Jr.
Among the missing
New England Review v20 no1 p159-72 Wint 1999
Deferment
Home and beyond; an anthology of Kentucky short stories; edited by Morris Allen Grubbs; with an introduction by Wade Hall and an afterword by Charles E. May
End of the steam age
New stories from the South: the year's best, 2002; edited by Shannon Ravenel; with a preface by Larry Brown
Succor
The Georgia Review v53 no1 p33-52 Spr 1999
Allen, Ed
A Foolish but Lovable Airport
The Antioch Review v61 no4 p692-700 Fall 2003
Allen, Henry W., 1912-1991
For works by this author under other names see Henry, Will, 1912-1991
Allen, Jeffery Renard
Bread and the Land
The Antioch Review v61 no4 p650-71 Fall 2003
Dog tags
Bomb no80 p98-102 Summ 2002
Holding Pattern
The Literary Review (Madison, N.J.) v46 no4 p590-616 Summ 2003
Liberty, equality, fraternity
African American Review v36 no1 p73-90 Spr 2002
Shadowboxing
Ploughshares v28 no2/3 p8-18 Fall 2002
Toilet training
The Antioch Review v59 no4 p700-17 Fall 2001
Allen, Lillian
In the beginning
Whispers from the cotton tree root; Caribbean fabulist fiction; edited by Nalo Hopkinson
Allen, Roberta
The one-armed man
The Ohio Review no60 p151-52 1999
Allen, Stephanie
Behind the black curtain
Allen, S. A place between stations; stories
Carved in vinyl
Allen, S. A place between stations; stories
Close to the body
Allen, S. A place between stations; stories
Keep looking
Allen, S. A place between stations; stories
Marisol's things
Allen, S. A place between stations; stories
Mud show
Allen, S. A place between stations; stories
Passage
Allen, S. A place between stations; stories
A place between stations
Allen, S. A place between stations; stories
Souvenir
Allen, S. A place between stations; stories
The Massachusetts Review v42 no3 p345-66 Aut 2001

Yearbook
Allen, S. A place between stations; stories
Allen, Woody
Retribution
The Best of The Kenyon review; edited by David Lynn; introduction by Joyce Carol Oates
Sing, you Sacher tortes
The New Yorker v78 no2 p34-6 Mr 4 2002
The whore of Mensa
Neurotica: Jewish writers on sex; edited by Melvin Jules Bukiet
Wonderful town; New York stories from The New Yorker; edited by David Remnick with Susan Choi
Allen, Paul
While the band played
Tetrick, B. In the shadow of the wall; an anthology of Vietnam stories that might have been; edited by Byron R. Tetrick
Allende, Isabel
An act of vengeance
Short stories by Latin American women; the magic and the real; edited by Celia Correas de Zapata; foreword by Isabel Allende
Wicked girl
Snapshots: 20th century mother-daughter fiction; edited by Joyce Carol Oates and Janet Berliner
Allergic reactions. Palomba, L.
Allerleirauh. Yolen, J.
Alley, Henry
The facts of life
The Virginia Quarterly Review v78 no3 p481-9 Summ 2002
The **allies.** Dunn, K.
Allie's girl. Amick, S.
Alligator tears. Crider, B.
ALLIGATORS
Crider, B. Alligator tears
Elrod, P. N. Izzy's shoe-in
Loeb, K. Fauna in Florida
Allingham, Margery
Money to burn
A moment on the edge; 100 years of crime stories by women; edited by Elizabeth George
One morning they'll hang him
Edwards, M. Mysterious pleasures; a celebration of the Crime Writers' Association's 50th anniversary; edited by Martin Edwards
Allison, Dorothy
Compassion
The Best American short stories, 2003; selected from U.S. and Canadian magazines by Walter Mosley with Katrina Kenison; with an introduction by Walter Mosley
New stories from the South: the year's best, 2003; edited by Shannon Ravenel; with a preface by Roy Blount Jr.
Allison, Will
Niernsee's Tower
The Kenyon Review v26 no2 p69-86 Spr 2004
Allog. Pearlman, E.
The **allotment.** Crowther, P.
All's well that ends. Hess, J.
Allures of grandeur. Kalman, J.

Allyn, Douglas
Black Irish
Murder most Celtic; tall tales of Irish may-
hem; edited by Martin H. Greenberg
The Christmas mitzvah
Browning, A. Murder is no mitzvah; edited
by Abigail Browning
The country of the blind
The World's finest mystery and crime stories,
second annual collection; edited by Ed
Gorman
The jukebox king
The Best American mystery stories, 2003; ed-
ited by Michael Connelly and Otto Penzler
Miracles! Happen!
The Best American mystery stories, 2000; ed-
ited and with an introduction by Donald E.
Westlake
Puppyland
Master's choice v2; mystery stories by to-
day's top writers and the masters who in-
spired them; edited by Lawrence Block
Saint Bobby
Crème de la crime; edited by Janet Hutchings
St. Margaret's kitten
Cat crimes through time; edited by Ed
Gorman, Martin H. Greenberg, and Larry
Segriff
The turncoat
The Blue and the gray undercover; edited by
Ed Gorman
Unchained melody
The World's finest mystery and crime stories,
first annual collection; edited by Ed
Gorman
Alma. Maleti, G.
Alma. Phillips, J. A.
Alma, meaning "To cherish". Aldrich, B. S.
Almánzar, José Alcántara *See* Alcántara
Almánzar, José, 1946-
Almog, Ruth
Shrinking
Six Israeli novellas; [by] Ruth Almog [et al.];
edited and with an introduction by Gershon
Shaked; translated from the Hebrew by
Dalya Bilu, Philip Simpson, and Marganit
Weinberger-Rotman
Almond, Steve
The Darkness Together
The Southern Review (Baton Rouge, La.) v40
no1 p73-84 Wint 2004
Divorcing Johnny Ponder
South Carolina Review v34 no1 p19-28 Fall
2001
A dream of sleep
Lost tribe; jewish fiction from the edge
The evil B. B. Chow
Francis Ford Coppola's Zoetrope all-story 2;
edited by Adrienne Brodeur and Samantha
Schnee; with an introduction by Francis
Ford Coppola
God bless America
The Southern Review (Baton Rouge, La.) v37
no1 p77-90 Wint 2001
Have a Coke and a Bullet
The Virginia Quarterly Review v80 no1 p80-
91 Wint 2004

I am as I am
New England Review v22 no1 p20-32 Wint
2001
Lincoln, arisen
The Antioch Review v59 no4 p767-82 Fall
2001
The most romantic story ever
The Southern Review (Baton Rouge, La.) v38
no1 p88-92 Wint 2002
The pass
New England Review v22 no4 p101-8 Fall
2001
Pushcart prize XXVII; best of the small
presses; edited by Bill Henderson with the
Pushcart prize editors
The President Returns
Harvard Review (1992) no22 p172-4 Spr
2002
The Problem of Human Consumption
The Virginia Quarterly Review v80 no3 p82-8
Summ 2004
Run away, my pale love
Ploughshares v28 no1 p35-52 Spr 2002
Saint Augustine Was a Player Once
New England Review v24 no3 p63-72 Summ
2003
Shotgun Wedding
New England Review v23 no4 p57-66 Fall
2002
The soul molecule
New stories from the South: the year's best,
2003; edited by Shannon Ravenel; with a
preface by Roy Blount Jr.
What It's Like to Be a Man
The Antioch Review v61 no2 p298-306 Spr
2003
Almond, Steven
The idea of sirloin
The Southern Review (Baton Rouge, La.) v35
no2 p253-59 Spr 1999
Almonds and cherries. Erian, A.
Almost Like Nowhere. Lamp, B.
An **almost** perfect heist. Hart, C. G.
An **almost** perfect murder. Hart, C. G.
Almost There. Kerley, J.
Almqvist, Éilís Ní Dhuibhne- *See* Ní Dhuibhne-
Almqvist, Éilís, 1954-
ALMSHOUSES
Singer, I. B. In the poorhouse
Singer, I. B. A night in the poorhouse
Aloha, Les. Burford, M.
Alone. Drake, R.
Alone. Garcia, L. G.
Alone. Gilchrist, E.
Alone. Schmid, W. A.
Alone in Africa. Rush, N.
Along for the ride. Schumacher, A.
Along the Frontage Road. Chabon, M.
Alonso, Dora
Sophie and the angel
Short stories by Latin American women; the
magic and the real; edited by Celia Correas
de Zapata; foreword by Isabel Allende
Alpha Romeo. Schwartz, J. B.
ALPHABET
Brockmeier, K. Small degrees
Alplax. Rejtman, M.
ALPS
Stanton, M. The cliffs of the moon

Already gone. Shepard, J.
Also a triangle. Lao She
Also Known as Alonzo Jones. Stamell, R. B.
Alsup, Benjamin
  So I've Got That Going for Me
    Esquire v141 no4 p68, 70, 72, 74, 76, 78-81,
    146-7 Ap 2004
Altamont Jones. Pollard, V.
Altar. Alcalá, K. J.
Las **Altas**. Gavell, M. L.
The **alternative**. Campbell, R.
Altman, Steven-Elliot
  A case of royal blood
    Shadows over Baker Street; edited by Michael
    Reaves and John Pelan
Alvarez, Aldo
  Death by bricolage
    Alvarez, A. Interesting monsters; fictions
  Ephemera
    Alvarez, A. Interesting monsters; fictions
  Fixing a shadow
    Alvarez, A. Interesting monsters; fictions
  Flatware
    Alvarez, A. Interesting monsters; fictions
  Ghosts, pockets, traces, necessary clouds
    Alvarez, A. Interesting monsters; fictions
  Heat rises
    Alvarez, A. Interesting monsters; fictions
  Index card, index finger
    Alvarez, A. Interesting monsters; fictions
  Losing count
    Alvarez, A. Interesting monsters; fictions
  Other people's complications
    Alvarez, A. Interesting monsters; fictions
  Property values
    Alvarez, A. Interesting monsters; fictions
  Public displays of affection
    Alvarez, A. Interesting monsters; fictions
  Quintessence
    Alvarez, A. Interesting monsters; fictions
  Rog & Venus become an item
    Alvarez, A. Interesting monsters; fictions
  A small indulgence
    Alvarez, A. Interesting monsters; fictions
  Up close
    Alvarez, A. Interesting monsters; fictions
Alvarez, Julia
  Amor divino
    The Art of the story; an international antholo-
    gy of contemporary short stories; edited by
    Daniel Halpern
  The blood of the Conquistadores
    Colchie, T. A whistler in the nightworld;
    short fiction from the Latin Americas; ed-
    ited by Thomas Colchie
  Consuelo's letter
    Snapshots: 20th century mother-daughter fic-
    tion; edited by Joyce Carol Oates and Janet
    Berliner
  Neighbors
    Américas v53 no1 p64 Ja/F 2001
Always Othello. Smith, J.
Always verbena. Garcia, L. G.
ALZHEIMER'S DISEASE
  Bradbury, R. The nineteenth
  Collins, B. and Collins, M. A. A cruise to forget
  Epstein, J. A loss for words
  Freudenberger, N. Outside the Eastern gate
  Gautreaux, T. Sunset in heaven

Gay, W. Those Deep Elm Brown's Ferry Blues
Gurganus, A. He's at the office
Händler, E.-W. Dissolution or for Mrs. Berta
  Zuckerkandl
Homes, A. M. The former First Lady and the
  football hero
Johnson-Davies, D. A short weekend
Krawiec, R. Rituals
McHugh, M. F. Presence
Munro, A. The bear came over the mountain
Norris, H. Niagara Falls
Schaeffer, S. F. The old farmhouse and the dog-
  wife
Smith, J. Cul-de-sac
Sosin, D. The only course
Van Winckel, N. Treat me nice
Watanabe McFerrin, L. The hand of Buddha
Wieland, L. Purgatory
AMALFI (ITALY) *See* Italy—Amalfi
Amanthis, Judith
  Down there undercover
    Valentine's Day: women against men; stories
    of revenge; introduction by Alice Thomas
Amar. Hoyt, D. A.
The **amateur** ventriloquist. Coshnear, D.
An **amateur's** guide to the night. Robison, M.
Amazon. Brownrigg, S.
AMAZON RIVER VALLEY
  Huttner, H. Dr. Cyclops
AMBASSADORS *See* Diplomatic life
The **ambassador's** son Fishman, B. Wild East;
    stories from the last frontier; edited with an
    introduction by Boris Fishman
The **ambassador's** son. Bissell, T.
Amber gate. Mosley, W.
The **amber** room. Watson, I.
AMBITION
  Auchincloss, L. The Devil and Guy Lansing
  Borges, J. L. The dead man
  Clarke, A. C. Death and the senator
  Delaney, E. J. The anchor and me
  Stern, D. Lunch with Gottlieb
  Winegardner, M. The untenured lecturer
The **ambitious** guest. Hawthorne, N.
Ambitious sophomore. Vonnegut, K.
Ambler, Eric
  The blood bargain
    Edwards, M. Mysterious pleasures; a celebra-
    tion of the Crime Writers' Association's
    50th anniversary; edited by Martin Edwards
AMBULANCES
  Foxwell, E. No man's land
  Wharton, E. Coming home
Ambush. Kohler, S.
Amdrup, Erik
  Chess on board
    Death cruise; crime stories on the open seas;
    edited by Lawrence Block
Amelia Earhart's coat. Knight, M.
Amen. Hogan, L.
Amen. Nash, S.
Amenhotep IV, King of Egypt *See* Akhenaton,
    King of Egypt, fl. ca. 1388-1358 B.C.
AMERICA
    See also South America
American Arms. Rinehart, S.
AMERICAN CIVIL WAR, 1861-1865 *See* Unit-
    ed States—Civil War, 1861-1865
An **American** couple. Yuknavitch, L.

American dead. Harrison, H.
The **American** embassy. Adichie, C. N.
American Falls. Gifford, B.
The **American** Hotel. Hashimoto, S.
American lottery. Nfah-Abbenyi, J. M.
American mandate Turtledove, H. Alternate generals II; ed. by Harry Turtledove
American model. Marshall, T.
American Overhaul. Villatoro, M.
American pastime. Macklin, T.
American primitive. Norris, L.
AMERICAN REVOLUTION, 1775-1783 *See* United States—Revolution, 1775-1783
AMERICAN SOLDIERS *See* Soldiers—United States
American Southwestern. Hyde, P. B.
AMERICANS
Panama
Kingsbury, Suzanne. Panama
Africa
Peterson, P. W. Africa
Tinti, H. Miss Waldron's red colobus
Argentina
Mueller, M. Exile
Belize
Abrams, T. Changing horses
Abrams, T. Joe Grind
Botswana
Luntta, K. A virgin twice
Rush, N. Alone in Africa
Whitty, J. Senti's last elephant
Bulgaria
Updike, J. The Bulgarian poetess
Cambodia
Salak, K. Beheadings
Tuck, L. Hotter
Caribbean region
Kurlansky, M. The deerness of life
Lopez, B. H. Light action in the Caribbean
López, L. Ivor's people
Central America
Pritchard, M. Funktionlust
China
Davidson, A. Dragon skin drum
Gambone, P. The singing boy
L'Amour, L. Beyond the Great Snow Mountains
McHugh, M. F. A foreigner's Christmas in China
Silber, J. Ideas of heaven
Colombia
Bowles, P. The echo
Costa Rica
Burgin, R. Bodysurfing
Cuba
Gifford, B. The old days
Menendez, A. Her mother's house
Czech Republic
Hamburger, A. Exile
Hamburger, A. Jerusalem
Hamburger, A. A man of the country
Hamburger, A. Sympathetic conversationalist
Hamburger, A. This ground you are standing on
Hamburger, A. You say you want a revolution
Phillips, A. Wenceslas Square
Eastern Europe
The ambassador's son
Egypt
Butler, R. O. The grotto
Updike, J. I am dying, Egypt, dying

England
Archer, J. Dougie Mortimer's right arm
Atkinson, K. Transparent fiction
Auchincloss, L. The Virginia redbird
Broughton, T. A. The burden of light
Carlson, R. The Hotel Eden
Drake, R. The cotton mill
Drake, R. Traveling companions
DuBois, B. Richard's children
Garner, J. Trick or treat
Holbrook, T. Drawing to a close
Jakes, J. Dr. Sweetkill
James, H. The author of "Beltraffio"
James, H. An international episode
James, H. Lady Barberina
James, H. A London life
James, H. The modern warning
James, H. A passionate pilgrim
Mason, B. A. Proper gypsies
O'Connell, M. The patron saint of travelers
Updike, J. Dentistry and doubt
Updike, J. A madman
Updike, J. Still life
Waugh, E. Out of depth
Yates, R. Liars in love
Ethiopia
Coskran, K. Sun
Coyne, J. Snow man
Updike, J. Ethiopia
Europe
Cooke, C. Bob darling
James, H. Daisy Miller: a study
James, H. Longstaff's marriage
James, H. Louisa Pallant
James, H. The siege of London
Wharton, E. Souls belated
Yates, R. A compassionate leave
France
Abrams, T. In the gare at Bayonne
Adams, A. Winter rain
Auchincloss, L. The veterans
Azadeh, C. A recitation of nomads
Bart, P. Power play
Bocock, M. Alice and me
Brackenbury, R. The forty-ninth lot joke
Brackenbury, R. Instead of the revolution
Butler, R. O. Mother in the trenches
Cohen, M. L. Polaroid
Dilworth, S. A little learning
Fairey, W. W. A hundred hearts
Fairey, W. W. Over the hill
Fitzgerald, F. S. The World's Fair
Foster, K. Happy people
Galef, D. Dear, dirty Paris
Greenberg, P. The subjunctive mood
Highsmith, P. A girl like Phyl
James, H. A bundle of letters
James, H. Madame de Mauves
James, H. Mrs. Temperly
L'Amour, L. The cross and the candle
Le Guin, U. K. April in Paris
Lee, A. In France
Lee, M. Oh, happy day
McGarry, J. Paris
Nissen, T. After twenty-five years, at the Palais Royale
Oppel, J.-H. A demon in my head
Patterson, K. Interposition
Prose, F. Three pigs in five days [excerpt]

AMERICANS—France—*Continued*
Robinson, P. April in Paris
Ryan, P. Second island
Shepard, S. It wasn't Proust
Silber, J. My shape
Stanton, M. Ping-pong
Stanton, M. The ugly virgin
Stern, D. The #63 bus from the Gare de Lyon
Stern, D. Time will tell
Swan, M. The deep
Updike, J. Avec la bébé-sitter
Vasseur, T. J. The woman who sugared straw-berries
Weihe, E. Another life
Wharton, E. The last asset
Wharton, E. Velvet ear-pads
Whitty, J. The story of the deep dark
Yates, R. Evening on the Côte d'Azur
Yates, R. A last fling, like
Yates, R. A really good jazz piano
Germany
Biguenet, J. I am not a Jew
Gilliland, G. News of the world
Griffin, W. E. B. Going back to the bridge in Berlin
Helms, B. American wives
Lowenthal, M. Infinity of angles
Michaels, L. A girl with a monkey
Rinehart, S. American Arms
Greece
Broughton, T. A. A tour of the islands
Campbell, R. The same in any language
Clark, J. The lotus-eater
Eakin, W. A god for delphi
Galef, D. All Cretans
Reifler, N. The splinter
Guatemala
Abrams, T. The king of everything
Brazaitis, M. The heroes of our stories
Honduras
Jacobs, M. Solidarity in green
Jacobs, M. The Telemachus box
Hong Kong
Row, J. The secrets of bats
Iceland
Richmond, M. Does anyone know you are going this way
India
Freudenberger, N. Lucky girls
Freudenberger, N. Outside the Eastern gate
Freudenberger, N. The tutor
Spencer, J. The robbers of Karnataka
Ireland
Boyle, T. C. The miracle at Ballinspittle
Bradbury, R. Getting through Sunday somehow
Bradbury, R. The great collision of Monday last
Bradbury, R. A wild night in Galway
Dorcey, M. A noise from the woodshed [ex-cerpt]
Honig, L. The sights of Cork
Lavin, M. Lemonade
Matthews, C. The moving statue of Ballinspittle
Mazor, J. Gray skies
Mazor, J. The munster final
Israel
Englander, N. In this way we are wise
Gabriel, D. Making peace with the Muslims
Goldstein, N. The conduct for consoling
Goldstein, N. Pickled sprouts

Goldstein, N. A pillar of a cloud
Hamburger, A. Law of return
Leegant, J. Seekers in the Holy Land
Papernick, J. The ascent of Eli Israel
Italy
Barolini, H. Bobbing
Barolini, H. Classic and good
Barolini, H. Diving into eternity
Barolini, H. Dr. Melfi in the morning
Barolini, H. Gianni on the rocks
Barolini, H. La giardiniera
Barolini, H. Henry and the miracle
Barolini, H. How to live in Rome and loathe it
Barolini, H. Michaelmas daisies
Barolini, H. More Italian hours
Barolini, H. Ms. Italia
Barolini, H. The Nordic type
Barolini, H. Of sketchbooks and millers, of Par-is and Rome
Barolini, H. Seven fishes
Barolini, H. Shores of light
Beattie, A. In Amalfi
Brady, C. Let my right hand forget her cunning
Brodkey, H. Verona: a young woman speaks
Broughton, T. A. Italian autumn
Bunin, I. A. The gentleman from San Francisco
Drake, R. The piazza
Egan, J. Goodbye, my love
Fulton, J. Iceland
Gilliland, G. Freedom
Girardi, R. Sunday evenings at Contessa Pasquali's
Helms, B. Men in Italy
James, H. Adina
James, H. The Aspern papers
James, H. At Isella
James, H. The last of the Valerii
James, H. The madonna of the future
James, H. The solution
James, H. Travelling companions
Kohler, S. The original
Leavitt, D. Crossing St. Gotthard
Leavitt, D. The marble quilt
Lee, A. About fog and cappuccino
Lee, A. The birthday present
Lee, A. Full moon over Milan
Lee, A. Sicily
Malamud, B. Still life
Roeske, P. The ecstasy of Magda Brummel
Schmidt, H. J. Songbirds
Silber, J. The dollar in Italy
Silber, J. Ragazzi
Spencer, E. The cousins
Spencer, E. The light in the piazza
Spencer, E. The visit
Spencer, E. The white azalea
Standiford, L. Succubus
Stern, D. Messenger
Tester, W. The living and the dead
Theroux, P. The stranger at the Palazzo d'Oro
Updike, J. Twin beds in Rome
Wharton, E. The daunt Diana
Wharton, E. Roman fever
White, E. A Venice story
Jamaica
Bowles, P. Pages from Cold Point
Japan
Blatnik, A. Kyoto
Browder, C. Fusuda the archer

AMERICANS—Japan—*Continued*
Browder, C. The missing day
Iyer, P. A walk in Kurama
Lee, D. Domo arigato
Packer, Z. Geese
Schmatz, P. Tokyo trains
Swain, H. Sushi
Kenya
Hunter, F. Laban and Murugi
Hunter, F. Night vigil
Hunter, F. North of Nairobi
Watanabe McFerrin, L. Masai heart
Korea
Byrd, Z. Of cabbages
Chamberlain, W. The trapped battalion
Depew, D. R. Indigenous girls
Givens, J. On the wheel of wandering-on
Pak, W.-S. Encounter at the airport
Sneider, V. A long way from home
Steiner, H. Rice
Majorca
Boylan, C. Villa Marta
Mexico
Adam, C. Vulture
Adams, A. The haunted beach
Adams, A. Mexican dust
Bowles, P. Tapiama
Boyle, T. C. Mexico
Bradbury, R. Where all is emptiness there is room to move
Browder, C. The juice-seller's bird
Butler, R. O. The one in white
Chacón, D. The biggest city in the world
Cobb, T. Las momias
Cohen, R. A flight of sparks
Crumley, J. Whores
Dickey, E. J. Café Piel
Flynn, T. T. Ghost guns for gold
Gilchrist, E. Mexico
Highsmith, P. In the plaza
Holleran, A. The ossuary
Kachtick, K. Hungry ghost
Lida, D. Acapulco gold
Lida, D. A beach day
Lida, D. Bewitched
Lida, D. Prenuptial agreement
Lida, D. The recruiting officer
Lida, D. Regrets
Lord, C. La Tortuga
Lutz, J. El Palacio
McBrearty, R. G. A night at the Y
McCourt, J. A plethora
Miller, A. L. Off-season travel
Nissen, T. The girl at Chichén Itzá
Otis, M. Aida South, flower
Richmond, M. Choose your travel partner wisely
Russo, R. The dowry
Spencer, E. The runaways
Treat, J. Not a chance
Wallace, R. The sacred well
Wheat, C. A bus called pity
White, E. Cinnamon skin
Morocco
Ardizzone, T. Larabi's ox
Azadeh, C. A recitation of nomads
Bocock, M. And silently steal away
Bowles, P. The dismissal
Bowles, P. Tea on the mountain

Netherlands
Coleman, J. Ten secrets of beauty
Holleran, A. Amsterdam
Lee, M. Wives, lovers, Maximilian
North Africa
Bowles, P. Too far from home
Norway
Earle, S. The internationale
Paraguay
Jacobs, M. Down in Paraguay
Jacobs, M. The egg queen rises
Philippines
Norris, L. American primitive
Norris, L. Stray dogs
Poland
Beckman, J. Babylon revisited redux
Michaels, L. Nachman
Seiffert, R. Field study
Portugal
Adams, A. Sintra
Greer, A. S. Lost causes
Russia
Bocock, M. A citizen of the world at large
De Waal, T. The English house: a story of Chechnya
Hays, D. Orphans
Lord, N. Behold
Shonk, K. The conversion
Shonk, K. Honey month
Shonk, K. Kitchen friends
Shonk, K. Our American
Simmons, D. The end of gravity
Scotland
Haslett, A. War's end
Knight, A. The deadly glen
Sierra Leone
Houghteling, M. K. Ma Kamanda's latrine
South America
Clark, J. Jungle wedding
Westlake, D. E. A good story
Spain
Abrams, T. The book of thieves
Abrams, T. The star train
Adams, A. Barcelona
Boswell, M. Spanish omens
Davis, L. Strays
Lord, N. Trip report (confidential)
Sweden
Furman, L. Hagalund
Switzerland
James, H. The pension Beaurepas
Tuck, L. Gold leaf
Thailand
Bowles, P. You have left your lotus pods on the bus
Freudenberger, N. The orphan
Lee, A. Interesting women
Tuck, L. Fortitude
Turkey
Gabriel, D. Necati Bey
Meredith, D. At the punishment cliff for women
Ukraine
Foer, J. S. The very rigid search
Vietnam
Barnes, H. L. The cat in the cage
Dinh, L. The hippie chick
Earle, S. The reunion
Hannah, B. Midnight and I'm not famous yet
O'Neill, S. Butch

AMERICANS—*Continued*
West Africa
Banks, R. Djinn
Drew, E. Mad dogs
Ekstrom, L. S. On Sunday there might be Americans
Hunter, F. Dr. Kleckner
Sumner, M. The guide
West Indies
Kurlansky, M. The unclean
Shacochis, B. Easy in the islands
Updike, J. The doctor's wife
Yugoslavia
Brkic, C. A. Where none is the number
Zaire
Hunter, F. Elizabeth who disappeared
Hunter, F. Waiting for the Mwami
Americans. Evans, E.
Amerikanski dead at the Moscow morgue. Newman, K.
Ames, Brian
Color separation
The Massachusetts Review v42 no1 p37-45 Spr 2001
The Last Living Elk in North America
The North American Review v289 no3/4 p46-9 My/Ag 2004
Ames, Jonathan
Lenore Malen
Bomb no81 p90-3 Fall 2002
Amichai, Yehuda
My father's deaths
When night fell; an anthology of Holocaust short stories; edited by Linda Schermer Raphael and Marc Lee Raphael
A poetry reading
The Yale Review v90 no3 p8-21 Jl 2002
Amick, Steve
Allie's girl
The Southern Review (Baton Rouge, La.) v37 no3 p526-58 Summ 2001
Animal Lover
New England Review v24 no1 p112-20 Wint 2003
Fat Tracy
New England Review v23 no1 p97-116 Wint 2002
Amihai, Yehuda *See* Amichai, Yehuda
Amin, Omnia
(jt. auth) *See* Kawar, Fakhri and Amin, Omnia
Aminoff, Jenise
Fate
Mojo: conjure stories; edited by Nalo Hopkinson
Amis, Martin
Career move
Amis, M. Heavy water and other stories
The coincidence of the arts
Amis, M. Heavy water and other stories
Denton's death
Amis, M. Heavy water and other stories
Heavy water
Amis, M. Heavy water and other stories
The immortals
The Art of the story; an international anthology of contemporary short stories; edited by Daniel Halpern

In the Palace of the End
The New Yorker v80 no4 p128-34 Mr 15 2004
The janitor on Mars
Amis, M. Heavy water and other stories
Let me count the times
Amis, M. Heavy water and other stories
Other people [excerpt]
The Vintage book of amnesia; an anthology; edited by Jonathan Lethem
State of England
Amis, M. Heavy water and other stories
Straight fiction
Amis, M. Heavy water and other stories
What happened to me on my holiday
Amis, M. Heavy water and other stories
AMISH
Myers, T. Chicken catch a tory
The **Amish**. Thompson, J.
AMNESIA
Amis, M. Other people [excerpt]
Bardin, J. F. The deadly percheron [excerpt]
Chesnutt, C. W. Cicely's dream
Cobb, W. J. Why you?
Erickson, S. Days between stations [excerpt]
Ha Jin. Alive
Kessel, J. A clean escape
Link, K. Carnation, Lily, Lily, Rose
Perabo, S. Reconstruction
Potter, D. Ticket to ride [excerpt]
Priest, C. The affirmation [excerpt]
Shainberg, L. Memories of amnesia [excerpt]
Thomas, J. The flaying season
White, E. Forgetting Elena [excerpt]
Woolrich, C. The black curtain [excerpt]
Amnesia. Kaminsky, S. M.
Amnesty. Browder, C.
Amnesty. Butler, O. E.
The **Amnesty** Barracks. Woodrell, D.
Amok. Zweig, S.
Among my souvenirs. McCrumb, S.
Among the blobs. Delany, S. R.
Among the dead. Chinodya, S.
Among the handlers; or, The Mark 16 Hands-on Assembly of Jesus Risen, formerly Snake-o-rama. Bishop, M.
Among the missing. Allen, D., Jr.
Among the missing. Chaon, D.
Among the mourners. Gilchrist, E.
Among the philistines. McGarry, J.
Among the Pomeranians. Lish, G.
Among the sick. Katowich, J.
Among the Tootalonians. Falco, E.
Amor de acuerdo—Arranged love. Martin, P. P.
Amor de madre—Mother's love. Martin, P. P.
Amor desesperado—Desperate love. Martin, P. P.
Amor divino. Alvarez, J.
Amor e ilusion—Love and illusion. Martin, P. P.
Amor encantado—Enchanted love. Martin, P. P.
Amor eterno—Eternal love. Martin, P. P.
Amor frustrado—Frustrated love. Martin, P. P.
Amor inolvidable—Unforgettable love. Martin, P. P.
Amor perdido—Lost love. Martin, P. P.
Amor prohibido—Forbidden love. Martin, P. P.
Amor sufrido—Long-suffering love. Martin, P. P.
Amos. Malzberg, B. N.
The **amount** to carry. Scholz, C.
Amphibians. Watanabe McFerrin, L.

Ampuero, Fernando
　Taxi driver, minus Robert De Niro
　　The Vintage book of Latin American stories;
　　edited by Carlos Fuentes and Julio Ortega
AMPUTATION
　Slavin, J. The woman who cut off her leg at the
　　Maidstone Club
AMPUTEES
　Aiyejina, F. The one-handed hero
　Alexie, S. One good man
　Chandra, V. Dharma
　Greer, R. O. Revision
　Packer, Z. Every tongue shall confess
Amras. Bernhard, T.
AMSTERDAM (NETHERLANDS) *See* Nether-
　lands—Amsterdam
Amsterdam. Holleran, A.
AMULETS *See* Charms
AMUSEMENT PARKS
　Abrams, T. The gaffer
　Bishop, M. Tithes of mint and rue
　Bradbury, R. The dwarf
　Bradbury, R. The illustrated man
　Chapman, C. M. It goes rickety
　Cody, L. K. K.
　Doctorow, C. Return to Pleasure Island
　Dowling, T. The saltimbanques
　Harrison, H. At last, the true story of Franken-
　　stein
　Jakes, J. The siren and the shill
　Loomis, N. M. The stick and the bearded lady
　Pronzini, B. and Malzberg, B. N. Another burnt-
　　out case
　Reid, E. Buffalo
　Rubin, L. D. The man at the beach
　Smith, M. M. What you make it
　Toft, M. Tourist trap
An-Ski, S. *See* Ansky, S., 1863-1920
Ana Maria. Donoso, J.
The **anachronism**. Brennan, M.
ANALYSTS *See* Psychoanalysts
ANARCHISM AND ANARCHISTS
　Paine, T. The spoon children
ANARCHISTS *See* Anarchism and anarchists
Anastas, Benjamin
　Falstaff, 193–
　　The Paris Review v44 p16-31 Fall 2002
Anastasia *See* Anastasiíà Nikolaevna, Grand
　Duchess, daughter of Nicholas II, Emperor
　of Russia, 1901-1918
**ANASTASIÍÀ NIKOLAEVNA, GRAND
　DUCHESS, DAUGHTER OF NICHO-
　LAS II, EMPEROR OF RUSSIA, 1901-
　1918**
About
　Llywelyn, M. Woman in a wheelchair
Anatomies. Hochman, A.
The **anatomy** and death of a dream. Auerbach, J.
The **anatomy** of a mermaid. Sharratt, M.
The **anchor** and me. Delaney, E. J.
ANCHOR PERSONS *See* Television announcing
Ancient fire. Fracis, S. H.
Ancient history. LaValle, V. D.
Ancient history. Thurm, M.
And. Davenport, G.
And Also with You. Perry, D.
And dwelt in a separate house. Galef, D.
"**—And** he built a crooked house". Heinlein, R. A.
And Here's to You, Mrs. Robinson.

And I, Isolde. Connor, J.
And in my heart. Cassill, R. V.
And king hereafter (a Boscobel League story).
　Edghill, R.
—and love them? Glave, T.
And maybe the horse will learn to sing. Fallis, G.
And never come up. Biguenet, J.
And now doth time waste me. Turner, G.
& other stories. Trudell, D.
And perhaps more. James, S.
And silently steal away. Bocock, M.
And still she sleeps. Costikyan, G.
And that's the name of that tune. Hribal, C. J.
And the glory of them Turtledove, H. Alternate
　generals II; ed. by Harry Turtledove
And the lillies-them a-blow. Hopkinson, N.
And the mothers stepped over their sons. Chap-
　man, C. M.
And the others. . . Ewing, C. D.
And the sea shall claim them. Costello, M. J. and
　Hautala, R.
And the shin bone's connected to the knee bone.
　Brady, C.
And the talk slid south. Mobilio, A.
And then there were nine. Babel´, I.
And then there were ten. Babel´, I.
And then we went to Venus. Pronzini, B.
. . . **And** thou!. Kilpatrick, N.
And when I should feel something. Paddock, J.
And Who Shall Provide the Lamb? Senstad, S. S.
Andahazi, Federico
　The sleep of the just
　　Colchie, T. A whistler in the nightworld;
　　short fiction from the Latin Americas; ed-
　　ited by Thomas Colchie
ANDALUSIA (SPAIN) *See* Spain—Andalusia
Andante lugubre. Malzberg, B. N.
Ander, Zed
　William and Antonio, Giotto and Mae
　　Iowa Review v29 no3 p70-1 Wint 1999
　Writing the body
　　Iowa Review v29 no3 p72-3 Wint 1999
Andersen, Kurt
　My people, your people
　　The New Yorker v75 no9 p162-73 Ap 26-My
　　3 1999
Andersen, Richard
　Melchior's Gift
　　Dalhousie Review v82 no2 p281-8 Summ
　　2002
Anderson, Barth
　Lark till dawn, princess
　　Mojo: conjure stories; edited by Nalo Hopkin-
　　son
Anderson, Cynthia
　Baker's helper
　　Iowa Review v32 no1 p50-1 Spr 2002
　Dance recital for the men of the American Le-
　　gion in April
　　Iowa Review v32 no1 p52-3 Spr 2002
　Pipe
　　The North American Review v284 no5 p21
　　S/O 1999
Anderson, Donald
　Accident
　　Anderson, D. Fire road
　Appendix
　　Anderson, D. Fire road

Anderson, Donald—*Continued*
The art of fiction
  Anderson, D. Fire road
Baby teeth
  Anderson, D. Fire road
Barrie (cont.)
  Anderson, D. Fire road
Barrie Hooper's dead
  Anderson, D. Fire road
Bliss
  Anderson, D. Fire road
The end of times
  Anderson, D. Fire road
Endnotes
  Anderson, D. Fire road
Fathers
  Anderson, D. Fire road
Fire road
  Anderson, D. Fire road
Luck
  Anderson, D. Fire road
mav.er.ick
  Anderson, D. Fire road
My name is Stephen Mann
  Anderson, D. Fire road
Overpass
  The North American Review v286 no3/4 p7
    My/Ag 2001
The peacock throne
  Anderson, D. Fire road
Quotidian
  Anderson, D. Fire road
sab.o.tage
  Anderson, D. Fire road
Scaling ice
  Anderson, D. Fire road
Twenty ways to look at fire
  Anderson, D. Fire road
Weather
  Anderson, D. Fire road
Wonder bread
  Anderson, D. Fire road
Would you feel better?
  Anderson, D. Fire road
Anderson, Frederick Irving
Blind man's buff
  The Best American mystery stories of the
    century; Tony Hillerman, editor; with an
    introduction by Tony Hillerman
Anderson, Jennifer
Things that make your heart beat faster
  The Best American mystery stories, 2001; ed-
    ited and with an Introduction by Lawrence
    Block
Anderson, Julian
The houses of double women
  The Pushcart prize XXIV: best of the small
    presses; an annual small press reader; ed-
    ited by Bill Henderson with the Pushcart
    prize editors
Anderson, Kent
Burglary in progress
  Murder and obsession; edited by Otto Penzler
Anderson, Poul
The big rain
  Worldmakers; SF adventures in terraforming;
    edited by Gardner Dozois

Call me Joe
  Masterpieces: the best science fiction of the
    century; edited by Orson Scott Card
Dead phone
  Anderson, P. Going for infinity; a literary
    journey
Death and the knight
  Anderson, P. Going for infinity; a literary
    journey
Delenda est
  One lamp; alternate history stories from The
    magazine of Fantasy & Science Fiction; ed-
    ited by Gordon van Gelder
Epilogue
  Anderson, P. Going for infinity; a literary
    journey
Eutopia
  The Best alternate history stories of the 20th
    century; edited by Harry Turtledove with
    Martin H. Greenberg
Goat song
  Anderson, P. Going for infinity; a literary
    journey
Gypsy
  Anderson, P. Going for infinity; a literary
    journey
The horn of time the hunter
  Anderson, P. Going for infinity; a literary
    journey
Journeys end
  Anderson, P. Going for infinity; a literary
    journey
Kyrie
  Anderson, P. Going for infinity; a literary
    journey
The martyr
  Nebula awards 33; the year's best SF and
    fantasy chosen by the science-fiction and
    fantasy writers of America; edited by
    Connie Willis
The master key
  Anderson, P. Going for infinity; a literary
    journey
A midsummer tempest
  Anderson, P. Going for infinity; a literary
    journey
The problem of pain
  Anderson, P. Going for infinity; a literary
    journey
The queen of air and darkness
  Anderson, P. Going for infinity; a literary
    journey
Quest
  Anderson, P. Going for infinity; a literary
    journey
Sam Hall
  Anderson, P. Going for infinity; a literary
    journey
The Saturn game
  Anderson, P. Going for infinity; a literary
    journey
The shrine for lost children
  Anderson, P. Going for infinity; a literary
    journey
The Sky People
  The Good old stuff; adventure SF in the
    grand tradition; edited by Gardner Dozois

Anderson, Poul—*Continued*

Three hearts and three lions

    Anderson, P. Going for infinity; a literary journey

Windmill

    Anderson, P. Going for infinity; a literary journey

Anderson, Robert

The angel of ubiquity

    Anderson, R. Ice age; stories

Death and the maid

    Anderson, R. Ice age; stories

Echo

    Anderson, R. Ice age; stories

Ice age

    Anderson, R. Ice age; stories

Mother tongue

    Anderson, R. Ice age; stories

The name of the dead

    Anderson, R. Ice age; stories

Photographs: rub Al Khali, 1990-91

    Anderson, R. Ice age; stories

The pyramid

    Anderson, R. Ice age; stories

Schism

    Anderson, R. Ice age; stories

    Iowa Review v29 no3 p94-120 Wint 1999

Slight return

    Anderson, R. Ice age; stories

Anderson, Sherwood

The other woman

    The Best American short stories of the century; John Updike, editor, Katrina Kenison, coeditor; with an introduction by John Updike

ANDES

Valenzuela, L. Up among the eagles

Andoe, Joe

Appreciation at the Door

    Bomb no84 p94 Summ 2003

Keepsake

    Bomb no84 p95 Summ 2003

The Rundown

    Bomb no84 p95 Summ 2003

The **Andrech** samples. Gores, J.

Andrews, Colin *See* Wilson, F. Paul (Francis Paul)

Andrews, Donna

The birthday dinner

    Bishop, C. and James, D. Death dines in; edited by Claudia Bishop and Dean James

Andrews, Mary Kay

Love at first byte

    Love and death; edited by Carolyn Hart

Andrézel, Pierre, 1885-1962

    For works written by this author under other names see Dinesen, Isak, 1885-1962

Andrić, Ivo

A letter from 1920

    Partisan Review v68 no2 p242-53 Spr 2001

Androgynous. Singer, I. B.

ANDROS, SIR EDMUND, 1637-1714

About

Hawthorne, N. The gray champion

Andy the office boy. Chacón, D.

The **Andy** Warhol sandcandle. Rucker, R. v. B.

The **anecdote** of the island. Connor, J.

Li **Ang**. Chang, L. S.

The **angel** at the grave. Wharton, E.

Angel dust. Aylett, S.

Angel of mercy. Pronzini, B.

The **angel** of the airwaves. Taylor, R. L.

The **angel** of ubiquity. Anderson, R.

Angelita y Rafael. Leff, V. A.

ANGELS

Alonso, D. Sophie and the angel

Chiang, T. Hell is the absence of God

Dyson, J. Love in the time of Molyneux

Fleming, R. The inhuman condition

Greenland, C. Wings

Jenkins, G. The reality of angels

Jones, G. The precision of angels

Matiella, A. C. Angels

Singer, I. B. Jachid and Jechidah

Spark, M. The Seraph and the Zambesi

Stern, S. The sin of Elijah

Stern, S. Sissman loses his way

Webb, J. Blake's angel

What, L. Smelling of earth, dreaming of sky

Willis, C. Miracle

Angels. Addonizio, K.

Angels. Matiella, A. C.

The **angels**. Vasseur, T. J.

Angel's island. Mosley, W.

Angels, saints and their friends. Broner, E. M.

ANGER

Aylett, S. Resenter

Bausch, R. Unjust

Boyle, T. C. Friendly skies

Dixon, S. Hand

Friedman, P. Dog days

Le Guin, U. K. The ire of the Veksi

Sammān, G. Thirty years of bees

Angie. Gorman, E.

Angie Luna. Troncoso, S.

Angkor Wat. West, K.

The **angled** city. Brkic, C. A.

Angles. Wuori, G. K.

ANGLICAN AND EPISCOPAL CLERGY

Auchincloss, L. The anniversary

Auchincloss, L. The Devil and Guy Lansing

Bennett, A. The laying on of hands

Berners, G. H. T.-W., Baron. The camel

Angrist, Misha

So much the better

    Best new American voices 2004; guest editor John Casey; series editors John Kulka and Natalie Danford

Swedish Bricks and Minerals

    Michigan Quarterly Review v42 no1 p178-94 Wint 2003

Aniebo, I. N. C.

Four dimensions

    The Anchor book of modern African stories; edited by Nadežda Obradovic ; with a foreword by Chinua Achebe

ANIMAL ABUSE *See* Animal welfare

ANIMAL COMMUNICATION

Lugones, L. Yzur

Animal heaven. Browder, C.

ANIMAL LANGUAGE *See* Animal communication

Animal Lover. Amick, S.

Animal rights. Wallace, R.

Animal rites. Kilpatrick, N.

Animal sounds. Strickland, L.

Animal stories. Brown, J.

ANIMAL WELFARE
See also Cockfighting
Block, L. How would you like it?
Ortiz, S. J. Distance
Wallace, R. Animal rights

ANIMALS
See also Extinct animals; Mythical animals; Taxidermy names of individual animals
Aylett, S. Bestiary
Boylan, C. L'amour
Browder, C. Animal heaven
Harris, J. C. How Mr. Rabbit was too sharp for Mr. Fox
Harris, J. C. Uncle Remus
Harris, J. C. Uncle Remus initiates the little boy
Harris, J. C. The wonderful Tar-Baby story
Heinlein, R. A. Jerry was a man
Le Guin, U. K. Buffalo gals, won't you come out tonight
MacLeod, A. Second spring
Oliver, C. Old four-eyes
Paschal, D. Sautéing the platygast
Perry, A. Daisy and the Christmas goose

Training
Chekhov, A. P. Kashtanka

Treatment
See Animal welfare

ANIMALS, MYTHICAL *See* Mythical animals
Animals. Estep, M.
The **animal's** best interest. Nissen, T.

ANKARA (TURKEY) *See* Turkey—Ankara
Anna around the neck. See Chekhov, A. P. "Anna on the neck"
"**Anna** on the neck". Chekhov, A. P.
Anna, Part I. Gilchrist, E.
Anna passes on. Gerber, M. J.
Anna round the neck. See Chekhov, A. P. "Anna on the neck"
Annals of the honorary secretary. Lasdun, J.
Anna's way. Schickler, D.

ANNE BOLEYN, QUEEN, CONSORT OF HENRY VIII, KING OF ENGLAND, 1507-1536
About
Carl, L. S. A rose with all its thorns
Wilson, D. A. The curse of the unborn dead
Anne's game. Le Clézio, J.-M. G.
Annibal, Lidiya Dmitrievna Zinovyeva- *See* Zinovyeva-Annibal, Lidiya Dmitrievna, 1866-1907
Annie's dream. Dadmun, B.

ANNIVERSARIES, WEDDING *See* Wedding anniversaries
The **anniversary.** Auchincloss, L.
The **anniversary** present. Heflin, R. V.
The **anniversary** waltz. Estleman, L. D.
The **Annunciation.** Wachtel, C.
The **anointed.** Hill, K.
Anomalies. Benford, G.
The **anomalist.** Brenner, W.
Anonymous. Carson, J.
An **anonymous** story. Chekhov, A. P.
Another Besting of Both Englishmen. Flannery, S.
Another day on Pegasus. Karnezis, P.
Another fine mess. Bradbury, R.
Another life. Weihe, E.
Another marvellous thing. Colwin, L.
Another memory. Proust, M.

Another night to remember. Chambers, W. E.
Another pair of hands. Spark, M.
Another place. Leslie, N.
Another pyramid scheme. Rinehart, S.
Another room. Hess, J.
Another shoot. Foster, K.
Another wonder of the world. Lee, M.

Ansa, Tina McElroy
Love
The Bluelight corner; black women writing on passion, sex, and romantic love; edited by Rosemarie Robotham

Ansay, A. Manette
Box
New stories from the South: the year's best, 2000; edited by Shannon Ravenel; with a preface by Ellen Douglas

Ansky, S.
Mendel the Turk
Neugroschel, J. No star too beautiful; Yiddish stories from 1382 to the present; compiled and translated by Joachim Neugroschel
The starveling
Neugroschel, J. No star too beautiful; Yiddish stories from 1382 to the present; compiled and translated by Joachim Neugroschel

Answer. Pourciau, G.
Answers. Powell, P.
Answers. Singleton, G.
The **ant** of the self. Packer, Z.
The **ant** trap. Engel, H.

ANTARCTIC REGIONS
See also Arctic regions
Campbell, J. W. Who goes there?
Green, Dominic. Send me a mentagram
Howard, C. The ice shelf
Vinge, V. Apartness
Whitty, J. Jimmy under water
Antarctica. Keegan, C.
Antarctica. Thompson, J.

ANTEUS (GREEK MYTHOLOGY)
Bowles, P. Afternoon with Antaeus
Anthem of the locusts. Cadle, D.

Anthony, Michael
They better don't stop the carnival
The Oxford book of Caribbean short stories; edited by Stewart Brown and John Wickham

ANTHROPOLOGISTS
Alexie, S. Dear John Wayne
Brackett, L. The last days of Shandakor
Delany, S. R. High weir
Oren, Y. The Cat Man
Anthropology. Lee, A.
Anthropology. Roorbach, B.
Antibodies. Stross, C.
Antic Light. Fowler, G.
Antigone. Bunin, I. A.

ANTIGRAVITY
See also Gravitation

ANTIGUA AND BARBUDA
Gonsalves, G. Tamarind stew
López, L. Ivor's people

Antin, David
California—the nervous camel
The Review of Contemporary Fiction v21 no1 p54-72 Spr 2001

ANTIQUE DEALERS
    See also Art dealers
    Rohmer, S. The death-ring of Sneferu
ANTIQUES
    Gavell, M. L. Yankee traders
    Taylor, T. L. Doves of Townsend
ANTIQUITIES
    See also Archeology
ANTISEMITISM
    See also Holocaust, Jewish (1933-1945);
      Jews—Persecutions
    Azadeh, C. A banal stain
    Biguenet, J. I am not a Jew
    Brownstein, G. Bachelor party
    Bukoski, A. Pesthouse
    Busch, F. A handbook for spies
    Epstein, J. The master's ring
    Foer, J. S. The very rigid search
    Hamburger, A. This ground you are standing on
    Highsmith, P. The returnees
    Horn, D. Barbarians at the gates
    Shapiro, G. Rosenthal unbound
    Singer, I. B. Pigeons
    Škvorecký, J. The cuckoo
    Škvorecký, J. Dr. Strass
    Škvorecký, J. My teacher, Mr. Katz
    Škvorecký, J. My Uncle Kohn
    Taylor, T. L. The resurrection plant
    Yates, R. Oh, Joseph, I'm so tired
Antoni, Robert
    My grandmother's tale of how Crab-o lost his
      head
      The Paris Review v41 no152 p225-54 Fall
      1999
    My grandmother's tale of the buried treasure
      and how she defeated the King of
      Chacachacari and the entire American
      Army with her venus-flytraps
      Whispers from the cotton tree root; Caribbean
      fabulist fiction; edited by Nalo Hopkinson
    A world of canes
      The Oxford book of Caribbean short stories;
      edited by Stewart Brown and John
      Wickham
Antony, who sought things that were lost. Waugh,
    E.
Antrim, Donald
    An actor prepares
      The New Yorker v75 no16 p162-65+ Je 21-28
      1999
    The pancake supper
      The New Yorker v75 no40 p100-09 D 27
      1999-Ja 3 2000
    Pond, With Mud
      The New Yorker v79 no31 p180-7 O 20 2003
ANTS
    Pohl, F. Let the ants try
Ants. Treat, J.
Antúnez, Rafael
    You Were a Better Liar in Paris
      Callaloo v26 no4 p962-8 Fall 2003
ANTWERP (BELGIUM) *See* Belgium—Antwerp
Antworth, Scott
    The tower pig
      Best new American voices 2000; guest editor
      Tobias Wolff; series editors John Kulka
      and Natalie Danford
Anubis. Murray, P.
ANXIETY *See* Fear

Anxious objects. Gartner, Z.
Any old mother. Hinger, C.
Any reasonable offer. Vonnegut, K.
Anya's angel. Lieberman, T.
Anyone's Venus. Spatz, G.
Anything. Ortiz, S. J.
Anything for a pal. L'Amour, L.
Anything for money. Bender, K. E.
Anything He Wants. Weems, R. K.
Anything That Floats. Johnston, B. A.
Anything you want, please. Eggers, P.
Anyuta. Chekhov, A. P.
Anzhelika, 13. Kalfus, K.
APACHE INDIANS
    Carney, O. How I happened to put on the blue
    Champlin, T. For the good of the service
    DeRosso, H. A. Witch
    Haycox, E. Stage to Lordsburg
    Henry, W. The legend of Trooper Hennepin
    Henry, W. River of decision
    L'Amour, L. The defense of Sentinel
    L'Amour, L. The gift of Cochise
    Swarthout, G. F. The attack on the mountain
    Wars, 1883-1886
    Swarthout, G. F. The attack on the mountain
    The **Apache** pest control. Clark, B. C.
APARTHEID *See* South Africa—Race relations
Apartheid, superstrings, and Mordecai Thubana.
    Bishop, M.
Apartment hotel. Benson, S.
APARTMENT HOUSES
    Barthelme, F. Pool lights
    Brennan, M. The gentleman in the pink-and-
      white striped shirt
    Brownstein, G. Wakefield, 7E
    Budnitz, J. Bruno
    Cohen, S. How much justice can you afford?
    Davies, Tristan. Grouper Schmidt
    Dixon, S. The elevator
    Hess, J. Another room
    Jackson, V. F. Living alone
    Lahiri, J. A real durwan
    McPherson, J. A. Gold Coast
    Tucci, N. The evolution of knowledge
APARTMENTS *See* Apartment houses
Apartness. Vinge, V.
An **ape** about the house. Clarke, A. C.
Apelman, Mark
    A visitor's guide to Berlin
      With signs and wonders; an international an-
      thology of Jewish fabulist fiction; edited by
      Daniel M. Jaffe
APES
    See also Gorillas
    Del Rey, L. The faithful
    Helprin, M. Letters from the Samantha
Aphrodite's vision. Georgiou, E.
The **apocalypse** museum. Gass, W. H.
Apocalypse noun. Grubb, G.
The **apocalypse** quatrain. Weinberg, R.
Apocrypha. Spielberg, P.
Apogee again. Aldiss, B. W.
Apollo Karamani. Markowsky, J.
Apologia. Devereaux, R.
The **Apology.** Clarke, B.
The **apology.** Loomis, C.
Apostasy. Robison, M.
APOTHECARIES *See* Pharmacists

APPALACHIAN HIGHLANDERS
  Wellman, M. W. O ugly bird!
APPALACHIAN MOUNTAINS
  Madden, D. The world's one breathing
APPALACHIAN REGION
  Clark, B. C. The Apache pest control
  Clark, B. C. Between girls and gamecocks
  Clark, B. C. By way of the forked stick
  Clark, B. C. The last picture show
The **apparition**. Gonzalez, R.
An **appeal**. Derby, M.
Appearance of Scandal. McGraw, E.
Appearances. Boylan, C.
Appel, Benjamin
  Murder of the frankfurter man
    Master's choice [v1]; mystery stories by to-
      day's top writers and the masters who in-
      spired them; edited by Lawrence Block
Appel, Jacob M.
  The Frying Finn
    Agni no59 p110-19 2004
  Grappling
    Southern Humanities Review v38 no2 p181-94
      Spr 2004
Appelfeld, Aharon *See* Appelfeld, Aron
Appelfeld, Aron
  Bertha
    When night fell; an anthology of Holocaust
      short stories; edited by Linda Schermer Ra-
      phael and Marc Lee Raphael
  In the isles of St. George
    Six Israeli novellas; [by] Ruth Almog [et al.];
      edited and with an introduction by Gershon
      Shaked; translated from the Hebrew by
      Dalya Bilu, Philip Simpson, and Marganit
      Weinberger-Rotman
  Kitty
    When night fell; an anthology of Holocaust
      short stories; edited by Linda Schermer Ra-
      phael and Marc Lee Raphael
Appendix. Anderson, D.
Apple, Max
  The eighth day
    Neurotica: Jewish writers on sex; edited by
      Melvin Jules Bukiet
  Gas stations
    Still wild; short fiction of the American West,
      1950 to the present; edited by Larry
      McMurtry
  Paddycake, paddycake—a memoir
    The Ohio Review no62/63 p32-43 2001
  Yao's Chick
    Atlantic Monthly (1993) v292 no4 p175-86 N
      2003
Apple pie. Nissen, T.
The **apple** tree. Trevanian
APPLE TREES
  Healy, J. F. Rotten to the core
  Trevanian. The apple tree
Apples. Brockmeier, K.
Apples from Shlitzbutter's garden. Rubina, D.
Apples in honey. Hendel, Y.
Applied aeronautics. Karnezis, P.
Appreciation at the Door. Andoe, J.
An **apprentice**. Bly, C.
The **apprentice**. Furman, L.
APPRENTICES
  Cai Cehai. The distant sound of tree-felling
  Chekhov, A. P. Vanka

The **approach** to Al-Mu'tasim. Borges, J. L.
Approaching Perimelasma. Landis, G. A.
Approximate to salvation. Joseph, D.
Approximations. Simpson, M.
Apraxia. Stern, D.
Apricots. Bingham, S.
April, Jean Pierre
  Rêve Canadien
    Northern suns; edited by David G. Hartwell
      & Glenn Grant
April. Noel, K.
April in Paris. Le Guin, U. K.
April in Paris. Robinson, P.
April: the story of a love affair. Roth, J.
Apukhtin, A. N.
  Between life and death: a fantastic story
    Apukhtin, A. N. Three tales; English transla-
      tions, notes and a foreword by Philip Tay-
      lor
  The diary of Pavlik Dolsky
    Apukhtin, A. N. Three tales; English transla-
      tions, notes and a foreword by Philip Tay-
      lor
  The papers of Countess D**: a tale in letters
    Apukhtin, A. N. Three tales; English transla-
      tions, notes and a foreword by Philip Tay-
      lor
Apukhtin, Alekseĭ Nikolaevich *See* Apukhtin, A.
  N., 1841-1893
Aqai, Farkhondeh
  One woman, one love
    A Feast in the mirror; stories by contempo-
      rary Iranian women; translated and edited
      by Mohammad Mehdi Khorrami, Shouleh
      Vatanabadi
Aqua Boulevard. Meloy, M.
Aquarium. Canty, K.
Aquerò. Hardy, M.
Aquin, Hubert
  Back on April eleventh
    Other people's mail; an anthology of letter
      stories; edited with an introduction by Gail
      Pool
Aquino, John T.
  The mysterious death of the shadow man
    Royal whodunnits; edited by Mike Ashley
ARAB-ISRAELI CONFLICT, 1948-1949 *See* Is-
  rael-Arab War, 1948-1949
ARAB-JEWISH RELATIONS *See* Jewish-Arab
  relations
ARAB WOMEN
  Raab, E. Rose Jam
  Shifra, S. The night of the kid [excerpt]
  Smilansky, M. Latifa
Arabella Leaves. Ciabattari, J.
ARABIA *See* Arabian Peninsula
ARABIAN PENINSULA
  Johnson-Davies, D. Deal concluded
  Johnson-Davies, D. Fate of a prisoner
  Lopez, B. H. Mornings in Quarain
ARABS
    See also Bedouins; Jewish-Arab rela-
      tions; Moors; Palestinian Arabs
  Borges, J. L. Hakim, the masked dyer of Merv
  Bowles, P. The story of Lahcen and Idir
  Gurnah, A. Bossy
  Papernick, J. An unwelcome guest
    United States
  Michaels, L. Nachman from Los Angeles

Aramaki, Yoshio
Soft clocks
The Review of Contemporary Fiction v22 no2
p36-52 Summ 2002
Arancio, Lawrence
Cross-fertilization
Iowa Review v29 no2 p70-79 Fall 1999
Arandi, Francisco Proaño
Final spells of vertigo in the vestibule
Bomb no78 p92-4 Wint 2001/2002
Arango, Angel
The cosmonaut
Cosmos latinos: an anthology of science fic-
tion from Latin America and Spain; trans-
lated, edited, & with an introduction &
notes by Andrea L. Bell & Yolanda Moli-
na-Gavilán
Arango, Arturo
The waiting room
Dream with no name; contemporary fiction
from Cuba; edited by Juana Ponce de León
and Esteban Ríos Rivera
Arastuyi, Shiva
I came to have tea with my daughter
A Feast in the mirror; stories by contempo-
rary Iranian women; translated and edited
by Mohammad Mehdi Khorrami, Shouleh
Vatanabadi
Araújo, Helena
Asthmatic
Short stories by Latin American women; the
magic and the real; edited by Celia Correas
de Zapata; foreword by Isabel Allende
Arbitration. Kirchheimer, G. D.
Arcana mundi. Girardi, R.
Archangela's place. Skinner, J.
ARCHEOLOGISTS
Clarke, A. C. History lesson
Fowler, K. J. Private grave 9
Gonzalez, R. Canyon de Kayenta
Herling, G. A hot breath from the desert
Oliver, C. If now you grieve a little
Simak, C. D. Grotto of the dancing deer
Vanderbes, J. The hatbox
Wharton, E. A bottle of Perrier
ARCHEOLOGY
See also Prehistoric man
Milletti, C. Villa of the veiled lady
Archeology. Wilson, B.
Archer, Jeffrey
Both sides against the middle
Archer, J. To cut a long story short
Chalk and cheese
Archer, J. To cut a long story short
A change of heart
Archer, J. To cut a long story short
Crime pays
Archer, J. To cut a long story short
Dougie Mortimer's right arm
Sports best short stories; edited by Paul D.
Staudohar
The endgame
Archer, J. To cut a long story short
The expert witness
Archer, J. To cut a long story short
The grass is always greener . . .
Archer, J. To cut a long story short
The letter
Archer, J. To cut a long story short

Love at first sight
Archer, J. To cut a long story short
Other blighters' efforts
Archer, J. To cut a long story short
The reclining woman
Archer, J. To cut a long story short
Something for nothing
Archer, J. To cut a long story short
Too many coincidences
Archer, J. To cut a long story short
A weekend to remember
Archer, J. To cut a long story short
ARCHERY
Browder, C. Fusuda the archer
ARCHITECTS
Blatnik, A. Scratches on the back
Chekhov, A. P. Old age
Lee, R. Fialta
Schlink, B. Sugar peas
Seiffert, R. Architect
Wharton, E. Sanctuary
**ARCHYTAS, OF TARENTUM, FL. 400-365
B.C.**
About
Rucker, R. v. B. The square root of Pythagoras
ARCTIC REGIONS
See also Alaska; Antarctic regions
DeAndrea, W. L. A friend of mine
Osgood, L. Great Sedna
Arden, William, 1924-
*For works written by this author under oth-
er names see* Collins, Michael, 1924-
Ardizzone, Tony
Larabi's ox
Best of Prairie schooner; fiction and poetry;
edited by Hilda Raz
Are these actual miles? Carver, R.
Are we almost there. Brenner, W.
Are we pleasing you tonight? Busch, F.
Arellano, Robert
One out of many
The Kenyon Review ns24 no1 p22-9 Wint
2002
Arena. Brown, F.
Arenas, Reinaldo
Alipio's kingdom
Arenas, R. Mona and other tales; selected and
translated from the Spanish by Dolores M.
Koch
Blacks
Arenas, R. Mona and other tales; selected and
translated from the Spanish by Dolores M.
Koch
End of a story
Arenas, R. Mona and other tales; selected and
translated from the Spanish by Dolores M.
Koch
The glass tower
Arenas, R. Mona and other tales; selected and
translated from the Spanish by Dolores M.
Koch
The Art of the story; an international antholo-
gy of contemporary short stories; edited by
Daniel Halpern
Goodbye mother
The Oxford book of Caribbean short stories;
edited by Stewart Brown and John
Wickham

Arenas, Reinaldo—*Continued*
The great force
    Arenas, R. Mona and other tales; selected and translated from the Spanish by Dolores M. Koch
Halley's comet
    Arenas, R. Mona and other tales; selected and translated from the Spanish by Dolores M. Koch
In the shade of the almond tree
    Arenas, R. Mona and other tales; selected and translated from the Spanish by Dolores M. Koch
Mona
    Arenas, R. Mona and other tales; selected and translated from the Spanish by Dolores M. Koch
The parade begins
    Arenas, R. Mona and other tales; selected and translated from the Spanish by Dolores M. Koch
The parade ends
    Arenas, R. Mona and other tales; selected and translated from the Spanish by Dolores M. Koch
Something is happening on the top floor
    Arenas, R. Mona and other tales; selected and translated from the Spanish by Dolores M. Koch
    Dream with no name; contemporary fiction from Cuba; edited by Juana Ponce de León and Esteban Ríos Rivera
Traitor
    Arenas, R. Mona and other tales; selected and translated from the Spanish by Dolores M. Koch
With my eyes closed
    Arenas, R. Mona and other tales; selected and translated from the Spanish by Dolores M. Koch
Aren't you happy for me? Bausch, R.
Argamak. Babel´, I.
Argelide. Viganò, R.
Argent blood. Hensley, J. L.
ARGENTINA
Borges, J. L. The congress
Borges, J. L. The south
Borges, J. L. There are more things
Gorriti, J. M. The black glove
Gorriti, J. M. The dead man's fiancée
Gorriti, J. M. Gubi Amaya
Gorriti, J. M. The mazorquero's daughter
Lojo, Maria Rosa. Compound eyes
Roffé, R. Transforming the desert
Politics
See Politics—Argentina
Rural life
Borges, J. L. The night of the gifts
Buenos Aires
Borges, J. L. The elderly lady
Borges, J. L. Juan Muraña
Borges, J. L. Man on pink corner
Borges, J. L. Pedro Salvadores
Borges, J. L. The story from Rosendo Juárez
Borges, J. L. Unworthy
Borges, J. L. The wait
Levrero, M. Notes from Buenos Aires
Mueller, M. Exile
The **Argentine**. Berberova, N.

ARGENTINE REPUBLIC *See* Argentina
ARGENTINES
France
Shua, A. M. The white Guanaco in the middle of France
New York (N.Y.)
Codrescu, A. Samba de los agentes
United States
Di Blasi, D. An interview with my husband
Uruguay
Borges, J. L. The dead man
ARGENTINIANS *See* Argentines
Argia. Maleti, G.
Argument and persuasion. Hall, D.
Argument outside a gin mill here. McNulty, J.
Ariadne. Chekhov, A. P.
Ariadne. Le Clézio, J.-M. G.
ARISTOCRACY
    See also Courts and courtiers
Avrich, J. The charwoman
Roth, J. The bust of the emperor
Waugh, E. A house of gentlefolks
England
Cannell, D. The gentleman's gentleman
James, H. An international episode
James, H. Lady Barberina
James, H. The path of duty
France
James, H. Gabrielle de Bergerac
Poland
Singer, I. B. The sorcerer
Russia
Pushkin, A. S. The guests were arriving at the dacha
Pushkin, A. S. In the corner of a small square
Pushkin, A. S. Roslavlev
Spain
Alarcón, P. A. d. The nun
ARISTOPHANES
About
Feeley, G. The crab lice
ARIZONA
Carlson, R. Oxygen
Cohen, S. Nadigo
Coleman, J. C. Ruby's cape
DeMarinis, R. Desert places
Gonzalez, R. Canyon de Kayenta
Guerrero, L. Blanca Rosa
Guerrero, L. Even in heaven
Guerrero, L. The girdle
Guerrero, L. Memories in white
Harty, R. Ongchoma
Harty, R. September
Jance, J. A. Death of a snowbird
Lawrence, D. H. St. Mawr
Sojourner, M. Absolute proof of the cosmos in life
Sojourner, M. Bear house
Sojourner, M. Delicate
Sojourner, M. Estrella Ranchos: where the real west begins
Sojourner, M. Hag
Swarthout, G. F. The ball really carries in the Cactus League because the air is dry
Swarthout, G. F. Going to see George
Vaswani, N. Blue, without sorrow
Winter, E. Blue-sky day
Winter, E. The price you pay

ARIZONA—*Continued*
Flagstaff
Matiella, A. C. The braid
Phoenix
Crane, M. The blood orange tree
Tucson
Evans, E. Suicide's girlfriend
Martin, P. P. Amor e ilusion—Love and illusion
Martin, P. P. Amor encantado—Enchanted love
Martin, P. P. Amor eterno—Eternal love
Poirier, M. J. Cul-de-sacs
Winter, E. Dragon box
Ark of bones. Dumas, H.
ARKANSAS
Gilchrist, E. The Southwest Experimental Fast
    Oxide Reactor
Gilchrist, E. The survival of the fittest
Gilchrist, E. Witness to the crucifixion
Holladay, C. C. Merry-go-sorry
Farm life
See Farm life—Arkansas
Arlo on the fence. Stefaniak, M. H.
Arm of the law. Harrison, H.
Armaments race. Clarke, A. C.
Der **Arme** Dolmetscher. Vonnegut, K.
ARMED FORCES
United States
See United States—Armed forces
ARMENIANS
Agabian, N. Ghosts and bags
Chekhov, A. P. The beauties
Gabrielyan, N. Hide and seek
Gabrielyan, N. The house in Metekhi Lane
Iran
Pirzad, Z. Sour cherry pits
United States
Saroyan, W. The pomegranate trees
Armistice. Berry, M. S.
ARMS AND ARMOR
See also Swords
Johnson-Davies, D. Deal concluded
Pronzini, B. Toy
Armstrong, Charlotte
The second commandment
    Murder most divine; ecclesiastical tales of un-
    holy crimes; edited by Ralph McInerny and
    Martin H. Greenberg
St. Patrick's Day in the morning
    A moment on the edge; 100 years of crime
    stories by women; edited by Elizabeth
    George
Armstrong, Kevin
The cane field
    Armstrong, K. Night watch
Drowning in air
    Armstrong, K. Night watch
The first motion of love
    Armstrong, K. Night watch
Hunga Pass
    Armstrong, K. Night watch
Inside passage
    Armstrong, K. Night watch
The legend of Kuop
    Armstrong, K. Night watch
Night watch
    Armstrong, K. Night watch

ARMSTRONG, LOUIS, 1900-1971
About
Di Filippo, P. And I think to myself, what a
    wonderful world
ARMSTRONG, NEIL, 1930-
About
Aylett, S. If Armstrong was interesting
ARMY HOSPITALS *See* Hospitals and sanatori-
ums
ARMY LIFE *See* Confederate States of America.
Army
ARMY OFFICERS *See* Germany—Army—Offi-
cers; Russia—Army—Officers
Arnason, Eleanor
Dapple: a hwarhath historical romance
    The Year's best science fiction, seventeenth
    annual collection; edited by Gardner Dozois
The grammarian's five daughters
    The Year's best fantasy & horror, thirteenth
    annual collection; edited by Ellen Datlow
    and Terri Windling
Moby Quilt
    The Year's best science fiction, nineteenth an-
    nual collection; edited by Gardner Dozois
The potter of bones
    The Year's best science fiction; twentieth an-
    nual collection; edited by Gardner Dozois
Stellar harvest
    Nebula awards showcase 2002; edited by Kim
    Stanley Robinson
ARNOLD, BENEDICT, 1741-1801
About
L'Amour, L. Meeting at Falmouth
Arnold, Hap *See* Arnold, Henry Harley, 1886-
1950
Arnold, Henry Harley
Bill's first airplane ride
    On glorious wings; the best flying stories of
    the century; edited and introduced by Ste-
    phen Coonts
Arnold, Miah
Losing the Dog's Paddle
    Confrontation no86/87 p177-86 Spr/Summ
    2004
The **Arnold** proof. Kane, J. F.
Arnold's number. Thompson, S.
Arnott, Marion
Marbles
    The best British mysteries; edited by Maxim
    Jakubowski
The **aroma** of Odessa. Babel', I.
Aronson, Heather
Elf consciousness
    American short fiction, vol. 8, no 29-32
Arraignment. Huffman, B., Jr.
Arrangement in black and white. Parker, D.
The **arrangement** of the night office in summer.
    Casey, M.
Arredondo, Inés
Subterranean river
    The Vintage book of Latin American stories;
    edited by Carlos Fuentes and Julio Ortega
Arreola, Juan José
Baby H. P.
    Cosmos latinos: an anthology of science fic-
    tion from Latin America and Spain; trans-
    lated, edited, & with an introduction &
    notes by Andrea L. Bell & Yolanda Moli-
    na-Gavilán

ARRESTS
Browder, C. Silver maple
Gates, D. George lassos moon
Leonard, E. Karen makes out
McNulty, J. Man here keeps getting arrested all the time
Nichols, J. Magic
Sojourner, M. Officer Magdalena, White Shell Woman, and me
Arrival. Vernon, D.
Arrow math. Haake, K.
The **Arrowmont** Prison riddle. Pronzini, B.
Arruda, Michael J.
Reconciliation
The Darkest thirst; a vampire anthology
Arsenault, Michael
A Halloween like any other
Witpunk; edited by Claude Lalumière and Marty Halpern
ARSON
Billman, J. Custer complex
Cohen, S. The battered mailbox
Gorman, E. All these condemned
Gorman, E. Sailing to Atlantis
Hoch, E. D. The Haggard Society
Johnston, B. A. Two liars
Lake, M. D. The tunnel
Lascaux, P. Fire works
Leonard, E. Sparks
Means, D. Assorted fire events
Nakagami, K. House on fire
Perabo, S. Some say the world
Phillips, S. Sockdolager
Pronzini, B. A taste of paradise
Resnick, R. Day 'n nite
Sanders, W. When this world is all on fire
Waugh, E. Love among the ruins
Wharton, E. Mrs. Manstey's view
White, M. C. Burn patterns
Wolven, S. Controlled burn
ART
Brkic, C. A. We will sleep in one nest
Cohen, R. Points of interest
Jenkins, G. Richard and poorer
Tillman, L. Madame Realism lies here
Touré. Solomon's big day
Art. Chekhov, A. P.
Art & craft. Westlake, D. E.
ART COLLECTORS
Bowles, P. Rumor and a ladder
Fish, R. L. The wager
Wharton, E. The daunt Diana
ART CRITICS
Malamud, B. Rembrandt's hat
Weldon, F. Inspector remorse
ART DEALERS
See also Antique dealers
Pearlman, D. D. The Vatican's secret cabinet
Raphael, F. An older woman
ART FORGERIES See Forgery of works of art
ART GALLERIES AND MUSEUMS
Hornby, N. NippleJesus
Krauss, N. Future emergencies
Muñoz, M. Museo de Bellas Artes
Smart, A. Posing
Smith, A. The shortlist season
Sosin, D. Still life
Updike, J. Still life
Art history. Wing, B.

Art in the blood. Stableford, B. M.
Art lesson. Budnitz, J.
Art lover. Davies, R.
ART OBJECTS
See also Antiques
Berkman, P. R. The falling nun
The **art** of correcting. Papernick, J.
The **art** of eating. Greer, A. S.
The **art** of fiction. Anderson, D.
The **art** of fiction. Barone, D.
The **Art** of Heroine Worship. Simms, R.
The **art** of losing. Lord, C.
The **Art** of Love. Xu Xi
The **Art** of Romance. Scott, J.
The **art** of the interview. Galef, D.
The **art** of the matter. Forsyth, F.
The **art** of the possible. Cavell, B.
ART TEACHERS
Budnitz, J. Art lesson
Dyson, J. A slate roof in the rain
ARTHUR, KING
About
Cornwell, B. Excalibur [excerpt]
Knowles, Sir J. King Arthur and his knights [excerpt]
Steinbeck, J. Morgan le Fay
Twain, M. A Connecticut Yankee at King Arthur's court [excerpt]
Articles of Faith. Ochsner, G.
Artie Glick in a family way. Epstein, J.
The **artificial** cloud. Tussing, J.
ARTIFICIAL INSEMINATION
Eugenides, J. Baster
O'Connell, M. Veronica's veil
ARTIFICIAL INTELLIGENCE
Aldiss, B. W. Supertoys in other seasons
Aldiss, B. W. Supertoys last all summer long
Aldiss, B. W. Supertoys when winter comes
Cherryh, C. J. Pots
Cherryh, C. J. Poys
Doctorow, C. All day sucker
Kelly, J. P. The prisoner of Chillon
Mixon, L. J. Proxies [excerpt]
Thomas, S. Correspondence [excerpt]
Thomson, A. Virtual girl [excerpt]
Waldrop, H. Sun's up!
Watson, I. Caucus winter
Watson, I. Three-legged dog
Zettel, S. Fool's errand
ARTIFICIAL LIFE
McAuley, P. J. Dr Pretorius and the lost temple
Pronzini, B. and Malzberg, B. N. A clone at last
Temple, W. F. The 4-sided triangle
ARTIFICIAL RESPIRATION
Fulton, J. Clean away
ARTIFICIAL SATELLITES
Clarke, A. C. Dial F for Frankenstein
Clarke, A. C. Hate
Clarke, A. C. I remember Babylon
ARTIST COLONIES
Summers, H. S. The vireo's nest
ARTIST LIFE
Bunin, I. A. Muza
The **artist** of the beautiful. Hawthorne, N.
ARTISTS
See also Artist life; Illustrators; Painters; Sculptors; Women artists
Alcott, L. M. A pair of eyes; or, Modern magic
Alcott, L. M. Victoria: a woman's statue

ARTISTS—*Continued*

Alexis, A. The third terrace

Archer, J. Chalk and cheese

Auchincloss, L. The Virginia redbird

Bail, M. A, B, C, D, E, F, G, H, I, J, K, L, M, N, O, P, Q, R, S, T, U, V, W, X, Y, Z

Bellow, S. Zetland: by a character witness

Bingham, S. Benjamin

Bingham, S. A remarkably pretty girl

Bocock, M. The face

Bradbury, R. Olé Orozco! Siqueiros, sí!

Brown, C. Miniature man

Butler, R. O. I got married to a milk can

Byatt, A. S. Christ in the house of Martha and Mary

Byatt, A. S. A lamia in the Cévennes

Campbell, R. The other woman

Carson, J. Flying apart

Chekhov, A. P. The grasshopper

Coleman, J. C. Borderlands

Erdrich, L. Revival Road

Fischer, T. Portrait of the artist as a foaming deathmonger

Fitzgerald, P. The red-haired girl

Fry, S. The impressionists in winter

Furman, L. The apprentice

Gabrielyan, N. The house in Metekhi Lane

Greer, R. O. Revision

Harrison, H. Portrait of the artist

Helms, B. Once

Helms, B. Oysters

Hermann, J. Camera obscura

Hermann, J. Sonja

Janowitz, T. Physics

Jesús, P. d. The portrait

Lee, M. Oh, happy day

Leong, R. Bodhi leaves

Linscott, G. For all the saints

Maddern, P. C. Things fall apart

McBain, E. Activity in the flood plain

Robison, M. Kite and paint

Roorbach, B. Thanksgiving

Schmidt, H. J. The funeral party

Scholz, C. Altamira

Shteyngart, G. Shylock on the Neva

Singer, I. B. Moishele

Singleton, G. Page-a-day

Singleton, G. Vietnam

Skillings, R. D. Paint

Spatz, G. Lisa picking cockles

Stern, D. Imperato placeless

Stern, D. Messenger

Taylor, T. L. Francisco's watch

Taylor, T. L. Newstart 2.0 TM

Tinti, H. Preservation

Updike, J. Avec la bébé-sitter

Wilson, A. Home, James, and don't spare the horses

Zabytko, I. The prodigal son enters heaven

Artists in the ghetto. Bryks, R.

The **artist's** life. Desai, A.

An **artist's** life. Harrison, H.

ARTISTS' MODELS

Budnitz, J. Art lesson

Chambers, R. W. The yellow sign

Fitzgerald, P. The red-haired girl

James, H. The sweetheart of M. Briseux

Leiber, F. The girl with the hungry eyes

Sandor, M. God's spies

Sandor, M. Portrait of my mother, who posed nude in wartime

Waugh, E. Essay

An **artist's** story. Chekhov, A. P.

Arvin, Nick

Aeronautics

Arvin, N. In the electric Eden; stories

Commemorating

Arvin, N. In the electric Eden; stories

Electric fence

Arvin, N. In the electric Eden; stories

In the electric Eden

Arvin, N. In the electric Eden; stories

The prototype

Arvin, N. In the electric Eden; stories

Radio ads

Arvin, N. In the electric Eden; stories

Take your child to work

Arvin, N. In the electric Eden; stories

Telescope

Arvin, N. In the electric Eden; stories

Two thousand Germans in Frankenmuth

Arvin, N. In the electric Eden; stories

What they teach you in engineering school

Arvin, N. In the electric Eden; stories

Arzola, Jorge Luis

Essential Things

Grand Street no71 p106-7 Spr 2003

The Night They Gave Orders for Us to Be Killed

Grand Street no71 p105-6 Spr 2003

As a Woman Grows Older. Coetzee, J. M.

As above, so below. Rucker, R. v. B.

As big as the Ritz. Benford, G.

As birds bring forth the sun. MacLeod, A.

As easy as ABC. Reiner, C.

As it is in heaven. Cherry, K.

As Kingfishers catch fire. McCann, C.

As luck would have it. Henley, P.

As the lord lives, he is one of our mother's children. Hopkins, P. E.

Asaro, Catherine

Ave de paso

Redshift; extreme visions of speculative fiction; edited by Al Sarrantonio

Dance in blue

Wondrous beginnings; edited by Steven H. Silver and Martin H. Greenberg

The quantum rose

Nebula Awards showcase 2003; edited by Nancy Kress

Ascent by balloon from the yard of Walnut Street Jail. Wideman, J. E.

The **ascent** of Eli Israel. Papernick, J.

Asch, Sholem

"Heil, Hitler!"

When night fell; an anthology of Holocaust short stories; edited by Linda Schermer Raphael and Marc Lee Raphael

The story of beautiful Marie

Neugroschel, J. No star too beautiful; Yiddish stories from 1382 to the present; compiled and translated by Joachim Neugroschel

Asendorf, Aracelis Gonzalez

The gossamer girl

100% pure Florida fiction; an anthology; edited by Susan Hubbard and Robley Wilson

ASEXUAL REPRODUCTION

Bisson, T. Macs

ASEXUAL REPRODUCTION—*Continued*
Butler, O. E. Bloodchild
Chiang, T. Seventy-two letters
Due, T. Like daughter
Dyer, S. N. Sins of the mothers
Eakin, W. Homesickness
Eakin, W. Roadkill Fred
Egan, G. Singleton
Egan, G. Wang's carpets
Ellison, H. Killing Bernstein
Hjortsberg, W. The clone who ran for congress
Jones, G. La Cenerentola
Latour, J. Golam
Leong, R. Hemispheres
Rusch, K. K. Millennium babies
Sheffield, C. Out of copyright
Sturgeon, T. The sex opposite
Thurm, M. Personal correspondence
Varley, J. Retrograde summer
Williams, W. J. Lethe
Ash. Billman, J.
Ash on Guavas. Scott, L.
ASH WEDNESDAY
Alas, L. The burial of the sardine
Ashes. Skillings, R. D.
Ashes: the fall of the House of Loris. Herling, G.
Ashputtle. Straub, P.
The **Ashtray**. Carpenter, R.
ASIA
    See also Southeast Asia
ASIA, SOUTHEASTERN *See* Southeast Asia
ASIA MINOR
    See also Troy (Ancient city)
ASIAN AMERICANS
Chan, D. M. Brilliant disguise
Chan, D. M. Falling
Chan, D. M. Goblin fruit
Chan, D. M. Lost years
Chan, D. M. Mystery boy
Chan, D. M. Open circles
Chan, D. M. Seven swans
Chan, D. M. Watchtower
Chee, A. Gold
Lee, D. Casul water
Lee, D. The Lone Night Cantina
Lee, D. The possible husband
Lee, D. The price of eggs in China
Leong, R. Camouflage
Leong, R. Daughters
Leong, R. Eclipse
Leong, R. No Bruce Lee
Leong, R. Runaways
Leong, R. Samsara
Leong, R. Virgins and Buddhas
Pittalwala, I. House of cards
Asimov, Isaac
The acquisitive chuckle
    Asimov, I. The return of the black widowers
Early Sunday morning
    Asimov, I. The return of the black widowers
The guest's guest
    Asimov, I. The return of the black widowers
The haunted cabin
    Asimov, I. The return of the black widowers
The iron gem
    Asimov, I. The return of the black widowers
It's such a beautiful day
    The SFWA grand masters v2; edited by
      Frederik Pohl

The last question
    The SFWA grand masters v2; edited by
      Frederik Pohl
The last story
    Asimov, I. The return of the black widowers
Lost in a space warp
    Asimov, I. The return of the black widowers
The Martian way
    The SFWA grand masters v2; edited by
      Frederik Pohl
The men who read Isaac Asimov
    Asimov, I. The return of the black widowers
Nightfall
    The Science fiction hall of fame: volume one,
      1929-1964; the greatest science fiction sto-
      ries of all time chosen by the members of
      the Science Fiction Writers of America; ed-
      ited by Robert Silverberg
Northwestward
    Asimov, I. The return of the black widowers
The obvious factor
    Asimov, I. The return of the black widowers
Ph as in Phony
    Asimov, I. The return of the black widowers
Police at the door
    Asimov, I. The return of the black widowers
The redhead
    Asimov, I. The return of the black widowers
Robot dreams
    Masterpieces: the best science fiction of the
      century; edited by Orson Scott Card
Sixty million trillion combinations
    Asimov, I. The return of the black widowers
Strikebreaker
    The SFWA grand masters v2; edited by
      Frederik Pohl
To the barest
    Asimov, I. The return of the black widowers
Triple devil
    Asimov, I. The return of the black widowers
The woman in the bar
    Asimov, I. The return of the black widowers
The wrong house
    Asimov, I. The return of the black widowers
Yes, but why?
    Asimov, I. The return of the black widowers
Ask Amelio. Carter, E.
Asleep. Yoshimoto, B.
ASP. Adam, C.
Aspects of motherhood. Casey, M.
The **Aspern** papers. James, H.
L'asphyxie [excerpt] Leduc, V.
Asplund, Russell William
The Rabbi and the sorcerer
    Browning, A. Murder is no mitzvah; edited
      by Abigail Browning
Assailable character. Daugherty, T.
The **assailant**. Oates, J. C.
ASSASSINATION
Albert, J. Byron
Borges, J. L. Avelino Arredondo
Borges, J. L. The theme of the traitor and the
    hero
Bradbury, R. Downwind from Gettysburg
Collins, M. A part of history
Davidson, A. The lineaments of gratified desire
Gordimer, N. Homage
Harrison, H. From fanaticism; or, For reward
Hoch, E. D. The day the dogs died

ASSASSINATION—*Continued*
Hodgen, C. Three parting shots and a forecast
Kaminsky, S. M. The buck stops here
Malzberg, B. N. Darwinian facts
Malzberg, B. N. Improvident excess
Malzberg, B. N. The intransigents
Marías, J. Broken binoculars
Ritchie, J. The little green book
Shteyngart, G. Shylock on the Neva
The **Assassination** Bureau. Nelson, R. F.
ASSAULT AND BATTERY
Michaels, L. The deal
Michaels, L. Going places
Oates, J. C. The assailant
Assemblies. Walser, M.
The **assembly** line. Klíma, I.
ASSES AND MULES
Doctorow, C. Return to Pleasure Island
Grey, Z. Tappan's burro
L'Amour, L. A mule for Santa Fe
Lansdale, J. R. The mule rustlers
Lincoln, C. A very close conspiracy
Wolfe, G. No planets strike
Asset. Wallace, D. F.
Assimilation. Alexie, S.
Assistance. Robinson, R.
The **assistant** murderer. Hammett, D.
The **assistant** to Dr. Jacob. Schaller, E.
Assisted living. Banks, R.
Assorted fire events. Means, D.
Assunta. Tozzi, F.
ASTEROIDS
Bear, G. The wind from a burning woman
Clarke, A. C. The hammer of God
Crowther, P. Songs of leaving
Kornbluth, C. M. That share of glory
Oliver, C. Didn't he ramble?
Sheckley, R. Mind-slaves of Manotori
ASTHMA
Eggers, P. Leo, chained
Asthmatic. Araújo, H.
The **astral** body of a U.S. mail truck. Herlihy, J. L.
The **astral** visitor Delta blues. Fleming, R.
Astro City. Peabody, R.
Astrolaters. MacGowan, R.
ASTROLOGY
Carl, L. S. The eye of the beholder
Crider, B. Out like a lion
Klíma, I. Uranus in the house of death
Lovesey, P. Star struck
Ponte, A. J. Heart of skitalietz
Winterson, J. Orion
Astronaut. Gussoff, C.
ASTRONAUTS
    See also Women astronauts
Adolph, J. B. The falsifier
Baxter, S. The Xeelee flower
Blish, J. Common time
Bradbury, R. June 2001: And the moon be still as bright
Clarke, A. C. Breaking strain
Clarke, A. C. Maelstrom II
DeAndrea, W. L. Sabotage
Delany, S. R. Aye, and Gomorrah. . .
DuBois, B. The star thief
Gores, J. Faulty register
Harrison, H. Down to earth
Harrison, H. Simulated trainer

McDonald, I. The old cosmonaut and the construction worker dream of Mars
Pohl, F. The gold at the starbow's end
Scholz, C. The eve of the last Apollo
Sturgeon, T. The man who lost the sea
Vance, J. Sail 25
Astronauts. Iribarne, M.
The **astronaut** tells of her love. Jones, G.
ASTRONOMERS
Benford, G. Anomalies
Clarke, A. C. Dog Star
Clarke, A. C. Let there be light
Jones, G. The astronomer tells of her love
ASTRONOMICAL OBSERVATORIES
Asimov, I. Nightfall
The **astronomical** scarf. Rendell, R.
ASTRONOMY
    See also Outer space; Stars; Telescope names of individual planets
Wilson, R. C. The Perseids
Asuquo; or, The winds of Harmattan. Okorafor, N.
Asylum [excerpt] McGrath, P.
At 15, he had been a leader in. Blitz, R.
At a country house. Chekhov, A. P.
At Celilo. Austin, S.
At Chênière Caminada. Chopin, K.
At Christmas time. Chekhov, A. P.
At Copper View. Carlson, R.
At Eventide. Koja, K.
At five in the afternoon. Steiner, G.
At grandmother's. Babel', I.
At Hiruharama. Fitzgerald, P.
At home. Chekhov, A. P.
At home in the pubs of old London. Fowler, C.
At Horseneck Beach. Orner, P.
At Isella. James, H.
At last. Dyson, J.
At last, the Ark. Clark, J.
At last, the true story of Frankenstein. Harrison, H.
At least. Skillings, R. D.
At Least It's Free. Albritton, L.
At life's limits. Salaam, K. I.
At Paso Jojo. Bowles, P.
At Prayerbook Cross. Harris, M.
At Random. Zacharias, L.
At Reparata. Ford, J.
At Saint Valentine's. Babel', I.
At Schindler's. Malouf, D.
At the bar. McIlvanney, W.
At the bath-house. Chekhov, A. P.
At the beach. Adams, A.
At the beach. Robinson, R.
At the Blue Breakers. Campbell, E.
At the bottom of the lake. Broyard, B.
At the 'Cadian ball. Chopin, K.
At the castle. Čapek, K.
At the "Changing Careers" conference. Kobin, J.
At the Conrad Hilton. Orner, P.
At the door. Yi, T.-H.
At the edge of the new world. Phillips, D. R.
At the El Sol. Carlson, R.
At the Four Seasons Hotel. Rawley, D.
At the great divide. Shapiro, G.
At the hop. Crider, B. and Crider, J.
At the huts of Ajala. Shawl, N.
At the Jim Bridger. Carlson, R.
At the Krungthep Plaza. Bowles, P.

At the lake. Drake, R.
At the manor. See Chekhov, A. P. At a country house
At the moment of destruction, you stop to examine the wreckage. Migdal, L.
At the money. Wadholm, R.
At the Motel Rainbow. Orner, P.
At the No. 1 Phoenix Garden. Nissen, T.
At the premier's literary awards. Chan, M.
At the punishment cliff for women. Meredith, D.
At the request of Ochun. Ponte, A. J.
At the river. Swan, M.
At the tent of Holofernes. Tremayne, P.
At the water's end. Lincoln, C.
At tide's turning. Mixon, L. J.
At Vega's taqueria. Lupoff, R. A.
Atasdi: fish story. Pettigrew, D. K.
ATHEISM
  Goran, L. A guest on Good Friday
Atheist hit by truck. McNulty, J.
The **atheist's** bible. Camenietzki, S.
Atheling, William, Jr. See Blish, James, 1921-1975
Athénaïse. Chopin, K.
Athill, Diana
  Alive, Alive-oh!
    Granta v85 p19-38 Spr 2004
ATHLETES
      See also Women athletes
  Greenberg, A. The high hard one
  Malone, M. The power
  Nailah, A. Bucket
  Swarthout, G. F. The ball really carries in the Cactus League because the air is dry
Atkins, Jack See Harris, Mark, 1922-
Atkins, Peter
  Adventures in further education
    Best new horror 10; edited and with an introduction by Stephen Jones
  King of outer space
    The Museum of horrors; edited by Dennis Etchison
Atkinson, Kate
  The bodies vest
    Atkinson, K. Not the end of the world; stories
  The cat lover
    Atkinson, K. Not the end of the world; stories
  Charlene and Trudi go shopping
    Atkinson, K. Not the end of the world; stories
  Dissonance
    Atkinson, K. Not the end of the world; stories
  Evil doppelgängers
    Atkinson, K. Not the end of the world; stories
  Pleasureland
    Atkinson, K. Not the end of the world; stories
  Sheer big waste of love
    Atkinson, K. Not the end of the world; stories
  Temporal anomaly
    Atkinson, K. Not the end of the world; stories
  Transparent fiction
    Atkinson, K. Not the end of the world; stories
  Tunnel of fish
    Atkinson, K. Not the end of the world; stories
  Unseen translation
    Atkinson, K. Not the end of the world; stories
  Wedding favors
    Atkinson, K. Not the end of the world; stories
ATLANTA (GA.) See Georgia—Atlanta

ATLANTIC CITY (N.J.) *See* New Jersey—Atlantic City
Atlantic City. Orner, P.
Atlantic crossing. Winterson, J.
The **atmosphere** of Vienna. Cobb, W. J.
The **atomic** age. Barkley, B.
Atomic Bar. Billman, J.
ATOMIC BOMB
  Butler, O. E. Speech sounds
  Kornbluth, C. M. Two dooms
  Leiber, F. A bad day for sales
  Robinson, K. S. The lucky strike
ATOMIC ENERGY *See* Nuclear energy
ATOMIC WARFARE *See* Nuclear warfare
ATONEMENT
  Doerr, A. The caretaker
  Singer, I. B. A crown of feathers
ATONEMENT, DAY OF *See* Yom Kippur
ATROCITIES
      See also Holocaust, Jewish (1933-1945); Jews—Persecutions; Massacres; Torture
  Kennedy, A. L. White house at night
  Murray, J. Watson and the shark
  Tran, V. The back streets of Hoi An
Atrophy. Wharton, E.
The **Attached** Couple. Fraterrigo, M.
Attachment. Lao She
Attack of the love dogma. Touré
The **attack** on the mountain. Swarthout, G. F.
The **attainable** border of the birds. Lord, N.
Attanasio, A. A.
  Hellbent
    The Crow; shattered lives & broken dreams; edited by J. O'Barr and Ed Kramer
ATTEMPTED MURDER *See* Murder stories
ATTEMPTED SUICIDE *See* Suicide
ATTITUDE (PSYCHOLOGY)
      See also Prejudices
ATTORNEYS *See* Law and lawyers
Atwell, Mary Stewart
  Blue night, Clover Lake
    Best new American voices 2004; guest editor John Casey; series editors John Kulka and Natalie Danford
Atwood, Margaret
  Death by landscape
    The Scribner anthology of contemporary short fiction; fifty North American stories since 1970; Lex Williford and Michael Martone, editors
  Freeforall
    Northern suns; edited by David G. Hartwell & Glenn Grant
  My life as a bat
    In our nature: stories of wildness; selected and introduced by Donna Seaman
  Significant moments in the life of my mother
    Snapshots: 20th century mother-daughter fiction; edited by Joyce Carol Oates and Janet Berliner
  Three Chronicles
    Ms. v12 no3 p30-4 Summ 2002
  Wilderness tips
    The Art of the story; an international anthology of contemporary short stories; edited by Daniel Halpern
AU PAIRS
  Bellow, S. A theft
  Chimera, B. July

AU PAIRS—*Continued*

Keegan, C. Where the water's deepest

Tamaro, S. Rispondimi

Au Sable. Oates, J. C.

Aub. Parker, G.

Auchincloss, Louis

All that may become a man

Auchincloss, L. Manhattan monologues

The anniversary

Auchincloss, L. The anniversary and other stories

Collaboration

Auchincloss, L. Manhattan monologues

DeCicco v. Schweizer

Auchincloss, L. The anniversary and other stories

The Devil and Guy Lansing

Auchincloss, L. The anniversary and other stories

The facts of fiction

Auchincloss, L. The anniversary and other stories

Harry's brother

Auchincloss, L. Manhattan monologues

He knew he was right

Auchincloss, L. Manhattan monologues

The heiress

Auchincloss, L. Manhattan monologues

The interlude

Auchincloss, L. The anniversary and other stories

The justice clerk

Auchincloss, L. Manhattan monologues

The last of the great courtesans

Auchincloss, L. The anniversary and other stories

Man of the Renaissance

Auchincloss, L. The anniversary and other stories

The marriage broker

Auchincloss, L. Manhattan monologues

The merger

Auchincloss, L. Manhattan monologues

The scarlet letters

Auchincloss, L. Manhattan monologues

The treacherous age

Auchincloss, L. Manhattan monologues

The veterans

Auchincloss, L. The anniversary and other stories

The Virginia redbird

Auchincloss, L. The anniversary and other stories

AUCTIONS

Bukiet, M. J. Splinters

Butler, R. O. Fair warning

Forsyth, F. The art of the matter

Lundquist, R. A free sinner

Auditor. Reifler, N.

Audrey. Phillips, M.

AUDUBON, JOHN JAMES, 1785-1851

About

Howard, M. Big as life

Auerbach, John

The anatomy and death of a dream

Auerbach, J. Tales of Grabowski; Transformations, Escape & other stories

The border incident

Auerbach, J. Tales of Grabowski; Transformations, Escape & other stories

Episodes in autobiography

Auerbach, J. Tales of Grabowski; Transformations, Escape & other stories

Escape

Auerbach, J. Tales of Grabowski; Transformations, Escape & other stories

Transformations

Auerbach, J. Tales of Grabowski; Transformations, Escape & other stories

August 1966. Waberi, A. A.

August 25, 1983. Borges, J. L.

August heat. Harvey, W. F.

AUGUSTINE, SAINT, BISHOP OF HIPPO

About

Updike, J. Augustine's concubine

Augustine de Villeblanche; or, Love's strategy. Sade, marquis de

Aunt Agatha leaving. Kenney, S.

Aunt Delia and her twins. Reiner, C.

Aunt Emma's defense. Collins, B.

Aunt Hester. Lumley, B.

Aunt Lympy's interference. Chopin, K.

Auntee and the two nieces. Drake, R.

Auntie Elspeth's Halloween story; or, The gourd, the bad, and the ugly. Friesner, E. M.

AUNTS

See also Nieces

Alcott, L. M. Lu Sing

Berberova, N. The little stranger

Bradbury, R. Autumn afternoon

Budnitz, J. Chaperone

Caspers, N. Vegetative states

Chopin, K. A family affair

Clarke, A. C. The reluctant orchid

Crowley, J. Her bounty to the dead

Danticat, E. Night talkers

De la Mare, W. Seaton's aunt

Deane, J. F. Big Lil

Drake, R. Graduation from the air

Edgerton, C. Lunch at the Piccadilly

Fischerová, D. My conversations with Aunt Marie

Flythe, S. A family of breast feeders

Frame, R. La Plume de ma tante

Gates, D. George lassos moon

Gunn, K. Visitor

Gurganus, A. The practical heart

Henley, P. Worship of the common heart

Hoffman, W. Humility

Honig, L. Hilda

Howard, M. Children with matches

Jaime-Becerra, M. Every night is ladies' night

Joseph, D. Shared and stolen

Lamé, A. Mapping

Lao She. Autobiography of a minor character

Lempel, Blume. The death of my aunt

Lerner, M. Little selves

Lewis, W. H. Germinating

Lieu, J. Always a descendant

Lincoln, C. A hook will sometimes keep you

Lumley, B. Aunt Hester

Magy, R. Family

Mastretta, A. Aunt Concha Esparza

McCracken, E. Here's your hat what's your hurry

Müller, H. Rotten pears

AUNTS—*Continued*
Munro, A. Family furnishings
Poirier, M. J. A note on the type
Robison, M. Happy boy, Allen
Senior, O. Do angels wear brassieres?
Singer, I. B. Guests on a winter night
Stefaniak, M. H. A note to biographers regarding famous author Flannery O'Connor
Troy, M. Mercy the midget
Vapnyar, L. Love lessons — Mondays, 9 A.M.
Youngblood, S. Triple X
Aura, cry, fall, and fit. Weingarten, R.
Auschwitz, our home (a letter). Borowski, T.
Ausherman, Stephen
Mistrals
New Letters v69 no1 p139-46 2002
Austerlitz. Sebald, W. G.
Austin, Mary Hunter
Old Spanish gardens
Of leaf and flower; stories and poems for gardeners; edited by Charles Dean and Clyde Wachsberger; illustrations by Clyde Wachsberger
Austin, Susan
At Celilo
Kulka, J. and Danford, N. The New American voices 2003; guest editor Joyce Carol Oates; series editors John Kulka and Natalie Danford
AUSTIN (TEX.) *See* Texas—Austin
AUSTRALIA
Brandt, W. Paradise Cove
Chandler, A. B. The mountain movers
Dowling, T. The saltimbanques
Fitzgerald, P. The means of escape
Frahm, L. Borderline
Jenkins, G. In the outback
Jones, G. Knowledge
Jones, G. These eyes
Jones, G. The word 'Ruby'
Lawson, C. Unborn again
Malouf, D. Great Day
Malouf, D. Jacko's reach
Malouf, D. Lone Pine
Sussex, L. Matilda told such dreadful lies
Native peoples
See Australian aborigines
Rural life
Malouf, D. Closer
Brisbane
Bail, M. Home ownership
Malouf, D. Dream stuff
The **Australia** stories. Pierce, T. J.
AUSTRALIAN ABORIGINES
Dedman, S. The wind shall blow for ever mair
Malouf, D. Blacksoil country
Vinge, V. Conquest by default
AUSTRALIAN SOLDIERS *See* Soldiers—Australia
AUSTRALIANS
China
Jones, G. Touching Tiananmen
India
Jones, G. Veronica
Thailand
Murray, S. Walkabout
AUSTRIA
Roth, J. Stationmaster Fallmerayer

Vienna
Jones, G. 'Life probably saved by imbecile dwarf'
Schnitzler, A. Baron von Leisenbohg's destiny
Schnitzler, A. The dead are silent
Shields, J. The Fig Eater [excerpt]
Zweig, S. Letter from an unknown woman
AUSTRIAN ALPS *See* Alps
Author, author. Linzner, G.
The **author** of "Beltraffio". James, H.
AUTHORITARIANISM *See* Totalitarianism
AUTHORS
See also Art critics; Authorship; Dramatists; Poets; Women authors names of individual authors, dramatists, poets, etc.
Adam, C. Lark
Alameddine, R. My grandmother, the grandmaster
Alas, L. Change of light
Alcott, L. M. Mark Field's mistake
Alcott, L. M. Mark Field's success
Alexie, S. Indian country
Anderson, D. Wonder bread
Arenas, R. The glass tower
Auerbach, J. The anatomy and death of a dream
Babel´, I. Inspiration
Babel´, I. Nine
Banville, J. Nightwind
Bart, P. The ghostwriter
Barth, J. A detective and a turtle
Bellow, S. What kind of day did you have?
Berry, R. M. Second story
Bisson, T. 10:07:24
Blatnik, A. Actually
Bocock, M. Alice and me
Bond, N. The bookshop
Borges, J. L. August 25, 1983
Borges, J. L. Pierre Menard, author of the Quixote
Borges, J. L. Shakespeare's memory
Borges, J. L. A survey of the works of Herbert Quain
Borges, J. L. Three versions of Judas
Borges, J. L. A weary man's utopia
Boylan, C. Bad-natured dog
Boylan, C. Perfect love
Boyle, T. C. Achates McNeil
Bradbury, R. Any friend of Nicholas Nickleby's is a friend of mine
Bradbury, R. Banshee
Bradbury, R. A careful man dies
Bradbury, R. The exiles
Bradbury, R. The R.B., G.K.C. and G.B.S. forever Orient
Bradbury, R. The F. Scott/Tolstoy/Ahab accumulator
Bradbury, R. Forever and the Earth
Bradbury, R. I get the blues when it rains (A remembrance)
Bradbury, R. Lafayette, farewell
Bradbury, R. Last rites
Bradbury, R. One more for the road
Bradbury, R. Quid pro quo
Bradbury, R. We'll just act natural
Bradbury, R. The wonderful death of Dudley Stone
Bryce Echenique, A. A brief reappearance by Florence, this autumn
Bukiet, M. J. Paper hero

AUTHORS—*Continued*

Bukoski, A. A philosophy of dust
Bullins, E. Support your local police
Campbell, R. Kill me hideously
Campbell, R. No story in it
Carver, R. Put yourself in my shoes
Casal, L. A love story according to Cyrano Prufrock
Cassill, R. V. And in my heart
Chan, M. At the premier's literary awards
Charteris, L. The mystery of the child's toy
Chaudhuri, A. Prelude to an autobiography: a fragment
Chesnutt, C. W. A grass widow
Clark, J. Spin-off
Codrescu, A. The babysitter
Codrescu, A. Samba de los agentes
Cohen, R. Influence
Cohen, S. Neville
Cole, C. B. Young Hemingways
Collins, M. Silent partner
Conlon, E. Telling
Connor, J. Writing the war novel
Coward, M. Twelve of the little buggers
Crowley, J. Novelty
D'Amato, B. Of course you know that chocolate is a vegetable
Davis, R. Fat Tuesday
De Lint, C. The words that remain
DeMarco, T. The Ninja
Di Filippo, P. Have gun, will edit
Disch, T. M. The squirrel cage
Dodd, S. M. Ethiopia
Dooling, R. Diary of an immortal man
Dunmore, H. Mason's mini-break
Dybek, S. Lunch at the Loyola Arms
Ellison, H. Tired old man
Englander, N. The twenty-seventh man
Epstein, J. Freddy Duchamp in action
Epstein, J. The master's ring
Evenson, B. Moran's Mexico: a refutation by C. Stelzmann
Evenson, B. One over twelve
Fitzgerald, F. S. Crazy Sunday
Flynn, R. Truth and beauty
Franzen, J. The failure
Freudenberger, N. Letter from the last bastion
Galef, D. The landlord
García Márquez, G. The ghosts of August
Garmendia, S. The melancholic pedestrian
Gash, J. Jack and Jill, R.I.P.
Gates, D. The bad thing
Gautreaux, T. The Pine Oil Writers' Conference
Glover, D. H. The obituary writer
Gray, A. Aiblins
Gray, A. Wellbeing
Greenberg, M. H. A literary death
Hammett, D. The second-story angel
Harrison, J. I forgot to go to Spain
Hartley, L. P. W.S.
Hawthorne, N. The Devil in manuscript
Hazel, R. White Anglo-Saxon Protestant
Hearon, S. A prince of a fellow [excerpt]
Hemon, A. Blind Jozef Pronek
Hemon, A. Blind Jozef Pronek & Dead Souls
Hermann, J. This side of the Oder
Highsmith, P. Variations on a game
Hinostroza, R. The benefactor
Hoffman, W. Tenant

James, H. The author of "Beltraffio"
James, H. The lesson of the master
Johnson-Davies, D. A short weekend
Kaplan, H. The spiral
Kawabata, Y. Nature
Kawabata, Y. Silence
Kawabata, Y. Yumiura
Kelly, J. P. Hubris
King, S. The Road Virus heads north
Klass, P. Dedication
Knight, M. Ellen's book
Kureishi, H. Strangers when we meet
Kureishi, H. Sucking stones
Kureishi, H. That was then
Lansdale, J. R. Bestsellers guaranteed
Lavin, M. A story with a pattern
Lavin, M. Trastevere
Leavitt, D. The term paper artist
Lee, A. Anthropology
Lefcourt, P. Thinning the herd
Locklin, G. Becalmed
Locklin, G. Fin de semestre
Locklin, G. The four-day workweek
Locklin, G. O Tannenbaum
Locklin, G. A sober reading of Dr. Sigmund Freud
Locklin, G. The story story
Lord, N. The census taker
Lupoff, R. A. Mr. Greene and the monster
Lustbader, E. V. An exaltation of termagants
Malouf, D. Dream stuff
Marechera, D. Thought tracks in the snow
Marías, J. Everything bad comes back
Maron, M. Craquelure
Maron, M. No, I'm not Jane Marple, but since you ask
Maron, M. Roman's holiday
Marston, E. Slaughter in the Strand
Massie, A. In the bare lands
Mazor, J. Durango
McBrearty, R. G. The things I don't know about
McDermid, V. The consolation blonde
McDermid, V. The wagon mound
Michaels, L. Tell me everything
Miller, R. Julianne
Moody, W. Matinee
Nesbitt, M. The children's book of victims
Nichols, J. Mackerel
Nolan, W. F. An act of violence
Oates, J. C. The high school sweetheart
Onions, O. The beckoning fair one
Ortiz, S. J. Anything
Painter, P. The real story
Paretsky, S. Heartbreak house
Paul, B. Stet
Pickard, N. Nine points for murder
Polansky, S. Beard
Pronzini, B. A craving for originality
Pronzini, B. and Malzberg, B. N. Prose bowl
Raphael, F. God and mammon
Raphael, F. L.S.D.
Raphael, F. An older woman
Raphael, F. Shared credit
Raphael, F. The siren's song
Raphael, F. Son of Enoch
Rosenfeld, S. The last known thing
Roth, J. Rare and ever rarer in this world of empirical facts. . .
Roth, P. Smart money

AUTHORS—*Continued*
Russell, R. Evil star
Russo, R. Poison
Saroyan, A. Hollywood lessons
Saroyan, A. My literary life
Saroyan, A. The war
Schmidt, H. J. Six figures in search of an author
Schoemperlen, D. The man of my dreams
Schoemperlen, D. Stranger than fiction
Scholz, C. Invisible ink
Schwartz, L. S. By a dimming light
Sheckley, R. The day the aliens came
Shrayer-Petrov, D. Dismemberers
Shrayer-Petrov, D. Old writer Foreman
Singer, I. B. The admirer
Singer, I. B. The adventure
Singer, I. B. The beard
Singer, I. B. The bird
Singer, I. B. The bond
Singer, I. B. The cabalist of East Broadway
Singer, I. B. The cafeteria
Singer, I. B. Caricature
Singer, I. B. Confused
Singer, I. B. A day in Coney Island
Singer, I. B. Dr. Beeber
Singer, I. B. Escape from civilization
Singer, I. B. Hanka
Singer, I. B. The joke
Singer, I. B. The lecture
Singer, I. B. The manuscript
Singer, I. B. The mentor
Singer, I. B. Morris and Timna
Singer, I. B. My adventures 25 as an idealist
Singer, I. B. The New Year party
Singer, I. B. One night in Brazil
Singer, I. B. A party in Miami Beach
Singer, I. B. Remnants
Singer, I. B. Sabbath in Portugal
Singer, I. B. Schloimele
Singer, I. B. Three encounters
Singer, I. B. Vanvild Kava
Singer, I. B. Why Heisherik was born
Singer, I. B. The yearning heifer
Singleton, G. I could've told you if you hadn't
    asked
Singleton, G. Raise children here
Skillings, R. D. The news
Škvorecký, J. How my literary career began
Smith, I. C. In the middle of the wood [excerpt]
Sorrentino, G. In loveland
Sorrentino, G. It's time to call it a day
Sorrentino, G. Land of cotton
Sorrentino, G. Life and letters
Stern, D. Apraxia
Stern, D. The exchange
Stern, S. Bruno's metamorphosis
Stern, S. The wedding jester
Stuart, J. The affair with Rachel Ware
Summers, H. S. The vireo's nest
Sumner, P. For your eyes only
Tessier, T. Lulu
Theroux, P. An African story
Tran, V. Nha Nam
Trevanian. The sacking of Miss Plimsoll
Updike, J. Bech noir
Updike, J. The Bulgarian poetess
Updike, J. His oeuvre
VanderMeer, J. Experiment #25 from the book
    of winter

VanderMeer, J. Learning to leave the flesh
Waugh, E. Excursion in reality
Waugh, E. Lucy Simmonds
Waugh, E. My father's house
Weaver, G. Gilded Quill: the story of Jones
Weaver, G. Solidarity forever!
Weihe, E. Another life
Weinberg, R. Chant
Weinberg, R. Elevator girls
Weinreb, M. Satisfaction
Wharton, E. The descent of man
Wharton, E. Full circle
Wharton, E. The legend
Whitty, J. Stealing from the dead
Wideman, J. E. Weight
Wilson, A. J. Under the bright and hollow sky
Wisniewski, M. Descending
Yates, R. Builders
Yates, R. Saying goodbye to Sally
Yoshimoto, B. Helix
Zweig, S. Letter from an unknown woman

AUTHORSHIP
    See also Authors
Agee, J. This is for Chet
Anderson, D. The art of fiction
Berry, R. M. Abandoned writing projects
Berry, R. M. History
Cady, J. On writing the ghost story
Davies, P. H. What you know
Eldridge, Courtney. Fits & starts
Fowler, C. Learning to let go
Galef, D. Metafiction
Hall, D. Argument and persuasion
Hunter, F. A newsman scratches an itch
Lee, M. Paradise dance
Melville, P. The fable of the two silver pens
Offutt, C. Chuck's bucket
Rabb, M. How to tell a story
Schmidt, H. J. Wild rice
Scholz, C. The nine billion names of God
Schwartz, L. S. The word
Sojourner, M. What they write in other coun-
    tries
Tillman, L. Come and go
Updike, J. The sea's green sameness
Volpi, J. Ars poetica
Wideman, J. E. Surfiction

AUTISTIC CHILDREN
Barth, J. Dead cat, floating boy

AUTOBIOGRAPHICAL STORIES
Atwood, M. Significant moments in the life of
    my mother
Babel´, I. At grandmother's
Borges, J. L. The other
Capote, T. A Christmas memory
Capote, T. One Christmas
Capote, T. The Thanksgiving visitor
Douglas, B. My childhood
Flynn, R. Truth and beauty
Gorriti, J. M. Gubi Amaya
Hemon, A. Imitation of life
Kavan, A. The zebra-struck
King, L. L. Three Letters
Lao She. Autobiography of a minor character
Reiner, C. How Paul Robeson saved my life
Shi Tiesheng. Fate
Singer, I. B. The bird
Singer, I. B. Confused
Singer, I. B. A day in Coney Island

AUTOBIOGRAPHICAL STORIES—*Continued*
Singer, I. B. Vanvild Kava
Škvorecký, J. Dr. Strass
Škvorecký, J. The end of Bull Macha
Škvorecký, J. Eve was naked
Škvorecký, J. How my literary career began
Škvorecký, J. My teacher, Mr. Katz
Škvorecký, J. My Uncle Kohn
Škvorecký, J. A remarkable chemical phenomenon
Škvorecký, J. Three bachelors in a fiery furnace
Škvorecký, J. Why do people have soft noses?
Škvorecký, J. Why I lernt how to reed
Viganò, R. Acquitted
Walker, A. To my young husband
Autobiography of a minor character. Lao She
The **autobiography** of my mother [excerpt] Kincaid, J.
The **autobiography** of Riva Jay. Barthelme, F.
AUTOMATA *See* Robots
AUTOMATION
Harrison, H. Portrait of the artist
Torrington, J. The fade
AUTOMOBILE ACCIDENTS *See* Traffic accidents
AUTOMOBILE DRIVERS
 See also Chauffeurs; Hit-and-run drivers
Adam, C. Impala
Cummins, A. Headhunter
Greenberg, A. Free-43
Hecht, J. Do the windows open?
King, S. Mrs. Todd's shortcut
AUTOMOBILE INDUSTRY
Carlson, R. The prisoner of Bluestone
Slezak, E. If you treat things right
AUTOMOBILE RACES
Agee, J. Dwight Tuggle
Agee, J. Flat spotting
Agee, J. Getting the heat up
Agee, J. The level of my uncertainty
Agee, J. Losing downforce
Agee, J. The luck of Junior Strong
Agee, J. Mile a mud
Agee, J. Omaha
Agee, J. Over the point of cohesion
Agee, J. The pop off valve
Agee, J. What's it take?
Jaime-Becerra, M. Georgie and Wanda
Love, R. Real men
Melchior, I. The racer
Purdy, K. W. Tell me the reason, do
AUTOMOBILES
Adams, A. The islands
Agee, J. Binding the devil
Agee, J. Good to go
Agee, J. Mercury
Arvin, N. The prototype
Barthelme, F. Driver
Berry, W. The lost bet
Berry, W. Nearly to the fair
Connolly, C. Paradise Drive
Daniels, J. Christmasmobile
Erdrich, L. The red convertible
Etchison, D. The detailer
Gifford, B. A fair price
Harrison, H. The greatest car in the world
Harrison, H. Speed of the cheetah, roar of the lion
McManus, J. Stop breakin down

Meredith, D. Chevy in the fast lane
Meyers, K. Light in the crossing
Phillips, G. '53 Buick
Rinehart, S. Funny cars
Scoville, S. The gift of a car
Shepard, J. First day she'd never see
Tabucchi, A. A riddle
Thomas, D. The car
Thomas, J. E. The Saturday Morning Car Wash Club
Touré. The Steviewondermobile
Updike, J. Packed dirt, churchgoing, a dying cat, a traded car
Vonnegut, K. The powder-blue dragon
Zabytko, I. My black Valiant
Accidents
 See Traffic accidents
Repairing
Greer, R. O. The ride
Service stations
Apple, M. Gas stations
Franklin, T. Dinosaurs
Grau, S. A. The last gas station
Shepard, S. The company's interest
Touring
Bonnie, F. Sign language
Butler, R. O. No chord of music
Daniels, J. Cross country
Desai, A. Five hours to Simla; or, Faisla
Gunn, K. Not that much to go on
Ryan, P. Before Las Blancas
Updike, J. How to love America and leave it at the same time
Autopsy Report. Purpura, L.
Autres temps . . . Wharton, E.
AUTUMN
Updike, J. In football season
Autumn afternoon. Bradbury, R.
Autumn night. Cheng, C.-W.
Avalli, Ippolita
Simena
 In the forbidden city; an anthology of erotic fiction by Italian women; edited by Maria Rosa Cutrufelli; translated by Vincent J. Bertolini
Avalon. Targan, B.
AVANT GARDE STORIES *See* Experimental stories
AVARICE
Alarcón, P. A. d. Moors and Christians
Arvin, N. Electric fence
Bail, M. Portrait of electricity
Banks, R. The fisherman
Block, L. Speaking of greed
Borges, J. L. The disk
Cannell, D. The high cost of living
Davidson, A. Mr. Folsom feels fine
Dunsany, E. J. M. D. P., Baron. The hoard of the Gibbelins
Gorriti, J. M. The quena
Gorriti, J. M. The treasure of the Incas
Gorriti, J. M. A year in California
Hambly, B. The horsemen and the morning star
Hamburger, A. Control
Hodgson, K. Requiem for Rosebud
Irsfeld, J. H. Finderkeepers
Kornbluth, C. M. The little black bag
Kruse, T. The good old German way
L'Amour, L. Off the Mangrove Coast

AVARICE—*Continued*
Meyers, A. and Meyers, M. The Daffodil
Pak, W.-S. A certain barbarity
Shawl, N. The tawny bitch
Wellen, E. A wreath for justice
Ave de paso. Asaro, C.
Avelino Arredondo. Borges, J. L.
Average Joe. Budnitz, J.
AVERROËS, 1126-1198
              About
Borges, J. L. Averroës' search
Averroës' search. Borges, J. L.
The **averted** strike. Chesnutt, C. W.
Avey, Laura
Perfect Planning
The North American Review v287 no6 p29-30
N/D 2002
AVIATION *See* Aeronautics
AVIATORS *See* Air pilots
Avrich, Jane
The banshee's song
Avrich, J. The winter without milk; stories
La belle dame sans merci
Avrich, J. The winter without milk; stories
The Paris Review v41 no152 p108-22 Fall
1999
The braid
Avrich, J. The winter without milk; stories
The census taker
Avrich, J. The winter without milk; stories
The charwoman
Avrich, J. The winter without milk; stories
Chez Oedipus
Avrich, J. The winter without milk; stories
The great flood
Avrich, J. The winter without milk; stories
Lady Macbeth, prickly pear queen
Avrich, J. The winter without milk; stories
Life in dearth
Avrich, J. The winter without milk; stories
Literary lonelyhearts
Avrich, J. The winter without milk; stories
Miss Carmichael's funeral
Avrich, J. The winter without milk; stories
Trash traders
Avrich, J. The winter without milk; stories
Ploughshares v28 no1 p74-6 Spr 2002
TrashTraders
Harper's v305 p30-1 Jl 2002
Waiting rooms
Avrich, J. The winter without milk; stories
The winter without milk
Avrich, J. The winter without milk; stories
Zanzibar
Avrich, J. The winter without milk; stories
Awaiting an adverse reaction. Kennedy, A. L.
The **awakening**. Chopin, K.
The **awakening**. Clarke, A. C.
Awareness. Brenner, W.
Away. Gonzalez, R.
Away Down in Jamaica. Sui Sin Far
Away for safekeeping. Dunlap, S.
Away with the fairies. Lovesey, P.
Awnings, bedspreads, combed yarns. Orner, P.
The **axe**. Fitzgerald, P.
Axton, David *See* Koontz, Dean R. (Dean Ray),
1945-

Axton, David, 1945-
*For works written by this author under oth-
er names see* Koontz, Dean R. (Dean
Ray), 1945-
Aye, and Gomorrah. . . Delany, S. R.
Ayers, Alice
Near miss
The Literary Review (Madison, N.J.) v44 no4
p664-75 Summ 2001
Ayers, Mary Alice
Works cited
American short fiction, vol. 8, no 29-32
Aylett, Steve
Angel dust
Aylett, S. Toxicology; stories
Bestiary
Aylett, S. Toxicology; stories
Dread honor
Aylett, S. Toxicology; stories
Gigantic
Aylett, S. Toxicology; stories
The idler
Aylett, S. Toxicology; stories
If Armstrong was interesting
Aylett, S. Toxicology; stories
Infestation
Aylett, S. Toxicology; stories
Jawbreaker
Aylett, S. Toxicology; stories
Maryland
Aylett, S. Toxicology; stories
The met are all for this
Aylett, S. Toxicology; stories
The passenger
Aylett, S. Toxicology; stories
Repeater
Aylett, S. Toxicology; stories
Resenter
Aylett, S. Toxicology; stories
Sampler
Aylett, S. Toxicology; stories
Shifa
Aylett, S. Toxicology; stories
The Siri gun
Aylett, S. Toxicology; stories
Tail
Aylett, S. Toxicology; stories
Tug of war
Aylett, S. Toxicology; stories
Tusk
Aylett, S. Toxicology; stories
The waffle code
Aylett, S. Toxicology; stories
Ayres, Noreen
Delta double-deal
The World's finest mystery and crime stories,
second annual collection; edited by Ed
Gorman
JoJo's gold
Blood on their hands; edited by Lawrence
Block
Azadeh, Carol
A banal stain
Azadeh, C. The marriage at Antibes; fiction
Bronagh
Azadeh, C. The marriage at Antibes; fiction
The country road
Azadeh, C. The marriage at Antibes; fiction

Azadeh, Carol—*Continued*
The marriage at Antibes
    Azadeh, C. The marriage at Antibes; fiction
A recitation of nomads
    Azadeh, C. The marriage at Antibes; fiction
Azélie. Chopin, K.
AZTECS
    Cortázar, J. The night face up
Aztlán, Oregon. Chacón, D.

B

B-17. Faust, I.
The **B.A.R.** man. Yates, R.
B. Horror. Mayo, W.
The **b-zone** open. Small, K.
Baader-Meinhof. DeLillo, D.
BAARTMAN, SAATJIE
           About
    Haskell, J. Elephant feelings
Babeau. Giono, J.
Babel', I. (Isaac)
Afonka bida
    Babel', I. The complete works of Isaac Babel;
      edited by Nathalie Babel; translated with
      notes by Peter Constantine; introduction by
      Cynthia Ozick
After the battle
    Babel', I. The complete works of Isaac Babel;
      edited by Nathalie Babel; translated with
      notes by Peter Constantine; introduction by
      Cynthia Ozick
And then there were nine
    Babel', I. The complete works of Isaac Babel;
      edited by Nathalie Babel; translated with
      notes by Peter Constantine; introduction by
      Cynthia Ozick
And then there were ten
    Babel', I. The complete works of Isaac Babel;
      edited by Nathalie Babel; translated with
      notes by Peter Constantine; introduction by
      Cynthia Ozick
Argamak
    Babel', I. The complete works of Isaac Babel;
      edited by Nathalie Babel; translated with
      notes by Peter Constantine; introduction by
      Cynthia Ozick
The aroma of Odessa
    Babel', I. The complete works of Isaac Babel;
      edited by Nathalie Babel; translated with
      notes by Peter Constantine; introduction by
      Cynthia Ozick
At grandmother's
    Babel', I. The complete works of Isaac Babel;
      edited by Nathalie Babel; translated with
      notes by Peter Constantine; introduction by
      Cynthia Ozick
At Saint Valentine's
    Babel', I. The complete works of Isaac Babel;
      edited by Nathalie Babel; translated with
      notes by Peter Constantine; introduction by
      Cynthia Ozick
Bagrat-Ogly and the eyes of his bull
    Babel', I. The complete works of Isaac Babel;
      edited by Nathalie Babel; translated with
      notes by Peter Constantine; introduction by
      Cynthia Ozick

The bathroom window
    Babel', I. The complete works of Isaac Babel;
      edited by Nathalie Babel; translated with
      notes by Peter Constantine; introduction by
      Cynthia Ozick
Beresteczko
    Babel', I. The complete works of Isaac Babel;
      edited by Nathalie Babel; translated with
      notes by Peter Constantine; introduction by
      Cynthia Ozick
The cemetery in Kozin
    Babel', I. The complete works of Isaac Babel;
      edited by Nathalie Babel; translated with
      notes by Peter Constantine; introduction by
      Cynthia Ozick
Chink
    Babel', I. The complete works of Isaac Babel;
      edited by Nathalie Babel; translated with
      notes by Peter Constantine; introduction by
      Cynthia Ozick
The church in Novograd
    Babel', I. The complete works of Isaac Babel;
      edited by Nathalie Babel; translated with
      notes by Peter Constantine; introduction by
      Cynthia Ozick
The commander of the second brigade
    Babel', I. The complete works of Isaac Babel;
      edited by Nathalie Babel; translated with
      notes by Peter Constantine; introduction by
      Cynthia Ozick
The continuation of The story of a horse
    Babel', I. The complete works of Isaac Babel;
      edited by Nathalie Babel; translated with
      notes by Peter Constantine; introduction by
      Cynthia Ozick
Crossing the River Zbrucz
    Babel', I. The complete works of Isaac Babel;
      edited by Nathalie Babel; translated with
      notes by Peter Constantine; introduction by
      Cynthia Ozick
Czesniki
    Babel', I. The complete works of Isaac Babel;
      edited by Nathalie Babel; translated with
      notes by Peter Constantine; introduction by
      Cynthia Ozick
Dante Street
    Babel', I. The complete works of Isaac Babel;
      edited by Nathalie Babel; translated with
      notes by Peter Constantine; introduction by
      Cynthia Ozick
The deserter
    Babel', I. The complete works of Isaac Babel;
      edited by Nathalie Babel; translated with
      notes by Peter Constantine; introduction by
      Cynthia Ozick
Dolgushov's death
    Babel', I. The complete works of Isaac Babel;
      edited by Nathalie Babel; translated with
      notes by Peter Constantine; introduction by
      Cynthia Ozick
Doudou
    Babel', I. The complete works of Isaac Babel;
      edited by Nathalie Babel; translated with
      notes by Peter Constantine; introduction by
      Cynthia Ozick

Babel´, I. (Isaac)—*Continued*

Elya Isaakovich and Margarita Prokofievna
  Babel´, I. The complete works of Isaac Babel;
    edited by Nathalie Babel; translated with
    notes by Peter Constantine; introduction by
    Cynthia Ozick
The end of St. Hypatius
  Babel´, I. The complete works of Isaac Babel;
    edited by Nathalie Babel; translated with
    notes by Peter Constantine; introduction by
    Cynthia Ozick
The end of the almshouse
  Babel´, I. The complete works of Isaac Babel;
    edited by Nathalie Babel; translated with
    notes by Peter Constantine; introduction by
    Cynthia Ozick
Evening
  Babel´, I. The complete works of Isaac Babel;
    edited by Nathalie Babel; translated with
    notes by Peter Constantine; introduction by
    Cynthia Ozick
An evening with the Empress
  Babel´, I. The complete works of Isaac Babel;
    edited by Nathalie Babel; translated with
    notes by Peter Constantine; introduction by
    Cynthia Ozick
The father
  Babel´, I. The complete works of Isaac Babel;
    edited by Nathalie Babel; translated with
    notes by Peter Constantine; introduction by
    Cynthia Ozick
First love
  Babel´, I. The complete works of Isaac Babel;
    edited by Nathalie Babel; translated with
    notes by Peter Constantine; introduction by
    Cynthia Ozick
Froim Grach
  Babel´, I. The complete works of Isaac Babel;
    edited by Nathalie Babel; translated with
    notes by Peter Constantine; introduction by
    Cynthia Ozick
Gapa guzhva
  Babel´, I. The complete works of Isaac Babel;
    edited by Nathalie Babel; translated with
    notes by Peter Constantine; introduction by
    Cynthia Ozick
Gedali
  Babel´, I. The complete works of Isaac Babel;
    edited by Nathalie Babel; translated with
    notes by Peter Constantine; introduction by
    Cynthia Ozick
Di Grasso
  Babel´, I. The complete works of Isaac Babel;
    edited by Nathalie Babel; translated with
    notes by Peter Constantine; introduction by
    Cynthia Ozick
Grishchuk
  Babel´, I. The complete works of Isaac Babel;
    edited by Nathalie Babel; translated with
    notes by Peter Constantine; introduction by
    Cynthia Ozick
Guy de Maupassant
  Babel´, I. The complete works of Isaac Babel;
    edited by Nathalie Babel; translated with
    notes by Peter Constantine; introduction by
    Cynthia Ozick

A hardworking woman
  Babel´, I. The complete works of Isaac Babel;
    edited by Nathalie Babel; translated with
    notes by Peter Constantine; introduction by
    Cynthia Ozick
How things were done in Odessa
  Babel´, I. The complete works of Isaac Babel;
    edited by Nathalie Babel; translated with
    notes by Peter Constantine; introduction by
    Cynthia Ozick
In the basement
  Babel´, I. The complete works of Isaac Babel;
    edited by Nathalie Babel; translated with
    notes by Peter Constantine; introduction by
    Cynthia Ozick
  New England Review v22 no4 p18-23 Fall
    2001
Information
  New England Review v22 no4 p8-10 Fall
    2001
Inspiration
  Babel´, I. The complete works of Isaac Babel;
    edited by Nathalie Babel; translated with
    notes by Peter Constantine; introduction by
    Cynthia Ozick
  New England Review v22 no4 p14-15 Fall
    2001
Italian sun
  Babel´, I. The complete works of Isaac Babel;
    edited by Nathalie Babel; translated with
    notes by Peter Constantine; introduction by
    Cynthia Ozick
Ivan and Ivan
  Babel´, I. The complete works of Isaac Babel;
    edited by Nathalie Babel; translated with
    notes by Peter Constantine; introduction by
    Cynthia Ozick
The Ivan and Maria
  Babel´, I. The complete works of Isaac Babel;
    edited by Nathalie Babel; translated with
    notes by Peter Constantine; introduction by
    Cynthia Ozick
Justice in parentheses
  Babel´, I. The complete works of Isaac Babel;
    edited by Nathalie Babel; translated with
    notes by Peter Constantine; introduction by
    Cynthia Ozick
Karl-Yankel
  Babel´, I. The complete works of Isaac Babel;
    edited by Nathalie Babel; translated with
    notes by Peter Constantine; introduction by
    Cynthia Ozick
The King
  Babel´, I. The complete works of Isaac Babel;
    edited by Nathalie Babel; translated with
    notes by Peter Constantine; introduction by
    Cynthia Ozick
The kiss
  Babel´, I. The complete works of Isaac Babel;
    edited by Nathalie Babel; translated with
    notes by Peter Constantine; introduction by
    Cynthia Ozick
Kolyvushka
  Babel´, I. The complete works of Isaac Babel;
    edited by Nathalie Babel; translated with
    notes by Peter Constantine; introduction by
    Cynthia Ozick

Babel´, I. (Isaac)—*Continued*

Konkin

Babel´, I. The complete works of Isaac Babel; edited by Nathalie Babel; translated with notes by Peter Constantine; introduction by Cynthia Ozick

A letter

Babel´, I. The complete works of Isaac Babel; edited by Nathalie Babel; translated with notes by Peter Constantine; introduction by Cynthia Ozick

A letter to the editor

Babel´, I. The complete works of Isaac Babel; edited by Nathalie Babel; translated with notes by Peter Constantine; introduction by Cynthia Ozick

The life story of Matvey Rodionovich Pavlichenko

Babel´, I. The complete works of Isaac Babel; edited by Nathalie Babel; translated with notes by Peter Constantine; introduction by Cynthia Ozick

Line and color

Babel´, I. The complete works of Isaac Babel; edited by Nathalie Babel; translated with notes by Peter Constantine; introduction by Cynthia Ozick

Lyubka the Cossack

Babel´, I. The complete works of Isaac Babel; edited by Nathalie Babel; translated with notes by Peter Constantine; introduction by Cynthia Ozick

Makhno's boys

Babel´, I. The complete works of Isaac Babel; edited by Nathalie Babel; translated with notes by Peter Constantine; introduction by Cynthia Ozick

Mama, Rimma, and Alla

Babel´, I. The complete works of Isaac Babel; edited by Nathalie Babel; translated with notes by Peter Constantine; introduction by Cynthia Ozick

My first fee

Babel´, I. The complete works of Isaac Babel; edited by Nathalie Babel; translated with notes by Peter Constantine; introduction by Cynthia Ozick

My first goose

Babel´, I. The complete works of Isaac Babel; edited by Nathalie Babel; translated with notes by Peter Constantine; introduction by Cynthia Ozick

New England Review v22 no4 p11-13 Fall 2001

Odessa

Babel´, I. The complete works of Isaac Babel; edited by Nathalie Babel; translated with notes by Peter Constantine; introduction by Cynthia Ozick

Old Shloyme

Babel´, I. The complete works of Isaac Babel; edited by Nathalie Babel; translated with notes by Peter Constantine; introduction by Cynthia Ozick

On the field of honor

Babel´, I. The complete works of Isaac Babel; edited by Nathalie Babel; translated with notes by Peter Constantine; introduction by Cynthia Ozick

Pan Apolek

Babel´, I. The complete works of Isaac Babel; edited by Nathalie Babel; translated with notes by Peter Constantine; introduction by Cynthia Ozick

Papa Marescot's family

Babel´, I. The complete works of Isaac Babel; edited by Nathalie Babel; translated with notes by Peter Constantine; introduction by Cynthia Ozick

Petroleum

Babel´, I. The complete works of Isaac Babel; edited by Nathalie Babel; translated with notes by Peter Constantine; introduction by Cynthia Ozick

Prishchepa

Babel´, I. The complete works of Isaac Babel; edited by Nathalie Babel; translated with notes by Peter Constantine; introduction by Cynthia Ozick

The public library

Babel´, I. The complete works of Isaac Babel; edited by Nathalie Babel; translated with notes by Peter Constantine; introduction by Cynthia Ozick

New England Review v22 no4 p16-17 Fall 2001

The Quaker

Babel´, I. The complete works of Isaac Babel; edited by Nathalie Babel; translated with notes by Peter Constantine; introduction by Cynthia Ozick

The rabbi

Babel´, I. The complete works of Isaac Babel; edited by Nathalie Babel; translated with notes by Peter Constantine; introduction by Cynthia Ozick

The rabbi's son

Babel´, I. The complete works of Isaac Babel; edited by Nathalie Babel; translated with notes by Peter Constantine; introduction by Cynthia Ozick

Red Army tales

Harper's v303 no1818 p23-5 N 2001

The reserve cavalry commander

Babel´, I. The complete works of Isaac Babel; edited by Nathalie Babel; translated with notes by Peter Constantine; introduction by Cynthia Ozick

The road

Babel´, I. The complete works of Isaac Babel; edited by Nathalie Babel; translated with notes by Peter Constantine; introduction by Cynthia Ozick

The road to Brody

Babel´, I. The complete works of Isaac Babel; edited by Nathalie Babel; translated with notes by Peter Constantine; introduction by Cynthia Ozick

Salt

Babel´, I. The complete works of Isaac Babel; edited by Nathalie Babel; translated with notes by Peter Constantine; introduction by Cynthia Ozick

Babel´, I. (Isaac)—*Continued*

Shabos-Nakhamu
  Babel´, I. The complete works of Isaac Babel; edited by Nathalie Babel; translated with notes by Peter Constantine; introduction by Cynthia Ozick

Shaska Christ
  Babel´, I. The complete works of Isaac Babel; edited by Nathalie Babel; translated with notes by Peter Constantine; introduction by Cynthia Ozick

The sin of Jesus
  Babel´, I. The complete works of Isaac Babel; edited by Nathalie Babel; translated with notes by Peter Constantine; introduction by Cynthia Ozick

The song
  Babel´, I. The complete works of Isaac Babel; edited by Nathalie Babel; translated with notes by Peter Constantine; introduction by Cynthia Ozick

Squadron Commander Trunov
  Babel´, I. The complete works of Isaac Babel; edited by Nathalie Babel; translated with notes by Peter Constantine; introduction by Cynthia Ozick

The story of a horse
  Babel´, I. The complete works of Isaac Babel; edited by Nathalie Babel; translated with notes by Peter Constantine; introduction by Cynthia Ozick

The story of my dovecote
  Babel´, I. The complete works of Isaac Babel; edited by Nathalie Babel; translated with notes by Peter Constantine; introduction by Cynthia Ozick

Sulak
  Babel´, I. The complete works of Isaac Babel; edited by Nathalie Babel; translated with notes by Peter Constantine; introduction by Cynthia Ozick

Sunset
  Babel´, I. The complete works of Isaac Babel; edited by Nathalie Babel; translated with notes by Peter Constantine; introduction by Cynthia Ozick

The tachanka theory
  Babel´, I. The complete works of Isaac Babel; edited by Nathalie Babel; translated with notes by Peter Constantine; introduction by Cynthia Ozick

A tale about a woman
  Babel´, I. The complete works of Isaac Babel; edited by Nathalie Babel; translated with notes by Peter Constantine; introduction by Cynthia Ozick

Treason
  Babel´, I. The complete works of Isaac Babel; edited by Nathalie Babel; translated with notes by Peter Constantine; introduction by Cynthia Ozick

The trial
  Babel´, I. The complete works of Isaac Babel; edited by Nathalie Babel; translated with notes by Peter Constantine; introduction by Cynthia Ozick

The widow
  Babel´, I. The complete works of Isaac Babel; edited by Nathalie Babel; translated with notes by Peter Constantine; introduction by Cynthia Ozick

You missed the boat, Captain!
  Babel´, I. The complete works of Isaac Babel; edited by Nathalie Babel; translated with notes by Peter Constantine; introduction by Cynthia Ozick

Zamosc
  Babel´, I. The complete works of Isaac Babel; edited by Nathalie Babel; translated with notes by Peter Constantine; introduction by Cynthia Ozick

Babel´, Isaac *See* Babel´, I. (Isaac), 1894-1940
Babes in the woods. Fitzgerald, F. S.
Babies. Jones, G.
Baby. Reifler, N.
Baby doll. LeRoy, J. T.
The **baby** in the box. Busch, F.
The **baby** in the icebox. Cain, J. M.
Baby Liz. Rawley, D.
BABY SITTERS
  Bauman, B. A. Stew
  Brockmeier, K. These hands
  Codrescu, A. The babysitter
  Gifford, B. The big love of Cherry Lane
  Harfenist, J. Body count
  Lahiri, J. Mrs. Sen's
  Lipsyte, S. The Drury girl
  Orner, P. Sitting Theodore
  Orringer, J. Care
  Svoboda, T. Polio
  Troy, M. Turning colder
  Updike, J. Avec la bébé-sitter
  Wexler, M. Waiting to discover electricity
Baby-sitting. Galloway, J.
Baby teeth. Anderson, D.
The **baby** who, according to his aunt, resembled his uncle. Lord, N.
Baby Wilson. Doctorow, E. L.
The **Babylon** lottery. See Borges, J. L. The lottery in Babylon
Babyproofing. Slavin, J.
The **babysitter**. Codrescu, A.
Baca, Jimmy Santiago
  Bull's blood
    Baca, J. S. The importance of a piece of paper
  Enemies
    Baca, J. S. The importance of a piece of paper
  The importance of a piece of paper
    Baca, J. S. The importance of a piece of paper
  Matilda's garden
    Baca, J. S. The importance of a piece of paper
  Mother's ashes
    Baca, J. S. The importance of a piece of paper
  Runaway
    Baca, J. S. The importance of a piece of paper
  The three sons of Julia
    Baca, J. S. The importance of a piece of paper

Baca, Jimmy Santiago—*Continued*
The Valentine's Day card
  Baca, J. S. The importance of a piece of paper
Bache, Ellyn
Raspberry Sherbet
  Good Housekeeping v235 no3 p181-2, 184-6
  S 2002
Shell Island
  This is where we live; short stories by 25
  contemporary North Carolina writers; edited by Michael McFee
Watching from the Wings
  Good Housekeeping v236 no1 p167-8, 170,
  172-5 Ja 2003
Bachelor party. Brownstein, G.
The **bachelor** party. Cohen, R.
BACHELORS *See* Single men
Bachman, Richard *See* King, Stephen, 1947-
Bachmann, Ingeborg
A site for contingencies
  Grand Street no69 p44-48 Summ 1999
Bacigalupi, Paolo
The fluted girl
  The year's best science fiction: twenty-first
  annual collection; edited by Gardner Dozois
Back. Straight, S.
Back east. Hammond, E.
Back in town. McBrearty, R. G.
The **back** nine in autumn. LaSalle, P.
Back on April eleventh. Aquin, H.
Back O'Town Blues. Fulmer, D.
The **back** streets of Hoi An. Tran, V.
Back to front. Barker, N.
Back to the future. Lisick, B.
Backdated. Johnson, L.
Backfield battering ram. L'Amour, L.
BACKGAMMON
Papernick, J. An unwelcome guest
BACKPACKING
Furman, L. The natural memory
Backtracking. Swan, G.
Backup. Greer, R. O.
Backyard burial. Matthews, C.
Bad. Gossy, D.
Bad ass Bob, a mug shot mug, a man. Goldner, B.
Bad bargain. Nevins, F. M., Jr.
Bad blood. DeRosso, H. A.
Bad boy number seventeen. Perillo, L. M.
Bad boy walking. Carter, E.
A **bad** business. Chekhov, A. P.
Bad day. Tester, W.
A **bad** day for sales. Leiber, F.
Bad debts and vindictive women. Reyes, S. R.
Bad form. See Bloom, A. Stars at elbow and foot
The **bad** hand. Fairey, W. W.
Bad Jews. Shapiro, G.
Bad john going down. Gentry, E.
A **bad** joke. Ha Jin
A **bad** man, so pretty. Knight, M.
Bad medicine. Dann, J.
Bad nature. Marías, J.
Bad-natured dog. Boylan, C.
Bad News. Cohen, G. K.
Bad news. O'Callaghan, M.
Bad news bridesmaid. Lisick, B.
Bad news of the heart. Glover, D. H.
Bad nose. Parker, G.
Bad review. Dunlap, S.

The **bad** seed: a guide. Mason, N.
The **Bad** Shepherd. Davies, P. H.
A **bad** son. Kennedy, A. L.
The **bad** thing. Gates, D.
The **Bad** Thing. Phillips, J. A.
Badlands bones. Sneve, V. D. H.
A **baffling** choice. Klíma, I.
Bag boy. Barthelme, F.
BAG LADIES *See* Homeless persons
Bagdasarian, Adam
Empty spaces
  The Antioch Review v59 no3 p564-8 Summ
  2001
The **bagel** murders. Kaufelt, D. A.
Baggage. Shrayer, M. D.
Baglady. Byatt, A. S.
Bagley, Julian Elihu
Children of chance
  The African American West; a century of
  short stories; edited by Bruce A. Glasrud
  and Laurie Champion
Bagombo snuff box. Vonnegut, K.
Bagrat-Ogly and the eyes of his bull. Babel´, I.
Bagworms. Nevins, F. M., Jr.
BAHAMAS
Lupoff, R. A. News from New Providence
Marsten, R. Every morning
Shaw, D. Diving with the devil
Bahr, Aida
Absences
  The Massachusetts Review v40 no2 p184-86
  Summ 1999
Imperfections
  The Massachusetts Review v40 no2 p186-88
  Summ 1999
Bahrami, Azardokht
Lida's cat, the bakery, and the streetlight pole
  A Feast in the mirror; stories by contemporary Iranian women; translated and edited
  by Mohammad Mehdi Khorrami, Shouleh
  Vatanabadi
Bahrami, Mihan
The end, a city
  A Feast in the mirror; stories by contemporary Iranian women; translated and edited
  by Mohammad Mehdi Khorrami, Shouleh
  Vatanabadi
Bai Xiao-Yi
Six short pieces
  The Vintage book of contemporary Chinese
  fiction; edited by Carolyn Choa and David
  Su Li-qun
Baida, Peter
Class warfare
  Baida, P. A nurse's story and others
A doctor's story
  Baida, P. A nurse's story and others
Family ties
  Baida, P. A nurse's story and others
Mr. Moth and Mr. Davenport
  Baida, P. A nurse's story and others
No place to hide
  Baida, P. A nurse's story and others
A nurse's story
  Baida, P. A nurse's story and others
  Prize stories, 1999; The O. Henry awards; edited and with an introduction by Larry
  Dark

Baida, Peter—*Continued*
Points of light
Baida, P. A nurse's story and others
The reckoning
Baida, P. A nurse's story and others
The rodent
Baida, P. A nurse's story and others
Bail, Murray
A, B, C, D, E, F, G, H, I, J, K, L, M, N, O, P, Q, R, S, T, U, V, W, X, Y, Z
Bail, M. Camouflage; stories
Camouflage
Bail, M. Camouflage; stories
Cul-de-sac (uncompleted)
Bail, M. Camouflage; stories
The drover's wife
Bail, M. Camouflage; stories
Healing
Bail, M. Camouflage; stories
Home ownership
Bail, M. Camouflage; stories
Huebler
Bail, M. Camouflage; stories
Life of the party
Bail, M. Camouflage; stories
Ore
Bail, M. Camouflage; stories
Paradise
Bail, M. Camouflage; stories
The partitions
Bail, M. Camouflage; stories
Portrait of electricity
Bail, M. Camouflage; stories
The seduction of my sister
Bail, M. Camouflage; stories
Zoellner's definition
Bail, M. Camouflage; stories
Bailey, Dale
Quinn's way
The Best from fantasy & science fiction: the fiftieth anniversary anthology; edited by Edward L. Ferman and Gordon Van Gelder
Bailey, Robin W.
Doing time
Past imperfect; edited by Martin H. Greenberg and Larry Segriff
Ring of sea and fire
Thieve's world: turning points; edited by Lynn Abbey
Bailey, Tom
Snow dreams
The Pushcart prize XXIV: best of the small presses; an annual small press reader; edited by Bill Henderson with the Pushcart prize editors
Bain, Terry
Don't move me
Gettysburg Review v14 no1 p65-70 Spr 2001
Still Life with Dog
Gettysburg Review v16 no3 p459-65 Aut 2003
This Is What You Owe Me
Gettysburg Review v16 no1 p111-26 Spr 2003
Baingana, Doreen
Questions of Home
Callaloo v27 no2 p413-28 Spr 2004
Tropical Fish
African American Review v37 no4 p629-36 Wint 2003

Ba'i's mourners. Naiyer Masud
Bake at 350°. Hoffman, A.
Baker, Alison
Happy Hour
Atlantic Monthly (1993) v291 no1 p147-52 Ja/F 2003
Baker, Jeffrey M.
Miss Mary Philpot
The Antioch Review v61 no3 p535-52 Summ 2003
Baker, Kage
The dust enclosed here
Baker, K. Black projects, white knights; the Company dossiers
Facts relating to the arrest of Dr. Kalugin
Baker, K. Black projects, white knights; the Company dossiers
Hanuman
Baker, K. Black projects, white knights; the Company dossiers
The hotel at Harlan's Landing
Baker, K. Black projects, white knights; the Company dossiers
The Year's best science fiction; twentieth annual collection; edited by Gardner Dozois
Lemuria will rise!
Baker, K. Black projects, white knights; the Company dossiers
The likely lad
Baker, K. Black projects, white knights; the Company dossiers
The literary agent
Baker, K. Black projects, white knights; the Company dossiers
Monster story
Baker, K. Black projects, white knights; the Company dossiers
Noble mold
Baker, K. Black projects, white knights; the Company dossiers
Old flat top
Baker, K. Black projects, white knights; the Company dossiers
The queen in yellow
Baker, K. Black projects, white knights; the Company dossiers
Smart Alec
Baker, K. Black projects, white knights; the Company dossiers
Son observe the time
The Year's best science fiction, seventeenth annual collection; edited by Gardner Dozois
Studio dick drowns near Malibu
Baker, K. Black projects, white knights; the Company dossiers
Welcome to Olympus, Mr. Hearst
The year's best science fiction: twenty-first annual collection; edited by Gardner Dozois
The wreck of the Gladstone
Baker, K. Black projects, white knights; the Company dossiers
Baker, Laura Jean
Nude portrait
Gettysburg Review v15 no1 p109-23 Spr 2002
Baker, Mike C.
(jt. auth) See Huber, Carol Y. and Baker, Mike C.

Baker, Paul
The actor
The Literary Review (Madison, N.J.) v42 no2 p288-92 Wint 1999
BAKERIES AND BAKERS
Weinstein, L. The Llipkin -Wexler affair
The **baker's** daughter. Bocock, M.
Baker's helper. Anderson, C.
The **baker's** wife. Powers, S.
Bakopoulos, Dean
Happy
The Virginia Quarterly Review v80 no3 p14-39 Summ 2004
Bakr, Salwá
Thirty-one beautiful green trees
The Anchor book of modern African stories; edited by Nadežda Obradovic ; with a fore-word by Chinua Achebe
The **Balance**. Barker, N.
The **balance**. Waugh, E.
Balázs, Thomas P.
My Secret War
The North American Review v289 no1 p16-23 Ja/F 2004
Balco, Július
Holes in the ground
In search of homo sapiens; twenty-five con-temporary Slovak short stories; editor, Pavol Hudík ; [translated by Heather Trebatická; American English editor, Lucy Bednár]
The **balcony**. Hernandez, F.
The **balcony**. King, G.
Baldry, Cherith
The friar's tale
Royal whodunnits; edited by Mike Ashley
Baldwin, Alex
For works written by this author under oth-er names see Griffin, W. E. B.
Baldwin, D. N.
Lamar ascending
American short fiction, vol. 8, no 29-32
Bali woman. Hermann, J.
Balint, Anna
Gypsies on the Lawn
Calyx v21 no2 p6-15 Summ 2003
Ball, Margaret
Shell game
Past lives, present tense; edited by Elizabeth Ann Scarborough
BALL GAMES
See also Baseball; Basketball; Bowling; Football; Rugby football; Soccer; Softball; Tennis
Ball peen. Nelson, A.
The **ball** really carries in the Cactus League be-cause the air is dry. Swarthout, G. F.
Ballad. Bunin, I. A.
Ballad for the new world. Scott, L.
The **ballad** of Duane Juarez. Franklin, T.
The **ballad** of my father's redneck wife. Davis, J. S.
The **ballad** of Rappy Valcour. Hill, I.
The **ballad** of Tony Nail. Jacobs, M.
BALLET
See also Dancers
Berkman, P. R. Witch
Matison, M. Rose into cauliflower
Mayhall, J. The men

The **balloon**. Barthelme, D.
BALLOON ASCENSIONS
Poe, E. A. The balloon hoax
Verne, J. Five weeks in a balloon
BALLOONS
Arvin, N. Aeronautics
Barthelme, D. The balloon
BALLS (PARTIES) *See* Parties
Balls, balls, balls. Cavell, B.
The **Ballyhooly** boy. Masterton, G.
The **balm** of Gilead tree. Morgan, R.
BALTIMORE (MD.) *See* Maryland—Baltimore
Balza, José
The stroke of midnight
The Vintage book of Latin American stories; edited by Carlos Fuentes and Julio Ortega
Bambara, Toni Cade
Gorilla, my love
The Art of the story; an international anthol-ogy of contemporary short stories; edited by Daniel Halpern
The hammer man
Crossing the color line; readings in Black and white; edited by Suzanne W. Jones
Maggie of the green bottles
Best of Prairie schooner; fiction and poetry; edited by Hilda Raz
Raymond's run
The Scribner anthology of contemporary short fiction; fifty North American stories since 1970; Lex Williford and Michael Martone, editors
A **bamboula**. Davis, M. M.
Bamforth, Iain
(jt. auth) *See* Weiss, Ernst
The **ban**. Tushnet, L.
A **banal** stain. Azadeh, C.
The **Banana** Pep Gal. Ritchie, E.
Banbury, Jen
Take, for example, meatpie
Tart noir; edited by Stella Duffy & Lauren Henderson
Bancroft, Laura *See* Baum, L. Frank (Lyman Frank), 1856-1919
Band day. Hardy, E.
The **bandit** who caught a killer. Ranieri, R.
BANDITS *See* Brigands and robbers
Bandolas, Banjo
One last soul
Dead on demand; the best of ghost story weekend; edited by Elizabeth Engstrom
BANDS (MUSIC)
Melville, P. Mrs. Da Silva's carnival
Vonnegut, K. Ambitious sophomore
Vonnegut, K. The boy who hated girls
Vonnegut, K. Find me a dream
Vonnegut, K. The no-talent kid
Bandyopadhyay, Bidisha *See* Bidisha
Bang, Nathan
That Awning on Third West
Western Humanities Review v58 no1 p8-11 Spr 2004
Bang bang bang. Cho, N.
BANGKOK (THAILAND) *See* Thailand—Bang-kok
Bangkok. Salter, J.

Banister, Manly Miles
Eena
The Literary werewolf; an anthology; edited by Charlotte F. Otten
Bank, Melissa
The girls' guide to hunting and fishing
Coppola, F. F. Francis Ford Coppola's Zoetrope: all story; edited by Adrienne Brodeur and Samantha Schnee; introduction by Francis Ford Coppola
The wonder spot
Speaking with the angel; original stories; edited by Nick Hornby
BANK CLERKS *See* Clerks
Bank job. Pronzini, B.
Bank job. Roche, T. S.
Bank of America. Singleton, G.
The **bank** president. Ebershoff, D.
BANK ROBBERS
Aldrich, B. S. How far is it to Hollywood?
Crumley, J. Hostages
Deaver, J. Wrong time, wrong place
Dixon, S. The tellers
Farrell, C. Day of the dedication
Holley, C. The island in the river
Humphrey, W. A voice from the woods
Leonard, E. Karen makes out
Lochte, D. Low Tide
MacDonald, J. D. The homesick Buick
Malone, M. Miss Mona's bank
Parker, T. J. Easy street
Pronzini, B. Bank job
Roche, T. S. Bank job
Westlake, D. E. Too many crooks
BANKERS
Aldrich, B. S. Alma, meaning "To cherish"
Aldrich, B. S. It's never too late to live
Archer, J. The grass is always greener . . .
Bonnie, F. In search of Number Seven
Dodd, S. M. So far you can't imagine
Mazor, J. The lost cause
Mazor, J. The modern age
Simpson, H. Burns and the bankers
Sturgeon, T. Microcosmic god
Swan, G. Sloan's daughter
Tilghman, C. Room for mistakes
Bankier, William
Child of another time
Master's choice v2; mystery stories by today's top writers and the masters who inspired them; edited by Lawrence Block
BANKRUPTCY
Carver, R. Are these actual miles?
Chabon, M. Mrs. Box
Mueller, D. Zero
Banks, Iain
The bridge [excerpt]
The Vintage book of contemporary Scottish fiction; edited and with an introduction by Peter Kravitz
The wasp factory [excerpt]
Dark: stories of madness, murder, and the supernatural; edited by Clint Willis
Banks, Leo W.
Goldie's gift
Arizona Highways v77 no12 p44-7 D 2001

Banks, Russell
Assisted living
Banks, R. The angel on the roof; the stories of Russell Banks
Black man and white woman in dark green rowboat
Banks, R. The angel on the roof; the stories of Russell Banks
The burden
Banks, R. The angel on the roof; the stories of Russell Banks
The caul
Banks, R. The angel on the roof; the stories of Russell Banks
The child screams and looks back at you
Banks, R. The angel on the roof; the stories of Russell Banks
Comfort
Banks, R. The angel on the roof; the stories of Russell Banks
Cow-cow
Banks, R. The angel on the roof; the stories of Russell Banks
Defenseman
Banks, R. The angel on the roof; the stories of Russell Banks
Dis bwoy, him gwan
Banks, R. The angel on the roof; the stories of Russell Banks
Djinn
Banks, R. The angel on the roof; the stories of Russell Banks
Firewood
Banks, R. The angel on the roof; the stories of Russell Banks
The fish
Banks, R. The angel on the roof; the stories of Russell Banks
The fisherman
Banks, R. The angel on the roof; the stories of Russell Banks
The guinea pig lady
Banks, R. The angel on the roof; the stories of Russell Banks
Indisposed
Banks, R. The angel on the roof; the stories of Russell Banks
The lie
Banks, R. The angel on the roof; the stories of Russell Banks
Lobster night
Banks, R. The angel on the roof; the stories of Russell Banks
The Best American mystery stories, 2001; edited and with an Introduction by Lawrence Block
Mistake
Banks, R. The angel on the roof; the stories of Russell Banks
The Moor
Banks, R. The angel on the roof; the stories of Russell Banks
The Pushcart prize XXVI; best of the small presses, an annual small press reader; edited by Bill Henderson and the Pushcart prize editors

Banks, Russell—*Continued*

My mother's memoirs, my father's lie, and other true stories

The Art of the story; an international anthology of contemporary short stories; edited by Daniel Halpern

The neighbor

Banks, R. The angel on the roof; the stories of Russell Banks

The outer banks

Esquire v135 no6 p150-1 Je 2001

New stories from the South: the year's best, 2002; edited by Shannon Ravenel; with a preface by Larry Brown

Plains of Abraham

Banks, R. The angel on the roof; the stories of Russell Banks

Esquire v132 no1 p78-85 Jl 1999

Prize stories, 2000; The O. Henry awards; edited and with an introduction by Larry Dark

Quality time

Banks, R. The angel on the roof; the stories of Russell Banks

Queen for a day

Banks, R. The angel on the roof; the stories of Russell Banks

Fault lines; stories of divorce; collected and edited by Caitlin Shetterly

The rise of the middle class

Banks, R. The angel on the roof; the stories of Russell Banks

Sarah Cole: a type of love story

Banks, R. The angel on the roof; the stories of Russell Banks

The Scribner anthology of contemporary short fiction; fifty North American stories since 1970; Lex Williford and Michael Martone, editors

Searching for survivors

Banks, R. The angel on the roof; the stories of Russell Banks

Success story

Banks, R. The angel on the roof; the stories of Russell Banks

Theory of flight

Banks, R. The angel on the roof; the stories of Russell Banks

The visit

Banks, R. The angel on the roof; the stories of Russell Banks

With Ché in New Hampshire

Banks, R. The angel on the roof; the stories of Russell Banks

Xmas

Banks, R. The angel on the roof; the stories of Russell Banks

BANKS

See also Bankers

Cohen, S. Those who appreciate money hate to touch the principal

Harris, M. Hi, Bob!

Lovesey, P. The man who jumped for England

The **banks** of the Vistula. Lee, R.

Banner, Keith

The one I remember

The Kenyon Review ns21 no3-4 p66-73 Summ/Fall 1999

The smallest people alive

The Kenyon Review ns21 no1 p185-98 Wint 1999

Prize stories, 2000; The O. Henry awards; edited and with an introduction by Larry Dark

The **banshee**. O'Malley, T.

BANSHEES

Kavanagh, H. T. The banshee's comb

The **banshee's** comb. Kavanagh, H. T.

The **banshee's** song. Avrich, J.

Banville, John

Nightwind

The Anchor book of new Irish writing; the new Gaelach ficsean; edited and with an introduction by John Somer and John J. Daly

Persona

The Anchor book of new Irish writing; the new Gaelach ficsean; edited and with an introduction by John Somer and John J. Daly

BAPTISM

Bly, C. After the baptism

Morrow, J. Auspicious eggs

A **bar** in Brooklyn. Codrescu, A.

The **bar** sinister. Davis, R. H.

BARA, THEDA, 1890-1955

About

Breen, J. L. Woollcott and the vamp

BARABBAS (BIBLICAL FIGURE)

Herling, G. The eyetooth of Barabbas

Baraka, Amiri *See* Baraka, Imamu Amiri, 1934-

Baraka, Imamu Amiri

Rhythm travel

Dark matter; a century of speculative fiction from the African diaspora; edited by Sheree R. Thomas

Barba, Rick

Guys

A different plain; contemporary Nebraska fiction writers; edited by Ladette Randolph ; introduction by Mary Pipher

BARBADOS

Clarke, A. Leaving this island place

Barbara. Roth, J.

Barbara's mother's rug. Davis, L.

Barbarese, J. T.

Where I come from

The North American Review v284 no2 p36-37 Mr/Ap 1999

The **barbarian** and the queen: thirteen interviews. Yolen, J.

The **barbarian** princess. Vinge, V.

Barber. Wilson, R., Jr.

BARBERS

Agee, J. The Jesus Barber Shop

Bradbury, R. The beautiful shave

Chekhov, A. P. At the bath-house

Chesnutt, C. W. The doll

Cooper, B. Bit-o-honey

Lardner, R. Haircut

Lovelace, E. Victory and the blight

Müller, H. About German mustaches and hair parts

Ponte, A. J. The summer in a barbershop

Vukcevich, R. The barber's theme

Wilson, R., Jr. Barber

The **barber's** theme. Vukcevich, R.

The **barber's** unhappiness. Saunders, G.
BARBIE DOLLS
  Barrett, L. Beauty
  Connor, J. Midlife Barbie
Barbosa Monteiro, Jerônimo *See* Monteiro,
    Jerônimo, 1908-1970
Barceló, Elia
  First time
    Cosmos latinos: an anthology of science fic-
      tion from Latin America and Spain; trans-
      lated, edited, & with an introduction &
      notes by Andrea L. Bell & Yolanda Moli-
      na-Gavilán
BARCELONA (SPAIN) *See* Spain—Barcelona
Barcelona. Adams, A.
Barcode Jesus. Evenson, B.
The **Bardalees** of Bordley Point. Ritchie, E.
Bardin, John Franklin
  The deadly percheron [excerpt]
    The Vintage book of amnesia; an anthology;
      edited by Jonathan Lethem
Bare. Connolly, C.
Bare bones. Bingham, S.
The **Bare** Manuscript. Miller, A.
Bare Ruined Choirs. Sullivan, W.
Bare ruined choirs, where late the sweet birds
    sang. Gilchrist, E.
The **Bargain**. Capote, T.
Baricco, Alessandro
  Without Blood
    The New Yorker v78 no40 p128-37, 139-42,
      145-7 D 23-30 2002
Bark. Barnes, J.
Barkeep won't let anybody at all shove this
    handyman around. McNulty, J.
BARKENTINES *See* Sailing vessels
Barker, Clive
  The age of desire
    Speaking of lust; stories of forbidden desire;
      edited by Lawrence Block
  The Yattering and Jack
    A yuletide universe; sixteen fantastical tales;
      edited by Brian M. Thomsen
Barker, Nicola
  Back to front
    Barker, N. The 3 button trick and other sto-
      ries
  The Balance
    Granta no81 p125-33 Spr 2003
  Bendy-Linda
    Barker, N. The 3 button trick and other sto-
      ries
  Blisters
    Barker, N. The 3 button trick and other sto-
      ries
  Braces
    Barker, N. The 3 button trick and other sto-
      ries
  The butcher's apprentice
    Barker, N. The 3 button trick and other sto-
      ries
  Dual balls
    Barker, N. The 3 button trick and other sto-
      ries
  G-string
    The Art of the story; an international antholo-
      gy of contemporary short stories; edited by
      Daniel Halpern

  Barker, N. The 3 button trick and other sto-
    ries
Gifts
  Barker, N. The 3 button trick and other sto-
    ries
Inside information
  Barker, N. The 3 button trick and other sto-
    ries
  Coppola, F. F. Francis Ford Coppola's
    Zoetrope: all story; edited by Adrienne
    Brodeur and Samantha Schnee; introduction
    by Francis Ford Coppola
Layla's nose job
  Barker, N. The 3 button trick and other sto-
    ries
Limpets
  Barker, N. The 3 button trick and other sto-
    ries
Mr. Lippy
  Barker, N. The 3 button trick and other sto-
    ries
Parker Swells
  Barker, N. The 3 button trick and other sto-
    ries
The Piazza Barberini
  Barker, N. The 3 button trick and other sto-
    ries
Popping corn
  Barker, N. The 3 button trick and other sto-
    ries
Skin
  Barker, N. The 3 button trick and other sto-
    ries
Symbiosis: class cestoda
  Barker, N. The 3 button trick and other sto-
    ries
The three button trick
  Barker, N. The 3 button trick and other sto-
    ries
Water marks
  Barker, N. The 3 button trick and other sto-
    ries
Barking at butterflies. McBain, E.
The **barking** dog. Hunter, F.
Barkley, Brad
  The atomic age
    The Southern Review (Baton Rouge, La.) v35
      no1 p75-91 Wint 1999
  Beneath the deep, slow motion
    New stories from the South: the year's best,
      2002; edited by Shannon Ravenel; with a
      preface by Larry Brown
    The Virginia Quarterly Review v77 no3 p470-
      91 Summ 2001
  Nineteen amenities
    The Southern Review (Baton Rouge, La.) v37
      no1 p91-102 Wint 2001
  The properties of stainless steel
    The Virginia Quarterly Review v75 no1 p136-
      50 Wint 1999
Barley. Salter, J.
Barlow, John
  Eating mammals
    The Paris Review v43 no160 p16-70 Wint
      2001

Barnard, Robert
Everybody's girl
  Edwards, M. Mysterious pleasures; a celebration of the Crime Writers' Association's 50th anniversary; edited by Martin Edwards
The gentleman in the lake
  A Century of great suspense stories; edited by Jeffery Deaver
Going through a phase
  The best British mysteries; edited by Maxim Jakubowski
Holy living and holy dying
  Murder most divine; ecclesiastical tales of unholy crimes; edited by Ralph McInerny and Martin H. Greenberg
Nothing to lose
  Malice domestic 9
  The World's finest mystery and crime stories, second annual collection; edited by Ed Gorman
Old dogs, new tricks
  The World's finest mystery and crime stories, third annual collection; edited by Ed Gorman and Martin H. Greenberg
Barnes, Eric Muss- *See* Muss-Barnes, Eric
Barnes, H. Lee
The cat in the cage
  Barnes, H. L. Gunning for Ho; Vietnam stories; afterword by John Clark Pratt
Gunning for Ho
  Barnes, H. L. Gunning for Ho; Vietnam stories; afterword by John Clark Pratt
A lovely day in the A Shau Valley
  Barnes, H. L. Gunning for Ho; Vietnam stories; afterword by John Clark Pratt
Plateau lands
  Barnes, H. L. Gunning for Ho; Vietnam stories; afterword by John Clark Pratt
A return
  Barnes, H. L. Gunning for Ho; Vietnam stories; afterword by John Clark Pratt
Stonehands and the tigress
  Barnes, H. L. Gunning for Ho; Vietnam stories; afterword by John Clark Pratt
Tunnel rat
  Barnes, H. L. Gunning for Ho; Vietnam stories; afterword by John Clark Pratt
Barnes, Jane
A Disney World
  Prairie Schooner v77 no2 p75-86 Summ 2003
Barnes, Jim
Pulpwood
  New Letters v67 no2 p19-31 2001
What They Lost
  Iowa Review v33 no2 p147-59 Fall 2003
Barnes, Julian
Bark
  The New Yorker v78 no27 p92-7 S 16 2002
Evermore
  The Art of the story; an international anthology of contemporary short stories; edited by Daniel Halpern
The fruit cage
  The New Yorker v78 no11 p78-85 My 13 2002
Hygiene
  The New Yorker v75 no25 p68-72 S 6 1999
Knowing French
  Granta v84 p237-53 Wint 2003

The silence
  Granta no76 p137-47 Wint 2001
Trespass
  The New Yorker v79 no36 p86-93 N 24 2003
Barnes, Steven
Heartspace
  Mojo: conjure stories; edited by Nalo Hopkinson
The woman in the wall
  Dark matter; a century of speculative fiction from the African diaspora; edited by Sheree R. Thomas
(jt. auth) See Niven, Larry and Barnes, Steven
Barnes, Vincent G.
The Melted Buddha
  Confrontation no86/87 p131-41 Spr/Summ 2004
Barnet, Miguel
Miosvatis
  Dream with no name; contemporary fiction from Cuba; edited by Juana Ponce de León and Esteban Ríos Rivera
Barnett, Paul
Two dead men
  Royal whodunnits; edited by Mike Ashley
Barnstorming. Davidson, R.
Barolini, Helen
Bobbing
  Barolini, H. More Italian hours and other stories
  New Letters v69 no1 p31-8 2002
Classic and good
  Barolini, H. More Italian hours and other stories
Diving into eternity
  Barolini, H. More Italian hours and other stories
Dr. Melfi in the morning
  Barolini, H. More Italian hours and other stories
Gianni on the rocks
  Barolini, H. More Italian hours and other stories
La giardiniera
  Barolini, H. More Italian hours and other stories
Henry and the miracle
  Barolini, H. More Italian hours and other stories
How to live in Rome and loathe it
  Barolini, H. More Italian hours and other stories
Michaelmas daisies
  Barolini, H. More Italian hours and other stories
More Italian hours
  Barolini, H. More Italian hours and other stories
Ms. Italia
  Barolini, H. More Italian hours and other stories
The Nordic type
  Barolini, H. More Italian hours and other stories
Of sketchbooks and millers, of Paris and Rome
  Barolini, H. More Italian hours and other stories

Barolini, Helen—*Continued*
  Seven fishes
    Barolini, H. More Italian hours and other stories
  Shores of light
    Barolini, H. More Italian hours and other stories
Baron, Devorah
  Aggravation
    Baron, D. "The first day" and other stories; translated by Naomi Seidman with Chana Kronfeld; edited by Chana Kronfeld and Naomi Seidman
  Bill of divorcement
    Baron, D. "The first day" and other stories; translated by Naomi Seidman with Chana Kronfeld; edited by Chana Kronfeld and Naomi Seidman
  Bubbe Henya
    Baron, D. "The first day" and other stories; translated by Naomi Seidman with Chana Kronfeld; edited by Chana Kronfeld and Naomi Seidman
  Burying the books
    Baron, D. "The first day" and other stories; translated by Naomi Seidman with Chana Kronfeld; edited by Chana Kronfeld and Naomi Seidman
  Deserted wife
    Baron, D. "The first day" and other stories; translated by Naomi Seidman with Chana Kronfeld; edited by Chana Kronfeld and Naomi Seidman
  The end of Sender Ziv
    Baron, D. "The first day" and other stories; translated by Naomi Seidman with Chana Kronfeld; edited by Chana Kronfeld and Naomi Seidman
  Family
    Baron, D. "The first day" and other stories; translated by Naomi Seidman with Chana Kronfeld; edited by Chana Kronfeld and Naomi Seidman
  Fedka
    Baron, D. "The first day" and other stories; translated by Naomi Seidman with Chana Kronfeld; edited by Chana Kronfeld and Naomi Seidman
  The first day
    Baron, D. "The first day" and other stories; translated by Naomi Seidman with Chana Kronfeld; edited by Chana Kronfeld and Naomi Seidman
  Fradl
    Baron, D. "The first day" and other stories; translated by Naomi Seidman with Chana Kronfeld; edited by Chana Kronfeld and Naomi Seidman
  Grandchildren
    Baron, D. "The first day" and other stories; translated by Naomi Seidman with Chana Kronfeld; edited by Chana Kronfeld and Naomi Seidman
  In the beginning
    Baron, D. "The first day" and other stories; translated by Naomi Seidman with Chana Kronfeld; edited by Chana Kronfeld and Naomi Seidman

Kaddish
    Baron, D. "The first day" and other stories; translated by Naomi Seidman with Chana Kronfeld; edited by Chana Kronfeld and Naomi Seidman
  Liska
    Baron, D. "The first day" and other stories; translated by Naomi Seidman with Chana Kronfeld; edited by Chana Kronfeld and Naomi Seidman
  An only daughter
    Baron, D. "The first day" and other stories; translated by Naomi Seidman with Chana Kronfeld; edited by Chana Kronfeld and Naomi Seidman
  Shifra
    Baron, D. "The first day" and other stories; translated by Naomi Seidman with Chana Kronfeld; edited by Chana Kronfeld and Naomi Seidman
  Sister
    Baron, D. "The first day" and other stories; translated by Naomi Seidman with Chana Kronfeld; edited by Chana Kronfeld and Naomi Seidman
  Ziva
    Baron, D. "The first day" and other stories; translated by Naomi Seidman with Chana Kronfeld; edited by Chana Kronfeld and Naomi Seidman
Baron, Dvora
  Bubbe Henya
    Beautiful as the moon, radiant as the stars; Jewish women in Yiddish stories : an anthology; edited by Sandra Bark; introduction by Francine Prose
  Kaddish
    Beautiful as the moon, radiant as the stars; Jewish women in Yiddish stories : an anthology; edited by Sandra Bark; introduction by Francine Prose
Baron von Leisenbohg's destiny. Schnitzler, A.
Barone, Dennis
  The art of fiction
    Chicago Review v45 no3/4 p153-54 1999
  My mausoleum
    Chicago Review v45 no3/4 p155-56 1999
  Savoir faire
    Chicago Review v45 no3/4 p151-52 1999
BARONS *See* Aristocracy
BARQUENTINES *See* Sailing vessels
Barr, Nevada
  Venus rising
    Malice domestic 8
Barred owl. Offutt, C.
Barrel racers: El Charro. Bowen, G.
Barren. Budnitz, J.
Barrett, Andrea
  The cure
    Barrett, A. Servants of the map; stories
  The forest
    Barrett, A. Servants of the map; stories
  The mysteries of ubiquitin
    Barrett, A. Servants of the map; stories
  The Other Williamsburg
    The Paris Review v45 p40-55 Wint 2003
  Servants of the map
    Barrett, A. Servants of the map; stories

Barrett, Andrea—*Continued*

The Best American short stories 2001; selected from U.S. and Canadian magazines by Barbara Kingsolver with Katrina Kenison; with an introduction by Barbara Kingsolver

Prize stories, 2001; The O. Henry awards; edited and with an introduction by Larry Dark

Salmagundi no124/125 p177-221 Fall 1999/Wint 2000

Theories of rain

Barrett, A. Servants of the map; stories

Prize stories, 2000; The O. Henry awards; edited and with an introduction by Larry Dark

The Southern Review (Baton Rouge, La.) v35 no3 p495-510 Summ 1999

Two rivers

Barrett, A. Servants of the map; stories

TriQuarterly no112 p214-52 Fall/Wint 2002

Barrett, Julie

A most electrifying evening

Dracula in London; edited by P. N. Elrod

Barrett, Lynne

Beauty

Barrett, L. The secret names of women; stories

Elvis lives

Barrett, L. The secret names of women; stories

The former Star Carlson

Barrett, L. The secret names of women; stories

Hush money

Barrett, L. The secret names of women; stories

Macy is the other woman

Barrett, L. The secret names of women; stories

Meet the impersonators! (1986)

Barrett, L. The secret names of women; stories

To go

Barrett, L. The secret names of women; stories

Twentieth century design

Barrett, L. The secret names of women; stories

Barrett, Neal, Jr.

Class of '61

Barrett, N., Jr. Perpetuity blues and other stories

Cush

Barrett, N., Jr. Perpetuity blues and other stories

"A day at the fair"

Barrett, N., Jr. Perpetuity blues and other stories

Diner

Barrett, N., Jr. Perpetuity blues and other stories

Ginny Sweethips' Flying Circus

Barrett, N., Jr. Perpetuity blues and other stories

Highbrow

Barrett, N., Jr. Perpetuity blues and other stories

Perpetuity blues

Barrett, N., Jr. Perpetuity blues and other stories

Rhido wars

Redshift; extreme visions of speculative fiction; edited by Al Sarrantonio

Sallie C.

Barrett, N., Jr. Perpetuity blues and other stories

Stairs

Barrett, N., Jr. Perpetuity blues and other stories

Trading post

Barrett, N., Jr. Perpetuity blues and other stories

Under old New York

Barrett, N., Jr. Perpetuity blues and other stories

Winter on the Belle Fourche

Barrett, N., Jr. Perpetuity blues and other stories

Barrett, Victoria

Gustavo's Wedding

The Massachusetts Review v44 no3 p497-504 Fall 2003

Barrie, J. M. (James Matthew)

Peter and Wendy [excerpt]

Swords and sorcerers; stories from the world of fantasy and adventure; edited by Clint Willis

BARRIE, J. M. (JAMES MATTHEW), 1860-1937

Parodies, imitations, etc.

Yolen, J. Lost girls

Barrie, James Matthew *See* Barrie, J. M. (James Matthew), 1860-1937

Barrie (cont.). Anderson, D.

Barrie Hooper's dead. Anderson, D.

Barrington, Judith

Nicolette: a memoir

Hers 3: brilliant new fiction by lesbian writers; edited by Terry Wolverton with Robert Drake

Barrio chronicle. Sánchez, R.

BARRISTERS *See* Law and lawyers

Barron, K. L.

First light

New Letters v68 no2 p17-33 2002

Barry, Desmond

Dalton's box

The New Yorker v77 no9 p178-81 Ap 23-30 2001

BARS *See* Hotels, taverns, etc.

Bars. Johnson, D.

Bart, David

Prom night

A Hot and sultry night for crime; edited by Jeffery Deaver

Bart, Peter

The arbiter

Bart, P. Dangerous company; dark tales from Tinseltown

Dangerous company

Bart, P. Dangerous company; dark tales from Tinseltown

Gentlemen's Quarterly v71 no7 p71-4 Jl 2001

Day of reckoning

Bart, P. Dangerous company; dark tales from Tinseltown

Bart, Peter—*Continued*

The founder

    Bart, P. Dangerous company; dark tales from Tinseltown

Friend of the family

    Bart, P. Dangerous company; dark tales from Tinseltown

The ghostwriter

    Bart, P. Dangerous company; dark tales from Tinseltown

Hard bargain

    Bart, P. Dangerous company; dark tales from Tinseltown

The makeover

    Bart, P. Dangerous company; dark tales from Tinseltown

The neighbors I

    Bart, P. Dangerous company; dark tales from Tinseltown

The neighbors II

    Bart, P. Dangerous company; dark tales from Tinseltown

The neighbors III

    Bart, P. Dangerous company; dark tales from Tinseltown

Power play

    Bart, P. Dangerous company; dark tales from Tinseltown

Second coming

    Bart, P. Dangerous company; dark tales from Tinseltown

Bartender here takes dislike to "Deep in the heart of Texas". McNulty, J.

BARTENDERS

Cady, J. Jeremiah

Engstrom, E. Crosley

Holman, J. Squabble

McNulty, J. Bartender here takes dislike to "Deep in the heart of Texas"

McNulty, J. It's hard to figure how they know

McNulty, J. People don't seem to think things out straight in this gin mill

McNulty, J. You can't tell how you'll get clobbered

Robinson, L. The toast

Skillings, R. D. Job ops

Barter. Bujold, L. M.

Barth, John

9999

    Barth, J. The book of ten nights and a night; eleven stories

And then there's the one

    Barth, J. The book of ten nights and a night; eleven stories

The big shrink

    Barth, J. The book of ten nights and a night; eleven stories

Click

    Barth, J. The book of ten nights and a night; eleven stories

    The Scribner anthology of contemporary short fiction; fifty North American stories since 1970; Lex Williford and Michael Martone, editors

Dead cat, floating boy

    Barth, J. The book of ten nights and a night; eleven stories

A detective and a turtle

    Barth, J. The book of ten nights and a night; eleven stories

Extension

    Barth, J. The book of ten nights and a night; eleven stories

    Writers harvest 3; edited and with an introduction by Tobias Wolff

Help

    Barth, J. The book of ten nights and a night; eleven stories

Landscape; the Eastern shore

    Barth, J. The book of ten nights and a night; eleven stories

The rest of your life

    Barth, J. The book of ten nights and a night; eleven stories

    New stories from the South: the year's best, 2001; edited by Shannon Ravenel; with a preface by Lee Smith

The ring

    Barth, J. The book of ten nights and a night; eleven stories

Barthelme, Donald

The balloon

    Wonderful town; New York stories from The New Yorker; edited by David Remnick with Susan Choi

A city of churches

    The Best American short stories of the century; John Updike, editor, Katrina Kenison, coeditor; with an introduction by John Updike

Game

    The Vintage book of amnesia; an anthology; edited by Jonathan Lethem

I bought a little city

    Graham, D. Lone Star literature; from the Red River to the Rio Grande; edited by Don Graham

The school

    The Scribner anthology of contemporary short fiction; fifty North American stories since 1970; Lex Williford and Michael Martone, editors

Barthelme, Frederick

The autobiography of Riva Jay

    Barthelme, F. The law of averages; new & selected stories

Bag boy

    Barthelme, F. The law of averages; new & selected stories

Chroma

    Barthelme, F. The law of averages; new & selected stories

Cooker

    Barthelme, F. The law of averages; new & selected stories

Domestic

    Barthelme, F. The law of averages; new & selected stories

Driver

    Barthelme, F. The law of averages; new & selected stories

Elroy Nights

    Barthelme, F. The law of averages; new & selected stories

Barthelme, Frederick—*Continued*

Export

   Barthelme, F. The law of averages; new & selected stories

From Mars

   Barthelme, F. The law of averages; new & selected stories

Galveston

   Barthelme, F. The law of averages; new & selected stories

Grapette

   Barthelme, F. The law of averages; new & selected stories

The great pyramids

   Barthelme, F. The law of averages; new & selected stories

Harmonic

   Barthelme, F. The law of averages; new & selected stories

Instructor

   Barthelme, F. The law of averages; new & selected stories

Larroquette

   100% pure Florida fiction; an anthology; edited by Susan Hubbard and Robley Wilson

   Barthelme, F. The law of averages; new & selected stories

Law of averages

   Barthelme, F. The law of averages; new & selected stories

Margaret & Bud

   Barthelme, F. The law of averages; new & selected stories

Pool lights

   Barthelme, F. The law of averages; new & selected stories

Pupil

   Barthelme, F. The law of averages; new & selected stories

Red Arrow

   Barthelme, F. The law of averages; new & selected stories

Reset

   Barthelme, F. The law of averages; new & selected stories

Retreat

   Barthelme, F. The law of averages; new & selected stories

Shopgirls

   Barthelme, F. The law of averages; new & selected stories

Spots

   Barthelme, F. The law of averages; new & selected stories

Tiny ape

   Barthelme, F. The law of averages; new & selected stories

Travel & leisure

   Barthelme, F. The law of averages; new & selected stories

Violet

   Barthelme, F. The law of averages; new & selected stories

War with Japan

   Barthelme, F. The law of averages; new & selected stories

With Ray & Judy

   Barthelme, F. The law of averages; new & selected stories

Barthelme, Steven

Claire

   The Yale Review v91 no4 p112-28 O 2003

Heaven

   Atlantic Monthly (1993) v289 no6 p78-80 Je 2002

Barton, Marlin

Final spring

   Stories from the Blue Moon Café; edited by Sonny Brewer

Slow waltz

   The Virginia Quarterly Review v77 no2 p230-46 Spr 2001

Barton, William

Down in the dark

   The Year's best science fiction, sixteenth annual collection; edited by Gardner Dozois

Off on a starship

   The year's best science fiction: twenty-first annual collection; edited by Gardner Dozois

Bartos, Eileen

The fisher

   The Georgia Review v55 no1 p29-41 Spr 2001

Baruth, Philip

Nancy & Tonya & the long hard rain

   New England Review v20 no1 p118-29 Wint 1999

Barwin, Gary

Defrosting Disney

   The Canadian Forum v78 no880 p32-33 Ag 1999

Base of a triangle. Kilpatrick, N.

The **base** of the triangle; a Father Dowling mystery. McInerny, R. M.

BASEBALL

   See also Softball

Barnes, H. L. A lovely day in the A Shau Valley

Bausch, R. Guatemala

Bausch, R. The last day of summer

Beaumont, Gerald. Tin Can Tommy

Billman, J. Indians

Boswell, M. Ready position

Breen, J. L. All-star team

Breen, J. L. The Babe Ruth murder case

Breen, J. L. The body in the bullpen

Breen, J. L. Designated murderer

Breen, J. L. Diamond Dick

Breen, J. L. Fall of a hero

Breen, J. L. Horsehide sleuth

Breen, J. L. Insider trading

Breen, J. L. Instant replay

Breen, J. L. Malice at the mike

Breen, J. L. The Mother's-Day doubleheader

Breen, J. L. The number 12 jinx

Breen, J. L. Old-timers' game

Breen, J. L. Streak to death

Brooks, N. Our base ball club

Broun, H. Mrs. Tiny Tyler

Bukoski, A. The tools of ignorance

Carlson, R. Sunny Billy Day

Carlson, R. Zanduce at second

Chadwick, Lester. Joe's run

Chance, F. The bride and the pennant

Chapman, A. The strange case of South-paw Skaggs: an odd story of the national game

Cooper, J. F. A game of ball

Day, C. The King and His Court

BASEBALL—*Continued*

Doble, J. Lefty
Dozois, G. R. The Mayan variation
DuBois, B. A family game
Evans, Frank Edgar. The diamond jester
Everett, W. The base ball match
Ferber, E. A bush league hero
Formichella, Joe. Lomax's trials
Fullerton, H. The insignificant "Dub"
Garrett, G. P. Feeling good, feeling fine
Graves, Louis. Fair-weather hits
Greenberg, A. The high hard one
Grey, Z. The redheaded outfield
Harris, M. The bonding
Iagnemma, K. Zilkowski's theorem
Johnson, Owen. The humming bird
Kinsella, W. P. Shoeless Joe Jackson comes to Iowa
Lardner, R. Back to Baltimore
Lardner, R. Hurry Kane
Lee, M. The Albright Kid
Leonard, E. Chickasaw Charlie Hoke
MacDonald, J. D. A young man's game
Malone, M. The power
Mathewson, C. The alumni game
Menendez, A. Baseball dreams
Needham, Henry Beach. The jinx
Norris, F. This animal of a Buldy Jones
O'Rourke, F. The catcher
O'Rourke, F. Close play at home
O'Rourke, F. Decision
O'Rourke, F. Flashing spikes
O'Rourke, F. The greatest victory
O'Rourke, F. The heavenly World Series
O'Rourke, F. Home game
O'Rourke, F. The impossible play
O'Rourke, F. The last pitch
O'Rourke, F. The last time around
O'Rourke, F. Look for the kid with the guts
O'Rourke, F. The magic circle
O'Rourke, F. The manager
O'Rourke, F. Moment of truth
O'Rourke, F. Nothing new
O'Rourke, F. One more inning
O'Rourke, F. One ounce of common sense
O'Rourke, F. The terrible-tempered rube
Perry, B. At the Polo Grounds
Pronzini, B. and Malzberg, B. N. On account of darkness
Ramírez Mercado, S. The centerfielder
Rusch, K. K. The young shall see visions, and the old dream dreams
Standish, B. L. Seeking the secret of the double shot
Swarthout, G. F. The ball really carries in the Cactus League because the air is dry
Touré. How Babe Ruth saved my life
Twain, M. This experiment was baseball
Updike, J. The slump
Van Loan, C. E. Mathewson, Incog.
Wilbur, R. A game of catch
Baseball dreams. Menendez, A.
Baseball[2270]— the A's versus the non-A's. Johnston, P. D.
Bashō *See* Matsuo, Bashō, 1644-1694
Basic black. Dowling, T.
Basil Seal rides again. Waugh, E.
Basil the dog. Sherwood, F.
The **basilisk**. Sada, D.

BASKETBALL

Alexie, S. Lawyer's League
Alexie, S. Saint Junior
Alexie, S. What ever happened to Frank Snake Church?
Bradbury, R. In memoriam
Greer, R. O. One-on-one
Nailah, A. Bucket
Rozan, S. J. Hoops
Stolar, D. Fundamentals
Touré. Falcon Malone can fly no mo
Wideman, J. E. Doc's story
BASQUES
Kennedy, A. In our part of the world
Moujan Otaño, M. Gu ta gutarrak (we and our own)
Trevanian. The apple tree
Trevanian. Minutes of a village meeting
Trevanian. That Fox-of-a-Beñat
Bass, Rick
Eating
The Southern Review (Baton Rouge, La.) v37 no1 p103-6 Wint 2001
The fireman
The Best American short stories 2001; selected from U.S. and Canadian magazines by Barbara Kingsolver with Katrina Kenison; with an introduction by Barbara Kingsolver
The Pushcart prize XXVI; best of the small presses, an annual small press reader; edited by Bill Henderson and the Pushcart prize editors
Her First Elk
The Paris Review v45 p14-29 Wint 2003
The hermit's story
The Best American short stories, 1999; selected from U.S. and Canadian magazines by Amy Tan with Katrina Kenison, with an introduction by Amy Tan
The legend of Pig-Eye
Boxing's best short stories; edited by Paul D. Staudohar
Mahatma Joe
Still wild; short fiction of the American West, 1950 to the present; edited by Larry McMurtry
Ogallala
Francis Ford Coppola's Zoetrope all-story 2; edited by Adrienne Brodeur and Samantha Schnee; with an introduction by Francis Ford Coppola
Pagans
New stories from the South; the year's best, 2004; edited by Shannon Ravenel; preface by Tim Gautreaux
President's Day
Southwest Review v86 no1 p81-104 Wint 2001
The river in winter
Gentlemen's Quarterly v69 no10 p177+ O 1999
Swamp Boy
In our nature: stories of wildness; selected and introduced by Donna Seaman
Wild horses
The Scribner anthology of contemporary short fiction; fifty North American stories since 1970; Lex Williford and Michael Martone, editors

BASS GUITARISTS *See* Guitarists

'Bassador. Wells, C.

Bassani, Giorgio
A plaque on Via Mazzini
When night fell; an anthology of Holocaust short stories; edited by Linda Schermer Raphael and Marc Lee Raphael

Basse Ville. Porter, J. A.

Basset hounds and Saint Bernards. Hauser, E.

Bastable, Bernard
See also Barnard, Robert

Bastard. Easter, C.

BASTARDY *See* Illegitimacy

Baster. Eugenides, J.

BASTILLE DAY
Berberova, N. Billancourt fiesta

Bastogne. McNally, T. M.

Bat. Adam, C.

Bates, H. E. (Herbert Ernest)
The lily
Of leaf and flower; stories and poems for gardeners; edited by Charles Dean and Clyde Wachsberger; illustrations by Clyde Wachsberger

Bates, Harry
Farewell to the master
Science-fiction classics; the stories that morphed into movies; compiled by Forrest J. Ackerman

Bates, Herbert Ernest *See* Bates, H. E. (Herbert Ernest), 1905-1974

The **bath**. Tawada, Y.

The **bathroom** window. Babel', I.

BATMAN (FICTITIOUS CHARACTER)
Lethem, J. The notebooks of Bob K.
Perabo, S. Retirement

Batman's helpers. Block, L.

Bátorová, Mária
Tells
In search of homo sapiens; twenty-five contemporary Slovak short stories; editor, Pavol Hudík ; [translated by Heather Trebatická; American English editor, Lucy Bednár]

BATS
Adam, C. Bat
Atwood, M. My life as a bat

Bats. Canovic, L. S.

The **battered** mailbox. Cohen, S.

BATTERED WIVES *See* Wife abuse

The **battle** of Gunsmoke Lode. Le May, A.

The **battle** of Khafji. Paine, T.

A **battlefield** in moonlight. Biguenet, J.

BATTLES
See also names of individual battles
Cornwell, B. Excalibur [excerpt]

Baucis. Gavell, M. L.

Baum, L. Frank (Lyman Frank)
The enchanted buffalo
The American fantasy tradition; edited by Brian M. Thomsen
Tales before Tolkien; the roots of modern fantasy; edited by Douglas A. Anderson
A kidnapped Santa Claus
A yuletide universe; sixteen fantastical tales; edited by Brian M. Thomsen

BAUM, L. FRANK (LYMAN FRANK), 1856-1919
Parodies, imitations, etc.
Connor, J. Under the rainbow

Baum, Lyman Frank *See* Baum, L. Frank (Lyman Frank), 1856-1919

Bauman, Beth Ann
Beautiful girls
Bauman, B. A. Beautiful girls; stories
Eden
Bauman, B. A. Beautiful girls; stories
The middle of the night
Bauman, B. A. Beautiful girls; stories
Safeway
Bauman, B. A. Beautiful girls; stories
Stew
Bauman, B. A. Beautiful girls; stories
True
Bauman, B. A. Beautiful girls; stories
Wash, rinse, spin
Bauman, B. A. Beautiful girls; stories
Wildlife of America
Bauman, B. A. Beautiful girls; stories

Bauman, Bruce
The Necklace
Confrontation no86/87 p212-20 Spr/Summ 2004

Baumer, Jennifer Rachel
The party over there
Ghost writing; haunted tales by contemporary writers; edited by Roger Weingarten

Bausch, Richard
1-900
Bausch, R. The stories of Richard Bausch
1951
Bausch, R. Someone to watch over me; stories
Bausch, R. The stories of Richard Bausch
Accuracy
Bausch, R. The stories of Richard Bausch
Ancient history
Bausch, R. The stories of Richard Bausch
Aren't you happy for me?
The Art of the story; an international anthology of contemporary short stories; edited by Daniel Halpern
Bausch, R. The stories of Richard Bausch
The Workshop; seven decades of the Iowa Writers' Workshop: 42 stories, recollections & essays on Iowa's place in 20th-century American literature; edited by Tom Grimes
Billboard
Bausch, R. The stories of Richard Bausch
The brace
Bausch, R. The stories of Richard Bausch
Consolation
Bausch, R. The stories of Richard Bausch
Contrition
Bausch, R. The stories of Richard Bausch
Design
Bausch, R. The stories of Richard Bausch
Equity
Bausch, R. The stories of Richard Bausch
Evening
Bausch, R. The stories of Richard Bausch
The eyes of love
Bausch, R. The stories of Richard Bausch

Bausch, Richard—*Continued*

Fatality
>Bausch, R. Someone to watch over me; stories
>
>Bausch, R. The stories of Richard Bausch

The fireman's wife
>Bausch, R. The stories of Richard Bausch

Glass meadow
>Bausch, R. Someone to watch over me; stories
>
>Bausch, R. The stories of Richard Bausch

Guatemala
>Bausch, R. The stories of Richard Bausch

High-heeled shoe
>Bausch, R. The stories of Richard Bausch

The last day of summer
>Bausch, R. The stories of Richard Bausch

Letter to the lady of the house
>Bausch, R. The stories of Richard Bausch

Luck
>Bausch, R. The stories of Richard Bausch

The man who knew Belle Starr
>Bausch, R. The stories of Richard Bausch
>
>The Scribner anthology of contemporary short fiction; fifty North American stories since 1970; Lex Williford and Michael Martone, editors

Missy
>New stories from the South: the year's best, 1999; edited by Shannon Ravenel; with a preface by Tony Earley

"My mistress' eyes are nothing like the sun"
>Bausch, R. The stories of Richard Bausch
>
>*Doubletake* v7 no2 p104-10 Spr 2001

Nobody in Hollywood
>Bausch, R. Someone to watch over me; stories
>
>Bausch, R. The stories of Richard Bausch

Not quite final
>Bausch, R. Someone to watch over me; stories
>
>Bausch, R. The stories of Richard Bausch

Old west
>Bausch, R. The stories of Richard Bausch

Par
>Bausch, R. Someone to watch over me; stories
>
>Bausch, R. The stories of Richard Bausch

The person I have mostly become
>Bausch, R. The stories of Richard Bausch

Police dreams
>Bausch, R. The stories of Richard Bausch

Rare & endangered species
>Bausch, R. Wives and lovers; three short novels; Richard Bausch

Requisite kindness
>Bausch, R. Wives and lovers; three short novels; Richard Bausch

Riches
>Bausch, R. Someone to watch over me; stories
>
>Bausch, R. The stories of Richard Bausch

Self knowledge
>Bausch, R. Someone to watch over me; stories
>
>Bausch, R. The stories of Richard Bausch

The Pushcart prize XXIV: best of the small presses; an annual small press reader; edited by Bill Henderson with the Pushcart prize editors

Someone to watch over me
>Bausch, R. Someone to watch over me; stories
>
>Bausch, R. The stories of Richard Bausch

Spirits

Tandolfo the Great
>Bausch, R. The stories of Richard Bausch

Two altercations
>Bausch, R. Someone to watch over me; stories
>
>Bausch, R. The stories of Richard Bausch

Unjust
>Bausch, R. The stories of Richard Bausch

Valor
>Bausch, R. Someone to watch over me; stories
>
>Bausch, R. The stories of Richard Bausch
>
>The Pushcart prize XXIII: best of the small presses; an annual small press reader; edited by Bill Henderson with the Pushcart prize editors

The voices from the other room
>Bausch, R. Someone to watch over me; stories
>
>Bausch, R. The stories of Richard Bausch

Weather
>Bausch, R. The stories of Richard Bausch

Wedlock
>Bausch, R. The stories of Richard Bausch

The weight
>Bausch, R. The stories of Richard Bausch
>
>Pushcart prize XXVII; best of the small presses; edited by Bill Henderson with the Pushcart prize editors
>
>*The Southern Review (Baton Rouge, La.)* v37 no2 p340-54 Spr 2001

What feels like the world
>Bausch, R. The stories of Richard Bausch

Wise men at their end
>Bausch, R. The stories of Richard Bausch

Baxter, Charles

Gryphon
>The Scribner anthology of contemporary short fiction; fifty North American stories since 1970; Lex Williford and Michael Martone, editors

Harry Ginsberg
>The Pushcart prize XXIV: best of the small presses; an annual small press reader; edited by Bill Henderson with the Pushcart prize editors

Innocent
>Politically inspired; edited by Stephen Elliott; assistant editor, Gabriel Kram; associate editors, Elizabeth Brooks [et al.]

Music for airports
>*Doubletake* v7 no2 p84-5 Spr 2001

Baxter, Stephen

Cilia-of-gold
>The Good new stuff; adventure SF in the grand tradition; edited by Gardner Dozois

In the un-black
>Redshift; extreme visions of speculative fiction; edited by Al Sarrantonio

Baxter, Stephen—*Continued*
Martian autumn
Mars probes; edited by Peter Crowther
The modern Cyrano
Royal whodunnits; edited by Mike Ashley
On the Orion line
The Year's best science fiction, eighteenth annual collection; edited by Gardner Dozois
People came from earth
Worldmakers; SF adventures in terraforming; edited by Gardner Dozois
The Year's best science fiction, seventeenth annual collection; edited by Gardner Dozois
Saddlepoint: roughneck
The Year's best science fiction, sixteenth annual collection; edited by Gardner Dozois
Sun-Cloud
Starlight 3; edited by Patrick Nielsen Hayden
The Xeelee flower
Wondrous beginnings; edited by Steven H. Silver and Martin H. Greenberg
Baxter's Procrustes. Chesnutt, C. W.
Bayam-sellam. Nfah-Abbenyi, J. M.
Beach, Rex
The weight of obligation
A Century of great Western stories; edited by John Jakes
The **beach** butler. Rendell, R.
A **beach** day. Lida, D.
Beach-Ferrara, Jasmine
The Last American Monkey
Harvard Review (1992) no24 p102-9 Spr 2003
A **beacon** shall I shine. Navarro, Y.
Beagan, Glenda
The great master of ecstasy
Mr. Roopratna's chocolate; the winning stories from the 1999 Rhys Davies competition
Beagle, Peter S.
My daughter's name is Sarah
Magical beginnings; edited by Steven H. Silver and Martin H. Greenberg
Bean, Barbara
Dancing naked
Bean, B. Dream house; stories
Dream house
Bean, B. Dream house; stories
Honey
Bean, B. Dream house; stories
Hunting
Bean, B. Dream house; stories
Lost children
Bean, B. Dream house; stories
Perfect heart
Bean, B. Dream house; stories
Rock star
Bean, B. Dream house; stories
Sugar Creek
Bean, B. Dream house; stories
There'll never be another you
Bean, B. Dream house; stories
Bear, Elizabeth
Tiger! tiger!
Shadows over Baker Street; edited by Michael Reaves and John Pelan
Bear, Greg
Blood music
Bear, G. The collected stories of Greg Bear

Darwin's radio [excerpt]
Nebula awards showcase 2002; edited by Kim Stanley Robinson
Dead run
The American fantasy tradition; edited by Brian M. Thomsen
Bear, G. The collected stories of Greg Bear
The fall of the house of Escher
Bear, G. The collected stories of Greg Bear
Hardfought
Bear, G. The collected stories of Greg Bear
Heads
Bear, G. The collected stories of Greg Bear
Judgment engine
Bear, G. The collected stories of Greg Bear
A Martian Ricorso
Bear, G. The collected stories of Greg Bear
MDIO ecosystems increase knowledge of DNA languages (2215 C.E.)
Bear, G. The collected stories of Greg Bear
Perihesperon
Bear, G. The collected stories of Greg Bear
Petra
Bear, G. The collected stories of Greg Bear
Plague of conscience
Bear, G. The collected stories of Greg Bear
Richie by the sea
Bear, G. The collected stories of Greg Bear
Scattershot
Bear, G. The collected stories of Greg Bear
Schrödinger's plague
Bear, G. The collected stories of Greg Bear
Sisters
Bear, G. The collected stories of Greg Bear
Sleepside story
Bear, G. The collected stories of Greg Bear
Tangents
Bear, G. The collected stories of Greg Bear
Through road, no whither
Bear, G. The collected stories of Greg Bear
The Best alternate history stories of the 20th century; edited by Harry Turtledove with Martin H. Greenberg
The venging
Bear, G. The collected stories of Greg Bear
The visitation
Bear, G. The collected stories of Greg Bear
The way of all ghosts
Bear, G. The collected stories of Greg Bear
Far horizons; all new tales from the greatest worlds of science fiction; edited by Robert Silverberg
Webster
Bear, G. The collected stories of Greg Bear
The white horse child
Bear, G. The collected stories of Greg Bear
The wind from a burning woman
Bear, G. The collected stories of Greg Bear
Bear. Doxey, W. S.
The **bear** came over the mountain. Munro, A.
The **bear** cubs. Zinovyeva-Annibal, L. D.
The **bear** hunters. Ely, S.
BEAR HUNTING
Sherman, J. The snows of August
Bear it away. Cadnum, M.
Bear the dead away. Sanford, A.
Beard. Polansky, S.
BEARS
Adam, C. Ursus horribilis

BEARS—*Continued*
  Bisson, T. Bears discover fire
  Cadnum, M. Bear it away
  Connor, J. Ursa major in Vermont
  Friesner, E. M. Trouble a-bruin
  Gilchrist, E. Fort Smith
  Jenkins, W. F. Exploration team
  Kittredge, W. We are not in this together
  Lord, N. The woman who would marry a bear
  Moffett, J. The bear's baby
  Powers, S. The wild
  Shade, E. Kaahumanu
  Steinbeck, T. The wool gatherer
  Vivante, A. Shelter
  Zinovyeva-Annibal, L. D. The bear cubs
Bears discover fire. Bisson, T.
Beast. Gruss, A. L. and Kingsgrave-Ernstein, C.
The **beast** God forgot to invent. Harrison, J.
Beastly heat. Vukcevich, R.
Beasts. Bradbury, R.
BEAT GENERATION *See* Bohemianism
Beata, Santa. Herling, G.
Beating. Gates, D.
Beatings. Yuknavitch, L.
BEATLES
  Bishop, M. With a little help from her friends
  Kirwan, Larry. Liverpool fantasy
BEATNIKS *See* Bohemianism
Beatniks with banjos. Vukcevich, R.
Beaton, M. C.
  Handle with care
    The Mysterious Press anniversary anthology;
      celebrating 25 years; by the editors of Mys-
      terious Press
Beatrice places a call. Ritchie, E.
Beatrice: the sacrifice. Klein, R. S.
Beattie, Ann
  The big-breasted pilgrim
    Beattie, A. Perfect recall; new stories
    The Pushcart prize XXVI; best of the small
      presses, an annual small press reader; ed-
      ited by Bill Henderson and the Pushcart
      prize editors
  The burning house
    Fault lines; stories of divorce; collected and
      edited by Caitlin Shetterly
  Cat people
    Beattie, A. Perfect recall; new stories
  Coydog
    Beattie, A. Perfect recall; new stories
  Distant music
    Wonderful town; New York stories from The
      New Yorker; edited by David Remnick
      with Susan Choi
  The famous poet, amid Bougainvillea
    Beattie, A. Perfect recall; new stories
  Find and replace
    The New Yorker v77 no34 p84-9 N 5 2001
  The Garden Game
    Ploughshares v29 no1 p38-43 Spr 2003
  Hurricane Carleyville
    Beattie, A. Perfect recall; new stories
  In Amalfi
    The Art of the story; an international antholo-
      gy of contemporary short stories; edited by
      Daniel Halpern
  In irons
    Beattie, A. Perfect recall; new stories

The infamous fall of Howell the clown
    Beattie, A. Perfect recall; new stories
  Janus
    The Best American short stories of the
      century; John Updike, editor, Katrina
      Kenison, coeditor; with an introduction by
      John Updike
  The last odd day in L.A.
    The New Yorker v77 no8 p66-77 Ap 16 2001
  Last scenes from single life
    The Southern Review (Baton Rouge, La.) v35
      no3 p511-24 Summ 1999
  Mermaids
    Beattie, A. Perfect recall; new stories
  Mostre
    Doubletake v7 no4 p93-8 Fall 2001
  Perfect recall
    Beattie, A. Perfect recall; new stories
  The Rabbit Hole as Likely Explanation
    The New Yorker v80 no8 p68-77 Ap 12 2004
  See the pyramids
    Beattie, A. Perfect recall; new stories
  The women of this world
    Beattie, A. Perfect recall; new stories
Beaty, David
  Ghosts
    The Best American mystery stories, 2000; ed-
      ited and with an introduction by Donald E.
      Westlake
Beaumont, Charles
  The howling man
    The American fantasy tradition; edited by Bri-
      an M. Thomsen
Beaumont, Gerald
  Tin Can Tommy
    Dead balls and double curves; an anthology
      of early baseball fiction; edited and with an
      introduction by Trey Strecker ; with a fore-
      word by Arnold Hano
The **beauties**. Chekhov, A. P.
Beautiful. Deaver, J.
Beautiful. Henríquez, C.
Beautiful baby. Furman, L.
The **beautiful** days. Byers, M.
Beautiful game. Lipsyte, S.
Beautiful girl. Adams, A.
Beautiful girls. Bauman, B. A.
Beautiful grade. Moore, L.
The **beautiful** inclination. Dwyer, M.
Beautiful land. Evans, E.
Beautiful Mayagüez women. Kurlansky, M.
The **beautiful** morning of almost June. Nelson, K.
The **Beautiful** One Has Come. Kamata, S.
A **beautiful** restoration. Rose, D.
BEAUTY *See* Aesthetics
BEAUTY, PERSONAL *See* Personal beauty
Beauty. Barrett, L.
Beauty. Yuknavitch, L.
Beauty and Rudy. Slavin, J.
Beauty and the beast. Rollins, H.
"**Beauty** as punishment". Hartzenbusch, J. E.
BEAUTY CONTESTS
  Bauman, B. A. Beautiful girls
  Friesner, E. M. Big hair
  Link, K. Shoe and marriage
  Poirier, M. J. Pageantry
  Polansky, S. Dating Miss Universe
  Reiner, C. G. G. Giggler
Beauty of blood. Thurmond, J.

BEAUTY SHOPS
Galloway, J. Waiting for Marilyn
Gilchrist, E. Remorse
Honig, L. No friends, all strangers
Mullen, H. R. Tenderhead
Seiffert, R. Reach
Valeri, L. A rafter in Miami Beach
                   Employees
Budnitz, J. Permanent wave
Frym, G. Nothing compared to
Mayo, W. Robert's bride
Beauty Spot. Grossman, J.
The **beauty** treatment. Richter, S.
BEAVERS
Lord, N. The man who swam with beavers
El **bebé** del vaquerón. Matiella, A. C.
Becalmed. Locklin, G.
Because it was there. Lovesey, P.
Because my father always said he was the only
    Indian who saw Jimi Hendrix play "The
    Star-Spangled Banner" at Woodstock.
    Alexie, S.
Because of men. Ponte, A. J.
Because the constable blundered. Nevins, F. M.,
    Jr.
Bech noir. Updike, J.
Beck, K. K.
The tell-tale tattoo
    Malice domestic 10; an anthology of original
    traditional mystery stories
Becker, Geoffrey
Black Elvis
    The Best American short stories, 2000; select-
    ed from U.S. and Canadian magazines by
    E. L. Doctorow with Katrina Kenison; with
    an introduction by E. L. Doctorow
    Ploughshares v25 no4 p119-29 Wint
    1999/2000
Great American
    The Antioch Review v61 no2 p307-18 Spr
    2003
Hot Springs
    Ploughshares v27 no1 p14-23 Spr 2001
Iowa winter
    Ploughshares v28 no1 p77-91 Spr 2002
Jimi Hendrix, Bluegrass Star
    Prairie Schooner v78 no1 p6-18 Spr 2004
Beckett, Chris
Marcher
    The Year's best science fiction, nineteenth an-
    nual collection; edited by Gardner Dozois
To become a warrior
    The Year's best science fiction; twentieth an-
    nual collection; edited by Gardner Dozois
BECKETT, SAMUEL, 1906-1989
                About
Berry, R. M. Samuel Beckett's Middlemarch
Beckman, John
Babylon revisited redux
    Fishman, B. Wild East; stories from the last
    frontier; edited with an introduction by Bo-
    ris Fishman
The **beckoning** fair one. Onions, O.
Becky. Gonzalez, R.
Becky Weed. Billman, J.
Become a warrior. Yolen, J.
The **becoming**. Hope, A. L.
Becoming the full butterfly. Aldiss, B. W.

Bécquer, Gustavo Adolfo
"Believe in God"
    Fedorchek, R. M. Stories of enchantment
    from nineteenth-century Spain; translated
    from the Spanish by Robert M. Fredorchek;
    introduction by Alan E. Smith
"The devil's cross"
    Fedorchek, R. M. Stories of enchantment
    from nineteenth-century Spain; translated
    from the Spanish by Robert M. Fredorchek;
    introduction by Alan E. Smith
Bed & breakfast. Burton, M.
Bed & breakfast. Wolfe, G.
Bed and breakfast. Stuart, D.
Bedfordshire. Crowther, P.
BEDOUINS
Oz, A. Nomad and viper
Bedtime story. Addonizio, K.
Bedtime story. Painter, P.
Bee moths. MacKenzie, G.
Beef. Aldiss, B. W.
Beef and pudding. Dwyer, M.
Beehernz. Fitzgerald, P.
Beekman, E. M.
The price
    The Massachusetts Review v43 no2 p304-12
    Summ 2002
Beeman, Robin
What she was doing
    The North American Review v284 no3-4 p20-
    23 My/Ag 1999
Beerbohm, Max
Enoch Soames
    Nightshade: 20th century ghost stories; edited
    by Robert Phillips
BEES
Brennan, M. A large bee
Mayo, W. Dance of eights
Sammān, G. Thirty years of bees
Young, T. In bed
The **bees**. Chaon, D.
The **Bees,** Part I. Hemon, A.
BEETLES
Murray, J. Acts of memory, wisdom of man
Stableford, B. M. Tenebrio
Before a fall. Hendee, B.
Before Eden. Clarke, A. C.
Before Las Blancas. Ryan, P.
Before Long. Laken, V.
Before the adventures. Carroll, L.
Before the change. Munro, A.
Before this day there were many days. Williams,
    A. J.
Before you leap. Lutz, J.
The **beggar**. Chekhov, A. P.
The **beggar** of Union Square. Dokey, R.
BEGGARS
Bowles, P. Mejdoub
Bradbury, R. The beggar on O'Connell Bridge
Brennan, M. The joker
Chekhov, A. P. The beggar
Dokey, R. The beggar of Union Square
Ferreira, R. Dream with no name
Modisane, B. The dignity of begging
Singer, I. B. The beggar said no
Singer, I. B. By the light of memorial candles
Beginner's luck. Cunningham, E.
Beginning. Engberg, S.
The **beginning**. Grau, S. A.

The **beginning** of a long story. Brennan, M.
Beginning with the letter. Cameron, P.
The **beginnings** of grief. Haslett, A.
Behar, Ruth
  I told you: love would last us
    Prairie Schooner v73 no4 p79-96 Wint 1999
Behavior pilot. Derby, M.
Beheading the cat. Sammăn, G.
Beheadings. Salak, K.
Behind sharp branches. Coyne, T.
Behind the black curtain. Allen, S.
Behind the blue curtain. Millhauser, S.
Behind the Suits I Wear to Work. Wisniewski, M.
Behold. Lord, N.
BEIJING (CHINA) *See* China—Beijing
Beijing opera [excerpt] Su, D. L.-q.
Being. Matheson, R.
Beinhart, Larry
  Funny story
    Browning, A. Murder is no mitzvah; edited
      by Abigail Browning
BEIRUT (LEBANON) *See* Lebanon—Beirut
Beisch, June
  The Doctor
    The Literary Review (Madison, N.J.) v46 no1
      p45-55 Fall 2002
Békés, Paul
  The age of discovery
    Iowa Review v29 no1 p121-26 Spr 1999
Belated revenge. Matthews, C.
Belfar, Edward
  Roman Honeymoon
    Confrontation no86/87 p236-43 Spr/Summ
      2004
Belfiore, Michael P.
  What's in a name
    Tetrick, B. In the shadow of the wall; an an-
      thology of Vietnam stories that might have
      been; edited by Byron R. Tetrick
BELGIAN CONGO *See* Zaire
The **Belgian** Governor and the Drunk. Alishan, L.
BELGIANS
         Africa
  Hunter, F. Africa, Africa!
         France
  Raphael, F. Emile
         Zaire
  Hunter, F. Lenoir
BELGIUM
         Antwerp
  Teigeler, P. The wind & Mary
         Bruges
  Hunter, F. Africa, Africa!
         Brussels
  Potvin, E. A. Assumptions
Belief. Cacek, P. D.
Belief. Evans, L. B.
"**Believe** in God". Bécquer, G. A.
Believers. Everett, P. L.
Belinda's world tour. Davenport, G.
BELIZE
  Ellis, Z. The waiting room
Bell, Derrick A.
  The space traders
    Dark matter; a century of speculative fiction
      from the African diaspora; edited by Sheree
      R. Thomas

Bell, Katherine
  What Remains
    Ploughshares v29 no4 p8-19 Wint 2003/2004
Bell, M. Shayne
  Anomalous structures of my dreams
    The year's best science fiction: twenty-first
      annual collection; edited by Gardner Dozois
  Mrs. Lincoln's china
    Circa 2000; gay fiction at the millennium; ed-
      ited by Robert Drake & Terry Wolverton
  The pagodas of Ciboure
    The Year's best fantasy & horror: sixteenth
      annual collection; edited by Ellen Datlow
      & Terri Windling
  The thing about Benny
    Vanishing acts; a science fiction anthology;
      edited by Ellen Datlow
    The Year's best science fiction, eighteenth an-
      nual collection; edited by Gardner Dozois
  (jt. auth) See Resnick, Mike and Bell, M.
    Shayne
Bell, Madison Smartt
  Customs of the country
    The Scribner anthology of contemporary short
      fiction; fifty North American stories since
      1970; Lex Williford and Michael Martone,
      editors
  Dead Letter
    The Virginia Quarterly Review v80 no4 p164-
      76 Fall 2004
  Labor
    The Pushcart prize XXVI; best of the small
      presses, an annual small press reader; ed-
      ited by Bill Henderson and the Pushcart
      prize editors
  The naked lady
    The Cry of an occasion; fiction from the Fel-
      lowship of Southern Writers; edited by
      Richard Bausch; with a foreword by
      George Garrett
  Petrified forest
    Daedalus v131 no3 p98-113 Summ 2002
  Two lives
    New stories from the South: the year's best,
      2001; edited by Shannon Ravenel; with a
      preface by Lee Smith
Bella Fleace gave a party. Waugh, E.
The **Bellarosa** connection. Bellow, S.
Bellatin, Mario
  Black ball
    Bomb no78 p96-8 Wint 2001/2002
Belle, Jennifer
  Book of Nick
    Typical girls; new stories by smart women;
      edited by Susan Corrigan
Belle bloody merciless dame. Yolen, J.
Belle Boyd, the rebel spy. Crider, B.
La **belle** dame sans merci. Avrich, J.
La **belle** Zorađe. Chopin, K.
La **Belle** Zoraïde. Chopin, K.
Beller, Thomas
  Caller I.D.
    Writers harvest 3; edited and with an intro-
      duction by Tobias Wolff
  A different kind of imperfection
    The Student body; short stories about college
      students and professors; edited by John
      McNally

Beller, Thomas—*Continued*
Sally the Slut
Ploughshares v30 no2/3 p7-25 Fall 2004
La **bellezza** delle bellezze. Pronzini, B.
Bellow, Saul
The Bellarosa connection
Bellow, S. Collected stories; preface by Janis
Bellow; introduction by James Wood
By the St. Lawrence
Bellow, S. Collected stories; preface by Janis
Bellow; introduction by James Wood
Cousins
Bellow, S. Collected stories; preface by Janis
Bellow; introduction by James Wood
A father-to-be
Wonderful town; New York stories from The
New Yorker; edited by David Remnick
with Susan Choi
Him with his foot in his mouth
Bellow, S. Collected stories; preface by Janis
Bellow; introduction by James Wood
Leaving the yellow house
Bellow, S. Collected stories; preface by Janis
Bellow; introduction by James Wood
Looking for Mr. Green
Bellow, S. Collected stories; preface by Janis
Bellow; introduction by James Wood
Mosby's memoirs
Bellow, S. Collected stories; preface by Janis
Bellow; introduction by James Wood
The old system
Bellow, S. Collected stories; preface by Janis
Bellow; introduction by James Wood
Ravelstein
The New Yorker v75 no32 p96-107 N 1 1999
A silver dish
Bellow, S. Collected stories; preface by Janis
Bellow; introduction by James Wood
The Best American short stories of the
century; John Updike, editor, Katrina
Kenison, coeditor; with an introduction by
John Updike
Something to remember me by
Bellow, S. Collected stories; preface by Janis
Bellow; introduction by James Wood
A theft
Bellow, S. Collected stories; preface by Janis
Bellow; introduction by James Wood
What kind of day did you have?
Bellow, S. Collected stories; preface by Janis
Bellow; introduction by James Wood
Zetland: by a character witness
Bellow, S. Collected stories; preface by Janis
Bellow; introduction by James Wood
Bellows, Nathaniel
First Four Measures
The Paris Review v46 p96-113 Summ 2004
Bells in the morning. Yates, R.
The **bells** of San Juan. Le May, A.
The **bells** of the "Laughing Sally". Hodgson, W.
H.
Belly Talk. Martin, L.
Below the sick water. Oaks, G.
Below the surface. Hart, R.
Beltran, Rosa
Scheheresade
Points of departure; new stories from Mexico;
edited by Mónica Lavín; translated by Gus-
tavo Segade

Beltway Dostoyevsky. Clark, J.
Bemelmans, Ludwig
Mespoulets of the Splendide
Wonderful town; New York stories from The
New Yorker; edited by David Remnick
with Susan Choi
Ben-Tov, Sharona
The invisible mine
Partisan Review v68 no4 p593-604 Fall 2001
Bench trial. Huffman, B., Jr.
A **bend** in the road. Sparks, N.
Bender, Aimee
The 20th-Century War Veteran Club
The Antioch Review v61 no2 p208-21 Spr
2003
The case of the salt and pepper shakers
McSweeney's mammoth treasury of thrilling
tales; edited by Michael Chabon
Dearth
On the rocks; the KGB Bar fiction anthology;
edited by Rebecca Donner ; foreword by
Denis Woychuk
Dreaming in Polish
Lost tribe; jewish fiction from the edge
Jinx
Pushcart prize XXVII; best of the small
presses; edited by Bill Henderson with the
Pushcart prize editors
What you left in the ditch
The Antioch Review v59 no2 p327-33 Spr
2001
Bender, Karen E.
Anything for money
Francis Ford Coppola's Zoetrope all-story 2;
edited by Adrienne Brodeur and Samantha
Schnee; with an introduction by Francis
Ford Coppola
Eternal love
LA shorts; edited by Steven Gilbar
The fourth Prussian dynasty
The New Yorker v75 no26 p88-92+ S 13
1999
Bendy-Linda. Barker, N.
Beneath the deep, slow motion. Barkley, B.
Beneath the moors. Lumley, B.
Beneath the planet of the compulsives. Alexander,
E.
Beneath the stars of winter. Landis, G. A.
Benedek, Dezsö
(jt. auth) See Spariosu, Mihai and Benedek,
Dezsö
Benedetti, Mario
From La muerte y otras sopresas: cuentos
The Kenyon Review ns21 no2 p82-83 Spr
1999
Lead Us Into
Michigan Quarterly Review v43 no1 p46-53
Wint 2004
Benedict, Pinckney
Miracle boy
Fishing for chickens; short stories about rural
youth; edited, with an introduction by Jim
Heynen
New stories from the South: the year's best,
1999; edited by Shannon Ravenel; with a
preface by Tony Earley
Prize stories, 1999; The O. Henry awards; ed-
ited and with an introduction by Larry
Dark

Benedict, Pinckney—*Continued*

The Sutton Pie Safe

The Workshop; seven decades of the Iowa Writers' Workshop: 42 stories, recollections & essays on Iowa's place in 20th-century American literature; edited by Tom Grimes

Zog-19: a scientific romance

Prize stories, 2001; The O. Henry awards; edited and with an introduction by Larry Dark

Benediction. Fitzgerald, F. S.

The **benefactor.** Hinostroza, R.

The **Benefit** of the Doubt. Wolff, T.

Benét, Stephen Vincent

Daniel Webster and the sea serpent

Fishing's best short stories; edited by Paul D. Staudohar

The Devil and Daniel Webster

The American fantasy tradition; edited by Brian M. Thomsen

Benford, Gregory

Anomalies

Redshift; extreme visions of speculative fiction; edited by Al Sarrantonio

As big as the Ritz

Benford, G. Worlds vast and various; stories

A calculus of desperation

Benford, G. Worlds vast and various; stories

The clear blue seas of Luna

The Year's best science fiction; twentieth annual collection; edited by Gardner Dozois

A dance to strange musics

Benford, G. Worlds vast and various; stories

Doing alien

Benford, G. Worlds vast and various; stories

A fairhope alien

Stories from the Blue Moon Cafe II; edited by Sonny Brewer

The goldilocks problem

Once upon a galaxy; edited by Will [sic] McCarthy, Martin H. Greenberg, and John Helfers

High abyss

Benford, G. Worlds vast and various; stories

A hunger for the infinite

Far horizons; all new tales from the greatest worlds of science fiction; edited by Robert Silverberg

In the dark backward

Benford, G. Worlds vast and various; stories

Kollapse

Benford, G. Worlds vast and various; stories

Manassas, again

The Best alternate history stories of the 20th century; edited by Harry Turtledove with Martin H. Greenberg

The scarred man

Benford, G. Worlds vast and various; stories

Shall we take a little walk?

Worldmakers; SF adventures in terraforming; edited by Gardner Dozois

The voice

Benford, G. Worlds vast and various; stories

World vast, world various

Benford, G. Worlds vast and various; stories

A worm in the well

Benford, G. Worlds vast and various; stories

Zoomers

Benford, G. Worlds vast and various; stories

Benigna Machiavelli. Gilman, C. P.

Benioff, David

The affairs of each beast

Francis Ford Coppola's Zoetrope all-story 2; edited by Adrienne Brodeur and Samantha Schnee; with an introduction by Francis Ford Coppola

When the nines roll over

Best new American voices 2000; guest editor Tobias Wolff; series editors John Kulka and Natalie Danford

Benítez-Rojo, Antonio

Buried statues

The Oxford book of Caribbean short stories; edited by Stewart Brown and John Wickham

Whispers from the cotton tree root; Caribbean fabulist fiction; edited by Nalo Hopkinson

The scissors

The Vintage book of Latin American stories; edited by Carlos Fuentes and Julio Ortega

Skin deep

Dream with no name; contemporary fiction from Cuba; edited by Juana Ponce de León and Esteban Ríos Rivera

The **Bênitous'** slave. Chopin, K.

Benjamin. Bingham, S.

Bennett, Alan

Father! Father! Burning bright

Bennett, A. The laying on of hands; stories

The laying on of hands

Bennett, A. The laying on of hands; stories

Miss Fozzard finds her feet

Bennett, A. The laying on of hands; stories

Bennett, Anna

Milk

The North American Review v284 no3-4 p60-63 My/Ag 1999

Bennett, Dwight, 1916-

For works by this author under other names see Newton, D. B. (Dwight Bennett), 1916-

Bennett, Gertrude Barrows *See* Stevens, Francis, b. 1884

Bennett, Hal

Miss Askew on ice

Callaloo v24 no2 p389-400 Spr 2001

Bennett, Nigel and Elrod, P. N.

Wolf and hound

Dracula in London; edited by P. N. Elrod

Benni, Stefano

The Year of Mad Weather

The Literary Review (Madison, N.J.) v46 no3 p533-6 Spr 2003

Benny's space. Muller, M.

Bensko, John

Creeping Things

New Letters v70 no2 p57-68 2004

Summer girls

Southwest Review v86 no2/3 p393-402 Spr/Summ 2001

Benson, Raymond

Live at five

TV Guide v47 no46 p36-38+ N 13-19 1999

Benson, Sally

Apartment hotel

Wonderful town; New York stories from The New Yorker; edited by David Remnick with Susan Choi

Bent Creek Burn. Palmer, S.
Benton, Caroline
Guardian angel
Murder most delectable; savory tales of culinary crimes; edited by Martin H. Greenberg
Benvenuto, Christine
Hindsight
Meridians v3 no1 p211-25 2002
Benvolio. James, H.
BEOWULF
Wägner, W. The legend of Beowulf
Berberova, Nina
About the hooks
Berberova, N. Billancourt tales; translated from the Russian with an introduction by Marian Schwartz
The Argentine
Berberova, N. Billancourt tales; translated from the Russian with an introduction by Marian Schwartz
Billancourt fiesta
Berberova, N. Billancourt tales; translated from the Russian with an introduction by Marian Schwartz
The Billancourt manuscript
Berberova, N. Billancourt tales; translated from the Russian with an introduction by Marian Schwartz
A gypsy romance
Berberova, N. Billancourt tales; translated from the Russian with an introduction by Marian Schwartz
An incident with music
Berberova, N. Billancourt tales; translated from the Russian with an introduction by Marian Schwartz
Kolka and Liusenka
Berberova, N. Billancourt tales; translated from the Russian with an introduction by Marian Schwartz
The little stranger
Berberova, N. Billancourt tales; translated from the Russian with an introduction by Marian Schwartz
The phantom of Billancourt
Berberova, N. Billancourt tales; translated from the Russian with an introduction by Marian Schwartz
Photogenique
Berberova, N. Billancourt tales; translated from the Russian with an introduction by Marian Schwartz
Ring of love
Berberova, N. Billancourt tales; translated from the Russian with an introduction by Marian Schwartz
Versts and sleeping cars
Berberova, N. Billancourt tales; translated from the Russian with an introduction by Marian Schwartz
The violin of Billancourt
Berberova, N. Billancourt tales; translated from the Russian with an introduction by Marian Schwartz
Berdine, Tom
Spring rite
The Best American mystery stories, 2000; edited and with an introduction by Donald E. Westlake

BEREAVEMENT
Alcott, L. M. Little Genevieve
Barnes, J. Evermore
Bass, R. Wild horses
Bausch, R. Ancient history
Blair, J. Julia loving the face of God
Bloom, A. Stars at elbow and foot
Carlson, R. Blazo
Casey, M. Talk show lady
Chekhov, A. P. Misery
Davis, L. Strays
Davis, M. K. Rachel
Desai, A. Underground
Di Filippo, P. Weeping walls
Eggers, P. A private space
Engel, M. P. What Addie wants
Gartner, Z. Odds that, all things considered, she'd someday be happy
Gilliland, G. Stones
Hall, D. The fifth box
Hendel, Y. The leter that came in time
Hirshberg, G. The two Sams
Hood, A. Lost parts
Hribal, C. J. The clouds in Memphis
Iribarne, M. Ross Willow's new and used cars
Johnson, A. The death-dealing Cassini satellite
Joseph, D. Bloodlines
Ketchum, J. Gone
Leslie, N. A little wild
Mayo, W. Jagged tooth, great tooth
Moore, L. Four calling birds, three French hens
Nietzke, A. Los Angeles here and now
Norris, H. The second shepherd
Oates, J. C. Cumberland breakdown
Ortiz, S. J. To change life in a good way
Perabo, S. Explaining death to the dog
Robison, M. I am twenty-one
Robison, M. I get by
Taylor, T. L. Doves of Townsend
Tilghman, C. Things left undone
West, M. Faces made of clay
Yoshimoto, B. Night and night's travelers
Berele in the ghetto. Bryks, R.
Berent, Mark
Raid on Thud Ridge
On glorious wings; the best flying stories of the century; edited and introduced by Stephen Coonts
Beresteczko. Babel´, I.
Berg, Elizabeth
Ordinary life: a love story
Good Housekeeping v232 no4 p183-94 Ap 2001
The Party
Ploughshares v29 no2/3 p8-11 Fall 2003
True to form
Good Housekeeping v234 no6 p175-91 Je 2002
BERG, MOE, 1902-1972
About
Irvine, A. Agent provocateur
Bergelson, David
The deal man
Neugroschel, J. No star too beautiful; Yiddish stories from 1382 to the present; compiled and translated by Joachim Neugroschel

Bergelson, David—*Continued*
  In the boardinghouse
    Beautiful as the moon, radiant as the stars;
      Jewish women in Yiddish stories : an an-
      thology; edited by Sandra Bark; introduc-
      tion by Francine Prose
  Spring
    Beautiful as the moon, radiant as the stars;
      Jewish women in Yiddish stories : an an-
      thology; edited by Sandra Bark; introduc-
      tion by Francine Prose
  Two roads
    Neugroschel, J. No star too beautiful; Yiddish
      stories from 1382 to the present; compiled
      and translated by Joachim Neugroschel
  Without a trace
    Neugroschel, J. No star too beautiful; Yiddish
      stories from 1382 to the present; compiled
      and translated by Joachim Neugroschel
Berger, John
  The courtesy
    The New Yorker v78 no16 p144-60 Je 17-24
      2002
  Passeur
    The New Yorker v77 no41 p92-7 D 24-31
      2001
  Woven, sir
    The New Yorker v77 no6 p76-81 Ap 2 2001
Bergeron, Alain
  The eighth register
    Northern suns; edited by David G. Hartwell
      & Glenn Grant
Bergman, Susan
  Try love
    TriQuarterly no106 p231-40 Fall 1999
Bergstrom, Elaine
  The three boxes
    Dracula in London; edited by P. N. Elrod
Berkeley, Anthony
  The avenging chance
    Berkeley, A. The avenging chance
  Double bluff
    Berkeley, A. The avenging chance
  "Mr. Bearstowe says ..."
    Berkeley, A. The avenging chance
  The mystery of Horne's Copse
    Berkeley, A. The avenging chance
  Perfect alibi
    Berkeley, A. The avenging chance
  Unsound mind
    Berkeley, A. The avenging chance
  White butterfly
    Berkeley, A. The avenging chance
  The wrong jar
    Berkeley, A. The avenging chance
BERKELEY (CALIF.) *See* California—Berkeley
Berkeley. Gilliland, G.
Berkeley house. Adams, A.
Berkley; or, Mariana of the universe. Heker, L.
Berkman, Pamela Rafael
  Bethlehem
    Berkman, P. The falling nun and other sto-
      ries; illustrations by Karen Roze
  Dark blue
    Berkman, P. R. Her infinite variety; stories of
      Shakespeare and the women he loved
  Diamonds at her fingertips
    Berkman, P. R. Her infinite variety; stories of
      Shakespeare and the women he loved

Duty
  Berkman, P. R. Her infinite variety; stories of
    Shakespeare and the women he loved
The falling nun
  Berkman, P. The falling nun and other sto-
    ries; illustrations by Karen Roze
February 14
  Berkman, P. The falling nun and other sto-
    ries; illustrations by Karen Roze
Gold
  Berkman, P. R. Her infinite variety; stories of
    Shakespeare and the women he loved
Gold glitter
  Berkman, P. The falling nun and other sto-
    ries; illustrations by Karen Roze
Holy holy holy
  Berkman, P. The falling nun and other sto-
    ries; illustrations by Karen Roze
In the bed
  Berkman, P. R. Her infinite variety; stories of
    Shakespeare and the women he loved
Jennet
  Berkman, P. R. Her infinite variety; stories of
    Shakespeare and the women he loved
Magic wand
  Berkman, P. R. Her infinite variety; stories of
    Shakespeare and the women he loved
Mary Mountjoy's dowry
  Berkman, P. R. Her infinite variety; stories of
    Shakespeare and the women he loved
Men have more upper-body strength
  Berkman, P. The falling nun and other sto-
    ries; illustrations by Karen Roze
Merry Christmas, Charlie Brown
  Berkman, P. The falling nun and other sto-
    ries; illustrations by Karen Roze
No cause
  Berkman, P. R. Her infinite variety; stories of
    Shakespeare and the women he loved
Playing crucifixion
  Berkman, P. The falling nun and other sto-
    ries; illustrations by Karen Roze
The Scottish wife
  Berkman, P. R. Her infinite variety; stories of
    Shakespeare and the women he loved
Snakes
  Berkman, P. The falling nun and other sto-
    ries; illustrations by Karen Roze
Tat
  Berkman, P. The falling nun and other sto-
    ries; illustrations by Karen Roze
Veronica
  Berkman, P. The falling nun and other sto-
    ries; illustrations by Karen Roze
Witch
  Berkman, P. The falling nun and other sto-
    ries; illustrations by Karen Roze
BERLIN (GERMANY) *See* Germany—Berlin
Berlin by heart. Heinold, T.
The **Berlin** Wall. Young, T.
Berlin Wall piece. Shepard, S.
Berliner, Janet
  Everything old is new again
    Snapshots: 20th century mother-daughter fic-
      tion; edited by Joyce Carol Oates and Janet
      Berliner
  Eye of the day
    Past lives, present tense; edited by Elizabeth
      Ann Scarborough

Berliner, Janet—*Continued*
Other.........1
   The Blue and the gray undercover; edited by
    Ed Gorman
Until the butterflies
   Lighthouse hauntings; 12 original tales of the
    supernatural; edited by Charles G. Waugh
    & Martin H. Greenberg
Berm. Levine, P.
Berman, Mitch
A walk in the park
   Southwest Review v84 no2 p297-303 1999
Bernard, Kenneth
A Leader of the People
   Salmagundi no137/138 p167-8 Wint/Spr 2003
Trimming Hedge
   Salmagundi no137/138 p164-6 Wint/Spr 2003
Berners, Gerald Hugh Tyrwhitt-Wilson, Baron
The camel
   Berners, G. H. T.-W., Baron. Collected tales
    and fantasies of Lord Berners
Count Omega
   Berners, G. H. T.-W., Baron. Collected tales
    and fantasies of Lord Berners
Far from the madding war
   Berners, G. H. T.-W., Baron. Collected tales
    and fantasies of Lord Berners
Mr. Pidger
   Berners, G. H. T.-W., Baron. Collected tales
    and fantasies of Lord Berners
Percy Wallingford
   Berners, G. H. T.-W., Baron. Collected tales
    and fantasies of Lord Berners
The romance of a nose
   Berners, G. H. T.-W., Baron. Collected tales
    and fantasies of Lord Berners
Berney, Louis
Stupid girl
   LA shorts; edited by Steven Gilbar
   The Pushcart prize XXIII: best of the small
    presses; an annual small press reader; ed-
    ited by Bill Henderson with the Pushcart
    prize editors
Bernhard, Thomas
Amras
   Bernhard, T. Three novellas; translated by Pe-
    ter Jansen and Kenneth J. Northcott; with
    a foreword by Brian Evenson
Playing Watten
   Bernhard, T. Three novellas; translated by Pe-
    ter Jansen and Kenneth J. Northcott; with
    a foreword by Brian Evenson
Walking
   Bernhard, T. Three novellas; translated by Pe-
    ter Jansen and Kenneth J. Northcott; with
    a foreword by Brian Evenson
Bernice bobs her hair. Fitzgerald, F. S.
Bernie and me. Raboteau, E. I.
Bernie the Faust. Tenn, W.
BERNSTEIN, LEONARD, 1918-1990
About
Anderson, R. Schism
Malzberg, B. N. Fugato
Bernstein, Leonard S.
Death by pastrami
   The Literary Review (Madison, N.J.) v44 no3
    p546-7 Spr 2001

Berrada, Mohammed
A life in detail
   The Anchor book of modern African stories;
    edited by Nadežda Obradovic ; with a fore-
    word by Chinua Achebe
Berriault, Gina
The infinite passion of expectation
   Breaking into print; early stories and insights
    into getting published; a Ploughshares an-
    thology; edited by DeWitt Henry
The **berries**. Tolstoy, L., graf
Berry, Minta Sue
Armistice
   Berry, M. S. Who is my neighbor?
Exit Miss Tish
   Berry, M. S. Who is my neighbor?
Final payment
   Berry, M. S. Who is my neighbor?
The four hundred ninety-first time
   Berry, M. S. Who is my neighbor?
The hawk
   Berry, M. S. Who is my neighbor?
The long dark hall
   Berry, M. S. Who is my neighbor?
The long view
   Berry, M. S. Who is my neighbor?
Next-door neighbors
   Berry, M. S. Who is my neighbor?
The passing night
   Berry, M. S. Who is my neighbor?
Philip's room
   Berry, M. S. Who is my neighbor?
The quantity of mercy
   Berry, M. S. Who is my neighbor?
Berry, R. M.
Abandoned writing projects
   Berry, R. M. Dictionary of modern anguish;
    fictions
'Bus
   Berry, R. M. Dictionary of modern anguish;
    fictions
Free enterprise
   Berry, R. M. Dictionary of modern anguish;
    fictions
(From) Frank
   Iowa Review v32 no1 p128-36 Spr 2002
The function of art at the present time
   Berry, R. M. Dictionary of modern anguish;
    fictions
History
   Berry, R. M. Dictionary of modern anguish;
    fictions
Knott unbound
   Berry, R. M. Dictionary of modern anguish;
    fictions
Mimesis
   Berry, R. M. Dictionary of modern anguish;
    fictions
(Paid advertisement)
   Berry, R. M. Dictionary of modern anguish;
    fictions
Pretense
   Berry, R. M. Dictionary of modern anguish;
    fictions
Samuel Beckett's Middlemarch
   Berry, R. M. Dictionary of modern anguish;
    fictions

Berry, R. M.—*Continued*
Second story
  Berry, R. M. Dictionary of modern anguish; fictions
The sentence
  Berry, R. M. Dictionary of modern anguish; fictions
A theory of fiction
  Berry, R. M. Dictionary of modern anguish; fictions
Torture!
  Berry, R. M. Dictionary of modern anguish; fictions
Berry, Wendell
Are you all right?
  Berry, W. That distant land; the collected stories of Wendell Berry
The boundary
  Berry, W. That distant land; the collected stories of Wendell Berry
A consent
  Berry, W. That distant land; the collected stories of Wendell Berry
The discovery of Kentucky
  Berry, W. That distant land; the collected stories of Wendell Berry
Don't send a boy to do a man's work
  Berry, W. That distant land; the collected stories of Wendell Berry
Fidelity
  Berry, W. That distant land; the collected stories of Wendell Berry
A friend of mine
  Berry, W. That distant land; the collected stories of Wendell Berry
A half-pint of Old Darling
  Berry, W. That distant land; the collected stories of Wendell Berry
The hurt man
  Berry, W. That distant land; the collected stories of Wendell Berry
  The Hudson Review v56 no3 p431-8 Aut 2003
The inheritors
  Berry, W. That distant land; the collected stories of Wendell Berry
It wasn't me
  Berry, W. That distant land; the collected stories of Wendell Berry
A jonquil for Mary Penn
  Berry, W. That distant land; the collected stories of Wendell Berry
The lost bet
  Berry, W. That distant land; the collected stories of Wendell Berry
Making it home
  Berry, W. That distant land; the collected stories of Wendell Berry
Nearly to the fair
  Berry, W. That distant land; the collected stories of Wendell Berry
Pray without ceasing
  Berry, W. That distant land; the collected stories of Wendell Berry
The solemn boy
  Berry, W. That distant land; the collected stories of Wendell Berry

That distant land
  Berry, W. That distant land; the collected stories of Wendell Berry
  Home and beyond; an anthology of Kentucky short stories; edited by Morris Allen Grubbs; with an introduction by Wade Hall and an afterword by Charles E. May
Thicker than liquor
  Berry, W. That distant land; the collected stories of Wendell Berry
Turn back the bed
  Berry, W. That distant land; the collected stories of Wendell Berry
Watch with me
  Berry, W. That distant land; the collected stories of Wendell Berry
Where did they go?
  Berry, W. That distant land; the collected stories of Wendell Berry
The wild birds
  Berry, W. That distant land; the collected stories of Wendell Berry
Berry, Betsy
Family and flood
  Graham, D. Lone Star literature; from the Red River to the Rio Grande; edited by Don Graham
Berserker. Kilpatrick, N.
Bertha. Alcott, L. M.
Bertha. Appelfeld, A.
Berthoff, Warner
(jt. auth) See Bulgheroni, Marisa
Bertie's box: a Christmas story. Alcott, L. M.
Bertles, Jeannette
Whileaway
  Gettysburg Review v12 no1 p65-83 Spr 1999
  Prize stories, 2000; The O. Henry awards; edited and with an introduction by Larry Dark
Beside ourselves. Van Winckel, N.
Bessette, Alicia
True north
  Yankee v65 no9 p98-103 N 2001
Best, Mireille
Stephanie's book [excerpt]
  The Vintage book of international lesbian fiction; edited and with an introduction by Naomi Holoch and Joan Nestle
Best behaviour. Brett, S.
The **best** friend. Offutt, C.
The **best** girlfriend you never had. Houston, P.
The **best-known** man in the world. Pearlman, D. D.
The **best** laid plans. Faulkner, J.
The **best** man. Wharton, E.
Best of. Lisick, B.
The **best** of everything. Yates, R.
The **best** way not to freeze. Levy, E. J.
The **Best** Years. Heidenreich, E.
Bester, Alfred
Disappearing act
  The SFWA grand masters v2; edited by Frederik Pohl
Fondly Fahrenheit
  The Science fiction hall of fame: volume one, 1929-1964; the greatest science fiction stories of all time chosen by the members of the Science Fiction Writers of America; edited by Robert Silverberg

Bester, Alfred—*Continued*
The SFWA grand masters v2; edited by Frederik Pohl
The four-hour fugue
The SFWA grand masters v2; edited by Frederik Pohl
Hobson's choice
The SFWA grand masters v2; edited by Frederik Pohl
The men who murdered Mohammed
One lamp; alternate history stories from The magazine of Fantasy & Science Fiction; edited by Gordon van Gelder
BESTIALITY
Kurahashi, Y. The house of the black cat
Bestiary. Aylett, S.
The **bet**. Chekhov, A. P.
The **bet**. Jenkins, G.
Betancourt, John Gregory
The devil's own
The Ultimate Halloween; edited by Marvin Kaye
Bête Noire. DeMarinis, R.
Betel nut town. Cheng, C.-W.
Betel Palm Village. See Cheng, C.-W. Betel nut town
Betelgeuse Bridge. Tenn, W.
Bethlehem. Berkman, P. R.
Bethune Street. Rowan, Q.
Betrayal. Duncker, P.
Betrayal. Sandifer, L.
Betrayals. Krawiec, R.
Betrayed. MacDonald, J. D.
BETROTHALS
Babel´, I. The father
Bellow, S. A father-to-be
DeLancey, K. Fast coming and then going
Galloway, J. Proposal
James, H. The story of a masterpiece
Martin, P. P. Amor de acuerdo—Arranged love
Robison, M. Pretty ice
Taylor, T. L. Prayers to Buxtehude
Yates, R. The best of everything
Betrothed. Chekhov, A. P.
BETS *See* Wagers
Better than counting sheep. Johnson, C.
Better than real. McGarry, J.
BETTING *See* Gambling
Betts, Doris
Aboveground
New stories from the South: the year's best, 2002; edited by Shannon Ravenel; with a preface by Larry Brown
Minding the graves
The Southern Review (Baton Rouge, La.) v38 no3 p522-35 Summ 2002
Three ghosts
The Cry of an occasion; fiction from the Fellowship of Southern Writers; edited by Richard Bausch; with a foreword by George Garrett
Betty Grace goes to county. Bleier, H.
Betty Hutton. Parvin, R.
Betty's cats. Shepard, S.
Between a white night and daybreak. Edwards, S.
Between disappearances. Hoffman, N. K.
Between girls and gamecocks. Clark, B. C.
Between hammers. Cohen, R.
Between life and death. Su Shuyang

Between life and death: a fantastic story. Apukhtin, A. N.
Between the floors. Campbell, R.
Between the lines. Smith, L.
Between the sheets. Cooper, B.
Between the teeth. Mann, J. H.
Between themselves. Wang Anyi
Between things. Boswell, M.
Between times. Deane, J. F.
Between two shores. MacLaverty, B.
Beveridge, Mary Ellen
A Late Spring
South Carolina Review v34 no1 p79-87 Fall 2001
BEVERLY HILLS (CALIF.) *See* California—Beverly Hills
Beware the gentle wife. Bosley, D.
Beware the pale horse comes riding. Wieland, M.
Bewitched. Lida, D.
Bewitched. Wharton, E.
Beyond eternity. Hart, E. T.
Beyond the barriers. Montpetit, C.
Beyond the Bayou. Chopin, K.
Beyond the border of love. O'Hara, M.
Beyond the Great Snow Mountains. L'Amour, L.
Beyond the point. Erard, M.
Beyond the Trees. Moose, R.
Beyond translation. Chaudhuri, A.
Bezmozgis, David
An animal to the memory
Bezmozgis, D. Natasha and other stories
Choynski
Bezmozgis, D. Natasha and other stories
Minyan
Bezmozgis, D. Natasha and other stories
Natasha
Bezmozgis, D. Natasha and other stories
Harper's v308 p69-77 My 2004
Roman Berman, massage therapist
Bezmozgis, D. Natasha and other stories
Harper's v306 p69-75 My 2003
The second strongest man
Bezmozgis, D. Natasha and other stories
Tapka
Bezmozgis, D. Natasha and other stories
The New Yorker v79 no12 p74-9 My 19 2003
Bhattacharyya, Roompa
Loss
Best new American voices 2001; guest editor Charles Baxter; series editors John Kulka and Natalie Danford
Bhêly-Quénum, Olympe
A child in the bush of ghosts
The Anchor book of modern African stories; edited by Nadežda Obradovic ; with a foreword by Chinua Achebe
Bi Shumin
One centimetre
The Vintage book of contemporary Chinese fiction; edited by Carolyn Choa and David Su Li-qun
Bialy Café. Simon, B.
Bianca's hands. Sturgeon, T.
Bianchini, Angela
Years later
In the forbidden city; an anthology of erotic fiction by Italian women; edited by Maria Rosa Cutrufelli; translated by Vincent J. Bertolini

BIBLE

Harris, M. From the desk of the troublesome editor

The **bible** of insects. Rawley, D.

BIBLICAL STORIES

Borges, J. L. The Gospel according to Mark

Chekhov, A. P. The student

Keret, E. Plague of the Firstborn

O'Connell, M. Saint Martha

Singer, I. B. The death of Methuselah

Vromen, G. Sarah's story

Zelitch, S. Ten plagues

Bicoastal. Saroyan, A.

BICYCLE RACING

McManus, J. The feed zone

Skármeta, A. The cyclist of San Cristóbal Hill

The **bicycle** rider. Davenport, G.

BICYCLES AND BICYCLING

Feitell, M. Bike New York!

Bidisha

Talking in bed

Typical girls; new stories by smart women; edited by Susan Corrigan

Bierce, Ambrose

The other lodgers

The American fantasy tradition; edited by Brian M. Thomsen

The story of a conscience

Death by espionage; intriguing stories of deception and betrayal; edited by Martin Cruz Smith

Big as life. Howard, M.

Big bang. Richmond, M.

Big Bear, California. Curtis, R.

The **big** bed. Bingham, S.

Big-bellied cow. Piñón, N.

Big bend. Roorbach, B.

The **big** bite. Pronzini, B.

The **big-breasted** pilgrim. Beattie, A.

The **Big** Broadcasts. Goran, L.

Big Brother. Peterson, P. W.

The **big** brown trout. Traver, R.

The **big** brush. Toscana, D.

The **big** buffalo bass. Stone, W.

Big bus. Hanna, J.

Big "C". Lumley, B.

Big Chan. Wang Cengqi

The **big** cheese. Jenkins, G.

Big city littles. De Lint, C.

The **big** cleanup. Gilchrist, E.

The **big** die-up. Smith, T. D.

Big-eyed women [excerpt] Mastretta, A.

Big game hunt. Clarke, A. C.

The **big** gift. Eggers, P.

The **big** green grin. Wilson, G.

Big hair. Friesner, E. M.

Big Jelly. Rucker, R. v. B.

Big Jesse, Little Jesse. Casares, O.

Big Joe. Harshbarger, K.

Big Lil. Deane, J. F.

The **big** love of Cherry Lane. Gifford, B.

Big me. Chaon, D.

The **big** nap. Breen, J. L.

The **big** opportunity. Viganò, R.

The **big** rain. Anderson, P.

Big ranch. Salter, J.

Big Ruthie imagines sex without pain. Wisenberg, S. L.

Big sister. Vachss, A. H.

The **big** sixtieth. Ritchie, E.

The **big** sky. De Lint, C.

Big Tim Magoon and the wild west. Estleman, L. D.

BIGAMY

James, H. Georgina's reasons

Smith, A. Believe me

Bigfoot. Aitken, M.

Bigfoot stole my wife. Carlson, R.

Bigger than life. Leslie, N.

The **biggest** city in the world. Chacón, D.

The **biggest** rat in the world. Abrams, T.

Biggle, Lloyd

The case of the headless witness

The World's finest mystery and crime stories, first annual collection; edited by Ed Gorman

Tunesmith

Masterpieces: the best science fiction of the century; edited by Orson Scott Card

BIGOTRY *See* Prejudices

Biguenet, John

And never come up

Biguenet, J. The torturer's apprentice; stories

A battlefield in moonlight

Biguenet, J. The torturer's apprentice; stories

Do me

Biguenet, J. The torturer's apprentice; stories

Fatherhood

Biguenet, J. The torturer's apprentice; stories

Gregory's fate

Biguenet, J. The torturer's apprentice; stories

I am not a Jew

Biguenet, J. The torturer's apprentice; stories

It is raining in Bejucal

The Best American mystery stories, 2002; edited and with an introduction by James Ellroy; Otto Penzler, series editor

Lunch with my daughter

Biguenet, J. The torturer's apprentice; stories

My slave

Biguenet, J. The torturer's apprentice; stories

The open curtain

Biguenet, J. The torturer's apprentice; stories

A plague of toads

Biguenet, J. The torturer's apprentice; stories

Rose

Biguenet, J. The torturer's apprentice; stories

Esquire v131 no1 p144 Ja 1999

Prize stories, 2000; The O. Henry awards; edited and with an introduction by Larry Dark

The torturer's apprentice

Biguenet, J. The torturer's apprentice; stories

The vulgar soul

Biguenet, J. The torturer's apprentice; stories

The work of art

Biguenet, J. The torturer's apprentice; stories

Bike New York!. Feitell, M.

Bikini. Erian, A.

Bikis, Gwendolyn

Cleo's back

Hers 3: brilliant new fiction by lesbian writers; edited by Terry Wolverton with Robert Drake

Bilgrey, Marc

Evening spirit

The Ultimate Halloween; edited by Marvin Kaye

Bilgrey, Marc—*Continued*

Living the lie

Cat crimes through time; edited by Ed Gorman, Martin H. Greenberg, and Larry Segriff

Bilick, Alison

The psychologist (who doesn't love me)

Virgin fiction 2

The **bill** collector's vacation. Hampl, P.

Bill of divorcement. Baron, D.

Billancourt fiesta. Berberova, N.

The **Billancourt** manuscript. Berberova, N.

BILLIARDS

Kelman, J. Remember Young Cecil

MacLeod, A. The golden gift of grey

Pronzini, B. The Hungarian cinch

Roche, T. S. Dirty pool

Tevis, W. S. The hustler

Billie Holiday. Blatnik, A.

Billman, Jon

Albatross

Billman, J. When we were wolves; stories

Ash

Billman, J. When we were wolves; stories

Atomic Bar

Billman, J. When we were wolves; stories

Becky Weed

Billman, J. When we were wolves; stories

Esquire v131 no4 p160 Ap 1999

Calcutta

Billman, J. When we were wolves; stories

Catfish

Esquire v132 no2 p144 Ag 1999

Custer complex

Billman, J. When we were wolves; stories

Custer on Mondays

Billman, J. When we were wolves; stories

Coppola, F. F. Francis Ford Coppola's Zoetrope: all story; edited by Adrienne Brodeur and Samantha Schnee; introduction by Francis Ford Coppola

Honeyville

Billman, J. When we were wolves; stories

Indians

Billman, J. When we were wolves; stories

Still wild; short fiction of the American West, 1950 to the present; edited by Larry McMurtry

Kerr's fault

Billman, J. When we were wolves; stories

Sugar City

Billman, J. When we were wolves; stories

When we were Wolves

Billman, J. When we were wolves; stories

Winter fat

Billman, J. When we were wolves; stories

Billy and Benjamin too. Doran, M. M.

Billy and Me. Mulhauser, T.

Billy by the bay. Cummins, A.

Billy Ducks among the pharaohs. DeMarinis, R.

Billy goats. McCorkle, J.

Billy Kitchen. Agee, J.

Billy Mason from Gloucester. James, S.

Billy the fetus. Sarrantonio, A.

Billy the Kid. Earle, S.

BILOXI (MISS.) *See* Mississippi—Biloxi

Bimko, Felix

The encounter

Neugroschel, J. No star too beautiful; Yiddish stories from 1382 to the present; compiled and translated by Joachim Neugroschel

Binchy, Maeve

Shepherd's Bush

The Anchor book of new Irish writing; the new Gaelach ficsean; edited and with an introduction by John Somer and John J. Daly

Victor and St. Valentine

Good Housekeeping v228 no4 p193-94 Ap 1999

Bing-bing and bong-bong. Rosenfeld, S.

Bingham, Sallie

Apricots

Bingham, S. Transgressions; stories

Bare bones

Home and beyond; an anthology of Kentucky short stories; edited by Morris Allen Grubbs; with an introduction by Wade Hall and an afterword by Charles E. May

Benjamin

Bingham, S. Transgressions; stories

The big bed

Bingham, S. Transgressions; stories

The hunt

Bingham, S. Transgressions; stories

Loving

Bingham, S. Transgressions; stories

The one true place

Bingham, S. Transgressions; stories

The pump

Bingham, S. Transgressions; stories

Rat

Bingham, S. Transgressions; stories

A remarkably pretty girl

Bingham, S. Transgressions; stories

Shall we dance?

Southwest Review v84 no4 p564-72 1999

The splinter

Bingham, S. Transgressions; stories

Calyx v21 no1 p9-20 Wint 2003

Stanley

Bingham, S. Transgressions; stories

What Men Don't Say

Southwest Review v88 no2/3 p200-20 2003

BIOGRAPHERS *See* Authors

Biography of a gallstone. Mayo, W.

A **biography** of Tadeo Isidoro Cruz (1829-1874). Borges, J. L.

BIOLOGISTS

Clarke, A. C. The next tenants

Hamilton, E. Devolution

Leslie, N. When lilacs last

Prose, F. Everything is about animals

Scholz, C. The menageries of Babel

Seiffert, R. Field study

BIOLOGY

Experiments

Oliver, C. Second nature

BIONICS

Vinge, V. "Bookworm, run!"

Biosphere. Lethem, J.

The **birch** grove. Iwaszkiewicz, J.

BIRCH SOCIETY *See* John Birch Society

Bird, Dick
TGE
Dalhousie Review v81 no2 p173-8 Summ 2001
Bird, Sarah
Bumfuzzled
Texas bound. Book III; 22 Texas stories; edited by Kay Cattarulla; foreword by Robert Flynn
Bird catcher. Somtow, S. P.
The **bird** chick. Brownrigg, S.
BIRD HUNTERS
McCorkle, J. Snipe
A **bird** in hand. Highsmith, P.
A **Bird** in My House. Kawar, F. and Amin, O.
The **Bird** in the Summer House. La Salle, P.
The **bird** market. Chekhov, A. P.
Bird of paradise. Harvey, J.
Bird of pardise. Troy, M.
Bird of passage. Bukoski, A.
Bird shadows. Meyers, K.
The **bird** that sings in the bamboo. Bukoski, A.
BIRD WATCHERS
Boyle, T. C. Swept away
Roorbach, B. Big Bend
Birdbath. Carter, C.
Birdland. Knight, M.
The **Birdman** of Cleveland. Parker, G.
BIRDS
See also Hawks; Ostriches; Owls; Parrots; Pigeons
Adam, C. Dove
Adam, C. Kestrel
Adam, C. Lark
Alcott, L. M. The eaglet in the dove's nest
Boyle, T. C. Rara avis
Bradbury, R. Once more, Legato
Brown, C. Wings
Brownrigg, S. The bird chick
Carl, L. S. A mimicry of mockingbirds
Dumas, H. The eagle the dove and the blackbird
Heynen, J. Who had good ears
Highsmith, P. A bird in hand
Hood, A. An ornithologist's guide to life
Johnston, B. A. Birds of Paradise
Lord, N. The attainable border of the birds
Parker, G. The sheld-duck of the Basingstoke Canal
Reed, R. Stride
Scoville, S. Pu'u Pu'iwa
Van Pelt, J. A flock of birds
VanderMeer, J. The Emperor's reply
Wilson, G. The big green grin
Birds. De Lint, C.
Birds. McKendry, J.
Birds. Mueller, D.
Birds of Paradise. Gordon, P.
Birds of paradise. Johnston, B. A.
Birdwell, Cleo *See* DeLillo, Don
Birkett, Terri
Horton hears a chainsaw
Harper's v303 no1814 p26-8 Jl 2001
Birmelin, Blair T.
In Her Time
Southwest Review v87 no4 p511-27 2002
Birmingham, Elizabeth
Falling away
Prairie Schooner v73 no1 p45-59 Spr 1999

The Year's best fantasy & horror, thirteenth annual collection; edited by Ellen Datlow and Terri Windling
Birnbaum, Alfred
(jt. auth) See Murakami, Haruki
Birobidzhan. Kalfus, K.
BIRTH CONTROL
See also Abortion
Henley, P. Love you can't imagine
Morrow, J. Auspicious eggs
Birth Mother. Durban, P.
Birth of a son-in-law. Orner, P.
A **birthday**. Friesner, E. M.
The **birthday**. Gilman, S. J.
Birthday. Mencken, S. H.
The **Birthday**. Petrakis, H. M.
Birthday Girl. Murakami, H.
The **birthday** of the world. Le Guin, U. K.
BIRTHDAY PARTIES *See* Birthdays
The **Birthday** Party. Denton, E.
The **birthday** presence. Allegra, D.
The **birthday** present. Lee, A.
BIRTHDAYS
Bausch, R. Letter to the lady of the house
Bausch, R. Tandolfo the Great
Cummins, A. Billy by the bay
Davies, Tristan. On the night before her birthday
Malouf, D. Great Day
Mencken, S. H. Little lady
Nabokov, V. V. Symbols and signs
Robinson, L. The toast
Wallace, D. F. Forever overhead
Wharton, E. Duration
The **birthing**. Henley, P.
Birthmark. Bowles, D.
The **birthmark**. Hawthorne, N.
Birthmark. July, M.
Birthmates. Jen, G.
Birthnight. West, M.
Bischoff, David
May oysters have legs
Mardi Gras madness; tales of terror and mayhem in New Orleans; edited by Martin H. Greenberg and Russell Davis
Sittin' on the dock
Past lives, present tense; edited by Elizabeth Ann Scarborough
Biscuit Baby. Harleman, A.
BISEXUALITY
See also Homosexuality
Fairey, W. W. A hundred hearts
Fairey, W. W. Mind and body
Jesús, P. d. The letter
LaValle, V. D. Slave
Parrish, T. Roustabout
Perkins, E. Her new life
Walker, A. Conscious birth
Walker, A. Growing out
Walker, A. This is how it happened
Bishop, Claudia
Dead and berried
Death dines at 8:30; edited by Claudia Bishop and Nick DiChario
Waiting for gateau
Bishop, C. and James, D. Death dines in; edited by Claudia Bishop and Dean James

Bishop, Elizabeth
The farmer's children
    The Best American short stories of the
    century; John Updike, editor, Katrina
    Kenison, coeditor; with an introduction by
    John Updike
Bishop, Michael
Among the handlers; or, The Mark 16 Hands-on
    Assembly of Jesus Risen, formerly Snake-
    o-rama
    The American fantasy tradition; edited by Bri-
    an M. Thomsen
Apartheid, superstrings, and Mordecai Thubana
    Bishop, M. Blue Kansas sky; four short nov-
    els of memory, magic, surmise & estrange-
    ment; with an introduction by James Mor-
    row
Blue Kansas sky
    Bishop, M. Blue Kansas sky; four short nov-
    els of memory, magic, surmise & estrange-
    ment; with an introduction by James Mor-
    row
Chihuahua Flats
    Bishop, M. Brighten to incandescence; 17 sto-
    ries
Cri de coeur
    Bishop, M. Blue Kansas sky; four short nov-
    els of memory, magic, surmise & estrange-
    ment; with an introduction by James Mor-
    row
Death and designation among the Asadi
    Bishop, M. Blue Kansas sky; four short nov-
    els of memory, magic, surmise & estrange-
    ment; with an introduction by James Mor-
    row
O happy day
    Bishop, M. Brighten to incandescence; 17 sto-
    ries
Help me, Rondo
    Bishop, M. Brighten to incandescence; 17 sto-
    ries
Herding with the hadrosaurs
    Bishop, M. Brighten to incandescence; 17 sto-
    ries
Icicle music
    A yuletide universe; sixteen fantastical tales;
    edited by Brian M. Thomsen
Last night out
    Bishop, M. Brighten to incandescence; 17 sto-
    ries
Of crystalline labyrinths and the new creation
    Bishop, M. Brighten to incandescence; 17 sto-
    ries
The procedure
    Bishop, M. Brighten to incandescence; 17 sto-
    ries
Sequel on Skorpios
    Bishop, M. Brighten to incandescence; 17 sto-
    ries
Simply indispensable
    Bishop, M. Brighten to incandescence; 17 sto-
    ries
A tapestry of little murders
    Bishop, M. Brighten to incandescence; 17 sto-
    ries
Thirteen lies about hummingbirds
    Bishop, M. Brighten to incandescence; 17 sto-
    ries

The tigers of hystria feed only on themselves
    Bishop, M. Brighten to incandescence; 17 sto-
    ries
Tithes of mint and rue
    Bishop, M. Brighten to incandescence; 17 sto-
    ries
The unexpected visit of a reanimated English-
    woman
    Bishop, M. Brighten to incandescence; 17 sto-
    ries
With a little help from her friends
    Bishop, M. Brighten to incandescence; 17 sto-
    ries
Bishop, Michael and DiFilippo, Paul
"We're all in this alone"
    Bishop, M. Brighten to incandescence; 17 sto-
    ries
Bishop, Michael and Page, Gerald W.
Murder on Lupozny Station
    Bishop, M. Brighten to incandescence; 17 sto-
    ries
Bishop, Paul
Celtic noir
    Murder most Celtic; tall tales of Irish may-
    hem; edited by Martin H. Greenberg
Concrete killer
    Bishop, P. Pattern of behavior; a short story
    collection
Dead easy
    Bishop, P. Pattern of behavior; a short story
    collection
Derringer
    Bishop, P. Pattern of behavior; a short story
    collection
Ebenezer
    Bishop, P. Pattern of behavior; a short story
    collection
The framing game
    Bishop, P. Pattern of behavior; a short story
    collection
Going postal
    Bishop, P. Pattern of behavior; a short story
    collection
The legend of Charlie McQuarkle
    Bishop, P. Pattern of behavior; a short story
    collection
The man who shot Trinity Valance
    Bishop, P. Pattern of behavior; a short story
    collection
    Speaking of lust; stories of forbidden desire;
    edited by Lawrence Block
Night of the Frankengolfer
    Bishop, P. Pattern of behavior; a short story
    collection
Pattern of behavior
    Bishop, P. Pattern of behavior; a short story
    collection
Quint and the braceros
    Bishop, P. Pattern of behavior; a short story
    collection
The samaritan
    Bishop, P. Pattern of behavior; a short story
    collection
Squeeze play
    Bishop, P. Pattern of behavior; a short story
    collection
The thief of Christmas
    Bishop, P. Pattern of behavior; a short story
    collection

The **bishop**. Chekhov, A. P.
The **bishop** and the hit man. Greeley, A. M.
BISHOPS
Chekhov, A. P. The bishop
BISHOPS, CATHOLIC *See* Catholic bishops
BISON
Reid, E. Buffalo
Biss, Gerald
The door of the unreal
The Literary werewolf; an anthology; edited
by Charlotte F. Otten
Bissell, Tom
The ambassador's son
Bomb no76 p104-11 Summ 2001
Death Defier
The Virginia Quarterly Review v80 no3 p136-68 Summ 2004
Bisson, Benoit
(jt. auth) See Kilpatrick, Nancy and Bisson, Benoit
Bisson, Terry
10:07:24
Bisson, T. In the upper room and other likely stories
Bears discover fire
Brown, C. N. and Strahan, J. The Locus awards; thirty years of the best in science fiction and fantasy; edited by Charles N. Brown and Jonathan Strahan
Masterpieces: the best science fiction of the century; edited by Orson Scott Card
Dead Man's Curve
Bisson, T. In the upper room and other likely stories
Dear Abbey
The year's best science fiction: twenty-first annual collection; edited by Gardner Dozois
The edge of the universe
Bisson, T. In the upper room and other likely stories
First fire
Bisson, T. In the upper room and other likely stories
Get me to the church on time
Bisson, T. In the upper room and other likely stories
He loved Lucy
Bisson, T. In the upper room and other likely stories
In the upper room
Bisson, T. In the upper room and other likely stories
Incident at Oak Ridge
Bisson, T. In the upper room and other likely stories
The Joe Show
Bisson, T. In the upper room and other likely stories
Macs
Bisson, T. In the upper room and other likely stories
Nebula awards showcase 2002; edited by Kim Stanley Robinson
Not this Virginia
Bisson, T. In the upper room and other likely stories
An office romance
Bisson, T. In the upper room and other likely stories

The old rugged cross
Starlight 3; edited by Patrick Nielsen Hayden
Partial people
The Best from fantasy & science fiction: the fiftieth anniversary anthology; edited by Edward L. Ferman and Gordon Van Gelder
The player
Bisson, T. In the upper room and other likely stories
Smoother
Bisson, T. In the upper room and other likely stories
Tell them they are all full of shit and they should fuck off
Bisson, T. In the upper room and other likely stories
There are no dead
Bisson, T. In the upper room and other likely stories
Bissoondath, Neil
The power of reason
Américas v53 no4 p64 Jl/Ag 2001
Sanctuary
Bomb no82 p88-9 Wint 2002/2003
Bit-o-honey. Cooper, B.
A **bit** on the side. Trevor, W.
The **bitang**. Spariosu, M. and Benedek, D.
Bite the hand. Cadnum, M.
Bitter grounds. Gaiman, N.
Bitter lemons. Kaminsky, S. M.
The **bitter** life of Shirin. Fadavi, P.
Bitterwater. Cummins, A.
Bix and Flannery. Miller, B.
Bixby, Jerome
It's a good life
The Science fiction hall of fame: volume one, 1929-1964; the greatest science fiction stories of all time chosen by the members of the Science Fiction Writers of America; edited by Robert Silverberg
The **bizarre** case expert. Collins, M.
Björkquist, Elena Díaz
Inocente's getaway
Fantasmas; supernatural stories by Mexican American writers; edited by Rob Johnson; introduction by Kathleen J. Alcalá
Bjorneby, Karen
Panther in the Woods
New Letters v69 no4 p177-91 2003
The **Blabber**. Vinge, V.
Black, Cara
Cabaret aux Assassins
My Sherlock Holmes; untold stories of the great detective; edited by Michael Kurland
Black, Carolyn
Trampoline lessons
Dalhousie Review v81 no2 p235-43 Summ 2001
Black, Michelle
The hundred day men
Westward; a fictional history of the American West : 28 original stories celebrating the 50th anniversary of the Western Writers of America; edited by Dale L. Walker
Black and white memories. Randisi, R. J.
The **Black** and White Museum. Dennis, F.
The **black** and white sisters. Boyle, T. C.
Black as the pit, from pole to pole. Waldrop, H.
Black ball. Bellatin, M.

Black bean soup. Smith, S. J.
The Black Bishop. Boito, A.
Black book. Cooke, C.
Black box. Leavitt, D.
The black cat. Poe, E. A.
Black cherries. Coates, G. S.
BLACK CHILDREN See African American children
The Black City. Alishan, L.
Black cowboy. Mitchell, C. E.
The black curtain [excerpt] Woolrich, C.
Black destroyer. Van Vogt, A. E.
Black Dorothea. Laikin, J.
A black dress. McGuane, T.
Black Dunstan's skull. Newton, D. B.
Black Elvis. Becker, G.
BLACK ENGLISH DIALECT See Dialect stories—Black English
The black ferris. Bradbury, R.
Black heart and cabin girl. Costa, S.
BLACK HOLES (ASTRONOMY)
    Bear, G. The venging
    Landis, G. A. Approaching Perimelasma
The black horn. Dann, J.
BLACK HUMOR See Humor; Satire
Black ice. Norris, L.
Black Irish. Allyn, D.
Black is the color of my true love's heart. O'Callaghan, M.
Black Jew. Toole, F. X.
Black Li and White Li. Lao She
BLACK MAGIC See Witchcraft
Black man and white woman in dark green rowboat. Banks, R.
BLACK MARKETS
    Hart, C. G. Spooked
    Kalfus, K. Pu-239
Black mist. Lupoff, R. A.
The black narcissus. Shepherd, R.
Black no more [excerpt] Schuyler, G. S.
Black out. Ungerer, K.
The black pig. Gonzalez, R.
The black prince. Grau, S. A.
BLACK SERVANTS See African American servants
BLACK SOLDIERS See African American soldiers
Black swan. Hoffman, W.
Black Sweater. McIlvoy, K.
Black tie and blue jeans. Fromm, P.
Black tulip. Turtledove, H.
Black walls. Liu Xinwu
BLACK WOMEN See African American women
The blackamoor of Peter the Great. Pushkin, A. S.
The blackberry season. Mazelis, J.
Blackberry winter. Warren, R. P.
Blackbird. Moss, B. R.
Blackbirds. Partridge, N.
Blackford, Russell
    The king with three daughters
        Black heart, ivory bones; [edited by] Ellen Datlow & Terri Windling
    Smoke City
        Gathering the bones; original stories from the world's masters of horror; edited by Dennis Etchison, Ramsey Campbell and Jack Dann

The soldier in the machine
    Centaurus: the best of Australian science fiction; edited by David G. Hartwell and Damien Broderick
    Dreaming down-under; edited by Jack Dann and Janeen Webb
BLACKMAIL
    See also Extortion
    Carter, C. Birdbath
    Coward, M. Too subtle for me
    Danihy, G. Jumping with Jim
    Deaver, J. For services rendered
    DuBois, B. Netmail
    Estleman, L. D. The man in the white hat
    Lee, M. Koza nights
    Vachss, A. H. Stuntman
    Westlake, D. E. Sniff
Blackmail. Yoder, E. M.
Blackmanwalkin. Touré
Blackness. Kincaid, J.
Blackout. Knight, M.
Blackout. Stanley, M. A.
BLACKS
    See also African Americans
    Allegra, D. God lies in the details
    Barnes, S. The woman in the wall
    Bell, D. A. The space traders
    Bowles, P. Too far from home
    Bradbury, R. June 2003: Way in the middle of the air
    Hopkinson, N. A habit of waste
    Johnson, C. R. A report from St. Domingue
    Johnson, C. R. A soldier for the crown
    Joseph, A. The African origins of UFOs [excerpt]
    Kincaid, J. Blackness
    Marshall, P. To Da-duh, in memoriam
    Melville, P. The president's exile
    Rossi, A. Orion's glow
    Sánchez, L. R. Getting even
                    Wales
    Lawrence, H. Pure Welsh
Blacks. Arenas, R.
Blacksoil country. Malouf, D.
Blackwell, Kate
    Duckie
        New Letters v67 no3 p129-39 2001
    To dance again
        The Literary Review (Madison, N.J.) v44 no4 p676-90 Summ 2001
Blackwood, Algernon
    Running wolf
        The Literary werewolf; an anthology; edited by Charlotte F. Otten
    The willows
        The 13 best horror stories of all time; edited by Leslie Pockell
Blackwood, Scott
    Alias
        Blackwood, S. In the shadow of our house; stories
    In the shadow of our house
        Blackwood, S. In the shadow of our house; stories
    New years
        Blackwood, S. In the shadow of our house; stories

Blackwood, Scott—*Continued*
Nostalgia
Blackwood, S. In the shadow of our house; stories
One flesh, one blood
Blackwood, S. In the shadow of our house; stories
One of us is hidden away
Blackwood, S. In the shadow of our house; stories
Prodigal fathers
Blackwood, S. In the shadow of our house; stories
Riverfest
Blackwood, S. In the shadow of our house; stories
See How Small
Southwest Review v88 no1 p168-71 2003
Worry
Blackwood, S. In the shadow of our house; stories
Bladder companion. Chapman, C. M.
Blagrave, Mark
Polyphemus
Dalhousie Review v79 no1 p87-108 Spr 1999
Blair, John
American standard
Blair, J. American standard
Bacon on the beach
Blair, J. American standard
Ghost river
Blair, J. American standard
The grove
Blair, J. American standard
Happy puppy
Blair, J. American standard
Julia loving the face of God
Blair, J. American standard
Memorial day
Blair, J. American standard
Moving man
Blair, J. American standard
Running away
Blair, J. American standard
A small church in the country
Blair, J. American standard
Swimming the cave
Blair, J. American standard
Trash fish
Blair, J. American standard
Blair, Sydney
The end of summer
Callaloo v24 no1 p18-22 Wint 2001
Blaise, Clark
The bridge
Blaise, C. Southern stories; with an introduction by Fenton Johnson
Broward Dowdy
Blaise, C. Southern stories; with an introduction by Fenton Johnson
Dunkelblau
The Workshop; seven decades of the Iowa Writers' Workshop: 42 stories, recollections & essays on Iowa's place in 20th-century American literature; edited by Tom Grimes
The fabulous Eddie Brewster
Blaise, C. Southern stories; with an introduction by Fenton Johnson

A fish like a buzzard
Blaise, C. Southern stories; with an introduction by Fenton Johnson
Giant turtles, gliding in the dark
Blaise, C. Southern stories; with an introduction by Fenton Johnson
How I became a Jew
Blaise, C. Southern stories; with an introduction by Fenton Johnson
Life Could Be a Dream (Sh-boom, Sh-boom)
Michigan Quarterly Review v42 no2 p293-303 Spr 2003
The Love God
Blaise, C. Southern stories; with an introduction by Fenton Johnson
A North American education
Blaise, C. Southern stories; with an introduction by Fenton Johnson
Notes beyond history
Blaise, C. Southern stories; with an introduction by Fenton Johnson
Relief
Blaise, C. Southern stories; with an introduction by Fenton Johnson
The salesman's son grows older
Blaise, C. Southern stories; with an introduction by Fenton Johnson
Sitting shivah with cousin Benny
Salmagundi no124/125 p238-55 Fall 1999/Wint 2000
Snow people
Blaise, C. Southern stories; with an introduction by Fenton Johnson
South
Blaise, C. Southern stories; with an introduction by Fenton Johnson
The waffle maker
Michigan Quarterly Review v41 no1 p95-113 Wint 2002
Blake, James Carlos
Aliens in the garden
Blake, J. C. Borderlands; short fictions
The house of Esperanza
Blake, J. C. Borderlands; short fictions
Referee
Blake, J. C. Borderlands; short fictions
Runaway horses
Blake, J. C. Borderlands; short fictions
Texas woman blues
Blake, J. C. Borderlands; short fictions
Three tales of the Revolution
Blake, J. C. Borderlands; short fictions
Under the sierra
Blake, J. C. Borderlands; short fictions
La vida loca
Blake, J. C. Borderlands; short fictions
Blake, Tobin
Grim's redemption
Dead on demand; the best of ghost story weekend; edited by Elizabeth Engstrom
Blakely, Mike
Laureano's wall
American West; twenty new stories from the Western Writers of America; edited with an introduction by Loren D. Estleman
Blake's angel. Webb, J.

Blaman, Anna
  Lonely adventure [excerpt]
    The Vintage book of international lesbian fiction; edited and with an introduction by Naomi Holoch and Joan Nestle
Blame it on my youth. Greer, A. S.
Blame the Tlaxcaltecs. Garro, E.
Blanca Rosa. Guerrero, L.
Bland, Eleanor Taylor
  The canasta club
    The World's finest mystery and crime stories, first annual collection; edited by Ed Gorman
Blasphemy. Tomlinson, T.
Blatnik, Andrej
  Actually
    Blatnik, A. Skinswaps; translated from the Slovenian by Tamara Soban
  Billie Holiday
    Blatnik, A. Skinswaps; translated from the Slovenian by Tamara Soban
  Damp walls
    Blatnik, A. Skinswaps; translated from the Slovenian by Tamara Soban
  His mother's voice
    Blatnik, A. Skinswaps; translated from the Slovenian by Tamara Soban
  Isaac
    Blatnik, A. Skinswaps; translated from the Slovenian by Tamara Soban
  Kyoto
    Blatnik, A. Skinswaps; translated from the Slovenian by Tamara Soban
  Scratches on the back
    Blatnik, A. Skinswaps; translated from the Slovenian by Tamara Soban
  The taste of blood
    Blatnik, A. Skinswaps; translated from the Slovenian by Tamara Soban
  Temporary residence
    Blatnik, A. Skinswaps; translated from the Slovenian by Tamara Soban
Blatty, William Peter
  Elsewhere
    999: new stories of horror and suspense; edited by Al Sarrantonio
Blau, Gala
  Outfangthief
    The Mammoth book of best horror 13; edited by Stephen Jones
Blavatsky, H. P. (Helena Petrovna)
  Can the double murder?
    Witches' brew; edited by Yvonne Jocks
Blavatsky, Helene Petrovna *See* Blavatsky, H. P. (Helena Petrovna), 1831-1891
Blaze. Smith, R. T.
Blaze. Walker, A.
The **blazing** sun. Yi, T.-H.
Blazo. Carlson, R.
A **bleak** future without thought-paper. Howells, R.
Bledsoe, Bob
  Who's Your Daddy?
    Ploughshares v30 no2/3 p26-41 Fall 2004
Bleed blue in Indonesia. Desnoyers, A.
The **bleeding** of Hauptmann Gehlen. Trotter, W. R.
Blegvad, Peter
  The free lunch
    Chicago Review v45 no3/4 p130-33 1999

  Hardware
    Chicago Review v45 no3/4 p126 1999
  Second person, secret self
    Chicago Review v45 no3/4 p115-16 1999
  Some kind of wonderful
    Chicago Review v45 no3/4 p117-20 1999
  The spoon
    Chicago Review v45 no3/4 p121-22 1999
  A visit from the king
    Chicago Review v45 no3/4 p127 1999
Bleier, Hannah
  Betty Grace goes to county
    Hers 2: brilliant new fiction by lesbian writers; edited by Terry Wolverton with Robert Drake
Blessed art thou among women. Desmond, K.
Blessed assurance: a moral tale. Gurganus, A.
Blessed event. Schow, D. J.
Blessed Virgin Mary, Saint *See* Mary, Blessed Virgin, Saint
The **blessing**. Gavell, M. L.
Blessing. Stuckey-French, E.
Blessington, Francis
  The clock
    Dalhousie Review v81 no2 p213-18 Summ 2001
Blest be the ties. Crider, B.
Blevins, Winfred
  Melodies the song dogs sing
    Westward; a fictional history of the American West : 28 original stories celebrating the 50th anniversary of the Western Writers of America; edited by Dale L. Walker
Blighted. Slavin, J.
Blighted cargo. Steinbeck, T.
BLIMPS *See* Airships
Blimunda. Stavans, I.
BLIND
  Alas, L. Change of light
  Borges, J. L. The maker
  Brown, J. The dog lover
  Chopin, K. The blind man
  Chopin, K. The recovery
  Danticat, E. Night talkers
  Doerr, A. The shell collector
  Ehlers, J. Golden Gate Bridge—a view from below
  Elkins, K. What is visible
  Georgiou, E. Aphrodite's vision
  Glover, D. H. Dog attempts to drown man in Saskatoon
  Goldner, B. Cardiff-by-the-Sea
  Gordon, M. The blind neighbor
  Hegi, U. The juggler
  King, L. R. Weaving the dark
  Kipling, R. They
  Klíma, I. The white house
  Lawrence, D. H. The blind man
  Morrow, B. Amazing Grace
  Schnitzler, A. Blind Geronimo and his brother
  Schwartz, L. S. By a dimming light
  Singleton, G. Rentals
  Spain, C. Scaring the baddest animal
  Swanwick, M. The blind minotaur
  Tran, V. Gunboat on the Yangtze
  Varley, J. The persistence of vision
  Weaver, G. Imagining the structure of free space on Pioneer Road
  Wells, H. G. The country of the blind

BLIND—*Continued*
  Wells, K. Hallie out of this world
  Wideman, J. E. Doc's story
Blind. Di Blasi, D.
Blind. Lachnit, C.
Blind alley. Maffini, M. J.
The **Blind** Calf. Shin, K.-S.
Blind Date. Vanderslice, J.
The **blind** gambler. Green, J.
The **blind** gambler. Greene, J.
Blind Geronimo and his brother. Schnitzler, A.
Blind Jozef Pronek. Hemon, A.
Blind Jozef Pronek & Dead Souls. Hemon, A.
Blind luck. Steinbeck, T.
Blind-Made Products. Lange, R.
Blind madness. Ponte Landa, M.
The **blind** man. Chopin, K.
The **blind** man. Lawrence, D. H.
Blind Man. Robinson, R.
A **blind** man can see how much I love you.
      Bloom, A.
Blind man's buff. Anderson, F. I.
The **blind** minotaur. Swanwick, M.
The **blind** mirror. Roth, J.
The **blind** neighbor. Gordon, M.
Blind shemmy. Dann, J.
Blind spot. Ziegler, I.
Blind willow, sleeping girl. Murakami, H.
The **blind** woman. Gabriel, D.
Blinkers. Shepard, J.
Blinking baby. Schulze, I.
Blinking eye. Shepard, S.
Blish, James
  Citadel of thought
      Blish, J. In this world, or another; stories
  Common time
      Blish, J. In this world, or another; stories
  A dusk of idols
      Blish, J. In this world, or another; stories
  Get out of my sky
      Blish, J. In this world, or another; stories
  How beautiful with banners
      Blish, J. In this world, or another; stories
  Nor iron bars
      Blish, J. In this world, or another; stories
  The oath
      Blish, J. In this world, or another; stories
  Surface tension
      Blish, J. In this world, or another; stories
      The Science fiction hall of fame: volume one,
         1929-1964; the greatest science fiction sto-
         ries of all time chosen by the members of
         the Science Fiction Writers of America; ed-
         ited by Robert Silverberg
  Testament of Andros
      Blish, J. In this world, or another; stories
  A work of art
      Blish, J. In this world, or another; stories
      Masterpieces: the best science fiction of the
         century; edited by Orson Scott Card
Bliss. Anderson, D.
Bliss. Peck, D.
Blissful. Huff, S.
Blisters. Barker, N.
Blitz, Renee
  At 15, he had been a leader in
      Blitz, R. In Berkeley's green and pleasant
         land; stories

Death to the fascist imperialist dogs
    Blitz, R. In Berkeley's green and pleasant
        land; stories
In Berkeley's green and pleasant land
    Blitz, R. In Berkeley's green and pleasant
        land; stories
Lies
    Blitz, R. In Berkeley's green and pleasant
        land; stories
Make haste, my beloved
    Blitz, R. In Berkeley's green and pleasant
        land; stories
The mother's wasteland
    Blitz, R. In Berkeley's green and pleasant
        land; stories
Notes from the tower of menopause
    Blitz, R. In Berkeley's green and pleasant
        land; stories
P.S. your thing is sticking out
    Blitz, R. In Berkeley's green and pleasant
        land; stories
The participant
    Blitz, R. In Berkeley's green and pleasant
        land; stories
She had mastered the art
    Blitz, R. In Berkeley's green and pleasant
        land; stories
The small revelation
    Blitz, R. In Berkeley's green and pleasant
        land; stories
This picnic you're having
    Blitz, R. In Berkeley's green and pleasant
        land; stories
Two women
    Blitz, R. In Berkeley's green and pleasant
        land; stories
The unuseable talent
    Blitz, R. In Berkeley's green and pleasant
        land; stories
Blitzed. Lovesey, P.
Blixen, Karen, Baroness, 1885-1962
      For works written by this author under oth-
      er names see Dinesen, Isak, 1885-1962
The **blizzard**. Pushkin, A. S.
Blizzard at Bald Rock. Henry, W.
BLIZZARDS *See* Storms
The **bloat-toad**. Lugones, L.
Bloch, Alice
  Learning the hula
      Hers 2: brilliant new fiction by lesbian writ-
         ers; edited by Terry Wolverton with Robert
         Drake
Bloch, Robert
  Life in our time
      A Century of great suspense stories; edited by
         Jeffery Deaver
Block, Francesca Lia
  Bones
      Death dines at 8:30; edited by Claudia Bishop
         and Nick DiChario
  Safe love
      Seventeen v58 no10 p106-07+ O 1999
Block, Lawrence
  Batman's helpers
      A Century of great suspense stories; edited by
         Jeffery Deaver

Block, Lawrence—*Continued*

By the dawn's early light
> The Best American mystery stories of the century; Tony Hillerman, editor; with an introduction by Tony Hillerman

How far it could go
> Master's choice [v1]; mystery stories by today's top writers and the masters who inspired them; edited by Lawrence Block

How would you like it?
> A Century of noir; thirty-two classic crime stories; edited by Mickey Spillane and Max Allan Collins

In for a penny
> Crème de la crime; edited by Janet Hutchings
> The World's finest mystery and crime stories, first annual collection; edited by Ed Gorman

Keller's last refuge
> The Best American mystery stories, 1999; edited and with an introduction by Ed McBain

Let's get lost
> The World's finest mystery and crime stories, second annual collection; edited by Ed Gorman

Like a bone in the throat
> Murder most postal; homicidal tales that deliver a message; edited by Martin H. Greenberg

A moment of wrong thinking
> Murder in the family; [by] the Adams Round Table

Sometimes they bite
> Master's choice v2; mystery stories by today's top writers and the masters who inspired them; edited by Lawrence Block

Speaking of greed
> The World's finest mystery and crime stories, third annual collection; edited by Ed Gorman and Martin H. Greenberg

Speaking of lust
> Speaking of lust; stories of forbidden desire; edited by Lawrence Block

Sweet little hands
> Flesh and blood; erotic tales of crime and passion; edited by Max Allan Collins and Jeff Gelb

Block, Ron

St. Anthony and the fish
> A different plain; contemporary Nebraska fiction writers; edited by Ladette Randolph ; introduction by Mary Pipher

Block party. Cherry, K.

BLOOD

Bowles, P. Hugh Harper

Gardner, J. A. Three hearings on the existence of snakes in the human bloodstream

Satterthwait, W. The cassoulet

Stableford, B. M. Hot blood

Blood. Carlson, R.

Blood. Hoffman, W.

Blood. Jackson, S.

Blood. Shade, E.

Blood and gore. Evans, E.

The **blood** bay. Proulx, A.

Blood Brothers. Kussi, P.

Blood brothers. Skiff, M.

Blood-burning moon. Toomer, J.

BLOOD DONORS

Updike, J. Giving blood

Blood knot. Westmoreland, T. A.

Blood knots. Burton, M.

Blood money. Pronzini, B.

Blood music. Bear, G.

Blood of a Mole. Evtimova, Z.

Blood opus. Yuknavitch, L.

The **blood** orange tree. Crane, M.

Blood poison. Schmidt, H. J.

The **blood-red** sea. Williamson, C.

Blood relations. Erwin, C.

Blood sister. Yolen, J.

Blood, snow, and classic cars. Hansen, J.

Blood sport. Lynch, T.

Blood trail. Rusch, K. K.

Blood types. Smith, J.

Blood work. Spencer, D.

Bloodknots. Brodoff, A. S.

Bloodlines. Hyde, C. R.

Bloodlines. Joseph, D.

Bloodlines: Conversations with my Mother. Taing, V.

A **Bloodsmoor** Romance. Oates, J. C.

The **Bloodthirsty** Witness (A mediocre variation on a hackneyed theme). Filatov, N.

Bloody knuckles. Boswell, M.

Bloody victims. Coward, M.

Bloom, Amy

A blind man can see how much I love you
> Bloom, A. A blind man can see how much I love you; stories

By-and-By
> *Ms.* v14 no2 p78-82 Summ 2004

The gates are closing
> Bloom, A. A blind man can see how much I love you; stories
> Coppola, F. F. Francis Ford Coppola's Zoetrope: all story; edited by Adrienne Brodeur and Samantha Schnee; introduction by Francis Ford Coppola

Hold tight
> Bloom, A. A blind man can see how much I love you; stories

Light into dark
> Bloom, A. A blind man can see how much I love you; stories

Night vision
> Bloom, A. A blind man can see how much I love you; stories

Rowing to Eden
> Bloom, A. A blind man can see how much I love you; stories

Silver water
> The Scribner anthology of contemporary short fiction; fifty North American stories since 1970; Lex Williford and Michael Martone, editors

Stars at elbow and foot
> Bloom, A. A blind man can see how much I love you; stories

The story
> The Best American short stories, 2000; selected from U.S. and Canadian magazines by E. L. Doctorow with Katrina Kenison; with an introduction by E. L. Doctorow
> Bloom, A. A blind man can see how much I love you; stories

Bloom, Amy—*Continued*
　Your borders, your rivers, your tiny villages
　　Ploughshares v28 no2/3 p19-25 Fall 2002
Bloom, John
　Pepper
　　Texas bound. Book III; 22 Texas stories; ed-
　　ited by Kay Cattarulla; foreword by Robert
　　Flynn
Bloom of Zenobia. Whittenberg, A.
The **blooming** season for cacti. Divakaruni, C. B.
Blorts. Holleran, A.
Blotting the triangle. Cunningham, E.
Blottner, Joseph
　The End of the Road
　　The Sewanee Review v110 no4 p596-613 Fall
　　2002
Blow-up. Cortázar, J.
Blowing shades. Dybek, S.
Blowing Up on the Spot. Wilson, K.
Blowout in Little Man Flats. Kaminsky, S. M.
Blue. Doyle, B.
Blue. Murray, J.
Blue boy. Dybek, S.
Blue Cadillac. Malone, M.
The **blue** carp. Zelinka, M.
Blue fly. Cummins, A.
Blue grotto. Händler, E.-W.
The **Blue** Hole. Krouse, E.
Blue horses. Franklin, T.
The **blue** hotel. Crane, S.
Blue Kansas sky. Bishop, M.
Blue Laws. Singleton, G.
Blue lightning. Mosley, W.
The **blue** line. Wegner, H.
The **blue** men. Williams, J.
The **blue** mirror. Gates, D. E.
Blue movie. Yuknavitch, L.
Blue Murder. Steele, W. D.
The **blue** Norton. Rinehart, S.
The **blue** of the Madrugada. Simonds, M.
Blue skin. Wells, K.
Blue-sky day. Winter, E.
Blue Springs. Ziegler, I.
Blue tigers. Borges, J. L.
Blue valentines. Davis, L.
Blue Willow. Kalpakian, L.
Blue yonder. Cavell, B.
Bluebeard's first wife. Connor, J.
Blues machine. Roorbach, B.
Blum, Ivon B.
　Inquest in Zion
　　Westward; a fictional history of the American
　　West : 28 original stories celebrating the
　　50th anniversary of the Western Writers of
　　America; edited by Dale L. Walker
Blum, Jenna
　Easter 1943
　　Prairie Schooner v77 no4 p134-48 Wint 2003
Blumfeld, an elderly bachelor. Kafka, F.
Blumfeld, an elderly bachelor. Scholz, C.
Blumlein, Michael
　Know how, can do
　　The Year's best science fiction, nineteenth an-
　　nual collection; edited by Gardner Dozois
　Paul and me
　　The Best from fantasy & science fiction: the
　　fiftieth anniversary anthology; edited by
　　Edward L. Ferman and Gordon Van Gelder

　Revenge
　　The Year's best fantasy & horror, twelfth an-
　　nual collection; edited by Ellen Datlow &
　　Terry Windling
A **blunder**. Chekhov, A. P.
Bly, Carol
　After the baptism
　　Bly, C. My Lord Bag of Rice; new and se-
　　lected stories
　An apprentice
　　Bly, C. My Lord Bag of Rice; new and se-
　　lected stories
　Chuck's money
　　Bly, C. My Lord Bag of Rice; new and se-
　　lected stories
　　TriQuarterly no104 p141-91 Wint 1999
　A committee of the whole
　　Bly, C. My Lord Bag of Rice; new and se-
　　lected stories
　The dignity of life
　　Bly, C. My Lord Bag of Rice; new and se-
　　lected stories
　Gunnar's sword
　　Bly, C. My Lord Bag of Rice; new and se-
　　lected stories
　The last of the gold star mothers
　　Bly, C. My Lord Bag of Rice; new and se-
　　lected stories
　Love in a Time of Empire
　　Prairie Schooner v77 no2 p172-83 Summ
　　2003
　My Lord Bag of Rice
　　Bly, C. My Lord Bag of Rice; new and se-
　　lected stories
　Renee: a war story
　　Bly, C. My Lord Bag of Rice; new and se-
　　lected stories
　The tender organizations
　　Bly, C. My Lord Bag of Rice; new and se-
　　lected stories
　The tomcat's wife
　　Bly, C. My Lord Bag of Rice; new and se-
　　lected stories
BOARDERS *See* Boarding houses
BOARDING HOUSES
　Aldrich, B. S. What God hath joined
　Allende, I. Wicked girl
　Barrett, A. The cure
　Bergelson, D. In the boardinghouse
　Bly, C. My Lord Bag of Rice
　Bradbury, R. Sometime before dawn
　Callaghan, M. Silk stockings
　Holleran, A. The boxer
　James, H. A bundle of letters
　James, H. The pension Beaurepas
　Pronzini, B. The dispatching of George Ferris
　Singer, I. B. Escape from civilization
　Sturgeon, T. The [widget], the [wadget], and
　　boff
　Wharton, E. Mrs. Manstey's view
BOARDING SCHOOLS *See* School life
The **boardinghouse**. Tozzi, F.
BOARS
　Gunn, K. The things he told her
Boarskin dances down the tables. Fischerová, D.
The **boat**. MacLeod, A.
BOAT RACING
　Archer, J. Dougie Mortimer's right arm

BOATBUILDING

Patterson, K. Boatbuilding

Boatbuilding. Patterson, K.

The **boathouse**. Bohart, L.

BOATS AND BOATING

See also Rafting (Sports); Sailing vessels; Tugboats

Banks, R. Black man and white woman in dark green rowboat

Brackenbury, R. At the reef

Brackenbury, R. Between man and woman keys

Cobb, T. Small-block chevy

Desplechin, M. At sea

Grau, S. A. The wind shifting west

MacLeod, A. The boat

Phillips, D. R. At the edge of the new world

Rodgers, S. J. The two husbands

Vonnegut, K. The cruise of The Jolly Roger

The **boats** of the "Glen Carrrig". Hodgson, W. H.

Bob darling. Cooke, C.

Bobbing. Barolini, H.

Bobby Angel. Williams, D.

Bobby Jackson. Silber, J.

Bobby Lee Carter and the hand of God. Schorn, S.

Bobes, Marilyn

Ten years later

Dream with no name; contemporary fiction from Cuba; edited by Juana Ponce de León and Esteban Ríos Rivera

Bobier, Michelle

The goddess of the moon

The Virginia Quarterly Review v75 no4 p758-71 Aut 1999

Bob's your uncle. Busch, F.

Bocock, Maclin

Alice and me

Bocock, M. A citizen of the world; short fiction

And silently steal away

Bocock, M. A citizen of the world; short fiction

The baker's daughter

Bocock, M. A citizen of the world; short fiction

A citizen of the world at large

Bocock, M. A citizen of the world; short fiction

Death is where you find it

Bocock, M. A citizen of the world; short fiction

Don't save your kisses

Bocock, M. A citizen of the world; short fiction

The face

Bocock, M. A citizen of the world; short fiction

The funeral

Bocock, M. A citizen of the world; short fiction

Heaven lies about

Bocock, M. A citizen of the world; short fiction

La humanidad

Bocock, M. A citizen of the world; short fiction

The Journey

Bocock, M. A citizen of the world; short fiction

Play me "Stormy weather," please

Bocock, M. A citizen of the world; short fiction

The tree

Bocock, M. A citizen of the world; short fiction

Bodhi leaves. Leong, R.

Bodies. Shattuck, J.

Body. Petrignani, S.

Body. Spatz, G.

Body and soul. McGarry, J.

Body count. Harfenist, J.

The **body** in the window. Campbell, R.

Body, mine. Fraterrigo, M.

Body, Numinous, Words. Wilhelm, V.

The **body** painters. McManus, J.

The **body** politic. Williams, T.

The **Body** Retriever. Steinkoler, M.

Body work. Davidson, R.

Body zone. Davis, L.

BODYBUILDING See Weight lifting

BODYGUARDS

Coward, M. Tall man, large cat

Marías, J. Broken binoculars

Parker, R. B. Harlem nocturne

Roberts, L. The gathering of the klan

Bodysurfing. Burgin, R.

BOERS See Afrikaners

Bogen, K. B.

Good help

Dracula in London; edited by P. N. Elrod

Boggs, Belle

Who is Beatrice?

Kulka, J. and Danford, N. The New American voices 2003; guest editor Joyce Carol Oates; series editors John Kulka and Natalie Danford

Boggs, Johnny D.

A piano at Dead Man's Crossing

American West; twenty new stories from the Western Writers of America; edited with an introduction by Loren D. Estleman

Bohart, Lynn

The boathouse

Dead on demand; the best of ghost story weekend; edited by Elizabeth Engstrom

Bohemia. Naipaul, V. S.

BOHEMIANISM

Henley, P. Aces

BOHEMIANS

United States

See Czechs—United States

The **Bohemians**. Brennan, M.

Bohemians. Saunders, G.

BOHEMOND I, PRINCE OF ANTIOCH, 1058?-1111

About

And the glory of them

Böhl von Faber, Cecilia See Caballero, Fernán, 1796-1877

Boilard, Jon

Two rules

Dalhousie Review v81 no2 p179-83 Summ 2001

Boito, Arrigo

The Black Bishop

New England Review v25 no1/2 p139-51 2004

Bojanowski, Marc
  The Showman
    The Literary Review (Madison, N.J.) v47 no3
    p15-17 Spr 2004
Bolaño, Roberto
  Phone calls
    Grand Street no67 p171-75 Wint 1999
    Grand Street no72 p34-8 Fall 2003
Boleyn, Anne *See* Anne Boleyn, Queen, consort
  of Henry VIII, King of England, 1507-1536
BOLÍVAR, SIMÓN, 1783-1830
               About
  Borges, J. L. Guayaquil
BOLIVIANS
          United States
  Di Blasi, D. I am telling you lies
BOLSHEVISM *See* Communism
Bomb scare. Vinge, V.
BOMB SHELTERS *See* Air raid shelters
Bombal, María Luisa
  The tree
    Short stories by Latin American women; the
    magic and the real; edited by Celia Correas
    de Zapata; foreword by Isabel Allende
Bombast von Hohenheim, Philipp Aureolus
  Theophrastus *See* Paracelsus, 1493-1541
BOMBAY (INDIA) *See* India—Bombay
Bombay talkies. Pittalwala, I.
BOMBING MISSIONS *See* World War, 1914-
  1918—Aerial operations; World War, 1939-
  1945—Aerial operations
The **Bombing** of Tripoli. McCauley, W.
BOMBS
      See also Atomic bomb
  Bradbury, R. The enemy in the wheat
  DuBois, B. Netmail
  Gartner, Z. The nature of pure evil
  Malzberg, B. N. The prince of the steppes
The **bombs**. Hogan, D.
Bonaparte, Napoleon *See* Napoleon I, Emperor of
  the French, 1769-1821
Bonaparte's dreams. Easton, R. O.
Bond, Nelson
  The bookshop
    Nebula awards 33; the year's best SF and
    fantasy chosen by the science-fiction and
    fantasy writers of America; edited by
    Connie Willis
Bondage. Koja, K.
Bondage. Lynn, D. H.
The **bonding**. Harris, M.
Bondurant, Matt
  The queen of Sparta
    Prairie Schooner v75 no4 p121-39 Wint 2001
  The Two Lands
    New England Review v24 no2 p35-48 Spr
    2003
Bone by bone. Matthiessen, P.
The **bone** divers. Koon, D.
Bone garden. Warren, D.
Bone key. Porter, J. A.
Bone orchards. McAuley, P. J.
The **bone** ship. Dowling, T.
Bonedaddy, Quincy Nell, and the fifteen thousand
  BTU electric chair. Gay, W.
Bones. Block, F. L.
Bones. Ferriss, L.
Bones. Kealey, T.
Bones for Dulath. Lindholm, M.

The **bones** of Garbo. Lewis, T.
Bones of the inner ear. Davenport, K.
Bonfires. Alcott, L. M.
The **bongo** bungler. Van de Wetering, J.
Bonham, Frank
  Burn him out
    A Century of great Western stories; edited by
    John Jakes
Bonman, Ina
  Mrs. Website's dance
    Death dance; suspenseful stories of the dance
    macabre; Trevanian, editor
Bonner, Paul Hyde
  John Monahan
    Fishing's best short stories; edited by Paul D.
    Staudohar
Bonner, Sherwood *See* MacDowell, Katherine
  Sherwood Bonner, 1849-1883
Le **Bonnet** Rouge. Coates, G. S.
Bonnie, Fred
  All-you-can-eat night
    Bonnie, F. Widening the road; stories
  The cookie trick
    Bonnie, F. Widening the road; stories
  Extreme unction
    Bonnie, F. Widening the road; stories
  Fifty winters
    Bonnie, F. Widening the road; stories
  Gone with wind—be back soon
    Bonnie, F. Widening the road; stories
  In search of Number Seven
    Bonnie, F. Widening the road; stories
  Nick the Russian
    Bonnie, F. Widening the road; stories
  Piano skirmish
    Bonnie, F. Widening the road; stories
  The race for last place
    Bonnie, F. Widening the road; stories
  Roland Fogg
    Bonnie, F. Widening the road; stories
  Screwdriver
    Bonnie, F. Widening the road; stories
  Selling delphinium
    Bonnie, F. Widening the road; stories
  Sign language
    Bonnie, F. Widening the road; stories
  Squatter's rights
    Bonnie, F. Widening the road; stories
  Widening the road
    Bonnie, F. Widening the road; stories
Bonnie Ledet. Parrish, T.
Bontemps, Arna Wendell
  Why I returned
    The African American West; a century of
    short stories; edited by Bruce A. Glasrud
    and Laurie Champion
Boo. Laymon, R.
Boo hoo hoo. Dinh, L.
Boobs. Charnas, S. M.
Boof, Kola
  The one you meet everywhere
    Politically inspired; edited by Stephen Elliott;
    assistant editor, Gabriel Kram; associate ed-
    itors, Elizabeth Brooks [et al.]
The **book** of irrational numbers. Smith, M. M.
A **Book** of Kells. Healy, J. F.
Book of Nick. Belle, J.
The **book** of sand. Borges, J. L.
The **book** of the dead. Danticat, E.

The **book** of thieves. Abrams, T.
BOOK RARITIES *See* Rare books
BOOK SHOPS *See* Booksellers and bookselling
Bookcruncher. Fischer, T.
Booker T's coming home. Butler, L. P.
Bookies, beware!. Heller, J.
BOOKS
        See also Books and reading; Manu-
        scripts; Rare books
  Cady, J. Science fiction, utopia, and the spirit
  Campbell, R. Worse than bones
  Chambers, R. W. The yellow sign
  DeMarco, T. Proper cover
  Milne, A. A. The rise and fall of Mortimer
    Scrivens
BOOKS, RARE *See* Rare books
BOOKS AND READING
  Benford, G. The voice
  Cady, J. Jacket copy
  Carson, J. Chosen
  Cherry, K. Chores
  Chesnutt, C. W. Baxter's procrustes
  Doyle, R. The slave
  Fischer, T. Bookcruncher
  Hand, E. The least trumps
  Irvine, A. The sea wind offers little relief
  Kelman, J. I was asking a question too
  Martin, V. Contraction
  Pronzini, B. and Malzberg, B. N. Reading day
  Rendell, R. Piranha to Scurfy
  Waugh, E. The man who liked Dickens
Books Never Written, Journeys Never Made.
  Tabucchi, A.
BOOKSELLERS AND BOOKSELLING
  Allen, S. Keep looking
  Bond, N. The bookshop
  Cady, J. Weird row
  Cherry, K. Tell her
  De Lint, C. Pixel pixies
  Fitzgerald, F. S. His russet witch
  Jacobsen, R. Encounter
  Maron, M. Till 3:45
  Moody, R. Surplus value books: catalogue num-
    ber 13
  Smith, A. Gothic
  Smith, A. The universal story
  Tea, M. 9/11 L.A. bookstore
  Vazquez, Maria Esther. Returning by train with
    Borges
  Wilson, R. C. The fields of Abraham
The **bookshop**. Bond, N.
"**Bookworm,** run!". Vinge, V.
BOOTH, JOHN WILKES, 1838-1865
        About
  Hodgen, C. Three parting shots and a forecast
Booth story. Cottle, T. J.
BOOTLEGGING *See* Liquor traffic
BOOTS AND SHOES
  Bradbury, R. The sound of summer running
  Buchanan, E. The red shoes
  Chenoweth, A. Wingtips
  Davis, A. Sticks and stones
  Dueñas, G. Shoes for the rest of my life
  Poirier, M. J. Gators
Border guards. Egan, G.
The **border** incident. Auerbach, J.
The **border** line. Lawrence, D. H.
Borderlands. Coleman, J. C.
Borderline. Frahm, L.

Bordiuk, Amy
  Lilly and Hanka
    The Massachusetts Review v42 no2 p289-99
    Summ 2001
  What if I had married you?
    Michigan Quarterly Review v38 no2 p260-69
    Spr 1999
BOREDOM
  Le Clézio, J.-M. G. The great life
  Leslie, N. Another place
  Warren, D. Bone garden
Borfka, David
  Next Day
    The Southern Review (Baton Rouge, La.) v39
    no1 p120-40 Wint 2003
Borges, Jorge Luis
  The aleph
    Borges, J. L. Collected fictions; translated by
    Andrew Hurley
    The Vintage book of Latin American stories;
    edited by Carlos Fuentes and Julio Ortega
  The approach to Al-Mu'tasim
    Borges, J. L. Collected fictions; translated by
    Andrew Hurley
  August 25, 1983
    Borges, J. L. Collected fictions; translated by
    Andrew Hurley
  Avelino Arredondo
    Borges, J. L. Collected fictions; translated by
    Andrew Hurley
  Averroës' search
    Borges, J. L. Collected fictions; translated by
    Andrew Hurley
  A biography of Tadeo Isidoro Cruz (1829-1874)
    Borges, J. L. Collected fictions; translated by
    Andrew Hurley
  Blue tigers
    Borges, J. L. Collected fictions; translated by
    Andrew Hurley
  The book of sand
    Borges, J. L. Collected fictions; translated by
    Andrew Hurley
  The bribe
    Borges, J. L. Collected fictions; translated by
    Andrew Hurley
  Brodie's report
    Borges, J. L. Collected fictions; translated by
    Andrew Hurley
  The circular ruins
    Borges, J. L. Collected fictions; translated by
    Andrew Hurley
  The congress
    Borges, J. L. Collected fictions; translated by
    Andrew Hurley
  The cruel redeemer Lazarus Morell
    Borges, J. L. Collected fictions; translated by
    Andrew Hurley
  The cult of the Phoenix
    Borges, J. L. Collected fictions; translated by
    Andrew Hurley
  The dead man
    Borges, J. L. Collected fictions; translated by
    Andrew Hurley
  Death and the compass
    Borges, J. L. Collected fictions; translated by
    Andrew Hurley
  Deutsches requiem
    Borges, J. L. Collected fictions; translated by
    Andrew Hurley

Borges, Jorge Luis—*Continued*
A dialog between dead men
　Borges, J. L. Collected fictions; translated by
　　Andrew Hurley
The disinterested killer Bill Harrigan
　Borges, J. L. Collected fictions; translated by
　　Andrew Hurley
The disk
　Borges, J. L. Collected fictions; translated by
　　Andrew Hurley
The duel
　Borges, J. L. Collected fictions; translated by
　　Andrew Hurley
The elderly lady
　Borges, J. L. Collected fictions; translated by
　　Andrew Hurley
Emma Zunz
　Borges, J. L. Collected fictions; translated by
　　Andrew Hurley
The encounter
　Borges, J. L. Collected fictions; translated by
　　Andrew Hurley
The end
　Borges, J. L. Collected fictions; translated by
　　Andrew Hurley
Et cetera
　Borges, J. L. Collected fictions; translated by
　　Andrew Hurley
Funes, his memory
　Borges, J. L. Collected fictions; translated by
　　Andrew Hurley
　The Vintage book of amnesia; an anthology;
　　edited by Jonathan Lethem
The garden of forking paths
　Borges, J. L. Collected fictions; translated by
　　Andrew Hurley
The Gospel according to Mark
　Borges, J. L. Collected fictions; translated by
　　Andrew Hurley
Guayaquil
　Borges, J. L. Collected fictions; translated by
　　Andrew Hurley
Hakim, the masked dyer of Merv
　Borges, J. L. Collected fictions; translated by
　　Andrew Hurley
The house of Asterion
　Borges, J. L. Collected fictions; translated by
　　Andrew Hurley
Ibn-Hakam al-Bokhari, murdered in his labyrinth
　Borges, J. L. Collected fictions; translated by
　　Andrew Hurley
The immortal
　Borges, J. L. Collected fictions; translated by
　　Andrew Hurley
The improbable impostor Tom Castro
　Borges, J. L. Collected fictions; translated by
　　Andrew Hurley
The interloper
　Borges, J. L. Collected fictions; translated by
　　Andrew Hurley
Juan Muraña
　Borges, J. L. Collected fictions; translated by
　　Andrew Hurley
The lottery in Babylon
　Borges, J. L. Collected fictions; translated by
　　Andrew Hurley
The maker
　Borges, J. L. Collected fictions; translated by
　　Andrew Hurley

Man on pink corner
　Borges, J. L. Collected fictions; translated by
　　Andrew Hurley
The man on the threshold
　Borges, J. L. Collected fictions; translated by
　　Andrew Hurley
The mirror and the mask
　Borges, J. L. Collected fictions; translated by
　　Andrew Hurley
Monk Eastman, purveyor of iniquities
　Borges, J. L. Collected fictions; translated by
　　Andrew Hurley
The night of the gifts
　Borges, J. L. Collected fictions; translated by
　　Andrew Hurley
The other
　Borges, J. L. Collected fictions; translated by
　　Andrew Hurley
The other death
　Borges, J. L. Collected fictions; translated by
　　Andrew Hurley
The other duel
　Borges, J. L. Collected fictions; translated by
　　Andrew Hurley
Pedro Salvadores
　Borges, J. L. Collected fictions; translated by
　　Andrew Hurley
Pierre Menard, author of the Quixote
　Borges, J. L. Collected fictions; translated by
　　Andrew Hurley
The rose of Paracelsus
　Borges, J. L. Collected fictions; translated by
　　Andrew Hurley
　The Year's best fantasy & horror, twelfth an-
　　nual collection; edited by Ellen Datlow &
　　Terry Windling
The secret miracle
　Borges, J. L. Collected fictions; translated by
　　Andrew Hurley
The Sect of the Thirty
　Borges, J. L. Collected fictions; translated by
　　Andrew Hurley
Shakespeare's memory
　Borges, J. L. Collected fictions; translated by
　　Andrew Hurley
The shape of the sword
　Borges, J. L. Collected fictions; translated by
　　Andrew Hurley
The south
　Borges, J. L. Collected fictions; translated by
　　Andrew Hurley
The story from Rosendo Juárez
　Borges, J. L. Collected fictions; translated by
　　Andrew Hurley
Story of the warrior and the captive maiden
　Borges, J. L. Collected fictions; translated by
　　Andrew Hurley
A survey of the works of Herbert Quain
　Borges, J. L. Collected fictions; translated by
　　Andrew Hurley
The theme of the traitor and the hero
　Borges, J. L. Collected fictions; translated by
　　Andrew Hurley
The theologians
　Borges, J. L. Collected fictions; translated by
　　Andrew Hurley
There are more things
　Borges, J. L. Collected fictions; translated by
　　Andrew Hurley

Borges, Jorge Luis—*Continued*
Three versions of Judas
    Borges, J. L. Collected fictions; translated by Andrew Hurley
Tlön, Uqbar, Orbis Tertius
    Borges, J. L. Collected fictions; translated by Andrew Hurley
Ulrikke
    Borges, J. L. Collected fictions; translated by Andrew Hurley
The uncivil teacher of court etiquette Kôtsuké no Suké
    Borges, J. L. Collected fictions; translated by Andrew Hurley
"Undr"
    Borges, J. L. Collected fictions; translated by Andrew Hurley
Unworthy
    Borges, J. L. Collected fictions; translated by Andrew Hurley
The wait
    Borges, J. L. Collected fictions; translated by Andrew Hurley
A weary man's utopia
    Borges, J. L. Collected fictions; translated by Andrew Hurley
The widow Ching—pirate
    Borges, J. L. Collected fictions; translated by Andrew Hurley
The writing of the god
    Borges, J. L. Collected fictions; translated by Andrew Hurley
The Zahir
    Borges, J. L. Collected fictions; translated by Andrew Hurley

BORGES, JORGE LUIS, 1899-1986
About
Vazquez, Maria Esther. Returning by train with Borges

BORGIA, CESARE, 1476?-1507
About
Griffen, C. Borgia by blood
Borgia by blood. Griffen, C.

BORMANN, MARTIN, 1900-1945
About
Kurlansky, M. Vertical administration
Born again. Boswell, M.
Born failure. Highsmith, P.
Born of man and woman. Matheson, R.
Born of the night. Muss-Barnes, E.
Born to the brand. Newton, D. B.
Born victims. Wellen, E.

BORNEO
L'Amour, L. The diamond of Jeru
L'Amour, L. Off the Mangrove Coast

Boroson, Rebecca
The roussalka
    With signs and wonders; an international anthology of Jewish fabulist fiction; edited by Daniel M. Jaffe

Borowski, Tadeusz
Auschwitz, our home (a letter)
    Other people's mail; an anthology of letter stories; edited with an introduction by Gail Pool
Borrowed hearts. DeMarinis, R.

BOSCH, HIERONYMUS, D. 1516
About
Yuknavitch, L. The garden of earthly delights

Bosch, Juan
Encarnación Mendoza's Christmas Eve
    The Oxford book of Caribbean short stories; edited by Stewart Brown and John Wickham

Bosley, Deborah
Beware the gentle wife
    Valentine's Day: women against men; stories of revenge; introduction by Alice Thomas

BOSNIA AND HERCEGOVINA
Canovic, L. S. Bats
Hemon, A. Exchange of pleasant words
        Sarajevo
Greenberg, P. The subjunctive mood
Hemon, A. A coin

BOSNIANS
        United States
Hemon, A. Blind Jozef Pronek
Hemon, A. Blind Jozef Pronek & Dead Souls
Novakovich, J. Spleen
Bosom companions. Jacobson, D.
The **Boss** in the Wall: a treatise on the house devil. Davidson, A. and Davis, G.

Bossert, Jill
Remaining in favor
    Ploughshares v25 no2/3 p9-19 Fall 1999
BOSTON (MASS.) *See* Massachusetts—Boston
The **Bostons**. Cooke, C.

Boswell, Marshall
Between things
    Boswell, M. Trouble with girls
Bloody knuckles
    Boswell, M. Trouble with girls
Born again
    Boswell, M. Trouble with girls
Grub worm
    Boswell, M. Trouble with girls
In between things
    New stories from the South: the year's best, 2001; edited by Shannon Ravenel; with a preface by Lee Smith
Karma wheel
    Boswell, M. Trouble with girls
New Wave
    Boswell, M. Trouble with girls
Ready position
    Boswell, M. Trouble with girls
Spanish omens
    Boswell, M. Trouble with girls
Stir crazy
    Boswell, M. Trouble with girls
Venus/Mars
    Boswell, M. Trouble with girls

Boswell, Robert
City Bus
    Ploughshares v30 no1 p37-48 Spr 2004
Glissando
    Still wild; short fiction of the American West, 1950 to the present; edited by Larry McMurtry
Miss Famous
    The Pushcart prize XXIV: best of the small presses; an annual small press reader; edited by Bill Henderson with the Pushcart prize editors

Bosworth, Beth
The year the world turned
    The Kenyon Review ns21 no3-4 p116-21 Summ/Fall 1999

BOTANISTS

Bell, M. S. The thing about Benny

Iagnemma, K. Kingdom, order, species

Both and. Fry, G.

Both sides against the middle. Archer, J.

BOTSWANA

Luntta, K. A virgin twice

Rush, N. Alone in Africa

Whitty, J. Senti's last elephant

Böttcher, Maximilian

The detective

Early German and Austrian detective fiction; an anthology; translated and edited by Mary W. Tannert and Henry Kratz

The **bottle** imp. Stevenson, R. L.

A **bottle** of Perrier. Wharton, E.

The **Bottom** of Things. Haigh, J.

Bottoms, Greg

1967

Bottoms, G. Sentimental, heartbroken rednecks; stories

Gray world

Bottoms, G. Sentimental, heartbroken rednecks; stories

Heroism

Bottoms, G. Sentimental, heartbroken rednecks; stories

Imaginary birds

Bottoms, G. Sentimental, heartbroken rednecks; stories

Intersections

Bottoms, G. Sentimental, heartbroken rednecks; stories

Levi's tongue

Bottoms, G. Sentimental, heartbroken rednecks; stories

LSD in Raleigh

Bottoms, G. Sentimental, heartbroken rednecks; stories

The metaphor

Bottoms, G. Sentimental, heartbroken rednecks; stories

Nostalgia for ghosts

Bottoms, G. Sentimental, heartbroken rednecks; stories

A seat for the coming savior

Bottoms, G. Sentimental, heartbroken rednecks; stories

Secret history of home cinema

Bottoms, G. Sentimental, heartbroken rednecks; stories

Sentimental, heartbroken rednecks

Bottoms, G. Sentimental, heartbroken rednecks; stories

A stupid story

Bottoms, G. Sentimental, heartbroken rednecks; stories

Bottoms. Gilb, D.

Bottomy, Hannah

The Revenant

South Carolina Review v35 no2 p67-70 Spr 2003

Botts and the biggest deal of all. Upson, W. H.

Botts at sea. Upson, W. H.

Botts Puts the Show on the Road. Upson, W. H.

Bouayad and the money. Bowles, P.

Boucher, Anthony

The girl who married a monster

A Century of great suspense stories; edited by Jeffery Deaver

The quest for Saint Aquin

The Science fiction hall of fame: volume one, 1929-1964; the greatest science fiction stories of all time chosen by the members of the Science Fiction Writers of America; edited by Robert Silverberg

The stripper

Murder most divine; ecclesiastical tales of unholy crimes; edited by Ralph McInerny and Martin H. Greenberg

Boucolon, Maryse *See* Condé, Maryse, 1937-

Bouldrey, Brian

The holy spirit bank

Men on men 2000; best new gay fiction for the millennium; edited and with an introduction by David Bergman and Karl Woelz

Boulevard. Grimsley, J.

Boulôt and Boulotte. Chopin, K.

Bouman, Ina

The deep blue sea

Death cruise; crime stories on the open seas; edited by Lawrence Block

The **bounce.** Connolly, C.

The **bouquet.** Chesnutt, C. W.

Bourke, Rita Welty

The excavator

The North American Review v286 no3/4 p8-12 My/Ag 2001

White Vitrock China

South Carolina Review v35 no2 p124-8 Spr 2003

Boutell, Amy

The Motion of Falling Bodies

New Letters v70 no1 p127-31 2003

Bova, Ben

The café coup

One lamp; alternate history stories from The magazine of Fantasy & Science Fiction; edited by Gordon van Gelder

Mount Olympus

The Year's best science fiction, seventeenth annual collection; edited by Gardner Dozois

BOW AND ARROW *See* Archery

Bow down. Kalam, M.

Bowen, Elizabeth

The happy autumn fields

Nightshade: 20th century ghost stories; edited by Robert Phillips

Summer night

The Anchor book of new Irish writing; the new Gaelach ficsean; edited and with an introduction by John Somer and John J. Daly

Bowen, Gary

Barrel racers: El Charro

His 3: brilliant new fiction by gay writers; edited by Robert Drake and Terry Wolverton

Bowen, Kevin

The thief of Tay Ninh

The Pushcart prize XXVI; best of the small presses, an annual small press reader; edited by Bill Henderson and the Pushcart prize editors

Bowen, Marjorie

The Crown Derby plate

Dark: stories of madness, murder, and the supernatural; edited by Clint Willis

Bowen, Rhys

Doppelganger

Blood on their hands; edited by Lawrence Block

The proof of the pudding

Bishop, C. and James, D. Death dines in; edited by Claudia Bishop and Dean James

Bowen, Robert O.

A matter of price

Retrieving bones; stories and poems of the Korean War; edited and with an introduction by W. D. Ehrhart and Philip K. Jason

Bower, B. M.

The lamb of the Flying U

A Century of great Western stories; edited by John Jakes

The **bower-bird**. Norris, H.

BOWIE, JAMES, 1799?-1836

About

Card, O. S. The Yazoo Queen

Bowles, David

Birthmark

South Carolina Review v33 no2 p62-7 Spr 2001

Bowles, Paul

Afternoon with Antaeus

Bowles, P. The stories of Paul Bowles; introduction by Robert Stone

Allal

Bowles, P. The stories of Paul Bowles; introduction by Robert Stone

At Paso Jojo

Bowles, P. The stories of Paul Bowles; introduction by Robert Stone

At the Krungthep Plaza

Bowles, P. The stories of Paul Bowles; introduction by Robert Stone

Bouayad and the money

Bowles, P. The stories of Paul Bowles; introduction by Robert Stone

By the water

Bowles, P. The stories of Paul Bowles; introduction by Robert Stone

Call at Corazón

Bowles, P. The stories of Paul Bowles; introduction by Robert Stone

The circular valley

Bowles, P. The stories of Paul Bowles; introduction by Robert Stone

The delicate prey

Bowles, P. The stories of Paul Bowles; introduction by Robert Stone

Dinner at Sir Nigel's

Bowles, P. The stories of Paul Bowles; introduction by Robert Stone

The dismissal

Bowles, P. The stories of Paul Bowles; introduction by Robert Stone

A distant episode

Bowles, P. The stories of Paul Bowles; introduction by Robert Stone

Dark: stories of madness, murder, and the supernatural; edited by Clint Willis

Doña Faustina

Bowles, P. The stories of Paul Bowles; introduction by Robert Stone

The echo

Bowles, P. The stories of Paul Bowles; introduction by Robert Stone

The empty amulet

Bowles, P. The stories of Paul Bowles; introduction by Robert Stone

The eye

Bowles, P. The stories of Paul Bowles; introduction by Robert Stone

The fourth day out from Santa Cruz

Bowles, P. The stories of Paul Bowles; introduction by Robert Stone

The fqih

Bowles, P. The stories of Paul Bowles; introduction by Robert Stone

A friend of the world

Bowles, P. The stories of Paul Bowles; introduction by Robert Stone

The frozen fields

Bowles, P. The stories of Paul Bowles; introduction by Robert Stone

The garden

Bowles, P. The stories of Paul Bowles; introduction by Robert Stone

He of the assembly

Bowles, P. The stories of Paul Bowles; introduction by Robert Stone

Here to learn

Bowles, P. The stories of Paul Bowles; introduction by Robert Stone

The hours after noon

Bowles, P. The stories of Paul Bowles; introduction by Robert Stone

How many midnights

Bowles, P. The stories of Paul Bowles; introduction by Robert Stone

Hugh Harper

Bowles, P. The stories of Paul Bowles; introduction by Robert Stone

The husband

Bowles, P. The stories of Paul Bowles; introduction by Robert Stone

The hyena

Bowles, P. The stories of Paul Bowles; introduction by Robert Stone

If I should open my mouth

Bowles, P. The stories of Paul Bowles; introduction by Robert Stone

In absentia

Bowles, P. The stories of Paul Bowles; introduction by Robert Stone

In the red room

Bowles, P. The stories of Paul Bowles; introduction by Robert Stone

An inopportune visit

Bowles, P. The stories of Paul Bowles; introduction by Robert Stone

Istikhara, Anaya, Medagan and the Medaganat

Bowles, P. The stories of Paul Bowles; introduction by Robert Stone

Julian Vreden

Bowles, P. The stories of Paul Bowles; introduction by Robert Stone

Kitty

Bowles, P. The stories of Paul Bowles; introduction by Robert Stone

Bowles, Paul—*Continued*

The little house
  Bowles, P. The stories of Paul Bowles; introduction by Robert Stone
Madame and Ahmed
  Bowles, P. The stories of Paul Bowles; introduction by Robert Stone
Massachusetts 1932
  Bowles, P. The stories of Paul Bowles; introduction by Robert Stone
Mejdoub
  Bowles, P. The stories of Paul Bowles; introduction by Robert Stone
Midnight mass
  Bowles, P. The stories of Paul Bowles; introduction by Robert Stone
New York 1965
  Bowles, P. The stories of Paul Bowles; introduction by Robert Stone
Pages from Cold Point
  Bowles, P. The stories of Paul Bowles; introduction by Robert Stone
Pastor Dowe at Tacate
  Bowles, P. The stories of Paul Bowles; introduction by Robert Stone
Reminders of Bouselham
  Bowles, P. The stories of Paul Bowles; introduction by Robert Stone
Rumor and a ladder
  Bowles, P. The stories of Paul Bowles; introduction by Robert Stone
The scorpion
  Bowles, P. The stories of Paul Bowles; introduction by Robert Stone
Señor Ong and Señor Ha
  Bowles, P. The stories of Paul Bowles; introduction by Robert Stone
The story of Lahcen and Idir
  Bowles, P. The stories of Paul Bowles; introduction by Robert Stone
The successor
  Bowles, P. The stories of Paul Bowles; introduction by Robert Stone
Tangier 1975
  Bowles, P. The stories of Paul Bowles; introduction by Robert Stone
Tapiama
  Bowles, P. The stories of Paul Bowles; introduction by Robert Stone
Tea on the mountain
  Bowles, P. The stories of Paul Bowles; introduction by Robert Stone
Things gone and things still here
  Bowles, P. The stories of Paul Bowles; introduction by Robert Stone
A thousand days for Mokhtar
  Bowles, P. The stories of Paul Bowles; introduction by Robert Stone
The time of friendship
  Bowles, P. The stories of Paul Bowles; introduction by Robert Stone
Too far from home
  Bowles, P. The stories of Paul Bowles; introduction by Robert Stone
Under the sky
  Bowles, P. The stories of Paul Bowles; introduction by Robert Stone

Unwelcome words
  Bowles, P. The stories of Paul Bowles; introduction by Robert Stone
The waters of Izli
  Bowles, P. The stories of Paul Bowles; introduction by Robert Stone
The wind at Beni Midar
  Bowles, P. The stories of Paul Bowles; introduction by Robert Stone
You are not I
  Bowles, P. The stories of Paul Bowles; introduction by Robert Stone
You have left your lotus pods on the bus
  Bowles, P. The stories of Paul Bowles; introduction by Robert Stone

Bowles, Scott Allen

Home improvement
  His 3: brilliant new fiction by gay writers; edited by Robert Drake and Terry Wolverton

BOWLING

Casares, O. Mrs. Perez
Singleton, G. Duke power
The **Bowlville** Cemetery. Connor, J.
Box. Ansay, A. M.
Box. Roderick, D.
Box number fifty. Saberhagen, F.
Boxcars, 1974. Stine, P.
The **boxer**. Holleran, A.
The **Boxer**. Simonetta, R.
A **boxer:** old. Sylvester, H. A.
BOXER REBELLION *See* China—Beijing—Siege, 1900

BOXING

Algren, N. He swung and he missed
Bass, R. The legend of Pig-Eye
Bezmozgis, D. Choynski
Blake, J. C. Referee
Cavell, B. Killing time
Cavell, B. The ropes
Cohen, O. R. The last blow
Cook, T. H. The fix
Davis, L. The kind of time you end up with
Doyle, Sir A. C. The Croxley Master
Farrell, J. T. Twenty-five bucks
Gallico, P. Thicker than water
Grady, J. The championship of nowhere
Hammett, D. His brother's keeper
Howard, C. Hit and run
Jones, T. My heroic mythic journey
Jones, T. Sonny Liston was a friend of mine
Katkov, N. Stop the fight!
Kittredge, W. Thirty-four seasons of winter
L'Amour, L. Fighter's fiasco
L'Amour, L. Fighters should be hungry
L'Amour, L. The ghost fighter
L'Amour, L. Making it the hard way
L'Amour, L. The money punch
L'Amour, L. The rounds don't matter
L'Amour, L. Sideshow champion
Lardner, R. Champion
London, J. A piece of steak
Matheson, R. Steel
Matison, M. Rose into cauliflower
McMahon, N. Heart
Meersch, M. v. d. Everything in the fifth
Mosley, W. The greatest
Offutt, C. Tough people
Paver, C. The boxing match
Queen, E. A matter of seconds

BOXING—*Continued*

Robinson, L. Fighting at night
Runyon, D. Bred for battle
Shaw, I. Return to Kansas City
Smart, A. Jersey Joe versus the Rock
Spencer, D. Pronto bucks
Switzer, R. Death of a prize fighter
Sylvester, H. A. A boxer: old
Sylvester, H. A. I won't do no dive
Toole, F. X. Black Jew
Toole, F. X. Fightin in Philly
Toole, F. X. Frozen water
Toole, F. X. Midnight emissions
Toole, F. X. Million $$$ baby
Toole, F. X. The monkey look
Toole, F. X. Rope burns
Van Loan, C. E. One-thirty-three—ringside
Witwer, H. C. The Chickasha Bone Crusher
Witwer, H. C. The leather pushers
Wodehouse, P. G. The debut of Battling Billson
Yuknavitch, L. Beatings

The **Boxing** Day bother. Guiver, P.

The **boxing** match. Paver, C.

The **boxroom**. Hird, L.

The **boy** from Montana. O'Neill, S.

The **boy** Gramophone and the pigeon man. Maraini, D.

A **boy** in the forest. O'Brien, E.

The **Boy** in the Tree. Spencer, E.

The **boy** next door. Goldberg, D. G. K.

The **Boy** on the Swing (Barcelona, 1981). Vila-Matas, E.

BOY SCOUTS

Dumas, H. Scout
Fulton, J. First sex
Rinehart, S. The order of the arrow
Weidman, J. Good man, bad man
Williamson, J. Jamboree

The **Boy** Who Hated Girls. Vonnegut, K.

The **boy** who lost an hour, the girl who lost her life. Watson, I.

The **boy** who would live forever. Pohl, F.

The **boy** who wrestled with angels. Hoffman, A.

Boy Wonder. Foley, S.

Boyczuk, Robert

Doing time
Northern suns; edited by David G. Hartwell & Glenn Grant

Boyd, William

Adult video
The New Yorker v75 no13 p88-92 My 31 1999
Fascination
The New Yorker v78 no2 p72-9 Mr 4 2002

Boyers, Robert

An Excitable Woman
Harvard Review (1992) no24 p6-17 Spr 2003
The visit
Parnassus: Poetry in Review v24 no1 p133-53 1999

The **Boyfriend**. Joseph, S.

Boyfriends. Weiner, C.

The **boyish** mulatto. Derby, M.

Boylan, Clare

Affairs in order
Boylan, C. The collected stories
Appearances
Boylan, C. The collected stories

Bad-natured dog
Boylan, C. The collected stories
The complete angler
Boylan, C. The collected stories
Concerning virgins
Boylan, C. The collected stories
Confession
Boylan, C. The collected stories
Ears
Boylan, C. The collected stories
Edna, back from America
Boylan, C. The collected stories
A funny thing happened
Boylan, C. The collected stories
Gods and slaves
Boylan, C. The collected stories
Horrible luck
Boylan, C. The collected stories
Housekeeper's cut
Boylan, C. The collected stories
It's her
Boylan, C. The collected stories
L'amour
Boylan, C. The collected stories
Life on Mars
Boylan, C. The collected stories
The Little Madonna
The Anchor book of new Irish writing; the new Gaelach ficsean; edited and with an introduction by John Somer and John J. Daly
Mama
Boylan, C. The collected stories
The miracle of life
Boylan, C. The collected stories
A model daughter
Boylan, C. The collected stories
My son the hero
Boylan, C. The collected stories
A nail on the head
Boylan, C. The collected stories
A particular calling
Boylan, C. The collected stories
Perfect love
Boylan, C. The collected stories
The picture house
Boylan, C. The collected stories
Poor old sod
Boylan, C. The collected stories
A reproduction
Boylan, C. The collected stories
The secret diary of Mrs Rochester
Boylan, C. The collected stories
Some retired ladies on a tour
Boylan, C. The collected stories
The spirit of the tree
Boylan, C. The collected stories
The stolen child
Boylan, C. The collected stories
Technical difficulties and the plague
Boylan, C. The collected stories
That bad woman
Boylan, C. The collected stories
Thatcher's Britain
Boylan, C. The collected stories
To tempt a woman
Boylan, C. The collected stories
Villa Marta
Boylan, C. The collected stories

Boylan, Clare—*Continued*
The wronged wife
  Boylan, C. The collected stories
You don't know you're alive
  Boylan, C. The collected stories
Boyle, T. Coraghessan
Achates McNeil
  Boyle, T. C. After the plague; stories
After the plague
  Boyle, T. C. After the plague; stories
The black and white sisters
  Boyle, T. C. After the plague; stories
Captured by the Indians
  Boyle, T. C. After the plague; stories
  The New Yorker v75 no28 p84-90 S 27 1999
Chicxulub
  The New Yorker v80 no2 p78-83 Mr 1 2004
Death of the cool
  Boyle, T. C. After the plague; stories
Dogology
  The New Yorker v78 no34 p130-2, 134,
    136-8, 140, 142-4, 147-8 N 11 2002
Fondue
  The Antioch Review v59 no2 p492-8 Spr 2001
  The Antioch Review v57 no4 p456-62 Fall
    1999
Friendly skies
  Boyle, T. C. After the plague; stories
Going down
  Boyle, T. C. After the plague; stories
  The Paris Review v41 no152 p63-78 Fall
    1999
Here Comes
  Harper's v305 p61-9 N 2002
Killing babies
  Boyle, T. C. After the plague; stories
The Kind Assassin
  Gentlemen's Quarterly v72 no11 p264-71,
    386-8 N 2002
The love of my life
  Boyle, T. C. After the plague; stories
  Prize stories, 2001; The O. Henry awards; ed-
    ited and with an introduction by Larry
    Dark
Mexico
  Boyle, T. C. After the plague; stories
The miracle at Ballinspittle
  Ghost writing; haunted tales by contemporary
    writers; edited by Roger Weingarten
My widow
  Boyle, T. C. After the plague; stories
  The New Yorker v76 no46 p80-7 F 12 2001
Peep Hall
  Boyle, T. C. After the plague; stories
Rara avis
  The Art of the story; an international antholo-
    gy of contemporary short stories; edited by
    Daniel Halpern
Rastrow's Island
  Harper's v308 p65-70 Mr 2004
Rust
  Boyle, T. C. After the plague; stories
She wasn't soft
  Boyle, T. C. After the plague; stories
Swept away
  The New Yorker v77 no44 p70-5 Ja 21 2002

The O. Henry Prize stories, 2003; edited and
    with an introduction by Laura Furman;
    jurers David Gutterson, Diane Johnson,
    Jennifer Egan
Termination dust
  Boyle, T. C. After the plague; stories
Tooth and Claw
  The New Yorker v79 no34 p106-15 N 10
    2003
The underground gardens
  Boyle, T. C. After the plague; stories
  Prize stories, 1999; The O. Henry awards; ed-
    ited and with an introduction by Larry
    Dark
When I Woke Up This Morning, Everything I
    Had Was Gone
  The New Yorker v79 no6 p86-8, 90-5 Mr 31
    2003
A women's restaurant
  The Workshop; seven decades of the Iowa
    Writers' Workshop: 42 stories, recollections
    & essays on Iowa's place in 20th-century
    American literature; edited by Tom Grimes
Boyne, Walter J.
Cleveland airport August 1933
  On glorious wings; the best flying stories of
    the century; edited and introduced by Ste-
    phen Coonts
BOYS
        See also Adolescence; Children; Youth
Abrams, T. The drinking of spirits
Abrams, T. Forgetting how to laugh
Alameddine, R. The changing room
Alcott, L. M. Bertie's box: a Christmas story
Alcott, L. M. Number eleven
Alcott, L. M. Uncles Smiley's boys
Aldrich, B. S. Ginger cookies
Aldrich, B. S. Last night when you kissed
    Blanche Thompson
Alexis, A. The night piece
Amis, M. What happened to me on my holiday
Appel, B. Murder of the frankfurter man
Arenas, R. In the shade of the almond tree
Arenas, R. With my eyes closed
Atkinson, K. Tunnel of fish
Bail, M. Healing
Bailey, D. Quinn's way
Barker, N. Back to front
Barker, N. Braces
Barker, N. The butcher's apprentice
Barrett, N., Jr. Cush
Barton, M. Final spring
Barton, W. Off on a starship
Bass, R. Swamp Boy
Bausch, R. Glass meadow
Benedict, P. Miracle boy
Berry, W. Don't send a boy to do a man's work
Berry, W. The hurt man
Berry, W. Where did they go?
Bezmozgis, D. Tapka
Bhêly-Quénum, O. A child in the bush of ghosts
Bishop, M. Blue Kansas sky
Bisson, T. There are no dead
Blaise, C. Dunkelblau
Blaise, C. Giant turtles, gliding in the dark
Blaise, C. Snow people
Bonnie, F. Fifty winters
Bonnie, F. Nick the Russian
Bonnie, F. Selling delphinium

BOYS—*Continued*

Boswell, M. Ready position
Bottoms, G. Nostalgia for ghosts
Bottoms, G. Secret history of home cinema
Brackenbury, R. The knowledge
Bradbury, R. Colonel Stonesteel's genuine home-made truly Egyptian mummy
Bradbury, R. Colonel Stonesteel's genuine homemade truly Egyptian mummy
Bradbury, R. With smiles as wide as summer
Brockmeier, K. Apples
Broughton, T. A. Leaving home
Brownstein, G. The inventor of love
Busch, F. The talking cure
Butler, R. O. Hiram the desperado
Callaghan, M. The white pony
Campbell, R. Feeling remains
Capote, T. The Thanksgiving visitor
Carlson, R. At Copper View
Casares, O. Mr. Z
Chabon, M. Spikes
Chabon, M. Werewolves in their youth
Chacón, D. Ofrenda
Chacón, D. Too white
Chan, D. M. Mystery boy
Chaon, D. Big me
Chapman, C. M. Johnny pumpkinseed
Chapman, C. M. The pool witch
Chappell, F. The encyclopedia Daniel
Chekhov, A. P. Boys
Chopin, K. Polydore
Chopin, K. A vacation and a voice
Chopin, K. A wizard from Gettysburg
Chwedyk, Richard. Bronte's egg
Clark, B. C. The Apache pest control
Clark, B. C. Between girls and gamecocks
Clark, B. C. By way of the forked stick
Clark, B. C. The last picture show
Cohen, R. Those kooks
Cohen, R. What makes you you
Condé, M. The breadnut and the breadfruit
Connolly, C. How I lost my vocation
Connolly, C. Indian summer
Cook, K. L. Breaking glass
Cummins, A. Crazy yellow
Dann, J. Voices
Davenport, G. Boys smell like oranges
Davenport, G. Wo es war, soll ich werden
Davidson, A. Captain Pasharooney
Deane, J. F. Big Lil
DeMarco, T. A boy's will is the winds's will
DeMarco, T. Prince of darkness
DeMarinis, R. The boys we were, the men we became
DeMarinis, R. Experience
DeMarinis, R. On the lam
Desaulniers, J. After Rosa Parks
Díaz, J. Ysrael
Doctorow, C. To market, to market: the re-branding of Billy Bailey
Dokey, R. Ace
Doran, M. M. Billy and Benjamin too
Doran, M. M. End October
Douglas, B. My childhood
Douglas, E. About loving women
Dozois, G. R. The clowns
Dozois, G. R. Playing the game
Drake, R. All that believe that, stand on their head!

Drake, R. The child prodigy
Drake, R. Let there be light
Drake, R. Shrouds with pockets in them
Dumas, H. Echo tree
Dumas, H. A Harlem game
Dumas, H. Rain God
Dumas, H. Thrust counter thrust
Dybek, S. Live from Dreamsville
Ebershoff, D. The dress
Egan, G. Oceanic
Ellison, R. Mister Toussan
Erickson, Ben. Floundering
Erofeev, V. The parakeet
Ferreira, R. Dream with no name
Firth, C. The Department of Nothing
Fischerová, D. A letter for President Eisenhower
Fitzgerald, P. Desideratus
Fleming, R. In my father's house
Fleming, R. Punish the young seed of Satan
Foley, S. Boy Wonder
Fulton, J. Braces
Gambone, P. The singing boy
Garrett, G. P. Feeling good, feeling fine
Gartner, Z. The tragedy of premature death among geniuses
Gilchrist, E. The stucco house
Godin, A. My dead brother comes to America
Gonzalez, R. Becky
Gonzalez, R. Eduardo
Gonzalez, R. Postcards
Gonzalez, R. Spanish
Gray, A. Sinkings
Greer, A. S. Cannibal kings
Greer, A. S. How it was for me
Greer, R. O. Grief
Gwyn, A. Against the pricks
Ha Jin. Emperor
Hall, D. Christmas snow
Hall, D. The Ideal Bakery
Hamburger, A. The view from Statlin's Head
Harris, M. Titwillow
Harte, B. How Santa Claus came to Simpson's Bar
Haslett, A. Divination
Hassler, J. Chief Larson
Hawthorne, N. The gentle boy
Hemon, A. Imitation of life
Hemon, A. The Sorge spy ring
Heynen, J. Who had good ears
Hill, J. Pop art
Hill, K. The anointed
Hirshberg, G. Dancing men
Hodge, B. Some other me
Hoffman, W. Blood
Hoffman, W. Roll call
Homes, A. M. Rockets round the moon
Horn, D. Barbarians at the gates
Howard, C. The last one to cry
Jaime-Becerra, M. La fiesta brava
Johnson-Davies, D. The garden of Sheikh Osman
Johnson-Davies, D. Two worlds
Joyce, G. The Coventry boy
Karnezis, P. Applied aeronautics
Keegan, C. The burning palms
Kelly, J. P. 1016 to 1
Kennedy, A. L. A bad son
Keret, E. Shoes
King, S. The man in the black suit

BOYS—*Continued*

Klass, P. Rainbow mama
Knight, M. A bad man, so pretty
Lansdale, J. R. Cowboy
LaValle, V. D. Chuckie
Lavín, G. Reaching the shore
Lee, M. The Albright Kid
Leff, R. J. Burn your maps
LeRoy, J. T. Baby doll
LeRoy, J. T. Coal
LeRoy, J. T. Disappearances
LeRoy, J. T. Foolishness is bound in the heart of a child
LeRoy, J. T. Lizards
Lida, D. Acapulco gold
Lincoln, C. Bug juice
Lincoln, C. Winter's wheat
Lipsyte, S. Admiral of the Swiss Navy
Lipsyte, S. The Drury girl
Lloyd, D. T. As always, Jason
Lloyd, D. T. The biggest
Lloyd, D. T. Boys only
Lloyd, D. T. Isaac and Abraham
Lloyd, D. T. No boundaries
Lloyd, D. T. Spider
Lloyd, D. T. Stain
Lloyd, D. T. Taking aim
Lloyd, D. T. Touch
Lloyd, D. T. Voodoo
Lord, N. The baby who, according to his aunt, resembled his uncle
Lord, N. Remaking the world
Lowenthal, M. Ordinary pain
Lundquist, R. Silence and slow time
MacLean, K. Games
MacLeod, A. The return
Maleti, G. David
Malouf, D. At Schindler's
Marshall, B. White sugar and red clay
Martin, P. P. Amor perdido—Lost love
Matthews, C. The dirt eaters
Matthews, C. To make a rabbit sing
Mazor, J. Friend of mankind
Mazor, J. On experience
Mazor, J. Storm
McBrearty, R. G. My life as a judo master
McCrumb, S. Foggy Mountain breakdown
McKnight, R. The kind of light that shines on Texas
McManus, J. June 1989
McManus, J. Megargel
McNally, J. The grand illusion
McNally, J. Smoke
McNally, J. The vomitorium
Meredith, D. Chevy in the fast lane
Metzger, T. Transorbital love probe
Meyers, K. Bird shadows
Michaels, L. Murderers
Mo Yan. Iron child
Morgan, R. Little Willie
Morgan, R. Pisgah
Moss, B. R. Blackbird
Muñoz, M. Campo
Muñoz, M. Not Nevada
Muñoz, M. Zigzagger
Nailah, A. My side of the story
Naiyer Masud. Sheesha ghat
Nawrocki, S. Farmer boy
Ndebele, N. S. The prophetess

Nordan, L. Sugar among the chickens
Norman, H. Unicycle
Oates, J. C. Cumberland breakdown
Oates, J. C. The ruins of Contracoeur
Oliver, C. A lake of summer
O'Neill, S. Butch
Ortiz, S. J. Something's going on
Padilla, M. Papel
Painter, P. No faith
Palwick, S. Going after Bobo
Papernick, J. Malchyk
Parker, G. The sheld-duck of the Basingstoke Canal
Parrish, T. Bonnie Ledet
Parrish, T. Complicity
Parrish, T. It pours
Partridge, N. Blackbirds
Penn, W. S. Cowboys and Indians
Penn, W. S. Neither
Perabo, S. Who I was supposed to be
Phillips, D. R. Why I'm talking
Phillips, R. S. Wolfie
Pirzad, Z. Sour cherry pits
Pittalwala, I. Ramadan
Prete, D. The biggest, most silent thing
Prete, D. No king, no puppy
Prete, D. Not because I'm thirsty
Puga, M. L. Naturally
Rawley, D. Baby Liz
Reifler, N. Upstream
Reiner, C. Heshie and Joey
Richter, S. A prodigy of longing
Ridgway, K. Fruit
Rifkin, A. The idols of sickness
Rinehart, S. American Arms
Roth, J. Youth
Rowell, J. The music of your life
Russo, R. Joy ride
Russo, R. The mysteries of Linwood Hart
Sánchez, R. Lucho
Saroyan, W. Resurrection of a life
Seepaul, L. Pan for Pockot
Seiffert, R. Dog-leg lane
Seiffert, R. Tentsmuir sands
Sharma, A. Surrounded by sleep
Sherwood, F. Basil the dog
Shonk, K. Our American
Singer, I. B. The power of darkness
Škvorecký, J. Feminine mystique
Slezak, E. By heart
Smith, M. M. Everybody goes
Smith, P. M. Oblivion, Nebraska
Sneve, V. D. H. Sun gazer
Spatz, G. Paradise was this
Spencer, E. First child
Spencer, E. The weekend travelers
Steavenson, W. Gika
Steele, M. The unripe heart
Steinbeck, T. The wool gatherer
Stollman, A. L. Enfleurage
Stollman, A. L. The little poet
Stollman, A. L. Mr. Mitochondria
Stollman, A. L. New memories
Straub, P. Bunny is good bread
Taylor, B. Walnuts, when the husks are green
Taylor, T. L. The resurrection plant
Theroux, P. A Judas memoir
Tinti, H. Slim's last ride
Tinti, H. Talk turkey

BOYS—*Continued*

Touré. Solomon's big day

Trevanian. Mrs. McGivney's nickel

Trevanian. Snatch off your cap, kid!

Ts'an-hsüeh. The child who raised poisonous snakes

Updike, J. Oliver's evolution

Vasseur, T. J. Noonan

Viganò, R. The big opportunity

Villanueva, A. Golden glass

Volkmer, J. The elevator man

Wang Anyi. Between themselves

Warren, R. P. Christmas gift

Waugh, E. Charles Ryder's schooldays

Waugh, E. Fragment of a novel

Waugh, E. A house of gentlefolks

Wells, K. Sherman and the swan

West, M. Diamonds

Wheat, C. Cousin Cora

White, E. Cinnamon skin

Wilbur, R. A game of catch

Williams, J. The last generation

Williams, M. The year Ward West took away the raccoon and Mr. Hanson's garage burneddown

Williamson, C. O come little children. . .

Williamson, J. The firefly tree

Wilson, R. C. The fields of Abraham

Wilson, R., Jr. Hard times

Winterson, J. The world and other places

Wolfe, G. The wrapper

Wolfe, T. O lost

Young, T. Kraut

Yuknavitch, L. The garden of earthly delights

Boys. Chekhov, A. P.

Boys. Gavell, M. L.

Boys. Moody, R.

Boys. Nawrocki, S.

The **boys**. Winter, E.

Boys: a new African fable. LaSalle, P.

The **boys** at night. Cohen, R.

Boys growing. Gartner, Z.

Boys keep being born. Frank, J.

Boys smell like oranges. Davenport, G.

The **boys** we were, the men we became. DeMarinis, R.

Braces. Barker, N.

Braces. Fulton, J.

Bracken, Michael

Feel the pain

Flesh and blood: guilty as sin; erotic tales of crime and passion; edited by Max Allan Collins and Jeff Gelb

Brackenbury, Rosalind

At the reef

Brackenbury, R. Between man and woman keys; stories

Between man and woman keys

Brackenbury, R. Between man and woman keys; stories

Chloe's pool

Brackenbury, R. Between man and woman keys; stories

Cuba run

Brackenbury, R. Between man and woman keys; stories

The forty-ninth lot joke

Brackenbury, R. Between man and woman keys; stories

Instead of the revolution

Brackenbury, R. Between man and woman keys; stories

The knowledge

Brackenbury, R. Between man and woman keys; stories

Nothing works in Homestead

Brackenbury, R. Between man and woman keys; stories

Brackett, Leigh

I feel bad killing you

A Century of noir; thirty-two classic crime stories; edited by Mickey Spillane and Max Allan Collins

The last days of Shandakor

The Good old stuff; adventure SF in the grand tradition; edited by Gardner Dozois

Bradbury, Ray

2004-05: The naming of names

Bradbury, R. Bradbury stories; 100 of his most celebrated tales

After the ball

Bradbury, R. One more for the road; a new short story collection

All my enemies are dead

Bradbury, R. The cat's pajamas; stories

All on a summer's night

Bradbury, R. Bradbury stories; 100 of his most celebrated tales

All summer in a day

The SFWA grand masters v2; edited by Frederik Pohl

Almost the end of the world

Bradbury, R. Bradbury stories; 100 of his most celebrated tales

And the rock cried out

Bradbury, R. Bradbury stories; 100 of his most celebrated tales

And the sailor, home from the sea

Bradbury, R. Bradbury stories; 100 of his most celebrated tales

Another fine mess

The Best from fantasy & science fiction: the fiftieth anniversary anthology; edited by Edward L. Ferman and Gordon Van Gelder

Bradbury, R. Bradbury stories; 100 of his most celebrated tales

Any friend of Nicholas Nickleby's is a friend of mine

Bradbury, R. Bradbury stories; 100 of his most celebrated tales

April 2005: Usher II

Bradbury, R. Bradbury stories; 100 of his most celebrated tales

April 2026: The long years

Bradbury, R. Bradbury stories; 100 of his most celebrated tales

At midnight, in the month of June

Bradbury, R. Bradbury stories; 100 of his most celebrated tales

Autumn afternoon

Bradbury, R. One more for the road; a new short story collection

Bang! You're dead!

Bradbury, R. Bradbury stories; 100 of his most celebrated tales

Banshee

Bradbury, R. Bradbury stories; 100 of his most celebrated tales

Bradbury, Ray—*Continued*

Beasts
  Bradbury, R. One more for the road; a new short story collection
The beautiful shave
  Bradbury, R. Bradbury stories; 100 of his most celebrated tales
The beggar on O'Connell Bridge
  Bradbury, R. Bradbury stories; 100 of his most celebrated tales
The black ferris
  The American fantasy tradition; edited by Brian M. Thomsen
A blade of grass
  Bradbury, R. Bradbury stories; 100 of his most celebrated tales
Bless me, Father, for I have sinned
  Bradbury, R. Bradbury stories; 100 of his most celebrated tales
Bright Phoenix
  Bradbury, R. Bradbury stories; 100 of his most celebrated tales
Bug
  Bradbury, R. Bradbury stories; 100 of his most celebrated tales
The burning man
  Bradbury, R. Bradbury stories; 100 of his most celebrated tales
By the numbers!
  Bradbury, R. Bradbury stories; 100 of his most celebrated tales
A careful man dies
  Bradbury, R. The cat's pajamas; stories
The cat's pajamas
  Bradbury, R. The cat's pajamas; stories
Changeling
  Bradbury, R. Bradbury stories; 100 of his most celebrated tales
Chrysalis
  Bradbury, R. The cat's pajamas; stories
The cistern
  Bradbury, R. Bradbury stories; 100 of his most celebrated tales
The city
  The SFWA grand masters v2; edited by Frederik Pohl
The cold wind and the warm
  Bradbury, R. Bradbury stories; 100 of his most celebrated tales
Colonel Stonesteel's genuine home-made truly Egyptian mummy
  Bradbury, R. Bradbury stories; 100 of his most celebrated tales
Colonel Stonesteel's genuine homemade truly Egyptian mummy
  Into the mummy's tomb; edited by John Richard Stephens
The completist
  Bradbury, R. The cat's pajamas; stories
The cricket on the hearth
  Bradbury, R. One more for the road; a new short story collection
Dark they were, and golden-eyed
  Masterpieces: the best science fiction of the century; edited by Orson Scott Card
The dead man
  Bradbury, R. Bradbury stories; 100 of his most celebrated tales

Death and the maiden
  Bradbury, R. Bradbury stories; 100 of his most celebrated tales
Diane de Forêt
  Bradbury, R. One more for the road; a new short story collection
Downwind from Gettysburg
  Bradbury, R. Bradbury stories; 100 of his most celebrated tales
The dragon
  Bradbury, R. Bradbury stories; 100 of his most celebrated tales
The dragon danced at midnight
  Bradbury, R. One more for the road; a new short story collection
The drummer boy of Shiloh
  Bradbury, R. Bradbury stories; 100 of his most celebrated tales
The dwarf
  Bradbury, R. Bradbury stories; 100 of his most celebrated tales
The enemy in the wheat
  Bradbury, R. One more for the road; a new short story collection
The exiles
  Bradbury, R. Bradbury stories; 100 of his most celebrated tales
Exorcism
  Witches' brew; edited by Yvonne Jocks
The R.B., G.K.C. and G.B.S. forever Orient
  Bradbury, R. The cat's pajamas; stories
The F. Scott/Tolstoy/Ahab accumulator
  Bradbury, R. One more for the road; a new short story collection
A far-away guitar
  Bradbury, R. Bradbury stories; 100 of his most celebrated tales
February 1999: Y11a
  Bradbury, R. Bradbury stories; 100 of his most celebrated tales
The Finnegan
  Bradbury, R. Bradbury stories; 100 of his most celebrated tales
First day
  Bradbury, R. One more for the road; a new short story collection
The first night of Lent
  Bradbury, R. Bradbury stories; 100 of his most celebrated tales
The flying machine
  Bradbury, R. Bradbury stories; 100 of his most celebrated tales
Fore!
  Bradbury, R. One more for the road; a new short story collection
Forever and the Earth
  Bradbury, R. Bradbury stories; 100 of his most celebrated tales
The fruit at the bottom of the bowl
  Bradbury, R. Bradbury stories; 100 of his most celebrated tales
G.B.S.- Mark V
  Bradbury, R. Bradbury stories; 100 of his most celebrated tales
The garbage collector
  Bradbury, R. Bradbury stories; 100 of his most celebrated tales

Bradbury, Ray—*Continued*

Getting through Sunday somehow
  Bradbury, R. Bradbury stories; 100 of his most celebrated tales
The ghosts
  Bradbury, R. The cat's pajamas; stories
The great collision of Monday last
  Bradbury, R. Bradbury stories; 100 of his most celebrated tales
Hail to the chief
  Bradbury, R. The cat's pajamas; stories
The handler
  Bradbury, R. Bradbury stories; 100 of his most celebrated tales
Heart transplant
  Bradbury, R. One more for the road; a new short story collection
Heavy set
  Bradbury, R. Bradbury stories; 100 of his most celebrated tales
Henry the Ninth
  Bradbury, R. Bradbury stories; 100 of his most celebrated tales
Hopscotch
  Bradbury, R. Bradbury stories; 100 of his most celebrated tales
The house
  Bradbury, R. The cat's pajamas; stories
I get the blues when it rains (A remembrance)
  Bradbury, R. The cat's pajamas; stories
I see you never
  Bradbury, R. Bradbury stories; 100 of his most celebrated tales
Icarus Montgolfier Wright
  Bradbury, R. Bradbury stories; 100 of his most celebrated tales
The illustrated man
  Bradbury, R. Bradbury stories; 100 of his most celebrated tales
In memoriam
  Bradbury, R. One more for the road; a new short story collection
The island
  Bradbury, R. The cat's pajamas; stories
The John Wilkes Booth/Warner Brothers/MGM/NBC funeral train
  Bradbury, R. The cat's pajamas; stories
June 2001: And the moon be still as bright
  Bradbury, R. Bradbury stories; 100 of his most celebrated tales
June 2003: Way in the middle of the air
  Bradbury, R. Bradbury stories; 100 of his most celebrated tales
Junior
  Bradbury, R. Bradbury stories; 100 of his most celebrated tales
The Kilimanjaro device
  Bradbury, R. Bradbury stories; 100 of his most celebrated tales
Lafayette, farewell
  Bradbury, R. Bradbury stories; 100 of his most celebrated tales
Last rites
  Bradbury, R. Bradbury stories; 100 of his most celebrated tales
The Laurel and Hardy Alpha Centauri farewell tour
  Bradbury, R. One more for the road; a new short story collection

The Laurel and Hardy love affair
  Bradbury, R. Bradbury stories; 100 of his most celebrated tales
Leftovers
  Bradbury, R. One more for the road; a new short story collection
Let's play poison
  Bradbury, R. Bradbury stories; 100 of his most celebrated tales
The lifework of Juan Diaz
  Bradbury, R. Bradbury stories; 100 of his most celebrated tales
A little journey
  Bradbury, R. Bradbury stories; 100 of his most celebrated tales
The lonely ones
  Bradbury, R. Bradbury stories; 100 of his most celebrated tales
The love affair
  Mars probes; edited by Peter Crowther
The machineries of joy
  Bradbury, R. Bradbury stories; 100 of his most celebrated tales
The Mafioso cement-mixing machine
  Bradbury, R. The cat's pajamas; stories
The man
  Bradbury, R. Bradbury stories; 100 of his most celebrated tales
The man in the Rorschach shirt
  Bradbury, R. Bradbury stories; 100 of his most celebrated tales
Mars is heaven!
  The Science fiction hall of fame: volume one, 1929-1964; the greatest science fiction stories of all time chosen by the members of the Science Fiction Writers of America; edited by Robert Silverberg
A matter of taste
  Bradbury, R. The cat's pajamas; stories
The meadow
  Bradbury, R. Bradbury stories; 100 of his most celebrated tales
Memento mori
  Gathering the bones; original stories from the world's masters of horror; edited by Dennis Etchison, Ramsey Campbell and Jack Dann
The Messiah
  Bradbury, R. Bradbury stories; 100 of his most celebrated tales
The million-year picnic
  The SFWA grand masters v2; edited by Frederik Pohl
The miracles of Jamie
  Bradbury, R. Bradbury stories; 100 of his most celebrated tales
My son, Max
  Bradbury, R. One more for the road; a new short story collection
The nineteenth
  Bradbury, R. One more for the road; a new short story collection
No news; or, What killed the dog?
  Bradbury, R. Bradbury stories; 100 of his most celebrated tales
Olé Orozco! Siqueiros, sí!
  Bradbury, R. The cat's pajamas; stories
On the Orient, North
  Bradbury, R. Bradbury stories; 100 of his most celebrated tales

Bradbury, Ray—*Continued*

Once more, Legato
  Bradbury, R. Bradbury stories; 100 of his most celebrated tales
One for his lordship, and one for the road
  Bradbury, R. Bradbury stories; 100 of his most celebrated tales
One more for the road
  Bradbury, R. One more for the road; a new short story collection
One-woman show
  Bradbury, R. One more for the road; a new short story collection
The pedestrian
  Bradbury, R. Bradbury stories; 100 of his most celebrated tales
The poems
  Bradbury, R. Bradbury stories; 100 of his most celebrated tales
The pumpernickel
  Bradbury, R. Bradbury stories; 100 of his most celebrated tales
Quid pro quo
  Bradbury, R. One more for the road; a new short story collection
Remember Sascha?
  Bradbury, R. Bradbury stories; 100 of his most celebrated tales
The rocket
  Bradbury, R. Bradbury stories; 100 of his most celebrated tales
The sea shell
  Bradbury, R. Bradbury stories; 100 of his most celebrated tales
Season of disbelief
  Bradbury, R. Bradbury stories; 100 of his most celebrated tales
Sixty-six
  Bradbury, R. The cat's pajamas; stories
The smile
  Bradbury, R. Bradbury stories; 100 of his most celebrated tales
The smiling people
  Bradbury, R. Bradbury stories; 100 of his most celebrated tales
Sometime before dawn
  Bradbury, R. The cat's pajamas; stories
The sound of summer running
  Bradbury, R. Bradbury stories; 100 of his most celebrated tales
The square pegs
  Bradbury, R. Bradbury stories; 100 of his most celebrated tales
The swan
  Bradbury, R. Bradbury stories; 100 of his most celebrated tales
Tangerine
  Bradbury, R. One more for the road; a new short story collection
Tête-à-tête
  Bradbury, R. One more for the road; a new short story collection
There will come soft rains
  The SFWA grand masters v2; edited by Frederik Pohl
Time in hy flight
  Bradbury, R. Bradbury stories; 100 of his most celebrated tales

Time intervening/interim
  Bradbury, R. Bradbury stories; 100 of his most celebrated tales
Time intervening
  Bradbury, R. One more for the road; a new short story collection
The Toynbee convection
  Bradbury, R. Bradbury stories; 100 of his most celebrated tales
The transformation
  Bradbury, R. The cat's pajamas; stories
Trapdoor
  Bradbury, R. Bradbury stories; 100 of his most celebrated tales
Triangle
  Bradbury, R. The cat's pajamas; stories
The trolley
  Bradbury, R. Bradbury stories; 100 of his most celebrated tales
Ulnterderseaboat dokfor
  Bradbury, R. Bradbury stories; 100 of his most celebrated tales
The veldt
  Science-fiction classics; the stories that morphed into movies; compiled by Forrest J. Ackerman
The visitor
  Bradbury, R. Bradbury stories; 100 of his most celebrated tales
The watchers
  Bradbury, R. Bradbury stories; 100 of his most celebrated tales
The watchful poker chip of H. Matisse
  Bradbury, R. Bradbury stories; 100 of his most celebrated tales
We'll just act natural
  Bradbury, R. The cat's pajamas; stories
Well, what do you have to say for yourself?
  Bradbury, R. One more for the road; a new short story collection
Where all is emptiness there is room to move
  Bradbury, R. One more for the road; a new short story collection
Where's my hat, what's my hurry?
  Bradbury, R. The cat's pajamas; stories
The whole town's sleeping
  Bradbury, R. Bradbury stories; 100 of his most celebrated tales
A wild night in Galway
  Bradbury, R. Bradbury stories; 100 of his most celebrated tales
The wind
  Bradbury, R. Bradbury stories; 100 of his most celebrated tales
The wish
  Bradbury, R. Bradbury stories; 100 of his most celebrated tales
The witch doctor
  Bradbury, R. Bradbury stories; 100 of his most celebrated tales
With smiles as wide as summer
  Bradbury, R. One more for the road; a new short story collection
The woman on the lawn
  Bradbury, R. Bradbury stories; 100 of his most celebrated tales
The wonderful death of Dudley Stone
  Bradbury, R. Bradbury stories; 100 of his most celebrated tales

Bradbury, Ray—*Continued*
Zero hour
    Bradbury, R. Bradbury stories; 100 of his
        most celebrated tales
Bradfield, Scott
Goldilocks tells all
    Black heart, ivory bones; [edited by] Ellen
        Datlow & Terri Windling
Bradford, Arthur
Dogs
    Esquire v132 no1 p92-97+ Jl 1999
Insects
    Esquire v135 no6 p152-3, 160-1 Je 2001
Little Rodney
    Bomb no76 p90-2 Summ 2001
South for the winter
    Esquire v131 no2 p152 F 1999
Brady, Catherine
And the shin bone's connected to the knee bone
    Brady, C. The end of the class war
Chatter
    Brady, C. The end of the class war
The custom of the country
    Brady, C. The end of the class war
Daley's girls
    Brady, C. The end of the class war
Don't run
    Brady, C. The end of the class war
Driving
    Brady, C. The end of the class war
The end of the class war
    Brady, C. The end of the class war
Home movies
    Brady, C. The end of the class war
Let my right hand forget her cunning
    Brady, C. The end of the class war
The lives of the saints
    Brady, C. The end of the class war
Pilgrimage
    Brady, C. The end of the class war
Rat
    Brady, C. The end of the class war
Rumpelstiltskin
    Brady, C. The end of the class war
Wild, wild horses
    Brady, C. The end of the class war
BRADY, MATHEW B., CA. 1823-1896
About
Rusch, K. K. The gallery of his dreams
Brady, William S., 1938-
    *For works written by this author under oth-
    er names see* Harvey, John, 1938-
BRAHE, TYCHO, 1546-1601
About
MacKay, S. The sages of Cassiopeia
Brahen, Marilyn Mattie
Trick or treat with Jesus
    The Ultimate Halloween; edited by Marvin
        Kaye
The **braid**. Avrich, J.
The **braid**. Matiella, A. C.
BRAIN
Blumlein, M. Know how, can do
Carneiro, A. Brain transplant
Chiang, T. Understand
Experiments
Keyes, D. Flowers for Algernon
The **brain's** closed castle. Sammān, G.
Brains of the Operation. McNally, J.

Brammer, Billy Lee
The Gay Place [excerpt]
    Graham, D. Lone Star literature; from the
        Red River to the Rio Grande; edited by
        Don Graham
Brammer, William *See* Brammer, Billy Lee,
1930-1978
Bramson. Chinodya, S.
Brand, Christianna
Clever and quick
    A moment on the edge; 100 years of crime
        stories by women; edited by Elizabeth
        George
Brand, Dionne
Madame Alaird's breasts
    The Vintage book of international lesbian fic-
        tion; edited and with an introduction by
        Naomi Holoch and Joan Nestle
Brand, Marlais Olmstead
Closer than you think
    Best new American voices 2000; guest editor
        Tobias Wolff; series editors John Kulka
        and Natalie Danford
Brand, Max
The bright face of danger
    Brand, M. The bright face of danger; a James
        Geraldi trio
Eagles over Crooked Creek
    The First Five Star western corral; western
        stories; edited by Jon Tuska and Vicki
        Piekarski
The Golden Horus
    Brand, M. The bright face of danger; a James
        Geraldi trio
Through steel and stone
    Brand, M. The bright face of danger; a James
        Geraldi trio
Wine on the desert
    A Century of great Western stories; edited by
        John Jakes
Brand, Rebecca *See* Charnas, Suzy McKee
The **brand** new suit. Sánchez, R.
Branded. Phillips, G.
Brandner, Gary
Heat lightning
    A Hot and sultry night for crime; edited by
        Jeffery Deaver
Brandon, Paul
The marsh runners
    Dreaming down-under; edited by Jack Dann
        and Janeen Webb
Brandt, William
All day sun
    Brandt, W. Alpha male
His father's shoes
    Brandt, W. Alpha male
The Jean-Paul Sartre experience
    Brandt, W. Alpha male
Paradise Cove
    Brandt, W. Alpha male
Rat
    Brandt, W. Alpha male
Brantenberg, Gerd
Four winds [excerpt]
    The Vintage book of international lesbian fic-
        tion; edited and with an introduction by
        Naomi Holoch and Joan Nestle

Brathwaite, Edward Kamau
Dream Haiti
The Oxford book of Caribbean short stories; edited by Stewart Brown and John Wickham
My funny Valentine
Whispers from the cotton tree root; Caribbean fabulist fiction; edited by Nalo Hopkinson
Brathwaite, Kamau *See* Brathwaite, Edward Kamau, 1930-
Brau, Edgar
The Child
The Literary Review (Madison, N.J.) v47 no2 p36-58 Wint 2004
The Forgotten God
The Antioch Review v61 no3 p569-71 Summ 2003
The Prisoner
The Literary Review (Madison, N.J.) v46 no1 p69-77 Fall 2002
Braun, Matthew
The stand
Westward; a fictional history of the American West : 28 original stories celebrating the 50th anniversary of the Western Writers of America; edited by Dale L. Walker
Braunbeck, Gary A.
Captain Jim's drunken dream
Lighthouse hauntings; 12 original tales of the supernatural; edited by Charles G. Waugh & Martin H. Greenberg
Curtain call
Dracula in London; edited by P. N. Elrod
Down in darkest Dixie where the dead don't dance
Mardi Gras madness; tales of terror and mayhem in New Orleans; edited by Martin H. Greenberg and Russell Davis
Mail-order Annie
Cat crimes through time; edited by Ed Gorman, Martin H. Greenberg, and Larry Segriff
Palimpsest day
Past imperfect; edited by Martin H. Greenberg and Larry Segriff
Safe
The Best American mystery stories, 1999; edited and with an introduction by Ed McBain
Small song
The Year's best fantasy & horror, thirteenth annual collection; edited by Ellen Datlow and Terri Windling
Who am a passer by
Past lives, present tense; edited by Elizabeth Ann Scarborough
Brave girl. Davies, P. H.
Brave newer world. Harrison, H.
The **braver** thing. Le May, A.
Braverman, Kate
Tall tales from the Mekong Delta
The Scribner anthology of contemporary short fiction; fifty North American stories since 1970; Lex Williford and Michael Martone, editors
Temporary light
LA shorts; edited by Steven Gilbar
Bravo America. Yuknavitch, L.
Brawith. Purdy, J.

Brazaitis, Mark
The heroes of our stories
Living on the edge; fiction by Peace Corps writers; edited by John Coyne
A kind of flight
U.S. Catholic v64 no6 p30-33 Je 1999
BRAZIL
L'Amour, L. Wings over Brazil
Waugh, E. The man who liked Dickens
Rio de Janeiro
Simonds, M. Nossa Senhora dos Remédios
BREACH OF PROMISE
Shade, E. Hoops and wires and plugs
Bread. Rachmil, B.
Bread and the Land. Allen, J. R.
Bread from a stone. Allegra, D.
Bread, money, and liberty. Raphael, F.
The **bread** of affliction. Kahn, M. A.
The **breadnut** and the breadfruit. Condé, M.
Break any woman down. Johnson, D.
Breakdown and bereavement [excerpt] Brenner, Y. H.
Breakfast at Woolworth's, 1956. Folayan, A.
Breakheart Valley. Newton, D. B.
Breaking and Entering. Pollack, E.
Breaking curfew. Doyle, M.
Breaking faith. Jackson, V. F.
Breaking strain. Clarke, A. C.
Breaking the pig. Keret, E.
Breaking the sabbath. Goliger, G.
Breaking the speed record. Peri Rossi, C.
Breakout. Vollmann, W. T.
The **breakup** ceremony. Touré
BREAST
Barker, N. Popping corn
Charnas, S. M. Boobs
D'Haene, E. Breasts
Flythe, S. A family of breast feeders
Goto, H. Tales from the breast
Hoffman, N. K. Savage breasts
Rodgers, S. J. Bust
Radiography
See Mammography
Breasts. D'Haene, E.
A **breath** holding contest. Vukcevich, R.
Breathe deep. Westlake, D. E.
Breathmoss. MacLeod, I.
Brecht, Bertolt
Etiquette in dark times
Harper's v303 no1814 p31-2 Jl 2001
Bred for battle. Runyon, D.
Breen, John V.
A man alone
Westward; a fictional history of the American West : 28 original stories celebrating the 50th anniversary of the Western Writers of America; edited by Dale L. Walker
Breen, Jon L.
The adventure of the mooning sentry
Murder, my dear Watson; new tales of Sherlock Holmes; edited by Martin H. Greenberg, Jon Lellenberg, Daniel Stashower
The adventures of the Cheshire Cheese
The World's finest mystery and crime stories, third annual collection; edited by Ed Gorman and Martin H. Greenberg
All-star team
Breen, J. L. Kill the umpire; the calls of Ed Gorgon

Breen, Jon L.—*Continued*
The Babe Ruth murder case
Breen, J. L. Kill the umpire; the calls of Ed Gorgon
The big nap
Breen, J. L. The drowning icecube and other stories
The body in the bullpen
Breen, J. L. Kill the umpire; the calls of Ed Gorgon
Captain Benvolio Bullhorner
Breen, J. L. The drowning icecube and other stories
The cat and the Kinetophone
Breen, J. L. The drowning icecube and other stories
Cat crimes through time; edited by Ed Gorman, Martin H. Greenberg, and Larry Segriff
Clever Hans
Breen, J. L. The drowning icecube and other stories
Credit the cat
Breen, J. L. The drowning icecube and other stories
Designated murderer
Breen, J. L. Kill the umpire; the calls of Ed Gorgon
Diamond Dick
Breen, J. L. Kill the umpire; the calls of Ed Gorgon
The drowning icecube
Breen, J. L. The drowning icecube and other stories
Fall of a hero
Breen, J. L. Kill the umpire; the calls of Ed Gorgon
Four views of justice
Breen, J. L. The drowning icecube and other stories
Horsehide sleuth
Breen, J. L. Kill the umpire; the calls of Ed Gorgon
Immortality
Breen, J. L. The drowning icecube and other stories
Insider trading
Breen, J. L. Kill the umpire; the calls of Ed Gorgon
Instant replay
Breen, J. L. Kill the umpire; the calls of Ed Gorgon
It's hard to dance with the devil on your back (with Rita A. Breen)
Breen, J. L. The drowning icecube and other stories
Jerry Brogan and the Kilkenny cats
Breen, J. L. The drowning icecube and other stories
Kill the umpire
Breen, J. L. Kill the umpire; the calls of Ed Gorgon
Longevity has its place
Breen, J. L. The drowning icecube and other stories
The male and female hogan
Murder most Celtic; tall tales of Irish mayhem; edited by Martin H. Greenberg

Malice at the mike
Breen, J. L. Kill the umpire; the calls of Ed Gorgon
The Mother's-Day doubleheader
Breen, J. L. Kill the umpire; the calls of Ed Gorgon
Breen, J. L. The drowning icecube and other stories
The number 12 jinx
Breen, J. L. Kill the umpire; the calls of Ed Gorgon
Old-timers' game
Breen, J. L. Kill the umpire; the calls of Ed Gorgon
A piece of the auction
Breen, J. L. The drowning icecube and other stories
The Pun Detective and the Danny Boy killer
Breen, J. L. The drowning icecube and other stories
Silver Spectre
Breen, J. L. The drowning icecube and other stories
Streak to death
Breen, J. L. Kill the umpire; the calls of Ed Gorgon
The tarnished star
Breen, J. L. The drowning icecube and other stories
Throw out the first ax
Breen, J. L. Kill the umpire; the calls of Ed Gorgon
Woollcott and the vamp
Breen, J. L. The drowning icecube and other stories
Breeze, Jean Binta
Sunday cricket
The Oxford book of Caribbean short stories; edited by Stewart Brown and John Wickham
Brenchley, Chaz
The keys to D'Espérance
Best new horror 10; edited and with an introduction by Stephen Jones
Brendan. Mathews, H.
Brenna, Duff
The law of falling bodies
New Letters v68 no1 p73-96 2001
Brennan, Karen
The man with the spotted dog
Ploughshares v25 no1 p118-20 Spr 1999
Mary Ann
Ploughshares v25 no1 p121-25 Spr 1999
The phantom ship
Ploughshares v25 no1 p126-28 Spr 1999
Brennan, Maeve
The anachronism
Brennan, M. The rose garden; short stories
The beginning of a long story
Brennan, M. The rose garden; short stories
The Bohemians
Brennan, M. The rose garden; short stories
The bride
Brennan, M. The rose garden; short stories
The children are there, trying not to laugh
Brennan, M. The rose garden; short stories
The children are very quiet when they are away
Brennan, M. The rose garden; short stories

Brennan, Maeve—*Continued*

The daughters
  Brennan, M. The rose garden; short stories
The divine fireplace
  Brennan, M. The rose garden; short stories
The door on West Tenth Street
  Brennan, M. The rose garden; short stories
The gentleman in the pink-and-white striped
    shirt
  Brennan, M. The rose garden; short stories
The holy terror
  Brennan, M. The rose garden; short stories
I see you, Bianca
  Brennan, M. The rose garden; short stories
  Wonderful town; New York stories from The
    New Yorker; edited by David Remnick
    with Susan Choi
In and out of never-never land
  Brennan, M. The rose garden; short stories
The joker
  Brennan, M. The rose garden; short stories
A large bee
  Brennan, M. The rose garden; short stories
The rose garden
  Brennan, M. The rose garden; short stories
The servants' dance
  Brennan, M. The rose garden; short stories
A snowy night on West Forty-ninth Street
  Brennan, M. The rose garden; short stories
The stone hot-water bottle
  Brennan, M. The rose garden; short stories
The view from the kitchen
  Brennan, M. The rose garden; short stories

Brenner, Wendy

The anomalist
  Brenner, W. Phone calls from the dead; sto-
    ries
Are we almost there
  Brenner, W. Phone calls from the dead; sto-
    ries
Awareness
  Brenner, W. Phone calls from the dead; sto-
    ries
The Cantankerous Judge
  Brenner, W. Phone calls from the dead; sto-
    ries
Four squirrels
  Brenner, W. Phone calls from the dead; sto-
    ries
The   human   side   of   instrumental
    transcommunication
  Brenner, W. Phone calls from the dead; sto-
    ries
  New stories from the South: the year's best,
    1999; edited by Shannon Ravenel; with a
    preface by Tony Earley
Mr. Meek
  Brenner, W. Phone calls from the dead; sto-
    ries
Mr. Puniverse
  Brenner, W. Phone calls from the dead; sto-
    ries
  New stories from the South: the year's best,
    2000; edited by Shannon Ravenel; with a
    preface by Ellen Douglas
Nipple
  Brenner, W. Phone calls from the dead; sto-
    ries
  Seventeen v60 no9 p190-2 S 2001

Remnants of Earl
  Brenner, W. Phone calls from the dead; sto-
    ries

Brenner, Yosef Haim

Breakdown and bereavement [excerpt]
  Sleepwalkers and other stories; the Arab in
    Hebrew fiction; edited by Ehud Ben-Ezer

Brennert, Alan

Her pilgrim soul
  The American fantasy tradition; edited by Bri-
    an M. Thomsen

Brett, Simon

Best behaviour
  Crème de la crime; edited by Janet Hutchings
Exit, pursued
  The best British mysteries; edited by Maxim
    Jakubowski
The girls in Villa Costas
  Speaking of lust; stories of forbidden desire;
    edited by Lawrence Block
Letter to his son
  Murder most postal; homicidal tales that de-
    liver a message; edited by Martin H.
    Greenberg
A note of note
  Malice domestic 10; an anthology of original
    traditional mystery stories

Brewer, Gil

The gesture
  A Century of noir; thirty-two classic crime
    stories; edited by Mickey Spillane and Max
    Allan Collins
Sauce for the goose
  Speaking of lust; stories of forbidden desire;
    edited by Lawrence Block

BREWSTER, SIR DAVID, 1781-1868
                    About
  Enright, A. Men and angels
The **bribe**. Borges, J. L.
BRIBERY
  Cherryh, C. J. Highliner
  Fuchs, D. Man in the middle of the ocean
  Hodgson, W. H. The red herring
Brickhouse, Robert
Night deposit
  The Virginia Quarterly Review v77 no1 p63-
    75 Wint 2001
BRICKLAYERS
  Morgan, R. Poinsett's Bridge
Bricolage; or, This side of the animal. Lish, G.
Bridal flowers. Cannell, D.
The **bride**. Brennan, M.
The **bride**. Callaghan, M.
The **bride**. Carter, E.
The **bride**. Dorrie, D.
The **bride**. See Chekhov, A. P. Betrothed
Bride of Angels. Mortaz, M.
The **bridegroom**. Ha Jin
Brides by night. Rosero Diago, E.
The **bride's** secret. Kohler, S.
The **bridesmaid**. Campbell, B. J.
The **bridge**. Dubnov, E.
The **bridge**. Galloway, J.
The **Bridge**. Holladay, C.
The **bridge**. Painter, P.
The **bridge** [excerpt] Banks, I.
The **Bridge** by Moonlight. Mayhoff, S.
The **bridge** players. Smart, A.
The **Bridge** Playing Ladies. Lear, P.

BRIDGER, JAMES, 1804-1881
About
House, R. Gabe and the doctor
Bridger, Jim *See* Bridger, James, 1804-1881
BRIDGES
Chekhov, A. P. The new villa
Morgan, R. Poinsett's Bridge
Nelson, K. Tides
Bridgford, Kim
Crazy people
Dalhousie Review v79 no2 p203-19 Summ
1999
In the Yellow House
Dalhousie Review v82 no2 p255-62 Summ
2002
A **brief** comedy. Régio, J.
The **brief** confession of an unrepentant erotic.
Gifford, B.
Brief Family Statment [i.e. Statement]. Bundy, A.
A **brief** geological guide to canyon country.
Hackbarth, P.
A **brief** history of condoms. Addonizio, K.
The **Brief** History of the Dead. Brockmeier, K.
Brief interviews with hideous men [I]. Wallace, D.
F.
Brief interviews with hideous men [II]. Wallace,
D. F.
Brief interviews with hideous men [III]. Wallace,
D. F.
Brief interviews with hideous men [IV]. Wallace,
D. F.
A **brief** reappearance by Florence, this autumn.
Bryce Echenique, A.
A **brief** spell by the river. McElroy, C. J.
A **brief** Washington-Mount Vernon chronology,
followed by an aborted picnic at the Holo-
caust Museum. Cheuse, A.
BRIGANDS AND ROBBERS
See also Outlaws; Robbery
Bowles, P. Istikhara, Anaya, Medagan and the
Medaganat
Fitzgerald, F. S. Dalyrimple goes wrong
Pushkin, A. S. Dubrovskii
Pushkin, A. S. Kirdzhali
Saro-Wiwa, K. Africa kills her sun
Spencer, J. The robbers of Karnataka
Briggs, Charles Frederick
Elegant Tom Dillar
PMLA v116 no2 p408-15 Mr 2001
Bright and morning star. Wright, R.
The **bright** face of danger. Brand, M.
Bright red apples. Carver, R.
Bright segment. Sturgeon, T.
A **brightness** new & welcoming. Morgan, R.
Brill, Toni
O! little town of Bedlam
Mystery midrash; an anthology of Jewish
mystery & detective fiction; [edited by]
Lawrence W. Raphael
Brilliant. Spence, A.
Brilliant company. Carson, J.
Brilliant disguise. Chan, D. M.
Brin, David
Temptation
Far horizons; all new tales from the greatest
worlds of science fiction; edited by Robert
Silverberg
Brina. Kilpatrick, N.
Bring the jubilee. Moore, W.

Bringing home the bones. Campbell, B. J.
Bringing in the sheaves. Rucker, R. v. B.
Bringing me up it never stops. Painter, P.
Brisa. Gilb, D.
Brite, Poppy Z.
O death, where is thy spatula?
The Mammoth book of best horror 13; edited
by Stephen Jones
Brite, Poppy Z. and Faust, Christa
Saved
Typical girls; new stories by smart women;
edited by Susan Corrigan
Brite, Poppy Z. and Ferguson, David
The curious case of Miss Violet Stone
Shadows over Baker Street; edited by Michael
Reaves and John Pelan
BRITISH
Africa
Gordimer, N. Mission statement
Haggard, H. R. Black heart and white heart: a
Zulu idyl
Arabian Peninsula
Johnson-Davies, D. Deal concluded
Johnson-Davies, D. Fate of a prisoner
Johnson-Davies, D. Oleanders pink and white
Argentina
Borges, J. L. Story of the warrior and the cap-
tive maiden
China
Su, D. L.-q. Beijing opera [excerpt]
Egypt
Johnson-Davies, D. Coffee at the Marriott
Johnson-Davies, D. A taxi to himself
Finland
Weldon, F. GUP—or, Falling in love in Helsin-
ki
France
Barnes, J. Evermore
Byatt, A. S. Crocodile tears
Byatt, A. S. A lamia in the Cévennes
Dunmore, H. Lisette
Fischer, T. We ate the chef
Hoch, E. D. The Club of Masks
Johnson-Davies, D. A short weekend
Kureishi, H. Midnight all day
Melville, P. Provenance of a face
India
Barrett, A. Servants of the map
Borges, J. L. The man on the threshold
Padilla, I. Darjeeling
Stevenson, J. The Colonel and Judy O'Grady
Italy
Barker, N. The Piazza Barberini
Lavin, M. Trastevere
Lebbon, T. The repulsion
Vivante, A. To mock the years
Java (Indonesia)
Padilla, I. Amends in Halak-Proot
Kenya
Johnson-Davies, D. Two worlds
Lebanon
Albert, J. Byron
Johnson-Davies, D. Open season in Beirut
Malaysia
Fowler, C. The green man
Mexico
Lida, D. Shuttered
Rendell, R. The beach butler

BRITISH—*Continued*
Middle East
Johnson-Davies, D. Slice of the cake
Morocco
Bowles, P. Dinner at Sir Nigel's
Bowles, P. Madame and Ahmed
Waugh, E. My father's house
Netherlands
Campbell, R. The body in the window
Nigeria
Kalu, Anthonia C. Angelus
Kalu, Anthonia C. Independence
Pakistan
Bail, M. A, B, C, D, E, F, G, H, I, J, K, L, M,
    N, O, P, Q, R, S, T, U, V, W, X, Y, Z
Sicily
Holliday, L. Provenance
Somalia
Farah, N. My father, the Englishman, and I
Spain
Bocock, M. Death is where you find it
O'Loughlin, M. The making of a bureaucrat
Sudan
Johnson-Davies, D. The garden of Sheikh Osman
Tanzania
Gurnah, A. Escort
Trinidad and Tobago
Sherwood, F. Basil the dog
Tunisia
Davis, C. A. Not long now
United States
Amis, M. The coincidence of the arts
Davies, P. H. How to be an expatriate
Hawthorne, N. Howe's masquerade
James, H. An international episode
Rendell, R. Catamount
Updike, J. A trillion feet of gas
Wharton, E. The pretext
West Indies
Rhys, J. Pioneers, oh, pioneers
Yugoslavia
Symons, J. A theme for Hyacinth
Zambia
Padilla, I. Rhodesia Express
BRITISH ARISTOCRACY *See* Aristocracy—
    England
BRITISH GUIANA *See* Guyana
BRITISH SOLDIERS *See* Soldiers—Great Britain
BRITISH WEST INDIES *See* West Indies
BRITTANY (FRANCE) *See* France—Brittany
Britto García, Luis
Future
    Cosmos latinos: an anthology of science fiction from Latin America and Spain; translated, edited, & with an introduction & notes by Andrea L. Bell & Yolanda Molina-Gavilán
Brkic, Courtney Angela
Adiyo, kerido
    Brkic, C. A. Stillness and other stories
Afterdamp
    Brkic, C. A. Stillness and other stories
The angled city
    Brkic, C. A. Stillness and other stories
Canis lupus
    Brkic, C. A. Stillness and other stories

The daughter
    Brkic, C. A. Stillness and other stories
In the jasmine shade
    Brkic, C. A. Stillness and other stories
Passage
    Brkic, C. A. Stillness and other stories
The peacebroker
    Brkic, C. A. Stillness and other stories
Remains
    Brkic, C. A. Stillness and other stories
Stillness
    Brkic, C. A. Stillness and other stories
Surveillance
    Brkic, C. A. Stillness and other stories
Suspension
    Brkic, C. A. Stillness and other stories
Swimming out
    Brkic, C. A. Stillness and other stories
We will sleep in one nest
    Brkic, C. A. Stillness and other stories
Where none is the number
    Brkic, C. A. Stillness and other stories
The **Broad** Estates of Death. Fox, P.
Broad from abroad. Brownrigg, S.
The **Broadcast**. Mathews, H.
Broadcasts from the flood. Chacko, M.
Broccoli. Vapnyar, L.
Brockmeier, Kevin
Apples
    Brockmeier, K. Things that fall from the sky
The Brief History of the Dead
    The New Yorker v79 no25 p76-83 S 8 2003
The ceiling
    Brockmeier, K. Things that fall from the sky
A day in the life of half of Rumpelstiltskin
    Brockmeier, K. Things that fall from the sky
The green children
    The Year's best fantasy & horror: sixteenth annual collection; edited by Ellen Datlow & Terri Windling
The house at the end of the world
    Brockmeier, K. Things that fall from the sky
The Jesus stories
    Brockmeier, K. Things that fall from the sky
The light through the window
    Brockmeier, K. Things that fall from the sky
The passenger
    Brockmeier, K. Things that fall from the sky
Small degrees
    Brockmeier, K. Things that fall from the sky
Space
    The Best American short stories, 2003; selected from U.S. and Canadian magazines by Walter Mosley with Katrina Kenison; with an introduction by Walter Mosley
    Brockmeier, K. Things that fall from the sky
    The Georgia Review v56 no2 p479-88 Summ 2002
These hands
    Brockmeier, K. Things that fall from the sky
    The Georgia Review v53 no3 p441-67 Fall 1999
    Prize stories, 2000; The O. Henry awards; edited and with an introduction by Larry Dark
Things that fall from the sky
    Brockmeier, K. Things that fall from the sky

Broderick, Damien
The Magi
Centaurus: the best of Australian science fiction; edited by David G. Hartwell and Damien Broderick
The womb
Dreaming down-under; edited by Jack Dann and Janeen Webb
Brodie's report. Borges, J. L.
Brodkey, Harold
Innocence
Neurotica: Jewish writers on sex; edited by Melvin Jules Bukiet
Verona: a young woman speaks
The Best American short stories of the century; John Updike, editor, Katrina Kenison, coeditor; with an introduction by John Updike
Brodoff, Ami Sands
Bloodknots
TriQuarterly no105 p125-44 Spr/Summ 1999
Brodsky, Louis Daniel
O.J., can you see?
The Literary Review (Madison, N.J.) v42 no2 p298-300 Wint 1999
Brokeback Mountain. Proulx, A.
Broken. Ha Jin
Broken binoculars. Marías, J.
Broken stone. O'Neill, S.
Broks, Paul
The sea horse and the almond
Granta no75 p237-55 Aut 2001
Bronagh. Azadeh, C.
El **Bronco** y La Lechuza. Saldaña, R.
Broner, E. M.
Angels, saints and their friends
The Massachusetts Review v40 no4 p503-19 Wint 1999/2000
BRONX (NEW YORK, N.Y.) *See* New York (N.Y.)—Bronx
Brookhouse, Christopher
Naked
Gettysburg Review v15 no3 p371-84 Aut 2002
Posing
Gettysburg Review v12 no3 p461-63 Aut 1999
BROOKLYN (NEW YORK, N.Y.) *See* New York (N.Y.)—Brooklyn
Brooklyn project. Tenn, W.
Brooklyn sestina. Mattison, A.
Brooks, Ben
Other people's lives
The Virginia Quarterly Review v78 no3 p540-58 Summ 2002
Songs and Sorrows
The Sewanee Review v111 no1 p94-115 Wint 2003
Brooks, Carrelin
The butcher's wife
Hers 3: brilliant new fiction by lesbian writers; edited by Terry Wolverton with Robert Drake
Brooks, Noah
Our base ball club
Dead balls and double curves; an anthology of early baseball fiction; edited and with an introduction by Trey Strecker ; with a foreword by Arnold Hano

Brooks, Terry
Indomitable
Silverberg, R. Legends II; new short novels by the masters of modern fantasy; edited by Robert Silverberg
Brooksmith. James, H.
Brossard, Nicole
Mauve desert [excerpt]
The Vintage book of international lesbian fiction; edited and with an introduction by Naomi Holoch and Joan Nestle
BROTHELS *See* Prostitution
Brother News from Home. Dinh, L.
Brother Orchid. Connell, R. E.
Brother to the machine. Matheson, R.
Brother, unadorned. Hagy, A. C.
Brotherhood. Graff, E. J.
The **brotherhood** of healing. Sutton, B.
The **brotherhood** of the saved. Walker, A.
BROTHERS
See also Brothers and sisters; Half-brothers; Stepbrothers; Twins
Adams, A. The swastika on our door
Alcott, L. M. Little sunbeam
Archer, J. Chalk and cheese
Auchincloss, L. Harry's brother
Baca, J. S. The three sons of Julia
Bausch, R. Nobody in Hollywood
Bausch, R. Riches
Berdine, T. Spring rite
Bernhard, T. Amras
Blaise, C. A fish like a buzzard
Borges, J. L. The interloper
Boswell, M. Bloody knuckles
Bowles, P. The fqih
Bowles, P. The successor
Boyle, T. C. Killing babies
Brkic, C. A. Passage
Brown, J. Afterlife
Brownstein, G. Bachelor party
Busch, F. Extra extra large
Busch, F. Vespers
Chan, D. M. Goblin fruit
Chan, D. M. Lost years
Chan, D. M. Open circles
Chekhov, A. P. Gooseberries
Cherryh, C. J. Sea change
Clark, B. C. Between girls and gamecocks
Clark, B. C. By way of the forked stick
Clark, B. C. The last picture show
Cooke, C. Twa Corbies
Cunningham, M. Mister Brother
Cunningham, M. White angel
D'Ambrosio, C., Jr. Open house
Daniels, J. Renegade
Davies, P. H. On the terraces
Delany, S. R. Dog in a fisherman's net
Díaz, J. Nilda
Díaz, J. Ysrael
Dinh, L. Fake House
Dokey, R. Pale morning dun
DuBois, B. The star thief
Dumas, H. My brother, my brother!
Dybek, S. Blue boy
Dybek, S. Live from Dreamsville
Dybek, S. Qué quieres
Dybek, S. Undertow
Dyson, J. At last
Earley, T. Quill

BROTHERS—*Continued*

Eggers, P. A private space
Ehlers, J. Golden Gate Bridge—a view from below
Engel, M. P. Let them big animals come back
Epstein, J. Family values
Erdrich, L. The red convertible
Fleming, J. H. Wind and rain
Franklin, T. The ballad of Duane Juarez
Franklin, T. Poachers
Galloway, J. Baby-sitting
Garrity, B. R. The holy boys
Glasgow, G. Home at last
Gorman, E. All these condemned
Gorman, E. Sailing to Atlantis
Grau, S. A. The last gas station
Greenberg, A. A couple of dead men
Greer, R. O. Backup
Guerrero, L. Cloud-shadow
Guerrero, L. The curse
Hammett, D. His brother's keeper
Harty, R. Crossroads
Harty, R. September
Harty, R. What can I tell you about my brother?
Hauptman, W. Good rockin' tonight
Haynes, M. Love like a bullet
Heim, S. Deep green, pale purple
Hickey, D. The closed season
Hodge, B. Some other me
Horgan, P. To the mountains
House, S. Gatlinburg
Iribarne, M. Astronauts
Iwaszkiewicz, J. The birch grove
Kees, W. The brothers
Keret, E. Korbi's girl
Knight, M. A bad man, so pretty
Lao She. Black Li and White Li
Lawrence, D. H. Love among the haystacks
Lee, D. Casul water
Lowenthal, M. Into a mirror
Lumley, B. A thing about cars!
Maleti, G. The house in the wood
Mayo, W. Dance of eights
McManus, J. The Magothy fires
McNally, J. The greatest goddamn thing
Moody, R. Boys
Morgan, R. The ratchet
Mungoshi, C. The brother
Murray, J. Acts of memory, wisdom of man
Nissen, T. Grover, king of Nebraska
Oates, J. C. Death cup
Oates, J. C. I'm not your son, I am no one you know
Ortiz, S. J. The end of Old Horse
Padilla, M. The king of snow
Padilla, M. Restoration
Patterson, K. Sick in public
Peery, J. Huevos
Penn, W. S. Storm watch
Poirier, M. J. Buttons
Polansky, S. Alarm
Ponte, A. J. A throw of the book of changes
Ramaya, S. Re:mohit
Raphael, F. All his sons
Reid, E. Dryfall
Richard, M. Strays
Robison, M. Doctor's sons
Schnitzler, A. Blind Geronimo and his brother
Shade, E. Kaahumanu

Shepard, J. Nurturer by nature
Shepard, J. 'Scuse me, while I kiss this guy
Singer, I. B. Fire
Singer, I. B. A nest egg for paradise
Tammuz, B. My brother
Tester, W. Wet
Tilghman, C. Something important
Touré. Young, black, and unstoppable; or, Death of a zeitgeist jockey
Tran, V. The coral reef
Watson, I. Such dedication
Waugh, E. Winner takes all
Weaver, G. And what should I do in Illyria?
Weaver, G. Without spot or wrinkle
White, M. C. Fugitives
The **brothers**. Kees, W.

BROTHERS AND SISTERS
See also Twins

Adam, C. Emu and elephant
Agee, J. The creek
Baca, J. S. The importance of a piece of paper
Bail, M. The seduction of my sister
Bambara, T. C. Raymond's run
Barthelme, F. The great pyramids
Bausch, R. Contrition
Bean, B. Dancing naked
Bingham, S. The hunt
Bowles, P. At Paso Jojo
Bowles, P. Reminders of Bouselham
Bowles, P. Too far from home
Brkic, C. A. Swimming out
Broughton, T. A. Living the revolution
Brown, J. Halloween
Brown, J. The naked running boy
Burgin, R. Miles
Cannell, D. The high cost of living
Caponegro, M. The son's burden
Carver, R. Furious seasons
Chapman, C. M. Spoonfed
Chopin, K. Cavanelle
Clark, J. K2
Cobb, W. J. Letting the dog out
Connor, J. The thief of flowers
Cook, K. L. Penance
Corcoran, T. The octopus alibi
Cummins, A. Blue fly
Daugharty, J. Name of love
Davis, A. Testimony
Davis, L. Scarecrow
Davis, W. The sharp light of trespassers
Desplechin, M. Taking it to heart
Dinesen, I. The supper at Elsinore
Divakaruni, C. B. The intelligence of wild things
Doran, M. M. A well-arranged life
Epstein, J. My little Marjie
Erian, A. When animals attack
Fairey, W. W. Family album
Fitzgerald, F. S. Benediction
Fromm, P. How all this started
Fromm, P. Night swimming
Gilchrist, E. Mexico
Gilchrist, E. Traceleen, she's still talking
Glover, D. A piece of the True Cross
Glover, D. H. The obituary writer
Glover, D. H. A piece of the true cross
Goran, L. The death of the quarterback
Gordon, M. Storytelling
Gorman, E. The way it used to be

BROTHERS AND SISTERS—*Continued*
Gray, A. Miss Kincaid's autumn
Grimsley, J. Into Greenwood
Grodstein, L. Family vacation
Guerrero, L. Love and happiness
Gunn, K. The swimming pool
Hagy, A. C. Brother, unadorned
Harfenist, J. Fully bonded by the state of Minnesota
Harrington, J. Sweet baby Jenny
Harty, R. Sarah at the Palace
Haslett, A. Devotion
Henley, P. The secret of cartwheels
Hochman, A. Nesting
Hodgen, C. The hero of loneliness
Hodgen, C. Sir Karl LaFong or current resident
Hodgen, C. What the rabbi said to the priest
Hoffman, A. The boy who wrestled with angels
Hoffman, A. Gretel
Hopkinson, N. Money tree
House, S. Coal house
Jackson, V. F. Imagining friends
James, H. The modern warning
Jones, T. Cold snap
Kalu, Anthonia C. Camwood
Kaminsky, S. M. Scorpion's kiss
Kavaler, R. Give brother my best
Kees, W. I should worry
Kittredge, W. Be careful what you want
Knight, M. Gerald's monkey
Krawiec, R. Accommodations
Lavin, M. The little prince
Laws, S. The song my sister sang
Leebron, F. G. That winter
Lipsyte, S. Old soul
Lloyd, D. T. Boys only
López, L. Frostbite
Malouf, M. From you know who
Mason, B. A. Wish
Matera, L. If it can't be true
Mayo, W. Mary Magdalena versus Godzilla
McManus, J. Scintilla
Moody, R. The Mansion on the Hill
Mueller, D. The night my brother worked the header
Muñoz, M. Good as yesterday
Nawrocki, S. Pampas grass day
Nelson, A. Ball peen
Nelson, A. Loose cannon
Oates, J. C. Curly Red
Oates, J. C. The deaths: an elegy
Oates, J. C. Fire
Orringer, J. The Isabel fish
Ortiz, S. J. Crossing
Osborn, C. My brother is a cowboy
Painter, P. Feeding the piranha
Painter, P. Sympathy
Powers, T. Itinerary
Reiner, C. G. G. Giggler
Reisman, N. Common light
Reisman, N. Edie in winter
Richmond, M. Does anyone know you are going this way
Rinehart, S. Another pyramid scheme
Robison, M. Smart
Robison, M. The Wellman twins
Robison, M. While home
Roorbach, B. Fredonia
Rosenfeld, S. Bing-bing and bong-bong

Rule, R. Walking the trapline
Sade, marquis de. Emilie de Tourville; or, Fraternal cruelty
Salak, K. Beheadings
Sandor, M. Annunciation
Sarrantonio, A. Wish
Saunders, G. My brother can tell
Scoville, S. Clara and Ben
Searle, E. Memoir of a soon-to-be star
Shippen, J. R. I am not like Nuñez
Smith, A. The universal story
Smith, Z. I'm the only one
Sojourner, M. Luzianne
Svoboda, T. Doll
Svoboda, T. Water
Swan, G. Backtracking
Taylor, P. H. Venus, cupid, folly and time
Tolstoy, L., graf. Sisters
Tran, V. Gunboat on the Yangtze
Trevor, W. Low Sunday, 1950
Vachss, A. H. Big sister
Vachss, A. H. Reaching back
VanderMeer, J. A heart for Lucretia
Varley, J. Retrograde summer
Weihe, E. Off season
Weingarten, R. Aura, cry, fall, and fit
Wells, K. Blue skin
Wells, K. Secession, XX
Wells, K. Sherman and the swan
Wharton, E. The pot-boiler
Wieland, L. Halloween
Williams, T. The resemblance between a violin case and a coffin
Wolff, T. The night in question
Yates, R. A compassionate leave
Yates, R. A private possession
Young, T. Yellow with black horns
Yuknavitch, L. Cusp
Brothers and sisters. Chinodya, S.
Brothers and sisters around the world. Lee, A.
Brothers Grimm
    See also Grimm, Jacob, 1785-1863;
    Grimm, Wilhelm, 1786-1859
BROTHERS-IN-LAW
Brown, C. Wings
Chaon, D. I demand to know where you're taking me
Davies, R. A human condition
Erdrich, L. Lulu's boys
Frym, G. Homologue
Grau, S. A. The wind shifting west
Leslie, N. Projectiles
Locklin, G. A sober reading of Dr. Sigmund Freud
Meredith, D. Desert music
Oates, J. C. Aiding and abetting
Oates, J. C. Fugitive
Offutt, C. Out of the woods
Silber, J. What lasts
Westlake, D. E. Nackles
Brotherton, Jim
Heat Death
    Gettysburg Review v15 no4 p662-3 Wint 2002
Brotherton, Michael
Blood bone tendon stone
    Tetrick, B. In the shadow of the wall; an anthology of Vietnam stories that might have been; edited by Byron R. Tetrick

Broudy, Oliver

My baby ran off with Edouard

American short fiction, vol. 8, no 29-32

Broughton, T. Alan (Thomas Alan)

Ashes

Broughton, T. A. Suicidal tendencies; stories

Bill's women

Broughton, T. A. Suicidal tendencies; stories

The burden of light

Broughton, T. A. Suicidal tendencies; stories

The Virginia Quarterly Review v79 no1 p51-69 Wint 2003

The classicist

Broughton, T. A. Suicidal tendencies; stories

Italian autumn

Broughton, T. A. Suicidal tendencies; stories

L'americana

Broughton, T. A. Suicidal tendencies; stories

Leaving home

Broughton, T. A. Suicidal tendencies; stories

Living the revolution

Broughton, T. A. Suicidal tendencies; stories

Spring cleaning

Broughton, T. A. Suicidal tendencies; stories

The terrorist

Broughton, T. A. Suicidal tendencies; stories

A tour of the islands

Broughton, T. A. Suicidal tendencies; stories

The wars I missed

Broughton, T. A. Suicidal tendencies; stories

Broughton, Thomas Alan *See* Broughton, T. Alan (Thomas Alan), 1936-

Broun, Heywood

Mrs. Tiny Tyler

Dead balls and double curves; an anthology of early baseball fiction; edited and with an introduction by Trey Strecker ; with a foreword by Arnold Hano

Broun, Matthew Heywood Campbell *See* Broun, Heywood, 1888-1939

Browder, Catherine

Amnesty

Browder, C. Secret lives; stories

Animal heaven

Browder, C. Secret lives; stories

Center zone

Browder, C. Secret lives; stories

Fusuda the archer

Browder, C. Secret lives; stories

Girls like us

Browder, C. Secret lives; stories

The juice-seller's bird

Browder, C. Secret lives; stories

The missing day

Browder, C. Secret lives; stories

Pizza man

Browder, C. Secret lives; stories

Secrets: three short stories

Browder, C. Secret lives; stories

Silver maple

Browder, C. Secret lives; stories

When Luz sings her solo

Browder, C. Secret lives; stories

Brown, Amy Knox

Strip Battleship

The Student body; short stories about college students and professors; edited by John McNally

Brown, Carrie

The correspondent

Brown, C. The house on Belle Isle and other stories

Father Judge Run

Brown, C. The house on Belle Isle and other stories

New stories from the South: the year's best, 2001; edited by Shannon Ravenel; with a preface by Lee Smith

Friend to women

Brown, C. The house on Belle Isle and other stories

The house on Belle Isle

Brown, C. The house on Belle Isle and other stories

Miniature man

Brown, C. The house on Belle Isle and other stories

Postman

Brown, C. The house on Belle Isle and other stories

Wings

Brown, C. The house on Belle Isle and other stories

The Georgia Review v56 no2 p537-57 Summ 2002

Brown, Cecil

Now is the time

The African American West; a century of short stories; edited by Bruce A. Glasrud and Laurie Champion

Brown, D. Winston

In the doorway of Rhee's Jazz Joint

New stories from the South: the year's best, 2000; edited by Shannon Ravenel; with a preface by Ellen Douglas

Brown, Dale

Powder River Moe

On glorious wings; the best flying stories of the century; edited and introduced by Stephen Coonts

Brown, Eric

Myths of the Martian future

Mars probes; edited by Peter Crowther

Brown, Fredric

Arena

The Science fiction hall of fame: volume one, 1929-1964; the greatest science fiction stories of all time chosen by the members of the Science Fiction Writers of America; edited by Robert Silverberg

Cry silence

Master's choice v2; mystery stories by today's top writers and the masters who inspired them; edited by Lawrence Block

Don't look behind you

A Century of noir; thirty-two classic crime stories; edited by Mickey Spillane and Max Allan Collins

The Geezenstacks

The American fantasy tradition; edited by Brian M. Thomsen

The wench is dead

A Century of great suspense stories; edited by Jeffery Deaver

Brown, J. Lorraine
Waterline
South Carolina Review v34 no2 p27-30 Spr 2002

Brown, Jason
Afterlife
Brown, J. Driving the heart and other stories
Afternoon of the Sassanoa
Atlantic Monthly v283 no4 p84-86+ Ap 1999
Writers harvest 3; edited and with an introduction by Tobias Wolff
Animal stories
Brown, J. Driving the heart and other stories
The coroner's report
Brown, J. Driving the heart and other stories
Detox
Brown, J. Driving the heart and other stories
The dog lover
Brown, J. Driving the heart and other stories
Driving the heart
Brown, J. Driving the heart and other stories
Halloween
Brown, J. Driving the heart and other stories
Head on
Brown, J. Driving the heart and other stories
Hydrophobia
Brown, J. Driving the heart and other stories
The Lake
TriQuarterly no117 p159-72 Fall 2003
The naked running boy
Brown, J. Driving the heart and other stories
Sadness of the body
Brown, J. Driving the heart and other stories
She
Harper's v302 no1810 p84-92 Mr 2001
On the rocks; the KGB Bar fiction anthology; edited by Rebecca Donner ; foreword by Denis Woychuk
The submariners
Brown, J. Driving the heart and other stories
Thief
Brown, J. Driving the heart and other stories

Brown, Larry
A roadside resurrection
Stories from the Blue Moon Cafe II; edited by Sonny Brewer

Brown, Nancy K.
Burn pile
Fishing for chickens; short stories about rural youth; edited, with an introduction by Jim Heynen

Brown, Peter
The Slaughterhouse
Harvard Review (1992) no26 p126-38 2004

Brown, Rebecca
The Last Time I Saw You
Ploughshares v30 no2/3 p42-50 Fall 2004
Other
Chicago Review v45 no2 p70-73 1999
Trying to Say
The Literary Review (Madison, N.J.) v46 no3 p435-42 Spr 2003

Brown, Rosellen
How to win
The Best American short stories of the century; John Updike, editor, Katrina Kenison, coeditor; with an introduction by John Updike

Brown, Simon
Love is a stone
Gathering the bones; original stories from the world's masters of horror; edited by Dennis Etchison, Ramsey Campbell and Jack Dann
With clouds at our feet
Dreaming down-under; edited by Jack Dann and Janeen Webb
(jt. auth) See Lawson, Chris and Brown, Simon

The **brown** cape. Gilchrist, E.

The **brown** coast. Tower, W.

Brownie and Montgomery. Latta, R.

Brownies. Packer, Z.

Browning, Sinclair
Neighborhood watch
A Hot and sultry night for crime; edited by Jeffery Deaver

Brownrigg, Sylvia
Amazon
Brownrigg, S. Ten women who shook the world
The bird chick
Brownrigg, S. Ten women who shook the world
The Year's best fantasy & horror, twelfth annual collection; edited by Ellen Datlow & Terry Windling
Broad from abroad
Brownrigg, S. Ten women who shook the world
A gal of ambition
Brownrigg, S. Ten women who shook the world
The girl in the red chair
Brownrigg, S. Ten women who shook the world
Hussy from the west
Brownrigg, S. Ten women who shook the world
The lady in the desert
Brownrigg, S. Ten women who shook the world
Mars needs women!
Brownrigg, S. Ten women who shook the world
Mistress of many moons
Brownrigg, S. Ten women who shook the world
She who caught buses
Brownrigg, S. Ten women who shook the world

Brownstein, Gabriel
Bachelor party
Brownstein, G. The curious case of Benjamin Button, Apt. 3W
Lost tribe; jewish fiction from the edge
The curious case of Benjamin Button, 3w
Brownstein, G. The curious case of Benjamin Button, Apt. 3W
The dead fiddler, 5E
Brownstein, G. The curious case of Benjamin Button, Apt. 3W
The inventor of love
Brownstein, G. The curious case of Benjamin Button, Apt. 3W
The Literary Review (Madison, N.J.) v44 no4 p642-57 Summ 2001

Brownstein, Gabriel—*Continued*
Musée des Beaux Arts
Brownstein, G. The curious case of Benjamin
Button, Apt. 3W
A penal colony all his own, 11E
Brownstein, G. The curious case of Benjamin
Button, Apt. 3W
Safety
Brownstein, G. The curious case of Benjamin
Button, Apt. 3W
The speedboat
Brownstein, G. The curious case of Benjamin
Button, Apt. 3W
Wakefield, 7E
Brownstein, G. The curious case of Benjamin
Button, Apt. 3W
Brownstone. Adler, R.
A **brownstone**, Park Slope. Nissen, T.
Brownsville. Piazza, T.
Broyard, Bliss
At the bottom of the lake
Broyard, B. My father, dancing; stories
A day in the country
Broyard, B. My father, dancing; stories
Loose talk
Broyard, B. My father, dancing; stories
Mr. Sweetly Indecent
Broyard, B. My father, dancing; stories
My father, dancing
Broyard, B. My father, dancing; stories
Snowed in
Broyard, B. My father, dancing; stories
The trouble with Mr. Leopold
Broyard, B. My father, dancing; stories
Ugliest faces
Broyard, B. My father, dancing; stories
Bruce, Colin
The adventure of the dying doctor
Murder, my dear Watson; new tales of Sher-
lock Holmes; edited by Martin H. Green-
berg, Jon Lellenberg, Daniel Stashower
Bruce, Robert *See* Robert I, King of Scotland,
1274-1329
Bruce Lee. Gussoff, C.
Bruchac, Joseph
The Hunter and the Walrus: Inuit
(Nunatsiaqmiut) of Baffin Island
Parabola v29 no2 p77-8 Summ 2004
Bruchac, Joseph and others
The Farmer Who Wanted to Be a Jaguar: Ma-
yan
Parabola v29 no2 p79-80 Summ 2004
Bruchman, Denise M.
Promises kept
Dead on demand; the best of ghost story
weekend; edited by Elizabeth Engstrom
Bruhl, Lucien Lévy- *See* Lévy-Bruhl, Lucien,
1857-1939
Brumbaugh, Sam
In the Nineties
Southwest Review v87 no2/3 p241-52 2002
BRUNEL, ISAMBARD KINGDOM, 1806-1859
About
Baxter, S. The modern Cyrano
Bruno. Budnitz, J.
Bruno's metamorphosis. Stern, S.

Bruns, Don
Sing for your supper
Bishop, C. and James, D. Death dines in; ed-
ited by Claudia Bishop and Dean James
Brunt, Carol Rifka
Negative Numbers
The North American Review v288 no3/4
p20-1 My/Ag 2003
BRUSSELS (BELGIUM) *See* Belgium—Brussels
The **brutal** language of love. Erian, A.
BRUTALITY *See* Cruelty; Violence
BRYAN, WILLIAM JENNINGS, 1860-1925
About
Landis, G. A. The eyes of America
BRYANT, BEAR
About
Vice, B. Report from Junction
Bryant, Edward
Styx and bones
999: new stories of horror and suspense; ed-
ited by Al Sarrantonio
The World's finest mystery and crime stories,
first annual collection; edited by Ed
Gorman
Bryant, Paul W. *See* Bryant, Bear
Bryce Echenique, Alfredo
A brief reappearance by Florence, this autumn
The Vintage book of Latin American stories;
edited by Carlos Fuentes and Julio Ortega
Bryks, Rachmil
Artists in the ghetto
When night fell; an anthology of Holocaust
short stories; edited by Linda Schermer Ra-
phael and Marc Lee Raphael
Berele in the ghetto
When night fell; an anthology of Holocaust
short stories; edited by Linda Schermer Ra-
phael and Marc Lee Raphael
Bryna. Miller, R.
Bubbe Henya. Baron, D.
BUBONIC PLAGUE *See* Plague
Bucak, Ayşe Papatya
Istanbul 11 April
The Literary Review (Madison, N.J.) v46 no1
p78-88 Fall 2002
Buchan, Jacob
Sleepwalkers
Sleepwalkers and other stories; the Arab in
Hebrew fiction; edited by Ehud Ben-Ezer
Buchan, John
The far islands
Tales before Tolkien; the roots of modern
fantasy; edited by Douglas A. Anderson
Buchanan, Edna
Goodnight, Irene
Esquire v135 no1 p80-1 Ja 2001
Miami heat
Irreconcilable differences; Lia Matera, editor
Rat boy
Esquire v137 no6 p106-9, 122 Je 2002
The red shoes
Murder and obsession; edited by Otto Penzler
Buchanan's head. Davidson, A.
Buchbinder, Jane
The first story
Prairie Schooner v75 no2 p99-112 Summ
2001

Buck, Charlie
Still-life with particle board
The New Yorker v75 no3 p78-83 Mr 15 1999
Buck, Pearl S. (Pearl Sydenstricker)
Ransom
The Best American mystery stories of the
century; Tony Hillerman, editor; with an
introduction by Tony Hillerman
The **buck** stops here. Kaminsky, S. M.
Buckell, Tobias S.
Death's dreadlocks
Mojo: conjure stories; edited by Nalo Hopkin-
son
Spurn Babylon
Whispers from the cotton tree root; Caribbean
fabulist fiction; edited by Nalo Hopkinson
Bucket. Nailah, A.
Buckeye the elder. Udall, B.
Buckhanon, Kalisha
Card Parties
Michigan Quarterly Review v42 no2 p365-84
Spr 2003
Buckley, Christopher
Royal Pain
Atlantic Monthly (1993) v293 no3 p94-8, 100,
102, 104, 106 Ap 2004
We Have a Pope!
Atlantic Monthly (1993) v291 no3 p70-4,
76-8, 80, 82, 84, 86 Ap 2003
Bucknell, Lucy
So You Can Stay
Southern Humanities Review v37 no2 p163-8
Spr 2003
BUDAPEST (HUNGARY) *See* Hungary—Buda-
pest
BUDDHISM
See also Buddhist priests; Buddhist tem-
ples
Cameron, S. Beautiful work
Dorrie, D. Where do we go from here
Gies, M. Zoo animal keeper 1, REC-SVC-ZK
Givens, J. On the wheel of wandering-on
Hampton, Francesca. Greyhound Bodhisatva
Heller, K. Memorizing the Buddha
Hodgman, J. Tanuki
Hodgman, Jan. Tanuki
Iyer, P. A walk in Kurama
Klein, Anne Carolyn. The mantra and the typist:
a story of east and west
Leong, R. Bodhi leaves
McLoughlin, M. In the sky there is no footstep
Stevenson, J. The Colonel and Judy O'Grady
Sukrungruang, I. The golden mix
Waller, Easton. The war against the lawns
Williams, W. J. Prayers on the wind
Wilson, Jeff. Buddherotica
Winston, D. Mi Mi May
BUDDHIST PRIESTS
Bowles, P. You have left your lotus pods on the
bus
BUDDHIST TEMPLES
Kawabata, Y. Chrysanthemum in the rock
Buddy. Furman, L.
Buddy Bolden. Kalamu ya Salaam
Budman, Mark
The land of dreams, the garden of insomnia
The Virginia Quarterly Review v78 no1 p79-
92 Wint 2002

Budnitz, Judy
Art lesson
Budnitz, J. Flying leap; stories
Average Joe
Budnitz, J. Flying leap; stories
Barren
Budnitz, J. Flying leap; stories
Bruno
Budnitz, J. Flying leap; stories
Burned
Budnitz, J. Flying leap; stories
Chaperone
Budnitz, J. Flying leap; stories
Composer
Budnitz, J. Flying leap; stories
Directions
Budnitz, J. Flying leap; stories
Dog days
Budnitz, J. Flying leap; stories
Flight
Budnitz, J. Flying leap; stories
Flush
Prize stories, 2000; The O. Henry awards; ed-
ited and with an introduction by Larry
Dark
Got spirit
Budnitz, J. Flying leap; stories
Guilt
Budnitz, J. Flying leap; stories
Hershel
Budnitz, J. Flying leap; stories
Lost tribe; jewish fiction from the edge
The Year's best fantasy & horror, twelfth an-
nual collection; edited by Ellen Datlow &
Terry Windling
Hook, line and sinker
On the rocks; the KGB Bar fiction anthology;
edited by Rebecca Donner ; foreword by
Denis Woychuk
Hundred-pound baby
Budnitz, J. Flying leap; stories
Lessons
Budnitz, J. Flying leap; stories
Miracle
The New Yorker v80 no19 p84-91 Jl 12-19
2004
Park bench
Budnitz, J. Flying leap; stories
Permanent wave
Budnitz, J. Flying leap; stories
Scenes from the fall fashion catalog
Budnitz, J. Flying leap; stories
Skin care
Budnitz, J. Flying leap; stories
Train
Budnitz, J. Flying leap; stories
Vacation
Budnitz, J. Flying leap; stories
Visiting hours
Harper's v304 p83-91 Ap 2002
What happened
Budnitz, J. Flying leap; stories
Yellville
Budnitz, J. Flying leap; stories
Budyonnovsk. Kalfus, K.
BUENOS AIRES (ARGENTINA) *See* Argenti-
na—Buenos Aires
Buenos Aires Side to Side. Shippen, J. R.
BUFFALO, AMERICAN *See* Bison

BUFFALO (N.Y.) *See* New York (State)—Buffalo
Buffalo. Kessel, J.
Buffalo. Reid, E.
Buffalo Boy. Janko, J.
Buffalo gals, won't you come out tonight. Le Guin, U. K.
Buffalo gals, won't you come out tonight. Monfredo, M. G.
The **buffalo** man. De Lint, C.
Buffalo Speedway. Farrin, S.
BUFFLO BILL
　　　　　　　　About
　Estleman, L. D. Big Tim Magoon and the wild west
The **Bufords.** Spencer, E.
Buford's last case. Nevins, F. M., Jr.
Bug day. Burgess, T.
Bug juice. Lincoln, C.
Buggé, Carole
　Uncle Evil Eye
　　The Ultimate Halloween; edited by Marvin Kaye
Buglesong. Stegner, W. E.
Bugtown. Pflug, U.
Builders. Yates, R.
The **building.** Le Guin, U. K.
The **Building** of Quality. Mayo, C. M.
Built upon the sand. Jacobs, J.
Bujold, Lois McMaster
　Barter
　　Wondrous beginnings; edited by Steven H. Silver and Martin H. Greenberg
Bukhara Nocturne. Pitol, S.
Bukiet, Melvin Jules
　But, Microsoft! what byte through yonder windows breaks?
　　Bukiet, M. J. A faker's dozen; stories
　Filophilia
　　Bukiet, M. J. A faker's dozen; stories
　Paper hero
　　Bukiet, M. J. A faker's dozen; stories
　　Southwest Review v87 no2/3 p206-20 2002
　The return of eros to academe
　　Bukiet, M. J. A faker's dozen; stories
　Splinters
　　Bukiet, M. J. A faker's dozen; stories
　　The Pushcart prize XXIII: best of the small presses; an annual small press reader; edited by Bill Henderson with the Pushcart prize editors
　Squeak, memory
　　Bukiet, M. J. A faker's dozen; stories
　The suburbiad
　　Bukiet, M. J. A faker's dozen; stories
　The swap
　　Bukiet, M. J. A faker's dozen; stories
　Tongue of the Jews
　　Bukiet, M. J. A faker's dozen; stories
　The two Franzes
　　Bukiet, M. J. A faker's dozen; stories
　　The Massachusetts Review v43 no3 p433-57 Aut 2002
　The war lovers
　　Bukiet, M. J. A faker's dozen; stories
Bukoski, Anthony
　The absolution of Hedda Borski
　　Bukoski, A. Polonaise; stories
　Bird of passage
　　Bukoski, A. Polonaise; stories

The bird that sings in the bamboo
　Bukoski, A. Time between trains; stories
Closing time
　Bukoski, A. Time between trains; stories
A concert of minor pieces
　Bukoski, A. Polonaise; stories
Dry spell
　Bukoski, A. Polonaise; stories
A geography of snow
　Bukoski, A. Time between trains; stories
Holy walker
　Bukoski, A. Time between trains; stories
Immigration and naturalization
　Bukoski, A. Polonaise; stories
It had to be you
　Bukoski, A. Time between trains; stories
The korporał's polonaise
　Bukoski, A. Polonaise; stories
Leaves that shimmer in the slightest breeze
　Bukoski, A. Time between trains; stories
Leokadia and fireflies
　Bukoski, A. Time between trains; stories
The month that brings winter; or, How Mr. Truzynski carried Vietnam home with him
　Bukoski, A. Polonaise; stories
The moon of the grass fires
　Bukoski, A. Time between trains; stories
Pesthouse
　Bukoski, A. Polonaise; stories
A philosophy of dust
　Bukoski, A. Time between trains; stories
President of the past
　Bukoski, A. Time between trains; stories
Private Tomaszewski
　Bukoski, A. Polonaise; stories
Time between trains
　Bukoski, A. Time between trains; stories
The tools of ignorance
　Bukoski, A. Polonaise; stories
The value of numbers
　Bukoski, A. Time between trains; stories
Winter weeds
　Bukoski, A. Time between trains; stories
The wood of such trees
　Bukoski, A. Polonaise; stories
The world at war
　Bukoski, A. Polonaise; stories
BULGARIA
Updike, J. The Bulgarian poetess
Bulgheroni, Marisa
　Letter from Persephone
　　The Sewanee Review v111 no3 p375-82 Summ 2003
BULIMIA
Millar, M. Dreams of sex and stage diving [excerpt]
Bull, Emma
　Rending dark
　　Magical beginnings; edited by Steven H. Silver and Martin H. Greenberg
Bull, Scott Emerson
　Mr. Sly stops for a cup of joe
　　Gathering the bones; original stories from the world's masters of horror; edited by Dennis Etchison, Ramsey Campbell and Jack Dann
Bulldog. Miller, A.
BULLDOZERS
Sturgeon, T. Killdozer!
Bullet train. Thien, M.

BULLFIGHTERS AND BULLFIGHTING
Baca, J. S. Bull's blood
Bocock, M. Death is where you find it
London, J. The madness of John Harned
Meredith, D. The horses speak French
BULLFIGHTING *See* Bullfighters and bullfighting
Bullies. DeWeese, D.
Bullies. Tanner, M.
Bullins, Ed
Support your local police
 The African American West; a century of short stories; edited by Bruce A. Glasrud and Laurie Champion
The **bullnoser**. Morgan, R.
BULLS
O'Connor, F. Greenleaf
The **bully**. Čapek, K.
Bumas, E. Shaskan
Love songs of fruit flies
 Gettysburg Review v12 no1 p27-41 Spr 1999
Song of the Chile bird
 Southwest Review v84 no3 p355-80 1999
Bumfuzzled. Bird, S.
Bummer. Henkel, V.
The **bummer**. Locklin, G.
The **bunchgrass** edge of the world. Proulx, A.
A **bundle** of letters. James, H.
The **Bundlelays**. Smith, C. W.
Bundy, Alison
Brief Family Statment [i.e. Statement]
 Chicago Review v49 no1 p90-2 Spr 2003
Episode from the History
 Harper's v308 p28-31 Ap 2004
 The Kenyon Review v26 no1 p46-54 Wint 2004
Family Statement
 Harper's v307 p31 S 2003
A **bungalow**, Koh Tao. Nissen, T.
Bunin, Ivan Alekseevich
Antigone
 Bunin, I. A. Sunstroke; selected stories; translated from the Russian and with an introduction by Graham Hettlinger
Ballad
 Bunin, I. A. Sunstroke; selected stories; translated from the Russian and with an introduction by Graham Hettlinger
Caucasus
 Bunin, I. A. Sunstroke; selected stories; translated from the Russian and with an introduction by Graham Hettlinger
Cold fall
 Bunin, I. A. Sunstroke; selected stories; translated from the Russian and with an introduction by Graham Hettlinger
The gentleman from San Francisco
 Bunin, I. A. Sunstroke; selected stories; translated from the Russian and with an introduction by Graham Hettlinger
Ida
 Bunin, I. A. Sunstroke; selected stories; translated from the Russian and with an introduction by Graham Hettlinger
In Paris
 Bunin, I. A. Sunstroke; selected stories; translated from the Russian and with an introduction by Graham Hettlinger

Late hour
 Bunin, I. A. Sunstroke; selected stories; translated from the Russian and with an introduction by Graham Hettlinger
Little fool
 Bunin, I. A. Sunstroke; selected stories; translated from the Russian and with an introduction by Graham Hettlinger
Muza
 Bunin, I. A. Sunstroke; selected stories; translated from the Russian and with an introduction by Graham Hettlinger
Old and young
 Bunin, I. A. Sunstroke; selected stories; translated from the Russian and with an introduction by Graham Hettlinger
On one familiar street
 Bunin, I. A. Sunstroke; selected stories; translated from the Russian and with an introduction by Graham Hettlinger
Raven
 Bunin, I. A. Sunstroke; selected stories; translated from the Russian and with an introduction by Graham Hettlinger
Rusya
 Bunin, I. A. Sunstroke; selected stories; translated from the Russian and with an introduction by Graham Hettlinger
 The Hudson Review v52 no1 p19-28 Spr 1999
Styopa
 Bunin, I. A. Sunstroke; selected stories; translated from the Russian and with an introduction by Graham Hettlinger
Sunstroke
 Bunin, I. A. Sunstroke; selected stories; translated from the Russian and with an introduction by Graham Hettlinger
Zoyka and Valeriya
 Bunin, I. A. Sunstroke; selected stories; translated from the Russian and with an introduction by Graham Hettlinger
Bunner Sisters. Wharton, E.
Bunny is good bread. Straub, P.
Buom. Nguyen, P.
The **burbot**. Chekhov, A. P.
The **burden**. Banks, R.
Burden. Marano, M.
The **Burden** of Light. Broughton, T. A.
Burdick, Eugene
Cold day, cold fear
 Retrieving bones; stories and poems of the Korean War; edited and with an introduction by W. D. Ehrhart and Philip K. Jason
Burdon, Eric
The Bukowski brothers
 Carved in rock; short stories by musicians; edited by Greg Kihn
BUREAUCRACY
 See also Civil service
Jones, E. P. Marie
Kurlansky, M. Naked
Shonk, K. Honey month
Weldon, F. A hard time to be a father
Burford, Miles
140 Sunset
 Burford, M. Flying lessons and other stories
Aloha, Les
 Burford, M. Flying lessons and other stories

Burford, Miles—*Continued*
David and Kitty
  Burford, M. Flying lessons and other stories
The faces of fear
  Burford, M. Flying lessons and other stories
Flying lessons
  Burford, M. Flying lessons and other stories
Out of the storm
  Burford, M. Flying lessons and other stories
Pesce volante
  Burford, M. Flying lessons and other stories
Burger, Wolfgang
Countdown
  The World's finest mystery and crime stories,
    third annual collection; edited by Ed
    Gorman and Martin H. Greenberg
Burgess, Anne
Just like your father
  U.S. Catholic v68 no10 p36-9 O 2003
Burgess, Tony
Bug day
  The Canadian Forum v78 no882 p26-33 O
    1999
Burgin, Richard
Bodysurfing
  The Pushcart prize XXIII: best of the small
    presses; an annual small press reader; ed-
    ited by Bill Henderson with the Pushcart
    prize editors
Cruise
  TriQuarterly no113 p97-111 Summ 2002
The endless visit
  The Ohio Review no62/63 p102-16 2001
The Identity Club
  TriQuarterly no118 p41-57 Wint 2004
Miles
  The Pushcart prize XXVI; best of the small
    presses, an annual small press reader; ed-
    ited by Bill Henderson and the Pushcart
    prize editors
The Second Floor
  The Antioch Review v62 no3 p519-33 Summ
    2004
The **burglar** and the whatsit. Westlake, D. E.
BURGLARS *See* Thieves
Burglary in progress. Anderson, K.
BURIAL *See* Funeral rites and ceremonies
The **burial**. Dixon, S.
Burial detail. Rusch, K. K.
The **burial** of Letty Strayhorn. Kelton, E.
The **burial** of the sardine. Alas, L.
The **buried** boy. Westmoreland, T. A.
Buried statues. Benítez-Rojo, A.
BURIED TREASURE
  Girardi, R. The primordial face
  Hawthorne, N. Peter Goldthwaite's treasure
  Hodgson, W. H. The adventure of the headland
  L'Amour, L. Off the Mangrove Coast
Buried treasure. Lovett, S.
Burke, James Lee
We Build Churches, Inc.
  Retrieving bones; stories and poems of the
    Korean War; edited and with an introduc-
    tion by W. D. Ehrhart and Philip K. Jason
Burke, Jan
The Abbey ghosts
  The World's finest mystery and crime stories,
    second annual collection; edited by Ed
    Gorman

The man in the civil suit
  Malice domestic 9
  The World's finest mystery and crime stories,
    second annual collection; edited by Ed
    Gorman
Mea culpa
  Murder most divine; ecclesiastical tales of un-
    holy crimes; edited by Ralph McInerny and
    Martin H. Greenberg
Miscalculation
  Death cruise; crime stories on the open seas;
    edited by Lawrence Block
An unsuspected condition of the heart
  Irreconcilable differences; Lia Matera, editor
Burke, Sue
Snare
  The Darkest thirst; a vampire anthology
Burleson, Donald R.
Pump Jack
  The Mammoth book of best horror 13; edited
    by Stephen Jones
The watcher at the window
  Gathering the bones; original stories from the
    world's masters of horror; edited by Dennis
    Etchison, Ramsey Campbell and Jack Dann
Burn him out. Bonham, F.
Burn patterns. White, M. C.
Burn pile. Brown, N. K.
Burn with me. Chaon, D.
Burn your maps. Leff, R. J.
Burnett, Elizabeth
Thieves
  New England Review v23 no2 p154-68 Spr
    2002
Burning. Schirmer, R.
Burning end. Rendell, R.
The **burning** forest. Tamaro, S.
The **burning** house. Beattie, A.
Burning luv. Rinehart, S.
The **burning** palms. Keegan, C.
The **burning** secret. Zweig, S.
Burning the commodity. Yuknavitch, L.
BURNS, ROBERT, 1759-1796
  About
  Simpson, H. Burns and the bankers
Burns, Tex, 1908-1988
  *For works written by this author under oth-
    er names see* L'Amour, Louis, 1908-
    1988
Burns. Keegan, C.
Burns and the bankers. Simpson, H.
Burrage, A. M. (Alfred McLelland)
Smee
  Dark: stories of madness, murder, and the su-
    pernatural; edited by Clint Willis
Burrage, Alfred McLelland *See* Burrage, A. M.
  (Alfred McLelland), 1889-1956
Burris, Jack
Judah's a two-way street running out
  The African American West; a century of
    short stories; edited by Bruce A. Glasrud
    and Laurie Champion
Burros gone bad. Schneider, P.
BURROUGHS, WILLIAM S., 1914-1997
  About
  Rucker, R. v. B. Instability
Burroway, Janet
Deconstruction
  Prairie Schooner v73 no4 p33-53 Wint 1999

Burroway, Janet—_Continued_
The Mandelbrot set
    Pushcart prize XXVII; best of the small
    presses; edited by Bill Henderson with the
    Pushcart prize editors
Oracles
    Prairie Schooner v78 no2 p70-85 Summ 2004
Regular
    New Letters v67 no3 p59-65 2001

Burstein, Michael A.
Teleabsence
    Wondrous beginnings; edited by Steven H.
    Silver and Martin H. Greenberg

Burstein, Michael A.
(jt. auth) See Resnick, Mike and Burstein,
    Michael A.

Burton, Mallory
Bed & breakfast
    Burton, M. Green River virgins and other
    passionate anglers; stories
Blood knots
    Burton, M. Green River virgins and other
    passionate anglers; stories
Casting blind
    Burton, M. Green River virgins and other
    passionate anglers; stories
The compleat adventures of Brooke E. Trout
    Burton, M. Green River virgins and other
    passionate anglers; stories
Degree days
    Burton, M. Green River virgins and other
    passionate anglers; stories
The facts
    Burton, M. Green River virgins and other
    passionate anglers; stories
Geoffrey's wife
    Burton, M. Green River virgins and other
    passionate anglers; stories
Green River virgins
    Burton, M. Green River virgins and other
    passionate anglers; stories
A guide's advice
    Burton, M. Green River virgins and other
    passionate anglers; stories
Home water
    Burton, M. Green River virgins and other
    passionate anglers; stories
In search of the holy grayling
    Burton, M. Green River virgins and other
    passionate anglers; stories
Messing with the river gods
    Burton, M. Green River virgins and other
    passionate anglers; stories
On a fly
    Burton, M. Green River virgins and other
    passionate anglers; stories
On becoming a fly-fishing artiste
    Burton, M. Green River virgins and other
    passionate anglers; stories
Quitting
    Burton, M. Green River virgins and other
    passionate anglers; stories
Reading the water
    Burton, M. Green River virgins and other
    passionate anglers; stories
Richard said that
    Burton, M. Green River virgins and other
    passionate anglers; stories

Timing the strike
    Burton, M. Green River virgins and other
    passionate anglers; stories
Why fly fishing ain't my cup a tea
    Burton, M. Green River virgins and other
    passionate anglers; stories

BURYING GROUNDS _See_ Cemeteries
Burying the books. Baron, D.
'Bus. Berry, R. M.
The **bus.** Jackson, S.
A **bus** called pity. Wheat, C.

BUS DRIVERS
Bail, M. Paradise
Burgin, R. Miles
Johnson, A. The death-dealing Cassini satellite
Karnezis, P. Another day on Pegasus
Keret, E. The story about a bus driver who
    wanted to be God
McNulty, J. Cluney McFarrar's hardtack
Murguía, A. Barrio lotto
Pittalwala, I. The change
Reisman, N. Strays
Saroyan, A. The genius

BUS TERMINALS
Arango, A. The waiting room
Thompson, S. Arnold's number

Busch, Frederick
Are we pleasing you tonight?
    Busch, F. Don't tell anyone
The baby in the box
    Busch, F. Don't tell anyone
Bob's your uncle
    Busch, F. Don't tell anyone
Debriefing
    Busch, F. Don't tell anyone
    Writers harvest 3; edited and with an intro-
    duction by Tobias Wolff
Domicile
    Busch, F. Don't tell anyone
Extra extra large
    What are you looking at?; the first fat fiction
    anthology; edited by Donna Jarrell and Ira
    Sukrungruang
A handbook for spies
    Busch, F. Don't tell anyone
The Hay behind the House
    Harper's v306 p81-8 Ja 2003
Heads
    Busch, F. Don't tell anyone
Joy of cooking
    Busch, F. Don't tell anyone
Laying the ghost
    Busch, F. Don't tell anyone
Machias
    Busch, F. Don't tell anyone
Malvasia
    Busch, F. Don't tell anyone
The ninth, in E minor
    Busch, F. Don't tell anyone
    The Pushcart prize XXIII: best of the small
    presses; an annual small press reader; ed-
    ited by Bill Henderson with the Pushcart
    prize editors
One Last Time, for Old Timaes' Sake
    The Georgia Review v56 no4 p881-91 Wint
    2002
Passengers
    Busch, F. Don't tell anyone

Busch, Frederick—*Continued*
The rescue mission
  Daedalus v131 no2 p115-25 Spr 2002
Still the same old story
  Busch, F. Don't tell anyone
The talking cure
  Busch, F. Don't tell anyone
  The Pushcart prize XXIV: best of the small
    presses; an annual small press reader; ed-
    ited by Bill Henderson with the Pushcart
    prize editors
Timberline
  Busch, F. Don't tell anyone
Vespers
  Busch, F. Don't tell anyone
The **busconductor** Hines [excerpt] Kelman, J.
BUSES
      See also Trolleys
  Abrams, T. Dream rider
  Berry, R. M. 'Bus
  Budnitz, J. Vacation
  Dodd, S. M. Adult education
  Hampton, Francesca. Greyhound Bodhisatva
  Hecht, J. Do the windows open?
  Hogan, E. Coyote goes Hollywood
  Jackson, S. The bus
  Kelman, J. The busconductor Hines [excerpt]
  Madden, D. The world's one breathing
  Mazelis, J. Over the rainbow
  Müller, H. The intervillage bus
  Oates, J. C. Secret, silent
  Ortiz, S. J. More than anything else in the world
  Reiner, C. Sissy Sue and the Reverend Rever-
    end
  Roeske, P. From this distance
  Singer, I. B. The bus
  Stefaniak, M. H. Believing Marina
  Taraqqi, G. The Shemiran bus
            Accidents
      See Traffic accidents
Bush, Gary R.
  The last reel
    Flesh and blood: guilty as sin; erotic tales of
      crime and passion; edited by Max Allan
      Collins and Jeff Gelb
BUSH, GEORGE, 1924-
            About
  Heller, J. The day Bush left
Bush, Mary
  Love
    Hers 2: brilliant new fiction by lesbian writ-
      ers; edited by Terry Wolverton with Robert
      Drake
BUSINESS
      See also Advertising; Department stores;
      Merchants
  Auchincloss, L. The merger
  Capanna, P. Acronia
  Girardi, R. Three ravens on a red ground
  Hawley, L. The good life
  Heinlein, R. A. Magic, inc.
  Kornbluth, C. M. That share of glory
  Thurber, J. The catbird seat
            Unscrupulous methods
  Baida, P. The rodent
  Beckman, J. Babylon revisited redux
  Singer, I. B. Tanhum
BUSINESS DEPRESSION, 1929
  Aldrich, B. S. Alma, meaning "To cherish"

Bellow, S. Looking for Mr. Green
Gautreaux, T. Same place, same things
Business must be picking up. Davidson, A.
The **business** of love. Kalotay, D. E.
The **business** venture. Spencer, E.
BUSINESSMEN
  Banks, R. Djinn
  Bart, P. Power play
  Davies, R. Mr. Pleasant
  DeMarco, T. The Ninja
  Doctorow, C. Power punctuation!
  Fawcett, B. Soul walker
  Fischer, T. We ate the chef
  Gabriel, D. Necati Bey
  Glover, D. H. The Indonesian client
  Gurganus, A. He's one, too
  Ha Jin. An entrepreneur's story
  Händler, E.-W. City with houses
  Händler, E.-W. The new guys
  Harris, M. Touching Idamae Low
  Highsmith, P. A girl like Phyl
  Johnson-Davies, D. Deal concluded
  Johnson-Davies, D. Slice of the cake
  Kaplan, H. Cuckle me
  Melville, P. The sparkling bitch
  Mueller, D. Zero
  Orner, P. Awnings, bedspreads, combed yarns
  Penn, W. S. Early age and late disorder
  Poirier, M. J. Buttons
  Roorbach, B. Big bend
  Shapiro, G. Shifman in paradise
  Shapiro, G. Worst-case scenarios
  Slavin, J. Lives of the invertebrates
  Sorrentino, G. Lost in the stars
  Spencer, D. Caution: men in trees
  Stern, D. Lunch with Gottlieb
  Stuart, J. Lost land of youth
  Tenn, W. Firewater
  Vonnegut, K. This son of mine
  Yates, R. The comptroller and the wild wind
BUSINESSWOMEN
  Auchincloss, L. The last of the great courtesans
  Bingham, S. Rat
  Brady, C. The end of the class war
  Gilman, C. P. What Diantha did
  Homes, A. M. Remedy
  Kane, J. F. Refuge
  Mercader, Mercer. The postponed journey
Buslik, Gary
  Killing sparrows
    Gettysburg Review v12 no4 p688-98 Wint
      1999
The **bust** of the emperor. Roth, J.
Busted blossoms. Kaminsky, S. M.
Bustle in the window. Meno, J.
But Little. Mysko, M.
But, Microsoft! what byte through yonder win-
  dows breaks? Bukiet, M. J.
But She's a Nice Girl and I Wish Her the Best.
  Henkin, J.
But you know us. McBain, E.
Butch. Galef, D.
Butch. O'Neill, S.
BUTCHERS
  Barker, N. The butcher's apprentice
  Brooks, C. The butcher's wife
  Doenges, J. God of gods
  Frym, G. Love
  Gifford, B. A really happy man

BUTCHERS—*Continued*

Nesbitt, M. Polly here somewhere

Ponte, A. J. At the request of Ochun

The **butcher's** apprentice. Barker, N.

The **butcher's** wife. Brooks, C.

The **butcher's** wife. Erdrich, L.

Butler, Laura Payne

Alice's Soulbath

South Carolina Review v34 no1 p54-61 Fall
2001

Booker T's coming home

New stories from the South: the year's best,
1999; edited by Shannon Ravenel; with a
preface by Tony Earley

Butler, Octavia E.

Amnesty

Callaloo v27 no3 p597-615 Summ 2004

Bloodchild

Brown, C. N. and Strahan, J. The Locus
awards; thirty years of the best in science
fiction and fantasy; edited by Charles N.
Brown and Jonathan Strahan

The evening and the morning and the night

Callaloo v24 no2 p401-18 Spr 2001

Dark matter; a century of speculative fiction
from the African diaspora; edited by Sheree
R. Thomas

Speech sounds

Reload: rethinking women + cyberculture; edited by Mary Flanagan and Austin Booth

A Woman's liberation; a choice of futures by
and about women; edited by Connie Willis
and Sheila Williams

Butler, Robert Olen

Carl and I

Butler, R. O. Had a good time; stories from
American postcards

Christmas 1910

Butler, R. O. Had a good time; stories from
American postcards

Fair warning

Coppola, F. F. Francis Ford Coppola's
Zoetrope: all story; edited by Adrienne
Brodeur and Samantha Schnee; introduction
by Francis Ford Coppola

A good scent from a strange mountain

The Scribner anthology of contemporary short
fiction; fifty North American stories since
1970; Lex Williford and Michael Martone,
editors

The grotto

Butler, R. O. Had a good time; stories from
American postcards

Ploughshares v30 no1 p49-62 Spr 2004

Heavy metal

New stories from the South: the year's best,
2000; edited by Shannon Ravenel; with a
preface by Ellen Douglas

Hiram the desperado

Butler, R. O. Had a good time; stories from
American postcards

Hotel Touraine

Butler, R. O. Had a good time; stories from
American postcards

I got married to a milk can

Butler, R. O. Had a good time; stories from
American postcards

The ironworkers' hayride

Butler, R. O. Had a good time; stories from
American postcards

Mother in the trenches

Butler, R. O. Had a good time; stories from
American postcards

Harper's v306 p26, 28-31 F 2003

Mr. Green

The Art of the story; an international anthology of contemporary short stories; edited by
Daniel Halpern

No chord of music

Butler, R. O. Had a good time; stories from
American postcards

The One in White

Atlantic Monthly (1993) v294 no1 p181-8
Jl/Ag 2004

Butler, R. O. Had a good time; stories from
American postcards

Severance: Three Fictions

Prairie Schooner v77 no4 p5-7 Wint 2003

Sunday

Butler, R. O. Had a good time; stories from
American postcards

This is Earl Sandt

Butler, R. O. Had a good time; stories from
American postcards

The Georgia Review v57 no4 p748-59 Wint
2003

Twins

Butler, R. O. Had a good time; stories from
American postcards

Prairie Schooner v78 no2 p3-10 Summ 2004

Uncle Andrew

Butler, R. O. Had a good time; stories from
American postcards

Up by heart

Butler, R. O. Had a good time; stories from
American postcards

BUTLERS

James, H. Brooksmith

Lavin, M. The joy-ride

Marías, J. What the butler said

Perabo, S. Retirement

Butta's backyard barbecue. Medina, T.

Buttenwieser, Sarah Werthan

Confluence

The Massachusetts Review v42 no1 p135-49
Spr 2001

BUTTERFLIES

Hand, E. Cleopatra Brimstone

Murray, J. A few short notes on tropical butterflies

Taylor, T. L. Doves of Townsend

Waterman, D. A lepidopterist's tale

Butterflies. Grace, P.

Butterflies. Sharifzadeh, M.

Butterfly. Guerrero, L.

Butterfly of illusion. Pak, W.-S.

Butterworth, W. E. (William Edmund), 1929-

*For works written by this author under oth-
er names see* Griffin, W. E. B.

Buttons. Adriázola, C.

Buttons. Poirier, M. J.

Buxton spice. Kempadoo, O.

Buying a Fishing Rod for My Grandfather. Gao
Xingjian

Buzz. Rucker, R. v. B.

Buzzard. Pilgrim, D.

By-and-By. Bloom, A.
By any other name. Donaldson, S. R.
By heart. Slezak, E.
By her hand, she draws you down. Smith, D.
By special request. Waugh, E.
By the dawn's early light. Block, L.
By the falls. Harrison, H.
By the light of the jukebox. Paschal, D.
By the sea. Adams, A.
By the sea, by the sea. Swan, M.
By the Sengsen Mountains, by the Dead Mountains. Händler, E.-W.
By the St. Lawrence. Bellow, S.
By the Time They Started First Grade. Carrollhach, H.
By the time we get to Uranus. Vukcevich, R.
By the water. Bowles, P.
By the waters of San Tadeo. L'Amour, L.
By way of the forked stick. Clark, B. C.
Byatt, A. S. (Antonia Susan)
　Baglady
　　Byatt, A. S. Elementals; stories of fire and ice
　Body art
　　Byatt, A. S. Little black book of stories; A.S. Byatt
　Christ in the house of Martha and Mary
　　Byatt, A. S. Elementals; stories of fire and ice
　Cold
　　Byatt, A. S. Elementals; stories of fire and ice
　　The Year's best fantasy & horror, twelfth annual collection; edited by Ellen Datlow & Terry Windling
　Crocodile tears
　　Byatt, A. S. Elementals; stories of fire and ice
　Jael
　　Byatt, A. S. Elementals; stories of fire and ice
　A lamia in the Cévennes
　　Byatt, A. S. Elementals; stories of fire and ice
　The pink ribbon
　　Byatt, A. S. Little black book of stories; A.S. Byatt
　Raw material
　　Atlantic Monthly (1993) v289 no4 p83-92 Ap 2002
　　Byatt, A. S. Little black book of stories; A.S. Byatt
　A stone woman
　　Byatt, A. S. Little black book of stories; A.S. Byatt
　　The New Yorker v79 no30 p90-6, 98-101 O 13 2003
　The thing in the forest
　　Byatt, A. S. Little black book of stories; A.S. Byatt
　　The New Yorker v78 no14 p80-9 Je 3 2002
　　The O. Henry Prize stories, 2003; edited and with an introduction by Laura Furman; jurers David Gutterson, Diane Johnson, Jennifer Egan
Byatt, Antonia Susan *See* Byatt, A. S. (Antonia Susan), 1936-
Byers, Michael
　The beautiful days
　　The Best American short stories, 2000; selected from U.S. and Canadian magazines by E. L. Doctorow with Katrina Kenison; with an introduction by E. L. Doctorow
　　Ploughshares v25 no2/3 p20-45 Fall 1999

Prize stories, 2000; The O. Henry awards; edited and with an introduction by Larry Dark
Bynum, Sarah Shun-Lien
　Accomplice
　　The Georgia Review v57 no1 p23-40 Spr 2003
Bypass. Koger, L.
Byrd, Ron D.
　Paradise
　　The Antioch Review v57 no2 p202-10 Spr 1999
Byrd, Zoey
　Of cabbages
　　Best new American voices 2001; guest editor Charles Baxter; series editors John Kulka and Natalie Danford
Byrne, Eugene
　Bagged 'n' tagged
　　Witpunk; edited by Claude Lalumière and Marty Halpern
BYRON, GEORGE GORDON BYRON, 6TH BARON, 1788-1824
About
　Crowley, J. Missolonghi 1824
Byron. Albert, J.

C

CAB DRIVERS
　Alexie, S. Flight patterns
　Bukiet, M. J. The swap
　Furman, L. Sympathy
　Hermann, J. Summerhouse, later
　Iribarne, M. The clear blue water
　Lida, D. Taxi
　Ludington, M. Thaw
　McNulty, J. An old college chum
　McNulty, J. The television helps, but not very much
　Moffett, M. Dead rock singer
　Nailah, A. The ride
　Polansky, S. Dating Miss Universe
　Yates, R. Builders
The **cabal**. Gilchrist, E.
Caballero, Fernán
　"The girl with three husbands"
　　Fedorchek, R. M. Stories of enchantment from nineteenth-century Spain; translated from the Spanish by Robert M. Fredorchek; introduction by Alan E. Smith
　"Lovely-flower"
　　Fedorchek, R. M. Stories of enchantment from nineteenth-century Spain; translated from the Spanish by Robert M. Fredorchek; introduction by Alan E. Smith
Caballero, Fernń
　"The wishes"
　　Fedorchek, R. M. Stories of enchantment from nineteenth-century Spain; translated from the Spanish by Robert M. Fredorchek; introduction by Alan E. Smith
Caban, Jennifer
　Moses and the Green Man
　　Parabola v28 no4 p32-5 Wint 2003
Cabaret aux Assassins. Black, C.

Cabell, James Branch
The thin queen of Elfhame
Tales before Tolkien; the roots of modern
fantasy; edited by Douglas A. Anderson
Cabeza de Vaca, Alvar Nuñez *See* Nuñez Cabeza
de Vaca, Alvar, 16th cent.
Cabeza de Vaca. Gonzalez, R.
Cabiles, Nelinia
Tsunami
Prairie Schooner v75 no4 p69-89 Wint 2001
Cable, George Washington
The story of Bras-Coupé
Southern local color; stories of region, race,
and gender; edited by Barbara C. Ewell and
Pamela Glenn Menke; with notes by An-
drea Humphrey
Caboose. Walden, S.
Cabrera Infante, G. (Guillermo)
The doors open at three
The Oxford book of Caribbean short stories;
edited by Stewart Brown and John
Wickham
The great ekbó
Cabrera Infante, G. Guilty of dancing the
chachachá; translated from Spanish by the
author
Guilty of dancing the chachachá
Cabrera Infante, G. Guilty of dancing the
chachachá; translated from Spanish by the
author
A woman saved from drowning
Cabrera Infante, G. Guilty of dancing the
chachachá; translated from Spanish by the
author
Cabrera Infante, Guillermo *See* Cabrera Infante,
G. (Guillermo), 1929-
Cacek, P. D. (Patricia D.)
Belief
Redshift; extreme visions of speculative fic-
tion; edited by Al Sarrantonio
The grave
999: new stories of horror and suspense; ed-
ited by Al Sarrantonio
Cacek, Patricia D. *See* Cacek, P. D. (Patricia D.)
The **Cactus** Kid. L'Amour, L.
CADETS
Harrison, H. Space rats of the CCC
Cadigan, Pat
Mother's milt
Witpunk; edited by Claude Lalumière and
Marty Halpern
Cadillac flambé. Ellison, R.
Cadle, Dean
Anthem of the locusts
Home and beyond; an anthology of Kentucky
short stories; edited by Morris Allen
Grubbs; with an introduction by Wade Hall
and an afterword by Charles E. May
Cadnum, Michael
Bear it away
Black heart, ivory bones; [edited by] Ellen
Datlow & Terri Windling
Bite the hand
Vanishing acts; a science fiction anthology;
edited by Ellen Datlow
Champion of the ocean floor
New England Review v20 no4 p34-35 Fall
1999

Cady, Jack
Daddy dearest
Cady, J. Ghosts of yesterday
The ghost of Dive Bomber Hill
Cady, J. Ghosts of yesterday
Halloween 1942
Cady, J. Ghosts of yesterday
Israel and Ernest
Cady, J. Ghosts of yesterday
Jacket copy
Cady, J. Ghosts of yesterday
Jeremiah
Cady, J. Ghosts of yesterday
Death dines at 8:30; edited by Claudia Bishop
and Nick DiChario
The lady with the blind dog
Cady, J. Ghosts of yesterday
On writing the ghost story
Cady, J. Ghosts of yesterday
Play like I'm sheriff
Home and beyond; an anthology of Kentucky
short stories; edited by Morris Allen
Grubbs; with an introduction by Wade Hall
and an afterword by Charles E. May
Science fiction, utopia, and the spirit
Cady, J. Ghosts of yesterday
Seven sisters
Datlow, E. The dark; new ghost stories; ed-
ited by Ellen Datlow
Support your local Griffin
Cady, J. Ghosts of yesterday
The time that time forgot
Cady, J. Ghosts of yesterday
Weird row
Cady, J. Ghosts of yesterday
Café Piel. Dickey, E. J.
Café society. Simpson, H.
CAFÉS *See* Restaurants, lunchrooms, etc.
The **cafeteria**. Singer, I. B.
The **Cafeteria** in the Evening and a Pool in the
Rain. Ogawa, Y.
Cage of brass. Delany, S. R.
Cai Cehai
The distant sound of tree-felling
The Vintage book of contemporary Chinese
fiction; edited by Carolyn Choa and David
Su Li-qun
Cain, James M. (James Mallahan)
The baby in the icebox
The Best American mystery stories of the
century; Tony Hillerman, editor; with an
introduction by Tony Hillerman
Cigarette girl
A Century of great suspense stories; edited by
Jeffery Deaver
A Century of noir; thirty-two classic crime
stories; edited by Mickey Spillane and Max
Allan Collins
Cain, Mary Ann
Maya
The North American Review v287 no1 p19-22
Ja/F 2002
CAIRO (EGYPT) *See* Egypt—Cairo
The **Cairo** cat caper. Schweighofer, P.
CAJUNS
Chopin, K. At the 'Cadian ball
Chopin, K. A gentleman of Bayou Têche
Chopin, K. The godmother
Chopin, K. A horse story

CAJUNS—*Continued*
  Chopin, K. In Sabine
  Chopin, K. A night in Acadie
  Chopin, K. The storm
  Chopin, K. Ti Démon
  Parrish, T. Bonnie Ledet
Cakes of baby. Davies, P. H.
Calbert, Cathleen
  Greece
    The Southern Review (Baton Rouge, La.) v39
      no4 p754-61 Aut 2003
The **calculator**. Hensley, J. L.
A **calculus** of desperation. Benford, G.
The **Calculus** of Felicity. Wahl, S.
CALCUTTA (INDIA) *See* India—Calcutta
Calcutta. Billman, J.
Calderon, Luna
  Day Ah Dallas Mare Toes
    Fantasmas; supernatural stories by Mexican
      American writers; edited by Rob Johnson;
      introduction by Kathleen J. Alcalá
Calendar waltz. Davis, L.
CALENDARS
  Sneve, V. D. H. The twelve moons
The **caliber**. Müllner, A.
Calibrations of latitude. Mathews, H.
Calico Rock Cave. Tillinghast, D.
CALIFORNIA
      See also Death Valley (Calif. and Nev.);
      Sierra Nevada Mountains (Calif. and Nev.)
  Barrett, N., Jr. Highbrow
  Canin, E. Where we are now
  Chacón, D. Slow and good
  Cooper, B. Intro to acting
  Gilchrist, E. The brown cape
  Gilchrist, E. Jade Buddhas, red bridges, fruits of
    love
  Gilchrist, E. The Starlight Express
  Gilchrist, E. You must change your life
  Kerouac, J. The Mexican girl
  Manzarek, R. The lady of the valley
  Muñoz, M. Anchorage
  Murray, Y. M. Girl on fire
  Rawley, D. The spells of an ordinary twilight
  Rucker, R. v. B. Chaos surfari
  Sánchez, R. Road detours
  Scoville, S. The dividing strand
  Steinbeck, J. The murder
            1800-1846
  Baker, K. Facts relating to the arrest of Dr.
    Kalugin
  Baker, K. Noble mold
            1846-1900
  Baker, K. Lemuria will rise!
  Dawson, J. What the cat dragged in
  Gorriti, J. M. A year in California
  Jakes, J. Jonas Crag
            20th century
  Adams, A. Greyhound people
  Barrett, L. Hush money
  Boyle, T. C. Death of the cool
  Carver, R. What would you like to see?
  Gilliland, G. Kindnesses
  Haake, K. The land of sculpture
  Haake, K. This is geology to us
  Lee, D. Casul water
  Lee, D. The Lone Night Cantina
  Lee, D. The price of eggs in China
  Lee, D. Voir dire

  Lee, D. Widowers
  Parker, T. J. Easy street
  Pronzini, B. Smuggler's island
  Rawley, D. A rumor of prayer
  Rawley, D. The tiger's tooth
  Rawley, D. Tina in the back seat
  Rawley, D. Vandeville
  Smart, A. The bridge players
  Smart, A. The Green Lantern
  Smart, A. Hunter
  Smart, A. Jersey Joe versus the Rock
  Smart, A. The wedding Dress
  Steinbeck, T. Sing Fat and the Imperial Duchess
    of Woo
  Wieland, L. Gray's anatomy
  Wilson, R., Jr. California
            Farm life
      See Farm life—California
          Frontier and pioneer life
      See Frontier and pioneer life—California
            Gold discoveries
      See California—1846-1900
            Bel Air
  Cooper, B. Night sky
            Berkeley
  Blitz, R. At 15, he had been a leader in
  Blitz, R. Death to the fascist imperialist dogs
  Blitz, R. In Berkeley's green and pleasant land
  Blitz, R. Lies
  Blitz, R. Make haste, my beloved
  Blitz, R. The mother's wasteland
  Blitz, R. Notes from the tower of menopause
  Blitz, R. P.S. your thing is sticking out
  Blitz, R. The participant
  Blitz, R. She had mastered the art
  Blitz, R. The small revelation
  Blitz, R. This picnic you're having
  Blitz, R. Two women
  Blitz, R. The unuseable talent
  Frym, G. Crime and punishment
  Frym, G. The oldest trick in the book
  Frym, G. Rosie since Vietnam
  Frym, G. SWAT
  Frym, G. Tagging
  Frym, G. "To see her in sunlight was to see
    Marxism die"
  Gilliland, G. Berkeley
  Scholz, C. The menageries of Babel
  Watanabe McFerrin, L. Khalida's dog
            Beverly Hills
  Braverman, K. Temporary light
  Gault, W. C. The Kerman kill
  Robison, M. Smoke
            Carmel
  Adams, A. Molly's dog
            Fresno
  Boyle, T. C. The underground gardens
  Chacón, D. Spring break
            Hollywood
  Bart, P. The founder
  Bart, P. The neighbors I
  Bart, P. The neighbors II
  Bart, P. The neighbors III
  Brown, C. Now is the time
  Clarke, A. C. Armaments race
  Collins, B. Cat got your tongue
  Collins, B. The ten lives of Talbert
  Cooper, B. Bit-o-honey
  Fitzgerald, F. S. Crazy Sunday

CALIFORNIA—Hollywood—*Continued*
Harrison, J. Westward ho
Kees, W. Do you like the mountains?
Perabo, S. Thick as thieves
Los Angeles
Adam, C. Cat
Alderete, P. Fire
Anderson, R. Slight return
Boyle, T. C. The black and white sisters
Bradbury, R. Another fine mess
Bradbury, R. Tangerine
Brown, F. The wench is dead
Chan, D. M. Goblin fruit
Chan, D. M. Seven swans
Cleaver, E. The flashlight
Davies, R. Celluloid heroes
Davies, R. The shirt
DeMarinis, R. The smile of a turtle
Etchison, D. The detailer
Himes, C. Lunching at the Ritzmore
Hood, A. Dropping bombs
Karbo, K. The palace of marriage
Leavitt, D. The term paper artist
Leong, R. Camouflage
Leong, R. Daughters
Leong, R. Geography one
Leong, R. Hemispheres
Leong, R. No Bruce Lee
Levinson, R. S. Good career moves
Locklin, G. Fin de semestre
Mathews, L. Crazy life
McNeal, T. Winter in Los Angeles
Mendoza, R. Traffic
Moody, R. On the carousel
Mosley, W. Blue lightning
Mosley, W. A day in the park
Mosley, W. Equal opportunity
Mosley, W. Mookie Kid
Mosley, W. Moving on
Mosley, W. The mugger
Mosley, W. Promise
Mosley, W. Rascals in the cane
Mosley, W. Rogue
Mosley, W. Shift, shift, shift
Mosley, W. That smell
Mosley, W. The thief
Mosley, W. Walkin' the dog
Mosley, W. What would you do?
Muñoz, M. By the time you get there, by the
    time you get back
Muñoz, M. Skyshot
Neri, K. Sentence imposed
Nietzke, A. Los Angeles here and now
Oates, J. C. The dark prince
Padilla, M. Restoration
Pak, T. The court interpreter
Rawley, D. Baby Liz
Rawley, D. The bible of insects
Rawley, D. Mother of pearl
Resnick, R. Day 'n nite
Rifkin, A. After the divorce
Rifkin, A. Signal Hill
Rusch, K. K. Spirit guides
Sánchez, R. He rolled up his sleeves
Saroyan, A. Hollywood lessons
Saroyan, A. My literary life
Scott, J. The coming of the Hoodlum
Skiff, M. Blood brothers
Tea, M. 9/11 L.A. bookstore
Toole, F. X. Rope burns
Vasseur, T. J. The angels
Vernon, D. Couple kills
Williams, J. A. Son in the afternoon
Yates, R. Saying goodbye to Sally
Malibu
Harrison, W. The rocky hills of Trancas
Monterey
Steinbeck, T. Blighted cargo
Steinbeck, T. The dark watcher
Steinbeck, T. The night guide
Steinbeck, T. An unbecoming grace
Steinbeck, T. The wool gatherer
Oakland
DeMarinis, R. Safe forever
Sacramento
Penn, W. S. Tarantulas
San Francisco
Adams, A. Earthquake damage
Adams, A. Fog
Adams, A. The last lovely city
Bagley, J. E. Children of chance
Baker, K. Son observe the time
Berriault, G. The infinite passion of expectation
Brady, C. And the shin bone's connected to the
    knee bone
Burford, M. The faces of fear
Burris, J. Judah's a two-way street running out
Chee, A. Gold
Chee, A. A pilgrimage of you
Cole, C. B. Foo dog
Davidson, A. Pebble in time
Dokey, R. The beggar of Union Square
Frym, G. Columbus Day
Gilchrist, E. Götterdämmerung, in which Nora
    Jane and Freddy Harwood confront evil in
    a world they never made
Gilchrist, E. Lunch at the best restaurant in the
    world
Gilchrist, E. Perhaps a miracle
Gilchrist, E. The sanguine blood of men
Gores, J. Inscrutable
Gores, J. Watch for it
Hayes, D. This world of ours
Hodgson, W. H. The adventure with the claim
    jumpers
Hogan, D. The bombs
Hood, A. Escapes
Houston, P. The best girlfriend you never had
Leavitt, D. The infection scene
Leong, R. Runaways
Leong, R. Sons
Leong, R. Virgins and Buddhas
Leong, R. The western paradise of Eddie Bin
Matera, L. Dream lawyer
McPherson, J. A. Elbow room
Michaels, L. Tell me everything
Murguía, A. Ofrendas
Murguía, A. El último round
Ortiz, S. J. The San Francisco Indians
Padilla, M. Who in the modern world can keep
    up with Julia Juárez?
Richmond, M. The girl in the fall-away dress
Richter, S. My date with Satan
Saroyan, A. The genius
Scoville, S. The pin collectors
Shapiro, G. Worst-case scenarios
Sorrentino, G. Perdído
Wheat, C. What the dormouse said

CALIFORNIA—San Francisco—*Continued*
Wieland, L. Cirque du Soleil
Santa Barbara
Boyle, T. C. She wasn't soft
Santa Cruz
Rucker, R. v. B. As above, so below
Venice
Clinton, M. T. Free your mind and your ass will follow
California. Wilson, R., Jr.
The **California** contact. Howard, C.
California fine view. Dinh, L.
The **California** Franchise Tax Board. Mayo, W.
California—the nervous camel. Antin, D.
Caline. Chopin, K.
Calisher, Hortense
In Greenwich, there are many gravelled walks
Wonderful town; New York stories from The New Yorker; edited by David Remnick with Susan Choi
Call at Corazón. Bowles, P.
CALL GIRLS *See* Escorts (Dating service)
Call if you need me. Carver, R.
The **call** in the dawn. Hodgson, W. H.
Call me Joe. Anderson, P.
Call me Ruby. Winter, E.
Call me Wiggins. Schreiber, N.
The **call** of cthulhu. Lovecraft, H. P.
Callaghan, Morley
Absolution
Callaghan, M. The New Yorker stories
All the years of her life
Callaghan, M. The New Yorker stories
The bride
Callaghan, M. The New Yorker stories
The chiseler
Callaghan, M. The New Yorker stories
Day by day
Callaghan, M. The New Yorker stories
The duel
Callaghan, M. The New Yorker stories
Ellen
Callaghan, M. The New Yorker stories
An escapade
Callaghan, M. The New Yorker stories
The faithful wife
Callaghan, M. The New Yorker stories
Lunch counter
Callaghan, M. The New Yorker stories
One spring night
Callaghan, M. The New Yorker stories
The red hat
Callaghan, M. The New Yorker stories
The rejected one
Callaghan, M. The New Yorker stories
The shining red apple
Callaghan, M. The New Yorker stories
Silk stockings
Callaghan, M. The New Yorker stories
The snob
Callaghan, M. The New Yorker stories
Their mother's purse
Callaghan, M. The New Yorker stories
Timothy Harshaw's flute
Callaghan, M. The New Yorker stories
The voyage out
Callaghan, M. The New Yorker stories
The white pony
Callaghan, M. The New Yorker stories

Younger brother
Callaghan, M. The New Yorker stories
Caller I.D. Beller, T.
Calling. Ford, R.
Calvino, Italo
Autumn; the rain and the leaves
The Best of The Kenyon review; edited by David Lynn; introduction by Joyce Carol Oates
CAMBODIANS
United States
Honig, L. Love, rescue, care, dream, sweep
Honig, L. Refuge
Miller, E. In memory of Chanveasna Chan, who is still alive
CAMBRIDGE (MASS.) *See* Massachusetts—Cambridge
The **camel**. Berners, G. H. T.-W., Baron
CAMELS
Berners, G. H. T.-W., Baron. The camel
Savage, L., Jr. The Lone Star camel corps
The **camel's** back. Fitzgerald, F. S.
Camenietzki, Shalom
The atheist's bible
Dalhousie Review v79 no3 p397-405 Aut 1999
Camera obscura. Hermann, J.
CAMERAS
Davidson, A. The Montavarde camera
Ziegler, I. Blind spot
Cameron, Peter
Beginning with the letter
New England Review v23 no1 p156-69 Wint 2002
Cameron, Sharon
Beautiful work
Nixon under the bodhi tree and other works of Buddhist fiction; edited by Kate Wheeler ; foreword by Charles Johnson
CAMEROON
April, J. P. Rêve Canadien
Mokoso, N. God of meme
Nfah-Abbenyi, J. M. Accidents are a sideshow
Nfah-Abbenyi, J. M. American lottery
Nfah-Abbenyi, J. M. Bayam-sellam
Nfah-Abbenyi, J. M. Election fever
Nfah-Abbenyi, J. M. The forest will claim you too
Nfah-Abbenyi, J. M. The healer
Nfah-Abbenyi, J. M. Market scene
Nfah-Abbenyi, J. M. Slow poison
Nfah-Abbenyi, J. M. Your madness, not mine
Camouflage. Bail, M.
Camouflage. Leong, R.
Camp. Winter, E.
Campalbo. Viganò, R.
Campbell, Bebe Moore
What you owe me
Essence v32 no3 p118 Jl 2001
Campbell, Bonnie Jo
The bridesmaid
Michigan Quarterly Review v38 no1 p29-34 Wint 1999
Bringing home the bones
Campbell, B. J. Women & other animals; stories
Celery fields
Campbell, B. J. Women & other animals; stories

Campbell, Bonnie Jo—*Continued*

Children of Transylvania
The Southern Review (Baton Rouge, La.) v38 no3 p536-55 Summ 2002

Circus matinee
Campbell, B. J. Women & other animals; stories

Eating Aunt Victoria
Campbell, B. J. Women & other animals; stories

The fishing dog
Campbell, B. J. Women & other animals; stories

Gorilla girl
Campbell, B. J. Women & other animals; stories

Old dogs
Campbell, B. J. Women & other animals; stories

The perfect lawn
Campbell, B. J. Women & other animals; stories

Rhyme game
Campbell, B. J. Women & other animals; stories

Running
Campbell, B. J. Women & other animals; stories

Shifting gears
Campbell, B. J. Women & other animals; stories

Shotgun wedding
Campbell, B. J. Women & other animals; stories

Sleeping sickness
Campbell, B. J. Women & other animals; stories

The smallest man in the world
Campbell, B. J. Women & other animals; stories
The Southern Review (Baton Rouge, La.) v35 no1 p92-100 Wint 1999

The sudden physical development of Debra Dupuis
Campbell, B. J. Women & other animals; stories

Taking care of the O'Learys
Campbell, B. J. Women & other animals; stories

Campbell, Ewing

At the Blue Breakers
The Georgia Review v56 no4 p994-1008 Wint 2002

Exposures
Southwest Review v84 no2 p205-18 1999

Campbell, Gabrielle Margaret Vere, 1886-1952
For works written by this author under other names see Bowen, Marjorie, 1886-1952

Campbell, John Wood

Twilight
The Science fiction hall of fame: volume one, 1929-1964; the greatest science fiction stories of all time chosen by the members of the Science Fiction Writers of America; edited by Robert Silverberg

Who goes there?
Science-fiction classics; the stories that morphed into movies; compiled by Forrest J. Ackerman

Campbell, Ramsey

All for sale
The Mammoth book of best horror 13; edited by Stephen Jones

The alternative
Campbell, R. Ghosts and grisly things

Between the floors
Campbell, R. Ghosts and grisly things

The body in the window
Campbell, R. Scared stiff; tales of sex and death

The change
Campbell, R. Ghosts and grisly things

The dead must die
Campbell, R. Ghosts and grisly things

Dolls
Campbell, R. Scared stiff; tales of sex and death

The entertainment
999: new stories of horror and suspense; edited by Al Sarrantonio
Best new horror 11; edited and with an introduction by Stephen Jones

Feeling remains
Datlow, E. The dark; new ghost stories; edited by Ellen Datlow

Going under
Campbell, R. Ghosts and grisly things

Kill me hideously
Campbell, R. Scared stiff; tales of sex and death

Lilith's
Campbell, R. Scared stiff; tales of sex and death

The limits of fantasy
Campbell, R. Scared stiff; tales of sex and death

Looking out
Campbell, R. Ghosts and grisly things

Loveman's comeback
Campbell, R. Scared stiff; tales of sex and death

McGonagall in the head
Campbell, R. Ghosts and grisly things

Merry May
Campbell, R. Scared stiff; tales of sex and death

Missed connection
Campbell, R. Ghosts and grisly things

No end of fun
The Year's best fantasy & horror: sixteenth annual collection; edited by Ellen Datlow & Terri Windling

No story in it
Death dines at 8:30; edited by Claudia Bishop and Nick DiChario

No strings
Best new horror 12; edited and with an introduction by Stephen Jones
Death dines at 8:30; edited by Claudia Bishop and Nick DiChario

The other woman
Campbell, R. Scared stiff; tales of sex and death

Campbell, Ramsey—*Continued*

Out of the woods

    Campbell, R. Ghosts and grisly things

Ra*e

    Best new horror 10; edited and with an introduction by Stephen Jones

    Campbell, R. Ghosts and grisly things

Root cause

    Campbell, R. Ghosts and grisly things

The same in any language

    Campbell, R. Ghosts and grisly things

The seductress

    Campbell, R. Scared stiff; tales of sex and death

See how they run

    Campbell, R. Ghosts and grisly things

A side of the sea

    Campbell, R. Ghosts and grisly things

The sneering

    Campbell, R. Ghosts and grisly things

Stages

    Campbell, R. Scared stiff; tales of sex and death

A street was chosen

    Campbell, R. Ghosts and grisly things

This time

    Campbell, R. Ghosts and grisly things

Through the walls

    Campbell, R. Ghosts and grisly things

Twice by fire

    The Crow; shattered lives & broken dreams; edited by J. O'Barr and Ed Kramer

The unbeheld

    The Mammoth book of best new horror 14; edited with an introduction by Stephen Jones

Welcomeland

    Campbell, R. Ghosts and grisly things

Where they lived

    Campbell, R. Ghosts and grisly things

Worse than bones

    The Museum of horrors; edited by Dennis Etchison

CAMPING

Adam, C. Ursus horribilis

Blackwood, A. The willows

Daniels, J. Fireworks

DeMarinis, R. Wilderness

Henley, P. Hard feelings

Henley, P. Same old big magic

Norris, L. Trailer people

Phillips, D. R. What we are up against

Potvin, E. A. Blue moon

Wallace, R. Logjam

Camping with strangers. Nawrocki, S.

Campo, Rafael

Mrs. Twomey

    The Georgia Review v57 no2 p328-32 Summ 2003

Campo, Rossana

Like a banana

    In the forbidden city; an anthology of erotic fiction by Italian women; edited by Maria Rosa Cutrufelli; translated by Vincent J. Bertolini

Campra, Rosalba

Dream tiger

    English translations of short stories by contemporary Argentine women writers; edited by Eliana Cazaubon Hermann ; translated by Sally Webb Thornton

CAMPS, SUMMER *See* Summer camps

Camps. Dann, J.

CAMPUS LIFE *See* College life

Can I forget you? Stewart, I.

Can I get a witness? Alexie, S.

The **can** men. Greer, R. O.

Can the double murder? Blavatsky, H. P.

Can we talk. Chinodya, S.

Can Xue *See* Ts'an-hsüeh, 1953-

Can you wave bye bye, baby? Gasco, E.

Can you wear my eyes. Kalamu ya Salaam

CANADA

April, J. P. Rêve Canadien

Choi, E. Divisions

Pflug, U. Bugtown

Schoemperlen, D. This town

Simonds, M. The blue of the Madrugada

Simonds, M. King of the Cowboys, Queen of the West

Warren, D. A reckless moon

    19th century

Hudgins, B. Fur bearing

Munro, A. Meneseteung

    20th century

Alexis, A. Despair: five stories of Ottawa

Alexis, A. Horse

Alexis, A. My Anabasis

Alexis, A. The night piece

Alexis, A. The road to Santiago de Compostela

Alexis, A. The third terrace

Johnson, A. The Canadanaut

Munro, A. Family furnishings

Munro, A. Hateship, friendship, courtship, loveship, marriage

Toft, M. Tourist trap

    College life

    See College life—Canada

    Farm life

    See Farm life—Canada

    Frontier and pioneer life

    See Frontier and pioneer life—Canada

    Rural life

Atwood, M. Wilderness tips

Munro, A. Save the reaper

    Alberta

Thomas, D. The Christmas whopper

Thomas, D. Flowers appear on the earth

    Edmonton

Forsyth, F. The veteran

    Manitoba

Norman, H. Unicycle

Patterson, K. Manitoba Avenue

Patterson, K. Saw marks

    Montreal

Bankier, W. Child of another time

Bonnie, F. Sign language

Ford, R. Dominion

Kalman, J. Ladies' wear

Kalman, J. The making of a Jew

Kalman, J. A reason to be

Spencer, E. I, Maureen

    Newfoundland

MacLeod, A. The lost salt gift of blood

CANADA—*Continued*

Nova Scotia

Gibson, W. The girl at Thorp's
MacLeod, A. The boat
MacLeod, A. Clearances
MacLeod, A. The closing down of summer
MacLeod, A. The return
MacLeod, A. The tuning of perfection
MacLeod, A. The vastness of the dark
Wuori, G. K. Mothers

Ontario

Hardy, M. The uncharted heart
MacLeod, A. Winter dog
Potvin, E. A. After hours, after years
Simonds, M. The day of the dead
Simonds, M. Taken for delirium

Québec (Province)

Bellow, S. By the St. Lawrence
Porter, J. A. Basse Ville
Vivante, A. The cove

Québec (Québec)

Glover, D. H. La Corriveau

Saskatchewan

Stegner, W. E. Buglesong

Toronto

Bezmozgis, D. An animal to the memory
Bezmozgis, D. Choynski
Bezmozgis, D. Minyan
Bezmozgis, D. Natasha
Bezmozgis, D. Roman Berman, massage therapist
Bezmozgis, D. The second strongest man
Bezmozgis, D. Tapka
Davis, L. Drop in any time
Doctorow, C. Shadow of mothaship
Munro, A. Queenie

Vancouver

Gartner, Z. City of my dreams
Munro, A. Post and beam
Taylor, T. L. Pope's own

Vancouver Island

See Vancouver Island (B.C.)

Victoria (B.C.)

Young, T. Too busy swimming

Yukon Territory

Kilpatrick, N. Snow angel
London, J. All Gold Canyon
Canada. Connolly, C.
Canada geese and apple chatney. Persaud, S.
The **Canadanaut**. Johnson, A.
CANADIAN SOLDIERS *See* Soldiers—Canada
CANADIANS

Bali

Paine, T. The hotel on Monkey Forest Road

Belgium

Swan, M. By the sea, by the sea

Brazil

Simonds, M. King of the Cowboys, Queen of the West
Simonds, M. The lion in the room next door

France

Potvin, E. A. After hours, after years

Greece

Simonds, M. The distance to Delphi

Guyana

Melville, P. Erzulie

Mexico

Simonds, M. In the city of the split sky
Simonds, M. The still point

New Zealand

Armstrong, K. The first motion of love

Spain

Swan, M. Spanish grammar

Sweden

Simonds, M. Navigating the Kattegat

United States

Jones, T. Tarantula
Skeet, M. Near enough to home
The **canal**. Yates, R.
Canal boat. Haskins, L.
The **canasta** club. Bland, E. T.
Cancellanda. Warner, M.
Cancelled friends. Disch, T. M.
CANCER

Baida, P. A nurse's story
Bellow, S. Something to remember me by
Blackwood, S. In the shadow of our house
Bloom, A. Hold tight
Bloom, A. Rowing to Eden
Broyard, B. My father, dancing
Canty, K. Carolina beach
Clyde, M. Krista had a treble clef rose
Clyde, M. Survival rates
Cobb, T. Oncology
Cohen, R. A flight of sparks
Connolly, C. How I lost my vocation
Davis, J. S. Some things collide
Deane, J. F. Between times
DeMarinis, R. Paraiso: an elegy
DeMarinis, R. The singular we
Desaulniers, J. After Rosa Parks
Díaz, J. Nilda
Dokey, R. A house in order
Fairey, W. W. The bad hand
Fraterrigo, M. Body, mine
Fulton, J. Retribution
Gay, W. My hand is just fine where it is
Greenberg, A. A couple of dead men
Grodstein, L. Yellow morning
Hoffman, A. Devotion
Hoffman, A. The rest of your life
Homes, A. M. Do not disturb
Howard, C. The cobalt blues
Jackson, S. Cancer
James, S. Love, lust, life
Johnson, A. The death-dealing Cassini satellite
Johnston, B. A. I see something you don't see
Jones, T. 40, still at home
Jones, T. I want to live!
Klíma, I. Rich men tend to be strange
Leebron, F. G. That winter
Lumley, B. Big "C"
McBain, E. But you know us
McGarry, J. Body and soul
Melville, P. Lucifer's shank
Moore, L. Real estate
Munro, A. Floating bridge
Newman, D. A. Mystery Spot
Nissen, T. Way back when in the now before now
Orringer, J. Pilgrims
Orringer, J. What we save
Pitt, M. The mean
Price, R. An evening meal
Reisman, N. Common light
Robinson, L. The toast
Rodgers, S. J. Bust
Singer, I. B. The witch

CANCER—*Continued*

Sojourner, M. Delicate

Stolar, D. Mourning

Sturgeon, T. Slow sculpture

Turchi, P. The night sky

Vachss, A. H. Dope fiend

Zabytko, I. Lavender soap

Candace counts coup. Lord, N.

Candie-gram. Garrett, M.

Candles in the bottom of the pool. Evans, M.

CANDLESTICKS

Chekhov, A. P. The objet d'art

Chekhov, A. P. A work of art

CANDY

Locklin, G. Candy bars

Candy art. Kelly, J. P.

Candy bars. Locklin, G.

The **cane** field. Armstrong, K.

Cane river. Tademy, L.

The **canebrake**. Mrabet, M.

Canin, Ethan

Vins fins

The New Yorker v75 no21 p66-76 Ag 2 1999

Vins fins (I)

The New Yorker v75 no16 p160-1 Je 21-28 1999

Where we are now

LA shorts; edited by Steven Gilbar

The year of getting to know us

The Scribner anthology of contemporary short fiction; fifty North American stories since 1970; Lex Williford and Michael Martone, editors

The Workshop; seven decades of the Iowa Writers' Workshop: 42 stories, recollections & essays on Iowa's place in 20th-century American literature; edited by Tom Grimes

Canis lupus. Brkic, C. A.

Canned foreign. Tawada, Y.

Cannell, Dorothy

Bridal flowers

Love and death; edited by Carolyn Hart

Come to Grandma

Cannell, D. The family jewels and other stories

Cupids arrow

Cannell, D. The family jewels and other stories

The family jewels: a moral tale

Cannell, D. The family jewels and other stories

Fetch

Cannell, D. The family jewels and other stories

The gentleman's gentleman

Cannell, D. The family jewels and other stories

The high cost of living

Cannell, D. The family jewels and other stories

The January sale stowaway

Cannell, D. The family jewels and other stories

One night at a time

Cannell, D. The family jewels and other stories

Poor Lincoln

Cannell, D. The family jewels and other stories

The purloined purple pearl

Cannell, D. The family jewels and other stories

Telling George

Cannell, D. The family jewels and other stories

What Mr. McGregor saw

Malice domestic 9

The World's finest mystery and crime stories, second annual collection; edited by Ed Gorman

CANNERIES

Tyau, K. Pick up your pine

Cannibal kings. Greer, A. S.

CANNIBALISM

Alexie, S. Ghost dance

Brown, S. With clouds at our feet

Chapman, C. M. Second helping

Gira, M. Why I ate my wife

Hayter, S. The diary of Sue Peaner, Marooned! contestant

Kilpatrick, N. Horrorscope

Kilpatrick, N. Snow angel

Kilpatrick, N. Youth not wasted

Russell, J. Hides

Somtow, S. P. Bird catcher

Cannon, Taffy

Restitution

Women before the bench; edited by Carolyn Wheat; introduction by Linda Fairstein

CANOES AND CANOEING

Gay, W. Charting the territories of the red

Hudgins, B. Fur bearing

Roorbach, B. Fog

Rosa, J. G. The third bank of the river

Canon. Vermeulen, J.

CANONIZATION

Hardy, M. Aquero

Canovic, Lidija S.

Bats

Best new American voices 2001; guest editor Charles Baxter; series editors John Kulka and Natalie Danford

Cantaloupes. Williams, M.

The **Cantankerous** Judge. Brenner, W.

The **Canterbury** pilgrims. Hawthorne, N.

Canticle. Frym, G.

A **canticle** for Wulfstan. Tremayne, P.

Cantinflas. Gutiérrez, S. D.

Canton, NY. Tait, J.

Cantor, Rachel

Hello, I'm Cora

New England Review v23 no3 p64-72 Summ 2002

Paige

The Antioch Review v61 no4 p687-91 Fall 2003

Rosaria 1988

New England Review v20 no4 p91-99 Fall 1999

Slave for a Day

New England Review v24 no4 p159-66 2003

Canty, Kevin

Aquarium

Canty, K. Honeymoon and other stories

Carolina beach

Canty, K. Honeymoon and other stories

Flipper

Canty, K. Honeymoon and other stories

Canty, Kevin—*Continued*
Girlfriend hit by bus
Canty, K. Honeymoon and other stories
Honeymoon
Canty, K. Honeymoon and other stories
Little Debbie
Canty, K. Honeymoon and other stories
Little palaces
Canty, K. Honeymoon and other stories
Red dress
Canty, K. Honeymoon and other stories
Scarecrow
Canty, K. Honeymoon and other stories
Sleepers holding hands
Canty, K. Honeymoon and other stories
Tokyo, my love
Canty, K. Honeymoon and other stories
Canyon de Kayenta. Gonzalez, R.
Capacity. Sandor, M.
Capanna, Pablo
Acronia
Cosmos latinos: an anthology of science fiction from Latin America and Spain; translated, edited, & with an introduction & notes by Andrea L. Bell & Yolanda Molina-Gavilán
The **cape**. Nakagami, K.
CAPE COD (MASS.) *See* Massachusetts—Cape Cod
Čapek, Karel
At the castle
Čapek, K. Cross roads; translated from the Czech and with an introduction by Norma Comrada; illustrated by Paul Hoffman
The bully
Čapek, K. Cross roads; translated from the Czech and with an introduction by Norma Comrada; illustrated by Paul Hoffman
Elegy (Footprint II)
Čapek, K. Cross roads; translated from the Czech and with an introduction by Norma Comrada; illustrated by Paul Hoffman
The footprint
Čapek, K. Cross roads; translated from the Czech and with an introduction by Norma Comrada; illustrated by Paul Hoffman
Grafitto
Čapek, K. Cross roads; translated from the Czech and with an introduction by Norma Comrada; illustrated by Paul Hoffman
Helena
Čapek, K. Cross roads; translated from the Czech and with an introduction by Norma Comrada; illustrated by Paul Hoffman
Help!
Čapek, K. Cross roads; translated from the Czech and with an introduction by Norma Comrada; illustrated by Paul Hoffman
Insulted
Čapek, K. Cross roads; translated from the Czech and with an introduction by Norma Comrada; illustrated by Paul Hoffman
Lida
Čapek, K. Cross roads; translated from the Czech and with an introduction by Norma Comrada; illustrated by Paul Hoffman
The lost way
Čapek, K. Cross roads; translated from the Czech and with an introduction by Norma Comrada; illustrated by Paul Hoffman
Love song (Lida II)
Čapek, K. Cross roads; translated from the Czech and with an introduction by Norma Comrada; illustrated by Paul Hoffman
Money
Čapek, K. Cross roads; translated from the Czech and with an introduction by Norma Comrada; illustrated by Paul Hoffman
The mountain
Čapek, K. Cross roads; translated from the Czech and with an introduction by Norma Comrada; illustrated by Paul Hoffman
Reflections
Čapek, K. Cross roads; translated from the Czech and with an introduction by Norma Comrada; illustrated by Paul Hoffman
The shirts
Čapek, K. Cross roads; translated from the Czech and with an introduction by Norma Comrada; illustrated by Paul Hoffman
Story without words
Čapek, K. Cross roads; translated from the Czech and with an introduction by Norma Comrada; illustrated by Paul Hoffman
Temptation
Čapek, K. Cross roads; translated from the Czech and with an introduction by Norma Comrada; illustrated by Paul Hoffman
Three
Čapek, K. Cross roads; translated from the Czech and with an introduction by Norma Comrada; illustrated by Paul Hoffman
Time stands still
Čapek, K. Cross roads; translated from the Czech and with an introduction by Norma Comrada; illustrated by Paul Hoffman
The tribunal
Čapek, K. Cross roads; translated from the Czech and with an introduction by Norma Comrada; illustrated by Paul Hoffman
Two fathers
Čapek, K. Cross roads; translated from the Czech and with an introduction by Norma Comrada; illustrated by Paul Hoffman
The waiting room
Čapek, K. Cross roads; translated from the Czech and with an introduction by Norma Comrada; illustrated by Paul Hoffman
Capers, I. Bennett
The Last Tenant
Callaloo v25 no3 p744-52 Summ 2002
Capital H. Deane, J. F.
CAPITAL PUNISHMENT
Chekhov, A. P. The bet
Downs, M. Prison food
Hillerman, T. First lead gasser
Oates, J. C. Death watch
Capitalism. Krawiec, R.
CAPITALISTS AND FINANCIERS
See also Bankers; Millionaires; Wealth
Doctorow, E. L. Loon lake
Evans, M. Candles in the bottom of the pool
Cap'n Bob and Gus. Crider, B.

Caponegro, Mary
The daughter's lamentation
Caponegro, M. The complexities of intimacy; stories
Epilogue of the progeny; or, Whoever is never born with the most toys wins
Caponegro, M. The complexities of intimacy; stories
The father's blessing
Caponegro, M. The complexities of intimacy; stories
The mother's mirror
Caponegro, M. The complexities of intimacy; stories
The son's burden
Caponegro, M. The complexities of intimacy; stories
Capote, Truman
Among the paths to Eden
Capote, T. and Price, R. The complete stories of Truman Capote; introduction by Reynolds Price
The bargain
Capote, T. and Price, R. The complete stories of Truman Capote; introduction by Reynolds Price
The New York Times Book Review v109 no37 p10-11 S 12 2004
Children on their birthdays
Capote, T. and Price, R. The complete stories of Truman Capote; introduction by Reynolds Price
A Christmas memory
Capote, T. and Price, R. The complete stories of Truman Capote; introduction by Reynolds Price
A diamond guitar
Capote, T. and Price, R. The complete stories of Truman Capote; introduction by Reynolds Price
The headless hawk
Capote, T. and Price, R. The complete stories of Truman Capote; introduction by Reynolds Price
House of flowers
Capote, T. and Price, R. The complete stories of Truman Capote; introduction by Reynolds Price
Jug of silver
Capote, T. and Price, R. The complete stories of Truman Capote; introduction by Reynolds Price
Master misery
Capote, T. and Price, R. The complete stories of Truman Capote; introduction by Reynolds Price
A mink of one's own
Capote, T. and Price, R. The complete stories of Truman Capote; introduction by Reynolds Price
Mojave
Capote, T. and Price, R. The complete stories of Truman Capote; introduction by Reynolds Price
My side of the matter
Capote, T. and Price, R. The complete stories of Truman Capote; introduction by Reynolds Price

One Christmas
Capote, T. and Price, R. The complete stories of Truman Capote; introduction by Reynolds Price
Preacher's legend
Capote, T. and Price, R. The complete stories of Truman Capote; introduction by Reynolds Price
Shut a final door
Capote, T. and Price, R. The complete stories of Truman Capote; introduction by Reynolds Price
The Thanksgiving visitor
Capote, T. and Price, R. The complete stories of Truman Capote; introduction by Reynolds Price
A tree of night
Capote, T. and Price, R. The complete stories of Truman Capote; introduction by Reynolds Price
The walls are cold
Capote, T. and Price, R. The complete stories of Truman Capote; introduction by Reynolds Price
CAPRA, FRANK, 1897-1991
About
Lethem, J. and Scholz, C. Receding horizon
The **caprices**. Murray, S.
Captain Bedlam. Harrison, H.
Captain Benvolio Bullhorner. Breen, J. L.
Captain Galaxy comes back to earth. Saknussemm, K.
Captain Honario Harpplayer, R.N. Harrison, H.
Captain Jim's drunken dream. Braunbeck, G. A.
Captain Pasharooney. Davidson, A.
Captain Poison. Alarcón, P. A. d.
The **captain's** daughter. Pushkin, A. S.
CAPTAINS OF SHIPS *See* Shipmasters
Captive kong. Reed, K.
Captives. Carson, J.
Captivity Narrative 109. Jones, S.
Captured by the Indians. Boyle, T. C.
CAPUCINE, 1933-1990
About
Haskell, J. Capucine
Capucine. Haskell, J.
The **car**. Highsmith, P.
The **car**. Strandquist, R.
Car frogs. Svoboda, T.
Caravan. Pearlberg, G.
Card, Orson Scott
50 WPM
Tetrick, B. In the shadow of the wall; an anthology of Vietnam stories that might have been; edited by Byron R. Tetrick
Ender's game
Wondrous beginnings; edited by Steven H. Silver and Martin H. Greenberg
Hatrack River
The American fantasy tradition; edited by Brian M. Thomsen
Investment counselor
Far horizons; all new tales from the greatest worlds of science fiction; edited by Robert Silverberg
Lost boys
Children of the night; stories of ghosts, vampires, werewolves, and "lost children"; edited by Martin H. Greenberg

Card, Orson Scott—*Continued*

The Yazoo Queen

Silverberg, R. Legends II; new short novels by the masters of modern fantasy; edited by Robert Silverberg

Card Parties. Buckhanon, K.

Card players. Hunter, F.

The **Card** Trick. Hadley, T.

CARDIFF (WALES) *See* Wales—Cardiff

Cardiff-by-the-Sea. Goldner, B.

CARDIFF GIANT

Twain, M. A ghost story

The **cardiologist's** house. White, M. C.

Cardoso, Onelio Jorge

The storyteller

Dream with no name; contemporary fiction from Cuba; edited by Juana Ponce de León and Esteban Ríos Rivera

CARDS

See also Tarot

Bernhard, T. Playing Watten

Chekhov, A. P. Vint

Dann, J. Blind shemmy

Care. Orringer, J.

Care. Robison, M.

Career. Roth, J.

Career move. Amis, M.

The **career** of Ivan Yakovlevich Antonov. Kharms, D.

Careful. Skinner, J.

The **caregiver**. Collier, E.

Carelessness. See Chekhov, A. P. An inadvertence

The **carer**. Rendell, R.

The **caretaker**. Doerr, A.

Carew, Jan

Tilson Ezekiel alias Ti-Zek

The Oxford book of Caribbean short stories; edited by Stewart Brown and John Wickham

Carey, Peter

The chance

Centaurus: the best of Australian science fiction; edited by David G. Hartwell and Damien Broderick

The fat man in history

The Art of the story; an international anthology of contemporary short stories; edited by Daniel Halpern

What are you looking at?; the first fat fiction anthology; edited by Donna Jarrell and Ira Sukrungruang

Cargo. Henley, P.

CARIB INDIANS

Harris, W. Yurokon

Caribbean chameleon. Silvera, M.

CARIBBEAN ISLANDS *See* West Indies

CARIBBEAN REGION

Antoni, R. My grandmother's tale of the buried treasure and how she defeated the King of Chacachacari and the entire American Army with her venus-flytraps

Bell, M. S. Labor

Chiappone, R. Q Roo

Foley, S. Off Grenada

Hopkinson, N. The glass bottle trick

Kurlansky, M. Naked

Kurlansky, M. Packets and paperscraps

Lansdale, J. R. Master of misery

Mastretta, A. Big-eyed women [excerpt]

Maxwell, M. A. O. Devil beads

McDonald, I. Pot O'Rice Horowitz's house of solace

Mordecai, P. Once on the shores of the stream Senegambia

Scott, L. Ballad for the new world

Senior, O. Mad Fish

Shacochis, B. Mundo's sign

Thomas, H. N. The village cock

Vega, A. L. Cloud cover Caribbean

Carl, Lillian Stewart

The eye of the beholder

The World's finest mystery and crime stories, third annual collection; edited by Ed Gorman and Martin H. Greenberg

A mimicry of mockingbirds

White House pet detectives; tales of crime and mystery at the White House from a pet's-eye view; edited by Carole Nelson Douglas

A rose with all its thorns

Past lives, present tense; edited by Elizabeth Ann Scarborough

Carl, under his car. Chambers, C.

Carleton, Michael R.

Conversations with a moose

Virgin fiction 2

Carley's knees. DeLancey, K.

Carlson, P. M.

The world is mine; or, Deeds that make heaven weep

Murder most Celtic; tall tales of Irish mayhem; edited by Martin H. Greenberg

Carlson, Ron

At Copper View

Carlson, R. At the Jim Bridger; stories

At the El Sol

Carlson, R. At the Jim Bridger; stories

At the Jim Bridger

Carlson, R. At the Jim Bridger; stories

Prize stories, 2001; The O. Henry awards; edited and with an introduction by Larry Dark

Bigfoot stole my wife

Carlson, R. A kind of flying; selected stories; with an introduction by the author

Blazo

Carlson, R. A kind of flying; selected stories; with an introduction by the author

Blood

Carlson, R. A kind of flying; selected stories; with an introduction by the author

The chromium hook

Carlson, R. A kind of flying; selected stories; with an introduction by the author

The clicker at Tips

Carlson, R. At the Jim Bridger; stories

DeRay

Carlson, R. A kind of flying; selected stories; with an introduction by the author

Disclaimer

Carlson, R. At the Jim Bridger; stories

Down the Green River

Carlson, R. A kind of flying; selected stories; with an introduction by the author

Dr. Slime

Carlson, R. A kind of flying; selected stories; with an introduction by the author

Carlson, Ron—*Continued*
Evil eye Allen
  Carlson, R. At the Jim Bridger; stories
Gary Garrison's wedding vows
  Carlson, R. At the Jim Bridger; stories
The Gold Lunch
  Ploughshares v30 no2/3 p51-5 Fall 2004
The governor's ball
  Carlson, R. A kind of flying; selected stories;
    with an introduction by the author
The H Street sledding record
  Carlson, R. A kind of flying; selected stories;
    with an introduction by the author
Hartwell
  Carlson, R. A kind of flying; selected stories;
    with an introduction by the author
  The Student body; short stories about college
    students and professors; edited by John
    McNally
The Hotel Eden
  Carlson, R. A kind of flying; selected stories;
    with an introduction by the author
I am Bigfoot
  Carlson, R. A kind of flying; selected stories;
    with an introduction by the author
Keith
  Carlson, R. A kind of flying; selected stories;
    with an introduction by the author
A kind of flying
  Carlson, R. A kind of flying; selected stories;
    with an introduction by the author
Life before science
  Carlson, R. A kind of flying; selected stories;
    with an introduction by the author
Max
  Carlson, R. A kind of flying; selected stories;
    with an introduction by the author
Milk
  Carlson, R. A kind of flying; selected stories;
    with an introduction by the author
Nightcap
  Carlson, R. A kind of flying; selected stories;
    with an introduction by the author
A note on the type
  Carlson, R. A kind of flying; selected stories;
    with an introduction by the author
Olympus Hills
  Carlson, R. A kind of flying; selected stories;
    with an introduction by the author
On the U.S.S. Fortitude
  Carlson, R. A kind of flying; selected stories;
    with an introduction by the author
The ordinary son
  The Best American short stories, 2000; select-
    ed from U.S. and Canadian magazines by
    E. L. Doctorow with Katrina Kenison; with
    an introduction by E. L. Doctorow
  Carlson, R. At the Jim Bridger; stories
Oxygen
  Carlson, R. A kind of flying; selected stories;
    with an introduction by the author
Phenomena
  Carlson, R. A kind of flying; selected stories;
    with an introduction by the author
Plan B for the middle class
  Carlson, R. A kind of flying; selected stories;
    with an introduction by the author
The potato gun
  Carlson, R. At the Jim Bridger; stories

Esquire v136 no6 p77-88, 160 D 2001
The prisoner of Bluestone
  Carlson, R. A kind of flying; selected stories;
    with an introduction by the author
Rocket Day
  Harper's v306 p60-6 F 2003
Santa Monica
  Carlson, R. A kind of flying; selected stories;
    with an introduction by the author
Single woman for long walks on the beach
  Carlson, R. At the Jim Bridger; stories
Some of our work with monsters
  Ploughshares v28 no2/3 p26-37 Fall 2002
The status quo
  Carlson, R. A kind of flying; selected stories;
    with an introduction by the author
The summer of vintage clothing
  Carlson, R. A kind of flying; selected stories;
    with an introduction by the author
Sunny Billy Day
  Carlson, R. A kind of flying; selected stories;
    with an introduction by the author
The Tablecloth of Turnin
  Carlson, R. A kind of flying; selected stories;
    with an introduction by the author
The time I died
  Carlson, R. A kind of flying; selected stories;
    with an introduction by the author
Towel season
  Carlson, R. At the Jim Bridger; stories
What we wanted to do
  Carlson, R. A kind of flying; selected stories;
    with an introduction by the author
Zanduce at second
  Carlson, R. A kind of flying; selected stories;
    with an introduction by the author
Carlyle tries polygamy. Kelley, W. M.
CARMEL (CALIF.) *See* California—Carmel
Carmelita's education for living. Harris, M.
Carmen Miranda's navel. Parris, P. B.
Carmody, Isobelle
  The dove game
    Gathering the bones; original stories from the
      world's masters of horror; edited by Dennis
      Etchison, Ramsey Campbell and Jack Dann
  The man who lost his shadow
    Dreaming down-under; edited by Jack Dann
      and Janeen Webb
Carnahan, Peter
  Things
    The North American Review v284 no3-4 p50-
      57 My/Ag 1999
Carnation, Lily, Lily, Rose. Link, K.
Carnegie's bones. Cliff, M.
Carneiro, André
  Brain transplant
    Cosmos latinos: an anthology of science fic-
      tion from Latin America and Spain; trans-
      lated, edited, & with an introduction &
      notes by Andrea L. Bell & Yolanda Moli-
      na-Gavilán
Carnevale: the first night. Swan, G.
Carney, Otis
  How I happened to put on the blue
    Westward; a fictional history of the American
      West : 28 original stories celebrating the
      50th anniversary of the Western Writers of
      America; edited by Dale L. Walker
Carnie. Means, D.

CARNIVAL
Anthony, M. They better don't stop the carnival
Melville, P. Mrs. Da Silva's carnival
Trevanian. Snatch off your cap, kid!
The **carnival**. Howard, C.
The **carnival** tradition. Moody, R.
CARNIVALS (CIRCUS) *See* Amusement parks
Carole Nelson Douglas
Sax and the single cat
  Felonious felines; edited by Carol and Ed Gorman
Carolina beach. Canty, K.
Caroline, Queen, consort of George IV, King of Great Britain, 1768-1821 *See* Caroline Amelia Elizabeth, Queen, consort of George IV, King of Great Britain, 1768-1821
CAROLINE AMELIA ELIZABETH, QUEEN, CONSORT OF GEORGE IV, KING OF GREAT BRITAIN, 1768-1821
About
Edwards, M. Natural causes
CAROLS
Updike, J. The carol sing
Carp fishing on valium. Parker, G.
Carp man. DiChario, N.
Carpenter, Rachel
The Ashtray
  Ploughshares v30 no1 p93-9 Spr 2004
The **carpenter** who looked like a boxer. Murray, J.
CARPENTERS
Alexie, S. One good man
Cai Cehai. The distant sound of tree-felling
Fromm, P. The raw material of ash
Lopez, B. H. In the great bend of the Souris River
Reid, E. Laura Borealis
Carpentier, Alejo
Journey back to the source
  Dream with no name; contemporary fiction from Cuba; edited by Juana Ponce de León and Esteban Ríos Rivera
Journey to the seed
  The Oxford book of Caribbean short stories; edited by Stewart Brown and John Wickham
CARPETS
Gault, W. C. The Kerman kill
Carr, Pat M.
Diary of a union soldier
  Home and beyond; an anthology of Kentucky short stories; edited by Morris Allen Grubbs; with an introduction by Wade Hall and an afterword by Charles E. May
An El Paso Idyll
  Graham, D. Lone Star literature; from the Red River to the Rio Grande; edited by Don Graham
CARRIACOU (GRENADA)
Davidson, R. A private life
Carrillo, H. G.
Abejas Rubias
  The Kenyon Review v26 no3 p75-90 Summ 2004
CARRINGTON, MARGARET IRVIN, 1831-1870
About
Carroll, L. Leaving paradise

Carrión, Carmen
Primavera
  Calyx v21 no2 p71-84 Summ 2003
Carrion crows. Yolen, J. and Harris, R. J.
Carroll, Jim
Curtis's charm
  Carved in rock; short stories by musicians; edited by Greg Kihn
Carroll, Jonathan
The Heidelberg cylinder
  Death dines at 8:30; edited by Claudia Bishop and Nick DiChario
Carroll, Lenore
Before the adventures
  Murder, my dear Watson; new tales of Sherlock Holmes; edited by Martin H. Greenberg, Jon Lellenberg, Daniel Stashower
Leaving paradise
  Westward; a fictional history of the American West : 28 original stories celebrating the 50th anniversary of the Western Writers of America; edited by Dale L. Walker
Traveling princess
  American West; twenty new stories from the Western Writers of America; edited with an introduction by Loren D. Estleman
Carrollhach, Haley
By the Time They Started First Grade
  Raritan v23 no1 p154-61 Summ 2003
Carry-on. Jakiela, L.
Carrying concealed. Scottoline, L.
Carrying Sergei. Padilla, M.
Carry's cat. Collins, B.
CARS (AUTOMOBILES) *See* Automobiles
Carson, Josephine
Anonymous
  Carson, J. Dog Star and other stories
Brilliant company
  Carson, J. Dog Star and other stories
Captives
  Carson, J. Dog Star and other stories
Chosen
  Carson, J. Dog Star and other stories
Dog Star
  Carson, J. Dog Star and other stories
Fair trades
  Carson, J. Dog Star and other stories
Flying apart
  Carson, J. Dog Star and other stories
Invaders
  Carson, J. Dog Star and other stories
Judgement
  Carson, J. Dog Star and other stories
Protective coloring
  Carson, J. Dog Star and other stories
Two thousand years of torture
  Carson, J. Dog Star and other stories
The virgin
  Carson, J. Dog Star and other stories
Carson, Michael
Peter's buddies
  Other people's mail; an anthology of letter stories; edited with an introduction by Gail Pool
The **cartel**. Roth, J.

Carter, Angela
  The courtship of Mr. Lyon
    The Art of the story; an international antholo-
      gy of contemporary short stories; edited by
      Daniel Halpern
Carter, Charlotte
  Birdbath
    The Mysterious Press anniversary anthology;
      celebrating 25 years; by the editors of Mys-
      terious Press
Carter, Emily
  A
    Carter, E. Glory goes and gets some; stories
  All the men are called McCabe
    Carter, E. Glory goes and gets some; stories
  Ask Amelio
    Carter, E. Glory goes and gets some; stories
  Bad boy walking
    Carter, E. Glory goes and gets some; stories
  The bride
    Carter, E. Glory goes and gets some; stories
  Clean clothes
    Carter, E. Glory goes and gets some; stories
  Cute in camouflage
    Carter, E. Glory goes and gets some; stories
  East on Houston
    Carter, E. Glory goes and gets some; stories
  Glory and the angels
    Carter, E. Glory goes and gets some; stories
  Glory B. and the baby Jesus
    Carter, E. Glory goes and gets some; stories
  Glory B. and the gentle art
    Carter, E. Glory goes and gets some; stories
  Glory B. and the ice-man
    Carter, E. Glory goes and gets some; stories
  Glory goes and gets some
    Carter, E. Glory goes and gets some; stories
  Luminous dial
    Carter, E. Glory goes and gets some; stories
  Minneapolis
    Carter, E. Glory goes and gets some; stories
  My big red heart
    Carter, E. Glory goes and gets some; stories
  New in north town
    Carter, E. Glory goes and gets some; stories
  Parachute silk
    Carter, E. Glory goes and gets some; stories
  Train line
    Carter, E. Glory goes and gets some; stories
  WLUV
    Carter, E. Glory goes and gets some; stories
  Zemecki's cat
    Carter, E. Glory goes and gets some; stories
Carter, Margaret L. (Margaret Louise)
  Mercy
    The Darkest thirst; a vampire anthology
CARTHAGE (ANCIENT CITY)
  Anderson, P. Delenda est
CARTOGRAPHERS
  Barrett, A. Servants of the map
CARTOONISTS
  Holbrook, T. Drawing to a close
CARUSO, ENRICO, 1873-1921
              About
  Paul, B. Portrait of the artist as a young corpse
Carved in vinyl. Allen, S.

Carver, Raymond
  The aficionados
    Carver, R. Call if you need me; the uncollect-
      ed fiction and other prose; edited by Wil-
      liam L. Stull; foreword by Tess Gallagher
  Are these actual miles?
    The Art of the story; an international antholo-
      gy of contemporary short stories; edited by
      Daniel Halpern
  Bright red apples
    Carver, R. Call if you need me; the uncollect-
      ed fiction and other prose; edited by Wil-
      liam L. Stull; foreword by Tess Gallagher
  Call if you need me
    The Best American short stories, 2000; select-
      ed from U.S. and Canadian magazines by
      E. L. Doctorow with Katrina Kenison; with
      an introduction by E. L. Doctorow
    Carver, R. Call if you need me; the uncollect-
      ed fiction and other prose; edited by Wil-
      liam L. Stull; foreword by Tess Gallagher
    Granta no68 p9-21 Wint 1999
  Dreams
    Carver, R. Call if you need me; the uncollect-
      ed fiction and other prose; edited by Wil-
      liam L. Stull; foreword by Tess Gallagher
  Errand
    The Scribner anthology of contemporary short
      fiction; fifty North American stories since
      1970; Lex Williford and Michael Martone,
      editors
  Fat
    What are you looking at?; the first fat fiction
      anthology; edited by Donna Jarrell and Ira
      Sukrungruang
  Furious seasons
    Carver, R. Call if you need me; the uncollect-
      ed fiction and other prose; edited by Wil-
      liam L. Stull; foreword by Tess Gallagher
  The hair
    Carver, R. Call if you need me; the uncollect-
      ed fiction and other prose; edited by Wil-
      liam L. Stull; foreword by Tess Gallagher
  Intimacy
    Fault lines; stories of divorce; collected and
      edited by Caitlin Shetterly
  Kindling
    Carver, R. Call if you need me; the uncollect-
      ed fiction and other prose; edited by Wil-
      liam L. Stull; foreword by Tess Gallagher
    Esquire v132 no1 p72-77 Jl 1999
    Prize stories, 2000; The O. Henry awards; ed-
      ited and with an introduction by Larry
      Dark
  Put yourself in my shoes
    The Workshop; seven decades of the Iowa
      Writers' Workshop: 42 stories, recollections
      & essays on Iowa's place in 20th-century
      American literature; edited by Tom Grimes
  The third thing that killed my father off
    Still wild; short fiction of the American West,
      1950 to the present; edited by Larry
      McMurtry
  Vandals
    Carver, R. Call if you need me; the uncollect-
      ed fiction and other prose; edited by Wil-
      liam L. Stull; foreword by Tess Gallagher
    Esquire v132 no4 p160-65 O 1999

Carver, Raymond—*Continued*
What would you like to see?
  Carver, R. Call if you need me; the uncollected fiction and other prose; edited by William L. Stull; foreword by Tess Gallagher
Where I'm calling from
  The Best American short stories of the century; John Updike, editor, Katrina Kenison, coeditor; with an introduction by John Updike
Casa, Ricard de la *See* Casa Pérez, Ricard de la, 1954-
La **casa** chica. Matiella, A. C.
Casa i Pérez, Ricard de la *See* Casa Pérez, Ricard de la, 1954-
Casa Pérez, Ricard de la
The day we went through the transition
  Cosmos latinos: an anthology of science fiction from Latin America and Spain; translated, edited, & with an introduction & notes by Andrea L. Bell & Yolanda Molina-Gavilán
Casal, Lourdes
A love story according to Cyrano Prufrock
Dream with no name; contemporary fiction from Cuba; edited by Juana Ponce de León and Esteban Ríos Rivera
CASANOVA, GIACOMO, 1725-1798
About
Reiner, C. Caz
Casares, Oscar
Big Jesse, Little Jesse
  Casares, O. Brownsville; stories
Chango
  Casares, O. Brownsville; stories
Charro
  Casares, O. Brownsville; stories
Domingo
  Casares, O. Brownsville; stories
Jerry Fuentes
  Casares, O. Brownsville; stories
Mr. Z
  Casares, O. Brownsville; stories
Mrs. Perez
  Casares, O. Brownsville; stories
RG
  Casares, O. Brownsville; stories
Ruben and Norma
  Iowa Review v32 no2 p111-25 Fall 2002
Yolanda
  Casares, O. Brownsville; stories
Case, David
Jimmy
  Best new horror 11; edited and with an introduction by Stephen Jones
A **case** of dementia. Kirchheimer, G. D.
The **case** of Grand Cru. Cohen, S.
A **case** of insomnia. Vourlis, J. P.
A **case** of royal blood. Altman, S.-E.
The **case** of the bloodless sock. Perry, A.
The **case** of the Chinese curio dealer. Hodgson, W. H.
The **case** of the discontented soldier. Christie, A.
The **case** of the headless witness. Biggle, L.
The **case** of the Highland hoax. Perry, A. and Saxon, M.
The **case** of the shaggy caps. Rendell, R.
The **case** of the wavy black dagger. Perry, S.

Casey, John
A more complete cross-section
  The Workshop; seven decades of the Iowa Writers' Workshop: 42 stories, recollections & essays on Iowa's place in 20th-century American literature; edited by Tom Grimes
Casey, Kevin
The coffin
  TriQuarterly no110/111 p372-6 Fall 2001
Refugees
  TriQuarterly no110/111 p377-81 Fall 2001
Casey, Maud
The arrangement of the night office in summer
  Casey, M. Drastic; stories
Aspects of motherhood
  Casey, M. Drastic; stories
Days at home
  Casey, M. Drastic; stories
Dirt
  Casey, M. Drastic; stories
Drastic
  Casey, M. Drastic; stories
Genealogy
  Casey, M. Drastic; stories
Indulgence
  Casey, M. Drastic; stories
Relief
  Casey, M. Drastic; stories
Rules to live
  Casey, M. Drastic; stories
Seaworthy
  Casey, M. Drastic; stories
  Gettysburg Review v14 no3 p382-93 Aut 2001
Talk show lady
  Casey, M. Drastic; stories
Trespassing
  Casey, M. Drastic; stories
  Prairie Schooner v75 no4 p140-51 Wint 2001
Casey, Paul
A Distant Death
  The Literary Review (Madison, N.J.) v46 no3 p521-32 Spr 2003
Cash crop: 1897. Pancake, A.
The **cash-point** oracle. Dyson, J.
Cashmere Christmas. Lombreglia, R.
The **Cask** of Amontillado. Flannery, S.
The **cask** of Amontillado. Poe, E. A.
Caspers, Nona
Country Girls
  Iowa Review v33 no3 p2-20 Wint 2003/2004
La maison de Madame Durard
  Hers 3: brilliant new fiction by lesbian writers; edited by Terry Wolverton with Robert Drake
Vegetative states
  Hers 2: brilliant new fiction by lesbian writers; edited by Terry Wolverton with Robert Drake
CASSADY, NEAL
About
Rucker, R. v. B. Instability
Cassandra is gone. Karnezis, P.
Cassandra mouth. Wells, K.

Cassill, R. V.
And in my heart
The Workshop; seven decades of the Iowa Writers' Workshop: 42 stories, recollections & essays on Iowa's place in 20th-century American literature; edited by Tom Grimes
Cassill, Ronald Verlin *See* Cassill, R. V., 1919-2002
Cassirer, Nadine Gordimer *See* Gordimer, Nadine, 1923-
The **cassoulet**. Satterthwait, W.
Cassutt, Michael
More adventures on other planets
The Year's best science fiction, nineteenth annual collection; edited by Gardner Dozois
A **cast** leaf. Coates, G. S.
Castaway. Clarke, A. C.
CASTE
Asimov, I. Strikebreaker
Castelgandolfo. Hill, I.
Castellanos, Rosario
Culinary lesson
Short stories by Latin American women; the magic and the real; edited by Celia Correas de Zapata; foreword by Isabel Allende
Castillo, Rafael
The battle of the Alamo
Graham, D. Lone Star literature; from the Red River to the Rio Grande; edited by Don Graham
Casting against type. Nye, J. L.
Casting blind. Burton, M.
Castle in the desert. Newman, K.
Castle of snow. Heller, J.
Castoro, Laura Parker
Christmas and Coconut Cake
Good Housekeeping v235 no6 p211-12, 214, 216, 218-19 D 2002
Castro, Adam-Troy
The funeral march of the Marionettes
Castro, A.-T. Tangled strings
The magic bullet theory
Castro, A.-T. Tangled strings
Sunday night yams at Minnie and Earl's
Castro, A.-T. Tangled strings
Nebula awards showcase 2004; edited by Vonda McIntyre
The tangled strings of the Marionettes
Castro, A.-T. Tangled strings
Unseen demons
Castro, A.-T. Tangled strings
CASTRO, FIDEL, 1927-
About
Arenas, R. Traitor
Castro, Joy
A notion I took
The North American Review v286 no6 p14-15 N/D 2001
Castro, Pablo A.
Exerion
Cosmos latinos: an anthology of science fiction from Latin America and Spain; translated, edited, & with an introduction & notes by Andrea L. Bell & Yolanda Molina-Gavilán
Castronuovo, David
(jt. auth) *See* Boito, Arrigo
Casualidades. Alessio, C.

CASUALTIES (WORLD WAR, 1914-1918) *See* World War, 1914-1918—Casualties
Casualty. Epstein, J.
Casul water. Lee, D.
Cat. Adam, C.
Cat. Johnson-Davies, D.
Cat and mouse. Metzgar, L.
The **cat** and the clown. Stanton, M.
The **cat** and the Kinetophone. Breen, J. L.
The **cat** garden. Setton, R. K.
Cat got your tongue. Collins, B.
A **cat** horror story. Dozois, G. R.
Cat in love. Scott, J.
The **cat** in the cage. Barnes, H. L.
The **Cat** Man. Oren, Y.
Cat 'N' Mouse. Millhauser, S.
Cat on an old school roof. Crowther, P.
Cat o'nine lives. Grape, J.
Cat people. Beattie, A.
Cat women of Rome. Gifford, B.
Catabolism. Van Belkom, E.
CATACOMBS
Poe, E. A. The cask of Amontillado
Catalano, Mark
Ted
Gettysburg Review v14 no2 p183-90 Summ 2001
Catalogues. Lippi, R.
Catamount. Rendell, R.
Cataract. Houston, P.
CATASTROPHES *See* Disasters
The **catbird** seat. Thurber, J.
Catch. Vukcevich, R.
Catch-23: Yossarian lives. Heller, J.
The **catcher**. O'Rourke, F.
Catching crumbs from the table. *See* Chiang, T. The evolution of human science
CATERERS AND CATERING
Moody, R. The Mansion on the Hill
Catfish. Billman, J.
Catfish gal blues. Collins, N. A.
Catgate. Collins, M. A.
Cathal's lake. McCann, C.
The **Catharine** wheel. McDonald, I.
CATHEDRALS
Bear, G. Petra
Friesner, E. M. Hallowmass
Cather, Willa
Double birthday
The Best American short stories of the century; John Updike, editor, Katrina Kenison, coeditor; with an introduction by John Updike
Paul's case
The Best American mystery stories of the century; Tony Hillerman, editor; with an introduction by Tony Hillerman
CATHERINE, OF SIENA, SAINT, 1347-1380
About
Anderson, R. Schism
Catherine, Saint *See* Labouré, Catherine, Saint, 1806-1876
CATHOLIC BISHOPS
Wharton, E. Expiation
CATHOLIC CHURCH *See* Catholic faith
CATHOLIC CLERGY *See* Catholic priests

CATHOLIC FAITH

See also Catholic bishops; Catholic priests; Convent life; Monasticism and religious orders

Alarcón, P. A. d. Moors and Christians
Alas, L. The golden rose
Arruda, M. J. Reconciliation
Barnard, R. Holy living and holy dying
Bukoski, A. A concert of minor pieces
Bukoski, A. Dry spell
Bukoski, A. The korporał's polonaise
Bukoski, A. The wood of such trees
Butler, R. O. Twins
Byatt, A. S. Body art
Chopin, K. Odalie misses mass
D'Ambrosio, C., Jr. Open house
Deane, J. F. Capital H
Deane, J. F. Poste restante
Foote, S. The sacred mound
Gardner, J. A. Three hearings on the existence of snakes in the human bloodstream
Gordon, M. Cleaning up
Gould, L. La Lloradora
Grau, S. A. Letting go
Hardy, M. Aquero
Herling, G. Beata, Santa
Herling, G. The eyetooth of Barabbas
Jacobs, M. Looking for Lourdes
Kalu, Anthonia C. Angelus
Mastretta, A. Aunt Verónica
McIntyre, V. N. The moon and the sun [excerpt]
Meade, D. Lost time
Morrow, J. Auspicious eggs
O'Connell, M. The patron saint of girls
O'Connell, M. Saint Anne
O'Connell, M. Saint Catherine Laboure
O'Connell, M. Saint Dymphna
O'Neill, S. Broken stone
Orringer, J. Stations of the cross
Scoville, S. The pin collectors
Smolens, J. Absolution
Smolens, J. The you is understood
Strauch, T. J. The Alberscine's vigil
Wharton, E. The duchess at prayer
Wharton, E. The hermit and the wild woman
Catholic guilt (you know you love it). Welsh, I.

CATHOLIC PRIESTS

See also Catholic bishops; Catholic faith

Alas, L. The lord
Babel', I. The church in Novograd
Block, L. Speaking of lust
Boucher, A. The quest for Saint Aquin
Bradbury, R. Bless me, Father, for I have sinned
Bradbury, R. The machineries of joy
Bukoski, A. The absolution of Hedda Borski
Bukoski, A. Winter weeds
Caponegro, M. The father's blessing
Davis, D. S. Now is forever
Deane, J. F. Big Lil
Delaney, E. J. The drowning
Dépestre, R. Rosena on the mountain
Gautreaux, T. Good for the soul
Giono, J. The solitude of compassion
Gonzalez, R. The garden of Padre Anselmo
Gorman, E. Judgment
Greeley, A. M. The bishop and the hit man
Hansen, R. My Communist
Hassler, J. Keepsakes
Hassler, J. Resident priest

Herling, G. The exorcist's brief confession
Iribarne, M. Make them laugh
Mastretta, A. Aunt Charo
McGraw, E. Ax of the Apostles
McInerny, R. M. The base of the triangle; a Father Dowling mystery
Morrow, J. Auspicious eggs
O'Connell, M. I fly unto you
O'Marie, C. A. Defender of the faith
Parks, J. A. The covenant of Il Vigneto
Powers, J. F. Death of a favorite
Sade, marquis de. The husband who turned priest: a tale of Provence
Sandlin, L. The saint of bilocation
Theroux, P. A Judas memoir

CATHOLIC RELIGION See Catholic faith
CATHOLICS See Catholic faith

Catlin, Alan

Death in Venice
The Literary Review (Madison, N.J.) v42 no3 p390-91 Spr 1999

CATS

Adam, C. Cat
Adam, C. Quail
Adams, A. The islands
Adams, A. Raccoons
Albert, J. Byron
Ansay, A. M. Box
Atkinson, K. The cat lover
Barth, J. Dead cat, floating boy
Bilgrey, M. Living the lie
Bowles, P. Kitty
Bradbury, R. The cat's pajamas
Braunbeck, G. A. Mail-order Annie
Breen, J. L. The cat and the Kinetophone
Breen, J. L. Credit the cat
Breen, J. L. Longevity has its place
Brennan, M. I see you, Bianca
Carole Nelson Douglas. Sax and the single cat
Channell, C. Coffee and murder
Chekhov, A. P. An incident
Collins, B. Aunt Emma's defense
Collins, B. Carry's cat
Collins, B. The night it rained cats and cats
Collins, B. A proper burial
Collins, B. The ten lives of Talbert
Collins, B. That damn cat
Collins, B. To kill a cat
Collins, B. Too many tomcats
Collins, M. A. Catgate
Collins, M. A. Cat's-eye witness
Compton, M. A. The fat cats' tale
Coward, M. Tall man, large cat
Coward, M. Three nil
Coward, M. Twelve of the little buggers
Crider, B. How I found a cat, lost true love, and broke the bank at Monte Carlo
Crowley, J. Antiquities
Crowther, P. Cat on an old school roof
Crowther, P. Shatsi
Dams, J. M. Remember the Maine?
Dawson, J. What the cat dragged in
DeAndrea, W. L. Killed in midstream
Dixon, S. The dat
Doran, M. M. The giver
Douglas, C. N. Licensed to koi
Douglas, C. N. The mummy case: a midnight Louie past life adventure
Douglas, C. N. Sax and the single cat

CATS—*Continued*

Dozois, G. R. Afternoon at Schraffts
Dozois, G. R. A cat horror story
Ebershoff, D. Living together
Edghill, R. The Maltese feline
Eldridge, Courtney. Young professionals
Ellis, A. T. The cat's whiskers
Estep, M. Animals
Franklin, T. The ballad of Duane Juarez
Gifford, B. Cat women of Rome
Grape, J. Cat o'nine lives
Grape, J. Tabby won't tell
Hershman, M. Slightly guilty
Hess, J. The Maggody files: Hillbilly cat
Hollon, F. T. Left behind
Houston, P. Waltzing the cat
Hudgins, B. Fur bearing
Jenkins, G. Richard and poorer
Johnson-Davies, D. Cat
Jones, T. Thorazine Johnny Felsun loves me
　　(from his permanent cage of lifelong con-
　　finement)
Kennett, S. A warm nest
Keret, E. Rabin's dead
Kohler, S. Light
Lawrence, B. Nothing but the best
Lee, W. W. Indiscreet
Lee, W. W. Letting the cat out of the bag
Lee, W. W. Life of Riley
Lee, W. W. Soft day
Linzner, G. Author, author
Little, B. Connie
Locklin, G. O Tannenbaum
Louise, D. D. Stitches in time
Maron, M. The stupid pet trick
Mason, B. A. Residents and transients
McGary, G. The cats and jammer
Moore, L. Four calling birds, three French hens
Nissen, T. The animal's best interest
Ortiz, S. J. Feathers
Pack, J. Impressions
Pack, J. The Secret Staff
Paul, B. Scat
Piccirilli, T. Diamond Mozzarella
Piccirilli, T. Of Persephone, Poe, and the Whis-
　　perer
Pickard, N. Dr. Couch saves a cat
Poe, E. A. The black cat
Porter, J. A. A man wanted to buy a cat
Porzecanski, T. The story of a cat
Powers, J. F. Death of a favorite
Ranieri, R. The bandit who caught a killer
Richter, S. Rats eat cats
Scarborough, E. A. Tinkler Tam and the body
　　snatchers
Schweighofer, P. The Cairo cat caper
Scott, J. Cat in love
Shepard, S. Betty's cats
Shonk, K. The death of Olga Vasilievna
Steiber, E. The cats of San Martino
Stoker, B. The Jewel of Seven Stars
Updike, J. The cats
Van Belkom, E. Catabolism
Vivante, A. Company
Watson, I. The last beast out of the box
Wheat, C. The princess and the pickle
Wilson, R. C. Ulysses sees the moon in the bed-
　　room window
Young, T. The new world

Cats. McCorkle, J.
The **cats**. Updike, J.
Cats and architecture. Kidd, C.
The **cats** and jammer. McGary, G.
Cat's-eye witness. Collins, M. A.
The **cats** of San Martino. Steiber, E.
Cat's out of the bag. Davis, L.
Cat's paw. Willis, C.
The **cat's** whiskers. Ellis, A. T.

CATSKILL MOUNTAINS (N.Y.)

Irving, W. Rip Van Winkle
Michaels, L. Honeymoon
Michaels, L. Second honeymoon

CATTLE

Banks, R. Cow-cow
Bausch, R. Glass meadow
Chacón, D. Spring break
Connor, J. The day the world declined to end
Cushman, D. Killers' country!
Easton, R. O. Bonaparte's dreams
Easton, R. O. Dynamite's day off
Easton, R. O. To find a place
Hardy, M. The heifer
Piñón, N. Big-bellied cow
Rhodes, E. M. The trouble man
Singer, I. B. The yearning heifer
The **cattle-dealers**. Chekhov, A. P.

CATTLE DRIVERS

L'Amour, L. Roundup in Texas
Le May, A. Eyes of doom
Le May, A. The little kid
Le May, A. Trail driver's luck
Loomis, N. M. Maverick factory
Newton, D. B. The taming of Johnny Peters
Smith, T. D. The big die-up

CATTLE THIEVES

DeRosso, H. A. Riders of the shadowlands
Kelton, E. North of the big river
L'Amour, L. Rustler roundup
Caucasus. Bunin, I. A.
Caucus winter. Watson, I.

Caudwell, Sarah

The triumph of Eve
　　Women before the bench; edited by Carolyn
　　　Wheat; introduction by Linda Fairstein
Caught. Goran, L.
Caught in the act. Pronzini, B.
The **caul**. Banks, R.
Caulk. Singleton, G.
Caution. Agee, J.
Caution: men in trees. Spencer, D.
Cavallo, Evelyn *See* Spark, Muriel
CAVALRY (U.S.) *See* United States. Army. Cav-
　　alry
Cavanelle. Chopin, K.
The **cave**. Dinh, L.
Cave fish. Foley, S.
Cave life. Svoboda, T.

Cavell, Benjamin

All the nights of the world
　　Cavell, B. Rumble, young man, rumble
The art of the possible
　　Cavell, B. Rumble, young man, rumble
Balls, balls, balls
　　Cavell, B. Rumble, young man, rumble
Blue yonder
　　Cavell, B. Rumble, young man, rumble
The death of cool
　　Cavell, B. Rumble, young man, rumble

Cavell, Benjamin—*Continued*
  Evolution
    Cavell, B. Rumble, young man, rumble
  Highway
    Cavell, B. Rumble, young man, rumble
  Killing time
    Cavell, B. Rumble, young man, rumble
  The ropes
    Cavell, B. Rumble, young man, rumble
The **cavemen** in the hedges. Richter, S.
CAVES
  Bowles, P. The scorpion
  Ellis, N. Dr. Livingston's grotto
  Mo Yan. Man and beast
  Ptacek, K. The grotto
  Simak, C. D. Grotto of the dancing deer
Cavin, Ruth
  The Mechanique affair
    Death dance; suspenseful stories of the dance
      macabre; Trevanian, editor
Caz. Reiner, C.
CCC *See* Civilian Conservation Corps (U.S.)
Ceauçsescu's cat. Paine, T.
Ceausescu's cat. Paine, T.
Cecil's highway. Hart, R.
The **ceiling**. Brockmeier, K.
Celebration. Searle, E.
CELEBRITIES
  Boylan, C. Perfect love
  Carlson, R. Zanduce at second
  Denton, B. We love Lydia love
  Richter, S. The ocean
  Searle, E. Celebrities in disgrace
  Walker, A. Nineteen fifty-five
Celebrities in disgrace. Searle, E.
Celebrity and justice for all. Jakes, J.
Celery fields. Campbell, B. J.
Celestial bodies. Davis, L.
The **celestial** railroad. Hawthorne, N.
CELIBACY
    See also Virginity
Cell phone. Schulze, I.
CELLISTS
  Link, K. Louise's ghost
  Tran, V. Gunboat on the Yangtze
Cells of knowledge [excerpt] Hayton, S.
Celluloid heroes. Davies, R.
Celtic noir. Bishop, P.
CEMETERIES
    See also Tombstones
  Almond, S. A dream of sleep
  Anderson, R. Death and the maid
  Babel´, I. Papa Marescot's family
  Bradbury, R. The handler
  Capote, T. Among the paths to Eden
  Chekhov, A. P. In the graveyard
  Dann, J. A quiet revolution for death
  Drake, R. The old cemetery
  Hendel, Y. Apples in honey
  Hensley, J. L. Watcher
  Herling, G. The Noonday Cemetery: an open
    story
  Lavin, M. Lemonade
  Lovecraft, H. P. The unnamable
  Lundquist, R. Now it looks respectable
  McAuley, P. J. Bone orchards
  Offutt, C. Moscow, Idaho
  Orner, P. High priest at the gates
  Porter, K. A. The grave

  Roth, J. The place I want to tell you about. . .
  Sinclair, I. The keeper of the Rothenstein tomb
  Slezak, E. Settled
  Stern, D. The #63 bus from the Gare de Lyon
The **cemetery** in Kozin. Babel´, I.
La **Cenerentola**. Jones, G.
The **census** taker. Avrich, J.
The **census** taker. Lord, N.
The **centaur-princess**. Zinovyeva-Annibal, L. D.
The **Center** of Everything. Moriarty, L.
The **Center** of the World. Clark, G. M.
Center zone. Browder, C.
The **centerfielder**. Ramírez Mercado, S.
Centipedes on skates. Robinson, J.
CENTRAL INTELLIGENCE AGENCY (U.S.)
    See United States. Central Intelligence
    Agency
CENTRAL PARK (NEW YORK, N.Y.) *See*
    New York (N.Y.)—Central Park
Central Square. Trevor, D.
CERAMICS *See* Pottery
CEREBROVASCULAR DISEASE
  Boyle, T. C. Rust
  DeMarco, T. Proper cover
  Gates, D. The mail lady
  Gautreaux, T. Sorry blood
  Kawabata, Y. Silence
  Oates, J. C. The assailant
  Ockert, J. Scarecrowed
  Yarbrough, S. The right kind of person
CEREMONIES *See* Rites and ceremonies
The **ceremony**. Kees, W.
Ceremony. Vukcevich, R.
Čeretková-Gállová, Marína
  The actress
    In search of homo sapiens; twenty-five con-
      temporary Slovak short stories; editor,
      Pavol Hudík ; [translated by Heather
      Trebatická; American English editor, Lucy
      Bednár]
Certain amazing adventures of Mr. Hoel. Darton,
    E.
A **certain** barbarity. Pak, W.-S.
A **certain** sense of place. Nair, M.
A **Certain** Weariness in Moonlight. Flannery, S.
Certificate of absence [excerpt] Molloy, S.
**CERVANTES SAAVEDRA, MIGUEL DE,
    1547-1616**
                    About
  Borges, J. L. Pierre Menard, author of the Qui-
    xote
C'est la vie. Nichols, J.
CESTODA
  Barker, N. Symbiosis: class cestoda
CEYLON *See* Sri Lanka
Cézanne in a soft hat. Hay, E.
Chabon, Michael
  Along the frontage road
    The Best American short stories, 2002; select-
      ed from U.S. and Canadian magazines by
      Sue Miller with Katrina Kenison, with an
      introduction by Sue Miller
    The New Yorker v77 no36 p74-7 N 19 2001
  The Final Solution
    The Paris Review v45 p64-144 Summ 2003
  The God of dark laughter
    The New Yorker v77 no7 p116-27 Ap 9 2001

Chabon, Michael—*Continued*
Green's book
  Chabon, M. Werewolves in their youth; stories
The Halloween party
  Fault lines; stories of divorce; collected and edited by Caitlin Shetterly
The Harris Fetko story
  Chabon, M. Werewolves in their youth; stories
The Hofzinser Club
  The New Yorker v75 no19 p78-84 Jl 19 1999
The Hofzinser Club (I)
  The New Yorker v75 no16 p154-5 Je 21-28 1999
House hunting
  Chabon, M. Werewolves in their youth; stories
In the black mill
  Chabon, M. Werewolves in their youth; stories
The Martian agent, a planetary romance
  McSweeney's mammoth treasury of thrilling tales; edited by Michael Chabon
Mrs. Box
  Chabon, M. Werewolves in their youth; stories
Son of the wolfman
  Chabon, M. Werewolves in their youth; stories
  Prize stories, 1999; The O. Henry awards; edited and with an introduction by Larry Dark
Spikes
  Chabon, M. Werewolves in their youth; stories
That was me
  Chabon, M. Werewolves in their youth; stories
Werewolves in their youth
  Chabon, M. Werewolves in their youth; stories
Chacko, Mathew
Broadcasts from the flood
  The Kenyon Review ns24 no1 p135-52 Wint 2002
Chacón, Daniel
Andy the office boy
  Chacón, D. Chicano chicanery; short stories
Aztlán, Oregon
  Chacón, D. Chicano chicanery; short stories
The biggest city in the world
  Chacón, D. Chicano chicanery; short stories
Epilogue: story #7 in D minor
  Chacón, D. Chicano chicanery; short stories
Expression of our people
  Chacón, D. Chicano chicanery; short stories
Godoy lives
  Chacón, D. Chicano chicanery; short stories
How hot was Mexicali?
  Chacón, D. Chicano chicanery; short stories
Mexican table
  Chacón, D. Chicano chicanery; short stories
Ofrenda
  Chacón, D. Chicano chicanery; short stories
Slow and good
  Chacón, D. Chicano chicanery; short stories
Spring break
  Chacón, D. Chicano chicanery; short stories

Too white
  Chacón, D. Chicano chicanery; short stories
Torture fantasy
  Chacón, D. Chicano chicanery; short stories
Chadwick, Lester
Joe's run
  Dead balls and double curves; an anthology of early baseball fiction; edited and with an introduction by Trey Strecker ; with a foreword by Arnold Hano
Chaikovsky, P. I. *See* Tchaikovsky, Peter Ilich, 1840-1893
The **chair**. Davenport, G.
Chair. Yuknavitch, L.
Chairman of the board. Di Blasi, D.
CHAIRS
  Yuknavitch, L. Chair
Chairs. Rose, C.
Chalk and cheese. Archer, J.
Chalker, Jack L.
Dance band on the Titanic
  The Best alternate history stories of the 20th century; edited by Harry Turtledove with Martin H. Greenberg
CHALLENGER (SPACE SHUTTLE)
  DeAndrea, W. L. Sabotage
Chamberlain, William
The trapped battalion
  Retrieving bones; stories and poems of the Korean War; edited and with an introduction by W. D. Ehrhart and Philip K. Jason
Chambers, Christopher
Aardvark to Aztec
  The Best American mystery stories, 2003; edited by Michael Connelly and Otto Penzler
Carl, under his car
  Gettysburg Review v14 no1 p39-49 Spr 2001
Chambers, Robert W. (Robert William)
The yellow sign
  The American fantasy tradition; edited by Brian M. Thomsen
Chambers, William E.
Another night to remember
  Blood on their hands; edited by Lawrence Block
A **chameleon**. Chekhov, A. P.
Chamois gloves. Lavin, M.
Chamoiseau, Patrick
The old man slave and the mastiff
  The Art of the story; an international anthology of contemporary short stories; edited by Daniel Halpern
Red hot peppers
  The Oxford book of Caribbean short stories; edited by Stewart Brown and John Wickham
Champagne. Chekhov, A. P.
Champion. Lardner, R.
Champion of the ocean floor. Cadnum, M.
The **championship** of nowhere. Grady, J.
Champlin, Tim
For the good of the service
  The First Five Star western corral; western stories; edited by Jon Tuska and Vicki Piekarski
Chan, David Marshall
Brilliant disguise
  Chan, D. M. Goblin fruit; stories

Chan, David Marshall—*Continued*
Empty houses
Chan, D. M. Goblin fruit; stories
Falling
Chan, D. M. Goblin fruit; stories
Goblin fruit
Chan, D. M. Goblin fruit; stories
Lost years
Chan, D. M. Goblin fruit; stories
Mystery boy
Chan, D. M. Goblin fruit; stories
Open circles
Chan, D. M. Goblin fruit; stories
Seven swans
Chan, D. M. Goblin fruit; stories
Watchtower
Chan, D. M. Goblin fruit; stories
Chan, Melissa
At the premier's literary awards
Brought to book; murderous stories from the
literary world; Penny Sumner, editor
Chan Koon Chung
Kamdu Tea Restaurant
The Literary Review (Madison, N.J.) v47 no4
p138-53 Summ 2004
Chance, Frank
The bride and the pennant
Dead balls and double curves; an anthology
of early baseball fiction; edited and with an
introduction by Trey Strecker ; with a fore-
word by Arnold Hano
CHANCE
De Lint, C. Wild horses
Hawthorne, N. David Swan
Mazelis, J. Flock
The **chance**. Carey, P.
Chance. Munro, A.
Chance. Pearlman, E.
Chance hospitality. Huber, C. Y. and Baker, M.
C.
Chance meeting. Karon, J.
Chandler, A. Bertram
The mountain movers
Centaurus: the best of Australian science fic-
tion; edited by David G. Hartwell and Da-
mien Broderick
Chandler, Raymond
Red wind
The Best American mystery stories of the
century; Tony Hillerman, editor; with an
introduction by Tony Hillerman
CHANDLER, RAYMOND, 1888-1959
About
Malzberg, B. N. The high purpose
Parodies, imitations, etc.
Kaminsky, S. M. Bitter lemons
Lochhead, L. Phyllis Marlowe: only diamonds
are forever
Nevins, F. M., Jr. Consultation in the dark
Chandra, Vikram
Dharma
The Art of the story; an international antholo-
gy of contemporary short stories; edited by
Daniel Halpern
Chaney, Gayal
Maggie's song of herself
U.S. Catholic v67 no11 p22-5 N 2002
Chang, Chieh *See* Zhang Jie, 1937-

Chang, Diana
Seeing Things
Confrontation no86/87 p109-12 Spr/Summ
2004
Chang, Lan Samantha
Li Ang
Harvard Review (1992) no26 p175-80 2004
The eve of the spirit festival
Best of Prairie schooner; fiction and poetry;
edited by Hilda Raz
Hangzhou 1925
Ploughshares v30 no1 p100-6 Spr 2004
Pipa's story
The Workshop; seven decades of the Iowa
Writers' Workshop: 42 stories, recollections
& essays on Iowa's place in 20th-century
American literature; edited by Tom Grimes
Chang, Leonard
Knives
The Literary Review (Madison, N.J.) v47 no3
p65-72 Spr 2004
The **change**. Campbell, R.
The **change**. Pittalwala, I.
A **change** of clients. O'Callaghan, M.
A **change** of face. Owens, A.
A **change** of heart. Archer, J.
Change of heart. Stewart, I.
CHANGE OF LIFE *See* Menopause
Change of light. Alas, L.
A **change** of lights. Pittalwala, I.
Change of season. Davis, L.
Change partners. Slesar, H.
Changeling. Mandelbaum, P.
Changelings. Kirchheimer, G. D.
Changer of worlds. Weber, D.
Changing horses. Abrams, T.
The **changing** room. Alameddine, R.
Chango. Casares, O.
Channel crossing. Kalman, J.
Channell, Carrie
Coffee and murder
Felonious felines; edited by Carol and Ed
Gorman
Channer, Colin
The High Priest of Love
Bomb no86 p98-102 Wint 2003/2004
I'm still waiting
Got to be real; four original love stories; [by]
E. Lynn Harris [et al.]
Rub me up, rub me down
Essence v32 no3 p114-16 Jl 2001
Chant. Weinberg, R.
Chanterelle. Stableford, B. M.
Chao, Ta-nien *See* Zhao Danian, 1931-
Chaon, Dan
Among the missing
Chaon, D. Among the missing
The bees
The Best American short stories, 2003; select-
ed from U.S. and Canadian magazines by
Walter Mosley with Katrina Kenison; with
an introduction by Walter Mosley
McSweeney's mammoth treasury of thrilling
tales; edited by Michael Chabon
Big me
Chaon, D. Among the missing
Prize stories, 2001; The O. Henry awards; ed-
ited and with an introduction by Larry
Dark

Chaon, Dan—*Continued*
Burn with me
  Chaon, D. Among the missing
Falling backwards
  Chaon, D. Among the missing
Fraternity
  The Student body; short stories about college
    students and professors; edited by John
    McNally
Here's a little something to remember me by
  Chaon, D. Among the missing
I demand to know where you're taking me
  Chaon, D. Among the missing
  A different plain; contemporary Nebraska fic-
    tion writers; edited by Ladette Randolph ;
    introduction by Mary Pipher
  Pushcart prize XXVII; best of the small
    presses; edited by Bill Henderson with the
    Pushcart prize editors
The illustrated encyclopedia of the animal king-
    dom
  Chaon, D. Among the missing
  The Pushcart prize XXIV: best of the small
    presses; an annual small press reader; ed-
    ited by Bill Henderson with the Pushcart
    prize editors
Late for the wedding
  Chaon, D. Among the missing
Passengers, remain calm
  Chaon, D. Among the missing
Prodigal
  Chaon, D. Among the missing
Prosthesis
  Chaon, D. Among the missing
Safety Man
  Chaon, D. Among the missing
Seven types of ambiguity
  The Pushcart prize XXVI; best of the small
    presses, an annual small press reader; ed-
    ited by Bill Henderson and the Pushcart
    prize editors
Thirteen windows
  The Ohio Review no62/63 p125-32 2001
Chaos. Stern, D.
Chaos surfari. Rucker, R. v. B.
The **chaperon**. James, H.
Chaperone. Budnitz, J.
Chaplin, Patrice
Pot luck
  Valentine's Day: women against men; stories
    of revenge; introduction by Alice Thomas
Chapman, Arthur
The strange case of South-paw Skaggs: an odd
    story of the national game
  Dead balls and double curves; an anthology
    of early baseball fiction; edited and with an
    introduction by Trey Strecker ; with a fore-
    word by Arnold Hano
Chapman, Clay McLeod
And the mothers stepped over their sons
  Chapman, C. M. Rest area; stories
Bladder companion
  Chapman, C. M. Rest area; stories
Chatterbox
  Chapman, C. M. Rest area; stories
Correspondence of corpses
  Chapman, C. M. Rest area; stories
Fox trot
  Chapman, C. M. Rest area; stories

Honey well hung
  Chapman, C. M. Rest area; stories
It goes rickety
  Chapman, C. M. Rest area; stories
Johnny pumpkinseed
  Chapman, C. M. Rest area; stories
The man corn triptych
  Chapman, C. M. Rest area; stories
Michelle
  Chapman, C. M. Rest area; stories
Milking cherry
  Chapman, C. M. Rest area; stories
Off-season spirits
  Chapman, C. M. Rest area; stories
The pool witch
  Chapman, C. M. Rest area; stories
Poor man's mermaid
  Chapman, C. M. Rest area; stories
Rest area
  Chapman, C. M. Rest area; stories
Rodeo inferno
  Chapman, C. M. Rest area; stories
Second helping
  Chapman, C. M. Rest area; stories
Spoonfed
  Chapman, C. M. Rest area; stories
A step off from fathering
  Chapman, C. M. Rest area; stories
The wheels on the bus go
  Chapman, C. M. Rest area; stories
Chapman, Maile
A love transaction
  Best new American voices 2000; guest editor
    Tobias Wolff; series editors John Kulka
    and Natalie Danford
Chappell, Fred
The encyclopedia Daniel
  The Cry of an occasion; fiction from the Fel-
    lowship of Southern Writers; edited by
    Richard Bausch; with a foreword by
    George Garrett
Chapter four. Morgan, K.
Chapter three. Morgan, K.
Chapters from **A dog's life**. Cherry, K.
Character flaw: a Robbie Stanton story. Mat-
    thews, C.
Character witness. Vinten, R.
Charades. Hart, R.
Charger. Mason, B. A.
The **chariot**. Mathews, H.
Charity. Ford, R.
Charles, Kate
The murder at the vicarage
  Malice domestic 9
CHARLES, RAY
                    About
Connor, J. Riding with Ray
Charles Ryder's schooldays. Waugh, E.
CHARLESTON (S.C.) *See* South Carolina—
    Charleston
Charlie. Chopin, K.
Charlie's game. Garfield, B.
The **charm**. Fernandez, P. A.
The **charm** bracelet. Ebershoff, D.
Charm incorporated. Wharton, E.
Charmed life. Vachss, A. H.
CHARMS
Davidson, A. The lineaments of gratified desire
Jacobs, W. W. The monkey's paw

Charms. Walker, A.
Charnas, Suzy McKee
Boobs
Children of the night; stories of ghosts, vampires, werewolves, and "lost children"; edited by Martin H. Greenberg
Listening to Brahms
Vanishing acts; a science fiction anthology; edited by Ellen Datlow
Charro. Casares, O.
Charteris, Leslie
The mugs' game
Sports best short stories; edited by Paul D. Staudohar
The mystery of the child's toy
Edwards, M. Mysterious pleasures; a celebration of the Crime Writers' Association's 50th anniversary; edited by Martin Edwards
Charting the territories of the red. Gay, W.
The **charwoman**. Avrich, J.
CHARWOMEN
See also Cleaning women
Charyn, Jerome
Countess Kathleen
The Mysterious Press anniversary anthology; celebrating 25 years; by the editors of Mysterious Press
Chase. Davis, A.
Chase. Hassler, J.
CHASIDISM *See* Hasidism
Chasing the moonlight. Williams, K.
The **chasm**. Swan, G.
Chaste Berry. Devine, M. R.
Chatter. Brady, C.
Chatterbox. Chapman, C. M.
CHAUCER, GEOFFREY, D. 1400
About
Baldry, C. The friar's tale
Chaudhuri, Amit
Beyond translation
Chaudhuri, A. Real time; stories and a reminiscence
Confession of a sacrifice
Chaudhuri, A. Real time; stories and a reminiscence
Four days before the Saturday night social
Chaudhuri, A. Real time; stories and a reminiscence
The great game
Chaudhuri, A. Real time; stories and a reminiscence
An infatuation
Chaudhuri, A. Real time; stories and a reminiscence
The man from Khurda district
Chaudhuri, A. Real time; stories and a reminiscence
The old masters
Chaudhuri, A. Real time; stories and a reminiscence
The party
Chaudhuri, A. Real time; stories and a reminiscence
Portrait of an artist
Chaudhuri, A. Real time; stories and a reminiscence
Prelude to an autobiography: a fragment
Chaudhuri, A. Real time; stories and a reminiscence

Real time
Chaudhuri, A. Real time; stories and a reminiscence
The second marriage
Chaudhuri, A. Real time; stories and a reminiscence
The wedding
Chaudhuri, A. Real time; stories and a reminiscence
White lies
Chaudhuri, A. Real time; stories and a reminiscence
Granta no76 p271-95 Wint 2001
Words, silences
Chaudhuri, A. Real time; stories and a reminiscence
CHAUFFEURS
Norris, H. A good shape
Rawley, D. Tina in the back seat
Weldon, F. Percentage trust
Chautauqua. Hart, R.
Chávez, Denise
Grand slam
Texas bound. Book III; 22 Texas stories; edited by Kay Cattarulla; foreword by Robert Flynn
Chaviano, Daína
The annunciation
Cosmos latinos: an anthology of science fiction from Latin America and Spain; translated, edited, & with an introduction & notes by Andrea L. Bell & Yolanda Molina-Gavilán
CHECHNYA (RUSSIA)
Benioff, D. The affairs of each beast
De Waal, T. The English house: a story of Chechnya
Kalfus, K. Budyonnovsk
Check up. Lee, W. W.
Checkmate. Goldner, B.
Chee, Alexander
Gold
Men on men 2000; best new gay fiction for the millennium; edited and with an introduction by David Bergman and Karl Woelz
A pilgrimage of you
His 3: brilliant new fiction by gay writers; edited by Robert Drake and Terry Wolverton
Cheers. Simpson, H.
CHEERS AND CHEERLEADING
Budnitz, J. Got spirit
Chee's witch. Hillerman, T.
Cheever, John
The country husband
The Best American short stories of the century; John Updike, editor, Katrina Kenison, coeditor; with an introduction by John Updike
The Enormous Radio
Doubletake v8 no3 p34-5 Summ 2002
The five-forty-eight
Wonderful town; New York stories from The New Yorker; edited by David Remnick with Susan Choi
Oh father, father, why have you come back?
Nightshade: 20th century ghost stories; edited by Robert Phillips

Cheever, John—*Continued*

The season of divorce

Fault lines; stories of divorce; collected and edited by Caitlin Shetterly

The swimmer

Sports best short stories; edited by Paul D. Staudohar

Chekhov, Anton Pavlovich

About love

Chekhov, A. P. Anton Chekhov: later short stories, 1888-1903; edited by Shelby Foote; translated by Constance Garnett

Chekhov, A. P. The essential tales of Chekhov; edited and with an introduction by Richard Ford; translated by Constance Garnett

After the theatre

Chekhov, A. P. Anton Chekhov: later short stories, 1888-1903; edited by Shelby Foote; translated by Constance Garnett

Agafya

Chekhov, A. P. Anton Chekhov: early short stories, 1883-1888; edited by Shelby Foote; translated by Constance Garnett

"Anna on the neck"

Chekhov, A. P. Anton Chekhov: later short stories, 1888-1903; edited by Shelby Foote; translated by Constance Garnett

An anonymous story

Chekhov, A. P. The essential tales of Chekhov; edited and with an introduction by Richard Ford; translated by Constance Garnett

Anyuta

Chekhov, A. P. Anton Chekhov: early short stories, 1883-1888; edited by Shelby Foote; translated by Constance Garnett

Ariadne

Chekhov, A. P. Anton Chekhov: later short stories, 1888-1903; edited by Shelby Foote; translated by Constance Garnett

Art

Chekhov, A. P. Anton Chekhov: early short stories, 1883-1888; edited by Shelby Foote; translated by Constance Garnett

An artist's story

Chekhov, A. P. Anton Chekhov: later short stories, 1888-1903; edited by Shelby Foote; translated by Constance Garnett

At a country house

Chekhov, A. P. Anton Chekhov: later short stories, 1888-1903; edited by Shelby Foote; translated by Constance Garnett

At Christmas time

Chekhov, A. P. Anton Chekhov: later short stories, 1888-1903; edited by Shelby Foote; translated by Constance Garnett

At home

Chekhov, A. P. Anton Chekhov: later short stories, 1888-1903; edited by Shelby Foote; translated by Constance Garnett

At the bath-house

Chekhov, A. P. The comic stories; translated from the Russian and with an introduction by Harvey Pitcher

A bad business

Chekhov, A. P. Anton Chekhov: early short stories, 1883-1888; edited by Shelby Foote; translated by Constance Garnett

The beauties

Chekhov, A. P. Anton Chekhov: later short stories, 1888-1903; edited by Shelby Foote; translated by Constance Garnett

The beggar

Chekhov, A. P. Anton Chekhov: early short stories, 1883-1888; edited by Shelby Foote; translated by Constance Garnett

The bet

Chekhov, A. P. Anton Chekhov: later short stories, 1888-1903; edited by Shelby Foote; translated by Constance Garnett

Betrothed

Chekhov, A. P. Anton Chekhov: later short stories, 1888-1903; edited by Shelby Foote; translated by Constance Garnett

The bird market

Chekhov, A. P. Anton Chekhov: early short stories, 1883-1888; edited by Shelby Foote; translated by Constance Garnett

The bishop

Chekhov, A. P. Anton Chekhov: later short stories, 1888-1903; edited by Shelby Foote; translated by Constance Garnett

A blunder

Chekhov, A. P. Anton Chekhov: early short stories, 1883-1888; edited by Shelby Foote; translated by Constance Garnett

Chekhov, A. P. The essential tales of Chekhov; edited and with an introduction by Richard Ford; translated by Constance Garnett

Boys

Chekhov, A. P. Anton Chekhov: early short stories, 1883-1888; edited by Shelby Foote; translated by Constance Garnett

Chekhov, A. P. The comic stories; translated from the Russian and with an introduction by Harvey Pitcher

The burbot

Chekhov, A. P. The comic stories; translated from the Russian and with an introduction by Harvey Pitcher

The cattle-dealers

Chekhov, A. P. Anton Chekhov: early short stories, 1883-1888; edited by Shelby Foote; translated by Constance Garnett

A chameleon

Chekhov, A. P. Anton Chekhov: early short stories, 1883-1888; edited by Shelby Foote; translated by Constance Garnett

Chekhov, A. P. The comic stories; translated from the Russian and with an introduction by Harvey Pitcher

Champagne

Chekhov, A. P. The essential tales of Chekhov; edited and with an introduction by Richard Ford; translated by Constance Garnett

Children

Chekhov, A. P. Anton Chekhov: early short stories, 1883-1888; edited by Shelby Foote; translated by Constance Garnett

Choristers

Chekhov, A. P. Anton Chekhov: early short stories, 1883-1888; edited by Shelby Foote; translated by Constance Garnett

Chekhov, Anton Pavlovich—*Continued*

The chorus girl
Chekhov, A. P. Anton Chekhov: early short stories, 1883-1888; edited by Shelby Foote; translated by Constance Garnett

The civil service exam
Chekhov, A. P. The comic stories; translated from the Russian and with an introduction by Harvey Pitcher

The complaints book
Chekhov, A. P. The comic stories; translated from the Russian and with an introduction by Harvey Pitcher

The cook's wedding
Chekhov, A. P. Anton Chekhov: early short stories, 1883-1888; edited by Shelby Foote; translated by Constance Garnett

The cossack
Chekhov, A. P. Anton Chekhov: early short stories, 1883-1888; edited by Shelby Foote; translated by Constance Garnett

The darling
Chekhov, A. P. Anton Chekhov: later short stories, 1888-1903; edited by Shelby Foote; translated by Constance Garnett
Chekhov, A. P. The essential tales of Chekhov; edited and with an introduction by Richard Ford; translated by Constance Garnett
Chekhov, A. P. The comic stories; translated from the Russian and with an introduction by Harvey Pitcher

A daughter of albion
Chekhov, A. P. Anton Chekhov: early short stories, 1883-1888; edited by Shelby Foote; translated by Constance Garnett
Chekhov, A. P. The comic stories; translated from the Russian and with an introduction by Harvey Pitcher

A day in the country
Chekhov, A. P. Anton Chekhov: early short stories, 1883-1888; edited by Shelby Foote; translated by Constance Garnett

A dead body
Chekhov, A. P. Anton Chekhov: early short stories, 1883-1888; edited by Shelby Foote; translated by Constance Garnett

The death of a civil servant
Chekhov, A. P. The comic stories; translated from the Russian and with an introduction by Harvey Pitcher

The death of a government clerk
Chekhov, A. P. Anton Chekhov: early short stories, 1883-1888; edited by Shelby Foote; translated by Constance Garnett

Difficult people
Chekhov, A. P. Anton Chekhov: early short stories, 1883-1888; edited by Shelby Foote; translated by Constance Garnett
Chekhov, A. P. The essential tales of Chekhov; edited and with an introduction by Richard Ford; translated by Constance Garnett

The doctor
Chekhov, A. P. Anton Chekhov: early short stories, 1883-1888; edited by Shelby Foote; translated by Constance Garnett

A doctor's visit
Chekhov, A. P. Anton Chekhov: later short stories, 1888-1903; edited by Shelby Foote; translated by Constance Garnett

A drama
Chekhov, A. P. The comic stories; translated from the Russian and with an introduction by Harvey Pitcher

A dreadful night
Chekhov, A. P. The comic stories; translated from the Russian and with an introduction by Harvey Pitcher

A dreary story
Chekhov, A. P. Anton Chekhov: later short stories, 1888-1903; edited by Shelby Foote; translated by Constance Garnett

Easter eve
Chekhov, A. P. Anton Chekhov: early short stories, 1883-1888; edited by Shelby Foote; translated by Constance Garnett

Encased
Chekhov, A. P. The comic stories; translated from the Russian and with an introduction by Harvey Pitcher

Enemies
Chekhov, A. P. The essential tales of Chekhov; edited and with an introduction by Richard Ford; translated by Constance Garnett

The exclamation mark
Chekhov, A. P. The comic stories; translated from the Russian and with an introduction by Harvey Pitcher

Fat and thin
Chekhov, A. P. Anton Chekhov: early short stories, 1883-1888; edited by Shelby Foote; translated by Constance Garnett
Chekhov, A. P. The comic stories; translated from the Russian and with an introduction by Harvey Pitcher

The fish
Chekhov, A. P. Anton Chekhov: early short stories, 1883-1888; edited by Shelby Foote; translated by Constance Garnett

Foiled!
Chekhov, A. P. The comic stories; translated from the Russian and with an introduction by Harvey Pitcher

From the diary of an assistant book-keeper
Chekhov, A. P. The comic stories; translated from the Russian and with an introduction by Harvey Pitcher

A gentleman friend
Chekhov, A. P. Anton Chekhov: early short stories, 1883-1888; edited by Shelby Foote; translated by Constance Garnett

Gooseberries
Chekhov, A. P. Anton Chekhov: later short stories, 1888-1903; edited by Shelby Foote; translated by Constance Garnett
Chekhov, A. P. The essential tales of Chekhov; edited and with an introduction by Richard Ford; translated by Constance Garnett

The grasshopper
Chekhov, A. P. Anton Chekhov: later short stories, 1888-1903; edited by Shelby Foote; translated by Constance Garnett

Chekhov, Anton Pavlovich—*Continued*

Chekhov, A. P. The essential tales of Chekhov; edited and with an introduction by Richard Ford; translated by Constance Garnett

Grisha

Chekhov, A. P. Anton Chekhov: early short stories, 1883-1888; edited by Shelby Foote; translated by Constance Garnett

Chekhov, A. P. The comic stories; translated from the Russian and with an introduction by Harvey Pitcher

Gusev

Chekhov, A. P. Anton Chekhov: later short stories, 1888-1903; edited by Shelby Foote; translated by Constance Garnett

Happiness

Chekhov, A. P. Anton Chekhov: early short stories, 1883-1888; edited by Shelby Foote; translated by Constance Garnett

He quarrelled with his wife

Chekhov, A. P. The comic stories; translated from the Russian and with an introduction by Harvey Pitcher

The head-gardener's story

Chekhov, A. P. Anton Chekhov: later short stories, 1888-1903; edited by Shelby Foote; translated by Constance Garnett

The head of the family

Chekhov, A. P. Anton Chekhov: early short stories, 1883-1888; edited by Shelby Foote; translated by Constance Garnett

The helpmate

Chekhov, A. P. Anton Chekhov: later short stories, 1888-1903; edited by Shelby Foote; translated by Constance Garnett

Home

Chekhov, A. P. Anton Chekhov: early short stories, 1883-1888; edited by Shelby Foote; translated by Constance Garnett

The horse-stealers

Chekhov, A. P. Anton Chekhov: later short stories, 1888-1903; edited by Shelby Foote; translated by Constance Garnett

A horsy name

Chekhov, A. P. The comic stories; translated from the Russian and with an introduction by Harvey Pitcher

The huntsman

Chekhov, A. P. Anton Chekhov: early short stories, 1883-1888; edited by Shelby Foote; translated by Constance Garnett

Hush!

Chekhov, A. P. The essential tales of Chekhov; edited and with an introduction by Richard Ford; translated by Constance Garnett

In exile

Chekhov, A. P. Anton Chekhov: later short stories, 1888-1903; edited by Shelby Foote; translated by Constance Garnett

In the court

Chekhov, A. P. Anton Chekhov: early short stories, 1883-1888; edited by Shelby Foote; translated by Constance Garnett

In the dark

Chekhov, A. P. The comic stories; translated from the Russian and with an introduction by Harvey Pitcher

In the graveyard

Chekhov, A. P. Anton Chekhov: early short stories, 1883-1888; edited by Shelby Foote; translated by Constance Garnett

In trouble

Chekhov, A. P. Anton Chekhov: early short stories, 1883-1888; edited by Shelby Foote; translated by Constance Garnett

An inadvertence

Chekhov, A. P. Anton Chekhov: early short stories, 1883-1888; edited by Shelby Foote; translated by Constance Garnett

An incident

Chekhov, A. P. Anton Chekhov: early short stories, 1883-1888; edited by Shelby Foote; translated by Constance Garnett

An incident at law

Chekhov, A. P. The comic stories; translated from the Russian and with an introduction by Harvey Pitcher

Ionitch

Chekhov, A. P. Anton Chekhov: later short stories, 1888-1903; edited by Shelby Foote; translated by Constance Garnett

A joke

Chekhov, A. P. Anton Chekhov: early short stories, 1883-1888; edited by Shelby Foote; translated by Constance Garnett

Joy

Chekhov, A. P. Anton Chekhov: early short stories, 1883-1888; edited by Shelby Foote; translated by Constance Garnett

Kashtanka

Chekhov, A. P. Anton Chekhov: early short stories, 1883-1888; edited by Shelby Foote; translated by Constance Garnett

Chekhov, A. P. The essential tales of Chekhov; edited and with an introduction by Richard Ford; translated by Constance Garnett

Chekhov, A. P. The comic stories; translated from the Russian and with an introduction by Harvey Pitcher

The kiss

Chekhov, A. P. Anton Chekhov: early short stories, 1883-1888; edited by Shelby Foote; translated by Constance Garnett

Chekhov, A. P. The essential tales of Chekhov; edited and with an introduction by Richard Ford; translated by Constance Garnett

The lady with the dog

Chekhov, A. P. Anton Chekhov: later short stories, 1888-1903; edited by Shelby Foote; translated by Constance Garnett

Chekhov, A. P. The essential tales of Chekhov; edited and with an introduction by Richard Ford; translated by Constance Garnett

A lady's story

Chekhov, A. P. Anton Chekhov: early short stories, 1883-1888; edited by Shelby Foote; translated by Constance Garnett

Lights

Chekhov, A. P. Anton Chekhov: early short stories, 1883-1888; edited by Shelby Foote; translated by Constance Garnett

Chekhov, Anton Pavlovich—*Continued*

The looking-glass
  Chekhov, A. P. Anton Chekhov: early short stories, 1883-1888; edited by Shelby Foote; translated by Constance Garnett

Love
  Chekhov, A. P. Anton Chekhov: early short stories, 1883-1888; edited by Shelby Foote; translated by Constance Garnett

A malefactor
  Chekhov, A. P. Anton Chekhov: early short stories, 1883-1888; edited by Shelby Foote; translated by Constance Garnett
  Chekhov, A. P. The comic stories; translated from the Russian and with an introduction by Harvey Pitcher

The man in a case
  Chekhov, A. P. Anton Chekhov: later short stories, 1888-1903; edited by Shelby Foote; translated by Constance Garnett

A man of ideas
  Chekhov, A. P. The comic stories; translated from the Russian and with an introduction by Harvey Pitcher

Mari d'elle
  Chekhov, A. P. Anton Chekhov: early short stories, 1883-1888; edited by Shelby Foote; translated by Constance Garnett

The marshal's widow
  Chekhov, A. P. Anton Chekhov: early short stories, 1883-1888; edited by Shelby Foote; translated by Constance Garnett

Minds in ferment
  Chekhov, A. P. Anton Chekhov: early short stories, 1883-1888; edited by Shelby Foote; translated by Constance Garnett

Misery
  Chekhov, A. P. Anton Chekhov: early short stories, 1883-1888; edited by Shelby Foote; translated by Constance Garnett

A misfortune
  Chekhov, A. P. Anton Chekhov: early short stories, 1883-1888; edited by Shelby Foote; translated by Constance Garnett
  Chekhov, A. P. The essential tales of Chekhov; edited and with an introduction by Richard Ford; translated by Constance Garnett

Neighbours
  Chekhov, A. P. Anton Chekhov: later short stories, 1888-1903; edited by Shelby Foote; translated by Constance Garnett
  Chekhov, A. P. The essential tales of Chekhov; edited and with an introduction by Richard Ford; translated by Constance Garnett

A nervous breakdown
  Chekhov, A. P. Anton Chekhov: later short stories, 1888-1903; edited by Shelby Foote; translated by Constance Garnett

The new villa
  Chekhov, A. P. Anton Chekhov: later short stories, 1888-1903; edited by Shelby Foote; translated by Constance Garnett
  Chekhov, A. P. The essential tales of Chekhov; edited and with an introduction by Richard Ford; translated by Constance Garnett

No comment
  Chekhov, A. P. The comic stories; translated from the Russian and with an introduction by Harvey Pitcher

Notes from the journal of a quick-tempered man
  Chekhov, A. P. The comic stories; translated from the Russian and with an introduction by Harvey Pitcher

Notes from the memoirs of a man of ideals
  Chekhov, A. P. The comic stories; translated from the Russian and with an introduction by Harvey Pitcher

The objet d'art
  Chekhov, A. P. The comic stories; translated from the Russian and with an introduction by Harvey Pitcher

Old age
  Chekhov, A. P. Anton Chekhov: early short stories, 1883-1888; edited by Shelby Foote; translated by Constance Garnett

On official duty
  Chekhov, A. P. Anton Chekhov: later short stories, 1888-1903; edited by Shelby Foote; translated by Constance Garnett
  Chekhov, A. P. The essential tales of Chekhov; edited and with an introduction by Richard Ford; translated by Constance Garnett

On the road
  Chekhov, A. P. Anton Chekhov: early short stories, 1883-1888; edited by Shelby Foote; translated by Constance Garnett

On the telephone
  Chekhov, A. P. The comic stories; translated from the Russian and with an introduction by Harvey Pitcher

The orator
  Chekhov, A. P. The comic stories; translated from the Russian and with an introduction by Harvey Pitcher

Overdoing it
  Chekhov, A. P. Anton Chekhov: early short stories, 1883-1888; edited by Shelby Foote; translated by Constance Garnett
  Chekhov, A. P. The comic stories; translated from the Russian and with an introduction by Harvey Pitcher

Oysters
  Chekhov, A. P. Anton Chekhov: early short stories, 1883-1888; edited by Shelby Foote; translated by Constance Garnett

The party
  Chekhov, A. P. Anton Chekhov: later short stories, 1888-1903; edited by Shelby Foote; translated by Constance Garnett

Peasant wives
  Chekhov, A. P. Anton Chekhov: later short stories, 1888-1903; edited by Shelby Foote; translated by Constance Garnett

Peasants
  Chekhov, A. P. The essential tales of Chekhov; edited and with an introduction by Richard Ford; translated by Constance Garnett

The Petchenyeg
  Chekhov, A. P. Anton Chekhov: later short stories, 1888-1903; edited by Shelby Foote; translated by Constance Garnett

Chekhov, Anton Pavlovich—*Continued*

The princess
  Chekhov, A. P. Anton Chekhov: later short stories, 1888-1903; edited by Shelby Foote; translated by Constance Garnett

The privy councillor
  Chekhov, A. P. Anton Chekhov: early short stories, 1883-1888; edited by Shelby Foote; translated by Constance Garnett

Rapture
  Chekhov, A. P. The comic stories; translated from the Russian and with an introduction by Harvey Pitcher

The requiem
  Chekhov, A. P. Anton Chekhov: early short stories, 1883-1888; edited by Shelby Foote; translated by Constance Garnett

Revenge
  Chekhov, A. P. The comic stories; translated from the Russian and with an introduction by Harvey Pitcher

Romance with double-bass
  Chekhov, A. P. The comic stories; translated from the Russian and with an introduction by Harvey Pitcher

Rothschild's fiddle
  Chekhov, A. P. Anton Chekhov: later short stories, 1888-1903; edited by Shelby Foote; translated by Constance Garnett

The runaway
  Chekhov, A. P. Anton Chekhov: early short stories, 1883-1888; edited by Shelby Foote; translated by Constance Garnett

The schoolmistress
  Chekhov, A. P. Anton Chekhov: later short stories, 1888-1903; edited by Shelby Foote; translated by Constance Garnett

Sergeant Prishibeyev
  Chekhov, A. P. The comic stories; translated from the Russian and with an introduction by Harvey Pitcher

The shoemaker and the devil
  Chekhov, A. P. Anton Chekhov: later short stories, 1888-1903; edited by Shelby Foote; translated by Constance Garnett

Shrove Tuesday
  Chekhov, A. P. Anton Chekhov: early short stories, 1883-1888; edited by Shelby Foote; translated by Constance Garnett

The siren
  Chekhov, A. P. The comic stories; translated from the Russian and with an introduction by Harvey Pitcher

Sleepy
  Chekhov, A. P. Anton Chekhov: later short stories, 1888-1903; edited by Shelby Foote; translated by Constance Garnett

Sorrow
  Chekhov, A. P. Anton Chekhov: early short stories, 1883-1888; edited by Shelby Foote; translated by Constance Garnett

The steppe
  Chekhov, A. P. Anton Chekhov: early short stories, 1883-1888; edited by Shelby Foote; translated by Constance Garnett

A story without a title
  Chekhov, A. P. Anton Chekhov: early short stories, 1883-1888; edited by Shelby Foote; translated by Constance Garnett

A story without an end
  Chekhov, A. P. Anton Chekhov: early short stories, 1883-1888; edited by Shelby Foote; translated by Constance Garnett

The student
  Chekhov, A. P. Anton Chekhov: later short stories, 1888-1903; edited by Shelby Foote; translated by Constance Garnett

Surgery
  Chekhov, A. P. The comic stories; translated from the Russian and with an introduction by Harvey Pitcher

The Swedish match
  Chekhov, A. P. The comic stories; translated from the Russian and with an introduction by Harvey Pitcher

The teacher of literature
  Chekhov, A. P. Anton Chekhov: later short stories, 1888-1903; edited by Shelby Foote; translated by Constance Garnett

Terror
  Chekhov, A. P. Anton Chekhov: later short stories, 1888-1903; edited by Shelby Foote; translated by Constance Garnett

A trifle from life
  Chekhov, A. P. Anton Chekhov: early short stories, 1883-1888; edited by Shelby Foote; translated by Constance Garnett
  Chekhov, A. P. The essential tales of Chekhov; edited and with an introduction by Richard Ford; translated by Constance Garnett

The two Volodyas
  Chekhov, A. P. Anton Chekhov: later short stories, 1888-1903; edited by Shelby Foote; translated by Constance Garnett

Typhus
  Chekhov, A. P. Anton Chekhov: early short stories, 1883-1888; edited by Shelby Foote; translated by Constance Garnett

An upheaval
  Chekhov, A. P. Anton Chekhov: early short stories, 1883-1888; edited by Shelby Foote; translated by Constance Garnett

Vanka
  Chekhov, A. P. Anton Chekhov: early short stories, 1883-1888; edited by Shelby Foote; translated by Constance Garnett

Verotchka
  Chekhov, A. P. Anton Chekhov: early short stories, 1883-1888; edited by Shelby Foote; translated by Constance Garnett

Vint
  Chekhov, A. P. The comic stories; translated from the Russian and with an introduction by Harvey Pitcher

Volodya
  Chekhov, A. P. Anton Chekhov: early short stories, 1883-1888; edited by Shelby Foote; translated by Constance Garnett

Ward no. 6
  Chekhov, A. P. The essential tales of Chekhov; edited and with an introduction by Richard Ford; translated by Constance Garnett

What you usually find in novels
  The Paris Review v41 no152 p206-07 Fall 1999

Chekhov, Anton Pavlovich—_Continued_
Whitebrow
  Chekhov, A. P. Anton Chekhov: later short
    stories, 1888-1903; edited by Shelby Foote;
    translated by Constance Garnett
The witch
  Chekhov, A. P. Anton Chekhov: early short
    stories, 1883-1888; edited by Shelby Foote;
    translated by Constance Garnett
  Witches' brew; edited by Yvonne Jocks
A woman without prejudices
  Chekhov, A. P. The comic stories; translated
    from the Russian and with an introduction
    by Harvey Pitcher
A work of art
  Chekhov, A. P. Anton Chekhov: early short
    stories, 1883-1888; edited by Shelby Foote;
    translated by Constance Garnett
Zinotchka
  Chekhov, A. P. Anton Chekhov: early short
    stories, 1883-1888; edited by Shelby Foote;
    translated by Constance Garnett
CHEKHOV, ANTON PAVLOVICH, 1860-1904
About
Carver, R. Errand
Chemistry. Kelly, J. P.
Ch'en, Shih-hsü _See_ Chen Shixu, 1948-
Chen, Willi
Trotters
  The Oxford book of Caribbean short stories;
    edited by Stewart Brown and John
    Wickham
Chen Shixu
The general and the small town
  The Vintage book of contemporary Chinese
    fiction; edited by Carolyn Choa and David
    Su Li-qun
Cheng, Ch'ing-wen
Autumn night
  Cheng, C.-W. Three-legged horse; edited by
    Pang-yuan Chi
Betel nut town
  Cheng, C.-W. Three-legged horse; edited by
    Pang-yuan Chi
The coconut palms on campus
  Cheng, C.-W. Three-legged horse; edited by
    Pang-yuan Chi
A fisherman's family
  Cheng, C.-W. Three-legged horse; edited by
    Pang-yuan Chi
God of thunder's gonna getcha
  Cheng, C.-W. Three-legged horse; edited by
    Pang-yuan Chi
Hair
  Cheng, C.-W. Three-legged horse; edited by
    Pang-yuan Chi
The last of the gentlemen
  Cheng, C.-W. Three-legged horse; edited by
    Pang-yuan Chi
The mosquito
  Cheng, C.-W. Three-legged horse; edited by
    Pang-yuan Chi
The river suite
  Cheng, C.-W. Three-legged horse; edited by
    Pang-yuan Chi
Secrets
  Cheng, C.-W. Three-legged horse; edited by
    Pang-yuan Chi

Spring rain
  Cheng, C.-W. Three-legged horse; edited by
    Pang-yuan Chi
The three-legged horse
  Cheng, C.-W. Three-legged horse; edited by
    Pang-yuan Chi
Cheng, Leslie Su
Points of Energy
  River Styx no67 p15-29 2004
Ch'eng, Nai-shan _See_ Cheng Naishan, 1946-
Cheng Naishan
Hong Taitai
  The Vintage book of contemporary Chinese
    fiction; edited by Carolyn Choa and David
    Su Li-qun
Chenoweth, Avery
Going back
  Chenoweth, A. Wingtips; stories
Housework
  Chenoweth, A. Wingtips; stories
I wish you wouldn't be that way
  Chenoweth, A. Wingtips; stories
If I were you
  Chenoweth, A. Wingtips; stories
Powerman
  Chenoweth, A. Wingtips; stories
Reunions
  Chenoweth, A. Wingtips; stories
The unfortunated city
  Chenoweth, A. Wingtips; stories
The visit
  Chenoweth, A. Wingtips; stories
Wingtips
  Chenoweth, A. Wingtips; stories
**CHERNOBYL NUCLEAR ACCIDENT,
  CHERNOBYL, UKRAINE, 1986**
Schroeder, K. The dragon of Pripyat
Chernoff, Maxine
The Living
  Prairie Schooner v77 no1 p162-5 Spr 2003
CHEROKEE INDIANS
Kingsolver, B. Homeland
Cherry, Kelly
As it is in heaven
  Cherry, K. The society of friends; stories
Block party
  Cherry, K. The society of friends; stories
Chapters from _A dog's life_
  Cherry, K. The society of friends; stories
Chores
  Cherry, K. The society of friends; stories
How it goes
  Cherry, K. The society of friends; stories
Love in the Middle Ages
  Cherry, K. The society of friends; stories
Lunachick
  Cherry, K. The society of friends; stories
Not the Phil Donahue show
  Cherry, K. The society of friends; stories
The prowler
  Cherry, K. The society of friends; stories
The society of friends
  Cherry, K. The society of friends; stories
Tell her
  Cherry, K. The society of friends; stories
The wedding cake in the middle of the road
  Cherry, K. The society of friends; stories
Your chances of getting married
  Cherry, K. The society of friends; stories

Cherry. Su Tong
Cherry Garcia, pistachio cream. Krysl, M.
Cherryh, C. J.
The brothers
  Cherryh, C. J. The collected short fiction of
  C.J. Cherryh
Cassandra
  Cherryh, C. J. The collected short fiction of
  C.J. Cherryh
Companions
  Cherryh, C. J. The collected short fiction of
  C.J. Cherryh
The dark king
  Cherryh, C. J. The collected short fiction of
  C.J. Cherryh
The dreamstone
  Cherryh, C. J. The collected short fiction of
  C.J. Cherryh
The general
  Cherryh, C. J. The collected short fiction of
  C.J. Cherryh
A gift of prophecy
  Cherryh, C. J. The collected short fiction of
  C.J. Cherryh
The haunted tower
  Cherryh, C. J. The collected short fiction of
  C.J. Cherryh
Highliner
  Cherryh, C. J. The collected short fiction of
  C.J. Cherryh
Homecoming
  Cherryh, C. J. The collected short fiction of
  C.J. Cherryh
Ice
  Cherryh, C. J. The collected short fiction of
  C.J. Cherryh
The last tower
  Cherryh, C. J. The collected short fiction of
  C.J. Cherryh
Masks
  Cherryh, C. J. The collected short fiction of
  C.J. Cherryh
Mech
  Cherryh, C. J. The collected short fiction of
  C.J. Cherryh
Nightgame
  Cherryh, C. J. The collected short fiction of
  C.J. Cherryh
Of law and magic
  Cherryh, C. J. The collected short fiction of
  C.J. Cherryh
The only death in the city
  Cherryh, C. J. The collected short fiction of
  C.J. Cherryh
Pots
  Masterpieces: the best science fiction of the
  century; edited by Orson Scott Card
Poys
  Cherryh, C. J. The collected short fiction of
  C.J. Cherryh
The Sandman, the Tinman, and Betty B.
  Cherryh, C. J. The collected short fiction of
  C.J. Cherryh
The scapegoat
  Cherryh, C. J. The collected short fiction of
  C.J. Cherryh
Sea change
  Cherryh, C. J. The collected short fiction of
  C.J. Cherryh

A thief in Korianth
  Cherryh, C. J. The collected short fiction of
  C.J. Cherryh
The Threads of time
  Cherryh, C. J. The collected short fiction of
  C.J. Cherryh
The unshadowed land
  Cherryh, C. J. The collected short fiction of
  C.J. Cherryh
Willow
  Cherryh, C. J. The collected short fiction of
  C.J. Cherryh
Wings
  Cherryh, C. J. The collected short fiction of
  C.J. Cherryh
Cheryl. Harvey, J.
CHESAPEAKE BAY (MD. AND VA.)
Hoffman, W. Landings
Tilghman, C. Something important
CHESHIRE (ENGLAND) *See* England—Chesh-
  ire
Chesnutt, Charles Waddell
The averted strike
  The African American West; a century of
  short stories; edited by Bruce A. Glasrud
  and Laurie Champion
A bad night
  Chesnutt, C. W. and Duncan, C. The northern
  stories of Charles W. Chesnutt; edited by
  Charles Duncan
Baxter's procrustes
  Chesnutt, C. W. and Duncan, C. The northern
  stories of Charles W. Chesnutt; edited by
  Charles Duncan
  Chesnutt, C. W. Stories, novels & essays;
  [by] Charles W. Chesnutt
The bouquet
  Chesnutt, C. W. Stories, novels & essays;
  [by] Charles W. Chesnutt
Cartwright's mistake
  Chesnutt, C. W. and Duncan, C. The northern
  stories of Charles W. Chesnutt; edited by
  Charles Duncan
Cicely's dream
  Chesnutt, C. W. Stories, novels & essays;
  [by] Charles W. Chesnutt
The conjurer's revenge
  Chesnutt, C. W. Stories, novels & essays;
  [by] Charles W. Chesnutt
Dave's neckliss
  Chesnutt, C. W. Stories, novels & essays;
  [by] Charles W. Chesnutt
  Southern local color; stories of region, race,
  and gender; edited by Barbara C. Ewell and
  Pamela Glenn Menke; with notes by An-
  drea Humphrey
A deep sleeper
  Chesnutt, C. W. Stories, novels & essays;
  [by] Charles W. Chesnutt
The doll
  Chesnutt, C. W. and Duncan, C. The northern
  stories of Charles W. Chesnutt; edited by
  Charles Duncan
  Chesnutt, C. W. Stories, novels & essays;
  [by] Charles W. Chesnutt
The dumb witness
  Chesnutt, C. W. Stories, novels & essays;
  [by] Charles W. Chesnutt

Chesnutt, Charles Waddell—*Continued*

The goophered grapevine
Chesnutt, C. W. Stories, novels & essays; [by] Charles W. Chesnutt
Dark matter; a century of speculative fiction from the African diaspora; edited by Sheree R. Thomas
Southern local color; stories of region, race, and gender; edited by Barbara C. Ewell and Pamela Glenn Menke; with notes by Andrea Humphrey

A grass widow
Chesnutt, C. W. and Duncan, C. The northern stories of Charles W. Chesnutt; edited by Charles Duncan

The gray wolf's ha'nt
Chesnutt, C. W. Stories, novels & essays; [by] Charles W. Chesnutt

Her Virginia Mammy
Chesnutt, C. W. and Duncan, C. The northern stories of Charles W. Chesnutt; edited by Charles Duncan
Chesnutt, C. W. Stories, novels & essays; [by] Charles W. Chesnutt

Hot-foot Hannibal
Chesnutt, C. W. Stories, novels & essays; [by] Charles W. Chesnutt

How he met her
Chesnutt, C. W. and Duncan, C. The northern stories of Charles W. Chesnutt; edited by Charles Duncan

The kiss
Chesnutt, C. W. and Duncan, C. The northern stories of Charles W. Chesnutt; edited by Charles Duncan
Chesnutt, C. W. Stories, novels & essays; [by] Charles W. Chesnutt

Lonesome Ben
Chesnutt, C. W. Stories, novels & essays; [by] Charles W. Chesnutt

The march of progress
Chesnutt, C. W. Stories, novels & essays; [by] Charles W. Chesnutt

Mars Jeems's nightmare
Chesnutt, C. W. Stories, novels & essays; [by] Charles W. Chesnutt

A matter of principle
Chesnutt, C. W. and Duncan, C. The northern stories of Charles W. Chesnutt; edited by Charles Duncan
Chesnutt, C. W. Stories, novels & essays; [by] Charles W. Chesnutt

A metropolitan experience
Chesnutt, C. W. and Duncan, C. The northern stories of Charles W. Chesnutt; edited by Charles Duncan

Mr. Taylor's funeral
Chesnutt, C. W. and Duncan, C. The northern stories of Charles W. Chesnutt; edited by Charles Duncan

The passing of Grandison
Chesnutt, C. W. and Duncan, C. The northern stories of Charles W. Chesnutt; edited by Charles Duncan
Chesnutt, C. W. Stories, novels & essays; [by] Charles W. Chesnutt

Southern local color; stories of region, race, and gender; edited by Barbara C. Ewell and Pamela Glenn Menke; with notes by Andrea Humphrey

Po' Sandy
Chesnutt, C. W. Stories, novels & essays; [by] Charles W. Chesnutt

The shadow of my past
Chesnutt, C. W. and Duncan, C. The northern stories of Charles W. Chesnutt; edited by Charles Duncan

The sheriff's children
Chesnutt, C. W. Stories, novels & essays; [by] Charles W. Chesnutt

Sis' Becky's pickaninny
Chesnutt, C. W. Stories, novels & essays; [by] Charles W. Chesnutt

Uncle Wellington's wives
Chesnutt, C. W. and Duncan, C. The northern stories of Charles W. Chesnutt; edited by Charles Duncan
Chesnutt, C. W. Stories, novels & essays; [by] Charles W. Chesnutt

The web of circumstance
Chesnutt, C. W. Stories, novels & essays; [by] Charles W. Chesnutt

White weeds
Chesnutt, C. W. and Duncan, C. The northern stories of Charles W. Chesnutt; edited by Charles Duncan
Chesnutt, C. W. Stories, novels & essays; [by] Charles W. Chesnutt

The wife of his youth
Chesnutt, C. W. and Duncan, C. The northern stories of Charles W. Chesnutt; edited by Charles Duncan
Chesnutt, C. W. Stories, novels & essays; [by] Charles W. Chesnutt

CHESS
Alameddine, R. My grandmother, the grandmaster
Amdrup, E. Chess on board
Archer, J. The endgame
Eggers, P. The big gift
Eggers, P. A private space
Eggers, P. Substitutes
Nemerov, H. and Johnson, W. R. Exchange of men
Wilson, R. C. The fields of Abraham
Zweig, S. The royal game
Chess on board. Amdrup, E.
Chest Pain. Love, M.
Chesterton, G. K. (Gilbert Keith)
The wrong shape
Murder most divine; ecclesiastical tales of unholy crimes; edited by Ralph McInerny and Martin H. Greenberg
Chesterton, Gilbert Keith *See* Chesterton, G. K. (Gilbert Keith), 1874-1936
Chetkovich, Kathryn
Envy
Granta no82 p67-87 Summ 2003
Cheuse, Alan
A brief Washington-Mount Vernon chronology, followed by an aborted picnic at the Holocaust Museum
The Antioch Review v59 no4 p749-66 Fall 2001

Cheuse, Alan—*Continued*
Days Given Over to Travel
  Prairie Schooner v77 no2 p144-71 Summ
    2003
Chevy in the fast lane. Meredith, D.
CHEYENNE INDIANS
  Alexie, S. Ghost dance
  Forsyth, F. Whispering wind
Chez Oedipus. Avrich, J.
Chi, Susan Y.
  Stormy Weather: Yin Tian
    Bomb no87 p102-5 Spr 2004
Chiang, Ted
  Division by zero
    Chiang, T. Stories of your life and others
  The evolution of human science
    Chiang, T. Stories of your life and others
  Hell is the absence of God
    Brown, C. N. and Strahan, J. The Locus
      awards; thirty years of the best in science
      fiction and fantasy; edited by Charles N.
      Brown and Jonathan Strahan
    Chiang, T. Stories of your life and others
    Nebula awards showcase 2004; edited by
      Vonda McIntyre
    Starlight 3; edited by Patrick Nielsen Hayden
  Liking what you see: a documentary
    Chiang, T. Stories of your life and others
  Seventy-two letters
    Chiang, T. Stories of your life and others
    Vanishing acts; a science fiction anthology;
      edited by Ellen Datlow
  Story of your life
    Chiang, T. Stories of your life and others
    Nebula awards showcase 2001; the year's best
      SF and fantasy chosen by the science fic-
      tion and fantasy writers of America; edited
      by Robert Silverberg
    The Year's best science fiction, sixteenth an-
      nual collection; edited by Gardner Dozois
  Tower of Babylon
    Chiang, T. Stories of your life and others
  Understand
    Chiang, T. Stories of your life and others
Chiappone, Richard
  The chubs
    Chiappone, R. Water of an undetermined
      depth
  Dealer's choice
    Chiappone, R. Water of an undetermined
      depth
  A girl, the jungle, monkeys
    Chiappone, R. Water of an undetermined
      depth
  Love A, love B
    Chiappone, R. Water of an undetermined
      depth
  Maximum reception
    Chiappone, R. Water of an undetermined
      depth
  Old friend
    Chiappone, R. Water of an undetermined
      depth
  Q Roo
    Chiappone, R. Water of an undetermined
      depth
  Raccoon
    Chiappone, R. Water of an undetermined
      depth

Sick baby
  Chiappone, R. Water of an undetermined
    depth
Side job
  Chiappone, R. Water of an undetermined
    depth
Things come to mind
  Chiappone, R. Water of an undetermined
    depth
Those little foreign beauties
  Chiappone, R. Water of an undetermined
    depth
Water of an undetermined depth
  Chiappone, R. Water of an undetermined
    depth
Winter fish
  Chiappone, R. Water of an undetermined
    depth
Chiarella, Tom
  Foley's confessions
    100% pure Florida fiction; an anthology; ed-
      ited by Susan Hubbard and Robley Wilson
CHICAGO (ILL.) *See* Illinois—Chicago
Chicago 1927. Gomez, J.
CHICANOS *See* Mexican Americans
Chickasaw Charlie Hoke. Leonard, E.
The **Chickasha** Bone Crusher. Witwer, H. C.
Chicken catch a tory. Myers, T.
Chicken Man. Rodgers, S. J.
CHICKENS
  Adam, C. Hen
  Kurlansky, M. The unclean
  Troncoso, S. Punching chickens
Chickens. McCorkle, J.
Chickens. Strom, D.
Chickensnake. Vice, B.
Chicxulub. Boyle, T. C.
The **chief** designer. Duncan, A.
Chief Larson. Hassler, J.
Chihuahua Flats. Bishop, M.
The **Child.** Brau, E.
CHILD ABUSE
  Bailey, D. Quinn's way
  Coberly, L. M. In which murder is done
  Donoso, J. Ana Maria
  Evans, E. Ransom
  Galloway, J. Someone had to
  Gunn, K. Grass, leaves
  Karnezis, P. A funeral of stones
  LeRoy, J. T. Disappearances
  LeRoy, J. T. Foolishness is bound in the heart
    of a child
  Maron, M. The choice
  Straub, P. Ashputtle
  Vachss, A. H. Dress-up day
  Wolff, T. The night in question
CHILD AND PARENT *See* Parent and child
The **child** borrows his uncle's gun and goes east
  to Safad. Kanafāni, G.
Child, Dead, in the Rose Garden. Doctorow, E. L.
The **child** discovers that the key looks like an axe.
  Kanafāni, G.
The **child** goes to the camp. Kanafāni, G.
The **child,** his father, and the gun go to the citadel
  at Jaddin. Kanafāni, G.
CHILD LABOR
  Boylan, C. A funny thing happened
The **child** Manuela [excerpt] Winsloe, C.
CHILD MOLESTING *See* Child sexual abuse

Child of another time. Bankier, W.
The **child** prodigy. Drake, R.
The **child** screams and looks back at you. Banks, R.

CHILD SEXUAL ABUSE
    Asendorf, A. G. The gossamer girl
    Ferriss, L. Mud time
    Hill, I. Pagan babies
    Joseph, D. Approximate to salvation
    LeRoy, J. T. Baby doll
    LeRoy, J. T. The heart is deceitful above all things
    LeRoy, J. T. Toyboxed
    Maraini, D. Alicetta
    Maraini, D. He is eleven years old, his name is Tano
    Nair, M. Summer
    Salaam, K. I. Rosamojo
    Sánchez, R. El tejón
    Simmons, D. Looking for Kelly Dahl
    Taylor, L. Unspeakable
    Thien, M. Alchemy
    Vachss, A. H. Curtains
    Vachss, A. H. The writing on the wall
    Ziegler, I. Hooked
The **child** that never was. Estenssoro, M. V.
The **child** that went with the fairies. Le Fanu, J. S.
The **child** who raised poisonous snakes. Ts'an-hsüeh
Child Widow. Marshall, A.

CHILDBIRTH
    Bell, M. S. Labor
    Carroll, L. Traveling princess
    Chekhov, A. P. The party
    Coates, G. S. A cast leaf
    Colwin, L. Another marvellous thing
    DeMarinis, R. Horizontal snow
    Hunter, F. Night vigil
    Klass, P. For women everywhere
    Le Clézio, J.-M. G. Moloch
    Mastretta, A. Aunt Eugenia
    McCaffrey, A. Freedom of the race
    Phillips, D. R. Everything quiet like church
    Wilmot, J. Dirt angel
    Zinovyeva-Annibal, L. D. Will
CHILDHOOD See Boys; Children; Girls
Childhood. Galaviz-Budziszewski, A.
Childhood. Rozan, S. J.
Childhood with grandmother. See Babel', I. At grandmother's

CHILDLESS MARRIAGE
    Beattie, A. Coydog
    Biguenet, J. Fatherhood
    Carlson, R. Life before science
    Chapman, C. M. Honey well hung
    Cheng, C.-W. Spring rain
    Cohen, R. Between hammers
    Fromm, P. Cowbird
    Goran, L. The chorus girl
    Graver, E. The mourning door
    Krawiec, R. Saving Saul
    Nelson, A. The unified front
    Schwartz, L. S. Hostages to fortune
    Tilghman, C. Mary in the mountains
CHILDLESSNESS
    See also Childless marriage
    Brady, C. Pilgrimage
    Budnitz, J. Barren

Connor, J. We who live apart
Grau, S. A. Home
Hoffman, A. Still among the living
Homes, A. M. Georgica
Martin, V. Contraction
Nfah-Abbenyi, J. M. The healer
O'Connell, M. Veronica's veil
Orner, P. Papa Gino's
Pittalwala, I. Kulsum, Nazia, and Ismail
Childproofing. Watanabe McFerrin, L.
CHILDREN
    See also Abandoned children; Adolescence; African American children; Boys; Emotionally disturbed children; Foster children; Girls; Jewish children; Lost children; Mentally handicapped children; Missing children; Orphans; Physically handicapped children; War and children; Wild children
    Adam, C. Watch dog
    Alcott, L. M. Mother's trial
    Alcott, L. M. Mrs. Gay's prescription
    Atkinson, K. Unseen translation
    Bambara, T. C. The hammer man
    Bausch, R. The weight
    Bishop, E. The farmer's children
    Bradbury, R. All summer in a day
    Bradbury, R. Let's play poison
    Bradbury, R. Season of disbelief
    Bradbury, R. Time in hy flight
    Bradbury, R. Zero hour
    Brennan, M. The children are there, trying not to laugh
    Brennan, M. In and out of never-never land
    Browder, C. Animal heaven
    Capote, T. Children on their birthdays
    Carlson, R. On the U.S.S. Fortitude
    Chekhov, A. P. Children
    Chekhov, A. P. A day in the country
    Chekhov, A. P. Grisha
    Chekhov, A. P. An incident
    Chopin, K. Regret
    Davies, P. H. Frogmen
    De Lint, C. There's no such thing
    Dumas, H. The crossing
    Ellison, H. Jeffty is five
    Faulkner, W. That evening sun go down
    Gallagher, S. The little dead girl singing
    Gilchrist, E. Summer, an elegy
    Gilman, C. P. Making a change
    Glave, T. The pit
    Greer, A. S. Life is over there
    Ha Jin. In the kindergarten
    Kalu, Anthonia C. Children's day
    Kawabata, Y. Raindrops
    King, S. Children of the corn
    LaValle, V. D. Who we did worship
    Mason, B. A. Three-wheeler
    McCorkle, J. Billy goats
    Mencken, S. H. Little lady
    Mencken, S. H. Tomboy
    Millar, M. The people across the canyon
    Muñoz, M. Campo
    Orringer, J. Pilgrims
    Robison, M. Seizing control
    Royle, N. Hide and seek
    Skillings, R. D. The sandbox
    Sneve, V. D. H. Clean hands
    Sneve, V. D. H. Jimmy Yellow Hawk
    Sneve, V. D. H. The slim butte ghost

CHILDREN—*Continued*

Svoboda, T. A mama

Svoboda, T. Trailer girl

Tem, M. Gardens

Tolstoy, L., graf. The power of childhood

Troy, M. The Alibi Café

Tucci, N. The evolution of knowledge

Updike, J. The alligators

Van Winckel, N. Beside ourselves

Watson, I. The boy who lost an hour, the girl who lost her life

Wolfe, G. Pocketful of diamonds

Yates, R. Doctor Jack-o'-Lantern

Yates, R. Fun with a stranger

Yates, R. A private possession

Adoption

See Adoption

CHILDREN, ABANDONED *See* Abandoned children

CHILDREN, ADOPTED *See* Adoption

CHILDREN, AUTISTIC *See* Autistic children

CHILDREN, CRUELTY TO *See* Child abuse

CHILDREN, GIFTED *See* Gifted children

CHILDREN, JEWISH *See* Jewish children

CHILDREN, LOST *See* Lost children

CHILDREN, SICK *See* Sick children

Children. Chekhov, A. P.

Children are bored on Sunday. Stafford, J.

The **children** are there, trying not to laugh. Brennan, M.

The **children** are very quiet when they are away. Brennan, M.

CHILDREN AS SLAVES *See* Slavery

Children of chance. Bagley, J. E.

The **children** of dead state troopers. Morris, K. L.

The **children** of Gael. Kilpatrick, N. and Bisson, B.

Children of hunger. Iagnemma, K.

Children of the corn. King, S.

Children of the Lodz, ghetto. Rachmil, B.

Children of Transylvania. Campbell, B. J.

The **children** stay. Munro, A.

Children with matches. Howard, M.

The **children's** book of victims. Nesbitt, M.

Child's play. Tenn, W.

The **child's** story. Lupoff, R. A.

A **child's** voice. Schiffman, C.

CHILE

L'Amour, L. By the waters of San Tadeo

Plager, S. A change of heart

Skármeta, A. The cyclist of San Cristóbal Hill

Chilson, Robert

This side of independence

The Year's best science fiction, sixteenth annual collection; edited by Gardner Dozois

Chimera, Beth

July

The Pushcart prize XXIII: best of the small presses; an annual small press reader; edited by Bill Henderson with the Pushcart prize editors

Chimera 8. Abraham, D.

CHIMNEY SWEEPS

Singer, I. B. The beggar said no

Singer, I. B. The chimney sweep

Chimp shrink and backwards. Nesbitt, M.

CHIMPANZEES

Clarke, A. C. An ape about the house

Lugones, L. Yzur

Murphy, P. Rachel in love

Oliver, C. Ghost town

Vinge, V. "Bookworm, run!"

Chin. Jen, G.

CHINA

To 1643

Bradbury, R. The flying machine

Painter, P. The story of Hu

1900-1949

L'Amour, L. Beyond the Great Snow Mountains

Lao She. Also a triangle

Lao She. Attachment

Lao She. Autobiography of a minor character

Lao She. Black Li and White Li

Lao She. Crooktails

Lao She. Ding

Lao She. The grand opening

Lao She. Hot dumplings

Lao She. Life choices

Lao She. A man who doesn't lie

Lao She. Neighbors

Lao She. No distance too far, no sacrifice too great

1949-

Bai Xiao-Yi. Six short pieces

Bi Shumin. One centimetre

Cai Cehai. The distant sound of tree-felling

Feng Jicai. The tall woman and her short husband

Gao Xingjian. The temple

Ha Jin. After Cowboy Chicken came to town

Ha Jin. Alive

Ha Jin. A bad joke

Ha Jin. The bridegroom

Ha Jin. Broken

Ha Jin. Emperor

Ha Jin. An entrepreneur's story

Ha Jin. Flame

Ha Jin. An official reply

Ha Jin. Saboteur

Ha Jin. A tiger-fighter is hard to find

Ha Jin. The woman from New York

Jen, G. Duncan in China

Leong, R. Where do people live who never die?

Liu Xinwu. Black walls

Min, A. Red azalea [excerpt]

Mo Shen. The window

Mo Yan. Abandoned child

Mo Yan. The cure

Mo Yan. Iron child

Mo Yan. Love story

Mo Yan. Shifu, you'll do anything for a laugh

Mo Yan. Soaring

Shi Tiesheng. Fate

Su Tong. Cherry

Su Tong. Young Muo

Wang Cengqi. Big Chan

Zhang Jie. Love must not be forgotten

Zhao Danian. Three sketches

Communism

See Communism—China

Peasant life

See Peasant life—China

Prisoners and prisons

See Prisoners and prisons—China

Rural life

Chen Shixu. The general and the small town

Fischerová, D. The thirty-sixth chicken of Master Wu

CHINA—Rural life—*Continued*
Ha Jin. In the kindergarten
Zhou Libo. The family on the other side of the mountain
Beijing
Siege, 1900
Silber, J. Ideas of heaven
Beijing
Cherryh, C. J. The general
Deng Youmei. Han the forger
Jones, G. Touching Tiananmen
Lao She. An old and established name
Lao She. An old man's romance
Lao She. Rabbit
Mo Yan. Shen Garden
Hong Kong
See Hong Kong
Peking
See China—Beijing
Shanghai
Chang, L. S. Pipa's story
Cheng Naishan. Hong Taitai
Padilla, I. The Chinaman with the heads
Wang Anyi. Life in a small courtyard
Tibet
L'Amour, L. May there be a road
The **China** cottage. Watson, I.
China doll. De Lint, C.
China Flats. Upton, J.
The **Chinaman**. See Babel', I. Chink
CHINATOWN (NEW YORK, N.Y.) *See* New York (N.Y.)—Chinatown
CHINESE
California
Leong, R. Geography one
Louis, L. G. Fur
Cuba
Ponte, A. J. At the request of Ochun
Japan
Mo Yan. Man and beast
Philippines
Murray, S. Yamashita's gold
Russia
Babel', I. Chink
United States
Davidson, A. The deed of the deft-footed dragon
Gilchrist, E. Light can be both wave and particle
Ha Jin. The woman from New York
Louie, D. W. Displacement
Martin, L. Bad family
Rogers, B. H. Cloud stalking mice
Steinbeck, T. Sing Fat and the Imperial Duchess of Woo
CHINESE AMERICANS
Chang, L. S. The eve of the spirit festival
Davies, P. H. The next life
Homes, A. M. The Chinese lesson
Jen, G. Birthmates
Jen, G. Chin
Jen, G. Duncan in China
Jen, G. House, house, home
Jen, G. In the American society
Jen, G. Just wait
Jen, G. The water faucet vision
Jen, G. Who's Irish?
Leong, R. The western paradise of Eddie Bin
Lieu, J. Always a descendant

Lieu, J. The children
Lieu, J. Potential weapons
Lieu, J. This world
Lieu, J. Troubles
Loh, S. T. My father's Chinese wives
Louis, L. G. Rudy's two wives
Louis, L. G. Tea
Louis, L. G. Thirty yards
Michaels, L. Tell me everything
Row, J. Heaven lake
Sandor, M. Annunciation
Tan, A. Two kinds
Vaswani, N. Bing-Chen
The **Chinese** lesson. Homes, A. M.
The **Chinese** restaurant. Gonzalez, R.
CHINESE SOLDIERS *See* Soldiers—China
Chink. Babel', I.
Chinodya, Shimmer
Among the dead
   Chinodya, S. Can we talk and other stories
Bramson
   Chinodya, S. Can we talk and other stories
Brothers and sisters
   Chinodya, S. Can we talk and other stories
Can we talk
   Chinodya, S. Can we talk and other stories
Going to see Mr. B. V.
   Chinodya, S. Can we talk and other stories
Hoffman Street
   Chinodya, S. Can we talk and other stories
The man who hanged himself
   Chinodya, S. Can we talk and other stories
Play your cards
   Chinodya, S. Can we talk and other stories
Snow
   Chinodya, S. Can we talk and other stories
Strays
   Chinodya, S. Can we talk and other stories
The waterfall
   Chinodya, S. Can we talk and other stories
Chinquee, Kim
Jesus
   South Carolina Review v35 no1 p19-26 Fall 2002
Chip. Pronzini, B.
Chip off the old block. Stegner, W. E.
CHIPPEWA INDIANS
Erdrich, L. Fleur
CHIROPODISTS
Bennett, A. Miss Fozzard finds her feet
CHIROPRACTIC
Papernick, J. The art of correcting
The **chiseler**. Callaghan, M.
Chislett, Michael
Off the map
   The Mammoth book of best horror 13; edited by Stephen Jones
Chittenden, Margaret
The spirit of Washington
   Bishop, C. and James, D. Death dines in; edited by Claudia Bishop and Dean James
Chitwood, Michael
The store
   The Ohio Review no62/63 p139-40 2001
CHIVALRY
   See also Knights and knighthood; Middle Ages

Chivers, Deborah
Radio baby
  Mr. Roopratna's chocolate; the winning sto-
  ries from the 1999 Rhys Davies competi-
  tion
Chloe. Saroyan, A.
Chloroform. Parker, G.
Cho, Natasha
Bang bang bang
  Hers 3: brilliant new fiction by lesbian writ-
  ers; edited by Terry Wolverton with Robert
  Drake
Chocolate mice. Spark, D.
Chocolate moose. Crider, B. and Crider, J.
CHOCTAW INDIANS
Chopin, K. Loka
Foote, S. The sacred mound
Choi, Eric
Divisions
  Northern suns; edited by David G. Hartwell
  & Glenn Grant
The **choice**. Collins, M.
The **choice**. Maron, M.
CHOLERA
Murray, J. The hill station
Choosing sides. Drake, D.
Choosing sides. Greer, R. O.
The **chop** girl. MacLeod, I.
Chopin, Kate
After the winter; In Chopin, K. Complete novels
  and stories
  Chopin, K. Complete novels and stories
Alexandre's wonderful experience
  Chopin, K. Complete novels and stories
At Chênière Caminada
  Chopin, K. Complete novels and stories
At the 'Cadian ball
  Chopin, K. Complete novels and stories
Athénaïse
  Chopin, K. Complete novels and stories
Aunt Lympy's interference
  Chopin, K. Complete novels and stories
The awakening
  Chopin, K. Complete novels and stories
Azélie
  Chopin, K. Complete novels and stories
La belle Zoraïde
  Chopin, K. Complete novels and stories
La Belle Zoraïde
  Southern local color; stories of region, race,
  and gender; edited by Barbara C. Ewell and
  Pamela Glenn Menke; with notes by An-
  drea Humphrey
The Bênitous' slave
  Chopin, K. Complete novels and stories
Beyond the Bayou
  Chopin, K. Complete novels and stories
The blind man
  Chopin, K. Complete novels and stories
Boulôt and Boulotte
  Chopin, K. Complete novels and stories
Caline
  Chopin, K. Complete novels and stories
Cavanelle
  Chopin, K. Complete novels and stories
Charlie
  Chopin, K. Complete novels and stories
Croque-Mitaine
  Chopin, K. Complete novels and stories

Dead men's shoes
  Chopin, K. Complete novels and stories
A December day in Dixie
  Chopin, K. Complete novels and stories
Désirée's baby
  Chopin, K. Complete novels and stories
  Southern local color; stories of region, race,
  and gender; edited by Barbara C. Ewell and
  Pamela Glenn Menke; with notes by An-
  drea Humphrey
Doctor Chevalier's lie
  Chopin, K. Complete novels and stories
A Dresden lady in Dixie
  Chopin, K. Complete novels and stories
An Egyptian ciagarette
  Chopin, K. Complete novels and stories
Elizabeth Stock's one story
  Chopin, K. Complete novels and stories
Emancipation. a life fable
  Chopin, K. Complete novels and stories
A family affair
  Chopin, K. Complete novels and stories
Fedora
  Chopin, K. Complete novels and stories
For Marse Chouchoute
  Chopin, K. Complete novels and stories
The gentleman from New Orleans
  Chopin, K. Complete novels and stories
A gentleman of Bayou Têche
  Chopin, K. Complete novels and stories
The godmother
  Chopin, K. Complete novels and stories
The going away of Liza
  Chopin, K. Complete novels and stories
A harbinger
  Chopin, K. Complete novels and stories
Her letters
  Chopin, K. Complete novels and stories
A horse story
  Chopin, K. Complete novels and stories
An idle fellow
  Chopin, K. Complete novels and stories
The impossible Miss Meadows
  Chopin, K. Complete novels and stories
In and out of old Natchitoches
  Chopin, K. Complete novels and stories
In Sabine
  Chopin, K. Complete novels and stories
  Southern local color; stories of region, race,
  and gender; edited by Barbara C. Ewell and
  Pamela Glenn Menke; with notes by An-
  drea Humphrey
Juanita
  Chopin, K. Complete novels and stories
The kiss
  Chopin, K. Complete novels and stories
A lady of bayou St. John
  Chopin, K. Complete novels and stories
Lilacs
  Chopin, K. Complete novels and stories
The lilies
  Chopin, K. Complete novels and stories
A little country girl
  Chopin, K. Complete novels and stories
A little free-mulatto
  Chopin, K. Complete novels and stories
The locket
  Chopin, K. Complete novels and stories

Chopin, Kate—*Continued*
Loka
Chopin, K. Complete novels and stories
Love on the Bon-Dieu
Chopin, K. Complete novels and stories
Ma'ame Pelagie
The American fantasy tradition; edited by Brian M. Thomsen
Chopin, K. Complete novels and stories
Madame Célestin's divorce
Chopin, K. Complete novels and stories
Madame Martel's Christmas Eve
Chopin, K. Complete novels and stories
The maid of Saint Phillippe
Chopin, K. Complete novels and stories
Mamouche
Chopin, K. Complete novels and stories
A matter of prejudice
Chopin, K. Complete novels and stories
A mental suggestion
Chopin, K. Complete novels and stories
Miss McEnders
Chopin, K. Complete novels and stories
Miss Witherwell's mistake
Chopin, K. Complete novels and stories
A morning walk
Chopin, K. Complete novels and stories
Mrs. Mobry's reason
Chopin, K. Complete novels and stories
Nég Créol
Chopin, K. Complete novels and stories
The night came slowly
Chopin, K. Complete novels and stories
A night in Acadie
Chopin, K. Complete novels and stories
A non-account Creole
Chopin, K. Complete novels and stories
Odalie misses mass
Chopin, K. Complete novels and stories
Old Aunt Peggy
Chopin, K. Complete novels and stories
Ozème's holiday
Chopin, K. Complete novels and stories
A pair of silk stockings
Chopin, K. Complete novels and stories
A point at issue!
Chopin, K. Complete novels and stories
Polly
Chopin, K. Complete novels and stories
Polydore
Chopin, K. Complete novels and stories
The recovery
Chopin, K. Complete novels and stories
A reflection
Chopin, K. Complete novels and stories
Regret
Chopin, K. Complete novels and stories
A respectable woman
Chopin, K. Complete novels and stories
The return of Alcibiade
Chopin, K. Complete novels and stories
Ripe figs
Chopin, K. Complete novels and stories
A rude awakening
Chopin, K. Complete novels and stories
A sentimental soul
Chopin, K. Complete novels and stories
A shameful affair
Chopin, K. Complete novels and stories

The storm
Chopin, K. Complete novels and stories
Southern local color; stories of region, race, and gender; edited by Barbara C. Ewell and Pamela Glenn Menke; with notes by Andrea Humphrey
The story of an hour
Chopin, K. Complete novels and stories
Suzette
Chopin, K. Complete novels and stories
Tante Cat'rinette
Chopin, K. Complete novels and stories
Ti Démon
Chopin, K. Complete novels and stories
Ti Frère
Chopin, K. Complete novels and stories
A turkey hunt
Chopin, K. Complete novels and stories
Two portraits
Chopin, K. Complete novels and stories
Two summers and two souls
Chopin, K. Complete novels and stories
The unexpected
Chopin, K. Complete novels and stories
A vacation and a voice
Chopin, K. Complete novels and stories
Vagabonds
Chopin, K. Complete novels and stories
A very fine fiddle
Chopin, K. Complete novels and stories
A visit to Avoyelles
Chopin, K. Complete novels and stories
The white eagle
Chopin, K. Complete novels and stories
Wiser than a god
Chopin, K. Complete novels and stories
With the violin
Chopin, K. Complete novels and stories
A wizard from Gettysburg
Chopin, K. Complete novels and stories
The wood-choopers
Chopin, K. Complete novels and stories
Chopped Steak Mountain. Dinh, L.
Chores. Cherry, K.
Choristers. Chekhov, A. P.
The **chorus** girl. Chekhov, A. P.
The **chorus** girl. Goran, L.
The **chorus** lady. See Chekhov, A. P. The chorus girl
Chosen. Carson, J.
Chosen. Shomer, E.
The **chosen** girl. Perrotta, T.
Chou, Li-po *See* Zhou Libo, 1908-1979
Christ *See* Jesus Christ
Christ in the house of Martha and Mary. Byatt, A. S.
Christ preaching at the Henley Regatta. Davenport, G.
CHRISTENINGS
Mencken, S. H. Namesake
A **Christian** education. Spencer, E.
CHRISTIAN LIFE
Bellow, S. A silver dish
Blair, J. Ghost river
Bly, C. Chuck's money
Lewis, Mark Ray. Scordatura
Tolstoy, L., graf. Divine and human
Tolstoy, L., graf. The poor people
Tolstoy, L., graf. The requirements of love

CHRISTIAN LIFE—*Continued*

Tolstoy, L., graf. The son of a thief

Vasseur, T. J. The sins of Jesus

CHRISTIANITY

    See also Catholic faith names of Christian churches or sects

Babel´, I. Pan Apolek

Harrison, H. The streets of Ashkelon

Lawrence, D. H. The man who died

Sneve, V. D. H. The first Christmas

Turtledove, H. Islands in the sea

CHRISTIANS, EARLY *See* Early Christians

Christie, Agatha

Accident

    Valentine's Day: women against men; stories of revenge; introduction by Alice Thomas

The adventure of the Egyptian tomb

    Into the mummy's tomb; edited by John Richard Stephens

The case of the discontented soldier

    Malice domestic 9

Problem at sea

    Death cruise; crime stories on the open seas; edited by Lawrence Block

CHRISTIE, AGATHA, 1890-1976

About

Kaminsky, S. M. Amnesia

Parodies, imitations, etc.

Cannell, D. What Mr. McGregor saw

Watson, I. The shape of murder

Wheat, C. Oh, to be in England!

Christie. Macy, C.

Christmas, Joyce

Takeout

    Murder most delectable; savory tales of culinary crimes; edited by Martin H. Greenberg

Christmas 1893. Franklin, T.

Christmas and Coconut Cake. Castoro, L. P.

A **Christmas** Carol. Heath, A. B.

Christmas gift. Warren, R. P.

A **Christmas** in Wyoming. Gilchrist, E.

Christmas snow. Hall, D.

CHRISTMAS STORIES

Agee, J. Mystery of numbers

Alcott, L. M. Bertie's box: a Christmas story

Allyn, D. The Christmas mitzvah

Asaro, C. Dance in blue

Beattie, A. Mermaids

Berkman, P. R. Merry Christmas, Charlie Brown

Bishop, M. Icicle music

Bishop, P. Ebenezer

Bishop, P. The thief of Christmas

Bosch, J. Encarnación Mendoza's Christmas Eve

Bowles, P. The frozen fields

Bradbury, R. Bless me, Father, for I have sinned

Brady, C. The custom of the country

Braverman, K. Temporary light

Brennan, M. The joker

Cannell, D. The January sale stowaway

Capote, T. A Christmas memory

Capote, T. One Christmas

Carlson, R. The H Street sledding record

Chopin, K. Madame Martel's Christmas Eve

Cohen, S. Just another New York Christmas story

Coward, M. No night by myself

Crider, B. The Santa Claus caper

Daniels, J. Christmasmobile

Davies, Tristan. Snapdragon

DeAndrea, W. L. The adventure of the Christmas tree

Doran, M. M. They shall have music

Edghill, R. The Christmas witch

Englander, N. Reb Kringle

Gifford, B. The lost Christmas

Gilchrist, E. A Christmas in Wyoming

Gilchrist, E. The golden bough

Hall, D. Christmas snow

Harte, B. How Santa Claus came to Simpson's Bar

Hinojosa, R. The Gulf Oil -Can Santa Claus

Kelly, J. P. Candy art

Kelly, J. P. Fruitcake theory

Klass, P. City sidewalks

Lee, M. A fresh start

Lewis, T. The marijuana tree

Lombreglia, R. Cashmere Christmas

MacLeod, A. To every thing there is a season

MacLeod, A. Winter dog

McBain, E. A very Merry Christmass

McHugh, M. F. A foreigner's Christmas in China

McNulty, J. Some nights when nothing happens are the best nights in this place

Morris, M. Coming home

Norris, H. The second shepherd

Paul, B. Ho ho ho

Pérez Galdós, B. "The mule and the ox"

Reed, I. Future Christmas

Reynolds, C. A train to catch

Rucker, R. v. B. Easy as pie

Salinger, J. D. Slight rebellion off Madison

Smiley, J. Long distance

Smith, A. The heat of the story

Sneve, V. D. H. The first Christmas

Spark, M. The leaf-sweeper

Spark, M. The Seraph and the Zambesi

Thomas, D. The Christmas whopper

Vukcevich, R. Beatniks with banjos

Vukcevich, R. The perfect gift

Waldrop, H. Household words; or, the powers-that-be

Weaver, G. Imagining the structure of free space on Pioneer Road

Wegner, H. Following the nun

Weldon, F. The ghost of potlatch past

West, M. Birthnight

West, M. Hunger

Westlake, D. E. Nackles

Willis, C. Adaptation

Willis, C. Cat's paw

Willis, C. In Coppelius's Toyshop

Willis, C. Inn

Willis, C. Miracle

Willis, C. Newsletter

Willis, C. The pony

Winterson, J. O'Brien's first Christmas

Yates, R. Out with the old

Christmas story. Rose, A.

CHRISTMAS TREES

Boylan, C. The spirit of the tree

Locklin, G. O Tannenbaum

The **Christmas** witch. Edghill, R.

Christopher, Constance

Get Well Soon

    Bomb no87 p96, 98-9 Spr 2004

Christopher, Peter
The Living
New Letters v70 no2 p37-55 2004
Christopher and Maggie. Davis, D. S.
Christopher, Moony, and the birds. Hassler, J.
Chroma. Barthelme, F.
The **chromium** hook. Carlson, R.
Chronicle of the ship of fools. Darton, E.
Chrysalis. Reed, R.
Chrysanthemum in the rock. Kawabata, Y.
The **chubs.** Chiappone, R.
Chuck Paa. Ebershoff, D.
Chuckie. LaValle, V. D.
Chuck's money. Bly, C.
Chuculate, Eddie D.
YoYo
Iowa Review v31 no1 p61-77 Summ 2001
Chudoba, Andrej
Snow and rooks
In search of homo sapiens; twenty-five contemporary Slovak short stories; editor, Pavol Hudík ; [translated by Heather Trebatická; American English editor, Lucy Bednár]
Church, Alfred
The Iliad for boys and girls [excerpt]
Swords and sorcerers; stories from the world of fantasy and adventure; edited by Clint Willis
CHURCH ATTENDANCE
Škvorecký, J. Why do people have soft noses?
Updike, J. The deacon
Updike, J. Packed dirt, churchgoing, a dying cat, a traded car
Yañez, R. Sacred Heart
The **church** in Novograd. Babel', I.
Church not made with hands. Wallace, D. F.
CHURCH SCHOOLS
See also School life
Bukoski, A. Leokadia and fireflies
Coyne, T. Behind sharp branches
Delaney, E. J. O beauty! o truth!
Potvin, E. A. Sister Marguerite
Pritchard, M. Salve Regina
Scoville, S. The pin collectors
Smolens, J. The you is understood
Vaswani, N. Where the long grass bends
CHURCHES
See also Cathedrals
Aickman, R. The cicerones
Babel', I. At Saint Valentine's
Babel', I. Pan Apolek
Barthelme, D. A city of churches
Bukoski, A. Holy walker
Coberly, L. M. Crisis at Bald Knob
Fitzgerald, P. The means of escape
Jackson, V. F. Breaking faith
Lee, V. The Virgin of the Seven Daggers
Willis, C. Inn
Chute, Carolyn
"Ollie, oh . . . "
Breaking into print; early stories and insights into getting published; a Ploughshares anthology; edited by DeWitt Henry
Chwedyk, Kathy
Dead women's things
Nightshade: 20th century ghost stories; edited by Robert Phillips

Chwedyk, Richard
Bronte's egg
Nebula awards showcase 2004; edited by Vonda McIntyre
CIA *See* United States. Central Intelligence Agency
Ciabattari, Jane
Arabella Leaves
Ms. v12 no4 p88-93 Wint 2002
How I Left Onondaga County and Found Peace and Contentment on 72nd Street
Ms. v14 no2 p84-5 Summ 2004
"**Ciccone** youths 1990". Morrow, B.
Cicely's dream. Chesnutt, C. W.
The **cicerones.** Aickman, R.
Cigarette girl. Cain, J. M.
Cigarette Love. Tenorio, G. A.
Cilia-of-gold. Baxter, S.
CINCINNATI (OHIO) *See* Ohio—Cincinnati
Cinderella. Rollins, H.
Cinnamon skin. White, E.
Cioffari, Philip
Dangerously the summer burns
100% pure Florida fiction; an anthology; edited by Susan Hubbard and Robley Wilson
A history of things lost or broken
The North American Review v284 no5 p14-20 S/O 1999
The **circle** of ink. Hoch, E. D.
Circling the drain. Davis, A.
Circling the hondo. Waters, M. Y.
Circling the tortilla dragon. Gonzalez, R.
The **circuit.** Foster, K.
Circuitry. Locklin, G.
Circuits. Garrett, C.
The **circular** ruins. Borges, J. L.
The **circular** valley. Bowles, P.
CIRCUMCISION
Apple, M. The eighth day
Babel', I. Karl-Yankel
What, L. The leap
The **circumcision.** Schlink, B.
CIRCUS
Allen, S. Mud show
Bailey, D. Quinn's way
Barker, N. Bendy-Linda
Carver, R. The aficionados
Day, C. The circus house
Day, C. Circus People
Day, C. Jennie Dixiana
Day, C. The Jungle Goolah Boy
Day, C. The last member of the Boela tribe
Day, C. The lone star cowboy
Day, C. Wallace Porter
Day, C. Winnesaw
Estep, M. Horses
Karnezis, P. A circus attraction
Keret, E. The flying Santinis
McBain, E. The fallen angel
Pearlman, D. D. The circus hand's desertion
Saunders, G. We'll get to now later
Schmitt, R. Leaving Venice, Florida
VanderMeer, J. Mahout
Circus. Estep, M.
A **circus** attraction. Karnezis, P.
The **circus** hand's desertion. Pearlman, D. D.
The **circus** house. Day, C.
Circus matinee. Campbell, B. J.
Cirque du Soleil. Wieland, L.

Cisneros, Sandra
Mericans
Ms. v12 no3 p62-3 Summ 2002
Never marry a Mexican
The Art of the story; an international antholo-gy of contemporary short stories; edited by Daniel Halpern
Woman Hollering Creek
The Scribner anthology of contemporary short fiction; fifty North American stories since 1970; Lex Williford and Michael Martone, editors
Citadel of thought. Blish, J.
Citations of a heretic. Yuknavitch, L.
CITIES AND TOWNS
See also Extinct cities; Imaginary cities; Metropolitan areas
Barthelme, D. I bought a little city
Bottoms, G. Intersections
Brownrigg, S. Broad from abroad
Clarke, A. C. The road to the sea
Le Clézio, J.-M. G. David
Le Clézio, J.-M. G. Villa Aurora
Rulfo, J. Luvina
Schoemperlen, D. This town
Yuknavitch, L. Bravo America
CITIES AND TOWNS, RUINED, EXTINCT, ETC. *See* Extinct cities
Cities of the plain. Peck, D.
The **citizen**. Forsyth, F.
A **citizen** of the world. Mosher, H. F.
A **citizen** of the world at large. Bocock, M.
Citizen of Vienna. McGraw, E.
Citizenship. Wexelblatt, R.
The **city**. Bradbury, R.
City boy. Michaels, L.
City Bus. Boswell, R.
City deep. Dyson, J.
City in aspic. Williams, C.
A **city** of churches. Barthelme, D.
City of Clowns. Alarcón, D.
City of my dreams. Gartner, Z.
City of refuge. Fulmer, J.
City of roses. Havazelet, E.
The **city** of the dead. Sheckley, R.
City sidewalks. Klass, P.
City with houses. Händler, E.-W.
CIVIL RIGHTS DEMONSTRATIONS *See* African Americans—Civil rights
CIVIL SERVICE
Avrich, J. The census taker
Chekhov, A. P. The civil service exam
Chekhov, A. P. The death of a civil servant
Chekhov, A. P. The death of a government clerk
Chekhov, A. P. The exclamation mark
Chekhov, A. P. Fat and thin
Chekhov, A. P. On official duty
Chekhov, A. P. The orator
The **civil** service exam. Chekhov, A. P.
A **civil** service servant. Harrison, H.
CIVIL WAR
England
See England—17th century
United States
See United States—Civil War, 1861-1865
CIVILIAN CONSERVATION CORPS (U.S.)
Kessel, J. Buffalo
CIVILIZATION *See* Social problems

CIVILIZATION AND TECHNOLOGY *See* Technology and civilization
Civilizations are islands. Gabriel, D.
Clair, Maxine
October Brown
The Bluelight corner; black women writing on passion, sex, and romantic love; edited by Rosemarie Robotham
Water seeks its own level
The African American West; a century of short stories; edited by Bruce A. Glasrud and Laurie Champion
Clair. Jannazzo, E.
Clair de lune. Millhauser, S.
Claire. Barthelme, S.
CLAIRVOYANCE
Avrich, J. The banshee's song
Bradbury, R. The illustrated man
Girardi, R. Arcana mundi
Singer, I. B. The chimney sweep
Svoboda, T. Psychic
Clamour. Frost, P. S.
CLANS
See also Tribes
Clarín *See* Alas, Leopoldo, 1852-1901
Clark, Alan M.
Constance
Dead on demand; the best of ghost story weekend; edited by Elizabeth Engstrom
Clark, Alfred Alexander Gordon *See* Hare, Cyr-il, 1900-1958
Clark, Billy C.
The Apache pest control
Clark, B. C. By way of the forked stick
Between girls and gamecocks
Clark, B. C. By way of the forked stick
By way of the forked stick
Clark, B. C. By way of the forked stick
Fur in the hickory
Home and beyond; an anthology of Kentucky short stories; edited by Morris Allen Grubbs; with an introduction by Wade Hall and an afterword by Charles E. May
The last picture show
Clark, B. C. By way of the forked stick
Clark, Carolyn A.
Kays and exes
Hers 3: brilliant new fiction by lesbian writ-ers; edited by Terry Wolverton with Robert Drake
Clark, Curt
For works written by this author under oth-er names see Westlake, Donald E.
Clark, George Makana
The Center of the World
The Georgia Review v57 no4 p679-91 Wint 2003
The Leopard Gang
Coppola, F. F. Francis Ford Coppola's Zoetrope: all story; edited by Adrienne Brodeur and Samantha Schnee; introduction by Francis Ford Coppola
Clark, Joseph
At last, the Ark
Clark, J. Jungle wedding; stories
Beltway Dostoyevsky
Clark, J. Jungle wedding; stories
Frazzle
Clark, J. Jungle wedding; stories

Clark, Joseph—*Continued*
Jungle wedding
  Clark, J. Jungle wedding; stories
K2
  Clark, J. Jungle wedding; stories
The lotus-eater
  Clark, J. Jungle wedding; stories
Mammals
  Clark, J. Jungle wedding; stories
Oasis
  Clark, J. Jungle wedding; stories
Public burning
  Clark, J. Jungle wedding; stories
Random access
  Clark, J. Jungle wedding; stories
Revenge
  Clark, J. Jungle wedding; stories
Spin-off
  Clark, J. Jungle wedding; stories
White Out
  Southwest Review v88 no4 p539-47 2003
Wild blue
  Clark, J. Jungle wedding; stories
Clark, Mary Higgins
The funniest thing has been happening lately
  Murder in the family; [by] the Adams Round
  Table
The man next door
  Master's choice v2; mystery stories by to-
  day's top writers and the masters who in-
  spired them; edited by Lawrence Block
Clark, Simon
Fenian ram
  Murder most Celtic; tall tales of Irish may-
  hem; edited by Martin H. Greenberg
Nightmare in wax
  Shadows over Baker Street; edited by Michael
  Reaves and John Pelan
Clark, William Lane
Quiet game
  Men on men 2000; best new gay fiction for
  the millennium; edited and with an intro-
  duction by David Bergman and Karl Woelz
Clarke, Arthur C.
All the time in the world
  Clarke, A. C. The collected stories of Arthur
  C. Clarke
An ape about the house
  Clarke, A. C. The collected stories of Arthur
  C. Clarke
Armaments race
  Clarke, A. C. The collected stories of Arthur
  C. Clarke
The awakening
  Clarke, A. C. The collected stories of Arthur
  C. Clarke
Before Eden
  Clarke, A. C. The collected stories of Arthur
  C. Clarke
  Worldmakers; SF adventures in terraforming;
  edited by Gardner Dozois
Big game hunt
  Clarke, A. C. The collected stories of Arthur
  C. Clarke
Breaking strain
  Clarke, A. C. The collected stories of Arthur
  C. Clarke

Castaway
  Clarke, A. C. The collected stories of Arthur
  C. Clarke
Cold war
  Clarke, A. C. The collected stories of Arthur
  C. Clarke
Cosmic Casanova
  Clarke, A. C. The collected stories of Arthur
  C. Clarke
Critical mass
  Clarke, A. C. The collected stories of Arthur
  C. Clarke
The cruel sky
  Clarke, A. C. The collected stories of Arthur
  C. Clarke
Crusade
  Clarke, A. C. The collected stories of Arthur
  C. Clarke
Death and the senator
  Clarke, A. C. The collected stories of Arthur
  C. Clarke
The deep range
  Clarke, A. C. The collected stories of Arthur
  C. Clarke
The defenestration of Ermintrude Inch
  Clarke, A. C. The collected stories of Arthur
  C. Clarke
Dial F for Frankenstein
  Clarke, A. C. The collected stories of Arthur
  C. Clarke
Dog Star
  Clarke, A. C. The collected stories of Arthur
  C. Clarke
Earthlight
  Clarke, A. C. The collected stories of Arthur
  C. Clarke
Encounter in the dawn
  Clarke, A. C. The collected stories of Arthur
  C. Clarke
The fires within
  Clarke, A. C. The collected stories of Arthur
  C. Clarke
The food of the gods
  Clarke, A. C. The collected stories of Arthur
  C. Clarke
The forgotten enemy
  Clarke, A. C. The collected stories of Arthur
  C. Clarke
Guardian angel
  Clarke, A. C. The collected stories of Arthur
  C. Clarke
The hammer of God
  Clarke, A. C. The collected stories of Arthur
  C. Clarke
Hate
  Clarke, A. C. The collected stories of Arthur
  C. Clarke
Hide-and-seek
  Clarke, A. C. The collected stories of Arthur
  C. Clarke
History lesson
  Clarke, A. C. The collected stories of Arthur
  C. Clarke
Holiday on the Moon
  Clarke, A. C. The collected stories of Arthur
  C. Clarke
How we went to Mars
  Clarke, A. C. The collected stories of Arthur
  C. Clarke

Clarke, Arthur C.—*Continued*

I remember Babylon
  Clarke, A. C. The collected stories of Arthur
  C. Clarke
'If I forget thee, oh Earth . . .'
  Clarke, A. C. The collected stories of Arthur
  C. Clarke
Inheritance
  Clarke, A. C. The collected stories of Arthur
  C. Clarke
Into the comet
  Clarke, A. C. The collected stories of Arthur
  C. Clarke
Jupiter five
  Clarke, A. C. The collected stories of Arthur
  C. Clarke
The last command
  Clarke, A. C. The collected stories of Arthur
  C. Clarke
Let there be light
  Clarke, A. C. The collected stories of Arthur
  C. Clarke
The light of darkness
  Clarke, A. C. The collected stories of Arthur
  C. Clarke
The lion of Comarre
  Clarke, A. C. The collected stories of Arthur
  C. Clarke
Loophole
  Clarke, A. C. The collected stories of Arthur
  C. Clarke
  Wondrous beginnings; edited by Steven H.
  Silver and Martin H. Greenberg
Love that Universe
  Clarke, A. C. The collected stories of Arthur
  C. Clarke
Maelstrom II
  Clarke, A. C. The collected stories of Arthur
  C. Clarke
The man who ploughed the sea
  Clarke, A. C. The collected stories of Arthur
  C. Clarke
A meeting with Medusa
  Clarke, A. C. The collected stories of Arthur
  C. Clarke
  The SFWA grand masters v2; edited by
  Frederik Pohl
Moving spirit
  Clarke, A. C. The collected stories of Arthur
  C. Clarke
Nemesis
  Clarke, A. C. The collected stories of Arthur
  C. Clarke
The next tenants
  Clarke, A. C. The collected stories of Arthur
  C. Clarke
Nightfall
  Clarke, A. C. The collected stories of Arthur
  C. Clarke
The nine billion names of God
  Clarke, A. C. The collected stories of Arthur
  C. Clarke
  Masterpieces: the best science fiction of the
  century; edited by Orson Scott Card
  The Science fiction hall of fame: volume one,
  1929-1964; the greatest science fiction sto-
  ries of all time chosen by the members of
  the Science Fiction Writers of America; ed-
  ited by Robert Silverberg

No morning after
  Clarke, A. C. The collected stories of Arthur
  C. Clarke
On golden seas
  Clarke, A. C. The collected stories of Arthur
  C. Clarke
The other side of the sky
  Clarke, A. C. The collected stories of Arthur
  C. Clarke
The other tiger
  Clarke, A. C. The collected stories of Arthur
  C. Clarke
Out of the cradle, endlessly orbiting
  Clarke, A. C. The collected stories of Arthur
  C. Clarke
Out of the sun
  Clarke, A. C. The collected stories of Arthur
  C. Clarke
The pacifist
  Clarke, A. C. The collected stories of Arthur
  C. Clarke
The parasite
  Clarke, A. C. The collected stories of Arthur
  C. Clarke
Patent pending
  Clarke, A. C. The collected stories of Arthur
  C. Clarke
Playback
  Clarke, A. C. The collected stories of Arthur
  C. Clarke
The possessed
  Clarke, A. C. The collected stories of Arthur
  C. Clarke
Publicity campaign
  Clarke, A. C. The collected stories of Arthur
  C. Clarke
Refugee
  Clarke, A. C. The collected stories of Arthur
  C. Clarke
The reluctant orchid
  Clarke, A. C. The collected stories of Arthur
  C. Clarke
Rescue party
  Clarke, A. C. The collected stories of Arthur
  C. Clarke
  The SFWA grand masters v2; edited by
  Frederik Pohl
Retreat from earth
  Clarke, A. C. The collected stories of Arthur
  C. Clarke
The road to the sea
  Clarke, A. C. The collected stories of Arthur
  C. Clarke
Saturn rising
  Clarke, A. C. The collected stories of Arthur
  C. Clarke
Second dawn
  Clarke, A. C. The collected stories of Arthur
  C. Clarke
The secret
  Clarke, A. C. The collected stories of Arthur
  C. Clarke
  The SFWA grand masters v2; edited by
  Frederik Pohl
Security check
  Clarke, A. C. The collected stories of Arthur
  C. Clarke

Clarke, Arthur C.—*Continued*

The sentinel
  Clarke, A. C. The collected stories of Arthur
    C. Clarke
The shining ones
  Clarke, A. C. The collected stories of Arthur
    C. Clarke
Silence please
  Clarke, A. C. The collected stories of Arthur
    C. Clarke
Sleeping beauty
  Clarke, A. C. The collected stories of Arthur
    C. Clarke
A slight case of sunstroke
  Clarke, A. C. The collected stories of Arthur
    C. Clarke
The songs of distant earth
  Clarke, A. C. The collected stories of Arthur
    C. Clarke
The star
  Clarke, A. C. The collected stories of Arthur
    C. Clarke
  The SFWA grand masters v2; edited by
    Frederik Pohl
The steam-powered word processor
  Clarke, A. C. The collected stories of Arthur
    C. Clarke
Summertime on Icarus
  Clarke, A. C. The collected stories of Arthur
    C. Clarke
Superiority
  Clarke, A. C. The collected stories of Arthur
    C. Clarke
Technical error
  Clarke, A. C. The collected stories of Arthur
    C. Clarke
Time's arrow
  Clarke, A. C. The collected stories of Arthur
    C. Clarke
Transience
  Clarke, A. C. The collected stories of Arthur
    C. Clarke
Transit of earth
  Clarke, A. C. The collected stories of Arthur
    C. Clarke
Travel by wire!
  Clarke, A. C. The collected stories of Arthur
    C. Clarke
Trouble with the natives
  Clarke, A. C. The collected stories of Arthur
    C. Clarke
Trouble with time
  Clarke, A. C. The collected stories of Arthur
    C. Clarke
The ultimate melody
  Clarke, A. C. The collected stories of Arthur
    C. Clarke
Venture to the Moon
  Clarke, A. C. The collected stories of Arthur
    C. Clarke
A walk in the dark
  Clarke, A. C. The collected stories of Arthur
    C. Clarke
The wall of darkness
  Clarke, A. C. The collected stories of Arthur
    C. Clarke
What goes up
  Clarke, A. C. The collected stories of Arthur
    C. Clarke

The wind from the sun
  Clarke, A. C. The collected stories of Arthur
    C. Clarke
The wire continuum
  Clarke, A. C. The collected stories of Arthur
    C. Clarke
Clarke, Austin
Leaving this island place
  The Oxford book of Caribbean short stories;
    edited by Stewart Brown and John
    Wickham
Clarke, Brock
The Apology
  New England Review v24 no3 p33-40 Summ
    2003
For Those of Us Who Need Such Things
  The Georgia Review v56 no3 p666-82 Fall
    2002
  New stories from the South: the year's best,
    2003; edited by Shannon Ravenel; with a
    preface by Roy Blount Jr.
The Fundraiser's Dance Card
  The Southern Review (Baton Rouge, La.) v40
    no1 p85-101 Wint 2004
The Lolita School
  New stories from the South; the year's best,
    2004; edited by Shannon Ravenel; preface
    by Tim Gautreaux
The Misunderstandings
  The Virginia Quarterly Review v80 no3 p54-
    66 Summ 2004
Plowing the secondaries
  New England Review v22 no4 p171-6 Fall
    2001
The Reason Was Us
  The Georgia Review v58 no1 p105-18 Spr
    2004
The Son's Point of View
  The Southern Review (Baton Rouge, La.) v39
    no3 p556-73 Summ 2003
Clarke, Susanna
The Duke of Wellington misplaces his horse
  The Year's best fantasy & horror, thirteenth
    annual collection; edited by Ellen Datlow
    and Terri Windling
Mr. Simonelli; or, The fairy widower
  Black heart, ivory bones; [edited by] Ellen
    Datlow & Terri Windling
  Death dines at 8:30; edited by Claudia Bishop
    and Nick DiChario
Mrs. Mabb
  The Year's best fantasy & horror, twelfth an-
    nual collection; edited by Ellen Datlow &
    Terry Windling
Tom Brightwind; or, How the fairy bridge was
    built at Thoresby
  Starlight 3; edited by Patrick Nielsen Hayden
Class. Alexie, S.
CLASS DISTINCTION
  See also Social classes
Chekhov, A. P. At a country house
Coates, G. S. Wild plums
Fitzgerald, F. S. Winter dreams
James, H. The Patagonia
Jen, G. In the American society
Lurie, A. The pool people
McBain, E. Happy New Year, Herbie
Mendes, A. H. Pablo's fandango
Nair, M. My grandfather dreams of fences

CLASS DISTINCTION—*Continued*
Taraqqi, G. The maid
Tolstoy, L., graf. The berries
Class of '61. Barrett, N., Jr.
Class Picture. Wolff, T.
Class reunion. Grass, G.
Class trip. LaValle, V. D.
Class warfare. Baida, P.
Classic and good. Barolini, H.
Claude comes and goes. Kaplan, H.
Clay, Heather
Original Beauty
The New Yorker v79 no16 p78, 80, 83-4, 89-90, 92-4 Je 16-23 2003
Clay, K. M.
Cowboys
Southern Humanities Review v36 no1 p30-41 Wint 2002
Clay pigeon. Collins, M.
Clay's thinking. Johnson, D.
Clayton, John J.
Adult Fiction: A Story
Commentary v115 no5 p45-51 My 2003
The Company You Keep: A Story
Commentary v117 no4 p42-50 Ap 2004
The Contract: A Story
Commentary v115 no2 p46-52 F 2003
Fables of the Erotic Other: A Story
Commentary v116 no3 p49-58 O 2003
The Promised Land
The Virginia Quarterly Review v79 no4 p662-89 Aut 2003
Clayton, John Jacob
Let's not talk politics, please
The Pushcart prize XXIII: best of the small presses; an annual small press reader; edited by Bill Henderson with the Pushcart prize editors
Clayton, Meg Waite
Low-floating balloons
The Literary Review (Madison, N.J.) v42 no2 p270-74 Wint 1999
Cleage, Pearl
The tree baby
Essence v32 no3 p120, 148 Jl 2001
Clean away. Fulton, J.
Clean clothes. Carter, E.
A **clean** escape. Kessel, J.
Clean hands. Sneve, V. D. H.
Clean room. Strandquist, R.
Cleaning Seed. Jolliff, W.
Cleaning up. Gordon, M.
CLEANING WOMEN
    See also Maids (Servants)
Adams, A. Alaska
Avrich, J. The charwoman
Bausch, R. "My mistress' eyes are nothing like the sun"
Boswell, R. Miss Famous
Dodd, S. M. Adult education
Lahiri, J. A real durwan
Mazelis, J. Mistaken identity
Sanford, A. The oil of gladness
Wellen, E. Mrs. Grady's swan song
The **clear** blue seas of Luna. Benford, G.
The **clear** blue water. Iribarne, M.
A **clear** record. Hay, E.
Clear sailing. Roberts, G.
Clearances. MacLeod, A.

CLEARY, BRIDGET, D. 1895
    About
Connor, J. Good people
Cleary, Rita
Horse tradin'
The First Five Star western corral; western stories; edited by Jon Tuska and Vicki Piekarski
Cleaver, Eldridge
The flashlight
The African American West; a century of short stories; edited by Bruce A. Glasrud and Laurie Champion
Cleft. Greisemer, J.
Cleft for me. Singleton, G.
Clemens, Matthew V.
(jt. auth) See Collins, Max Allan and Clemens, Matthew V.
Clemens, Samuel Langhorne *See* Twain, Mark, 1835-1910
Clement, Hal
Exchange rate
The Year's best science fiction, seventeenth annual collection; edited by Gardner Dozois
Proof
Wondrous beginnings; edited by Steven H. Silver and Martin H. Greenberg
Uncommon sense
Nebula awards showcase 2000; the year's best SF and fantasy chosen by the science fiction and fantasy writers of america; edited by Gregory Benford
CLEOPATRA, QUEEN OF EGYPT, D. 30 B.C.
    About
Berners, G. H. T.-W., Baron. The romance of a nose
Pushkin, A. S. Egyptian nights
Pushkin, A. S. We were spending the evening at Princess D.'s dacha
Cleopatra Brimstone. Hand, E.
Cleo's back. Bikis, G.
CLEPTOMANIA *See* Kleptomania
CLERGY
    See also Evangelists; Rabbis; Women clergy
Alcott, L. M. John Marlow's victory
Aniebo, I. N. C. Four dimensions
Armstrong, C. The second commandment
Bausch, R. Design
Blair, J. A small church in the country
Bly, C. The tender organizations
Bradbury, R. The Messiah
Cady, J. Jeremiah
Daniels, J. The Jimmy Stewart story
Del Rey, L. For I am a jealous people!
DeMarco, T. Prince of darkness
DeMarco, T. The rose festival boxed lunch
Donnelly, Marcos. Café con leche
Drake, R. All under one roof
Engel, M. P. All that we need
Engel, M. P. You got to learn how to read things right
Ford, N. A. Let the church roll on
Garnett, R. The demon pope
Gautreaux, T. The Pine Oil Writers' Conference
Greer, R. O. Choosing sides
Gwyn, A. In tongues
Hawthorne, N. The minister's black veil
Hoffman, W. Prodigal

CLERGY—_Continued_
Hood, A. Total cave darkness
Hopkins, P. E. As the lord lives, he is one of our mother's children
Jacobs, M. How birds communicate
Kenan, R. The foundations of the earth
L'Amour, L. Elisha comes to Red Horse
Le Fanu, J. S. Green tea
Lundquist, R. The motions of love
Martin, G. R. R. The way of cross and dragon
Perry, A. The end of innocence
Sade, marquis de. An eye for an eye
Skillings, R. D. Tabletalk
Stockton, F. The Griffin and the minor canon
Tilghman, C. A gracious rain
Trevor, W. Of the cloth
Wallace, R. The night nurse
Westlake, D. E. Sinner or saint
Williams, J. Taking care
Willis, C. Epiphany
CLERGY, ANGLICAN AND EPISCOPAL _See_ Anglican and Episcopal clergy
CLERGY, CATHOLIC _See_ Catholic priests
CLERKS
> _See also_ Civil service

Daniels, J. Minding the store
Fitzgerald, F. S. Dalyrimple goes wrong
Smith, A. Gothic
CLEVELAND (OHIO) _See_ Ohio—Cleveland
Clever Hans. Breen, J. L.
Click. Barth, J.
The **clicker** at Tips. Carlson, R.
Cliff, Michelle
Carnegie's bones
> _Southwest Review_ v84 no3 p381-85 1999

Cliff dweller. Rosenfeld, S.
Cliff gods of Acapulco. Johnson, A.
Cliff gods of Acapulco. Johnson, A. M.
Clifford, William
Scoring
> Pieces; a collection of new voices; edited by Stephen Chbosky

Cliffs notes. Ziegler, I.
The **cliffs** of the moon. Stanton, M.
Clift, G. W.
Great Plain
> _The North American Review_ v286 no2 p31-6 Mr/Ap 2001

Climb aboard the mighty flea. Shepard, J.
Climbing down from heaven. Lamsley, T.
Cling to life with your whole body. Hejazi, K.
Clinging to a thread. What, L.
Clinging vine. Mencken, S. H.
Clingman, Stephen
(jt. auth) See Heller, Yehudit Ben-Zvi
A **clinical** romance. Yates, R.
CLINICS
Leong, R. Runaways
Leong, R. Virgins and Buddhas
Maraini, D. Alicetta
CLINTON, BILL, 1946-
> **About**

Nair, M. A warm welcome to the President, insh'allah!
Clinton, Michelle T.
Free your mind and your ass will follow
> LA shorts; edited by Steven Gilbar

Clinton, William Jefferson _See_ Clinton, Bill, 1946-

CLIPPER SHIPS _See_ Sailing vessels
Cloak and digger. Jakes, J.
The **clock**. Blessington, F.
Clocking the world on cue: the chronogram for 2001. Mathews, H.
The **clocks**. Tozzi, F.
CLOCKS AND WATCHES
Ellison, H. Paladin of the lost hour
Hawthorne, N. The artist of the beautiful
Lee, T. The ghost of the clock
Mastretta, A. Aunt Cecilia
Taylor, T. L. Francisco's watch
Vonnegut, K. Souvenir
CLONES _See_ Asexual reproduction
Close. Dark, A. E.
A **close** encounter. Deane, J. F.
Close play at home. O'Rourke, F.
Close to the body. Allen, S.
Close to the water's edge. Keegan, C.
Closed Mondays. Greenberg, A.
The **closed** season. Hickey, D.
Closer. Malouf, D.
The **closer**. Meredith, D.
Closer than you think. Brand, M. O.
The **closest** thing to God. Rawley, D.
The **closet**. Wexler, M.
The **closing** down of summer. MacLeod, A.
Closing the gap. Morris, W.
Closing time. Bukoski, A.
Closure and roadkill on the life's highway. Gay, W.
CLOTHING AND DRESS
Davies, L. Run ragged
Deb, A. The three-piece suit
McGarry, J. Moon, June
Singer, I. B. The primper
Tenn, W. The masculinist revolt
Cloud cover Caribbean. Vega, A. L.
Cloud-shadow. Guerrero, L.
Cloud stalking mice. Rogers, B. H.
Cloudland. Foley, S.
Cloudland. Hanley, N.
CLOUDS
Mathews, H. The ledge
Clouds. Draitser, E.
Clouds. Griner, P.
The **clouds** in Memphis. Hribal, C. J.
Clough, B. W.
Home is the sailor
> Starlight 3; edited by Patrick Nielsen Hayden

May be some time
> The Year's best science fiction, nineteenth annual collection; edited by Gardner Dozois

Times fifty
> _Christianity Today_ v45 no12 p48-50 O 1 2001

Cloutier, Naini
Searching for Mahesh
> _Dalhousie Review_ v82 no2 p263-72 Summ 2002

CLOWNS
Chapman, C. M. Rodeo inferno
Day, C. The bullhook
Dozois, G. R. The clowns
Greenberg, P. The subjunctive mood
Howard, C. The carnival
Piñera, V. The Great Baro
Robison, M. For real
The **clowns**. Dozois, G. R.

The **Club** of Masks. Hoch, E. D.
CLUBS

> *See also* Country clubs

Asimov, I. The acquisitive chuckle
Asimov, I. Early Sunday morning
Asimov, I. The guest's guest
Asimov, I. The haunted cabin
Asimov, I. The iron gem
Asimov, I. The last story
Asimov, I. Lost in a space warp
Asimov, I. The men who read Isaac Asimov
Asimov, I. Northwestward
Asimov, I. The obvious factor
Asimov, I. Ph as in Phony
Asimov, I. Police at the door
Asimov, I. The redhead
Asimov, I. Sixty million trillion combinations
Asimov, I. To the barest
Asimov, I. Triple devil
Asimov, I. The woman in the bar
Asimov, I. The wrong house
Asimov, I. Yes, but why?
Boyle, T. C. A women's restaurant
Chesnutt, C. W. Baxter's procrustes
Drake, R. The girls
Weaver, G. Gilded Quill: the story of Jones
Wharton, E. Xingu

Cluccellas, Maria Isabel
Tango and feathers
> English translations of short stories by contemporary Argentine women writers; edited by Eliana Cazaubon Hermann ; translated by Sally Webb Thornton

Cluney McFarrar's hardtack. McNulty, J.

Clyde, Mary
Farming butterflies
> Clyde, M. Survival rates; stories

A good paved road
> Clyde, M. Survival rates; stories

Heartbreak house
> Clyde, M. Survival rates; stories

Howard Johnson's house
> Clyde, M. Survival rates; stories

Jumping
> Clyde, M. Survival rates; stories

Krista had a treble clef rose
> Clyde, M. Survival rates; stories
> New stories from the South: the year's best, 1999; edited by Shannon Ravenel; with a preface by Tony Earley

Pruitt love
> Clyde, M. Survival rates; stories

Survival rates
> Clyde, M. Survival rates; stories

Victor's funeral urn
> Clyde, M. Survival rates; stories

Clynes, Michael
> *For works written by this author under other names see* Doherty, P. C.

Coach. Robison, M.
COACHING (ATHLETICS)
Chabon, M. The Harris Fetko story
Robison, M. Coach
Spatz, G. Walking in my sleep
Verghese, A. Tension
Wright, D. Dialogue of men and boys

Coake, Christopher
All through the House
> *Gettysburg Review* v16 no2 p257-93 Summ 2003

Coal. LeRoy, J. T.
COAL MINERS *See* Coal mines and mining
Coal miner's holiday. DeLancey, K.
COAL MINES AND MINING
Lawrence, D. H. Odour of chrysanthemums
Lawrence, D. H. Strike-pay
COAL TOWNS *See* Coal mines and mining
Coalinga 1/2 way. Shepard, S.
COAST GUARD (U.S.) *See* United States. Coast Guard
Coast patrol. L'Amour, L.
Coates, Grace Stone
Black cherries
> Coates, G. S. Black cherries; introduction to the Bison Books edition by Mary Clearman Blew

Le Bonnet Rouge
> Coates, G. S. Black cherries; introduction to the Bison Books edition by Mary Clearman Blew

A cast leaf
> Coates, G. S. Black cherries; introduction to the Bison Books edition by Mary Clearman Blew

The corn knife
> Coates, G. S. Black cherries; introduction to the Bison Books edition by Mary Clearman Blew

Crickets
> Coates, G. S. Black cherries; introduction to the Bison Books edition by Mary Clearman Blew

The flyleaf in the book of disillusion
> Coates, G. S. Black cherries; introduction to the Bison Books edition by Mary Clearman Blew

Glass
> Coates, G. S. Black cherries; introduction to the Bison Books edition by Mary Clearman Blew

The horn
> Coates, G. S. Black cherries; introduction to the Bison Books edition by Mary Clearman Blew

Late fruit
> Coates, G. S. Black cherries; introduction to the Bison Books edition by Mary Clearman Blew

The nymphs and pan
> Coates, G. S. Black cherries; introduction to the Bison Books edition by Mary Clearman Blew

A pine tree
> Coates, G. S. Black cherries; introduction to the Bison Books edition by Mary Clearman Blew

Plaster of Paris
> Coates, G. S. Black cherries; introduction to the Bison Books edition by Mary Clearman Blew

Promises
> Coates, G. S. Black cherries; introduction to the Bison Books edition by Mary Clearman Blew

Coates, Grace Stone—*Continued*
Spring beauties
  Coates, G. S. Black cherries; introduction to
    the Bison Books edition by Mary Clearman
    Blew
Trees of heaven
  Coates, G. S. Black cherries; introduction to
    the Bison Books edition by Mary Clearman
    Blew
The truth
  Coates, G. S. Black cherries; introduction to
    the Bison Books edition by Mary Clearman
    Blew
The way of the transgressor
  Coates, G. S. Black cherries; introduction to
    the Bison Books edition by Mary Clearman
    Blew
Wild plums
  The Best American short stories of the
    century; John Updike, editor, Katrina
    Kenison, coeditor; with an introduction by
    John Updike
  Coates, G. S. Black cherries; introduction to
    the Bison Books edition by Mary Clearman
    Blew
The **cobalt** blues. Howard, C.
Cobb, James H.
Monica Van Telflin and the proper application
    of pressure
  The Blue and the gray undercover; edited by
    Ed Gorman
Cobb, Thomas
Acts of contrition
  Cobb, T. Acts of contrition
Adultery
  Cobb, T. Acts of contrition
Ball hawks
  Cobb, T. Acts of contrition
A cold, cotton shirt
  Cobb, T. Acts of contrition
Face the music
  Cobb, T. Acts of contrition
Getting bud
  Cobb, T. Acts of contrition
I'll never get out of this world alive
  Cobb, T. Acts of contrition
Las momias
  Cobb, T. Acts of contrition
Newswatch
  Cobb, T. Acts of contrition
Oncology
  Cobb, T. Acts of contrition
Real stories of true crime
  Cobb, T. Acts of contrition
Skeletons
  Cobb, T. Acts of contrition
Small-block chevy
  Cobb, T. Acts of contrition
Vinson, in passing
  Cobb, T. Acts of contrition
Vinson, in Passing homage à Don
  Literature and Psychology v48 no1/2 p115-19
    2002
Cobb, William
Walking strawberry
  Southern Humanities Review v35 no1 p64-70
    Wint 2001

When we were cool
  Texas bound. Book III; 22 Texas stories; ed-
    ited by Kay Cattarulla; foreword by Robert
    Flynn
Cobb, William J.
The atmosphere of Vienna
  Cobb, W. J. The white tattoo; a collection of
    short stories
Dark matter
  Cobb, W. J. The white tattoo; a collection of
    short stories
The decline of King Fabulous
  Cobb, W. J. The white tattoo; a collection of
    short stories
Father tongue
  Cobb, W. J. The white tattoo; a collection of
    short stories
For all you dorks, blah blah blah
  Cobb, W. J. The white tattoo; a collection of
    short stories
Letting the dog out
  Cobb, W. J. The white tattoo; a collection of
    short stories
Marathon
  Cobb, W. J. The white tattoo; a collection of
    short stories
Mergers & acquisitions
  Cobb, W. J. The white tattoo; a collection of
    short stories
Motel ice
  Cobb, W. J. The white tattoo; a collection of
    short stories
The Queen of Fruit Cocktail
  The Antioch Review v61 no1 p27-43 Wint
    2003
There's nothing the matter with Gwen
  Cobb, W. J. The white tattoo; a collection of
    short stories
Three feet of water
  Cobb, W. J. The white tattoo; a collection of
    short stories
The white tatto
  Cobb, W. J. The white tattoo; a collection of
    short stories
Why you?
  Cobb, W. J. The white tattoo; a collection of
    short stories
The wishes
  Cobb, W. J. The white tattoo; a collection of
    short stories
The **cobblestones** of Saratoga Street. Davidson, A.
Coberly, Lenore M.
Crisis at Bald Knob
  Coberly, L. M. The handywoman stories
The death of Alma Ruth
  Coberly, L. M. The handywoman stories
Early transparent
  Coberly, L. M. The handywoman stories
The evidence of things not seen
  Coberly, L. M. The handywoman stories
The fellowsip at Wysong's Clearing
  Coberly, L. M. The handywoman stories
Garnet
  Coberly, L. M. The handywoman stories
Going over
  Coberly, L. M. The handywoman stories
Growing up in the Navy
  Coberly, L. M. The handywoman stories

Coberly, Lenore M.—*Continued*

The handywoman
  Coberly, L. M. The handywoman stories
In which murder is done
  Coberly, L. M. The handywoman stories
Just a love story
  Coberly, L. M. The handywoman stories
Miss Carrollene tells a story
  Coberly, L. M. The handywoman stories
Night-blooming cereus
  Coberly, L. M. The handywoman stories
Over Sulphur Mountain
  Coberly, L. M. The handywoman stories
The sighting
  Coberly, L. M. The handywoman stories
Snap beans and petits fours
  Coberly, L. M. The handywoman stories
Sweet shrub
  Coberly, L. M. The handywoman stories
Tears need shedding
  Coberly, L. M. The handywoman stories
Will's Valentine
  Coberly, L. M. The handywoman stories
Willy Mae goes north
  Coberly, L. M. The handywoman stories

COBRAS

Rifaat, A. My world of the unknown

COCAINE

Anderson, K. Burglary in progress
Dozois, G. R. Snow job
Reilly, L. 1984
Villane, M. The color of rain

COCHISE, APACHE CHIEF, D. 1874
About

L'Amour, L. The gift of Cochise

Cocked and locked. Keret, E.

COCKFIGHTING

Clark, B. C. Between girls and gamecocks

COCKROACHES

Jenkins, G. Something to cling to
Keegan, C. Burns
Reiner, C. How could this happen?

Cockshut light. Wegner, H.

COCKTAIL PARTIES *See* Parties

The **Cocktail** Party. Wong, D. T. K.

The **coconut** palms on campus. Cheng, C.-W.

Coda. Linney, R.

Coda. Polansky, S.

Code. Crouse, D.

Codrescu, Andrei

The babysitter
  Codrescu, A. A bar in Brooklyn; novellas & stories, 1970-1978
A bar in Brooklyn
  Codrescu, A. A bar in Brooklyn; novellas & stories, 1970-1978
The herald
  Codrescu, A. A bar in Brooklyn; novellas & stories, 1970-1978
Julie
  Codrescu, A. A bar in Brooklyn; novellas & stories, 1970-1978
Monsieur Teste in America
  Codrescu, A. A bar in Brooklyn; novellas & stories, 1970-1978
The old couple
  Codrescu, A. A bar in Brooklyn; novellas & stories, 1970-1978

Perfume: a tale of felicity
  Codrescu, A. A bar in Brooklyn; novellas & stories, 1970-1978
Petra
  Codrescu, A. A bar in Brooklyn; novellas & stories, 1970-1978
Samba de los agentes
  Codrescu, A. A bar in Brooklyn; novellas & stories, 1970-1978
Tenderness
  Codrescu, A. A bar in Brooklyn; novellas & stories, 1970-1978
Three simple hearts
  Codrescu, A. A bar in Brooklyn; novellas & stories, 1970-1978

Cody, Liza

A card or a kitten
  Cody, L. Lucky dip and other stories
Chalk mother
  Cody, L. Lucky dip and other stories
Doing it under the table
  Cody, L. Lucky dip and other stories
In those days
  Cody, L. Lucky dip and other stories
Indian throw
  Cody, L. Lucky dip and other stories
K. K.
  Cody, L. Lucky dip and other stories
Listen
  Cody, L. Lucky dip and other stories
Love in vain
  Cody, L. Lucky dip and other stories
Lucky dip
  Cody, L. Lucky dip and other stories
Queen of mean
  Cody, L. Lucky dip and other stories
  Tart noir; edited by Stella Duffy & Lauren Henderson
Reconstruction
  Cody, L. Lucky dip and other stories
Solar zits
  Cody, L. Lucky dip and other stories
Spasmo
  Cody, L. Lucky dip and other stories
The uniform
  Cody, L. Lucky dip and other stories
Walking blues
  Cody, L. Lucky dip and other stories
Where's Stacey?
  Cody, L. Lucky dip and other stories
Woke up this morning
  Cody, L. Lucky dip and other stories

Coe, Tucker

  For works written by this author under other names see Westlake, Donald E.

Coel, Margaret

A well-respected man
  Women before the bench; edited by Carolyn Wheat; introduction by Linda Fairstein
  The World's finest mystery and crime stories, third annual collection; edited by Ed Gorman and Martin H. Greenberg

Coelacanths. Reed, R.

Coetzee, J. M.

As a Woman Grows Older
  The New York Review of Books v51 no1 p11-14 Ja 15 2004

Coffee and murder. Channell, C.

Coffee at the Marriott. Johnson-Davies, D.

A **coffeehouse** in the city of Surat. Tolstoy, L., graf

Coffey, Brian *See* Koontz, Dean R. (Dean Ray), 1945-

Coffey, Brian, 1945-
> *For works written by this author under other names see* Koontz, Dean R. (Dean Ray), 1945-

The **coffin**. Casey, K.

The **coffin** master. Deane, J. F.

COFFINS
Chekhov, A. P. A dreadful night
Ritchie, E. Shopping expedition

Cogitor, ergo sum. Pearlman, D. D.

Cognitive ability and the light bulb. Aldiss, B. W.

Cohen, Bernard
Kafka's diary
> *The Literary Review (Madison, N.J.)* v45 no1 p138-42 Fall 2001

Cohen, Garnett Kilberg
Afterlife
> *TriQuarterly* no113 p190-8 Summ 2002
Bad News
> *Michigan Quarterly Review* v42 no3 p522-32 Summ 2003

Cohen, Matthew Loren
Polaroid
> Pieces; a collection of new voices; edited by Stephen Chbosky

Cohen, Michael
Alice's ground
> Virgin fiction 2

Cohen, Michael D.
Kytzvinyne's 7th symphony
> *Gettysburg Review* v12 no3 p473-79 Aut 1999

Cohen, Octavus Roy
The last blow
> Boxing's best short stories; edited by Paul D. Staudohar

Cohen, Richard
Cousin Gemma
> Cohen, R. Pronoun music; stories
Delicate destinies
> Cohen, R. Pronoun music; stories
Dream group forming
> Cohen, R. Pronoun music; stories
Good with girls
> Cohen, R. Pronoun music; stories
On the flight path
> Cohen, R. Pronoun music; stories
Possible future stepmother
> Cohen, R. Pronoun music; stories
Putting up signs
> Cohen, R. Pronoun music; stories
Refuge
> Cohen, R. Pronoun music; stories
Theme from a summer place
> Cohen, R. Pronoun music; stories
Those kooks
> Cohen, R. Pronoun music; stories
Uncle Wolfie
> Cohen, R. Pronoun music; stories
What makes you you
> Cohen, R. Pronoun music; stories

Cohen, Robert
Adult education
> Cohen, R. The varieties of romantic experience; stories

The bachelor party
> Cohen, R. The varieties of romantic experience; stories
Between hammers
> Cohen, R. The varieties of romantic experience; stories
The boys at night
> Cohen, R. The varieties of romantic experience; stories
A flight of sparks
> Cohen, R. The varieties of romantic experience; stories
Influence
> Cohen, R. The varieties of romantic experience; stories
The next big thing
> Cohen, R. The varieties of romantic experience; stories
Oscillations
> Cohen, R. The varieties of romantic experience; stories
Points of interest
> Cohen, R. The varieties of romantic experience; stories
The varieties of romantic experience: an introduction
> Cohen, R. The varieties of romantic experience; stories

Cohen, Stanley
The battered mailbox
> Cohen, S. A night in the Manchester store and other stories
The case of Grand Cru
> Cohen, S. A night in the Manchester store and other stories
The everlasting Jug
> Cohen, S. A night in the Manchester store and other stories
A girl named Charlie
> Murder in the family; [by] the Adams Round Table
Hello! my name is Irving Wasserman
> Cohen, S. A night in the Manchester store and other stories
Homeless, hungry, please help
> Cohen, S. A night in the Manchester store and other stories
How much justice can you afford?
> Cohen, S. A night in the Manchester store and other stories
I'm sorry, Mr. Griggs
> Cohen, S. A night in the Manchester store and other stories
I'm sorry, Mr. Turini
> Cohen, S. A night in the Manchester store and other stories
Just another New York Christmas story
> Cohen, S. A night in the Manchester store and other stories
Nadigo
> Cohen, S. A night in the Manchester store and other stories
Neville
> Cohen, S. A night in the Manchester store and other stories
A night in the Manchester store
> Cohen, S. A night in the Manchester store and other stories

Cohen, Stanley—*Continued*
>   The World's finest mystery and crime stories, second annual collection; edited by Ed Gorman
>   The ransom of Retta Chiefman
>>   Cohen, S. A night in the Manchester store and other stories
>   Six-four, four-three, deuce, a ghost story of sorts
>>   Cohen, S. A night in the Manchester store and other stories
>   Those who appreciate money hate to touch the principal
>>   Cohen, S. A night in the Manchester store and other stories

A **coin**. Hemon, A.

The **coin** collector. Finney, J.

Coin of the realm. Fesler, P. J.

The **coincidence** of the arts. Amis, M.

Coins. Simpson, M.

Coitus. Means, D.

Cold. Byatt, A. S.

Cold. Smolens, J.

Cold. Thurm, M.

Cold comfort. Kilpatrick, N.

Cold day, cold fear. Burdick, E.

The **cold** equations. Godwin, T.

Cold fall. Bunin, I. A.

Cold snap. Jones, T.

Cold turkey. Davidson, D. M.

Cold war. Clarke, A. C.

A **cold** winter light. Miller, A. L.

A **colder** war. Stross, C.

Coldsmith, Don
>   First horse
>>   Westward; a fictional history of the American West : 28 original stories celebrating the 50th anniversary of the Western Writers of America; edited by Dale L. Walker
>   The guardians
>>   American West; twenty new stories from the Western Writers of America; edited with an introduction by Loren D. Estleman

Cole, C. Bard
>   Additional selected lives in brief
>>   Cole, C. B. Briefly told lives
>   Foo dog
>>   Cole, C. B. Briefly told lives
>   Michael Mc:_____ a case study
>>   Cole, C. B. Briefly told lives
>   More Selected lives in brief
>>   Cole, C. B. Briefly told lives
>   The mother
>>   Cole, C. B. Briefly told lives
>   On a railroad bridge, throwing stones
>>   Cole, C. B. Briefly told lives
>   Selected lives in brief
>>   Cole, C. B. Briefly told lives
>   That's how straight boys dance
>>   Cole, C. B. Briefly told lives
>   Used to dream
>>   Cole, C. B. Briefly told lives
>   Young Hemingways
>>   Cole, C. B. Briefly told lives

Cole, Isabel Fargo
>   A Strange Place
>>   *The Antioch Review* v60 no4 p603-20 Fall 2002
>   (jt. auth) See Hilbig, Wolfgang

Cole, Martina
>   Enough was enough
>>   The best British mysteries; edited by Maxim Jakubowski
>>   Tart noir; edited by Stella Duffy & Lauren Henderson

Colebatch, Hal G. P.
>   The colonel's tiger
>>   Centaurus: the best of Australian science fiction; edited by David G. Hartwell and Damien Broderick

Coleman, Anita Scott
>   The little grey house
>>   The African American West; a century of short stories; edited by Bruce A. Glasrud and Laurie Champion

Coleman, Jane Candia
>   Borderlands
>>   Coleman, J. C. Borderlands; western stories
>   Fiddle case
>>   Coleman, J. C. Borderlands; western stories
>   Loner
>>   Coleman, J. C. Borderlands; western stories
>   Marvel Bird
>>   Coleman, J. C. Borderlands; western stories
>   A pair to draw to
>>   Coleman, J. C. Borderlands; western stories
>   The Perseid meteors
>>   Coleman, J. C. Borderlands; western stories
>   Rodeo
>>   Coleman, J. C. Borderlands; western stories
>   Ruby's cape
>>   The First Five Star western corral; western stories; edited by Jon Tuska and Vicki Piekarski
>   Sandhill cranes
>>   Coleman, J. C. Borderlands; western stories
>   Wild flower
>>   Coleman, J. C. Borderlands; western stories

Coleman, Jason
>   Ten secrets of beauty
>>   Best new American voices 2000; guest editor Tobias Wolff; series editors John Kulka and Natalie Danford

Coleman, Wanda
>   The Friday night shift at the Taco House blues (wah-wah)
>>   The African American West; a century of short stories; edited by Bruce A. Glasrud and Laurie Champion

COLERIDGE, SAMUEL TAYLOR, 1772-1834
>   **About**
>   Davidson, A. One morning with Samuel, Dorothy, and William

Coley, David
>   The Reach of Wonder
>>   *Harper's* v307 p26-32 O 2003
>>   *Southwest Review* v86 no4 p581-94 2001

Coley's war. Williams, M.

Colford, Ian
>   The comfort of knowing
>>   *Dalhousie Review* v81 no2 p185-212 Summ 2001

Colgan, Jenny
>   The wrong train
>>   Tart noir; edited by Stella Duffy & Lauren Henderson

Collaboration. Auchincloss, L.

The **collaboration**. Wallace, M.

Collaborators. See Hegi, U. A woman's perfume
Collapsing into a Story. Martin, S.-P.
Collecting shadows. Strandquist, R.
COLLECTION AGENCIES
Hampl, P. The bill collector's vacation
COLLECTIVE SETTLEMENTS
Brackenbury, R. The forty-ninth lot joke
Hand, E. Last summer at Mars Hill
Henley, P. As luck would have it
Henley, P. The birthing
Henley, P. Let me call you sweetheart
Van Winckel, N. Beside ourselves
Van Winckel, N. The expectation of abundance
Van Winckel, N. Immunity
Van Winckel, N. The land of anarchy
Van Winckel, N. The lap of luxury
Van Winckel, N. Making headway
Van Winckel, N. Sometimes he borrowed a horse
Van Winckel, N. Treat me nice
Israel
Oz, A. Nomad and viper
Oz, A. Where the jackals howl
Shomer, E. The problem with Yosi
Swan, M. On the border
United States
Varley, J. The persistence of vision
COLLECTORS AND COLLECTING
Bradbury, R. Autumn afternoon
Bradbury, R. The completist
Bukiet, M. J. Splinters
Doctorow, C. Craphound
Lao She. Attachment
Mendes, B. Noble causes
Parker, G. The sheld-duck of the Basingstoke Canal
Pronzini, B. The man who collected "The Shadow"
Singleton, G. How to collect fishing lures
COLLEGE LIFE
See also College students; School life; Students; Teachers
Gordimer, N. Look-alikes
Canada
Škvorecký, J. According to Poe
Škvorecký, J. Jezebel from Forest Hill (A love story)
Škvorecký, J. Wayne's hero (An English story)
Wuori, G. K. Mothers
England
Archer, J. Dougie Mortimer's right arm
Trevor, W. Death of a professor
Waugh, E. Edward of unique achievement
Waugh, E. Portrait of young man with career
Netherlands
Stevenson, J. Law and order
United States
Brown, A. K. Strip Battleship
Broyard, B. Ugliest faces
Gavell, M. L. The rotifer
Griffith, M. Bibliophilia
Harris, M. Carmelita's education for living
Harris, M. Flattery
King, S. Strawberry spring
Lee, R. The banks of the Vistula
Locklin, G. The English girl
Matheson, R. C. Graduation
Packer, Z. Drinking coffee elsewhere
Schraufnagel, J. Like whiskey for Christmas

Stuckey-French, E. Famous poets
Updike, J. The Christian roommates
Vivante, A. Stones aplenty
Whalen, T. Professors
Williams, M. The journal
Winter, E. Full moon howl
COLLEGE STUDENTS
See also College life
Alexie, S. The search engine
Allen, S. Souvenir
Azadeh, C. A banal stain
Beller, T. A different kind of imperfection
Berkman, P. R. Bethlehem
Boswell, M. Between things
Boswell, M. Grub worm
Bukiet, M. J. The return of eros to academe
Byers, M. The beautiful days
Chiarella, T. Foley's confessions
Cobb, T. Las momias
Daniels, J. Middle of the mitten
Doble, J. The mind reader
Gilchrist, E. Lunch at the best restaurant in the world
Goldstein, N. Barbary apes
Gray, A. Lanark [excerpt]
Holleran, A. The man who got away
Hood, A. Inside Gorbachev's head
Huffman, B., Jr. Mutuality of interests
Iagnemma, K. On the nature of human romantic interaction
Keegan, C. Close to the water's edge
Klíma, I. Lingula
Lahiri, J. Nobody's business
Mazor, J. Skylark
McManus, J. Gegenschein
McManus, J. Stop breakin down
Michaels, L. Nachman from Los Angeles
Miller, E. In memory of Chanveasna Chan, who is still alive
Nelson, A. Stitches
Nissen, T. 819 Walnut
Nissen, T. Grog
Nissen, T. Jono, an elegy
Nissen, T. Mailing incorrectly
Oates, J. C. Three girls
Ramaya, S. Destiny
Rinehart, S. Kick in the head
Robison, M. I am twenty-one
Smolens, J. Absolution
Sojourner, M. Monsters
Taylor, P. H. A sentimental journey
Thompson, C. Judgment
Vice, B. Report from Junction
Weinreb, M. The last American virgin
Zabytko, I. My black Valiant
COLLEGE TEACHERS *See* Teachers
Collier, Eugenia
The caregiver
African American Review v36 no1 p65-72 Spr 2002
Collier, Eugenia W.
Marigolds
Of leaf and flower; stories and poems for gardeners; edited by Charles Dean and Clyde Wachsberger; illustrations by Clyde Wachsberger

Collins, Barbara

Aunt Emma's defense

Collins, B. Too many tomcats and other feline tales of suspense; edited and introduced by Max Allan Collins

Carry's cat

Cat crimes through time; edited by Ed Gorman, Martin H. Greenberg, and Larry Segriff

Collins, B. Too many tomcats and other feline tales of suspense; edited and introduced by Max Allan Collins

Cat got your tongue

Collins, B. Too many tomcats and other feline tales of suspense; edited and introduced by Max Allan Collins

Dalliance at Sunnydale

Flesh and blood: guilty as sin; erotic tales of crime and passion; edited by Max Allan Collins and Jeff Gelb

Dead and breakfast

Collins, B. and Collins, M. A. Murder—his and hers; short stories; [by] Barbara Collins & Max Allan Collins

Murder most delectable; savory tales of culinary crimes; edited by Martin H. Greenberg

The night it rained cats and cats

Collins, B. Too many tomcats and other feline tales of suspense; edited and introduced by Max Allan Collins

Obeah, my love

Collins, B. Too many tomcats and other feline tales of suspense; edited and introduced by Max Allan Collins

A proper burial

Collins, B. Too many tomcats and other feline tales of suspense; edited and introduced by Max Allan Collins

Reunion queen

Collins, B. and Collins, M. A. Murder—his and hers; short stories; [by] Barbara Collins & Max Allan Collins

Seeing red

Collins, B. and Collins, M. A. Murder—his and hers; short stories; [by] Barbara Collins & Max Allan Collins

The ten lives of Talbert

Collins, B. Too many tomcats and other feline tales of suspense; edited and introduced by Max Allan Collins

That damn cat

Collins, B. Too many tomcats and other feline tales of suspense; edited and introduced by Max Allan Collins

To grandmother's house we go

Collins, B. Too many tomcats and other feline tales of suspense; edited and introduced by Max Allan Collins

To kill a cat

Collins, B. Too many tomcats and other feline tales of suspense; edited and introduced by Max Allan Collins

Too many tomcats

Collins, B. Too many tomcats and other feline tales of suspense; edited and introduced by Max Allan Collins

World's greatest mother

Collins, B. and Collins, M. A. Murder—his and hers; short stories; [by] Barbara Collins & Max Allan Collins

Collins, Barbara and Collins, Max Allan

A cruise to forget

Collins, B. and Collins, M. A. Murder—his and hers; short stories; [by] Barbara Collins & Max Allan Collins

Death cruise; crime stories on the open seas; edited by Lawrence Block

Eddie Haskell in a short skirt

Collins, B. and Collins, M. A. Murder—his and hers; short stories; [by] Barbara Collins & Max Allan Collins

Collins, Kelly

Love notes

'Teen v43 no11 p102-03 N 1999

Collins, Max Allan

Catgate

Collins, B. and Collins, M. A. Murder—his and hers; short stories; [by] Barbara Collins & Max Allan Collins

Cat's-eye witness

Collins, B. and Collins, M. A. Murder—his and hers; short stories; [by] Barbara Collins & Max Allan Collins

Flowers for Bill O'Reilly

Flesh and blood; erotic tales of crime and passion; edited by Max Allan Collins and Jeff Gelb

Inconvenience store

Collins, B. and Collins, M. A. Murder—his and hers; short stories; [by] Barbara Collins & Max Allan Collins

Kaddish for the kid

Browning, A. Murder is no mitzvah; edited by Abigail Browning

A Century of noir; thirty-two classic crime stories; edited by Mickey Spillane and Max Allan Collins

A matter of principal

A Century of great suspense stories; edited by Jeffery Deaver

Unreasonable doubt

The World's finest mystery and crime stories, third annual collection; edited by Ed Gorman and Martin H. Greenberg

(jt. auth) See Collins, Barbara and Collins, Max Allan

Collins, Max Allan and Clemens, Matthew V.

Lie beside me

Flesh and blood: guilty as sin; erotic tales of crime and passion; edited by Max Allan Collins and Jeff Gelb

Collins, Merle

The walk

The Oxford book of Caribbean short stories; edited by Stewart Brown and John Wickham

Collins, Michael

The bizarre case expert

Collins, M. Spies and thieves, cops and killers, etc

The choice

Collins, M. Spies and thieves, cops and killers, etc

Collins, Michael—*Continued*
  Clay pigeon
    Collins, M. Spies and thieves, cops and kill-
      ers, etc
  Death, my love
    Collins, M. Spies and thieves, cops and kill-
      ers, etc
  Freedom fighter
    Collins, M. Spies and thieves, cops and kill-
      ers, etc
  Hard cop
    Collins, M. Spies and thieves, cops and kill-
      ers, etc
  Harness bull
    Collins, M. Spies and thieves, cops and kill-
      ers, etc
  Homecoming
    Collins, M. Spies and thieves, cops and kill-
      ers, etc
  Hot night homicide
    Collins, M. Spies and thieves, cops and kill-
      ers, etc
  Man on the run
    Collins, M. Spies and thieves, cops and kill-
      ers, etc
  Nobody frames Big Sam
    Collins, M. Spies and thieves, cops and kill-
      ers, etc
  Occupational hazard
    Collins, M. Spies and thieves, cops and kill-
      ers, etc
  A part of history
    Collins, M. Spies and thieves, cops and kill-
      ers, etc
    Death by espionage; intriguing stories of de-
      ception and betrayal; edited by Martin Cruz
      Smith
  The savage
    Collins, M. Spies and thieves, cops and kill-
      ers, etc
  Silent partner
    Collins, M. Spies and thieves, cops and kill-
      ers, etc
  The sleeper
    Collins, M. Spies and thieves, cops and kill-
      ers, etc
  Success of a mission
    Collins, M. Spies and thieves, cops and kill-
      ers, etc
Collins, Michael and Lynds, Gayle
  A delicate mission
    Flesh and blood: guilty as sin; erotic tales of
      crime and passion; edited by Max Allan
      Collins and Jeff Gelb
Collins, Nancy A.
  Catfish gal blues
    999: new stories of horror and suspense; ed-
      ited by Al Sarrantonio
  Variations on a theme
    The Crow; shattered lives & broken dreams;
      edited by J. O'Barr and Ed Kramer
Collins, Paul
  Wired dreaming
    Dreaming down-under; edited by Jack Dann
      and Janeen Webb
Collins, Stephen
  Ace's big entrance
    Good Housekeeping v238 no6 p223-6, 228-30
    Je 2004

Collusions. Helms, B.
Collymore, Frank
  Some people are meant to live alone
    The Oxford book of Caribbean short stories;
      edited by Stewart Brown and John
      Wickham
Coloma, Luis
  "Green bird"
    Fedorchek, R. M. Stories of enchantment
      from nineteenth-century Spain; translated
      from the Spanish by Robert M. Fredorchek;
      introduction by Alan E. Smith
  "Pérez the Mouse"
    Fedorchek, R. M. Stories of enchantment
      from nineteenth-century Spain; translated
      from the Spanish by Robert M. Fredorchek;
      introduction by Alan E. Smith
COLOMBIANS
England
  Borges, J. L. Ulrikke
United States
  Leonard, E. When the women come out to
    dance
Colombo, Cristoforo *See* Columbus, Christopher
The **Colonel** and Judy O'Grady. Stevenson, J.
Colonel Stonesteel's genuine homemade truly
    Egyptian mummy. Bradbury, R.
The **colonel's** jeep. Pearlman, D. D.
The **colonel's** tiger. Colebatch, H. G. P.
COLONIES
Great Britain
    See Great Britain—Colonies
COLONIES, ARTIST *See* Artist colonies
The **color** of death. Howard, C.
The **Color** of My Eyes. Moyer, K.
The **color** of rain. Villane, M.
A **color** of sky. Winter, E.
Color separation. Ames, B.
COLORADO
  Greer, R. O. One-on-one
  Mazor, J. Durango
  Offutt, C. Barred owl
  Overholser, W. D. The leather slapper
  Pritchett, L. Dry roots
  Pritchett, L. An easy birth
  Pritchett, L. A fine white dust
  Pritchett, L. Grayblue day
  Pritchett, L. Hell's bottom
  Pritchett, L. Jailbird gone songbird
  Pritchett, L. A new name each day
  Pritchett, L. Rattlesnake fire
  Pritchett, L. The record keeper
  Pritchett, L. Summer flood
  Swan, G. Backtracking
Denver
  Greer, R. O. The can men
Colorado. Taylor, R. L.
Colossus. Murray, S.
Colouring mother. Horton, B.
The **colt**. Stegner, W. E.
COLUMBUS, CHRISTOPHER
About
  Malzberg, B. N. Ship full of Jews
Columbus Day. Frym, G.
COLUMNISTS *See* Journalists
Colvin, Clare
  The sound of the horn
    Valentine's Day: women against men; stories
      of revenge; introduction by Alice Thomas

Colwin, Laurie
  Another marvellous thing
    Wonderful town; New York stories from The
      New Yorker; edited by David Remnick
      with Susan Choi
COMANCHE INDIANS
  Braun, M. The stand
  Farrell, C. Desperate journey
  Graves, J. The last running
  Henry, W. Comanche passport
  Loomis, N. M. Grandfather out of the past
Comanche passport. Henry, W.
Come again? Westlake, D. E.
Come and go. Tillman, L.
Come fly with me. Schmand, T.
Come home, come home, it's suppertime. Gay, W.
O **come** little children. . . Williamson, C.
Come live with me and be my love. Greer, A. S.
Come on, everyone!. Weldon, F.
Come sta? Come va? Gildner, G.
Come to Grandma. Cannell, D.
COMEDIANS
  Dann, J. Fairy tale
  Fischer, T. I like being killed
  Parker, G. The Birdman of Cleveland
Comer, Brooke
  Life and death in Bab-el-Louq
    The Massachusetts Review v42 no4 p644-61
    Wint 2001/2002
The **comet**. Du Bois, W. E. B.
COMETS
  Clarke, A. C. Into the comet
  Du Bois, W. E. B. The comet
Comfort. Banks, R.
The **comfort**. Kelman, J.
Comfort. Munro, A.
Comfort. Stern, D.
Comfort me with apples. Daugherty, T.
The **comfort** of knowing. Colford, I.
Comforts. Silber, J.
The **comforts** of home. O'Connor, F.
Comic cuts. Kelman, J.
Comic Valentine. Meredith, D.
Coming. Ponte, A. J.
Coming around the mountain. Crumley, J.
Coming attraction. Leiber, F.
Coming Clean. Stein, D. B.
The **coming** home. Loomis, N. M.
Coming home. Morris, M.
Coming home. Wharton, E.
Coming in with their hands up. Epstein, J.
Coming of age. Lane, J.
COMING OF AGE STORIES *See* Adolescence;
  Youth
The **coming** of the clan. Karon, J.
The **coming** of the Hoodlum. Scott, J.
COMMANCHE INDIANS *See* Comanche Indi-
  ans
The **commander**. Viganò, R.
The **commander** of the second brigade. Babel´, I.
Commemorating. Arvin, N.
The **commemorative**. Goldberg, M.
Commencement. Mencken, S. H.
Commencement. Oates, J. C.
COMMENCEMENTS
  Mencken, S. H. Commencement
  Oates, J. C. Commencement
Commendable. Silber, J.
Commendation. O'Neill, S.

The **commercial** channel: a unique business op-
  portunity. Touré
COMMERCIAL TRAVELERS
  DeMarinis, R. The smile of a turtle
  Welty, E. The hitch-hikers
Commission. Winton, T.
Commit to memory. Parker, M.
Commitment. Glave, T.
A **committee** of the whole. Bly, C.
Common light. Reisman, N.
Common time. Blish, J.
COMMUNES *See* Collective settlements
COMMUNICATION
    See also Telecommunication
  Cohen, R. Oscillations
  Harris, M. Conversation on southern Honshu
  Leiber, F. Moon duel
COMMUNICATION OF ANIMALS *See* Animal
  communication
Communion. Smith, S.
COMMUNISM
    See also Totalitarianism
  Bellow, S. Mosby's memoirs
  Hamburger, A. The view from Statlin's Head
  Paz, S. Don't tell her you love her
  Sekaran, S. Stalin
  Shaw, I. Sailor off the Bremen
            China
  Ha Jin. Broken
  Ha Jin. An official reply
  Ha Jin. Saboteur
        Czechoslovakia
  Škvorecký, J. The end of Bull Macha
  Škvorecký, J. An insoluble problem of genetics
  Škvorecký, J. Laws of the jungle
  Škvorecký, J. Song of forgotten years
  Škvorecký, J. Spectator on a February night
           Korea
  Jung, H.-Y. Our lady of the height
          Romania
  Paine, T. Ceauçsescu's cat
           Russia
  Babel´, I. Evening
  Babel´, I. Italian sun
  Babel´, I. Petroleum
  Babel´, I. Salt
  Frym, G. "To see her in sunlight was to see
    Marxism die"
        United States
  Wright, R. Bright and morning star
COMMUNISTS *See* Communism
Community. Dozois, G. R.
Community of victims. Thelwell, M.
Community property. Saer, J. J.
The **commuter**. Harrison, C.
COMMUTERS
  McBain, E. The sharers
Compadres Turtledove, H. Alternate generals II;
  ed. by Harry Turtledove
Companion Animal. Kaplan, H.
COMPANIONS
  Greer, A. S. The art of eating
  Kaplan, H. Cuckle me
  Ocampo, Flaminia. Crossing oceans
  Roeske, P. The ecstasy of Magda Brummel
  Wharton, E. Confession
  Wharton, E. The introducers
  Willis, M. S. Tales of the abstract expressionists
Company wife. Hager, J.

The **Company** You Keep: A Story. Clayton, J. J.
The **company's** interest. Shepard, S.
Comparative religion. Williams, L.
Comparing. Dixon, S.
Compass Rose. Gates, D. E.
COMPASSION *See* Sympathy
Compassion. Allison, D.
Compassion. Waugh, E.
A **compassionate** leave. Yates, R.
Compelle intrare. Seltz, E.
COMPETITION
  Bonnie, F. The race for last place
  Doerr, A. July fourth
  L'Amour, L. It's your move
  Slesar, H. Change partners
  Vance, J. The new prime
  Wallace, R. Cross country
The **complaints** book. Chekhov, A. P.
The **compleat** adventures of Brooke E. Trout. Burton, M.
The **complete** angler. Boylan, C.
Completely overloaded. Kieser, C.
Complicity. Parrish, T.
Composer. Budnitz, J.
COMPOSERS
  Berners, G. H. T.-W., Baron. Count Omega
  Biggle, L. Tunesmith
  Blish, J. A work of art
  Dunn, D. The political piano
  Nevins, F. M., Jr. Funeral music
  Oates, J. C. Summer sweat
  Wilson, R., Jr. A simple elegy
COMPOST
  Graves, R. Earth to earth
Compression scars. Wells, K.
Compton, D. G. (David Guy)
  In which Avu Giddy tries to stop dancing
    Starlight 3; edited by Patrick Nielsen Hayden
Compton, David Guy *See* Compton, D. G. (David Guy), 1930-
Compton, Martha A.
  The fat cats' tale
  Such a pretty face; edited by Lee Martindale
Compton, Valerie
  Sound Advice
    Dalhousie Review v83 no2 p273-81 Summ 2003
The **comptroller** and the wild wind. Yates, R.
COMPULSORY MILITARY SERVICE *See* Draft
COMPUTER SIMULATION *See* Virtual reality
Computer virus. Kress, N.
COMPUTERS
  Anderson, P. Goat song
  Andrews, M. K. Love at first byte
  Asimov, I. The last question
  Aylett, S. The idler
  Barr, N. Venus rising
  Barth, J. Click
  Barth, J. The rest of your life
  Benford, G. The scarred man
  Bisson, T. An office romance
  Boyle, T. C. Peep Hall
  Bukiet, M. J. But, Microsoft! what byte through yonder windows breaks?
  Burstein, M. A. Teleabsence
  Card, O. S. Investment counselor
  Clarke, A. C. The nine billion names of God
  Clarke, A. C. The pacifist

Cohen, S. Those who appreciate money hate to touch the principal
  Costello, M. J. Someone who understands me
  Dickson, G. R. Computers don't argue
  Dix, S. Matters of consequence
  Dorsey, C. J. (Learning about) machine sex
  DuBois, B. Netmail
  Kress, N. Computer virus
  Landis, G. A. Ouroboros
  LaValle, V. D. Getting ugly
  Leavitt, D. The list
  Lupoff, R. A. The adventures of Mr. Tindle
  Lupoff, R. A. The turret
  Ramaya, S. Re:mohit
  Reed, R. R. On line
  Richter, S. My date with Satan
  Roberts, A. Swiftly
  Rucker, R. v. B. As above, so below
  Rucker, R. v. B. Soft Death
  Ryman, G. Fan
  Scholz, C. Travels
  Smith, M. M. Welcome
  Sterling, B. Maneki Neko
  Stross, C. Antibodies
  Taylor, T. L. Newstart 2.0 TM
  Updike, J. Bech noir
  Van Winckel, N. Making headway
  Vinge, V. The accomplice
Computers don't argue. Dickson, G. R.
CON MEN *See* Swindlers and swindling
CONCENTRATION CAMPS
    See also Political prisoners; World War, 1939-1945—Prisoners and prisons
  Borowski, T. Auschwitz, our home (a letter)
  Dann, J. Camps
  Dozois, G. R. Down among the dead men
  Gascar, P. The season of the dead
  Lustig, A. Stephen and Anne
  Nomberg-Przytyk, S. Old words—new meanings
  Ozick, C. The shawl
  Paver, C. The boxing match
  Zabytko, I. Obligation
Concepción. Shepard, S.
Concerning love. Wallenstein, J.
Concerning virgins. Boylan, C.
A **concert** of minor pieces. Bukoski, A.
Concerto accademico. Malzberg, B. N.
CONCERTS
  Charnas, S. M. Listening to Brahms
Concessions. Rodburg, M.
CONCIENTIOUS OBJECTORS
  Babel´, I. The Quaker
The **Concord** sonata. Davenport, G.
Concrete killer. Bishop, P.
The **concrete** puppy. Vachss, A. H.
Condé, Maryse
  The breadnut and the breadfruit
    Callaloo v24 no2 p419-26 Spr 2001
    The Oxford book of Caribbean short stories; edited by Stewart Brown and John Wickham
Conde, Rosina
  Morente
    Points of departure; new stories from Mexico; edited by Mónica Lavín; translated by Gustavo Segade
CONDOMS
  Addonizio, K. A brief history of condoms
Condoms. Wuori, G. K.

CONDUCT OF LIFE *See* Ethics
CONDUCTORS (MUSIC)
Devereaux, R. Nocturne a tre in b-double-sharp
    minor
Fitzgerald, P. Beehernz
Rowell, J. Saviors
Vaswani, N. Bolero
Cones. Ronk, M.
CONEY ISLAND (NEW YORK, N.Y.) *See* New
    York (N.Y.)—Coney Island
CONFEDERACY *See* Confederate States of
    America
CONFEDERATE AGENTS *See* Spies
Confederate flag. Pinson, H.
CONFEDERATE STATES OF AMERICA
Hoffman, L. The third nation
Knight, M. Killing Stonewall Jackson
CONFEDERATE STATES OF AMERICA.
    ARMY
Swarthout, G. F. O captain, my captain
CONFESSION
Chekhov, A. P. An incident at law
Hensley, J. L. Paint doctor
Russell, R. Evil star
Tuma, H. The Waldiba story
CONFESSION (CATHOLIC)
Boylan, C. Confession
Bradbury, R. Bless me, Father, for I have sinned
Bukoski, A. Winter weeds
Burke, J. Mea culpa
Gorman, E. Judgment
Reach, A. S. In the confessional
Smolens, J. Absolution
Confession. Boylan, C.
Confession. Johnson, C. R.
Confession. Kaminsky, S. M.
The **confession**. Rankin, I.
Confession. Wharton, E.
Confession of a sacrifice. Chaudhuri, A.
The **confessional** approach. Iagnemma, K.
Confessions. Reisman, N.
Confirmation. Harvey, J.
CONFLICT OF GENERATIONS
Armstrong, K. Drowning in air
Barthelme, F. Grapette
Gilchrist, E. Music
Updike, J. The hillies
Confluence. Buttenwieser, S. W.
CONFORMITY
Asimov, I. It's such a beautiful day
Dozois, G. R. Community
Gores, J. The criminal
Hernandez-Ramdwar, C. Soma
Confusing the dog. Painter, P.
Confusing the saints. Menendez, A.
Confusion cargo. Tenn, W.
Confusions of Uñi. Le Guin, U. K.
CONGO (DEMOCRATIC REPUBLIC) *See*
    Zaire
CONGRESS (U.S.) *See* United States. Congress
The **congress**. Borges, J. L.
CONGRESSES AND CONFERENCES
    See also Meetings
Borges, J. L. The congress
Singer, I. B. The conference
CONGRESSMEN *See* United States. Congress.
    House
Conjugal conversations. Klíma, I.
The **conjurer's** revenge. Chesnutt, C. W.

Conlon, Evelyn
Telling
    The Anchor book of new Irish writing; the
    new Gaelach ficsean; edited and with an
    introduction by John Somer and John J.
    Daly
CONNECTICUT
Bloom, A. The story
Gates, D. Saturn
Gates, D. Vigil
McBain, E. Activity in the flood plain
    New Haven
Dodd, S. M. Adult education
A **Connecticut** Yankee at King Arthur's court [ex-
    cerpt] Twain, M.
Connections. Drake, R.
Connell, Evan S.
Election eve
    The O. Henry Prize stories, 2003; edited and
    with an introduction by Laura Furman;
    jurers David Gutterson, Diane Johnson,
    Jennifer Egan
Connell, Richard Edward
Brother Orchid
    Murder most divine; ecclesiastical tales of un-
    holy crimes; edited by Ralph McInerny and
    Martin H. Greenberg
Connelly, Michael
Two-bagger
    The Best American mystery stories, 2002; ed-
    ited and with an introduction by James
    Ellroy; Otto Penzler, series editor
Connie. Little, B.
Connoisseur. Pronzini, B.
Connolly, Cressida
Bare
    Connolly, C. The happiest days
The bounce
    Connolly, C. The happiest days
Canada
    Connolly, C. The happiest days
Granville Hill
    Connolly, C. The happiest days
Greengages
    Connolly, C. The happiest days
How I lost my vocation
    Connolly, C. The happiest days
Indian summer
    Connolly, C. The happiest days
Paradise Drive
    Connolly, C. The happiest days
The pleasure gardens
    Connolly, C. The happiest days
Connor, Joan
Adam and Eve at the automat
    Connor, J. History lessons; stories
And I, Isolde
    Connor, J. We who live apart; stories
The anecdote of the island
    Connor, J. We who live apart; stories
Bluebeard's first wife
    Connor, J. We who live apart; stories
The Bowlville Cemetery
    Connor, J. We who live apart; stories
The butterfly effect
    Connor, J. History lessons; stories
The day the world declined to end
    Connor, J. History lessons; stories

Connor, Joan—*Continued*
The deposition of the prince of whales
Connor, J. History lessons; stories
Florida
Connor, J. History lessons; stories
Good people
Connor, J. History lessons; stories
Halfbaby
The Southern Review (Baton Rouge, La.) v38 no3 p556-69 Summ 2002
I wouldn't do that if I were you
Connor, J. History lessons; stories
Juana La Loca
Connor, J. History lessons; stories
The Southern Review (Baton Rouge, La.) v35 no2 p260-79 Spr 1999
The last native
Connor, J. We who live apart; stories
Let us now praise dead white men
Connor, J. History lessons; stories
Midlife Barbie
Connor, J. History lessons; stories
The mystery of Thomas Power James
Connor, J. History lessons; stories
October
Connor, J. We who live apart; stories
The parrot man
Connor, J. History lessons; stories
The poet's lobster
Connor, J. History lessons; stories
Riding with Ray
Connor, J. History lessons; stories
Second nature
Connor, J. We who live apart; stories
Stone man
Connor, J. History lessons; stories
Summer girls
Connor, J. We who live apart; stories
Tea and comfortable advice
Connor, J. We who live apart; stories
The thief of flowers
Connor, J. We who live apart; stories
This one fact
Connor, J. History lessons; stories
Under the rainbow
Connor, J. History lessons; stories
Ursa major in Vermont
Connor, J. We who live apart; stories
Victor learns to speak
Connor, J. History lessons; stories
We who live apart
Connor, J. We who live apart; stories
What It Is
TriQuarterly no113 p199-212 Summ 2002
Women's problems
Connor, J. We who live apart; stories
Writing the war novel
Connor, J. History lessons; stories
The year of no weather
Connor, J. History lessons; stories
Connors, Philip
Help
Utne Reader no109 p70-6 Ja/F 2002
Conquest by default. Vinge, V.
CONRAD, JOSEPH, 1857-1924
About
Zawieyski, J. Conrad in the ghetto

Conrad, Roxanne Longstreet
The dark downstairs
Dracula in London; edited by P. N. Elrod
Conrad in the ghetto. Zawieyski, J.
Conroy, Alicia L.
Mud-Colored Beauties of the Plains
Ploughshares v29 no4 p20-37 Wint 2003/2004
Conroy, Frank
Midair
Wonderful town; New York stories from The New Yorker; edited by David Remnick with Susan Choi
Conroy, Thom
The infinite shades of white
Prairie Schooner v75 no4 p111-20 Wint 2001
Conroy-Goldman, Melanie
The first old
Virgin fiction 2
CONSCIENCE
See also Ethics; Guilt
Stevenson, R. L. Markheim
Wharton, E. The touchstone
Conscience. Rykena, S.
Conscious birth. Walker, A.
Consent. Hribal, C. J.
Consider the Dilemma Facing an Ovulating Cavewoman Who Has Just Been Fertilised. Joseph, A.
Consideration. Strauss, B.
CONSPIRACIES
Baker, K. Son observe the time
Baldry, C. The friar's tale
Benford, G. A calculus of desperation
De Camp, L. S. The isolinguals
DuBois, B. Old soldiers
DuBois, B. Richard's children
Francis, D. The gift
L'Amour, L. Wings over Brazil
Malzberg, B. N. All assassins
Malzberg, B. N. In the stone house
Mosley, W. Doctor Kismet
Mosley, W. En masse
Wellen, E. Experiment
Conspiracy buffs. Delaney, E. J.
Conspiracy to murder. Waugh, E.
Constance. Clark, A. M.
Constant concupiscence. Skillings, R. D.
Constantine, Storm
Paragenesis
The Crow; shattered lives & broken dreams; edited by J. O'Barr and Ed Kramer
CONSTANTINOPLE *See* Turkey—Istanbul
Constellation. Kelman, J.
CONSTRUCTION INDUSTRY
Bonnie, F. Roland Fogg
Cherryh, C. J. Highliner
Kelman, J. Pulped sandwiches
Lavin, M. The girders
Means, D. What they did
Schumacher, A. Along for the ride
The **construction** of the Rachel. Lopez, B. H.
Construction zone. Greenberg, A.
Consuelo's letter. Alvarez, J.
Consulate. Tenn, W.
CONSULS *See* Diplomatic life
Consultation in the dark. Nevins, F. M., Jr.
The **container.** Unferth, D. O.

CONTENTMENT
See also Happiness
The **Contest**. Proulx, A.
CONTESTS
Patterson, K. Sick in public
Sterling, B. Sunken gardens
Vukcevich, R. A breath holding contest
Continental Divide. Lindner, V.
The **continuation** of The story of a horse. Babel´, I.
Contra dance. Winter, E.
Contraband of war. Hodgson, W. H.
CONTRACEPTION *See* Birth control
The **Contract**: A Story. Clayton, J. J.
Contraction. Martin, V.
Contrary to democracy. Hajizadeh, F.
Contrary to the manifest tenor. Huffman, B., Jr.
Contributor's Note. Martone, M.
Contributor's Notes. McNally, J.
The **control** device. Patton, F.
CONVALESCENCE
Yates, R. A convalescent ego
A **convalescent** ego. Yates, R.
The **convenience** boy. Massey, S.
The **convent**. Lavin, M.
CONVENT LIFE
See also Nuns
Appelfeld, A. Kitty
Chopin, K. The lilies
Deane, J. F. From a walled garden
Dougherty, K. When your breath freezes
Gomes, M. T. Dead woman's grove
Lavin, M. Chamois gloves
Maraini, D. Sister Attanasia's chickens
Newman, S. Conventual spirit
Newman, S. Death before compline
Conventional wisdom. Talley, M.
CONVENTS *See* Convent life
CONVENTS AND NUNNERIES *See* Convent life
Conventual spirit. Newman, S.
CONVERSATION
Clarke, A. C. The defenestration of Ermintrude Inch
Harris, M. Conversation on southern Honshu
James, H. A day of days
Roeske, P. Four characters, three small stories
Weaver, G. A dialogue
Conversation on southern Honshu. Harris, M.
Conversations with a moose. Carleton, M. R.
Conversations with the Doge of Venice. Alexander, D.
CONVERSION
Conroy-Goldman, M. The first old
Singer, I. B. Blood
Singer, I. B. A crown of feathers
Singer, I. B. The primper
Singer, I. B. Zeidlus the Pope
The **conversion** of Millicent Vernon. Melville, P.
The **Convert**. Friedman, B. J.
The **convertible**. Drake, R.
CONVICTS *See* Crime and criminals; Ex-convicts; Prisoners and prisons
CONVICTS, ESCAPED *See* Escaped convicts
Convolution. Hogan, J. P.
Convulsion. Shepard, S.

Cook, Alan
Hot days, cold nights
A Hot and sultry night for crime; edited by Jeffery Deaver
Cook, Christopher
The pickpocket
The Best American mystery stories, 2003; edited by Michael Connelly and Otto Penzler
Cook, John Estes *See* Baum, L. Frank (Lyman Frank), 1856-1919
Cook, K. L.
Breaking glass
Cook, K. L. Last call
Costa Rica
Cook, K. L. Last call
Easter weekend
Cook, K. L. Last call
Gone
Cook, K. L. Last call
Knock down, drag out
Cook, K. L. Last call
Last call
Cook, K. L. Last call
Marty
Cook, K. L. Last call
Nature's way
Cook, K. L. Last call
Penance
Cook, K. L. Last call
Pool boy
Cook, K. L. Last call
Texas moon
Cook, K. L. Last call
Thrumming
Cook, K. L. Last call
Cook, Rick and Hogan, Ernest
Obsidian harvest
The Year's best science fiction, eighteenth annual collection; edited by Gardner Dozois
Cook, Thomas H.
Fatherhood
The Best American mystery stories, 1999; edited and with an introduction by Ed McBain
The fix
The Best American mystery stories, 2002; edited and with an introduction by James Ellroy; Otto Penzler, series editor
Cooke, Carolyn
Black book
Cooke, C. The Bostons
Bob darling
Cooke, C. The Bostons
The Bostons
Cooke, C. The Bostons
New England Review v22 no1 p166-75 Wint 2001
Dirt-eaters
Cooke, C. The Bostons
Girl of their dreams
Cooke, C. The Bostons
Mourning party
Cooke, C. The Bostons
Ploughshares v25 no4 p142-54 Wint 1999/2000
The sugar-tit
Cooke, C. The Bostons
The trouble with money
Cooke, C. The Bostons

Cooke, Carolyn—*Continued*
Twa Corbies
  Cooke, C. The Bostons
Cooke, John Peyton
After you've gone
  The Best American mystery stories, 2003; edited by Michael Connelly and Otto Penzler
Cooker. Barthelme, F.
COOKERY
Beattie, A. The big-breasted pilgrim
Bishop, C. Dead and berried
Delllamonica, A. M. Cooking creole
Mathews, H. Country cooking from central France: roast boned rolled stuffed shoulder of lamb (farce double)
Mazelis, J. The blackberry season
Paschal, D. Sautéing the platygast
Porzecanski, T. The seder
Satterthwait, W. The cassoulet
Wolzien, V. Just one bite won't kill you
Cookie and me. Turner, G.
The **cookie** trick. Bonnie, F.
Cooking creole. Delllamonica, A. M.
The **cooking** lessons. Murabito, S.
COOKS
Bocock, M. The funeral
Byatt, A. S. Christ in the house of Martha and Mary
Chekhov, A. P. The cook's wedding
Chekhov, A. P. In the dark
Davis, A. Spice
Downs, M. Prison food
Dunmore, H. My Polish teacher's tie
Fischerová, D. The thirty-sixth chicken of Master Wu
Hughes, K. B. Roam
Kelton, E. Hewey and the wagon cook
Mayo, W. Day cook
McNulty, J. Barkeep won't let anybody at all shove this handyman around
Ramaya, S. Gopal's kitchen
Smith, G. Last requests
Taylor, T. L. The Boar's Head Easter
The **cook's** wedding. Chekhov, A. P.
The **cool**. Lisick, B.
Cool blues. Harvey, J.
Cool wedding. Viswanathan, L.
Cooley, Nicole
Stories that could not be true
  Southwest Review v84 no4 p479-91 1999
Coolhunting. Rusch, K. K.
COOLIDGE, CALVIN, 1872-1933
                    About
Friesner, E. M. Trouble a-bruin
Coonts, Stephen
Corey Ford buys the farm
  On glorious wings; the best flying stories of the century; edited and introduced by Stephen Coonts
Cooper, Bernard
Between the sheets
  Cooper, B. Guess again
Bit-o-honey
  Cooper, B. Guess again
  The Pushcart prize XXVI; best of the small presses, an annual small press reader; edited by Bill Henderson and the Pushcart prize editors

Exterior decoration
  Cooper, B. Guess again
Graphology
  Cooper, B. Guess again
Hunters and gatherers
  Circa 2000; gay fiction at the millennium; edited by Robert Drake & Terry Wolverton
  Cooper, B. Guess again
  Ploughshares v25 no1 p25-49 Spr 1999
Intro to acting
  Cooper, B. Guess again
  The North American Review v284 no6 p31-37 N/D 1999
A man in the making
  Cooper, B. Guess again
Night sky
  Cooper, B. Guess again
  LA shorts; edited by Steven Gilbar
Old birds
  Cooper, B. Guess again
  The Paris Review v41 no153 p212-19 Wint 1999
What to name the baby
  Cooper, B. Guess again
X
  Cooper, B. Guess again
Cooper, Brandt Jesus
A new night of long knives
  Fantasmas; supernatural stories by Mexican American writers; edited by Rob Johnson; introduction by Kathleen J. Alcalá
Cooper, Brenda
(jt. auth) See Niven, Larry and Cooper, Brenda
Cooper, J. California
The eagle flies
  Cooper, J. C. The future has a past; stories
A filet of soul
  Cooper, J. C. The future has a past; stories
The lost and the found
  Cooper, J. C. The future has a past; stories
A shooting star
  Cooper, J. C. The future has a past; stories
Cooper, James Fenimore
A game of ball
  Dead balls and double curves; an anthology of early baseball fiction; edited and with an introduction by Trey Strecker ; with a foreword by Arnold Hano
Cooper, Rand Richards
Heroes of 1974
  Iowa Review v33 no1 p122-37 Spr 2003
Johnny Hamburger
  The Best American short stories, 2003; selected from U.S. and Canadian magazines by Walter Mosley with Katrina Kenison; with an introduction by Walter Mosley
  Esquire v137 no3 p112-17, 178 Mr 2002
Coover, Robert
The Return of the Dark Children
  Harvard Review (1992) no23 p104-13 Fall 2002
The sheriff goes to church
  The Pushcart prize XXIV: best of the small presses; an annual small press reader; edited by Bill Henderson with the Pushcart prize editors
Stick man
  Harper's v303 no1815 p39-45 Ag 2001

Coover, Robert—*Continued*
Visitation
Ghost writing; haunted tales by contemporary writers; edited by Roger Weingarten
Copper, Basil
Ill met by daylight
The Mammoth book of best new horror 14; edited with an introduction by Stephen Jones
The **copper** kings. Wolven, S.
COPPER MINES AND MINING
Miller, R. The darkness of the deep
The **coppersmith**. Del Rey, L.
Copycat. Myers, J.
The **coral** reef. Tran, V.
CORBETT, BOSTON, B. 1832
About
Hodgen, C. Three parting shots and a forecast
Corbett, Thomas P. *See* Corbett, Boston, b. 1832
The **Corbett** correspondence: "Agent no. 5 & Agent no. 6". Marston, E. and Lovesey, P.
Corcoran, Tom
The octopus alibi
Stories from the Blue Moon Café; edited by Sonny Brewer
Cordelia. Gomes, M. T.
Corin, Lucy
My Favorite Dentist
The Southern Review (Baton Rouge, La.) v40 no2 p304-13 Spr 2004
Rich people
New stories from the South: the year's best, 2003; edited by Shannon Ravenel; with a preface by Roy Blount Jr.
Who buried the baby
Ploughshares v27 no1 p28-36 Spr 2001
CORK (IRELAND: COUNTY) *See* Ireland—Cork (County)
The **corn** bin. Heynen, J.
The **corn** knife. Coates, G. S.
Cornwell, Bernard
Excalibur [excerpt]
Swords and sorcerers; stories from the world of fantasy and adventure; edited by Clint Willis
Corona. Delany, S. R.
CORONERS
See also Medical examiners
Brown, J. The coroner's report
Oates, J. C. The skull
The **coroner's** report. Brown, J.
Corporal Lewis. Dubus, A.
Corporal love. Phillips, D. R.
CORPORATIONS *See* Business
CORPULENCE *See* Obesity
Corpus. Johnston, B. A.
Correa, Arnaldo
The merry ghosts of the Grampus
Death cruise; crime stories on the open seas; edited by Lawrence Block
Spy's fate
Death by espionage; intriguing stories of deception and betrayal; edited by Martin Cruz Smith

Correa, Hugo
When Pilate said no
Cosmos latinos: an anthology of science fiction from Latin America and Spain; translated, edited, & with an introduction & notes by Andrea L. Bell & Yolanda Molina-Gavilán
Correspondence. Kline, D.
Correspondence [excerpt] Thomas, S.
Correspondence I. Kohler, S.
Correspondence II. Kohler, S.
Correspondence of corpses. Chapman, C. M.
The **correspondent**. Brown, C.
La **Corriveau**. Glover, D. H.
CORRUPTION (IN POLITICS)
See also Bribery
CORSAIRS *See* Pirates
Cortados on the quai. Greenberg, K. J.
Cortázar, Julio
Blow-up
The Vintage book of Latin American stories; edited by Carlos Fuentes and Julio Ortega
Letter to a young lady in Paris
Other people's mail; an anthology of letter stories; edited with an introduction by Gail Pool
The night face up
The Vintage book of amnesia; an anthology; edited by Jonathan Lethem
Summer
The Best of The Kenyon review; edited by David Lynn; introduction by Joyce Carol Oates
Il **Cortigiano** of Thomas Avenue. Miner, V.
Cory, Rowena *See* Lindquist, Rowena Cory, 1958-
COSA NOSTRA *See* Mafia
Cosas, Inc. Skinner, J.
Coshnear, Daniel
The amateur ventriloquist
Coshnear, D. Jobs & other preoccupations; stories; with an introduction by Rosellen Brown
A day at the beach
Coshnear, D. Jobs & other preoccupations; stories; with an introduction by Rosellen Brown
Double shift
Coshnear, D. Jobs & other preoccupations; stories; with an introduction by Rosellen Brown
The full six
Coshnear, D. Jobs & other preoccupations; stories; with an introduction by Rosellen Brown
Gauge
Coshnear, D. Jobs & other preoccupations; stories; with an introduction by Rosellen Brown
How we remember you
Coshnear, D. Jobs & other preoccupations; stories; with an introduction by Rosellen Brown
The logic of the heart
Coshnear, D. Jobs & other preoccupations; stories; with an introduction by Rosellen Brown

Coshnear, Daniel—*Continued*

Mr. Passion
  Coshnear, D. Jobs & other preoccupations; stories; with an introduction by Rosellen Brown

New job
  Coshnear, D. Jobs & other preoccupations; stories; with an introduction by Rosellen Brown

The resolution of nothing
  Coshnear, D. Jobs & other preoccupations; stories; with an introduction by Rosellen Brown

The right-hand man
  Coshnear, D. Jobs & other preoccupations; stories; with an introduction by Rosellen Brown

The smilies meet the brooders
  Coshnear, D. Jobs & other preoccupations; stories; with an introduction by Rosellen Brown

Toxic round-up
  Coshnear, D. Jobs & other preoccupations; stories; with an introduction by Rosellen Brown

Transactional paralysis
  Coshnear, D. Jobs & other preoccupations; stories; with an introduction by Rosellen Brown

What to say when you talk to yourself
  Coshnear, D. Jobs & other preoccupations; stories; with an introduction by Rosellen Brown

Where's Fran Haynes?
  Coshnear, D. Jobs & other preoccupations; stories; with an introduction by Rosellen Brown

White veil
  Coshnear, D. Jobs & other preoccupations; stories; with an introduction by Rosellen Brown

Coskran, Kathleen

Sun
  Living on the edge; fiction by Peace Corps writers; edited by John Coyne

Cosmic Casanova. Clarke, A. C.

The **cosmic** frame. Fairman, P. W.

The **cosmology** of Bing [excerpt] Cullin, M.

The **cossack**. Chekhov, A. P.

COSSACKS

Babel´, I. Afonka bida

Babel´, I. My first goose

Babel´, I. Shaska Christ

Pushkin, A. S. The captain's daughter

Cossío, Alicia Yánez *See* Yánez Cossío, Alicia, 1929-

The **cost** of doing business. What, L.

The **cost** of Kent Castwell. Davidson, A.

Costa, Margaret Jull

(jt. auth) *See* Arzola, Jorge Luis

(jt. auth) *See* Lemebel, Pedro

(jt. auth) *See* Vila-Matas, Enrique

Costa, Shelley

Black heart and cabin girl
  Blood on their hands; edited by Lawrence Block

Getting the story
  The Georgia Review v55 no3 p479-97 Fall 2001

Costello, Matthew J.

Someone who understands me
  Murder most postal; homicidal tales that deliver a message; edited by Martin H. Greenberg

Costello, Matthew J. and Hautala, Rick

And the sea shall claim them
  Lighthouse hauntings; 12 original tales of the supernatural; edited by Charles G. Waugh & Martin H. Greenberg

Costikyan, Greg

And still she sleeps
  Black heart, ivory bones; [edited by] Ellen Datlow & Terri Windling

Costume drama. Simpson, H.

COSTUME PARTIES *See* Parties

COTTAGES

Willis, M. S. Dwight's house

The **cottagette**. Gilman, C. P.

Cotter, John

Good Morning, New Jersey
  Hanging Loose no84 p13-14 2004

Nights Out
  Hanging Loose no84 p16 2004

Someone Else's Mouth
  Hanging Loose no84 p15 2004

Cottle, Thomas J.

Booth story
  The Antioch Review v59 no1 p58-66 Wint 2001

Final Concert
  The Antioch Review v61 no4 p624-38 Fall 2003

The **cotton** field. Gavell, M. L.

The **cotton** mill. Drake, R.

The **Cougar** Ladies. Roberts, S.

Coughlan Dice at his closet window. Skillings, R. D.

Could be better. Duffy, S.

Coulter, Kristi

Normalcy
  Virgin fiction 2

Counsel for the defense. Matera, L.

Count Omega. Berners, G. H. T.-W., Baron

Countdown. Burger, W.

COUNTER CULTURE

Hochman, A. Liability

Lipsyte, S. Ergo, ice pick

Paine, T. The spoon children

COUNTERESPIONAGE *See* International intrigue; Spies

The **counterfeit** copperhead. Hoch, E. D.

COUNTERFEITERS

Allingham, M. Money to burn

Brown, F. Don't look behind you

Davidson, A. Business must be picking up

The **counterlife** [excerpt] Roth, P.

Counterplot. Nevins, F. M., Jr.

The **counterpuncher**. Jenkins, G.

Countess Kathleen. Charyn, J.

Counting. Melton, F.

Counting Sheep. Rice, R.

Counting the ways. Perabo, S.

Country Boy. Nyi Pu Lay

COUNTRY CLUBS

Slavin, J. The woman who cut off her leg at the Maidstone Club

Country cooking from central France: roast boned rolled stuffed shoulder of lamb (farce double). Mathews, H.
Country Girls. Caspers, N.
The country husband. Cheever, J.
COUNTRY LIFE
   See also Farm life; Mountain life; Outdoor life; Plantation life; Ranch life; Small town life
Agee, J. The land you claim
Banks, R. The neighbor
Bass, R. The legend of Pig-Eye
Benedict, P. The Sutton Pie Safe
Berry, W. Are you all right?
Berry, W. Fidelity
Berry, W. A jonquil for Mary Penn
Berry, W. Making it home
Berry, W. Pray without ceasing
Bingham, S. Apricots
Bonnie, F. Extreme unction
Bonnie, F. Widening the road
Chute, C. "Ollie, oh . . . "
Coates, G. S. Trees of heaven
Coberly, L. M. Garnet
Gunn, K. Everyone is sleeping
Hall, J. B. If you can't win
Hoffman, W. Humility
Hoffman, W. Tenant
Jackson, V. F. A little kingdom
Leslie, N. Lost
Linney, R. The widow
Proulx, A. On the antler
Sanford, A. Helens and Roses
Strom, D. Chickens
Updike, J. The gun shop
Warren, R. P. Christmas gift
Westmoreland, T. A. Winter Island
Youmans, M. A girl in summer
COUNTRY MUSIC
Earle, S. Billy the Kid
King, C. My life is a country song
Country of cold. Patterson, K.
The country of the blind. Allyn, D.
The country of the blind. Wells, H. G.
The country of the kind. Knight, D. F.
The country road. Azadeh, C.
Country Sleep. Fitzpatrick, T.
Countrymen: A Story. Aizman, D.
The county of birches. Kalman, J.
County Road G. Orner, P.
Couple kills. Vernon, D.
The couple next door. McBain, E.
The couple next door. Millar, M.
A couple of dead men. Greenberg, A.
COUPS D'ÉTAT
Ambler, E. The blood bargain
Davenport, K. Fork used in eating Reverend Baker
Škvorecký, J. Spectator on a February night
COURAGE
Henry, O. The higher pragmatism
The court interpreter. Pak, T.
COURT LIFE See Courts and courtiers
Court of palms. Epstein, L.
Courtesan with a Lover. Storey, D. G.
COURTESANS
   See also Prostitutes
The courtesy. Berger, J.
COURTROOM SCENES See Trials

COURTS AND COURTIERS
   See also names of individual kings, queens, and rulers; also subdivision Kings and rulers under names of countries
      France
Dumas, A. The three musketeers [excerpt]
      Japan
Borges, J. L. The uncivil teacher of court etiquette Kôtsuké no Suké
      Russia
Pushkin, A. S. The blackamoor of Peter the Great
Van Belkom, E. The debauched one
COURTSHIP
Barrett, A. Theories of rain
Berry, W. A consent
Chekhov, A. P. Encased
Chekhov, A. P. The teacher of literature
Craddock, C. E. The star in the valley
Donaldson, S. R. Reave the Just
Dove, R. Second-hand man
Fitzgerald, F. S. The camel's back
Jaime-Becerra, M. Media vuelta
James, H. Guest's confession
James, H. A landscape painter
James, H. Longstaff's marriage
James, H. Poor Richard
James, H. Sir Edmund Orme
James, H. The story of a year
L'Amour, L. The courting of Griselda
Pushkin, A. S. The squire's daughter
Régio, J. They used to go for long walks on Sundays . . .
Spencer, E. First dark
Thomas, D. The Steckley girls
The courtship. Goldstein, R.
The courtship of Captain Swenk. Nagle, P. G.
The courtship of Mr. Lyon. Carter, A.
Cousin Cora. Wheat, C.
Cousin Gemma. Cohen, R.
Cousin Tuck's. Orner, P.
COUSINS
Alameddine, R. Remembering Nasser
Allen, D., Jr. End of the steam age
Bellow, S. By the St. Lawrence
Bellow, S. Cousins
Bezmozgis, D. Natasha
Boucher, A. The girl who married a monster
Bukoski, A. A concert of minor pieces
Burke, J. Miscalculation
Capote, T. A Christmas memory
Capote, T. One Christmas
Capote, T. The Thanksgiving visitor
Cohen, R. Cousin Gemma
Daniels, J. Bonus
Davidson, R. Barnstorming
Desplechin, M. My cousin Gérard
Drake, R. All that believe that, stand on their head!
Drake, R. The child prodigy
Drake, R. Shrouds with pockets in them
Dropkin, Celia. At the rich relatives
Dunmore, H. Lilac
Gavell, M. L. The rotifer
Gay, W. Homecoming
Gilchrist, E. Mexico
Gilchrist, E. The sanguine blood of men
Goldstein, N. A pillar of a cloud
Havazelet, E. Leah

COUSINS—*Continued*

Hirshberg, G. Shipwreck beach

Hoffman, A. The rest of your life

Hoffman, A. Still among the living

Hoffman, A. True confession

Howard, M. The Magdalene

James, H. Four meetings

James, H. The impressions of a cousin

James, H. Mrs. Temperly

Johnson, D. Something to remember me by

Jones, Tayari. Best cousin

Kelman, J. The grapes of Roth

Kohler, S. Poor cousins

Kress, N. The most famous little girl in the world

Lear, P. Nirvana

Lee, A. Anthropology

Malouf, D. Dream stuff

Mastretta, A. Aunt Carmen

Mastretta, A. Aunt Leonor

McDowell, I. Sunflowers

McManus, J. Megargel

Munro, A. Family furnishings

Munro, A. Post and beam

Murguía, A. Ofrendas

Nair, M. Summer

Norman, G. Maxine

Orringer, J. When she is old and I am famous

Ramaya, S. Operation monsoon

Reifler, N. Julian

Sandor, M. Capacity

Sanford, A. Strangers and pilgrims

Slezak, E. Lucky

Spencer, E. The cousins

Stollman, A. L. New memories

Tester, W. Cousins

Van Winckel, N. Sometimes he borrowed a horse

Vasseur, T. J. First love

Vasseur, T. J. Pig summer

Walbert, K. The gardens of Kyoto

Yoshimoto, B. Night and night's travelers

Cousins. Bellow, S.

The **Cousins**. Oates, J. C.

The **cousins**. Spencer, E.

Cousins. Tester, W.

The **cove**. Levinson, L. M.

The **covenant** of Il Vigneto. Parks, J. A.

The **Coventry** boy. Joyce, G.

Covered. Silber, J.

Covered. Slavin, J.

The **coveted** correspondence. McInerny, R. M.

Cow-cow. Banks, R.

Cowan, Judith

Laiah and the Sun King

The Canadian Forum v78 no884 p28-32 D 1999

Coward, Mat

Bloody victims

Blood on their hands; edited by Lawrence Block

No night by myself

Master's choice v2; mystery stories by today's top writers and the masters who inspired them; edited by Lawrence Block

The shortest distance

The World's finest mystery and crime stories, first annual collection; edited by Ed Gorman

So where've you buried the missus then, Paddy?

Murder most Celtic; tall tales of Irish mayhem; edited by Martin H. Greenberg

Tall man, large cat

Felonious felines; edited by Carol and Ed Gorman

Three nil

The World's finest mystery and crime stories, second annual collection; edited by Ed Gorman

Too hot to die

A Hot and sultry night for crime; edited by Jeffery Deaver

Too subtle for me

The best British mysteries; edited by Maxim Jakubowski

Twelve of the little buggers

The World's finest mystery and crime stories, second annual collection; edited by Ed Gorman

You can jump

Death dance; suspenseful stories of the dance macabre; Trevanian, editor

COWARDICE

Babel', I. On the field of honor

Borges, J. L. The other death

Borges, J. L. The shape of the sword

Lawrence, D. H. The thorn in the flesh

Cowbird. Fromm, P.

COWBOYS

Bird, S. Bumfuzzled

Bowen, G. Barrel racers: El Charro

Bower, B. M. The lamb of the Flying U

Coleman, J. C. Rodeo

Davis, A. Chase

Davis, A. Fairy tale

Day, C. The lone star cowboy

DeRosso, H. A. Witch

Easton, R. O. Death in October

Easton, R. O. The legend of Shorm

Giles, J. H. The gift

Greer, R. O. Spoon

Henry, W. Rough Riders of Arizona

Hickey, D. I'm bound to follow the longhorn cows

L'Amour, L. End of the drive

L'Amour, L. Rustler roundup

Lansdale, J. R. Cowboy

Leonard, E. Hurrah for Capt. Early

Leonard, E. Tenkiller

Osborn, C. My brother is a cowboy

Proulx, A. The blood bay

Proulx, A. The mud below

Shepard, J. Night shot

Shepard, J. Thirty head of killers

Thompson, J. Heart of gold

Cowboys. Clay, K. M.

Cowboys. Norman, G.

Cowboys and Indians. Penn, W. S.

Cowboys don't cry [excerpt] Davis, L. J.

Cowdrey, Albert E.

Crux

The Year's best science fiction, eighteenth annual collection; edited by Gardner Dozois

Cowgirl. Hay, E.

COWHANDS *See* Cowboys

COWS *See* Cattle

Cox, Anthony Berkeley *See* Berkeley, Anthony, 1893-1971

Coydog. Beattie, A.
Coyne, John
  Snow man
    Living on the edge; fiction by Peace Corps
      writers; edited by John Coyne
Coyne, Stephen
  Hollowed Be Thy Name
    The North American Review v289 no2 p25-7
      Mr/Ap 2004
  Hunting country
    New stories from the South: the year's best,
      2001; edited by Shannon Ravenel; with a
      preface by Lee Smith
  The visitation
    The North American Review v286 no3/4
      p41-6 My/Ag 2001
Coyne, Tom
  Behind sharp branches
    Virgin fiction 2
Coyote. Villoro, J.
Coyote comes calling. Watanabe McFerrin, L.
Coyotes. Porter, A.
Crab. Russell, C.
The **crab** lice. Feeley, G.
The **crab** with the green mango belly. Ramos, M.
CRABS
  Hodgson, W. H. From the tideless sea, part one
  Hodgson, W. H. From the tideless sea, part two:
    further news of the Homebird
  Hoffman, W. Landings
Crace, Jim
  Digestions
    The New Yorker v77 no10 p78-83 My 7 2001
  The prospect from the silver hills
    The Art of the story; an international anthology of contemporary short stories; edited by
      Daniel Halpern
Crack. Hall, J.
Cracks. Kohler, S.
Craddock, Charles Egbert
  The star in the valley
    Southern local color; stories of region, race,
      and gender; edited by Barbara C. Ewell and
      Pamela Glenn Menke; with notes by Andrea Humphrey
Craig, Amanda
  The French Boy
    Valentine's Day: women against men; stories
      of revenge; introduction by Alice Thomas
Craig, Chauna
  Pluma Piluma and the Utopian Turtle Top: A
    Bedtime Story for Women Writers
    Calyx v21 no2 p96-106 Summ 2003
Craig, Kit, 1932-
    See also Reed, Kit, 1932-
Crane, Dede
  Inviting Blindness
    Dalhousie Review v83 no1 p99-116 Spr 2003
Crane, Hamilton
    See also Mason, Sarah J.
Crane, Marian
  The blood orange tree
    Such a pretty face; edited by Lee Martindale
Crane, Stephen
  The blue hotel
    Master's choice [v1]; mystery stories by today's top writers and the masters who inspired them; edited by Lawrence Block

CRANES (BIRDS)
  Zinovyeva-Annibal, L. D. Zhurya
The **cranes**. Meinke, P.
Crane's grace. Devine, M. R.
Cranley Meadows. Lasdun, J.
Craphound. Doctorow, C.
Crash. Davis, A.
Crash landing. L'Amour, L.
Crashing. Krawiec, R.
A **craving** for originality. Pronzini, B.
Crawford, Dan
  Guile is where it goes
    Blood on their hands; edited by Lawrence
      Block
Crawford, F. Marion (Francis Marion)
  The upper berth
    Nightshade: 20th century ghost stories; edited
      by Robert Phillips
Crawford, Francis Marion *See* Crawford, F.
    Marion (Francis Marion), 1854-1909
Crawford's consistency. James, H.
Crawl space. Singleton, G.
Crawley, Dan
  Derrick was right
    The North American Review v287 no3/4 p28-
      33 My/Ag 2002
Crayencour, Marguerite De *See* Yourcenar, Marguerite
Crazy. Swenson, L.
Crazy dead kid lady. DeLancey, K.
**CRAZY HORSE, SIOUX CHIEF, CA. 1842-
1877**

About
  Graebner, J. E. The whispering
  Waldrop, H. Custer's last jump!
Crazy life. Mathews, L.
Crazy people. Bridgford, K.
Crazy Sunday. Fitzgerald, F. S.
The **crazy** thought. Gates, D.
Crazy yellow. Cummins, A.
Cream of kohlrabi. Skloot, F.
Creasey, John
  The chief witness
    Edwards, M. Mysterious pleasures; a celebration of the Crime Writers' Association's
      50th anniversary; edited by Martin Edwards
CREATION
  Crowley, J. The nightingale sings at night
CREATION (LITERARY, ARTISTIC, ETC.)
    See also Authorship
  Crowley, J. Novelty
Creation. Ford, J.
Creation. Reiner, C.
The **creation** of Anat. Stollman, A. L.
Creationism: an illustrated lecture in two parts.
    Yolen, J.
The **creator** has a master plan. Martin, V.
Creature comforts. Kilpatrick, N.
Crèche. Ford, R.
CREDIBILITY *See* Truthfulness and falsehood
Credit card test. Lisick, B.
Credit the cat. Breen, J. L.
CREE INDIANS
  Norman, H. Unicycle
Creeping Things. Bensko, J.
Cremains. Lipsyte, S.
CREMATION
  Cady, J. Daddy dearest

CREMATORIUMS
Su Shuyang. Between life and death
Crenshaw, Paul
Missing
The North American Review v286 no3/4 p63-6 My/Ag 2001
A **Creole** mystery. Hearn, L.
CREOLES
Cable, G. W. The story of Bras-Coupé
Chen, W. Trotters
Chopin, K. At Chênière Caminada
Chopin, K. The awakening
Chopin, K. Azélie
Chopin, K. La belle Zorađe
Chopin, K. La Belle Zoraïde
Chopin, K. Beyond the Bayou
Chopin, K. Caline
Chopin, K. A Dresden lady in Dixie
Chopin, K. For Marse Chouchoute
Chopin, K. Love on the Bon-Dieu
Chopin, K. Madame Célestin's divorce
Chopin, K. Madame Martel's Christmas Eve
Chopin, K. Mamouche
Chopin, K. A matter of prejudice
Chopin, K. Nég Créol
Chopin, K. A night in Acadie
Chopin, K. A non-account Creole
Chopin, K. Odalie misses mass
Chopin, K. Ozème's holiday
Chopin, K. Ti Frère
Chopin, K. A wizard from Gettysburg
Ellis, Z. The waiting room
King, G. La grande demoiselle
Scott, L. Ballad for the new world
Crespi, Camilla T.
The fixer
Death dines at 8:30; edited by Claudia Bishop and Nick DiChario
Cri de coeur. Bishop, M.
Crichton, Michael
Blood doesn't come out
McSweeney's mammoth treasury of thrilling tales; edited by Michael Chabon
CRICKET
Breeze, J. B. Sunday cricket
Chaudhuri, A. The great game
Selvon, S. The cricket match
Waugh, E. The national game
The **cricket** match. Selvon, S.
The **cricket** on the hearth. Bradbury, R.
CRICKETS
Vivante, A. The cricket
Crickets. Coates, G. S.
Crider, Bill
The adventure of the young British soldier
Murder, my dear Watson; new tales of Sherlock Holmes; edited by Martin H. Greenberg, Jon Lellenberg, Daniel Stashower
Alligator tears
White House pet detectives; tales of crime and mystery at the White House from a pet's-eye view; edited by Carole Nelson Douglas
Belle Boyd, the rebel spy
The Blue and the gray undercover; edited by Ed Gorman
Blest be the ties
Crider, B. The nighttime is the right time; a collection of stories

Cap'n Bob and Gus
Crider, B. The nighttime is the right time; a collection of stories
An evening out with Carl
Crider, B. The nighttime is the right time; a collection of stories
Gored
Crider, B. The nighttime is the right time; a collection of stories
Murder most delectable; savory tales of culinary crimes; edited by Martin H. Greenberg
How I found a cat, lost true love, and broke the bank at Monte Carlo
Crider, B. The nighttime is the right time; a collection of stories
It happened at grandmother's house
Crider, B. The nighttime is the right time; a collection of stories
King of the night
Crider, B. The nighttime is the right time; a collection of stories
The nighttime is the right time
Crider, B. The nighttime is the right time; a collection of stories
One of our leprechauns is missing
Murder most Celtic; tall tales of Irish mayhem; edited by Martin H. Greenberg
Out like a lion
The World's finest mystery and crime stories, third annual collection; edited by Ed Gorman and Martin H. Greenberg
Poo-Poo
Crider, B. The nighttime is the right time; a collection of stories
The Santa Claus caper
Crider, B. The nighttime is the right time; a collection of stories
See what the boys in the locked room will have
Crider, B. The nighttime is the right time; a collection of stories
Tinseltown Follies of 1948
Cat crimes through time; edited by Ed Gorman, Martin H. Greenberg, and Larry Segriff
The true facts about the death of Wes Hardin
Westward; a fictional history of the American West : 28 original stories celebrating the 50th anniversary of the Western Writers of America; edited by Dale L. Walker
Crider, Bill and Crider, Judy
At the hop
Death dance; suspenseful stories of the dance macabre; Trevanian, editor
Chocolate moose
Death dines at 8:30; edited by Claudia Bishop and Nick DiChario
Crider, Judy
(jt. auth) See Crider, Bill and Crider, Judy
Criers and kibitzers, kibitzers and criers. Elkin, S.
Crime. Wuori, G. K.

CRIME AND CRIMINALS

See also Arson; Atrocities; Bank robbers; Brigands and robbers; Child abuse; Counterfeiters; Escaped convicts; Extortion; Gangs; Gangsters; Hostages; Juvenile delinquency; Kidnapping; Kleptomania; Mafia; Murder stories; Rape; Smuggling; Swindlers and swindling; Thieves; Underworld; Vandalism; Vigilance committees; War criminals; Wife abuse

Agee, J. The god of gestures
Aldiss, B. W. Judas danced
Archer, J. Crime pays
Beinhart, L. Funny story
Borges, J. L. Juan Muraña
Brett, S. Letter to his son
Brett, S. A note of note
Cobb, T. Real stories of true crime
Cody, L. Lucky dip
Collins, B. That damn cat
Collins, M. Nobody frames Big Sam
Connell, R. E. Brother Orchid
Correa, A. The merry ghosts of the Grampus
Coward, M. Bloody victims
Crider, B. An evening out with Carl
Crumley, J. Hot Springs
Davidson, A. The importance of trifles
Davidson, A. The singular incident of the dog on the beach
De Noux, O. Death on denial
Deaver, J. The weekender
Delaney, E. J. O beauty! o truth!
Delany, S. R. Time considered as a helix of semi-precious stones
Dilts, Tyler. Thug: signification and the (de) constuction of self
Dokey, R. Monkey
Doolittle, S. Summa mathematica
Drake, D. Nation without walls
Drake, D. The predators
Drake, D. Underground
DuBois, B. A family game
DuBois, B. The star thief
DuBois, B. The summer people
Dunlap, S. Away for safekeeping
Ellison, H. Sensible city
Fischer, T. Then they say you're drunk
Fitzgerald, F. S. Tarquin of cheapside
Fleming, R. Punish the young seed of Satan
Forsyth, F. The veteran
Gifford, B. Vendetta
Goodis, D. The plunge
Gores, J. Inscrutable
Gorman, E. Out there in the darkness
Groves, J. W. Stop, thief!
Hammett, D. Afraid of a gun
Hammett, D. His brother's keeper
Hammett, D. Ruffian's wife
Hansen, R. His dog
Harrison, H. A criminal act
Healy, J. F. The safest little town in Texas
Henry, O. A retrieved reformation
Hinger, C. Any old mother
Hornsby, W. New moon and rattlesnakes
Howard, C. The cobalt blues
Howard, C. Out of control
Howard, C. When the black shadows die
Kelly, J. P. The prisoner of Chillon
L'Amour, L. Down Paagumene way

Lane, J. The receivers
Lee, W. W. Dying for sin
Leonard, E. Fire in the hole
Leonard, E. How Carlos Webster changed his name to Carl and became a famous Oklahoma lawman
Lochte, D. In the city of angels
Maraini, D. The boy Gramophone and the pigeon man
Matera, L. Performance crime
McInerny, R. M. Mutiny of the bounty hunter
McNally, J. The greatest goddamn thing
Oates, J. C. The girl with the blackened eye
Oates, J. C. The stalker
Painter, P. Murder one
Rick, M. Next time
Roth, J. Strawberries
Savage, L., Jr. The sting of Señorita Scorpion
Shepard, J. Dade County, November 2000
Shepard, L. Limbo
Silverstein, S. The guilty party
Smith, J. Crime wave in Pinhole
Strauss, A. The way you left
Tenn, W. Party of the two parts
Vachss, A. H. Everybody pays
Vachss, A. H. Going home
Wellen, E. Inside evidence
Westlake, D. E. Art & craft
Westlake, D. E. Art and craft
Westlake, D. E. Ask a silly question
Westlake, D. E. The Dortmunder workout
Westlake, D. E. Fugue for felons
Westlake, D. E. Give till it hurts
Westlake, D. E. Horse laugh
Westlake, D. E. Jumble sale
Westlake, D. E. A midsummer daydream
Westlake, D. E. Now what?
Westlake, D. E. Party animal
Westlake, D. E. Take it away
Westlake, D. E. Too many crooks
Westlake, D. E. You put on some weight
What, L. The cost of doing business
Wolven, S. Controlled burn
Wood, M. That one autumn
Crime and punishment. Frym, G.
The **crime** of Miss Oyster Brown. Lovesey, P.
Crime pays. Archer, J.
Crime wave in Pinhole. Smith, J.
Crimes against humanity. Greenberg, A.
Crimes at midnight. Haskell, J.

CRIMES OF PASSION

See also Murder stories
The **criminal**. Gores, J.
A **criminal** act. Harrison, H.

CRIMINAL INVESTIGATION

Chekhov, A. P. A malefactor
Cody, L. Reconstruction
Evenson, B. White square
Nevins, F. M., Jr. Fair game
Shields, J. The Fig Eater [excerpt]
The **Criminal** Mastermind Is Confined. Davies, P. H.

CRIMINALLY INSANE See Insane, Criminal and dangerous
CRIMINALS See Crime and criminals
Crimson stain. Mosley, W.
Crisis at Bald Knob. Coberly, L. M.
Crisis in the Life of an Actor. Indiana, G.
Critical mass. Clarke, A. C.

Critterworld. Watkins, S.
CRO-MAGNON MAN *See* Prehistoric man
CROATIA
    See also Mljet Island (Croatia)
CROCKETT, DAVY, 1786-1836
              About
  Empire
Crocodile lady. Fowler, C.
Crocodile tears. Byatt, A. S.
CROCODILES
  VanderMeer, J. Experiment #25 from the book
    of winter
  Wolfe, G. The dead man
Crone, Moira
  The kudzu
    The Ohio Review no62/63 p153-9 2001
  Where what gets into people comes from
    New stories from the South: the year's best,
    2001; edited by Shannon Ravenel; with a
    preface by Lee Smith
Crooks. Doenges, J.
Crooktails. Lao She
Croque-Mitaine. Chopin, K.
CROQUET
  Maron, M. Croquet summer
Crosley. Engstrom, E.
Cross, Amanda
  The double-barreled gun
    Murder and obsession; edited by Otto Penzler
  My dinner with Aunt Kate
    Malice domestic 8
  The perfect revenge
    Irreconcilable differences; Lia Matera, editor
The **cross** and the candle. L'Amour, L.
Cross country. Wallace, R.
Cross-fertilization. Arancio, L.
The **cross** on the church tower. Alcott, L. M.
Crossbones. Michaels, L.
Crossing. Ortiz, S. J.
Crossing. White, M. C.
Crossing. See Divakaruni, C. B. The intelligence
  of wild things
Crossing over. Stolar, D.
Crossing Shattuck Bridge. Sanford, A.
Crossing St. Gotthard. Leavitt, D.
Crossing the River Zbrucz. Babel´, I.
Crossing the water. Stevenson, J.
Crossroads blues. Gay, W.
CROSSWORD PUZZLES
  Paz Soldán, E. Dochera
Crouse, David
  Code
    The Massachusetts Review v45 no1 p108-28
    Spr 2004
Crow girls. De Lint, C.
CROW INDIANS
  Aadland, D. East breeze
Crowded lives. Howard, C.
Crowe, John, 1924-
    For works written by this author under oth-
    er names see Collins, Michael, 1924-
Crowell, Elizabeth
  Perfectly good
    Hers 2: brilliant new fiction by lesbian writ-
    ers; edited by Terry Wolverton with Robert
    Drake

Crowley, John
  Antiquities
    Crowley, J. Novelties and souvenirs; collected
    short fiction; John Crowley
  An earthly mother sits and sings
    Crowley, J. Novelties and souvenirs; collected
    short fiction; John Crowley
    Death dines at 8:30; edited by Claudia Bishop
    and Nick DiChario
  Exogamy
    Crowley, J. Novelties and souvenirs; collected
    short fiction; John Crowley
  Gone
    The Best from fantasy & science fiction: the
    fiftieth anniversary anthology; edited by
    Edward L. Ferman and Gordon Van Gelder
    Brown, C. N. and Strahan, J. The Locus
    awards; thirty years of the best in science
    fiction and fantasy; edited by Charles N.
    Brown and Jonathan Strahan
    Crowley, J. Novelties and souvenirs; collected
    short fiction; John Crowley
  Great work of time
    Crowley, J. Novelties and souvenirs; collected
    short fiction; John Crowley
  The green child
    Crowley, J. Novelties and souvenirs; collected
    short fiction; John Crowley
  Her bounty to the dead
    Crowley, J. Novelties and souvenirs; collected
    short fiction; John Crowley
  In blue
    Crowley, J. Novelties and souvenirs; collected
    short fiction; John Crowley
  Lost and abandoned
    Crowley, J. Novelties and souvenirs; collected
    short fiction; John Crowley
  Missolonghi 1824
    Crowley, J. Novelties and souvenirs; collected
    short fiction; John Crowley
  The nightingale sings at night
    Crowley, J. Novelties and souvenirs; collected
    short fiction; John Crowley
  Novelty
    Crowley, J. Novelties and souvenirs; collected
    short fiction; John Crowley
  The reason for the visit
    Crowley, J. Novelties and souvenirs; collected
    short fiction; John Crowley
  Snow
    Crowley, J. Novelties and souvenirs; collected
    short fiction; John Crowley
    Masterpieces: the best science fiction of the
    century; edited by Orson Scott Card
  The war between the objects and the subjects
    Crowley, J. Novelties and souvenirs; collected
    short fiction; John Crowley
Crowley, Kathleen
Listening for Carl
    The Literary Review (Madison, N.J.) v44 no3
    p475-84 Spr 2001
The **Crown** Derby plate. Bowen, M.
The **crown** on prince. López, L.
Crownfield, David
  Reasons
    The North American Review v284 no5 p22
    S/O 1999
CROWS
  Frazier, I. Tomorrow's bird

CROWS—*Continued*
Yasrebi, C. Love and scream
Crowther, Peter
The allotment
  The World's finest mystery and crime stories, second annual collection; edited by Ed Gorman
Bedfordshire
  Gathering the bones; original stories from the world's masters of horror; edited by Dennis Etchison, Ramsey Campbell and Jack Dann
Cat on an old school roof
  Cat crimes through time; edited by Ed Gorman, Martin H. Greenberg, and Larry Segriff
Dark times
  The World's finest mystery and crime stories, first annual collection; edited by Ed Gorman
The main event
  Murder most delectable; savory tales of culinary crimes; edited by Martin H. Greenberg
Shatsi
  The Year's best fantasy & horror, thirteenth annual collection; edited by Ellen Datlow and Terri Windling
Songs of leaving
  Mardi Gras madness; tales of terror and mayhem in New Orleans; edited by Martin H. Greenberg and Russell Davis
Things I didn't know my father knew
  Past imperfect; edited by Martin H. Greenberg and Larry Segriff
The **Croxley** Master. Doyle, Sir A. C.
Crucible. Lisberger, J.
The **crucifix**. Tozzi, F.
CRUCIFIXION
Bisson, T. The old rugged cross
The **cruel** redeemer Lazarus Morell. Borges, J. L.
The **cruel** sky. Clarke, A. C.
The **cruelest** month. Kelly, J. P.
CRUELTY
  See also Atrocities; Violence
Alderete, P. Fire
Borges, J. L. The cruel redeemer Lazarus Morell
Cobb, W. J. The white tatto
Coyne, J. Snow man
Doran, M. M. End October
Gunn, K. Visitor
Gwyn, A. Dog on the cross
Ha Jin. Emperor
Jones, T. The roadrunner
Matthews, C. To make a rabbit sing
Mayo, W. Overtures
McBain, E. Happy New Year, Herbie
Swanwick, M. Radiant doors
CRUELTY TO CHILDREN *See* Child abuse
Cruise, Cathy
Other people's lives
  Michigan Quarterly Review v40 no1 p101-18 Wint 2001
Cruise. Burgin, R.
Cruise. Waugh, E.
The **cruise** of The **Jolly Roger**. Vonnegut, K.
A **cruise** to forget. Collins, B. and Collins, M. A.

Crumey, Andrew
Pfitz [excerpt]
  The Vintage book of contemporary Scottish fiction; edited and with an introduction by Peter Kravitz
Crumley, James
Coming around the mountain
  The Mysterious Press anniversary anthology; celebrating 25 years; by the editors of Mysterious Press
Hostages
  The Best American mystery stories, 2003; edited by Michael Connelly and Otto Penzler
Hot Springs
  The Best American mystery stories of the century; Tony Hillerman, editor; with an introduction by Tony Hillerman
  Speaking of lust; stories of forbidden desire; edited by Lawrence Block
The Mexican pig bandit
  Murder and obsession; edited by Otto Penzler
Motherlove
  Esquire v135 no1 p82-3 Ja 2001
Whores
  Graham, D. Lone Star literature; from the Red River to the Rio Grande; edited by Don Graham
Crusade. Clarke, A. C.
CRUSADES
  See also Knights and knighthood
Crush. Foster, K.
Crutches used as weapon. Derby, M.
Crux. Cowdrey, A. E.
The **crux**. Gilman, C. P.
The **cry**. Robotham, R.
Cry about a nickel. Everett, P. L.
Cry silence. Brown, F.
Cry wolf. Spielberg, P.
Crybaby butch. Frank, J.
CRYOGENICS *See* Low temperatures
CRYONICS
Dick, P. K. I hope I shall arrive soon
Morrell, D. Resurrection
Cryptology. Michaels, L.
CUBA
Arango, A. The waiting room
Arenas, R. Traitor
Benítez-Rojo, A. Skin deep
Brackenbury, R. Cuba run
Cardoso, O. J. The storyteller
Correa, A. Spy's fate
Fernandez, P. A. The charm
Kurlansky, M. Devaluation
Mejides, M. The tropics
Menendez, A. Her mother's house
Michaels, L. Viva la Tropicana
Obejas, A. Waters
Piñera, V. The Great Baro
Ponte Landa, M. Blind madness
Sarduy, S. Curriculum cubense
       Prisoners and prisons
      See Prisoners and prisons—Cuba
          Havana
Arenas, R. In the shade of the almond tree
Arenas, R. The parade begins
Barnet, M. Miosvatis
Benítez-Rojo, A. Buried statues
Cabrera Infante, G. The great ekbó

CUBA—Havana—*Continued*

Cabrera Infante, G. Guilty of dancing the chachachá

Cabrera Infante, G. A woman saved from drowning

Gifford, B. The old days

Gutiérrez, P. J. Nothing to do

Padura Fuentes, L. The hunter

Pearlman, D. D. The drang of speaking forth

Ponte, A. J. Coming

Ponte, A. J. Heart of skitalietz

CUBAN AMERICANS

Asendorf, A. G. The gossamer girl

Menendez, A. Baseball dreams

Menendez, A. Confusing the saints

Menendez, A. In Cuba I was a German shepherd

Menendez, A. The last rescue

Menendez, A. The party

Menendez, A. The perfect fruit

Menendez, A. Story of a parrot

Mestre, E. After Elián

CUBAN REFUGEES

Arenas, R. End of a story

Arenas, R. The parade begins

CUBANS

Italy

Bobes, M. Ten years later

Russia

Ponte, A. J. Coming

Ponte, A. J. Tears in the Congri

United States

Arenas, R. End of a story

Arenas, R. The glass tower

Casal, L. A love story according to Cyrano Prufrock

Michaels, L. Viva la Tropicana

Valeri, L. A rafter in Miami Beach

Valeri, L. Whatever he did, he did enough

Cubicles. Maliszewski, P.

Cuckle me. Kaplan, H.

The **cuckoo**. Škvorecký, J.

The **cuckoo's** boys. Reed, R.

Cuddling. Walker, A.

Cul-de-sac. Smith, J.

Cul-de-sac (uncompleted). Bail, M.

Cul-de-sacs. Poirier, M. J.

Culinary lesson. Castellanos, R.

Cullin, Mitch

The cosmology of Bing [excerpt]

Circa 2000; gay fiction at the millennium; edited by Robert Drake & Terry Wolverton

The **cult** of the Phoenix. Borges, J. L.

CULTS

Borges, J. L. The cult of the Phoenix

Doctorow, E. L. Walter John Harmon

Helfers, J. Farewell to the flesh

Henley, P. The birthing

Lovecraft, H. P. The call of cthulhu

McBrearty, R. G. The unfolding

Mokoso, N. God of meme

Pickard, N. Speak no evil

Weinberg, R. Chant

Westlake, D. E. Come again?

CULTURE CONFLICT

Bowles, P. Here to learn

Bowles, P. Pastor Dowe at Tacate

Byatt, A. S. Crocodile tears

Coskran, K. Sun

Depew, D. R. Indigenous girls

Desai, A. Winterscape

Divakaruni, C. B. Mrs. Dutta writes a letter

Ekstrom, L. S. On Sunday there might be Americans

Gabriel, D. The kapici's wife

Ha Jin. After Cowboy Chicken came to town

Houghteling, M. K. Ma Kamanda's latrine

Jen, G. Who's Irish?

Johnson-Davies, D. Two worlds

Kurlansky, M. Packets and paperscraps

Kurlansky, M. The white man in the tree

Lahiri, J. Mrs. Sen's

Luntta, K. A virgin twice

Marshall, T. American model

Oz, A. Nomad and viper

Packer, G. The water-girl

Silko, L. Lullaby

Steiner, H. Rice

Sumner, M. The guide

Thien, M. A map of the city

Vinge, V. Conquest by default

A **cultured** boy. Dinh, L.

Culver, Timothy J.

For works written by this author under other names see Westlake, Donald E.

Cummings, John Michael

Fourteen seconds

The North American Review v286 no3/4 p26-31 My/Ag 2001

Cummins, Ann

Billy by the bay

Cummins, A. Red ant house; stories

Bitterwater

Cummins, A. Red ant house; stories

Blue fly

Cummins, A. Red ant house; stories

Crazy yellow

Cummins, A. Red ant house; stories

Dr. War is a voice on the phone

Cummins, A. Red ant house; stories

Headhunter

Cummins, A. Red ant house; stories

The hypnotist's trailer

Cummins, A. Red ant house; stories

The red ant house

The Best American short stories, 2002; selected from U.S. and Canadian magazines by Sue Miller with Katrina Kenison, with an introduction by Sue Miller

Cummins, A. Red ant house; stories

The Shiprock Fair

Cummins, A. Red ant house; stories

Starburst

Cummins, A. Red ant house; stories

Trapeze

Cummins, A. Red ant house; stories

Where I work

Cummins, A. Red ant house; stories

Cunningham, Eugene

Beginner's luck

Cunningham, E. Trails west; western stories

Blotting the triangle

Cunningham, E. Trails west; western stories

The hammer thumb

Cunningham, E. Trails west; western stories

The hermit of Tigerhead Butte

Cunningham, E. Trails west; western stories

Cunningham, Eugene—*Continued*

The ranger way
  Cunningham, E. Trails west; western stories
Spiderweb trail
  Cunningham, E. Trails west; western stories
The trail of a fool
  Cunningham, E. Trails west; western stories
Wanted—?
  Cunningham, E. Trails west; western stories
Ware calls it a day
  Cunningham, E. Trails west; western stories

Cunningham, John M.

The tin star
  A Century of great Western stories; edited by
  John Jakes

Cunningham, Michael

Mister Brother
  Prize stories, 1999; The O. Henry awards; ed-
  ited and with an introduction by Larry
  Dark
White angel
  The Scribner anthology of contemporary short
  fiction; fifty North American stories since
  1970; Lex Williford and Michael Martone,
  editors
  The Workshop; seven decades of the Iowa
  Writers' Workshop: 42 stories, recollections
  & essays on Iowa's place in 20th-century
  American literature; edited by Tom Grimes

Cunningham, Michael and others

Murder at the Beau Rivage
  The Paris Review v44 p217-36 Wint 2002

A **cup** of cold water. Wharton, E.

A **cup** of tea. Lavin, M.

Cupids arrow. Cannell, D.

The **cure**. Barrett, A.

The **cure**. Mo Yan

The **cure** for everything. Park, S.

Cures. Hunt, S.

The **curious** case of Benjamin Button. Fitzgerald,
  F. S.

The **curious** case of Benjamin Button, 3w. Brownstein, G.

The **curious** case of Miss Violet Stone. Brite, P.
  Z. and Ferguson, D.

A **curious** experience. Twain, M.

The **curious** facts preceding my execution. Westlake, D. E.

Curly Hamson Learns How to Eat. Schiffman, C.

Curly red. Oates, J. C.

Currency. Alessio, C.

Curriculum cubense. Sarduy, S.

Currier, Jameson

Pasta night
  Circa 2000; gay fiction at the millennium; edited by Robert Drake & Terry Wolverton

Curry, Peggy Simson

Geranium house
  A Century of great Western stories; edited by
  John Jakes

The **curry** leaf tree. Nair, M.

The **curse**. Guerrero, L.

The **curse**. See Clarke, A. C. Nightfall

The **curse** of the horse race. Waugh, E.

The **curse** of the unborn dead. Wilson, D. A.

CURSES

Alcott, L. M. Lost in a pyramid; or, The Mummy's Curse
Edghill, R. Haut-Clare

Greenberg, M. H. A literary death
Guerrero, L. The curse
Kelly, J. P. Hubris
Kilpatrick, N. and Bisson, B. The children of
  Gael
Rice, A. The mummy; or, Ramses the damned
Scarborough, E. A. Worse than the curse

Curtain call. Braunbeck, G. A.

Curtains. Nyren, R.

Curtains. Vachss, A. H.

Curtis, Rebecca

Big Bear, California
  Harper's v305 p82-7 Jl 2002
The deep red cremation of Isaac and Grace
  The Antioch Review v60 no2 p287-91 Spr
  2002
Hungry self
  The New Yorker v77 no17 p70-5 Jl 2 2001

Curtis, Rebecca

Hungry self
  What are you looking at?; the first fat fiction
  anthology; edited by Donna Jarrell and Ira
  Sukrungruang

Curvature. Richmond, M.

Curved is the line of beauty. Mantel, H.

Cush. Barrett, N., Jr.

Cushman, Dan

Killers' country!
  A Century of great Western stories; edited by
  John Jakes

Cushman, Steve

Me and Dr. Bob
  100% pure Florida fiction; an anthology; edited by Susan Hubbard and Robley Wilson

Cusk, Rachel

After Caravaggio's Sacrifice of Isaac
  Granta no81 p101-6 Spr 2003
The way you do it
  Granta no78 p85-96 Summ 2002

Cusp. Yuknavitch, L.

CUSTER, ELIZABETH BACON, 1842-1933
                   About
Salzer, S. K. Miss Libbie tells all

CUSTER, GEORGE ARMSTRONG, 1839-1876
                   About
Billman, J. Custer on Mondays
Salzer, S. K. Miss Libbie tells all
Swarthout, G. F. A horse for Mrs. Custer
Tarnished glory
Waldrop, H. Custer's last jump!

Custer complex. Billman, J.

Custer on Mondays. Billman, J.

Custer's last jump!. Waldrop, H.

Custody. Painter, P.

CUSTODY OF CHILDREN
Bell, M. S. Customs of the country
Stuckey-French, E. Plywood rabbit

Custom-made bride. Vonnegut, K.

The **custom** of the country. Brady, C.

Customs of the country. Bell, M. S.

The **cut-glass** bowl. Fitzgerald, F. S.

Cute in camouflage. Carter, E.

Cutler, Judith

Doctor's orders
  The best British mysteries; edited by Maxim
  Jakubowski

Cutrufelli, Maria Rosa
Happiness
In the forbidden city; an anthology of erotic fiction by Italian women; edited by Maria Rosa Cutrufelli; translated by Vincent J. Bertolini
Cutter, Leah
The red boots
Black heart, ivory bones; [edited by] Ellen Datlow & Terri Windling
Cutter, Leah R.
Obsessions
Tetrick, B. In the shadow of the wall; an anthology of Vietnam stories that might have been; edited by Byron R. Tetrick
Cuxabexis, Cuxabexis. Robinson, L.
Cyber-Claus. Gibson, W.
Cybermorphic beat-up get-down subterranean homesick reality-sandwich blues. Olsen, L.
CYBERNETICS
See also Bionics
Oliver, C. Blood's a rover
Rojo, P. Gray noise
CYBORGS *See* Bionics
The **cyclist** from San Cristóbal. See Skármeta, A. The cyclist of San Cristóbal Hill
The **cyclist** of San Cristóbal Hill. Skármeta, A.
CYPRUS
Davidson, A. The ikon of Elijah
The **Cyrillic** Alphabet. Thirlwell, A.
CZECH REPUBLIC
See also Czechoslovakia
Davenport, G. The chair
Fischerová, D. My conversations with Aunt Marie
Hamburger, A. The view from Statlin's Head
Shepley, J. A golem in Prague
Politics
See Politics—Czech Republic
Prague
Bukiet, M. J. The two Franzes
Fischerová, D. Boarskin dances down the tables
Fischerová, D. Far and near
Fischerová, D. A letter for President Eisenhower
Hamburger, A. Control
Hamburger, A. Exile
Hamburger, A. Garage sale
Hamburger, A. Jerusalem
Hamburger, A. A man of the country
Hamburger, A. Sympathetic conversationalist
Hamburger, A. This ground you are standing on
Hamburger, A. You say you want a revolution
Melville, P. The migration of ghosts
Phillips, A. Wenceslas Square
Škvorecký, J. The end of Bull Macha
Škvorecký, J. Filthy cruel world
Škvorecký, J. My Uncle Kohn
Škvorecký, J. Pink champagne
Škvorecký, J. Song of forgotten years
Škvorecký, J. Spectator on a February night
CZECHOSLOVAKIA
See also Czech Republic
Hamburger, A. The view from Statlin's Head
Škvorecký, J. A magic mountain and a willowy wench
Škvorecký, J. A remarkable chemical phenomenon
Škvorecký, J. Three bachelors in a fiery furnace
Škvorecký, J. Why do people have soft noses?

CZECHS
Canada
Škvorecký, J. According to Poe
Škvorecký, J. Jezebel from Forest Hill (A love story)
Škvorecký, J. A magic mountain and a willowy wench
Škvorecký, J. The mysterious events at night
Škvorecký, J. Wayne's hero (An English story)
India
Fischerová, D. Dhum
Scotland
Dunn, D. The political piano
United States
Bradbury, R. The watchful poker chip of H. Matisse
Cherry, K. Chores
Czerneda, Julie
First Contact Inc.
Wondrous beginnings; edited by Steven H. Silver and Martin H. Greenberg
Czesniki. Babel′, I.
Czezarley Zoo gets out. Skillings, R. D.
Czuchlewski, David
The theory of everything
The Kenyon Review ns24 no2 p135-49 Spr 2002

D

Da capo. LaPierre, J.
Da Vinci, Leonardo *See* Leonardo, da Vinci, 1452-1519
Da Vinci rising. Dann, J.
Dabydeen, Cyril
Swimming with Chairman Mao
World Literature Today v78 no2 p63-6 My/Ag 2004
Daddy dearest. Cady, J.
Daddy Mention and the Monday skull. Duncan, A.
Daddy's girl. Jones, T.
Daddy's world. Williams, W. J.
Dadmun, Bentley
Annie's dream
The Best American mystery stories, 2000; edited and with an introduction by Donald E. Westlake
The **Daffodil.** Meyers, A. and Meyers, M.
Dagger. Jakes, J.
Dagon's bell. Lumley, B.
Daguerreotypy. Scheid, S.
The **daguerrotype.** Whitty, J.
D'Aguiar, Fred
Triptych
Bomb no82 p90-4 Wint 2002/2003
Daheim, Mary
Just so much garbage
Malice domestic 8
Dahlie, Michael
Young Collectors' Day
Ploughshares v28 no2/3 p38-60 Fall 2002
Daily Double. MacAvoy, S.
Dain, Catherine
Mirror, mirror
Flesh and blood: guilty as sin; erotic tales of crime and passion; edited by Max Allan Collins and Jeff Gelb
Daisy. Lee, C.-R.

Daisy and the Christmas goose. Perry, A.

Daisy Miller: a study. James, H.

DAKOTA INDIANS
    Graebner, J. E. The whispering
    Power, S. A hole in the sheets

Daldorph, Brian
    On the road
        The North American Review v287 no2 p27-9
        Mr/Ap 2002

Daley's girls. Brady, C.

DALLAS (TEX.) *See* Texas—Dallas

Dallas. Sánchez, R.

Dalliance at Sunnydale. Collins, B.

Dalton, Quinn
    Lennie Remembers the Angels
        The Kenyon Review v26 no2 p38-55 Spr 2004

Dalton's box. Barry, D.

Daly, Carroll John
    Just another stiff
        A Century of noir; thirty-two classic crime
        stories; edited by Mickey Spillane and Max
        Allan Collins

Dalyrimple goes wrong. Fitzgerald, F. S.

Damage. Stephens, M.

D'Amato, Barbara
    Motel 66
        The Best American mystery stories, 2000; ed-
        ited and with an introduction by Donald E.
        Westlake
    Of course you know that chocolate is a vegeta-
    ble
        Crème de la crime; edited by Janet Hutchings
        Murder most delectable; savory tales of culi-
        nary crimes; edited by Martin H. Greenberg
    Steak tartare
        Death dines at 8:30; edited by Claudia Bishop
        and Nick DiChario

D'Ambrosio, Charles
    The High Divide
        The New Yorker v78 no45 p76-83 F 3 2003
    Screenwriter
        The New Yorker v79 no38 p112-21 D 8 2003

D'Ambrosio, Charles, Jr.
    Drummond & Son
        The New Yorker v78 no30 p84-92 O 7 2002
    Open house
        The Workshop; seven decades of the Iowa
        Writers' Workshop: 42 stories, recollections
        & essays on Iowa's place in 20th-century
        American literature; edited by Tom Grimes

Damon and Vandalia. Dove, R.

Damp walls. Blatnik, A.

Dams, Jeanne M.
    Remember the Maine?
        White House pet detectives; tales of crime
        and mystery at the White House from a
        pet's-eye view; edited by Carole Nelson
        Douglas

DAMS
    Earley, T. The prophet from Jupiter

Dance band on the Titanic. Chalker, J. L.

DANCE HALLS
    DeLancey, K. Swingtime
    Kees, W. Gents 50/Ladies 25

Dance in blue. Asaro, C.

Dance of eights. Mayo, W.

The **dance** of the Apsara. Richter, J.

Dance of the cranes. Allegra, D.

Dance of the dolphins. Mattingly, K.

Dance of the yellow-breasted Luddites. Shunn, W.

Dance recital for the men of the American Legion
    in April. Anderson, C.

A **dance** to strange musics. Benford, G.

Dance with death. Tarrera, C.

The **dancer**. Parekh, A.

DANCERS
    Allegra, D. The birthday presence
    Allegra, D. Bread from a stone
    Allegra, D. Dance of the cranes
    Allegra, D. Einbahnstrasse
    Allegra, D. God lies in the details
    Allegra, D. In a pig's eye
    Allegra, D. Low-impact aerobics
    Allegra, D. Me and Mrs. Jones
    Allegra, D. Navigating by stars
    Allegra, D. Sacrament in the wind and the storm
    Allegra, D. Snatched
    Allegra, D. Witness to the league of blond hip
        hop dancers
    Cavin, R. The Mechanique affair
    Davies, R. The forty-eight-bar bridge
    Kennedy, A. In our part of the world
    Leong, R. Camouflage
    Melville, P. The duende
    Nissen, T. The mushroom girl
    Silber, J. The high road
    Silber, J. My shape
    Smith, B. B. Death of a damn moose
    Solwitz, S. Ballerina
    Vasseur, T. J. The woman who sugared straw-
        berries
    Wang Anyi. Life in a small courtyard
    Whitaker, A. The trespasser

DANCING
    Bloch, A. Learning the hula
    Bonman, I. Mrs. Website's dance
    Bradbury, R. Bug
    Bukoski, A. It had to be you
    Coward, M. You can jump
    Crider, B. and Crider, J. At the hop
    Davies, R. Holiday romance
    Douglas, C. N. Dirty dancing
    DuBois, B. Dancing the night away
    Easton, R. O. Nobody danced
    Friedman, M. Tango is my life
    Goldner, B. Taxi dancer
    Kerslake, L. Lookin' 'n' jivin'
    Lee, A. Dancing with Josefina
    Leslie, N. Rain dance
    Lutz, J. Tango was her life
    Murguía, A. A lesson in merengue
    Richter, J. The dance of the Apsara
    Richter, S. Prom night
    Slesar, H. Change partners
    Tarrera, C. Dance with death
    Vaswani, N. The rigors of dance lessons
    Watanabe McFerrin, L. Khalida's dog

The **Dancing** Floor. Wilder, C.

Dancing in the ashes. Friesen, R. E.

Dancing Lessons. Ward, L.

Dancing men. Hirshberg, G.

Dancing naked. Bean, B.

The **Dancing** Party. Gordon, M.

Dancing the night away. DuBois, B.

Dancing with father. Flynt, C.

Dancing with Josefina. Lee, A.

Dancing with Lawrence of Arabia. Leslie, N.

Dancing with the one-armed gal. Gautreaux, T.

Dandelion Summer. Malin, A.
DANES

    See also Vikings
Haiti
Kurlansky, M. The white man in the tree
Danger, Nick
  8-3-oh
    Death dines at 8:30; edited by Claudia Bishop
    and Nick DiChario
Dangerous company. Bart, P.
A **dangerous** hobby. Highsmith, P.
Dangerous waters. Painter, P.
Dangerously the summer burns. Cioffari, P.
Daniel, Susanna
  We are cartographers
    Best new American voices 2001; guest editor
    Charles Baxter; series editors John Kulka
    and Natalie Danford
Daniel, Tony
  A dry, quiet war
    The Good new stuff; adventure SF in the
    grand tradition; edited by Gardner Dozois
  Grist
    The Year's best science fiction, sixteenth an-
    nual collection; edited by Gardner Dozois
Daniel Webster and the sea serpent. Benét, S. V.
Daniels, Jim
  Bonus
    Daniels, J. Detroit tales; [by] Jim Ray Daniels
  Christmasmobile
    Daniels, J. Detroit tales; [by] Jim Ray Daniels
  Cross country
    Daniels, J. Detroit tales; [by] Jim Ray Daniels
  Fireworks
    Daniels, J. Detroit tales; [by] Jim Ray Daniels
  Good neighbor
    Daniels, J. Detroit tales; [by] Jim Ray Daniels
  Islands
    Daniels, J. Detroit tales; [by] Jim Ray Daniels
  The Jimmy Stewart story
    Daniels, J. Detroit tales; [by] Jim Ray Daniels
  Karaoke moon
    Daniels, J. Detroit tales; [by] Jim Ray Daniels
  Middle of the mitten
    Daniels, J. Detroit tales; [by] Jim Ray Daniels
  Minding the store
    Daniels, J. Detroit tales; [by] Jim Ray Daniels
  Renegade
    Daniels, J. Detroit tales; [by] Jim Ray Daniels
  Sugar water
    Daniels, J. Detroit tales; [by] Jim Ray Daniels
Daniels, Lucy
  Virtuoso
    Confrontation no86/87 p96-108 Spr/Summ
    2004
Danihy, Geary
  Jumping with Jim
    The Best American mystery stories, 2000; ed-
    ited and with an introduction by Donald E.
    Westlake
Dann, Jack
  Bad medicine
    Dann, J. Jubilee
  The black horn
    Dann, J. Jubilee
  Blind shemmy
    Dann, J. Jubilee
  Camps
    Dann, J. Jubilee

Da Vinci rising
  Dann, J. Jubilee
The diamond pit
  Dann, J. Jubilee
The extra
  Dann, J. Jubilee
Fairy tale
  Dann, J. Jubilee
Going under
  Dann, J. Jubilee
Jubilee
  Dann, J. Jubilee
Jumping the road
  Dann, J. Jubilee
Kaddish
  Dann, J. Jubilee
Marilyn
  Dann, J. Jubilee
  Death dines at 8:30; edited by Claudia Bishop
  and Nick DiChario
A quiet revolution for death
  Dann, J. Jubilee
Spirit dog
  The Crow; shattered lives & broken dreams;
  edited by J. O'Barr and Ed Kramer
Tattoos
  Dann, J. Jubilee
Tea
  Dann, J. Jubilee
Ting-a-ling
  Redshift; extreme visions of speculative fic-
  tion; edited by Al Sarrantonio
Voices
  Dann, J. Jubilee
Dann. Gold, M. A.
Dannay, Frederic, 1905-1982
    *For works written by this author in collab-
    oration with Manfred Lee see Queen,
    Ellery*
Danny and me. Evanier, D.
DANTE ALIGHIERI, 1265-1321
About
  Vivante, A. Dante
Dante Street. Babel´, I.
Danticat, Edwidge
  The book of the dead
    The New Yorker v75 no16 p194-99 Je 21-28
    1999
  Night talkers
    The Best American short stories, 2003; select-
    ed from U.S. and Canadian magazines by
    Walter Mosley with Katrina Kenison; with
    an introduction by Walter Mosley
    Callaloo v25 no4 p1007-20 Fall 2002
  Night women
    The Art of the story; an international antholo-
    gy of contemporary short stories; edited by
    Daniel Halpern
    The Bluelight corner; black women writing on
    passion, sex, and romantic love; edited by
    Rosemarie Robotham
  Nineteen thirty-seven
    The Oxford book of Caribbean short stories;
    edited by Stewart Brown and John
    Wickham

Danticat, Edwidge—*Continued*
Seven
The Best American short stories, 2002; selected from U.S. and Canadian magazines by Sue Miller with Katrina Kenison, with an introduction by Sue Miller
The New Yorker v77 no29 p88-97 O 1 2001
Tatiana, Mon Amour
Callaloo v27 no2 p439-53 Spr 2004
DANUBE RIVER
Blackwood, A. The willows
Dapple: a hwarhath historical romance. Arnason, E.
Darby, Ann
Pity My Simplicity
Prairie Schooner v77 no2 p3-14 Summ 2003
Dark, Alice Elliott
Close
Fault lines; stories of divorce; collected and edited by Caitlin Shetterly
In the gloaming
The Best American short stories of the century; John Updike, editor, Katrina Kenison, coeditor; with an introduction by John Updike
Watch the animals
Harper's v299 no1792 p91-96 S 1999
Prize stories, 2000; The O. Henry awards; edited and with an introduction by Larry Dark
DARK AGES *See* Middle Ages
Dark blue. Berkman, P. R.
Dark corner. Morgan, R.
The **dark** downstairs. Conrad, R. L.
A **dark** fire, burning from within. What, L.
Dark is not a single shade of gray. Hochman, A.
Dark lady. Landis, G. A.
Dark matter. Cobb, W. J.
Dark mirror. Henderson, L.
A **dark** night. Jones, E. P.
The **dark** prince. Oates, J. C.
Dark purpose. DeRosso, H. A.
The **dark** snow. DuBois, B.
Dark society. Aldiss, B. W.
The **dark** star. Tenn, W.
Dark they were, and golden-eyed. Bradbury, R.
Dark times. Crowther, P.
Dark times. Jones, G.
The **dark** tower. Moffat, G.
The **Dark** Tower. Pipik, J. and Vargo, J.
Dark valley. Yi, T.-H.
The **dark** watcher. Steinbeck, T.
Darkening of the world. Westmoreland, T. A.
Darkness. McKiernan, D. L.
The **darkness** of the deep. Miller, R.
The **Darkness** Together. Almond, S.
Darkrose and Diamond. Le Guin, U. K.
The **darling**. Chekhov, A. P.
Darling?. Schmidt, H. J.
Darlington, Tenaya
Preservation
Bomb no75 p102-5 Spr 2001
Darrell's garage. Jackson, V. F.
Darton, Eric
Certain amazing adventures of Mr. Hoel
New England Review v22 no2 p165-76 Spr 2001

Chronicle of the ship of fools
New England Review v20 no2 p138-46 Spr 1999
Darvasi, László
Pages from the black notebook
Grand Street no69 p6-14 Summ 1999
DARWIN, CHARLES, 1809-1882
About
Gardner, J. A. Three hearings on the existence of snakes in the human bloodstream
Whitty, J. Darwin in heaven
Darwin in heaven. Whitty, J.
Darwinian facts. Malzberg, B. N.
The **dat**. Dixon, S.
DATING (SOCIAL CUSTOMS)
Almond, S. The evil B. B. Chow
Avrich, J. Literary lonelyhearts
Bank, M. The wonder spot
Barker, N. G-string
Barker, N. Limpets
Boswell, M. Venus/Mars
Budnitz, J. Hook, line and sinker
Carter, E. Glory goes and gets some
Cohen, R. Good with girls
De Lint, C. Trading hearts at the Half Kaffe Cafe
Doble, J. After six weeks in New York
Edgerton, C. Debra's flap and snap
Grau, S. A. Homecoming
Hayes, D. Twenty-six hours, twenty-five minutes
Holman, J. Squabble
Keegan, C. Ride if you dare
Kusel, L. SWM
Porter, J. A. Schrekx and son
Richter, S. My date with Satan
Smith, J. Where the boys are
Spencer, E. A southern landscape
Strauss, A. Post-dated
Valeri, L. A rafter in Miami Beach
Valeri, L. She's anonymous
Weinreb, M. Bear claws the size of her head
Wexler, M. Helen of Alexandria
Zabytko, I. John Mars, all-American
Dating Miss Universe. Polansky, S.
Datum centurio. Wallace, D. F.
Dauenhauer, Nora
Egg boat
Fishing for chickens; short stories about rural youth; edited, with an introduction by Jim Heynen
Daugharty, Janice
Name of love
New stories from the South: the year's best, 1999; edited by Shannon Ravenel; with a preface by Tony Earley
Daugherty, Tracy
Assailable character
Texas bound. Book III; 22 Texas stories; edited by Kay Cattarulla; foreword by Robert Flynn
Comfort me with apples
The Southern Review (Baton Rouge, La.) v35 no4 p709-45 Aut 1999
The leavings of panic
Southwest Review v86 no2/3 p332-59 Spr/Summ 2001

Daugherty, Tracy—*Continued*

Superman
    The Southern Review (Baton Rouge, La.) v38
    no1 p93-100 Wint 2002

The **daughter**. Brkic, C. A.

A **daughter** of albion. Chekhov, A. P.

The **daughter** of Kadmos. Grushin, O.

DAUGHTERS *See* Fathers and daughters; Mothers and daughters; Stepdaughters

The **daughters**. Brennan, M.

Daughters. Leong, R.

Daughters. Orner, P.

Daughters. Robison, M.

DAUGHTERS-IN-LAW

  Aldrich, B. S. The runaway judge

  Chen, W. Trotters

  Cody, L. Indian throw

  Gavell, M. L. The last daughter-in-law

  Moss, B. K. Rug weaver

  Murphy, W. Motherly love

  Pak, W.-S. She knows, I know, and heaven knows

  Rash, R. Last rite

  Ritchie, E. A lovely day for tennis

  Waters, M. Y. Since my house burned down

  Willis, M. S. Tiny gorillas

The **daughter's** lamentation. Caponegro, M.

Daum, Meghan

Alternative lifestyle alert
    A different plain; contemporary Nebraska fiction writers; edited by Ladette Randolph ; introduction by Mary Pipher

The **daunt** Diana. Wharton, E.

Dave, Laura

London is the best city in America
    Gettysburg Review v14 no4 p561-5 Wint 2001

Davenport, Diana *See* Davenport, Kiana

Davenport, Guy

The aeroplanes at Brescia
    Davenport, G. The death of Picasso; new and selected writing

And
    Davenport, G. The death of Picasso; new and selected writing

Belinda's world tour
    Davenport, G. The death of Picasso; new and selected writing
    Home and beyond; an anthology of Kentucky short stories; edited by Morris Allen Grubbs; with an introduction by Wade Hall and an afterword by Charles E. May

The bicycle rider
    Davenport, G. The death of Picasso; new and selected writing

Boys smell like oranges
    Davenport, G. The death of Picasso; new and selected writing

The chair
    Davenport, G. The death of Picasso; new and selected writing

Christ preaching at the Henley Regatta
    Davenport, G. The death of Picasso; new and selected writing

The Concord sonata
    Davenport, G. The death of Picasso; new and selected writing

The death of Picasso
    Davenport, G. The death of Picasso; new and selected writing

Dinner at the Bank of England
    Davenport, G. The death of Picasso; new and selected writing

Gunnar and Nikolai
    Davenport, G. The death of Picasso; new and selected writing

The Jules Verne Steam balloon
    Davenport, G. The death of Picasso; new and selected writing

The messengers
    Davenport, G. The death of Picasso; new and selected writing

Mr. Churchyard and the troll
    Davenport, G. The death of Picasso; new and selected writing

The owl of Minerva
    Davenport, G. The death of Picasso; new and selected writing
    The Georgia Review v56 no2 p573-93 Summ 2002

The playing field
    Davenport, G. The death of Picasso; new and selected writing

The ringdove sign
    Davenport, G. The death of Picasso; new and selected writing

We often think of Lenin at the clothespin factory
    Davenport, G. The death of Picasso; new and selected writing

Wo es war, soll ich werden
    Davenport, G. The death of Picasso; new and selected writing

Davenport, Kiana

Bones of the inner ear
    The Best American short stories, 2000; selected from U.S. and Canadian magazines by E. L. Doctorow with Katrina Kenison; with an introduction by E. L. Doctorow
    Prize stories, 2000; The O. Henry awards; edited and with an introduction by Larry Dark

Fork used in eating Reverend Baker
    Prize stories, 1999; The O. Henry awards; edited and with an introduction by Larry Dark

Davenport, Stirling

Abba's mark
    The Darkest thirst; a vampire anthology

Dave's neckliss. Chesnutt, C. W.

David. Le Clézio, J.-M. G.

David. Maleti, G.

David and Alice: Seventeen Lines about the End of the World. Goldman, A. S.

David and Kitty. Burford, M.

David Swan. Hawthorne, N.

David's worm. Lumley, B.

Davidson, Avram

The account of Mr. Ira Davidson
    Davidson, A. The other nineteenth century; a story collection; edited by Grania Davis and Henry Wessells

Buchanan's head
    Davidson, A. The other nineteenth century; a story collection; edited by Grania Davis and Henry Wessells

Davidson, Avram—*Continued*
Business must be picking up
  Davidson, A. The other nineteenth century; a
    story collection; edited by Grania Davis
    and Henry Wessells
Captain Pasharooney
  Davidson, A. The investigations of Avram
    Davidson; edited by Grania Davis and
    Richard A. Lupoff
The cobblestones of Saratoga Street
  Davidson, A. The investigations of Avram
    Davidson; edited by Grania Davis and
    Richard A. Lupoff
The cost of Kent Castwell
  Davidson, A. The investigations of Avram
    Davidson; edited by Grania Davis and
    Richard A. Lupoff
The deed of the deft-footed dragon
  Davidson, A. The other nineteenth century; a
    story collection; edited by Grania Davis
    and Henry Wessells
  Davidson, A. The investigations of Avram
    Davidson; edited by Grania Davis and
    Richard A. Lupoff
Dr. Bhumbo Singh
  Davidson, A. The other nineteenth century; a
    story collection; edited by Grania Davis
    and Henry Wessells
Dragon skin drum
  Davidson, A. The other nineteenth century; a
    story collection; edited by Grania Davis
    and Henry Wessells
The engine of Samoset Erastus Hale, and one
    other, unknown
  Davidson, A. The other nineteenth century; a
    story collection; edited by Grania Davis
    and Henry Wessells
Great is Diana
  Davidson, A. The other nineteenth century; a
    story collection; edited by Grania Davis
    and Henry Wessells
The ikon of Elijah
  Davidson, A. The investigations of Avram
    Davidson; edited by Grania Davis and
    Richard A. Lupoff
The importance of trifles
  Davidson, A. The investigations of Avram
    Davidson; edited by Grania Davis and
    Richard A. Lupoff
The lineaments of gratified desire
  Davidson, A. The other nineteenth century; a
    story collection; edited by Grania Davis
    and Henry Wessells
The lord of Central Park
  Davidson, A. The investigations of Avram
    Davidson; edited by Grania Davis and
    Richard A. Lupoff
The man who saw the elephant
  Davidson, A. The other nineteenth century; a
    story collection; edited by Grania Davis
    and Henry Wessells
Mickelrede; or, The slayer and the staff
  Davidson, A. The other nineteenth century; a
    story collection; edited by Grania Davis
    and Henry Wessells
The Montavarde camera
  Davidson, A. The other nineteenth century; a
    story collection; edited by Grania Davis
    and Henry Wessells

Mr. Folsom feels fine
  Davidson, A. The investigations of Avram
    Davidson; edited by Grania Davis and
    Richard A. Lupoff
Murder is murder
  Davidson, A. The investigations of Avram
    Davidson; edited by Grania Davis and
    Richard A. Lupoff
The necessity of his condition
  Davidson, A. The investigations of Avram
    Davidson; edited by Grania Davis and
    Richard A. Lupoff
Now let us sleep
  Vanishing acts; a science fiction anthology;
    edited by Ellen Datlow
O brave old world!
  Davidson, A. The other nineteenth century; a
    story collection; edited by Grania Davis
    and Henry Wessells
The odd old bird
  Davidson, A. The other nineteenth century; a
    story collection; edited by Grania Davis
    and Henry Wessells
One morning with Samuel, Dorothy, and Wil-
    liam
  Davidson, A. The other nineteenth century; a
    story collection; edited by Grania Davis
    and Henry Wessells
Pebble in time
  Davidson, A. The other nineteenth century; a
    story collection; edited by Grania Davis
    and Henry Wessells
The Peninsula
  Davidson, A. The other nineteenth century; a
    story collection; edited by Grania Davis
    and Henry Wessells
A quiet room with a view
  Davidson, A. The investigations of Avram
    Davidson; edited by Grania Davis and
    Richard A. Lupoff
The singular incident of the dog on the beach
  Davidson, A. The other nineteenth century; a
    story collection; edited by Grania Davis
    and Henry Wessells
Summon the watch!
  Davidson, A. The other nineteenth century; a
    story collection; edited by Grania Davis
    and Henry Wessells
The third sacred well of the temple
  Davidson, A. The investigations of Avram
    Davidson; edited by Grania Davis and
    Richard A. Lupoff
Thou still unravished bride
  Davidson, A. The investigations of Avram
    Davidson; edited by Grania Davis and
    Richard A. Lupoff
Traveller from an antique land
  Davidson, A. The other nineteenth century; a
    story collection; edited by Grania Davis
    and Henry Wessells
Twenty-three
  The American fantasy tradition; edited by Bri-
    an M. Thomsen
  Davidson, A. The other nineteenth century; a
    story collection; edited by Grania Davis
    and Henry Wessells

Davidson, Avram—*Continued*

El Vilvoy de las islas

    Davidson, A. The other nineteenth century; a story collection; edited by Grania Davis and Henry Wessells

What strange stars and skies

    Davidson, A. The other nineteenth century; a story collection; edited by Grania Davis and Henry Wessells

Davidson, Avram and Davis, Grania

The Boss in the Wall: a treatise on the house devil

    Best new horror 10; edited and with an introduction by Stephen Jones

Davidson, Chad

(jt. auth) *See* Benni, Stefano

Davidson, Diane Mott

Cold turkey

    Death dines at 8:30; edited by Claudia Bishop and Nick DiChario

Davidson, Jean

A stone of destiny

    Royal whodunnits; edited by Mike Ashley

Davidson, Kurtis

Man with a Gun

    The North American Review v289 no3/4 p41-3 My/Ag 2004

Davidson, Lionel

Indian rope trick

    Edwards, M. Mysterious pleasures; a celebration of the Crime Writers' Association's 50th anniversary; edited by Martin Edwards

Davidson, Rob

Barnstorming

    Davidson, R. Field observations; stories

Body work

    Davidson, R. Field observations; stories

Field observations

    Davidson, R. Field observations; stories

The Hillside Slasher

    Davidson, R. Field observations; stories

Inventory

    Davidson, R. Field observations; stories

Maintenance

    Davidson, R. Field observations; stories

A private life

    Davidson, R. Field observations; stories

What we leave behind

    Davidson, R. Field observations; stories

You have to say something

    Davidson, R. Field observations; stories

Davies, Denys Johnson- *See* Johnson-Davies, Denys

Davies, Laurence

Run ragged

    Ghost writing; haunted tales by contemporary writers; edited by Roger Weingarten

Davies, Lewis

Mr. Roopratna's chocolate

    Mr. Roopratna's chocolate; the winning stories from the 1999 Rhys Davies competition

Davies, Peter Ho

The Bad Shepherd

    Ploughshares v29 no2/3 p12-20 Fall 2003

Brave girl

    Davies, P. H. Equal love; stories

Cakes of baby

    Davies, P. H. Equal love; stories

The ends

    The Paris Review v44 no162 p10-14 Summ 2002

Equal love

    Davies, P. H. Equal love; stories

Everything you can remember in thirty seconds is yours to keep

    Davies, P. H. Equal love; stories

Fit mother

    Granta no68 p93-104 Wint 1999

Frogmen

    Davies, P. H. Equal love; stories

How to be an expatriate

    Davies, P. H. Equal love; stories

The Hull case

    Davies, P. H. Equal love; stories

    Ploughshares v25 no2/3 p46-60 Fall 1999

The New Corporal

    The Virginia Quarterly Review v80 no3 p90-107 Summ 2004

The next life

    Davies, P. H. Equal love; stories

    Harper's v298 no1786 p72-75+ Mr 1999

On the terraces

    Davies, P. H. Equal love; stories

Sales

    Davies, P. H. Equal love; stories

Small world

    Davies, P. H. Equal love; stories

    Fault lines; stories of divorce; collected and edited by Caitlin Shetterly

Think of England

    The Best American short stories 2001; selected from U.S. and Canadian magazines by Barbara Kingsolver with Katrina Kenison; with an introduction by Barbara Kingsolver

Today is Sunday

    Davies, P. H. Equal love; stories

The ugliest house in the world

    The Antioch Review v59 no2 p208-23 Spr 2001

What you know

    Harper's v302 no1808 p82-9 Ja 2001

    On the rocks; the KGB Bar fiction anthology; edited by Rebecca Donner ; foreword by Denis Woychuk

Davies, Peter Ho.

The Criminal Mastermind Is Confined

    Harper's v308 p71-3 Ja 2004

Davies, Ray

Afternoon tea

    Davies, R. Waterloo sunset

Art lover

    Davies, R. Waterloo sunset

Celluloid heroes

    Davies, R. Waterloo sunset

The deal

    Davies, R. Waterloo sunset

Dreams

    Davies, R. Waterloo sunset

The forty-eight-bar bridge

    Davies, R. Waterloo sunset

Holiday romance

    Davies, R. Waterloo sunset

Home

    Davies, R. Waterloo sunset

A little bit of abuse

    Carved in rock; short stories by musicians; edited by Greg Kihn

Davies, Ray—*Continued*
Misfits
Davies, R. Waterloo sunset
Missing person
Davies, R. Waterloo sunset
Mr. Pleasant
Davies, R. Waterloo sunset
No more looking back
Davies, R. Waterloo sunset
Return to Waterloo
Davies, R. Waterloo sunset
Rock-and-roll fantasy
Davies, R. Waterloo sunset
The shirt
Davies, R. Waterloo sunset
Still searching
Davies, R. Waterloo sunset
Voices in the dark
Davies, R. Waterloo sunset
Waterloo sunset
Davies, R. Waterloo sunset
Where are they now?
Davies, R. Waterloo sunset

Davies, Rhys
The darling of her heart
Davies, R. A human condition
The dilemma of Catherine Fuchsias
Davies, R. A human condition
The Fashion Plate
Davies, R. A human condition
A human condition
Davies, R. A human condition
I will keep her company
Davies, R. A human condition
The sisters
Davies, R. A human condition
The song of songs
Davies, R. A human condition

Davies, Robertson
Offer of immortality
Northern suns; edited by David G. Hartwell
& Glenn Grant

Davies, William Robertson *See* Davies, Robertson, 1913-1995

Davies, Tristan
Alfalfa valve
Davies, Tristan. Cake; stories
Alias
Davies, Tristan. Cake; stories
Buena Vista notebook
Davies, Tristan. Cake; stories
Cake
Davies, Tristan. Cake; stories
Counterfactuals
Davies, Tristan. Cake; stories
Crazy Yvonne
Davies, Tristan. Cake; stories
Dan, Astrid says
Davies, Tristan. Cake; stories
Grouper Schmidt
Davies, Tristan. Cake; stories
In the woodlands
Davies, Tristan. Cake; stories
A night dive
Davies, Tristan. Cake; stories
On the night before her birthday
Davies, Tristan. Cake; stories

Personals
Davies, Tristan. Cake; stories
Snapdragon
Davies, Tristan. Cake; stories
Snowflake
Davies, Tristan. Cake; stories
Talent show
Davies, Tristan. Cake; stories
The tning itself
Davies, Tristan. Cake; stories

Davila, Amparo
The end of a struggle
Short stories by Latin American women; the
magic and the real; edited by Celia Correas
de Zapata; foreword by Isabel Allende

Davis, Amanda
Chase
Davis, A. Circling the drain; stories
Circling the drain
Davis, A. Circling the drain; stories
Crash
Davis, A. Circling the drain; stories
Ending things
Davis, A. Circling the drain; stories
Fairy tale
Davis, A. Circling the drain; stories
Faith; or, Tips for the successful young lady
Davis, A. Circling the drain; stories
Fat ladies floated in the sky like balloons
Davis, A. Circling the drain; stories
Louisiana loses its cricket hum
Best new American voices 2001; guest editor
Charles Baxter; series editors John Kulka
and Natalie Danford
Prints
Davis, A. Circling the drain; stories
Red lights like laughter
Davis, A. Circling the drain; stories
Spice
Davis, A. Circling the drain; stories
Sticks and stones
Davis, A. Circling the drain; stories
Testimony
Davis, A. Circling the drain; stories
True story
Davis, A. Circling the drain; stories
The very moment they're about
Davis, A. Circling the drain; stories
The visit
Davis, A. Circling the drain; stories

Davis, Carol Anne
Brand new boyfriend
The best British mysteries; edited by Maxim
Jakubowski
Not long now
The World's finest mystery and crime stories,
first annual collection; edited by Ed
Gorman

Davis, Claire
Labors of the heart
The Best American short stories 2001; select-
ed from U.S. and Canadian magazines by
Barbara Kingsolver with Katrina Kenison;
with an introduction by Barbara Kingsolver

Davis, Dorothy Salisbury
Christopher and Maggie
Davis, D. S. In the still of the night; tales to
lock your doors by

Davis, Dorothy Salisbury—*Continued*

Justina
  Davis, D. S. In the still of the night; tales to lock your doors by
The letter
  Murder in the family; [by] the Adams Round Table
Miles to go
  Davis, D. S. In the still of the night; tales to lock your doors by
Now is forever
  Davis, D. S. In the still of the night; tales to lock your doors by
The puppet
  Davis, D. S. In the still of the night; tales to lock your doors by
The purple is everything
  A moment on the edge; 100 years of crime stories by women; edited by Elizabeth George
The scream
  Davis, D. S. In the still of the night; tales to lock your doors by
Till death do us part
  Davis, D. S. In the still of the night; tales to lock your doors by
To forget Mary Ellen
  Davis, D. S. In the still of the night; tales to lock your doors by

Davis, Frances Pettey

Rest Stop
  Calyx v21 no3 p73-80 Wint 2004

Davis, Grania

(jt. auth) See Davidson, Avram and Davis, Grania

DAVIS, JEFFERSON, 1808-1889
About
DuBois, B. The greatest sacrifice

Davis, Jennifer S.

The ballad of my father's redneck wife
  Davis, J. S. Her kind of want
The one thing God'll give you
  Davis, J. S. Her kind of want
Only ends
  Davis, J. S. Her kind of want
Pojo's and the buttery slope
  Davis, J. S. Her kind of want
Reckonings
  Grand Street no73 p151-60 Spr 2004
Some things collide
  Davis, J. S. Her kind of want
Tammy, imagined
  Davis, J. S. Her kind of want
What kind of man
  Davis, J. S. Her kind of want
When you see
  Davis, J. S. Her kind of want

Davis, Kathryn

Floggings
  Ghost writing; haunted tales by contemporary writers; edited by Roger Weingarten

Davis, L. J. (Lawrence J.)

Cowboys don't cry [excerpt]
  The Vintage book of amnesia; an anthology; edited by Jonathan Lethem

Davis, Lauren

Barbara's mother's rug
  Davis, L. Rat medicine & other unlikely curatives

Blue valentines
  Davis, L. Rat medicine & other unlikely curatives
Calendar waltz
  Davis, L. Rat medicine & other unlikely curatives
Cat's out of the bag
  Davis, L. Rat medicine & other unlikely curatives
Celestial bodies
  Davis, L. Rat medicine & other unlikely curatives
Change of season
  Davis, L. Rat medicine & other unlikely curatives
Drop in any time
  Davis, L. Rat medicine & other unlikely curatives
The Golden Benefactors of Brewster McMahon
  Davis, L. Rat medicine & other unlikely curatives
Harold Luddock's decision
  Davis, L. Rat medicine & other unlikely curatives
In the memory house
  Davis, L. Rat medicine & other unlikely curatives
The kind of time you end up with
  Davis, L. Rat medicine & other unlikely curatives
A man like that
  Davis, L. Rat medicine & other unlikely curatives
Party girls
  Davis, L. Rat medicine & other unlikely curatives
The poet's corner
  Davis, L. Rat medicine & other unlikely curatives
Rat medicine
  Davis, L. Rat medicine & other unlikely curatives
Scarecrow
  Davis, L. Rat medicine & other unlikely curatives
Sensitive things
  Davis, L. Rat medicine & other unlikely curatives
Smoke and ash
  Davis, L. Rat medicine & other unlikely curatives
Strays
  Davis, L. Rat medicine & other unlikely curatives
Yours truly
  Davis, L. Rat medicine & other unlikely curatives

Davis, Lawrence J. *See* Davis, L. J. (Lawrence J.)

Davis, Lindsey

Body zone
  The Mysterious Press anniversary anthology; celebrating 25 years; by the editors of Mysterious Press
Something spooky on Geophys
  Edwards, M. Mysterious pleasures; a celebration of the Crime Writers' Association's 50th anniversary; edited by Martin Edwards

Davis, Lydia
The furnace
  Granta no68 p205-18 Wint 1999
Grammar Questions
  Harper's v305 p24-6 Ag 2002
The house behind
  The Art of the story; an international antholo-
  gy of contemporary short stories; edited by
  Daniel Halpern
Davis, Martha K.
Rachel
  Hers 2: brilliant new fiction by lesbian writ-
  ers; edited by Terry Wolverton with Robert
  Drake
Davis, Mollie Moore
A bamboula
  Southern local color; stories of region, race,
  and gender; edited by Barbara C. Ewell and
  Pamela Glenn Menke; with notes by An-
  drea Humphrey
Davis, Norbert
Something for the sweeper
  A Century of noir; thirty-two classic crime
  stories; edited by Mickey Spillane and Max
  Allan Collins
Davis, R.
Fat Tuesday
  Mardi Gras madness; tales of terror and may-
  hem in New Orleans; edited by Martin H.
  Greenberg and Russell Davis
Davis, Richard Harding
The bar sinister
  Sports best short stories; edited by Paul D.
  Staudohar
Davis, Whitney
The sharp light of trespassers
  Best new American voices 2001; guest editor
  Charles Baxter; series editors John Kulka
  and Natalie Danford
Daviu, Matilde
Midday
  Bomb no81 p102-5 Fall 2002
Dawn of the endless night. Harrison, H.
Dawn Venus. Nordley, G. D.
Dawson, Janet
What the cat dragged in
  Cat crimes through time; edited by Ed
  Gorman, Martin H. Greenberg, and Larry
  Segriff
Dawson, Peter
Night ride
  The First Five Star western corral; western
  stories; edited by Jon Tuska and Vicki
  Piekarski
Day, Barry
The adventure of the curious canary
  Murder, my dear Watson; new tales of Sher-
  lock Holmes; edited by Martin H. Green-
  berg, Jon Lellenberg, Daniel Stashower
Day, Cathy
Boss man
  Day, C. The circus in winter
The bullhook
  Day, C. The circus in winter
The circus house
  Day, C. The circus in winter
  New stories from the South: the year's best,
  2000; edited by Shannon Ravenel; with a
  preface by Ellen Douglas

Circus People
  Day, C. The circus in winter
The girl with big hair
  Gettysburg Review v12 no2 p251-61 Summ
  1999
Jennie Dixiana
  Day, C. The circus in winter
The Jungle Goolah Boy
  Day, C. The circus in winter
The King and His Court
  Day, C. The circus in winter
The Last Member of the Boela Tribe
  The Antioch Review v61 no4 p598-619 Fall
  2003
  Day, C. The circus in winter
The lone star cowboy
  Day, C. The circus in winter
Wallace Porter
  Day, C. The circus in winter
Wallace Porter sees the elephant
  The Southern Review (Baton Rouge, La.) v37
  no1 p107-20 Wint 2001
Winnesaw
  Day, C. The circus in winter
Day, Richard Cortez
The fugitive
  Home and beyond; an anthology of Kentucky
  short stories; edited by Morris Allen
  Grubbs; with an introduction by Wade Hall
  and an afterword by Charles E. May
The **day** after the end of the world. Harrison, H.
Day Ah Dallas Mare Toes. Calderon, L.
A **day** at the beach. Coshnear, D.
"A **day** at the fair". Barrett, N., Jr.
A **day** at the lake. Goran, L.
The **day** Bush left. Heller, J.
Day by day. Callaghan, M.
Day cook. Mayo, W.
Day for a picnic. Hoch, E. D.
The **day** ghost. Huddle, D.
The **day** his wife's face froze. Tanner, R.
A **Day** in Paradise. Rackstraw, L.
A **day** in the country. Broyard, B.
A **day** in the country. Chekhov, A. P.
A **Day** in the Country. Feliu-Pettet, R.
A **day** in the country. Heller, J.
A **day** in the countryside. See Chekhov, A. P. A
  day in the country
A **day** in the life of half of Rumpelstiltskin.
  Brockmeier, K.
A **day** in the park. Mosley, W.
A **day** laborer. Alas, L.
Day million. Pohl, F.
Day 'n nite. Resnick, R.
A **day** of days. James, H.
DAY OF JUDGMENT *See* Judgment Day
The **day** of retaliation. Aldrich, B. S.
A **day** of splendid omens. Wilson, R., Jr.
A **day** of sunshine and tears. Edwards, S.
The **day** of the 31st. Slesar, H.
The **day** of the beast. Karnezis, P.
Day of the butterfly. Peñaranda, O.
The **day** of the dance. Tomlinson, N. C.
The **day** of the dead. Simonds, M.
Day of the dead. Troncoso, S.
Day of the dead. Wallington, A.
Day of the dedication. Farrell, C.
The **day** of the execution. Slesar, H.
The **day** of the funeral. Wharton, E.

The **day** the aliens came. Sheckley, R.

The **day** the dogs died. Hoch, E. D.

The **day** the lake went down. Young, T.

The **day** the outlaws came. Farrell, C.

The **day** they took my uncle. Garcia, L. G.

A **day** without Dad. Watson, I.

Daynard, Jodi

No survivors

New England Review v22 no1 p144-54 Wint 2001

Days at home. Casey, M.

The **days** between. Steele, A. M.

Days between stations [excerpt] Erickson, S.

Days Given Over to Travel. Cheuse, A.

Days of awe. Rodburg, M.

Days of dear death. Tomioka, T.

The **days** of Solomon Gursky. McDonald, I.

De Alarcón, Pedro Antonio *See* Alarcón, Pedro Antonio de, 1833-1891

De Camp, L. Sprague

The Galton whistle

The Good old stuff; adventure SF in the grand tradition; edited by Gardner Dozois

A gun for dinosaur

The SFWA grand masters v1; edited by Frederik Pohl

The isolinguals

Wondrous beginnings; edited by Steven H. Silver and Martin H. Greenberg

Living fossil

The SFWA grand masters v1; edited by Frederik Pohl

De Camp, Lyon Sprague *See* De Camp, L. Sprague, 1907-2000

De Crayencour, Marguerite *See* Yourcenar, Marguerite

De Grey: a romance. James, H.

De Ferrari, Gabriella

A House

Bomb no84 p98-9 Summ 2003

De Jesús, Pedro *See* Jesús, Pedro de

De la Mare, Walter

Seaton's aunt

Dark: stories of madness, murder, and the supernatural; edited by Clint Willis

De Leon, Aya *See* Leon, Aya de

De Lint, Charles

Big city littles

De Lint, C. Tapping the dream tree

The big sky

De Lint, C. Moonlight and vines; a Newford collection

Birds

De Lint, C. Moonlight and vines; a Newford collection

The buffalo man

De Lint, C. Tapping the dream tree

China doll

The Crow; shattered lives & broken dreams; edited by J. O'Barr and Ed Kramer

De Lint, C. Moonlight and vines; a Newford collection

Crow girls

De Lint, C. Moonlight and vines; a Newford collection

Embracing the mystery

De Lint, C. Tapping the dream tree

The fane of the Grey Rose

Magical beginnings; edited by Steven H. Silver and Martin H. Greenberg

The fields beyond the fields

De Lint, C. Moonlight and vines; a Newford collection

Forest of stone

De Lint, C. Tapping the dream tree

Freak

De Lint, C. Tapping the dream tree

Granny Weather

Death dines at 8:30; edited by Claudia Bishop and Nick DiChario

De Lint, C. Tapping the dream tree

Heartfires

De Lint, C. Moonlight and vines; a Newford collection

Held safe by moonlight and vines

De Lint, C. Moonlight and vines; a Newford collection

If I close my eyes forever

De Lint, C. Moonlight and vines; a Newford collection

In the land of the unforgiven

De Lint, C. Moonlight and vines; a Newford collection

In the pines

De Lint, C. Moonlight and vines; a Newford collection

In the quiet after midnight

De Lint, C. Moonlight and vines; a Newford collection

In this soul of a woman

De Lint, C. Moonlight and vines; a Newford collection

The invisibles

De Lint, C. Moonlight and vines; a Newford collection

Making a noise in this world

De Lint, C. Tapping the dream tree

Many worlds are born

De Lint, C. Tapping the dream tree

Masking Indian

De Lint, C. Tapping the dream tree

Mardi Gras madness; tales of terror and mayhem in New Orleans; edited by Martin H. Greenberg and Russell Davis

My life as a bird

Black heart, ivory bones; [edited by] Ellen Datlow & Terri Windling

De Lint, C. Moonlight and vines; a Newford collection

Passing

De Lint, C. Moonlight and vines; a Newford collection

The pennymen

De Lint, C. Moonlight and vines; a Newford collection

Pixel pixies

De Lint, C. Tapping the dream tree

The Year's best fantasy & horror, thirteenth annual collection; edited by Ellen Datlow and Terri Windling

Saskia

De Lint, C. Moonlight and vines; a Newford collection

Second chances

De Lint, C. Tapping the dream tree

De Lint, Charles—*Continued*

Seven for a secret
De Lint, C. Moonlight and vines; a Newford collection
Seven wild sisters
De Lint, C. Tapping the dream tree
Shining nowhere but in the dark
De Lint, C. Moonlight and vines; a Newford collection
Sign here
De Lint, C. Tapping the dream tree
Sweet forget-me-not
Greenberg, M. H. Faerie tales
Ten for the devil
De Lint, C. Tapping the dream tree
There's no such thing
Children of the night; stories of ghosts, vampires, werewolves, and "lost children"; edited by Martin H. Greenberg
Trading hearts at the Half Kaffe Cafe
De Lint, C. Tapping the dream tree
Twa corbies
De Lint, C. Moonlight and vines; a Newford collection
The Year's best fantasy & horror, twelfth annual collection; edited by Ellen Datlow & Terry Windling
Wild horses
De Lint, C. Moonlight and vines; a Newford collection
Wingless angels
De Lint, C. Tapping the dream tree
The witching hour
De Lint, C. Tapping the dream tree
The words that remain
De Lint, C. Tapping the dream tree

De Noux, O'Neil

Death on denial
The Best American mystery stories, 2003; edited by Michael Connelly and Otto Penzler
The Iberville mistress
Flesh and blood: guilty as sin; erotic tales of crime and passion; edited by Max Allan Collins and Jeff Gelb

DE QUILLE, DAN, 1829-1898
About
Wheeler, R. S. The square reporter

De Rosas, Juan Manuel José Domingo Ortiz *See* Rosas, Juan Manuel José Domingo Ortiz de, 1793-1877

De San Martín, José *See* San Martín, José de, 1778?-1850

De Soto, Hernando *See* Soto, Hernando de, ca. 1500-1542

De Trueba, Antonio *See* Trueba, Antonio de

De Vallbona, Rima *See* Vallbona, Rima de, 1931-

De Varennes, Monique

Cabeza
Pushcart prize XXVII; best of the small presses; edited by Bill Henderson with the Pushcart prize editors

De Waal, Thomas

The English house: a story of Chechnya
Fishman, B. Wild East; stories from the last frontier; edited with an introduction by Boris Fishman

The **deacon**. Gordon, M.

DEACONS

Chekhov, A. P. The witch

Updike, J. The deacon

DEAD

See also Funeral rites and ceremonies

Bear, G. Dead run
Bradbury, R. Diane de Forêt
Bradbury, R. The lifework of Juan Diaz
Budnitz, J. Permanent wave
Campbell, R. Loveman's comeback
Carroll, J. The Heidelberg cylinder
Chekhov, A. P. A dead body
Chekhov, A. P. The requiem
Connor, J. The Bowlville Cemetery
Crowther, P. Songs of leaving
Fleming, R. The tenderness of Monsieur Blanc
Godwin, P. A matter of taste
Gurganus, A. Reassurance
Harrison, H. At last, the true story of Frankenstein
Hoffman, L. The third nation
Kees, W. The ceremony
Llano, M. E. In the family
Mayo, W. The California Franchise Tax Board
Newman, K. Amerikanski dead at the Moscow morgue
Richter, S. Rules for being human
Rogers, B. H. The dead boy at your window
Shacochis, B. Easy in the islands
Travis, T. V. The kiss
VanderMeer, J. The General who is dead
Vonnegut, K. Thanasphere
Wuori, G. K. Golden

The **dead**. Saroyan, A.
The **dead**. Swanwick, M.
Dead. Young, T.
Dead and berried. Bishop, C.
Dead and breakfast. Collins, B.
The **dead** are silent. Schnitzler, A.
A **dead** body. Chekhov, A. P.
The **dead** boy at your window. Rogers, B. H.
Dead Dog Lying. German, N.
Dead drunk. Matera, L.
Dead Duck. Lawson, P.
Dead easy. Bishop, P.
Dead Eddy. Lumley, B.
Dead end. Treat, J.
The **dead** fiddler, 5E. Brownstein, G.
Dead game man. Zanjani, S. S.
The **dead** girl. Watson, B.
Dead in the net. Hart, C. G.
Dead Letter. Bell, M. S.
The **dead** line. Rusch, K. K.
The **dead** man. Borges, J. L.
The **dead** man. Harmon, J.
The **dead** man. Wolfe, G.
Dead man in the oven. Tozzi, F.
The **dead** man of St. Anne's Chapel. Ludwig, O.
Dead Man's Curve. Bisson, T.
Dead Man's Hollow. Reasoner, J.
Dead man's slough. Pronzini, B.
Dead Men. DeMarinis, R.
Dead men don't dream. Hunter, E.
Dead men's shoes. Chopin, K.
The **dead** must die. Campbell, R.
Dead on arrival. Dinh, L.
The **dead** past. Pickard, N.
Dead phone. Anderson, P.
Dead rock singer. Moffett, M.
Dead run. Bear, G.
Dead sleep. Tillman, L.

Dead woman's grove. Gomes, M. T.
Dead women's things. Chwedyk, K.
Deadlier than the mail. Hunter, E.
Deadly city. Jorgenson, I.
The **deadly** egg. Van de Wetering, J.
The **deadly** glen. Knight, A.
Deadly hunger. Hensley, J. L.
The **deadly** percheron [excerpt] Bardin, J. F.
DEAF
    Atkinson, K. Tunnel of fish
    Chapman, C. M. The wheels on the bus go
    Davis, L. The Golden Benefactors of Brewster
       McMahon
    Dokey, R. A house in order
    Elkins, K. What is visible
    Kees, W. I should worry
    Lopez, B. H. The deaf girl
    Spencer, D. Caution: men in trees
    Thomas, D. The girl from follow
    Zinovyeva-Annibal, L. D. Deaf Dasha
Deaf Dasha. Zinovyeva-Annibal, L. D.
The **deaf** girl. Lopez, B. H.
The **Deaf** Musician. Haake, K.
Deaf mute. Siasoco, R. V.
DEAFNESS *See* Deaf
The **deal**. Davies, R.
The **deal**. Michaels, L.
Deal concluded. Johnson-Davies, D.
Deal me jacks or better. Kudritzki, J.
Deal with the Devil. O'Callaghan, M.
Dealer's choice. Chiappone, R.
DEAN, JAMES, 1931-1955
                About
    Dann, J. Ting-a-ling
    Des Barres, P. The James Dean diaries
DeAndrea, William L.
    The adventure of the Christmas tree
       DeAndrea, W. L. Murder-all kinds; introduc-
       tion by Jane Haddam
    The adventure of the cripple parade
       DeAndrea, W. L. Murder-all kinds; introduc-
       tion by Jane Haddam
    A friend of mine
       DeAndrea, W. L. Murder-all kinds; introduc-
       tion by Jane Haddam
    Hero's welcome
       DeAndrea, W. L. Murder-all kinds; introduc-
       tion by Jane Haddam
    Killed in good company
       DeAndrea, W. L. Murder-all kinds; introduc-
       tion by Jane Haddam
    Killed in midstream
       DeAndrea, W. L. Murder-all kinds; introduc-
       tion by Jane Haddam
    Killed top to bottom
       DeAndrea, W. L. Murder-all kinds; introduc-
       tion by Jane Haddam
    Murder at the end of the world
       DeAndrea, W. L. Murder-all kinds; introduc-
       tion by Jane Haddam
    Prince Charming
       DeAndrea, W. L. Murder-all kinds; introduc-
       tion by Jane Haddam
    Sabotage
       DeAndrea, W. L. Murder-all kinds; introduc-
       tion by Jane Haddam
    Snowy reception
       DeAndrea, W. L. Murder-all kinds; introduc-
       tion by Jane Haddam

Deane, John F.
    Between times
       Deane, J. F. The coffin master and other sto-
       ries
    Big Lil
       Deane, J. F. The coffin master and other sto-
       ries
    Capital H
       Deane, J. F. The coffin master and other sto-
       ries
    A close encounter
       Deane, J. F. The coffin master and other sto-
       ries
    The coffin master
       Deane, J. F. The coffin master and other sto-
       ries
    The experience of what is beautiful
       Deane, J. F. The coffin master and other sto-
       ries
    From a walled garden
       Deane, J. F. The coffin master and other sto-
       ries
    Lawrence
       Deane, J. F. The coffin master and other sto-
       ries
    A migrant bird
       Deane, J. F. The coffin master and other sto-
       ries
       Death dines at 8:30; edited by Claudia Bishop
       and Nick DiChario
    Nighthawk
       Deane, J. F. The coffin master and other sto-
       ries
    Poste restante
       Deane, J. F. The coffin master and other sto-
       ries
    Rituals of departure
       Deane, J. F. The coffin master and other sto-
       ries
    The sins of the fathers
       Deane, J. F. The coffin master and other sto-
       ries
    Twenty-three
       Deane, J. F. The coffin master and other sto-
       ries
DEANS (CATHEDRAL AND COLLEGIATE)
    See Anglican and Episcopal clergy
The **dean's** widow. Frym, G.
Dear darling Mr. Ramage. See Rhys, J. Pioneers,
    oh, pioneers
Dear diary. Hoffman, A.
Dear, dirty Paris. Galef, D.
Dear floods of her hair. Sallis, J.
Dear John. Reiner, C.
Dear John Wayne. Alexie, S.
Dear Lottie. Matthews, C.
Dear mother. Mathews, H.
Dear Mr. Bernard Shaw. Proctor, J.
Dear Mr. President. Hudson, G.
Dear Paramont Pictures. Pittalwala, I.
Dear pen pal. Van Vogt, A. E.
Dearest Roland. Grimm, J. and Grimm, W.
Dearth. Bender, A.
Deas, Nilo MarX̆ia Fabra y *See* Fabra, Nilo Ma-
    ría, 1843-1903
Deason, Lisa
    Lady Emerdirael's rescue
       Such a pretty face; edited by Lee Martindale

DEATH

See also Bereavement; Dead; Deathbed scenes

Adams, A. Waiting for Stella
Agee, J. Stiller's pond
Alarcón, P. A. d. "Death's friend"
Alcott, L. M. Lost in a pyramid; or, The Mummy's Curse
Alexie, S. This is what it means to say Phoenix, Arizona
Amichai, Y. My father's deaths
Amis, M. Denton's death
Anderson, D. Accident
Anderson, R. The pyramid
Apukhtin, A. N. Between life and death: a fantastic story
Arenas, R. Goodbye mother
Atkinson, K. The bodies vest
Atkinson, K. Temporal anomaly
Atwood, M. Death by landscape
Babel', I. Dolgushov's death
Banks, R. The child screams and looks back at you
Barrett, L. To go
Bausch, R. Requisite kindness
Bezmozgis, D. Choynski
Biguenet, J. Rose
Bishop, M. Chihuahua Flats
Bisson, T. Dead Man's Curve
Blackwood, S. In the shadow of our house
Blatnik, A. Isaac
Blumlein, M. Revenge
Bly, C. After the baptism
Bly, C. An apprentice
Boggs, B. Who is Beatrice?
Bond, N. The bookshop
Bonnie, F. Selling delphinium
Bosch, J. Encarnación Mendoza's Christmas Eve
Bradbury, R. All my enemies are dead
Bradbury, R. Death and the maiden
Bradbury, R. In memoriam
Bradbury, R. The Kilimanjaro device
Bradbury, R. The miracles of Jamie
Bradbury, R. No news; or, What killed the dog?
Bradbury, R. Tête-à-tête
Brockmeier, K. Apples
Brockmeier, K. Space
Broughton, T. A. Ashes
Brown, J. The coroner's report
Brown, J. The submariners
Brownrigg, S. A gal of ambition
Brownstein, G. Safety
Buckell, T. S. Death's dreadlocks
Bunin, I. A. The gentleman from San Francisco
Cabrera Infante, G. The doors open at three
Cacek, P. D. Belief
Canty, K. Girlfriend hit by bus
Carlson, R. The time I died
Carlson, R. Zanduce at second
Carroll, L. Traveling princess
Carson, J. Fair trades
Carson, J. Two thousand years of torture
Casey, M. Trespassing
Chan, D. M. Goblin fruit
Chang, L. S. The eve of the spirit festival
Chekhov, A. P. Gusev
Cheng, C.-W. The last of the gentlemen
Cherryh, C. J. The dark king
Cherryh, C. J. The only death in the city

Chopin, K. Suzette
Clark, J. Frazzle
Clarke, A. C. Death and the senator
Coberly, L. M. The death of Alma Ruth
Compton, D. G. In which Avu Giddy tries to stop dancing
Coskran, K. Sun
Crowley, J. Her bounty to the dead
Dann, J. The black horn
Dann, J. Kaddish
Dann, J. A quiet revolution for death
Dann, J. Voices
Danticat, E. Night talkers
Davies, R. No more looking back
Davis, L. Harold Luddock's decision
Deane, J. F. Rituals of departure
Delaney, E. J. What I have noticed
DeMarinis, R. Paraiso: an elegy
Denton, B. The hero of the night
DeRosso, H. A. The happy death
Di Blasi, D. Chairman of the board
Dixon, S. Sleep
Dixon, S. Survivors
Dozois, G. R. Down among the dead men
Drake, R. The convertible
Dybek, S. Blue boy
Edugyan, E. The woman who tasted of rose oil
Eisenberg, D. The girl who left her sock on the floor
Enstice, A. Dream, until god burns
Erdrich, L. Le mooz
Evans, E. A new life
Evenson, B. Garker's aestheticals
Evenson, B. The installation
Evenson, B. Virtual
Ferriss, L. Bones
Fink, I. The death of Tsaritsa
Firth, C. The Department of Nothing
Fleming, R. The inhuman condition
Ford, R. Abyss
Foster, K. Things you can make something out of
Franklin, T. Christmas 1893
Freudenberger, N. Lucky girls
Fromm, P. Night swimming
Furman, L. Sunny
Furman, L. Sympathy
Gaitskill, M. Dream of men
Gao Xingjian. The accident
Gavell, M. L. Baucis
Gay, W. Come home, come home, it's suppertime
Gay, W. A death in the woods
Gay, W. My hand is just fine where it is
Gay, W. Standing by peaceful waters
Gay, W. Sugarbaby
Gilchrist, E. A tree to be desired
Glave, T. The final inning
Glover, D. H. La Corriveau
Glover, D. H. My romance
Godin, A. My dead brother comes to America
Gonzalez, R. The garden of Padre Anselmo
Gonzalez, R. The legend
Goran, L. The inheritance
Grau, S. A. Flight
Grau, S. A. Hunter
Grau, S. A. One summer
Grau, S. A. Widow's walk
Greenberg, A. Gruber in traffic

DEATH—*Continued*

Gunn, K. The swimming pool
Harris, M. At Prayerbook Cross
Harrison, H. No me, not Amos Cabot!
Harty, R. September
Haynes, M. Love like a bullet
Hempel, A. In the cemetery where Al Jolson is buried
Hendel, Y. Low, close to the floor
Hendel, Y. My friend B's feast
Hendel, Y. A story with no address
Henley, P. Sun damage
Herling, G. Ashes: the fall of the House of Loris
Highsmith, P. Nothing that meets the eye
Hirshberg, G. The two Sams
Hodge, B. Some other me
Hoffman, A. How to talk to the dead
Honig, L. After
Hood, A. The language of sorrow
Horgan, P. The peach stone
Houarner, G. She'd make a dead man crawl
Houston, P. Waltzing the cat
Iribarne, M. The gift
Irsfeld, J. H. Death of a soldier
Irsfeld, J. H. My neighbor Mr. Young
Iwaszkiewicz, J. The birch grove
Jacobs, M. Two dead Indians
James, S. And perhaps more
James, S. John Hedward
Jenkins, G. Something to cling to
Johnson, D. Train dreams
Johnston, B. A. Buy for me the rain
Johnston, B. A. Waterwalkers
Jones, T. I want to live!
Kanafāni, G. The death of bed number 12
Kane, J. F. Pantomime
Karnezis, P. Jeremiad
Keegan, C. The burning palms
Kemper, M. God's goodness
Kittredge, W. Momentum is always the weapon
Kittredge, W. The van Gogh field
Kociancich, V. Knight, death and the devil
Kohler, S. The adulterous woman
Kohler, S. Ambush
Kohler, S. Water Baby
Lao She. Autobiography of a minor character
Lao She. Ding
Lavin, M. The convent
Lavin, M. A gentle soul
Lawrence, D. H. Odour of chrysanthemums
Leavitt, D. Black box
Lee, M. A king's epitaph
Lempel, Blume. The death of my aunt
Lieu, J. The children
Lincoln, C. Acorn pipes
Lincoln, C. A very close conspiracy
Link, K. The specialist's hat
Lipenga, K. Wainting for a turn
Lundquist, R. The visitation
Malzberg, B. N. Understanding entropy
Mastretta, A. Aunt Concha
Mastretta, A. Aunt Isabel
Matiella, A. C. Angels
Mayo, W. Jagged tooth, great tooth
Mazor, J. On experience
McBrearty, R. G. The things I don't know about
McCrumb, S. Foggy Mountain breakdown
McDonald, I. The days of Solomon Gursky

McGarry, M. J. The mercy gate
McKay, K. Pie Row Joe
McManus, J. Die like a lobster
Meade, D. Lost time
Means, D. Sleeping Bear lament
Means, D. Tahorah
Melville, P. The president's exile
Meyers, K. The smell of the deer
Moody, R. Demonology
Moody, R. The Mansion on the Hill
Morgan, R. Little Willie
Moss, B. R. Blackbird
Murguía, A. Ofrendas
Nailah, A. Free
Naiyer Masud. Interregnum
Nfah-Abbenyi, J. M. Slow poison
Nissen, T. When the rain washes you clean you'll know
Norris, H. The second shepherd
Oates, J. C. Fire
Oates, J. C. Subway
O'Callaghan, M. Exit
Offutt, C. Out of the woods
Orner, P. Atlantic City
Orner, P. Papa Gino's
Orner, P. Pile of clothes
Otis, M. Aida South, flower
Paredes, A. The hammon and the beans
Paver, C. The boxing match
Pearlman, D. D. Over the H.I.L.L.
Perabo, S. Explaining death to the dog
Peretz, I. L. Bryna's Mendl
Piñera, V. The one who came to save me
Poirier, M. J. Worms
Porter, K. A. The grave
Porzecanski, T. The story of a cat
Rachmil, B. The last journey
Rawley, D. The spells of an ordinary twilight
Rawley, D. Tim
Reisman, N. House fires
Richter, S. A groupie, a rock star
Ritchie, E. The big sixtieth
Rodburg, M. The orphan
Rogers, B. H. Lifeboat on a burning sea
Rucker, R. v. B. Soft Death
Salak, K. Beheadings
Sánchez, R. The brand new suit
Schnitzler, A. Dying
Schoemperlen, D. The antonyms of fiction
Schoemperlen, D. Losing ground
Scholz, C. A draft of Canto CI
Schwartz, L. S. What I did for love
Seiffert, R. The last spring
Shackelford, R. T. From Tucson to Tucumcari, from Tehachapi to Tonopah
Sheckley, R. The city of the dead
Sherman, J. The snows of August
Shishin, A. Mr. Eggplant goes home
Simonds, M. The day of the dead
Singer, I. B. Joy
Singer, I. B. The lecture
Singer, I. B. The reencounter
Singer, I. B. Short Friday
Singer, I. B. Strong as death is love
Sinor, B. H. Eleven to seven
Skillings, R. D. Ashes
Skillings, R. D. Here I am
Slavin, J. Covered
Smith, A. Being quick

DEATH—*Continued*

Sobott-Mogwe, G. Smile of fortune
Sosin, D. You're so simple
Steiber, E. The shape of things
Stolar, D. Mourning
Stollman, A. L. Mr. Mitochondria
Stollman, A. L. New memories
Sturgeon, T. The man who lost the sea
Su Shuyang. Between life and death
Swick, M. A. Crete
Switzer, R. Death of a prize fighter
Thompson, J. Mercy
Tilghman, C. A gracious rain
Tillman, L. Dead sleep
Tolstoy, L., graf. The poor people
Tolstoy, L., graf. The prayer
Troncoso, S. The abuelita
Troncoso, S. The last tortilla
Troncoso, S. A rock trying to be a stone
Van Winckel, N. Immunity
Vasseur, T. J. The angels
Watson, B. The dead girl
Watson, I. The China cottage
Weldon, F. Noisy into the night
West, M. Faces made of clay
Westlake, D. E. Good night, good night
Westmoreland, T. A. Darkening of the world
Wharton, E. The duchess at prayer
Wharton, E. The fulness of life
Wharton, E. A journey
What, L. The sacred society
Whitty, J. The daguerrotype
Williams, M. One Saturday afternoon
Williams, M. The year Ward West took away the raccoon and Mr. Hanson's garage burneddown
Wilson, R., Jr. A day of splendid omens
Wilson, R., Jr. Grief
Wilson, R., Jr. A simple elegy
Wilson, R., Jr. Trespass
Winegardner, M. How we came to Indiana
Wright, D. Dialogue of men and boys
Wuori, G. K. Family
Wuori, G. K. Nude
Yi, T.-H. Perspiration
Yi, T.-H. Shrapnel
Yolen, J. Godmother death
Yoshimoto, B. Asleep
Zinovyeva-Annibal, L. D. Will
Death and designation among the Asadi. Bishop, M.
Death and joy. Hannah, B.
Death and taxes. Wellen, E.
Death and the compass. Borges, J. L.
Death and the knight. Anderson, P.
Death and the maid. Anderson, R.
Death and the senator. Clarke, A. C.
Death and transfiguration of a teacher. Solari, M. T.
Death before compline. Newman, S.
Death by bricolage. Alvarez, A.
Death by landscape. Atwood, M.
Death by pastrami. Bernstein, L. S.
Death by reputation. Gerard, P.
The **Death** Cat of Hester Street. Gorman, C.
Death comes gift-wrapped. McGivern, W. P.
Death crown. Morgan, R.
Death cup. Oates, J. C.
The **death-dealing** Cassini satellite. Johnson, A.

Death Defier. Bissell, T.
Death did not become him. Wilson, D. N. and Macomber, P. L.
Death In Naples. Gordon, M.
Death in October. Easton, R. O.
Death in Rome. Kohler, S.
Death in the des(s)ert. Pearlman, D. D.
A **death** in the woods. Gay, W.
Death in Venice. Catlin, A.
Death is not the end. Wallace, D. F.
Death is where you find it. Bocock, M.
Death mother. Oates, J. C.
Death, my love. Collins, M.
Death of a bachelor. Schnitzler, A.
The **death** of a civil servant. Chekhov, A. P.
Death of a damn moose. Smith, B. B.
Death of a favorite. Powers, J. F.
Death of a glamour cat. Matthews, C.
The **death** of a government clerk. Chekhov, A. P.
Death of a mother. Viganò, R.
Death of a prize fighter. Switzer, R.
Death of a professor. Trevor, W.
Death of a street dog. Paschal, D.
The **death** of Alma Ruth. Coberly, L. M.
Death of an official. See Chekhov, A. P. The death of a civil servant See Chekhov, A. P. The death of a government clerk
The **death** of Baldassare Silvande, Viscount of Sylvania. Proust, M.
The **death** of bed number 12. Kanafānī, G.
The **death** of Captain Future. Steele, A. M.
The **Death** of Colonel Thoureau Master's choice v2; mystery stories by today's top writers and the masters who inspired them; edited by Lawrence Block
The **death** of cool. Cavell, B.
The **death** of Dolgushov. See Babel′, I. Dolgushov's death
The **death** of Jack Hamilton. King, S.
The **death** of Olga Vasilievna. Shonk, K.
The **death** of Picasso. Davenport, G.
Death of the cool. Boyle, T. C.
The **death** of the Duke. Kushner, E.
The **death** of the dying swan. Heller, J.
The **death** of the quarterback. Goran, L.
Death of the Rabbits. Romo-Carmona, M.
The **death** of Tsaritsa. Fink, I.
Death on Pine Street. Hammett, D.
A **death** on the Ho Chi Minh Trail. Harford, D. K.
The **death-ring** of Sneferu. Rohmer, S.
Death ship. Matheson, R.
Death takes the veil. Quill, M.
Death to everybody over thirty. Swarthout, G. F.
Death to the fascist imperialist dogs. Blitz, R.
DEATH VALLEY (CALIF. AND NEV.)
L'Amour, L. Sand trap
Rifkin, A. The honor system
Death watch. Oates, J. C.
O **death,** where is thy spatula? Brite, P. Z.
DEATHBED SCENES
Allison, D. Compassion
Babel′, I. The widow
Bennett, A. Father! Father! Burning bright
Brennan, M. The rose garden
Bukoski, A. The absolution of Hedda Borski
Carver, R. Errand
Clarke, A. Leaving this island place
Dark, A. E. In the gloaming

DEATHBED SCENES—*Continued*

DeLancey, K. Washed

Gores, J. Goodbye, Pops

Lerner, M. Little selves

McCorkle, J. Fish

Morgan, R. Death crown

Plá, J. To seize the earth

Schnitzler, A. A farewell

Sontag, S. The way we live now

Death's dreadlocks. Buckell, T. S.

"Death's friend". Alarcón, P. A. d.

Deaver, Jeff

Beautiful

The World's finest mystery and crime stories, third annual collection; edited by Ed Gorman and Martin H. Greenberg

Eye to eye

Irreconcilable differences; Lia Matera, editor

For services rendered

The World's finest mystery and crime stories, first annual collection; edited by Ed Gorman

Ninety-eight point six

A Hot and sultry night for crime; edited by Jeffery Deaver

A simple question

Esquire v135 no1 p85-7 Ja 2001

Triangle

The Best American mystery stories, 2000; edited and with an introduction by Donald E. Westlake

Crème de la crime; edited by Janet Hutchings

The weekender

A Century of great suspense stories; edited by Jeffery Deaver

Wrong time, wrong place

The Best American mystery stories, 1999; edited and with an introduction by Ed McBain

Deaver, Jeffery *See* Deaver, Jeff

Deb, Ali

The three-piece suit

The Anchor book of modern African stories; edited by Nadežda Obradovic ; with a foreword by Chinua Achebe

Debarking. Moore, L.

The **debauched** one. Van Belkom, E.

DeBoer, Jason

Godless in India

Iowa Review v32 no2 p142-4 Fall 2002

Debra's flap and snap. Edgerton, C.

Debriefing. Busch, F.

The **debt.** Wharton, E.

DEBTOR AND CREDITOR

Ṣāliḥ, al-Ṭ. A handful of dates

DEBTS

Lutz, J. High stakes

The **debut** of Battling Billson. Wodehouse, P. G.

DECADENCE *See* Degeneration

December birthday. Moss, B. K.

A **December** day in Dixie. Chopin, K.

Decency. Reed, R.

Deceptions. Muller, M.

DeChoudhury, Sujata

Forbidden fate

Pieces; a collection of new voices; edited by Stephen Chbosky

DeCicco v. Schweizer. Auchincloss, L.

Decision. Hensley, J. L.

Decision. O'Rourke, F.

Deck, John

Sailors at their mourning: a memory

Retrieving bones; stories and poems of the Korean War; edited and with an introduction by W. D. Ehrhart and Philip K. Jason

Deck ape. Reid, E.

Deck load strike. Green, R. J.

The **decline** of King Fabulous. Cobb, W. J.

Deconstruction. Burroway, J.

Decoys. Devane, T.

Dedication. Klass, P.

Dedman, Stephen

From whom all blessings flow

Centaurus: the best of Australian science fiction; edited by David G. Hartwell and Damien Broderick

A walk-on part in the war

Dreaming down-under; edited by Jack Dann and Janeen Webb

The wind shall blow for ever mair

Gathering the bones; original stories from the world's masters of horror; edited by Dennis Etchison, Ramsey Campbell and Jack Dann

The **deed** of the deft-footed dragon. Davidson, A.

Deena. Nailah, A.

Deep. Juska, E.

The **deep.** Swan, M.

The **deep** blue sea. Bouman, I.

Deep Blue Sleep. Sheckley, R.

Deep down to the bottom of this. Goldner, B.

Deep green, pale purple. Heim, S.

A **deep** hole. Rankin, I.

The **deep** range. Clarke, A. C.

Deep red. Heldrich, P.

The **deep** red cremation of Isaac and Grace. Curtis, R.

A **deep** sleeper. Chesnutt, C. W.

Deeper than the world. Strandquist, R.

The **deepest** dive. Gussoff, C.

DEER

Bell, M. S. Two lives

Kingrea, Eric. A waltz in the snow

Offill, J. The deer

Watanabe McFerrin, L. Childproofing

The **deer.** Offill, J.

Deer gone. Singleton, G.

DEER HUNTING

Bailey, T. Snow dreams

Evans, M. The heart of the matter

Henley, P. The late hunt

Kaplan, D. M. Doe season

Proulx, A. On the antler

A **deer** on the lawn. Malone, M.

The **deerness** of life. Kurlansky, M.

DEFECTORS

DeAndrea, W. L. Hero's welcome

Defender of the faith. O'Marie, C. A.

Defender of the faith. Roth, P.

The **defenestration** of Aba Sid. Girardi, R.

The **defenestration** of Ermintrude Inch. Clarke, A. C.

Defenseman. Banks, R.

Deferment. Allen, D., Jr.

DEFORMITIES

See also Face—Abnormalities and deformities; Monsters

Fitzgerald, F. S. The curious case of Benjamin Button

DEFORMITIES—*Continued*
Hawthorne, N. The birthmark
Merril, J. That only a mother
Defrosting Disney. Barwin, G.
DEGENERACY *See* Degeneration
DEGENERATION
Girardi, R. The dinner party
Degollado, Rubén
Our story frays
Fantasmas; supernatural stories by Mexican
American writers; edited by Rob Johnson;
introduction by Kathleen J. Alcalá
Degree days. Burton, M.
Deibenquist sounds famous. Reiner, C.
Deighton, Len
Hell over Germany
On glorious wings; the best flying stories of
the century; edited and introduced by Ste-
phen Coonts
Del Giudice, Daniele
All because of the mistake
The Art of the story; an international antholo-
gy of contemporary short stories; edited by
Daniel Halpern
Del Rey, Lester
The coppersmith
The SFWA grand masters; edited by Frederik
Pohl
The faithful
The SFWA grand masters; edited by Frederik
Pohl
For I am a jealous people!
The SFWA grand masters; edited by Frederik
Pohl
Helen O'Loy
The Science fiction hall of fame: volume one,
1929-1964; the greatest science fiction sto-
ries of all time chosen by the members of
the Science Fiction Writers of America; ed-
ited by Robert Silverberg
The pipes of Pan
The SFWA grand masters; edited by Frederik
Pohl
La **del** Sapo. Jiménez, K. P.
DELACROIX, EUGÈNE, 1798-1863
About
Baker, K. The wreck of the Gladstone
DeLancey, Kiki
Carley's knees
DeLancey, K. Coal miner's holiday; stories
Coal miner's holiday
DeLancey, K. Coal miner's holiday; stories
Crazy dead kid lady
DeLancey, K. Coal miner's holiday; stories
Dinger and Blacker
DeLancey, K. Coal miner's holiday; stories
Fast coming and then going
DeLancey, K. Coal miner's holiday; stories
Great ones
DeLancey, K. Coal miner's holiday; stories
A hole in the wall of noise
DeLancey, K. Coal miner's holiday; stories
I loved the squire
DeLancey, K. Coal miner's holiday; stories
It's dark
DeLancey, K. Coal miner's holiday; stories
Jules Jr Michael Jules Jr
DeLancey, K. Coal miner's holiday; stories

The mystery of George Jones
DeLancey, K. Coal miner's holiday; stories
The seven pearls
DeLancey, K. Coal miner's holiday; stories
Swingtime
DeLancey, K. Coal miner's holiday; stories
Two strippers
DeLancey, K. Coal miner's holiday; stories
Washed
DeLancey, K. Coal miner's holiday; stories
The Welsh engineer
DeLancey, K. Coal miner's holiday; stories
What the hell
DeLancey, K. Coal miner's holiday; stories
Delancey Place. Holleran, A.
Delaney, Edward J.
The anchor and me
Delaney, E. J. The drowning and other stories
Conspiracy buffs
Delaney, E. J. The drowning and other stories
The drowning
Delaney, E. J. The drowning and other stories
Hero
Delaney, E. J. The drowning and other stories
Notes toward my absolution
Delaney, E. J. The drowning and other stories
O beauty! o truth!
Delaney, E. J. The drowning and other stories
Travels with Mr. Slush
Delaney, E. J. The drowning and other stories
A visit to my uncle
Delaney, E. J. The drowning and other stories
The warp and the weft
Atlantic Monthly v288 no4 p111-18 N 2001
What I have noticed
Delaney, E. J. The drowning and other stories
Delany, Samuel R.
Among the blobs
Delany, S. R. Aye, and Gomorrah; stories
Aye, and Gomorrah . . .
Dark matter; a century of speculative fiction
from the African diaspora; edited by Sheree
R. Thomas
Delany, S. R. Aye, and Gomorrah; stories
Cage of brass
Delany, S. R. Aye, and Gomorrah; stories
Corona
Delany, S. R. Aye, and Gomorrah; stories
Dog in a fisherman's net
Delany, S. R. Aye, and Gomorrah; stories
Driftglass
Delany, S. R. Aye, and Gomorrah; stories
High weir
Delany, S. R. Aye, and Gomorrah; stories
Night and the loves of Joe Dicostanzo
Delany, S. R. Aye, and Gomorrah; stories
Omegahelm
Delany, S. R. Aye, and Gomorrah; stories
Prismatica
Delany, S. R. Aye, and Gomorrah; stories
Ruins
Delany, S. R. Aye, and Gomorrah; stories
The star pit
Delany, S. R. Aye, and Gomorrah; stories
Tapestry
Delany, S. R. Aye, and Gomorrah; stories
Time considered as a helix of semi-precious
stones
Delany, S. R. Aye, and Gomorrah; stories

Delany, Samuel R.—*Continued*
  We, in some strange power's employ, move on
    a rigorous line
    Delany, S. R. Aye, and Gomorrah; stories
Delbanco, Nicholas
  Night and fog
    Salmagundi no124/125 p228-37 Fall
    1999/Wint 2000
Delegates. Rowell, J.
Delfigo Street. Thomas, M. W.
DELHI (INDIA) *See* India—Delhi
Delia. Miller, R.
Delicate. Sojourner, M.
Delicate destinies. Cohen, R.
A **delicate** mission. Collins, M. and Lynds, G.
The **delicate** prey. Bowles, P.
Delicate Wives. Updike, J.
DeLillo, Don
  Baader-Meinhof
    The New Yorker v78 no6 p78-82 Ap 1 2002
Delivering meat. Garcia, L. G.
Delllamonica, A. M.
  Cooking creole
    Mojo: conjure stories; edited by Nalo Hopkin-
    son
Dell'Oro, Erminia
  The red bathrobe
    In the forbidden city; an anthology of erotic
    fiction by Italian women; edited by Maria
    Rosa Cutrufelli; translated by Vincent J.
    Bertolini
DeLoach, Nora
  Victim by consent
    Women before the bench; edited by Carolyn
    Wheat; introduction by Linda Fairstein
Delta double-deal. Ayres, N.
Delta Interval. Johnson, D.
DeMarco, Tom
  A boy's will is the winds's will
    DeMarco, T. Lieutenant America and Miss
    Apple Pie; stories; Tom DeMarco
  Dancing bare
    DeMarco, T. Lieutenant America and Miss
    Apple Pie; stories; Tom DeMarco
  Down at the end of lonely street
    DeMarco, T. Lieutenant America and Miss
    Apple Pie; stories; Tom DeMarco
  Jasper
    DeMarco, T. Lieutenant America and Miss
    Apple Pie; stories; Tom DeMarco
  Lieutenant America and Miss Apple Pie
    DeMarco, T. Lieutenant America and Miss
    Apple Pie; stories; Tom DeMarco
  Nahigian's Day in court
    DeMarco, T. Lieutenant America and Miss
    Apple Pie; stories; Tom DeMarco
  The needle in the haystack
    DeMarco, T. Lieutenant America and Miss
    Apple Pie; stories; Tom DeMarco
  The Ninja
    DeMarco, T. Lieutenant America and Miss
    Apple Pie; stories; Tom DeMarco
  P-413: Psycho-Sociology
    DeMarco, T. Lieutenant America and Miss
    Apple Pie; stories; Tom DeMarco
  Prince of darkness
    DeMarco, T. Lieutenant America and Miss
    Apple Pie; stories; Tom DeMarco

  Proper cover
    DeMarco, T. Lieutenant America and Miss
    Apple Pie; stories; Tom DeMarco
  The rose festival boxed lunch
    DeMarco, T. Lieutenant America and Miss
    Apple Pie; stories; Tom DeMarco
DeMarinis, Rick
  An airman's goodbye
    DeMarinis, R. Borrowed hearts; new and se-
    lected stories
  Aliens
    DeMarinis, R. Borrowed hearts; new and se-
    lected stories
  Bête Noire
    The Antioch Review v62 no3 p447-57 Summ
    2004
  Billy Ducks among the pharaohs
    DeMarinis, R. Borrowed hearts; new and se-
    lected stories
  Borrowed hearts
    The Antioch Review v59 no2 p408-15 Spr
    2001
    DeMarinis, R. Borrowed hearts; new and se-
    lected stories
    New stories from the South: the year's best,
    1999; edited by Shannon Ravenel; with a
    preface by Tony Earley
  The boys we were, the men we became
    DeMarinis, R. Borrowed hearts; new and se-
    lected stories
  Dead Men
    The Antioch Review v61 no2 p251-4 Spr 2003
  Desert places
    DeMarinis, R. Borrowed hearts; new and se-
    lected stories
  Disneyland
    DeMarinis, R. Borrowed hearts; new and se-
    lected stories
  Experience
    DeMarinis, R. Borrowed hearts; new and se-
    lected stories
  Fault lines
    DeMarinis, R. Borrowed hearts; new and se-
    lected stories
  Feet
    DeMarinis, R. Borrowed hearts; new and se-
    lected stories
  The handgun
    DeMarinis, R. Borrowed hearts; new and se-
    lected stories
  Horizontal snow
    DeMarinis, R. Borrowed hearts; new and se-
    lected stories
  Hormone X
    DeMarinis, R. Borrowed hearts; new and se-
    lected stories
  Insulation
    DeMarinis, R. Borrowed hearts; new and se-
    lected stories
  Life between meals
    DeMarinis, R. Borrowed hearts; new and se-
    lected stories
  Medicine man
    DeMarinis, R. Borrowed hearts; new and se-
    lected stories
  Novias
    DeMarinis, R. Borrowed hearts; new and se-
    lected stories

DeMarinis, Rick—*Continued*

Texas bound. Book III; 22 Texas stories; edited by Kay Cattarulla; foreword by Robert Flynn

On the lam

DeMarinis, R. Borrowed hearts; new and selected stories

Pagans

DeMarinis, R. Borrowed hearts; new and selected stories

Paraiso: an elegy

DeMarinis, R. Borrowed hearts; new and selected stories

Romance: a prose villanelle

DeMarinis, R. Borrowed hearts; new and selected stories

A romantic interlude

DeMarinis, R. Borrowed hearts; new and selected stories

Safe forever

DeMarinis, R. Borrowed hearts; new and selected stories

Seize the day

DeMarinis, R. Borrowed hearts; new and selected stories

The singular we

DeMarinis, R. Borrowed hearts; new and selected stories

The smile of a turtle

DeMarinis, R. Borrowed hearts; new and selected stories

Under the wheat

DeMarinis, R. Borrowed hearts; new and selected stories

The Voice of America

DeMarinis, R. Borrowed hearts; new and selected stories

Weeds

DeMarinis, R. Borrowed hearts; new and selected stories

In our nature: stories of wildness; selected and introduced by Donna Seaman

Why the Tears, Miss Earhart?

The Paris Review v46 p160-70 Summ 2004

Wilderness

DeMarinis, R. Borrowed hearts; new and selected stories

Your burden is lifted, love returns

DeMarinis, R. Borrowed hearts; new and selected stories

Your story

DeMarinis, R. Borrowed hearts; new and selected stories

Dembo, Margot Bettauer

(jt. auth) See Hremann, Judith

Deming, Richard

Honeymoon cruise

Death cruise; crime stories on the open seas; edited by Lawrence Block

Demiurg. Händler, E.-W.

Demon bone. Roberts, T. N.

A **demon** in my head. Oppel, J.-H.

The **demon** of longing. Gilliland, G.

The **Demon-possessed** princess Into the mummy's tomb; edited by John Richard Stephens

DEMONIAC POSSESSION

See also Exorcism

Singer, I. B. The dead fiddler

Singer, I. B. Esther Kreindel the second

Singer, I. B. The lantuch

Singer, I. B. Lost

Singer, I. B. A night in the poorhouse

Vaswani, N. Possession at the tomb of Sayyed Pir Hazrat Baba Bahadur Saheed Rah Aleh

DEMONOLOGY

See also Demoniac possession; Witchcraft

Lovecraft, H. P. The call of cthulhu

Singer, I. B. The black wedding

Vance, J. The miracle workers

Demonology. Moody, R.

Demons, dreamers, and madmen. Goldstein, R.

The **demons** tormenting Untersturmführer Hans Otto Graebner. Girardi, R.

DEMONSTRATIONS

Erian, A. The winning side

Gray, A. 15 February 2003

Sojourner, M. Binky

Sojourner, M. Officer Magdalena, White Shell Woman, and me

The **Denali** Widows' Club. Lynch, D.

Dendel, Esther Warner

Only brotherness can warm a cold heart

Parabola v26 no4 p37-8 N 2001

Denevi, Marco

Journey to Port Adventure

Michigan Quarterly Review v40 no4 p643-63 Fall 2001

Deng Xiaohua *See* Ts'an-hsüeh, 1953-

Deng Youmei

Han the forger

The Vintage book of contemporary Chinese fiction; edited by Carolyn Choa and David Su Li-qun

Denis the Pirate. Johnson, D.

DENMARK

Davenport, G. Wo es war, soll ich werden

Høeg, P. Portrait of the avant-garde

Dennis, Douglas

(jt. auth) See Padgett, Abigail and Dennis, Douglas

Dennis, Ferdinand

The Black and White Museum

Critical Quarterly v41 no4 p28-34 Wint 1999

Dentaphilia. Slavin, J.

DENTISTS

Bail, M. The drover's wife

Davies, P. H. Brave girl

Davis, L. Sensitive things

Dodd, S. M. Lady Chatterley's root canal

Highsmith, P. Man's best friend

Kornegay, Jamie. Dog days

Roth, P. The counterlife [excerpt]

Schwartz, L. S. Referred pain

Thurm, M. Cold

Updike, J. Dentistry and doubt

Denton, Bradley

The hero of the night

The American fantasy tradition; edited by Brian M. Thomsen

The territory

One lamp; alternate history stories from The magazine of Fantasy & Science Fiction; edited by Gordon van Gelder

Timmy and Tommy's Thanksgiving secret

Witpunk; edited by Claude Lalumière and Marty Halpern

Denton, Bradley—*Continued*
  We love Lydia love
    The Best from fantasy & science fiction: the
      fiftieth anniversary anthology; edited by
      Edward L. Ferman and Gordon Van Gelder
Denton, Elizabeth
  The Birthday Party
    The Yale Review v92 no3 p107-28 Jl 2004
  Lice
    The Massachusetts Review v43 no1 p17-41
      Spr 2002
  Mick Jagger's green-eyed daughter
    The Yale Review v90 no4 p112-23 O 2002
  Taco Bell
    The Virginia Quarterly Review v78 no2 p304-
      11 Spr 2002
The **Denton** mare. Lanham, E.
Denton's death. Amis, M.
DeNunzio, Roy
  Mrs. Margolis' Garden
    South Carolina Review v33 no2 p39-51 Spr
      2001
DENVER (COLO.) *See* Colorado—Denver
The **Department** of Nothing. Firth, C.
DEPARTMENT STORES
  Banks, R. Success story
  Cohen, S. A night in the Manchester store
  Gilb, D. Maria de Covina
  Kees, W. So cold outside
  Paul, B. Ho ho ho
  Pronzini, B. and Kurland, M. Quicker than the
    eye
  Rendell, R. The professional
Dependents. Simpson, M.
Dépestre, René
  A return to Jacmel
    Callaloo v24 no4 p983-90 Fall 2001
  Rosena on the mountain
    The Oxford book of Caribbean short stories;
      edited by Stewart Brown and John
      Wickham
Depew, Donald R.
  Indigenous girls
    Retrieving bones; stories and poems of the
      Korean War; edited and with an introduc-
      tion by W. D. Ehrhart and Philip K. Jason
The **depressed** person. Wallace, D. F.
DEPRESSION, 1929 *See* Business depression,
  1929
DEPRESSIONS, BUSINESS *See* Business de-
  pression, 1929
Der Nister
  Beheaded
    Neugroschel, J. No star too beautiful; Yiddish
      stories from 1382 to the present; compiled
      and translated by Joachim Neugroschel
DeRay. Carlson, R.
**DERBY, FERDINANDO STANLEY, 5TH
  EARL OF, 1559?-1594**
                    About
  Lane, A. The gaze of the falcon
Derby, Matthew
  An appeal
    Derby, M. Super flat times; stories
  Behavior pilot
    Derby, M. Super flat times; stories
  The boyish mulatto
    Derby, M. Super flat times; stories

Crutches used as weapon
    Derby, M. Super flat times; stories
The end of men
    Derby, M. Super flat times; stories
The father helmet
    Derby, M. Super flat times; stories
First
    Derby, M. Super flat times; stories
Gantry's last
    Derby, M. Super flat times; stories
Home recordings
    Derby, M. Super flat times; stories
Instructions
    Derby, M. Super flat times; stories
Joy of eating
    Derby, M. Super flat times; stories
The life jacket
    Derby, M. Super flat times; stories
Meat tower
    Derby, M. Super flat times; stories
Night watchmen
    Derby, M. Super flat times; stories
Sky harvest
    Derby, M. Super flat times; stories
The sound gun
    Derby, M. Super flat times; stories
Stupid animals
    Derby, M. Super flat times; stories
Derleth, August William
  The adventure of the Penny Magenta
    Murder most postal; homicidal tales that de-
      liver a message; edited by Martin H.
      Greenberg
Derleth, August William and Schorer, Mark
  The woman at Loon Point
    The Literary werewolf; an anthology; edited
      by Charlotte F. Otten
Dermont, Amber
  Merchants
    Gettysburg Review v16 no4 p653-61 Wint
      2003
DeRosso, H. A. (Henry Andrew)
  Bad blood
    DeRosso, H. A. Riders of the shadowlands;
      western stories; edited by Bill Pronzini
  Dark purpose
    DeRosso, H. A. Riders of the shadowlands;
      western stories; edited by Bill Pronzini
  Endless trail
    DeRosso, H. A. Riders of the shadowlands;
      western stories; edited by Bill Pronzini
  Fear in the saddle
    DeRosso, H. A. Riders of the shadowlands;
      western stories; edited by Bill Pronzini
  The happy death
    DeRosso, H. A. Riders of the shadowlands;
      western stories; edited by Bill Pronzini
  Killer
    DeRosso, H. A. Riders of the shadowlands;
      western stories; edited by Bill Pronzini
  The return of the Arapaho Kid
    DeRosso, H. A. Riders of the shadowlands;
      western stories; edited by Bill Pronzini
  Riders of the shadowlands
    DeRosso, H. A. Riders of the shadowlands;
      western stories; edited by Bill Pronzini
  The ways of vengeance
    DeRosso, H. A. Riders of the shadowlands;
      western stories; edited by Bill Pronzini

DeRosso, H. A. (Henry Andrew)—*Continued*
  Witch
    DeRosso, H. A. Riders of the shadowlands; western stories; edited by Bill Pronzini
DeRosso, Henry Andrew *See* DeRosso, H. A. (Henry Andrew), 1917-1960
Derrick was right. Crawley, D.
Derrida's sandwich. Targan, B.
Derringer. Bishop, P.
Des Barres, Pamela
  The James Dean diaries
    Carved in rock; short stories by musicians; edited by Greg Kihn
Des saucisses, sans doute. Schneider, P.
Desai, Anita
  The artist's life
    Desai, A. Diamond dust; stories
  Diamond dust, a tragedy
    Desai, A. Diamond dust; stories
  Five hours to Simla; or, Faisla
    Desai, A. Diamond dust; stories
  The man who saw himself drown
    Desai, A. Diamond dust; stories
  The rooftop dwellers
    Desai, A. Diamond dust; stories
  Royalty
    Desai, A. Diamond dust; stories
  Tepoztlan tomorrow
    Desai, A. Diamond dust; stories
  Underground
    Desai, A. Diamond dust; stories
  Winterscape
    Desai, A. Diamond dust; stories
Desaparecidos. Kurlansky, M.
Desaulniers, Janet
  After Rosa Parks
    Breaking into print; early stories and insights into getting published; a Ploughshares anthology; edited by DeWitt Henry
DESCARTES, RENÉ, 1596-1650
  About
  Melville, P. The parrot and Descartes
Descending. Wisniewski, M.
Descent. Scutt, C.
The **descent**. Watson, I.
The **descent** of man. Wharton, E.
Deseret. McManus, J.
Desert. Epstein, L.
The **desert** limited. Pronzini, B.
Desert music. Meredith, D.
Desert places. DeMarinis, R.
DESERTED HOUSES
  Händler, E.-W. Morgenthau
Deserted wife. Baron, D.
The **deserter**. Babel´, I.
The **deserter**. Tenn, W.
DESERTION, MILITARY *See* Military desertion
Desertion. Simak, C. D.
DESERTION AND NONSUPPORT
  Davis, J. S. The one thing God'll give you
  Grau, S. A. The man outside
  Hawthorne, N. Wakefield
  Hodgen, C. A jeweler's eye for flaw
  Singer, I. B. Altele
  Singer, I. B. Disguised
DESERTS
  See also Sahara
  Anderson, P. Windmill
  Brand, M. Wine on the desert

  Coleman, J. C. The Perseid meteors
  Grey, Z. Tappan's burro
  Hirshberg, G. Dancing men
  Iribarne, M. The clear blue water
  L'Amour, L. Desperate men
  L'Amour, L. The lonesome gods
  Padilla, I. The antipodes and the century
  Rinehart, S. Burning luv
  Wolfe, G. A traveler in desert lands
Desideratus. Fitzgerald, P.
Desire. Kim, N. J.
Desire lines. Frank, M.
Desire lines. Molyneux, J.
Désirée's baby. Chopin, K.
Desiring desire. Skinner, J.
Desleal, Alvaro Menen *See* Menen Desleal, Alvaro
Desmond, Kristen
  Blessed art thou among women
    Gettysburg Review v12 no3 p387-401 Aut 1999
Desnoyers, Adam
  Bleed blue in Indonesia
    The O. Henry Prize stories, 2003; edited and with an introduction by Laura Furman; jurers David Gutterson, Diane Johnson, Jennifer Egan
Desolation. Jones, G.
DESPAIR
  Bakr, S. Thirty-one beautiful green trees
  Gussoff, C. The wave: a novella
  Händler, E.-W. Morgenthau
  Ponte, A. J. Because of men
Despair: five stories of Ottawa. Alexis, A.
Desperate journey. Farrell, C.
The **desperate** ones. Pronzini, B.
Desplechin, Marie
  At sea
    Desplechin, M. Taking it to heart; translated from the French by Will Hobson
  Haiku
    Desplechin, M. Taking it to heart; translated from the French by Will Hobson
  An important question
    Desplechin, M. Taking it to heart; translated from the French by Will Hobson
  Joy
    Desplechin, M. Taking it to heart; translated from the French by Will Hobson
  The kiwi-seller
    Desplechin, M. Taking it to heart; translated from the French by Will Hobson
  My cousin Gérard
    Desplechin, M. Taking it to heart; translated from the French by Will Hobson
  Something's wrong
    Desplechin, M. Taking it to heart; translated from the French by Will Hobson
  Taking it to heart
    Desplechin, M. Taking it to heart; translated from the French by Will Hobson
Dessen, Sarah
  Umbrella
    This is where we live; short stories by 25 contemporary North Carolina writers; edited by Michael McFee
DESTINY *See* Fate and fatalism
Destiny. Ramaya, S.
Destroying angel. Matera, L.

DESTRUCTION OF EARTH *See* Earth, Destruction of
The **destruction** of Paris. Giono, J.
DESTRUCTION OF THE JEWS *See* Holocaust, Jewish (1933-1945)
The **detailer**. Etchison, D.
Details. Miéville, C.
Details. Rusch, K. K.
Details. Tarses, M.
The **detective**. Böttcher, M.
DETECTIVE AND MYSTERY STORIES *See* Mystery and detective stories
DETECTIVES
Alleyn, Superintendent Roderick. See stories by Marsh, Dame N.
Archer, Lew. See stories by Macdonald, R.
Axton, R. B. See stories by Allyn, D.
Barlow, Hannah. See stories by Lachnit, C.
Bartholomew, Matthew. See stories by Gregory, S.
Bascombe, Special Constable Frank. See stories by Robinson, P.
Bayles, China. See stories by Albert, S. W.
Bear, Goldy. See stories by Davidson, D. M.
Birch, Jefferson. See stories by Lee, W. W.
Bloodworth, Leo. See stories by Lochte, D.
Blue, Sebastian. See stories by Hoch, E. D.
Bohannon, Hack. See stories by Hansen, J.
Boore, Clement. See stories by Breen, J. L.
Breedlove, Pete. See stories by Kaminsky, S. M.
Brogan, Jerry. See stories by Breen, J. L.
Brown, Father. See stories by Chesterton, G. K.
Calhoun, Rory. See stories by Healy, J. F.
Campion, Albert. See stories by Allingham, M.
Cannon, Curt. See stories by Hunter, E.
Carmody. See stories by Pronzini, B.
Cavanaugh, Robert. See stories by Kress, N.
Charme, Laura. See stories by Hoch, E. D.
Chee, Corporal Jim. See stories by Hillerman, T.
Chin, Lydia. See stories by Rozan, S. J.
Cohen, Midge. See stories by Brill, T.
Connell, Dan. See stories by Pronzini, B.
Continental Op. See stories by Hammett, D.
Cooperman, Benny. See stories by Engel, H.
Cordell, Matt. See stories by Hunter, E.
Croaker, Fey. See stories by Bishop, P.
Crowne, Rachel. See stories by Rawlings, E.
Cuddy, John Francis. See stories by Healy, J. F.
Dahlquist, Serendipity. See stories by Lochte, D.
Dalziel, Inspector. See stories by Hill, R.
Darling, Annie. See stories by Hart, C. G.
Darling, Max. See stories by Hart, C. G.
Darwin, Erasmus. See stories by Sheffield, C.
De Gier, Sergeant Rinus. See stories by Van de Wetering, J.
Dortmunder. See stories by Westlake, D. E.
Dowling, Father. See stories by McInerny, R. M.
Drum, Chester. See stories by Marlowe, S.
Dupin, C. Auguste. See stories by Poe, E. A.
Dwyer, Jack. See stories by Gorman, E.
Ellis, Trade. See stories by Browning, S.
Fansler, Kate. See stories by Cross, A.
Fidelma, Sister. See stories by Tremayne, P.
Floyd, C. J. See stories by Greer, R. O.
Flynn, Judith McMonigle. See stories by Daheim, M.
Fonesca, Lew. See stories by Kaminsky, S. M.

Frevisse, Sister. See stories by Frazer, M.
Ghote, Inspector Ganesh. See stories by Keating, H. R. F.
Gold, Rachel. See stories by Kahn, M. A.
Gordianus the Finder. See stories by Saylor, S.
Gorgon, Ed. See stories by Breen, J. L.
Grijpstra, Adjutant Henk. See stories by Van de Wetering, J.
Gunther, Joe. See stories by Mayor, A.
Haggerty, Leo. See stories by Schutz, B. M.
Hanks, Arly. See stories by Hess, J.
Hasp, Al. See stories by Breen, J. L.
Havoc, Johnny. See stories by Jakes, J.
Hawthorne, Dr. Sam. See stories by Hoch, E. D.
Heller, Nate. See stories by Collins, M. A.
Hennings, Rachel. See stories by Breen, J. L.
Henrie O. See stories by Hart, C. G.
Holmes, Sherlock. See stories by Altman, S.-E.
Holmes, Sherlock. See stories by Bear, E.
Holmes, Sherlock. See stories by Black, C.
Holmes, Sherlock. See stories by Breen, J. L.
Holmes, Sherlock. See stories by Brite, P. Z. and Ferguson, D.
Holmes, Sherlock. See stories by Bruce, C.
Holmes, Sherlock. See stories by Carroll, L.
Holmes, Sherlock. See stories by Clark, S.
Holmes, Sherlock. See stories by Crider, B.
Holmes, Sherlock. See stories by Day, B.
Holmes, Sherlock. See stories by DeAndrea, W. L.
Holmes, Sherlock. See stories by Dôle, G.
Holmes, Sherlock. See stories by Doyle, Sir A. C.
Holmes, Sherlock. See stories by Effinger, G. A.
Holmes, Sherlock. See stories by Estleman, L. D.
Holmes, Sherlock. See stories by Ewing, C. D.
Holmes, Sherlock. See stories by Finch, P.
Holmes, Sherlock. See stories by Gaiman, N.
Holmes, Sherlock. See stories by Gilden, M.
Holmes, Sherlock. See stories by Hambly, B.
Holmes, Sherlock. See stories by Kiernan, C. R.
Holmes, Sherlock. See stories by Kurland, M.
Holmes, Sherlock. See stories by Landis, G. A.
Holmes, Sherlock. See stories by Lebbon, T.
Holmes, Sherlock. See stories by Linscott, G.
Holmes, Sherlock. See stories by Lovisi, G.
Holmes, Sherlock. See stories by Lowder, J.
Holmes, Sherlock. See stories by Lupoff, R. A.
Holmes, Sherlock. See stories by MacIntyre, F. G.
Holmes, Sherlock. See stories by Mallory, M.
Holmes, Sherlock. See stories by McCrumb, S.
Holmes, Sherlock. See stories by Pelan, J.
Holmes, Sherlock. See stories by Perry, A.
Holmes, Sherlock. See stories by Perry, A. and Saxon, M.
Holmes, Sherlock. See stories by Perry, S.
Holmes, Sherlock. See stories by Reaves, M.
Holmes, Sherlock. See stories by Robertson, L.
Holmes, Sherlock. See stories by Schreiber, N.
Holmes, Sherlock. See stories by Stableford, B. M.
Holmes, Sherlock. See stories by Stashower, D.
Holmes, Sherlock. See stories by Tremayne, P.
Holmes, Sherlock. See stories by Vourlis, J. P.
Holmes, Sherlock. See stories by Wheat, C.
Holmes, Sherlock. See stories by Wilson, D. N. and Macomber, P. L.

DETECTIVES—*Continued*

Hood, John. See stories by Jakes, J.
Howard, Roz. See stories by Kenney, S.
Howe, Emma. See stories by Roberts, G.
James, Nathan. See stories by Danger, N.
Keane, Owen. See stories by Faherty, T.
Knott, Deborah. See stories by Maron, M.
Krajewski, Bonecrack. See stories by Gores, J.
Lake, Barrett. See stories by Singer, S.
Langdon, Skip. See stories by Smith, J.
Langtry, Janice. See stories by Crider, B.
Legendre, J. J. See stories by Lochte, D.
Lieberman, Abe. See stories by Kaminsky, S. M.
Lindsey, Hobart. See stories by Lupoff, R. A.
Lynley, Detective Inspector Thomas. See stories by George, E.
MacAlister, Marti. See stories by Bland, E. T.
Macbeth, Hamish. See stories by Beaton, M. C.
Mackenzie, Blue. See stories by Bishop, P.
Magnum, Cuddy. See stories by Malone, M.
Manion, Terry. See stories by Lochte, D.
Marlowe, Philip. See stories by Chandler, R.
Marlowe, Philip. See stories by Nevins, F. M., Jr.
Marx, Detective Sergeant Joseph. See stories by Collins, M.
Mary Teresa, Sister. See stories by Quill, M.
Mastro, Lieutenant. See stories by Collins, M.
Matelli, Angela. See stories by Lee, W. W.
McCone, Sharon. See stories by Muller, M.
Mensing, Loren. See stories by Nevins, F. M., Jr.
Millhone, Kinsey. See stories by Grafton, S.
Monk, Ivan. See stories by Phillips, G.
Murphy, Molly. See stories by Bowen, R.
Noble, Nick. See stories by Boucher, A.
Noone, Father David. See stories by Hoch, E. D.
Nudger, Alo. See stories by Lutz, J.
O'Hara, Fergus. See stories by Pronzini, B.
O'Malley, Father John. See stories by Coel, M.
O'Malley, Maggie. See stories by Lee, W. W.
Paris, Charles. See stories by Brett, S.
Pascoe, Inspector. See stories by Hill, R.
Perkins, Ben. See stories by Kantner, R.
Peters, Toby. See stories by Kaminsky, S. M.
Pink, Miss. See stories by Moffat, G.
Plum, Marvia. See stories by Lupoff, R. A.
Po, Henry. See stories by Randisi, R. J.
Poirot, Hercule. See stories by Christie, A.
Poirot, Hercule. See stories by Watson, I.
Pons, Solar. See stories by Derleth, A. W.
Pope, Blaine. See stories by Bishop, P.
Private. See stories by Coward, M.
Quade, Theolonius. See stories by Perry, A.
Queen, Ellery. See stories by Hoch, E. D.
Queen, Ellery. See stories by Queen, E.
Quincannon, John. See stories by Pronzini, B.
Quintana, Ramon. See stories by Bishop, P.
Rawlings, Easy. See stories by Mosley, W.
Rawlins, Easy. See stories by Mosley, W.
Rebus, Detective Inspector John. See stories by Rankin, I.
Resnick, Inspector Charlie. See stories by Harvey, J.
Rhodes, Sheriff Dan. See stories by Crider, B.
Rhodes, Sheriff Dan. See stories by Crider, B. and Crider, J.

Rosen, Nate. See stories by Levitsky, R.
Rostnikov, Inspector Porfiry. See stories by Kaminsky, S. M.
Saint, The. See stories by Charteris, L.
Scott, Shell. See stories by Prather, R. S.
Scudder, Matt. See stories by Block, L.
Shelley, Mary. See stories by Morgan, D.
Sheringham, Roger. See stories by Berkeley, A.
Shore, Jemima. See stories by Fraser, A.
Simon, Margo. See stories by Steinberg, J.
Smith, Bill. See stories by Rozan, S. J.
Smith, Grace. See stories by Evans, L.
Smith, Patience. See stories by LaPierre, J.
Smith, Truman. See stories by Crider, B.
Spade, Sam. See stories by Hammett, D.
Stanton, Roberta. See stories by Matthews, C.
Steele, Christopher. See stories by Pronzini, B. and Kurland, M.
Stone, Richard. See stories by Collins, M. A.
Strange, Violet. See stories by Green, A. K.
Sughrue, C. W. See stories by Crumley, J.
Taine, Sidney. See stories by Weinberg, R.
Tanner, John Marshall. See stories by Greenleaf, S.
Thinking Machine. See stories by Futrelle, J.
Tramwell, Hyacinth. See stories by Cannell, D.
Tramwell, Primrose. See stories by Cannell, D.
Tree, Ms. See stories by Collins, M. A.
Ursula, Sister. See stories by Boucher, A.
Velvet, Nick. See stories by Hoch, E. D.
Wagner, Bo. See stories by Crider, B.
Walker, Amos. See stories by Estleman, L. D.
Warshawski, V. I. See stories by Paretsky, S.
Welt, Nicky. See stories by Kemelman, H.
Wennick, Peter. See stories by Gardner, E. S.
West, Delilah. See stories by O'Callaghan, M.
Wexford, Chief Inspector. See stories by Rendell, R.
Williams, Race. See stories by Daly, C. J.
Wolfe, Nero. See stories by Stout, R.
Yamamura, Trygve. See stories by Anderson, P.

DETECTIVES, PRIVATE

Allyn, D. Unchained melody
Anderson, P. The queen of air and darkness
Ayres, N. Delta double-deal
Bishop, P. Ebenezer
Bishop, P. Night of the Frankengolfer
Bracken, M. Feel the pain
Collins, B. and Collins, M. A. Eddie Haskell in a short skirt
Coward, M. The shortest distance
Crichton, M. Blood doesn't come out
Crider, B. One of our leprechauns is missing
Danihy, G. Jumping with Jim
Davis, L. Body zone
De Lint, C. If I close my eyes forever
De Noux, O. The Iberville mistress
Estleman, L. D. A hatful of Ralph
Fallis, G. And maybe the horse will learn to sing
Fesler, P. J. Coin of the realm
Fulmer, D. Back O'Town Blues
Gates, D. E. The blue mirror
Gores, J. Inscrutable
Gores, J. Sleep the big sleep
Gores, J. Summer fog
Grape, J. Cat o'nine lives
Groller, B. The vault break-in
Hammett, D. The assistant murderer

DETECTIVES, PRIVATE—*Continued*

Hammett, D. House dick
Herbert, J. Others
Hoch, E. D. V-2
Howard, C. The Dublin eye
L'Amour, L. A friend of a hero
L'Amour, L. Under the hanging wall
L'Amour, L. The unexpected corpse
L'Amour, L. The vanished blonde
Little, B. Maya's mother
Lochte, D. Sad-eyed blonde
Lupoff, R. A. The second drug
MacDonald, J. D. Murder for money
Matthews, C. I'm a dirty girl
McAuley, P. J. Naming the dead
Moorcock, M. The case of the Nazi canary
Mosley, W. The electric eye
Perelman, S. J. Farewell, my lovely appetizer
Phillips, G. '53 Buick
Pickard, N. Dust devil
Pickard, N. A rock and a hard place
Pronzini, B. La bellezza delle bellezze
Pronzini, B. The big bite
Pronzini, B. Dead man's slough
Pronzini, B. A killing in Xanadu
Pronzini, B. One night at Dolores Park
Pronzini, B. One of those cases
Pronzini, B. Shade work
Pronzini, B. Souls burning
Pronzini, B. Stacked deck
Pronzini, B. Stakeout
Redman, B. R. The perfect crime
Resnick, M. Even butterflies can sting
Rozan, S. J. Hoops
Schwarz, M.-J. Glimmerings on blue glass
Sumner, P. For your eyes only
Thrasher, L. L. Sacrifice
Townshend, P. The plate from horse's neck
Traylor, J. L. Dicks are blind
VanderMeer, J. Corpse mouth and spore nose
Vinge, V. The Science Fair
Wellen, E. Inside evidence

The **detective's** wife. Hoch, E. D.
Detour Drive. Lankford, T.
Detox. Brown, J.
DETROIT (MICH.) *See* Michigan—Detroit
Deus ex machina. Gomes, M. T.
Deus ex machina. Karnezis, P.
Deutchman, Joshua
  Swimming upstream
    Prairie Schooner v73 no1 p96-104 Spr 1999
Deutsches requiem. Borges, J. L.
Devaluation. Kurlansky, M.
Devane, Terry
  Decoys
    Women before the bench; edited by Carolyn
    Wheat; introduction by Linda Fairstein
Devassie, Thad
  Earthtonium and other white lies
    The North American Review v286 no3/4 p55
    My/Ag 2001
Development. Milliken, J.
Devereaux, Robert
  Apologia
    The Museum of horrors; edited by Dennis
    Etchison

Li'l Miss Ultrasound
    Gathering the bones; original stories from the
    world's masters of horror; edited by Dennis
    Etchison, Ramsey Campbell and Jack Dann
Nocturne a tre in b-double-sharp minor
    The Darkest thirst; a vampire anthology
Devi, Jyotirmoyee
  "That Little Boy": An English Translation of
    Jyotirmoyee Devi's Bengali Short Story
    "Shei Chheleta"
    Meridians v2 no2 p128-45 2002
DEVIL
  Barker, C. The Yattering and Jack
  Beaumont, C. The howling man
  Beerbohm, M. Enoch Soames
  Benét, S. V. The Devil and Daniel Webster
  Bradbury, R. The burning man
  De Lint, C. Sign here
  De Lint, C. Ten for the devil
  Dumas, H. The bewitching bag; or, How the
    man escaped from Hell
  Dumas, H. Devil bird
  Garnett, R. The demon pope
  Gores, J. Speak of the Devil
  Grau, S. A. The black prince
  Groom, W. Just a little closer to the Lord
  Hawthorne, N. Ethan Brand
  Hawthorne, N. Young Goodman Brown
  Heinlein, R. A. Magic, inc.
  King, S. The man in the black suit
  Lee, V. A wicked voice
  Lewis, R. J. Into the abyss
  Machen, A. The great god Pan
  McBain, E. The fallen angel
  Padilla, I. Hagiography of the apostate
  Pronzini, B. and Malzberg, B. N. Opening a
    vein
  Singer, I. B. A cage for Satan
  Singer, I. B. The destruction of Kreshev
  Singer, I. B. From the diary of one not born
  Singer, I. B. The gentleman from Crakow
  Singer, I. B. The last demon
  Singer, I. B. The mirror
  Singer, I. B. Shiddah and Kuziba
  Singer, I. B. A tale of two liars
  Singer, I. B. The unseen
The **devil**. Zinovyeva-Annibal, L. D.
The **Devil** and Daniel Webster. Benét, S. V.
The **Devil** and Guy Lansing. Auchincloss, L.
Devil beads. Maxwell, M. A. O.
Devil Dogs. Svoboda, T.
The **Devil** in manuscript. Hawthorne, N.
The **devil** in the valley. Rice, D.
The **devil** is a busy man. Wallace, D. F.
The **devil**, lightning, and policemen. Drake, R.
The **devil** of Malkirk. Sheffield, C.
The **Devil** Swims Across the Anacostia River.
    Jones, E. P.
Devilishly. Westlake, D. E.
Devil's bargain Turtledove, H. Alternate generals
    II; ed. by Harry Turtledove
"The **devil's** cross". Bécquer, G. A.
The **devil's** hop yard. Lupoff, R. A.
The **devil's** own. Betancourt, J. G.
Devil's pass. Wellen, E.
Devine, Maija Rhee
  Chaste Berry
    The Kenyon Review v26 no3 p118-30 Summ
    2004

Devine, Maija Rhee—*Continued*
  Crane's grace
    The Kenyon Review ns21 no3-4 p22-33
    Summ/Fall 1999
Devine, Thea
  The pleasure game
    Fascinated; [by] Bertrice Small, Susan John-
    son, Thea Devine and Robin Schone
Devlin, Anne
  Naming the names
    The Anchor book of new Irish writing; the
    new Gaelach ficsean; edited and with an
    introduction by John Somer and John J.
    Daly
Devolution. Hamilton, E.
DEVON (ENGLAND) *See* England—Devon
Devotion. Haslett, A.
Devotion. Hoffman, A.
DeVries, Melanie
  Of Death and Diners
    The North American Review v287 no6 p26-8
    N/D 2002
DeWeese, Dan
  Bullies
    New England Review v23 no3 p76-86 Summ
    2002
  The Problem of the House
    New England Review v24 no3 p134-43 Summ
    2003
DeWeese, Gene
  An essay on containment
    Dracula in London; edited by P. N. Elrod
Dexter, Colin
  The double crossing
    Edwards, M. Mysterious pleasures; a celebra-
    tion of the Crime Writers' Association's
    50th anniversary; edited by Martin Edwards
Dexter, Pete
  The jeweler
    The Best American mystery stories, 2003; ed-
    ited by Michael Connelly and Otto Penzler
Dexterity. Harvey, J.
D'Haene, Elise
  Breasts
    Hers 2: brilliant new fiction by lesbian writ-
    ers; edited by Terry Wolverton with Robert
    Drake
Dharma. Chandra, V.
Dhuibhne-Almqvist, Éilís Ní *See* Ní Dhuibhne-
    Almqvist, Éilís, 1954-
Dhum. Fischerová, D.
Di Blasi, Debra
  Blind
    Di Blasi, D. Prayers of an accidental nature;
    stories
  Chairman of the board
    Di Blasi, D. Prayers of an accidental nature;
    stories
  Drowning hard
    Di Blasi, D. Prayers of an accidental nature;
    stories
  Fog
    Di Blasi, D. Prayers of an accidental nature;
    stories
  Glauke's gown: the function of myth
    Iowa Review v32 no1 p137-53 Spr 2002
  I am telling you lies
    Di Blasi, D. Prayers of an accidental nature;
    stories

An interview with my husband
    Di Blasi, D. Prayers of an accidental nature;
    stories
An obscure geography
    Di Blasi, D. Prayers of an accidental nature;
    stories
Our perversions
    Di Blasi, D. Prayers of an accidental nature;
    stories
Pavlov's smile
    Di Blasi, D. Prayers of an accidental nature;
    stories
Prayers of an accidental nature
    Di Blasi, D. Prayers of an accidental nature;
    stories
The season's condition
    Di Blasi, D. Prayers of an accidental nature;
    stories
Where all things converge
    Di Blasi, D. Prayers of an accidental nature;
    stories
Di Filippo, Paul
  Ailoura
    Once upon a galaxy; edited by Will [sic]
    McCarthy, Martin H. Greenberg, and John
    Helfers
  And I think to myself, what a wonderful world
    One lamp; alternate history stories from The
    magazine of Fantasy & Science Fiction; ed-
    ited by Gordon van Gelder
  And the dish ran away with the spoon
    The year's best science fiction: twenty-first
    annual collection; edited by Gardner Dozois
  Have gun, will edit
    The Best from fantasy & science fiction: the
    fiftieth anniversary anthology; edited by
    Edward L. Ferman and Gordon Van Gelder
  A Martian theodicy
    Mars probes; edited by Peter Crowther
  Neutrino drag
    The Year's best science fiction, nineteenth an-
    nual collection; edited by Gardner Dozois
  Weeping walls
    Redshift; extreme visions of speculative fic-
    tion; edited by Al Sarrantonio
DIABETES
  Schmidt, H. J. A girl like you
  Westmoreland, T. A. Blood knot
  Westmoreland, T. A. The buried boy
Diaconú, Alina
  Blue lagoon
    English translations of short stories by con-
    temporary Argentine women writers; edited
    by Eliana Cazaubon Hermann ; translated
    by Sally Webb Thornton
Dial 411 for legal smut. Reiner, C.
Dial F for Frankenstein. Clarke, A. C.
Dial your dreams. Weinberg, R.
The **dialect** of the tribe. Mathews, H.
DIALECT STORIES
                    Australian
  McKay, K. Pie Row Joe
                    Black English
  Bambara, T. C. Gorilla, my love
  Chesnutt, C. W. The goophered grapevine
  Dumas, H. Ark of bones
  Ellison, R. Mister Toussan
  Glave, T. The final inning

DIALECT STORIES—Black English—*Continued*
Harris, J. C. How Mr. Rabbit was too sharp for Mr. Fox
Harris, J. C. Uncle Remus initiates the little boy
Harris, J. C. The wonderful Tar-Baby story
Jones, G. White rat
MacDowell, K. S. B. Gran'mammy
MacDowell, K. S. B. Why Gran'mammy didn't like pound-cake
McKnight, R. Quitting smoking
Page, T. N. Unc' Edinburg's drowndin'
Twain, M. A true story, repeated word for word as I heard it
Wright, R. Bright and morning star
Scottish
Healy, T. It might have been Jerusalem [excerpt]
Jamieson, R. A. The last black hoose
Kelman, J. The comfort
Kelman, J. Comic cuts
Kelman, J. Every fucking time
Kelman, J. Gardens go on forever
Kelman, J. It happened to me once
Kelman, J. Joe laughed
Kelman, J. Oh my darling
Kelman, J. Pulped sandwiches
Kelman, J. Then later
Kelman, J. The wey it can turn
Leonard, T. Honest
Owens, A. When Shankland comes
Robertson, S. A monk's tail
Scarborough, E. A. Tinkler Tam and the body snatchers
Spence, A. Brilliant
Southern States
Morgan, R. Dark corner
Smith, J. Crime wave in Pinhole
West Indian
Adisa, O. P. Widows' walk
Antoni, R. A world of canes
Breeze, J. B. Sunday cricket
Chen, W. Trotters
Lovelace, E. Victory and the blight
Murray, M. Shame the devil
Persaud, S. Canada geese and apple chatney
Salkey, A. A proper Anno Domini feeling
Shacochis, B. Easy in the islands
Shacochis, B. Mundo's sign
Walrond, E. Drought
Dialectic, abrasions, the backs of heads again. Singleton, G.
A **dialog** between dead men. Borges, J. L.
DIALOGUE *See* Conversation
The **dialogues** of time and entropy. Stollman, A. L.

Diamond, Pamela
Whitey
Southwest Review v84 no2 p251-68 1999
Texas bound. Book III; 22 Texas stories; edited by Kay Cattarulla; foreword by Robert Flynn
The **diamond** as big as the Ritz. Fitzgerald, F. S.
Diamond dust, a tragedy. Desai, A.
The **diamond** mine. Gordimer, N.
Diamond Mozzarella. Piccirilli, T.
The **diamond** of Jeru. L'Amour, L.
The **diamond** pit. Dann, J.
The **diamond** spy. Hodgson, W. H.

DIAMONDS
Fitzgerald, F. S. The diamond as big as the Ritz
L'Amour, L. The diamond of Jeru
Teigeler, P. The wind & Mary
Diamonds. Kobin, J.
Diamonds. West, M.
Diamonds are a girl's best friend. Hochman, A.
Diamonds are for never. O'Callaghan, M.
Diamonds at her fingertips. Berkman, P. R.
DIANA, PRINCESS OF WALES, 1961-1997
About
Perabo, S. Counting the ways
Diane de Forêt. Bradbury, R.
DIARIES (STORIES ABOUT)
Carr, P. M. Diary of a union soldier
Crider, B. Tinseltown Follies of 1948
Kusel, L. Juvenile hall
Kusel, L. The other side
Taylor, T. L. The Boar's Head Easter
DIARIES (STORIES IN DIARY FORM)
See also Letters (Stories in letter form)
Apukhtin, A. N. The diary of Pavlik Dolsky
Arnott, Marion. Marbles
Barceló, E. First time
Baxter, S. The modern Cyrano
Bowles, P. If I should open my mouth
Broughton, T. A. A tour of the islands
Carroll, L. Traveling princess
Charnas, S. M. Listening to Brahms
Chekhov, A. P. From the diary of an assistant book-keeper
Clark, J. Public burning
Connor, J. The day the world declined to end
Crowther, P. Bedfordshire
Davenport, G. The death of Picasso
Doble, J. Entries from Skipper Bitwell's journal
Dooling, R. Diary of an immortal man
Gaiman, N. Pages from a journal found in a shoebox left in a Greyhound bus somewhere between Tulsa, Oklahoma, and Louisville, Kentucky
George Patton slept here
Gies, M. Zoo animal keeper 1, REC-SVC-ZK
Gifford, B. The Tunisian notebook
Gilman, C. P. The yellow wallpaper
Gunthorp, D. Pikeman and the Bagwoman
Herling, G. Notebook of William Moulding, pensioner
James, H. The diary of a man of fifty
James, H. The impressions of a cousin
James, H. A landscape painter
James, H. A light man
Keyes, D. Flowers for Algernon
Knight, P. Set in stone
Lee, T. Yellow and red
Lee, V. Amour dure
Levrero, M. Notes from Buenos Aires
Naipaul, V. S. The night watchman's occurrence book
Olsen, S. S. Free writing
Reifler, N. Personal foundations of self-forming through auto-identification with otherness
Turzillo, M. A. Mars is no place for children
Williamson, C. Excerpts from the Records of the New Zodiac and the diaries of Henry Watson Fairfax
The **diary** of a man of fifty. James, H.
Diary of a union soldier. Carr, P. M.
Diary of an explorer. Accame, J.

The **diary** of Pavlik Dolsky. Apukhtin, A. N.
The **diary** of Sue Peaner, Marooned! contestant.
  Hayter, S.
Díaz, Junot
  The brief wondrous life of Oscar Wao
    What are you looking at?; the first fat fiction
    anthology; edited by Donna Jarrell and Ira
    Sukrungruang
  Edison, New Jersey
    Colchie, T. A whistler in the nightworld;
    short fiction from the Latin Americas; ed-
    ited by Thomas Colchie
  Fiesta 1980
    The Scribner anthology of contemporary short
    fiction; fifty North American stories since
    1970; Lex Williford and Michael Martone,
    editors
  Nilda
    The Best American short stories, 2000; select-
    ed from U.S. and Canadian magazines by
    E. L. Doctorow with Katrina Kenison; with
    an introduction by E. L. Doctorow
    The New Yorker v75 no29 p92-97 O 4 1999
  Otravida, otravez
    The New Yorker v75 no16 p186-89+ Je 21-28
    1999
  The sun, the moon, the stars
    The Best American short stories, 1999; select-
    ed from U.S. and Canadian magazines by
    Amy Tan with Katrina Kenison, with an in-
    troduction by Amy Tan
  Ysrael
    The Art of the story; an international antholo-
    gy of contemporary short stories; edited by
    Daniel Halpern
Dib, Mohammed
  The station of the cow
    The Hudson Review v54 no3 p367-70 Aut
    2001
DiChario, Nick
  Carp man
    The Year's best fantasy & horror, twelfth an-
    nual collection; edited by Ellen Datlow &
    Terry Windling
  Dragonhead
    The year's best science fiction: twenty-first
    annual collection; edited by Gardner Dozois
  The one-half boy
    Tetrick, B. In the shadow of the wall; an an-
    thology of Vietnam stories that might have
    been; edited by Byron R. Tetrick
  Where the wildflowers bloom
    Bishop, C. and James, D. Death dines in; ed-
    ited by Claudia Bishop and Dean James
  The winterberry
    The Best alternate history stories of the 20th
    century; edited by Harry Turtledove with
    Martin H. Greenberg
Dick, Philip K.
  I hope I shall arrive soon
    The Vintage book of amnesia; an anthology;
    edited by Jonathan Lethem
    About
  McAuley, P. J. The two Dicks
  The two dicks
Dick. Nelson, A.
A **Dick** and Jane story. Kelly, J.
Dick W. and his Pussy; or, Tess and her Adequate
  Dick. Yolen, J.

DICKENS, CHARLES, 1812-1870
About
  Bradbury, R. Any friend of Nicholas Nickleby's
    is a friend of mine
  Connor, J. The mystery of Thomas Power James
  Waldrop, H. Household words; or, the powers-
    that-be
Parodies, imitations, etc.
  Bishop, P. Ebenezer
  Willis, C. Adaptation
Dickerson, D. Ellis
  Mom, Having Died
    Gettysburg Review v17 no1 p65-75 Spr 2004
Dickey, Eric Jerome
  Café Piel
    Got to be real; four original love stories; [by]
    E. Lynn Harris [et al.]
DICKINSON, EMILY, 1830-1886
About
  Barrett, N., Jr. Winter on the Belle Fourche
  Malzberg, B. N. Standards & practices
  Yolen, J. Sister Emily's lightship
Dickinson, Marc
  Momentary Darkness
    The North American Review v288 no6 p24-5
    N/D 2003
Dickinson, Peter
  Mermaid song
    The Year's best fantasy & horror: sixteenth
    annual collection; edited by Ellen Datlow
    & Terri Windling
Dickinson, Stephanie
  A Lynching in Stereoscope
    African American Review v38 no1 p35-43 Spr
    2004
Dicks are blind. Traylor, J. L.
Dickson, Gordon R.
  Computers don't argue
    Murder most postal; homicidal tales that de-
    liver a message; edited by Martin H.
    Greenberg
  The man in the mailbag
    The Good old stuff; adventure SF in the
    grand tradition; edited by Gardner Dozois
DICTATORS
  See also Totalitarianism
  Clarke, A. C. The light of darkness
  Jenkins, G. Gotta sing
DICTATORSHIP *See* Dictators
Die **like** a lobster. McManus, J.
Dies Irae. Koskinen, M.
DIETING *See* Reducing
A **different** kind of courage. Lackey, M.
A **different** kind of imperfection. Beller, T.
Difficult people. Chekhov, A. P.
The **difficulty** of translation. Ferriss, L.
DiFilippo, Paul
  Science fiction
    Witpunk; edited by Claude Lalumière and
    Marty Halpern
  (jt. auth) See Bishop, Michael and DiFilippo,
    Paul
Digestions. Crace, J.
Digging. Lordan, B.
Digging the hole. Zafris, N.
The **dignity** of life. Bly, C.

Dik, Aizik-Meyer
The panic; or, The town of Hérres
Neugroschel, J. No star too beautiful; Yiddish stories from 1382 to the present; compiled and translated by Joachim Neugroschel
Dildo. Jackson, S.
Dillard, Annie
The Two of Them
Harper's v307 p61-5 N 2003
Dillard, R. H. W. (Richard H. W.)
Forgetting the end of the world
New stories from the South: the year's best, 2000; edited by Shannon Ravenel; with a preface by Ellen Douglas
The Virginia Quarterly Review v75 no4 p649-55 Aut 1999
Dillard, Richard H. W. *See* Dillard, R. H. W. (Richard H. W.), 1937-
A **diller**, a daughter. Lewis, T.
Dillingham, Dennis G.
The white carousel horse
Pieces; a collection of new voices; edited by Stephen Chbosky
Dillon, Millicent
Mingling
Southwest Review v86 no4 p500-9 2001
Staying
Michigan Quarterly Review v41 no1 p127-35 Wint 2002
The **Dilly**. Nichols, J.
Dilts, Tyler
Thug: signification and the (de) constuction of self
The Best American mystery stories, 2003; edited by Michael Connelly and Otto Penzler
Dilworth, Sharon
A little learning
The Pushcart prize XXVI; best of the small presses, an annual small press reader; edited by Bill Henderson and the Pushcart prize editors
The **diminishing** draft. Haempffert, W.
Diner. Barrett, N., Jr.
Dinesen, Isak
The supper at Elsinore
Nightshade: 20th century ghost stories; edited by Robert Phillips
Dinezon, Yankev
The crisis [excerpt]
Neugroschel, J. No star too beautiful; Yiddish stories from 1382 to the present; compiled and translated by Joachim Neugroschel
Ding. Lao She
Dinger and Blacker. DeLancey, K.
Dinh, Linh
!
The American Poetry Review v30 no5 p17-18 S/O 2001
10X50
Dinh, L. Fake House; stories
555
Dinh, L. Fake House; stories
Boo hoo hoo
Dinh, L. Fake House; stories
Brother News from Home
Dinh, L. Fake House; stories
California fine view
Dinh, L. Fake House; stories

The cave
Dinh, L. Fake House; stories
Chopped Steak Mountain
Dinh, L. Fake House; stories
A cultured boy
Dinh, L. Fake House; stories
Dead on arrival
Dinh, L. Fake House; stories
Fake House
Dinh, L. Fake House; stories
For gristles
Dinh, L. Fake House; stories
Fritz Glatman
Dinh, L. Fake House; stories
The hippie chick
Dinh, L. Fake House; stories
Hope and standards
Dinh, L. Fake House; stories
In the vein
Dinh, L. Fake House; stories
Saigon Pull
Dinh, L. Fake House; stories
Two who forgot
Dinh, L. Fake House; stories
The ugliest girl
Dinh, L. Fake House; stories
Uncle Tom's cabin
Dinh, L. Fake House; stories
Val
Dinh, L. Fake House; stories
Western music
Dinh, L. Fake House; stories
Dinh, Viet
Parts of Speech
Chicago Review v49 no2 p77-93 Summ 2003
The **dinner**. Doyle, R.
Dinner at Sir Nigel's. Bowles, P.
Dinner at the Bank of England. Davenport, G.
A **dinner** in high society. Proust, M.
DINNER PARTIES *See* Dinners
Dinner party. Dozois, G. R.
The **dinner** party. Girardi, R.
Dinner with Dr Azad. Ali, M.
DINNERS
Adams, A. Fog
Bowles, P. Dinner at Sir Nigel's
Boylan, C. A nail on the head
Brennan, M. The joker
Di Blasi, D. Prayers of an accidental nature
Godwin, P. A matter of taste
McGarry, J. Among the Philistines
Moore, L. Beautiful grade
Dinosaur. Troy, M.
Dinosaur dreams. Lumley, B.
DINOSAURS
Bishop, M. Herding with the hadrosaurs
Clarke, A. C. Time's arrow
De Camp, L. S. A gun for dinosaur
Emshwiller, C. Creature
Harrison, H. Dawn of the endless night
Lumley, B. Dinosaur dreams
Malzberg, B. N. Major league triceratops
Swanwick, M. Scherzo with tyrannosaur
Updike, J. During the Jurassic
Dinosaurs. Franklin, T.
Dinsmore's Paradox. McBrearty, R. G.
Dio. Knight, D. F.
DIPLOMATIC LIFE
The ambassador's son

DIPLOMATIC LIFE—*Continued*
Archer, J. Other blighters' efforts
Gabriel, D. The kapici's wife
Hunter, F. Dr. Kleckner
Hunter, F. Pepper
James, H. Pandora
Lida, D. The recruiting officer
Phillips, A. Wenceslas Square
DIPLOMATS *See* Diplomatic life
Direct action. Thelwell, M.
Direct male. Mickenberg, R.
Directions. Budnitz, J.
Directions for seeing, directions for singing. Singleton, G.
DIRECTORS, MOTION PICTURE *See* Motion picture producers and directors
DIRIGIBLES *See* Airships
Dirt. Casey, M.
Dirt angel. Wilmot, J.
Dirt-eaters. Cooke, C.
The **dirt** eaters. Matthews, C.
Dirty dancing. Douglas, C. N.
Dirty pool. Roche, T. S.
Dis bwoy, him gwan. Banks, R.
Disappearance I. Winterson, J.
Disappearance II. Winterson, J.
Disappearance of an ordinary woman. Alavi, T.
The **disappearance** of Edna Guberman. Lee, W. W.
The **disappearance** of Elaine Coleman. Millhauser, S.
DISAPPEARANCES *See* Missing persons
Disappearances. LeRoy, J. T.
Disappearing act. Bester, A.
The **disapproval** of Jeremy Cleave. Lumley, B.
Disaster. Doenges, J.
DISASTERS
See also Earthquakes; Epidemics; Floods; Shipwrecks and castaways
Avrich, J. The great flood
DeAndrea, W. L. Sabotage
DISC JOCKEYS
Leslie, N. Rain dance
Disch, Thomas M.
Cancelled friends
The Hudson Review v54 no2 p237-43 Summ 2001
The first annual performance art festival at the Slaughter Rock Battlefield
The Pushcart prize XXIII: best of the small presses; an annual small press reader; edited by Bill Henderson with the Pushcart prize editors
In Xanadu
Redshift; extreme visions of speculative fiction; edited by Al Sarrantonio
The owl and the pussycat
999: new stories of horror and suspense; edited by Al Sarrantonio
The squirrel cage
The Vintage book of amnesia; an anthology; edited by Jonathan Lethem
Disciple pigeons. Smolens, J.
Discipline and will. Kobin, J.
Disclaimer. Carlson, R.
A **discourse** on history. Lock, N.
The **discovery** of Morniel Mathaway. Tenn, W.
Discovery of the Ghooric Zone. Lupoff, R. A.

DISEASES
See also AIDS (Disease); Alzheimer's disease; Sexually transmitted diseases; Tuberculosis; Typhus fever
Bear, G. Darwin's radio [excerpt]
Butler, O. E. The evening and the morning and the night
Green, Dominic. Send me a mentagram
Holt, T. E. 'O
Kress, N. Inertia
Link, K. Louise's ghost
Stableford, B. M. The house of mourning
Theroux, P. White lies
Tremain, R. John-Jin
DISGUISES *See* Impersonations
The **dishwasher**. McBrearty, R. G.
The **disinterested** killer Bill Harrigan. Borges, J. L.
The **disk**. Borges, J. L.
The **dismissal**. Bowles, P.
DISMISSAL OF EMPLOYEES
Bowles, P. The dismissal
Cummins, A. Billy by the bay
Ellin, S. Reasons unknown
Harrison, H. Portrait of the artist
Dismissed, with prejudice. Huffman, B., Jr.
A **Disney** World. Barnes, J.
DISNEYLAND (ANAHEIM, CALIF.)
Berney, L. Stupid girl
Howard, C. The California contact
Vernon, D. Arrival
Disneyland. DeMarinis, R.
DISORDERS OF PERSONALITY *See* Personality disorders
Dispatch. Thien, M.
The **dispatching** of George Ferris. Pronzini, B.
Displacement. Louie, D. W.
Dispossessed. Honig, L.
Dissections. Lobenstine, D. M.
DISSENTERS
Brkic, C. A. Surveillance
Singer, I. B. The blasphemer
DISSIDENTS *See* Dissenters
Dissolution or for Mrs. Berta Zuckerkandl. Händler, E.-W.
Distance. Ortiz, S. J.
Distance man. Schwarzschild, E. L.
Distance no object. Frym, G.
The **distance** to Delphi. Simonds, M.
A **Distant** Death. Casey, M.
A **distant** episode. Bowles, P.
Distant music. Beattie, A.
The **distant** sound of tree-felling. Cai Cehai
DISTILLING, ILLICIT *See* Moonshiners
DISTRICT OF COLUMBIA *See* Washington (D.C.)
Disturbances. White, M. C.
Disturbing the peace. Granelli, R.
The **ditch**. Sánchez, R.
Divakaruni, Chitra Banerjee
The blooming season for cacti
Divakaruni, C. B. The unknown errors of our lives; stories
The forgotten children
Divakaruni, C. B. The unknown errors of our lives; stories
The intelligence of wild things
Divakaruni, C. B. The unknown errors of our lives; stories

Divakaruni, Chitra Banerjee—*Continued*
  The lives of strangers
    Divakaruni, C. B. The unknown errors of our
      lives; stories
    Pushcart prize XXVII; best of the small
      presses; edited by Bill Henderson with the
      Pushcart prize editors
  The love of a good man
    Divakaruni, C. B. The unknown errors of our
      lives; stories
  Mrs. Dutta writes a letter
    The Best American short stories, 1999; select-
      ed from U.S. and Canadian magazines by
      Amy Tan with Katrina Kenison, with an in-
      troduction by Amy Tan
    Divakaruni, C. B. The unknown errors of our
      lives; stories
  The names of stars in Bengali
    Divakaruni, C. B. The unknown errors of our
      lives; stories
  The unknown errors of our lives
    Divakaruni, C. B. The unknown errors of our
      lives; stories
    Prairie Schooner v75 no1 p7-19 Spr 2001
  What the body knows
    Divakaruni, C. B. The unknown errors of our
      lives; stories
The **diver**. Robinson, L.
Divertimento Number III. Doderer, H. v.
Divided by infinity. Wilson, R. C.
Divided highway. Painter, P.
Dividends and distributions. Pearson, T. R.
Dividing by zero. Nyren, R.
Divination. Haslett, A.
Divine and human. Tolstoy, L., graf
The **divine** fireplace. Brennan, M.
Divine guidance. Newman, S.
Divine Thanks for Packaged Light. Means, D. R.
The **diviners**. Kinsella, J.
The **diving** girls. Mazelis, J.
Diving into eternity. Barolini, H.
A **diving** rock on the Hudson [excerpt] Roth, H.
Divining the waters. Louis, L. G.
Division by zero. Chiang, T.
Divisions. Choi, E.
DIVORCE
        See also Desertion and nonsupport; Di-
        vorced persons; Marriage problems
  Abbott, L. K. Once upon a time
  Alvarez, J. Amor divino
  Archer, J. Too many coincidences
  Auchincloss, L. DeCicco v. Schweizer
  Bingham, S. Bare bones
  Chabon, M. Spikes
  Chekhov, A. P. Old age
  Chenoweth, A. Reunions
  Chopin, K. Madame Célestin's divorce
  Cobb, W. J. There's nothing the matter with
    Gwen
  Cook, K. L. Breaking glass
  D'Ambrosio, C., Jr. Open house
  Devane, T. Decoys
  Epstein, J. Saturday afternoon at the zoo with
    dad
  Fulton, J. Braces
  Giles, M. Pie dance
  Grau, S. A. Letting go
  Hall, D. From Willow Temple
  Homes, A. M. Rockets round the moon

  James, H. The chaperon
  Kane, J. F. Refuge
  Klíma, I. It's raining out
  McCorkle, J. Crash diet
  McKee, J. Under the influence
  Murakami, H. Honey Pie
  Nailah, A. My side of the story
  Onetti, J. C. Hell most feared
  Painter, P. Custody
  Painter, P. Divided highway
  Painter, P. Feeding the piranha
  Painter, P. New family car
  Phillips, D. R. When love gets worn
  Reifler, N. The splinter
  Reifler, N. Upstream
  Rodgers, S. J. Fits and starts
  Singer, I. B. The divorce
  Singer, I. B. The fast
  Sosin, D. You're so simple
  Stafford, J. Children are bored on Sunday
  Stollman, A. L. If I have found favor in your
    eyes
  Thurm, M. Passenger
  Updike, J. The orphaned swimming pool
  Walker, A. Kindred spirits
  Walton, A. Divorce education
  Weldon, F. Move out: move on
  Wexler, M. Pink is for punks
  Wharton, E. Autres temps . . .
  Wharton, E. The other two
  Wharton, E. The reckoning
  Wharton, E. Souls belated
  White, M. C. Voices
  Winegardner, M. Halftime
Divorce. Klíma, I.
Divorce education. Walton, A.
The **divorced** men's mall walkers club. Weaver,
  G.
DIVORCED PERSONS
  Abraham, D. An amicable divorce
  Adam, C. Fox
  Adams, A. Greyhound people
  Agee, J. And blue
  Agee, J. Dwight Tuggle
  Allyn, D. Unchained melody
  Almond, S. The evil B. B. Chow
  Aqai, F. One woman, one love
  Arvin, N. Take your child to work
  Atkinson, K. Wedding favors
  Bache, E. Shell Island
  Baida, P. No place to hide
  Banks, R. Plains of Abraham
  Banks, R. Sarah Cole: a type of love story
  Banks, R. Xmas
  Barthelme, F. Export
  Barthelme, F. Larroquette
  Barthelme, F. Law of averages
  Bauman, B. A. Safeway
  Bausch, R. Not quite final
  Beattie, A. In Amalfi
  Beattie, A. In irons
  Bellow, S. What kind of day did you have?
  Boylan, C. The wronged wife
  Busch, F. Machias
  Busch, F. The ninth, in E minor
  Capote, T. The bargain
  Carson, J. Protective coloring
  Carver, R. Intimacy
  Chabon, M. Green's book

DIVORCED PERSONS—*Continued*

Channer, C. I'm still waiting
Clark, J. Revenge
Clyde, M. Victor's funeral urn
Coberly, L. M. Snap beans and petits fours
Cody, L. A card or a kitten
Cohen, R. Dream group forming
Cohen, R. The bachelor party
Connor, J. Tea and comfortable advice
Cooper, B. Night sky
Crowley, J. Lost and abandoned
Davis, L. Sensitive things
DeLancey, K. It's dark
DeMarco, T. Dancing bare
DeMarinis, R. Novias
DeMarinis, R. Romance: a prose villanelle
Dinh, L. Fritz Glatman
Dodd, S. M. I married a space alien
Dokey, R. Hampstead's folly
Dokey, R. Vital statistics
Dubus, A. The winter father
Dunmore, H. Be vigilant, rejoice, eat plenty
Etchison, D. My present wife
Foster, K. Remainders
Fulton, J. Clean away
Fulton, J. Liars
Gabrielyan, N. Happiness
Gay, W. The man who knew Dylan
Gray, A. My ex husband
Greenberg, A. Crimes against humanity
Greenberg, A. How the dead live
Greenberg, A. No loose ends
Greer, A. S. The art of eating
Harty, R. Sarah at the Palace
Hendel, Y. Late revenge
Henley, P. Same old big magic
Highsmith, P. The second cigarette
Hribal, C. J. The clouds in Memphis
Iribarne, M. Astronauts
Jen, G. Birthmates
Johnson-Davies, D. A short weekend
Johnston, B. A. Waterwalkers
Kaufman, W. Helen on Eighty-Sixth Street
Kawabata, Y. First snow on Fuji
Kelman, J. Just desserts
Kenan, R. Hobbits and hobgoblins
Kennedy, A. L. Touch positive
Klass, P. Rainbow mama
Knight, M. The end of everything
Knight, M. Feeling lucky
Leslie, N. Poker face
Lombreglia, R. Cashmere Christmas
Lord, N. Wolverine grudge
Louis, L. G. Rudy's two wives
Lundquist, R. Now it looks respectable
Malone, M. The power
Malone, M. Winners and losers
Martin, L. Bad family
Mason, B. A. The funeral side
Mason, B. A. Tobrah
Mason, B. A. Tunica
Mason, B. A. With jazz
Matera, L. Counsel for the defense
Mattison, A. In case we're separated
Mazor, J. The munster final
McCorkle, J. Cats
McGarry, J. Paris
Meredith, D. Wing walking
Miller, S. Expensive gifts

Murakami, H. Thailand
Nevai, L. Step men
Norris, L. Self-defense
Oates, J. C. In hiding
Oates, J. C. A Manhattan romance
Oates, J. C. Physical
Oates, J. C. The vigil
Offutt, C. Two-eleven all around
Otis, M. Five-minute hearts
Painter, P. Going wild
Penn, W. S. In dreams begins reality
Peterson, P. W. Cherry's ghost
Phillips, D. R. My people's waltz
Phillips, D. R. What we are up against
Potvin, E. A. Wings
Proulx, A. Pair a spurs
Reid, E. All that good stuff
Rifkin, A. The honor system
Robison, M. An amateur's guide to the night
Robison, M. Daughters
Robison, M. In the woods
Robison, M. Kite and paint
Robison, M. Your errant mom
Rodgers, S. J. Bones and flowers
Rodgers, S. J. The two husbands
Rosenfeld, S. Grasp special comb
Rosenfeld, S. The last known thing
Sánchez, R. Three generations
Schwartz, L. S. The trip to Halawa Valley
Silber, J. The dollar in Italy
Singer, I. B. Androgynous
Singer, I. B. Exes
Smith, J. Fresh paint
Smith, J. Where the boys are
Sosin, D. Internal medicine
Spencer, E. I, Maureen
Stanton, M. Marie Antoinette's harp
Stuckey-French, E. Scavenger hunt
Svoboda, T. What did you bring me?
Swan, M. In the story that won't be written
Swick, M. A. The rhythm of disintegration
Swick, M. A. The zealous mourner
Thompson, J. Mother nature
Tinti, H. Animal crackers
Tuck, L. Dream house
Tuck, L. Rue Guynemer
Tuck, L. Verdi
Updike, J. Nevada
Valeri, L. She's anonymous
Weaver, G. The divorced men's mall walkers
    club
Weihe, E. All clear
Weldon, F. Noisy into the night
Wexler, M. The Maginot Line
Wilson, R., Jr. Florida
Wilson, R., Jr. Parts runner
Wilson, R., Jr. Trespass
Yates, R. Trying out for the race
DIVORCÉES *See* Divorced persons
DIVORCÉS *See* Divorced persons
Divorcing Johnny Ponder. Almond, S.
Diwakar, S.
    The Vow
        Iowa Review v33 no2 p121-3 Fall 2003
Dix, Shane
    Matters of consequence
        Centaurus: the best of Australian science fic-
        tion; edited by David G. Hartwell and Da-
        mien Broderick

DIXON, BILLY, 1850-1913
              About
  Braun, M. The stand
Dixon, Stephen
  Again—Part II
    TriQuarterly no113 p112-47 Summ 2002
  The burial
    The Pushcart prize XXIII: best of the small
      presses; an annual small press reader; ed-
      ited by Bill Henderson with the Pushcart
      prize editors
  Comparing
    Dixon, S. Sleep; stories
  The dat
    Dixon, S. Sleep; stories
  The elevator
    Dixon, S. Sleep; stories
  Game
    Dixon, S. Sleep; stories
  Give and take
    Dixon, S. Sleep; stories
  The hairpiece
    Dixon, S. Sleep; stories
  Hand
    Dixon, S. Sleep; stories
  Heat
    Dixon, S. Sleep; stories
  The knife
    Dixon, S. Sleep; stories
  Man of letters
    Other people's mail; an anthology of letter
      stories; edited with an introduction by Gail
      Pool
  Many Janes
    Dixon, S. Sleep; stories
  My life up till now
    Dixon, S. Sleep; stories
  Never ends
    Dixon, S. Sleep; stories
  On a windy night
    Dixon, S. Sleep; stories
  Other way
    Dixon, S. Sleep; stories
  The Party
    TriQuarterly no115 p165-73 Spr 2003
  The rehearsal
    Dixon, S. Sleep; stories
  The school bus
    Dixon, S. Sleep; stories
  Sleep
    Dixon, S. Sleep; stories
  Speed bump
    TriQuarterly no105 p98-104 Spr/Summ 1999
  The stranded man
    Dixon, S. Sleep; stories
  Survivors
    Dixon, S. Sleep; stories
  Tails
    Dixon, S. Sleep; stories
  The tellers
    Dixon, S. Sleep; stories
  To Tom
    Dixon, S. Sleep; stories
Djemai, Abdelkader
  No Way Out
    College Literature v30 no1 p153-6 Wint 2003
Djinn. Banks, R.
The **djinn** game. Sarath, P. E.

The **djinn** who watches over the accursed.
  Donaldson, S. R.
Djinni. Gussoff, C.
Do angels wear brassieres? Senior, O.
Do me. Biguenet, J.
Do me a favor. Paolucci, A.
Do not attempt to climb out. Hochman, A.
Do not concern yourself with things Lee Nading
  has left out. Roberge, R.
Do not disturb. Homes, A. M.
Do not go gentle. Alexie, S.
Do not resuscitate. Matera, L.
Do the dark dance. Knight, A. W.
Do the windows open? Hecht, J.
Do with me what you will. Oates, J. C.
Do you believe in the chicken hanger? Troy, M.
Do you know where I am? Alexie, S.
Do you like the mountains? Kees, W.
Dobbs, Kevin
  Table Fifteen
    Raritan v23 no3 p75-91 Wint 2004
Doble, John
  The accordian's greatest hits
  After six weeks in New York
  Entries from Skipper Bitwell's journal
  Lefty
  The magic show
  The mind reader
  Two letters from the doctor
Dobychin, Leonid
  Lyoshka
    The Kenyon Review ns23 no1 p31-5 Wint
    2001
  Ninon
    The Kenyon Review ns23 no1 p29-31 Wint
    2001
Dobyns, Stephen
  Kansas
    The Best American short stories, 1999; select-
      ed from U.S. and Canadian magazines by
      Amy Tan with Katrina Kenison, with an in-
      troduction by Amy Tan
  Part of the story
    The Pushcart prize XXVI; best of the small
      presses, an annual small press reader; ed-
      ited by Bill Henderson and the Pushcart
      prize editors
  Saying hello
    Esquire v135 no1 p83-4 Ja 2001
Doc's Boy. Linney, R.
Doc's story. Wideman, J. E.
The **Doctor**. Beisch, J.
The **doctor**. Chekhov, A. P.
The **Doctor**. Wilbur, E.
Doctor Chevalier's lie. Chopin, K.
Doctor Jack-o'-Lantern. Yates, R.
Doctor Kismet. Mosley, W.
Doctor Weltschmerz, I presume. Dwyer, M.
Doctorow, Cory
  All day sucker
    Doctorow, C. A place so foreign and eight
      more stories; introduction by Bruce Sterling
  Craphound
    Doctorow, C. A place so foreign and eight
      more stories; introduction by Bruce Sterling
    Northern suns; edited by David G. Hartwell
      & Glenn Grant
    The Year's best science fiction, sixteenth an-
      nual collection; edited by Gardner Dozois

Doctorow, Cory—*Continued*
Home again, home again
    Doctorow, C. A place so foreign and eight
        more stories; introduction by Bruce Sterling
OwnzOred
    Doctorow, C. A place so foreign and eight
        more stories; introduction by Bruce Sterling
A place so foreign
    Doctorow, C. A place so foreign and eight
        more stories; introduction by Bruce Sterling
Power punctuation!
    Starlight 3; edited by Patrick Nielsen Hayden
Return to Pleasure Island
    Doctorow, C. A place so foreign and eight
        more stories; introduction by Bruce Sterling
Shadow of mothaship
    Doctorow, C. A place so foreign and eight
        more stories; introduction by Bruce Sterling
The Super Man and the bugout
    Doctorow, C. A place so foreign and eight
        more stories; introduction by Bruce Sterling
To market, to market: the re-branding of Billy
    Bailey
    Doctorow, C. A place so foreign and eight
        more stories; introduction by Bruce Sterling
(jt. auth) See Skeet, Michael
Doctorow, E. L.
Baby Wilson
    The Best American short stories, 2003; select-
        ed from U.S. and Canadian magazines by
        Walter Mosley with Katrina Kenison; with
        an introduction by Walter Mosley
    Doctorow, E. L. Sweet land stories
    The New Yorker v78 no5 p76-84 Mr 25 2002
Child, dead, in the rose garden
    Doctorow, E. L. Sweet land stories
    The Virginia Quarterly Review v80 no2 p176-
        94 Spr 2004
A house on the plains
    The Best American short stories, 2002; select-
        ed from U.S. and Canadian magazines by
        Sue Miller with Katrina Kenison, with an
        introduction by Sue Miller
    Doctorow, E. L. Sweet land stories
    The New Yorker v77 no16 p138-51 Je 18-25
        2001
Jolene: a life
    Doctorow, E. L. Sweet land stories
    The New Yorker v78 no40 p102-7, 109-13 D
        23-30 2002
Loon lake
    The Best of The Kenyon review; edited by
        David Lynn; introduction by Joyce Carol
        Oates
Walter John Harmon
    Doctorow, E. L. Sweet land stories
    The New Yorker v79 no11 p88-99 My 12
        2003
Willi
    In our nature: stories of wildness; selected
        and introduced by Donna Seaman
DOCTORS *See* Physicians; Surgeons; Women
    physicians
Doctor's sons. Robison, M.
A **doctor's** story. Baida, P.
A **doctor's** visit. Chekhov, A. P.
The **documentary** artist. Manrique, J.
DOCUMENTS *See* Manuscripts

Documents in the case of Elizabeth Akeley.
    Lupoff, R. A.
Dodd, Susan
Lokey man
    The Ohio Review no62/63 p171-92 2001
Dodd, Susan M.
Adult education
    Dodd, S. M. O careless love; stories and a
        novella
Ethiopia
    Dodd, S. M. O careless love; stories and a
        novella
I married a space alien
    Dodd, S. M. O careless love; stories and a
        novella
In France they turn to stone when they die
    Dodd, S. M. O careless love; stories and a
        novella
Lady Chatterley's root canal
    Dodd, S. M. O careless love; stories and a
        novella
Lokey man
    Dodd, S. M. O careless love; stories and a
        novella
The lost art of sleep
    Dodd, S. M. O careless love; stories and a
        novella
So far you can't imagine
    Dodd, S. M. O careless love; stories and a
        novella
Song-and-dance man
    Dodd, S. M. O careless love; stories and a
        novella
What I remember now
    Dodd, S. M. O careless love; stories and a
        novella
Doderer, Heimito von
Divertimento Number III
    Southern Humanities Review v37 no1 p36-62
        Wint 2003
**DODGER STADIUM (LOS ANGELES,
    CALIF.)**
Connelly, M. Two-bagger
Doe season. Kaplan, D. M.
Doelwijt, Thea
In foreign parts
    The Oxford book of Caribbean short stories;
        edited by Stewart Brown and John
        Wickham
Doenges, Judy
Crooks
    Doenges, J. What she left me; stories and a
        novella
Disaster
    Doenges, J. What she left me; stories and a
        novella
God of gods
    Doenges, J. What she left me; stories and a
        novella
Incognito
    Doenges, J. What she left me; stories and a
        novella
MIB
    Doenges, J. What she left me; stories and a
        novella
The money stays, the people go
    Doenges, J. What she left me; stories and a
        novella

Doenges, Judy—*Continued*

Occidental
  Doenges, J. What she left me; stories and a
    novella
Solved
  Doenges, J. What she left me; stories and a
    novella
What she left me
  Doenges, J. What she left me; stories and a
    novella
The whole numbers of families
  Doenges, J. What she left me; stories and a
    novella

Doerr, Anthony

The caretaker
  Doerr, A. The shell collector; stories
  The Paris Review v43 no159 p236-70 Fall
    2001
For a long time this was Griselda's story
  Doerr, A. The shell collector; stories
  The North American Review v284 no6 p11-17
    N/D 1999
The hunter's wife
  Atlantic Monthly v287 no5 p77-86 My 2001
  Doerr, A. The shell collector; stories
July fourth
  Doerr, A. The shell collector; stories
Mkondo
  Doerr, A. The shell collector; stories
River run
  The Sewanee Review v109 no3 p321-30 Jl/S
    2001
The shell collector
  The Best American short stories, 2003; select-
    ed from U.S. and Canadian magazines by
    Walter Mosley with Katrina Kenison; with
    an introduction by Walter Mosley
  Chicago Review v47 no4/48 no1 p225-50
    Wint 2001/Spr 2002
  Doerr, A. The shell collector; stories
  The O. Henry Prize stories, 2003; edited and
    with an introduction by Laura Furman;
    jurers David Gutterson, Diane Johnson,
    Jennifer Egan
So many chances
  Doerr, A. The shell collector; stories
A tangle by the rapid river
  Doerr, A. The shell collector; stories
Does anyone know you are going this way. Rich-
  mond, M.
Dog attempts to drown man in Saskatoon. Glover,
  D. H.
Dog days. Budnitz, J.
Dog days. Friedman, P.
The **dog** fight. Hines, J.
Dog in a fisherman's net. Delany, S. R.
The **dog** lover. Brown, J.
The **dog** said bow-wow. Swanwick, M.
DOG SLED RACING *See* Sled dog racing
Dog Star. Carson, J.
Dog Star. Clarke, A. C.
Dog stories. Gilliland, G.
Dog tags. Allen, J. R.
Dogfight. Foley, S.
Dogfight. Gibson, W. and Swanwick, M.
Dogfight. Knight, M.
Doggy. Skillings, R. D.
Doghouse roses. Earle, S.
Dogology. Boyle, T. C.

DOGS

Abbott, L. K. Once upon a time
Adam, C. Josie
Adam, C. Watch dog
Adams, A. Molly's dog
Adams, A. A very nice dog
Agee, J. Carl Millennium
Allyn, D. Puppyland
Banks, R. The outer banks
Barnard, R. Old dogs, new tricks
Beattie, A. Distant music
Berners, G. H. T.-W., Baron. Mr. Pidger
Bezmozgis, D. Tapka
Billman, J. Albatross
Bishop, M. Chihuahua Flats
Blair, J. Happy puppy
Bradbury, R. No news; or, What killed the dog?
Bradbury, R. With smiles as wide as summer
Brady, C. The end of the class war
Brennan, M. The children are very quiet when
  they are away
Brennan, M. The door on West Tenth Street
Brennan, M. In and out of never-never land
Browder, C. Secrets: three short stories
Brown, J. The dog lover
Cady, J. The lady with the blind dog
Cannell, D. Fetch
Carlson, R. Max
Casares, O. Charro
Chamoiseau, P. The old man slave and the mas-
  tiff
Chekhov, A. P. A chameleon
Chekhov, A. P. Kashtanka
Chekhov, A. P. Whitebrow
Cherry, K. Chapters from *A dog's life*
Chiappone, R. Side job
Clark, B. C. The Apache pest control
Clarke, A. C. Dog Star
Cobb, T. Small-block chevy
Cody, L. Listen
Cook, K. L. Nature's way
Coyne, S. Hunting country
Daniels, J. Middle of the mitten
Dann, J. Spirit dog
Davis, R. H. The bar sinister
Del Rey, L. The faithful
DeMarinis, R. The handgun
Desai, A. Diamond dust, a tragedy
Doran, M. M. Showdown
DuBois, B. The greatest sacrifice
Dufresne, J. Johnny too bad
Eggers, D. After I was thrown in the river and
  before I drowned
Fairey, W. W. Family pets
Ford, R. Puppy
Friedman, P. Dog days
Fulton, J. The troubled dog
Gay, W. Sugarbaby
Gilliland, G. Dog stories
Glover, D. H. Dog attempts to drown man in
  Saskatoon
Gwyn, A. Dog on the cross
Hansen, R. His dog
Harris, M. The iron fist of oligarchy
Haskell, J. Good world
Hegi, U. Lower Crossing
Henry, W. Wolf-Eye
Highsmith, P. Man's best friend
Hodgson, W. H. The adventure of the headland

DOGS—*Continued*
Hoffman, A. Tell the truth
Hunter, F. The barking dog
Kavaler, R. Pets
Kelly, J. A Dick and Jane story
Kelner, T. L. P. Old dog days
Kennedy, A. In our part of the world
Knight, M. Dogfight
Knight, M. Poker
Knight, M. Sleeping with my dog
Knight, M. Tenant
Kornegay, Jamie. Dog days
Lansdale, J. R. Fire dog
Lansdale, J. R. and Lansdale, Karen. A change
   of lifestyle
Le Clézio, J.-M. G. Moloch
Lewis, W. H. The trip back from Whidbey
Link, K. The hortlak
MacLeod, A. As birds bring forth the sun
Marías, J. Unfinished figures
Maron, M. Shaggy dog
Marshall, B. White sugar and red clay
Mathews, H. Mr. Smathers
Matiella, A. C. Twice-cooked Yorky
McBain, E. Barking at butterflies
McGuane, T. Dogs
McNally, J. Roger's new life
Meyers, K. Easter dresses
Miller, A. Bulldog
Morris, M. Just an old cur
Norris, L. Stray dogs
Norris, L. Trailer people
Offutt, C. The best friend
Ortiz, S. J. The end of Old Horse
Painter, P. Confusing the dog
Pancake, A. Dog song
Paschal, D. Death of a street dog
Paschal, D. The puppies
Perabo, S. Explaining death to the dog
Phillips, R. S. Wolfie
Pickard, N. Dr. Couch saves a president
Randolph, L. The girls
Richard, M. Strays
Richter, S. Sally's story
Shrayer-Petrov, D. Rusty
Skillings, R. D. Doggy
Smart, A. Vincent
Spedding, Sally. Strangers waiting
Spencer, D. The 12-inch dog
Spiegel, I. A ghetto dog
Steele, A. M. Jake and the enemy
Strom, D. Chickens
Sukrungruang, I. The golden mix
Swanwick, M. The dog said bow-wow
Taylor, T. L. Smoke's fortune
Tinti, H. Home sweet home
Wallace, R. Quick bright things
Watanabe McFerrin, L. Khalida's dog
Watson, B. Last days of the dog-men
Waugh, E. On guard
Westlake, D. E. Skeeks
Westmoreland, T. A. Darkening of the world
Westmoreland, T. A. Good as any
Wharton, E. Kerfol
Whitty, J. The dreams of dogs
Willis, M. S. Tales of the abstract expressionists
Wilson, R., Jr. Grief
Winter, E. The boys
Winter, E. Full moon howl

Winter, E. Love in the desert
Winter, E. The planting
Winterson, J. The 24-hour dog
Yi, T.-H. Perspiration
Ziegler, I. Nobody home: an epilogue
   Training
Bass, R. The hermit's story
Dogs. Bradford, A.
Dogs. McCorkle, J.
Dogs. McGuane, T.
Dogs. Nawrocki, S.
Dogs. Skinner, J.
A **dog's** eye view. Tomioka, T.
Dogs of autumn. Wegner, H.
The **dog's** visit. Duve, K.
Doherty, Michael
   Those Tender Mayfly Childhood Sweetheart
      Games
      South Carolina Review v36 no2 p47-59 Spr
      2004
Doherty, P. C.
   The monk's tale
      Murder most divine; ecclesiastical tales of un-
         holy crimes; edited by Ralph McInerny and
         Martin H. Greenberg
Doing alien. Benford, G.
Doing the gods' work. Nye, J. L.
Doing time. Bailey, R. W.
Doing time. Boyczuk, R.
Doing time. Vukcevich, R.
Dokey, Richard
   Ace
      Dokey, R. Pale morning dun; stories
   The beggar of Union Square
      Dokey, R. Pale morning dun; stories
      The Literary Review (Madison, N.J.) v44 no4
         p726-34 Summ 2001
   Electric dog
      Dokey, R. Pale morning dun; stories
   Hampstead's folly
      Dokey, R. Pale morning dun; stories
   A house in order
      Dokey, R. Pale morning dun; stories
   Monkey
      Dokey, R. Pale morning dun; stories
   The monster
      Dokey, R. Pale morning dun; stories
   The mouse
      Dokey, R. Pale morning dun; stories
   Never trust the weatherman
      Dokey, R. Pale morning dun; stories
   Pale morning dun
      Dokey, R. Pale morning dun; stories
   The shopper
      Dokey, R. Pale morning dun; stories
   The suicide
      Dokey, R. Pale morning dun; stories
   Vital statistics
      Dokey, R. Pale morning dun; stories
Dôle, Gérard
   The witch of Greenwich
      My Sherlock Holmes; untold stories of the
         great detective; edited by Michael Kurland
Dolgushov's death. Babel', I.
The **doll**. Chesnutt, C. W.
The **doll**. Oates, J. C.
Doll. Svoboda, T.
The **doll**. Welty, E.
Doll: A Romance of the Mississippi. Oates, J. C.

The **dollar** in Italy. Silber, J.
The **dollmaker** of Marigold Walk. Hambly, B.
DOLLS
 See also Barbie dolls
Brown, F. The Geezenstacks
Campbell, R. Lilith's
Davenport, G. Belinda's world tour
Matheson, R. Prey
Paschal, D. Moriya
Smart, A. Emily
Wellen, E. Sanity clause
Dolls. Campbell, R.
The **dolphin**. Hopkins, G. M.
The **dolphin** story. Renwick, J.
DOLPHINS
Clark, J. Mammals
Hendricks, V. Stormy, mon amour
Renwick, J. The dolphin story
Domecq, Alcina Lubitch *See* Lubitch Domecq, Alcina, 1953-
Domestic. Barthelme, F.
DOMESTIC RELATIONS *See* Family life
Domestic slash and thrust. Jensen, J. L.
Domicile. Busch, F.
The **dominant** style. McMullen, S.
Domingo. Casares, O.
DOMINICAN AMERICANS
Díaz, J. The brief wondrous life of Oscar Wao
DOMINICAN REPUBLIC
Alvarez, J. Amor divino
Bosch, J. Encarnación Mendoza's Christmas Eve
Díaz, J. The sun, the moon, the stars
Díaz, J. Ysrael
   Santo Domingo
Johnson, C. R. A report from St. Domingue
DOMINICANS
   United States
Díaz, J. Fiesta 1980
Díaz, J. The sun, the moon, the stars
Dominion. Ford, R.
Dominion. Stone, R.
Domo arigato. Lee, D.
Don Giovanni in the tub. Wexler, M.
Don Ildebrando. Herling, G.
DON JUAN (LEGENDARY CHARACTER)
Lee, V. The Virgin of the Seven Daggers
Don Juan Zimmerman. Epstein, J.
Don Salomón. Sánchez, R.
Doña Berta. Alas, L.
Doña Faustina. Bowles, P.
Donaldson, Stephen R.
By any other name
 Donaldson, S. R. Reave the Just and other tales; stories
The djinn who watches over the accursed
 Donaldson, S. R. Reave the Just and other tales; stories
The killing stroke
 Donaldson, S. R. Reave the Just and other tales; stories
The kings of tarshish shall bring gifts
 Donaldson, S. R. Reave the Just and other tales; stories
Penance
 Donaldson, S. R. Reave the Just and other tales; stories
Reave the Just
 Donaldson, S. R. Reave the Just and other tales; stories

What makes us human
 Donaldson, S. R. Reave the Just and other tales; stories
The woman who loved pigs
 Donaldson, S. R. Reave the Just and other tales; stories
Donigyan, Hovaness
Legacy
 New Letters v70 no1 p55-9 2003
DONKEYS *See* Asses and mules
Donnelly, Marcos
Café con leche
 Bishop, C. and James, D. Death dines in; edited by Claudia Bishop and Dean James
DONNER PARTY
Travis, T. V. Down here in the garden
Tuck, L. Verdi
Donoghue, Emma
How a lady dies
 Hers 3: brilliant new fiction by lesbian writers; edited by Terry Wolverton with Robert Drake
Looking for Petronilla
 The Vintage book of international lesbian fiction; edited and with an introduction by Naomi Holoch and Joan Nestle
Seven pictures not taken
 The Anchor book of new Irish writing; the new Gaelach ficsean; edited and with an introduction by John Somer and John J. Daly
The **Donoghues** of Dunno Weir. Galton, Sir F.
Donoso, José
Ana Maria
 The Vintage book of Latin American stories; edited by Carlos Fuentes and Julio Ortega
DONS *See* Teachers
Don't give me your sad stories. Melville, P.
Don't look behind you. Brown, F.
Don't mean nothing. O'Neill, S.
Don't move me. Bain, T.
Don't run. Brady, C.
Don't save your kisses. Bocock, M.
Don't say sorry. Stewart, I.
Don't scrub off these names. McNulty, J.
Don't tell her you love her. Paz, S.
Doodlebug. Stuckey-French, E.
Doogan, Mike
War can be murder
 The Best American mystery stories, 2003; edited by Michael Connelly and Otto Penzler
Dooling, Richard
Diary of an immortal man
 A different plain; contemporary Nebraska fiction writers; edited by Ladette Randolph ; introduction by Mary Pipher
Doolittle, Sean
Summa mathematica
 The Best American mystery stories, 2002; edited and with an introduction by James Ellroy; Otto Penzler, series editor
DOOMSDAY *See* Judgment Day
The **door** of the unreal. Biss, G.
The **door** on West Tenth Street. Brennan, M.
The **door** to women. Shepard, S.
Doorbell for Louisa. Highsmith, P.
The **Doorman**. Yardumian, R.
Doors. Fromm, P.
Doors. Hoffman, W.

Doors. Painter, P.

The **doors** of his face, the lamps of his mouth. Zelazny, R.

The **doors** open at three. Cabrera Infante, G.

Dope fiend. Vachss, A. H.

Doppelganger. Bowen, R.

The **doppelganger** effect. Strasser, D.

Doran, Maggie Morgan

Billy and Benjamin too

Dead on demand; the best of ghost story weekend; edited by Elizabeth Engstrom

Doran, M. M. Gentle hearts, guilty sins

End October

Doran, M. M. Gentle hearts, guilty sins

The estate of Joseph P. Bosley

Doran, M. M. Gentle hearts, guilty sins

A family in winter

Doran, M. M. Gentle hearts, guilty sins

The giver

Doran, M. M. Gentle hearts, guilty sins

Golden anniversary

Doran, M. M. Gentle hearts, guilty sins

Showdown

Doran, M. M. Gentle hearts, guilty sins

They shall have music

Doran, M. M. Gentle hearts, guilty sins

Wedding at the Gormay Cafe

Doran, M. M. Gentle hearts, guilty sins

A well-arranged life

Doran, M. M. Gentle hearts, guilty sins

Dorbin, Sariah

Shelter

The Antioch Review v61 no4 p742-51 Fall 2003

Dorcey, Mary

A noise from the woodshed [excerpt]

The Vintage book of international lesbian fiction; edited and with an introduction by Naomi Holoch and Joan Nestle

A sense of humour

The Anchor book of new Irish writing; the new Gaelach ficsean; edited and with an introduction by John Somer and John J. Daly

Doris is coming. Packer, Z.

Dormen, Lesley

The old economy husband

Atlantic Monthly v288 no5 p98-106 D 2001

Dorothy and her friends. Wilson, R., Jr.

Dorrie, Doris

The bride

Southern Humanities Review v33 no4 p375-86 Fall 1999

Where do we go from here

Nixon under the bodhi tree and other works of Buddhist fiction; edited by Kate Wheeler ; foreword by Charles Johnson

DORSET (ENGLAND) *See* England—Dorset

Dorsey, Candas Jane

(Learning about) machine sex

Reload: rethinking women + cyberculture; edited by Mary Flanagan and Austin Booth

Dorst, Doug

Vikings

Ploughshares v25 no2/3 p61-78 Fall 1999

Dou you spik Frrench? Saumont, A.

Double act in Soho. Zinik, Z.

The **double-barreled** gun. Cross, A.

Double birthday. Cather, W.

Double-crossing Delancey. Rozan, S. J.

Double fries. Saroyan, A.

Double Helix. Magee, R. M.

Double shift. Coshnear, D.

The **double** take. Prather, R. S.

Double Whammy. Klass, P.

The **double** zero. Moody, R.

Doubt. Shields, D.

Doucette, Rita J.

The Last Cat

Michigan Quarterly Review v43 no1 p94-105 Wint 2004

Doudou. Babel´, I.

Dougherty, Kathleen

When your breath freezes

Murder most divine; ecclesiastical tales of unholy crimes; edited by Ralph McInerny and Martin H. Greenberg

DOUGHTY-TICHBORNE,   ROGER CHARLES, 1829-1854

About

Borges, J. L. The improbable impostor Tom Castro

Dougie. Ma, K.

Dougie Mortimer's right arm. Archer, J.

DOUGLAS, ALFRED BRUCE, LORD, 1870-1945

About

Leavitt, D. The infection scene

Douglas, Bill

My childhood

The Vintage book of contemporary Scottish fiction; edited and with an introduction by Peter Kravitz

Douglas, Carole Nelson

Dirty dancing

Death dance; suspenseful stories of the dance macabre; Trevanian, editor

Licensed to koi

Bishop, C. and James, D. Death dines in; edited by Claudia Bishop and Dean James

The mummy case: a midnight Louie past life adventure

Cat crimes through time; edited by Ed Gorman, Martin H. Greenberg, and Larry Segriff

The World's finest mystery and crime stories, first annual collection; edited by Ed Gorman

Night owl

Past lives, present tense; edited by Elizabeth Ann Scarborough

Sax and the single cat

White House pet detectives; tales of crime and mystery at the White House from a pet's-eye view; edited by Carole Nelson Douglas

Douglas, Ellen

About loving women

The Cry of an occasion; fiction from the Fellowship of Southern Writers; edited by Richard Bausch; with a foreword by George Garrett

I just love Carrie Lee

Crossing the color line; readings in Black and white; edited by Suzanne W. Jones

Douglas, Marcia
Notes from a writer's book of cures and spells
Mojo: conjure stories; edited by Nalo Hopkinson
What the periwinkle remember
Whispers from the cotton tree root; Caribbean fabulist fiction; edited by Nalo Hopkinson
Douglas, Michael *See* Crichton, Michael, 1942-
DOUGLASS, FREDERICK, 1817?-1895
About
Johnson, C. R. A lion at Pendleton
Douglass, Sara
The evil within
Dreaming down-under; edited by Jack Dann and Janeen Webb
The Year's best fantasy & horror, twelfth annual collection; edited by Ellen Datlow & Terry Windling
The mistress of Marwood Hagg
Gathering the bones; original stories from the world's masters of horror; edited by Dennis Etchison, Ramsey Campbell and Jack Dann
Dove, Rita
Damon and Vandalia
The African American West; a century of short stories; edited by Bruce A. Glasrud and Laurie Champion
Second-hand man
The Bluelight corner; black women writing on passion, sex, and romantic love; edited by Rosemarie Robotham
Dove. Adam, C.
The **dove** game. Carmody, I.
Dove of the back streets. Jacobs, M.
Doves. Hegi, U.
Dove's song. Eickhoff, R. L.
Dowd, Catherine
Mourning has broken
U.S. Catholic v69 no1 p39-41 Ja 2004
DOWDING, HUGH CASWALL TREMENHEERE DOWDING, 1ST BARON, 1882-1970
About
Twelve legions of angels
Dowling, Terry
Basic black
Death dines at 8:30; edited by Claudia Bishop and Nick DiChario
The bone ship
Gathering the bones; original stories from the world's masters of horror; edited by Dennis Etchison, Ramsey Campbell and Jack Dann
Flashmen
The year's best science fiction: twenty-first annual collection; edited by Gardner Dozois
He tried to catch the light
Dreaming down-under; edited by Jack Dann and Janeen Webb
Jenny come to play
The Year's best fantasy & horror, twelfth annual collection; edited by Ellen Datlow & Terry Windling
One thing about the night
Datlow, E. The dark; new ghost stories; edited by Ellen Datlow
Privateer's moon
Centaurus: the best of Australian science fiction; edited by David G. Hartwell and Damien Broderick

The saltimbanques
Death dines at 8:30; edited by Claudia Bishop and Nick DiChario
Stitch
The Year's best fantasy & horror: sixteenth annual collection; edited by Ellen Datlow & Terri Windling
Down among the dead men. Dozois, G. R.
Down among the dead men. Tenn, W.
Down by the lake. Swan, M.
Down here in the garden. Travis, T. V.
Down in darkest Dixie where the dead don't dance. Braunbeck, G. A.
Down in Paraguay. Jacobs, M.
Down in the dark. Barton, W.
Down Paagumene way. L'Amour, L.
Down the garden path. Squire, E. D.
Down the Green River. Carlson, R.
Down the shore everything's all right. Richmond, M.
Down there undercover. Amanthis, J.
Down through the valley. Tower, W.
Down to earth. Harrison, H.
Downfall. Masuri, N.
Downs, Greg
Driving Lessons
The Literary Review (Madison, N.J.) v46 no1 p31-40 Fall 2002
Downs, Michael
193 Barker Street
New Letters v68 no1 p27-45 2001
Man kills wife, two dogs
The Best American mystery stories, 2002; edited and with an introduction by James Ellroy; Otto Penzler, series editor
Prison food
The Best American mystery stories, 2001; edited and with an Introduction by Lawrence Block
DOWN'S SYNDROME
Cohen, R. The boys at night
Downsized. Stern, R. G.
DOWRY *See* Marriage customs
The **dowry**. Russo, R.
Doxey, W. S.
Bear
South Carolina Review v36 no2 p111-14 Spr 2004
Doyle, Sir Arthur Conan
The adventure of Silver Blaze
Sports best short stories; edited by Paul D. Staudohar
The adventure of the Bruce-Partington plans
Death by espionage; intriguing stories of deception and betrayal; edited by Martin Cruz Smith
The Croxley Master
Boxing's best short stories; edited by Paul D. Staudohar
The horror of the heights
On glorious wings; the best flying stories of the century; edited and introduced by Stephen Coonts
The Jew's breastplate
Browning, A. Murder is no mitzvah; edited by Abigail Browning
The leather funnel
Witches' brew; edited by Yvonne Jocks

Doyle, Sir Arthur Conan—*Continued*
Lot no. 249
> Into the mummy's tomb; edited by John Richard Stephens

DOYLE, SIR ARTHUR CONAN, 1859-1930
Parodies, imitations, etc.
Altman, S.-E. A case of royal blood
Bear, E. Tiger! tiger!
Black, C. Cabaret aux Assassins
Böttcher, M. The detective
Breen, J. L. The adventure of the mooning sentry
Breen, J. L. The adventures of the Cheshire Cheese
Brite, P. Z. and Ferguson, D. The curious case of Miss Violet Stone
Bruce, C. The adventure of the dying doctor
Carroll, L. Before the adventures
Clark, S. Nightmare in wax
Crider, B. The adventure of the young British soldier
Davidson, A. The singular incident of the dog on the beach
Day, B. The adventure of the curious canary
DeAndrea, W. L. The adventure of the Christmas tree
DeAndrea, W. L. The adventure of the cripple parade
Dôle, G. The witch of Greenwich
Effinger, G. A. The adventure of the celestial snows
Estleman, L. D. The riddle of the golden monkeys
Ewing, C. D. And the others. . .
Finch, P. The mystery of the hanged man's puzzle
Gaiman, N. A study in emerald
Gilden, M. The adventure of the forgotten umbrella
Hambly, B. The adventure of the antiquarian's niece
Hambly, B. The dollmaker of Marigold Walk
Kaminsky, S. M. The final toast
Kiernan, C. R. The drowned geologist
Kurland, M. Years ago and in a different place
Landis, G. A. The singular habits of wasps
Lebbon, T. The horror of the many faces
Linscott, G. A scandal in winter
Lovisi, G. Mycroft's great game
Lowder, J. The weeping masks
Lupoff, R. A. The adventure of the Voorish Sign
Lupoff, R. A. The adventures of the boulevard assassin
Lupoff, R. A. The incident of the impecunious chevalier
MacIntyre, F. G. The adventure of Exham Priory
Mallory, M. The riddle of the young protestor
McCrumb, S. The vale of the white horse
Pelan, J. The mystery of the worm
Perry, A. The case of the bloodless sock
Perry, A. and Saxon, M. The case of the Highland hoax
Perry, S. The case of the wavy black dagger
Reaves, M. The adventure of the Arab's manuscript
Robertson, L. Mrs. Hudson reminisces
Schreiber, N. Call me Wiggins

Stableford, B. M. Art in the blood
Stashower, D. The adventure of the agitated actress
Tremayne, P. A study in orange
Vourlis, J. P. A case of insomnia
Wheat, C. The adventure of the rara avis
Wilson, D. N. and Macomber, P. L. Death did not become him

Doyle, Brian
Blue
> *U.S. Catholic* v67 no7 p38-40 Jl 2002

Lucy
> *U.S. Catholic* v66 no8 p36-7 Ag 2001

Yoda
> *U.S. Catholic* v69 no4 p42-4 Ap 2004

Doyle, Conan *See* Doyle, Sir Arthur Conan, 1859-1930

Doyle, Miranda
Breaking curfew
> *'Teen* v43 no1 p100-02 Ja 1999

Doyle, Roddy
The dinner
> *The New Yorker* v76 no45 p72-81 F 5 2001

Recuperation
> *The New Yorker* v79 no39 p98-102 D 15 2003

The slave
> Speaking with the angel; original stories; edited by Nick Hornby

Dozois, Gardner R.
Afternoon at Schraffts
> Dozois, G. R. Strange days; fabulous journeys with Gardner Dozois; edited by Tim Szczesuil and Ann Broomhead

A cat horror story
> Dozois, G. R. Strange days; fabulous journeys with Gardner Dozois; edited by Tim Szczesuil and Ann Broomhead

The clowns
> Dozois, G. R. Strange days; fabulous journeys with Gardner Dozois; edited by Tim Szczesuil and Ann Broomhead

Community
> Dozois, G. R. Strange days; fabulous journeys with Gardner Dozois; edited by Tim Szczesuil and Ann Broomhead

Dinner party
> Dozois, G. R. Strange days; fabulous journeys with Gardner Dozois; edited by Tim Szczesuil and Ann Broomhead

Down among the dead men
> Dozois, G. R. Strange days; fabulous journeys with Gardner Dozois; edited by Tim Szczesuil and Ann Broomhead

Executive clemency
> Dozois, G. R. Strange days; fabulous journeys with Gardner Dozois; edited by Tim Szczesuil and Ann Broomhead

Flash point
> Dozois, G. R. Strange days; fabulous journeys with Gardner Dozois; edited by Tim Szczesuil and Ann Broomhead

The gods of Mars
> Dozois, G. R. Strange days; fabulous journeys with Gardner Dozois; edited by Tim Szczesuil and Ann Broomhead

Dozois, Gardner R.—*Continued*
Golden apples of the sun
  Dozois, G. R. Strange days; fabulous journeys with Gardner Dozois; edited by Tim Szczesuil and Ann Broomhead
A knight of ghosts and shadows
  Dozois, G. R. Strange days; fabulous journeys with Gardner Dozois; edited by Tim Szczesuil and Ann Broomhead
  Nebula awards showcase 2002; edited by Kim Stanley Robinson
The last day of July
  Dozois, G. R. Strange days; fabulous journeys with Gardner Dozois; edited by Tim Szczesuil and Ann Broomhead
The Mayan variation
  Dozois, G. R. Strange days; fabulous journeys with Gardner Dozois; edited by Tim Szczesuil and Ann Broomhead
Passage
  Dozois, G. R. Strange days; fabulous journeys with Gardner Dozois; edited by Tim Szczesuil and Ann Broomhead
Playing the game
  Dozois, G. R. Strange days; fabulous journeys with Gardner Dozois; edited by Tim Szczesuil and Ann Broomhead
Send no money
  Dozois, G. R. Strange days; fabulous journeys with Gardner Dozois; edited by Tim Szczesuil and Ann Broomhead
Snow job
  Dozois, G. R. Strange days; fabulous journeys with Gardner Dozois; edited by Tim Szczesuil and Ann Broomhead
Solace
  Dozois, G. R. Strange days; fabulous journeys with Gardner Dozois; edited by Tim Szczesuil and Ann Broomhead
The storm
  Dozois, G. R. Strange days; fabulous journeys with Gardner Dozois; edited by Tim Szczesuil and Ann Broomhead
Strangers
  Dozois, G. R. Strange days; fabulous journeys with Gardner Dozois; edited by Tim Szczesuil and Ann Broomhead
Touring
  Dozois, G. R. Strange days; fabulous journeys with Gardner Dozois; edited by Tim Szczesuil and Ann Broomhead
The visible man
  Dozois, G. R. Strange days; fabulous journeys with Gardner Dozois; edited by Tim Szczesuil and Ann Broomhead
Dr. Bhumbo Singh. Davidson, A.
Dr. Couch saves a cat. Pickard, N.
Dr. Couch saves a president. Pickard, N.
Dr. Cyclops. Huttner, H.
Dr. Heidegger's experiment. Hawthorne, N.
Dr. Kleckner. Hunter, F.
Dr. Leopold on the loose. Kobin, J.
Dr. Leopold's Problem with Contentment. Kobin, J.
Dr. Livingston's grotto. Ellis, N.
Dr. Melfi in the morning. Barolini, H.
Dr. Qassim talks to Eva about Mansur who has arrived in Safad. Kanafāni, G.
Dr. Slime. Carlson, R.

Dr. Strass. Škvorecký, J.
Dr. Sweetkill. Jakes, J.
Dr. War is a voice on the phone. Cummins, A.
Dracula's guest. Stoker, B.
DRAFT
  Ortiz, S. J. Kaiser and the War
DRAFT, MILITARY *See* Draft
DRAFT RESISTERS *See* Draft
Dragon box. Winter, E.
The **dragon** danced at midnight. Bradbury, R.
The **dragon** hunt. Tran, V.
A **dragon** of conspiracy. Eakin, W.
The **dragon** of Pripyat. Schroeder, K.
Dragon skin drum. Davidson, A.
DRAGONS
  Eakin, W. A dragon of conspiracy
  Edghill, R. Lizzie Fair and the dragon of heart's desire
  McCaffrey, A. Beyond between
  Nesbit, E. The dragon tamers
  Shepard, L. The scalehunter's beautiful daughter
  Swanwick, M. King dragon
The **dragons** of Springplace. Reed, R.
Draitser, Emil
Clouds
  The Literary Review (Madison, N.J.) v44 no3 p447-64 Spr 2001
Faithful Masha
  Partisan Review v68 no3 p416-24 Summ 2001
Zugzwang
  The Kenyon Review ns21 no3-4 p74-90 Summ/Fall 1999
Drake, David
Choosing sides
  Drake, D. Paying the piper
Coming up against it
  Drake, D. Grimmer than hell
The end
  Drake, D. Grimmer than hell
Facing the enemy
  Drake, D. Grimmer than hell
Failure mode
  Drake, D. Grimmer than hell
The fool
  The American fantasy tradition; edited by Brian M. Thomsen
Mission accomplished
  Drake, D. Grimmer than hell
Nation without walls
  Drake, D. Grimmer than hell
Neck or nothing
  Drake, D. Paying the piper
The political process
  Drake, D. Paying the piper
The predators
  Drake, D. Grimmer than hell
Rescue mission
  Drake, D. Grimmer than hell
Smash and grab
  Drake, D. Grimmer than hell
Team effort
  Drake, D. Grimmer than hell
The tradesmen
  Drake, D. Grimmer than hell
Underground
  Drake, D. Grimmer than hell
When the devil drives
  Drake, D. Grimmer than hell

Drake, David—*Continued*
With the sword he must be slain
  Drake, D. Grimmer than hell
Drake, Robert
All that believe that, stand on their head!
  Drake, R. The picture frame and other stories
All under one roof
  Drake, R. The picture frame and other stories
Alone
  Drake, R. The picture frame and other stories
At the lake
  Drake, R. The picture frame and other stories
Auntee and the two nieces
  Drake, R. The picture frame and other stories
The child prodigy
  Drake, R. The picture frame and other stories
Connections
  Drake, R. The picture frame and other stories
  Modern Age v41 no4 p343-47 Fall 1999
The convertible
  Drake, R. The picture frame and other stories
The cotton mill
  Drake, R. The picture frame and other stories
The devil, lightning, and policemen
  Drake, R. The picture frame and other stories
The election
  Drake, R. The picture frame and other stories
Every Friday afternoon
  Drake, R. The picture frame and other stories
The girls
  Drake, R. The picture frame and other stories
Graduation from the air
  Drake, R. The picture frame and other stories
How come you reckon he did that?
  Drake, R. The picture frame and other stories
I've got a sneaking idea; or, I'd just get me a
    lawyer
  The Christian Century v116 no21 p747-48 Jl
    28-Ag 4 1999
I've got a sneaking idea that . . .; or, I'd just
    get me a lawyer
  Drake, R. The picture frame and other stories
The last day, an epilogue
  Drake, R. The picture frame and other stories
The last old maid in town
  Drake, R. The picture frame and other stories
Let there be light
  Drake, R. The picture frame and other stories
The little girl with the blue eyes
  Drake, R. The picture frame and other stories
The old cemetery
  Drake, R. The picture frame and other stories
The Peabody ducks and all the rest
  Drake, R. The picture frame and other stories
The piazza
  Drake, R. The picture frame and other stories
The pickup truck
  Drake, R. The picture frame and other stories
Power
  Circa 2000; gay fiction at the millennium; ed-
    ited by Robert Drake & Terry Wolverton
A short horse
  Drake, R. The picture frame and other stories
Shrouds with pockets in them
  Drake, R. The picture frame and other stories
Stardust
  Drake, R. The picture frame and other stories
Traveling companions
  Drake, R. The picture frame and other stories

A **drama**. Chekhov, A. P.
DRAMA CRITICS
  Bradbury, R. One-woman show
DRAMATISTS
  See also Women dramatists
  Armstrong, C. St. Patrick's Day in the morning
  Bausch, R. The brace
  Borges, J. L. The secret miracle
  Cohen, S. The case of Grand Cru
  Schoemperlen, D. Tickets to Spain
The **drang** of speaking forth. Pearlman, D. D.
Drastic. Casey, M.
Drawer. Moody, R.
Drawing room B. O'Hara, J.
Drawing to a close. Holbrook, T.
Dread honor. Aylett, S.
Dread Inlet. Mosiman, B. S.
A **dreadful** night. Chekhov, A. P.
The **dream**. Johnson-Davies, D.
Dream Boy. Kaplan, D. M.
Dream group forming. Cohen, R.
Dream Haiti. Brathwaite, E. K.
Dream house. Bean, B.
Dream house. Tuck, L.
Dream lawyer. Matera, L.
A **dream,** not alone. Iribarne, M.
The **dream** of a beast. Jordan, N.
Dream of a clean slate. Haskell, J.
Dream of men. Gaitskill, M.
The **dream** of misunderstanding. Sheckley, R.
Dream of Venus. Sargent, P.
Dream rider. Abrams, T.
Dream science [excerpt] Palmer, T.
Dream story. Schnitzler, A.
Dream stuff. Malouf, D.
Dream, until god burns. Enstice, A.
Dream with no name. Ferreira, R.
Dreaming among men. Kanar, B.
Dreaming of the snail life. Reisman, N.
DREAMS
  Alvarez, J. Consuelo's letter
  Asimov, I. Robot dreams
  Austin, S. At Celilo
  Barth, J. A detective and a turtle
  Bausch, R. Billboard
  Bender, A. Dreaming in Polish
  Borges, J. L. The circular ruins
  Borges, J. L. The other
  Bowles, P. A thousand days for Mokhtar
  Campbell, R. The alternative
  Cherryh, C. J. Nightgame
  Chesnutt, C. W. Mars Jeems's nightmare
  Clarke, A. C. Inheritance
  Cohen, R. Dream group forming
  Cortázar, J. The night face up
  Dann, J. Camps
  Doyle, Sir A. C. The leather funnel
  Enstice, A. Dream, until god burns
  Gutiérrez, S. D. Cantinflas
  Hawthorne, N. The celestial railroad
  Himes, C. The meanest cop in the world
  Hjortsberg, W. Symbiography
  Hopkinson, N. Money tree
  Kalamu ya Salaam. Buddy Bolden
  Karnezis, P. Stella the spinster's afternoon
    dreams
  Kornbluth, C. M. Two dooms
  Kusel, L. Other fish in the sea
  Lansdale, J. R. The man who dreamed

DREAMS—*Continued*
Le Guin, U. K. Social dreaming of the Frin
Lord, N. The girl who dreamed only geese
Lumley, B. The statement of Henry Worthy
Meinke, P. Unheard music
Mordecai, P. Once on the shores of the stream Senegambia
Müller, H. The funeral sermon
Schlink, B. The woman at the gas station
Schoemperlen, D. A change is as good as a rest
Schoemperlen, D. The man of my dreams
Sheckley, R. The dream of misunderstanding
Talbot, N. The latest dream I ever dreamed
Vigano, V. Giraglia
Walker, A. There was a river
Watson, I. The amber room
Wellen, E. Spur the nightmare
Westlake, D. E. The girl of my dreams
Wolfe, G. Houston, 1943
Dreams. Carver, R.
Dreams. Davies, R.
The **dreams** of dogs. Whitty, J.
Dreams of sex and stage diving [excerpt] Millar, M.
A **dreary** story. Chekhov, A. P.
A **Dresden** lady in Dixie. Chopin, K.
The **dress**. Ebershoff, D.
Dress-up day. Vachss, A. H.
Dressing down. Shields, C.
DRESSMAKERS
Hudson, Suzanne. The seamstress
Winter, E. Pretty please
Drew, Eileen
Mad dogs
Living on the edge; fiction by Peace Corps writers; edited by John Coyne
Dreyer, Eileen
Fun with forensics
Irreconcilable differences; Lia Matera, editor
Drift. Goto, H.
Drift. Sarah, R.
Driftglass. Delany, S. R.
The **drinking** club. Adams, A.
Drinking coffee elsewhere. Packer, Z.
The **drinking** of spirits. Abrams, T.
Drinking with the cook. Furman, L.
Driskell, Leon V.
A fellow making himself up
Home and beyond; an anthology of Kentucky short stories; edited by Morris Allen Grubbs; with an introduction by Wade Hall and an afterword by Charles E. May
Drive. Henríquez, C.
DRIVE-IN THEATERS
Shade, E. Eyesores
Driven to kill. Wallace, J.
Driven woman. McCourt, J.
Driver. Barthelme, F.
Driver, Wilsonia Benita *See* Sanchez, Sonia, 1934-
Driving. Brady, C.
Driving Lessons. Downs, G.
Driving the heart. Brown, J.
Drop in any time. Davis, L.

Dropkin, Celia
At the rich relatives
Beautiful as the moon, radiant as the stars; Jewish women in Yiddish stories : an anthology; edited by Sandra Bark; introduction by Francine Prose
Bella fell in love
Beautiful as the moon, radiant as the stars; Jewish women in Yiddish stories : an anthology; edited by Sandra Bark; introduction by Francine Prose
Drought, James
The secret [excerpt]
Retrieving bones; stories and poems of the Korean War; edited and with an introduction by W. D. Ehrhart and Philip K. Jason
The **Drought**. Gates, D.
Drought. Walrond, E.
DROUGHTS
Bukoski, A. Dry spell
Gautreaux, T. Same place, same things
Walrond, E. Drought
The **drover's** wife. Bail, M.
The **drowned** geologist. Kiernan, C. R.
Drowne's wooden image. Hawthorne, N.
DROWNING
Bart, P. The neighbors III
Bass, R. Mahatma Joe
Brackenbury, R. Between man and woman keys
Carson, J. Judgement
Cherryh, C. J. Sea change
Davidson, A. Traveller from an antique land
Davies, P. H. Frogmen
DeLancey, K. Crazy dead kid lady
Desai, A. The man who saw himself drown
Foster, P. The girl from Soldier Creek
Gao Xingjian. Cramp
García Márquez, G. The handsomest drowned man in the world
Hagy, A. C. Semper paratus
Hall, L. S. The ledge
Harrison, J. The beast God forgot to invent
Hribal, C. J. Consent
Laws, S. The song my sister sang
Leslie, N. A little wild
Mazelis, J. Running away with the hairdresser
McGrath, P. Asylum [excerpt]
Norman, H. Unicycle
Rinehart, S. Another pyramid scheme
Rippen, C. Under my skin
Sanford, A. In the Little Hunky River
Svoboda, T. Water
Westmoreland, T. A. The buried boy
Ziegler, I. Nobody home: an epilogue
The **drowning**. Delaney, E. J.
Drowning hard. Di Blasi, D.
The **drowning** icecube. Breen, J. L.
Drowning in air. Armstrong, K.
Drowning the Charge. Grimmett, N.
DRUG ABUSE
See also Drugs; Marijuana
Bernhard, T. Playing Watten
Evenson, B. One over twelve
Gates, D. Saturn
Henley, P. Aces
Krawiec, R. Betrayals
McKnight, R. Quitting smoking
Wilmot, J. Dirt angel

DRUG ADDICTION

Braverman, K. Tall tales from the Mekong Delta

Brown, J. Head on

Carter, E. Ask Amelio

Carter, E. Bad boy walking

Carter, E. The bride

Carter, E. Cute in camouflage

Carter, E. Parachute silk

Carter, E. WLUV

Carter, E. Zemecki's cat

D'Ambrosio, C., Jr. Open house

Davies, P. H. Everything you can remember in thirty seconds is yours to keep

Davis, L. The kind of time you end up with

Earle, S. Doghouse roses

Earle, S. A eulogy of sorts

Fischerová, D. Dhum

Foster, K. Another shoot

Frym, G. Where she stays

Gates, D. George lassos moon

Gates, D. Star baby

Gorman, E. Such a good girl

Greene, B. An ordinary woman

Heller, J. A day in the country

Heller, J. To laugh in the morning

Hoffman, A. The boy who wrestled with angels

Krawiec, R. Capitalism

LeRoy, J. T. Coal

Lipsyte, S. Beautiful game

Lipsyte, S. Cremains

Mosley, W. Voices

Oates, J. C. Me & Wolfie, 1979

Paschal, D. Genesis (The G.I. bleed)

Richter, S. The first men

Richter, S. A groupie, a rock star

Silber, J. Bobby Jackson

Strike, Johnny. Crazy Carl's thing

Thon, M. R. Little white sister

Werve, S. If I were lemon pie

Wharton, E. Bunner Sisters

Yuknavitch, L. Bravo America

Yuknavitch, L. Shooting

DRUG INDUSTRY See Drug trade; Pharmaceutical industry

DRUG TRADE

Gores, J. Smart guys don't snore

DRUG TRAFFIC

Banks, R. Dis bwoy, him gwan

Bishop, P. The samaritan

Chambers, W. E. Another night to remember

Daniels, J. Islands

Earle, S. Jaguar dance

Forsyth, F. The citizen

Gates, D. E. The blue mirror

Gonzalez, R. Invisible country

Harty, R. Between Tubac and Tumacacori

Heller, J. A man named Flute

Jones, E. P. A rich man

Kelly, J. P. Rat

Lansdale, J. R. The mule rustlers

McManus, J. What I remember about the cold war

Padilla, M. The king of snow

Prete, D. Green

Roberts, G. Clear sailing

Shaw, D. Diving with the devil

Westlake, D. E. A good story

Winter, E. A color of sky

Wolven, S. The copper kings

DRUGGISTS See Pharmacists

DRUGS

See also Drug addiction; Drug traffic

Aylett, S. Sampler

Brown, R. How to win

Campbell, R. Stages

Clark, J. Jungle wedding

Clark, J. The lotus-eater

Harfenist, J. Pixie dust

McManus, J. Deseret

Mead, H. Wednesday night, Thursday morning

Moody, R. The Albertine notes

Orringer, J. Care

Parker, G. Carp fishing on valium

Parker, G. The evening before . . .

Pitt, M. The mean

Wilson, R. C. Protocols of consumption

Drugs. O'Neill, S.

Drugs and you. Krouse, E.

DRUGSTORES See Pharmacists

The **drum** of saccharine. Hodgson, W. H.

DRUMMERS

Barrett, L. Meet the impersonators! (1986)

Bradbury, R. The drummer boy of Shiloh

Drummond, Laurie Lynn

Absolutes

Drummond, L. L. Anything you say can and will be used against you; Laurie Lynn Drummond

Cleaning your gun

Drummond, L. L. Anything you say can and will be used against you; Laurie Lynn Drummond

Finding a place

Drummond, L. L. Anything you say can and will be used against you; Laurie Lynn Drummond

Katherine's elegy

Drummond, L. L. Anything you say can and will be used against you; Laurie Lynn Drummond

Keeping the dead alive

Drummond, L. L. Anything you say can and will be used against you; Laurie Lynn Drummond

Lemme tell you something

Drummond, L. L. Anything you say can and will be used against you; Laurie Lynn Drummond

Something about a scar

Drummond, L. L. Anything you say can and will be used against you; Laurie Lynn Drummond

Taste, touch, sight, sound, smell

Drummond, L. L. Anything you say can and will be used against you; Laurie Lynn Drummond

Under control

Drummond, L. L. Anything you say can and will be used against you; Laurie Lynn Drummond

Where I come from

Drummond, L. L. Anything you say can and will be used against you; Laurie Lynn Drummond

Drummond & Son. D'Ambrosio, C.

Drunk with love. Gilchrist, E.

DRUNKARDS

See also Alcoholism; Temperance

Alexie, S. Because my father always said he was the only Indian who saw Jimi Hendrix play "The Star-Spangled Banner" at Woodstock

Bukoski, A. A geography of snow

Chekhov, A. P. Sorrow

Cummins, A. Headhunter

Davis, L. Barbara's mother's rug

DeLancey, K. Carley's knees

Gass, W. H. The Pedersen kid

L'Amour, L. The defense of Sentinel

Lee, M. Wives, lovers, Maximilian

McKee, J. Under the influence

McNulty, J. Atheist hit by truck

Mrabet, M. The canebrake

Ortiz, S. J. The panther waits

Spencer, E. The fishing lake

Spencer, E. A southern landscape

Swarthout, G. F. A glass of blessings

Thelwell, M. Community of victims

DRUNKENNESS

Abrams, T. A tale of two losers

Banks, I. The bridge [excerpt]

Boyle, T. C. Mexico

Carlson, R. DeRay

Carter, E. Glory and the angels

Chaon, D. Fraternity

Chekhov, A. P. A man of ideas

Chekhov, A. P. Rapture

Chesnutt, C. W. A bad night

Cobb, T. I'll never get out of this world alive

Cobb, T. Small-block chevy

Evans, E. Voodoo girls on ice

Fielding, H. Luckybitch

Gay, W. Crossroads blues

Gonzalez, R. Away

Grodstein, L. Lonely planet

Henry, W. The true friends

Hobson, C. The bottle: a provincial tale

House, S. Gatlinburg

Hughes, J. Forbidden fruits

Iribarne, M. Make them laugh

Jones, T. The roadrunner

McManus, J. The Magothy fires

McManus, J. Stop breakin down

Morgan, R. A taxpayer & a citizen

Muñoz, M. Zigzagger

Shade, E. Stability

Smith, A. The heat of the story

Smolens, J. Snow

Updike, J. The taste of metal

Yañez, R. Rio Bravo

Zinik, Z. A pickled nose

DRUP number one. Kaminsky, S. M.

Drury, Joan M.

Murder at the sales meeting

Brought to book; murderous stories from the literary world; Penny Sumner, editor

The **Drury** girl. Lipsyte, S.

Dry ice. Hackbarth, P.

A **dry**, quiet war. Daniel, T.

Dry roots. Pritchett, L.

Dry spell. Bukoski, A.

Dry whiskey. Silva, D. B.

DRYADS

Yolen, J. The sleep of trees

Dryfall. Reid, E.

Drywall, plaster, and the things that cover them. Prinzo, D.

Du Bois, W. E. B. (William Edward Burghardt)

The comet

Dark matter; a century of speculative fiction from the African diaspora; edited by Sheree R. Thomas

Jesus Christ in Texas

The African American West; a century of short stories; edited by Bruce A. Glasrud and Laurie Champion

Du Bois, William Edward Burghardt *See* Du Bois, W. E. B. (William Edward Burghardt), 1868-1963

Dual balls. Barker, N.

DUAL PERSONALITY

See also Personality disorders

James, H. Benvolio

Nolan, W. F. An act of violence

Duane, Diane

In the company of heroes

Past imperfect; edited by Martin H. Greenberg and Larry Segriff

Dubinsky on the loose. Epstein, J.

DUBLIN (IRELAND) *See* Ireland—Dublin

The **Dublin** eye. Howard, C.

Dubnov, Eugene

The bridge

Chicago Review v47 no2 p61-2 Summ 2001

The red horse

Chicago Review v47 no2 p50-60 Summ 2001

The Second Sunday in October

South Carolina Review v36 no1 p19-28 Fall 2003

So to speak

Dalhousie Review v79 no3 p389-95 Aut 1999

DuBois, Brendan

Dancing the night away

Death dance; suspenseful stories of the dance macabre; Trevanian, editor

The dark snow

The Best American mystery stories of the century; Tony Hillerman, editor; with an introduction by Tony Hillerman

A family game

The Best American mystery stories, 2002; edited and with an introduction by James Ellroy; Otto Penzler, series editor

The greatest sacrifice

White House pet detectives; tales of crime and mystery at the White House from a pet's-eye view; edited by Carole Nelson Douglas

Her last gift

Blood on their hands; edited by Lawrence Block

The invisible spy

The Blue and the gray undercover; edited by Ed Gorman

Netmail

The Best American mystery stories, 1999; edited and with an introduction by Ed McBain

Old soldiers

The World's finest mystery and crime stories, second annual collection; edited by Ed Gorman

DuBois, Brendan—*Continued*
Richard's children
    The Best American mystery stories, 2003; edited by Michael Connelly and Otto Penzler
The star thief
    The World's finest mystery and crime stories, third annual collection; edited by Ed Gorman and Martin H. Greenberg
The summer people
    The World's finest mystery and crime stories, second annual collection; edited by Ed Gorman
The tourist who wasn't there
    Lighthouse hauntings; 12 original tales of the supernatural; edited by Charles G. Waugh & Martin H. Greenberg
Trade wars
    Crème de la crime; edited by Janet Hutchings
The wearing of the green
    Murder most Celtic; tall tales of Irish mayhem; edited by Martin H. Greenberg
Dubois, Jocelyne
Silence
    Dalhousie Review v81 no1 p95-100 Spr 2001
Dubrovskii. Pushkin, A. S.
Dubus, Andre
An afternoon with the old man
    Sports best short stories; edited by Paul D. Staudohar
Corporal Lewis
    Writers harvest 3; edited and with an introduction by Tobias Wolff
Falling in love
    The Workshop; seven decades of the Iowa Writers' Workshop: 42 stories, recollections & essays on Iowa's place in 20th-century American literature; edited by Tom Grimes
The fat girl
    What are you looking at?; the first fat fiction anthology; edited by Donna Jarrell and Ira Sukrungruang
The winter father
    Fault lines; stories of divorce; collected and edited by Caitlin Shetterly
The **duchess** at prayer. Wharton, E.
Duck. Alameddine, R.
DUCK HUNTING
    Hall, L. S. The ledge
    Lansdale, J. R. Duck hunt
    Robinson, L. Eiders
Duck season. Harfenist, J.
Duckie. Blackwell, K.
Dud. Painter, P.
Dud. Tenn, W.
Due, Tananarive
Like daughter
    Dark matter; a century of speculative fiction from the African diaspora; edited by Sheree R. Thomas
Patient zero
    The Year's best science fiction, eighteenth annual collection; edited by Gardner Dozois
Trial day
    Mojo: conjure stories; edited by Nalo Hopkinson
Due west. Kennett, R.
The **duel**. Borges, J. L.
The **duel**. Callaghan, M.
Duel. Matheson, R.

Duel. McKiernan, D. L.
DUELING
    Borges, J. L. The encounter
    Borges, J. L. The other duel
    Borges, J. L. The south
    Edghill, R. The long divorce of steel
    Pushkin, A. S. The shot
    Schnitzler, A. The second
Dueling grandmothers. Wu, C. H.
DUELS *See* Dueling
Dueñas, Guadalupe
In heaven
    Short stories by Latin American women; the magic and the real; edited by Celia Correas de Zapata; foreword by Isabel Allende
Shoes for the rest of my life
    Short stories by Latin American women; the magic and the real; edited by Celia Correas de Zapata; foreword by Isabel Allende
The **duende**. Melville, P.
Duff, Gerald
Texas Wherever You Look
    Southwest Review v87 no4 p565-84 2002
Duffy, Maureen
The microcosm [excerpt]
    The Vintage book of international lesbian fiction; edited and with an introduction by Naomi Holoch and Joan Nestle
Duffy, Stella
Could be better
    Brought to book; murderous stories from the literary world; Penny Sumner, editor
Martha Grace
    The best British mysteries; edited by Maxim Jakubowski
    Tart noir; edited by Stella Duffy & Lauren Henderson
Duffy, Steve
Running dogs
    The Year's best fantasy & horror, twelfth annual collection; edited by Ellen Datlow & Terry Windling
(jt. auth) See Rodwell, Ian and Duffy, Steve
Dufresne, Frank
The Kelly rainbow
    Sports best short stories; edited by Paul D. Staudohar
Dufresne, John
Johnny too bad
    New stories from the South: the year's best, 2003; edited by Shannon Ravenel; with a preface by Roy Blount Jr.
    TriQuarterly no112 p174-213 Fall/Wint 2002
Duggin, Richard
Why won't you talk to me?
    A different plain; contemporary Nebraska fiction writers; edited by Ladette Randolph ; introduction by Mary Pipher
DUKAKIS, MICHAEL
About
    Sheckley, R. Dukakis and the aliens
Dukakis and the aliens. Sheckley, R.
The **Duke** of Wellington misplaces his horse. Clarke, S.
Duke power. Singleton, G.
Dukthas, Ann
    For works written by this author under other names see Doherty, P. C.

Dulac, Brion
What I was thinking
The Antioch Review v60 no1 p56-66 Wint
2002
A **dull,** orderly job. Williams, D.
Duluth. Hubbard, S.
Dumas, Alexandre
The three musketeers [excerpt]
Swords and sorcerers; stories from the world
of fantasy and adventure; edited by Clint
Willis
Dumas, Henry
Ark of bones
Dark matter; a century of speculative fiction
from the African diaspora; edited by Sheree
R. Thomas
Dumas, H. and Redmond, E. B. Echo tree;
the collected short fiction of Henry Dumas;
edited and with a foreword by Eugene B.
Redmond ; critical introduction by John S.
Wright
The bewitching bag; or, How the man escaped
from Hell
Dumas, H. and Redmond, E. B. Echo tree;
the collected short fiction of Henry Dumas;
edited and with a foreword by Eugene B.
Redmond ; critical introduction by John S.
Wright
A boll of roses
Dumas, H. and Redmond, E. B. Echo tree;
the collected short fiction of Henry Dumas;
edited and with a foreword by Eugene B.
Redmond ; critical introduction by John S.
Wright
Children of the sun
Dumas, H. and Redmond, E. B. Echo tree;
the collected short fiction of Henry Dumas;
edited and with a foreword by Eugene B.
Redmond ; critical introduction by John S.
Wright
The crossing
Dumas, H. and Redmond, E. B. Echo tree;
the collected short fiction of Henry Dumas;
edited and with a foreword by Eugene B.
Redmond ; critical introduction by John S.
Wright
Devil bird
Dumas, H. and Redmond, E. B. Echo tree;
the collected short fiction of Henry Dumas;
edited and with a foreword by Eugene B.
Redmond ; critical introduction by John S.
Wright
The distributors
Dumas, H. and Redmond, E. B. Echo tree;
the collected short fiction of Henry Dumas;
edited and with a foreword by Eugene B.
Redmond ; critical introduction by John S.
Wright
Double nigger
Dumas, H. and Redmond, E. B. Echo tree;
the collected short fiction of Henry Dumas;
edited and with a foreword by Eugene B.
Redmond ; critical introduction by John S.
Wright

The eagle the dove and the blackbird
Dumas, H. and Redmond, E. B. Echo tree;
the collected short fiction of Henry Dumas;
edited and with a foreword by Eugene B.
Redmond ; critical introduction by John S.
Wright
Echo tree
Dumas, H. and Redmond, E. B. Echo tree;
the collected short fiction of Henry Dumas;
edited and with a foreword by Eugene B.
Redmond ; critical introduction by John S.
Wright
Fon
Dumas, H. and Redmond, E. B. Echo tree;
the collected short fiction of Henry Dumas;
edited and with a foreword by Eugene B.
Redmond ; critical introduction by John S.
Wright
Goodbye, sweetwater
Dumas, H. and Redmond, E. B. Echo tree;
the collected short fiction of Henry Dumas;
edited and with a foreword by Eugene B.
Redmond ; critical introduction by John S.
Wright
Harlem
Dumas, H. and Redmond, E. B. Echo tree;
the collected short fiction of Henry Dumas;
edited and with a foreword by Eugene B.
Redmond ; critical introduction by John S.
Wright
A Harlem game
Dumas, H. and Redmond, E. B. Echo tree;
the collected short fiction of Henry Dumas;
edited and with a foreword by Eugene B.
Redmond ; critical introduction by John S.
Wright
Invasion
Dumas, H. and Redmond, E. B. Echo tree;
the collected short fiction of Henry Dumas;
edited and with a foreword by Eugene B.
Redmond ; critical introduction by John S.
Wright
The lake
Dumas, H. and Redmond, E. B. Echo tree;
the collected short fiction of Henry Dumas;
edited and with a foreword by Eugene B.
Redmond ; critical introduction by John S.
Wright
The man who could see through fog
Dumas, H. and Redmond, E. B. Echo tree;
the collected short fiction of Henry Dumas;
edited and with a foreword by Eugene B.
Redmond ; critical introduction by John S.
Wright
The marchers
Dumas, H. and Redmond, E. B. Echo tree;
the collected short fiction of Henry Dumas;
edited and with a foreword by Eugene B.
Redmond ; critical introduction by John S.
Wright
The metagensesis of Sunra
Dumas, H. and Redmond, E. B. Echo tree;
the collected short fiction of Henry Dumas;
edited and with a foreword by Eugene B.
Redmond ; critical introduction by John S.
Wright

Dumas, Henry—*Continued*

My brother, my brother!

Dumas, H. and Redmond, E. B. Echo tree; the collected short fiction of Henry Dumas; edited and with a foreword by Eugene B. Redmond ; critical introduction by John S. Wright

Rain God

Dumas, H. and Redmond, E. B. Echo tree; the collected short fiction of Henry Dumas; edited and with a foreword by Eugene B. Redmond ; critical introduction by John S. Wright

Riot or revolt?

Dumas, H. and Redmond, E. B. Echo tree; the collected short fiction of Henry Dumas; edited and with a foreword by Eugene B. Redmond ; critical introduction by John S. Wright

Rope of wind

Dumas, H. and Redmond, E. B. Echo tree; the collected short fiction of Henry Dumas; edited and with a foreword by Eugene B. Redmond ; critical introduction by John S. Wright

Scout

Dumas, H. and Redmond, E. B. Echo tree; the collected short fiction of Henry Dumas; edited and with a foreword by Eugene B. Redmond ; critical introduction by John S. Wright

Six days you shall labor

Dumas, H. and Redmond, E. B. Echo tree; the collected short fiction of Henry Dumas; edited and with a foreword by Eugene B. Redmond ; critical introduction by John S. Wright

Strike and fade

Dumas, H. and Redmond, E. B. Echo tree; the collected short fiction of Henry Dumas; edited and with a foreword by Eugene B. Redmond ; critical introduction by John S. Wright

Thalia

Dumas, H. and Redmond, E. B. Echo tree; the collected short fiction of Henry Dumas; edited and with a foreword by Eugene B. Redmond ; critical introduction by John S. Wright

Thrust counter thrust

Dumas, H. and Redmond, E. B. Echo tree; the collected short fiction of Henry Dumas; edited and with a foreword by Eugene B. Redmond ; critical introduction by John S. Wright

The university of man

Dumas, H. and Redmond, E. B. Echo tree; the collected short fiction of Henry Dumas; edited and with a foreword by Eugene B. Redmond ; critical introduction by John S. Wright

The voice

Dumas, H. and Redmond, E. B. Echo tree; the collected short fiction of Henry Dumas; edited and with a foreword by Eugene B. Redmond ; critical introduction by John S. Wright

Will the circle be unbroken?

Dumas, H. and Redmond, E. B. Echo tree; the collected short fiction of Henry Dumas; edited and with a foreword by Eugene B. Redmond ; critical introduction by John S. Wright

The **dumb** witness. Chesnutt, C. W.

Dummies, Shakers, Barkers, Wanderers. Martin, L.

Dummy. See Carver, R. The third thing that killed my father off

The **dummy** ward. Nickle, D.

Dumpster diving. Yeager, L.

Dunbar, Paul Laurence

The ingrate

The African American West; a century of short stories; edited by Bruce A. Glasrud and Laurie Champion

The lynching of Jube Benson

Southern local color; stories of region, race, and gender; edited by Barbara C. Ewell and Pamela Glenn Menke; with notes by Andrea Humphrey

Nelse Hatton's vengeance

Southern local color; stories of region, race, and gender; edited by Barbara C. Ewell and Pamela Glenn Menke; with notes by Andrea Humphrey

Dunbar-Nelson, Alice Moore

The praline woman

Southern local color; stories of region, race, and gender; edited by Barbara C. Ewell and Pamela Glenn Menke; with notes by Andrea Humphrey

Sister Josepha

Southern local color; stories of region, race, and gender; edited by Barbara C. Ewell and Pamela Glenn Menke; with notes by Andrea Humphrey

Tony's wife

Southern local color; stories of region, race, and gender; edited by Barbara C. Ewell and Pamela Glenn Menke; with notes by Andrea Humphrey

Duncan, Andy

The chief designer

The Year's best science fiction, nineteenth annual collection; edited by Gardner Dozois

Daddy Mention and the Monday skull

Mojo: conjure stories; edited by Nalo Hopkinson

The Pottawatomie Giant

Death dines at 8:30; edited by Claudia Bishop and Nick DiChario

Senator Bilbo

Starlight 3; edited by Patrick Nielsen Hayden

Duncan in China. Jen, G.

Duncker, Patricia

Betrayal

The Art of the story; an international anthology of contemporary short stories; edited by Daniel Halpern

Dundee. Harmon, J.

Dunkelblau. Blaise, C.

Dunlap, Murray

A Wolf in Virginia

The Virginia Quarterly Review v79 no3 p469-81 Summ 2003

Dunlap, Susan
Away for safekeeping
  Love and death; edited by Carolyn Hart
Bad review
  Brought to book; murderous stories from the
    literary world; Penny Sumner, editor
People who sit in glass houses
  Malice domestic 10; an anthology of original
    traditional mystery stories
A worm in the winesap
  Mom, apple pie, and murder; edited by Nancy
    Pickard
Dunmore, Helen
Be vigilant, rejoice, eat plenty
  Dunmore, H. Ice cream
The clear and rolling water
  Dunmore, H. Ice cream
Coosing
  Dunmore, H. Ice cream
Emily's ring
  Dunmore, H. Ice cream
The fag
  Dunmore, H. Ice cream
Ice cream
  Dunmore, H. Ice cream
The icon room
  Dunmore, H. Ice cream
The Kiwi-fruit arbour
  Dunmore, H. Ice cream
Leonardo, Michelangelo, SuperStork
  Dunmore, H. Ice cream
The lighthouse keeper's wife
  Dunmore, H. Ice cream
Lilac
  Dunmore, H. Ice cream
Lisette
  Dunmore, H. Ice cream
Living out
  Dunmore, H. Ice cream
Mason's mini-break
  Dunmore, H. Ice cream
My Polish teacher's tie
  Dunmore, H. Ice cream
Salmon
  Dunmore, H. Ice cream
Swimming into the millennium
  Dunmore, H. Ice cream
You stayed awake with me
  Dunmore, H. Ice cream
Dunn, Douglas
The political piano
  The Vintage book of contemporary Scottish
    fiction; edited and with an introduction by
    Peter Kravitz
Dunn, Katherine
The allies
  Snapshots: 20th century mother-daughter fic-
    tion; edited by Joyce Carol Oates and Janet
    Berliner
**Dunsany, Edward John Moreton Drax Plunkett,
Baron**
Chu-bu and Sheemish
  Tales before Tolkien; the roots of modern
    fantasy; edited by Douglas A. Anderson
The hoard of the Gibbelins
  Swords and sorcerers; stories from the world
    of fantasy and adventure; edited by Clint
    Willis

Duong, Thu Huong
Reflections of spring
  The Art of the story; an international antholo-
    gy of contemporary short stories; edited by
    Daniel Halpern
Durando, Neal
Notes to Chris concerning household conduct
  while I am away in Buenos Aires
  Chicago Review v45 no2 p17-18 1999
Duras, Mireille
The Sanitorium Syndrome
  The Literary Review (Madison, N.J.) v47 no1
    p118-20 Fall 2003
Duration. Wharton, E.
Durban, Pam
Soon
  The Best American short stories of the
    century; John Updike, editor, Katrina
    Kenison, coeditor; with an introduction by
    John Updike
Dusk. Powell, P.
A **dusk** of idols. Blish, J.
Dust. Rose, P. S.
Dust and ashes. Lee, W. W.
Dust and joys: a tale from the alternative archives.
  Maya, G.
Dust devil. Pickard, N.
Dust devils. Lundquist, R.
The **dust** enclosed here. Baker, K.
Dusty loves. Yolen, J.
DUTCH
                    Indonesia
  Murray, S. Folly
Duty. Berkman, P. R.
Duve, Karen
The dog's visit
  Chicago Review v48 no2/3 p62-6 Summ 2002
DWARFS
  Al-Shaykh, H. The keeper of the virgins
  Bradbury, R. The dwarf
  Jones, G. 'Life probably saved by imbecile
    dwarf'
  McClanahan, E. The little-known bird of the in-
    ner eye
  Orozco, O. The midgets
  Pearlman, D. D. The circus hand's desertion
  Rawley, D. Baby Liz
  Singleton, G. Crawl space
  VanderMeer, J. Learning to leave the flesh
  Wharton, E. The young gentlemen
Dwight Tuggle. Agee, J.
Dworkin, Susan
The World Famous Tightrope Walker
  Ms. v12 no3 p54-9 Summ 2002
Dwyer, Deanna *See* Koontz, Dean R. (Dean Ray),
  1945-
Dwyer, K. R. *See* Koontz, Dean R. (Dean Ray),
  1945-
Dwyer, K. R., 1945-
  *For works written by this author under oth-
    er names see* Koontz, Dean R. (Dean
    Ray), 1945-
Dwyer, Maggie
After Chernobyl
  Dwyer, M. Misplaced love; short stories
The beautiful inclination
  Dwyer, M. Misplaced love; short stories
Beef and pudding
  Dwyer, M. Misplaced love; short stories

Dwyer, Maggie—*Continued*
  Doctor Weltschmerz, I presume
    Dwyer, M. Misplaced love; short stories
  Lot's wife
    Dwyer, M. Misplaced love; short stories
  May 22, 1954
    Dwyer, M. Misplaced love; short stories
  Once more with feeling
    Dwyer, M. Misplaced love; short stories
  The sweet science
    Dwyer, M. Misplaced love; short stories
  This bitter earth
    Dwyer, M. Misplaced love; short stories
  Wrap your troubles in dreams
    Dwyer, M. Misplaced love; short stories
Dybek, Stuart
  Blowing shades
    The Pushcart prize XXIII: best of the small
      presses; an annual small press reader; ed-
      ited by Bill Henderson with the Pushcart
      prize editors
  Blue boy
    Dybek, S. I sailed with Magellan
    TriQuarterly no110/111 p12-50 Fall 2001
  Breasts
    Dybek, S. I sailed with Magellan
  Je reviens
    Dybek, S. I sailed with Magellan
  Live from Dreamsville
    Dybek, S. I sailed with Magellan
  Lunch at the Loyola Arms
    Dybek, S. I sailed with Magellan
  A minor mood
    Dybek, S. I sailed with Magellan
  Orchids
    Dybek, S. I sailed with Magellan
  Paper lantern
    The Workshop; seven decades of the Iowa
      Writers' Workshop: 42 stories, recollections
      & essays on Iowa's place in 20th-century
      American literature; edited by Tom Grimes
  Pet milk
    The Scribner anthology of contemporary short
      fiction; fifty North American stories since
      1970; Lex Williford and Michael Martone,
      editors
  Qué quieres
    Dybek, S. I sailed with Magellan
    TriQuarterly no117 p9-30 Fall 2003
  Song
    Dybek, S. I sailed with Magellan
    Harper's v307 p87-92 O 2003
  A Steamer Trunk
    The Virginia Quarterly Review v80 no2 p85-
      97 Spr 2004
  Swing
    Ploughshares v30 no1 p107-14 Spr 2004
  Undertow
    Dybek, S. I sailed with Magellan
  We didn't
    Dybek, S. I sailed with Magellan
Dyer, Geoff
  Hotel Oblivion
    Granta no79 p81-95 Aut 2002
Dyer, S. N.
  The July Ward
    A Woman's liberation; a choice of futures by
      and about women; edited by Connie Willis
      and Sheila Williams

  Sins of the mothers
    The Best from fantasy & science fiction: the
      fiftieth anniversary anthology; edited by
      Edward L. Ferman and Gordon Van Gelder
Dying. Schnitzler, A.
Dying for sin. Lee, W. W.
Dying light. Hays, D.
Dykstra, Emily Mills
  One-match fire
    The North American Review v287 no3/4
      p61-8 My/Ag 2002
Dynamite's day off. Easton, R. O.
Dysaesthesia. Kaplan, H.
Dyson, Jeremy
  £250,000 electrical clearance
    Dyson, J. Never trust a rabbit
  All in the telling
    Dyson, J. Never trust a rabbit
  At last
    Dyson, J. Never trust a rabbit
  The cash-point oracle
    Dyson, J. Never trust a rabbit
  City deep
    Dyson, J. Never trust a rabbit
  The engine of desire
    Dyson, J. Never trust a rabbit
  A last look at the sea
    Dyson, J. Never trust a rabbit
  Love in the time of Molyneux
    Dyson, J. Never trust a rabbit
  The maze
    Dyson, J. Never trust a rabbit
  A slate roof in the rain
    Dyson, J. Never trust a rabbit
  A visit from Val Koran
    Dyson, J. Never trust a rabbit
  We who walk through walls
    Dyson, J. Never trust a rabbit

E

Each in her own day. Mencken, S. H.
The **eagle** flies. Cooper, J. C.
EAGLES
  Chopin, K. The white eagle
  Cooper, J. C. The eagle flies
Eagles over Crooked Creek. Brand, M.
The **eaglet** in the dove's nest. Alcott, L. M.
Eakin, William
  A dragon of conspiracy
    Eakin, W. Redgunk tales; apocalypse and
      kudzu from Redgunk, Mississippi
  Encounter in Redgunk
    Eakin, W. Redgunk tales; apocalypse and
      kudzu from Redgunk, Mississippi
  A god for delphi
    Eakin, W. Redgunk tales; apocalypse and
      kudzu from Redgunk, Mississippi
  Homesickness
    Eakin, W. Redgunk tales; apocalypse and
      kudzu from Redgunk, Mississippi
  How Boy Howdy saved the world
    Eakin, W. Redgunk tales; apocalypse and
      kudzu from Redgunk, Mississippi
  Lawnmower Moe
    Eakin, W. Redgunk tales; apocalypse and
      kudzu from Redgunk, Mississippi

Eakin, William—_Continued_
  Meadow song
    Eakin, W. Redgunk tales; apocalypse and
      kudzu from Redgunk, Mississippi
  The miracle of Swamp Gas Jackson
    Eakin, W. Redgunk tales; apocalypse and
      kudzu from Redgunk, Mississippi
  Plain female seeks nice guy
    Eakin, W. Redgunk tales; apocalypse and
      kudzu from Redgunk, Mississippi
  Redgunk, Texas
    Eakin, W. Redgunk tales; apocalypse and
      kudzu from Redgunk, Mississippi
  Roadkill Fred
    Eakin, W. Redgunk tales; apocalypse and
      kudzu from Redgunk, Mississippi
  The secret of the mummy's brain
    Eakin, W. Redgunk tales; apocalypse and
      kudzu from Redgunk, Mississippi
  Unicorn stew
    Eakin, W. Redgunk tales; apocalypse and
      kudzu from Redgunk, Mississippi
EAR
  Tawada, Y. A guest
  Tawada, Y. Spores
EARHART, AMELIA, 1898-1937
                  About
  Gilliland, G. When Amelia smiled
  Knight, M. Amelia Earhart's coat
  Murray, S. Position
Earle, Steve
  Billy the Kid
    Earle, S. Doghouse roses; stories
  Doghouse roses
    Earle, S. Doghouse roses; stories
  A eulogy of sorts
    Carved in rock; short stories by musicians;
      edited by Greg Kihn
    Earle, S. Doghouse roses; stories
  The internationale
    Earle, S. Doghouse roses; stories
  Jaguar dance
    Earle, S. Doghouse roses; stories
  The red suitcase
    Earle, S. Doghouse roses; stories
  The reunion
    Earle, S. Doghouse roses; stories
  Taneytown
    Earle, S. Doghouse roses; stories
  A well-tempered heart
    Earle, S. Doghouse roses; stories
  Wheeler County
    Earle, S. Doghouse roses; stories
  The witness
    Earle, S. Doghouse roses; stories
Earley, Tony
  Aliceville
    Fishing for chickens; short stories about rural
      youth; edited, with an introduction by Jim
      Heynen
  Have You Seen the Stolen Girl?
    The New Yorker v79 no33 p78-83 N 3 2003
  Just married
    Esquire v131 no5 p144 My 1999
    New stories from the South: the year's best,
      2000; edited by Shannon Ravenel; with a
      preface by Ellen Douglas
  The Prophet from Jupiter
    The Scribner anthology of contemporary short
      fiction; fifty North American stories since
      1970; Lex Williford and Michael Martone,
      editors
    This is where we live; short stories by 25
      contemporary North Carolina writers; ed-
      ited by Michael McFee
  Quill
    New stories from the South: the year's best,
      1999; edited by Shannon Ravenel; with a
      preface by Tony Earley
  The wide sea
    The New Yorker v75 no16 p172-76 Je 21-28
      1999
Earling, Debra Magpie
  Real Indians
    Prairie Schooner v77 no2 p15-20 Summ 2003
Early age and late disorder. Penn, W. S.
EARLY CHRISTIANS
  Borges, J. L. The Sect of the Thirty
An **early** death. Schmidt, H. J.
Early, in the evening. Watson, I.
Early November. Orner, P.
Early transparent. Coberly, L. M.
EARP, LOUISA HOUSTON
                  About
  Coleman, J. C. Wild flower
EARRINGS
  Tawada, Y. The talisman
Earrings. Hay, E.
Ears. Boylan, C.
EARTH
  Chilson, R. This side of independence
  Clarke, A. C. The fires within
  Clarke, A. C. History lesson
  Niven, L. Inconstant moon
EARTH, DESTRUCTION OF
  Anderson, P. Epilogue
  Bradbury, R. The million-year picnic
  Clarke, A. C. 'If I forget thee, oh Earth . . .'
  Clarke, A. C. The last command
  Clarke, A. C. Nightfall
  Clarke, A. C. No morning after
  Clarke, A. C. Rescue party
  Clarke, A. C. The road to the sea
  Oliver, C. King of the hill
  Pohl, F. The gold at the starbow's end
  Pronzini, B. and Malzberg, B. N. Inaugural
  Tenn, W. The liberation of earth
Earth to earth. Graves, R.
Earthbound. Thurm, M.
Earthlight. Clarke, A. C.
An **earthly** mother sits and sings. Crowley, J.
Earthquake damage. Adams, A.
EARTHQUAKES
          See also Disasters
  Blake, J. C. Under the sierra
  Burford, M. The faces of fear
  Chee, A. A pilgrimage of you
  Clarke, A. C. Dog Star
  Ha Jin. Alive
  Haake, K. This is geology to us
  Murakami, H. Honey Pie
  Murakami, H. Super-Frog saves Tokyo
  Murakami, H. UFO in Kushiro
  Wilson, R., Jr. California
Earthtonium and other white lies. Devassie, T.

EAST AFRICA
Vanderbes, J. The hatbox
Waugh, E. Incident in Azania
East Bay Grease. Vaz, K.
East breeze. Aadland, D.
EAST INDIAN AMERICANS
Lahiri, J. Nobody's business
Sharma, A. Surrounded by sleep
EAST INDIAN SOLDIERS *See* Soldiers—India
EAST INDIANS
Canada
Desai, A. Winterscape
Mukherjee, B. The management of grief
England
Chaudhuri, A. The second marriage
Cutler, J. Doctor's orders
New York (N.Y.)
Vaswani, N. Domestication of an imaginary goat
Trinidad and Tobago
Hosein, C. Morris, Bhaiya
United States
Bhattacharyya, R. Loss
Divakaruni, C. B. The blooming season for cacti
Divakaruni, C. B. The intelligence of wild things
Divakaruni, C. B. The love of a good man
Divakaruni, C. B. Mrs. Dutta writes a letter
Divakaruni, C. B. The unknown errors of our lives
Divakaruni, C. B. What the body knows
Kavaler, R. Pigeons
Lahiri, J. Mrs. Sen's
Lahiri, J. The third and final continent
Lahiri, J. This blessed house
Lahiri, J. When Mr. Pirzada came to dine
Mukherjee, B. Happiness
Pittalwala, I. Lost in the U.S.A.
Ramaya, S. The matchmakers
Ramaya, S. Re:mohit
Vaswani, N. Five objects in Queens
Viswanathan, L. Cool wedding
East on Houston. Carter, E.
EAST SIDE, LOWER (NEW YORK, N.Y.) *See* New York (N.Y.)—Lower East Side
EAST TIMOR (INDONESIA)
Jones, G. Other places
Easter, Chuck
Bastard
The Literary Review (Madison, N.J.) v44 no4 p662-3 Summ 2001
EASTER
Skillings, R. D. Easter at the old homestead
Yates, R. Bells in the morning
Easter. McGahern, J.
Easter, 1939. Powers, R.
Easter 1943. Blum, J.
Easter at the old homestead. Skillings, R. D.
Easter dresses. Meyers, K.
Easter Egg Hunt. Klise, J.
Easter eve. Chekhov, A. P.
Easter night. See Chekhov, A. P. Easter eve
Easter story. Trevanian
Easton, Robert Olney
Bonaparte's dreams
Easton, R. O. To find a place; western stories
Death in October
Easton, R. O. To find a place; western stories
Dynamite's day off
Easton, R. O. To find a place; western stories

First dawning
Easton, R. O. To find a place; western stories
The happy man
Easton, R. O. To find a place; western stories
Jim Magee's sand
Easton, R. O. To find a place; western stories
The legend of Shorm
Easton, R. O. To find a place; western stories
Nobody danced
Easton, R. O. To find a place; western stories
Quick and the cat
Easton, R. O. To find a place; western stories
To find a place
Easton, R. O. To find a place; western stories
Wild challenge
The First Five Star western corral; western stories; edited by Jon Tuska and Vicki Piekarski
The wind of Pelican Island
Easton, R. O. To find a place; western stories
Women and Dynamite
Easton, R. O. To find a place; western stories
Eastward ho!. Tenn, W.
EASTWOOD, CLINT
About
Tillman, L. The undiagnosed
Easy as pie. Rucker, R. v. B.
An **easy** birth. Pritchett, L.
Easy go. Matera, L.
Easy in the islands. Shacochis, B.
Easy pickings. Gautreaux, T.
Easy street. Parker, T. J.
Easy Street. Purdy, J.
Eater. Hansen, J.
Eating. Bass, R.
Eating Aunt Victoria. Campbell, B. J.
EATING DISORDERS
Thien, M. Alchemy
Eating mammals. Barlow, J.
Eating out. Michaels, L.
Eating Vic. Weiner, S.
EAVESDROPPING
Chaon, D. Big me
Singer, I. B. Not for the Sabbath
Ebenezer. Bishop, P.
Ebershoff, David
The bank president
His 3: brilliant new fiction by gay writers; edited by Robert Drake and Terry Wolverton
The charm bracelet
Ebershoff, D. The Rose City; stories
Chuck Paa
Ebershoff, D. The Rose City; stories
The dress
Ebershoff, D. The Rose City; stories
Living together
Ebershoff, D. The Rose City; stories
Regime
Ebershoff, D. The Rose City; stories
The rose city
Circa 2000; gay fiction at the millennium; edited by Robert Drake & Terry Wolverton
Ebershoff, D. The Rose City; stories
Trespass
Ebershoff, D. The Rose City; stories
Eberts, Gerik R. *See* Eberts, Max

Eberts, Max
Lost lives
  Nightshade: 20th century ghost stories; edited
    by Robert Phillips
ECCENTRICS AND ECCENTRICITIES
  See also Recluses
Bambara, T. C. Maggie of the green bottles
Banks, R. The guinea pig lady
Baxter, C. Gryphon
Berners, G. H. T.-W., Baron. Mr. Pidger
Bowles, P. Hugh Harper
Boylan, C. Appearances
Boyle, T. C. The underground gardens
Brenner, W. The anomalist
Brockmeier, K. Things that fall from the sky
Brownstein, G. A penal colony all his own, 11E
Brownstein, G. Wakefield, 7E
Budnitz, J. Vacation
Burke, J. The man in the civil suit
Clyde, M. Pruitt love
Dark, A. E. Watch the animals
Dybek, S. Breasts
Gifford, B. The lonely and the lost
Goldberg, M. Bee season
Gonzalez, R. The scorpion eater
Greenberg, A. The life of the mind
Hamburger, A. Exile
Hansen, R. His dog
Hill, I. The ballad of Rappy Valcour
Homes, A. M. Remedy
Link, K. Water off a black dog's back
Means, D. The gesture hunter
Muñoz, M. Loco
Oliver, C. Pilgrimage
Pancake, A. Dog song
Poirier, M. J. Buttons
Poirier, M. J. A note on the type
Poirier, M. J. Worms
Porter, J. A. A pear-shaped woman and a fuddy-
  duddy
Régio, J. Miss Olimpia and her maid Belarmina
Richter, S. Rats eat cats
Sanford, A. Goose girl
Scoville, S. Pu'u Pu'iwa
Singer, I. B. A pair
Smith, A. Gothic
Smith, A. The universal story
Stefaniak, M. H. Believing Marina
Treat, J. Walking
Trevanian. Mrs. McGivney's nickel
Urrea, L. A. Mr. Mendoza's paintbrush
Vivante, A. The foundling
Waugh, E. A house of gentlefolks
Weaver, G. Viewed from Lanta & Wally's
Wharton, E. The House of the Dead Hand
Williams, J. The blue men
Wuori, G. K. Condoms
Wuori, G. K. Glory
Wuori, G. K. Skunk
Eccles, Marjorie
Peril at Melford house
  Malice domestic 9
Echea. Rusch, K. K.
Echenique, Alfredo Bryce *See* Bryce Echenique,
  Alfredo, 1939-
Echo. Anderson, R.
The **echo.** Bowles, P.

Eckhardt, C. F. (Charley F.)
The fevers
  Westward; a fictional history of the American
    West : 28 original stories celebrating the
    50th anniversary of the Western Writers of
    America; edited by Dale L. Walker
Eckhardt, Charley F. *See* Eckhardt, C. F. (Char-
  ley F.)
Eclipse. Leong, R.
Eclipse. McGlynn, D.
The **eclipse.** Spencer, E.
ECLIPSES
Updike, J. Eclipse
ECOLOGY
Anderson, P. Windmill
ECONOMISTS
Varley, J. Goodbye, Robinson Crusoe
Ecopoiesis. Landis, G. A.
The **ecstasy** of Magda Brummel. Roeske, P.
ECUADOR
London, J. The madness of John Harned
Ed Stein, Ed Stein, speak to me!. Weaver, G.
Eddie Haskell in a short skirt. Collins, B. and
  Collins, M. A.
Edelman, Scott
Eros and agape among the asteroids
  Once upon a galaxy; edited by Will [sic]
    McCarthy, Martin H. Greenberg, and John
    Helfers
Mom, the Martians, and me
  Mars probes; edited by Peter Crowther
Edelstein, June R.
On Florentine Road
  New England Review v22 no4 p112-28 Fall
    2001
Eden. Bauman, B. A.
The **edge** of marriage. Kaplan, H.
The **edge** of the forest and the edge of the ocean.
  Robinson, L.
The **edge** of the universe. Bisson, T.
Edgerton, Clyde
Debra's flap and snap
  New stories from the South: the year's best,
    2000; edited by Shannon Ravenel; with a
    preface by Ellen Douglas
Lunch at the Piccadilly
  New stories from the South: the year's best,
    1999; edited by Shannon Ravenel; with a
    preface by Tony Earley
Edgerton, Leslie
In the zone
  The Best American mystery stories, 2001; ed-
    ited and with an Introduction by Lawrence
    Block
Edghill, Rosemary
And king hereafter (a Boscobel League story)
  Edghill, R. Paying the piper at the gates of
    dawn
The Christmas witch
  Witches' brew; edited by Yvonne Jocks
The fairy ring
  Edghill, R. Paying the piper at the gates of
    dawn
For I have sworn thee fair
  Edghill, R. Paying the piper at the gates of
    dawn
A gift of two grey horses
  Edghill, R. Paying the piper at the gates of
    dawn

Edghill, Rosemary—*Continued*
Haut-Clare
  Edghill, R. Paying the piper at the gates of
    dawn
The intersection of Anastasia Yeoman and light
  Edghill, R. Paying the piper at the gates of
    dawn
Killer in the reign
  Edghill, R. Paying the piper at the gates of
    dawn
Lizzie Fair and the dragon of heart's desire
  Edghill, R. Paying the piper at the gates of
    dawn
The long divorce of steel
  Edghill, R. Paying the piper at the gates of
    dawn
The Maltese feline
  Edghill, R. Paying the piper at the gates of
    dawn
May Eve
  Edghill, R. Paying the piper at the gates of
    dawn
The piper at the gate
  Edghill, R. Paying the piper at the gates of
    dawn
Prince of exiles
  Edghill, R. Paying the piper at the gates of
    dawn
Scandal
  Edghill, R. Paying the piper at the gates of
    dawn
The Sword of the North
  Edghill, R. Paying the piper at the gates of
    dawn
War of the roses
  Edghill, R. Paying the piper at the gates of
    dawn
We have met the enemy
  Edghill, R. Paying the piper at the gates of
    dawn
Edie in winter. Reisman, N.
EDINBURGH (SCOTLAND) *See* Scotland—Ed-
  inburgh
**EDISON, THOMAS A. (THOMAS ALVA),
1847-1931**
  About
  Landis, G. A. The eyes of America
Edith Teilheimer's war. Goliger, G.
EDITORS
  See also Journalists; Women editors
  Adams, A. An unscheduled stop
  Berry, R. M. History
  Carson, J. Invaders
  Codrescu, A. The herald
  Cross, A. The perfect revenge
  Gartner, Z. Measuring death in column inches (a
    nine-week manual for girl rim pigs)
  Harris, M. From the desk of the troublesome ed-
    itor
  James, H. The Aspern papers
  Paul, B. Stet
  Scholz, C. The nine billion names of God
  Taylor, T. L. Newstart 2.0 TM
EDMONTON *See* Canada—Edmonton
Edmundson, Mark
  Game time
    The Yale Review v90 no1 p92-105 Ja 2002
Edna, back from America. Boylan, C.
Eduardo. Gonzalez, R.

EDUCATION
  See also Books and reading; Literacy;
    Teachers
  Coates, G. S. Promises
An **Education** in the Faith. Sayers, V.
EDUCATORS *See* Teachers
Edugyan, Esi
  The woman who tasted of rose oil
    Kulka, J. and Danford, N. The New American
    voices 2003; guest editor Joyce Carol
    Oates; series editors John Kulka and
    Natalie Danford
EDWARD II, KING OF ENGLAND, 1284-1327
  About
  Marston, E. Perfect shadows
Edward VIII, King of Great Britain *See* Wind-
  sor, Edward, Duke of, 1894-1972
Edward, Duke of Windsor *See* Windsor, Edward,
  Duke of, 1894-1972
Edward Albert, Prince of Wales *See* Windsor,
  Edward, Duke of, 1894-1972
Edward of unique achievement. Waugh, E.
Edwards, Kim
  In the Garden
    Ploughshares v29 no2/3 p21-42 Fall 2003
  The story of my life
    The Workshop; seven decades of the Iowa
    Writers' Workshop: 42 stories, recollections
    & essays on Iowa's place in 20th-century
    American literature; edited by Tom Grimes
  The way it felt to be falling
    Home and beyond; an anthology of Kentucky
    short stories; edited by Morris Allen
    Grubbs; with an introduction by Wade Hall
    and an afterword by Charles E. May
Edwards, Malon
  The scissors lady and the green man
    African American Review v33 no4 p609-11
    Wint 1999
Edwards, Martin
  24 hours from Tulsa
    The best British mysteries; edited by Maxim
    Jakubowski
  Natural causes
    Royal whodunnits; edited by Mike Ashley
Edwards, Sonia
  Between a white night and daybreak
    Edwards, S. A white veil for tomorrow
  A day of sunshine and tears
    Edwards, S. A white veil for tomorrow
  The girl who saw the colours of the rain
    Edwards, S. A white veil for tomorrow
  A half-sinner
    Edwards, S. A white veil for tomorrow
  Like the sun itself
    Edwards, S. A white veil for tomorrow
  A penance
    Edwards, S. A white veil for tomorrow
  A pleasant room
    Edwards, S. A white veil for tomorrow
  A white veil for tomorrow
    Edwards, S. A white veil for tomorrow
Eena. Banister, M. M.
Effinger, George Alec
  The adventure of the celestial snows
    My Sherlock Holmes; untold stories of the
    great detective; edited by Michael Kurland

Effinger, George Alec—*Continued*

One

Masterpieces: the best science fiction of the century; edited by Orson Scott Card

Egan, Greg

Border guards

The Year's best science fiction, seventeenth annual collection; edited by Gardner Dozois

Oceanic

The Year's best science fiction, sixteenth annual collection; edited by Gardner Dozois

Oracle

The Year's best science fiction, eighteenth annual collection; edited by Gardner Dozois

Singleton

The Year's best science fiction; twentieth annual collection; edited by Gardner Dozois

Wang's carpets

Centaurus: the best of Australian science fiction; edited by David G. Hartwell and Damien Broderick

Egan, Jennifer

Forty-minute lunch

Harper's v229 no1791 p90-96 Ag 1999

Goodbye, my love

Francis Ford Coppola's Zoetrope all-story 2; edited by Adrienne Brodeur and Samantha Schnee; with an introduction by Francis Ford Coppola

Egg. Jackson, S.

Egg boat. Dauenhauer, N.

Egg-face. Waters, M. Y.

The **egg** lady. Stuart, D.

The **egg** queen rises. Jacobs, M.

Eggers, Dave

After I was thrown in the river and before I drowned

Speaking with the angel; original stories; edited by Nick Hornby

Measuring the Jump

The New Yorker v79 no24 p114-21 S 1 2003

Up the mountain coming down slowly

McSweeney's mammoth treasury of thrilling tales; edited by Michael Chabon

Where Were We

The New Yorker v78 no23 p62-75 Ag 12 2002

Eggers, Paul

Anything you want, please

A different plain; contemporary Nebraska fiction writers; edited by Ladette Randolph ; introduction by Mary Pipher

Eggers, P. How the water feels; stories

The big gift

Eggers, P. How the water feels; stories

How the water feels

Eggers, P. How the water feels; stories

Leo, chained

Eggers, P. How the water feels; stories

A private space

Eggers, P. How the water feels; stories

Proof

Eggers, P. How the water feels; stories

The public spectacle

Prairie Schooner v75 no2 p123-33 Summ 2001

Substitutes

Eggers, P. How the water feels; stories

The year five

Eggers, P. How the water feels; stories

The **Eggplant** Legacy. Shishin, A.

EGGS

Jackson, S. Egg

Jacobs, M. The egg queen rises

Parker, G. The sheld-duck of the Basingstoke Canal

EGOISM

Hawthorne, N. Egotism; or, The bosom serpent

Su Tong. Young Muo

Egotism; or, The bosom serpent. Hawthorne, N.

EGYPT

Baker, K. The queen in yellow

Gabriel, D. Civilizations are islands

Posadas, Carmen. The Nubian lover

To 640

The Demon-possessed princess

Douglas, C. N. The mummy case: a midnight Louie past life adventure

Haggard, H. R. Smith and the pharaohs

Horizon

Lovecraft, H. P. Under the pyramids

Poe, E. A. Some words with a mummy

Rice, A. The mummy; or, Ramses the damned

Rohmer, S. The death-ring of Sneferu

Stoker, B. The Jewel of Seven Stars

Williams, T. The vengeance of Nitocris

Kings and rulers

Williams, T. The vengeance of Nitocris

Cairo

Hoch, E. D. The day the dogs died

Johnson-Davies, D. Coffee at the Marriott

Johnson-Davies, D. The dream

Johnson-Davies, D. Garbage girl

Johnson-Davies, D. A taxi to himself

Raab, E. Rose Jam

Sinai

See Sinai (Egypt)

Egyptian Avenue. Newman, K.

An **Egyptian** ciagarette. Chopin, K.

Egyptian nights. Pushkin, A. S.

EGYPTIANS

England

Aboulela, L. The museum

Saudi Arabia

Megid, Ibrahim Abdel. The other city

Ehlers, Jürgen

Golden Gate Bridge—a view from below

The World's finest mystery and crime stories, second annual collection; edited by Ed Gorman

"Wangeroog, de schone . . ."

Death by espionage; intriguing stories of deception and betrayal; edited by Martin Cruz Smith

Ehrenreich, Ben

What You Eat

Bomb no83 p96-9 Spr 2003

Eichmann's monogram. Kalman, J.

Eickhoff, Randy Lee

Dove's song

American West; twenty new stories from the Western Writers of America; edited with an introduction by Loren D. Estleman

Eiders. Robinson, L.

Eidus, Janice
  Elvis, Axl, and me
    Neurotica: Jewish writers on sex; edited by
    Melvin Jules Bukiet
EIFFEL TOWER (PARIS, FRANCE)
  Cohen, M. L. Polaroid
Eight o'clock in the morning. Nelson, R. F.
Eight Pieces for the Left Hand. Lennon, J. R.
The **eighth** day. Apple, M.
The **eighth** register. Bergeron, A.
The **eighth** sacrament. Rogers, E. M.
The **eighth** sea. Johnson, A.
The **eighty-yard** run. Shaw, I.
Einbahnstrasse. Allegra, D.
EINSTEIN, ALBERT, 1879-1955
About
  Pearlman, D. D. The Einstein-Jung connection
  Reiner, C. The Heidi and Albert correspondence
  What, L. Nothing without a name
The **Einstein-Jung** connection. Pearlman, D. D.
Eisenberg, Deborah
  The girl who left her sock on the floor
    The Art of the story; an international antholo-
    gy of contemporary short stories; edited by
    Daniel Halpern
  Some Other, Better Otto
    The Yale Review v91 no1 p123-55 Ja 2003
  What it was like, seeing Chris
    Wonderful town; New York stories from The
    New Yorker; edited by David Remnick
    with Susan Choi
Ekstrom, Leslie Simmonds
  On Sunday there might be Americans
    Living on the edge; fiction by Peace Corps
    writers; edited by John Coyne
EL PASO (TEX.) *See* Texas—El Paso
EL SALVADOR
  Howard, C. When the black shadows die
  Robinson, R. The face-lift
Eladio comes home. Garcia, L. G.
Elberg, Yehuda
  The empire of Kalman the Cripple
    Neugroschel, J. No star too beautiful; Yiddish
    stories from 1382 to the present; compiled
    and translated by Joachim Neugroschel
Elbow room. McPherson, J. A.
ELDERLY
See also Old age
  Bly, C. A committee of the whole
  Irsfeld, J. H. My neighbor Mr. Young
  Weaver, G. Learst's last stand
  Willis, M. S. Tales of the abstract expressionists
The **elderly** lady. Borges, J. L.
Eldridge, Courtney
  Becky
    Eldridge, Courtney. Unkempt
  Fits & starts
    Eldridge, Courtney. Unkempt
  The former world record holder settles down
    Eldridge, Courtney. Unkempt
  Sharks
    Eldridge, Courtney. Unkempt
  Summer of mopeds
    Eldridge, Courtney. Unkempt
  Thieves
    Eldridge, Courtney. Unkempt
  Unkempt
    Eldridge, Courtney. Unkempt

  Young professionals
    Eldridge, Courtney. Unkempt
The **election**. Drake, R.
Election. Struthers, A.
Election eve. Connell, E. S.
Election fever. Nfah-Abbenyi, J. M.
ELECTIONS
See also Presidents—Election
  Drake, R. The election
  Nfah-Abbenyi, J. M. Election fever
Electric brae [excerpt] Greig, A.
The **electric** eye. Mosley, W.
Electric fence. Arvin, N.
Electric wizard. Stuckey-French, E.
ELECTRICITY
  Arvin, N. In the electric Eden
  Delany, S. R. We, in some strange power's em-
    ploy, move on a rigorous line
Electricity. Svoboda, T.
ELECTRONIC COMPUTERS *See* Computers
Elegant Tom Dillar. Briggs, C. F.
Elegy. West, M.
Elegy (Footprint II). Čapek, K.
Elemenopy. Foley, S.
Elemental. Landis, G. A.
Elements. Gasco, E.
Elephant Feelings. Haskell, J.
The **elephant** vanishes. Murakami, H.
ELEPHANTS
  Arvin, N. In the electric Eden
  Bausch, R. The weight
  Haskell, J. Elephant feelings
  Resnick, M. The elephants on Neptune
  Tinti, H. Animal crackers
  VanderMeer, J. Mahout
  Watkins, S. Critterworld
The **elephants** on Neptune. Resnick, M.
The **elevator**. Dixon, S.
Elevator girls. Weinberg, R.
The **elevator** man. Volkmer, J.
ELEVATORS
  Dixon, S. The elevator
  Hochman, A. Do not attempt to climb out
Eleven o'clock bulletin. Turner, R.
Eleven to seven. Sinor, B. H.
Eleven Trials. Ng, K.-H.
Elf consciousness. Aronson, H.
ELIZABETH I, QUEEN OF ENGLAND, 1533-1603
About
  Franks, R. A secret murder
Elizabeth. Adams, A.
The **Elizabeth** complex. Fowler, K. J.
Elizabeth Stock's one story. Chopin, K.
Elizabeth who disappeared. Hunter, F.
Elizondo, Salvador
  The founding of Rome
    Bomb no74 p90-1 Wint 2001
    Harper's v303 no1819 p29-31 D 2001
Elkin, Stanley
  Criers and kibitzers, kibitzers and criers
    The Best American short stories of the
    century; John Updike, editor, Katrina
    Kenison, coeditor; with an introduction by
    John Updike
Elkins, Kimberly
  What Is Visible
    Atlantic Monthly (1993) v291 no2 p84, 86-8,
    90, 92 Mr 2003

Elkins, Kimberly—*Continued*

Best new American voices 2004; guest editor John Casey; series editors John Kulka and Natalie Danford

The **Elk's** Funeral. McEwen, T.

Ellen. Callaghan, M.

Ellen's book. Knight, M.

Ellin, Stanley

The last bottle in the world

Murder most delectable; savory tales of culinary crimes; edited by Martin H. Greenberg

The moment of decision

The Best American mystery stories of the century; Tony Hillerman, editor; with an introduction by Tony Hillerman

Reasons unknown

A Century of great suspense stories; edited by Jeffery Deaver

You can't be a little girl all your life

Master's choice v2; mystery stories by today's top writers and the masters who inspired them; edited by Lawrence Block

Elliott, Bruce

Wolves don't cry

The Literary werewolf; an anthology; edited by Charlotte F. Otten

Elliott, Sarah Barnwell

The heart of it

Southern local color; stories of region, race, and gender; edited by Barbara C. Ewell and Pamela Glenn Menke; with notes by Andrea Humphrey

Elliott, Stephen

The patriot actor

Politically inspired; edited by Stephen Elliott; assistant editor, Gabriel Kram; associate editors, Elizabeth Brooks [et al.]

Ellis, Alice Thomas

The cat's whiskers

Valentine's Day: women against men; stories of revenge; introduction by Alice Thomas

Ellis, Maeve Mullen

All Her Dreams

Calyx v22 no1 p41-8 Summ 2004

Ellis, Normandi

Dr. Livingston's grotto

Home and beyond; an anthology of Kentucky short stories; edited by Morris Allen Grubbs; with an introduction by Wade Hall and an afterword by Charles E. May

Ellis, Zoila

The waiting room

The Oxford book of Caribbean short stories; edited by Stewart Brown and John Wickham

Ellison, Harlan

The goddess in the ice

Witches' brew; edited by Yvonne Jocks

Goodbye to all that

McSweeney's mammoth treasury of thrilling tales; edited by Michael Chabon

Incognita, Inc.

Death dines at 8:30; edited by Claudia Bishop and Nick DiChario

Jeffty is five

Brown, C. N. and Strahan, J. The Locus awards; thirty years of the best in science fiction and fantasy; edited by Charles N. Brown and Jonathan Strahan

Killing Bernstein

A Century of great suspense stories; edited by Jeffery Deaver

Objects of desire in the mirror are closer than they appear

Best new horror 10; edited and with an introduction by Stephen Jones

Paladin of the lost hour

The American fantasy tradition; edited by Brian M. Thomsen

"Repent, Harlequin!" said the Ticktockman

Masterpieces: the best science fiction of the century; edited by Orson Scott Card

Santa Claus vs. S.P.I.D.E.R.

A yuletide universe; sixteen fantastical tales; edited by Brian M. Thomsen

Sensible city

The Best from fantasy & science fiction: the fiftieth anniversary anthology; edited by Edward L. Ferman and Gordon Van Gelder

Tired old man

Master's choice [v1]; mystery stories by today's top writers and the masters who inspired them; edited by Lawrence Block

The whimper of whipped dogs

The American fantasy tradition; edited by Brian M. Thomsen

The Best American mystery stories of the century; Tony Hillerman, editor; with an introduction by Tony Hillerman

Ellison, Ralph

Cadillac flambé

Callaloo v24 no2 p442-53 Spr 2001

Mister Toussan

The African American West; a century of short stories; edited by Bruce A. Glasrud and Laurie Champion

Ellroy, James

Tijuana, mon amour

Gentlemen's Quarterly v69 no2 p150-57+ F 1999

Tijuana, mon amour 2

Gentlemen's Quarterly v69 no3 p274-82+ Mr 1999

ELOPEMENTS

Bausch, R. Billboard

Chopin, K. A night in Acadie

James, H. Adina

Orner, P. Providence

Orringer, J. Stars of Motown shining bright

Eloy. Skinner, J.

Elphinstone, Margaret

A sparrow's flight [excerpt]

The Vintage book of contemporary Scottish fiction; edited and with an introduction by Peter Kravitz

Elrod, P. N.

Izzy's shoe-in

White House pet detectives; tales of crime and mystery at the White House from a pet's-eye view; edited by Carole Nelson Douglas

The tea room beasts

Witches' brew; edited by Yvonne Jocks

(jt. auth) See Bennett, Nigel and Elrod, P. N.

Elroy Nights. Barthelme, F.

Elsa. Werner, I.

Elsewhere. Blatty, W. P.

Elsewhere. Kennedy, A. L.

Elvis, Axl, and me. Eidus, J.
Elvis lives. Barrett, L.
Ely, Scott
  The bear hunters
    The Southern Review (Baton Rouge, La.) v37
    no2 p355-67 Spr 2001
  Pine Cones
    New Letters v69 no1 p101-17 2002
  Stalingrad
    The Antioch Review v60 no3 p425-37 Summ
    2002
  The sweeper
    The Antioch Review v57 no4 p530-39 Fall
    1999
  Walking to Carcassonne
    The Southern Review (Baton Rouge, La.) v37
    no4 p686-96 Aut 2001
Elya Isaakovich and Margarita Prokofievna. Ba-
  bel´, I.
Emancipation. a life fable. Chopin, K.
EMBEZZLEMENT
  Estleman, L. D. The used
  Hughes, J. Forbidden fruits
  Pronzini, B. Bank job
  Toes, J. Rhine Ablaze
  Vachss, A. H. Time share
  Wharton, E. A cup of cold water
Embracing the mystery. De Lint, C.
Emerald City: Third & Pike. Sherman, C. W.
Emergency. Johnson, D.
Emergency room. Addonizio, K.
The **emergency** room. Garcia, L. G.
EMERSON, RALPH WALDO, 1803-1882
               About
  McDevitt, J. The Emerson effect
The **Emerson** effect. McDevitt, J.
EMIGRÉS *See* Refugees
Emile. Raphael, F.
Emilie de Tourville; or, Fraternal cruelty. Sade,
  marquis de
Emilie de Tourville; or, The cruel brothers. See
  Sade, marquis de. Emilie de Tourville; or,
  Fraternal cruelty
Emily. Smart, A.
Emily: How Far Will a Boy Go to Find the Girl
  of His Dreams? Bagdasarian, A.
Emin, Tracey
  Albert Bert and Andy
    Typical girls; new stories by smart women;
    edited by Susan Corrigan
Eminent Domain. Nelson, A.
An **emissary.** Gordimer, N.
Emissary from a green and yellow world.
  Sheckley, R.
Emma Zunz. Borges, J. L.
Emma's hands. Swan, M.
Emory Bear Hands' birds. Lopez, B. H.
EMOTIONALLY DISTURBED CHILDREN
  DeLancey, K. I loved the squire
  DeMarinis, R. Aliens
  Di Blasi, D. An obscure geography
  Gunn, K. Grass, leaves
  Hunter, F. Pepper
  Tenn, W. The malted milk monsters
  Vasseur, T. J. The sins of Jesus
  Wuori, G. K. Madness
The **emperor's** new (and improved) clothes. What,
  L.
The **Emperor's** Old Bones. Files, G.

The **emperor's** revenge. Schmidt, S.
Empire Turtledove, H. Alternate generals II; ed.
  by Harry Turtledove
EMPLOYEES, DISMISSAL OF *See* Dismissal
  of employees
EMPLOYMENT INTERVIEWING
  Gussoff, C. Love story
The **empress's** new lingerie. Rollins, H.
The **empty** amulet. Bowles, P.
Empty arms. Wings, M.
Empty houses. Chan, D. M.
Empty Nest. Lab, O. K.
The **empty** quarter. Porto, E.
The **empty** rocker. Spivack, K.
Empty spaces. Bagdasarian, A.
Empty stations. Royle, N.
Emshwiller, Carol
  Creature
    Nebula awards showcase 2004; edited by
    Vonda McIntyre
  The general
    McSweeney's mammoth treasury of thrilling
    tales; edited by Michael Chabon
Emu and elephant. Adam, C.
En **famille.** Gorman, E.
En **famille.** Kelly, R.
En **route** to the congress of dreams; or, The
  zipless fuck. Jong, E.
Encarnación Mendoza's Christmas Eve. Bosch, J.
Encased. Chekhov, A. P.
Enchanté. Marsella, A.
The **enchanted** buffalo. Baum, L. F.
Encinosa, Michel *See* Encinosa Fú, Michel
Encinosa Fú, Michel
  Like the roses had to die
    Cosmos latinos: an anthology of science fic-
    tion from Latin America and Spain; trans-
    lated, edited, & with an introduction &
    notes by Andrea L. Bell & Yolanda Moli-
    na-Gavilán
The **encounter.** Borges, J. L.
Encounter. Jacobsen, R.
Encounter at dawn. See Clarke, A. C. Encounter
  in the dawn
Encounter at the airport. Pak, W.-S.
Encounter in Redgunk. Eakin, W.
Encounter in the dawn. Clarke, A. C.
An **Encounter** on a Train. Suárez, P.
Encounter on Horse-Killed Creek. Gulick, B.
The **encyclopedia** Daniel. Chappell, F.
ENCYCLOPEDIAS AND DICTIONARIES
  Wallace, D. F. Datum centurio
The **end.** Borges, J. L.
The **end,** a city. Bahrami, M.
The **end** of a good party. Justice, J. R.
End of a story. Arenas, R.
The **end** of a struggle. Davila, A.
The **end** of all sadness. Hegi, U.
The **end** of Bull Macha. Škvorecký, J.
The **end** of everything. Knight, M.
The **end** of gravity. Simmons, D.
The **end** of it all. Gorman, E.
The **end** of jealousy. Proust, M.
The **end** of men. Derby, M.
The **end** of Old Horse. Ortiz, S. J.
The **end** of romance. McNally, J.
The **end** of Sender Ziv. Baron, D.
The **end** of something. Hermann, J.
The **end** of St. Hypatius. Babel´, I.

The **end** of summer. Blair, S.
The **end** of the almshouse. Babel´, I.
The **end** of the class war. Brady, C.
The **end** of the earth. Smith, J.
End of the line. Franzen, J.
The **End** of the Road. Blottner, J.
End of the steam age. Allen, D., Jr.
END OF THE WORLD
    See also Earth, Destruction of
Atkinson, K. Pleasureland
Barton, W. Down in the dark
Bradbury, R. There will come soft rains
Campbell, J. W. Twilight
Clarke, A. C. The forgotten enemy
Clarke, A. C. The nine billion names of God
Connor, J. The day the world declined to end
DeAndrea, W. L. Murder at the end of the
    world
Du Bois, W. E. B. The comet
Harrison, H. The day after the end of the world
Knight, D. F. Not with a bang
Le Guin, U. K. The birthday of the world
Malzberg, B. N. The only thing you learn
Matheson, R. The last day
Mosley, W. The nig in me
O'Callaghan, M. Survival instinct
Waldrop, H. Willow Beeman
The **end** of the world. Adams, A.
The **end** of times. Anderson, D.
The **end** zone. Gilley, T.
ENDANGERED SPECIES
Abraham, D. Chimera 8
McAuley, P. J. The Rift
Morlan, A. R. Fast glaciers
ENDECOTT, JOHN, 1588?-1665
          About
Hawthorne, N. Endicott and the Red Cross
Enders, Alexandra
Where the f stops
    Bomb no79 p103-11 Spr 2002
Ender's game. Card, O. S.
The **endgame**. Archer, J.
Endicott, John *See* Endecott, John, 1588?-1665
Endicott and the Red Cross. Hawthorne, N.
Ending things. Davis, A.
Endless summer. O'Nan, S.
Endless trail. DeRosso, H. A.
The **endless** visit. Burgin, R.
Endnotes. Anderson, D.
Endrezze, Anita
The humming of stars and bees and waves
    Witches' brew; edited by Yvonne Jocks
The **ends**. Davies, P. H.
Endure the night. Weinberg, R.
The **enduring** nights of Sidney Wingcloud.
    Vasseur, T. J.
Enekwe, Ossie Onuora
The last battle
    The Anchor book of modern African stories;
        edited by Nadežda Obradovic ; with a fore-
        word by Chinua Achebe
Enemies. Chekhov, A. P.
The **Enemy**. Hadley, T.
The **enemy** in the wheat. Bradbury, R.
Enemy territory. Hoch, E. D.
Enfleurage. Stollman, A. L.
ENGAGEMENTS *See* Betrothals
Engaging Diane. Jones, B.

Engberg, Susan
Beginning
    The Sewanee Review v111 no1 p1-31 Wint
    2003
Fortune
    Michigan Quarterly Review v42 no3 p496-
    506 Summ 2003
Rain
    Southwest Review v88 no1 p95-117 2003
Reunion
    The Southern Review (Baton Rouge, La.) v39
    no4 p762-81 Aut 2003
Engel, Howard
The ant trap
    Death by espionage; intriguing stories of de-
    ception and betrayal; edited by Martin Cruz
    Smith
The reading
    Mystery midrash; an anthology of Jewish
    mystery & detective fiction; [edited by]
    Lawrence W. Raphael
Engel, Mary Potter
All that we need
    Engel, M. P. Strangers and sojourners; stories
    from the lowcountry
A better man
    Engel, M. P. Strangers and sojourners; stories
    from the lowcountry
Dis aliter visum
    Engel, M. P. Strangers and sojourners; stories
    from the lowcountry
Epiphany
    Engel, M. P. Strangers and sojourners; stories
    from the lowcountry
Let them big animals come back
    Engel, M. P. Strangers and sojourners; stories
    from the lowcountry
Lot's wife
    The North American Review v287 no1 p30-5
    Ja/F 2002
Lowcountry cold
    Engel, M. P. Strangers and sojourners; stories
    from the lowcountry
M to F
    Engel, M. P. Strangers and sojourners; stories
    from the lowcountry
Philosophy of education
    Engel, M. P. Strangers and sojourners; stories
    from the lowcountry
Queen Esther Coosawaw
    Engel, M. P. Strangers and sojourners; stories
    from the lowcountry
Rat
    Engel, M. P. Strangers and sojourners; stories
    from the lowcountry
Redeeming the dead
    Engel, M. P. Strangers and sojourners; stories
    from the lowcountry
A soldier's disease
    Engel, M. P. Strangers and sojourners; stories
    from the lowcountry
Strangers and sojourners
    Engel, M. P. Strangers and sojourners; stories
    from the lowcountry
Those who shine like the stars
    Engel, M. P. Strangers and sojourners; stories
    from the lowcountry

Engel, Mary Potter—*Continued*
  Unnatural acts
    Engel, M. P. Strangers and sojourners; stories
      from the lowcountry
  What Addie wants
    Engel, M. P. Strangers and sojourners; stories
      from the lowcountry
  What we ought to be
    Engel, M. P. Strangers and sojourners; stories
      from the lowcountry
  Who calls each one by name
    Engel, M. P. Strangers and sojourners; stories
      from the lowcountry
  Why
    Engel, M. P. Strangers and sojourners; stories
      from the lowcountry
  You got to learn how to read things right
    Engel, M. P. Strangers and sojourners; stories
      from the lowcountry
The **engine** of desire. Dyson, J.
The **engine** of fate. Trevanian
The **engine** of Samoset Erastus Hale, and one oth-
  er, unknown. Davidson, A.
ENGINEERS
  Arvin, N. What they teach you in engineering
    school
  Chekhov, A. P. Lights
  Clarke, A. C. Saturn rising
  Fuchs, D. Man in the middle of the ocean
  Harrar, G. The 5:22
ENGLAND
  Bradbury, R. Henry the Ninth
  Davidson, A. O brave old world!
    Anglo-Saxon period, 449-1066
  Cornwell, B. Excalibur [excerpt]
  Knowles, Sir J. King Arthur and his knights
    [excerpt]
  Steinbeck, J. Morgan le Fay
  Twain, M. A Connecticut Yankee at King Ar-
    thur's court [excerpt]
    11th century
  Holt, T. Accidental death
  Reed, M. and Mayer, E. Even kings die
    12th century
  Crowley, J. The green child
  Gregory, S. The White Ship murders
  Rath, T. and Rath, T. Who killed fair
    Rosamund?
    13th century
  Pulver, M. M. To whom the victory?
    14th century
  Baldry, C. The friar's tale
    15th century
  Frazer, M. Neither pity, love nor fear
  Lawrence, D. H. A fragment of stained glass
  Myers, A. Happy the man . . .
    16th century
  Douglass, S. The mistress of Marwood Hagg
  Franks, R. A secret murder
  Lane, A. The gaze of the falcon
    17th century
  Aquino, J. T. The mysterious death of the shad-
    ow man
    18th century
  Gabaldon, D. Lord John and the succubus
  Small, B. Mastering Lady Lucinda
    19th century
  Devine, T. The pleasure game
  Edwards, M. Natural causes

James, H. The path of duty
Newman, K. A Victorian ghost story
    20th century
Amis, M. State of England
Berners, G. H. T.-W., Baron. Far from the mad-
  ding war
Berners, G. H. T.-W., Baron. Percy Wallingford
Di Blasi, D. Fog
Guiver, P. The Boxing Day bother
Lake, D. J. Re-deem the time
Parker, G. Aub
Parker, G. Bad nose
Parker, G. The sheld-duck of the Basingstoke
  Canal
Rankin, I. Adventures in babysitting
Spark, M. The Portobello Road
Waugh, E. Basil Seal rides again
Waugh, E. Lucy Simmonds
    Aristocracy
    See Aristocracy—England
    Civil War
    See England—17th century
    College life
    See College life—England
    Farm life
    See Farm life—England
    Politics
    See Politics—England
    Prisoners and prisons
    See Prisoners and prisons—England
    Race relations
Lessing, D. M. Victoria and the Staveneys
    Rural life
Berners, G. H. T.-W., Baron. The camel
Bowen, E. The happy autumn fields
Bowen, M. The Crown Derby plate
Cannell, D. The purloined purple pearl
Fitzgerald, P. Not shown
James, H. A passionate pilgrim
James, M. R. Oh, whistle and I'll come to you,
  my lad
Kipling, R. Mary Postgate
Kipling, R. They
Lawrence, D. H. England, my England
Lovesey, P. Away with the fairies
Lumley, B. The statement of Henry Worthy
Rendell, R. High mysterious union
Waugh, E. An Englishman's home
Waugh, E. Period piece
Waugh, E. Winner takes all
Wharton, E. Mr. Jones
    World War, 1914-1918
    See World War, 1914-1918—England
    World War, 1939-1945
    See World War, 1939-1945—England
    Cheshire
Crowley, J. Antiquities
    Devon
McManus, J. The Magothy fires
    Dorset
Wharton, E. Afterward
    London
Atkinson, K. Transparent fiction
Brackenbury, R. The knowledge
Carlson, R. The Hotel Eden
Cherryh, C. J. The haunted tower
Gordimer, N. Visiting George
Harrison, M. J. Suicide coast

ENGLAND—London—*Continued*

Jurado, A. Saying goodbye through twenty-five centuries

Lessing, D. M. Victoria and the Staveneys

Marston, E. Slaughter in the Strand

Nevins, F. M., Jr. The other man in the pin-stripe

Royle, N. Standard gauge

16th century

Fitzgerald, F. S. Tarquin of cheapside

Sherman, D. The faerie cony-catcher

19th century

Auchincloss, L. The Virginia redbird

Beerbohm, M. Enoch Soames

Davidson, A. What strange stars and skies

Goulart, R. The phantom highwayman

James, H. The chaperon

James, H. A London life

Paul, B. Jack be quick

20th century

Amis, M. Other people [excerpt]

Barker, N. The butcher's apprentice

Davies, R. Afternoon tea

Davies, R. Art lover

Davies, R. Home

Davies, R. Misfits

Davies, R. Missing person

Davies, R. Mr. Pleasant

Davies, R. Return to Waterloo

Davies, R. Voices in the dark

Davies, R. Waterloo sunset

Dyson, J. City deep

Forsyth, F. The art of the matter

Gunthorp, D. Pikeman and the Bagwoman

Kalman, J. Allures of grandeur

Kalman, J. Flight

Kalman, J. Monahan Avenue

Kalman, J. Rain

Kimber, J. Having myself a time

Kureishi, H. That was then

Mason, B. A. Proper gypsies

McAuley, P. J. Naming the dead

McEwan, I. Pornography

Meloy, M. Red

Melville, P. Don't give me your sad stories

Melville, P. Lucifer's shank

Raphael, F. An older woman

Simpson, H. Cheers

Simpson, H. Golden apples

Simpson, H. Millennium blues

Simpson, H. Opera

Starr, G. Tuberama: a musical on the Northern Line (or how to be in touch with your emotions)

Yates, R. Liars in love

Zinik, Z. Double act in Soho

Zinik, Z. No cause for alarm

Zinik, Z. A pickled nose

Norfolk

Duffy, S. Running dogs

Oxford

Doyle, Sir A. C. Lot no. 249

Oxfordshire

Davenport, G. Christ preaching at the Henley Regatta

Suffolk

Stevenson, J. Crossing the water

England, I give this cigarette. Faulkner, J.

England, my England. Lawrence, D. H.

Englander, Nathan

For the relief of unbearable urges

  Englander, N. For the relief of unbearable urges

The gilgul of Park Avenue

  Atlantic Monthly v283 no3 p77-80+ Mr 1999

  The Best American short stories, 2000; selected from U.S. and Canadian magazines by E. L. Doctorow with Katrina Kenison; with an introduction by E. L. Doctorow

  Englander, N. For the relief of unbearable urges

  Prize stories, 2000; The O. Henry awards; edited and with an introduction by Larry Dark

In this way we are wise

  Englander, N. For the relief of unbearable urges

The last one way

  Englander, N. For the relief of unbearable urges

Lost tribe; jewish fiction from the edge

  The New Yorker v74 no42 p64-70 Ja 18 1999

Peep show

  Neurotica: Jewish writers on sex; edited by Melvin Jules Bukiet

  The New Yorker v75 no20 p78-82 Jl 26 1999

Peep show (I)

  The New Yorker v75 no16 p202-3 Je 21-28 1999

Reb Kringle

  Englander, N. For the relief of unbearable urges

Reunion

  Englander, N. For the relief of unbearable urges

The tumblers

  American short fiction, vol. 8, no 29-32

  The Best American short stories, 1999; selected from U.S. and Canadian magazines by Amy Tan with Katrina Kenison, with an introduction by Amy Tan

  Englander, N. For the relief of unbearable urges

The twenty-seventh man

  The Art of the story; an international anthology of contemporary short stories; edited by Daniel Halpern

  Englander, N. For the relief of unbearable urges

The wig

  Englander, N. For the relief of unbearable urges

English as a second language. Evans, E.

English as a second language. Honig, L.

ENGLISH CIVIL WAR *See* England—17th century

The **English** girl. Locklin, G.

ENGLISH LANGUAGE

Bezmozgis, D. Tapka

Honig, L. English as a second language

ENGLISH PEOPLE *See* British

English table wuk. Melville, P.

An **Englishman's** home. Waugh, E.

Engstrom, Elizabeth

Crosley

  The Year's best fantasy & horror, thirteenth annual collection; edited by Ellen Datlow and Terri Windling

Engstrom, Elizabeth—*Continued*
Purple shards
Dead on demand; the best of ghost story weekend; edited by Elizabeth Engstrom
Riding the black horse
Death dines at 8:30; edited by Claudia Bishop and Nick DiChario
Enlightenment Rabies. Rucker, R. v. B.
ENNUI *See* Boredom
Enoch Soames. Beerbohm, M.
The **Enormous** Radio. Cheever, J.
Enough was enough. Cole, M.
Enright, Anne
In the bed department
The New Yorker v77 no11 p92-5 My 14 2001
Little sister
Granta no75 p169-77 Aut 2001
Men and angels
The Anchor book of new Irish writing; the new Gaelach ficsean; edited and with an introduction by John Somer and John J. Daly
Shaft
Granta v85 p249-55 Spr 2004
What are cicadas?
The Anchor book of new Irish writing; the new Gaelach ficsean; edited and with an introduction by John Somer and John J. Daly
Ensenada. McCourt, J.
ENSOR, JAMES, 1860-1949
About
Girardi, R. The demons tormenting Untersturmführer Hans Otto Graebner
Enstice, Andrew
Dream, until god burns
Dreaming down-under; edited by Jack Dann and Janeen Webb
Enter the Ford. Agee, J.
ENTERTAINERS
See also Acrobats; Actors; Actresses; Clowns; Ventriloquists
Allen, S. Behind the black curtain
Anderson, R. The pyramid
Barrett, L. Elvis lives
Boylan, C. A funny thing happened
Brown, C. Now is the time
Capote, T. A tree of night
Collins, B. Cat got your tongue
Fischer, T. Fifty uselessnesses
Fitzgerald, F. S. Head and shoulders
Knight, D. F. The handler
Mann, A. Taking care of Frank
ENTERTAINING *See* Parties
The **entertainment**. Campbell, R.
ENTOMOLOGISTS
Barrett, A. The mysteries of ubiquitin
Theroux, P. White lies
Entrada. Rosenblum, M. H.
Entre les beaux morts en vie (Among the beautiful living dead). Williams, S.
An **entrepreneur's** story. Ha Jin
Entropy. Gilchrist, E.
ENVIRONMENTALISTS
Bisson, T. Dear Abbey
ENVY *See* Jealousy
Envy. Chetkovich, K.
Envy. Pasquali, M. d.
Ephemera. Alvarez, A.

EPIDEMICS
See also Plague
Benford, G. A calculus of desperation
Johnson, C. R. The plague
Wideman, J. E. Fever
EPILEPTICS
Alessio, Carolyn. Casualidades
Bernhard, T. Amras
Epilogue. Anderson, P.
Epilogue of the progeny; or, Whoever is never born with the most toys wins. Caponegro, M.
Epilogue: story #7 in D minor. Chacón, D.
Epiphany. Willis, C.
EPISCOPAL CLERGY *See* Anglican and Episcopal clergy
Episode from the History. Bundy, A.
Episodes in autobiography. Auerbach, J.
The **epistemology**. Saunders, G.
Epitaph. Longstreet, K. A.
Epstein, Joseph
Artie Glick in a family way
Epstein, J. Fabulous small Jews
Casualty
The Sewanee Review v112 no1 p73-91 Wint 2004
Coming in with their hands up
Epstein, J. Fabulous small Jews
Don Juan Zimmerman
Epstein, J. Fabulous small Jews
Dubinsky on the loose
Epstein, J. Fabulous small Jews
The executor
Epstein, J. Fabulous small Jews
Family values
Epstein, J. Fabulous small Jews
Felix emeritus
Epstein, J. Fabulous small Jews
Freddy Duchamp in action
Commentary v108 no3 p41-7 O 1999
Epstein, J. Fabulous small Jews
Howie's gift
Epstein, J. Fabulous small Jews
Howie's gift: a story
Commentary v111 no6 p41-7 Je 2001
A loss for words
Epstein, J. Fabulous small Jews
A loss for words: a story
Commentary v112 no3 p58-63 O 2001
Love and The Guinness book of records
Epstein, J. Fabulous small Jews
The master's ring
Epstein, J. Fabulous small Jews
Moe
Epstein, J. Fabulous small Jews
My little Marjie
Epstein, J. Fabulous small Jews
My little Marjie: a story
Commentary v112 no4 p42-8 N 2001
Postcards
Epstein, J. Fabulous small Jews
Postcards: a story
Commentary v111 no3 p42-9 Mr 2001
Saturday afternoon at the zoo with dad
Epstein, J. Fabulous small Jews
The third Mrs. Kessler
Epstein, J. Fabulous small Jews
Uncle Jack
Commentary v113 no5 p46-52 My 2002

Epstein, Joseph—*Continued*
  Epstein, J. Fabulous small Jews
Epstein, Leslie
  Court of palms
    Harper's v298 no1787 p75-81 Ap 1999
  Desert
    Partisan Review v70 no1 p34-60 Wint 2003
Equal love. Davies, P. H.
Equal opportunity. Mosley, W.
Equateur. Hunter, F.
Erard, Michael
  Beyond the point
    New stories from the South: the year's best,
      1999; edited by Shannon Ravenel; with a
      preface by Tony Earley
Erasing Sonny. McQuain, K.
Erdrich, Louise
  The butcher's wife
    The New Yorker v77 no31 p188-200 O 15
      2001
  Fleur
    Witches' brew; edited by Yvonne Jocks
  Love Snares
    The New Yorker v79 no32 p88-97 O 27 2003
  Lulu's boys
    The Best of The Kenyon review; edited by
      David Lynn; introduction by Joyce Carol
      Oates
  Le mooz
    Death dines at 8:30; edited by Claudia Bishop
      and Nick DiChario
    Ghost writing; haunted tales by contemporary
      writers; edited by Roger Weingarten
  The Painted Drum
    The New Yorker v79 no2 p74-81 Mr 3 2003
  The Plague of Doves
    The New Yorker v80 no17 p90-7 Je 28 2004
  The red convertible
    Still wild; short fiction of the American West,
      1950 to the present; edited by Larry
      McMurtry
  Revival Road
    Prize stories, 2001; The O. Henry awards; ed-
      ited and with an introduction by Larry
      Dark
  Saint Marie
    The Scribner anthology of contemporary short
      fiction; fifty North American stories since
      1970; Lex Williford and Michael Martone,
      editors
  Shamengwa
    The Best American short stories, 2003; select-
      ed from U.S. and Canadian magazines by
      Walter Mosley with Katrina Kenison; with
      an introduction by Walter Mosley
    The New Yorker v78 no37 p94-101 D 2 2002
  The shawl
    The New Yorker v77 no2 p84-7 Mr 5 2001
  Sister Godzilla
    Atlantic Monthly v287 no2 p96-9 F 2001
Erens, Pamela
  Gaarg. Gaarrgh. Gak.
    The Literary Review (Madison, N.J.) v44 no4
      p615-29 Summ 2001
Ergo, ice pick. Lipsyte, S.
Erian, Alicia
  Alcatraz
    Erian, A. The brutal language of love; stories

Almonds and cherries
  Erian, A. The brutal language of love; stories
    Iowa Review v31 no1 p153-68 Summ 2001
Bikini
  Erian, A. The brutal language of love; stories
The brutal language of love
  Erian, A. The brutal language of love; stories
Lass
  Erian, A. The brutal language of love; stories
On the occasion of my ruination
  Erian, A. The brutal language of love; stories
Standing up to the superpowers
  Erian, A. The brutal language of love; stories
Still life with plaster
  Erian, A. The brutal language of love; stories
When animals attack
  Erian, A. The brutal language of love; stories
The winning side
  Politically inspired; edited by Stephen Elliott;
    assistant editor, Gabriel Kram; associate ed-
    itors, Elizabeth Brooks [et al.]
You
  Francis Ford Coppola's Zoetrope all-story 2;
    edited by Adrienne Brodeur and Samantha
    Schnee; with an introduction by Francis
    Ford Coppola
Erickson, Steve
  Days between stations [excerpt]
    The Vintage book of amnesia; an anthology;
      edited by Jonathan Lethem
Erickson, Ben
  Floundering
    Stories from the Blue Moon Cafe II; edited
      by Sonny Brewer
Erie's last day. Hockensmith, S.
Ernie's ark. Wood, M.
Erofeev, Viktor
  The parakeet
    The Art of the story; an international antholo-
      gy of contemporary short stories; edited by
      Daniel Halpern
Erofeyev, Victor *See* Erofeev, Viktor, 1947-
Eros and agape among the asteroids. Edelman, S.
Erosion. Hunt, S.
EROTICISM *See* Sex
Erpenbeck, Jenny
  Siberia
    Chicago Review v48 no2/3 p71-9 Summ 2002
Errand. Carver, R.
An errand. Porter, J. A.
The errand. Smolens, J.
Errand boy. Tenn, W.
Erratics. Hart, R.
An error in chemistry. Faulkner, W.
An error of desire. Freed, L.
ERRORS
  Singer, I. B. Errors
  Singer, I. B. The mistake
Eruption. Hammond, E.
Erwin, Christine
  Blood relations
    The Canadian Forum v78 no875 p28-31 Mr
      1999
Erzulie. Melville, P.
Esarhaddon, King of Assyria. Tolstoy, L., graf
Esbaum, Jill
  I was a teenage beauty queen
    'Teen v45 no5 p102-5 My 2001
An escapade. Callaghan, M.

Escape. Auerbach, J.
Escape. Nelson, R. F.
The **escape**. Perry, A.
Escape artist. Grut, V.
Escape route. Hamilton, P. F.
ESCAPED CONVICTS
    Carlson, R. A note on the type
    Du Bois, W. E. B. Jesus Christ in Texas
    Fitzgerald, P. The means of escape
    Gores, J. Goodbye, Pops
    L'Amour, L. Desperate men
    Madden, D. The world's one breathing
    O'Connor, F. A good man is hard to find
    Savage, L., Jr. The hangman's segundo
    Singleton, G. Deer gone
    Smolens, J. Cold
The **escapee**. Le Clézio, J.-M. G.
ESCAPES
    Capote, T. A diamond guitar
    Deaver, J. Ninety-eight point six
    Duncan, A. Daddy Mention and the Monday skull
    Fitzgerald, F. S. Tarquin of cheapside
    Kaminsky, S. M. DRUP number one
    Pronzini, B. The Arrowmont Prison riddle
    Rucker, R. v. B. Tales of Houdini
Escapes. Powers, R.
Escort. Gurnah, A.
An **Escort**. Martin, D. A.
Escort service. Vachss, A. H.
ESCORTS (DATING SERVICE)
    Hodgen, C. Take them in, please
    Olsen, L. Cybermorphic beat-up get-down subterranean homesick reality-sandwich blues
Escrava Anastácia Speaks. Watson-Aifah, J.
ESKIMOS *See* Aleuts; Inuit
ESP *See* Extrasensory perception
ESPIONAGE *See* International intrigue; Spies
Espiritu Santo. Troncoso, S.
Esquivel, Laura
    Blessed reality
        Colchie, T. A whistler in the nightworld; short fiction from the Latin Americas; edited by Thomas Colchie
Essay. Waugh, E.
An **essay** on containment. DeWeese, G.
Essence of camphor. Naiyer Masud
Essential Things. Arzola, J. L.
The **Estate**. Nissen, T.
ESTATES *See* Houses
Estenssoro, Maria Virginia
    The child that never was
        Short stories by Latin American women; the magic and the real; edited by Celia Correas de Zapata; foreword by Isabel Allende
Estep, Maggie
    Animals
        Estep, M. Soft maniacs; stories
    Circus
        Estep, M. Soft maniacs; stories
    Horses
        Estep, M. Soft maniacs; stories
    The messenger
        Estep, M. Soft maniacs; stories
    Monkeys
        Estep, M. Soft maniacs; stories
    One of us
        Estep, M. Soft maniacs; stories

The patient
    Estep, M. Soft maniacs; stories
Teeth
    Estep, M. Soft maniacs; stories
Tools
    Estep, M. Soft maniacs; stories
Esterházy, Péter
    Roberto narrates
        The Art of the story; an international anthology of contemporary short stories; edited by Daniel Halpern
Esther stories. Orner, P.
ESTHETICS *See* Aesthetics
Estleman, Loren D.
    The anniversary waltz
        The Mysterious Press anniversary anthology; celebrating 25 years; by the editors of Mysterious Press
    Big Tim Magoon and the wild west
        Westward; a fictional history of the American West : 28 original stories celebrating the 50th anniversary of the Western Writers of America; edited by Dale L. Walker
    Evil grows
        Flesh and blood; erotic tales of crime and passion; edited by Max Allan Collins and Jeff Gelb
    A hatful of Ralph
        Flesh and blood: guilty as sin; erotic tales of crime and passion; edited by Max Allan Collins and Jeff Gelb
    Hell on the draw
        A Century of great Western stories; edited by John Jakes
    I'm in the book
        Speaking of lust; stories of forbidden desire; edited by Lawrence Block
    Lady on ice
        A Hot and sultry night for crime; edited by Jeffery Deaver
    The man in the white hat
        The World's finest mystery and crime stories, first annual collection; edited by Ed Gorman
    Redneck
        The Best American mystery stories, 1999; edited and with an introduction by Ed McBain
    The riddle of the golden monkeys
        Murder, my dear Watson; new tales of Sherlock Holmes; edited by Martin H. Greenberg, Jon Lellenberg, Daniel Stashower
    South Georgia crossing
        The Blue and the gray undercover; edited by Ed Gorman
    State of grace
        Murder most divine; ecclesiastical tales of unholy crimes; edited by Ralph McInerny and Martin H. Greenberg
    Thirteen coils
        American West; twenty new stories from the Western Writers of America; edited with an introduction by Loren D. Estleman
    The used
        A Century of noir; thirty-two classic crime stories; edited by Mickey Spillane and Max Allan Collins

Estrada, Josefina
June gave him the voice
  Points of departure; new stories from Mexico;
    edited by Mónica Lavín; translated by Gus-
    tavo Segade
Et **cetera**. Borges, J. L.
Etchison, Dennis
The detailer
  Best new horror 12; edited and with an intro-
    duction by Stephen Jones
Got to kill them all
  The Mammoth book of best horror 13; edited
    by Stephen Jones
Inside the cackle factory
  Best new horror 10; edited and with an intro-
    duction by Stephen Jones
  The Year's best fantasy & horror, twelfth an-
    nual collection; edited by Ellen Datlow &
    Terry Windling
My present wife
  Death dines at 8:30; edited by Claudia Bishop
    and Nick DiChario
Eternal love. Bender, K. E.
Ethan Brand. Hawthorne, N.
ETHICS
        See also Conscience; Medical ethics; Sin;
        Truthfulness and falsehood
Alcott, L. M. Marion Earle; or, Only an actress!
Chopin, K. Miss McEnders
Martini, S. Poetic justice
Wharton, E. Sanctuary
ETHIOPIA
Coskran, K. Sun
Tuma, H. The Waldiba story
Ethiopia. Dodd, S. M.
ETHNOLOGISTS
Davidson, A. and Davis, G. The Boss in the
  Wall: a treatise on the house devil
Etiquette in dark times. Brecht, B.
Etta Mae Johnson. Naylor, G.
Eugene Pickering. James, H.
The **Eugenic** College of Kantsaywhere. Galton, Sir
  F.
Eugenides, Jeffrey
Baster
  Wonderful town; New York stories from The
    New Yorker; edited by David Remnick
    with Susan Choi
The Obscure Object
  The New Yorker v78 no21 p66-81 Jl 29 2002
The oracular vulva
  The New Yorker v75 no16 p178-85 Je 21-28
    1999
Timeshare
  The Pushcart prize XXIII: best of the small
    presses; an annual small press reader; ed-
    ited by Bill Henderson with the Pushcart
    prize editors
A **eulogy** of sorts. Earle, S.
Eurema's dam. Lafferty, R. A.
EUROPE
        See also Danube River; Rhine River
                   20th century
Lawrence, D. H. The border line
EUROPEANS
                        Zaire
Hunter, F. Card players
EUTHANASIA
Matheson, R. The test

Resnick, M. Hothouse flowers
Robinson, L. The toast
Vonnegut, K. 2BRO2B
Eutopia. Anderson, P.
Eva O. *See* Brantenberg, Gerd, 1941-
EVANGELISTS
Bass, R. Mahatma Joe
Bear, G. The white horse child
Evenson, B. Barcode Jesus
Newman, S. Divine guidance
Reiner, C. Sissy Sue and the Reverend Rever-
  end
Wilson, R., Jr. Dorothy and her friends
Evanier, David
Danny and me
  TriQuarterly no110/111 p382-91 Fall 2001
Evans, Elizabeth
Americans
  Evans, E. Suicide's girlfriend; a novella and
    short stories
Beautiful land
  Evans, E. Suicide's girlfriend; a novella and
    short stories
Blood and gore
  Evans, E. Suicide's girlfriend; a novella and
    short stories
English as a second language
  Evans, E. Suicide's girlfriend; a novella and
    short stories
Home ec
  Evans, E. Suicide's girlfriend; a novella and
    short stories
A new life
  Evans, E. Suicide's girlfriend; a novella and
    short stories
Ransom
  Evans, E. Suicide's girlfriend; a novella and
    short stories
Suicide's girlfriend
  Evans, E. Suicide's girlfriend; a novella and
    short stories
Thieves
  Evans, E. Suicide's girlfriend; a novella and
    short stories
Voodoo girls on ice
  Evans, E. Suicide's girlfriend; a novella and
    short stories
Evans, Lawrence Watt- *See* Watt-Evans, Law-
  rence, 1954-
Evans, Linda
The stray
  Worlds of Honor
Evans, Linda Baker
Belief
  Women's Studies v28 no6 p703-10 D 1999
Evans, Liz
Pussy Galore
  Tart noir; edited by Stella Duffy & Lauren
    Henderson
Evans, Max
Candles in the bottom of the pool
  A Century of great Western stories; edited by
    John Jakes
The heart of the matter
  American West; twenty new stories from the
    Western Writers of America; edited with an
    introduction by Loren D. Estleman

Evans, Richard Paul

The Light of Christmas

   Ladies' Home Journal v119 no12 p100-6 D 2002

Evans, Frank Edgar

The diamond jester

   Dead balls and double curves; an anthology of early baseball fiction; edited and with an introduction by Trey Strecker ; with a foreword by Arnold Hano

EVE (BIBLICAL FIGURE)

About

Connor, J. Adam and Eve at the automat

The **eve** of the spirit festival. Chang, L. S.

Eve was naked. Škvorecký, J.

Eveline. Flannery, S.

Even butterflies can sting. Resnick, M.

Even Further. Pilgrim, K.

Even if it's Mexico nothing flashy ever happens to Grogan. McNulty, J.

Even in heaven. Guerrero, L.

Even kings die. Reed, M. and Mayer, E.

Even the queen. Willis, C.

Evening. Babel´, I.

The **evening** and the morning and the night. Butler, O. E.

An **evening** at the Blackstone. Keeley, C.

The **evening** before . . . Parker, G.

An **evening** meal. Price, R.

An **evening** of Eliot. Ritchie, E.

The **evening** of the Fourth of July. Kees, W.

Evening on the Côte d'Azur. Yates, R.

An **evening** out with Carl. Crider, B.

Evening spirit. Bilgrey, M.

An **evening** with the Empress. Babel´, I.

Evenings at home. Hardwick, E.

Evenson, Brian

   Evenson, B. The wavering knife; stories

Barcode Jesus

   Evenson, B. The wavering knife; stories

   The Southern Review (Baton Rouge, La.) v35 no4 p746-55 Aut 1999

Body

   Evenson, B. The wavering knife; stories

Calling the hour

   Evenson, B. The wavering knife; stories

The ex-father

   Evenson, B. The wavering knife; stories

Garker's aestheticals

   Evenson, B. The wavering knife; stories

The gravediggers

   Evenson, B. The wavering knife; stories

House rules

   Evenson, B. The wavering knife; stories

The installation

   Evenson, B. The wavering knife; stories

   The Paris Review v44 p18-27 Wint 2002

The intricacies of post-shooting etiquette

   Evenson, B. The wavering knife; stories

Moran's Mexico: a refutation by C. Stelzmann

   Evenson, B. The wavering knife; stories

Müller

   Evenson, B. The wavering knife; stories

One over twelve

   Evenson, B. The wavering knife; stories

The progenitor

   Evenson, B. The wavering knife; stories

Promisekeepers

   Evenson, B. The wavering knife; stories

The prophets

   Evenson, B. The wavering knife; stories

Stockwell

   Evenson, B. The wavering knife; stories

Virtual

   Evenson, B. The wavering knife; stories

   Prairie Schooner v76 no4 p5-17 Wint 2002

The wavering knife

   Evenson, B. The wavering knife; stories

White square

   Evenson, B. The wavering knife; stories

Evensong. Nevins, F. M., Jr.

The **Events** Leading Up to the Accident. Koven, S.

The **ever-branching** tree. Harrison, H.

Everett, Percival

The Last Heat of Summer

   Ploughshares v29 no1 p44-56 Spr 2003

A Stiffer Breeze

   Callaloo v27 no3 p616-20 Summ 2004

Everett, Percival L.

Believers

   Callaloo v24 no4 p1000-14 Fall 2001

Cry about a nickel

   The African American West; a century of short stories; edited by Bruce A. Glasrud and Laurie Champion

The fix

   The Best American short stories, 2000; selected from U.S. and Canadian magazines by E. L. Doctorow with Katrina Kenison; with an introduction by E. L. Doctorow

Meiosis

   Callaloo v24 no2 p454-67 Spr 2001

Wolf at the door

   In our nature: stories of wildness; selected and introduced by Donna Seaman

Everett, William

The base ball match

   Dead balls and double curves; an anthology of early baseball fiction; edited and with an introduction by Trey Strecker ; with a foreword by Arnold Hano

The **everlasting** Jug. Cohen, S.

The **everlasting** light. Spencer, E.

Evermore. Barnes, J.

Evermore. Williams, S.

Every angel is terrifying. Kessel, J.

Every day a little death. Rao, H.

Every Friday afternoon. Drake, R.

Every fucking time. Kelman, J.

Every head's a world. Skinner, J.

Every morning. Marsten, R.

Every time my lil' world seems blue. Shange, N.

Every tongue shall confess. Packer, Z.

Every year they came out. Kees, W.

Everybody goes. Smith, M. M.

Everybody loves Irving Bommer. Tenn, W.

Everybody pays. Vachss, A. H.

Everybody's Alien. Turchi, P.

Everyday use. Walker, A.

Everyone is sleeping. Gunn, K.

Everything bad comes back. Marías, J.

Everything in the fifth. Meersch, M. v. d.

Everything in this country must. McCann, C.

Everything is about animals. Prose, F.

Everything is different in your house. Mars-Jones, A.

Everything must go. Gilbert, J.

Everything must go. Matthews, B.
Everything old is new again. Berliner, J.
Everything quiet like church. Phillips, D. R.
Everything to order. Nye, J. L.
Everything you can remember in thirty seconds is yours to keep. Davies, P. H.
Everywhere. Ryman, G.
Evidence of old repairs. Kane, J. F.
The **evidence** of things not seen. Coberly, L. M.
EVIL *See* Good and evil
The **evil** B. B. Chow. Almond, S.
Evil eye Allen. Carlson, R.
Evil grows. Estleman, L. D.
Evil star. Russell, R.
The **evil** within. Douglass, S.
EVOLUTION
   Anderson, P. Epilogue
   Anderson, P. The horn of time the hunter
   Baxter, S. Cilia-of-gold
   Blish, J. How beautiful with banners
   Clarke, A. C. Second dawn
   Hamilton, E. Devolution
   Oliver, C. Transfusion
   Sturgeon, T. The golden helix
   Tiedemann, M. W. Links
Evolution. Cavell, B.
The **evolution** of human science. Chiang, T.
The **evolution** of knowledge. Tucci, N.
Evtimova, Zdravka
   Blood of a Mole
      The Antioch Review v61 no4 p620-3 Fall 2003
Ewing, C. D.
   And the others. . .
      My Sherlock Holmes; untold stories of the great detective; edited by Michael Kurland
EX-CONVICTS
   Allyn, D. Unchained melody
   Baca, J. S. Enemies
   Billman, J. Winter fat
   Bishop, M. Blue Kansas sky
   Block, L. In for a penny
   Carlson, R. At the El Sol
   Collins, M. The choice
   Davidson, R. Body work
   Davies, R. A little bit of abuse
   Davis, L. Scarecrow
   Delaney, E. J. Travels with Mr. Slush
   Dinh, L. In the vein
   Gaiman, N. American gods [excerpt]
   Hegi, U. The end of all sadness
   Howard, C. Crowded lives
   Howard, C. Hanging it on a limb
   Howard, C. New Orleans getaway
   Jaime-Becerra, M. The corrido of Hector Cruz
   Kaminsky, S. M. Scorpion's kiss
   L'Amour, L. Beyond the chaparral
   Mosley, W. Blue lightning
   Mosley, W. A day in the park
   Mosley, W. Equal opportunity
   Mosley, W. Mookie Kid
   Mosley, W. Moving on
   Mosley, W. The mugger
   Mosley, W. Promise
   Mosley, W. Rascals in the cane
   Mosley, W. Rogue
   Mosley, W. Shift, shift, shift
   Mosley, W. That smell
   Mosley, W. The thief

   Mosley, W. Walkin' the dog
   Mosley, W. What would you do?
   Oates, J. C. The instructor
   Oates, J. C. Mark of satan
   Offutt, C. Moscow, Idaho
   Paine, T. Scar Vegas
   Parvin, R. Betty Hutton
   Peck, D. Bliss
   Thon, M. R. Little white sister
   Toes, J. Known unto God
   Vachss, A. H. Proving it
   Vachss, A. H. The real world
   Vachss, A. H. Summer girl
   Wallace, D. F. Philosophy and the mirror of nature
EX-HUSBANDS *See* Divorced persons
EX-NAZIS *See* National socialism
EX-NUNS
   Carter, E. Glory B. and the baby Jesus
   Scoville, S. The gift of a car
EX-WIVES
   Lee, A. The visit
Exact change. Klass, P.
Exactly the size of life. Rosenfeld, S.
An **exaltation** of termagants. Lustbader, E. V.
EXAMINATIONS
   Matheson, R. The test
   Robison, M. I am twenty-one
Examining the evidence. Hoffman, A.
Excalibur [excerpt] Cornwell, B.
The **excavator**. Bourke, R. W.
Excellence. Rowan, Q.
Excerpts from the Records of the New Zodiac and the diaries of Henry Watson Fairfax. Williamson, C.
The **exchange**. Stern, D.
Exchange of men. Nemerov, H. and Johnson, W. R.
Exchange of pleasant words. Hemon, A.
Exchange rate. Clement, H.
Exchanges. Morris, M.
An **Excitable** Woman. Boyers, R.
The **exclamation** mark. Chekhov, A. P.
Excursion. Oliver, B.
Excursion in reality. Waugh, E.
Execution of a horse. Klíma, I.
EXECUTIONS AND EXECUTIONERS
      See also Hangings
   Borges, J. L. The man on the threshold
   Borges, J. L. The secret miracle
   Earle, S. The witness
   Estleman, L. D. Thirteen coils
   Gores, J. The second coming
   Gorman, E. That day at Eagle's Point
   Herling, G. Notebook of William Moulding, pensioner
   Howard, C. The marksman
   Maupassant, G. d. A fishing excursion
   Maupassant, G. d. Two fishers
   Mo Yan. The cure
   Pronzini, B. The Arrowmont Prison riddle
   Saro-Wiwa, K. Africa kills her sun
   Wellen, E. The last mile
Executive clemency. Dozois, G. R.
EXECUTIVES
   Girardi, R. Three ravens on a red ground
   Händler, E.-W. The new guys
The **executor**. Epstein, J.
The **executor**. Spark, M.

EXERCISE

> *See also* Weight lifting

Heller, J. Yossarian survives

Exhibit A. Frank, J.

Exile. Mueller, M.

Exile of the eons. See Clarke, A. C. Nemesis

EXILES

> *See also* Refugees

Azadeh, C. The marriage at Antibes

Bellow, S. Him with his foot in his mouth

Chekhov, A. P. In exile

Hamburger, A. Exile

Mueller, M. Exile

Roffé, R. Transforming the desert

Taraqqi, G. The bizarre comportment of Mr. Alpha in exile

Exit. O'Callaghan, M.

Exit Miss Tish. Berry, M. S.

EXORCISM

> *See also* Demoniac possession

Herling, G. The exorcist's brief confession

Singer, I. B. The dead fiddler

Exorcism. Bradbury, R.

The **exorcism**. O'Neill, S.

The **exorcist's** brief confession. Herling, G.

Expanses of white. Meddeb, A.

EXPATRIATES *See* Exiles

Expatriates. Goldner, B.

Expatriates. Joseph, D.

The **expectation** of abundance. Van Winckel, N.

Expensive gifts. Miller, S.

Experience. DeMarinis, R.

The **experience** of what is beautiful. Deane, J. F.

Experiment. Wellen, E.

EXPERIMENTAL DRUGS *See* Drugs

EXPERIMENTAL MEDICINE *See* Medicine—Research

EXPERIMENTAL STORIES

> *See also* Surrealism

Adler, R. Brownstone

Alexis, A. My Anabasis

Amis, M. What happened to me on my holiday

Arenas, R. Goodbye mother

Arenas, R. Mona

Aylett, S. Bestiary

Bail, M. Cul-de-sac (uncompleted)

Bail, M. Zoellner's definition

Barth, J. 9999

Barth, J. Click

Barth, J. Help

Berry, R. M. Abandoned writing projects

Berry, R. M. 'Bus

Berry, R. M. Free enterprise

Berry, R. M. Knott unbound

Berry, R. M. Mimesis

Berry, R. M. (Paid advertisement)

Berry, R. M. The sentence

Berry, R. M. Torture!

Bisson, T. Incident at Oak Ridge

Brathwaite, E. K. Dream Haiti

Brathwaite, E. K. My funny Valentine

Campbell, R. A street was chosen

Chacón, D. Epilogue: story #7 in D minor

Cho, N. Bang bang bang

Codrescu, A. Samba de los agentes

Cortázar, J. Letter to a young lady in Paris

Davenport, G. Belinda's world tour

Davenport, G. The bicycle rider

Davenport, G. Christ preaching at the Henley Regatta

Davenport, G. The Concord sonata

Davenport, G. The death of Picasso

Davenport, G. Gunnar and Nikolai

Davenport, G. The Jules Verne Steam balloon

Davenport, G. The playing field

Davenport, G. The ringdove sign

Davenport, G. We often think of Lenin at the clothespin factory

Davenport, G. Wo es war, soll ich werden

Davies, R. Celluloid heroes

DiFilippo, P. Science fiction

Dinh, L. Val

Foley, S. Y's story

Galloway, J. After the rains

Galloway, J. He dreams of pleasing his mother

Galloway, J. Last thing

Galloway, J. Six horses

Glave, T. A real place

Glover, D. H. A man in a box

Händler, E.-W. Demiurg

Hayton, S. Cells of knowledge [excerpt]

Hemon, A. The life and work of Alphonse Kauders

Hemon, A. The Sorge spy ring

Joseph, A. The African origins of UFOs [excerpt]

Leong, R. Eclipse

Link, K. The girl detective

Lopez, B. H. Ruben Mendoza Vega, Suzuki professor of early Caribbean history, University of Florida at Gainesville, offers a history of the United States based on personal experience

Mathews, H. Clocking the world on cue: the chronogram for 2001

Mathews, H. The way home

Michaels, L. Eating out

Murakami, H. The fall of the Roman Empire, the 1881 Indian uprising, Hitler's invasion of Poland, and the realm of raging winds

Sanchez, S. Wounded in the house of a friend

Sarduy, S. Curriculum cubense

Schoemperlen, D. The antonyms of fiction

Schoemperlen, D. Five small rooms (A murder mystery)

Schoemperlen, D. How deep is the river?

Schoemperlen, D. Mastering effective English (A linguistic fable)

Schoemperlen, D. Railroading; or, Twelve small stories with the word train in the title

Schoemperlen, D. A simple story

Schoemperlen, D. Weights and measures

Skillings, R. D. The spiritus step

Sorrentino, G. Allegory of innocence

Sorrentino, G. Sample writing sample

Sorrentino, G. The sea, caught in roses

Sorrentino, G. Times without number

Steinberg, S. Away!

Steinberg, S. The end of free love

Steinberg, S. Far

Steinberg, S. Forward

Steinberg, S. Isla

Steinberg, S. Life

Steinberg, S. Nothing

Steinberg, S. Opening

Steinberg, S. Saturday

Steinberg, S. Standstill

EXPERIMENTAL STORIES—*Continued*

Steinberg, S. Start

Steinberg, S. Stay with me

Steinberg, S. Testing,

Steinberg, S. There's a window

Steinberg, S. Trees

Steinberg, S. Vulgar

Steinberg, S. What makes you think

Steinberg, S. Winner

Tillman, L. Flowers

Tillman, L. Hold me

Tillman, L. Snow-job

Vaswani, N. An outline of no direction

Volpi, J. Ars poetica

Wallace, D. F. Adult world [II]

Wallace, D. F. Church not made with hands

Wallace, D. F. Octet

Wallace, D. F. Tri-stan: I sold sissee nar to Ecko

Wells, K. Secession, XX

Wideman, J. E. Surfiction

Yuknavitch, L. Beauty

Yuknavitch, L. Burning the commodity

Yuknavitch, L. Citations of a heretic

Yuknavitch, L. From the boy stories

Yuknavitch, L. Outtakes

Yuknavitch, L. Scripted

Yuknavitch, L. Signification

Yuknavitch, L. Three studies for figures on beds after Francis Bacon and Antonin Artaud

EXPERIMENTS, SCIENTIFIC *See* Scientific experiments

Experiments. Flann, K.

The **expert** witness. Archer, J.

Expiation. Wharton, E.

Explaining death to the dog. Perabo, S.

Exploration. Pittard, S.

Exploration team. Jenkins, W. F.

EXPLORERS

Cady, J. The time that time forgot

Clough, B. W. May be some time

Padilla, I. The antipodes and the century

Padilla, I. Darjeeling

Shepard, J. Tedford and the megalodon

EXPLOSIONS

Crowther, P. The main event

Powers, T. Itinerary

Export. Barthelme, F.

Exposure. George, E.

Exposure. Kane, J. F.

Exposures. Campbell, E.

Expression of our people. Chacón, D.

Exquisite. Frank, J.

Extension. Barth, J.

Exterior decoration. Cooper, B.

EXTERMINATION *See* Pests—Control

EXTERMINATION, JEWISH *See* Holocaust, Jewish (1933-1945)

Exterminator. Parrish, T.

EXTINCT ANIMALS

Fowler, K. J. Faded roses

EXTINCT CITIES

See also Troy (Ancient city)

Ponte, A. J. A knack for making ruins

EXTORTION

Bishop, P. Going postal

Franklin, T. Grit

Krist, G. An innocent bystander

Trevor, W. Against the odds

The **extra.** Dann, J.

Extra. Li, Y.

The **extraordinary** member of Carlos Artiga. Frank, J.

EXTRASENSORY PERCEPTION

See also Clairvoyance; Telepathy

Anderson, P. The Saturn game

Card, O. S. Hatrack River

Haslett, A. Divination

Moody, R. Forecast from the retail desk

Rusch, K. K. Burial detail

Spencer, E. The finder

Wilson, R. C. Ulysses sees the moon in the bedroom window

Extreme unction. Bonnie, F.

EYE

Hogan, L. Amen

Wharton, E. The eyes

Diseases

Gordimer, N. Message in a bottle

Newman, D. A. Mystery Spot

The **eye.** Bowles, P.

An **eye** for an eye. Kilpatrick, N.

An **eye** for an eye. Sade, marquis de

The **eye** of God. Rosenblum, M. H.

The **eye** of the beholder. Carl, L. S.

Eye of the beholder. Gorman, E.

Eye of the day. Berliner, J.

Eye-openers. Vega, A. L.

Eye to eye. Deaver, J.

EYEGLASSES

Hill, I. The more they stay the same

The **eyes.** Wharton, E.

Eyes of doom. Le May, A.

Eyesores. Shade, E.

The **eyetooth** of Barabbas. Herling, G.

EYEWITNESSES *See* Witnesses

F

Fm. Matheson, R.

The **F.** Scott/Tolstoy/Ahab accumulator. Bradbury, R.

F-stops. Jones, C.

Faber, Cecilia Böhl von *See* Caballero, Fernán, 1796-1877

The **fable** of the two silver pens. Melville, P.

FABLES

See also Allegories

Alcott, L. M. The eaglet in the dove's nest

Bail, M. Huebler

Biguenet, J. The torturer's apprentice

Bocock, M. The baker's daughter

Bowles, P. The hyena

Hartzenbusch, J. E. "Beauty as punishment"

Lindgren, T. The stump-grubber

Lugones, L. The horses of Abdera

Nair, M. The curry leaf tree

Nichols, I. The last dance

Škvorecký, J. The cuckoo

Tolstoy, L., graf. A grain of rye the size of a chicken egg

Wang Meng. The lovesick crow and other fables

Williamson, D. Mary and the seal

Fables of the Erotic Other: A Story. Clayton, J. J.

Fabra, Nilo María
  On the planet Mars
    Cosmos latinos: an anthology of science fiction from Latin America and Spain; translated, edited, & with an introduction & notes by Andrea L. Bell & Yolanda Molina-Gavilán
Fabra y Deas, Nilo MarXia *See* Fabra, Nilo María, 1843-1903
FACE
    Abnormalities and deformities
  Cody, L. K. K.
The **face**. Bocock, M.
The **face-lift**. Robinson, R.
The **face** of the Mesquaki woman. Roemer, A.
Face value. Fowler, K. J.
Faces made of clay. West, M.
The **faces** of fear. Burford, M.
The **faces** of Joan of Arc. Haskell, J.
Facing the forests. Yehoshua, A. B.
FACTORIES
      See also Labor and laboring classes
  Chekhov, A. P. A doctor's visit
  Chesnutt, C. W. The averted strike
  Franklin, T. Grit
  Hribal, C. J. War babies
  Klíma, I. The assembly line
  Mason, B. A. Charger
  Mayo, W. Robert's bride
  Parker, G. Bad nose
  Reid, E. Overtime
  Sumner, M. Good-hearted woman
  Torrington, J. The fade
  Vasilenko, S. Shamara
  Wallace, R. The little woman
  Wuori, G. K. Parents
The **facts**. Burton, M.
The **facts** of fiction. Auchincloss, L.
The **facts** of life. Alley, H.
The **facts** of life. Rucker, R. v. B.
Facts relating to the arrest of Dr. Kalugin. Baker, K.
FACULTY (EDUCATION) *See* Teachers
Fadavi, Parvin
  The bitter life of Shirin
    A Feast in the mirror; stories by contemporary Iranian women; translated and edited by Mohammad Mehdi Khorrami, Shouleh Vatanabadi
The **fade**. Torrington, J.
Faded roses. Fowler, K. J.
The **faerie** cony-catcher. Sherman, D.
Fagan, Eleanora *See* Holiday, Billie, 1915-1959
Faherty, Terence
  The third Manny
    Crème de la crime; edited by Janet Hutchings
FAILURE
  Alexis, A. The third terrace
  Blair, J. Bacon on the beach
  Blaise, C. Giant turtles, gliding in the dark
  Epstein, J. Postcards
  Fairey, W. W. Grace
  Fischer, T. We ate the chef
  Harris, M. The bonding
  Hodgen, C. The great Americans
  Lipsyte, S. My life, for promotional use only
  Perabo, S. Reconstruction
  Poirier, M. J. Buttons
  Slavin, J. Covered

  Troy, M. Dinosaur
  Weaver, G. And what should I do in Illyria?
  Weaver, G. The emancipation of hoytie rademacher
  Yates, R. A glutton for punishment
The **failure**. Franzen, J.
The **failure** (I). Franzen, J.
Fair and impartial. Huffman, B., Jr.
Fair exchange. Rendell, R.
Fair exchange. Wellen, E.
Fair game. Nevins, F. M., Jr.
A **fair** price. Gifford, B.
Fair trades. Carson, J.
Fair warning. Butler, R. O.
Fairey, Wendy W.
  The bad hand
    Fairey, W. W. Full house; stories
  Family album
    Fairey, W. W. Full house; stories
  Family pets
    Fairey, W. W. Full house; stories
  Grace
    Fairey, W. W. Full house; stories
  Her hair
    Fairey, W. W. Full house; stories
  Hermes
    Fairey, W. W. Full house; stories
  House of cards
    Fairey, W. W. Full house; stories
  A hundred hearts
    Fairey, W. W. Full house; stories
  Menopause and poker
    Fairey, W. W. Full house; stories
  Mind and body
    Fairey, W. W. Full house; stories
  Over the hill
    Fairey, W. W. Full house; stories
The **fairground** horror. Lumley, B.
FAIRIES
  Blackford, R. The king with three daughters
  Boylan, C. Ears
  Clarke, S. Mr. Simonelli; or, The fairy widower
  Dann, J. Fairy tale
  Davenport, G. Mr. Churchyard and the troll
  De Lint, C. Big city littles
  De Lint, C. Seven wild sisters
  De Lint, C. Sweet forget-me-not
  Fiscus, J. A very special relativity
  Helfers, J. Changeling
  Hoyt, S. A. Yellow tide foam
  Huff, T. He said, sidhe said
  Le Fanu, J. S. The child that went with the fairies
  Lindskold, J. M. Witche's-broom, apple soon
  Rusch, K. K. Judgment
  Scarborough, E. A. The filial fiddler
  Schweitzer, D. Tom O'bedlam's night out
  Singer, I. B. The lantuch
  Spencer, W. Wyvern
  Stemple, A. A piece of flesh
  Waggoner, T. The September people
  West, M. The stolen child
  Winterson, J. O'Brien's first Christmas
  Yolen, J. Belle bloody merciless dame
  Yolen, J. Dusty loves
  Yolen, J. The thirteenth fey
  Yolen, J. The uncorking of Uncle Finn

Fairman, Paul W.
  The cosmic frame
    Science-fiction classics; the stories that morphed into movies; compiled by Forrest J. Ackerman
FAIRS
  Bradbury, R. The black ferris
  Cummins, A. The Shiprock Fair
  Shade, E. The last night of the county fair
  Tillman, L. Thrilled to death
  Updike, J. You'll never know, dear, how much I love you
The **fairy** ring. Edghill, R.
Fairy tale. Dann, J.
Fairy tale. Davis, A.
FAIRY TALES *See* Fantasies
FAITH
  Anderson, P. The problem of pain
  Auchincloss, L. The Devil and Guy Lansing
  Avrich, J. The winter without milk
  Berkman, P. R. Holy holy holy
  Berkman, P. R. Veronica
  Boucher, A. The quest for Saint Aquin
  Butler, R. O. Up by heart
  Capote, T. Preacher's legend
  Coates, G. S. The truth
  Connolly, C. How I lost my vocation
  Del Rey, L. For I am a jealous people!
  Egan, G. Oceanic
  Highsmith, P. The hollow oracle
  Iwaszkiewicz, J. The mill on the River Utrata
  Jackson, V. F. Breaking faith
  Jen, G. The water faucet vision
  Kemper, M. God's goodness
  Martin, G. R. R. The way of cross and dragon
  Mastretta, A. Aunt Isabel
  Morrow, J. Auspicious eggs
  Rogers, B. H. Cloud stalking mice
  Singer, I. B. The blasphemer
  Singer, I. B. Jachid and Jechidah
  Singer, I. B. The pocket remembered
  Singer, I. B. Something is there
  Tolstoy, L., graf. A coffeehouse in the city of Surat
  Tolstoy, L., graf. Divine and human
  Tolstoy, L., graf. The prayer
  Updike, J. Believers
  Wells, K. Godlight
  Wells, K. Swallowing angels whole
Faith and lightning. Saknussemm, K.
FAITH CURE
  Brown, L. A roadside resurrection
  Cody, L. Doing it under the table
  Engel, M. P. You got to learn how to read things right
  Koja, K. Road trip
  Ndebele, N. S. The prophetess
  Setton, R. K. The cat garden
  Wildgen, M. Healer
Faith healer. Nevai, L.
FAITH HEALERS *See* Faith cure
Faith; or, Tips for the successful young lady. Davis, A.
The **faithful**. Del Rey, L.
The **faithful**. Prather, P.
Faithful Masha. Draitser, E.
The **faithful** wife. Callaghan, M.
FAITHFULNESS
  McEwan, I. Pornography

Schoemperlen, D. Forms of devotion
Faithless. Oates, J. C.
Fake House. Dinh, L.
Fake man. See McCorkle, J. Toads
Falco, Edward
  Among the Tootalonians
    Gettysburg Review v16 no3 p351-65 Aut 2003
  The instruments of peace
    The Best American mystery stories, 2000; edited and with an introduction by Donald E. Westlake
  The revenant
    The Pushcart prize XXIII: best of the small presses; an annual small press reader; edited by Bill Henderson with the Pushcart prize editors
  Sweet
    TriQuarterly no105 p86-97 Spr/Summ 1999
Falcon Malone can fly no mo. Touré
The **fall** of Saigon. Addonizio, K.
The **fall** of the house. Pearlman, D. D.
The **fall** of the house of Escher. Bear, G.
The **fall** of the Nixon administration. Hudson, S.
The **fall** of the Roman Empire, the 1881 Indian uprising, Hitler's invasion of Poland, and the realm of raging winds. Murakami, H.
The **fallen** angel. McBain, E.
Falling. Chan, D. M.
Falling. Fracis, S. H.
Falling away. Birmingham, E.
Falling backwards. Chaon, D.
Falling in love. Dubus, A.
Falling in Love During Wartime. Tucker, S. B.
The **falling** love of Flora: a sketch. See Chopin, K. Fedora
The **falling** nun. Berkman, P. R.
Falling Sky. Garcia, C.
Falling umbrella. Whitty, J.
Fallis, Greg
  And maybe the horse will learn to sing
    The Best American mystery stories, 1999; edited and with an introduction by Ed McBain
  Comes the revolution
    Browning, A. Murder is no mitzvah; edited by Abigail Browning
FALSE ACCUSATION
  Banks, R. The lie
  Bishop, P. The framing game
  Fairman, P. W. The cosmic frame
  Feng Jicai. The tall woman and her short husband
  L'Amour, L. Sand trap
  L'Amour, L. Waltz him around again, Shadow
  Matera, L. Destroying angel
  Matiella, A. C. The ring
  Mosley, W. Pet fly
  Ritchie, J. The absence of Emily
  Schutz, B. M. Not enough monkeys
False confessions. Garrett, G. P.
False lights. Godwin, G.
Falstaff, 193–. Anastas, B.
Fam da Sham. King, A. B.
FAME
  DeMarco, T. Lieutenant America and Miss Apple Pie
  Sykes, J. Seduced
Fame and Fortune. Kobin, J.

Familiar noise. Mazza, C.
Family. Baron, D.
Family. Leone, D.
Family. Magy, R.
Family. Makuck, P.
Family. Sherwood, F.
Family. Wuori, G. K.
A **family** affair. Chopin, K.
Family album. Fairey, W. W.
FAMILY CHRONICLES
    See also Family life
Alvarez, J. The blood of the Conquistadores
Bottoms, G. Levi's tongue
Durban, P. Soon
MacLeod, A. Clearances
Proulx, A. The bunchgrass edge of the world
Family furnishings. Munro, A.
A **family** game. DuBois, B.
The **family** jewels: a moral tale. Cannell, D.
FAMILY LIFE
    See also Aunts; Brothers; Brothers and
    sisters; Family chronicles; Fathers; Fathers
    and sons; Fathers-in-law; Grandchildren;
    Granddaughters; Grandfathers; Grandmoth-
    ers; Grandparents; Grandsons; Half-
    brothers; Half-sisters; Marriage; Marriage
    problems; Mothers and daughters; Mothers
    and sons; Mothers-in-law; Nephews;
    Nieces; Parent and child; Sisters; Stepbroth-
    ers; Stepdaughters; Stepfathers; Stepmoth-
    ers; Stepsisters; Stepsons; Twins; Uncles
Adisa, O. P. Widows' walk
Agee, J. The first obligation
Agee, J. The level of my uncertainty
Agee, J. You know I am lying
Alameddine, R. My grandmother, the
    grandmaster
Alameddine, R. Whore
Aldrich, B. S. The great wide world of men
Aldrich, B. S. Will the romance be the same?
Allen, S. Carved in vinyl
Avrich, J. The banshee's song
Banks, R. The visit
Barrett, A. The cure
Bausch, R. The brace
Bausch, R. Evening
Bausch, R. Rare & endangered species
Beattie, A. Perfect recall
Beaty, D. Ghosts
Bellow, S. Him with his foot in his mouth
Bellow, S. The old system
Bender, A. Dreaming in Polish
Benítez-Rojo, A. Buried statues
Berry, W. Pray without ceasing
Berry, W. Turn back the bed
Berry, Betsy. Family and flood
Bezmozgis, D. Roman Berman, massage thera-
    pist
Biguenet, J. The open curtain
Blaise, C. South
Bocock, M. Don't save your kisses
Bowen, E. The happy autumn fields
Brady, C. The custom of the country
Budnitz, J. Dog days
Budnitz, J. Hundred-pound baby
Budnitz, J. What happened
Budnitz, J. Yellville
Bukoski, A. The wood of such trees
Busch, F. The talking cure

Butler, L. P. Booker T's coming home
Callaghan, M. Their mother's purse
Capote, T. My side of the matter
Carlson, R. The H Street sledding record
Carlson, R. The ordinary son
Carlson, R. The status quo
Carlson, R. The summer of vintage clothing
Carlson, R. Towel season
Chacón, D. How hot was Mexicali?
Chaon, D. Here's a little something to remem-
    ber me by
Chávez, D. Grand slam
Chekhov, A. P. Betrothed
Chekhov, A. P. Boys
Chekhov, A. P. Difficult people
Chekhov, A. P. A dreary story
Chekhov, A. P. The head of the family
Chekhov, A. P. Shrove Tuesday
Cheng, C.-W. A fisherman's family
Cheng, C.-W. The mosquito
Chenoweth, A. If I were you
Chenoweth, A. The unfortunate city
Chenoweth, A. The visit
Chimera, B. July
Chopin, K. Mrs. Mobry's reason
Chute, C. "Ollie, oh . . . "
Clark, J. Public burning
Coates, G. S. Black cherries
Coates, G. S. A cast leaf
Coates, G. S. The corn knife
Coates, G. S. Crickets
Coates, G. S. Glass
Coates, G. S. The horn
Coates, G. S. Late fruit
Coates, G. S. The nymphs and pan
Coates, G. S. A pine tree
Coates, G. S. Plaster of Paris
Coates, G. S. Promises
Coates, G. S. Spring beauties
Coates, G. S. Trees of heaven
Coates, G. S. The truth
Coates, G. S. The way of the transgressor
Cohen, R. The boys at night
Cook, K. L. Easter weekend
Cook, K. L. Gone
Cook, K. L. Nature's way
Cook, K. L. Thrumming
Cooke, C. Dirt-eaters
Coyne, T. Behind sharp branches
Daniels, J. Fireworks
Dauenhauer, N. Egg boat
Davenport, K. Bones of the inner ear
Davidson, A. Twenty-three
Davis, D. S. The letter
Davis, J. S. The ballad of my father's redneck
    wife
De Varennes, Monique. Cabeza
DeLancey, K. The Welsh engineer
Delaney, E. J. Hero
Delaney, E. J. A visit to my uncle
DeMarinis, R. Desert places
Desai, A. The artist's life
Desai, A. Five hours to Simla; or, Faisla
Divakaruni, C. B. The forgotten children
Divakaruni, C. B. The love of a good man
Divakaruni, C. B. Mrs. Dutta writes a letter
Dixon, S. My life up till now
Emshwiller, C. The general
Eugenides, J. Timeshare

FAMILY LIFE—*Continued*

Evans, E. Ransom
Fairey, W. W. A hundred hearts
Fischerová, D. Two revolts in one family
Foley, S. Elemenopy
Foley, S. Off Grenada
Ford, R. Crèche
Ford, R. Optimists
Furman, L. Sunny
Gass, W. H. The Pedersen kid
Gates, D. Star baby
Gavell, M. L. The blessing
Gavell, M. L. Lois in the country
Gilchrist, E. Entropy
Gilchrist, E. Fort Smith
Gilchrist, E. The golden bough
Gilman, C. P. Benigna Machiavelli
Gingher, M. Teen angel
Godwin, G. A sorrowful woman
Goldberg, M. Bee season
Goliger, G. Song of ascent
Grau, S. A. The man outside
Greer, A. S. The future of the Flynns
Grodstein, L. Family vacation
Gunn, K. Grass, leaves
Gunn, K. This place you return to is home
Gunn, K. Tinsel bright
Haake, K. All the water in the world
Hall, D. From Willow Temple
Hall, D. New England primer
Harfenist, J. Floating
Harfenist, J. The gift
Harfenist, J. The history of the flood
Harfenist, J. Safety off, not a shot fired
Havazelet, E. Leah
Hegi, U. A town like ours
Hemon, A. Exchange of pleasant words
Henley, P. Sun damage
Henley, P. Victory
Hodgen, C. Going out of business forever
Hodgen, C. A jeweler's eye for flaw
Hodgen, C. Sir Karl LaFong or current resident
Honwana, L. B. Papa, snake & I
Horgan, P. The peach stone
Howard, M. The Magdalene
Hwang, F. Transparency
Iribarne, M. Ross Willow's new and used cars
Iribarne, M. Wedding dance
Isaacs, S. My cousin Rachel's Uncle Murray
Jackson, V. F. Darrell's garage
Jackson, V. F. Telling stories
Jackson, V. F. What I cannot say to you
Jaime-Becerra, M. Practice tattoos
Jen, G. House, house, home
Jen, G. In the American society
Jen, G. Just wait
Jen, G. Who's Irish?
Johnson, A. Trauma plate
Joseph, D. Many will enter, few will win
Kalman, J. Allures of grandeur
Kalman, J. Channel crossing
Kalman, J. Eichmann's monogram
Kalman, J. Flight
Kalman, J. Ladies' wear
Kalman, J. The making of a Jew
Kalman, J. Monahan Avenue
Kalman, J. Not for me a crown of thorns
Kalman, J. Personal effects
Kalman, J. A reason to be

Kalman, J. What's in a name?
Kaplan, H. Would you know it wasn't love?
Kavaler, R. Give brother my best
Kim, Junse. Yangban
Kirchheimer, G. D. A case of dementia
Kirchheimer, G. D. Feast of Lights
Kirshenbaum, B. Who knows Kaddish
Lawrence, D. H. England, my England
Lawrence, D. H. Odour of chrysanthemums
Leslie, N. Lost
Lieu, J. Troubles
Lincoln, C. At the water's end
Lincoln, C. Winter's wheat
Lombreglia, R. Cashmere Christmas
MacLeod, A. The boat
MacLeod, A. In the fall
MacLeod, A. The vastness of the dark
MacLeod, A. Winter dog
Malouf, D. Great Day
Maron, M. Croquet summer
Mathews, A. The story of the German parachut-
   ist who landed forty-two years late
Maxwell, W. Over by the river
McCorkle, J. Snipe
McCorkle, J. Toads
McNally, J. Roger's new life
McNally, J. Torture
Menendez, A. Miami relatives
Menendez, A. The perfect fruit
Meyers, K. The heart of the sky
Mirvis, T. A Poland, a Lithuania, a Galicia
Moody, R. Boys
Moore, L. Four calling birds, three French hens
Morgan, R. Dark corner
Morrow, B. Amazing Grace
Muñoz, M. The third myth
Munro, A. Family furnishings
Munro, A. Save the reaper
Murguía, A. Rose-colored dreams
Nakagami, K. The cape
Nawrocki, S. Hovercraft
Naylor, G. Kiswana Browne
Nelson, A. Irony, irony, irony
Newman, D. A. Good news and bad news
Oates, J. C. We were worried about you
O'Connor, F. A good man is hard to find
Orner, P. Esther stories
Orringer, J. Pilgrims
Orringer, J. What we save
Painter, P. New family car
Pak, W.-S. A certain barbarity
Pak, W.-S. Mr. Hong's medals
Pearlman, D. D. The fall of the house
Perabo, S. The rocks over Kyburz
Peretz, I. L. Bryna's Mendl
Pesetsky, B. Offspring of the first generation
Phillips, D. R. What men love for
Phillips, D. R. The woods at the back of our
   houses
Prose, F. Talking dog
Proulx, A. The bunchgrass edge of the world
Reifler, N. Sugar
Reisman, N. House fires
Reisman, N. Illumination
Robison, M. An amateur's guide to the night
Robison, M. Coach
Robison, M. Doctor's sons
Rodburg, M. Concessions
Rodburg, M. Days of awe

FAMILY LIFE—*Continued*
Rodburg, M. Keer Avenue, July 1967
Rodburg, M. The law of return
Rodburg, M. The orphan
Rodburg, M. Pochantas in Camelot
Rodburg, M. The widower Visarrion
Roorbach, B. Thanksgiving
Rubin, L. D. The man at the beach
Rusch, K. K. Harvest
Russo, R. The farther you go
Sandor, M. The handcuff king
Schmidt, H. J. The funeral party
Schoemperlen, D. Hockey night in Canada
Scibona, S. The plateform
Searle, E. The young and the rest of us
Seiffert, R. Tentsmuir sands
Sharma, A. Surrounded by sleep
Shepard, S. Concepción
Singer, I. B. Guests on a winter night
Škvorecký, J. A remarkable chemical phenomenon
Slavin, J. Pudding
Smiley, J. Long distance
Smith, L. Between the lines
Smith, S. J. Black bean soup
Smith, S. J. Gar fishing
Smith, S. J. Healing the mare
Smith, S. J. Jack in Chicago
Smith, S. J. Looping
Smith, S. J. Metamorphose, oboe
Smith, S. J. My father weeping
Smith, S. J. No thanks
Smith, S. J. Selling the house
Smith, S. J. Turtle hunting with black
Smith, S. J. Valerie rakes the leaves
Sosin, D. What Mark couldn't see
Spencer, E. The adult holiday
Spencer, E. The girl who loved horses
Spencer, E. Indian summer
Stanton, M. How to converse in Italian
Stanton, M. My death
Stern, D. Comfort
Stolar, D. Home in New Hampshire
Stollman, A. L. The seat of higher consciousness
Swan, M. At the river
Tanaka, S. Video ame
Taraqqi, G. The maid
Thomas, D. The car
Thomas, D. The girl from follow
Thompson, J. The Amish
Tinti, H. Home sweet home
Tomioka, T. Days of dear death
Troncoso, S. The last tortilla
Troy, J. Ramone
Troy, M. We're still Keeneys
Tuck, L. La Mayonette
Turchi, P. The night sky
Udall, B. Buckeye the elder
Updike, J. Daughter, Last glimpses of
Updike, J. The day of the dying rabbit
Updike, J. Incest
Updike, J. Pigeon feathers
Updike, J. Plumbing
Updike, J. Rabbit remembered
Updike, J. Sublimating
Vasilenko, S. Piggy
Vaswani, N. Blue, without sorrow
Vaswani, N. Five objects in Queens

Wallace, R. Logjam
Walrond, E. Drought
Weaver, G. Looking for the lost Eden
West, D. My baby . . .
Wharton, E. Charm incorporated
What, L. The sweet and sour tongue
Whisnant, L. Across from the Motoheads
White, M. C. Three whacks a buck
Wieland, L. Purgatory
Williams, J. Taking care
Willis, M. S. Dwight's house
Winegardner, M. How we came to Indiana
Yates, R. Oh, Joseph, I'm so tired
Young, T. Sometimes night never ends
Ziegler, I. Rules of the lake
Zinovyeva-Annibal, L. D. The bear cubs
Zinovyeva-Annibal, L. D. Wolves
A **family** likeness. Lavin, M.
The **family** on the other side of the mountain. Zhou Libo
Family pets. Fairey, W. W.
FAMILY REUNIONS
Baca, J. S. The three sons of Julia
Bausch, R. The eyes of love
Beattie, A. Coydog
Bingham, S. The hunt
Bowles, P. The frozen fields
Chenoweth, A. Powerman
Gordon, C. The petrified woman
Grau, S. A. Summer shore
Hardwick, E. Evenings at home
Lewis, W. H. Germinating
López, L. Love can make you sick
MacLeod, A. The return
Updike, J. The family meadow
Updike, J. Home
Wallace, R. A trick of memory
Yates, R. A compassionate leave
FAMILY SAGAS *See* Family chronicles
Family Statement. Bundy, A.
A **family** supper. Ishiguro, K.
Family ties. Baida, P.
Family vacation. Grodstein, L.
Family values. Epstein, J.
Famous builder. Lisicky, P.
Famous people. Pamuk, O.
The **famous** poet, amid Bougainvillea. Beattie, A.
Famous poets. Stuckey-French, E.
The **famous** poll at Jody's Bar. Gilchrist, E.
Fan. Ryman, G.
A **fan** despite himself. Wallenstein, J.
FANATICISM
Dozois, G. R. Community
Evenson, B. The prophets
McAuley, P. J. Sea change, with monsters
FANATICS *See* Fanaticism
Fancy pants. Vukcevich, R.
The **fane** of the Grey Rose. De Lint, C.
FANTASIES
See also Allegories; End of the world; Experimental stories; Future; Improbable stories; Science fiction; Utopias Queen of soulmates
Abbey, L. The red lucky
Addison, L. Twice, at once, separated
Adriázola, C. Buttons
Aickman, R. The cicerones
Alarcón, P. A. d. "Death's friend"
Alas, L. "My funeral"

FANTASIES—See also—*Continued*

Alas, L. "Socrates' rooster"
Alcalá, K. J. Altar
Alcott, L. M. Rosy's journey
Aldiss, B. W. Becoming the full butterfly
Allen, Paul. While the band played
American mandate
And the glory of them
Anderson, P. A midsummer tempest
Anderson, P. The Sky People
Anderson, P. Three hearts and three lions
Arenas, R. Halley's comet
Arnason, E. The grammarian's five daughters
Arsenault, Michael. A Halloween like any other
Atkinson, K. The cat lover
Attanasio, A. A. Hellbent
Bailey, R. W. Ring of sea and fire
Barceló, E. First time
Barrett, N., Jr. Stairs
Barrett, N., Jr. Winter on the Belle Fourche
Barrie, J. M. Peter and Wendy [excerpt]
Barthelme, D. The balloon
Baum, L. F. The enchanted buffalo
Baum, L. F. A kidnapped Santa Claus
Beagle, P. S. My daughter's name is Sarah
Bear, G. Petra
Bear, G. Webster
Bear, G. The white horse child
Beaumont, C. The howling man
Bécquer, G. A. "Believe in God"
Bécquer, G. A. "The devil's cross"
Belfiore, Michael P. What's in a name
Bell, M. S. The pagodas of Ciboure
Bender, A. Dearth
Benét, S. V. Daniel Webster and the sea serpent
Benford, G. The goldilocks problem
Bester, A. Disappearing act
Birmingham, E. Falling away
Bishop, M. Among the handlers; or, The Mark 16 Hands-on Assembly of Jesus Risen, formerly Snake-o-rama
Bishop, M. Thirteen lies about hummingbirds
Bishop, M. The tigers of hystria feed only on themselves
Bishop, M. and DiFilippo, P. "We're all in this alone"
Bisson, T. Partial people
Bixby, J. It's a good life
Björkquist, E. D. Inocente's getaway
Blackford, R. The king with three daughters
Block, F. L. Bones
Blumlein, M. Paul and me
Blumlein, M. Revenge
Bond, N. The bookshop
Borges, J. L. The aleph
Borges, J. L. The approach to Al-Mu'tasim
Borges, J. L. The book of sand
Borges, J. L. Funes, his memory
Borges, J. L. The house of Asterion
Borges, J. L. The rose of Paracelsus
Borges, J. L. Tlön, Uqbar, Orbis Tertius
Borges, J. L. A weary man's utopia
Boroson, R. The roussalka
Boylan, C. A model daughter
Bradbury, R. After the ball
Bradbury, R. Almost the end of the world
Bradbury, R. Another fine mess
Bradbury, R. Bang! You're dead!
Bradbury, R. The cold wind and the warm

Bradbury, R. The dragon
Bradbury, R. A far-away guitar
Bradbury, R. Fore!
Bradbury, R. The meadow
Bradbury, R. Once more, Legato
Bradbury, R. The sea shell
Bradbury, R. Season of disbelief
Bradbury, R. The swan
Bradbury, R. Time intervening/interim
Bradbury, R. Ulnterderseaboat dokfor
Bradbury, R. The watchful poker chip of H. Matisse
Bradbury, R. The wonderful death of Dudley Stone
Bradfield, S. Goldilocks tells all
Braunbeck, G. A. Small song
Brockmeier, K. The ceiling
Brockmeier, K. A day in the life of half of Rumpelstiltskin
Brockmeier, K. The green children
Brockmeier, K. The passenger
Brooks, T. Indomitable
Brotherton, Michael. Blood bone tendon stone
Brown, F. The Geezenstacks
Brownrigg, S. Amazon
Brownrigg, S. The bird chick
Brownrigg, S. Broad from abroad
Brownrigg, S. Mars needs women!
Brownrigg, S. Mistress of many moons
Brownstein, G. The curious case of Benjamin Button, 3w
Buchan, J. The far islands
Bull, E. Rending dark
Byatt, A. S. Cold
Byatt, A. S. A lamia in the Cévennes
Caballero, F. "The girl with three husbands"
Caballero, F. "Lovely-flower"
Caballero, F. "The wishes"
Cabell, J. B. The thin queen of Elfhame
Cadnum, M. Bear it away
Calderon, L. Day Ah Dallas Mare Toes
Campbell, R. No story in it
Campra, Rosalba. Dream tiger
Card, O. S. 50 WPM
Card, O. S. Hatrack River
Card, O. S. The Yazoo Queen
Carpentier, A. Journey back to the source
Carpentier, A. Journey to the seed
Carter, A. The courtship of Mr. Lyon
Chapman, C. M. Poor man's mermaid
Charnas, S. M. Boobs
Chaviano, D. The annunciation
Cherryh, C. J. The brothers
Cherryh, C. J. The dark king
Cherryh, C. J. The dreamstone
Cherryh, C. J. The last tower
Cherryh, C. J. Of law and magic
Cherryh, C. J. Sea change
Cherryh, C. J. A thief in Korianth
Cherryh, C. J. The Threads of time
Cherryh, C. J. The unshadowed land
Cherryh, C. J. Willow
Chiang, T. Hell is the absence of God
Chivers, D. Radio baby
Chwedyk, Richard. Bronte's egg
Clarke, A. C. The wall of darkness
Clarke, S. The Duke of Wellington misplaces his horse
Clarke, S. Mr. Simonelli; or, The fairy widower

FANTASIES—See also—*Continued*

Clarke, S. Mrs. Mabb
Clarke, S. Tom Brightwind; or, How the fairy bridge was built at Thoresby
Colgan, J. The wrong train
Coloma, L. "Green bird"
Coloma, L. "Pérez the Mouse"
Compadres
Compton, M. A. The fat cats' tale
Connor, J. Bluebeard's first wife
Connor, J. The butterfly effect
Connor, J. The year of no weather
Constantine, S. Paragenesis
Cook, R. and Hogan, E. Obsidian harvest
Cooper, B. J. A new night of long knives
Costikyan, G. And still she sleeps
Crowley, J. An earthly mother sits and sings
Crowley, J. Exogamy
Crowley, J. The green child
Crowley, J. Lost and abandoned
Crowley, J. Missolonghi 1824
Crowley, J. The nightingale sings at night
Crumey, A. Pfitz [excerpt]
Cutter, L. The red boots
Cutter, Leah R. Obsessions
Dann, J. The black horn
Dann, J. Da Vinci rising
Dann, J. The extra
Dann, J. Jubilee
Dann, J. Marilyn
Dann, J. Spirit dog
Dann, J. Ting-a-ling
Davidson, A. The account of Mr. Ira Davidson
Davidson, A. Buchanan's head
Davidson, A. Dr. Bhumbo Singh
Davidson, A. The engine of Samoset Erastus Hale, and one other, unknown
Davidson, A. Great is Diana
Davidson, A. The Montavarde camera
Davidson, A. O brave old world!
Davidson, A. The odd old bird
Davidson, A. Pebble in time
Davidson, A. The Peninsula
Davidson, A. Twenty-three
Davidson, A. El Vilvoy de las islas
Davidson, A. What strange stars and skies
De Lint, C. Big city littles
De Lint, C. The big sky
De Lint, C. Birds
De Lint, C. The buffalo man
De Lint, C. China doll
De Lint, C. Crow girls
De Lint, C. Embracing the mystery
De Lint, C. The fane of the Grey Rose
De Lint, C. The fields beyond the fields
De Lint, C. Forest of stone
De Lint, C. Granny weather
De Lint, C. Heartfires
De Lint, C. Held safe by moonlight and vines
De Lint, C. If I close my eyes forever
De Lint, C. In the land of the unforgiven
De Lint, C. In the pines
De Lint, C. In the quiet after midnight
De Lint, C. The invisibles
De Lint, C. Making a noise in this world
De Lint, C. Many worlds are born
De Lint, C. My life as a bird
De Lint, C. Passing
De Lint, C. The pennymen

De Lint, C. Pixel pixies
De Lint, C. Saskia
De Lint, C. Seven for a secret
De Lint, C. Seven wild sisters
De Lint, C. Shining nowhere but in the dark
De Lint, C. Sign here
De Lint, C. Ten for the devil
De Lint, C. Twa Corbies
De Lint, C. Wild horses
De Lint, C. Wingless angels
Deane, J. F. A migrant bird
Deason, L. Lady Emerdirael's rescue
Degollado, R. Our story frays
Del Rey, L. The coppersmith
Del Rey, L. The pipes of Pan
Delany, S. R. Cage of brass
Delany, S. R. Omegahelm
Delany, S. R. Prismatica
Delany, S. R. Ruins
Delany, S. R. Tapestry
DeMarinis, R. Your story
Denton, B. The hero of the night
Denton, B. We love Lydia love
Devil's bargain
Di Filippo, P. Ailoura
Diaconú, A. Blue lagoon
DiChario, N. Carp man
DiChario, N. The one-half boy
Dinesen, I. The supper at Elsinore
Disch, T. M. In Xanadu
Doctorow, C. Return to Pleasure Island
Doelwijt, T. In foreign parts
Donaldson, S. R. By any other name
Donaldson, S. R. The djinn who watches over the accursed
Donaldson, S. R. The kings of tarshish shall bring gifts
Donaldson, S. R. Reave the Just
Donaldson, S. R. The woman who loved pigs
Douglass, S. The evil within
Dozois, G. R. Golden apples of the sun
Dozois, G. R. Passage
Dozois, G. R. Playing the game
Dozois, G. R. Send no money
Drake, D. The fool
Duncan, A. The Pottawatomie Giant
Duncan, A. Senator Bilbo
Dunsany, E. J. M. D. P., Baron. Chu-bu and Sheemish
Dunsany, E. J. M. D. P., Baron. The hoard of the Gibbelins
Dyson, J. The engine of desire
Edelman, S. Eros and agape among the asteroids
Edghill, R. And king hereafter (a Boscobel League story)
Edghill, R. The fairy ring
Edghill, R. For I have sworn thee fair
Edghill, R. A gift of two grey horses
Edghill, R. Haut-Clare
Edghill, R. The intersection of Anastasia Yeoman and light
Edghill, R. Killer in the reign
Edghill, R. Lizzie Fair and the dragon of heart's desire
Edghill, R. The long divorce of steel
Edghill, R. The Maltese feline
Edghill, R. May Eve
Edghill, R. The piper at the gate
Edghill, R. Prince of exiles

FANTASIES—See also—*Continued*

Edghill, R. Scandal
Edghill, R. The Sword of the North
Edghill, R. War of the roses
Ellison, H. The goddess in the ice
Ellison, H. Incognita, Inc.
Ellison, H. Jeffty is five
Ellison, H. Objects of desire in the mirror are closer than they appear
Ellison, H. Santa Claus vs. S.P.I.D.E.R.
Empire
Evans, M. Candles in the bottom of the pool
Evenson, B. The progenitor
Feist, R. E. The messenger
Feist, R. E. One to go
Fintushel, E. Milo and Sylvie
Fiscus, J. A very special relativity
Fitzgerald, F. S. The curious case of Benjamin Button
Fitzgerald, F. S. The diamond as big as the Ritz
Ford, J. At Reparata
Ford, J. Creation
Ford, J. The green word
Foster, A. D. Jackalope
Fowler, C. Learning to let go
Fowler, K. J. What I didn't see
Friesen, R. E. Dancing in the ashes
Friesner, E. M. Big hair
Friesner, E. M. Hallowmass
Friesner, E. M. The stuff of heroes
Gabaldon, D. Lord John and the succubus
Gaiman, N. American gods [excerpt]
Gaiman, N. October in the chair
Gaiman, N. Pages from a journal found in a shoebox left in a Greyhound bus somewhere between Tulsa, Oklahoma, and Louisville, Kentucky
Gaiman, N. The wedding present
Galeano, E. H. The story of the lizard who had the habit of dining on his wives
Gallagher, S. The little dead girl singing
García Márquez, G. The handsomest drowned man in the world
Garfinkle, R. The last invasion of Ireland
George Patton slept here
Gilchrist, E. You must change your life
Gilchrist, E. The young man
Gilman, C. P. If I were a man
Gilman, G. Jack Daw's pack
Glassco, B. Taking loup
Golden, C. Lament for the gunwitch
Goldman, W. The princess bride [excerpt]
Goldstein, L. The fantasma of Q_____
Goliger, G. One morning in Prague
Goss, T. The rose in twelve petals
Goto, H. Tales from the breast
Goytisolo, J. The stork-men
Grant, G. J. and Link, K. Ship, sea, mountain, sky
Gray, N. S. Grimbold's other world [excerpt]
Grimm, J. and Grimm, W. The fisherman and his wife
Grimm, J. and Grimm, W. The gallant tailor
Grubb, J. Apocalypse noun
Haldeman, J. W. Names in marble
Hand, E. Last summer at Mars Hill
Hand, E. The least trumps
Hardesty, E. Rosie's dance
Hardy, M. Aquero

Harrison, H. Incident in the IND
Hart, E. T. Beyond eternity
Hartzenbusch, J. E. "Beauty as punishment"
Hawthorne, N. Drowne's wooden image
Hawthorne, N. Feathertop
Hawthorne, N. Feathertop: a moralized legend
Haydon, E. Threshold
Heinlein, R. A. The man who traveled in elephants
Heinlein, R. A. Our fair city
Heinlein, R. A. The unpleasant profession of Jonathan Hoag
Helfers, J. Changeling
Hendricks, V. Stormy, mon amour
Hill, J. Pop art
Hobb, R. Homecoming
Hodgman, J. Tanuki
Hodgman, Jan. Tanuki
Hodgson, W. H. The Baumoff explpsive
Hodgson, W. H. The island of the Ud
Hogan, E. Coyote goes Hollywood
Hope, A. L. The becoming
Hopkinson, N. The glass bottle trick
Hopkinson, N. Riding the red
Hopkinson, N. Under glass
Horizon
Housman, C. The drawn arrow
Howells, R. A bleak future without thought-paper
Hoyt, S. A. Yellow tide foam
Huff, T. He said, sidhe said
Huff, T. Nanite, star bright
Huff, T. Third time lucky
In the prison of his days
Jacobs, J. The story of rough niall of the speckled rock
Jacquez, K. Michelle's miracle
Jewell, L. Labia Lobelia
Jiménez, K. P. La del Sapo
Jordan, N. The dream of a beast
Joyce, G. First, catch your demon
Kaminsky, S. M. In thunder, lightning or in rain
Kanar, B. Dreaming among men
Kenan, R. Hobbits and hobgoblins
Keret, E. Kneller's happy campers
Keret, E. One last story and that's it
King, S. The tale of the Gray Dick
King, S. That feeling, you can only say what it is in French
Kinsella, W. P. Shoeless Joe Jackson comes to Iowa
Kinsella, W. P. Things invisible to see
Knatchbull-Hugessen, Sir H. Puss-cat Mew
Kornbluth, C. M. The words of Guru
Kushner, E. The death of the Duke
Kuttner, H. We are the dead
Labor relations
Lackey, M. A different kind of courage
Laidlaw, M. and Shirley, J. Pearlywhite
Landis, G. A. Elemental
Landis, G. A. The eyes of America
Lane, J. The hunger of the leaves
Lang, A. The story of Sigurd
Lansdale, J. R. Last of the hopeful
Le Guin, U. K. Buffalo gals, won't you come out tonight
Le Guin, U. K. The building
Le Guin, U. K. Confusions of Uñi
Le Guin, U. K. Darkrose and Diamond

FANTASIES—See also—*Continued*

Le Guin, U. K. Feeling at home with the Hennebet
Le Guin, U. K. The fliers of Gy
Le Guin, U. K. Great joy
Le Guin, U. K. The ire of the Veksi
Le Guin, U. K. The Island of the Immortals
Le Guin, U. K. The Nna Mmoy language
Le Guin, U. K. Porridge on Islac
Le Guin, U. K. The royals of Hegn
Le Guin, U. K. Seasons of the Ansarac
Le Guin, U. K. Semley's necklace
Le Guin, U. K. The silence of the Asonu
Le Guin, U. K. Sita Dulip's Method
Le Guin, U. K. Social dreaming of the Frin
Le Guin, U. K. Wake Island
Le Guin, U. K. Woeful tales from Mahigul
Lee, D. Sailing the painted ocean
Lee, S. and Miller, S. Naratha's shadow
Lee, T. All the birds of hell
Lee, T. Rapunzel
Lee, V. Prince Alberic and the snake lady
Leiber, F. The mer she
Lindholm, M. Bones for Dulath
Lindskold, J. M. Witche's-broom, apple soon
Link, K. The girl detective
Link, K. Travels with the Snow Queen
Lojo, Maria Rosa. Compound eyes
Lopez, B. H. In the Garden of the Lords of War
Love, R. Two recipes for magic beans
Lugones, L. The bloat-toad
Lugones, L. The firestorm
Lugones, L. Metamusic
Lugones, L. The Omega Force
Lugones, L. Origins of the flood
Lugones, L. Viola acherontia
Lumley, B. The stealer of dreams
Lumley, B. The weird wines of Naxas Niss
Lundoff, C. Vadija
Lupoff, R. A. A freeway for Draculas
Lustbader, E. V. An exaltation of termagants
MacDonald, G. The golden key
Machen, A. The coming of the terror
MacLean, K. The kidnapping of Baroness 5
MacLeod, I. Isabel of the fall
Malzberg, B. N. Allegro marcato
Malzberg, B. N. Andante lugubre
Malzberg, B. N. Concerto accademico
Malzberg, B. N. Fugato
Malzberg, B. N. Getting there
Malzberg, B. N. Hieractic realignment
Malzberg, B. N. The high purpose
Malzberg, B. N. In the stone house
Malzberg, B. N. Standards & practices
Malzberg, B. N. Understanding entropy
Manzarek, R. The lady of the valley
Martin, G. R. R. The sworn sword
Maxwell, M. A. O. Devil beads
McCaffrey, A. Beyond between
McCaffrey, A. A proper Santa Claus
McCarthy, W. He died that day, in thirty years
McIntyre, V. N. The moon and the sun [excerpt]
McIntyre, V. N. Of mist, and grass, and sand
McKiernan, D. L. Duel
McKillip, P. A. Oak Hill
McKillip, P. A. Toad
McKinley, R. A pool in the desert
McQuillin, C. Seliki
Medina, T. Butta's backyard barbecue

Merritt, A.
Millar, M. The people across the canyon
Millhauser, S. Behind the blue curtain
Millhauser, S. The disappearance of Elaine Coleman
Modesitt, L. E., Jr. The pilots
Montaño, G. G. Maldicion
Moody, J. The gift
Moody, R. Pan's fair throng
Moorcock, M. A slow Saturday night at the Surrealist Sporting Club
Morris, W. The folk of the mountain door
Mungan, M. Muradhan and selvihan; or, The tale of the Crystal Kiosk
Murakami, H. The elephant vanishes
Naiyer Masud. The myna from Peacock Garden
Newman, K. Egyptian Avenue
Niven, L. Loki
Niven, L. and Pournelle, J. The burning city [excerpt]
Nogueira, C. B. Maria de Jesus
Norman, L. The jewel and the demon
Norton, A. People of the crater
Norton, A. Serpent's tooth
Norton, A. Were-wrath
Nye, J. L. Doing the gods' work
Oates, J. C. The sky-blue ball
Oates, J. C. You, little match-girl
Offutt, A. J. Role model
Olivas, D. A. The plumed serpent of Los Angeles
Oliver, C. Transformer
Olson, T. Tear out my heart
Osgood, L. Great Sedna
Padilla, I. About our flour
Park, S. The golem
Patterson, A. Hussy Strutt
Patton, F. The control device
Patton, F. The raven's quest
Paxson, D. L. The prisoner in the jewel
Pérez Galdós, B. "The mule and the ox"
Pérez Galdós, B. "The princess and the street urchin"
Perrault, C. Toads and diamonds
Pettigrew, D. K. Atasdi: fish story
Pickard, N. It had to be you
Pohl, F. Day million
Pollack, R. The fool, the stick, and the princess
Powell, J. The plot against Santa Claus
Power, S. Roofwalker
Powers, T. Itinerary
Reed, R. Raven dream
Reichert, M. Z. Home is where the hate is
Reichert, M. Z. The Ulfjarl's stone
Resnick, L. Wallgate
Resnick, M. and Burstein, Michael A. Reflections in black granite
Reyes, S. R. Bad debts and vindictive women
Rice, D. The devil in the valley
Richter, S. The cavemen in the hedges
Richter, S. Rules for being human
Roberts, A. Swiftly
Roberts, R. Second chance
Roberts, T. N. Demon bone
Rogers, B. H. The dead boy at your window
Rogers, B. H. Sleeping Beauty
Rogoff, R. E. The princess and the accountant
Rollins, H. Beauty and the beast
Rollins, H. Cinderella

FANTASIES—See also—*Continued*

Rollins, H. The empress's new lingerie
Rollins, H. Goldie and the three bare bachelors
Rollins, H. Hansel and Gretel
Rollins, H. Jackie and the beanstalk
Rollins, H. The miller's daughter (Rumpelstiltskin)
Rollins, H. Rapunzel
Rollins, H. Red
Rollins, H. The sleeping beauty
Rollins, H. Snow White and the seven dwarves
Rollins, H. The three little pigs
Rosen, S. Ritual evolution
Rosenblum, M. H. The rainmaker
Roth, J. The leviathan
Routley, J. To avalon
Rucker, R. v. B. The Andy Warhol sandcandle
Rucker, R. v. B. Chaos surfari
Rucker, R. v. B. Instability
Rucker, R. v. B. Monument to the Third International
Rucker, R. v. B. A new experiment with time
Rusch, K. K. Harvest
Rusch, K. K. Monuments to the dead
Rusch, K. K. Sing
Rusch, K. K. Spirit guides
Saldaña, R. El Bronco y La Lechuza
Sánchez, R. Road detours
Sarath, P. E. The djinn game
Saunders, C. R. Gimmile's songs
Sawyer, R. J. Black reflection
Scarborough, E. A. Worse than the curse
Scarborough, E. A. and Reaser, Rick. Long time coming home
Schmidt, S. The emperor's revenge
Scholz, C. The amount to carry
Schuyler, G. S. Black no more [excerpt]
Schwartz, L. S. Deadly nightshade
Schwartz, L. S. Twisted tales
Scutt, C. Descent
Seagren, R. Of wood and stone
Sharratt, M. The anatomy of a mermaid
Shawl, N. At the huts of Ajala
Sheckley, R. Agamemnon's run
Sheckley, R. The city of the dead
Sheckley, R. Pandora's box—open with care
Sheckley, R. The Universal Karmic Clearing House
Shepard, L. The scalehunter's beautiful daughter
Sherman, D. The faerie cony-catcher
Sherman, D. The Parwat Ruby
Sherman, J. The magic-stealer
Shirley, J. Wings burnt black
Shmuelian, A. Moonstruck sunflowers
Shrayer-Petrov, D. Dismemberers
Shrayer-Petrov, D. Jonah and Sarah
Shua, A. M. The white Guanaco in the middle of France
Shwartz, S. The fires of her vengeance
Silverberg, R. The book of changes
Silverberg, R. Getting to know the dragon
Singer, I. B. Jachid and Jechidah
Slavin, J. Dentaphilia
Southern strategy
Spark, M. The house of the famous poet
Spencer, W. Wyvern
Stableford, B. M. Chanterelle
Steiber, E. The cats of San Martino
Stemple, A. A piece of flesh

Stern, S. The sin of Elijah
Stern, S. Sissman loses his way
Stern, S. A string around the moon: a children's story
Stevens, F. The elf trap
Stevenson, J. Notes from a bottle
Stockton, F. The Griffin and the minor canon
Straub, P. Ashputtle
Sussex, L. My lady tongue
Swanwick, M. The blind minotaur
Swanwick, M. Dirty little war
Swanwick, M. The dog said bow-wow
Swanwick, M. King dragon
Swanwick, M. The raggle taggle gypsy-o
Tafolla, C. Tia
Tarnished glory
Taylor, L. The wedding at Esperanza
Tenn, W. Everybody loves Irving Bommer
Tenn, W. She only goes out at night . . .
Tetrick, B. The angel of the wall
Thomas, J. The flaying season
Tieck, L. The elves
Tiedemann, M. W. Psyché
Tillman, L. Madame Realism: a fairy tale
Touré. Falcon Malone can fly no mo
Trueba, A. d. "The king's son-in-law"
Turtledove, H. Black tulip
Turtledove, H. Joe Steele
Tussing, J. The artificial cloud
Twain, M. A Connecticut Yankee at King Arthur's court [excerpt]
Twelve legions of angels
Uncle Alf
Underwood, L. J. The wife of Ben-y-ghloe
Updike, J. The baluchitherium
Valera, J. "The green bird"
Valera, J. "The wizard"
Van Eekhout, G. Wolves till the world goes down
VanderMeer, J. Corpse mouth and spore nose
VanderMeer, J. Exhibit H: torn pages discovered in the vest pocket of an unidentified tourist
VanderMeer, J. Experiment #25 from the book of winter
VanderMeer, J. The Festival of the Freshwater Squid
VanderMeer, J. Greensleeves
VanderMeer, J. Learning to leave the flesh
VanderMeer, J. London burning
VanderMeer, J. The machine
VanderMeer, J. The mansions of the moon (A cautionary tale)
Vasilenko, S. Going after goat antelopes
Vaughn, E. Winter solstice
Vinge, V. Bomb scare
Vinge, V. The peddler's apprentice
Vis, J. The mermaid
Vivante, A. Dante
Vonnegut, K. The powder-blue dragon
Vukcevich, R. By the time we get to Uranus
Vukcevich, R. The finger
Waldrop, H. Custer's last jump!
Waldrop, H. Our mortal span
Watson, I. The boy who lost an hour, the girl who lost her life
Watson, I. A day without Dad
Watson, I. Early, in the evening
Watson, I. The great escape
Watson, I. The last beast out of the box

FANTASIES—See also—*Continued*
Watson, I. Such dedication
Watson, I. Tulips from Amsterdam
Watson, I. What actually happened in Docklands
Weinberg, R. Riverworld roulette
Weinberg, R. Unfinished business
Wellman, M. W. O ugly bird!
Wellman, M. W. The valley was still
Wentworth, K. D. A taste of song
West, M. Birthnight
West, M. Diamonds
West, M. Elegy
West, M. Four attempts at a letter
West, M. Gifted
West, M. The law of man
West, M. The nightingale
West, M. Return of the king
West, M. Sunrise
West, M. To speak with angels
West, M. Under the skin
West, M. Winter
Westlake, D. E. Nackles
Wharton, T. The paper-thin garden
What, L. A dark fire, burning from within
What, L. How to feed your inner troll
What, L. The man I loved was an elf
What, L. You are who you eat
Wheeler, W. Skin so green and fine
Wilkins, C. Meluse's counsel
Williams, C. The machine
Williams, T. The happiest dead boy in the world
Williamson, C. The blood-red sea
Williamson, J. The firefly tree
Willis, C. Miracle
Wilson, R. C. The inner inner city
Winterson, J. The green man
Winterson, J. Lives of saints
Winterson, J. Orion
Winterson, J. The three friends
Winterson, J. Turn of the world
Wolfe, G. Bed & breakfast
Wolfe, G. Copperhead
Wolfe, G. The dead man
Wolfe, G. The eleventh city
Wolfe, G. How the bishop sailed to Inniskeen
Wolfe, G. The legend of Xi Cygnus
Wolfe, G. The night chough
Wolfe, G. No planets strike
Wolfe, G. The old woman whose rolling pin is the sun
Wolfe, G. Pocketful of diamonds
Wolfe, G. Queen
Wolfe, G. Slow children at play
Wolfe, G. A traveler in desert lands
Wolfe, G. Under hill
Wolfe, G. The waif
Wolfe, G. Wolfer
Wolfe, G. The wrapper
Wright, A. T. The story of Alwina
Wright, J. C. Awake in the night
Wu, C.-E. Monkey [excerpt]
Wyke-Smith, E. A. Golithos the ogre
Wylde, T. Spinning kingdoms, two
Yolen, J. The barbarian and the queen: thirteen interviews
Yolen, J. Become a warrior
Yolen, J. Belle bloody merciless dame
Yolen, J. Blood sister

Yolen, J. Dick W. and his Pussy; or, Tess and her Adequate Dick
Yolen, J. Dusty loves
Yolen, J. Granny rumple
Yolen, J. Green messiah
Yolen, J. Journey into the dark
Yolen, J. Lost girls
Yolen, J. Memoirs of a bottle djinn
Yolen, J. The singer and the song
Yolen, J. The sleep of trees
Yolen, J. Snow in summer
Yolen, J. Speaking to the wind
Yolen, J. Sun/flight
Yolen, J. The thirteenth fey
Yolen, J. The uncorking of Uncle Finn
Yolen, J. Under the hill
Yolen, J. Words of power
Yolen, J. and Harris, R. J. Carrion crows
Zinovyeva-Annibal, L. D. The centaur-princess
The **fantasma** of Q_____. Goldstein, L.
FANTASTIC FICTION *See* Fantasies; Science fiction
Fantastic Yellow Sun. De Gramont, N.
Fantasy for Eleven Fingers. Fountain, B.
A **fantasy** in memory of the Anglesey bone doctors. Rowlands, S. P.
Far and near. Fischerová, D.
Far centaurus. Van Vogt, A. E.
Far from the madding war. Berners, G. H. T.-W., Baron
Farah, Nuruddin
My father, the Englishman, and I
The Art of the story; an international anthology of contemporary short stories; edited by Daniel Halpern
Farangs. Lapcharoensap, R.
Faraway eyes. Rucker, R. v. B.
The **fare** to the moon. Price, R.
A **farewell**. Schnitzler, A.
Farewell, Angelina. Rutherglen, S.
Farewell at Kimpo Airport. Pak, W.-S.
Farewell, my lovely appetizer. Perelman, S. J.
Farewell to Frognall. Kees, W.
Farewell to the flesh. Helfers, J.
Farewell to the master. Bates, H.
FAREWELLS
Clarke, A. Leaving this island place
Kees, W. Farewell to Frognall
Farkašová, Etela
A sky full of migrating birds
In search of homo sapiens; twenty-five contemporary Slovak short stories; editor, Pavol Hudík ; [translated by Heather Trebatická; American English editor, Lucy Bednár]
The **farm**. Williams, J.
FARM HANDS *See* Farm workers
FARM LIFE
See also Peasant life
Agee, J. The creek
Agee, J. You know I am lying
Aldrich, B. S. Romance in G minor
Baca, J. S. The importance of a piece of paper
Benedict, P. Miracle boy
Bishop, E. The farmer's children
Boggs, B. Who is Beatrice?
Chapman, C. M. Honey well hung
Chopin, K. A shameful affair
Coates, G. S. The corn knife

FARM LIFE—*Continued*
Coates, G. S. Glass
Coates, G. S. Promises
Connor, J. The day the world declined to end
Gavell, M. L. Lois in the country
Gay, W. I hate to see that evening sun go down
Gay, W. Standing by peaceful waters
Gunn, K. The things he told her
Hoover, M. The quickening
Kauffman, J. Patriotic
Kittredge, W. Agriculture
Lincoln, C. Sap rising
MacLeod, A. As birds bring forth the sun
MacLeod, A. In the fall
MacLeod, A. Second spring
MacLeod, A. To every thing there is a season
Meyers, K. Bird shadows
Meyers, K. Easter dresses
Meyers, K. Glacierland
Meyers, K. The heart of the sky
Meyers, K. The husker tender
Meyers, K. A strange brown fruit
Meyers, K. Wind rower
Miller, R. Bryna
Muñoz, M. The unimportant Lila Parr
Noel, K. April
Peck, D. Cities of the plain
Perry, G. S. Hold autumn in your hand
Rosenblum, M. H. The rainmaker
Sosin, D. Ice age
Spatz, G. Paradise was this
Swarthout, G. F. Gersham and the saber
Tilghman, C. Things left undone
Wicks, V. I have the serpent brought
Alabama
Vice, B. Chickensnake
Arkansas
Bishop, M. The tigers of hystria feed only on themselves
California
Brown, N. K. Burn pile
Yamamoto, H. Seventeen syllables
Canada
Hardy, M. The heifer
Stegner, W. E. Buglesong
England
Lawrence, D. H. Love among the haystacks
Iowa
Kinsella, W. P. Shoeless Joe Jackson comes to Iowa
Ireland
Boylan, C. Concerning virgins
Boylan, C. To tempt a woman
Lavin, M. In the middle of the fields
Trevor, W. The hill bachelors
Kentucky
Berry, W. The boundary
Berry, W. A consent
Berry, W. A friend of mine
Berry, W. A half-pint of Old Darling
Berry, W. It wasn't me
Berry, W. The lost bet
Berry, W. Nearly to the fair
Berry, W. The solemn boy
Berry, W. Turn back the bed
Berry, W. Watch with me
Louisiana
Gautreaux, T. Same place, same things

Maine
Wuori, G. K. Family
Massachusetts
Hall, D. The figure of the woods
Michigan
Hall, D. From Willow Temple
Middle Western States
Gass, W. H. The Pedersen kid
Minnesota
Bly, C. The tomcat's wife
Nebraska
Aldrich, B. S. The day of retaliation
Block, R. St. Anthony and the fish
New York (State)
Singer, I. B. The yearning heifer
Traver, R. The big brown trout
North Carolina
Kenan, R. The foundations of the earth
Oregon
Kittredge, W. The van Gogh field
Russia
Chekhov, A. P. The cossack
Scotland
Shon, F. The farmer's wife
Southern States
Grau, S. A. The man outside
Taiwan
Cheng, C.-W. Betel nut town
Tennessee
Warren, R. P. Blackberry winter
Texas
Williams, M. Grazing in good pastures
Vermont
Stegner, L. Hired man
Washington (State)
Melton, F. Counting
Western States
DeMarinis, R. Weeds
Wisconsin
Bukoski, A. Leaves that shimmer in the slightest breeze
Farm wife. Goldner, B.
Farm wife. Kilpatrick, N.
FARM WORKERS
Dumas, H. A boll of roses
Reid, E. Lime
Sánchez, R. The fields
Sánchez, R. Like I was telling you . . .
Troncoso, S. Punching chickens
FARMER, PHILIP JOSÉ
Parodies, imitations, etc.
Steele, A. M. Graceland
Farmer. Holbert, B.
Farmer boy. Nawrocki, S.
The **Farmer** Who Wanted to Be a Jaguar: Mayan. Bruchac, J. and others
FARMERS *See* Farm life
The **farmer's** children. Bishop, E.
The **farmer's** wife. Shon, F.
Farming butterflies. Clyde, M.
FARMWORKERS *See* Farm workers
Farnham, Brian
Midnight trash
Virgin fiction 2
FAROUK I, KING OF EGYPT, 1920-1965
About
Gifford, B. The yellow palace
Farouq *See* Farouk I, King of Egypt, 1920-1965

Farrell, Cliff
Day of the dedication
  The First Five Star western corral; western
    stories; edited by Jon Tuska and Vicki
    Piekarski
The day the outlaws came
  Farrell, C. Desperate journey; edited by R.E.
    Briney
Desperate journey
  Farrell, C. Desperate journey; edited by R.E.
    Briney
Fire in their stacks
  Farrell, C. Desperate journey; edited by R.E.
    Briney
Five aces west
  Farrell, C. Desperate journey; edited by R.E.
    Briney
He knew all about women
  Farrell, C. Desperate journey; edited by R.E.
    Briney
Hung up at Parley's store
  Farrell, C. Desperate journey; edited by R.E.
    Briney
I'm going to California
  Farrell, C. Desperate journey; edited by R.E.
    Briney
The lady was a dude
  Farrell, C. Desperate journey; edited by R.E.
    Briney
The pay-back race
  Farrell, C. Desperate journey; edited by R.E.
    Briney
Picture bride
  Farrell, C. Desperate journey; edited by R.E.
    Briney
River ambush
  Farrell, C. Desperate journey; edited by R.E.
    Briney
The shining mountains
  Farrell, C. Desperate journey; edited by R.E.
    Briney
Thorns for Johnny Spring
  Farrell, C. Desperate journey; edited by R.E.
    Briney
Farrell, James T. (James Thomas)
Twenty-five bucks
  Boxing's best short stories; edited by Paul D.
    Staudohar
Farren, Mick
Again the last plane out?
  Carved in rock; short stories by musicians;
    edited by Greg Kihn
Farrin, Scott
Buffalo Speedway
  South Carolina Review v35 no1 p29-37 Fall
    2002
Faruk See Farouk I, King of Egypt, 1920-1965
Fascination. Boyd, W.
Fascination. O'Dell, C. D.
FASCISM
  See also Communism; Dictators; Nation-
    al socialism; Totalitarianism
FASHION INDUSTRY AND TRADE
Budnitz, J. Scenes from the fall fashion catalog
FASHION MODELS
Dunmore, H. Ice cream
Matthews, C. The moving statue of Ballinspittle
Weldon, F. What the papers say
Fast. Jaffe, H.

The **fast**. Krouse, E.
Fast. Young, T.
Fast coming and then going. DeLancey, K.
Fast glaciers. Morlan, A. R.
Fast love. Malone, M.
Fast Sunday. Standing, S.
Fast times at Fairmont High. Vinge, V.
FASTING
  Singer, I. B. The fast
Fat. Jackson, S.
Fat and thin. Chekhov, A. P.
The **fat** cats' tale. Compton, M. A.
Fat ladies floated in the sky like balloons. Davis,
    A.
The **fat** magician. Wolfe, G.
The **fat** man in history. Carey, P.
Fat Tracy. Amick, S.
Fat Tuesday. Davis, R.
Fat Tuesday. Rudd, K.
Fata morgana across the street. Hendel, Y.
The **fatal** success. Van Dyke, H.
Fatal tears. Nikas, E.
Fatality. Bausch, R.
Fate. Aminoff, J.
Fate. Hoffman, A.
Fate. Shi Tiesheng
FATE AND FATALISM
  Borges, J. L. A biography of Tadeo Isidoro
    Cruz (1829-1874)
  Harvey, W. F. August heat
  James, H. De Grey: a romance
  Morton, L. Pound rots in Fragrant Harbour
  Ramaya, S. Destiny
  Singer, I. B. The fatalist
  Singer, I. B. Fate
  Singer, I. B. There are no coincidences
Fate of a prisoner. Johnson-Davies, D.
The **father**. Babel', I.
The **father**. Pickering, J.
Father Daughter. Harrison, J.
Father! Father! Burning bright. Bennett, A.
Father, grandfather. Robison, M.
The **father** helmet. Derby, M.
Father Judge Run. Brown, C.
Father of the family. See Chekhov, A. P. The
    head of the family
A **father-to-be**. Bellow, S.
Father tongue. Cobb, W. J.
Fatherhood. Biguenet, J.
Fatherhood. Cook, T. H.
Fatherland. Hemon, A.
FATHERS
  See also Fathers and daughters; Fathers
    and sons; Fathers-in-law; Stepfathers
  Baida, P. The rodent
  Brown, J. The naked running boy
  Carlson, R. Blazo
  Dubus, A. The winter father
  Epstein, J. Saturday afternoon at the zoo with
    dad
  Galef, D. The inner child
  Hirshberg, G. The two Sams
  Leslie, N. Bigger than life
  Lipsyte, S. The wrong arm
  Nawrocki, S. Hovercraft
  Nichols, J. The rain barrel
  Ribeyro, J. R. The wardrobe, the old man and
    death
  Richter, S. Goodnight

FATHERS—*Continued*
Shepard, S. A frightening seizure
Stern, R. G. The illegibility of this world
Taraqqi, G. Father
Tawada, Y. Raisin eyes
Weldon, F. A hard time to be a father
Wieland, L. Purgatory
Wolff, T. The night in question
Fathers. Anderson, D.
Fathers. Munro, A.

FATHERS AND DAUGHTERS
See also Fathers and sons; Parent and child
Agee, J. Asparagus
Alcott, L. M. A New Year's blessing
Alderete, P. Victor the Bear
Alexie, S. Indian country
Anderson, D. Fire road
Arvin, N. Take your child to work
Auchincloss, L. The heiress
Auchincloss, L. The scarlet letters
Avrich, J. The braid
Babel´, I. The father
Baida, P. Family ties
Banks, R. Quality time
Barnard, R. Everybody's girl
Barthelme, F. Law of averages
Bass, R. The fireman
Bauman, B. A. The middle of the night
Bauman, B. A. Wash, rinse, spin
Bausch, R. Aren't you happy for me?
Bausch, R. Missy
Bausch, R. Not quite final
Bausch, R. Unjust
Beagle, P. S. My daughter's name is Sarah
Biguenet, J. Lunch with my daughter
Blackwood, S. One flesh, one blood
Blackwood, S. One of us is hidden away
Blumlein, M. Revenge
Bocock, M. The tree
Brady, C. Daley's girls
Brennan, M. The daughters
Brkic, C. A. The daughter
Brockmeier, K. The house at the end of the world
Broughton, T. A. The classicist
Brown, N. K. Burn pile
Broyard, B. At the bottom of the lake
Broyard, B. Mr. Sweetly Indecent
Broyard, B. My father, dancing
Broyard, B. The trouble with Mr. Leopold
Buggé, C. Uncle Evil Eye
Bukoski, A. Pesthouse
Busch, F. Malvasia
Busch, F. The ninth, in E minor
Butler, R. O. Heavy metal
Cai Cehai. The distant sound of tree-felling
Callaghan, M. Ellen
Canty, K. Sleepers holding hands
Caponegro, M. The daughter's lamentation
Carlson, R. The prisoner of Bluestone
Casey, M. Seaworthy
Chabon, M. Green's book
Chang, L. S. The eve of the spirit festival
Chaon, D. Seven types of ambiguity
Chapman, C. M. Rest area
Chekhov, A. P. At a country house
Chekhov, A. P. The requiem
Chenoweth, A. I wish you wouldn't be that way
Chopin, K. Charlie
Clark, J. Oasis
Coates, G. S. Plaster of Paris
Cobb, W. J. Father tongue
Cohen, R. Putting up signs
Collins, B. and Collins, M. A. Eddie Haskell in a short skirt
Colvin, C. The sound of the horn
Connolly, C. The pleasure gardens
Conroy-Goldman, M. The first old
Cooper, B. What to name the baby
Cummins, A. The Shiprock Fair
Davies, P. H. Brave girl
Davies, R. The song of songs
Day, C. Circus People
Dixon, S. The school bus
Dokey, R. Hampstead's folly
Due, T. Trial day
Erian, A. The brutal language of love
Evenson, B. The ex-father
Falco, E. The instruments of peace
Fleming, R. The garden of evil
Flynt, C. Dancing with father
Foley, S. Cloudland
Foster, P. The girl from Soldier Creek
Fowler, K. J. The Elizabeth complex
Freudenberger, N. Outside the Eastern gate
Freudenberger, N. The tutor
Furman, L. The apprentice
Furman, L. Melville's house
Gaitskill, M. Dream of men
Gallagher, S. Doctor Hood
Gasco, E. The spider of Bumba
Gautreaux, T. Resistance
Gay, W. The man who knew Dylan
Gilchrist, E. The brown cape
Gilchrist, E. A Christmas in Wyoming
Gilchrist, E. I, Rhoda Manning, go hunting with my daddy
Gilchrist, E. On the Wind River in Wyoming
Gilliland, G. The Texas Ranger
Gilliland, G. When Amelia smiled
Girardi, R. Arcana mundi
Goldner, B. Cardiff-by-the-Sea
Goliger, G. In this corner
Goliger, G. A man who has brothers
Gordimer, N. L. U. C. I. E.
Gorriti, J. M. The mazorquero's daughter
Grodstein, L. Satellites or airplanes
Guerrero, L. Memories in white
Harrington, J. A letter to Amy
Hawthorne, N. Rappaccini's daughter
Hegi, U. A woman's perfume
Hendel, Y. Low, close to the floor
Hernandez, F. The balcony
Hochman, A. Aggiornamento
Hoffman, N. K. Gone
Hoffman, W. Place
Iribarne, M. The sun in the sky
James, H. The ghostly rental
James, H. Guest's confession
James, H. The marriages
James, H. Professor Fargo
Johnson, A. The Jughead of Berlin
Johnson, L. Backdated
Joseph, D. Approximate to salvation
Joseph, D. Shared and stolen
Kaplan, H. Goodwill
Karnezis, P. A funeral of stones

FATHERS AND DAUGHTERS—*Continued*
Kelly, J. P. Itsy bitsy spider
Kendall, G. In loco parentis
Kennedy, A. L. Looking for the possible dance [excerpt]
Kirchheimer, G. D. Arbitration
Kirchheimer, G. D. Traffic manager
Kirchheimer, G. D. The voyager
Knight, M. Amelia Earhart's coat
Knight, M. Feeling lucky
Knight, M. Mitchell's girls
Kohler, S. Peaches and plums
L'Amour, L. By the waters of San Tadeo
Lavin, M. Tom
Lawson, C. Written in blood
Lincoln, C. Acorn pipes
Locklin, G. Swing shift
Loh, S. T. My father's Chinese wives
López, L. After Dad shot Jesus
Mahmudi, S. The Fin Garden of Kashan
Maleti, G. Adornato and Venus
Maleti, G. The precipice
Mason, B. A. The funeral side
Mason, B. A. Tobrah
Massie, A. In the bare lands
Mastretta, A. Aunt Elena
McCann, C. Everything in this country must
McCorkle, J. Fish
McWhorter, C. T. Silent protest
Mehra, D. The garden
Meloy, M. A stakes horse
Miller, A. L. A cold winter light
Montero, M. That man, Pollack
Müller, H. Rotten pears
Munro, A. Before the change
Munro, A. Fathers
Nair, M. Sixteen days in December
Nawrocki, S. Pressure
Nelson, A. The other daughter
Norris, H. One day in the life of a born again loser
Oates, J. C. The assailant
Oates, J. C. A Manhattan romance
O'Connell, M. Saint Therese of Lisieux
Ortiz, S. J. Distance
Oz, A. Where the jackals howl
Paddock, J. And when I should feel something
Patterson, K. Interposition
Pittalwala, I. Bombay talkies
Pittalwala, I. Trivedi Park
Polansky, S. Sleights
Ponte Landa, M. Blind madness
Potvin, E. A. Assumptions
Pushkin, A. S. The stationmaster
Reed, R. A place with shade
Reifler, N. The splinter
Richmond, M. Intermittent waves of unusual size and force
Richmond, M. Satellite
Ritchie, E. Re-inventing the archives
Row, J. Heaven lake
Rule, R. Walking the trapline
Salaam, K. I. Rosamojo
Sánchez, L. R. Getting even
Schmidt, H. J. Blood poison
Schwartz, L. S. Francesca
Segriff, L. Specters in the moonlight
Sellers, H. Fla. boys
Sholem Aleichem. Hodel

Simonds, M. King of the Cowboys, Queen of the West
Simpson, M. Approximations
Slater, Judy. The glass house
Smart, A. The bridge players
Smart, A. The Green Lantern
Smart, A. Hunter
Smart, A. Jersey Joe versus the Rock
Smart, A. The turtle
Spencer, E. The everlasting light
Stern, D. Messenger
Stolar, D. Marriage lessons
Stollman, A. L. The creation of Anat
Stollman, A. L. The dialogues of time and entropy
Stuckey-French, E. Doodlebug
Swan, G. Sloan's daughter
Tamaro, S. The burning forest
Taylor, T. L. Doves of Townsend
Thien, M. Simple recipes
Thomas, D. Flowers appear on the earth
Thurm, M. Earthbound
Tinti, H. Preservation
Trevor, W. Three people
Troy, M. Mercy the midget
Tuck, L. Horses
Tuck, L. Ouarzazate
Updike, J. Daughter, Last glimpses of
Updike, J. Killing
Updike, J. Man and daughter in the cold
Updike, J. Nevada
Updike, J. Should wizard hit mommy?
Vaughn, S. Able, Baker, Charlie, Dog
Vivante, A. The homing pigeon
Waggoner, T. Picking up Courtney
Warren, D. Michelangelo
Weldon, F. GUP—or, Falling in love in Helsinki
Wells, K. Godlight
Wendling, L. Inappropriate babies
Wexler, M. The closet
Wharton, E. The House of the Dead Hand
Wharton, E. The last asset
What, L. Uncle Gorby and the baggage ghost
White, M. C. Instincts
Wicks, V. I have the serpent brought
Wilson, A. Home, James, and don't spare the horses
Wilson, R., Jr. California
Winegardner, M. The visiting poet
Wolitzer, M. Tea at the house
Yañez, R. Amoroza Tires
Yates, R. A natural girl
Young, T. In bed
Ziegler, I. Blind spot
Ziegler, I. My last deer
Ziegler, I. The treasure hunter's daughter
FATHERS AND SONS
        See also Fathers and daughters; Parent and child
Agee, J. Mystery of numbers
Alameddine, R. A flight to Paris
Aldrich, B. S. The weakling
Alexie, S. Because my father always said he was the only Indian who saw Jimi Hendrix play "The Star-Spangled Banner" at Woodstock
Alexie, S. Do not go gentle
Alexie, S. One good man

FATHERS AND SONS—*Continued*

Alexie, S. This is what it means to say Phoenix, Arizona

Alexie, S. What ever happened to Frank Snake Church?

Alexis, A. Kuala Lumpur

Amichai, Y. My father's deaths

Amis, M. State of England

Anderson, D. Accident

Anderson, D. My name is Stephen Mann

Anderson, D. Weather

Armstrong, K. Drowning in air

Arvin, N. What they teach you in engineering school

Atkinson, K. Sheer big waste of love

Auchincloss, L. All that may become a man

Auchincloss, L. Man of the Renaissance

Babel´, I. The end of the almshouse

Babel´, I. A letter

Babel´, I. Sunset

Bache, E. Shell Island

Baida, P. The reckoning

Bailey, D. Quinn's way

Bailey, T. Snow dreams

Banks, R. The burden

Banks, R. Defenseman

Banks, R. Firewood

Banks, R. The lie

Barnes, H. L. The cat in the cage

Barnes, H. L. A return

Barnes, S. Heartspace

Bart, P. The ghostwriter

Bass, R. Ogallala

Bausch, R. The last day of summer

Bausch, R. Luck

Bausch, R. Police dreams

Beinhart, L. Funny story

Bellow, S. A silver dish

Benedict, P. The Sutton Pie Safe

Bennett, A. Father! Father! Burning bright

Berry, W. Don't send a boy to do a man's work

Berry, W. Fidelity

Berry, W. The solemn boy

Berry, W. Where did they go?

Biguenet, J. It is raining in Bejucal

Bishop, M. Icicle music

Blackwood, S. Prodigal fathers

Blackwood, S. Worry

Blair, J. The grove

Blair, J. Happy puppy

Blair, J. Trash fish

Blaise, C. The bridge

Blaise, C. A North American education

Blaise, C. The salesman's son grows older

Bonnie, F. Screwdriver

Boswell, R. Glissando

Bottoms, G. 1967

Bottoms, G. A stupid story

Bowles, P. The frozen fields

Bowles, P. Pages from Cold Point

Boylan, C. L'amour

Boyle, T. C. Achates McNeil

Boyle, T. C. Going down

Bradbury, R. By the numbers!

Bradbury, R. The completist

Bradbury, R. In memoriam

Bradbury, R. My son, Max

Bradbury, R. The nineteenth

Bradbury, R. The wish

Brandt, W. His father's shoes

Brkic, C. A. Afterdamp

Brkic, C. A. Suspension

Brockmeier, K. Space

Broughton, T. A. Ashes

Brown, J. Afternoon of the Sassanoa

Brown, J. The dog lover

Brown, J. The submariners

Brown, S. With clouds at our feet

Brownstein, G. Musée des Beaux Arts

Bukoski, A. The world at war

Bunin, I. A. Raven

Busch, F. Passengers

Busch, F. The talking cure

Busch, F. Timberline

Cady, J. Daddy dearest

Callaghan, M. The snob

Canin, E. The year of getting to know us

Caponegro, M. The son's burden

Carlson, R. Blood

Carlson, R. The potato gun

Casares, O. Big Jesse, Little Jesse

Casares, O. Chango

Cavell, B. All the nights of the world

Chabon, M. Along the frontage road

Chabon, M. The Harris Fetko story

Chan, D. M. Brilliant disguise

Chaon, D. The bees

Chaon, D. Burn with me

Chaon, D. Prodigal

Chekhov, A. P. At home

Chekhov, A. P. Home

Chekhov, A. P. Oysters

Chenoweth, A. Reunions

Chiappone, R. The chubs

Chiappone, R. Old friend

Chiappone, R. Things come to mind

Chiappone, R. Water of an undetermined depth

Clark, W. L. Quiet game

Clarke, A. Leaving this island place

Coates, G. S. Crickets

Cobb, T. Getting bud

Cohen, R. On the flight path

Cohen, R. Possible future stepmother

Cohen, R. Those kooks

Coleman, J. C. Rodeo

Condé, M. The breadnut and the breadfruit

Conroy, F. Midair

Cook, K. L. Pool boy

Cooper, B. Bit-o-honey

Cooper, B. Old birds

Dann, J. Voices

Davidson, A. Captain Pasharooney

Davies, P. H. Today is Sunday

Deane, J. F. A close encounter

Deane, J. F. The sins of the fathers

DeLancey, K. A hole in the wall of noise

DeLancey, K. I loved the squire

DeLancey, K. It's dark

DeLancey, K. Jules Jr Michael Jules Jr

Delaney, E. J. The drowning

DeMarinis, R. Disneyland

DeMarinis, R. Weeds

Díaz, J. Fiesta 1980

DuBois, B. A family game

Dubus, A. An afternoon with the old man

Ebershoff, D. The bank president

Ebershoff, D. The dress

FATHERS AND SONS—*Continued*

Elkin, S. Criers and kibitzers, kibitzers and criers
Engel, M. P. All that we need
Enright, A. What are cicadas?
Everett, P. L. Cry about a nickel
Farah, N. My father, the Englishman, and I
Farrell, C. The day the outlaws came
Ford, R. Calling
Franklin, T. Dinosaurs
Fromm, P. Doors
Fromm, P. The investigator
Fromm, P. The Thatch weave
Fulton, J. Liars
Fulton, J. Stealing
Gao Xingjian. The accident
Gautreaux, T. Sorry blood
Gay, W. I hate to see that evening sun go down
Gay, W. Those Deep Elm Brown's Ferry Blues
Glave, T. Commitment
Godfrey, D. O. Inland, shoreline
Goldner, B. Checkmate
Goliger, G. Who you are
Gonzalez, R. The Chinese restaurant
Gonzalez, R. Fishing
Gonzalez, R. The grandfather horse
Gordimer, N. Letter from his father
Gores, J. Goodbye, Pops
Gorman, E. Mom and Dad at home
Grau, S. A. The patriarch
Gray, A. Job's skin game
Greenberg, A. Oedipus at Columbus
Gunn, K. The meatyard
Gurganus, A. He's at the office
Gurganus, A. Saint monster
Hall, D. The figure of the woods
Hall, D. The Ideal Bakery
Harrison, W. The rocky hills of Trancas
Harty, R. Why the sky turns red when the sun goes down
Haschemeyer, O. The storekeeper
Haslett, A. My father's business
Haslett, A. Notes to my biographer
Hassler, J. Christopher, Moony, and the birds
Hegi, U. Moonwalkers
Heller, J. Love, Dad
Hemon, A. Fatherland
Hemon, A. The Sorge spy ring
Hickey, D. The closed season
Hoffman, W. Blood
Hoffman, W. Prodigal
Holbrook, C. The idea of it
Howard, C. McCulla's kid
Hribal, C. J. And that's the name of that tune
Hribal, C. J. The last great dream of my father
Huffman, B., Jr. Mutuality of interests
Iribarne, M. The gift
Jackson, V. F. Victoria and Albert I: Running away to sea
Jacobs, M. Down in Paraguay
Jaime-Becerra, M. La fiesta brava
Jamieson, R. A. The last black hoose
Johnson, A. Cliff gods of Acapulco
Johnson, A. Your own backyard
Johnston, B. A. In the tall grass
Johnston, B. A. Two liars
Johnston, T. Irish girl
Joseph, D. Bloodlines
Kaplan, H. Cuckle me

Kaplan, H. From where we've fallen
Katkov, N. Stop the fight!
Kavaler, R. The inheritance
Kay, J. Trumpet [excerpt]
Kelman, J. My eldest
Kennedy, A. L. A little like light
Keret, E. Breaking the pig
Keret, E. The son of the Head of the Mossad
Kirchheimer, G. D. Silver screen
Kittredge, W. The waterfowl tree
Koja, K. Velocity
Kooker, J. Pretend I've died
Koon, D. The bone divers
Kureishi, H. Morning in the bowl of night
Kureishi, H. The umbrella
L'Amour, L. Caprock rancher
L'Amour, L. From the listening hills
Lansdale, J. R. Walks
Lao She. A man who doesn't lie
LaValle, V. D. Pops
Lavin, M. A story with a pattern
Lee, M. Glory
Leonard, E. How Carlos Webster changed his name to Carl and became a famous Oklahoma lawman
Leong, R. Sons
Leslie, N. Projectiles
Lipsyte, S. The Drury girl
Loomis, N. M. The fighting road
Lopez, B. H. The letters of heaven
MacLeod, A. The lost salt gift of blood
Makuck, P. Piecework
Maleti, G. David
Malouf, D. Blacksoil country
Matheson, R. The test
Mazelis, J. The game
Mazor, J. Friend of mankind
McNally, J. The New Year
Meyers, K. Two-speed
Millhauser, S. Behind the blue curtain
Mo Yan. The cure
Monteleone, T. F. Rehearsals
Moriconi, V. Simple arithmetic
Morrell, D. Resurrection
Muñoz, M. By the time you get there, by the time you get back
Muñoz, M. Skyshot
Murray, J. All the rivers in the world
Murray, J. Blue
Murray, J. White flour
Naiyer Masud. Interregnum
Nakagami, K. House on fire
Nesbitt, M. What good is you anyway?
Nguyen, D. T. Peace
Nichols, J. Giant
Nichols, J. Jon-clod
Nordan, L. Tombstone
Oates, J. C. I'm not your son, I am no one you know
Oates, J. C. Questions
Offutt, C. Target practice
Okri, B. In the shadow of war
Oliver, C. The gift
Orner, P. The house on Lunt Avenue
Ortiz, S. J. Feathers
Ortiz, S. J. The way you see horses
Packer, Z. The ant of the self
Parker, M. Commit to memory
Parrish, T. Hardware man

FATHERS AND SONS—*Continued*

Parrish, T. It pours
Patterson, K. The Perseid shower
Perabo, S. Thick as thieves
Perabo, S. Who I was supposed to be
Percy, W. The second coming [excerpt]
Phillips, D. R. At the edge of the new world
Phillips, D. R. What men love for
Phillips, D. R. What we are up against
Phillips, L. In the house of simple sentences
Polansky, S. Acts
Polansky, S. Leg
Porter, J. A. Schrekx and son
Posey, J. R. Ticket to freedom
Price, R. The fare to the moon
Pronzini, B. Chip
Pronzini, B. Epitaph
Pronzini, B. and Malzberg, B. N. On the nature
    of time
Provenzano, J. Quality time
Raphael, F. All his sons
Reisman, N. Sharks
Richter, S. A prodigy of longing
Rifkin, A. After the divorce
Robinson, L. Eiders
Robinson, L. Ride
Roffé, R. Transforming the desert
Rosa, J. G. The third bank of the river
Sagstetter, K. The thing with Willie
Schlink, B. Girl with lizard
Schlink, B. The son
Schrank, B. Consent
Seiffert, R. Dimitroff
Shapiro, G. Bad Jews
Shaw, D. Any myth you can imagine
Shepard, J. Dade County, November 2000
Silva, D. B. Dry whiskey
Singer, I. B. The son
Singleton, G. Fossils
Singleton, G. The ruptures and limits of absence
Singleton, G. Show-and-tell
Slezak, E. By heart
Smolens, J. The errand
Sorrentino, G. Things that have stopped moving
Spatz, G. Lisa picking cockles
Spatz, G. Stone fish
Stern, D. Apraxia
Stolar, D. Fundamentals
Stolar, D. Second son
Stollman, A. L. New memories
Stuckey-French, E. Blessing
Su Tong. Young Muo
Svoboda, T. Leadership
Swan, M. Max-1970
Swarthout, G. F. What every man knows
Tester, W. Floridita
Thurm, M. Ancient history
Tuma, H. The Waldiba story
Turner, R. Eleven o'clock bulletin
Updike, J. The gun shop
Updike, J. The lucid eye in silver town
Updike, J. My father on the verge of disgrace
Updike, J. Son
Valeri, L. Turn these stones into bread
Vasseur, T. J. The windmill of happiness
Volkmer, J. The elevator man
Vonnegut, K. This son of mine

Wallace, D. F. On his deathbed, holding your
    hand, the acclaimed new young off-
    Broadway playwright's father begs a boon
Wallace, D. F. Signifying nothing
Wallace, D. F. The soul is not a smithy
Wallace, R. Talking
Waters, M. Y. Rationing
Watson, I. A day without Dad
Watson, I. Early, in the evening
Waugh, E. Too much tolerance
Wegner, H. The blue line
Weihe, E. All clear
Wharton, E. His father's son
Wharton, E. The young gentlemen
White, E. Cinnamon skin
White, M. C. Marked men
White, M. C. The smell of life
Wieland, L. You can sleep while I drive
Williams, J. The last generation
Wilson, R., Jr. A simple elegy
Wilson, R., Jr. Trespass
Yarbrough, S. Veneer
Yi, T.-H. At the door
Young, T. Kraut
Young, T. Pig on a spit
The **father's** blessing. Caponegro, M.
Father's Day. Schaefer, W. D.
FATHERS-IN-LAW

Bausch, R. Consolation
Dilworth, S. A little learning
Erian, A. Lass
Grau, S. A. Letting go
Ha Jin. The bridegroom
Knight, M. Ellen's book
O'Callaghan, M. An insignificant crime
Simonds, M. Navigating the Kattegat
Singer, I. B. A piece of advice
The **father's** story. Zaimoglu, F.
Fatso. Keret, E.
Faulkner, John
The best laid plans
    The Mississippi Quarterly v54 no4 p465-76
    Fall 2001
England, I give this cigarette
    The Mississippi Quarterly v54 no4 p453-64
    Fall 2001
Treasure hunt
    The Mississippi Quarterly v54 no4 p477-91
    Fall 2001
Untitled prose sketch
    The Mississippi Quarterly v54 no4 p449-52
    Fall 2001
Faulkner, William
All the dead pilots
    On glorious wings; the best flying stories of
    the century; edited and introduced by Ste-
    phen Coonts
An error in chemistry
    The Best American mystery stories of the
    century; Tony Hillerman, editor; with an
    introduction by Tony Hillerman
Lucas Beauchamp
    The Virginia Quarterly Review v75 no3 p417-
    37 Summ 1999
That evening sun go down
    The Best American short stories of the
    century; John Updike, editor, Katrina
    Kenison, coeditor; with an introduction by
    John Updike

Fault lines. DeMarinis, R.
Faulty register. Gores, J.
Fauna in Florida. Loeb, K.
Faust, Christa
    (jt. auth) See Brite, Poppy Z. and Faust, Christa
Faust, Frederick, 1892-1944
    See also Brand, Max, 1892-1944
Faust, Irvin
    B-17
        The Literary Review (Madison, N.J.) v46 no3
        p537-55 Spr 2003
    Starring Nohj Anyew
        The Literary Review (Madison, N.J.) v44 no3
        p548-67 Spr 2001
The **favor**. Paul, B.
Favorite son. Haseloff, C. H.
Favors. Adams, A.
Fawcett, Brian
    Soul walker
        The Vintage book of amnesia; an anthology;
        edited by Jonathan Lethem
Fayer, Steve
    The Vision of Mr. Brand
        The North American Review v288 no5 p10-20
        S/O 2003
Faygenberg, Rochel
    My first readers
        Beautiful as the moon, radiant as the stars;
        Jewish women in Yiddish stories : an an-
        thology; edited by Sandra Bark; introduc-
        tion by Francine Prose
FBI *See* United States. Federal Bureau of Investi-
    gation
FEAR
    Adams, A. Alaska
    Allen, S. Keep looking
    Bear, G. The fall of the house of Escher
    Bowles, P. He of the assembly
    Bradbury, R. The whole town's sleeping
    Bradbury, R. The wind
    Chopin, K. Beyond the Bayou
    Drake, R. The devil, lightning, and policemen
    Eldridge, Courtney. Sharks
    Faulkner, W. That evening sun go down
    Irsfeld, J. H. The man who watched airplanes
    Jackson, S. The bus
    Krouse, E. Too big to float
    Lebbon, T. White
    Lundquist, R. Silence and slow time
    Mayo, W. Mary Magdalena versus Godzilla
    McKiernan, D. L. Darkness
    Michaels, L. Going places
    Naiyer Masud. Ba'i's mourners
    Nesbitt, M. Quality fuel for electric living
    Oates, J. C. First views of the enemy
    Oates, J. C. The mutants
    Pickard, N. Afraid all the time
    Pickard, N. The dead past
    Pronzini, B. Under the skin
    Schwartz, L. S. Intrusions
    Spencer, E. The weekend travelers
    Tester, W. Where the dark ended
    Tinti, H. Preservation
    Vivante, A. The foghorn
    Weinberg, R. Endure the night
    Wharton, E. All Souls'
    Willis, M. S. Attack
    Zweig, S. Fear
Fear. Halvoník, A.

Fear. Pronzini, B.
Fear. Zweig, S.
Fear in the saddle. DeRosso, H. A.
A **Fear** of Falling. Jablonsky, W.
The **feast**. Varon, P.
Feast of Lights. Kirchheimer, G. D.
Feathers. Ortiz, S. J.
Feathers on the solar wind. Wood, D.
Feathertop. Hawthorne, N.
Feathertop: a moralized legend. Hawthorne, N.
Febres, Mayra Santos- *See* Santos-Febres, Mayra,
    1966-
February 14. Berkman, P. R.
February, cycle of the werewolf. King, S.
FEDERAL BUREAU OF INVESTIGATION
    (U.S.) *See* United States. Federal Bureau of
    Investigation
Fedka. Baron, D.
Fedora. Chopin, K.
Feed the City. Hubbard, J. R.
The **feed** zone. McManus, J.
Feedback. Vardeman, R. E.
Feeders and eaters. Gaiman, N.
Feeding the piranha. Painter, P.
Feel the pain. Bracken, M.
Feel the zaz. Kelly, J. P.
Feeley, Gregory
    The crab lice
        Nebula awards 33; the year's best SF and
        fantasy chosen by the science-fiction and
        fantasy writers of America; edited by
        Connie Willis
Feeling at home with the Hennebet. Le Guin, U.
    K.
Feeling good, feeling fine. Garrett, G. P.
Feeling Lucky. Knight, M.
Feeling old. Ortiz, S. J.
Feet. DeMarinis, R.
The **Feigenbaum** Foundation. Shapiro, G.
Feis. Lee, W. W.
Feist, Raymond E.
    The messenger
        Silverberg, R. Legends II; new short novels
        by the masters of modern fantasy; edited
        by Robert Silverberg
    One to go
        Thieve's world: turning points; edited by
        Lynn Abbey
Feitell, Merrill
    Bike New York!
        Best new American voices 2000; guest editor
        Tobias Wolff; series editors John Kulka
        and Natalie Danford
    It Couldn't Be More Beautiful
        The Virginia Quarterly Review v80 no3 p40-
        53 Summ 2004
Felipa. Woolson, C. F.
Feliu-Pettet, Rosebud
    A Day in the Country
        Hanging Loose no83 p23-5 2003
    Stevie
        Hanging Loose no83 p20-2 2003
Felix emeritus. Epstein, J.
Feliz Navidad. Matiella, A. C.
Fell, Alison
    There's tradition for you
        The Vintage book of contemporary Scottish
        fiction; edited and with an introduction by
        Peter Kravitz

A **fellow** making himself up. Driskell, L. V.

The **fellowship**. Stern, D.

The **fellowsip** at Wysong's Clearing. Coberly, L. M.

Felsenfeld, Judith

Her Lover

Chicago Review v48 no4 p63-4 Wint 2002/2003

Shayna Kupp

Southwest Review v87 no4 p528-37 2002

Felthousen, Robert Arthur

Questionnaire

The North American Review v289 no3/4 p20-4 My/Ag 2004

Feltrin-Morris, Marella

(jt. auth) See Benni, Stefano

Female trouble. Nelson, A.

Feminine mystique. Škvorecký, J.

FEMINISM

Carl, L. S. A rose with all its thorns

Carter, E. The bride

Cody, L. Queen of mean

Fowler, K. J. What I didn't see

Gilman, C. P. Benigna Machiavelli

Gilman, C. P. Herland

Gilman, C. P. Moving the mountain

Gilman, C. P. With her in Ourland

Gilman, C. P. The yellow wallpaper

Sussex, L. My lady tongue

Walker, A. Conscious birth

Willis, C. Even the queen

The **fence**. Hart, R.

The **fence**. Overholser, W. D.

FENCING

Moon, E. Silver lining

Feng, Chi-ts'ai *See* Feng Jicai

Feng Jicai

The tall woman and her short husband

The Vintage book of contemporary Chinese fiction; edited by Carolyn Choa and David Su Li-qun

Fenian ram. Clark, S.

Fennelly, Beth Ann and Franklin, Tom

The saint of broken objects

The Southern Review (Baton Rouge, La.) v38 no3 p570-1 Summ 2002

FERAL CHILDREN *See* Wild children

Ferber, Edna

A bush league hero

Dead balls and double curves; an anthology of early baseball fiction; edited and with an introduction by Trey Strecker ; with a foreword by Arnold Hano

Ferch, Kathleen M. Massie- *See* Massie-Ferch, Kathleen M., 1954-2002

The **Ferdinand** Magellan. Snyder, W., Jr.

Fergus O'Hara, detective. Pronzini, B.

Ferguson, David

(jt. auth) See Brite, Poppy Z. and Ferguson, David

Ferko, Andrej

Intra muros populis

In search of homo sapiens; twenty-five contemporary Slovak short stories; editor, Pavol Hudík ; [translated by Heather Trebatická; American English editor, Lucy Bednár]

Fernandez, Pablo Armando

The charm

Dream with no name; contemporary fiction from Cuba; edited by Juana Ponce de León and Esteban Ríos Rivera

Fernández, Roberto G.

Is in the stars (for Lisa Photos)

Callaloo v24 no1 p64-6 Wint 2001

Ferré, Rosario

A poisoned tale

Short stories by Latin American women; the magic and the real; edited by Celia Correas de Zapata; foreword by Isabel Allende

When women love men

The Oxford book of Caribbean short stories; edited by Stewart Brown and John Wickham

Ferreira, Ramón

Dream with no name

Dream with no name; contemporary fiction from Cuba; edited by Juana Ponce de León and Esteban Ríos Rivera

Ferrell, Carolyn

Proper library

The Best American short stories of the century; John Updike, editor, Katrina Kenison, coeditor; with an introduction by John Updike

Breaking into print; early stories and insights into getting published; a Ploughshares anthology; edited by DeWitt Henry

Truth or consequences

The Bluelight corner; black women writing on passion, sex, and romantic love; edited by Rosemarie Robotham

Wonderful teen

The African American West; a century of short stories; edited by Bruce A. Glasrud and Laurie Champion

FERRETS

Saki. Sredni Vashtar

FERRIES

Chalker, J. L. Dance band on the Titanic

Chekhov, A. P. Easter eve

Cheng, C.-W. The river suite

Ferris, Joshua

Mrs. Blue

Iowa Review v29 no2 p34-46 Fall 1999

Ferriss, Lucy

Bones

Ferriss, L. Leaving the neighborhood and other stories

The difficulty of translation

Michigan Quarterly Review v40 no3 p518-30 Summ 2001

Husband material

Ferriss, L. Leaving the neighborhood and other stories

Leaving the neighborhood

Ferriss, L. Leaving the neighborhood and other stories

Mud time

Ferriss, L. Leaving the neighborhood and other stories

Over the Cliff

The Georgia Review v58 no1 p63-70 Spr 2004

Ferriss, Lucy—*Continued*
  Politics
    Ferriss, L. Leaving the neighborhood and other stories
  Purring
    Ferriss, L. Leaving the neighborhood and other stories
  Rumpelstiltskin
    Ferriss, L. Leaving the neighborhood and other stories
  Safe-T-Man
    Ferriss, L. Leaving the neighborhood and other stories
  Stampede
    Ferriss, L. Leaving the neighborhood and other stories
  Time-share
    Ferriss, L. Leaving the neighborhood and other stories
  The vortex
    Ferriss, L. Leaving the neighborhood and other stories
  The woman who said no
    Ferriss, L. Leaving the neighborhood and other stories
Ferry from Kabatas. Meredith, D.
Ferryman. Watson, I.
Fesler, Pamela J.
  Coin of the realm
    Mom, apple pie, and murder; edited by Nancy Pickard
Fessel, Karen-Susan
  Lost faces
    The Vintage book of international lesbian fiction; edited and with an introduction by Naomi Holoch and Joan Nestle
FESTIVALS
  DeMarco, T. The rose festival boxed lunch
  Hawthorne, N. The Maypole of Merry Mount
  VanderMeer, J. The Festival of the Freshwater Squid
Fetch. Cannell, D.
FETUS
        See also Pregnancy
  Jackson, S. Foetus
  Sarrantonio, A. Billy the fetus
  Singleton, G. Outlaw head and tail
Feud of the maids. Ziegler, I.
FEUDS
  Fitzgerald, F. S. Jemina, the mountain girl
  Hegi, U. A town like ours
  MacLeod, A. Vision
  Offutt, C. Melungeons
  Weinstein, L. The Llipkin -Wexler affair
Fever, Buck *See* Anderson, Sherwood, 1876-1941
FEVER
  Bottoms, G. Nostalgia for ghosts
  DeLancey, K. Washed
Fever. McKinley, J. C.
Fever. Wideman, J. E.
The **fevers**. Eckhardt, C. F.
A **few** short notes on tropical butterflies. Murray, J.
Fewer scruples. Marías, J.
FEYNMAN, RICHARD PHILLIPS, 1918-1988
                  About
  Rucker, R. v. B. Instability
Fialta. Lee, R.
Fictions. Morse, S.

FICTITIOUS ANIMALS *See* Mythical animals
Fiddle case. Coleman, J. C.
Fiddler on the roof. Morris, M. V.
FIDDLERS *See* Violinists
Fidon's confetion. Waugh, E.
Field, Eugene
  The werewolf
    The Literary werewolf; an anthology; edited by Charlotte F. Otten
Field observations. Davidson, R.
Field Study. Seiffert, R.
Fielding, Helen
  Luckybitch
    Speaking with the angel; original stories; edited by Nick Hornby
Fields. Giono, J.
The **fields**. Sánchez, R.
The **fields** beyond the fields. De Lint, C.
The **fields** of Abraham. Wilson, R. C.
Fields of purple forever. Jones, T.
Fiesta 1980. Díaz, J.
The **fifth** box. Hall, D.
Fifth grade: a criminal history. Richmond, M.
The **fifth** Mrs. Hughes. Joseph, D.
Fifty Chinese. Hensley, J. L.
The **fifty-seventh** Franz Kafka. Rucker, R. v. B.
Fifty uselessnesses. Fischer, T.
Fifty winters. Bonnie, F.
Fig. Williams, S. P.
The **fight**. Hay, E.
The **fight** in the hallway. McNulty, J.
Fighter's fiasco. L'Amour, L.
Fighters should be hungry. L'Amour, L.
Fightin in Philly. Toole, F. X.
FIGHTING, COCK *See* Cockfighting
FIGHTING, HAND-TO-HAND *See* Hand-to-hand fighting
Fighting at night. Robinson, L.
The **fighting** road. Loomis, N. M.
The **figure** of the woods. Hall, D.
FIGURINES *See* Art objects
FIJI
  Davenport, K. Fork used in eating Reverend Baker
FIJI ISLANDS *See* Fiji
Filatov, Nikita
  The Bloodthirsty Witness (A mediocre variation on a hackneyed theme)
    World Literature Today v78 no1 p64-6 Ja/Ap 2004
Filer, Tomás
  Mr. Schoenberg, the 12-tone scale, Marlene, Tarzan and me
    American short fiction, vol. 8, no 29-32
Files, Gemma
  The Emperor's Old Bones
    Best new horror 11; edited and with an introduction by Stephen Jones
    The Year's best fantasy & horror, thirteenth annual collection; edited by Ellen Datlow and Terri Windling
A **filet** of soul. Cooper, J. C.
FILICIDE
  Bukiet, M. J. Filophilia
Filipak, Christine and Vargo, Joseph
  Vampire's kiss
    Tales from The Dark Tower; illustrated by Joseph Vargo; edited by Joseph Vargo and Christine Filipak

FILIPINOS
United States
Simpson, M. Coins
Filophilia. Bukiet, M. J.
Filthy cruel world. Škvorecký, J.
Fin de semestre. Locklin, G.
The **Fin** Garden of Kashan. Mahmudi, S.
Final acquittal. Wellen, E.
Final Concert. Cottle, T. J.
Final encounter. Harrison, H.
The **final** inning. Glave, T.
Final judgment. Peri Rossi, C.
A **final** midrash. Fliegel, R.
Final payment. Berry, M. S.
A **final** reunion. Shade, E.
The **Final** Solution. Chabon, M.
Final spells of vertigo in the vestibule. Arandi, F. P.
Final spring. Barton, M.
The **final** toast. Kaminsky, S. M.
Finally fruit. Vukcevich, R.
FINANCE
>*See also* Banks; Taxation
Paine, T. A predictable nightmare on the eve of the stock market first breaking 6,000
FINANCIERS *See* Capitalists and financiers
Finch, Paul
>The mystery of the hanged man's puzzle
>>Shadows over Baker Street; edited by Michael Reaves and John Pelan
Finch, Sheila
>Reading the bones
>>Nebula awards showcase 2000; the year's best SF and fantasy chosen by the science fiction and fantasy writers of america; edited by Gregory Benford
Finch. Levin, A.
Finches. Robinson, L.
Find and replace. Beattie, A.
Find me a dream. Vonnegut, K.
The **finder**. Spencer, E.
Finding my faith. Trollope, J.
The **finding** of the Graiken. Hodgson, W. H.
The **fine** art of watching. Steele, A. M.
A **fine** white dust. Pritchett, L.
Finger, Anne
>Gloucester
>>*The Southern Review (Baton Rouge, La.)* v35 no2 p280-94 Spr 1999
>Goliath's Story
>>*The Southern Review (Baton Rouge, La.)* v40 no1 p102-16 Wint 2004
The **finger**. Vukcevich, R.
FINGERS
Parker, G. Well well well
Finishing school. Wilder, C.
Fink, Ida
>The death of Tsaritsa
>>When night fell; an anthology of Holocaust short stories; edited by Linda Schermer Raphael and Marc Lee Raphael
Finkelstein, Mark Harris *See* Harris, Mark, 1922-
FINLAND
Helsinki
Weldon, F. GUP—or, Falling in love in Helsinki

Finlay, Charles Coleman
>The political officer
>>The Year's best science fiction; twentieth annual collection; edited by Gardner Dozois
>We come not to praise Washington
>>One lamp; alternate history stories from The magazine of Fantasy & Science Fiction; edited by Gordon van Gelder
Finn, Patrick Michael
>Where Beautiful Ladies Dance for You
>>*Ploughshares* v29 no4 p38-58 Wint 2003/2004
Finney, Jack
>The coin collector
>>The American fantasy tradition; edited by Brian M. Thomsen
FINNS
Germany
Koskinen, M. Dies Irae
Fintushel, Eliot
>Franis
>>*The Ohio Review* no60 p27-42 1999
>Milo and Sylvie
>>The Year's best science fiction, eighteenth annual collection; edited by Gardner Dozois
>White man's trick
>>Mojo: conjure stories; edited by Nalo Hopkinson
Fiorani, Sílvio
>The taste of revenge
>>*Prairie Schooner* v73 no1 p137-39 Spr 1999
>To remember is to relive
>>*Prairie Schooner* v73 no1 p140-42 Spr 1999
Fioravanti, Valerie
>Garbage Night at the Opera
>>*The North American Review* v287 no6 p13-17 N/D 2002
Fiorello. Pennee, R.
Fioretos, Aris
>Release from Russia
>>*The Antioch Review* v60 no3 p396-408 Summ 2002
Firan, Carmen
>A Trio for Inferno
>>*The Literary Review (Madison, N.J.)* v46 no2 p249-55 Wint 2003
Fire. Alderete, P.
Fire. Hart, R.
The **fire**. Hay, E.
Fire. Moss, R.
Fire. Oates, J. C.
Fire. Wuori, G. K.
Fire and Sand. Halaby, L.
Fire dreams. Thompson, J.
Fire in the hole. Leonard, E.
Fire in their stacks. Farrell, C.
FIRE ISLAND (N.Y.)
Holleran, A. In September, the light changes
Holleran, A. Petunias
Fire Patrol. House, T.
Fire road. Anderson, D.
Fire works. Lascaux, P.
FIREARMS
Agee, J. The gun
Archer, J. The expert witness
Aylett, S. The Siri gun
Brite, P. Z. and Faust, C. Saved
Cross, A. The double-barreled gun
DeMarinis, R. The handgun

FIREARMS—*Continued*

DeMarinis, R. Hormone X

Franklin, T. Blue horses

Greer, R. O. Grief

Haschemeyer, O. The storekeeper

Healy, J. F. The safest little town in Texas

Le May, A. The loan of a gun

Lieu, J. Safety

Lombreglia, R. Cashmere Christmas

Lundquist, R. Into this house

Martin, V. The creator has a master plan

Norris, L. Toy guns

Oates, J. C. Gunlove

Piper, H. B. Gunpowder god

Robinson, P. The wrong hands

Shepard, S. An unfair question

Simonds, M. King of the Cowboys, Queen of the West

Smart, A. Raccoon

Updike, J. The gun shop

Van Vogt, A. E. The weapon shop

Ziegler, I. My last deer

The **Firebird**. Hodges, E. L.

". . . Fired by the hand of Robert Ford". Henry, W.

FIREFIGHTERS

Bass, R. The fireman

Bausch, R. The fireman's wife

Billman, J. Ash

Billman, J. Custer complex

Giles, M. Two words

Lansdale, J. R. Fire dog

Thompson, J. Fire dreams

The **firefly** tree. Williamson, J.

The **fireman**. Bass, R.

Fireman. Vachss, A. H.

FIRES

See also Arson; Disasters

Arredondo, I. Subterranean river

Bisson, T. Bears discover fire

Bisson, T. First fire

Brown, N. K. Burn pile

Cady, J. Jeremiah

Chesnutt, C. W. How he met her

Clark, J. Public burning

Dybek, S. Paper lantern

Ferriss, L. Purring

Gomes, M. T. Cordelia

Haake, K. The land of sculpture

Hardy, M. The heifer

Hawthorne, N. The Devil in manuscript

Johnson, D. Train dreams

Lindskold, J. M. It must burn

Mazelis, J. On the edge

McKay, K. Pie Row Joe

Murakami, H. Landscape with flatiron

Oates, J. C. Fire

Painter, P. The house that burned

Reisman, N. House fires

Rendell, R. Burning end

Richard, M. Strays

Schirmer, R. Burning

Schmidt, H. J. An early death

Singer, I. B. Henne fire

Tillman, L. Madame Realism's torch song

Troncoso, S. A rock trying to be a stone

Fires of Dreams. Kübler, R.

The **fires** of her vengeance. Shwartz, S.

The **fires** within. Clarke, A. C.

The **firestorm**. Lugones, L.

Firewater. Tenn, W.

Fireweed. Rowell, C.

Firewood. Banks, R.

FIREWORKS

Brennan, M. In and out of never-never land

Casares, O. Mr. Z

First. Derby, M.

The **first** annual performance art festival at the Slaughter Rock Battlefield. Disch, T. M.

First, body. Thon, M. R.

First, catch your demon. Joyce, G.

First child. Spencer, E.

The **first** Christmas. Sneve, V. D. H.

First contact. Jenkins, W. F.

First Contact Inc. Czerneda, J.

First dark. Spencer, E.

First dawning. Easton, R. O.

The **first** day. Baron, D.

First day. Bradbury, R.

The **first** day. Jones, E. P.

First day. McBrearty, R. G.

First day she'd never see. Shepard, J.

First fire. Bisson, T.

First Four Measures. Bellows, N.

First Hair. Sherman, S.

First horse. Coldsmith, D.

First in flight. Hunt, S.

First lead gasser. Hillerman, T.

First light. Barron, K. L.

First love. Babel´, I.

First love. Tozzi, F.

First love. Vasseur, T. J.

First marriage. Silber, J.

The **first** men. Richter, S.

The **first** motion of love. Armstrong, K.

The **first** obligation. Agee, J.

The **first** of your last chances. McNally, J.

First offense. Hunter, E.

The **first** old. Conroy-Goldman, M.

The **first** one to blink. Haywood, G. A.

The **first** paper girl in Red Oak, Iowa. Stuckey-French, E.

The **First** Punch. McGregor, J.

First sale. Kane, J. F.

First sex. Fulton, J.

First Snow. Groves, D. R.

First snow. Rothbart, D.

First snow on Fuji. Kawabata, Y.

The **first** story. Buchbinder, J.

First surmise. Johnson, G.

The **first** thin man. Hammett, D.

First Tuesday. Reed, R.

First views of the enemy. Oates, J. C.

The **First** Wedding. Schwartz, H.

The **first** woman. Hall, D.

Firth, Colin

The Department of Nothing

Speaking with the angel; original stories; edited by Nick Hornby

Fischer, Tibor

Bookcruncher

Fischer, T. I like being killed; stories

Fifty uselessnesses

Fischer, T. I like being killed; stories

I like being killed

Fischer, T. I like being killed; stories

Ice tonight in the hearts of young visitors

Fischer, T. I like being killed; stories

Fischer, Tibor—*Continued*
Portrait of the artist as a foaming deathmonger
    Fischer, T. I like being killed; stories
Then they say you're drunk
    Fischer, T. I like being killed; stories
We ate the chef
    Fischer, T. I like being killed; stories
Fischerová, Daniela
Boarskin dances down the tables
    Fischerová, D. Fingers pointing somewhere
    else; stories; translated from the Czech by
    Neil Bermel
Dhum
    Fischerová, D. Fingers pointing somewhere
    else; stories; translated from the Czech by
    Neil Bermel
Far and near
    Fischerová, D. Fingers pointing somewhere
    else; stories; translated from the Czech by
    Neil Bermel
A letter for President Eisenhower
    Fischerová, D. Fingers pointing somewhere
    else; stories; translated from the Czech by
    Neil Bermel
My conversations with Aunt Marie
    Fischerová, D. Fingers pointing somewhere
    else; stories; translated from the Czech by
    Neil Bermel
The thirty-sixth chicken of Master Wu
    Fischerová, D. Fingers pointing somewhere
    else; stories; translated from the Czech by
    Neil Bermel
Two revolts in one family
    Fischerová, D. Fingers pointing somewhere
    else; stories; translated from the Czech by
    Neil Bermel
Fiscus, Jim
A very special relativity
    Greenberg, M. H. Faerie tales
Fish, Robert L.
The wager
    The Best American mystery stories of the
    century; Tony Hillerman, editor; with an
    introduction by Tony Hillerman
The **fish**. Banks, R.
The **fish**. Chekhov, A. P.
Fish. McCorkle, J.
Fish. Schulze, I.
Fish story. Golden, K.
Fish Story. Moody, R.
A **fish** story. Wolfe, G.
Fish tales. Abrams, T.
Fisher, Clay, 1912-1991
    For works by this author under other
    names see Henry, Will, 1912-1991
FISHER, KING, 1854-1884
        About
Froh, R. I killed King Fisher
Fisher, Lou
A kiss and no goodbye
    New Letters v67 no2 p117-32 2001
The **fisher**. Bartos, E.
The **fisherman**. Banks, R.
Fisherman. Hopkinson, N.
The **fisherman** and his wife. Grimm, J. and
    Grimm, W.
The **fisherman** who got away. Williams, T.
A **fisherman's** family. Cheng, C.-W.
Fisherman's terrace. Vivante, A.

FISHERMEN
    See also Fishing
Carlson, R. At the Jim Bridger
Cheng, C.-W. A fisherman's family
Delany, S. R. Dog in a fisherman's net
Frym, G. Distance no object
Grimm, J. and Grimm, W. The fisherman and
    his wife
Hagy, A. C. North of Fear, south of Kill Devil
Hagy, A. C. Sharking
Jacobsen, R. Encounter
Koon, D. The bone divers
Lord, N. What was washing around out there
MacLeod, A. The lost salt gift of blood
Parker, M. Off island
Porter, J. A. Naufrage and diapason
Pronzini, B. Smuggler's island
Proulx, A. The wer-trout
Renwick, J. The dolphin story
Senior, O. Mad Fish
Shacochis, B. Mundo's sign
FISHES
Banks, R. The fish
Hogan, L. Amen
Lumley, B. Beneath the moors
Pettigrew, D. K. Atasdi: fish story
Swain, H. Sushi
Vukcevich, R. Message in a fish
FISHING
    See also Fishermen; Salmon fishing
Abrams, T. Fish tales
Adam, C. Nightcrawler
Banks, R. The fisherman
Blair, J. Trash fish
Blaise, C. A fish like a buzzard
Block, L. Sometimes they bite
Bonner, P. H. John Monahan
Burton, M. Bed & breakfast
Burton, M. Blood knots
Burton, M. Casting blind
Burton, M. The compleat adventures of Brooke
    E. Trout
Burton, M. Degree days
Burton, M. The facts
Burton, M. Geoffrey's wife
Burton, M. Green River virgins
Burton, M. A guide's advice
Burton, M. Home water
Burton, M. In search of the holy grayling
Burton, M. Messing with the river gods
Burton, M. On a fly
Burton, M. On becoming a fly-fishing artiste
Burton, M. Quitting
Burton, M. Reading the water
Burton, M. Richard said that
Burton, M. Timing the strike
Burton, M. Why fly fishing ain't my cup a tea
Chekhov, A. P. The burbot
Chekhov, A. P. A daughter of albion
Chekhov, A. P. The fish
Chiappone, R. The chubs
Chiappone, R. Q Roo
Collins, N. A. Catfish gal blues
Davidson, L. Indian rope trick
Delany, S. R. Driftglass
Doerr, A. July fourth
Doerr, A. So many chances
Doerr, A. A tangle by the rapid river
Dokey, R. Pale morning dun

FISHING—*Continued*

Dokey, R. The suicide
Dufresne, F. The Kelly rainbow
Erickson, Ben. Floundering
Foote, J. T. A wedding gift
Gibson, W. The girl at Thorp's
Gilchrist, J. Opening day
Gonzalez, R. Fishing
Hackle, S. G. Murder
Hall, D. The figure of the woods
Jenkins, G. The big cheese
Lansdale, J. R. Old Charlie
Lucas, J. Old Croc
MacLeod, A. The boat
MacLeod, A. The road to Rankin's Point
MacLeod, A. Vision
Maupassant, G. d. A fishing excursion
McGuane, T. Skelton's party
Nichols, J. Orion
Norman, G. Cowboys
O'Rourke, P. J. Fly-fishing
Parker, G. Carp fishing on valium
Pertwee, R. The river god
Peterson, E. L. The Parmachene Belle
Ransom, E. Fishing's just luck
Rash, R. Speckled trout
Ribeiro, E. T. The turn in the river
Shacochis, B. Squirrelly's grouper
Singleton, G. How to collect fishing lures
Stone, W. The big buffalo bass
Traver, R. The big brown trout
Traver, R. The intruder
Van Dyke, H. The fatal success
Westmoreland, T. A. Blood knot
Williams, T. The fisherman who got away
Wylie, P. Light tackle
Wylie, P. Spare the rod
Zelazny, R. The doors of his face, the lamps of
   his mouth
Fishing. Gonzalez, R.
The **fishing** dog. Campbell, B. J.
A **fishing** excursion. Maupassant, G. d.
The **fishing** lake. Spencer, E.
Fishing the sloe-black river. McCann, C.
Fishing's just luck. Ransom, E.
Fishman's fascination. Schmidt, H. J.
The **fit**. See Chekhov, A. P. A nervous breakdown
Fit mother. Davies, P. H.
Fitch, Brian
Gilpin Street
   The North American Review v288 no3/4
   p22-7 My/Ag 2003
Yankee Doodle dandy
   The North American Review v286 no3/4
   p20-5 My/Ag 2001
Fitzgerald, Captain Hugh *See* Baum, L. Frank
   (Lyman Frank), 1856-1919
Fitzgerald, F. Scott (Francis Scott)
Babes in the woods
   Fitzgerald, F. S. Before Gatsby; the first
   twenty-six stories; edited by Matthew J.
   Bruccoli with the assistance of Judith S.
   Baughman
Benediction
   Fitzgerald, F. S. Before Gatsby; the first
   twenty-six stories; edited by Matthew J.
   Bruccoli with the assistance of Judith S.
   Baughman

Bernice bobs her hair
   Fitzgerald, F. S. Before Gatsby; the first
   twenty-six stories; edited by Matthew J.
   Bruccoli with the assistance of Judith S.
   Baughman
The camel's back
   Fitzgerald, F. S. Before Gatsby; the first
   twenty-six stories; edited by Matthew J.
   Bruccoli with the assistance of Judith S.
   Baughman
Crazy Sunday
   The Best American short stories of the
   century; John Updike, editor, Katrina
   Kenison, coeditor; with an introduction by
   John Updike
The curious case of Benjamin Button
   Fitzgerald, F. S. Before Gatsby; the first
   twenty-six stories; edited by Matthew J.
   Bruccoli with the assistance of Judith S.
   Baughman
The cut-glass bowl
   Fitzgerald, F. S. Before Gatsby; the first
   twenty-six stories; edited by Matthew J.
   Bruccoli with the assistance of Judith S.
   Baughman
Dalyrimple goes wrong
   Fitzgerald, F. S. Before Gatsby; the first
   twenty-six stories; edited by Matthew J.
   Bruccoli with the assistance of Judith S.
   Baughman
The diamond as big as the Ritz
   Fitzgerald, F. S. Before Gatsby; the first
   twenty-six stories; edited by Matthew J.
   Bruccoli with the assistance of Judith S.
   Baughman
The four fists
   Fitzgerald, F. S. Before Gatsby; the first
   twenty-six stories; edited by Matthew J.
   Bruccoli with the assistance of Judith S.
   Baughman
Head and shoulders
   Fitzgerald, F. S. Before Gatsby; the first
   twenty-six stories; edited by Matthew J.
   Bruccoli with the assistance of Judith S.
   Baughman
His russet witch
   Fitzgerald, F. S. Before Gatsby; the first
   twenty-six stories; edited by Matthew J.
   Bruccoli with the assistance of Judith S.
   Baughman
The ice palace
   Fitzgerald, F. S. Before Gatsby; the first
   twenty-six stories; edited by Matthew J.
   Bruccoli with the assistance of Judith S.
   Baughman
The jelly-bean
   Fitzgerald, F. S. Before Gatsby; the first
   twenty-six stories; edited by Matthew J.
   Bruccoli with the assistance of Judith S.
   Baughman
Jemina, the mountain girl
   Fitzgerald, F. S. Before Gatsby; the first
   twenty-six stories; edited by Matthew J.
   Bruccoli with the assistance of Judith S.
   Baughman

Fitzgerald, F. Scott (Francis Scott)—*Continued*
The lees of happiness
    Fitzgerald, F. S. Before Gatsby; the first twenty-six stories; edited by Matthew J. Bruccoli with the assistance of Judith S. Baughman
May Day
    Fitzgerald, F. S. Before Gatsby; the first twenty-six stories; edited by Matthew J. Bruccoli with the assistance of Judith S. Baughman
Myra meets his family
    Fitzgerald, F. S. Before Gatsby; the first twenty-six stories; edited by Matthew J. Bruccoli with the assistance of Judith S. Baughman
The offshore pirate
    Fitzgerald, F. S. Before Gatsby; the first twenty-six stories; edited by Matthew J. Bruccoli with the assistance of Judith S. Baughman
The popular girl
    Fitzgerald, F. S. Before Gatsby; the first twenty-six stories; edited by Matthew J. Bruccoli with the assistance of Judith S. Baughman
The smilers
    Fitzgerald, F. S. Before Gatsby; the first twenty-six stories; edited by Matthew J. Bruccoli with the assistance of Judith S. Baughman
Tarquin of cheapside
    Fitzgerald, F. S. Before Gatsby; the first twenty-six stories; edited by Matthew J. Bruccoli with the assistance of Judith S. Baughman
Two for a cent
    Fitzgerald, F. S. Before Gatsby; the first twenty-six stories; edited by Matthew J. Bruccoli with the assistance of Judith S. Baughman
Winter dreams
    Fitzgerald, F. S. Before Gatsby; the first twenty-six stories; edited by Matthew J. Bruccoli with the assistance of Judith S. Baughman
The World's Fair
    The Best of The Kenyon review; edited by David Lynn; introduction by Joyce Carol Oates

FITZGERALD, F. SCOTT (FRANCIS SCOTT), 1896-1940
          About
Bradbury, R. The Mafioso cement-mixing machine
Smith, A. The universal story
        Parodies, imitations, etc.
Irsfeld, J. H. Interview with Jordan Baker
Fitzgerald, Francis Scott *See* Fitzgerald, F. Scott (Francis Scott), 1896-1940
Fitzgerald, Penelope
At Hiruharama
    Fitzgerald, P. The means of escape
The axe
    Fitzgerald, P. The means of escape
Beehernz
    Fitzgerald, P. The means of escape
Desideratus
    Fitzgerald, P. The means of escape

The means of escape
    Fitzgerald, P. The means of escape
Not shown
    Fitzgerald, P. The means of escape
Our lives are only lent to us
    Granta no74 p241-55 Summ 2001
The prescription
    Fitzgerald, P. The means of escape
The red-haired girl
    Fitzgerald, P. The means of escape
Fitzpatrick, Tony
Country Sleep
    U.S. Catholic v69 no8 p36-9 Ag 2004
FitzSimons, Molly
It Loses Its Grandeur
    The Massachusetts Review v43 no3 p486-97 Aut 2002
Five aces west. Farrell, C.
Five dreams of falling. Rosenfeld, S.
The **five-forty-eight**. Cheever, J.
Five fucks. Lethem, J.
Five hours to Simla. See Desai, A. Five hours to Simla; or, Faisla
Five hours to Simla; or, Faisla. Desai, A.
The **five** seasons of a writer. Skwar, H.
The **five** twenty two. See Harrar, G. The 5:22
The **fix**. Cook, T. H.
The **fix**. Everett, P. L.
The **fixer**. Crespi, C. T.
Fixing a shadow. Alvarez, A.
Fla. boys. Sellers, H.
Flagg, Fannie
Rome, Italy
    Stories from the Blue Moon Cafe II; edited by Sonny Brewer
Flame. Ha Jin
The **flame-coloured** dress. Régio, J.
FLAMENCO DANCERS *See* Dancers
Flamingo. French, E. K.
Flanagan, Erin
Honda People
    South Carolina Review v34 no2 p109-18 Spr 2002
Intervention
    Best new American voices 2001; guest editor Charles Baxter; series editors John Kulka and Natalie Danford
Flann, Kathy
Experiments
    The North American Review v286 no2 p24-9 Mr/Ap 2001
Flannery, Silas
Another Besting of Both Englishmen
    The Review of Contemporary Fiction v23 no2 p89-90 Summ 2003
The Cask of Amontillado
    The Review of Contemporary Fiction v23 no2 p103-6 Summ 2003
A Certain Weariness in Moonlight
    The Review of Contemporary Fiction v23 no2 p96-7 Summ 2003
Eveline
    The Review of Contemporary Fiction v23 no2 p111-13 Summ 2003
The Man at Night's Window
    The Review of Contemporary Fiction v23 no2 p94-5 Summ 2003
A **flash** of chrysanthemum. Jance, J. A.
Flash point. Dozois, G. R.

Flashing spikes. O'Rourke, F.
The **flashlight**. Cleaver, E.
The **flat-eyed** monster. Tenn, W.
Flat spotting. Agee, J.
Flattery. Harris, M.
Flatware. Alvarez, A.
Flaw in the shelter. Shepard, J.
The **flaying** season. Thomas, J.
FLEA MARKETS
   Singleton, G. What slide rules can't measure
Fledgling Magic. Gotera, A. B.
Fleischman, Cyrille
   One day, Victor Hugo. . .
      With signs and wonders; an international anthology of Jewish fabulist fiction; edited by Daniel M. Jaffe
Fleming, John Henry
   Weighing of the heart
      The North American Review v284 no6 p18-24 N/D 1999
   Wind and rain
      100% pure Florida fiction; an anthology; edited by Susan Hubbard and Robley Wilson
Fleming, Mark
   St. Andrew's day
      The Vintage book of contemporary Scottish fiction; edited and with an introduction by Peter Kravitz
Fleming, Paula L.
   Polyformus perfectus
      Such a pretty face; edited by Lee Martindale
Fleming, Peter
   The kill
      The Literary werewolf; an anthology; edited by Charlotte F. Otten
Fleming, Robert
   Arbeit Macht Frei
      Fleming, R. Havoc after dark; tales of terror; foreword by Tananarive Due
   The astral visitor Delta blues
      Dark matter; a century of speculative fiction from the African diaspora; edited by Sheree R. Thomas
   The blasphemer
      Fleming, R. Havoc after dark; tales of terror; foreword by Tananarive Due
   Bordering on the divine
      Fleming, R. Havoc after dark; tales of terror; foreword by Tananarive Due
   The garden of evil
      Fleming, R. Havoc after dark; tales of terror; foreword by Tananarive Due
   Havoc after dark
      Fleming, R. Havoc after dark; tales of terror; foreword by Tananarive Due
   In my father's house
      Fleming, R. Havoc after dark; tales of terror; foreword by Tananarive Due
   The inhuman condition
      Fleming, R. Havoc after dark; tales of terror; foreword by Tananarive Due
   Life after bas
      Fleming, R. Havoc after dark; tales of terror; foreword by Tananarive Due
   A lizard's kiss
      Fleming, R. Havoc after dark; tales of terror; foreword by Tananarive Due

Punish the young seed of Satan
      Fleming, R. Havoc after dark; tales of terror; foreword by Tananarive Due
Speak no evil
      Fleming, R. Havoc after dark; tales of terror; foreword by Tananarive Due
The tenderness of Monsieur Blanc
      Fleming, R. Havoc after dark; tales of terror; foreword by Tananarive Due
The ultimate bad luck
      Fleming, R. Havoc after dark; tales of terror; foreword by Tananarive Due
The wisdom of the serpents
      Fleming, R. Havoc after dark; tales of terror; foreword by Tananarive Due
Fleming, Robert Peter *See* Fleming, Peter, 1907-1971
Flesh of leaves, bones of desire. Jacob, C.
Flesh Sunday. Marías, J.
Fleur. Erdrich, L.
Fleurette bleu. Longstreet, K. A.
Fliegel, Richard
   A final midrash
      Mystery midrash; an anthology of Jewish mystery & detective fiction; [edited by] Lawrence W. Raphael
FLIERS *See* Air pilots
The **fliers** of Gy. Le Guin, U. K.
FLIGHT
   Bradbury, R. The flying machine
   Burford, M. Flying lessons
   Dann, J. Da Vinci rising
   Jensen, J. L. The secret history of the ornithopter
   VanderMeer, J. Flight is for those who have not yet crossed over
Flight. Budnitz, J.
Flight. Grau, S. A.
Flight. Hoffman, A.
Flight. Kalman, J.
Flight. Lennon, J. R.
Flight. Nixon, C.
Flight. Skinner, J.
Flight into darkness. Schnitzler, A.
A **flight** of sparks. Cohen, R.
The **flight** of the elephant. Salvatori, C.
Flight patterns. Alexie, S.
A **flight** to Paris. Alameddine, R.
Flight to the north. L'Amour, L.
Flights. Adams, A.
Flipper. Canty, K.
Flirleflip. Tenn, W.
Floating. Harfenist, J.
Floating. Thompson, S.
Floating bridge. Munro, A.
Flock. Mazelis, J.
A **flock** of birds. Van Pelt, J.
Floggings. Davis, K.
Flood. Pronzini, B.
Flood. Vasseur, T. J.
FLOODS
      See also Disasters
   Agee, J. The land you claim
   Avrich, J. The great flood
   Berry, W. Are you all right?
   Berry, Betsy. Family and flood
   Clair, M. Water seeks its own level
   Clark, J. At last, the Ark
   Day, C. Winnesaw

FLOODS—*Continued*

Karnezis, P. The legend of Atlantis
Morgan, R. 1916 flood
Morgan, R. Poinsett's Bridge
Offutt, C. High water everywhere
Parrish, T. It pours
Pronzini, B. Flood
Rusch, K. K. Strange creatures
Stevenson, J. Notes from a bottle
Vasseur, T. J. Flood

Flora fountain. Fracis, S. H.
Flora in shadows. Padilla, M.
FLORENCE (ITALY) *See* Italy—Florence
FLORIDA

Abrams, T. Fish tales
Abrams, T. The gaffer
Abrams, T. Monroe Puckett
Allen, S. Souvenir
Arvin, N. Commemorating
Barthelme, F. The autobiography of Riva Jay
Barthelme, F. From Mars
Beaty, D. Ghosts
Blair, J. American standard
Blair, J. Bacon on the beach
Blair, J. Moving man
Blair, J. Running away
Blaise, C. Broward Dowdy
Blaise, C. The fabulous Eddie Brewster
Blaise, C. A fish like a buzzard
Blaise, C. Giant turtles, gliding in the dark
Blaise, C. Notes beyond history
Blaise, C. Relief
Blake, J. C. Aliens in the garden
Blake, J. C. The house of Esperanza
Connor, J. Florida
Cushman, S. Me and Dr. Bob
Eugenides, J. Timeshare
Gordon, M. Storytelling
Green, J. The blind gambler
Hendricks, V. Gators
Kaminsky, S. M. Adele
Leavitt, D. The scruff of the neck
Loeb, K. Fauna in Florida
Mayo, W. Jagged tooth, great tooth
McCorkle, J. Migration of the love bugs
McGuane, T. Skelton's party
Meinke, P. Unheard music
Murphy, P. J. The flower's noiseless hunger, the tree's clandestine tide
Nelson, A. The unified front
Nichols, J. Slow monkeys
Phillips, L. In the house of simple sentences
Polansky, S. Alarm
Sellers, H. Fla. boys
Sellers, H. Florida law
Sellers, H. The Gulf of Mexico
Sellers, H. In the drink
Sellers, H. It's water, it's not going to kill you
Sellers, H. Myself as a delicious peach
Sellers, H. Sinking
Sellers, H. Sleep creep leap
Sellers, H. Spurt
Tester, W. Wet
VanderMeer, J. The Festival of the Freshwater Squid
Williams, J. The blue men
Wilson, R., Jr. Florida
Woolson, C. F. Felipa
Ziegler, I. Blue Springs

Ziegler, I. Feud of the maids
Ziegler, I. Hooked
Ziegler, I. How to breathe underwater
Ziegler, I. Nobody home: an epilogue
Ziegler, I. Rules of the lake
Ziegler, I. The treasure hunter's daughter
Ziegler, I. The waiting list

Fort Lauderdale

Blaise, C. The bridge

Jacksonville

Chenoweth, A. If I were you
Chenoweth, A. The visit
Watkins, S. Critterworld

Key West

Arenas, R. End of a story
Beattie, A. Mermaids
Brackenbury, R. Between man and woman keys
Brackenbury, R. Chloe's pool
Brackenbury, R. Nothing works in Homestead
Healy, J. F. Food for thought
Holleran, A. Sunday morning: Key West
Porter, J. A. Bone key
Spencer, E. The legacy

Miami

Buchanan, E. Miami heat
Hochman, A. Local currency
Menendez, A. Confusing the saints
Menendez, A. In Cuba I was a German shepherd
Menendez, A. The party
Mestre, E. After Elián
Pearlman, E. Skin deep
Rodburg, M. The orphan
Singer, I. B. Alone
Walker, A. Kindred spirits

Palm Beach

Leonard, E. When the women come out to dance

Saint Petersburg

Banks, R. Success story
Chiarella, T. Foley's confessions
Lardner, R. The golden honeymoon

Tampa

Abrams, T. A small thing that mattered greatly
Abrams, T. A tale of two losers

Venice

Schmitt, R. Leaving Venice, Florida

Florida. Wilson, R., Jr.
Florida law. Sellers, H.
Floridita. Tester, W.
Flotsam and jetsam. Lutz, J.
Flower children. Swann, M.
Flower children of Mars. Resnick, M. and Bell, M. S.
A **Flower** for Ginette. Vreeland, S.
The **flower** nation. Sneve, V. D. H.
Flowering mandrake. Turner, G.
FLOWERS

See also Orchids

Sorrentino, G. The sea, caught in roses
Flowers. Tillman, L.
The **flowers**. Walker, A.
Flowers for Algernon. Keyes, D.
Flowers for Bill O'Reilly. Collins, M. A.
Flowers in the dustbin, poison in the human machine. Nissen, T.
The **flower's** noiseless hunger, the tree's clandestine tide. Murphy, P. J.
The **flowers** of Aulit Prison. Kress, N.

Flush. Budnitz, J.
Fly-fishing. O'Rourke, P. J.
"A **fly** struck—". Kharms, D.
FLYING *See* Flight
Flying. Glave, T.
Flying apart. Carson, J.
The **flying** camel spin. Leff, V. A.
The **flying** hawk. Norris, H.
Flying lessons. Burford, M.
Flying lessons. Link, K.
The **flying** Santinis. Keret, E.
FLYING SAUCERS
  Clarke, A. C. Trouble with the natives
  Davies, P. H. The Hull case
  Sturgeon, T. A saucer of loneliness
The **flyleaf** in the book of disillusion. Coates, G. S.
Flynn, Robert
  Truth and beauty
    Texas bound. Book III; 22 Texas stories; edited by Kay Cattarulla; foreword by Robert Flynn
Flynn, T. T.
  Ghost guns for gold
    Flynn, T. T. Ride to glory; a Western quartet
  The gun wolf
    Flynn, T. T. Ride to glory; a Western quartet
  Half interest in hell
    Flynn, T. T. Ride to glory; a Western quartet
  Ride to glory
    Flynn, T. T. Ride to glory; a Western quartet
  So wild, so free
    The First Five Star western corral; western stories; edited by Jon Tuska and Vicki Piekarski
Flynt, Candace
  Dancing with father
    This is where we live; short stories by 25 contemporary North Carolina writers; edited by Michael McFee
Flythe, Starkey
  A family of breast feeders
    New stories from the South; the year's best, 2004; edited by Shannon Ravenel; preface by Tim Gautreaux
Fo Nut X. Sanford, A.
Foaling Season. Kyle, A.
Foer, Jonathan Safran
  A primer for the punctuation of heart disease
    The New Yorker v78 no15 p82-5 Je 10 2002
  The very rigid search
    Lost tribe; jewish fiction from the edge
    The New Yorker v77 no16 p116-28 Je 18-25 2001
FOETUS *See* Fetus
Foetus. Jackson, S.
FOG
  Di Blasi, D. Fog
Fog. Adams, A.
Fog. Di Blasi, D.
Fog. Penn, W. S.
Fog. Roorbach, B.
The **Fog** Sleepers. Vivian, R.
Foggy Mountain breakdown. McCrumb, S.
A **foggy** walk. Odell, B.
Foiled!. Chekhov, A. P.

Folayan, Ayofemi
  Breakfast at Woolworth's, 1956
    Hers 2: brilliant new fiction by lesbian writers; edited by Terry Wolverton with Robert Drake
Foley, Sylvia
  Boy Wonder
    Foley, S. Life in the air ocean; stories
  Cave fish
    Foley, S. Life in the air ocean; stories
  Cloudland
    The Antioch Review v57 no1 p74-82 Wint 1999
    Foley, S. Life in the air ocean; stories
  Dogfight
    Foley, S. Life in the air ocean; stories
  Elemenopy
    Foley, S. Life in the air ocean; stories
  A history of sex
    Foley, S. Life in the air ocean; stories
  Life in the air ocean
    Foley, S. Life in the air ocean; stories
  Off Grenada
    Foley, S. Life in the air ocean; stories
  The state of union
    Foley, S. Life in the air ocean; stories
  Y's story
    On the rocks; the KGB Bar fiction anthology; edited by Rebecca Donner ; foreword by Denis Woychuk
Foley's confessions. Chiarella, T.
FOLK MEDICINE
  DeMarinis, R. Medicine man
The **Folklore** of Our Times. Murakami, H.
The **Following** Fifteen Things, A Love Story. Levine, S.
Following Leuda. Weathers, S.
Following the nun. Wegner, H.
Folly. Murray, S.
Folsom, Heather
  The House of Inspection
    Tikkun v17 no6 p57-60 N/D 2002
Fondly Fahrenheit. Bester, A.
Fondue. Boyle, T. C.
Fonseca, Angelo
  (jt. auth) *See* Lazo, Norma
Fontanel. Haverty, C.
Foo dog. Cole, C. B.
FOOD
  Chekhov, A. P. The siren
  Clarke, A. C. The food of the gods
  DeMarinis, R. Life between meals
  Greer, A. S. The art of eating
  Stableford, B. M. The last supper
Food chain. Hoffman, N. K.
Food, Clothing, Shelter. Middleton, N.
Food of love. Kirchheimer, G. D.
The **food** of the gods. Clarke, A. C.
Food that pleases, food to take home. Grooms, A.
The **fool**. Drake, D.
Fool Radiance. Heuler, K.
Fool soldiers. Sneve, V. D. H.
The **fool,** the stick, and the princess. Pollack, R.
A **Foolish** but Lovable Airport. Allen, E.
Foolishness is bound in the heart of a child. LeRoy, J. T.
FOOLS AND JESTERS
  Ellison, H. "Repent, Harlequin!" said the Ticktockman

FOOLS AND JESTERS—*Continued*

Singer, I. B. Gimpel the fool

Fool's errand. Zettel, S.

The **fool's** proxy. Lennon, J. R.

The **foot** of Saint Catherine. Kennedy, T. E.

FOOTBALL

Chabon, M. The Harris Fetko story

Clarke, A. C. A slight case of sunstroke

Jenkins, G. Fumble

L'Amour, L. Backfield battering ram

L'Amour, L. Moran of the Tigers

Mayo, W. Going long

Mazor, J. The lone star kid

Nichols, J. C'est la vie

Robison, M. Coach

Shaw, I. Whispers in bedlam

Shepard, S. Lajitas and the NFL

Vice, B. Report from Junction

Wright, D. Dialogue of men and boys

Foote, John Taintor

A wedding gift

Fishing's best short stories; edited by Paul D. Staudohar

Foote, Shelby

The sacred mound

The Cry of an occasion; fiction from the Fellowship of Southern Writers; edited by Richard Bausch; with a foreword by George Garrett

The **footprint**. Čapek, K.

For a long time, this was Griselda's story. Doerr, A.

For Alice to the fourth floor. Knight, M.

For all the saints. Linscott, G.

For all you dorks, blah blah blah. Cobb, W. J.

For as long as the lamp is burning. Papernick, J.

For good. Adams, A.

For gristles. Dinh, L.

For I am a jealous people!. Del Rey, L.

For I have sworn thee fair. Edghill, R.

For Marse Chouchoute. Chopin, K.

For real. Robison, M.

For services rendered. Deaver, J.

For the good of the service. Champlin, T.

For the love of vampires. Markus, D.

For the relief of unbearable urges. Englander, N.

For the Solitary Soul. Rabasa, G.

For their own survival. Hegi, U.

For this we give thanks. Gifford, B.

For Those of Us Who Need Such Things. Clarke, B.

For White Hill. Haldeman, J. W.

For women everywhere. Klass, P.

For your eyes only. Sumner, P.

Forbes, Charlotte

On the Way to the Dewberry Gardens

New Letters v69 no4 p99-115 2003

Sign

Prize stories, 1999; The O. Henry awards; edited and with an introduction by Larry Dark

Forbidden. Mazelis, J.

Forbidden fate. DeChoudhury, S.

Forbidden fruits. Hughes, J.

Forbidden planet. McGruder, K.

Ford, Elaine

Suicide

The North American Review v286 no3/4 p48-54 My/Ag 2001

Ford, Jeffrey

At Reparata

The Year's best fantasy & horror, thirteenth annual collection; edited by Ellen Datlow and Terri Windling

Creation

The Year's best fantasy & horror: sixteenth annual collection; edited by Ellen Datlow & Terri Windling

The green word

The Year's best fantasy & horror: sixteenth annual collection; edited by Ellen Datlow & Terri Windling

Tje Trentino kid

Datlow, E. The dark; new ghost stories; edited by Ellen Datlow

The Trentino kid

Datlow, E. The dark; new ghost stories; edited by Ellen Datlow

FORD, JOHN SALMON, 1815-1897

About

Reasoner, J. Dead Man's Hollow

Ford, Judith

Upper Captiva

Southern Humanities Review v37 no3 p249-55 Summ 2003

Ford, Nick Aaron

Let the church roll on

The African American West; a century of short stories; edited by Bruce A. Glasrud and Laurie Champion

Ford, Richard

Abyss

Ford, R. A multitude of sins; stories

Calling

Ford, R. A multitude of sins; stories

Charity

Ford, R. A multitude of sins; stories

Crèche

Ford, R. A multitude of sins; stories

Dominion

Ford, R. A multitude of sins; stories

Optimists

The Art of the story; an international anthology of contemporary short stories; edited by Daniel Halpern

Privacy

Ford, R. A multitude of sins; stories

Puppy

The Best American short stories, 2003; selected from U.S. and Canadian magazines by Walter Mosley with Katrina Kenison; with an introduction by Walter Mosley

Ford, R. A multitude of sins; stories

The Southern Review (Baton Rouge, La.) v37 no4 p697-723 Aut 2001

Quality time

Ford, R. A multitude of sins; stories

Reunion

Fault lines; stories of divorce; collected and edited by Caitlin Shetterly

Ford, R. A multitude of sins; stories

Rock Springs

The Scribner anthology of contemporary short fiction; fifty North American stories since 1970; Lex Williford and Michael Martone, editors

Ford, Richard—*Continued*
Still wild; short fiction of the American West, 1950 to the present; edited by Larry McMurtry
The Shore
The New Yorker v80 no21 p64-8, 70-5 Ag 2 2004
Under the radar
Ford, R. A multitude of sins; stories
Ford, Robert
The oboist
American short fiction, vol. 8, no 29-32
FORD, ROBERT, 1862-1892
About
Henry, W. ". . . Fired by the hand of Robert Ford"
Ford, Val
Gingerbread and men
Dead on demand; the best of ghost story weekend; edited by Elizabeth Engstrom
Fore!. Bradbury, R.
Forecast from the retail desk. Moody, R.
FOREIGN SERVICE *See* Diplomatic life
FOREIGN VISITORS
Brownrigg, S. Broad from abroad
Valenzuela, L. Up among the eagles
Foreigners. Shepard, S.
A **foreigner's** Christmas in China. McHugh, M. F.
Foreman, Walt
Happy birthday
Ploughshares v25 no4 p92-94 Wint 1999/2000
White fang
Ploughshares v25 no4 p95-101 Wint 1999/2000
The **forest**. Barrett, A.
Forest of stone. De Lint, C.
The **Forest** of Titles. LaSalle, P.
The **forest** will claim you too. Nfah-Abbenyi, J. M.
FORESTER, C. S. (CECIL SCOTT), 1899-1966
Parodies
Harrison, H. Captain Honario Harpplayer, R.N.
Parodies, imitations, etc.
Breen, J. L. Captain Benvolio Bullhorner
Forester, Cecil Scott *See* Forester, C. S. (Cecil Scott), 1899-1966
FORESTIERE, BALDASARE, 1879-1946
About
Boyle, T. C. The underground gardens
FORESTS AND FORESTRY
Brownrigg, S. Broad from abroad
Gay, W. A death in the woods
Iagnemma, K. Kingdom, order, species
Iwaszkiewicz, J. The birch grove
Kessel, J. Buffalo
West, M. Ghostwood
Yehoshua, A. B. Facing the forests
Forever. Thompson, J.
Forever free. Garcia y Robertson, R.
Forever Gramma. Garris, M.
Forever lasts only a full moon. Roffiel, R. M.
Forever overhead. Wallace, D. F.
Forever peace [excerpt] Haldeman, J. W.
FORGERY OF WORKS OF ART
Deng Youmei. Han the forger
Highsmith, P. The great cardhouse
Meredith, D. The closer
Forget luck. Wilhelm, K.

Forgetting Elena [excerpt] White, E.
Forgetting how to laugh. Abrams, T.
Forgetting the end of the world. Dillard, R. H. W.
Forgetting the girl. Smith, P. M.
FORGIVENESS
Banks, R. The child screams and looks back at you
Dunbar, P. L. Nelse Hatton's vengeance
Tolstoy, L., graf. Kornei Vasiliev
The **forgotten** children. Divakaruni, C. B.
The **forgotten** enemy. Clarke, A. C.
The **Forgotten** God. Brau, E.
Fork. Karasu, B.
Fork used in eating Reverend Baker. Davenport, K.
The **form** of a fish is its knowledge of the water. Schuemmer, S. A.
The **form** of the sword. See Borges, J. L. The shape of the sword
The **former** First Lady and the football hero. Homes, A. M.
The **former** Star Carlson. Barrett, L.
Formichella, Joe
Lomax's trials
Stories from the Blue Moon Cafe II; edited by Sonny Brewer
Forrest, Felix C., 1913-1966
For works written by this author under other names see Smith, Cordwainer, 1913-1966
Forsyth, Frederick
Alone
On glorious wings; the best flying stories of the century; edited and introduced by Stephen Coonts
The art of the matter
Forsyth, F. The veteran; five heart-stopping stories
The citizen
Forsyth, F. The veteran; five heart-stopping stories
The miracle
Forsyth, F. The veteran; five heart-stopping stories
The veteran
Forsyth, F. The veteran; five heart-stopping stories
Whispering wind
Forsyth, F. The veteran; five heart-stopping stories
FORT LAUDERDALE (FLA.) *See* Florida—Fort Lauderdale
Fort Smith. Gilchrist, E.
Fortitude. Tuck, L.
The **fortunate** ruse. Sade, marquis de
Fortune. Engberg, S.
A **fortune**. Sakaguchi, J. M. T.
Fortune. Williams, S. P.
FORTUNE TELLING
Chopin, K. A vacation and a voice
Dyson, J. The cash-point oracle
Gorman, C. The Death Cat of Hester Street
Pak, W.-S. Butterfly of illusion
Rankin, I. The hanged man
Sammān, G. The metallic crocodile
Singleton, G. When children count
FORTUNES *See* Wealth
Forty Acres and a Pool. Johnson, L.
The **forty-eight-bar** bridge. Davies, R.

Forty-minute lunch. Egan, J.
FOSSILS
  Keith, W. H. Fossils
  Oliver, C. Transfusion
  Updike, J. The man who loved extinct mammals
Fossils. Keith, W. H.
Fossils. Singleton, G.
Foster, Alan Dean
  Jackalope
    The American fantasy tradition; edited by Brian M. Thomsen
  Procrastinator
    The Crow; shattered lives & broken dreams; edited by J. O'Barr and Ed Kramer
Foster, Cindy
  Some breed of magic
    Dead on demand; the best of ghost story weekend; edited by Elizabeth Engstrom
Foster, Ken
  Another shoot
    Foster, K. The kind I'm likely to get; a collection
  The circuit
    Foster, K. The kind I'm likely to get; a collection
  Crush
    Foster, K. The kind I'm likely to get; a collection
  Happy people
    Foster, K. The kind I'm likely to get; a collection
  Indelible
    Foster, K. The kind I'm likely to get; a collection
  Keep it from the flame
    Foster, K. The kind I'm likely to get; a collection
  The kind I'm likely to get
    Foster, K. The kind I'm likely to get; a collection
  Like incest
    Foster, K. The kind I'm likely to get; a collection
  Red dresses
    Foster, K. The kind I'm likely to get; a collection
  Remainders
    Foster, K. The kind I'm likely to get; a collection
  Running in place
    Foster, K. The kind I'm likely to get; a collection
  A story about someone else
    Foster, K. The kind I'm likely to get; a collection
  Things you can make something out of
    Foster, K. The kind I'm likely to get; a collection
  Two windows
    Foster, K. The kind I'm likely to get; a collection
Foster, Patricia
  The girl from Soldier Creek
    Stories from the Blue Moon Café; edited by Sonny Brewer
  I'll Be Watching You
    The Antioch Review v62 no3 p549-65 Summ 2004

Foster, Phoebe Kate
  Naming the Monster
    Prairie Schooner v78 no2 p147-59 Summ 2004
FOSTER CHILDREN
    See also Adoption
  Henley, P. The secret of cartwheels
  LeRoy, J. T. Disappearances
  Morrison, T. Recitatif
  Thien, M. House
  Wharton, E. The mission of Jane
Found. Greenberg, A.
The **foundations** of the earth. Kenan, R.
Founding father. Simak, C. D.
The **founding** of Rome. Elizondo, S.
FOUNDLINGS *See* Abandoned children
Fountain, III Ben
  Fantasy for Eleven Fingers
    Southwest Review v88 no1 p123-43 2003
Four. Nailah, A.
Four attempts at a letter. West, M.
Four bites. Greer, A. S.
Four blue chairs. Kureishi, H.
Four calling birds, three French hens. Moore, L.
Four characters, four lunches. Moorhead, F.
Four characters, three small stories. Roeske, P.
The **Four** Daughters. Leegant, J.
The **four-day** workweek. Locklin, G.
Four days before the Saturday night social. Chaudhuri, A.
Four days from Oregon. Thien, M.
The **four** fists. Fitzgerald, F. S.
The **four-hour** fugue. Bester, A.
The **four** hundred ninety-first time. Berry, M. S.
Four lean hounds, CA. 1976. Meloy, M.
Four meetings. James, H.
Four older men. Swarthout, G. F.
The **four-sided** triangle. See Temple, W. F. The 4-sided triangle
Four squirrels. Brenner, W.
Four views of justice. Breen, J. L.
Four winds [excerpt] Brantenberg, G.
Fourteen seconds. Cummings, J. M.
The **fourth** at Getup. Guthrie, A. B.
The **fourth** day out from Santa Cruz. Bowles, P.
FOURTH DIMENSION
  Bear, G. Tangents
  Clarke, A. C. Technical error
  Heinlein, R. A. "—And he built a crooked house"
  Kalamu ya Salaam. Can you wear my eyes
FOURTH OF JULY
  Kees, W. The evening of the Fourth of July
  Yarbrough, S. Veneer
Fourth of July. Mathes, T. S.
Fourth of July picnic. Stout, R.
The **fourth** Prussian dynasty. Bender, K. E.
Fowler, Christopher
  At home in the pubs of old London
    Best new horror 12; edited and with an introduction by Stephen Jones
  Crocodile lady
    The Mammoth book of best horror 13; edited by Stephen Jones
  The green man
    The Year's best fantasy & horror: sixteenth annual collection; edited by Ellen Datlow & Terri Windling

Fowler, Christopher—*Continued*
Learning to let go
Best new horror 10; edited and with an intro-
duction by Stephen Jones
Fowler, Giles
Antic Light
The Sewanee Review v111 no4 p530-46 Fall
2003
Fowler, Karen Joy
The Elizabeth complex
Nebula awards 33; the year's best SF and
fantasy chosen by the science-fiction and
fantasy writers of America; edited by
Connie Willis
Face value
Masterpieces: the best science fiction of the
century; edited by Orson Scott Card
Faded roses
Vanishing acts; a science fiction anthology;
edited by Ellen Datlow
Private grave 9
McSweeney's mammoth treasury of thrilling
tales; edited by Michael Chabon
Sarah Canary [excerpt]
The Vintage book of amnesia; an anthology;
edited by Jonathan Lethem
The travails
The Year's best fantasy & horror, twelfth an-
nual collection; edited by Ellen Datlow &
Terry Windling
What I didn't see
The Year's best fantasy & horror: sixteenth
annual collection; edited by Ellen Datlow
& Terri Windling
Fox, Paula
The Broad Estates of Death
Harper's v308 p72-8 Ap 2004
Grace
Harper's v306 p63-70 Je 2003
Fox. Adam, C.
The **fox**. Lawrence, D. H.
Fox Hill. Winter, E.
Fox trot. Chapman, C. M.
FOXES
Adam, C. Fox
Chapman, C. M. Fox trot
Lawrence, D. H. The fox
Wicks, V. I have the serpent brought
Foxwell, Elizabeth
Alice and the agent of the Hun
Bishop, C. and James, D. Death dines in; ed-
ited by Claudia Bishop and Dean James
No man's land
Blood on their hands; edited by Lawrence
Block
A Roman of no importance
Cat crimes through time; edited by Ed
Gorman, Martin H. Greenberg, and Larry
Segriff
Foxx hunting. Stern, D.
FP 1 does not reply. Siodmak, C.
The **fqih**. Bowles, P.
Fracis, Sohrab Homi
Ancient fire
Fracis, S. H. Ticket to Minto; stories of India
and America
Falling
Fracis, S. H. Ticket to Minto; stories of India
and America

Flora fountain
Fracis, S. H. Ticket to Minto; stories of India
and America
Hamid gets his hair cut
Fracis, S. H. Ticket to Minto; stories of India
and America
Holy cow
Fracis, S. H. Ticket to Minto; stories of India
and America
Keeping time
Fracis, S. H. Ticket to Minto; stories of India
and America
The Mark Twain overlook
Fracis, S. H. Ticket to Minto; stories of India
and America
Matters of balance
Fracis, S. H. Ticket to Minto; stories of India
and America
Rabbit's foot
Fracis, S. H. Ticket to Minto; stories of India
and America
Stray
Fracis, S. H. Ticket to Minto; stories of India
and America
Ticket to Minto
Fracis, S. H. Ticket to Minto; stories of India
and America
Who's your authority?
Fracis, S. H. Ticket to Minto; stories of India
and America
The **Fractious** South. Ochsner, G.
Fradl. Baron, D.
Fragment. Wedler, R.
Fragment of a novel. Waugh, E.
A **fragment** of stained glass. Lawrence, D. H.
Fragments about Rebecca. Škvorecký, J.
Fragments of commedia dell'arte. Proust, M.
Fragments: they dine with the past. Waugh, E.
The **fragrance** of orchids. McBride, S.
Frahm, Leanne
Borderline
Centaurus: the best of Australian science fic-
tion; edited by David G. Hartwell and Da-
mien Broderick
A **frail** young life. Vink, R.
Frame, Ronald
La Plume de ma tante
The Vintage book of contemporary Scottish
fiction; edited and with an introduction by
Peter Kravitz
Siren Song
The Antioch Review v62 no3 p466-86 Summ
2004
Frames and wonders. Hospital, J. T.
The **framing** game. Bishop, P.
FRANCE
Desplechin, M. Taking it to heart
17th century
Dumas, A. The three musketeers [excerpt]
18th century
Sade, marquis de. The Gascon wit
Sade, marquis de. The mystified magistrate
1789-1799
Perry, A. The escape
19th century
Fitzgerald, P. The red-haired girl
James, H. A tragedy of error
1940-1945
L'Amour, L. The cross and the candle

FRANCE—*Continued*
Aristocracy
See Aristocracy—France
Courts and courtiers
See Courts and courtiers—France
German occupation, 1940-1945
See France—1940-1945
Peasant life
See Peasant life—France
Prisoners and prisons
See Prisoners and prisons—France
Rural life
Giono, J. Jofroi de Maussan
Giono, J. Sylvie
James, H. Gabrielle de Bergerac
Leduc, V. L'asphyxie [excerpt]
Trevanian. The apple tree
Trevanian. Minutes of a village meeting
Trevanian. That Fox-of-a-Beñat
Tuck, L. La Mayonette
World War, 1914-1918
See World War, 1914-1918—France
Antibes
Azadeh, C. The marriage at Antibes
Brittany
Wharton, E. Kerfol
Lyons
Azadeh, C. A banal stain
Nice
Johnson-Davies, D. A short weekend
Nimes
Byatt, A. S. Crocodile tears
Paris
Adams, A. Winter rain
Avrich, J. The braid
Azadeh, C. A recitation of nomads
Babel', I. Dante Street
Bocock, M. Alice and me
Bova, B. The café coup
Boylan, C. L'amour
Bunin, I. A. In Paris
Cherryh, C. J. The only death in the city
Fitzgerald, F. S. The World's Fair
Fleischman, C. One day, Victor Hugo. . .
Foster, K. Happy people
Galef, D. Dear, dirty Paris
Greenberg, P. The subjunctive mood
Kohler, S. The bride's secret
Kohler, S. Trust
Kureishi, H. Midnight all day
Le Guin, U. K. April in Paris
Marías, J. The night doctor
Melville, P. Provenance of a face
Robinson, P. April in Paris
Rucker, R. v. B. The Indian rope trick explained
Sade, marquis de. Thieves and swindlers
Sammān, G. The swan genie
Shua, A. M. The white Guanaco in the middle of France
Silber, J. My shape
Skeet, Michael. I love Paree
Stern, D. The #63 bus from the Gare de Lyon
Tuck, L. Rue Guynemer
Weihe, E. Another life
19th century
Auchincloss, L. The veterans
20th century
Meloy, M. Aqua Boulevard
Waugh, E. The manager of "The Kremlin"

Provence
Giono, J. Fields
Giono, J. The hand
Giono, J. Ivan Ivanovitch Kossiakoff
Giono, J. Joselet
Giono, J. Lost rafts
Giono, J. On the side of the road
Giono, J. Philemon
Giono, J. Prelude to pan
Giono, J. The solitude of compassion
Tuscany
Ptacek, K. The grotto
Versailles
McIntyre, V. N. The moon and the sun [excerpt]
Francis, Dick
The gift
  Edwards, M. Mysterious pleasures; a celebration of the Crime Writers' Association's 50th anniversary; edited by Martin Edwards
Francis, H. E. (Herbert Edward)
Señor Alvaro
  The Literary Review (Madison, N.J.) v46 no1 p124-32 Fall 2002
Francis, Patry
Limbe
  The Antioch Review v59 no3 p613-27 Summ 2001
FRANCO-GERMAN WAR, 1870-1871
Maupassant, G. d. A fishing excursion
Maupassant, G. d. Two fishers
Frangello, Gina
Truck stop
  Prairie Schooner v75 no4 p152-66 Wint 2001
Franis. Fintushel, E.
Frank, Joan
Boys keep being born
  Frank, J. Boys keep being born; stories
Exhibit A
  Frank, J. Boys keep being born; stories
Exquisite
  The Antioch Review v57 no4 p540-46 Fall 1999
  Frank, J. Boys keep being born; stories
The extraordinary member of Carlos Artiga
  Frank, J. Boys keep being born; stories
Green fruit
  Frank, J. Boys keep being born; stories
  South Carolina Review v33 no2 p25-30 Spr 2001
The guardian
  Frank, J. Boys keep being born; stories
The queen of worldly graces
  Frank, J. Boys keep being born; stories
The scanner
  Frank, J. Boys keep being born; stories
The sounds that arrive in the present
  Frank, J. Boys keep being born; stories
  The Ohio Review no62/63 p225-40 2001
A stalwart girl
  Frank, J. Boys keep being born; stories
  Salmagundi no130/131 p177-88 Spr/Summ 2001
The waiting room
  Frank, J. Boys keep being born; stories
What winter brings
  Frank, J. Boys keep being born; stories
When the universe was young
  Frank, J. Boys keep being born; stories

Frank, Judith
Crybaby butch
  The Massachusetts Review v40 no3 p410-19
  Aut 1999
Frank, Michael
Desire lines
  Salmagundi no124/125 p256-77 Fall
  1999/Wint 2000
Frank, Orsolya
(jt. auth) See Szántó, Gábor
**FRANKENSTEIN (FICTITIOUS CHARAC-
  TER)**
DeAndrea, W. L. A friend of mine
Lansdale, J. R. Personality problem
Franklin, Tom
Alaska
  Franklin, T. Poachers; stories
The ballad of Duane Juarez
  Franklin, T. Poachers; stories
Blue horses
  Franklin, T. Poachers; stories
Christmas 1893
  Stories from the Blue Moon Café; edited by
  Sonny Brewer
Dinosaurs
  Franklin, T. Poachers; stories
Grit
  The Best American mystery stories, 2000; ed-
  ited and with an introduction by Donald E.
  Westlake
  Franklin, T. Poachers; stories
Instinct
  Franklin, T. Poachers; stories
Nap Time
  The Georgia Review v58 no1 p99-102 Spr
  2004
Poachers
  The Best American mystery stories of the
  century; Tony Hillerman, editor; with an
  introduction by Tony Hillerman
  The Best American mystery stories, 1999; ed-
  ited and with an introduction by Ed
  McBain
  Franklin, T. Poachers; stories
  New stories from the South: the year's best,
  1999; edited by Shannon Ravenel; with a
  preface by Tony Earley
Shubuta
  Franklin, T. Poachers; stories
A tiny history
  Franklin, T. Poachers; stories
Triathlon
  Franklin, T. Poachers; stories
(jt. auth) See Fennelly, Beth Ann and Franklin,
  Tom
Franks, Robert
A secret murder
  Royal whodunnits; edited by Mike Ashley
Frank's friends. Strandquist, R.
Frannycam.net/diary. Hrbek, G.
Franz, Carlos
Circle
  Colchie, T. A whistler in the nightworld;
  short fiction from the Latin Americas; ed-
  ited by Thomas Colchie
**FRANZ FERDINAND, ARCHDUKE OF AUS-
  TRIA, 1863-1914**
  About
Hemon, A. The accordion

Franz Kafka in Riga. Mathews, H.
Franzen, Jonathan
End of the line
  The New Yorker v77 no15 p72-81 Je 11 2001
The failure
  The New Yorker v75 no17 p68-74 Jl 5 1999
  Wonderful town; New York stories from The
  New Yorker; edited by David Remnick
  with Susan Choi
The failure (I)
  The New Yorker v75 no16 p192-3 Je 21-28
  1999
Fraser, Antonia
Jemima Shore at the sunny grave
  A moment on the edge; 100 years of crime
  stories by women; edited by Elizabeth
  George
Jemima Shore's first case
  Murder most divine; ecclesiastical tales of un-
  holy crimes; edited by Ralph McInerny and
  Martin H. Greenberg
The twist
  Edwards, M. Mysterious pleasures; a celebra-
  tion of the Crime Writers' Association's
  50th anniversary; edited by Martin Edwards
Fraternité. Némirovsky, I.
Fraternity. Chaon, D.
Fraterrigo, Melissa
The Attached Couple
  The Massachusetts Review v44 no3 p399-415
  Fall 2003
Body, mine
  Virgin fiction 2
FRAUD
Asplund, Russell William. The Rabbi and the
  sorcerer
Boylan, C. A model daughter
Dokey, R. The beggar of Union Square
Hoch, E. D. Great day for the Irish
Lovesey, P. The man who jumped for England
Pronzini, B. Caught in the act
Singer, I. B. The bishop's robe
Singer, I. B. The captive
Singer, I. B. The seance
Westlake, D. E. The sweetest man in the world
Fräulein Else. Schnitzler, A.
Frazer, Margaret
Neither pity, love nor fear
  Royal whodunnits; edited by Mike Ashley
The witch's tale
  Murder most divine; ecclesiastical tales of un-
  holy crimes; edited by Ralph McInerny and
  Martin H. Greenberg
Frazier, Ian
Tomorrow's bird
  The Pushcart prize XXVI; best of the small
  presses, an annual small press reader; ed-
  ited by Bill Henderson and the Pushcart
  prize editors
Frazier, Kevin
The White Bows
  Dalhousie Review v83 no1 p87-97 Spr 2003
Frazier-DeLoach, Nora L. See DeLoach, Nora
Frazzle. Clark, J.
Freak. De Lint, C.
Freddy Duchamp in action. Epstein, J.
Fredonia. Roorbach, B.
Free. Nailah, A.
Free. Updike, J.

Free-43. Greenberg, A.

Free enterprise. Berry, R. M.

Free fall. Parrish, T.

Free in Asveroth. Grimsley, J.

The **Free** Library. Moody, R.

The **free** lunch. Blegvad, P.

The **free** radio. Rushdie, S.

A **free** royal town. Hykisch, A.

A **free** sinner. Lundquist, R.

Free trade. Lida, D.

Free writing. Olsen, S. S.

Free your mind and your ass will follow. Clinton, M. T.

Freed, Lynn
  An error of desire
    Michigan Quarterly Review v41 no2 p289-98 Spr 2002
  Twilight
    Harper's v298 no1788 p71-72+ My 1999
  The Widow's Daughter
    Southwest Review v87 no4 p438-48 2002

Freedom. Galaviz-Budziszewski, A.

Freedom. Gilliland, G.

Freedom fighter. Collins, M.

Freedom fighter. Klass, P.

FREEDOM OF RELIGION *See* Religious liberty

Freedom of the race. McCaffrey, A.

The **Freedom** Pig. Sim, A.

Freeforall. Atwood, M.

The **freelance** demolitionist. Wayman, T.

Freeman, Castle
  The Gift of Loneliness
    Southwest Review v88 no2/3 p262-71 2003
  Round Mountain
    American short fiction, vol. 8, no 29-32

Freeman, Mary Eleanor Wilkins
  The witch's daughter
    Witches' brew; edited by Yvonne Jocks

A **freeway** for Draculas. Lupoff, R. A.

Freezeout. Fromm, P.

FREEZING OF HUMAN BODIES *See* Cryonics

Freidson, Matt
  Strange new homeland
    The Virginia Quarterly Review v78 no3 p413-26 Summ 2002

FREIGHTERS *See* Ships

Freitod. Hegi, U.

French, Elizabeth Kemper
  Flamingo
    Ploughshares v27 no2/3 p55-70 Fall 2001

French, Elizabeth Stuckey- *See* Stuckey-French, Elizabeth

FRENCH
            Caribbean region
  Kurlansky, M. Packets and paperscraps
            Egypt
  Hoch, E. D. The day the dogs died
            Morocco
  Bowles, P. Midnight mass
            Norway
  Earle, S. The internationale
            Spain
  Marías, J. Everything bad comes back
            United States
  Chopin, K. A lady of bayou St. John
  Chopin, K. The maid of Saint Phillippe

French. Nailah, A.

French asparagus. Paul, B.

The **French** Boy. Craig, A.

FRENCH CAMEROONS *See* Cameroon

FRENCH CANADIANS
            United States
  Blaise, C. The fabulous Eddie Brewster
  Blaise, C. Snow people

FRENCH GUIANA
  Kurlansky, M. Vertical administration

FRENCH LANGUAGE
            Study and teaching
  Bemelmans, L. Mespoulets of the Splendide
  Erian, A. You

French letters. Meredith, D.

French press. Munro, K. E.

FRENCH REVOLUTION *See* France—1789-1799

FRENCH SOLDIERS *See* Soldiers—France

Fresan, Rodrigo
  National sovereignty
    The Vintage book of Latin American stories; edited by Carlos Fuentes and Julio Ortega

Fresh paint. Smith, J.

A **fresh** start. Lee, M.

A **fresh** start. Packer, A.

FREUD, SIGMUND, 1856-1939
            About
  Jones, G. 'Life probably saved by imbecile dwarf'

Freudenberger, Nell
  Letter from the last bastion
    Freudenberger, N. Lucky girls; stories
    The Paris Review v44 p269-329 Wint 2002
  Lucky girls
    Freudenberger, N. Lucky girls; stories
    The New Yorker v77 no16 p68-80 Je 18-25 2001
  The orphan
    Freudenberger, N. Lucky girls; stories
  Outside the Eastern gate
    Freudenberger, N. Lucky girls; stories
  The tutor
    Freudenberger, N. Lucky girls; stories
    Granta no82 p161-202 Summ 2003

Freund, Charles Paul
  The Tale of Many Jersualems
    Reason v34 no6 p26-34 N 2002

The **friar's** tale. Baldry, C.

Frick, Thomas
  The Picture House
    Agni no57 p154-5 2003

Friday night at Silver Star. Henley, P.

The **Friday** night shift at the Taco House blues (wah-wah). Coleman, W.

Friedman, Bruce Jay
  The Convert
    The Antioch Review v62 no3 p392-400 Summ 2004

Friedman, Kinky
  Don't forget
    Carved in rock; short stories by musicians; edited by Greg Kihn

Friedman, Mickey
  Tango is my life
    Murder in the family; [by] the Adams Round Table

Friedman, Philip
  Dog days
    Murder and obsession; edited by Otto Penzler

The **friend**. Hay, E.

A **friend** in need. Maugham, W. S.

A **friend** in the trade. Trevor, W.
A **friend** of a hero. L'Amour, L.
A **friend** of the world. Bowles, P.
Friend to women. Brown, C.
Friendly skies. Boyle, T. C.
FRIENDS *See* Friendship
FRIENDS, SOCIETY OF *See* Society of Friends
Friends and oranges. Moose, R.
The **friends** of the friends. James, H.
FRIENDSHIP
> *See also* Love

Aboulela, L. The museum
Adams, A. Elizabeth
Adams, A. New best friends
Adams, A. Roses, rhododendron
Adams, A. Tide pools
Adams, A. Waiting for Stella
Alas, L. Two scholars
Aldrich, B. S. Juno's swans
Allen, S. Souvenir
Almond, S. The soul molecule
Atwood, M. Death by landscape
Barthelme, F. Shopgirls
Bass, R. Pagans
Bausch, R. Accuracy
Bausch, R. The fireman's wife
Beach, R. The weight of obligation
Beattie, A. The burning house
Berkman, P. R. Merry Christmas, Charlie Brown
Berkman, P. R. Playing crucifixion
Bernhard, T. Walking
Bingham, S. Apricots
Bingham, S. The big bed
Bingham, S. Rat
Bloom, A. Rowing to Eden
Bly, C. The tomcat's wife
Bocock, M. Play me "Stormy weather," please
Bonnie, F. Gone with wind—be back soon
Bowles, P. He of the assembly
Bowles, P. The story of Lahcen and Idir
Bowles, P. The time of friendship
Boylan, C. The miracle of life
Boylan, C. Poor old sod
Bradbury, R. All my enemies are dead
Bradbury, R. The pumpernickel
Brenner, W. Remnants of Earl
Broughton, T. A. The wars I missed
Burford, M. Aloha, Les
Cady, J. Weird row
Carey, P. The fat man in history
Carlson, R. Santa Monica
Carlson, R. The time I died
Carver, R. Where I'm calling from
Cavell, B. Blue yonder
Chan, D. M. Falling
Chaudhuri, A. Words, silences
Chekhov, A. P. Fat and thin
Coberly, L. M. The death of Alma Ruth
Davies, P. H. Equal love
Desai, A. Royalty
Di Blasi, D. I am telling you lies
Di Blasi, D. Prayers of an accidental nature
Doenges, J. MIB
Dokey, R. Ace
Dokey, R. The mouse
Dunmore, H. The clear and rolling water
Dybek, S. Orchids
Eldridge, Courtney. Sharks
Evans, E. Voodoo girls on ice

Fairey, W. W. Grace
Fairey, W. W. Over the hill
Fitzgerald, F. S. The lees of happiness
Gilb, D. The pillows
Gilchrist, E. Alone
Gilchrist, E. The brown cape
Gilchrist, E. Summer, an elegy
Gilchrist, E. You must change your life
Goran, L. Alias Eleanor Roosevelt
Grodstein, L. Yellow morning
Gurnah, A. Bossy
Gussoff, C. Djinni
Gussoff, C. The wave: a novella
Hay, E. Cézanne in a soft hat
Hay, E. A clear record
Hay, E. Cowgirl
Hay, E. Earrings
Hay, E. The fight
Hay, E. The fire
Hay, E. The friend
Hay, E. Hand games
Hay, E. January through March
Hay, E. Johnny's smile
Hay, E. The kiss
Hay, E. Makeup
Hay, E. Overnight visitor
Hay, E. The parents
Hay, E. A personal letter
Hay, E. Purge me with hyssop
Hay, E. The reader
Hay, E. Sayonara
Hay, E. Secondhand Rose
Hay, E. Several losses
Hempel, A. In the cemetery where Al Jolson is buried
Hill, J. Pop art
Hoffman, A. Dear diary
Hoffman, A. Fate
Hoffman, A. Local girls
Houston, P. The best girlfriend you never had
Hunter, F. Africa, Africa!
Irsfeld, J. H. Death of a soldier
Irsfeld, J. H. My neighbor Mr. Young
Jackson, V. F. Darrell's garage
Jackson, V. F. A little kingdom
Jackson, V. F. On the road to Greater Bishop
Jackson, V. F. The outing
James, H. A light man
James, H. My friend Bingham
James, H. Osborne's revenge
Joseph, D. Expatriates
Karodia, F. The woman in green
Klass, P. The province of the bearded fathers
Kohler, S. Death in Rome
Lao She. Crooktails
LaValle, V. D. Ancient history
LaValle, V. D. Getting paid
LaValle, V. D. Ghost story
Lawrence, D. H. The blind man
Lee, M. Another wonder of the world
Leslie, N. Another place
Lessing, D. M. The grandmothers
Lethem, J. Planet Big Zero
Link, K. Most of my friends are two-thirds water
Marías, J. Everything bad comes back
Mazelis, J. The blackberry season
Mazelis, J. Over the rainbow
Mazelis, J. Setting

FRIENDSHIP—*Continued*
Means, D. McGregor's day on
Means, D. Sleeping Bear lament
Mitchell, C. E. Black cowboy
Moose, R. Friends and oranges
Murakami, H. Honey Pie
Nair, M. A certain sense of place
Nelson, A. Incognito
Nelson, A. Palisades
Norman, G. Cowboys
Norris, H. A good shape
Orner, P. Melba Kuperchmid returns
Orner, P. Melba Kuperschmid returns
Ortiz, S. J. To change life in a good way
Padilla, M. Carrying Sergei
Patterson, K. Country of cold
Pronzini, B. Under the skin
Reiner, C. Heshie and Joey
Ritchie, E. The big sixtieth
Roberts, N. This is not skin
Robinson, L. The edge of the forest and the
    edge of the ocean
Robinson, L. Seeing the world
Robison, M. Mirror
Roeske, P. Smaller than life
Roorbach, B. Taughannock Falls
Rosenfeld, S. Good for the frog
Rosenfeld, S. How I went (recipe for lime curd)
Rosenfeld, S. To Sarah, wherever you are
Russo, R. Poison
Sandlin, L. Another exciting day in Santa Fe
Sanford, A. Crossing Shattuck Bridge
Schlink, B. A little fling
Scholz, C. The menageries of Babel
Shepard, S. Great dream of heaven
Silber, J. Partners
Singer, I. B. The New Year party
Singleton, G. Bank of America
Smith, A. The heat of the story
Sojourner, M. Armageddon coffee
Sojourner, M. Huevos
Sontag, S. The way we live now
Sorrentino, G. Things that have stopped moving
Spark, M. The Portobello Road
Stanton, M. The cat and the clown
Stanton, M. The ugly virgin
Steiber, E. The shape of things
Stolar, D. Jack Landers is my friend
Stolar, D. Mourning
Taraqqi, G. My little friend
Thurm, M. Ancient history
Trevor, W. A friend in the trade
Troncoso, S. The gardener
Troy, M. The Alibi Café
Troy, M. A little zip
Updike, J. Who made yellow roses yellow?
Valeri, L. The kind of things saints do
Vapnyar, L. There are Jews in my house
Vernon, D. Arrival
Vivante, A. The cricket
Walker, A. There was a river
Warren, D. Tuxedo
Waugh, E. Lucy Simmonds
Weaver, G. Learst's last stand
Wexler, M. Save yourself
Wilson, R., Jr. A day of splendid omens
Wolff, T. Hunters in the snow
Yates, R. A really good jazz piano
Yates, R. Regards at home

Yates, R. Trying out for the race
Frierson, Eugene P.
An adventure in the Big Horn Mountains; or,
    The trials and tribulations of a recruit
    The African American West; a century of
    short stories; edited by Bruce A. Glasrud
    and Laurie Champion
Friesen, Richard E.
Dancing in the ashes
    Once upon a galaxy; edited by Will [sic]
    McCarthy, Martin H. Greenberg, and John
    Helfers
Friesner, Esther M.
Auntie Elspeth's Halloween story; or, The
    gourd, the bad, and the ugly
    The Ultimate Halloween; edited by Marvin
    Kaye
Big hair
    Black heart, ivory bones; [edited by] Ellen
    Datlow & Terri Windling
A birthday
    The Best from fantasy & science fiction: the
    fiftieth anniversary anthology; edited by
    Edward L. Ferman and Gordon Van Gelder
Hallowmass
    Death dines at 8:30; edited by Claudia Bishop
    and Nick DiChario
The stuff of heroes
    Magical beginnings; edited by Steven H. Sil-
    ver and Martin H. Greenberg
Trouble a-bruin
    White House pet detectives; tales of crime
    and mystery at the White House from a
    pet's-eye view; edited by Carole Nelson
    Douglas
A **frightening** seizure. Shepard, S.
Frisch, Wendi
Safe sex
    Hers 2: brilliant new fiction by lesbian writ-
    ers; edited by Terry Wolverton with Robert
    Drake
Fritz Glatman. Dinh, L.
Froggies. Whitton, L.
Frogmen. Davies, P. H.
FROGS
Murakami, H. Super-Frog saves Tokyo
VanderMeer, J. Greensleeves
Froh, Riley
I killed King Fisher
    Westward; a fictional history of the American
    West : 28 original stories celebrating the
    50th anniversary of the Western Writers of
    America; edited by Dale L. Walker
The two trail ride tricksters
    American West; twenty new stories from the
    Western Writers of America; edited with an
    introduction by Loren D. Estleman
Froim Grach. Babel´, I.
From a walled garden. Deane, J. F.
From Basra to Bethlehem. See Paine, T. The bat-
    tle of Khafji
From dawn to dusk. Heller, J.
From fanaticism; or, For reward. Harrison, H.
From foe to friend. Agnon, S. Y.
(From) Frank. Berry, R. M.
From information received. Hodgson, W. H.
From La muerte y otras sopresas: cuentos.
    Benedetti, M.
From Mars. Barthelme, F.

From Mutton Island. Lordan, B.
From parts unknown. Wellen, E.
From Tanga, a girl from Hamburg. Lustig, A.
From the boy stories. Yuknavitch, L.
From the desk of the troublesome editor. Harris, M.
From the diary of an assistant book-keeper. Chekhov, A. P.
From the highlands. Weber, D.
From the listening hills. L'Amour, L.
From the tideless sea, part one. Hodgson, W. H.
From the tideless sea, part two: further news of the Homebird. Hodgson, W. H.
From this distance. Roeske, P.
From Tikal. McRandle, P.
From Tucson to Tucumcari, from Tehachapi to Tonopah. Shackelford, R. T.
From where we've fallen. Kaplan, H.
From whom all blessings flow. Dedman, S.
From Willow Temple. Hall, D.
From you know who. Malouf, M.
Fromm, Pete
Black tie and blue jeans
Fromm, P. Night swimming; stories
Cowbird
Fromm, P. Night swimming; stories
Doors
Fromm, P. Night swimming; stories
Freezeout
Fromm, P. Night swimming; stories
Gluttony
Fromm, P. Night swimming; stories
The gravy on the cake
Fromm, P. Night swimming; stories
How all this started
Fromm, P. Night swimming; stories
The investigator
Fromm, P. Night swimming; stories
Night swimming
Fromm, P. Night swimming; stories
The raw material of ash
Fromm, P. Night swimming; stories
The Thatch weave
Fromm, P. Night swimming; stories
Willowy-wisps
Fromm, P. Night swimming; stories
Wind
Fromm, P. Night swimming; stories
FRONTIER AND PIONEER LIFE
Card, O. S. Hatrack River
Alaska
DeRosso, H. A. Endless trail
California
Levy, J. A woman 49er
Canada
Hudgins, B. Fur bearing
Munro, A. A wilderness station
Patterson, K. Boatbuilding
Idaho
Sherlock, P. Mother George, midwife
Kansas
Coldsmith, D. The guardians
Lilly, J. M. Going home money
Montana
Coleman, J. C. Loner
O'Callaghan, M. Wolf winter
New England
Hawthorne, N. Roger Malvin's burial

North Carolina
Morgan, R. Kuykendall's gold
Ohio
Braunbeck, G. A. Mail-order Annie
Ohio River Valley
Farrell, C. River ambush
Western States
Farrell, C. The shining mountains
Henry, W. Jefferson's captains
Johnson, D. Train dreams
Long, E. Letters to the stove
Wyoming
Le May, A. The bells of San Juan
Frost, Gregory
The prowl
Mojo: conjure stories; edited by Nalo Hopkinson
Frost, Pablo Soler
Clamour
The Vintage book of Latin American stories; edited by Carlos Fuentes and Julio Ortega
Frostbite. López, L.
Frostbite. López, L. M.
The **frozen** fields. Bowles, P.
Frozen water. Toole, F. X.
FRUIT
Sorrentino, G. Pastilles
Fruit. Ridgway, K.
The **fruit** cage. Barnes, J.
FRUIT PICKERS See Migrant labor
Fruitcake theory. Kelly, J. P.
Fry, Gary
Both and
Gathering the bones; original stories from the world's masters of horror; edited by Dennis Etchison, Ramsey Campbell and Jack Dann
Fry, Susan
The impressionists in winter
The Museum of horrors; edited by Dennis Etchison
The **Frying** Finn. Appel, J. M.
Frym, Gloria
Canticle
Frym, G. Distance no object; stories
Columbus Day
Frym, G. Distance no object; stories
Crime and punishment
Frym, G. Distance no object; stories
The dean's widow
Frym, G. Distance no object; stories
Distance no object
Frym, G. Distance no object; stories
Homologue
Frym, G. Distance no object; stories
Infant sorrow
Frym, G. Distance no object; stories
A little window
Frym, G. Distance no object; stories
Live oak
Frym, G. Distance no object; stories
Loosestrife
Frym, G. Distance no object; stories
Love
Frym, G. Distance no object; stories
No clubs allowed
Frym, G. Distance no object; stories
Nothing compared to
Frym, G. Distance no object; stories

Frym, Gloria—*Continued*
The oldest trick in the book
Frym, G. Distance no object; stories
Rosie since Vietnam
Frym, G. Distance no object; stories
Sleepy
Frym, G. Distance no object; stories
The social contract
Frym, G. Distance no object; stories
The stick
Frym, G. Distance no object; stories
SWAT
Frym, G. Distance no object; stories
Tagging
Frym, G. Distance no object; stories
"To see her in sunlight was to see Marxism die"
Frym, G. Distance no object; stories
Where she stays
Frym, G. Distance no object; stories
Fú, Michel Encinosa *See* Encinosa Fú, Michel
Fuchs, Daniel
Man in the middle of the ocean
Wonderful town; New York stories from The
New Yorker; edited by David Remnick
with Susan Choi
Fugato. Malzberg, B. N.
The **fugitive**. Day, R. C.
Fugitive Color. Gardiner, J. R.
FUGITIVE SLAVES
Johnson, C. R. The soulcatcher
Morgan, R. Little Willie
Wellen, E. The postmaster & the slave
FUGITIVES
See also Escaped convicts; Fugitive
slaves; Manhunts; Outlaws
Babel´, I. Sulak
Bilgrey, M. Living the lie
Bosch, J. Encarnación Mendoza's Christmas Eve
Davis, A. Red lights like laughter
Ford, R. Rock Springs
Matiella, A. C. The braid
Fugitives. White, M. C.
Fugue. Reed, S.
Full circle. Wharton, E.
Full moon howl. Winter, E.
Full moon over Milan. Lee, A.
Full Replacement Value. Nevai, L.
The **full** six. Coshnear, D.
Fullerton, Hugh
The insignificant "Dub"
Dead balls and double curves; an anthology
of early baseball fiction; edited and with an
introduction by Trey Strecker ; with a fore-
word by Arnold Hano
Fully bonded by the state of Minnesota. Harfenist,
J.
Fulmer, David
Back O'Town Blues
Flesh and blood: guilty as sin; erotic tales of
crime and passion; edited by Max Allan
Collins and Jeff Gelb
Fulmer, John
City of refuge
The Hudson Review v55 no2 p253-67 Summ
2002
The **fulness** of life. Wharton, E.

Fulton, Alice
If It's Not Too Much to Ask
The Georgia Review v57 no1 p100-26 Spr
2003
The Real Eleanor Rigby
Gettysburg Review v16 no4 p521-42 Wint
2003
Fulton, John
Braces
Fulton, J. Retribution
Clean away
Fulton, J. Retribution
First sex
Fulton, J. Retribution
Iceland
Fulton, J. Retribution
Liars
Fulton, J. Retribution
Outlaws
Fulton, J. Retribution
Retribution
Fulton, J. Retribution
Rose
Fulton, J. Retribution
The Southern Review (Baton Rouge, La.) v35
no4 p756-59 Aut 1999
Stealing
Fulton, J. Retribution
The troubled dog
Fulton, J. Retribution
Visions
Fulton, J. Retribution
Fumble. Jenkins, G.
Fun with a stranger. Yates, R.
Fun with forensics. Dreyer, E.
Fun with Problems. Stone, R.
The **function** of art at the present time. Berry, R.
M.
FUNDAMENTALISM *See* Fundamentalists
FUNDAMENTALISTS
Butler, R. O. Up by heart
Walker, A. The brotherhood of the saved
Fundamentals. Stolar, D.
Fundamentals of communication. Nissen, T.
The **Fundraiser's** Dance Card. Clarke, B.
The **funeral**. Bocock, M.
The **Funeral**. Harshbarger, K.
Funeral. Holbert, B.
The **Funeral**. Szántó, G.
FUNERAL DIRECTORS *See* Undertakers and
undertaking
The **funeral** march of the Marionettes. Castro,
A.-T.
Funeral music. Nevins, F. M., Jr.
The **funeral** of a giraffe. Tomioka, T.
A **funeral** of stones. Karnezis, P.
Funeral of the Virgin. Van Winckel, N.
The **funeral** party. Schmidt, H. J.
FUNERAL RITES AND CEREMONIES
Agee, J. Dead space
Agee, J. Time only adds to the blame
Alameddine, R. Whore
Alexis, A. Kuala Lumpur
Avrich, J. Miss Carmichael's funeral
Bocock, M. The funeral
Bradbury, R. Memento mori
Bradbury, R. One for his lordship, and one for
the road
Chekhov, A. P. The orator

FUNERAL RITES AND CEREMONIES—*Continued*

Chenoweth, A. The visit
Chesnutt, C. W. Mr. Taylor's funeral
Cooke, C. Mourning party
Crowley, J. Snow
Davies, P. H. The next life
Davies, R. A human condition
DeMarco, T. Jasper
Dixon, S. The burial
Dixon, S. The hairpiece
Doran, M. M. The estate of Joseph P. Bosley
Evenson, B.
Evenson, B. The gravediggers
Garrity, B. R. The holy boys
Grant, G. J. and Link, K. Ship, sea, mountain, sky
Hawthorne, N. The wedding knell
Hollon, F. T. The scrapbook
López, L. Mother-in-law tongue
Offutt, C. Inside out
Padilla, M. Papel
Padilla, M. The reason for angels
Rawley, D. Tim
Robison, M. I get by
Shapiro, G. Bad Jews
Shepard, S. Blinking eye
Singer, I. B. The last gaze
Strauss, A. Addressing the dead
Strauss, A. The joy of funerals
Stuart, J. Lost land of youth
Wallace, R. The night nurse
Weaver, G. Dirt
Weaver, G. Without spot or wrinkle
The **funeral** sermon. Müller, H.
The **funeral** side. Mason, B. A.
Funes, his memory. Borges, J. L.
Funes the memorious. See Borges, J. L. Funes, his memory
Fungi. Mayhar, A.
Funktionlust. Pritchard, M.
Funktionslust. Pritchard, M.
The **funniest** thing has been happening lately. Clark, M. H.
Funny cars. Rinehart, S.
A **funny** thing happened. Boylan, C.
Funny Valentine. Udall, B.
Fur. Louis, L. G.
Fur bearing. Hudgins, B.
FUR GARMENTS
Capote, T. A mink of one's own
Fur in the hickory. Clark, B. C.
The **Furies** of Menlo Park. Padilla, I.
Furious seasons. Carver, R.
Furman, Laura
The apprentice
    Furman, L. Drinking with the cook
Beautiful baby
    Furman, L. Drinking with the cook
    The Yale Review v89 no1 p89-103 Ja 2001
Buddy
    Furman, L. Drinking with the cook
Drinking with the cook
    Furman, L. Drinking with the cook
Hagalund
    Furman, L. Drinking with the cook
Melville's house
    Furman, L. Drinking with the cook

The natural memory
    Furman, L. Drinking with the cook
The Right Place For A Widow
    Southwest Review v88 no4 p503-13 2003
Sunny
    Furman, L. Drinking with the cook
Sympathy
    Furman, L. Drinking with the cook
That boy
    Furman, L. Drinking with the cook
What would Buddha do?
    Furman, L. Drinking with the cook
Wonderful gesture
    Furman, L. Drinking with the cook
The woods
    Furman, L. Drinking with the cook
The **furnace**. Davis, L.
FURNITURE
    See also Chairs
Hayes, D. This world of ours
Fusuda the archer. Browder, C.
Futrelle, Jacques
The problem of cell 13
    The Best American mystery stories of the century; Tony Hillerman, editor; with an introduction by Tony Hillerman
    Master's choice [v1]; mystery stories by today's top writers and the masters who inspired them; edited by Lawrence Block
FUTURE
    See also Science fiction
Aldiss, B. W. Beef
Aldiss, B. W. Headless
Aldiss, B. W. Supertoys in other seasons
Aldiss, B. W. Supertoys last all summer long
Aldiss, B. W. Supertoys when winter comes
Aldiss, B. W. A whiter Mars
Amis, M. The immortals
Anderson, P. Goat song
Anderson, P. The horn of time the hunter
Anderson, P. Windmill
Asimov, I. It's such a beautiful day
Asimov, I. The last question
Atkinson, K. Charlene and Trudi go shopping
Atwood, M. Freeforall
Barrett, N., Jr. Ginny Sweethips' Flying Circus
Barrett, N., Jr. Highbrow
Baxter, S. People came from earth
Bear, G. Judgment engine
Bear, G. MDIO ecosystems increase knowledge of DNA languages (2215 C.E.)
Bear, G. Petra
Bear, G. Sisters
Bear, G. The venging
Beckett, C. Marcher
Bell, M. S. Mrs. Lincoln's china
Bell, M. S. The thing about Benny
Benford, G. A hunger for the infinite
Bester, A. The four-hour fugue
Bester, A. Hobson's choice
Biggle, L. Tunesmith
Bishop, M. Simply indispensable
Bisson, T. Tell them they are all full of shit and they should fuck off
Bisson, T. There are no dead
Blish, J. A work of art
Boucher, A. The quest for Saint Aquin
Boyle, T. C. After the plague
Bradbury, R. And the rock cried out

FUTURE—*Continued*

Bradbury, R. Bright Phoenix
Bradbury, R. Forever and the Earth
Bradbury, R. Henry the Ninth
Bradbury, R. The man
Bradbury, R. The pedestrian
Bradbury, R. The smile
Bradbury, R. There will come soft rains
Bradbury, R. The Toynbee convection
Britto García, L. Future
Butler, O. E. The evening and the morning and the night
Campbell, J. W. Twilight
Capanna, P. Acronia
Castro, A.-T. The funeral march of the Marionettes
Castro, A.-T. The tangled strings of the Marionettes
Castro, A.-T. Unseen demons
Cherryh, C. J. The general
Cherryh, C. J. The haunted tower
Cherryh, C. J. Highliner
Cherryh, C. J. Ice
Cherryh, C. J. Masks
Cherryh, C. J. Mech
Cherryh, C. J. Nightgame
Cherryh, C. J. The only death in the city
Cherryh, C. J. Wings
Chiang, T. The evolution of human science
Chilson, R. This side of independence
Clarke, A. C. Death and the senator
Clarke, A. C. The fires within
Clarke, A. C. Guardian angel
Clarke, A. C. The hammer of God
Clarke, A. C. History lesson
Clarke, A. C. 'If I forget thee, oh Earth . . .'
Clarke, A. C. The lion of Comarre
Clarke, A. C. Nemesis
Clarke, A. C. The other side of the sky
Clarke, A. C. The songs of distant earth
Clarke, A. C. Transience
Cowdrey, A. E. Crux
Crowley, J. Snow
Daniel, T. A dry, quiet war
Daniel, T. Grist
Dann, J. Blind shemmy
Dann, J. Going under
Dann, J. A quiet revolution for death
De Camp, L. S. The Galton whistle
De Camp, L. S. Living fossil
Del Rey, L. The faithful
Delany, S. R. Corona
Delany, S. R. Driftglass
Delany, S. R. Time considered as a helix of semi-precious stones
Delany, S. R. We, in some strange power's employ, move on a rigorous line
Derby, M. An appeal
Derby, M. Behavior pilot
Derby, M. The boyish mulatto
Derby, M. Crutches used as weapon
Derby, M. The end of men
Derby, M. The father helmet
Derby, M. First
Derby, M. Gantry's last
Derby, M. Home recordings
Derby, M. Instructions
Derby, M. Joy of eating
Derby, M. The life jacket

Derby, M. Meat tower
Derby, M. Night watchmen
Derby, M. Sky harvest
Derby, M. The sound gun
Derby, M. Stupid animals
Di Filippo, P. And the dish ran away with the spoon
Doctorow, C. Craphound
Doctorow, C. Home again, home again
Doctorow, C. OwnzOred
Dozois, G. R. Dinner party
Dozois, G. R. Executive clemency
Dozois, G. R. A knight of ghosts and shadows
Dozois, G. R. Solace
Drake, D. Nation without walls
Drake, D. The predators
Drake, D. Underground
Due, T. Like daughter
Egan, G. Border guards
Egan, G. Oceanic
Egan, G. Singleton
Ellison, H. "Repent, Harlequin!" said the Ticktockman
Gibson, W. and Swanwick, M. Dogfight
Gilman, C. The real thing
Girardi, R. Arcana mundi
Girardi, R. The dinner party
Gores, J. The criminal
Green, Dominic. Send me a mentagram
Grossbach, R. Of scorned women and causal loops
Haldeman, J. W. For White Hill
Haldeman, J. W. Forever peace [excerpt]
Haldeman, J. W. A separate war
Hamilton, P. F. The suspect genome
Harrison, H. After the storm
Harrison, H. Brave newer world
Harrison, H. A criminal act
Harrison, H. I always do what Teddy says
Harrison, H. The road to the year 3000
Harrison, H. Roommates
Harrison, M. J. Suicide coast
Heinlein, R. A. The roads must roll
Hjortsberg, W. Gray matters
Hjortsberg, W. Symbiography
Hodgson, W. H. The Baumoff explpsive
Hornby, N. Otherwise pandemonium
Howells, R. A bleak future without thought-paper
Jakes, J. The man who wanted to be in the movies
Jennings, P. C. The road to reality
Johnson, A. Trauma plate
Kelly, J. P. Chemistry
Kelly, J. P. Glass cloud
Kelly, J. P. Itsy bitsy spider
Kelly, J. P. The prisoner of Chillon
Kelly, J. P. Rat
Kelly, J. P. Undone
Kelly, J. P. Unique visitors
Kessel, J. A clean escape
Knight, D. F. The country of the kind
Knight, D. F. Dio
Knight, D. F. I see you
Kornbluth, C. M. Two dooms
Kress, N. Inertia
Landis, G. A. Elemental
Landis, G. A. Impact parameter
Landis, G. A. Winter fire

FUTURE—*Continued*

Lansdale, J. R. In the cold, dark time
Leiber, F. Coming attraction
Lindquist, R. C. Prelude to a nocturne
Lopez, B. H. In the Garden of the Lords of War
Lupoff, R. A. The child's story
MacLeod, I. Breathmoss
MacLeod, I. Isabel of the fall
MacLeod, I. New light on the Drake equation
Maddern, P. C. Things fall apart
Malzberg, B. N. Police actions
Martin, G. R. R. The way of cross and dragon
Marusek, D. The wedding album
Matheson, R. The test
Matheson, R. When the waker sleeps
McAllister, B. The girl who loved animals
McAuley, P. J. All tomorrow's parties
McBride, S. The fragrance of orchids
McDonald, I. Tendeléo's story
McHugh, M. F. Interview: on any given day
Melchior, I. The racer
Melko, Paul. Singletons in love
Montpetit, C. Beyond the barriers
Mordecai, P. Once on the shores of the stream Senegambia
Morrow, J. Auspicious eggs
Mosley, W. Angel's island
Mosley, W. Doctor Kismet
Mosley, W. The electric eye
Mosley, W. The greatest
Mosley, W. En masse
Mosley, W. Voices
Mosley, W. Whispers in the dark
Murphy, D. The history of photography
Niven, L. and Barnes, S. Saturn's race
Oliver, C. End of the line
Oliver, C. Far from this earth
Oliver, C. Field expedient
Oliver, C. King of the hill
Palwick, S. Going after Bobo
Park, S. The cure for everything
Peters, R. Retaliation
Pflug, U. Bugtown
Pohl, F. The boy who would live forever
Pohl, F. Day million
Pronzini, B. and Malzberg, B. N. On account of darkness
Pronzini, B. and Malzberg, B. N. Prose bowl
Reed, I. Future Christmas
Reed, R. Coelacanths
Reed, R. First Tuesday
Reed, R. The shape of everything
Reed, R. Winemaster
Resnick, M. Hothouse flowers
Rojo, P. Gray noise
Rosenblum, M. H. Entrada
Rucker, R. v. B. Enlightenment Rabies
Rucker, R. v. B. The man who ate himself
Rucker, R. v. B. Rapture in space
Rusch, K. K. Millennium babies
Ryman, G. Birth days
Ryman, G. Everywhere
Scott, M. Trouble and her friends [excerpt]
Sheckley, R. Sightseeing, 2179
Sheffield, C. Out of copyright
Shepard, L. Radiant green star
Shockley, E. Separation anxiety
Shunn, W. Dance of the yellow-breasted Luddites

Shunn, W. Strong medicine
Silva Román, E. The death star
Silverberg, R. Passengers
Simak, C. D. Huddling place
Simmons, D. The ninth of av
Simmons, D. Orphans of the Helix
Skeet, Michael. I love Paree
Smith, C. Mother Hitton's littul kittons
Smith, D. A. The pretended
Spencer, W. B. The halfway house at the heart of darkness
Stableford, B. M. Another branch of the family tree
Stableford, B. M. The facts of life
Stableford, B. M. The house of mourning
Stableford, B. M. The last supper
Stableford, B. M. The milk of human kindness
Sterling, B. Maneki Neko
Sterling, B. and Shiner, L. Mozart in mirrorshades
Stross, C. Halo
Stross, C. Lobsters
Stross, C. Rogue farm
Swanwick, M. Radiant doors
Tenn, W. Eastward ho!
Tenn, W. The jester
Tenn, W. A man of family
Tenn, W. The masculinist revolt
Tenn, W. Null-P
Tenn, W. The servant problem
Tenn, W. The sickness
Tiptree, J. Mother in the sky with diamonds
Vachss, A. H. Charmed life
Vachss, A. H. Curtains
Vachss, A. H. Gamblers
Vachss, A. H. Safe sex
Vachss, A. H. The writing on the wall
Van Pelt, J. A flock of birds
Van Pelt, J. The long way home
Van Vogt, A. E. Far centaurus
Van Vogt, A. E. The weapon shop
Vanasco, A. Post-boomboom
Vance, J. Ullward's retreat
VanderMeer, J. The city
VanderMeer, J. A heart for Lucretia
Varley, J. Goodbye, Robinson Crusoe
Varley, J. The persistence of vision
Vinge, V. "Bookworm, run!"
Vinge, V. Conquest by default
Vinge, V. Fast times at Fairmont High
Vonnegut, K. 2BRO2B
Wadholm, R. At the money
Wadholm, R. Green tea
Waldrop, H. Willow Beeman
Watson, I. Ahead!
Watson, I. Nanunculus
Waugh, E. Love among the ruins
Westlake, D. E. The risk profession
What, L. Is that hard science; or, Are you just happy to see me
Williams, L. Voivodoi
Williams, T. The body politic
Williams, W. J. Lethe
Williams, W. J. The millennium party
Williams, W. J. Prayers on the wind
Williamson, J. Jamboree
Williamson, J. The ultimate earth
Williamson, J. With folded hands
Wilson, R. C. The great goodbye

FUTURE—*Continued*
Yánez Cossío, A. The IWM 1000
Future Christmas. Reed, I.
Future emergencies. Krauss, N.
The **future** is orange. McManus, J.
FUTURE LIFE
Carmody, I. The man who lost his shadow
Collins, P. Wired dreaming
Disch, T. M. In Xanadu
Rucker, R. v. B. In frozen time
Wharton, E. The fulness of life
Williams, S. Entre les beaux morts en vie
(Among the beautiful living dead)
Williams, T. The happiest dead boy in the world
The **future** of the Flynns. Greer, A. S.
The **Futurist**. Othmer, J. P.
Fuzzyland. Lange, R.

G

G. G. Giggler. Reiner, C.
G-string. Barker, N.
Gaarg. Gaarrgh. Gak. Erens, P.
Gabaldon, Diana
Lord John and the succubus
Silverberg, R. Legends II; new short novels
by the masters of modern fantasy; edited
by Robert Silverberg
Gabe and the doctor. House, R.
Gabriel, David
The blind woman
Gabriel, D. Making peace with the Muslims;
stories
Civilizations are islands
Gabriel, D. Making peace with the Muslims;
stories
Irina's lullaby
Gabriel, D. Making peace with the Muslims;
stories
The kapici's wife
Gabriel, D. Making peace with the Muslims;
stories
Making peace with the Muslims
Gabriel, D. Making peace with the Muslims;
stories
Necati Bey
Gabriel, D. Making peace with the Muslims;
stories
The reincarnation of Donaldo Fuertes
Gabriel, D. Making peace with the Muslims;
stories
Gabriel-Ernest. Saki
Gabriella: parts one and two. Patterson, K.
Gabrielle de Bergerac. James, H.
Gabrielyan, Nina
Bee heaven
Gabrielyan, N. Master of the grass; translated
by Kathleen Cook, Joanne Turnbull, Jean
MacKenzie, and Sofi Cook
Happiness
Gabrielyan, N. Master of the grass; translated
by Kathleen Cook, Joanne Turnbull, Jean
MacKenzie, and Sofi Cook
Hide and seek
Gabrielyan, N. Master of the grass; translated
by Kathleen Cook, Joanne Turnbull, Jean
MacKenzie, and Sofi Cook

The house in Metekhi Lane
Gabrielyan, N. Master of the grass; translated
by Kathleen Cook, Joanne Turnbull, Jean
MacKenzie, and Sofi Cook
The lilac dressing gown
Gabrielyan, N. Master of the grass; translated
by Kathleen Cook, Joanne Turnbull, Jean
MacKenzie, and Sofi Cook
Master of the grass
Gabrielyan, N. Master of the grass; translated
by Kathleen Cook, Joanne Turnbull, Jean
MacKenzie, and Sofi Cook
The studio apartment
Gabrielyan, N. Master of the grass; translated
by Kathleen Cook, Joanne Turnbull, Jean
MacKenzie, and Sofi Cook
Gaede, Dixie
The punishment
Dead on demand; the best of ghost story
weekend; edited by Elizabeth Engstrom
The **gaffer**. Abrams, T.
Gaffney, Elizabeth
Jerusalem
The North American Review v284 no3-4 p44-
47 My/Ag 1999
GAGARIN, YURI, 1934-1968
About
Kalfus, K. Orbit
Gahunia, Vivek
Little arrow
Iowa Review v29 no1 p168-69 Spr 1999
Gaiman, Neil
American gods [excerpt]
Nebula awards showcase 2004; edited by
Vonda McIntyre
Bitter grounds
Mojo: conjure stories; edited by Nalo Hopkin-
son
Closing time
McSweeney's mammoth treasury of thrilling
tales; edited by Michael Chabon
Feeders and eaters
The Year's best fantasy & horror: sixteenth
annual collection; edited by Ellen Datlow
& Terri Windling
Harlequin Valentine
Best new horror 11; edited and with an intro-
duction by Stephen Jones
The Year's best fantasy & horror, thirteenth
annual collection; edited by Ellen Datlow
and Terri Windling
Keepsakes and treasures: a love story
999: new stories of horror and suspense; ed-
ited by Al Sarrantonio
The Year's best fantasy & horror, thirteenth
annual collection; edited by Ellen Datlow
and Terri Windling
The Monarch of the Glen
Silverberg, R. Legends II; new short novels
by the masters of modern fantasy; edited
by Robert Silverberg
Murder mysteries
Murder most divine; ecclesiastical tales of unholy crimes; edited by Ralph McInerny and
Martin H. Greenberg
Nicholas was. . .
A yuletide universe; sixteen fantastical tales;
edited by Brian M. Thomsen

Gaiman, Neil—*Continued*
  October in the chair
    Brown, C. N. and Strahan, J. The Locus
      awards; thirty years of the best in science
      fiction and fantasy; edited by Charles N.
      Brown and Jonathan Strahan
    The Mammoth book of best new horror 14;
      edited with an introduction by Stephen
      Jones
  Pages from a journal found in a shoebox left in
      a Greyhound bus somewhere between Tul-
      sa, Oklahoma, and Louisville, Kentucky
    The Year's best fantasy & horror: sixteenth
      annual collection; edited by Ellen Datlow
      & Terri Windling
  Shoggoth's old peculiar
    The Year's best fantasy & horror, twelfth an-
      nual collection; edited by Ellen Datlow &
      Terry Windling
  A study in emerald
    Shadows over Baker Street; edited by Michael
      Reaves and John Pelan
  The wedding present
    Best new horror 10; edited and with an intro-
      duction by Stephen Jones
Gaitskill, Mary
  Dream of men
    On the rocks; the KGB Bar fiction anthology;
      edited by Rebecca Donner ; foreword by
      Denis Woychuk
  Processing
    Hers 2: brilliant new fiction by lesbian writ-
      ers; edited by Terry Wolverton with Robert
      Drake
A **gal** of ambition. Brownrigg, S.
Galactic north. Reynolds, A.
Galang, M. Evelina
  Labandera
    Prairie Schooner v76 no3 p5-19 Fall 2002
Galaviz-Budziszewski, Alexai
  Childhood
    Ploughshares v29 no4 p59-73 Wint
      2003/2004
  Freedom
    TriQuarterly no118 p170-81 Wint 2004
  Supernatural
    TriQuarterly no118 p182-4 Wint 2004
Galaxy Zee. Aldiss, B. W.
Galdós, Benito Pérez *See* Pérez Galdós, Benito,
      1843-1920
Galeano, Eduardo H.
  The story of the lizard who had the habit of din-
      ing on his wives
    The Art of the story; an international antholo-
      gy of contemporary short stories; edited by
      Daniel Halpern
Galeazzi, Jean
  Little Water
    The Literary Review (Madison, N.J.) v46 no1
      p137-46 Fall 2002
Galef, David
  All Cretans
    Galef, D. Laugh track
  And dwelt in a separate house
    Galef, D. Laugh track
  The art of the interview
    Galef, D. Laugh track
  Butch
    Galef, D. Laugh track

Dear, dirty Paris
    Galef, D. Laugh track
  The inner child
    Galef, D. Laugh track
  The jury
    Galef, D. Laugh track
  The landlord
    Galef, D. Laugh track
  Laugh track
    Galef, D. Laugh track
  Metafiction
    Galef, D. Laugh track
  Portrait of a portrayal
    Galef, D. Laugh track
  Triptych
    Galef, D. Laugh track
  The web of Möbius
    Galef, D. Laugh track
  The work of art in the age of mechanical repro-
      duction
    Galef, D. Laugh track
  You
    Galef, D. Laugh track
GALES *See* Storms
Gallagher, Stephen
  Doctor Hood
    Datlow, E. The dark; new ghost stories; ed-
      ited by Ellen Datlow
  Jailbird for Jesus
    The best British mysteries; edited by Maxim
      Jakubowski
  The little dead girl singing
    The Mammoth book of best new horror 14;
      edited with an introduction by Stephen
      Jones
    The Year's best fantasy & horror: sixteenth
      annual collection; edited by Ellen Datlow
      & Terri Windling
Gallagher, Tess
  Her speaking, her silence
    TriQuarterly no110/111 p59-70 Fall 2001
  I got a guy once
    In our nature: stories of wildness; selected
      and introduced by Donna Seaman
  (jt. auth) *See* Gray, Josie and Gallagher, Tess
The **gallant** tailor. Grimm, J. and Grimm, W.
Gallatin Canyon. McGuane, T.
The **gallery** of his dreams. Rusch, K. K.
Gallico, Paul
  Thicker than water
    Boxing's best short stories; edited by Paul D.
      Staudohar
Gállová, Marína Čeretková- *See*
      Čeretková-Gállová, Marína, 1931-
Galloway, Janice
  After the rains
    Galloway, J. Where you find it; stories
  Baby-sitting
    Galloway, J. Where you find it; stories
  The bridge
    Galloway, J. Where you find it; stories
  He dreams of pleasing his mother
    Galloway, J. Where you find it; stories
  Hope
    Galloway, J. Where you find it; stories
  Last thing
    Galloway, J. Where you find it; stories
  A night in
    Galloway, J. Where you find it; stories

Galloway, Janice—*Continued*

Not flu
    Galloway, J. Where you find it; stories
Peeping Tom
    Galloway, J. Where you find it; stories
A proper respect
    Galloway, J. Where you find it; stories
Proposal
    Galloway, J. Where you find it; stories
    The Literary Review (Madison, N.J.) v45 no2
      p250-63 Wint 2002
Six horses
    Galloway, J. Where you find it; stories
Someone had to
    Galloway, J. Where you find it; stories
Sonata form
    Galloway, J. Where you find it; stories
Test
    Galloway, J. Where you find it; stories
Tourists from the south arrive in the indepen-
    dent state
    Galloway, J. Where you find it; stories
The trick is to keep breathing [excerpt]
    The Vintage book of contemporary Scottish
      fiction; edited and with an introduction by
      Peter Kravitz
Valentine
    Galloway, J. Where you find it; stories
Waiting for Marilyn
    Galloway, J. Where you find it; stories
Where you find it
    Galloway, J. Where you find it; stories

Galton, Sir Francis

The Donoghues of Dunno Weir
    Utopian Studies v12 no2 p210-33 2001
The Eugenic College of Kantsaywhere
    Utopian Studies v12 no2 p191-209 2001
The **Galton** whistle. De Camp, L. S.
Galveston. Barthelme, F.
GAMBLERS *See* Gambling
Gamblers. Vachss, A. H.
Gamblin' man. Swain, D. V.
GAMBLING

        See also Lotteries; Wagers
Barthelme, F. Tiny ape
Bradbury, R. Hail to the chief
Cain, J. M. Cigarette girl
Chekhov, A. P. The bet
Cohen, R. The next big thing
Crane, S. The blue hotel
Crider, B. How I found a cat, lost true love, and
    broke the bank at Monte Carlo
DeLancey, K. Dinger and Blacker
Dumas, H. A Harlem game
Fitzgerald, F. S. The jelly-bean
Francis, D. The gift
Franklin, T. Grit
Gorman, E. En famille
Heller, J. Bookies, beware!
Heller, J. Nothing to be done
Irsfeld, J. H. The chance
Johnson, S. Risking it all
L'Amour, L. Moran of the Tigers
Lumley, B. Dead Eddy
Lupoff, R. A. The Tootsie Roll factor
Lutz, J. High stakes
Mason, B. A. Tunica
McNulty, J. Don't scrub off these names

McNulty, J. Even if it's Mexico nothing flashy
    ever happens to Grogan
McNulty, J. They don't seem to be talking to
    Grogan
Newton, D. B. Tinhorn trouble
Paul, B. The favor
Pronzini, B. Liar's dice
Rawley, D. The tiger's tooth
Rodgers, S. J. Luck
Schnitzler, A. Night games
Singer, I. B. Dr. Beeber
Swain, D. V. Gamblin' man
Taylor, T. L. Silent cruise
Tevis, W. S. The hustler
Touré. How Babe Ruth saved my life
Vachss, A. H. Gamblers
Waugh, E. The curse of the horse race
Wharton, E. Velvet ear-pads

Gambone, Philip

The singing boy
    His 3: brilliant new fiction by gay writers; ed-
      ited by Robert Drake and Terry Wolverton

Gambrell, Jamey

(jt. auth) See Sorokin, Vladimir
Game. Barthelme, D.
Game. Dixon, S.
The **game**. Mazelis, J.
A **game** of catch. Wilbur, R.
GAME PROTECTION
    Franklin, T. Poachers
Game time. Edmundson, M.
GAME WARDENS *See* Game protection
Gamelli, Ralph

A hero, plain and simple
    Such a pretty face; edited by Lee Martindale
GAMES

        See also Video games
Brown, A. K. Strip Battleship
Burrage, A. M. Smee
Chekhov, A. P. Children
Cooper, B. Hunters and gatherers
Gibson, W. and Swanwick, M. Dogfight
Kawabata, Y. Raindrops
Locklin, G. The monopoly story
Pronzini, B. and Malzberg, B. N. Fascination
Straub, P. Perdido: a fragment from a work in
    progress
GAMES, WAR *See* War games
Ganger (ball lightning). Hopkinson, N.
GANGS

        See also Juvenile delinquency
Cleaver, E. The flashlight
Daniels, J. Renegade
Delany, S. R. We, in some strange power's em-
    ploy, move on a rigorous line
Le Clézio, J.-M. G. Ariadne
Mathews, L. Crazy life
McBain, E. The last spin
Murray, Y. M. Girl on fire
Newhouse, E. The Mentocrats
Richards, T. The lords of zero
Vachss, A. H. Charmed life
Vachss, A. H. True colors
Yañez, R. Good time
GANGSTERS

        See also Mafia
Babel´, I. How things were done in Odessa
Babel´, I. The King
Block, L. How far it could go

GANGSTERS—*Continued*

Borges, J. L. Monk Eastman, purveyor of iniquities

DeMarinis, R. On the lam

Galef, D. Butch

Gifford, B. The old days

Girardi, R. The defenestration of Aba Sid

Goran, L. Caught

Gores, J. Quit screaming

Gorman, E. A new man

Heinlein, R. A. Magic, inc.

Hemingway, E. The killers

King, S. The wedding gig

L'Amour, L. Sideshow champion

McBain, E. Running from Legs

Paul, B. Scat

Pronzini, B. Chip

Runyon, D. Sense of humor

Gann, Ernest Kellogg

An hour to San Francisco

On glorious wings; the best flying stories of the century; edited and introduced by Stephen Coonts

Gansworth, Eric L.

The Raleigh Man

Fishing for chickens; short stories about rural youth; edited, with an introduction by Jim Heynen

Gantry's last. Derby, M.

GANYMEDE (SATELLITE)

Benford, G. Shall we take a little walk?

Gao Xingjian

The accident

Gao, X. and Lee, M. Buying a fishing rod for my grandfather; stories; Gao Xingjian ; translated from the Chinese by Mabel Lee

The New Yorker v79 no14 p82-7 Je 2003

Buying a fishing rod for my grandfather

Gao, X. and Lee, M. Buying a fishing rod for my grandfather; stories; Gao Xingjian ; translated from the Chinese by Mabel Lee

Grand Street no72 p108-23 Fall 2003

Cramp

Gao, X. and Lee, M. Buying a fishing rod for my grandfather; stories; Gao Xingjian ; translated from the Chinese by Mabel Lee

In an instant

Gao, X. and Lee, M. Buying a fishing rod for my grandfather; stories; Gao Xingjian ; translated from the Chinese by Mabel Lee

In the park

Gao, X. and Lee, M. Buying a fishing rod for my grandfather; stories; Gao Xingjian ; translated from the Chinese by Mabel Lee

The Kenyon Review v26 no1 p6-15 Wint 2004

The temple

Gao, X. and Lee, M. Buying a fishing rod for my grandfather; stories; Gao Xingjian ; translated from the Chinese by Mabel Lee

The New Yorker v79 no1 p178-83 F 14-24 2003

Gapa guzhva. Babel´, I.

Gaps. Addonizio, K.

Gar fishing. Smith, S. J.

Garbage girl. Johnson-Davies, D.

Garbage Night at the Opera. Fioravanti, V.

Garcia, Christina

Falling Sky

Bomb no86 p88-91 Wint 2003/2004

Garcia, Lionel G.

Alone

Garcia, L. G. The day they took my uncle and other stories

Always verbena

Garcia, L. G. The day they took my uncle and other stories

The day they took my uncle

Garcia, L. G. The day they took my uncle and other stories

Delivering meat

Garcia, L. G. The day they took my uncle and other stories

Eladio comes home

Garcia, L. G. The day they took my uncle and other stories

The emergency room

Garcia, L. G. The day they took my uncle and other stories

Girl

Garcia, L. G. The day they took my uncle and other stories

Mammogram

Garcia, L. G. The day they took my uncle and other stories

Mister Tyrone

Garcia, L. G. The day they took my uncle and other stories

Nano returns

Garcia, L. G. The day they took my uncle and other stories

Parents

Garcia, L. G. The day they took my uncle and other stories

The sergeant

Garcia, L. G. The day they took my uncle and other stories

Uncle Willy

Garcia, L. G. The day they took my uncle and other stories

The wedding

Garcia, L. G. The day they took my uncle and other stories

West Texas cowboys

Garcia, L. G. The day they took my uncle and other stories

García, Luis Britto *See* Britto García, Luis, 1940-

GARCÍA LORCA, FEDERICO, 1898-1936

Parodies, imitations, etc.

Arenas, R. Halley's comet

García Márquez, Gabriel

The ghosts of August

Nightshade: 20th century ghost stories; edited by Robert Phillips

The handsomest drowned man in the world

The Vintage book of Latin American stories; edited by Carlos Fuentes and Julio Ortega

The last voyage of the ghost ship

The Oxford book of Caribbean short stories; edited by Stewart Brown and John Wickham

Meeting in August

The New Yorker v75 no37 p126-28+ D 6 1999

Garcia y Robertson, R.
Forever free
    Past lives, present tense; edited by Elizabeth Ann Scarborough
Gone to glory
    The Good new stuff; adventure SF in the grand tradition; edited by Gardner Dozois
The **garden**. Bowles, P.
The **Garden**. Mehra, D.
A **Garden** Amid Fires. Swan, G.
The **Garden** Game. Beattie, A.
The **garden** of earthly delights. Yuknavitch, L.
The **Garden** of Eden. Ní Dhuibhne-Almqvist, É.
The **garden** of forking paths. Borges, J. L.
The **garden** of Padre Anselmo. Gonzalez, R.
The **garden** of Sheikh Osman. Johnson-Davies, D.
GARDEN PARTIES *See* Parties
Garden primitives. Sosin, D.
The **gardener**. Troncoso, S.
GARDENERS
Barrett, L. Hush money
Bowles, P. Madame and Ahmed
Bowles, P. Reminders of Bouselham
Boyle, T. C. The black and white sisters
Davies, L. Mr. Roopratna's chocolate
Lopez, B. H. Thomas Lowdermilk's generosity
Lugones, L. Viola acherontia
Mais, R. Red dirt don't wash
Troncoso, S. The gardener
GARDENING *See* Gardens
GARDENS
Austin, M. H. Old Spanish gardens
Bowles, P. The garden
Hawthorne, N. Rappaccini's daughter
Hoffman, W. The secret garden
Jacobsen, J. Jack Frost
Jewett, S. O. Mrs. Todd
Kelman, J. Gardens go on forever
Leavitt, D. Route 80
Mo Yan. Shen Garden
Naslund, S. J. The perfecting of the Chopin Valse No. 14 in E Minor
Saidi, W. The garden of evil
Saki. The occasional garden
Vivante, A. Fisherman's terrace
Gardens. Tem, M.
Gardens go on forever. Kelman, J.
The **gardens** of Kyoto. Walbert, K.
Gardiner, John Rolfe
Fugitive Color
    Southwest Review v88 no4 p454-82 2003
Gardner, Erle Stanley
Leg man
    A Century of great suspense stories; edited by Jeffery Deaver
Gardner, James Alan
Three hearings on the existence of snakes in the human bloodstream
    Nebula awards 33; the year's best SF and fantasy chosen by the science-fiction and fantasy writers of America; edited by Connie Willis
Garfield, Brian
Charlie's game
    Death by espionage; intriguing stories of deception and betrayal; edited by Martin Cruz Smith

Peace officer
    A Century of great Western stories; edited by John Jakes
Garfinkle, Richard
The last invasion of Ireland
    Once upon a galaxy; edited by Will [sic] McCarthy, Martin H. Greenberg, and John Helfers
Garmendia, Salvador
The melancholic pedestrian
    The Vintage book of Latin American stories; edited by Carlos Fuentes and Julio Ortega
Garner, Judith
Trick or treat
    Master's choice [v1]; mystery stories by today's top writers and the masters who inspired them; edited by Lawrence Block
Garnet. Coberly, L. M.
Garnett, Richard
The demon pope
    Tales before Tolkien; the roots of modern fantasy; edited by Douglas A. Anderson
Garrett, Caimeen
Circuits
    Kulka, J. and Danford, N. The New American voices 2003; guest editor Joyce Carol Oates; series editors John Kulka and Natalie Danford
Garrett, George P.
False confessions
    Ploughshares v25 no4 p172-78 Wint 1999/2000
Feeling good, feeling fine
    The Cry of an occasion; fiction from the Fellowship of Southern Writers; edited by Richard Bausch; with a foreword by George Garrett
Garrett, Michael
Candie-gram
    Flesh and blood; erotic tales of crime and passion; edited by Max Allan Collins and Jeff Gelb
Sex crimes
    Flesh and blood: guilty as sin; erotic tales of crime and passion; edited by Max Allan Collins and Jeff Gelb
Garris, Mick
Forever Gramma
    Best new horror 12; edited and with an introduction by Stephen Jones
Garrison Junction. Meloy, M.
Garrity, Bridget Rohan
The holy boys
    Writers harvest 3; edited and with an introduction by Tobias Wolff
Garro, Elena
Blame the Tlaxcaltecs
    Short stories by Latin American women; the magic and the real; edited by Celia Correas de Zapata; foreword by Isabel Allende
Gartner, Zsuzsi
Anxious objects
    Gartner, Z. All the anxious girls on earth
Boys growing
    Gartner, Z. All the anxious girls on earth
City of my dreams
    Gartner, Z. All the anxious girls on earth
How to survive in the bush
    Gartner, Z. All the anxious girls on earth

Gartner, Zsuzsi—*Continued*

Measuring death in column inches (a nine-week manual for girl rim pigs)
    Gartner, Z. All the anxious girls on earth
The nature of pure evil
    Gartner, Z. All the anxious girls on earth
Odds that, all things considered, she'd someday be happy
    Gartner, Z. All the anxious girls on earth
Pest control for dummies
    Gartner, Z. All the anxious girls on earth
The tragedy of premature death among geniuses
    Gartner, Z. All the anxious girls on earth

Gary Garrison's wedding vows. Carlson, R.

Garza, Daniel L.

Saturday belongs to the palomía
    Texas bound. Book III; 22 Texas stories; edited by Kay Cattarulla; foreword by Robert Flynn

Gas. Addonizio, K.

Gas stations. Apple, M.

Gascar, Pierre

The season of the dead
    When night fell; an anthology of Holocaust short stories; edited by Linda Schermer Raphael and Marc Lee Raphael

Gasco, Elyse

Can you wave bye bye, baby?
    Gasco, E. Can you wave bye bye, baby?; stories
Elements
    Gasco, E. Can you wave bye bye, baby?; stories
Mother: not a true story
    Gasco, E. Can you wave bye bye, baby?; stories
The spider of Bumba
    Gasco, E. Can you wave bye bye, baby?; stories
The third person
    Gasco, E. Can you wave bye bye, baby?; stories
A well-imagined life
    Gasco, E. Can you wave bye bye, baby?; stories
You have the body
    Gasco, E. Can you wave bye bye, baby?; stories

The Gascon wit. Sade, marquis de

Gash, Jonathan

Jack and Jill, R.I.P.
    Malice domestic 8

GASOLINE STATIONS *See* Automobiles—Service stations

Gass, William H.

The apocalypse museum
    Harper's v304 p25-9 My 2002
The Pedersen kid
    Still wild; short fiction of the American West, 1950 to the present; edited by Larry McMurtry

Gaston, Bill

The Kite Trick
    Granta no82 p225-37 Summ 2003
Where it comes from, where it goes
    Saturday Night v114 no4 p82-85+ My 1999

Gate of ivory, gate of horn. Swan, G.

Gates, David

The bad thing
    Gates, D. The wonders of the invisible world; stories
Beating
    Gates, D. The wonders of the invisible world; stories
The crazy thought
    Gates, D. The wonders of the invisible world; stories
The Drought
    Ploughshares v30 no2/3 p82-97 Fall 2004
George lassos moon
    Gentlemen's Quarterly v71 no12 p180-8, 268-70 D 2001
    On the rocks; the KGB Bar fiction anthology; edited by Rebecca Donner ; foreword by Denis Woychuk
The intruder
    Gates, D. The wonders of the invisible world; stories
The mail lady
    Gates, D. The wonders of the invisible world; stories
    The Scribner anthology of contemporary short fiction; fifty North American stories since 1970; Lex Williford and Michael Martone, editors
Monsalvat
    Gentlemen's Quarterly v72 no12 p228-36, 306-9 D 2002
Round on Both Ends and High in the Middle
    Ploughshares v30 no2/3 p70-81 Fall 2004
Saturn
    Gates, D. The wonders of the invisible world; stories
Side Angle Side
    Gentlemen's Quarterly v73 no6 p166, 168-70, 172, 174, 256-7 Je 2003
Star baby
    Gates, D. The wonders of the invisible world; stories
Vigil
    Gates, D. The wonders of the invisible world; stories
The wonders of the invisible world
    Gates, D. The wonders of the invisible world; stories
A wronged husband
    Breaking into print; early stories and insights into getting published; a Ploughshares anthology; edited by DeWitt Henry
    Gates, D. The wonders of the invisible world; stories

Gates, David Edgerley

The blue mirror
    The Best American mystery stories, 2002; edited and with an introduction by James Ellroy; Otto Penzler, series editor
Compass Rose
    The Best American mystery stories, 2000; edited and with an introduction by Donald E. Westlake

The gates are closing. Bloom, A.

Gates of Saigon. Phan, A.

Gatewood, Robert

Down in New Orleans
    Stories from the Blue Moon Cafe II; edited by Sonny Brewer

A **Gathering** of Kites. Parotti, P.
The **gathering** of the klan. Roberts, L.
Gator green. Mosley, W.
Gators. Hendricks, V.
Gators. Poirier, M. J.
Gauge. Coshnear, D.
Gault, William Campbell
  The Kerman kill
    A Century of noir; thirty-two classic crime
    stories; edited by Mickey Spillane and Max
    Allan Collins
Gautier, Amina
  Yearn
    African American Review v38 no1 p127-34
    Spr 2004
Gautier, Amina Lolita
  On Fridays
    Callaloo v25 no3 p753-8 Summ 2002
Gautreaux, Tim
  Dancing with the one-armed gal
    Coppola, F. F. Francis Ford Coppola's
    Zoetrope: all story; edited by Adrienne
    Brodeur and Samantha Schnee; introduction
    by Francis Ford Coppola
    Gautreaux, T. Welding with children
    New stories from the South: the year's best,
    2000; edited by Shannon Ravenel; with a
    preface by Ellen Douglas
  Easy pickings
    Gautreaux, T. Welding with children
    Gentlemen's Quarterly v69 no8 p103-04+ Ag
    1999
    Prize stories, 2000; The O. Henry awards; ed-
    ited and with an introduction by Larry
    Dark
  Good for the soul
    The Best American short stories, 2000; select-
    ed from U.S. and Canadian magazines by
    E. L. Doctorow with Katrina Kenison; with
    an introduction by E. L. Doctorow
    Gautreaux, T. Welding with children
  Misuse of light
    Gautreaux, T. Welding with children
  The piano tuner
    The Best American short stories, 1999; select-
    ed from U.S. and Canadian magazines by
    Amy Tan with Katrina Kenison, with an in-
    troduction by Amy Tan
    Gautreaux, T. Welding with children
  The Pine Oil Writers' Conference
    Gautreaux, T. Welding with children
  Resistance
    Gautreaux, T. Welding with children
  Rodeo parole
    Gautreaux, T. Welding with children
  Rodeo patrol
    Writers harvest 3; edited and with an intro-
    duction by Tobias Wolff
  Same place, same things
    The Scribner anthology of contemporary short
    fiction; fifty North American stories since
    1970; Lex Williford and Michael Martone,
    editors
  Something for Nothing
    Harper's v305 p66-72 S 2002
  Sorry blood
    Gautreaux, T. Welding with children
  Sunset in heaven
    Gautreaux, T. Welding with children

  Welding with children
    Gautreaux, T. Welding with children
Gavell, Mary Ladd
  Las Altas
    Gavell, M. L. I cannot tell a lie, exactly and
    other stories
  Baucis
    Gavell, M. L. I cannot tell a lie, exactly and
    other stories
  The blessing
    Gavell, M. L. I cannot tell a lie, exactly and
    other stories
  Boys
    Gavell, M. L. I cannot tell a lie, exactly and
    other stories
  The cotton field
    Gavell, M. L. I cannot tell a lie, exactly and
    other stories
  His beautiful handwriting
    Gavell, M. L. I cannot tell a lie, exactly and
    other stories
  I cannot tell a lie, exactly
    Gavell, M. L. I cannot tell a lie, exactly and
    other stories
  The infant
    Gavell, M. L. I cannot tell a lie, exactly and
    other stories
  The last daughter-in-law
    Gavell, M. L. I cannot tell a lie, exactly and
    other stories
  Lois in the country
    Gavell, M. L. I cannot tell a lie, exactly and
    other stories
  Penelope
    Gavell, M. L. I cannot tell a lie, exactly and
    other stories
  The rotifer
    The Best American short stories of the
    century; John Updike, editor, Katrina
    Kenison, coeditor; with an introduction by
    John Updike
    Gavell, M. L. I cannot tell a lie, exactly and
    other stories
  The school bus
    Gavell, M. L. I cannot tell a lie, exactly and
    other stories
    Graham, D. Lone Star literature; from the
    Red River to the Rio Grande; edited by
    Don Graham
  Sober, exper., work guar.
    Gavell, M. L. I cannot tell a lie, exactly and
    other stories
  The swing
    Gavell, M. L. I cannot tell a lie, exactly and
    other stories
  Yankee traders
    Gavell, M. L. I cannot tell a lie, exactly and
    other stories
Gay, Rafael Perez
  Night calls
    Points of departure; new stories from Mexico;
    edited by Mónica Lavín; translated by Gus-
    tavo Segade
Gay, William
  Bonedaddy, Quincy Nell, and the fifteen thou-
    sand BTU electric chair
    Gay, W. I hate to see that evening sun go
    down; collected stories

Gay, William—*Continued*

Charting the territories of the red

New stories from the South: the year's best, 2002; edited by Shannon Ravenel; with a preface by Larry Brown

The Southern Review (Baton Rouge, La.) v37 no2 p368-81 Spr 2001

Closure and roadkill on the life's highway

Atlantic Monthly v284 no4 p83-88+ O 1999

Gay, W. I hate to see that evening sun go down; collected stories

Come home, come home, it's suppertime

Stories from the Blue Moon Café; edited by Sonny Brewer

Crossroads blues

Gay, W. I hate to see that evening sun go down; collected stories

A death in the woods

Gay, W. I hate to see that evening sun go down; collected stories

Good 'til now

Gay, W. I hate to see that evening sun go down; collected stories

Homecoming

Stories from the Blue Moon Cafe II; edited by Sonny Brewer

I hate to see that evening sun go down

Gay, W. I hate to see that evening sun go down; collected stories

The lightpainter

Gay, W. I hate to see that evening sun go down; collected stories

The man who knew Dylan

Gay, W. I hate to see that evening sun go down; collected stories

My hand is just fine where it is

Gay, W. I hate to see that evening sun go down; collected stories

New stories from the South: the year's best, 2000; edited by Shannon Ravenel; with a preface by Ellen Douglas

The paperhanger

The Best American mystery stories, 2001; edited and with an Introduction by Lawrence Block

Gay, W. I hate to see that evening sun go down; collected stories

New stories from the South: the year's best, 2001; edited by Shannon Ravenel; with a preface by Lee Smith

Prize stories, 2001; The O. Henry awards; edited and with an introduction by Larry Dark

The paperhanger, the doctor's wife, and the child who went into the abstract

Best new American voices 2000; guest editor Tobias Wolff; series editors John Kulka and Natalie Danford

Standing by peaceful waters

Gay, W. I hate to see that evening sun go down; collected stories

Sugarbaby

Gay, W. I hate to see that evening sun go down; collected stories

Those Deep Elm Brown's Ferry Blues

Gay, W. I hate to see that evening sun go down; collected stories

New stories from the South: the year's best, 1999; edited by Shannon Ravenel; with a preface by Tony Earley

GAY MEN *See* Homosexuality

GAY WOMEN *See* Lesbianism

Gayle, Aisha D.

Mother

Pieces; a collection of new voices; edited by Stephen Chbosky

The **gaze** of the falcon. Lane, A.

Gazelles. Grodstein, L.

Geary, Tracy Miller

How to Be a Beekeeper

Harvard Review (1992) no23 p147-9 Fall 2002

Gedali. Babel', I.

Geeks dream. Jaffe, H.

GEESE

Adam, C. Goose

Earley, T. Aliceville

Lord, N. The girl who dreamed only geese

Meyers, K. The heart of the sky

Geese. Packer, Z.

The **geese** at Mayville. Slezak, E.

The **Geezenstacks.** Brown, F.

Gegenschein. McManus, J.

Geist, Ellen

Mistaking one man for another: a story

Commentary v111 no2 p41-9 F 2001

Gelb, Jeff

Perfection

Flesh and blood: guilty as sin; erotic tales of crime and passion; edited by Max Allan Collins and Jeff Gelb

Trophy wife

Flesh and blood; erotic tales of crime and passion; edited by Max Allan Collins and Jeff Gelb

Gellhorn, Martha

Miami—New York

The Best American short stories of the century; John Updike, editor, Katrina Kenison, coeditor; with an introduction by John Updike

Gemcrack. Phillips, J. A.

GEMS *See* Diamonds; Rubies

Gemstone. Vinge, V.

Gene and Nikki, Nikki and Gene. Meads, K.

GENEALOGY

Mathews, H. Tradition and the individual talent:the "Bratislava spiccato"

Westlake, D. E. Never shake a family tree

Genealogy. Casey, M.

Gener. Steward, D. E.

The **general** and the small town. Chen Shixu

General Markman's last stand. Paine, T.

GENERALS

Bester, A. Disappearing act

Bradbury, R. The drummer boy of Shiloh

Chen Shixu. The general and the small town

Clarke, A. C. The pacifist

Mencken, S. H. Twilight of chivalry

Paine, T. General Markman's last stand

GENERATION GAP *See* Conflict of generations

The **generation** gap. Gordimer, N.

Generation of Noah. Tenn, W.

Generation why. Kilpatrick, N.

Genesis (The G.I. bleed). Paschal, D.

GENETIC EXPERIMENTATION *See* Genetics

GENETIC RESEARCH *See* Genetics

GENETICS

Bear, G. MDIO ecosystems increase knowledge of DNA languages (2215 C.E.)

Bear, G. Sisters

Gores, J. The criminal

Kress, N. Sleeping dogs

Lawson, C. Written in blood

Le Guin, U. K. Porridge on Islac

Le Guin, U. K. Wake Island

Lindholm, M. Cut

Oliver, C. King of the hill

Park, S. The cure for everything

Stableford, B. M. The milk of human kindness

Williams, L. Voivodoi

Williamson, J. Jamboree

Wolfe, G. The fat magician

Geng, Veronica

Partners

    Wonderful town; New York stories from The New Yorker; edited by David Remnick with Susan Choi

GENIUS

See also Gifted children

Carlson, R. The ordinary son

Gartner, Z. The tragedy of premature death among geniuses

The **genius**. Saroyan, A.

The **gentle** boy. Hawthorne, N.

Gentle insanities. Matthews, C.

A **gentle** soul. Lavin, M.

A **gentleman** friend. Chekhov, A. P.

The **gentleman** from New Orleans. Chopin, K.

The **gentleman** from San Francisco. Bunin, I. A.

The **gentleman** in the lake. Barnard, R.

The **gentleman** in the pink-and-white striped shirt. Brennan, M.

A **gentleman** of Bayou Têche. Chopin, K.

A **gentleman** on the train. Palacios, A.

The **gentleman's** gentleman. Cannell, D.

Gentry, Erika

Bad john going down

    Iowa Review v29 no2 p128-45 Fall 1999

Gents 50/Ladies 25. Kees, W.

Geoff and Kurt. Reiner, C.

Geoffrey Sonnabend's obliscence: theories of forgetting and the problem of matter—an encapsulation. Worth, V.

Geoffrey's wife. Burton, M.

GEOGRAPHERS

Lopez, B. H. The mappist

A **geography** of snow. Bukoski, A.

The **geography** of the body. Shapcott, T.

Geography one. Leong, R.

GEOLOGISTS

Hardy, M. The uncharted heart

GEORGE IV, KING OF GREAT BRITAIN, 1762-1830

About

Edwards, M. Natural causes

George, Elizabeth

Exposure

    George, E. I, Richard; stories of suspense

Good fences aren't always enough

    George, E. I, Richard; stories of suspense

I, Richard

    George, E. I, Richard; stories of suspense

    Murder and obsession; edited by Otto Penzler

Remember, I'll always love you

    George, E. I, Richard; stories of suspense

The surprise of his life

    George, E. I, Richard; stories of suspense

George is all right. Wandrei, H.

George lassos moon. Gates, D.

George Patton slept here Turtledove, H. Alternate generals II; ed. by Harry Turtledove

George Washington crashed here. Hager, J.

GEORGIA

Fitzgerald, F. S. The jelly-bean

Harris, J. C. Where's Duncan?

Hoffman, L. The third nation

Kessel, J. Every angel is terrifying

McManus, J. Scintilla

O'Connor, F. A good man is hard to find

Ponder, D. U. The rat spoon

Atlanta

Becker, G. Black Elvis

Grimsley, J. Jesus is sending you this message

Packer, Z. Speaking in tongues

Savannah

Clarke, B. For those of us who need such things

GEORGIA (REPUBLIC)

Steavenson, W. Gika

Georgica. Homes, A. M.

Georgie [excerpt] Jutras, J. d.

Georgina's reasons. James, H.

Georgiou, Elena

Aphrodite's vision

    The Vintage book of international lesbian fiction; edited and with an introduction by Naomi Holoch and Joan Nestle

Geraldine Loves. Morris, K. L.

Gerald's monkey. Knight, M.

Geranium house. Curry, P. S.

Gerard, Philip

Death by reputation

    This is where we live; short stories by 25 contemporary North Carolina writers; edited by Michael McFee

Gérard de Nerval *See* Nerval, Gérard de, 1808-1855

Gerber, Merrill Joan

Anna passes on

    Southwest Review v86 no2/3 p284-92 Spr/Summ 2001

A great miracle

    Good Housekeeping v229 no6 p101-02+ D 1999

German, Norman

Dead Dog Lying

    The Virginia Quarterly Review v78 no4 p710-27 Aut 2002

GERMAN AMERICANS

Wegner, H. Cockshut light

Wegner, H. Dogs of autumn

Wegner, H. Following the nun

Wegner, H. On the road to Szkaradowo

Wegner, H. The pilots of the rose trellis

GERMAN EAST AFRICA *See* East Africa

The **German** refugee. Malamud, B.

GERMAN REFUGEES

Meyers, K. Abiding by law

GERMAN SOLDIERS *See* Soldiers—Germany

The **German** spy. Hodgson, W. H.

GERMAN WEST AFRICA *See* Cameroon

GERMANS
Argentina
Maraini, D. A number on her arm
Caribbean region
Hermann, J. Hurricane (something farewell)
Czechoslovakia
Škvorecký, J. The cuckoo
England
Trevor, W. The telephone game
Italy
Hegi, U. A woman's perfume
Mexico
Hegi, U. Freitod
Paraguay
Jacobs, M. Dove of the back streets
Russia
Hermann, J. The red coral bracelet
South America
Schlink, B. The son
United States
Aldrich, B. S. The day of retaliation
Arvin, N. Two thousand Germans in Frankenmuth
Harrison, H. Down to earth
James, H. Pandora
Malamud, B. The German refugee
Robison, M. For real
Schlink, B. The circumcision
Seiffert, R. Dimitroff
Young, T. The Berlin Wall
GERMANY
19th century
Ludwig, O. The dead man of St. Anne's Chapel
Pushkin, A. S. Maria Schoning
1918-1945
Borges, J. L. Deutsches requiem
1945-
Biguenet, J. I am not a Jew
Händler, E.-W. City with houses
Highsmith, P. The returnees
Schlink, B. Sugar peas
American occupation, 1945-1955
See Germany—1945-
Army
Officers
Lawrence, D. H. The Prussian officer
Rural life
Hegi, U. A town like ours
Hermann, J. This side of the Oder
World War, 1939-1945
See World War, 1939-1945—Germany
Berlin
Apelman, M. A visitor's guide to Berlin
Schlink, B. A little fling
Germinating. Lewis, W. H.
GERONTOLOGISTS *See* Physicians
Gerrold, David
The spell
Witches' brew; edited by Yvonne Jocks
Gersham and the saber. Swarthout, G. F.
Gershon, Ruth
Habibi
Granta no68 p23-68 Wint 1999
Gessen, Keith
The Right of Return
Agni no59 p6-24 2004
GESTAPO *See* National socialism
Gestella. Palwick, S.
The **gesture**. Brewer, G.

The **gesture** hunter. Means, D.
Gesturing. Updike, J.
GESUALDO, CARLO, PRINCE OF VENOSA, CA. 1560-1613
About
Herling, G. A madrigal of mourning
Get a lifestyle. Renado, T.
Get Away from Me, David. Reinhorn, H.
Get lost. Meek, J.
Get me to the church on time. Bisson, T.
Get out of my sky. Blish, J.
Get the message. Lochte, D.
Get Well Soon. Christopher, C.
Getaway. Whiton, T.
Getel's story. Luxenberg, H.
Getting a life. Simpson, H.
Getting even. Sánchez, L. R.
Getting Heavy with Fate. Ryan, P.
Getting Mario. Shapiro, J.
Getting Mother's Body. Parks, S.-L.
Getting paid. LaValle, V. D.
Getting the heat up. Agee, J.
Getting the story. Costa, S.
Getting to know the dragon. Silverberg, R.
Getting ugly. LaValle, V. D.
GETTYSBURG, BATTLE OF, 1863
Wolfe, T. O lost
GHANA
Aidoo, A. A. A gift from somewhere
Packer, G. The water-girl
A **ghetto** dog. Spiegel, I.
Ghost-Birds. Pizzolatto, N.
The **ghost** fighter. L'Amour, L.
Ghost girls. Oates, J. C.
Ghost guns for gold. Flynn, T. T.
Ghost knife. Pomerantz, S.
Ghost of a chance. Gorman, E.
A **ghost** of an affair. Yolen, J.
The **ghost** of Dive Bomber Hill. Cady, J.
The **ghost** of John Wayne. Gonzalez, R.
The **ghost** of potlatch past. Weldon, F.
GHOST SHIPS
García Márquez, G. The last voyage of the ghost ship
Hodgson, W. H. The call in the dawn
Hodgson, W. H. The mystery of the derelict
The **ghost** standard. Tenn, W.
GHOST STORIES
See also Horror stories; Supernatural phenomena
Abraham, D. An amicable divorce
Aichinger, I. Ghosts on the lake
Aiken, J. Sonata for harp and bicycle
Aikman, S. Pia
Alexie, S. Ghost dance
Bandolas, B. One last soul
Barker, C. The Yattering and Jack
Barrett, N., Jr. Class of '61
Bear, G. Sleepside story
Berliner, J. Until the butterflies
Betts, D. Three ghosts
Bierce, A. The other lodgers
Bilgrey, M. Evening spirit
Birmingham, E. Falling away
Bishop, M. Icicle music
Blake, T. Grim's redemption
Blatty, W. P. Elsewhere
Bohart, L. The boathouse
Bottoms, G. Nostalgia for ghosts

GHOST STORIES—*Continued*

Bowen, E. The happy autumn fields
Bowen, M. The Crown Derby plate
Boylan, C. Life on Mars
Boyle, T. C. My widow
Bradbury, R. The ghosts
Bradbury, R. Lafayette, farewell
Bradbury, R. On the Orient, North
Bradbury, R. The witch doctor
Bradbury, R. The woman on the lawn
Braunbeck, G. A. Captain Jim's drunken dream
Braunbeck, G. A. Safe
Breen, J. L. Silver Spectre
Bruchman, D. M. Promises kept
Burke, J. The Abbey ghosts
Burrage, A. M. Smee
Cady, J. Daddy dearest
Cady, J. The ghost of Dive Bomber Hill
Cady, J. Israel and Ernest
Cady, J. On writing the ghost story
Cady, J. Seven sisters
Cady, J. The time that time forgot
Cannell, D. Come to Grandma
Card, O. S. Lost boys
Chandra, V. Dharma
Cheever, J. Oh father, father, why have you come back?
Cherry, K. As it is in heaven
Cherryh, C. J. The haunted tower
Cherryh, C. J. Wings
Chesnutt, C. W. Hot-foot Hannibal
Chesnutt, C. W. Po' Sandy
Clark, A. M. Constance
Cohen, S. Six-four, four-three, deuce, a ghost story of sorts
Coover, R. Visitation
Copper, B. Ill met by daylight
Crawford, F. M. The upper berth
Davidson, A. Mickelrede; or, The slayer and the staff
Davis, K. Floggings
Davis, L. Something spooky on Geophys
De la Mare, W. Seaton's aunt
De Lint, C. Many worlds are born
De Lint, C. Masking Indian
De Lint, C. The witching hour
De Lint, C. The words that remain
Doran, M. M. Billy and Benjamin too
Dowling, T. One thing about the night
DuBois, B. The tourist who wasn't there
Duffy, S. Running dogs
Eakin, W. Lawnmower Moe
Eakin, W. The miracle of Swamp Gas Jackson
Eberts, M. Lost lives
Engstrom, E. Purple shards
Fitzgerald, P. The axe
Ford, J. Tje Trentino kid
Ford, J. The Trentino kid
Ford, V. Gingerbread and men
Foster, C. Some breed of magic
Frost, G. The prowl
Gaede, D. The punishment
Gaiman, N. Closing time
Gallagher, S. Doctor Hood
García Márquez, G. The ghosts of August
Gilliland, G. Witches
Glasgow, E. The shadowy third
Glover, D. A piece of the True Cross
Goran, L. Jenny and the Episcopalian

Gorman, E. Ghost of a chance
Gorman, E. Ghosts
Goulart, R. The phantom highwayman
Goyen, W. A shape of light
Grant, C. L. Brownie, and me
Grant, C. L. Whose ghosts these are
Griffith, N. A troll story: lesson in what matters, No. 1
Hautala, R. The Nephews
Hawthorne, N. The gray champion
Herber, P. J. True colors
Herlihy, J. L. The astral body of a U.S. mail truck
Hill, J. 20th century ghost
Hirshberg, G. Dancing men
Hirshberg, G. Mr. Dark's carnival
Hirshberg, G. Shipwreck beach
Hirshberg, G. Struwwelpeter
Hirshberg, G. The two Sams
Hoffman, N. K. Gone
Iorillo, J. and Pipik, J. Shadows
Jackson, S. The haunting of Hill House [excerpt]
Jacobs, W. W. The monkey's paw
James, H. The friends of the friends
James, H. The ghostly rental
James, H. The jolly corner
James, H. The romance of certain old clothes
James, H. Sir Edmund Orme
James, M. R. Oh, whistle and I'll come to you, my lad
Joyce, G. Tiger moth
Kelly, J. P. The cruelest month
Kennett, R. Due west
Kilpatrick, N. Megan's spirit
Kipling, R. They
Koja, K. Velocity
Lawrence, D. H. The border line
Lawson, C. and Brown, S. No Man's Land
Lay, C. Windigo
Lee, T. The ghost of the clock
Lee, T. Jedella ghost
Lee, V. Amour dure
Lindskold, J. M. It must burn
Link, K. Louise's ghost
Lott, B. The train, the lake, the bridge
Lurie, A. The highboy
Lurie, A. The pool people
Marías, J. No more loves
Marías, J. When I was mortal
Matiella, A. C. Feliz Navidad
Mattingly, K. Dance of the dolphins
McAuley, P. J. Bone orchards
McAuley, P. J. Naming the dead
McCrumb, S. The gallows necklace
Michaels, R. Noctem Aeternus
Monteleone, T. F. Lux et veritas
Morris, M. Coming home
Mosiman, B. S. Dread Inlet
Myrmo, M. Mama dear
Newman, K. Egyptian Avenue
Newman, K. A Victorian ghost story
Oates, J. C. Ghost girls
Odell, B. A foggy walk
O'Driscoll, M. The silence of the falling stars
Oliver, C. A lake of summer
Oltion, J. Abandon in place
Onions, O. The beckoning fair one
Palmer, S. Bent Creek Burn

GHOST STORIES—*Continued*

Pastor, B. Achilles' grave
Peterson, P. W. Cherry's ghost
Phillips, R. S. Wolfie
Rodgers, D. Star Woman's child
Rodwell, I. and Duffy, S. The penny drops
Rudd, K. Fat Tuesday
Rusch, K. K. The light in Whale Cove
Sammān, G. The other side of the door
Sammān, G. Register: I'm not an Arab woman
Segriff, L. Specters in the moonlight
Shawl, N. The tawny bitch
Shepard, L. Limbo
Singer, I. B. The shadow of a crib
Singer, I. B. Two corpses go dancing
Smee, B. The old ones cast
Sneve, V. D. H. The slim butte ghost
Spark, M. Another pair of hands
Spark, M. The executor
Spark, M. The leaf-sweeper
Spark, M. The Portobello Road
Spencer, E. Owl
Stavans, I. Blimunda
Straub, P. Hunger, an introduction
Su Tong. Cherry
Swarthout, G. F. Gersham and the saber
Tangh, J. The Skinned
Tawada, Y. The bath
Tessier, T. Lulu
Thomas, H. N. The village cock
Van Pelt, L. River watch
Vukcevich, R. Pretending
Watt-Evans, L. Upstairs
Weinberg, R. Three steps back
Weingarten, R. Aura, cry, fall, and fit
Weldon, F. Spirits fly south
West, M. Ghostwood
West, M. Hunger
Westlake, D. E. This is death
Wharton, E. All Souls'
Wharton, E. Bewitched
Wharton, E. Kerfol
Wharton, E. The lady's maid's bell
Wharton, E. Miss Mary Pask
Wharton, E. Mr. Jones
Wharton, E. Pomegranate seed
Wharton, E. The triumph of night
What, L. Clinging to a thread
What, L. Uncle Gorby and the baggage ghost
What, L. You gotta believe
Willis, C. Adaptation
Wilson, F. P. Aftershock
Wilson, G. The dead ghost
Yolen, J. A ghost of an affair
Zind, Rick. The way he knew it
Ghost story. LaValle, V. D.
A **ghost** story. Twain, M.
GHOST TOWNS *See* Extinct cities
The **ghost** village. Straub, P.
Ghost wolf of Thunder Mountain. Henry, W.
The **ghostly** rental. James, H.
GHOSTS *See* Ghost stories
Ghosts. Beaty, D.
Ghosts. Gorman, E.
Ghosts and bags. Agabian, N.
The **ghosts** of August. García Márquez, G.
Ghosts on the lake. Aichinger, I.
Ghosts, pockets, traces, necessary clouds. Alvarez, A.

Ghostwood. West, M.
Ghostwriter. Nelson, K.
GHOULS AND OGRES
Weinberg, R. The silent majority
Giacobino, Margherita
Mermaids, and other sea creatures
In the forbidden city; an anthology of erotic fiction by Italian women; edited by Maria Rosa Cutrufelli; translated by Vincent J. Bertolini
Gianni on the rocks. Barolini, H.
Giant. Nichols, J.
Giant step. Vukcevich, R.
La **giardiniera**. Barolini, H.
Gibbons, Reginald
What happened
The Ohio Review no60 p47-50 1999
Gibbons, Robert
Venice via hell & Belgrade
The Literary Review (Madison, N.J.) v42 no3 p383-84 Spr 1999
Giberga, Jane Sughrue
The implausible blonde
Good Housekeeping v229 no2 p174+ Ag 1999
Gibson, Stephen
Occam's razor
The Georgia Review v53 no2 p290-98 Summ 1999
Gibson, Warren
The girl at Thorp's
Fishing's best short stories; edited by Paul D. Staudohar
Gibson, William
Cyber-Claus
A yuletide universe; sixteen fantastical tales; edited by Brian M. Thomsen
Gibson, William and Swanwick, Michael
Dogfight
Masterpieces: the best science fiction of the century; edited by Orson Scott Card
Gies, Martha
Zoo animal keeper 1, REC-SVC-ZK
Nixon under the bodhi tree and other works of Buddhist fiction; edited by Kate Wheeler ; foreword by Charles Johnson
Gifford, Barry
American Falls
Gifford, B. American Falls; the collected short stories
The big love of Cherry Lane
Gifford, B. American Falls; the collected short stories
The brief confession of an unrepentant erotic
Gifford, B. American Falls; the collected short stories
Cat women of Rome
Gifford, B. American Falls; the collected short stories
A fair price
Gifford, B. American Falls; the collected short stories
For this we give thanks
Gifford, B. American Falls; the collected short stories
The lonely and the lost
Gifford, B. American Falls; the collected short stories

Gifford, Barry—*Continued*
The lost Christmas
  Gifford, B. American Falls; the collected short stories
My last martini
  Gifford, B. American Falls; the collected short stories
New mysteries of Paris
  Gifford, B. American Falls; the collected short stories
The old days
  Gifford, B. American Falls; the collected short stories
Only you
  Gifford, B. American Falls; the collected short stories
A really happy man
  Gifford, B. American Falls; the collected short stories
Romantica
  Gifford, B. American Falls; the collected short stories
Room 584, the Starr Hotel
  Gifford, B. American Falls; the collected short stories
The Tunisian notebook
  Gifford, B. American Falls; the collected short stories
Two border stories
  Gifford, B. American Falls; the collected short stories
The unspoken (Il nondetto)
  Gifford, B. American Falls; the collected short stories
Vendetta
  Gifford, B. American Falls; the collected short stories
The winner
  Gifford, B. American Falls; the collected short stories
Wrap it up
  Gifford, B. American Falls; the collected short stories
The yellow palace
  Gifford, B. American Falls; the collected short stories
The **gift**. Addonizio, K.
The **gift**. Giles, J. H.
The **gift**. Harfenist, J.
The **gift**. Iribarne, M.
The **gift**. Janicke, G.
The **gift**. Moody, J.
Gift. Roscoe, P.
A **gift** from somewhere. Aidoo, A. A.
The **gift** of a dream. Smith, D. W.
The **gift** of Cochise. L'Amour, L.
The **Gift** of Her Hands. Hanson, J.
The **Gift** of Loneliness. Freeman, C.
The **gift** of the magi. Henry, O.
The **gift** of the magicians, with apologies to you know who. Yolen, J.
A **gift** of two grey horses. Edghill, R.
Gifted. West, M.
GIFTED CHILDREN
  Kornbluth, C. M. The words of Guru
  Padgett, L. Mimsy were the borogoves
GIFTS
  Chacón, D. Andy the office boy
Gifts. Barker, N.

Gifts & grace. Taylor, J.
Gigantic. Aylett, S.
Gigantic. Nesbitt, M.
GIGOLOS
  Gabrielyan, N. Happiness
Gilb, Dagoberto
About Tere who was in Palomas
  Gilb, D. Woodcuts of women
  The Pushcart prize XXVI; best of the small presses, an annual small press reader; edited by Bill Henderson and the Pushcart prize editors
Bottoms
  Gilb, D. Woodcuts of women
Brisa
  Gilb, D. Woodcuts of women
Hueco
  Gilb, D. Woodcuts of women
Maria de Covina
  Gilb, D. Woodcuts of women
Mayela one day in 1989
  Gilb, D. Woodcuts of women
A painting in Santa Fe
  Gilb, D. Woodcuts of women
The pillows
  Gilb, D. Woodcuts of women
Romero's shirt
  Still wild; short fiction of the American West, 1950 to the present; edited by Larry McMurtry
Shout
  Gilb, D. Woodcuts of women
Snow
  Gilb, D. Woodcuts of women
Gilbert, Jim
Everything must go
  Stories from the Blue Moon Café; edited by Sonny Brewer
Gilbert, Michael
Judith
  Edwards, M. Mysterious pleasures; a celebration of the Crime Writers' Association's 50th anniversary; edited by Martin Edwards
Gilbert, Shloyme
Canary
  Neugroschel, J. No star too beautiful; Yiddish stories from 1382 to the present; compiled and translated by Joachim Neugroschel
Gilchrist, Ellen
1944
  Gilchrist, E. Collected stories
The abortion
  Gilchrist, E. I, Rhoda Manning, go hunting with my daddy, & other stories
Alone
  Gilchrist, E. I, Rhoda Manning, go hunting with my daddy, & other stories
Among the mourners
  Gilchrist, E. Collected stories
Anna, Part I
  Gilchrist, E. Collected stories
Bare ruined choirs, where late the sweet birds sang
  Gilchrist, E. The cabal and other stories
The big cleanup
  Gilchrist, E. The cabal and other stories
The brown cape
  Gilchrist, E. Collected stories

Gilchrist, Ellen—*Continued*
The cabal
  Gilchrist, E. The cabal and other stories
A Christmas in Wyoming
  Gilchrist, E. I, Rhoda Manning, go hunting
    with my daddy, & other stories
Drunk with love
  Gilchrist, E. Collected stories
Entropy
  Gilchrist, E. I, Rhoda Manning, go hunting
    with my daddy, & other stories
The famous poll at Jody's Bar
  Gilchrist, E. Collected stories
Fort Smith
  Gilchrist, E. Collected stories
The golden bough
  Gilchrist, E. I, Rhoda Manning, go hunting
    with my daddy, & other stories
Götterdämmerung, in which Nora Jane and
    Freddy Harwood confront evil in a world
    they never made
  Gilchrist, E. I, Rhoda Manning, go hunting
    with my daddy, & other stories
Hearts of Dixie
  Gilchrist, E. The cabal and other stories
I, Rhoda Manning, go hunting with my daddy
  Gilchrist, E. I, Rhoda Manning, go hunting
    with my daddy, & other stories
In the land of dreamy dreams
  Gilchrist, E. Collected stories
Jade Buddhas, red bridges, fruits of love
  Gilchrist, E. Collected stories
A lady with pearls
  Gilchrist, E. Collected stories
Light can be both wave and particle
  Gilchrist, E. Collected stories
Light shining through a honey jar
  Gilchrist, E. I, Rhoda Manning, go hunting
    with my daddy, & other stories
Lunch at the best restaurant in the world
  Gilchrist, E. Collected stories
Mexico
  Gilchrist, E. Collected stories
Miss Crystal's maid name Traceleen, she's talk-
    ing, she's telling everything she knows
  Gilchrist, E. Collected stories
Music
  Gilchrist, E. Collected stories
On the Wind River in Wyoming
  Gilchrist, E. I, Rhoda Manning, go hunting
    with my daddy, & other stories
Perhaps a miracle
  Gilchrist, E. Collected stories
Remorse
  Gilchrist, E. I, Rhoda Manning, go hunting
    with my daddy, & other stories
Revenge
  Gilchrist, E. Collected stories
The sanguine blood of men
  Gilchrist, E. The cabal and other stories
Some blue hills at sundown
  Gilchrist, E. Collected stories
The Southwest Experimental Fast Oxide Reactor
  Gilchrist, E. Collected stories
The Starlight Express
  Gilchrist, E. Collected stories
A statue of Aphrodite
  Gilchrist, E. Collected stories

The stucco house
  Gilchrist, E. Collected stories
Summer, an elegy
  Gilchrist, E. Collected stories
The survival of the fittest
  Gilchrist, E. The cabal and other stories
There's a Garden of Eden
  Gilchrist, E. Collected stories
Traceleen at dawn
  Gilchrist, E. Collected stories
Traceleen, she's still talking
  Gilchrist, E. Collected stories
Traceleen turns east
  Gilchrist, E. Collected stories
A tree to be desired
  Gilchrist, E. Collected stories
The uninsured
  Gilchrist, E. Collected stories
Victory over Japan
  Gilchrist, E. Collected stories
Witness to the crucifixion
  Gilchrist, E. Collected stories
You must change your life
  Gilchrist, E. Collected stories
The young man
  Gilchrist, E. Collected stories
Gilchrist, Jack
Opening day
  Fishing's best short stories; edited by Paul D.
    Staudohar
Gilded Quill: the story of Jones. Weaver, G.
Gilden, Mel
The adventure of the forgotten umbrella
  My Sherlock Holmes; untold stories of the
    great detective; edited by Michael Kurland
Gilders, Adam
One Theory about my Marriage
  The Paris Review v45 p149-52 Wint 2003
Parrot
  The Paris Review v45 p147-8 Wint 2003
Gildner, Gary
Come sta? Come va?
  The Kenyon Review ns24 no1 p119-34 Wint
    2002
The inheritance
  The Georgia Review v55 no3 p598-617 Fall
    2001
Leaving
  The North American Review v287 no1 p26-7
    Ja/F 2002
A picture postcard
  The Ohio Review no62/63 p253-7 2001
Giles, Janice Holt
The gift
  Home and beyond; an anthology of Kentucky
    short stories; edited by Morris Allen
    Grubbs; with an introduction by Wade Hall
    and an afterword by Charles E. May
Giles, Molly
Pie dance
  Fault lines; stories of divorce; collected and
    edited by Caitlin Shetterly
Two words
  The O. Henry Prize stories, 2003; edited and
    with an introduction by Laura Furman;
    jurers David Gutterson, Diane Johnson,
    Jennifer Egan
The **gilgul** of Park Avenue. Englander, N.

Gilley, Ted
The end zone
Prairie Schooner v75 no4 p35-47 Wint 2001
Gilliland, Gail
All their secrets
Gilliland, G. The demon of longing; short stories
Berkeley
Gilliland, G. The demon of longing; short stories
The demon of longing
Gilliland, G. The demon of longing; short stories
Dog stories
Gilliland, G. The demon of longing; short stories
Freedom
Gilliland, G. The demon of longing; short stories
Kindnesses
Gilliland, G. The demon of longing; short stories
News of the world
Gilliland, G. The demon of longing; short stories
Permanence
Gilliland, G. The demon of longing; short stories
Purple Heart
Gilliland, G. The demon of longing; short stories
Stones
Gilliland, G. The demon of longing; short stories
The Sturbridge tale
Gilliland, G. The demon of longing; short stories
The Texas Ranger
Gilliland, G. The demon of longing; short stories
When Amelia smiled
Gilliland, G. The demon of longing; short stories
Witches
Gilliland, G. The demon of longing; short stories
Gilman, Carolyn
The real thing
The Year's best science fiction, nineteenth annual collection; edited by Gardner Dozois
Gilman, Charlotte Perkins
Benigna Machiavelli
Gilman, C. P. The Charlotte Perkins Gilman reader; edited and introduced by Ann J. Lane
The cottagette
Gilman, C. P. The Charlotte Perkins Gilman reader; edited and introduced by Ann J. Lane
The crux
Gilman, C. P. The Charlotte Perkins Gilman reader; edited and introduced by Ann J. Lane
The girl in the pink hat
Gilman, C. P. The Charlotte Perkins Gilman reader; edited and introduced by Ann J. Lane

Herland
Gilman, C. P. The Charlotte Perkins Gilman reader; edited and introduced by Ann J. Lane
An honest woman
Gilman, C. P. The Charlotte Perkins Gilman reader; edited and introduced by Ann J. Lane
If I were a man
Gilman, C. P. The Charlotte Perkins Gilman reader; edited and introduced by Ann J. Lane
Making a change
Gilman, C. P. The Charlotte Perkins Gilman reader; edited and introduced by Ann J. Lane
Moving the mountain
Gilman, C. P. The Charlotte Perkins Gilman reader; edited and introduced by Ann J. Lane
Mr. Peebles heart
Gilman, C. P. The Charlotte Perkins Gilman reader; edited and introduced by Ann J. Lane
Turned
Gilman, C. P. The Charlotte Perkins Gilman reader; edited and introduced by Ann J. Lane
The unnatural mother
Gilman, C. P. The Charlotte Perkins Gilman reader; edited and introduced by Ann J. Lane
Unpunished
Gilman, C. P. The Charlotte Perkins Gilman reader; edited and introduced by Ann J. Lane
What Diantha did
Gilman, C. P. The Charlotte Perkins Gilman reader; edited and introduced by Ann J. Lane
When I was a witch
Gilman, C. P. The Charlotte Perkins Gilman reader; edited and introduced by Ann J. Lane
The widow's might
Gilman, C. P. The Charlotte Perkins Gilman reader; edited and introduced by Ann J. Lane
With her in Ourland
Gilman, C. P. The Charlotte Perkins Gilman reader; edited and introduced by Ann J. Lane
The yellow wallpaper
The 13 best horror stories of all time; edited by Leslie Pockell
The American fantasy tradition; edited by Brian M. Thomsen
Dark: stories of madness, murder, and the supernatural; edited by Clint Willis
Gilman, C. P. The Charlotte Perkins Gilman reader; edited and introduced by Ann J. Lane
Gilman, Greer
Jack Daw's pack
Death dines at 8:30; edited by Claudia Bishop and Nick DiChario

Gilman, Jeremy
　The Real World School of Law
　　New England Review v20 no2 p115-26 Spr
　　1999
Gilman, Susan Jane
　The birthday
　　The Virginia Quarterly Review v75 no2 p334-
　　59 Spr 1999
Gilpin Street. Fitch, B.
Gimmile's songs. Saunders, C. R.
Ginger cookies. Aldrich, B. S.
The **Ginger** Rogers sermon. Keegan, C.
Gingerbread and men. Ford, V.
Gingher, Marianne
　Teen angel
　　This is where we live; short stories by 25
　　contemporary North Carolina writers; ed-
　　ited by Michael McFee
Ginny Sweethips' Flying Circus. Barrett, N., Jr.
Ginsberg's tie. Acosta, J.
Giono, Jean
　Babeau
　　Giono, J. The solitude of compassion; trans-
　　lated by Edward Ford
　The destruction of Paris
　　Giono, J. The solitude of compassion; trans-
　　lated by Edward Ford
　Fields
　　Giono, J. The solitude of compassion; trans-
　　lated by Edward Ford
　The great fence
　　Giono, J. The solitude of compassion; trans-
　　lated by Edward Ford
　The hand
　　Giono, J. The solitude of compassion; trans-
　　lated by Edward Ford
　In the land of the tree cutters
　　Giono, J. The solitude of compassion; trans-
　　lated by Edward Ford
　Ivan Ivanovitch Kossiakoff
　　Giono, J. The solitude of compassion; trans-
　　lated by Edward Ford
　Jofroi de Maussan
　　Giono, J. The solitude of compassion; trans-
　　lated by Edward Ford
　Joselet
　　Giono, J. The solitude of compassion; trans-
　　lated by Edward Ford
　Lost rafts
　　Giono, J. The solitude of compassion; trans-
　　lated by Edward Ford
　Magnestism
　　Giono, J. The solitude of compassion; trans-
　　lated by Edward Ford
　On the side of the road
　　Giono, J. The solitude of compassion; trans-
　　lated by Edward Ford
　Philemon
　　Giono, J. The solitude of compassion; trans-
　　lated by Edward Ford
　Prelude to pan
　　Giono, J. The solitude of compassion; trans-
　　lated by Edward Ford
　The sheep
　　Giono, J. The solitude of compassion; trans-
　　lated by Edward Ford
　The solitude of compassion
　　Giono, J. The solitude of compassion; trans-
　　lated by Edward Ford

　Sylvie
　　Giono, J. The solitude of compassion; trans-
　　lated by Edward Ford
GIPSIES *See* Gypsies
Gira, M.
　Why I ate my wife
　　Carved in rock; short stories by musicians;
　　edited by Greg Kihn
GIRAFFES
　Tinti, H. Reasonable terms
Giraglia. Vigano, V.
Girardi, Robert
　Arcana mundi
　　Girardi, R. A vaudeville of devils; 7 moral
　　tales
　The defenestration of Aba Sid
　　The Best American mystery stories, 2000; ed-
　　ited and with an introduction by Donald E.
　　Westlake
　　Girardi, R. A vaudeville of devils; 7 moral
　　tales
　The demons tormenting Untersturmführer Hans
　　Otto Graebner
　　Girardi, R. A vaudeville of devils; 7 moral
　　tales
　The dinner party
　　Girardi, R. A vaudeville of devils; 7 moral
　　tales
　　The Year's best fantasy & horror, thirteenth
　　annual collection; edited by Ellen Datlow
　　and Terri Windling
　The primordial face
　　Girardi, R. A vaudeville of devils; 7 moral
　　tales
　Sunday evenings at Contessa Pasquali's
　　Girardi, R. A vaudeville of devils; 7 moral
　　tales
　Three ravens on a red ground
　　Girardi, R. A vaudeville of devils; 7 moral
　　tales
The **girders**. Lavin, M.
The **girdle**. Guerrero, L.
Girl. Garcia, L. G.
Girl. Kincaid, J.
Girl. Kureishi, H.
The **girl** across the room. Adams, A.
The **girl** at Chichén Itzá. Nissen, T.
The **girl** at Thorp's. Gibson, W.
The **girl** behind the hedge. Spillane, M.
The **girl** detective. Link, K.
Girl from Greenwich. Heller, J.
The **girl** from Soldier Creek. Foster, P.
The **Girl** in Snow. Stringer, S.
A **girl** in summer. Youmans, M.
Girl in the coat. Weihe, E.
The **girl** in the fall-away dress. Richmond, M.
The **girl** in the golden cage. Jakes, J.
The **girl** in the pink hat. Gilman, C. P.
The **girl** in the red chair. Brownrigg, S.
A **Girl** Like Me. Xi Xi
A **girl** like Phyl. Highsmith, P.
A **Girl** Like Summer. Goodman, L.
A **girl** like you. Gorman, E.
A **girl** like you. Schmidt, H. J.
A **girl** named Charlie. Cohen, S.
The **girl** of my dreams. Westlake, D. E.
Girl of their dreams. Cooke, C.
Girl on a couch. Reisman, N.
Girl on fire. Murray, Y. M.

GIRL SCOUTS
   Packer, Z. Brownies
   Ziegler, I. The waiting list
A **girl,** the jungle, monkeys. Chiappone, R.
The **girl** typist who worked for a provincial ministry of culture. Nuñez, M. E. A.
The **girl** who dreamed only geese. Lord, N.
The **girl** who killed Santa Claus. McDermid, V.
The **girl** who left her sock on the floor. Eisenberg, D.
The **girl** who loved animals. McAllister, B.
The **girl** who loved horses. Spencer, E.
The **girl** who married a monster. Boucher, A.
The **girl** who saw the colours of the rain. Edwards, S.
The **girl** who was plugged in. Tiptree, J.
A **girl** with a monkey. Michaels, L.
The **girl** with big hair. Day, C.
Girl with lizard. Schlink, B.
The **girl** with some kind of past. And George. Tenn, W.
The **girl** with the blackened eye. Oates, J. C.
The **girl** with the hungry eyes. Leiber, F.
"The **girl** with three husbands". Caballero, F.
Girlfriend hit by bus. Canty, K.
GIRLS
        See also Adolescence; Children; Youth
   Adam, C. Opossum
   Adam, C. Yellow jacket
   Adams, A. For good
   Adams, A. Roses, rhododendron
   Alcott, L. M. Bonfires
   Alcott, L. M. Grandmama's pearls
   Alcott, L. M. A little Cinderella
   Alcott, L. M. Little Genevieve
   Alcott, L. M. Little Robin
   Alcott, L. M. Milly's messenger
   Alcott, L. M. Lu Sing
   Aldrich, B. S. Across the smiling meadow
   Aldrich, B. S. How far is it to Hollywood?
   Aldrich, B. S. Juno's swans
   Antoni, R. A world of canes
   Atkinson, K. Dissonance
   Atwell, M. S. Blue night, Clover Lake
   Azadeh, C. The country road
   Bambara, T. C. Raymond's run
   Barker, N. Layla's nose job
   Baron, Dvora. Kaddish
   Barrett, N., Jr. "A day at the fair"
   Barrett, N., Jr. Perpetuity blues
   Bauman, B. A. Beautiful girls
   Bauman, B. A. The middle of the night
   Bausch, R. 1951
   Bausch, R. Missy
   Beattie, A. See the pyramids
   Bender, A. Jinx
   Bender, K. E. Anything for money
   Bly, C. Renee: a war story
   Bocock, M. The funeral
   Bocock, M. Heaven lies about
   Bocock, M. The tree
   Bowles, P. Here to learn
   Boylan, C. Gods and slaves
   Brady, C. Daley's girls
   Brady, C. Home movies
   Brand, D. Madame Alaird's breasts
   Brenner, W. Are we almost there
   Brenner, W. Nipple
   Brockmeier, K. These hands

   Brossard, N. Mauve desert [excerpt]
   Brown, C. Father Judge Run
   Brown, J. The submariners
   Brownstein, G. Safety
   Broyard, B. A day in the country
   Bukoski, A. Leokadia and fireflies
   Bush, M. Love
   Byatt, A. S. Jael
   Byatt, A. S. The thing in the forest
   Carson, J. Two thousand years of torture
   Caspers, N. La maison de Madame Durard
   Chopin, K. Charlie
   Chopin, K. A little country girl
   Chopin, K. Loka
   Chopin, K. A morning walk
   Clair, M. October Brown
   Clarke, B. The Lolita School
   Coates, G. S. Wild plums
   Cobb, W. J. The atmosphere of Vienna
   Connor, J. The thief of flowers
   Cook, K. L. Easter weekend
   Cook, K. L. Gone
   Cook, K. L. Nature's way
   Cook, K. L. Thrumming
   Corin, L. Rich people
   Craddock, C. E. The star in the valley
   Crone, M. Where what gets into people comes from
   Cummins, A. Dr. War is a voice on the phone
   Cummins, A. Red ant house
   Cummins, A. Trapeze
   Cutrufelli, M. R. Happiness
   Davenport, G. Belinda's world tour
   Davidson, A. The deed of the deft-footed dragon
   Davis, C. A. Brand new boyfriend
   Davis, L. Barbara's mother's rug
   Davis, L. In the memory house
   DeChoudhury, S. Forbidden fate
   Desai, A. The artist's life
   Díaz, J. Nilda
   Dillingham, D. G. The white carousel horse
   Doenges, J. Disaster
   Doerr, A. So many chances
   Doran, M. M. The estate of Joseph P. Bosley
   Doran, M. M. They shall have music
   Drake, R. The convertible
   Dropkin, Celia. At the rich relatives
   Eisenberg, D. The girl who left her sock on the floor
   Elrod, P. N. Izzy's shoe-in
   Emin, T. Albert Bert and Andy
   Erian, A. Alcatraz
   Erian, A. Still life with plaster
   Faygenberg, Rochel. My first readers
   Ferrell, C. Truth or consequences
   Ferrell, C. Wonderful teen
   Fischerová, D. Boarskin dances down the tables
   Fischerová, D. My conversations with Aunt Marie
   Foley, S. Elemenopy
   Franz, Carlos. Circle
   Frym, G. Canticle
   Frym, G. Infant sorrow
   Frym, G. No clubs allowed
   Frym, G. The stick
   Gabriel, D. Civilizations are islands
   Gabrielyan, N. The lilac dressing gown
   Galef, D. Dear, dirty Paris

GIRLS—*Continued*

Gansworth, E. L. The Raleigh Man
Gautreaux, T. Resistance
Gavell, M. L. The cotton field
Gavell, M. L. Penelope
Gilchrist, E. 1944
Gilchrist, E. Alone
Gilchrist, E. Revenge
Gilchrist, E. Victory over Japan
Gingher, M. Teen angel
Goldberg, M. Bee season
Goldstein, N. The conduct for consoling
Goldstein, N. Pickled sprouts
Goldstein, N. The Roberto touch
Goldstein, N. The verse in the margins
Goliger, G. Breaking the sabbath
Gonzalez, R. The garden of Padre Anselmo
Gordon, C. The petrified woman
Guerrero, L. Butterfly
Händler, E.-W. Language game
Harfenist, J. Body count
Harfenist, J. Duck season
Harfenist, J. The road out of Acorn Lake
Harfenist, J. Salad girls
Harfenist, J. Voluntary breathers
Hart, C. G. Spooked
Henley, P. Slinkers
Highsmith, P. The mightiest mornings
Highsmith, P. A mighty nice man
Highsmith, P. Miss Juste and the green rompers
Hill, I. Jolie-Gray
Hill, I. Pagan babies
Hill, I. Valor
Hird, L. The boxroom
Hochman, A. Diamonds are a girl's best friend
Hochman, A. Good with animals
Hochman, A. The whole truth and nothing but
Hoffman, A. Bake at 350°
Hoffman, A. Dear diary
Hoffman, A. Fate
Hoffman, A. Flight
Hoffman, A. How to talk to the dead
Hoffman, A. Rose red
Hoffman, A. Tell the truth
Homes, A. M. Things you should know
Honig, L. After
Hood, A. An ornithologist's guide to life
Horton, B. Colouring mother
Hughes, J. Forbidden fruits
Hyde, M. Her Hollywood
Jackson, V. F. Grandmother's footsteps
James, S. Hester and Louise
James, S. John Hedward
James, S. Mountain air
James, S. Outside paradise
James, S. Strawberry cream
Jen, G. The water faucet vision
Jimenez, K. P. The lake at the end of the wash
Johnson, D. Hot pepper
Johnson, D. Melvin in the sixth grade
Johnson, G. C. The obedient child
Johnson-Davies, D. Garbage girl
Jones, G. Knowledge
Jones, G. Modernity
Jones, G. The word 'Ruby'
Jones, T. Thorazine Johnny Felsun loves me (from his permanent cage of lifelong confinement)
Jones, Tayari. Best cousin

Kalfus, K. Anzhelika, 13
Kalman, J. Eichmann's monogram
Kalman, J. Personal effects
Kalman, J. A property of childhood
Kalu, Anthonia C. Angelus
Kalu, Anthonia C. Independence
Kaminsky, S. M. Hidden
Kaplan, D. M. Doe season
Kaufman, W. Helen on Eighty-Sixth Street
Kavaler, R. Pets
Keegan, C. The Ginger Rogers sermon
Keegan, C. Men and women
Keegan, C. The singing cashier
King, G. The little convent girl
Knight, M. Amelia Earhart's coat
Kohler, S. Cracks
Kohler, S. Luck
Kohler, S. Poor cousins
Kohler, S. Underworld
Kortes, Mary Lee. Summer vacation
Krawiec, R. The house of women
Lamé, A. Mapping
Lavin, M. Lemonade
Le Guin, U. K. Buffalo gals, won't you come out tonight
Lear, P. Nirvana
Leduc, V. L'asphyxie [excerpt]
Lessing, D. M. Victoria and the Staveneys
Lincoln, C. A hook will sometimes keep you
Link, K. Vanishing act
Lipsyte, S. The morgue rollers
Londynski, Helen. The four-ruble war
Lopez, B. H. The deaf girl
López, L. Sophia
Lord, N. The girl who dreamed only geese
Louis, L. G. Thirty yards
Lundquist, R. Grounded
Maleti, G. Lime-tree
Maleti, G. The precipice
Maraini, D. Viollca, the child from Albania
Marías, J. Unfinished figures
Maron, M. Till 3:45
Marshall, P. Bunnymoon
Martin, P. P. Amor desesperado—Desperate love
Martin, P. P. Amor prohibido—Forbidden love
Mastretta, A. Aunt Elvira
Mastretta, A. Aunt Verónica
Matiella, A. C. Feliz Navidad
Maxwell, M. A. O. Devil beads
McDonald, I. Tendeléo's story
McKenzie, A. Private school
Mencken, S. H. Birthday
Mencken, S. H. Grown-up
Mencken, S. H. Little white girl
Mencken, S. H. Tomboy
Meredith, D. The recital
Miller, R. Nancy
Mirvis, T. A Poland, a Lithuania, a Galicia
Moses, J. Girls like you
Müller, H. Nadirs
Murray, S. The caprices
Murray, Y. M. Girl on fire
Nailah, A. French
Nawrocki, S. Boys
Nawrocki, S. Dogs
Neri, K. Sentence imposed
Nissen, T. Flowers in the dustbin, poison in the human machine

GIRLS—*Continued*

Nissen, T. Out of the girls' room and into the night

Nissen, T. When the rain washes you clean you'll know

Norris, H. The great and small

Norris, L. American primitive

Norris, L. Stray dogs

Oates, J. C. Ghost girls

Oates, J. C. The sky-blue ball

Oates, J. C. Upholstery

O'Connell, M. The patron saint of girls

O'Connell, M. The patron saint of travelers

O'Connell, M. Saint Catherine Laboure

O'Connell, M. Saint Dymphna

Offutt, C. The best friend

Offutt, C. Second hand

O'Nan, S. 20 burgers

Orringer, J. Note to sixth-grade self

Orringer, J. Stars of Motown shining bright

Orringer, J. Stations of the cross

Packer, Z. Brownies

Packer, Z. Speaking in tongues

Parris, P. B. Carmen Miranda's navel

Perabo, S. Gravity

Perkins, E. The indelible hulk

Philip, M. N. Stop frame

Phillips, J. A. Alma

Piñón, N. House of passion

Poirier, M. J. Gators

Potvin, E. A. Invert and multiply

Potvin, E. A. Sister Marguerite

Power, S. Roofwalker

Pritchard, M. Salve Regina

Rabb, M. My mother's first lover

Reifler, N. The river and Una

Reifler, N. Sugar

Reifler, N. Teeny

Richmond, M. Big bang

Richmond, M. Mathematics and acrobatics

Richter, S. The beauty treatment

Rinehart, S. Another pyramid scheme

Robison, M. Trying

Rodgers, S. J. Fits and starts

Rodgers, S. J. Lost spirits

Roemer, A. The inheritance of my father: a story for listening

Roth, J. The blind mirror

Sandlin, L. Beautiful

Sandor, M. Capacity

Sanford, A. Fo Nut X

Sanford, A. In the Little Hunky River

Sanford, A. Mr. Moore's old car

Sanford, A. Nobody listens when I talk

Sanford, A. One summer

Schmidt, H. J. A girl like you

Schoemperlen, D. Losing ground

Schtok, F. At the mill

Schtok, F. Winter berries

Scoville, S. The dividing strand

Scoville, S. The pin collectors

Searle, E. Memoir of a soon-to-be star

Sekaran, S. Stalin

Sellers, H. Florida law

Sellers, H. The Gulf of Mexico

Sellers, H. In the drink

Sellers, H. It's water, it's not going to kill you

Sellers, H. Myself as a delicious peach

Sellers, H. Sinking

Sellers, H. Sleep creep leap

Sellers, H. Spurt

Senior, O. Do angels wear brassieres?

Shippen, J. R. I am not like Nuñez

Shoemaker, Karen. Playing horses

Shonk, K. My mother's garden

Shrayer-Petrov, D. Young Jews and two gymnasium girls

Simonds, M. King of the Cowboys, Queen of the West

Simonds, M. The lion in the room next door

Simonds, M. Nossa Senhora dos Remédios

Simpson, H. Golden apples

Slaughter, K. Necessary women

Slezak, E. Head, heart, legs or arms

Slezak, E. Last year's Jesus (or Passion play)

Smart, A. The bridge players

Smart, A. Emily

Smart, A. The Green Lantern

Smart, A. Hunter

Smart, A. Mud and strawberries

Smart, A. The turtle

Smart, A. The wedding Dress

Smith, A. The unthinkable happens to people every day

Sojourner, M. Betabank

Soukup, M. Up above Diamond City

Spedding, Sally. Strangers waiting

Spencer, E. The legacy

Spencer, E. Sharon

Stableford, B. M. The pipes of Pan

Stableford, B. M. What can Chloe want?

Stahl, Anna Kazumi. Natural disasters

Stuckey-French, E. Junior

Svoboda, T. Party girl

Svoboda, T. Polio

Swan, G. Gate of ivory, gate of horn

Thomas, D. The Christmas whopper

Thomas, D. Flowers appear on the earth

Thomas, D. Frost in the morning

Thompson, J. The Amish

Tippens, E. Make a wish

Trevor, W. Good news

Tuck, L. Gold leaf

Tyau, K. Pick up your pine

Umansky, E. M. How to make it to the promised land

Vapnyar, L. Ovrashki's trains

Vapnyar, L. A question for Vera

Vaswani, N. Sita and Ms. Durber

Vaswani, N. Where the long grass bends

Verolin, Irma. The stairway in the gray patio

Vivante, A. The foghorn

Ward, L. Dancing lessons

Watanabe McFerrin, L. God and all the angels

Wells, K. A. wonderland

West, D. My baby . . .

West, M. The stolen child

Wexler, M. Save yourself

White, M. C. Three whacks a buck

White, M. C. Voices

Wicks, V. I have the serpent brought

Winsloe, C. The child Manuela [excerpt]

Woolson, C. F. Felipa

Yolen, J. Lost girls

Yolen, J. Speaking to the wind

Youmans, M. A girl in summer

Young, T. Yellow with black horns

Youngblood, S. Triple X

GIRLS—*Continued*

Zabytko, I. My black Valiant
Zabytko, I. Saint Sonya
Ziegler, I. Feud of the maids
Ziegler, I. Hooked
Ziegler, I. How to breathe underwater
Ziegler, I. The raft
Ziegler, I. Rules of the lake
Ziegler, I. The waiting list
Zinovyeva-Annibal, L. D. The centaur-princess
Zinovyeva-Annibal, L. D. Deaf Dasha
Zinovyeva-Annibal, L. D. The devil
Zinovyeva-Annibal, L. D. The midge
Zinovyeva-Annibal, L. D. Zhurya

The **girls**. Drake, R.
The **girls**. Randolph, L.
The **girls'** guide to hunting and fishing. Bank, M.
The **girls** in Villa Costas. Brett, S.
Girls like us. Browder, C.
Girls like you. Moses, J.

Gischler, Victor

Hitting Rufus
The Best American mystery stories, 1999; edited and with an introduction by Ed McBain

"Give-a-Damn" Jones. Pronzini, B.
Give and take. Dixon, S.
Give brother my best. Kavaler, R.
Give it up for Billy. White, E.
Give me a sign. Leslie, N.
Given. McNally, T. M.

Givens, John

On the wheel of wandering-on
Living on the edge; fiction by Peace Corps writers; edited by John Coyne

Glacial. Reynolds, A.
Glacierland. Meyers, K.
GLADNESS *See* Happiness

Glasgow, Ellen

The shadowy third
Nightshade: 20th century ghost stories; edited by Robert Phillips

Glasgow, Greg

Home at last
Virgin fiction 2

GLASGOW (SCOTLAND) *See* Scotland—Glasgow

Glaspell, Susan

A jury of her peers
The Best American mystery stories of the century; Tony Hillerman, editor; with an introduction by Tony Hillerman
The Best American short stories of the century; John Updike, editor, Katrina Kenison, coeditor; with an introduction by John Updike
Master's choice v2; mystery stories by today's top writers and the masters who inspired them; edited by Lawrence Block
A moment on the edge; 100 years of crime stories by women; edited by Elizabeth George

Glass. Coates, G. S.
The **glass** bottle trick. Hopkinson, N.
Glass cheques. O'Hagan, A.
Glass cloud. Kelly, J. P.
Glass house. Stanton, M.
Glass meadow. Bausch, R.
A **glass** of blessings. Swarthout, G. F.

The **glass** tower. Arenas, R.

Glassco, Bruce

Taking loup
The Year's best fantasy & horror, twelfth annual collection; edited by Ellen Datlow & Terry Windling

GLAUCUS, FL. CA. 80 B.C.
About
Rucker, R. v. B. The square root of Pythagoras

Glauke's gown: the function of myth. Di Blasi, D.

Glave, Thomas

Accidents
Glave, T. Whose song? and other stories
—and love them?
Glave, T. Whose song? and other stories
Commitment
Glave, T. Whose song? and other stories
The final inning
The Best of The Kenyon review; edited by David Lynn; introduction by Joyce Carol Oates
Glave, T. Whose song? and other stories
Flying
Glave, T. Whose song? and other stories
The pit
Glave, T. Whose song? and other stories
The Kenyon Review ns21 no1 p51-72 Wint 1999
A real place
Glave, T. Whose song? and other stories
South Beach, 1992
Callaloo v26 no2 p417-30 Spr 2003
Their story
Glave, T. Whose song? and other stories
Whose song?
Callaloo v24 no2 p478-86 Spr 2001
Circa 2000; gay fiction at the millennium; edited by Robert Drake & Terry Wolverton
Glave, T. Whose song? and other stories

Glenn Gould in six parts. Haskell, J.

Glickmann, Nora

The last emigrant
Short stories by Latin American women; the magic and the real; edited by Celia Correas de Zapata; foreword by Isabel Allende

Glidden, Frederick Dilley *See* Short, Luke, 1908-1975

A **glimpse**. Wharton, E.
Glissando. Boswell, R.

Gloeggler, Tony

The Way a World Can Change
The Massachusetts Review v44 no3 p416-18 Fall 2003

Glorious Days. Yoshimura, A.
Glory. Lee, M.
Glory. Wuori, G. K.
Glory and the angels. Carter, E.
Glory B. and the baby Jesus. Carter, E.
Glory B. and the gentle art. Carter, E.
Glory B. and the ice-man. Carter, E.
Glory goes and gets some. Carter, E.

Gloss, Molly

Lambing season
The Year's best science fiction; twentieth annual collection; edited by Gardner Dozois

Gloucester. Finger, A.

Glover, Douglas
  A piece of the True Cross
    Ghost writing; haunted tales by contemporary
      writers; edited by Roger Weingarten
Glover, Douglas H.
  Abrupt extinctions at the end of the Triassic
    The Canadian Forum v78 no877 p34-35 My
      1999
  Bad news of the heart
    Glover, D. H. Bad news of the heart
  La Corriveau
    Glover, D. H. Bad news of the heart
  Dog attempts to drown man in Saskatoon
    Glover, D. H. Bad news of the heart
  A guide to animal behaviour
    Glover, D. H. Bad news of the heart
  Iglaf and Swan
    Glover, D. H. Bad news of the heart
  The Indonesian client
    Glover, D. H. Bad news of the heart
  A man in a box
    Glover, D. H. Bad news of the heart
  My romance
    Glover, D. H. Bad news of the heart
  The obituary writer
    Glover, D. H. Bad news of the heart
  A piece of the true cross
    Glover, D. H. Bad news of the heart
  State of the nation
    Glover, D. H. Bad news of the heart
  Why I decide to kill myself and other jokes
    Glover, D. H. Bad news of the heart
Gloves of her own. Guerrero, L.
A **Glue-Related** Problem. Haines, L.
Glut your soul on my accursed ugliness. Shepard,
  J.
A **glutton** for punishment. Yates, R.
Gluttony. Fromm, P.
GNOMES *See* Fairies
Goal 666. Richter, S.
Goat song. Anderson, P.
GOATS
  Bowles, P. The husband
  Ortiz, S. J. Distance
Goblin fruit. Chan, D. M.
GOD
  Aldiss, B. W. Steppenpferd
  Bradbury, R. The man
  Dowling, T. He tried to catch the light
  Dubus, A. Corporal Lewis
  Kelly, J. P. Proof of the existence of God
  Moorcock, M. A slow Saturday night at the Sur-
    realist Sporting Club
  Peterson, P. W. A miracle
  Reiner, C. Creation
God and all the angels. Watanabe McFerrin, L.
God and mammon. Raphael, F.
God bless America. Almond, S.
God bless America. Killens, J. O.
A **god** for delphi. Eakin, W.
God knows. Skillings, R. D.
God lies in the details. Allegra, D.
The **God** of dark laughter. Chabon, M.
God of gods. Doenges, J.
God of thunder's gonna getcha. Cheng, C.-W.
The **goddess** in the ice. Ellison, H.
The **goddess** of the moon. Bobier, M.

Godfrey, Darren O.
  Inland, shoreline
    The Museum of horrors; edited by Dennis
      Etchison
Godin, Alexander
  My dead brother comes to America
    The Best American short stories of the
      century; John Updike, editor, Katrina
      Kenison, coeditor; with an introduction by
      John Updike
Godless in India. DeBoer, J.
Godlight. Wells, K.
The **godmother**. Chopin, K.
Godmother death. Yolen, J.
Godoy lives. Chacón, D.
GODS
  Gaiman, N. The Monarch of the Glen
Gods and slaves. Boylan, C.
God's goodness. Kemper, M.
The **gods** of Mars. Dozois, G. R.
The **gods** themselves throw incense. Harrison, H.
Godwin, Gail
  False lights
    Other people's mail; an anthology of letter
      stories; edited with an introduction by Gail
      Pool
  Largesse
    TriQuarterly no110/111 p71-82 Fall 2001
  A sorrowful woman
    The Workshop; seven decades of the Iowa
      Writers' Workshop: 42 stories, recollections
      & essays on Iowa's place in 20th-century
      American literature; edited by Tom Grimes
Godwin, Parke
  A matter of taste
    The Ultimate Halloween; edited by Marvin
      Kaye
Godwin, Tom
  The cold equations
    The Science fiction hall of fame: volume one,
      1929-1964; the greatest science fiction sto-
      ries of all time chosen by the members of
      the Science Fiction Writers of America; ed-
      ited by Robert Silverberg
GODZILLA (FICTITIOUS CHARACTER)
  Canty, K. Tokyo, my love
GOEBBELS, JOSEPH, 1897-1945
                  About
  Linaweaver, B. Moon of ice
Goebbels, Paul Joseph *See* Goebbels, Joseph,
  1897-1945
Goering, Hermann *See* Göring, Hermann, 1893-
  1946
Gogol. Lahiri, J.
Goin' down slow. Vachss, A. H.
Going after Bobo. Palwick, S.
Going after Cacciato. O'Brien, T.
Going after goat antelopes. Vasilenko, S.
The **going** away of Liza. Chopin, K.
Going back. Chenoweth, A.
Going back to the bridge in Berlin. Griffin, W. E.
  B.
Going down. Boyle, T. C.
Going home. Vachss, A. H.
Going home money. Lilly, J. M.
Going into hiding. Kercheval, J. L.
Going long. Mayo, W.
Going native. Rusch, K. K.
Going out of business forever. Hodgen, C.

Going over. Coberly, L. M.
Going places. Michaels, L.
Going postal. Bishop, P.
Going to see George. Swarthout, G. F.
Going to see Mr. B. V. Chinodya, S.
Going under. Campbell, R.
Going under. Dann, J.
Going wild. Painter, P.
Golam. Latour, J.
Gold, Glen David
   The tears of squonk, and what happened thereaf-
      ter
      McSweeney's mammoth treasury of thrilling
         tales; edited by Michael Chabon
Gold, Herbert
   My Mafia moll
      Modern Maturity v42R no5 p70-73 S/O 1999
   Religion: Goy
      Michigan Quarterly Review v41 no4 p522-6
         Fall 2002
   When Love dies, Where Is It Buried?
      Michigan Quarterly Review v43 no3 p350-8
         Summ 2004
Gold, Michael Anthony
   Dann
      His 3: brilliant new fiction by gay writers; ed-
         ited by Robert Drake and Terry Wolverton
GOLD
   Clarke, A. C. On golden seas
   Flynn, T. T. Ghost guns for gold
   L'Amour, L. By the waters of San Tadeo
   L'Amour, L. Trap of gold
   Locklin, G. The gold rush
   Wellen, E. The whisper of gold
Gold. Berkman, P. R.
Gold. Chee, A.
The gold at the starbow's end. Pohl, F.
Gold Coast. McPherson, J. A.
Gold glitter. Berkman, P. R.
Gold leaf. Tuck, L.
The Gold Lunch. Carlson, R.
GOLD MINES AND MINING
   Hodgson, K. Requiem for Rosebud
   Jakes, J. Jonas Crag
   L'Amour, L. Under the hanging wall
   London, J. All Gold Canyon
GOLD RUSH See California—1846-1900
The gold rush. Locklin, G.
Goldberg, D. G. K.
   The boy next door
      The Darkest thirst; a vampire anthology
Goldberg, Myla
   Bee season
      Lost tribe; jewish fiction from the edge
   The commemorative
      Harper's v302 no1812 p71-8 My 2001
Golden, Christopher
   Lament for the gunwitch
      The Crow; shattered lives & broken dreams;
         edited by J. O'Barr and Ed Kramer
Golden, Karris
   Fish story
      The North American Review v286 no6 p24-7
         N/D 2001
Golden. Wuori, G. K.
Golden apples. Simpson, H.
Golden apples of the sun. Dozois, G. R.
The Golden Benefactors of Brewster McMahon.
   Davis, L.

The golden bough. Gilchrist, E.
The golden bullet. Groner, A.
The golden chariot. Lee, A.
The Golden Cradle mystery. Morris, M. V.
Golden Gate Bridge—a view from below. Ehlers,
   J.
The golden gift of grey. MacLeod, A.
Golden glass. Villanueva, A.
The golden helix. Sturgeon, T.
The golden honeymoon. Lardner, R.
The Golden Horus. Brand, M.
The golden rose. Alas, L.
The golden rounds. Holtzer, S.
A golden wedding: and what came of it. Alcott, L.
   M.
Goldfaden, Josh
   The Veronese Circle
      New England Review v24 no1 p204-19 Wint
         2003
A goldfish, a plant, a bowl of fresh fruit. Strick-
   land, L.
Goldhagen, Shari
   The Next Generation of Dead Kennedys
      Confrontation no86/87 p25-42 Spr/Summ
         2004
Goldhammer, Arthur
   (jt. auth) See Waberi, Abdourahman A.
Goldie and the three bare bachelors. Rollins, H.
Goldie's gift. Banks, L. W.
The goldilocks problem. Benford, G.
Goldilocks tells all. Bradfield, S.
Goldman, Arthur Steven
   David and Alice: Seventeen Lines about the End
      of the World
      Gettysburg Review v17 no1 p109-20 Spr 2004
Goldman, William
   The princess bride [excerpt]
      Swords and sorcerers; stories from the world
         of fantasy and adventure; edited by Clint
         Willis
Goldner, Beth
   Bad ass Bob, a mug shot mug, a man
      Goldner, B. Wake; stories
   Cardiff-by-the-Sea
      Goldner, B. Wake; stories
   Checkmate
      Goldner, B. Wake; stories
   Deep down to the bottom of this
      Goldner, B. Wake; stories
   Expatriates
      Goldner, B. Wake; stories
   Farm wife
      Goldner, B. Wake; stories
   Outcomes
      Goldner, B. Wake; stories
   Plan B
      Goldner, B. Wake; stories
   Taxi dancer
      Goldner, B. Wake; stories
   Wake
      Goldner, B. Wake; stories
   Waxing
      Goldner, B. Wake; stories
Goldstein, Lisa
   The fantasma of Q_____
      The Year's best fantasy & horror, twelfth an-
         nual collection; edited by Ellen Datlow &
         Terry Windling

Goldstein, Lisa—*Continued*

Tourists
  Masterpieces: the best science fiction of the century; edited by Orson Scott Card

Goldstein, Naama

Anatevka tender
  Goldstein, N. The place will comfort you; stories
Barbary apes
  Goldstein, N. The place will comfort you; stories
The conduct for consoling
  Goldstein, N. The place will comfort you; stories
Pickled sprouts
  Goldstein, N. The place will comfort you; stories
A pillar of a cloud
  Goldstein, N. The place will comfort you; stories
The Roberto touch
  Goldstein, N. The place will comfort you; stories
The verse in the margins
  Goldstein, N. The place will comfort you; stories
The worker rests under the hero trees
  Goldstein, N. The place will comfort you; stories

Goldstein, Rebecca

The courtship
  Neurotica: Jewish writers on sex; edited by Melvin Jules Bukiet
Demons, dreamers, and madmen
  Tikkun v14 no2 p58-65 Mr/Ap 1999

Goldstein, Yael

When Skeptics Die: A Story
  Commentary v117 no3 p41-7 Mr 2004

GOLEM

Shepley, J. A golem in Prague
Weiss, Bernice F. Where does a golem go?
The **golem**. Park, S.
A **golem** in Prague. Shepley, J.

GOLF

Bausch, R. Accuracy
Bausch, R. Par
Bishop, P. Night of the Frankengolfer
Bradbury, R. Fore!
Canin, E. The year of getting to know us
Cobb, T. Ball hawks
Dubus, A. An afternoon with the old man
Fitzgerald, F. S. Winter dreams
McBrearty, R. G. Soft song of the sometimes sane
Swarthout, G. F. Mulligans
Wodehouse, P. G. The heart of a goof

Goliath's Story. Finger, A.

Goliger, Gabriella

Air and earth
  Goliger, G. Song of ascent; stories
Breaking the sabbath
  Goliger, G. Song of ascent; stories
Edith Teilheimer's war
  Goliger, G. Song of ascent; stories
In this corner
  Goliger, G. Song of ascent; stories

Maedele
  Best new American voices 2000; guest editor Tobias Wolff; series editors John Kulka and Natalie Danford
  Goliger, G. Song of ascent; stories
Maladies of the inner ear
  Goliger, G. Song of ascent; stories
A man who has brothers
  Goliger, G. Song of ascent; stories
Mother tongue
  Goliger, G. Song of ascent; stories
One morning in Prague
  Goliger, G. Song of ascent; stories
Song of ascent
  Goliger, G. Song of ascent; stories
Who you are
  Goliger, G. Song of ascent; stories

Goligorsky, Eduardo

The last refuge
  Cosmos latinos: an anthology of science fiction from Latin America and Spain; translated, edited, & with an introduction & notes by Andrea L. Bell & Yolanda Molina-Gavilán

Gombrowicz, Witold

The Rat
  New England Review v25 no1/2 p78-86 2004

Gomes, Manuel Teixeira

Cordelia
  Gomes, M. T. Erotic stories; translated by Alison Aiken
Dead woman's grove
  Gomes, M. T. Erotic stories; translated by Alison Aiken
Deus ex machina
  Gomes, M. T. Erotic stories; translated by Alison Aiken
The gypsy: a letter to Antonio Patricio
  Gomes, M. T. Erotic stories; translated by Alison Aiken
Margareta
  Gomes, M. T. Erotic stories; translated by Alison Aiken
Question mark
  Gomes, M. T. Erotic stories; translated by Alison Aiken

Gomez, Jewelle

Chicago 1927
  Dark matter; a century of speculative fiction from the African diaspora; edited by Sheree R. Thomas

Gone. Crowley, J.
Gone. Hoffman, N. K.
Gone. Ketchum, J.
Gone girl. Macdonald, R.
Gone to glory. Garcia y Robertson, R.
Gone with wind—be back soon. Bonnie, F.

Gonsalves, Gayle

Tamarind stew
  The Bluelight corner; black women writing on passion, sex, and romantic love; edited by Rosemarie Robotham

González, Federico Schaffler *See* Schaffler González, Federico, 1959-

Gonzalez, Ray

The apparition
  Gonzalez, R. The ghost of John Wayne and other stories

Gonzalez, Ray—*Continued*

Away
    Gonzalez, R. The ghost of John Wayne and
      other stories

Becky
    Gonzalez, R. The ghost of John Wayne and
      other stories

The black pig
    Gonzalez, R. The ghost of John Wayne and
      other stories

Cabeza de Vaca
    Gonzalez, R. The ghost of John Wayne and
      other stories

Canyon de Kayenta
    Gonzalez, R. The ghost of John Wayne and
      other stories

The Chinese restaurant
    Gonzalez, R. The ghost of John Wayne and
      other stories

Circling the tortilla dragon
    Gonzalez, R. The ghost of John Wayne and
      other stories

Eduardo
    Gonzalez, R. The ghost of John Wayne and
      other stories

Fishing
    Gonzalez, R. The ghost of John Wayne and
      other stories

The garden of Padre Anselmo
    Gonzalez, R. The ghost of John Wayne and
      other stories

The ghost of John Wayne
    Gonzalez, R. The ghost of John Wayne and
      other stories

The grandfather horse
    Gonzalez, R. The ghost of John Wayne and
      other stories

How the brujo stole the moon
    Gonzalez, R. The ghost of John Wayne and
      other stories

In the ruins
    Gonzalez, R. The ghost of John Wayne and
      other stories

Invisible country
    Gonzalez, R. The ghost of John Wayne and
      other stories

The jalapeño contest
    Gonzalez, R. The ghost of John Wayne and
      other stories

The legend
    Gonzalez, R. The ghost of John Wayne and
      other stories

Mountain
    Gonzalez, R. The ghost of John Wayne and
      other stories

Postcards
    Gonzalez, R. The ghost of John Wayne and
      other stories

The properties of magic
    Gonzalez, R. The ghost of John Wayne and
      other stories

The scorpion eater
    Gonzalez, R. The ghost of John Wayne and
      other stories

Spaceship
    Gonzalez, R. The ghost of John Wayne and
      other stories

    Poets & Writers v29 no6 p39 N/D 2001

Spanish
    Gonzalez, R. The ghost of John Wayne and
      other stories

Train station
    Gonzalez, R. The ghost of John Wayne and
      other stories

Good. Strayed, C.

GOOD AND EVIL
    See also Sin; Suffering
    Alas, L. The golden rose
    Brooks, T. Indomitable
    Chekhov, A. P. A story without a title
    Donaldson, S. R. The djinn who watches over
      the accursed
    Drake, D. With the sword he must be slain
    Hawthorne, N. The great stone face
    Hawthorne, N. Young Goodman Brown
    Russ, J. Souls
    Singer, I. B. The jew from Babylon
    Stevenson, R. L. Markheim
    Troncoso, S. Espiritu Santo

Good as any. Westmoreland, T. A.

Good, brothers. Markus, P.

Good-by, Grandma. Bradbury, R.

Good-bye, Emily Dickinson. Trudeau, S.

GOOD-BYES *See* Farewells

Good career moves. Levinson, R. S.

A **Good,** Cheap Thrill. Wisniewski, M.

A **Good** Country. Jensen, G. S.

The **good** doctor. Abrams, T.

The **good** doctor. Haslett, A.

Good Fences. Meacham, R.

Good fences aren't always enough. George, E.

Good for the frog. Rosenfeld, S.

Good for the soul. Gautreaux, T.

Good for the soul. Vachss, A. H.

Good Friday. Wilson, F. P.

The **Good** Friday procession. Huffman, M.

Good-hearted woman. Sumner, M.

Good help. Bogen, K. B.

Good intentions. Keret, E.

The **good** life. Hawley, L.

The **good** life. Reisman, N.

Good man, bad man. Weidman, J.

A **good** man is hard to find. O'Connor, F.

Good Morning, New Jersey. Cotter, J.

Good news. Trevor, W.

Good news and bad news. Newman, D. A.

Good news in Culver Bend. Hassler, J.

Good night, good night. Westlake, D. E.

Good night, Mr. Khrushchev. Saum, S. B.

The **good** old German way. Kruse, T.

A **good** paved road. Clyde, M.

The **good** rabbi. Sloan, B.

Good rockin' tonight. Hauptman, W.

A **good** scent from a strange mountain. Butler, R.
    O.

A **good** shape. Norris, H.

The **good** shopkeeper. Upadhyay, S.

A **good** story. Westlake, D. E.

Good 'til now. Gay, W.

The **good** times. Kelman, J.

The **good** times are killing me. Krouse, E.

Good to go. Agee, J.

Good with animals. Hochman, A.

Good with girls. Cohen, R.

Good world. Haskell, J.

Goodbye, evil eye. Kirchheimer, G. D.

Goodbye mother. Arenas, R.

Goodbye, my love. Egan, J.
Goodbye, Oscar. Linney, R.
Goodbye party. Pietrzyk, L.
Goodbye, Pops. Gores, J.
Goodbye, Robinson Crusoe. Varley, J.
GOODBYES *See* Farewells
Goodfellows. Nelson, A.
Goodis, David
  The plunge
    A Century of noir; thirty-two classic crime
      stories; edited by Mickey Spillane and Max
      Allan Collins
Goodman, Allegra
  The local production of Cinderella
    The New Yorker v75 no16 p118+ Je 21-28
      1999
Goodman, Lee
  A Girl Like Summer
    Iowa Review v32 no2 p2-19 Fall 2002
Goodman. Keret, E.
Goodnight. Richter, S.
Goodnight, Irene. Buchanan, E.
GoodWeather, Hartley *See* King, Thomas, 1943-
Goodwill. Kaplan, H.
The **goophered** grapevine. Chesnutt, C. W.
Goose. Adam, C.
The **Goose** and the Moon.
Goose girl. Sanford, A.
Gooseberries. Chekhov, A. P.
Gopaleen, Myles Na *See* O'Brien, Flann, 1911-
      1966
Gopaleen, Myles *See* O'Brien, Flann, 1911-1966
Gopal's kitchen. Ramaya, S.
The **gopher**. Vasilenko, S.
GOPHERS
  Vasilenko, S. The gopher
Goran, Lester
  Adventurer
    Goran, L. Outlaws of the Purple Cow and
      other stories
  Alias Eleanor Roosevelt
    Goran, L. Outlaws of the Purple Cow and
      other stories
  The Big Broadcasts
    Goran, L. Outlaws of the Purple Cow and
      other stories
  Caught
    Goran, L. Outlaws of the Purple Cow and
      other stories
  The chorus girl
    Goran, L. Outlaws of the Purple Cow and
      other stories
  A day at the lake
    Goran, L. Outlaws of the Purple Cow and
      other stories
  The death of the quarterback
    Goran, L. Outlaws of the Purple Cow and
      other stories
  A guest on Good Friday
    Goran, L. Outlaws of the Purple Cow and
      other stories
  Hello, good-bye
    Goran, L. Outlaws of the Purple Cow and
      other stories
  The inheritance
    Goran, L. Outlaws of the Purple Cow and
      other stories

Jenny and the Episcopalian
  Goran, L. Outlaws of the Purple Cow and
    other stories
Keeping count
  Goran, L. Outlaws of the Purple Cow and
    other stories
O'Casey and the career
  Goran, L. Outlaws of the Purple Cow and
    other stories
An old man and three whores
  Goran, L. Outlaws of the Purple Cow and
    other stories
Outlaws of the Purple Cow
  Goran, L. Outlaws of the Purple Cow and
    other stories
The priest of storms
  Goran, L. Outlaws of the Purple Cow and
    other stories
Say something to Miss Kathleen Lacey
  Goran, L. Outlaws of the Purple Cow and
    other stories
Shannon made of sunlight and bones
  Goran, L. Outlaws of the Purple Cow and
    other stories
Why he never left his wife
  Goran, L. Outlaws of the Purple Cow and
    other stories
Goranson, Aaron
  When the Aliens Came
    The Literary Review (Madison, N.J.) v47 no2
      p139-43 Wint 2004
Gordimer, Nadine
  Country lovers
    A moment on the edge; 100 years of crime
      stories by women; edited by Elizabeth
      George
  The diamond mine
    Gordimer, N. Loot and other stories
    The New Yorker v75 no10 p82-85 My 10
      1999
  An emissary
    Gordimer, N. Loot and other stories
  The generation gap
    Gordimer, N. Loot and other stories
  History
    Harper's v308 p61-3 F 2004
  Homage
    Gordimer, N. Loot and other stories
  Karma
    Gordimer, N. Loot and other stories
  L. U. C. I. E.
    Gordimer, N. Loot and other stories
  Letter from his father
    Other people's mail; an anthology of letter
      stories; edited with an introduction by Gail
      Pool
  Look-alikes
    Gordimer, N. Loot and other stories
  Loot
    The New Yorker v75 no4 p104-05 Mr 22
      1999
  Message in a bottle
    The Best of The Kenyon review; edited by
      David Lynn; introduction by Joyce Carol
      Oates
  Mission statement
    Gordimer, N. Loot and other stories
  Safety Procedures
    The New Yorker v78 no28 p78-80 S 23 2002

Gordimer, Nadine—*Continued*

Visiting George

 Gordimer, N. Loot and other stories

Gordin, Jacob

Moses, Jesus Christ and Karl Marx Visit New York

 MELUS v28 no2 p224-35 Summ 2003

Gordon, Bill

Home

 Men on men 2000; best new gay fiction for the millennium; edited and with an introduction by David Bergman and Karl Woelz

Gordon, Caroline

The petrified woman

 Home and beyond; an anthology of Kentucky short stories; edited by Morris Allen Grubbs; with an introduction by Wade Hall and an afterword by Charles E. May

Gordon, Mary

The blind neighbor

 Writers harvest 3; edited and with an introduction by Tobias Wolff

Cleaning up

 Snapshots: 20th century mother-daughter fiction; edited by Joyce Carol Oates and Janet Berliner

The Dancing Party

 Ms. v12 no3 p40-4 Summ 2002

The deacon

 Atlantic Monthly v283 no5 p94-96+ My 1999

 Prize stories, 2000; The O. Henry awards; edited and with an introduction by Larry Dark

Death In Naples

 Salmagundi no137/138 p99-119 Wint/Spr 2003

Storytelling

 New stories from the South: the year's best, 1999; edited by Shannon Ravenel; with a preface by Tony Earley

The Translator's Husband

 Ms. v12 no4 p86-7 Wint 2002

Gordon, Peter

Birds of Paradise

 Ploughshares v29 no1 p79-89 Spr 2003

Swimmer

 Gettysburg Review v15 no2 p195-227 Summ 2002

Gored. Crider, B.

Gores, Joe

The Andrech samples

 Gores, J. Speak of the Devil; 14 tales of crimes and their punishments

The criminal

 Master's choice v2; mystery stories by today's top writers and the masters who inspired them; edited by Lawrence Block

Faulty register

 Gores, J. Speak of the Devil; 14 tales of crimes and their punishments

Goodbye, Pops

 The Best American mystery stories of the century; Tony Hillerman, editor; with an introduction by Tony Hillerman

 Gores, J. Speak of the Devil; 14 tales of crimes and their punishments

 Master's choice [v1]; mystery stories by today's top writers and the masters who inspired them; edited by Lawrence Block

Inscrutable

 The Best American mystery stories, 2002; edited and with an introduction by James Ellroy; Otto Penzler, series editor

 The Mysterious Press anniversary anthology; celebrating 25 years; by the editors of Mysterious Press

Killer man

 Gores, J. Speak of the Devil; 14 tales of crimes and their punishments

Night out

 Gores, J. Speak of the Devil; 14 tales of crimes and their punishments

Plot it yourself

 Gores, J. Speak of the Devil; 14 tales of crimes and their punishments

Quit screaming

 Gores, J. Speak of the Devil; 14 tales of crimes and their punishments

Raptor

 Gores, J. Speak of the Devil; 14 tales of crimes and their punishments

The second coming

 Gores, J. Speak of the Devil; 14 tales of crimes and their punishments

Sleep the big sleep

 Gores, J. Speak of the Devil; 14 tales of crimes and their punishments

Smart guys don't snore

 Gores, J. Speak of the Devil; 14 tales of crimes and their punishments

Speak of the Devil

 Gores, J. Speak of the Devil; 14 tales of crimes and their punishments

Summer fog

 Flesh and blood; erotic tales of crime and passion; edited by Max Allan Collins and Jeff Gelb

Watch for it

 Gores, J. Speak of the Devil; 14 tales of crimes and their punishments

You're putting me on, aren't you?

 Gores, J. Speak of the Devil; 14 tales of crimes and their punishments

Gores, Joseph N. *See* Gores, Joe

Gorey, Edward

The admonitory hippopotamus: or, Angelica and Sneezby

 The Paris Review v44 no162 p144-7 Summ 2002

Gorilla girl. Campbell, B. J.

Gorilla, my love. Bambara, T. C.

GORILLAS

Pritchard, M. Funktionlust

GÖRING, HERMANN, 1893-1946

    About

Twelve legions of angels

Gorky, Maksim

Song of the blind

 The Yale Review v89 no2 p104-11 Ap 2001

Gorman, Carol

The Death Cat of Hester Street

 Cat crimes through time; edited by Ed Gorman, Martin H. Greenberg, and Larry Segriff

 The World's finest mystery and crime stories, first annual collection; edited by Ed Gorman

Gorman, Edward
Aftermath
  Gorman, E. Such a good girl and other crime
    stories; with an introduction by Richard
    Laymon
All these condemned
  Gorman, E. Such a good girl and other crime
    stories; with an introduction by Richard
    Laymon
Angie
  999: new stories of horror and suspense; ed-
    ited by Al Sarrantonio
  Gorman, E. Such a good girl and other crime
    stories; with an introduction by Richard
    Laymon
En famille
  Master's choice [v1]; mystery stories by to-
    day's top writers and the masters who in-
    spired them; edited by Lawrence Block
The end of it all
  Speaking of lust; stories of forbidden desire;
    edited by Lawrence Block
Eye of the beholder
  Gorman, E. Such a good girl and other crime
    stories; with an introduction by Richard
    Laymon
Ghost of a chance
  Lighthouse hauntings; 12 original tales of the
    supernatural; edited by Charles G. Waugh
    & Martin H. Greenberg
Ghosts
  Gorman, E. Such a good girl and other crime
    stories; with an introduction by Richard
    Laymon
A girl like you
  Gorman, E. Such a good girl and other crime
    stories; with an introduction by Richard
    Laymon
  Love and death; edited by Carolyn Hart
Judgment
  Gorman, E. Such a good girl and other crime
    stories; with an introduction by Richard
    Laymon
Mom and Dad at home
  Mom, apple pie, and murder; edited by Nancy
    Pickard
A new man
  Gorman, E. Such a good girl and other crime
    stories; with an introduction by Richard
    Laymon
One of those days, one of those nights
  A Century of great suspense stories; edited by
    Jeffery Deaver
Out there in the darkness
  The Best American mystery stories, 1999; ed-
    ited and with an introduction by Ed
    McBain
The reason why
  A Century of noir; thirty-two classic crime
    stories; edited by Mickey Spillane and Max
    Allan Collins
Sailing to Atlantis
  Flesh and blood; erotic tales of crime and
    passion; edited by Max Allan Collins and
    Jeff Gelb
A small and private war
  The Blue and the gray undercover; edited by
    Ed Gorman

Such a good girl
  Gorman, E. Such a good girl and other crime
    stories; with an introduction by Richard
    Laymon
That day at Eagle's Point
  Gorman, E. Such a good girl and other crime
    stories; with an introduction by Richard
    Laymon
The way it used to be
  Gorman, E. Such a good girl and other crime
    stories; with an introduction by Richard
    Laymon
Wolf moon
  A Century of great Western stories; edited by
    John Jakes
Gorodischer, Angélica
The violet's embryos
  Cosmos latinos: an anthology of science fic-
    tion from Latin America and Spain; trans-
    lated, edited, & with an introduction &
    notes by Andrea L. Bell & Yolanda Moli-
    na-Gavilán
Gorriti, Juana Manuela
The black glove
  Gorriti, J. M. and others. Dreams and reali-
    ties; selected fiction of Juana Manuela
    Gorriti; translated from the Spanish by
    Sergio Waisman ; edited, with an introduc-
    tion and notes by Francine Masiello
The dead man's fiancée
  Gorriti, J. M. and others. Dreams and reali-
    ties; selected fiction of Juana Manuela
    Gorriti; translated from the Spanish by
    Sergio Waisman ; edited, with an introduc-
    tion and notes by Francine Masiello
Gubi Amaya
  Gorriti, J. M. and others. Dreams and reali-
    ties; selected fiction of Juana Manuela
    Gorriti; translated from the Spanish by
    Sergio Waisman ; edited, with an introduc-
    tion and notes by Francine Masiello
If you do wrong, expect no good
  Gorriti, J. M. and others. Dreams and reali-
    ties; selected fiction of Juana Manuela
    Gorriti; translated from the Spanish by
    Sergio Waisman ; edited, with an introduc-
    tion and notes by Francine Masiello
The mazorquero's daughter
  Gorriti, J. M. and others. Dreams and reali-
    ties; selected fiction of Juana Manuela
    Gorriti; translated from the Spanish by
    Sergio Waisman ; edited, with an introduc-
    tion and notes by Francine Masiello
The quena
  Gorriti, J. M. and others. Dreams and reali-
    ties; selected fiction of Juana Manuela
    Gorriti; translated from the Spanish by
    Sergio Waisman ; edited, with an introduc-
    tion and notes by Francine Masiello
The treasure of the Incas
  Gorriti, J. M. and others. Dreams and reali-
    ties; selected fiction of Juana Manuela
    Gorriti; translated from the Spanish by
    Sergio Waisman ; edited, with an introduc-
    tion and notes by Francine Masiello

Gorriti, Juana Manuela—*Continued*

A year in California

Gorriti, J. M. and others. Dreams and realities; selected fiction of Juana Manuela Gorriti; translated from the Spanish by Sergio Waisman ; edited, with an introduction and notes by Francine Masiello

Gorshman, Shira

Bubbe Malke

Beautiful as the moon, radiant as the stars; Jewish women in Yiddish stories : an anthology; edited by Sandra Bark; introduction by Francine Prose

Gosling, Patricia

Hurricane season

The Virginia Quarterly Review v78 no1 p109-22 Wint 2002

Scorched Earth

The Literary Review (Madison, N.J.) v47 no1 p126-38 Fall 2003

The **Gospel** according to Mark. Borges, J. L.

The **Gospel** of Mark Schneider. Vollmer, M.

Goss, Theodora

The rose in twelve petals

The Year's best fantasy & horror: sixteenth annual collection; edited by Ellen Datlow & Terri Windling

The **gossamer** girl. Asendorf, A. G.

GOSSIP

Brennan, M. The divine fireplace

Brennan, M. The view from the kitchen

Chávez, D. Grand slam

Davies, R. The dilemma of Catherine Fuchsias

Hawthorne, N. Mr. Higginbotham's catastrophe

James, H. The Patagonia

Lopez, B. H. Thomas Lowdermilk's generosity

Singer, I. B. On a wagon

Spence, J. Missing women

Gossy, Dorian

Bad

The North American Review v287 no3/4 p9-15 My/Ag 2002

Got spirit. Budnitz, J.

Got to kill them all. Etchison, D.

Gotera, Amanda Blue

Fledgling Magic

The North American Review v287 no6 p32-6 N/D 2002

GOTHIC ROMANCES

See also Horror stories

Goto, Hiromi

Drift

Ms. v9 no3 p82-87 Ap/My 1999

Tales from the breast

Witpunk; edited by Claude Lalumière and Marty Halpern

Gotta sing. Jenkins, G.

Götterdämmerung, in which Nora Jane and Freddy Harwood confront evil in a world they never made. Gilchrist, E.

Goudsward, Scott T.

Trailer trash

The Darkest thirst; a vampire anthology

Goulart, Ron

The phantom highwayman

The Ultimate Halloween; edited by Marvin Kaye

GOULD, GLENN, 1932-1982

About

Haskell, J. Glenn Gould in six parts

Gould, Lois

La Lloradora

Snapshots: 20th century mother-daughter fiction; edited by Joyce Carol Oates and Janet Berliner

Gould, Philip

A Mediterranean Goddess on the James

The Virginia Quarterly Review v78 no4 p616-35 Aut 2002

Meg O'Fallon

The Virginia Quarterly Review v79 no4 p635-50 Aut 2003

A nest of mares

The Virginia Quarterly Review v77 no4 p625-41 Aut 2001

Gourevitch, Philip

Mortality check

Coppola, F. F. Francis Ford Coppola's Zoetrope: all story; edited by Adrienne Brodeur and Samantha Schnee; introduction by Francis Ford Coppola

On the rocks; the KGB Bar fiction anthology; edited by Rebecca Donner ; foreword by Denis Woychuk

Goussier. See Chekhov, A. P. Gusev

GOVERNESSES

See also Housekeepers

Chekhov, A. P. A daughter of albion

Chekhov, A. P. An upheaval

Chekhov, A. P. Zinotchka

Kincaid, J. Poor Visitor

Wexler, M. The nanny trap

GOVERNORS

Wharton, E. The best man

The **governor's** ball. Carlson, R.

The **governors** of Wyoming. Proulx, A.

Goyen, William

A shape of light

Nightshade: 20th century ghost stories; edited by Robert Phillips

Goytisolo, Juan

The stork-men

The Year's best fantasy & horror, thirteenth annual collection; edited by Ellen Datlow and Terri Windling

Grab hold. Penn, W. S.

Grace, C. L.

For works written by this author under other names see Doherty, P. C.

Grace, Patricia

Butterflies

Ms. v12 no3 p78-9 Summ 2002

Grace. Alameddine, R.

Grace. Fairey, W. W.

Grace. Fox, P.

Grace notes. Paretsky, S.

GRACELAND

Hodgen, C. The hero of loneliness

Graceland. Steele, A. M.

A **gracious** rain. Tilghman, C.

Grade, Chaim

My quarrel with Hersh Rasseyner

When night fell; an anthology of Holocaust short stories; edited by Linda Schermer Raphael and Marc Lee Raphael

Grading the lilies. McIntosh, C. C.

GRADUATION *See* Commencements
Graduation. Matheson, R. C.
Graduation from the air. Drake, R.
Grady, James
  The championship of nowhere
    The Best American mystery stories, 2002; edited and with an introduction by James Ellroy; Otto Penzler, series editor
Graebner, Janet E.
  The living land
    American West; twenty new stories from the Western Writers of America; edited with an introduction by Loren D. Estleman
  The whispering
    Westward; a fictional history of the American West : 28 original stories celebrating the 50th anniversary of the Western Writers of America; edited by Dale L. Walker
Graff, E. J.
  Brotherhood
    Iowa Review v31 no2 p143-5 Fall 2001
GRAFFITI
  Bradbury, R. Olé Orozco! Siqueiros, sí!
  Urrea, L. A. Mr. Mendoza's paintbrush
  Vachss, A. H. Tag
Grafitto. Čapek, K.
Grafting. Nagai, M.
Grafton, Sue
  The Parker shotgun
    The Best American mystery stories of the century; Tony Hillerman, editor; with an introduction by Tony Hillerman
Graham, Philip
  My Miracle
    Western Humanities Review v57 no2 p32-40 Fall 2003
Grahn, Judy
  Green toads of the high desert
    Hers 2: brilliant new fiction by lesbian writers; edited by Terry Wolverton with Robert Drake
GRAIL
  Edghill, R. Prince of exiles
A **grain** of rye the size of a chicken egg. Tolstoy, L., graf
Grammar Questions. Davis, L.
The **grammarian's** five daughters. Arnason, E.
GRANADA (SPAIN) *See* Spain—Granada
Grand, David
  Louse [excerpt]
    The Vintage book of amnesia; an anthology; edited by Jonathan Lethem
The **grand** house opposite. Roth, J.
The **grand** illusion. McNally, J.
The **grand** opening. Lao She
Grand slam. Chávez, D.
Grand Street. Saroyan, A.
GRANDCHILDREN
    See also Granddaughters; Grandsons
  Gautreaux, T. Welding with children
Grandchildren. Baron, D.
GRANDDAUGHTERS
  Bender, K. E. Anything for money
  Farrell, C. Day of the dedication
  Jaime-Becerra, M. Lopez Trucking Incorporated
  Joseph, D. What remains
  Thompson, J. Antarctica
  Vinge, V. Gemstone
  Wharton, E. The angel at the grave

La **grande** demoiselle. King, G.
The **grandfather** horse. Gonzalez, R.
Grandfather out of the past. Loomis, N. M.
GRANDFATHERS
    See also Great-grandfathers
  Alvarez, J. Amor divino
  Anderson, D. My name is Stephen Mann
  Baida, P. A doctor's story
  Baron, Dvora. Kaddish
  Beinhart, L. Funny story
  Bezmozgis, D. Minyan
  Breen, J. L. Credit the cat
  Broughton, T. A. Italian autumn
  Butler, R. O. Mr. Green
  Clark, B. C. Fur in the hickory
  DeMarco, T. A boy's will is the winds's will
  Dunmore, H. Lisette
  Erickson, Ben. Floundering
  Evenson, B. Müller
  Gao Xingjian. Buying a fishing rod for my grandfather
  Gautreaux, T. Welding with children
  Gilchrist, E. A tree to be desired
  Greenberg, A. Tremors
  Greer, R. O. Isolation
  Hirshberg, G. Dancing men
  Hoch, E. D. Day for a picnic
  Kees, W. Letter from Maine
  LeRoy, J. T. Foolishness is bound in the heart of a child
  Matiella, A. C. Feliz Navidad
  Matiella, A. C. Nana's trilogy
  Mo Yan. Man and beast
  Murray, J. A few short notes on tropical butterflies
  Nair, M. My grandfather dreams of fences
  Oliver, C. Pilgrimage
  Orner, P. The raft
  Ortiz, S. J. Feeling old
  Ortiz, S. J. Men on the moon
  Ortiz, S. J. The San Francisco Indians
  Phillips, D. R. Why I'm talking
  Rendell, R. Walter's leg
  Rosenblatt, B. Zelig
  Shepard, S. The door to women
  Singer, I. B. A crown of feathers
  Singer, I. B. Grandfather and grandson
  Slezak, E. Tomato watch
  Smith, T. D. The purification of Jim Barnes
  Sneve, V. D. H. Grandpa was a cowboy and an Indian
  Sneve, V. D. H. Jimmy Yellow Hawk
  Sneve, V. D. H. The slim butte ghost
  Spencer, E. A Christian education
  Svoboda, T. White
  Tessier, T. Lulu
  Vapnyar, L. Mistress
  Wang Anyi. Between themselves
  Wharton, E. The angel at the grave
  Williams, M. The year Ward West took away the raccoon and Mr. Hanson's garage burneddown
Grandmama's pearls. Alcott, L. M.
GRANDMOTHERS
    See also Great-grandmothers
  Agabian, N. Ghosts and bags
  Alameddine, R. My grandmother, the grandmaster
  Alcott, L. M. Grandmama's pearls

GRANDMOTHERS—Continued

Aldrich, B. S. He whom a dream hath possest
Babel´, I. At grandmother's
Bambara, T. C. Maggie of the green bottles
Barrett, L. Twentieth century design
Berry, W. Pray without ceasing
Brady, C. Rat
Brown, C. The house on Belle Isle
Burke, J. Miscalculation
Chenoweth, A. If I were you
Chopin, K. A matter of prejudice
Collins, B. To grandmother's house we go
Connor, J. The thief of flowers
Desplechin, M. Taking it to heart
Dixon, S. The burial
Eickhoff, R. L. Dove's song
Faygenberg, Rochel. My first readers
Fernandez, P. A. The charm
Firth, C. The Department of Nothing
Franz, Carlos. Circle
Gay, W. Come home, come home, it's supper-time
Gilchrist, E. Bare ruined choirs, where late the sweet birds sang
Gonzalez, R. The black pig
Guerrero, L. Gloves of her own
Hermann, J. The end of something
Hermann, J. The red coral bracelet
Hoffman, A. How to talk to the dead
Hopkinson, N. Riding the red
Jackson, V. F. Grandmother's footsteps
James, S. Hester and Louise
Joseph, D. What remains
Keegan, C. The burning palms
Kenan, R. Hobbits and hobgoblins
Korn, R. H. The sack with pink stripes
Krawiec, R. The house of women
Lieu, J. The children
López, L. Soy la Avon lady
Lord, N. Remaking the world
Maraini, D. Shadows
Marshall, P. To Da-duh, in memoriam
Mastretta, A. Aunt Leonor
Mastretta, A. Aunt Rebeca
Meade, D. Lost time
Mencken, S. H. Each in her own day
Mogan, J. Mrs. Bajon says
Oates, J. C. What then, my life?
O'Connor, F. A good man is hard to find
Peck, D. Cities of the plain
Penn, W. S. Interlude
Rodgers, S. J. Lost spirits
Roemer, A. The inheritance of my father: a story for listening
Rossi, A. Orion's glow
Sandor, M. Legend
Sanford, A. In the Little Hunky River
Sanford, A. One summer
Shonk, K. My mother's garden
Singer, I. B. A crown of feathers
Smart, A. Emily
Smith, B. B. Death of a damn moose
Sneve, V. D. H. Clean hands
Spatz, G. Paradise was this
Swan, M. Emma's hands
Taraqqi, G. Grandma's house
Thomas, D. Grandma and the sentimental travler
Thomas, D. Grandma Hotel Adams
Thompson, J. Antarctica

Tomioka, T. Days of dear death
Troncoso, S. The abuelita
Updike, J. The blessed man of Boston, my grandmother's thimble, and Fanning Island
Vinge, V. Gemstone
Wegner, H. The pilots of the rose trellis
Weinreb, M. Pictures of my family
Williams, J. The blue men

Grandmother's footsteps. Jackson, V. F.

Grandpa. Stern, R. G.

Grandpa was a cowboy and an Indian. Sneve, V. D. H.

GRANDPARENTS

Brand, M. O. Closer than you think
Brown, J. The submariners
Brownstein, G. Safety
Erian, A. Still life with plaster
Jackson, V. F. Telling stories
MacLeod, A. The road to Rankin's Point
MacLeod, A. Vision
Müller, H. Nadirs
Parris, P. B. Carmen Miranda's navel
Stanton, M. My death
Yañez, R. Sacred Heart

GRANDSONS

Canty, K. Sleepers holding hands
Epstein, J. Moe
Hood, A. The language of sorrow
Iribarne, M. A dream, not alone
Reiner, C. Hampa Ham
Somtow, S. P. Bird catcher

Granelli, Roger

Disturbing the peace
    Mr. Roopratna's chocolate; the winning stories from the 1999 Rhys Davies competition

Granger, Ann

Murder at midday
    Malice domestic 9

Granja Carneiro, André See Carneiro, André, 1922-

Gran'mammy. MacDowell, K. S. B.

Grannie. Šikula, V.

Granny flowers in those heartless days. Pak, W.-S.

Granny rumple. Yolen, J.

Granny weather. De Lint, C.

The **Granny** Woman. Hughes, D. B.

Grant, Charles L.

Brownie, and me
    Datlow, E. The dark; new ghost stories; edited by Ellen Datlow
Whose ghosts are these
    The Mammoth book of best horror 13; edited by Stephen Jones
Whose ghosts these are
    The Museum of horrors; edited by Dennis Etchison

Grant, Gavin J. and Link, Kelly

Ship, sea, mountain, sky
    Death dines at 8:30; edited by Claudia Bishop and Nick DiChario

Grant, John See Gash, Jonathan, 1933-

Grant, John, 1949-
    See also Barnett, Paul, 1949-

Grant, Linda

The second-oldest profession
    Mom, apple pie, and murder; edited by Nancy Pickard

Grant, Linda—*Continued*
Murder most delectable; savory tales of culinary crimes; edited by Martin H. Greenberg
GRANT, ULYSSES S. (ULYSSES SIMPSON), 1822-1885
About
Marks, J. Under hoof
Granville Hill. Connolly, C.
Grape, Jan
Cat o'nine lives
Cat crimes through time; edited by Ed Gorman, Martin H. Greenberg, and Larry Segriff
Tabby won't tell
White House pet detectives; tales of crime and mystery at the White House from a pet's-eye view; edited by Carole Nelson Douglas
Grape Bay (1941). Maxwell, W.
GRAPES
Baker, K. Noble mold
The **grapes** of Roth. Kelman, J.
Grapette. Barthelme, F.
Graphology. Cooper, B.
Grappling. Appel, J. M.
Grasp special comb. Rosenfeld, S.
Grass, Günter
Class reunion
The New Yorker v75 no30 p86-92 O 11 1999
Grass. Roderick, D.
The **grass** is always greener . . . Archer, J.
Grass, leaves. Gunn, K.
The **grasshopper**. Chekhov, A. P.
Di **Grasso**. Babel', I.
GRATEFUL DEAD (MUSICAL GROUP)
Nissen, T. Grover, king of Nebraska
Grau, Shirley Ann
The beginning
Grau, S. A. Selected stories; with a foreword by Robert Phillips
The black prince
Grau, S. A. Selected stories; with a foreword by Robert Phillips
Flight
Grau, S. A. Selected stories; with a foreword by Robert Phillips
Home
Grau, S. A. Selected stories; with a foreword by Robert Phillips
Homecoming
Grau, S. A. Selected stories; with a foreword by Robert Phillips
Housekeeper
Grau, S. A. Selected stories; with a foreword by Robert Phillips
Hunter
Grau, S. A. Selected stories; with a foreword by Robert Phillips
The last gas station
Grau, S. A. Selected stories; with a foreword by Robert Phillips
Letting go
Grau, S. A. Selected stories; with a foreword by Robert Phillips
The lovely April
Grau, S. A. Selected stories; with a foreword by Robert Phillips

The man outside
Grau, S. A. Selected stories; with a foreword by Robert Phillips
One summer
Grau, S. A. Selected stories; with a foreword by Robert Phillips
The patriarch
Grau, S. A. Selected stories; with a foreword by Robert Phillips
Sea change
Grau, S. A. Selected stories; with a foreword by Robert Phillips
Summer shore
Grau, S. A. Selected stories; with a foreword by Robert Phillips
Three
Grau, S. A. Selected stories; with a foreword by Robert Phillips
Widow's walk
Grau, S. A. Selected stories; with a foreword by Robert Phillips
The wind shifting west
Grau, S. A. Selected stories; with a foreword by Robert Phillips
The **grave**. Cacek, P. D.
A **grave** in two places. Honigmann, B.
Grave Love: A Story. McAuliffe, J. D.
GRAVE ROBBERS
Arenas, R. End of a story
Evenson, B. The prophets
GRAVEDIGGERS
Bradbury, R. The lifework of Juan Diaz
Evenson, B.
Evenson, B. The gravediggers
Singer, I. B. By the light of memorial candles
Singer, I. B. The gravedigger
The **gravel** pit. L'Amour, L.
Graver, Elizabeth
The mourning door
The Best American short stories 2001; selected from U.S. and Canadian magazines by Barbara Kingsolver with Katrina Kenison; with an introduction by Barbara Kingsolver
Prize stories, 2001; The O. Henry awards; edited and with an introduction by Larry Dark
The Pushcart prize XXVI; best of the small presses, an annual small press reader; edited by Bill Henderson and the Pushcart prize editors
Graves, John
The last running
Graham, D. Lone Star literature; from the Red River to the Rio Grande; edited by Don Graham
Graves, Robert
Earth to earth
Of leaf and flower; stories and poems for gardeners; edited by Charles Dean and Clyde Wachsberger; illustrations by Clyde Wachsberger
Graves. Power, M.
Graves, Louis
Fair-weather hits
Dead balls and double curves; an anthology of early baseball fiction; edited and with an introduction by Trey Strecker ; with a foreword by Arnold Hano
GRAVESTONES *See* Tombstones

Graveyard of the Atlantic. Hagy, A. C.
GRAVEYARDS *See* Cemeteries
GRAVITATION

> *See also* Relativity (Physics); Weightless-
> ness

Clarke, A. C. What goes up
GRAVITY *See* Gravitation
Gravity. Henry, D.
Gravity. Perabo, S.
The **gravy** on the cake. Fromm, P.
Gray, Alasdair
15 February 2003
    Gray, A. The Ends of Our Tethers; thirteen
      sorry stories
Aiblins
    Gray, A. The Ends of Our Tethers; thirteen
      sorry stories
Big pockets with buttoned flaps
    Gray, A. The Ends of Our Tethers; thirteen
      sorry stories
Job's skin game
    Gray, A. The Ends of Our Tethers; thirteen
      sorry stories
Lanark [excerpt]
    The Vintage book of contemporary Scottish
      fiction; edited and with an introduction by
      Peter Kravitz
Miss Kincaid's autumn
    Gray, A. The Ends of Our Tethers; thirteen
      sorry stories
Moral philosophy exam
    Gray, A. The Ends of Our Tethers; thirteen
      sorry stories
My ex husband
    Gray, A. The Ends of Our Tethers; thirteen
      sorry stories
A night off
    The Literary Review (Madison, N.J.) v45 no2
      p264-87 Wint 2002
No bluebeard
    Gray, A. The Ends of Our Tethers; thirteen
      sorry stories
Pillow talk
    Gray, A. The Ends of Our Tethers; thirteen
      sorry stories
Property
    Gray, A. The Ends of Our Tethers; thirteen
      sorry stories
Sinkings
    Gray, A. The Ends of Our Tethers; thirteen
      sorry stories
Swan burial
    Gray, A. The Ends of Our Tethers; thirteen
      sorry stories
Wellbeing
    Gray, A. The Ends of Our Tethers; thirteen
      sorry stories
Gray, Gallagher *See* Munger, Katy
Gray, Josie and Gallagher, Tess
A Lake in the Boat
    Doubletake v8 no3 p85-6 Summ 2002
The Rate Collector
    Doubletake v8 no3 p86-7 Summ 2002
Gray, Muriel
Shite hawks
    The Mammoth book of best horror 13; edited
      by Stephen Jones

Gray, Nicholas Stuart
Grimbold's other world [excerpt]
    Swords and sorcerers; stories from the world
      of fantasy and adventure; edited by Clint
      Willis
The **gray** champion. Hawthorne, N.
Gray-eyed death. Mosley, W.
Gray rider. Le May, A.
The **gray** wolf's ha'nt. Chesnutt, C. W.
Gray world. Bottoms, G.
Grayblue day. Pritchett, L.
Gray's anatomy. Wieland, L.
Grazing in good pastures. Williams, M.
Greaney, Áine
A loveless match
    The Literary Review (Madison, N.J.) v44 no4
      p638-41 Summ 2001
Great American. Becker, G.
The **great** Americans. Hodgen, C.
The **great** and small. Norris, H.
A **great** antipodean scandal. Weldon, F.
GREAT AUNTS *See* Aunts
The **Great** Baro. Piñera, V.
GREAT BARRIER REEF (AUSTRALIA)
Clarke, A. C. Hate
GREAT BRITAIN

> *See also* England; Northern Ireland;
> Scotland; Wales

MacLeod, I. R. The summer isles
Colonies
Crowley, J. Great work of time
The **great** carbuncle. Hawthorne, N.
The **great** cardhouse. Highsmith, P.
Great Day. Malouf, D.
Great day for the Irish. Hoch, E. D.
Great dream of heaven. Shepard, S.
The **great** ekbó. Cabrera Infante, G.
The **great** escape. Watson, I.
The **great** fence. Giono, J.
The **great** flood. Avrich, J.
The **great** force. Arenas, R.
The **great** game. Chaudhuri, A.
The **great** god Pan. Machen, A.
The **great** goodbye. Wilson, R. C.
GREAT-GRANDFATHERS
Jenkins, G. The reality of angels
Sneve, V. D. H. The medicine bag
GREAT-GRANDMOTHERS
Kingsolver, B. Homeland
Whitty, J. The daguerrotype
Great gray. Yolen, J.
Great Guruji. Pittalwala, I.
Great is Diana. Davidson, A.
Great joy. Le Guin, U. K.
The **great** life. Le Clézio, J.-M. G.
The **great** master of ecstasy. Beagan, G.
A **great** miracle. Gerber, M. J.
Great Moments in Psychotherapy, Number 39.
    Moody, R.
The **great** Northfield raid. Henry, W.
Great ones. DeLancey, K.
Great Plain. Clift, G. W.
The **great** pyramids. Barthelme, F.
The **great** return. Kundera, M.
Great Sedna. Osgood, L.
Great sex. Adams, A.
The **great** stone face. Hawthorne, N.
The **Great** Wall of California. Solomon, R.
Great walls of Mars. Reynolds, A.

The **great** wide world of men. Aldrich, B. S.
The **greater** grace of Carlisle. Perabo, S.
The **greatest**. Mosley, W.
The **greatest** car in the world. Harrison, H.
The **greatest** goddamn thing. McNally, J.
The **greatest** sacrifice. DuBois, B.
The **greatest** victory. O'Rourke, F.
GREECE
  Crowley, J. Missolonghi 1824
  Delany, S. R. Dog in a fisherman's net
  Joyce, G. First, catch your demon
  Pearlman, D. D. Zeno evil
  Rucker, R. v. B. The square root of Pythagoras
  Simonds, M. The distance to Delphi
    Rural life
  Karnezis, P. Another day on Pegasus
  Karnezis, P. Applied aeronautics
  Karnezis, P. Cassandra is gone
  Karnezis, P. A circus attraction
  Karnezis, P. The day of the beast
  Karnezis, P. Deus ex machina
  Karnezis, P. A funeral of stones
  Karnezis, P. The hunters in winter
  Karnezis, P. Immortality
  Karnezis, P. Jeremiad
  Karnezis, P. The legend of Atlantis
  Karnezis, P. Sacrifice
  Karnezis, P. Sins of a harvest god
  Karnezis, P. Stella the spinster's afternoon
    dreams
  Karnezis, P. Whale on the beach
  Karnezis, P. Wilt thou be made whole?
Greece. Calbert, C.
GREED *See* Avarice
Greedy choke puppy. Hopkinson, N.
GREEK AMERICANS
  DeLancey, K. Swingtime
  Pelecanos, G. P. The dead their eyes implore us
GREEKS
    Turkey
  Fitzgerald, P. The prescription
Greeley, Andrew M.
  The bishop and the hit man
    Murder most divine; ecclesiastical tales of un-
      holy crimes; edited by Ralph McInerny and
      Martin H. Greenberg
Green, Anna Katharine
  Missing: page thirteen
    A Century of great suspense stories; edited by
      Jeffery Deaver
Green, Jeffrey
  The blind gambler
    100% pure Florida fiction; an anthology; ed-
      ited by Susan Hubbard and Robley Wilson
Green, Roland J.
  Deck load strike
    Worlds of Honor
Green. Shaw, C. E.
Green acres. Steele, A. M.
"**Green** bird". Coloma, L.
"The **green** bird". Valera, J.
The **green** children. Brockmeier, K.
Green, Dominic
  Send me a mentagram
    The year's best science fiction: twenty-first
      annual collection; edited by Gardner Dozois
Green Fruit. Frank, J.
Green ice. Lupoff, R. A.
Green Lake. Weihe, E.

The **Green** Lantern. Smart, A.
Green legs and glam. Randisi, R. J.
The **green** man. Fowler, C.
The **green** man. Winterson, J.
Green messiah. Yolen, J.
Green River virgins. Burton, M.
A **green** square. Winterson, J.
Green tea. Le Fanu, J. S.
Green tea. Wadholm, R.
Green toads of the high desert. Grahn, J.
The **green** word. Ford, J.
Green world. Hrbek, G.
Greenberg, Alvin
  Closed Mondays
    Greenberg, A. How the dead live; stories
  Construction zone
    Greenberg, A. How the dead live; stories
  A couple of dead men
    Greenberg, A. How the dead live; stories
  Crimes against humanity
    Greenberg, A. How the dead live; stories
  Found
    Greenberg, A. How the dead live; stories
  Free-43
    Greenberg, A. How the dead live; stories
  Gruber in traffic
    Greenberg, A. How the dead live; stories
  The high hard one
    Greenberg, A. How the dead live; stories
  How the dead live
    Greenberg, A. How the dead live; stories
  Immersion
    Greenberg, A. How the dead live; stories
  The life of the mind
    Greenberg, A. How the dead live; stories
  No loose ends
    Greenberg, A. How the dead live; stories
  Oedipus at Columbus
    Greenberg, A. How the dead live; stories
  Scholars and lovers
    Greenberg, A. How the dead live; stories
  Tremors
    Greenberg, A. How the dead live; stories
Greenberg, Karen J.
  Cortados on the quai
    Partisan Review v69 no1 p79-88 Wint 2002
Greenberg, Martin Harry
  A literary death
    Murder most postal; homicidal tales that de-
      liver a message; edited by Martin H.
      Greenberg
Greenberg, Paul
  The subjunctive mood
    Fishman, B. Wild East; stories from the last
      frontier; edited with an introduction by Bo-
      ris Fishman
Greene, A. C.
  The girl at Cabe ranch
    Graham, D. Lone Star literature; from the
      Red River to the Rio Grande; edited by
      Don Graham
Greene, Bette
  An ordinary woman
    Snapshots: 20th century mother-daughter fic-
      tion; edited by Joyce Carol Oates and Janet
      Berliner

Greene, Jeffrey
The blind gambler
The North American Review v284 no2 p18-25 Mr/Ap 1999
The **greener** pasture. Lundquist, R.
Greengages. Connolly, C.
The **greening** of the green. Harrison, H.
Greenland, Colin
Wings
Starlight 3; edited by Patrick Nielsen Hayden
Greenleaf, Stephen
Iris
The Best American mystery stories of the century; Tony Hillerman, editor; with an introduction by Tony Hillerman
Greenleaf. O'Connor, F.
Greenman, Ben
Mr. Mxyzptlk's opus
Politically inspired; edited by Stephen Elliott; assistant editor, Gabriel Kram; associate editors, Elizabeth Brooks [et al.]
No Friend of Mine
The Paris Review v45 p241-55 Wint 2003
Green's book. Chabon, M.
Greenside, Mark
Penny For My Thoughts
The Literary Review (Madison, N.J.) v46 no3 p513-16 Spr 2003
GREENWICH VILLAGE (NEW YORK, N.Y.)
See New York (N.Y.)—Greenwich Village
Greenwood, Kerry
Jetsam
Dreaming down-under; edited by Jack Dann and Janeen Webb
Greenwood, T. (Tammy)
Instruments of torture
Western Humanities Review v55 no2 p164-78 Fall 2001
Greenwood, Tammy *See* Greenwood, T. (Tammy)
Greer, Andrew Sean
The art of eating
Greer, A. S. How it was for me
Blame it on my youth
Greer, A. S. How it was for me
Cannibal kings
Greer, A. S. How it was for me
Come live with me and be my love
Greer, A. S. How it was for me
Four bites
Greer, A. S. How it was for me
The future of the Flynns
Greer, A. S. How it was for me
How it was for me
Greer, A. S. How it was for me
The Islanders
The New Yorker v80 no12 p86-91 My 17 2004
Life is over there
Greer, A. S. How it was for me
The Paris Review v41 no153 p164-74 Wint 1999
Lost causes
Greer, A. S. How it was for me
Titipu
Greer, A. S. How it was for me
The walker
Greer, A. S. How it was for me

Greer, Robert O.
Backup
Greer, R. O. Isolation, and other stories
The can men
Greer, R. O. Isolation, and other stories
Choosing sides
Greer, R. O. Isolation, and other stories
Grief
Greer, R. O. Isolation, and other stories
Isolation
Greer, R. O. Isolation, and other stories
One-on-one
Greer, R. O. Isolation, and other stories
Prime
Greer, R. O. Isolation, and other stories
The real thing
Greer, R. O. Isolation, and other stories
Red-nickel rhythms
Greer, R. O. Isolation, and other stories
Revision
The Mysterious Press anniversary anthology; celebrating 25 years; by the editors of Mysterious Press
The ride
Greer, R. O. Isolation, and other stories
Spoon
Greer, R. O. Isolation, and other stories
Gregory, Susanna
The trebuchet murder
The World's finest mystery and crime stories, third annual collection; edited by Ed Gorman and Martin H. Greenberg
The White Ship murders
Royal whodunnits; edited by Mike Ashley
Gregory's fate. Biguenet, J.
Greig, Andrew
Electric brae [excerpt]
The Vintage book of contemporary Scottish fiction; edited and with an introduction by Peter Kravitz
Greisemer, John
Cleft
Gettysburg Review v12 no1 p152-56 Spr 1999
Grenville, Kate
Jacob's Ladder
Harvard Review (1992) no23 p23-31 Fall 2002
Greta. Miller, R.
Gretel. Hoffman, A.
Grey, Zane
The redheaded outfield
Dead balls and double curves; an anthology of early baseball fiction; edited and with an introduction by Trey Strecker ; with a foreword by Arnold Hano
Tappan's burro
A Century of great Western stories; edited by John Jakes
Greyhound people. Adams, A.
GRIEF *See* Bereavement
Grief. Greer, R. O.
Grief. Painter, P.
Grief. Wilson, R., Jr.
Grief counselor. Smith, J.
Griesemer, John
The Isle of Dogs
The Paris Review v45 p302-31 Spr 2003

Griffen, Claire
  Borgia by blood
    Royal whodunnits; edited by Mike Ashley
Griffin, Daniel
  Mercedes Buyer's Guide
    Dalhousie Review v83 no3 p391-403 Aut
    2003
  A perfect circle
    The Massachusetts Review v42 no3 p441-51
    Aut 2001
Griffin, W. E. B.
  Going back to the bridge in Berlin
    Stories from the Blue Moon Café; edited by
    Sonny Brewer
The **Griffin** and the minor canon. Stockton, F.
GRIFFINS
  Cady, J. Support your local Griffin
  Stockton, F. The Griffin and the minor canon
Griffith, David
  Neighbors
    Gettysburg Review v15 no1 p153-60 Spr 2002
  Termite colonies
    New England Review v23 no2 p186-95 Spr
    2002
Griffith, Michael
  Bibliophilia
    Griffith, M. Bibliophilia; a novella and stories
  Hooper gets a perm
    Griffith, M. Bibliophilia; a novella and stories
    Southwest Review v84 no4 p536-63 1999
  Kidnapped (A romance)
    Griffith, M. Bibliophilia; a novella and stories
  The trichologist's rug
    Griffith, M. Bibliophilia; a novella and stories
  Zugzwang
    New England Review v22 no3 p91-104 Summ
    2001
Griffith, Nicola
  A troll story: lesson in what matters, No. 1
    Ghost writing; haunted tales by contemporary
    writers; edited by Roger Weingarten
Griffith, Vivé
  October
    Gettysburg Review v14 no4 p586-95 Wint
    2001
Grilled Shrimp Pasta. Sariol, J. P.
Grillo, Art
  What my boss is thinking
    The Student body; short stories about college
    students and professors; edited by John
    McNally
GRILLPARZER, FRANZ, 1791-1872
          About
  Bukiet, M. J. The two Franzes
Grimbold's other world [excerpt] Gray, N. S.
Grimm, Jacob and Grimm, Wilhelm
  Dearest Roland
    The Literary Review (Madison, N.J.) v45 no3
    p435-7 Spr 2002
  The fisherman and his wife
    Fishing's best short stories; edited by Paul D.
    Staudohar
  The gallant tailor
    Swords and sorcerers; stories from the world
    of fantasy and adventure; edited by Clint
    Willis
Grimm, Mary
  Here, at last
    New Letters v67 no4 p21-36 2001

Grimm, Wilhelm
  (jt. auth) See Grimm, Jacob and Grimm, Wil-
    helm
  (jt. auth) See Grimm, Jacob and Grimm, Wil-
    helm
Grimmett, Neil
  Drowning the Charge
    Doubletake v8 no2 p98-101 Spr 2002
  In pursuit of monsters
    The Southern Review (Baton Rouge, La.) v38
    no2 p299-306 Spr 2002
Grim's redemption. Blake, T.
Grimsley, Jim
  Boulevard
    Men on men 2000; best new gay fiction for
    the millennium; edited and with an intro-
    duction by David Bergman and Karl Woelz
  Free in Asveroth
    The Year's best science fiction, sixteenth an-
    nual collection; edited by Gardner Dozois
  Into Greenwood
    The Year's best science fiction, nineteenth an-
    nual collection; edited by Gardner Dozois
  Jesus is sending you this message
    New stories from the South: the year's best,
    2001; edited by Shannon Ravenel; with a
    preface by Lee Smith
Grimson, Todd
  I, Osiris
    Bomb no85 p111 Fall 2003
  Orzoura
    Bomb no85 p110 Fall 2003
Griner, Paul
  Clouds
    Home and beyond; an anthology of Kentucky
    short stories; edited by Morris Allen
    Grubbs; with an introduction by Wade Hall
    and an afterword by Charles E. May
The **grip**. Means, D.
Grisha. Chekhov, A. P.
Grishchuk. Babel´, I.
Grist. Daniel, T.
Grit. Franklin, T.
Grit in the oil. Lisick, B.
GROCERS
  McDonald, I. Pot O'Rice Horowitz's house of
    solace
  McPherson, J. A. A loaf of bread
GROCERY TRADE
  Elkin, S. Criers and kibitzers, kibitzers and cri-
    ers
  Harris, M. The self-made brain surgeon
Grodstein, Lauren
  Family vacation
    Grodstein, L. The best of animals; stories
    Virgin fiction 2
  Gazelles
    Grodstein, L. The best of animals; stories
  Hey, beautiful
    Grodstein, L. The best of animals; stories
  How the stars live
    Grodstein, L. The best of animals; stories
  John on the train: a fable for our cynical friends
    Grodstein, L. The best of animals; stories
  Lonely planet
    Grodstein, L. The best of animals; stories
  On the side
    Grodstein, L. The best of animals; stories

Grodstein, Lauren—_Continued_
Satellites or airplanes
Grodstein, L. The best of animals; stories
Such a pretty face
Grodstein, L. The best of animals; stories
Yellow morning
Grodstein, L. The best of animals; stories
Groff, David
The third person
Men on men 2000; best new gay fiction for the millennium; edited and with an introduction by David Bergman and Karl Woelz
Grog. Nissen, T.
Groller, Balduin
The vault break-in
Early German and Austrian detective fiction; an anthology; translated and edited by Mary W. Tannert and Henry Kratz
Groman Creek. Strandquist, R.
Groner, Auguste
The golden bullet
Early German and Austrian detective fiction; an anthology; translated and edited by Mary W. Tannert and Henry Kratz
Groom, Winston
Just a little closer to the Lord
Stories from the Blue Moon Café; edited by Sonny Brewer
Grooms, Anthony
Food that pleases, food to take home
Crossing the color line; readings in Black and white; edited by Suzanne W. Jones
Grooms, Tony _See_ Grooms, Anthony
Grossbach, Robert
Of scorned women and causal loops
The Year's best science fiction, seventeenth annual collection; edited by Gardner Dozois
Die **grosse** Liebe. Stollman, A. L.
Grossman, David
Yani on the mountain
Six Israeli novellas; [by] Ruth Almog [et al.]; edited and with an introduction by Gershon Shaked; translated from the Hebrew by Dalya Bilu, Philip Simpson, and Marganit Weinberger-Rotman
Grossman, Judith
Beauty Spot
Western Humanities Review v58 no1 p109-16 Spr 2004
How aliens think
Ploughshares v25 no1 p146-61 Spr 1999
The **Grotto.** Butler, R. O.
The **grotto.** Ptacek, K.
Grotto of the dancing deer. Simak, C. D.
Ground Control. Ryan, P.
Grounded. Lundquist, R.
A **groupie,** a rock star. Richter, S.
GROUPS, SOCIAL _See_ Social groups
Grout. Mooney, B. D.
Grove, Fred
The Mystery Dogs
The First Five Star western corral; western stories; edited by Jon Tuska and Vicki Piekarski
Grover, king of Nebraska. Nissen, T.
Groves, Donnie Ray
First Snow
South Carolina Review v33 no2 p85-9 Spr 2001

Groves, John Wesley
Stop, thief!
The African American West; a century of short stories; edited by Bruce A. Glasrud and Laurie Champion
Growing out. Walker, A.
Growing things. Klein, T. E. D.
Growing up in the Navy. Coberly, L. M.
Growing up north. Hodgson, M. H.
Grown-up. Mencken, S. H.
The **growth** and death of Buddy Gardner. Mesler, C.
Growth marks. Maron, M.
Grub worm. Boswell, M.
Grubb, Jeff
Apocalypse noun
Thieve's world: turning points; edited by Lynn Abbey
Gruber in traffic. Greenberg, A.
Grushin, Olga
The daughter of Kadmos
Partisan Review v69 no3 p374-401 Summ 2002
Seven variations on the theme of untied shoelaces
The Massachusetts Review v43 no1 p141-52 Spr 2002
Gruss, Amy L. and Kingsgrave-Ernstein, Catt
Beast
Dracula in London; edited by P. N. Elrod
Grut, Vicky
Escape artist
Valentine's Day: women against men; stories of revenge; introduction by Alice Thomas
Grynberg, Henryk
Uncle Aron
When night fell; an anthology of Holocaust short stories; edited by Linda Schermer Raphael and Marc Lee Raphael
Gryphon. Baxter, C.
GUADELOUPE
Condé, M. The breadnut and the breadfruit
Warner-Vieyra, M. Passport to paradise
The **guardian.** Frank, J.
GUARDIAN AND WARD
See also Adoption
Saki. Sredni Vashtar
Guardian angel. Benton, C.
Guardian angel. Clarke, A. C.
Guardian angel. Togneri, E.
The **guardians.** Coldsmith, D.
The **guardians.** Updike, J.
GUATEMALA
Brazaitis, M. The heroes of our stories
GUATEMALANS
United States
Honig, L. English as a second language
Guayaquil. Borges, J. L.
Guerra, Lucia
The virgin's passion
Short stories by Latin American women; the magic and the real; edited by Celia Correas de Zapata; foreword by Isabel Allende
Guerrero, Lucrecia
Blanca Rosa
Guerrero, L. Chasing shadows; stories
Butterfly
Guerrero, L. Chasing shadows; stories

Guerrero, Lucrecia—*Continued*
Cloud-shadow
　Guerrero, L. Chasing shadows; stories
The curse
　Guerrero, L. Chasing shadows; stories
Even in heaven
　Guerrero, L. Chasing shadows; stories
The girdle
　Guerrero, L. Chasing shadows; stories
Gloves of her own
　Guerrero, L. Chasing shadows; stories
Hotel Arco Iris
　Fantasmas; supernatural stories by Mexican
　　American writers; edited by Rob Johnson;
　　introduction by Kathleen J. Alcalá
　Guerrero, L. Chasing shadows; stories
Love and happiness
　Guerrero, L. Chasing shadows; stories
Memories in white
　Guerrero, L. Chasing shadows; stories
Return of the spirit
　Guerrero, L. Chasing shadows; stories
GUERRILLAS
　See also World War, 1939-1945—Under-
　　ground movements
Harrison, H. American dead
A **guest**. Tawada, Y.
A **guest!**. Touré
Guest of honor. Reed, R.
A **guest** on Good Friday. Goran, L.
GUESTS
Adams, A. Favors
Brennan, M. The stone hot-water bottle
Brennan, M. The view from the kitchen
Carlson, R. Max
Chekhov, A. P. The Petchenyeg
Chopin, K. A respectable woman
Furman, L. Wonderful gesture
Hawthorne, N. The ambitious guest
Hermann, J. This side of the Oder
Spencer, E. The master of Shongalo
Tomioka, T. A dog's eye view
Guest's confession. James, H.
Guests of the Or Tog Bar. Tashi, P.
The **guests** were arriving at the dacha. Pushkin, A.
　S.
Guian, Stephen
The Age of Enlightenment
　South Carolina Review v34 no1 p93-101 Fall
　　2001
Guibert, Hervé
The Hammam
　The Art of the story; an international antholo-
　　gy of contemporary short stories; edited by
　　Daniel Halpern
The **guide**. Sumner, M.
A **guide** to animal behaviour. Glover, D. H.
GUIDED MISSILE BASES
Barthelme, D. Game
A **guide's** advice. Burton, M.
Guile is where it goes. Crawford, D.
GUILT
　See also Sin
Allende, I. An act of vengeance
Armstrong, C. The second commandment
Banks, R. Djinn
Chaon, D. Here's a little something to remem-
　ber me by
Cheng, C.-W. The three-legged horse

Clyde, M. Jumping
Cobb, T. Face the music
Costa, S. Black heart and cabin girl
Dunmore, H. Emily's ring
Griner, P. Clouds
Harty, R. Sarah at the Palace
Hawthorne, N. The minister's black veil
Hawthorne, N. Roger Malvin's burial
Hirshberg, G. Shipwreck beach
Keegan, C. Passport soup
Kohler, S. All the days of my life
Koja, K. Road trip
Krouse, E. No universe
Lee, A. Anthropology
Leegant, J. How to comfort the sick and dying
Leslie, N. Poker face
Lumley, B. Vanessa's voice
McKee, Robert. The confession
Michaels, L. Nachman from Los Angeles
Monteleone, T. F. Rehearsals
Oates, J. C. Curly Red
Orringer, J. The Isabel fish
Pittalwala, I. Trivedi Park
Poe, E. A. The tell-tale heart
Pronzini, B. and Malzberg, B. N. Night rider
Reid, E. Overtime
Richmond, M. Mathematics and acrobatics
Saunders, G. We'll get to now later
Scholz, C. A catastrophe machine
Schwartz, L. S. Referred pain
Schwartz, L. S. Sightings of Loretta
Silva, D. B. Dry whiskey
Singer, I. B. A boy knows the truth
Singer, I. B. Her son
Swan, M. On the border
Wallace, M. Thinking
What, L. Clinging to a thread
Williams, M. The wall
Yuknavitch, L. How to lose an eye
Guilt. Budnitz, J.
Guilt-edged blonde. Macdonald, R.
Guilty of dancing the chachachá. Cabrera Infante,
　G.
The **guilty** party. Silverstein, S.
Guimarães Rosa, João *See* Rosa, João
　Guimarães, 1908-1967
Guinea. Murray, S.
The **guinea** pig lady. Banks, R.
GUINEA PIGS
Banks, R. The guinea pig lady
Schwartz, L. S. What I did for love
Guista, Michael
A walk outside
　The North American Review v284 no3-4 p38-
　　43 My/Ag 1999
GUITARISTS
Cain, J. M. Cigarette girl
De Lint, C. In the pines
Jaime-Becerra, M. Media vuelta
Guiver, Patricia
The Boxing Day bother
　Death dines at 8:30; edited by Claudia Bishop
　　and Nick DiChario
The **gulf**. Oguine, I.
Gulf Breeze. White, J.
The **Gulf** of Mexico. Sellers, H.
GULF WAR, 1991 *See* Persian Gulf War, 1991

Gulick, Bill
 Encounter on Horse-Killed Creek
  Westward; a fictional history of the American
   West : 28 original stories celebrating the
   50th anniversary of the Western Writers of
   America; edited by Dale L. Walker
 The shaming of broken horn
  A Century of great Western stories; edited by
   John Jakes
The **gun**. Hughes, L.
A **gun** for dinosaur. De Camp, L. S.
Gun job. Thompson, T.
The **gun** lobby. Shephard, J.
The **gun** wolf. Flynn, T. T.
Gunboat on the Yangtze. Tran, V.
Gunlove. Oates, J. C.
Gunn, Kirsty
 Everyone is sleeping
  Gunn, K. This place you return to is home
 Grass, leaves
  Gunn, K. This place you return to is home
 Jesus, I know that guy
  Gunn, K. This place you return to is home
 The meatyard
  Gunn, K. This place you return to is home
 Not that much to go on
  Gunn, K. This place you return to is home
 Not that much to go on: 2
  Gunn, K. This place you return to is home
 The swimming pool
  Gunn, K. This place you return to is home
 The things he told her
  Gunn, K. This place you return to is home
 This place you return to is home
  Gunn, K. This place you return to is home
 Tinsel bright
  Gunn, K. This place you return to is home
 Visitor
  Gunn, K. This place you return to is home
Gunnar and Nikolai. Davenport, G.
Gunnar's sword. Bly, C.
Gunning for Ho. Barnes, H. L.
Gunpowder god. Piper, H. B.
GUNS *See* Firearms
Guns in the camp. Kanafāni, G.
The **guns** of William Longley. Hamilton, D.
Guns went off. Rinehart, S.
Gunsmoke. Silver, M.
Gunthorp, Dale
 Gypsophila
  The Vintage book of international lesbian fic-
   tion; edited and with an introduction by
   Naomi Holoch and Joan Nestle
 Pikeman and the Bagwoman
  Brought to book; murderous stories from the
   literary world; Penny Sumner, editor
GUP—or, Falling in love in Helsinki. Weldon, F.
Gurganus, Allan
 Blessed assurance: a moral tale
  The Workshop; seven decades of the Iowa
   Writers' Workshop: 42 stories, recollections
   & essays on Iowa's place in 20th-century
   American literature; edited by Tom Grimes
 He's at the office
  The Best American short stories, 2000; select-
   ed from U.S. and Canadian magazines by
   E. L. Doctorow with Katrina Kenison; with
   an introduction by E. L. Doctorow

New stories from the South: the year's best,
 2000; edited by Shannon Ravenel; with a
 preface by Ellen Douglas
The New Yorker v74 no46 p72-79 F 15 1999
Prize stories, 2000; The O. Henry awards; ed-
 ited and with an introduction by Larry
 Dark
He's one, too
 Gurganus, A. The practical heart; four novel-
  las
The practical heart
 Gurganus, A. The practical heart; four novel-
  las
Preservation news
 Gurganus, A. The practical heart; four novel-
  las
Reassurance
 The Cry of an occasion; fiction from the Fel-
  lowship of Southern Writers; edited by
  Richard Bausch; with a foreword by
  George Garrett
Saint monster
 Gurganus, A. The practical heart; four novel-
  las
Gurnah, Abdulrazak
 Bossy
  The Anchor book of modern African stories;
   edited by Nadežda Obradovic ; with a fore-
   word by Chinua Achebe
 Escort
  The Art of the story; an international antholo-
   gy of contemporary short stories; edited by
   Daniel Halpern
Gusev. Chekhov, A. P.
Gussler, Phyllis Sanchez
 An in-between season
  Prairie Schooner v73 no2 p36-48 Summ 1999
Gussoff, Caren
 Astronaut
  Gussoff, C. The wave; a novella and other
   stories
 Bruce Lee
  Gussoff, C. The wave; a novella and other
   stories
 The deepest dive
  Gussoff, C. The wave; a novella and other
   stories
 Djinni
  Gussoff, C. The wave; a novella and other
   stories
 Love story
  Gussoff, C. The wave; a novella and other
   stories
 Sight unseen
  Gussoff, C. The wave; a novella and other
   stories
 Spark
  Gussoff, C. The wave; a novella and other
   stories
 Stealing purses
  Gussoff, C. The wave; a novella and other
   stories
 Surface reading
  Gussoff, C. The wave; a novella and other
   stories
 Unpretty
  Gussoff, C. The wave; a novella and other
   stories

Gussoff, Caren—_Continued_
  The wave: a novella
    Gussoff, C. The wave; a novella and other
    stories
Gustavo's Wedding. Barrett, V.
Guthrie, A. B. (Alfred Bertram)
  The fourth at Getup
    Home and beyond; an anthology of Kentucky
    short stories; edited by Morris Allen
    Grubbs; with an introduction by Wade Hall
    and an afterword by Charles E. May
Guthrie, Alfred Bertram _See_ Guthrie, A. B. (Alfred Bertram), 1901-1991
Gutiérrez, Pedro Juan
  Nothing to do
    Colchie, T. A whistler in the nightworld;
    short fiction from the Latin Americas; edited by Thomas Colchie
Gutiérrez, Stephen D.
  Cantinflas
    Fantasmas; supernatural stories by Mexican
    American writers; edited by Rob Johnson;
    introduction by Kathleen J. Alcalá
The **gutting** of Couffignal. Hammett, D.
Guy de Maupassant. Babel', I.
GUYANA
  Harris, W. Yurokon
  Melville, P. The conversion of Millicent Vernon
  Melville, P. English table wuk
  Melville, P. Erzulie
GUYANESE
Canada
  Persaud, S. Canada geese and apple chatney
Gwyn, Aaron
  Against the pricks
    Gwyn, A. Dog on the cross; stories; by Aaron
    Gwyn
  The backsliders
    Gwyn, A. Dog on the cross; stories; by Aaron
    Gwyn
  Courtship
    Gwyn, A. Dog on the cross; stories; by Aaron
    Gwyn
  Dog on the cross
    Gwyn, A. Dog on the cross; stories; by Aaron
    Gwyn
  In tongues
    Gwyn, A. Dog on the cross; stories; by Aaron
    Gwyn
  Of falling
    Gwyn, A. Dog on the cross; stories; by Aaron
    Gwyn
    New stories from the South: the year's best,
    2002; edited by Shannon Ravenel; with a
    preface by Larry Brown
  The offering
    Gwyn, A. Dog on the cross; stories; by Aaron
    Gwyn
  Truck
    Gwyn, A. Dog on the cross; stories; by Aaron
    Gwyn
GYNECOLOGISTS
  Byatt, A. S. Body art
  Desplechin, M. Joy
  Sosin, D. Internal medicine
GYPSIES
  Blaise, C. Dunkelblau
  Day, C. Boss man
  Gomes, M. T. The gypsy: a letter to Antonio
  Patricio
  Hoch, E. D. A wall too high
  Shepard, S. Concepción
  Winterson, J. The green man
Gypsies on the Lawn. Balint, A.
Gypsophila. Gunthorp, D.
Gypsy. Anderson, P.
The **gypsy:** a letter to Antonio Patricio. Gomes, M. T.
A **gypsy** romance. Berberova, N.

H

The **H** Street sledding record. Carlson, R.
Ha Jin
  After Cowboy Chicken came to town
    The Best American short stories 2001; selected from U.S. and Canadian magazines by
    Barbara Kingsolver with Katrina Kenison;
    with an introduction by Barbara Kingsolver
    Ha Jin. The bridegroom; stories
  Alive
    Ha Jin. The bridegroom; stories
  A bad joke
    Ha Jin. The bridegroom; stories
  The bridegroom
    The Best American short stories, 2000; selected from U.S. and Canadian magazines by
    E. L. Doctorow with Katrina Kenison; with
    an introduction by E. L. Doctorow
    Ha Jin. The bridegroom; stories
    Harper's v299 no1790 p80-88 Jl 1999
  Broken
    Ha Jin. The bridegroom; stories
  Emperor
    The Best of The Kenyon review; edited by
    David Lynn; introduction by Joyce Carol
    Oates
  An entrepreneur's story
    Ha Jin. The bridegroom; stories
  Flame
    Ha Jin. The bridegroom; stories
  In the kindergarten
    The Best American short stories, 1999; selected from U.S. and Canadian magazines by
    Amy Tan with Katrina Kenison, with an introduction by Amy Tan
    Ha Jin. The bridegroom; stories
  An official reply
    Ha Jin. The bridegroom; stories
    The Pushcart prize XXVI; best of the small
    presses, an annual small press reader; edited by Bill Henderson and the Pushcart
    prize editors
  Saboteur
    The Antioch Review v59 no2 p271-80 Spr
    2001
    Ha Jin. The bridegroom; stories
  A tiger-fighter is hard to find
    Ha Jin. The bridegroom; stories
  The woman from New York
    Ha Jin. The bridegroom; stories
Haake, Katharine
  All the water in the world
    Haake, K. The height and depth of everything; stories

Haake, Katharine—*Continued*
All this land
  Haake, K. The height and depth of every-
    thing; stories
Arrow math
  Haake, K. The height and depth of every-
    thing; stories
The Deaf Musician
  Iowa Review v32 no3 p169-88 Wint
  2002/2003
The land of sculpture
  Haake, K. The height and depth of every-
    thing; stories
The laying on of hands
  Haake, K. The height and depth of every-
    thing; stories
A small measure of safety
  Haake, K. The height and depth of every-
    thing; stories
This is geology to us
  Haake, K. The height and depth of every-
    thing; stories
The woman in the water
  Haake, K. The height and depth of every-
    thing; stories
Haardt, Sara *See* Mencken, Sara Haardt, 1898-
  1935
Haas, Elizabeth
Horses, not reindeer
  The Antioch Review v57 no4 p552-64 Fall
  1999
Habeas Corpus. Henkin, J.
Habibi. Gershon, R.
Habila, Helon
My Uncle Ezekiel
  The Virginia Quarterly Review v80 no3 p124-
  35 Summ 2004
A **habit** of waste. Hopkinson, N.
Hackbarth, Patricia
A brief geological guide to canyon country
  The Georgia Review v55 no2 p314-28 Summ
  2001
Dry ice
  The North American Review v287 no3/4 p16-
  21 My/Ag 2002
Hacker, Ute *See* Rubin, Billie
Hackle, Sparse Grey
Murder
  Fishing's best short stories; edited by Paul D.
  Staudohar
Haddam, Jane
Port Tobacco
  The Blue and the gray undercover; edited by
  Ed Gorman
Hadley, Tessa
The Card Trick
  The New Yorker v78 no43 p74-81 Ja 20 2003
The Enemy
  Granta v86 p53-66 Summ 2004
Lost and found
  The New Yorker v78 no1 p168-75 F 18-25
  2002
Mother's Son
  The New Yorker v80 no24 p84-6, 88-91 Ag
  30 2004
Sunstroke
  The New Yorker v79 no37 p88-90, 92-9 D 1
  2003

The Surrogate
  The New Yorker v79 no26 p82-7 S 15 2003
Haempffert, Waldemar
The diminishing draft
  Science-fiction classics; the stories that
  morphed into movies; compiled by Forrest
  J. Ackerman
Haessig, Jalone J.
Sorrow's end
  Tales from The Dark Tower; illustrated by
  Joseph Vargo; edited by Joseph Vargo and
  Christine Filipak
Hagalund. Furman, L.
Hagenston, Becky
Trafalgar
  Gettysburg Review v15 no4 p571-90 Wint
  2002
Hager, Jean
Company wife
  Love and death; edited by Carolyn Hart
George Washington crashed here
  Death dines at 8:30; edited by Claudia Bishop
  and Nick DiChario
Haggard, H. Rider (Henry Rider)
Black heart and white heart: a Zulu idyl
  Tales before Tolkien; the roots of modern
  fantasy; edited by Douglas A. Anderson
Smith and the pharaohs
  Into the mummy's tomb; edited by John
  Richard Stephens
Haggard, Henry Rider *See* Haggard, H. Rider
  (Henry Rider), 1856-1925
The **Haggard** Society. Hoch, E. D.
Hagy, Alyson
Snow, ashes
  The Virginia Quarterly Review v77 no3 p406-
  23 Summ 2001
Hagy, Alyson Carol
Brother, unadorned
  Hagy, A. C. Graveyard of the Atlantic; short
  stories
Graveyard of the Atlantic
  Hagy, A. C. Graveyard of the Atlantic; short
  stories
North of Fear, south of Kill Devil
  Hagy, A. C. Graveyard of the Atlantic; short
  stories
Search bay
  Hagy, A. C. Graveyard of the Atlantic; short
  stories
Semper paratus
  Hagy, A. C. Graveyard of the Atlantic; short
  stories
  The Pushcart prize XXVI; best of the small
  presses, an annual small press reader; ed-
  ited by Bill Henderson and the Pushcart
  prize editors
Sharking
  Hagy, A. C. Graveyard of the Atlantic; short
  stories
The snake hunters
  Hagy, A. C. Graveyard of the Atlantic; short
  stories
Hahn, Beth
The Story of the Crooked Woman
  South Carolina Review v34 no1 p88-92 Fall
  2001

Haigh, Jennifer
  The Bottom of Things
    The Virginia Quarterly Review v80 no3 p214-
    32 Summ 2004
  What I should have said
    Good Housekeeping v237 no3 p106, 108-10
    Ag 2003
The **Haight**. Svoboda, T.
Hail. Novakovich, J.
Haines, Lise
  A Glue-Related Problem
    Ploughshares v29 no1 p90-6 Spr 2003
  Stolen Photo
    Agni no57 p138-48 2003
HAIR
  Dixon, S. The hairpiece
  Friesner, E. M. Big hair
  Griffith, M. The trichologist's rug
  Jackson, S. Hair
  Quan, A. Hair
  Schmand, T. Come fly with me
  Stefaniak, M. H. Believing Marina
The **hair**. Carver, R.
Hair. Cheng, C.-W.
Hair. Quan, A.
Haircut. Lardner, R.
HAIRDRESSERS *See* Beauty shops
The **hairpiece**. Dixon, S.
HAITI
  Brathwaite, E. K. Dream Haiti
  Capote, T. House of flowers
  Danticat, E. Night talkers
  Danticat, E. Night women
  Danticat, E. Nineteen thirty-seven
  Dépestre, R. Rosena on the mountain
  Hayden, G. M. The maids
      Port-au-Prince
  Kurlansky, M. The white man in the tree
HAITIAN AMERICANS
  Danticat, E. Seven
HAITIAN REFUGEES
  Dodd, S. M. The lost art of sleep
  Paine, T. Will you say something, Monsieur El-
    iot?
HAITIANS
      United States
  Phipps, M. Marie-Ange's ginen
Hajizadeh, Farkhondeh
  Contrary to democracy
    A Feast in the mirror; stories by contempo-
    rary Iranian women; translated and edited
    by Mohammad Mehdi Khorrami, Shouleh
    Vatanabadi
Hajjaj, Nasri
  I believe I'm in love with the government
    Politically inspired; edited by Stephen Elliott;
    assistant editor, Gabriel Kram; associate ed-
    itors, Elizabeth Brooks [et al.]
Hakim, the masked dyer of Merv. Borges, J. L.
Hal Irwin's magic lamp. Vonnegut, K.
Halaby, Laila
  Fire and Sand
    Meridians v1 no2 p53-64 Spr 2001
Haldeman, Joe W.
  For White Hill
    Worldmakers; SF adventures in terraforming;
    edited by Gardner Dozois

Forever peace [excerpt]
    Nebula awards showcase 2000; the year's best
    SF and fantasy chosen by the science fic-
    tion and fantasy writers of america; edited
    by Gregory Benford
Names in marble
    Tetrick, B. In the shadow of the wall; an an-
    thology of Vietnam stories that might have
    been; edited by Byron R. Tetrick
Road kill
    Redshift; extreme visions of speculative fic-
    tion; edited by Al Sarrantonio
A separate war
    Far horizons; all new tales from the greatest
    worlds of science fiction; edited by Robert
    Silverberg
The **half**. Sher, I.
Half a story, a third of the pie. Paolucci, A.
HALF-BROTHERS
  Coates, G. S. The flyleaf in the book of disillu-
    sion
  Philp, G. My brother's keeper
HALF-CASTES *See* Mixed bloods
Half gone. O'Brien, T.
Half interest in hell. Flynn, T. T.
The **half-mammals** of Dixie. Singleton, G.
Half of something. Maron, M.
A **half-sinner**. Edwards, S.
HALF-SISTERS
  Coates, G. S. The flyleaf in the book of disillu-
    sion
  Coates, G. S. The way of the transgressor
  Gasco, E. Can you wave bye bye, baby?
  Mason, B. A. Tobrah
  Ritchie, E. Inventories
  Tomlinson, N. C. The pretty surprise
The **half-skinned** steer. Proulx, A.
Half-states & curses. Haynes, M.
Halfbaby. Connor, J.
Halftime. Winegardner, M.
The **halfway** house at the heart of darkness. Spen-
  cer, W. B.
Hall, Cedelas
  Potato Eyes
    Calyx v21 no3 p49-59 Wint 2004
Hall, Donald
  The accident
    Hall, D. Willow Temple; new and selected
    stories
  Argument and persuasion
    Hall, D. Willow Temple; new and selected
    stories
  Christmas snow
    Hall, D. Willow Temple; new and selected
    stories
  The fifth box
    Hall, D. Willow Temple; new and selected
    stories
  The figure of the woods
    Hall, D. Willow Temple; new and selected
    stories
  The first woman
    Hall, D. Willow Temple; new and selected
    stories
  From Willow Temple
    Hall, D. Willow Temple; new and selected
    stories

Hall, Donald—*Continued*
I never looked
  Gettysburg Review v14 no2 p294-5 Summ
    2001
The Ideal Bakery
  Hall, D. Willow Temple; new and selected
    stories
Lake Paradise
  Hall, D. Willow Temple; new and selected
    stories
New England primer
  Atlantic Monthly (1993) v289 no5 p67-76 My
    2002
  Hall, D. Willow Temple; new and selected
    stories
Roast suckling pig
  Hall, D. Willow Temple; new and selected
    stories
  The Yale Review v90 no2 p121-39 Ap 2002
The tattered man
  Yankee v63 no6 p74-75+ Je 1999
Widowers' woods
  Hall, D. Willow Temple; new and selected
    stories
Hall, H. Palmer
The home front
  The North American Review v286 no1 p25-30
    Ja/F 2001
Hall, James Baker
If you can't win
  Home and beyond; an anthology of Kentucky
    short stories; edited by Morris Allen
    Grubbs; with an introduction by Wade Hall
    and an afterword by Charles E. May
Hall, James W. *See* Hall, Jim, 1947-
Hall, Jim
Crack
  Murder and obsession; edited by Otto Penzler
  Speaking of lust; stories of forbidden desire;
    edited by Lawrence Block
  The World's finest mystery and crime stories,
    first annual collection; edited by Ed
    Gorman
Hall, Lawrence Sargent
The ledge
  The Best American short stories of the
    century; John Updike, editor, Katrina
    Kenison, coeditor; with an introduction by
    John Updike
Hall, Martha L.
The Snakeshooter
  The Sewanee Review v110 no3 p345-55
    Summ 2002
Hall, Mary Ann Taylor- *See* Taylor-Hall, Mary
  Ann
Hall, Parnell
Lethal luncheon
  Bishop, C. and James, D. Death dines in; ed-
    ited by Claudia Bishop and Dean James
Hall, Rachel
Saint-Malo, 1939
  Gettysburg Review v14 no2 p301-3 Summ
    2001
Surrogates
  New Letters v70 no2 p81-100 2004
Hall, Robert Lee
No lie
  A Hot and sultry night for crime; edited by
    Jeffery Deaver

Halley's comet. Arenas, R.
Hallie out of this world. Wells, K.
Hallock's madness. Tenn, W.
Halloff, Patricia
Tenants
  New England Review v23 no2 p171-8 Spr
    2002
HALLOWEEN
Arsenault, Michael. A Halloween like any other
Berkman, P. R. Snakes
Brahen, M. M. Trick or treat with Jesus
Buggé, C. Uncle Evil Eye
Cady, J. Halloween 1942
Cannell, D. One night at a time
Chabon, M. Along the frontage road
Chiappone, R. Love A, love B
Cooper, B. Bit-o-honey
Friesner, E. M. Auntie Elspeth's Halloween sto-
  ry; or, The gourd, the bad, and the ugly
Gaiman, N. October in the chair
Garner, J. Trick or treat
Hirshberg, G. Mr. Dark's carnival
Hirshberg, G. Struwwelpeter
Hoch, E. D. The theft of the Halloween pump-
  kin
Jacob, C. Flesh of leaves, bones of desire
Kavanagh, H. T. The banshee's comb
Kaye, T. The witch who hated Halloween
Ketchum, J. Gone
Laymon, R. Boo
Lewis, R. J. Into the abyss
McNally, J. The vomitorium
Moody, R. The carnival tradition
Nolan, W. E. The Halloween man
Schow, D. J. The absolute last of the ultra-
  spooky, super-scary Hallowe'en horror
  nights
Tem, S. R. Halloween Street
Tem, S. R. Tricks & treats one night on Hal-
  loween Street
Wieland, L. Halloween
Halloween. Brown, J.
Halloween. Wieland, L.
Halloween 1942. Cady, J.
The **Halloween** man. Nolan, W. E.
Halloween notes. Nelson, V.
The **Halloween** party. Chabon, M.
Halloween Street. Tem, S. R.
Hallowmass. Friesner, E. M.
HALLUCINATIONS AND ILLUSIONS
  See also Personality disorders
Biguenet, J. Fatherhood
Borges, J. L. The circular ruins
Bradbury, R. The cistern
Brown, F. Don't look behind you
Campbell, R. Through the walls
Cheever, J. The swimmer
Chopin, K. An Egyptian ciagarette
Evenson, B. One over twelve
Gay, W. Crossroads blues
Grau, S. A. Three
Kittredge, W. Momentum is always the weapon
Kornbluth, C. M. The words of Guru
Le Fanu, J. S. Green tea
Martin, V. Messengers
Simak, C. D. Founding father
Singer, I. B. The cafeteria
Stern, S. Bruno's metamorphosis
Trevor, W. Mrs. Acland's ghosts

HALLUCINATIONS AND ILLUSIONS—*Continued*

Wharton, E. The eyes

Halo. Schroeder, K.

Halo. Stross, C.

Halpern, Nick

Temping

American short fiction, vol. 8, no 29-32

Halpern, Frume

Dog Blood

Neugroschel, J. No star too beautiful; Yiddish stories from 1382 to the present; compiled and translated by Joachim Neugroschel

Halvoník, Alexander

Fear

In search of homo sapiens; twenty-five contemporary Slovak short stories; editor, Pavol Hudík ; [translated by Heather Trebatická; American English editor, Lucy Bednár]

The **ham** theory. Ludmerer, N.

Hambly, Barbara

The adventure of the antiquarian's niece

Shadows over Baker Street; edited by Michael Reaves and John Pelan

The dollmaker of Marigold Walk

My Sherlock Holmes; untold stories of the great detective; edited by Michael Kurland

The horsemen and the morning star

Mojo: conjure stories; edited by Nalo Hopkinson

Hamburger, Aaron

Control

Hamburger, A. The view from Stalin's Head; stories

Exile

Hamburger, A. The view from Stalin's Head; stories

Garage sale

Hamburger, A. The view from Stalin's Head; stories

Jerusalem

Hamburger, A. The view from Stalin's Head; stories

Law of return

Hamburger, A. The view from Stalin's Head; stories

A man of the country

Hamburger, A. The view from Stalin's Head; stories

Sympathetic conversationalist

Hamburger, A. The view from Stalin's Head; stories

This ground you are standing on

Hamburger, A. The view from Stalin's Head; stories

The view from Statlin's Head

Hamburger, A. The view from Stalin's Head; stories

You say you want a revolution

Hamburger, A. The view from Stalin's Head; stories

The **hamburger** man. Holleran, A.

Hamby, Barbara

Iniki Chicken

Southwest Review v89 no1 p95-108 2004

Hamel, Ruth

My favorite lies

Prairie Schooner v75 no3 p104-17 Fall 2001

Hamer-Jacklyn, Sarah

She's found an audience

Neugroschel, J. No star too beautiful; Yiddish stories from 1382 to the present; compiled and translated by Joachim Neugroschel

Hamid gets his hair cut. Fracis, S. H.

Hamid stops listening to the uncles' stories. Kanafāni, G.

Hamilton, Donald

The guns of William Longley

A Century of great Western stories; edited by John Jakes

Hamilton, Edmond

Devolution

Masterpieces: the best science fiction of the century; edited by Orson Scott Card

Hamilton, Lyn

Stark terror at tea-time

Bishop, C. and James, D. Death dines in; edited by Claudia Bishop and Dean James

Hamilton, Peter F.

Escape route

The Good new stuff; adventure SF in the grand tradition; edited by Gardner Dozois

The suspect genome

The Year's best science fiction, eighteenth annual collection; edited by Gardner Dozois

The **Hammam**. Guibert, H.

Hammer, Melanie

Moving violations

The Ohio Review no62/63 p317-30 2001

The **hammer** man. Bambara, T. C.

The **hammer** of God. Clarke, A. C.

The **hammer** thumb. Cunningham, E.

Hammerhead. Laymon, R.

Hammett, Dashiell

Afraid of a gun

Hammett, D. Nightmare town; stories; edited by Kirby McCauley, Martin H. Greenberg, and Ed Gorman

The assistant murderer

Hammett, D. Nightmare town; stories; edited by Kirby McCauley, Martin H. Greenberg, and Ed Gorman

Death on Pine Street

Hammett, D. Nightmare town; stories; edited by Kirby McCauley, Martin H. Greenberg, and Ed Gorman

The first thin man

Hammett, D. Nightmare town; stories; edited by Kirby McCauley, Martin H. Greenberg, and Ed Gorman

The gutting of Couffignal

The Best American mystery stories of the century; Tony Hillerman, editor; with an introduction by Tony Hillerman

His brother's keeper

Hammett, D. Nightmare town; stories; edited by Kirby McCauley, Martin H. Greenberg, and Ed Gorman

House dick

Hammett, D. Nightmare town; stories; edited by Kirby McCauley, Martin H. Greenberg, and Ed Gorman

A man called Spade

Hammett, D. Nightmare town; stories; edited by Kirby McCauley, Martin H. Greenberg, and Ed Gorman

Hammett, Dashiell—*Continued*

A man named Thin
  Hammett, D. Nightmare town; stories; edited by Kirby McCauley, Martin H. Greenberg, and Ed Gorman
The man who killed Dan Odams
  Hammett, D. Nightmare town; stories; edited by Kirby McCauley, Martin H. Greenberg, and Ed Gorman
Night shots
  Hammett, D. Nightmare town; stories; edited by Kirby McCauley, Martin H. Greenberg, and Ed Gorman
Nightmare town
  Hammett, D. Nightmare town; stories; edited by Kirby McCauley, Martin H. Greenberg, and Ed Gorman
One hour
  Hammett, D. Nightmare town; stories; edited by Kirby McCauley, Martin H. Greenberg, and Ed Gorman
Ruffian's wife
  Hammett, D. Nightmare town; stories; edited by Kirby McCauley, Martin H. Greenberg, and Ed Gorman
The second-story angel
  Hammett, D. Nightmare town; stories; edited by Kirby McCauley, Martin H. Greenberg, and Ed Gorman
They only hang you once
  Hammett, D. Nightmare town; stories; edited by Kirby McCauley, Martin H. Greenberg, and Ed Gorman
Tom, Dick, or Harry
  Hammett, D. Nightmare town; stories; edited by Kirby McCauley, Martin H. Greenberg, and Ed Gorman
Too many have lived
  Hammett, D. Nightmare town; stories; edited by Kirby McCauley, Martin H. Greenberg, and Ed Gorman
Two sharp knives
  Hammett, D. Nightmare town; stories; edited by Kirby McCauley, Martin H. Greenberg, and Ed Gorman
Who killed Bob Teal?
  Hammett, D. Nightmare town; stories; edited by Kirby McCauley, Martin H. Greenberg, and Ed Gorman
Zigzags of treachery
  Hammett, D. Nightmare town; stories; edited by Kirby McCauley, Martin H. Greenberg, and Ed Gorman

HAMMETT, DASHIELL, 1894-1961
About
Doogan, M. War can be murder
Malzberg, B. N. The high purpose

Hammett, Samuel Dashiell *See* Hammett, Dashiell, 1894-1961

Hammond, Emily
Back east
  Ploughshares v25 no2/3 p79-95 Fall 1999
Eruption
  Ploughshares v27 no4 p33-45 Wint 2001/2002

Hampa Ham. Reiner, C.

Hampl, Patricia
The bill collector's vacation
  The Pushcart prize XXIII: best of the small presses; an annual small press reader; edited by Bill Henderson with the Pushcart prize editors

HAMPTON, JAMES, 1909-1964
About
Bottoms, G. A seat for the coming savior

Hampton, Francesca
Greyhound Bodhisatva
  Nixon under the bodhi tree and other works of Buddhist fiction; edited by Kate Wheeler ; foreword by Charles Johnson

Han the forger. Deng Youmei

Hand, Elizabeth
Cleopatra Brimstone
  The Mammoth book of best horror 13; edited by Stephen Jones
  Redshift; extreme visions of speculative fiction; edited by Al Sarrantonio
Last summer at Mars Hill
  The Best from fantasy & science fiction: the fiftieth anniversary anthology; edited by Edward L. Ferman and Gordon Van Gelder
The least trumps
  The Year's best fantasy & horror: sixteenth annual collection; edited by Ellen Datlow & Terri Windling

HAND
Sturgeon, T. Bianca's hands
Hand. Dixon, S.
The **hand**. Giono, J.
Hand games. Hay, E.
The **hand** of Buddha. Watanabe McFerrin, L.
The **hand** of Kuan-yin. L'Amour, L.

HAND-TO-HAND FIGHTING
See also Karate; Wrestling
Crane, S. The blue hotel
Fitzgerald, F. S. The four fists
Lansdale, J. R. Master of misery
Lloyd, D. T. The biggest
Perry, G. S. Hold autumn in your hand
Weinreb, M. The fox hunters

Hand-to-mouth. Ritchie, E.
A **handbook** for spies. Busch, F.
Handel's Father. Oliver, B.
The **handgun**. DeMarinis, R.
A **handgun** for protection. Lutz, J.
Handle with care. Beaton, M. C.

Handler, David
The last of the bad girls
  A Hot and sultry night for crime; edited by Jeffery Deaver

Händler, Ernst-Wilhelm
Blue grotto
  Händler, E.-W. City with houses; translated from the German and with an afterword by Martin Klebes
By the Sengsen Mountains, by the Dead Mountains
  Händler, E.-W. City with houses; translated from the German and with an afterword by Martin Klebes
City with houses
  Händler, E.-W. City with houses; translated from the German and with an afterword by Martin Klebes

Händler, Ernst-Wilhelm—*Continued*
  Demiurg
    Händler, E.-W. City with houses; translated from the German and with an afterword by Martin Klebes
  Dissolution or for Mrs. Berta Zuckerkandl
    Händler, E.-W. City with houses; translated from the German and with an afterword by Martin Klebes
  Language game
    Händler, E.-W. City with houses; translated from the German and with an afterword by Martin Klebes
  Max
    Händler, E.-W. City with houses; translated from the German and with an afterword by Martin Klebes
  Morgenthau
    Händler, E.-W. City with houses; translated from the German and with an afterword by Martin Klebes
  The new guys
    Händler, E.-W. City with houses; translated from the German and with an afterword by Martin Klebes
  A story from the eighties
    Händler, E.-W. City with houses; translated from the German and with an afterword by Martin Klebes
  Trigger
    Händler, E.-W. City with houses; translated from the German and with an afterword by Martin Klebes
The **handler**. Knight, D. F.
The **handover**. Smith, M. M.
Hands in Pockets. Miano, S. E.
Hands no good. McNulty, J.
The **hands** of Dingo Deery. McCabe, P.
The **handsomest** drowned man in the world. García Márquez, G.
HANDYMEN *See* Hired men
The **handywoman**. Coberly, L. M.
The **hanged** man. Rankin, I.
The **Hanged** Man of Oz. Nagy, S.
The **hanging** girl. Smith, A.
Hanging it on a limb. Howard, C.
The **hanging** judge. Spark, M.
Hanging on. Mobilio, A.
Hanging out at the Buena Vista. Leonard, E.
HANGINGS
  Gores, J. You're putting me on, aren't you?
  Pronzini, B. The Arrowmont Prison riddle
The **hangman's** segundo. Savage, L., Jr.
Hangover. Wellen, E.
Hangzhou 1925. Chang, L. S.
Hanley, Nell
  Cloudland
    The Southern Review (Baton Rouge, La.) v40 no3 p539-54 Summ 2004
Hanna, Julia
  Big bus
    The Massachusetts Review v40 no2 p265-72 Summ 1999
Hannah, Barry
  Death and joy
    The Cry of an occasion; fiction from the Fellowship of Southern Writers; edited by Richard Bausch; with a foreword by George Garrett

Midnight and I'm not famous yet
  The Art of the story; an international anthology of contemporary short stories; edited by Daniel Halpern
A small madness
  Harper's v303 no1814 p28-31 Jl 2001
HANOI (VIETNAM) *See* Vietnam—Hanoi
Hansel and Gretel. Rollins, H.
Hansen, Jon
  Eater
    Such a pretty face; edited by Lee Martindale
Hansen, Joseph
  Blood, snow, and classic cars
    The World's finest mystery and crime stories, third annual collection; edited by Ed Gorman and Martin H. Greenberg
  Survival
    The Best American mystery stories, 1999; edited and with an introduction by Ed McBain
  Widower's walk
    The World's finest mystery and crime stories, second annual collection; edited by Ed Gorman
Hansen, Ron
  His dog
    The Workshop; seven decades of the Iowa Writers' Workshop: 42 stories, recollections & essays on Iowa's place in 20th-century American literature; edited by Tom Grimes
  My Communist
    A different plain; contemporary Nebraska fiction writers; edited by Ladette Randolph ; introduction by Mary Pipher
    Harper's v303 no1818 p85-7 N 2001
  My Kid's Dog
    Harper's v306 p71-3 Mr 2003
  Nebraska
    Best of Prairie schooner; fiction and poetry; edited by Hilda Raz
    The Scribner anthology of contemporary short fiction; fifty North American stories since 1970; Lex Williford and Michael Martone, editors
  True romance
    Still wild; short fiction of the American West, 1950 to the present; edited by Larry McMurtry
Hanson, Jean
  The Gift of Her Hands
    New Letters v69 no4 p155-73 2003
Hanson, Robert
  Actaeon in the studio of Diana
    Iowa Review v32 no1 p171-2 Spr 2002
HANUKKAH
  Kirchheimer, G. D. Feast of Lights
A **Hanukkah** miracle. Hope, T. G.
Hanuman. Baker, K.
A **happening**. Spielberg, P.
HAPPINESS
    See also Joy and sorrow
  Brodkey, H. Verona: a young woman speaks
Happiness. Chekhov, A. P.
Happiness. Cutrufelli, M. R.
Happiness. Mukherjee, B.
Happiness. Oates, J. C.
Happy. Bakopoulos, D.
Happy as Saturday night. James, S.
The **happy** autumn fields. Bowen, E.

Happy birthday. Foreman, W.
Happy birthday. Tomioka, T.
Happy birthday, Gabriella. Scott, J.
Happy boy, Allen. Robison, M.
O **happy** day. Bishop, M.
The **happy** death. DeRosso, H. A.
Happy Hour. Baker, A.
Happy hour. Nelson, A.
Happy Jack. Reid, E.
The **happy** man. Easton, R. O.
Happy New Year, Herbie. McBain, E.
Happy people. Foster, K.
Happy the man . . . Myers, A.
Haram. Harris, R. M.
HARASSMENT, SEXUAL See Sexual harassment
A **harbinger**. Chopin, K.
HARBORS
                     Massachusetts
   Lovecraft, H. P. The shadow over Innsmouth
Hard cop. Collins, M.
The **hard** fact. Roeske, P.
Hard feelings. Henley, P.
Hard language. Padilla, M.
A **hard** time to be a father. Weldon, F.
Hard times. Wilson, R., Jr.
The **hard** way home. Weber, D.
Hardening of the arteries. Krawiec, R.
Hardesty, Emma
   Rosie's dance
      Black heart, ivory bones; [edited by] Ellen
      Datlow & Terri Windling
Hardfought. Bear, G.
HARDIN, WES
                     About
   Crider, B. The true facts about the death of Wes
   Hardin
Harding, Eliza
   After Dark
      Good Housekeeping v238 no3 p198, 200,
      203-8 Mr 2004
Harding, Paul
   Walter, Charmed
      Harvard Review (1992) no22 p46-53 Spr
      2002
      *For works written by this author under oth-
      er names see* Doherty, P. C.
Hardinge, Elmer
   Nicodemus, the detective from Africa
      American Visions v14 no1 p16-20 F/Mr 1999
Hardware. Blegvad, P.
Hardware man. Parrish, T.
Hardwick, Elizabeth
   Evenings at home
      Home and beyond; an anthology of Kentucky
      short stories; edited by Morris Allen
      Grubbs; with an introduction by Wade Hall
      and an afterword by Charles E. May
   Shot: a New York story
      Wonderful town; New York stories from The
      New Yorker; edited by David Remnick
      with Susan Choi
A **hardworking** woman. Babel´, I.
Hardy, Edward
   Band day
      Prairie Schooner v73 no4 p120-34 Wint 1999
   The Oort cloud
      New England Review v23 no2 p73-85 Spr
      2002

Hardy, Melissa
   Aquerò
      Atlantic Monthly (1993) v290 no5 p113-16,
      119-20, 122 D 2002
      The Year's best fantasy & horror: sixteenth
      annual collection; edited by Ellen Datlow
      & Terri Windling
   The heifer
      The Best American short stories, 2002; select-
      ed from U.S. and Canadian magazines by
      Sue Miller with Katrina Kenison, with an
      introduction by Sue Miller
   Imposters in love
      Dalhousie Review v81 no2 p221-31 Summ
      2001
   Strays
      Dalhousie Review v79 no2 p232-44 Summ
      1999
   The uncharted heart
      The Best American short stories, 1999; select-
      ed from U.S. and Canadian magazines by
      Amy Tan with Katrina Kenison, with an in-
      troduction by Amy Tan
HARDY, OLIVER, 1892-1957
                     About
   Bradbury, R. The Laurel and Hardy Alpha
   Centauri farewell tour
Hare, Cyril
   Name of Smith
      Edwards, M. Mysterious pleasures; a celebra-
      tion of the Crime Writers' Association's
      50th anniversary; edited by Martin Edwards
The **Hare**. Litt, T.
HARELIP See Face—Abnormalities and deformi-
   ties
Harfenist, Jean
   Body count
      Harfenist, J. A brief history of the flood; sto-
      ries
   Duck season
      Harfenist, J. A brief history of the flood; sto-
      ries
   Floating
      Harfenist, J. A brief history of the flood; sto-
      ries
   Fully bonded by the state of Minnesota
      Harfenist, J. A brief history of the flood; sto-
      ries
   The gift
      Harfenist, J. A brief history of the flood; sto-
      ries
   The history of the flood
      Harfenist, J. A brief history of the flood; sto-
      ries
   Pixie dust
      Harfenist, J. A brief history of the flood; sto-
      ries
   The road out of Acorn Lake
      Harfenist, J. A brief history of the flood; sto-
      ries
   Safety off, not a shot fired
      Harfenist, J. A brief history of the flood; sto-
      ries
   Salad girls
      Harfenist, J. A brief history of the flood; sto-
      ries
   Voluntary breathers
      Harfenist, J. A brief history of the flood; sto-
      ries

Harford, David K.

A death on the Ho Chi Minh Trail

The Best American mystery stories, 1999; edited and with an introduction by Ed McBain

HARLEM (NEW YORK, N.Y.) *See* New York (N.Y.)—Harlem

Harlem nocturne. Parker, R. B.

Harleman, Ann

Biscuit Baby

Ms. v14 no1 p80-2 Spr 2004

Meanwhile

The O. Henry Prize stories, 2003; edited and with an introduction by Laura Furman; jurers David Gutterson, Diane Johnson, Jennifer Egan

Southwest Review v87 no1 p49-61 2002

Harlequin Valentine. Gaiman, N.

Harman, Christopher

Jackdaw Jack

The Year's best fantasy & horror, twelfth annual collection; edited by Ellen Datlow & Terry Windling

Harman, Matthew

Honeymoon

Gettysburg Review v12 no4 p618-27 Wint 1999

Harmon, Joshua

The dead man

Bomb no75 p96-8 Spr 2001

Dundee

The Massachusetts Review v40 no1 p64-70 Spr 1999

The lighthouse keeper

The Antioch Review v57 no4 p509-29 Fall 1999

Rope

TriQuarterly no118 p10-26 Wint 2004

Harmonic. Barthelme, F.

Harms, James

Saw you see me

The Antioch Review v59 no4 p718-23 Fall 2001

Harness bull. Collins, M.

Harold Luddock's decision. Davis, L.

HARPISTS

Bradbury, R. Getting through Sunday somehow

Harrar, George

The 5:22

The Best American short stories, 1999; selected from U.S. and Canadian magazines by Amy Tan with Katrina Kenison, with an introduction by Amy Tan

Harriet Munro: the untold story. Masters, H.

Harrington, Joyce

In the merry month of mayhem

Murder in the family; [by] the Adams Round Table

A letter to Amy

Murder most postal; homicidal tales that deliver a message; edited by Martin H. Greenberg

Sweet baby Jenny

A moment on the edge; 100 years of crime stories by women; edited by Elizabeth George

Harris, E. Lynn

Money can't buy me love

Got to be real; four original love stories; [by] E. Lynn Harris [et al.]

Harris, Joel Chandler

How Mr. Rabbit was too sharp for Mr. Fox

Southern local color; stories of region, race, and gender; edited by Barbara C. Ewell and Pamela Glenn Menke; with notes by Andrea Humphrey

Uncle Remus

The American fantasy tradition; edited by Brian M. Thomsen

Uncle Remus initiates the little boy

Southern local color; stories of region, race, and gender; edited by Barbara C. Ewell and Pamela Glenn Menke; with notes by Andrea Humphrey

Where's Duncan?

Southern local color; stories of region, race, and gender; edited by Barbara C. Ewell and Pamela Glenn Menke; with notes by Andrea Humphrey

The wonderful Tar-Baby story

Southern local color; stories of region, race, and gender; edited by Barbara C. Ewell and Pamela Glenn Menke; with notes by Andrea Humphrey

Harris, Mark

At Prayerbook Cross

Harris, M. The self-made brain surgeon and other stories; with an introduction by Jon Surgal

The bonding

Harris, M. The self-made brain surgeon and other stories; with an introduction by Jon Surgal

Carmelita's education for living

Harris, M. The self-made brain surgeon and other stories; with an introduction by Jon Surgal

Conversation on southern Honshu

Harris, M. The self-made brain surgeon and other stories; with an introduction by Jon Surgal

Flattery

Harris, M. The self-made brain surgeon and other stories; with an introduction by Jon Surgal

From the desk of the troublesome editor

Harris, M. The self-made brain surgeon and other stories; with an introduction by Jon Surgal

Hi, Bob!

Harris, M. The self-made brain surgeon and other stories; with an introduction by Jon Surgal

The iron fist of oligarchy

Harris, M. The self-made brain surgeon and other stories; with an introduction by Jon Surgal

La Lumiére

Harris, M. The self-made brain surgeon and other stories; with an introduction by Jon Surgal

The self-made brain surgeon

Harris, M. The self-made brain surgeon and other stories; with an introduction by Jon Surgal

Harris, Mark—*Continued*

Titwillow

   Harris, M. The self-made brain surgeon and other stories; with an introduction by Jon Surgal

Touching Idamae Low

   Harris, M. The self-made brain surgeon and other stories; with an introduction by Jon Surgal

Harris, Reginald M.

Haram

   His 3: brilliant new fiction by gay writers; edited by Robert Drake and Terry Wolverton

Harris, Robert

PMQ

   Speaking with the angel; original stories; edited by Nick Hornby

Harris, Robert J.

(jt. auth) See Yolen, Jane and Harris, Robert J.

Harris, Theodore Wilson *See* Harris, Wilson, 1921-

Harris, Webb, Jr.

Why It Remains Unfinished

   The Southern Review (Baton Rouge, La.) v40 no3 p529-38 Summ 2004

Harris, Wilson

Yurokon

   Whispers from the cotton tree root; Caribbean fabulist fiction; edited by Nalo Hopkinson

The **Harris** Fetko story. Chabon, M.

Harrison, Colin

The commuter

   The Workshop; seven decades of the Iowa Writers' Workshop: 42 stories, recollections & essays on Iowa's place in 20th-century American literature; edited by Tom Grimes

Harrison, Harry

After the storm

   Harrison, H. 50 in 50; a collection of short stories, one for each of fifty years

American dead

   Harrison, H. 50 in 50; a collection of short stories, one for each of fifty years

Arm of the law

   Harrison, H. 50 in 50; a collection of short stories, one for each of fifty years

An artist's life

   Harrison, H. 50 in 50; a collection of short stories, one for each of fifty years

At last, the true story of Frankenstein

   Harrison, H. 50 in 50; a collection of short stories, one for each of fifty years

Brave newer world

   Harrison, H. 50 in 50; a collection of short stories, one for each of fifty years

By the falls

   Harrison, H. 50 in 50; a collection of short stories, one for each of fifty years

Captain Bedlam

   Harrison, H. 50 in 50; a collection of short stories, one for each of fifty years

Captain Honario Harpplayer, R.N.

   Harrison, H. 50 in 50; a collection of short stories, one for each of fifty years

A civil service servant

   Harrison, H. 50 in 50; a collection of short stories, one for each of fifty years

A criminal act

   Harrison, H. 50 in 50; a collection of short stories, one for each of fifty years

Dawn of the endless night

   Harrison, H. 50 in 50; a collection of short stories, one for each of fifty years

The day after the end of the world

   Harrison, H. 50 in 50; a collection of short stories, one for each of fifty years

Down to earth

   Harrison, H. 50 in 50; a collection of short stories, one for each of fifty years

The ever-branching tree

   Harrison, H. 50 in 50; a collection of short stories, one for each of fifty years

Final encounter

   Harrison, H. 50 in 50; a collection of short stories, one for each of fifty years

From fanaticism; or, For reward

   Harrison, H. 50 in 50; a collection of short stories, one for each of fifty years

The gods themselves throw incense

   Harrison, H. 50 in 50; a collection of short stories, one for each of fifty years

The greatest car in the world

   Harrison, H. 50 in 50; a collection of short stories, one for each of fifty years

The greening of the green

   Harrison, H. 50 in 50; a collection of short stories, one for each of fifty years

Heavy duty

   Harrison, H. 50 in 50; a collection of short stories, one for each of fifty years

An honest day's work

   Harrison, H. 50 in 50; a collection of short stories, one for each of fifty years

How the old world died

   Harrison, H. 50 in 50; a collection of short stories, one for each of fifty years

I always do what Teddy says

   Harrison, H. 50 in 50; a collection of short stories, one for each of fifty years

I have my vigil

   Harrison, H. 50 in 50; a collection of short stories, one for each of fifty years

I see you

   Harrison, H. 50 in 50; a collection of short stories, one for each of fifty years

If

   Harrison, H. 50 in 50; a collection of short stories, one for each of fifty years

Incident in the IND

   Harrison, H. 50 in 50; a collection of short stories, one for each of fifty years

The k-factor

   Harrison, H. 50 in 50; a collection of short stories, one for each of fifty years

The man from P.I.G.

   Harrison, H. 50 in 50; a collection of short stories, one for each of fifty years

Mute Milton

   Harrison, H. 50 in 50; a collection of short stories, one for each of fifty years

No me, not Amos Cabot!

   Harrison, H. 50 in 50; a collection of short stories, one for each of fifty years

The pliable animal

   Harrison, H. 50 in 50; a collection of short stories, one for each of fifty years

Harrison, Harry—*Continued*

Portrait of the artist

Harrison, H. 50 in 50; a collection of short stories, one for each of fifty years

Pressure

Harrison, H. 50 in 50; a collection of short stories, one for each of fifty years

The repairman

Harrison, H. 50 in 50; a collection of short stories, one for each of fifty years

Rescue operation

Harrison, H. 50 in 50; a collection of short stories, one for each of fifty years

The road to the year 3000

Harrison, H. 50 in 50; a collection of short stories, one for each of fifty years

The robot who wanted to know

Harrison, H. 50 in 50; a collection of short stories, one for each of fifty years

Rock diver

Harrison, H. 50 in 50; a collection of short stories, one for each of fifty years

Roommates

Harrison, H. 50 in 50; a collection of short stories, one for each of fifty years

Simulated trainer

Harrison, H. 50 in 50; a collection of short stories, one for each of fifty years

Space rats of the CCC

Harrison, H. 50 in 50; a collection of short stories, one for each of fifty years

Speed of the cheetah, roar of the lion

Harrison, H. 50 in 50; a collection of short stories, one for each of fifty years

The streets of Ashkelon

Harrison, H. 50 in 50; a collection of short stories, one for each of fifty years

Survival planet

Harrison, H. 50 in 50; a collection of short stories, one for each of fifty years

Toy shop

Harrison, H. 50 in 50; a collection of short stories, one for each of fifty years

The velvet glove

Harrison, H. 50 in 50; a collection of short stories, one for each of fifty years

Welcoming committee

Harrison, H. 50 in 50; a collection of short stories, one for each of fifty years

You men of violence

Harrison, H. 50 in 50; a collection of short stories, one for each of fifty years

Harrison, Jim

The beast God forgot to invent

Harrison, J. The beast God forgot to invent

Father Daughter

The New Yorker v80 no6 p86-90 Mr 29 2004

I forgot to go to Spain

Harrison, J. The beast God forgot to invent

Westward ho

Harrison, J. The beast God forgot to invent

Harrison, Kathryn

Planting

The Workshop; seven decades of the Iowa Writers' Workshop: 42 stories, recollections & essays on Iowa's place in 20th-century American literature; edited by Tom Grimes

Harrison, M. John (Michael John)

Science and the arts

The Times Literary Supplement no5031 p15 S 3 1999

Suicide coast

The Year's best science fiction, seventeenth annual collection; edited by Gardner Dozois

Harrison, Marshall

LZ ambush

On glorious wings; the best flying stories of the century; edited and introduced by Stephen Coonts

Harrison, Michael John *See* Harrison, M. John (Michael John), 1945-

Harrison, Payne

Zero-G dogfight

On glorious wings; the best flying stories of the century; edited and introduced by Stephen Coonts

Harrison, Wayne

Wrench

New Letters v70 no2 p181-98 2004

Harrison, William

The rocky hills of Trancas

LA shorts; edited by Steven Gilbar

Harry at Crossroads. Aizley, H.

Harry Bellefield. Pozzi, L.

Harry Ginsberg. Baxter, C.

Harry's brother. Auchincloss, L.

Harshbarger, Karl

Big Joe

The Antioch Review v61 no1 p116-30 Wint 2003

The Funeral

Iowa Review v32 no2 p135-41 Fall 2002

The mail in the morning

Iowa Review v31 no2 p60-6 Fall 2001

The photograph

Prairie Schooner v73 no3 p77-81 Fall 1999

Train to Chinko

Ploughshares v29 no2/3 p43-66 Fall 2003

Hart, Carolyn G.

Accidents happen

Hart, C. G. Crime on her mind; a collection of short stories

An almost perfect heist

Hart, C. G. Crime on her mind; a collection of short stories

An almost perfect murder

Hart, C. G. Crime on her mind; a collection of short stories

Dead in the net

Hart, C. G. Crime on her mind; a collection of short stories

Henrie O's holiday

Hart, C. G. Crime on her mind; a collection of short stories

Her good name

Hart, C. G. Crime on her mind; a collection of short stories

Life-interest

Hart, C. G. Crime on her mind; a collection of short stories

None of my business, but . . .

Hart, C. G. Crime on her mind; a collection of short stories

Nothing ventured

Hart, C. G. Crime on her mind; a collection of short stories

Hart, Carolyn G.—*Continued*
Out of the ashes
  Hart, C. G. Crime on her mind; a collection
    of short stories
Remembrance
  Hart, C. G. Crime on her mind; a collection
    of short stories
Secrets
  Love and death; edited by Carolyn Hart
Spooked
  Crème de la crime; edited by Janet Hutchings
  The World's finest mystery and crime stories,
    first annual collection; edited by Ed
    Gorman
Turnaround
  Malice domestic 10; an anthology of original
    traditional mystery stories
  The World's finest mystery and crime stories,
    third annual collection; edited by Ed
    Gorman and Martin H. Greenberg
Upstaging murder
  Hart, C. G. Crime on her mind; a collection
    of short stories

Hart, Elva Trevino
Beyond eternity
  Fantasmas; supernatural stories by Mexican
    American writers; edited by Rob Johnson;
    introduction by Kathleen J. Alcalá

Hart, Maarten 't
Midsummer in April
  Granta no83 p13-28 Fall 2003

Hart, Roger
Below the surface
  Hart, R. Erratics
Cecil's highway
  Hart, R. Erratics
Charades
  Hart, R. Erratics
Chautauqua
  Hart, R. Erratics
Erratics
  Hart, R. Erratics
The fence
  Hart, R. Erratics
Fire
  Hart, R. Erratics
Lines
  Hart, R. Erratics
Lubing: sex and symbolism beneath an '88
    Buick
  Hart, R. Erratics
My stuff
  Hart, R. Erratics
Numbers
  Hart, R. Erratics
The woman in the front seat
  Hart, R. Erratics

Harte, Bret
How Santa Claus came to Simpson's Bar
  A yuletide universe; sixteen fantastical tales;
    edited by Brian M. Thomsen

Hartley, L. P. (Leslie Poles)
W.S.
  Nightshade: 20th century ghost stories; edited
    by Robert Phillips
Hartley, Leslie Poles *See* Hartley, L. P. (Leslie
    Poles), 1895-1972
Hartwell. Carlson, R.

Harty, Ryan
Between Tubac and Tumacacori
  Harty, R. Bring me your saddest Arizona
Crossroads
  Harty, R. Bring me your saddest Arizona
Don't call it Christmas
  Harty, R. Bring me your saddest Arizona
Ongchoma
  Harty, R. Bring me your saddest Arizona
Sarah at the Palace
  Harty, R. Bring me your saddest Arizona
September
  Harty, R. Bring me your saddest Arizona
What can I tell you about my brother?
  Harty, R. Bring me your saddest Arizona
Why the sky turns red when the sun goes down
  The Best American short stories, 2003; select-
    ed from U.S. and Canadian magazines by
    Walter Mosley with Katrina Kenison; with
    an introduction by Walter Mosley
  Harty, R. Bring me your saddest Arizona

Hartzenbusch, Juan Eugenio
"Beauty as punishment"
  Fedorchek, R. M. Stories of enchantment
    from nineteenth-century Spain; translated
    from the Spanish by Robert M. Fredorchek;
    introduction by Alan E. Smith

Haruf, Kent
Dancing
  A different plain; contemporary Nebraska fic-
    tion writers; edited by Ladette Randolph ;
    introduction by Mary Pipher

Harvard 1917. Lohier, P.
HARVARD UNIVERSITY
Reisman, N. Girl on a couch
Updike, J. The Christian roommates
Harvest. Rusch, K. K.
Harvest the wind. Nesset, K.
Harvest time. Vachss, A. H.
Harvesttime. Ritchie, E.
Harvey, Caroline *See* Trollope, Joanna
Harvey, Jack *See* Rankin, Ian, 1960-
Harvey, John
Bird of paradise
  Harvey, J. Now's the time
Cheryl
  Harvey, J. Now's the time
Confirmation
  Harvey, J. Now's the time
Cool blues
  Harvey, J. Now's the time
Dexterity
  Harvey, J. Now's the time
Due North
  The best British mysteries; edited by Maxim
    Jakubowski
My little suede shoes
  Harvey, J. Now's the time
Now's the time
  Harvey, J. Now's the time
She rote
  Harvey, J. Now's the time
Slow burn
  Harvey, J. Now's the time
Stupendous
  Harvey, J. Now's the time
Work
  Harvey, J. Now's the time

Harvey, Miles

Why I Married My Wife

Michigan Quarterly Review v42 no4 p690-703 Fall 2003

Harvey, W. F. (William Fryer)

August heat

Master's choice [v1]; mystery stories by today's top writers and the masters who inspired them; edited by Lawrence Block

Harvey, William Fryer *See* Harvey, W. F. (William Fryer), 1885-1937

Hasak-Lowy, Todd

On the grounds of the complex commemorating the Nazis' treatment of the Jews

Iowa Review v31 no2 p67-80 Fall 2001

Haschemeyer, Otis

The designated marksman

Politically inspired; edited by Stephen Elliott; assistant editor, Gabriel Kram; associate editors, Elizabeth Brooks [et al.]

The storekeeper

Kulka, J. and Danford, N. The New American voices 2003; guest editor Joyce Carol Oates; series editors John Kulka and Natalie Danford

Haseloff, C. H. (Cynthia H.)

Favorite son

The First Five Star western corral; western stories; edited by Jon Tuska and Vicki Piekarski

Haseloff, Cynthia H. *See* Haseloff, C. H. (Cynthia H.)

Hashimoto, Sharon

The American Hotel

The North American Review v286 no5 p27-9 S/O 2001

Part of Their Nature

The North American Review v288 no6 p10-18 N/D 2003

HASIDISM

Englander, N. For the relief of unbearable urges

Englander, N. The tumblers

Malzberg, B. N. Ship full of Jews

Singer, I. B. A boy knows the truth

Singer, I. B. Yochna and Schmelke

Haskell, John

Capucine

Haskell, J. I am not Jackson Pollock

The Paris Review v44 p88-95 Fall 2002

Crimes at midnight

Haskell, J. I am not Jackson Pollock

Dream of a clean slate

Haskell, J. I am not Jackson Pollock

Elephant feelings

Haskell, J. I am not Jackson Pollock

Ploughshares v29 no1 p97-105 Spr 2003

The faces of Joan of Arc

Haskell, J. I am not Jackson Pollock

Glenn Gould in six parts

Haskell, J. I am not Jackson Pollock

Good world

Haskell, J. I am not Jackson Pollock

The judgment of Psycho

Haskell, J. I am not Jackson Pollock

Narrow road

Haskell, J. I am not Jackson Pollock

Haskins, Lola

Canal boat

The Ohio Review no59 p101 1999

Haslem, Steven

The Very Thought of You

South Carolina Review v33 no2 p52-9 Spr 2001

Haslett, Adam

The beginnings of grief

Haslett, A. You are not a stranger here

Devotion

The Best American short stories, 2003; selected from U.S. and Canadian magazines by Walter Mosley with Katrina Kenison; with an introduction by Walter Mosley

Haslett, A. You are not a stranger here

The Yale Review v90 no3 p103-18 Jl 2002

Divination

Haslett, A. You are not a stranger here

The good doctor

Haslett, A. You are not a stranger here

My father's business

Haslett, A. You are not a stranger here

Notes to my biographer

Coppola, F. F. Francis Ford Coppola's Zoetrope: all story; edited by Adrienne Brodeur and Samantha Schnee; introduction by Francis Ford Coppola

Haslett, A. You are not a stranger here

Reunion

Haslett, A. You are not a stranger here

The volunteer

Haslett, A. You are not a stranger here

War's end

Haslett, A. You are not a stranger here

Hassler, Jon

Chase

Hassler, J. Keepsakes & other stories; wood engravings by Gaylord Schanilec

Chief Larson

Hassler, J. Keepsakes & other stories; wood engravings by Gaylord Schanilec

Christopher, Moony, and the birds

Hassler, J. Keepsakes & other stories; wood engravings by Gaylord Schanilec

Good news in Culver Bend

Hassler, J. Keepsakes & other stories; wood engravings by Gaylord Schanilec

Keepsakes

Hassler, J. Keepsakes & other stories; wood engravings by Gaylord Schanilec

Resident priest

Hassler, J. Keepsakes & other stories; wood engravings by Gaylord Schanilec

Yesterday's garbage

Hassler, J. Keepsakes & other stories; wood engravings by Gaylord Schanilec

The **hatbox**. Vanderbes, J.

Hatching the Phoenix. Pohl, F.

HATE

Bradbury, R. All my enemies are dead

Engel, M. P. What Addie wants

Hensley, J. L. Shut the final door

Knight, D. F. The country of the kind

Levinson, L. M. The cove

Proulx, A. On the antler

Hate. Clarke, A. C.

Hate. Landis, D.

Hateship, friendship, courtship, loveship, marriage. Munro, A.

A **hatful** of Ralph. Estleman, L. D.

HATHAWAY, ANNE, 1556?-1623
About
Berkman, P. R. In the bed
Hathway, Agnes *See* Hathaway, Anne, 1556?-
1623
Hating yourself in the morning. Limsky, D.
Hatrack River. Card, O. S.
HATRED *See* Hate
HATS
Coates, G. S. Le Bonnet Rouge
Malamud, B. Rembrandt's hat
HATTON, RONDO, 1894-1946
About
Bishop, M. Help me, Rondo
Haunted. Cabot, M.
The **haunted** beach. Adams, A.
HAUNTED HOUSES *See* Ghost stories
The **haunting** of Hill House [excerpt] Jackson, S.
Hauptman, William
Good rockin' tonight
Still wild; short fiction of the American West,
1950 to the present; edited by Larry
McMurtry
Hauser, Ethan
Basset hounds and Saint Bernards
The Antioch Review v60 no1 p28-41 Wint
2002
Lightning Over the Lake
Ploughshares v28 no4 p52-62 Wint
2002/2003
Haut-Clare. Edghill, R.
Hautala, Rick
Knocking
999: new stories of horror and suspense; ed-
ited by Al Sarrantonio
The Nephews
Lighthouse hauntings; 12 original tales of the
supernatural; edited by Charles G. Waugh
& Martin H. Greenberg
(jt. auth) *See* Costello, Matthew J. and Hautala,
Rick
Hautman, Pete
Showdown at the Terminal Oasis
Irreconcilable differences; Lia Matera, editor
HAVANA (CUBA) *See* Cuba—Havana
Havanightmare. Latour, J.
Havazelet, Ehud
City of roses
The Southern Review (Baton Rouge, La.) v38
no1 p101-37 Wint 2002
Leah
Lost tribe; jewish fiction from the edge
Have a Coke and a Bullet. Almond, S.
Have a prayer. Winter, E.
Have gun, will edit. Di Filippo, P.
Have not have. Ryman, G.
Have you decided to love me yet? Morrison, B.
Have you seen me? Addonizio, K.
Have You Seen the Stolen Girl? Earley, T.
Haven, Chris
Sitcom Mom
Confrontation no86/87 p164-74 Spr/Summ
2004
Haverty, Charles
Fontanel
Gettysburg Review v17 no1 p33-45 Spr 2004
Having myself a time. Kimber, J.
HAWAII
Adams, A. Flights

Davenport, K. Bones of the inner ear
Gies, M. Zoo animal keeper 1, REC-SVC-ZK
Hirshberg, G. Shipwreck beach
L'Amour, L. The hand of Kuan-yin
Pronzini, B. A taste of paradise
Schwartz, L. S. The trip to Halawa Valley
Scoville, S. Pu'u Pu'iwa
Scoville, S. Ulu's dog
Simonds, M. Song of the Japanese white-eye
Stevenson, R. L. The bottle imp
Theroux, P. Disheveled nymphs
Todd, R. L. Vinegar
Tyau, K. Pick up your pine
Honolulu
Jones, T. You cheated, you lied
HAWAIIAN ISLANDS *See* Hawaii
Hawaiian night. Moody, R.
Hawk, Alex, 1926-
*For works written by this author under oth-
er names see* Kelton, Elmer, 1926-
Hawk, Brandon W.
The Marriage of Siddhartha Gautama Buddha
Parabola v29 no1 p46-8 Spr 2004
The **hawk**. Berry, M. S.
Hawk. Williams, J.
Hawkins, Tom
Wedding night
This is where we live; short stories by 25
contemporary North Carolina writers; ed-
ited by Michael McFee
HAWKS
Shepard, S. Blinking eye
Hawk's landing. Warren, D.
Hawley, Ellen
What we forgot to tell Tina about boys
Hers 3: brilliant new fiction by lesbian writ-
ers; edited by Terry Wolverton with Robert
Drake
Hawley, Laura
The good life
Kulka, J. and Danford, N. The New American
voices 2003; guest editor Joyce Carol
Oates; series editors John Kulka and
Natalie Danford
Hawley, Noah
In the air
The Paris Review v41 no151 p260-72 Summ
1999
Hawthorne, Nathaniel
The ambitious guest
Hawthorne, N. The Hawthorne treasury
The artist of the beautiful
Hawthorne, N. The Hawthorne treasury
The birthmark
Hawthorne, N. The Hawthorne treasury
The Canterbury pilgrims
Hawthorne, N. The Hawthorne treasury
The celestial railroad
Hawthorne, N. The Hawthorne treasury
David Swan
Hawthorne, N. The Hawthorne treasury
The Devil in manuscript
Hawthorne, N. The Hawthorne treasury
Dr. Heidegger's experiment
Hawthorne, N. The Hawthorne treasury
Drowne's wooden image
Hawthorne, N. The Hawthorne treasury
Egotism; or, The bosom serpent
Hawthorne, N. The Hawthorne treasury

Hawthorne, Nathaniel—*Continued*
  Endicott and the Red Cross
    Hawthorne, N. The Hawthorne treasury
  Ethan Brand
    Hawthorne, N. The Hawthorne treasury
  Feathertop
    The American fantasy tradition; edited by Brian M. Thomsen
    Witches' brew; edited by Yvonne Jocks
  Feathertop: a moralized legend
    Hawthorne, N. The Hawthorne treasury
  The gentle boy
    Hawthorne, N. The Hawthorne treasury
  The gray champion
    Hawthorne, N. The Hawthorne treasury
  The great carbuncle
    Hawthorne, N. The Hawthorne treasury
  The great stone face
    Hawthorne, N. The Hawthorne treasury
  The hollow of the three hills
    Hawthorne, N. The Hawthorne treasury
  Howe's masquerade
    Hawthorne, N. The Hawthorne treasury
  The Maypole of Merry Mount
    Hawthorne, N. The Hawthorne treasury
  The minister's black veil
    Hawthorne, N. The Hawthorne treasury
  Mr. Higginbotham's catastrophe
    Hawthorne, N. The Hawthorne treasury
  Mrs. Bullfrog
    Hawthorne, N. The Hawthorne treasury
  My kinsman, Major Molineux
    Hawthorne, N. The Hawthorne treasury
  Peter Goldthwaite's treasure
    Hawthorne, N. The Hawthorne treasury
  The procession of life
    Hawthorne, N. The Hawthorne treasury
  Rappaccini's daughter
    Hawthorne, N. The Hawthorne treasury
  Roger Malvin's burial
    Hawthorne, N. The Hawthorne treasury
  The Shaker bridal
    Hawthorne, N. The Hawthorne treasury
  The snow image: a childish miracle
    Hawthorne, N. The Hawthorne treasury
  Wakefield
    Hawthorne, N. The Hawthorne treasury
  The wedding knell
    Hawthorne, N. The Hawthorne treasury
  Young Goodman Brown
    Hawthorne, N. The Hawthorne treasury
HAWTHORNE, NATHANIEL, 1804-1864
    Parodies, imitations, etc.
  Avrich, J. Literary lonelyhearts
Haxton, Josephine *See* Douglas, Ellen
Hay, Elizabeth
  Cézanne in a soft hat
    Hay, E. Small change
  A clear record
    Hay, E. Small change
  Cowgirl
    Hay, E. Small change
  Earrings
    Hay, E. Small change
  The fight
    Hay, E. Small change
  The fire
    Hay, E. Small change

  The friend
    Hay, E. Small change
  Hand games
    Hay, E. Small change
  January through March
    Hay, E. Small change
  Johnny's smile
    Hay, E. Small change
  The kiss
    Hay, E. Small change
  Makeup
    Hay, E. Small change
  Overnight visitor
    Hay, E. Small change
  The parents
    Hay, E. Small change
  A personal letter
    Hay, E. Small change
  Purge me with hyssop
    Hay, E. Small change
  The reader
    Hay, E. Small change
  Sayonara
    Hay, E. Small change
  Secondhand Rose
    Hay, E. Small change
  Several losses
    Hay, E. Small change
The **Hay** behind the House. Busch, F.
Haycox, Ernest
  Stage to Lordsburg
    A Century of great Western stories; edited by John Jakes
Hayden, G. Miki
  The maids
    Blood on their hands; edited by Lawrence Block
  War crimes
    A Hot and sultry night for crime; edited by Jeffery Deaver
Haydon, Elizabeth
  Threshold
    Silverberg, R. Legends II; new short novels by the masters of modern fantasy; edited by Robert Silverberg
Hayes, Daniel
  Anything but a gentleman
    Hayes, D. Kissing you; stories
  Hope
    Hayes, D. Kissing you; stories
  Kissing you
    Hayes, D. Kissing you; stories
    The Massachusetts Review v42 no1 p75-91 Spr 2001
  Motormouth
    Hayes, D. Kissing you; stories
  Prayers
    Hayes, D. Kissing you; stories
  Shakedown
    Hayes, D. Kissing you; stories
  Sweet nothings
    Hayes, D. Kissing you; stories
  This world of ours
    Hayes, D. Kissing you; stories
  Twenty-six hours, twenty-five minutes
    Hayes, D. Kissing you; stories
  What I wanted most of all
    Hayes, D. Kissing you; stories

Hayes, J. G.
Regular Flattop
Men on men 2000; best new gay fiction for the millennium; edited and with an introduction by David Bergman and Karl Woelz
HAYES, RUTHERFORD B., 1822-1893
About
Wheat, C. The princess and the pickle
Haynes, Melinda
Half-states & curses
Ms. v9 no4 p90-94 Je/Jl 1999
Love like a bullet
Stories from the Blue Moon Café; edited by Sonny Brewer
Hays, Donald
Dying light
The Southern Review (Baton Rouge, La.) v38 no3 p572-86 Summ 2002
Orphans
Stories from the Blue Moon Cafe II; edited by Sonny Brewer
Private Dance
The Southern Review (Baton Rouge, La.) v40 no1 p132-52 Wint 2004
Hayter, Sparkle
The diary of Sue Peaner, Marooned! contestant
Tart noir; edited by Stella Duffy & Lauren Henderson
Hayton, Sian
Cells of knowledge [excerpt]
The Vintage book of contemporary Scottish fiction; edited and with an introduction by Peter Kravitz
Haywood, Gar Anthony
The first one to blink
Love and death; edited by Carolyn Hart
Hazel, Robert
White Anglo-Saxon Protestant
Home and beyond; an anthology of Kentucky short stories; edited by Morris Allen Grubbs; with an introduction by Wade Hall and an afterword by Charles E. May
He and she at the end of an afternoon. Alcántara Almánzar, J.
He came apart. Slavin, J.
He Did It for Morgan. Watterson, K.
He died that day, in thirty years. McCarthy, W.
He dreams of pleasing his mother. Galloway, J.
He is eleven years old, his name is Tano. Maraini, D.
He knew all about women. Farrell, C.
He knew German. Viganò, R.
He knew he was right. Auchincloss, L.
He loved Lucy. Bisson, T.
He of the assembly. Bowles, P.
He quarrelled with his wife. Chekhov, A. P.
He rolled up his sleeves. Sánchez, R.
He should have left him have it anyway. McNulty, J.
He swung and he missed. Algren, N.
He tried to catch the light. Dowling, T.
He walked in and sat down. Sánchez, R.
He was a child that day. Kanafāni, G.
He whom a dream hath possest. Aldrich, B. S.
He wouldn't give up his turn. Rivas, H.
Head and shoulders. Fitzgerald, F. S.
The **head-gardener's** story. Chekhov, A. P.
Head, heart, legs or arms. Slezak, E.
The **head** of the family. Chekhov, A. P.

Head on. Brown, J.
Headhunter. Cummins, A.
Headless. Aldiss, B. W.
Headlong. Rees, R.
HEADMASTERS *See* School superintendents and principals; Teachers
HEADMISTRESSES *See* School superintendents and principals; Teachers
Heads. Bear, G.
Heads. Busch, F.
The **healer.** Nfah-Abbenyi, J. M.
Healing. Bail, M.
Healing the mare. Smith, S. J.
Health card. Yerby, F.
HEALTH RESORTS
See also Summer resorts
Healy, J. F. (Jeremiah F.)
A Book of Kells
The Best American mystery stories, 2001; edited and with an Introduction by Lawrence Block
Murder most Celtic; tall tales of Irish mayhem; edited by Martin H. Greenberg
Food for thought
Bishop, C. and James, D. Death dines in; edited by Claudia Bishop and Dean James
Hero
Speaking of lust; stories of forbidden desire; edited by Lawrence Block
Hodegetria
Death cruise; crime stories on the open seas; edited by Lawrence Block
The lady from yesterday
Blood on their hands; edited by Lawrence Block
Legacy
Irreconcilable differences; Lia Matera, editor
Rotten to the core
Mom, apple pie, and murder; edited by Nancy Pickard
The safest little town in Texas
Crème de la crime; edited by Janet Hutchings
The slow blink
A Hot and sultry night for crime; edited by Jeffery Deaver
Voir dire
A Century of great suspense stories; edited by Jeffery Deaver
Healy, Jeremiah F. *See* Healy, J. F. (Jeremiah F.), 1948-
Healy, Thomas
It might have been Jerusalem [excerpt]
The Vintage book of contemporary Scottish fiction; edited and with an introduction by Peter Kravitz
Heaped earth. Leavitt, D.
Hearn, Lafcadio
A Creole mystery
Southern local color; stories of region, race, and gender; edited by Barbara C. Ewell and Pamela Glenn Menke; with notes by Andrea Humphrey
Why crabs are boiled alive
Southern local color; stories of region, race, and gender; edited by Barbara C. Ewell and Pamela Glenn Menke; with notes by Andrea Humphrey

Hearon, Shelby

Order

Ghost writing; haunted tales by contemporary writers; edited by Roger Weingarten

A prince of a fellow [excerpt]

Graham, D. Lone Star literature; from the Red River to the Rio Grande; edited by Don Graham

HEARST, WILLIAM RANDOLPH, 1863-1951
About

Baker, K. Welcome to Olympus, Mr. Hearst

HEART

Diseases

Budnitz, J. Guilt

Chopin, K. The story of an hour

Clarke, A. C. Death and the senator

Cooke, C. The trouble with money

Davies, R. Dreams

Dokey, R. Electric dog

Ohlin, A. Transcription

Heart. Jackson, S.

Heart. McMahon, N.

Heart break. Roberts, G.

The **heart** hankers. Shade, E.

The **heart** is deceitful above all things. LeRoy, J. T.

The **heart** never fits its wanting. Abbott, L. K.

The **heart** of a goof. Wodehouse, P. G.

The **heart** of Ahura Mazda. Sheffield, C.

Heart of gold. Thompson, J.

Heart of hearts. Reisman, N.

The **heart** of it. Elliott, S. B.

Heart of skitalietz. Ponte, A. J.

The **heart** of the matter. Evans, M.

The **heart** of the sky. Meyers, K.

Heart Suture. Weiss, E.

Heart transplant. Bradbury, R.

Heartaches. Hodgen, P.

Heartbeat. Kilpatrick, N.

Heartbreak house. Clyde, M.

Heartbreak house. Paretsky, S.

Heartfires. De Lint, C.

Hearts of Dixie. Gilchrist, E.

Heartspace. Barnes, S.

HEAT

Tem, S. R. Heat

Heat. Dixon, S.

Heat. Tem, S. R.

Heat Death. Brotherton, J.

Heat of the day. Junger, S.

Heat rises. Alvarez, A.

Heath, Aloise Buckley

A Christmas Carol

National Review v54 no25 p33-5 D 31 2002

It Says Here . . .

National Review v55 no25 p31-3 D 31 2003

Heath, Roy A. K.

The master tailor and the teacher's skirt

The Oxford book of Caribbean short stories; edited by Stewart Brown and John Wickham

Heathcock, Alan

Our Summarative History of Quixotica: Krafton, Indiana, 1987-1991

Harvard Review (1992) no22 p34-45 Spr 2002

The **heather** blazing [excerpt] Tóibín, C.

HEAVEN

Alvarez, A. A small indulgence

Singer, I. B. The warehouse

Whitty, J. Darwin in heaven

Heaven. Barthelme, S.

Heaven, hell, paradise. Klíma, I.

Heaven Lake. Row, J.

Heaven lies about. Bocock, M.

Heavenly Creatures: For Wandering Children and Their Delinquent Mother. Thon, M. R.

The **heavenly** World Series. O'Rourke, F.

Heavy duty. Harrison, H.

Heavy metal. Butler, R. O.

Heavy metal. Malzberg, B. N.

Heavy water. Amis, M.

Hecht, Julie

Do the windows open?

Wonderful town; New York stories from The New Yorker; edited by David Remnick with Susan Choi

Mind on fire

Harper's v298 no1789 p85-91 Je 1999

Hecht, Tobias

(jt. auth) See Millás, Juan José

(jt. auth) See Rossi, Cristina Peri

Heed. Pease, E.

Heflin, Robin Valaitis

The anniversary present

Good Housekeeping v239 no1 p169-73 Jl 2004

The **Hegeling** legend [excerpt] Wägner, W.

Hegi, Ursula

Doves

Hegi, U. Hotel of the saints; stories

The end of all sadness

Hegi, U. Hotel of the saints; stories

For their own survival

Hegi, U. Hotel of the saints; stories

Freitod

Hegi, U. Hotel of the saints; stories

Ms. v12 no3 p46-50 Summ 2002

Hotel of the saints

Hegi, U. Hotel of the saints; stories

Jamesey, Jamesey

Ms. v14 no3 p74-8 Fall 2004

The juggler

Hegi, U. Hotel of the saints; stories

Lower Crossing

Hegi, U. Hotel of the saints; stories

Moonwalkers

Hegi, U. Hotel of the saints; stories

Stolen chocolates

Hegi, U. Hotel of the saints; stories

A town like ours

Hegi, U. Hotel of the saints; stories

A woman's perfume

Hegi, U. Hotel of the saints; stories

The **Heidelberg** cylinder. Carroll, J.

Heidenreich, Elke

The Best Years

Southern Humanities Review v38 no2 p157-78 Spr 2004

The **Heidi** and Albert correspondence. Reiner, C.

The **heifer**. Hardy, M.

The **height** of summer: a Roman story. Herling, G.

Heights. White, M. C.

"**Heil**, Hitler!". Asch, S.

Heilbrun, Carolyn G., 1926-

For works written by this author under other names see Cross, Amanda, 1926-2003

Heim, Scott
Deep green, pale purple
  Circa 2000; gay fiction at the millennium; edited by Robert Drake & Terry Wolverton
Heinlein, Robert A. (Robert Anson)
"—All you zombies—"
  Heinlein, R. A. The fantasies of Robert A. Heinlein
  Masterpieces: the best science fiction of the century; edited by Orson Scott Card
"—And he built a crooked house"
  Heinlein, R. A. The fantasies of Robert A. Heinlein
Jerry was a man
  The SFWA grand masters v1; edited by Frederik Pohl
The long watch
  The SFWA grand masters v1; edited by Frederik Pohl
Magic, inc.
  Heinlein, R. A. The fantasies of Robert A. Heinlein
The man who traveled in elephants
  Heinlein, R. A. The fantasies of Robert A. Heinlein
Our fair city
  Heinlein, R. A. The fantasies of Robert A. Heinlein
The roads must roll
  The Science fiction hall of fame: volume one, 1929-1964; the greatest science fiction stories of all time chosen by the members of the Science Fiction Writers of America; edited by Robert Silverberg
  The SFWA grand masters v1; edited by Frederik Pohl
"They—"
  Heinlein, R. A. The fantasies of Robert A. Heinlein
The unpleasant profession of Jonathan Hoag
  Heinlein, R. A. The fantasies of Robert A. Heinlein
Waldo
  Heinlein, R. A. The fantasies of Robert A. Heinlein
The year of the jackpot
  The SFWA grand masters v1; edited by Frederik Pohl
Heinold, Thomas
Berlin by heart
  Prairie Schooner v73 no3 p37-43 Fall 1999
The **heiress.** Auchincloss, L.
HEIRESSES *See* Inheritance and succession; Wealth
HEIRS *See* Inheritance and succession; Wealth
The **heirs.** Aldrich, B. S.
Hejazi, Banafsheh
The pool
  A Feast in the mirror; stories by contemporary Iranian women; translated and edited by Mohammad Mehdi Khorrami, Shouleh Vatanabadi
Hejazi, Khatereh
Cling to life with your whole body
  A Feast in the mirror; stories by contemporary Iranian women; translated and edited by Mohammad Mehdi Khorrami, Shouleh Vatanabadi

Heker, Liliana
Berkley; or, Mariana of the universe
  Short stories by Latin American women; the magic and the real; edited by Celia Correas de Zapata; foreword by Isabel Allende
A morning made for happiness
  Bomb no78 p100-2 Wint 2001/2002
Held safe by moonlight and vines. De Lint, C.
Heldrich, Philip
Deep red
  Texas bound. Book III; 22 Texas stories; edited by Kay Cattarulla; foreword by Robert Flynn
Helen of Alexandria. Wexler, M.
HELEN OF TROY (LEGENDARY CHARACTER)
Dedman, S. A walk-on part in the war
Helen O'Loy. Del Rey, L.
Helen on Eighty-Sixth Street. Kaufman, W.
Helena. Čapek, K.
Helena and the babies. Mina, D.
Helens and Roses. Sanford, A.
Helfers, John
Changeling
  Greenberg, M. H. Faerie tales
Farewell to the flesh
  Mardi Gras madness; tales of terror and mayhem in New Orleans; edited by Martin H. Greenberg and Russell Davis
Helix. Yoshimoto, B.
Hell, Richard
A novel in progress
  Carved in rock; short stories by musicians; edited by Greg Kihn
HELL
Aldiss, B. W. Dark society
Bear, G. Dead run
Cacek, P. D. Belief
Carroll, J. The Heidelberg cylinder
Scutt, C. Descent
Singer, I. B. Sabbath in Gehanna
Stevenson, R. L. The bottle imp
Watson, I. The great escape
Hell does not exist. Tamaro, S.
Hell-Heaven. Lahiri, J.
Hell is the absence of God. Chiang, T.
Hell most feared. Onetti, J. C.
Hell on the draw. Estleman, L. D.
Hell on wheels. Roche, T. S.
Hellbent. Attanasio, A. A.
Heller, Joseph
Bookies, beware!
  Heller, J. Catch as catch can; the collected stories and other writings; edited by Matthew J. Bruccoli and Park Bucker
Castle of snow
  Heller, J. Catch as catch can; the collected stories and other writings; edited by Matthew J. Bruccoli and Park Bucker
Catch-23: Yossarian lives
  Heller, J. Catch as catch can; the collected stories and other writings; edited by Matthew J. Bruccoli and Park Bucker
Chief White Halfoat
  On glorious wings; the best flying stories of the century; edited and introduced by Stephen Coonts

Heller, Joseph—*Continued*
The day Bush left
  Heller, J. Catch as catch can; the collected stories and other writings; edited by Matthew J. Bruccoli and Park Bucker
A day in the country
  Heller, J. Catch as catch can; the collected stories and other writings; edited by Matthew J. Bruccoli and Park Bucker
The death of the dying swan
  Heller, J. Catch as catch can; the collected stories and other writings; edited by Matthew J. Bruccoli and Park Bucker
From dawn to dusk
  Heller, J. Catch as catch can; the collected stories and other writings; edited by Matthew J. Bruccoli and Park Bucker
Girl from Greenwich
  Heller, J. Catch as catch can; the collected stories and other writings; edited by Matthew J. Bruccoli and Park Bucker
I don't love you any more
  Heller, J. Catch as catch can; the collected stories and other writings; edited by Matthew J. Bruccoli and Park Bucker
Lot's wife
  Heller, J. Catch as catch can; the collected stories and other writings; edited by Matthew J. Bruccoli and Park Bucker
Love, Dad
  Heller, J. Catch as catch can; the collected stories and other writings; edited by Matthew J. Bruccoli and Park Bucker
Macadam's log
  Heller, J. Catch as catch can; the collected stories and other writings; edited by Matthew J. Bruccoli and Park Bucker
A man named Flute
  Heller, J. Catch as catch can; the collected stories and other writings; edited by Matthew J. Bruccoli and Park Bucker
Nothing to be done
  Heller, J. Catch as catch can; the collected stories and other writings; edited by Matthew J. Bruccoli and Park Bucker
The sound of asthma
  Heller, J. Catch as catch can; the collected stories and other writings; edited by Matthew J. Bruccoli and Park Bucker
To laugh in the morning
  Heller, J. Catch as catch can; the collected stories and other writings; edited by Matthew J. Bruccoli and Park Bucker
World full of great cities
  Heller, J. Catch as catch can; the collected stories and other writings; edited by Matthew J. Bruccoli and Park Bucker
Yossarian survives
  Heller, J. Catch as catch can; the collected stories and other writings; edited by Matthew J. Bruccoli and Park Bucker
Heller, Keith
Memorizing the Buddha
  Nixon under the bodhi tree and other works of Buddhist fiction; edited by Kate Wheeler ; foreword by Charles Johnson

Heller, Yehudit Ben-Zvi
Salt Women
  The Massachusetts Review v44 no1/2 p314-15 Spr/Summ 2003
Hello?. Zeman, A.
Hello, good-bye. Goran, L.
Hello, I'm Cora. Cantor, R.
Hello! my name is Irving Wasserman. Cohen, S.
The **hellraiser**. McBrearty, R. G.
Hell's bottom. Pritchett, L.
Helms, Beth
American wives
  Helms, B. American wives
Antique map collecting
  Helms, B. American wives
Collected stories
  Helms, B. American wives
Collusions
  Bomb no88 p90-6 Summ 2004
The confines of civilized behavior
  Helms, B. American wives
Glazing
  Helms, B. American wives
Men in Italy
  Helms, B. American wives
Once
  Helms, B. American wives
Oysters
  Helms, B. American wives
Telling stories
  Helms, B. American wives
Help!. Čapek, K.
Help. Connors, P.
The **help**. Robison, M.
Help me, Rondo. Bishop, M.
The **helpmate**. Chekhov, A. P.
Helprin, Mark
Letters from the Samantha
  Other people's mail; an anthology of letter stories; edited with an introduction by Gail Pool
HELSINKI (FINLAND) *See* Finland—Helsinki
Hemingway, Ernest
The killers
  The Best American short stories of the century; John Updike, editor, Katrina Kenison, coeditor; with an introduction by John Updike
HEMINGWAY, ERNEST, 1899-1961
About
  Bradbury, R. The F. Scott/Tolstoy/Ahab accumulator
  Bradbury, R. The Kilimanjaro device
  Pearlman, D. D. The drang of speaking forth
  Weihe, E. Another life
Hemispheres. Leong, R.
Hemlock at Vespers. Tremayne, P.
Hemon, Aleksandar
The accordion
  Hemon, A. The question of Bruno
The Bees, Part I
  The New Yorker v78 no31 p196-205 O 14-21 2002
Blind Jozef Pronek
  The Best American short stories, 2000; selected from U.S. and Canadian magazines by E. L. Doctorow with Katrina Kenison; with an introduction by E. L. Doctorow
  The New Yorker v75 no8 p86-93 Ap 19 1999

Hemon, Aleksandar—*Continued*

Blind Jozef Pronek & Dead Souls
  Hemon, A. The question of Bruno
A coin
  Hemon, A. The question of Bruno
Exchange of pleasant words
  Hemon, A. The question of Bruno
Fatherland
  Fishman, B. Wild East; stories from the last
    frontier; edited with an introduction by Bo-
    ris Fishman
  The Paris Review v44 no162 p178-220 Summ
    2002
Imitation of life
  Hemon, A. The question of Bruno
Islands
  The Best American short stories, 1999; select-
    ed from U.S. and Canadian magazines by
    Amy Tan with Katrina Kenison, with an in-
    troduction by Amy Tan
  Hemon, A. The question of Bruno
The life and work of Alphonse Kauders
  Hemon, A. The question of Bruno
Passover
  Ploughshares v28 no2/3 p61-78 Fall 2002
The Sorge spy ring
  Hemon, A. The question of Bruno
Szmura's Room
  The New Yorker v80 no16 p96, 98, 101-2,
    105-7 Je 14-21 2004
Hemophage. Spruill, S. G.
Hempel, Amy
In the cemetery where Al Jolson is buried
  The Scribner anthology of contemporary short
    fiction; fifty North American stories since
    1970; Lex Williford and Michael Martone,
    editors
Hen. Adam, C.
Hendee, Barb
Before a fall
  The Darkest thirst; a vampire anthology
Hendel, Judith *See* Hendel, Yehudit, 1926-
Hendel, Yehudit
Apples in honey
  Hendel, Y. Small change; a collection of sto-
    ries
Fata morgana across the street
  Hendel, Y. Small change; a collection of sto-
    ries
Late revenge
  Hendel, Y. Small change; a collection of sto-
    ries
The leter that came in time
  Hendel, Y. Small change; a collection of sto-
    ries
Low, close to the floor
  Hendel, Y. Small change; a collection of sto-
    ries
My friend B's feast
  Hendel, Y. Small change; a collection of sto-
    ries
Small change
  Hendel, Y. Small change; a collection of sto-
    ries
  Six Israeli novellas; [by] Ruth Almog [et al.];
    edited and with an introduction by Gershon
    Shaked; translated from the Hebrew by
    Dalya Bilu, Philip Simpson, and Marganit
    Weinberger-Rotman

A story with no address
  Hendel, Y. Small change; a collection of sto-
    ries
Henderson, Bill
A powerful salvo
  Model Railroader v68 no9 p80-3 S 2001
Henderson, Gretchen E.
Las Vueltas
  Iowa Review v34 no2 p70-7 Fall 2004
Henderson, Lauren
Dark mirror
  The World's finest mystery and crime stories,
    third annual collection; edited by Ed
    Gorman and Martin H. Greenberg
Tragic heroines tell all
  Tart noir; edited by Stella Duffy & Lauren
    Henderson
Hendricks, Vicki
Gators
  Flesh and blood; erotic tales of crime and
    passion; edited by Max Allan Collins and
    Jeff Gelb
Stormy, mon amour
  Tart noir; edited by Stella Duffy & Lauren
    Henderson
HENDRIX, JIMI
        About
Alexie, S. Because my father always said he
  was the only Indian who saw Jimi Hendrix
  play "The Star-Spangled Banner" at Wood-
  stock
Anderson, R. Slight return
Vanderhaeghe, G. The Jimi Hendrix experience
Henkel, Vera
Bummer
  Prairie Schooner v73 no3 p71 Fall 1999
Singles' club
  Prairie Schooner v73 no3 p70 Fall 1999
Henkin, Joshua
But She's a Nice Girl and I Wish Her the Best
  TriQuarterly no115 p136-49 Spr 2003
Habeas Corpus
  Doubletake v8 no2 p93-8 Spr 2002
Oh, Canada
  Southwest Review v86 no1 p147-59 Wint
    2001
References available upon request
  The Yale Review v89 no4 p74-95 O 2001
Summer People
  New England Review v23 no3 p134-42 Summ
    2002
Henley, Patricia
Aces
  Henley, P. Worship of the common heart;
    new and selected stories
As luck would have it
  Henley, P. Worship of the common heart;
    new and selected stories
The birthing
  Henley, P. Worship of the common heart;
    new and selected stories
Cargo
  Henley, P. Worship of the common heart;
    new and selected stories
Friday night at Silver Star
  Henley, P. Worship of the common heart;
    new and selected stories

Henley, Patricia—*Continued*
Hard feelings
  Henley, P. Worship of the common heart; new and selected stories
Labrador
  Henley, P. Worship of the common heart; new and selected stories
The late hunt
  Henley, P. Worship of the common heart; new and selected stories
Lessons in joy
  Henley, P. Worship of the common heart; new and selected stories
Let me call you sweetheart
  Henley, P. Worship of the common heart; new and selected stories
Love you can't imagine
  Henley, P. Worship of the common heart; new and selected stories
Picking time
  Henley, P. Worship of the common heart; new and selected stories
The pleasure of pears
  Henley, P. Worship of the common heart; new and selected stories
Same old big magic
  Henley, P. Worship of the common heart; new and selected stories
The secret of cartwheels
  Henley, P. Worship of the common heart; new and selected stories
Slinkers
  Henley, P. Worship of the common heart; new and selected stories
Sun damage
  Henley, P. Worship of the common heart; new and selected stories
Victory
  Henley, P. Worship of the common heart; new and selected stories
Worship of the common heart
  Henley, P. Worship of the common heart; new and selected stories

HENLEY ROYAL REGATTA (ENGLAND)
Davenport, G. Christ preaching at the Henley Regatta

Henrie O's holiday. Hart, C. G.

Henríquez, Cristina
Beautiful
  TriQuarterly no117 p173-80 Fall 2003
Drive
  The Virginia Quarterly Review v80 no3 p68-81 Summ 2004

HENRY II, KING OF ENGLAND, 1133-1189
About
Rath, T. and Rath, T. Who killed fair Rosamund?

HENRY VI, KING OF ENGLAND, 1421-1471
About
Frazer, M. Neither pity, love nor fear

HENRY VII, KING OF ENGLAND, 1457-1509
About
Wilson, D. A. The curse of the unborn dead

Henry, DeWitt
Gravity
  Iowa Review v31 no2 p53-9 Fall 2001

Henry, Gray
That the heart no longer moves
  Parabola v26 no4 p55 N 2001

Henry, Jim
There's Nothing
  South Carolina Review v35 no1 p94-106 Fall 2002

Henry, O.
Art and the bronco
  Graham, D. Lone Star literature; from the Red River to the Rio Grande; edited by Don Graham
The gift of the magi
  The Saturday Evening Post v273 no6 p50-1, 54 N/D 2001
The higher pragmatism
  Boxing's best short stories; edited by Paul D. Staudohar
The last leaf
  Of leaf and flower; stories and poems for gardeners; edited by Charles Dean and Clyde Wachsberger; illustrations by Clyde Wachsberger
A retrieved reformation
  The Best American mystery stories of the century; Tony Hillerman, editor; with an introduction by Tony Hillerman

Henry, Will
Blizzard at Bald Rock
  Henry, W. Tumbleweeds; frontier stories
Comanche passport
  Henry, W. Tumbleweeds; frontier stories
". . . Fired by the hand of Robert Ford"
  Henry, W. Tumbleweeds; frontier stories
Ghost wolf of Thunder Mountain
  Henry, W. Ghost wolf of Thunder Mountain; frontier stories
The great Northfield raid
  Henry, W. Tumbleweeds; frontier stories
Home place
  Henry, W. Tumbleweeds; frontier stories
Jefferson's captains
  Henry, W. Tumbleweeds; frontier stories
The legend of Trooper Hennepin
  Henry, W. Ghost wolf of Thunder Mountain; frontier stories
Not wanted dead or alive
  Henry, W. Tumbleweeds; frontier stories
River of decision
  Henry, W. Ghost wolf of Thunder Mountain; frontier stories
Rough Riders of Arizona
  Henry, W. Ghost wolf of Thunder Mountain; frontier stories
The skinning of Black Coyote
  Henry, W. Tumbleweeds; frontier stories
The Streets of Laredo
  Henry, W. Tumbleweeds; frontier stories
The tallest Indian in Toltepec
  Henry, W. Tumbleweeds; frontier stories
The true friends
  Henry, W. Tumbleweeds; frontier stories
Wolf-Eye
  Henry, W. Ghost wolf of Thunder Mountain; frontier stories

Henry and the miracle. Barolini, H.

Hensher, Philip
In Time of War
  Granta no81 p275-98 Spr 2003
To feed the night
  Granta no65 p241-54 Spr 1999

Hensley, Joe L.

Argent blood

    Hensley, J. L. Deadly hunger and other tales

The calculator

    Hensley, J. L. Deadly hunger and other tales

Deadly hunger

    Hensley, J. L. Deadly hunger and other tales

Decision

    Hensley, J. L. Deadly hunger and other tales

Fifty Chinese

    Hensley, J. L. Deadly hunger and other tales

The home

    Hensley, J. L. Deadly hunger and other tales

Killer scent

    Hensley, J. L. Deadly hunger and other tales

A lot of sense

    Hensley, J. L. Deadly hunger and other tales

On the rocks

    Hensley, J. L. Deadly hunger and other tales

Paint doctor

    Hensley, J. L. Deadly hunger and other tales

The retiree

    Hensley, J. L. Deadly hunger and other tales

Savant

    Hensley, J. L. Deadly hunger and other tales

Shut the final door

    Hensley, J. L. Deadly hunger and other tales

Trial

    Hensley, J. L. Deadly hunger and other tales

Truly yours, John R. Jacks

    Hensley, J. L. Deadly hunger and other tales

Watcher

    Hensley, J. L. Deadly hunger and other tales

Whistler

    Hensley, J. L. Deadly hunger and other tales

Widow

    Hensley, J. L. Deadly hunger and other tales

Her birthday suit. Weihe, E.

Her Father's Voice. Silman, R.

Her First Elk. Bass, R.

Her good name. Hart, C. G.

Her hair. Fairey, W. W.

Her hair is red. Williams, D.

Her Hollywood. Hyde, M.

Her husband didn't. Kawabata, Y.

Her last gift. DuBois, B.

Her letters. Chopin, K.

Her Lover. Felsenfeld, J.

Her mother's house. Menendez, A.

Her new life. Perkins, E.

Her own private sitcom. Steele, A. M.

Her pilgrim soul. Brennert, A.

Her slow and steady. Louis, L. G.

Her son. Wharton, E.

Her speaking, her silence. Gallagher, T.

Her unmentionables. Adams, A.

Her Virginia mammy. Chesnutt, C. W.

HERACLES (LEGENDARY CHARACTER)

    See Hercules (Legendary character)

The **herald**. Codrescu, A.

Herber, Pamela Jean

True colors

    Dead on demand; the best of ghost story weekend; edited by Elizabeth Engstrom

Herbert, James

Others

    Best new horror 11; edited and with an introduction by Stephen Jones

Herbert, Joyce

The sadness of Doctor Mendoza

    Mr. Roopratna's chocolate; the winning stories from the 1999 Rhys Davies competition

Herbert, Wesley

Twilight of the real

    Northern suns; edited by David G. Hartwell & Glenn Grant

Herbert, Zbigniew

Securitas

    Parnassus: Poetry in Review v24 no1 p188-92 1999

HERBS

Austin, M. H. Old Spanish gardens

Jewett, S. O. Mrs. Todd

HERCEGOVINA *See* Bosnia and Hercegovina

HERCULES (LEGENDARY CHARACTER)

Bowles, P. Afternoon with Antaeus

Herding with the hadrosaurs. Bishop, M.

Herdman, John

Original sin

    The Vintage book of contemporary Scottish fiction; edited and with an introduction by Peter Kravitz

Here. Petty, A.

Here, at last. Grimm, M.

Here beneath low-flying planes. Feitell, M.

Here Comes. Boyle, T. C.

Here comes Glad. Magrs, P.

Here I am. Skillings, R. D.

Here in car city. Slezak, E.

Here to learn. Bowles, P.

Here we are. Parker, D.

Here's a little something to remember me by. Chaon, D.

Here's to Abundance. Leary, J.

Here's your hat what's your hurry. McCracken, E.

HERESIES AND HERETICS

Borges, J. L. The Sect of the Thirty

Borges, J. L. The theologians

Douglass, S. The evil within

Martin, G. R. R. The way of cross and dragon

Herko, Milos

Rapid-fire love in Automonster

    Gettysburg Review v12 no1 p47-53 Spr 1999

Herland. Gilman, C. P.

Herlihy, James Leo

The astral body of a U.S. mail truck

    Nightshade: 20th century ghost stories; edited by Robert Phillips

Herling, Gustaw

Ashes: the fall of the House of Loris

    Herling, G. The Noonday Cemetery and other stories; translated from the Polish by Bill Johnston

Beata, Santa

    Herling, G. The Noonday Cemetery and other stories; translated from the Polish by Bill Johnston

Don Ildebrando

    Herling, G. The Noonday Cemetery and other stories; translated from the Polish by Bill Johnston

The exorcist's brief confession

    Herling, G. The Noonday Cemetery and other stories; translated from the Polish by Bill Johnston

Herling, Gustaw—*Continued*

The eyetooth of Barabbas
  Herling, G. The Noonday Cemetery and other
    stories; translated from the Polish by Bill
    Johnston
The height of summer: a Roman story
  Herling, G. The Noonday Cemetery and other
    stories; translated from the Polish by Bill
    Johnston
A hot breath from the desert
  Herling, G. The Noonday Cemetery and other
    stories; translated from the Polish by Bill
    Johnston
A madrigal of mourning
  Herling, G. The Noonday Cemetery and other
    stories; translated from the Polish by Bill
    Johnston
The Noonday Cemetery: an open story
  Herling, G. The Noonday Cemetery and other
    stories; translated from the Polish by Bill
    Johnston
Notebook of William Moulding, pensioner
  Herling, G. The Noonday Cemetery and other
    stories; translated from the Polish by Bill
    Johnston
The Silver Coffer
  Herling, G. The Noonday Cemetery and other
    stories; translated from the Polish by Bill
    Johnston
Suor Strega
  Herling, G. The Noonday Cemetery and other
    stories; translated from the Polish by Bill
    Johnston
Ugolone da Todi: obituary of a philosopher
  Herling, G. The Noonday Cemetery and other
    stories; translated from the Polish by Bill
    Johnston
Herling-Grudzinski, Gustaw *See* Herling,
  Gustaw, 1919-2000
Herman, William
I'm Not Gloria
  Hanging Loose no84 p31-42 2004
Hermann, Judith
Bali woman
  Hermann, J. Summerhouse, later; stories;
    translated from the German by Margot
    Bettauer Dembo
Camera obscura
  Hermann, J. Summerhouse, later; stories;
    translated from the German by Margot
    Bettauer Dembo
The end of something
  Hermann, J. Summerhouse, later; stories;
    translated from the German by Margot
    Bettauer Dembo
Hunter Johnson music
  Hermann, J. Summerhouse, later; stories;
    translated from the German by Margot
    Bettauer Dembo
Hurricane (something farewell)
  Hermann, J. Summerhouse, later; stories;
    translated from the German by Margot
    Bettauer Dembo
The red coral bracelet
  Hermann, J. Summerhouse, later; stories;
    translated from the German by Margot
    Bettauer Dembo

Sonja
  Hermann, J. Summerhouse, later; stories;
    translated from the German by Margot
    Bettauer Dembo
A summer house, later
  Grand Street no69 p139-50 Summ 1999
Summerhouse, later
  Hermann, J. Summerhouse, later; stories;
    translated from the German by Margot
    Bettauer Dembo
This side of the Oder
  Granta no74 p115-29 Summ 2001
  Hermann, J. Summerhouse, later; stories;
    translated from the German by Margot
    Bettauer Dembo
HERMAPHRODITISM
Heinlein, R. A. "All you zombies—"
Hermes. Fairey, W. W.
The **hermit** and the wild woman. Wharton, E.
The **hermit** of Tigerhead Butte. Cunningham, E.
HERMITS
        See also Recluses
Johnson, D. Train dreams
Sinclair, I. The keeper of the Rothenstein tomb
Updike, J. The hermit
Wharton, E. The hermit and the wild woman
The **hermit's** story. Bass, R.
Hernández, Claudia
Highway without an ox
  Bomb no78 p82 Wint 2001/2002
Sewer fauna
  Bomb no78 p83 Wint 2001/2002
Hernandez, Filisberto
The balcony
  The Vintage book of Latin American stories;
    edited by Carlos Fuentes and Julio Ortega
Hernández, Gary G.
Lilith's dance
  Fantasmas; supernatural stories by Mexican
    American writers; edited by Rob Johnson;
    introduction by Kathleen J. Alcalá
Hernandez-Ramdwar, Camille
Soma
  Whispers from the cotton tree root; Caribbean
    fabulist fiction; edited by Nalo Hopkinson
Hero. Delaney, E. J.
Hero. Healy, J. F.
The **hero**. Martin, G. R. R.
The **hero** of loneliness. Hodgen, C.
A **hero** of the Empire. Silverberg, R.
The **hero** of the night. Denton, B.
A **hero,** plain and simple. Gamelli, R.
HEROES
Borges, J. L. The elderly lady
Doctorow, C. The Super Man and the bugout
Heroes. Perry, A.
Heroes of 1974. Cooper, R. R.
The **heroes** of our stories. Brazaitis, M.
HEROIN
Canty, K. Aquarium
Harty, R. Between Tubac and Tumacacori
Krouse, E. Drugs and you
Landis, G. A. Dark lady
O'Loughlin, M. The making of a bureaucrat
Thompson, J. All shall love me and despair
HEROISM
        See also Courage; Heroes
Heroism. Bottoms, G.

Heron, Liz
Undue haste
The Vintage book of contemporary Scottish fiction; edited and with an introduction by Peter Kravitz
Heron Island. Van de Wetering, J.
Herranz Brooks, Jacqueline
An unexpected interlude between two characters
Dream with no name; contemporary fiction from Cuba; edited by Juana Ponce de León and Esteban Ríos Rivera
Herring, Jane
Sunday in the Park With Boy
Critical Quarterly v46 no1 p64-72 Spr 2004
Hersey, John
The raid
On glorious wings; the best flying stories of the century; edited and introduced by Stephen Coonts
Hersh, Kristin
The snowballing of Alt.Rock
Typical girls; new stories by smart women; edited by Susan Corrigan
Hershel. Budnitz, J.
Hershman, Morris
Letter to the editor
Murder most postal; homicidal tales that deliver a message; edited by Martin H. Greenberg
Slightly guilty
Cat crimes through time; edited by Ed Gorman, Martin H. Greenberg, and Larry Segriff
Hervey, Evelyn *See* Keating, H. R. F. (Henry Reymond Fitzwalter), 1926-
He's at the office. Gurganus, A.
He's back. Redel, V.
He's one, too. Gurganus, A.
Heshie and Joey. Reiner, C.
Hess, Joan
All that glitters
Speaking of lust; stories of forbidden desire; edited by Lawrence Block
All's well that ends
Irreconcilable differences; Lia Matera, editor
Another room
Master's choice [v1]; mystery stories by today's top writers and the masters who inspired them; edited by Lawrence Block
The Maggody files: Death in bloom
Mom, apple pie, and murder; edited by Nancy Pickard
The Maggody files: Hillbilly cat
Felonious felines; edited by Carol and Ed Gorman
Make yourselves at home
Murder most postal; homicidal tales that deliver a message; edited by Martin H. Greenberg
Hester, Katherine L.
Märchen
The Yale Review v89 no3 p104-27 Jl 2001
The shoals
Southwest Review v86 no4 p599-609 2001
Hester and Louise. James, S.
Heuler, Karen
Fool Radiance
The Literary Review (Madison, N.J.) v46 no1 p105-13 Fall 2002

Hewett, Greg
Ruins
Prairie Schooner v77 no2 p126-43 Summ 2003
Hewey and the wagon cook. Kelton, E.
Hey, beautiful. Grodstein, L.
Heynen, Jim
The corn bin
Ploughshares v27 no2/3 p75-7 Fall 2001
Kickers
Ploughshares v27 no2/3 p73-4 Fall 2001
Watched and listened: stories about the boys
The Georgia Review v55 no2 p199-203 Summ 2001
What happened during the ice storm
Fishing for chickens; short stories about rural youth; edited, with an introduction by Jim Heynen
Who had good ears
Fishing for chickens; short stories about rural youth; edited, with an introduction by Jim Heynen
Winter chores
Ploughshares v27 no2/3 p78 Fall 2001
The **Heyworth** Fragment. Lupoff, R. A.
Hi, Bob!. Harris, M.
Hickey, Dave
The closed season
Still wild; short fiction of the American West, 1950 to the present; edited by Larry McMurtry
I'm bound to follow the longhorn cows
Graham, D. Lone Star literature; from the Red River to the Rio Grande; edited by Don Graham
Hickman, Martha Whitmore
The lost son
The Christian Century v119 no2 p29-31 Ja 16-23 2002
Hidden. Kaminsky, S. M.
Hide. Pourciau, G.
Hide-and-seek. Clarke, A. C.
Hide and seek. Royle, N.
Hides. Russell, J.
Hiding, west of here. Ortiz, S. J.
Hieractic realignment. Malzberg, B. N.
Higgins, George V.
An interview with Diane Fox
The Sewanee Review v107 no1 p7-17 Wint 1999
High abyss. Benford, G.
The **high** cost of living. Cannell, D.
High crimes. Torockio, C.
The **High** Divide. D'Ambrosio, C.
The **high** hard one. Greenberg, A.
The **High** King's sword. Tremayne, P.
High maintenance. Saulnier, B.
High mysterious union. Rendell, R.
High priest at the gates. Orner, P.
The **High** Priest of Love. Channer, C.
The **high** purpose. Malzberg, B. N.
The **high** road. Silber, J.
The **high** school sweetheart. Oates, J. C.
HIGH SCHOOLS *See* School life
High stakes. Lutz, J.
High tea. Perillo, L. M.
High water everywhere. Offutt, C.
High weir. Delany, S. R.
The **highbinders**. Pronzini, B.

The **highboy**. Lurie, A.
Highbrow. Barrett, N., Jr.
The **higher** pragmatism. Henry, O.
Highsmith, Patricia
A bird in hand
Highsmith, P. Nothing that meets the eye; the
uncollected stories of Patricia Highsmith
Born failure
Highsmith, P. Nothing that meets the eye; the
uncollected stories of Patricia Highsmith
The car
Highsmith, P. Nothing that meets the eye; the
uncollected stories of Patricia Highsmith
A dangerous hobby
Highsmith, P. Nothing that meets the eye; the
uncollected stories of Patricia Highsmith
Doorbell for Louisa
Highsmith, P. Nothing that meets the eye; the
uncollected stories of Patricia Highsmith
A girl like Phyl
Highsmith, P. Nothing that meets the eye; the
uncollected stories of Patricia Highsmith
The great cardhouse
Highsmith, P. Nothing that meets the eye; the
uncollected stories of Patricia Highsmith
The hollow oracle
Highsmith, P. Nothing that meets the eye; the
uncollected stories of Patricia Highsmith
In the plaza
Highsmith, P. Nothing that meets the eye; the
uncollected stories of Patricia Highsmith
It's a deal
Highsmith, P. Nothing that meets the eye; the
uncollected stories of Patricia Highsmith
Magic casements
Highsmith, P. Nothing that meets the eye; the
uncollected stories of Patricia Highsmith
Man's best friend
Highsmith, P. Nothing that meets the eye; the
uncollected stories of Patricia Highsmith
The mightiest mornings
Highsmith, P. Nothing that meets the eye; the
uncollected stories of Patricia Highsmith
A mighty nice man
Highsmith, P. Nothing that meets the eye; the
uncollected stories of Patricia Highsmith
Miss Juste and the green rompers
Highsmith, P. Nothing that meets the eye; the
uncollected stories of Patricia Highsmith
Music to die by
Highsmith, P. Nothing that meets the eye; the
uncollected stories of Patricia Highsmith
Nothing that meets the eye
Highsmith, P. Nothing that meets the eye; the
uncollected stories of Patricia Highsmith
The pianos of the Steinachs
Highsmith, P. Nothing that meets the eye; the
uncollected stories of Patricia Highsmith
Quiet night
Highsmith, P. Nothing that meets the eye; the
uncollected stories of Patricia Highsmith
The returnees
Highsmith, P. Nothing that meets the eye; the
uncollected stories of Patricia Highsmith
The second cigarette
Highsmith, P. Nothing that meets the eye; the
uncollected stories of Patricia Highsmith

The still point of the turning world
Highsmith, P. Nothing that meets the eye; the
uncollected stories of Patricia Highsmith
The terrapin
The Best American mystery stories of the
century; Tony Hillerman, editor; with an
introduction by Tony Hillerman
Things had gone badly
Highsmith, P. Nothing that meets the eye; the
uncollected stories of Patricia Highsmith
The trouble with Mrs. Blynn, the trouble with
the world
Highsmith, P. Nothing that meets the eye; the
uncollected stories of Patricia Highsmith
The New Yorker v78 no13 p106-11 My 27
2002
Two disagreeable pigeons
Highsmith, P. Nothing that meets the eye; the
uncollected stories of Patricia Highsmith
Uncertain treasure
Highsmith, P. Nothing that meets the eye; the
uncollected stories of Patricia Highsmith
Variations on a game
Highsmith, P. Nothing that meets the eye; the
uncollected stories of Patricia Highsmith
Where the door is always open and the welcome
mat is out
Highsmith, P. Nothing that meets the eye; the
uncollected stories of Patricia Highsmith
Highway. Cavell, B.
Highway without an ox. Hernández, C.
HIJACKING OF TRUCKS
Crawford, D. Guile is where it goes
Hilbig, Wolfgang
The Abandoned Factory
Agni no57 p128-9 2003
Hilda. Honig, L.
Hildt, Robert
Orbit
Gettysburg Review v15 no3 p441-5 Aut 2002
Slice
Gettysburg Review v12 no1 p105-16 Spr 1999
Working without a Net
The Virginia Quarterly Review v79 no3 p523-
33 Summ 2003
Hill, Ingrid
The ballad of Rappy Valcour
New stories from the South: the year's best,
2003; edited by Shannon Ravenel; with a
preface by Roy Blount Jr.
Castelgandolfo
The Southern Review (Baton Rouge, La.) v40
no2 p314-42 Spr 2004
Jolie-Gray
New stories from the South: the year's best,
2001; edited by Shannon Ravenel; with a
preface by Lee Smith
The more they stay the same
New stories from the South: the year's best,
2002; edited by Shannon Ravenel; with a
preface by Larry Brown
Pagan babies
New stories from the South: the year's best,
1999; edited by Shannon Ravenel; with a
preface by Tony Earley
Valor
New stories from the South; the year's best,
2004; edited by Shannon Ravenel; preface
by Tim Gautreaux

Hill, Joe
20th century ghost
The Mammoth book of best new horror 14; edited with an introduction by Stephen Jones
Pop art
With signs and wonders; an international anthology of Jewish fabulist fiction; edited by Daniel M. Jaffe
Hill, John *See* Koontz, Dean R. (Dean Ray), 1945-
Hill, Kathleen
The anointed
The Best American short stories, 2000; selected from U.S. and Canadian magazines by E. L. Doctorow with Katrina Kenison; with an introduction by E. L. Doctorow
Hill, Reginald
The game of dog
Edwards, M. Mysterious pleasures; a celebration of the Crime Writers' Association's 50th anniversary; edited by Martin Edwards
True Thomas
Master's choice v2; mystery stories by today's top writers and the masters who inspired them; edited by Lawrence Block
The **hill** bachelors. Trevor, W.
The **hill** station. Murray, J.
Hillerman, Tony
Chee's witch
A Century of great suspense stories; edited by Jeffery Deaver
First lead gasser
Master's choice [v1]; mystery stories by today's top writers and the masters who inspired them; edited by Lawrence Block
Hills like white hills. Wetherell, W. D.
The **Hillside** Slasher. Davidson, R.
Him with his foot in his mouth. Bellow, S.
HIMALAYA MOUNTAINS
Barrett, A. Servants of the map
Murray, J. Blue
Himes, Chester
Lunching at the Ritzmore
The African American West; a century of short stories; edited by Bruce A. Glasrud and Laurie Champion
The meanest cop in the world
A Century of noir; thirty-two classic crime stories; edited by Mickey Spillane and Max Allan Collins
HINDENBURG (AIRSHIP)
Shepard, J. Love and hydrogen
Hindsight. Benvenuto, C.
HINDUS
Nair, M. Sixteen days in December
England
See also East Indians—England
Hines, James
The dog fight
New Letters v67 no4 p59-70 2001
Hines, Valerie
Three Women by the River—At One Time or Another
Ms. v13 no3 p81-2 Fall 2003
Hinger, Charlotte
Any old mother
Blood on their hands; edited by Lawrence Block

Hinojosa, Francisco
Marina Dosal, juice vendor
Points of departure; new stories from Mexico; edited by Mónica Lavín; translated by Gustavo Segade
Hinojosa, Rolando
The Gulf Oil -Can Santa Claus
Graham, D. Lone Star literature; from the Red River to the Rio Grande; edited by Don Graham
Hoengsong
Retrieving bones; stories and poems of the Korean War; edited and with an introduction by W. D. Ehrhart and Philip K. Jason
Hinojosa-Smith, R. Rolando *See* Hinojosa, Rolando, 1929-
Hinostroza, Rodolfo
The benefactor
The Vintage book of Latin American stories; edited by Carlos Fuentes and Julio Ortega
The **hippie** chick. Dinh, L.
The **hippie** shirt. Locklin, G.
HIPPIES
See also Bohemianism
Clinton, M. T. Free your mind and your ass will follow
Coberly, L. M. The fellowsip at Wysong's Clearing
Little, B. Connie
Locklin, G. The hippie shirt
Locklin, G. Return of the hippie shirt
Swann, M. Flower children
Taylor, P. E. Leaping Leo
Wheat, C. What the dormouse said
Hird, Laura
The boxroom
Typical girls; new stories by smart women; edited by Susan Corrigan
The last supper
Grand Street no67 p6-21 Wint 1999
Meat
The Literary Review (Madison, N.J.) v45 no2 p288-300 Wint 2002
Hired Hand. Pourciau, G.
HIRED KILLERS
Bishop, P. The man who shot Trinity Valance
Block, L. Keller's last refuge
Cavell, B. Evolution
Collins, M. Man on the run
Connelly, M. Two-bagger
Davis, D. S. To forget Mary Ellen
Di Filippo, P. Have gun, will edit
DuBois, B. Trade wars
Dybek, S. Breasts
Gischler, V. Hitting Rufus
Gores, J. Killer man
Gores, J. Raptor
Grant, L. The second-oldest profession
Greeley, A. M. The bishop and the hit man
Hager, J. Company wife
Johnson, A. Teen sniper
Kelman, J. The grapes of Roth
Keret, E. Good intentions
L'Amour, L. Anything for a pal
Lansdale, J. R. Bestsellers guaranteed
Lee, W. W. The right thing to do
Mann, A. Taking care of Frank
Mosley, W. Doctor Kismet
Nevins, F. M., Jr. Evensong

HIRED KILLERS—*Continued*
O'Callaghan, M. It takes one to kill one
O'Callaghan, M. The sweet old lady who sits in the park
Pelegrimas, M. and Randisi, R. J. I love everything about you
Rankin, I. The hanged man
Smith, J. Strangers on a plane
Straub, P. Isn't it romantic?
Tinti, H. Hit man of the year
Vachss, A. H. Everybody pays
Vachss, A. H. Harvest time
Vachss, A. H. Hit man
Vachss, A. H. Pigeon drop
Vachss, A. H. Two-way radio
Weaver, G. A dialogue
Zeman, A. Green heat
Hired man. Stegner, L.
HIRED MEN
Aldrich, B. S. Romance in G minor
Bowles, P. The dismissal
Busch, F. Domicile
Casares, O. Domingo
Chenoweth, A. Housework
Chute, C. "Ollie, oh . . . "
Everett, P. L. Cry about a nickel
Falco, E. The instruments of peace
Forbes, C. Sign
Gavell, M. L. Sober, exper., work guar.
Hoffman, W. Tenant
Lundquist, R. Silence and slow time
O'Connor, F. Greenleaf
Robinson, L. The diver
Roorbach, B. A job at Little Henry's
Spencer, E. The girl who loved horses
Stegner, L. Hired man
Stegner, L. Pipers at the gates of dawn
Tester, W. Who's your daddy now?
Wells, K. Godlight
Hiroshima. Sorokin, V.
Hirsch and Bratinsky. Lynn, D. H.
Hirshberg, Glen
Dancing men
    Datlow, E. The dark; new ghost stories; edited by Ellen Datlow
    Hirshberg, G. The two Sams; ghost stories
Mr. Dark's carnival
    Death dines at 8:30; edited by Claudia Bishop and Nick DiChario
    Hirshberg, G. The two Sams; ghost stories
Shipwreck beach
    Hirshberg, G. The two Sams; ghost stories
Struwwelpeter
    Hirshberg, G. The two Sams; ghost stories
    The Mammoth book of best horror 13; edited by Stephen Jones
The two Sams
    Hirshberg, G. The two Sams; ghost stories
    The Mammoth book of best new horror 14; edited with an introduction by Stephen Jones
His beautiful handwriting. Gavell, M. L.
His brother's keeper. Hammett, D.
His dog. Hansen, R.
His father's shoes. Brandt, W.
His father's son. Wharton, E.
His mother's voice. Blatnik, A.
His oeuvre. Updike, J.
His personal prisoner. Savage, L., Jr.

His russet witch. Fitzgerald, F. S.
His sweater. Treat, J.
His wife. See Chekhov, A. P. The helpmate
His women. Adams, A.
HISPANIC AMERICANS
Baca, J. S. The importance of a piece of paper
Baca, J. S. Matilda's garden
Baca, J. S. The three sons of Julia
Garcia, L. G. Alone
Garcia, L. G. Always verbena
Garcia, L. G. Delivering meat
Garcia, L. G. Eladio comes home
Garcia, L. G. The emergency room
Garcia, L. G. Girl
Garcia, L. G. Mammogram
Garcia, L. G. Mister Tyrone
Garcia, L. G. Nano returns
Garcia, L. G. Parents
Garcia, L. G. The sergeant
Garcia, L. G. Uncle Willy
Garcia, L. G. West Texas cowboys
Gonzalez, R. Eduardo
Gonzalez, R. The garden of Padre Anselmo
Gonzalez, R. Mountain
Gonzalez, R. The scorpion eater
Gonzalez, R. Spanish
Jaime-Becerra, M. Buena Suerte Airlines
Jaime-Becerra, M. The corrido of Hector Cruz
Jaime-Becerra, M. Every night is ladies' night
Jaime-Becerra, M. La fiesta brava
Jaime-Becerra, M. Georgie and Wanda
Jaime-Becerra, M. Gina and Max
Jaime-Becerra, M. Lopez Trucking Incorporated
Jaime-Becerra, M. Media vuelta
Jaime-Becerra, M. Practice tattoos
Jaime-Becerra, M. Riding with Lencho
HISTORIANS
Bellow, S. By the St. Lawrence
Borges, J. L. Guayaquil
MacLeod, I. R. The summer isles
Waugh, E. Scott-King's modern Europe
History. Berry, R. M.
History. Gordimer, N.
History. Sherwood, F.
History lesson. Clarke, A. C.
The **history** of cancer. Johnson, A.
The **history** of photography. Murphy, D.
A **history** of sex. Foley, S.
A **history** of swimming. Roeske, P.
The **history** of the flood. Harfenist, J.
A **history** of the village of Goriukhino. Pushkin, A. S.
A **history** of things lost or broken. Cioffari, P.
Hit and run. Howard, C.
HIT-AND-RUN DRIVERS
Davis, D. S. The scream
Hit man. Vachss, A. H.
The **hitch-hikers**. Welty, E.
Hitchcock, Robyn
Narcissus
    Carved in rock; short stories by musicians; edited by Greg Kihn
HITCHHIKERS
Alexie, S. The toughest Indian in the world
Bausch, R. The man who knew Belle Starr
Bishop, P. The samaritan
Bullins, E. Support your local police
Dobyns, S. Kansas
Earle, S. Wheeler County

HITCHHIKERS—*Continued*
Gautreaux, T. Dancing with the one-armed gal
Irsfeld, J. H. Have you knocked on Cleopatra?
Jenkins, G. Strange attractors
Miller, R. Paula
Murguía, A. A toda máquina
Nakagami, K. Red hair
Oates, J. C. We were worried about you
O'Callaghan, M. Exit
O'Connor, J. The long way home
Rinehart, S. Burning luv
Skillings, R. D. No escape for yours truly
Tester, W. The living and the dead
Welty, E. The hitch-hikers
White, M. C. Burn patterns
Winter, E. The price you pay
HITLER, ADOLF, 1889-1945
About
Asch, S. "Heil, Hitler!"
Malzberg, B. N. Hitler at Nuremberg
Uncle Alf
Hitler at Nuremberg. Malzberg, B. N.
Hitting Into the Wind. Meissner, B.
Hitting Rufus. Gischler, V.
Hjortsberg, William
The clone who ran for congress
Hjortsberg, W. Odd corners
Gray matters
Hjortsberg, W. Odd corners
Homecoming
Hjortsberg, W. Odd corners
Symbiography
Hjortsberg, W. Odd corners
HO, CHÍ MINH, 1890-1969
About
Butler, R. O. A good scent from a strange
mountain
HO CHI MINH CITY (VIETNAM) *See* Vietnam—Ho Chi Minh City
Ho **ho** ho. Paul, B.
The **hoard** of the Gibbelins. Dunsany, E. J. M. D.
P., Baron
HOAXES
Anderson, F. I. Blind man's buff
Babel´, I. Shabos-Nakhamu
Bowles, P. Madame and Ahmed
Fitzgerald, F. S. Myra meets his family
Fitzgerald, F. S. The offshore pirate
Singer, I. B. Taibele and her demon
Stevenson, J. The island of the day before yesterday
Taylor, P. H. Venus, cupid, folly and time
Trevor, W. Death of a professor
Wharton, E. Her son
Wharton, E. Miss Mary Pask
Hoban, Russell
Kleinzeit [excerpt]
The Vintage book of amnesia; an anthology;
edited by Jonathan Lethem
Hobb, Robin
Homecoming
Silverberg, R. Legends II; new short novels
by the masters of modern fantasy; edited
by Robert Silverberg
Hobbits and hobgoblins. Kenan, R.
Hobby Division. Allison, W.
HOBOKEN (N.J.) *See* New Jersey—Hoboken

Hobson, Charlotte
The bottle: a provincial tale
Fishman, B. Wild East; stories from the last
frontier; edited with an introduction by Boris Fishman
Hobson's choice. Bester, A.
Hobson's choice. Lutz, J.
Hoch, Edward D.
The circle of ink
The World's finest mystery and crime stories,
first annual collection; edited by Ed
Gorman
The Club of Masks
Flesh and blood; erotic tales of crime and
passion; edited by Max Allan Collins and
Jeff Gelb
The counterfeit copperhead
The Blue and the gray undercover; edited by
Ed Gorman
Day for a picnic
Murder most delectable; savory tales of culinary crimes; edited by Martin H. Greenberg
The day the dogs died
Royal whodunnits; edited by Mike Ashley
The detective's wife
Master's choice v2; mystery stories by today's top writers and the masters who inspired them; edited by Lawrence Block
Enemy territory
Death by espionage; intriguing stories of deception and betrayal; edited by Martin Cruz
Smith
Great day for the Irish
Murder most Celtic; tall tales of Irish mayhem; edited by Martin H. Greenberg
The Haggard Society
The World's finest mystery and crime stories,
second annual collection; edited by Ed
Gorman
Interpol: the case of the modern medusa
A Century of great suspense stories; edited by
Jeffery Deaver
Martha's parrot
White House pet detectives; tales of crime
and mystery at the White House from a
pet's-eye view; edited by Carole Nelson
Douglas
One bag of coconuts
Crème de la crime; edited by Janet Hutchings
The problem of the yellow wallpaper
The World's finest mystery and crime stories,
third annual collection; edited by Ed
Gorman and Martin H. Greenberg
The sweating statue
Murder most divine; ecclesiastical tales of unholy crimes; edited by Ralph McInerny and
Martin H. Greenberg
The theft of the bingo card
Death cruise; crime stories on the open seas;
edited by Lawrence Block
The theft of the Halloween pumpkin
The Ultimate Halloween; edited by Marvin
Kaye
The theft of the sandwich board
Death dines at 8:30; edited by Claudia Bishop
and Nick DiChario
V-2
Malice domestic 8

Hoch, Edward D.—*Continued*
A wall too high
  The World's finest mystery and crime stories, second annual collection; edited by Ed Gorman
Hochman, Anndee
Aggiornamento
  Hochman, A. Anatomies; a novella and stories
Anatomies
  Hochman, A. Anatomies; a novella and stories
Dark is not a single shade of gray
  Hochman, A. Anatomies; a novella and stories
Diamonds are a girl's best friend
  Hochman, A. Anatomies; a novella and stories
Do not attempt to climb out
  Hochman, A. Anatomies; a novella and stories
Good with animals
  Hochman, A. Anatomies; a novella and stories
The honor of your presence is requested
  Hochman, A. Anatomies; a novella and stories
I seen some stuf horabl stuf lisen
  Hochman, A. Anatomies; a novella and stories
In case of emergency
  Hochman, A. Anatomies; a novella and stories
Liability
  Hochman, A. Anatomies; a novella and stories
Local currency
  Hochman, A. Anatomies; a novella and stories
Nesting
  Hochman, A. Anatomies; a novella and stories
Underneath
  Hochman, A. Anatomies; a novella and stories
What's more
  Hochman, A. Anatomies; a novella and stories
The whole truth and nothing but
  Hochman, A. Anatomies; a novella and stories
Hochstein, Rolaine
The Woman Who Tortured and Nurtured Turgenev
  The Antioch Review v60 no4 p640-8 Fall 2002
Hockensmith, Steve
Erie's last day
  The Best American mystery stories, 2001; edited and with an Introduction by Lawrence Block
HOCKEY
Angrist, M. So much the better
Billman, J. When we were Wolves
LaSalle, P. Hockey
Robinson, L. Puckheads
Schoemperlen, D. Hockey night in Canada
Hockey. LaSalle, P.

Hoddeson, Bob
How to play the twelve-bar blues
  The North American Review v287 no3/4 p22-7 My/Ag 2002
Hodegetria. Healy, J. F.
Hodge, Brian
Nesting instincts
  The Mammoth book of best new horror 14; edited with an introduction by Stephen Jones
  The Year's best fantasy & horror: sixteenth annual collection; edited by Ellen Datlow & Terri Windling
Some other me
  The Year's best fantasy & horror: sixteenth annual collection; edited by Ellen Datlow & Terri Windling
Hodgen, Christie
Going out of business forever
  Hodgen, C. A jeweler's eye for flaw; stories
The great Americans
  Hodgen, C. A jeweler's eye for flaw; stories
The hero of loneliness
  Hodgen, C. A jeweler's eye for flaw; stories
  New stories from the South: the year's best, 2001; edited by Shannon Ravenel; with a preface by Lee Smith
A jeweler's eye for flaw
  The Georgia Review v56 no2 p438-55 Summ 2002
  Hodgen, C. A jeweler's eye for flaw; stories
Sir Karl LaFong or current resident
  Hodgen, C. A jeweler's eye for flaw; stories
Take them in, please
  Hodgen, C. A jeweler's eye for flaw; stories
The tender of unmarked graves
  Hodgen, C. A jeweler's eye for flaw; stories
Three parting shots and a forecast
  Hodgen, C. A jeweler's eye for flaw; stories
What the rabbi said to the priest
  Hodgen, C. A jeweler's eye for flaw; stories
Hodgen, Page
Heartaches
  South Carolina Review v35 no1 p111-17 Fall 2002
Hodges, Elizabeth L.
The Firebird
  Ploughshares v29 no2/3 p67-72 Fall 2003
HODGKIN'S DISEASE
Shapiro, G. At the great divide
Shapiro, G. Shifman in paradise
Hodgman, Jan
Tanuki
  The Year's best fantasy & horror, thirteenth annual collection; edited by Ellen Datlow and Terri Windling
Hodgman, Jan
Tanuki
  Nixon under the bodhi tree and other works of Buddhist fiction; edited by Kate Wheeler ; foreword by Charles Johnson
Hodgson, Ken
Requiem for Rosebud
  American West; twenty new stories from the Western Writers of America; edited with an introduction by Loren D. Estleman
Hodgson, M. H.
Growing up north
  U.S. Catholic v67 no3 p34-7 Mr 2002

Hodgson, William Hope
The adventure of the garter
  Hodgson, W. H. The boats of the "Glen
    Carrig" and other nautical adventures; be-
    ing the first volume of The collected fiction
    of William Hope Hodgson; edited by
    Jeremy Lessen
The adventure of the headland
  Hodgson, W. H. The boats of the "Glen
    Carrig" and other nautical adventures; be-
    ing the first volume of The collected fiction
    of William Hope Hodgson; edited by
    Jeremy Lessen
The adventure with the claim jumpers
  Hodgson, W. H. The boats of the "Glen
    Carrig" and other nautical adventures; be-
    ing the first volume of The collected fiction
    of William Hope Hodgson; edited by
    Jeremy Lessen
The Baumoff explpsive
  Tales before Tolkien; the roots of modern
    fantasy; edited by Douglas A. Anderson
The bells of the "Laughing Sally"
  Hodgson, W. H. The boats of the "Glen
    Carrig" and other nautical adventures; be-
    ing the first volume of The collected fiction
    of William Hope Hodgson; edited by
    Jeremy Lessen
The boats of the "Glen Carrrig"
  Hodgson, W. H. The boats of the "Glen
    Carrig" and other nautical adventures; be-
    ing the first volume of The collected fiction
    of William Hope Hodgson; edited by
    Jeremy Lessen
The call in the dawn
  Hodgson, W. H. The boats of the "Glen
    Carrig" and other nautical adventures; be-
    ing the first volume of The collected fiction
    of William Hope Hodgson; edited by
    Jeremy Lessen
The case of the Chinese curio dealer
  Hodgson, W. H. The boats of the "Glen
    Carrig" and other nautical adventures; be-
    ing the first volume of The collected fiction
    of William Hope Hodgson; edited by
    Jeremy Lessen
Contraband of war
  Hodgson, W. H. The boats of the "Glen
    Carrig" and other nautical adventures; be-
    ing the first volume of The collected fiction
    of William Hope Hodgson; edited by
    Jeremy Lessen
The diamond spy
  Hodgson, W. H. The boats of the "Glen
    Carrig" and other nautical adventures; be-
    ing the first volume of The collected fiction
    of William Hope Hodgson; edited by
    Jeremy Lessen
The drum of saccharine
  Hodgson, W. H. The boats of the "Glen
    Carrig" and other nautical adventures; be-
    ing the first volume of The collected fiction
    of William Hope Hodgson; edited by
    Jeremy Lessen

The finding of the Graiken
  Hodgson, W. H. The boats of the "Glen
    Carrig" and other nautical adventures; be-
    ing the first volume of The collected fiction
    of William Hope Hodgson; edited by
    Jeremy Lessen
From information received
  Hodgson, W. H. The boats of the "Glen
    Carrig" and other nautical adventures; be-
    ing the first volume of The collected fiction
    of William Hope Hodgson; edited by
    Jeremy Lessen
From the tideless sea, part one
  Hodgson, W. H. The boats of the "Glen
    Carrig" and other nautical adventures; be-
    ing the first volume of The collected fiction
    of William Hope Hodgson; edited by
    Jeremy Lessen
From the tideless sea, part two: further news of
  the Homebird
  Hodgson, W. H. The boats of the "Glen
    Carrig" and other nautical adventures; be-
    ing the first volume of The collected fiction
    of William Hope Hodgson; edited by
    Jeremy Lessen
The German spy
  Hodgson, W. H. The boats of the "Glen
    Carrig" and other nautical adventures; be-
    ing the first volume of The collected fiction
    of William Hope Hodgson; edited by
    Jeremy Lessen
The island of the Ud
  Hodgson, W. H. The boats of the "Glen
    Carrig" and other nautical adventures; be-
    ing the first volume of The collected fiction
    of William Hope Hodgson; edited by
    Jeremy Lessen
My lady's jewels
  Hodgson, W. H. The boats of the "Glen
    Carrig" and other nautical adventures; be-
    ing the first volume of The collected fiction
    of William Hope Hodgson; edited by
    Jeremy Lessen
The mystery of the derelict
  Hodgson, W. H. The boats of the "Glen
    Carrig" and other nautical adventures; be-
    ing the first volume of The collected fiction
    of William Hope Hodgson; edited by
    Jeremy Lessen
The painted lady
  Hodgson, W. H. The boats of the "Glen
    Carrig" and other nautical adventures; be-
    ing the first volume of The collected fiction
    of William Hope Hodgson; edited by
    Jeremy Lessen
The plans of the reefing bi-plane
  Hodgson, W. H. The boats of the "Glen
    Carrig" and other nautical adventures; be-
    ing the first volume of The collected fiction
    of William Hope Hodgson; edited by
    Jeremy Lessen
The problem of the pearls
  Hodgson, W. H. The boats of the "Glen
    Carrig" and other nautical adventures; be-
    ing the first volume of The collected fiction
    of William Hope Hodgson; edited by
    Jeremy Lessen

Hodgson, William Hope—*Continued*

The red herring
    Hodgson, W. H. The boats of the "Glen Carrig" and other nautical adventures; being the first volume of The collected fiction of William Hope Hodgson; edited by Jeremy Lessen

The thing in the weeds
    Hodgson, W. H. The boats of the "Glen Carrig" and other nautical adventures; being the first volume of The collected fiction of William Hope Hodgson; edited by Jeremy Lessen

Trading with the enemy
    Hodgson, W. H. The boats of the "Glen Carrig" and other nautical adventures; being the first volume of The collected fiction of William Hope Hodgson; edited by Jeremy Lessen

HODGSON, WILLIAM HOPE, 1877-1918
Parodies, imitations, etc.
Wright, J. C. Awake in the night

Hodson, Ed
Son of man
    Iowa Review v32 no1 p173-4 Spr 2002

Høeg, Peter
Portrait of the avant-garde
    The Art of the story; an international anthology of contemporary short stories; edited by Daniel Halpern

Hoehling, Annaliese
(jt. auth) See Suárez, Patricia

Hoengsong. Hinojosa, R.

Hoffman, Alice
Bake at 350°
    Hoffman, A. Local girls
The boy who wrestled with angels
    Hoffman, A. Local girls
Dear diary
    Hoffman, A. Local girls
Devotion
    Hoffman, A. Local girls
Examining the evidence
    Hoffman, A. Local girls
Fate
    Hoffman, A. Local girls
Flight
    Hoffman, A. Local girls
Gretel
    Hoffman, A. Local girls
How to talk to the dead
    Hoffman, A. Local girls
Insulting the Angels
    Prairie Schooner v78 no2 p22-33 Summ 2004
Local girls
    Hoffman, A. Local girls
The rest of your life
    Hoffman, A. Local girls
Rose red
    Hoffman, A. Local girls
Still among the living
    Hoffman, A. Local girls
Tell the truth
    Hoffman, A. Local girls
True confession
    Hoffman, A. Local girls
The Witch of Truro
    The Kenyon Review v26 no2 p8-16 Spr 2004

Hoffman, Lee
The third nation
    Children of the night; stories of ghosts, vampires, werewolves, and "lost children"; edited by Martin H. Greenberg

Hoffman, Nina Kiriki
Between disappearances
    Redshift; extreme visions of speculative fiction; edited by Al Sarrantonio
Food chain
    Children of the night; stories of ghosts, vampires, werewolves, and "lost children"; edited by Martin H. Greenberg
Gone
    Lighthouse hauntings; 12 original tales of the supernatural; edited by Charles G. Waugh & Martin H. Greenberg
Mint condition
    Past imperfect; edited by Martin H. Greenberg and Larry Segriff
Savage breasts
    Witpunk; edited by Claude Lalumière and Marty Halpern
Voyage of discovery
    Past lives, present tense; edited by Elizabeth Ann Scarborough

Hoffman, William
Black swan
    The Sewanee Review v107 no1 p18-31 Wint 1999
Blood
    Hoffman, W. Doors; stories
Doors
    Hoffman, W. Doors; stories
Humility
    Hoffman, W. Doors; stories
Landings
    Hoffman, W. Doors; stories
Place
    Hoffman, W. Doors; stories
Prodigal
    Hoffman, W. Doors; stories
Pursuit
    The Sewanee Review v107 no4 p499-512 Fall 1999
Roll call
    Hoffman, W. Doors; stories
The secret garden
    The Cry of an occasion; fiction from the Fellowship of Southern Writers; edited by Richard Bausch; with a foreword by George Garrett
Stones
    Hoffman, W. Doors; stories
Tenant
    Hoffman, W. Doors; stories
Tribute
    The Virginia Quarterly Review v75 no1 p19-30 Wint 1999
Winter wheat
    Hoffman, W. Doors; stories

Hoffman Street. Chinodya, S.
The **Hofzinser** Club. Chabon, M.
The **Hofzinser** Club (I). Chabon, M.

Hogan, Desmond
 The bombs
  The Anchor book of new Irish writing; the
   new Gaelach ficsean; edited and with an
   introduction by John Somer and John J.
   Daly
Hogan, Ernest
 Coyote goes Hollywood
  Witpunk; edited by Claude Lalumière and
   Marty Halpern
 (jt. auth) See Cook, Rick and Hogan, Ernest
Hogan, James P.
 Convolution
  Past imperfect; edited by Martin H. Green-
   berg and Larry Segriff
Hogan, Linda
 Amen
  In our nature: stories of wildness; selected
   and introduced by Donna Seaman
Hogan, Ray
 A question of faith
  The First Five Star western corral; western
   stories; edited by Jon Tuska and Vicki
   Piekarski
Hogan, Robert Ray See Hogan, Ray, 1908-
Hoggard, James
 The scapegoat
  Graham, D. Lone Star literature; from the
   Red River to the Rio Grande; edited by
   Don Graham
**Hohenheim, Philipp Aureolus Theophrastus
  Bombast von** See Paracelsus, 1493-1541
Holbert, Bruce
 Farmer
  Iowa Review v29 no1 p37-45 Spr 1999
 Funeral
  The Antioch Review v60 no3 p500-10 Summ
   2002
Holbrook, Chris
 The idea of it
  Home and beyond; an anthology of Kentucky
   short stories; edited by Morris Allen
   Grubbs; with an introduction by Wade Hall
   and an afterword by Charles E. May
Holbrook, Teri
 Drawing to a close
  Malice domestic 9
Hold me. Tillman, L.
Hold tight. Bloom, A.
Holdefer, Charles
 Letter of rec
  The North American Review v284 no5 p22
   S/O 1999
Holder, Nancy
 Skeleton krewe
  Mardi Gras madness; tales of terror and may-
   hem in New Orleans; edited by Martin H.
   Greenberg and Russell Davis
Holding Cells. Marinara, M.
Holding Pattern. Allen, J. R.
Holding pattern. Scollins-Mantha, B.
Holdstock, Pauline
 Sitting pretty
  Valentine's Day: women against men; stories
   of revenge; introduction by Alice Thomas
HOLDUPS See Robbery
Hole in the head. Strieber, W.
A **hole** in the sheets. Power, S.
Hole in the wall. Keret, E.

A **hole** in the wall of noise. DeLancey, K.
Holes in the ground. Balco, J.
HOLIDAY, BILLIE, 1915-1959
     About
 Blatnik, A. Billie Holiday
Holiday. Matheson, R. C.
A **holiday** junket. Vukcevich, R.
Holiday on the Moon. Clarke, A. C.
Holiday patrol. Van de Wetering, J.
Holiday romance. Davies, R.
HOLIDAYS
     See also Bastille Day; Christmas stories;
      Fourth of July; New Year; Passover; Saint
      Patrick's Day; Thanksgiving Day; Vaca-
      tions; Valentine's Day; Yom Kippur
A **holier** temple. Spatz, G.
Holka, Peter
 Love as a crime
  In search of homo sapiens; twenty-five con-
   temporary Slovak short stories; editor,
   Pavol Hudík ; [translated by Heather
   Trebatická; American English editor, Lucy
   Bednár]
Holladay, Cary
 The Bridge
  The Hudson Review v56 no4 p605-23 Wint
   2004
Holladay, Cary C.
 Merry-go-sorry
  Prize stories, 1999; The O. Henry awards; ed-
   ited and with an introduction by Larry
   Dark
HOLLAND See Netherlands
Holleran, Andrew
 Amsterdam
  Holleran, A. In September, the light changes;
   the stories of Andrew Holleran
 Blorts
  Holleran, A. In September, the light changes;
   the stories of Andrew Holleran
 The boxer
  Holleran, A. In September, the light changes;
   the stories of Andrew Holleran
 Delancey Place
  Holleran, A. In September, the light changes;
   the stories of Andrew Holleran
 The hamburger man
  Holleran, A. In September, the light changes;
   the stories of Andrew Holleran
 The housesitter
  Holleran, A. In September, the light changes;
   the stories of Andrew Holleran
 In September, the light changes
  Holleran, A. In September, the light changes;
   the stories of Andrew Holleran
 Innocence and longing
  Holleran, A. In September, the light changes;
   the stories of Andrew Holleran
 Joshua & Clark
  Holleran, A. In September, the light changes;
   the stories of Andrew Holleran
 The man who got away
  Holleran, A. In September, the light changes;
   the stories of Andrew Holleran
 The ossuary
  Holleran, A. In September, the light changes;
   the stories of Andrew Holleran

Holleran, Andrew—*Continued*
The penthouse
    Holleran, A. In September, the light changes; the stories of Andrew Holleran
Petunias
    Holleran, A. In September, the light changes; the stories of Andrew Holleran
The sentimental education
    Holleran, A. In September, the light changes; the stories of Andrew Holleran
Someone is crying in the chateau de Berne
    Holleran, A. In September, the light changes; the stories of Andrew Holleran
Sunday morning: Key West
    Holleran, A. In September, the light changes; the stories of Andrew Holleran
Holley, Chad
The island in the river
    The Best American mystery stories, 2000; edited and with an introduction by Donald E. Westlake
Holliday, Doc *See* Holliday, John Henry, 1851-1887
HOLLIDAY, JOHN HENRY, 1851-1887
About
    Knight, A. W. Do the dark dance
    Knowles, T. W. Luck of the draw
Holliday, Liz
Provenance
    Royal whodunnits; edited by Mike Ashley
Hollo, Anselm
    (jt. auth) *See* Liksom, Rosa
Hollon, Frank Turner
Left behind
    Stories from the Blue Moon Café; edited by Sonny Brewer
The scrapbook
    Stories from the Blue Moon Cafe II; edited by Sonny Brewer
The **hollow** of the three hills. Hawthorne, N.
The **hollow** oracle. Highsmith, P.
Hollowbrook. Wisniewski, M.
Hollowed Be Thy Name. Coyne, S.
HOLLY, BUDDY, 1936-1959
About
    Dozois, G. R. Touring
HOLLYWOOD (CALIF.) *See* California—Hollywood
Hollywood lessons. Saroyan, A.
Holman, John
Squabble
    This is where we live; short stories by 25 contemporary North Carolina writers; edited by Michael McFee
Wave
    New stories from the South: the year's best, 2000; edited by Shannon Ravenel; with a preface by Ellen Douglas
Holmes, A. M.
Things You Should Know
    Harper's v305 p31 Ag 2002
Holmes, Charlotte
Songs Without Words
    New Letters v69 no2/3 p59-64 2003
HOLOCAUST, JEWISH (1933-1945)
    See also Jews—Persecutions
    Amichai, Y. My father's deaths
    Appelfeld, A. Kitty
    Asch, S. "Heil, Hitler!"

Bellow, S. The Bellarosa connection
Bender, A. Dreaming in Polish
Blatnik, A. Isaac
Bryks, R. Artists in the ghetto
Bryks, R. Berele in the ghetto
Dunmore, H. Lisette
Fink, I. The death of Tsaritsa
Fleming, R. Arbeit Macht Frei
Gascar, P. The season of the dead
Grynberg, H. Uncle Aron
Kalman, J. Not for me a crown of thorns
Kalman, J. What's in a name?
Keret, E. Shoes
Kirshenbaum, B. Who knows Kaddish
Korn, R. H. The road of no return
Lowenthal, M. Ordinary pain
Lustig, A. The lemon
Lustig, A. Stephen and Anne
Morgan, E. S. Saturday afternoon in the Holocaust Museum
Nomberg-Przytyk, S. Old words—new meanings
Ozick, C. The shawl
Paver, C. The boxing match
Rachmil, B. Bread
Rachmil, B. Children of the Lodz, ghetto
Rachmil, B. The last journey
Schlink, B. Girl with lizard
Umansky, E. M. How to make it to the promised land
Wegner, H. A ransom for Tedek
Wisenberg, S. L. Liberator
Wisenberg, S. L. My mother's war
Zawieyski, J. Conrad in the ghetto
HOLOCAUST SURVIVORS
Agnon, S. Y. The night
Almond, S. A dream of sleep
Appelfeld, A. Bertha
Appelfeld, A. In the isles of St. George
Auerbach, J. The border incident
Bassani, G. A plaque on Via Mazzini
Bukiet, M. J. Tongue of the Jews
Cohen, R. Refuge
Epstein, J. Felix emeritus
Grynberg, H. Uncle Aron
Hirshberg, G. Dancing men
Kalman, J. Allures of grandeur
Kalman, J. Channel crossing
Kalman, J. The county of birches
Kalman, J. Eichmann's monogram
Kalman, J. Flight
Kalman, J. Monahan Avenue
Kalman, J. Rain
Kalman, J. A reason to be
Krawiec, R. Hardening of the arteries
Maraini, D. A number on her arm
Rykena, S. Conscience
Schwartz, L. S. Referred pain
Singer, I. B. The bird
Škvorecký, J. Fragments about Rebecca
Tushnet, L. The ban
Holt, H. A.
Notes on My Leprosy
    Confrontation no86/87 p81-9 Spr/Summ 2004
Holt, Rochelle Lynn
Pride Cometh Before a Fall
    Meridians v3 no1 p253-64 2002

Holt, T. E.
'O
  Francis Ford Coppola's Zoetrope all-story 2;
    edited by Adrienne Brodeur and Samantha
    Schnee; with an introduction by Francis
    Ford Coppola
Holt, Tom
Accidental death
  Royal whodunnits; edited by Mike Ashley
Holtzer, Susan
The golden rounds
  Malice domestic 8
Holy blood. Tremayne, P.
The **holy** boys. Garrity, B. R.
Holy cow. Fracis, S. H.
HOLY GRAIL *See* Grail
Holy holy holy. Berkman, P. R.
Holy living and holy dying. Barnard, R.
Holy matrimony. Winterson, J.
HOLY SHROUD
Rusch, K. K. Relics
The **holy** spirit bank. Bouldrey, B.
The **holy** terror. Brennan, M.
Holy walker. Bukoski, A.
Holy water. Kellerman, F.
Homage. Gordimer, N.
Home. Chekhov, A. P.
Home. Davies, R.
Home. Gordon, B.
Home. Grau, S. A.
The **home**. Hensley, J. L.
Home. Matiella, A. C.
Home. Tushinski, J.
Home. See Chekhov, A. P. At home
Home at last. Glasgow, G.
Home-cooked. Mazelis, J.
Home cooking. Sack, D. U.
Home country. Ortiz, S. J.
Home ec. Evans, E.
HOME ECONOMICS
Gilman, C. P. The cottagette
Gilman, C. P. What Diantha did
The **home** front. Hall, H. P.
Home game. O'Rourke, F.
Home improvement. Bowles, S. A.
Home Improvements. Wortman-Wunder, E.
Home in New Hampshire. Stolar, D.
Home is the sailor. Clough, B. W.
Home is where. Adams, A.
Home is where the hate is. Reichert, M. Z.
Home, James, and don't spare the horses. Wilson, A.
Home movies. Brady, C.
Home ownership. Bail, M.
Home place. Henry, W.
Home recordings. Derby, M.
Home remedy. Vukcevich, R.
Home water. Burton, M.
Homecoming. Collins, M.
Homecoming. Grau, S. A.
The **homecoming**. Stewart, I.
HOMECOMINGS
Banks, R. With Ché in New Hampshire
Berry, W. That distant land
Boylan, C. Edna, back from America
Chopin, K. After the winter
Fitzgerald, F. S. Two for a cent
Giono, J. On the side of the road
Ishiguro, K. A family supper

Jafta, M. The home-coming
Miller, J. W. The taste of ironwater
Morgan, R. The welcome
Singer, I. B. The son from America
Updike, J. Home
Wharton, E. Coming home
Wharton, E. Joy in the house
Homeland. Kingsolver, B.
Homeless. Vachss, A. H.
Homeless, hungry, please help. Cohen, S.
HOMELESS PERSONS
Alexie, S. What you pawn I will redeem
Allen, S. Yearbook
Ayres, N. JoJo's gold
Baida, P. No place to hide
Barker, N. Gifts
Berry, W. The solemn boy
Bradbury, R. The dead man
Cody, L. Lucky dip
Cohen, S. Homeless, hungry, please help
Davis, L. The poet's corner
De Lint, C. Birds
De Lint, C. Freak
De Lint, C. Heartfires
Dixon, S. The knife
Dodd, S. M. In France they turn to stone when
  they die
Emin, T. Albert Bert and Andy
Gates, D. Beating
Gordimer, N. Look-alikes
Gunthorp, D. Pikeman and the Bagwoman
Harty, R. Don't call it Christmas
Honig, L. The truly needy
Matera, L. Dead drunk
Means, D. The grip
Means, D. The interruption
Mendoza, R. Traffic
Nichols, J. Slow monkeys
Nietzke, A. Los Angeles here and now
O'Connor, F. The life you save may be your
  own
Pittalwala, I. A change of lights
Reiner, C. That SOB bastard Eddie
Richter, S. The cavemen in the hedges
Shepard, J. First day she'd never see
Sherman, C. W. Emerald City: Third & Pike
Svoboda, T. Car frogs
Svoboda, T. Sundress
Thompson, M. Jesus, beans, and butter rum life-
  savers
Warren, R. P. Blackberry winter
Welty, E. The hitch-hikers
Zabytko, I. Obligation
HOMER
                    About
Borges, J. L. The maker
                Parodies, imitations, etc.
Church, A. The Iliad for boys and girls [ex-
  cerpt]
Homes, A. M.
The Chinese lesson
  Granta no74 p193-210 Summ 2001
  Homes, A. M. Things you should know; a
    collection of stories
Do not disturb
  Homes, A. M. Things you should know; a
    collection of stories

Homes, A. M.—*Continued*
The former First Lady and the football hero
  Homes, A. M. Things you should know; a collection of stories
Georgica
  Homes, A. M. Things you should know; a collection of stories
Please remain calm
  Homes, A. M. Things you should know; a collection of stories
Raft in water, floating
  Homes, A. M. Things you should know; a collection of stories
  The New Yorker v75 no16 p112+ Je 21-28 1999
Remedy
  Bomb no80 p82-5, 106-11 Summ 2002
  Homes, A. M. Things you should know; a collection of stories
Rockets round the moon
  Homes, A. M. Things you should know; a collection of stories
Things you should know
  Homes, A. M. Things you should know; a collection of stories
The weather outside is sunny and bright
  Homes, A. M. Things you should know; a collection of stories
The whiz kids
  Homes, A. M. Things you should know; a collection of stories
HOMES *See* Houses
HOMES FOR THE ELDERLY *See* Old age homes
The **homesick** Buick. MacDonald, J. D.
Homesickness. Eakin, W.
HOMESTEADING
  See also Frontier and pioneer life
Butler, R. O. Christmas 1910
Curry, P. S. Geranium house
Kittredge, W. Breaker of horses
Lilly, J. M. Going home money
Overholser, W. D. The leather slapper
Thomas, D. The girl from follow
Thomas, D. Up in the hills
Hominids. McCorkle, J.
Homologue. Frym, G.
HOMOSEXUALITY
  See also Bisexuality; Lesbianism
Alameddine, R. The changing room
Alameddine, R. Duck
Alameddine, R. A flight to Paris
Alameddine, R. The perv
Alameddine, R. Remembering Nasser
Alexander, E. Beneath the planet of the compulsives
Alexie, S. The toughest Indian in the world
Alvarez, A. Ephemera
Alvarez, A. Fixing a shadow
Alvarez, A. Flatware
Alvarez, A. Ghosts, pockets, traces, necessary clouds
Alvarez, A. Heat rises
Alvarez, A. Losing count
Alvarez, A. Other people's complications
Alvarez, A. Property values
Alvarez, A. Public displays of affection
Alvarez, A. Quintessence
Alvarez, A. Up close

Amis, M. Straight fiction
Anderson, B. Lark till dawn, princess
Arenas, R. End of a story
Banks, R. Comfort
Banner, K. The smallest people alive
Bart, P. Day of reckoning
Beattie, A. The infamous fall of Howell the clown
Bennett, A. The laying on of hands
Bingham, S. The one true place
Bingham, S. The splinter
Bouldrey, B. The holy spirit bank
Bowen, G. Barrel racers: El Charro
Bowles, P. Pages from Cold Point
Bowles, S. A. Home improvement
Brenner, W. Mr. Puniverse
Brenner, W. Remnants of Earl
Broughton, T. A. The wars I missed
Brownstein, G. The inventor of love
Chee, A. Gold
Chee, A. A pilgrimage of you
Clark, W. L. Quiet game
Cole, C. B. Additional selected lives in brief
Cole, C. B. Foo dog
Cole, C. B. Michael Mc:_____ a case study
Cole, C. B. More Selected lives in brief
Cole, C. B. The mother
Cole, C. B. On a railroad bridge, throwing stones
Cole, C. B. Selected lives in brief
Cole, C. B. That's how straight boys dance
Cole, C. B. Used to dream
Cole, C. B. Young Hemingways
Cook, K. L. Penance
Cooper, B. Between the sheets
Cooper, B. Bit-o-honey
Cooper, B. Exterior decoration
Cooper, B. Graphology
Cooper, B. Hunters and gatherers
Cooper, B. Intro to acting
Cooper, B. A man in the making
Cooper, B. Night sky
Cooper, B. Old birds
Cooper, B. What to name the baby
Cooper, B. X
Cullin, M. The cosmology of Bing [excerpt]
Cunningham, M. Mister Brother
Currier, J. Pasta night
Daniels, J. Minding the store
Davenport, G. Gunnar and Nikolai
Davenport, G. The owl of Minerva
Davenport, G. The playing field
Davenport, G. Wo es war, soll ich werden
Davis, A. Circling the drain
Dinh, L. Western music
Doenges, J. God of gods
Doenges, J. MIB
Drake, R. Power
Dunmore, H. Swimming into the millennium
Ebershoff, D. The bank president
Ebershoff, D. The charm bracelet
Ebershoff, D. Chuck Paa
Ebershoff, D. The dress
Ebershoff, D. Living together
Ebershoff, D. Regime
Ebershoff, D. The Rose City
Ebershoff, D. Trespass
Evenson, B. The intricacies of post-shooting etiquette

HOMOSEXUALITY—*Continued*

Evenson, B. Promisekeepers
Ferrell, C. Proper library
Ferriss, L. Leaving the neighborhood
Galef, D. All Cretans
Galloway, J. Not flu
Gambone, P. The singing boy
Gates, D. The intruder
Gates, D. Star baby
Gilchrist, E. Remorse
Glave, T. Accidents
Glave, T. Commitment
Glave, T. Flying
Glave, T. Their story
Gold, M. A. Dann
Gordon, B. Home
Gordon, M. Storytelling
Gorodischer, A. The violet's embryos
Greer, A. S. Blame it on my youth
Greer, A. S. Come live with me and be my love
Greer, A. S. Lost causes
Griffith, M. Hooper gets a perm
Grimsley, J. Boulevard
Groff, D. The third person
Guibert, H. The Hammam
Gunn, K. Tinsel bright
Gurganus, A. He's one, too
Gurganus, A. Preservation news
Gwyn, A. The backsliders
Gwyn, A. Courtship
Ha Jin. The bridegroom
Hamburger, A. Exile
Hamburger, A. Garage sale
Hamburger, A. Law of return
Hamburger, A. A man of the country
Hannah, B. Death and joy
Harris, E. L. Money can't buy me love
Harris, R. M. Haram
Harty, R. Ongchoma
Haslett, A. The beginnings of grief
Haslett, A. Notes to my biographer
Haslett, A. Reunion
Hayes, D. Kissing you
Hayes, D. This world of ours
Hayes, J. G. Regular Flattop
Hell, R. A novel in progress
Hochman, A. The honor of your presence is requested
Holleran, A. Amsterdam
Holleran, A. Blorts
Holleran, A. Delancey Place
Holleran, A. The hamburger man
Holleran, A. The housesitter
Holleran, A. In September, the light changes
Holleran, A. Innocence and longing
Holleran, A. Joshua & Clark
Holleran, A. The man who got away
Holleran, A. The ossuary
Holleran, A. The penthouse
Holleran, A. Petunias
Holleran, A. The sentimental education
Holleran, A. Someone is crying in the chateau de Berne
Holleran, A. Sunday morning: Key West
Homes, A. M. The whiz kids
Horton, H. The year draws in the day
House, T. Scarecrow
Hudson, S. The fall of the Nixon administration
Huffman, B., Jr. Some due process

Ingenito-DeSio, L. A really weird thing happened recently
James, H. The pupil
Jesús, P. d. Instructions for a single man
Jesús, P. d. The letter
Jesús, P. d. Oh, that music (the importance of going on until the end)
Jesús, P. d. The portrait
Johnson, D. Something to remember me by
Jones, G. Other places
Kenan, R. The foundations of the earth
Kennedy, A. L. An immaculate man
Kennedy, A. L. A wrong thing
Krawiec, R. Listening to the gay boys fight
Kuhr, J. We're all chicken here
Lane, J. The window
Lao She. Rabbit
LaValle, V. D. Trinidad
Lawrence, D. H. The Prussian officer
Leavitt, D. Black box
Leavitt, D. Crossing St. Gotthard
Leavitt, D. The infection scene
Leavitt, D. The list
Leavitt, D. The marble quilt
Leavitt, D. The term paper artist
Leavitt, D. Territory
Leong, R. Camouflage
Leong, R. Eclipse
Leong, R. Geography one
Leong, R. Hemispheres
Leong, R. No Bruce Lee
Leong, R. Phoenix eyes
Lewis, Mark Ray. Scordatura
Lida, D. Regrets
Livingood, J. Oh, Albany, my love
Lord, C. La Tortuga
Lowenthal, M. Infinity of angles
Lowenthal, M. Into a mirror
MacLeod, I. R. The summer isles
Mann, W. J. Say goodbye to Middletown
Manrique, J. The documentary artist
Marano, M. Burden
McCann, R. The universe, concealed
McManus, J. Scintilla
McQuain, K. Erasing Sonny
McWhorter, C. T. Silent protest
Mills, J. Watch out, the world's behind you
Monardo, A. Our passion
Morrow, B. "Ciccone youths 1990"
Mueller, D. Ice breaking
Mueller, D. Zero
Muñoz, M. By the time you get there, by the time you get back
Muñoz, M. Everything the white boy told you
Muñoz, M. Good as yesterday
Muñoz, M. Monkey, Sí
Muñoz, M. Skyshot
Muñoz, M. The third myth
Muñoz, M. Zigzagger
Newman, D. A. Good news and bad news
Ordoña, R. World without end
Padura Fuentes, L. The hunter
Patterson, K. Sick in public
Peck, D. Bliss
Peck, D. Cities of the plain
Pratt, D. Series
Price, R. An evening meal
Proulx, A. Brokeback Mountain
Provenzano, J. Quality time

HOMOSEXUALITY—*Continued*
Quan, A. Hair
Rawley, D. Mother of pearl
Rawley, D. Saigon
Reilly, L. 1984
Reiner, C. Aunt Delia and her twins
Reisman, N. Confessions
Renado, T. Get a lifestyle
Roberts, N. This is not skin
Ronan, F. The last innocence of Simeon
Rosenfeld, S. How I went (recipe for lime curd)
Rowell, J. Delegates
Rowell, J. The mother-of-the-groom and I
Rowell, J. The music of your life
Rowell, J. Saviors
Rowell, J. Spectators in love
Rowell, J. Who lives you?
Rowell, J. Wildlife of Coastal Carolina
Ryan, P. Before Las Blancas
Ryan, P. Second island
Ryman, G. Birth days
Sade, marquis de. Augustine de Villeblanche; or, Love's strategy
Sandford, R. Manifest white
Shepherd, R. The black narcissus
Silber, J. The high road
Singer, I. B. Two
Skiff, M. Blood brothers
Skillings, R. D. At least
Skillings, R. D. God knows
Skillings, R. D. The spiritus step
Skillings, R. D. Theatre of the real
Smart, A. Posing
Smart, A. Vincent
Smyth, C. Near the bone
Strober, R. Poker face
Thurm, M. Ancient history
Thurmond, J. Beauty of blood
Tran, H. Little murmurs
Treat, J. Ants
Tuller, D. Sperm-and-egg tango
Tushinski, J. Home
Updike, J. Scenes from the fifties
Verghese, A. Lilacs
Vernon, D. Arrival
Vernon, D. Couple kills
Villane, M. The color of rain
Watmough, D. Sharing Hale-Bopp
Welsh, I. Catholic guilt (you know you love it)
Wheat, C. A bus called pity
White, E. Cinnamon skin
White, E. A Venice story
Willis, M. S. Another perversion
Ziegler, I. Cliffs notes
HOMOSEXUALS *See* Homosexuality; Lesbianism
Honda. Treat, J.
Honda People. Flanagan, E.
HONDURAN SOLDIERS *See* Soldiers—Honduras
HONDURAS
Jacobs, M. Looking for Lourdes
Honest. Leonard, T.
An **honest** day's work. Harrison, H.
An **honest** woman. Gilman, C. P.
HONESTY
     See also Truthfulness and falsehood
Honey. Bean, B.
Honey pie. Murakami, H.

Honey well hung. Chapman, C. M.
Honeydew. Reid, N. L.
Honeymoon. Canty, K.
Honeymoon. Harman, M.
Honeymoon. Klíma, I.
Honeymoon. Michaels, L.
Honeymoon cruise. Deming, R.
HONEYMOONS
Bausch, R. Wedlock
Boswell, M. Spanish omens
Bowles, P. Call at Corazón
Deming, R. Honeymoon cruise
Gao Xingjian. The temple
Klíma, I. Honeymoon
Marías, J. On the honeymoon
McCorkle, J. Chickens
Parker, D. Here we are
Standiford, L. Succubus
Vivante, A. Honeymoon
Honeyville. Billman, J.
HONG KONG
Morton, L. Pound rots in Fragrant Harbour
Hong Taitai. Cheng Naishan
HONGKONG *See* Hong Kong
Honig, Lucy
After
    Honig, L. The truly needy and other stories
Dispossessed
    Honig, L. The truly needy and other stories
English as a second language
    Honig, L. The truly needy and other stories
Hilda
    Honig, L. The truly needy and other stories
Love, rescue, care, dream, sweep
    Honig, L. The truly needy and other stories
No friends, all strangers
    Honig, L. The truly needy and other stories
Refuge
    Honig, L. The truly needy and other stories
The sights of Cork
    Honig, L. The truly needy and other stories
The truly needy
    Honig, L. The truly needy and other stories
Honigmann, Barbara
A grave in two places
    Prairie Schooner v73 no3 p47-52 Fall 1999
HONOLULU (HAWAII) *See* Hawaii—Honolulu
The **honor** of your presence is requested. Hochman, A.
The **honor** system. Rifkin, A.
Honors. Kercheval, J. L.
The **honors** student. Roth, J.
Honwana, Luís Bernardo
Papa, snake & I
    The Anchor book of modern African stories; edited by Nadežda Obradovic ; with a foreword by Chinua Achebe
Hood, Ann
After Zane
    Hood, A. An ornithologist's guide to life; Ann Hood
Dropping bombs
    Hood, A. An ornithologist's guide to life; Ann Hood
Escapes
    Hood, A. An ornithologist's guide to life; Ann Hood

Hood, Ann—*Continued*
  Imagining Africa
    Good Housekeeping v229 no2 p165-69 Ag
    1999
  Inside Gorbachev's head
    Hood, A. An ornithologist's guide to life;
    Ann Hood
  Joelle's mother
    Hood, A. An ornithologist's guide to life;
    Ann Hood
  The language of sorrow
    Hood, A. An ornithologist's guide to life;
    Ann Hood
  Lost parts
    Hood, A. An ornithologist's guide to life;
    Ann Hood
  The mystery of Joelle
    Good Housekeeping v233 no4 p236-43 O
    2001
  New people
    Hood, A. An ornithologist's guide to life;
    Ann Hood
  An ornithologist's guide to life
    Hood, A. An ornithologist's guide to life;
    Ann Hood
  The rightness of things
    Hood, A. An ornithologist's guide to life;
    Ann Hood
  Total cave darkness
    Hood, A. An ornithologist's guide to life;
    Ann Hood
Hood, Robert
  Tamed
    Dreaming down-under; edited by Jack Dann
    and Janeen Webb
Hook, line and sinker. Budnitz, J.
A **hook** will sometimes keep you. Lincoln, C.
Hooked. Ziegler, I.
Hoopa, the white deer dance. Salisbury, R.
Hooper, Chloe
  Stolen Kisses
    Gentlemen's Quarterly v73 no5 p193-5 My
    2003
Hooper gets a perm. Griffith, M.
Hoops. Rozan, S. J.
Hoops and wires and plugs. Shade, E.
HOOVER, LOU HENRY, 1874-1944
                    About
  Elrod, P. N. Izzy's shoe-in
Hoover, Michelle
  The quickening
    Best new American voices 2004; guest editor
    John Casey; series editors John Kulka and
    Natalie Danford
  Sausages
    The Massachusetts Review v42 no3 p385-90
    Aut 2001
Hoover, Paul
  Lesson of the billboard dogs
    The Ohio Review no62/63 p359-60 2001
Hope, Akua Lezli
  The becoming
    Dark matter; a century of speculative fiction
    from the African diaspora; edited by Sheree
    R. Thomas
HOPE, BOB, 1903-2003
                    About
  O'Neill, S. Hope is the thing with a golf club

Hope, Toni Gerber
  A Hanukkah miracle
    Good Housekeeping v233 no6 p225-9 D 2001
Hope. Galloway, J.
Hope. Leary, J.
Hope and standards. Dinh, L.
Hope is the thing with a golf club. O'Neill, S.
Hopkins, Gerard Manley
  The dolphin
    The Times Literary Supplement no5000 p14
    Ja 29 1999
Hopkins, James *See* Nolan, William F., 1928-
Hopkins, Pauline Elizabeth
  As the lord lives, he is one of our mother's chil-
  dren
    The African American West; a century of
    short stories; edited by Bruce A. Glasrud
    and Laurie Champion
Hopkinson, Nalo
  And the lillies-them a-blow
    Hopkinson, N. Skin folk
  Fisherman
    Hopkinson, N. Skin folk
  Ganger (ball lightning)
    Dark matter; a century of speculative fiction
    from the African diaspora; edited by Sheree
    R. Thomas
    Hopkinson, N. Skin folk
  The glass bottle trick
    Hopkinson, N. Skin folk
    Whispers from the cotton tree root; Caribbean
    fabulist fiction; edited by Nalo Hopkinson
  Greedy choke puppy
    Dark matter; a century of speculative fiction
    from the African diaspora; edited by Sheree
    R. Thomas
    Death dines at 8:30; edited by Claudia Bishop
    and Nick DiChario
    Hopkinson, N. Skin folk
  A habit of waste
    Hopkinson, N. Skin folk
    Northern suns; edited by David G. Hartwell
    & Glenn Grant
  Money tree
    Hopkinson, N. Skin folk
  Precious
    Hopkinson, N. Skin folk
  Riding the red
    Hopkinson, N. Skin folk
  Slow cold chick
    Hopkinson, N. Skin folk
  Snake
    Hopkinson, N. Skin folk
  Something to hitch meat to
    Hopkinson, N. Skin folk
  Tan-Tan and Dry Bone
    Hopkinson, N. Skin folk
  Under glass
    Hopkinson, N. Skin folk
  Whose upward flight I love
    Hopkinson, N. Skin folk
Hopley, George, 1903-1968
    For works written by this author under oth-
    er names see Woolrich, Cornell, 1903-
    1968
Hopley-Woolrich, Cornell George *See* Woolrich,
    Cornell, 1903-1968

Hoppe, Felicitas
  Knights and duellists
    Chicago Review v48 no2/3 p149-50 Summ 2002
  The left shoe
    Grand Street no69 p75-78 Summ 1999
Horgan, Paul
  The peach stone
    The Best American short stories of the century; John Updike, editor, Katrina Kenison, coeditor; with an introduction by John Updike
  To the mountains
    Sports best short stories; edited by Paul D. Staudohar
Horizon Turtledove, H. Alternate generals II; ed. by Harry Turtledove
Horizontal snow. DeMarinis, R.
Hormone X. DeMarinis, R.
Horn, Dara
  Barbarians at the gates
  Lost tribe; jewish fiction from the edge
Horn, Michiel
  (jt. auth) See Hart, Maarten 't
The **horn**. Coates, G. S.
The **horn** of time the hunter. Anderson, P.
Hornby, Nick
  NippleJesus
    Speaking with the angel; original stories; edited by Nick Hornby
  Otherwise pandemonium
    McSweeney's mammoth treasury of thrilling tales; edited by Michael Chabon
The **horned** women. Wilde, Lady
Hornosty, Cornelia C.
  Millefiori beads
    Dalhousie Review v81 no2 p303-4 Summ 2001
  Room full of Cosmos
    Dalhousie Review v79 no2 p227-8 Summ 1999
Hornsby, Wendy
  New moon and rattlesnakes
    A moment on the edge; 100 years of crime stories by women; edited by Elizabeth George
Horrible but true things you'd rather not know. Hurley, V.
Horrible luck. Boylan, C.
The **horror** of the many faces. Lebbon, T.
HORROR STORIES
    See also Ghost stories; Murder stories; Supernatural phenomena; Vampires; Werewolves
  Altman, S.-E. A case of royal blood
  Atkins, P. Adventures in further education
  Atkins, P. King of outer space
  Barker, C. The age of desire
  Bear, E. Tiger! tiger!
  Bear, G. Richie by the sea
  Bishop, M. Help me, Rondo
  Bishop, M. A tapestry of little murders
  Blackford, R. Smoke City
  Blatnik, A. His mother's voice
  Blatty, W. P. Elsewhere
  Blau, G. Outfangthief
  Borges, J. L. The Gospel according to Mark
  Borges, J. L. There are more things
  Bowles, P. The circular valley

  Bowles, P. A distant episode
  Bradbury, R. April 2005: Usher II
  Bradbury, R. Beasts
  Bradbury, R. The black ferris
  Bradbury, R. The Finnegan
  Bradbury, R. Heavy set
  Bradbury, R. The island
  Bradbury, R. Let's play poison
  Bradbury, R. Trapdoor
  Bradbury, R. The veldt
  Bradbury, R. The watchers
  Bradbury, R. The whole town's sleeping
  Bradbury, R. Zero hour
  Brenchley, C. The keys to D'Espérance
  Brite, P. Z. and Ferguson, D. The curious case of Miss Violet Stone
  Brown, F. The Geezenstacks
  Brown, S. Love is a stone
  Bryant, E. Styx and bones
  Bull, S. E. Mr. Sly stops for a cup of joe
  Burleson, D. R. Pump Jack
  Burleson, D. R. The watcher at the window
  Cacek, P. D. The grave
  Campbell, R. All for sale
  Campbell, R. The alternative
  Campbell, R. Between the floors
  Campbell, R. The change
  Campbell, R. The dead must die
  Campbell, R. Dolls
  Campbell, R. The entertainment
  Campbell, R. Feeling remains
  Campbell, R. Going under
  Campbell, R. Kill me hideously
  Campbell, R. Looking out
  Campbell, R. Loveman's comeback
  Campbell, R. Merry May
  Campbell, R. Missed connection
  Campbell, R. No end of fun
  Campbell, R. No strings
  Campbell, R. Out of the woods
  Campbell, R. Root cause
  Campbell, R. The same in any language
  Campbell, R. The seductress
  Campbell, R. See how they run
  Campbell, R. A side of the sea
  Campbell, R. The sneering
  Campbell, R. A street was chosen
  Campbell, R. This time
  Campbell, R. Through the walls
  Campbell, R. The unbeheld
  Campbell, R. Welcomeland
  Campbell, R. Where they lived
  Campbell, R. Worse than bones
  Carmody, I. The dove game
  Carroll, J. The Heidelberg cylinder
  Case, D. Jimmy
  Castro, A.-T. The magic bullet theory
  Chabon, M. In the black mill
  Chambers, R. W. The yellow sign
  Chislett, M. Off the map
  Chwedyk, K. Dead women's things
  Clark, S. Nightmare in wax
  Clarke, A. C. A walk in the dark
  Collins, B. Dead and breakfast
  Collins, N. A. Catfish gal blues
  Costello, M. J. and Hautala, R. And the sea shall claim them
  Coyne, J. Snow man
  Crawford, F. M. The upper berth

HORROR STORIES—*Continued*

Crowther, P. Bedfordshire
Crowther, P. Dark times
Dann, J. A quiet revolution for death
Davidson, A. The ikon of Elijah
Davidson, A. and Davis, G. The Boss in the Wall: a treatise on the house devil
Davis, R. Fat Tuesday
Denton, B. Timmy and Tommy's Thanksgiving secret
Devereaux, R. Li'l Miss Ultrasound
Disch, T. M. The owl and the pussycat
Douglass, S. The mistress of Marwood Hagg
Dowling, T. Basic black
Dowling, T. The bone ship
Dowling, T. Jenny come to play
Doyle, Sir A. C. The horror of the heights
Doyle, Sir A. C. Lot no. 249
Dozois, G. R. The clowns
Dyson, J. City deep
Ellison, H. Sensible city
Ellison, H. The whimper of whipped dogs
Engstrom, E. Riding the black horse
Etchison, D. The detailer
Etchison, D. Got to kill them all
Etchison, D. Inside the cackle factory
Etchison, D. My present wife
Files, G. The Emperor's Old Bones
Finch, P. The mystery of the hanged man's puzzle
Fleming, R. The garden of evil
Fleming, R. In my father's house
Fleming, R. The wisdom of the serpents
Fowler, C. At home in the pubs of old London
Fowler, C. Crocodile lady
Fowler, C. The green man
Fowler, K. J. What I didn't see
Friesner, E. M. Auntie Elspeth's Halloween story; or, The gourd, the bad, and the ugly
Fry, G. Both and
Fry, S. The impressionists in winter
Gaiman, N. Feeders and eaters
Gaiman, N. Harlequin Valentine
Gaiman, N. Shoggoth's old peculiar
Gaiman, N. A study in emerald
Garner, J. Trick or treat
Garris, M. Forever Gramma
Gores, J. Quit screaming
Grant, C. L. Whose ghosts are these
Graves, R. Earth to earth
Gray, M. Shite hawks
Hambly, B. The adventure of the antiquarian's niece
Harman, C. Jackdaw Jack
Harrison, H. At last, the true story of Frankenstein
Harvey, W. F. August heat
Hautala, R. Knocking
Helfers, J. Farewell to the flesh
Herbert, J. Others
Hirshberg, G. Mr. Dark's carnival
Hodge, B. Nesting instincts
Hodgson, W. H. From the tideless sea, part one
Hodgson, W. H. The mystery of the derelict
Hodgson, W. H. The thing in the weeds
Hoffman, N. K. Food chain
Hoffman, N. K. Savage breasts
Holder, N. Skeleton krewe
Hopkinson, N. Slow cold chick

Hopkinson, N. Something to hitch meat to
Iorillo, J. Vesper tolls
Jackson, S. The lottery
Jackson, S. Nightmare
Jacob, C. Flesh of leaves, bones of desire
Jakes, J. The opener of the crypt
Jensen, J. L. Domestic slash and thrust
Joyce, G. First, catch your demon
Joyce, G. Xenos Beach
Kessel, J. Every angel is terrifying
Ketchum, J. Gone
Kidd, C. Cats and architecture
Kidd, C. Mark of the beast
Kiernan, C. R. The drowned geologist
Kiernan, C. R. In the water works (Birmingham, Alabama 1888)
Kiernan, C. R. The long hall on the top floor
Kiernan, C. R. Nor the demons down under the sea
Kiernan, C. R. Postcards from the King of Tides
Kilpatrick, N. . . . And thou!
Kilpatrick, N. Animal rites
Kilpatrick, N. Base of a triangle
Kilpatrick, N. Cold comfort
Kilpatrick, N. Creature comforts
Kilpatrick, N. Farm wife
Kilpatrick, N. Horrorscope
Kilpatrick, N. Inspiriter
Kilpatrick, N. Metal fatigue
Kilpatrick, N. The middle of nowhere
Kilpatrick, N. The power of one
Kilpatrick, N. Projections
Kilpatrick, N. Punkins
Kilpatrick, N. Rural legend
Kilpatrick, N. Truth
Kilpatrick, N. Vermiculture
Kilpatrick, N. When shadows come back
Kilpatrick, N. Whitelight
Kilpatrick, N. Woodworker
Kilpatrick, N. Youth not wasted
Kilpatrick, N. and Bisson, B. The children of Gael
King, S. Children of the corn
King, S. Mrs. Todd's shortcut
King, S. Quitters, inc.
King, S. The Road Virus heads north
Klass, F. Jennifer's turn
Klein, T. E. D. Growing things
Koja, K. At Eventide
Koontz, D. R. Snatcher
Lamsley, T. Climbing down from heaven
Lamsley, T. The stunted house
Lamsley, T. Suburban blight
Landis, G. A. The singular habits of wasps
Lane, J. Coming of age
Lane, J. The hunger of the leaves
Lane, J. The lost district
Lane, J. The receivers
Lansdale, J. R. Chompers
Lansdale, J. R. The dump
Lansdale, J. R. The Fat Man
Lansdale, J. R. Fish night
Lansdale, J. R. On a dark October
Lansdale, J. R. The shaggy house
Lansdale, J. R. and others. The companion
Lansdale, J. R. and Lowry, D. Pilots
Laws, S. The song my sister sang
Lawson, C. and Brown, S. No Man's Land
Lebbon, T. The horror of the many faces

HORROR STORIES—*Continued*

Lebbon, T. The repulsion
Lebbon, T. White
Lee, E. ICU
Lee, T. The abortionist's horse (a nightmare)
Lee, T. Where all things perish
Lee, T. Yellow and red
Leiber, F. The girl with the hungry eyes
Libling, M. Puce Boy
Ligotti, T. I have a special plan for this world
Ligotti, T. The shadow, the darkness
Link, K. Catskin
Link, K. The hortlak
Link, K. The specialist's hat
Linzner, G. Author, author
Little, B. The theater
Love, R. The raptures of the deep
Lovecraft, H. P. The call of cthulhu
Lovecraft, H. P. The shadow over Innsmouth
Lovecraft, H. P. Witches' Hollow
Lowder, J. The weeping masks
Lumley, B. Beneath the moors
Lumley, B. Dagon's bell
Lumley, B. David's worm
Lumley, B. The disapproval of Jeremy Cleave
Lumley, B. The fairground horror
Lumley, B. Lord of the worms
Lumley, B. The luststone
Lumley, B. Name and number
Lumley, B. No sharks in the Med
Lumley, B. Resurrection
Lumley, B. The return of the Deep Ones
Lumley, B. The second wish
Lumley, B. Snarker's son
Lumley, B. The statement of Henry Worthy
Lumley, B. The sun, the sea, and the silent scream
Lumley, B. A thing about cars!
Lumley, B. The whisperer
Lupoff, R. A. The adventure of the Voorish Sign
Lupoff, R. A. The devil's hop yard
Lupoff, R. A. Documents in the case of Elizabeth Akeley
Lupoff, R. A. Simeon Dimsby's workshop
Machen, A. The great god Pan
MacIntyre, F. G. The adventure of Exham Priory
Marano, M. Burden
Masterton, G. The Ballyhooly boy
Matera, L. The river mouth
Matheson, R. Duel
Matheson, R. Little girl lost
Matheson, R. Prey
Mayo, W. B. Horror
McAuley, P. J. Bone orchards
McAuley, P. J. Dr Pretorius and the lost temple
McGarry, T. Miasma
Mellick, C. Porno in August
Metzger, T. Transorbital love probe
Miéville, C. Details
Morrell, D. Rio Grande gothic
Morton, L. Pound rots in Fragrant Harbour
Moser, Elise. The seven-day itch
Muss-Barnes, E. Born of the night
Nagy, S. The Hanged Man of Oz
Nevill, A. L. G. Mother's milk
Newman, K. Amerikanski dead at the Moscow morgue

Newman, K. Castle in the desert
Newman, K. The intervention
Newman, K. The other side of midnight
Nickle, D. The dummy ward
Novotny, R. Sanctuary
Oates, J. C. The museum of Dr. Moses
Oates, J. C. The ruins of Contracoeur
Oates, J. C. You, little match-girl
O'Driscoll, M. Sounds like
Oliver, C. The boy next door
Olsen, L. Cybermorphic beat-up get-down subterranean homesick reality-sandwich blues
Onions, O. The beckoning fair one
Partridge, N. Blackbirds
Pelan, J. The mystery of the worm
Perry, S. The case of the wavy black dagger
Piccirilli, T. Those vanished I recognize
Pipik, J. Nightwatcher
Pipik, J. and Vargo, J. The Dark Tower
Pipik, J. and Vargo, J. Sentinels
Poe, E. A. The black cat
Poe, E. A. The cask of Amontillado
Poe, E. A. The tell-tale heart
Pohl, F. Let the ants try
Ptacek, K. The grotto
Reaves, M. The adventure of the Arab's manuscript
Richards, T. The lords of zero
Rogers, B. H. King Corpus
Royle, N. Empty stations
Royle, N. Hide and seek
Royle, N. Standard gauge
Rozanski, J. M. The search for a sipping house
Rucker, L. E. No more a-roving
Rucker, R. v. B. Bringing in the sheaves
Sallis, J. Dear floods of her hair
Sarrantonio, A. Pumpkin head
Sarrantonio, A. The ropy thing
Sarrantonio, A. Wish
Schneider, P. Des saucisses, sans doute
Schow, D. J. The absolute last of the ultra-spooky, super-scary Hallowe'en horror nights
Schow, D. J. Unhasped
Sheckley, R. The new Horla
Sheckley, R. Warm
Sinclair, I. The keeper of the Rothenstein tomb
Smith, D. By her hand, she draws you down
Smith, M. M. Everybody goes
Smith, M. M. The handover
Smith, M. M. The Right Men
Smith, M. M. Welcome
Smith, M. M. What you make it
Somtow, S. P. Bird catcher
Spruill, S. G. Hemophage
Stableford, B. M. Art in the blood
Sterns, A. The third rail
Sterns, A. Watchmen
Stoker, B. Dracula's guest
Stoker, B. The Jewel of Seven Stars
Straub, P. Ashputtle
Straub, P. The ghost village
Sturgeon, T. Bianca's hands
Sturgeon, T. Bright segment
Sturgeon, T. It
Taylor, L. Unspeakable
Tem, M. Gardens
Tem, S. R. Halloween Street
Tem, S. R. Heat

HORROR STORIES—*Continued*
Tem, S. R. Out late in the park
Tem, S. R. Pareidolia
Tem, S. R. Tricks & treats one night on Halloween Street
Tem, S. R. What slips away
Tenn, W. The malted milk monsters
Tessier, T. Moments of change
Travis, T. V. Down here in the garden
Tumasonis, D. The prospect cards
Tumasonis, D. The wretched thicket of thorn
Tuttle, L. "The mezzotint"
Van Pelt, J. The boy behind the gate
VanderMeer, J. The bone carver's tale
VanderMeer, J. The cage
Vargo, J. Lilith
Vargo, J. Watcher at the gate
Vourlis, J. P. A case of insomnia
Waggoner, T. Picking up Courtney
Wagner, K. E. Where the summer ends
Waldrop, H. Black as the pit, from pole to pole
Wandrei, H. George is all right
Warburton, G. Merry Roderick
Webb, J. Blake's angel
Weinberg, R. Chant
Weinberg, R. Dial your dreams
Weinberg, R. Elevator girls
Weinberg, R. Endure the night
Wellen, E. Spur the nightmare
Wilder, C. Finishing school
Williams, C. City in aspic
Williamson, C. Excerpts from the Records of the New Zodiac and the diaries of Henry Watson Fairfax
Wilson, A. J. Under the bright and hollow sky
Wilson, D. N. and Macomber, P. L. Death did not become him
Wilson, F. P. Good Friday
Wilson, G. The big green grin
Wilson, G. The dead ghost
Wilson, R. C. Pearl baby
Wolfe, G. A fish story
Wolfe, G. Houston, 1943
Wolfe, G. The Monday man
Wolfe, G. The tree is my hat
Wuori, G. K. Illusions
Yolen, J. Great gray
Yolen, J. Sister death
Horrorscope. Kilpatrick, N.
Horse. Alexis, A.
A **horse** for Mrs. Custer. Swarthout, G. F.
HORSE RACING
Breen, J. L. Silver Spectre
Francis, D. The gift
Gorman, E. En famille
Heller, J. Bookies, beware!
Lanham, E. The Denton mare
McNulty, J. Don't scrub off these names
McNulty, J. Even if it's Mexico nothing flashy ever happens to Grogan
McNulty, J. Man here keeps getting arrested all the time
Meloy, M. A stakes horse
Oates, J. C. Raven's Wing
Taylor, T. L. Silent cruise
Waugh, E. The curse of the horse race
The **horse-stealers**. Chekhov, A. P.
A **horse** story. Chopin, K.
The **horse** that died for shame. Tremayne, P.

HORSE THIEVES
Chekhov, A. P. The horse-stealers
Lopez, B. H. Stolen horses
Horse tradin'. Cleary, R.
HORSEMANSHIP
Spencer, E. The girl who loved horses
The **horsemen** and the morning star. Hambly, B.
HORSES
Abrams, T. Changing horses
Adam, C. Red pony
Agee, J. The creek
Agee, J. The October horse
Babel', I. Afonka bida
Babel', I. Argamak
Babel', I. The continuation of The story of a horse
Babel', I. The Quaker
Babel', I. The story of a horse
Banks, R. The neighbor
Bass, R. Wild horses
Billman, J. Atomic Bar
Bowles, P. The waters of Izli
Chopin, K. A horse story
Cleary, R. Horse tradin'
Coldsmith, D. First horse
Davis, A. Chase
DeRosso, H. A. Fear in the saddle
Dillingham, D. G. The white carousel horse
Edghill, R. A gift of two grey horses
Estep, M. Animals
Estep, M. Monkeys
Gonzalez, R. The grandfather horse
Hoffman, W. Place
Karnezis, P. Deus ex machina
Lawrence, D. H. St. Mawr
Lorfing, Jake. Old horse
Lugones, L. The horses of Abdera
Lundquist, R. Dust devils
Lundquist, R. A free sinner
MacLeod, A. In the fall
Marks, J. Under hoof
McCann, C. Everything in this country must
McNulty, J. They don't seem to be talking to Grogan
Meloy, M. Kite Whistler Aquamarine
Oliver, C. A star above it
Oz, A. Where the jackals howl
Robison, M. In the woods
Shepard, J. Blinkers
Shepard, J. Jubilee King
Shepard, J. Night shot
Shepard, J. Thirty head of killers
Shepard, S. The remedy man
Shepard, S. The stout of heart
Shoemaker, Karen. Playing horses
Steele, W. D. Blue Murder
Stegner, W. E. The colt
Warren, D. A reckless moon
Horses. Estep, M.
Horses. Tuck, L.
Horses, not reindeer. Haas, E.
The **horses** of Abdera. Lugones, L.
The **horses** speak French. Meredith, D.
A **horsy** name. Chekhov, A. P.
Horton, Babs
Colouring mother
    Mr. Roopratna's chocolate; the winning stories from the 1999 Rhys Davies competition

Horton, Hal

The year draws in the day

Kulka, J. and Danford, N. The New American voices 2003; guest editor Joyce Carol Oates; series editors John Kulka and Natalie Danford

Horton hears a chainsaw. Birkett, T.

Hosein, Clyde

Morris, Bhaiya

The Oxford book of Caribbean short stories; edited by Stewart Brown and John Wickham

HOSPICES (TERMINAL CARE)

Gabriel, D. The blind woman

Goldner, B. Outcomes

Horton, H. The year draws in the day

Hospital, Janette Turner

Frames and wonders

The Literary Review (Madison, N.J.) v45 no1 p36-51 Fall 2001

HOSPITALS AND SANATORIUMS

Aldrich, B. S. Across the smiling meadow

Angrist, M. So much the better

Babel´, I. Doudou

Banks, R. Plains of Abraham

Bell, M. S. Anomalous structures of my dreams

Bennett, A. Father! Father! Burning bright

Bowen, R. O. A matter of price

Brady, C. Rumpelstiltskin

Brown, J. Animal stories

Bukoski, A. Pesthouse

Butler, O. E. The evening and the morning and the night

Carver, R. Where I'm calling from

Chekhov, A. P. The runaway

Coleman, J. C. A pair to draw to

Dann, J. Camps

Deane, J. F. Between times

Dyer, S. N. The July Ward

Gates, D. Vigil

Greenberg, A. Immersion

Greer, R. O. The can men

Harleman, A. Meanwhile

Howard, C. Old soldiers

Johnson, D. Emergency

Johnston, B. A. Corpus

Johnston, B. A. Corpus Christi

Jones, H. Tom's homecoming

Kanafāni, G. The death of bed number 12

Kirchheimer, G. D. The voyager

Klass, P. Exact change

Knight, M. Keeper of secrets, teller of lies

Lavin, M. The girders

López, L. Walking circles

Love, M. Nightfloat

Mastretta, A. Aunt Eugenia

Means, D. Tahorah

Ortiz, S. J. Where o where

Paschal, D. Genesis (The G.I. bleed)

Roth, J. Sick people

Sandor, M. Malingerer

Scarborough, E. A. The filial fiddler

Shapiro, G. At the great divide

Shaw, D. A cure for gravity

Sinor, B. H. Eleven to seven

Smith, L. Intensive care

Stafford, J. The interior castle

Svoboda, T. Electricity

Thon, M. R. First, body

VanderMeer, J. London burning

Vasseur, T. J. The life and death of stars

Wegner, H. Cockshut light

Weldon, F. A hard time to be a father

Weldon, F. Noisy into the night

What, L. Clinging to a thread

Yates, R. A clinical romance

Yates, R. Out with the old

Yates, R. Thieves

Zabytko, I. Lavender soap

The **hostage**. Uribe, A.

HOSTAGES

Waugh, E. The man who liked Dickens

A **hot** breath from the desert. Herling, G.

Hot dumplings. Lao She

Hot-foot Hannibal. Chesnutt, C. W.

Hot night homicide. Collins, M.

Hot night in the city. Trevanian

Hot night in the city II. Trevanian

Hot pepper. Johnson, D.

Hot Spring. Storey, D. G.

Hot Springs. Becker, G.

Hot Springs. Crumley, J.

A **hot** time at the Church of Kentucky Fried Souls and the spectacular final Sunday sermon of the Right Revren Daddy Love. Touré

Hotel Arco Iris. Guerrero, L.

The **hotel** at Harlan's Landing. Baker, K.

The **Hotel** Eden. Carlson, R.

Hotel Oblivion. Dyer, G.

Hotel of the saints. Hegi, U.

The **hotel** on Monkey Forest Road. Paine, T.

HOTELS, TAVERNS, ETC.

See also Motels

Abrams, T. Monroe Puckett

Abrams, T. A small thing that mattered greatly

Adams, A. The end of the world

Adams, A. La Señora

Addonizio, K. Angels

Agee, J. How good I am to you

Allyn, D. The jukebox king

Anderson, R. The name of the dead

Bagley, J. E. Children of chance

Baker, K. The hotel at Harlan's Landing

Bausch, R. Valor

Benson, S. Apartment hotel

Berkman, P. R. Snakes

Bierce, A. The other lodgers

Bishop, C. Waiting for gateau

Bonnie, F. In search of Number Seven

Bowles, P. At the Krungthep Plaza

Boyle, T. C. Death of the cool

Brennan, M. The holy terror

Broughton, T. A. Spring cleaning

Brown, C. Father Judge Run

Brown, D. W. In the doorway of Rhee's Jazz Joint

Bukoski, A. The tools of ignorance

Butler, R. O. Hotel Touraine

Carlson, R. The clicker at Tips

Carson, J. Two thousand years of torture

Chabon, M. That was me

Chekhov, A. P. The horse-stealers

Chesnutt, C. W. How he met her

Clarke, A. C. Silence please

Cobb, T. Adultery

Cobb, T. Getting bud

Codrescu, A. A bar in Brooklyn

Collins, B. Dead and breakfast

HOTELS, TAVERNS, ETC.—*Continued*

Cook, K. L. Last call
Cooper, B. Intro to acting
Crane, S. The blue hotel
Cummins, A. Billy by the bay
Daniels, J. Karaoke moon
Davies, P. H. Think of England
Davies, R. Holiday romance
Davis, A. Fairy tale
De Lint, C. The words that remain
Deane, J. F. A migrant bird
DeLancey, K. Carley's knees
Delaney, E. J. Hero
DeMarinis, R. A romantic interlude
Desai, A. Underground
Dinh, L. In the vein
Dinh, L. Saigon Pull
Dorcey, M. A sense of humour
Dybek, S. Song
Earle, S. The internationale
Engstrom, E. Crosley
Eugenides, J. Timeshare
Fowler, C. At home in the pubs of old London
Fulmer, D. Back O'Town Blues
Gifford, B. My last martini
Gifford, B. Room 584, the Starr Hotel
Gilchrist, E. The famous poll at Jody's Bar
Gilman, C. P. An honest woman
Gores, J. Night out
Guthrie, A. B. The fourth at Getup
Hautman, P. Showdown at the Terminal Oasis
Healy, T. It might have been Jerusalem [excerpt]
Hegi, U. Hotel of the saints
Henley, P. Friday night at Silver Star
Hermann, J. Hunter Johnson music
Highsmith, P. Magic casements
Highsmith, P. Nothing that meets the eye
Holman, J. Squabble
House, S. Coal house
Hribal, C. J. And that's the name of that tune
Jen, G. Birthmates
Jenkins, G. Night game
Kaplan, H. Live life king-sized
Kees, W. Every year they came out
Kelman, J. Every fucking time
Kennedy, A. L. A wrong thing
Kureishi, H. Strangers when we meet
Lacy, M. No fools, no fun
Lee, D. The Lone Night Cantina
Lee, M. Glory
Lee, M. Territorial rights
Locklin, G. To the shores of San Clemente
López, L. Ivor's people
Lundquist, R. The greener pasture
McBain, E. A very Merry Christmass
McClanahan, E. The little-known bird of the inner eye
McIlvanney, W. At the bar
McManus, J. The future is orange
McNulty, J. Barkeep won't let anybody at all shove this handyman around
McNulty, J. Bartender here takes dislike to "Deep in the heart of Texas"
McNulty, J. The fight in the hallway
McNulty, J. Hands no good
McNulty, J. It's hard to figure how they know
McNulty, J. A man like Grady, you got to know him first

McNulty, J. A man's going into the Army what can you do about it?
McNulty, J. People don't seem to think things out straight in this gin mill
McNulty, J. Some nights when nothing happens are the best nights in this place
McNulty, J. Tell him what happen, Joe, see will he believe you
McNulty, J. They'd have taken him if he was only a torso
McNulty, J. Third Avenue medicine
McNulty, J. Two bums here would spend freely except for poverty
McNulty, J. You can't tell how you'll get clobbered
Meissner, J. Placedo junction
Melville, P. Don't give me your sad stories
Myers, T. Chicken catch a tory
Naipaul, V. S. The night watchman's occurrence book
Nair, M. The lodger in room 726
Nichols, J. Magic
Niven, L. Smut talk
Orner, P. The Moraine on the lake
Orner, P. Thursday night at the Gopher Hole, April 1992
Owens, A. When Shankland comes
Painter, P. The second night of a one night stand
Paschal, D. By the light of the jukebox
Perillo, L. M. Bad boy number seventeen
Phillips, S. Sockdolager
Plager, S. A change of heart
Pronzini, B. Liar's dice
Rawley, D. At the Four Seasons Hotel
Reid, E. Random beatings and you
Rendell, R. The beach butler
Rinehart, S. Mr. Big Stuff
Roeske, P. Smaller than life
Schaffert, T. Sound from the courtyard
Sheehan, R. Telescope
Simonds, M. The lion in the room next door
Singer, I. B. Alone
Singleton, G. Outlaw head and tail
Skillings, R. D. Czezarley Zoo gets out
Slezak, E. Here in car city
Smyth, C. Near the bone
Spence, A. Brilliant
Steeves, Rafael Franco. The couple and the stranger
Straub, P. Perdido: a fragment from a work in progress
Thompson, J. Poor Helen
Trevanian. After hours at Rick's
Turner, R. Eleven o'clock bulletin
Updike, J. At a bar in Charlotte Amalie
Walters, M. English autumn-American fall
Warren, D. Bone garden
Weaver, G. The white elephant
Wellen, E. Hangover
Wells, K. Godlight
Winter, E. Spin cycle
Yañez, R. Rio Bravo
Zabytko, I. John Mars, all-American
Zabytko, I. Steve's bar
Ziegler, I. Cliffs notes
Zinik, Z. A pickled nose
Zivkovic, Z. The violin-maker

Hothouse flowers. Resnick, M.

Hotter. Tuck, L.

Houarner, Gerard
She'd make a dead man crawl
  Mojo: conjure stories; edited by Nalo Hopkinson

HOUDINI, HARRY, 1874-1926
About
Duncan, A. The Pottawatomie Giant
Leslie, N. Give me a sign

Houghteling, Marla Kay
Ma Kamanda's latrine
  Living on the edge; fiction by Peace Corps
  writers; edited by John Coyne

The **hound**. Leiber, F.

Hour of lead. Swan, M.

The **hours** after noon. Bowles, P.

Hours of darkness. McLean, D.

House, Richard
Gabe and the doctor
  Westward; a fictional history of the American
  West : 28 original stories celebrating the
  50th anniversary of the Western Writers of
  America; edited by Dale L. Walker

House, Silas
Coal house
  New stories from the South; the year's best,
  2004; edited by Shannon Ravenel; preface
  by Tim Gautreaux
Gatlinburg
  Stories from the Blue Moon Cafe II; edited
  by Sonny Brewer
The last days
  Stories from the Blue Moon Café; edited by
  Sonny Brewer

House, Tom
Fire Patrol
  Chicago Review v48 no4 p32-62 Wint
  2002/2003
Princes, very late
  The Literary Review (Madison, N.J.) v42 no2
  p283-87 Wint 1999
Rush
  Southwest Review v87 no2/3 p253-66 2002
Scarecrow
  Men on men 2000; best new gay fiction for
  the millennium; edited and with an intro-
  duction by David Bergman and Karl Woelz
To my former mother, Mrs. Callahan
  The Antioch Review v60 no2 p301-11 Spr
  2002

A **House**. De Ferrari, G.

House. Thien, M.

The **house**: an anti-climax. Waugh, E.

The **house** at the end of the world. Brockmeier, K.

The **house** behind. Davis, L.

House dick. Hammett, D.

The **house** dutiful. Tenn, W.

House fires. Reisman, N.

House for sale. Tozzi, F.

House, house, home. Jen, G.

House hunting. Chabon, M.

The **house** in the wood. Maleti, G.

House in the woods. Winter, E.

The **house** of Asterion. Borges, J. L.

The **house** of breathing. Jones, G.

House of cards. Fairey, W. W.

House of cards. Pittalwala, I.

The **house** of Esperanza. Blake, J. C.

A **house** of gentlefolks. Waugh, E.

The **House** of Inspection. Folsom, H.

A **house** of one's own. James, S.

House of passion. Piñón, N.

HOUSE OF REPRESENTATIVES (U.S.) *See*
  United States. Congress. House

The **house** of the black cat. Kurahashi, Y.

The **House** of the Dead Hand. Wharton, E.

The **house** of the famous poet. Spark, M.

The **house** of women. Krawiec, R.

The **house** on Belle Isle. Brown, C.

House on fire. Nakagami, K.

The **house** on Lunt Avenue. Orner, P.

The **house** on the ice. Viganò, R.

A **house** on the plains. Doctorow, E. L.

HOUSE SITTING
Dunlap, S. People who sit in glass houses
Gilb, D. About Tere who was in Palomas
Holleran, A. The housesitter

The **house** that burned. Painter, P.

The **house** with a mezzanine. See Chekhov, A. P.
  An artist's story

The **house** with the attic room. See Chekhov, A.
  P. An artist's story

The **house** with the mansard. See Chekhov, A. P.
  An artist's story

Housecleaning. Thurm, M.

Houseful of mussels. Van de Wetering, J.

HOUSEHOLD EMPLOYEES
  See also Au pairs; Butlers; Cooks; Hired
  men; Housekeepers; Maids (Servants);
  Nursemaids
Aldrich, B. S. Will the romance be the same?
Bellow, S. A theft
Fitzgerald, P. Not shown
Johnson-Davies, D. The dream
Kavaler, R. Servants
Kohler, S. On the money
Malone, M. The rising of the South and Flonnie
  Rogers
Melville, P. Erzulie
Pearlman, E. Allog
Robison, M. The help

Household words; or, the powers-that-be.
  Waldrop, H.

Housekeeper. Grau, S. A.

HOUSEKEEPERS
Agee, J. Invisible
Grau, S. A. Housekeeper
Munro, A. Hateship, friendship, courtship,
  loveship, marriage
O'Marie, C. A. Defender of the faith
Thurm, M. Housecleaning

Housekeeper's cut. Boylan, C.

Housekeeping. Sanford, A.

HOUSEMAIDS *See* Maids (Servants)

HOUSES
  See also Apartment houses; Summer
  homes
Adams, A. Berkeley house
Arredondo, I. Subterranean river
Barth, J. Extension
Bean, B. Dream house
Bellow, S. Leaving the yellow house
Bertles, J. Whileaway
Borges, J. L. There are more things
Boylan, C. Mama
Bradbury, R. The house
Bradbury, R. Trapdoor
Brennan, M. I see you, Bianca

HOUSES—*Continued*

Burford, M. 140 Sunset
Burrage, A. M. Smee
Cherry, K. Chores
Chopin, K. Ma'ame Pélagie
Coleman, A. S. The little grey house
Gurganus, A. Preservation news
Händler, E.-W. City with houses
Hawley, L. The good life
Heinlein, R. A. "—And he built a crooked house"
Helms, B. Glazing
Hermann, J. Summerhouse, later
Jackson, V. F. A little kingdom
Kalam, M. Bow down
Matiella, A. C. Home
McBrearty, R. G. The yellow house
Oates, J. C. The doll
Painter, P. Doors
Painter, P. The house that burned
Pearlman, D. D. The fall of the house
Rifaat, A. My world of the unknown
Roth, J. The grand house opposite
Sanford, A. Housekeeping
Schaeffer, S. F. The old farmhouse and the dog-wife
Singleton, G. Crawl space
Smith, C. W. The Bundlelays
Spark, M. The house of the famous poet
Tem, S. R. What slips away
Thompson, J. The rich man's house
Thompson, J. The widower
Updike, J. Plumbing
Waugh, E. The house: an anti-climax
Weldon, F. Spirits fly south

HOUSES, DESERTED *See* Deserted houses

The **houses** of double women. Anderson, J.

The **housesitter**. Holleran, A.

Housework. Chenoweth, A.

Housman, Clemence

The drawn arrow
    Tales before Tolkien; the roots of modern fantasy; edited by Douglas A. Anderson
The were-wolf
    The Literary werewolf; an anthology; edited by Charlotte F. Otten

Houston, Pam

The best girlfriend you never had
    The Best American short stories, 1999; selected from U.S. and Canadian magazines by Amy Tan with Katrina Kenison, with an introduction by Amy Tan
    The Pushcart prize XXIV: best of the small presses; an annual small press reader; edited by Bill Henderson with the Pushcart prize editors
Cataract
    Prize stories, 1999; The O. Henry awards; edited and with an introduction by Larry Dark
Waltzing the cat
    What are you looking at?; the first fat fiction anthology; edited by Donna Jarrell and Ira Sukrungruang

HOUSTON (TEX.) *See* Texas—Houston

Hovercraft. Nawrocki, S.

How a lady dies. Donoghue, E.

How aliens think. Grossman, J.

How all this started. Fromm, P.

How animals mate. Mueller, D.

How Babe Ruth saved my life. Touré

How beautiful with banners. Blish, J.

How beautifully resilient the human being. Nissen, T.

How birds communicate. Jacobs, M.

How Boy Howdy saved the world. Eakin, W.

How Brando was made. McMahon, P.

How come you reckon he did that? Drake, R.

How could this happen? Reiner, C.

"How did I get away with killing one of the biggest lawyers in the state? It was easy.". Walker, A.

How far is it to Hollywood? Aldrich, B. S.

How far it could go. Block, L.

How hot was Mexicali? Chacón, D.

How I came to love books. Rothschild, V.

How I found a cat, lost true love, and broke the bank at Monte Carlo. Crider, B.

How I happened to put on the blue. Carney, O.

How I Left Onondaga County and Found Peace and Contentment on 72nd Street. Ciabattari, J.

How I lost my inheritance. LaValle, V. D.

How I lost my vocation. Connolly, C.

How I met my second wife. Singleton, G.

How I went (recipe for lime curd). Rosenfeld, S.

How in a lifetime? Lea, S.

How it goes. Cherry, K.

How it was done in Odessa. *See* Babel', I. How things were done in Odessa

How it was for me. Greer, A. S.

How many midnights. Bowles, P.

How Mr. Rabbit was too sharp for Mr. Fox. Harris, J. C.

How much justice can you afford? Cohen, S.

How my literary career began. Škvorecký, J.

How Paul Robeson saved my life. Reiner, C.

How Pinkie killed a man. Maja-Pearce, A.

How Santa Claus came to Simpson's Bar. Harte, B.

How Sin Is Unsaid. Ortale, J.

How Sukie Come Free. Thomas, S. R.

How Sukie cross de big wata. Thomas, S. R.

How the animals got their voices. Trevanian

How the brujo stole the moon. Gonzalez, R.

How the crow became black and the culeta lost his crown of feathers. Ramos, M.

How the dead live. Greenberg, A.

How the old world died. Harrison, H.

How the stars live. Grodstein, L.

How the water feels. Eggers, P.

How things were done in Odessa. Babel', I.

How this song ends. Richards, J.

How to act in 1830. Jesús, P. d.

How to Be a Beekeeper. Geary, T. M.

How to be an expatriate. Davies, P. H.

How to become a publicist. Kane, J. F.

How to breathe underwater. Ziegler, I.

How to collect fishing lures. Singleton, G.

How to converse in Italian. Stanton, M.

How to fall in love. Watanabe McFerrin, L.

How to feed your inner troll. What, L.

How to find your way in woods. Kennedy, A. L.

How to live in Rome and loathe it. Barolini, H.

How to lose an eye. Yuknavitch, L.

How to play the twelve-bar blues. Hoddeson, B.

How to survive in the bush. Gartner, Z.

How to talk to the dead. Hoffman, A.

How to talk to your mother (notes). Moore, L.

How to tell a story. Rabb, M.

How to win. Brown, R.

How to write a successful short story. Rooke, L.

How was it, really? Updike, J.

How we came to Indiana. Winegardner, M.

How we lost the moon, a true story by Frank W. Allen. McAuley, P. J.

How we remember you. Coshnear, D.

How we went to Mars. Clarke, A. C.

How would you like it? Block, L.

Howard, Clark

The California contact

The World's finest mystery and crime stories, third annual collection; edited by Ed Gorman and Martin H. Greenberg

The cobalt blues

The Best American mystery stories, 2002; edited and with an introduction by James Ellroy; Otto Penzler, series editor

The color of death

Howard, C. Crowded lives and other stories of desperation and danger

Crowded lives

Howard, C. Crowded lives and other stories of desperation and danger

The Dublin eye

Murder most Celtic; tall tales of Irish mayhem; edited by Martin H. Greenberg

Hanging it on a limb

Howard, C. Crowded lives and other stories of desperation and danger

Hit and run

Howard, C. Crowded lives and other stories of desperation and danger

The ice shelf

The World's finest mystery and crime stories, first annual collection; edited by Ed Gorman

The last one to cry

Master's choice v2; mystery stories by today's top writers and the masters who inspired them; edited by Lawrence Block

The marksman

Howard, C. Crowded lives and other stories of desperation and danger

McCulla's kid

Howard, C. Crowded lives and other stories of desperation and danger

New Orleans getaway

Howard, C. Crowded lives and other stories of desperation and danger

Old soldiers

Howard, C. Crowded lives and other stories of desperation and danger

Out of control

Crème de la crime; edited by Janet Hutchings

Under suspicion

The Best American mystery stories, 2001; edited and with an Introduction by Lawrence Block

The World's finest mystery and crime stories, second annual collection; edited by Ed Gorman

When the black shadows die

The World's finest mystery and crime stories, second annual collection; edited by Ed Gorman

Wild things

Howard, C. Crowded lives and other stories of desperation and danger

Howard, Clementyne

The carnival

Pieces; a collection of new voices; edited by Stephen Chbosky

Howard, Joanna

Now You Can Hear Us, Our Stiff Wings Flapping

Chicago Review v49 no1 p93-7 Spr 2003

Howard, Maureen

Big as life

Howard, M. Big as life; three tales for spring

Children with matches

Howard, M. Big as life; three tales for spring

The Magdalene

Howard, M. Big as life; three tales for spring

Vernissage

Agni no57 p158-61 2003

Howard, Ravi

Ways of the World

The Massachusetts Review v44 no3 p383-93 Fall 2003

Howard Johnson's house. Clyde, M.

Howbah Indians. Ortiz, S. J.

Howe, Fanny

Lotto

Chicago Review v47 no3 p54-66 Fall 2001

HOWE, GORDIE

About

Popkes, S. The ice

Howe, Melodie Johnson

Acting tips

Malice domestic 10; an anthology of original traditional mystery stories

Killing the sixties

Crème de la crime; edited by Janet Hutchings

Howells, Rae

A bleak future without thought-paper

Mr. Roopratna's chocolate; the winning stories from the 1999 Rhys Davies competition

Howe's masquerade. Hawthorne, N.

Howie's gift. Epstein, J.

Howie's gift: a story. Epstein, J.

The **howling** man. Beaumont, C.

Hoyt, Daniel A.

Amar

The Kenyon Review v25 no3/4 p63-71 Summ/Fall 2003

Hoyt, Sarah A.

Yellow tide foam

Greenberg, M. H. Faerie tales

Hrbek, Greg

Frannycam.net/diary

Salmagundi no141/142 p199-226 Wint/Spr 2004

Green world

Harper's v299 no1795 p104-08+ D 1999

Hremann, Judith

Nothing but Ghosts

Granta v84 p161-85 Wint 2003

Hribal, C. J.

And that's the name of that tune

Hribal, C. J. The clouds in Memphis; stories and novellas

Hribal, C. J.—*Continued*
  The clouds in Memphis
    Hribal, C. J. The clouds in Memphis; stories
    and novellas
  Consent
    Hribal, C. J. The clouds in Memphis; stories
    and novellas
  The last great dream of my father
    Hribal, C. J. The clouds in Memphis; stories
    and novellas
  War babies
    Hribal, C. J. The clouds in Memphis; stories
    and novellas
Hsueh, Mabelle
  Spillage
    Ploughshares v25 no2/3 p96-103 Fall 1999
Huang, M. J.
  Martyr
    Nixon under the bodhi tree and other works
    of Buddhist fiction; edited by Kate Wheeler
    ; foreword by Charles Johnson
Hubbard, Jennifer R.
  Feed the City
    The North American Review v289 no2 p20-2
    Mr/Ap 2004
Hubbard, Susan
  Duluth
    TriQuarterly no113 p167-77 Summ 2002
HUBBLE, EDWIN POWELL, 1889-1953
    1
    Wilson, R. C. The observer
Huber, Carol Y. and Baker, Mike C.
  Chance hospitality
    Such a pretty face; edited by Lee Martindale
Hubris. Kelly, J. P.
Huddle, David
  The day ghost
    Ghost writing; haunted tales by contemporary
    writers; edited by Roger Weingarten
  The story of the door
    The Pushcart prize XXVI; best of the small
    presses, an annual small press reader; ed-
    ited by Bill Henderson and the Pushcart
    prize editors
  La Tour dreams of the wolf girl
    American short fiction, vol. 8, no 29-32
Huddling place. Simak, C. D.
Hudec, Ivan
  The undeniable likeness of twins
    In search of homo sapiens; twenty-five con-
    temporary Slovak short stories; editor,
    Pavol Hudík ; [translated by Heather
    Trebatická; American English editor, Lucy
    Bednár]
Hudgins, Al
  The librarian's farewell
    The Georgia Review v53 no1 p73-95 Spr
    1999
Hudgins, Brett
  Fur bearing
    Cat crimes through time; edited by Ed
    Gorman, Martin H. Greenberg, and Larry
    Segriff
Hudson, Gabe
  Dear Mr. President
    The New Yorker v77 no16 p100-15 Je 18-25
    2001
Hudson, Jeffery *See* Crichton, Michael, 1942-

Hudson, Suzanne
  The fall of the Nixon administration
    Stories from the Blue Moon Café; edited by
    Sonny Brewer
HUDSON BAY
    Patterson, K. Hudson Bay in winter
Hudson Bay in winter. Patterson, K.
Hudson, Suzanne
  The seamstress
    Stories from the Blue Moon Cafe II; edited
    by Sonny Brewer
Huebler. Bail, M.
Hueco. Gilb, D.
Huelle, Pawel
  Moving house
    The Art of the story; an international antholo-
    gy of contemporary short stories; edited by
    Daniel Halpern
Huevos. Peery, J.
Huff, Steven
  Blissful
    The Hudson Review v54 no1 p39-56 Spr 2001
Huff, Tanya
  He said, sidhe said
    Greenberg, M. H. Faerie tales
  Nanite, star bright
    Once upon a galaxy; edited by Will [sic]
    McCarthy, Martin H. Greenberg, and John
    Helfers
  Third time lucky
    Magical beginnings; edited by Steven H. Sil-
    ver and Martin H. Greenberg
  To each his own kind
    Dracula in London; edited by P. N. Elrod
Huffman, Bob, Jr.
  Acceptance of responsibility
    Huffman, B., Jr. Legal fiction
  Arraignment
    Huffman, B., Jr. Legal fiction
  Bench trial
    Huffman, B., Jr. Legal fiction
  Contrary to the manifest tenor
    Huffman, B., Jr. Legal fiction
  Dismissed, with prejudice
    Huffman, B., Jr. Legal fiction
  Fair and impartial
    Huffman, B., Jr. Legal fiction
  Initial consultation
    Huffman, B., Jr. Legal fiction
  Judicial economy
    Huffman, B., Jr. Legal fiction
  Maintaining integrity
    Huffman, B., Jr. Legal fiction
  Mutuality of interests
    Huffman, B., Jr. Legal fiction
  Some due process
    Huffman, B., Jr. Legal fiction
  Synthesis of the community standard
    Huffman, B., Jr. Legal fiction
  Yielding to science
    Huffman, B., Jr. Legal fiction
  Zealous representation
    Huffman, B., Jr. Legal fiction
Huffman, Michael
  The Good Friday procession
    Ploughshares v27 no4 p75-83 Wint
    2001/2002
Hugessen, Hughe Knatchbull- *See* Knatchbull-
    Hugessen, Sir Hughe, 1886-1971

Hugh Harper. Bowles, P.
Hughes, Dorothy B.
  The Granny Woman
    A Century of noir; thirty-two classic crime
    stories; edited by Mickey Spillane and Max
    Allan Collins
Hughes, Jo
  Forbidden fruits
    Mr. Roopratna's chocolate; the winning sto-
    ries from the 1999 Rhys Davies competi-
    tion
Hughes, Kathleen Bedwell
  Roam
    Pieces; a collection of new voices; edited by
    Stephen Chbosky
Hughes, Langston
  The gun
    The African American West; a century of
    short stories; edited by Bruce A. Glasrud
    and Laurie Champion
Hughes, Mary-Beth
  Israel
    Ploughshares v25 no4 p108-11 Wint
    1999/2000
  Pelican Song
    The Paris Review v46 p191-203 Summ 2004
Hughes, Ryan *See* Oltion, Jerry
HUGO, VICTOR, 1802-1885
        About
  Fleischman, C. One day, Victor Hugo. . .
Hugo, Arthur, and Bobby Joe. Valeri, L.
The **Hull** case. Davies, P. H.
Hulme, Juliet *See* Perry, Anne, 1938-
HUMAN ANATOMY
    See also Eye; Nose; Teeth
The **human** angle. Tenn, W.
The **human** front. MacLeod, K.
HUMAN SACRIFICE
  Campbell, R. Merry May
  Cortázar, J. The night face up
  Dozois, G. R. The Mayan variation
  King, S. Children of the corn
  Lawrence, D. H. The woman who rode away
  Lovecraft, H. P. The shadow over Innsmouth
  Oates, J. C. Commencement
The **human** side of instrumental
  transcommunication. Brenner, W.
La **humanidad**. Bocock, M.
Humfrey, Michael
  A Sense of Colour
    Dalhousie Review v83 no2 p251-9 Summ
    2003
Humility. Hoffman, W.
Humming back yesterday. Wilkinson, C. E.
The **humming** of stars and bees and waves.
  Endrezze, A.
HUMMINGBIRDS
  Bishop, M. Thirteen lies about hummingbirds
Hummingbirds. Ackerman, D.
HUMOR
    See also Parodies; Practical jokes; Satire
  Allen, W. Retribution
  Allen, W. The whore of Mensa
  Babel´, I. Shabos-Nakhamu
  Barrett, N., Jr. Perpetuity blues
  Bausch, R. Nobody in Hollywood
  Bausch, R. Riches
  Butler, R. O. The ironworkers' hayride
  Butler, R. O. Up by heart

Capote, T. Among the paths to Eden
Capote, T. My side of the matter
Carter, E. Glory goes and gets some
Chekhov, A. P. At the bath-house
Chekhov, A. P. The burbot
Chekhov, A. P. The exclamation mark
Chekhov, A. P. Foiled!
Chekhov, A. P. From the diary of an assistant
  book-keeper
Chekhov, A. P. In the dark
Chekhov, A. P. Notes from the journal of a
  quick-tempered man
Chekhov, A. P. Notes from the memoirs of a
  man of ideals
Chekhov, A. P. The objet d'art
Chekhov, A. P. On the telephone
Chekhov, A. P. Romance with double-bass
Chekhov, A. P. The siren
Chekhov, A. P. A work of art
Chesnutt, C. W. The shadow of my past
Clarke, A. C. The reluctant orchid
Clarke, A. C. Sleeping beauty
Cody, L. Where's Stacey?
Desplechin, M. At sea
Dozois, G. R. Afternoon at Schraffts
Englander, N. The gilgul of Park Avenue
Fitzgerald, P. At Hiruharama
Flagg, F. Rome, Italy
Froh, R. The two trail ride tricksters
Galef, D. Laugh track
Gautreaux, T. Welding with children
Gilchrist, E. The cabal
Gilman, C. P. When I was a witch
Harris, M. The iron fist of oligarchy
Harrison, H. The day after the end of the world
Harrison, H. The greening of the green
James, H. The solution
Lao She. The grand opening
Lardner, R. Hurry Kane
Mickenberg, R. Direct male
Proulx, A. The blood bay
Reiner, C. Deibenquist sounds famous
Reiner, C. Yehudah Benjamin Aronowitz
Sade, marquis de. The Gascon wit
Saki. The occasional garden
Shaw, I. Whispers in bedlam
Singer, I. B. Cockadoodledoo
Singleton, G. Outlaw head and tail
Tenn, W. Venus and the seven sexes
Thurber, J. The catbird seat
Trevanian. The sacking of Miss Plimsoll
Tucci, N. The evolution of knowledge
Updike, J. The baluchitherium
Westlake, D. E. Art and craft
Westlake, D. E. Ask a silly question
Westlake, D. E. The Dortmunder workout
Westlake, D. E. Fugue for felons
Westlake, D. E. Give till it hurts
Westlake, D. E. Horse laugh
Westlake, D. E. Jumble sale
Westlake, D. E. Love in the lean years
Westlake, D. E. A midsummer daydream
Westlake, D. E. Now what?
Westlake, D. E. Party animal
Westlake, D. E. Too many crooks
Wodehouse, P. G. The heart of a goof
HUMOROUS STORIES *See* Humor

Humphrey, William

A voice from the woods

Graham, D. Lone Star literature; from the Red River to the Rio Grande; edited by Don Graham

HUNCHBACKS

Singer, I. B. Alone

Singer, I. B. Two markets

The **hundred** day men. Black, M.

A **hundred** hearts. Fairey, W. W.

Hundred-pound baby. Budnitz, J.

Hung up at Parley's store. Farrell, C.

Hunga Pass. Armstrong, K.

HUNGARIANS

United States

Collins, M. Freedom fighter

Updike, J. The astronomer

HUNGARY

Budapest

Kalman, J. Personal effects

HUNGER

See also Starvation

Rachmil, B. Bread

Wallace, D. F. Mister Squishy

Williams, W. J. The Green Leopard Plague

Hunger. Stevens, J. D.

Hunger. West, M.

Hunger, an introduction. Straub, P.

A **hunger** for the infinite. Benford, G.

The **hunger** of the leaves. Lane, J.

Hungry everywhere. Shepherd, P.

Hungry self. Curtis, R.

Hunnicutt, Ellen

Radio room

Prairie Schooner v75 no1 p152-71 Spr 2001

Hunt, Samantha

Cures

Iowa Review v29 no2 p80-81 Fall 1999

Erosion

Iowa Review v29 no2 p82 Fall 1999

First in flight

The Literary Review (Madison, N.J.) v45 no3 p539 Spr 2002

In between the storm and the window

The Literary Review (Madison, N.J.) v45 no3 p537-8 Spr 2002

Language

The Literary Review (Madison, N.J.) v45 no3 p540 Spr 2002

Why

The Literary Review (Madison, N.J.) v45 no3 p538 Spr 2002

The **hunt**. Bingham, S.

Hunter, Evan

Dead men don't dream

A Century of noir; thirty-two classic crime stories; edited by Mickey Spillane and Max Allan Collins

Deadlier than the mail

Murder most postal; homicidal tales that deliver a message; edited by Martin H. Greenberg

First offense

The Best American mystery stories of the century; Tony Hillerman, editor; with an introduction by Tony Hillerman

The killing at Triple Tree

A Century of great Western stories; edited by John Jakes

Hunter, Evan, 1926-

For works written by this author under other names see Marsten, Richard, 1926-; McBain, Ed, 1926-

Hunter, Frederic

Africa, Africa!

Hunter, F. Africa, Africa!; fifteen stories

The barking dog

Hunter, F. Africa, Africa!; fifteen stories

Card players

Hunter, F. Africa, Africa!; fifteen stories

Dr. Kleckner

Hunter, F. Africa, Africa!; fifteen stories

Elizabeth who disappeared

Hunter, F. Africa, Africa!; fifteen stories

Equateur

Hunter, F. Africa, Africa!; fifteen stories

Laban and Murugi

Hunter, F. Africa, Africa!; fifteen stories

Lenoir

Hunter, F. Africa, Africa!; fifteen stories

Madagascar

Hunter, F. Africa, Africa!; fifteen stories

A newsman scratches an itch

Hunter, F. Africa, Africa!; fifteen stories

Night vigil

Hunter, F. Africa, Africa!; fifteen stories

North of Nairobi

Hunter, F. Africa, Africa!; fifteen stories

Pepper

Hunter, F. Africa, Africa!; fifteen stories

Waiting for the Mwami

Hunter, F. Africa, Africa!; fifteen stories

Hunter, Jack D.

For want of a Fokker

On glorious wings; the best flying stories of the century; edited and introduced by Stephen Coonts

Hunter. Grau, S. A.

The **hunter**. Padura Fuentes, L.

Hunter. Smart, A.

The **Hunter** and the Walrus: Inuit (Nunatsiaqmiut) of Baffin Island. Bruchac, J.

Hunter, come home. McKenna, R.

Hunter Johnson music. Hermann, J.

HUNTERS See Hunting

Hunters and gatherers. Cooper, B.

The **Hunter's** Freedom. Werner, J.

The **hunters** in winter. Karnezis, P.

The **hunter's** wife. Doerr, A.

HUNTING

See also Duck hunting; Trappers and trapping

Adam, C. Dove

Cherryh, C. J. Ice

Chiappone, R. Raccoon

Clark, B. C. Fur in the hickory

Coyne, S. Hunting country

De Camp, L. S. A gun for dinosaur

Doerr, A. The hunter's wife

Gilchrist, E. I, Rhoda Manning, go hunting with my daddy

Gulick, B. Encounter on Horse-Killed Creek

Gunn, K. The meatyard

Hickey, D. The closed season

Horgan, P. To the mountains

Jenkins, G. In the outback

Karnezis, P. The hunters in winter

Kittredge, W. We are not in this together

HUNTING—*Continued*

Lincoln, C. Winter's wheat
Meyers, K. The smell of the deer
Nichols, J. Jade
Percy, W. The second coming [excerpt]
Shade, E. Blood
Small, K. The b-zone open
Steele, A. M. The teb hunter
Wolff, T. Hunters in the snow
Ziegler, I. My last deer
Zinovyeva-Annibal, L. D. Wolves
Hunting. Bean, B.

HUNTING ACCIDENTS

Kittredge, W. The waterfowl tree
Hunting country. Coyne, S.
Hunting icebergs. Lock, N.
Hunting Knife. Murakami, H.
Hunting mother. Walker, S.
The **huntsman**. Chekhov, A. P.
Huo Mu *See* Chen Shixu, 1948-
Hup three. Van de Wetering, J.

Hurley, Valerie

Alice, rolling down the mountainside
  The Literary Review (Madison, N.J.) v44 no3
  p490-5 Spr 2001
Horrible but true things you'd rather not know
  The North American Review v286 no3/4 p56-
  62 My/Ag 2001
Ruby, Wanda and Me, Late at Night, in the
  County Jail
  Iowa Review v32 no2 p92-9 Fall 2002

Hurrah for Capt. Early. Leonard, E.
Hurrah for the hols. Simpson, H.
Hurricane Carleyville. Beattie, A.
Hurricane season. Gosling, P.
Hurricane (something farewell). Hermann, J.
Hurricane stories. Menendez, A.

HURRICANES

Blaise, C. Relief
Brackenbury, R. Nothing works in Homestead
Kurlansky, M. Naked
Robison, M. Kite and paint
Sanabria Santaliz, E. After the hurricane
Stahl, Anna Kazumi. Natural disasters
Hurry Kane. Lardner, R.
The **Hurt** Man. Berry, W.
The **husband**. Bowles, P.
Husband. Jackson, S.

HUSBAND AND WIFE

  See also Desertion and nonsupport; Mar-
    riage
Adam, C. ASP
Adam, C. Cat
Adam, C. Dove
Adam, C. Quail
Adam, C. Turtle
Adams, A. The girl across the room
Agee, J. Earl
Agee, J. The only thing different
Agee, J. A pleasant story
Alcott, L. M. The lady and the woman
Alcott, L. M. Lost in a pyramid; or, The Mum-
  my's Curse
Alcott, L. M. A pair of eyes; or, Modern magic
Aldrich, B. S. The day of retaliation
Alexie, S. Saint Junior
Amis, M. Let me count the times
Ansay, A. M. Box
Arvin, N. Commemorating

Austin, S. At Celilo
Banks, R. Cow-cow
Banks, R. The outer banks
Barth, J. The rest of your life
Barthelme, F. Cooker
Barthelme, F. Domestic
Bausch, R. The eyes of love
Bausch, R. The fireman's wife
Bausch, R. Letter to the lady of the house
Bausch, R. Spirits
Bausch, R. Two altercations
Berry, W. A half-pint of Old Darling
Berry, W. Nearly to the fair
Biguenet, J. Fatherhood
Bingham, S. Loving
Blair, J. Julia loving the face of God
Block, L. A moment of wrong thinking
Bocock, M. Death is where you find it
Bocock, M. The face
Bocock, M. The Journey
Bowles, P. Call at Corazón
Bowles, P. Julian Vreden
Boylan, C. A nail on the head
Boyle, T. C. Rust
Bradbury, R. And the sailor, home from the sea
Bradbury, R. The house
Bradbury, R. In memoriam
Bradbury, R. Leftovers
Bradbury, R. Remember Sascha?
Bradbury, R. Tête-à-tête
Bradbury, R. Where's my hat, what's my hurry?
Brandt, W. All day sun
Brennan, M. The Bohemians
Browder, C. When Luz sings her solo
Brown, C. Friend to women
Busch, F. Bob's your uncle
Butler, R. O. Carl and I
Butler, R. O. I got married to a milk can
Butler, R. O. No chord of music
Byatt, A. S. The pink ribbon
Byrd, Z. Of cabbages
Callaghan, M. The bride
Callaghan, M. Day by day
Campra, Rosalba. Dream tiger
Canin, E. Where we are now
Canty, K. Little Debbie
Canty, K. Scarecrow
Capote, T. Mojave
Carlson, R. DeRay
Carlson, R. The Hotel Eden
Carlson, R. Life before science
Carlson, R. Plan B for the middle class
Carlson, R. The prisoner of Bluestone
Carlson, R. The time I died
Carson, J. Dog Star
Carver, R. Are these actual miles?
Carver, R. Dreams
Carver, R. The hair
Cassill, R. V. And in my heart
Castellanos, R. Culinary lesson
Chekhov, A. P. "Anna on the neck"
Chekhov, A. P. The chorus girl
Chekhov, A. P. In the dark
Chekhov, A. P. The party
Chekhov, A. P. Revenge
Chekhov, A. P. The witch
Chekhov, A. P. A woman without prejudices
Chesnutt, C. W. The kiss
Chesnutt, C. W. The wife of his youth

HUSBAND AND WIFE—*Continued*

Chiappone, R. Things come to mind
Chiappone, R. Winter fish
Chittenden, M. The spirit of Washington
Chopin, K. A point at issue!
Clark, J. At last, the Ark
Clarke, A. C. The defenestration of Ermintrude Inch
Cobb, W. J. Why you?
Coleman, J. C. Marvel Bird
Coleman, J. Ten secrets of beauty
Cooke, C. The Bostons
Cortázar, J. Summer
Crowther, P. The allotment
Cummins, A. Starburst
Daniels, J. Karaoke moon
Danticat, E. Seven
Davidson, R. The Hillside Slasher
Davies, R. I will keep her company
Davies, Tristan. On the night before her birthday
Davies, Tristan. Snowflake
Davis, J. S. What kind of man
Davis, L. Strays
Deane, J. F. The experience of what is beautiful
Delaney, E. J. The anchor and me
Delaney, E. J. Conspiracy buffs
DeMarco, T. Down at the end of lonely street
DeMarinis, R. Borrowed hearts
DeMarinis, R. The handgun
DeMarinis, R. Your burden is lifted, love returns
DeMarinis, R. Your story
Dixon, S. The stranded man
Doble, J. The accordian's greatest hits
Dodd, S. M. Lokey man
Dodd, S. M. The lost art of sleep
Doran, M. M. Golden anniversary
Dunbar, P. L. The ingrate
Dunmore, H. Coosing
Dunmore, H. The lighthouse keeper's wife
Eggers, P. Substitutes
Ellin, S. You can't be a little girl all your life
Ellis, A. T. The cat's whiskers
Ellis, N. Dr. Livingston's grotto
Engel, M. P. Philosophy of education
Erdrich, L. Le mooz
Erian, A. The winning side
Evenson, B. The installation
Evenson, B. Virtual
Feng Jicai. The tall woman and her short husband
Fitzgerald, F. S. Head and shoulders
Fitzgerald, F. S. The lees of happiness
Ford, R. Puppy
Foster, K. Happy people
Fraterrigo, M. Body, mine
Frym, G. Tagging
Fulton, J. Rose
Furman, L. The natural memory
Gabrielyan, N. Hide and seek
Gabrielyan, N. Master of the grass
Galef, D. You
Gates, D. Beating
Gates, D. The mail lady
Gavell, M. L. The infant
Gavell, M. L. Yankee traders
Gilchrist, E. Lunch at the best restaurant in the world

Gilchrist, E. Traceleen at dawn
Gilman, C. P. Mr. Peebles heart
Gilman, C. P. The yellow wallpaper
Gray, A. Pillow talk
Griffith, M. The trichologist's rug
Gunn, K. Everyone is sleeping
Hagy, A. C. Graveyard of the Atlantic
Hampl, P. The bill collector's vacation
Hardy, M. The heifer
Harleman, A. Meanwhile
Hawthorne, N. The birthmark
Hawthorne, N. Mrs. Bullfrog
Hays, D. Orphans
Heller, J. The death of the dying swan
Heller, J. I don't love you any more
Heller, J. Lot's wife
Helms, B. Antique map collecting
Helms, B. Collected stories
Henley, P. The late hunt
Herling, G. A hot breath from the desert
Highsmith, P. Born failure
Hodgen, C. What the rabbi said to the priest
Holdstock, P. Sitting pretty
Homes, A. M. Please remain calm
Howard, M. Big as life
Iagnemma, K. Children of hunger
Iagnemma, K. The confessional approach
Iagnemma, K. The ore miner's wife
Irsfeld, J. H. The marriage auditors
Jackson, S. The summer people
Jackson, V. F. Victoria and Albert II: Daytrippers
James, H. The author of "Beltraffio"
James, H. Crawford's consistency
James, H. The liar
James, H. The modern warning
James, H. A problem
Jance, J. A. Death of a snowbird
Jenkins, G. Something to cling to
Kane, J. F. Paris
Kaplan, H. Claude comes and goes
Karbo, K. The palace of marriage
Kelly, J. P. The propagation of light in a vacuum
Kelman, J. The good times
Kelman, J. Oh my darling
Kelman, J. Strength
Kittredge, W. Kissing
Klíma, I. Conjugal conversations
Knight, M. The man who went out for cigarettes
Kohler, S. Baboons
Kohler, S. The bride's secret
Kohler, S. Light
Kohler, S. On the money
Kohler, S. Structure
Kureishi, H. Four blue chairs
Kurlansky, M. The deerness of life
Lahiri, J. A temporary matter
Lao She. Life choices
Lawrence, D. H. The blind man
Lee, A. The birthday present
Lee, M. A fresh start
Lee, M. The secrets of Cooperstown
Lewis, T. The marijuana tree
Lindgren, T. The stump-grubber
Lindgren, T. Water
Link, K. Shoe and marriage
Lippman, L. What he needed
Locklin, G. The monopoly story

HUSBAND AND WIFE—*Continued*

Lord, N. What was washing around out there
Lordan, B. The man with the lapdog
Louis, L. G. Her slow and steady
Marías, J. On the honeymoon
Mason, B. A. Thunder snow
Mastretta, A. Aunt Laura
Mastretta, A. Aunt Magdalena
Matteson, S. The trouble with Harry
Mayo, W. Going long
Mayo, W. Jagged tooth, great tooth
McBain, E. The couple next door
McCorkle, J. Chickens
McCorkle, J. Intervention
McGarry, J. With her
Meacock, N. The mole trap
Meinke, P. The cranes
Melville, P. Erzulie
Melville, P. The migration of ghosts
Menendez, A. Story of a parrot
Miller, R. Bryna
Mo Yan. Abandoned child
Morgan, R. Kuykendall's gold
Murguía, A. Barrio lotto
Nabokov, V. V. "That in Aleppo once . . . "
Nair, M. The curry leaf tree
Nair, M. Video
Nair, M. Vishnukumar's Valentine's Day
Naumoff, L. Moon pie over Miami
Nelson, A. The unified front
Nissen, T. 29th Street Playground, September 1968
Nissen, T. After twenty-five years, at the Palais Royale
Nissen, T. At the No. 1 Phoenix Garden
Norris, L. Wind across the breaks
O'Hara, J. In a grove
Orner, P. The waters
Painter, P. Confusing the dog
Painter, P. Doors
Painter, P. The house that burned
Pearlman, E. The story
Porter, J. A. A man wanted to buy a cat
Potvin, E. A. You are here
Powers, S. The baker's wife
Pronzini, B. Mrs. Rakubian
Pronzini, B. and Malzberg, B. N. Multiples
Rendell, R. Fair exchange
Reynolds, A. Alcestis
Richmond, M. Choose your travel partner wisely
Robison, M. Yours
Robotham, R. The cry
Rodgers, S. J. Luck
Rodgers, S. J. The rice in question
Rodgers, S. J. The two husbands
Rosenfeld, S. Exactly the size of life
Roth, J. The triumph of beauty
Sandor, M. Gravity
Schlink, B. The woman at the gas station
Schnitzler, A. Dream story
Schwartz, L. S. Hostages to fortune
Schwartz, L. S. Twisted tales
Searle, E. Celebration
Shade, E. The heart hankers
Shepard, J. We'll talk later
Shon, F. The farmer's wife
Shonk, K. The death of Olga Vasilievna
Shteyngart, G. Several anecdotes about my wife
Singer, I. B. The brooch

Singer, I. B. Esther Kreindel the second
Singer, I. B. The man who came back
Singer, I. B. Short Friday
Singer, I. B. The unseen
Singer, I. B. The wife killer
Singleton, G. Answers
Singleton, G. Remember why we're here
Singleton, G. These people are us
Singleton, G. Vietnam
Smith, L. Intensive care
Sojourner, M. Absolute proof of the cosmos in life
Sojourner, M. Riv
Stern, D. The #63 bus from the Gare de Lyon
Straight, S. Back
Swick, M. A. Crete
Thurm, M. Miss Grace at her best
Tilghman, C. Mary in the mountains
Todd, R. L. Vinegar
Tolstoy, L., graf. Kornei Vasiliev
Tomioka, T. A dog's eye view
Tomioka, T. Yesteryear
Updike, J. Ace in the hole
Updike, J. Giving blood
Updike, J. His finest hour
Updike, J. Marching through Boston
Updike, J. Nakedness
Updike, J. The rescue
Updike, J. Separating
Updike, J. Sunday teasing
Updike, J. Unstuck
Updike, J. Walter Briggs
Updike, J. Wife-wooing
Vasseur, T. J. The most beautiful day of your life
Vaswani, N. The rigors of dance lessons
Vermeulen, J. Canon
Viets, E. Red meat
Vivante, A. Can-can
Vivante, A. Company
Vivante, A. Escapes
Vivante, A. Musico
Vonnegut, K. A night for love
Walker, A. Olive oil
Wallace, D. Slippered feet
Wallace, D. F. Adult world [I]
Wallace, D. F. Adult world [II]
Wallace, D. F. Oblivion
Wallace, R. The sacred well
Watanabe McFerrin, L. Amphibians
Waugh, E. Tactical exercise
Weihe, E. Her birthday suit
Weihe, E. Love spots
Weihe, E. The morning room
Weiner, S. Eating Vic
Westlake, D. E. Love in the lean years
Wharton, E. Afterward
Wharton, E. The best man
Wharton, E. Bewitched
Wharton, E. Charm incorporated
Wharton, E. A journey
Wharton, E. The lamp of Psyche
Wharton, E. The mission of Jane
Wharton, E. The reckoning
Wharton, E. The recovery
Wharton, E. The twilight of the God
What, L. Those who know
White, M. C. Heights
White, M. C. Ray's shoes

HUSBAND AND WIFE—*Continued*
  Williams, M. Grazing in good pastures
  Wood, M. Ernie's ark
  Wood, M. That one autumn
  Yañez, R. I&M Plumbing
  Yates, R. The B.A.R. man
  Yates, R. A convalescent ego
  Yates, R. A glutton for punishment
  Yates, R. A natural girl
  Yates, R. Regards at home
  Young, T. Fast
Husband material. Ferriss, L.
The **husband** who played priest. See Sade, marquis de. The husband who turned priest: a tale of Provence
The **husband** who turned priest: a tale of Provence. Sade, marquis de
The **husbands**. Krouse, E.
Hush!. Chekhov, A. P.
Hush. Roensch, R.
Hush money. Barrett, L.
The **husker** tender. Meyers, K.
Huss, Sandy
  Scissors kick
    Prairie Schooner v75 no2 p5-11 Summ 2001
Hussy from the west. Brownrigg, S.
Hussy Strutt. Patterson, A.
The **hustler**. Tevis, W. S.
Huttner, Henry
  Dr. Cyclops
    Science-fiction classics; the stories that morphed into movies; compiled by Forrest J. Ackerman
Hwang, Frances
  Transparency
    Kulka, J. and Danford, N. The New American voices 2003; guest editor Joyce Carol Oates; series editors John Kulka and Natalie Danford
Hyannis boat. Wetherell, W. D.
Hyde, Catherine Ryan
  Bloodlines
    Ploughshares v27 no1 p66-79 Spr 2001
  Witness to breath
    New Letters v67 no3 p27-37 2001
Hyde, Michael
  Her Hollywood
    The Best American mystery stories, 2001; edited and with an Introduction by Lawrence Block
Hyde, Phoebe Baker
  American Southwestern
    Confrontation no86/87 p187-201 Spr/Summ 2004
HYDROGEN BOMB *See* Atomic bomb
HYDROPHOBIA *See* Rabies
Hydrophobia. Brown, J.
The **hyena**. Bowles, P.
HYENAS
  Bowles, P. The hyena
Hygiene. Barnes, J.
Hykisch, Anton
  A free royal town
    In search of homo sapiens; twenty-five contemporary Slovak short stories; editor, Pavol Hudík ; [translated by Heather Trebatická; American English editor, Lucy Bednár]

HYPERACTIVE CHILDREN
  Brown, R. How to win
HYPERHIDROSIS
  Ross, L. Tasting songs
Hypertension. Moya, H. C.
HYPNOSIS *See* Hypnotism
HYPNOTISM
  Chopin, K. A mental suggestion
  Cummins, A. The hypnotist's trailer
  Dann, J. Marilyn
  Knight, M. The mesmerist
  Nelson, R. F. Eight o'clock in the morning
  Pickard, N. The dead past
The **hypnotist's** trailer. Cummins, A.
HYPOCHONDRIA
  Roth, J. The triumph of beauty

I

I always do what Teddy says. Harrison, H.
I am as I am. Almond, S.
I am Bigfoot. Carlson, R.
I am not a Jew. Biguenet, J.
I am not like Nuñez. Shippen, J. R.
I Am Not Your Mother. Mattison, A.
I am telling you lies. Di Blasi, D.
I am twenty-one. Robison, M.
I Brake for Moose. Kothari, G.
I came to have tea with my daughter. Arastuyi, S.
I can speak!™. Saunders, G.
I cannot tell a lie, exactly. Gavell, M. L.
I could've told you if you hadn't asked. Singleton, G.
I demand to know where you're taking me. Chaon, D.
I didn't do it. Pronzini, B.
I do like to be beside the seaside. Adams, J.
I do not have herpes. Locklin, G.
I don't love you any more. Heller, J.
I don't tell lies. Lupoff, R. A.
I dreamt he fell three floors and lived. Svoboda, T.
I feel bad killing you. Brackett, L.
I fly unto you. O'Connell, M.
I Forbid You This Recurring Dream. Willoughby, J.
I forgot to go to Spain. Harrison, J.
I get by. Robison, M.
I got a guy once. Gallagher, T.
I Got Somebody in Staunton. Lewis, W. H.
I got something with your name on it. Nesbitt, M.
I got the beat. Lisick, B.
I hate to see that evening sun go down. Gay, W.
I have a special plan for this world. Ligotti, T.
I have lost my right. Smith, R. T.
I have my vigil. Harrison, H.
I have the serpent brought. Wicks, V.
I hope I shall arrive soon. Dick, P. K.
I is for impala. Adam, C.
I just love Carrie Lee. Douglas, E.
I killed King Fisher. Froh, R.
I like being killed. Fischer, T.
I love everything about you. Pelegrimas, M. and Randisi, R. J.
I LOVE LUCY (TELEVISION PROGRAM)
  Rowell, J. Who lives you?
I love you, Sophie Western. Jones, T.
I loved the squire. DeLancey, K.

I married a space alien. Dodd, S. M.
I, Maureen. Spencer, E.
I never looked. Hall, D.
I, Osiris. Grimson, T.
I remember Babylon. Clarke, A. C.
I, Rhoda Manning, go hunting with my daddy. Gilchrist, E.
I, Richard. George, E.
I see you. Harrison, H.
I see you. Knight, D. F.
I see you, Bianca. Brennan, M.
I seen some stuf horabl stuf lisen. Hochman, A.
I should worry. Kees, W.
I think I will not hang myself today. Pronzini, B.
I told you: love would last us. Behar, R.
I want to live!. Jones, T.
I was a teenage beauty queen. Esbaum, J.
I was asking a question too. Kelman, J.
I was in love. Oates, J. C.
I Will Clean Your Attic. Parker, M.
I will hide in God. Abrams, T.
I wish you wouldn't be that way. Chenoweth, A.
I won't do no dive. Sylvester, H. A.

Iagnemma, Karl
  Children of hunger
    Iagnemma, K. On the nature of human romantic interaction
  The confessional approach
    Iagnemma, K. On the nature of human romantic interaction
    The Paris Review v43 no160 p246-64 Wint 2001
  The Indian agent
    Iagnemma, K. On the nature of human romantic interaction
  Kingdom, Order, Species
    The Antioch Review v61 no2 p269-87 Spr 2003
    Iagnemma, K. On the nature of human romantic interaction
  On the nature of human romantic interaction
    Iagnemma, K. On the nature of human romantic interaction
    Pushcart prize XXVII; best of the small presses; edited by Bill Henderson with the Pushcart prize editors
  The ore miner's wife
    Iagnemma, K. On the nature of human romantic interaction
    The Virginia Quarterly Review v78 no2 p324-41 Spr 2002
  The phrenologist's dream
    Iagnemma, K. On the nature of human romantic interaction
  Zilkowski's theorem
    The Best American short stories, 2002; selected from U.S. and Canadian magazines by Sue Miller with Katrina Kenison, with an introduction by Sue Miller
    Iagnemma, K. On the nature of human romantic interaction

Iarrera, Carmen
  A telephone call too many
    Death by espionage; intriguing stories of deception and betrayal; edited by Martin Cruz Smith
The **Iberville** mistress. De Noux, O.
Ibn-Hakam al-Bokhari, murdered in his labyrinth. Borges, J. L.

Ibn-Hakkan al Bokhari, dead in his labyrinth. See Borges, J. L. Ibn-Hakam al-Bokhari, murdered in his labyrinth
Ibn Rushd *See* Averroës, 1126-1198
ICARUS (GREEK MYTHOLOGY)
  Brownstein, G. Musée des Beaux Arts
ICE
  Meloy, M. The ice harvester
  Whitty, J. Jimmy under water
Ice. Shields, D.
Ice age. Anderson, R.
Ice age. Sosin, D.
Ice angels. Thompson, J.
Ice breaking. Mueller, D.
The **ice** harvester. Meloy, M.
ICE HOCKEY *See* Hockey
Ice Man. Murakami, H.
The **ice** palace. Fitzgerald, F. S.
The **ice** shelf. Howard, C.
ICE SKATING
  Banks, R. Defenseman
  Slezak, E. Patch
Ice tonight in the hearts of young visitors. Fischer, T.
ICEBERGS
  Clarke, A. C. Cold war
Icehouse Burgess. Porter, J. A.
Iceland. Fulton, J.
ICELANDERS
                              United States
  Borges, J. L. The bribe
Icicle music. Bishop, M.
ICU. Lee, E.
Ida. Bunin, I. A.
IDAHO
  Wolven, S. The copper kings
The **idea** of it. Holbrook, C.
The **idea** of sirloin. Almond, S.
The **Ideal** Bakery. Hall, D.
IDEALISM
  Hawthorne, N. The great stone face
Ideas of home, but not the thing itself. Kane, J. F.
IDENTITY *See* Personality
The **Identity** Club. Burgin, R.
Identity crisis. West, K.
The **idiot**. Tozzi, F.
An **idle** fellow. Chopin, K.
The **idler**. Aylett, S.
The **idols** of sickness. Rifkin, A.
If. Harrison, H.
If Armstrong was interesting. Aylett, S.
If I close my eyes forever. De Lint, C.
If I close them. Joseph, D.
'**If** I forget thee, oh Earth . . .'. Clarke, A. C.
If I have found favor in your eyes. Stollman, A. L.
If I Have to Hit One of You, I'll Hit You Both. Shopper, E.
If I should open my mouth. Bowles, P.
"**If** I should wake. . . .". Paolucci, A.
If I were a man. Gilman, C. P.
If I were lemon pie. Werve, S.
If I were you. Chenoweth, A.
If it can't be true. Matera, L.
If It's Not Too Much to Ask. Fulton, A.
If My Mother's Soul Can Hear. Spraker, S.
If there be any praise. Wadsworth, S.
If you can't take the heat. Shankman, S.
If you can't win. Hall, J. B.

If you treat things right. Slezak, E.
Iglaf and Swan. Glover, D. H.
Igloria, Luisa A.
  Wedding night
    The North American Review v286 no1 p8-12
    Ja/F 2001
Iguana boy. Rawley, D.
III. Aldiss, B. W.
Ikhnaton *See* Akhenaton, King of Egypt, fl. ca.
    1388-1358 B.C.
The **ikon** of Elijah. Davidson, A.
Iles, Francis *See* Berkeley, Anthony, 1893-1971
The **Iliad** for boys and girls [excerpt] Church, A.
I'll Be Watching You. Foster, P.
ILLEGAL ALIENS *See* Undocumented aliens
The **illegibility** of this world. Stern, R. G.
ILLEGITIMACY
        See also Unmarried mothers
  Atkinson, K. Sheer big waste of love
  Babel´, I. The sin of Jesus
  Bowles, P. Allal
  Bunin, I. A. Little fool
  Harrington, J. Sweet baby Jenny
  Murakami, H. All God's children can dance
  Nakagami, K. The cape
  Oz, A. Where the jackals howl
  Updike, J. Rabbit remembered
  Vachss, A. H. Searcher
  Van Winckel, N. Sometimes he borrowed a
    horse
  Warren, R. P. Christmas gift
ILLINOIS
  Thompson, J. The Amish
                    Chicago
  Bellow, S. Cousins
  Bellow, S. Looking for Mr. Green
  Bellow, S. A silver dish
  Bellow, S. Something to remember me by
  Bellow, S. What kind of day did you have?
  Bellow, S. Zetland: by a character witness
  Brady, C. The end of the class war
  Chesnutt, C. W. How he met her
  Doenges, J. God of gods
  Doenges, J. Incognito
  Dybek, S. Blue boy
  Dybek, S. Breasts
  Dybek, S. Je reviens
  Dybek, S. Lunch at the Loyola Arms
  Dybek, S. A minor mood
  Dybek, S. Orchids
  Dybek, S. Pet milk
  Dybek, S. Qué quieres
  Dybek, S. Song
  Dybek, S. Undertow
  Epstein, J. Uncle Jack
  Gifford, B. The lost Christmas
  Hemon, A. Blind Jozef Pronek
  Hemon, A. Blind Jozef Pronek & Dead Souls
  McNally, J. The grand illusion
  McNally, J. Limbs
  McNally, J. Torture
  Orner, P. Daughters
  Orner, P. Esther stories
  Orner, P. The house on Lunt Avenue
  Slezak, E. By heart
  Taylor, T. L. The Boar's Head Easter
  Wieland, L. The loop, the snow, their daughters,
    the rain
  Zabytko, I. The celebrity

  Zabytko, I. John Mars, all-American
  Zabytko, I. The last boat
  Zabytko, I. Lavender soap
  Zabytko, I. My black Valiant
  Zabytko, I. Obligation
  Zabytko, I. Pani Ryhotska in love
  Zabytko, I. The prodigal son enters heaven
  Zabytko, I. Saint Sonya
  Zabytko, I. Steve's bar
ILLITERACY *See* Literacy
ILLNESS
        See also Invalids; Mental illness; Termi-
    nal illness
  Adams, A. A pale and perfectly oval moon
  Aldrich, B. S. Across the smiling meadow
  Allen, S. Behind the black curtain
  Allen, S. Close to the body
  Banks, R. Indisposed
  Beattie, A. The famous poet, amid Bougainvil-
    lea
  Bingham, S. Rat
  Chekhov, A. P. A doctor's visit
  Chekhov, A. P. A dreary story
  DeMarinis, R. Borrowed hearts
  Divakaruni, C. B. What the body knows
  Gayle, A. D. Mother
  Henley, P. Cargo
  Henley, P. The secret of cartwheels
  Henry, O. The last leaf
  Hwang, F. Transparency
  Jacobs, M. Looking for Lourdes
  Kennedy, A. L. A wrong thing
  Mazelis, J. Seven thousand flowers
  Nfah-Abbenyi, J. M. Slow poison
  O'Connell, M. Saint Ursula and her maidens
  Ponte, A. J. Heart of skitalietz
  Reifler, N. Memoir
  Roorbach, B. Taughannock Falls
  Singer, I. B. The letter writer
  Stegner, W. E. Chip off the old block
  Waters, M. Y. Rationing
  Wharton, E. Atrophy
Illumination. Reisman, N.
ILLUSIONS *See* Hallucinations and illusions
Illusions. Wuori, G. K.
The **illustrated** encyclopedia of the animal king-
    dom. Chaon, D.
ILLUSTRATORS
  Dodd, S. M. What I remember now
Ilya Isaakovich and Margarita Prokofyeuna. *See*
    Babel´, I. Elya Isaakovich and Margarita
    Prokofievna
I'm a dirty girl. Matthews, C.
I'm getting married tomorrow. Moses, J.
I'm going to California. Farrell, C.
I'm in the book. Estleman, L. D.
I'm Not Gloria. Herman, W.
I'm not that kind of girl. Matthews, C.
I'm not that kind of girl. Pelegrimas, M.
I'm slavering. Lipsyte, S.
I'm sorry, Mr. Griggs. Cohen, S.
I'm sorry, Mr. Turini. Cohen, S.
I'm still waiting. Channer, C.
I'm the only one. Smith, Z.
Images, questions re: beautiful dead woman. Je-
    sús, P. d.
IMAGINARY ANIMALS *See* Mythical animals
Imaginary birds. Bottoms, G.

IMAGINARY CITIES
  Eakin, W. How Boy Howdy saved the world
  Wells, H. G. The country of the blind
IMAGINARY KINGDOMS
  Brooks, T. Indomitable
  Ford, J. At Reparata
IMAGINARY PLAYMATES
  Barker, N. Braces
  Millar, M. The people across the canyon
  Spencer, E. The little brown girl
IMAGINARY WARS AND BATTLES
  Anderson, P. The Sky People
  Clarke, A. C. Superiority
  Edghill, R. War of the roses
Imagining Africa. Hood, A.
Imagining friends. Jackson, V. F.
Imagining the structure of free space on Pioneer
    Road. Weaver, G.
Imbroglio. Williams, C.
Imitation of life. Hemon, A.
Immaculate. Tester, W.
An **immaculate** man. Kennedy, A. L.
Immersion. Greenberg, A.
IMMIGRANTS
  Bhattacharyya, R. Loss
  Bukoski, A. Immigration and naturalization
  Butler, R. O. Sunday
  Codrescu, A. Monsieur Teste in America
  Glickmann, N. The last emigrant
  Godin, A. My dead brother comes to America
  Honig, L. English as a second language
  Karbo, K. The palace of marriage
  Steinbeck, T. Sing Fat and the Imperial Duchess
    of Woo
  Troncoso, S. Day of the dead
Immigration and naturalization. Bukoski, A.
The **immortal**. Borges, J. L.
Immortal. Sneed, C.
IMMORTALITY
  Amis, M. The immortals
  Baker, K. The likely lad
  Baker, K. Monster story
  Baker, K. Old flat top
  Baker, K. Smart Alec
  Bear, G. Heads
  Borges, J. L. The immortal
  Davies, R. Offer of immortality
  Knight, D. F. Dio
  Le Guin, U. K. The Island of the Immortals
  Lupoff, R. A. I don't tell lies
  McAuley, P. J. All tomorrow's parties
  Simak, C. D. Grotto of the dancing deer
  Williams, S. Entre les beaux morts en vie
    (Among the beautiful living dead)
  Wilson, R. C. Divided by infinity
  Wilson, R. C. The fields of Abraham
  Wu, C.-E. Monkey [excerpt]
Immortality. Breen, J. L.
Immortality. Karnezis, P.
Immortality. Li, Y.
The **immortals**. Amis, M.
The **Immortals**. McNally, J.
The **immortals**. Ross, J.
Immunity. Van Winckel, N.
Impact parameter. Landis, G. A.
Impala. Adam, C.
Imperato placeless. Stern, D.
Imperfections. Bahr, A.
Imperialistas. Lee, D.

IMPERSONATIONS
    See also Impostors; Mistaken identity;
    Transvestism
  Bradbury, R. Any friend of Nicholas Nickleby's
    is a friend of mine
  Chacón, D. Godoy lives
  Chopin, K. The return of Alcibiade
  Cobb, W. J. The decline of King Fabulous
  DeLancey, K. The mystery of George Jones
  Delany, S. R. Time considered as a helix of
    semi-precious stones
  Gorriti, J. M. Gubi Amaya
  Hauptman, W. Good rockin' tonight
  Johnson, C. R. A soldier for the crown
  Knight, D. F. The handler
  Orner, P. Two Poes
  Singer, I. B. Taibele and her demon
  Singer, I. B. Yentl the yeshiva boy
  Wharton, E. Her son
Impersonators. Krouse, E.
The **implausible** blonde. Giberga, J. S.
The **Importance** of Cardboard Boxes. Salinas, K.
The **importance** of trifles. Davidson, A.
Impossible. Martin, S.-P.
The **impossible** Miss Meadows. Chopin, K.
The **impossible** play. O'Rourke, F.
Imposters in love. Hardy, M.
The **impostor**. Muller, M.
IMPOSTORS
    See also Impersonations
  Borges, J. L. The improbable impostor Tom
    Castro
  Bowles, P. Mejdoub
  James, H. The Aspern papers
  McCracken, E. Here's your hat what's your hur-
    ry
  Singleton, G. When children count
  Vink, R. A frail young life
The **impressionists** in winter. Fry, S.
Impressions. Pack, J.
The **impressions** of a cousin. James, H.
The **improbable** impostor Tom Castro. Borges, J.
    L.
IMPROBABLE STORIES
    See also Fantasies
  Carmody, I. The man who lost his shadow
  Foster, A. D. Jackalope
  Lansdale, J. R. Fire dog
  Llano, M. E. In the family
  Pronzini, B. The man who collected "The Shad-
    ow"
Improvident excess. Malzberg, B. N.
Improvising. McBrearty, R. G.
Impurities. Singleton, G.
In a café. Lavin, M.
In a danger zone. Rothmayerová, G.
In a grove. O'Hara, J.
In a pig's eye. Allegra, D.
In a Siberian town. Rasputin, V. G.
In absentia. Bowles, P.
In Amalfi. Beattie, A.
In and out of never-never land. Brennan, M.
In and out of old Natchitoches. Chopin, K.
In bed. Young, T.
In Berkeley's green and pleasant land. Blitz, R.
An **in-between** season. Gussler, P. S.
In between talking about the elephant. Kay, J.
In between the storm and the window. Hunt, S.
In between things. Boswell, M.

In Black and White. Svoboda, T.
In case of emergency. Hochman, A.
In case we're separated. Mattison, A.
In Copland. Oates, J. C.
In Coppelius's Toyshop. Willis, C.
In Cuba I was a German shepherd. Menendez, A.
In Defiance of Club Rules. Parks, T.
In dreams begins reality. Penn, W. S.
In exile. Chekhov, A. P.
In Flanders Fields. Robinson, P.
In for a penny. Block, L.
In foreign parts. Doelwijt, T.
In France. Lee, A.
In France they turn to stone when they die. Dodd, S. M.
In frozen time. Rucker, R. v. B.
In Greenwich, there are many gravelled walks. Calisher, H.
"In haste I write you this note—". Ritchie, E.
In heaven. Dueñas, G.
In Her Time. Birmelin, B. T.
In hiding. Oates, J. C.
In Hot May. Oates, J. C.
In irons. Beattie, A.
In Jewel. Robison, M.
In loco parentis. Kendall, G.
In memoriam. Bradbury, R.
In My Movie. Prince, R.
In our part of the world. Kennedy, A.
In Paris. Bunin, I. A.
In pursuit of monsters. Grimmett, N.
In real life. Nolan, W. F.
In Sabine. Chopin, K.
In search of Number Seven. Bonnie, F.
In search of the holy grayling. Burton, M.
In September, the light changes. Holleran, A.
In Spain There Was Revolution. Williams, T.
In the air. Hawley, N.
In the American society. Jen, G.
In the bare lands. Massie, A.
In the basement. Babel´, I.
In the bed. Berkman, P. R.
In the bed department. Enright, A.
In the beginning. Allen, L.
In the beginning. Baron, D.
In the belly of the cat. Libman, D. S.
In the black mill. Chabon, M.
In the box called pleasure. Addonizio, K.
In the cage. Wright, A.
In the cart. See Chekhov, A. P. The schoolmistress
In the cemetery. See Chekhov, A. P. In the graveyard
In the cemetery where Al Jolson is buried. Hempel, A.
In the city of angels. Lochte, D.
In the city of the split sky. Simonds, M.
In the city of X. Jacobs, M.
In the cold of the Malecón. Ponte, A. J.
In the company of heroes. Duane, D.
In the confessional. Reach, A. S.
In the corner of a small square. Pushkin, A. S.
In the country of the young. Stern, D.
In the court. Chekhov, A. P.
In the dark. Chekhov, A. P.
In the dark. Orner, P.
In the dark backward. Benford, G.
In the doorway of Rhee's Jazz Joint. Brown, D. W.

In the drink. Sellers, H.
In the electric Eden. Arvin, N.
In the fall. MacLeod, A.
In the family. Llano, M. E.
In the family. Rayford, P. R.
In the fifties. Michaels, L.
In the Garden. Edwards, K.
In the Garden of the Lords of War. Lopez, B. H.
In the gare at Bayonne. Abrams, T.
In the gloaming. Dark, A. E.
In the graveyard. Chekhov, A. P.
In the great bend of the Souris River. Lopez, B. H.
In the horsecart. See Chekhov, A. P. The schoolmistress
In the house of simple sentences. Phillips, L.
In the house of the child. Sadoff, I.
In the isles of St. George. Appelfeld, A.
In the jasmine shade. Brkic, C. A.
In the kindergarten. Ha Jin
In the land of dreamy dreams. Gilchrist, E.
In the land of the tree cutters. Giono, J.
In the land of the unforgiven. De Lint, C.
In the Little Hunky River. Sanford, A.
In the memory house. Davis, L.
In the merry month of mayhem. Harrington, J.
In the middle of the fields. Lavin, M.
In the middle of the wood [excerpt] Smith, I. C.
In the mind. Porter, J. A.
In the Nineties. Brumbaugh, S.
In the open. Shepard, J.
In the outback. Jenkins, G.
In the Palace of the End. Amis, M.
In the Park. Gao Xingjian
In the pines. De Lint, C.
In the plaza. Highsmith, P.
In the prison of his days Turtledove, H. Alternate generals II; ed. by Harry Turtledove
In the quiet after midnight. De Lint, C.
In the red room. Bowles, P.
In the Reeds. Shrayer-Petrov, D.
In the refrigerator. Vukcevich, R.
In the ruins. Gonzalez, R.
In the shade of the almond tree. Arenas, R.
In the shadow of our house. Blackwood, S.
In the shadow of war. Okri, B.
In the stone house. Malzberg, B. N.
In the story that won't be written. Swan, M.
In the un-black. Baxter, S.
In the upper room. Bisson, T.
In the valley of the shadow. Stewart, T. L.
In the vein. Dinh, L.
In the walls. Orner, P.
In the water works (Birmingham, Alabama 1888). Kiernan, C. R.
In the woods. Robison, M.
In the Yellow House. Bridgford, K.
In the zone. Edgerton, L.
In this corner. Goliger, G.
In this soul of a woman. De Lint, C.
In this way we are wise. Englander, N.
In thunder, lightning or in rain. Kaminsky, S. M.
In Time of War. Hensher, P.
In Tir na nOg. McCourt, J.
In trouble. Chekhov, A. P.
In uncertain time. Marías, J.
In which Avu Giddy tries to stop dancing. Compton, D. G.
In which murder is done. Coberly, L. M.

In Xanadu. Disch, T. M.
An **inadvertence**. Chekhov, A. P.
The **inanimate** world. Strandquist, R.
Inappropriate babies. Wendling, L.
INCAS
  Adolph, J. B. The falsifier
  Gorriti, J. M. If you do wrong, expect no good
  Gorriti, J. M. The quena
  Gorriti, J. M. The treasure of the Incas
  VanderMeer, J. The compass of his bones
  VanderMeer, J. The Emperor's reply
  VanderMeer, J. Ghost dancing with Manco
    Tupac
Inception. Lumley, B.
INCEST
  Brandon, P. The marsh runners
  Canty, K. Aquarium
  Connolly, C. The pleasure gardens
  Fairey, W. W. Family album
  Foley, S. Cloudland
  Gould, L. La Lloradora
  Malamud, B. Still life
  Naiyer Masud. Obscure domains of fear and de-
    sire
  O'Connell, M. Saint Therese of Lisieux
  Oz, A. Where the jackals howl
  Roth, H. A diving rock on the Hudson [excerpt]
  Sade, marquis de. Emilie de Tourville; or, Fra-
    ternal cruelty
  Slaughter, K. Necessary women
  Thompson, S. Ernest
  Tomaso, C. Rain
  Tran, V. Gunboat on the Yangtze
  Watanabe McFerrin, L. How to fall in love
  Yolen, J. Allerleirauh
An **incident**. Chekhov, A. P.
An **incident** at law. Chekhov, A. P.
Incident at Oak Ridge. Bisson, T.
Incident in Azania. Waugh, E.
Incident in the IND. Harrison, H.
The **incident** of the impecunious chevalier. Lupoff,
  R. A.
An **incident** with music. Berberova, N.
Incidents on the road. Penney, B.
Incognita, Inc. Ellison, H.
Incognito. Doenges, J.
Incognito. Nelson, A.
Incognito. Nelson, A.
Incognito with My Brother. Shepard, K.
An **Incomplete** Map of the Northern Polarity.
  Roberts, N.
Inconstant moon. Niven, L.
Inconvenience store. Collins, M. A.
Indelible. Foster, K.
Indelible acts. Kennedy, A. L.
The **indelible** hulk. Perkins, E.
INDEPENDENCE DAY (UNITED STATES)
  See Fourth of July
Independence day. Robison, M.
Index card, index finger. Alvarez, A.
INDIA
  Tolstoy, L., graf. A coffeehouse in the city of
    Surat
  Vaswani, N. Possession at the tomb of Sayyed
    Pir Hazrat Baba Bahadur Saheed Rah Aleh
  Vaswani, N. Sita and Ms. Durber
  Vaswani, N. Where the long grass bends
  1947-
  Chaudhuri, A. The great game

Chaudhuri, A. The old masters
Chaudhuri, A. The party
Chaudhuri, A. Real time
Chaudhuri, A. Words, silences
Desai, A. Diamond dust, a tragedy
Desai, A. Five hours to Simla; or, Faisla
Desai, A. The man who saw himself drown
Desai, A. Royalty
Divakaruni, C. B. The forgotten children
Lahiri, J. Interpreter of maladies
Lahiri, J. The treatment of Bibi Haldar
Nair, M. A certain sense of place
Nair, M. The lodger in room 726
Nair, M. My grandfather dreams of fences
Nair, M. The sculptor of sands
Nair, M. Sixteen days in December
Nair, M. Summer
Nair, M. Video
Nair, M. Vishnukumar's Valentine's Day
Nair, M. A warm welcome to the President,
  insh'allah!
Pittalwala, I. The change
Pittalwala, I. Great Guruji
Ramaya, S. Destiny
Rushdie, S. The free radio
Sekaran, S. Stalin
Spencer, J. The robbers of Karnataka
  Marriage customs
  See Marriage customs—India
  Rural life
Borges, J. L. Blue tigers
Divakaruni, C. B. The names of stars in Bengali
  Bombay
Chandra, V. Dharma
Chaudhuri, A. White lies
Mehra, D. The garden
Murray, J. The hill station
Murray, J. White flour
Pittalwala, I. Bombay talkies
Pittalwala, I. A change of lights
Pittalwala, I. Dear Paramont Pictures
Pittalwala, I. Kulsum, Nazia, and Ismail
Pittalwala, I. Mango season
  Calcutta
Chaudhuri, A. The man from Khurda district
Chaudhuri, A. Portrait of an artist
DeChoudhury, S. Forbidden fate
Lahiri, J. A real durwan
Ramaya, S. The matchmakers
  Delhi
Desai, A. The rooftop dwellers
Freudenberger, N. Lucky girls
  Vale of Kashmir
Divakaruni, C. B. The lives of strangers
The **Indian**. Updike, J.
The **Indian** agent. Iagnemma, K.
Indian country. Alexie, S.
The **Indian** rope trick explained. Rucker, R. v. B.
Indian summer. Connolly, C.
Indian summer. Spencer, E.
Indian summer. Stegner, L.
INDIANA
  Burford, M. David and Kitty
  Day, C. Boss man
  Day, C. The bullhook
  Day, C. Circus People
  Day, C. Jennie Dixiana
  Day, C. The King and His Court
  Day, C. The lone star cowboy

INDIANA—*Continued*
Day, C. Wallace Porter
Day, C. Winnesaw
Ebershoff, D. The bank president
Stuckey-French, E. Leufredus
Indians. Billman, J.
INDIANS OF CENTRAL AMERICA
See also Mayas
INDIANS OF MEXICO
See also Aztecs; Incas
Bowles, P. Pastor Dowe at Tacate
Henry, W. The tallest Indian in Toltepec
Lawrence, D. H. The woman who rode away
INDIANS OF NORTH AMERICA
See also names of specific tribes or nations
Alexie, S. Assimilation
Alexie, S. Because my father always said he was the only Indian who saw Jimi Hendrix play "The Star-Spangled Banner" at Woodstock
Alexie, S. Can I get a witness?
Alexie, S. Do you know where I am?
Alexie, S. Flight patterns
Alexie, S. Indian country
Alexie, S. The life and times of Estelle Walks Above
Alexie, S. Saint Junior
Alexie, S. The search engine
Alexie, S. The sin eaters
Alexie, S. South by Southwest
Alexie, S. This is what it means to say Phoenix, Arizona
Alexie, S. The toughest Indian in the world
Alexie, S. What ever happened to Frank Snake Church?
Alexie, S. What you pawn I will redeem
Barrett, N., Jr. Winter on the Belle Fourche
Bradbury, R. Hail to the chief
Brand, M. O. Closer than you think
Carroll, L. Leaving paradise
Chacón, D. Expression of our people
Coldsmith, D. First horse
Coldsmith, D. The guardians
Cummins, A. Bitterwater
Cummins, A. The Shiprock Fair
Cummins, A. Trapeze
De Lint, C. Making a noise in this world
Eickhoff, R. L. Dove's song
Endrezze, A. The humming of stars and bees and waves
Erdrich, L. Le mooz
Erdrich, L. Saint Marie
Erdrich, L. Shamengwa
Gansworth, E. L. The Raleigh Man
Gulick, B. The shaming of broken horn
Haake, K. All this land
Harrison, J. Westward ho
Henry, W. The skinning of Black Coyote
Hogan, L. Amen
Iagnemma, K. The Indian agent
Jakes, J. Manitow and Ironhand
Kees, W. The ceremony
L'Amour, L. The moon of the trees broken by snow
Lopez, B. H. Emory Bear Hands' birds
Lopez, B. H. In the great bend of the Souris River
Ludington, M. Thaw

Morgan, R. The tracks of Chief de Soto
Ortiz, S. J. Crossing
Ortiz, S. J. Hiding, west of here
Ortiz, S. J. Home country
Ortiz, S. J. Howbah Indians
Ortiz, S. J. Kaiser and the War
Ortiz, S. J. The killing of a state cop
Ortiz, S. J. Loose
Ortiz, S. J. Men on the moon
Ortiz, S. J. More than anything else in the world
Ortiz, S. J. The panther waits
Ortiz, S. J. Pennstuwehniyaahtse: Quuti's story
Ortiz, S. J. Something's going on
Ortiz, S. J. To change life in a good way
Ortiz, S. J. What Indians do
Ortiz, S. J. Woman singing
Ortiz, S. J. You were real, the white radical said to me
Penn, W. S. This is the world
Penn, W. S. Toothpaste
Power, S. Roofwalker
Rusch, K. K. Monuments to the dead
Salisbury, R. Hoopa, the white deer dance
Sanders, W. The undiscovered
Sanders, W. When this world is all on fire
Savage, L., Jr. The Lone Star camel corps
Singleton, G. Public relations
Smith, T. D. The purification of Jim Barnes
Sneve, V. D. H. Clean hands
Sneve, V. D. H. The first Christmas
Sneve, V. D. H. Fool soldiers
Sneve, V. D. H. Jimmy Yellow Hawk
Sneve, V. D. H. The medicine bag
Sneve, V. D. H. The slim butte ghost
Sneve, V. D. H. The twelve moons
Tenn, W. Eastward ho!
Vasseur, T. J. The enduring nights of Sidney Wingcloud
Winter, E. A color of sky
Winter, E. Spin cycle
Captivities
Schaefer, J. W. Sergeant Houck
Legends
Cady, J. The time that time forgot
Momaday, N. S. The transformation
Sneve, V. D. H. All the time in the world
Sneve, V. D. H. Badlands bones
Sneve, V. D. H. The flower nation
Sneve, V. D. H. The speck in the sky
Sneve, V. D. H. Sun gazer
Sneve, V. D. H. Takoza said "goo"
Sneve, V. D. H. The tribe of the burnt thigh
Sneve, V. D. H. The white buffalo calf woman
Trevanian. How the animals got their voices
Rites and ceremonies
Dann, J. Bad medicine
California
Ortiz, S. J. The San Francisco Indians
Steinbeck, T. The dark watcher
Maine
Wuori, G. K. Golden
Wuori, G. K. Skunk
Massachusetts
Updike, J. The Indian
Updike, J. the Indian
New Mexico
Tomlinson, N. C. The pretty surprise
Pacific Northwest
Dauenhauer, N. Egg boat

INDIANS OF NORTH AMERICA—*Continued*
South Dakota
Sneve, V. D. H. Grandpa was a cowboy and an Indian

INDIANS OF SOUTH AMERICA
Lojo, Maria Rosa. Compound eyes
Shua, A. M. The white Guanaco in the middle of France

The **indifferent** man. Proust, M.
Indigenous girls. Depew, D. R.
Indiscreet. Lee, W. W.
Indisposed. Banks, R.

INDOCHINA
See also Vietnam

The **Indonesian** client. Glover, D. H.
Indra Gets Caught. Kapur, K.
Indulgence. Casey, M.

INDUSTRIAL PAINTERS
Bausch, R. Luck
Michaels, L. Going places
Reid, E. Dryfall
Singleton, G. Caulk

INDUSTRIALISTS See Capitalists and financiers
Ineluctable modality of the vaginal. Moody, R.
Inertia. Kress, N.
Inertia. Rucker, R. v. B.
Inertia. Wunder, W.
An **inexplicable** phenomenon. Lugones, L.
The **infamous** fall of Howell the clown. Beattie, A.
The **infant**. Gavell, M. L.
Infant sorrow. Frym, G.
Infante, G. Cabrera See Cabrera Infante, G. (Guillermo), 1929-

INFANTICIDE
Boyle, T. C. The love of my life
Cacek, P. D. The grave
Chekhov, A. P. Sleepy
Jackson, V. F. Imagining friends
James, H. The author of "Beltraffio"
LaValle, V. D. Kids on Colden Street
Maraini, D. He is eleven years old, his name is Tano
Nailah, A. Sunday visit
Thrasher, L. L. Sacrifice

INFANTS
Anderson, P. The queen of air and darkness
Boylan, C. The stolen child
Budnitz, J. Hershel
Busch, F. The baby in the box
Carlson, R. Blood
Evenson, B. Virtual
Kalu, Anthonia C. Ogbanje father
Klass, P. Dedication
Norris, L. Wind across the breaks
Potvin, E. A. Infant colic: What it is and what you can do about it
Reifler, N. Baby
Slavin, J. Babyproofing
Sneve, V. D. H. Takoza said "goo"
Svoboda, T. Lost the baby
Vukcevich, R. Poop
White, M. C. The smell of life
Whitty, J. The daguerrotype
An **infatuation**. Chaudhuri, A.
The **infection** scene. Leavitt, D.
Infestation. Aylett, S.
The **infiltrator**. Shirazi, S.
The **infinite** passion of expectation. Berriault, G.

The **infinite** shades of white. Conroy, T.
Infinity of angles. Lowenthal, M.
Influence. Cohen, R.
Information. Babel´, I.

INFORMERS
See also Treason
Kress, N. The flowers of Aulit Prison

Ingenito-DeSio, Len
A really weird thing happened recently
Men on men 2000; best new gay fiction for the millennium; edited and with an introduction by David Bergman and Karl Woelz

Ingram, Willis J. *See* Harris, Mark, 1922-
The **ingrate**. Dunbar, P. L.

Ings, Simon
Russian vine
The Year's best science fiction, nineteenth annual collection; edited by Gardner Dozois

Inheritance. Clarke, A. C.
The **inheritance**. Gildner, G.
The **inheritance**. Goran, L.
The **inheritance**. Kavaler, R.

INHERITANCE AND SUCCESSION
See also Wills
Aldrich, B. S. The heirs
Archer, J. The endgame
Baca, J. S. The importance of a piece of paper
Beck, K. K. The tell-tale tattoo
Cannon, T. Restitution
Caudwell, S. The triumph of Eve
Collins, B. The night it rained cats and cats
Collins, B. The ten lives of Talbert
Davidson, A. The deed of the deft-footed dragon
Davidson, A. Murder is murder
Davies, R. The dilemma of Catherine Fuchsias
Hamilton, L. Stark terror at tea-time
Highsmith, P. Born failure
Jacobs, J. Built upon the sand
James, D. All in the family
James, H. A passionate pilgrim
James, S. A house of one's own
Kelman, J. The grapes of Roth
Lee, W. W. Life of Riley
Nichols, J. The rain barrel
Nikas, E. Fatal tears
Reiner, C. Hampa Ham
Shawl, N. The tawny bitch
Spencer, E. The legacy
Swan, G. Backtracking
Waugh, E. Period piece
Wharton, E. Sanctuary
Youmans, C. Mortmain
The **inheritance** of my father: a story for listening. Roemer, A.
Iniki Chicken. Hamby, B.
Initial consultation. Huffman, B., Jr.
Initials etched on a dining-room table, Lockeport, Nova Scotia. Orner, P.
Intimate obsession. Randisi, R. J.
Inland, shoreline. Godfrey, D. O.
Inn. Willis, C.
Inner Chesapeake. Luther, J.
The **inner** child. Galef, D.
The **inner** inner city. Wilson, R. C.
INNKEEPERS See Hotels, taverns, etc.
Innocence. Brodkey, H.
Innocence and longing. Holleran, A.
An **innocent** bystander. Krist, G.

Innocents abroad. Rowan, Q.

INNS *See* Hotels, taverns, etc.

Inocente's getaway. Björkquist, E. D.

An **inopportune** visit. Bowles, P.

Inquest in Zion. Blum, I. B.

INSANE, CRIMINAL AND DANGEROUS
 See also Insanity; Mentally ill
 Carlson, R. The chromium hook
 Correa, A. The merry ghosts of the Grampus
 Davies, R. Return to Waterloo
 Davis, D. S. Miles to go
 Hensley, J. L. Argent blood
 Hensley, J. L. Whistler
 King, S. The shining [excerpt]
 Lansdale, J. R. God of the razor
 Laymon, R. Hammerhead
 Newman, K. You don't have to be mad . . .
 Pronzini, B. Mrs. Rakubian
 Smith, M. M. The book of irrational numbers

INSANE ASYLUMS *See* Mentally ill—Care and treatment

INSANITY
 See also Insane, Criminal and dangerous; Mental illness; Personality disorders
 Alas, L. "My funeral"
 Anderson, R. Ice age
 Bernhard, T. Amras
 Bernhard, T. Walking
 Bowles, P. If I should open my mouth
 Bowles, P. You are not I
 Bradbury, R. The smiling people
 Bradbury, R. The square pegs
 Burleson, D. R. The watcher at the window
 Collins, M. Homecoming
 Connor, J. The poet's lobster
 Evenson, B. The installation
 Fleming, R. Bordering on the divine
 Fleming, R. Life after bas
 Hautala, R. Knocking
 Hawthorne, N. Egotism; or, The bosom serpent
 Leiber, F. Sanity
 Lugones, L. Psychon
 Malzberg, B. N. Final war
 Pronzini, B. The REC field
 Pronzini, B. and Malzberg, B. N. Another burnt-out case
 Singer, I. B. The slaughterer
 Spark, M. The leaf-sweeper
 Watson, I. Tulips from Amsterdam
 Westlake, D. E. One on a desert island

Inscrutable. Gores, J.

INSECTS
 Barrett, N., Jr. Diner
 Butler, O. E. Bloodchild
 Chiappone, R. A girl, the jungle, monkeys
 Clarke, A. C. The awakening
 Wilson, R. C. Protocols of consumption

Insects. Bradford, A.

Insects in amber. Rosenfeld, S.

INSEMINATION, ARTIFICIAL *See* Artificial insemination

Inside evidence. Wellen, E.

Inside her, in heaven. Painter, P.

Inside information. Barker, N.

Inside out. Addonizio, K.

Inside out. Nailah, A.

Inside out. Offutt, C.

Inside out. Rucker, R. v. B.

Inside passage. Armstrong, K.

Inside the cackle factory. Etchison, D.

Inside the whale; or, I don't know but I've been told. Weldon, F.

An **insignificant** crime. O'Callaghan, M.

An **insoluble** problem of genetics. Škvorecký, J.

INSOMNIA
 Meinke, P. Unheard music
 Millhauser, S. Clair de lune
 Patterson, K. Insomnia, infidelity, and the leopard seal
 Shankman, S. Love thy neighbor
 Tillman, L. Dead sleep
 White, M. C. The cardiologist's house

Insomnia. Smith, C.

Insomnia, infidelity, and the leopard seal. Patterson, K.

An **Inspector** in Palestine. Wilson, J.

Inspector remorse. Weldon, F.

INSPIRATION *See* Creation (Literary, artistic, etc.)

Inspiration. Babel', I.

Inspiriter. Kilpatrick, N.

Instability. Rucker, R. v. B.

The **Installation**. Evenson, B.

Instinct. Franklin, T.

Instinct. Mayor, A.

Instincts. White, M. C.

Instructions. Derby, M.

Instructions for a single man. Jesús, P. d.

Instructor. Barthelme, F.

The **instructor**. Oates, J. C.

INSTRUCTORS *See* Teachers

The **instrumentalina**. Jorge, L.

The **instruments** of peace. Falco, E.

Instruments of torture. Greenwood, T.

Insulation. DeMarinis, R.

Insulted. Čapek, K.

Insulting the Angels. Hoffman, A.

INSURANCE
 Gilchrist, E. The uninsured
 Gurganus, A. Blessed assurance: a moral tale
 Johnston, B. A. Two liars
 Scholz, C. The amount to carry

INSURANCE BROKERS
 Cavell, B. The death of cool
 Gordimer, N. Karma
 Rinehart, S. LeSabre
 Westlake, D. E. The risk profession

INTELLECTUALS
 See also Scholars
 Alas, L. A day laborer
 Bellow, S. Mosby's memoirs
 Herling, G. Ashes: the fall of the House of Loris
 Škvorecký, J. Filthy cruel world

INTELLIGENCE AGENTS *See* Secret service

The **intelligence** of wild things. Divakaruni, C. B.

Intensive care. Smith, L.

Intent to kill. Quill, M.

INTER-RACIAL MARRIAGE *See* Interracial marriage

Interesting women. Lee, A.

The **interior** castle. Stafford, J.

Interior country. Norris, L.

The **interloper**. Borges, J. L.

The **interlude**. Auchincloss, L.

Interlude. Penn, W. S.

Intermittent waves of unusual size and force. Richmond, M.

Internal medicine. Sosin, D.
An **international** episode. James, H.
INTERNATIONAL INTRIGUE
    See also Adventure; Secret service; Spies
  Garfield, B. Charlie's game
  Harrison, P. Zero-G dogfight
INTERNATIONAL MARRIAGES
  Browder, C. When Luz sings her solo
  Desai, A. Winterscape
  Gabriel, D. Irina's lullaby
  Jacobs, M. Down in Paraguay
  James, H. Lady Barberina
  James, H. The last of the Valerii
  James, H. Madame de Mauves
  James, H. The siege of London
  Johnson-Davies, D. Coffee at the Marriott
  Lee, A. Brothers and sisters around the world
  Melville, P. The migration of ghosts
  Viswanathan, L. Cool wedding
The **internationale**. Earle, S.
INTERPLANETARY TRAVEL *See* Interplanetary voyages
INTERPLANETARY VISITORS
    See also Martians
  Aldrich, B. S. The outsider
  Almond, S. The soul molecule
  Anderson, P. Delenda est
  Anderson, P. The shrine for lost children
  Barrett, N., Jr. Class of '61
  Barrett, N., Jr. Perpetuity blues
  Bates, H. Farewell to the master
  Baxter, S. Cilia-of-gold
  Bell, D. A. The space traders
  Benedict, P. Zog-19: a scientific romance
  Benford, G. Doing alien
  Benford, G. A fairhope alien
  Bisson, T. Tell them they are all full of shit and they should fuck off
  Blish, J. Get out of my sky
  Bradbury, R. The city
  Bradbury, R. February 1999: Y11a
  Bradbury, R. Mars is heaven!
  Bradbury, R. A matter of taste
  Bradbury, R. Zero hour
  Broderick, D. The womb
  Campbell, J. W. Who goes there?
  Charnas, S. M. Listening to Brahms
  Chiang, T. Story of your life
  Clarke, A. C. Guardian angel
  Clarke, A. C. The possessed
  Clarke, A. C. Publicity campaign
  Clarke, A. C. Rescue party
  Clarke, A. C. Security check
  Clarke, A. C. Trouble with the natives
  Correa, H. When Pilate said no
  Crane, M. The blood orange tree
  Crowley, J. Gone
  Del Rey, L. For I am a jealous people!
  Doctorow, C. Craphound
  Dowling, T. Flashmen
  Dozois, G. R. A cat horror story
  Eakin, W. Encounter in Redgunk
  Eakin, W. Homesickness
  Eakin, W. Plain female seeks nice guy
  Edghill, R. We have met the enemy
  Effinger, G. A. One
  Fairman, P. W. The cosmic frame
  Fleming, R. The astral visitor Delta blues
  Frahm, L. Borderline

  Gloss, M. Lambing season
  Hamilton, E. Devolution
  Harrison, H. An artist's life
  Harrison, H. Rescue operation
  Harrison, H. Survival planet
  Hoffman, N. K. Between disappearances
  Ings, S. Russian vine
  Jorgenson, I. Deadly city
  Kilpatrick, N. Alien love
  Kilpatrick, N. Metal fatigue
  Koja, K. and Malzberg, B. N. What we did that summer
  Kress, N. The most famous little girl in the world
  Kress, N. Savior
  Landis, G. A. Impact parameter
  Link, K. Most of my friends are two-thirds water
  Lupoff, R. A. Documents in the case of Elizabeth Akeley
  Lupoff, R. A. Lux was dead right
  Lupoff, R. A. The turret
  MacLeod, K. The human front
  Malzberg, B. N. Something from the seventies
  Matera, L. If it can't be true
  Matheson, R. Being
  Matheson, R. One for the books
  Matheson, R. Trespass
  McBride, S. The fragrance of orchids
  McDonald, I. Tendeléo's story
  Nelson, R. F. Eight o'clock in the morning
  Niven, L. Smut talk
  Oliver, C. The ant and the eye
  Oliver, C. Of course
  Oliver, C. The one that got away
  Oliver, C. RIte of passage
  Oliver, C. To whom it may concern
  Oliver, C. Transfusion
  Oltion, J. Much ado about nothing
  Padgett, L. The twonky
  Philp, G. Uncle Obadiah and the alien
  Pronzini, B. The Hungarian cinch
  Pronzini, B. and Malzberg, B. N. Fascination
  Pronzini, B. and Malzberg, B. N. In our image
  Pronzini, B. and Malzberg, B. N. The last one left
  Reed, R. Decency
  Reed, R. Guest of honor
  Reed, R. To church with Mr. Multhiford
  Reed, R. The utility man
  Richter, S. A prodigy of longing
  Rucker, R. v. B. The facts of life
  Rucker, R. v. B. Inside out
  Rucker, R. v. B. Jumpin' Jack Flash
  Rucker, R. v. B. Pac-Man
  Rucker, R. v. B. Pi in the sky
  Rucker, R. v. B. Plastic letters
  Rucker, R. v. B. Wishloop
  Russ, J. Souls
  Sheckley, R. The day the aliens came
  Sheckley, R. Dukakis and the aliens
  Sheckley, R. Emissary from a green and yellow world
  Silverberg, R. Amanda and the alien
  Simmons, D. On K2 with kanakaredes
  Tavares, B. Stuntmind
  Tenn, W. Bernie the Faust
  Tenn, W. Betelgeuse Bridge
  Tenn, W. Firewater

INTERPLANETARY VISITORS—*Continued*
  Tenn, W. The flat-eyed monster
  Tenn, W. The liberation of earth
  Tenn, W. "Will you walk a little faster"
  Tiptree, J. The only neat thing to do
  Turner, G. Flowering mandrake
  Turtledove, H. The road not taken
  Vinge, V. Conquest by default
  Vinge, V. Gemstone
  Vinge, V. Original sin
  Watson, I. The descent
  Watson, I. Such dedication
  Wilson, R. C. The Perseids
  Yolen, J. Sister Emily's lightship
INTERPLANETARY VOYAGES
        See also Science fiction; Space flight
  Anderson, P. Gypsy
  Bear, G. Perihesperon
  Bradbury, R. G.B.S.- Mark V
  Cherryh, C. J. Pots
  Cherryh, C. J. Poys
  Clarke, A. C. Breaking strain
  Clarke, A. C. Crusade
  Finlay, C. C. The political officer
  Godwin, T. The cold equations
  Pohl, F. The gold at the starbow's end
  Reynolds, A. Galactic north
  Tenn, W. Alexander the bait
  Tenn, W. Venus is a man's world
  Van Vogt, A. E. Far centaurus
INTERPLANETARY WARS
  Bear, G. Hardfought
  Brown, F. Arena
  Card, O. S. Ender's game
  Daniel, T. A dry, quiet war
  Drake, D. Choosing sides
  Drake, D. The end
  Drake, D. Mission accomplished
  Drake, D. Neck or nothing
  Drake, D. The political process
  Drake, D. Rescue mission
  Drake, D. Smash and grab
  Drake, D. Team effort
  Drake, D. When the devil drives
  Green, R. J. Deck load strike
  Martin, G. R. R. The hero
  McAuley, P. J. The passenger
  Reed, R. Waging good
  Van Vogt, A. E. The rull
  Vance, J. The miracle workers
  Waldrop, H. Men of Greywater Station
Interpol: the case of the modern medusa. Hoch, E. D.
Interposition. Patterson, K.
Interpreter of maladies. Lahiri, J.
INTERPRETERS *See* Translators
INTERRACIAL MARRIAGE
  Alexie, S. Assimilation
  Chopin, K. Désirée's baby
  Davies, P. H. The Hull case
  Gilliland, G. News of the world
  Jen, G. House, house, home
  Jen, G. Who's Irish?
  Karodia, F. The woman in green
  Lee, A. Brothers and sisters around the world
  McPherson, J. A. Elbow room
  Miller, A. L. A cold winter light
  Oates, J. C. Fugitive

  Roemer, A. The inheritance of my father: a story for listening
  Sherwood, F. History
  Shwartz, S. Suppose they gave a peace
  Walker, A. Kindred spirits
  Walker, A. To my young husband
Interregnum. Naiyer Masud
The **interruption**. Means, D.
Intersection. Liu Yichang
Intersection. Robinson, R.
The **intersection** of Anastasia Yeoman and light. Edghill, R.
Intersections. Bottoms, G.
Interstate. Kudritzki, J.
INTERSTELLAR COLONIES *See* Space colonies
Intervention. Flanagan, E.
Intervention. McCorkle, J.
The **intervention**. Newman, K.
The **intervention**. Walbert, K.
The **interview**. McBain, E.
Interview: on any given day. McHugh, M. F.
An **interview** with Diane Fox. Higgins, G. V.
An **interview** with my husband. Di Blasi, D.
INTERVIEWING
  Boylan, C. Bad-natured dog
  Hearon, S. A prince of a fellow [excerpt]
  Lessing, D. M. One off the short list
  McBain, E. The interview
INTERVIEWS (STORIES IN INTERVIEW FORM)
  Irsfeld, J. H. Interview with Jordan Baker
The **intervillage** bus. Müller, H.
Intimacy. Carver, R.
Intimacy. Klass, P.
Intimacy. Kureishi, H.
Into a mirror. Lowenthal, M.
Into Greenwood. Grimsley, J.
Into many a green valley. Kennedy, R.
Into the abyss. Lewis, R. J.
Into the blue abyss. Landis, G. A.
Into the comet. Clarke, A. C.
Into the house of desire: a Ceylonese riddle in fourteen parts. Meidav, E.
Into the rhythm. Kelman, J.
Into the Standing Corn. Rybicki, J.
Into this house. Lundquist, R.
Intra muros populis. Ferko, A.
Intramuros. Murray, S.
The **intransigents**. Malzberg, B. N.
Intro to acting. Cooper, B.
The **introducers**. Wharton, E.
The **intruder**. Gates, D.
The **intruder**. Traver, R.
INUIT
  Osgood, L. Great Sedna
Invaders. Carson, J.
INVALIDS
        See also Paraplegics
  Borges, J. L. The south
  Bowen, R. O. A matter of price
  Boylan, C. Mama
  Chopin, K. A family affair
  Cobb, W. J. Father tongue
  Fitzgerald, F. S. The lees of happiness
  Highsmith, P. The pianos of the Steinachs
  James, H. Longstaff's marriage
  James, H. A most extraordinary case
  James, H. A passionate pilgrim

INVALIDS—*Continued*
Reid, E. No strings attached
Rendell, R. Burning end
Troy, J. Ramone
INVENTIONS
Clarke, A. C. Patent pending
Clarke, A. C. Silence please
Clarke, A. C. The steam-powered word processor
Clarke, A. C. The ultimate melody
Harrison, H. Toy shop
Lugones, L. The Omega Force
Sturgeon, T. Microcosmic god
Updike, J. The invention of the horse collar
Westlake, D. E. The burglar and the whatsit
The **inventor** of love. Brownstein, G.
Inventories. Ritchie, E.
INVENTORS
Clarke, A. C. Moving spirit
Davidson, A. The engine of Samoset Erastus Hale, and one other, unknown
Haslett, A. Notes to my biographer
Jensen, J. L. The secret history of the ornithopter
Knight, D. F. I see you
Lafferty, R. A. Eurema's dam
Lugones, L. Psychon
Sturgeon, T. Slow sculpture
Wieland, L. Gray's anatomy
Williamson, J. With folded hands
Inventory. Davidson, R.
Inversion. Rosenfeld, S.
Inversion. Spatz, G.
The **investigation.** Saer, J. J.
Investigations of a tourist by Mrs. Wendell A. Prescott. Zadoorian, M.
The **investigator.** Fromm, P.
Investment counselor. Card, O. S.
INVESTMENTS
Bail, M. Ore
Beaty, D. Ghosts
DeMarco, T. Dancing bare
Vonnegut, K. Custom-made bride
Vonnegut, K. Unpaid consultant
INVISIBILITY
Dozois, G. R. The visible man
Lansdale, J. R. Listen
Link, K. Vanishing act
Pronzini, B. The man who collected "The Shadow"
Scarborough, E. A. The invisible woman's clever disguise
Invisible country. Gonzalez, R.
The **invisible** Dutchman and his dog. Lock, N.
The **invisible** mine. Ben-Tov, S.
The **invisible** spy. DuBois, B.
The **invisible** woman's clever disguise. Scarborough, E. A.
The **invisibles.** De Lint, C.
Invitation to a poisoning. Tremayne, P.
Invitation to the ball. Malone, M.
Inviting Blindness. Crane, D.
Inyama, Nnadozie
Hot days, long nights
The Anchor book of modern African stories; edited by Nadežda Obradovic ; with a foreword by Chinua Achebe
The **Ionian** cycle. Tenn, W.
Ionitch. Chekhov, A. P.

Iorillo, Joseph
Vesper tolls
Tales from The Dark Tower; illustrated by Joseph Vargo; edited by Joseph Vargo and Christine Filipak
Iorillo, Joseph and Pipik, James
Shadows
Tales from The Dark Tower; illustrated by Joseph Vargo; edited by Joseph Vargo and Christine Filipak
IOWA
Agee, J. Aronson's Orchard
Agee, J. What the Fall brings
Evans, E. Beautiful land
Gorman, E. The way it used to be
Holleran, A. The boxer
Wilson, R., Jr. Parts runner
Farm life
See Farm life—Iowa
Iowa winter. Becker, G.
IRA *See* Irish Republican Army
IRAN
Ahmadi Khorasani, N. That day
Aqai, F. One woman, one love
Arastuyi, S. I came to have tea with my daughter
Bahrami, A. Lida's cat, the bakery, and the streetlight pole
Bahrami, M. The end, a city
Fadavi, P. The bitter life of Shirin
Hajizadeh, F. Contrary to democracy
Hejazi, K. Cling to life with your whole body
Mahmudi, S. The Fin Garden of Kashan
Sari, F. The absent soldier
Sharifzadeh, M. Butterflies
Tabatabai, N. The lark
Taraqqi, G. Father
Taraqqi, G. Grandma's house
Taraqqi, G. The maid
Taraqqi, G. A mansion in the sky
Taraqqi, G. The Shemiran bus
Yasrebi, C. Love and scream
Prisoners and prisons
See Prisoners and prisons—Iran
IRANIANS
France
Taraqqi, G. The bizarre comportment of Mr. Alpha in exile
Taraqqi, G. My little friend
United States
Anderson, D. The peacock throne
Moss, B. K. Rug weaver
Mullins, M. The rug
IRAQ
Haschemeyer, O. The storekeeper
The **ire** of the Veksi. Le Guin, U. K.
IRELAND
See also Northern Ireland
Boylan, C. A particular calling
Bradbury, R. Banshee
Bradbury, R. One for his lordship, and one for the road
Connor, J. Good people
Trevor, W. Sacred statues
Trevor, W. The Virgin's gift
To 1172
Borges, J. L. The mirror and the mask
19th century
Clark, S. Fenian ram

IRELAND—*Continued*

20th century

Adams, J. Stealing the dark

Deane, J. F. Nighthawk

Donoghue, E. Looking for Petronilla

Lavin, M. The convent

Lavin, M. The joy-ride

Lavin, M. Lemonade

Lavin, M. Tom

Ryan, M. Murder in Kilcurry

Smyth, C. Near the bone

Trevor, W. Low Sunday, 1950

Farm life

See Farm life—Ireland

Rural life

Bradbury, R. The first night of Lent

Bradbury, R. The great collision of Monday last

Deane, J. F. Capital H

Deane, J. F. The coffin master

Deane, J. F. A migrant bird

Kavanagh, H. T. The banshee's comb

Keegan, C. The burning palms

Keegan, C. The Ginger Rogers sermon

Keegan, C. Love in the tall grass

Keegan, C. Men and women

Keegan, C. Sisters

Keegan, C. Storms

Le Fanu, J. S. The child that went with the fairies

Masterton, G. The Ballyhooly boy

McCabe, P. The hands of Dingo Deery

McCann, C. As Kingfishers catch fire

McCann, C. Fishing the sloe-black river

O'Brien, E. A rose in the heart of New York

Trevor, W. Of the cloth

Waugh, E. Bella Fleace gave a party

Cork (County)

Honig, L. The sights of Cork

Dublin

Bradbury, R. The beggar on O'Connell Bridge

Bradbury, R. The cold wind and the warm

Bradbury, R. Getting through Sunday somehow

Brennan, M. The beginning of a long story

Brennan, M. The holy terror

Doyle, R. The slave

In the prison of his days

Lavin, M. In a café

Tóibín, C. The heather blazing [excerpt]

Galway

Bradbury, R. A wild night in Galway

Lordan, B. The man with the lapdog

Iribarne, Matthew

Astronauts

  Iribarne, M. Astronauts & other stories

The clear blue water

  Iribarne, M. Astronauts & other stories

A dream, not alone

  Iribarne, M. Astronauts & other stories

The gift

  Iribarne, M. Astronauts & other stories

Make them laugh

  Iribarne, M. Astronauts & other stories

Ross Willow's new and used cars

  Iribarne, M. Astronauts & other stories

Sudden mysteries

  Iribarne, M. Astronauts & other stories

  New England Review v22 no2 p187-201 Spr 2001

The sun in the sky

  Iribarne, M. Astronauts & other stories

Wedding dance

  Iribarne, M. Astronauts & other stories

Irina's lullaby. Gabriel, D.

Iris. Greenleaf, S.

Irish, William, 1903-1968

  For works written by this author under other names see Woolrich, Cornell, 1903-1968

IRISH

Egypt

Johnson-Davies, D. The dream

England

Binchy, M. Shepherd's Bush

Boylan, C. Thatcher's Britain

Coward, M. So where've you buried the missus then, Paddy?

MacLaverty, B. Between two shores

Trevor, W. The mourning

Spain

Azadeh, C. Bronagh

United States

Carlson, P. M. The world is mine; or, Deeds that make heaven weep

Delaney, E. J. The drowning

Delaney, E. J. A visit to my uncle

Hogan, D. The bombs

Howard, M. The Magdalene

Lavin, M. The little prince

Lavin, M. Tom

Lerner, M. Little selves

Sweeney, E. Lord McDonald

IRISH AMERICANS

Aldrich, B. S. Trust the Irish for that

Allyn, D. Black Irish

Brady, C. And the shin bone's connected to the knee bone

Brady, C. Don't run

Brady, C. Rumpelstiltskin

Delaney, E. J. Hero

Delaney, E. J. O beauty! o truth!

DuBois, B. The wearing of the green

Goran, L. Adventurer

Goran, L. Alias Eleanor Roosevelt

Goran, L. The Big Broadcasts

Goran, L. The chorus girl

Goran, L. The death of the quarterback

Goran, L. A guest on Good Friday

Goran, L. The inheritance

Goran, L. Keeping count

Goran, L. O'Casey and the career

Goran, L. An old man and three whores

Goran, L. Outlaws of the Purple Cow

Goran, L. Say something to Miss Kathleen Lacey

Goran, L. Why he never left his wife

Hayes, J. G. Regular Flattop

Hoch, E. D. Great day for the Irish

Jen, G. Who's Irish?

Lordan, B. Digging

Irish girl. Johnston, T.

Irish Lesson. Mullen, J.

IRISH REPUBLICAN ARMY

Devlin, A. Naming the names

Iron child. Mo Yan

The **iron** fist of oligarchy. Harris, M.

IRONY

Avrich, J. The charwoman

IRONY—*Continued*

Bester, A. Disappearing act

Borges, J. L. The Sect of the Thirty

Bowles, P. The wind at Beni Midar

Byatt, A. S. Baglady

Capote, T. A mink of one's own

Chekhov, A. P. The bet

Davidson, A. The cost of Kent Castwell

Davidson, A. The necessity of his condition

Fitzgerald, F. S. The smilers

Grau, S. A. Homecoming

Lutz, J. Pure rotten

Pronzini, B. Bank job

Pronzini, B. Connoisseur

Roth, J. Stationmaster Fallmerayer

Scholz, C. The menageries of Babel

Slesar, H. The day of the execution

Tenn, W. Eastward ho!

Tyre, N. A nice place to stay

Valenzuela, L. Who, me a bum?

Waugh, E. Bella Fleace gave a party

Waugh, E. Love in the slump

Wharton, E. A cup of cold water

Irony, irony, irony. Nelson, A.

Irradiation. Wieland, L.

Irsfeld, John H.

Ambivalence Hardy Fire

Irsfeld, J. H. Radio Elvis and other stories

The chance

Irsfeld, J. H. Radio Elvis and other stories

Death of a soldier

Irsfeld, J. H. Radio Elvis and other stories

Finderkeepers

Irsfeld, J. H. Radio Elvis and other stories

Have you knocked on Cleopatra?

Irsfeld, J. H. Radio Elvis and other stories

The horse fountain

Irsfeld, J. H. Radio Elvis and other stories

Interview with Jordan Baker

Irsfeld, J. H. Radio Elvis and other stories

It's fun to say yes, but sometimes you just got to say no

Irsfeld, J. H. Radio Elvis and other stories

The man who watched airplanes

Irsfeld, J. H. Radio Elvis and other stories

The marriage auditors

Irsfeld, J. H. Radio Elvis and other stories

My neighbor Mr. Young

Irsfeld, J. H. Radio Elvis and other stories

Puerto Rico '61

Irsfeld, J. H. Radio Elvis and other stories

Radio Elvis

Irsfeld, J. H. Radio Elvis and other stories

Stop, rewind, and play

Irsfeld, J. H. Radio Elvis and other stories

Irvine, Alex

The sea wind offers little relief

Starlight 3; edited by Patrick Nielsen Hayden

Irvine, Alexander

Agent provocateur

The Year's best science fiction; twentieth annual collection; edited by Gardner Dozois

Irving, Washington

Rip Van Winkle

The American fantasy tradition; edited by Brian M. Thomsen

Is in the stars (for Lisa Photos). Fernández, R. G.

Les **is** more. Patterson, K.

Is you is or is you ain't Miranda? O'Callaghan, M.

Isaac. Blatnik, A.

Isaacs, Neil D.

The Swannanoa review

The Virginia Quarterly Review v75 no2 p280-91 Spr 1999

Isaacs, Susan

My cousin Rachel's Uncle Murray

Murder in the family; [by] the Adams Round Table

The **Isabel** Fish. Orringer, J.

Isabel of the fall. MacLeod, I.

Isaiah vll, 14. Krauze, E.

Ishiguro, Kazuo

A family supper

The Art of the story; an international anthology of contemporary short stories; edited by Daniel Halpern

A village after dark

The New Yorker v77 no12 p86-91 My 21 2001

ISLAM

See also Muslims

Kvashay-Boyle, K. Da bomb

Lawson, C. Written in blood

Turtledove, H. Islands in the sea

Island. MacLeod, A.

The **island** in the river. Holley, C.

An **island** of boyfriends. Richter, S.

The **island** of the day before yesterday. Stevenson, J.

The **Island** of the Immortals. Le Guin, U. K.

The **island** of the Ud. Hodgson, W. H.

Island of Three Pines. Walpole, P.

Island tales. Painter, P.

The **Islanders.** Greer, A. S.

ISLANDS

See also names of individual islands and groups of islands

Boyle, T. C. Swept away

Connor, J. The anecdote of the island

Connor, J. The last native

Connor, J. Summer girls

Deane, J. F. Capital H

Deane, J. F. The coffin master

DuBois, B. The tourist who wasn't there

Herling, G. Ashes: the fall of the House of Loris

Hermann, J. Hurricane (something farewell)

Hodgson, W. H. The call in the dawn

Høeg, P. Portrait of the avant-garde

Kaplan, H. Live life king-sized

Lawrence, D. H. The man who loved islands

Lumley, B. Rising with Surtsey

MacLeod, A. Island

Padilla, I. Time regained

Parker, M. Off island

Pronzini, B. Smuggler's island

Sandstrom, E. K. The people's way

Siodmak, C. FP 1 does not reply

Winterson, J. Turn of the world

Wolfe, G. The death of Doctor Island

The **islands.** Adams, A.

Islands. Hemon, A.

Islands in the sea. Turtledove, H.

ISLANDS OF THE PACIFIC

See also Solomon Islands

Armstrong, K. The cane field

ISLANDS OF THE PACIFIC—*Continued*
Hodgson, W. H. The island of the Ud
Russell, J. The knife
Van de Wetering, J. Lady Hillary
Isle, Ray
Wild turkey
  Texas bound. Book III; 22 Texas stories; ed-
  ited by Kay Cattarulla; foreword by Robert
  Flynn
The **Isle** of Dogs. Griesemer, J.
Isn't it romantic? Straub, P.
Isolation. Greer, R. O.
The **isolinguals**. De Camp, L. S.
ISRAEL
       See also Jerusalem
Appelfeld, A. Bertha
Buchan, J. Sleepwalkers
Englander, N. For the relief of unbearable urges
Goldstein, N. The conduct for consoling
Goldstein, N. A pillar of a cloud
Goldstein, N. The Roberto touch
Goldstein, N. The verse in the margins
Grossman, D. Yani on the mountain
Hendel, Y. Apples in honey
Hendel, Y. Fata morgana across the street
Hendel, Y. Late revenge
Hendel, Y. The leter that came in time
Hendel, Y. Low, close to the floor
Hendel, Y. My friend B's feast
Hendel, Y. Small change
Keret, E. Cocked and locked
Keret, E. The son of the Head of the Mossad
Latour, J. Golam
Leegant, J. The seventh year
Papernick, J. For as long as the lamp is burning
Papernick, J. The King of the King of Falafel
Papernick, J. Lucky eighteen
Papernick, J. Malchyk
Seltz, E. Compelle intrare
Setton, R. K. The cat garden
Shechter, Y. Midday
Singer, I. B. The mentor
Singer, I. B. The psychic journey
Stollman, A. L. The dialogues of time and en-
  tropy
Stollman, A. L. Mr. Mitochondria
Tammuz, B. The swimming race
Yehoshua, A. B. Facing the forests
       Tel Aviv
Almog, R. Shrinking
Lempel, Blume. Scenes on a bare canvas
Singer, I. B. Brother Beetle
Singer, I. B. Two markets
Israel. Hughes, M.-B.
Israel and Ernest. Cady, J.
ISRAEL-ARAB WAR, 1948-1949
Yizhar, S. The prisoner
ISRAELI SOLDIERS *See* Soldiers—Israel
ISRAELIS
       Canada
Auerbach, J. The border incident
       United States
Goldstein, N. The worker rests under the hero
  trees
Keret, E. Goodman
ISRAELITES *See* Jews
Issues I dealt with in therapy. Klam, M.
Issues I dealt with in therapy (I). Klam, M.
ISTANBUL (TURKEY) *See* Turkey—Istanbul

Istanbul 11 April. Bucak, A. P.
Istikhara, Anaya, Medagan and the Medaganat.
  Bowles, P.
It. Sturgeon, T.
It ain't hay. Wellen, E.
It comes back. Struloeff, J.
It comes with the badge. Kaminsky, S. M.
It Couldn't Be More Beautiful. Feitell, M.
It ends with a flicker. Tenn, W.
It goes rickety. Chapman, C. M.
It had to be you. Bukoski, A.
It had to be you. Pickard, N.
It happened at grandmother's house. Crider, B.
It happened to me once. Kelman, J.
It Is Not Entirely My Fault. Willoughby, J.
It is raining in Bejucal. Biguenet, J.
It Loses Its Grandeur. FitzSimons, M.
It might have been Jerusalem [excerpt] Healy, T.
It must burn. Lindskold, J. M.
It pours. Parrish, T.
It Says Here . . . Heath, A. B.
It takes one to kill one. O'Callaghan, M.
It wasn't Proust. Shepard, S.
ITALIAN AMERICANS
Hill, I. The ballad of Rappy Valcour
Hochman, A. Aggiornamento
Johnson, D. Markers
Lombreglia, R. Cashmere Christmas
Prete, D. After we left Yonkers and before we
  came back
Prete, D. The biggest, most silent thing
Prete, D. Bleachers
Prete, D. The itch
Prete, D. No king, no puppy
Prete, D. Not because I'm thirsty
Prete, D. Say that to my face
Prete, D. Self-respecting Neapolitans
Scibona, S. The plateform
Stanton, M. My death
Stanton, M. Squash flowers
The **Italian** legacy. Marías, J.
Italian sun. Babel´, I.
ITALIANS
       England
Foxwell, E. A Roman of no importance
Raphael, F. L.S.D.
       France
Marías, J. The Italian legacy
Marías, J. The night doctor
       Russia
Pushkin, A. S. Egyptian nights
ITALY
       See also Sicily
       15th century
Dann, J. Da Vinci rising
Griffen, C. Borgia by blood
       19th century
Davidson, A. Traveller from an antique land
James, H. Travelling companions
Lee, V. A wicked voice
Wharton, E. The letters
       20th century
Broughton, T. A. The terrorist
Calvino, I. Autumn
Gifford, B. A fair price
Maraini, D. Letters to Marina [excerpt]
Parks, J. A. The covenant of Il Vigneto
Steiber, E. The cats of San Martino

ITALY—*Continued*

Rural life

Herling, G. A hot breath from the desert

Herling, G. The Noonday Cemetery: an open story

James, H. At Isella

Lee, V. Amour dure

Vivante, A. Solitude

World War, 1939-1945

See World War, 1939-1945—Italy

Amalfi

Beattie, A. In Amalfi

Brescia

Davenport, G. The aeroplanes at Brescia

Florence

Bobes, M. Ten years later

Broughton, T. A. Italian autumn

Herling, G. Ashes: the fall of the House of Loris

James, H. The diary of a man of fifty

James, H. The madonna of the future

Milan

Lee, A. About fog and cappuccino

Lee, A. Full moon over Milan

Milletti, C. Villa of the veiled lady

Naples

Egan, J. Goodbye, my love

Girardi, R. Sunday evenings at Contessa Pasquali's

Herling, G. Don Ildebrando

Padua

Hawthorne, N. Rappaccini's daughter

Rome

Alcott, L. M. The rival painters: a tale of Rome

Barker, N. The Piazza Barberini

Cherryh, C. J. Nightgame

Gifford, B. Cat women of Rome

Herling, G. The height of summer: a Roman story

James, H. Daisy Miller: a study

James, H. The solution

Kennedy, A. L. Indelible acts

Kohler, S. The adulterous woman

Kohler, S. The original

Malamud, B. Still life

Tuck, L. L'Esprit de L'Escalier

Wharton, E. Roman fever

Siena

Boylan, C. Technical difficulties and the plague

Wharton, E. The House of the Dead Hand

Turin

Gomes, M. T. Cordelia

Tuscany

Meredith, D. The closer

Vivante, A. Fisherman's terrace

Vivante, A. The park

Vivante, A. Train ride of a faun

Venice

Cherryh, C. J. Masks

Delany, S. R. Cage of brass

James, H. The Aspern papers

Sheckley, R. Sightseeing, 2179

Wharton, E. A glimpse

White, E. A Venice story

Whitty, J. Stealing from the dead

Iterations. Keith, W. H.

Itinerary. Powers, T.

It's a deal. Highsmith, P.

It's a good life. Bixby, J.

It's a lot scarier if you take Jesus out. Spencer, D.

It's a wise child who knows. Kaminsky, S. M.

IT'S A WONDERFUL LIFE (MOTION PICTURE)

Willis, C. Miracle

It's a wonderful miracle on 34th Street's Christmas carol. Thomsen, B.

It's dark. DeLancey, K.

It's hard to dance with the devil on your back (with Rita A. Breen). Breen, J. L.

It's hard to figure how they know. McNulty, J.

It's her. Boylan, C.

It's life and death at the Slush Puppie Open. Touré

It's never too late to live. Aldrich, B. S.

It's raining out. Klíma, I.

It's such a beautiful day. Asimov, I.

It's water, it's not going to kill you. Sellers, H.

It's your move. L'Amour, L.

Itsy bitsy spider. Kelly, J. P.

Ivan and Ivan. Babel', I.

The **Ivan** and Maria. Babel', I.

Ivan Ivanovitch Kossiakoff. Giono, J.

"**Ivan** Yakovelevich Bobov woke up—". Kharms, D.

The **Ivans**. See Babel', I. Ivan and Ivan

I've got a sneaking idea; or, I'd just get me a lawyer. Drake, R.

I've got a sneaking idea that . . .; or, I'd just get me a lawyer. Drake, R.

IVES, CHARLES EDWARD, 1874-1954

About

Scholz, C. The amount to carry

Ivor's people. López, L.

Iwaszkiewicz, Jarosław

The birch grove

Iwaszkiewicz, J. The birch grove and other stories; translated by Antonia Lloyd-Jones ; with an introduction by Leszek Kołakowski

The mill on the River Utrata

Iwaszkiewicz, J. The birch grove and other stories; translated by Antonia Lloyd-Jones ; with an introduction by Leszek Kołakowski

A new love

Iwaszkiewicz, J. The birch grove and other stories; translated by Antonia Lloyd-Jones ; with an introduction by Leszek Kołakowski

The Wilko girls

Iwaszkiewicz, J. The birch grove and other stories; translated by Antonia Lloyd-Jones ; with an introduction by Leszek Kołakowski

The **IWM** 1000. Yánez Cossío, A.

Ixion. Swarthout, G. F.

Iyer, Pico

A walk in Kurama

Nixon under the bodhi tree and other works of Buddhist fiction; edited by Kate Wheeler ; foreword by Charles Johnson

Izzy's shoe-in. Elrod, P. N.

J

J. D. Rooke, L.

Jablonsky, William

A Fear of Falling

Southern Humanities Review v36 no4 p363-73 Fall 2002

Jack and Jill, R.I.P. Gash, J.

Jack and the mountain pink. MacDowell, K. S. B.

Jack be quick. Paul, B.

Jack Daw's pack. Gilman, G.

Jack Frost. Jacobsen, J.

Jack in Chicago. Smith, S. J.

The **Jack** Kerouac disembodied school of poetics. Rucker, R. v. B.

Jack Landers is my friend. Stolar, D.

Jack of diamonds. Spencer, E.

JACK THE RIPPER

About

Hensley, J. L. Truly yours, John R. Jacks

Paul, B. Jack be quick

Jackalope. Foster, A. D.

JACKALS

Oz, A. Where the jackals howl

Jackdaw Jack. Harman, C.

Jacket copy. Cady, J.

Jackie and the beanstalk. Rollins, H.

Jacko's reach. Malouf, D.

Jackson, Carla Jean *See* Tangh, Jarla

Jackson, Gale

Wedding symphony

The Bluelight corner; black women writing on passion, sex, and romantic love; edited by Rosemarie Robotham

Jackson, Kerri Anne

Natsumi Quarra

The North American Review v288 no6 p32-5 N/D 2003

Jackson, Shelley

Blood

Jackson, S. The melancholy of anatomy; stories

Cancer

Jackson, S. The melancholy of anatomy; stories

Dildo

Jackson, S. The melancholy of anatomy; stories

Egg

Grand Street no70 p202-19 Spr/Summ 2002

Jackson, S. The melancholy of anatomy; stories

Fat

Jackson, S. The melancholy of anatomy; stories

The Kenyon Review ns24 no1 p1-9 Wint 2002

Foetus

Jackson, S. The melancholy of anatomy; stories

Hair

Jackson, S. The melancholy of anatomy; stories

Heart

Jackson, S. The melancholy of anatomy; stories

Milk

Jackson, S. The melancholy of anatomy; stories

Nerve

Jackson, S. The melancholy of anatomy; stories

Phlegm

Jackson, S. The melancholy of anatomy; stories

Sleep

Jackson, S. The melancholy of anatomy; stories

Sperm

Jackson, S. The melancholy of anatomy; stories

Jackson, Shirley

The bus

Nightshade: 20th century ghost stories; edited by Robert Phillips

The haunting of Hill House [excerpt]

Dark: stories of madness, murder, and the supernatural; edited by Clint Willis

Husband

The Paris Review v44 p158-66 Wint 2002

The lottery

The 13 best horror stories of all time; edited by Leslie Pockell

The American fantasy tradition; edited by Brian M. Thomsen

Nightmare

The Vintage book of amnesia; an anthology; edited by Jonathan Lethem

The possibility of evil

The Best American mystery stories of the century; Tony Hillerman, editor; with an introduction by Tony Hillerman

The summer people

A moment on the edge; 100 years of crime stories by women; edited by Elizabeth George

The very strange house next door

Witches' brew; edited by Yvonne Jocks

JACKSON, STONEWALL, 1824-1863

About

Knight, M. Killing Stonewall Jackson

Smith, R. T. I have lost my right

Jackson, Thomas Jonathan *See* Jackson, Stonewall, 1824-1863

Jackson, Tim

Reef Line

Confrontation no86/87 p90-5 Spr/Summ 2004

Jackson, Vanessa Furse

Breaking faith

Jackson, V. F. What I cannot say to you; stories

Darrell's garage

Jackson, V. F. What I cannot say to you; stories

Grandmother's footsteps

Jackson, V. F. What I cannot say to you; stories

Imagining friends

Jackson, V. F. What I cannot say to you; stories

A little kingdom

Jackson, V. F. What I cannot say to you; stories

Living alone

Jackson, V. F. What I cannot say to you; stories

On the road to Greater Bishop

Jackson, V. F. What I cannot say to you; stories

The outing

Jackson, V. F. What I cannot say to you; stories

A small independence

Jackson, V. F. What I cannot say to you; stories

Jackson, Vanessa Furse—*Continued*

Telling stories

Jackson, V. F. What I cannot say to you; stories

Victoria and Albert I: Running away to sea

Jackson, V. F. What I cannot say to you; stories

Victoria and Albert II: Day-trippers

Jackson, V. F. What I cannot say to you; stories

What I cannot say to you

Jackson, V. F. What I cannot say to you; stories

White sandals

Jackson, V. F. What I cannot say to you; stories

Jackson, Yvonne

Jesus Jones

Gettysburg Review v14 no3 p422-4 Aut 2001

JACKSON (MISS.) *See* Mississippi—Jackson

Jacob, Charlee

Flesh of leaves, bones of desire

Best new horror 12; edited and with an introduction by Stephen Jones

Jacobs, Jonnie

Built upon the sand

Women before the bench; edited by Carolyn Wheat; introduction by Linda Fairstein

Jacobs, Joseph

Nix Nought Nothing

New England Review v24 no3 p217-20 Summ 2003

The story of rough niall of the speckled rock

The Literary werewolf; an anthology; edited by Charlotte F. Otten

Jacobs, Mark

The ballad of Tony Nail

Jacobs, M. The liberation of little heaven and other stories

Dove of the back streets

Jacobs, M. The liberation of little heaven and other stories

Down in Paraguay

Jacobs, M. The liberation of little heaven and other stories

The egg queen rises

Living on the edge; fiction by Peace Corps writers; edited by John Coyne

How birds communicate

Jacobs, M. The liberation of little heaven and other stories

In the city of X

The Southern Review (Baton Rouge, La.) v35 no4 p760-71 Aut 1999

The liberation of little heaven

Jacobs, M. The liberation of little heaven and other stories

Looking for Lourdes

Jacobs, M. The liberation of little heaven and other stories

Marina in the key of blue flat

Jacobs, M. The liberation of little heaven and other stories

Mengele dies again

Jacobs, M. The liberation of little heaven and other stories

Mud Man

Jacobs, M. The liberation of little heaven and other stories

The rape of reason

Jacobs, M. The liberation of little heaven and other stories

Solidarity in green

Jacobs, M. The liberation of little heaven and other stories

The Telemachus box

Jacobs, M. The liberation of little heaven and other stories

Thirsty deer

Southwest Review v86 no2/3 p214-27 Spr/Summ 2001

Two dead Indians

Jacobs, M. The liberation of little heaven and other stories

Uncle Joe's Old-Time Communist Nostalgia Bar

The Southern Review (Baton Rouge, La.) v35 no1 p101-13 Wint 1999

White cloud

The Southern Review (Baton Rouge, La.) v38 no1 p138-48 Wint 2002

Witness Protection

The Southern Review (Baton Rouge, La.) v39 no3 p574-86 Summ 2003

Jacobs, W. W. (William Wymark)

The monkey's paw

The 13 best horror stories of all time; edited by Leslie Pockell

Dark: stories of madness, murder, and the supernatural; edited by Clint Willis

Jacobs, William Wymark *See* Jacobs, W. W. (William Wymark), 1863-1943

Jacob's Ladder. Grenville, K.

Jacob's voice. Levitsky, R.

Jacobsen, Josephine

Jack Frost

Of leaf and flower; stories and poems for gardeners; edited by Charles Dean and Clyde Wachsberger; illustrations by Clyde Wachsberger

Jacobsen, Roy

Encounter

The Art of the story; an international anthology of contemporary short stories; edited by Daniel Halpern

Jacobson, Dan

Bosom companions

The Times Literary Supplement no5009 p14 Ap 2 1999

Jacquez, Kelley

Michelle's miracle

Fantasmas; supernatural stories by Mexican American writers; edited by Rob Johnson; introduction by Kathleen J. Alcalá

Jade. Nichols, J.

Jade. Pronzini, B.

Jade Buddhas, red bridges, fruits of love. Gilchrist, E.

JAEL (BIBLICAL FIGURE)

s

Byatt, A. S. Jael

Jael. Byatt, A. S.

Jaffe, Daniel M.

Sarrushka and her daughter

With signs and wonders; an international anthology of Jewish fabulist fiction; edited by Daniel M. Jaffe

Jaffe, Harold
Fast
Western Humanities Review v53 no4 p340-43
Wint 1999/2000
Geeks dream
Western Humanities Review v53 no4 p346-48
Wint 1999/2000
Severed hand
Western Humanities Review v53 no4 p349-54
Wint 1999/2000
Jafta, Milly
The home-coming
The Anchor book of modern African stories;
edited by Nadežda Obradović ; with a fore-
word by Chinua Achebe
Jagged tooth, great tooth. Mayo, W.
JAGGER, MICK
About
Magnuson, A. Mom comes home
Jaguar dance. Earle, S.
Jailbird gone songbird. Pritchett, L.
The **jailhouse** lawyer. Margolin, P.
Jaime-Becerra, M.
Buena Suerte Airlines
Jaime-Becerra, M. Every night is ladies'
night; stories; Michael Jaime-Beccerra
The corrido of Hector Cruz
Jaime-Becerra, M. Every night is ladies'
night; stories; Michael Jaime-Beccerra
Every night is ladies' night
Jaime-Becerra, M. Every night is ladies'
night; stories; Michael Jaime-Beccerra
La fiesta brava
Jaime-Becerra, M. Every night is ladies'
night; stories; Michael Jaime-Beccerra
Georgie and Wanda
Jaime-Becerra, M. Every night is ladies'
night; stories; Michael Jaime-Beccerra
Gina and Max
Jaime-Becerra, M. Every night is ladies'
night; stories; Michael Jaime-Beccerra
Lopez Trucking Incorporated
Jaime-Becerra, M. Every night is ladies'
night; stories; Michael Jaime-Beccerra
Media vuelta
Jaime-Becerra, M. Every night is ladies'
night; stories; Michael Jaime-Beccerra
Practice tattoos
Jaime-Becerra, M. Every night is ladies'
night; stories; Michael Jaime-Beccerra
Riding with Lencho
Jaime-Becerra, M. Every night is ladies'
night; stories; Michael Jaime-Beccerra
Jaiser, Ingeborg
Lara
Prairie Schooner v73 no3 p107-08 Fall 1999
Jake and the enemy. Steele, A. M.
Jakes, John
Celebrity and justice for all
Jakes, J. Crime time: mystery and suspense
stories
Cloak and digger
Jakes, J. Crime time: mystery and suspense
stories
Dagger
Jakes, J. Crime time: mystery and suspense
stories

Dr. Sweetkill
Death by espionage; intriguing stories of de-
ception and betrayal; edited by Martin Cruz
Smith
Jakes, J. Crime time: mystery and suspense
stories
The girl in the golden cage
Jakes, J. Crime time: mystery and suspense
stories
Jonas Crag
Westward; a fictional history of the American
West : 28 original stories celebrating the
50th anniversary of the Western Writers of
America; edited by Dale L. Walker
Little man—It's been a busy day
Jakes, J. Crime time: mystery and suspense
stories
The man who wanted to be in the movies
Jakes, J. Crime time: mystery and suspense
stories
Manitow and Ironhand
A Century of great Western stories; edited by
John Jakes
No comment
A Century of noir; thirty-two classic crime
stories; edited by Mickey Spillane and Max
Allan Collins
The opener of the crypt
Jakes, J. Crime time: mystery and suspense
stories
The siren and the shill
Jakes, J. Crime time: mystery and suspense
stories
Tex
Jakes, J. Crime time: mystery and suspense
stories
Unc foils show foe
Jakes, J. Crime time: mystery and suspense
stories
Unc probes pickle plot
Jakes, J. Crime time: mystery and suspense
stories
Jakiela, Lori
Carry-on
Doubletake v7 no5 p107-8 2001 Special Edi-
tion
Jakober, Marie
Slither
The Blue and the gray undercover; edited by
Ed Gorman
The **jalapeño** contest. Gonzalez, R.
JAMAICA
Bowles, P. Pages from Cold Point
Channer, C. I'm still waiting
Cohen, S. Neville
Douglas, M. What the periwinkle remember
Hopkinson, N. Money tree
McTair, R. Just a lark; or, The crypt of Mat-
thew Ashdown
Philp, G. My brother's keeper
Senior, O. Do angels wear brassieres?
Silvera, M. Caribbean chameleon
Kingston
Banks, R. The rise of the middle class
McKenzie, A. Private school
Jamaica. Schickler, D.
JAMAICANS
England
Murray, M. Shame the devil

JAMAICANS—*Continued*
United States
Banks, R. Dis bwoy, him gwan
Glave, T. Their story
Jamboree. Williamson, J.
JAMES I, KING OF GREAT BRITAIN, 1566-1625
About
Aquino, J. T. The mysterious death of the shadow man
James VI, King of Scotland *See* James I, King of Great Britain, 1566-1625
James, Bill
Big city
   The best British mysteries; edited by Maxim Jakubowski
James, C. L. R. (Cyril Lionel Robert)
Triumph
   The Oxford book of Caribbean short stories; edited by Stewart Brown and John Wickham
James, Cyril Lionel Robert *See* James, C. L. R. (Cyril Lionel Robert), 1901-1989
James, Dean
All in the family
   Bishop, C. and James, D. Death dines in; edited by Claudia Bishop and Dean James
James, Henry
Adina
   James, H. Complete stories, 1864-1874
The Aspern papers
   James, H. Complete stories, 1884-1891
At Isella
   James, H. Complete stories, 1864-1874
The author of "Beltraffio"
   James, H. Complete stories, 1874-1884
Benvolio
   James, H. Complete stories, 1874-1884
Brooksmith
   James, H. Complete stories, 1884-1891
A bundle of letters
   James, H. Complete stories, 1874-1884
The chaperon
   James, H. Complete stories, 1884-1891
Crawford's consistency
   James, H. Complete stories, 1874-1884
Daisy Miller: a study
   James, H. Complete stories, 1874-1884
A day of days
   James, H. Complete stories, 1864-1874
De Grey: a romance
   James, H. Complete stories, 1864-1874
The diary of a man of fifty
   James, H. Complete stories, 1874-1884
Eugene Pickering
   James, H. Complete stories, 1874-1884
Four meetings
   James, H. Complete stories, 1874-1884
The friends of the friends
   Nightshade: 20th century ghost stories; edited by Robert Phillips
Gabrielle de Bergerac
   James, H. Complete stories, 1864-1874
Georgina's reasons
   James, H. Complete stories, 1884-1891
The ghostly rental
   James, H. Complete stories, 1874-1884
Guest's confession
   James, H. Complete stories, 1864-1874

The impressions of a cousin
   James, H. Complete stories, 1874-1884
An international episode
   James, H. Complete stories, 1874-1884
The jolly corner
   The American fantasy tradition; edited by Brian M. Thomsen
Lady Barberina
   James, H. Complete stories, 1874-1884
A landscape painter
   James, H. Complete stories, 1864-1874
The last of the Valerii
   James, H. Complete stories, 1864-1874
The lesson of the master
   James, H. Complete stories, 1884-1891
The liar
   James, H. Complete stories, 1884-1891
A light man
   James, H. Complete stories, 1864-1874
A London life
   James, H. Complete stories, 1884-1891
Longstaff's marriage
   James, H. Complete stories, 1874-1884
Louisa Pallant
   James, H. Complete stories, 1884-1891
Madame de Mauves
   James, H. Complete stories, 1864-1874
The madonna of the future
   James, H. Complete stories, 1864-1874
The marriages
   James, H. Complete stories, 1884-1891
Master Eustace
   James, H. Complete stories, 1864-1874
The modern warning
   James, H. Complete stories, 1884-1891
A most extraordinary case
   James, H. Complete stories, 1864-1874
Mrs. Temperly
   James, H. Complete stories, 1884-1891
My friend Bingham
   James, H. Complete stories, 1864-1874
A New England winter
   James, H. Complete stories, 1884-1891
Osborne's revenge
   James, H. Complete stories, 1864-1874
Pandora
   James, H. Complete stories, 1874-1884
A passionate pilgrim
   James, H. Complete stories, 1864-1874
The Patagonia
   James, H. Complete stories, 1884-1891
The path of duty
   James, H. Complete stories, 1884-1891
The pension Beaurepas
   James, H. Complete stories, 1874-1884
The point of view
   James, H. Complete stories, 1874-1884
Poor Richard
   James, H. Complete stories, 1864-1874
A problem
   James, H. Complete stories, 1864-1874
Professor Fargo
   James, H. Complete stories, 1874-1884
The pupil
   James, H. Complete stories, 1884-1891
The romance of certain old clothes
   James, H. Complete stories, 1864-1874
Rose-Agathe
   James, H. Complete stories, 1874-1884

James, Henry—*Continued*
The siege of London
  James, H. Complete stories, 1874-1884
Sir Edmund Orme
  James, H. Complete stories, 1884-1891
The solution
  James, H. Complete stories, 1884-1891
The story of a masterpiece
  James, H. Complete stories, 1864-1874
The story of a year
  James, H. Complete stories, 1864-1874
The sweetheart of M. Briseux
  James, H. Complete stories, 1864-1874
A tragedy of error
  James, H. Complete stories, 1864-1874
Travelling companions
  James, H. Complete stories, 1864-1874
JAMES, JESSE, 1847-1882
About
Henry, W. ". . . Fired by the hand of Robert Ford"
Henry, W. The great Northfield raid
Henry, W. Not wanted dead or alive
James, Kelvin Christopher
Shopping Trip
  The Literary Review (Madison, N.J.) v46 no2 p293-6 Wint 2003
James, M. R. (Montague Rhodes)
Oh, whistle and I'll come to you, my lad
  The 13 best horror stories of all time; edited by Leslie Pockell
James, Montague Rhodes *See* James, M. R. (Montague Rhodes), 1862-1936
James, Siân
And perhaps more
  James, S. Outside paradise
  The Literary Review (Madison, N.J.) v44 no2 p261-7 Wint 2001
Billy Mason from Gloucester
  James, S. Outside paradise
Happy as Saturday night
  James, S. Outside paradise
Hester and Louise
  James, S. Outside paradise
A house of one's own
  James, S. Outside paradise
John Hedward
  James, S. Outside paradise
Love, lust, life
  James, S. Outside paradise
Mountain air
  James, S. Outside paradise
Not singing exactly
  James, S. Outside paradise
Outside paradise
  James, S. Outside paradise
Strawberry cream
  James, S. Outside paradise
Jamesey, Jamesey. Hegi, U.
James's story. Zane, D.
Jamieson, Robert Alan
The last black hoose
  The Vintage book of contemporary Scottish fiction; edited and with an introduction by Peter Kravitz
Jamir, Suzanne
New Again
  South Carolina Review v35 no2 p149-56 Spr 2003

Jančar, Drago
Joyce's pupil
  The Kenyon Review ns23 no1 p86-98 Wint 2001
Jance, Judith A.
Death of a snowbird
  A moment on the edge; 100 years of crime stories by women; edited by Elizabeth George
A flash of chrysanthemum
  The World's finest mystery and crime stories, first annual collection; edited by Ed Gorman
Janda's sister. Winegardner, M.
Janicke, Gregory
The gift
  Mom, apple pie, and murder; edited by Nancy Pickard
The **janitor** on Mars. Amis, M.
JANITORS
Amis, M. The janitor on Mars
Davis, C. Labors of the heart
Fromm, P. Night swimming
Kennedy, A. L. A little like light
Lloyd, D. T. Portraits
McPherson, J. A. Gold Coast
Shade, E. The heart hankers
Troncoso, S. Time magician
Janko, James
Buffalo Boy
  The Massachusetts Review v44 no4 p649-59 Wint 2003/2004
Jannazzo, Eric
Clair
  Confrontation no86/87 p229-35 Spr/Summ 2004
Janowitz, Tama
Physics
  Wonderful town; New York stories from The New Yorker; edited by David Remnick with Susan Choi
The **January** Man. Mitchell, D.
The **January** sale stowaway. Cannell, D.
January through March. Hay, E.
Janus. Beattie, A.
JAPAN
Sterling, B. Maneki Neko
Yoshikawa, E. Musashi [excerpt]
11th century
Waldrop, H. The latter days of the law
20th century
Ishiguro, K. A family supper
Kawabata, Y. This country, that country
1945-
Browder, C. Fusuda the archer
Massey, S. The convenience boy
Murakami, H. All God's children can dance
Murakami, H. The elephant vanishes
Murakami, H. Honey Pie
Murakami, H. Landscape with flatiron
Murakami, H. UFO in Kushiro
Nakagami, K. The cape
Nakagami, K. House on fire
Nakagami, K. Red hair
Shishin, A. Mr. Eggplant goes home
Tomioka, T. Days of dear death
Tomioka, T. A dog's eye view
Tomioka, T. The funeral of a giraffe
Tomioka, T. Happy birthday

JAPAN—1945-—*Continued*
Tomioka, T. Yesterday's girl
Waters, M. Y. Circling the hondo
Waters, M. Y. Egg-face
Waters, M. Y. Kami
Waters, M. Y. The laws of evening
Waters, M. Y. Rationing
Waters, M. Y. The way love works
Yoshimoto, B. Asleep
Yoshimoto, B. Love songs
Yoshimoto, B. Night and night's travelers
Courts and courtiers
See Courts and courtiers—Japan
Rural life
Tomioka, T. Yesteryear
Waters, M. Y. Mirror studies
Kyoto
Blatnik, A. Kyoto
Waters, M. Y. Since my house burned down
Nagasaki
Tuck, L. The view from Madama Butterfly's house
Tokyo
Davies, R. Still searching
Murakami, H. Super-Frog saves Tokyo
JAPANESE
China
Lao She. Attachment
Waters, M. Y. Seed
France
Tomioka, T. Time table
Philippines
Murray, S. The caprices
Murray, S. Yamashita's gold
Thailand
Murakami, H. Thailand
United States
Yamamoto, H. Seventeen syllables
JAPANESE AMERICANS
Gifford, B. American Falls
Tanaka, S. Video ame
Waters, M. Y. The way love works
JAPANESE SOLDIERS *See* Soldiers—Japan
Jaroš, Peter
Making faces
In search of homo sapiens; twenty-five contemporary Slovak short stories; editor, Pavol Hudík ; [translated by Heather Trebatická; American English editor, Lucy Bednár]
Jarrad, Kyle
Mercy
The North American Review v284 no1 p25-30 Ja/F 1999
Jarrar, Randa
The Lunatics' Eclipse
Ploughshares v30 no2/3 p98-105 Fall 2004
Jarrell, Donna
The displaced overweight homemaker's guide to finding a man
What are you looking at?; the first fat fiction anthology; edited by Donna Jarrell and Ira Sukrungruang
Jarvis. Nailah, A.
Jawbreaker. Aylett, S.
JAZZ MUSIC
Carter, C. Birdbath
DeLancey, K. Swingtime

Di Filippo, P. And I think to myself, what a wonderful world
Moody, W. Matinee
Oliver, C. Didn't he ramble?
Saroyan, A. The shape of jazz to come
Škvorecký, J. The end of Bull Macha
Škvorecký, J. Song of forgotten years
Straub, P. Pork pie hat
Touré. The sad, sweet story of Sugar Lips Shinehot, the man with the portable promised land
Yates, R. A really good jazz piano
JEALOUSY
Alas, L. Two scholars
Alcott, L. M. Agatha's confession
Babel´, I. Bagrat-Ogly and the eyes of his bull
Bausch, R. Billboard
Boyle, T. C. Termination dust
Brady, C. Let my right hand forget her cunning
Davies, R. The sisters
Douglas, E. About loving women
Eldridge, Courtney. Becky
Friedman, M. Tango is my life
Gorman, E. One of those days, one of those nights
Gray, A. Aiblins
Howard, C. The ice shelf
Humphrey, W. A voice from the woods
Jakes, J. The siren and the shill
James, C. L. R. Triumph
James, H. Master Eustace
James, H. The romance of certain old clothes
Johnson, D. Mouthful of sorrow
Knight, M. Sundays
Mazelis, J. The blackberry season
Mazelis, J. Running away with the hairdresser
McGarry, J. Moon, June
Padilla, M. Hard language
Pasquali, M. d. Envy
Reiner, C. G. G. Giggler
Rivera Valdés, S. Little poisons
Schnitzler, A. Dream story
Singer, I. B. The impresario
Singer, I. B. The prodigy
Weldon, F. Inspector remorse
Wellen, E. Born victims
Wexler, M. The nanny trap
Zabytko, I. Pani Ryhotska in love
The **Jean-Paul** Sartre experience. Brandt, W.
Jedella ghost. Lee, T.
Jeffers, Honorée Fanonne
Sister Lilith
Dark matter; a century of speculative fiction from the African diaspora; edited by Sheree R. Thomas
JEFFERSON, THOMAS, 1743-1826
About
Carl, L. S. A mimicry of mockingbirds
Henry, W. Jefferson's captains
Johnson, C. R. A report from St. Domingue
Jefferson's captains. Henry, W.
Jeff's best joke. Lindskold, J. M.
JEHOVAH'S WITNESSES
Chan, D. M. Watchtower
Young, T. Sometimes night never ends
The **jelly-bean**. Fitzgerald, F. S.
Jemima Shore's first case. Fraser, A.
Jemina, the mountain girl. Fitzgerald, F. S.

Jen, Gish
Birthmates
　The Best American short stories of the
　　century; John Updike, editor, Katrina
　　Kenison, coeditor; with an introduction by
　　John Updike
　Jen, G. Who's Irish?; stories
　The Workshop; seven decades of the Iowa
　　Writers' Workshop: 42 stories, recollections
　　& essays on Iowa's place in 20th-century
　　American literature; edited by Tom Grimes
Chin
　Jen, G. Who's Irish?; stories
Duncan in China
　Jen, G. Who's Irish?; stories
House, house, home
　Jen, G. Who's Irish?; stories
In the American society
　Jen, G. Who's Irish?; stories
Just wait
　Jen, G. Who's Irish?; stories
The water faucet vision
　Jen, G. Who's Irish?; stories
Who's Irish?
　Jen, G. Who's Irish?; stories
Jen. Rosovsky, M.
Jenkins, Greg
The bet
　Jenkins, G. Night game; stories
The big cheese
　Jenkins, G. Night game; stories
The counterpuncher
　Jenkins, G. Night game; stories
Fumble
　Jenkins, G. Night game; stories
Gotta sing
　Jenkins, G. Night game; stories
In the outback
　Jenkins, G. Night game; stories
Night game
　Jenkins, G. Night game; stories
The Person
　Jenkins, G. Night game; stories
A portrait of the artist at Warner Bros.
　Jenkins, G. Night game; stories
Private places
　Jenkins, G. Night game; stories
The reality of angels
　Jenkins, G. Night game; stories
Red roses and cognac
　Jenkins, G. Night game; stories
Richard and poorer
　Jenkins, G. Night game; stories
Something to cling to
　Jenkins, G. Night game; stories
Spin
　Jenkins, G. Night game; stories
Strange attractors
　Jenkins, G. Night game; stories
Jenkins, Will F.
Exploration team
　The Good old stuff; adventure SF in the
　　grand tradition; edited by Gardner Dozois
First contact
　The Science fiction hall of fame: volume one,
　　1929-1964; the greatest science fiction sto-
　　ries of all time chosen by the members of
　　the Science Fiction Writers of America; ed-
　　ited by Robert Silverberg

The runaway skyscraper
　Wondrous beginnings; edited by Steven H.
　　Silver and Martin H. Greenberg
Jennet. Berkman, P. R.
Jennifer's turn. Klass, F.
Jennings, Phillip C.
The road to reality
　Worldmakers; SF adventures in terraforming;
　　edited by Gardner Dozois
Jenny and the Episcopalian. Goran, L.
Jenny come to play. Dowling, T.
Jensen, Geeta Sharma
A Good Country
　Atlantic Monthly (1993) v291 no4 p93-101
　　My 2003
Jensen, Jan Lars
Domestic slash and thrust
　Northern suns; edited by David G. Hartwell
　　& Glenn Grant
The secret history of the ornithopter
　One lamp; alternate history stories from The
　　magazine of Fantasy & Science Fiction; ed-
　　ited by Gordon van Gelder
Jenz, Thomas
The makeover
　The Virginia Quarterly Review v77 no1 p110-
　　26 Wint 2001
Jeremiad. Karnezis, P.
Jeremiah. Cady, J.
Jergović, Miljenko
The Condor
　Fishman, B. Wild East; stories from the last
　　frontier; edited with an introduction by Bo-
　　ris Fishman
Jerry Brogan and the Kilkenny cats. Breen, J. L.
Jerry Fuentes. Casares, O.
Jerry was a man. Heinlein, R. A.
Jersey Joe versus the Rock. Smart, A.
JERUSALEM
Englander, N. In this way we are wise
Goliger, G. Edith Teilheimer's war
Goliger, G. Song of ascent
Leegant, J. The diviners of desire: a modern fa-
　　ble
Leegant, J. The seventh year
Pearlman, E. Allog
Stollman, A. L. The adornment of days
Svirsky, G. Meeting Natalia
Zinik, Z. The notification
Jerusalem. Gaffney, E.
The **jester**. Tenn, W.
JESTERS *See* Fools and jesters
JESUITS
Fitzgerald, F. S. Benediction
McIntyre, V. N. The moon and the sun [excerpt]
Jesús, Pedro de
How to act in 1830
　Jesús, P. d. Frigid tales; translated from the
　　Spanish by Dick Cluster
Images, questions re: beautiful dead woman
　Jesús, P. d. Frigid tales; translated from the
　　Spanish by Dick Cluster
Instructions for a single man
　Jesús, P. d. Frigid tales; translated from the
　　Spanish by Dick Cluster
The letter
　Jesús, P. d. Frigid tales; translated from the
　　Spanish by Dick Cluster

Jesús, Pedro de—*Continued*
  Oh, that music (the importance of going on until the end)
    Jesús, P. d. Frigid tales; translated from the Spanish by Dick Cluster
  The portrait
    Jesús, P. d. Frigid tales; translated from the Spanish by Dick Cluster
Jesus. Chinquee, K.
Jesus, beans, and butter rum lifesavers. Thompson, M.
JESUS CHRIST
About
  Babel´, I. The sin of Jesus
  Ball, M. Shell game
  Bishop, M. Sequel on Skorpios
  Brahen, M. M. Trick or treat with Jesus
  Brockmeier, K. The Jesus stories
  Cook, T. H. Fatherhood
  Davenport, G. And
  Lawrence, D. H. The man who died
  Malzberg, B. N. Understanding entropy
  Updike, J. Jesus on Honshu
  Watson, I. Such dedication
  Williamson, C. O come little children. . .
Crucifixion
  Devereaux, R. Apologia
  Trevanian. Easter story
Jesus Christ in Texas. Du Bois, W. E. B.
Jesus, I know that guy. Gunn, K.
Jesus is sending you this message. Grimsley, J.
Jesus Jones. Jackson, Y.
Jesus of Nazareth. Singleton, G.
The **Jesus** stories. Brockmeier, K.
Jesus Wept. Smith, R. T.
Jetlag. Keret, E.
Jetsam. Greenwood, K.
Jett, Joan and Kihn, Greg
  Bad reputation
    Carved in rock; short stories by musicians; edited by Greg Kihn
The **jewel** and the demon. Norman, L.
The **Jewel** of Seven Stars. Stoker, B.
JEWEL ROBBERIES *See* Robbery
The **jeweler**. Dexter, P.
A **jeweler's** eye for flaw. Hodgen, C.
Jewell, Lisa
  Labia Lobelia
    Tart noir; edited by Stella Duffy & Lauren Henderson
JEWELRY
    See also Diamonds; Necklaces; Pearls; Rings; Rubies
  Bellow, S. A theft
  Hodgson, W. H. My lady's jewels
  Maron, M. Virgo in sapphires
Jewett, Sarah Orne
  Mrs. Todd
    Of leaf and flower; stories and poems for gardeners; edited by Charles Dean and Clyde Wachsberger; illustrations by Clyde Wachsberger
  New Neighbors
    American Literary Realism v36 no3 p260-8 Spr 2004
JEWISH-ARAB RELATIONS
  Agnon, S. Y. Under the tree
  Buchan, J. Sleepwalkers
  Goldstein, N. A pillar of a cloud

  Keret, E. Cocked and locked
  Michael, S. Refuge [excerpt]
  Shmuelian, A. Moonstruck sunflowers
  Smilansky, M. Latifa
  Tammuz, B. The swimming race
  Yehoshua, A. B. Facing the forests
JEWISH CHILDREN
  Appelfeld, A. Kitty
  Bryks, R. Berele in the ghetto
  Grynberg, H. Uncle Aron
  Lustig, A. The lemon
  Rachmil, B. Children of the Lodz, ghetto
  Sher, S. Tsuris
JEWISH HOLOCAUST (1933-1945) *See* Holocaust, Jewish (1933-1945)
JEWISH REFUGEES
    See also Holocaust survivors
  Malamud, B. The German refugee
  Singer, I. B. The cafeteria
  Singer, I. B. A day in Coney Island
  Singer, I. B. The joke
  Singer, I. B. The seance
JEWISH WOMEN
  Baron, Dvora. Bubbe Henya
  Bergelson, D. In the boardinghouse
  Bergelson, D. Spring
  Dropkin, Celia. Bella fell in love
  Engel, M. P. Redeeming the dead
  Englander, N. The last one way
  Englander, N. The wig
  Fink, I. The death of Tsaritsa
  Gorshman, Shira. Bubbe Malke
  Korn, R. H. The sack with pink stripes
  Kreitman, Esther Singer. A satin coat
  Lempel, Blume. The death of my aunt
  Lempel, Blume. Scenes on a bare canvas
  Miller, E. In memory of Chanveasna Chan, who is still alive
  Molodowsky, K. The fourth Mitzvah
  Park, S. The golem
  Serdatzky, Yente. Rosh Hashanah
  Singer, I. B. Yochna and Schmelke
JEWS
    See also Antisemitism; Hasidism; Israelis; Jewish-Arab relations; Jewish women; Judaism; Sephardim; World War, 1939-1945—Jews
  Almond, S. A dream of sleep
  Amichai, Y. My father's deaths
  Appelfeld, A. Bertha
  Baron, Dvora. Kaddish
  Baxter, C. Harry Ginsberg
  Beinhart, L. Funny story
  Bellow, S. The Bellarosa connection
  Bellow, S. Him with his foot in his mouth
  Bocock, M. A citizen of the world at large
  Brownstein, G. Bachelor party
  Dann, J. Fairy tale
  Dann, J. Jumping the road
  Dann, J. Kaddish
  Dyson, J. At last
  Engel, M. P. Dis aliter visum
  Engel, M. P. Strangers and sojourners
  Engel, M. P. Those who shine like the stars
  Englander, N. Peep show
  Englander, N. The tumblers
  Faygenberg, Rochel. My first readers
  Gabriel, D. Making peace with the Muslims
  Goldstein, N. The conduct for consoling

JEWS—*Continued*
Goldstein, N. Pickled sprouts
Goliger, G. Edith Teilheimer's war
Goliger, G. Maladies of the inner ear
Goliger, G. A man who has brothers
Goliger, G. Mother tongue
Greenberg, A. Gruber in traffic
Kadish, R. The argument
Kalman, J. Channel crossing
Kirshenbaum, B. Jews have no business being enamored of Germans
Leegant, J. Accounting
Leegant, J. The diviners of desire: a modern fable
Leegant, J. How to comfort the sick and dying
Leegant, J. Seekers in the Holy Land
Leegant, J. The seventh year
Malzberg, B. N. Ship full of Jews
McCann, R. The universe, concealed
Michaels, L. Nachman
Papernick, J. The art of correcting
Papernick, J. The ascent of Eli Israel
Papernick, J. For as long as the lamp is burning
Papernick, J. An unwelcome guest
Roth, P. Defender of the faith
Schlink, B. The circumcision
Schtok, F. Winter berries
Shapiro, G. At the great divide
Shapiro, G. Shifman in paradise
Shrayer-Petrov, D. David and Goliath
Singer, I. B. Brother Beetle
Singer, I. B. The bus
Singer, I. B. The dead fiddler
Singer, I. B. Henne fire
Singer, I. B. Miracles
Singer, I. B. My adventures 25 as an idealist
Singer, I. B. The needle
Singer, I. B. One day of happiness
Singer, I. B. A pair
Singer, I. B. A piece of advice
Singer, I. B. The plagiarist
Singer, I. B. Strangers
Singer, I. B. Three encounters
Singer, I. B. Two markets
Singer, I. B. Two weddings and one divorce
Singer, I. B. Zeidlus the Pope
Singer, I. B. Zeitl and Rickel
Stern, D. Apraxia
Stern, S. Bruno's metamorphosis
Stern, S. Romance
Stern, S. Sissman loses his way
Stollman, A. L. The adornment of days
Stollman, A. L. Enfleurage
Stollman, A. L. The seat of higher consciousness
Swan, G. Gate of ivory, gate of horn
Tenn, W. On Venus, have we got a rabbi
What, L. How to feed your inner troll
What, L. The man I loved was an elf
What, L. Smelling of earth, dreaming of sky
What, L. The sweet and sour tongue
What, L. You gotta believe
Wisenberg, S. L. Liberator
Zelitch, S. Ten plagues
Marriage customs
See Marriage customs—Jews
Persecutions
See also Holocaust, Jewish (1933-1945)
Babel´, I. First love
Babel´, I. The story of my dovecote
Englander, N. The twenty-seventh man
Richter, H. P. The teacher
Škvorecký, J. Dr. Strass
Škvorecký, J. My teacher, Mr. Katz
Spiegel, I. A ghetto dog
Religion
See Judaism
Argentina
Glickmann, N. The last emigrant
Singer, I. B. Hanka
Singer, I. B. A tale of two sisters
Brazil
Scliar, M. The prophets of Benjamin Bok
Singer, I. B. One night in Brazil
Buffalo (N.Y.)
Reisman, N. Illumination
Canada
Bezmozgis, D. An animal to the memory
Bezmozgis, D. Choynski
Bezmozgis, D. Minyan
Bezmozgis, D. Natasha
Bezmozgis, D. Roman Berman, massage therapist
Bezmozgis, D. Tapka
Goliger, G. Air and earth
Goliger, G. Maedele
Goliger, G. Song of ascent
Goliger, G. Who you are
Kalman, J. Eichmann's monogram
Kalman, J. Ladies' wear
Kalman, J. The making of a Jew
Kalman, J. A reason to be
Singer, I. B. The lecture
Škvorecký, J. Jezebel from Forest Hill (A love story)
Taylor, T. L. The resurrection plant
Chicago (Ill.)
Epstein, J. Artie Glick in a family way
Epstein, J. Don Juan Zimmerman
Epstein, J. Family values
Epstein, J. Freddy Duchamp in action
Epstein, J. Howie's gift
Epstein, J. Love and The Guinness book of records
Epstein, J. Moe
Czech Republic
Hamburger, A. Exile
Hamburger, A. Jerusalem
Hamburger, A. This ground you are standing on
Škvorecký, J. The cuckoo
Škvorecký, J. Dr. Strass
Škvorecký, J. Feminine mystique
Škvorecký, J. Filthy cruel world
Škvorecký, J. Fragments about Rebecca
Škvorecký, J. My teacher, Mr. Katz
Škvorecký, J. My Uncle Kohn
Eastern Europe
Baron, D. Aggravation
Baron, D. Bill of divorcement
Baron, D. Bubbe Henya
Baron, D. Burying the books
Baron, D. Deserted wife
Baron, D. The end of Sender Ziv
Baron, D. Family
Baron, D. Fedka
Baron, D. The first day
Baron, D. Fradl
Baron, D. Grandchildren

JEWS—Eastern Europe—*Continued*
Baron, D. In the beginning
Baron, D. Kaddish
Baron, D. Liska
Baron, D. An only daughter
Baron, D. Shifra
Baron, D. Sister
Baron, D. Ziva
Stern, S. Yiddish twilight
England
Kalman, J. Allures of grandeur
Kalman, J. Flight
Kalman, J. Monahan Avenue
Kalman, J. Rain
Waugh, E. Essay
Florida
Rodburg, M. The orphan
France
Dunmore, H. Lisette
Germany
Apelman, M. A visitor's guide to Berlin
Asch, S. "Heil, Hitler!"
Bowen, R. Doppelganger
Goliger, G. Breaking the sabbath
Richter, H. P. The teacher
Hungary
Kalman, J. The county of birches
Kalman, J. Not for me a crown of thorns
Kalman, J. Personal effects
Kalman, J. What's in a name?
Illinois
Orner, P. Esther stories
Italy
Bassani, G. A plaque on Via Mazzini
Louisiana
Orringer, J. Stations of the cross
Massachusetts
Orner, P. Birth of a son-in-law
Rodburg, M. Concessions
Mexico
Lida, D. La quedada
Mastretta, A. Aunt Paulina
Miami Beach (Fla.)
Kaufelt, D. A. The bagel murders
Singer, I. B. The hotel
Singer, I. B. Old love
Singer, I. B. A party in Miami Beach
Missouri
Shapiro, G. The tutor
Morocco
Bowles, P. A friend of the world
Nebraska
Shapiro, G. The Feigenbaum Foundation
Netherlands
Horn, D. Barbarians at the gates
New Jersey
Rodburg, M. Days of awe
Rodburg, M. Keer Avenue, July 1967
Rodburg, M. The law of return
Rodburg, M. March of Dimes
Rodburg, M. Pochantas in Camelot
Rodburg, M. The widower Visarrion
New York (N.Y.)
Allen, W. Retribution
Baida, P. No place to hide
Baida, P. Points of light
Brownstein, G. The curious case of Benjamin
    Button, 3w
Brownstein, G. The dead fiddler, 5E

Dann, J. Tea
Englander, N. The last one way
Englander, N. Reb Kringle
Englander, N. Reunion
Englander, N. The wig
Fallis, G. Comes the revolution
Fliegel, R. A final midrash
Goldstein, N. Barbary apes
Goldstein, N. The worker rests under the hero
    trees
Gorman, C. The Death Cat of Hester Street
Kirchheimer, G. D. Arbitration
Kirchheimer, G. D. A case of dementia
Kirchheimer, G. D. Changelings
Kirchheimer, G. D. Feast of Lights
Kirchheimer, G. D. Food of love
Kirchheimer, G. D. Goodbye, evil eye
Kirchheimer, G. D. Rafi
Kirchheimer, G. D. Silver screen
Kirchheimer, G. D. A skirmish in the desert
Kirchheimer, G. D. Traffic manager
Kirchheimer, G. D. The voyager
Levitsky, R. A Sabbath flame
Lieberman, T. Anya's angel
Michaels, L. Murderers
Reiner, C. Sorry Solomon and Guey Jew
Rosenbaum, T. Romancing the yohrzeit light
Rosenblatt, B. Zelig
Roth, H. A diving rock on the Hudson [excerpt]
Shteyngart, G. Several anecdotes about my wife
Singer, I. B. The admirer
Singer, I. B. Advice
Singer, I. B. The bird
Singer, I. B. The cabalist of East Broadway
Singer, I. B. The cafeteria
Singer, I. B. A day in Coney Island
Singer, I. B. Escape from civilization
Singer, I. B. Fate
Singer, I. B. The joke
Singer, I. B. The Key
Singer, I. B. The last gaze
Singer, I. B. The letter writer
Singer, I. B. Morris and Timna
Singer, I. B. The New Year party
Singer, I. B. The painting
Singer, I. B. Property
Singer, I. B. The safe deposit
Singer, I. B. Sam Palka and David Vishkover
Singer, I. B. Schloimele
Singer, I. B. The seance
Singer, I. B. The son
Singer, I. B. The yearning heifer
Stern, S. The wedding jester
Yasgur, B. S. Kaddish
New York (State)
Allyn, D. The Christmas mitzvah
Michaels, L. Honeymoon
Michaels, L. Second honeymoon
Reisman, N. Common light
Reisman, N. Confessions
Reisman, N. Edie in winter
Reisman, N. Heart of hearts
Weinstein, L. The Llipkin -Wexler affair
Poland
Auerbach, J. Transformations
Babel´, I. Beresteczko
Babel´, I. Gedali
Bryks, R. Artists in the ghetto
Bryks, R. Berele in the ghetto

JEWS—Poland—*Continued*
Grynberg, H. Uncle Aron
Korn, R. H. The road of no return
Londynski, Helen. The four-ruble war
Rachmil, B. Bread
Rachmil, B. Children of the Lodz, ghetto
Rachmil, B. The last journey
Roth, J. Strawberries
Singer, I. B. The adventure
Singer, I. B. Altele
Singer, I. B. Androgynous
Singer, I. B. The angry man
Singer, I. B. The beggar said no
Singer, I. B. The betrayer of Israel
Singer, I. B. Big and little
Singer, I. B. The black wedding
Singer, I. B. The blasphemer
Singer, I. B. Blood
Singer, I. B. The building project
Singer, I. B. Caricature
Singer, I. B. The chimney sweep
Singer, I. B. A crown of feathers
Singer, I. B. A dance and a hop
Singer, I. B. The destruction of Kreshev
Singer, I. B. The divorce
Singer, I. B. Dr. Beeber
Singer, I. B. Elka and Meier
Singer, I. B. Errors
Singer, I. B. Esther Kreindel the second
Singer, I. B. The fast
Singer, I. B. The fatalist
Singer, I. B. A friend of Kafka
Singer, I. B. Getzel the monkey
Singer, I. B. Gimpel the fool
Singer, I. B. Grandfather and grandson
Singer, I. B. The gravedigger
Singer, I. B. Guests on a winter night
Singer, I. B. I place my reliance on no man
Singer, I. B. The image
Singer, I. B. The jew from Babylon
Singer, I. B. The lantuch
Singer, I. B. The little shoemakers
Singer, I. B. The man who came back
Singer, I. B. The manuscript
Singer, I. B. The mathematician
Singer, I. B. The mirror
Singer, I. B. The mistake
Singer, I. B. Moishele
Singer, I. B. Moon and madness
Singer, I. B. A nest egg for paradise
Singer, I. B. A night in the poorhouse
Singer, I. B. Not for the Sabbath
Singer, I. B. The old man
Singer, I. B. On a wagon
Singer, I. B. On the way to the poorhouse
Singer, I. B. Passions
Singer, I. B. Pigeons
Singer, I. B. The pocket remembered
Singer, I. B. The power of darkness
Singer, I. B. Powers
Singer, I. B. The primper
Singer, I. B. The recluse
Singer, I. B. Remnants
Singer, I. B. The riddle
Singer, I. B. The secret
Singer, I. B. The shadow of a crib
Singer, I. B. Short Friday
Singer, I. B. Something is there
Singer, I. B. The son from America

Singer, I. B. The Spinoza of Market Street
Singer, I. B. Stories from behind the stove
Singer, I. B. Taibele and her demon
Singer, I. B. A tale of two liars
Singer, I. B. A tale of two sisters
Singer, I. B. Tanhum
Singer, I. B. Three tales
Singer, I. B. A tutor in the village
Singer, I. B. Two
Singer, I. B. The unseen
Singer, I. B. Vanvild Kava
Singer, I. B. The wager
Singer, I. B. Why Heisherik was born
Singer, I. B. The wife killer
Singer, I. B. The witch
Singer, I. B. Yentl the yeshiva boy
Tushnet, L. The ban
What, L. The sacred society
Zawieyski, J. Conrad in the ghetto
Portugal
Singer, I. B. Sabbath in Portugal
Russia
Babel', I. At grandmother's
Babel', I. Elya Isaakovich and Margarita Prokofievna
Babel', I. The end of the almshouse
Babel', I. The father
Babel', I. First love
Babel', I. How things were done in Odessa
Babel', I. In the basement
Babel', I. Karl-Yankel
Babel', I. The King
Babel', I. Old Shloyme
Babel', I. The rabbi
Babel', I. The rabbi's son
Babel', I. Shabos-Nakhamu
Babel', I. The story of my dovecote
Babel', I. Sunset
Dropkin, Celia. At the rich relatives
Englander, N. The twenty-seventh man
Kalfus, K. Birobidzhan
Rubina, D. Apples from Shlitzbutter's garden
Schtok, F. At the mill
Sholem Aleichem. Hodel
Shrayer-Petrov, D. He, she and the others
Shrayer-Petrov, D. Tsukerman and his children
Shrayer-Petrov, D. Young Jews and two gymnasium girls
Vapnyar, L. A question for Vera
Vapnyar, L. There are Jews in my house
Ukraine
Jaffe, D. M. Sarrushka and her daughter
United States
Apple, M. The eighth day
Bellow, S. Cousins
Bellow, S. The old system
Bloom, A. The gates are closing
Bukoski, A. Time between trains
Cohen, R. Refuge
Elkin, S. Criers and kibitzers, kibitzers and criers
Goldberg, M. Bee season
Goldstein, N. Anatevka tender
Havazelet, E. Leah
Kirshenbaum, B. Who knows Kaddish
Leegant, J. Lucky in love
Leegant, J. Mezivosky
Leegant, J. The tenth
Lieu, J. This world

JEWS—United States—*Continued*

Lowenthal, M. Ordinary pain

Michaels, L. Reflections of a wild kid

Miller, E. In memory of Chanveasna Chan, who is still alive

Mirvis, T. A Poland, a Lithuania, a Galicia

Shapiro, G. Bad Jews

Shapiro, G. Rosenthal unbound

Shapiro, G. Suskind, the impresario

Shapiro, G. The twelve plagues

Shouse, D. A portrait of angels

Shrayer-Petrov, D. Hände hoch!

Singer, I. B. Alone

Singer, I. B. Confused

Singer, I. B. Exes

Singer, I. B. The little shoemakers

Singer, I. B. A peephole in the gate

Singer, I. B. A telephone call on Yom Kippur

Stern, S. Swan song

Stern, S. The tale of a kite

Stollman, A. L. If I have found favor in your eyes

Umansky, E. M. How to make it to the promised land

Wisenberg, S. L. My mother's war

Jews have no business being enamored of Germans. Kirshenbaum, B.

Jezebel from Forest Hill (A love story). Škvorecký, J.

JILTING

Boswell, R. Glissando

Fitzgerald, F. S. Myra meets his family

Gilman, C. P. The girl in the pink hat

Honig, L. Refuge

Reiner, C. Dear John

Jim Crow in Texas. Pickens, W.

Jim Magee's sand. Easton, R. O.

Jiménez, Karleen Pendleton

La del Sapo

Fantasmas; supernatural stories by Mexican American writers; edited by Rob Johnson; introduction by Kathleen J. Alcalá

The lake at the end of the wash

Hers 3: brilliant new fiction by lesbian writers; edited by Terry Wolverton with Robert Drake

Jimi Hendrix, Bluegrass Star. Becker, G.

The **Jimi** Hendrix experience. Vanderhaeghe, G.

Jimmy. Case, D.

Jimmy under water. Whitty, J.

Jimmy Yellow Hawk. Sneve, V. D. H.

Jimmy's Pearl. Mundy, R.

Jimtown Road. McFadden, D.

Jin, Ha *See* Ha Jin, 1956-

JINGU, EMPRESS OF JAPAN, 170-269
About

Labor relations

JINN

West, M. Gifted

The **job**. Rao, K.

A **job** at Little Henry's. Roorbach, B.

Job history. Proulx, A.

Job ops. Skillings, R. D.

Jobs. Saroyan, A.

Jody rolled the bones. Yates, R.

Joe Grind. Abrams, T.

Joe laughed. Kelman, J.

Joe Moore and Callie Blasingame. Mencken, S. H.

The **Joe** Show. Bisson, T.

Joey falling. Nailah, A.

Jofroi de Maussan. Giono, J.

JOHANNESBURG (SOUTH AFRICA) *See* South Africa—Johannesburg

JOHN, KING OF ENGLAND, 1167-1216
About

Pulver, M. M. To whom the victory?

JOHN BIRCH SOCIETY

Bullins, E. Support your local police

John Gardner's Ghost. Wyatt, C.

John Hedward. James, S.

John-Jin. Tremain, R.

John Marlow's victory. Alcott, L. M.

John Monahan. Bonner, P. H.

John on the train: a fable for our cynical friends. Grodstein, L.

Johnny Hamburger. Cooper, R. R.

Johnny pumpkinseed. Chapman, C. M.

Johnny Too Bad. Dufresne, J.

Johnny's smile. Hay, E.

Johnson, Adam

The Canadanaut

Johnson, A. Emporium; stories

Cliff gods of Acapulco

Best new American voices 2000; guest editor Tobias Wolff; series editors John Kulka and Natalie Danford

Johnson, A. Emporium; stories

The death-dealing Cassini satellite

Johnson, A. Emporium; stories

The eighth sea

Johnson, A. Emporium; stories

The history of cancer

Johnson, A. Emporium; stories

The Jughead of Berlin

Johnson, A. Emporium; stories

Teen sniper

Johnson, A. Emporium; stories

Trauma plate

Johnson, A. Emporium; stories

Your own backyard

Johnson, A. Emporium; stories

Johnson, Adam Marshall

Cliff gods of Acapulco

Esquire v131 no4 p138-43+ Ap 1999

Trauma plate

The Virginia Quarterly Review v75 no3 p544-57 Summ 1999

Johnson, Brady

Michiganders, 1979

Best new American voices 2004; guest editor John Casey; series editors John Kulka and Natalie Danford

Johnson, Charles

Better than counting sheep

Callaloo v24 no4 p1058-60 Fall 2001

The sorcerer's apprentice

Callaloo v24 no2 p495-503 Spr 2001

Johnson, Charles Richard

Confession

Johnson, C. R. Soulcatcher and other stories

A lion at Pendleton

Johnson, C. R. Soulcatcher and other stories

Martha's dilemma

Johnson, C. R. Soulcatcher and other stories

The mayor's tale

Johnson, C. R. Soulcatcher and other stories

Murderous thoughts

Johnson, C. R. Soulcatcher and other stories

Johnson, Charles Richard—*Continued*
The people speak
  Johnson, C. R. Soulcatcher and other stories
The plague
  Johnson, C. R. Soulcatcher and other stories
Poetry and politics
  Johnson, C. R. Soulcatcher and other stories
A report from St. Domingue
  Johnson, C. R. Soulcatcher and other stories
A soldier for the crown
  Johnson, C. R. Soulcatcher and other stories
The soulcatcher
  Johnson, C. R. Soulcatcher and other stories
The transmission
  Johnson, C. R. Soulcatcher and other stories
Johnson, Chelsey
Pinhead, moonhead
  Ploughshares v27 no4 p84-95 Wint
    2001/2002
Johnson, Dana
Bars
  Johnson, D. Break any woman down; stories
Break any woman down
  Johnson, D. Break any woman down; stories
Clay's thinking
  Johnson, D. Break any woman down; stories
Hot pepper
  Johnson, D. Break any woman down; stories
Markers
  Johnson, D. Break any woman down; stories
Melvin in the sixth grade
  Johnson, D. Break any woman down; stories
Mouthful of sorrow
  Johnson, D. Break any woman down; stories
Something to remember me by
  Johnson, D. Break any woman down; stories
Three ladies sipping tea in a Persian garden
  Johnson, D. Break any woman down; stories
Johnson, Denis
Denis the Pirate
  The Paris Review v45 p261-4 Fall 2003
Emergency
  The Scribner anthology of contemporary short
    fiction; fifty North American stories since
    1970; Lex Williford and Michael Martone,
    editors
Train dreams
  The O. Henry Prize stories, 2003; edited and
    with an introduction by Laura Furman;
    jurers David Gutterson, Diane Johnson,
    Jennifer Egan
  The Paris Review v44 no162 p250-312 Summ
    2002
Work
  The Workshop; seven decades of the Iowa
    Writers' Workshop: 42 stories, recollections
    & essays on Iowa's place in 20th-century
    American literature; edited by Tom Grimes
Johnson, Drew
Delta Interval
  Harper's v308 p29-34 Je 2004
Johnson, George Clayton
The obedient child
  Gathering the bones; original stories from the
    world's masters of horror; edited by Dennis
    Etchison, Ramsey Campbell and Jack Dann

Johnson, Greg
First surmise
  Michigan Quarterly Review v41 no2 p201-16
    Spr 2002
The man next door
  Southern Humanities Review v35 no3 p272-86
    Summ 2001
Shining city
  Prairie Schooner v75 no3 p131-50 Fall 2001
Sticky kisses
  TriQuarterly no110/111 p392-404 Fall 2001
Zelda, Zelda
  Southern Humanities Review v38 no1 p45-56
    Wint 2004
Johnson, Keith Leslie
(jt. auth) See Yoshimura, Akira
Johnson, Linnea
Forty Acres and a Pool
  The Antioch Review v61 no1 p109-15 Wint
    2003
Johnson, Lisa
Backdated
  Virgin fiction 2
Johnson, Rebecca
Twilight
  The Hudson Review v55 no1 p63-74 Spr 2002
Johnson, Susan
Phoca the waiter
  The Massachusetts Review v42 no2 p202-5
    Summ 2001
Risking it all
  Fascinated; [by] Bertrice Small, Susan John-
    son, Thea Devine and Robin Schone
The salad diet
  The Massachusetts Review v42 no2 p199-202
    Summ 2001
The thrill of a good ride
  The Massachusetts Review v42 no2 p205-7
    Summ 2001
Johnson, Suzanne C.
Body in the pond
  A Hot and sultry night for crime; edited by
    Jeffery Deaver
Johnson, W. R. (Walter Ralph)
(jt. auth) See Nemerov, Howard and Johnson,
  W. R. (Walter Ralph)
Johnson, Walter Ralph *See* Johnson, W. R.
  (Walter Ralph), 1933-
Johnson, Willis
Vienna, City of My Dreams
  TriQuarterly no113 p75-96 Summ 2002
Johnson-Davies, Denys
Cat
  Johnson-Davies, D. Fate of a prisoner and
    other stories
Coffee at the Marriott
  Johnson-Davies, D. Fate of a prisoner and
    other stories
Deal concluded
  Johnson-Davies, D. Fate of a prisoner and
    other stories
The dream
  Johnson-Davies, D. Fate of a prisoner and
    other stories
Fate of a prisoner
  Johnson-Davies, D. Fate of a prisoner and
    other stories

Johnson-Davies, Denys—*Continued*
  Garbage girl
    Johnson-Davies, D. Fate of a prisoner and
      other stories
  The garden of Sheikh Osman
    Johnson-Davies, D. Fate of a prisoner and
      other stories
  Mr. Pritchard
    Johnson-Davies, D. Fate of a prisoner and
      other stories
  Oleanders pink and white
    Johnson-Davies, D. Fate of a prisoner and
      other stories
  Open season in Beirut
    Johnson-Davies, D. Fate of a prisoner and
      other stories
  A short weekend
    Johnson-Davies, D. Fate of a prisoner and
      other stories
  Slice of the cake
    Johnson-Davies, D. Fate of a prisoner and
      other stories
  A smile from the past
    Johnson-Davies, D. Fate of a prisoner and
      other stories
  A taxi to himself
    Johnson-Davies, D. Fate of a prisoner and
      other stories
  Two worlds
    Johnson-Davies, D. Fate of a prisoner and
      other stories
Johnson, Owen
  The humming bird
    Dead balls and double curves; an anthology
      of early baseball fiction; edited and with an
      introduction by Trey Strecker ; with a fore-
      word by Arnold Hano
Johnston, Bill
  (jt. auth) See Gombrowicz, Witold
Johnston, Bret Anthony
  Anything that floats
    Johnston, B. A. Corpus Christi; stories; Bret
      Anthony Johnston
    The Paris Review v45 p169-77 Wint 2003
  Birds of Paradise
    Johnston, B. A. Corpus Christi; stories; Bret
      Anthony Johnston
    Southwest Review v86 no4 p519-32 2001
  Buy for me the rain
    Johnston, B. A. Corpus Christi; stories; Bret
      Anthony Johnston
  Corpus
    New stories from the South: the year's best,
      2003; edited by Shannon Ravenel; with a
      preface by Roy Blount Jr.
  Corpus Christi
    Johnston, B. A. Corpus Christi; stories; Bret
      Anthony Johnston
  I see something you don't see
    Johnston, B. A. Corpus Christi; stories; Bret
      Anthony Johnston
  In the tall grass
    Johnston, B. A. Corpus Christi; stories; Bret
      Anthony Johnston
  Two liars
    Johnston, B. A. Corpus Christi; stories; Bret
      Anthony Johnston

Waterwalkers
    Johnston, B. A. Corpus Christi; stories; Bret
      Anthony Johnston
  The widow
    Johnston, B. A. Corpus Christi; stories; Bret
      Anthony Johnston
    New England Review v24 no2 p134-46 Spr
      2003
    New stories from the South; the year's best,
      2004; edited by Shannon Ravenel; preface
      by Tim Gautreaux
Johnston, Paul Dennithorne
  Baseball[2270]— the A's versus the non-A's
    Etc. v58 no4 p454-62 Wint 2001/2002
  The right to life?
    Etc. v58 no2 p185-93 Summ 2001
  Silent night: non-verbal sex at the Galactic Cafe
    Etc. v56 no1 p25-35 Spr 1999
  Today never happened before
    Etc. v58 no3 p294-306 Fall 2001
Johnston, Tim
  Irish girl
    Doubletake v8 no1 p95-9 Wint 2002
    The O. Henry Prize stories, 2003; edited and
      with an introduction by Laura Furman;
      jurers David Gutterson, Diane Johnson,
      Jennifer Egan
  State v. Stucky
    Iowa Review v32 no3 p134-46 Wint
      2002/2003
JoJo's gold. Ayres, N.
A **joke**. Chekhov, A. P.
The **joker**. Brennan, M.
JOKES, PRACTICAL *See* Practical jokes
Jolene: A Life. Doctorow, E. L.
Jolie-Gray. Hill, I.
Jolliff, William
  Cleaning Seed
    Southern Humanities Review v38 no2 p195
      Spr 2004
The **jolly** corner. James, H.
Jon. Saunders, G.
Jon-clod. Nichols, J.
Jonas Crag. Jakes, J.
Jones, Adam Mars- *See* Mars-Jones, Adam,
  1954-
Jones, Bethalee
  Engaging Diane
    Ploughshares v25 no4 p15-23 Wint
      1999/2000
JONES, BRIAN, 1943-1969
                  About
  Kihn, G. Mirror gazing with Brian Jones
Jones, Cori
  F-stops
    The North American Review v284 no2 p26-34
      Mr/Ap 1999
Jones, Courtney
  Irregularities
    Best new American voices 2004; guest editor
      John Casey; series editors John Kulka and
      Natalie Danford
Jones, Edward P.
  All Aunt Hagar's Children
    The New Yorker v79 no40 p128-32, 134-40,
      142, 144, 146-7 D 22-29 2003

Jones, Edward P.—*Continued*
A dark night
  Breaking into print; early stories and insights into getting published; a Ploughshares anthology; edited by DeWitt Henry
The Devil Swims Across the Anacostia River
  Grand Street no73 p8-26 Spr 2004
The first day
  The Art of the story; an international anthology of contemporary short stories; edited by Daniel Halpern
Marie
  The Scribner anthology of contemporary short fiction; fifty North American stories since 1970; Lex Williford and Michael Martone, editors
Old Boys, Old Girls
  The New Yorker v80 no10 p86-97 My 3 2004
A rich man
  New stories from the South; the year's best, 2004; edited by Shannon Ravenel; preface by Tim Gautreaux
  The New Yorker v79 no21 p64-73 Ag 4 2003

Jones, Gail
The astronomer tells of her love
  Jones, G. The house of breathing; stories
Babies
  Jones, G. The house of breathing; stories
Dark times
  Jones, G. The house of breathing; stories
Desolation
  The Kenyon Review v25 no1 p9-17 Wint 2003
The house of breathing
  Jones, G. The house of breathing; stories
Knowledge
  Jones, G. The house of breathing; stories
'Life probably saved by imbecile dwarf'
  Jones, G. The house of breathing; stories
Modernity
  Jones, G. The house of breathing; stories
On the piteous death of Mary Wollstonecraft
  Jones, G. The house of breathing; stories
Other places
  Jones, G. The house of breathing; stories
The precision of angels
  Jones, G. The house of breathing; stories
These eyes
  Jones, G. The house of breathing; stories
Touching Tiananmen
  Jones, G. The house of breathing; stories
Veronica
  Jones, G. The house of breathing; stories
The word 'Ruby'
  Jones, G. The house of breathing; stories

Jones, Gayl
White rat
  Home and beyond; an anthology of Kentucky short stories; edited by Morris Allen Grubbs; with an introduction by Wade Hall and an afterword by Charles E. May

Jones, Gwyneth
La Cenerentola
  The Year's best science fiction, sixteenth annual collection; edited by Gardner Dozois

Jones, Harri Pritchard *See* Pritchard Jones, Harri, 1933-

Jones, Heather
Tom's homecoming
  Mr. Roopratna's chocolate; the winning stories from the 1999 Rhys Davies competition

Jones, LeRoi *See* Baraka, Imamu Amiri, 1934-

Jones, Madison
Sim Denny
  The Cry of an occasion; fiction from the Fellowship of Southern Writers; edited by Richard Bausch; with a foreword by George Garrett

Jones, Raki
8 A.M.
  African American Review v36 no1 p91-9 Spr 2002

Jones, Raymond F.
The alien machine
  Science-fiction classics; the stories that morphed into movies; compiled by Forrest J. Ackerman

Jones, Ron
Meredith Evans' kiss
  Mr. Roopratna's chocolate; the winning stories from the 1999 Rhys Davies competition

Jones, Stephen
Captivity Narrative 109
  South Carolina Review v36 no2 p19-23 Spr 2004
The Nature of Man
  South Carolina Review v35 no2 p165-6 Spr 2003

Jones, Thom
40, still at home
  Jones, T. Sonny Liston was a friend of mine; stories
Cold snap
  The Scribner anthology of contemporary short fiction; fifty North American stories since 1970; Lex Williford and Michael Martone, editors
Daddy's girl
  Jones, T. Sonny Liston was a friend of mine; stories
Fields of purple forever
  Jones, T. Sonny Liston was a friend of mine; stories
I love you, Sophie Western
  Jones, T. Sonny Liston was a friend of mine; stories
I want to live!
  The Best American short stories of the century; John Updike, editor, Katrina Kenison, coeditor; with an introduction by John Updike
A midnight clear
  Jones, T. Sonny Liston was a friend of mine; stories
Mouses
  Jones, T. Sonny Liston was a friend of mine; stories
The Workshop; seven decades of the Iowa Writers' Workshop: 42 stories, recollections & essays on Iowa's place in 20th-century American literature; edited by Tom Grimes
My heroic mythic journey
  Jones, T. Sonny Liston was a friend of mine; stories

Jones, Thom—*Continued*

Night Train

Doubletake v8 no4 p110-15 Spr 2003

The roadrunner

Jones, T. Sonny Liston was a friend of mine; stories

A run through the jungle

Jones, T. Sonny Liston was a friend of mine; stories

Sonny Liston was a friend of mine

Boxing's best short stories; edited by Paul D. Staudohar

Jones, T. Sonny Liston was a friend of mine; stories

Tarantula

Jones, T. Sonny Liston was a friend of mine; stories

Thorazine Johnny Felsun loves me (from his permanent cage of lifelong confinement)

On the rocks; the KGB Bar fiction anthology; edited by Rebecca Donner ; foreword by Denis Woychuk

You cheated, you lied

Jones, T. Sonny Liston was a friend of mine; stories

Jones, Tayari

Best cousin

New stories from the South; the year's best, 2004; edited by Shannon Ravenel; preface by Tim Gautreaux

Jong, Erica

En route to the congress of dreams; or, The zipless fuck

Neurotica: Jewish writers on sex; edited by Melvin Jules Bukiet

Jono, an elegy. Nissen, T.

JOPLIN, JANIS, 1943-1970

About

Dozois, G. R. Touring

Jordan, Jennifer

The wife

The Bluelight corner; black women writing on passion, sex, and romantic love; edited by Rosemarie Robotham

Jordan, Neil

The dream of a beast

The Anchor book of new Irish writing; the new Gaelach ficsean; edited and with an introduction by John Somer and John J. Daly

Jorge, Lídia

The instrumentalina

Grand Street no68 p121-36 Spr 1999

Jorgenson, Ivar

Deadly city

Science-fiction classics; the stories that morphed into movies; compiled by Forrest J. Ackerman

Jorie (& Jamie). Oates, J. C.

Joselet. Giono, J.

Joseph, Alison

Consider the Dilemma Facing an Ovulating Cavewoman Who Has Just Been Fertilised

Critical Quarterly v44 no3 p99-105 Aut 2002

Joseph, Anthony

The African origins of UFOs [excerpt]

Dark matter; a century of speculative fiction from the African diaspora; edited by Sheree R. Thomas

Joseph, Diana

Approximate to salvation

Joseph, D. Happy or otherwise

Bloodlines

Joseph, D. Happy or otherwise

Expatriates

Joseph, D. Happy or otherwise

The fifth Mrs. Hughes

Joseph, D. Happy or otherwise

If I close them

Joseph, D. Happy or otherwise

Many will enter, few will win

Joseph, D. Happy or otherwise

Naming stories

Joseph, D. Happy or otherwise

Schandorsky's mother

Joseph, D. Happy or otherwise

Shared and stolen

Joseph, D. Happy or otherwise

Sick child

Joseph, D. Happy or otherwise

What remains

Joseph, D. Happy or otherwise

Windows and words

Joseph, D. Happy or otherwise

Joseph, Sheri

The Boyfriend

The Kenyon Review v25 no1 p128-43 Wint 2003

Rest stop

The Virginia Quarterly Review v78 no3 p517-37 Summ 2002

The waiting room

The Georgia Review v53 no3 p497-512 Fall 1999

Joseph. Maleti, G.

Joshua. Maleti, G.

Joshua & Clark. Holleran, A.

Joshua's holiday. Van Daele, R.

Josie. Adam, C.

Josué Chili-Mazel meets himself. Lubitch Domecq, A.

The **journal.** Williams, M.

JOURNALISM

Carlson, R. I am Bigfoot

Singer, I. B. The missing line

JOURNALISTS

See also Women journalists

Adams, A. The last lovely city

Adams, A. Old love affairs

Atkinson, K. Evil doppelgängers

Bates, H. Farewell to the master

Boylan, C. Perfect love

Bradbury, R. The swan

Brenner, W. Mr. Puniverse

Campbell, R. McGonagall in the head

Carlson, R. Plan B for the middle class

Chekhov, A. P. Hush!

Coleman, J. C. Borderlands

Davidson, A. The third sacred well of the temple

Davies, R. Misfits

De Waal, T. The English house: a story of Chechnya

Engel, H. The ant trap

Fischer, T. Ice tonight in the hearts of young visitors

Fleming, R. The blasphemer

Francis, D. The gift

JOURNALISTS—*Continued*

Gamelli, R. A hero, plain and simple
Gilchrist, E. You must change your life
Girardi, R. The dinner party
Grodstein, L. John on the train: a fable for our cynical friends
Harrison, H. American dead
Harrison, H. At last, the true story of Frankenstein
Harrison, H. By the falls
Hassler, J. Good news in Culver Bend
Hautala, R. The Nephews
Hess, J. All's well that ends
Hillerman, T. First lead gasser
Hunter, F. Madagascar
Hunter, F. A newsman scratches an itch
Hunter, F. North of Nairobi
Hunter, F. Waiting for the Mwami
Jacobs, M. The rape of reason
Jenkins, G. Richard and poorer
Johnson-Davies, D. Open season in Beirut
Kurlansky, M. Desaparecidos
Lee, M. Memo to our journalists
Lovesey, P. Star struck
Madden, D. The world's one breathing
Melville, P. Provenance of a face
Oates, J. C. Death watch
O'Faoláin, S. Persecution mania
Onetti, J. C. Hell most feared
Paine, T. Ceauçsescu's cat
Popkes, S. Winters are hard
Roth, J. The cartel
Royle, N. The Inland Waterways Association
Rusch, K. K. Going native
Shonk, K. Kitchen friends
Singer, I. B. The interview
Smith, L. Between the lines
Squire, E. D. A passion for the cook
Taylor, Nick. The smell of despair
Tenn, W. The human angle
Thompson, J. Forever
Watson, B. Last days of the dog-men
Westlake, D. E. Come again?
Westlake, D. E. Skeeks
Wharton, E. The last asset
Wheeler, R. S. The square reporter
Yates, R. A wrestler with sharks

JOURNALS *See* Diaries (Stories about); Diaries (Stories in diary form)

The **Journey**. Bocock, M.
A **journey**. Wharton, E.
Journey back to the source. Carpentier, A.
A **journey** by cart. See Chekhov, A. P. The schoolmistress
Journey into the dark. Yolen, J.
Journey to Port Adventure. Denevi, M.
Journey to the seed. Carpentier, A.
JOURNEYS *See* Voyages and travels
Journeys end. Anderson, P.
Journeys to six lands. Mathews, H.
Joy. Chekhov, A. P.
JOY AND SORROW
    See also Happiness
Kittredge, W. Momentum is always the weapon
Joy in the house. Wharton, E.
Joy of cooking. Busch, F.
Joy of eating. Derby, M.
The **joy-ride**. Lavin, M.

Joyce, Graham
The Coventry boy
    The Mammoth book of best new horror 14; edited with an introduction by Stephen Jones
    The Year's best fantasy & horror: sixteenth annual collection; edited by Ellen Datlow & Terri Windling
First, catch your demon
    The Mammoth book of best horror 13; edited by Stephen Jones
Tiger moth
    Gathering the bones; original stories from the world's masters of horror; edited by Dennis Etchison, Ramsey Campbell and Jack Dann
Xenos Beach
    Best new horror 12; edited and with an introduction by Stephen Jones
JOYCE, JAMES, 1882-1941
    About
    Jenkins, G. A portrait of the artist at Warner Bros.
Joyce, Michael
Storm-tossed
    Iowa Review v29 no1 p64-69 Spr 1999
White moths
    Iowa Review v29 no1 p70-74 Spr 1999
Joyce's children. Kaminsky, S. M.
Joyce's pupil. Jančar, D.
Joyeux Noël. Korner, S.
Juan Muraña. Borges, J. L.
JUANA, LA LOCA, QUEEN OF CASTILE, 1479-1555
    About
    Connor, J. Juana La Loca
Juana la Loca. Connor, J.
Juanita. Chopin, K.
JUÁREZ, BENITO, 1806-1872
    About
    Henry, W. The tallest Indian in Toltepec
Jubilee. Dann, J.
Jubilee. Lupoff, R. A.
Jubilee King. Shepard, J.
Judah's a two-way street running out. Burris, J.
JUDAISM
    See also Hasidism; Jews; Synagogues; Yom Kippur
Bukiet, M. J. Tongue of the Jews
Englander, N. The gilgul of Park Avenue
Grade, C. My quarrel with Hersh Rasseyner
Leegant, J. The lament of the rabbi's daughters
Malzberg, B. N. Hieractic realignment
Orringer, J. The smoothest way is full of stones
Schmidt, H. J. Fishman's fascination
Schrank, B. Consent
What, L. The leap
What, L. Those who know
Judas danced. Aldiss, B. W.
JUDAS ISCARIOT
    About
    Borges, J. L. Three versions of Judas
    Devereaux, R. Apologia
Judgement. Carson, J.
The **Judgement** of Paris. Longstreet, K. A.
JUDGES
Aldrich, B. S. The runaway judge
Aldrich, B. S. The weakling
Allen, D., Jr. End of the steam age
Auchincloss, L. The justice clerk

JUDGES—*Continued*
Brenner, W. The Cantankerous Judge
Huffman, B., Jr. Contrary to the manifest tenor
Huffman, B., Jr. Synthesis of the community standard
Huffman, B., Jr. Zealous representation
Klíma, I. It's raining out
Lupoff, R. A. The monster and Mr. Greene
Post, M. D. Naboth's vineyard
Reiner, C. The people versus De Marco
Reiner, C. Warren Waits and the spaghetti-strap girl
Sade, marquis de. The mystified magistrate
Sade, marquis de. The windbags of Provence
Savage, L., Jr. The hangman's segundo
Silverstein, S. The guilty party
Spark, M. The hanging judge
Tóibín, C. The heather blazing [excerpt]
Wheat, C. The only good judge
Judgment. Gorman, E.
Judgment. Thompson, C.
JUDGMENT DAY
Peri Rossi, C. Final judgment
Judgment day. Norris, H.
Judgment engine. Bear, G.
The **judgment** of Psycho. Haskell, J.
Judicial economy. Huffman, B., Jr.
Juergensmeyer, Jane Stuart *See* Stuart, Jane, 1942-
Juggernaut. O'Shaughnessy, P.
Juggernaut. Springer, N.
The **juggler**. Hegi, U.
The **Jughead** of Berlin. Johnson, A.
The **juice-seller's** bird. Browder, C.
Julavits, Heidi
Marry the one who gets there first
The Best American short stories, 1999; selected from U.S. and Canadian magazines by Amy Tan with Katrina Kenison, with an introduction by Amy Tan
Jules Jr Michael Jules Jr. DeLancey, K.
The **Jules** Verne Steam balloon. Davenport, G.
Julian. Reifler, N.
Julian Vreden. Bowles, P.
Julianne. Miller, R.
Julie. Codrescu, A.
Julius. Lass, A.
July, Miranda
Birthmark
The Paris Review v45 p45-51 Spr 2003
Making Love in 2003
The Paris Review v45 p164-81 Fall 2003
July. Chimera, B.
JULY FOURTH *See* Fourth of July
July fourth. Doerr, A.
The **July** Ward. Dyer, S. N.
Jumpin' Jack Flash. Rucker, R. v. B.
Jumping. Clyde, M.
Jumping ship. Thurm, M.
Jumping the road. Dann, J.
Jumping with Jim. Danihy, G.
June 1989. McManus, J.
June gave him the voice. Estrada, J.
JUNG, C. G. (CARL GUSTAV), 1875-1961
About
Pearlman, D. D. The Einstein-Jung connection
Jung, Carl Gustav *See* Jung, C. G. (Carl Gustav), 1875-1961

Jung, Ha-Yun
Our lady of the height
Best new American voices 2001; guest editor Charles Baxter; series editors John Kulka and Natalie Danford
Prairie Schooner v75 no2 p67-80 Summ 2001
Junger, Sebastian
Heat of the day
The Ohio Review no62/63 p399-404 2001
Jungle wedding. Clark, J.
JUNGLES
Fowler, C. The green man
Junior. Stuckey-French, E.
Junior high samurai. Massey, S.
The **juniper** tree. Kessel, J.
Juno's swans. Aldrich, B. S.
JUPITER (PLANET)
Anderson, P. Call me Joe
Clarke, A. C. A meeting with Medusa
Simak, C. D. Desertion
Tenn, W. The deserter
Jupiter five. Clarke, A. C.
Jupiter V. See Clarke, A. C. Jupiter five
Jurado, Alicia
Saying goodbye through twenty-five centuries
English translations of short stories by contemporary Argentine women writers; edited by Eliana Cazaubon Hermann ; translated by Sally Webb Thornton
Jurík, Luboš
The road sweeper
In search of homo sapiens; twenty-five contemporary Slovak short stories; editor, Pavol Hudík ; [translated by Heather Trebatická; American English editor, Lucy Bednár]
The **jury**. Galef, D.
JURY DUTY *See* Trials
A **jury** of her peers. Glaspell, S.
Juska, Elise
Deep
Salmagundi no124/125 p278-87 Fall 1999/Wint 2000
Like Two People Who Have Never Met
Calyx v21 no1 p54-67 Wint 2003
Northeast Philly girls
The Hudson Review v55 no1 p31-44 Spr 2002
Just a lark; or, The crypt of Matthew Ashdown. McTair, R.
Just a little closer to the Lord. Groom, W.
Just a love story. Coberly, L. M.
Just another New York Christmas story. Cohen, S.
Just another stiff. Daly, C. J.
Just desserts. Kelman, J.
Just like Eddy. Newman, K.
Just like your father. Burgess, A.
Just married. Earley, T.
Just one bite won't kill you. Wolzien, V.
Just only one little mystery-pistery. Keating, H. R. F.
Just peace. Vinge, V.
Just so much garbage. Daheim, M.
Just stunning. Padgett, A. and Dennis, D.
Just the ticket. Vachss, A. H.
Just wait. Jen, G.
Justice, Jean Ross
The end of a good party
The Yale Review v90 no3 p119-27 Jl 2002

Justice, Jean Ross—*Continued*
  The Next to Last Line
    The Antioch Review v61 no3 p498-505 Summ
      2003
  Night thoughts
    The Antioch Review v57 no2 p232-36 Spr
      1999
  Three Sisters
    Southwest Review v88 no2/3 p350-66 2003
JUSTICE
  Bowles, P. Bouayad and the money
  Chekhov, A. P. An incident at law
Justice. Wuori, G. K.
Justice—A Beginning. Paley, G.
The **justice** clerk. Auchincloss, L.
Justice in brackets. See Babel´, I. Justice in paren-
    theses
Justice in parentheses. Babel´, I.
Justina. Davis, D. S.
Justina's priest. Trevor, W.
Jutras, Jeanne d'Arc
  Georgie [excerpt]
    The Vintage book of international lesbian fic-
      tion; edited and with an introduction by
      Naomi Holoch and Joan Nestle
JUVENILE DELINQUENCY
  Cather, W. Paul's case
  Doenges, J. Crooks
  Hunter, E. First offense
  Kalam, M. Bow down
  Shade, E. A rage forever
  Symons, J. The tigers of Subtopia

K

The **k-factor**. Harrison, H.
K fof fake. Lethem, J.
K2. Clark, J.
Ka-man, Shirley Poon
  (jt. auth) See Chan Koon Chung
Kaahumanu. Shade, E.
The **Kabuliwallah** (The Fruitseller from Kabul).
    Tagore, Sir R. and Noble, M. E.
Kachtick, Keith
  Hungry ghost
    Nixon under the bodhi tree and other works
      of Buddhist fiction; edited by Kate Wheeler
      ; foreword by Charles Johnson
Kaddish. Baron, D.
Kaddish. Dann, J.
Kaddish. Yasgur, B. S.
Kaddish for the kid. Collins, M. A.
Kadetsky, Elizabeth
  The Poison That Purifies You
    Gettysburg Review v16 no1 p49-64 Spr 2003
Kadish, Rachel
  The argument
    Lost tribe; jewish fiction from the edge
KAFIRS (AFRICAN PEOPLE) *See* Zulus
    (African people)
Kafka, Franz
  Blumfeld, an elderly bachelor
    Nightshade: 20th century ghost stories; edited
      by Robert Phillips
KAFKA, FRANZ, 1883-1924
                    About
  Bukiet, M. J. The two Franzes
  Davenport, G. The aeroplanes at Brescia

  Davenport, G. Belinda's world tour
  Davenport, G. The chair
  Davenport, G. The messengers
  Goliger, G. One morning in Prague
  Lethem, J. and Scholz, C. Receding horizon
  Mathews, H. Franz Kafka in Riga
  Rucker, R. v. B. The fifty-seventh Franz Kafka
  Scholz, C. The amount to carry
  Singer, I. B. A friend of Kafka
                Parodies, imitations, etc.
  Lethem, J. K fof fake
  Lethem, J. The notebooks of Bob K.
  Scholz, C. Blumfeld, an elderly bachelor
Kafka's diary. Cohen, B.
Kagan, Janet
  The return of the kangaroo rex
    The Good new stuff; adventure SF in the
      grand tradition; edited by Gardner Dozois
Kahanovitch, Pinhas *See* Der Nister, 1884-1950
Kahn, Michael A.
  The bread of affliction
    Browning, A. Murder is no mitzvah; edited
      by Abigail Browning
    Mystery midrash; an anthology of Jewish
      mystery & detective fiction; [edited by]
      Lawrence W. Raphael
  Strange bedfellows
    Women before the bench; edited by Carolyn
      Wheat; introduction by Linda Fairstein
Kaiser and the War. Ortiz, S. J.
Kajane, Jiri
  The usual trickery!
    Michigan Quarterly Review v40 no3 p582-93
      Summ 2001
Kalam, Murad
  Bow down
    Prize stories, 2001; The O. Henry awards; ed-
      ited and with an introduction by Larry
      Dark
Kalamu ya Salaam
  Buddy Bolden
    Dark matter; a century of speculative fiction
      from the African diaspora; edited by Sheree
      R. Thomas
  Can you wear my eyes
    Dark matter; a century of speculative fiction
      from the African diaspora; edited by Sheree
      R. Thomas
Kaleidoscope. Paolucci, A.
Kalfus, Ken
  Anzhelika, 13
    Kalfus, K. Pu-239 and other Russian fantasies
  Birobidzhan
    Kalfus, K. Pu-239 and other Russian fantasies
  Budyonnovsk
    Kalfus, K. Pu-239 and other Russian fantasies
  The Moment They Were Waiting For
    Harper's v307 p72-5 S 2003
  Orbit
    Kalfus, K. Pu-239 and other Russian fantasies
  Peredelkino
    Kalfus, K. Pu-239 and other Russian fantasies
  Pu-239
    Kalfus, K. Pu-239 and other Russian fantasies
  A remembrance of ink past
    Harper's v299 no1790 p36-37 Jl 1999
  Salt
    Kalfus, K. Pu-239 and other Russian fantasies

Kalman, Judith

Allures of grandeur
   Kalman, J. The county of birches; stories
Channel crossing
   Kalman, J. The county of birches; stories
The county of birches
   Kalman, J. The county of birches; stories
Eichmann's monogram
   Kalman, J. The county of birches; stories
Flight
   Kalman, J. The county of birches; stories
Ladies' wear
   Kalman, J. The county of birches; stories
The making of a Jew
   Kalman, J. The county of birches; stories
Monahan Avenue
   Kalman, J. The county of birches; stories
Not for me a crown of thorns
   Kalman, J. The county of birches; stories
Personal effects
   Kalman, J. The county of birches; stories
A property of childhood
   Kalman, J. The county of birches; stories
Rain
   Kalman, J. The county of birches; stories
A reason to be
   Kalman, J. The county of birches; stories
What's in a name?
   Kalman, J. The county of birches; stories

Kalotay, Daphne

All Life's Grandeur
   Prairie Schooner v78 no2 p128-40 Summ 2004

Kalotay, Daphne Eva

The business of love
   The Virginia Quarterly Review v75 no2 p360-74 Spr 1999
Snapshots
   The Literary Review (Madison, N.J.) v42 no4 p503-15 Summ 1999

Kalpakian, Laura

Blue Willow
   Good Housekeeping v236 no4 p203-4, 207, 210, 212-16 Ap 2003
A long story short
   Iowa Review v31 no3 p130-42 Wint 2001/2002
The nine-year-old who stole Christmas
   Good Housekeeping v237 no6 p205-6, 208-10, 212-14 D 2003
The talking kimono
   Good Housekeeping v238 no2 p193-4, 196, 198, 200, 204-5 F 2004
Unforeseen Circumstances
   Good Housekeeping v235 no1 p191-6 Jl 2002
What to bring to an American picnic
   Good Housekeeping v239 no2 p173-4, 176, 178-81 Ag 2004

Kalu, Anthonia C.

Angelus
   Kalu, Anthonia C. Broken lives and other stories; foreword by Emmanuel N. Obiechina
Broken lives
   Kalu, Anthonia C. Broken lives and other stories; foreword by Emmanuel N. Obiechina
Camwood
   Kalu, Anthonia C. Broken lives and other stories; foreword by Emmanuel N. Obiechina

Children's day
   Kalu, Anthonia C. Broken lives and other stories; foreword by Emmanuel N. Obiechina
The gift
   Kalu, Anthonia C. Broken lives and other stories; foreword by Emmanuel N. Obiechina
Independence
   Kalu, Anthonia C. Broken lives and other stories; foreword by Emmanuel N. Obiechina
The last push
   Kalu, Anthonia C. Broken lives and other stories; foreword by Emmanuel N. Obiechina
Ogbanje father
   Kalu, Anthonia C. Broken lives and other stories; foreword by Emmanuel N. Obiechina
Osondu
   Kalu, Anthonia C. Broken lives and other stories; foreword by Emmanuel N. Obiechina
Relief duty
   Kalu, Anthonia C. Broken lives and other stories; foreword by Emmanuel N. Obiechina

Kamata, Suzanne

The Beautiful One Has Come
   Meridians v3 no2 p132-8 2003

Kamdu Tea Restaurant. Chan Koon Chung

Kami. Waters, M. Y.

Kaminer, Wladimir

Suleyman and Salieri
   Chicago Review v48 no2/3 p153-4 Summ 2002

Kaminsky, Stuart M.

Adele
   Master's choice v2; mystery stories by today's top writers and the masters who inspired them; edited by Lawrence Block
Amnesia
   Kaminsky, S. M. Hidden and other stories
Bitter lemons
   Kaminsky, S. M. Hidden and other stories
Blowout in Little Man Flats
   Kaminsky, S. M. Hidden and other stories
The buck stops here
   Kaminsky, S. M. Hidden and other stories
Busted blossoms
   A Century of noir; thirty-two classic crime stories; edited by Mickey Spillane and Max Allan Collins
   Kaminsky, S. M. Hidden and other stories
Confession
   Mystery midrash; an anthology of Jewish mystery & detective fiction; [edited by] Lawrence W. Raphael
DRUP number one
   Kaminsky, S. M. Hidden and other stories
The final toast
   Kaminsky, S. M. Hidden and other stories
Hidden
   Kaminsky, S. M. Hidden and other stories
In thunder, lightning or in rain
   Kaminsky, S. M. Hidden and other stories
It comes with the badge
   Kaminsky, S. M. Hidden and other stories
It's a wise child who knows
   Kaminsky, S. M. Hidden and other stories
Joyce's children
   Crème de la crime; edited by Janet Hutchings
Listen, my children
   Kaminsky, S. M. Hidden and other stories

Kaminsky, Stuart M.—*Continued*

The man who shot Lewis Vance
Kaminsky, S. M. Hidden and other stories
Punishment
Kaminsky, S. M. Hidden and other stories
Scorpion's kiss
Flesh and blood; erotic tales of crime and passion; edited by Max Allan Collins and Jeff Gelb
The World's finest mystery and crime stories, second annual collection; edited by Ed Gorman
Snow
The World's finest mystery and crime stories, first annual collection; edited by Ed Gorman
Sometimes something goes wrong
The Best American mystery stories, 2002; edited and with an introduction by James Ellroy; Otto Penzler, series editor
The Mysterious Press anniversary anthology; celebrating 25 years; by the editors of Mysterious Press
The voice of a child
Kaminsky, S. M. Hidden and other stories
What you don't know
Death by espionage; intriguing stories of deception and betrayal; edited by Martin Cruz Smith

Kamov, Janko Polić

Sorrow
Partisan Review v66 no2 p310-26 Spr 1999

Kanafāni, Ghassān

Abu al-Hassan ambushes an English car
Kanafāni, G. Palestine's children; returning to Haifa & other stories; translated by Barbara Harlow & Karen E. Riley, with an introduction and a biographical essay on Ghassan Kanafani
The child borrows his uncle's gun and goes east to Safad
Kanafāni, G. Palestine's children; returning to Haifa & other stories; translated by Barbara Harlow & Karen E. Riley, with an introduction and a biographical essay on Ghassan Kanafani
The child discovers that the key looks like an axe
Kanafāni, G. Palestine's children; returning to Haifa & other stories; translated by Barbara Harlow & Karen E. Riley, with an introduction and a biographical essay on Ghassan Kanafani
The child goes to the camp
Kanafāni, G. Palestine's children; returning to Haifa & other stories; translated by Barbara Harlow & Karen E. Riley, with an introduction and a biographical essay on Ghassan Kanafani
The child, his father, and the gun go to the citadel at Jaddin
Kanafāni, G. Palestine's children; returning to Haifa & other stories; translated by Barbara Harlow & Karen E. Riley, with an introduction and a biographical essay on Ghassan Kanafani

The death of bed number 12
Other people's mail; an anthology of letter stories; edited with an introduction by Gail Pool
Dr. Qassim talks to Eva about Mansur who has arrived in Safad
Kanafāni, G. Palestine's children; returning to Haifa & other stories; translated by Barbara Harlow & Karen E. Riley, with an introduction and a biographical essay on Ghassan Kanafani
Guns in the camp
Kanafāni, G. Palestine's children; returning to Haifa & other stories; translated by Barbara Harlow & Karen E. Riley, with an introduction and a biographical essay on Ghassan Kanafani
Hamid stops listening to the uncles' stories
Kanafāni, G. Palestine's children; returning to Haifa & other stories; translated by Barbara Harlow & Karen E. Riley, with an introduction and a biographical essay on Ghassan Kanafani
He was a child that day
Kanafāni, G. Palestine's children; returning to Haifa & other stories; translated by Barbara Harlow & Karen E. Riley, with an introduction and a biographical essay on Ghassan Kanafani
Paper from Ramleh
Kanafāni, G. Palestine's children; returning to Haifa & other stories; translated by Barbara Harlow & Karen E. Riley, with an introduction and a biographical essay on Ghassan Kanafani
A present for the holiday
Kanafāni, G. Palestine's children; returning to Haifa & other stories; translated by Barbara Harlow & Karen E. Riley, with an introduction and a biographical essay on Ghassan Kanafani
Returning to Haifa
Kanafāni, G. Palestine's children; returning to Haifa & other stories; translated by Barbara Harlow & Karen E. Riley, with an introduction and a biographical essay on Ghassan Kanafani
Six eagles and a child
Kanafāni, G. Palestine's children; returning to Haifa & other stories; translated by Barbara Harlow & Karen E. Riley, with an introduction and a biographical essay on Ghassan Kanafani
The slope
Kanafāni, G. Palestine's children; returning to Haifa & other stories; translated by Barbara Harlow & Karen E. Riley, with an introduction and a biographical essay on Ghassan Kanafani
Suliman's friend learns many things in one night
Kanafāni, G. Palestine's children; returning to Haifa & other stories; translated by Barbara Harlow & Karen E. Riley, with an introduction and a biographical essay on Ghassan Kanafani

Kanar, Bryn
Dreaming among men
    Black heart, ivory bones; [edited by] Ellen
        Datlow & Terri Windling
Kane, Jessica Francis
The Arnold proof
    Kane, J. F. Bending heaven; stories
    Michigan Quarterly Review v40 no2 p355-72
        Spr 2001
Evidence of old repairs
    Kane, J. F. Bending heaven; stories
Exposure
    Kane, J. F. Bending heaven; stories
First sale
    Kane, J. F. Bending heaven; stories
How to become a publicist
    Kane, J. F. Bending heaven; stories
Ideas of home, but not the thing itself
    Kane, J. F. Bending heaven; stories
Pantomime
    Kane, J. F. Bending heaven; stories
Paris
    Kane, J. F. Bending heaven; stories
Refuge
    Kane, J. F. Bending heaven; stories
The trailing spouse
    Kane, J. F. Bending heaven; stories
Wreckers
    Kane, J. F. Bending heaven; stories
KANGAROOS
Davidson, A. The man who saw the elephant
Jenkins, G. In the outback
KANSAS
Agee, J. Binding the devil
Bishop, M. Blue Kansas sky
Denton, B. The territory
Doctorow, E. L. Walter John Harmon
Frontier and pioneer life
See Frontier and pioneer life—Kansas
Kansas City
Clair, M. October Brown
Clair, M. Water seeks its own level
Kansas. Dobyns, S.
Kansas. Robinson, M.
KANSAS CITY (KAN.) *See* Kansas—Kansas
    City
KANSAS CITY (MO.) *See* Missouri—Kansas
    City
Kantner, Rob
Something simple
    The World's finest mystery and crime stories,
        first annual collection; edited by Ed
        Gorman
Kao, Hsing-chien *See* Gao Xingjian, 1940-
Kapel, Alexander
How long does a pogrom last?
    Neugroschel, J. No star too beautiful; Yiddish
        stories from 1382 to the present; compiled
        and translated by Joachim Neugroschel
The **kapici's** wife. Gabriel, D.
Kaplan, David Michael
Doe season
    The Scribner anthology of contemporary short
        fiction; fifty North American stories since
        1970; Lex Williford and Michael Martone,
        editors
Dream Boy
    TriQuarterly no117 p181-217 Fall 2003

Kaplan, Hester
Claude comes and goes
    Kaplan, H. The edge of marriage
Companion Animal
    Ploughshares v29 no1 p131-48 Spr 2003
Cuckle me
    Kaplan, H. The edge of marriage
Dysaesthesia
    Kaplan, H. The edge of marriage
The edge of marriage
    Kaplan, H. The edge of marriage
From where we've fallen
    Kaplan, H. The edge of marriage
Goodwill
    Kaplan, H. The edge of marriage
Live life king-sized
    The Best American short stories, 1999; select-
        ed from U.S. and Canadian magazines by
        Amy Tan with Katrina Kenison, with an in-
        troduction by Amy Tan
    Kaplan, H. The edge of marriage
The spiral
    Kaplan, H. The edge of marriage
Would you know it wasn't love?
    Kaplan, H. The edge of marriage
Kapur, Kamla
Indra Gets Caught
    Parabola v28 no4 p71-3 Wint 2003
Karampur, Farzaneh
Refugee
    A Feast in the mirror; stories by contempo-
        rary Iranian women; translated and edited
        by Mohammad Mehdi Khorrami, Shouleh
        Vatanabadi
Karasu, Bilge
Fork
    Grand Street no67 p78-91 Wint 1999
KARATE
Southgate, M. The kick inside
Karbo, Karen
The palace of marriage
    LA shorts; edited by Steven Gilbar
Karen makes out. Leonard, E.
Karl-Yankel. Babel´, I.
Karlin, Katherine
Midnight shift
    The North American Review v286 no5 p16-25
        S/O 2001
Karma. Gordimer, N.
Karma. Reddi, R. P.
Karma wheel. Boswell, M.
Karnezis, Panos
Another day on Pegasus
    Karnezis, P. Little infamies; stories
Applied aeronautics
    Karnezis, P. Little infamies; stories
Cassandra is gone
    Karnezis, P. Little infamies; stories
A circus attraction
    Karnezis, P. Little infamies; stories
The day of the beast
    Karnezis, P. Little infamies; stories
Deus ex machina
    Karnezis, P. Little infamies; stories
A funeral of stones
    Karnezis, P. Little infamies; stories
The hunters in winter
    Karnezis, P. Little infamies; stories

Karnezis, Panos—*Continued*
Immortality
Karnezis, P. Little infamies; stories
Jeremiad
Karnezis, P. Little infamies; stories
The legend of Atlantis
Karnezis, P. Little infamies; stories
Medical ethics
Karnezis, P. Little infamies; stories
On the first day of Lent
Karnezis, P. Little infamies; stories
Sacrifice
Karnezis, P. Little infamies; stories
Sins of a harvest god
Karnezis, P. Little infamies; stories
Stella the spinster's afternoon dreams
Karnezis, P. Little infamies; stories
Whale on the beach
Karnezis, P. Little infamies; stories
Wilt thou be made whole?
Karnezis, P. Little infamies; stories

Karodia, Farida
The woman in green
The Anchor book of modern African stories;
edited by Nadežda Obradovic ; with a foreword by Chinua Achebe

Karon, Jan
Chance meeting
Good Housekeeping v229 no5 p222+ N 1999
The coming of the clan
Good Housekeeping v228 no2 p159-61+ F
1999

Karp-Gendre, Jacqueline
Sans paroles
Dalhousie Review v79 no2 p229-31 Summ
1999

Karpinovitsh, Avrom
Zubak
Neugroschel, J. No star too beautiful; Yiddish
stories from 1382 to the present; compiled
and translated by Joachim Neugroschel

Kasai, Kiyoshi
Oedipus city
The Review of Contemporary Fiction v22 no2
p60-74 Summ 2002

KASHMIR VALLEY (INDIA) *See* India—Vale
of Kashmir

Kashtanka. Chekhov, A. P.

Katkov, Norman
Stop the fight!
Boxing's best short stories; edited by Paul D.
Staudohar

Katowich, James
Among the sick
Southern Humanities Review v36 no2 p148-59
Spr 2002

Katz, David
The Rachel Weisz Experiment
Esquire v141 no4 p92-7 Ap 2004

Katzenstein. Keret, E.

Kaufelt, David A.
The bagel murders
Death dines at 8:30; edited by Claudia Bishop
and Nick DiChario

Kauffman, Janet
Patriotic
The Scribner anthology of contemporary short
fiction; fifty North American stories since
1970; Lex Williford and Michael Martone,
editors

Kaufman, Wendi
Helen on Eighty-Sixth Street
Fault lines; stories of divorce; collected and
edited by Caitlin Shetterly

Kavaler, Rebecca
Give brother my best
Kavaler, R. A little more than kin; a collec-
tion of short stories
The inheritance
Kavaler, R. A little more than kin; a collec-
tion of short stories
Mother
Kavaler, R. A little more than kin; a collec-
tion of short stories
Mysteries
Kavaler, R. A little more than kin; a collec-
tion of short stories
Pets
Kavaler, R. A little more than kin; a collec-
tion of short stories
Pigeons
Kavaler, R. A little more than kin; a collec-
tion of short stories
Servants
Kavaler, R. A little more than kin; a collec-
tion of short stories
Sisters
Kavaler, R. A little more than kin; a collec-
tion of short stories

Kavan, Anna
The zebra-struck
The Vintage book of amnesia; an anthology;
edited by Jonathan Lethem

Kavanagh, Herminie Templeton
The banshee's comb
The Ultimate Halloween; edited by Marvin
Kaye

Kavita through glass. Raboteau, E. I.

Kawabata, Yasunari
Chrysanthemum in the rock
Kawabata, Y. First snow on Fuji; translated
by Michael Emmerich
First snow on Fuji
Kawabata, Y. First snow on Fuji; translated
by Michael Emmerich
Her husband didn't
Kawabata, Y. First snow on Fuji; translated
by Michael Emmerich
Nature
Kawabata, Y. First snow on Fuji; translated
by Michael Emmerich
Raindrops
Kawabata, Y. First snow on Fuji; translated
by Michael Emmerich
A row of trees
Kawabata, Y. First snow on Fuji; translated
by Michael Emmerich
Silence
Kawabata, Y. First snow on Fuji; translated
by Michael Emmerich
This country, that country
Kawabata, Y. First snow on Fuji; translated
by Michael Emmerich

Kawabata, Yasunari—*Continued*
Yumiura
  Kawabata, Y. First snow on Fuji; translated
    by Michael Emmerich
Kawar, Fakhri and Amin, Omnia
A Bird in My House
  World Literature Today v78 no1 p62-3 Ja/Ap
    2004
Kay, Jackie
In between talking about the elephant
  Granta no75 p179-89 Aut 2001
Trumpet [excerpt]
  The Vintage book of contemporary Scottish
    fiction; edited and with an introduction by
    Peter Kravitz
You Go When You Can No Longer Stay
  Granta v85 p69-78 Spr 2004
Kaye, Terry
The witch who hated Halloween
  The Ultimate Halloween; edited by Marvin
    Kaye
Kays and exes. Clark, C. A.
Kealey, Tom
Bones
  Prairie Schooner v77 no4 p94-113 Wint 2003
Keating, H. R. F. (Henry Reymond Fitzwalter)
The hound of the hanging gardens
  Edwards, M. Mysterious pleasures; a celebra-
    tion of the Crime Writers' Association's
    50th anniversary; edited by Martin Edwards
Just only one little mystery-pistery
  Malice domestic 8
Keating, Henry Reymond Fitzwalter *See*
  Keating, H. R. F. (Henry Reymond
    Fitzwalter), 1926-
KEATS, JOHN, 1795-1821
        About
Haskell, J. Narrow road
Keegan, Claire
Antarctica
  Keegan, C. Antarctica
The burning palms
  Keegan, C. Antarctica
Burns
  Keegan, C. Antarctica
Close to the water's edge
  Keegan, C. Antarctica
The Ginger Rogers sermon
  Keegan, C. Antarctica
Love in the tall grass
  Keegan, C. Antarctica
Men and women
  Keegan, C. Antarctica
Passport soup
  Keegan, C. Antarctica
Quare name for a boy
  Keegan, C. Antarctica
Ride if you dare
  Keegan, C. Antarctica
The scent of winter
  Keegan, C. Antarctica
The singing cashier
  Keegan, C. Antarctica
Sisters
  Keegan, C. Antarctica
Storms
  Keegan, C. Antarctica
Where the water's deepest
  Keegan, C. Antarctica

You can't be too careful
  Keegan, C. Antarctica
Keegan's load. Winegardner, M.
Keeley, Carol
An evening at the Blackstone
  The Antioch Review v57 no3 p426-31 Summ
    1999
Keene, Jarret
Son of Mogar
  New England Review v22 no2 p148-63 Spr
    2001
Keep it from the flame. Foster, K.
Keep looking. Allen, S.
Keeper of secrets, teller of lies. Knight, M.
The **keeper** of the Rothenstein tomb. Sinclair, I.
The **keeper** of the virgins. Al-Shaykh, H.
Keeping count. Goran, L.
Keeping time. Fracis, S. H.
Keepsake. Andoe, J.
Keepsakes. Hassler, J.
Keepsakes and treasures: a love story. Gaiman, N.
Keer Avenue, July 1967. Rodburg, M.
Kees, Weldon
The brothers
  Kees, W. Selected short stories of Weldon
    Kees; edited and with an introduction by
    Dana Gioia
The ceremony
  Kees, W. Selected short stories of Weldon
    Kees; edited and with an introduction by
    Dana Gioia
Do you like the mountains?
  Kees, W. Selected short stories of Weldon
    Kees; edited and with an introduction by
    Dana Gioia
The evening of the Fourth of July
  Kees, W. Selected short stories of Weldon
    Kees; edited and with an introduction by
    Dana Gioia
Every year they came out
  Kees, W. Selected short stories of Weldon
    Kees; edited and with an introduction by
    Dana Gioia
Farewell to Frognall
  Kees, W. Selected short stories of Weldon
    Kees; edited and with an introduction by
    Dana Gioia
Gents 50/Ladies 25
  Kees, W. Selected short stories of Weldon
    Kees; edited and with an introduction by
    Dana Gioia
I should worry
  Kees, W. Selected short stories of Weldon
    Kees; edited and with an introduction by
    Dana Gioia
Letter from Maine
  Kees, W. Selected short stories of Weldon
    Kees; edited and with an introduction by
    Dana Gioia
The library: four sketches
  Kees, W. Selected short stories of Weldon
    Kees; edited and with an introduction by
    Dana Gioia
The life of the mind
  Kees, W. Selected short stories of Weldon
    Kees; edited and with an introduction by
    Dana Gioia

Kees, Weldon—*Continued*
Mrs. Lutz
Kees, W. Selected short stories of Weldon Kees; edited and with an introduction by Dana Gioia
Public library
Kees, W. Selected short stories of Weldon Kees; edited and with an introduction by Dana Gioia
The Purcells
Kees, W. Selected short stories of Weldon Kees; edited and with an introduction by Dana Gioia
The sign
Kees, W. Selected short stories of Weldon Kees; edited and with an introduction by Dana Gioia
So cold outside
Kees, W. Selected short stories of Weldon Kees; edited and with an introduction by Dana Gioia

Keith, William H.
Fossils
Worldmakers; SF adventures in terraforming; edited by Gardner Dozois
Iterations
Past imperfect; edited by Martin H. Greenberg and Larry Segriff

Keith. Carlson, R.

Kelin, Daniel A.
Uom and Tak
Parabola v28 no4 p84-5 Wint 2003

Keller, Christoph
So, Sweetie, what's your Wilhelm been up to?
The Paris Review v43 no160 p169-79 Wint 2001

Kellerman, Faye
Holy water
Mystery midrash; an anthology of Jewish mystery & detective fiction; [edited by] Lawrence W. Raphael

Keller's last refuge. Block, L.

Kelley, Douglas
A modern tragedy
Stories from the Blue Moon Café; edited by Sonny Brewer

Kelley, William Melvin
Carlyle tries polygamy
Wonderful town; New York stories from The New Yorker; edited by David Remnick with Susan Choi

Kelly, Jack
A Dick and Jane story
Flesh and blood: guilty as sin; erotic tales of crime and passion; edited by Max Allan Collins and Jeff Gelb

Kelly, James Patrick
1016 to 1
Kelly, J. P. Strange but not a stranger; with an introduction by Connie Willis
The Year's best science fiction, seventeenth annual collection; edited by Gardner Dozois
Candy art
Kelly, J. P. Strange but not a stranger; with an introduction by Connie Willis
Chemistry
Kelly, J. P. Strange but not a stranger; with an introduction by Connie Willis

The cruelest month
Kelly, J. P. Strange but not a stranger; with an introduction by Connie Willis
Feel the zaz
Kelly, J. P. Strange but not a stranger; with an introduction by Connie Willis
Fruitcake theory
Kelly, J. P. Strange but not a stranger; with an introduction by Connie Willis
Glass cloud
Kelly, J. P. Strange but not a stranger; with an introduction by Connie Willis
Hubris
Kelly, J. P. Strange but not a stranger; with an introduction by Connie Willis
Itsy bitsy spider
Nebula awards 33; the year's best SF and fantasy chosen by the science-fiction and fantasy writers of America; edited by Connie Willis
Lovestory
Kelly, J. P. Strange but not a stranger; with an introduction by Connie Willis
The prisoner of Chillon
Kelly, J. P. Strange but not a stranger; with an introduction by Connie Willis
Proof of the existence of God
Kelly, J. P. Strange but not a stranger; with an introduction by Connie Willis
The propagation of light in a vacuum
Kelly, J. P. Strange but not a stranger; with an introduction by Connie Willis
The Pyramid of Amirah
Kelly, J. P. Strange but not a stranger; with an introduction by Connie Willis
Rat
Masterpieces: the best science fiction of the century; edited by Orson Scott Card
Undone
Kelly, J. P. Strange but not a stranger; with an introduction by Connie Willis
Nebula Awards showcase 2003; edited by Nancy Kress
The Year's best science fiction, nineteenth annual collection; edited by Gardner Dozois
Unique visitors
Kelly, J. P. Strange but not a stranger; with an introduction by Connie Willis
Redshift; extreme visions of speculative fiction; edited by Al Sarrantonio

Kelly, Rita
En famille
The Anchor book of new Irish writing; the new Gaelach ficsean; edited and with an introduction by John Somer and John J. Daly

The **Kelly** rainbow. Dufresne, F.

Kelman, James
The busconductor Hines [excerpt]
The Vintage book of contemporary Scottish fiction; edited and with an introduction by Peter Kravitz
The comfort
Kelman, J. The good times; stories
Comic cuts
Kelman, J. The good times; stories
Constellation
Kelman, J. The good times; stories

Kelman, James—*Continued*
Every fucking time
Kelman, J. The good times; stories
Gardens go on forever
Kelman, J. The good times; stories
The good times
Kelman, J. The good times; stories
I was asking a question too
Kelman, J. The good times; stories
Into the rhythm
Kelman, J. The good times; stories
It happened to me once
Kelman, J. The good times; stories
Joe laughed
Kelman, J. The good times; stories
My eldest
Kelman, J. The good times; stories
Naval history
The Literary Review (Madison, N.J.) v45 no2
p304-14 Wint 2002
The norwest reaches
Kelman, J. The good times; stories
Oh my darling
Kelman, J. The good times; stories
Pulped sandwiches
Kelman, J. The good times; stories
Remember Young Cecil
The Art of the story; an international antholo-
gy of contemporary short stories; edited by
Daniel Halpern
Some thoughts that morning
Kelman, J. The good times; stories
Strength
Kelman, J. The good times; stories
Sustenance sustenance
Kelman, J. The good times; stories
Then later
Kelman, J. The good times; stories
The wey it can turn
Kelman, J. The good times; stories
Yeh, these stages
Kelman, J. The good times; stories
Kelman, Judith
The grapes of Roth
Murder in the family; [by] the Adams Round
Table
Just desserts
Irreconcilable differences; Lia Matera, editor
Kelner, Toni L. P.
Old dog days
A Hot and sultry night for crime; edited by
Jeffery Deaver
Kelton, Elmer
The burial of Letty Strayhorn
A Century of great Western stories; edited by
John Jakes
Hewey and the wagon cook
American West; twenty new stories from the
Western Writers of America; edited with an
introduction by Loren D. Estleman
North of the big river
Graham, D. Lone Star literature; from the
Red River to the Rio Grande; edited by
Don Graham
Kemelman, Harry
The nine mile walk
The Best American mystery stories of the
century; Tony Hillerman, editor; with an
introduction by Tony Hillerman

Kempadoo, Oonya
Buxton spice
Seventeen v58 no6 p140-41 Je 1999
Was Me Mudda
Bomb no86 p94-7 Wint 2003/2004
Kemper, Marjorie
God's goodness
Atlantic Monthly (1993) v289 no3 p81-9 Mr
2002
The O. Henry Prize stories, 2003; edited and
with an introduction by Laura Furman;
jurers David Gutterson, Diane Johnson,
Jennifer Egan
Poetic License
The Southern Review (Baton Rouge, La.) v40
no3 p516-28 Summ 2004
Kempker, Birgit
The root of the free radical is heart
Chicago Review v48 no2/3 p155-61 Summ
2002
Kenagy, Mary
Meeting the family
The Georgia Review v55 no2 p271-87 Summ
2001
Kenan, Randall
The foundations of the earth
Crossing the color line; readings in Black and
white; edited by Suzanne W. Jones
Hobbits and hobgoblins
Fault lines; stories of divorce; collected and
edited by Caitlin Shetterly
Now why come that is?
Callaloo v24 no2 p510-23 Spr 2001
Kendall, Gillian
In loco parentis
The Student body; short stories about college
students and professors; edited by John
McNally
Kenemore, Scott
The lizard boy
The Kenyon Review ns24 no2 p96-7 Spr 2002
Kennedy, A. L.
Awaiting an adverse reaction
Kennedy, A. L. Indelible acts; stories
A bad son
Kennedy, A. L. Indelible acts; stories
Elsewhere
Kennedy, A. L. Indelible acts; stories
How to find your way in woods
Kennedy, A. L. Indelible acts; stories
An immaculate man
Kennedy, A. L. Indelible acts; stories
Indelible acts
Kennedy, A. L. Indelible acts; stories
A Little Like Light
Grand Street no71 p75-90 Spr 2003
Kennedy, A. L. Indelible acts; stories
Looking for the possible dance [excerpt]
The Vintage book of contemporary Scottish
fiction; edited and with an introduction by
Peter Kravitz
Made over, made out
The Literary Review (Madison, N.J.) v45 no2
p315-28 Wint 2002
Not anything to do with love
Kennedy, A. L. Indelible acts; stories
Spared
Kennedy, A. L. Indelible acts; stories

Kennedy, A. L.—*Continued*
  Touch positive
    Kennedy, A. L. Indelible acts; stories
  White house at night
    Kennedy, A. L. Indelible acts; stories
  A wrong thing
    Kennedy, A. L. Indelible acts; stories
Kennedy, Andrew
  In our part of the world
    Death dance; suspenseful stories of the dance
      macabre; Trevanian, editor
**KENNEDY, JOHN F. (JOHN FITZGERALD),
  1917-1963**
                     About
  DiChario, N. The winterberry
  Malzberg, B. N. Heavy metal
                  Assassination
  Barthelme, F. Bag boy
  Delaney, E. J. Conspiracy buffs
  Malzberg, B. N. All assassins
  Malzberg, B. N. In the stone house
KENNEDY, JOSEPH PATRICK, 1915-1944
                     About
  Malzberg, B. N. In the stone house
Kennedy, Leigh
  (jt. auth) See Waldrop, Howard and Kennedy,
    Leigh
Kennedy, Raymond
  Into many a green valley
    The Massachusetts Review v40 no4 p585-95
      Wint 1999/2000
KENNEDY, ROBERT F., 1925-1968
                     About
  Malzberg, B. N. Heavy metal
Kennedy, Thomas E.
  The foot of Saint Catherine
    The Literary Review (Madison, N.J.) v42 no3
      p394-99 Spr 1999
  The Pleasure of Man And Woman Together on
    Earth
    New Letters v69 no2/3 p215-39 2003
  Surprise endings
    New Letters v68 no1 p107-26 2001
Kennett, Rick
  Due west
    The Year's best fantasy & horror, twelfth an-
      nual collection; edited by Ellen Datlow &
      Terry Windling
Kennett, Shirley
  A warm nest
    Cat crimes through time; edited by Ed
      Gorman, Martin H. Greenberg, and Larry
      Segriff
Kenney, Susan
  Aunt Agatha leaving
    Malice domestic 8
KENTUCKY
  Allen, D., Jr. Deferment
  Berry, W. Are you all right?
  Berry, W. The discovery of Kentucky
  Berry, W. Fidelity
  Berry, W. The inheritors
  Berry, W. A jonquil for Mary Penn
  Berry, W. Making it home
  Berry, W. Pray without ceasing
  Berry, W. That distant land
  Berry, W. The wild birds
  Bisson, T. Bears discover fire
  Day, R. C. The fugitive

  Fitzgerald, F. S. Jemina, the mountain girl
  Gilchrist, E. Music
  Hardwick, E. Evenings at home
  Holbrook, C. The idea of it
  House, S. Coal house
  Mason, B. A. Charger
  Mason, B. A. The funeral side
  Mason, B. A. Night flight
  Mason, B. A. Three-wheeler
  Mason, B. A. Thunder snow
  Miller, J. W. The taste of ironwater
  Offutt, C. Melungeons
  Porter, J. A. Yours
  Vasseur, T. J. Flood
  Vasseur, T. J. Noonan
  Vasseur, T. J. Pig summer
                  Farm life
    See Farm life—Kentucky
                  Lexington
  Mason, B. A. Window lights
KENYA
  Doerr, A. The shell collector
  Hunter, F. North of Nairobi
  Ng'ugĩ wa Thiong'o. Minutes of glory
  Oliver, C. Far from this earth
  Richter, J. The ones left behind
                   Nairobi
  Hunter, F. Laban and Murugi
  Hunter, F. Night vigil
Kenya and Amir. Major, M.
Keppel, Tim
  The Old Year
    The Literary Review (Madison, N.J.) v47 no1
      p146-56 Fall 2003
Kercheval, Jesse Lee
  Going into hiding
    Good Housekeeping v229 no5 p231-34+ N
      1999
  Honors
    Prairie Schooner v77 no2 p87-106 Summ
      2003
Keret, Etgar
  Breaking the pig
    Keret, E. The bus driver who wanted to be
      God and other stories
  Cocked and locked
    Keret, E. The bus driver who wanted to be
      God and other stories
    Sleepwalkers and other stories; the Arab in
      Hebrew fiction; edited by Ehud Ben-Ezer
  Fatso
    Iowa Review v32 no2 p37-9 Fall 2002
  The flying Santinis
    Keret, E. The bus driver who wanted to be
      God and other stories
  Good intentions
    Keret, E. The bus driver who wanted to be
      God and other stories
  Goodman
    Keret, E. The bus driver who wanted to be
      God and other stories
  Hole in the wall
    Keret, E. The bus driver who wanted to be
      God and other stories
  Jetlag
    Keret, E. The bus driver who wanted to be
      God and other stories

Keret, Etgar—*Continued*

Katzenstein

Keret, E. The bus driver who wanted to be God and other stories

Kneller's happy campers

Keret, E. The bus driver who wanted to be God and other stories

Korbi's girl

Keret, E. The bus driver who wanted to be God and other stories

Missing Kissinger

Keret, E. The bus driver who wanted to be God and other stories

The mysterious disappearance of Alon Shemesh

Keret, E. The bus driver who wanted to be God and other stories

One last story and that's it

Keret, E. The bus driver who wanted to be God and other stories

Pipes

Keret, E. The bus driver who wanted to be God and other stories

Plague of the Firstborn

Keret, E. The bus driver who wanted to be God and other stories

Rabin's dead

Keret, E. The bus driver who wanted to be God and other stories

Shoes

Keret, E. The bus driver who wanted to be God and other stories

Siren

Keret, E. The bus driver who wanted to be God and other stories

The son of the Head of the Mossad

Keret, E. The bus driver who wanted to be God and other stories

A souvenir of Hell

Keret, E. The bus driver who wanted to be God and other stories

The story about a bus driver who wanted to be God

Keret, E. The bus driver who wanted to be God and other stories

Uterus

Keret, E. The bus driver who wanted to be God and other stories

Kerfol. Wharton, E.

Kerley, Jack

Almost There

The Southern Review (Baton Rouge, La.) v40 no2 p291-4 Spr 2004

The **Kerman** kill. Gault, W. C.

Kern, Nancy

Pranks

The Antioch Review v60 no3 p459-72 Summ 2002

Kerouac, Jack

The Mexican girl

Still wild; short fiction of the American West, 1950 to the present; edited by Larry McMurtry

KEROUAC, JACK, 1922-1969

About

Rucker, R. v. B. Instability

Rucker, R. v. B. The Jack Kerouac disembodied school of poetics

Parodies, imitations, etc.

Lupoff, R. A. The adventures of the boulevard assassin

Kerr, James B.

The Veil of Things

The Sewanee Review v111 no1 p73-93 Wint 2003

Kerr's fault. Billman, J.

Kerschen, Paul

Let the Day Perish

The Southern Review (Baton Rouge, La.) v40 no3 p500-15 Summ 2004

Kerslake, Linda

Lookin' 'n' jivin'

Death dance; suspenseful stories of the dance macabre; Trevanian, editor

Kessel, John

Buffalo

Brown, C. N. and Strahan, J. The Locus awards; thirty years of the best in science fiction and fantasy; edited by Charles N. Brown and Jonathan Strahan

This is where we live; short stories by 25 contemporary North Carolina writers; edited by Michael McFee

A clean escape

Masterpieces: the best science fiction of the century; edited by Orson Scott Card

Every angel is terrifying

The Year's best fantasy & horror, twelfth annual collection; edited by Ellen Datlow & Terry Windling

It's all true

The year's best science fiction: twenty-first annual collection; edited by Gardner Dozois

The juniper tree

The Year's best science fiction, eighteenth annual collection; edited by Gardner Dozois

Stories for men

The Year's best science fiction; twentieth annual collection; edited by Gardner Dozois

Kestrel. Adam, C.

Ketchum, Jack

Gone

Death dines at 8:30; edited by Claudia Bishop and Nick DiChario

Kettler, Georgie

What Was Meant to Be

Good Housekeeping v235 no5 p199-200, 202, 204, 206, 210 N 2002

The **key**. Singer, I. B.

KEY WEST (FLA.) *See* Florida—Key West

Keyes, Daniel

Flowers for Algernon

The Science fiction hall of fame: volume one, 1929-1964; the greatest science fiction stories of all time chosen by the members of the Science Fiction Writers of America; edited by Robert Silverberg

Keyes, John

The story that won't go away

Gettysburg Review v12 no2 p309-24 Summ 1999

Where It Is That Things Go

The Massachusetts Review v43 no4 p676-87 Wint 2002/2003

You Have Never Heard Their Voices

Gettysburg Review v15 no2 p257-73 Summ 2002

The **keys** to December. Zelazny, R.

The **keys** to D'Espérance. Brenchley, C.

Keys to the city. Wald, M.

Khadra, Yasmina See Moulessehoul, Mohammed, 1955-

Khalida's dog. Watanabe McFerrin, L.

Khan, Ismith
  Shadows move in the Britannia Bar
    The Oxford book of Caribbean short stories; edited by Stewart Brown and John Wickham
    Whispers from the cotton tree root; Caribbean fabulist fiction; edited by Nalo Hopkinson

Kharms, Daniel
  The career of Ivan Yakovlevich Antonov
    The Kenyon Review ns21 no3-4 p125-26 Summ/Fall 1999
  "A fly struck—"
    The Kenyon Review ns21 no3-4 p122-25 Summ/Fall 1999
  "Ivan Yakovelevich Bobov woke up—"
    The Kenyon Review ns21 no3-4 p126-28 Summ/Fall 1999
  "Once Andre Vasilevich—"
    The Kenyon Review ns21 no3-4 p129-30 Summ/Fall 1999
  Thing
    The Kenyon Review ns21 no3-4 p130-34 Summ/Fall 1999

Khaury, Herbert See Tiny Tim, d. 1996

Kheradmand, Farideh
  Smile!
    A Feast in the mirror; stories by contemporary Iranian women; translated and edited by Mohammad Mehdi Khorrami, Shouleh Vatanabadi

Khorasani, Nushin Ahmadi See Ahmadi Khorasani, Nushin, 1969-

KIBBUTZIM See Collective settlements—Israel

Kick in the head. Rinehart, S.

The **kick** inside. Southgate, M.

Kickers. Heynen, J.

Kidd, Chico
  Cats and architecture
    The Mammoth book of best horror 13; edited by Stephen Jones
  Mark of the beast
    The Mammoth book of best horror 13; edited by Stephen Jones

A **kidnapped** Santa Claus. Baum, L. F.

KIDNAPPING
    See also Hostages
  Anderson, P. The queen of air and darkness
  Araújo, H. Asthmatic
  Baum, L. F. A kidnapped Santa Claus
  Bear, G. Sleepside story
  Blackwood, S. Alias
  Boylan, C. The stolen child
  Buck, P. S. Ransom
  Cohen, S. The ransom of Retta Chiefman
  Collins, M. A. A matter of principal
  Connolly, C. Greengages
  Davis, D. S. The puppet
  DeAndrea, W. L. Prince Charming
  Deaver, J. The weekender
  Doctorow, E. L. Baby Wilson
  Gasco, E. The spider of Bumba
  Gorriti, J. M. If you do wrong, expect no good
  House, S. The last days

  Iribarne, M. A dream, not alone
  Jacobs, M. Solidarity in green
  Johnson, G. C. The obedient child
  Kellerman, F. Holy water
  Knight, M. Feeling lucky
  Knight, M. The mesmerist
  Latour, J. Havanightmare
  Le Fanu, J. S. The child that went with the fairies
  Lutz, J. Pure rotten
  Mastretta, A. Aunt Elvira
  Morgan, C. What I eat
  Oates, J. C. The girl with the blackened eye
  Reed, R. R. Moving toward the light
  Roche, T. S. Bank job
  Shawl, N. The tawny bitch
  Swarthout, G. F. Ixion
  Thompson, J. The lost child
  Waugh, E. Incident in Azania
  Wings, M. Empty arms

The **kidnapping** of Baroness 5. MacLean, K.

Kids. See Chekhov, A. P. Children

Kids on Colden Street. LaValle, V. D.

KIERKEGAARD, SØREN, 1813-1855
    About
  Baxter, C. Harry Ginsberg

Kiernan, Caitlín R.
  The drowned geologist
    Shadows over Baker Street; edited by Michael Reaves and John Pelan
  In the water works (Birmingham, Alabama 1888)
    Best new horror 12; edited and with an introduction by Stephen Jones
  The king of birds
    The Crow; shattered lives & broken dreams; edited by J. O'Barr and Ed Kramer
  The long hall on the top floor
    Best new horror 11; edited and with an introduction by Stephen Jones
  Nor the demons down under the sea
    The Mammoth book of best new horror 14; edited with an introduction by Stephen Jones
  Postcards from the King of Tides
    Best new horror 10; edited and with an introduction by Stephen Jones

Kieser, Christine
  Completely overloaded
    Typical girls; new stories by smart women; edited by Susan Corrigan

Kihn, Greg
  Mirror gazing with Brian Jones
    Carved in rock; short stories by musicians; edited by Greg Kihn
  (jt. auth) See Jett, Joan and Kihn, Greg

KIKUYU (AFRICAN PEOPLE)
  Hunter, F. Laban and Murugi

The **kill**. Fleming, P.

Kill me hideously. Campbell, R.

Killdozer!. Sturgeon, T.

Killens, John Oliver
  God bless America
    The African American West; a century of short stories; edited by Bruce A. Glasrud and Laurie Champion

Killer. DeRosso, H. A.

Killer in the reign. Edghill, R.

Killer man. Gores, J.

Killer Miller. P´yetsukh, V.
Killer scent. Hensley, J. L.
The **killers**. Hemingway, E.
Killers' country!. Cushman, D.
The **killing** at Triple Tree. Hunter, E.
Killing babies. Boyle, T. C.
Killing Bernstein. Ellison, H.
A **killing** in Xanadu. Pronzini, B.
The **killing** of a state cop. Ortiz, S. J.
Killing sparrows. Buslik, G.
Killing Stonewall Jackson. Knight, M.
The **killing** stroke. Donaldson, S. R.
Killing the sixties. Howe, M. J.
Killing time. Cavell, B.
Kilpatrick, Nancy
Alien love
   Kilpatrick, N. Cold comfort
. . . And thou!
   Kilpatrick, N. Cold comfort
Animal rites
   Kilpatrick, N. Cold comfort
Base of a triangle
   Kilpatrick, N. Cold comfort
Berserker
   Dracula in London; edited by P. N. Elrod
Brina
   Kilpatrick, N. Cold comfort
Cold comfort
   Kilpatrick, N. Cold comfort
Creature comforts
   Kilpatrick, N. Cold comfort
An eye for an eye
   Kilpatrick, N. Cold comfort
Farm wife
   Northern suns; edited by David G. Hartwell
     & Glenn Grant
Generation why
   Kilpatrick, N. Cold comfort
Heartbeat
   Kilpatrick, N. Cold comfort
Horrorscope
   Kilpatrick, N. Cold comfort
Inspiriter
   Kilpatrick, N. Cold comfort
Megan's spirit
   Kilpatrick, N. Cold comfort
Metal fatigue
   Kilpatrick, N. Cold comfort
The middle of nowhere
   Kilpatrick, N. Cold comfort
The power of one
   Kilpatrick, N. Cold comfort
Projections
   Kilpatrick, N. Cold comfort
Punkins
   Kilpatrick, N. Cold comfort
Rural legend
   Kilpatrick, N. Cold comfort
Snow angel
   Kilpatrick, N. Cold comfort
Truth
   Kilpatrick, N. Cold comfort
Vermiculture
   Kilpatrick, N. Cold comfort
What matters
   Kilpatrick, N. Cold comfort
When shadows come back
   Kilpatrick, N. Cold comfort

Whitelight
   Kilpatrick, N. Cold comfort
Woodworker
   Kilpatrick, N. Cold comfort
Youth not wasted
   Kilpatrick, N. Cold comfort
Kilpatrick, Nancy and Bisson, Benoit
The children of Gael
   Kilpatrick, N. Cold comfort
Kim, Chungmi
A Stranger in America
   Amerasia Journal v30 no1 p200-7 2004
Kim, Nancy Jooyoun
Desire
   Amerasia Journal v27 no2 p135-44 2001
Kim, Junse
Yangban
   Pushcart prize XXVII; best of the small
     presses; edited by Bill Henderson with the
     Pushcart prize editors
Kimber, Josie
Having myself a time
   Typical girls; new stories by smart women;
     edited by Susan Corrigan
Kincaid, Jamaica
The autobiography of my mother [excerpt]
   The Bluelight corner; black women writing on
     passion, sex, and romantic love; edited by
     Rosemarie Robotham
Blackness
   The Oxford book of Caribbean short stories;
     edited by Stewart Brown and John
     Wickham
Girl
   The Scribner anthology of contemporary short
     fiction; fifty North American stories since
     1970; Lex Williford and Michael Martone,
     editors
   Snapshots: 20th century mother-daughter fic-
     tion; edited by Joyce Carol Oates and Janet
     Berliner
My mother
   Whispers from the cotton tree root; Caribbean
     fabulist fiction; edited by Nalo Hopkinson
Poor Visitor
   Wonderful town; New York stories from The
     New Yorker; edited by David Remnick
     with Susan Choi
Kincaid, Nanci
Krystal Lynn
   Southern Humanities Review v37 no4 p352-62
     Fall 2003
The **Kind** Assassin. Boyle, T. C.
The **kind** I'm likely to get. Foster, K.
A **kind** of artistry. Aldiss, B. W.
A **kind** of flight. Brazaitis, M.
A **kind** of flying. Carlson, R.
The **kind** of light that shines on Texas. McKnight,
   R.
The **kind** of things saints do. Valeri, L.
The **kind** of time you end up with. Davis, L.
Kinder, Chuck
The wife in the story
   New England Review v22 no2 p16-21 Spr
     2001
You are not your characters
   New England Review v22 no2 p22-34 Spr
     2001

KINDERGARTEN
Ha Jin. In the kindergarten
Kalman, J. A property of childhood
Klass, P. The trouble with Sophie
Kindertotenlieder or, Daycare among the Paste-
eaters. Skibell, J.
Kindling. Carver, R.
Kindnesses. Gilliland, G.
Kindred. McKinnon, K.
Kindred spirits. Walker, A.
King, Amanda Brauman
Fam da Sham
The Massachusetts Review v44 no3 p494-6
Fall 2003
King, Cassandra
My life is a country song
Stories from the Blue Moon Cafe II; edited
by Sonny Brewer
King, Grace
The balcony
Southern local color; stories of region, race,
and gender; edited by Barbara C. Ewell and
Pamela Glenn Menke; with notes by An-
drea Humphrey
La grande demoiselle
Southern local color; stories of region, race,
and gender; edited by Barbara C. Ewell and
Pamela Glenn Menke; with notes by An-
drea Humphrey
The little convent girl
Southern local color; stories of region, race,
and gender; edited by Barbara C. Ewell and
Pamela Glenn Menke; with notes by An-
drea Humphrey
King, Larry L.
Three Letters
Texas bound. Book III; 22 Texas stories; ed-
ited by Kay Cattarulla; foreword by Robert
Flynn
King, Laurie R.
Paleta man
Irreconcilable differences; Lia Matera, editor
The World's finest mystery and crime stories,
first annual collection; edited by Ed
Gorman
Weaving the dark
McSweeney's mammoth treasury of thrilling
tales; edited by Michael Chabon
KING, MARTIN LUTHER, 1929-1968
About
Breen, J. L. Longevity has its place
King, Stephen
All that you love will be carried away
The New Yorker v76 no44 p74-80 Ja 29 2001
Children of the corn
The American fantasy tradition; edited by Bri-
an M. Thomsen
The death of Jack Hamilton
The New Yorker v77 no41 p76-81, 84-7, 89-
91 D 24-31 2001
February, cycle of the werewolf
The Literary werewolf; an anthology; edited
by Charlotte F. Otten
The man in the black suit
Fishing's best short stories; edited by Paul D.
Staudohar
Mrs. Todd's shortcut
The American fantasy tradition; edited by Bri-
an M. Thomsen

Quitters, Inc.
The Best American mystery stories of the
century; Tony Hillerman, editor; with an
introduction by Tony Hillerman
A Century of great suspense stories; edited by
Jeffery Deaver
Rest Stop
Esquire v140 no6 p133-4, 136, 138, 142,
145-7 D 2003
The Road Virus heads north
999: new stories of horror and suspense; ed-
ited by Al Sarrantonio
The shining [excerpt]
Dark: stories of madness, murder, and the su-
pernatural; edited by Clint Willis
Strawberry spring
The Student body; short stories about college
students and professors; edited by John
McNally
The tale of the Gray Dick
McSweeney's mammoth treasury of thrilling
tales; edited by Michael Chabon
That feeling, you can only say what it is in
French
The Year's best fantasy & horror, twelfth an-
nual collection; edited by Ellen Datlow &
Terry Windling
The wedding gig
Master's choice [v1]; mystery stories by to-
day's top writers and the masters who in-
spired them; edited by Lawrence Block
KING, STEPHEN, 1947-
About
Wuori, G. K. Parents
King, Thomas
A short history of Indians in Canada
Canadian Literature no161/162 p62-64
Summ/Aut 1999
The **King**. Babel´, I.
King Arthur and his knights [excerpt] Knowles,
Sir J.
King Corpus. Rogers, B. H.
The **king** of birds. Kiernan, C. R.
The **king** of everything. Abrams, T.
King of Handcuffs. Savage, R.
The **King** of Infinite Space. Wieland, M.
King of outer space. Atkins, P.
The **king** of snow. Padilla, M.
King of the buckskin breed. Savage, L., Jr.
King of the Cowboys, Queen of the West.
Simonds, M.
The **King** of the King of Falafel. Papernick, J.
King of the night. Crider, B.
The **king** with three daughters. Blackford, R.
Kingdom, Order, Species. Iagnemma, K.
Kingrea, Eric
A waltz in the snow
Stories from the Blue Moon Cafe II; edited
by Sonny Brewer
KINGS AND RULERS
See also Courts and courtiers names of
kings and rulers
Borges, J. L. The disk
Borges, J. L. The mirror and the mask
Donaldson, S. R. The kings of tarshish shall
bring gifts
Frost, P. S. Clamour
Vance, J. The new prime
Wägner, W. The Hegeling legend [excerpt]

KINGS AND RULERS—*Continued*

What, L. The emperor's new (and improved) clothes

Yolen, J. Allerleirauh

A **king's** epitaph. Lee, M.

The **kings** of tarshish shall bring gifts. Donaldson, S. R.

"The **king's** son-in-law". Trueba, A. d.

Kingsbury, Kate

A nice cup of tea

Murder most postal; homicidal tales that deliver a message; edited by Martin H. Greenberg

Kingsbury, Suzanne

Panama

Stories from the Blue Moon Cafe II; edited by Sonny Brewer

Kingsgrave-Ernstein, Catt

(jt. auth) See Gruss, Amy L. and Kingsgrave-Ernstein, Catt

Kingsolver, Barbara

Homeland

Home and beyond; an anthology of Kentucky short stories; edited by Morris Allen Grubbs; with an introduction by Wade Hall and an afterword by Charles E. May

KINGSTON (JAMAICA) *See* Jamaica—Kingston

Kinman, Gay Toltl

Miss Parker & the Cutter-Sanborn tables

A Deadly dozen; tales of murder from members of Sisters in Crime/Los Angeles; edited by Susan B. Casmier, Aljean Harmetz and Cynthia Lawrence

Kinsella, John

The diviners

The Kenyon Review ns24 no1 p33-5 Wint 2002

The well

The Kenyon Review ns24 no1 p30-2 Wint 2002

Kinsella, W. P.

Shoeless Joe Jackson comes to Iowa

The American fantasy tradition; edited by Brian M. Thomsen

Things invisible to see

Northern suns; edited by David G. Hartwell & Glenn Grant

KIOWA INDIANS

Haseloff, C. H. Favorite son

Loomis, N. M. When the children cry for meat

Kipling, Rudyard

The mark of the beast

The Literary werewolf; an anthology; edited by Charlotte F. Otten

Mary Postgate

On glorious wings; the best flying stories of the century; edited and introduced by Stephen Coonts

They

Dark: stories of madness, murder, and the supernatural; edited by Clint Willis

Nightshade: 20th century ghost stories; edited by Robert Phillips

Kipnis, Menakhem

What became of the fools of Khelm?

Neugroschel, J. No star too beautiful; Yiddish stories from 1382 to the present; compiled and translated by Joachim Neugroschel

Kirchheimer, Gloria DeVidas

Arbitration

Kirchheimer, G. D. Goodbye, evil eye; stories

A case of dementia

Kirchheimer, G. D. Goodbye, evil eye; stories

With signs and wonders; an international anthology of Jewish fabulist fiction; edited by Daniel M. Jaffe

Changelings

Kirchheimer, G. D. Goodbye, evil eye; stories

Feast of Lights

Kirchheimer, G. D. Goodbye, evil eye; stories

Food of love

Kirchheimer, G. D. Goodbye, evil eye; stories

Goodbye, evil eye

Kirchheimer, G. D. Goodbye, evil eye; stories

Lost tribe; jewish fiction from the edge

Rafi

Kirchheimer, G. D. Goodbye, evil eye; stories

Silver screen

Kirchheimer, G. D. Goodbye, evil eye; stories

A skirmish in the desert

Kirchheimer, G. D. Goodbye, evil eye; stories

Traffic manager

Kirchheimer, G. D. Goodbye, evil eye; stories

The voyager

Kirchheimer, G. D. Goodbye, evil eye; stories

Kirdjali. See Pushkin, A. S. Kirdzhali

Kirdzhali. Pushkin, A. S.

Kirn, Walter

The Lost Continent

Gentlemen's Quarterly v72 no8 p96-107 Ag 2002

Up in the air

Gentlemen's Quarterly v71 no5 p151-7 My 2001

Kirshenbaum, Binnie

Jews have no business being enamored of Germans

Neurotica: Jewish writers on sex; edited by Melvin Jules Bukiet

Who knows Kaddish

Lost tribe; jewish fiction from the edge

Kirwan, Larry

Liverpool fantasy

Carved in rock; short stories by musicians; edited by Greg Kihn

Kismet. Odishoo, S. A.

The **kiss**. Babel', I.

The **kiss**. Chekhov, A. P.

The **kiss**. Chesnutt, C. W.

The **kiss**. Chopin, K.

The **kiss**. Hay, E.

The **kiss**. Painter, P.

The **kiss**. Travis, T. V.

Kiss. Wolff, T.

A **kiss** and no goodbye. Fisher, L.

KISSING

Brockmeier, K. Apples

Galloway, J. Where you find it

Hoffman, A. Bake at 350°

Painter, P. The kiss

Kissing. Kittredge, W.

Kissing you. Hayes, D.

Kiswana Browne. Naylor, G.

Kite and paint. Robison, M.

The **Kite** Trick. Gaston, B.

Kite Whistler Aquamarine. Meloy, M.

KITES

Ortiz, S. J. The way you see horses

Robison, M. Kite and paint

Kittredge, William

Agriculture

Kittredge, W. The best short stories of William Kittredge

Balancing water

Kittredge, W. The best short stories of William Kittredge

Be careful what you want

Kittredge, W. The best short stories of William Kittredge

Breaker of horses

Kittredge, W. The best short stories of William Kittredge

Do you hear your mother talking?

Kittredge, W. The best short stories of William Kittredge

Kissing

Kittredge, W. The best short stories of William Kittredge

The O. Henry Prize stories, 2003; edited and with an introduction by Laura Furman; jurers David Gutterson, Diane Johnson, Jennifer Egan

Momentum is always the weapon

Kittredge, W. The best short stories of William Kittredge

The soap bear

Kittredge, W. The best short stories of William Kittredge

The stone corral

Kittredge, W. The best short stories of William Kittredge

Thirty-four seasons of winter

Kittredge, W. The best short stories of William Kittredge

The Workshop; seven decades of the Iowa Writers' Workshop: 42 stories, recollections & essays on Iowa's place in 20th-century American literature; edited by Tom Grimes

The van Gogh field

Kittredge, W. The best short stories of William Kittredge

The waterfowl tree

Kittredge, W. The best short stories of William Kittredge

We are not in this together

Kittredge, W. The best short stories of William Kittredge

Kitty. Appelfeld, A.

Kitty. Bowles, P.

KKK *See* Ku Klux Klan

Klam, Matthew

Issues I dealt with in therapy

The New Yorker v75 no18 p64-73 Jl 12 1999

Issues I dealt with in therapy (I)

The New Yorker v75 no16 p218 Je 21-28 1999

Klaskin, Ronnie

Child support

A Hot and sultry night for crime; edited by Jeffery Deaver

Klass, Fruma

Jennifer's turn

Gathering the bones; original stories from the world's masters of horror; edited by Dennis Etchison, Ramsey Campbell and Jack Dann

Klass, Perri

City sidewalks

Klass, P. Love and modern medicine; stories

Dedication

Klass, P. Love and modern medicine; stories

Double Whammy

Ploughshares v29 no2/3 p73-88 Fall 2003

Exact change

Klass, P. Love and modern medicine; stories

For women everywhere

Klass, P. Love and modern medicine; stories

Freedom fighter

Klass, P. Love and modern medicine; stories

Intimacy

Klass, P. Love and modern medicine; stories

Love and modern medicine

Klass, P. Love and modern medicine; stories

Necessary risks

Klass, P. Love and modern medicine; stories

The province of the bearded fathers

Klass, P. Love and modern medicine; stories

Rainbow mama

Klass, P. Love and modern medicine; stories

The trouble with Sophie

Klass, P. Love and modern medicine; stories

Klass, Philip *See* Tenn, William, 1920-

KLEE, PAUL, 1879-1940

About

Gifford, B. The Tunisian notebook

Klein, Rachel S.

Beatrice: the sacrifice

The Literary Review (Madison, N.J.) v42 no4 p580-93 Summ 1999

Klein, T. E. D.

Growing things

999: new stories of horror and suspense; edited by Al Sarrantonio

Best new horror 11; edited and with an introduction by Stephen Jones

Klein, Ted *See* Klein, T. E. D., 1947-

Klein, Anne Carolyn

The mantra and the typist: a story of east and west

Nixon under the bodhi tree and other works of Buddhist fiction; edited by Kate Wheeler ; foreword by Charles Johnson

Kleinman, Liza

What went wrong

The Hudson Review v51 no4 p666-80 Wint 1999

Kleinzeit [excerpt] Hoban, R.

KLEPTOMANIA

Brown, J. Thief

Perabo, S. Thick as thieves

Vukcevich, R. Pink smoke

Klíma, Ivan

The assembly line

Klíma, I. Lovers for a day; translated from the Czech by Gerald Turner

A baffling choice

Klíma, I. Lovers for a day; translated from the Czech by Gerald Turner

Conjugal conversations

Klíma, I. Lovers for a day; translated from the Czech by Gerald Turner

Divorce

The New Yorker v75 no23 p76-78 Ag 16 1999

Klíma, Ivan—*Continued*
  Execution of a horse
    Klíma, I. Lovers for a day; translated from
      the Czech by Gerald Turner
  Heaven, hell, paradise
    Klíma, I. Lovers for a day; translated from
      the Czech by Gerald Turner
  Honeymoon
    Klíma, I. Lovers for a day; translated from
      the Czech by Gerald Turner
  It's raining out
    Klíma, I. Lovers for a day; translated from
      the Czech by Gerald Turner
  Lingula
    Klíma, I. Lovers for a day; translated from
      the Czech by Gerald Turner
  Long-distance conversations
    Klíma, I. Lovers for a day; translated from
      the Czech by Gerald Turner
  Rich men tend to be strange
    Klíma, I. Lovers for a day; translated from
      the Czech by Gerald Turner
  Uranus in the house of death
    Klíma, I. Lovers for a day; translated from
      the Czech by Gerald Turner
  The washing machine
    Best of Prairie schooner; fiction and poetry;
      edited by Hilda Raz
  The white house
    Klíma, I. Lovers for a day; translated from
      the Czech by Gerald Turner
Klimasewiski, Marshall N.
  Nobile's airship
    The Yale Review v87 no1 p111-31 Ja 1999
Kline, Donna
  Correspondence
    Other people's mail; an anthology of letter
      stories; edited with an introduction by Gail
      Pool
Kling, Vincent
  (jt. auth) See Doderer, Heimito von
Klise, James
  Easter Egg Hunt
    Southern Humanities Review v38 no1 p60-76
      Wint 2004
A **knack** for making ruins. Ponte, A. J.
Knatchbull-Hugessen, Sir Hughe
  Puss-cat Mew
    Tales before Tolkien; the roots of modern
      fantasy; edited by Douglas A. Anderson
Kneller's happy campers. Keret, E.
The **knife**. Dixon, S.
The **knife**. Russell, J.
Knight, Alanna
  The deadly glen
    Malice domestic 8
Knight, Arthur Winfield
  Do the dark dance
    Westward; a fictional history of the American
      West : 28 original stories celebrating the
      50th anniversary of the Western Writers of
      America; edited by Dale L. Walker
Knight, Damon Francis
  The country of the kind
    The Science fiction hall of fame: volume one,
      1929-1964; the greatest science fiction sto-
      ries of all time chosen by the members of
      the Science Fiction Writers of America; ed-
      ited by Robert Silverberg

Dio
    The SFWA grand masters; edited by Frederik
      Pohl
  The handler
    The SFWA grand masters; edited by Frederik
      Pohl
  I see you
    The SFWA grand masters; edited by Frederik
      Pohl
  Masks
    The SFWA grand masters; edited by Frederik
      Pohl
  Not with a bang
    The SFWA grand masters; edited by Frederik
      Pohl
Knight, Jenny
  Schering PC4—a love story
    Typical girls; new stories by smart women;
      edited by Susan Corrigan
Knight, Michael
  Amelia Earhart's coat
    Knight, M. Dogfight and other stories
  A bad man, so pretty
    Knight, M. Dogfight and other stories
  Birdland
    Knight, M. Goodnight, nobody
    New stories from the South: the year's best,
      1999; edited by Shannon Ravenel; with a
      preface by Tony Earley
  Blackout
    Knight, M. Goodnight, nobody
  Dogfight
    Knight, M. Dogfight and other stories
  Ellen's book
    Knight, M. Goodnight, nobody
    New stories from the South: the year's best,
      2003; edited by Shannon Ravenel; with a
      preface by Roy Blount Jr.
  The end of everything
    Gentlemen's Quarterly v69 no12 p171+ D
      1999
    Knight, M. Goodnight, nobody
  Feeling lucky
    Knight, M. Goodnight, nobody
    New stories from the South; the year's best,
      2004; edited by Shannon Ravenel; preface
      by Tim Gautreaux
    The Virginia Quarterly Review v79 no1 p124-
      33 Wint 2003
  For Alice to the fourth floor
    The Cry of an occasion; fiction from the Fel-
      lowship of Southern Writers; edited by
      Richard Bausch; with a foreword by
      George Garrett
  Gerald's monkey
    Knight, M. Dogfight and other stories
  Keeper of secrets, teller of lies
    Knight, M. Goodnight, nobody
    The Virginia Quarterly Review v77 no4 p603-
      14 Aut 2001
  Killing Stonewall Jackson
    Knight, M. Goodnight, nobody
    Stories from the Blue Moon Café; edited by
      Sonny Brewer
  The man who went out for cigarettes
    Knight, M. Dogfight and other stories
  The mesmerist
    Esquire v131 no3 p180 Mr 1999
    Knight, M. Goodnight, nobody

Knight, Michael—*Continued*

Mitchell's girls
  Knight, M. Goodnight, nobody
Now you see her
  Knight, M. Dogfight and other stories
Poker
  Knight, M. Dogfight and other stories
Sleeping with my dog
  Knight, M. Dogfight and other stories
Sundays
  Knight, M. Dogfight and other stories
Tenant
  Knight, M. Dogfight and other stories

Knight, Pat

Set in stone
  Valentine's Day: women against men; stories of revenge; introduction by Alice Thomas

Knight, Tracy

A trail of mirrors
  Blood on their hands; edited by Lawrence Block

Knight, death and the devil. Kociancich, V.

A **knight** of ghosts and shadows. Dozois, G. R.

KNIGHTHOOD *See* Knights and knighthood

Knights and duellists. Hoppe, F.

KNIGHTS AND KNIGHTHOOD

  See also Middle Ages

  Anderson, P. Death and the knight
  Cornwell, B. Excalibur [excerpt]
  Dunsany, E. J. M. D. P., Baron. The hoard of the Gibbelins
  Girardi, R. Three ravens on a red ground
  Knowles, Sir J. King Arthur and his knights [excerpt]
  Kociancich, V. Knight, death and the devil
  Trevanian. Sir Gervais in the enchanted forest
  Wolfe, G. Under hill

The **Knights** of Liberty. Randisi, R. J.

Knives. Chang, L.

Knocking. Hautala, R.

Knoderer, Tony

About the grass
  Iowa Review v29 no2 p121-27 Fall 1999

Knott unbound. Berry, R. M.

Know how, can do. Blumlein, M.

Knowall, George *See* O'Brien, Flann, 1911-1966

Knowing French. Barnes, J.

Knowledge. Jones, G.

Knowles, Sir James

King Arthur and his knights [excerpt]
  Swords and sorcerers; stories from the world of fantasy and adventure; edited by Clint Willis

Knowles, Thomas W.

Luck of the draw
  Past lives, present tense; edited by Elizabeth Ann Scarborough

Known unto God. Toes, J.

KNOXVILLE (TENN.) *See* Tennessee—Knoxville

Kobin, Joann

At the "Changing Careers" conference
  New England Review v22 no2 p84-92 Spr 2001
Diamonds
  New England Review v23 no1 p53-62 Wint 2002

Discipline and will
  The Virginia Quarterly Review v77 no2 p299-312 Spr 2001
Dr. Leopold on the loose
  New England Review v20 no1 p132-43 Wint 1999
Dr. Leopold's Problem with Contentment
  New England Review v25 no1/2 p288-98 2004
Fame and Fortune
  New England Review v24 no1 p191-200 Wint 2003
What I learned from Clara
  New England Review v20 no3 p52-65 Summ 1999

Kobrin, Leon

Apartment no. four
  Neugroschel, J. No star too beautiful; Yiddish stories from 1382 to the present; compiled and translated by Joachim Neugroschel

Kociancich, Vlady

Knight, death and the devil
  Short stories by Latin American women; the magic and the real; edited by Celia Correas de Zapata; foreword by Isabel Allende

Koehler, Jamison

Toasting the Bride
  The Literary Review (Madison, N.J.) v46 no1 p114-23 Fall 2002

Koger, Lisa

Bypass
  Home and beyond; an anthology of Kentucky short stories; edited by Morris Allen Grubbs; with an introduction by Wade Hall and an afterword by Charles E. May

Kohler, Sheila

The adulterous woman
  Doubletake v7 no4 p90-2 Fall 2001
  Kohler, S. Stories from another world
Africans
  The Best American short stories, 1999; selected from U.S. and Canadian magazines by Amy Tan with Katrina Kenison, with an introduction by Amy Tan
  Kohler, S. One girl; a novel in stories
All the days of my life
  Kohler, S. Stories from another world
Ambush
  Kohler, S. One girl; a novel in stories
Baboons
  Kohler, S. Stories from another world
The bride's secret
  Kohler, S. One girl; a novel in stories
Casualty
  Kohler, S. Stories from another world
Correspondence I
  Kohler, S. One girl; a novel in stories
Correspondence II
  Kohler, S. One girl; a novel in stories
Cracks
  Kohler, S. One girl; a novel in stories
Death in Rome
  The Antioch Review v59 no1 p26-39 Wint 2001
  Kohler, S. Stories from another world
Light
  Kohler, S. One girl; a novel in stories
Luck
  Kohler, S. One girl; a novel in stories

Kohler, Sheila—*Continued*

Lunch with mother

Kohler, S. Stories from another world

The Yale Review v91 no2 p134-47 Ap 2003

The mask

Kohler, S. Stories from another world

On the money

Kohler, S. One girl; a novel in stories

The original

Kohler, S. One girl; a novel in stories

Paris by night

Kohler, S. Stories from another world

The Paris Review v43 no159 p122-30 Fall 2001

Peaches and plums

Kohler, S. One girl; a novel in stories

Poor cousins

Kohler, S. Stories from another world

Rain check

Kohler, S. Stories from another world

Structure

Kohler, S. One girl; a novel in stories

Trust

Kohler, S. One girl; a novel in stories

Underworld

Kohler, S. Stories from another world

Violence

The Antioch Review v62 no3 p401-15 Summ 2004

Water Baby

Kohler, S. One girl; a novel in stories

Youth

Kohler, S. Stories from another world

Koizumi, Yakumo *See* Hearn, Lafcadio, 1850-1904

Koja, Kathe

At Eventide

Best new horror 12; edited and with an introduction by Stephen Jones

Death dines at 8:30; edited by Claudia Bishop and Nick DiChario

Bondage

Best new horror 10; edited and with an introduction by Stephen Jones

Road trip

The Year's best fantasy & horror: sixteenth annual collection; edited by Ellen Datlow & Terri Windling

Velocity

Datlow, E. The dark; new ghost stories; edited by Ellen Datlow

Koja, Kathe and Malzberg, Barry N.

What we did that summer

Redshift; extreme visions of speculative fiction; edited by Al Sarrantonio

Koldys, Sayzie

On a Bus to St. Cloud

The North American Review v288 no5 p20-5 S/O 2003

Kolka and Liusenka. Berberova, N.

Kollapse. Benford, G.

Kolyvushka. Babel´, I.

Konkin. Babel´, I.

Konzapas' commander. See Babel´, I. The commander of the second brigade

Kooker, Jonathan

Pretend I've died

Virgin fiction 2

Koon, David

The bone divers

New stories from the South: the year's best, 2002; edited by Shannon Ravenel; with a preface by Larry Brown

Koontz, Dean R. (Dean Ray)

Snatcher

Witches' brew; edited by Yvonne Jocks

Korbi's girl. Keret, E.

KOREA

Depew, D. R. Indigenous girls

Givens, J. On the wheel of wandering-on

Labor relations

Pak, W.-S. Butterfly of illusion

Pak, W.-S. A certain barbarity

Pak, W.-S. Encounter at the airport

Pak, W.-S. My very last possession

Pak, W.-S. She knows, I know, and heaven knows

Pak, W.-S. Three days in that autumn

Pak, W.-S. Thus ended my days of watching over the house

Steiner, H. Rice

Yi, T.-H. Shrapnel

Communism

See Communism—Korea

Rural life

Pak, W.-S. Granny flowers in those heartless days

Yi, T.-H. The blazing sun

Yi, T.-H. Dark valley

KOREAN AMERICANS

Kim, Junse. Yangban

Lee, D. Domo arigato

Lee, D. Voir dire

Lee, D. Yellow

Pak, T. The court interpreter

KOREAN WAR, 1950-1953

Burdick, E. Cold day, cold fear

Burke, J. L. We Build Churches, Inc.

Chamberlain, W. The trapped battalion

Deck, J. Sailors at their mourning: a memory

Drought, J. The secret [excerpt]

Hinojosa, R. Hoengsong

Martin, P. P. Amor de madre—Mother's love

Pak, W.-S. Granny flowers in those heartless days

Pak, W.-S. Mr. Hong's medals

Power, M. Graves

Sneider, V. A long way from home

VanderMeer, J. The General who is dead

Whitmore, S. Lost soldier

KOREANS

United States

Pak, W.-S. Farewell at Kimpo Airport

Wallace, R. Wordplay

Korn, Rachel H.

The road of no return

When night fell; an anthology of Holocaust short stories; edited by Linda Schermer Raphael and Marc Lee Raphael

The sack with pink stripes

Beautiful as the moon, radiant as the stars; Jewish women in Yiddish stories : an anthology; edited by Sandra Bark; introduction by Francine Prose

Korn, Rokhl

The end of the road

Neugroschel, J. No star too beautiful; Yiddish stories from 1382 to the present; compiled and translated by Joachim Neugroschel

Kornbluth, C. M. (Cyril M.)

The little black bag

The Science fiction hall of fame: volume one, 1929-1964; the greatest science fiction stories of all time chosen by the members of the Science Fiction Writers of America; edited by Robert Silverberg

That share of glory

The Good old stuff; adventure SF in the grand tradition; edited by Gardner Dozois

Two dooms

One lamp; alternate history stories from The magazine of Fantasy & Science Fiction; edited by Gordon van Gelder

The words of Guru

Children of the night; stories of ghosts, vampires, werewolves, and "lost children"; edited by Martin H. Greenberg

Kornbluth, Cyril M. *See* Kornbluth, C. M. (Cyril M.), 1923-1958

Kornegay, Jamie

Dog days

Stories from the Blue Moon Cafe II; edited by Sonny Brewer

Kornei Vasiliev. Tolstoy, L., graf

Korner, Simon

Joyeux Noël

Dalhousie Review v83 no1 p117-26 Spr 2003

The **korporał's** polonaise. Bukoski, A.

Kortes, Mary Lee

Summer vacation

Carved in rock; short stories by musicians; edited by Greg Kihn

Koschei the deathless. Sherman, J.

Kosinski, Jerzy N.

Steps [excerpt]

Neurotica: Jewish writers on sex; edited by Melvin Jules Bukiet

Koskinen, Marjatta

Dies Irae

With signs and wonders; an international anthology of Jewish fabulist fiction; edited by Daniel M. Jaffe

Kothari, Geeta

I Brake for Moose

The Massachusetts Review v44 no4 p660-76 Wint 2003/2004

Koven, Stephanie

The Events Leading Up to the Accident

The Antioch Review v61 no1 p149-52 Wint 2003

Koza nights. Lee, M.

Kramer, Wayne

East Side story

Carved in rock; short stories by musicians; edited by Greg Kihn

Krasnoff, Barbara

Stoop ladies

Such a pretty face; edited by Lee Martindale

Krauss, Nicole

Future emergencies

The Best American short stories, 2003; selected from U.S. and Canadian magazines by Walter Mosley with Katrina Kenison; with an introduction by Walter Mosley

The Last Words On Earth

The New Yorker v79 no46 p64-73 F 9 2004

Kraut. Young, T.

Krauze, Ethel

Isaiah vll, 14

Points of departure; new stories from Mexico; edited by Mónica Lavín; translated by Gustavo Segade

Krawiec, Richard

Accommodations

Krawiec, R. And fools of God; stories

Betrayals

Krawiec, R. And fools of God; stories

Capitalism

Krawiec, R. And fools of God; stories

Crashing

Krawiec, R. And fools of God; stories

Hardening of the arteries

Krawiec, R. And fools of God; stories

The house of women

Krawiec, R. And fools of God; stories

Listening to the gay boys fight

Krawiec, R. And fools of God; stories

Lovers

Krawiec, R. And fools of God; stories

Maggots, infidelity, and the oyster roast

Krawiec, R. And fools of God; stories

Rituals

Krawiec, R. And fools of God; stories

Saving Saul

Krawiec, R. And fools of God; stories

Troubles on Morning Glory Road

Krawiec, R. And fools of God; stories

Kreitman, Esther Singer

A satin coat

Beautiful as the moon, radiant as the stars; Jewish women in Yiddish stories : an anthology; edited by Sandra Bark; introduction by Francine Prose

Kress, Nancy

Computer virus

The Year's best science fiction, nineteenth annual collection; edited by Gardner Dozois

Ej-es

The year's best science fiction: twenty-first annual collection; edited by Gardner Dozois

The flowers of Aulit Prison

Nebula awards 33; the year's best SF and fantasy chosen by the science-fiction and fantasy writers of America; edited by Connie Willis

Inertia

A Woman's liberation; a choice of futures by and about women; edited by Connie Willis and Sheila Williams

The most famous little girl in the world

The Year's best science fiction; twentieth annual collection; edited by Gardner Dozois

Plant engineering

Death dines at 8:30; edited by Claudia Bishop and Nick DiChario

Kress, Nancy—*Continued*
Savior
  The Year's best science fiction, eighteenth annual collection; edited by Gardner Dozois
Sleeping dogs
  Far horizons; all new tales from the greatest worlds of science fiction; edited by Robert Silverberg

Krich, Rochelle Majer
"You win some . . . "
  Women before the bench; edited by Carolyn Wheat; introduction by Linda Fairstein

Krieger, Elliot
My Only Jew
  Michigan Quarterly Review v42 no1 p60-78 Wint 2003

KRIS KRINGLE *See* Santa Claus

Kriseová, Eda
A whirl of witches
  Partisan Review v66 no4 p611-24 Fall 1999

Krist, Gary
An innocent bystander
  The Best American mystery stories, 1999; edited and with an introduction by Ed McBain

Krista had a treble clef rose. Clyde, M.

Krouse, Erika
Drugs and you
  Krouse, E. Come up and see me sometime
The fast
  Krouse, E. Come up and see me sometime
The good times are killing me
  Ploughshares v28 no1 p120-35 Spr 2002
The husbands
  Krouse, E. Come up and see me sometime
  The New Yorker v77 no16 p132-7 Je 18-25 2001
Impersonators
  Krouse, E. Come up and see me sometime
Mercy
  Krouse, E. Come up and see me sometime
Momentum
  Krouse, E. Come up and see me sometime
My weddings
  Krouse, E. Come up and see me sometime
No universe
  Krouse, E. Come up and see me sometime
Other people's mothers
  Krouse, E. Come up and see me sometime
  Ploughshares v25 no4 p33-42 Wint 1999/2000
Too big to float
  Krouse, E. Come up and see me sometime
What I wore
  Krouse, E. Come up and see me sometime

Krout-Hasegawa, Ellen
Noise
  Hers 2: brilliant new fiction by lesbian writers; edited by Terry Wolverton with Robert Drake

Kruse, Tatjana
The good old German way
  The World's finest mystery and crime stories, third annual collection; edited by Ed Gorman and Martin H. Greenberg

Krysl, Marilyn
Cherry Garcia, pistachio cream
  Prairie Schooner v75 no4 p167-81 Wint 2001

The thing around them
  The Best American short stories, 2000; selected from U.S. and Canadian magazines by E. L. Doctorow with Katrina Kenison; with an introduction by E. L. Doctorow

Krystal Lynn. Kincaid, N.

KU KLUX KLAN
Berry, W. Don't send a boy to do a man's work
Lieu, J. Potential weapons
Roberts, L. The gathering of the klan

Kuala Lumpur. Alexis, A.

Kübler, Roland
Fires of Dreams
  Southern Humanities Review v36 no3 p254-60 Summ 2002

Kudritzki, Julian
Deal me jacks or better
  Chicago Review v47 no3 p114-20 Fall 2001
Interstate
  Chicago Review v47 no3 p112-13 Fall 2001
Sogged
  Chicago Review v47 no3 p111 Fall 2001

The **kudzu**. Crone, M.

Kudzu. Lewis, W. H.

Kuhr, Jeff
We're all chicken here
  Men on men 2000; best new gay fiction for the millennium; edited and with an introduction by David Bergman and Karl Woelz

Kulbak, Moyshe
Zelmenyaners
  Neugroschel, J. No star too beautiful; Yiddish stories from 1382 to the present; compiled and translated by Joachim Neugroschel

Kulsum, Nazia, and Ismail. Pittalwala, I.

The **kumquats** affairs. Nevins, F. M., Jr.

Kundera, Milan
The great return
  The New Yorker v78 no12 p96-105 My 20 2002

Kunin, Carolyn
(jt. auth) See Lichberg, Heinz von

Kunz, Don
The: Dancer's Hand
  South Carolina Review v35 no2 p50-7 Spr 2003

Kuo, Alex
10,000 Dildoes
  Amerasia Journal v29 no2 p254-63 2003

Kuppner, Frank
A very quiet street [excerpt]
  The Vintage book of contemporary Scottish fiction; edited and with an introduction by Peter Kravitz

Kurahashi, Yumiko
The house of the black cat
  The Year's best fantasy & horror, twelfth annual collection; edited by Ellen Datlow & Terry Windling

Kureishi, Hanif
Four blue chairs
  Kureishi, H. Intimacy; a novel; and, Midnight all day: stories
Girl
  Kureishi, H. Intimacy; a novel; and, Midnight all day: stories

Kureishi, Hanif—*Continued*
Intimacy
The Art of the story; an international antholo-
gy of contemporary short stories; edited by
Daniel Halpern
Kureishi, H. Intimacy; a novel; and, Midnight
all day: stories
Long Ago Yesterday
The New Yorker v80 no3 p74-8 Mr 8 2004
A meeting, at last
Kureishi, H. Intimacy; a novel; and, Midnight
all day: stories
Midnight all day
Kureishi, H. Intimacy; a novel; and, Midnight
all day: stories
Morning in the bowl of night
Kureishi, H. Intimacy; a novel; and, Midnight
all day: stories
The penis
Kureishi, H. Intimacy; a novel; and, Midnight
all day: stories
Strangers when we meet
Kureishi, H. Intimacy; a novel; and, Midnight
all day: stories
Sucking stones
Kureishi, H. Intimacy; a novel; and, Midnight
all day: stories
That was then
Kureishi, H. Intimacy; a novel; and, Midnight
all day: stories
Touched
The New Yorker v77 no27 p152-7 S 17 2001
The umbrella
Granta no65 p227-37 Spr 1999
Kureishi, H. Intimacy; a novel; and, Midnight
all day: stories
Kurland, Michael
Years ago and in a different place
My Sherlock Holmes; untold stories of the
great detective; edited by Michael Kurland
(jt. auth) See Pronzini, Bill and Kurland,
Michael
Kurlansky, Mark
Beautiful Mayagüez women
Kurlansky, M. The white man in the tree and
other stories
The deerness of life
Kurlansky, M. The white man in the tree and
other stories
Desaparecidos
Kurlansky, M. The white man in the tree and
other stories
Devaluation
Kurlansky, M. The white man in the tree and
other stories
Naked
Kurlansky, M. The white man in the tree and
other stories
Packets and paperscraps
Kurlansky, M. The white man in the tree and
other stories
The unclean
Kurlansky, M. The white man in the tree and
other stories
Vertical administration
Kurlansky, M. The white man in the tree and
other stories

The white man in the tree
Kurlansky, M. The white man in the tree and
other stories
Kuryla, Mary
Mis-sayings
The Pushcart prize XXIII: best of the small
presses; an annual small press reader; ed-
ited by Bill Henderson with the Pushcart
prize editors
Kusel, Lisa
Bars
Kusel, L. Other fish in the sea
Bones
Kusel, L. Other fish in the sea
Craps
Kusel, L. Other fish in the sea
Juvenile hall
Kusel, L. Other fish in the sea
Other fish in the sea
Kusel, L. Other fish in the sea
The other side
Kusel, L. Other fish in the sea
Perdition
Kusel, L. Other fish in the sea
Prairie dogs
Kusel, L. Other fish in the sea
Single white female
Kusel, L. Other fish in the sea
SWM
Kusel, L. Other fish in the sea
Kushner, Ellen
The death of the Duke
The Year's best fantasy & horror, twelfth an-
nual collection; edited by Ellen Datlow &
Terry Windling
The unicorn masque
Magical beginnings; edited by Steven H. Sil-
ver and Martin H. Greenberg
Kussi, Peter
Blood Brothers
Southwest Review v88 no2/3 p301-14 2003
Kůstka. Lustig, A.
Kuttner, Henry
We are the dead
The American fantasy tradition; edited by Bri-
an M. Thomsen
Kuttner, Henry, 1915-1958
*For works written by this author in collab-
oration with C. L. Moore see* Padgett,
Lewis
KUWAIT
Kanafāni, G. The death of bed number 12
Kuykendall's gold. Morgan, R.
Kvashay-Boyle, K.
Da bomb
Politically inspired; edited by Stephen Elliott;
assistant editor, Gabriel Kram; associate ed-
itors, Elizabeth Brooks [et al.]
Kyle, Aryn
Foaling Season
Atlantic Monthly (1993) v293 no4 p149-54,
156-62 My 2004
KYOTO (JAPAN) *See* Japan—Kyoto
Kyoto. Blatnik, A.
Kyrie. Anderson, P.
Kytzvinyne's 7th symphony. Cohen, M. D.

L

L.S.D.. Raphael, F.

L. U. C. I. E. Gordimer, N.

La Salle, Peter

The Bird in the Summer House

Southwest Review v87 no2/3 p310-26 2002

La Spina, Silvana

The night of crossed destinies

In the forbidden city; an anthology of erotic fiction by Italian women; edited by Maria Rosa Cutrufelli; translated by Vincent J. Bertolini

Lab, Olivia Kennedy

Empty Nest

The North American Review v288 no5 p8-9 S/O 2003

Laban and Murugi. Hunter, F.

Labandera. Galang, M. E.

Labia Lobelia. Jewell, L.

Labor. Bell, M. S.

LABOR AND LABORING CLASSES

See also Apprentices; Farm workers; Labor unions; Migrant labor; Strikes and lockouts

Calvino, I. Autumn

Cummins, A. Where I work

Sorrentino, G. The dignity of labor

Trevor, W. The mourning

United States

Chesnutt, C. W. The averted strike

Labor relations Turtledove, H. Alternate generals II; ed. by Harry Turtledove

LABOR UNIONS

See also Labor and laboring classes; Strikes and lockouts

Baida, P. Class warfare

Burton, M. Timing the strike

Labors of the heart. Davis, C.

LABOURÉ, CATHERINE, SAINT, 1806-1876

About

O'Connell, M. Saint Catherine Laboure

Labrador. Henley, P.

Labrunie, Gérard *See* Nerval, Gérard de, 1808-1855

LaBute, Neil

Layover

The New Yorker v77 no13 p120-1 My 28 2001

LABYRINTHS

Borges, J. L. The garden of forking paths

Borges, J. L. Ibn-Hakam al-Bokhari, murdered in his labyrinth

Lac Noir. LaSalle, P.

Lachnit, Carroll

Blind

Women before the bench; edited by Carolyn Wheat; introduction by Linda Fairstein

Lackey, Mercedes

A different kind of courage

Magical beginnings; edited by Steven H. Silver and Martin H. Greenberg

Nightside

Witches' brew; edited by Yvonne Jocks

Lackland, John *See* John, King of England, 1167-1216

Lacy, March

No fools, no fun

The African American West; a century of short stories; edited by Bruce A. Glasrud and Laurie Champion

Ladies and lovers. Mencken, S. H.

Ladies' man. Sanderson, J.

Ladies' wear. Kalman, J.

The **lady** and the woman. Alcott, L. M.

Lady Barberina. James, H.

Lady Chatterley's root canal. Dodd, S. M.

Lady Emerdirael's rescue. Deason, L.

The **lady** from yesterday. Healy, J. F.

Lady Hillary. Van de Wetering, J.

The **lady** in the desert. Brownrigg, S.

The **lady** in the looking-glass: a reflection. Woolf, V.

Lady Macbeth, prickly pear queen. Avrich, J.

Lady M's story. See Chekhov, A. P. A lady's story

A **lady** of bayou St. John. Chopin, K.

Lady of the Wild Beasts. Spark, D.

The **lady** was a dude. Farrell, C.

The **lady** with a pet dog. See Chekhov, A. P. The lady with the dog

A **lady** with pearls. Gilchrist, E.

The **lady** with the blind dog. Cady, J.

The **lady** with the dog. Chekhov, A. P.

The **lady** with the lap dog. See Chekhov, A. P. The lady with the dog

The **lady** with the little dog. See Chekhov, A. P. The lady with the dog

The **lady** with the pet dog. See Chekhov, A. P. The lady with the dog

The **lady** with the toy dog. See Chekhov, A. P. The lady with the dog

The **lady's** maid's bell. Wharton, E.

A **lady's** story. Chekhov, A. P.

LaFarge, Paul

Lamentation over the destruction of Ur

Politically inspired; edited by Stephen Elliott; assistant editor, Gabriel Kram; associate editors, Elizabeth Brooks [et al.]

Lafferty, R. A.

Eurema's dam

Masterpieces: the best science fiction of the century; edited by Orson Scott Card

Narrow Valley

The American fantasy tradition; edited by Brian M. Thomsen

LAGOS

Adichie, C. N. The American embassy

Lahiri, Jhumpa

Gogol

The New Yorker v79 no16 p170-87 Je 16-23 2003

Hell-Heaven

The New Yorker v80 no13 p72-81 My 24 2004

Interpreter of maladies

The Best American short stories, 1999; selected from U.S. and Canadian magazines by Amy Tan with Katrina Kenison, with an introduction by Amy Tan

Lahiri, J. Interpreter of maladies; stories

Prize stories, 1999; The O. Henry awards; edited and with an introduction by Larry Dark

Lahiri, Jhumpa—*Continued*
Mrs. Sen's
Lahiri, J. Interpreter of maladies; stories
Nobody's business
The Best American short stories, 2002; select-
ed from U.S. and Canadian magazines by
Sue Miller with Katrina Kenison, with an
introduction by Sue Miller
The New Yorker v77 no3 p78-95 Mr 12 2001
A real durwan
Lahiri, J. Interpreter of maladies; stories
Sexy
Lahiri, J. Interpreter of maladies; stories
A temporary matter
Fault lines; stories of divorce; collected and
edited by Caitlin Shetterly
Lahiri, J. Interpreter of maladies; stories
The third and final continent
The Best American short stories, 2000; select-
ed from U.S. and Canadian magazines by
E. L. Doctorow with Katrina Kenison; with
an introduction by E. L. Doctorow
Lahiri, J. Interpreter of maladies; stories
The New Yorker v75 no16 p200-08+ Je 21-28
1999
This blessed house
Lahiri, J. Interpreter of maladies; stories
The treatment of Bibi Haldar
Lahiri, J. Interpreter of maladies; stories
When Mr. Pirzada came to dine
Lahiri, J. Interpreter of maladies; stories
Laiah and the Sun King. Cowan, J.
Laidlaw, Marc and Shirley, John
Pearlywhite
Carved in rock; short stories by musicians;
edited by Greg Kihn
Laikin, Judith
Black Dorothea
The Ohio Review no59 p107-20 1999
Lajitas and the NFL. Shepard, S.
Lake, David J.
Re-deem the time
Centaurus: the best of Australian science fic-
tion; edited by David G. Hartwell and Da-
mien Broderick
The truth about Weena
Dreaming down-under; edited by Jack Dann
and Janeen Webb
Lake, M. D.
A. B. C. D. E. A. T. H.
Malice domestic 10; an anthology of original
traditional mystery stories
Tea for two
Murder most delectable; savory tales of culi-
nary crimes; edited by Martin H. Greenberg
The tunnel
Love and death; edited by Carolyn Hart
Lake, Robert
When, Before and After She Learned About
Trudy
Dalhousie Review v83 no2 p239-50 Summ
2003
The **Lake**. Brown, J.
Lake. Olivera, F.
The **lake** at the end of the wash. Jimenez, K. P.
A **Lake** in the Boat. Gray, J. and Gallagher, T.
Lake Natasink. Silber, J.
Lake Paradise. Hall, D.

LAKE TAHOE (CALIF. AND NEV.)
O'Shaughnessy, P. Juggernaut
Laken, Valerie
Before Long
Ploughshares v28 no4 p85-100 Wint
2002/2003
LAKES
Aichinger, I. Ghosts on the lake
Drake, R. At the lake
Oliver, C. A lake of summer
Vivante, A. The cove
Willis, M. S. Attack
Willis, M. S. Tiny gorillas
Ziegler, I. The stranger
Lamar ascending. Baldwin, D. N.
LAMAS
Clarke, A. C. The nine billion names of God
Lamb, Mike
The Painter
New Letters v69 no4 p41-51 2003
The **lamb** of the Flying U. Bower, B. M.
The **Lambeth** immortal. Sheffield, C.
Lambing season. Gloss, M.
The **lambs** on the boulder. Wright, J. A.
Lamé, Amy
Mapping
Typical girls; new stories by smart women;
edited by Susan Corrigan
Lament for the gunwitch. Golden, C.
A **lamia** in the Cévennes. Byatt, A. S.
L'Amore. Tozzi, F.
L'Amour, Louis
Alkali Basin
L'Amour, L. The collected short stories of
Louis L'Amour; The frontier stories: vol-
ume 1
Anything for a pal
L'Amour, L. From the listening hills
Backfield battering ram
L'Amour, L. From the listening hills
Beyond the chaparral
L'Amour, L. The collected short stories of
Louis L'Amour; The frontier stories: vol-
ume 1
Beyond the Great Snow Mountains
L'Amour, L. Beyond the Great Snow Moun-
tains
Booty for a badman
L'Amour, L. The collected short stories of
Louis L'Amour; The frontier stories: vol-
ume 1
By the waters of San Tadeo
L'Amour, L. Beyond the Great Snow Moun-
tains
The Cactus Kid
L'Amour, L. May there be a road
Caprock rancher
L'Amour, L. The collected short stories of
Louis L'Amour; The frontier stories: vol-
ume 1
Coast patrol
L'Amour, L. Beyond the Great Snow Moun-
tains
The courting of Griselda
L'Amour, L. The collected short stories of
Louis L'Amour; The frontier stories: vol-
ume 1

L'Amour, Louis—*Continued*

Crash landing
L'Amour, L. Beyond the Great Snow Mountains

The cross and the candle
L'Amour, L. Off the Mangrove Coast

Dead-end drift
L'Amour, L. The collected short stories of Louis L'Amour; The frontier stories: volume 1

The defense of Sentinel
L'Amour, L. The collected short stories of Louis L'Amour; The frontier stories: volume 1

Desperate men
L'Amour, L. The collected short stories of Louis L'Amour; The frontier stories: volume 1

The diamond of Jeru
L'Amour, L. Off the Mangrove Coast

Down Paagumene way
L'Amour, L. From the listening hills

Duffy's man
L'Amour, L. The collected short stories of Louis L'Amour; The frontier stories: volume 1

Dutchman's Flat
L'Amour, L. The collected short stories of Louis L'Amour; The frontier stories: volume 1

Elisha comes to Red Horse
L'Amour, L. The collected short stories of Louis L'Amour; The frontier stories: volume 1

End of the drive
L'Amour, L. The collected short stories of Louis L'Amour; The frontier stories: volume 1

Fighter's fiasco
L'Amour, L. May there be a road

Fighters should be hungry
L'Amour, L. Off the Mangrove Coast

Flight to the north
L'Amour, L. From the listening hills

A friend of a hero
L'Amour, L. May there be a road

From the listening hills
L'Amour, L. From the listening hills
L'Amour, L. The collected short stories of Louis L'Amour; The frontier stories: volume 1

Get out of town
L'Amour, L. The collected short stories of Louis L'Amour; The frontier stories: volume 1

The ghost fighter
L'Amour, L. May there be a road

The gift of Cochise
A Century of great Western stories; edited by John Jakes
L'Amour, L. The collected short stories of Louis L'Amour; The frontier stories: volume 1

The gravel pit
L'Amour, L. Beyond the Great Snow Mountains

The hand of Kuan-yin
L'Amour, L. May there be a road

Home is the hunter
L'Amour, L. The collected short stories of Louis L'Amour; The frontier stories: volume 1

A huband for Janey
L'Amour, L. The collected short stories of Louis L'Amour; The frontier stories: volume 1

Ironwood Station
L'Amour, L. The collected short stories of Louis L'Amour; The frontier stories: volume 1

It's your move
L'Amour, L. Off the Mangrove Coast

Let the cards decide
L'Amour, L. The collected short stories of Louis L'Amour; The frontier stories: volume 1

The lonesome gods
L'Amour, L. The collected short stories of Louis L'Amour; The frontier stories: volume 1

Making it the hard way
L'Amour, L. May there be a road

Marshal of Canyon Gap
L'Amour, L. The collected short stories of Louis L'Amour; The frontier stories: volume 1

May there be a road
L'Amour, L. May there be a road

Meeting at Falmouth
L'Amour, L. Beyond the Great Snow Mountains

The money punch
L'Amour, L. Beyond the Great Snow Mountains

The moon of the trees broken by snow
L'Amour, L. From the listening hills
L'Amour, L. The collected short stories of Louis L'Amour; The frontier stories: volume 1

Moran of the Tigers
L'Amour, L. From the listening hills

A mule for Santa Fe
L'Amour, L. The collected short stories of Louis L'Amour; The frontier stories: volume 1

Murphy plays his hand
L'Amour, L. From the listening hills

A night at wagon camp
L'Amour, L. From the listening hills

Off the Mangrove Coast
L'Amour, L. Off the Mangrove Coast

The one for the Mohave Kid
L'Amour, L. The collected short stories of Louis L'Amour; The frontier stories: volume 1

One for the pot
L'Amour, L. The collected short stories of Louis L'Amour; The frontier stories: volume 1

One night stand
L'Amour, L. The collected short stories of Louis L'Amour; The frontier stories: volume 1

Red butte showdown
L'Amour, L. May there be a road

L'Amour, Louis—_Continued_

Riches beyond dream
L'Amour, L. The collected short stories of Louis L'Amour; The frontier stories: volume 1

The rounds don't matter
L'Amour, L. Off the Mangrove Coast

Roundup in Texas
L'Amour, L. Beyond the Great Snow Mountains

Rustler roundup
L'Amour, L. The collected short stories of Louis L'Amour; The frontier stories: volume 1

Sand trap
L'Amour, L. From the listening hills

Secret of Silver Springs
L'Amour, L. Off the Mangrove Coast

Sideshow champion
L'Amour, L. Beyond the Great Snow Mountains

The skull and the arrow
L'Amour, L. The collected short stories of Louis L'Amour; The frontier stories: volume 1

Stage to Willowspring
L'Amour, L. The collected short stories of Louis L'Amour; The frontier stories: volume 1

That man from the bitter sands
L'Amour, L. The collected short stories of Louis L'Amour; The frontier stories: volume 1

Time of terror
L'Amour, L. Off the Mangrove Coast

To make a stand
L'Amour, L. The collected short stories of Louis L'Amour; The frontier stories: volume 1

Too tough to kill
L'Amour, L. From the listening hills

Trap of gold
L'Amour, L. The collected short stories of Louis L'Amour; The frontier stories: volume 1

Under the hanging wall
L'Amour, L. Beyond the Great Snow Mountains

The unexpected corpse
L'Amour, L. Off the Mangrove Coast

The vanished blonde
L'Amour, L. May there be a road

Waltz him around again, Shadow
L'Amour, L. From the listening hills

War party
L'Amour, L. The collected short stories of Louis L'Amour; The frontier stories: volume 1

Wings over Brazil
L'Amour, L. May there be a road

Wings over Khabarovsk
On glorious wings; the best flying stories of the century; edited and introduced by Stephen Coonts

L'amour. Boylan, C.

Lamp, Bill

Almost Like Nowhere
The Kenyon Review v25 no3/4 p135-51 Summ/Fall 2003

On Impulse
Confrontation no86/87 p69-80 Spr/Summ 2004

A **lamp** for Medusa. Tenn, W.

The **lamp** of Psyche. Wharton, E.

Lamsley, Terry

Climbing down from heaven
Best new horror 12; edited and with an introduction by Stephen Jones
Death dines at 8:30; edited by Claudia Bishop and Nick DiChario

The stunted house
Best new horror 11; edited and with an introduction by Stephen Jones

Suburban blight
The Year's best fantasy & horror, twelfth annual collection; edited by Ellen Datlow & Terry Windling

Lanark [excerpt] Gray, A.

Lance and Gwendolyn. Reiner, C.

The **land** of anarchy. Van Winckel, N.

The **land** of dreams, the garden of insomnia. Budman, M.

The **land** of sculpture. Haake, K.

Landing. McGarry, J.

Landings. Hoffman, W.

Landis, Dylan

Hate
Bomb no88 p106-10 Summ 2004

Landis, Geoffrey A.

Across the darkness
Landis, G. A. Impact parameter and other quantum realities; with a foreword by Joe Haldeman

Approaching Perimelasma
Landis, G. A. Impact parameter and other quantum realities; with a foreword by Joe Haldeman
The Year's best science fiction, sixteenth annual collection; edited by Gardner Dozois

Beneath the stars of winter
Landis, G. A. Impact parameter and other quantum realities; with a foreword by Joe Haldeman

Dark lady
Landis, G. A. Impact parameter and other quantum realities; with a foreword by Joe Haldeman

Ecopoiesis
Landis, G. A. Impact parameter and other quantum realities; with a foreword by Joe Haldeman
Worldmakers; SF adventures in terraforming; edited by Gardner Dozois

Elemental
Landis, G. A. Impact parameter and other quantum realities; with a foreword by Joe Haldeman

The eyes of America
The year's best science fiction: twenty-first annual collection; edited by Gardner Dozois

Impact parameter
Landis, G. A. Impact parameter and other quantum realities; with a foreword by Joe Haldeman

Into the blue abyss
Landis, G. A. Impact parameter and other quantum realities; with a foreword by Joe Haldeman

Landis, Geoffrey A.—*Continued*

Ouroboros

    Landis, G. A. Impact parameter and other quantum realities; with a foreword by Joe Haldeman

Outsider's chance

    Landis, G. A. Impact parameter and other quantum realities; with a foreword by Joe Haldeman

Rorvik's war

    Landis, G. A. Impact parameter and other quantum realities; with a foreword by Joe Haldeman

The secret egg of the clouds

    Starlight 3; edited by Patrick Nielsen Hayden

The singular habits of wasps

    Landis, G. A. Impact parameter and other quantum realities; with a foreword by Joe Haldeman

Snow

    Landis, G. A. Impact parameter and other quantum realities; with a foreword by Joe Haldeman

A walk in the sun

    Landis, G. A. Impact parameter and other quantum realities; with a foreword by Joe Haldeman

What we really do here at NASA

    Landis, G. A. Impact parameter and other quantum realities; with a foreword by Joe Haldeman

Winter fire

    Landis, G. A. Impact parameter and other quantum realities; with a foreword by Joe Haldeman

    Nebula awards showcase 2000; the year's best SF and fantasy chosen by the science fiction and fantasy writers of america; edited by Gregory Benford

LANDLADIES *See* Landlord and tenant

The **landlord**. Galef, D.

LANDLORD AND TENANT

Barthelme, F. Elroy Nights

Carver, R. What would you like to see?

Casey, M. Relief

Chekhov, A. P. Notes from the memoirs of a man of ideals

Cohen, S. How much justice can you afford?

Dixon, S. Heat

Galef, D. The landlord

Gilb, D. Hueco

Knight, M. Tenant

Krouse, E. Mercy

Morgan, R. The bullnoser

Orner, P. Pile of clothes

Pushkin, A. S. Dubrovskii

Rubin, B. Living next door to malice

Tenn, W. The tenants

LANDLORDS *See* Landlord and tenant

LANDSCAPE GARDENING

    See also Trees

Waller, Easton. The war against the lawns

A **landscape** painter. James, H.

Landscape with flatiron. Murakami, H.

LANDSLIDES

Hawthorne, N. The ambitious guest

Landwehr, Al

Seasons

    New Letters v68 no3/4 p9-15 Spr/Summ 2002

Lane, Andrew

The gaze of the falcon

    Royal whodunnits; edited by Mike Ashley

Lane, Joel

Coming of age

    Gathering the bones; original stories from the world's masters of horror; edited by Dennis Etchison, Ramsey Campbell and Jack Dann

The hunger of the leaves

    Best new horror 12; edited and with an introduction by Stephen Jones

The lost district

    The Mammoth book of best horror 13; edited by Stephen Jones

The receivers

    The Year's best fantasy & horror: sixteenth annual collection; edited by Ellen Datlow & Terri Windling

The window

    The Museum of horrors; edited by Dennis Etchison

Lang, Andrew

The story of Sigurd

    Tales before Tolkien; the roots of modern fantasy; edited by Douglas A. Anderson

Lange, John *See* Crichton, Michael, 1942-

Lange, Richard

Blind-Made Products

    Iowa Review v32 no3 p157-68 Wint 2002/2003

Fuzzyland

    The Georgia Review v56 no3 p727-46 Fall 2002

Langford, David

Encounter of another kind

    Witpunk; edited by Claude Lalumière and Marty Halpern

Language. Hunt, S.

LANGUAGE AND LANGUAGES

    See also English language; French language

Arnason, E. The grammarian's five daughters

Chiang, T. Story of your life

Cohen, R. Oscillations

De Camp, L. S. The isolinguals

Le Guin, U. K. The Nna Mmoy language

Le Guin, U. K. The silence of the Asonu

Mathews, H. The dialect of the tribe

Mathews, H. Remarks of the scholar graduate

Montpetit, C. Beyond the barriers

Tawada, Y. Canned foreign

Touré. Afrolexicology today's biannual list of the top fifty words in African-American

Touré. We words

Wallace, D. Slippered feet

Language game. Händler, E.-W.

Language of the self. Villani, L.

Lanham, Edwin

The Denton mare

    Sports best short stories; edited by Paul D. Staudohar

Lankford, Terrill

Detour Drive

    Flesh and blood; erotic tales of crime and passion; edited by Max Allan Collins and Jeff Gelb

L'Annonciation. Paschal, D.

Lansdale, Joe R.
Bar talk
  Lansdale, J. R. Bumper crop / Joe R. Lansdale
Bestsellers guaranteed
  Lansdale, J. R. Bumper crop / Joe R. Lansdale
Billie Sue
  Lansdale, J. R. Bumper crop / Joe R. Lansdale
Chompers
  Lansdale, J. R. Bumper crop / Joe R. Lansdale
Cowboy
  Lansdale, J. R. Bumper crop / Joe R. Lansdale
Down by the sea near the great big rock
  Lansdale, J. R. Bumper crop / Joe R. Lansdale
Duck hunt
  Lansdale, J. R. Bumper crop / Joe R. Lansdale
The dump
  Lansdale, J. R. Bumper crop / Joe R. Lansdale
The Fat Man
  Lansdale, J. R. Bumper crop / Joe R. Lansdale
Fire dog
  Lansdale, J. R. Bumper crop / Joe R. Lansdale
Fish night
  Lansdale, J. R. Bumper crop / Joe R. Lansdale
God of the razor
  Lansdale, J. R. Bumper crop / Joe R. Lansdale
I tell you it's love
  Lansdale, J. R. Bumper crop / Joe R. Lansdale
In the cold, dark time
Last of the hopeful
  Lansdale, J. R. Bumper crop / Joe R. Lansdale
Listen
  Lansdale, J. R. Bumper crop / Joe R. Lansdale
Mad dog summer
  999: new stories of horror and suspense; edited by Al Sarrantonio
The man who dreamed
  Lansdale, J. R. Bumper crop / Joe R. Lansdale
Master of misery
  Lansdale, J. R. Bumper crop / Joe R. Lansdale
The mule rustlers
  The Best American mystery stories, 2002; edited and with an introduction by James Ellroy; Otto Penzler, series editor
  The Mysterious Press anniversary anthology; celebrating 25 years; by the editors of Mysterious Press
Old Charlie
  Lansdale, J. R. Bumper crop / Joe R. Lansdale
On a dark October
  Lansdale, J. R. Bumper crop / Joe R. Lansdale

Personality problem
  Lansdale, J. R. Bumper crop / Joe R. Lansdale
The shaggy house
  Lansdale, J. R. Bumper crop / Joe R. Lansdale
Walks
  Lansdale, J. R. Bumper crop / Joe R. Lansdale
Lansdale, Joe R. and Lansdale, Karen
A change of lifestyle
  Lansdale, J. R. Bumper crop / Joe R. Lansdale
Lansdale, Joe R. and Lowry, Dan
Pilots
  Lansdale, J. R. Bumper crop / Joe R. Lansdale
Lansdale, Joe R. and others
The companion
  Lansdale, J. R. Bumper crop / Joe R. Lansdale
Lansdale, Karen
(jt. auth) See Lansdale, Joe R. and Lansdale, Karen
Lao, She *See* Lao She, 1899-1966
Lao She
Also a triangle
  Lao She. Blades of grass; the stories of Lao She; translated from the Chinese by William A. Lyell and Sarah Wei-ming Chen; general editor, Howard Goldblatt
Attachment
  Lao She. Blades of grass; the stories of Lao She; translated from the Chinese by William A. Lyell and Sarah Wei-ming Chen; general editor, Howard Goldblatt
Autobiography of a minor character
  Lao She. Blades of grass; the stories of Lao She; translated from the Chinese by William A. Lyell and Sarah Wei-ming Chen; general editor, Howard Goldblatt
Black Li and White Li
  Lao She. Blades of grass; the stories of Lao She; translated from the Chinese by William A. Lyell and Sarah Wei-ming Chen; general editor, Howard Goldblatt
Crooktails
  Lao She. Blades of grass; the stories of Lao She; translated from the Chinese by William A. Lyell and Sarah Wei-ming Chen; general editor, Howard Goldblatt
Ding
  Lao She. Blades of grass; the stories of Lao She; translated from the Chinese by William A. Lyell and Sarah Wei-ming Chen; general editor, Howard Goldblatt
The grand opening
  Lao She. Blades of grass; the stories of Lao She; translated from the Chinese by William A. Lyell and Sarah Wei-ming Chen; general editor, Howard Goldblatt
Hot dumplings
  Lao She. Blades of grass; the stories of Lao She; translated from the Chinese by William A. Lyell and Sarah Wei-ming Chen; general editor, Howard Goldblatt

Lao She—*Continued*

Life choices

Lao She. Blades of grass; the stories of Lao She; translated from the Chinese by William A. Lyell and Sarah Wei-ming Chen; general editor, Howard Goldblatt

A man who doesn't lie

Lao She. Blades of grass; the stories of Lao She; translated from the Chinese by William A. Lyell and Sarah Wei-ming Chen; general editor, Howard Goldblatt

Neighbors

Lao She. Blades of grass; the stories of Lao She; translated from the Chinese by William A. Lyell and Sarah Wei-ming Chen; general editor, Howard Goldblatt

No distance too far, no sacrifice too great

Lao She. Blades of grass; the stories of Lao She; translated from the Chinese by William A. Lyell and Sarah Wei-ming Chen; general editor, Howard Goldblatt

An old and established name

Lao She. Blades of grass; the stories of Lao She; translated from the Chinese by William A. Lyell and Sarah Wei-ming Chen; general editor, Howard Goldblatt

An old man's romance

Lao She. Blades of grass; the stories of Lao She; translated from the Chinese by William A. Lyell and Sarah Wei-ming Chen; general editor, Howard Goldblatt

Rabbit

Lao She. Blades of grass; the stories of Lao She; translated from the Chinese by William A. Lyell and Sarah Wei-ming Chen; general editor, Howard Goldblatt

The **lap** of luxury. Van Winckel, N.

Lapcharoensap, Rattawut

Farangs

Granta v84 p187-203 Wint 2003

LaPierre, Janet

Da capo

Crème de la crime; edited by Janet Hutchings

Sex, lies, and apple pie

Mom, apple pie, and murder; edited by Nancy Pickard

Lara. Jaiser, I.

Larabi's ox. Ardizzone, T.

Laramie. Wieland, L.

LARCENY *See* Theft

Lardner, Ring

Back to Baltimore

Dead balls and double curves; an anthology of early baseball fiction; edited and with an introduction by Trey Strecker ; with a foreword by Arnold Hano

Champion

Boxing's best short stories; edited by Paul D. Staudohar

The golden honeymoon

The Best American short stories of the century; John Updike, editor, Katrina Kenison, coeditor; with an introduction by John Updike

Haircut

The Best American mystery stories of the century; Tony Hillerman, editor; with an introduction by Tony Hillerman

Hurry Kane

Sports best short stories; edited by Paul D. Staudohar

A **large** bee. Brennan, M.

Largesse. Godwin, G.

Lark. Adam, C.

The **lark**. Tabatabai, N.

Lark till dawn, princess. Anderson, B.

Larminie, Margaret Beda *See* Yorke, Margaret

Larroquette. Barthelme, F.

Larry's words, 1983. Shields, C.

LAS VEGAS (NEV.) *See* Nevada—Las Vegas

LaSalle, Peter

The Absent Painter

The Antioch Review v62 no3 p430-46 Summ 2004

The admissions officer

The Antioch Review v59 no2 p434-50 Spr 2001

The Antioch Review v57 no1 p5-21 Wint 1999

The back nine in autumn

Western Humanities Review v53 no4 p359-65 Wint 1999/2000

Boys: a new African fable

The Literary Review (Madison, N.J.) v44 no3 p496-508 Spr 2001

The Forest of Titles

The Massachusetts Review v45 no1 p33-50 Spr 2004

A guide to some small border airports

Graham, D. Lone Star literature; from the Red River to the Rio Grande; edited by Don Graham

Hockey

Sports best short stories; edited by Paul D. Staudohar

Lac Noir

The Ohio Review no62/63 p448-65 2001

Murdering the Moonlight

New England Review v24 no1 p22-35 Wint 2003

Nocturne

The Antioch Review v60 no3 p438-58 Summ 2002

Sleeping Mask

Western Humanities Review v57 no2 p91-5 Fall 2003

Snug Harbor

New England Review v22 no4 p42-55 Fall 2001

Tell Borges If You See Him

New England Review v25 no1/2 p210-22 2004

Lascaux, Paul

Fire works

The World's finest mystery and crime stories, third annual collection; edited by Ed Gorman and Martin H. Greenberg

Lasdun, James

Annals of the honorary secretary

The Times Literary Supplement no5000 p15-16 Ja 29 1999

Cranley Meadows

The Times Literary Supplement no5043 p18-19 N 26 1999

Lass, Andrew
Julius
The Massachusetts Review v44 no1/2 p331-46
Spr/Summ 2003
Lass. Erian, A.
The **last** action. Viganò, R.
The **Last** American Monkey. Beach-Ferrara, J.
The **last** asset. Wharton, E.
The **last** bad thing. Richmond, M.
The **last** beast out of the box. Watson, I.
The **last** black hoose. Jamieson, R. A.
The **last** blow. Cohen, O. R.
The **last** bottle in the world. Ellin, S.
The **last** bounce. Tenn, W.
The **Last** Cat. Doucette, R. J.
Last Chance Gravity Fill Station. Allen, C.
The **last** command. Clarke, A. C.
The **last** dance. Nichols, I.
Last date. Vachss, A. H.
The **last** daughter-in-law. Gavell, M. L.
The **last** day. Matheson, R.
The **last** day, an epilogue. Drake, R.
The **last** day of July. Dozois, G. R.
The **last** days. House, S.
The **last** days of Dominic Prince. Wheeler, R. S.
The **last** days of Shandakor. Brackett, L.
The **last** Einstein-Rosen bridge. Rucker, R. v. B.
The **last** emigrant. Glickmann, N.
The **Last** Field Marshal. Vollmann, W. T.
A **last** fling, like. Yates, R.
The **last** gas station. Grau, S. A.
The **last** generation. Williams, J.
The **last** great dream of my father. Hribal, C. J.
The **Last** Heat of Summer. Everett, P.
The **last** innocence of Simeon. Ronan, F.
The **last** invasion of Ireland. Garfinkle, R.
The **last** journey. Rachmil, B.
The **last** known thing. Rosenfeld, S.
The **last** leaf. Henry, O.
The **Last** Living Elk in North America. Ames, B.
A **last** look at the sea. Dyson, J.
Last love song at the Valentine. Winegardner, M.
The **last** lovely city. Adams, A.
The **Last** Member of the Boela Tribe. Day, C.
The **last** mile. Wellen, E.
Last-minute shopping. Westlake, D. E.
The **last** native. Connor, J.
Last Night. Salter, J.
The **last** night of the county fair. Shade, E.
Last night out. Bishop, M.
Last night when you kissed Blanche Thompson.
Aldrich, B. S.
The **last** odd day in L.A. Beattie, A.
The **last** of the beaux. Mencken, S. H.
The **last** of the gentlemen. Cheng, C.-W.
The **last** of the gold star mothers. Bly, C.
The **last** of the great courtesans. Auchincloss, L.
The **last** of the traveling picture shows. Levit, D. J.
The **last** of the Valerii. James, H.
Last of the white slaves. Meloy, M.
The **last** old maid in town. Drake, R.
The **last** one to cry. Howard, C.
The **last** one way. Englander, N.
The **last** passenger. Nevins, F. M., Jr.
The **last** picture show. Clark, B. C.
The **last** pitch. O'Rourke, F.
The **last** question. Asimov, I.
The **last** reel. Bush, G. R.

Last requests. Smith, G.
The **last** rescue. Menendez, A.
The **last** ride of Gunplay Maxwell. Overholser, S.
Last rite. Rash, R.
Last scenes from single life. Beattie, A.
The **last** spin. McBain, E.
Last summer at Mars Hill. Hand, E.
The **last** supper. Hird, L.
The **Last** Tenant. Capers, I. B.
Last thing. Galloway, J.
The **last** time. McGarry, J.
The **last** time around. O'Rourke, F.
The **Last** Time I Saw You. Brown, R.
The **last** tortilla. Troncoso, S.
The **last** voyage of the ghost ship. García Márquez, G.
Last will. Lincoln, C.
The **last** word. Painter, P.
The **Last** Words On Earth. Krauss, N.
Last year's Jesus (or Passion play). Slezak, E.
Late for the wedding. Chaon, D.
Late fruit. Coates, G. S.
Late hour. Bunin, I. A.
The **late** hunt. Henley, P.
The **late** night news. Tilghman, C.
Late-night TV. Spencer, D.
Late revenge. Hendel, Y.
A **Late** Spring. Beveridge, M. E.
The **latest** dream I ever dreamed. Talbot, N.
Latifa. Smilansky, M.
Latimer, Renate
(jt. auth) See Heidenreich, Elke
LATIN AMERICA
Williams, M. Coley's war
Politics
See Politics—Latin America
LATINOS (U.S.) *See* Hispanic Americans
Latour, José
Golam
Death by espionage; intriguing stories of deception and betrayal; edited by Martin Cruz Smith
Havanightmare
Death cruise; crime stories on the open seas; edited by Lawrence Block
Latta, Ruth
Brownie and Montgomery
Dalhousie Review v81 no1 p117-22 Spr 2001
The **latter** days of the law. Waldrop, H.
Latty, Yvonne
Margie
Callaloo v26 no3 p622-8 Summ 2003
Laugh track. Galef, D.
Laughter. Wuori, G. K.
The **laughter** of the gods. Updike, J.
LAUNDRESSES
Butler, R. O. The one in white
Laundromat. Stuckrad-Barre, B. v.
LAUNDROMATS *See* Self-service laundries
Laura Borealis. Reid, E.
Laureano's wall. Blakely, M.
LAUREL, STAN, 1890-1965
About
Bradbury, R. The Laurel and Hardy Alpha Centauri farewell tour
The **Laurel** and Hardy Alpha Centauri farewell tour. Bradbury, R.

Laurence, Janet

Time share

Malice domestic 8

Lavalle, Victor

Times Square Romance

Gentlemen's Quarterly v73 no5 p195 My 2003

LaValle, Victor D.

Ancient history

LaValle, V. D. Slapboxing with Jesus; stories

Chuckie

LaValle, V. D. Slapboxing with Jesus; stories

Class trip

LaValle, V. D. Slapboxing with Jesus; stories

Getting paid

On the rocks; the KGB Bar fiction anthology; edited by Rebecca Donner ; foreword by Denis Woychuk

Getting ugly

LaValle, V. D. Slapboxing with Jesus; stories

Ghost story

LaValle, V. D. Slapboxing with Jesus; stories

How I lost my inheritance

LaValle, V. D. Slapboxing with Jesus; stories

Kids on Colden Street

LaValle, V. D. Slapboxing with Jesus; stories

Pops

LaValle, V. D. Slapboxing with Jesus; stories

Raw daddy

LaValle, V. D. Slapboxing with Jesus; stories

Slave

LaValle, V. D. Slapboxing with Jesus; stories

Trinidad

LaValle, V. D. Slapboxing with Jesus; stories

Who we did worship

LaValle, V. D. Slapboxing with Jesus; stories

Lavare. McGarry, J.

Lavender. Mosley, W.

Lavers, Norman

My life

The North American Review v284 no3-4 p32-33 My/Ag 1999

Lavín, Guillermo

Reaching the shore

Cosmos latinos: an anthology of science fiction from Latin America and Spain; translated, edited, & with an introduction & notes by Andrea L. Bell & Yolanda Molina-Gavilán

Lavin, Mary

Chamois gloves

Lavin, M. In a café; selected stories; edited by Elizabeth Walsh Peavoy; foreword by Thomas Kilroy

The convent

Lavin, M. In a café; selected stories; edited by Elizabeth Walsh Peavoy; foreword by Thomas Kilroy

A cup of tea

Lavin, M. In a café; selected stories; edited by Elizabeth Walsh Peavoy; foreword by Thomas Kilroy

A family likeness

Lavin, M. In a café; selected stories; edited by Elizabeth Walsh Peavoy; foreword by Thomas Kilroy

A gentle soul

Lavin, M. In a café; selected stories; edited by Elizabeth Walsh Peavoy; foreword by Thomas Kilroy

The girders

Lavin, M. In a café; selected stories; edited by Elizabeth Walsh Peavoy; foreword by Thomas Kilroy

In a café

Lavin, M. In a café; selected stories; edited by Elizabeth Walsh Peavoy; foreword by Thomas Kilroy

In the middle of the fields

Lavin, M. In a café; selected stories; edited by Elizabeth Walsh Peavoy; foreword by Thomas Kilroy

The joy-ride

Lavin, M. In a café; selected stories; edited by Elizabeth Walsh Peavoy; foreword by Thomas Kilroy

Lemonade

Lavin, M. In a café; selected stories; edited by Elizabeth Walsh Peavoy; foreword by Thomas Kilroy

The little prince

Lavin, M. In a café; selected stories; edited by Elizabeth Walsh Peavoy; foreword by Thomas Kilroy

A story with a pattern

Lavin, M. In a café; selected stories; edited by Elizabeth Walsh Peavoy; foreword by Thomas Kilroy

Tom

Lavin, M. In a café; selected stories; edited by Elizabeth Walsh Peavoy; foreword by Thomas Kilroy

Trastevere

Lavin, M. In a café; selected stories; edited by Elizabeth Walsh Peavoy; foreword by Thomas Kilroy

The widow's son

Lavin, M. In a café; selected stories; edited by Elizabeth Walsh Peavoy; foreword by Thomas Kilroy

The will

Lavin, M. In a café; selected stories; edited by Elizabeth Walsh Peavoy; foreword by Thomas Kilroy

Lavín, Mónica

Why come back?

Points of departure; new stories from Mexico; edited by Mónica Lavín; translated by Gustavo Segade

LAW AND LAWYERS

See also Judges; Trials; Women lawyers

Adams, A. A pale and perfectly oval moon

Agee, J. The world. The text. The crime.

Archer, J. The expert witness

Auchincloss, L. DeCicco v. Schweizer

Auchincloss, L. The interlude

Auchincloss, L. The justice clerk

Auchincloss, L. The scarlet letters

Baca, J. S. Mother's ashes

Berry, W. The inheritors

Berry, W. It wasn't me

Berry, W. Thicker than liquor

Berry, W. The wild birds

Biguenet, J. The work of art

Borges, J. L. The man on the threshold

LAW AND LAWYERS—*Continued*

Brownstein, G. Wakefield, 7E

Bukiet, M. J. Tongue of the Jews

Canty, K. Carolina beach

Carlson, R. Nightcap

Chekhov, A. P. At home

Chekhov, A. P. An incident at law

Chekhov, A. P. Old age

Chekhov, A. P. The Petchenyeg

Chekhov, A. P. The siren

Dinh, L. Fritz Glatman

Doenges, J. The money stays, the people go

Epstein, J. Coming in with their hands up

Fischer, T. Then they say you're drunk

Forsyth, F. The veteran

Galef, D. All Cretans

Girardi, R. The defenestration of Aba Sid

Gores, J. Plot it yourself

Greenberg, A. Gruber in traffic

Hare, C. Name of Smith

Hensley, J. L. Fifty Chinese

Hensley, J. L. The home

Hensley, J. L. Trial

Hensley, J. L. Whistler

Hensley, J. L. Widow

Huffman, B., Jr. Acceptance of responsibility

Huffman, B., Jr. Arraignment

Huffman, B., Jr. Bench trial

Huffman, B., Jr. Contrary to the manifest tenor

Huffman, B., Jr. Dismissed, with prejudice

Huffman, B., Jr. Initial consultation

Huffman, B., Jr. Maintaining integrity

Huffman, B., Jr. Mutuality of interests

Huffman, B., Jr. Some due process

Huffman, B., Jr. Synthesis of the community standard

Huffman, B., Jr. Yielding to science

Huffman, B., Jr. Zealous representation

Jakes, J. Celebrity and justice for all

Joyce, G. Tiger moth

Kennedy, A. L. An immaculate man

Lee, D. Voir dire

Lopez, B. H. The construction of the Rachel

Margolin, P. The jailhouse lawyer

Martini, S. Poetic justice

McDermid, V. Metamorphosis

McNeely, T. H. Sheep

Meloy, M. Kite Whistler Aquamarine

Mortimer, J. C. Rumpole and the absence of body

Mortimer, J. C. Rumpole and the actor laddie

Mortimer, J. C. Rumpole and the asylum seekers

Mortimer, J. C. Rumpole and the Camberwell

Mortimer, J. C. Rumpole and the old familiar faces

Mortimer, J. C. Rumpole and the remembrance of things past

Mortimer, J. C. Rumpole and the teenage werewolf

Mortimer, J. C. Rumpole at sea

Mortimer, J. C. Rumpole rests his case

Nelson, K. Tides

Painter, P. Murder one

Reeve, A. B. The poisoned pen

Scottoline, L. Carrying concealed

Singer, I. B. The litigants

Slesar, H. The day of the execution

Tenn, W. Child's play

Wuori, G. K. Justice

Law and order. Stevenson, J.

Law of averages. Barthelme, F.

The **law** of diminishing returns. Peck, D.

The **law** of falling bodies. Brenna, D.

The **law** of man. West, M.

The **law** of return. Rodburg, M.

Lawman's debt. Le May, A.

Lawnmower Moe. Eakin, W.

Lawrence, Brian

Nothing but the best

Felonious felines; edited by Carol and Ed Gorman

Lawrence, D. H. (David Herbert)

The blind man

Lawrence, D. H. Selected short stories of D. H. Lawrence; edited, with an introduction by James Wood

The border line

Lawrence, D. H. Selected short stories of D. H. Lawrence; edited, with an introduction by James Wood

England, my England

Lawrence, D. H. Selected short stories of D. H. Lawrence; edited, with an introduction by James Wood

The fox

Lawrence, D. H. Selected short stories of D. H. Lawrence; edited, with an introduction by James Wood

A fragment of stained glass

Lawrence, D. H. Selected short stories of D. H. Lawrence; edited, with an introduction by James Wood

Love among the haystacks

Lawrence, D. H. Selected short stories of D. H. Lawrence; edited, with an introduction by James Wood

The man who died

Lawrence, D. H. Selected short stories of D. H. Lawrence; edited, with an introduction by James Wood

The man who loved islands

Lawrence, D. H. Selected short stories of D. H. Lawrence; edited, with an introduction by James Wood

Odour of chrysanthemums

Lawrence, D. H. Selected short stories of D. H. Lawrence; edited, with an introduction by James Wood

The Prussian officer

Lawrence, D. H. Selected short stories of D. H. Lawrence; edited, with an introduction by James Wood

St. Mawr

Lawrence, D. H. Selected short stories of D. H. Lawrence; edited, with an introduction by James Wood

Strike-pay

Lawrence, D. H. Selected short stories of D. H. Lawrence; edited, with an introduction by James Wood

The thorn in the flesh

Lawrence, D. H. Selected short stories of D. H. Lawrence; edited, with an introduction by James Wood

Lawrence, D. H. (David Herbert)—*Continued*
The woman who rode away
　Lawrence, D. H. Selected short stories of D.
　H. Lawrence; edited, with an introduction
　by James Wood
Lawrence, David Herbert *See* Lawrence, D. H.
　(David Herbert), 1885-1930
Lawrence, Huw
Pure Welsh
　Mr. Roopratna's chocolate; the winning sto-
　ries from the 1999 Rhys Davies competi-
　tion
Lawrence, Martha C.
The sea cave
　Malice domestic 10; an anthology of original
　traditional mystery stories
Lawrence. Deane, J. F.
Laws, Stephen
The song my sister sang
　Best new horror 10; edited and with an intro-
　duction by Stephen Jones
The **laws** of evening. Waters, M. Y.
Laws of the jungle. Škvorecký, J.
Lawson, Chris
Unborn again
　Dreaming down-under; edited by Jack Dann
　and Janeen Webb
　The Year's best science fiction, sixteenth an-
　nual collection; edited by Gardner Dozois
Written in blood
　Centaurus: the best of Australian science fic-
　tion; edited by David G. Hartwell and Da-
　mien Broderick
　The Year's best science fiction, seventeenth
　annual collection; edited by Gardner Dozois
Lawson, Chris and Brown, Simon
No Man's Land
　Gathering the bones; original stories from the
　world's masters of horror; edited by Dennis
　Etchison, Ramsey Campbell and Jack Dann
Lawson, Patricia
Dead Duck
　Dalhousie Review v84 no2 p285-97 Summ
　2004
LAWSUITS *See* Law and lawyers
LAWYERS *See* Law and lawyers
Lawyer's League. Alexie, S.
Lay, Christina
Windigo
　Dead on demand; the best of ghost story
　weekend; edited by Elizabeth Engstrom
The **lay** of the were-wolf. Marie
The **laying** on of hands. Bennett, A.
The **laying** on of hands. Haake, K.
Laying the ghost. Busch, F.
Layla's nose job. Barker, N.
Laymon, Richard
Boo
　The World's finest mystery and crime stories,
　second annual collection; edited by Ed
　Gorman
Hammerhead
　The Museum of horrors; edited by Dennis
　Etchison
Layover. LaBute, N.
Layover. Paolucci, A.
Lazo, Norma
The Taxidermist (The Father)
　Callaloo v26 no4 p969-71 Fall 2003

Lê, Linda
Voice crisis
　Grand Street no67 p27-33 Wint 1999
Le Clézio, J.-M. G. (Jean-Marie Gustave)
Anne's game
　Le Clézio, J.-M. G. The round & other cold
　hard facts; translated by C. Dickson
Ariadne
　Le Clézio, J.-M. G. The round & other cold
　hard facts; translated by C. Dickson
David
　Le Clézio, J.-M. G. The round & other cold
　hard facts; translated by C. Dickson
The escapee
　Le Clézio, J.-M. G. The round & other cold
　hard facts; translated by C. Dickson
The great life
　Chicago Review v47 no2 p13-38 Summ 2001
　Le Clézio, J.-M. G. The round & other cold
　hard facts; translated by C. Dickson
Moloch
　Le Clézio, J.-M. G. The round & other cold
　hard facts; translated by C. Dickson
The round
　Le Clézio, J.-M. G. The round & other cold
　hard facts; translated by C. Dickson
The runner
　Le Clézio, J.-M. G. The round & other cold
　hard facts; translated by C. Dickson
O thief, what is the life you lead?
　Le Clézio, J.-M. G. The round & other cold
　hard facts; translated by C. Dickson
Villa Aurora
　Le Clézio, J.-M. G. The round & other cold
　hard facts; translated by C. Dickson
Le Clézio, Jean-Marie Gustave *See* Le Clézio,
　J.-M. G. (Jean-Marie Gustave), 1940-
Le Fanu, Joseph Sheridan
The child that went with the fairies
　Children of the night; stories of ghosts, vam-
　pires, werewolves, and "lost children"; ed-
　ited by Martin H. Greenberg
Green tea
　The 13 best horror stories of all time; edited
　by Leslie Pockell
Le Guin, Ursula K.
April in Paris
　Magical beginnings; edited by Steven H. Sil-
　ver and Martin H. Greenberg
　Witches' brew; edited by Yvonne Jocks
The birthday of the world
　The Year's best science fiction, eighteenth an-
　nual collection; edited by Gardner Dozois
Buffalo gals, won't you come out tonight
　The American fantasy tradition; edited by Bri-
　an M. Thomsen
The building
　Le Guin, U. K. Changing planes; illustrated
　by Eric Beddows
　Redshift; extreme visions of speculative fic-
　tion; edited by Al Sarrantonio
Confusions of Uñi
　Le Guin, U. K. Changing planes; illustrated
　by Eric Beddows
Darkrose and Diamond
　The Year's best fantasy & horror, thirteenth
　annual collection; edited by Ellen Datlow
　and Terri Windling

Le Guin, Ursula K.—*Continued*

The day before the revolution

  Brown, C. N. and Strahan, J. The Locus awards; thirty years of the best in science fiction and fantasy; edited by Charles N. Brown and Jonathan Strahan

Feeling at home with the Hennebet

  Le Guin, U. K. Changing planes; illustrated by Eric Beddows

The fliers of Gy

  Le Guin, U. K. Changing planes; illustrated by Eric Beddows

Great joy

  Le Guin, U. K. Changing planes; illustrated by Eric Beddows

The ire of the Veksi

  Le Guin, U. K. Changing planes; illustrated by Eric Beddows

The Island of the Immortals

  Le Guin, U. K. Changing planes; illustrated by Eric Beddows

  The Year's best science fiction, sixteenth annual collection; edited by Gardner Dozois

The Nna Mmoy language

  Le Guin, U. K. Changing planes; illustrated by Eric Beddows

Old Music and the slave women

  Far horizons; all new tales from the greatest worlds of science fiction; edited by Robert Silverberg

The ones who walk away from Omelas

  Masterpieces: the best science fiction of the century; edited by Orson Scott Card

Porridge on Islac

  Le Guin, U. K. Changing planes; illustrated by Eric Beddows

The royals of Hegn

  Le Guin, U. K. Changing planes; illustrated by Eric Beddows

Seasons of the Ansarac

  Le Guin, U. K. Changing planes; illustrated by Eric Beddows

Semley's necklace

  The Good old stuff; adventure SF in the grand tradition; edited by Gardner Dozois

The silence of the Asonu

  Le Guin, U. K. Changing planes; illustrated by Eric Beddows

Sita Dulip's Method

  Le Guin, U. K. Changing planes; illustrated by Eric Beddows

  Nebula awards showcase 2004; edited by Vonda McIntyre

Social dreaming of the Frin

  Le Guin, U. K. Changing planes; illustrated by Eric Beddows

Solitude

  The Best from fantasy & science fiction: the fiftieth anniversary anthology; edited by Edward L. Ferman and Gordon Van Gelder

  Snapshots: 20th century mother-daughter fiction; edited by Joyce Carol Oates and Janet Berliner

Standing Ground

  Ms. v12 no3 p82-8 Summ 2002

Wake Island

  Le Guin, U. K. Changing planes; illustrated by Eric Beddows

Woeful tales from Mahigul

  Le Guin, U. K. Changing planes; illustrated by Eric Beddows

A woman's liberation

  A Woman's liberation; a choice of futures by and about women; edited by Connie Willis and Sheila Williams

Le May, Alan

The battle of Gunsmoke Lode

  Le May, A. The bells of San Juan; western stories

The bells of San Juan

  Le May, A. The bells of San Juan; western stories

The braver thing

  Le May, A. The bells of San Juan; western stories

Eyes of doom

  Le May, A. The bells of San Juan; western stories

Gray rider

  Le May, A. The bells of San Juan; western stories

Lawman's debt

  Le May, A. The bells of San Juan; western stories

The little kid

  Le May, A. The bells of San Juan; western stories

The loan of a gun

  Le May, A. The bells of San Juan; western stories

Star on his heart

  Le May, A. The bells of San Juan; western stories

Sundown Corral

  Le May, A. The bells of San Juan; western stories

Tombstone's daughter

  Le May, A. The bells of San Juan; western stories

Trail driver's luck

  Le May, A. The bells of San Juan; western stories

Lea, Sydney

How in a lifetime?

  New England Review v20 no3 p182-91 Summ 1999

Lead Us Into. Benedetti, M.

A **Leader** of the People. Bernard, K.

Leadership. Svoboda, T.

The **leaf-sweeper**. Spark, M.

Leal, Alvaro Menendez *See* Menen Desleal, Alvaro

Lean and fat. See Chekhov, A. P. Fat and thin

The **leap**. What, L.

Leap day. Nevins, F. M., Jr.

Lear, Patricia

After Memphis

  The Antioch Review v59 no2 p137-61 Spr 2001

The Bridge Playing Ladies

  The Antioch Review v61 no1 p5-26 Wint 2003

Nirvana

  New stories from the South: the year's best, 2003; edited by Shannon Ravenel; with a preface by Roy Blount Jr.

Lear, Patricia—*Continued*
  Summer party
    TriQuarterly no105 p145-62 Spr/Summ 1999
Lear, Peter *See* Lovesey, Peter
(Learning about) machine sex. Dorsey, C. J.
LEARNING AND SCHOLARSHIP *See* Scholars
Learning the hula. Bloch, A.
Learning to let go. Fowler, C.
Learning to smoke. Moyer, K.
Learning to speak Klingon. Merriman, C.
Learning to swim. Swift, G.
Learst, Allen
  Shadowboxing
    The Literary Review (Madison, N.J.) v43 no1
      p83-86 Fall 1999
  A sheet, a clothesline, a bed
    The Literary Review (Madison, N.J.) v43 no1
      p80-82 Fall 1999
Leary, Jan English
  Rabbit's foot
    The Literary Review (Madison, N.J.) v44 no3
      p513-22 Spr 2001
Leary, John
  Here's to Abundance
    Gettysburg Review v16 no4 p625-33 Wint
      2003
  Hope
    Gettysburg Review v14 no4 p631-7 Wint
      2001
The **least** trumps. Hand, E.
The **least** you need to know about radio. Marcus,
  B.
The **leather** funnel. Doyle, Sir A. C.
The **leather** pushers. Witwer, H. C.
The **leather** slapper. Overholser, W. D.
LEAVE-TAKINGS *See* Farewells
Leaves. Updike, J.
Leaves that shimmer in the slightest breeze.
  Bukoski, A.
Leaving. Gildner, G.
Leaving paradise. Carroll, L.
Leaving Reseda. Tarses, M.
Leaving the neighborhood. Ferriss, L.
Leaving the yellow house. Bellow, S.
Leaving this island place. Clarke, A.
Leaving Venice, Florida. Schmitt, R.
The **leavings** of panic. Daugherty, T.
Leavitt, David
  Black box
    Leavitt, D. The marble quilt; stories
  Crossing St. Gotthard
    Leavitt, D. The marble quilt; stories
  Heaped earth
    Leavitt, D. The marble quilt; stories
  The infection scene
    Leavitt, D. The marble quilt; stories
  The list
    Leavitt, D. The marble quilt; stories
  The marble quilt
    Leavitt, D. The marble quilt; stories
  Route 80
    Leavitt, D. The marble quilt; stories
  The scruff of the neck
    Leavitt, D. The marble quilt; stories
    Southwest Review v86 no1 p47-63 Wint 2001
  Speonk
    Doubletake v7 no2 p99-104 Spr 2001
    Leavitt, D. The marble quilt; stories

The term paper artist
  Circa 2000; gay fiction at the millennium; ed-
    ited by Robert Drake & Terry Wolverton
Territory
  The Scribner anthology of contemporary short
    fiction; fifty North American stories since
    1970; Lex Williford and Michael Martone,
    editors
LEBANESE
                    Czech Republic
  Alameddine, R. Grace
                    England
  Alameddine, R. The changing room
  Sammān, G. The plot against Badi'
                    France
  Sammān, G. Beheading the cat
  Sammān, G. The metallic crocodile
  Sammān, G. The other side of the door
  Sammān, G. Register: I'm not an Arab woman
  Sammān, G. The swan genie
  Sammān, G. Thirty years of bees
  Sammān, G. Visitors of a dying person
                    United States
  Alameddine, R. The perv
  Alameddine, R. Remembering Nasser
LEBANON
  Alameddine, R. My grandmother, the
    grandmaster
                    Beirut
  Alameddine, R. Grace
  Alameddine, R. Whore
  Albert, J. Byron
  Johnson-Davies, D. Open season in Beirut
Lebbon, Tim
  The horror of the many faces
    Shadows over Baker Street; edited by Michael
      Reaves and John Pelan
  The repulsion
    Best new horror 12; edited and with an intro-
      duction by Stephen Jones
  White
    Best new horror 11; edited and with an intro-
      duction by Stephen Jones
    The Year's best fantasy & horror, thirteenth
      annual collection; edited by Ellen Datlow
      and Terri Windling
LECTURES AND LECTURING
    See also Speeches, addresses, etc.
  Wharton, E. The pelican
  Yolen, J. Creationism: an illustrated lecture in
    two parts
LED ZEPPELIN (MUSICAL GROUP)
  Harty, R. Crossroads
Leda and the swan. Weldon, F.
The **ledge**. Hall, L. S.
The **ledge**. Mathews, H.
Leduc, Violette
  L'asphyxie [excerpt]
    The Vintage book of international lesbian fic-
      tion; edited and with an introduction by
      Naomi Holoch and Joan Nestle
Lee, Andrea
  About fog and cappuccino
    Lee, A. Interesting women; stories
  Anthropology
    Lee, A. Interesting women; stories
    New stories from the South: the year's best,
      2002; edited by Shannon Ravenel; with a
      preface by Larry Brown

Lee, Andrea—*Continued*
The birthday present
  Lee, A. Interesting women; stories
  The New Yorker v76 no43 p72-9 Ja 22 2001
Brothers and sisters around the world
  The Best American short stories 2001; select-
    ed from U.S. and Canadian magazines by
    Barbara Kingsolver with Katrina Kenison;
    with an introduction by Barbara Kingsolver
  Lee, A. Interesting women; stories
Dancing with Josefina
  Lee, A. Interesting women; stories
Full moon over Milan
  Lee, A. Interesting women; stories
The golden chariot
  Lee, A. Interesting women; stories
In France
  The Bluelight corner; black women writing on
    passion, sex, and romantic love; edited by
    Rosemarie Robotham
Interesting women
  Lee, A. Interesting women; stories
Un petit d'un petit
  Lee, A. Interesting women; stories
The Prior's room
  The New Yorker v78 no10 p120-7 My 6 2002
The pulpit
  Lee, A. Interesting women; stories
La Ragazza
  The New Yorker v80 no1 p174-6, 178-87 F
    16-23 2004
Sicily
  Lee, A. Interesting women; stories
The visit
  Lee, A. Interesting women; stories
Winter barley
  Lee, A. Interesting women; stories
Lee, Chang-Rae
Daisy
  The New Yorker v79 no42 p66-75 Ja 12 2004
The volunteers
  The New Yorker v75 no16 p150-55+ Je 21-28
    1999
Lee, Christina
Luisa
  Brought to book; murderous stories from the
    literary world; Penny Sumner, editor
Lee, Denise
Sailing the painted ocean
  The Year's best fantasy & horror, thirteenth
    annual collection; edited by Ellen Datlow
    and Terri Windling
Lee, Don
Casul water
  Lee, D. Yellow; stories
Domo arigato
  Lee, D. Yellow; stories
  New England Review v22 no1 p90-100 Wint
    2001
Imperialistas
  The North American Review v284 no3-4 p64-
    67+ My/Ag 1999
The Lone Night Cantina
  Lee, D. Yellow; stories
The possible husband
  Lee, D. Yellow; stories
The price of eggs in China
  Lee, D. Yellow; stories

The Pushcart prize XXVI; best of the small
    presses, an annual small press reader; ed-
    ited by Bill Henderson and the Pushcart
    prize editors
Voir dire
  Lee, D. Yellow; stories
Widowers
  Lee, D. Yellow; stories
Yellow
  Lee, D. Yellow; stories
Lee, Dong-Ha *See* Yi, Tong-Ha, 1942-
Lee, Edward
ICU
  999: new stories of horror and suspense; ed-
    ited by Al Sarrantonio
  The Best American mystery stories, 2000; ed-
    ited and with an introduction by Donald E.
    Westlake
Lee, Helen Elaine
The serpent's gift [excerpt]
  The Bluelight corner; black women writing on
    passion, sex, and romantic love; edited by
    Rosemarie Robotham
Silences
  Callaloo v24 no2 p524-30 Spr 2001
Lee, Mabel
(jt. auth) See Gao Xingjian
Lee, Manfred, 1905-1971
  For works written by this author in collab-
    oration with Frederic Dannay see Queen,
    Ellery
Lee, Mark
Memo to our journalists
  Politically inspired; edited by Stephen Elliott;
    assistant editor, Gabriel Kram; associate ed-
    itors, Elizabeth Brooks [et al.]
Lee, Michael
The Albright Kid
  Lee, M. Paradise dance; stories; with an intro-
    duction by James Carroll
Another wonder of the world
  Lee, M. Paradise dance; stories; with an intro-
    duction by James Carroll
A fresh start
  Lee, M. Paradise dance; stories; with an intro-
    duction by James Carroll
Glory
  Lee, M. Paradise dance; stories; with an intro-
    duction by James Carroll
A king's epitaph
  Lee, M. Paradise dance; stories; with an intro-
    duction by James Carroll
Koza nights
  Lee, M. Paradise dance; stories; with an intro-
    duction by James Carroll
Oh, happy day
  Lee, M. Paradise dance; stories; with an intro-
    duction by James Carroll
Paradise dance
  Lee, M. Paradise dance; stories; with an intro-
    duction by James Carroll
The secrets of Cooperstown
  Lee, M. Paradise dance; stories; with an intro-
    duction by James Carroll
Territorial rights
  Lee, M. Paradise dance; stories; with an intro-
    duction by James Carroll

Lee, Michael—*Continued*

Wives, lovers, Maximilian

Lee, M. Paradise dance; stories; with an introduction by James Carroll

Lee, Nancy

Young love

Dalhousie Review v79 no3 p355-65 Aut 1999

Lee, Rebecca

The banks of the Vistula

The Student body; short stories about college students and professors; edited by John McNally

Fialta

Francis Ford Coppola's Zoetrope all-story 2; edited by Adrienne Brodeur and Samantha Schnee; with an introduction by Francis Ford Coppola

Lee, Sharon and Miller, Steve

Naratha's shadow

Such a pretty face; edited by Lee Martindale

Lee, Tanith

The abortionist's horse (a nightmare)

Death dines at 8:30; edited by Claudia Bishop and Nick DiChario

All the birds of hell

The Best from fantasy & science fiction: the fiftieth anniversary anthology; edited by Edward L. Ferman and Gordon Van Gelder

The ghost of the clock

Datlow, E. The dark; new ghost stories; edited by Ellen Datlow

Jedella ghost

The Year's best science fiction, sixteenth annual collection; edited by Gardner Dozois

Rapunzel

Black heart, ivory bones; [edited by] Ellen Datlow & Terri Windling

The sky-green blues

The Year's best science fiction, seventeenth annual collection; edited by Gardner Dozois

Where all things perish

The Mammoth book of best horror 13; edited by Stephen Jones

Yellow and red

Best new horror 10; edited and with an introduction by Stephen Jones

Lee, Vernon

Amour dure

Lee, V. Supernatural tales; excursions into fantasy; with an introduction by I. Cooper Willis

The legend of Madame Krasinska

Lee, V. Supernatural tales; excursions into fantasy; with an introduction by I. Cooper Willis

Prince Alberic and the snake lady

Lee, V. Supernatural tales; excursions into fantasy; with an introduction by I. Cooper Willis

The Virgin of the Seven Daggers

Lee, V. Supernatural tales; excursions into fantasy; with an introduction by I. Cooper Willis

A wedding chest

Lee, V. Supernatural tales; excursions into fantasy; with an introduction by I. Cooper Willis

A wicked voice

Lee, V. Supernatural tales; excursions into fantasy; with an introduction by I. Cooper Willis

Lee, W. W. (Wendi W.)

Check up

Lee, W. W. Check up and other stories

The disappearance of Edna Guberman

Lee, W. W. Check up and other stories

Dust and ashes

Lee, W. W. Check up and other stories

Dying for sin

Flesh and blood; erotic tales of crime and passion; edited by Max Allan Collins and Jeff Gelb

Feis

Lee, W. W. Check up and other stories

Indiscreet

Lee, W. W. Check up and other stories

Letting the cat out of the bag

Felonious felines; edited by Carol and Ed Gorman

Life of Riley

Lee, W. W. Check up and other stories

Miami

Lee, W. W. Check up and other stories

Miles deep

Lee, W. W. Check up and other stories

The other woman

Lee, W. W. Check up and other stories

Red Feather's daughter

Lee, W. W. Check up and other stories

The right thing to do

Lee, W. W. Check up and other stories

Salad days

Lee, W. W. Check up and other stories

Skiv

Murder most Celtic; tall tales of Irish mayhem; edited by Martin H. Greenberg

Soft day

Lee, W. W. Check up and other stories

Winston's wife

Lee, W. W. Check up and other stories

Lee, Wendi W. *See* Lee, W. W. (Wendi W.), 1956-

The **Lee** Marvins. Whitton, D.

Leebron, Fred G.

That winter

Prize stories, 2001; The O. Henry awards; edited and with an introduction by Larry Dark

Leegant, Joan

Accounting

Leegant, J. An hour in paradise; stories

The diviners of desire: a modern fable

Leegant, J. An hour in paradise; stories

The Four Daughters

New England Review v23 no4 p87-101 Fall 2002

Henny's wedding

Leegant, J. An hour in paradise; stories

How to comfort the sick and dying

Leegant, J. An hour in paradise; stories

The lament of the rabbi's daughters

Leegant, J. An hour in paradise; stories

Lucky in love

Leegant, J. An hour in paradise; stories

Mezivosky

Leegant, J. An hour in paradise; stories

Leegant, Joan—_Continued_
Seekers in the Holy Land
  Leegant, J. An hour in paradise; stories
  Lost tribe; jewish fiction from the edge
The seventh year
  Leegant, J. An hour in paradise; stories
  Prairie Schooner v76 no2 p5-21 Summ 2002
The tenth
  Leegant, J. An hour in paradise; stories
  With signs and wonders; an international anthology of Jewish fabulist fiction; edited by Daniel M. Jaffe
The **lees** of happiness. Fitzgerald, F. S.
LEEUWENHOEK, ANTONI VAN, 1632-1723
About
  Gardner, J. A. Three hearings on the existence of snakes in the human bloodstream
LeFanu, Joseph Sheridan _See_ Le Fanu, Joseph Sheridan, 1814-1873
Lefcourt, Peter
Thinning the herd
  Coppola, F. F. Francis Ford Coppola's Zoetrope: all story; edited by Adrienne Brodeur and Samantha Schnee; introduction by Francis Ford Coppola
Leff, Robyn Joy
Burn your maps
  Atlantic Monthly (1993) v289 no1 p94-102 Ja 2002
  The O. Henry Prize stories, 2003; edited and with an introduction by Laura Furman; jurers David Gutterson, Diane Johnson, Jennifer Egan
Leff, Valerie Ann
Angelita y Rafael
  The Antioch Review v61 no3 p442-61 Summ 2003
The flying camel spin
  The Antioch Review v60 no1 p42-55 Wint 2002
Left behind. Hollon, F. T.
The **left** shoe. Hoppe, F.
Leftovers. Bradbury, R.
Leg. Polansky, S.
Leg man. Gardner, E. S.
LEGACIES _See_ Inheritance and succession
Legacy. Donigyan, H.
Legacy. Healy, J. F.
The **legacy**. Spencer, E.
LEGAL PROFESSION _See_ Law and lawyers
LEGAL STORIES _See_ Law and lawyers
The **legend**. Gonzalez, R.
The **legend**. Wharton, E.
The **legend** of Atlantis. Karnezis, P.
The **legend** of Beowulf. Wägner, W.
The **legend** of Charlie McQuarkle. Bishop, P.
The **legend** of Kuop. Armstrong, K.
The **legend** of Pig-Eye. Bass, R.
The **legend** of Shorm. Easton, R. O.
The **legend** of Trooper Hennepin. Henry, W.
Legends. Adams, A.
LEGENDS AND FOLK TALES
  See also Grail
  Collins, N. A. Catfish gal blues
  Harris, J. C. How Mr. Rabbit was too sharp for Mr. Fox
  Harris, J. C. Uncle Remus initiates the little boy
  Harris, J. C. The wonderful Tar-Baby story
  Singer, I. B. Three tales

Sussex, L. Matilda told such dreadful lies
Wiggin, K. D. S. and Smith, N. A. The story of Ali Baba and the forty thieves
India
Chaudhuri, A. An infatuation
Chaudhuri, A. The wedding
Japan
Updike, J. Jesus on Honshu
Morocco
Bowles, P. Things gone and things still here
Polynesia
Armstrong, K. The legend of Kuop
United States
Harris, J. C. Uncle Remus
Hawthorne, N. The great carbuncle
Irving, W. Rip Van Winkle
O'Reilly, E. The saga of Pecos Bill
West Indies
Hopkinson, N. Greedy choke puppy
Hopkinson, N. Precious
Hopkinson, N. Tan-Tan and Dry Bone
Legends of West Street. Marshall, T.
Legge, Gordon
Life on a Scottish council estate vol. 1
  The Vintage book of contemporary Scottish fiction; edited and with an introduction by Peter Kravitz
Legs shimmering under moonlight. McGowan, J. T.
LeGuin, Ursula _See_ Le Guin, Ursula K., 1929-
Lehane, Dennis
Running out of dog
  The Best American mystery stories, 2000; edited and with an introduction by Donald E. Westlake
  The Best American mystery stories of the century; Tony Hillerman, editor; with an introduction by Tony Hillerman
  Murder and obsession; edited by Otto Penzler
Until Gwen
  Atlantic Monthly (1993) v293 no5 p143-52 Je 2004
Lehner, Christine
Lost in the mail
  Southwest Review v87 no1 p106-20 2002
Leiber, Fritz
A bad day for sales
  The SFWA grand masters v1; edited by Frederik Pohl
Coming attraction
  The Science fiction hall of fame: volume one, 1929-1964; the greatest science fiction stories of all time chosen by the members of the Science Fiction Writers of America; edited by Robert Silverberg
The girl with the hungry eyes
  Children of the night; stories of ghosts, vampires, werewolves, and "lost children"; edited by Martin H. Greenberg
The hound
  The Literary werewolf; an anthology; edited by Charlotte F. Otten
The mer she
  The SFWA grand masters v1; edited by Frederik Pohl
Moon duel
  The Good old stuff; adventure SF in the grand tradition; edited by Gardner Dozois

Leiber, Fritz—*Continued*

Sanity

The SFWA grand masters v1; edited by Frederik Pohl

Leinster, Murray *See* Jenkins, Will F., 1896-1975

Lelchuk, Bertha

The aunt from Norfolk

Neugroschel, J. No star too beautiful; Yiddish stories from 1382 to the present; compiled and translated by Joachim Neugroschel

Lemebel, Pedro

Loba Lamar's Last Kiss (Silk Crepe Ribbons at my Funeral...Please)

Grand Street no70 p156-62 Spr/Summ 2002

LEMMINGS

Clarke, A. C. The possessed

The **lemon**. Lustig, A.

The **lemon-green** spaghetti-loud dynamite-dribble day. Tenn, W.

Lemon scent. Mootoo, S.

Lemonade. Lavin, M.

Lempel, Blume

The death of my aunt

Beautiful as the moon, radiant as the stars; Jewish women in Yiddish stories : an anthology; edited by Sandra Bark; introduction by Francine Prose

Scenes on a bare canvas

Beautiful as the moon, radiant as the stars; Jewish women in Yiddish stories : an anthology; edited by Sandra Bark; introduction by Francine Prose

Lemuria will rise!. Baker, K.

Lenčo, Ján

On the way to P.

In search of homo sapiens; twenty-five contemporary Slovak short stories; editor, Pavol Hudík ; [translated by Heather Trebatická; American English editor, Lucy Bednár]

LENINGRAD (SOVIET UNION) *See* Russia— St. Petersburg

Lennie Remembers the Angels. Dalton, Q.

Lennon, J. Robert

Eight Pieces for the Left Hand

Granta v85 p39-49 Spr 2004

Flight

The New Yorker v75 no15 p72-77 Je 14 1999

The fool's proxy

Harper's v299 no1793 p84-92+ O 1999

Prize stories, 2000; The O. Henry awards; edited and with an introduction by Larry Dark

The Missing Man

Harper's v307 p30-1 Ag 2003

Lenoir. Hunter, F.

Lenore Malen. Ames, J.

LENT

Bradbury, R. The first night of Lent

Leo, chained. Eggers, P.

Leokadia and fireflies. Bukoski, A.

Leon, Aya de

Tell me Moore

The African American West; a century of short stories; edited by Bruce A. Glasrud and Laurie Champion

Leonard, Elmore

Chickasaw Charlie Hoke

Leonard, E. When the women come out to dance; stories

Fire in the hole

Leonard, E. When the women come out to dance; stories

Hanging out at the Buena Vista

Leonard, E. When the women come out to dance; stories

How Carlos Webster changed his name to Carl and became a famous Oklahoma lawman

McSweeney's mammoth treasury of thrilling tales; edited by Michael Chabon

Hurrah for Capt. Early

Leonard, E. When the women come out to dance; stories

Karen makes out

Leonard, E. When the women come out to dance; stories

Sparks

Leonard, E. When the women come out to dance; stories

Murder and obsession; edited by Otto Penzler

Tenkiller

Leonard, E. When the women come out to dance; stories

The Tonto woman

Leonard, E. When the women come out to dance; stories

When the women come out to dance

The Best American mystery stories, 2003; edited by Michael Connelly and Otto Penzler

Leonard, E. When the women come out to dance; stories

Leonard, Tom

Honest

The Vintage book of contemporary Scottish fiction; edited and with an introduction by Peter Kravitz

LEONARDO, DA VINCI, 1452-1519

About

Arenas, R. Mona

Dann, J. Da Vinci rising

Gilchrist, E. You must change your life

Oltion, J. Renaissance man

Leone, Dan

Family

The Best American mystery stories, 2001; edited and with an Introduction by Lawrence Block

Leong, Russell

Bodhi leaves

Leong, R. Phoenix eyes and other stories

Camouflage

Leong, R. Phoenix eyes and other stories

Daughters

Leong, R. Phoenix eyes and other stories

Eclipse

Leong, R. Phoenix eyes and other stories

Geography one

Leong, R. Phoenix eyes and other stories

Hemispheres

Leong, R. Phoenix eyes and other stories

No Bruce Lee

Leong, R. Phoenix eyes and other stories

Phoenix eyes

Leong, R. Phoenix eyes and other stories

Leong, Russell—*Continued*

Runaways
> Leong, R. Phoenix eyes and other stories

Samsara
> Leong, R. Phoenix eyes and other stories

Sons
> Leong, R. Phoenix eyes and other stories

Virgins and Buddhas
> Circa 2000; gay fiction at the millennium; edited by Robert Drake & Terry Wolverton

The western paradise of Eddie Bin
> Leong, R. Phoenix eyes and other stories

Where do people live who never die?
> Leong, R. Phoenix eyes and other stories

A yin and her man
> Leong, R. Phoenix eyes and other stories

Leong, Sandra

Repulsion
> *Southwest Review* v88 no1 p62-78 2003

The **Leopard** Gang. Clark, G. M.

A **lepidopterist's** tale. Waterman, D.

LEPROSY

Borges, J. L. Hakim, the masked dyer of Merv
Budnitz, J. Skin care
Campbell, R. The same in any language
Galef, D. And dwelt in a separate house

Lerner, Mary

Little selves
> The Best American short stories of the century; John Updike, editor, Katrina Kenison, coeditor; with an introduction by John Updike

LeRoy, J. T.

Baby doll
> LeRoy, J. T. The heart is deceitful above all things

Coal
> LeRoy, J. T. The heart is deceitful above all things

Disappearances
> LeRoy, J. T. The heart is deceitful above all things

Foolishness is bound in the heart of a child
> LeRoy, J. T. The heart is deceitful above all things

The heart is deceitful above all things
> LeRoy, J. T. The heart is deceitful above all things

Lizards
> LeRoy, J. T. The heart is deceitful above all things

Meteors
> LeRoy, J. T. The heart is deceitful above all things

Natoma Street
> LeRoy, J. T. The heart is deceitful above all things

Salve Regina
> *Film Comment* v38 no4 p20-1 Jl/Ag 2002

Toyboxed
> LeRoy, J. T. The heart is deceitful above all things

Viva Las Vegas
> LeRoy, J. T. The heart is deceitful above all things

LeSabre. Rinehart, S.

Lesbian bedrooms. Price, C.

LESBIANISM

> *See also* Homosexuality

Agabian, N. Ghosts and bags
Alexie, S. Indian country
Allegra, D. The birthday presence
Allegra, D. Bread from a stone
Allegra, D. Dance of the cranes
Allegra, D. Einbahnstrasse
Allegra, D. God lies in the details
Allegra, D. In a pig's eye
Allegra, D. Low-impact aerobics
Allegra, D. Me and Mrs. Jones
Allegra, D. The moon in cancer
Allegra, D. Navigating by stars
Allegra, D. Sacrament in the wind and the storm
Allegra, D. Snatched
Allegra, D. Witness to the league of blond hip hop dancers
Anderson, J. The houses of double women
Barrington, J. Nicolette: a memoir
Bikis, G. Cleo's back
Blaman, A. Lonely adventure [excerpt]
Bleier, H. Betty Grace goes to county
Bloch, A. Learning the hula
Bloom, A. Rowing to Eden
Brand, D. Madame Alaird's breasts
Brantenberg, G. Four winds [excerpt]
Brooks, C. The butcher's wife
Busch, F. The baby in the box
Canty, K. Honeymoon
Carson, J. The virgin
Cherry, K. Not the Phil Donahue show
Cho, N. Bang bang bang
Chopin, K. Fedora
Clark, C. A. Kays and exes
Cohen, M. Alice's ground
Cooke, C. Black book
Crowell, E. Perfectly good
Curtis, Rebecca. Hungry self
Daniel, S. We are cartographers
Davis, M. K. Rachel
D'Haene, E. Breasts
Doenges, J. Incognito
Doenges, J. The whole numbers of families
Donoghue, E. How a lady dies
Donoghue, E. Looking for Petronilla
Donoghue, E. Seven pictures not taken
Dorcey, M. A noise from the woodshed [excerpt]
Duffy, M. The microcosm [excerpt]
Duncker, P. Betrayal
Erian, A. Almonds and cherries
Evans, E. Home ec
Fessel, K.-S. Lost faces
Fitzgerald, F. S. The World's Fair
Frisch, W. Safe sex
Gaitskill, M. Processing
Gautreaux, T. Dancing with the one-armed gal
Georgiou, E. Aphrodite's vision
Giacobino, M. Mermaids, and other sea creatures
Gilb, D. Bottoms
Glave, T. Whose song?
Gordimer, N. Karma
Grahn, J. Green toads of the high desert
Grau, S. A. Home
Greer, A. S. Come live with me and be my love
Gunthorp, D. Gypsophila
Hall, R. L. No lie

LESBIANISM—*Continued*

Hawley, E. What we forgot to tell Tina about boys

Hochman, A. In case of emergency

Hochman, A. Liability

Jesús, P. d. How to act in 1830

Jimenez, K. P. The lake at the end of the wash

Joseph, D. If I close them

Jutras, J. d. Georgie [excerpt]

Kahn, M. A. Strange bedfellows

Kendall, G. In loco parentis

Kieser, C. Completely overloaded

Kohler, S. Underworld

Krouse, E. Impersonators

Lawrence, D. H. The fox

Lee, C. Luisa

Lord, C. The art of losing

Lord, N. The baby who, according to his aunt, resembled his uncle

Luz Montes, A. M. d. l. While Pilar Tobillo sleeps

Magy, R. Family

Maraini, D. Letters to Marina [excerpt]

Min, A. Red azalea [excerpt]

Molloy, S. Certificate of absence [excerpt]

Mootoo, S. Lemon scent

Mueller, D. Birds

Munson, P. Teratophobia

Nissen, T. The animal's best interest

Nissen, T. Apple pie

Obejas, A. Waters

Orner, P. Sitting Theodore

Packer, Z. Drinking coffee elsewhere

Pearlberg, G. Caravan

Penney, B. Incidents on the road

Podolsky, R. Memory like ash borne on air

Price, C. Lesbian bedrooms

Rawley, D. The closest thing to God

Reisman, N. The good life

Richmond, M. Intermittent waves of unusual size and force

Richmond, M. The world's greatest pants

Roberts, N. This is not skin

Robyn, K. L. They've got my (wrong) number

Roffiel, R. M. Forever lasts only a full moon

Sade, marquis de. Augustine de Villeblanche; or, Love's strategy

Schein, G. Minnie gets married

Silber, J. Lake Natasink

Silber, J. Ordinary

Singer, I. B. Zeitl and Rickel

Smyth, C. Sand and other grit

Southgate, M. The kick inside

Strauss, A. Swimming without Annette

Strober, R. Poker face

Sussex, L. My lady tongue

Svirsky, G. Meeting Natalia

Te Awekotuku, N. Paretipua

Thurm, M. Personal correspondence

Thurmond, J. Beauty of blood

Tomaso, C. Rain

Tomioka, T. Yesterday's girl

Tratnik, S. Under the ironwood trees

Tuller, D. Sperm-and-egg tango

Turner, G. Cookie and me

Tusquets, E. The same sea as every summer [excerpt]

Valeri, L. The kind of things saints do

Vinten, R. Character witness

Walker, A. The brotherhood of the saved

Wheat, C. Cousin Cora

Williams, K. They came at dawn

Wilson, B. Archeology

Wilson, B. Wie bitte?

Winterson, J. Atlantic crossing

Winterson, J. The poetics of sex

Wolverton, T. Sex less

Yourcenar, M. Sappho; or, Suicide

Leslie, Nan

Quixotic

The North American Review v289 no1 p25-8 Ja/F 2004

Leslie, Naton

Another place

Leslie, N. Marconi's dream

Bigger than life

Leslie, N. Marconi's dream

Dancing with Lawrence of Arabia

Leslie, N. Marconi's dream

Give me a sign

Leslie, N. Marconi's dream

A little wild

Leslie, N. Marconi's dream

Lost

Leslie, N. Marconi's dream

Marconi's dream

Leslie, N. Marconi's dream

Poker face

Leslie, N. Marconi's dream

Prayer wheel

Leslie, N. Marconi's dream

Projectiles

Leslie, N. Marconi's dream

Rain dance

Leslie, N. Marconi's dream

The scavenger's eye

Leslie, N. Marconi's dream

When lilacs last

Leslie, N. Marconi's dream

Leslie and Sam. Unger, D.

L'Esprit de L'Escalier. Tuck, L.

Less tar. Lipsyte, S.

The **lesser** half of the world. Walser, A.

Lessing, Doris May

The grandmothers

Lessing, D. M. The grandmothers; [by] Doris Lessing

A letter from home

Other people's mail; an anthology of letter stories; edited with an introduction by Gail Pool

A love child

Lessing, D. M. The grandmothers; [by] Doris Lessing

One off the short list

The Best of The Kenyon review; edited by David Lynn; introduction by Joyce Carol Oates

The reason for it

Lessing, D. M. The grandmothers; [by] Doris Lessing

Victoria and the Staveneys

Lessing, D. M. The grandmothers; [by] Doris Lessing

Lesson of the billboard dogs. Hoover, P.

The **lesson** of the master. James, H.

Lessons. Budnitz, J.

Lessons in another language. Staffel, M.

Lessons in fire. Slowik, M.
Lessons in joy. Henley, P.
Let me call you sweetheart. Henley, P.
Let me count the times. Amis, M.
Let me sleep. See Chekhov, A. P. Sleepy
Let my right hand forget her cunning. Brady, C.
Let the ants try. Pohl, F.
Let the church roll on. Ford, N. A.
Let the Day Perish. Kerschen, P.
Let there be light. Clarke, A. C.
Let there be light. Drake, R.
The **leter** that came in time. Hendel, Y.
Lethe. Williams, W. J.
Lethem, Jonathan
   Biosphere
     Esquire v132 no3 p216 S 1999
   Five fucks
     The Vintage book of amnesia; an anthology;
     edited by Jonathan Lethem
   K fof fake
     Lethem, J. and Scholz, C. Kafka Americana;
     [by] Jonathan Lethem [and] Carter Scholz
   The notebooks of Bob K.
     Lethem, J. and Scholz, C. Kafka Americana;
     [by] Jonathan Lethem [and] Carter Scholz
   Planet Big Zero
     On the rocks; the KGB Bar fiction anthology;
     edited by Rebecca Donner ; foreword by
     Denis Woychuk
   Super Goat Man
     The New Yorker v80 no7 p68-75 Ap 5 2004
   View From a Headlock
     The New Yorker v79 no20 p68-77 Jl 28 2003
Lethem, Jonathan and Scholz, Carter
   Receding horizon
     Lethem, J. and Scholz, C. Kafka Americana;
     [by] Jonathan Lethem [and] Carter Scholz
Let's get lost. Block, L.
Let's not talk politics, please. Clayton, J. J.
The **letter**. Archer, J.
A **letter**. Babel', I.
The **letter**. Davis, D. S.
The **letter**. Jesús, P. d.
A **letter** for President Eisenhower. Fischerová, D.
A **letter** from 1920. Andrić, I.
Letter from a very worried man. Slesar, H.
Letter from an unknown woman. Zweig, S.
Letter from—Dresden. Schulze, I.
Letter from his father. Gordimer, N.
A **letter** from home. Lessing, D. M.
Letter from Maine. Kees, W.
A **letter** from paradise. Ritchie, E.
Letter from Persephone. Bulgheroni, M.
Letter from the Last Bastion. Freudenberger, N.
The **letter** in the peppermint jar. Van de Wetering,
   J.
Letter of rec. Holdefer, C.
Letter present. Van de Wetering, J.
Letter to a young lady in Paris. Cortázar, J.
A **letter** to Amy. Harrington, J.
Letter to his son. Brett, S.
A **letter** to the editor. Babel', I.
Letter to the editor. Hershman, M.
LETTERS (STORIES ABOUT)
   Alvarez, J. Consuelo's letter
   Archer, J. The letter
   Babel', I. A letter
   Borges, J. L. Guayaquil
   Brown, C. The correspondent

Chekhov, A. P. At Christmas time
Chekhov, A. P. Vanka
Chopin, K. Her letters
Davis, D. S. The letter
Davis, J. S. Tammy, imagined
Dinh, L. Brother News from Home
Doble, J. Two letters from the doctor
Faygenberg, Rochel. My first readers
Gilchrist, E. Hearts of Dixie
Jackson, S. The possibility of evil
Kees, W. Letter from Maine
Kohler, S. Rain check
Lopez, B. H. The letters of heaven
Malouf, M. From you know who
Painter, P. The last word
Penn, W. S. Tarantulas
Poe, E. A. The purloined letter
Reeve, A. B. The poisoned pen
Ruy Sánchez, A. Voices of the water
Schnitzler, A. Death of a bachelor
Schnitzler, A. The widower
Slesar, H. Letter from a very worried man
Sloan, B. The good rabbi
Spencer, E. The white azalea
Trevor, W. Mrs. Acland's ghosts
Westlake, D. E. Sniff
Wharton, E. His father's son
Wharton, E. Pomegranate seed
Wharton, E. The touchstone
Zinik, Z. The notification
Zweig, S. Letter from an unknown woman
LETTERS (STORIES IN LETTER FORM)
   Alameddine, R. The perv
   Alvarez, A. Index card, index finger
   Apukhtin, A. N. The papers of Countess D**:
     a tale in letters
   Aquin, H. Back on April eleventh
   Armstrong, K. The first motion of love
   Auchincloss, L. The Devil and Guy Lansing
   Bausch, R. Letter to the lady of the house
   Berkman, P. R. No cause
   Borowski, T. Auschwitz, our home (a letter)
   Bowles, P. In absentia
   Bowles, P. Unwelcome words
   Brett, S. Letter to his son
   Carson, M. Peter's buddies
   Clark, S. Fenian ram
   Clarke, A. C. Loophole
   Coberly, L. M. Willy Mae goes north
   Cody, L. In those days
   Coleman, J. C. Wild flower
   Cortázar, J. Letter to a young lady in Paris
   Davenport, G. Belinda's world tour
   Davidson, R. The Hillside Slasher
   Day, C. The Jungle Goolah Boy
   Dickson, G. R. Computers don't argue
   Dixon, S. Man of letters
   Doctorow, C. Power punctuation!
   Eldridge, Courtney. Thieves
   Engel, M. P. Who calls each one by name
   Fowler, K. J. The travails
   Freudenberger, N. Letter from the last bastion
   Gilchrist, E. The uninsured
   Godwin, G. False lights
   Gomes, M. T. The gypsy: a letter to Antonio
     Patricio
   Gordimer, N. Letter from his father
   Greenberg, M. H. A literary death
   Gurganus, A. Reassurance

LETTERS (STORIES IN LETTER FORM)—
Continued
Ha Jin. An official reply
Harris, M. From the desk of the troublesome editor
Harris, M. Hi, Bob!
Helprin, M. Letters from the Samantha
Hershman, M. Letter to the editor
James, H. A bundle of letters
James, H. The point of view
Johnson, C. R. A report from St. Domingue
Kanafāni, G. The death of bed number 12
King, L. L. Three Letters
Kline, D. Correspondence
Kohler, S. Correspondence I
Kohler, S. Correspondence II
La Spina, S. The night of crossed destinies
Leavitt, D. The list
Lessing, D. M. A letter from home
Link, K. Carnation, Lily, Lily, Rose
Lutz, J. Pure rotten
Malzberg, B. N. Agony column
Malzberg, B. N. We're coming through the window
Maraini, D. Letters to Marina [excerpt]
Marston, E. and Lovesey, P. The Corbett correspondence: "Agent no. 5 & Agent no. 6"
Martin, P. P. Amor de acuerdo—Arranged love
Matheson, R. C. Graduation
Matthews, C. Dear Lottie
McKnight, R. Quitting smoking
Mickenberg, R. Direct male
Milne, A. A. The rise and fall of Mortimer Scrivens
Moriconi, V. Simple arithmetic
Munro, A. Before the change
Munro, A. A wilderness station
Nabokov, V. V. "That in Aleppo once . . . "
Nolan, W. F. An act of violence
Pittalwala, I. Dear Paramount Pictures
Poniatowska, E. Park Cinema
Porter, J. A. Yours
Porzecanski, T. Rochel Eisips
Potvin, E. A. The traveller's hat
Pushkin, A. S. Maria Schoning
Pushkin, A. S. A novel in letters
Reiner, C. Dear John
Reiner, C. The Heidi and Albert correspondence
Rogers, B. H. Cloud stalking mice
Russell, R. Evil star
Saro-Wiwa, K. Africa kills her sun
Scholz, C. The nine billion names of God
Searle, E. What it's worth
Shawl, N. The tawny bitch
Shepard, S. Tinnitus
Treat, J. Dead end
Uncle Alf
Updike, J. Dear Alexandros
Updike, J. Four sides of one story
Van Vogt, A. E. Dear pen pal
Vinge, V. Win a Nobel Prize!
Viswanathan, L. Cool wedding
Waugh, E. Cruise
West, M. Four attempts at a letter
Wilson, A. J. Under the bright and hollow sky
Wolfe, G. The eleventh city
Wolfe, G. The fat magician
The **letters**. Wharton, E.
Letters from the Samantha. Helprin, M.

Letters from Yerevan. Mathews, H.
The **letters** of heaven. Lopez, B. H.
LETTERS OF THE ALPHABET *See* Alphabet
Letters to Marina [excerpt] Maraini, D.
Letters to the stove. Long, E.
Letting go. Grau, S. A.
Letting the cat out of the bag. Lee, W. W.
Letting the dog out. Cobb, W. J.
Leufredus. Stuckey-French, E.
LEUKEMIA
Clyde, M. Howard Johnson's house
Rawley, D. Tim
The **level** of my uncertainty. Agee, J.
Leventhal, Alice Walker *See* Walker, Alice, 1944-
The **leviathan**. Roth, J.
Levin, Adam
Finch
New England Review v23 no2 p128-44 Spr 2002
Levine, Philip
Berm
The Paris Review v45 p265-6 Fall 2003
Levine, Sara
The Following Fifteen Things, A Love Story
Iowa Review v32 no3 p56-60 Wint 2002/2003
Levinson, Luisa Mercedes
The cove
Short stories by Latin American women; the magic and the real; edited by Celia Correas de Zapata; foreword by Isabel Allende
The violated dream
Michigan Quarterly Review v40 no4 p640-2 Fall 2001
Levinson, Robert S.
Good career moves
Flesh and blood: guilty as sin; erotic tales of crime and passion; edited by Max Allan Collins and Jeff Gelb
Levi's tongue. Bottoms, G.
Levit, Donald J.
The last of the traveling picture shows
Culturefront v8 no3/4 p23-4, 75 Fall 1999
LEVITATION
Clarke, A. C. The cruel sky
Levitsky, Ronald
Jacob's voice
Mystery midrash; an anthology of Jewish mystery & detective fiction; [edited by] Lawrence W. Raphael
A Sabbath flame
Browning, A. Murder is no mitzvah; edited by Abigail Browning
Levrero, Mario
Notes from Buenos Aires
The Vintage book of Latin American stories; edited by Carlos Fuentes and Julio Ortega
Levy, E. J.
The best way not to freeze
Gettysburg Review v15 no1 p35-54 Spr 2002
Small Bright Thing
The North American Review v288 no2 p27-31 Mr/Ap 2003
Theory of the Leisure Class
The Paris Review v45 p261-76 Summ 2003

Levy, JoAnn
  A woman 49er
    American West; twenty new stories from the
      Western Writers of America; edited with an
      introduction by Loren D. Estleman
LÉVY-BRUHL, LUCIEN, 1857-1939
           About
  Davenport, G. Boys smell like oranges
Lewis, Jim
  Stay up Late
    Granta v86 p197-214 Summ 2004
Lewis, Mary *See* Brand, Christianna, 1907-1988
Lewis, Mary Christianna Milne *See* Brand,
  Christianna, 1907-1988
LEWIS, MERIWETHER, 1774-1809
           About
  Hoffman, N. K. Voyage of discovery
Lewis, R. J.
  Into the abyss
    The Ultimate Halloween; edited by Marvin
      Kaye
Lewis, Trudy
  The bones of Garbo
    New England Review v20 no1 p56-80 Wint
    1999
  A diller, a daughter
    Atlantic Monthly v287 no1 p65-74 Ja 2001
  The marijuana tree
    A different plain; contemporary Nebraska fic-
      tion writers; edited by Ladette Randolph ;
      introduction by Mary Pipher
  West Wind
    New England Review v25 no1/2 p235-45
    2004
Lewis, William Henry
  Germinating
    The Cry of an occasion; fiction from the Fel-
      lowship of Southern Writers; edited by
      Richard Bausch; with a foreword by
      George Garrett
  I Got Somebody in Staunton
    Callaloo v26 no3 p595-606 Summ 2003
  Kudzu
    Ploughshares v28 no1 p136-44 Spr 2002
  The trip back from Whidbey
    The African American West; a century of
      short stories; edited by Bruce A. Glasrud
      and Laurie Champion
LEWIS AND CLARK EXPEDITION (1804-1806)
  Gulick, B. Encounter on Horse-Killed Creek
  Henry, W. Jefferson's captains
  Walker, D. L. York's story
Lewis, Mark Ray
  Scordatura
    Pushcart prize XXVII; best of the small
      presses; edited by Bill Henderson with the
      Pushcart prize editors
Lewitt, Shariann
  A real girl
    Reload: rethinking women + cyberculture; ed-
      ited by Mary Flanagan and Austin Booth
Li, Nancy
  (jt. auth) *See* Liu Yichang
Li, Yiyun
  Extra
    The New Yorker v79 no40 p120-4, 126-7 D
    22-29 2003

Immortality
    The Paris Review v45 p24-43 Fall 2003
Liability. Hochman, A.
The **liar**. James, H.
LIARS
  Banks, R. The burden
  Di Blasi, D. I am telling you lies
  James, H. The liar
  Singer, I. B. A tale of two liars
  Theroux, P. White lies
  Troy, M. A little zip
Liars. Fulton, J.
Liar's dice. Pronzini, B.
Liars in love. Yates, R.
A **libation** of blood. Weldon, F.
The **liberation** of a face. Min, K.
The **liberation** of earth. Tenn, W.
The **liberation** of little heaven. Jacobs, M.
Liberator. Wisenberg, S. L.
LIBERIA
  Doerr, A. The caretaker
Liberty, Hilary James
  Under Number Nine
    Dalhousie Review v81 no1 p101-16 Spr 2001
Liberty, equality, fraternity. Allen, J. R.
Libling, Michael
  Puce Boy
    The Year's best fantasy & horror: sixteenth
      annual collection; edited by Ellen Datlow
      & Terri Windling
Libman, Daniel S.
  In the belly of the cat
    The Paris Review v41 no150 p30-44 Spr
    1999
LIBRARIANS
  Brockmeier, K. Things that fall from the sky
  Griffith, M. Bibliophilia
  Gunn, K. Not that much to go on: 2
  Kees, W. The sign
  Marston, E. Slaughter in the Strand
  Mason, S. J. With thanks to Agatha Christie
  Mayhall, J. The men
  Norris, H. The flying hawk
  Talley, M. Safety first
The **librarian's** farewell. Hudgins, A.
LIBRARIES
  Babel', I. The public library
  Bradbury, R. Bright Phoenix
  Harrison, H. The robot who wanted to know
  Kees, W. The library: four sketches
  Kees, W. Public library
  Kinman, G. T. Miss Parker & the Cutter-
    Sanborn tables
  VanderMeer, J. Greensleeves
The **library:** four sketches. Kees, W.
LICE
  Rosenfeld, S. Grasp special comb
  Singleton, G. This itches, y'all
Lice. Denton, E.
Lichberg, Heinz von
  Lolita
    The Times Literary Supplement no5286 p14-
    15 Jl 23 2004
Lichtenstein, Alfred
  The virgin
    Partisan Review v66 no3 p468-71 Summ
    1999

Lichtenstein, Alfred—*Continued*

The winner

Partisan Review v66 no3 p472-81 Summ 1999

Licks of love in the heart of the Cold War. Updike, J.

Lida, David

Acapulco gold

Lida, D. Travel advisory; stories of Mexico

A beach day

Lida, D. Travel advisory; stories of Mexico

Bewitched

Lida, D. Travel advisory; stories of Mexico

Free trade

Lida, D. Travel advisory; stories of Mexico

Prenuptial agreement

Lida, D. Travel advisory; stories of Mexico

La quedada

Lida, D. Travel advisory; stories of Mexico

The recruiting officer

Lida, D. Travel advisory; stories of Mexico

Regrets

Lida, D. Travel advisory; stories of Mexico

Shuttered

Lida, D. Travel advisory; stories of Mexico

Taxi

Lida, D. Travel advisory; stories of Mexico

The Literary Review (Madison, N.J.) v42 no2 p252-61 Wint 1999

Lida. Čapek, K.

Lida's cat, the bakery, and the streetlight pole. Bahrami, A.

Liddle, Rod

What the Thunder Said

Esquire v142 no4 p138, 140, 142, 212, 216, 218 O 2004

The **lie**. Banks, R.

Lie beside me. Collins, M. A. and Clemens, M. V.

Lieberman, Lisa

My Ex-Boyfriend's Wife

Gettysburg Review v16 no3 p391-400 Aut 2003

Lieberman, Tehila

Anya's angel

With signs and wonders; an international anthology of Jewish fabulist fiction; edited by Daniel M. Jaffe

Lies. Blitz, R.

Lieu, Jocelyn

Always a descendant

Lieu, J. Potential weapons

The children

Lieu, J. Potential weapons

Potential weapons

Lieu, J. Potential weapons

Safety

Lieu, J. Potential weapons

This world

Lieu, J. Potential weapons

Troubles

Lieu, J. Potential weapons

LIFE (PHILOSOPHY OF LIFE)

Bernhard, T. Walking

Chekhov, A. P. About love

Chekhov, A. P. Gooseberries

Chekhov, A. P. The man in a case

Fitzgerald, F. S. The smilers

Life. Tozzi, F.

Life #5. Aldrich, M.

The **life** and adventures of shed number XII. Pelevin, V.

Life and death in Bab-el-Louq. Comer, B.

The **Life** and Death of Sally Brand, Part 1. Banks, L. W.

The **Life** and Death of Sally Brand, Part 2. Banks, L. W.

The **life** and death of stars. Vasseur, T. J.

The **life** and times of Estelle Walks Above. Alexie, S.

The **life** and work of Alphonse Kauders. Hemon, A.

Life before science. Carlson, R.

Life between meals. DeMarinis, R.

Life choices. Lao She

Life Could Be a Dream (Sh-boom, Sh-boom). Blaise, C.

Life in a small courtyard. Wang Anyi

Life in dearth. Avrich, J.

Life in our time. Bloch, R.

Life in the air ocean. Foley, S.

Life-interest. Hart, C. G.

Life is a highway. Ryan, P. L.

Life is over there. Greer, A. S.

The **life** jacket. Derby, M.

Life of Riley. Lee, W. W.

The **life** of the mind. Greenberg, A.

The **life** of the mind. Kees, W.

Life of the party. Bail, M.

Life on a Scottish council estate vol. 1. Legge, G.

Life on Mars. Boylan, C.

LIFE ON OTHER PLANETS

See also Interplanetary visitors

Amis, M. The janitor on Mars

Anderson, P. Kyrie

Anderson, P. The martyr

Anderson, P. The master key

Anderson, P. The queen of air and darkness

Arango, A. The cosmonaut

Arnason, E. Dapple: a hwarhath historical romance

Arnason, E. Moby Quilt

Arnason, E. The potter of bones

Asaro, C. The quantum rose

Asimov, I. Strikebreaker

Barrett, N., Jr. "A day at the fair"

Bear, G. Hardfought

Bear, G. The way of all ghosts

Benedict, P. Zog-19: a scientific romance

Bishop, M. Death and designation among the Asadi

Blish, J. Citadel of thought

Blish, J. Surface tension

Brin, D. Temptation

Brown, F. Arena

Butler, O. E. Bloodchild

Cherryh, C. J. Companions

Cherryh, C. J. The scapegoat

Clarke, A. C. Before Eden

Clarke, A. C. Crusade

Clarke, A. C. A meeting with Medusa

Clarke, A. C. A walk in the dark

Clement, H. Exchange rate

Clement, H. Uncommon sense

Czerneda, J. First Contact Inc.

Dann, J. Jumping the road

Davidson, A. Now let us sleep

Delany, S. R. The star pit

Dickson, G. R. The man in the mailbag

LIFE ON OTHER PLANETS—*Continued*

Dozois, G. R. Strangers
Drake, D. Choosing sides
Drake, D. Neck or nothing
Drake, D. The political process
Effinger, G. A. One
Evans, L. The stray
Finch, S. Reading the bones
Fowler, K. J. Face value
Grimsley, J. Free in Asveroth
Haldeman, J. W. For White Hill
Harrison, H. Final encounter
Harrison, H. Heavy duty
Harrison, H. The repairman
Harrison, H. The streets of Ashkelon
Harrison, H. Welcoming committee
Hood, R. Tamed
Jenkins, W. F. First contact
Jones, R. F. The alien machine
Kagan, J. The return of the kangaroo rex
Kelly, J. P. Lovestory
Kress, N. The flowers of Aulit Prison
Le Guin, U. K. The building
Le Guin, U. K. Semley's necklace
Le Guin, U. K. Solitude
Le Guin, U. K. A woman's liberation
MacLeod, I. Breathmoss
MacLeod, I. New light on the Drake equation
Martin, G. R. R. Sandkings
Martin, G. R. R. The way of cross and dragon
McAuley, P. J. Reef
McCaffrey, A. Beyond between
McDevitt, J. Nothing ever happens in Rock City
McGarry, M. J. The mercy gate
McKenna, R. Hunter, come home
Niven, L. and Cooper, B. Ice and mirrors
Nordley, G. D. Poles apart
Norton, A. Mousetrap
Oliver, C. Between the thunder and the sun
Oliver, C. Blood's a rover
Oliver, C. The edge of forever
Oliver, C. The gift
Oliver, C. Guardian spirit
Oliver, C. Just like a man
Oliver, C. Let me live in a house
Oliver, C. Night
Oliver, C. North wind
Oliver, C. RIte of passage
Oliver, C. Second nature
Pronzini, B. And then we went to Venus
Pronzini, B. and Malzberg, B. N. "Do I dare to eat a peach?"
Reed, R. Night of time
Resnick, M. The elephants on Neptune
Rosenblum, M. H. The eye of God
Rusch, K. K. Skin deep
Sheckley, R. Mind-slaves of Manotori
Shunn, W. Dance of the yellow-breasted Luddites
Sterling, B. Sunken gardens
Sterling, B. Swarm
Sturgeon, T. The golden helix
Swanwick, M. Slow life
Tenn, W. On Venus, have we got a rabbi
Tenn, W. Venus and the seven sexes
Tiptree, J. The only neat thing to do
Van Vogt, A. E. Black destroyer
Van Vogt, A. E. The rull
Vinge, V. The Blabber

Waldrop, H. Lunchbox
Weber, D. Changer of worlds
Weber, D. The hard way home
Weber, D. Ms. Midshipwoman Harrington
Whitton, L. Froggies
Williams, W. J. Prayers on the wind
Zelazny, R. The keys to December
Life prerecorded. McCorkle, J.
'Life probably saved by imbecile dwarf'. Jones, G.
Life sentences. Lynn, D. H.
The **life** story of Matvey Rodionovich Pavlichenko. Babel´, I.
Life without Valentino. Tyennick, J.
Lifeboat on a burning sea. Rogers, B. H.
The **lifeguard**. Morris, M.
LIFESAVING
Hoffman, W. Landings
Morris, M. The lifeguard
Steinwachs, M. Swimming out to Holly
Updike, J. Lifeguard
Light, Douglas
Three days. a month. more.
The O. Henry Prize stories, 2003; edited and with an introduction by Laura Furman; jurers David Gutterson, Diane Johnson, Jennifer Egan
Light. Kohler, S.
Light. Montemarano, N.
Light action in the Caribbean. Lopez, B. H.
Light can be both wave and particle. Gilchrist, E.
LIGHT HOUSES *See* Lighthouses
Light in the crossing. Meyers, K.
The **light** in the piazza. Spencer, E.
The **light** in Whale Cove. Rusch, K. K.
Light into dark. Bloom, A.
A **light** man. James, H.
The **Light** of Christmas. Evans, R. P.
The **light** of darkness. Clarke, A. C.
The **light** on the sea. Wickham, J.
Light shining through a honey jar. Gilchrist, E.
Light Skin. Adichie, C. N.
Light tackle. Wylie, P.
The **light** through the window. Brockmeier, K.
The **lighthouse** keeper. Harmon, J.
LIGHTHOUSES
Berliner, J. Until the butterflies
Braunbeck, G. A. Captain Jim's drunken dream
Costello, M. J. and Hautala, R. And the sea shall claim them
DuBois, B. The tourist who wasn't there
Gorman, E. Ghost of a chance
Hautala, R. The Nephews
Hoffman, N. K. Gone
Lindskold, J. M. It must burn
MacLeod, A. Island
Monteleone, T. F. Lux et veritas
Mosiman, B. S. Dread Inlet
Navarro, Y. A beacon shall I shine
Porter, J. A. Scrupulous Amédée
Rusch, K. K. The light in Whale Cove
LIGHTNING CONDUCTORS
DeMarinis, R. Insulation
Lightning man. Means, D.
Lightning Over the Lake. Hauser, E.
The **lightpainter**. Gay, W.
Lights. Chekhov, A. P.
The **lights** below [excerpt] MacDougall, C.

Ligotti, Thomas
I have a special plan for this world
Best new horror 12; edited and with an introduction by Stephen Jones
Our temporary supervisor
The Mammoth book of best horror 13; edited by Stephen Jones
The shadow, the darkness
999: new stories of horror and suspense; edited by Al Sarrantonio
Like a banana. Campo, R.
Like a bone in the throat. Block, L.
Like daughter. Due, T.
Like dove wings. Lincoln, C.
Like I was telling you . . . Sánchez, R.
Like incest. Foster, K.
Like something in this world. Thurm, M.
Like the sun itself. Edwards, S.
Like Two People Who Have Never Met. Juska, E.
Like whiskey for Christmas. Schraufnagel, J.
The **likely** lad. Baker, K.
Likely Lake. Robison, M.
Liking what you see: a documentary. Chiang, T.
Liksom, Rosa
"We Got Married"
CLCWeb: Comparative Literature and Culture v4 no4 p1 2002
Li'l Miss Ultrasound. Devereaux, R.
Lilacs. Chopin, K.
Lilacs. Verghese, A.
Liliane's Sunday. Vega, A. L.
LILIES
Bates, H. E. The lily
The **lilies.** Chopin, K.
LILITH (SEMITIC MYTHOLOGY)
Jeffers, H. F. Sister Lilith
Lilith. Vargo, J.
Lilith's. Campbell, R.
Lilith's dance. Hernández, G. G.
Lilly, Judy Magnuson
Going home money
American West; twenty new stories from the Western Writers of America; edited with an introduction by Loren D. Estleman
Lilly and Hanka. Bordiuk, A.
The **lily.** Bates, H. E.
LIMA (PERU) *See* Peru—Lima
Lima, Peru, July 28, 1979. Alarcón, D.
Limbe. Francis, P.
Limbo. Tuck, L.
Limbs. McNally, J.
Lime. Reid, E.
LIME-KILNS
Hawthorne, N. Ethan Brand
Lime-tree. Maleti, G.
The **limits** of fantasy. Campbell, R.
Limpets. Barker, N.
Limsky, Drew
Hating yourself in the morning
His 3: brilliant new fiction by gay writers; edited by Robert Drake and Terry Wolverton
Linaweaver, Brad
Moon of ice
The Best alternate history stories of the 20th century; edited by Harry Turtledove with Martin H. Greenberg
LINCOLN, ABRAHAM, 1809-1865
About
Bradbury, R. Downwind from Gettysburg

Card, O. S. The Yazoo Queen
Grape, J. Tabby won't tell
Hodgen, C. Three parting shots and a forecast
Wellen, E. The postmaster & the slave
Lincoln, Christine
Acorn pipes
Lincoln, C. Sap rising
All that's left
Lincoln, C. Sap rising
At the water's end
Lincoln, C. Sap rising
Bug juice
Lincoln, C. Sap rising
A hook will sometimes keep you
Lincoln, C. Sap rising
Last will
Lincoln, C. Sap rising
Like dove wings
Lincoln, C. Sap rising
More like us
Lincoln, C. Sap rising
Sap rising
Lincoln, C. Sap rising
A very close conspiracy
Lincoln, C. Sap rising
Winter's wheat
Lincoln, C. Sap rising
Wishes
Lincoln, C. Sap rising
Lincoln, arisen. Almond, S.
The **Lincoln** Train. McHugh, M. F.
LINDBERGH, CHARLES, JR.
About
Waldrop, H. Us
Lindbergh Baby *See* Lindbergh, Charles, Jr.
Lindgren, Torgny
The stump-grubber
The Art of the story; an international anthology of contemporary short stories; edited by Daniel Halpern
Water
Other people's mail; an anthology of letter stories; edited with an introduction by Gail Pool
Lindholm, Megan
Bones for Dulath
Magical beginnings; edited by Steven H. Silver and Martin H. Greenberg
Cut
Nebula awards showcase 2004; edited by Vonda McIntyre
Lindner, Vicki
Continental Divide
Ploughshares v27 no1 p86-99 Spr 2001
Lindquist, Rowena Cory
Prelude to a nocturne
Dreaming down-under; edited by Jack Dann and Janeen Webb
Lindskold, Jane M.
It must burn
Lighthouse hauntings; 12 original tales of the supernatural; edited by Charles G. Waugh & Martin H. Greenberg
Jeff's best joke
Past imperfect; edited by Martin H. Greenberg and Larry Segriff
Queen's gambit
Worlds of Honor

Lindskold, Jane M.—*Continued*
The road to Stony Creek
   The Blue and the gray undercover; edited by
      Ed Gorman
Sacrifice
   Mardi Gras madness; tales of terror and may-
      hem in New Orleans; edited by Martin H.
      Greenberg and Russell Davis
Witche's-broom, apple soon
   Greenberg, M. H. Faerie tales
The **line**. Skillings, R. D.
Line and color. Babel´, I.
The **lineaments** of gratified desire. Davidson, A.
Linebarger, Paul M. A., 1913-1966
   *For works written by this author under oth-
      er names see* Smith, Cordwainer, 1913-
      1966
Lines. Hart, R.
Lingard, Joan
After Colette [excerpt]
   The Vintage book of contemporary Scottish
      fiction; edited and with an introduction by
      Peter Kravitz
Lingula. Klíma, I.
Link, Kelly
Carnation, Lily, Lily, Rose
   Link, K. Stranger things happen
   The Vintage book of amnesia; an anthology;
      edited by Jonathan Lethem
Catskin
   The Mammoth book of best new horror 14;
      edited with an introduction by Stephen
      Jones
   McSweeney's mammoth treasury of thrilling
      tales; edited by Michael Chabon
Flying lessons
   Link, K. Stranger things happen
The girl detective
   Link, K. Stranger things happen
   The Year's best fantasy & horror, thirteenth
      annual collection; edited by Ellen Datlow
      and Terri Windling
The hortlak
   Datlow, E. The dark; new ghost stories; ed-
      ited by Ellen Datlow
Louise's ghost
   Link, K. Stranger things happen
   Nebula Awards showcase 2003; edited by
      Nancy Kress
Lull
   The Year's best fantasy & horror: sixteenth
      annual collection; edited by Ellen Datlow
      & Terri Windling
Most of my friends are two-thirds water
   Link, K. Stranger things happen
   The Mammoth book of best horror 13; edited
      by Stephen Jones
Shoe and marriage
   Link, K. Stranger things happen
The specialist's hat
   Best new horror 10; edited and with an intro-
      duction by Stephen Jones
   Link, K. Stranger things happen
   The Year's best fantasy & horror, twelfth an-
      nual collection; edited by Ellen Datlow &
      Terry Windling
Survivor's ball; or, The Donner party
   Link, K. Stranger things happen

Travels with the Snow Queen
   Link, K. Stranger things happen
   The Year's best fantasy & horror, twelfth an-
      nual collection; edited by Ellen Datlow &
      Terry Windling
Vanishing act
   Link, K. Stranger things happen
Water off a black dog's back
   Link, K. Stranger things happen
(jt. auth) See Grant, Gavin J. and Link, Kelly
Links. Tiedemann, M. W.
Linney, Romulus
Coda
   Bomb no85 p88-91 Fall 2003
Doc's Boy
   The Southern Review (Baton Rouge, La.) v39
      no2 p336-9 Spr 2003
Goodbye, Oscar
   Bomb no79 p82-4 Spr 2002
Tennessee
   New stories from the South: the year's best,
      2002; edited by Shannon Ravenel; with a
      preface by Larry Brown
   The Southern Review (Baton Rouge, La.) v37
      no2 p382-403 Spr 2001
The widow
   New stories from the South: the year's best,
      2000; edited by Shannon Ravenel; with a
      preface by Ellen Douglas
Linscott, Gillian
For all the saints
   The World's finest mystery and crime stories,
      second annual collection; edited by Ed
      Gorman
Poison peach
   Murder most delectable; savory tales of culi-
      nary crimes; edited by Martin H. Greenberg
A scandal in winter
   A moment on the edge; 100 years of crime
      stories by women; edited by Elizabeth
      George
Linzner, Gordon
Author, author
   The Museum of horrors; edited by Dennis
      Etchison
A **lion** at Pendleton. Johnson, C. R.
The **lion** in the room next door. Simonds, M.
The **lion** of Comarre. Clarke, A. C.
LIONS
Carter, A. The courtship of Mr. Lyon
Simonds, M. The lion in the room next door
Lipenga, Ken
Wainting for a turn
   The Anchor book of modern African stories;
      edited by Nadežda Obradovic ; with a fore-
      word by Chinua Achebe
Lippi, Rosina
Catalogues
   Ploughshares v30 no2/3 p106-15 Fall 2004
Lippman, Laura
What he needed
   Tart noir; edited by Stella Duffy & Lauren
      Henderson
Lipsyte, Sam
Admiral of the Swiss Navy
   Lipsyte, S. Venus drive; stories
Beautiful game
   Lipsyte, S. Venus drive; stories

Lipsyte, Sam—*Continued*
Cremains
Lipsyte, S. Venus drive; stories
The Drury girl
Lipsyte, S. Venus drive; stories
Ergo, ice pick
Lipsyte, S. Venus drive; stories
I'm slavering
Lipsyte, S. Venus drive; stories
Less tar
Lipsyte, S. Venus drive; stories
The morgue rollers
Lipsyte, S. Venus drive; stories
My life, for promotional use only
Lipsyte, S. Venus drive; stories
Old soul
Lipsyte, S. Venus drive; stories
Probe to the negative
Lipsyte, S. Venus drive; stories
The relentless approximation of feeling
Film Comment v38 no3 p20-1 My/Je 2002
Torquemada
Lipsyte, S. Venus drive; stories
The wrong arm
Lipsyte, S. Venus drive; stories
LIQUOR INDUSTRY *See* Liquor traffic
LIQUOR TRAFFIC
See also Moonshiners
Billman, J. Honeyville
Hershman, M. Slightly guilty
Lisa picking cockles. Spatz, G.
Lisberger, Jody
Crucible
Michigan Quarterly Review v41 no1 p61-77 Wint 2002
LISBON (PORTUGAL) *See* Portugal—Lisbon
Lisbon cubed. Tenn, W.
Lish, Gordon
Among the Pomeranians
The Ohio Review no62/63 p490-509 2001
The Ohio Review no59 p79-95 1999
Bricolage; or, This side of the animal
Salmagundi no124/125 p222-27 Fall 1999/Wint 2000
Mercantilism
The Ohio Review no60 p7-12 1999
Narratology to the people!
The Ohio Review no62/63 p487-9 2001
Physis versus nomos versus storytime
The Antioch Review v57 no2 p159-64 Spr 1999
The positions
Salmagundi no123 p96-100 Summ 1999
Squeak in the sycamore
The Antioch Review v59 no2 p231-3 Spr 2001
Lisick, Beth
Aerosol halo
Lisick, B. This too can be yours
Back to the future
Lisick, B. This too can be yours
Bad news bridesmaid
Lisick, B. This too can be yours
Best of
Lisick, B. This too can be yours
The cool
Lisick, B. This too can be yours
Credit card test
Lisick, B. This too can be yours

Grit in the oil
Lisick, B. This too can be yours
I got the beat
Lisick, B. This too can be yours
Maneuvers
Lisick, B. This too can be yours
Mass theft
Lisick, B. This too can be yours
Nancy Druid
Lisick, B. This too can be yours
Old school ex
Lisick, B. This too can be yours
The other cheers
Lisick, B. This too can be yours
Punchlining
Lisick, B. This too can be yours
A skill you'll develop
Lisick, B. This too can be yours
Someone to contact
Lisick, B. This too can be yours
We call it blog
Lisick, B. This too can be yours
What you're worth
Lisick, B. This too can be yours
What's up there
Lisick, B. This too can be yours
Lisicky, Paul
Famous builder
Ploughshares v28 no1 p165-7 Spr 2002
Liska. Baron, D.
Lispector, Clarice
Looking for some dignity
Short stories by Latin American women; the magic and the real; edited by Celia Correas de Zapata; foreword by Isabel Allende
Love
The Vintage book of Latin American stories; edited by Carlos Fuentes and Julio Ortega
The **list**. Leavitt, D.
Listen, my children. Kaminsky, S. M.
Listening. Wyatt, C.
Listening for Carl. Crowley, K.
Listening to Brahms. Charnas, S. M.
Listening to the gay boys fight. Krawiec, R.
LITERACY
Aldrich, B. S. Trust the Irish for that
The **literary** agent. Baker, K.
LITERARY CRITICS
Berry, R. M. A theory of fiction
Brennan, M. The stone hot-water bottle
Chekhov, A. P. A drama
D'Amato, B. Of course you know that chocolate is a vegetable
Epstein, J. The executor
Evenson, B. The wavering knife
Gilb, D. Bottoms
Michaels, L. Some laughed
Singer, I. B. The beard
Singer, I. B. Vanvild Kava
Wharton, E. The legend
A **literary** death. Greenberg, M. H.
LITERARY LIFE
See also Authors
Amis, M. Career move
Amis, M. The coincidence of the arts
Chan, M. At the premier's literary awards
Heller, J. Girl from Greenwich
Kalfus, K. Peredelkino
Sorrentino, G. Perdído

LITERARY LIFE—*Continued*

Zawieyski, J. Conrad in the ghetto

Literary lonelyhearts. Avrich, J.

Literary lunch. Wilding, M.

LITHUANIA

Vilnius

Mayo, W. Overtures

Mayo, W. What rough beasts

The **litigants**. Lutz, J.

Litt, Toby

The Hare

Granta no81 p89-99 Spr 2003

Little, Benilde

The yellow sweater

The Bluelight corner; black women writing on
passion, sex, and romantic love; edited by
Rosemarie Robotham

Little, Bentley

Connie

Cat crimes through time; edited by Ed
Gorman, Martin H. Greenberg, and Larry
Segriff

Maya's mother

The Year's best fantasy & horror: sixteenth
annual collection; edited by Ellen Datlow
& Terri Windling

The theater

999: new stories of horror and suspense; edited by Al Sarrantonio

Little arrow. Gahunia, V.

LITTLE BIG HORN, BATTLE OF THE, 1876

Billman, J. Custer on Mondays

Salzer, S. K. Miss Libbie tells all

Swarthout, G. F. A horse for Mrs. Custer

A **little** bit of abuse. Davies, R.

Little bitty pretty one. Alexander, A.

The **little** black bag. Kornbluth, C. M.

Little brother. Mosley, W.

The **little** brown girl. Spencer, E.

A **little** Cinderella. Alcott, L. M.

The **little** convent girl. King, G.

A **little** country girl. Chopin, K.

Little dead girl singing. Gallagher, S.

Little Debbie. Canty, K.

Little Edens. Moss, B. K.

A **little** fling. Schlink, B.

Little fool. Bunin, I. A.

Little fool. Vasilenko, S.

A **little** free-mulatto. Chopin, K.

Little Genevieve. Alcott, L. M.

Little girl lost. Matheson, R.

The **little** girl with the blue eyes. Drake, R.

The **little** green book. Ritchie, J.

The **little** grey house. Coleman, A. S.

The **little** heart. Thompson, J.

The **little** house. Bowles, P.

The **little** house at Croix-Rousse. Simenon, G.

A **little** joke. See Chekhov, A. P. A joke

The **little** kid. Le May, A.

A **little** kingdom. Jackson, V. F.

The **little-known** bird of the inner eye.
McClanahan, E.

Little lady. Mencken, S. H.

A **little** learning. Dilworth, S.

A **Little** Like Light. Kennedy, A. L.

The **Little** Madonna. Boylan, C.

Little man—It's been a busy day. Jakes, J.

Little murmurs. Tran, H.

Little palaces. Canty, K.

Little people. O'Brien, T.

The **little** poet. Stollman, A. L.

Little poisons. Rivera Valdés, S.

The **little** prince. Lavin, M.

Little Robin. Alcott, L. M.

Little Rodney. Bradford, A.

The **little** seed. Alcott, L. M.

Little selves. Lerner, M.

Little sister. Enright, A.

The **little** stranger. Berberova, N.

Little sunbeam. Alcott, L. M.

A **little** variety. Watanabe McFerrin, L.

Little Water. Galeazzi, J.

Little white girl. Mencken, S. H.

Little white sister. Thon, M. R.

A **little** wild. Leslie, N.

Little Willie. Morgan, R.

A **little** window. Frym, G.

The **little** woman. Wallace, R.

A **little** zip. Troy, M.

The **littlest** guest uninvited. Walz, T.

Litzky, Tsaurah

End-of-the-world sex

Politically inspired; edited by Stephen Elliott;
assistant editor, Gabriel Kram; associate editors, Elizabeth Brooks [et al.]

Liu, Hsin-wu *See* Liu Xinwu, 1942-

Liu Xinwu

Black walls

The Vintage book of contemporary Chinese
fiction; edited by Carolyn Choa and David
Su Li-qun

Liu Yichang

Intersection

The Literary Review (Madison, N.J.) v47 no4
p10-42 Summ 2004

Live at five. Benson, R.

Live life king-sized. Kaplan, H.

Live oak. Frym, G.

The **Lives** of Pioneers. Thomas, R.

Lives of saints. Winterson, J.

The **lives** of strangers. Divakaruni, C. B.

Lives of the invertebrates. Slavin, J.

The **lives** of the saints. Brady, C.

Livesey, Margot

The Niece

The New Yorker v79 no7 p80-7 Ap 7 2003

The **Living**. Chernoff, M.

The **Living**. Christopher, P.

Living alone. Jackson, V. F.

The **living** and the dead. Tester, W.

Living fossil. De Camp, L. S.

The **living** land. Graebner, J. E.

Living next door to malice. Rubin, B.

Living the lie. Bilgrey, M.

Living the sign. Shepard, S.

Living together. Ebershoff, D.

Living with contradictions. Tillman, L.

Livingood, Jeb

Oh, Albany, my love

Best new American voices 2001; guest editor
Charles Baxter; series editors John Kulka
and Natalie Danford

Liyong, Taban lo

Princess, won by a bull

The Literary Review (Madison, N.J.) v45 no3
p438-43 Spr 2002

The **lizard** boy. Kenemore, S.

LIZARDS
Huff, T. Third time lucky
Ziegler, I. The stranger
Lizards. LeRoy, J. T.
Lizzie Fair and the dragon of heart's desire.
Edghill, R.
Llano, Maria Elena
In the family
Short stories by Latin American women; the
magic and the real; edited by Celia Correas
de Zapata; foreword by Isabel Allende
La **Lloradora**. Gould, L.
La **Llorona**. Lubitch Domecq, A.
Lloyd, David T.
As always, Jason
Lloyd, D. T. Boys; stories and a novella; [by]
David Lloyd
The biggest
Lloyd, D. T. Boys; stories and a novella; [by]
David Lloyd
Boys only
Lloyd, D. T. Boys; stories and a novella; [by]
David Lloyd
Isaac and Abraham
Lloyd, D. T. Boys; stories and a novella; [by]
David Lloyd
No boundaries
Lloyd, D. T. Boys; stories and a novella; [by]
David Lloyd
Portraits
Lloyd, D. T. Boys; stories and a novella; [by]
David Lloyd
Shortcut
Lloyd, D. T. Boys; stories and a novella; [by]
David Lloyd
Snow
Lloyd, D. T. Boys; stories and a novella; [by]
David Lloyd
Women's Studies v28 no5 p575-78 S/O 1999
Spider
Lloyd, D. T. Boys; stories and a novella; [by]
David Lloyd
Stain
Lloyd, D. T. Boys; stories and a novella; [by]
David Lloyd
Taking aim
Lloyd, D. T. Boys; stories and a novella; [by]
David Lloyd
Touch
Lloyd, D. T. Boys; stories and a novella; [by]
David Lloyd
Voodoo
Lloyd, D. T. Boys; stories and a novella; [by]
David Lloyd
Llywelyn, Morgan
Woman in a wheelchair
Royal whodunnits; edited by Mike Ashley
Lo Liyong, Taban *See* Liyong, Taban lo
A **loaf** of bread. McPherson, J. A.
A **loaf** of bread, a jug of wine. Olsen, S. S.
The **loan** of a gun. Le May, A.
LOANS
See also Moneylenders
Casares, O. RG
Loayza, Luis
A new man
The Vintage book of Latin American stories;
edited by Carlos Fuentes and Julio Ortega

Loba Lamar's Last Kiss (Silk Crepe Ribbons at
my Funeral...Please). Lemebel, P.
Lobenstine, David M.
Dissections
The Antioch Review v61 no4 p672-86 Fall
2003
Lobster night. Banks, R.
LOBSTERS
MacLeod, A. Vision
Slavin, J. Lives of the invertebrates
Lobsters. Stross, C.
Local currency. Hochman, A.
Local girls. Hoffman, A.
The **local** production of Cinderella. Goodman, A.
LOCH NESS MONSTER
Smith, A. Paradise
Lochhead, Liz
Phyllis Marlowe: only diamonds are forever
The Vintage book of contemporary Scottish
fiction; edited and with an introduction by
Peter Kravitz
Lochte, Dick
Get the message
Lochte, D. Lucky dog and other tales of mur-
der
In the city of angels
Flesh and blood; erotic tales of crime and
passion; edited by Max Allan Collins and
Jeff Gelb
The World's finest mystery and crime stories,
third annual collection; edited by Ed
Gorman and Martin H. Greenberg
Low Tide
Flesh and blood: guilty as sin; erotic tales of
crime and passion; edited by Max Allan
Collins and Jeff Gelb
Lucky dog
Lochte, D. Lucky dog and other tales of mur-
der
Mad Dog
Lochte, D. Lucky dog and other tales of mur-
der
Murder at Mardi Gras
Lochte, D. Lucky dog and other tales of mur-
der
A murder of import
Lochte, D. Lucky dog and other tales of mur-
der
Rappin' dog
Lochte, D. Lucky dog and other tales of mur-
der
The World's finest mystery and crime stories,
first annual collection; edited by Ed
Gorman
Sad-eyed blonde
Lochte, D. Lucky dog and other tales of mur-
der
A tough case to figure
Lochte, D. Lucky dog and other tales of mur-
der
Vampire dreams
Lochte, D. Lucky dog and other tales of mur-
der
Lock, Norman
A discourse on history
The North American Review v284 no2 p12-15
Mr/Ap 1999

Lock, Norman—*Continued*

Hunting icebergs

The Literary Review (Madison, N.J.) v42 no2
p293-97 Wint 1999

The **invisible** Dutchman and his dog

New England Review v23 no2 p52-4 Spr
2002

Marco and Marian take a vacation

New England Review v23 no2 p48-51 Spr
2002

Tango in Amsterdam

New England Review v24 no4 p152-7 2003

The **locked** tomb mystery. Peters, E.

The **locket**. Chopin, K.

Locklin, Gerald

Becalmed

Locklin, G. Candy bars; selected stories

The bummer

Locklin, G. Candy bars; selected stories

Candy bars

Locklin, G. Candy bars; selected stories

Circuitry

Locklin, G. Candy bars; selected stories

The English girl

Locklin, G. Candy bars; selected stories

Fin de semestre

Locklin, G. Candy bars; selected stories

The four-day workweek

Locklin, G. Candy bars; selected stories

The gold rush

Locklin, G. Candy bars; selected stories

The hippie shirt

Locklin, G. Candy bars; selected stories

I do not have herpes

Locklin, G. Candy bars; selected stories

The monopoly story

Locklin, G. Candy bars; selected stories

Not to worry

Locklin, G. Candy bars; selected stories

O Tannenbaum

Locklin, G. Candy bars; selected stories

Return of the hippie shirt

Locklin, G. Candy bars; selected stories

A sober reading of Dr. Sigmund Freud

Locklin, G. Candy bars; selected stories

The story story

Locklin, G. Candy bars; selected stories

Swing shift

Locklin, G. Candy bars; selected stories

To the shores of San Clemente

Locklin, G. Candy bars; selected stories

Turkey Day

Locklin, G. Candy bars; selected stories

LOCUSTS

Stollman, A. L. Mr. Mitochondria

Locusts. Nawrocki, S.

The **lodger** in room 726. Nair, M.

LODZ (POLAND) *See* Poland—Lodz

Loeb, Karen

Fauna in Florida

100% pure Florida fiction; an anthology; edited by Susan Hubbard and Robley Wilson

Loebel-Fried, Caren

The Sacred Tree: Hawaiian

Parabola v29 no2 p71-5 Summ 2004

LOGGERS

Gallagher, T. I got a guy once

Loomis, N. M. The fighting road

The **logic** of the heart. Coshnear, D.

Logjam. Wallace, R.

Loh, Sandra Tsing

My father's Chinese wives

LA shorts; edited by Steven Gilbar

Lohafer, Susan

The Man Who Understood Everybody

The Southern Review (Baton Rouge, La.) v40
no1 p117-31 Wint 2004

Lohier, Patrick

Harvard 1917

African American Review v38 no1 p87-98 Spr
2004

Lois in the country. Gavell, M. L.

Lojo, Maria Rosa

Compound eyes

English translations of short stories by contemporary Argentine women writers; edited
by Eliana Cazaubon Hermann ; translated
by Sally Webb Thornton

Loka. Chopin, K.

Lokey man. Dodd, S.

Lokey man. Dodd, S. M.

Lolita. Lichberg, H. von

Lolly. Solotaroff, V.

Lombreglia, Ralph

Cashmere Christmas

Writers harvest 3; edited and with an introduction by Tobias Wolff

London, Jack

All Gold Canyon

A Century of great Western stories; edited by
John Jakes

The madness of John Harned

Sports best short stories; edited by Paul D.
Staudohar

A piece of steak

Boxing's best short stories; edited by Paul D.
Staudohar

LONDON (ENGLAND) *See* England—London

London is the best city in America. Dave, L.

A **London** life. James, H.

Londynski, Helen

The four-ruble war

Beautiful as the moon, radiant as the stars;
Jewish women in Yiddish stories : an anthology; edited by Sandra Bark; introduction by Francine Prose

The **Lone** Night Cantina. Lee, D.

Lone Pine. Malouf, D.

The **Lone** Star camel corps. Savage, L., Jr.

LONELINESS

Almog, R. Shrinking

Avrich, J. La belle dame sans merci

Berkman, P. R. Merry Christmas, Charlie Brown

Bingham, S. Bare bones

Bingham, S. The pump

Bingham, S. Stanley

Bottoms, G. The metaphor

Boylan, C. Thatcher's Britain

Bradbury, R. Where all is emptiness there is
room to move

Burford, M. Out of the storm

Butler, R. O. Christmas 1910

Cady, J. Jeremiah

Cady, J. Play like I'm sheriff

Capote, T. Shut a final door

Carter, E. Zemecki's cat

Chaon, D. The illustrated encyclopedia of the
animal kingdom

LONELINESS—*Continued*

Chekhov, A. P. Misery

Connor, J. I wouldn't do that if I were you

Connor, J. Summer girls

Davidson, R. A private life

Davies, R. The song of songs

Day, C. The circus house

Desplechin, M. The kiwi-seller

Engel, M. P. Redeeming the dead

Epstein, J. Postcards

Gabrielyan, N. Bee heaven

Gilchrist, E. The young man

Goran, L. Keeping count

Grau, S. A. The beginning

Grau, S. A. Sea change

Grodstein, L. John on the train: a fable for our cynical friends

Hamburger, A. Sympathetic conversationalist

Hayes, D. Sweet nothings

Highsmith, P. Magic casements

Highsmith, P. Where the door is always open and the welcome mat is out

Jackson, V. F. White sandals

Kennedy, A. L. Elsewhere

Lavin, M. In a café

Mazelis, J. Setting

Patterson, K. Country of cold

Patterson, K. Les is more

Patterson, K. Structure is constant

Roorbach, B. Loneliness

Seiffert, R. The last spring

Serdatzky, Yente. Two heads

Shepard, S. The company's interest

Stafford, J. Children are bored on Sunday

Sturgeon, T. A saucer of loneliness

Thompson, J. The widower

Troncoso, S. The gardener

Troncoso, S. My life in the city

Vivante, A. The cricket

Vivante, A. Fall and rise

Vivante, A. Osage orange

Vivante, A. Solitude

Wallace, D. F. The soul is not a smithy

Yates, R. Doctor Jack-o'-Lantern

Loneliness. Roorbach, B.

Lonely adventure [excerpt] Blaman, A.

The **lonely** and the lost. Gifford, B.

A **lonely** coast. Proulx, A.

The **lonely** doll. Nelson, A.

Lonely planet. Grodstein, L.

Loner. Coleman, J. C.

Lonesome Ben. Chesnutt, C. W.

Long, Amelia Reynolds

The thought-monster

Science-fiction classics; the stories that morphed into movies; compiled by Forrest J. Ackerman

Long, Elaine

Letters to the stove

Westward; a fictional history of the American West : 28 original stories celebrating the 50th anniversary of the Western Writers of America; edited by Dale L. Walker

Long, Gabrielle Margaret Vere Campbell, 1886-1952

For works written by this author under other names see Bowen, Marjorie, 1886-1952

Long Ago Yesterday. Kureishi, H.

The **long** dark hall. Berry, M. S.

Long distance. Smiley, J.

Long-distance conversations. Klíma, I.

Long distances. Rhodes, J. P.

The **long** divorce of steel. Edghill, R.

The **long** game. Pneuman, A.

Long gone and Mister Lonely. Warren, D.

The **long** hall on the top floor. Kiernan, C. R.

LONG ISLAND (N.Y.)

Hecht, J. Do the windows open?

Long odds. Weaver, G.

The **long** run. Wharton, E.

Long shot. Vinge, V.

A **long** story short. Kalpakian, L.

Long-term investment. Yarbro, C. Q.

The **long** view. Berry, M. S.

The **long** watch. Heinlein, R. A.

A **long** way from home. Sneider, V.

The **long** way home. O'Connor, J.

LONGEVITY

See also Aging; Rejuvenation

Clarke, A. C. The secret

Longevity has its place. Breen, J. L.

Longstaff's marriage. James, H.

Longstreet, K. A.

Epitaph

New England Review v24 no3 p145-55 Summ 2003

Fleurette bleu

The Georgia Review v55 no1 p97-109 Spr 2001

The judgement of Paris

New stories from the South; the year's best, 2004; edited by Shannon Ravenel; preface by Tim Gautreaux

The Virginia Quarterly Review v79 no2 p249-64 Spr 2003

Luxor

The Southern Review (Baton Rouge, La.) v39 no1 p141-54 Wint 2003

Provenance

The Sewanee Review v109 no2 p185-97 Spr 2001

LONGWORTH, ALICE ROOSEVELT, 1884-1980

About

Foxwell, E. Alice and the agent of the Hun

Look-alikes. Gordimer, N.

Look at Me, I'm Beautiful!. Rice, B.

Look for the kid with the guts. O'Rourke, F.

Look Into Their Own Dark Places. Sides, D. L.

Lookin' 'n' jivin'. Kerslake, L.

Looking for Kelly Dahl. Simmons, D.

Looking for Lourdes. Jacobs, M.

Looking for Mr. Green. Bellow, S.

Looking for Petronilla. Donoghue, E.

Looking for some dignity. Lispector, C.

Looking for the possible dance [excerpt] Kennedy, A. L.

Looking for War. Unger, D.

Looking forward to the harvest. Wilder, C.

The **looking-glass.** Chekhov, A. P.

The **looking-glass.** Wharton, E.

Looking out. Campbell, R.

Loomis, Craig

The apology

Iowa Review v31 no3 p143-53 Wint 2001/2002

Loomis, Noel M.

The coming home
Loomis, N. M. Heading west; western stories; edited by Bill Pronzini

The fighting road
Loomis, N. M. Heading west; western stories; edited by Bill Pronzini

Grandfather out of the past
Loomis, N. M. Heading west; western stories; edited by Bill Pronzini

The man who had no thumbs
Loomis, N. M. Heading west; western stories; edited by Bill Pronzini

Maverick factory
Loomis, N. M. Heading west; western stories; edited by Bill Pronzini

The St. Louis salesman
Loomis, N. M. Heading west; western stories; edited by Bill Pronzini

The stick and the bearded lady
Loomis, N. M. Heading west; western stories; edited by Bill Pronzini

Tough hombre
Loomis, N. M. Heading west; western stories; edited by Bill Pronzini

When the children cry for meat
Loomis, N. M. Heading west; western stories; edited by Bill Pronzini

Looney, George

What gives us voice
New England Review v20 no2 p99-111 Spr 1999

Loons. Nichols, J.

The **loop**, the snow, their daughters, the rain. Wieland, L.

Loophole. Clarke, A. C.

Looping. Smith, S. J.

Loose. Ortiz, S. J.

Loose cannon. Nelson, A.

Loose ends. Stuart, D.

Loose talk. Broyard, B.

Loosestrife. Frym, G.

Loot. Gordimer, N.

Lopes, Henri

The advance
The Anchor book of modern African stories; edited by Nadežda Obradović ; with a foreword by Chinua Achebe

Lopez, Barry Holstun

The construction of the Rachel
Lopez, B. H. Light action in the Caribbean; stories

The deaf girl
Lopez, B. H. Light action in the Caribbean; stories

Emory Bear Hands' birds
Lopez, B. H. Light action in the Caribbean; stories

In the Garden of the Lords of War
Lopez, B. H. Light action in the Caribbean; stories

In the great bend of the Souris River
Lopez, B. H. Light action in the Caribbean; stories

The letters of heaven
Lopez, B. H. Light action in the Caribbean; stories

Light action in the Caribbean
Lopez, B. H. Light action in the Caribbean; stories

The mappist
Lopez, B. H. Light action in the Caribbean; stories

Mornings in Quarain
Lopez, B. H. Light action in the Caribbean; stories

The open lot
In our nature: stories of wildness; selected and introduced by Donna Seaman

Remembering orchards
Lopez, B. H. Light action in the Caribbean; stories

Ruben Mendoza Vega, Suzuki professor of early Caribbean history, University of Florida at Gainesville, offers a history of the United States based on personal experience
Lopez, B. H. Light action in the Caribbean; stories

Stolen horses
Lopez, B. H. Light action in the Caribbean; stories

Writers harvest 3; edited and with an introduction by Tobias Wolff

Thomas Lowdermilk's generosity
Lopez, B. H. Light action in the Caribbean; stories

López, Lorraine

After Dad shot Jesus
López, L. Soy la Avon lady and other stories

The crown on prince
López, L. Soy la Avon lady and other stories

Frostbite
López, L. Soy la Avon lady and other stories

Ivor's people
López, L. Soy la Avon lady and other stories

Love can make you sick
López, L. Soy la Avon lady and other stories

Mother-in-law tongue
López, L. Soy la Avon lady and other stories

Sophia
López, L. Soy la Avon lady and other stories

Soy la Avon lady
López, L. Soy la Avon lady and other stories

A tatting man
López, L. Soy la Avon lady and other stories

To control a rabid rodent
López, L. Soy la Avon lady and other stories

Walking circles
López, L. Soy la Avon lady and other stories

López, Lorraine M.

Frostbite
Prairie Schooner v75 no4 p20-34 Wint 2001

Lorca, Federico García *See* García Lorca, Federico, 1898-1936

Lord, Catherine

The art of losing
Hers 3: brilliant new fiction by lesbian writers; edited by Terry Wolverton with Robert Drake

Lord, Christopher

La Tortuga
His 3: brilliant new fiction by gay writers; edited by Robert Drake and Terry Wolverton

Lord, Nancy
  Afterlife
    Lord, N. The man who swam with beavers; stories
  The attainable border of the birds
    Lord, N. The man who swam with beavers; stories
  The baby who, according to his aunt, resembled his uncle
    Lord, N. The man who swam with beavers; stories
  Behold
    Lord, N. The man who swam with beavers; stories
  Candace counts coup
    Lord, N. The man who swam with beavers; stories
    Pushcart prize XXVII; best of the small presses; edited by Bill Henderson with the Pushcart prize editors
  The census taker
    Lord, N. The man who swam with beavers; stories
  The girl who dreamed only geese
    Lord, N. The man who swam with beavers; stories
  The man who swam with beavers
    Lord, N. The man who swam with beavers; stories
  The man who went through everything
    Lord, N. The man who swam with beavers; stories
  Recall of the wild
    Lord, N. The man who swam with beavers; stories
  Remaking the world
    Lord, N. The man who swam with beavers; stories
  Trip report (confidential)
    Lord, N. The man who swam with beavers; stories
  What was washing around out there
    Lord, N. The man who swam with beavers; stories
  White bird
    Lord, N. The man who swam with beavers; stories
  Why owls die with wings outspread
    Lord, N. The man who swam with beavers; stories
  Wolverine grudge
    Lord, N. The man who swam with beavers; stories
  The woman who would marry a bear
    Lord, N. The man who swam with beavers; stories
The **lord**. Alas, L.
Lord McDonald. Sweeney, E.
The **lord** of Central Park. Davidson, A.
Lord of the worms. Lumley, B.
Lordan, Beth
  Digging
    Atlantic Monthly v288 no2 p110-16 S 2001
    The Best American short stories, 2002; selected from U.S. and Canadian magazines by Sue Miller with Katrina Kenison, with an introduction by Sue Miller
  From Mutton Island
    Atlantic Monthly v284 no1 p74-76+ Jl 1999

The man with the lapdog
    Atlantic Monthly v283 no2 p78-80+ F 1999
    Prize stories, 2000; The O. Henry awards; edited and with an introduction by Larry Dark
  Penumbra
    Atlantic Monthly (1993) v289 no2 p73-9 F 2002
The **lords** of zero. Richards, T.
LORD'S SUPPER
    Carlson, R. The Tablecloth of Turnin
Lorenz, Elizabeth
  Tinkering with What's Left
    Gettysburg Review v15 no4 p623-8 Wint 2002
Lorfing, Jake
  Old horse
    Nixon under the bodhi tree and other works of Buddhist fiction; edited by Kate Wheeler ; foreword by Charles Johnson
LOS ANGELES (CALIF.) *See* California—Los Angeles
Los **Angeles** here and now. Nietzke, A.
Losing count. Alvarez, A.
Losing downforce. Agee, J.
Losing the Dog's Paddle. Arnold, M.
Losing Zan Gambol. McGinn, J. M.
Loss. Bhattacharyya, R.
A **loss** for words. Epstein, J.
A **loss** for words: a story. Epstein, J.
Losses. Sullivan, W.
Lost. Leslie, N.
O **lost**. Wolfe, T.
Lost and found. Hadley, T.
Lost and found. Schutz, B. M.
The **lost** and the found. Cooper, J. C.
The **lost** art of sleep. Dodd, S. M.
Lost boys. Card, O. S.
Lost causes. Greer, A. S.
The **lost** child. Thompson, J.
LOST CHILDREN
    Orringer, J. Care
    Still, J. The nest
Lost children. Bean, B.
The **lost** Christmas. Gifford, B.
The **lost** city of words. Tillman, L.
The **Lost** Continent. Kirn, W.
The **lost** district. Lane, J.
Lost faces. Fessel, K.-S.
Lost girls. Yolen, J.
Lost in a pyramid; or, The Mummy's Curse. Alcott, L. M.
Lost in the mail. Lehner, C.
Lost in the U.S.A. Pittalwala, I.
Lost land of youth. Stuart, J.
Lost lives. Eberts, M.
Lost luggage. Adams, A.
Lost polars. Singer, S.
Lost rafts. Giono, J.
The **lost** salt gift of blood. MacLeod, A.
Lost soldier. Whitmore, S.
The **lost** son. Hickman, M. W.
Lost sorceress of the silent citadel. Moorcock, M.
Lost the baby. Svoboda, T.
Lost time. Meade, D.
The **lost** way. Čapek, K.
Lost years. Chan, D. M.
Lot no. 249. Doyle, Sir A. C.
A **lot** of sense. Hensley, J. L.

Lot's wife. Dwyer, M.
Lot's wife. Engel, M. P.
Lot's wife. Heller, J.
Lott, Bret
  The train, the lake, the bridge
    Death dines at 8:30; edited by Claudia Bishop
      and Nick DiChario
    Ghost writing; haunted tales by contemporary
      writers; edited by Roger Weingarten
LOTTERIES
  Banks, R. The fisherman
  Bausch, R. Riches
  Biguenet, J. It is raining in Bejucal
  Borges, J. L. The lottery in Babylon
  Capote, T. Jug of silver
  Carey, P. The chance
  Jackson, S. The lottery
  Jaime-Becerra, M. Buena Suerte Airlines
  Perabo, S. The greater grace of Carlisle
  Reiner, C. Xavier
The **lottery**. Jackson, S.
The **lottery** in Babylon. Borges, J. L.
Lotto. Howe, F.
The **lotus-eater**. Clark, J.
Louie, David Wong
  Displacement
    Breaking into print; early stories and insights
      into getting published; a Ploughshares an-
      thology; edited by DeWitt Henry
Louis, Laura Glen
  Divining the waters
    Louis, L. G. Talking in the dark; stories
  Fur
    Louis, L. G. Talking in the dark; stories
  Her slow and steady
    Louis, L. G. Talking in the dark; stories
  The quiet at the bottom of the pool
    Louis, L. G. Talking in the dark; stories
  Rudy's two wives
    Louis, L. G. Talking in the dark; stories
  Talking in the dark
    Louis, L. G. Talking in the dark; stories
  Tea
    Louis, L. G. Talking in the dark; stories
  Thirty yards
    Louis, L. G. Talking in the dark; stories
Louisa. Miller, R.
Louisa Pallant. James, H.
Louise, Debbie De
  Stitches in time
    Cat crimes through time; edited by Ed
      Gorman, Martin H. Greenberg, and Larry
      Segriff
Louise and Al get married. Nawrocki, S.
Louise's ghost. Link, K.
LOUISIANA
  Chabon, M. The Martian agent, a planetary ro-
    mance
  Chopin, K. Desirée's baby
  Chopin, K. In Sabine
  Diamond, P. Whitey
  Gautreaux, T. Dancing with the one-armed gal
  Gautreaux, T. Easy pickings
  Gautreaux, T. Good for the soul
  Gautreaux, T. The piano tuner
  Gautreaux, T. The Pine Oil Writers' Conference
  Gautreaux, T. Resistance
  Gautreaux, T. Sorry blood
  Gautreaux, T. Sunset in heaven

  Gautreaux, T. Welding with children
  Hannah, B. Death and joy
  Keegan, C. You can't be too careful
  Mogan, J. Mrs. Bajon says
  Poirier, M. J. Gators
  Stahl, Anna Kazumi. Natural disasters
  Wendling, L. Inappropriate babies
        18th century
  Chopin, K. The maid of Saint Phillippe
        19th century
  Chopin, K. Desirée's baby
  Chopin, K. In and out of old Natchitoches
  Chopin, K. A lady of bayou St. John
  Chopin, K. A non-account Creole
  Chopin, K. Polydore
  Chopin, K. The return of Alcibiade
        Farm life
    See Farm life—Louisiana
        Baton Rouge
  Parrish, T. After the river
  Parrish, T. Bonnie Ledet
  Parrish, T. Complicity
  Parrish, T. Exterminator
  Parrish, T. Free fall
  Parrish, T. Hardware man
  Parrish, T. It pours
  Parrish, T. The smell of a car
        New Orleans
  Bischoff, D. May oysters have legs
  Braunbeck, G. A. Down in darkest Dixie where
    the dead don't dance
  Cable, G. W. The story of Bras-Coupé
  Chopin, K. The awakening
  Chopin, K. Cavanelle
  Chopin, K. A matter of prejudice
  Crowther, P. Songs of leaving
  Davis, R. Fat Tuesday
  De Noux, O. Death on denial
  Dunbar-Nelson, A. M. Tony's wife
  Fleming, R. Life after bas
  Ford, R. Puppy
  Foster, K. The kind I'm likely to get
  Gautreaux, T. Misuse of light
  Gilchrist, E. The big cleanup
  Gilchrist, E. In the land of dreamy dreams
  Gilchrist, E. Light shining through a honey jar
  Gilchrist, E. The stucco house
  Gilchrist, E. There's a Garden of Eden
  Helfers, J. Farewell to the flesh
  Hill, I. The ballad of Rappy Valcour
  Hill, I. Pagan babies
  Hill, I. Valor
  Holder, N. Skeleton krewe
  Howard, C. McCulla's kid
  King, G. La grande demoiselle
  Lindskold, J. M. Sacrifice
  Orringer, J. Pilgrims
  Piazza, T. Brownsville
  Rogers, B. H. King Corpus
  Scarborough, E. A. The invisible woman's clev-
    er disguise
  Smith, M. M. A place to stay
  Thompson, J. The little heart
  Thompson, M. Jesus, beans, and butter rum life-
    savers
  VanderMeer, J. Black Duke blues
  West, M. Faces made of clay
Louisiana loses its cricket hum. Davis, A.
Louse [excerpt] Grand, D.

Love, Matthew
Chest Pain
  The Antioch Review v61 no3 p462-76 Summ
  2003
Nightfloat
  Best new American voices 2004; guest editor
  John Casey; series editors John Kulka and
  Natalie Danford
Love, Rosaleen
The raptures of the deep
  Gathering the bones; original stories from the
  world's masters of horror; edited by Dennis
  Etchison, Ramsey Campbell and Jack Dann
Real men
  Dreaming down-under; edited by Jack Dann
  and Janeen Webb
The Total Devotion Machine
  Centaurus: the best of Australian science fic-
  tion; edited by David G. Hartwell and Da-
  mien Broderick
Two recipes for magic beans
  Dreaming down-under; edited by Jack Dann
  and Janeen Webb
LOVE
Alas, L. The lord
Chekhov, A. P. Love
Lawrence, D. H. St. Mawr
Williams, J. Taking care
Love. Ansa, T. M.
Love. Bush, M.
Love. Chekhov, A. P.
Love. Frym, G.
Love. Lispector, C.
Love. Martin, V.
Love A, love B. Chiappone, R.
The **love** affair. Bradbury, R.
LOVE AFFAIRS
    See also Courtship; Love stories; Lovers;
  Marriage problems
Adams, A. The haunted beach
Adams, A. Home is where
Adams, A. Legends
Adams, A. Old love affairs
Adams, A. Sintra
Agee, J. Invisible
Agee, J. My last try
Allen, D., Jr. Deferment
Allen, W. Retribution
Anderson, D. Would you feel better?
Apple, M. The eighth day
Aquin, H. Back on April eleventh
Archer, J. The letter
Auchincloss, L. He knew he was right
Auchincloss, L. The scarlet letters
Azadeh, C. A recitation of nomads
Bail, M. A, B, C, D, E, F, G, H, I, J, K, L, M,
  N, O, P, Q, R, S, T, U, V, W, X, Y, Z
Bank, M. The girls' guide to hunting and fish-
  ing
Banks, R. Black man and white woman in dark
  green rowboat
Banks, R. Sarah Cole: a type of love story
Barrett, A. The mysteries of ubiquitin
Barrett, L. Macy is the other woman
Bart, P. Hard bargain
Barthelme, F. The autobiography of Riva Jay
Barthelme, F. Bag boy
Barthelme, F. Red Arrow
Barthelme, F. Spots

Bauman, B. A. Eden
Bausch, R. High-heeled shoe
Bausch, R. The voices from the other room
Beattie, A. Distant music
Beattie, A. Janus
Belle, J. Book of Nick
Bellow, S. What kind of day did you have?
Benítez-Rojo, A. Skin deep
Berkman, P. R. The falling nun
Berkman, P. R. Jennet
Billman, J. Ash
Blackwood, S. Prodigal fathers
Blatnik, A. Billie Holiday
Block, F. L. Bones
Bocock, M. Alice and me
Bonman, I. Mrs. Website's dance
Boswell, M. Grub worm
Boswell, M. In between things
Bowles, P. Here to learn
Boylan, C. Affairs in order
Boylan, C. Housekeeper's cut
Boylan, C. It's her
Bradbury, R. Heart transplant
Brand, C. Clever and quick
Brewer, G. Sauce for the goose
Brodkey, H. Innocence
Browder, C. Girls like us
Brownrigg, S. The girl in the red chair
Brownstein, G. Bachelor party
Bunin, I. A. Antigone
Bunin, I. A. Muza
Bunin, I. A. Raven
Busch, F. Debriefing
Busch, F. A handbook for spies
Butler, R. O. Fair warning
Carlson, R. Gary Garrison's wedding vows
Carlson, R. Hartwell
Carlson, R. Oxygen
Carter, E. A
Carter, E. Glory B. and the ice-man
Chambers, C. Aardvark to Aztec
Chamoiseau, P. Red hot peppers
Channer, C. I'm still waiting
Chaon, D. Late for the wedding
Chekhov, A. P. The grasshopper
Cherry, K. Lunachick
Chesnutt, C. W. A grass widow
Chiappone, R. Love A, love B
Cisneros, S. Never marry a Mexican
Cobb, W. J. The decline of King Fabulous
Cobb, W. J. There's nothing the matter with
  Gwen
Cohen, R. A flight of sparks
Cohen, R. The varieties of romantic experience:
  an introduction
Coleman, J. C. Marvel Bird
Colvin, C. The sound of the horn
Connolly, C. The bounce
Dark, A. E. Close
Davies, R. Afternoon tea
Davies, R. Art lover
Davies, R. The forty-eight-bar bridge
Davies, R. A little bit of abuse
Davies, R. Missing person
Davies, Tristan. Snapdragon
Davis, A. Circling the drain
Davis, A. Ending things
Davis, A. Fat ladies floated in the sky like bal-
  loons

LOVE AFFAIRS—*Continued*

Davis, D. S. Now is forever
Davis, L. Smoke and ash
Deaver, J. Triangle
DeMarinis, R. An airman's goodbye
DeMarinis, R. Novias
DeMarinis, R. Seize the day
Desplechin, M. Haiku
Desplechin, M. My cousin Gérard
Devlin, A. Naming the names
Diamond, P. Whitey
Díaz, J. The sun, the moon, the stars
Dodd, S. M. What I remember now
Doerr, A. A tangle by the rapid river
Dokey, R. Never trust the weatherman
Dove, R. Damon and Vandalia
Dubus, A. Falling in love
Dybek, S. Blowing shades
Dybek, S. Paper lantern
Eisenberg, D. What it was like, seeing Chris
Engstrom, E. Crosley
Epstein, J. Love and The Guinness book of records
Epstein, J. Uncle Jack
Erdrich, L. Revival Road
Erian, A. The brutal language of love
Estep, M. Horses
Estep, M. Monkeys
Estep, M. The patient
Estep, M. Tools
Estleman, L. D. Evil grows
Fairey, W. W. Hermes
Ferriss, L. Purring
Ferriss, L. Time-share
Ferriss, L. The vortex
Ferriss, L. The woman who said no
Fischerová, D. Far and near
Flanagan, E. Intervention
Ford, R. Abyss
Ford, R. Dominion
Ford, R. Quality time
Ford, R. Reunion
Ford, R. Under the radar
Foster, K. Indelible
Foster, K. Running in place
Foster, K. A story about someone else
Freudenberger, N. Lucky girls
Garrett, C. Circuits
Garro, E. Blame the Tlaxcaltecs
Gates, D. The wonders of the invisible world
Gay, W. Good 'til now
Gilb, D. Brisa
Gilb, D. Hueco
Gilb, D. Maria de Covina
Gilb, D. The pillows
Gilchrist, E. Anna, Part I
Gilchrist, E. Drunk with love
Gilchrist, E. Jade Buddhas, red bridges, fruits of love
Gilchrist, E. A statue of Aphrodite
Gilchrist, E. There's a Garden of Eden
Gilchrist, E. A tree to be desired
Gilliland, G. Kindnesses
Goldner, B. Taxi dancer
Goliger, G. Maedele
Gomes, M. T. The gypsy: a letter to Antonio Patricio
Gordimer, N. The generation gap
Gordimer, N. Mission statement

Gorman, E. En famille
Gorman, E. The end of it all
Gorman, E. Eye of the beholder
Grau, S. A. The wind shifting west
Grodstein, L. How the stars live
Gussoff, C. Love story
Hall, D. From Willow Temple
Hall, D. Lake Paradise
Hall, D. Roast suckling pig
Harrison, W. The rocky hills of Trancas
Harty, R. Don't call it Christmas
Harty, R. September
Haskell, J. Dream of a clean slate
Hayes, D. Anything but a gentleman
Healy, J. F. Hero
Heldrich, P. Deep red
Helms, B. American wives
Helms, B. Oysters
Henley, P. Lessons in joy
Henley, P. Love you can't imagine
Henley, P. Same old big magic
Heron, L. Undue haste
Highsmith, P. In the plaza
Highsmith, P. Variations on a game
Hoffman, A. True confession
Hood, A. Inside Gorbachev's head
Hood, A. New people
Houston, P. The best girlfriend you never had
Hunter, F. Madagascar
Iagnemma, K. Zilkowski's theorem
James, H. A tragedy of error
Jesús, P. d. The letter
Johnson, D. Break any woman down
Johnson, D. Clay's thinking
Johnson, D. Markers
Jones, G. Other places
Kawabata, Y. Her husband didn't
Kawabata, Y. This country, that country
Kelman, J. Constellation
Kelman, J. Just desserts
Kennedy, A. L. Indelible acts
Kennedy, A. L. A little like light
Kennedy, A. L. Not anything to do with love
Kennedy, A. L. Spared
Kennedy, A. L. White house at night
Kerouac, J. The Mexican girl
Kingsbury, Suzanne. Panama
Klíma, I. The assembly line
Klíma, I. Execution of a horse
Klíma, I. Heaven, hell, paradise
Klíma, I. Honeymoon
Klíma, I. Long-distance conversations
Knight, M. Birdland
Knight, M. Sleeping with my dog
Kohler, S. Youth
Kureishi, H. A meeting, at last
Kusel, L. Perdition
Kusel, L. Single white female
Lahiri, J. Sexy
LaValle, V. D. Getting ugly
Lee, A. Dancing with Josefina
Lee, A. In France
Lee, A. Winter barley
Lee, D. The possible husband
Lee, D. The price of eggs in China
Lee, H. E. The serpent's gift [excerpt]
Lee, W. W. The right thing to do
Lessing, D. M. The grandmothers
Lessing, D. M. A love child

LOVE AFFAIRS—*Continued*
Lida, D. Prenuptial agreement
Lieberman, T. Anya's angel
Link, K. Louise's ghost
Livingood, J. Oh, Albany, my love
Locklin, G. The story story
Martin, V. The creator has a master plan
Mason, B. A. Charger
Mason, B. A. Residents and transients
Mason, B. A. With jazz
Mason, N. The bad seed: a guide
Mastretta, A. Aunt Celia
Mastretta, A. Aunt Fernanda
Mastretta, A. Aunt Mariana
Mazor, J. Durango
McDermid, V. The wagon mound
McGarry, J. Body and soul
McManus, J. Reaffirmation
McManus, J. Sleep on stones
McMillan, T. Quilting on the rebound
Mead, H. Wednesday night, Thursday morning
Means, D. Coitus
Meredith, D. Parade's end
Michaels, L. Crossbones
Michaels, L. Honeymoon
Michaels, L. Mildred
Michaels, L. Second honeymoon
Michaels, L. Tell me everything
Miner, C. Rhonda and her children
Moffett, M. Dead rock singer
Moore, L. Beautiful grade
Moore, L. Willing
Moore, L. You're ugly, too
Mueller, D. The night my brother worked the header
Mueller, D. The start of something
Mukherjee, B. Saints
Muñoz, M. The unimportant Lila Parr
Munro, K. E. French press
Murguía, A. Lucky Alley
Nawrocki, S. Camping with strangers
Nawrocki, S. Star seed
Naylor, G. Etta Mae Johnson
Nelson, A. Female trouble
Nesbitt, M. Chimp shrink and backwards
Nesbitt, M. Man in towel with gun
Nissen, T. Grog
Norris, H. The bower-bird
Norris, L. Swimmers
Oates, J. C. Gunlove
Oates, J. C. I was in love
Oates, J. C. Mrs. Halifax and Rickie Swann: a ballad
Oates, J. C. Questions
Oates, J. C. Summer sweat
Offutt, C. Two-eleven all around
Orner, P. Cousin Tuck's
Paine, T. The hotel on Monkey Forest Road
Painter, P. The second night of a one night stand
Palacios, A. A gentleman on the train
Paschal, D. L'Annonciation
Penn, W. S. Fog
Penn, W. S. Star Lake, long ago
Perkins, E. Her new life
Phillips, D. R. At the edge of the new world
Phillips, D. R. Corporal love
Phillips, D. R. What it cost travelers
Pickard, N. Tea for two
Pickard, N. Valentine's night
Pickering, J. The father
Polansky, S. Pantalone
Pomerantz, S. Ghost knife
Porter, J. A. Scrupulous Amédée
Price, R. The fare to the moon
Puga, M. L. Naturally
Pushkin, A. S. In the corner of a small square
Reid, E. No strings attached
Reisman, N. Heart of hearts
Reisman, N. Rubies
Reisman, N. Strays
Richmond, M. Down the shore everything's all right
Rifkin, A. Sonority
Rinehart, S. Guns went off
Rinehart, S. Kick in the head
Rinehart, S. Make me
Robinson, L. The edge of the forest and the edge of the ocean
Robinson, L. Finches
Robison, M. For real
Roche, T. S. Hell on wheels
Rodgers, S. J. How I spent my summer vacation
Rodgers, S. J. Remembering Tom Blake
Rodgers, S. J. The trouble with you is
Rosenbaum, T. Romancing the yohrzeit light
Rosenfeld, S. Five dreams of falling
Rosenfeld, S. Good for the frog
Ross, L. Tasting songs
Roth, J. April: the story of a love affair
Roth, P. The counterlife [excerpt]
Sammān, G. The brain's closed castle
Sanderson, J. Ladies' man
Schlink, B. Sugar peas
Schnitzler, A. Baron von Leisenbohg's destiny
Schnitzler, A. The dead are silent
Schoemperlen, D. Frogs
Schoemperlen, D. In a dark season
Schoemperlen, D. Red plaid shirt
Schoemperlen, D. Stranger than fiction
Schwartz, L. S. Francesca
Shade, E. A final reunion
Shange, N. Every time my lil' world seems blue
Shapiro, G. Shifman in paradise
Shapiro, G. The tutor
Shepard, J. Love and hydrogen
Shepard, S. Coalinga 1/2 way
Silber, J. My shape
Singer, I. B. Brother Beetle
Singer, I. B. Confused
Singer, I. B. Elka and Meier
Singer, I. B. The house friend
Singer, I. B. The manuscript
Singer, I. B. Miracles
Singer, I. B. Morris and Timna
Singer, I. B. A night in the poorhouse
Singer, I. B. A quotation from Klopstock
Singer, I. B. The reencounter
Singer, I. B. Remnants
Singer, I. B. A telephone call on Yom Kippur
Singer, I. B. The trap
Skillings, R. D. Constant concupiscence
Slater, Judy. The glass house
Slavin, J. He came apart
Slavin, J. The woman who cut off her leg at the Maidstone Club
Smiley, J. Long distance
Smolens, J. The Meetinghouse

LOVE AFFAIRS—Continued

Smolens, J. My one and only bomb shelter
Solwitz, S. Ballerina
Sorrentino, G. Decades
Sorrentino, G. Things that have stopped moving
Sosin, D. There are no green butterflies
Spatz, G. Anyone's Venus
Spatz, G. Plenty of pools in Texas
Spatz, G. Walking in my sleep
Spatz, G. Zigzag cabinet
Spencer, D. Caution: men in trees
Spencer, E. The skater
Stolar, D. Home in New Hampshire
Strayed, C. Good
Stuart, J. The affair with Rachel Ware
Swain, H. Sushi
Swan, M. The manual of remote sensing
Swan, M. Spanish grammar
Symons, J. A theme for Hyacinth
Tabucchi, A. A riddle
Tester, W. Bad day
Theroux, P. An African story
Theroux, P. White lies
Thompson, J. Fire dreams
Thon, M. R. First, body
Thurm, M. Mourners
Toomer, J. Blood-burning moon
Touré. The breakup ceremony
Tran, V. The back streets of Hoi An
Troncoso, S. Angie Luna
Updike, J. Augustine's concubine
Updike, J. A constellation of events
Updike, J. Gesturing
Updike, J. His oeuvre
Updike, J. Licks of love in the heart of the Cold War
Updike, J. Love song, for a moog synthesizer
Updike, J. Natural color
Updike, J. New York Girl
Updike, J. The women who got away
Valeri, L. She's anonymous
Valeri, L. Whatever he did, he did enough
Van Winckel, N. Making headway
Viganò, R. Partisan wedding
Wallace, R. Topless in Tucson
Warren, D. Michelangelo
Watanabe McFerrin, L. God and all the angels
Watanabe McFerrin, L. How to fall in love
Watson, B. Last days of the dog-men
Waugh, E. Excursion in reality
Weinreb, M. All I know about it
Weldon, F. Inspector remorse
Weldon, F. New Year's Day
Weldon, F. Once in love in Oslo
Weldon, F. Percentage trust
Weldon, F. What the papers say
Westlake, D. E. The girl of my dreams
Wexler, M. Solomon and his wives
Wexler, M. Waiting to discover electricity
Wharton, E. Souls belated
Whitaker, A. The trespasser
White, M. C. The cardiologist's house
Wieland, L. Cirque du Soleil
Wilson, R. C. The Perseids
Wilson, R., Jr. Dorothy and her friends
Wilson, R., Jr. Parts runner
Winegardner, M. Rain itself
Winegardner, M. Song for a certain girl
Winegardner, M. The untenured lecturer

Winter, E. Contra dance
Winter, E. The planting
Winter, E. Spring
Yates, R. No pain whatsoever
Yates, R. Saying goodbye to Sally
Yolen, J. A ghost of an affair
Yolen, J. Sun/flight
Yoshimoto, B. Asleep
Yoshimoto, B. Love songs
Young, T. Dead
Love among the haystacks. Lawrence, D. H.
Love among the records. Mallon, T.
Love among the ruins. Waugh, E.
Love and happiness. Guerrero, L.
Love and hydrogen. Shepard, J.
Love and modern medicine. Klass, P.
Love and other crimes. Malone, M.
Love and scream. Yasrebi, C.
Love and self-love. Alcott, L. M.
Love and The Guinness book of records. Epstein, J.
Love as a crime. Holka, P.
Love at first byte. Andrews, M. K.
Love at first sight. Archer, J.
Love can make you sick. López, L.
Love, Dad. Heller, J.
Love in a Time of Empire. Bly, C.
Love in the desert. Winter, E.
Love in the lean years. Westlake, D. E.
Love in the Middle Ages. Cherry, K.
Love in the slump. Waugh, E.
Love in the tall grass. Keegan, C.
Love in the time of Molyneux. Dyson, J.
Love in vain. Tozzi, F.
Love is a stone. Brown, S.
Love Lessons Mondays, 9 A.M. Vapnyar, L.
Love like a bullet. Haynes, M.
Love lottery. Tinsley, M. B.
Love, lust, life. James, S.
Love must not be forgotten. Zhang Jie
Love notes. Collins, K.
The **love** of a good man. Divakaruni, C. B.
The **love** of my life. Boyle, T. C.
Love on the Bon-Dieu. Chopin, K.
Love, rescue, care, dream, sweep. Honig, L.
Love scenes. Saroyan, A.
Love, sin and forgiveness at the Village Café. Passaro, V.
Love Snares. Erdrich, L.
Love song (Lida II). Čapek, K.
Love songs. Yoshimoto, B.
Love songs of fruit flies. Bumas, E. S.
Love spots. Weihe, E.
LOVE STORIES
See also Courtship; Love affairs; Lovers
Adams, A. Verlie I say unto you
Agee, J. Cleveland Pinkney
Agee, J. The luck of Junior Strong
Alarcón, P. A. d. Captain Poison
Alas, L. Doña Berta
Alcott, L. M. Agatha's confession
Alcott, L. M. Bertha
Alcott, L. M. Love and self-love
Alcott, L. M. Mark Field's mistake
Alcott, L. M. Mark Field's success
Alcott, L. M. The masked marriage
Alcott, L. M. The monk's island: a legend of the Rhine
Alcott, L. M. Ruth's secret

LOVE STORIES—*Continued*

Aldrich, B. S. Romance in G minor
Aldrich, B. S. The victory of Connie Lee
Alexie, S. Do you know where I am?
Allende, I. An act of vengeance
Anderson, P. The Saturn game
Ansa, T. M. Love
Appelfeld, A. Bertha
Archer, J. Love at first sight
Auchincloss, L. Collaboration
Baca, J. S. Bull's blood
Balza, J. The stroke of midnight
Banks, R. Success story
Barthelme, F. Reset
Bass, R. Pagans
Bausch, R. Par
Bausch, R. Wise men at their end
Bergelson, D. Spring
Berkman, P. R. Tat
Berriault, G. The infinite passion of expectation
Billman, J. Honeyville
Blair, J. Moving man
Blair, J. Swimming the cave
Blatnik, A. Actually
Borges, J. L. Ulrikke
Boswell, M. Between things
Boyle, T. C. After the plague
Boyle, T. C. The underground gardens
Bradbury, R. Hopscotch
Bradbury, R. The Laurel and Hardy love affair
Bradbury, R. Well, what do you have to say for yourself?
Brady, C. And the shin bone's connected to the knee bone
Brandt, W. Rat
Brenner, W. The Cantankerous Judge
Brennert, A. Her pilgrim soul
Brown, C. Postman
Brown, J. She
Bunin, I. A. Caucasus
Bunin, I. A. Cold fall
Bunin, I. A. In Paris
Bunin, I. A. On one familiar street
Bunin, I. A. Rusya
Bunin, I. A. Sunstroke
Bunin, I. A. Zoyka and Valeriya
Burford, M. Flying lessons
Burford, M. Pesce volante
Burton, M. Green River virgins
Butler, R. O. The ironworkers' hayride
Cain, J. M. Cigarette girl
Canty, K. Carolina beach
Carey, P. The chance
Carleton, M. R. Conversations with a moose
Carlson, R. At the Jim Bridger
Carlson, R. Nightcap
Carter, E. Train line
Casal, L. A love story according to Cyrano Prufrock
Chekhov, A. P. About love
Chekhov, A. P. Ariadne
Chekhov, A. P. A joke
Chekhov, A. P. The lady with the dog
Chekhov, A. P. Notes from the journal of a quick-tempered man
Chekhov, A. P. Verotchka
Cheng, C.-W. The river suite
Cherry, K. Love in the Middle Ages
Cherryh, C. J. Sea change

Chesnutt, C. W. Her Virginia Mammy
Chesnutt, C. W. How he met her
Chesnutt, C. W. The shadow of my past
Chopin, K. At Chênière Caminada
Chopin, K. At the 'Cadian ball
Chopin, K. Aunt Lympy's interference
Chopin, K. The awakening
Chopin, K. La belle Zorade
Chopin, K. La Belle Zoraïde
Chopin, K. The kiss
Chopin, K. The locket
Chopin, K. Love on the Bon-Dieu
Chopin, K. Miss Witherwell's mistake
Chopin, K. A non-account Creole
Chopin, K. Two summers and two souls
Clyde, M. Pruitt love
Cobb, W. J. The white tatto
Coberly, L. M. Early transparent
Coberly, L. M. Just a love story
Coberly, L. M. Night-blooming cereus
Coberly, L. M. Will's Valentine
Coleman, J. C. The Perseid meteors
Connor, J. The anecdote of the island
Cooper, J. C. A filet of soul
Cooper, J. C. The lost and the found
Coulter, K. Normalcy
Dann, J. Going under
Davies, P. H. Think of England
Davies, R. The song of songs
Davis, A. Chase
Davis, A. Fairy tale
Davis, A. Sticks and stones
Davis, C. Labors of the heart
Davis, L. The kind of time you end up with
Day, C. The King and His Court
De Lint, C. Sweet forget-me-not
DeLancey, K. Coal miner's holiday
DeLancey, K. Fast coming and then going
DeLancey, K. Great ones
DeLancey, K. The mystery of George Jones
DeLancey, K. What the hell
DeMarco, T. Lieutenant America and Miss Apple Pie
DeMarinis, R. Romance: a prose villanelle
Dépestre, R. Rosena on the mountain
Desnoyers, A. Bleed blue in Indonesia
Díaz, J. The brief wondrous life of Oscar Wao
Dickey, E. J. Café Piel
Doble, J. Entries from Skipper Bitwell's journal
Dodd, S. M. Ethiopia
Doerr, A. For a long time this was Griselda's story
Dokey, R. The shopper
Dropkin, Celia. Bella fell in love
Dubus, A. An afternoon with the old man
Dufresne, J. Johnny too bad
Duong, T. H. Reflections of spring
Dybek, S. Je reviens
Dybek, S. Pet milk
Dyson, J. The cash-point oracle
Eakin, W. Plain female seeks nice guy
Earle, S. A well-tempered heart
Eggers, P. Proof
Elkins, K. What is visible
Estep, M. Circus
Fitzgerald, F. S. His russet witch
Fitzgerald, F. S. The offshore pirate
Fitzgerald, F. S. The popular girl
Fitzgerald, F. S. Winter dreams

LOVE STORIES—*Continued*

Fitzgerald, F. S. The World's Fair
Foster, K. Crush
Frym, G. Love
Frym, G. The oldest trick in the book
Gabriel, D. Making peace with the Muslims
Galloway, J. Proposal
Gartner, Z. How to survive in the bush
Gibson, W. The girl at Thorp's
Gifford, B. The big love of Cherry Lane
Gilb, D. Snow
Gilchrist, E. Light can be both wave and particle
Gilchrist, E. The Starlight Express
Giles, J. H. The gift
Gilliland, G. Permanence
Gilman, C. P. The cottagette
Girardi, R. The primordial face
Goldstein, N. The worker rests under the hero trees
Goldstein, R. The courtship
Gomes, M. T. Cordelia
Gomes, M. T. Dead woman's grove
Gomes, M. T. Deus ex machina
Gomes, M. T. Margareta
Gomes, M. T. Question mark
Gonsalves, G. Tamarind stew
Gonzalez, R. Becky
Goran, L. The chorus girl
Goran, L. Say something to Miss Kathleen Lacey
Gorman, E. A girl like you
Gorman, E. That day at Eagle's Point
Gorriti, J. M. The dead man's fiancée
Grau, S. A. The lovely April
Grau, S. A. Three
Händler, E.-W. By the Sengsen Mountains, by the Dead Mountains
Hardy, M. The uncharted heart
Hayes, D. Motormouth
Hayes, D. Shakedown
Henley, P. As luck would have it
Henry, O. The higher pragmatism
Henry, W. River of decision
Herling, G. A madrigal of mourning
Highsmith, P. A girl like Phyl
Høeg, P. Portrait of the avant-garde
Hunter, F. Elizabeth who disappeared
Iagnemma, K. On the nature of human romantic interaction
Iwaszkiewicz, J. A new love
Jacobs, M. Looking for Lourdes
Jaime-Becerra, M. Georgie and Wanda
Jaime-Becerra, M. Media vuelta
Jaime-Becerra, M. Riding with Lencho
James, H. De Grey: a romance
James, H. Gabrielle de Bergerac
James, H. My friend Bingham
James, H. Poor Richard
James, H. Travelling companions
Jones, T. My heroic mythic journey
Jones, T. You cheated, you lied
Kelly, J. P. Chemistry
Kittredge, W. Do you hear your mother talking?
Klíma, I. Lingula
Klíma, I. Uranus in the house of death
Klíma, I. The white house
Knight, D. F. Dio
Knight, M. Birdland

Knight, M. Sundays
Koon, D. The bone divers
Krouse, E. Drugs and you
Kureishi, H. Girl
Kurlansky, M. The white man in the tree
Kusel, L. Bars
Kusel, L. Craps
Kushner, E. The unicorn masque
L'Amour, L. The cross and the candle
Lao She. Hot dumplings
Lawrence, D. H. Love among the haystacks
Lawrence, D. H. The thorn in the flesh
Lee, D. Widowers
Link, K. Water off a black dog's back
Little, B. The yellow sweater
Lord, C. The art of losing
Major, M. Kenya and Amir
Malone, M. Fast love
Martin, P. P. Amor encantado—Enchanted love
Martin, P. P. Amor eterno—Eternal love
Martin, P. P. Amor frustrado—Frustrated love
Martin, P. P. Amor perdido—Lost love
Mason, B. A. Night flight
Mastretta, A. Aunt Clemencia
Mastretta, A. Aunt Daniela
Mastretta, A. Aunt Fátima
Mastretta, A. Aunt Leonor
Mastretta, A. Aunt Mercedes
Mastretta, A. Aunt Paulina
Mazor, J. Skylark
McInerny, R. M. Mutiny of the bounty hunter
McKenna, R. Hunter, come home
McKinney-Whetstone, D. Moon penitent
McKinnon, K. Kindred
Mencken, S. H. Joe Moore and Callie Blasingame
Mencken, S. H. Twilight of chivalry
Metzgar, L. Cat and mouse
Mo Yan. Love story
Murakami, H. Honey Pie
Murguía, A. This war called love
Nissen, T. Accidental love
Nissen, T. Mailing incorrectly
Nissen, T. The mushroom girl
Nissen, T. The rather unlikely courtship of Edwin Anderson and Roz Rosenzweig
Olsen, S. S. Free writing
O'Neill, S. Three minor love stories
Orner, P. At the Motel Rainbow
Packer, Z. Every tongue shall confess
Penn, W. S. Talking turkey, not goose
Pushkin, A. S. The blizzard
Pushkin, A. S. A novel in letters
Pushkin, A. S. The squire's daughter
Régio, J. The flame-coloured dress
Régio, J. A sad smile
Régio, J. The story of Rosa Brava
Reiner, C. Lance and Gwendolyn
Richmond, M. The last bad thing
Richter, J. The dance of the Apsara
Richter, S. The cavemen in the hedges
Rinehart, S. Outstanding in my field
Robinson, L. Cuxabexis, Cuxabexis
Robinson, L. Fighting at night
Robinson, P. April in Paris
Roorbach, B. Big bend
Rossi, A. Orion's glow
Roth, J. Stationmaster Fallmerayer
Ruy Sánchez, A. Voices of the water

LOVE STORIES—*Continued*

Sandor, M. Annunciation

Sanford, A. Bear the dead away

Schlink, B. The circumcision

Schoemperlen, D. Mastering effective English (A linguistic fable)

Scoville, S. The gift of a car

Silber, J. The high road

Silber, J. The same ground

Singer, I. B. Burial at sea

Singer, I. B. Dazzled

Singer, I. B. Hershele and Hanele' or, The power of a dream

Singer, I. B. The last gaze

Singer, I. B. Neighbors

Singer, I. B. Pity

Singer, I. B. Property

Singer, I. B. Sam Palka and David Vishkover

Singer, I. B. Strong as death is love

Škvorecký, J. Jezebel from Forest Hill (A love story)

Škvorecký, J. A magic mountain and a willowy wench

Smith, A. Erosive

Smith, A. May

Sorrentino, G. The moon in its flight

Spencer, E. The cousins

Spencer, E. The eclipse

Spencer, E. The light in the piazza

Steinbeck, T. Sing Fat and the Imperial Duchess of Woo

Stuart, J. Lost land of youth

Swan, M. Hour of lead

Tallent, E. Eight hundred pages

Thien, M. Dispatch

Thompson, J. All shall love me and despair

Tinti, H. How to revitalize the snake in your life

Trevanian. The engine of fate

Troncoso, S. Remembering possibilities

Updike, J. Four sides of one story

Updike, J. The morning

Van Winckel, N. The lap of luxury

Vasseur, T. J. The angels

Vasseur, T. J. The woman who sugared strawberries

Vaswani, N. Domestication of an imaginary goat

Vivante, A. The cove

Vivante, A. Doves

Vivante, A. The Italian class

Vivante, A. The park

Vivante, A. To mock the years

Vonnegut, K. Find me a dream

Vonnegut, K. A night for love

Vonnegut, K. Runaways

Vukcevich, R. Jumping

Vukcevich, R. Meet me in the moon room

Wallington, A. Day of the dead

Wang Anyi. Life in a small courtyard

Watanabe McFerrin, L. A little variety

Waugh, E. Lucy Simmonds

Weinreb, M. The fox hunters

Weinreb, M. Girl boy etc.

Weinreb, M. L.A., baby

Weinreb, M. Radio radio

Weinreb, M. What I would tell her

Westmoreland, T. A. They have numbered all my bones

Wharton, E. Confession

Wharton, E. The introducers

Wharton, E. The lamp of Psyche

Wharton, E. The letters

Wharton, E. The long run

Wharton, E. The muse's tragedy

Wharton, E. The pot-boiler

Wharton, E. The pretext

Wharton, E. The touchstone

Wicomb, Z. You can't get lost in Cape Town

Williams, M. Truth and goodness

Wilson, R., Jr. Remembered names

Winter, E. Fox Hill

Winter, E. Pretty please

Winterson, J. O'Brien's first Christmas

Woolson, C. F. Felipa

Yañez, R. Desert Vista

Zabytko, I. Pani Ryhotska in love

Zabytko, I. The prodigal son enters heaven

Zhang Jie. Love must not be forgotten

Zinik, Z. The notification

Zweig, S. Letter from an unknown woman

Love story. Gussoff, C.

Love story. Mo Yan

A **love** story according to Cyrano Prufrock. Casal, L.

Love that Universe. Clarke, A. C.

Love thy neighbor. Shankman, S.

A **love** transaction. Chapman, M.

Love you can't imagine. Henley, P.

Lovecraft, H. P. (Howard Phillips)

The call of cthulhu

    The 13 best horror stories of all time; edited by Leslie Pockell

The shadow over Innsmouth

    The American fantasy tradition; edited by Brian M. Thomsen

Under the pyramids

    Into the mummy's tomb; edited by John Richard Stephens

The unnamable

    The Ultimate Halloween; edited by Marvin Kaye

Witches' Hollow

    Witches' brew; edited by Yvonne Jocks

LOVECRAFT, H. P. (HOWARD PHILLIPS), 1890-1937

    Parodies, imitations, etc.

Altman, S.-E. A case of royal blood

Bear, E. Tiger! tiger!

Brite, P. Z. and Ferguson, D. The curious case of Miss Violet Stone

Clark, S. Nightmare in wax

Finch, P. The mystery of the hanged man's puzzle

Gaiman, N. A study in emerald

Hambly, B. The adventure of the antiquarian's niece

Kiernan, C. R. The drowned geologist

Lebbon, T. The horror of the many faces

Lowder, J. The weeping masks

Lupoff, R. A. The adventure of the Voorish Sign

Lupoff, R. A. The devil's hop yard

Lupoff, R. A. Documents in the case of Elizabeth Akeley

MacIntyre, F. G. The adventure of Exham Priory

Pelan, J. The mystery of the worm

Perry, S. The case of the wavy black dagger

LOVECRAFT, H. P. (HOWARD PHILLIPS), 1890-1937—Parodies, imitations, etc.—*Continued*
Reaves, M. The adventure of the Arab's manuscript
Stableford, B. M. Art in the blood
Vourlis, J. P. A case of insomnia
Wilson, D. N. and Macomber, P. L. Death did not become him
Lovecraft, Howard Phillips *See* Lovecraft, H. P. (Howard Phillips), 1890-1937
Lovegrove, James
Out of the blue, into the red
Mars probes; edited by Peter Crowther
Lovelace, Earl
Victory and the blight
The Oxford book of Caribbean short stories; edited by Stewart Brown and John Wickham
A **loveless** match. Greaney, Á.
The **lovely** April. Grau, S. A.
A **lovely** day for tennis. Ritchie, E.
A **lovely** day in the A Shau Valley. Barnes, H. L.
"Lovely-flower". Caballero, F.
Loveman's comeback. Campbell, R.
Lover. Oates, J. C.
Lover when you're near me. Matheson, R.
LOVERS
Adams, A. The haunted beach
Addonizio, K. Scores
Agee, J. You belong to me
Allende, I. Wicked girl
Banks, R. The moor
Beller, T. Caller I.D.
Bianchini, A. Years later
Blatnik, A. Scratches on the back
Bloom, A. The gates are closing
Boof, Kola. The one you meet everywhere
Boylan, C. The complete angler
Boylan, C. A reproduction
Boyle, T. C. The love of my life
Boyle, T. C. She wasn't soft
Brkic, C. A. Surveillance
Budnitz, J. Burned
Budnitz, J. Park bench
Canty, K. Girlfriend hit by bus
Canty, K. Honeymoon
Capote, T. Mojave
Carson, J. Flying apart
Carter, E. All the men are called McCabe
Clark, G. M. The Leopard Gang
Cobb, W. J. The wishes
Connor, J. And I, Isolde
Connor, J. October
Connor, J. Women's problems
Cooper, R. R. Johnny Hamburger
Davies, Tristan. Crazy Yvonne
Davies, Tristan. In the woodlands
Davis, L. Celestial bodies
Dell'Oro, E. The red bathrobe
Desplechin, M. An important question
Desplechin, M. Something's wrong
Di Blasi, D. Our perversions
Di Blasi, D. Pavlov's smile
Di Blasi, D. Where all things converge
Dunmore, H. Living out
Dybek, S. Lunch at the Loyola Arms
Evenson, B. Calling the hour
Fernandez, P. A. The charm
Foster, K. Like incest

Furman, L. Drinking with the cook
Gay, W. My hand is just fine where it is
Gifford, B. Only you
Gonzalez, R. Canyon de Kayenta
Greenberg, P. The subjunctive mood
Greer, A. S. Blame it on my youth
Gussoff, C. The deepest dive
Haake, K. Arrow math
Hall, D. The first woman
Helms, B. Once
Henley, P. Cargo
Hood, A. Total cave darkness
Howard, M. Children with matches
Howe, M. J. Killing the sixties
Irsfeld, J. H. The horse fountain
Johnston, B. A. Buy for me the rain
Jones, G. The astronomer tells of her love
Kaplan, H. Claude comes and goes
Kavan, A. The zebra-struck
Kawabata, Y. First snow on Fuji
Kawabata, Y. Yumiura
Keegan, C. Love in the tall grass
Kelman, J. The wey it can turn
Kennedy, A. L. How to find your way in woods
Kincaid, J. The autobiography of my mother [excerpt]
Kohler, S. Water Baby
Kureishi, H. Midnight all day
Kureishi, H. Strangers when we meet
Kureishi, H. Sucking stones
Kureishi, H. That was then
Link, K. Flying lessons
Martin, V. Contraction
Mastretta, A. Aunt Teresa
Mathews, H. Their words, for you
Mattison, A. In case we're separated
Mazelis, J. Running away with the hairdresser
Mazelis, J. Tongue
McGarry, J. Landing
McNally, J. The first of your last chances
Merriman, C. Painting Juliet
Moody, R. The carnival tradition
Moody, R. Ineluctable modality of the vaginal
Murguía, A. El último round
Naranjo, C. Symbiotic encounter
Nissen, T. How beautifully resilient the human being
Oates, J. C. Fire
Packer, G. The water-girl
Painter, P. Dangerous waters
Parrish, T. Exterminator
Patterson, K. Interposition
Penn, W. S. Grab hold
Peterson, P. W. Alfie and Grace
Petrignani, S. Body
Pickard, N. Sex and violence
Porter, J. A. Touch wood
Posadas, Carmen. The Nubian lover
Potvin, E. A. After hours, after years
Prose, F. Everything is about animals
Prose, F. Three pigs in five days [excerpt]
Proulx, A. A lonely coast
Resnick, R. Day 'n nite
Restrepo, L. The scent of invisible roses
Richmond, M. The girl in the fall-away dress
Richmond, M. Satellite
Rifkin, A. Signal Hill
Ritchie, E. The view from seven
Rodgers, S. J. Women of will

LOVERS—*Continued*
Roeske, P. A history of swimming
Roeske, P. Open arms
Schnitzler, A. A farewell
Schoemperlen, D. Nothing happens
Scoville, S. Waiting for Zilly Finkbine
Shade, E. Stability
Shaw, D. Diving with the devil
Shepard, J. Already gone
Shrayer-Petrov, D. Jonah and Sarah
Silber, J. Ashes of love
Simonds, M. Song of the Japanese white-eye
Singer, I. B. Two
Singleton, G. I could've told you if you hadn't asked
Skillings, R. D. Here I am
Sojourner, M. Delicate
Sojourner, M. Luzianne
Sorrentino, G. Facts and their manifestations
Sorrentino, G. Land of cotton
Sorrentino, G. Times without number
Spencer, D. It's a lot scarier if you take Jesus out
Stern, D. Messenger
Stern, D. Time will tell
Strauss, A. Shrinking away
Sucher, C. P. The quality of being a Ruby
Taylor, T. L. Francisco's watch
Thomas, D. The getaway
Thomas, D. My pigeon pair
Thompson, J. The little heart
Tillman, L. Living with contradictions
Treat, J. His sweater
Treat, J. Not a chance
Updike, J. Bech noir
Walker, A. Charms
Walker, A. Conscious birth
Walker, A. Cuddling
Walker, A. This is how it happened
Waugh, E. Antony, who sought things that were lost
Wieland, L. Laramie
Winter, E. Dragon box
Lovers. Krawiec, R.
The **lovers**. Tozzi, F.
Lovers Anonymous. Vonnegut, K.
Love's mysteries. Sullivan, W.
Love's Triangle Lost. Shteyngart, G.
Lovesey, Peter
Away with the fairies
  Malice domestic 10; an anthology of original traditional mystery stories
Because it was there
  Crème de la crime; edited by Janet Hutchings
The crime of Miss Oyster Brown
  Master's choice [v1]; mystery stories by today's top writers and the masters who inspired them; edited by Lawrence Block
The man who jumped for England
  Edwards, M. Mysterious pleasures; a celebration of the Crime Writers' Association's 50th anniversary; edited by Martin Edwards
The perfectionist
  The best British mysteries; edited by Maxim Jakubowski
  The World's finest mystery and crime stories, second annual collection; edited by Ed Gorman

Star struck
  The World's finest mystery and crime stories, third annual collection; edited by Ed Gorman and Martin H. Greenberg
The usual table
  The Mysterious Press anniversary anthology; celebrating 25 years; by the editors of Mysterious Press
(jt. auth) See Marston, Edward and Lovesey, Peter
Lovesey, Phil
Blitzed
  The World's finest mystery and crime stories, first annual collection; edited by Ed Gorman
Under the knife
  Crème de la crime; edited by Janet Hutchings
The **lovesick** crow and other fables. Wang Meng
Lovestory. Kelly, J. P.
Lovett, Sarah
Buried treasure
  Irreconcilable differences; Lia Matera, editor
Loving. Bingham, S.
Lovisi, Gary
Mycroft's great game
  My Sherlock Holmes; untold stories of the great detective; edited by Michael Kurland
Service
  Flesh and blood: guilty as sin; erotic tales of crime and passion; edited by Max Allan Collins and Jeff Gelb
Low, close to the floor. Hendel, Y.
Low-floating balloons. Clayton, M. W.
Low-impact aerobics. Allegra, D.
Low Sunday, 1950. Trevor, W.
LOW TEMPERATURES
Cherryh, C. J. Ice
Ross, J. The immortals
Low Tide. Lochte, D.
Lowder, James
The weeping masks
  Shadows over Baker Street; edited by Michael Reaves and John Pelan
Lowenthal, Michael
Infinity of angles
  Neurotica: Jewish writers on sex; edited by Melvin Jules Bukiet
Into a mirror
  Circa 2000; gay fiction at the millennium; edited by Robert Drake & Terry Wolverton
Ordinary pain
  Lost tribe; jewish fiction from the edge
You are here
  The Southern Review (Baton Rouge, La.) v38 no1 p149-75 Wint 2002
Lower Crossing. Hegi, U.
LOWER EAST SIDE (NEW YORK, N.Y.) *See* New York (N.Y.)—Lower East Side
LOWRY, DAN
About
Lansdale, J. R. and Lowry, D. Pilots
(jt. auth) See Lansdale, Joe R. and Lowry, Dan
LSD (DRUG)
Bottoms, G. LSD in Raleigh
Campbell, R. Through the walls
Cunningham, M. White angel
Huffman, B., Jr. Yielding to science
Jones, T. I love you, Sophie Western
Paine, T. The spoon children

LSD (DRUG)—*Continued*
  Tenn, W. The lemon-green spaghetti-loud dyna-
    mite-dribble day
LSD in Raleigh. Bottoms, G.
Lubing: sex and symbolism beneath an '88 Buick.
  Hart, R.
Lubitch Domecq, Alcina
  Josué Chili-Mazel meets himself
    The Literary Review (Madison, N.J.) v43 no1
    p19-20 Fall 1999
  La Llorona
    The Literary Review (Madison, N.J.) v43 no1
    p17-18 Fall 1999
LUBLIN (POLAND) *See* Poland—Lublin
Lucas, Jason
  Old Croc
    Fishing's best short stories; edited by Paul D.
    Staudohar
Lucas Beauchamp. Faulkner, W.
Lucho. Sánchez, R.
Lucifer's alligator. Whitty, J.
Lucifer's shank. Melville, P.
Lucinda. Swan, G.
Luck. Anderson, D.
Luck. Kohler, S.
The **luck** of Junior Strong. Agee, J.
Luck of the dead. Nevins, F. M., Jr.
Luck of the draw. Knowles, T. W.
Lucky. Slezak, E.
Lucky. Strand, G.
Lucky devil. Pickard, N.
Lucky dog. Lochte, D.
Lucky eighteen. Papernick, J.
Lucky girls. Freudenberger, N.
The **lucky** strike. Robinson, K. S.
Luckybitch. Fielding, H.
Lucy. Doyle, B.
Lucy Simmonds. Waugh, E.
Luddy, Karon G.
  Ticket to Ride
    South Carolina Review v36 no1 p115-21 Fall
    2003
Ludington, Max
  Thaw
    On the rocks; the KGB Bar fiction anthology;
    edited by Rebecca Donner ; foreword by
    Denis Woychuk
Ludmerer, Nancy
  The ham theory
    The Kenyon Review ns24 no2 p24-40 Spr
    2002
Ludwig, Otto
  The dead man of St. Anne's Chapel
    Early German and Austrian detective fiction;
    an anthology; translated and edited by
    Mary W. Tannert and Henry Kratz
Lugones, Leopoldo
  The bloat-toad
    Lugones, L. Strange forces; translated by Gil-
    bert Alter-Gilbert
  The firestorm
    Lugones, L. Strange forces; translated by Gil-
    bert Alter-Gilbert
  The horses of Abdera
    Lugones, L. Strange forces; translated by Gil-
    bert Alter-Gilbert
  An inexplicable phenomenon
    Lugones, L. Strange forces; translated by Gil-
    bert Alter-Gilbert

  Metamusic
    Lugones, L. Strange forces; translated by Gil-
    bert Alter-Gilbert
  The miracle of Saint Wilfred
    Lugones, L. Strange forces; translated by Gil-
    bert Alter-Gilbert
  The Omega Force
    Lugones, L. Strange forces; translated by Gil-
    bert Alter-Gilbert
  Origins of the flood
    Lugones, L. Strange forces; translated by Gil-
    bert Alter-Gilbert
  The pillar of salt
    Lugones, L. Strange forces; translated by Gil-
    bert Alter-Gilbert
  Psychon
    Lugones, L. Strange forces; translated by Gil-
    bert Alter-Gilbert
  Viola acherontia
    Lugones, L. Strange forces; translated by Gil-
    bert Alter-Gilbert
  Yzur
    Lugones, L. Strange forces; translated by Gil-
    bert Alter-Gilbert
Luisa. Lee, C.
Lull. Link, K.
Lullaby. Silko, L.
Lulu. Tessier, T.
LUMBER INDUSTRY
    See also Loggers
  Nfah-Abbenyi, J. M. The forest will claim you
    too
LUMBERJACKS *See* Loggers
LUMBERMEN *See* Loggers
La **Lumiére.** Harris, M.
Luminous dial. Carter, E.
Lumley, Brian
  Aunt Hester
    Lumley, B. The whisperer and other voices
  Beneath the moors
    Lumley, B. Beneath the moors and darker
    places
  Big "C"
    Lumley, B. Beneath the moors and darker
    places
  Dagon's bell
    Lumley, B. Beneath the moors and darker
    places
  David's worm
    Lumley, B. Beneath the moors and darker
    places
  Dead Eddy
    Lumley, B. Harry Keogh; necroscope and oth-
    er weird heroes!
  Dinosaur dreams
    Lumley, B. Harry Keogh; necroscope and oth-
    er weird heroes!
  The disapproval of Jeremy Cleave
    Lumley, B. The whisperer and other voices
  The fairground horror
    Lumley, B. Beneath the moors and darker
    places
  Inception
    Lumley, B. Harry Keogh; necroscope and oth-
    er weird heroes!
  Lord of the worms
    Lumley, B. Harry Keogh; necroscope and oth-
    er weird heroes!

Lumley, Brian—*Continued*
The luststone
Lumley, B. The whisperer and other voices
Name and number
Lumley, B. Harry Keogh; necroscope and other weird heroes!
No sharks in the Med
Lumley, B. The whisperer and other voices
Resurrection
Lumley, B. Harry Keogh; necroscope and other weird heroes!
The return of the Deep Ones
Lumley, B. The whisperer and other voices
Rising with Surtsey
Lumley, B. Beneath the moors and darker places
The second wish
Lumley, B. Beneath the moors and darker places
Snarker's son
Lumley, B. The whisperer and other voices
The statement of Henry Worthy
Lumley, B. The whisperer and other voices
The stealer of dreams
Lumley, B. Harry Keogh; necroscope and other weird heroes!
The sun, the sea, and the silent scream
Lumley, B. Beneath the moors and darker places
A thing about cars!
Lumley, B. Beneath the moors and darker places
Vanessa's voice
Lumley, B. The whisperer and other voices
The weird wines of Naxas Niss
Lumley, B. Harry Keogh; necroscope and other weird heroes!
The whisperer
Lumley, B. The whisperer and other voices
Lumley, Dorothy *See* Davidson, Jean
Lunachick. Cherry, K.
The **Lunatics'** Eclipse. Jarrar, R.
Lunch, Lydia
The devil's racetrack: Ray trailer
Carved in rock; short stories by musicians; edited by Greg Kihn
Lunch at the best restaurant in the world. Gilchrist, E.
Lunch at the Blacksmith. Nixon, C.
Lunch at the Piccadilly. Edgerton, C.
Lunch counter. Callaghan, M.
Lunch hour. Updike, J.
Lunch time. Ritchie, E.
Lunch with Gottlieb. Stern, D.
Lunch with Mother. Kohler, S.
Lunch with my daughter. Biguenet, J.
Lunchbox. Waldrop, H.
LUNCHEONS
Adams, A. Waiting for Stella
Brennan, M. The gentleman in the pink-and-white striped shirt
Lunching at the Ritzmore. Himes, C.
Lundoff, Catherine
Vadija
Such a pretty face; edited by Lee Martindale
Lundquist, Richard
Dust devils
Lundquist, R. What we come in for; stories

A free sinner
Lundquist, R. What we come in for; stories
The greener pasture
Lundquist, R. What we come in for; stories
Grounded
Lundquist, R. What we come in for; stories
Into this house
Lundquist, R. What we come in for; stories
The motions of love
Lundquist, R. What we come in for; stories
Now it looks respectable
Lundquist, R. What we come in for; stories
Silence and slow time
Lundquist, R. What we come in for; stories
A stone house of many rooms
Lundquist, R. What we come in for; stories
The visitation
Lundquist, R. What we come in for; stories
When the blood came faster than the water
Lundquist, R. What we come in for; stories
Luntta, Karl
A virgin twice
Living on the edge; fiction by Peace Corps writers; edited by John Coyne
Lupoff, Richard A.
31.12.99
Lupoff, R. A. Claremont tales II
The adventure of the Voorish Sign
Shadows over Baker Street; edited by Michael Reaves and John Pelan
The adventures of Mr. Tindle
Lupoff, R. A. Claremont tales
The adventures of the boulevard assassin
Lupoff, R. A. Claremont tales II
At Vega's taqueria
Lupoff, R. A. Claremont tales
Black mist
Lupoff, R. A. Claremont tales
The child's story
Lupoff, R. A. Claremont tales
The devil's hop yard
Lupoff, R. A. Claremont tales II
Discovery of the Ghooric Zone
Lupoff, R. A. Claremont tales
Documents in the case of Elizabeth Akeley
Lupoff, R. A. Claremont tales
A freeway for Draculas
Lupoff, R. A. Claremont tales II
Green ice
Lupoff, R. A. Claremont tales II
The Heyworth Fragment
Lupoff, R. A. Claremont tales II
I don't tell lies
Lupoff, R. A. Claremont tales
The incident of the impecunious chevalier
My Sherlock Holmes; untold stories of the great detective; edited by Michael Kurland
Jubilee
Lupoff, R. A. Claremont tales II
Lux was dead right
Lupoff, R. A. Claremont tales
The monster and Mr. Greene
Lupoff, R. A. Claremont tales
Mr. Greene and the monster
Lupoff, R. A. Claremont tales
News from New Providence
Lupoff, R. A. Claremont tales II
Royal whodunnits; edited by Mike Ashley

Lupoff, Richard A.—*Continued*
  Old folks at home
    Lupoff, R. A. Claremont tales II
  The second drug
    Lupoff, R. A. Claremont tales
  Simeon Dimsby's workshop
    The Mammoth book of best horror 13; edited
      by Stephen Jones
  Stream of consciousness
    Lupoff, R. A. Claremont tales II
  The Tootsie Roll factor
    Lupoff, R. A. Claremont tales
  The turret
    Lupoff, R. A. Claremont tales II
  Whatever happened to Nick Neptune?
    Lupoff, R. A. Claremont tales II
  You don't know me, Charlie
    Lupoff, R. A. Claremont tales II
LUPUS
  Van Winckel, N. The expectation of abundance
Lurie, Alison
  The highboy
    Nightshade: 20th century ghost stories; edited
      by Robert Phillips
  The pool people
    100% pure Florida fiction; an anthology; ed-
      ited by Susan Hubbard and Robley Wilson
Lush. Morrow, B.
Lust for love. Tillman, L.
Lustbader, Eric Van
  An exaltation of termagants
    999: new stories of horror and suspense; ed-
      ited by Al Sarrantonio
  Slow burn
    Murder and obsession; edited by Otto Penzler
Lustig, Arnošt
  From Tanga, a girl from Hamburg
    The Kenyon Review ns24 no2 p65-75 Spr
      2002
  Kůstka
    The Kenyon Review ns21 no2 p90-123 Spr
      1999
  The lemon
    When night fell; an anthology of Holocaust
      short stories; edited by Linda Schermer Ra-
      phael and Marc Lee Raphael
  Stephen and Anne
    When night fell; an anthology of Holocaust
      short stories; edited by Linda Schermer Ra-
      phael and Marc Lee Raphael
The **luststone**. Lumley, B.
Luther, John
  Inner Chesapeake
    Doubletake v8 no3 p88-91 Summ 2002
Lutz, John
  Before you leap
    Lutz, J. The Nudger dilemmas; a short story
      collection
  Flotsam and jetsam
    Lutz, J. The Nudger dilemmas; a short story
      collection
  A handgun for protection
    Speaking of lust; stories of forbidden desire;
      edited by Lawrence Block
  High stakes
    Master's choice [v1]; mystery stories by to-
      day's top writers and the masters who in-
      spired them; edited by Lawrence Block

  Hobson's choice
    The Blue and the gray undercover; edited by
      Ed Gorman
  The litigants
    Lutz, J. The Nudger dilemmas; a short story
      collection
  The man in the morgue
    Lutz, J. The Nudger dilemmas; a short story
      collection
  Nighthawks
    Flesh and blood: guilty as sin; erotic tales of
      crime and passion; edited by Max Allan
      Collins and Jeff Gelb
  Only one way to land
    Lutz, J. The Nudger dilemmas; a short story
      collection
  El Palacio
    A Hot and sultry night for crime; edited by
      Jeffery Deaver
  Pure rotten
    Murder most postal; homicidal tales that de-
      liver a message; edited by Martin H.
      Greenberg
  The real shape of the coast
    A Century of noir; thirty-two classic crime
      stories; edited by Mickey Spillane and Max
      Allan Collins
  Ride the lightning
    Lutz, J. The Nudger dilemmas; a short story
      collection
  The right to sing the blues
    Lutz, J. The Nudger dilemmas; a short story
      collection
  The romantics
    Lutz, J. The Nudger dilemmas; a short story
      collection
  S.O.S.
    Death cruise; crime stories on the open seas;
      edited by Lawrence Block
  So young, so fair, so dead
    A Century of great suspense stories; edited by
      Jeffery Deaver
  Stutter step
    Irreconcilable differences; Lia Matera, editor
  Tango was her life
    Death dance; suspenseful stories of the dance
      macabre; Trevanian, editor
  The thunder of guilt
    Lutz, J. The Nudger dilemmas; a short story
      collection
  Time exposure
    Lutz, J. The Nudger dilemmas; a short story
      collection
  Typographical error
    Lutz, J. The Nudger dilemmas; a short story
      collection
  Veterans
    The World's finest mystery and crime stories,
      second annual collection; edited by Ed
      Gorman
  What you don't know can hurt you
    Lutz, J. The Nudger dilemmas; a short story
      collection
  Where is Harry Beal?
    Lutz, J. The Nudger dilemmas; a short story
      collection

Lutz, John—*Continued*
Winds of change
Death by espionage; intriguing stories of deception and betrayal; edited by Martin Cruz Smith
Luvaas, William
A Working Man's Apocrypha
The Antioch Review v62 no3 p534-48 Summ 2004
Luvina. Rulfo, J.
Lux et veritas. Monteleone, T. F.
Lux was dead right. Lupoff, R. A.
Luxenberg, Howard
Getel's story
Iowa Review v31 no2 p116-18 Fall 2001
Tag Sale
Gettysburg Review v15 no4 p555-67 Wint 2002
Luxor. Longstreet, K. A.
Luz Montes, Amelia Maria de la
While Pilar Tobillo sleeps
Hers 3: brilliant new fiction by lesbian writers; edited by Terry Wolverton with Robert Drake
Lycanthropy. Moyer, K.
Lycaon's punishment. Ovid
Lychack, William
Thin end of the wedge
TriQuarterly no105 p163-72 Spr/Summ 1999
Lynch, Doris
The Denali Widows' Club
Calyx v22 no1 p88-99 Summ 2004
Lynch, Thomas
Blood sport
The Best American mystery stories, 2001; edited and with an Introduction by Lawrence Block
The Pushcart prize XXVI; best of the small presses, an annual small press reader; edited by Bill Henderson and the Pushcart prize editors
LYNCHING
Dumas, H. Rope of wind
Dunbar, P. L. The lynching of Jube Benson
Fleming, R. The ultimate bad luck
A **Lynching** in Stereoscope. Dickinson, S.
The **lynching** of Jube Benson. Dunbar, P. L.
Lynds, Dennis, 1924-
For works written by this author under other er names see Collins, Michael, 1924-
Lynds, Gayle
(jt. auth) See Collins, Michael and Lynds, Gayle
Lynn, David H.
Bondage
Michigan Quarterly Review v43 no2 p263-4 Spr 2004
Hirsch and Bratinsky
New England Review v23 no1 p91-4 Wint 2002
Life sentences
The Virginia Quarterly Review v77 no4 p701-18 Aut 2001
Mistaken Identity
TriQuarterly no113 p53-74 Summ 2002
Mt. Pleasant
Michigan Quarterly Review v43 no2 p265-8 Spr 2004
Muggings
TriQuarterly no118 p235-48 Wint 2004

Naming the stones
Salmagundi no130/131 p160-76 Spr/Summ 2001
Lyon, Annabel
Saturday Night Function
Harvard Review (1992) no26 p25-35 2004
LYONS (FRANCE) *See* France—Lyons
Lyoshka. Dobychin, L.
LYSERGIC ACID DIETHYLAMIDE *See* LSD (Drug)
Lyubka Kozak. See Babel', I. Lyubka the Cossack
Lyubka the Cossack. Babel', I.

M

M. Saroyan, A.
Ma, Kathryn
Dougie
Southwest Review v88 no2/3 p315-28 2003
What I Know Now
The Antioch Review v61 no1 p68-87 Wint 2003
Ma Jian
The Abandoner
The New Yorker v80 no11 p92-4, 96-7 My 10 2004
Ma Kamanda's latrine. Houghteling, M. K.
Ma rung. Paulsen, S.
Ma'ame Pélagie. Chopin, K.
Maartiens, glory and me. Shir-Jacob, A.
Mabel's May day. Alcott, L. M.
MACABRE STORIES *See* Horror stories
MacAdam, Alfred J.
(jt. auth) See Pitol, Sergio
Macadam's log. Heller, J.
Macaque. Maraini, D.
MacAvoy, Sheila
Daily Double
Iowa Review v34 no1 p157-69 Spr 2004
MACBETH, KING OF SCOTLAND, D. 1057
About
Tremayne, P. Night's black agents
MacDonald, George
The golden key
Tales before Tolkien; the roots of modern fantasy; edited by Douglas A. Anderson
MacDonald, John D. (John Dann)
Betrayed
Death by espionage; intriguing stories of deception and betrayal; edited by Martin Cruz Smith
The homesick Buick
The Best American mystery stories of the century; Tony Hillerman, editor; with an introduction by Tony Hillerman
Murder for money
A Century of noir; thirty-two classic crime stories; edited by Mickey Spillane and Max Allan Collins
Nor iron bars
A Century of great suspense stories; edited by Jeffery Deaver
A young man's game
Sports best short stories; edited by Paul D. Staudohar

Macdonald, Ross

Gone girl

The Best American mystery stories of the century; Tony Hillerman, editor; with an introduction by Tony Hillerman

Guilt-edged blonde

A Century of great suspense stories; edited by Jeffery Deaver

A Century of noir; thirty-two classic crime stories; edited by Mickey Spillane and Max Allan Collins

MACDONALD, ROSS, 1915-1983

Parodies, imitations, etc.

Breen, J. L. The drowning icecube

MacDougall, Carl

The lights below [excerpt]

The Vintage book of contemporary Scottish fiction; edited and with an introduction by Peter Kravitz

MacDowell, Katherine Sherwood Bonner

Gran'mammy

Southern local color; stories of region, race, and gender; edited by Barbara C. Ewell and Pamela Glenn Menke; with notes by Andrea Humphrey

Jack and the mountain pink

Southern local color; stories of region, race, and gender; edited by Barbara C. Ewell and Pamela Glenn Menke; with notes by Andrea Humphrey

Why Gran'mammy didn't like pound-cake

Southern local color; stories of region, race, and gender; edited by Barbara C. Ewell and Pamela Glenn Menke; with notes by Andrea Humphrey

MacGowan, Robert

Astrolaters

The North American Review v287 no6 p38-42 N/D 2002

Machen, Arthur

The coming of the terror

Tales before Tolkien; the roots of modern fantasy; edited by Douglas A. Anderson

The great god Pan

The 13 best horror stories of all time; edited by Leslie Pockell

Machias. Busch, F.

The **machine**. Williams, C.

The **machine** gun and the mannequin. Van de Wetering, J.

MACHINERY AND CIVILIZATION *See* Technology and civilization

MACHINERY AND MACHINISTS

Lafferty, R. A. Eurema's dam

MacIntyre, F. Gwynplaine

The adventure of Exham Priory

Shadows over Baker Street; edited by Michael Reaves and John Pelan

MacKay, Scott

The sages of Cassiopeia

Northern suns; edited by David G. Hartwell & Glenn Grant

MACKE, AUGUST, 1887-1914

About

Gifford, B. The Tunisian notebook

MacKenzie, Ginny

Bee moths

New Letters v68 no2 p53-66 2002

Mackerel. Nichols, J.

Mackin, Edward, 1929-

For works written by this author under other names see McInerny, Ralph M., 1929-; Quill, Monica, 1929-

Macklin, Tony

American pastime

The North American Review v284 no3-4 p14-18 My/Ag 1999

Maclaren-Ross, J.

Some time I shall sleep out

The Times Literary Supplement no5202 [5203] p13-14 D 20 2002

MacLaverty, Bernard

Between two shores

The Anchor book of new Irish writing; the new Gaelach ficsean; edited and with an introduction by John Somer and John J. Daly

MacLean, Katherine

Games

Nebula awards showcase 2004; edited by Vonda McIntyre

The kidnapping of Baroness 5

A Woman's liberation; a choice of futures by and about women; edited by Connie Willis and Sheila Williams

MacLeod, Alistair

As birds bring forth the sun

MacLeod, A. Island; the complete stories

The boat

MacLeod, A. Island; the complete stories

Clearances

MacLeod, A. Island; the complete stories

The closing down of summer

MacLeod, A. Island; the complete stories

The golden gift of grey

MacLeod, A. Island; the complete stories

In the fall

MacLeod, A. Island; the complete stories

Island

MacLeod, A. Island; the complete stories

The lost salt gift of blood

MacLeod, A. Island; the complete stories

The return

MacLeod, A. Island; the complete stories

The road to Rankin's Point

MacLeod, A. Island; the complete stories

Second spring

MacLeod, A. Island; the complete stories

To every thing there is a season

MacLeod, A. Island; the complete stories

The tuning of perfection

MacLeod, A. Island; the complete stories

The vastness of the dark

MacLeod, A. Island; the complete stories

Vision

MacLeod, A. Island; the complete stories

Winter dog

MacLeod, A. Island; the complete stories

MacLeod, Ian

Breathmoss

The Year's best science fiction; twentieth annual collection; edited by Gardner Dozois

The chop girl

The Year's best fantasy & horror, thirteenth annual collection; edited by Ellen Datlow and Terri Windling

MacLeod, Ian—*Continued*
Isabel of the fall
The Year's best science fiction, nineteenth annual collection; edited by Gardner Dozois
New light on the Drake equation
The Year's best science fiction, nineteenth annual collection; edited by Gardner Dozois
MacLeod, Ian R.
The summer isles
The Year's best science fiction, sixteenth annual collection; edited by Gardner Dozois
MacLeod, Ken
The human front
The Year's best science fiction, nineteenth annual collection; edited by Gardner Dozois
Macomber, Patricia Lee
(jt. auth) See Wilson, David Niall and Macomber, Patricia Lee
Macs. Bisson, T.
Macy, Caitlin
Christie
The New Yorker v79 no3 p72-7 Mr 10 2003
Macy is the other woman. Barrett, L.
Mad Dog. Lochte, D.
Mad dog summer. Lansdale, J. R.
Mad dogs. Drew, E.
Mad dogs. See McCorkle, J. Dogs
Mad Fish. Senior, O.
Mad for music. Tozzi, F.
MADAGASCAR
Hunter, F. Madagascar
Lee, A. Brothers and sisters around the world
Madagascar. Hunter, F.
Madame Alaird's breasts. Brand, D.
Madame and Ahmed. Bowles, P.
Madame Célestin's divorce. Chopin, K.
Madame de Mauves. James, H.
Madame Martel's Christmas Eve. Chopin, K.
Madame Realism. Tillman, L.
Madame Realism: a fairy tale. Tillman, L.
Madame Realism lies here. Tillman, L.
Madame Realism looks for relief. Tillman, L.
Madame Realism's torch song. Tillman, L.
Madden, David
The world's one breathing
Home and beyond; an anthology of Kentucky short stories; edited by Morris Allen Grubbs; with an introduction by Wade Hall and an afterword by Charles E. May
Maddern, Philippa C.
Things fall apart
Centaurus: the best of Australian science fiction; edited by David G. Hartwell and Damien Broderick
Made over, made out. Kennedy, A. L.
Ma'dear. McMillan, T.
Madison at Guignol. Oates, J. C.
The **Madman**. Achebe, C.
MADNESS *See* Insanity; Mental illness
Madness. Wuori, G. K.
The **madness** of John Harned. London, J.
The **madonna** of the future. James, H.
MADRID (SPAIN) *See* Spain—Madrid
A **madrigal** of mourning. Herling, G.
Maedele. Goliger, G.
Maelstrom II. Clarke, A. C.
The **maestro**. McGarry, J.

Maffini, Mary Jane
Blind alley
The World's finest mystery and crime stories, third annual collection; edited by Ed Gorman and Martin H. Greenberg
Cocktails with the corpse
Bishop, C. and James, D. Death dines in; edited by Claudia Bishop and Dean James
MAFIA
See also Gangsters
Allyn, D. The jukebox king
Anderson, R. The name of the dead
Bischoff, D. May oysters have legs
Davidson, A. The lord of Central Park
Healy, J. F. Food for thought
Maron, M. The early retirement of Mario Colletti
Piccirilli, T. Diamond Mozzarella
Vonnegut, K. A present for Big Saint Nick
MAGAZINES *See* Periodicals
The **Magdalene**. Howard, M.
Maggie of the green bottles. Bambara, T. C.
Maggie's song of herself. Chaney, G.
The **Maggody** files: Death in bloom. Hess, J.
The **Maggody** files: Hillbilly cat. Hess, J.
Maggots, infidelity, and the oyster roast. Krawiec, R.
MAGI
Broderick, D. The Magi
Willis, C. Epiphany
The **Magi**. Broderick, D.
Magi Dogs. Rooke, L.
MAGIC
See also Supernatural phenomena; Witchcraft Queen of soulmates
Anderson, B. Lark till dawn, princess
Bear, G. The fall of the house of Escher
Bixby, J. It's a good life
Bowles, P. A friend of the world
Bowles, P. The wind at Beni Midar
Card, O. S. The Yazoo Queen
Carlson, R. Evil eye Allen
Cherryh, C. J. Of law and magic
De Lint, C. Big city littles
De Lint, C. The buffalo man
De Lint, C. Embracing the mystery
De Lint, C. Forest of stone
De Lint, C. Granny weather
De Lint, C. Seven wild sisters
De Lint, C. Sign here
Delllamonica, A. M. Cooking creole
Donaldson, S. R. The killing stroke
Douglas, M. Notes from a writer's book of cures and spells
Edghill, R. The piper at the gate
Elrod, P. N. The tea room beasts
Gerrold, D. The spell
Huber, C. Y. and Baker, M. C. Chance hospitality
Jackson, S. The very strange house next door
James, H. Professor Fargo
Landis, G. A. Elemental
Martin, P. P. Amor frustrado—Frustrated love
Roberts, T. N. Demon bone
Salaam, K. I. Rosamojo
Sarath, P. E. The djinn game
Sheckley, R. Magic, maples, and Maryanne
Sherman, J. The magic-stealer
Stevenson, R. L. The bottle imp

MAGIC—See also—*Continued*
  Tangh, J. The Skinned
  Valera, J. "The wizard"
  Yolen, J. The gift of the magicians, with apologies to you know who
Magic. Nichols, J.
The **magic** bullet theory. Castro, A.-T.
Magic casements. Highsmith, P.
The **magic** circle. O'Rourke, F.
Magic, inc. Heinlein, R. A.
Magic, maples, and Maryanne. Sheckley, R.
A **magic** mountain and a willowy wench. Skvorecký, J.
The **magic-stealer**. Sherman, J.
Magic wand. Berkman, P. R.
MAGICIANS
  Anderson, F. I. Blind man's buff
  Bausch, R. Tandolfo the Great
  Chesnutt, C. W. The conjurer's revenge
  Dozois, G. R. Afternoon at Schraffts
  Dyson, J. We who walk through walls
  Edghill, R. Haut-Clare
  Ellin, S. The moment of decision
  Lovecraft, H. P. Under the pyramids
  Polansky, S. Sleights
  Pronzini, B. and Kurland, M. Quicker than the eye
  Vukcevich, R. Pink smoke
The **Maginot** Line. Wexler, M.
The **Magisterium**. Rutkowski, E.
Magnestism. Giono, J.
Magnifying glass. Stösser, A.
Magnolia stellata. Stypes, A.
Magnuson, Ann
  Mom comes home
    Carved in rock; short stories by musicians; edited by Greg Kihn
Magona, Sindiwe
  It was Easter Sunday the day I went to Netreg
    The Anchor book of modern African stories; edited by Nadežda Obradovic ; with a foreword by Chinua Achebe
The **Magothy** fires. McManus, J.
Magrs, Paul
  Here comes Glad
    The Times Literary Supplement no5136 p14-15 S 7 2001
Magruder, James
  You've Really Learned How
    Gettysburg Review v17 no2 p263-81 Summ 2004
Maguire, Gregory
  Precision Marching at the Orphanage, 1890
    Ploughshares v29 no2/3 p89-91 Fall 2003
Maguire, Jim
  Quiet people
    The Literary Review (Madison, N.J.) v44 no4 p735-49 Summ 2001
Magy, Ronna
  Family
    Hers 2: brilliant new fiction by lesbian writers; edited by Terry Wolverton with Robert Drake
Mahatma Joe. Bass, R.
Mahfouz, Naguib *See* Maḥfūẓ, Najīb, 1912-
Maḥfūẓ, Najīb
  The mummy awakens
    The Massachusetts Review v42 no4 p507-23 Wint 2001/2002

A voice from the other world
    The Kenyon Review ns23 no2 p122-35 Spr 2001
Mahmudi, Sofia
  The Fin Garden of Kashan
    A Feast in the mirror; stories by contemporary Iranian women; translated and edited by Mohammad Mehdi Khorrami, Shouleh Vatanabadi
The **maid** of Saint Phillippe. Chopin, K.
MAIDS (SERVANTS)
    See also Cleaning women
  Adams, A. La Señora
  Adams, A. Verlie I say unto you
  Babel´, I. The sin of Jesus
  Bausch, R. 1951
  Brantenberg, G. Four winds [excerpt]
  Brennan, M. The anachronism
  Brennan, M. The bride
  Brennan, M. The divine fireplace
  Brennan, M. The view from the kitchen
  Chopin, K. A Dresden lady in Dixie
  Gilchrist, E. The big cleanup
  Gilchrist, E. Light shining through a honey jar
  Gilchrist, E. Miss Crystal's maid name Traceleen, she's talking, she's telling everything she knows
  Gilchrist, E. Traceleen, she's still talking
  Gilchrist, E. Traceleen turns east
  Hardwick, E. Shot: a New York story
  Harrington, J. Sweet baby Jenny
  Hearn, L. A Creole mystery
  Jacobs, M. Marina in the key of blue flat
  Leonard, E. When the women come out to dance
  Lida, D. Free trade
  Mais, R. Red dirt don't wash
  Matiella, A. C. El bebé del vaquerón
  Matiella, A. C. The ring
  Régio, J. Miss Olimpia and her maid Belarmina
  Singer, I. B. Dazzled
  Taraqqi, G. The maid
  Theroux, P. Disheveled nymphs
  Watanabe McFerrin, L. Los mariachis del muerto
  Wharton, E. All Souls'
  Wharton, E. The lady's maid's bell
The **maids**. Hayden, G. M.
The **mail** in the morning. Harshbarger, K.
The **mail** lady. Gates, D.
Mail-order Annie. Braunbeck, G. A.
MAILER, NORMAN
    About
  Anderson, R. Mother tongue
Mailing incorrectly. Nissen, T.
The **main** event. Crowther, P.
MAINE
    See also White Mountains (N.H. and Me.)
  Bonnie, F. Selling delphinium
  Busch, F. Machias
  Connor, J. The anecdote of the island
  Connor, J. The last native
  Connor, J. We who live apart
  Costello, M. J. and Hautala, R. And the sea shall claim them
  DeMarco, T. Down at the end of lonely street
  DeMarco, T. Prince of darkness
  DeMarco, T. The rose festival boxed lunch

MAINE—*Continued*
 Ford, R. Charity
 Gorman, E. Ghost of a chance
 Hand, E. Last summer at Mars Hill
 Robinson, L. Cuxabexis, Cuxabexis
 Robinson, L. The diver
 Robinson, L. The edge of the forest and the
  edge of the ocean
 Robinson, L. Finches
 Robinson, L. Officer Friendly
 Robinson, L. Seeing the world
 Roorbach, B. Fog
 Russo, R. Joy ride
 Wilson, R., Jr. Remembered names
 Wood, M. That one autumn
 Wuori, G. K. Angles
 Wuori, G. K. Condoms
 Wuori, G. K. Crime
 Wuori, G. K. Family
 Wuori, G. K. Fire
 Wuori, G. K. Glory
 Wuori, G. K. Golden
 Wuori, G. K. Illusions
 Wuori, G. K. Justice
 Wuori, G. K. Laughter
 Wuori, G. K. Madness
 Wuori, G. K. Murder
 Wuori, G. K. Nose
 Wuori, G. K. Nude
 Wuori, G. K. Parents
 Wuori, G. K. Revenge
 Wuori, G. K. Skunk
   Farm life
   See Farm life—Maine
MAINE (BATTLESHIP)
 Dams, J. M. Remember the Maine?
Maintaining integrity. Huffman, B., Jr.
Maintenance. Davidson, R.
Maintenance. Young, T.
Mais, Roger
 Red dirt don't wash
  The Oxford book of Caribbean short stories;
   edited by Stewart Brown and John
   Wickham
Maisie's foot. See Slavin, J. The woman who cut
  off her leg at the Maidstone Club
La **maison** de Madame Durard. Caspers, N.
Maja-Pearce, Adewale
 Civil War I-VII
  The Anchor book of modern African stories;
   edited by Nadežda Obradovic ; with a fore-
   word by Chinua Achebe
 How Pinkie killed a man
  Granta no66 p199-206 Summ 1999
The **majesty**. Tomlinson, N. C.
Major, Devorah
 Shining through 24/7
  Mojo: conjure stories; edited by Nalo Hopkin-
   son
Major, Marcus
 Kenya and Amir
  Got to be real; four original love stories; [by]
   E. Lynn Harris [et al.]
Major league triceratops. Malzberg, B. N.
MAJORCA (SPAIN)
 Boylan, C. Villa Marta
Make a wish. Tippens, E.
Make haste, my beloved. Blitz, R.
Make me. Rinehart, S.

Make them laugh. Iribarne, M.
Make yourselves at home. Hess, J.
The **makeover**. Jenz, T.
The **maker**. Borges, J. L.
Makeup. Hay, E.
Makhno's boys. Babel´, I.
Making a change. Gilman, C. P.
Making a noise in this world. De Lint, C.
Making faces. Jaroš, P.
Making headway. Van Winckel, N.
Making it the hard way. L'Amour, L.
Making Love in 2003. July, M.
The **making** of a bureaucrat. O'Loughlin, M.
The **making** of a Jew. Kalman, J.
Making peace with the Muslims. Gabriel, D.
Making the news. Meyers, K.
Making the weight. Steckevicz, E. M.
Makuchi *See* Nfah-Abbenyi, Juliana Makuchi,
 1958-
Makuck, Peter
 Family
  The Hudson Review v55 no3 p385-402 Aut
   2002
 Piecework
  This is where we live; short stories by 25
   contemporary North Carolina writers; ed-
   ited by Michael McFee
Maladies of the inner ear. Goliger, G.
MALADJUSTED CHILDREN *See* Emotionally
 disturbed children
Malamud, Bernard
 The German refugee
  The Best American short stories of the
   century; John Updike, editor, Katrina
   Kenison, coeditor; with an introduction by
   John Updike
 Rembrandt's hat
  Wonderful town; New York stories from The
   New Yorker; edited by David Remnick
   with Susan Choi
 Still life
  Neurotica: Jewish writers on sex; edited by
   Melvin Jules Bukiet
MALANGA, GERARD
   About
 Rucker, R. v. B. The Andy Warhol sandcandle
MALARIA
 Gordimer, N. An emissary
MALAWI
 Hunter, F. Pepper
 Lipenga, K. Wainting for a turn
 Weiner, S. Eating Vic
MALAYA
   See also Malaysia
MALAYSIA
 Eggers, P. How the water feels
 Eggers, P. Leo, chained
 Eggers, P. The year five
MALAYSIANS
   Canada
 Thien, M. Simple recipes
Malchyk. Papernick, J.
Maldicion. Montaño, G. G.
The **male** and female hogan. Breen, J. L.
Male lead. Yuknavitch, L.
A **malefactor**. Chekhov, A. P.

Maleti, Gabriella
Acedia
Maleti, G. Bitter asylum; translated by Sharon
Wood
Adornato and Venus
Maleti, G. Bitter asylum; translated by Sharon
Wood
Agognata
Maleti, G. Bitter asylum; translated by Sharon
Wood
Alma
Maleti, G. Bitter asylum; translated by Sharon
Wood
Argia
Maleti, G. Bitter asylum; translated by Sharon
Wood
David
Maleti, G. Bitter asylum; translated by Sharon
Wood
The house in the wood
Maleti, G. Bitter asylum; translated by Sharon
Wood
Joseph
Maleti, G. Bitter asylum; translated by Sharon
Wood
Joshua
Maleti, G. Bitter asylum; translated by Sharon
Wood
Lime-tree
Maleti, G. Bitter asylum; translated by Sharon
Wood
Mirta
Maleti, G. Bitter asylum; translated by Sharon
Wood
Odilia and Liberato
Maleti, G. Bitter asylum; translated by Sharon
Wood
The precipice
Maleti, G. Bitter asylum; translated by Sharon
Wood
Sempiterno's fears
Maleti, G. Bitter asylum; translated by Sharon
Wood
Vidor and Mummy
Maleti, G. Bitter asylum; translated by Sharon
Wood
The visit
Maleti, G. Bitter asylum; translated by Sharon
Wood
The word
Maleti, G. Bitter asylum; translated by Sharon
Wood
MALIBU (CALIF.) *See* California—Malibu
MALICIOUS MISCHIEF
Jackson, S. The possibility of evil
Malingerer. Sandor, M.
Maliszewski, Paul
After the Mailman
The Paris Review v44 p211-19 Fall 2002
Cubicles
Gettysburg Review v16 no2 p201-10 Summ
2003
News junkie
The Antioch Review v59 no1 p40-7 Wint
2001
Prayer against the experts and their ways
Harper's v303 no1819 p26 D 2001

Prayer for the driver at night
Western Humanities Review v53 no4 p375-76
Wint 1999/2000
Prayer for the first balance
Gettysburg Review v12 no1 p131-32 Spr 1999
Prayer for the safety of the mother
Western Humanities Review v53 no4 p377
Wint 1999/2000
Prayer for the safety of the public screamer
Western Humanities Review v53 no4 p373-74
Wint 1999/2000
Maliszewski, Paul
Prayer against the experts and their ways
Pushcart prize XXVII; best of the small
presses; edited by Bill Henderson with the
Pushcart prize editors
Mallon, Thomas
Love among the records
Gentlemen's Quarterly v69 no11 p333-34+ N
1999
Mallory, Michael
The riddle of the young protestor
My Sherlock Holmes; untold stories of the
great detective; edited by Michael Kurland
Malololailai; or, Discovering the world. Vasseur,
T. J.
Malone, Michael
Blue Cadillac
Malone, M. Red clay, blue Cadillac; stories of
twelve Southern women
A deer on the lawn
Malone, M. Red clay, blue Cadillac; stories of
twelve Southern women
Fast love
Malone, M. Red clay, blue Cadillac; stories of
twelve Southern women
Invitation to the ball
Malone, M. Red clay, blue Cadillac; stories of
twelve Southern women
Murder and obsession; edited by Otto Penzler
Love and other crimes
Malone, M. Red clay, blue Cadillac; stories of
twelve Southern women
Maniac loose
The Best American mystery stories, 2002; ed-
ited and with an introduction by James
Ellroy; Otto Penzler, series editor
Malone, M. Red clay, blue Cadillac; stories of
twelve Southern women
Miss Mona's bank
Malone, M. Red clay, blue Cadillac; stories of
twelve Southern women
The power
Malone, M. Red clay, blue Cadillac; stories of
twelve Southern women
Red clay
The Best American mystery stories of the
century; Tony Hillerman, editor; with an
introduction by Tony Hillerman
A Century of great suspense stories; edited by
Jeffery Deaver
Malone, M. Red clay, blue Cadillac; stories of
twelve Southern women
The rising of the South and Flonnie Rogers
Malone, M. Red clay, blue Cadillac; stories of
twelve Southern women
White trash noir
Malone, M. Red clay, blue Cadillac; stories of
twelve Southern women

Malone, Michael—*Continued*

Winners and losers

Malone, M. Red clay, blue Cadillac; stories of twelve Southern women

Malone, Paul Scott

Memorial Day, 1987: a holiday story

Southern Humanities Review v33 no2 p131-42 Spr 1999

Malouf, David

At Schindler's

Malouf, D. Dream stuff; stories

Blacksoil country

Malouf, D. Dream stuff; stories

Closer

Granta no68 p219-25 Wint 1999

Malouf, D. Dream stuff; stories

Dream stuff

Malouf, D. Dream stuff; stories

Great Day

Malouf, D. Dream stuff; stories

Jacko's reach

Malouf, D. Dream stuff; stories

Lone Pine

Malouf, D. Dream stuff; stories

Night training

Malouf, D. Dream stuff; stories

Sally's story

Malouf, D. Dream stuff; stories

Malouf, Melissa

From you know who

This is where we live; short stories by 25 contemporary North Carolina writers; edited by Michael McFee

The **malted** milk monsters. Tenn, W.

The **Maltese** feline. Edghill, R.

Malvasia. Busch, F.

Malzberg, Barry N.

Agony column

Murder most postal; homicidal tales that deliver a message; edited by Martin H. Greenberg

All assassins

Malzberg, B. N. In the stone house

Allegro marcato

Malzberg, B. N. In the stone house

Amos

Malzberg, B. N. In the stone house

Andante lugubre

Malzberg, B. N. In the stone house

Concerto accademico

Malzberg, B. N. In the stone house

Darwinian facts

Malzberg, B. N. In the stone house

Final war

Pronzini, B. and Malzberg, B. N. On account of darkness and other SF stories; [by] Bill Pronzini and Barry N. Malzberg

Fugato

Malzberg, B. N. In the stone house

Getting there

Tetrick, B. In the shadow of the wall; an anthology of Vietnam stories that might have been; edited by Byron R. Tetrick

Heavy metal

Malzberg, B. N. In the stone house

Hieractic realignment

Malzberg, B. N. In the stone house

The high purpose

Malzberg, B. N. In the stone house

Hitler at Nuremberg

Malzberg, B. N. In the stone house

Improvident excess

Malzberg, B. N. In the stone house

In the stone house

Malzberg, B. N. In the stone house

The intransigents

Malzberg, B. N. In the stone house

Major league triceratops

Malzberg, B. N. In the stone house

The only thing you learn

Malzberg, B. N. In the stone house

Police actions

Malzberg, B. N. In the stone house

The prince of the steppes

Malzberg, B. N. In the stone house

Quartermain

Malzberg, B. N. In the stone house

Ship full of Jews

Malzberg, B. N. In the stone house

Something from the seventies

Malzberg, B. N. In the stone house

Standards & practices

Malzberg, B. N. In the stone house

Turpentine

Malzberg, B. N. In the stone house

Understanding entropy

Malzberg, B. N. In the stone house

We're coming through the window

Wondrous beginnings; edited by Steven H. Silver and Martin H. Greenberg

(jt. auth) See Koja, Kathe and Malzberg, Barry N.

(jt. auth) See Pronzini, Bill and Malzberg, Barry N.

(jt. auth) See Yasgur, Batya Swift and Malzberg, Barry N.

Mama. Boylan, C.

A **mama**. Svoboda, T.

Mama dear. Myrmo, M.

Mama, Rimma, and Alla. Babel´, I.

Mama's gift. Pratt, M.

MAMMALS, FOSSIL *See* Fossils

Mammals. Clark, J.

Mammie's form at the post office. Markham, E. A.

Mammogram. Garcia, L. G.

MAMMOGRAPHY

Swick, M. A. The zealous mourner

Mamouche. Chopin, K.

MAN

Bocock, M. La humanidad

De Camp, L. S. Living fossil

Del Rey, L. The faithful

Oliver, C. End of the line

MAN, PREHISTORIC *See* Prehistoric man

The **man**. Munger, K.

A **man** alone. Breen, J. V.

A **man** and a woman. Schone, R.

Man and beast. Mo Yan

The **Man** and the Muskrat: African (from Botswana). Sherman, J.

The **Man** at Night's Window. Flannery, S.

The **man** at the beach. Rubin, L. D.

Man bites dog. Queen, E.

A **man** called Spade. Hammett, D.

The **man** corn triptych. Chapman, C. M.

Man Crawling Out of Trees. Proulx, A.

The **man** from Khurda district. Chaudhuri, A.

The **man** from P.I.G. Harrison, H.
Man here keeps getting arrested all the time.
    McNulty, J.
The **man** I loved was an elf. What, L.
A **Man** Identifies A Body. Waters, J.
A **man** in a box. Glover, D. H.
The **man** in a case. Chekhov, A. P.
The **man** in a shell. See Chekhov, A. P. The man
    in a case
The **Man** in the Back Row Has a Question: VIII.
    Akunin, B. and others
The **man** in the black suit. King, S.
The **man** in the civil suit. Burke, J.
The **man** in the mailbag. Dickson, G. R.
A **man** in the making. Cooper, B.
Man in the middle of the ocean. Fuchs, D.
The **man** in the morgue. Lutz, J.
The **man** in the white hat. Estleman, L. D.
Man in towel with gun. Nesbitt, M.
Man kills wife, two dogs. Downs, M.
A **man** like Grady, you got to know him first.
    McNulty, J.
A **man** like that. Davis, L.
A **man** named Flute. Heller, J.
A **man** named Thin. Hammett, D.
The **man** next door. Clark, M. H.
The **man** next door. Johnson, G.
A **man** of family. Tenn, W.
A **man** of ideas. Chekhov, A. P.
Man of letters. Dixon, S.
Man of the Renaissance. Auchincloss, L.
Man on pink corner. Borges, J. L.
Man on the run. Collins, M.
Man on the run. Morábito, F.
The **man** on the threshold. Borges, J. L.
The **man** outside. Grau, S. A.
Man overboard. Wagner, B.
A **man** wanted to buy a cat. Porter, J. A.
The **man** who ate himself. Rucker, R. v. B.
The **Man** Who Became Himself. Yu, C.
The **man** who caught the weather. Aldrich, B. S.
The **man** who collected "The Shadow". Pronzini,
    B.
The **man** who died. Lawrence, D. H.
A **man** who doesn't lie. Lao She
The **man** who dreaded to go home. Aldrich, B. S.
The **man** who got away. Holleran, A.
The **man** who had no thumbs. Loomis, N. M.
The **man** who hanged himself. Chinodya, S.
A **man** who has brothers. Goliger, G.
The **man** who killed Dan Odams. Hammett, D.
The **man** who knew Belle Starr. Bausch, R.
The **man** who knew Dylan. Gay, W.
The **man** who liked Dickens. Waugh, E.
The **man** who lost his shadow. Carmody, I.
The **man** who lost the sea. Sturgeon, T.
The **man** who loved islands. Lawrence, D. H.
The **man** who never was. Todd, C.
The **man** who ploughed the sea. Clarke, A. C.
The **man** who saw himself drown. Desai, A.
The **man** who saw the elephant. Davidson, A.
The **man** who shot Lewis Vance. Kaminsky, S. M.
The **man** who shot Trinity Valance. Bishop, P.
The **man** who swam with beavers. Lord, N.
The **man** who traveled in elephants. Heinlein, R.
    A.
The **Man** Who Understood Everybody. Lohafer, S.
The **man** who walks. Warner, A.

The **man** who wanted to be in the movies. Jakes,
    J.
The **man** who was a cosmic string. Rucker, R. v.
    B.
The **man** who went out for cigarettes. Knight, M.
The **man** who went through everything. Lord, N.
Man with a Gun. Davidson, K.
The **Man** with the Gun Waits for Me to Talk.
    Vida, V.
The **man** with the lapdog. Lordan, B.
The **Man** with the Movie Camera. Brownstein, G.
The **man** with the spotted dog. Brennan, K.
The **man** with the weak heart. Mikolaj, D.
The **management** of grief. Mukherjee, B.
The **manager**. O'Rourke, F.
The **manager** of "The Kremlin". Waugh, E.
Manang. Peralejo, C.
Manassas, again. Benford, G.
Mandela Was Late. Mehlman, P.
Mandelbaum, Paul
    Changeling
        New England Review v22 no1 p101-13 Wint
        2001
    The omelet king
        The Massachusetts Review v40 no2 p229-44
        Summ 1999
    Several answers
        New Letters v67 no2 p95-108 2001
    Sweet thunderous twilight
        Poets & Writers v27 no1 p88 Ja/F 1999
Mandelman, Avner
    Pangs
        Prairie Schooner v73 no1 p86-87 Spr 1999
Mandelstam in Exile. Shirazi, S.
Mandrell, Liz
    Passing for faith
        The Georgia Review v55 no3 p589-95 Fall
        2001
Maneki Neko. Sterling, B.
Maneuvers. Lisick, B.
Mango season. Pittalwala, I.
Mangum, Bryant
    The Palms
        South Carolina Review v36 no1 p30-7 Fall
        2003
MANHATTAN (NEW YORK, N.Y.) *See* New
    York (N.Y.)—Manhattan
A **Manhattan** romance. Oates, J. C.
MANHUNTS
    See also Adventure
    Anderson, P. Eutopia
Maniac loose. Malone, M.
Manifest white. Sandford, R.
Manikin. Michaels, L.
MANILA (PHILIPPINES) *See* Philippines—Ma-
    nila
MANITOBA *See* Canada—Manitoba
Manitoba Avenue. Patterson, K.
Manitow and Ironhand. Jakes, J.
Manley, Michael S.
    My secret life with Amy
        Gettysburg Review v12 no2 p327-31 Summ
        1999
Mann, Antony
    Taking care of Frank
        The World's finest mystery and crime stories,
        first annual collection; edited by Ed
        Gorman

Mann, Joy Hewitt

Between the teeth

Dalhousie Review v79 no1 p109-18 Spr 1999

Mann, Phil

Touch of a vanish'd hand

A Deadly dozen; tales of murder from members of Sisters in Crime/Los Angeles; edited by Susan B. Casmier, Aljean Harmetz and Cynthia Lawrence

Mann, William J.

Say goodbye to Middletown

Circa 2000; gay fiction at the millennium; edited by Robert Drake & Terry Wolverton

Mannequin. Weaver, G.

MANORS *See* Houses

Manrique, Jaime

The documentary artist

Circa 2000; gay fiction at the millennium; edited by Robert Drake & Terry Wolverton

Colchie, T. A whistler in the nightworld; short fiction from the Latin Americas; edited by Thomas Colchie

Man's best friend. Highsmith, P.

A **man's** book. Wilkinson, M.

A **man's** going into the Army what can you do about it? McNulty, J.

MANSFIELD, KATHERINE, 1888-1923

About

Stanton, M. The cliffs of the moon

Mansfield, Kathleen Beauchamp *See* Mansfield, Katherine, 1888-1923

The **Mansion** on the Hill. Moody, R.

MANSIONS *See* Houses

Mantel, Hilary

Curved is the line of beauty

The Times Literary Supplement no5157 p13-15 F 1 2002

Mantel, Tara

Walking on Water

TriQuarterly no118 p224-34 Wint 2004

MANTLE, MICKEY, 1931-1995

About

Jenkins, G. Night game

The **manual** of remote sensing. Swan, M.

MANUSCRIPTS

Borges, J. L. The immortal

Evenson, B. The wavering knife

Hawthorne, N. The Devil in manuscript

Many Janes. Dixon, S.

Many-splendored things. Reisman, N.

Many will enter, few will win. Joseph, D.

Many worlds are born. De Lint, C.

Manzarek, Ray

The lady of the valley

Carved in rock; short stories by musicians; edited by Greg Kihn

MAP DRAWING

Barrett, A. Servants of the map

Ellison, H. Incognita, Inc.

A **Map** of Stars. Shannahan, M.

A **map** of the city. Thien, M.

A **map** of the mines of Barnath. Williams, S.

Mapping. Lamé, A.

The **mappist.** Lopez, B. H.

Maraini, Dacia

Alicetta

Maraini, D. Darkness; fiction; translated by Martha King

The boy Gramophone and the pigeon man

Maraini, D. Darkness; fiction; translated by Martha King

He is eleven years old, his name is Tano

Maraini, D. Darkness; fiction; translated by Martha King

Letters to Marina [excerpt]

The Vintage book of international lesbian fiction; edited and with an introduction by Naomi Holoch and Joan Nestle

Macaque

Maraini, D. Darkness; fiction; translated by Martha King

A number on her arm

Maraini, D. Darkness; fiction; translated by Martha King

Shadows

Maraini, D. Darkness; fiction; translated by Martha King

Sister Attanasia's chickens

Maraini, D. Darkness; fiction; translated by Martha King

Today is today is today

Maraini, D. Darkness; fiction; translated by Martha King

Viollca, the child from Albania

Maraini, D. Darkness; fiction; translated by Martha King

Walls of darkness

Maraini, D. Darkness; fiction; translated by Martha King

The zipper

In the forbidden city; an anthology of erotic fiction by Italian women; edited by Maria Rosa Cutrufelli; translated by Vincent J. Bertolini

Marano, Michael

Burden

Best new horror 11; edited and with an introduction by Stephen Jones

Marathon. Cobb, W. J.

Marber, Patrick

Peter Shelley

Speaking with the angel; original stories; edited by Nick Hornby

The **marble** quilt. Leavitt, D.

March of Dimes. Rodburg, M.

The **march** of progress. Chesnutt, C. W.

Märchen. Hester, K. L.

Marcher. Beckett, C.

Marching as to war. Ritchie, E.

Marco and Marian take a vacation. Lock, N.

Marconi's dream. Leslie, N.

Marcus, Ben

The least you need to know about radio

On the rocks; the KGB Bar fiction anthology; edited by Rebecca Donner ; foreword by Denis Woychuk

Pushcart prize XXVII; best of the small presses; edited by Bill Henderson with the Pushcart prize editors

The new female head

Harper's v304 no1820 p84-7 Ja 2002

MARDI GRAS

Bischoff, D. May oysters have legs

Braunbeck, G. A. Down in darkest Dixie where the dead don't dance

Crowther, P. Songs of leaving

Davis, R. Fat Tuesday

MARDI GRAS—Continued
De Lint, C. Masking Indian
Helfers, J. Farewell to the flesh
Holder, N. Skeleton krewe
Hudson, Suzanne. The seamstress
Lindskold, J. M. Sacrifice
Rogers, B. H. King Corpus
Scarborough, E. A. The invisible woman's clever disguise
West, M. Faces made of clay

Marechera, Dambudzo
Thought tracks in the snow
The Anchor book of modern African stories; edited by Nadežda Obradovic ; with a foreword by Chinua Achebe

Marffin, Kyle
Waiting for the 400
The Darkest thirst; a vampire anthology

MARGARET, QUEEN OF SCOTLAND, 1283-1290
About
Vink, R. A frail young life

Margaret & Bud. Barthelme, F.
Margareta. Gomes, M. T.
Margie. Latty, Y.

Margolin, Phillip
The jailhouse lawyer
The Best American mystery stories, 1999; edited and with an introduction by Ed McBain

Mari d'elle. Chekhov, A. P.
Maria de Covina. Gilb, D.
Maria de Jesus. Nogueira, C. B.
Maria do Ahu. Régio, J.
Maria Schoning. Pushkin, A. S.
Los **mariachis** del muerto. Watanabe McFerrin, L.

Marías, Javier
Bad nature
Granta no66 p67-105 Summ 1999
Broken binoculars
Marías, J. When I was mortal; translated by Margaret Jull Costa
Everything bad comes back
Marías, J. When I was mortal; translated by Margaret Jull Costa
Fewer scruples
Marías, J. When I was mortal; translated by Margaret Jull Costa
Flesh Sunday
Marías, J. When I was mortal; translated by Margaret Jull Costa
In uncertain time
Marías, J. When I was mortal; translated by Margaret Jull Costa
The Italian legacy
Marías, J. When I was mortal; translated by Margaret Jull Costa
The night doctor
Marías, J. When I was mortal; translated by Margaret Jull Costa
No more loves
Marías, J. When I was mortal; translated by Margaret Jull Costa
On the honeymoon
Marías, J. When I was mortal; translated by Margaret Jull Costa
Spear blood
Marías, J. When I was mortal; translated by Margaret Jull Costa

Unfinished figures
Marías, J. When I was mortal; translated by Margaret Jull Costa
What the butler said
Coppola, F. F. Francis Ford Coppola's Zoetrope: all story; edited by Adrienne Brodeur and Samantha Schnee; introduction by Francis Ford Coppola
When I was mortal
Marías, J. When I was mortal; translated by Margaret Jull Costa

Marie
The lay of the were-wolf
The Literary werewolf; an anthology; edited by Charlotte F. Otten

Marie. Jones, E. P.
Marie-Ange's Ginen. Phipps, M.
Marie Antoinette's harp. Stanton, M.
Marigolds. Collier, E. W.
MARIHUANA *See* Marijuana

MARIJUANA
Banks, R. Dis bwoy, him gwan
Bowles, P. He of the assembly
Bowles, P. Under the sky
Daniels, J. Christmasmobile
Harrison, H. The velvet glove
Rash, R. Speckled trout
Steele, A. M. Green acres

Marilyn. Dann, J.
Marina Dosal, juice vendor. Hinojosa, F.
Marina in the key of blue flat. Jacobs, M.

Marinara, Martha
Holding Cells
The Massachusetts Review v44 no4 p689-706 Wint 2003/2004

MARINE BIOLOGY
Lumley, B. The return of the Deep Ones

MARINE CORPS (U.S.) *See* United States. Marine Corps

MARINES (U.S.) *See* United States. Marine Corps

Marion Earle; or, Only an actress!. Alcott, L. M.
Marisol's things. Allen, S.

Maristed, Kai
The mercenary's song
The Kenyon Review ns21 no2 p64-75 Spr 1999

Mark Field's mistake. Alcott, L. M.
Mark Field's success. Alcott, L. M.
Mark of satan. Oates, J. C.
Mark of the beast. Kidd, C.
The **mark** of the beast. Kipling, R.
The **Mark** Twain overlook. Fracis, S. H.
Marked men. White, M. C.
Markers. Johnson, D.
Market scene. Nfah-Abbenyi, J. M.

MARKETS
Bauman, B. A. Safeway
Chekhov, A. P. The bird market
Ekstrom, L. S. On Sunday there might be Americans
Inyama, N. Hot days, long nights
Singer, I. B. Two markets
Updike, J. A & P

Markham, Edward Archibald
Mammie's form at the post office
The Oxford book of Caribbean short stories; edited by Stewart Brown and John Wickham

Markheim. Stevenson, R. L.
Markowsky, Jason
  Apollo Karamani
    Dalhousie Review v84 no2 p251-9 Summ
    2004
Marks, Jeffrey
  Under hoof
    White House pet detectives; tales of crime
    and mystery at the White House from a
    pet's-eye view; edited by Carole Nelson
    Douglas
Marks, Melanie
  Noah's walls
    'Teen v43 no5 p122-24 My 1999
The **marksman**. Howard, C.
Markus, Deborah
  For the love of vampires
    The Darkest thirst; a vampire anthology
Markus, Peter
  Good, brothers
    The Massachusetts Review v43 no2 p257-9
    Summ 2002
Marlowe, Stephen
  Wanted—dead and alive
    A Century of noir; thirty-two classic crime
    stories; edited by Mickey Spillane and Max
    Allan Collins
The **Marne**. Wharton, E.
Maron, Margaret
  The choice
    Malice domestic 10; an anthology of original
    traditional mystery stories
    Maron, M. Suitable for hanging
  Craquelure
    Maron, M. Suitable for hanging
  Croquet summer
    Maron, M. Suitable for hanging
  The dog that didn't bark
    Maron, M. Suitable for hanging
  The early retirement of Mario Colletti
    Maron, M. Suitable for hanging
  Growth marks
    Maron, M. Suitable for hanging
    Mom, apple pie, and murder; edited by Nancy
    Pickard
  Half of something
    Irreconcilable differences; Lia Matera, editor
    Maron, M. Suitable for hanging
  Lost and found
    Maron, M. Suitable for hanging
  Mixed blessings
    Maron, M. Suitable for hanging
    Women before the bench; edited by Carolyn
    Wheat; introduction by Linda Fairstein
  No, I'm not Jane Marple, but since you ask
    Maron, M. Suitable for hanging
  Roman's holiday
    Maron, M. Suitable for hanging
  Shaggy dog
    Maron, M. Suitable for hanging
  The stupid pet trick
    Maron, M. Suitable for hanging
  That married dear old dad
    Maron, M. Suitable for hanging
  The third element
    Maron, M. Suitable for hanging
  Till 3:45
    Love and death; edited by Carolyn Hart
    Maron, M. Suitable for hanging

To hide a tree
  Maron, M. Suitable for hanging
Virgo in sapphires
  Maron, M. Suitable for hanging
What's in a name?
  Maron, M. Suitable for hanging
  The Mysterious Press anniversary anthology;
  celebrating 25 years; by the editors of Mys-
  terious Press
Márquez, Gabriel García *See* García Márquez,
  Gabriel, 1928-
Marquise. Thurm, M.
MARRIAGE
    See also Childless marriage; Divorce;
    Family life; Husband and wife; Interracial
    marriage; Marriage problems; Weddings
Adams, A. The end of the world
Adams, A. Favors
Agee, J. The pop off valve
Agee, J. The trouble with the truth
Agee, J. Winter dreaming
Alcott, L. M. Mabel's May day
Alcott, L. M. The masked marriage
Aldrich, B. S. What God hath joined
Auchincloss, L. The interlude
Auchincloss, L. The marriage broker
Barrett, L. The former Star Carlson
Barth, J. Extension
Barthelme, F. Harmonic
Bass, R. The fireman
Bausch, R. Aren't you happy for me?
Bean, B. Hunting
Bean, B. Lost children
Bean, B. Rock star
Bean, B. There'll never be another you
Beattie, A. The burning house
Beattie, A. Mermaids
Berry, W. A jonquil for Mary Penn
Billman, J. Sugar City
Boylan, C. A nail on the head
Boylan, C. The secret diary of Mrs Rochester
Brennan, M. The bride
Brown, J. Hydrophobia
Bukoski, A. Bird of passage
Burford, M. 140 Sunset
Carson, J. The virgin
Carver, R. Vandals
Casey, M. Aspects of motherhood
Chekhov, A. P. The teacher of literature
Cheng, C.-W. The mosquito
Cheng, C.-W. Secrets
Cherry, K. Tell her
Chesnutt, C. W. A metropolitan experience
Chesnutt, C. W. Uncle Wellington's wives
Chopin, K. The going away of Liza
Daugherty, T. Assailable character
DeChoudhury, S. Forbidden fate
DeMarinis, R. Fault lines
Dixon, S. Give and take
Dokey, R. Electric dog
Doyle, R. The slave
Drake, R. The last old maid in town
Earley, T. Just married
Eldridge, Courtney. The former world record
  holder settles down
Ellin, S. The last bottle in the world
Epstein, J. Artie Glick in a family way
Epstein, J. The third Mrs. Kessler
Estep, M. Tools

MARRIAGE—*Continued*

Fairey, W. W. Mind and body
Farrell, C. The shining mountains
Fitzgerald, F. S. The cut-glass bowl
Foley, S. Dogfight
Ford, R. Privacy
Gaiman, N. The wedding present
Gavell, M. L. Baucis
Gavell, M. L. The blessing
Glave, T. Commitment
Goran, L. A guest on Good Friday
Goran, L. Why he never left his wife
Gourevitch, P. Mortality check
Gray, A. No bluebeard
Greer, A. S. Come live with me and be my love
Huddle, D. The day ghost
Jaime-Becerra, M. The corrido of Hector Cruz
James, H. The lesson of the master
Jordan, N. The dream of a beast
Joseph, D. Windows and words
Kane, J. F. Ideas of home, but not the thing itself
Kane, J. F. The trailing spouse
Kohler, S. Paris by night
Kreitman, Esther Singer. A satin coat
Lordan, B. Digging
Marías, J. In uncertain time
Maron, M. Half of something
Martin, P. P. Amor sufrido—Long-suffering love
Mastretta, A. Aunt Cristina
Mastretta, A. Aunt Eugenia
Mastretta, A. Aunt Valeria
Mathews, A. The strangest feeling in Bernard's bathroom
Mazor, J. The lost cause
McCorkle, J. Snakes
Miller, R. Julianne
Mo Yan. Soaring
Munro, A. Post and beam
Pak, W.-S. Thus ended my days of watching over the house
Paley, G. Wants
Poirier, M. J. Worms
Polansky, S. Rein
Rawley, D. The bible of insects
Régio, J. A brief comedy
Reisman, N. Confessions
Rose, D. All the little loved ones
Russo, R. Poison
Sanford, A. Helens and Roses
Silber, J. First marriage
Silver, M. What I saw from where I stood
Simonds, M. Navigating the Kattegat
Singer, I. B. Two weddings and one divorce
Slavin, J. Babyproofing
Spencer, E. Jack of diamonds
Stern, D. Apraxia
Stern, S. Romance
Swan, M. The new wife
Thien, M. A map of the city
Thomas, D. Grandma Hotel Adams
Thurm, M. Housecleaning
Tolstoy, L., graf. Why did it happen?
Vivante, A. Honeymoon
Vonnegut, K. Lovers Anonymous
Waugh, E. Love in the slump
Weldon, F. A great antipodean scandal
Weldon, F. Spirits fly south

Wharton, E. Bunner Sisters
Wilkinson, C. E. Humming back yesterday
Winterson, J. Holy matrimony
Yates, R. No pain whatsoever

MARRIAGE, CHILDLESS *See* Childless marriage

MARRIAGE, INTERRACIAL *See* Interracial marriage

The **marriage** at Antibes. Azadeh, C.
The **marriage** broker. Auchincloss, L.

MARRIAGE BROKERS

Avrich, J. Literary lonelyhearts
Sammān, G. Beheading the cat

MARRIAGE COUNSELING *See* Marriage problems

MARRIAGE CUSTOMS

Jews

Singer, I. B. The destruction of Kreshev
Singer, I. B. The needle
Singer, I. B. Yochna and Schmelke

India

Mukherjee, B. Happiness

Marriage lessons. Stolar, D.

The **Marriage** of Siddhartha Gautama Buddha. Hawk, B. W.

MARRIAGE PROBLEMS

See also Divorce; Family life; Love affairs

Adams, A. The drinking club
Adams, A. His women
Adams, A. Ocracoke Island
Adams, A. Your doctor loves you
Addonizio, K. In the box called pleasure
Agee, J. Adjusting the bite
Agee, J. The god of gestures
Agee, J. What's it take?
Alexie, S. Assimilation
Alexie, S. Class
Amanthis, J. Down there undercover
Amis, M. State of England
Anderson, D. Wonder bread
Anderson, S. The other woman
Arastuyi, S. I came to have tea with my daughter
Archer, J. Too many coincidences
Atwood, M. Wilderness tips
Auchincloss, L. The anniversary
Auchincloss, L. The scarlet letters
Auchincloss, L. The Virginia redbird
Avrich, J. La belle dame sans merci
Avrich, J. Lady Macbeth, prickly pear queen
Azadeh, C. The marriage at Antibes
Bahrami, A. Lida's cat, the bakery, and the streetlight pole
Banks, R. Indisposed
Banks, R. Mistake
Banks, R. Queen for a day
Banks, R. Theory of flight
Banville, J. Nightwind
Barker, N. The three button trick
Bart, P. The neighbors I
Barthelme, F. Chroma
Barthelme, F. Galveston
Barthelme, F. War with Japan
Barthelme, F. With Ray & Judy
Bauman, B. A. The middle of the night
Bausch, R. Contrition
Bausch, R. Evening
Bausch, R. The eyes of love

MARRIAGE PROBLEMS—*Continued*

Bausch, R. "My mistress' eyes are nothing like the sun"

Bausch, R. Police dreams

Bausch, R. Requisite kindness

Bausch, R. Someone to watch over me

Bausch, R. Valor

Bausch, R. Weather

Bean, B. Dream house

Blackwood, S. New years

Blackwood, S. Nostalgia

Blair, J. Bacon on the beach

Blair, J. Happy puppy

Blair, J. A small church in the country

Blaman, A. Lonely adventure [excerpt]

Bloch, R. Life in our time

Bocock, M. Alice and me

Bombal, M. L. The tree

Bonnie, F. All-you-can-eat night

Bosley, D. Beware the gentle wife

Bowen, E. Summer night

Bowles, P. The empty amulet

Bowles, P. The husband

Bowles, P. Reminders of Bouselham

Boylan, C. The complete angler

Boylan, C. Horrible luck

Boylan, C. It's her

Boylan, C. Technical difficulties and the plague

Boylan, C. That bad woman

Boylan, C. The wronged wife

Boylan, C. You don't know you're alive

Brady, C. Driving

Brady, C. Wild, wild horses

Brennan, M. The divine fireplace

Brockmeier, K. The ceiling

Broyard, B. Mr. Sweetly Indecent

Buchanan, E. Miami heat

Bukoski, A. Dry spell

Bunin, I. A. Caucasus

Burford, M. David and Kitty

Busch, F. Joy of cooking

Busch, F. Still the same old story

Busch, F. The talking cure

Cain, J. M. The baby in the icebox

Carlson, R. At the Jim Bridger

Carlson, R. Bigfoot stole my wife

Carver, R. Call if you need me

Carver, R. The third thing that killed my father off

Carver, R. What would you like to see?

Carver, R. Where I'm calling from

Cassill, R. V. And in my heart

Chabon, M. House hunting

Chabon, M. Son of the wolfman

Chabon, M. That was me

Chambers, C. Aardvark to Aztec

Chaon, D. I demand to know where you're taking me

Chaplin, P. Pot luck

Cheever, J. The country husband

Cheever, J. The five-forty-eight

Cheever, J. The season of divorce

Chekhov, A. P. Agafya

Chekhov, A. P. An anonymous story

Chekhov, A. P. The grasshopper

Chekhov, A. P. He quarrelled with his wife

Chekhov, A. P. The helpmate

Chekhov, A. P. The huntsman

Chekhov, A. P. The lady with the dog

Chekhov, A. P. Mari d'elle

Chekhov, A. P. Neighbours

Chekhov, A. P. Peasant wives

Chekhov, A. P. Revenge

Chekhov, A. P. Terror

Chekhov, A. P. The two Volodyas

Chekhov, A. P. The witch

Cherry, K. How it goes

Chiang, T. Division by zero

Chopin, K. Athénaïse

Chopin, K. Her letters

Chopin, K. In Sabine

Chopin, K. The storm

Clarke, B. For those of us who need such things

Clyde, M. Survival rates

Cobb, T. Adultery

Cobb, T. Face the music

Cobb, T. I'll never get out of this world alive

Cobb, W. When we were cool

Cobb, W. J. Marathon

Cohen, M. Alice's ground

Cohen, R. Theme from a summer place

Cohen, R. Between hammers

Cohen, R. Influence

Cohen, R. The varieties of romantic experience: an introduction

Connell, E. S. Election eve

Connolly, C. Canada

Connolly, C. Indian summer

Cook, K. L. Breaking glass

Cook, K. L. Knock down, drag out

Cook, K. L. Texas moon

Cooke, C. The sugar-tit

Costello, M. J. Someone who understands me

Cummins, A. Bitterwater

Cutler, J. Doctor's orders

Dark, A. E. Close

Davidson, L. Indian rope trick

Davidson, R. Maintenance

Davidson, R. You have to say something

Davies, Tristan. Snapdragon

Davis, A. Louisiana loses its cricket hum

Davis, D. S. Till death do us part

Davis, J. S. The ballad of my father's redneck wife

Davis, J. S. The one thing God'll give you

Davis, L. Cat's out of the bag

Day, C. The bullhook

Deaver, J. Triangle

DeLancey, K. Jules Jr Michael Jules Jr

DeMarco, T. Down at the end of lonely street

DeMarinis, R. The boys we were, the men we became

DeMarinis, R. Seize the day

DeMarinis, R. Under the wheat

DeMarinis, R. Wilderness

DeMarinis, R. Your burden is lifted, love returns

Dessen, S. Umbrella

Di Blasi, D. An interview with my husband

Dilworth, S. A little learning

Dixon, S. Comparing

Dixon, S. Never ends

Doctorow, E. L. Jolene: a life

Doenges, J. Occidental

Doerr, A. The hunter's wife

Doerr, A. Mkondo

Dokey, R. The monster

Dubus, A. The fat girl

MARRIAGE PROBLEMS—*Continued*

Earle, S. Doghouse roses
Engel, M. P. All that we need
Englander, N. For the relief of unbearable urges
Englander, N. The last one way
Epstein, J. Coming in with their hands up
Evenson, B. Virtual
Everett, P. L. Wolf at the door
Fadavi, P. The bitter life of Shirin
Fairey, W. W. Hermes
Falco, E. The revenant
Ferriss, L. Mud time
Ferriss, L. Politics
Ferriss, L. Safe-T-Man
Ferriss, L. The vortex
Ferriss, L. The woman who said no
Foley, S. Life in the air ocean
Foley, S. The state of union
Ford, R. Charity
Ford, R. Puppy
Ford, R. Reunion
Ford, R. Under the radar
Franklin, T. A tiny history
Franklin, T. Triathlon
Fromm, P. The gravy on the cake
Fromm, P. The raw material of ash
Frym, G. Loosestrife
Frym, G. "To see her in sunlight was to see Marxism die"
Fuchs, D. Man in the middle of the ocean
Furman, L. What would Buddha do?
Garro, E. Blame the Tlaxcaltecs
Gates, D. The bad thing
Gates, D. The crazy thought
Gates, D. Saturn
Gates, D. Vigil
Gates, D. A wronged husband
Gay, W. Closure and roadkill on the life's highway
Gay, W. Come home, come home, it's suppertime
Gay, W. Crossroads blues
Gay, W. A death in the woods
Gay, W. Good 'til now
Gay, W. Sugarbaby
Gilb, D. Shout
Gilchrist, E. A lady with pearls
Gilchrist, E. Miss Crystal's maid name Traceleen, she's talking, she's telling everything she knows
Gilman, C. P. Turned
Glave, T. Flying
Glover, D. H. Iglaf and Swan
Goldner, B. Plan B
Gordimer, N. The generation gap
Grau, S. A. Sea change
Grau, S. A. The wind shifting west
Grodstein, L. On the side
Grut, V. Escape artist
Guerrero, L. The girdle
Gunn, K. Not that much to go on
Gunn, K. The things he told her
Haake, K. A small measure of safety
Hager, J. Company wife
Hansen, R. True romance
Harfenist, J. Safety off, not a shot fired
Harrison, C. The commuter
Haruf, K. Dancing
Hayes, D. Prayers

Healy, J. F. Food for thought
Hegi, U. For their own survival
Helms, B. The confines of civilized behavior
Helms, B. Glazing
Hendricks, V. Gators
Henley, P. Labrador
Hensley, J. L. Widow
Highsmith, P. The returnees
Hoffman, A. Dear diary
Hoffman, W. Winter wheat
Homes, A. M. The Chinese lesson
Hood, A. New people
Hornsby, W. New moon and rattlesnakes
Hudson, S. The fall of the Nixon administration
Hunter, F. Pepper
Jacobs, M. The ballad of Tony Nail
Jacobs, M. Down in Paraguay
James, B. Big city
James, H. At Isella
James, H. The last of the Valerii
James, H. Madame de Mauves
Jenkins, G. Fumble
Johnston, B. A. Birds of Paradise
Jones, G. White rat
Jordan, J. The wife
Joseph, D. Many will enter, few will win
Jung, H.-Y. Our lady of the height
Kalfus, K. Budyonnovsk
Kane, J. F. Wreckers
Kaplan, H. Dysaesthesia
Kaplan, H. The edge of marriage
Kaplan, H. The spiral
Kawabata, Y. This country, that country
Keegan, C. Antarctica
Keegan, C. Men and women
Kees, W. The life of the mind
Kees, W. The Purcells
Kennedy, A. L. Spared
Kennedy, A. In our part of the world
King, C. My life is a country song
Kittredge, W. Agriculture
Klíma, I. A baffling choice
Klíma, I. Honeymoon
Klíma, I. Long-distance conversations
Klíma, I. The washing machine
Knight, M. Dogfight
Knight, M. Ellen's book
Knight, M. Poker
Knight, P. Set in stone
Koger, L. Bypass
Kohler, S. Casualty
Kohler, S. Rain check
Kohler, S. Trust
Krawiec, R. Maggots, infidelity, and the oyster roast
Krawiec, R. Troubles on Morning Glory Road
Kureishi, H. Intimacy
Kureishi, H. A meeting, at last
Kureishi, H. The umbrella
Lahiri, J. Interpreter of maladies
Lahiri, J. A temporary matter
Lankford, T. Detour Drive
Lawrence, D. H. Strike-pay
Leavitt, D. Route 80
Lee, M. Oh, happy day
Loayza, L. A new man
Locklin, G. The story story
Lopez, B. H. The construction of the Rachel
Louis, L. G. Divining the waters

MARRIAGE PROBLEMS—*Continued*

Louis, L. G. The quiet at the bottom of the pool
Lundquist, R. The motions of love
MacLaverty, B. Between two shores
Malone, M. A deer on the lawn
Maraini, D. Macaque
Martin, V. Transposing
Mason, B. A. Window lights
Mastretta, A. Aunt Carmen
Mastretta, A. Aunt Chila
Mastretta, A. Aunt Mariana
Matiella, A. C. Size does matter
Matiella, A. C. The truth about Alicia
Mayo, W. Mortal sins
Mazelis, J. Seven thousand flowers
Mazelis, J. Too perfect
Mazor, J. Gray skies
Mazor, J. The modern age
McBain, E. The victim
McCabe, B. Not about the kids
McCorkle, J. Migration of the love bugs
McGarry, J. Among the Philistines
McGarry, J. The Maestro
McManus, J. The future is orange
McNally, J. The end of romance
McNally, J. Limbs
McNeal, T. Watermelon Days
McNeal, T. Winter in Los Angeles
McWilliam, C. Seven magpies
Meloy, M. Four lean hounds, CA. 1976
Melville, P. The sparkling bitch
Menendez, A. The last rescue
Millar, M. The couple next door
Miller, A. L. Off-season travel
Miller, R. Greta
Miner, C. Rhonda and her children
Moore, L. Real estate
Morris, M. Just an old cur
Mrabet, M. The canebrake
Mukherjee, B. Happiness
Munro, A. The bear came over the mountain
Munro, A. The children stay
Munro, A. What is remembered
Murakami, H. UFO in Kushiro
Murray, J. The carpenter who looked like a boxer
Nawrocki, S. Louise and Al get married
Nelson, A. Happy hour
Nelson, A. Palisades
Ní Dhuibhne-Almqvist, É. The Garden of Eden
Norris, H. Judgment day
Norris, H. One day in the life of a born again loser
Norris, L. Swimmers
Norris, L. Trailer people
Oates, J. C. Raven's Wing
O'Callaghan, M. Black is the color of my true love's heart
O'Callaghan, M. Sorry, Frank
O'Connor, J. The long way home
Ortiz, S. J. 3 women
Ortiz, S. J. Anything
Ossana, D. White line fever
Padilla, M. Hard language
Painter, P. Bedtime story
Patterson, K. Insomnia, infidelity, and the leopard seal
Patterson, K. Les is more
Penn, W. S. So much water, underground

Perabo, S. Counting the ways
Phillips, D. R. What it cost travelers
Phillips, D. R. The woods at the back of our houses
Pittalwala, I. House of cards
Pittalwala, I. Kulsum, Nazia, and Ismail
Pittalwala, I. Ramadan
Poirier, M. J. Cul-de-sacs
Polansky, S. Pantalone
Pollard, V. Altamont Jones
Ponte, A. J. Because of men
Potvin, E. A. Blue moon
Potvin, E. A. Deflection
Potvin, E. A. Ghost
Potvin, E. A. Riding to Tibet
Powers, S. The wild
Pronzini, B. Wishful thinking
Prose, F. The witch
Proulx, A. The wer-trout
Reid, E. No strings attached
Richards, J. How this song ends
Ritchie, E. Telling Mr. M.
Rivera Valdés, S. Little poisons
Robison, M. Care
Robison, M. Independence day
Rucker, R. v. B. Inside out
Russo, R. Buoyancy
Sade, marquis de. An eye for an eye
Sade, marquis de. The fortunate ruse
Sade, marquis de. The husband who turned priest: a tale of Provence
Sade, marquis de. Room for two
Sánchez, R. El tejón
Saunders, G. No money for stamps
Savage, T. One of us
Schlink, B. A little fling
Schmidt, H. J. Songbirds
Schnitzler, A. Death of a bachelor
Scholz, C. The eve of the last Apollo
Scoville, S. Clara and Ben
Seiffert, R. Second best
Shabtai, Y. Uncle Peretz takes flight
Shaw, D. Any myth you can imagine
Shepard, J. In the open
Shepard, S. The stout of heart
Shields, C. Larry's words, 1983
Shrayer-Petrov, D. He, she and the others
Shrayer-Petrov, D. Rusty
Simonds, M. Taken for delirium
Simpson, H. Cheers
Singer, I. B. Advice
Singer, I. B. Big and little
Singer, I. B. Blood
Singer, I. B. Burial at sea
Singer, I. B. The bus
Singer, I. B. The destruction of Kreshev
Singer, I. B. Disguised
Singer, I. B. Dr. Beeber
Singer, I. B. Gimpel the fool
Singer, I. B. Her son
Singer, I. B. The image
Singer, I. B. The impresario
Singer, I. B. The mathematician
Singer, I. B. The mentor
Singer, I. B. The mistake
Singer, I. B. Moishele
Singer, I. B. On a wagon
Singer, I. B. The prodigy
Singer, I. B. The riddle

MARRIAGE PROBLEMS—*Continued*

Singer, I. B. The third one
Singer, I. B. The unseen
Singer, I. B. The witch
Singleton, G. Answers
Singleton, G. Caulk
Singleton, G. Deer gone
Singleton, G. Dialectic, abrasions, the backs of heads again
Singleton, G. Directions for seeing, directions for singing
Skillings, R. D. Outcomes
Slavin, J. Pudding
Slesar, H. Change partners
Smart, A. The wedding Dress
Smith, A. Believe me
Sobott-Mogwe, G. Smile of fortune
Sorrentino, G. In loveland
Sorrentino, G. Land of cotton
Sorrentino, G. Perdído
Sosin, D. This third year of returning
Spatz, G. Body
Spatz, G. Inversion
Spatz, G. Plenty of pools in Texas
Spatz, G. Wonderful tricks
Spencer, B. This is the last of the nice
Spencer, D. The 12-inch dog
Spencer, D. Park host
Spencer, E. The business venture
Spencer, E. The finder
Stegner, L. Pipers at the gates of dawn
Steinbeck, J. The murder
Stollman, A. L. The dialogues of time and entropy
Straub, P. Mr. Clubb and Mr. Cuff
Straub, P. Perdido: a fragment from a work in progress
Strauss, A. Still life
Stuckey-French, E. The first paper girl in Red Oak, Iowa
Swift, G. Learning to swim
Taylor, T. L. Francisco's watch
Thompson, J. Poor Helen
Thompson, J. The rich man's house
Thurm, M. Cold
Thurm, M. Moonlight
Thurm, M. Mourners
Tilghman, C. Mary in the mountains
Tilghman, C. Something important
Tilghman, C. Things left undone
Tinti, H. Gallus, gallus
Todd, R. L. Vinegar
Tomioka, T. Time table
Tomioka, T. Yesteryear
Troy, M. Bird of pardise
Troy, M. Do you believe in the chicken hanger?
Tuck, L. Hotter
Tuck, L. Next of kin
Tuck, L. Second wife
Tyre, N. Recipe for a happy marriage
Upadhyay, S. The good shopkeeper
Upidke, J. Avec la bébé-sitter
Updike, J. Dear Alexandros
Updike, J. Eros rampant
Updike, J. Four sides of one story
Updike, J. Gesturing
Updike, J. Killing
Updike, J. Leaves
Updike, J. The man who loved extinct mammals

Updike, J. My lover has dirty fingernails
Updike, J. Separating
Updike, J. Snowing in Greenwich Village
Updike, J. Solitaire
Updike, J. The stare
Updike, J. Sublimating
Updike, J. Twin beds in Rome
Updike, J. Your lover just called
Vivante, A. Can-can
Vivante, A. The homing pigeon
Vonnegut, K. Custom-made bride
Vonnegut, K. Hal Irwin's magic lamp
Wallace, R. Topless in Tucson
Warren, D. Long gone and Mister Lonely
Warren, Lee Gay. Vials of life
Watson, B. Last days of the dog-men
Waugh, E. By special request
Waugh, E. Period piece
Waugh, E. Too much tolerance
Weldon, F. Leda and the swan
Weldon, F. My mother said
Weldon, F. Once in love in Oslo
Westlake, D. E. The mother of invention is worth a pound of cure
Wharton, E. Atrophy
Wharton, E. The day of the funeral
Wharton, E. The duchess at prayer
Wharton, E. Joy in the house
White, M. C. Burn patterns
White, M. C. Three whacks a buck
Williams, J. The farm
Winegardner, M. Song for a certain girl
Yamamoto, H. Seventeen syllables
Yates, R. The comptroller and the wild wind
Yates, R. Evening on the Côte d'Azur
Yates, R. Liars in love
Yates, R. A natural girl
Yi, T.-H. Dark valley
Young, T. Yellow with black horns
Zweig, S. Fear

MARRIAGE PROPOSALS

Boylan, C. To tempt a woman
Chekhov, A. P. Foiled!
Karnezis, P. Medical ethics
Thomas, D. The joybell
The **marriages**. James, H.
Marric, J. J., 1908-1973
> *For works written by this author under other names see Creasey, John, 1908-1973*

Marry the one who gets there first. Julavits, H.
The **Marrying** Kind. Feitell, M.

MARS (PLANET)

Aldiss, B. W. Near earth object
Aldiss, B. W. A whiter Mars
Amis, M. The janitor on Mars
Asimov, I. The Martian way
Baxter, S. Martian autumn
Bear, G. A Martian Ricorso
Bova, B. Mount Olympus
Brackett, L. The last days of Shandakor
Bradbury, R. 2004-05: The naming of names
Bradbury, R. April 2005: Usher II
Bradbury, R. April 2026: The long years
Bradbury, R. Dark they were, and golden-eyed
Bradbury, R. June 2001: And the moon be still as bright
Bradbury, R. June 2003: Way in the middle of the air
Bradbury, R. A little journey

MARS (PLANET)—*Continued*

Bradbury, R. The lonely ones
Bradbury, R. The love affair
Bradbury, R. Mars is heaven!
Bradbury, R. The Messiah
Bradbury, R. The million-year picnic
Bradbury, R. The visitor
Brown, E. Myths of the Martian future
Clarke, A. C. Transit of earth
Delany, S. R. High weir
Di Filippo, P. A Martian theodicy
Dozois, G. R. The gods of Mars
Edelman, S. Mom, the Martians, and me
Fabra, N. M. On the planet Mars
Harrison, H. Simulated trainer
Harrison, H. Welcoming committee
Keith, W. H. Fossils
Landis, G. A. Ecopoiesis
Lovegrove, J. Out of the blue, into the red
Lupoff, R. A. Black mist
McAuley, P. J. Under Mars
McDonald, I. The old cosmonaut and the construction worker dream of Mars
Moorcock, M. Lost sorceress of the silent citadel
Morrow, J. The war of the worldviews
Norton, A. Mousetrap
O'Leary, P. The me after the rock
Oliver, C. Artifact
Pronzini, B. Epitaph
Resnick, M. and Bell, M. S. Flower children of Mars
Reynolds, A. Great walls of Mars
Reynolds, A. The real story
Robinson, K. S. A Martian romance
Steele, A. M. A walk across Mars
Sterling, B. Sunken gardens
Tenn, W. The sickness
Turzillo, M. A. Mars is no place for children
Waldrop, H. Lunchbox
Weinbaum, S. G. A Martian odyssey
Wolfe, G. Shields of Mars
Mars is heaven!. Bradbury, R.
Mars is no place for children. Turzillo, M. A.
Mars Jeems's nightmare. Chesnutt, C. W.
Mars-Jones, Adam

Everything is different in your house
Granta no75 p191-216 Aut 2001
Mars needs women!. Brownrigg, S.
Marsella, Anne

Enchanté
The Southern Review (Baton Rouge, La.) v39 no2 p340-54 Spr 2003
Marsh, Geoffrey *See* Grant, Charles L.
Marsh, Dame Ngaio

I can find my way out
A moment on the edge; 100 years of crime stories by women; edited by Elizabeth George
The **marsh** runners. Brandon, P.
Marshall, Alexandra

Child Widow
Ploughshares v29 no2/3 p92-102 Fall 2003
Marshall, Bevlyn

White sugar and red clay
Stories from the Blue Moon Café; edited by Sonny Brewer

Marshall, Paule

To Da-duh, in memoriam
The Oxford book of Caribbean short stories; edited by Stewart Brown and John Wickham
Marshall, Peyton

Bunnymoon
Best new American voices 2004; guest editor John Casey; series editors John Kulka and Natalie Danford
Marshall, Terry

American model
Living on the edge; fiction by Peace Corps writers; edited by John Coyne
Marshall, Tom

Legends of West Street
The Canadian Forum v78 no878 p28-30 Je 1999
Marshall, William Leonard

Them!
The Mysterious Press anniversary anthology; celebrating 25 years; by the editors of Mysterious Press
The **marshal's** widow. Chekhov, A. P.
Marsten, Richard

Every morning
Speaking of lust; stories of forbidden desire; edited by Lawrence Block
Marsten, Richard, 1926-

For works written by this author under other names see Hunter, Evan, 1926-; McBain, Ed, 1926-
Marston, Edward

Perfect shadows
Royal whodunnits; edited by Mike Ashley
Slaughter in the Strand
The best British mysteries; edited by Maxim Jakubowski
Marston, Edward and Lovesey, Peter

The Corbett correspondence: "Agent no. 5 & Agent no. 6"
Murder most postal; homicidal tales that deliver a message; edited by Martin H. Greenberg
MARTHA, SAINT

About

O'Connell, M. Saint Martha
Martha, Henry *See* Harris, Mark, 1922-
Martha Grace. Duffy, S.
Martha, Martha. Smith, Z.
Martha's dilemma. Johnson, C. R.
Martha's parrot. Hoch, E. D.
MARTHA'S VINEYARD (MASS.)

Chenoweth, A. Housework
MARTIAL ARTS

Donaldson, S. R. The killing stroke
Lansdale, J. R. Master of misery
Reid, E. Happy Jack
Vachss, A. H. Mission
Martian autumn. Baxter, S.
A **Martian** odyssey. Weinbaum, S. G.
A **Martian** Ricorso. Bear, G.
A **Martian** romance. Robinson, K. S.
A **Martian** theodicy. Di Filippo, P.
The **Martian** way. Asimov, I.
MARTIANS

See also Interplanetary visitors; Mars (Planet)
Boylan, C. Life on Mars

MARTIANS—*Continued*
Bradbury, R. Dark they were, and golden-eyed
Bradbury, R. February 1999: Y11a
Bradbury, R. The Messiah
Clarke, A. C. Jupiter five
Clarke, A. C. Loophole
Lansdale, J. R. Bar talk
Matheson, R. Trespass
McCaffrey, A. Freedom of the race
Zelazny, R. A rose for Ecclesiastes
MARTIN, BILLY, 1928-1989
About
Jenkins, G. Night game
Martin, Douglas A.
An Escort
The Literary Review (Madison, N.J.) v46 no4 p672-6 Summ 2003
Martin, George R. R.
The hero
Wondrous beginnings; edited by Steven H. Silver and Martin H. Greenberg
Sandkings
Masterpieces: the best science fiction of the century; edited by Orson Scott Card
The sworn sword
Silverberg, R. Legends II; new short novels by the masters of modern fantasy; edited by Robert Silverberg
The way of cross and dragon
Brown, C. N. and Strahan, J. The Locus awards; thirty years of the best in science fiction and fantasy; edited by Charles N. Brown and Jonathan Strahan
The Good new stuff; adventure SF in the grand tradition; edited by Gardner Dozois
Martin, Lee
Bad family
A different plain; contemporary Nebraska fiction writers; edited by Ladette Randolph ; introduction by Mary Pipher
Belly Talk
The Southern Review (Baton Rouge, La.) v39 no1 p155-67 Wint 2003
Dummies, Shakers, Barkers, Wanderers
The Kenyon Review v26 no1 p129-43 Wint 2004
Martin, Patricia Preciado
Amor de acuerdo—Arranged love
Martin, P. P. Amor eterno; eleven lessons in love
Amor de madre—Mother's love
Martin, P. P. Amor eterno; eleven lessons in love
Amor desesperado—Desperate love
Martin, P. P. Amor eterno; eleven lessons in love
Amor e ilusion—Love and illusion
Martin, P. P. Amor eterno; eleven lessons in love
Amor encantado—Enchanted love
Martin, P. P. Amor eterno; eleven lessons in love
Amor eterno—Eternal love
Martin, P. P. Amor eterno; eleven lessons in love
Amor frustrado—Frustrated love
Martin, P. P. Amor eterno; eleven lessons in love

Amor inolvidable—Unforgettable love
Martin, P. P. Amor eterno; eleven lessons in love
Amor perdido—Lost love
Martin, P. P. Amor eterno; eleven lessons in love
Amor prohibido—Forbidden love
Martin, P. P. Amor eterno; eleven lessons in love
Amor sufrido—Long-suffering love
Martin, P. P. Amor eterno; eleven lessons in love
Martin, Stephen-Paul
Collapsing into a Story
Western Humanities Review v57 no1 p54-65 Spr 2003
Impossible
Western Humanities Review v58 no1 p78-87 Spr 2004
The Possibility of Music
Western Humanities Review v58 no1 p88-98 Spr 2004
Martin, Tom
Witness
Ploughshares v29 no2/3 p103-11 Fall 2003
Martin, Valerie
Contraction
Martin, V. Love; short stories
The creator has a master plan
Martin, V. Love; short stories
Love
Martin, V. Love; short stories
The mechanics of it
Martin, V. Love; short stories
Messengers
Martin, V. Love; short stories
The open door
The Massachusetts Review v43 no2 p190-212 Summ 2002
Surface calm
Martin, V. Love; short stories
Transposing
Martin, V. Love; short stories
Martin. Mayhall, J.
Martini, Steve
Poetic justice
A Century of great suspense stories; edited by Jeffery Deaver
Martone, Michael
Contributor's Note
The Literary Review (Madison, N.J.) v46 no4 p639-41 Summ 2003
The Literary Review (Madison, N.J.) v46 no4 p642-4 Summ 2003
The Literary Review (Madison, N.J.) v46 no4 p639-41 Summ 2003
The Literary Review (Madison, N.J.) v46 no4 p642-4 Summ 2003
The **martyr**. Anderson, P.
Marusek, David
The wedding album
Nebula awards showcase 2001; the year's best SF and fantasy chosen by the science fiction and fantasy writers of America; edited by Robert Silverberg
The Year's best science fiction, seventeenth annual collection; edited by Gardner Dozois
Marvel Bird. Coleman, J. C.
Marvells of Utopia. Aldiss, B. W.

MARY, BLESSED VIRGIN, SAINT
About
Chaviano, D. The annunciation
MARY, QUEEN OF SCOTS, 1542-1587
About
Barnett, P. Two dead men
Mary. Monardo, A.
Mary and the seal. Williamson, D.
Mary Ann. Brennan, K.
Mary in the mountains. Tilghman, C.
Mary Magdalena versus Godzilla. Mayo, W.
Mary Mountjoy's dowry. Berkman, P. R.
Mary, Staring at Me. Shah, S.
MARYLAND
       See also Chesapeake Bay (Md. and Va.)
Baltimore
Baida, P. Family ties
Davies, Tristan. Grouper Schmidt
Jenkins, G. Red roses and cognac
McManus, J. Stop breakin down
McManus, J. Vlad the nefarious
Maryland. Aylett, S.
MASAI (AFRICAN PEOPLE)
Watanabe McFerrin, L. Masai heart
Masai heart. Watanabe McFerrin, L.
The **masculinist** revolt. Tenn, W.
Masiki, Trent
  With myth and fire
    Callaloo v25 no2 p407-15 Spr 2002
The **masked** dyer, Hakim of Merv. See Borges, J.
    L. Hakim, the masked dyer of Merv
The **masked** marriage. Alcott, L. M.
Masking Indian. De Lint, C.
Masks. Knight, D. F.
Maso, Carole
  The names
    The Pushcart prize XXVI; best of the small
    presses, an annual small press reader; ed-
    ited by Bill Henderson and the Pushcart
    prize editors
MASOCHISM
Biguenet, J. Do me
Campbell, R. The body in the window
Lane, J. The window
Lansdale, J. R. I tell you it's love
Leiber, F. Coming attraction
Martin, V. Surface calm
Mason, Bobbie Ann
  Charger
    Mason, B. A. Zigzagging down a wild trail;
    stories
  The funeral side
    Mason, B. A. Zigzagging down a wild trail;
    stories
    The Southern Review (Baton Rouge, La.) v35
    no3 p525-43 Summ 1999
  Night flight
    Mason, B. A. Zigzagging down a wild trail;
    stories
  Proper gypsies
    Mason, B. A. Zigzagging down a wild trail;
    stories
  Residents and transients
    Home and beyond; an anthology of Kentucky
    short stories; edited by Morris Allen
    Grubbs; with an introduction by Wade Hall
    and an afterword by Charles E. May

  Rolling into Atlanta
    Mason, B. A. Zigzagging down a wild trail;
    stories
  Three-wheeler
    Atlantic Monthly v287 no6 p76-80 Je 2001
    Mason, B. A. Zigzagging down a wild trail;
    stories
  Thunder snow
    Mason, B. A. Zigzagging down a wild trail;
    stories
  Tobrah
    Mason, B. A. Zigzagging down a wild trail;
    stories
  Tunica
    Mason, B. A. Zigzagging down a wild trail;
    stories
  Window lights
    Mason, B. A. Zigzagging down a wild trail;
    stories
  Wish
    The Art of the story; an international antholo-
    gy of contemporary short stories; edited by
    Daniel Halpern
  With jazz
    Mason, B. A. Zigzagging down a wild trail;
    stories
Mason, Nicola
  The bad seed: a guide
    The Pushcart prize XXVI; best of the small
    presses, an annual small press reader; ed-
    ited by Bill Henderson and the Pushcart
    prize editors
  The whimsied world
    New stories from the South: the year's best,
    2001; edited by Shannon Ravenel; with a
    preface by Lee Smith
Mason, Sarah J.
  With thanks to Agatha Christie
    Mom, apple pie, and murder; edited by Nancy
    Pickard
MASQUERADES
Fitzgerald, F. S. The camel's back
Westlake, D. E. Devilishly
Mass theft. Lisick, B.
MASSACHUSETTS
       See also Martha's Vineyard (Mass.)
Gates, D. E. The blue mirror
Lee, M. A king's epitaph
Smolens, J. My one and only bomb shelter
Theroux, P. A Judas memoir
Updike, J. The hillies
Yolen, J. Great gray
17th century
Hawthorne, N. The gentle boy
Hawthorne, N. My kinsman, Major Molineux
Boston
Davies, P. H. Small world
The Death of Colonel Thoureau
Delaney, E. J. Hero
Dodd, S. M. So far you can't imagine
Greer, R. O. The real thing
Hawthorne, N. The gray champion
James, H. A New England winter
Johnson, C. R. Murderous thoughts
Johnson, C. R. The soulcatcher
Landis, G. A. Impact parameter
Lee, M. A fresh start
McPherson, J. A. Gold Coast
Reisman, N. Rubies

MASSACHUSETTS—Boston—*Continued*
Rodburg, M. Concessions
Searle, E. Celebrities in disgrace
Verghese, A. Lilacs
Wharton, E. Duration
Wilson, R., Jr. Dorothy and her friends
     18th century
Hawthorne, N. Howe's masquerade
        Cambridge
Lahiri, J. Nobody's business
        Cape Cod
Smolens, J. The errand
Smolens, J. The Meetinghouse
        Provincetown
Shrayer-Petrov, D. Hurricane Bob
Skillings, R. D. Ashes
Skillings, R. D. At least
Skillings, R. D. Constant concupiscence
Skillings, R. D. Coughlan Dice at his closet
    window
Skillings, R. D. Czezarley Zoo gets out
Skillings, R. D. Doggy
Skillings, R. D. Job ops
Skillings, R. D. The line
Skillings, R. D. No escape for yours truly
Skillings, R. D. Noon, afternoon, night
Skillings, R. D. Paint
Skillings, R. D. Tabletalk
Massachusetts 1932. Bowles, P.
Massachusetts, California, Timbuktoo. Rosenfeld,
    S.
MASSACRES
Carroll, L. Leaving paradise
Kalu, Anthonia C. Osondu
Wuori, G. K. Parents
En **masse**. Mosley, W.
Massey, Sujata
The convenience boy
    Tart noir; edited by Stella Duffy & Lauren
      Henderson
Junior high samurai
    Malice domestic 10; an anthology of original
      traditional mystery stories
Massie, Allan
In the bare lands
    The Vintage book of contemporary Scottish
      fiction; edited and with an introduction by
      Peter Kravitz
Massie-Ferch, Kathleen M.
A touch through time
    Past imperfect; edited by Martin H. Green-
      berg and Larry Segriff
Master Eustace. James, H.
The **master** key. Anderson, P.
The **master** of Shongalo. Spencer, E.
The **master** tailor and the teacher's skirt. Heath,
    R. A. K.
Mastering Lady Lucinda. Small, B.
Masters, Hilary
Harriet Munro: the untold story
    The Virginia Quarterly Review v77 no4
      p680-7 Aut 2001
The **master's** ring. Epstein, J.
Masterton, Graham
The Ballyhooly boy
    Best new horror 11; edited and with an intro-
      duction by Stephen Jones

Mastretta, Angeles
Aunt Amanda
    Mastretta, A. Women with big eyes; {translat-
      ed by Amy Schildhouse Greenberg}
Aunt Carmen
    Mastretta, A. Women with big eyes; {translat-
      ed by Amy Schildhouse Greenberg}
Aunt Cecilia
    Mastretta, A. Women with big eyes; {translat-
      ed by Amy Schildhouse Greenberg}
Aunt Celia
    Mastretta, A. Women with big eyes; {translat-
      ed by Amy Schildhouse Greenberg}
Aunt Charo
    Mastretta, A. Women with big eyes; {translat-
      ed by Amy Schildhouse Greenberg}
Aunt Chila
    Mastretta, A. Women with big eyes; {translat-
      ed by Amy Schildhouse Greenberg}
Aunt Clemencia
    Mastretta, A. Women with big eyes; {translat-
      ed by Amy Schildhouse Greenberg}
Aunt Concha
    Mastretta, A. Women with big eyes; {translat-
      ed by Amy Schildhouse Greenberg}
Aunt Concha Esparza
    Colchie, T. A whistler in the nightworld;
      short fiction from the Latin Americas; ed-
      ited by Thomas Colchie
Aunt Cristina
    Mastretta, A. Women with big eyes; {translat-
      ed by Amy Schildhouse Greenberg}
Aunt Daniela
    Mastretta, A. Women with big eyes; {translat-
      ed by Amy Schildhouse Greenberg}
Aunt Elena
    Mastretta, A. Women with big eyes; {translat-
      ed by Amy Schildhouse Greenberg}
Aunt Elvira
    Mastretta, A. Women with big eyes; {translat-
      ed by Amy Schildhouse Greenberg}
Aunt Eugenia
    Mastretta, A. Women with big eyes; {translat-
      ed by Amy Schildhouse Greenberg}
Aunt Fátima
    Mastretta, A. Women with big eyes; {translat-
      ed by Amy Schildhouse Greenberg}
Aunt Fernanda
    Mastretta, A. Women with big eyes; {translat-
      ed by Amy Schildhouse Greenberg}
Aunt Isabel
    Mastretta, A. Women with big eyes; {translat-
      ed by Amy Schildhouse Greenberg}
Aunt Jose
    Mastretta, A. Women with big eyes; {translat-
      ed by Amy Schildhouse Greenberg}
Aunt Laura
    Mastretta, A. Women with big eyes; {translat-
      ed by Amy Schildhouse Greenberg}
Aunt Leonor
    Mastretta, A. Women with big eyes; {translat-
      ed by Amy Schildhouse Greenberg}
Aunt Magdalena
    Mastretta, A. Women with big eyes; {translat-
      ed by Amy Schildhouse Greenberg}
Aunt Marcela and Aunt Jacinta
    Mastretta, A. Women with big eyes; {translat-
      ed by Amy Schildhouse Greenberg}

Mastretta, Angeles—_Continued_
Aunt Mariana
Mastretta, A. Women with big eyes; {translated by Amy Schildhouse Greenberg}
Aunt Mercedes
Mastretta, A. Women with big eyes; {translated by Amy Schildhouse Greenberg}
Aunt Natalia
Mastretta, A. Women with big eyes; {translated by Amy Schildhouse Greenberg}
Aunt Paulina
Mastretta, A. Women with big eyes; {translated by Amy Schildhouse Greenberg}
Aunt Pilar and Aunt Marta
Mastretta, A. Women with big eyes; {translated by Amy Schildhouse Greenberg}
Aunt Rebeca
Mastretta, A. Women with big eyes; {translated by Amy Schildhouse Greenberg}
Aunt Teresa
Mastretta, A. Women with big eyes; {translated by Amy Schildhouse Greenberg}
Aunt Valeria
Mastretta, A. Women with big eyes; {translated by Amy Schildhouse Greenberg}
Aunt Verónica
Mastretta, A. Women with big eyes; {translated by Amy Schildhouse Greenberg}
Big-eyed women [excerpt]
The Vintage book of Latin American stories; edited by Carlos Fuentes and Julio Ortega
MASTURBATION
Amis, M. Let me count the times
Edgerton, C. Debra's flap and snap
Hayes, D. This world of ours
Homes, A. M. Georgica
Johnson, A. The Canadanaut
Schmatz, P. Tokyo trains
Taylor, B. Walnuts, when the husks are green
Masud, Naiyer _See_ Naiyer Masud
Masuri, Nosrat
Downfall
A Feast in the mirror; stories by contemporary Iranian women; translated and edited by Mohammad Mehdi Khorrami, Shouleh Vatanabadi
MATA HARI, 1876-1917
About
Berliner, J. Eye of the day
MATCHMAKERS _See_ Marriage brokers
The **matchmakers**. Ramaya, S.
MATCHMAKING
Leegant, J. The diviners of desire: a modern fable
Ramaya, S. The matchmakers
Waters, M. Y. Egg-face
Matera, Lia
Counsel for the defense
Matera, L. Counsel for the defense and other stories
Dead drunk
A Century of noir; thirty-two classic crime stories; edited by Mickey Spillane and Max Allan Collins
Matera, L. Counsel for the defense and other stories
Destroying angel
Matera, L. Counsel for the defense and other stories

Do not resuscitate
Matera, L. Counsel for the defense and other stories
Dream lawyer
Matera, L. Counsel for the defense and other stories
The World's finest mystery and crime stories, first annual collection; edited by Ed Gorman
Easy go
Matera, L. Counsel for the defense and other stories
If it can't be true
Irreconcilable differences; Lia Matera, editor
Matera, L. Counsel for the defense and other stories
Performance crime
Matera, L. Counsel for the defense and other stories
The river mouth
Matera, L. Counsel for the defense and other stories
A moment on the edge; 100 years of crime stories by women; edited by Elizabeth George
The **Mathematician** Repents. Nagy, E.
MATHEMATICIANS
Carlson, R. Towel season
Clarke, A. C. The pacifist
Doolittle, S. Summa mathematica
Goldstein, R. The courtship
Iagnemma, K. On the nature of human romantic interaction
Iagnemma, K. The ore miner's wife
Iagnemma, K. Zilkowski's theorem
Kane, J. F. The Arnold proof
Michaels, L. Nachman
Singer, I. B. The mathematician
Whitty, J. Falling umbrella
MATHEMATICS
Chiang, T. Division by zero
Rucker, R. v. B. A new golden age
Rucker, R. v. B. Pi in the sky
Rucker, R. v. B. The square root of Pythagoras
Watson, I. Nanunculus
Mathematics and acrobatics. Richmond, M.
Mathes, Teresa S.
Fourth of July
South Carolina Review v36 no1 p127-39 Fall 2003
The sound is so shallow here
The Georgia Review v53 no3 p529-45 Fall 1999
Matheson, Richard
Being
Matheson, R. Duel; terror stories
Born of man and woman
Matheson, R. Duel; terror stories
The Science fiction hall of fame: volume one, 1929-1964; the greatest science fiction stories of all time chosen by the members of the Science Fiction Writers of America; edited by Robert Silverberg
Brother to the machine
Matheson, R. Duel; terror stories
Death ship
Matheson, R. Duel; terror stories
Duel
Matheson, R. Duel; terror stories

Matheson, Richard—*Continued*

Fm
Matheson, R. Duel; terror stories
The last day
Matheson, R. Duel; terror stories
Little girl lost
Matheson, R. Duel; terror stories
Lover when you're near me
Matheson, R. Duel; terror stories
One for the books
Matheson, R. Duel; terror stories
Prey
The American fantasy tradition; edited by Brian M. Thomsen
Return
Matheson, R. Duel; terror stories
Shipshape home
Matheson, R. Duel; terror stories
SRL ad
Matheson, R. Duel; terror stories
Steel
Matheson, R. Duel; terror stories
The test
Matheson, R. Duel; terror stories
Third from the sun
Matheson, R. Duel; terror stories
Trespass
Matheson, R. Duel; terror stories
When the waker sleeps
Matheson, R. Duel; terror stories

Matheson, Richard Christian

Graduation
Murder most postal; homicidal tales that deliver a message; edited by Martin H. Greenberg
Holiday
A yuletide universe; sixteen fantastical tales; edited by Brian M. Thomsen

Mathews, Aidan

The story of the German parachutist who landed forty-two years late
The Anchor book of new Irish writing; the new Gaelach ficsean; edited and with an introduction by John Somer and John J. Daly
The strangest feeling in Bernard's bathroom
The Anchor book of new Irish writing; the new Gaelach ficsean; edited and with an introduction by John Somer and John J. Daly

Mathews, Harry

Brendan
Mathews, H. The human country; new and collected stories
The Broadcast
Harvard Review (1992) no23 p114-15 Fall 2002
Mathews, H. The human country; new and collected stories
Calibrations of latitude
Mathews, H. The human country; new and collected stories
The chariot
Mathews, H. The human country; new and collected stories
Clocking the world on cue: the chronogram for 2001
Mathews, H. The human country; new and collected stories

Country cooking from central France: roast boned rolled stuffed shoulder of lamb (farce double)
Mathews, H. The human country; new and collected stories
Dear mother
Mathews, H. The human country; new and collected stories
The Pushcart prize XXIV: best of the small presses; an annual small press reader; edited by Bill Henderson with the Pushcart prize editors
The dialect of the tribe
Mathews, H. The human country; new and collected stories
Franz Kafka in Riga
Mathews, H. The human country; new and collected stories
Journeys to six lands
Chicago Review v47 no3 p5-13 Fall 2001
Mathews, H. The human country; new and collected stories
The ledge
Mathews, H. The human country; new and collected stories
Letters from Yerevan
Mathews, H. The human country; new and collected stories
Mr. Smathers
Mathews, H. The human country; new and collected stories
The network
Mathews, H. The human country; new and collected stories
The novel as history
Mathews, H. The human country; new and collected stories
One-way mirror
Mathews, H. The human country; new and collected stories
Remarks of the scholar graduate
Mathews, H. The human country; new and collected stories
Soap opera
Mathews, H. The human country; new and collected stories
Still life
Mathews, H. The human country; new and collected stories
The taxidermist
Mathews, H. The human country; new and collected stories
Tear sheet
Mathews, H. The human country; new and collected stories
Their words, for you
Mathews, H. The human country; new and collected stories
Tradition and the individual talent:the "Bratislava spiccato"
Mathews, H. The human country; new and collected stories
The way home
Mathews, H. The human country; new and collected stories

Mathews, Lou

Crazy life
LA shorts; edited by Steven Gilbar

Mathewson, Christy
The alumni game
Dead balls and double curves; an anthology of early baseball fiction; edited and with an introduction by Trey Strecker ; with a foreword by Arnold Hano

Matiella, Ana Consuelo
Angels
Matiella, A. C. The truth about Alicia and other stories
El bebé del vaquerón
Matiella, A. C. The truth about Alicia and other stories
The braid
Matiella, A. C. The truth about Alicia and other stories
La casa chica
Matiella, A. C. The truth about Alicia and other stories
Feliz Navidad
Matiella, A. C. The truth about Alicia and other stories
Home
Matiella, A. C. The truth about Alicia and other stories
Nana's trilogy
Matiella, A. C. The truth about Alicia and other stories
Polvito de amor
Matiella, A. C. The truth about Alicia and other stories
Rat roulette
Matiella, A. C. The truth about Alicia and other stories
The ring
Matiella, A. C. The truth about Alicia and other stories
Sana, sana, colita de rana
Matiella, A. C. The truth about Alicia and other stories
Size does matter
Matiella, A. C. The truth about Alicia and other stories
The truth about Alicia
Matiella, A. C. The truth about Alicia and other stories
Twice-cooked Yorky
Matiella, A. C. The truth about Alicia and other stories
Tying St. Anthony's feet
Matiella, A. C. The truth about Alicia and other stories

Matilda told such dreadful lies. Sussex, L.
Matison, Mel
Rose into cauliflower
Boxing's best short stories; edited by Paul D. Staudohar
MATRIARCHS *See* Mothers
MATRICIDE *See* Parricide
MATSUO, BASHŌ, 1644-1694
About
Haskell, J. Narrow road
A **matter** of days before the collapse. Akins, E.
A **matter** of frequency. Tenn, W.
A **matter** of mathematics. Aldiss, B. W.
A **matter** of prejudice. Chopin, K.
A **matter** of price. Bowen, R. O.
A **matter** of principal. Collins, M. A.
A **matter** of principle. Chesnutt, C. W.

A **matter** of seconds. Queen, E.
A **matter** of taste. Godwin, P.
Matter of time. Powell, P.
Matters of balance. Fracis, S. H.
Matters of consequence. Dix, S.
Matteson, Stefanie
The trouble with Harry
Blood on their hands; edited by Lawrence Block
Matthews, A. J. *See* Hautala, Rick
Matthews, Barry
Everything must go
Kulka, J. and Danford, N. The New American voices 2003; guest editor Joyce Carol Oates; series editors John Kulka and Natalie Danford
Matthews, Christine
Backyard burial
Matthews, C. Gentle insanities and other states of mind
Belated revenge
Matthews, C. Gentle insanities and other states of mind
Character flaw: a Robbie Stanton story
Matthews, C. Gentle insanities and other states of mind
The World's finest mystery and crime stories, second annual collection; edited by Ed Gorman
Dear Lottie
Matthews, C. Gentle insanities and other states of mind
Death of a glamour cat
Matthews, C. Gentle insanities and other states of mind
The dirt eaters
Matthews, C. Gentle insanities and other states of mind
Gentle insanities
Matthews, C. Gentle insanities and other states of mind
I'm a dirty girl
Matthews, C. Gentle insanities and other states of mind
I'm not that kind of girl
Matthews, C. Gentle insanities and other states of mind
The moving statue of Ballinspittle
Matthews, C. Gentle insanities and other states of mind
Niiice
Matthews, C. Gentle insanities and other states of mind
Promises made and broken
Matthews, C. Gentle insanities and other states of mind
The tailor of Yuma
Matthews, C. Gentle insanities and other states of mind
To make a rabbit sing
Matthews, C. Gentle insanities and other states of mind
(jt. auth) See Randisi, Robert J. and Matthews, Christine
Matthiessen, Peter
Bone by bone
The Paris Review v41 no150 p216-21 Spr 1999

Mattingly, Kathryn
Dance of the dolphins
Dead on demand; the best of ghost story weekend; edited by Elizabeth Engstrom
Mattison, Alice
Brooklyn sestina
Michigan Quarterly Review v41 no3 p400-12 Summ 2002
I Am Not Your Mother
Ploughshares v29 no2/3 p112-27 Fall 2003
In case we're separated
The Best American short stories, 2002; selected from U.S. and Canadian magazines by Sue Miller with Katrina Kenison, with an introduction by Sue Miller
Ploughshares v27 no2/3 p102-14 Fall 2001
Maugham, Somerset *See* Maugham, W. Somerset (William Somerset), 1874-1965
Maugham, W. Somerset (William Somerset)
A friend in need
Sports best short stories; edited by Paul D. Staudohar
Maugham, William Somerset *See* Maugham, W. Somerset (William Somerset), 1874-1965
Maupassant, Guy de
A fishing excursion
Fishing's best short stories; edited by Paul D. Staudohar
Two fishers
Death by espionage; intriguing stories of deception and betrayal; edited by Martin Cruz Smith
The wolf
The Literary werewolf; an anthology; edited by Charlotte F. Otten
MAUPASSANT, GUY DE, 1850-1893
About
Babel´, I. Guy de Maupassant
Parodies, imitation, etc.
Sheckley, R. The new Horla
Mauve desert [excerpt] Brossard, N.
mav.er.ick. Anderson, D.
Maverick factory. Loomis, N. M.
Max. Carlson, R.
Max. Händler, E.-W.
Max-1970. Swan, M.
Maximum reception. Chiappone, R.
Maximum sunlight. Small, K.
Maxine. Norman, G.
Maxwell, Marina Ama Omowale
Devil beads
Whispers from the cotton tree root; Caribbean fabulist fiction; edited by Nalo Hopkinson
Maxwell, William
Grape Bay (1941)
The New Yorker v75 no14 p76-80 Je 7 1999
Over by the river
Wonderful town; New York stories from The New Yorker; edited by David Remnick with Susan Choi
May, Rachel
(jt. auth) See Xi Xi
May 22, 1954. Dwyer, M.
May be some time. Clough, B. W.
MAY DAY
Robison, M. May Queen
May Day. Fitzgerald, F. S.
May Eve. Edghill, R.
May oysters have legs. Bischoff, D.

May Queen. Robison, M.
May there be a road. L'Amour, L.
Maya, Gabriela
Dust and joys: a tale from the alternative archives
Iowa Review v32 no1 p159-70 Spr 2002
Maya. Cain, M. A.
The **Mayan** variation. Dozois, G. R.
MAYAS
Simonds, M. In the city of the split sky
Maya's mother. Little, B.
Maybe, Maybe Not. Sutton, B.
Mayela one day in 1989. Gilb, D.
Mayer, Eric
(jt. auth) See Reed, Mary and Mayer, Eric
Mayhall, Jane
Martin
New Letters v68 no1 p97-9 2001
The men
Home and beyond; an anthology of Kentucky short stories; edited by Morris Allen Grubbs; with an introduction by Wade Hall and an afterword by Charles E. May
Mayhar, Ardath
Fungi
Redshift; extreme visions of speculative fiction; edited by Al Sarrantonio
Mayo, C. M.
The Building of Quality
The Kenyon Review v26 no3 p30-42 Summ 2004
Mayo, Jim, 1908-1988
For works written by this author under other names see L'Amour, Louis, 1908-1988
Mayo, Wendell
B. Horror
Mayo, W. B. Horror and other stories
Biography of a gallstone
The North American Review v287 no3/4 p41-7 My/Ag 2002
The California Franchise Tax Board
Mayo, W. B. Horror and other stories
Dance of eights
Mayo, W. B. Horror and other stories
Day cook
Mayo, W. B. Horror and other stories
Going long
Mayo, W. B. Horror and other stories
Jagged tooth, great tooth
100% pure Florida fiction; an anthology; edited by Susan Hubbard and Robley Wilson
Mary Magdalena versus Godzilla
Mayo, W. B. Horror and other stories
Mortal sins
Mayo, W. B. Horror and other stories
Overtures
Chicago Review v45 no1 p17-26 1999
Mayo, W. B. Horror and other stories
Robert's bride
Mayo, W. B. Horror and other stories
What rough beasts
Mayo, W. B. Horror and other stories
Who made you
Mayo, W. B. Horror and other stories
Woman without arms
Mayo, W. B. Horror and other stories

Mayoff, Steven
  The Bridge by Moonlight
    Dalhousie Review v83 no2 p283-90 Summ
    2003
La **Mayonette**. Tuck, L.
Mayor, Archer
  Instinct
    The Mysterious Press anniversary anthology;
    celebrating 25 years; by the editors of Mys-
    terious Press
The **mayor** of St. John. Paine, T.
MAYORS
  Paine, T. The mayor of St. John
  Wald, M. Keys to the city
The **mayor's** tale. Johnson, C. R.
The **Maypole** of Merry Mount. Hawthorne, N.
The **maze**. Dyson, J.
Mazelis, Jo
  The blackberry season
    Mazelis, J. Diving girls
  The diving girls
    Mazelis, J. Diving girls
  Flock
    Mazelis, J. Diving girls
  Forbidden
    Mazelis, J. Diving girls
  The game
    Mazelis, J. Diving girls
  Home-cooked
    Mazelis, J. Diving girls
  Mistaken identity
    Mazelis, J. Diving girls
  On the edge
    Mazelis, J. Diving girls
  Over the rainbow
    Mazelis, J. Diving girls
  Peaches
    Mazelis, J. Diving girls
  Running away with the hairdresser
    Mazelis, J. Diving girls
  Setting
    Mazelis, J. Diving girls
  Seven thousand flowers
    Mazelis, J. Diving girls
  Siriol, she-devil of naked madness
    Mazelis, J. Diving girls
  Snakeskin becomes her
    Mazelis, J. Diving girls
  Tongue
    Mazelis, J. Diving girls
  Too perfect
    Mazelis, J. Diving girls
Mazor, Julian
  Durango
    Mazor, J. Friend of mankind and other sto-
    ries; by Julian Mazor
  Friend of mankind
    Mazor, J. Friend of mankind and other sto-
    ries; by Julian Mazor
  Gray skies
    Mazor, J. Friend of mankind and other sto-
    ries; by Julian Mazor
  The lone star kid
    Mazor, J. Friend of mankind and other sto-
    ries; by Julian Mazor
  The lost cause
    Mazor, J. Friend of mankind and other sto-
    ries; by Julian Mazor

The modern age
    Mazor, J. Friend of mankind and other sto-
    ries; by Julian Mazor
The munster final
    Mazor, J. Friend of mankind and other sto-
    ries; by Julian Mazor
On experience
    Mazor, J. Friend of mankind and other sto-
    ries; by Julian Mazor
Skylark
    Mazor, J. Friend of mankind and other sto-
    ries; by Julian Mazor
Storm
    Mazor, J. Friend of mankind and other sto-
    ries; by Julian Mazor
Mazza, Cris
  Familiar noise
    TriQuarterly no110/111 p83-101 Fall 2001
McAllister, Bruce
  The girl who loved animals
    Vanishing acts; a science fiction anthology;
    edited by Ellen Datlow
McAllister, Laurent
  Kapuzine and the wolf: a hortatory tale
    Witpunk; edited by Claude Lalumière and
    Marty Halpern
McAuley, Paul J.
  All tomorrow's parties
    The Good new stuff; adventure SF in the
    grand tradition; edited by Gardner Dozois
  Bone orchards
    Best new horror 12; edited and with an intro-
    duction by Stephen Jones
    Death dines at 8:30; edited by Claudia Bishop
    and Nick DiChario
  Dr Pretorius and the lost temple
    The Mammoth book of best new horror 14;
    edited with an introduction by Stephen
    Jones
  How we lost the moon, a true story by Frank
    W. Allen
    The Year's best science fiction, seventeenth
    annual collection; edited by Gardner Dozois
  Naming the dead
    Best new horror 11; edited and with an intro-
    duction by Stephen Jones
    The Year's best fantasy & horror, thirteenth
    annual collection; edited by Ellen Datlow
    and Terri Windling
  The passenger
    The Year's best science fiction; twentieth an-
    nual collection; edited by Gardner Dozois
  Reef
    The Year's best science fiction, eighteenth an-
    nual collection; edited by Gardner Dozois
  The Rift
    Vanishing acts; a science fiction anthology;
    edited by Ellen Datlow
  Sea change, with monsters
    The Year's best science fiction, sixteenth an-
    nual collection; edited by Gardner Dozois
  The two Dicks
    The Mammoth book of best horror 13; edited
    by Stephen Jones
    The Year's best science fiction, nineteenth an-
    nual collection; edited by Gardner Dozois
  Under Mars
    Mars probes; edited by Peter Crowther

McAuliffe, J. D.

Grave Love: A Story

The South Atlantic Quarterly v103 no1 p265-70 Wint 2004

McBain, Ed

Activity in the flood plain

The Mysterious Press anniversary anthology; celebrating 25 years; by the editors of Mysterious Press

The World's finest mystery and crime stories, third annual collection; edited by Ed Gorman and Martin H. Greenberg

Barking at butterflies

Murder and obsession; edited by Otto Penzler

The World's finest mystery and crime stories, first annual collection; edited by Ed Gorman

But you know us

McBain, E. Running from Legs and other stories; [by] Ed McBain a.k.a. Evan Hunter

The couple next door

McBain, E. Running from Legs and other stories; [by] Ed McBain a.k.a. Evan Hunter

The fallen angel

McBain, E. Running from Legs and other stories; [by] Ed McBain a.k.a. Evan Hunter

Happy New Year, Herbie

McBain, E. Running from Legs and other stories; [by] Ed McBain a.k.a. Evan Hunter

The interview

Edwards, M. Mysterious pleasures; a celebration of the Crime Writers' Association's 50th anniversary; edited by Martin Edwards

Master's choice v2; mystery stories by today's top writers and the masters who inspired them; edited by Lawrence Block

McBain, E. Running from Legs and other stories; [by] Ed McBain a.k.a. Evan Hunter

The last spin

McBain, E. Running from Legs and other stories; [by] Ed McBain a.k.a. Evan Hunter

The prisoner

McBain, E. Running from Legs and other stories; [by] Ed McBain a.k.a. Evan Hunter

Running from Legs

McBain, E. Running from Legs and other stories; [by] Ed McBain a.k.a. Evan Hunter

The sharers

McBain, E. Running from Legs and other stories; [by] Ed McBain a.k.a. Evan Hunter

Terminal misunderstanding

McBain, E. Running from Legs and other stories; [by] Ed McBain a.k.a. Evan Hunter

A very Merry Christmass

A Century of great suspense stories; edited by Jeffery Deaver

The victim

McBain, E. Running from Legs and other stories; [by] Ed McBain a.k.a. Evan Hunter

The World's finest mystery and crime stories, second annual collection; edited by Ed Gorman

McBain, Ed, 1926-

For works written by this author under other names see Hunter, Evan, 1926-; Marsten, Richard, 1926-

McBrearty, Robert Garner

Back in town

McBrearty, R. G. A night at the Y; a collection of short stories

Dinsmore's Paradox

The North American Review v289 no2 p16-19 Mr/Ap 2004

The dishwasher

McBrearty, R. G. A night at the Y; a collection of short stories

First day

McBrearty, R. G. A night at the Y; a collection of short stories

The hellraiser

McBrearty, R. G. A night at the Y; a collection of short stories

Improvising

McBrearty, R. G. A night at the Y; a collection of short stories

My life as a judo master

McBrearty, R. G. A night at the Y; a collection of short stories

A night at the Y

McBrearty, R. G. A night at the Y; a collection of short stories

The pearl diver

McBrearty, R. G. A night at the Y; a collection of short stories

Soft song of the sometimes sane

McBrearty, R. G. A night at the Y; a collection of short stories

The things I don't know about

McBrearty, R. G. A night at the Y; a collection of short stories

The unfolding

McBrearty, R. G. A night at the Y; a collection of short stories

The yellow house

McBrearty, R. G. A night at the Y; a collection of short stories

McBride, Sally

The fragrance of orchids

Northern suns; edited by David G. Hartwell & Glenn Grant

McCabe, Brian

Not about the kids

The Vintage book of contemporary Scottish fiction; edited and with an introduction by Peter Kravitz

McCabe, Patrick

The hands of Dingo Deery

The Anchor book of new Irish writing; the new Gaelach ficsean; edited and with an introduction by John Somer and John J. Daly

McCaffrey, Anne

Beyond between

Silverberg, R. Legends II; new short novels by the masters of modern fantasy; edited by Robert Silverberg

Freedom of the race

Wondrous beginnings; edited by Steven H. Silver and Martin H. Greenberg

A proper Santa Claus

A yuletide universe; sixteen fantastical tales; edited by Brian M. Thomsen

McCaffrey, Anne—*Continued*

The ship that returned

Far horizons; all new tales from the greatest worlds of science fiction; edited by Robert Silverberg

The ship who mourned

A Woman's liberation; a choice of futures by and about women; edited by Connie Willis and Sheila Williams

The ship who sang

Reload: rethinking women + cyberculture; edited by Mary Flanagan and Austin Booth

McCann, Colum

As Kingfishers catch fire

The Pushcart prize XXIII: best of the small presses; an annual small press reader; edited by Bill Henderson with the Pushcart prize editors

Cathal's lake

The Anchor book of new Irish writing; the new Gaelach ficsean; edited and with an introduction by John Somer and John J. Daly

Everything in this country must

The Art of the story; an international anthology of contemporary short stories; edited by Daniel Halpern

Fishing the sloe-black river

The Anchor book of new Irish writing; the new Gaelach ficsean; edited and with an introduction by John Somer and John J. Daly

Wood

The New Yorker v75 no36 p108-14 N 29 1999

McCann, Richard

The universe, concealed

Men on men 2000; best new gay fiction for the millennium; edited and with an introduction by David Bergman and Karl Woelz

McCarthy, Wil

He died that day, in thirty years

Once upon a galaxy; edited by Will [sic] McCarthy, Martin H. Greenberg, and John Helfers

McCauley, William

The Bombing of Tripoli

New Letters v69 no1 p167-74 2002

McClanahan, Ed

The little-known bird of the inner eye

Home and beyond; an anthology of Kentucky short stories; edited by Morris Allen Grubbs; with an introduction by Wade Hall and an afterword by Charles E. May

McCorkle, Jill

Billy goats

The Best American short stories, 2003; selected from U.S. and Canadian magazines by Walter Mosley with Katrina Kenison; with an introduction by Walter Mosley

Bomb no77 p81-5 Fall 2001

McCorkle, J. Creatures of habit; stories

Cats

McCorkle, J. Creatures of habit; stories

Chickens

McCorkle, J. Creatures of habit; stories

The Southern Review (Baton Rouge, La.) v37 no4 p724-38 Aut 2001

Crash diet

What are you looking at?; the first fat fiction anthology; edited by Donna Jarrell and Ira Sukrungruang

Dogs

McCorkle, J. Creatures of habit; stories

Fish

McCorkle, J. Creatures of habit; stories

The Southern Review (Baton Rouge, La.) v37 no4 p738-45 Aut 2001

Hominids

McCorkle, J. Creatures of habit; stories

Intervention

New stories from the South; the year's best, 2004; edited by Shannon Ravenel; preface by Tim Gautreaux

Ploughshares v29 no2/3 p128-44 Fall 2003

Life prerecorded

The Cry of an occasion; fiction from the Fellowship of Southern Writers; edited by Richard Bausch; with a foreword by George Garrett

Migration of the love bugs

100% pure Florida fiction; an anthology; edited by Susan Hubbard and Robley Wilson

Monkeys

McCorkle, J. Creatures of habit; stories

Snakes

McCorkle, J. Creatures of habit; stories

Snipe

McCorkle, J. Creatures of habit; stories

Starlings

McCorkle, J. Creatures of habit; stories

Toads

McCorkle, J. Creatures of habit; stories

Turtles

McCorkle, J. Creatures of habit; stories

McCormack, Judith

A Theory of Probability

Harvard Review (1992) no26 p6-24 2004

McCourt, James

Driven woman

McCourt, J. Wayfaring at Waverly in Silver Lake; stories

Ensenada

McCourt, J. Wayfaring at Waverly in Silver Lake; stories

In Tir na nOg

McCourt, J. Wayfaring at Waverly in Silver Lake; stories

New York lit up that way at night

McCourt, J. Wayfaring at Waverly in Silver Lake; stories

A plethora

McCourt, J. Wayfaring at Waverly in Silver Lake; stories

Principal photography

McCourt, J. Wayfaring at Waverly in Silver Lake; stories

Wayfaring at Waverly in Silver Lake

McCourt, J. Wayfaring at Waverly in Silver Lake; stories

McCracken, Elizabeth

Here's your hat what's your hurry

The Workshop; seven decades of the Iowa Writers' Workshop: 42 stories, recollections & essays on Iowa's place in 20th-century American literature; edited by Tom Grimes

McCrumb, Sharyn

Among my souvenirs

A Century of great suspense stories; edited by Jeffery Deaver

Foggy Mountain breakdown

Master's choice v2; mystery stories by today's top writers and the masters who inspired them; edited by Lawrence Block

The gallows necklace

Datlow, E. The dark; new ghost stories; edited by Ellen Datlow

A predatory woman

A moment on the edge; 100 years of crime stories by women; edited by Elizabeth George

The vale of the white horse

Murder, my dear Watson; new tales of Sherlock Holmes; edited by Martin H. Greenberg, Jon Lellenberg, Daniel Stashower

McCuaig, Andrew

The only woman in the orchestra

Prairie Schooner v75 no4 p90-110 Wint 2001

McCulla's kid. Howard, C.

McDermid, Val

The consolation blonde

Edwards, M. Mysterious pleasures; a celebration of the Crime Writers' Association's 50th anniversary; edited by Martin Edwards

The girl who killed Santa Claus

The World's finest mystery and crime stories, third annual collection; edited by Ed Gorman and Martin H. Greenberg

Metamorphosis

Tart noir; edited by Stella Duffy & Lauren Henderson

The wagon mound

The best British mysteries; edited by Maxim Jakubowski

McDevitt, Jack

The Emerson effect

Wondrous beginnings; edited by Steven H. Silver and Martin H. Greenberg

Nothing ever happens in Rock City

Nebula awards showcase 2004; edited by Vonda McIntyre

McDonald, Ian

The Catharine wheel

Worldmakers; SF adventures in terraforming; edited by Gardner Dozois

The days of Solomon Gursky

The Year's best science fiction, sixteenth annual collection; edited by Gardner Dozois

The old cosmonaut and the construction worker dream of Mars

Mars probes; edited by Peter Crowther

The Year's best science fiction; twentieth annual collection; edited by Gardner Dozois

Pot O'Rice Horowitz's house of solace

Whispers from the cotton tree root; Caribbean fabulist fiction; edited by Nalo Hopkinson

Tendeléo's story

The Year's best science fiction, eighteenth annual collection; edited by Gardner Dozois

McDowell, Ian

Sunflowers

Vanishing acts; a science fiction anthology; edited by Ellen Datlow

McDowell, Katherine Sherwood Bonner *See* MacDowell, Katherine Sherwood Bonner, 1849-1883

McElroy, Colleen J.

A brief spell by the river

The African American West; a century of short stories; edited by Bruce A. Glasrud and Laurie Champion

McElroy, Lee, 1926-

For works written by this author under other names see Kelton, Elmer, 1926-

McEwan, Ian

Pornography

The Art of the story; an international anthology of contemporary short stories; edited by Daniel Halpern

McEwen, Todd

The Elk's Funeral

Granta v80 p235-9 Wint 2002

McFadden, Dennis

Jimtown Road

New England Review v23 no3 p89-97 Summ 2002

McFerrin, Linda Watanabe *See* Watanabe McFerrin, Linda, 1953-

McGahern, John

Easter

The Times Literary Supplement no5013 p16-17 Ap 30 1999

McGarry, Jean

Among the Philistines

McGarry, J. Dream date; stories

The Yale Review v87 no2 p119-41 Ap 1999

Better than real

McGarry, J. Dream date; stories

Body and soul

McGarry, J. Dream date; stories

Landing

McGarry, J. Dream date; stories

The last time

McGarry, J. Dream date; stories

Lavare

McGarry, J. Dream date; stories

The Maestro

McGarry, J. Dream date; stories

The Yale Review v89 no2 p118-26 Ap 2001

Moon, June

McGarry, J. Dream date; stories

Paris

McGarry, J. Dream date; stories

Partly him

McGarry, J. Dream date; stories

The secret of his sleep

McGarry, J. Dream date; stories

The thin man

McGarry, J. Dream date; stories

The Wedding Gowns

The Yale Review v92 no1 p137-49 Ja 2004

With her

McGarry, J. Dream date; stories

Southwest Review v86 no2/3 p186-93 Spr/Summ 2001

McGarry, Mark J.

The mercy gate

Nebula awards showcase 2000; the year's best SF and fantasy chosen by the science fiction and fantasy writers of america; edited by Gregory Benford

McGarry, Terry
Miasma
The Ultimate Halloween; edited by Marvin Kaye
McGary, Gayle
The cats and jammer
A Deadly dozen; tales of murder from members of Sisters in Crime/Los Angeles; edited by Susan B. Casmier, Aljean Harmetz and Cynthia Lawrence
McGill, Robert
The Widower's House
Dalhousie Review v83 no2 p261-72 Summ 2003
McGinn, Judith Moore
Losing Zan Gambol
South Carolina Review v34 no2 p78-87 Spr 2002
McGivern, William P.
Death comes gift-wrapped
A Century of noir; thirty-two classic crime stories; edited by Mickey Spillane and Max Allan Collins
McGlynn, David
Eclipse
Western Humanities Review v56 no1 p32-42 Spr 2002
McGonagall in the head. Campbell, R.
McGowan, James T.
Legs shimmering under moonlight
The North American Review v286 no3/4 p68-73 My/Ag 2001
McGrath, Patrick
Asylum [excerpt]
Dark: stories of madness, murder, and the supernatural; edited by Clint Willis
McGraw, Erin
Appearance of Scandal
Daedalus v133 no2 p94-104 Spr 2004
Ax of the Apostles
What are you looking at?; the first fat fiction anthology; edited by Donna Jarrell and Ira Sukrungruang
Citizen of Vienna
The Southern Review (Baton Rouge, La.) v38 no2 p307-20 Spr 2002
The Penance Practicum
The Kenyon Review v26 no1 p18-35 Wint 2004
A whole new man
Good Housekeeping v239 no4 p245-6, 248, 251-2, 254-7 O 2004
McGregor, Jon
The First Punch
Granta no83 p183-92 Fall 2003
What the sky sees
Granta no78 p33-55 Summ 2002
McGregor's day on. Means, D.
McGruder, Krista
Forbidden planet
The North American Review v287 no3/4 p34-40 My/Ag 2002
McGuane, Thomas
A black dress
Gentlemen's Quarterly v71 no8 p101-9 Ag 2001

Dogs
Still wild; short fiction of the American West, 1950 to the present; edited by Larry McMurtry
Gallatin Canyon
The New Yorker v78 no42 p72-7 Ja 13 2003
Skelton's party
Fishing's best short stories; edited by Paul D. Staudohar
Vicious Circle
The New Yorker v79 no27 p135-6, 140, 142, 144, 146, 157-8 S 22 2003
McGuire, Ian
The red monk
The Paris Review v43 no158 p85-117 Spr/Summ 2001
McHugh, Maureen F.
A foreigner's Christmas in China
A yuletide universe; sixteen fantastical tales; edited by Brian M. Thomsen
Interview: on any given day
Starlight 3; edited by Patrick Nielsen Hayden
The Year's best science fiction, nineteenth annual collection; edited by Gardner Dozois
The Lincoln Train
The Best from fantasy & science fiction: the fiftieth anniversary anthology; edited by Edward L. Ferman and Gordon Van Gelder
One lamp; alternate history stories from The magazine of Fantasy & Science Fiction; edited by Gordon van Gelder
The missionary's child
The Good new stuff; adventure SF in the grand tradition; edited by Gardner Dozois
Presence
The Year's best science fiction; twentieth annual collection; edited by Gardner Dozois
McIlvanney, William
At the bar
The Vintage book of contemporary Scottish fiction; edited and with an introduction by Peter Kravitz
McIlvoy, Kevin
Black Sweater
Western Humanities Review v57 no2 p21-2 Fall 2003
Miss Luck
Western Humanities Review v57 no2 p23-7 Fall 2003
Smoke, ice
The Southern Review (Baton Rouge, La.) v37 no4 p746-54 Aut 2001
McInerny, Ralph M.
The base of the triangle; a Father Dowling mystery
Murder most divine; ecclesiastical tales of unholy crimes; edited by Ralph McInerny and Martin H. Greenberg
The coveted correspondence
Murder most postal; homicidal tales that deliver a message; edited by Martin H. Greenberg
Mutiny of the bounty hunter
Death cruise; crime stories on the open seas; edited by Lawrence Block
McInerny, Ralph M., 1929-
For works written by this author under other names see Quill, Monica, 1929-

McIntosh, Carol C.

Grading the lilies

The Virginia Quarterly Review v75 no3 p573-82 Summ 1999

McIntyre, Vonda N.

The moon and the sun [excerpt]

Nebula awards 33; the year's best SF and fantasy chosen by the science-fiction and fantasy writers of America; edited by Connie Willis

Of mist, and grass, and sand

A Woman's liberation; a choice of futures by and about women; edited by Connie Willis and Sheila Williams

McKay, Kevin

Pie Row Joe

Centaurus: the best of Australian science fiction; edited by David G. Hartwell and Damien Broderick

McKean, Robert

Ralphie's Clarinet

The Kenyon Review v26 no1 p100-19 Wint 2004

McKee, Jenn

Under the influence

Kulka, J. and Danford, N. The New American voices 2003; guest editor Joyce Carol Oates; series editors John Kulka and Natalie Danford

Prairie Schooner v76 no3 p65-84 Fall 2002

McKee, Robert

The confession

The Best American mystery stories, 2003; edited by Michael Connelly and Otto Penzler

McKendry, Jo

Birds

Southwest Review v88 no2/3 p373-9 2003

Uncle Gerard

The Antioch Review v61 no1 p88-94 Wint 2003

McKenna, Richard

Hunter, come home

Worldmakers; SF adventures in terraforming; edited by Gardner Dozois

McKenzie, Alecia

Private school

The Oxford book of Caribbean short stories; edited by Stewart Brown and John Wickham

McKiernan, Dennis L.

Darkness

999: new stories of horror and suspense; edited by Al Sarrantonio

Duel

Thieve's world: turning points; edited by Lynn Abbey

McKillip, Patricia A.

Oak Hill

The Year's best fantasy & horror, twelfth annual collection; edited by Ellen Datlow & Terri Windling

Toad

The Year's best fantasy & horror, thirteenth annual collection; edited by Ellen Datlow and Terri Windling

McKinley, James Conrad

Fever

The Virginia Quarterly Review v78 no3 p457-71 Summ 2002

McKinley, Robin

A pool in the desert

The Year's best fantasy & horror: sixteenth annual collection; edited by Ellen Datlow & Terri Windling

MCKINLEY, WILLIAM, 1843-1901

About

Dams, J. M. Remember the Maine?

McKinney-Whetstone, Diane

Moon penitent

The Bluelight corner; black women writing on passion, sex, and romantic love; edited by Rosemarie Robotham

McKinnon, Karen

Kindred

On the rocks; the KGB Bar fiction anthology; edited by Rebecca Donner ; foreword by Denis Woychuk

McKnight, Reginald

The kind of light that shines on Texas

The African American West; a century of short stories; edited by Bruce A. Glasrud and Laurie Champion

The Best of The Kenyon review; edited by David Lynn; introduction by Joyce Carol Oates

The Scribner anthology of contemporary short fiction; fifty North American stories since 1970; Lex Williford and Michael Martone, editors

Palm wine

Callaloo v24 no2 p551-61 Spr 2001

Quitting smoking

Crossing the color line; readings in Black and white; edited by Suzanne W. Jones

Other people's mail; an anthology of letter stories; edited with an introduction by Gail Pool

McLaglen, John J., 1938-

For works written by this author under other names see Harvey, John, 1938-

McLean, Duncan

Hours of darkness

The Vintage book of contemporary Scottish fiction; edited and with an introduction by Peter Kravitz

McLellan, Don

Mother's Day

Dalhousie Review v81 no3 p429-36 Aut 2001

McLoughlin, Margo

In the sky there is no footstep

Nixon under the bodhi tree and other works of Buddhist fiction; edited by Kate Wheeler ; foreword by Charles Johnson

McMahon, Neil

Heart

Boxing's best short stories; edited by Paul D. Staudohar

McMahon, Pat *See* Hoch, Edward D., 1930-

McMahon, Paul

How Brando was made

The Darkest thirst; a vampire anthology

McManus, John

The body painters

McManus, J. Stop breakin down; stories

Deseret

McManus, J. Stop breakin down; stories

Die like a lobster

McManus, J. Stop breakin down; stories

McManus, John—*Continued*

The feed zone
   McManus, J. Stop breakin down; stories
The future is orange
   McManus, J. Stop breakin down; stories
Gegenschein
   McManus, J. Stop breakin down; stories
June 1989
   McManus, J. Stop breakin down; stories
The Magothy fires
   McManus, J. Stop breakin down; stories
Megargel
   McManus, J. Stop breakin down; stories
Reaffirmation
   McManus, J. Stop breakin down; stories
Scintilla
   McManus, J. Stop breakin down; stories
Sleep on stones
   McManus, J. Stop breakin down; stories
Stop breakin down
   McManus, J. Stop breakin down; stories
Stop breaking down
   Ploughshares v25 no4 p190-204 Wint
   1999/2000
Vlad the nefarious
   McManus, J. Stop breakin down; stories
What I remember about the cold war
   McManus, J. Stop breakin down; stories

McMillan, Terry

Ma'dear
   Callaloo v24 no2 p562-8 Spr 2001
Quilting on the rebound
   The African American West; a century of
   short stories; edited by Bruce A. Glasrud
   and Laurie Champion

McMullan, Margaret

Museum Piece
   TriQuarterly no115 p150-9 Spr 2003
Pi
   Michigan Quarterly Review v42 no4 p616-30
   Fall 2003

McMullen, Sean

The dominant style
   Centaurus: the best of Australian science fiction; edited by David G. Hartwell and Damien Broderick

McMurtry, Larry

The last picture show [excerpt]
   Graham, D. Lone Star literature; from the
   Red River to the Rio Grande; edited by
   Don Graham

McNally, John

Brains of the Operation
   New England Review v24 no4 p38-96 2003
Contributor's Notes
   The Virginia Quarterly Review v80 no3 p234-
   52 Summ 2004
The end of romance
   McNally, J. Troublemakers
The first of your last chances
   McNally, J. Troublemakers
The grand illusion
   McNally, J. Troublemakers
The greatest goddamn thing
   McNally, J. Troublemakers
The Immortals
   The Virginia Quarterly Review v80 no2 p136-
   53 Spr 2004

Limbs
   McNally, J. Troublemakers
The New Year
   A different plain; contemporary Nebraska fic-
   tion writers; edited by Ladette Randolph ;
   introduction by Mary Pipher
   McNally, J. Troublemakers
The politics of correctness
   McNally, J. Troublemakers
Roger's new life
   McNally, J. Troublemakers
Smoke
   McNally, J. Troublemakers
Torture
   McNally, J. Troublemakers
The vomitorium
   McNally, J. Troublemakers

McNally, Richard

The people in room 3P
   Iowa Review v29 no3 p46-52 Wint 1999

McNally, T. M.

Bastogne
   Doubletake v7 no3 p96-102 Summ 2001
Given
   Gettysburg Review v15 no3 p453-70 Aut
   2002
Open my heart
   The Yale Review v89 no2 p131-49 Ap 2001

McNamer, Deirdre

Water thieves
   Ploughshares v28 no2/3 p79-91 Fall 2002

McNeal, Tom

Watermelon days
   The Best American short stories, 2002; select-
   ed from U.S. and Canadian magazines by
   Sue Miller with Katrina Kenison, with an
   introduction by Sue Miller
   A different plain; contemporary Nebraska fic-
   tion writers; edited by Ladette Randolph ;
   introduction by Mary Pipher
Winter in Los Angeles
   LA shorts; edited by Steven Gilbar

McNeely, Thomas H.

Sheep
   Atlantic Monthly v283 no6 p106-14+ Je 1999
   The Best American mystery stories, 2000; ed-
   ited and with an introduction by Donald E.
   Westlake
   New stories from the South: the year's best,
   2000; edited by Shannon Ravenel; with a
   preface by Ellen Douglas
Snow, Houston, 1974
   The Virginia Quarterly Review v78 no1 p26-
   40 Wint 2002
Tickle torture
   Ploughshares v27 no4 p135-51 Wint
   2001/2002

MCNELLY, LEANDER H., 1843 OR 4-1877
About

Smith, C. Thirty rangers

McNulty, John

Argument outside a gin mill here
   McNulty, J. This place on Third Avenue; the
   New York stories of John McNulty; memoir by Faith McNulty; photographs by Morris Engel

McNulty, John—*Continued*

Atheist hit by truck

  McNulty, J. This place on Third Avenue; the New York stories of John McNulty; memoir by Faith McNulty; photographs by Morris Engel

Barkeep won't let anybody at all shove this handyman around

  McNulty, J. This place on Third Avenue; the New York stories of John McNulty; memoir by Faith McNulty; photographs by Morris Engel

Bartender here takes dislike to "Deep in the heart of Texas"

  McNulty, J. This place on Third Avenue; the New York stories of John McNulty; memoir by Faith McNulty; photographs by Morris Engel

Cluney McFarrar's hardtack

  McNulty, J. This place on Third Avenue; the New York stories of John McNulty; memoir by Faith McNulty; photographs by Morris Engel

Don't scrub off these names

  McNulty, J. This place on Third Avenue; the New York stories of John McNulty; memoir by Faith McNulty; photographs by Morris Engel

Even if it's Mexico nothing flashy ever happens to Grogan

  McNulty, J. This place on Third Avenue; the New York stories of John McNulty; memoir by Faith McNulty; photographs by Morris Engel

The fight in the hallway

  McNulty, J. This place on Third Avenue; the New York stories of John McNulty; memoir by Faith McNulty; photographs by Morris Engel

Hands no good

  McNulty, J. This place on Third Avenue; the New York stories of John McNulty; memoir by Faith McNulty; photographs by Morris Engel

He should have left him have it anyway

  McNulty, J. This place on Third Avenue; the New York stories of John McNulty; memoir by Faith McNulty; photographs by Morris Engel

It's hard to figure how they know

  McNulty, J. This place on Third Avenue; the New York stories of John McNulty; memoir by Faith McNulty; photographs by Morris Engel

Man here keeps getting arrested all the time

  McNulty, J. This place on Third Avenue; the New York stories of John McNulty; memoir by Faith McNulty; photographs by Morris Engel

A man like Grady, you got to know him first

  McNulty, J. This place on Third Avenue; the New York stories of John McNulty; memoir by Faith McNulty; photographs by Morris Engel

A man's going into the Army what can you do about it?

  McNulty, J. This place on Third Avenue; the New York stories of John McNulty; memoir by Faith McNulty; photographs by Morris Engel

An old college chum

  McNulty, J. This place on Third Avenue; the New York stories of John McNulty; memoir by Faith McNulty; photographs by Morris Engel

Peether is full of blather

  McNulty, J. This place on Third Avenue; the New York stories of John McNulty; memoir by Faith McNulty; photographs by Morris Engel

People don't seem to think things out straight in this gin mill

  McNulty, J. This place on Third Avenue; the New York stories of John McNulty; memoir by Faith McNulty; photographs by Morris Engel

The Slugger comes into his own

  McNulty, J. This place on Third Avenue; the New York stories of John McNulty; memoir by Faith McNulty; photographs by Morris Engel

Some nights when nothing happens are the best nights in this place

  McNulty, J. This place on Third Avenue; the New York stories of John McNulty; memoir by Faith McNulty; photographs by Morris Engel

  Wonderful town; New York stories from The New Yorker; edited by David Remnick with Susan Choi

The television helps, but not very much

  McNulty, J. This place on Third Avenue; the New York stories of John McNulty; memoir by Faith McNulty; photographs by Morris Engel

Tell him what happen, Joe, see will he believe you

  McNulty, J. This place on Third Avenue; the New York stories of John McNulty; memoir by Faith McNulty; photographs by Morris Engel

They don't seem to be talking to Grogan

  McNulty, J. This place on Third Avenue; the New York stories of John McNulty; memoir by Faith McNulty; photographs by Morris Engel

They'd have taken him if he was only a torso

  McNulty, J. This place on Third Avenue; the New York stories of John McNulty; memoir by Faith McNulty; photographs by Morris Engel

Third Avenue medicine

  McNulty, J. This place on Third Avenue; the New York stories of John McNulty; memoir by Faith McNulty; photographs by Morris Engel

This lady was a Bostonian they call them

  McNulty, J. This place on Third Avenue; the New York stories of John McNulty; memoir by Faith McNulty; photographs by Morris Engel

McNulty, John—_Continued_

Two bums here would spend freely except for poverty

McNulty, J. This place on Third Avenue; the New York stories of John McNulty; memoir by Faith McNulty; photographs by Morris Engel

You can't tell how you'll get clobbered

McNulty, J. This place on Third Avenue; the New York stories of John McNulty; memoir by Faith McNulty; photographs by Morris Engel

McPherson, James Alan

Elbow room

The African American West; a century of short stories; edited by Bruce A. Glasrud and Laurie Champion

Gold Coast

The Best American short stories of the century; John Updike, editor, Katrina Kenison, coeditor; with an introduction by John Updike

A loaf of bread

Crossing the color line; readings in Black and white; edited by Suzanne W. Jones

A solo song: for Doc

The Workshop; seven decades of the Iowa Writers' Workshop: 42 stories, recollections & essays on Iowa's place in 20th-century American literature; edited by Tom Grimes

McQuain, Kelly

Erasing Sonny

Men on men 2000; best new gay fiction for the millennium; edited and with an introduction by David Bergman and Karl Woelz

McQuillin, Cynthia

Seliki

Such a pretty face; edited by Lee Martindale

McRandle, Paul

From Tikal

New England Review v20 no3 p18-19 Summ 1999

McTair, Roger

Just a lark; or, The crypt of Matthew Ashdown

Whispers from the cotton tree root; Caribbean fabulist fiction; edited by Nalo Hopkinson

McWhorter, Craig T.

Silent protest

Men on men 2000; best new gay fiction for the millennium; edited and with an introduction by David Bergman and Karl Woelz

McWilliam, Candia

Seven magpies

The Vintage book of contemporary Scottish fiction; edited and with an introduction by Peter Kravitz

MDIO ecosystems increase knowledge of DNA languages (2215 C.E.). Bear, G.

The **me** after the rock. O'Leary, P.

Me and Dr. Bob. Cushman, S.

Me and Mrs. Jones. Allegra, D.

Me and the sea. P'yetsukh, V.

Me and the Stones. Parker, G.

Me, myself, and I. Tenn, W.

Mea culpa. Burke, J.

Meacham, Rebecca

Good Fences

Michigan Quarterly Review v43 no2 p187-202 Spr 2004

Meacock, Norma

The mole trap

Valentine's Day: women against men; stories of revenge; introduction by Alice Thomas

Mead, Helen

Wednesday night, Thursday morning

Typical girls; new stories by smart women; edited by Susan Corrigan

Meade, Declan

Lost time

His 3: brilliant new fiction by gay writers; edited by Robert Drake and Terry Wolverton

Meadow song. Eakin, W.

Meads, Kat

Gene and Nikki, Nikki and Gene

Southern Humanities Review v35 no2 p153-81 Spr 2001

The **mean**. Pitt, M.

The **meanest** cop in the world. Himes, C.

Meaney, John

The whisper of disks

The Year's best science fiction; twentieth annual collection; edited by Gardner Dozois

Means, David

Assorted fire events

Means, D. Assorted fire events; stories

Carnie

The Best American mystery stories, 2001; edited and with an Introduction by Lawrence Block

Coitus

Means, D. Assorted fire events; stories

The gesture hunter

Means, D. Assorted fire events; stories

The grip

The Antioch Review v57 no4 p463-70 Fall 1999

Means, D. Assorted fire events; stories

The interruption

Means, D. Assorted fire events; stories

Lightning man

Esquire v135 no4 p88-92, 166 Ap 2001

McGregor's day on

Crossing the color line; readings in Black and white; edited by Suzanne W. Jones

The Project

Harper's v306 p30-2 Ja 2003

Railroad incident, August 1995

Means, D. Assorted fire events; stories

The reaction

Means, D. Assorted fire events; stories

Sault Ste. Marie

Harper's v309 p63-7 Ag 2004

The Secret Goldfish

The New Yorker v80 no14 p70-5 My 31 2004

Sleeping Bear lament

Means, D. Assorted fire events; stories

Tahorah

Means, D. Assorted fire events; stories

What I hope for

Means, D. Assorted fire events; stories

What they did

Means, D. Assorted fire events; stories

The Pushcart prize XXIV: best of the small presses; an annual small press reader; edited by Bill Henderson with the Pushcart prize editors

The widow predicament

Means, D. Assorted fire events; stories

Means, David—*Continued*
 The woodcutter
  Means, D. Assorted fire events; stories
Means, David R.
 Divine Thanks for Packaged Light
  Doubletake v8 no2 p80-1 Spr 2002
The **means** of escape. Fitzgerald, P.
Meanwhile. Harleman, A.
The **measure**. Phillips, G.
The **measure** of devotion. Perabo, S.
Measuring death in column inches (a nine-week
  manual for girl rim pigs). Gartner, Z.
Measuring the Jump. Eggers, D.
Meat. Hird, L.
Meat Squad, 1982. Stine, P.
Meat tower. Derby, M.
The **meatyard**. Gunn, K.
MECHANICS (PERSONS)
 Iribarne, M. The gift
 Jaime-Becerra, M. The corrido of Hector Cruz
 Jaime-Becerra, M. Riding with Lencho
The **mechanics** of it. Martin, V.
The **Mechanique** affair. Cavin, R.
MEDALS
 Fitzgerald, P. Desideratus
Medcap. O'Neill, S.
Meddeb, Abdelwahab
 Expanses of white
  Parnassus: Poetry in Review v25 no1/2 p81-3
  2001
MEDEA (GREEK MYTHOLOGY)
 Henderson, L. Tragic heroines tell all
MEDICAL ETHICS
 Karnezis, P. Medical ethics
Medical ethics. Karnezis, P.
MEDICAL EXAMINERS
 Sturgeon, T. The sex opposite
MEDICAL LIFE *See* Physicians
MEDICAL RESEARCH *See* Medicine—Re-
 search
MEDICAL STUDENTS *See* Students
MEDICINE
      See also Surgery
           Research
 Davidson, A. Now let us sleep
 Kress, N. Inertia
MEDICINE, EXPERIMENTAL *See* Medicine—
 Research
MEDICINE, PRACTICE OF *See* Physicians
The **medicine** bag. Sneve, V. D. H.
Medicine man. DeMarinis, R.
MEDIEVAL LIFE *See* Middle Ages
Medina, Tony
 Butta's backyard barbecue
  Dark matter; a century of speculative fiction
  from the African diaspora; edited by Sheree
  R. Thomas
MEDITATION
 Cameron, S. Beautiful work
 Dorrie, D. Where do we go from here
 Fischerová, D. Dhum
 Gilchrist, E. Traceleen turns east
A **Mediterranean** Goddess on the James. Gould,
 P.
MEDITERRANEAN REGION
 Rippen, C. Under my skin
Medium rare. Pronzini, B.
MEDIUMS *See* Spiritualism

Mee, Susie
 Playing Hedda
  The Virginia Quarterly Review v77 no1 p36-
  48 Wint 2001
Meek, Ed
 Out west
  The North American Review v284 no3-4 p10-
  13 My/Ag 1999
Meek, James
 Get lost
  The Vintage book of contemporary Scottish
  fiction; edited and with an introduction by
  Peter Kravitz
MEEK, JOE
           About
 Sykes, J. Symptoms of loss
Meersch, Maxence van der
 Everything in the fifth
  Boxing's best short stories; edited by Paul D.
  Staudohar
Meet me in the moon room. Vukcevich, R.
Meet the impersonators! (1986). Barrett, L.
Meeting at Falmouth. L'Amour, L.
A **meeting**, at last. Kureishi, H.
Meeting in August. García Márquez, G.
Meeting Natalia. Svirsky, G.
Meeting the family. Kenagy, M.
A **meeting** with Medusa. Clarke, A. C.
The **Meetinghouse**. Smolens, J.
MEETINGS
 Barthelme, F. Retreat
Meg O'Fallon. Gould, P.
Megan's spirit. Kilpatrick, N.
Megargel. McManus, J.
Megid, Ibrahim Abdel
 The other city
  The Anchor book of modern African stories;
  edited by Nadežda Obradovic ; with a fore-
  word by Chinua Achebe
Mehlman, Peter
 Mandela Was Late
  Esquire v140 no2 p124 Ag 2003
Mehor, Emery L.
 Noah
  Westward; a fictional history of the American
  West : 28 original stories celebrating the
  50th anniversary of the Western Writers of
  America; edited by Dale L. Walker
Mehra, Devika
 The garden
  Best new American voices 2004; guest editor
  John Casey; series editors John Kulka and
  Natalie Danford
  Ploughshares v29 no1 p149-70 Spr 2003
Meidav, Edie
 Into the house of desire: a Ceylonese riddle in
  fourteen parts
  The Kenyon Review ns21 no1 p105-18 Wint
  1999
Meier, Emily
 The Temple of Amun
  Prairie Schooner v73 no1 p6-26 Spr 1999
Meinke, Peter
 The cranes
  100% pure Florida fiction; an anthology; ed-
  ited by Susan Hubbard and Robley Wilson
 Unheard Music
  Gettysburg Review v15 no2 p185-90 Summ
  2002

Meinke, Peter—*Continued*

New stories from the South: the year's best, 2003; edited by Shannon Ravenel; with a preface by Roy Blount Jr.

Meiosis. Everett, P. L.

MEIR, GOLDA, 1898-1978

About

West, M. Four attempts at a letter

Meissner, Bill

Hitting Into the Wind

New Letters v68 no3/4 p79-86 Spr/Summ 2002

The Outfielder

New Letters v68 no3/4 p87-91 Spr/Summ 2002

Meissner, Jan

Placedo junction

Texas bound. Book III; 22 Texas stories; edited by Kay Cattarulla; foreword by Robert Flynn

Mejdoub. Bowles, P.

Mejides, Miguel

The tropics

Dream with no name; contemporary fiction from Cuba; edited by Juana Ponce de León and Esteban Ríos Rivera

Mekler, Dovid Leyb

The Dybbuk

Neugroschel, J. No star too beautiful; Yiddish stories from 1382 to the present; compiled and translated by Joachim Neugroschel

The **melancholic** pedestrian. Garmendia, S.

The **melancholy** summer of Madame de Breyves. Proust, M.

Melba Kuperchmid returns. Orner, P.

Melba Kuperschmid returns. Orner, P.

Melchior, Ib

The racer

Science-fiction classics; the stories that morphed into movies; compiled by Forrest J. Ackerman

Melchior's Gift. Andersen, R.

Melko, Paul

Singletons in love

The year's best science fiction: twenty-first annual collection; edited by Gardner Dozois

Mellick, Carlton

Porno in August

The Year's best fantasy & horror: sixteenth annual collection; edited by Ellen Datlow & Terri Windling

Melnyczuk, Askold

Starting with Sneakers

The Antioch Review v62 no3 p487-500 Summ 2004

Melodies the song dogs sing. Blevins, W.

Meloy, Maile

Accidents

Meloy, M. Half in love; stories

Aqua Boulevard

The Paris Review v43 no158 p20-8 Spr/Summ 2001

Four lean hounds, CA. 1976

Meloy, M. Half in love; stories

Garrison Junction

Meloy, M. Half in love; stories

The ice harvester

Meloy, M. Half in love; stories

Kite Whistler Aquamarine

Meloy, M. Half in love; stories

Last of the white slaves

Meloy, M. Half in love; stories

Native sandstone

Meloy, M. Half in love; stories

Ploughshares v28 no1 p168-75 Spr 2002

Ranch girl

Meloy, M. Half in love; stories

Red

Meloy, M. Half in love; stories

Red from Green

The New Yorker v79 no8 p70-5 Ap 14 2003

The river

Meloy, M. Half in love; stories

A stakes horse

Meloy, M. Half in love; stories

Thirteen & a half

Meloy, M. Half in love; stories

Tome

Best new American voices 2000; guest editor Tobias Wolff; series editors John Kulka and Natalie Danford

Meloy, M. Half in love; stories

Travis, B.

The New Yorker v78 no32 p94-101 O 28 2002

The **Melted** Buddha. Barnes, V. G.

The **Melting** Queen. Bordeau, J.

Melton, Fred

Counting

The Best American mystery stories, 2002; edited and with an introduction by James Ellroy; Otto Penzler, series editor

Melungeons. Offutt, C.

Meluse's counsel. Wilkins, C.

MELVILLE, HERMAN, 1819-1891

About

Bradbury, R. The F. Scott/Tolstoy/Ahab accumulator

Melville, Pauline

The conversion of Millicent Vernon

The Oxford book of Caribbean short stories; edited by Stewart Brown and John Wickham

Don't give me your sad stories

Melville, P. The migration of ghosts

The duende

Melville, P. The migration of ghosts

English table wuk

Melville, P. The migration of ghosts

Erzulie

In our nature: stories of wildness; selected and introduced by Donna Seaman

Melville, P. The migration of ghosts

The fable of the two silver pens

Melville, P. The migration of ghosts

Lucifer's shank

Melville, P. The migration of ghosts

The migration of ghosts

Melville, P. The migration of ghosts

Mrs. Da Silva's carnival

Melville, P. The migration of ghosts

The parrot and Descartes

Melville, P. The migration of ghosts

The president's exile

Melville, P. The migration of ghosts

Provenance of a face

Melville, P. The migration of ghosts

Melville, Pauline—*Continued*
  The sparkling bitch
    Melville, P. The migration of ghosts
Melville's house. Furman, L.
Melvin in the sixth grade. Johnson, D.
Memento mori. Bradbury, R.
Memento mori. Nolan, J.
Memoir. Reifler, N.
Memoir of a soon-to-be star. Searle, E.
Memoirs of a bottle djinn. Yolen, J.
Memoirs of an amnesiac. Williamson, G.
Memorial Day, 1987: a holiday story. Malone, P. S.
MEMORIAL SERVICE
  Bennett, A. The laying on of hands
  Chekhov, A. P. The marshal's widow
Memories in white. Guerrero, L.
Memories of amnesia [excerpt] Shainberg, L.
MEMORY
      See also Amnesia
  Adams, A. 1940: fall
  Allen, S. Carved in vinyl
  Allen, S. Passage
  Anderson, R. The angel of ubiquity
  Barnes, J. Evermore
  Berkman, P. R. February 14
  Berkman, P. R. Snakes
  Borges, J. L. Funes, his memory
  Bradbury, R. I get the blues when it rains (A remembrance)
  Bradbury, R. The pumpernickel
  Bradbury, R. Time intervening
  Braunbeck, G. A. Small song
  Bunin, I. A. Cold fall
  Bunin, I. A. Late hour
  Busch, F. Machias
  Cluccellas, Maria Isabel. Tango and feathers
  Cobb, T. Face the music
  Davis, J. S. When you see
  Dillard, R. H. W. Forgetting the end of the world
  Duong, T. H. Reflections of spring
  Dybek, S. Pet milk
  Fawcett, B. Soul walker
  Ferriss, L. Stampede
  Gabrielyan, N. Hide and seek
  Gao Xingjian. Buying a fishing rod for my grandfather
  Garcia, L. G. The wedding
  Gordimer, N. Visiting George
  Grau, S. A. Flight
  Hall, D. Widowers' woods
  Harris, M. La Lumiére
  Herling, G. A hot breath from the desert
  Hoban, R. Kleinzeit [excerpt]
  Johnson, L. Backdated
  Johnson-Davies, D. A smile from the past
  Jones, T. Daddy's girl
  Kadish, R. The argument
  Kerslake, L. Lookin' 'n' jivin'
  King, S. That feeling, you can only say what it is in French
  Le Clézio, J.-M. G. Villa Aurora
  Lerner, M. Little selves
  Leslie, N. Give me a sign
  Lovesey, P. Away with the fairies
  Maleti, G. Odilia and Liberato
  Mayhall, J. The men
  Moody, R. The Albertine notes

  Oates, J. C. The doll
  Oates, J. C. Upholstery
  Pak, W.-S. Butterfly of illusion
  Palmer, T. Dream science [excerpt]
  Rawley, D. Iguana boy
  Reed, R. Night of time
  Reynolds, C. A train to catch
  Roorbach, B. Taughannock Falls
  Smith, A. The book club
  Swan, M. Hour of lead
  Swarthout, G. F. Four older men
  Vivante, A. Reflection
  Vonnegut, K. Mnemonics
  Wallace, R. The new sidewalks
  Waters, M. Y. The laws of evening
  Weaver, G. Looking for the lost Eden
  Wegner, H. Dogs of autumn
  Wegner, H. On the road to Szkaradowo
  Wilde, Dana. The green moon
  Worth, V. Geoffrey Sonnabend's obliscence: theories of forgetting and the problem of matter—an encapsulation
Memory. Proust, M.
Memory like ash borne on air. Podolsky, R.
MEMPHIS (TENN.) *See* Tennessee—Memphis
MEN
      See also Single men
  Connor, J. Let us now praise dead white men
  Davies, P. H. Small world
  DeMarinis, R. The boys we were, the men we became
  McBrearty, R. G. The hellraiser
  McCorkle, J. Hominids
  Meloy, M. Aqua Boulevard
  Nesset, K. Mr. Agreeable
  Polansky, S. Coda
  Tilghman, C. The late night news
  Vukcevich, R. The finger
  Wallace, D. F. Brief interviews with hideous men [I]
  Wallace, D. F. Brief interviews with hideous men [II]
  Wallace, D. F. Brief interviews with hideous men [III]
  Wallace, D. F. Brief interviews with hideous men [IV]
  Weaver, G. Long odds
The **men**. Mayhall, J.
Men and angels. Enright, A.
Men and women. Keegan, C.
Men have more upper-body strength. Berkman, P. R.
Men of Greywater Station. Waldrop, H.
Men of rough persuasion. Abbott, L. K.
Men on the moon. Ortiz, S. J.
Menaker, Daniel
  The treatment
      Wonderful town; New York stories from The New Yorker; edited by David Remnick with Susan Choi
Mencken, Sara Haardt
  Absolutely perfect
      Mencken, S. H. Southern souvenirs; selected stories and essays; edited with an introduction by Ann Henley
  Alabama April
      Mencken, S. H. Southern souvenirs; selected stories and essays; edited with an introduction by Ann Henley

Mencken, Sara Haardt—*Continued*

Birthday

Mencken, S. H. Southern souvenirs; selected stories and essays; edited with an introduction by Ann Henley

Clinging vine

Mencken, S. H. Southern souvenirs; selected stories and essays; edited with an introduction by Ann Henley

Commencement

Mencken, S. H. Southern souvenirs; selected stories and essays; edited with an introduction by Ann Henley

Each in her own day

Mencken, S. H. Southern souvenirs; selected stories and essays; edited with an introduction by Ann Henley

Grown-up

Mencken, S. H. Southern souvenirs; selected stories and essays; edited with an introduction by Ann Henley

Joe Moore and Callie Blasingame

Mencken, S. H. Southern souvenirs; selected stories and essays; edited with an introduction by Ann Henley

Ladies and lovers

Mencken, S. H. Southern souvenirs; selected stories and essays; edited with an introduction by Ann Henley

The last of the beaux

Mencken, S. H. Southern souvenirs; selected stories and essays; edited with an introduction by Ann Henley

Little lady

Mencken, S. H. Southern souvenirs; selected stories and essays; edited with an introduction by Ann Henley

Little white girl

Mencken, S. H. Southern souvenirs; selected stories and essays; edited with an introduction by Ann Henley

Miss Rebecca

Mencken, S. H. Southern souvenirs; selected stories and essays; edited with an introduction by Ann Henley

Namesake

Mencken, S. H. Southern souvenirs; selected stories and essays; edited with an introduction by Ann Henley

Solitaire

Mencken, S. H. Southern souvenirs; selected stories and essays; edited with an introduction by Ann Henley

Southern town

Mencken, S. H. Southern souvenirs; selected stories and essays; edited with an introduction by Ann Henley

Tomboy

Mencken, S. H. Southern souvenirs; selected stories and essays; edited with an introduction by Ann Henley

Twilight of chivalry

Mencken, S. H. Southern souvenirs; selected stories and essays; edited with an introduction by Ann Henley

Mendes, Alfred H.

Pablo's fandango

The Oxford book of Caribbean short stories; edited by Stewart Brown and John Wickham

Mendes, Bob

Noble causes

The World's finest mystery and crime stories, second annual collection; edited by Ed Gorman

Tooth marks

Death by espionage; intriguing stories of deception and betrayal; edited by Martin Cruz Smith

Mendez. Stepto, R. B.

Mendoza, Rubén

Traffic

LA shorts; edited by Steven Gilbar

Menen Desleal, Alvaro

A cord made of nylon and gold

Cosmos latinos: an anthology of science fiction from Latin America and Spain; translated, edited, & with an introduction & notes by Andrea L. Bell & Yolanda Molina-Gavilán

Menendez, Ana

Baseball dreams

Menendez, A. In Cuba I was a German shepherd

Confusing the saints

Menendez, A. In Cuba I was a German shepherd

Her mother's house

Menendez, A. In Cuba I was a German shepherd

Hurricane stories `

Menendez, A. In Cuba I was a German shepherd

In Cuba I was a German shepherd

Best new American voices 2000; guest editor Tobias Wolff; series editors John Kulka and Natalie Danford

Menendez, A. In Cuba I was a German shepherd

The last rescue

Menendez, A. In Cuba I was a German shepherd

Miami relatives

Menendez, A. In Cuba I was a German shepherd

The party

Menendez, A. In Cuba I was a German shepherd

The perfect fruit

Menendez, A. In Cuba I was a German shepherd

Story of a parrot

Menendez, A. In Cuba I was a German shepherd

Why we left

Menendez, A. In Cuba I was a German shepherd

Menendez Leal, Alvaro *See* Menen Desleal, Alvaro

Meneseteung. Munro, A.

MENGELE, JOSEF

About

Jacobs, M. Mengele dies again

Scholz, C. Mengele's Jew

Mengele dies again. Jacobs, M.
Meno, Joe
  Bustle in the window
    TriQuarterly no110/111 p405-12 Fall 2001
MENOPAUSE
  Fairey, W. W. Menopause and poker
Menopause and poker. Fairey, W. W.
MENSERVANTS
  Pushkin, A. S. The captain's daughter
MENSTRUATION
  Jackson, S. Blood
  Kalfus, K. Anzhelika, 13
  Willis, C. Even the queen
Mental. Welch, N.
MENTAL DEPRESSION
  Brady, C. Don't run
  Cortázar, J. Letter to a young lady in Paris
  Erdrich, L. The red convertible
  Galloway, J. The trick is to keep breathing [excerpt]
  Jones, T. Cold snap
  Polansky, S. Rein
  Robison, M. An amateur's guide to the night
  Rowell, J. Wildlife of Coastal Carolina
  Singer, I. B. The building project
  Thompson, J. Who do you love
MENTAL DISORDERS *See* Mental illness
The **mental** female. Ohara, M.
MENTAL HOSPITALS *See* Mentally ill—Care and treatment
MENTAL ILLNESS
    See also Dual personality; Hallucinations and illusions; Nervous breakdown; Paranoia; Personality disorders; Schizophrenia
  Agee, J. Each time we meet
  Agee, J. What the Fall brings
  Arenas, R. Mona
  Arnott, Marion. Marbles
  Arredondo, I. Subterranean river
  Bakr, S. Thirty-one beautiful green trees
  Blair, J. Julia loving the face of God
  Bloom, A. Silver water
  Boylan, C. My son the hero
  Brenner, Y. H. Breakdown and bereavement [excerpt]
  Brett, S. Best behaviour
  Brown, J. Afterlife
  Brown, J. Thief
  Bukoski, A. Private Tomaszewski
  Canovic, L. S. Bats
  Cheever, J. The five-forty-eight
  Chopin, K. La belle Zorađe
  Chopin, K. La Belle Zoraïde
  Cody, L. Listen
  Conroy, F. Midair
  Davies, R. Voices in the dark
  Davis, A. Faith; or, Tips for the successful young lady
  Davis, A. True story
  De Lint, C. Freak
  DeMarinis, R. Pagans
  Doble, J. The magic show
  Dozois, G. R. Executive clemency
  Dozois, G. R. The last day of July
  Englander, N. Reunion
  Friedman, K. Don't forget
  Gifford, B. New mysteries of Paris
  Gilman, C. P. The yellow wallpaper
  Glover, D. H. Bad news of the heart

Godwin, G. A sorrowful woman
Goldner, B. Wake
Harty, R. September
Haslett, A. My father's business
Haslett, A. Notes to my biographer
Haslett, A. War's end
Henley, P. Labrador
Hensley, J. L. The retiree
Hodgen, C. The great Americans
Hodgen, C. What the rabbi said to the priest
Jones, G. Babies
Jones, T. You cheated, you lied
Keegan, C. Storms
Mathews, H. The broadcast
Miller, H. R. Monette's fingers
Murray, S. The caprices
Nabokov, V. V. Symbols and signs
Naiyer Masud. Obscure domains of fear and desire
Nissen, T. Grover, king of Nebraska
Oates, J. C. Death mother
O'Callaghan, M. Is you is or is you ain't Miranda?
Perabo, S. Some say the world
Phillips, D. R. What men love for
Richard, N. The order of things
Robins, M. E. La vie en ronde
Schnitzler, A. Flight into darkness
Scoville, S. Ulu's dog
Slezak, E. Lucky
Sosin, D. Submersion
Svoboda, T. Trailer girl
Yañez, R. Lucero's Mkt.
A **mental** suggestion. Chopin, K.
MENTAL TELEPATHY *See* Telepathy
MENTALLY HANDICAPPED
    See also Mentally handicapped children
Amis, M. Heavy water
Banner, K. The smallest people alive
Bender, K. E. Eternal love
Carson, J. Judgement
Cooke, C. Twa Corbies
Daugharty, J. Name of love
Davis, J. S. Only ends
Earle, S. The red suitcase
Gartner, Z. The tragedy of premature death among geniuses
Grau, S. A. The lovely April
Harrington, J. In the merry month of mayhem
Hensley, J. L. Savant
Keyes, D. Flowers for Algernon
Lardner, R. Haircut
Morgan, R. Death crown
Parker, G. Chloroform
Perillo, L. M. Bad boy number seventeen
Proulx, A. People in hell just want a drink of water
Reid, E. Buffalo
Searle, E. Memoir of a soon-to-be star
Spatz, G. Wonderful tricks
Spencer, E. The light in the piazza
Thompson, S. Ernest
MENTALLY HANDICAPPED CHILDREN
    See also Autistic children
Fromm, P. Cowbird
Gunn, K. This place you return to is home
Sagstetter, K. The thing with Willie
Wharton, E. The young gentlemen

MENTALLY ILL

    See also Insane, Criminal and dangerous

    Care and treatment

Bakr, S. Thirty-one beautiful green trees

Chekhov, A. P. Ward no. 6

Chiang, T. Division by zero

Dowling, T. Basic black

Evenson, B. House rules

Fowler, K. J. Sarah Canary [excerpt]

Galef, D. The web of Möbius

Garcia, L. G. The day they took my uncle

Haslett, A. The volunteer

Heinlein, R. A. "They—"

Johnston, B. A. Corpus

Johnston, B. A. Corpus Christi

Jones, T. A midnight clear

Jones, T. Thorazine Johnny Felsun loves me
    (from his permanent cage of lifelong confinement)

Kaminsky, S. M. DRUP number one

Kohler, S. The mask

Lutz, J. The real shape of the coast

Noel, K. April

Ortiz, S. J. A story of Rios and Juan Jesus

Ortiz, S. J. Where o where

Padilla, I. Amends in Halak-Proot

Smith, I. C. In the middle of the wood [excerpt]

Waugh, E. Mr. Loveday's little outing

Wolfe, G. The death of Doctor Island

Wolitzer, M. Tea at the house

The **Mentocrats**. Newhouse, E.

The **mer** she. Leiber, F.

Mercader, Mercer

    The postponed journey

        English translations of short stories by contemporary Argentine women writers; edited by Eliana Cazaubon Hermann ; translated by Sally Webb Thornton

Mercado, Sergio Ramírez *See* Ramírez Mercado, Sergio, 1942-

Mercantilism. Lish, G.

Mercedes Buyer's Guide. Griffin, D.

MERCENARIES *See* Soldiers of fortune

The **Mercenary** Goes to Church. Southwick, S.

The **mercenary's** song. Maristed, K.

MERCHANT MARINE *See* Seamen

MERCHANTS

    See also Department stores

Chekhov, A. P. In trouble

Donaldson, S. R. By any other name

Highsmith, P. Born failure

Kees, W. I should worry

Lavin, M. The little prince

Roth, J. The leviathan

Merchants. Dermont, A.

MERCURY (PLANET)

Baxter, S. Cilia-of-gold

Benford, G. A worm in the well

Varley, J. Retrograde summer

Mercy. Carter, M. L.

Mercy. Jarrad, K.

Mercy. Krouse, E.

Mercy. Thompson, J.

MERCY DEATH *See* Euthanasia

The **mercy** gate. McGarry, M. J.

Mercy the midget. Troy, M.

Meredith, Don

    At the punishment cliff for women

        Meredith, D. Wing walking

Chevy in the fast lane

    Meredith, D. Wing walking

The closer

    Meredith, D. Wing walking

Comic Valentine

    Meredith, D. Wing walking

Desert music

    Meredith, D. Wing walking

Ferry from Kabatas

    Meredith, D. Wing walking

French letters

    Meredith, D. Wing walking

The horses speak French

    Meredith, D. Wing walking

Parade's end

    Meredith, D. Wing walking

The recital

    Meredith, D. Wing walking

Wanamaker

    Meredith, D. Wing walking

Wing walking

    Meredith, D. Wing walking

Meredith Evans' kiss. Jones, R.

The **merger**. Auchincloss, L.

Mergers & acquisitions. Cobb, W. J.

Mericans. Cisneros, S.

The **mermaid**. Vis, J.

Mermaid song. Dickinson, P.

MERMAIDS

Dickinson, P. Mermaid song

Sharratt, M. The anatomy of a mermaid

Vis, J. The mermaid

Mermaids. Beattie, A.

Mermaids, and other sea creatures. Giacobino, M.

Mermaids of the Saluda. Presnell, D.

Merril, Judith

    That only a mother

        The Science fiction hall of fame: volume one, 1929-1964; the greatest science fiction stories of all time chosen by the members of the Science Fiction Writers of America; edited by Robert Silverberg

Merrill, Christopher

    (jt. auth) See Diwakar, S.

Merriman, Catherine

    Learning to speak Klingon

        The Literary Review (Madison, N.J.) v44 no2 p311-17 Wint 2001

    Painting Juliet

        Mr. Roopratna's chocolate; the winning stories from the 1999 Rhys Davies competition

Merritt, Abraham

    Tales before Tolkien; the roots of modern fantasy; edited by Douglas A. Anderson

The **merry** adventures of Robin Hood [excerpt]. Pyle, H.

Merry Christmas, Charlie Brown. Berkman, P. R.

The **merry** ghosts of the Grampus. Correa, A.

MERRY-GO-ROUNDS

Dillingham, D. G. The white carousel horse

Merry-go-sorry. Holladay, C. C.

Merry May. Campbell, R.

Merry Roderick. Warburton, G.

Mertz, Barbara, 1927-

    For works written by this author under other names see Peters, Elizabeth, 1927-

Mesler, Corey
The growth and death of Buddy Gardner
New stories from the South: the year's best, 2002; edited by Shannon Ravenel; with a preface by Larry Brown
The **mesmerist**. Knight, M.
Mespoulets of the Splendide. Bemelmans, L.
Message found in a copy of Flatland. Rucker, R. v. B.
Message in a fish. Vukcevich, R.
The **messenger**. Estep, M.
Messenger. Stern, D.
MESSENGERS
Estep, M. The messenger
Heller, J. World full of great cities
The **messengers**. Davenport, G.
Messengers. Martin, V.
Messing with the river gods. Burton, M.
Mestre, Ernesto
After Elián
Colchie, T. A whistler in the nightworld; short fiction from the Latin Americas; edited by Thomas Colchie
The **met** are all for this. Aylett, S.
Metafiction. Galef, D.
Metal fatigue. Kilpatrick, N.
The **metallic** crocodile. Sammān, G.
Metamorphose, oboe. Smith, S. J.
METAMORPHOSIS
Addonizio, K. The gift
Atkinson, K. Transparent fiction
Biguenet, J. Gregory's fate
Bowles, P. Allal
Bowles, P. Kitty
Byatt, A. S. A stone woman
Carey, P. The chance
Kurahashi, Y. The house of the black cat
Lumley, B. The statement of Henry Worthy
Paschal, D. Python
Yolen, J. Words of power
Metamorphosis. McDermid, V.
Metamorphosis. Updike, J.
Metamusic. Lugones, L.
The **metaphor**. Bottoms, G.
Metaphysics of morals. Alexis, A.
Metcalf, suzanne *See* Baum, L. Frank (Lyman Frank), 1856-1919
METEORITES
Coleman, J. C. The Perseid meteors
Meteors. LeRoy, J. T.
Méthode champenoise. Wieland, L.
METROPOLITAN AREAS
Budnitz, J. Directions
Metzgar, Lisa
Cat and mouse
Best new American voices 2000; guest editor Tobias Wolff; series editors John Kulka and Natalie Danford
Metzger, Th.
Transorbital love probe
The Museum of horrors; edited by Dennis Etchison
MEXICAN AMERICANS
See also Mexicans—United States
Alderete, P. Fire
Alderete, P. Victor the Bear
Blake, J. C. Referee
Browder, C. Amnesty
Casares, O. Charro

Casares, O. Domingo
Castillo, R. The battle of the Alamo
Chacón, D. Aztlán, Oregon
Chacón, D. How hot was Mexicali?
Chacón, D. Mexican table
Chacón, D. Slow and good
Chacón, D. Spring break
Chacón, D. Too white
Cisneros, S. Never marry a Mexican
Cisneros, S. Woman Hollering Creek
Garcia, L. G. The day they took my uncle
Garcia, L. G. The wedding
Gifford, B. Two border stories
Gilb, D. About Tere who was in Palomas
Gilb, D. Brisa
Gilb, D. A painting in Santa Fe
Gilb, D. The pillows
Gilb, D. Romero's shirt
Guerrero, L. Blanca Rosa
Guerrero, L. Cloud-shadow
Guerrero, L. The curse
Guerrero, L. The girdle
Guerrero, L. Gloves of her own
Guerrero, L. Hotel Arco Iris
Guerrero, L. Love and happiness
Guerrero, L. Memories in white
Guerrero, L. Return of the spirit
Hinojosa, R. The Gulf Oil -Can Santa Claus
López, L. After Dad shot Jesus
López, L. The crown on prince
López, L. Frostbite
López, L. Love can make you sick
López, L. Sophia
López, L. Soy la Avon lady
López, L. A tatting man
López, L. To control a rabid rodent
Martin, P. P. Amor de madre—Mother's love
Martin, P. P. Amor desesperado—Desperate love
Martin, P. P. Amor e ilusion—Love and illusion
Martin, P. P. Amor encantado—Enchanted love
Martin, P. P. Amor eterno—Eternal love
Martin, P. P. Amor prohibido—Forbidden love
Mathews, L. Crazy life
Matiella, A. C. The braid
Matiella, A. C. La casa chica
Matiella, A. C. Rat roulette
Matiella, A. C. The ring
Matiella, A. C. Sana, sana, colita de rana
Matiella, A. C. The truth about Alicia
Matiella, A. C. Tying St. Anthony's feet
Muñoz, M. Anchorage
Murguía, A. Barrio lotto
Murguía, A. A lesson in merengue
Murguía, A. Ofrendas
Murguía, A. Rose-colored dreams
Murguía, A. This war called love
Murguía, A. A toda máquina
Murguía, A. El último round
Murray, Y. M. Girl on fire
Padilla, M. Flora in shadows
Padilla, M. Hard language
Padilla, M. The king of snow
Padilla, M. Papel
Padilla, M. The reason for angels
Padilla, M. Restoration
Padilla, M. Who in the modern world can keep up with Julia Juárez?
Paredes, A. The hammon and the beans

MEXICAN AMERICANS—*Continued*

Rivera, T. The salamanders
Saenz, B. A. Exile
Sánchez, R. Barrio chronicle
Sánchez, R. Dallas
Sánchez, R. Don Salomón
Sánchez, R. He rolled up his sleeves
Sánchez, R. Lucho
Sánchez, R. One morning: 1952
Sánchez, R. One night
Sánchez, R. Road detours
Sanderson, J. Commerce Street
Troncoso, S. The abuelita
Troncoso, S. Angie Luna
Troncoso, S. Espiritu Santo
Troncoso, S. The gardener
Troncoso, S. The last tortilla
Troncoso, S. My life in the city
Troncoso, S. Punching chickens
Troncoso, S. Remembering possibilities
Troncoso, S. A rock trying to be a stone
Troncoso, S. The snake
Troncoso, S. Time magician
Vaswani, N. Blue, without sorrow
Yañez, R. Amoroza Tires
Yañez, R. Desert Vista
Yañez, R. Good time
Yañez, R. I&M Plumbing
Yañez, R. Lucero's Mkt.
Yañez, R. Rio Bravo
Yañez, R. Rio Grande
Yañez, R. Sacred Heart
Mexican dust. Adams, A.
The **Mexican** girl. Kerouac, J.
The **Mexican** pig bandit. Crumley, J.
MEXICAN REVOLUTION *See* Mexico—20th
    century
Mexican table. Chacón, D.
MEXICANS
California
Cleaver, E. The flashlight
Japan
Zavala, H. L. Mirror images
United States
Blake, J. C. Aliens in the garden
Blake, J. C. La vida loca
Blakely, M. Laureano's wall
Bradbury, R. I see you never
Chacón, D. Godoy lives
DeMarinis, R. Novias
Garza, D. L. Saturday belongs to the palomía
Kelton, E. North of the big river
Kerouac, J. The Mexican girl
Sánchez, R. The fields
Sánchez, R. Like I was telling you . . .
Shepard, S. Lajitas and the NFL
Troncoso, S. Angie Luna
Troncoso, S. Day of the dead
Vasseur, T. J. The angels
Watanabe McFerrin, L. Los mariachis del
    muerto
MEXICO
Bradbury, R. The lifework of Juan Diaz
Mastretta, A. Aunt Cristina
Mastretta, A. Aunt Elena
19th century
Loomis, N. M. Tough hombre
Martin, P. P. Amor de acuerdo—Arranged love

20th century
Adams, A. At the beach
Adams, A. The end of the world
Adams, A. The haunted beach
Adams, A. The wrong Mexico
Bellow, S. Mosby's memoirs
Blake, J. C. Three tales of the Revolution
Bowles, P. Doña Faustina
Bowles, P. Señor Ong and Señor Ha
Lawrence, D. H. The woman who rode away
Luz Montes, A. M. d. l. While Pilar Tobillo
    sleeps
Matiella, A. C. Angels
Miller, A. L. Off-season travel
Murguía, A. Lucky Alley
Roffiel, R. M. Forever lasts only a full moon
Spencer, E. The runaways
Swarthout, G. F. Ixion
Swarthout, G. F. Pancho Villa's one-man war
Urrea, L. A. Mr. Mendoza's paintbrush
Rural life
Bowles, P. Pastor Dowe at Tacate
Desai, A. Tepoztlan tomorrow
Martin, P. P. Amor perdido—Lost love
Mastretta, A. Aunt Charo
Rulfo, J. Luvina
Taylor, L. The wedding at Esperanza
Acapulco
Lida, D. Acapulco gold
Mexico City
Chacón, D. The biggest city in the world
Lida, D. Free trade
Lida, D. Regrets
Lida, D. Taxi
Murguía, A. Boy on a wooden horse
White, E. Cinnamon skin
Oaxaca
Raphael, F. Bread, money, and liberty
Mexico. Boyle, T. C.
Mexico. Gilchrist, E.
MEXICO CITY (MEXICO) *See* Mexico—Mexi-
    co City
Meyers, Annette
You don't know me
    The Best American mystery stories, 2002; ed-
      ited and with an introduction by James
      Ellroy; Otto Penzler, series editor
    Flesh and blood; erotic tales of crime and
      passion; edited by Max Allan Collins and
      Jeff Gelb
Meyers, Annette and Meyers, Martin
The Daffodil
    Flesh and blood: guilty as sin; erotic tales of
      crime and passion; edited by Max Allan
      Collins and Jeff Gelb
Meyers, Kent
Abiding by law
    Meyers, K. Light in the crossing; stories
Bird shadows
    Meyers, K. Light in the crossing; stories
Easter dresses
    Meyers, K. Light in the crossing; stories
Glacierland
    Meyers, K. Light in the crossing; stories
The heart of the sky
    In our nature: stories of wildness; selected
      and introduced by Donna Seaman
    Meyers, K. Light in the crossing; stories

Meyers, Kent—*Continued*
The husker tender
Meyers, K. Light in the crossing; stories
Light in the crossing
Meyers, K. Light in the crossing; stories
Making the news
Meyers, K. Light in the crossing; stories
The smell of the deer
Meyers, K. Light in the crossing; stories
The Year's best fantasy & horror, thirteenth
annual collection; edited by Ellen Datlow
and Terri Windling
A strange brown fruit
Meyers, K. Light in the crossing; stories
Two-speed
Meyers, K. Light in the crossing; stories
Wind rower
Meyers, K. Light in the crossing; stories
Meyers, Martin
(jt. auth) See Meyers, Annette and Meyers, Mar-
tin
Meyerson, Golda *See* Meir, Golda, 1898-1978
"The **mezzotint**". Tuttle, L.
MIAMI (FLA.) *See* Florida—Miami
Miami. Lee, W. W.
Miami heat. Buchanan, E.
Miami—New York. Gellhorn, M.
Miami relatives. Menendez, A.
Miano, Sarah Emily
Hands in Pockets
Grand Street no72 p164-73 Fall 2003
Miasma. McGarry, T.
MIB. Doenges, J.
MICE
Jones, T. Mouses
Metzgar, L. Cat and mouse
Michael, Sami
Refuge [excerpt]
Sleepwalkers and other stories; the Arab in
Hebrew fiction; edited by Ehud Ben-Ezer
Michael Mc:_____ a case study. Cole, C. B.
Michaelmas daisies. Barolini, H.
Michaels, Barbara, 1927-
*For works written by this author under oth-
er names see* Peters, Elizabeth, 1927-
Michaels, Leonard
City boy
Michaels, L. A girl with a monkey; new and
selected stories
Crossbones
Michaels, L. A girl with a monkey; new and
selected stories
Cryptology
The New Yorker v79 no13 p82-4, 86-9 My 26
2003
The deal
Michaels, L. A girl with a monkey; new and
selected stories
Eating out
Michaels, L. A girl with a monkey; new and
selected stories
A girl with a monkey
Michaels, L. A girl with a monkey; new and
selected stories
Going places
Michaels, L. A girl with a monkey; new and
selected stories

Honeymoon
Michaels, L. A girl with a monkey; new and
selected stories
In the fifties
Michaels, L. A girl with a monkey; new and
selected stories
Manikin
Michaels, L. A girl with a monkey; new and
selected stories
Mildred
Michaels, L. A girl with a monkey; new and
selected stories
Murderers
Michaels, L. A girl with a monkey; new and
selected stories
Neurotica: Jewish writers on sex; edited by
Melvin Jules Bukiet
Nachman
The Pushcart prize XXIV: best of the small
presses; an annual small press reader; ed-
ited by Bill Henderson with the Pushcart
prize editors
Nachman at the races
Partisan Review v66 no3 p398-403 Summ
1999
Nachman from Los Angeles
The Best American short stories, 2002; select-
ed from U.S. and Canadian magazines by
Sue Miller with Katrina Kenison, with an
introduction by Sue Miller
The New Yorker v77 no35 p110-21 N 12
2001
Of mystery there is no end
The New Yorker v78 no7 p74-81 Ap 8 2002
The penultimate conjecture
The New Yorker v74 no44 p64-68 F 1 1999
Reflections of a wild kid
Michaels, L. A girl with a monkey; new and
selected stories
Second honeymoon
Michaels, L. A girl with a monkey; new and
selected stories
Some laughed
Michaels, L. A girl with a monkey; new and
selected stories
Tell me everything
Michaels, L. A girl with a monkey; new and
selected stories
Viva la Tropicana
Michaels, L. A girl with a monkey; new and
selected stories
Michaels, Robert
Noctem Aeternus
Tales from The Dark Tower; illustrated by
Joseph Vargo; edited by Joseph Vargo and
Christine Filipak
Michaud, Jon
The night the clocks go back
The North American Review v286 no6 p18-22
N/D 2001
Michelangelo. Warren, D.
Michelle. Chapman, C. M.
Michelle's miracle. Jacquez, K.
Michener, James A.
The milk run
On glorious wings; the best flying stories of
the century; edited and introduced by Ste-
phen Coonts

MICHIGAN
Daniels, J. Good neighbor
Daniels, J. Middle of the mitten
Hagy, A. C. Search bay
Harrison, J. The beast God forgot to invent
Smith, S. J. Black bean soup
Smith, S. J. Gar fishing
Smith, S. J. Healing the mare
Smith, S. J. Jack in Chicago
Smith, S. J. Looping
Smith, S. J. Metamorphose, oboe
Smith, S. J. My father weeping
Smith, S. J. No thanks
Smith, S. J. Selling the house
Smith, S. J. Turtle hunting with black
Smith, S. J. Valerie rakes the leaves
Detroit
Allyn, D. Black Irish
Allyn, D. The jukebox king
Daniels, J. Christmasmobile
Daniels, J. Cross country
Daniels, J. Islands
Daniels, J. Minding the store
Daniels, J. Renegade
Jones, T. Tarantula
Kramer, W. East Side story
Slezak, E. Head, heart, legs or arms
Slezak, E. Here in car city
Slezak, E. If you treat things right
Slezak, E. Last year's Jesus (or Passion play)
Slezak, E. Patch
Slezak, E. Settled
Slezak, E. Tomato watch
Michigan City, Indiana. Orner, P.
Mick Jagger's green-eyed daughter. Denton, E.
Mickelrede; or, The slayer and the staff. Davidson, A.
Mickenberg, Risa
Direct male
The Pushcart prize XXIII: best of the small presses; an annual small press reader; edited by Bill Henderson with the Pushcart prize editors
The **microcosm** [excerpt] Duffy, M.
Microcosmic god. Sturgeon, T.
Midair. Conroy, F.
Midday. Daviu, M.
Midday. Shechter, Y.
MIDDLE AGE
See also Aging
Bausch, R. Design
Boyle, T. C. Death of the cool
Carleton, M. R. Conversations with a moose
DeMarinis, R. Desert places
McBrearty, R. G. The yellow house
Mencken, S. H. The last of the beaux
Robison, M. Your errant mom
Updike, J. The persistence of desire
Winegardner, M. Obvious questions
MIDDLE AGES
See also Knights and knighthood
Allyn, D. The country of the blind
Allyn, D. St. Margaret's kitten
Borges, J. L. "Undr"
Douglass, S. The evil within
Friesner, E. M. Hallowmass
Hendee, B. Before a fall
Newman, S. Death before compline
The **middle** of nowhere. Kilpatrick, N.

The **middle** of the night. Bauman, B. A.
The **Middle** of the Night. Stolar, D.
MIDDLE WESTERN STATES
Evans, E. Americans
Moody, R. The double zero
Farm life
See Farm life—Middle Western States
Middleton, Nancy
Food, Clothing, Shelter
South Carolina Review v36 no1 p87-95 Fall 2003
Shipbuilding
South Carolina Review v34 no2 p47-58 Spr 2002
The **midge.** Zinovyeva-Annibal, L. D.
MIDGETS *See* Dwarfs
The **midgets.** Orozco, O.
Midnight. Rellas, D.
Midnight all day. Kureishi, H.
Midnight and I'm not famous yet. Hannah, B.
A **midnight** clear. Jones, T.
The **midnight** el. Weinberg, R.
Midnight emissions. Toole, F. X.
Midnight mass. Bowles, P.
Midnight shift. Karlin, K.
Midnight trash. Farnham, B.
Midsummer in April. Hart, M. 't
A **midsummer** tempest. Anderson, P.
MIDWEST *See* Middle Western States
MIDWIVES
Phillips, D. R. Everything quiet like church
Sherlock, P. Mother George, midwife
Miéville, China
Details
The Mammoth book of best new horror 14; edited with an introduction by Stephen Jones
The Year's best fantasy & horror: sixteenth annual collection; edited by Ellen Datlow & Terri Windling
Migdal, Laura
At the moment of destruction, you stop to examine the wreckage
Bomb no79 p86-7 Spr 2002
The **mightiest** mornings. Highsmith, P.
A **mighty** nice man. Highsmith, P.
A **migrant** bird. Deane, J. F.
MIGRANT LABOR
Blaise, C. Broward Dowdy
Blake, J. C. Aliens in the garden
Blake, J. C. The house of Esperanza
Garza, D. L. Saturday belongs to the palomía
Henley, P. Picking time
Muñoz, M. Campo
Nichols, J. Slow monkeys
Oates, J. C. First views of the enemy
Penn, W. S. Rosa
Rivera, T. The salamanders
The **migration** of ghosts. Melville, P.
Migration of the love bugs. McCorkle, J.
Mikolaj, Dušan
The man with the weak heart
In search of homo sapiens; twenty-five contemporary Slovak short stories; editor, Pavol Hudík ; [translated by Heather Trebatická; American English editor, Lucy Bednár]
MILAN (ITALY) *See* Italy—Milan
Mildred. Michaels, L.

Mile a mud. Agee, J.
Miles. Burgin, R.
Miles deep. Lee, W. W.
Miles to go. Davis, D. S.
MILITARISM
  Clark, J. Wild blue
MILITARY AERONAUTICS
     See also World War, 1914-1918—Aerial
    operations; World War, 1939-1945—Aerial
    operations
  Brown, D. Powder River Moe
  Harrison, P. Zero-G dogfight
  Peters, R. Retaliation
MILITARY DESERTION
  Babel´, I. The deserter
  James, S. Billy Mason from Gloucester
  O'Brien, T. Going after Cacciato
MILITARY EDUCATION
  Longstreet, K. A. The judgement of Paris
MILITARY MANEUVERS
     See also War games
MILITARY OCCUPATION
  Malzberg, B. N. Police actions
MILITARY SCHOOLS *See* Military education
MILITARY SERVICE, COMPULSORY *See*
  Draft
MILITARY TRAINING CAMPS
  Casey, J. A more complete cross-section
  Yates, R. Jody rolled the bones
Milk. Bennett, A.
Milk. Carlson, R.
Milk. Jackson, S.
Milking cherry. Chapman, C. M.
The **mill** on the River Utrata. Iwaszkiewicz, J.
Millar, Kenneth *See* Macdonald, Ross, 1915-1983
Millar, Margaret
  The couple next door
    The Best American mystery stories of the
    century; Tony Hillerman, editor; with an
    introduction by Tony Hillerman
  The people across the canyon
    A Century of great suspense stories; edited by
    Jeffery Deaver
Millar, Martin
  Dreams of sex and stage diving [excerpt]
    The Vintage book of contemporary Scottish
    fiction; edited and with an introduction by
    Peter Kravitz
Millás, Juan José
  Other Persons
    The Antioch Review v61 no3 p577-9 Summ
    2003
Millefiori beads. Hornosty, C. C.
Millennium babies. Rusch, K. K.
Millennium blues. Simpson, H.
The **millennium** party. Williams, W. J.
Miller, Alyce L.
  A cold winter light
    Crossing the color line; readings in Black and
    white; edited by Suzanne W. Jones
  Off-season travel
    Crossing the color line; readings in Black and
    white; edited by Suzanne W. Jones
  Winter
    Prairie Schooner v76 no2 p63-86 Summ 2002
Miller, Arthur
  The Bare Manuscript
    The New Yorker v78 no39 p82-93 D 16 2002

Bulldog
    The Best American short stories, 2002; select-
    ed from U.S. and Canadian magazines by
    Sue Miller with Katrina Kenison, with an
    introduction by Sue Miller
    The New Yorker v77 no23 p72-6 Ag 13 2001
  The performance
    The New Yorker v78 no9 p176-88 Ap 22-29
    2002
  Presence
    Esquire v140 no1 p106-9 Jl 2003
Miller, Ben
  #361
    Western Humanities Review v55 no2 p190-1
    Fall 2001
  Bix and Flannery
    Raritan v22 no4 p4-11 Spr 2003
  Spike song
    American short fiction, vol. 8, no 29-32
Miller, Ellen
  In memory of Chanveasna Chan, who is still
    alive
  Lost tribe; jewish fiction from the edge
Miller, Emily
  #4. Leave
    The North American Review v288 no1 p22-7
    Ja/F 2003
Miller, Heather Ross
  Monette's fingers
    This is where we live; short stories by 25
    contemporary North Carolina writers; ed-
    ited by Michael McFee
Miller, Jim Wayne
  The taste of ironwater
    Home and beyond; an anthology of Kentucky
    short stories; edited by Morris Allen
    Grubbs; with an introduction by Wade Hall
    and an afterword by Charles E. May
Miller, Rebecca
  Bryna
    Miller, R. Personal velocity
  Delia
    Miller, R. Personal velocity
  Greta
    Miller, R. Personal velocity
  Julianne
    Miller, R. Personal velocity
  Louisa
    Miller, R. Personal velocity
  Nancy
    Miller, R. Personal velocity
  Paula
    Miller, R. Personal velocity
Miller, Rex
  Spike team
    The Crow; shattered lives & broken dreams;
    edited by J. O'Barr and Ed Kramer
  Walking to Paris
    Flesh and blood: guilty as sin; erotic tales of
    crime and passion; edited by Max Allan
    Collins and Jeff Gelb
Miller, Rod
  The darkness of the deep
    Westward; a fictional history of the American
    West : 28 original stories celebrating the
    50th anniversary of the Western Writers of
    America; edited by Dale L. Walker
Miller, Steve
  (jt. auth) *See* Lee, Sharon and Miller, Steve

Miller, Sue

Expensive gifts

Breaking into print; early stories and insights into getting published; a Ploughshares anthology; edited by DeWitt Henry

The world below

Good Housekeeping v233 no5 p231-41 N 2001

MILLER, WILLIAM, 1782-1849

About

Connor, J. The day the world declined to end

The **miller's** daughter (Rumpelstiltskin). Rollins, H.

Milletti, Christina

The search for Anna Boubouli

Chicago Review v45 no3/4 p77-88 1999

Villa of the veiled lady

Best new American voices 2001; guest editor Charles Baxter; series editors John Kulka and Natalie Danford

Millhauser, Steven

Behind the blue curtain

The Art of the story; an international anthology of contemporary short stories; edited by Daniel Halpern

Cat 'N' Mouse

The New Yorker v80 no9 p174-6, 178-83 Ap 19-26 2004

Clair de lune

The Year's best fantasy & horror, twelfth annual collection; edited by Ellen Datlow & Terry Windling

The disappearance of Elaine Coleman

The New Yorker v75 no35 p176-82+ N 22 1999

The Year's best fantasy & horror, thirteenth annual collection; edited by Ellen Datlow and Terri Windling

Revenge

Harper's v303 no1814 p37-56 Jl 2001

Milliken, Josie

Development

The Antioch Review v57 no1 p88-98 Wint 1999

Million $$$ baby. Toole, F. X.

The **million-year** picnic. Bradbury, R.

MILLIONAIRES

See also Capitalists and financiers; Wealth

Barthelme, D. I bought a little city

Clarke, A. C. The man who ploughed the sea

Mills, Joseph

Watch out, the world's behind you

The Vintage book of contemporary Scottish fiction; edited and with an introduction by Peter Kravitz

Milly's messenger. Alcott, L. M.

Milne, A. A. (Alan Alexander)

The rise and fall of Mortimer Scrivens

Other people's mail; an anthology of letter stories; edited with an introduction by Gail Pool

Milne, Alan Alexander *See* Milne, A. A. (Alan Alexander), 1882-1956

Milo and Sylvie. Fintushel, E.

The **Milqueiest** Piece of Toast. Power, N.

Milt and Moose. Pollack, E.

MIMES

Melville, P. Provenance of a face

Mimesis. Berry, R. M.

A **mimicry** of mockingbirds. Carl, L. S.

Mimsy were the borogoves. Padgett, L.

Min, Anchee

Red azalea [excerpt]

The Vintage book of international lesbian fiction; edited and with an introduction by Naomi Holoch and Joan Nestle

Min, Katherine

The liberation of a face

TriQuarterly no110/111 p102-6 Fall 2001

Mina, Denise

Alice opens the box

The best British mysteries; edited by Maxim Jakubowski

Tart noir; edited by Stella Duffy & Lauren Henderson

Helena and the babies

The World's finest mystery and crime stories, second annual collection; edited by Ed Gorman

MIND AND BODY

Dann, J. Blind shemmy

Sheckley, R. Warm

Silverberg, R. Passengers

Mind and body. Fairey, W. W.

Mind of Winter. Wei, J.

Mind on fire. Hecht, J.

MIND READING *See* Telepathy

Mind-slaves of Manotori. Sheckley, R.

Mind the doors. Zinik, Z.

Minding the graves. Betts, D.

Minding the Store. Mogan, J.

Minds in ferment. Chekhov, A. P.

Mindt, Alex

Stories of the hunt

The Literary Review (Madison, N.J.) v42 no4 p561-75 Summ 1999

MINE ACCIDENTS

L'Amour, L. Dead-end drift

Miner, Christopher

Rhonda and her children

New stories from the South: the year's best, 2000; edited by Shannon Ravenel; with a preface by Ellen Douglas

Miner, Valerie

All the way

Salmagundi no124/125 p288-301 Fall 1999/Wint 2000

Il Cortigiano of Thomas Avenue

The Georgia Review v57 no2 p245-50 Summ 2003

Percussion

Prairie Schooner v77 no3 p87-103 Fall 2003

Veranda

Southwest Review v87 no4 p484-508 2002

Vital signs

New Letters v67 no2 p39-64 2001

MINERS *See* Coal mines and mining; Copper mines and mining; Gold mines and mining; Mines and mining

Mines. Straight, S.

MINES AND MINING

See also Coal mines and mining; Copper mines and mining; Gold mines and mining

Bail, M. Ore

Brkic, C. A. Afterdamp

Chiang, T. Tower of Babylon

DeLancey, K. Coal miner's holiday

MINES AND MINING—*Continued*
DeLancey, K. Dinger and Blacker
DeLancey, K. It's dark
DeLancey, K. Two strippers
DeLancey, K. The Welsh engineer
Harrison, H. Rock diver
MacLeod, A. The closing down of summer
MacLeod, A. The vastness of the dark
Williams, S. A map of the mines of Barnath
Mingling. Dillon, M.
Miniature man. Brown, C.
MINING TOWNS
Bradbury, R. Almost the end of the world
Crumley, J. Coming around the mountain
Steinbeck, T. Blighted cargo
MINISTERS *See* Clergy
The **minister's** black veil. Hawthorne, N.
MINNEAPOLIS (MINN.) *See* Minnesota—
Minneapolis
Minneapolis. Carter, E.
Minneapolis & The Flattening of the Vault of
Heaven. Willoughby, J.
MINNESOTA
Bly, C. An apprentice
Bly, C. Chuck's money
Bly, C. A committee of the whole
Bly, C. The dignity of life
Bly, C. Gunnar's sword
Bly, C. The last of the gold star mothers
Bly, C. My Lord Bag of Rice
Bly, C. The tender organizations
Harfenist, J. Body count
Harfenist, J. Duck season
Harfenist, J. Floating
Harfenist, J. Fully bonded by the state of Min-
nesota
Harfenist, J. The gift
Harfenist, J. The history of the flood
Harfenist, J. Pixie dust
Harfenist, J. The road out of Acorn Lake
Harfenist, J. Salad girls
Mueller, D. How animals mate
Mueller, D. Ice breaking
Farm life
See Farm life—Minnesota
Minneapolis
Carter, E. Minneapolis
Carter, E. New in north town
St. Paul
Murphy, N. The butterfly garden
Murphy, N. The catcher
Murphy, N. Miini-Giizi
Rawson, J. Eleven ways to live in the city
Rawson, J. The interview
Rawson, J. A working history of the alley
Singer, Julia Klatt. Chicken
Singer, Julia Klatt. From one window
Singer, Julia Klatt. Translations
Vázquez, D., Jr. The fat-brush painter
Vázquez, D., Jr. The first time I saw St. Paul
Vázquez, D., Jr. My friend Cintia
Minnie gets married. Schein, G.
MINOR PLANETS *See* Asteroids
The **minstrel** tree. Shayne, A.
MINSTRELS
Allyn, D. The country of the blind
Allyn, D. St. Margaret's kitten
Mint condition. Hoffman, N. K.
Minutes of a village meeting. Trevanian

Minutes of glory. Ng'ugĩ wa Thiong'o
Miosvatis. Barnet, M.
Miracle. Budnitz, J.
The **miracle**. Forsyth, F.
The **miracle**. Tozzi, F.
Miracle. Willis, C.
The **miracle** at Ballinspittle. Boyle, T. C.
Miracle boy. Benedict, P.
The **miracle** of life. Boylan, C.
The **miracle** of Saint Wilfred. Lugones, L.
The **miracle** of Swamp Gas Jackson. Eakin, W.
The **miracle** workers. Vance, J.
MIRACLES
Borges, J. L. The secret miracle
Boyle, T. C. The miracle at Ballinspittle
Chwedyk, Richard. Bronte's egg
Erdrich, L. Saint Marie
Hawthorne, N. The snow image: a childish mir-
acle
Lugones, L. The miracle of Saint Wilfred
Matthews, C. The moving statue of Ballinspittle
Sandlin, L. The saint of bilocation
Miracles! Happen!. Allyn, D.
Mirosevich, Toni
The Whole Story
Western Humanities Review v57 no2 p4-12
Fall 2003
Mirror. Robison, M.
The **mirror** and the mask. Borges, J. L.
Mirror games. Sheckley, R.
Mirror images. Zavala, H. L.
Mirror, mirror. Dain, C.
Mirror studies. Waters, M. Y.
MIRRORS
Delany, S. R. Prismatica
Dowling, T. One thing about the night
Greenberg, A. The life of the mind
Llano, M. E. In the family
Ribeyro, J. R. The wardrobe, the old man and
death
Sheckley, R. Mirror games
Singer, I. B. The mirror
Tawada, Y. The reflection
Mirta. Maleti, G.
Mirvis, Tova
A Poland, a Lithuania, a Galicia
Lost tribe; jewish fiction from the edge
Mis-sayings. Kuryla, M.
Miscalculation. Burke, J.
MISCARRIAGE
McMillan, T. Quilting on the rebound
Ockert, J. Scarecrowed
Silver, M. What I saw from where I stood
Whittenberg, A. Bloom of Zenobia
MISCEGENATION
See also Interracial marriage
Elliott, S. B. The heart of it
Gordimer, N. Country lovers
Rhys, J. Pioneers, oh, pioneers
Misery. Chekhov, A. P.
Misfits. Davies, R.
A **misfortune**. Chekhov, A. P.
A **mishap** at the manor. Satterthwait, W.
Miss Askew on ice. Bennett, H.
Miss Butterfingers. Quill, M.
Miss Carmichael's funeral. Avrich, J.
Miss Carrollene tells a story. Coberly, L. M.
Miss Ellen Jameson Is Not Deceased.
Schottenfeld, S.

Miss Famous. Boswell, R.
Miss Fozzard finds her feet. Bennett, A.
Miss Grace at her best. Thurm, M.
Miss Juste and the green rompers. Highsmith, P.
Miss Libbie tells all. Salzer, S. K.
Miss Lien. Phan, A.
Miss Luck. McIlvoy, K.
Miss Mary Pask. Wharton, E.
Miss Mary Philpot. Baker, J. M.
Miss McEnders. Chopin, K.
Miss Mona's bank. Malone, M.
Miss Olimpia and her maid Belarmina. Régio, J.
Miss Parker & the Cutter-Sanborn tables. Kinman, G. T.
Miss Rebecca. Mencken, S. H.
Miss Witherwell's mistake. Chopin, K.
Missed connection. Campbell, R.
Missing. Crenshaw, P.
Missing. Winn, T.
MISSING CHILDREN
See also Lost children
Barth, J. Dead cat, floating boy
Cohen, R. Putting up signs
Davies, P. H. Frogmen
Dunmore, H. Emily's ring
Gay, W. The paperhanger, the doctor's wife, and the child who went into the abstract
Keegan, C. Passport soup
Wheat, C. Show me the bones
The missing day. Browder, C.
Missing in action. Robinson, P.
Missing Kissinger. Keret, E.
The Missing Man. Lennon, J. R.
Missing: page thirteen. Green, A. K.
Missing person. Davies, R.
MISSING PERSONS
See also Missing children
Arvin, N. Commemorating
Bester, A. Disappearing act
Bradbury, R. The poems
Budnitz, J. What happened
Chan, D. M. Open circles
Chaon, D. Among the missing
Chaon, D. Here's a little something to remember me by
Chapman, C. M. Rest area
Chesnutt, C. W. Mr. Taylor's funeral
Cohen, S. Just another New York Christmas story
Davidson, A. Thou still unravished bride
Gault, W. C. The Kerman kill
Hawthorne, N. Wakefield
Kaminsky, S. M. Adele
Millhauser, S. The disappearance of Elaine Coleman
Padilla, I. Ever wrest: log of the journey
Pearlman, D. D. Cogitor, ergo sum
Roth, J. The cartel
Singer, I. B. Lost
Spence, J. Missing women
Thompson, J. The rich man's house
Treat, J. Not a chance
VanderMeer, J. Corpse mouth and spore nose
Winegardner, M. Thirty-year-old
Wolven, S. The copper kings
Missing Sam. Reed, K.
Missing time. Steele, A. M.
Missing women. Spence, J.
Mission. Vachss, A. H.

The mission of Jane. Wharton, E.
Mission statement. Gordimer, N.
MISSIONARIES
Bowles, P. Pastor Dowe at Tacate
Harrison, H. The streets of Ashkelon
L'Amour, L. Beyond the Great Snow Mountains
Lord, N. Behold
Rogers, B. H. Cloud stalking mice
Silber, J. Ideas of heaven
Wharton, E. The seed of the faith
The missionary's child. McHugh, M. F.
MISSISSIPPI
Bass, R. The legend of Pig-Eye
Brown, L. A roadside resurrection
Douglas, E. I just love Carrie Lee
Eakin, W. Lawnmower Moe
Foote, S. The sacred mound
Franklin, T. Shubuta
Gilchrist, E. Bare ruined choirs, where late the sweet birds sang
Gilchrist, E. A lady with pearls
Gilchrist, E. Summer, an elegy
Hill, I. Jolie-Gray
McManus, J. Megargel
Nordan, L. Sugar among the chickens
Spencer, E. The business venture
Spencer, E. The finder
Spencer, E. First dark
Spencer, E. The master of Shongalo
Spencer, E. Sharon
Spencer, E. Ship island: the story of a mermaid
Spencer, E. A southern landscape
Walker, A. To my young husband
Weaver, G. Without spot or wrinkle
Williams, J. Spring is now
Biloxi
Porter, J. A. A pear-shaped woman and a fuddy-duddy
Jackson
Gilchrist, E. The cabal
Gilchrist, E. Hearts of Dixie
MISSISSIPPI RIVER
Farrell, C. Fire in their stacks
Parrish, T. After the river
MISSISSIPPI RIVER VALLEY
Borges, J. L. The cruel redeemer Lazarus Morell
MISSOURI
McElroy, C. J. A brief spell by the river
Smart, A. Raccoon
Thelwell, M. Direct action
Kansas City
Shapiro, G. The tutor
Saint Louis
Stolar, D. Crossing over
Stolar, D. Jack Landers is my friend
Missy. Bausch, R.
Mistake. Banks, R.
MISTAKEN IDENTITY
See also Impersonations
Boylan, C. Edna, back from America
Jackson, S. Nightmare
Leone, D. Family
Mistaken Identity. Lynn, D. H.
Mistaken identity. Mazelis, J.
Mistaking one man for another: a story. Geist, E.
Mister Brother. Cunningham, M.
Mister Toussan. Ellison, R.
Mister Tyrone. Garcia, L. G.
Mistrals. Ausherman, S.

Mistress Morgana
All in a day's work
Politically inspired; edited by Stephen Elliott; assistant editor, Gabriel Kram; associate editors, Elizabeth Brooks [et al.]
Mistress of many moons. Brownrigg, S.
The **mistress** of Marwood Hagg. Douglass, S.
The **Mistress** of the Horse God. Wieland, M.
Mistress Sary. Tenn, W.
MISTRESSES
Bean, B. Perfect heart
Chopin, K. A sentimental soul
Collins, M. Death, my love
De Noux, O. The Iberville mistress
Matiella, A. C. La casa chica
McGarry, J. Paris
Painter, P. The story of Hu
Phillips, D. R. Why I'm talking
Régio, J. A brief comedy
Vapnyar, L. Mistress
The **Misunderstandings**. Clarke, B.
Misuse of light. Gautreaux, T.
Mitchell, Carmen Elena
Black cowboy
Pieces; a collection of new voices; edited by Stephen Chbosky
Mitchell, David
The January Man
Granta no81 p135-48 Spr 2003
MITCHELL, JONI
About
Young, T. Rhymes with useless
Mitchell, Judith Claire
Unknown donor
Iowa Review v31 no2 p23-41 Fall 2001
Mitchell's girls. Knight, M.
Mitchum, Hank, 1916-
For works by this author under other names see Newton, D. B. (Dwight Bennett), 1916-
Mixed blessings. Maron, M.
MIXED BLOODS
See also Mulattoes
Alexie, S. Lawyer's League
Buckell, T. S. Spurn Babylon
Chopin, K. Loka
Greer, R. O. Spoon
Lieu, J. Potential weapons
Murray, S. Intramuros
Penn, W. S. Cowboys and Indians
Steinbeck, T. The night guide
Mixed Emotions. Trager-Mendel, L.
Mixon, Laura J.
At tide's turning
Worldmakers; SF adventures in terraforming; edited by Gardner Dozois
Proxies [excerpt]
Reload: rethinking women + cyberculture; edited by Mary Flanagan and Austin Booth
Mizelle, Tim
Washerbaum the crestfallen
The Paris Review v41 no150 p181-85 Spr 1999
Mkondo. Doerr, A.
MLJET ISLAND (CROATIA)
Hemon, A. Islands
Mnemonics. Vonnegut, K.
Mo, Yen *See* Mo Yan, 1956-

Mo Shen
The window
The Vintage book of contemporary Chinese fiction; edited by Carolyn Choa and David Su Li-qun
Mo Yan
Abandoned child
Mo Yan. Shifu, you'll do anything for a laugh; translated from the Chinese by Howard Goldblatt
The cure
Mo Yan. Shifu, you'll do anything for a laugh; translated from the Chinese by Howard Goldblatt
Iron child
Mo Yan. Shifu, you'll do anything for a laugh; translated from the Chinese by Howard Goldblatt
Love story
Mo Yan. Shifu, you'll do anything for a laugh; translated from the Chinese by Howard Goldblatt
Man and beast
Mo Yan. Shifu, you'll do anything for a laugh; translated from the Chinese by Howard Goldblatt
Shen Garden
Mo Yan. Shifu, you'll do anything for a laugh; translated from the Chinese by Howard Goldblatt
Shifu, you'll do anything for a laugh
Mo Yan. Shifu, you'll do anything for a laugh; translated from the Chinese by Howard Goldblatt
Soaring
Mo Yan. Shifu, you'll do anything for a laugh; translated from the Chinese by Howard Goldblatt
MOBILE (ALA.) *See* Alabama—Mobile
Mobilio, Albert
And the talk slid south
Bomb no77 p86 Fall 2001
Hanging on
Bomb no77 p87 Fall 2001
Moby Quilt. Arnason, E.
A **model** daughter. Boylan, C.
MODELS, ARTISTS' *See* Artists' models
MODELS, FASHION *See* Fashion models
MODELS AND MODELMAKING
Dowling, T. The bone ship
Gibson, W. and Swanwick, M. Dogfight
Hodgson, W. H. The plans of the reefing biplane
Oliver, C. Transformer
Padilla, I. The antipodes and the century
The **modern** Cyrano. Baxter, S.
A **modern** tragedy. Kelley, D.
The **modern** warning. James, H.
Modernity. Jones, G.
Modesitt, L. E., Jr.
The pilots
Tetrick, B. In the shadow of the wall; an anthology of Vietnam stories that might have been; edited by Byron R. Tetrick
Modisane, Bloke
The dignity of begging
The Anchor book of modern African stories; edited by Nadežda Obradovic ; with a foreword by Chinua Achebe

Moe. Epstein, J.

Moffat, Gwen
   The dark tower
      Malice domestic 9

Moffett, Judith
   The bear's baby
      The year's best science fiction: twenty-first annual collection; edited by Gardner Dozois

Moffett, Martha
   Dead rock singer
      The Best American mystery stories, 2000; edited and with an introduction by Donald E. Westlake

Mogan, Jewel
   Minding the Store
      The Southern Review (Baton Rouge, La.) v40 no2 p295-303 Spr 2004
   Mrs. Bajon says
      Texas bound. Book III; 22 Texas stories; edited by Kay Cattarulla; foreword by Robert Flynn
   X and O
      Texas bound. Book III; 22 Texas stories; edited by Kay Cattarulla; foreword by Robert Flynn

Mogwe, Gaele Sobott- *See* Sobott-Mogwe, Gaele, 1956-

MOHAMMEDANISM *See* Islam

MOHAMMEDANS *See* Muslims

Mokoso, Ndeley
   God of meme
      The Anchor book of modern African stories; edited by Nadežda Obradovic ; with a foreword by Chinua Achebe

MOLDAVIA *See* Moldova

MOLDOVA
   Pushkin, A. S. Kirdzhali

The mole trap. Meacock, N.

Moline, Karen
   No parachutes
      Tart noir; edited by Stella Duffy & Lauren Henderson

Mollel, Tololwa M. (Tololwa Marti)
   A night out
      The Anchor book of modern African stories; edited by Nadežda Obradovic ; with a foreword by Chinua Achebe

Molloy, Sylvia
   Certificate of absence [excerpt]
      The Vintage book of international lesbian fiction; edited and with an introduction by Naomi Holoch and Joan Nestle

Molly's dog. Adams, A.

Moloch. Le Clézio, J.-M. G.

Molodowsky, Kadya
   The fourth Mitzvah
      Beautiful as the moon, radiant as the stars; Jewish women in Yiddish stories : an anthology; edited by Sandra Bark; introduction by Francine Prose

Molyneux, Jacob
   Desire lines
      Writers harvest 3; edited and with an introduction by Tobias Wolff

Mom and Dad at home. Gorman, E.

Mom, Having Died. Dickerson, D. E.

Mom remembers. Yaffe, J.

Mom, the Martians, and me. Edelman, S.

Momaday, N. Scott
   The transformation
      The Year's best fantasy & horror, thirteenth annual collection; edited by Ellen Datlow and Terri Windling

The moment of decision. Ellin, S.

Moment of truth. O'Rourke, F.

A moment of wrong thinking. Block, L.

The Moment They Were Waiting For. Kalfus, K.

Momentary Darkness. Dickinson, M.

Moments of change. Tessier, T.

Momentum. Agee, D.

Momentum. Krouse, E.

Mom's little friends. Vukcevich, R.

Mon Pere, Claudia
   All Sweet Things Float
      Prairie Schooner v77 no1 p129-37 Spr 2003

Mona. Arenas, R.

MONACO
Monte Carlo
   Crider, B. How I found a cat, lost true love, and broke the bank at Monte Carlo
   Johnson, S. Risking it all

Monahan Avenue. Kalman, J.

Monardo, Anna
   Mary
      Prairie Schooner v78 no1 p65-80 Spr 2004
   Our passion
      A different plain; contemporary Nebraska fiction writers; edited by Ladette Randolph ; introduction by Mary Pipher

MONASTERIES *See* Monasticism and religious orders

MONASTICISM AND RELIGIOUS ORDERS
      See also Convent life; Jesuits; Monks
   Al-Shaykh, H. The keeper of the virgins
   Babel´, I. The end of St. Hypatius
   Chekhov, A. P. The princess

Monette's fingers. Miller, H. R.

MONEY
      See also Finance
   Borges, J. L. The Zahir
   Brett, S. A note of note
   Harris, M. Hi, Bob!
   Kees, W. Letter from Maine
   Klíma, I. Rich men tend to be strange
   Maron, M. Lost and found

Money. Čapek, K.

Money-back guarantee. Pelegrimas, M. and Randisi, R. J.

Money can't buy me love. Harris, E. L.

The money punch. L'Amour, L.

The money stays, the people go. Doenges, J.

Money tree. Hopkinson, N.

MONEYLENDERS
      See also Loans; Pawnbrokers
   Shteyngart, G. Shylock on the Neva
   Singer, I. B. Getzel the monkey

Monfredo, Miriam Grace
   Buffalo gals, won't you come out tonight
      Malice domestic 8

MONGOLISM (DISEASE) *See* Down's syndrome

MONGOLS
      See also Tatars

Monhegan light. Russo, R.

Monica Van Telflin and the proper application of pressure. Cobb, J. H.

Monk Eastman, purveyor of iniquities. Borges, J. L.
Monkey [excerpt] Wu, C.-E.
The **monkey** look. Toole, F. X.
Monkey on our backs. O'Neill, S.
Monkey stew. Richmond, M.
MONKEYS
    Alexander, A. Little bitty pretty one
    Knight, M. Gerald's monkey
    O'Neill, S. Monkey on our backs
    Tinti, H. Miss Waldron's red colobus
    Vaswani, N. The pelvis series
    Wu, C.-E. Monkey [excerpt]
Monkeys. Estep, M.
Monkeys. McCorkle, J.
The **monkey's** paw. Jacobs, W. W.
MONKS
    See also Monasticism and religious orders
    Aldiss, B. W. Steppenpferd
    Chekhov, A. P. Easter eve
    Chekhov, A. P. No comment
    Chekhov, A. P. A story without a title
    Davidson, A. The ikon of Elijah
    Doherty, P. C. The monk's tale
    Hendee, B. Before a fall
    Leong, R. Bodhi leaves
    Lugones, L. The pillar of salt
    McAuley, P. J. Sea change, with monsters
    Owen, M. G. The snows of Saint Stephen
    Padilla, I. Hagiography of the apostate
    Robertson, S. A monk's tail
    Škvorecký, J. Laws of the jungle
    Tawada, Y. The reflection
    Trevor, W. The Virgin's gift
The **monk's** island: a legend of the Rhine. Alcott, L. M.
A **monk's** tail. Robertson, S.
The **monk's** tale. Doherty, P. C.
The **monopoly** story. Locklin, G.
MonPere, Claudia
    What the sky delivers
        The Kenyon Review ns23 no3/4 p31-44 Summ/Fall 2001
Monroe, Debra
    Shambles
        Prairie Schooner v77 no2 p38-59 Summ 2003
MONROE, MARILYN, 1926-1962
          About
    Barrett, L. Hush money
    Dann, J. Marilyn
    Dann, J. Ting-a-ling
    Oates, J. C. The photographer
    Oates, J. C. Three girls
    Pickard, N. It had to be you
Monroe Puckett. Abrams, T.
Monroe Service. Rawlins, P.
Monsalvat. Gates, D.
Monsieur Marty: a Tale of Southwestern France. Rendall, S.
Monsieur Teste in America. Codrescu, A.
The **monsoon** season. Sweeney, J. E.
The **monster.** Zinovyeva-Annibal, L. D.
The **monster** and Mr. Greene. Lupoff, R. A.
Monster story. Baker, K.
MONSTERS
    Bradbury, R. The dragon danced at midnight
    Brandon, P. The marsh runners
    Byatt, A. S. The thing in the forest

    Clement, H. Uncommon sense
    De Lint, C. Granny weather
    De Lint, C. Wingless angels
    Dunsany, E. J. M. D. P., Baron. The hoard of the Gibbelins
    Jordan, N. The dream of a beast
    Lovecraft, H. P. The call of cthulhu
    Lovecraft, H. P. The unnamable
    Matheson, R. Born of man and woman
    Nolan, W. E. The Halloween man
    Rucker, R. v. B. Bringing in the sheaves
    Shepard, J. Tedford and the megalodon
    Sturgeon, T. It
    Tumasonis, D. The wretched thicket of thorn
    Van Vogt, A. E. Vault of the beast
    Wägner, W. The legend of Beowulf
    Waldrop, H. Black as the pit, from pole to pole
Monstress. Tenorio, L.
MONTANA
    Bass, R. Mahatma Joe
    Billman, J. Custer on Mondays
    Cushman, D. Killers' country!
    Doerr, A. The hunter's wife
    Frierson, E. P. An adventure in the Big Horn Mountains; or, The trials and tribulations of a recruit
    Grady, J. The championship of nowhere
    Greer, R. O. Spoon
    Guthrie, A. B. The fourth at Getup
    Haake, K. All this land
    Henley, P. Aces
    Henley, P. The late hunt
    Henley, P. Slinkers
    Hirshberg, G. Mr. Dark's carnival
    Kittredge, W. Balancing water
    Meloy, M. Tome
    Parvin, R. Betty Hutton
    Rendell, R. Catamount
    Tilghman, C. Room for mistakes
        Frontier and pioneer life
        See Frontier and pioneer life—Montana
Montaño, Guadalupe García
    Maldicion
        Fantasmas; supernatural stories by Mexican American writers; edited by Rob Johnson; introduction by Kathleen J. Alcalá
The **Montavarde** camera. Davidson, A.
MONTE CARLO (MONACO) *See* Monaco—Monte Carlo
Monteiro, Jerônimo
    The crystal goblet
        Cosmos latinos: an anthology of science fiction from Latin America and Spain; translated, edited, & with an introduction & notes by Andrea L. Bell & Yolanda Molina-Gavilán
Monteleone, Thomas F.
    Lux et veritas
        Lighthouse hauntings; 12 original tales of the supernatural; edited by Charles G. Waugh & Martin H. Greenberg
    Rehearsals
        999: new stories of horror and suspense; edited by Al Sarrantonio
Montemarano, Nicholas
    Light
        The Massachusetts Review v42 no2 p271-87 Summ 2001

Montemarano, Nicholas—*Continued*
The November Fifteen
  Esquire v142 no3 p152, 154, 156, 158, 160,
    162-3, 226-7 S 2004
Story
  Doubletake v8 no1 p91-5 Wint 2002
The Usual Human Disabilities
  Agni no57 p100-17 2003
The worst degree of unforgivable
  The Antioch Review v59 no1 p48-57 Wint
    2001
  Pushcart prize XXVII; best of the small
    presses; edited by Bill Henderson with the
    Pushcart prize editors
MONTEREY (CALIF.) *See* California—Monte-
  rey
Montero, Mayra
That man, Pollack
  Colchie, T. A whistler in the nightworld;
    short fiction from the Latin Americas; ed-
    ited by Thomas Colchie
Montezuma's other revenge. Smith, J.
MONTGOMERY (ALA.) *See* Alabama—Mont-
  gomery
The **month** that brings winter; or, How Mr.
  Truzynski carried Vietnam home with him.
  Bukoski, A.
Montiel, Mauricio
Olga; or, The darkest mambo
  Points of departure; new stories from Mexico;
    edited by Mónica Lavín; translated by Gus-
    tavo Segade
Montoya, M. J. R.
The Tears of Cortés
  Bomb no83 p86-8, 90 Spr 2003
Montpetit, Charles
Beyond the barriers
  Northern suns; edited by David G. Hartwell
    & Glenn Grant
MONTREAL (QUÉBEC) *See* Canada—Montreal
Monument to the Third International. Rucker, R.
  v. B.
MONUMENTS
  See also Sculpture
Monuments to the dead. Rusch, K. K.
Moody, Jacquie
The gift
  Fantasmas; supernatural stories by Mexican
    American writers; edited by Rob Johnson;
    introduction by Kathleen J. Alcalá
Moody, Nancy Carol
About the man who jumped from the bridge
  The Massachusetts Review v40 no3 p406-09
    Aut 1999
Moody, Rick
The Albertine notes
  McSweeney's mammoth treasury of thrilling
    tales; edited by Michael Chabon
Boys
  The Best American short stories 2001; select-
    ed from U.S. and Canadian magazines by
    Barbara Kingsolver with Katrina Kenison;
    with an introduction by Barbara Kingsolver
  Moody, R. Demonology; stories
The carnival tradition
  Moody, R. Demonology; stories
Demonology
  Moody, R. Demonology; stories

The double zero
  Moody, R. Demonology; stories
Drawer
  Moody, R. Demonology; stories
Fish Story
  Daedalus v132 no2 p118-30 Spr 2003
Forecast from the retail desk
  Moody, R. Demonology; stories
The Free Library
  Ploughshares v30 no1 p146-57 Spr 2004
Great Moments in Psychotherapy, Number 39
  The Literary Review (Madison, N.J.) v46 no3
    p425-8 Spr 2003
Hawaiian Night
  Moody, R. Demonology; stories
  The New Yorker v75 no16 p108-11 Je 21-28
    1999
Ineluctable modality of the vaginal
  Moody, R. Demonology; stories
The Mansion on the Hill
  Moody, R. Demonology; stories
  The Pushcart prize XXIV: best of the small
    presses; an annual small press reader; ed-
    ited by Bill Henderson with the Pushcart
    prize editors
On the carousel
  Moody, R. Demonology; stories
Pan's fair throng
  Moody, R. Demonology; stories
Savasana
  The Paris Review v46 p101-13 Spr 2004
Surplus value books: catalogue number 13
  Moody, R. Demonology; stories
Wilkie Fahnstock, the boxed set
  Moody, R. Demonology; stories
Moody, Susan
Oliphants can remember
  Malice domestic 9
Moody, William
Matinee
  Bishop, C. and James, D. Death dines in; ed-
    ited by Claudia Bishop and Dean James
Mookerjea, Debali
(jt. auth) *See* Devi, Jyotirmoyee
Mookie Kid. Mosley, W.
Moon, Elizabeth
Silver lining
  Past lives, present tense; edited by Elizabeth
    Ann Scarborough
Moon, Steve Hosik
Mountains and Fire
  Amerasia Journal v30 no1 p191-9 2004
MOON
  See also Space flight to the moon
  Baxter, S. Saddlepoint: roughneck
  Benford, G. The clear blue seas of Luna
  Clarke, A. C. Earthlight
  Clarke, A. C. Holiday on the Moon
  Clarke, A. C. The secret
  Clarke, A. C. Venture to the Moon
  Harrison, H. Down to earth
  Heinlein, R. A. The long watch
  Kessel, J. The juniper tree
  Kessel, J. Stories for men
  Landis, G. A. A walk in the sun
  Leiber, F. Moon duel
  McAuley, P. J. How we lost the moon, a true
    story by Frank W. Allen
  Niven, L. The woman in Del Rey crater

MOON—*Continued*

Sturgeon, T. The man who lost the sea

Varley, John. The Bellman

Vukcevich, R. Meet me in the moon room

Wilde, Dana. The green moon

Moon. Potok, C.

The **moon** and the sun [excerpt] McIntyre, V. N.

Moon duel. Leiber, F.

The **moon** in cancer. Allegra, D.

The **moon** in its flight. Sorrentino, G.

Moon, June. McGarry, J.

Moon of ice. Linaweaver, B.

The **moon** of the grass fires. Bukoski, A.

The **moon** of the trees broken by snow. L'Amour, L.

Moon penitent. McKinney-Whetstone, D.

Moon pie over Miami. Naumoff, L.

Mooney, Brian David

Grout

Chicago Review v48 no4 p117-26 Wint 2002/2003

Moonlight. Thurm, M.

MOONSHINERS

Clarke, A. C. Moving spirit

Moonstruck sunflowers. Shmuelian, A.

Moonwalkers. Hegi, U.

The **moor**. Banks, R.

The **Moor** of Peter the Great. See Pushkin, A. S. The blackamoor of Peter the Great

Moorcock, Michael

The case of the Nazi canary

McSweeney's mammoth treasury of thrilling tales; edited by Michael Chabon

Lost sorceress of the silent citadel

Mars probes; edited by Peter Crowther

A slow Saturday night at the Surrealist Sporting Club

Redshift; extreme visions of speculative fiction; edited by Al Sarrantonio

Moore, C. L. (Catherine Lucille)

No woman born

Reload: rethinking women + cyberculture; edited by Mary Flanagan and Austin Booth

Moore, C. L. (Catherine Lucille), 1911-

For works written by this author in collaboration with Henry Kuttner see Padgett, Lewis

Moore, Catherine Lucille *See* Moore, C. L. (Catherine Lucille), 1911-

Moore, Idora McClellan

Two Betsy Hamilton Letters

Studies in American Humor ns3 no10 p73-6 2003

Moore, Lorrie

Beautiful grade

Fault lines; stories of divorce; collected and edited by Caitlin Shetterly

Debarking

The New Yorker v79 no40 p104-8, 110-13, 115-19 D 22-29 2003

Four calling birds, three French hens

In our nature: stories of wildness; selected and introduced by Donna Seaman

How to talk to your mother (notes)

Snapshots: 20th century mother-daughter fiction; edited by Joyce Carol Oates and Janet Berliner

Real estate

The Best American short stories, 1999; selected from U.S. and Canadian magazines by Amy Tan with Katrina Kenison, with an introduction by Amy Tan

Willing

The Art of the story; an international anthology of contemporary short stories; edited by Daniel Halpern

You're ugly, too

The Best American short stories of the century; John Updike, editor, Katrina Kenison, coeditor; with an introduction by John Updike

The Scribner anthology of contemporary short fiction; fifty North American stories since 1970; Lex Williford and Michael Martone, editors

Wonderful town; New York stories from The New Yorker; edited by David Remnick with Susan Choi

Moore, Phyllis

Rembrandt's bones

The Georgia Review v53 no4 p673-88 Wint 1999

Moore, Ward

Bring the jubilee

The Best alternate history stories of the 20th century; edited by Harry Turtledove with Martin H. Greenberg

Moorhead, Finola

Four characters, four lunches

Brought to book; murderous stories from the literary world; Penny Sumner, editor

MOORS

Alarcón, P. A. d. Moors and Christians

Pushkin, A. S. The blackamoor of Peter the Great

Moors and Christians. Alarcón, P. A. d.

Moose, Ruth

Beyond the Trees

The North American Review v289 no3/4 p52-6 My/Ag 2004

Friends and oranges

This is where we live; short stories by 25 contemporary North Carolina writers; edited by Michael McFee

Moose. Adam, C.

Mootoo, Shani

Lemon scent

The Vintage book of international lesbian fiction; edited and with an introduction by Naomi Holoch and Joan Nestle

Le **mooz**. Erdrich, L.

Mora, Terézia

Ophelia

Grand Street no70 p74-85 Spr/Summ 2002

Strange matter

Chicago Review v48 no2/3 p205-12 Summ 2002

Morábito, Fabio

Man on the run

Grand Street no68 p72-77 Spr 1999

The **Moraine** on the lake. Orner, P.

Morales, Harry

(jt. auth) See Benedetti, Mario

MORALITY

Alcott, L. M. Marion Earle; or, Only an actress!

Moran of the Tigers. L'Amour, L.

MORAVIA, ALBERTO, 1907-1990
About
Tuck, L. L'Esprit de L'Escalier
Mordecai, Pamela
Once on the shores of the stream Senegambia
　Whispers from the cotton tree root; Caribbean
　fabulist fiction; edited by Nalo Hopkinson
More. Wideman, J. E.
More adventures on other planets. Cassutt, M.
A **more** complete cross-section. Casey, J.
More Italian hours. Barolini, H.
More like us. Lincoln, C.
More Selected lives in brief. Cole, C. B.
More than anything else in the world. Ortiz, S. J.
The **more** they stay the same. Hill, I.
Morente. Conde, R.
Morgan, Charlotte
What I eat
　The Pushcart prize XXIV: best of the small
　presses; an annual small press reader; ed-
　ited by Bill Henderson with the Pushcart
　prize editors
Morgan, Deborah
Sepia sun
　American West; twenty new stories from the
　Western Writers of America; edited with an
　introduction by Loren D. Estleman
The Windsor ballet
　Flesh and blood: guilty as sin; erotic tales of
　crime and passion; edited by Max Allan
　Collins and Jeff Gelb
Morgan, Elizabeth Seydel
Saturday afternoon in the Holocaust Museum
　New stories from the South; the year's best,
　2004; edited by Shannon Ravenel; preface
　by Tim Gautreaux
　The Southern Review (Baton Rouge, La.) v39
　no4 p794-805 Aut 2003
Morgan, Kitty
Chapter four
　Cincinnati Magazine v35 no4 p8-10 Ja 2002
Chapter three
　Cincinnati Magazine v35 no3 p10-13 D 2001
Morgan, Robert
1916 flood
　Morgan, R. The balm of Gilead tree; new and
　selected stories
The balm of Gilead tree
　Morgan, R. The balm of Gilead tree; new and
　selected stories
A brightness new & welcoming
　Morgan, R. The balm of Gilead tree; new and
　selected stories
The bullnoser
　Morgan, R. The balm of Gilead tree; new and
　selected stories
Dark corner
　Morgan, R. The balm of Gilead tree; new and
　selected stories
Death crown
　Morgan, R. The balm of Gilead tree; new and
　selected stories
Kuykendall's gold
　Morgan, R. The balm of Gilead tree; new and
　selected stories
Little Willie
　Morgan, R. The balm of Gilead tree; new and
　selected stories

Murals
　Morgan, R. The balm of Gilead tree; new and
　selected stories
Pisgah
　Morgan, R. The balm of Gilead tree; new and
　selected stories
Poinsett's Bridge
　Morgan, R. The balm of Gilead tree; new and
　selected stories
The ratchet
　Morgan, R. The balm of Gilead tree; new and
　selected stories
Sleepy Gap
　Morgan, R. The balm of Gilead tree; new and
　selected stories
Tailgunner
　Morgan, R. The balm of Gilead tree; new and
　selected stories
A taxpayer & a citizen
　Morgan, R. The balm of Gilead tree; new and
　selected stories
The tracks of Chief de Soto
　Morgan, R. The balm of Gilead tree; new and
　selected stories
The welcome
　Morgan, R. The balm of Gilead tree; new and
　selected stories
Morgan le Fay. Steinbeck, J.
Morgenthau. Händler, E.-W.
The **morgue** rollers. Lipsyte, S.
MORGUES
Lipsyte, S. The morgue rollers
Mori, Kyoko
The world of weather
　Prairie Schooner v75 no4 p48-68 Wint 2001
Moriah. Stewart, T. L.
Moriconi, Virginia
Simple arithmetic
　Other people's mail; an anthology of letter
　stories; edited with an introduction by Gail
　Pool
MORISOT, BERTHE, 1841-1895
About
Tiedemann, M. W. Psyché
Moriya. Paschal, D.
Morlan, A. R.
Fast glaciers
　Vanishing acts; a science fiction anthology;
　edited by Ellen Datlow
MORMONISM *See* Mormons and Mormonism
MORMONS AND MORMONISM
Billman, J. Winter fat
Blum, I. B. Inquest in Zion
Clyde, M. A good paved road
Cooper, B. Hunters and gatherers
Davidson, A. Pebble in time
Engel, M. P. Redeeming the dead
Spencer, D. Blood work
Udall, B. Buckeye the elder
Morning glory Harley. Svoboda, T.
Morning in the bowl of night. Kureishi, H.
A **morning** made for happiness. Heker, L.
The **morning** room. Weihe, E.
A **morning** walk. Chopin, K.
Mornings in Quarain. Lopez, B. H.
MOROCCO
Ardizzone, T. Larabi's ox
Azadeh, C. A recitation of nomads
Berrada, Mohammed. A life in detail

MOROCCO—*Continued*
Bowles, P. Allal
Bowles, P. Bouayad and the money
Bowles, P. The empty amulet
Bowles, P. The fqih
Bowles, P. A friend of the world
Bowles, P. He of the assembly
Bowles, P. Here to learn
Bowles, P. The hours after noon
Bowles, P. The husband
Bowles, P. The little house
Bowles, P. Mejdoub
Bowles, P. Things gone and things still here
Bowles, P. The wind at Beni Midar
Mrabet, M. The canebrake
Wharton, E. The seed of the faith
          Tangier
Bowles, P. Dinner at Sir Nigel's
Bowles, P. The dismissal
Bowles, P. The eye
Bowles, P. Midnight mass
Bowles, P. Reminders of Bouselham
Bowles, P. Tea on the mountain
MORPHINE
Vachss, A. H. Dope fiend
Morrell, David
Resurrection
   Redshift; extreme visions of speculative fiction; edited by Al Sarrantonio
Rio Grande gothic
   999: new stories of horror and suspense; edited by Al Sarrantonio
   The World's finest mystery and crime stories, first annual collection; edited by Ed Gorman
Morris, Irvin
The sleeping Picasso
   Iowa Review v31 no1 p103-11 Summ 2001
Morris, J. M. *See* Morris, Mark, 1963-
Morris, Keith Lee
The children of dead state troopers
   New England Review v23 no1 p11-19 Wint 2002
Geraldine Loves
   New England Review v23 no4 p121-8 Fall 2002
Notes for an Aborted Story Called "The Cyclist" That Turned Out to Be Too Much Like "The Swimmer"
   New England Review v24 no4 p187-94 2003
Morris, Kenneth
The regent of the north
   Tales before Tolkien; the roots of modern fantasy; edited by Douglas A. Anderson
Morris, Mark
Coming home
   Best new horror 12; edited and with an introduction by Stephen Jones
Morris, Mary
Exchanges
   Daedalus v132 no1 p106-20 Wint 2003
The lifeguard
   The Art of the story; an international anthology of contemporary short stories; edited by Daniel Halpern
Morris, Michael
Just an old cur
   Stories from the Blue Moon Cafe II; edited by Sonny Brewer

Morris, Mildred Verba
Fiddler on the roof
   Iowa Review v29 no1 p56-63 Spr 1999
The Golden Cradle mystery
   Michigan Quarterly Review v41 no3 p388-99 Summ 2002
The Ultimate Film Writing Exercise
   New Letters v70 no1 p153-7 2003
Morris, William
The folk of the mountain door
   Tales before Tolkien; the roots of modern fantasy; edited by Douglas A. Anderson
Morris, Wright
Closing the gap
   The Ohio Review no64/65 p115-21 2001
Morris, Bhaiya. Hosein, C.
Morrison, Blake
Have you decided to love me yet?
   Granta no77 p193-221 Spr 2002
Morrison, James
Stalker
   Ploughshares v25 no2/3 p104-23 Fall 1999
Morrison, Marion Michael *See* Wayne, John, 1907-1979
Morrison, Toni
Recitatif
   Crossing the color line; readings in Black and white; edited by Suzanne W. Jones
Morrow, Bradford
Amazing Grace
   Pushcart prize XXVII; best of the small presses; edited by Bill Henderson with the Pushcart prize editors
Lush
   The O. Henry Prize stories, 2003; edited and with an introduction by Laura Furman; jurers David Gutterson, Diane Johnson, Jennifer Egan
Morrow, Bruce
"Ciccone youths 1990"
   Men on men 2000; best new gay fiction for the millennium; edited and with an introduction by David Bergman and Karl Woelz
Morrow, James
Auspicious eggs
   One lamp; alternate history stories from The magazine of Fantasy & Science Fiction; edited by Gordon van Gelder
   Witpunk; edited by Claude Lalumière and Marty Halpern
The war of the worldviews
   Mars probes; edited by Peter Crowther
Morse, Sandell
Fictions
   Ploughshares v28 no1 p176-92 Spr 2002
Mortal sins. Mayo, W.
MORTALITY
Bausch, R. Design
Oliver, C. Field expedient
Wells, K. Compression scars
Mortality check. Gourevitch, P.
Mortaz, Maryam
Bride of Angels
   Bomb no83 p92-4 Spr 2003
MORTICIANS *See* Undertakers and undertaking
Mortimer, John Clifford
Rumpole and the absence of body
   Crème de la crime; edited by Janet Hutchings

Mortimer, John Clifford—*Continued*
  Rumpole and the actor laddie
    Mortimer, J. C. Rumpole rests his case; [by]
      John Mortimer
  Rumpole and the asylum seekers
    Mortimer, J. C. Rumpole rests his case; [by]
      John Mortimer
  Rumpole and the Camberwell
    Mortimer, J. C. Rumpole rests his case; [by]
      John Mortimer
  Rumpole and the old familiar faces
    Mortimer, J. C. Rumpole rests his case; [by]
      John Mortimer
  Rumpole and the remembrance of things past
    Mortimer, J. C. Rumpole rests his case; [by]
      John Mortimer
  Rumpole and the teenage werewolf
    Mortimer, J. C. Rumpole rests his case; [by]
      John Mortimer
  Rumpole at sea
    Death cruise; crime stories on the open seas;
      edited by Lawrence Block
  Rumpole rests his case
    Mortimer, J. C. Rumpole rests his case; [by]
      John Mortimer
Mortmain. Youmans, C.
Morton, Anthony, 1908-1973
    *For works written by this author under oth-
      er names see* Creasey, John, 1908-1973
Morton, Lisa
  Pound rots in Fragrant Harbour
    The Museum of horrors; edited by Dennis
      Etchison
The **Morton's** Salt Boy. Singleton, G.
Mosby's memoirs. Bellow, S.
MOSCOW (RUSSIA) *See* Russia—Moscow
Moscow, Idaho. Offutt, C.
Moser, Elise
  The seven-day itch
    Witpunk; edited by Claude Lalumière and
      Marty Halpern
Moses, Jennifer
  Girls like you
    The Pushcart prize XXIII: best of the small
      presses; an annual small press reader; ed-
      ited by Bill Henderson with the Pushcart
      prize editors
  I'm getting married tomorrow
    Commentary v108 no5 p43-48 D 1999
  Next of Kin: A Story
    Commentary v117 no1 p35-42 Ja 2004
Moses and the Green Man. Caban, J.
Moses, Jesus Christ and Karl Marx Visit New
    York. Gordin, J.
Mosher, Howard Frank
  A citizen of the world
    Yankee v66 no1 p110-18 Ja/F 2002
  On Kingdom Mountain
    Yankee v65 no3 p100-5, 156 Ap 2001
Mosiman, Billie Sue
  Dread Inlet
    Lighthouse hauntings; 12 original tales of the
      supernatural; edited by Charles G. Waugh
      & Martin H. Greenberg
Mosley, Walter
  Amber gate
    Mosley, W. Six Easy pieces; Easy Rawlins
      stories

Angel's island
  Mosley, W. Futureland
Blue lightning
  Mosley, W. Walkin' the dog
Crimson stain
  Mosley, W. Six Easy pieces; Easy Rawlins
    stories
A day in the park
  Mosley, W. Walkin' the dog
Doctor Kismet
  Mosley, W. Futureland
The electric eye
  Mosley, W. Futureland
Equal opportunity
  The African American West; a century of
    short stories; edited by Bruce A. Glasrud
    and Laurie Champion
Gator green
  Mosley, W. Six Easy pieces; Easy Rawlins
    stories
Gray-eyed death
  Mosley, W. Six Easy pieces; Easy Rawlins
    stories
The greatest
  Mosley, W. Futureland
Lavender
  The Best American mystery stories, 2003; ed-
    ited by Michael Connelly and Otto Penzler
  Mosley, W. Six Easy pieces; Easy Rawlins
    stories
Little brother
  Mosley, W. Futureland
En masse
  Mosley, W. Futureland
Mookie Kid
  Mosley, W. Walkin' the dog
Moving on
  Mosley, W. Walkin' the dog
The mugger
  Mosley, W. Walkin' the dog
The nig in me
  Mosley, W. Futureland
Pet fly
  The Best American short stories, 2000; select-
    ed from U.S. and Canadian magazines by
    E. L. Doctorow with Katrina Kenison; with
    an introduction by E. L. Doctorow
  The New Yorker v75 no38 p90-97 D 13 1999
Promise
  Mosley, W. Walkin' the dog
Rascals in the cane
  Mosley, W. Walkin' the dog
Rogue
  Mosley, W. Walkin' the dog
Shift, shift, shift
  Mosley, W. Walkin' the dog
Silver lining
  Mosley, W. Six Easy pieces; Easy Rawlins
    stories
Smoke
  Mosley, W. Six Easy pieces; Easy Rawlins
    stories
That smell
  Mosley, W. Walkin' the dog
The thief
  LA shorts; edited by Steven Gilbar
Voices
  Mosley, W. Futureland

Mosley, Walter—*Continued*
  Walkin' the dog
    Mosley, W. Walkin' the dog
  What would you do?
    Mosley, W. Walkin' the dog
  Whispers in the dark
    Mosley, W. Futureland
The **mosquito**. Cheng, C.-W.
MOSQUITOES
  Gordimer, N. An emissary
Moss, Barbara Klein
  December birthday
    New England Review v20 no4 p6-16 Fall 1999
  Little Edens
    Southwest Review v88 no4 p424-48 2003
  Rug weaver
    The Best American short stories 2001; selected from U.S. and Canadian magazines by Barbara Kingsolver with Katrina Kenison; with an introduction by Barbara Kingsolver
Moss, Barbara Robinette
  Blackbird
    Stories from the Blue Moon Café; edited by Sonny Brewer
Moss, Rose
  Fire
    Prairie Schooner v77 no1 p143-55 Spr 2003
  The widow's widow
    Southwest Review v84 no4 p594-600 1999
The **most** beautiful day of your life. Vasseur, T. J.
The **Most** Beautiful Girl in the World. Troy, M.
A **most** electrifying evening. Barrett, J.
A **most** extraordinary case. James, H.
The **most** famous little girl in the world. Kress, N.
Most Likely to Be Remembered. Raymond, M.
Most of my friends are two-thirds water. Link, K.
The **most** romantic story ever. Almond, S.
Mostre. Beattie, A.
Motel 66. D'Amato, B.
Motel ice. Cobb, W. J.
MOTELS
  Andrews, M. K. Love at first byte
  Barthelme, F. Bag boy
  Barthelme, F. Travel & leisure
  Bell, M. S. Two lives
  Gifford, B. American Falls
  Smart, A. The bridge players
  Smart, A. The Green Lantern
  Smart, A. Hunter
  Smart, A. The wedding Dress
  Updike, J. How to love America and leave it at the same time
The **mother**. Cole, C. B.
Mother. Gayle, A. D.
Mother. Kavaler, R.
Mother bother. Neudecker, C.
Mother, father, and the little one. Müller, H.
Mother George, midwife. Sherlock, P.
Mother Hitton's littul kittons. Smith, C.
Mother-in-law tongue. López, L.
Mother in the sky with diamonds. Tiptree, J.
Mother in the Trenches. Butler, R. O.
Mother nature. Thompson, J.
Mother: not a true story. Gasco, E.
The **mother** of invention is worth a pound of cure. Westlake, D. E.
Mother of pearl. Rawley, D.

The **mother-of-the-groom** and I. Rowell, J.
Mother Superior. Sosin, D.
Mother tongue. Anderson, R.
Mother tongue. Goliger, G.
MOTHERHOOD *See* Mothers
Motherlove. Crumley, J.
Motherly love. Murphy, W.
MOTHERS
  See also Mothers and daughters; Mothers and sons; Mothers-in-law; Stepmothers; Surrogate mothers
  Banks, R. The caul
  Caponegro, M. The mother's mirror
  Carlson, R. On the U.S.S. Fortitude
  Chacón, D. Ofrenda
  Chivers, D. Radio baby
  Coates, G. S. Black cherries
  Coates, G. S. Spring beauties
  Desplechin, M. An important question
  Dobyns, S. Part of the story
  Erian, A. When animals attack
  Fitzgerald, F. S. The cut-glass bowl
  Foley, S. Life in the air ocean
  Fromm, P. Night swimming
  Gilman, C. P. Making a change
  Gilman, C. P. The unnatural mother
  Hood, A. The rightness of things
  Kalu, Anthonia C. The gift
  Klass, P. Love and modern medicine
  Krouse, E. Other people's mothers
  Markham, E. A. Mammie's form at the post office
  Matthews, C. Death of a glamour cat
  McCann, C. Fishing the sloe-black river
  Miller, R. Delia
  Mina, D. Alice opens the box
  Naslund, S. J. The perfecting of the Chopin Valse No. 14 in E Minor
  Papernick, J. For as long as the lamp is burning
  Robison, M. Your errant mom
  Seiffert, R. The crossing
  Simpson, H. Café society
  Simpson, H. Getting a life
  Sojourner, M. Officer Magdalena, White Shell Woman, and me
  Thompson, J. Poor Helen
  Vallbona, R. d. Penelope's silver wedding anniversary
  Wexler, M. The nanny trap
  Wexler, M. The porno girl
  What, L. Is that hard science; or, Are you just happy to see me
  Yates, R. Oh, Joseph, I'm so tired
  Young, T. The Berlin Wall
Mothers. Wuori, G. K.
MOTHERS AND DAUGHTERS
  See also Parent and child
  Adam, C. Josie
  Adam, C. Opossum
  Adams, A. 1940: fall
  Adams, A. By the sea
  Addonizio, K. Gas
  Agee, J. Adjusting the bite
  Agee, J. Caution
  Agee, J. Each time we meet
  Agee, J. Good to go
  Alcott, L. M. Little Genevieve
  Aldrich, B. S. Across the smiling meadow
  Allende, I. Wicked girl

MOTHERS AND DAUGHTERS—*Continued*

Allison, D. Compassion
Alvarez, J. Consuelo's letter
Arenas, R. Goodbye mother
Arvin, N. Two thousand Germans in Frankenmuth
Asendorf, A. G. The gossamer girl
Atwood, M. Significant moments in the life of my mother
Banks, R. Theory of flight
Barnard, R. Going through a phase
Bart, D. Prom night
Bausch, R. Equity
Bausch, R. Guatemala
Bausch, R. Weather
Berliner, J. Everything old is new again
Betts, D. Aboveground
Betts, D. Three ghosts
Bowles, P. The echo
Bowles, P. The hours after noon
Boylan, C. The Little Madonna
Boylan, C. A model daughter
Brackenbury, R. The forty-ninth lot joke
Brackenbury, R. Instead of the revolution
Bradbury, R. We'll just act natural
Brady, C. Rat
Brady, C. Wild, wild horses
Brennan, M. The beginning of a long story
Broughton, T. A. L'americana
Brown, C. The correspondent
Budnitz, J. Flush
Busch, F. Heads
Busch, F. Still the same old story
Carson, J. Fair trades
Carson, J. Judgement
Carter, E. The bride
Carter, E. Train line
Casey, M. Days at home
Caspers, N. Vegetative states
Chaon, D. Safety Man
Cherry, K. As it is in heaven
Cherry, K. Lunachick
Cherry, K. Not the Phil Donahue show
Cherry, K. The society of friends
Cherry, K. Your chances of getting married
Chiang, T. Story of your life
Clark, J. Frazzle
Clyde, M. Heartbreak house
Coates, G. S. Late fruit
Cody, L. Chalk mother
Cody, L. Love in vain
Cohen, R. Cousin Gemma
Coleman, J. C. Fiddle case
Collins, M. The walk
Connolly, C. Greengages
Connor, J. Women's problems
Cooke, C. The trouble with money
Cooper, J. C. A filet of soul
Coulter, K. Normalcy
Daniel, S. We are cartographers
Danticat, E. Nineteen thirty-seven
Davies, P. H. Cakes of baby
Davies, P. H. Everything you can remember in thirty seconds is yours to keep
Davis, A. The visit
Davis, J. S. The one thing God'll give you
Davis, L. Party girls
DeLancey, K. Crazy dead kid lady
DeLancey, K. Washed

Doenges, J. What she left me
Doenges, J. The whole numbers of families
Due, T. Like daughter
Dunn, K. The allies
Edwards, K. The story of my life
Eldridge, Courtney. Unkempt
Engel, M. P. You got to learn how to read things right
Fairey, W. W. Family album
Fairey, W. W. Her hair
Ferrell, C. Wonderful teen
Freeman, M. E. W. The witch's daughter
Freudenberger, N. The orphan
Friesner, E. M. Big hair
Friesner, E. M. A birthday
Fromm, P. Freezeout
Fromm, P. The gravy on the cake
Frym, G. Sleepy
Fulton, J. Retribution
Gabriel, D. Civilizations are islands
Gabrielyan, N. Bee heaven
Gabrielyan, N. The lilac dressing gown
Gartner, Z. Odds that, all things considered, she'd someday be happy
Gasco, E. Elements
Gasco, E. Mother: not a true story
Gasco, E. You have the body
Gayle, A. D. Mother
Gilliland, G. The Sturbridge tale
Gilliland, G. Witches
Glasgow, E. The shadowy third
Goldner, B. Expatriates
Goldner, B. Waxing
Goliger, G. Air and earth
Goliger, G. Mother tongue
Gordon, M. Cleaning up
Gorman, E. Eye of the beholder
Gorman, E. Such a good girl
Gould, L. La Lloradora
Grau, S. A. The beginning
Grau, S. A. Homecoming
Greene, B. An ordinary woman
Guerrero, L. Gloves of her own
Gussoff, C. The deepest dive
Gussoff, C. Surface reading
Haake, K. The laying on of hands
Händler, E.-W. By the Sengsen Mountains, by the Dead Mountains
Harfenist, J. Pixie dust
Harty, R. Ongchoma
Hegi, U. The juggler
Helms, B. Glazing
Helms, B. Men in Italy
Helms, B. Telling stories
Henley, P. Cargo
Henley, P. Hard feelings
Highsmith, P. The car
Highsmith, P. The pianos of the Steinachs
Hoffman, A. The rest of your life
Hoffman, W. The secret garden
Horton, B. Colouring mother
Jackson, V. F. Telling stories
Jaffe, D. M. Sarrushka and her daughter
Jafta, M. The home-coming
James, H. The chaperon
James, H. Louisa Pallant
James, H. Mrs. Temperly
James, H. Sir Edmund Orme
James, S. Happy as Saturday night

MOTHERS AND DAUGHTERS—*Continued*

Johnson, D. Markers
Jones, E. P. The first day
Jones, G. Babies
Jones, G. The precision of angels
Joseph, D. The fifth Mrs. Hughes
Kalman, J. A property of childhood
Kaplan, H. Dysaesthesia
Kaufman, W. Helen on Eighty-Sixth Street
Keegan, C. Storms
Kincaid, J. Girl
Kincaid, J. My mother
Kirchheimer, G. D. Food of love
Kirchheimer, G. D. Goodbye, evil eye
Kirchheimer, G. D. A skirmish in the desert
Klass, P. Necessary risks
Knight, M. Sundays
Kohler, S. Casualty
Kohler, S. The original
Kohler, S. Water Baby
Korn, R. H. The sack with pink stripes
Kortes, Mary Lee. Summer vacation
Krout-Hasegawa, E. Noise
Kureishi, H. Girl
Kureishi, H. Sucking stones
Landis, G. A. Snow
Lavin, M. A cup of tea
Lavin, M. A family likeness
Lavin, M. The will
Leavitt, D. The scruff of the neck
Lee, A. Interesting women
Leegant, J. Lucky in love
Lieu, J. The children
Lieu, J. Potential weapons
Lindholm, M. Cut
Lingard, J. After Colette [excerpt]
López, L. Walking circles
Magnuson, A. Mom comes home
Magona, S. It was Easter Sunday the day I went to Netreg
Maleti, G. Alma
Mason, S. J. With thanks to Agatha Christie
Mastretta, A. Aunt Amanda
Mastretta, A. Aunt Jose
Matheson, R. Prey
Matiella, A. C. The braid
Mazelis, J. Forbidden
Mazelis, J. Home-cooked
Mazelis, J. On the edge
Mazelis, J. Peaches
McGarry, J. Partly him
McKenzie, A. Private school
Mencken, S. H. Birthday
Miller, H. R. Monette's fingers
Miller, R. Louisa
Mina, D. Helena and the babies
Monardo, A. Our passion
Moore, L. How to talk to your mother (notes)
Müller, H. Oppressive tango
Müller, H. The window
Nagai, M. Grafting
Nailah, A. Free
Nailah, A. Sunday visit
Nawrocki, S. Camping with strangers
Nawrocki, S. Star seed
Naylor, G. Kiswana Browne
Nelson, A. Stitches
Nissen, T. 3 ½ x 5
Nissen, T. Think about if you want

Norman, G. Maxine
Oates, J. C. Death mother
Oates, J. C. Faithless
Oates, J. C. Mark of satan
Oates, J. C. The museum of Dr. Moses
Oates, J. C. The scarf
Oates, J. C. Tell me you forgive me?
O'Brien, E. A rose in the heart of New York
O'Connell, M. Saint Anne
Orner, P. Sarah
Ozick, C. The shawl
Packer, Z. Speaking in tongues
Patterson, K. Interposition
Perabo, S. The greater grace of Carlisle
Perabo, S. The measure of devotion
Peterson, P. W. Big brother
Peterson, P. W. Song of Camille
Philip, M. N. Stop frame
Phillips, J. A. Alma
Phipps, M. Marie-Ange's ginen
Poirier, M. J. Pageantry
Ponder, D. U. The rat spoon
Potvin, E. A. Infant colic: What it is and what you can do about it
Rabb, M. My mother's first lover
Rainwater, A. Night rose
Rawley, D. The spells of an ordinary twilight
Reisman, N. The good life
Richard, N. The order of things
Richmond, M. Mathematics and acrobatics
Ritchie, E. Marching as to war
Ritchie, E. Shopping expedition
Robison, M. Daughters
Robison, M. Father, grandfather
Robison, M. Pretty ice
Roche, S. Love
Rodgers, S. J. Lost spirits
Roeske, P. The hard fact
Rosenfeld, S. Grasp special comb
Rosenfeld, S. Insects in amber
Rosenfeld, S. Inversion
Sánchez, R. Three generations
Sandor, M. God's spies
Sandor, M. Legend
Sandor, M. Portrait of my mother, who posed nude in wartime
Sari, F. The absent soldier
Saunders, G. The epistemology
Schmidt, H. J. A girl like you
Schwartz, L. S. What I did for love
Seiffert, R. Reach
Setton, R. K. The cat garden
Shapiro, J. Mousetrap
Sheffield, C. Phallicide
Shonk, K. My mother's garden
Shonk, K. The wooden village of Kizhi
Silber, J. The dollar in Italy
Simonds, M. The day of the dead
Simpson, H. Golden apples
Singer, I. B. The mentor
Slaughter, K. Necessary women
Slezak, E. Patch
Smart, A. Mud and strawberries
Smith, J. Too mean to die
Sojourner, M. Estrella Ranchos: where the real west begins
Sojourner, M. The most amazing thing
Soukup, M. Up above Diamond City
Spencer, E. First dark

MOTHERS AND DAUGHTERS—*Continued*

Spencer, E. The light in the piazza
Steele, C. Respiration
Stollman, A. L. If I have found favor in your eyes
Strauss, A. Addressing the dead
Strayed, C. Good
Stuckey-French, E. Electric wizard
Stuckey-French, E. Plywood rabbit
Stuckey-French, E. Professor claims he found formula for ancient steel
Sullivan, W. Losses
Svoboda, T. Petrified woman
Swan, M. In the story that won't be written
Tan, A. Two kinds
Tangh, J. The Skinned
Taraqqi, G. The Shemiran bus
Thien, M. Bullet train
Thien, M. Four days from Oregon
Thien, M. House
Thompson, J. Mother nature
Thurm, M. Jumping ship
Thurm, M. Passenger
Tomioka, T. The funeral of a giraffe
Trevor, W. Good news
Tuck, L. Limbo
Vafi, F. My mother, behind the glass
Van Winckel, N. Treat me nice
Vanderbes, J. The hatbox
Vapnyar, L. Lydia's Grove
Vasseur, T. J. Talk, talk, talk
Vaswani, N. Twang (Release)
Walker, A. The brotherhood of the saved
Walker, A. Everyday use
Warren, D. Hawk's landing
Watanabe McFerrin, L. The hand of Buddha
Waters, M. Y. The laws of evening
Waters, M. Y. The way love works
Wegner, H. The stone girl
Weldon, F. A libation of blood
Weldon, F. My mother said
Wells, K. My guardian, Claire
Wexler, M. Pink is for punks
Wharton, E. Autres temps . . .
What, L. Clinging to a thread
Wieland, L. The loop, the snow, their daughters, the rain
Wieland, L. Salt Lake
Willis, C. Even the queen
Wilson, R., Jr. Barber
Wilson, R., Jr. Dorothy and her friends
Winterson, J. Psalms
Wisenberg, S. L. My mother's war
Yarbrough, S. The right kind of person
Young, T. The new world
Zhang Jie. Love must not be forgotten

MOTHERS AND SONS

See also Parent and child

Alexie, S. The life and times of Estelle Walks Above
Alvarez, A. Heat rises
Aminoff, J. Fate
Amis, M. Heavy water
Auchincloss, L. The marriage broker
Baca, J. S. The three sons of Julia
Banks, R. Assisted living
Banks, R. The child screams and looks back at you

Banks, R. My mother's memoirs, my father's lie, and other true stories
Banks, R. Queen for a day
Barthelme, F. Larroquette
Bausch, R. Ancient history
Bausch, R. "My mistress' eyes are nothing like the sun"
Bausch, R. Old west
Bausch, R. Requisite kindness
Bell, M. S. Mrs. Lincoln's china
Beller, T. A different kind of imperfection
Berkman, P. R. Gold
Berry, W. The hurt man
Bi Shumin. One centimetre
Bingham, S. Stanley
Blaise, C. Dunkelblau
Blatnik, A. His mother's voice
Bonnie, F. Nick the Russian
Bowles, P. The scorpion
Bowles, S. A. Home improvement
Boylan, C. My son the hero
Brown, J. Animal stories
Brown, J. Thief
Budnitz, J. Composer
Budnitz, J. Guilt
Bukiet, M. J. Filophilia
Bukoski, A. The month that brings winter; or, How Mr. Truzynski carried Vietnam home with him
Butler, R. O. Mother in the trenches
Calisher, H. In Greenwich, there are many gravelled walks
Callaghan, M. All the years of her life
Canty, K. Red dress
Carson, J. Invaders
Carson, J. Protective coloring
Chaon, D. Among the missing
Chaon, D. Seven types of ambiguity
Chapman, C. M. And the mothers stepped over their sons
Chappell, F. The encyclopedia Daniel
Chekhov, A. P. The bishop
Chekhov, A. P. Volodya
Cheng, C.-W. God of thunder's gonna getcha
Chopin, K. The going away of Liza
Clyde, M. Howard Johnson's house
Cody, L. Solar zits
Collins, M. Homecoming
Connor, J. Florida
Cook, K. L. Last call
Cook, K. L. Marty
Cooper, B. Between the sheets
Crichton, M. Blood doesn't come out
Danticat, E. Night women
Dark, A. E. In the gloaming
Davies, R. The darling of her heart
Deaver, J. Triangle
DeMarinis, R. On the lam
Desaulniers, J. After Rosa Parks
Divakaruni, C. B. The names of stars in Bengali
Downs, M. Prison food
Drake, R. I've got a sneaking idea that . . .; or, I'd just get me a lawyer
Drake, R. The little girl with the blue eyes
Drake, R. The piazza
Dyer, S. N. Sins of the mothers
Epstein, J. Uncle Jack
Erdrich, L. Lulu's boys
Ferriss, L. Rumpelstiltskin

MOTHERS AND SONS—*Continued*

Fischerová, D. Boarskin dances down the tables
Foley, S. Boy Wonder
Franklin, T. Christmas 1893
Fulton, J. Outlaws
Fulton, J. The troubled dog
Furman, L. Beautiful baby
Furman, L. The woods
Gavell, M. L. Baucis
Gavell, M. L. Boys
Gavell, M. L. I cannot tell a lie, exactly
Gavell, M. L. The swing
Gifford, B. The winner
Gilchrist, E. The abortion
Gilliland, G. Stones
Goldstein, N. Anatevka tender
Gorman, E. The way it used to be
Greer, A. S. Titipu
Gwyn, A. Truck
Haake, K. Arrow math
Harrington, J. In the merry month of mayhem
Harty, R. Don't call it Christmas
Healy, J. F. Rotten to the core
Highsmith, P. The still point of the turning world
Highsmith, P. The terrapin
Hochman, A. I seen some stuf horabl stuf lisen
Hood, A. Dropping bombs
Hood, A. The language of sorrow
House, S. The last days
Hribal, C. J. The clouds in Memphis
Jaime-Becerra, M. Buena Suerte Airlines
James, H. Master Eustace
James, H. A New England winter
James, H. The siege of London
James, S. And perhaps more
Janicke, G. The gift
Johnston, B. A. Anything that floats
Johnston, B. A. Buy for me the rain
Johnston, B. A. I see something you don't see
Johnston, B. A. The widow
Jones, T. 40, still at home
Joseph, D. Schandorsky's mother
Joseph, D. Sick child
Joyce, G. Tiger moth
Kane, J. F. First sale
Kavaler, R. Mother
Kennedy, A. L. A bad son
Kirchheimer, G. D. Changelings
Kittredge, W. Do you hear your mother talking?
Klass, P. Rainbow mama
Klíma, I. A baffling choice
Kohler, S. Ambush
Kohler, S. Lunch with mother
Kohler, S. Trust
Krysl, M. The thing around them
L'Amour, L. Beyond the Great Snow Mountains
Lao She. Autobiography of a minor character
LaValle, V. D. How I lost my inheritance
Lavin, M. The widow's son
Leavitt, D. Crossing St. Gotthard
Leavitt, D. Territory
Lee, M. A king's epitaph
LeRoy, J. T. Baby doll
LeRoy, J. T. Coal
LeRoy, J. T. Lizards
LeRoy, J. T. Meteors
LeRoy, J. T. Viva Las Vegas
Lipsyte, S. Cremains

Lloyd, D. T. Snow
Lopes, H. The advance
Lopez, B. H. Mornings in Quarain
Lundquist, R. The visitation
Maleti, G. Sempiterno's fears
Maleti, G. Vidor and Mummy
Maleti, G. The visit
Malouf, D. At Schindler's
Maron, M. Growth marks
Martin, P. P. Amor de madre—Mother's love
Matiella, A. C. Sana, sana, colita de rana
Matthews, B. Everything must go
Mazelis, J. Running away with the hairdresser
Mazor, J. The lost cause
McBrearty, R. G. The unfolding
McGrath, P. Asylum [excerpt]
Michaels, L. Eating out
Miller, S. Expensive gifts
Mukherjee, B. Saints
Murguía, A. Boy on a wooden horse
Murphy, P. J. The flower's noiseless hunger, the tree's clandestine tide
Murphy, W. Motherly love
Nailah, A. Joey falling
Nailah, A. My side of the story
Nevai, L. Step men
Newman, D. A. Mystery Spot
Norris, L. Toy guns
Oates, J. C. First views of the enemy
Oates, J. C. I was in love
Oates, J. C. In hiding
Oates, J. C. Me & Wolfie, 1979
Ockert, J. Scarecrowed
O'Connor, F. The comforts of home
O'Connor, F. Greenleaf
Olivares Baró, C. Small creatures
Painter, P. Bringing me up it never stops
Pak, W.-S. My very last possession
Penn, W. S. Cowboys and Indians
Peterson, P. W. In the grove
Phillips, D. R. My people's waltz
Pittalwala, I. Lost in the U.S.A.
Polansky, S. Alarm
Potvin, E. A. Sunday
Rankin, I. The hanged man
Rash, R. Last rite
Rawley, D. Tim
Redel, V. He's back
Régio, J. Maria do Ahu
Reifler, N. Baby
Riahi, M. War letters
Rifkin, A. The idols of sickness
Rodgers, S. J. Still life
Roth, J. Barbara
Rowell, J. The mother-of-the-groom and I
Russo, R. Joy ride
Russo, R. The mysteries of Linwood Hart
Schmidt, H. J. An early death
Schoemperlen, D. In a dark season
Seiffert, R. Field study
Seiffert, R. Second best
Shapiro, D. Plane crash theory
Shapiro, G. Suskind, the impresario
Shrayer-Petrov, D. David and Goliath
Silber, J. Ragazzi
Simonds, M. In the city of the split sky
Simonds, M. Navigating the Kattegat
Singer, I. B. The dance
Škvorecký, J. Why I lernt how to reed

MOTHERS AND SONS—*Continued*

Slavin, J. Covered
Slavin, J. He came apart
Smart, A. Posing
Sojourner, M. Messin' with the kid
Spatz, G. Walking in my sleep
Steinbeck, T. The night guide
Stolar, D. Mourning
Stollman, A. L. The adornment of days
Stollman, A. L. Die grosse Liebe
Svoboda, T. Car frogs
Svoboda, T. Water
Taraqqi, G. A mansion in the sky
Taylor, T. L. The Boar's Head Easter
Thomas, D. The getaway
Thompson, J. Mercy
Tilghman, C. A suitable good-bye
Tolstoy, L., graf. The prayer
Tran, H. Little murmurs
Trevor, W. The hill bachelors
Troy, M. Bird of pardise
Tushinski, J. Home
Updike, J. The cats
Updike, J. Flight
Viganò, R. Death of a mother
Villanueva, A. Golden glass
Walker, S. Hunting mother
Wallace, D. F. Philosophy and the mirror of nature
Wallace, D. F. Suicide as a sort of present
Wallace, M. Thinking
Waters, M. Y. Aftermath
Waters, M. Y. Shibusa
Watson, I. The China cottage
Waugh, E. Winner takes all
Weaver, G. Dirt
Weaver, G. The emancipation of hoytie rademacher
Wegner, H. Off Paradise
Weinreb, M. Pictures of my family
Weldon, F. Stasi
Wexler, M. Don Giovanni in the tub
Wharton, E. Her son
Wharton, E. The pelican
Wharton, E. Sanctuary
Wheat, C. A bus called pity
Wideman, J. E. Weight
Wieland, L. Cirque du Soleil
Williams, J. A. Son in the afternoon
Winter, E. A color of sky
Yaffe, J. Mom remembers
Yates, R. Regards at home
Zweig, S. The burning secret
Mother's Day. McLellan, D.
Mother's Day. Plant, R.
The **Mother's-Day** doubleheader. Breen, J. L.
MOTHERS-IN-LAW

Bausch, R. Consolation
Bottoms, G. A stupid story
Bowles, P. The little house
Cannell, D. Come to Grandma
Cheng, C.-W. Autumn night
Cutler, J. Doctor's orders
Grau, S. A. Letting go
Ha Jin. An entrepreneur's story
Homes, A. M. The Chinese lesson
López, L. Mother-in-law tongue
Quill, M. A sound investment
Quill, M. The visitor

Rodgers, S. J. Bones and flowers
Willis, M. S. Tiny gorillas
Yaffe, J. Mom remembers
Mother's milk. Nevill, A. L. G.
The **mother's** mirror. Caponegro, M.
Mother's Son. Hadley, T.
Mother's trial. Alcott, L. M.
The **mother's** wasteland. Blitz, R.
The **Motion** of Falling Bodies. Boutell, A.
MOTION PICTURE ACTORS AND ACTRESSES

Anderson, R. The angel of ubiquity
Bart, P. Dangerous company
Bart, P. The makeover
Bart, P. Second coming
Bauman, B. A. Wash, rinse, spin
Brandt, W. Paradise Cove
Breen, J. L. Immortality
Estleman, L. D. The man in the white hat
Handler, D. The last of the bad girls
Haskell, J. The faces of Joan of Arc
McCourt, J. Driven woman
McCourt, J. Ensenada
McCourt, J. In Tir na nOg
McCourt, J. New York lit up that way at night
McCourt, J. A plethora
McCourt, J. Principal photography
McCourt, J. Wayfaring at Waverly in Silver Lake
Moore, L. Willing
Nye, J. L. Casting against type
O'Hara, J. Drawing room B
Rankin, I. Adventures in babysitting
Stern, D. Foxx hunting
Straub, P. Ronald, D_____!
Trevor, W. Good news
Weldon, F. Stasi
Weldon, F. What the papers say
Yolen, J. The sleep of trees
MOTION PICTURE CRITICS

Rowell, J. Spectators in love
MOTION PICTURE DIRECTORS *See* Motion picture producers and directors
MOTION PICTURE PRODUCERS AND DIRECTORS

Bart, P. Day of reckoning
Bart, P. Friend of the family
Bart, P. Hard bargain
Bart, P. The neighbors I
Bart, P. The neighbors II
Bradbury, R. The cricket on the hearth
Crider, B. Cap'n Bob and Gus
Crowther, P. Shatsi
Fitzgerald, F. S. Crazy Sunday
Gilchrist, E. The sanguine blood of men
Handler, D. The last of the bad girls
Kurlansky, M. The white man in the tree
Leong, R. Hemispheres
Manrique, J. The documentary artist
McBain, E. The interview
Perkins, E. Her new life
Raphael, F. All his sons
Raphael, F. An older woman
Raphael, F. Who whom?
Russo, R. Monhegan light
MOTION PICTURE THEATERS

Clark, B. C. The last picture show
Millhauser, S. Behind the blue curtain

MOTION PICTURES

Anderson, D. Baby teeth
Arnason, E. Stellar harvest
Baker, K. Studio dick drowns near Malibu
Bart, P. The arbiter
Bart, P. The ghostwriter
Berberova, N. Photogenique
Bishop, M. Help me, Rondo
Blatnik, A. His mother's voice
Bradbury, R. Another fine mess
Bradbury, R. The dragon danced at midnight
Bradbury, R. The meadow
Bradbury, R. Where all is emptiness there is room to move
Breen, J. L. The cat and the Kinetophone
Breen, J. L. Credit the cat
Breen, J. L. The tarnished star
Bush, G. R. The last reel
Clark, J. Random access
Clarke, A. C. Armaments race
Clarke, A. C. History lesson
Cooper, B. Intro to acting
Crider, B. Out like a lion
Crider, B. Tinseltown Follies of 1948
Dann, J. The extra
Davies, R. Celluloid heroes
Erian, A. Almonds and cherries
Erian, A. The brutal language of love
Harrison, W. The rocky hills of Trancas
Haskell, J. Crimes at midnight
Jakes, J. The man who wanted to be in the movies
Jenkins, G. A portrait of the artist at Warner Bros.
Jones, G. Modernity
Lethem, J. and Scholz, C. Receding horizon
Lochte, D. Vampire dreams
Lupoff, R. A. The Heyworth Fragment
Murguía, A. Lucky Alley
Nevins, F. M., Jr. Bagworms
Nolan, W. F. In real life
Oliver, C. Anachronism
Oliver, C. Technical advisor
Painter, P. Dud
Pittalwala, I. Bombay talkies
Pittalwala, I. Dear Paramont Pictures
Raphael, F. Shared credit
Robinson, L. Seeing the world
Rucker, R. v. B. Tales of Houdini
Shepard, J. Night shot
Singleton, G. I could've told you if you hadn't asked
Stollman, A. L. Die grosse Liebe
Waugh, E. Excursion in reality
Weldon, F. GUP—or, Falling in love in Helsinki
Winegardner, M. Last love song at the Valentine
Yates, R. Saying goodbye to Sally
Yuknavitch, L. Blue movie
Yuknavitch, L. From the boy stories
Yuknavitch, L. Outtakes
The **motions** of love. Lundquist, R.

MOTOR BUSES See Buses

MOTOR INNS See Motels

MOTORCYCLE DRIVERS

Carlson, R. DeRay
Meyers, K. The husker tender

MOTORCYCLES

Blair, J. American standard
Cortázar, J. The night face up
Le Clézio, J.-M. G. The round
Parker, G. Chloroform
Rinehart, S. The blue Norton

Motz, Dorin

(jt. auth) See Firan, Carmen

Moujan Otaño, Magdalena

Gu ta gutarrak (we and our own)
    Cosmos latinos: an anthology of science fiction from Latin America and Spain; translated, edited, & with an introduction & notes by Andrea L. Bell & Yolanda Molina-Gavilán

Moulessehoul, Mohammed

The wicked tongue
    The Anchor book of modern African stories; edited by Nadežda Obradovic ; with a foreword by Chinua Achebe

Moulton, Muriel

Reaching for Sunlight
    Calyx v21 no1 p74-82 Wint 2003

MOUNT EVEREST (CHINA AND NEPAL)

Clarke, A. C. The cruel sky
Padilla, I. Ever wrest: log of the journey
Simmons, D. On K2 with kanakaredes
Mount Olympus. Bova, B.

MOUNT SAINT HELENS (WASH.)

Haake, K. Arrow math
The **mountain**. Čapek, K.
Mountain. Gonzalez, R.
Mountain air. James, S.

MOUNTAIN CLIMBING See Mountaineering

MOUNTAIN LIFE

Southern States

See also Appalachian highlanders
Cadle, D. Anthem of the locusts
Craddock, C. E. The star in the valley
Hughes, D. B. The Granny Woman
Linney, R. Tennessee
MacDowell, K. S. B. Jack and the mountain pink
O'Connor, F. The life you save may be your own
Offutt, C. Melungeons

MOUNTAIN LIONS See Pumas

MOUNTAIN MEADOWS MASSACRE, 1857

Blum, I. B. Inquest in Zion
The **mountain** movers. Chandler, A. B.

MOUNTAIN WHITES (SOUTHERN STATES)

See Appalachian highlanders

MOUNTAINEERING

Clarke, A. C. The cruel sky
Eggers, D. Up the mountain coming down slowly
Greig, A. Electric brae [excerpt]
Murray, J. Blue
Padilla, I. Ever wrest: log of the journey
Simmons, D. On K2 with kanakaredes

MOUNTAINS

See also Adirondack Mountains (N.Y.); Andes; Appalachian Mountains; Catskill Mountains (N.Y.); Himalaya Mountains; Rocky Mountains; Sierra Nevada Mountains (Calif. and Nev.); Volcanoes; White Mountains (N.H. and Me.)
Mungan, M. Muradhan and selvihan; or, The tale of the Crystal Kiosk

Mountains and Fire. Moon, S. H.
Mourners. Thurm, M.
MOURNING *See* Bereavement
Mourning. Stolar, D.
The mourning. Trevor, W.
MOURNING CUSTOMS *See* Funeral rites and ceremonies
The mourning door. Graver, E.
Mourning has broken. Dowd, C.
The mourning party. Cooke, C.
MOURNING RITES AND CEREMONIES
Hendel, Y. The leter that came in time
Mouses. Jones, T.
Mousetrap. Norton, A.
Mousetrap. Shapiro, J.
Mouthful of sorrow. Johnson, D.
Move out: move on. Weldon, F.
Movie Beast. Woronov, M.
MOVING (HOUSEHOLD GOODS)
Bausch, R. Spirits
Rhodes, J. P. Long distances
Weaver, G. Looking for the lost Eden
Moving. Reid, N. L.
The moving finger. Wharton, E.
Moving house. Huelle, P.
Moving on. Mosley, W.
MOVING PICTURE INDUSTRY *See* Motion pictures
MOVING PICTURES *See* Motion pictures
Moving pictures. Warren, D.
Moving spirit. Clarke, A. C.
The moving statue of Ballinspittle. Matthews, C.
Moving the mountain. Gilman, C. P.
Moving toward the light. Reed, R. R.
Moving violations. Hammer, M.
Moya, Horacio Castellanos
Hypertension
Bomb no78 p107-10 Wint 2001/2002
Moyer, Kermit
The Color of My Eyes
The Hudson Review v56 no4 p647-51 Wint 2004
Learning to smoke
The Hudson Review v55 no2 p268-76 Summ 2002
Lycanthropy
The Hudson Review v52 no2 p249-67 Summ 1999
Mozart, Johann Chrysostom Wolfgang Amadeus *See* Mozart, Wolfgang Amadeus, 1756-1791
MOZART, WOLFGANG AMADEUS, 1756-1791
About
Sterling, B. and Shiner, L. Mozart in mirrorshades
Mozart in mirrorshades. Sterling, B. and Shiner, L.
Mr. Agreeable. Nesset, K.
Mr. Antler's princess dust. Weber, K.
Mr. Big Stuff. Rinehart, S.
Mr. Churchyard and the troll. Davenport, G.
Mr. Clubb and Mr. Cuff. Straub, P.
Mr. Connaughton (From the Song by Ralph McTell). Welshons, R.
Mr. Costello, hero. Sturgeon, T.
Mr. Dark's carnival. Hirshberg, G.
Mr. Destitute. Nesset, K.
Mr. Eggplant goes home. Shishin, A.

Mr. Folsom feels fine. Davidson, A.
Mr. Gold. Paolucci, A.
Mr. Green. Butler, R. O.
Mr. Greene and the monster. Lupoff, R. A.
Mr. Gutman and Dr. Magic. Reiner, C.
Mr. Higginbotham's catastrophe. Hawthorne, N.
Mr. Hong's medals. Pak, W.-S.
Mr. Jones. Wharton, E.
Mr. Lippy. Barker, N.
Mr. Loveday's little outing. Waugh, E.
Mr. Meek. Brenner, W.
Mr. Mendoza's paintbrush. Urrea, L. A.
Mr. Mitochondria. Stollman, A. L.
Mr. Moore's old car. Sanford, A.
Mr. Moth and Mr. Davenport. Baida, P.
Mr. Passion. Coshnear, D.
Mr. Peebles heart. Gilman, C. P.
Mr. Pidger. Berners, G. H. T.-W., Baron
Mr. Pleasant. Davies, R.
Mr. Pritchard. Johnson-Davies, D.
Mr. Puniverse. Brenner, W.
Mr. Roopratna's chocolate. Davies, L.
Mr. Schoenberg, the 12-tone scale, Marlene, Tarzan and me. Filer, T.
Mr. Simmons Takes a Prisoner. Unferth, D. O.
Mr. Simonelli; or, The fairy widower. Clarke, S.
Mr. Sly stops for a cup of joe. Bull, S. E.
Mr. Smathers. Mathews, H.
Mr. Sweetly Indecent. Broyard, B.
Mr. Z. Casares, O.
Mrabet, Mohammed
The canebrake
The Art of the story; an international anthology of contemporary short stories; edited by Daniel Halpern
Mrs. Acland's ghosts. Trevor, W.
Mrs. Bajon says. Mogan, J.
Mrs. Blue. Ferris, J.
Mrs. Box. Chabon, M.
Mrs. Bullfrog. Hawthorne, N.
Mrs. Da Silva's carnival. Melville, P.
Mrs. Dutta writes a letter. Divakaruni, C. B.
Mrs. Gay's hint, and how it was taken. Alcott, L. M.
Mrs. Gay's prescription. Alcott, L. M.
Mrs. Grady's swan song. Wellen, E.
Mrs. Holland. Walker, B.
Mrs. Hudson reminisces. Robertson, L.
Mrs. Lincoln's china. Bell, M. S.
Mrs. Lutz. Kees, W.
Mrs. Mabb. Clarke, S.
Mrs. Manstey's view. Wharton, E.
Mrs. Margolis' Garden. DeNunzio, R.
Mrs. McGivney's nickel. Trevanian
Mrs. Mobry's reason. Chopin, K.
Mrs. Perez. Casares, O.
Mrs. Rakubian. Pronzini, B.
Mrs. Sen's. Lahiri, J.
Mrs. Temperly. James, H.
Mrs. Todd. Jewett, S. O.
Mrs. Todd's shortcut. King, S.
Mrs. Twomey. Campo, R.
Mrs. Website's dance. Bonman, I.
Ms. Italia. Barolini, H.
Ms. Midshipwoman Harrington. Weber, D.
Mt Fuji. Walker, B.
Mt. Pleasant. Lynn, D. H.
Much ado about nothing. Oltion, J.
Mud and strawberries. Smart, A.

The **mud** below. Proulx, A.
Mud-Colored Beauties of the Plains. Conroy, A. L.
Mud Man. Jacobs, M.
Mud show. Allen, S.
Mud time. Ferriss, L.
Mudlavia. Stuckey-French, E.
Mueller, Daniel
  Birds
    Mueller, D. How animals mate; stories
  How animals mate
    Mueller, D. How animals mate; stories
  Ice breaking
    Mueller, D. How animals mate; stories
  The night my brother worked the header
    Mueller, D. How animals mate; stories
  P. M. R. C.
    Mueller, D. How animals mate; stories
  The start of something
    Mueller, D. How animals mate; stories
  Torturing creatures at night
    Mueller, D. How animals mate; stories
  Zero
    Mueller, D. How animals mate; stories
Mueller, Marnie
  Exile
    Living on the edge; fiction by Peace Corps writers; edited by John Coyne
The **mugger**. Mosley, W.
MUGGING
  Frym, G. A little window
  Gourevitch, P. Mortality check
  Griffith, M. Kidnapped (A romance)
  Troncoso, S. Espiritu Santo
Muggings. Lynn, D. H.
The **mugs'** game. Charteris, L.
Mujica, Barbara
  Xelipe
    Southern Humanities Review v35 no4 p369-91 Fall 2001
Mukherjee, Bharati
  Happiness
    The Pushcart prize XXIII: best of the small presses; an annual small press reader; edited by Bill Henderson with the Pushcart prize editors
  The management of grief
    The Art of the story; an international anthology of contemporary short stories; edited by Daniel Halpern
    The Scribner anthology of contemporary short fiction; fifty North American stories since 1970; Lex Williford and Michael Martone, editors
  Saints
    The Workshop; seven decades of the Iowa Writers' Workshop: 42 stories, recollections & essays on Iowa's place in 20th-century American literature; edited by Tom Grimes
MULATION (BIOLOGY)
  Le Guin, U. K. The fliers of Gy
MULATTOES
  Chesnutt, C. W. The goophered grapevine
  Chopin, K. In and out of old Natchitoches
  Elliott, S. B. The heart of it
  Jones, G. White rat
  Lessing, D. M. Victoria and the Staveneys
  Shawl, N. The tawny bitch
"The **mule** and the ox". Pérez Galdós, B.

The **mule** rustlers. Lansdale, J. R.
Mulekwa, Charles
  Time is Strange
    Iowa Review v33 no2 p125-6 Fall 2003
Mulhauser, Travis
  Billy and Me
    The Literary Review (Madison, N.J.) v46 no4 p733-48 Summ 2003
Mullen, Harryette Romell
  Tenderhead
    The African American West; a century of short stories; edited by Bruce A. Glasrud and Laurie Champion
Mullen, Jane
  Irish Lesson
    New England Review v24 no3 p43-59 Summ 2003
  Two for One
    The North American Review v287 no5 p21-5 S/O 2002
Müller, Herta
  About German mustaches and hair parts
    Müller, H. Nadirs; (Niederungen); translated and with an afterword by Sieglinde Lug
  The funeral sermon
    Müller, H. Nadirs; (Niederungen); translated and with an afterword by Sieglinde Lug
  The intervillage bus
    Müller, H. Nadirs; (Niederungen); translated and with an afterword by Sieglinde Lug
  Mother, father, and the little one
    Müller, H. Nadirs; (Niederungen); translated and with an afterword by Sieglinde Lug
  Nadirs
    Müller, H. Nadirs; (Niederungen); translated and with an afterword by Sieglinde Lug
  Oppressive tango
    Müller, H. Nadirs; (Niederungen); translated and with an afterword by Sieglinde Lug
  Rotten pears
    Müller, H. Nadirs; (Niederungen); translated and with an afterword by Sieglinde Lug
  Village chronicle
    Müller, H. Nadirs; (Niederungen); translated and with an afterword by Sieglinde Lug
  The window
    Müller, H. Nadirs; (Niederungen); translated and with an afterword by Sieglinde Lug
Muller, Marcia
  Benny's space
    A Century of great suspense stories; edited by Jeffery Deaver
  Deceptions
    A Century of noir; thirty-two classic crime stories; edited by Mickey Spillane and Max Allan Collins
  The impostor
    The Mysterious Press anniversary anthology; celebrating 25 years; by the editors of Mysterious Press
    The World's finest mystery and crime stories, third annual collection; edited by Ed Gorman and Martin H. Greenberg
  Recycle
    The World's finest mystery and crime stories, first annual collection; edited by Ed Gorman

Muller, Marcia—*Continued*

Sweet cactus wine

A Century of great Western stories; edited by John Jakes

Up at the Riverside

Irreconcilable differences; Lia Matera, editor

Wild mustard

A moment on the edge; 100 years of crime stories by women; edited by Elizabeth George

Muller, Robert

The question

In search of homo sapiens; twenty-five contemporary Slovak short stories; editor, Pavol Hudík ; [translated by Heather Trebatická; American English editor, Lucy Bednár]

Mulligan, Sheila

What Flows Through Me That You Call Time

New England Review v24 no4 p139-48 2003

Mulligans. Swarthout, G. F.

Mullins, Meg

The rug

The Best American short stories, 2002; selected from U.S. and Canadian magazines by Sue Miller with Katrina Kenison, with an introduction by Sue Miller

Iowa Review v31 no3 p47-60 Wint 2001/2002

Müllner, Adolph

The caliber

Early German and Austrian detective fiction; an anthology; translated and edited by Mary W. Tannert and Henry Kratz

Multa Pecunia. Waugh, E.

MULTIPLE PERSONALITY

> *See also* Dual personality; Personality disorders

MULTIPLE SCLEROSIS

Harleman, A. Meanwhile

Wallace, R. Talking

MUMMIES

Alcott, L. M. Lost in a pyramid; or, The mummy's curse

Baker, K. The queen in yellow

Bradbury, R. Colonel Stonesteel's genuine home-made truly Egyptian mummy

Bradbury, R. Colonel Stonesteel's genuine homemade truly Egyptian mummy

Connor, J. Stone man

Crowley, J. Antiquities

Douglas, C. N. The mummy case: a midnight Louie past life adventure

Doyle, Sir A. C. Lot no. 249

Eakin, W. The secret of the mummy's brain

Fowler, K. J. Private grave 9

Haggard, H. R. Smith and the pharaohs

Lovecraft, H. P. Under the pyramids

Poe, E. A. Some words with a mummy

Rice, A. The mummy; or, Ramses the damned

Stoker, B. The Jewel of Seven Stars

The **mummy** awakens. Mahfūz, N.

The **mummy** case: a midnight Louie past life adventure. Douglas, C. N.

The **mummy**; or, Ramses the damned. Rice, A.

Mun, Nami

On the Bus

Iowa Review v34 no2 p56-64 Fall 2004

Mundo's sign. Shacochis, B.

Mundy, Robyn

Jimmy's Pearl

Iowa Review v33 no3 p67-84 Wint 2003/2004

Mungan, Murathan

Muradhan and selvihan; or, The tale of the Crystal Kiosk

The Art of the story; an international anthology of contemporary short stories; edited by Daniel Halpern

This side of the legend

Grand Street no68 p157-73 Spr 1999

Munger, Katy

The man

Tart noir; edited by Stella Duffy & Lauren Henderson

Mungoshi, Charles

The brother

The Anchor book of modern African stories; edited by Nadežda Obradovic ; with a foreword by Chinua Achebe

Munich. Wickersham, J.

MUNITIONS INDUSTRY

Kennett, S. A warm nest

Muñiz-Huberman, Angelina,

The tower of Gallipoli

With signs and wonders; an international anthology of Jewish fabulist fiction; edited by Daniel M. Jaffe

Muñoz, Manuel

Anchorage

Muñoz, M. Zigzagger

By the time you get there, by the time you get back

Muñoz, M. Zigzagger

Campo

Muñoz, M. Zigzagger

Everything the white boy told you

Muñoz, M. Zigzagger

Good as yesterday

Muñoz, M. Zigzagger

Loco

Muñoz, M. Zigzagger

Monkey, Sí

Muñoz, M. Zigzagger

Museo de Bellas Artes

Muñoz, M. Zigzagger

Not Nevada

Muñoz, M. Zigzagger

Skyshot

Muñoz, M. Zigzagger

The third myth

Muñoz, M. Zigzagger

The unimportant Lila Parr

The Massachusetts Review v40 no3 p375-85 Aut 1999

Muñoz, M. Zigzagger

Zigzagger

Muñoz, M. Zigzagger

Munro, Alice

The bear came over the mountain

Munro, A. Hateship, friendship, courtship, loveship, marriage; stories

The New Yorker v75 no40 p110-21+ D 27 1999-Ja 3 2000

Before the change

Valentine's Day: women against men; stories of revenge; introduction by Alice Thomas

Munro, Alice—_Continued_
Chance
  The New Yorker v80 no16 p130-42 Je 14-21
    2004
The children stay
  Fault lines; stories of divorce; collected and
    edited by Caitlin Shetterly
Comfort
  Munro, A. Hateship, friendship, courtship,
    loveship, marriage; stories
  The New Yorker v77 no30 p66-77 O 8 2001
Family furnishings
  The Best American short stories, 2002; select-
    ed from U.S. and Canadian magazines by
    Sue Miller with Katrina Kenison, with an
    introduction by Sue Miller
  Munro, A. Hateship, friendship, courtship,
    loveship, marriage; stories
  The New Yorker v77 no20 p64-77 Jl 23 2001
Fathers
  The New Yorker v78 no22 p64-71 Ag 5 2002
  The O. Henry Prize stories, 2003; edited and
    with an introduction by Laura Furman;
    jurers David Gutterson, Diane Johnson,
    Jennifer Egan
Floating bridge
  Munro, A. Hateship, friendship, courtship,
    loveship, marriage; stories
  Prize stories, 2001; The O. Henry awards; ed-
    ited and with an introduction by Larry
    Dark
Hateship, friendship, courtship, loveship, mar-
    riage
  Munro, A. Hateship, friendship, courtship,
    loveship, marriage; stories
Meneseteung
  The Best American short stories of the
    century; John Updike, editor, Katrina
    Kenison, coeditor; with an introduction by
    John Updike
  The Scribner anthology of contemporary short
    fiction; fifty North American stories since
    1970; Lex Williford and Michael Martone,
    editors
Nettles
  Munro, A. Hateship, friendship, courtship,
    loveship, marriage; stories
Passion
  The New Yorker v80 no5 p76-89 Mr 22 2004
Post and beam
  The Best American short stories 2001; select-
    ed from U.S. and Canadian magazines by
    Barbara Kingsolver with Katrina Kenison;
    with an introduction by Barbara Kingsolver
  Munro, A. Hateship, friendship, courtship,
    loveship, marriage; stories
Queenie
  Munro, A. Hateship, friendship, courtship,
    loveship, marriage; stories
Runaway
  The New Yorker v79 no22 p62-75 Ag 11
    2003
Save the reaper
  The Best American short stories, 1999; select-
    ed from U.S. and Canadian magazines by
    Amy Tan with Katrina Kenison, with an in-
    troduction by Amy Tan

Prize stories, 1999; The O. Henry awards; ed-
    ited and with an introduction by Larry
    Dark
Silence
  The New Yorker v80 no16 p157-8, 160,
    163-4, 166, 168-72, 175-6, 178-80, 183 Je
    14-21 2004
Soon
  The New Yorker v80 no16 p142-9, 151-7 Je
    14-21 2004
What is remembered
  Munro, A. Hateship, friendship, courtship,
    loveship, marriage; stories
  The New Yorker v77 no1 p196-207 F 19-26
    2001
A wilderness station
  Other people's mail; an anthology of letter
    stories; edited with an introduction by Gail
    Pool
Munro, H. H. (Hector Hugh) _See_ Saki, 1870-
    1916
Munro, K. E.
French press
  Hers 3: brilliant new fiction by lesbian writ-
    ers; edited by Terry Wolverton with Robert
    Drake
Munson, Peggy
Teratophobia
  Hers 3: brilliant new fiction by lesbian writ-
    ers; edited by Terry Wolverton with Robert
    Drake
Murabito, Stephen
The cooking lessons
  The North American Review v287 no3/4 p55-
    60 My/Ag 2002
Muradhan and selvihan; or, The tale of the Crys-
    tal Kiosk. Mungan, M.
Murakami, Haruki
Airplane
  The New Yorker v78 no17 p78-81 Jl 1 2002
All God's children can dance
  Harper's v303 no1817 p74-82 O 2001
  Murakami, H. After the earthquake; stories;
    translated from the Japanese by Jay Rubin
Birthday Girl
  Harper's v307 p75-80 Jl 2003
Blind willow, sleeping girl
  Harper's v304 p67-73 Je 2002
The elephant vanishes
  The Art of the story; an international antholo-
    gy of contemporary short stories; edited by
    Daniel Halpern
The fall of the Roman Empire, the 1881 Indian
    uprising, Hitler's invasion of Poland, and
    the realm of raging winds
  The Vintage book of amnesia; an anthology;
    edited by Jonathan Lethem
The Folklore of Our Times
  The New Yorker v79 no15 p90-7 Je 9 2003
Honey Pie
  Murakami, H. After the earthquake; stories;
    translated from the Japanese by Jay Rubin
  The New Yorker v77 no24 p146-55 Ag 20-27
    2001
Hunting Knife
  The New Yorker v79 no35 p140-9 N 17 2003
Ice Man
  The New Yorker v78 no46 p80-5 F 10 2003

Murakami, Haruki—*Continued*

Landscape with flatiron
Murakami, H. After the earthquake; stories; translated from the Japanese by Jay Rubin
Ploughshares v28 no2/3 p92-106 Fall 2002

New York mining disaster
The New Yorker v74 no41 p74-79 Ja 11 1999

A poor-aunt story
The New Yorker v77 no38 p86-93 D 3 2001

Super-Frog save Tokyo
Gentlemen's Quarterly v72 no6 p154-66, 265 Je 2002

Super-Frog saves Tokyo
Murakami, H. After the earthquake; stories; translated from the Japanese by Jay Rubin

Thailand
Granta no74 p61-77 Summ 2001
Murakami, H. After the earthquake; stories; translated from the Japanese by Jay Rubin
The Year's best fantasy & horror: sixteenth annual collection; edited by Ellen Datlow & Terri Windling

Three German fantasies
The Review of Contemporary Fiction v22 no2 p120-7 Summ 2002

Tony Takitani
The New Yorker v78 no8 p74-81 Ap 15 2002

U.F.O. in Kushiro
The New Yorker v77 no4 p130-5 Mr 19 2001

UFO in Kushiro
Murakami, H. After the earthquake; stories; translated from the Japanese by Jay Rubin

Murals. Morgan, R.
Murder. Hackle, S. G.
The **murder**. Steinbeck, J.
Murder. Wuori, G. K.
A **murder,** a mystery, and a marriage. Twain, M.
Murder at Mardi Gras. Lochte, D.
Murder at midday. Granger, A.
Murder at the Beau Rivage. Cunningham, M. and others
Murder at the sales meeting. Drury, J. M.
The **murder** at the vicarage. Charles, K.
Murder by miracle. Tremayne, P.
Murder for money. MacDonald, J. D.
Murder in Kilcurry. Ryan, M.
Murder in repose. Tremayne, P.
Murder is murder. Davidson, A.
Murder mysteries. Gaiman, N.
A **murder** of import. Lochte, D.
Murder of the frankfurter man. Appel, B.
Murder on Lupozny Station. Bishop, M. and Page, G. W.
Murder one. Painter, P.

MURDER STORIES
See also Assassination; Crime and criminals; Filicide; Infanticide; International intrigue; Murderers; Mystery and detective stories; Parricide; Poisons; Violence

Agee, J. Aronson's Orchard
Agee, J. The gun
Agustí, M. Rebirth [Cain and Abel]
Allyn, D. Black Irish
Allyn, D. The Christmas mitzvah
Allyn, D. The country of the blind
Allyn, D. The jukebox king
Allyn, D. Puppyland
Allyn, D. Saint Bobby
Amdrup, E. Chess on board

Andrews, M. K. Love at first byte
Aquino, J. T. The mysterious death of the shadow man
Ayres, N. JoJo's gold
Babel', I. Dante Street
Bailey, D. Quinn's way
Bankier, W. Child of another time
Banks, R. The lie
Banks, R. Lobster night
Barker, N. The Piazza Barberini
Barnard, R. Everybody's girl
Barnard, R. The gentleman in the lake
Barnard, R. Holy living and holy dying
Barnard, R. Nothing to lose
Barnett, P. Two dead men
Barrett, L. Elvis lives
Bart, D. Prom night
Bausch, R. Fatality
Bausch, R. The man who knew Belle Starr
Bender, A. The case of the salt and pepper shakers
Berdine, T. Spring rite
Berners, G. H. T.-W., Baron. Percy Wallingford
Berry, W. Pray without ceasing
Bester, A. Fondly Fahrenheit
Bester, A. The four-hour fugue
Betts, D. Aboveground
Biguenet, J. It is raining in Bejucal
Bishop, C. Dead and berried
Bishop, C. Waiting for gateau
Bishop, M. Icicle music
Bishop, M. and Page, G. W. Murder on Lupozny Station
Bishop, P. Dead easy
Blavatsky, H. P. Can the double murder?
Bloch, R. Life in our time
Block, L. How would you like it?
Block, L. Sometimes they bite
Block, L. Speaking of lust
Block, L. Sweet little hands
Bocock, M. The Journey
Bonman, I. Mrs. Website's dance
Borges, J. L. The dead man
Borges, J. L. Death and the compass
Borges, J. L. Emma Zunz
Borges, J. L. Ibn-Hakam al-Bokhari, murdered in his labyrinth
Borges, J. L. The interloper
Borges, J. L. Juan Muraña
Borges, J. L. The wait
Bouman, I. The deep blue sea
Bowles, P. In the red room
Brackett, L. I feel bad killing you
Bradbury, R. A careful man dies
Bradbury, R. The Finnegan
Bradbury, R. The fruit at the bottom of the bowl
Bradbury, R. The illustrated man
Bradbury, R. Sixty-six
Bradbury, R. The smiling people
Brand, C. Clever and quick
Brandner, G. Heat lightning
Brandon, P. The marsh runners
Braunbeck, G. A. Down in darkest Dixie where the dead don't dance
Braunbeck, G. A. Mail-order Annie
Braunbeck, G. A. Safe
Breen, J. L. The cat and the Kinetophone
Breen, J. L. Clever Hans
Breen, J. L. Four views of justice

MURDER STORIES—*Continued*

Brett, S. Best behaviour
Brewer, G. Sauce for the goose
Brite, P. Z. O death, where is thy spatula?
Brown, F. The wench is dead
Bruns, Don. Sing for your supper
Buchanan, E. The red shoes
Bukiet, M. J. The war lovers
Burke, J. The man in the civil suit
Burke, J. Miscalculation
Burke, J. An unsuspected condition of the heart
Bush, G. R. The last reel
Cain, J. M. The baby in the icebox
Campbell, R. Lilith's
Campbell, R. The other woman
Campbell, R. Ra*e
Cannell, D. Cupids arrow
Cannell, D. The family jewels: a moral tale
Cannell, D. Fetch
Cannell, D. The January sale stowaway
Cannell, D. Poor Lincoln
Cannell, D. The purloined purple pearl
Cannell, D. Telling George
Cannell, D. What Mr. McGregor saw
Cannon, T. Restitution
Carlson, P. M. The world is mine; or, Deeds that make heaven weep
Carver, R. Furious seasons
Carver, R. The third thing that killed my father off
Chambers, C. Aardvark to Aztec
Channell, C. Coffee and murder
Chapman, C. M. Michelle
Charles, K. The murder at the vicarage
Charteris, L. The mystery of the child's toy
Chekhov, A. P. A drama
Chesnutt, C. W. The sheriff's children
Chittenden, M. The spirit of Washington
Christie, A. Accident
Clarke, A. C. Let there be light
Cobb, W. J. Dark matter
Coberly, L. M. Over Sulphur Mountain
Codrescu, A. Samba de los agentes
Cody, L. In those days
Cody, L. Reconstruction
Cody, L. Walking blues
Cody, L. Woke up this morning
Cohen, S. The case of Grand Cru
Cohen, S. Homeless, hungry, please help
Cohen, S. A night in the Manchester store
Cole, M. Enough was enough
Collins, B. Aunt Emma's defense
Collins, B. Carry's cat
Collins, B. Cat got your tongue
Collins, B. Dalliance at Sunnydale
Collins, B. Dead and breakfast
Collins, B. A proper burial
Collins, B. Seeing red
Collins, B. To grandmother's house we go
Collins, B. To kill a cat
Collins, B. World's greatest mother
Collins, B. and Collins, M. A. A cruise to forget
Collins, B. and Collins, M. A. Eddie Haskell in a short skirt
Collins, M. A. Catgate
Collins, M. A. Cat's-eye witness
Collins, M. Death, my love
Collins, M. Nobody frames Big Sam
Collins, M. Occupational hazard

Collins, M. Silent partner
Collymore, F. Some people are meant to live alone
Connor, J. Good people
Cook, A. Hot days, cold nights
Cooke, J. P. After you've gone
Corcoran, T. The octopus alibi
Costa, S. Black heart and cabin girl
Costello, M. J. Someone who understands me
Coward, M. So where've you buried the missus then, Paddy?
Coward, M. Too hot to die
Coward, M. Twelve of the little buggers
Coward, M. You can jump
Creasey, J. The chief witness
Crider, B. Blest be the ties
Crider, B. Out like a lion
Crider, B. The Santa Claus caper
Crider, B. and Crider, J. At the hop
Crone, M. Where what gets into people comes from
Cross, A. The double-barreled gun
Crowther, P. The allotment
Crowther, P. The main event
Crumley, J. Hot Springs
Cutler, J. Doctor's orders
Dadmun, B. Annie's dream
Dain, C. Mirror, mirror
D'Amato, B. Motel 66
Davidson, A. The cobblestones of Saratoga Street
Davidson, A. The cost of Kent Castwell
Davidson, A. Murder is murder
Davidson, A. A quiet room with a view
Davidson, A. The third sacred well of the temple
Davidson, A. Thou still unravished bride
Davidson, J. A stone of destiny
Davidson, L. Indian rope trick
Davis, A. Prints
Davis, C. A. Not long now
Davis, D. S. The letter
Davis, D. S. Till death do us part
Davis, D. S. To forget Mary Ellen
Davis, L. Something spooky on Geophys
Davis, L. The house behind
Dawson, J. What the cat dragged in
De Noux, O. Death on denial
De Noux, O. The Iberville mistress
DeAndrea, W. L. Killed in good company
DeAndrea, W. L. Killed in midstream
DeAndrea, W. L. Killed top to bottom
DeAndrea, W. L. Murder at the end of the world
The Death of Colonel Thoureau
Deaver, J. For services rendered
Deaver, J. Triangle
Deaver, J. The weekender
Dedman, S. The wind shall blow for ever mair
DeLancey, K. I loved the squire
DeLoach, N. Victim by consent
Deming, R. Honeymoon cruise
Devane, T. Decoys
Dexter, C. The double crossing
Díaz, J. The brief wondrous life of Oscar Wao
Doctorow, E. L. Child, dead, in the rose garden
Doctorow, E. L. A house on the plains
Donnelly, Marcos. Café con leche
Doogan, M. War can be murder

MURDER STORIES—*Continued*

Dougherty, K. When your breath freezes
Dowling, T. Basic black
Dowling, T. Stitch
Downs, M. Man kills wife, two dogs
Dreyer, E. Fun with forensics
Drury, J. M. Murder at the sales meeting
DuBois, B. The wearing of the green
Duffy, S. Could be better
Duffy, S. Martha Grace
Dunlap, S. Bad review
Edwards, M. 24 hours from Tulsa
Ehlers, J. Golden Gate Bridge—a view from below
Ellin, S. The last bottle in the world
Ellin, S. Reasons unknown
Ellison, H. Killing Bernstein
Engstrom, E. Crosley
Estleman, L. D. A hatful of Ralph
Evans, M. Candles in the bottom of the pool
Evenson, B. The intricacies of post-shooting etiquette
Evenson, B. Stockwell
Falco, E. The instruments of peace
Fesler, P. J. Coin of the realm
Fliegel, R. A final midrash
Fowler, K. J. Private grave 9
Foxwell, E. A Roman of no importance
Franklin, T. Poachers
Franks, R. A secret murder
Fraser, A. The twist
Frazer, M. Neither pity, love nor fear
Friedman, M. Tango is my life
Friedman, P. Dog days
Gaiman, N. Murder mysteries
Garrett, M. Candie-gram
Garrett, M. Sex crimes
Gash, J. Jack and Jill, R.I.P.
Gates, D. E. Compass Rose
Gay, W. The paperhanger
Gelb, J. Perfection
Gelb, J. Trophy wife
George, E. I, Richard
George, E. The surprise of his life
Gerard, P. Death by reputation
Gilbert, J. Everything must go
Gilbert, M. Judith
Glaspell, S. A jury of her peers
Godfrey, D. O. Inland, shoreline
Gonzalez, R. Invisible country
Goran, L. The priest of storms
Gordimer, N. Country lovers
Gores, J. The Andrech samples
Gores, J. Night out
Gores, J. Plot it yourself
Gores, J. Quit screaming
Gores, J. Watch for it
Gorman, E. Angie
Gorman, E. En famille
Gorman, E. The end of it all
Gorman, E. Judgment
Gorman, E. A new man
Gorman, E. Out there in the darkness
Gorman, E. Such a good girl
Gregory, S. The White Ship murders
Griffen, C. Borgia by blood
Guiver, P. The Boxing Day bother
Gwyn, A. The backsliders
Hackle, S. G. Murder

Hager, J. George Washington crashed here
Hall, P. Lethal luncheon
Hall, R. L. No lie
Hamilton, L. Stark terror at tea-time
Hammett, D. His brother's keeper
Hammett, D. The man who killed Dan Odams
Handler, D. The last of the bad girls
Hansen, J. Blood, snow, and classic cars
Hardy, M. The heifer
Harford, D. K. A death on the Ho Chi Minh Trail
Harrington, J. In the merry month of mayhem
Hart, C. G. Accidents happen
Hart, C. G. Life-interest
Hart, C. G. Turnaround
Hartley, L. P. W.S.
Harvey, J. Due North
Hassler, J. Yesterday's garbage
Hayter, S. The diary of Sue Peaner, Marooned! contestant
Haywood, G. A. The first one to blink
Healy, J. F. Food for thought
Healy, J. F. Hero
Healy, J. F. Rotten to the core
Henderson, L. Dark mirror
Hensley, J. L. The calculator
Hensley, J. L. Decision
Hensley, J. L. Fifty Chinese
Hensley, J. L. On the rocks
Hensley, J. L. The retiree
Hensley, J. L. Widow
Herling, G. The Noonday Cemetery: an open story
Hershman, M. Letter to the editor
Hess, J. All that glitters
Hess, J. Another room
Highsmith, P. It's a deal
Highsmith, P. Music to die by
Highsmith, P. The terrapin
Highsmith, P. Things had gone badly
Highsmith, P. Variations on a game
Hoch, E. D. The Club of Masks
Hoch, E. D. The detective's wife
Hoch, E. D. Great day for the Irish
Hoch, E. D. One bag of coconuts
Hoch, E. D. A wall too high
Hockensmith, S. Erie's last day
Hoffman, W. Winter wheat
Holladay, C. C. Merry-go-sorry
Holliday, L. Provenance
Holt, T. Accidental death
Howard, C. The California contact
Howard, C. Hit and run
Howard, C. The ice shelf
Howard, C. The last one to cry
Howard, C. Under suspicion
Howard, C. Wild things
Howe, M. J. Killing the sixties
Hudgins, B. Fur bearing
Hunter, E. The killing at Triple Tree
Hyde, M. Her Hollywood
Isaacs, S. My cousin Rachel's Uncle Murray
Jacobs, M. The ballad of Tony Nail
Jakes, J. Dagger
Jakes, J. No comment
Jakes, J. Tex
James, B. Big city
James, D. All in the family
James, H. A tragedy of error

MURDER STORIES—Continued

Johnson, D. Mouthful of sorrow
Johnson, S. C. Body in the pond
Kaminsky, S. M. Hidden
Kaminsky, S. M. It comes with the badge
Karnezis, P. The day of the beast
Kaufelt, D. A. The bagel murders
Keegan, C. The singing cashier
Kelner, T. L. P. Old dog days
Kennett, S. A warm nest
Kerslake, L. Lookin' 'n' jivin'
Kilpatrick, N. An eye for an eye
King, S. Strawberry spring
Kingsbury, K. A nice cup of tea
Kinman, G. T. Miss Parker & the Cutter-Sanborn tables
Kittredge, W. The soap bear
Klaskin, R. Child support
Knight, A. The deadly glen
Knight, T. A trail of mirrors
Kohler, S. Correspondence I
Kohler, S. Correspondence II
Kruse, T. The good old German way
Kuppner, F. A very quiet street [excerpt]
Lake, M. D. A. B. C. D. E. A. T. H.
Lake, M. D. The tunnel
L'Amour, L. The gravel pit
L'Amour, L. The hand of Kuan-yin
L'Amour, L. The money punch
L'Amour, L. Off the Mangrove Coast
L'Amour, L. Too tough to kill
Lane, A. The gaze of the falcon
Lane, J. The window
Lansdale, J. R. Down by the sea near the great big rock
Lansdale, J. R. Duck hunt
Lansdale, J. R. Mad dog summer
Lansdale, J. R. Old Charlie
Lansdale, J. R. Walks
LaPierre, J. Da capo
Laurence, J. Time share
Lawrence, B. Nothing but the best
Lawrence, M. C. The sea cave
Laymon, R. Boo
Leavitt, D. The marble quilt
Lee, C. Luisa
Lee, M. Koza nights
Lee, V. Amour dure
Lee, W. W. Indiscreet
Lee, W. W. Miles deep
Lee, W. W. Soft day
Lehane, D. Running out of dog
Leonard, E. When the women come out to dance
Levinson, L. M. The cove
Levinson, R. S. Good career moves
Levitsky, R. A Sabbath flame
Lippman, L. What he needed
Little, B. Connie
Lochte, D. Mad Dog
Lovesey, P. Because it was there
Lovesey, P. The perfectionist
Lovesey, P. The usual table
Lovesey, P. Blitzed
Lovett, S. Buried treasure
Lovisi, G. Service
Ludwig, O. The dead man of St. Anne's Chapel
Lumley, B. Vanessa's voice
Lupoff, R. A. Black mist

Lupoff, R. A. News from New Providence
Lustbader, E. V. Slow burn
Lutz, J. A handgun for protection
Lutz, J. Nighthawks
Lutz, J. El Palacio
Lutz, J. The real shape of the coast
Lutz, J. S.O.S.
Lutz, J. Stutter step
Lutz, J. Tango was her life
Lutz, J. Veterans
Lynch, T. Blood sport
Maffini, M. J. Blind alley
Maffini, M. J. Cocktails with the corpse
Malone, M. Invitation to the ball
Malone, M. Maniac loose
Malone, M. Red clay
Malone, M. White trash noir
Malouf, D. Blacksoil country
Malouf, D. Lone Pine
Malzberg, B. N. Agony column
Mann, P. Touch of a vanish'd hand
Maraini, D. Alicetta
Maraini, D. The boy Gramophone and the pigeon man
Maraini, D. Walls of darkness
Marías, J. Flesh Sunday
Marías, J. The night doctor
Marías, J. Spear blood
Maron, M. The dog that didn't bark
Maron, M. Growth marks
Maron, M. Half of something
Maron, M. The stupid pet trick
Maron, M. That married dear old dad
Maron, M. To hide a tree
Maron, M. Virgo in sapphires
Marston, E. Perfect shadows
Marston, E. Slaughter in the Strand
Mason, S. J. With thanks to Agatha Christie
Matera, L. Counsel for the defense
Matera, L. Dead drunk
Matera, L. Do not resuscitate
Matheson, R. C. Graduation
Matiella, A. C. The truth about Alicia
Matteson, S. The trouble with Harry
Matthews, C. Backyard burial
Matthews, C. Dear Lottie
Matthews, C. Death of a glamour cat
McAuley, P. J. Naming the dead
McBain, E. Activity in the flood plain
McBain, E. Barking at butterflies
McBain, E. Running from Legs
McBain, E. A very Merry Christmass
McDermid, V. The consolation blonde
McDermid, V. The girl who killed Santa Claus
McDermid, V. The wagon mound
McGary, G. The cats and jammer
McKee, Robert. The confession
McNally, J. Limbs
McNeely, T. H. Sheep
Meacock, N. The mole trap
Means, D. Carnie
Melton, F. Counting
Melville, P. Erzulie
Meyers, A. You don't know me
Mina, D. Helena and the babies
Moffett, M. Dead rock singer
Mokoso, N. God of meme
Moody, W. Matinee
Moorcock, M. The case of the Nazi canary

MURDER STORIES—Continued

Mortimer, J. C. Rumpole and the absence of body
Muller, M. Sweet cactus wine
Munger, K. The man
Murray, M. Shame the devil
Myers, A. Happy the man . . .
Myers, A. The Rightful King of England
Myers, J. Copycat
Myers, T. Chicken catch a tory
Neri, K. Sentence imposed
Nevins, F. M., Jr. Bad bargain
Nevins, F. M., Jr. Because the constable blundered
Nevins, F. M., Jr. Buford's last case
Nevins, F. M., Jr. Funeral music
Nevins, F. M., Jr. The last passenger
Nevins, F. M., Jr. Leap day
Nevins, F. M., Jr. Luck of the dead
Newman, C. Wifely duties
Newman, S. Death before compline
Newton, D. B. Born to the brand
Nikas, E. Fatal tears
Niles, C. Revenge is the best revenge
Nolan, W. F. In real life
Norris, L. Interior country
Oates, J. C. Curly Red
Oates, J. C. The deaths: an elegy
Oates, J. C. Faithless
Oates, J. C. Happiness
Oates, J. C. The high school sweetheart
Oates, J. C. The skull
Oates, J. C. Tell me you forgive me?
Oates, J. C. The vampire
O'Callaghan, M. Black is the color of my true love's heart
O'Callaghan, M. It takes one to kill one
O'Callaghan, M. The sweet old lady who sits in the park
O'Connor, F. The comforts of home
O'Connor, F. A good man is hard to find
Offutt, C. Out of the woods
O'Hara, J. In a grove
Orner, P. County Road G
Orner, P. Daughters
Ortiz, S. J. The killing of a state cop
O'Shaughnessy, P. Juggernaut
Overholser, W. D. The fence
Owen, M. G. The snows of Saint Stephen
Pack, J. Impressions
Page, K. H. The would-be widower
Painter, P. Sympathy
Paretsky, S. At the Century of Progress
Paretsky, S. Heartbreak house
Parrish, T. The smell of a car
Paul, B. French asparagus
Paul, B. Ho ho ho
Paul, B. Jack be quick
Paul, B. Okay, Diogenes, you can stop looking—we found him
Paul, B. Portrait of the artist as a young corpse
Paul, B. Scat
Paul, B. Stet
Pelecanos, G. P. The dead their eyes implore us
Pelegrimas, M. I'm not that kind of girl
Pelegrimas, M. and Randisi, R. J. I love everything about you
Pelegrimas, M. and Randisi, R. J. Money-back guarantee

Perry, A. The end of innocence
Perry, A. The escape
Perry, A. Heroes
Petter, S. Widow's peak
Piccirilli, T. Of Persephone, Poe, and the Whisperer
Pickard, N. The dead past
Pickard, N. Dr. Couch saves a cat
Pickard, N. Lucky devil
Pickard, N. Sex and violence
Pickard, N. Speak no evil
Poe, E. A. The cask of Amontillado
Poe, E. A. The tell-tale heart
Popkes, S. Winters are hard
Post, M. D. Naboth's vineyard
Powell, T. Somebody cares
Pronzini, B. The Arrowmont Prison riddle
Pronzini, B. Connoisseur
Pronzini, B. Flood
Pronzini, B. I didn't do it
Pronzini, B. Mrs. Rakubian
Pronzini, B. Putting the pieces back
Pronzini, B. Under the skin
Pronzini, B. Wishful thinking
Pronzini, B. and Kurland, M. Quicker than the eye
Pronzini, B. and Malzberg, B. N. Another burnt-out case
Pronzini, B. and Malzberg, B. N. Multiples
Pronzini, B. and Malzberg, B. N. Night rider
Proulx, A. 55 miles to the gas pump
Pryor, J. Wrong numbers
Pulver, M. M. To whom the victory?
Quill, M. Intent to kill
Quill, M. A sound investment
Quill, M. The visitor
Rainwater, A. Night rose
Randisi, R. J. and Matthews, C. A night at the love nest resort
Ranieri, R. The bandit who caught a killer
Rankin, I. A deep hole
Rankin, I. The serpent's back
Rash, R. Last rite
Rath, T. and Rath, T. Who killed fair Rosamund?
Reach, A. S. In the confessional
Reeve, A. B. The poisoned pen
Reid, E. Overtime
Rellas, D. Midnight
Rendell, R. The carer
Rendell, R. The irony of hate
Rendell, R. The professional
Resnick, M. Even butterflies can sting
Richter, J. The ones left behind
Robinson, P. The Duke's wife
Robinson, P. The wrong hands
Roche, T. S. Hell on wheels
Rogers, B. H. Cloud stalking mice
Royle, N. The Inland Waterways Association
Rozan, S. J. Childhood
Rubin, B. Living next door to malice
Runyon, D. Sense of humor
Rusch, K. K. Details
Rusch, K. K. The silence
Rusch, K. K. Spinning
Rusch, K. K. The young shall see visions, and the old dream dreams
Ryan, M. Murder in Kilcurry
Rykena, S. Conscience

MURDER STORIES—*Continued*

Sammān, G. The brain's closed castle
Sammān, G. The metallic crocodile
Sammān, G. The plot against Badi'
Sarrantonio, A. Pumpkin head
Saulnier, B. High maintenance
Savage, T. One of us
Sayers, D. L. The man who knew how
Scarborough, E. A. Tinkler Tam and the body snatchers
Schoemperlen, D. The look of the lightning, the sound of the birds
Schumacher, A. Along for the ride
Schutz, B. M. Not enough monkeys
Scott, J. Cat in love
Scoville, S. The dividing strand
Seidman, L. Over my shoulder
Shankman, S. Love thy neighbor
Shields, J. The Fig Eater [excerpt]
Silber, J. Without Ellie
Siler, J. Africa
Singer, I. B. Under the knife
Slaughter, K. Necessary women
Slesar, H. Letter from a very worried man
Smith, B. B. Death of a damn moose
Smith, J. Blood types
Smith, J. Grief counselor
Smith, J. Montezuma's other revenge
Smith, J. Silk strands
Solari, M. T. Death and transfiguration of a teacher
Spillane, M. Tomorrow I die
Squire, E. D. Down the garden path
Squire, E. D. A passion for the cook
Steele, W. D. Blue Murder
Steinbeck, J. The murder
Stevenson, R. L. Markheim
Straub, P. Mr. Clubb and Mr. Cuff
Straub, P. Perdido: a fragment from a work in progress
Straub, P. Pork pie hat
Straub, P. Ronald, D_____!
Strauss, A. Post-dated
Strauss, A. Swimming without Annette
Strieber, W. Hole in the head
Sumner, P. For your eyes only
Sykes, J. Seduced
Sykes, J. Symptoms of loss
Symons, J. A theme for Hyacinth
Talley, M. Conventional wisdom
Talley, M. Safety first
Tarrera, C. Dance with death
Teigeler, P. The wind & Mary
Tem, M. Piano bar blues
Thompson, J. Forever
Thornton, K. Ai witness
Tinti, H. Home sweet home
Togneri, E. Guardian angel
Toole, F. X. Midnight emissions
Touré. It's life and death at the Slush Puppie Open
Tremayne, P. Night's black agents
Trevanian. Hot night in the city
Trevanian. Hot night in the city II
Turnbull, P. Weasal and the fish
Turner, G. And now doth time waste me
Tyre, N. A nice place to stay
Tyre, N. Recipe for a happy marriage
Vachss, A. H. Dope fiend
Vachss, A. H. Goin' down slow
Van de Wetering, J. Lady Hillary
VanderMeer, J. Black Duke blues
Varley, John. The Bellman
Vermeulen, J. Canon
Viets, E. Red meat
Vinten, R. Character witness
Vis, J. The mermaid
Wallace, J. Driven to kill
Wallace, M. Splitting
Walpow, N. Push comes to shove
Walters, M. English autumn-American fall
Walters, M. The tinder box
Wandrei, H. George is all right
Waterman, D. A lepidopterist's tale
Watson, B. Water dog god
Watson, I. The shape of murder
Watson, I. Three-legged dog
Waugh, E. Fidon's confetion
Waugh, E. Mr. Loveday's little outing
Weinberg, R. Ro Erg
Wellen, E. Born victims
Wellen, E. Fair exchange
Wellen, E. Final acquittal
Wellen, E. Play death
Wellen, E. A wreath for justice
Westlake, D. E. The curious facts preceding my execution
Westlake, D. E. Good night, good night
Westlake, D. E. Never shake a family tree
Westlake, D. E. The sweetest man in the world
Wharton, E. A bottle of Perrier
Wheat, C. A bus called pity
Wheat, C. Ghost Station
Wheat, C. The only good judge
Wheat, C. The time of his life
White, M. C. Disturbances
Williams, D. A nose for murder
Wolzien, V. Just one bite won't kill you
Woolrich, C. Rear window
Wright, J. B. Stitch and bitch
Yarbrough, S. The rest of her life
Yasgur, B. S. Kaddish
Youmans, C. Mortmain
Zind, Rick. The way he knew it

MURDER TRIALS *See* Trials

Murder-two. Oates, J. C.

MURDERERS

See also Murder stories

Allende, I. An act of vengeance
Appel, B. Murder of the frankfurter man
Banks, I. The wasp factory [excerpt]
Bishop, M. and DiFilippo, P. "We're all in this alone"
Bisson, T. The old rugged cross
Block, L. Like a bone in the throat
Boylan, C. My son the hero
Bradbury, R. At midnight, in the month of June
Campbell, R. Twice by fire
Carlson, R. The chromium hook
Cavell, B. Highway
Clark, M. H. The man next door
Cody, L. K. K.
Cohen, S. I'm sorry, Mr. Griggs
Connor, J. This one fact
Crowther, P. Shatsi
Davies, R. Return to Waterloo
Davis, A. Red lights like laughter
Davis, D. S. Miles to go

MURDERERS—*Continued*

De Lint, C. Freak
De Lint, C. The witching hour
DeLancey, K. Dinger and Blacker
DuBois, B. Dancing the night away
Foote, S. The sacred mound
Foster, A. D. Procrastinator
Fulmer, D. Back O'Town Blues
Gaiman, N. Keepsakes and treasures: a love story
Garmendia, S. The melancholic pedestrian
Gautreaux, T. Same place, same things
Gay, W. Crossroads blues
Gifford, B. Room 584, the Starr Hotel
Glasgow, E. The shadowy third
Gorman, E. Ghosts
Gorman, E. Mom and Dad at home
Haldeman, J. W. Road kill
Hensley, J. L. Killer scent
Hernández, G. G. Lilith's dance
Hodge, B. Some other me
Hopkinson, N. Snake
Johnson-Davies, D. Fate of a prisoner
Keegan, C. You can't be too careful
Keret, E. Goodman
Kessel, J. Every angel is terrifying
Lansdale, J. R. I tell you it's love
Laymon, R. Hammerhead
Lee, D. Voir dire
Lefcourt, P. Thinning the herd
Linscott, G. For all the saints
Matthews, C. I'm not that kind of girl
Matthews, C. Niiice
Matthews, C. To make a rabbit sing
McCrumb, S. A predatory woman
Miller, R. Spike team
Mina, D. Alice opens the box
Oates, J. C. Death watch
O'Callaghan, M. Wolf winter
O'Nan, S. Endless summer
Orner, P. Thumbs
Padilla, I. The Chinaman with the heads
Peck, D. Bliss
Phillips, J. A. Gemcrack
Pickard, N. Afraid of the dark
Pickard, N. Nine points for murder
Poe, E. A. The black cat
Pronzini, B. I think I will not hang myself today
Pronzini, B. Liar's dice
Régio, J. Maria do Ahu
Sánchez, R. El tejón
Schaller, E. The assistant to Dr. Jacob
Schow, D. J. Unhasped
Shirley, J. Wings burnt black
Smith, M. M. The book of irrational numbers
Smith, P. M. Forgetting the girl
Spark, M. The hanging judge
Straub, P. Bunny is good bread
Svoboda, T. Psychic
Tamaro, S. The burning forest
Turner, R. Eleven o'clock bulletin
Vachss, A. H. Big sister
Vachss, A. H. Good for the soul
Vachss, A. H. Homeless
Vachss, A. H. Mission
Vachss, A. H. Perp walk
Vachss, A. H. Reaching back
Vachss, A. H. Slow motion
Vachss, A. H. Summer girl

Welty, E. The hitch-hikers
Williams, C. Imbroglio
Wuori, G. K. Justice
Zeman, A. Hello?
Murderers. Michaels, L.
Murdering the Moonlight. LaSalle, P.
Murderous thoughts. Johnson, C. R.
Murfree, Mary Noailles *See* Craddock, Charles Egbert, 1850-1922
Murguía, Alejandro
Barrio lotto
   Murguía, A. This war called love; nine stories
Boy on a wooden horse
   Murguía, A. This war called love; nine stories
A lesson in merengue
   Murguía, A. This war called love; nine stories
Lucky Alley
   Murguía, A. This war called love; nine stories
Ofrendas
   Murguía, A. This war called love; nine stories
Rose-colored dreams
   Murguía, A. This war called love; nine stories
This war called love
   Murguía, A. This war called love; nine stories
A toda máquina
   Murguía, A. This war called love; nine stories
El último round
   Murguía, A. This war called love; nine stories
A **murmur.** Tužinský, J.
Murmuring. Sucher, C. P.
Murphy, Derryl
The history of photography
   Northern suns; edited by David G. Hartwell & Glenn Grant
Murphy, Nora
The butterfly garden
   Murphy, N. Twelve branches; stories from St. Paul; [by] Nora Murphy ... {et al.}
The catcher
   Murphy, N. Twelve branches; stories from St. Paul; [by] Nora Murphy ... {et al.}
Miini-Giizi
   Murphy, N. Twelve branches; stories from St. Paul; [by] Nora Murphy ... {et al.}
Murphy, Pat
Rachel in love
   Brown, C. N. and Strahan, J. The Locus awards; thirty years of the best in science fiction and fantasy; edited by Charles N. Brown and Jonathan Strahan
   A Woman's liberation; a choice of futures by and about women; edited by Connie Willis and Sheila Williams
Wild girls
   Witpunk; edited by Claude Lalumière and Marty Halpern
Murphy, Patrick J.
The flower's noiseless hunger, the tree's clandestine tide
   100% pure Florida fiction; an anthology; edited by Susan Hubbard and Robley Wilson
Murphy, Warren
Motherly love
   Murder in the family; [by] the Adams Round Table
Murphy plays his hand. L'Amour, L.

Murr, Naeem
Nude
  Gettysburg Review v12 no4 p559-92 Wint
    1999
Murray, John
Acts of memory, wisdom of man
  Murray, J. A few short notes on tropical but-
    terflies; stories
All the rivers in the world
  Murray, J. A few short notes on tropical but-
    terflies; stories
Blue
  Murray, J. A few short notes on tropical but-
    terflies; stories
The carpenter who looked like a boxer
  Murray, J. A few short notes on tropical but-
    terflies; stories
A few short notes on tropical butterflies
  Kulka, J. and Danford, N. The New American
    voices 2003; guest editor Joyce Carol
    Oates; series editors John Kulka and
    Natalie Danford
  Murray, J. A few short notes on tropical but-
    terflies; stories
The hill station
  Murray, J. A few short notes on tropical but-
    terflies; stories
Watson and the shark
  Murray, J. A few short notes on tropical but-
    terflies; stories
White flour
  Murray, J. A few short notes on tropical but-
    terflies; stories
Murray, Millie
Shame the devil
  Brought to book; murderous stories from the
    literary world; Penny Sumner, editor
Murray, Paul
Anubis
  Granta no82 p45-66 Summ 2003
Murray, Peter, 1952-
  See also Hautman, Pete, 1952-
Murray, Sabina
The caprices
  Murray, S. The caprices
  New England Review v20 no3 p20-32 Summ
    1999
Colossus
  Murray, S. The caprices
Folly
  Murray, S. The caprices
Guinea
  Murray, S. The caprices
Intramuros
  Murray, S. The caprices
The naked ape
  The Massachusetts Review v40 no2 p288-300
    Summ 1999
Order of precedence
  Murray, S. The caprices
Position
  Murray, S. The caprices
Walkabout
  Murray, S. The caprices
Yamashita's gold
  Murray, S. The caprices
Murray, Yxta Maya
Girl on fire
  LA shorts; edited by Steven Gilbar

Musashi [excerpt] Yoshikawa, E.
Musée des Beaux Arts. Brownstein, G.
The **muse's** tragedy. Wharton, E.
Museum. Rabb, M.
The **museum** of Dr. Moses. Oates, J. C.
Museum Piece. McMullan, M.
MUSEUMS
  Avrich, J. Chez Oedipus
  Bail, M. Portrait of electricity
  Doyle, Sir A. C. The Jew's breastplate
  Frym, G. Distance no object
  Horn, D. Barbarians at the gates
  Jurado, A. Saying goodbye through twenty-five
    centuries
  Morgan, E. S. Saturday afternoon in the Holo-
    caust Museum
  Rosenfeld, S. Insects in amber
  Shapiro, G. Suskind, the impresario
  Somtow, S. P. Bird catcher
  Tinti, H. Preservation
  Tuck, L. The view from Madama Butterfly's
    house
  Updike, J. Museums and women
The **mushroom** girl. Nissen, T.
MUSIC
  See also Popular music
  Clarke, A. C. The ultimate melody
  De Lint, C. Seven for a secret
  Gilchrist, E. 1944
  Huelle, P. Moving house
  Lugones, L. Metamusic
  Naslund, S. J. The perfecting of the Chopin
    Valse No. 14 in E Minor
MUSIC, POPULAR *See* Popular music
Music. Gilchrist, E.
Music for airports. Baxter, C.
MUSIC HALL ENTERTAINERS *See* Entertain-
  ers
MUSIC LESSONS
  Greer, A. S. How it was for me
The **music** of your life. Rowell, J.
MUSIC TEACHERS
  Avrich, J. Miss Carmichael's funeral
  Hill, K. The anointed
  Jacobs, M. Dove of the back streets
  Perabo, S. The rocks over Kyburz
  Sandor, M. Elegy for Miss Beagle
  Taylor, T. L. Prayers to Buxtehude
  Vonnegut, K. The no-talent kid
Music to die by. Highsmith, P.
MUSICAL INSTRUMENTS
  Coates, G. S. The horn
The **musician**. Saroyan, A.
MUSICIANS
  See also Accordionists; Cellists; Conduc-
    tors (Music); Drummers; Guitarists; Harp-
    ists; Oboe players; Pianists; Trombonists;
    Trumpet players; Violinists
  Alvarez, A. Heat rises
  Anderson, D. Barrie (cont.)
  Baca, J. S. Bull's blood
  Becker, G. Black Elvis
  Bryks, R. Artists in the ghetto
  Budnitz, J. Composer
  Chekhov, A. P. Romance with double-bass
  Chekhov, A. P. Rothschild's fiddle
  Cody, L. Walking blues
  Cody, L. Woke up this morning
  De Lint, C. Ten for the devil

MUSICIANS—*Continued*

Dumas, H. Will the circle be unbroken?

Eakin, W. The miracle of Swamp Gas Jackson

Earle, S. Doghouse roses

Fleming, R. Speak no evil

Gates, D. The wonders of the invisible world

Gay, W. Good 'til now

Greer, R. O. The real thing

Hegi, U. The juggler

Howard, C. McCulla's kid

Johnson, D. Clay's thinking

Kelman, J. Comic cuts

King, S. The wedding gig

Kohler, S. Youth

Levinson, R. S. Good career moves

Mastretta, A. Aunt Paulina

Mesler, C. The growth and death of Buddy Gardner

Packer, Z. Every tongue shall confess

Parker, G. Bad nose

Shrayer-Petrov, D. Jonah and Sarah

Smith, S. J. Oboe camp

Spatz, G. Zigzag cabinet

Stern, D. In the country of the young

Vachss, A. H. Goin' down slow

VanderMeer, J. Black Duke blues

Wharton, E. A glimpse

MUSLIM WOMEN

Moulessehoul, M. The wicked tongue

MUSLIMS

See also Islam; Muslim women

Aidoo, A. A. A gift from somewhere

Azadeh, C. The marriage at Antibes

Berrada, Mohammed. A life in detail

Bowles, P. A friend of the world

Bowles, P. He of the assembly

Bowles, P. The time of friendship

Gabriel, D. The blind woman

Gabriel, D. The reincarnation of Donaldo Fuertes

Nair, M. Sixteen days in December

Pittalwala, I. Ramadan

Raboteau, E. I. Kavita through glass

Ṣāliḥ, al-Ṭ. A handful of dates

Wharton, E. The seed of the faith

Muss-Barnes, Eric

Born of the night

Tales from The Dark Tower; illustrated by Joseph Vargo; edited by Joseph Vargo and Christine Filipak

MUTATION (BIOLOGY)

Bear, G. Blood music

Long, A. R. The thought-monster

Lumley, B. David's worm

Reed, R. The remoras

Sturgeon, T. The golden helix

Weinbaum, S. G. The adaptive ultimate

Mute Milton. Harrison, H.

MUTE PERSONS

Girardi, R. The primordial face

Gwyn, A. The offering

Thomas, D. The girl from follow

MUTILATION

Evenson, B.

Evenson, B. The gravediggers

MUTINY

Clement, H. Uncommon sense

Mutiny of the bounty hunter. McInerny, R. M.

Mutuality of interests. Huffman, B., Jr.

Muza. Bunin, I. A.

My Anabasis. Alexis, A.

My baby . . . West, D.

My baby ran off with Edouard. Broudy, O.

My Bear. Rosenblatt, R.

My Berlin. Özdamar, E. S.

My big red heart. Carter, E.

My brother. Tammuz, B.

My brother can tell. Saunders, G.

My brother's keeper. Philp, G.

My childhood. Douglas, B.

My Communist. Hansen, R.

My Confession. Phillian, G. S.

My conversations with Aunt Marie. Fischerová, D.

My cousin Rachel's Uncle Murray. Isaacs, S.

My date with Satan. Richter, S.

My daughter's name is Sarah. Beagle, P. S.

My dead brother comes to America. Godin, A.

My death. Stanton, M.

My dinner with Aunt Kate. Cross, A.

My eldest. Kelman, J.

My Ex-Boyfriend's Wife. Lieberman, L.

My fabulous Baku fortune. Ripp, V.

My family, posing for Rodin. Vaz, K.

My father addresses me on the facts of old age. Paley, G.

My father, dancing. Broyard, B.

My father in an elevator with Anita Fanska, August 1976. Orner, P.

My father on the verge of disgrace. Updike, J.

My father, the Englishman, and I. Farah, N.

My Father, the Perfect Man. Narayanan, V.

My father weeping. Smith, S. J.

My father's business. Haslett, A.

My father's Chinese wives. Loh, S. T.

My father's deaths. Amichai, Y.

My father's house. Waugh, E.

My Favorite Dentist. Corin, L.

My favorite lies. Hamel, R.

My first fee. Babel´, I.

My first goose. Babel´, I.

My flamboyant grandson. Saunders, G.

My friend Bingham. James, H.

My friend B's feast. Hendel, Y.

"My funeral". Alas, L.

My funny Valentine. Brathwaite, E. K.

My grandfather dreams of fences. Nair, M.

My grandmother, the grandmaster. Alameddine, R.

My grandmother's tale of how Crab-o lost his head. Antoni, R.

My grandmother's tale of the buried treasure and how she defeated the King of Chacachacari and the entire American Army with her venus-flytraps. Antoni, R.

My guardian, Claire. Wells, K.

My hand is just fine where it is. Gay, W.

My heroic mythic journey. Jones, T.

My history. Touré

My idea of fun [excerpt] Self, W.

My Kid's Dog. Hansen, R.

My Kingdom for Jones. Schramm, W.

My kinsman, Major Molineux. Hawthorne, N.

My lady tongue. Sussex, L.

My lady's jewels. Hodgson, W. H.

My last deer. Ziegler, I.

My last essay. Singleton, G.

My last martini. Gifford, B.

My life. Lavers, N.

My life as a bat. Atwood, M.

My life as a bird. De Lint, C.
My life as a judo master. McBrearty, R. G.
My life, for promotional use only. Lipsyte, S.
My life in the city. Troncoso, S.
My life up till now. Dixon, S.
My literary life. Saroyan, A.
My little Marjie. Epstein, J.
My little Marjie: a story. Epstein, J.
My little suede shoes. Harvey, J.
My Lord Bag of Rice. Bly, C.
My Mafia moll. Gold, H.
My mausoleum. Barone, D.
My Miracle. Graham, P.
My mistress' eyes are nothing like the sun. Bausch, R.
My mother. Kincaid, J.
My mother, behind the glass. Vafi, F.
My mother said. Weldon, F.
My mother was a witch. Tenn, W.
My mother's first lover. Rabb, M.
My mother's garden. Shonk, K.
My mother's heart. Wolfe, S.
My mother's memoirs, my father's lie, and other true stories. Banks, R.
My mother's war. Wisenberg, S. L.
My Mother's Wedding Dress. Williford, L.
My mustache. Vukcevich, R.
My name is Stephen Mann. Anderson, D.
My one and only bomb shelter. Smolens, J.
My Only Jew. Krieger, E.
My people, your people. Andersen, K.
My people's waltz. Phillips, D. R.
My present wife. Etchison, D.
My quarrel with Hersh Rasseyner. Grade, C.
My romance. Glover, D. H.
My secret life with Amy. Manley, M. S.
My Secret War. Balázs, T. P.
My side of the story. Nailah, A.
My singular Irene. Alcántara Almánzar, J.
My sister Alice. Stewart, I.
My sister's novel. Stanton, M.
My slave. Biguenet, J.
My son, Max. Bradbury, R.
My son the hero. Boylan, C.
My stuff. Hart, R.
My teacher, Mr. Katz. Škvorecký, J.
My Uncle Ezekiel. Habila, H.
My Uncle Kohn. Škvorecký, J.
My vampire cake. Watson, I.
My very last possession. Pak, W.-S.
My weddings. Krouse, E.
My widow. Boyle, T. C.
My world of the unknown. Rifaat, A.
Mycroft's great game. Lovisi, G.
Myers, Amy
    Happy the man . . .
        Royal whodunnits; edited by Mike Ashley
    The Rightful King of England
        The best British mysteries; edited by Maxim Jakubowski
Myers, Joan
    Copycat
        A Deadly dozen; tales of murder from members of Sisters in Crime/Los Angeles; edited by Susan B. Casmier, Aljean Harmetz and Cynthia Lawrence

Myers, Tamar
    Chicken catch a tory
        Death dines at 8:30; edited by Claudia Bishop and Nick DiChario
Myers, Tim
    The stay-at-home thief
        A Hot and sultry night for crime; edited by Jeffery Deaver
The myna from Peacock Garden. Naiyer Masud
Myra meets his family. Fitzgerald, F. S.
Myrmo, Millen
    Mama dear
        Dead on demand; the best of ghost story weekend; edited by Elizabeth Engstrom
Myself as a delicious peach. Sellers, H.
Mysko, Madeleine
    But Little
        The Hudson Review v57 no2 p259-70 Summ 2004
Mysteries. Kavaler, R.
The mysteries of ubiquitin. Barrett, A.
The mysterious death of the shadow man. Aquino, J. T.
The mysterious disappearance of Alon Shemesh. Keret, E.
The mysterious events at night. Škvorecký, J.
MYSTERY AND DETECTIVE STORIES
        See also Crime and criminals; International intrigue; Murder stories
Asimov, I. The men who read Isaac Asimov
Breen, J. L. The Pun Detective and the Danny Boy killer
Chan, D. M. Mystery boy
Christie, A. Problem at sea
Cook, R. and Hogan, E. Obsidian harvest
Hodgson, W. H. The finding of the Graiken
Lupoff, R. A. Green ice
Paul, B. Play nice
Pronzini, B. and Malzberg, B. N. The Lyran case
Pronzini, B. and Malzberg, B. N. Prose bowl
Pronzini, B. and Malzberg, B. N. Vanishing point
Pronzini, B. and Malzberg, B. N. Whither thou, ghost
Wellen, E. The adventure of the blind alley
        Afghanistan
Crider, B. The adventure of the young British soldier
        Algeria
Pronzini, B. The desperate ones
        Antarctic regions
Smith, J. The end of the earth
        Austria
Groller, B. The vault break-in
Groner, A. The golden bullet
        Canada
Engel, H. The reading
        Caribbean Region
Hart, C. G. Henrie O's holiday
Hoch, E. D. The theft of the bingo card
Pronzini, B. Out of the depths
        Egypt
Christie, A. The adventure of the Egyptian tomb
Douglas, C. N. The mummy case: a midnight Louie past life adventure
Peters, E. The locked tomb mystery
Schweighofer, P. The Cairo cat caper

MYSTERY AND DETECTIVE STORIES—
Continued

England

Adams, J. I do like to be beside the seaside
Allingham, M. One morning they'll hang him
Altman, S.-E. A case of royal blood
Bear, E. Tiger! tiger!
Berkeley, A. The avenging chance
Berkeley, A. Double bluff
Berkeley, A. "Mr. Bearstowe says ..."
Berkeley, A. The mystery of Horne's Copse
Berkeley, A. Perfect alibi
Berkeley, A. Unsound mind
Berkeley, A. White butterfly
Berkeley, A. The wrong jar
Biggle, L. The case of the headless witness
Black, C. Cabaret aux Assassins
Breen, J. L. The adventure of the mooning sentry
Breen, J. L. The adventures of the Cheshire Cheese
Brett, S. Exit, pursued
Brite, P. Z. and Ferguson, D. The curious case of Miss Violet Stone
Bruce, C. The adventure of the dying doctor
Cannell, D. Bridal flowers
Cannell, D. One night at a time
Carroll, L. Before the adventures
Chesterton, G. K. The wrong shape
Christie, A. The case of the discontented soldier
Clark, S. Nightmare in wax
Cody, L. Spasmo
Coward, M. The shortest distance
Coward, M. Three nil
Davis, L. Body zone
Day, B. The adventure of the curious canary
DeAndrea, W. L. The adventure of the Christmas tree
DeAndrea, W. L. The adventure of the cripple parade
Derleth, A. W. The adventure of the Penny Magenta
Doherty, P. C. The monk's tale
Dôle, G. The witch of Greenwich
Doyle, Sir A. C. The adventure of Silver Blaze
Doyle, Sir A. C. The adventure of the Bruce-Partington plans
Eccles, M. Peril at Melford house
Effinger, G. A. The adventure of the celestial snows
Estleman, L. D. The riddle of the golden monkeys
Evans, L. Pussy Galore
Ewing, C. D. And the others. . .
Finch, P. The mystery of the hanged man's puzzle
Fraser, A. Jemima Shore at the sunny grave
Fraser, A. Jemima Shore's first case
Frazer, M. The witch's tale
Gaiman, N. A study in emerald
George, E. Exposure
Gilden, M. The adventure of the forgotten umbrella
Granger, A. Murder at midday
Gregory, S. The trebuchet murder
Hambly, B. The adventure of the antiquarian's niece
Hambly, B. The dollmaker of Marigold Walk
Hamilton, P. F. The suspect genome

Harvey, J. Bird of paradise
Harvey, J. Cheryl
Harvey, J. Confirmation
Harvey, J. Cool blues
Harvey, J. Dexterity
Harvey, J. My little suede shoes
Harvey, J. Now's the time
Harvey, J. She rote
Harvey, J. Slow burn
Harvey, J. Stupendous
Harvey, J. Work
Hill, R. The game of dog
Hill, R. True Thomas
Hoch, E. D. V-2
Kaminsky, S. M. The final toast
Kiernan, C. R. The drowned geologist
Kurland, M. Years ago and in a different place
Landis, G. A. The singular habits of wasps
Lebbon, T. The horror of the many faces
Linscott, G. A scandal in winter
Lovesey, P. The crime of Miss Oyster Brown
Lovisi, G. Mycroft's great game
Lowder, J. The weeping masks
Lupoff, R. A. The adventure of the Voorish Sign
Lupoff, R. A. The adventures of the boulevard assassin
Lupoff, R. A. The incident of the impecunious chevalier
MacIntyre, F. G. The adventure of Exham Priory
Mallory, M. The riddle of the young protestor
Marsh, Dame N. I can find my way out
McCrumb, S. The vale of the white horse
Moffat, G. The dark tower
Moody, S. Oliphants can remember
Pelan, J. The mystery of the worm
Perry, A. The case of the bloodless sock
Perry, A. Sing a song of sixpence
Perry, S. The case of the wavy black dagger
Reaves, M. The adventure of the Arab's manuscript
Rendell, R. The case of the shaggy caps
Rendell, R. When the wedding was over
Robertson, L. Mrs. Hudson reminisces
Robinson, P. In Flanders Fields
Robinson, P. Missing in action
Satterthwait, W. A mishap at the manor
Schreiber, N. Call me Wiggins
Sheffield, C. The devil of Malkirk
Sheffield, C. The heart of Ahura Mazda
Sheffield, C. The Lambeth immortal
Sheffield, C. The phantom of Dunwell Cove
Sheffield, C. The Solborne vampire
Sheffield, C. The treasure of Odirex
Stableford, B. M. Art in the blood
Stashower, D. The adventure of the agitated actress
Todd, C. The man who never was
Tremayne, P. A study in orange
Tremayne, P. Those that trespass
Vourlis, J. P. A case of insomnia
Wheat, C. The adventure of the rara avis
Wheat, C. Oh, to be in England!
Willis, C. Cat's paw
Wilson, D. N. and Macomber, P. L. Death did not become him

France

Alvarez, A. Death by bricolage

MYSTERY AND DETECTIVE STORIES—
France—*Continued*

Poe, E. A. The purloined letter
Simenon, G. The little house at Croix-Rousse

Germany
Böttcher, M. The detective
Müllner, A. The caliber
Streckfuss, A. The Star Tavern

Greece
Brett, S. The girls in Villa Costas

Hong Kong
Marshall, W. L. Them!

India
Keating, H. R. F. The hound of the hanging gardens
Keating, H. R. F. Just only one little mystery-pistery

Ireland
Bishop, P. Celtic noir
Breen, J. L. Jerry Brogan and the Kilkenny cats
Lee, W. W. Feis
Lee, W. W. Skiv
Tremayne, P. Abbey sinister
Tremayne, P. At the tent of Holofernes
Tremayne, P. A canticle for Wulfstan
Tremayne, P. Hemlock at Vespers
Tremayne, P. The High King's sword
Tremayne, P. Holy blood
Tremayne, P. The horse that died for shame
Tremayne, P. Invitation to a poisoning
Tremayne, P. Murder by miracle
Tremayne, P. Murder in repose
Tremayne, P. Our lady of death
Tremayne, P. The poisoned chalice
Tremayne, P. Scattered thorns
Tremayne, P. A scream from the sepulcher
Tremayne, P. Tarnished halo
Tremayne, P. Those that trespass

Italy
Maraini, D. Today is today is today
Marlowe, S. Wanted—dead and alive
Maron, M. Roman's holiday
Pronzini, B. Blood money

Japan
Waldrop, H. The latter days of the law

Kenya
Collins, M. The savage

Netherlands
Van de Wetering, J. The bongo bungler
Van de Wetering, J. The deadly egg
Van de Wetering, J. Heron Island
Van de Wetering, J. Holiday patrol
Van de Wetering, J. Houseful of mussels
Van de Wetering, J. Hup three
Van de Wetering, J. The letter in the peppermint jar
Van de Wetering, J. Letter present
Van de Wetering, J. The machine gun and the mannequin
Van de Wetering, J. Non-interference
Van de Wetering, J. The sergeant's cat
Van de Wetering, J. Six this, six that
Van de Wetering, J. Sure, blue, and dead, too
Van de Wetering, J. There goes Ravelaar

Northern Ireland
Howard, C. The Dublin eye

Rome
Saylor, S. Poppy and the poisoned cake

Russia
Chekhov, A. P. The Swedish match
Kaminsky, S. M. Punishment
Kaminsky, S. M. Snow

Scotland
Allyn, D. St. Margaret's kitten
Beaton, M. C. Handle with care
Perry, A. and Saxon, M. The case of the Highland hoax
Rankin, I. Saint Nicked
Rankin, I. Tell me who to kill

Singapore
Pronzini, B. Jade

Switzerland
Hoch, E. D. Interpol: the case of the modern medusa

United States
Albert, S. W. Bloom where you're planted
Albert, S. W. A deadly chocolate valentine
Albert, S. W. Death of a Rose Rustler
Albert, S. W. Ivy's wild, wonderful weeds
Albert, S. W. The knat who became a hero
Albert, S. W. Mustard madness
Albert, S. W. The pennyroyal plot
Albert, S. W. The Rosemary caper
Albert, S. W. An unthymely death
Albert, S. W. A violet death
Allingham, M. Money to burn
Allyn, D. Miracles! Happen!
Anderson, P. Dead phone
Armstrong, C. St. Patrick's Day in the morning
Asimov, I. The acquisitive chuckle
Asimov, I. Early Sunday morning
Asimov, I. The guest's guest
Asimov, I. The haunted cabin
Asimov, I. The iron gem
Asimov, I. The last story
Asimov, I. Lost in a space warp
Asimov, I. Northwestward
Asimov, I. The obvious factor
Asimov, I. Ph as in Phony
Asimov, I. Police at the door
Asimov, I. The redhead
Asimov, I. Sixty million trillion combinations
Asimov, I. To the barest
Asimov, I. Triple devil
Asimov, I. The woman in the bar
Asimov, I. The wrong house
Asimov, I. Yes, but why?
Ayres, N. Delta double-deal
Bishop, P. Derringer
Bishop, P. Ebenezer
Bishop, P. Quint and the braceros
Bland, E. T. The canasta club
Block, L. Batman's helpers
Block, L. By the dawn's early light
Block, L. Let's get lost
Boucher, A. The girl who married a monster
Boucher, A. The stripper
Bowen, R. The proof of the pudding
Breen, J. L. All-star team
Breen, J. L. The Babe Ruth murder case
Breen, J. L. The big nap
Breen, J. L. The body in the bullpen
Breen, J. L. The cat and the Kinetophone
Breen, J. L. Designated murderer
Breen, J. L. Diamond Dick
Breen, J. L. The drowning icecube
Breen, J. L. Fall of a hero

MYSTERY AND DETECTIVE STORIES—

United States—*Continued*

Breen, J. L. Horsehide sleuth
Breen, J. L. Insider trading
Breen, J. L. Instant replay
Breen, J. L. Kill the umpire
Breen, J. L. The male and female hogan
Breen, J. L. Malice at the mike
Breen, J. L. The Mother's-Day doubleheader
Breen, J. L. The number 12 jinx
Breen, J. L. Old-timers' game
Breen, J. L. A piece of the auction
Breen, J. L. Streak to death
Breen, J. L. Throw out the first ax
Brill, T. O! little town of Bedlam
Brown, F. Cry silence
Browning, S. Neighborhood watch
Carole Nelson Douglas. Sax and the single cat
Chandler, R. Red wind
Charteris, L. The mugs' game
Christmas, J. Takeout
Coel, M. A well-respected man
Cohen, S. Hello! my name is Irving Wasserman
Collins, M. A. Flowers for Bill O'Reilly
Collins, M. A. Inconvenience store
Collins, M. A. Kaddish for the kid
Collins, M. A. Unreasonable doubt
Collins, M. The bizarre case expert
Collins, M. Hot night homicide
Crider, B. Cap'n Bob and Gus
Crider, B. Gored
Crider, B. One of our leprechauns is missing
Crider, B. Poo-Poo
Crider, B. See what the boys in the locked room
    will have
Crider, B. and Crider, J. Chocolate moose
Cross, A. My dinner with Aunt Kate
Crumley, J. The Mexican pig bandit
Daheim, M. Just so much garbage
Daly, C. J. Just another stiff
Danger, N. 8-3-oh
Davidson, D. M. Cold turkey
Davis, D. S. Justina
Davis, D. S. The puppet
Davis, N. Something for the sweeper
DeAndrea, W. L. Snowy reception
Douglas, C. N. Licensed to koi
Douglas, C. N. Sax and the single cat
Estleman, L. D. The anniversary waltz
Estleman, L. D. I'm in the book
Estleman, L. D. Lady on ice
Estleman, L. D. Redneck
Estleman, L. D. State of grace
Faherty, T. The third Manny
Fallis, G. And maybe the horse will learn to
    sing
Faulkner, W. An error in chemistry
Futrelle, J. The problem of cell 13
Gardner, E. S. Leg man
Gores, J. Sleep the big sleep
Gores, J. Smart guys don't snore
Gorman, E. The reason why
Grafton, S. The Parker shotgun
Grape, J. Cat o'nine lives
Green, A. K. Missing: page thirteen
Greenleaf, S. Iris
Greer, R. O. Red-nickel rhythms
Hammett, D. The assistant murderer
Hammett, D. Death on Pine Street

Hammett, D. The first thin man
Hammett, D. The gutting of Couffignal
Hammett, D. House dick
Hammett, D. A man called Spade
Hammett, D. A man named Thin
Hammett, D. Night shots
Hammett, D. Nightmare town
Hammett, D. One hour
Hammett, D. They only hang you once
Hammett, D. Tom, Dick, or Harry
Hammett, D. Too many have lived
Hammett, D. Two sharp knives
Hammett, D. Who killed Bob Teal?
Hammett, D. Zigzags of treachery
Hansen, J. Survival
Hansen, J. Widower's walk
Hart, C. G. An almost perfect heist
Hart, C. G. An almost perfect murder
Hart, C. G. Dead in the net
Hart, C. G. Her good name
Hart, C. G. None of my business, but . . .
Hart, C. G. Nothing ventured
Hart, C. G. Out of the ashes
Hart, C. G. Remembrance
Hart, C. G. Upstaging murder
Healy, J. F. A Book of Kells
Healy, J. F. Hodegetria
Healy, J. F. The lady from yesterday
Healy, J. F. Legacy
Healy, J. F. The slow blink
Healy, J. F. Voir dire
Hess, J. The Maggody files: Death in bloom
Hess, J. The Maggody files: Hillbilly cat
Hillerman, T. Chee's witch
Hoch, E. D. The circle of ink
Hoch, E. D. The problem of the yellow wallpa-
    per
Hoch, E. D. The sweating statue
Hoch, E. D. The theft of the Halloween pump-
    kin
Hoch, E. D. The theft of the sandwich board
Hodgson, W. H. The case of the Chinese curio
    dealer
Hunter, E. Dead men don't dream
Hunter, E. Deadlier than the mail
Jakes, J. The girl in the golden cage
Jakes, J. Little man—It's been a busy day
Jakes, J. Unc foils show foe
Jakes, J. Unc probes pickle plot
Kahn, M. A. The bread of affliction
Kaminsky, S. M. Bitter lemons
Kaminsky, S. M. Blowout in Little Man Flats
Kaminsky, S. M. Busted blossoms
Kaminsky, S. M. Confession
Kaminsky, S. M. It's a wise child who knows
Kaminsky, S. M. Joyce's children
Kaminsky, S. M. Listen, my children
Kaminsky, S. M. The man who shot Lewis
    Vance
Kaminsky, S. M. The voice of a child
Kantner, R. Something simple
Kemelman, H. The nine mile walk
Kenney, S. Aunt Agatha leaving
Kress, N. Plant engineering
Lachnit, C. Blind
L'Amour, L. A friend of a hero
L'Amour, L. Time of terror
L'Amour, L. The unexpected corpse
L'Amour, L. The vanished blonde

MYSTERY AND DETECTIVE STORIES—

United States—*Continued*

LaPierre, J. Sex, lies, and apple pie
Lee, W. W. Check up
Lee, W. W. The disappearance of Edna Guberman
Lee, W. W. Dust and ashes
Lee, W. W. The other woman
Lee, W. W. Red Feather's daughter
Lee, W. W. Salad days
Lee, W. W. Winston's wife
Leon, A. d. Tell me Moore
Levitsky, R. Jacob's voice
Little, B. Maya's mother
Lochte, D. Get the message
Lochte, D. Lucky dog
Lochte, D. Murder at Mardi Gras
Lochte, D. A murder of import
Lochte, D. Rappin' dog
Lochte, D. Sad-eyed blonde
Lochte, D. A tough case to figure
Lupoff, R. A. Old folks at home
Lupoff, R. A. The second drug
Lupoff, R. A. You don't know me, Charlie
Lutz, J. Before you leap
Lutz, J. Flotsam and jetsam
Lutz, J. The litigants
Lutz, J. The man in the morgue
Lutz, J. Only one way to land
Lutz, J. Ride the lightning
Lutz, J. The right to sing the blues
Lutz, J. The romantics
Lutz, J. So young, so fair, so dead
Lutz, J. The thunder of guilt
Lutz, J. Time exposure
Lutz, J. Typographical error
Lutz, J. What you don't know can hurt you
Lutz, J. Where is Harry Beal?
MacDonald, J. D. Murder for money
Macdonald, R. Gone girl
Macdonald, R. Guilt-edged blonde
Malone, M. Love and other crimes
Maron, M. Mixed blessings
Maron, M. The third element
Maron, M. What's in a name?
Matthews, C. Character flaw: a Robbie Stanton story
Matthews, C. Gentle insanities
Matthews, C. Promises made and broken
Mayor, A. Instinct
McGivern, W. P. Death comes gift-wrapped
McInerny, R. M. The base of the triangle; a Father Dowling mystery
McInerny, R. M. The coveted correspondence
Monfredo, M. G. Buffalo gals, won't you come out tonight
Morgan, D. The Windsor ballet
Mosley, W. Amber gate
Mosley, W. Crimson stain
Mosley, W. Gator green
Mosley, W. Gray-eyed death
Mosley, W. Lavender
Mosley, W. Silver lining
Mosley, W. Smoke
Muller, M. Benny's space
Muller, M. Deceptions
Muller, M. The impostor
Muller, M. Recycle
Muller, M. Up at the Riverside

Muller, M. Wild mustard
Nevins, F. M., Jr. Consultation in the dark
Nevins, F. M., Jr. Counterplot
Nevins, F. M., Jr. The kumquats affairs
O'Callaghan, M. Bad news
O'Callaghan, M. A change of clients
O'Callaghan, M. Deal with the Devil
O'Callaghan, M. Diamonds are for never
O'Callaghan, M. Somewhere South of Melrose
Padgett, A. and Dennis, D. Just stunning
Paretsky, S. The case of the Pietro Andromache
Paretsky, S. Grace notes
Paretsky, S. Three-Dot Po
Perelman, S. J. Farewell, my lovely appetizer
Phillips, G. The sleeping detective
Pickard, N. Dust devil
Pickard, N. A rock and a hard place
Pickard, N. Sign of the times
Prather, R. S. The double take
Pronzini, B. La bellezza delle bellezze
Pronzini, B. The big bite
Pronzini, B. Dead man's slough
Pronzini, B. The desert limited
Pronzini, B. Fergus O'Hara, detective
Pronzini, B. The highbinders
Pronzini, B. A killing in Xanadu
Pronzini, B. Medium rare
Pronzini, B. One night at Dolores Park
Pronzini, B. One of those cases
Pronzini, B. Shade work
Pronzini, B. Smuggler's island
Pronzini, B. Souls burning
Pronzini, B. Stacked deck
Pronzini, B. Stakeout
Pronzini, B. and Kurland, M. Vanishing act
Queen, E. The adventure of the Dauphin doll
Queen, E. The adventure of the one-penny black
Queen, E. The adventure of the President's half disme
Queen, E. Man bites dog
Queen, E. A matter of seconds
Quill, M. Death takes the veil
Quill, M. Miss Butterfingers
Quill, M. The other urn
Quill, M. A rose is a rose is a rose
Randisi, R. J. Green legs and glam
Randisi, R. J. The nickel Derby
Rawlings, E. Poison
Redman, B. R. The perfect crime
Roberts, G. Heart break
Rozan, S. J. Double-crossing Delancey
Rozan, S. J. Hoops
Schutz, B. M. Lost and found
Singer, S. Lost polars
Smith, J. Always Othello
Steinberg, J. Wailing reed
Stout, R. Fourth of July picnic
Stout, R. Poison à la carte
Vachss, A. H. Everybody pays
Van Belkom, E. Catabolism
Weinberg, R. The apocalypse quatrain
Weinberg, R. The midnight el
Weinberg, R. Seven drops of blood
Weinberg, R. Terror by night
Westlake, D. E. Now what?
Westlake, D. E. Sinner or saint
Yaffe, J. Mom remembers
Mystery boy. Chan, D. M.
The **Mystery** Dogs. Grove, F.

The **mystery** of George Jones. DeLancey, K.
The **mystery** of Joelle. Hood, A.
Mystery of numbers. Agee, J.
The **mystery** of the derelict. Hodgson, W. H.
The **mystery** of the hanged man's puzzle. Finch,
    P.
The **mystery** of the worm. Pelan, J.
Mystery Play. Shepley, J.
Mystery Spot. Newman, D. A.
MYSTICISM
    De Lint, C. Second chances
    Girardi, R. Arcana mundi
The **mystified** magistrate. Sade, marquis de
MYTHICAL ANIMALS
        See also Dragons; Griffins; Unicorns;
      Vampires; Werewolves
    Borges, J. L. The house of Asterion
    Cadnum, M. Bite the hand
    De Lint, C. The buffalo man
    De Lint, C. Embracing the mystery
    De Lint, C. Trading hearts at the Half Kaffe
    Cafe
    Lindholm, M. Bones for Dulath
MYTHOLOGY
        See also Helen of Troy (Legendary char-
      acter); Medea (Greek mythology); Mythical
      animals
    Gaiman, N. The Monarch of the Glen
    Kelly, J. P. Hubris
    Morris, K. The regent of the north
    Ovid. Lycaon's punishment
    Williamson, C. The blood-red sea
Myths of the Martian future. Brown, E.

N

Na gCopaleen, Myles *See* O'Brien, Flann, 1911-
    1966
Na Gopaleen, Myles *See* O'Brien, Flann, 1911-
    1966
Nabokov, Vladimir Vladimirovich
    Symbols and signs
        Wonderful town; New York stories from The
        New Yorker; edited by David Remnick
        with Susan Choi
    "That in Aleppo once. . . "
        The Best American short stories of the
        century; John Updike, editor, Katrina
        Kenison, coeditor; with an introduction by
        John Updike
        The Vintage book of amnesia; an anthology;
        edited by Jonathan Lethem
NABOKOV, VLADIMIR VLADIMIROVICH,
    1899-1977
           About
    Bukiet, M. J. Squeak, memory
Naboth's vineyard. Post, M. D.
Nachman, of Bratslav *See* Naḥman, of Bratslav,
    1772-1811
Nachman. Michaels, L.
Nachman at the races. Michaels, L.
Nachman ben Simchah *See* Naḥman, of Bratslav,
    1772-1811
Nachman from Los Angeles. Michaels, L.
Nackles. Westlake, D. E.
Nadigo. Cohen, S.
Nadirs. Müller, H.

Nagai, Mariko
    Grafting
        The Pushcart prize XXVI; best of the small
        presses, an annual small press reader; ed-
        ited by Bill Henderson and the Pushcart
        prize editors
NAGASAKI (JAPAN) *See* Japan—Nagasaki
Nagata, Linda
    Goddesses
        Nebula awards showcase 2002; edited by Kim
        Stanley Robinson
Nagle, P. G.
    The courtship of Captain Swenk
        The Blue and the gray undercover; edited by
        Ed Gorman
Nagy, Estep
    The Mathematician Repents
        Southwest Review v89 no1 p37-46 2004
Nagy, Steve
    The Hanged Man of Oz
        Gathering the bones; original stories from the
        world's masters of horror; edited by Dennis
        Etchison, Ramsey Campbell and Jack Dann
Naḥman, of Bratslav
    A tale of a king's son who was switched at
        birth with a maidservant's son
        Neugroschel, J. No star too beautiful; Yiddish
        stories from 1382 to the present; compiled
        and translated by Joachim Neugroschel
A **nail** on the head. Boylan, C.
Nailah, Anika
    Alice & Jesse
        Nailah, A. Free and other stories
    Bucket
        Nailah, A. Free and other stories
    Deena
        Nailah, A. Free and other stories
    Four
        Nailah, A. Free and other stories
    Free
        Nailah, A. Free and other stories
    French
        Nailah, A. Free and other stories
    Inside out
        Nailah, A. Free and other stories
    Jarvis
        Nailah, A. Free and other stories
    Joey falling
        Nailah, A. Free and other stories
    My side of the story
        Nailah, A. Free and other stories
    Professor
        Nailah, A. Free and other stories
    The ride
        Nailah, A. Free and other stories
    Sunday visit
        Nailah, A. Free and other stories
    Trudy
        Nailah, A. Free and other stories
Naipaul, V. S. (Vidiadhar Surajprasad)
    Bohemia
        The New Yorker v77 no32 p66-71 O 22 2001
    The night watchman's occurrence book
        The Oxford book of Caribbean short stories;
        edited by Stewart Brown and John
        Wickham
    Suckers
        The New Yorker v80 no15 p76-85 Je 7 2004

Naipaul, Vidiadhar Surajprasad *See* Naipaul, V.
  S. (Vidiadhar Surajprasad), 1932-
Nair, Meera
  A certain sense of place
    Nair, M. Video; stories
  The curry leaf tree
    Nair, M. Video; stories
  The lodger in room 726
    Nair, M. Video; stories
  My grandfather dreams of fences
    Nair, M. Video; stories
  The sculptor of sands
    Nair, M. Video; stories
  Sixteen days in December
    Nair, M. Video; stories
  Summer
    Nair, M. Video; stories
  Video
    Nair, M. Video; stories
  Vishnukumar's Valentine's Day
    Nair, M. Video; stories
  A warm welcome to the President, insh'allah!
    Nair, M. Video; stories
Naiyer Masud
  Ba'i's mourners
    Naiyer Masud. Essence of camphor; translated
      from the Urdu by Muhammad Umar
      Memon and others
  Essence of camphor
    Naiyer Masud. Essence of camphor; translated
      from the Urdu by Muhammad Umar
      Memon and others
  Interregnum
    Naiyer Masud. Essence of camphor; translated
      from the Urdu by Muhammad Umar
      Memon and others
  The myna from Peacock Garden
    Naiyer Masud. Essence of camphor; translated
      from the Urdu by Muhammad Umar
      Memon and others
  Obscure domains of fear and desire
    Naiyer Masud. Essence of camphor; translated
      from the Urdu by Muhammad Umar
      Memon and others
  Remains of the Ray family
    Naiyer Masud. Essence of camphor; translated
      from the Urdu by Muhammad Umar
      Memon and others
  Sheesha ghat
    Naiyer Masud. Essence of camphor; translated
      from the Urdu by Muhammad Umar
      Memon and others
Nakagami, Kenji
  The cape
    Nakagami, K. The cape and other stories
      from the Japanese ghetto; translated, with a
      preface and afterword by Eve Zimmerman
  House on fire
    Nakagami, K. The cape and other stories
      from the Japanese ghetto; translated, with a
      preface and afterword by Eve Zimmerman
  Red hair
    Nakagami, K. The cape and other stories
      from the Japanese ghetto; translated, with a
      preface and afterword by Eve Zimmerman
Naked. Brookhouse, C.
Naked. Kurlansky, M.
The **naked** ape. Murray, S.
The **naked** lady. Bell, M. S.

The **naked** running boy. Brown, J.
Nakhman *See* Naḥman, of Bratslav, 1772-1811
NAME, BILLY, 1940-
About
  Rucker, R. v. B. The Andy Warhol sandcandle
Name and number. Lumley, B.
Name of love. Daugharty, J.
The **name** of the dead. Anderson, R.
NAMES, PERSONAL *See* Personal names
The **names.** Maso, C.
The **names** of stars in Bengali. Divakaruni, C. B.
Namesake. Mencken, S. H.
NAMIBIA
  Jafta, M. The home-coming
Naming stories. Joseph, D.
Naming the dead. McAuley, P. J.
Naming the Monster. Foster, P. K.
Naming the names. Devlin, A.
Naming the stones. Lynn, D. H.
Nana's trilogy. Matiella, A. C.
Nancy. Miller, R.
Nancy & Tonya & the long hard rain. Baruth, P.
Nancy Druid. Lisick, B.
Nangle, Paula
  Svikiro
    Michigan Quarterly Review v40 no1 p223-37
      Wint 2001
Nanite, star bright. Huff, T.
NANNIES *See* Governesses; Nursemaids
The **nanny** trap. Wexler, M.
Nano returns. Garcia, L. G.
Nanunculus. Watson, I.
Nap Time. Franklin, T.
NAPLES (ITALY) *See* Italy—Naples
NAPOLEON I, EMPEROR OF THE FRENCH,
  1769-1821
About
  Empire
  Hoch, E. D. The day the dogs died
Naranjo, Alberto Guerra
  There are blows in life so hard—
    Grand Street no68 p10-22 Spr 1999
Naranjo, Carmen
  Symbiotic encounter
    Short stories by Latin American women; the
      magic and the real; edited by Celia Correas
      de Zapata; foreword by Isabel Allende
Naratha's shadow. Lee, S. and Miller, S.
Narayanan, Vivek
  My Father, the Perfect Man
    Agni no59 p34-69 2004
NARCISSISM
  Gabrielyan, N. Master of the grass
  Willis, C. In Coppelius's Toyshop
NARCOTIC HABIT *See* Drug addiction
NARCOTICS, CONTROL OF *See* Drug traffic
NARCOTICS AGENTS *See* Drug traffic
Narratology to the people!. Lish, G.
Narrow road. Haskell, J.
Narrow Valley. Lafferty, R. A.
NASA *See* United States. National Aeronautics
  and Space Administration
Nash, Sunny
  Amen
    The African American West; a century of
      short stories; edited by Bruce A. Glasrud
      and Laurie Champion

Naslund, Sena Jeter

The perfecting of the Chopin Valse No. 14 in E Minor

Home and beyond; an anthology of Kentucky short stories; edited by Morris Allen Grubbs; with an introduction by Wade Hall and an afterword by Charles E. May

Natasha. Bezmozgis, D.

Nath, Michael

To Philosophise with a Hammer

Critical Quarterly v45 no1/2 p203-11 Spr/Summ 2003

NATION, CARRY AMELIA MOORE, 1846-1911

About

Collins, B. Carry's cat

NATIONAL AERONAUTICS AND SPACE ADMINISTRATION (U.S.) *See* United States. National Aeronautics and Space Administration

The **national** game. Waugh, E.

NATIONAL SOCIALISM

See also Germany—1918-1945

Bear, G. Through road, no whither

Borges, J. L. Deutsches requiem

Bowen, R. Doppelganger

Girardi, R. The demons tormenting Untersturmführer Hans Otto Graebner

Harrison, H. Down to earth

Kurlansky, M. Vertical administration

Linaweaver, B. Moon of ice

Lupoff, R. A. News from New Providence

Moorcock, M. The case of the Nazi canary

Pearlman, D. D. The drang of speaking forth

Shaw, I. Sailor off the Bremen

Škvorecký, J. My teacher, Mr. Katz

Turtledove, H. The last article

Vapnyar, L. There are Jews in my house

National sovereignty. Fresan, R.

Native sandstone. Meloy, M.

Natoma Street. LeRoy, J. T.

Natsumi Quarra. Jackson, K. A.

Natural causes. Edwards, M.

Natural color. Updike, J.

A **natural** girl. Yates, R.

The **natural** memory. Furman, L.

Naturalezas menores [excerpt] Ortega, A. L.

NATURALISTS

See also Paleontologists

Clement, H. Uncommon sense

Naturally. Puga, M. L.

NATURE

Lopez, B. H. The open lot

Reed, R. A place with shade

Zinovyeva-Annibal, L. D. The monster

Nature. Kawabata, Y.

The **Nature** of Man. Jones, S.

The **nature** of pure evil. Gartner, Z.

Naufrage and diapason. Porter, J. A.

Naumoff, Lawrence

Moon pie over Miami

This is where we live; short stories by 25 contemporary North Carolina writers; edited by Michael McFee

NAVAHO INDIANS *See* Navajo Indians

NAVAJO INDIANS

Grove, F. The Mystery Dogs

Hillerman, T. Chee's witch

Silko, L. Lullaby

NAVAL BATTLES

See also Sea stories

Naval history. Kelman, J.

Navarro, Yvonne

A beacon shall I shine

Lighthouse hauntings; 12 original tales of the supernatural; edited by Charles G. Waugh & Martin H. Greenberg

Navigating by stars. Allegra, D.

Navigating the Kattegat. Simonds, M.

Nawrocki, Sarah

Boys

Nawrocki, S. Camping with strangers; stories

Camping with strangers

Nawrocki, S. Camping with strangers; stories

Dogs

Nawrocki, S. Camping with strangers; stories

Farmer boy

Nawrocki, S. Camping with strangers; stories

Hovercraft

Nawrocki, S. Camping with strangers; stories

Locusts

Nawrocki, S. Camping with strangers; stories

Louise and Al get married

Nawrocki, S. Camping with strangers; stories

Pampas grass day

Nawrocki, S. Camping with strangers; stories

Pressure

Nawrocki, S. Camping with strangers; stories

Star seed

Nawrocki, S. Camping with strangers; stories

Naylor, Gloria

Etta Mae Johnson

The Bluelight corner; black women writing on passion, sex, and romantic love; edited by Rosemarie Robotham

Kiswana Browne

Snapshots: 20th century mother-daughter fiction; edited by Joyce Carol Oates and Janet Berliner

NAZIS *See* National socialism

NAZISM *See* National socialism

Ndebele, Njabulo S. (Njabulo Simakahle)

The prophetess

The Anchor book of modern African stories; edited by Nadežda Obradovic ; with a foreword by Chinua Achebe

Neal Pollack's Passage to Iraq. Pollack, N.

NEANDERTHAL RACE

See also Prehistoric man

Richter, S. The cavemen in the hedges

Near earth object. Aldiss, B. W.

Near enough to home. Skeet, M.

Near miss. Ayers, A.

Near the bone. Smyth, C.

Near to eternity. Ševčovič, P.

Near to gone. Westmoreland, T. A.

Neather, Robert

(jt. auth) See Chan Koon Chung

NEBRASKA

Agee, J. The October horse

Block, R. St. Anthony and the fish

Crane, S. The blue hotel

Hansen, R. Nebraska

King, S. Children of the corn

Martin, L. Bad family

Thomas, D. Frost in the morning

Thomas, D. The getaway

Thomas, D. Grandma Hotel Adams

NEBRASKA—*Continued*

Thomas, D. The joybell

Thomas, D. The Steckley girls

Farm life

See Farm life—Nebraska

Nebraska. Hansen, R.

Necati Bey. Gabriel, D.

Necessary risks. Klass, P.

Necessary women. Slaughter, K.

The **necessity** of his condition. Davidson, A.

Neck or nothing. Drake, D.

The **Necklace**. Bauman, B.

NECKLACES

Le Guin, U. K. Semley's necklace

NECROPHILIA

Swanwick, M. The dead

Needham, Henry Beach

The jinx

Dead balls and double curves; an anthology of early baseball fiction; edited and with an introduction by Trey Strecker ; with a foreword by Arnold Hano

NEEDLEWORK

Traba, M. The tale of the velvet pillows

Nég Créol. Chopin, K.

Negative Numbers. Brunt, C. R.

NEGROES *See* African Americans

The **neighbor**. Banks, R.

Neighborhood. Rheinheimer, K.

NEIGHBORS

Abrams, T. The drinking of spirits

Agee, J. Dwight Tuggle

Agee, J. I can't stop loving you

Aldrich, B. S. The man who caught the weather

Anderson, J. The houses of double women

Arnott, Marion. Marbles

Avrich, J. La belle dame sans merci

Bail, M. Life of the party

Bart, P. The neighbors I

Bart, P. The neighbors II

Bart, P. The neighbors III

Barthelme, F. Elroy Nights

Barthelme, F. Larroquette

Barthelme, F. Pool lights

Baxter, C. Harry Ginsberg

Beattie, A. Cat people

Berdine, T. Spring rite

Berry, W. Are you all right?

Berry, W. Watch with me

Bingham, S. The splinter

Blackwood, S. In the shadow of our house

Boswell, M. Stir crazy

Boyle, T. C. Peep Hall

Brackenbury, R. Chloe's pool

Brownstein, G. The speedboat

Budnitz, J. Bruno

Busch, F. Machias

Carver, R. Dreams

Casares, O. Charro

Casares, O. RG

Casares, O. Yolanda

Casey, M. Relief

Chaon, D. Big me

Chaon, D. The illustrated encyclopedia of the animal kingdom

Chapman, C. M. Michelle

Cherry, K. Block party

Cherry, K. The society of friends

Clark, M. H. The man next door

Crone, M. Where what gets into people comes from

Cummins, A. Crazy yellow

Cushman, S. Me and Dr. Bob

Daniels, J. Good neighbor

Dark, A. E. Watch the animals

Davis, L. The house behind

Downs, M. Man kills wife, two dogs

DuBois, B. The dark snow

Duggin, Richard. Why won't you talk to me?

Ellin, S. The moment of decision

Fallis, G. Comes the revolution

Farnham, B. Midnight trash

Frym, G. Loosestrife

Furman, L. That boy

Gautreaux, T. Easy pickings

Gautreaux, T. Resistance

George, E. Good fences aren't always enough

Gilchrist, E. Perhaps a miracle

Goldner, B. Bad ass Bob, a mug shot mug, a man

Gordon, M. The blind neighbor

Harrison, H. Speed of the cheetah, roar of the lion

Henley, P. Slinkers

Hodge, B. Some other me

Huelle, P. Moving house

Hughes, J. Forbidden fruits

Hunter, F. The barking dog

Irsfeld, J. H. My neighbor Mr. Young

Jackson, V. F. Living alone

James, S. A house of one's own

Jen, G. Chin

Kavaler, R. Pigeons

Kawabata, Y. Raindrops

Kelly, J. A Dick and Jane story

Knight, M. Blackout

Knight, M. Now you see her

Knight, M. Sundays

Krawiec, R. Listening to the gay boys fight

Kurlansky, M. Devaluation

Lamsley, T. Climbing down from heaven

Lansdale, J. R. Billie Sue

Lao She. Neighbors

Leegant, J. Mezivosky

Liu Xinwu. Black walls

López, L. To control a rabid rodent

Lundquist, R. Grounded

Lutz, J. So young, so fair, so dead

Mathews, H. Mr. Smathers

Mazelis, J. Forbidden

McNally, J. Torture

Means, D. The reaction

Muñoz, M. Anchorage

Munro, K. E. French press

Nawrocki, S. Dogs

Nietzke, A. Los Angeles here and now

Novakovich, J. Spleen

Oates, J. C. Upholstery

Parrish, T. Complicity

Penn, W. S. Neither

Perabo, S. The rocks over Kyburz

Pittalwala, I. Mango season

Pronzini, B. Wishful thinking

Proulx, A. People in hell just want a drink of water

Reisman, N. Dreaming of the snail life

Richmond, M. Propaganda

Ritchie, E. "In haste I write you this note—"

NEIGHBORS—*Continued*

Ritchie, E. Shopping expedition
Ritchie, E. The view from seven
Scoville, S. Pu'u Pu'iwa
Shankman, S. Love thy neighbor
Shapiro, G. Rosenthal unbound
Singer, I. B. Old love
Singleton, G. Rentals
Slezak, E. The geese at Mayville
Spencer, D. Blood work
Spencer, D. Late-night TV
Spencer, D. There's too much news
Strom, D. Chickens
Stuart, J. The affair with Rachel Ware
Thompson, J. The rich man's house
Treat, J. Walking
Tucci, N. The evolution of knowledge
Updike, J. Eclipse
Updike, J. His finest hour
Wallace, R. The quarry
Warren, D. Michelangelo
Weaver, G. On watch for Big Red
Weihe, E. The morning room
Wellen, E. Waswolf
White, M. C. The cardiologist's house
Wilson, R., Jr. Grief
Winterson, J. Newton
Wolfe, G. The wrapper
Yañez, R. Lucero's Mkt.

Neighbors. Alvarez, J.
Neighbors. Griffith, D.
Neighbors. Lao She
Neighbours. Chekhov, A. P.
Neither. Penn, W. S.
Neither pity, love nor fear. Frazer, M.
Nelse Hatton's vengeance. Dunbar, P. L.
Nelson, Alice Moore Dunbar- *See* Dunbar-
 Nelson, Alice Moore, 1875-1935
Nelson, Antony
 Incognito
  American short fiction, vol. 8, no 29-32
Nelson, Antonya
 Ball peen
  Harper's v304 no1821 p77-83 F 2002
  Nelson, A. Female trouble; a collection of
   short stories
 Dick
  The New Yorker v79 no10 p82-93 My 5 2003
 Eminent Domain
  The New Yorker v79 no44 p74-83 Ja 26 2004
 Female trouble
  Nelson, A. Female trouble; a collection of
   short stories
  Prize stories, 2001; The O. Henry awards; ed-
   ited and with an introduction by Larry
   Dark
 Goodfellows
  Nelson, A. Female trouble; a collection of
   short stories
 Happy hour
  Nelson, A. Female trouble; a collection of
   short stories
 Incognito
  Nelson, A. Female trouble; a collection of
   short stories
 Irony, irony, irony
  Nelson, A. Female trouble; a collection of
   short stories

The lonely doll
 Nelson, A. Female trouble; a collection of
  short stories
Loose cannon
 Nelson, A. Female trouble; a collection of
  short stories
One dog is people
 Nelson, A. Female trouble; a collection of
  short stories
Only a Thing
 The New Yorker v78 no33 p83-91 N 4 2002
The other daughter
 Nelson, A. Female trouble; a collection of
  short stories
Palisades
 Nelson, A. Female trouble; a collection of
  short stories
 Ploughshares v25 no2/3 p124-39 Fall 1999
Party of one
 The New Yorker v75 no16 p140+ Je 21-28
  1999
Rear View
 Ploughshares v29 no2/3 p145-62 Fall 2003
Stitches
 Nelson, A. Female trouble; a collection of
  short stories
 The New Yorker v75 no27 p112-19 S 20 1999
The unified front
 Nelson, A. Female trouble; a collection of
  short stories
Nelson, Kent
 The beautiful morning of almost June
  The Virginia Quarterly Review v78 no2 p207-
   17 Spr 2002
 Ghostwriter
  Southern Humanities Review v33 no3 p263-75
   Summ 1999
 Ringo Bingo
  Prairie Schooner v77 no2 p60-72 Summ 2003
 Swimming in Moonlight
  Southern Humanities Review v37 no2 p141-58
   Spr 2003
 Tides
  The Best American mystery stories, 2001; ed-
   ited and with an Introduction by Lawrence
   Block
Nelson, Randy F.
 The Assassination Bureau
  Gettysburg Review v16 no3 p441-53 Aut
   2003
 Escape
  The Georgia Review v55 no3 p400-12 Fall
   2001
 Refiner's fire
  The Southern Review (Baton Rouge, La.) v38
   no2 p321-33 Spr 2002
Nelson, Ray Faraday
 Eight o'clock in the morning
  Science-fiction classics; the stories that
   morphed into movies; compiled by Forrest
   J. Ackerman
Nelson, Victoria
 Halloween notes
  Southwest Review v86 no2/3 p403-11
   Spr/Summ 2001
 Wild California
  Raritan v22 no4 p40-64 Spr 2003

Nemerov, Howard and Johnson, W. R. (Walter Ralph)
Exchange of men
Sports best short stories; edited by Paul D. Staudohar
Nemesis. Clarke, A. C.
Némirovsky, Irène
Fraternité
Prairie Schooner v76 no2 p137-46 Summ 2002
NEO-NAZIS *See* Skinheads
NEPAL
Upadhyay, S. The good shopkeeper
NEPHEWS
Canty, K. Aquarium
Chaon, D. Passengers, remain calm
Clarke, A. C. The reluctant orchid
Jaime-Becerra, M. The corrido of Hector Cruz
Leslie, N. Prayer wheel
McCourt, J. A plethora
Mosley, W. Whispers in the dark
Porter, J. A. Naufrage and diapason
Robison, M. Happy boy, Allen
Stegner, L. Indian summer
The **Nephews.** Hautala, R.
NEPTUNE (PLANET)
Resnick, M. The elephants on Neptune
Neri, Kris
Sentence imposed
A Deadly dozen; tales of murder from members of Sisters in Crime/Los Angeles; edited by Susan B. Casmier, Aljean Harmetz and Cynthia Lawrence
NERVAL, GÉRARD DE, 1808-1855
About
Connor, J. The poet's lobster
Nerve. Jackson, S.
NERVOUS BREAKDOWN
Broughton, T. A. Ashes
Chekhov, A. P. A nervous breakdown
Delany, S. R. High weir
Dodd, S. M. Ethiopia
Falco, E. The revenant
Mazelis, J. On the edge
White, M. C. Fugitives
A **nervous** breakdown. Chekhov, A. P.
The **Nervous** Person. Shohei, O.
Nesbit, E. (Edith)
The dragon tamers
Tales before Tolkien; the roots of modern fantasy; edited by Douglas A. Anderson
Nesbit, Edith *See* Nesbit, E. (Edith), 1858-1924
Nesbitt, Marc
The children's book of victims
Nesbitt, M. Gigantic; stories
Chimp shrink and backwards
Nesbitt, M. Gigantic; stories
Gigantic
Nesbitt, M. Gigantic; stories
The New Yorker v77 no18 p76-81 Jl 9 2001
I got something with your name on it
Nesbitt, M. Gigantic; stories
Man in towel with gun
Nesbitt, M. Gigantic; stories
The ones who may kill you in the morning
Nesbitt, M. Gigantic; stories
Polly here somewhere
Nesbitt, M. Gigantic; stories

Quality fuel for electric living
Nesbitt, M. Gigantic; stories
Thursday the sixteenth
Nesbitt, M. Gigantic; stories
What good is you anyway?
Nesbitt, M. Gigantic; stories
Nesset, Kirk
Harvest the wind
The North American Review v284 no2 p40-44 Mr/Ap 1999
Mr. Agreeable
The Pushcart prize XXIII: best of the small presses; an annual small press reader; edited by Bill Henderson with the Pushcart prize editors
Mr. Destitute
New England Review v20 no2 p179-81 Spr 1999
The **nest.** Still, J.
A **nest** of mares. Gould, P.
Nesting. Hochman, A.
Nesting instincts. Hodge, B.
NETHERLANDS
Amsterdam
Campbell, R. The body in the window
Carson, J. Two thousand years of torture
Gomes, M. T. Deus ex machina
Holleran, A. Amsterdam
Horn, D. Barbarians at the gates
Netmail. DuBois, B.
Nettles. Munro, A.
The **network.** Mathews, H.
Neudecker, Christiane
Mother bother
Prairie Schooner v73 no3 p82-89 Fall 1999
Neumann, Anne Waldron
The Turtle That Had Elevated Thoughts
Harvard Review (1992) no23 p120-2 Fall 2002
Neumann, John Von *See* Von Neumann, John, 1903-1957
NEURASTHENIA *See* Nervous breakdown
NEUROSES
Alexis, A. The third terrace
Cather, W. Paul's case
Phillips, J. A. Gemcrack
Spillane, M. The girl behind the hedge
Sturgeon, T. Bianca's hands
NEUROTICS *See* Neuroses
Neutrino drag. Di Filippo, P.
NEVADA
See also Death Valley (Calif. and Nev.); Sierra Nevada Mountains (Calif. and Nev.)
Kittredge, W. The stone corral
Rusch, K. K. Details
Tuck, L. Verdi
Updike, J. Nevada
Las Vegas
Cook, K. L. Costa Rica
Cook, K. L. Pool boy
Doenges, J. The money stays, the people go
Harty, R. Sarah at the Palace
Irsfeld, J. H. The chance
Irsfeld, J. H. Have you knocked on Cleopatra?
Irsfeld, J. H. Stop, rewind, and play
Lumley, B. Dead Eddy
Paine, T. Scar Vegas
Rodgers, S. J. Luck
Spencer, D. Caution: men in trees

NEVADA—Las Vegas—*Continued*
Strober, R. Poker face
Weaver, G. Solidarity forever!
Wegner, H. Following the nun
Weinreb, M. Girl boy etc.
Westlake, D. E. Breathe deep
Nevai, Lucia
Faith healer
Iowa Review v31 no1 p1-15 Summ 2001
New stories from the South: the year's best, 2002; edited by Shannon Ravenel; with a preface by Larry Brown
Full Replacement Value
New England Review v24 no1 p82-7 Wint 2003
Step men
Coppola, F. F. Francis Ford Coppola's Zoetrope: all story; edited by Adrienne Brodeur and Samantha Schnee; introduction by Francis Ford Coppola
Fault lines; stories of divorce; collected and edited by Caitlin Shetterly
Never ends. Dixon, S.
Never marry a Mexican. Cisneros, S.
Never shake a family tree. Westlake, D. E.
Nevill, Adam L. G.
Mother's milk
Gathering the bones; original stories from the world's masters of horror; edited by Dennis Etchison, Ramsey Campbell and Jack Dann
Neville. Cohen, S.
Nevins, Francis M., Jr.
Bad bargain
Nevins, F. M., Jr. Leap day and other stories
Bagworms
Nevins, F. M., Jr. Leap day and other stories
Because the constable blundered
Nevins, F. M., Jr. Leap day and other stories
Buford's last case
Nevins, F. M., Jr. Leap day and other stories
Consultation in the dark
Nevins, F. M., Jr. Leap day and other stories
Counterplot
Nevins, F. M., Jr. Leap day and other stories
Evensong
Nevins, F. M., Jr. Leap day and other stories
Fair game
Nevins, F. M., Jr. Leap day and other stories
Funeral music
Nevins, F. M., Jr. Leap day and other stories
The kumquats affairs
Nevins, F. M., Jr. Leap day and other stories
The last passenger
Nevins, F. M., Jr. Leap day and other stories
Leap day
Nevins, F. M., Jr. Leap day and other stories
Luck of the dead
Nevins, F. M., Jr. Leap day and other stories
The other man in the pinstripe
Nevins, F. M., Jr. Leap day and other stories
New Again. Jamir, S.
The **New** and Best Rule for Sandwich. Toutonghi, P.
New best friends. Adams, A.
The **New** Cat. Feitell, M.
The **New** Corporal. Davies, P. H.
The **New** Currency. Kane, J. F.
NEW ENGLAND
Banks, R. Defenseman

Davidson, A. Twenty-three
Hall, D. New England primer
Klass, P. Freedom fighter
Westmoreland, T. A. Winter Island
17th century
Hawthorne, N. Endicott and the Red Cross
19th century
Davidson, A. Twenty-three
James, H. A landscape painter
Wharton, E. The angel at the grave
Frontier and pioneer life
See Frontier and pioneer life—New England
New England primer. Hall, D.
A **New** England winter. James, H.
A **new** experiment with time. Rucker, R. v. B.
New family car. Painter, P.
The **new** female head. Marcus, B.
A **new** golden age. Rucker, R. v. B.
The **new** guy. Toscana, D.
The **new** guys. Händler, E.-W.
NEW HAMPSHIRE
See also White Mountains (N.H. and Me.)
Banks, R. Black man and white woman in dark green rowboat
Banks, R. The burden
Banks, R. Comfort
Banks, R. Dis bwoy, him gwan
Banks, R. Firewood
Banks, R. The fisherman
Banks, R. The guinea pig lady
Banks, R. Sarah Cole: a type of love story
Banks, R. With Ché in New Hampshire
Hall, D. Christmas snow
Updike, J. The women who got away
Wolven, S. Controlled burn
The **new** Horla. Sheckley, R.
New Husband. Adichie, C. N.
New in north town. Carter, E.
NEW JERSEY
Chenoweth, A. The unfortunated city
Davis, W. The sharp light of trespassers
Díaz, J. Edison, New Jersey
Gordon, B. Home
Atlantic City
Toole, F. X. Black Jew
Hoboken
Moody, R. The carnival tradition
Newark
Rodburg, M. Days of awe
Rodburg, M. Keer Avenue, July 1967
Rodburg, M. The law of return
Rodburg, M. March of Dimes
Rodburg, M. Pochantas in Camelot
Rodburg, M. The widower Visarrion
New job. Coshnear, D.
A **new** life. Evans, E.
New light on the Drake equation. MacLeod, I.
A **new** love. Iwaszkiewicz, J.
The **new** maid. Schlaks, M.
A **new** man. Gorman, E.
A **new** man. Loayza, L.
The **New** Map. Parameswaran, R.
New memories. Stollman, A. L.
NEW MEXICO
Adam, C. Quail
Barrett, N., Jr. Sallie C.
Barthelme, F. Travel & leisure

NEW MEXICO—*Continued*
Coleman, J. C. Borderlands
Evans, M. The heart of the matter
Grahn, J. Green toads of the high desert
Hirshberg, G. Dancing men
Horgan, P. The peach stone
Kaminsky, S. M. Blowout in Little Man Flats
Meredith, D. Comic Valentine
Sandlin, L. Beautiful
Sandlin, L. Everything moves
Sandlin, L. I loved you then, I love you still
Sandlin, L. 'Orita on the road to Chimayó
Sandlin, L. The saint of bilocation
Sojourner, M. What they write in other countries
Swan, G. Gate of ivory, gate of horn
Vasseur, T. J. The enduring nights of Sidney Wingcloud
Albuquerque
Gilliland, G. Witches
Mueller, D. Birds
Santa Fe
Matiella, A. C. Tying St. Anthony's feet
Morrell, D. Rio Grande gothic
Sandlin, L. Another exciting day in Santa Fe
Sandlin, L. Night class
Watanabe McFerrin, L. Los mariachis del muerto
New mysteries of Paris. Gifford, B.
A new name each day. Pritchett, L.
New Neighbors. Jewett, S. O.
A new night of long knives. Cooper, B. J.
The New Optics Technician. Doerr, A.
NEW ORLEANS (LA.) *See* Louisiana—New Orleans
New Orleans getaway. Howard, C.
The new prime. Vance, J.
The new sidewalks. Wallace, R.
NEW SOUTHWEST *See* Southwestern States
The new villa. Chekhov, A. P.
New Wave. Boswell, M.
The new wife. Swan, M.
The new world. Young, T.
NEW YEAR
DeMarinis, R. Pagans
Weinreb, M. Girl boy etc.
Yates, R. Out with the old
The new year. McNally, J.
New years. Blackwood, S.
A New Year's blessing. Alcott, L. M.
New Year's Day. Weldon, F.
NEW YORK (N.Y.)
Barrett, N., Jr. Under old New York
Borges, J. L. Monk Eastman, purveyor of iniquities
Cherryh, C. J. Highliner
De Camp, L. S. The isolinguals
Finney, J. The coin collector
Gilman, C. P. When I was a witch
Harrison, H. Roommates
Kelly, J. P. Rat
Malzberg, B. N. The prince of the steppes
Sterns, A. The third rail
19th century
Chesnutt, C. W. A metropolitan experience
Davidson, A. The importance of trifles
James, H. Crawford's consistency
James, H. Georgina's reasons
James, H. The jolly corner

Wharton, E. Bunner Sisters
20th century
Bowles, P. If I should open my mouth
Carter, E. Glory and the angels
Davies, R. Rock-and-roll fantasy
Du Bois, W. E. B. The comet
Estep, M. Animals
Estep, M. Monkeys
Feitell, M. Bike New York!
Fitzgerald, F. S. May Day
Foster, K. A story about someone else
Franzen, J. The failure
Godin, A. My dead brother comes to America
Hershman, M. Slightly guilty
Honig, L. Dispossessed
Honig, L. Hilda
Honig, L. Love, rescue, care, dream, sweep
Honig, L. No friends, all strangers
Honig, L. Refuge
Honig, L. The truly needy
LaValle, V. D. Class trip
LaValle, V. D. Getting ugly
LaValle, V. D. Ghost story
Lopez, B. H. The open lot
Malone, M. Invitation to the ball
McBain, E. Happy New Year, Herbie
Miller, R. Nancy
Nissen, T. The rather unlikely courtship of Edwin Anderson and Roz Rosenzweig
Oates, J. C. The museum of Dr. Moses
Runyon, D. Sense of humor
Smyth, C. Sand and other grit
Sorrentino, G. Decades
Spain, C. Scaring the baddest animal
Straub, P. Pork pie hat
Tester, W. Where the dark ended
Turner, G. Cookie and me
Updike, J. A gift from the city
Wheat, C. Ghost Station
Yates, R. Regards at home
Politics
See Politics—New York (N.Y.)
Bronx
Cohen, R. Those kooks
Eidus, J. Elvis, Axl, and me
Ferrell, C. Proper library
Ferrell, C. Truth or consequences
Gifford, B. Vendetta
Glave, T. Their story
Glave, T. Whose song?
Phillips, J. A. Gemcrack
Rozan, S. J. Hoops
Sweeney, E. Lord McDonald
Wexler, M. Solomon and his wives
Brooklyn
Bank, M. The wonder spot
Busch, F. Vespers
Hood, A. An ornithologist's guide to life
LaValle, V. D. Raw daddy
Singer, I. B. A wedding in Brownsville
Vapnyar, L. Mistress
Central Park
Davidson, A. The lord of Central Park
Chinatown
Lieu, J. Always a descendant
Vaswani, N. Bing-Chen
Coney Island
Arvin, N. In the electric Eden
Butler, R. O. Sunday

NEW YORK (N.Y.)—Coney Island—*Continued*

Hershman, M. Letter to the editor

Greenwich Village

Allegra, D. The moon in cancer

Allegra, D. Witness to the league of blond hip hop dancers

Amis, M. Straight fiction

Carter, E. East on Houston

Carter, E. Glory B. and the ice-man

Hazel, R. White Anglo-Saxon Protestant

Henry, O. The last leaf

Hughes, K. B. Roam

Leong, R. Eclipse

Oates, J. C. Three girls

Perkins, E. Her new life

Roorbach, B. Loneliness

Sorrentino, G. Perdído

Updike, J. Snowing in Greenwich Village

Villane, M. The color of rain

Yates, R. Oh, Joseph, I'm so tired

Harlem

Dumas, H. Harlem

Dumas, H. A Harlem game

Dumas, H. Riot or revolt?

Dumas, H. Scout

Kelley, W. M. Carlyle tries polygamy

McNulty, J. Cluney McFarrar's hardtack

Lower East Side

Gorman, C. The Death Cat of Hester Street

Weidman, J. Good man, bad man

Manhattan

Adler, R. Brownstone

Amis, M. The coincidence of the arts

Auchincloss, L. The treacherous age

Bank, M. The girls' guide to hunting and fishing

Barthelme, D. The balloon

Bellow, S. A theft

Bemelmans, L. Mespoulets of the Splendide

Benson, S. Apartment hotel

Block, L. How would you like it?

Block, L. In for a penny

Bowles, P. How many midnights

Brennan, M. The daughters

Brennan, M. I see you, Bianca

Brennan, M. A snowy night on West Forty-ninth Street

Brownstein, G. The curious case of Benjamin Button, 3w

Brownstein, G. The dead fiddler, 5E

Brownstein, G. Musée des Beaux Arts

Bukiet, M. J. Squeak, memory

Cohen, S. How much justice can you afford?

Cohen, S. Just another New York Christmas story

Davis, D. S. Now is forever

Delaney, E. J. Conspiracy buffs

Dixon, S. The hairpiece

Dixon, S. Heat

Dixon, S. To Tom

Doble, J. After six weeks in New York

Eldridge, Courtney. Young professionals

Ellison, H. The whimper of whipped dogs

Estep, M. Circus

Estep, M. The messenger

Fitzgerald, F. S. The popular girl

Fitzgerald, F. S. The smilers

Gates, D. Beating

Gates, D. The wonders of the invisible world

Gates, D. A wronged husband

Gilb, D. Snow

Hardwick, E. Shot: a New York story

Hermann, J. Hunter Johnson music

Highsmith, P. Uncertain treasure

Highsmith, P. Where the door is always open and the welcome mat is out

Hoch, E. D. Great day for the Irish

Holleran, A. The housesitter

Holleran, A. The penthouse

Jenkins, W. F. The runaway skyscraper

Kane, J. F. How to become a publicist

Kaufman, W. Helen on Eighty-Sixth Street

Krouse, E. Mercy

LaValle, V. D. Slave

Leiber, F. A bad day for sales

Leiber, F. Coming attraction

Maxwell, W. Over by the river

McNulty, J. Argument outside a gin mill here

McNulty, J. Barkeep won't let anybody at all shove this handyman around

McNulty, J. He should have left him have it anyway

McNulty, J. Man here keeps getting arrested all the time

McNulty, J. A man like Grady, you got to know him first

McNulty, J. A man's going into the Army what can you do about it?

McNulty, J. An old college chum

McNulty, J. Peether is full of blather

McNulty, J. Some nights when nothing happens are the best nights in this place

McNulty, J. This lady was a Bostonian they call them

McNulty, J. Two bums here would spend freely except for poverty

Means, D. McGregor's day on

Menaker, D. The treatment

Meyers, A. and Meyers, M. The Daffodil

Nissen, T. The mushroom girl

Nissen, T. When the rain washes you clean you'll know

Oates, J. C. A Manhattan romance

Oates, J. C. The mutants

Penn, W. S. In dreams begins reality

Penn, W. S. Toothpaste

Pronzini, B. The man who collected "The Shadow"

Roth, P. Smart money

Salinger, J. D. Slight rebellion off Madison

Sorrentino, G. Subway

Stern, D. Lunch with Gottlieb

Stevenson, J. Notes from a bottle

Taylor, P. H. A sentimental journey

Tevis, W. S. Rent control

Touré. The playground of the ecstatically blasé

Troncoso, S. My life in the city

Troncoso, S. Remembering possibilities

Turner, R. Eleven o'clock bulletin

Updike, J. The astronomer

Updike, J. The lucid eye in silver town

Updike, J. The stare

Wexler, M. Save yourself

Wexler, M. What Marcia wanted

Wharton, E. After Holbein

Wharton, E. A cup of cold water

Wisniewski, M. Descending

NEW YORK (N.Y.)—*Continued*

Queens

Baida, P. Points of light

Grodstein, L. John on the train: a fable for our cynical friends

LaValle, V. D. Ancient history

LaValle, V. D. Chuckie

LaValle, V. D. Kids on Colden Street

Sharma, A. Surrounded by sleep

Vaswani, N. Five objects in Queens

NEW YORK (STATE)

See also Adirondack Mountains (N.Y.); Long Island (N.Y.)

20th century

Bailey, T. Snow dreams

Banks, R. Lobster night

Banks, R. Plains of Abraham

Bishop, C. Dead and berried

Brennan, M. The view from the kitchen

Busch, F. Bob's your uncle

Busch, F. Domicile

Busch, F. A handbook for spies

Busch, F. The talking cure

Gates, D. The bad thing

Means, D. The gesture hunter

Means, D. Railroad incident, August 1995

Moody, R. The Mansion on the Hill

Mukherjee, B. Saints

Oates, J. C. Faithless

Oates, J. C. Secret, silent

Oates, J. C. We were worried about you

Prete, D. After we left Yonkers and before we came back

Prete, D. The biggest, most silent thing

Prete, D. Bleachers

Prete, D. The itch

Prete, D. No king, no puppy

Prete, D. Not because I'm thirsty

Prete, D. Say that to my face

Prete, D. Self-respecting Neapolitans

Trevanian. Mrs. McGivney's nickel

Farm life

See Farm life—New York (State)

Albany

Gates, D. Star baby

Livingood, J. Oh, Albany, my love

Buffalo

Kessel, J. Buffalo

Reisman, N. Common light

Reisman, N. Illumination

Rucker, R. v. B. A new experiment with time

Fire Island

See Fire Island (N.Y.)

New York City

See New York (N.Y.)

Newburgh

Morrison, T. Recitatif

Westchester County

Fitzgerald, F. S. Myra meets his family

Knight, M. Amelia Earhart's coat

New York 1965. Bowles, P.

New York Girl. Updike, J.

New York lit up that way at night. McCourt, J.

New York mining disaster. Murakami, H.

NEW ZEALAND

Weldon, F. Spirits fly south

Rural life

Fitzgerald, P. At Hiruharama

NEWARK (N.J.) *See* New Jersey—Newark

NEWFOUNDLAND *See* Canada—Newfoundland

NEWHART, BOB

s

Harris, M. Hi, Bob!

Newhouse, Edward

The Mentocrats

Wonderful town; New York stories from The New Yorker; edited by David Remnick with Susan Choi

Newman, Cory

Wifely duties

A Deadly dozen; tales of murder from members of Sisters in Crime/Los Angeles; edited by Susan B. Casmier, Aljean Harmetz and Cynthia Lawrence

Newman, David A.

Good news and bad news

His 3: brilliant new fiction by gay writers; edited by Robert Drake and Terry Wolverton

Mystery Spot

Circa 2000; gay fiction at the millennium; edited by Robert Drake & Terry Wolverton

Newman, Kim

Amerikanski dead at the Moscow morgue

999: new stories of horror and suspense; edited by Al Sarrantonio

Castle in the desert

Best new horror 12; edited and with an introduction by Stephen Jones

Egyptian Avenue

The Mammoth book of best new horror 14; edited with an introduction by Stephen Jones

The Year's best fantasy & horror: sixteenth annual collection; edited by Ellen Datlow & Terri Windling

The intervention

Gathering the bones; original stories from the world's masters of horror; edited by Dennis Etchison, Ramsey Campbell and Jack Dann

Just like Eddy

Best new horror 11; edited and with an introduction by Stephen Jones

The other side of midnight

Best new horror 12; edited and with an introduction by Stephen Jones

A Victorian ghost story

Best new horror 10; edited and with an introduction by Stephen Jones

You don't have to be mad . . .

The Year's best fantasy & horror, thirteenth annual collection; edited by Ellen Datlow and Terri Windling

Newman, Sharan

Conventual spirit

Murder most divine; ecclesiastical tales of unholy crimes; edited by Ralph McInerny and Martin H. Greenberg

Death before compline

Death dines at 8:30; edited by Claudia Bishop and Nick DiChario

Divine guidance

Past lives, present tense; edited by Elizabeth Ann Scarborough

NEWPORT (R.I.) *See* Rhode Island—Newport

The **news**. Skillings, R. D.

News from New Providence. Lupoff, R. A.

News from the volcano. Swan, G.

News junkie. Maliszewski, P.

News of the world. Gilliland, G.

Newsletter. Willis, C.

A newsman scratches an itch. Hunter, F.

NEWSPAPER PUBLISHERS *See* Publishers and publishing

NEWSPAPER VENDORS
Hawkins, T. Wedding night
Saroyan, W. Resurrection of a life

NEWSPAPERMEN *See* Journalists

NEWSPAPERS
Chekhov, A. P. Rapture
Codrescu, A. The herald
Singleton, G. Fossils
Weldon, F. What the papers say

Newsworld. Pierce, T. J.

Newton, D. B. (Dwight Bennett)
Black Dunstan's skull
Newton, D. B. Born to the brand; western stories
Born to the brand
Newton, D. B. Born to the brand; western stories
Breakheart Valley
Newton, D. B. Born to the brand; western stories
Reach high, top hand!
Newton, D. B. Born to the brand; western stories
The taming of Johnny Peters
Newton, D. B. Born to the brand; western stories
Tinhorn trouble
Newton, D. B. Born to the brand; western stories

Newton, Dwight Bennett *See* Newton, D. B. (Dwight Bennett), 1916-

Newton. Winterson, J.

The next best kiss. Shields, C.

The next best thing. Vukcevich, R.

The next big thing. Cohen, R.

Next Day. Borfka, D.

Next-door neighbors. Berry, M. S.

The Next Generation of Dead Kennedys. Goldhagen, S.

The next greatest thing. Tachick, C.

The next life. Davies, P. H.

Next of kin. Tuck, L.

Next of Kin: A Story. Moses, J.

The next tenants. Clarke, A. C.

Next time. Rick, M.

The Next to Last Line. Justice, J. R.

Nfah-Abbenyi, Juliana Makuchi
Accidents are a sideshow
Nfah-Abbenyi, J. M. Your madness, not mine: stories of Cameroon; with an introduction by Eloise A. Brière
American lottery
Nfah-Abbenyi, J. M. Your madness, not mine: stories of Cameroon; with an introduction by Eloise A. Brière
Bayam-sellam
Nfah-Abbenyi, J. M. Your madness, not mine: stories of Cameroon; with an introduction by Eloise A. Brière
Election fever
Nfah-Abbenyi, J. M. Your madness, not mine: stories of Cameroon; with an introduction by Eloise A. Brière

The forest will claim you too
Nfah-Abbenyi, J. M. Your madness, not mine: stories of Cameroon; with an introduction by Eloise A. Brière
The healer
Nfah-Abbenyi, J. M. Your madness, not mine: stories of Cameroon; with an introduction by Eloise A. Brière
Market scene
Nfah-Abbenyi, J. M. Your madness, not mine: stories of Cameroon; with an introduction by Eloise A. Brière
Slow poison
The Anchor book of modern African stories; edited by Nadežda Obradovic ; with a foreword by Chinua Achebe
Nfah-Abbenyi, J. M. Your madness, not mine: stories of Cameroon; with an introduction by Eloise A. Brière
Your madness, not mine
Nfah-Abbenyi, J. M. Your madness, not mine: stories of Cameroon; with an introduction by Eloise A. Brière

Ng, Kum-Hoon
Eleven Trials
Parabola v28 no4 p58-60 Wint 2003

Ngugi, James *See* Ng'ugĩ wa Thiong'o, 1938-

Ng'ugĩ wa Thiong'o
Minutes of glory
The Art of the story; an international anthology of contemporary short stories; edited by Daniel Halpern

Nguyen, Dylan Tai
Peace
Kulka, J. and Danford, N. The New American voices 2003; guest editor Joyce Carol Oates; series editors John Kulka and Natalie Danford

Nguyen, Phoenix
Buom
The Paris Review v41 no150 p69-115 Spr 1999

Nguyen Tat Thành *See* Ho, Chí Minh, 1890-1969

Nguyen Van Thieu Is Dead at 78. Welsch, G.

Nha Nam. Tran, V.

Ní Dhuibhne-Almqvist, Éilís
The Garden of Eden
The Anchor book of new Irish writing; the new Gaelach ficsean; edited and with an introduction by John Somer and John J. Daly

Niagara Falls. Norris, H.

Nicaraguan birds. Treat, J.

Nicastro, Laura
Haguit
English translations of short stories by contemporary Argentine women writers; edited by Eliana Cazaubon Hermann ; translated by Sally Webb Thornton

NICE (FRANCE) *See* France—Nice

A nice cup of tea. Kingsbury, K.

Nicholas was. . . Gaiman, N.

Nichols, Ian
The last dance
Dreaming down-under; edited by Jack Dann and Janeen Webb

Nichols, Jim
C'est la vie
Nichols, J. Slow monkeys and other stories

Nichols, Jim—*Continued*
  The Dilly
    Nichols, J. Slow monkeys and other stories
  Giant
    Nichols, J. Slow monkeys and other stories
  Jade
    Nichols, J. Slow monkeys and other stories
  Jon-clod
    Nichols, J. Slow monkeys and other stories
  Loons
    Nichols, J. Slow monkeys and other stories
  Mackerel
    Nichols, J. Slow monkeys and other stories
  Magic
    Nichols, J. Slow monkeys and other stories
  Orion
    Nichols, J. Slow monkeys and other stories
  The rain barrel
    Nichols, J. Slow monkeys and other stories
  Slow monkeys
    Nichols, J. Slow monkeys and other stories
Nichols, Leigh *See* Koontz, Dean R. (Dean Ray), 1945-
Nichols, Leigh, 1945-
    For works written by this author under oth-er names see Koontz, Dean R. (Dean Ray), 1945-
Nicholson, Margaret Beda *See* Yorke, Margaret
Nick the Russian. Bonnie, F.
The **nickel** Derby. Randisi, R. J.
Nickle, David
  The dummy ward
    Northern suns; edited by David G. Hartwell & Glenn Grant
Nicodemus, the detective from Africa. Hardinge, E.
Nicolette: a memoir. Barrington, J.
The **Niece.** Livesey, M.
NIECES
  Agee, J. The presence of absence
  Chopin, K. Ma'ame Pélagie
  Chopin, K. Miss Witherwell's mistake
  Egan, J. Goodbye, my love
  Fitzgerald, F. S. The offshore pirate
  Hawley, E. What we forgot to tell Tina about boys
  Hood, A. Escapes
  Malouf, D. Closer
  Martin, P. P. Amor prohibido—Forbidden love
  Poirier, M. J. Cul-de-sacs
  Watson, B. Water dog god
Niernsee's Tower. Allison, W.
Nieson, M. S.
  What I did on my summer vacation
    The Literary Review (Madison, N.J.) v42 no3 p455-68 Spr 1999
Nietzke, Ann
  Los Angeles here and now
    LA shorts; edited by Steven Gilbar
The **nig** in me. Mosley, W.
NIGERIA
  Aiyejina, F. The one-handed hero
  Aniebo, I. N. C. Four dimensions
    Civil War, 1967-1970
  Kalu, Anthonia C. Angelus
  Kalu, Anthonia C. Broken lives
  Kalu, Anthonia C. Camwood
  Kalu, Anthonia C. Children's day
  Kalu, Anthonia C. The gift

  Kalu, Anthonia C. Independence
  Kalu, Anthonia C. The last push
  Kalu, Anthonia C. Ogbanje father
  Kalu, Anthonia C. Osondu
  Kalu, Anthonia C. Relief duty
  Maja-Pearce, A. Civil War I-VII
NIGERIANS
    United States
  Evans, E. Americans
  Fintushel, E. White man's trick
NIGHT
  Chekhov, A. P. A dreadful night
The **night**. Agnon, S. Y.
Night and fog. Delbanco, N.
Night and night's travelers. Yoshimoto, B.
Night and the loves of Joe Dicostanzo. Delany, S. R.
A **night** at the love nest resort. Randisi, R. J. and Matthews, C.
A **night** at the Y. McBrearty, R. G.
A **night** at wagon camp. L'Amour, L.
Night-blooming cereus. Coberly, L. M.
Night calls. Gay, R. P.
The **night** came slowly. Chopin, K.
The **night** chough. Wolfe, G.
NIGHT CLUBS
  Becker, G. Black Elvis
  Cain, J. M. Cigarette girl
  DeLancey, K. Swingtime
  DuBois, B. Dancing the night away
  Nesbitt, M. Thursday the sixteenth
  Waugh, E. The manager of "The Kremlin"
Night deposit. Brickhouse, R.
The **night** doctor. Marías, J.
The **night** face up. Cortázar, J.
Night flight. Mason, B. A.
A **night** for love. Vonnegut, K.
Night Frames. Yourgrau, B.
Night game. Jenkins, G.
Night games. Schnitzler, A.
Night guests. Novakovich, J.
The **night** guide. Steinbeck, T.
A **night** in. Galloway, J.
A **night** in Acadie. Chopin, K.
The **night** in question. Wolff, T.·
A **night** in the Manchester store. Cohen, S.
The **night** it rained cats and cats. Collins, B.
The **night** my brother worked the header. Mueller, D.
The **night** nurse. Wallace, R.
The **night** of crossed destinies. La Spina, S.
Night of the Frankengolfer. Bishop, P.
The **night** of the gifts. Borges, J. L.
The **night** of the kid [excerpt] Shifra, S.
Night of the wandjina. Whiteford, W.
A **night** off. Gray, A.
Night out. Gores, J.
Night owl. Douglas, C. N.
The **night** piece. Alexis, A.
Night ride. Dawson, P.
Night shot. Shepard, J.
Night shots. Hammett, D.
Night sky. Cooper, B.
The **night** sky. Turchi, P.
Night swimming. Fromm, P.
Night Talkers. Danticat, E.
The **night** the clocks go back. Michaud, J.
The **Night** They Gave Orders for Us to Be Killed. Arzola, J. L.

Night thoughts. Justice, J. R.
A night to remember. Sullivan, M.
Night Train. Jones, T.
Night train to Chicago. Smolens, J.
Night Train to Napa. Weinstein, R.
Night training. Malouf, D.
Night, truck, two lights burning. Turchi, P.
Night vigil. Hunter, F.
Night vision. Bloom, A.
Night watch. Armstrong, K.
The night watchman's occurrence book. Naipaul, V. S.
Night watchmen. Derby, M.
Night women. Danticat, E.
Nightcap. Carlson, R.
Nightcrawler. Adam, C.
Nightfall. Asimov, I.
Nightfall. Clarke, A. C.
Nightfall. Weber, D.
Nighthawk. Deane, J. F.
Nighthawks. Lutz, J.
NIGHTINGALE, FLORENCE, 1820-1910
About
Douglas, C. N. Night owl
The nightingale. West, M.
Nightmare. Jackson, S.
Nightmare in wax. Clark, S.
Nightmare town. Hammett, D.
Night's black agents. Tremayne, P.
Nights Out. Cotter, J.
Nightside. Lackey, M.
The nighttime is the right time. Crider, B.
Nightwatcher. Pipik, J.
Nightwind. Banville, J.
NIHILISM
See also Anarchism and anarchists
Niiice. Matthews, C.
Nikas, Ekaterine
Fatal tears
A Deadly dozen; tales of murder from members of Sisters in Crime/Los Angeles; edited by Susan B. Casmier, Aljean Harmetz and Cynthia Lawrence
Nilda. Díaz, J.
Nile, Willie
The cracks
Carved in rock; short stories by musicians; edited by Greg Kihn
Niles, Chris
Revenge is the best revenge
Tart noir; edited by Stella Duffy & Lauren Henderson
Nilon, Joan
Venice unbound
The Literary Review (Madison, N.J.) v42 no3 p483-90 Spr 1999
Nine. Babel', I.
The nine billion names of God. Clarke, A. C.
The nine mile walk. Kemelman, H.
Nine points for murder. Pickard, N.
The nine-year-old who stole Christmas. Kalpakian, L.
Nineteen amenities. Barkley, B.
Nineteen fifty-five. Walker, A.
Nineteen thirty-seven. Danticat, E.
The nineteenth. Bradbury, R.
Ninon. Dobychin, L.
The ninth, in E minor. Busch, F.
The ninth of av. Simmons, D.

Nipple. Brenner, W.
NippleJesus. Hornby, N.
Nirvana. Lear, P.
Nissen, Thisbe
3 ½ x 5
Nissen, T. Out of the girls' room and into the night
29th Street Playground, September 1968
Nissen, T. Out of the girls' room and into the night
819 Walnut
Nissen, T. Out of the girls' room and into the night
Accidental love
Nissen, T. Out of the girls' room and into the night
After twenty-five years, at the Palais Royale
Nissen, T. Out of the girls' room and into the night
The animal's best interest
Nissen, T. Out of the girls' room and into the night
Apple pie
Nissen, T. Out of the girls' room and into the night
At the No. 1 Phoenix Garden
Nissen, T. Out of the girls' room and into the night
A brownstone, Park Slope
The North American Review v284 no3-4 p26-31 My/Ag 1999
A bungalow, Koh Tao
Nissen, T. Out of the girls' room and into the night
The Estate
Nissen, T. Out of the girls' room and into the night
Flowers in the dustbin, poison in the human machine
Nissen, T. Out of the girls' room and into the night
Fundamentals of communication
Nissen, T. Out of the girls' room and into the night
The Student body; short stories about college students and professors; edited by John McNally
The girl at Chichén Itzá
Nissen, T. Out of the girls' room and into the night
Grog
Nissen, T. Out of the girls' room and into the night
Grover, king of Nebraska
Nissen, T. Out of the girls' room and into the night
How beautifully resilient the human being
Nissen, T. Out of the girls' room and into the night
Jono, an elegy
Nissen, T. Out of the girls' room and into the night
Mailing incorrectly
Nissen, T. Out of the girls' room and into the night
The mushroom girl
Nissen, T. Out of the girls' room and into the night

Nissen, Thisbe—*Continued*

Out of the girls' room and into the night
  Nissen, T. Out of the girls' room and into the night

The rather unlikely courtship of Edwin Anderson and Roz Rosenzweig
  Nissen, T. Out of the girls' room and into the night

Think about if you want
  Nissen, T. Out of the girls' room and into the night

Way back when in the now before now
  Nissen, T. Out of the girls' room and into the night

What safety is
  Nissen, T. Out of the girls' room and into the night

When the rain washes you clean you'll know
  Nissen, T. Out of the girls' room and into the night

Wrestling jailbait
  Seventeen v60 no6 p164-7 Je 2001

You Were My Favorite Scarecrow
  The Virginia Quarterly Review v80 no3 p108-22 Summ 2004

Nister *See* Der Nister, 1884-1950

Niven, Larry

All the myriad ways
  The Best alternate history stories of the 20th century; edited by Harry Turtledove with Martin H. Greenberg

Destiny's road [excerpt]
  Niven, L. Scatterbrain; Larry Niven

Inconstant moon
  Masterpieces: the best science fiction of the century; edited by Orson Scott Card

Loki
  Niven, L. Scatterbrain; Larry Niven

Procrustes
  Niven, L. Scatterbrain; Larry Niven

Smut talk
  Niven, L. Scatterbrain; Larry Niven

Ssoroghod's people
  Redshift; extreme visions of speculative fiction; edited by Al Sarrantonio

The woman in Del Rey crater
  Niven, L. Scatterbrain; Larry Niven

Niven, Larry and Barnes, Steven

Saturn's race
  Niven, L. Scatterbrain; Larry Niven

Niven, Larry and Cooper, Brenda

Ice and mirrors
  Niven, L. Scatterbrain; Larry Niven

Niven, Larry and Pournelle, Jerry

The burning city [excerpt]
  Niven, L. Scatterbrain; Larry Niven

Nix Nought Nothing. Jacobs, J.

Nixon, Cornelia

After the beep
  Gettysburg Review v12 no3 p425-38 Aut 1999

Flight
  Iowa Review v29 no1 p25-36 Spr 1999

Lunch at the Blacksmith
  Ploughshares v27 no2/3 p122-41 Fall 2001
  Pushcart prize XXVII; best of the small presses; edited by Bill Henderson with the Pushcart prize editors

NIXON, RICHARD M. (RICHARD MILHOUS), 1913-1994
About

Barrett, N., Jr. Highbrow
McAuley, P. J. The two Dicks
Reilly, G. Nixon under the bodhi tree
The two dicks

Nixon under the bodhi tree. Reilly, G.
The **Nna** Mmoy language. Le Guin, U. K.
No Bruce Lee. Leong, R.
No cause. Berkman, P. R.
No cause for alarm. Zinik, Z.
No clubs allowed. Frym, G.
No comet. Vukcevich, R.
No comment. Chekhov, A. P.
No comment. Jakes, J.
No distance too far, no sacrifice too great. Lao She
No end of fun. Campbell, R.
No escape for yours truly. Skillings, R. D.
No faith. Painter, P.
No fools, no fun. Lacy, M.
No Friend of Mine. Greenman, B.
No friends, all strangers. Honig, L.
No loose ends. Greenberg, A.
No man's land. Foxwell, E.
No Man's Land. Lawson, C. and Brown, S.
No me, not Amos Cabot!. Harrison, H.
No money for stamps. Saunders, G.
No more a-roving. Rucker, L. E.
No more looking back. Davies, R.
No more loves. Marías, J.
No morning after. Clarke, A. C.
No night by myself. Coward, M.
No pain whatsoever. Yates, R.
No parachutes. Moline, K.
No place to hide. Baida, P.
No planets strike. Wolfe, G.
No sharks in the Med. Lumley, B.
No story in it. Campbell, R.
No stranger to Luke. Purdy, J.
No strings. Campbell, R.
No strings attached. Reid, E.
No survivors. Daynard, J.
The **no-talent** kid. Vonnegut, K.
No thanks. Smith, S. J.
No universe. Krouse, E.
No visible means of support. Stuart, D.
No Way Out. Djemai, A.
No woman born. Moore, C. L.
Noah. Mehor, E. L.
Noah's walls. Marks, M.
Nobile's airship. Klimasewiski, M. N.
NOBILITY *See* Aristocracy
Noble, Margaret Elizabeth
  (jt. auth) See Tagore, Sir Rabindranath and Noble, Margaret Elizabeth
Noble causes. Mendes, B.
Noble mold. Baker, K.
Nobody danced. Easton, R. O.
Nobody frames Big Sam. Collins, M.
Nobody home: an epilogue. Ziegler, I.
Nobody in Hollywood. Bausch, R.
Nobody listens when I talk. Sanford, A.
Nobody's business. Lahiri, J.
The **noctambulists**. Spielberg, P.
Noctem Aeternus. Michaels, R.
Nocturne. LaSalle, P.

Nocturne a tre in b-double-sharp minor. Devereaux, R.

Noel, Katharine
April
Kulka, J. and Danford, N. The New American voices 2003; guest editor Joyce Carol Oates; series editors John Kulka and Natalie Danford

Nogales. O'Brien, T.

Nogueira, Claudia Barbosa
Maria de Jesus
Death dines at 8:30; edited by Claudia Bishop and Nick DiChario

Noise. Krout-Hasegawa, E.

A **noise** from the woodshed [excerpt] Dorcey, M.

Noisy into the night. Weldon, F.

Nolan, Jonathan
Memento mori
Esquire v135 no3 p186-91 Mr 2001

Nolan, William E.
The Halloween man
The Ultimate Halloween; edited by Marvin Kaye

Nolan, William F.
An act of violence
Murder most postal; homicidal tales that deliver a message; edited by Martin H. Greenberg
In real life
The Museum of horrors; edited by Dennis Etchison

Nomad and viper. Oz, A.

Nomberg, Hersh Dovid
In the mountains
Neugroschel, J. No star too beautiful; Yiddish stories from 1382 to the present; compiled and translated by Joachim Neugroschel

Nomberg-Przytyk, Sara
Old words—new meanings
When night fell; an anthology of Holocaust short stories; edited by Linda Schermer Raphael and Marc Lee Raphael

A **non-account** Creole. Chopin, K.

The **non-cultural** man. Saer, J. J.

Non-interference. Van de Wetering, J.

None of my business, but . . . Hart, C. G.

NONVIOLENCE
Turtledove, H. The last article

Noon, afternoon, night. Skillings, R. D.

Noonan. Vasseur, T. J.

The **Noonday** Cemetery: an open story. Herling, G.

Nor iron bars. Blish, J.

Nor iron bars. MacDonald, J. D.

Nordan, Lewis
Owling
Southern Quarterly v41 no3 p92-4 Spr 2003
Sugar among the chickens
Fishing for chickens; short stories about rural youth; edited, with an introduction by Jim Heynen
Tombstone
The Cry of an occasion; fiction from the Fellowship of Southern Writers; edited by Richard Bausch; with a foreword by George Garrett

The **Nordic** type. Barolini, H.

Nordley, G. David
Dawn Venus
Worldmakers; SF adventures in terraforming; edited by Gardner Dozois
Poles apart
The Good new stuff; adventure SF in the grand tradition; edited by Gardner Dozois

NORFOLK (ENGLAND) *See* England—Norfolk

Normal. Singleton, G.

Normalcy. Coulter, K.

Norman, Geoffrey
Cowboys
Fishing's best short stories; edited by Paul D. Staudohar

Norman, Gurney
Maxine
Home and beyond; an anthology of Kentucky short stories; edited by Morris Allen Grubbs; with an introduction by Wade Hall and an afterword by Charles E. May

Norman, Howard
Unicycle
Breaking into print; early stories and insights into getting published; a Ploughshares anthology; edited by DeWitt Henry

Norman, Lisanne
The jewel and the demon
Magical beginnings; edited by Steven H. Silver and Martin H. Greenberg

Norman things. Proust, M.

Norris, Benjamin Franklin *See* Norris, Frank, 1870-1902

Norris, Frank
This animal of a Buldy Jones
Dead balls and double curves; an anthology of early baseball fiction; edited and with an introduction by Trey Strecker ; with a foreword by Arnold Hano

Norris, Helen
The bower-bird
Norris, H. One day in the life of a born again loser and other stories
The flying hawk
Norris, H. One day in the life of a born again loser and other stories
A good shape
Norris, H. One day in the life of a born again loser and other stories
The great and small
Norris, H. One day in the life of a born again loser and other stories
Judgment day
Norris, H. One day in the life of a born again loser and other stories
Niagara Falls
Norris, H. One day in the life of a born again loser and other stories
One day in the life of a born again loser
Norris, H. One day in the life of a born again loser and other stories
The second shepherd
Norris, H. One day in the life of a born again loser and other stories
Tutankhamen Calhoun
Norris, H. One day in the life of a born again loser and other stories

Norris, Lisa
American primitive
Norris, L. Toy guns; stories

Norris, Lisa—*Continued*
Black ice
    Norris, L. Toy guns; stories
Interior country
    Norris, L. Toy guns; stories
Prisoner of war
    Norris, L. Toy guns; stories
Self-defense
    Norris, L. Toy guns; stories
Stray dogs
    Norris, L. Toy guns; stories
Swimmers
    Norris, L. Toy guns; stories
Toy guns
    Norris, L. Toy guns; stories
Trailer people
    Norris, L. Toy guns; stories
Wind across the breaks
    Norris, L. Toy guns; stories
North, Anthony *See* Koontz, Dean R. (Dean
    Ray), 1945-
NORTH AFRICA
    See also Sahara
Bowles, P. By the water
Bowles, P. The delicate prey
Bowles, P. A distant episode
Bowles, P. Istikhara, Anaya, Medagan and the
    Medaganat
Bowles, P. The story of Lahcen and Idir
Bowles, P. The successor
Bowles, P. A thousand days for Mokhtar
Bowles, P. The waters of Izli
NORTH CAROLINA
Bache, E. Shell Island
Banks, R. The outer banks
Bottoms, G. Levi's tongue
Burford, M. Flying lessons
Chesnutt, C. W. Cicely's dream
Crone, M. Where what gets into people comes
    from
Earley, T. Aliceville
Earley, T. The prophet from Jupiter
Gurganus, A. Blessed assurance: a moral tale
Gurganus, A. He's one, too
Gurganus, A. The practical heart
Gurganus, A. Preservation news
Gurganus, A. Saint monster
Hagy, A. C. Graveyard of the Atlantic
Hagy, A. C. North of Fear, south of Kill Devil
Hagy, A. C. The snake hunters
Lee, A. Anthropology
Linney, R. The widow
Malone, M. A deer on the lawn
Malone, M. Fast love
Morgan, R. The ratchet
Morgan, R. Sleepy Gap
Parker, M. Commit to memory
Parker, M. Off island
Phillips, D. R. At the edge of the new world
Phillips, D. R. Why I'm talking
Phillips, D. R. The woods at the back of our
    houses
Rash, R. Last rite
Singleton, G. I could've told you if you hadn't
    asked
    Farm life
    See Farm life—North Carolina
    Kitty Hawk
Banks, R. Theory of flight

    Raleigh
Bottoms, G. LSD in Raleigh
NORTH DAKOTA
Butler, R. O. Christmas 1910
Erdrich, L. Fleur
Lopez, B. H. In the great bend of the Souris
    River
Lopez, B. H. The mappist
North of Fear, south of Kill Devil. Hagy, A. C.
North of Nairobi. Hunter, F.
Northeast Philly girls. Juska, E.
NORTHERN IRELAND
Azadeh, C. The country road
Devlin, A. Naming the names
McCann, C. Cathal's lake
Trevor, W. Against the odds
NORTHERN RHODESIA *See* Zambia
NORTHMEN *See* Vikings
NORTHWEST, PACIFIC *See* Pacific Northwest
Norton, Alice Mary *See* Norton, Andre, 1912-
Norton, Andre
All cats are gray
    The SFWA grand masters v2; edited by
    Frederik Pohl
Mousetrap
    The SFWA grand masters v2; edited by
    Frederik Pohl
People of the crater
    Magical beginnings; edited by Steven H. Sil-
    ver and Martin H. Greenberg
Serpent's tooth
    The SFWA grand masters v2; edited by
    Frederik Pohl
Were-wrath
    The SFWA grand masters v2; edited by
    Frederik Pohl
NORWAY
    Rural life
Griffith, N. A troll story: lesson in what matters,
    No. 1
NORWEGIAN AMERICANS
Aadland, D. East breeze
NORWEGIANS
    See also Vikings
    England
Borges, J. L. Ulrikke
    France
Byatt, A. S. Crocodile tears
The **norwest** reaches. Kelman, J.
NOSE
Barker, N. Layla's nose job
Link, K. Water off a black dog's back
Nose. Wuori, G. K.
Nossa Senhora dos Remédios. Simonds, M.
NOSTALGIA
Bowles, P. Unwelcome words
Ellison, H. Jeffty is five
Lao She. Hot dumplings
Nostalgia. Blackwood, S.
Nostalgia for ghosts. Bottoms, G.
Not a chance. Treat, J.
Not about the kids. McCabe, B.
Not anything to do with love. Kennedy, A. L.
Not enough monkeys. Schutz, B. M.
Not flu. Galloway, J.
Not for me a crown of thorns. Kalman, J.
Not long now. Davis, C. A.
Not quite final. Bausch, R.
Not shown. Fitzgerald, P.

Not singing exactly. James, S.

Not that much to go on. Gunn, K.

Not that much to go on: 2. Gunn, K.

Not the Phil Donahue show. Cherry, K.

Not this Virginia. Bisson, T.

Not to worry. Locklin, G.

Not wanted dead or alive. Henry, W.

Not with a bang. Knight, D. F.

Not Your Personal Ashtray. Paterson, M.

A note of note. Brett, S.

A note on the type. Carlson, R.

A note on the type. Poirier, M. J.

A note to biographers regarding famous author Flannery O'Connor. Stefaniak, M. H.

Note to sixth-grade self. Orringer, J.

Notebook of William Moulding, pensioner. Herling, G.

The notebooks of Bob K. Lethem, J.

Notes for an Aborted Story Called "The Cyclist" That Turned Out to Be Too Much Like "The Swimmer". Morris, K. L.

Notes from a bottle. Stevenson, J.

Notes from a writer's book of cures and spells. Douglas, M.

Notes from Buenos Aires. Levrero, M.

Notes from the journal of a quick-tempered man. Chekhov, A. P.

Notes from the memoirs of a man of ideals. Chekhov, A. P.

Notes from the tower of menopause. Blitz, R.

Notes on My Leprosy. Holt, H. A.

Notes recorded on the Lofoten Islands. Tawada, Y.

Notes to Chris concerning household conduct while I am away in Buenos Aires. Durando, N.

Notes to my biographer. Haslett, A.

Notes toward my absolution. Delaney, E. J.

Nothing but Ghosts. Hremann, J.

Nothing but the best. Lawrence, B.

Nothing compared to. Frym, G.

Nothing in life is ever enough. Aldiss, B. W.

Nothing new. O'Rourke, F.

Nothing that meets the eye. Highsmith, P.

Nothing to be done. Heller, J.

Nothing to lose. Barnard, R.

Nothing ventured. Hart, C. G.

Nothing without a name. What, L.

The notification. Zinik, Z.

A notion I took. Castro, J.

NOVA SCOTIA See Canada—Nova Scotia

Novakovich, Josip

Hail

TriQuarterly no115 p9-24 Spr 2003

Night guests

The Antioch Review v59 no4 p783-97 Fall 2001

Spleen

Fishman, B. Wild East; stories from the last frontier; edited with an introduction by Boris Fishman

The Paris Review v45 p245-59 Spr 2003

The Stamp

Ploughshares v28 no4 p101-18 Wint 2002/2003

The novel as history. Mathews, H.

A novel in letters. Pushkin, A. S.

NOVELISTS See Authors

November 1943. Viganò, R.

The November Fifteen. Montemarano, N.

Novias. DeMarinis, R.

Novotny, Russell

Sanctuary

Tales from The Dark Tower; illustrated by Joseph Vargo; edited by Joseph Vargo and Christine Filipak

Now is forever. Davis, D. S.

Now is the time. Brown, C.

Now it looks respectable. Lundquist, R.

Now let us sleep. Davidson, A.

Now that I'm Back. Afolabi, S. A.

Now That They Are Dead. Wyatt, J.

Now what? Westlake, D. E.

Now why come that is? Kenan, R.

Now You Can Hear Us, Our Stiff Wings Flapping. Howard, J.

Now you see her. Knight, M.

Now's the time. Harvey, J.

NUCLEAR BOMB See Atomic bomb

NUCLEAR ENERGY

Kalfus, K. Pu-239

NUCLEAR POWER See Nuclear energy

NUCLEAR POWER PLANTS

Shonk, K. My mother's garden

NUCLEAR WARFARE

See also Atomic bomb

Barthelme, D. Game

Bocock, M. La humanidad

Bradbury, R. The garbage collector

Menen Desleal, A. A cord made of nylon and gold

Monteiro, J. The crystal goblet

Rosen, S. Nuclear winter

Scholz, C. A draft of Canto CI

Sturgeon, T. Thunder and roses

Van Pelt, J. The long way home

Vanasco, A. Post-boomboom

NUCLEAR WEAPONS

Eakin, W. Redgunk, Texas

Rucker, R. v. B. Instability

Nuclear winter. Rosen, S.

Nude. Murr, N.

Nude. Wuori, G. K.

Nude portrait. Baker, L. J.

NUDITY

Budnitz, J. Art lesson

Mueller, D. Birds

Searle, E. 101

Tuck, L. Horses

Updike, J. Nakedness

Null-P. Tenn, W.

Number eleven. Alcott, L. M.

A number on her arm. Maraini, D.

Numbers. Hart, R.

Numbers. Redwood, J. D.

The nun. Alarcón, P. A. d.

Nuñez, Maria Eugenia Alegria

The girl typist who worked for a provincial ministry of culture

The Vintage book of international lesbian fiction; edited and with an introduction by Naomi Holoch and Joan Nestle

NUÑEZ CABEZA DE VACA, ALVAR, 16TH CENT.

About

Gonzalez, R. Cabeza de Vaca

NUNS

See also Ex-nuns

Alarcón, P. A. d. The nun

NUNS—*Continued*
Appelfeld, A. Kitty
Berkman, P. R. Veronica
Block, R. St. Anthony and the fish
Browder, C. The juice-seller's bird
Bukoski, A. Leokadia and fireflies
Chopin, K. Lilacs
Chopin, K. The lilies
Chopin, K. Two portraits
Delaney, E. J. O beauty! o truth!
Dougherty, K. When your breath freezes
Dunbar-Nelson, A. M. Sister Josepha
Erdrich, L. Saint Marie
Gonzalez, R. Spanish
Gordon, M. The deacon
Henley, P. Worship of the common heart
Herling, G. Suor Strega
Lee, V. The legend of Madame Krasinska
Maleti, G. Joseph
Maraini, D. Sister Attanasia's chickens
Newman, S. Conventual spirit
Potvin, E. A. Sister Marguerite
Robison, M. Sisters
Russ, J. Souls
Russo, R. The whore's child
Sandlin, L. The saint of bilocation
Scoville, S. The pin collectors
Smolens, J. Disciple pigeons
NURSEMAIDS
Atkinson, K. Unseen translation
Chekhov, A. P. Sleepy
Simpson, M. Coins
NURSES AND NURSING
See also Orderlies
Babel', I. Doudou
Baida, P. A nurse's story
Dann, J. Camps
Davies, R. I will keep her company
Ebershoff, D. Chuck Paa
Engel, M. P. What we ought to be
Gabriel, D. The blind woman
Gilchrist, E. The survival of the fittest
Glasgow, E. The shadowy third
Ha Jin. Flame
Highsmith, P. The trouble with Mrs. Blynn, the trouble with the world
Jones, G. 'Life probably saved by imbecile dwarf'
Klíma, I. Rich men tend to be strange
Kosinski, J. N. Steps [excerpt]
McCann, C. As Kingfishers catch fire
McEwan, I. Pornography
Mina, D. Helena and the babies
O'Neill, S. The boy from Montana
O'Neill, S. Commendation
O'Neill, S. Drugs
O'Neill, S. The exorcism
O'Neill, S. Hope is the thing with a golf club
O'Neill, S. Monkey on our backs
O'Neill, S. One positive thing
O'Neill, S. The perils of Pappy
O'Neill, S. Perquisites
O'Neill, S. Prometheus burned
O'Neill, S. Psychic hand
O'Neill, S. Three minor love stories
O'Neill, S. What dreams may come
Packer, Z. Every tongue shall confess
Pickard, N. Out of Africa
Sandor, M. Malingerer

Thurmond, J. Beauty of blood
Wharton, E. Writing a war story
The **nurses'** house. Tomlinson, N. C.
A **nurse's** story. Baida, P.
NURSING HOMES
Barnard, R. Nothing to lose
Collins, B. Dalliance at Sunnydale
Davidson, A. A quiet room with a view
Herbert, J. Others
Lee, M. Paradise dance
McCorkle, J. Turtles
Mestre, E. After Elián
Munro, A. The bear came over the mountain
Quill, M. A sound investment
Reynolds, C. A train to catch
Thompson, J. Antarctica
Yañez, R. I&M Plumbing
Nurturer by nature. Shepard, J.
Nye, Jody Lynn
Casting against type
    Such a pretty face; edited by Lee Martindale
Doing the gods' work
    Thieve's world: turning points; edited by Lynn Abbey
Everything to order
    Dracula in London; edited by P. N. Elrod
Theory of relativity
    Past imperfect; edited by Martin H. Greenberg and Larry Segriff
Nyi Pu Lay
Country Boy
    The Kenyon Review v24 no3/4 p80-9 Summ/Fall 2002
NYMPHOMANIA
Estep, M. The patient
O'Connor, F. The comforts of home
The **nymphs** and pan. Coates, G. S.
Nyren, Ron
Curtains
    The North American Review v284 no3-4 p24-25 My/Ag 1999
Dividing by zero
    The North American Review v284 no3-4 p25 My/Ag 1999
The yearbook
    The Paris Review v41 no150 p151-69 Spr 1999

O

O., Eva *See* Brantenberg, Gerd, 1941-
'O. Holt, T. E.
O **is** for opossum. Adam, C.
O.J., can you see? Brodsky, L. D.
O! little town of Bedlam. Brill, T.
O **beauty!** o truth!. Delaney, E. J.
O **brave** old world!. Davidson, A.
O **captain,** my captain. Swarthout, G. F.
O **Tannenbaum.** Locklin, G.
Oak Hill. McKillip, P. A.
OAKLAND (CALIF.) *See* California—Oakland
Oaks, Greg
Below the sick water
    Gettysburg Review v14 no1 p121-7 Spr 2001
Oasis. Clark, J.
Oates, Joyce Carol
Aiding and abetting
    Oates, J. C. I am no one you know; stories

Oates, Joyce Carol—*Continued*

The assailant
>   Best of Prairie schooner; fiction and poetry; edited by Hilda Raz

Au Sable
>   *Harper's* v298 no1785 p72-74+ F 1999
>   Oates, J. C. Faithless: tales of transgression

A Bloodsmoor Romance
>   *Ms.* v12 no3 p66-70 Summ 2002

Commencement
>   Redshift; extreme visions of speculative fiction; edited by Al Sarrantonio

The Cousins
>   *Harper's* v309 p59-68 Jl 2004

Cumberland breakdown
>   Oates, J. C. I am no one you know; stories

Curly red
>   *Harper's* v302 no1811 p86-94 Ap 2001
>   Oates, J. C. I am no one you know; stories

The dark prince
>   The World's finest mystery and crime stories, first annual collection; edited by Ed Gorman

Death cup
>   Murder most delectable; savory tales of culinary crimes; edited by Martin H. Greenberg

Death mother
>   The Best of The Kenyon review; edited by David Lynn; introduction by Joyce Carol Oates
>   Snapshots: 20th century mother-daughter fiction; edited by Joyce Carol Oates and Janet Berliner

Death watch
>   Oates, J. C. Faithless: tales of transgression

The deaths: an elegy
>   Oates, J. C. I am no one you know; stories

Do with me what you will
>   The Best American mystery stories of the century; Tony Hillerman, editor; with an introduction by Tony Hillerman
>   Speaking of lust; stories of forbidden desire; edited by Lawrence Block

The doll
>   Nightshade: 20th century ghost stories; edited by Robert Phillips

Doll: A Romance of the Mississippi
>   *Gettysburg Review* v16 no1 p5-22 Spr 2003

Faithless
>   Oates, J. C. Faithless: tales of transgression
>   The Pushcart prize XXIII: best of the small presses; an annual small press reader; edited by Bill Henderson with the Pushcart prize editors

Fire
>   Oates, J. C. I am no one you know; stories
>   *TriQuarterly* no115 p193-210 Spr 2003

First views of the enemy
>   Best of Prairie schooner; fiction and poetry; edited by Hilda Raz

Fugitive
>   Oates, J. C. I am no one you know; stories

Ghost girls
>   The Scribner anthology of contemporary short fiction; fifty North American stories since 1970; Lex Williford and Michael Martone, editors

The girl with the blackened eye
>   The Best American mystery stories, 2001; edited and with an Introduction by Lawrence Block
>   Oates, J. C. I am no one you know; stories
>   Prize stories, 2001; The O. Henry awards; edited and with an introduction by Larry Dark

Gunlove
>   Oates, J. C. Faithless: tales of transgression

Happiness
>   Oates, J. C. I am no one you know; stories
>   The World's finest mystery and crime stories, second annual collection; edited by Ed Gorman

The high school sweetheart
>   The Best American mystery stories, 2002; edited and with an introduction by James Ellroy; Otto Penzler, series editor
>   Oates, J. C. Faithless: tales of transgression

I was in love
>   Valentine's Day: women against men; stories of revenge; introduction by Alice Thomas

I'm not your son, I am no one you know
>   Oates, J. C. I am no one you know; stories

In Copland
>   Oates, J. C. Faithless: tales of transgression

In hiding
>   *Michigan Quarterly Review* v40 no2 p373-9 Spr 2001
>   Oates, J. C. I am no one you know; stories
>   On the rocks; the KGB Bar fiction anthology; edited by Rebecca Donner ; foreword by Denis Woychuk

In Hot May
>   *The Georgia Review* v58 no1 p43-55 Spr 2004

The instructor
>   Oates, J. C. I am no one you know; stories
>   Pushcart prize XXVII; best of the small presses; edited by Bill Henderson with the Pushcart prize editors
>   *Salmagundi* no132 p44-75 Fall 2001

Jorie (& Jamie)
>   *The Yale Review* v91 no3 p131-42 Jl 2003

Lover
>   Master's choice v2; mystery stories by today's top writers and the masters who inspired them; edited by Lawrence Block
>   Oates, J. C. Faithless: tales of transgression

Madison at Guignol
>   *The Kenyon Review* ns24 no1 p43-50 Wint 2002

A Manhattan romance
>   Oates, J. C. Faithless: tales of transgression

Mark of satan
>   The Art of the story; an international anthology of contemporary short stories; edited by Daniel Halpern

Me & Wolfie, 1979
>   Oates, J. C. I am no one you know; stories

Mrs. Halifax and Rickie Swann: a ballad
>   Oates, J. C. I am no one you know; stories

Murder-two
>   Master's choice [v1]; mystery stories by today's top writers and the masters who inspired them; edited by Lawrence Block

Oates, Joyce Carol—*Continued*

A moment on the edge; 100 years of crime stories by women; edited by Elizabeth George
    Oates, J. C. Faithless: tales of transgression

The museum of Dr. Moses
    The Museum of horrors; edited by Dennis Etchison

The mutants
    Oates, J. C. I am no one you know; stories

Panic
    Michigan Quarterly Review v43 no3 p413-21 Summ 2004

The photographer
    Writers harvest 3; edited and with an introduction by Tobias Wolff

Physical
    Oates, J. C. Faithless: tales of transgression

Questions
    Oates, J. C. Faithless: tales of transgression

Raven's Wing
    Sports best short stories; edited by Paul D. Staudohar

The ruins of Contracoeur
    999: new stories of horror and suspense; edited by Al Sarrantonio

The scarf
    Oates, J. C. Faithless: tales of transgression

Secret, silent
    The Best American mystery stories, 1999; edited and with an introduction by Ed McBain
    Oates, J. C. Faithless: tales of transgression

Shot
    The Ohio Review no64/65 p134-43 2001

The skull
    The Best American mystery stories, 2003; edited by Michael Connelly and Otto Penzler
    Harper's v304 p63-9 My 2002; a love story
    Oates, J. C. I am no one you know; stories

The sky-blue ball
    Crème de la crime; edited by Janet Hutchings

Soft Core
    Granta v80 p155-67 Wint 2002

Spider Boy
    The New Yorker v80 no27 p88-95 S 20 2004

The stalker
    Oates, J. C. Faithless: tales of transgression

Subway
    Datlow, E. The dark; new ghost stories; edited by Ellen Datlow

Summer sweat
    Oates, J. C. Faithless: tales of transgression

Tell me you forgive me?
    The World's finest mystery and crime stories, third annual collection; edited by Ed Gorman and Martin H. Greenberg

Three Girls
    The Georgia Review v56 no3 p771-9 Fall 2002
    Oates, J. C. I am no one you know; stories

Tusk
    Irreconcilable differences; Lia Matera, editor
    Oates, J. C. Faithless: tales of transgression

Ugly
    Oates, J. C. Faithless: tales of transgression

Upholstery
    The New Yorker v78 no4 p128-33 Mr 18 2002

Oates, J. C. I am no one you know; stories
The vampire
    Murder and obsession; edited by Otto Penzler
    Oates, J. C. Faithless: tales of transgression

The vigil
    Oates, J. C. Faithless: tales of transgression

We were worried about you
    Oates, J. C. Faithless: tales of transgression

What then, my life?
    Oates, J. C. Faithless: tales of transgression

Where are you going, where have you been?
    The Best American short stories of the century; John Updike, editor, Katrina Kenison, coeditor; with an introduction by John Updike

You, little match-girl
    Black heart, ivory bones; [edited by] Ellen Datlow & Terri Windling

Oates, Nathan

Running Rapids
    The Antioch Review v61 no4 p701-12 Fall 2003

The **oath**. Blish, J.

O'Bannion, Seamus

A singular indiscretion
    New Letters v67 no4 p121-36 2001

O'Barr, J. (James)

Spooky, Codeine, and the dead man
    The Crow; shattered lives & broken dreams; edited by J. O'Barr and Ed Kramer

O'Barr, James *See* O'Barr, J. (James)

Obeah, my love. Collins, B.

The **obedient** child. Johnson, G. C.

Obejas, Achy

Waters
    The Vintage book of international lesbian fiction; edited and with an introduction by Naomi Holoch and Joan Nestle

OBESITY

Bausch, R. What feels like the world
Bishop, M. Tithes of mint and rue
Canty, K. Flipper
Carey, P. The fat man in history
Carver, R. Fat
Chesnutt, C. W. Cartwright's mistake
Connolly, C. Indian summer
Davis, A. Faith; or, Tips for the successful young lady
Davis, C. Labors of the heart
DeMarinis, R. Life between meals
Dubus, A. The fat girl
Duffy, S. Martha Grace
Ebershoff, D. Regime
Fleming, P. L. Polyformus perfectus
Hegi, U. Stolen chocolates
Hochman, A. What's more
Holdstock, P. Sitting pretty
Huber, C. Y. and Baker, M. C. Chance hospitality
Jackson, S. Fat
Jarrell, D. The displaced overweight homemaker's guide to finding a man
King, S. Quitters, inc.
King, S. The wedding gig
López, L. Sophia
McQuillin, C. Seliki
Mueller, D. Torturing creatures at night
Nye, J. L. Casting against type
Pacheco, J. E. The queen

OBESITY—*Continued*

Rosen, S. Nuclear winter

Scarborough, E. A. Worse than the curse

Stamell, R. B. Love for a fat man

Strauss, A. Versions of you

Tenn, W. The malted milk monsters

Wisenberg, S. L. Big Ruthie imagines sex without pain

Wisenberg, S. L. Big Ruthie imagines sex without pain

Wolfe, G. The fat magician

Wolff, T. Hunters in the snow

OBITUARIES

Campbell, R. McGonagall in the head

Obituaries. Schottenfeld, S.

The **obituary** writer. Glover, D. H.

Objects of desire in the mirror are closer than they appear. Ellison, H.

The **objet** d'art. Chekhov, A. P.

Oblivion, Nebraska. Smith, P. M.

Oboe camp. Smith, S. J.

OBOE PLAYERS

Mathews, H. Brendan

The **oboist**. Ford, R.

O'Brien, Edna

A boy in the forest

The New Yorker v77 no46 p64-71 F 4 2002

A rose in the heart of New York

Snapshots: 20th century mother-daughter fiction; edited by Joyce Carol Oates and Janet Berliner

O'Brien, Flann

The third policeman [excerpt]

The Vintage book of amnesia; an anthology; edited by Jonathan Lethem

O'Brien, Tim

Going after Cacciato

Breaking into print; early stories and insights into getting published; a Ploughshares anthology; edited by DeWitt Henry

Half gone

The New Yorker v78 no18 p66-71 Jl 8 2002

Little people

Esquire v136 no4 p98-108, 188 O 2001

Nogales

The New Yorker v75 no2 p68-73 Mr 8 1999

The things they carried

The Best American short stories of the century; John Updike, editor, Katrina Kenison, coeditor; with an introduction by John Updike

The Scribner anthology of contemporary short fiction; fifty North American stories since 1970; Lex Williford and Michael Martone, editors

Too skinny

The New Yorker v77 no26 p92-100 S 10 2001

What went wrong

Esquire v138 no2 p124-8 Ag 2002

The O. Henry Prize stories, 2003; edited and with an introduction by Laura Furman; jurers David Gutterson, Diane Johnson, Jennifer Egan

O'Brien's first Christmas. Winterson, J.

Obscure domains of fear and desire. Naiyer Masud

An **obscure** geography. Di Blasi, D.

The **Obscure** Object. Eugenides, J.

The **observer**. Wilson, R. C.

Obsidian harvest. Cook, R. and Hogan, E.

OBSTETRICIANS *See* Physicians

Obvious questions. Winegardner, M.

O'Callaghan, Maxine

Bad news

O'Callaghan, M. Deal with the Devil and other stories

Black is the color of my true love's heart

O'Callaghan, M. Deal with the Devil and other stories

A change of clients

O'Callaghan, M. Deal with the Devil and other stories

Deal with the Devil

O'Callaghan, M. Deal with the Devil and other stories

Diamonds are for never

O'Callaghan, M. Deal with the Devil and other stories

Exit

O'Callaghan, M. Deal with the Devil and other stories

An insignificant crime

O'Callaghan, M. Deal with the Devil and other stories

Is you is or is you ain't Miranda?

O'Callaghan, M. Deal with the Devil and other stories

It takes one to kill one

O'Callaghan, M. Deal with the Devil and other stories

Somewhere South of Melrose

O'Callaghan, M. Deal with the Devil and other stories

Sorry, Frank

O'Callaghan, M. Deal with the Devil and other stories

Survival instinct

O'Callaghan, M. Deal with the Devil and other stories

The sweet old lady who sits in the park

O'Callaghan, M. Deal with the Devil and other stories

Wolf winter

O'Callaghan, M. Deal with the Devil and other stories

Ocampo, Flaminia

Crossing oceans

English translations of short stories by contemporary Argentine women writers; edited by Eliana Cazaubon Hermann ; translated by Sally Webb Thornton

O'Casey and the career. Goran, L.

Occam's razor. Gibson, S.

The **occasional** garden. Saki

Occidental. Doenges, J.

OCCULTISM

See also Fortune telling; Supernatural phenomena; Superstition; Witchcraft

Doyle, Sir A. C. The leather funnel

Lumley, B. Aunt Hester

McAuley, P. J. Dr Pretorius and the lost temple

Scoville, S. The dividing strand

Singer, I. B. The bishop's robe

Occupational hazard. Collins, M.

OCEAN

Clarke, A. C. The deep range

Clarke, A. C. The man who ploughed the sea

Clarke, A. C. The shining ones

OCEAN—*Continued*
Delany, S. R. Driftglass
Rucker, R. v. B. Probability pipeline
Updike, J. The sea's green sameness
The **Ocean**. Reiken, F.
The **ocean**. Richter, S.
OCEAN TRAVEL
    See also Yachts and yachting
Amis, M. Heavy water
Bauman, B. A. Eden
Bouman, I. The deep blue sea
Bunin, I. A. The gentleman from San Francisco
Burke, J. Miscalculation
Christie, A. Problem at sea
Collins, B. and Collins, M. A. A cruise to forget
Correa, A. The merry ghosts of the Grampus
Crawford, F. M. The upper berth
James, H. Pandora
James, H. The Patagonia
Latour, J. Havanightmare
Lee, D. Sailing the painted ocean
Lutz, J. S.O.S.
Malzberg, B. N. Ship full of Jews
McInerny, R. M. Mutiny of the bounty hunter
Mortimer, J. C. Rumpole at sea
Ocampo, Flaminia. Crossing oceans
Painter, P. Island tales
Pickard, N. Nine points for murder
Rippen, C. Under my skin
Ruy Sánchez, A. Voices of the water
Singer, I. B. The enemy
Teigeler, P. The wind & Mary
Vis, J. The mermaid
Vivante, A. The foghorn
Waugh, E. Cruise
Wheat, C. The time of his life
Winterson, J. Atlantic crossing
Zweig, S. Amok
OCEANIA *See* Islands of the Pacific
Oceanic. Egan, G.
Ochoa, George
This Island Queens
    The North American Review v287 no6 p8-12
    N/D 2002
Ochsner, Gina
Articles of Faith
    The Kenyon Review v25 no3/4 p1-15
    Summ/Fall 2003
The Fractious South
    The New Yorker v80 no23 p70-7 Ag 23 2004
Second skin
    New Letters v68 no2 p129-38 2002
Ockert, Jason
Scarecrowed
    Virgin fiction 2
O'Connell, Mary
I fly unto you
    O'Connell, M. Living with saints
The patron saint of girls
    O'Connell, M. Living with saints
The patron saint of travelers
    O'Connell, M. Living with saints
Saint Anne
    O'Connell, M. Living with saints
Saint Catherine Laboure
    O'Connell, M. Living with saints
Saint Dymphna
    O'Connell, M. Living with saints

Saint Martha
    O'Connell, M. Living with saints
Saint Therese of Lisieux
    O'Connell, M. Living with saints
Saint Ursula and her maidens
    O'Connell, M. Living with saints
Veronica's veil
    O'Connell, M. Living with saints
O'Connor, Flannery
The comforts of home
    The Best American mystery stories of the
    century; Tony Hillerman, editor; with an
    introduction by Tony Hillerman
    The Workshop; seven decades of the Iowa
    Writers' Workshop: 42 stories, recollections
    & essays on Iowa's place in 20th-century
    American literature; edited by Tom Grimes
A good man is hard to find
    Dark: stories of madness, murder, and the su-
    pernatural; edited by Clint Willis
Greenleaf
    The Best American short stories of the
    century; John Updike, editor, Katrina
    Kenison, coeditor; with an introduction by
    John Updike
The life you save may be your own
    The Best of The Kenyon review; edited by
    David Lynn; introduction by Joyce Carol
    Oates
        About
Stefaniak, M. H. A note to biographers regard-
    ing famous author Flannery O'Connor
O'Connor, Joseph
The long way home
    The Anchor book of new Irish writing; the
    new Gaelach ficsean; edited and with an
    introduction by John Somer and John J.
    Daly
O'Connor, Mary Beth
The story of my travels
    The Massachusetts Review v42 no2 p239-52
    Summ 2001
O'Connor, Mary Flannery *See* O'Connor,
    Flannery
Ocracoke Island. Adams, A.
Octet. Wallace, D. F.
October. Connor, J.
October. Griffith, V.
October Brown. Clair, M.
OCTOPUS
Hodgson, W. H. From the tideless sea, part one
Hodgson, W. H. The thing in the weeds
The **octopus** alibi. Corcoran, T.
Odalie misses mass. Chopin, K.
The **odd** old bird. Davidson, A.
Odds that, all things considered, she'd someday be
    happy. Gartner, Z.
Ode to Le Petomane. Tillman, L.
Odell, Bill
A foggy walk
    Dead on demand; the best of ghost story
    weekend; edited by Elizabeth Engstrom
ODESSA (UKRAINE) *See* Ukraine—Odessa
Odessa. Babel´, I.
Odilia and Liberato. Maleti, G.
Odishoo, Sarah A.
Kismet
    New Letters v69 no2/3 p65-71 2003
Odour of chrysanthemums. Lawrence, D. H.

O'Driscoll, Mike
The silence of the falling stars
  Datlow, E. The dark; new ghost stories; edited by Ellen Datlow
Sounds like
  Gathering the bones; original stories from the world's masters of horror; edited by Dennis Etchison, Ramsey Campbell and Jack Dann
ODYSSEUS (GREEK MYTHOLOGY)
Clough, B. W. Home is the sailor
Dedman, S. A walk-on part in the war
OEDIPUS (GREEK MYTHOLOGY)
Avrich, J. Chez Oedipus
Oedipus at Columbus. Greenberg, A.
Oedipus city. Kasai, K.
Of cabbages. Byrd, Z.
Of course you know that chocolate is a vegetable. D'Amato, B.
Of crystalline labyrinths and the new creation. Bishop, M.
Of Death and Diners. DeVries, M.
Of falling. Gwyn, A.
Of mist, and grass, and sand. McIntyre, V. N.
Of mystery there is no end. Michaels, L.
Of Persephone, Poe, and the Whisperer. Piccirilli, T.
Of scorned women and causal loops. Grossbach, R.
Of sketchbooks and millers, of Paris and Rome. Barolini, H.
Of the cloth. Trevor, W.
Of two minds. Weissman, B.
Of wood and stone. Seagren, R.
O'Faoláin, Seán
Persecution mania
  The Best of The Kenyon review; edited by David Lynn; introduction by Joyce Carol Oates
O'Farrell, John
Walking into the wind
  Speaking with the angel; original stories; edited by Nick Hornby
Off Grenada. Foley, S.
Off island. Parker, M.
Off Paradise. Wegner, H.
Off season. Weihe, E.
Off-season spirits. Chapman, C. M.
Off-season travel. Miller, A. L.
Off the C-47: stories from Goas Farm. Orner, P.
Off the Mangrove Coast. L'Amour, L.
Off the map. Chislett, M.
Offer of immortality. Davies, R.
An **office** romance. Bisson, T.
OFFICE WORKERS
Arvin, N. Take your child to work
Berkman, P. R. The falling nun
Berkman, P. R. Holy holy holy
Chacón, D. Andy the office boy
DeLancey, K. Great ones
Dokey, R. The mouse
Foster, K. Things you can make something out of
Gurganus, A. He's at the office
Harfenist, J. Fully bonded by the state of Minnesota
Klass, P. Exact change
Ligotti, T. Our temporary supervisor
Martin, V. Love
Mosley, W. Pet fly

Strauss, A. Versions of you
Stuckey-French, E. Search and rescue
Tester, W. Bad day
VanderMeer, J. Secret life
Officer Friendly. Robinson, L.
Officers Weep. Orozco, D.
An **official** reply. Ha Jin
Offill, Jenny
The deer
  This is where we live; short stories by 25 contemporary North Carolina writers; edited by Michael McFee
The **offshore** pirate. Fitzgerald, F. S.
Offspring of the first generation. Pesetsky, B.
Offutt, Andrew J.
Role model
  Thieve's world: turning points; edited by Lynn Abbey
Offutt, Chris
Barred owl
  Home and beyond; an anthology of Kentucky short stories; edited by Morris Allen Grubbs; with an introduction by Wade Hall and an afterword by Charles E. May
  In our nature: stories of wildness; selected and introduced by Donna Seaman
  Offutt, C. Out of the woods; stories
The best friend
  New stories from the South: the year's best, 2000; edited by Shannon Ravenel; with a preface by Ellen Douglas
Chuck's bucket
  McSweeney's mammoth treasury of thrilling tales; edited by Michael Chabon
High water everywhere
  Offutt, C. Out of the woods; stories
Inside out
  New stories from the South: the year's best, 2003; edited by Shannon Ravenel; with a preface by Roy Blount Jr.
Melungeons
  Offutt, C. Out of the woods; stories
Moscow, Idaho
  Offutt, C. Out of the woods; stories
Out of the woods
  Offutt, C. Out of the woods; stories
  The Workshop; seven decades of the Iowa Writers' Workshop: 42 stories, recollections & essays on Iowa's place in 20th-century American literature; edited by Tom Grimes
  Writers harvest 3; edited and with an introduction by Tobias Wolff
Second Hand
  Iowa Review v33 no1 p12-20 Spr 2003
  New stories from the South; the year's best, 2004; edited by Shannon Ravenel; preface by Tim Gautreaux
Target practice
  Offutt, C. Out of the woods; stories
Tough people
  Offutt, C. Out of the woods; stories
Two-eleven all around
  Offutt, C. Out of the woods; stories
Ofrenda. Chacón, D.
Ogallala. Bass, R.
Ogawa, Yoko
The Cafeteria in the Evening and a Pool in the Rain
  The New Yorker v80 no25 p146-54 S 6 2004

OGLALA INDIANS
Graebner, J. E. The living land
O'Grady, Thomas
Underfoot
Harvard Review (1992) no26 p158 2004
Oguine, Ike
The gulf
The Times Literary Supplement no5133 p8 Ag 17 2001
Oh, Albany, my love. Livingood, J.
Oh, Canada. Henkin, J.
Oh father, father, why have you come back? Cheever, J.
Oh, happy day. Lee, M.
Oh, Joseph, I'm so tired. Yates, R.
Oh land of national paradise, how glorious are thy bounties. Vollmer, M.
Oh my darling. Kelman, J.
Oh, that music (the importance of going on until the end). Jesús, P. d.
Oh, to be in England!. Wheat, C.
Oh, whistle and I'll come to you, my lad. James, M. R.
O'Hagan, Andrew
Glass cheques
The Vintage book of contemporary Scottish fiction; edited and with an introduction by Peter Kravitz
The sea shore
Grand Street no67 p147-59 Wint 1999
O'Hara, John
Drawing room B
Wonderful town; New York stories from The New Yorker; edited by David Remnick with Susan Choi
In a grove
Master's choice [v1]; mystery stories by today's top writers and the masters who inspired them; edited by Lawrence Block
Ohara, Mariko
The mental female
The Review of Contemporary Fiction v22 no2 p134-55 Summ 2002
O'Hara, Maryanne
Beyond the border of love
The North American Review v287 no1 p10-17 Ja/F 2002
OHIO
Byers, M. The beautiful days
Dunbar, P. L. Nelse Hatton's vengeance
Greer, R. O. Choosing sides
Leslie, N. Another place
Spencer, D. There's too much news
Frontier and pioneer life
See Frontier and pioneer life—Ohio
Cincinnati
Blaise, C. How I became a Jew
Greenberg, A. Tremors
Cleveland
Roberts, L. The gathering of the klan
OHIO RIVER VALLEY
Leslie, N. The scavenger's eye
Frontier and pioneer life
See Frontier and pioneer life—Ohio River Valley

Ohlin, Alix
Transcription
Best new American voices 2004; guest editor John Casey; series editors John Kulka and Natalie Danford
OIL INDUSTRY *See* Petroleum industry
The **oil** of gladness. Sanford, A.
OIL WELLS *See* Petroleum industry
OJIBWA INDIANS *See* Chippewa Indians
Okay, Diogenes, you can stop looking—we found him. Paul, B.
OKLAHOMA
Greer, R. O. Isolation
Heldrich, P. Deep red
Leonard, E. How Carlos Webster changed his name to Carl and became a famous Oklahoma lawman
Okorafor, Nnedima
Asuquo; or, The winds of Harmattan
Mojo: conjure stories; edited by Nalo Hopkinson
Okri, Ben
In the shadow of war
The Art of the story; an international anthology of contemporary short stories; edited by Daniel Halpern
What the tapster saw
The Anchor book of modern African stories; edited by Nadežda Obradovic ; with a foreword by Chinua Achebe
OLD AGE
See also Aging; Elderly
Adams, A. The girl across the room
Aldrich, B. S. He whom a dream hath possest
Aldrich, B. S. The heirs
Aldrich, B. S. The man who dreaded to go home
Aldrich, B. S. Trust the Irish for that
Alonso, D. Sophie and the angel
Anderson, R. The angel of ubiquity
Azadeh, C. A banal stain
Baida, P. Mr. Moth and Mr. Davenport
Baida, P. Points of light
Banks, R. The fisherman
Banks, R. The moor
Barker, N. Gifts
Baron, Dvora. Bubbe Henya
Bausch, R. Equity
Bausch, R. Letter to the lady of the house
Bausch, R. Wise men at their end
Bellow, S. By the St. Lawrence
Bellow, S. Leaving the yellow house
Berriault, G. The infinite passion of expectation
Berry, W. The inheritors
Bingham, S. Benjamin
Bingham, S. The splinter
Blaise, C. Notes beyond history
Bly, C. Gunnar's sword
Bocock, M. Play me "Stormy weather," please
Bonnie, F. Piano skirmish
Bonnie, F. Squatter's rights
Borges, J. L. The elderly lady
Bowles, P. The little house
Bowles, P. The scorpion
Boylan, C. Poor old sod
Bradbury, R. After the ball
Bradbury, R. All my enemies are dead
Bradbury, R. Autumn afternoon
Bradbury, R. A far-away guitar

OLD AGE—*Continued*

Bradbury, R. First day
Bradbury, R. Junior
Bradbury, R. The nineteenth
Bradbury, R. Season of disbelief
Bradbury, R. The swan
Bradbury, R. Time intervening/interim
Bradbury, R. Time intervening
Budnitz, J. Burned
Bukoski, A. The absolution of Hedda Borski
Bukoski, A. Holy walker
Bukoski, A. It had to be you
Bunin, I. A. Old and young
Burford, M. Out of the storm
Butler, R. O. A good scent from a strange mountain
Butler, R. O. Uncle Andrew
Cady, J. The lady with the blind dog
Capote, T. Preacher's legend
Carlson, R. Oxygen
Carson, J. Anonymous
Chabon, M. Mrs. Box
Chapman, C. M. Fox trot
Chekhov, A. P. Old age
Cheng, C.-W. The last of the gentlemen
Cohen, R. The next big thing
Collins, B. Dalliance at Sunnydale
Connor, J. Ursa major in Vermont
Cooke, C. The Bostons
Coward, M. Bloody victims
Davidson, A. El Vilvoy de las islas
Davies, R. I will keep her company
Davis, L. Harold Luddock's decision
DeMarinis, R. Borrowed hearts
Di Blasi, D. Blind
Dixon, S. To Tom
Dodd, S. M. In France they turn to stone when they die
Donoso, J. Ana Maria
Doran, M. M. End October
Eakin, W. Meadow song
Earley, T. Just married
Edgerton, C. Lunch at the Piccadilly
Ellison, H. Paladin of the lost hour
Engel, M. P. Queen Esther Coosawaw
Fairey, W. W. Her hair
Fielding, H. Luckybitch
Gabrielyan, N. Bee heaven
Garcia, L. G. The wedding
Gautreaux, T. Sunset in heaven
Gay, W. Closure and roadkill on the life's highway
Gifford, B. The old days
Giono, J. Jofroi de Maussan
Goran, L. An old man and three whores
Gorshman, Shira. Bubbe Malke
Grau, S. A. Flight
Grau, S. A. The patriarch
Greenberg, A. Oedipus at Columbus
Griner, P. Clouds
Hagy, A. C. Search bay
Harrison, H. No me, not Amos Cabot!
Hermann, J. The end of something
Honig, L. Hilda
Jackson, S. The summer people
Jacobsen, J. Jack Frost
James, H. A light man
Johnson-Davies, D. Cat
Jones, E. P. A dark night

Jones, E. P. Marie
Jones, H. Tom's homecoming
Jones, T. Daddy's girl
Kadish, R. The argument
Kane, J. F. Pantomime
Kaplan, H. Cuckle me
Kittredge, W. Breaker of horses
Klass, F. Jennifer's turn
Klíma, I. A baffling choice
Krawiec, R. Hardening of the arteries
Lao She. An old man's romance
Lardner, R. The golden honeymoon
Le Guin, U. K. The day before the revolution
Leavitt, D. The scruff of the neck
Leonard, E. Hanging out at the Buena Vista
Lipsyte, S. Cremains
Lispector, C. Looking for some dignity
Loomis, N. M. Grandfather out of the past
López, L. A tatting man
Lord, N. The attainable border of the birds
Lorfing, Jake. Old horse
MacLeod, A. The tuning of perfection
Maleti, G. Argia
Maleti, G. Joseph
Maleti, G. Joshua
Maleti, G. Mirta
Maleti, G. Odilia and Liberato
Malouf, D. Great Day
Mason, B. A. Wish
Mastretta, A. Aunt Cecilia
Mastretta, A. Aunt Concha
Mastretta, A. Aunt Rebeca
Matheson, R. The test
Mazelis, J. Seven thousand flowers
Mazelis, J. Siriol, she-devil of naked madness
McCorkle, J. Migration of the love bugs
McCorkle, J. Starlings
McCorkle, J. Turtles
McPherson, J. A. Gold Coast
Meinke, P. The cranes
Menendez, A. In Cuba I was a German shepherd
Mestre, E. After Elián
Muñoz, M. Anchorage
Nichols, J. The rain barrel
Ortiz, S. J. Feeling old
Pak, W.-S. Butterfly of illusion
Pak, W.-S. Farewell at Kimpo Airport
Pearlman, E. Allog
Porter, J. A. Basse Ville
Porzecanski, T. Rochel Eisips
Proulx, A. The half-skinned steer
Raphael, F. Emile
Rawley, D. Iguana boy
Rendell, R. Burning end
Rendell, R. Walter's leg
Reynolds, C. A train to catch
Rusch, K. K. The young shall see visions, and the old dream dreams
Ryman, G. V.A.O.
Saidi, W. The garden of evil
Schaeffer, S. F. The old farmhouse and the dog-wife
Seiffert, R. Francis John Jones, 1924-
Seiffert, R. The last spring
Shepard, S. Betty's cats
Shepard, S. Great dream of heaven
Shonk, K. The young people of Moscow
Singer, I. B. The hotel

OLD AGE—*Continued*

Singer, I. B. The Key
Singer, I. B. Old love
Singer, I. B. The old man
Singer, I. B. The painting
Singer, I. B. The safe deposit
Singer, I. B. The seance
Singer, I. B. The secret
Singer, I. B. The Spinoza of Market Street
Skillings, R. D. Paint
Slesar, H. The day of the execution
Slezak, E. The geese at Mayville
Smith, C. When the people fell
Sneve, V. D. H. The medicine bag
Sosin, D. The only course
Stern, S. Swan song
Swan, M. Down by the lake
Taraqqi, G. A mansion in the sky
Updike, J. A madman
Updike, J. Personal archaeology
Vivante, A. The Italian class
Walters, M. English autumn-American fall
Waters, M. Y. Circling the hondo
Waters, M. Y. The laws of evening
Watmough, D. Sharing Hale-Bopp
Watson, I. The last beast out of the box
Waugh, E. Bella Fleace gave a party
Wegner, H. The blue line
Wegner, H. Cockshut light
Wharton, E. After Holbein
Wharton, E. Duration
Wharton, E. Mrs. Manstey's view
Whitty, J. Falling umbrella
Wickham, J. The light on the sea
Yañez, R. Lucero's Mkt.
Yi, T.-H. At the door
Yi, T.-H. Perspiration
Zabytko, I. Pani Ryhotska in love
Old age. Chekhov, A. P.

OLD AGE HOMES

See also Nursing homes; Retirement communities

Bly, C. Gunnar's sword
Epstein, J. Felix emeritus
Hensley, J. L. The home
Johnson-Davies, D. A smile from the past
Kosinski, J. N. Steps [excerpt]
Norris, H. Niagara Falls
Rendell, R. The wink
Tomioka, T. Happy birthday
Vivante, A. Fall and rise
An old and established name. Lao She
Old and young. Bunin, I. A.
Old Aunt Peggy. Chopin, K.
Old birds. Cooper, B.
Old Boys, Old Girls. Jones, E. P.
The old cemetery. Drake, R.
An old college chum. McNulty, J.
The old cosmonaut and the construction worker dream of Mars. McDonald, I.
The old couple. Codrescu, A.
Old Croc. Lucas, J.
The old days. Gifford, B.
Old dogs. Campbell, B. J.
Old dogs, new tricks. Barnard, R.
The old economy husband. Dormen, L.
The old farmhouse and the dog-wife. Schaeffer, S. F.
Old flat top. Baker, K.

Old folks at home. Lupoff, R. A.
Old friend. Chiappone, R.
OLD LADIES *See* Old age
The Old Lady in the Cave. Yolen, J.
Old love affairs. Adams, A.
OLD MAIDS *See* Single women
An old man and three whores. Goran, L.
The old man slave and the mastiff. Chamoiseau, P.
An old man's romance. Lao She
The old masters. Chaudhuri, A.
OLD MEN *See* Old age
The old men used to dance. Stewart, J.
Old Music and the slave women. Le Guin, U. K.
The old mythology. Aldiss, B. W.
The old ones cast. Smee, B.
The old rugged cross. Bisson, T.
Old school ex. Lisick, B.
Old Shloyme. Babel´, I.
Old soldiers. DuBois, B.
Old soldiers. Howard, C.
Old soul. Lipsyte, S.
Old Spanish gardens. Austin, M. H.
The old system. Bellow, S.
OLD WOMEN *See* Old age
Old words—new meanings. Nomberg-Przytyk, S.
The Old Year. Keppel, T.
An older woman. Raphael, F.
The oldest trick in the book. Frym, G.
Oleanders pink and white. Johnson-Davies, D.
O'Leary, Patrick
The me after the rock
  Mars probes; edited by Peter Crowther
Olga; or, The darkest mambo. Montiel, M.
Oliphants can remember. Moody, S.
Olivares Baró, Carlos
Small creatures
  Dream with no name; contemporary fiction from Cuba; edited by Juana Ponce de León and Esteban Ríos Rivera
Olivas, Daniel A.
The plumed serpent of Los Angeles
  Fantasmas; supernatural stories by Mexican American writers; edited by Rob Johnson; introduction by Kathleen J. Alcalá
Olive oil. Walker, A.
Oliver, Bill
Excursion
  The Virginia Quarterly Review v77 no2 p339-54 Spr 2001
Handel's Father
  New Letters v69 no1 p119-37 2002
Oliver, Chad
Anachronism
  Oliver, C. Far from this earth and other stories; volume 2 of selected stories
The ant and the eye
  Oliver, C. A star above it and other stories; volume 1 of selected stories
Any more at home like you?
  Oliver, C. A star above it and other stories; volume 1 of selected stories
Artifact
  Oliver, C. A star above it and other stories; volume 1 of selected stories
Between the thunder and the sun
  Oliver, C. A star above it and other stories; volume 1 of selected stories

Oliver, Chad—_Continued_

Blood's a rover

Oliver, C. A star above it and other stories; volume 1 of selected stories

The boy next door

Oliver, C. A star above it and other stories; volume 1 of selected stories

Didn't he ramble?

Oliver, C. Far from this earth and other stories; volume 2 of selected stories

The edge of forever

Oliver, C. A star above it and other stories; volume 1 of selected stories

End of the line

Oliver, C. Far from this earth and other stories; volume 2 of selected stories

Far from this earth

Oliver, C. Far from this earth and other stories; volume 2 of selected stories

Field expedient

Oliver, C. Far from this earth and other stories; volume 2 of selected stories

Ghost town

Oliver, C. Far from this earth and other stories; volume 2 of selected stories

The gift

Oliver, C. A star above it and other stories; volume 1 of selected stories

Guardian spirit

Oliver, C. A star above it and other stories; volume 1 of selected stories

If now you grieve a little

Oliver, C. Far from this earth and other stories; volume 2 of selected stories

Just like a man

Oliver, C. Far from this earth and other stories; volume 2 of selected stories

King of the hill

Oliver, C. Far from this earth and other stories; volume 2 of selected stories

A lake of summer

Oliver, C. Far from this earth and other stories; volume 2 of selected stories

The land of lost content

Oliver, C. A star above it and other stories; volume 1 of selected stories

Let me live in a house

Oliver, C. Far from this earth and other stories; volume 2 of selected stories

Meanwhile, back on the reservation

Oliver, C. Far from this earth and other stories; volume 2 of selected stories

The mother of necessity

Oliver, C. A star above it and other stories; volume 1 of selected stories

Night

Oliver, C. A star above it and other stories; volume 1 of selected stories

North wind

Oliver, C. Far from this earth and other stories; volume 2 of selected stories

Of course

Oliver, C. Far from this earth and other stories; volume 2 of selected stories

Old four-eyes

Oliver, C. A star above it and other stories; volume 1 of selected stories

The one that got away

Oliver, C. A star above it and other stories; volume 1 of selected stories

Pilgrimage

Oliver, C. Far from this earth and other stories; volume 2 of selected stories

Rewrite man

Oliver, C. A star above it and other stories; volume 1 of selected stories

RIte of passage

Oliver, C. Far from this earth and other stories; volume 2 of selected stories

Second nature

Oliver, C. Far from this earth and other stories; volume 2 of selected stories

A star above it

Oliver, C. A star above it and other stories; volume 1 of selected stories

Stardust

Oliver, C. Far from this earth and other stories; volume 2 of selected stories

A stick for Harry Eddington

Oliver, C. A star above it and other stories; volume 1 of selected stories

Technical advisor

Oliver, C. A star above it and other stories; volume 1 of selected stories

To whom it may concern

Oliver, C. A star above it and other stories; volume 1 of selected stories

Transformer

Oliver, C. Far from this earth and other stories; volume 2 of selected stories

Transfusion

Oliver, C. A star above it and other stories; volume 1 of selected stories

The wind blows free

Oliver, C. Far from this earth and other stories; volume 2 of selected stories

Oliver, Symmes Chadwick _See_ Oliver, Chad, 1928-1993

Olivera, Felicia

Lake

Western Humanities Review v56 no2 p4-13 Fall 2002

Oliver's evolution. Updike, J.

"Ollie, oh . . . ". Chute, C.

O'Loughlin, Michael

The making of a bureaucrat

The Anchor book of new Irish writing; the new Gaelach ficsean; edited and with an introduction by John Somer and John J. Daly

Olsen, Lance

Cybermorphic beat-up get-down subterranean homesick reality-sandwich blues

The Pushcart prize XXIII: best of the small presses; an annual small press reader; edited by Bill Henderson with the Pushcart prize editors

Sixteen Jackies

New Letters v69 no4 p87-97 2003

The Wounded Angel

Iowa Review v33 no1 p109-21 Spr 2003

Olsen, Paul

She wore a yellow ribbon

We (New York, N.Y.) v3 no3 p78-81 My/Je 1999

Olsen, Sondra Spatt
Free writing
The Student body; short stories about college students and professors; edited by John McNally
A loaf of bread, a jug of wine
The Antioch Review v59 no3 p608-12 Summ 2001
Shrink
Iowa Review v31 no1 p25-32 Summ 2001
Submarine races
Southwest Review v84 no2 p269-75 1999
Olson, Torie
Tear out my heart
Fantasmas; supernatural stories by Mexican American writers; edited by Rob Johnson; introduction by Kathleen J. Alcalá
Oltion, Jerry
Abandon in place
Nebula awards 33; the year's best SF and fantasy chosen by the science-fiction and fantasy writers of America; edited by Connie Willis
Much ado about nothing
Wondrous beginnings; edited by Steven H. Silver and Martin H. Greenberg
Renaissance man
Past lives, present tense; edited by Elizabeth Ann Scarborough
Olympus Hills. Carlson, R.
Omaha. Agee, J.
O'Malley, Thomas
The banshee
Ploughshares v27 no4 p158-70 Wint 2001/2002
O'Marie, Carol Anne
Defender of the faith
Malice domestic 8
The **Omega** Force. Lugones, L.
Omegahelm. Delany, S. R.
The **omelet** king. Mandelbaum, P.
On a bridge over the Homochitto. Orner, P.
On a Bus to St. Cloud. Koldys, S.
On a fly. Burton, M.
On a railroad bridge, throwing stones. Cole, C. B.
On a windy night. Dixon, S.
On becoming a fly-fishing artiste. Burton, M.
On Florentine Road. Edelstein, J. R.
On Fridays. Gautier, A. L.
On Fridays. Raymer, R.
On golden seas. Clarke, A. C.
On guard. Waugh, E.
On his deathbed, holding your hand, the acclaimed new young off-Broadway playwright's father begs a boon. Wallace, D. F.
On Impulse. Lamp, B.
On K2 with kanakaredes. Simmons, D.
On Kingdom Mountain. Mosher, H. F.
On line. Reed, R. R.
On official business. See Chekhov, A. P. On official duty
On official duty. Chekhov, A. P.
On one familiar street. Bunin, I. A.
On Sunday there might be Americans. Ekstrom, L. S.
On the antler. Proulx, A.
On the border. Swan, M.
On the Bus. Mun, N.
On the carousel. Moody, R.

On the edge. Mazelis, J.
On the field of honor. Babel', I.
On the first day of Lent. Karnezis, P.
On the flight path. Cohen, R.
On the golden porch. TolstaıSaS, T.
On the grounds of the complex commemorating the Nazis' treatment of the Jews. Hasak-Lowy, T.
On the honeymoon. Marías, J.
On the lam. DeMarinis, R.
On the money. Kohler, S.
On the nature of human romantic interaction. Iagnemma, K.
On the occasion of my ruination. Erian, A.
On the Orion line. Baxter, S.
On the piteous death of Mary Wollstonecraft. Jones, G.
On the road. Chekhov, A. P.
On the road. Daldorph, B.
On the road to Greater Bishop. Jackson, V. F.
On the road to Szkaradowo. Wegner, H.
On the rocks. Hensley, J. L.
On the Russian River. Tatum, R.
On the side. Grodstein, L.
On the side of the road. Giono, J.
On the Streets. Trevor, W.
On the telephone. Chekhov, A. P.
On the terraces. Davies, P. H.
On the U.S.S. Fortitude. Carlson, R.
On the way to P. Lenčo, J.
On the Way to the Dewberry Gardens. Forbes, C.
On the wheel of wandering-on. Givens, J.
On the Wind River in Wyoming. Gilchrist, E.
On Venus, have we got a rabbi. Tenn, W.
On watch for Big Red. Weaver, G.
On writing the ghost story. Cady, J.
O'Nan, Stewart
20 burgers
Writers harvest 3; edited and with an introduction by Tobias Wolff
Endless summer
Death dines at 8:30; edited by Claudia Bishop and Nick DiChario
The great Rushdie
Politically inspired; edited by Stephen Elliott; assistant editor, Gabriel Kram; associate editors, Elizabeth Brooks [et al.]
Please help find
Ploughshares v25 no2/3 p140-49 Fall 1999
Once an oreo, always an oreo. Touré
"**Once** Andre Vasilevich—". Kharms, D.
Once in love in Oslo. Weldon, F.
Once more with feeling. Dwyer, M.
Once on the shores of the stream Senegambia. Mordecai, P.
Once upon a time. Abbott, L. K.
One. Effinger, G. A.
The **one-armed** man. Allen, R.
One bag of coconuts. Hoch, E. D.
One centimetre. Bi Shumin
One day in the life of a born again loser. Norris, H.
One day, Victor Hugo. . . Fleischman, C.
One dog is people. Nelson, A.
One evening, on the banks of the Tiber. Tozzi, F.
One flesh, one blood. Blackwood, S.
One for the books. Matheson, R.
One good man. Alexie, S.
One good turn. Stuart, D.

One horse town. Waldrop, H.

One-horse town. Waldrop, H. and Kennedy, L.

One hour. Hammett, D.

The **one** I remember. Banner, K.

The **One** in White. Butler, R. O.

One last soul. Bandolas, B.

One last story and that's it. Keret, E.

One Last Time, for Old Timaes' Sake. Busch, F.

One man on a desert island. See Westlake, D. E. One on a desert island

One-match fire. Dykstra, E. M.

One more for the road. Bradbury, R.

One more inning. O'Rourke, F.

One morning: 1952. Sánchez, R.

One morning in Prague. Goliger, G.

One morning with Samuel, Dorothy, and William. Davidson, A.

One night. Sánchez, R.

One night at a time. Cannell, D.

One night at Dolores Park. Pronzini, B.

One of our leprechauns is missing. Crider, B.

One of Star wars, one of Doom. Abbott, L. K.

One of those cases. Pronzini, B.

One of those days, one of those nights. Gorman, E.

One of us. Estep, M.

One of us. Savage, T.

One of us is hidden away. Blackwood, S.

One on a desert island. Westlake, D. E.

One-on-one. Greer, R. O.

One ounce of common sense. O'Rourke, F.

One out of many. Arellano, R.

One positive thing. O'Neill, S.

One Saturday afternoon. Williams, M.

One spring night. Callaghan, M.

One summer. Grau, S. A.

One Theory about my Marriage. Gilders, A.

The **one** thing God'll give you. Davis, J. S.

One-thirty-three—ringside. Van Loan, C. E.

One to go. Feist, R. E.

The **one** true place. Bingham, S.

One-way mirror. Mathews, H.

The **one** who came to save me. Piñera, V.

One woman, one love. Aqai, F.

One-woman show. Bradbury, R.

O'Neill, Susan

The boy from Montana
   O'Neill, S. Don't mean nothing; short stories of Vietnam

Broken stone
   O'Neill, S. Don't mean nothing; short stories of Vietnam

Butch
   O'Neill, S. Don't mean nothing; short stories of Vietnam

Commendation
   O'Neill, S. Don't mean nothing; short stories of Vietnam

Don't mean nothing
   O'Neill, S. Don't mean nothing; short stories of Vietnam

Drugs
   O'Neill, S. Don't mean nothing; short stories of Vietnam

The exorcism
   O'Neill, S. Don't mean nothing; short stories of Vietnam

Hope is the thing with a golf club
   O'Neill, S. Don't mean nothing; short stories of Vietnam

Medcap
   O'Neill, S. Don't mean nothing; short stories of Vietnam

Monkey on our backs
   O'Neill, S. Don't mean nothing; short stories of Vietnam

One positive thing
   O'Neill, S. Don't mean nothing; short stories of Vietnam

The perils of Pappy
   O'Neill, S. Don't mean nothing; short stories of Vietnam

Perquisites
   O'Neill, S. Don't mean nothing; short stories of Vietnam

Prometheus burned
   O'Neill, S. Don't mean nothing; short stories of Vietnam

Psychic hand
   O'Neill, S. Don't mean nothing; short stories of Vietnam

This rough magic
   O'Neill, S. Don't mean nothing; short stories of Vietnam

Three minor love stories
   O'Neill, S. Don't mean nothing; short stories of Vietnam

What dreams may come
   O'Neill, S. Don't mean nothing; short stories of Vietnam

The **ones** left behind. Richter, J.

The **Ones** Who Are Holding Things Up. Paddock, J.

The **ones** who may kill you in the morning. Nesbitt, M.

The **ones** who walk away from Omelas. Le Guin, U. K.

Onetti, Juan Carlos

Hell most feared
   The Vintage book of Latin American stories; edited by Carlos Fuentes and Julio Ortega

Onions, Oliver

The beckoning fair one
   The 13 best horror stories of all time; edited by Leslie Pockell
   Dark: stories of madness, murder, and the supernatural; edited by Clint Willis

Only a Thing. Nelson, A.

Only brotherness can warm a cold heart. Dendel, E. W.

The **only** course. Sosin, D.

An **only** daughter. Baron, D.

Only ends. Davis, J. S.

The **only** good judge. Wheat, C.

Only one way to land. Lutz, J.

Only Sons. Passanante, J.

Only the dance. Sullivan, W.

The **only** thing you learn. Malzberg, B. N.

The **only** woman in the orchestra. McCuaig, A.

Only you. Gifford, B.

O'Nolan, Brian See O'Brien, Flann, 1911-1966

ONTARIO See Canada—Ontario

The **Oort** cloud. Hardy, E.

Open arms. Roeske, P.

Open circles. Chan, D. M.

The **open** curtain. Biguenet, J.

The **open** door. Martin, V.
Open house. D'Ambrosio, C., Jr.
The **open** lot. Lopez, B. H.
Open my heart. McNally, T. M.
Open season in Beirut. Johnson-Davies, D.
The **opener** of the crypt. Jakes, J.
Opening day. Gilchrist, J.
OPERA
  Alas, L. Queen Margaret
  Alcott, L. M. The rival prima donnas
  Dixon, S. The rehearsal
  Lao She. Rabbit
  Paul, B. Portrait of the artist as a young corpse
  Schnitzler, A. Baron von Leisenbohg's destiny
  Simpson, H. Opera
  Stanton, M. Marie Antoinette's harp
  Su, D. L.-q. Beijing opera [excerpt]
Opera. Simpson, H.
OPERATION DESERT STORM *See* Persian
  Gulf War, 1991
Operation monsoon. Ramaya, S.
OPERATIONS, SURGICAL *See* Surgery
Ophelia. Mora, T.
OPIUM TRADE
  Bowles, P. Señor Ong and Señor Ha
Opossum. Adam, C.
Oppel, Jean-Hugues
  A demon in my head
    Death by espionage; intriguing stories of deception and betrayal; edited by Martin Cruz Smith
Opportunity. Pronzini, B.
Oppressive tango. Müller, H.
Optimists. Ford, R.
OPTOMETRISTS
  Chabon, M. Mrs. Box
  Updike, J. The persistence of desire
Oracle. Egan, G.
ORACLES
  Borges, J. L. The rose of Paracelsus
Oracles. Burroway, J.
The **oracular** vulva. Eugenides, J.
ORANGE
  Crane, M. The blood orange tree
The **orange** bird. Swan, G.
The **orator**. Chekhov, A. P.
Orbit. Hildt, R.
Orbit. Kalfus, K.
ORCHIDS
  Clarke, A. C. The reluctant orchid
  Dybek, S. Orchids
Order. Hearon, S.
Order of precedence. Murray, S.
The **order** of St. Anne. See Chekhov, A. P. "Anna on the neck"
The **order** of the arrow. Rinehart, S.
The **order** of things. Richard, N.
The **order** of wolves. Zelinová, H.
ORDERLIES
  Johnson, D. Emergency
Ordinary. Silber, J.
Ordinary life: a love story. Berg, E.
Ordinary Mortals. Winch, T.
The **ordinary** son. Carlson, R.
An **ordinary** woman. Greene, B.
Ordoña, Robert
  World without end
    His 3: brilliant new fiction by gay writers; edited by Robert Drake and Terry Wolverton

Ore. Bail, M.
The **ore** miner's wife. Iagnemma, K.
OREGON
  Doerr, A. The caretaker
  Kittredge, W. Breaker of horses
  Loomis, N. M. The fighting road
  Offutt, C. High water everywhere
  Overholser, W. D. The fence
  Small, K. The b-zone open
      Farm life
      See Farm life—Oregon
      Portland
  Chacón, D. Aztlán, Oregon
  Foster, K. The circuit
  Hochman, A. Liability
  McManus, J. Die like a lobster
O'Reilly, Edward
  The saga of Pecos Bill
    The American fantasy tradition; edited by Brian M. Thomsen
Oren, Yizhak
  The Cat Man
    With signs and wonders; an international anthology of Jewish fabulist fiction; edited by Daniel M. Jaffe
ORGASM
  Brodkey, H. Innocence
The **original**. Kohler, S.
Original Beauty. Clay, H.
Original sin. Herdman, J.
Original sin. Vinge, V.
Origins of the flood. Lugones, L.
Orion. Nichols, J.
Orion. Winterson, J.
Orion's glow. Rossi, A.
Orner, Peter
  At Horseneck Beach
    Orner, P. Esther stories
  At the Conrad Hilton
    Orner, P. Esther stories
  At the Motel Rainbow
    Orner, P. Esther stories
  Atlantic City
    Orner, P. Esther stories
  Awnings, bedspreads, combed yarns
    Orner, P. Esther stories
  Birth of a son-in-law
    Orner, P. Esther stories
  County Road G
    Orner, P. Esther stories
  Cousin Tuck's
    The North American Review v284 no3-4 p35-37 My/Ag 1999
    Orner, P. Esther stories
  Daughters
    Orner, P. Esther stories
  Early November
    Orner, P. Esther stories
  Esther stories
    Orner, P. Esther stories
  High priest at the gates
    Orner, P. Esther stories
  The house on Lunt Avenue
    Orner, P. Esther stories
  In the dark
    Orner, P. Esther stories
  In the walls
    Orner, P. Esther stories

Orner, Peter—*Continued*

Initials etched on a dining-room table, Lockeport, Nova Scotia
  Orner, P. Esther stories
  The Southern Review (Baton Rouge, La.) v37 no1 p121-2 Wint 2001
Melba Kuperchmid returns
  The Pushcart prize XXVI; best of the small presses, an annual small press reader; edited by Bill Henderson and the Pushcart prize editors
Melba Kuperschmid returns
  Orner, P. Esther stories
Michigan City, Indiana
  Orner, P. Esther stories
The Moraine on the lake
  Orner, P. Esther stories
My father in an elevator with Anita Fanska, August 1976
  Orner, P. Esther stories
Off the C-47: stories from Goas Farm
  Ploughshares v28 no2/3 p107-22 Fall 2002
On a bridge over the Homochitto
  Orner, P. Esther stories
Papa Gino's
  Orner, P. Esther stories
Pile of clothes
  Orner, P. Esther stories
Providence
  Orner, P. Esther stories
The raft
  The Best American short stories 2001; selected from U.S. and Canadian magazines by Barbara Kingsolver with Katrina Kenison; with an introduction by Barbara Kingsolver
  Orner, P. Esther stories
Sarah
  Orner, P. Esther stories
Seymour
  Orner, P. Esther stories
Seymour Rising
  Bomb no83 p84-5 Spr 2003
Shoe story
  Orner, P. Esther stories
Sitting Theodore
  Orner, P. Esther stories
Story of a Teacher's Wife
  The Paris Review v45 p12-15 Summ 2003
Thumbs
  Orner, P. Esther stories
Thursday night at the Gopher Hole, April 1992
  Orner, P. Esther stories
Two Poes
  Orner, P. Esther stories
Walt Kaplan reads Hiroshima, March 1947
  Lost tribe; jewish fiction from the edge
  Orner, P. Esther stories
Walter Kaplan reads John Hersey's Hiroshima, March 1947
  Michigan Quarterly Review v38 no3 p466-70 Summ 1999
The waters
  Orner, P. Esther stories

ORNITHOLOGISTS
Knight, M. Birdland

O'Rourke, Frank

The catcher
  O'Rourke, F. The heavenly World Series; timeless baseball fiction; edited by Edith Carlson; introduction by Darryl Brock
Close play at home
  O'Rourke, F. The heavenly World Series; timeless baseball fiction; edited by Edith Carlson; introduction by Darryl Brock
Decision
  O'Rourke, F. The heavenly World Series; timeless baseball fiction; edited by Edith Carlson; introduction by Darryl Brock
Flashing spikes
  O'Rourke, F. The heavenly World Series; timeless baseball fiction; edited by Edith Carlson; introduction by Darryl Brock
The greatest victory
  O'Rourke, F. The heavenly World Series; timeless baseball fiction; edited by Edith Carlson; introduction by Darryl Brock
The heavenly World Series
  O'Rourke, F. The heavenly World Series; timeless baseball fiction; edited by Edith Carlson; introduction by Darryl Brock
Home game
  O'Rourke, F. The heavenly World Series; timeless baseball fiction; edited by Edith Carlson; introduction by Darryl Brock
The impossible play
  O'Rourke, F. The heavenly World Series; timeless baseball fiction; edited by Edith Carlson; introduction by Darryl Brock
The last pitch
  O'Rourke, F. The heavenly World Series; timeless baseball fiction; edited by Edith Carlson; introduction by Darryl Brock
The last time around
  O'Rourke, F. The heavenly World Series; timeless baseball fiction; edited by Edith Carlson; introduction by Darryl Brock
Look for the kid with the guts
  O'Rourke, F. The heavenly World Series; timeless baseball fiction; edited by Edith Carlson; introduction by Darryl Brock
The magic circle
  O'Rourke, F. The heavenly World Series; timeless baseball fiction; edited by Edith Carlson; introduction by Darryl Brock
The manager
  O'Rourke, F. The heavenly World Series; timeless baseball fiction; edited by Edith Carlson; introduction by Darryl Brock
Moment of truth
  O'Rourke, F. The heavenly World Series; timeless baseball fiction; edited by Edith Carlson; introduction by Darryl Brock
Nothing new
  O'Rourke, F. The heavenly World Series; timeless baseball fiction; edited by Edith Carlson; introduction by Darryl Brock
One more inning
  O'Rourke, F. The heavenly World Series; timeless baseball fiction; edited by Edith Carlson; introduction by Darryl Brock
One ounce of common sense
  O'Rourke, F. The heavenly World Series; timeless baseball fiction; edited by Edith Carlson; introduction by Darryl Brock

O'Rourke, Frank—*Continued*

The terrible-tempered rube

    O'Rourke, F. The heavenly World Series; timeless baseball fiction; edited by Edith Carlson; introduction by Darryl Brock

O'Rourke, P. J.

Fly-fishing

    Fishing's best short stories; edited by Paul D. Staudohar

Orozco, Daniel

Officers Weep

    Harper's v308 p81-4 Je 2004

Orozco, Olga

The midgets

    Short stories by Latin American women; the magic and the real; edited by Celia Correas de Zapata; foreword by Isabel Allende

The **orphan**. Freudenberger, N.

The **orphan**. Rodburg, M.

The **orphan** lover. Rosen, N. G.

ORPHANS

Alcott, L. M. A New Year's blessing

Baca, J. S. Runaway

Baca, J. S. The Valentine's Day card

Browder, C. The juice-seller's bird

Cheng, C.-W. Spring rain

Coleman, J. C. Sandhill cranes

Gartner, Z. The tragedy of premature death among geniuses

Goldstein, N. The conduct for consoling

Gorriti, J. M. A year in California

Haslett, A. The beginnings of grief

Hays, D. Orphans

Le May, A. The little kid

Munro, A. A wilderness station

Norris, H. The second shepherd

Sanford, A. In the Little Hunky River

Singer, I. B. A crown of feathers

Steinbeck, T. Blind luck

Tamaro, S. Rispondimi

Vasilenko, S. Little fool

Vaswani, N. Where the long grass bends

Verolin, Irma. The stairway in the gray patio

Orphans of the Helix. Simmons, D.

Orphée, Elvira

The journey of Amatista and the dirty prince

    English translations of short stories by contemporary Argentine women writers; edited by Eliana Cazaubon Hermann ; translated by Sally Webb Thornton

Orringer, Julie

Care

    Orringer, J. How to breathe underwater; stories

The Isabel fish

    Orringer, J. How to breathe underwater; stories

    The Yale Review v91 no3 p106-30 Jl 2003

Note to sixth-grade self

    Orringer, J. How to breathe underwater; stories

Pilgrims

    Best new American voices 2001; guest editor Charles Baxter; series editors John Kulka and Natalie Danford

    New stories from the South: the year's best, 2002; edited by Shannon Ravenel; with a preface by Larry Brown

Orringer, J. How to breathe underwater; stories

    Ploughshares v27 no1 p133-49 Spr 2001

    Pushcart prize XXVII; best of the small presses; edited by Bill Henderson with the Pushcart prize editors

The smoothest way is full of stones

    Orringer, J. How to breathe underwater; stories

Stars of Motown shining bright

    Orringer, J. How to breathe underwater; stories

Stations of the cross

    Orringer, J. How to breathe underwater; stories

What we save

    Orringer, J. How to breathe underwater; stories

When she is old and I am famous

    Orringer, J. How to breathe underwater; stories

Ortale, Julianne

How Sin Is Unsaid

    Salmagundi no137/138 p179-87 Wint/Spr 2003

Ortega, Antonio Lopez

Naturalezas menores [excerpt]

    The Vintage book of Latin American stories; edited by Carlos Fuentes and Julio Ortega

Ortiz, Simon J.

3 women

    Ortiz, S. J. Men on the moon; collected short stories

Anything

    Ortiz, S. J. Men on the moon; collected short stories

Crossing

    Ortiz, S. J. Men on the moon; collected short stories

Distance

    Ortiz, S. J. Men on the moon; collected short stories

The end of Old Horse

    Ortiz, S. J. Men on the moon; collected short stories

Feathers

    Ortiz, S. J. Men on the moon; collected short stories

Feeling old

    Ortiz, S. J. Men on the moon; collected short stories

Hiding, west of here

    Ortiz, S. J. Men on the moon; collected short stories

Home country

    Ortiz, S. J. Men on the moon; collected short stories

Howbah Indians

    Ortiz, S. J. Men on the moon; collected short stories

Kaiser and the War

    Ortiz, S. J. Men on the moon; collected short stories

The killing of a state cop

    Ortiz, S. J. Men on the moon; collected short stories

Loose

    Ortiz, S. J. Men on the moon; collected short stories

Ortiz, Simon J.—*Continued*
Men on the moon
In our nature: stories of wildness; selected
and introduced by Donna Seaman
Ortiz, S. J. Men on the moon; collected short
stories
More than anything else in the world
Ortiz, S. J. Men on the moon; collected short
stories
The panther waits
Ortiz, S. J. Men on the moon; collected short
stories
Pennstuwehniyaahtse: Quuti's story
Ortiz, S. J. Men on the moon; collected short
stories
The San Francisco Indians
Ortiz, S. J. Men on the moon; collected short
stories
Something's going on
Ortiz, S. J. Men on the moon; collected short
stories
A story of Rios and Juan Jesus
Ortiz, S. J. Men on the moon; collected short
stories
To change life in a good way
Ortiz, S. J. Men on the moon; collected short
stories
The way you see horses
Ortiz, S. J. Men on the moon; collected short
stories
What Indians do
Ortiz, S. J. Men on the moon; collected short
stories
Where o where
Ortiz, S. J. Men on the moon; collected short
stories
Woman singing
Ortiz, S. J. Men on the moon; collected short
stories
You were real, the white radical said to me
Ortiz, S. J. Men on the moon; collected short
stories
ORTON, ARTHUR, 1834-1898
About
Borges, J. L. The improbable impostor Tom
Castro
Orzoura. Grimson, T.
Osborn, Carolyn
My brother is a cowboy
Graham, D. Lone Star literature; from the
Red River to the Rio Grande; edited by
Don Graham
The Weak Sister
The Antioch Review v61 no3 p506-15 Summ
2003
Osborn, William P.
Perfect
Southern Humanities Review v33 no3 p278-85
Summ 1999
Osborne, Karen Lee
Spectacles
The North American Review v288 no3/4 p9-
18 My/Ag 2003
Osborne's revenge. James, H.
Oscillations. Cohen, R.

Osgood, Lawrence
Great Sedna
The Year's best fantasy & horror, twelfth an-
nual collection; edited by Ellen Datlow &
Terry Windling
O'Shaughnessy, Mary
*For works written by this author in collab-
oration with Pamela O'Shaughnessy see*
O'Shaughnessy, Perri
O'Shaughnessy, Pamela
*For works written by this author in collab-
oration with Mary O'Shaughnessy see*
O'Shaughnessy, Perri
O'Shaughnessy, Perri
Juggernaut
Women before the bench; edited by Carolyn
Wheat; introduction by Linda Fairstein
Ossana, Diana
White line fever
Still wild; short fiction of the American West,
1950 to the present; edited by Larry
McMurtry
The **ossuary**. Holleran, A.
OSTRICHES
Kahn, M. A. Strange bedfellows
Moody, R. The double zero
Otaño, Magdalena Moujan *See* Moujan Otaño,
Magdalena
Other........1. Berliner, J.
The **other**. Borges, J. L.
Other. Brown, R.
Other blighters' efforts. Archer, J.
The **other** cheers. Lisick, B.
The **other** daughter. Nelson, A.
The **other** death. Borges, J. L.
The **other** duel. Borges, J. L.
The **other** lodgers. Bierce, A.
The **other** man. Schlink, B.
The **other** man in the pinstripe. Nevins, F. M., Jr.
Other people [excerpt] Amis, M.
Other people's complications. Alvarez, A.
Other people's lives. Brooks, B.
Other people's lives. Cruise, C.
Other people's mothers. Krouse, E.
Other Persons. Millás, J. J.
Other places. Jones, G.
The **Other** Side. Reene, D.
The **other** side of midnight. Newman, K.
The **other** side of the door. Sammãn, G.
The **other** side of the sky. Clarke, A. C.
The **other** tiger. Clarke, A. C.
The **other** two. Wharton, E.
The **other** urn. Quill, M.
Other way. Dixon, S.
The **Other** Williamsburg. Barrett, A.
The **other** woman. Anderson, S.
The **other** woman. Campbell, R.
The **other** woman. Lee, W. W.
The **other** woman. Raymond, I.
Others. Herbert, J.
Othmer, James P.
The Futurist
The Virginia Quarterly Review v80 no4 p100-
14 Fall 2004
Othón, the Waiter Who Lost his Memory. Ramos,
L. A.

Otis, Martha
Aida South, flower
Best new American voices 2000; guest editor Tobias Wolff; series editors John Kulka and Natalie Danford
Otis, Mary
Five-minute hearts
Best new American voices 2004; guest editor John Casey; series editors John Kulka and Natalie Danford
Otravida, otravez. Díaz, J.
Ott, Paul *See* Lascaux, Paul, 1955-
Otto, Lon
The Urban Forest
Prairie Schooner v77 no2 p27-37 Summ 2003
Ouarzazate. Tuck, L.
Our fair city. Heinlein, R. A.
Our house. Roper, M.
Our lady of death. Tremayne, P.
Our Lady of Peace. Packer, Z.
Our Lady of the Height. Jung, H.-Y.
Our lives are only lent to us. Fitzgerald, P.
Our mortal span. Waldrop, H.
Our perversions. Di Blasi, D.
Our story frays. Degollado, R.
Our Summarative History of Quixotica: Krafton, Indiana, 1987-1991. Heathcock, A.
Our temporary supervisor. Ligotti, T.
Ouroboros. Landis, G. A.
Ousmane, Sembène
Her three days
The Anchor book of modern African stories; edited by Nadežda Obradovic ; with a fore-word by Chinua Achebe
Out late in the park. Tem, S. R.
Out like a lion. Crider, B.
Out of Africa. Pickard, N.
Out of control. Howard, C.
Out of copyright. Sheffield, C.
Out of depth. Waugh, E.
Out of Purmort. Schmidt, H. J.
Out of the ashes. Hart, C. G.
Out of the blue, into the red. Lovegrove, J.
Out of the cradle, endlessly orbiting. Clarke, A. C.
Out of the depths. Pronzini, B.
Out of the girls' room and into the night. Nissen, T.
Out of the storm. Burford, M.
Out of the sun. Clarke, A. C.
Out of the woods. Campbell, R.
Out of the woods. Offutt, C.
Out-of-Work Line, 1980. Stine, P.
Out there in the darkness. Gorman, E.
Out there, in the desert. Rickstad, E.
Out west. Meek, E.
Out with the old. Yates, R.
Outcomes. Goldner, B.
Outcomes. Skillings, R. D.
OUTDOOR LIFE
See also Country life
Carlson, R. At the Jim Bridger
Henley, P. Hard feelings
Meloy, M. The river
The **outer** banks. Banks, R.
OUTER SPACE
See also Space flight
Clarke, A. C. Cosmic Casanova
Hamilton, P. F. Escape route

Exploration
Anderson, P. Gypsy
Anderson, P. Kyrie
Anderson, P. The Saturn game
Blish, J. How beautiful with banners
Clarke, A. C. Encounter in the dawn
Clarke, A. C. Jupiter five
Clarke, A. C. Rescue party
Harrison, H. Final encounter
Kornbluth, C. M. That share of glory
Van Vogt, A. E. Black destroyer
Vinge, V. Long shot
Outfangthief. Blau, G.
The **Outfielder**. Meissner, B.
The **outing**. Jackson, V. F.
Outlaw head and tail. Singleton, G.
OUTLAWS
See also Brigands and robbers
Borges, J. L. The disinterested killer Bill Harrigan
Borges, J. L. The night of the gifts
Coleman, J. C. A pair to draw to
DeRosso, H. A. The return of the Arapaho Kid
Farrell, C. The day the outlaws came
Flynn, T. T. The gun wolf
Henry, W. ". . . Fired by the hand of Robert Ford"
Henry, W. The great Northfield raid
Henry, W. Not wanted dead or alive
Henry, W. The Streets of Laredo
L'Amour, L. Booty for a badman
L'Amour, L. Caprock rancher
L'Amour, L. From the listening hills
L'Amour, L. The one for the Mohave Kid
L'Amour, L. Secret of Silver Springs
Leonard, E. The Tonto woman
McBrearty, R. G. Back in town
Overholser, S. The last ride of Gunplay Maxwell
Sandifer, L. Betrayal
Savage, L., Jr. His personal prisoner
Outlaws. Fulton, J.
Outlaws of the Purple Cow. Goran, L.
Outside paradise. James, S.
Outside The Crowded Bus. Alishan, L.
Outside the Eastern gate. Freudenberger, N.
Outside Valentine. Ward, A.
The **outsider**. Aldrich, B. S.
Outsider's chance. Landis, G. A.
Outstanding in my field. Rinehart, S.
Outtakes. Yuknavitch, L.
Over by the river. Maxwell, W.
Over my shoulder. Seidman, L.
Over Sulphur Mountain. Coberly, L. M.
Over the Cliff. Ferriss, L.
Over the H.I.L.L. Pearlman, D. D.
Over the hill. Fairey, W. W.
Over the point of cohesion. Agee, J.
Over the rainbow. Mazelis, J.
Overdoing it. Chekhov, A. P.
Overholser, Stephen
The last ride of Gunplay Maxwell
The First Five Star western corral; western stories; edited by Jon Tuska and Vicki Piekarski
Overholser, Wayne D.
The fence
Overholser, W. D. Rainbow rider; a western trio

Overholser, Wayne D.—*Continued*
The leather slapper
Overholser, W. D. Rainbow rider; a western trio
Rainbow rider
Overholser, W. D. Rainbow rider; a western trio
Overnight visitor. Hay, E.
Overpass. Anderson, D.
Overseasoned. See Chekhov, A. P. Overdoing it
Overspiced. See Chekhov, A. P. Overdoing it
Overtime. Reid, E.
Overtures. Mayo, W.
Ovid
Lycaon's punishment
The Literary werewolf; an anthology; edited by Charlotte F. Otten
Owen, M. G.
The snows of Saint Stephen
Royal whodunnits; edited by Mike Ashley
Owens, Agnes
A change of face
The Literary Review (Madison, N.J.) v45 no2 p360-6 Wint 2002
When Shankland comes
The Vintage book of contemporary Scottish fiction; edited and with an introduction by Peter Kravitz
Owl. Spencer, E.
The **owl** and the pussycat. Disch, T. M.
The **owl** of Minerva. Davenport, G.
Owling. Nordan, L.
OWLS
Barker, N. Mr. Lippy
Disch, T. M. The owl and the pussycat
Offutt, C. Barred owl
Yolen, J. Great gray
OXFORD (ENGLAND) *See* England—Oxford
OXFORDSHIRE (ENGLAND) *See* England—Oxfordshire
Oxygen. Carlson, R.
Oysters. Chekhov, A. P.
Oz, Amos
Nomad and viper
Sleepwalkers and other stories; the Arab in Hebrew fiction; edited by Ehud Ben-Ezer
Where the jackals howl
The Art of the story; an international anthology of contemporary short stories; edited by Daniel Halpern
Özdamar, Emine Sevgi
My Berlin
Chicago Review v48 no2/3 p226-30 Summ 2002
Ozème's holiday. Chopin, K.
Ozick, Cynthia
The pagan rabbi
Neurotica: Jewish writers on sex; edited by Melvin Jules Bukiet
The shawl
The Best American short stories of the century; John Updike, editor, Katrina Kenison, coeditor; with an introduction by John Updike
The Scribner anthology of contemporary short fiction; fifty North American stories since 1970; Lex Williford and Michael Martone, editors

P

P. M. R. C. Mueller, D.
P.S.. Schulman, H.
P.S. your thing is sticking out. Blitz, R.
Pablo's fandango. Mendes, A. H.
Pac-Man. Rucker, R. v. B.
Pacheco, José Emilio
The queen
The Vintage book of Latin American stories; edited by Carlos Fuentes and Julio Ortega
PACIFIC NORTHWEST
Davidson, A. The Peninsula
Gallagher, T. I got a guy once
Hirshberg, G. Struwwelpeter
Whitty, J. The dreams of dogs
PACIFIC OCEAN
World War, 1939-1945
See World War, 1939-1945—Pacific Ocean
The **pacifist**. Clarke, A. C.
Pack, Janet
Impressions
Felonious felines; edited by Carol and Ed Gorman
The Secret Staff
White House pet detectives; tales of crime and mystery at the White House from a pet's-eye view; edited by Carole Nelson Douglas
The **package**. Vonnegut, K.
Packer, Ann
A fresh start
Good Housekeeping v234 no2 p171-9 F 2002
Packer, George
The water-girl
Living on the edge; fiction by Peace Corps writers; edited by John Coyne
Packer, Nancy Huddleston
The Pioneer Women
The North American Review v287 no6 p18-24 N/D 2002
Packer, ZZ
The ant of the self
The New Yorker v78 no36 p86-95 N 25 2002
Packer, Z. Drinking coffee elsewhere
Brownies
The Best American short stories, 2000; selected from U.S. and Canadian magazines by E. L. Doctorow with Katrina Kenison; with an introduction by E. L. Doctorow
Harper's v299 no1794 p92-100 N 1999
Packer, Z. Drinking coffee elsewhere
Doris is coming
Packer, Z. Drinking coffee elsewhere
Drinking coffee elsewhere
Packer, Z. Drinking coffee elsewhere
Every tongue shall confess
The Best American short stories, 2003; selected from U.S. and Canadian magazines by Walter Mosley with Katrina Kenison; with an introduction by Walter Mosley
New stories from the South: the year's best, 2003; edited by Shannon Ravenel; with a preface by Roy Blount Jr.
Packer, Z. Drinking coffee elsewhere
Ploughshares v28 no2/3 p123-37 Fall 2002
Geese
Packer, Z. Drinking coffee elsewhere

Packer, ZZ—*Continued*
Our Lady of Peace
Packer, Z. Drinking coffee elsewhere
Speaking in tongues
Packer, Z. Drinking coffee elsewhere
The Workshop; seven decades of the Iowa Writers' Workshop: 42 stories, recollections & essays on Iowa's place in 20th-century American literature; edited by Tom Grimes
Where Eric fell
Politically inspired; edited by Stephen Elliott; assistant editor, Gabriel Kram; associate editors, Elizabeth Brooks [et al.]
Packets and paperscraps. Kurlansky, M.
Paddock, Jennifer
And when I should feel something
Stories from the Blue Moon Café; edited by Sonny Brewer
The Ones Who Are Holding Things Up
South Carolina Review v35 no2 p142-8 Spr 2003
Something temporary
The North American Review v287 no3/4 p50-4 My/Ag 2002
Paddycake, paddycake—a memoir. Apple, M.
Padgett, Abigail and Dennis, Douglas
Just stunning
Malice domestic 8
Padgett, Lewis
Mimsy were the borogoves
The Science fiction hall of fame: volume one, 1929-1964; the greatest science fiction stories of all time chosen by the members of the Science Fiction Writers of America; edited by Robert Silverberg
The twonky
Science-fiction classics; the stories that morphed into movies; compiled by Forrest J. Ackerman
Padilla, Ignacio
About our flour
Padilla, I. and Reid, A. Antipodes; Ignacio Padilla ; translated by Alastair Reid
Amends in Halak-Proot
Padilla, I. and Reid, A. Antipodes; Ignacio Padilla ; translated by Alastair Reid
The antipodes and the century
Colchie, T. A whistler in the nightworld; short fiction from the Latin Americas; edited by Thomas Colchie
Padilla, I. and Reid, A. Antipodes; Ignacio Padilla ; translated by Alastair Reid
Ballistics: some notes
Padilla, I. and Reid, A. Antipodes; Ignacio Padilla ; translated by Alastair Reid
A bestiary
Padilla, I. and Reid, A. Antipodes; Ignacio Padilla ; translated by Alastair Reid
The Chinaman with the heads
Padilla, I. and Reid, A. Antipodes; Ignacio Padilla ; translated by Alastair Reid
Chronicle of the second plague
Padilla, I. and Reid, A. Antipodes; Ignacio Padilla ; translated by Alastair Reid
Darjeeling
Padilla, I. and Reid, A. Antipodes; Ignacio Padilla ; translated by Alastair Reid

Ever wrest: log of the journey
Padilla, I. and Reid, A. Antipodes; Ignacio Padilla ; translated by Alastair Reid
The Furies of Menlo Park
The Paris Review v46 p12-18 Summ 2004
Hagiography of the apostate
Padilla, I. and Reid, A. Antipodes; Ignacio Padilla ; translated by Alastair Reid
Rhodesia Express
Padilla, I. and Reid, A. Antipodes; Ignacio Padilla ; translated by Alastair Reid
Time regained
Padilla, I. and Reid, A. Antipodes; Ignacio Padilla ; translated by Alastair Reid
Padilla, Mike
Carrying Sergei
Padilla, M. Hard language
Flora in shadows
Padilla, M. Hard language
Hard language
Padilla, M. Hard language
The king of snow
Padilla, M. Hard language
Papel
Padilla, M. Hard language
The reason for angels
Padilla, M. Hard language
Restoration
Padilla, M. Hard language
Who in the modern world can keep up with Julia Juárez?
Padilla, M. Hard language
PADUA (ITALY) *See* Italy—Padua
Padura Fuentes, Leonardo
The hunter
Dream with no name; contemporary fiction from Cuba; edited by Juana Ponce de León and Esteban Ríos Rivera
Pagan babies. Hill, I.
The **pagan** rabbi. Ozick, C.
PAGANISM
Ozick, C. The pagan rabbi
Pagano, Mabel
A death in June
English translations of short stories by contemporary Argentine women writers; edited by Eliana Cazaubon Hermann ; translated by Sally Webb Thornton
Pagans. DeMarinis, R.
Page, Gerald W.
(jt. auth) See Bishop, Michael and Page, Gerald W.
Page, Katherine Hall
The would-be widower
Malice domestic 10; an anthology of original traditional mystery stories
Page, Thomas Nelson
Unc' Edinburg's drowndin'
Southern local color; stories of region, race, and gender; edited by Barbara C. Ewell and Pamela Glenn Menke; with notes by Andrea Humphrey
Page-a-day. Singleton, G.
Pageantry. Poirier, M. J.
Pages from a journal found in a shoebox left in a Greyhound bus somewhere between Tulsa, Oklahoma, and Louisville, Kentucky. Gaiman, N.
Pages from Cold Point. Bowles, P.

Pages from the black notebook. Darvasi, L.

Paget, Violet *See* Lee, Vernon, 1856-1935

The **pagodas** of Ciboure. Bell, M. S.

(Paid advertisement). Berry, R. M.

Paige. Cantor, R.

PAIN
> *See also* Suffering

Martin, V. Messengers

Paine, Tom
> The battle of Khafji
>> Paine, T. Scar Vegas and other stories
> Ceauçsescu's cat
>> Paine, T. Scar Vegas and other stories
> Ceausescu's cat
>> *New England Review* v20 no3 p161-72 Summ 1999
> General Markman's last stand
>> Paine, T. Scar Vegas and other stories
> The hotel on Monkey Forest Road
>> Paine, T. Scar Vegas and other stories
> The mayor of St. John
>> Paine, T. Scar Vegas and other stories
> A predictable nightmare on the eve of the stock market first breaking 6,000
>> Paine, T. Scar Vegas and other stories
> Scar Vegas
>> Paine, T. Scar Vegas and other stories
> The spoon children
>> Paine, T. Scar Vegas and other stories
> Unapproved minutes of the Carthage, Vermont, Zoning Board of Adjustment
>> Paine, T. Scar Vegas and other stories
> Will you say something, Monsieur Eliot?
>> Paine, T. Scar Vegas and other stories

Paint. Skillings, R. D.

Paint doctor. Hensley, J. L.

PAINTBALL (GAME)
> Norris, L. Prisoner of war

The **Painted** Drum. Erdrich, L.

The **painted** lady. Hodgson, W. H.

Painter, Pamela
> Bedtime story
>> Painter, P. The long and short of it; short stories
> The bridge
>> Painter, P. The long and short of it; short stories
> Bringing me up it never stops
>> Painter, P. The long and short of it; short stories
> Confusing the dog
>> Painter, P. The long and short of it; short stories
> Custody
>> Painter, P. The long and short of it; short stories
> Dangerous waters
>> Painter, P. The long and short of it; short stories
> Divided highway
>> Painter, P. The long and short of it; short stories
> Doors
>> Ghost writing; haunted tales by contemporary writers; edited by Roger Weingarten
> Dud
>> Painter, P. The long and short of it; short stories

Feeding the piranha
> Painter, P. The long and short of it; short stories
Going wild
> Painter, P. The long and short of it; short stories
Grief
> The Pushcart prize XXVI; best of the small presses, an annual small press reader; edited by Bill Henderson and the Pushcart prize editors
The house that burned
> Painter, P. The long and short of it; short stories
Inside her, in heaven
> Painter, P. The long and short of it; short stories
Island tales
> Painter, P. The long and short of it; short stories
The kiss
> Painter, P. The long and short of it; short stories
The last word
> Painter, P. The long and short of it; short stories
Murder one
> Painter, P. The long and short of it; short stories
New family car
> Painter, P. The long and short of it; short stories
No faith
> Painter, P. The long and short of it; short stories
Reading in His Wake
> *Ploughshares* v29 no2/3 p163-7 Fall 2003
The real story
> Painter, P. The long and short of it; short stories
The second night of a one night stand
> Painter, P. The long and short of it; short stories
The story of Hu
> Painter, P. The long and short of it; short stories
Sympathy
> Painter, P. The long and short of it; short stories

The **Painter**. Lamb, M.

PAINTERS
> *See also* Women painters

Alcott, L. M. The rival painters: a tale of Rome

Babel´, I. Pan Apolek

Brady, C. Let my right hand forget her cunning

Chambers, R. W. The yellow sign

Chekhov, A. P. An artist's story

Cisneros, S. Never marry a Mexican

Davidson, R. Maintenance

Davies, L. Mr. Roopratna's chocolate

Davies, R. A little bit of abuse

Henry, O. Art and the bronco

Henry, O. The last leaf

Høeg, P. Portrait of the avant-garde

James, H. A landscape painter

James, H. The liar

James, H. The madonna of the future

James, H. The story of a masterpiece

James, H. The sweetheart of M. Briseux

PAINTERS—*Continued*
Kusel, L. Prairie dogs
Malamud, B. Still life
Merriman, C. Painting Juliet
Padilla, I. The Chinaman with the heads
Rosenbaum, T. Romancing the yohrzeit light
Shapiro, G. Rosenthal unbound
Shapiro, G. The twelve plagues
Singer, I. B. The captive
Wharton, E. The pot-boiler
Wharton, E. The recovery
PAINTERS, INDUSTRIAL *See* Industrial painters

The **painting**. States, B. O.
Painting house. Slavin, J.
A **painting** in Santa Fe. Gilb, D.
Painting Juliet. Merriman, C.
PAINTINGS
Arenas, R. Mona
Auchincloss, L. The last of the great courtesans
Bail, M. The drover's wife
Baker, K. The wreck of the Gladstone
Baxter, C. Harry Ginsberg
Bradbury, R. The smile
Byatt, A. S. Jael
Clarke, A. C. An ape about the house
Clarke, A. C. The road to the sea
Coates, G. S. The nymphs and pan
Davis, D. S. The purple is everything
Dunmore, H. Coosing
Forsyth, F. The art of the matter
Gilb, D. A painting in Santa Fe
Hodgson, W. H. The painted lady
King, S. The Road Virus heads north
Kittredge, W. The van Gogh field
Lee, V. A wedding chest
Marías, J. Unfinished figures
Maron, M. Craquelure
Reiner, C. Deibenquist sounds famous
Schlink, B. Girl with lizard
Singer, I. B. The painting
Stevenson, J. Crossing the water
Tiedemann, M. W. Psyché
Wharton, E. The House of the Dead Hand
Wharton, E. The moving finger
Wharton, E. The Rembrandt
Pair a spurs. Proulx, A.
A **pair** of eyes; or, Modern magic. Alcott, L. M.
A **pair** of silk stockings. Chopin, K.
A **pair** to draw to. Coleman, J. C.
Pak, Ty
The court interpreter
LA shorts; edited by Steven Gilbar
Pak, Wan-So
Butterfly of illusion
Pak, W.-S. My very last possession and other stories; translated by Chun Kyung-Ja et al.
A certain barbarity
Pak, W.-S. My very last possession and other stories; translated by Chun Kyung-Ja et al.
Encounter at the airport
Pak, W.-S. My very last possession and other stories; translated by Chun Kyung-Ja et al.
Farewell at Kimpo Airport
Pak, W.-S. My very last possession and other stories; translated by Chun Kyung-Ja et al.
Granny flowers in those heartless days
Pak, W.-S. My very last possession and other stories; translated by Chun Kyung-Ja et al.

Mr. Hong's medals
Pak, W.-S. My very last possession and other stories; translated by Chun Kyung-Ja et al.
My very last possession
Pak, W.-S. My very last possession and other stories; translated by Chun Kyung-Ja et al.
She knows, I know, and heaven knows
Pak, W.-S. My very last possession and other stories; translated by Chun Kyung-Ja et al.
Three days in that autumn
Pak, W.-S. My very last possession and other stories; translated by Chun Kyung-Ja et al.
Thus ended my days of watching over the house
Pak, W.-S. My very last possession and other stories; translated by Chun Kyung-Ja et al.
PAKISTANIS
United States
Gay, W. The paperhanger
Lahiri, J. When Mr. Pirzada came to dine
Potok, C. Moon
The **palace** of marriage. Karbo, K.
PALACES
Babel', I. An evening with the Empress
Palacios, Antonia
A gentleman on the train
Short stories by Latin American women; the magic and the real; edited by Celia Correas de Zapata; foreword by Isabel Allende
Paladin of the lost hour. Ellison, H.
A **pale** and perfectly oval moon. Adams, A.
PALEONTOLOGISTS
Lopez, B. H. The open lot
PALESTINE
See also Israel; Jerusalem
Agnon, S. Y. From foe to friend
Agnon, S. Y. Under the tree
Brenner, Y. H. Breakdown and bereavement [excerpt]
Shabtai, Y. Uncle Peretz takes flight
Smilansky, M. Latifa
Tammuz, B. My brother
PALESTINIAN ARABS
See also Jewish-Arab relations
Gabriel, D. Making peace with the Muslims
Michael, S. Refuge [excerpt]
Paleta man. King, L. R.
Paley, Grace
Justice—A Beginning
Ploughshares v29 no2/3 p168-9 Fall 2003
My father addresses me on the facts of old age
The New Yorker v78 no16 p76-83 Je 17-24 2002
Two Ways of Telling
Ms. v12 no3 p72-5 Summ 2002
Wants
Fault lines; stories of divorce; collected and edited by Caitlin Shetterly
Palimpsest day. Braunbeck, G. A.
Palisades. Nelson, A.
PALM BEACH (FLA.) *See* Florida—Palm Beach
Palm wine. McKnight, R.
Palmer, Karen
Virtuoso Mio
The Kenyon Review v25 no2 p103-17 Spr 2003
Palmer, Susan
Bent Creek Burn
Dead on demand; the best of ghost story weekend; edited by Elizabeth Engstrom

Palmer, Thomas
Dream science [excerpt]
  The Vintage book of amnesia; an anthology; edited by Jonathan Lethem
The **Palms**. Mangum, B.
Palomba, Lauro
Allergic reactions
  Dalhousie Review v79 no3 p375-87 Aut 1999
Palwick, Susan
Gestella
  Starlight 3; edited by Patrick Nielsen Hayden
Going after Bobo
  The Year's best science fiction, eighteenth annual collection; edited by Gardner Dozois
Pampas grass day. Nawrocki, S.
Pamuk, Orhan
Famous people
  Granta no68 p69-92 Wint 1999
PAN (DEITY)
Del Rey, L. The pipes of Pan
Pan Apolek. Babel´, I.
Pan for Pockot. Seepaul, L.
PANAMA
Kingsbury, Suzanne. Panama
Pancake, Ann
Cash crop: 1897
  The Massachusetts Review v40 no1 p11-25 Spr 1999
Dog song
  New stories from the South; the year's best, 2004; edited by Shannon Ravenel; preface by Tim Gautreaux
PANCAKE, BREECE D'J, D. 1979
About
Bottoms, G. Sentimental, heartbroken rednecks
The **pancake** supper. Antrim, D.
Pancho Villa's one-man war. Swarthout, G. F.
Pandora. James, H.
Pandora. Thompson, A.
Pandora's box—open with care. Sheckley, R.
The **Pang** of Queer. Winner, D.
Pangs. Mandelman, A.
Panic. Oates, J. C.
Pan's fair throng. Moody, R.
Pantalone. Polansky, S.
Panther eyes. Valenzuela, L.
Panther in the Woods. Bjorneby, K.
The **panther** waits. Ortiz, S. J.
Pantomime. Kane, J. F.
The **Pantomine** [i.e. Pantomime] Horse. Sanders, G.
The **Pantyhose** Man. Soppe, R.
Paolucci, Anne
Do me a favor
  Paolucci, A. Do me a favor and other short stories
Half a story, a third of the pie
  Paolucci, A. Do me a favor and other short stories
"If I should wake. . . ."
  Paolucci, A. Do me a favor and other short stories
Kaleidoscope
  Paolucci, A. Do me a favor and other short stories
Layover
  Paolucci, A. Do me a favor and other short stories

Mr. Gold
  Paolucci, A. Do me a favor and other short stories
Play it again!
  Paolucci, A. Do me a favor and other short stories
Soho revisited
  Paolucci, A. Do me a favor and other short stories
Summer solstice
  Paolucci, A. Do me a favor and other short stories
A tape for Bronko
  Paolucci, A. Do me a favor and other short stories
Papa Gino's. Orner, P.
Papa Marescot's family. Babel´, I.
PAPACY *See* Catholic faith; Popes
Papel. Padilla, M.
Paper from Ramleh. Kanafāni, G.
Paper Hero. Bukiet, M. J.
Paper lantern. Dybek, S.
The **paper-thin** garden. Wharton, T.
Paper trail. Strickland, L.
The **paperhanger**. Gay, W.
The **paperhanger**, the doctor's wife, and the child who went into the abstract. Gay, W.
Papernick, Jon
The art of correcting
  Papernick, J. The ascent of Eli Israel and other stories
The ascent of Eli Israel
  Papernick, J. The ascent of Eli Israel and other stories
For as long as the lamp is burning
  Papernick, J. The ascent of Eli Israel and other stories
The King of the King of Falafel
  Lost tribe; jewish fiction from the edge
  Papernick, J. The ascent of Eli Israel and other stories
Lucky eighteen
  Papernick, J. The ascent of Eli Israel and other stories
Malchyk
  Papernick, J. The ascent of Eli Israel and other stories
An unwelcome guest
  Papernick, J. The ascent of Eli Israel and other stories
PAPERS *See* Manuscripts
The **papers** of Countess D**: a tale in letters. Apukhtin, A. N.
Par. Bausch, R.
PARABLES
  See also Allegories
Avrich, J. Life in dearth
Banks, R. The fish
Borges, J. L. The lottery in Babylon
Bunin, I. A. Old and young
Byatt, A. S. Christ in the house of Martha and Mary
Davenport, G. And
Pak, W.-S. Granny flowers in those heartless days
Roth, J. The bust of the emperor
Singer, I. B. Logorihims

PARACELSUS, 1493-1541
About
Borges, J. L. The rose of Paracelsus

Paracelsus and the rose. See Borges, J. L. The rose of Paracelsus

Parachute silk. Carter, E.

The **parade**. Abrams, T.

The **parade** begins. Arenas, R.

The **parade** ends. Arenas, R.

PARADES
Abrams, T. The parade

Meredith, D. Parade's end

Parade's end. Meredith, D.

Paradise. Bail, M.

Paradise. Byrd, R. D.

Paradise. Ryan, J.

Paradise Cove. Brandt, W.

Paradise dance. Lee, M.

Paradise Drive. Connolly, C.

Paradise was this. Spatz, G.

Paragenesis. Constantine, S.

PARAGUAY
Jacobs, M. The egg queen rises

Jacobs, M. How birds communicate

Jacobs, M. The liberation of little heaven

Jacobs, M. Marina in the key of blue flat

Jacobs, M. Mengele dies again

Jacobs, M. Mud Man

Paraiso: an elegy. DeMarinis, R.

The **parakeet**. Erofeev, V.

PARAKEETS
Erofeev, V. The parakeet

Sanford, A. One summer

PARALYSIS
See also Paraplegics

PARANOIA
Blish, J. Testament of Andros

Bradbury, R. The island

Cavell, B. The death of cool

McGarry, T. Miasma

McKiernan, D. L. Darkness

Newman, K. The intervention

Schnitzler, A. Flight into darkness

Schwartz, L. S. By a dimming light

Waugh, E. Conspiracy to murder

PARAPLEGICS
Shi Tiesheng. Fate

The **parasite**. Clarke, A. C.

Paredes, Américo
The hammon and the beans

Graham, D. Lone Star literature; from the Red River to the Rio Grande; edited by Don Graham

Pareidolia. Tem, S. R.

Parekh, Asha
The dancer

Prairie Schooner v76 no2 p36-40 Summ 2002

PARENT AND CHILD
See also Conflict of generations; Fathers and daughters; Fathers and sons; Mothers and daughters; Mothers and sons

Adams, A. For good

Alcott, L. M. Mark Field's success

Arvin, N. Telescope

Bankier, W. Child of another time

Bausch, R. Fatality

Bausch, R. Glass meadow

Bausch, R. The person I have mostly become

Bausch, R. What feels like the world

Bean, B. Lost children

Bellow, S. Something to remember me by

Bender, K. E. Eternal love

Berberova, N. Kolka and Liusenka

Berkman, P. R. Jennet

Biguenet, J. Rose

Bloom, A. A blind man can see how much I love you

Bloom, A. Hold tight

Boggs, B. Who is Beatrice?

Bowles, P. In the red room

Brady, C. The end of the class war

Brady, C. The lives of the saints

Brenner, W. The human side of instrumental transcommunication

Brodkey, H. Verona: a young woman speaks

Brownstein, G. A penal colony all his own, 11E

Caponegro, M. Epilogue of the progeny; or, Whoever is never born with the most toys wins

Card, O. S. Lost boys

Carlson, R. Milk

Chabon, M. Werewolves in their youth

Chaon, D. Falling backwards

Chaon, D. The illustrated encyclopedia of the animal kingdom

Cohen, R. What makes you you

Crowell, E. Perfectly good

Daugherty, T. Assailable character

Davies, P. H. Everything you can remember in thirty seconds is yours to keep

Davies, P. H. Today is Sunday

Davies, Tristan. Alfalfa valve

Davis, L. A man like that

Dix, S. Matters of consequence

Dixon, S. On a windy night

Doctorow, E. L. Willi

Dodd, S. M. The lost art of sleep

Doran, M. M. A family in winter

Drake, R. The last old maid in town

Dubus, A. The winter father

Dunmore, H. Lisette

Egan, G. Singleton

Evans, E. Home ec

Franzen, J. The failure

Fulton, J. Braces

Gartner, Z. Anxious objects

Gilchrist, E. Perhaps a miracle

Glover, D. H. Iglaf and Swan

Glover, D. H. My romance

Gordimer, N. The generation gap

Gorman, E. En famille

Grau, S. A. Letting go

Greenberg, A. Crimes against humanity

Greer, A. S. Four bites

Gunn, K. Not that much to go on

Gunn, K. Not that much to go on: 2

Hall, D. The accident

Harris, M. At Prayerbook Cross

Houston, P. Waltzing the cat

Johnson, A. The history of cancer

Johnston, B. A. Waterwalkers

Joseph, D. Naming stories

Kalu, Anthonia C. Ogbanje father

Kavaler, R. Pets

Kenan, R. Hobbits and hobgoblins

Klass, P. Dedication

Klass, P. The trouble with Sophie

Leegant, J. Accounting

PARENT AND CHILD—*Continued*

Leff, R. J. Burn your maps

Leong, R. Where do people live who never die?

Lewis, Mark Ray. Scordatura

López, L. To control a rabid rodent

Malouf, D. Closer

Matheson, R. Little girl lost

Mayo, W. Jagged tooth, great tooth

McKee, J. Under the influence

McManus, J. June 1989

McWilliam, C. Seven magpies

Michaels, L. City boy

Müller, H. Mother, father, and the little one

Müller, H. Nadirs

Muñoz, M. Zigzagger

Murakami, H. All God's children can dance

Nabokov, V. V. Symbols and signs

Nawrocki, S. Boys

Painter, P. Divided highway

Painter, P. The real story

Perabo, S. Some say the world

Ponte, A. J. In the cold of the Malecón

Richmond, M. Monkey stew

Richmond, M. The world's greatest pants

Ritchie, E. Telling Mr. M.

Robison, M. May Queen

Rodgers, S. J. Fits and starts

Sanford, A. Strangers and pilgrims

Saroyan, A. Chloe

Schwartz, L. S. Referred pain

Seiffert, R. The crossing

Seiffert, R. Dog-leg lane

Škvorecký, J. The mysterious events at night

Smart, A. The wedding Dress

Spencer, D. Blood work

Spencer, E. Jack of diamonds

Stableford, B. M. The milk of human kindness

Sumner, M. Good-hearted woman

Svoboda, T. Lost the baby

Swann, M. Flower children

Swift, G. Learning to swim

Thomas, D. Grandma Hotel Adams

Tinti, H. Bloodworks

Updike, J. How was it, really?

Wallace, D. F. Incarnations of burned children

Wallace, R. Animal rights

Ward, L. Dancing lessons

Weaver, G. Imagining the structure of free space on Pioneer Road

Wegner, H. Cockshut light

Weldon, F. A great antipodean scandal

Wells, K. Star-dogged moon

West, M. Under the skin

Wilson, R., Jr. Grief

Wood, M. That one autumn

Yates, R. Trying out for the race

Parents. Garcia, L. G.

The **parents**. Hay, E.

Parents. Wuori, G. K.

Paretipua. Te Awekotuku, N.

Paretsky, Sara

At the Century of Progress

Edwards, M. Mysterious pleasures; a celebration of the Crime Writers' Association's 50th anniversary; edited by Martin Edwards

The case of the Pietro Andromache

A moment on the edge; 100 years of crime stories by women; edited by Elizabeth George

Grace notes

A Century of noir; thirty-two classic crime stories; edited by Mickey Spillane and Max Allan Collins

Heartbreak house

A Century of great suspense stories; edited by Jeffery Deaver

Three-Dot Po

The Best American mystery stories of the century; Tony Hillerman, editor; with an introduction by Tony Hillerman

Pargeter, Edith, 1913-1995

For works written by this author under other names see Peters, Ellis, 1913-1995

Pariahs. Wisniewski, M.

PARIS (FRANCE) *See* France—Paris

PARIS (FRANCE). EIFFEL TOWER *See* Eiffel Tower (Paris, France)

PARIS (LEGENDARY CHARACTER)

Haskell, J. The judgment of Psycho

Paris. Kane, J. F.

Paris. McGarry, J.

Paris. Rawson, E.

Paris by night. Kohler, S.

A **Paris** Story. Sloan, L. L.

Park, Severna

The cure for everything

Nebula Awards showcase 2003; edited by Nancy Kress

The Year's best science fiction, eighteenth annual collection; edited by Gardner Dozois

The golem

Black heart, ivory bones; [edited by] Ellen Datlow & Terri Windling

Park bench. Budnitz, J.

Park Cinema. Poniatowska, E.

Park host. Spencer, D.

Parker, Dorothy

Arrangement in black and white

Wonderful town; New York stories from The New Yorker; edited by David Remnick with Susan Choi

Here we are

The Best American short stories of the century; John Updike, editor, Katrina Kenison, coeditor; with an introduction by John Updike

Parker, Graham

Aub

Parker, G. Carp fishing on valium and other tales of the stranger road traveled

Bad nose

Parker, G. Carp fishing on valium and other tales of the stranger road traveled

The Birdman of Cleveland

Parker, G. Carp fishing on valium and other tales of the stranger road traveled

Carp fishing on valium

Parker, G. Carp fishing on valium and other tales of the stranger road traveled

Chloroform

Parker, G. Carp fishing on valium and other tales of the stranger road traveled

The evening before . . .

Parker, G. Carp fishing on valium and other tales of the stranger road traveled

Me and the Stones

Parker, G. Carp fishing on valium and other tales of the stranger road traveled

Parker, Graham—*Continued*
  Scenes from new Europe
    Carved in rock; short stories by musicians;
      edited by Greg Kihn
  The sheld-duck of the Basingstoke Canal
    Parker, G. Carp fishing on valium and other
      tales of the stranger road traveled
  Tinseltown, Morocco
    Parker, G. Carp fishing on valium and other
      tales of the stranger road traveled
  Well well well
    Parker, G. Carp fishing on valium and other
      tales of the stranger road traveled
Parker, Jeff
  The Taste of Penny
    Ploughshares v29 no4 p74-90 Wint
      2003/2004
Parker, Michael
  Commit to memory
    This is where we live; short stories by 25
      contemporary North Carolina writers; ed-
      ited by Michael McFee
  I Will Clean Your Attic
    The Literary Review (Madison, N.J.) v46 no3
      p408-24 Spr 2003
  Off island
    New stories from the South: the year's best,
      2003; edited by Shannon Ravenel; with a
      preface by Roy Blount Jr.
    Pushcart prize XXVII; best of the small
      presses; edited by Bill Henderson with the
      Pushcart prize editors
Parker, Robert B.
  Harlem nocturne
    The Best American mystery stories, 2002; ed-
      ited and with an introduction by James
      Ellroy; Otto Penzler, series editor
Parker, T. Jefferson
  Easy street
    The Best American mystery stories, 2001; ed-
      ited and with an Introduction by Lawrence
      Block
The **Parker** shotgun. Grafton, S.
Parker Swells. Barker, N.
PARKINSONISM
  Bloom, A. The gates are closing
  Lawson, C. Unborn again
  Nissen, T. 29th Street Playground, September
    1968
  Nissen, T. At the No. 1 Phoenix Garden
Parkison, Aimee
  Warnings
    The North American Review v289 no3/4 p3-8
      My/Ag 2004
Parks, Julie Anne
  The covenant of Il Vigneto
    The Darkest thirst; a vampire anthology
Parks, Tim
  In Defiance of Club Rules
    The New Yorker v79 no29 p106-11 O 6 2003
PARKS
    See also Amusement parks; Zoos
  Brownrigg, S. The bird chick
  Dixon, S. The rehearsal
  Frym, G. Live oak
  Gao Xingjian. In the park
  Menendez, A. In Cuba I was a German shep-
    herd
  Vivante, A. The park

Weihe, E. Green Lake
The **Parmachene** Belle. Peterson, E. L.
PAROCHIAL SCHOOLS *See* Church schools
PARODIES
    See also names of prominent authors
      with the subdivision Parodies, imitations,
      etc.
  Alvarez, A. Death by bricolage
  Breen, J. L. The big nap
  Coover, R. The sheriff goes to church
  Davenport, G. Mr. Churchyard and the troll
  Fitzgerald, F. S. Jemina, the mountain girl
  Marston, E. and Lovesey, P. The Corbett corre-
    spondence: "Agent no. 5 & Agent no. 6"
  Perelman, S. J. Farewell, my lovely appetizer
  Schneider, P. Des saucisses, sans doute
  Updike, J. Commercial
  Wallace, D. F. Datum centurio
  Wellen, E. The adventure of the blind alley
Parotti, Phillip
  A Gathering of Kites
    The Sewanee Review v110 no4 p513-30 Fall
      2002
  Spot of Trouble
    The Sewanee Review v112 no1 p1-21 Wint
      2004
Parra, Eduardo Antonio
  Real life
    Points of departure; new stories from Mexico;
      edited by Mónica Lavín; translated by Gus-
      tavo Segade
PARRICIDE
  Blatnik, A. His mother's voice
  Oates, J. C. Murder-two
  Rendell, R. Piranha to Scurfy
Parris, P. B.
  Carmen Miranda's navel
    This is where we live; short stories by 25
      contemporary North Carolina writers; ed-
      ited by Michael McFee
Parrish, Tim
  After the river
    Parrish, T. Red stick men; stories
  Bonnie Ledet
    Parrish, T. Red stick men; stories
  Complicity
    Parrish, T. Red stick men; stories
  Exterminator
    Parrish, T. Red stick men; stories
  Free fall
    Parrish, T. Red stick men; stories
  Hardware man
    Parrish, T. Red stick men; stories
  It pours
    Parrish, T. Red stick men; stories
  Roustabout
    New England Review v20 no4 p23-33 Fall
      1999
    Parrish, T. Red stick men; stories
  The smell of a car
    Parrish, T. Red stick men; stories
Parrot. Gilders, A.
The **parrot** and Descartes. Melville, P.
PARROTS
  Brown, C. Father Judge Run
  Butler, R. O. Mr. Green
  Chaon, D. I demand to know where you're tak-
    ing me
  Hoch, E. D. Martha's parrot

PARROTS—*Continued*
Knight, M. Birdland
Lopez, B. H. Mornings in Quarain
Melville, P. The parrot and Descartes
Porter, J. A. Basse Ville
Singer, I. B. The parrot
Parry, Owen, 1952-
    See also Peters, Ralph, 1952-
A **part** of history. Collins, M.
Part of the story. Dobyns, S.
Part of Their Nature. Hashimoto, S.
Partial people. Bisson, T.
The **participant**. Blitz, R.
A **particular** calling. Boylan, C.
PARTIES
    See also Dinners
Bank, M. The wonder spot
Barthelme, F. With Ray & Judy
Bingham, S. Benjamin
Bowles, P. Midnight mass
Brennan, M. The servants' dance
Brownrigg, S. Mars needs women!
Broyard, B. Snowed in
Capote, T. The walls are cold
Carlson, R. Olympus Hills
Chaudhuri, A. The party
Chekhov, A. P. "Anna on the neck"
Chopin, K. At the 'Cadian ball
Cobb, T. Small-block chevy
Cohen, R. The bachelor party
DeMarinis, R. Feet
Etchison, D. My present wife
Evans, M. Candles in the bottom of the pool
Fitzgerald, F. S. Babes in the woods
Foster, K. Red dresses
Girardi, R. The dinner party
Heller, J. The death of the dying swan
Heller, J. Girl from Greenwich
Holleran, A. The hamburger man
Lee, M. A fresh start
McBain, E. Happy New Year, Herbie
McNally, J. The politics of correctness
Menendez, A. The party
Moody, R. The carnival tradition
Orner, P. Daughters
Penn, W. S. Cowboys and Indians
Penn, W. S. Toothpaste
Pynchon, T. Entropy
Reilly, L. 1984
Shepard, S. An unfair question
Singer, I. B. The New Year party
Singer, I. B. There are no coincidences
Taylor, P. H. Venus, cupid, folly and time
Tillman, L. The undiagnosed
Updike, J. During the Jurassic
Updike, J. The happiest I've been
Updike, J. I will not let thee go, except thou
    bless me
Updike, J. A trillion feet of gas
Waugh, E. Bella Fleace gave a party
Yates, R. The best of everything
Yates, R. The canal
A **parting** gift. Ťažký, L.
PARTINGS (FAREWELLS) *See* Farewells
Partisan wedding. Viganò, R.
PARTISANS *See* Guerrillas
The **partitions**. Bail, M.
Partly him. McGarry, J.
Partners. Geng, V.

Partners. Silber, J.
Partridge, Norman
Blackbirds
    The Year's best fantasy & horror, twelfth an-
    nual collection; edited by Ellen Datlow &
    Terry Windling
Parts and labor. Schaffert, T.
Parts of Speech. Dinh, V.
Parts runner. Wilson, R., Jr.
The **Party**. Berg, E.
The **party**. Chaudhuri, A.
The **party**. Chekhov, A. P.
The **Party**. Dixon, S.
The **party**. Menendez, A.
Party girl. Svoboda, T.
Party girls. Davis, L.
Party of one. Nelson, A.
Party of the two parts. Tenn, W.
The **party** over there. Baumer, J. R.
Parvin, Roy
Betty Hutton
    The Best American short stories 2001; select-
    ed from U.S. and Canadian magazines by
    Barbara Kingsolver with Katrina Kenison;
    with an introduction by Barbara Kingsolver
The **Parwat** Ruby. Sherman, D.
Paschal, Dean
By the light of the jukebox
    Paschal, D. By the light of the jukebox
Death of a street dog
    Paschal, D. By the light of the jukebox
Genesis (The G.I. bleed)
    Paschal, D. By the light of the jukebox
L'Annonciation
    Paschal, D. By the light of the jukebox
Moriya
    The Best American short stories, 2003; select-
    ed from U.S. and Canadian magazines by
    Walter Mosley with Katrina Kenison; with
    an introduction by Walter Mosley
    Paschal, D. By the light of the jukebox
The puppies
    Paschal, D. By the light of the jukebox
Python
    Paschal, D. By the light of the jukebox
Sautéing the platygast
    Paschal, D. By the light of the jukebox
Pasquali, Marc de'
Envy
    In the forbidden city; an anthology of erotic
    fiction by Italian women; edited by Maria
    Rosa Cutrufelli; translated by Vincent J.
    Bertolini
The **pass**. Almond, S.
Passage. Allen, S.
Passage. Brkic, C. A.
Passage. Dozois, G. R.
Passanante, Joy
Only Sons
    Gettysburg Review v15 no2 p299-309 Summ
    2002
Passaro, Vince
Love, sin and forgiveness at the Village Café
    Gentlemen's Quarterly v71 no6 p138-48 Je
    2001
The **passenger**. Aylett, S.
The **passenger**. Brockmeier, K.
The **passenger**. McAuley, P. J.
Passenger. Thurm, M.

Passengers. Busch, F.
Passengers. Schumacher, J.
Passengers. Silverberg, R.
Passengers, remain calm. Chaon, D.
Passeur. Berger, J.
Passing. De Lint, C.
Passing for faith. Mandrell, L.
The **passing** night. Berry, M. S.
The **passing** of Grandison. Chesnutt, C. W.
Passion. Munro, A.
A **passion** for the cook. Squire, E. D.
A **passionate** pilgrim. James, H.
PASSOVER
What, L. The man I loved was an elf
Passover. Hemon, A.
Passport soup. Keegan, C.
Passport to paradise. Warner-Vieyra, M.
Pasta night. Currier, J.
Pastor, Ben
Achilles' grave
Death dines at 8:30; edited by Claudia Bishop and Nick DiChario
Ghost writing; haunted tales by contemporary writers; edited by Roger Weingarten
Pastor Dowe at Tacate. Bowles, P.
Pastoralia. Saunders, G.
PASTORS *See* Clergy
Pasulka, Brigid K.
What We Do To Ourselves (1994)
Confrontation no86/87 p43-68 Spr/Summ 2004
The **Patagonia**. James, H.
Patch. Slezak, E.
Patch. See Chekhov, A. P. Whitebrow
Patent pending. Clarke, A. C.
Paterson, Mark
Not Your Personal Ashtray
Dalhousie Review v83 no3 p415-25 Aut 2003
The **path** of duty. James, H.
PATHOLOGISTS *See* Physicians
The **patient**. Estep, M.
Patient zero. Due, T.
Patients. Adams, A.
The **patriarch**. Grau, S. A.
Patriotic. Kauffman, J.
PATRIOTISM
Wharton, E. The letters
The **patron** saint of girls. O'Connell, M.
The **patron** saint of travelers. O'Connell, M.
Patten, Gilbert *See* Standish, Burt L., 1866-1945
Pattern of behavior. Bishop, P.
Patterson, Ama
Hussy Strutt
Dark matter; a century of speculative fiction from the African diaspora; edited by Sheree R. Thomas
Patterson, Kevin
Boatbuilding
Patterson, K. Country of cold; stories of sex and death
Country of cold
Patterson, K. Country of cold; stories of sex and death
Gabriella: parts one and two
Patterson, K. Country of cold; stories of sex and death
Hudson Bay in winter
Patterson, K. Country of cold; stories of sex and death
Insomnia, infidelity, and the leopard seal
Patterson, K. Country of cold; stories of sex and death
Interposition
Patterson, K. Country of cold; stories of sex and death
Les is more
Patterson, K. Country of cold; stories of sex and death
Manitoba Avenue
Patterson, K. Country of cold; stories of sex and death
The Perseid shower
Patterson, K. Country of cold; stories of sex and death
Saw marks
Patterson, K. Country of cold; stories of sex and death
Sick in public
Patterson, K. Country of cold; stories of sex and death
Starlight, starbright
Patterson, K. Country of cold; stories of sex and death
Structure is constant
Patterson, K. Country of cold; stories of sex and death
Patterson, Steven
Aground and Aloft
Iowa Review v34 no1 p26-42 Spr 2004
Patton, Fiona
The control device
Once upon a galaxy; edited by Will [sic] McCarthy, Martin H. Greenberg, and John Helfers
The raven's quest
Magical beginnings; edited by Steven H. Silver and Martin H. Greenberg
PATTON, GEORGE S. (GEORGE SMITH), 1885-1945
About
George Patton slept here
Paul, Barbara
The favor
Paul, B. Jack be quick and other crime stories
French asparagus
Paul, B. Jack be quick and other crime stories
Ho ho ho
Paul, B. Jack be quick and other crime stories
Jack be quick
A moment on the edge; 100 years of crime stories by women; edited by Elizabeth George
Paul, B. Jack be quick and other crime stories
Okay, Diogenes, you can stop looking—we found him
Paul, B. Jack be quick and other crime stories
Play nice
Paul, B. Jack be quick and other crime stories
Portrait of the artist as a young corpse
Paul, B. Jack be quick and other crime stories
Scat
Paul, B. Jack be quick and other crime stories
Stet
Brought to book; murderous stories from the literary world; Penny Sumner, editor
Paul, B. Jack be quick and other crime stories
Paul and me. Blumlein, M.

PAUL BUNYAN (LEGENDARY CHARACTER)

Blumlein, M. Paul and me

Paula. Miller, R.

Paul's case. Cather, W.

Paulsen, Steven

Ma rung

Dreaming down-under; edited by Jack Dann and Janeen Webb

The **pause** button. Aldiss, B. W.

Paver, Chaver

The boxing match

When night fell; an anthology of Holocaust short stories; edited by Linda Schermer Raphael and Marc Lee Raphael

Pavlov's smile. Di Blasi, D.

PAWNBROKERS

Offutt, C. Second hand

Vonnegut, K. Souvenir

PAWNEE INDIANS

Lafferty, R. A. Narrow Valley

Paxson, Diana L.

The prisoner in the jewel

Thieve's world: turning points; edited by Lynn Abbey

The **pay-back** race. Farrell, C.

Paz, Senel

Don't tell her you love her

The Vintage book of Latin American stories; edited by Carlos Fuentes and Julio Ortega

Paz Soldán, Edmundo

Dochera

Colchie, T. A whistler in the nightworld; short fiction from the Latin Americas; edited by Thomas Colchie

Peabody, Richard

Astro City

The North American Review v288 no3/4 p28-37 My/Ag 2003

The **Peabody** ducks and all the rest. Drake, R.

Peace. Nguyen, D. T.

PEACE CORPS (U.S.)

Abrams, T. Joe Grind

Brazaitis, M. The heroes of our stories

Coyne, J. Snow man

Davidson, R. A private life

Eggers, P. Anything you want, please

Eggers, P. Leo, chained

Houghteling, M. K. Ma Kamanda's latrine

Nissen, T. A bungalow, Koh Tao

Peace officer. Garfield, B.

The **peacebroker**. Brkic, C. A.

Peach. Swan, M.

The **peach** stone. Horgan, P.

Peaches. Mazelis, J.

Peaches and plums. Kohler, S.

The **peacock** throne. Anderson, D.

Peanuts. Schweikert, R.

A **pear-shaped** woman and a fuddy-duddy. Porter, J. A.

Pearce, Adewale Maja- *See* Maja-Pearce, Adewale

Pearl baby. Wilson, R. C.

The **pearl** diver. McBrearty, R. G.

Pearlberg, Gerry

Caravan

Hers 2: brilliant new fiction by lesbian writers; edited by Terry Wolverton with Robert Drake

Pearlman, Daniel D.

The best-known man in the world

Pearlman, D. D. The best-known man in the world and other misfits

The circus hand's desertion

Pearlman, D. D. The best-known man in the world and other misfits

Cogitor, ergo sum

Pearlman, D. D. The best-known man in the world and other misfits

The colonel's jeep

Pearlman, D. D. The best-known man in the world and other misfits

Death in the des(s)ert

Pearlman, D. D. The best-known man in the world and other misfits

The drang of speaking forth

Pearlman, D. D. The best-known man in the world and other misfits

The Einstein-Jung connection

Pearlman, D. D. The best-known man in the world and other misfits

The fall of the house

Pearlman, D. D. The best-known man in the world and other misfits

Over the H.I.L.L.

Pearlman, D. D. The best-known man in the world and other misfits

Spellchecked

Pearlman, D. D. The best-known man in the world and other misfits

The Vatican's secret cabinet

Pearlman, D. D. The best-known man in the world and other misfits

Zeno evil

Pearlman, D. D. The best-known man in the world and other misfits

Pearlman, Edith

Accommodators

The Antioch Review v57 no4 p482-92 Fall 1999

Allog

The Best American short stories, 2000; selected from U.S. and Canadian magazines by E. L. Doctorow with Katrina Kenison; with an introduction by E. L. Doctorow

Chance

The Antioch Review v59 no2 p334-46 Spr 2001

Prodigal Niece

The Antioch Review v62 no3 p458-65 Summ 2004

Skin deep

New stories from the South: the year's best, 2001; edited by Shannon Ravenel; with a preface by Lee Smith

The story

The O. Henry Prize stories, 2003; edited and with an introduction by Laura Furman; jurers David Gutterson, Diane Johnson, Jennifer Egan

PEARLS

Hodgson, W. H. The problem of the pearls

Taylor, T. L. Pope's own

Pearson, T. R.

Dividends and distributions

Esquire v135 no6 p151-2 Je 2001

PEASANT LIFE
Caribbean region
Chamoiseau, P. Red hot peppers
China
Fischerová, D. The thirty-sixth chicken of Master Wu
France
Giono, J. The great fence
Giono, J. The hand
Giono, J. In the land of the tree cutters
Giono, J. Lost rafts
Giono, J. Magnestism
Giono, J. Philemon
Giono, J. Prelude to pan
Giono, J. The sheep
Russia
Chekhov, A. P. The burbot
Chekhov, A. P. A malefactor
Chekhov, A. P. Peasants
Chekhov, A. P. Sorrow
Peasant wives. Chekhov, A. P.
Peasant women. See Chekhov, A. P. Peasant wives

PEASANTS
Peasants
Kreitman, Esther Singer. A satin coat
Peasants. Chekhov, A. P.

Pease, Emily
Heed
The Georgia Review v55 no3 p545-62 Fall 2001

Pebble in time. Davidson, A.

Peck, Dale
Bliss
Prize stories, 2001; The O. Henry awards; edited and with an introduction by Larry Dark
Cities of the plain
On the rocks; the KGB Bar fiction anthology; edited by Rebecca Donner ; foreword by Denis Woychuk
The law of diminishing returns
Granta no65 p48-64 Spr 1999

PEDDLERS AND PEDDLING
Hawthorne, N. Mr. Higginbotham's catastrophe
Vinge, V. The peddler's apprentice
The **peddler's** apprentice. Vinge, V.
The **Pedersen** kid. Gass, W. H.

PEDIATRICIANS *See* Physicians

PEDOPHILIA
Maraini, D. The boy Gramophone and the pigeon man
Theroux, P. A Judas memoir
Willis, M. S. Another perversion
Young, T. Too busy swimming
Pedro Salvadores. Borges, J. L.

Peel, John
Toccata and feud
The Literary Review (Madison, N.J.) v42 no3 p423-32 Spr 1999

Peep Hall. Boyle, T. C.
Peep show. Englander, N.
Peep show (I). Englander, N.
Peeping Tom. Galloway, J.

Peery, Janet
Huevos
Texas bound. Book III; 22 Texas stories; edited by Kay Cattarulla; foreword by Robert Flynn

Peether is full of blather. McNulty, J.
PEKING (CHINA) *See* China—Beijing
Pelan, John
The mystery of the worm
Shadows over Baker Street; edited by Michael Reaves and John Pelan
Pelecanos, George P.
The dead their eyes implore us
The Best American mystery stories, 2003; edited by Michael Connelly and Otto Penzler
Pelegrimas, Marthayn
I'm not that kind of girl
Speaking of lust; stories of forbidden desire; edited by Lawrence Block
Pelegrimas, Marthayn and Randisi, Robert J.
I love everything about you
The World's finest mystery and crime stories, first annual collection; edited by Ed Gorman
Money-back guarantee
Flesh and blood: guilty as sin; erotic tales of crime and passion; edited by Max Allan Collins and Jeff Gelb
Pelevin, Victor
The life and adventures of shed number XII
The Art of the story; an international anthology of contemporary short stories; edited by Daniel Halpern
The **pelican**. Wharton, E.
Pelican Song. Hughes, M.-B.
A **penal** colony all his own, 11E. Brownstein, G.
Penance. Donaldson, S. R.
A **penance**. Edwards, S.
The **Penance** Practicum. McGraw, E.
Peñaranda, Oscar
Day of the butterfly
The North American Review v286 no1 p34-41 Ja/F 2001
Pendarvis, Jack
Escape by Zebra
Stories from the Blue Moon Cafe II; edited by Sonny Brewer
Pendleton, Jan
Truly great people
The Antioch Review v60 no3 p511-22 Summ 2002
Penelope. Gavell, M. L.
Penelope's silver wedding anniversary. Vallbona, R. d.
The **Penguin** Parade. Wallace, R.
The **Peninsula**. Davidson, A.
PENIS
Kureishi, H. The penis
Phillips, G. Branded
Silverstein, S. The guilty party
The **penis**. Kureishi, H.
Penn, W. S. (William S.)
Cowboys and Indians
Penn, W. S. This is the world
Early age and late disorder
Penn, W. S. This is the world
Fog
Penn, W. S. This is the world
Grab hold
Penn, W. S. This is the world
In dreams begins reality
Penn, W. S. This is the world
Interlude
Penn, W. S. This is the world

Penn, W. S. (William S.)—*Continued*
Neither
  Penn, W. S. This is the world
Rosa
  Penn, W. S. This is the world
So much water, underground
  Penn, W. S. This is the world
Star Lake, long ago
  Penn, W. S. This is the world
Storm watch
  Penn, W. S. This is the world
Talking turkey, not goose
  Penn, W. S. This is the world
Tarantulas
  Penn, W. S. This is the world
This is the world
  Penn, W. S. This is the world
Toothpaste
  Penn, W. S. This is the world
Penn, William S. *See* Penn, W. S. (William S.),
  1949-
Pennee, Robert
Fiorello
  Dalhousie Review v79 no3 p367-73 Aut 1999
Penney, Bridget
Incidents on the road
  The Vintage book of contemporary Scottish
  fiction; edited and with an introduction by
  Peter Kravitz
Pennstuwehniyaahtse: Quuti's story. Ortiz, S. J.
PENNSYLVANIA
Banks, R. The visit
O'Nan, S. 20 burgers
Updike, J. The gun shop
Updike, J. The happiest I've been
Updike, J. My father on the verge of disgrace
        Gettysburg
Perabo, S. The measure of devotion
        Philadelphia
Johnson, C. R. The plague
Major, M. Kenya and Amir
McQuain, K. Erasing Sonny
Wideman, J. E. Fever
        Pittsburgh
Blaise, C. Dunkelblau
Goran, L. Adventurer
Goran, L. Alias Eleanor Roosevelt
Goran, L. The Big Broadcasts
Goran, L. Caught
Goran, L. The chorus girl
Goran, L. A day at the lake
Goran, L. The death of the quarterback
Goran, L. A guest on Good Friday
Goran, L. The inheritance
Goran, L. Jenny and the Episcopalian
Goran, L. Keeping count
Goran, L. O'Casey and the career
Goran, L. An old man and three whores
Goran, L. Outlaws of the Purple Cow
Goran, L. The priest of storms
Goran, L. Say something to Miss Kathleen
  Lacey
Goran, L. Shannon made of sunlight and bones
Goran, L. Why he never left his wife
Paul, B. The favor
PENNSYLVANIA DUTCH
Joseph, D. Expatriates
The **penny** drops. Rodwell, I. and Duffy, S.
Penny For My Thoughts. Greenside, M.

The **pennymen**. De Lint, C.
The **pension** Beaurepas. James, H.
PENSIONS
Bowles, P. The hours after noon
The **penthouse**. Holleran, A.
Penuel, John
(jt. auth) *See* Ribeyro, Julio Ramón
The **penultimate** conjecture. Michaels, L.
Penumbra. Lordan, B.
The **people** across the canyon. Millar, M.
People came from earth. Baxter, S.
People don't seem to think things out straight in
  this gin mill. McNulty, J.
People in hell just want a drink of water. Proulx,
  A.
The **people** in room 3P. McNally, R.
People of the crater. Norton, A.
The **people** speak. Johnson, C. R.
The **people** versus De Marco. Reiner, C.
People who sit in glass houses. Dunlap, S.
The **people's** way. Sandstrom, E. K.
Pepper. Bloom, J.
Pepper. Hunter, F.
Perabo, Susan
Counting the ways
  Perabo, S. Who I was supposed to be; short
  stories
Explaining death to the dog
  Perabo, S. Who I was supposed to be; short
  stories
Gravity
  Perabo, S. Who I was supposed to be; short
  stories
The greater grace of Carlisle
  Perabo, S. Who I was supposed to be; short
  stories
The measure of devotion
  Perabo, S. Who I was supposed to be; short
  stories
Reconstruction
  Perabo, S. Who I was supposed to be; short
  stories
Retirement
  Perabo, S. Who I was supposed to be; short
  stories
The rocks over Kyburz
  Perabo, S. Who I was supposed to be; short
  stories
Some say the world
  Perabo, S. Who I was supposed to be; short
  stories
Thick as thieves
  Perabo, S. Who I was supposed to be; short
  stories
Who I was supposed to be
  Perabo, S. Who I was supposed to be; short
  stories
Peralejo, Cristina
Manang
  Calyx v22 no1 p23-34 Summ 2004
Percentage trust. Weldon, F.
Percussion. Miner, V.
Percy, Walker
The second coming [excerpt]
  The Vintage book of amnesia; an anthology;
  edited by Jonathan Lethem
Percy Wallingford. Berners, G. H. T.-W., Baron
Perdído. Sorrentino, G.

Perdido: a fragment from a work in progress. Straub, P.

Perdita's wrapper. Woodrow, M.

Peredelkino. Kalfus, K.

Perelman, S. J. (Sidney Joseph)
Farewell, my lovely appetizer
 Wonderful town; New York stories from The New Yorker; edited by David Remnick with Susan Choi

Perelman, Sidney Joseph *See* Perelman, S. J. (Sidney Joseph), 1904-1979

Peretz, Isaac Leib
Bryna's Mendl
 Beautiful as the moon, radiant as the stars; Jewish women in Yiddish stories : an anthology; edited by Sandra Bark; introduction by Francine Prose
Cabalists
 Neugroschel, J. No star too beautiful; Yiddish stories from 1382 to the present; compiled and translated by Joachim Neugroschel
Hear, o Israel; or, The bassist
 Neugroschel, J. No star too beautiful; Yiddish stories from 1382 to the present; compiled and translated by Joachim Neugroschel
On the stagecoach
 Neugroschel, J. No star too beautiful; Yiddish stories from 1382 to the present; compiled and translated by Joachim Neugroschel
Stories
 Neugroschel, J. No star too beautiful; Yiddish stories from 1382 to the present; compiled and translated by Joachim Neugroschel

Pérez, Ricard de la Casa *See* Casa Pérez, Ricard de la, 1954-

Pérez Galdós, Benito
"The mule and the ox"
 Fedorchek, R. M. Stories of enchantment from nineteenth-century Spain; translated from the Spanish by Robert M. Fredorchek; introduction by Alan E. Smith
"The princess and the street urchin"
 Fedorchek, R. M. Stories of enchantment from nineteenth-century Spain; translated from the Spanish by Robert M. Fredorchek; introduction by Alan E. Smith

"**Pérez** the Mouse". Coloma, L.

Perfect. Osborn, W. P.

A **perfect** circle. Griffin, D.

The **perfect** crime. Redman, B. R.

The **perfect** fruit. Menendez, A.

The **perfect** gift. Vukcevich, R.

Perfect heart. Bean, B.

The **perfect** lawn. Campbell, B. J.

Perfect love. Boylan, C.

The **perfect** man. Rusch, K. K.

Perfect Planning. Avey, L.

Perfect recall. Beattie, A.

The **perfect** revenge. Cross, A.

The **perfect** rotter. Wellen, E.

Perfect shadows. Marston, E.

The **perfecting** of the Chopin Valse No. 14 in E Minor. Naslund, S. J.

PERFECTION
Brennan, M. The gentleman in the pink-and-white striped shirt
Hawthorne, N. The birthmark

Perfection. Gelb, J.

The **perfectionist.** Lovesey, P.

Perfectly good. Crowell, E.

The **performance.** Miller, A.

PERFORMANCE ART
Disch, T. M. The first annual performance art festival at the Slaughter Rock Battlefield
Hochman, A. Local currency
Leong, R. Samsara
Matera, L. Performance crime
Richter, S. Sally's story
Weaver, G. Mannequin

Performance crime. Matera, L.

PERFORMERS *See* Entertainers

Perfume: a tale of felicity. Codrescu, A.

PERFUMES
Dueñas, G. In heaven
Naiyer Masud. Essence of camphor

Perhaps a miracle. Gilchrist, E.

Peri Rossi, Cristina
Breaking the speed record
 Short stories by Latin American women; the magic and the real; edited by Celia Correas de Zapata; foreword by Isabel Allende
Final judgment
 The Vintage book of international lesbian fiction; edited and with an introduction by Naomi Holoch and Joan Nestle
Singing in the desert
 The Vintage book of international lesbian fiction; edited and with an introduction by Naomi Holoch and Joan Nestle

Perihesperon. Bear, G.

Peril at Melford house. Eccles, M.

Perillo, Lucia Maria
Bad boy number seventeen
 The Pushcart prize XXIII: best of the small presses; an annual small press reader; edited by Bill Henderson with the Pushcart prize editors
High tea
 New England Review v20 no2 p167-76 Spr 1999
Slash (1976)
 The North American Review v288 no1 p29-31 Ja/F 2003
The wife of the Indian
 The Student body; short stories about college students and professors; edited by John McNally

The **perils** of Pappy. O'Neill, S.

Period piece. Waugh, E.

PERIODICALS
Harrison, H. No me, not Amos Cabot!
Lupoff, R. A. Whatever happened to Nick Neptune?
Wallace, D. F. The Suffering Channel

Perkins, Emily
Her new life
 Coppola, F. F. Francis Ford Coppola's Zoetrope: all story; edited by Adrienne Brodeur and Samantha Schnee; introduction by Francis Ford Coppola
The indelible hulk
 Typical girls; new stories by smart women; edited by Susan Corrigan

Perle, Yeshue
A legend
 Neugroschel, J. No star too beautiful; Yiddish stories from 1382 to the present; compiled and translated by Joachim Neugroschel

Permanence. Gilliland, G.
Permanent wave. Budnitz, J.
Perp walk. Vachss, A. H.
Perpetuity blues. Barrett, N., Jr.
Perquisites. O'Neill, S.
Perrault, Charles
  Toads and diamonds
    Witches' brew; edited by Yvonne Jocks
Perrotta, Tom
  The chosen girl
    Gettysburg Review v14 no2 p211-24 Summ
    2001
Perry, Anne
  The case of the bloodless sock
    The World's finest mystery and crime stories,
    third annual collection; edited by Ed
    Gorman and Martin H. Greenberg
  Daisy and the Christmas goose
    Malice domestic 10; an anthology of original
    traditional mystery stories
  The end of innocence
    The best British mysteries; edited by Maxim
    Jakubowski
  The escape
    Crème de la crime; edited by Janet Hutchings
  Heroes
    Murder and obsession; edited by Otto Penzler
    The World's finest mystery and crime stories,
    first annual collection; edited by Ed
    Gorman
  Sing a song of sixpence
    Bishop, C. and James, D. Death dines in; ed-
    ited by Claudia Bishop and Dean James
Perry, Anne and Saxon, Malachi
  The case of the Highland hoax
    Murder, my dear Watson; new tales of Sher-
    lock Holmes; edited by Martin H. Green-
    berg, Jon Lellenberg, Daniel Stashower
Perry, Bliss
  At the Polo Grounds
    Dead balls and double curves; an anthology
    of early baseball fiction; edited and with an
    introduction by Trey Strecker ; with a fore-
    word by Arnold Hano
Perry, Drew
  And Also with You
    South Carolina Review v34 no1 p134-49 Fall
    2001
  Love is gnats today
    New stories from the South; the year's best,
    2004; edited by Shannon Ravenel; preface
    by Tim Gautreaux
Perry, George Sessions
  Hold autumn in your hand
    Graham, D. Lone Star literature; from the
    Red River to the Rio Grande; edited by
    Don Graham
Perry, Steve
  The case of the wavy black dagger
    Shadows over Baker Street; edited by Michael
    Reaves and John Pelan
Persaud, Sasenarine
  Canada geese and apple chatney
    The Oxford book of Caribbean short stories;
    edited by Stewart Brown and John
    Wickham
PERSECUTION
    See also Atrocities; Jews—Persecutions
  Hawthorne, N. The gentle boy

The **Perseid** meteors. Coleman, J. C.
The **Perseid** shower. Patterson, K.
The **Perseids**. Wilson, R. C.
**PERSHING, JOHN J. (JOHN JOSEPH), 1860-
1948**
      About
  American mandate
PERSIA *See* Iran
PERSIAN GULF WAR, 1991
  Anderson, R. Photographs: rub Al Khali, 1990-
  91
The **Person**. Jenkins, G.
Persona. Banville, J.
PERSONAL ADVERTISING *See* Personals
Personal archaeology. Updike, J.
PERSONAL BEAUTY
  Bauman, B. A. True
  Chiang, T. Liking what you see: a documentary
  García Márquez, G. The handsomest drowned
    man in the world
  Goldner, B. Waxing
  Gorman, E. Eye of the beholder
  Mayo, W. Robert's bride
  Nailah, A. Deena
  Orringer, J. When she is old and I am famous
  Richter, S. The beauty treatment
  Wharton, E. The looking-glass
Personal correspondence. Thurm, M.
Personal effects. Kalman, J.
Personal foundations of self-forming through auto-
  identification with otherness. Reifler, N.
A **personal** letter. Hay, E.
PERSONAL NAMES
  Clarke, A. C. Sleeping beauty
  Driskell, L. V. A fellow making himself up
  Sneve, V. D. H. Jimmy Yellow Hawk
PERSONALITY
  Dann, J. Camps
PERSONALITY DISORDERS
    See also Dual personality; Hallucinations
    and illusions; Insane, Criminal and danger-
    ous
  Barker, N. Parker Swells
  Barthelme, D. Game
  Berners, G. H. T.-W., Baron. Percy Wallingford
  Chute, C. "Ollie, oh . . . "
  Cohen, R. Oscillations
  Crace, J. The prospect from the silver hills
  Davila, A. The end of a struggle
  Harrison, K. Planting
  Knight, D. F. The country of the kind
  LaValle, V. D. Ghost story
  McGuane, T. Dogs
  O'Connor, F. A good man is hard to find
  Searle, E. Celebrities in disgrace
  Singer, I. B. The admirer
  Wharton, E. The House of the Dead Hand
PERSONALS
  Boylan, C. Concerning virgins
Perspiration. Yi, T.-H.
Pertwee, Roland
  The river god
    Fishing's best short stories; edited by Paul D.
    Staudohar
PERU
      Lima
  Loayza, L. A new man
  Lopez, B. H. The letters of heaven
  Taylor, Nick. The smell of despair

PERU—Lima—*Continued*
Tuck, L. Limbo
The **perv**. Alameddine, R.
Pesce volante. Burford, M.
Pesetsky, Bette
Offspring of the first generation
The Workshop; seven decades of the Iowa
Writers' Workshop: 42 stories, recollections
& essays on Iowa's place in 20th-century
American literature; edited by Tom Grimes
Peshkov, Alekseĭ Maksimovich *See* Gorky,
Maksim, 1868-1936
Pest control for dummies. Gartner, Z.
Pesthouse. Bukoski, A.
PESTS
Control
Parrish, T. Exterminator
Sanders, W. The scuttling; or, Down by the sea
with Marvin and Pamela
Pet fly. Mosley, W.
Pet milk. Dybek, S.
The **Petchenyeg**. Chekhov, A. P.
**PETER I, THE GREAT, EMPEROR OF RUS-
SIA, 1672-1725**
About
Pushkin, A. S. The blackamoor of Peter the
Great
Peter. Viganò, R.
Peter and Wendy [excerpt] Barrie, J. M.
Peter Goldthwaite's treasure. Hawthorne, N.
PETER PAN (FICTITIOUS CHARACTER)
Barrie, J. M. Peter and Wendy [excerpt]
Peter Shelley. Marber, P.
Peter the Great's negro. See Pushkin, A. S. The
blackamoor of Peter the Great
Peters, Elizabeth
The locked tomb mystery
Into the mummy's tomb; edited by John
Richard Stephens
Peters, Ellis
Guide to doom
Edwards, M. Mysterious pleasures; a celebra-
tion of the Crime Writers' Association's
50th anniversary; edited by Martin Edwards
Peters, Ralph
Retaliation
On glorious wings; the best flying stories of
the century; edited and introduced by Ste-
phen Coonts
Peter's buddies. Carson, M.
Peterson, Edwin L.
The Parmachene Belle
Fishing's best short stories; edited by Paul D.
Staudohar
Peterson, Paula W.
Africa
Peterson, P. W. Women in the grove; Paula
W. Peterson
Alfie and Grace
Peterson, P. W. Women in the grove; Paula
W. Peterson
The as and is
Peterson, P. W. Women in the grove; Paula
W. Peterson
Big Brother
Iowa Review v33 no2 p45-57 Fall 2003
Peterson, P. W. Women in the grove; Paula
W. Peterson

Cherry's ghost
Peterson, P. W. Women in the grove; Paula
W. Peterson
In the grove
Peterson, P. W. Women in the grove; Paula
W. Peterson
A miracle
Peterson, P. W. Women in the grove; Paula
W. Peterson
Song of Camille
Peterson, P. W. Women in the grove; Paula
W. Peterson
The woman in the long green coat
Peterson, P. W. Women in the grove; Paula
W. Peterson
Un **petit** d'un petit. Lee, A.
Petra. Bear, G.
Petra. Codrescu, A.
Petrakis, Harry Mark
The Birthday
New Letters v69 no1 p57-73 2002
Petrified forest. Bell, M. S.
The **petrified** woman. Gordon, C.
Petrified woman. Svoboda, T.
Petrignani, Sandra
Body
In the forbidden city; an anthology of erotic
fiction by Italian women; edited by Maria
Rosa Cutrufelli; translated by Vincent J.
Bertolini
Petroglyphs. Thomas, S. P.
Petroleum. Babel´, I.
PETROLEUM INDUSTRY
Burleson, D. R. Pump Jack
Johnson-Davies, D. Oleanders pink and white
Parrish, T. Roustabout
Swofford, A. Freedom Oil
PETRONIUS ARBITER
About
Pushkin, A. S. A tale of Roman life
Petrov, David Shrayer- *See* Shrayer-Petrov, Da-
vid, 1936-
PETS
See also names of individual pets
Delany, S. R. The star pit
Martin, G. R. R. Sandkings
Škvorecký, J. The mysterious events at night
Winterson, J. Psalms
Pets. Kavaler, R.
Petter, Sylvia
Widow's peak
Valentine's Day: women against men; stories
of revenge; introduction by Alice Thomas
Pettigrew, Dawn Karima
Atasdi: fish story
Death dines at 8:30; edited by Claudia Bishop
and Nick DiChario
Petty, Audrey
Here
African American Review v35 no1 p73-6 Spr
2001
PETTY, RICHARD
About
Singleton, G. Richard Petty accepts national
book ward
Petty theft. Wilson, M.
Petunias. Holleran, A.
Pfitz [excerpt] Crumey, A.

Pflug, Ursula
  Bugtown
    Northern suns; edited by David G. Hartwell
      & Glenn Grant
PHAEDRA (GREEK MYTHOLOGY)
  Henderson, L. Tragic heroines tell all
Phallicide. Sheffield, C.
Phan, Aimee
  Gates of Saigon
    The Virginia Quarterly Review v80 no1 p144-
      61 Wint 2004
  Miss Lien
    Prairie Schooner v77 no4 p8-22 Wint 2003
The **phantom** farmhouse. Quinn, S.
The **phantom** highwayman. Goulart, R.
The **phantom** of Billancourt. Berberova, N.
The **phantom** of Dunwell Cove. Sheffield, C.
The **phantom** ship. Brennan, K.
Phantoms. Tillman, L.
Pharaoh's smile. Švenková, V.
PHARMACEUTICAL INDUSTRY
  Baida, P. The rodent
PHARMACISTS
  Steinbeck, T. Sing Fat and the Imperial Duchess
    of Woo
PHAROAHS *See* Egypt—Kings and rulers
Phenomena. Carlson, R.
PHILADELPHIA (PA.) *See* Pennsylvania—Phila-
  delphia
PHILANTHROPISTS
  Davidson, A. What strange stars and skies
  Singer, I. B. There are no coincidences
  Wharton, E. The Rembrandt
PHILANTHROPY *See* Philanthropists
Philemon. Giono, J.
Philip, Marlene Nourbese
  Stop frame
    Best of Prairie schooner; fiction and poetry;
      edited by Hilda Raz
PHILIPPINES
                            Manila
  Murray, S. The caprices
  Murray, S. Intramuros
  Murray, S. Yamashita's gold
Philip's room. Berry, M. S.
Phillian, Gregory S.
  My Confession
    South Carolina Review v36 no1 p52-63 Fall
      2003
Phillips, Arthur
  Wenceslas Square
    Fishman, B. Wild East; stories from the last
      frontier; edited with an introduction by Bo-
      ris Fishman
Phillips, Dale Ray
  At the edge of the new world
    Phillips, D. R. My people's waltz
  Corporal love
    Phillips, D. R. My people's waltz
  Everything quiet like church
    Phillips, D. R. My people's waltz
  My people's waltz
    Phillips, D. R. My people's waltz
  What it cost travelers
    Phillips, D. R. My people's waltz
  What men love for
    Phillips, D. R. My people's waltz
  What we are up against
    Phillips, D. R. My people's waltz

  When love gets worn
    Phillips, D. R. My people's waltz
  Why I'm talking
    Phillips, D. R. My people's waltz
  The woods at the back of our houses
    Phillips, D. R. My people's waltz
    This is where we live; short stories by 25
      contemporary North Carolina writers; ed-
      ited by Michael McFee
Phillips, Gary
  '53 Buick
    The World's finest mystery and crime stories,
      first annual collection; edited by Ed
      Gorman
  Branded
    Flesh and blood; erotic tales of crime and
      passion; edited by Max Allan Collins and
      Jeff Gelb
  The measure
    The Blue and the gray undercover; edited by
      Ed Gorman
  The raiders
    Flesh and blood: guilty as sin; erotic tales of
      crime and passion; edited by Max Allan
      Collins and Jeff Gelb
  The sleeping detective
    The World's finest mystery and crime stories,
      second annual collection; edited by Ed
      Gorman
Phillips, Jayne Anne
  Alma
    The Workshop; seven decades of the Iowa
      Writers' Workshop: 42 stories, recollections
      & essays on Iowa's place in 20th-century
      American literature; edited by Tom Grimes
  The Bad Thing
    Ploughshares v29 no2/3 p170-2 Fall 2003
  Gemcrack
    Breaking into print; early stories and insights
      into getting published; a Ploughshares an-
      thology; edited by DeWitt Henry
Phillips, Louis
  In the house of simple sentences
    100% pure Florida fiction; an anthology; ed-
      ited by Susan Hubbard and Robley Wilson
Phillips, Michael
  Audrey
    Dalhousie Review v84 no2 p261-75 Summ
      2004
Phillips, Robert S.
  Wolfie
    Nightshade: 20th century ghost stories; edited
      by Robert Phillips
Phillips, Scott
  Sockdolager
    The Best American mystery stories, 2003; ed-
      ited by Michael Connelly and Otto Penzler
PHILOSOPHERS
  Evenson, B. The wavering knife
  Pearlman, D. D. Zeno evil
  Singer, I. B. Caricature
  Singer, I. B. The Spinoza of Market Street
A **philosophy** of dust. Bukoski, A.
PHILOSOPHY OF LIFE *See* Life (Philosophy of
  life)
PHILOSPHERS
  Herling, G. Ugolone da Todi: obituary of a phi-
    losopher

Philp, Geoffrey
  My brother's keeper
    The Oxford book of Caribbean short stories;
      edited by Stewart Brown and John
      Wickham
  Uncle Obadiah and the alien
    Whispers from the cotton tree root; Caribbean
      fabulist fiction; edited by Nalo Hopkinson
Phipps, Marilene
  Marie-Ange's ginen
    The Best American short stories, 2003; select-
      ed from U.S. and Canadian magazines by
      Walter Mosley with Katrina Kenison; with
      an introduction by Walter Mosley
    Callaloo v25 no4 p1075-82 Fall 2002
The **Phlebotomist's** Boyfriend. Schoech, S.
Phlegm. Jackson, S.
Phoca the waiter. Johnson, S.
PHOENIX (ARIZ.) *See* Arizona—Phoenix
Phoenix eyes. Leong, R.
Phone calls. Bolaño, R.
Photogenique. Berberova, N.
The **photograph**. Harshbarger, K.
The **photographer**. Oates, J. C.
PHOTOGRAPHERS
    See also Women photographers
  Bail, M. Huebler
  Bowles, P. Tapiama
  Bukiet, M. J. The war lovers
  Campbell, R. The limits of fantasy
  Cohen, R. Points of interest
  Corcoran, T. The octopus alibi
  Cortázar, J. Blow-up
  DeMarinis, R. Billy Ducks among the pharaohs
  Dickey, E. J. Café Piel
  Kachtick, K. Hungry ghost
  Kosinski, J. N. Steps [excerpt]
  Leiber, F. The girl with the hungry eyes
  Lida, D. Shuttered
  Marshall, T. American model
  Muñoz, M. Not Nevada
  Murphy, D. The history of photography
  Oates, J. C. The photographer
  Potvin, E. A. You are here
  Ross, L. Tasting songs
  Rusch, K. K. Burial detail
  Rusch, K. K. The gallery of his dreams
  Santos-Febres, M. Flight
  Smith, P. M. Forgetting the girl
  Updike, J. Ethiopia
PHOTOGRAPHS
  Adams, J. Stealing the dark
  Chacón, D. Ofrenda
  Evenson, B. The installation
  Gautreaux, T. Misuse of light
  Hayes, D. Motormouth
  Julavits, H. Marry the one who gets there first
  Karnezis, P. Immortality
  Kheradmand, F. Smile!
  Mathews, H. Letters from Yerevan
  Rivera, T. The portrait
  Tuttle, L. "The mezzotint"
  Whitty, J. The daguerrotype
The **phrenologist's** dream. Iagnemma, K.
PHRENOLOGY
  Iagnemma, K. The phrenologist's dream
Phyllis Marlowe: only diamonds are forever.
    Lochhead, L.
Physical. Oates, J. C.

PHYSICALLY HANDICAPPED
    See also Blind; Deaf; Hunchbacks; Para-
    plegics; Physically handicapped children
  Abrams, T. The gaffer
  Barker, N. Back to front
  Benedict, P. Miracle boy
  Brackenbury, R. The knowledge
  Brady, C. Rumpelstiltskin
  Burke, J. Mea culpa
  Butler, R. O. The ironworkers' hayride
  Canty, K. Little palaces
  Cheng, C.-W. The coconut palms on campus
  Clarke, A. C. The cruel sky
  Davis, L. Smoke and ash
  Day, R. C. The fugitive
  Deane, J. F. The coffin master
  Deane, J. F. The sins of the fathers
  Díaz, J. Ysrael
  Eldridge, Courtney. Becky
  Epstein, J. A loss for words
  Gilman, C. P. Unpunished
  Hensley, J. L. Shut the final door
  Highsmith, P. Uncertain treasure
  Hoffman, N. K. Voyage of discovery
  Knight, M. The man who went out for cigarettes
  Mayo, W. Woman without arms
  McCaffrey, A. The ship who sang
  Modisane, B. The dignity of begging
  Pittalwala, I. A change of lights
  Rawley, D. Saigon
  Self, W. My idea of fun [excerpt]
  Spencer, E. The legacy
  Ward, C. Wolf Man
  White, M. C. Heights
  Zeman, A. Hello?
PHYSICALLY HANDICAPPED CHILDREN
  Bloom, A. Stars at elbow and foot
  Brady, C. The lives of the saints
  Hensley, J. L. Deadly hunger
  Potvin, E. A. Sunday
PHYSICIANS
    See also Gynecologists; Psychiatrists;
    Surgeons; Veterinarians; Women physicians
  Adams, A. The last lovely city
  Alexis, A. Horse
  Amdrup, E. Chess on board
  Baida, P. A doctor's story
  Bail, M. Ore
  Bernhard, T. Playing Watten
  Blackwood, S. In the shadow of our house
  Blish, J. A dusk of idols
  Blish, J. The oath
  Block, L. Speaking of lust
  Bowles, P. Rumor and a ladder
  Brown, C. Miniature man
  Brown, J. Hydrophobia
  Bukoski, A. Private Tomaszewski
  Busch, F. Laying the ghost
  Canty, K. Sleepers holding hands
  Carson, J. Brilliant company
  Carson, J. Fair trades
  Cather, W. Double birthday
  Cheever, J. The season of divorce
  Chekhov, A. P. The doctor
  Chekhov, A. P. A doctor's visit
  Chekhov, A. P. Enemies
  Chekhov, A. P. The grasshopper
  Chekhov, A. P. The helpmate
  Chekhov, A. P. Ionitch

PHYSICIANS—*Continued*
Chesnutt, C. W. A metropolitan experience
Chopin, K. Mamouche
Cohen, R. Dream group forming
Collins, B. and Collins, M. A. A cruise to forget
Delaney, E. J. What I have noticed
Doyle, Sir A. C. The Croxley Master
Drew, E. Mad dogs
Dunbar, P. L. The lynching of Jube Benson
Dunmore, H. Lisette
Dyer, S. N. The July Ward
Eckhardt, C. F. The fevers
Engel, M. P. A better man
Engel, M. P. M to F
Engel, M. P. A soldier's disease
Engel, M. P. Who calls each one by name
Epstein, J. Howie's gift
Ferriss, L. Bones
Fitzgerald, P. The prescription
Foster, A. D. Procrastinator
Greenberg, A. Tremors
Groff, D. The third person
Gunn, K. Tinsel bright
Harris, E. L. Money can't buy me love
Harrison, H. Brave newer world
Hawthorne, N. Dr. Heidegger's experiment
Hensley, J. L. Savant
Herbert, J. The sadness of Doctor Mendoza
Hodgen, C. What the rabbi said to the priest
James, H. Lady Barberina
Jones, G. Other places
Jones, T. Cold snap
Jones, T. A midnight clear
Karnezis, P. Medical ethics
Kennedy, A. L. Awaiting an adverse reaction
Klíma, I. Heaven, hell, paradise
Kornbluth, C. M. The little black bag
Kress, N. Ej-es
Lao She. A man who doesn't lie
Le Fanu, J. S. Green tea
Louis, L. G. Talking in the dark
Love, M. Nightfloat
Lovesey, P. Under the knife
Marías, J. The night doctor
McCorkle, J. Chickens
Means, D. The reaction
Munro, A. Before the change
Murray, J. Acts of memory, wisdom of man
Murray, J. Watson and the shark
Murray, J. White flour
Oates, J. C. The museum of Dr. Moses
Peterson, P. W. The woman in the long green coat
Ponte, A. J. This life
Régio, J. The flame-coloured dress
Rhys, J. Pioneers, oh, pioneers
Robinson, L. Cuxabexis, Cuxabexis
Singer, I. B. The shadow of a crib
Singer, I. B. A wedding in Brownsville
Škvorecký, J. Dr. Strass
Steinbeck, T. An unbecoming grace
Su Tong. Young Muo
Warren, R. P. Christmas gift
Wharton, E. The angel at the grave
White, M. C. The cardiologist's house
White, M. C. Disturbances
Zweig, S. Amok
PHYSICISTS
Bester, A. The men who murdered Mohammed
Clarke, A. C. Technical error
Cobb, W. J. The atmosphere of Vienna
Harrison, H. The greening of the green
Johnson, A. The Canadanaut
Kornbluth, C. M. Two dooms
Landis, G. A. Dark lady
PHYSICS
Jenkins, G. Strange attractors
Rucker, R. v. B. Inertia
Physics. Janowitz, T.
Physis versus nomos versus storytime. Lish, G.
Pi. McMullan, M.
Pi in the sky. Rucker, R. v. B.
Pia. Aikman, S.
PIANISTS
Adams, A. The drinking club
Berberova, N. An incident with music
Chopin, K. Wiser than a god
Drake, R. The child prodigy
Epstein, J. The third Mrs. Kessler
Galloway, J. Sonata form
Hernandez, F. The balcony
Highsmith, P. The pianos of the Steinachs
Leavitt, D. Heaped earth
Williams, T. The resemblance between a violin case and a coffin
Yates, R. A really good jazz piano
PIANO
Boggs, J. D. A piano at Dead Man's Crossing
Dixon, S. On a windy night
Doran, M. M. They shall have music
Tan, A. Two kinds
A **piano** at Dead Man's Crossing. Boggs, J. D.
Piano bar blues. Tem, M.
A **piano** shudders. Webster, B.
Piano skirmish. Bonnie, F.
The **piano** tuner. Gautreaux, T.
PIANO TUNERS
Bail, M. Camouflage
Gautreaux, T. The piano tuner
The **pianos** of the Steinachs. Highsmith, P.
Piazza, Tom
Brownsville
The Workshop; seven decades of the Iowa Writers' Workshop: 42 stories, recollections & essays on Iowa's place in 20th-century American literature; edited by Tom Grimes
The **piazza**. Drake, R.
The **Piazza** Barberini. Barker, N.
Piccirilli, Tom
Diamond Mozzarella
Felonious felines; edited by Carol and Ed Gorman
Of Persephone, Poe, and the Whisperer
Cat crimes through time; edited by Ed Gorman, Martin H. Greenberg, and Larry Segriff
Those vanished I recognize
The Museum of horrors; edited by Dennis Etchison
Pick up your pine. Tyau, K.
Pickard, Nancy
Afraid all the time
A moment on the edge; 100 years of crime stories by women; edited by Elizabeth George

Pickard, Nancy—*Continued*
Afraid of the dark
The World's finest mystery and crime stories, second annual collection; edited by Ed Gorman
The dead past
Pickard, N. Storm warnings
Dr. Couch saves a cat
Felonious felines; edited by Carol and Ed Gorman
Dr. Couch saves a president
White House pet detectives; tales of crime and mystery at the White House from a pet's-eye view; edited by Carole Nelson Douglas
Dust devil
Pickard, N. Storm warnings
It had to be you
Pickard, N. Storm warnings
Lucky devil
Malice domestic 10; an anthology of original traditional mystery stories
The World's finest mystery and crime stories, third annual collection; edited by Ed Gorman and Martin H. Greenberg
Nine points for murder
Death cruise; crime stories on the open seas; edited by Lawrence Block
Out of Africa
Mom, apple pie, and murder; edited by Nancy Pickard
A rock and a hard place
Pickard, N. Storm warnings
Sex and violence
Pickard, N. Storm warnings
Sign of the times
Pickard, N. Storm warnings
Speak no evil
Pickard, N. Storm warnings
Storm warnings
Pickard, N. Storm warnings
Tea for two
Love and death; edited by Carolyn Hart
Valentine's night
Pickard, N. Storm warnings
Pickens, William
Jim Crow in Texas
The African American West; a century of short stories; edited by Bruce A. Glasrud and Laurie Champion
Pickering, Jean
The father
Valentine's Day: women against men; stories of revenge; introduction by Alice Thomas
Picking time. Henley, P.
Picking up Courtney. Waggoner, T.
Pickled eggs. Watanabe McFerrin, L.
A **pickled** nose. Zinik, Z.
PICKPOCKETS See Thieves
Pickup. Skinner, J.
The **pickup** truck. Drake, R.
PICNICS
Bradbury, R. The pumpernickel
The **picture**. Tomlinson, N. C.
Picture bride. Farrell, C.
The **picture** house. Boylan, C.
The **Picture** House. Frick, T.
A **picture** of time. Tillman, L.
A **picture** postcard. Gildner, G.

Pictures of Darlene. Robbins, J.
Pie. Aldrich, B. S.
Pie dance. Giles, M.
Pie Row Joe. McKay, K.
A **piece** of steak. London, J.
A **piece** of the auction. Breen, J. L.
A **piece** of the True Cross. Glover, D.
A **piece** of the true cross. Glover, D. H.
Piecework. Makuck, P.
Piecework. Vachss, A. H.
Pierce, Todd James
The Australia stories
The Literary Review (Madison, N.J.) v44 no3 p417-33 Spr 2001
Newsworld
The Georgia Review v57 no2 p339-44 Summ 2003
Wrestling Al Gore
The North American Review v289 no1 p30-5 Ja/F 2004
Pierre Menard, author of the Quixote. Borges, J. L.
Pietrzyk, Leslie
Goodbye party
Washingtonian v36 no5 p29-33 F 2001
Pirates
Gettysburg Review v14 no3 p491-6 Aut 2001
Slumber party, 1975
TriQuarterly no110/111 p413-43 Fall 2001
Pig on a spit. Young, T.
Pig summer. Vasseur, T. J.
Pigeon drop. Vachss, A. H.
PIGEONS
Highsmith, P. Two disagreeable pigeons
Pigeons. Kavaler, R.
Piggies. Walters, M.
Piggy. Vasilenko, S.
PIGS
Gonzalez, R. The black pig
Harrison, H. The man from P.I.G.
Maleti, G. Joshua
Stableford, B. M. What can Chloe want?
Vasilenko, S. Piggy
Pikeman and the Bagwoman. Gunthorp, D.
PILATE, PONTIUS, 1ST CENT.
About
Trevanian. Easter story
Pile of clothes. Orner, P.
Pilgrim, David
Buzzard
African American Review v35 no4 p651-4 Wint 2001
Pilgrim, Kari
Even Further
The Literary Review (Madison, N.J.) v47 no3 p132-44 Spr 2004
Pilgrimage. Brady, C.
A **pilgrimage** of you. Chee, A.
PILGRIMAGES See Pilgrims and pilgrimages
Pilgrims. Orringer, J.
PILGRIMS AND PILGRIMAGES
Divakaruni, C. B. The lives of strangers
Hawthorne, N. The Canterbury pilgrims
Sandlin, L. Everything moves
Sandlin, L. I loved you then, I love you still
Sandlin, L. 'Orita on the road to Chimayó
The **pillar** of salt. Lugones, L.
The **pillows**. Gilb, D.
PILOTS, AIRPLANE See Air pilots

The **pilots** of the rose trellis. Wegner, H.

PIMPS

See also Prostitutes

Pinball. Rekulak, J.

Pinch, Alan

(jt. auth) See Tolstoy, Leo, graf

Pincherle, Alberto *See* Moravia, Alberto, 1907-1990

Pine Cones. Ely, S.

Pine Hill. Walcott-Hackshaw, E.

The **Pine** Oil Writers' Conference. Gautreaux, T.

A **pine** tree. Coates, G. S.

PINEAPPLE

Tyau, K. Pick up your pine

Piñera, Virgilio

The Great Baro

Dream with no name; contemporary fiction from Cuba; edited by Juana Ponce de León and Esteban Ríos Rivera

The one who came to save me

The Vintage book of Latin American stories; edited by Carlos Fuentes and Julio Ortega

Ping-pong. Stanton, M.

Pinhead, moonhead. Johnson, C.

Pink champagne. Škvorecký, J.

Pink is for punks. Wexler, M.

Pink Miracle in East Tennessee. Taylor, R. L.

Pink smoke. Vukcevich, R.

Piñón, Nélida

Big-bellied cow

Short stories by Latin American women; the magic and the real; edited by Celia Correas de Zapata; foreword by Isabel Allende

House of passion

The Vintage book of Latin American stories; edited by Carlos Fuentes and Julio Ortega

Pinsky, David

In the madhouse

Neugroschel, J. No star too beautiful; Yiddish stories from 1382 to the present; compiled and translated by Joachim Neugroschel

Pinson, Hermine

Confederate flag

Callaloo v24 no1 p144-54 Wint 2001

PIONEER LIFE *See* Frontier and pioneer life

The **Pioneer** Women. Packer, N. H.

Pioneers, oh, pioneers. Rhys, J.

Pipa's story. Chang, L. S.

Pipe. Anderson, C.

Piper, H. Beam

Gunpowder god

The Good old stuff; adventure SF in the grand tradition; edited by Gardner Dozois

The **piper** at the gate. Edghill, R.

Pipers at the gates of dawn. Stegner, L.

Pipes. Keret, E.

The **pipes** of Pan. Del Rey, L.

Pipik, James

Nightwatcher

Tales from The Dark Tower; illustrated by Joseph Vargo; edited by Joseph Vargo and Christine Filipak

(jt. auth) See Iorillo, Joseph and Pipik, James

Pipik, James and Vargo, Joseph

The Dark Tower

Tales from The Dark Tower; illustrated by Joseph Vargo; edited by Joseph Vargo and Christine Filipak

Sentinels

Tales from The Dark Tower; illustrated by Joseph Vargo; edited by Joseph Vargo and Christine Filipak

Piranha to Scurfy. Rendell, R.

PIRATES

Anderson, P. The Sky People

Baker, K. The likely lad

Borges, J. L. The widow Ching—pirate

Davidson, A. The lord of Central Park

Fitzgerald, F. S. The offshore pirate

Pirates. Pietrzyk, L.

Pirzad, Zoya

Sour cherry pits

A Feast in the mirror; stories by contemporary Iranian women; translated and edited by Mohammad Mehdi Khorrami, Shouleh Vatanabadi

Pisgah. Morgan, R.

The **pit**. Glave, T.

Pitol, Sergio

Bukhara Nocturne

Callaloo v26 no4 p940-53 Fall 2003

The Vintage book of Latin American stories; edited by Carlos Fuentes and Julio Ortega

Pitt, Matthew

The mean

Best new American voices 2001; guest editor Charles Baxter; series editors John Kulka and Natalie Danford

Pittalwala, Iqbal

Bombay talkies

Pittalwala, I. Dear Paramount Pictures; stories

The change

Pittalwala, I. Dear Paramount Pictures; stories

A change of lights

Pittalwala, I. Dear Paramount Pictures; stories

Dear Paramont Pictures

Pittalwala, I. Dear Paramount Pictures; stories

Great Guruji

Pittalwala, I. Dear Paramount Pictures; stories

House of cards

Pittalwala, I. Dear Paramount Pictures; stories

Kulsum, Nazia, and Ismail

Pittalwala, I. Dear Paramount Pictures; stories

Lost in the U.S.A.

Pittalwala, I. Dear Paramount Pictures; stories

Mango season

Pittalwala, I. Dear Paramount Pictures; stories

Ramadan

Pittalwala, I. Dear Paramount Pictures; stories

Trivedi Park

Pittalwala, I. Dear Paramount Pictures; stories

Pittard, Shawn

Exploration

Confrontation no86/87 p175-6 Spr/Summ 2004

PITTSBURGH (PA.) *See* Pennsylvania—Pittsburgh

PITY *See* Sympathy

Pity My Simplicity. Darby, A.

Pixel pixies. De Lint, C.

Pixie dust. Harfenist, J.

PIXIES *See* Fairies

Pizza man. Browder, C.

Pizzolatto, Nicolas

Ghost-Birds

Atlantic Monthly (1993) v292 no3 p147-58 O 2003

Plá, Josefina
  To seize the earth
    Short stories by Latin American women; the
      magic and the real; edited by Celia Correas
      de Zapata; foreword by Isabel Allende
Place. Hoffman, W.
A **place** between stations. Allen, S.
The **place** I want to tell you about. . . Roth, J.
A **place** to stay. Smith, M. M.
A **place** with shade. Reed, R.
Placedo junction. Meissner, J.
"**Places** for act two!". Sinor, B. H.
Plager, Silvia
  A change of heart
    English translations of short stories by con-
      temporary Argentine women writers; edited
      by Eliana Cazaubon Hermann ; translated
      by Sally Webb Thornton
PLAGIARISM
  Lee, R. The banks of the Vistula
  Singer, I. B. The plagiarist
PLAGUE
    See also Disasters
  Herbert, W. Twilight of the real
  Padilla, I. Chronicle of the second plague
The **plague**. Johnson, C. R.
Plague of conscience. Bear, G.
The **Plague** of Doves. Erdrich, L.
Plague of the Firstborn. Keret, E.
A **plague** of toads. Biguenet, J.
Plain female seeks nice guy. Eakin, W.
Plains of Abraham. Banks, R.
Plan B. Goldner, B.
Plan B for the middle class. Carlson, R.
The **plan** of the snake. Wellen, E.
Plane crash theory. Shapiro, D.
Planet Big Zero. Lethem, J.
PLANETS, MINOR *See* Asteroids
The **plans** of the reefing bi-plane. Hodgson, W. H.
Plant, Richard
  Mother's Day
    U.S. Catholic v66 no5 p39-42 My 2001
Plant engineering. Kress, N.
PLANTATION LIFE
  Bell, M. S. Labor
  Chesnutt, C. W. Dave's neckliss
  Chopin, K. Azélie
  Chopin, K. A non-account Creole
  Chopin, K. A respectable woman
Planted. Sosin, D.
Planting. Harrison, K.
The **planting**. Winter, E.
PLANTS
  Bell, M. S. The thing about Benny
  Calvino, I. Autumn
Plants and ghosts. Woodward, S. T.
A **plaque** on Via Mazzini. Bassani, G.
Plaster of Paris. Coates, G. S.
Plastic letters. Rucker, R. v. B.
PLASTIC SURGERY
  Barker, N. Layla's nose job
  Berners, G. H. T.-W., Baron. The romance of a
    nose
  Clyde, M. Howard Johnson's house
  Cody, L. Solar zits
  Gorman, E. The end of it all
  Reiner, C. Too damned handsome
  Updike, J. Metamorphosis

Wallace, D. F. Philosophy and the mirror of na-
    ture
Plateau lands. Barnes, H. L.
PLATONIC LOVE *See* Love
Plato's mirror. Wilson, R. C.
Play death. Wellen, E.
Play it again!. Paolucci, A.
Play like I'm sheriff. Cady, J.
Play me "Stormy weather," please. Bocock, M.
Play nice. Paul, B.
Play your cards. Chinodya, S.
Playback. Clarke, A. C.
The **player**. Bisson, T.
The **playground** of the ecstatically blasé. Touré
PLAYING CARDS *See* Cards
Playing crucifixion. Berkman, P. R.
The **playing** field. Davenport, G.
Playing Hedda. Mee, S.
Playing Holi. Tomlinson, N. C.
Playing horses. Shoemaker, K. G.
Playing the Angles. Pomerantz, S.
Playing the game. Dozois, G. R.
Playing Watten. Bernhard, T.
PLAYWRIGHTS *See* Dramatists
A **pleasant** room. Edwards, S.
Please help find. O'Nan, S.
Please remain calm. Homes, A. M.
Please to forgive sloppiness. Spencer, D.
PLEASURE *See* Happiness
The **pleasure** game. Devine, T.
The **pleasure** gardens. Connolly, C.
Pleasure isn't a pretty picture. Tillman, L.
The **Pleasure** of Man And Woman Together on
    Earth. Kennedy, T. E.
The **pleasure** of pears. Henley, P.
Pleasure palace. Thurm, M.
Plenty of pools in Texas. Spatz, G.
A **plethora**. McCourt, J.
The **pliable** animal. Harrison, H.
Plinking. Smith, R. T.
The **plot** against Badi'. Sammān, G.
The **plot** against Santa Claus. Powell, J.
Plot it yourself. Gores, J.
Plowing the secondaries. Clarke, B.
Pluma Piluma and the Utopian Turtle Top: A
    Bedtime Story for Women Writers. Craig,
    C.
PLUMBERS
  Chiappone, R. Side job
  Yañez, R. I&M Plumbing
La **Plume** de ma tante. Frame, R.
The **plumed** serpent of Los Angeles. Olivas, D. A.
The **plunge**. Goodis, D.
**Plunkett, Edward John Moreton Drax, Baron
    Dunsany** *See* Dunsany, Edward John More-
    ton Drax Plunkett, Baron, 1878-1957
PLUTO (PLANET)
  Varley, J. Goodbye, Robinson Crusoe
Plywood rabbit. Stuckey-French, E.
PMQ. Harris, R.
Pneuman, Angela
  All Saints Day
    The Virginia Quarterly Review v79 no4 p716-
      34 Aut 2003
  The long game
    Ploughshares v28 no2/3 p138-59 Fall 2002
Po' Sandy. Chesnutt, C. W.
Poachers. Franklin, T.

POACHING

See also Hunting

Franklin, T. Poachers

Pochantas in Camelot. Rodburg, M.

Pockets. Rucker, R. v. B. and Shirley, J.

Podolsky, Robin

Memory like ash borne on air

Hers 2: brilliant new fiction by lesbian writers; edited by Terry Wolverton with Robert Drake

Poe, Edgar Allan

The balloon hoax

On glorious wings; the best flying stories of the century; edited and introduced by Stephen Coonts

The black cat

Master's choice v2; mystery stories by today's top writers and the masters who inspired them; edited by Lawrence Block

The cask of Amontillado

Dark: stories of madness, murder, and the supernatural; edited by Clint Willis

The purloined letter

Murder most postal; homicidal tales that deliver a message; edited by Martin H. Greenberg

Some words with a mummy

Into the mummy's tomb; edited by John Richard Stephens

The tell-tale heart

The 13 best horror stories of all time; edited by Leslie Pockell

Master's choice v2; mystery stories by today's top writers and the masters who inspired them; edited by Lawrence Block

POE, EDGAR ALLAN, 1809-1849

About

Banks, R. The caul

Braunbeck, G. A. Who am a passer by

Fleming, R. Bordering on the divine

Jenkins, G. Red roses and cognac

Newman, K. Just like Eddy

Orner, P. Two Poes

Parodies, imitations, etc.

Jakes, J. The opener of the crypt

Poetic justice. Martini, S.

Poetic License. Kemper, M.

The **poetics** of sex. Winterson, J.

POETRY

Boggs, B. Who is Beatrice?

Bradbury, R. The poems

Desplechin, M. Haiku

Jones, G. Dark times

Joseph, D. Schandorsky's mother

Shonk, K. The young people of Moscow

Poetry and politics. Johnson, C. R.

A **poetry** reading. Amichai, Y.

POETS

See also Women poets

Agee, J. Cupid

Alexie, S. The search engine

Auchincloss, L. Man of the Renaissance

Beerbohm, M. Enoch Soames

Blish, J. The oath

Borges, J. L. The aleph

Borges, J. L. The maker

Borges, J. L. The mirror and the mask

Borges, J. L. "Undr"

Bryks, R. Artists in the ghetto

Connor, J. The poet's lobster

Davis, L. The poet's corner

Dunmore, H. The icon room

Dunmore, H. My Polish teacher's tie

Epstein, J. Postcards

Gilchrist, E. Among the mourners

Glover, D. H. Iglaf and Swan

Hagy, A. C. Graveyard of the Atlantic

Hell, R. A novel in progress

Iwaszkiewicz, J. The mill on the River Utrata

Jacobs, M. The Telemachus box

Lessing, D. M. A letter from home

Michael, S. Refuge [excerpt]

Mueller, M. Exile

Munro, A. Meneseteung

Nesbitt, M. Chimp shrink and backwards

Ortiz, S. J. You were real, the white radical said to me

Pearlman, D. D. The best-known man in the world

Pushkin, A. S. Egyptian nights

Pushkin, A. S. A tale of Roman life

Ritchie, E. An evening of Eliot

Singer, I. B. Her son

Singer, I. B. A pair

Singer, I. B. A tale of two sisters

Sorrentino, G. Perdído

Stollman, A. L. The little poet

Stuckey-French, E. Famous poets

Taylor, P. E. Leaping Leo

Wallace, D. F. Death is not the end

Wharton, E. The muse's tragedy

Winegardner, M. The visiting poet

Wuori, G. K. Fire

The **poet's** corner. Davis, L.

POGROMS *See* Jews—Persecutions

Pohl, Frederik

The boy who would live forever

Far horizons; all new tales from the greatest worlds of science fiction; edited by Robert Silverberg

Day million

The SFWA grand masters; edited by Frederik Pohl

The gold at the starbow's end

The SFWA grand masters; edited by Frederik Pohl

Hatching the Phoenix

The Year's best science fiction, seventeenth annual collection; edited by Gardner Dozois

Let the ants try

The SFWA grand masters; edited by Frederik Pohl

The tunnel under the world

Masterpieces: the best science fiction of the century; edited by Orson Scott Card

The SFWA grand masters; edited by Frederik Pohl

Poinsett's Bridge. Morgan, R.

A **point** at issue!. Chopin, K.

The **point** of view. James, H.

Points of Energy. Cheng, L. S.

Points of interest. Cohen, R.

Points of light. Baida, P.

Poirier, Mark Jude

Buttons

Poirier, M. J. Unsung heroes of American industry; stories

Poirier, Mark Jude—*Continued*
  Cul-de-sacs
    Still wild; short fiction of the American West, 1950 to the present; edited by Larry McMurtry
  Gators
    Poirier, M. J. Unsung heroes of American industry; stories
  A note on the type
    Poirier, M. J. Unsung heroes of American industry; stories
  Pageantry
    Poirier, M. J. Unsung heroes of American industry; stories
  Worms
    Poirier, M. J. Unsung heroes of American industry; stories
    The Southern Review (Baton Rouge, La.) v37 no1 p123-40 Wint 2001

POISON *See* Poisons
Poison. Rawlings, E.
Poison à la carte. Stout, R.
Poison peach. Linscott, G.
POISON PEN LETTERS *See* Letters (Stories about)
The **Poison** That Purifies You. Kadetsky, E.
The **poisoned** chalice. Tremayne, P.
The **poisoned** pen. Reeve, A. B.
A **poisoned** tale. Ferré, R.

POISONING
    See also Poisons
  Andrews, D. The birthday dinner
  Benton, C. Guardian angel
  Bowles, P. The little house
  Chaplin, P. Pot luck
  Christie, A. Accident
  Cobb, W. J. Father tongue
  Crespi, C. T. The fixer
  DiChario, N. Where the wildflowers bloom
  Dunlap, S. A worm in the winesap
  Edwards, M. Natural causes
  Foxwell, E. Alice and the agent of the Hun
  Hayden, G. M. The maids
  Hensley, J. L. Argent blood
  Hensley, J. L. Deadly hunger
  Hensley, J. L. The home
  Hoch, E. D. Day for a picnic
  Janicke, G. The gift
  Lake, M. D. Tea for two
  Lindholm, M. Bones for Dulath
  Linscott, G. Poison peach
  Matera, L. Destroying angel
  Miller, R. Walking to Paris
  Moorhead, F. Four characters, four lunches
  Murphy, W. Motherly love
  Nolan, W. F. In real life
  O'Marie, C. A. Defender of the faith
  Pickard, N. Out of Africa
  Pickard, N. Valentine's night
  Quill, M. The visitor
  Shankman, S. If you can't take the heat
  Smith, J. Project Mushroom
  Wheat, C. What the dormouse said

POISONOUS SNAKES *See* Snakes
POISONS
    See also Poisoning
  LeRoy, J. T. Coal
  Westlake, D. E. Skeeks
Pojo's and the buttery slope. Davis, J. S.

POKER (GAME)
  Agee, J. Omaha
  Block, L. Speaking of greed
  Chiappone, R. Dealer's choice
  Fairey, W. W. House of cards
  Fairey, W. W. Menopause and poker
  Green, J. The blind gambler
  Knight, M. Poker
  L'Amour, L. Let the cards decide
  Leslie, N. Poker face
  Link, K. Lull
  Swain, D. V. Gamblin' man
Poker. Knight, M.
Poker face. Leslie, N.
Poker face. Strober, R.
POLAND
  Huelle, P. Moving house
  Singer, I. B. The pocket remembered
      20th century
  Babel', I. Afonka bida
  Babel', I. Beresteczko
  Babel', I. The kiss
  Babel', I. The reserve cavalry commander
  Babel', I. Squadron Commander Trunov
  Babel', I. Zamosc
  Iwaszkiewicz, J. The birch grove
  Iwaszkiewicz, J. The mill on the River Utrata
  Iwaszkiewicz, J. The Wilko girls
  Singer, I. B. The bond
  Singer, I. B. The conference
  Singer, I. B. Dazzled
  Singer, I. B. The interview
      Aristocracy
    See Aristocracy—Poland
      Rural life
  Roth, J. The bust of the emperor
  Singer, I. B. The blizzard
  Singer, I. B. A dance and a hop
  Singer, I. B. The divorce
  Singer, I. B. The litigants
  Singer, I. B. Passions
  Singer, I. B. The son from America
  Singer, I. B. The sorcerer
  Singer, I. B. Strong as death is love
  Singer, I. B. Yanda
      Krakow
  Michaels, L. Nachman
      Lodz
  Bryks, R. Berele in the ghetto
  Lustig, A. The lemon
  Rachmil, B. Bread
  Rachmil, B. Children of the Lodz, ghetto
  Rachmil, B. The last journey
      Lublin
  Singer, I. B. Hershele and Hanele' or, The power of a dream
  Singer, I. B. A nest egg for paradise
      Prague
  Goliger, G. One morning in Prague
      Warsaw
  Pitol, S. Bukhara nocturne
  Singer, I. B. Between shadows
  Singer, I. B. The bitter truth
  Singer, I. B. Grandfather and grandson
  Singer, I. B. Loshikl
  Singer, I. B. Moishele

Polansky, Steven

Acts
  Polansky, S. Dating Miss Universe; nine stories

Alarm
  Polansky, S. Dating Miss Universe; nine stories

Beard
  Polansky, S. Dating Miss Universe; nine stories

Coda
  Polansky, S. Dating Miss Universe; nine stories

Dating Miss Universe
  Polansky, S. Dating Miss Universe; nine stories

Leg
  Polansky, S. Dating Miss Universe; nine stories

Pantalone
  Polansky, S. Dating Miss Universe; nine stories

Rein
  Polansky, S. Dating Miss Universe; nine stories

Sleights
  Polansky, S. Dating Miss Universe; nine stories

POLAR REGIONS *See* Antarctic regions; Arctic regions

Polaroid. Cohen, M. L.

POLES

England

Dunmore, H. My Polish teacher's tie

Germany

Seiffert, R. Second best

Italy

Lee, V. Amour dure

United States

Barrett, A. The forest
Hansen, R. My Communist
Singer, I. B. The smuggler

Poles apart. Nordley, G. D.

POLICE

Anderson, K. Burglary in progress
Aylett, S. Maryland
Aylett, S. Repeater
Aylett, S. The Siri gun
Aylett, S. The waffle code
Blatnik, A. The taste of blood
Block, L. Speaking of lust
Cavell, B. Highway
Collins, B. World's greatest mother
Collins, M. Harness bull
Cooke, J. P. After you've gone
Coward, M. Bloody victims
Cummins, A. Starburst
Davis, L. The kind of time you end up with
Ellison, H. Objects of desire in the mirror are closer than they appear
Estleman, L. D. Evil grows
Gallagher, S. Jailbird for Jesus
Gorman, E. Aftermath
Harrison, H. Arm of the law
Hockensmith, S. Erie's last day
Huffman, B., Jr. Dismissed, with prejudice
Lustbader, E. V. Slow burn
Maron, M. Lost and found
Morgan, R. A taxpayer & a citizen

Prose, F. The witch
Randisi, R. J. Black and white memories
Robinson, L. Officer Friendly
Rozan, S. J. Childhood
Saulnier, B. High maintenance
Schaller, E. The assistant to Dr. Jacob
Sloan, B. The good rabbi
Updike, J. The tarbox police
Varon, P. The feast
Vukcevich, R. Giant step
Wellen, E. It ain't hay
Wolfe, G. The Monday man

California

See also Police—Los Angeles (Calif.)

Anderson, J. Things that make your heart beat faster
Ayres, N. JoJo's gold
Collins, M. Occupational hazard
Frym, G. Crime and punishment
Harris, M. The self-made brain surgeon
Pronzini, B. Opportunity

Canada

Forsyth, F. The veteran

Chicago (Ill.)

Howard, C. Under suspicion

Dallas (Tex.)

Cherryh, C. J. Mech

Edinburgh (Scotland)

Rankin, I. The confession

England

See also Police—London (England)

Florida

Cioffari, P. Dangerously the summer burns
Fleming, J. H. Wind and rain

Hollywood (Calif.)

See Police—Los Angeles (Calif.)

Illinois

Thompson, J. Ice angels

Ireland

O'Brien, F. The third policeman [excerpt]

London (England)

Cody, L. The uniform
Harvey, J. Due North

Los Angeles (Calif.)

Bishop, P. Concrete killer
Bishop, P. The legend of Charlie McQuarkle
Bishop, P. Pattern of behavior
Bishop, P. Squeeze play
Bishop, P. The thief of Christmas
Brackett, L. I feel bad killing you
Connelly, M. Two-bagger
Kaminsky, S. M. It comes with the badge
Lankford, T. Detour Drive

Louisiana

Drummond, L. L. Absolutes
Drummond, L. L. Cleaning your gun
Drummond, L. L. Finding a place
Drummond, L. L. Katherine's elegy
Drummond, L. L. Keeping the dead alive
Drummond, L. L. Lemme tell you something
Drummond, L. L. Something about a scar
Drummond, L. L. Taste, touch, sight, sound, smell
Drummond, L. L. Under control
Drummond, L. L. Where I come from

Mexico

Lida, D. A beach day

Michigan

Johnson, B. Michiganders, 1979

POLICE—*Continued*
Mississippi
Smith, J. Crime wave in Pinhole
New Jersey
Lipsyte, S. Torquemada
Oates, J. C. In Copland
New Mexico
Morrell, D. Rio Grande gothic
New Orleans (La.)
Braunbeck, G. A. Down in darkest Dixie where
the dead don't dance
New York (N.Y.)
Bambara, T. C. The hammer man
Charteris, L. The mystery of the child's toy
Cross, A. The double-barreled gun
Davidson, A. The importance of trifles
Fliegel, R. A final midrash
Hunter, E. First offense
McNulty, J. An old college chum
Nevins, F. M., Jr. Because the constable blun-
dered
Rusch, K. K. The silence
Wheat, C. Ghost Station
Yaffe, J. Mom remembers
Yasgur, B. S. Kaddish
New York (State)
Busch, F. The baby in the box
Northern Ireland
Archer, J. Both sides against the middle
Ohio
DeLancey, K. Carley's knees
Pittsburgh (Pa.)
Goran, L. Keeping count
Syracuse (N.Y.)
Collins, M. Hard cop
Texas
Matiella, A. C. The truth about Alicia
United States
Goodis, D. The plunge
McBain, E. The prisoner
Molyneux, J. Desire lines
Powell, T. Somebody cares
Thompson, J. Mercy
Vienna (Austria)
Shields, J. The Fig Eater [excerpt]
Virginia
Deaver, J. Eye to eye
West Virginia
Coberly, L. M. In which murder is done
Coberly, L. M. Will's Valentine
Police actions. Malzberg, B. N.
Poliner, Elizabeth
Unfinished Symphony
The Kenyon Review v24 no3/4 p49-62
Summ/Fall 2002
Polio. Svoboda, T.
POLIOMYELITIS
Abrams, T. Forgetting how to laugh
POLISH AMERICANS
Bukoski, A. Bird of passage
Bukoski, A. Closing time
Bukoski, A. A concert of minor pieces
Bukoski, A. Dry spell
Bukoski, A. A geography of snow
Bukoski, A. Holy walker
Bukoski, A. Immigration and naturalization
Bukoski, A. It had to be you
Bukoski, A. The korporał's polonaise

Bukoski, A. Leaves that shimmer in the slightest
breeze
Bukoski, A. The month that brings winter; or,
How Mr. Truzynski carried Vietnam home
with him
Bukoski, A. The moon of the grass fires
Bukoski, A. Pesthouse
Bukoski, A. A philosophy of dust
Bukoski, A. President of the past
Bukoski, A. Private Tomaszewski
Bukoski, A. Time between trains
Bukoski, A. The tools of ignorance
Bukoski, A. The value of numbers
Bukoski, A. Winter weeds
Bukoski, A. The wood of such trees
Bukoski, A. The world at war
Slezak, E. Tomato watch
POLISH REFUGEES
Singer, I. B. The lecture
Singer, I. B. Runners to nowhere
POLITICAL CAMPAIGNS *See* Politics
POLITICAL CRIMES AND OFFENSES
See also Assassination; Political prison-
ers; Terrorism
POLITICAL DEFECTORS *See* Defectors
POLITICAL ETHICS
See also Power (Social sciences)
POLITICAL INTRIGUE *See* International in-
trigue; Politics
The **political** officer. Finlay, C. C.
The **political** piano. Dunn, D.
POLITICAL PRISONERS
Barnes, S. The woman in the wall
Brkic, C. A. Canis lupus
Jones, G. Dark times
Nguyen, D. T. Peace
Ritchie, E. Wild garlic: the journal of Maria X.
VanderMeer, J. Flight is for those who have not
yet crossed over
Yuknavitch, L. Blood opus
The **political** process. Drake, D.
POLITICIANS *See* Politics
POLITICS
See also Suffrage; Utopias; Women in
politics
Ambler, E. The blood bargain
Oliver, C. Meanwhile, back on the reservation
Singer, I. B. Sabbath in Gehanna
Argentina
Gorriti, J. M. The black glove
Gorriti, J. M. The dead man's fiancée
Gorriti, J. M. The mazorquero's daughter
Bolivia
Jacobs, M. The rape of reason
Czech Republic
Škvorecký, J. Spectator on a February night
England
Cherryh, C. J. The haunted tower
Latin America
Melville, P. The president's exile
New York (N.Y.)
Weidman, J. Good man, bad man
Texas
Brammer, B. L. The Gay Place [excerpt]
Trinidad and Tobago
Hosein, C. Morris, Bhaiya
United States
Cavell, B. The art of the possible
Charyn, J. Countess Kathleen

POLITICS—United States—*Continued*
Connell, E. S. Election eve
Heller, J. The day Bush left
Hoch, E. D. Day for a picnic
Pomerantz, S. Ghost knife
Updike, J. Licks of love in the heart of the Cold War
Wharton, E. The best man
1900-
Landis, G. A. The eyes of America
Updike, J. A trillion feet of gas
Zimbabwe
Marechera, D. Thought tracks in the snow
Politics. Ferriss, L.
The **politics** of correctness. McNally, J.
Pollack, Eileen
Breaking and Entering
Prairie Schooner v78 no2 p95-114 Summ 2004
Milt and Moose
Michigan Quarterly Review v38 no1 p66-83 Wint 1999
Pollack, Helen Alene
The Adeline Shop
Calyx v21 no3 p60-7 Wint 2004
Pollack, Neal
Neal Pollack's Passage to Iraq
Vanity Fair no518 p264 O 2003
Pollack, Rachel
The fool, the stick, and the princess
The Best from fantasy & science fiction: the fiftieth anniversary anthology; edited by Edward L. Ferman and Gordon Van Gelder
Pollard, Velma
Altamont Jones
The Oxford book of Caribbean short stories; edited by Stewart Brown and John Wickham
POLLOCK, JACKSON, 1912-1956
About
Haskell, J. Dream of a clean slate
Pollock, Paul Jackson *See* Pollock, Jackson, 1912-1956
POLLUTION
Franklin, T. Dinosaurs
Hansen, J. Eater
Seiffert, R. Field study
Polly. Chopin, K.
Polly here somewhere. Nesbitt, M.
POLO, MARCO, 1254-1323?
About
Scholz, C. Travels
Polvito de amor. Matiella, A. C.
Polydore. Chopin, K.
Polyformus perfectus. Fleming, P. L.
POLYGAMY
See also Mormons and Mormonism
Kelley, W. M. Carlyle tries polygamy
Ousmane, Sembène. Her three days
Singer, I. B. The betrayer of Israel
POLYNESIA
Vasseur, T. J. Malololailai; or, Discovering the world
POLYNESIANS
United States
Armstrong, K. Hunga Pass
Polyphemus. Blagrave, M.
Pomegranate seed. Wharton, E.
The **pomegranate** trees. Saroyan, W.

Pomerantz, Sharon
Ghost knife
The Best American short stories, 2003; selected from U.S. and Canadian magazines by Walter Mosley with Katrina Kenison; with an introduction by Walter Mosley
Ploughshares v28 no2/3 p160-77 Fall 2002
Playing the Angles
Michigan Quarterly Review v41 no4 p612-29 Fall 2002
Pond, With Mud. Antrim, D.
Ponder, Dulane Upshaw
The rat spoon
New stories from the South: the year's best, 2002; edited by Shannon Ravenel; with a preface by Larry Brown
South Carolina Review v34 no1 p45-53 Fall 2001
Poniatowska, Elena
Park Cinema
Short stories by Latin American women; the magic and the real; edited by Celia Correas de Zapata; foreword by Isabel Allende
Ponte, Antonio José
At the request of Ochun
Ponte, A. J. Tales from the Cuban empire; translated from the Spanish by Cola Franzen
Because of men
Ponte, A. J. Tales from the Cuban empire; translated from the Spanish by Cola Franzen
Coming
Ponte, A. J. In the cold of the Malecón & other stories; translated from the Spanish by Cola Franzen and Dick Cluster
Heart of skitalietz
Ponte, A. J. In the cold of the Malecón & other stories; translated from the Spanish by Cola Franzen and Dick Cluster
In the cold of the Malecón
Ponte, A. J. In the cold of the Malecón & other stories; translated from the Spanish by Cola Franzen and Dick Cluster
A knack for making ruins
Ponte, A. J. Tales from the Cuban empire; translated from the Spanish by Cola Franzen
Station H
Ponte, A. J. In the cold of the Malecón & other stories; translated from the Spanish by Cola Franzen and Dick Cluster
The summer in a barbershop
Ponte, A. J. Tales from the Cuban empire; translated from the Spanish by Cola Franzen
Tears in the Congri
Ponte, A. J. Tales from the Cuban empire; translated from the Spanish by Cola Franzen
This life
Ponte, A. J. In the cold of the Malecón & other stories; translated from the Spanish by Cola Franzen and Dick Cluster
A throw of the book of changes
Ponte, A. J. In the cold of the Malecón & other stories; translated from the Spanish by Cola Franzen and Dick Cluster

Ponte Landa, Miguelina
Blind madness
Dream with no name; contemporary fiction from Cuba; edited by Juana Ponce de León and Esteban Ríos Rivera
Pontius Pilate *See* Pilate, Pontius, 1st cent.
The **pony**. Willis, C.
Poo-Poo. Crider, B.
The **pool**. Hejazi, B.
A **pool** in the desert. McKinley, R.
Pool lights. Barthelme, F.
The **pool** people. Lurie, A.
The **pool** witch. Chapman, C. M.
Poop. Vukcevich, R.
POOR *See* Poverty
A **poor-aunt** story. Murakami, H.
Poor Helen. Thompson, J.
Poor Lincoln. Cannell, D.
Poor little rich town. Vonnegut, K.
Poor man's mermaid. Chapman, C. M.
Poor old sod. Boylan, C.
The **poor** people. Tolstoy, L., graf
POOR RELIEF *See* Public welfare
Poor Richard. James, H.
Poor Visitor. Kincaid, J.
Poore, Michael
Six Chinese Cooks Rose into the Air
The Southern Review (Baton Rouge, La.) v39 no3 p587-95 Summ 2003
Pop art. Hill, J.
The **pop** off valve. Agee, J.
POPES
Flagg, F. Rome, Italy
Popkes, Steven
The ice
The year's best science fiction: twenty-first annual collection; edited by Gardner Dozois
Winters are hard
The Year's best science fiction; twentieth annual collection; edited by Gardner Dozois
Poplar, poplar's daughter. Vasilenko, S.
Poppies. Smith, S.
Popping corn. Barker, N.
Poppy and the poisoned cake. Saylor, S.
Pops. LaValle, V. D.
The **popular** girl. Fitzgerald, F. S.
Popular girls. Shepard, K.
POPULAR MUSIC
Walker, A. Nineteen fifty-five
POPULAR SONGS *See* Popular music
POPULATION
Barth, J. And then there's the one
Harrison, H. A criminal act
Harrison, H. The pliable animal
Harrison, H. Roommates
Vance, J. Ullward's retreat
Porcelain. Zaiman, E.
Porcupine. Adam, C.
Pork pie hat. Straub, P.
The **porno** girl. Wexler, M.
Porno in August. Mellick, C.
PORNOGRAPHY
Bush, G. R. The last reel
Cody, L. Indian throw
Eldridge, Courtney. The former world record holder settles down
Grimsley, J. Boulevard
Lee, E. ICU
Marías, J. Fewer scruples

McCabe, P. The hands of Dingo Deery
Stern, D. Foxx hunting
Tenn, W. Party of the two parts
Vachss, A. H. The real thing
Wexler, M. The porno girl
Youngblood, S. Triple X
Zinik, Z. Double act in Soho
Pornography. McEwan, I.
Porridge on Islac. Le Guin, U. K.
PORT-AU-PRINCE (HAITI) *See* Haiti—Port-au-Prince
PORT OF SPAIN (TRINIDAD AND TOBAGO) *See* Trinidad and Tobago—Port of Spain
Port Tobacco. Haddam, J.
Porter, Andrew
Coyotes
The Antioch Review v61 no1 p153-67 Wint 2003
Porter, Joseph Ashby
Basse Ville
This is where we live; short stories by 25 contemporary North Carolina writers; edited by Michael McFee
Bone key
Porter, J. A. Touch wood; short stories
An errand
Porter, J. A. Touch wood; short stories
Icehouse Burgess
Porter, J. A. Touch wood; short stories
In the mind
Porter, J. A. Touch wood; short stories
A man wanted to buy a cat
The Kenyon Review ns24 no2 p127-34 Spr 2002
Porter, J. A. Touch wood; short stories
Naufrage and diapason
Porter, J. A. Touch wood; short stories
A pear-shaped woman and a fuddy-duddy
Porter, J. A. Touch wood; short stories
Schrekx and son
Porter, J. A. Touch wood; short stories
Scrupulous Amédée
The Kenyon Review v24 no3/4 p190-217 Summ/Fall 2002
Porter, J. A. Touch wood; short stories
Touch wood
Porter, J. A. Touch wood; short stories
Yours
Home and beyond; an anthology of Kentucky short stories; edited by Morris Allen Grubbs; with an introduction by Wade Hall and an afterword by Charles E. May
Porter, Katherine Anne
The grave
Graham, D. Lone Star literature; from the Red River to the Rio Grande; edited by Don Graham
Theft
The Best American short stories of the century; John Updike, editor, Katrina Kenison, coeditor; with an introduction by John Updike
Porter, William Sydney *See* Henry, O., 1862-1910
PORTLAND (OR.) *See* Oregon—Portland
Porto, Elizabeth
The empty quarter
Western Humanities Review v55 no1 p65-74 Spr 2001

The **Portobello** Road. Spark, M.

The **portrait**. Jesús, P. d.

Portrait of a portrayal. Galef, D.

Portrait of an artist. Chaudhuri, A.

A **portrait** of angels. Shouse, D.

Portrait of electricity. Bail, M.

The **portrait** of Garibaldi. Viganò, R.

Portrait of Madame X. Proust, M.

Portrait of the artist. Harrison, H.

Portrait of the artist as a foaming deathmonger. Fischer, T.

Portrait of the artist as a young corpse. Paul, B.

A **portrait** of the artist at Warner Bros. Jenkins, G.

Portrait of the avant-garde. Høeg, P.

Portrait of young man with career. Waugh, E.

PORTRAITS
  James, H. The story of a masterpiece
  Warburton, G. Merry Roderick

Portraits of painters and composers. Proust, M.

PORTUGAL
  Adams, A. Sintra
  Gomes, M. T. Dead woman's grove
  Herbert, J. The sadness of Doctor Mendoza
  Régio, J. A brief comedy
  Régio, J. Maria do Ahu
  Régio, J. Miss Olimpia and her maid Belarmina
  Régio, J. A sad smile
  Régio, J. The story of Rosa Brava
  Régio, J. They used to go for long walks on Sundays . . .

  Lisbon
  Greer, A. S. Lost causes
  Régio, J. The flame-coloured dress
  Singer, I. B. Sabbath in Portugal

PORTUGUESE

  Italy
  Gomes, M. T. Cordelia
  Gomes, M. T. Margareta

Porzecanski, Teresa
  Rochel Eisips
    With signs and wonders; an international anthology of Jewish fabulist fiction; edited by Daniel M. Jaffe
  The seder
    With signs and wonders; an international anthology of Jewish fabulist fiction; edited by Daniel M. Jaffe
  The story of a cat
    Short stories by Latin American women; the magic and the real; edited by Celia Correas de Zapata; foreword by Isabel Allende

Posadas, Carmen
  The Nubian lover
    Colchie, T. A whistler in the nightworld; short fiction from the Latin Americas; edited by Thomas Colchie

Posey, John R.
  Ticket to freedom
    The African American West; a century of short stories; edited by Bruce A. Glasrud and Laurie Champion

Posing. Brookhouse, C.

Posing. Smart, A.

Position. Murray, S.

The **positions**. Lish, G.

The **possessed**. Clarke, A. C.

POSSESSION, DEMONIAC *See* Demoniac possession

The **possibility** of evil. Jackson, S.

The **Possibility** of Music. Martin, S.-P.

Possible future stepmother. Cohen, R.

The **possible** husband. Lee, D.

Post, Melville Davisson
  Naboth's vineyard
    The Best American mystery stories of the century; Tony Hillerman, editor; with an introduction by Tony Hillerman

Post and beam. Munro, A.

POSTAGE STAMPS
  Pronzini, B. and Kurland, M. Quicker than the eye
  Wellen, E. Fair exchange

POSTAL CARDS
  Rawley, D. Iguana boy
  Tumasonis, D. The prospect cards

POSTAL SERVICE
  Bishop, P. Going postal
  Chopin, K. For Marse Chouchoute
  Harrison, H. A civil service servant
  Herlihy, J. L. The astral body of a U.S. mail truck
  Kingsbury, K. A nice cup of tea
  Kline, D. Correspondence
  Markham, E. A. Mammie's form at the post office
  McDevitt, J. The Emerson effect
  Penn, W. S. Tarantulas
  Wellen, E. The postmaster & the slave

Postcards. Epstein, J.

Postcards. Gonzalez, R.

Postcards: a story. Epstein, J.

Postcards from the King of Tides. Kiernan, C. R.

Poste restante. Deane, J. F.

Postman. Brown, C.

The **postmaster** & the slave. Wellen, E.

The **pot-boiler**. Wharton, E.

Pot luck. Chaplin, P.

Pot O'Rice Horowitz's house of solace. McDonald, I.

Potato Eyes. Hall, C.

The **potato** gun. Carlson, R.

Poteet caught up in lust and history. Swarthout, G. F.

Potok, Chaim
  Moon
    Prize stories, 1999; The O. Henry awards; edited and with an introduction by Larry Dark

Pots. Cherryh, C. J.

The **Pottawatomie** Giant. Duncan, A.

Potter, Dennis
  Ticket to ride [excerpt]
    The Vintage book of amnesia; an anthology; edited by Jonathan Lethem

The **potter** of bones. Arnason, E.

POTTERS AND POTTERY
  Mason, B. A. Three-wheeler

POTTERY
  Krawiec, R. Rituals

Potvin, Elizabeth Ann
  After hours, after years
    Potvin, E. A. The traveller's hat; [by] Liza Potvin
  Assumptions
    Potvin, E. A. The traveller's hat; [by] Liza Potvin

Potvin, Elizabeth Ann—*Continued*

Blue moon
   Potvin, E. A. The traveller's hat; [by] Liza
   Potvin
The death of a husband
   Potvin, E. A. The traveller's hat; [by] Liza
   Potvin
Deflection
   Potvin, E. A. The traveller's hat; [by] Liza
   Potvin
Ghost
   Potvin, E. A. The traveller's hat; [by] Liza
   Potvin
Infant colic: What it is and what you can do
   about it
   Potvin, E. A. The traveller's hat; [by] Liza
   Potvin
Invert and multiply
   Potvin, E. A. The traveller's hat; [by] Liza
   Potvin
Open skies
   Potvin, E. A. The traveller's hat; [by] Liza
   Potvin
Riding to Tibet
   Potvin, E. A. The traveller's hat; [by] Liza
   Potvin
Sister Marguerite
   Potvin, E. A. The traveller's hat; [by] Liza
   Potvin
Sunday
   Potvin, E. A. The traveller's hat; [by] Liza
   Potvin
To rise above
   Potvin, E. A. The traveller's hat; [by] Liza
   Potvin
The traveller's hat
   Potvin, E. A. The traveller's hat; [by] Liza
   Potvin
The way home
   Potvin, E. A. The traveller's hat; [by] Liza
   Potvin
Wings
   Potvin, E. A. The traveller's hat; [by] Liza
   Potvin
You are here
   Potvin, E. A. The traveller's hat; [by] Liza
   Potvin
Potvin, Liza *See* Potvin, Elizabeth Ann, 1958-
POULTRY
Singer, I. B. Cockadoodledoo
Pound rots in Fragrant Harbour. Morton, L.
Pourciau, Glen
Answer
   New England Review v23 no3 p111-15 Summ
   2002
Hide
   New England Review v25 no1/2 p131-6 2004
Hired Hand
   New England Review v24 no2 p165-7 Spr
   2003
Sleep
   New England Review v22 no3 p84-6 Summ
   2001
Pournelle, Jerry
(jt. auth) *See* Niven, Larry and Pournelle, Jerry
POVERTY
Alcott, L. M. The cross on the church tower
Anderson, R. Death and the maid
Bell, M. S. The naked lady

Blaise, C. South
Bottoms, G. The metaphor
Browder, C. Secrets: three short stories
Chekhov, A. P. Anyuta
Chopin, K. A pair of silk stockings
Davidson, A. What strange stars and skies
Dumas, H. A boll of roses
Ferreira, R. Dream with no name
Greer, R. O. The can men
Lao She. Life choices
Lopes, H. The advance
Lutz, J. Tango was her life
McManus, J. June 1989
Melville, P. The conversion of Millicent Vernon
Mo Yan. Iron child
Mollel, T. M. A night out
Morgan, R. Dark corner
Morgan, R. Pisgah
Régio, J. Miss Olimpia and her maid Belarmina
Rulfo, J. Luvina
Slezak, E. Patch
Svoboda, T. Trailer girl
Tolstoy, L., graf. The requirements of love
Valenzuela, L. Who, me a bum?
Vice, B. Chickensnake
Vukcevich, R. The perfect gift
Walrond, E. Drought
Wharton, E. Full circle
Wharton, E. The pot-boiler
Poverty. Tozzi, F.
The **powder-blue** dragon. Vonnegut, K.
Powell, James
The plot against Santa Claus
   A yuletide universe; sixteen fantastical tales;
   edited by Brian M. Thomsen
Powell, Padgett
Answers
   New England Review v23 no2 p146 Spr 2002
Dusk
   New England Review v23 no2 p147-8 Spr
   2002
Matter of time
   New England Review v23 no2 p149-51 Spr
   2002
Sermon
   New England Review v22 no3 p146-50 Summ
   2001
Powell, Talmage
Somebody cares
   A Century of noir; thirty-two classic crime
   stories; edited by Mickey Spillane and Max
   Allan Collins
Power, Mark
Graves
   Retrieving bones; stories and poems of the
   Korean War; edited and with an introduc-
   tion by W. D. Ehrhart and Philip K. Jason
Power, Nani
The Milqueiest Piece of Toast
   The Paris Review v44 p145-50 Fall 2002
Power, Susan
A hole in the sheets
   The Workshop; seven decades of the Iowa
   Writers' Workshop: 42 stories, recollections
   & essays on Iowa's place in 20th-century
   American literature; edited by Tom Grimes

Power, Susan—*Continued*

Roofwalker

The Year's best fantasy & horror: sixteenth annual collection; edited by Ellen Datlow & Terri Windling

Watermelon seeds

Best of Prairie schooner; fiction and poetry; edited by Hilda Raz

POWER (SOCIAL SCIENCES)

Sturgeon, T. Microcosmic god

Power. Drake, R.

The **power**. Malone, M.

The **power** of childhood. Tolstoy, L., graf

The **power** of one. Kilpatrick, N.

The **power** of reason. Bissoondath, N.

Power punctuation!. Doctorow, C.

A **powerful** salvo. Henderson, B.

Powerman. Chenoweth, A.

Powers, J. F. (James Farl)

Death of a favorite

The Best American short stories of the century; John Updike, editor, Katrina Kenison, coeditor; with an introduction by John Updike

Powers, James Farl *See* Powers, J. F. (James Farl), 1917-1999

Powers, Richard

Easter, 1939

The Paris Review v44 p93-105 Wint 2002

Escapes

Esquire v132 no1 p86-91+ Jl 1999

Powers, Sara

The baker's wife

Coppola, F. F. Francis Ford Coppola's Zoetrope: all story; edited by Adrienne Brodeur and Samantha Schnee; introduction by Francis Ford Coppola

The wild

Texas bound. Book III; 22 Texas stories; edited by Kay Cattarulla; foreword by Robert Flynn

Powers, Tim

Itinerary

999: new stories of horror and suspense; edited by Al Sarrantonio

Pozzi, Lucio

Harry Bellefield

Bomb no76 p86-9 Summ 2001

The **practical** heart. Gurganus, A.

PRACTICAL JOKES

D'Amato, B. Steak tartare

Kelman, J. Joe laughed

Lardner, R. Haircut

Lovesey, P. The perfectionist

Pronzini, B. The dispatching of George Ferris

Runyon, D. Sense of humor

Singer, I. B. The wager

Whittenberg, A. Bloom of Zenobia

PRAGUE (CZECH REPUBLIC) *See* Czech Republic—Prague

PRAIRIE LIFE

Pickard, N. Afraid all the time

The **praline** woman. Dunbar-Nelson, A. M.

PRANKS *See* Practical jokes

Pranks. Kern, N.

Prather, Paul

The faithful

New stories from the South: the year's best, 2003; edited by Shannon Ravenel; with a preface by Roy Blount Jr.

Prather, Richard S.

The double take

A Century of noir; thirty-two classic crime stories; edited by Mickey Spillane and Max Allan Collins

Pratt, David

Series

His 3: brilliant new fiction by gay writers; edited by Robert Drake and Terry Wolverton

Pratt, Laura

Something like friends

'Teen v43 no6 p116-18 Je 1999

Pratt, Mary

Mama's gift

Arizona Highways v75 no12 p38-41 D 1999

Pray for the dead. Tristram, C.

The **prayer**. Tolstoy, L., graf

Prayer against the experts and their ways. Maliszewski, P.

Prayer for the driver at night. Maliszewski, P.

Prayer for the first balance. Maliszewski, P.

Prayer for the safety of the mother. Maliszewski, P.

Prayer for the safety of the public screamer. Maliszewski, P.

Prayer wheel. Leslie, N.

PRAYERS

Chekhov, A. P. The requiem

Norris, H. The great and small

Tolstoy, L., graf. The prayer

Prayers of an accidental nature. Di Blasi, D.

Prayers on the wind. Williams, W. J.

Precht, Vincent

Pull

Western Humanities Review v56 no1 p68-75 Spr 2002

Precious. Hopkinson, N.

Precious Blood. Wisniewski, M.

The **precipice**. Maleti, G.

Precision Marching at the Orphanage, 1890. Maguire, G.

The **precision** of angels. Jones, G.

Predation. Shapiro, J.

PREDESTINATION

Gaiman, N. Murder mysteries

A **predictable** nightmare on the eve of the stock market first breaking 6,000. Paine, T.

PREDICTIONS *See* Prophecies

PREGNANCY

See also Abortion

Ansay, A. M. Box

Atkinson, K. The cat lover

Banks, R. Black man and white woman in dark green rowboat

Barker, N. Inside information

Barrett, L. Beauty

Bear, G. Darwin's radio [excerpt]

Bell, M. S. Labor

Blackwood, S. One of us is hidden away

Bly, C. The tender organizations

Boylan, C. A reproduction

Boyle, T. C. Captured by the Indians

Bradbury, R. Remember Sascha?

Brkic, C. A. In the jasmine shade

PREGNANCY—*Continued*
Broughton, T. A. The classicist
Browder, C. Girls like us
Carson, J. Judgement
Casey, M. Aspects of motherhood
Chabon, M. Son of the wolfman
Coates, G. S. Late fruit
Cooper, B. What to name the baby
Day, C. The King and His Court
Dixon, S. Comparing
Doenges, J. Solved
Dunmore, H. The Kiwi-fruit arbour
Dyer, S. N. Sins of the mothers
Furman, L. Buddy
Galloway, J. A proper respect
Gasco, E. Can you wave bye bye, baby?
Gasco, E. The third person
Gasco, E. A well-imagined life
Gasco, E. You have the body
Gay, W. Bonedaddy, Quincy Nell, and the fif-
    teen thousand BTU electric chair
Gilchrist, E. Drunk with love
Gilchrist, E. The Starlight Express
Gilchrist, E. The survival of the fittest
Grodstein, L. Family vacation
Harfenist, J. Salad girls
Highsmith, P. The hollow oracle
Hochman, A. Underneath
Hoffman, A. Fate
Hood, A. After Zane
Jaime-Becerra, M. The corrido of Hector Cruz
Jen, G. Just wait
Jones, C. Irregularities
Kelly, R. En famille
Klass, P. For women everywhere
Klass, P. Freedom fighter
Krauss, N. Future emergencies
Kureishi, H. Midnight all day
Lee, T. The abortionist's horse (a nightmare)
Leegant, J. Henny's wedding
Lieu, J. Troubles
López, L. Walking circles
Maraini, D. Sister Attanasia's chickens
Martin, V. The creator has a master plan
Matheson, R. Trespass
Matiella, A. C. El bebé del vaquerón
McCorkle, J. Life prerecorded
McNally, J. The New Year
Meyers, K. The heart of the sky
Michaels, L. Mildred
Miller, R. Paula
Murray, J. A few short notes on tropical butter-
    flies
Murray, J. The hill station
Nailah, A. Joey falling
Naranjo, C. Symbiotic encounter
O'Neill, S. One positive thing
Ossana, D. White line fever
Pickering, J. The father
Power, S. Watermelon seeds
Raboteau, E. I. Kavita through glass
Robinson, L. Cuxabexis, Cuxabexis
Robison, M. Smart
Robotham, R. The cry
Rucker, R. v. B. Rapture in space
Sandor, M. Portrait of my mother, who posed
    nude in wartime
Searle, E. Celebration
Silber, J. Ashes of love

Slezak, E. Tomato watch
Stuckey-French, E. Leufredus
Thien, M. Bullet train
Tuller, D. Sperm-and-egg tango
Vasseur, T. J. The most beautiful day of your
    life
Weldon, F. A libation of blood
Winter, E. Blue-sky day
PREHISTORIC ANIMALS *See* Fossils
PREHISTORIC MAN
Baker, K. Hanuman
Clarke, A. C. Encounter in the dawn
Connor, J. Stone man
Nicastro, Laura. Haguit
Simak, C. D. Grotto of the dancing deer
The **Prehistoric** Producer. Bradbury, R.
PREJUDICES
        See also Antisemitism; Race relations
Alexie, S. Lawyer's League
Archer, J. A change of heart
Brownrigg, S. She who caught buses
Chesnutt, C. W. Cartwright's mistake
De Lint, C. Making a noise in this world
Dumas, H. Double nigger
Dunmore, H. Coosing
Gifford, B. American Falls
Gorman, E. The way it used to be
Hazel, R. White Anglo-Saxon Protestant
Honwana, L. B. Papa, snake & I
Hopkinson, N. A habit of waste
Jen, G. Chin
Lee, D. Yellow
McKnight, R. The kind of light that shines on
    Texas
McPherson, J. A. Elbow room
Parker, D. Arrangement in black and white
Parrish, T. Bonnie Ledet
Potok, C. Moon
Reiner, C. How Paul Robeson saved my life
Sandlin, L. Beautiful
Schoemperlen, D. Losing ground
Silber, J. Ordinary
Skillings, R. D. Czezarley Zoo gets out
Williams, J. Spring is now
Prelude to a nocturne. Lindquist, R. C.
Prelude to an autobiography: a fragment.
    Chaudhuri, A.
Prelude to pan. Giono, J.
Prenuptial agreement. Lida, D.
The **prescription**. Fitzgerald, P.
Presence. McHugh, M. F.
Presence. Miller, A.
The **present**. Skillings, R. D.
A **present** for Big Saint Nick. Vonnegut, K.
A **present** for the holiday. Kanafāni, G.
Preservation. Darlington, T.
Preservation news. Gurganus, A.
President of the past. Bukoski, A.
The **President** Returns. Almond, S.
PRESIDENTS
Bisson, T. Tell them they are all full of shit and
    they should fuck off
Melville, P. The president's exile
Wolfe, G. Copperhead
                    Election
Malzberg, B. N. Heavy metal
                United States
Dozois, G. R. Executive clemency
Martini, S. Poetic justice

PRESIDENTS—United States—*Continued*
Reed, R. First Tuesday
Turtledove, H. Joe Steele
Ursu, Anne. The president's new clothes
PRESIDENTS
United States
Bradbury, R. Hail to the chief
The **president's** cold legs. Ross, S.
President's Day. Bass, R.
The **president's** exile. Melville, P.
PRESLEY, ELVIS, 1935-1977
About
Barrett, L. Elvis lives
Crider, B. King of the night
Dozois, G. R. Touring
Eidus, J. Elvis, Axl, and me
Hauptman, W. Good rockin' tonight
Irsfeld, J. H. Radio Elvis
Malone, M. Blue Cadillac
Presnell, Daniel
Mermaids of the Saluda
South Carolina Review v36 no2 p161-3 Spr 2004
Pressure. Harrison, H.
Pressure. Nawrocki, S.
Prete, David
After we left Yonkers and before we came back
Prete, D. Say that to my face; fiction
The biggest, most silent thing
Prete, D. Say that to my face; fiction
Bleachers
Prete, D. Say that to my face; fiction
Green
Prete, D. Say that to my face; fiction
The itch
Prete, D. Say that to my face; fiction
No king, no puppy
Prete, D. Say that to my face; fiction
Not because I'm thirsty
Prete, D. Say that to my face; fiction
Say that to my face
Prete, D. Say that to my face; fiction
Self-respecting Neapolitans
Prete, D. Say that to my face; fiction
Pretend I've died. Kooker, J.
The **pretended.** Smith, D. A.
Pretending. Vukcevich, R.
Pretense. Berry, R. M.
The **pretext.** Wharton, E.
Pretty ice. Robison, M.
Pretty please. Winter, E.
The **pretty** surprise. Tomlinson, N. C.
Prevost, Claude-Michel
Tears for Ersulie Freda: men without shadow
Whispers from the cotton tree root; Caribbean fabulist fiction; edited by Nalo Hopkinson
Prey. Matheson, R.
Price, Cynthia
Lesbian bedrooms
The Vintage book of international lesbian fiction; edited and with an introduction by Naomi Holoch and Joan Nestle
Price, Reynolds
An evening meal
Best of Prairie schooner; fiction and poetry; edited by Hilda Raz
The fare to the moon
Crossing the color line; readings in Black and white; edited by Suzanne W. Jones

The **price.** Beekman, E. M.
The **price** of a charm. See Davidson, A. The lineaments of gratified desire
The **price** of eggs in China. Lee, D.
The **price** you pay. Winter, E.
PRIDE AND VANITY
Alarcón, P. A. d. Captain Poison
Alas, L. Two scholars
Borges, J. L. The bribe
Cutter, L. The red boots
Fitzgerald, F. S. The popular girl
Singer, I. B. The mirror
Singer, I. B. Zeidlus the Pope
West, M. To speak with angels
Pride Cometh Before a Fall. Holt, R. L.
Priest, Christopher
The affirmation [excerpt]
The Vintage book of amnesia; an anthology; edited by Jonathan Lethem
The **priest** of storms. Goran, L.
PRIESTS *See* Anglican and Episcopal clergy; Catholic priests; Clergy
PRIESTS, BUDDHIST *See* Buddhist priests
PRIESTS, CATHOLIC *See* Catholic priests
Primavera. Carrión, C.
Prime. Greer, R. O.
PRIME MINISTERS
Harris, R. PMQ
A **primer** for the punctuation of heart disease. Foer, J. S.
PRIMITIVE RELIGION *See* Religion
The **primordial** face. Girardi, R.
Prince of exiles. Edghill, R.
The **prince** of the steppes. Malzberg, B. N.
PRINCES
See also Princesses
Lee, V. Prince Alberic and the snake lady
Princes, very late. House, T.
The **princess.** Chekhov, A. P.
The **princess** and the accountant. Rogoff, R. E.
The **princess** and the pickle. Wheat, C.
"The **princess** and the street urchin". Pérez Galdós, B.
The **princess** bride [excerpt] Goldman, W.
Princess Di *See* Diana, Princess of Wales, 1961-1997
Princess Diana *See* Diana, Princess of Wales, 1961-1997
Princess, won by a bull. Liyong, T. l.
PRINCESSES
Byatt, A. S. Cold
Chekhov, A. P. The princess
Chekhov, A. P. Romance with double-bass
Principal photography. McCourt, J.
PRINTERS AND PRINTING
Singer, I. B. The adventure
PRINTING *See* Printers and printing
Prints. Davis, A.
Prinzo, D.
Drywall, plaster, and the things that cover them
Gettysburg Review v12 no1 p169-78 Spr 1999
The **Prior's** room. Lee, A.
Prishchepa. Babel´, I.
Prismatica. Delany, S. R.
PRISON CAMPS *See* Vietnamese War, 1961-1975—Prisoners and prisons; World War, 1939-1945—Prisoners and prisons
PRISON ESCAPES *See* Escapes
Prison food. Downs, M.

The **Prisoner**. Brau, E.
The **prisoner**. McBain, E.
The **prisoner**. Yizhar, S.
The **prisoner** in the jewel. Paxson, D. L.
The **prisoner** of Bluestone. Carlson, R.
The **prisoner** of Chillon. Kelly, J. P.
Prisoner of war. Norris, L.
PRISONERS, POLITICAL *See* Political prisoners
PRISONERS AND PRISONS
>   *See also* Ex-convicts; Political prisoners; Prisoners of war

Borges, J. L. The writing of the god
Bottoms, G. Gray world
Chekhov, A. P. A man of ideas
Delany, S. R. Cage of brass
Disch, T. M. The squirrel cage
Harrison, H. You men of violence
Kress, N. The flowers of Aulit Prison
Lee, V. Prince Alberic and the snake lady
Lunch, L. The devil's racetrack: Ray trailer
Mosley, W. Angel's island
Pronzini, B. and Malzberg, B. N. "Do I dare to eat a peach?"
Ramírez Mercado, S. The centerfielder
Singer, I. B. Loshikl
Singer, I. B. The parrot
Tenn, W. Time in advance
Tolstoy, L., graf. The power of childhood
VanderMeer, J. Flight is for those who have not yet crossed over
Waugh, E. Love among the ruins
China
Ha Jin. A bad joke
Ha Jin. Saboteur
Cuba
Benítez-Rojo, A. Buried statues
England
Cherryh, C. J. The haunted tower
Smith, G. Last requests
France
Perry, A. The escape
Greece
Karnezis, P. On the first day of Lent
Haiti
Danticat, E. Nineteen thirty-seven
Iran
Vafi, F. My mother, behind the glass
Russia
>   *See also* Prisoners and prisons—Siberia (Russia)

Siberia (Russia)
Landis, G. A. Beneath the stars of winter
Yuknavitch, L. Siberia: still life of a moving image
United States
Antworth, S. The tower pig
Capote, T. A diamond guitar
Chaon, D. I demand to know where you're taking me
Connell, R. E. Brother Orchid
Downs, M. Prison food
Duncan, A. Daddy Mention and the Monday skull
Earle, S. The witness
Edgerton, L. In the zone
Gautreaux, T. Rodeo parole
Gautreaux, T. Rodeo patrol
Harrington, J. A letter to Amy

Himes, C. The meanest cop in the world
Krawiec, R. Accommodations
Lopez, B. H. Emory Bear Hands' birds
Mathews, L. Crazy life
Matthews, C. The tailor of Yuma
McKinnon, K. Kindred
McMahon, N. Heart
Morgan, R. Sleepy Gap
Muñoz, M. Good as yesterday
Nailah, A. Sunday visit
Oates, J. C. In hiding
Ortiz, S. J. Kaiser and the War
Richmond, M. Fifth grade: a criminal history
Rothbart, D. First snow
Straight, S. Mines
Vachss, A. H. Good for the soul
Vachss, A. H. Word play
Wood, D. Feathers on the solar wind
PRISONERS OF WAR
>   *See also* Concentration camps; World War, 1939-1945—Prisoners and prisons

Babel´, I. Squadron Commander Trunov
Carson, J. Captives
Coberly, L. M. Early transparent
Gascar, P. The season of the dead
Murray, S. Order of precedence
Viganò, R. Peter
PRISONS *See* Prisoners and prisons
Pritchard, Melissa
Funktionlust
>   The Pushcart prize XXVI; best of the small presses, an annual small press reader; edited by Bill Henderson and the Pushcart prize editors

Funktionslust
>   *The Paris Review* v41 no153 p95-108 Wint 1999

Salve regina
>   *Gettysburg Review* v12 no2 p197-217 Summ 1999

>   Prize stories, 2000; The O. Henry awards; edited and with an introduction by Larry Dark

Pritchard Jones, Harri
The stranger
>   *The Literary Review (Madison, N.J.)* v44 no2 p274-83 Wint 2001

Pritchett, Laura
Dry roots
>   Pritchett, L. Hell's bottom, Colorado
An easy birth
>   Pritchett, L. Hell's bottom, Colorado
A fine white dust
>   Pritchett, L. Hell's bottom, Colorado
Grayblue day
>   Pritchett, L. Hell's bottom, Colorado
Hell's bottom
>   Pritchett, L. Hell's bottom, Colorado
Jailbird gone songbird
>   Pritchett, L. Hell's bottom, Colorado
A new name each day
>   Pritchett, L. Hell's bottom, Colorado
Rattlesnake fire
>   Pritchett, L. Hell's bottom, Colorado
The record keeper
>   Pritchett, L. Hell's bottom, Colorado
Summer flood
>   Pritchett, L. Hell's bottom, Colorado

Pritchett, Laura—*Continued*
This imaginary me
U.S. Catholic v68 no3 p36-9 Mr 2003
Privacy. Ford, R.
Private Dance. Hays, D.
PRIVATE DETECTIVES *See* Detectives, Private
A **Private** Experience. Adichie, C. N.
PRIVATE EYE STORIES *See* Detectives, Private; Mystery and detective stories
A **private** life. Davidson, R.
Private places. Jenkins, G.
A **private** possession. Yates, R.
Private school. McKenzie, A.
PRIVATE SCHOOLS *See* School life
A **private** space. Eggers, P.
Private Tomaszewski. Bukoski, A.
Privateer's moon. Dowling, T.
The **privy** councillor. Chekhov, A. P.
Probability pipeline. Rucker, R. v. B.
PROBATION OFFICERS
Huffman, B., Jr. Acceptance of responsibility
Probe to the negative. Lipsyte, S.
A **problem**. James, H.
Problem at sea. Christie, A.
PROBLEM CHILDREN *See* Emotionally disturbed children
The **problem** of cell 13. Futrelle, J.
The **Problem** of Human Consumption. Almond, S.
The **problem** of pain. Anderson, P.
The **Problem** of the House. DeWeese, D.
The **problem** of the pearls. Hodgson, W. H.
The **problem** of the yellow wallpaper. Hoch, E. D.
The **problem** with Yosi. Shomer, E.
Problems for Self-Study. Yu, C.
The **procedure**. Bishop, M.
Processing. Gaitskill, M.
The **procession** of life. Hawthorne, N.
Procrastinator. Foster, A. D.
Proctor, Judith
Dear Mr. Bernard Shaw
Dracula in London; edited by P. N. Elrod
Proctor, Minna
(jt. auth) *See* Tabucchi, Antonio
Prodigal. Chaon, D.
Prodigal. Hoffman, W.
Prodigal fathers. Blackwood, S.
Prodigal Niece. Pearlman, E.
The **prodigy** of longing. Richter, S.
The **professional**. Rendell, R.
Professor. Nailah, A.
Professor claims he found formula for ancient steel. Stuckey-French, E.
Professor Fargo. James, H.
PROFESSORS *See* Teachers
Professors. Whalen, T.
PROGERIA
Stableford, B. M. The pipes of Pan
The **Project**. Means, D.
Project Hush. Tenn, W.
Project Mushroom. Smith, J.
Projectiles. Leslie, N.
Projections. Kilpatrick, N.
Prom night. Richter, S.
Prometheus burned. O'Neill, S.
PROMISCUITY
Cooper, J. C. A shooting star
Dinh, L. The ugliest girl
Ebershoff, D. The Rose City
Foley, S. A history of sex

Fromm, P. Wind
Krouse, E. The husbands
Miller, R. Louisa
Oates, J. C. Me & Wolfie, 1979
Promise. Mosley, W.
The **Promised** Land. Clayton, J. J.
Promises. Coates, G. S.
Promises kept. Bruchman, D. M.
Promises made and broken. Matthews, C.
Pronto bucks. Spencer, D.
Pronzini, Bill
And then we went to Venus
Pronzini, B. Oddments; a short story collection
Angel of mercy
Pronzini, B. More oddments
The Arrowmont Prison riddle
Pronzini, B. Oddments; a short story collection
Bank job
Pronzini, B. Oddments; a short story collection
La bellezza delle bellezze
Pronzini, B. Sleuths
The big bite
The Best American mystery stories, 2001; edited and with an Introduction by Lawrence Block
Pronzini, B. Oddments; a short story collection
The World's finest mystery and crime stories, second annual collection; edited by Ed Gorman
Blood money
Pronzini, B. Sleuths
Caught in the act
Pronzini, B. Oddments; a short story collection
Chip
Pronzini, B. More oddments
The World's finest mystery and crime stories, third annual collection; edited by Ed Gorman and Martin H. Greenberg
Connoisseur
Murder most delectable; savory tales of culinary crimes; edited by Martin H. Greenberg
Pronzini, B. More oddments
A craving for originality
Pronzini, B. More oddments
Dead man's slough
Pronzini, B. Sleuths
The desert limited
Pronzini, B. Sleuths
The desperate ones
Pronzini, B. Sleuths
The dispatching of George Ferris
Pronzini, B. Oddments; a short story collection
Epitaph
Pronzini, B. and Malzberg, B. N. On account of darkness and other SF stories; [by] Bill Pronzini and Barry N. Malzberg
Fear
A Century of great Western stories; edited by John Jakes
Fergus O'Hara, detective
Pronzini, B. More oddments
Pronzini, B. Sleuths

Pronzini, Bill—*Continued*

Flood
The World's finest mystery and crime stories, first annual collection; edited by Ed Gorman

"Give-a-Damn" Jones
The First Five Star western corral; western stories; edited by Jon Tuska and Vicki Piekarski

The highbinders
Pronzini, B. Oddments; a short story collection

The Hungarian cinch
Pronzini, B. and Malzberg, B. N. On account of darkness and other SF stories; [by] Bill Pronzini and Barry N. Malzberg

I didn't do it
Pronzini, B. More oddments

I think I will not hang myself today
Pronzini, B. Oddments; a short story collection

Jade
Pronzini, B. Sleuths

A killing in Xanadu
Pronzini, B. Sleuths

Liar's dice
Pronzini, B. Oddments; a short story collection

The man who collected "The Shadow"
Pronzini, B. Oddments; a short story collection

Medium rare
Pronzini, B. Sleuths

Mrs. Rakubian
Pronzini, B. More oddments

One night at Dolores Park
A Century of noir; thirty-two classic crime stories; edited by Mickey Spillane and Max Allan Collins

One of those cases
Pronzini, B. More oddments

Opportunity
Pronzini, B. More oddments

Out of the depths
Pronzini, B. Oddments; a short story collection

Putting the pieces back
Pronzini, B. Oddments; a short story collection

The REC field
Pronzini, B. and Malzberg, B. N. On account of darkness and other SF stories; [by] Bill Pronzini and Barry N. Malzberg

Shade work
Pronzini, B. Oddments; a short story collection

Smuggler's island
Pronzini, B. More oddments

Souls burning
Master's choice [v1]; mystery stories by today's top writers and the masters who inspired them; edited by Lawrence Block

Stacked deck
A Century of great suspense stories; edited by Jeffery Deaver

Stakeout
Pronzini, B. Sleuths

A taste of paradise
Pronzini, B. More oddments

Toy
Pronzini, B. and Malzberg, B. N. On account of darkness and other SF stories; [by] Bill Pronzini and Barry N. Malzberg

Under the skin
Pronzini, B. More oddments

Wishful thinking
Irreconcilable differences; Lia Matera, editor
Pronzini, B. Oddments; a short story collection

Pronzini, Bill and Kurland, Michael

Quicker than the eye
Pronzini, B. More oddments

Vanishing act
Pronzini, B. Sleuths

Pronzini, Bill and Malzberg, Barry N.

Another burnt-out case
Pronzini, B. and Malzberg, B. N. On account of darkness and other SF stories; [by] Bill Pronzini and Barry N. Malzberg

A clone at last
Pronzini, B. and Malzberg, B. N. On account of darkness and other SF stories; [by] Bill Pronzini and Barry N. Malzberg

"Do I dare to eat a peach?"
Pronzini, B. and Malzberg, B. N. On account of darkness and other SF stories; [by] Bill Pronzini and Barry N. Malzberg

Fascination
Pronzini, B. and Malzberg, B. N. On account of darkness and other SF stories; [by] Bill Pronzini and Barry N. Malzberg

In our image
Pronzini, B. and Malzberg, B. N. On account of darkness and other SF stories; [by] Bill Pronzini and Barry N. Malzberg

Inaugural
Pronzini, B. and Malzberg, B. N. On account of darkness and other SF stories; [by] Bill Pronzini and Barry N. Malzberg

The last one left
Pronzini, B. and Malzberg, B. N. On account of darkness and other SF stories; [by] Bill Pronzini and Barry N. Malzberg

The Lyran case
Pronzini, B. and Malzberg, B. N. On account of darkness and other SF stories; [by] Bill Pronzini and Barry N. Malzberg

Multiples
Pronzini, B. and Malzberg, B. N. On account of darkness and other SF stories; [by] Bill Pronzini and Barry N. Malzberg

Night rider
Pronzini, B. and Malzberg, B. N. On account of darkness and other SF stories; [by] Bill Pronzini and Barry N. Malzberg

On account of darkness
Pronzini, B. and Malzberg, B. N. On account of darkness and other SF stories; [by] Bill Pronzini and Barry N. Malzberg

On the nature of time
Pronzini, B. and Malzberg, B. N. On account of darkness and other SF stories; [by] Bill Pronzini and Barry N. Malzberg

Opening a vein
Pronzini, B. and Malzberg, B. N. On account of darkness and other SF stories; [by] Bill Pronzini and Barry N. Malzberg

Pronzini, Bill and Malzberg, Barry N.—*Continued*

Out of quarantine
  Pronzini, B. and Malzberg, B. N. On account of darkness and other SF stories; [by] Bill Pronzini and Barry N. Malzberg
Prose bowl
  Pronzini, B. and Malzberg, B. N. On account of darkness and other SF stories; [by] Bill Pronzini and Barry N. Malzberg
Pronzini, B. More oddments
Reading day
  Pronzini, B. and Malzberg, B. N. On account of darkness and other SF stories; [by] Bill Pronzini and Barry N. Malzberg
Shakespeare MCMLXXXV
  Pronzini, B. and Malzberg, B. N. On account of darkness and other SF stories; [by] Bill Pronzini and Barry N. Malzberg
Vanishing point
  Pronzini, B. and Malzberg, B. N. On account of darkness and other SF stories; [by] Bill Pronzini and Barry N. Malzberg
Whither thou, ghost
  Pronzini, B. and Malzberg, B. N. On account of darkness and other SF stories; [by] Bill Pronzini and Barry N. Malzberg

Proof. Clement, H.

Proof. Eggers, P.

Proof of the existence of God. Kelly, J. P.

Propaganda. Richmond, M.

The **propagation** of light in a vacuum. Kelly, J. P.

A **proper** Anno Domini feeling. Salkey, A.

A **proper** burial. Collins, B.

Proper gypsies. Mason, B. A.

Proper library. Ferrell, C.

A **proper** respect. Galloway, J.

A **proper** Santa Claus. McCaffrey, A.

The **properly** punished pimp. Sade, marquis de

Properties of language. Shields, D.

The **properties** of magic. Gonzalez, R.

The **properties** of stainless steel. Barkley, B.

PROPERTY
  See also Real estate
  Vivante, A. Fisherman's terrace
  Weaver, G. The white elephant

A **property** of childhood. Kalman, J.

Property values. Alvarez, A.

PROPHECIES
  Cherryh, C. J. A gift of prophecy
  Haggard, H. R. Black heart and white heart: a Zulu idyl
  Hawthorne, N. The great stone face
  James, H. A problem

The **prophet** from Jupiter. Earley, T.

PROPHETS
  Borges, J. L. Hakim, the masked dyer of Merv

The **prophets** of Benjamin Bok. Scliar, M.

Proposal. Galloway, J.

Proposals and advice. Schwarzschild, E. L.

Prose, Francine
  Everything is about animals
    In our nature: stories of wildness; selected and introduced by Donna Seaman
  Talking dog
    The Art of the story; an international anthology of contemporary short stories; edited by Daniel Halpern

Three pigs in five days [excerpt]
  Neurotica: Jewish writers on sex; edited by Melvin Jules Bukiet
The witch
  Francis Ford Coppola's Zoetrope all-story 2; edited by Adrienne Brodeur and Samantha Schnee; with an introduction by Francis Ford Coppola
  On the rocks; the KGB Bar fiction anthology; edited by Rebecca Donner ; foreword by Denis Woychuk

Prose bowl. Pronzini, B. and Malzberg, B. N.

The **prospect** cards. Tumasonis, D.

The **prospect** from the silver hills. Crace, J.

PROSPECTORS
  Crace, J. The prospect from the silver hills
  Dawson, J. What the cat dragged in
  Grey, Z. Tappan's burro
  L'Amour, L. Trap of gold
  London, J. All Gold Canyon
  Wellen, E. The whisper of gold

Prosthesis. Chaon, D.

PROSTITUTES
    See also Escorts (Dating service)
  Anderson, R. Echo
  Babel´, I. Chink
  Babel´, I. Elya Isaakovich and Margarita Prokofievna
  Babel´, I. A hardworking woman
  Bahrami, M. The end, a city
  Barnet, M. Miosvatis
  Bear, G. Sleepside story
  Bellow, S. Something to remember me by
  Blake, J. C. The house of Esperanza
  Borges, J. L. The night of the gifts
  Bowles, P. The story of Lahcen and Idir
  Brenner, W. Mr. Meek
  Brite, P. Z. and Faust, C. Saved
  Canty, K. Sleepers holding hands
  Chapman, C. M. Milking cherry
  Chekhov, A. P. A nervous breakdown
  Chopin, K. Two portraits
  Cohen, S. A girl named Charlie
  Crumley, J. Coming around the mountain
  Crumley, J. Whores
  Danticat, E. Night women
  De Lint, C. In this soul of a woman
  Díaz, J. The brief wondrous life of Oscar Wao
  Dinh, L. 555
  Englander, N. For the relief of unbearable urges
  Ferré, R. When women love men
  Foster, K. Two windows
  Galloway, J. Where you find it
  Goldstein, N. The verse in the margins
  Goran, L. An old man and three whores
  Gurnah, A. Escort
  Händler, E.-W. Trigger
  Haycox, E. Stage to Lordsburg
  Hoch, E. D. The Club of Masks
  Hopkinson, N. Fisherman
  Irsfeld, J. H. Stop, rewind, and play
  Kohler, S. Lunch with mother
  Krawiec, R. Troubles on Morning Glory Road
  LaValle, V. D. Class trip
  LaValle, V. D. Getting ugly
  LaValle, V. D. Slave
  Lee, A. The birthday present
  Lee, W. W. Indiscreet
  LeRoy, J. T. Natoma Street

PROSTITUTES—*Continued*
Malouf, D. Sally's story
Michaels, L. A girl with a monkey
Nakagami, K. The cape
Paul, B. Jack be quick
Peterson, P. W. The woman in the long green coat
Ponte, A. J. In the cold of the Malecón
Rawley, D. Tina in the back seat
Reiner, C. Warren Waits and the spaghetti-strap girl
Salter, J. Big ranch
Shomer, E. The problem with Yosi
Singer, I. B. In the poorhouse
Singer, I. B. On the way to the poorhouse
Singer, I. B. Yanda
Stableford, B. M. The house of mourning
Tolstoy, L., graf. Sisters
Updike, J. Transaction
Vachss, A. H. Last date
Vachss, A. H. Summer girl
Vachss, A. H. Time share
Yates, R. Liars in love
PROSTITUTION
   See also Prostitutes
Alameddine, R. Grace
Barrett, N., Jr. Ginny Sweethips' Flying Circus
Danihy, G. Jumping with Jim
Jacobs, M. The liberation of little heaven
Lee, W. W. Dying for sin
Leong, R. Daughters
Leong, R. Phoenix eyes
Maraini, D. Shadows
Maraini, D. Viollca, the child from Albania
McBain, E. The prisoner
Mollel, T. M. A night out
Sade, marquis de. The properly punished pimp
Vachss, A. H. Escort service
Vachss, A. H. Searcher
Protective coloring. Carson, J.
Protocols of consumption. Wilson, R. C.
The **prototype**. Arvin, N.
Proudflesh. Robertson, D.
Proulx, Annie
55 miles to the gas pump
   Proulx, A. Close range; Wyoming stories
The blood bay
   Proulx, A. Close range; Wyoming stories
Brokeback Mountain
   Proulx, A. Close range; Wyoming stories
   The Scribner anthology of contemporary short fiction; fifty North American stories since 1970; Lex Williford and Michael Martone, editors
   Still wild; short fiction of the American West, 1950 to the present; edited by Larry McMurtry
The bunchgrass edge of the world
   The Best American short stories, 1999; selected from U.S. and Canadian magazines by Amy Tan with Katrina Kenison, with an introduction by Amy Tan
   Proulx, A. Close range; Wyoming stories
The Contest
   The Virginia Quarterly Review v80 no4 p233-42 Fall 2004
The governors of Wyoming
   Proulx, A. Close range; Wyoming stories

The half-skinned steer
   The Best American short stories of the century; John Updike, editor, Katrina Kenison, coeditor; with an introduction by John Updike
   Proulx, A. Close range; Wyoming stories
Job history
   Proulx, A. Close range; Wyoming stories
A lonely coast
   Proulx, A. Close range; Wyoming stories
Man Crawling Out of Trees
   The New Yorker v80 no20 p72-83 Jl 26 2004
The mud below
   Prize stories, 1999; The O. Henry awards; edited and with an introduction by Larry Dark
   Proulx, A. Close range; Wyoming stories
On the antler
   Sports best short stories; edited by Paul D. Staudohar
Pair a spurs
   Proulx, A. Close range; Wyoming stories
People in hell just want a drink of water
   The Best American short stories, 2000; selected from U.S. and Canadian magazines by E. L. Doctorow with Katrina Kenison; with an introduction by E. L. Doctorow
   Gentlemen's Quarterly v69 no4 p117-18+ Ap 1999
   Proulx, A. Close range; Wyoming stories
Summer of the Hot Tubs
   The New Yorker v78 no24 p158-60 Ag 19-26 2002
The Trickle-Down Effect
   The New Yorker v78 no40 p124-7 D 23-30 2002
The wer-trout
   Fishing's best short stories; edited by Paul D. Staudohar
What Kind of Furniture Would Jesus Pick?
   The New Yorker v79 no23 p126-34, 136-7 Ag 18-25 2003
Proust, Marcel
Another memory
   Proust, M. The complete short stories of Marcel Proust; compiled and translated by Joachim Neugroschel; foreword by Roger Shattuck
The death of Baldassare Silvande, Viscount of Sylvania
   Proust, M. The complete short stories of Marcel Proust; compiled and translated by Joachim Neugroschel; foreword by Roger Shattuck
A dinner in high society
   Proust, M. The complete short stories of Marcel Proust; compiled and translated by Joachim Neugroschel; foreword by Roger Shattuck
The end of jealousy
   Proust, M. The complete short stories of Marcel Proust; compiled and translated by Joachim Neugroschel; foreword by Roger Shattuck
Fragments of commedia dell'arte
   Proust, M. The complete short stories of Marcel Proust; compiled and translated by Joachim Neugroschel; foreword by Roger Shattuck

Proust, Marcel—*Continued*

The indifferent man
Proust, M. The complete short stories of Marcel Proust; compiled and translated by Joachim Neugroschel; foreword by Roger Shattuck

The melancholy summer of Madame de Breyves
Proust, M. The complete short stories of Marcel Proust; compiled and translated by Joachim Neugroschel; foreword by Roger Shattuck

Memory
Harper's v302 no1810 p17-18 Mr 2001

Norman things
Proust, M. The complete short stories of Marcel Proust; compiled and translated by Joachim Neugroschel; foreword by Roger Shattuck

Portrait of Madame X.
Proust, M. The complete short stories of Marcel Proust; compiled and translated by Joachim Neugroschel; foreword by Roger Shattuck

Portraits of painters and composers
Proust, M. The complete short stories of Marcel Proust; compiled and translated by Joachim Neugroschel; foreword by Roger Shattuck

Regrets, reveries the color of time
Proust, M. The complete short stories of Marcel Proust; compiled and translated by Joachim Neugroschel; foreword by Roger Shattuck

Social ambitions and musical tastes of Bouvard and Pécuchet
Proust, M. The complete short stories of Marcel Proust; compiled and translated by Joachim Neugroschel; foreword by Roger Shattuck

Violante or high society
Proust, M. The complete short stories of Marcel Proust; compiled and translated by Joachim Neugroschel; foreword by Roger Shattuck

A young girl's confession
Proust, M. The complete short stories of Marcel Proust; compiled and translated by Joachim Neugroschel; foreword by Roger Shattuck

Provenance. Holliday, L.

Provenance. Longstreet, K. A.

Provenance of a face. Melville, P.

PROVENCE (FRANCE) *See* France—Provence

Provenzano, Jim

Quality time
Men on men 2000; best new gay fiction for the millennium; edited and with an introduction by David Bergman and Karl Woelz

PROVIDENCE (R.I.) *See* Rhode Island—Providence

Providence. Orner, P.

The **province** of the bearded fathers. Klass, P.

PROVINCETOWN (MASS.) *See* Massachusetts—Provincetown

Proving it. Vachss, A. H.

The **prowl**. Frost, G.

The **prowler**. Cherry, K.

Proxies [excerpt] Mixon, L. J.

Pruitt love. Clyde, M.

Prum, Deborah

Searching for Arthur's Stone
The Virginia Quarterly Review v79 no3 p438-58 Summ 2003

The **Prussian** officer. Lawrence, D. H.

Pryor, Josh

Wrong numbers
The Best American mystery stories, 2000; edited and with an introduction by Donald E. Westlake

Przytyk, Sara Nomberg- *See* Nomberg-Przytyk, Sara, 1915-

Psalms. Winterson, J.

Psyché. Tiedemann, M. W.

PSYCHIATRISTS
See also Mentally ill—Care and treatment; Psychoanalysts; Women psychiatrists

Abrams, T. The good doctor
Adams, A. The drinking club
Adams, A. Earthquake damage
Adams, A. Patients
Adams, A. The wrong Mexico
Bradbury, R. The man in the Rorschach shirt
Brownstein, G. The dead fiddler, 5E
Clifford, W. Scoring
Curtis, Rebecca. Hungry self
Deaver, J. For services rendered
Estep, M. Teeth
Gilchrist, E. The cabal
Haslett, A. The good doctor
Jenkins, G. The counterpuncher
Kessel, J. A clean escape
Klass, P. Exact change
Kohler, S. The mask
Kooker, J. Pretend I've died
Lansdale, J. R. Listen
Lovett, S. Buried treasure
Martin, V. Transposing
Newman, K. You don't have to be mad . . .
Thomsen, B. It's a wonderful miracle on 34th Street's Christmas carol
White, E. B. The second tree from the corner

Psychic. Svoboda, T.

Psychic hand. O'Neill, S.

PSYCHIC PHENOMENA *See* Extrasensory perception; Occultism; Spiritualism; Supernatural phenomena

PSYCHICAL RESEARCH
Gonzalez, R. The ghost of John Wayne

PSYCHO (MOTION PICTURE: 1960)
Haskell, J. The judgment of Psycho

PSYCHOANALYSIS
Galef, D. Laugh track

PSYCHOANALYSTS
Jong, E. En route to the congress of dreams; or, The zipless fuck
Locklin, G. A sober reading of Dr. Sigmund Freud
Updike, J. My lover has dirty fingernails

The **psychologist** (who doesn't love me). Bilick, A.

PSYCHOLOGISTS
Berriault, G. The infinite passion of expectation
Bilick, A. The psychologist (who doesn't love me)
Bly, C. The tomcat's wife
Knight, T. A trail of mirrors
Lutz, J. S.O.S.
Pickard, N. The dead past

PSYCHOLOGISTS—*Continued*
Reisman, N. Rubies
Schmidt, H. J. Darling?
Sheckley, R. The dream of misunderstanding
Smith, I. C. In the middle of the wood [excerpt]
Wallace, M. Splitting
Psychon. Lugones, L.
PSYCHOPATHS *See* Insane, Criminal and dangerous; Personality disorders
PSYCHOTHERAPISTS *See* Psychotherapy
PSYCHOTHERAPY
Epstein, J. Artie Glick in a family way
Estep, M. One of us
Klass, P. The trouble with Sophie
Menaker, D. The treatment
Strauss, A. Shrinking away
Treat, J. Radio disturbance
Wallace, D. F. The depressed person
Ptacek, Kathryn
The grotto
Best new horror 12; edited and with an introduction by Stephen Jones
Reunion
Witches' brew; edited by Yvonne Jocks
Pu-239. Kalfus, K.
Public burning. Clark, J.
Public defenders and other fossils. Singleton, G.
Public displays of affection. Alvarez, A.
The **public** library. Babel´, I.
Public library. Kees, W.
A **public** pool. Adams, A.
PUBLIC PROSECUTORS
Krich, R. M. "You win some . . . "
PUBLIC RELATIONS
Painter, P. Dud
Public relations. Singleton, G.
PUBLIC SCHOOLS *See* School life
The **public** spectacle. Eggers, P.
PUBLIC UTILITIES
See also Electricity
PUBLIC WELFARE
Bellow, S. Looking for Mr. Green
Martin, V. Love
Publicity campaign. Clarke, A. C.
PUBLISHERS AND PUBLISHING
See also Newspapers; Periodicals
Bradbury, R. One more for the road
Desai, A. The rooftop dwellers
Drury, J. M. Murder at the sales meeting
Kane, J. F. How to become a publicist
Marston, E. Slaughter in the Strand
Moorhead, F. Four characters, four lunches
Paretsky, S. Heartbreak house
Singer, I. B. The joke
Singer, I. B. The magazine
Trevor, W. A friend in the trade
Wallace, D. F. The Suffering Channel
Wallace, R. Wordplay
Wharton, E. The descent of man
PUBS *See* Hotels, taverns, etc.
Puce Boy. Libling, M.
Puckheads. Robinson, L.
Pudding. Slavin, J.
PUERTO RICANS
New York (N.Y.)
Michaels, L. The deal
United States
Vega Yunqué, E. Eight morenos

PUERTO RICO
Alvarez, A. Property values
Ferré, R. When women love men
Irsfeld, J. H. Puerto Rico '61
Kurlansky, M. Beautiful Mayagüez women
Ortiz, S. J. A story of Rios and Juan Jesus
Vega, A. L. Eye-openers
Puga, María Luisa
Naturally
The Vintage book of Latin American stories; edited by Carlos Fuentes and Julio Ortega
PUGILISM *See* Boxing
Pull. Precht, V.
Pulped sandwiches. Kelman, J.
The **pulpit**. Lee, A.
Pulpwood. Barnes, J.
Pulver, Mary Monica
To whom the victory?
Royal whodunnits; edited by Mike Ashley
PUMAS
Easton, R. O. Quick and the cat
Van Winckel, N. The land of anarchy
The **pump**. Bingham, S.
Pump Jack. Burleson, D. R.
PUMPING IRON *See* Weight lifting
Pumpkin head. Sarrantonio, A.
The **Pun** Detective and the Danny Boy killer. Breen, J. L.
Punching chickens. Troncoso, S.
Punchlining. Lisick, B.
PUNIC WAR, 2D, 218-201 B.C.
Anderson, P. Delenda est
PUNISHMENT
Cheng, C.-W. Hair
DeLancey, K. A hole in the wall of noise
Harrison, H. I see you
Tenn, W. Time in advance
Yolen, J. Sun/flight
The **punishment**. Gaede, D.
Punishment. Kaminsky, S. M.
The **punishment**. Tani, C.
Punkins. Kilpatrick, N.
PUNS
Breen, J. L. The Pun Detective and the Danny Boy killer
The **pup**. See Chekhov, A. P. Whitebrow
Pupil. Barthelme, F.
The **pupil**. James, H.
The **puppet**. Davis, D. S.
PUPPETS AND PUPPET PLAYS
Gutiérrez, S. D. Cantinflas
The **puppies**. Paschal, D.
Puppy. Ford, R.
Puppyland. Allyn, D.
The **Purcells**. Kees, W.
Purdy, James
Brawith
The Antioch Review v59 no2 p196-205 Spr 2001
Easy Street
The Antioch Review v60 no3 p377-95 Summ 2002
No stranger to Luke
The Antioch Review v59 no1 p13-25 Wint 2001
Purdy, Ken W.
Tell me the reason, do
Sports best short stories; edited by Paul D. Staudohar

Pure rotten. Lutz, J.
Pure Welsh. Lawrence, H.
Purgatory. Wieland, L.
Purge me with hyssop. Hay, E.
The **purification** of Jim Barnes. Smith, T. D.
PURITANS
    Hawthorne, N. The gentle boy
    Hawthorne, N. The Maypole of Merry Mount
The **purloined** letter. Poe, E. A.
The **purloined** purple pearl. Cannell, D.
Purple Heart. Gilliland, G.
Purple shards. Engstrom, E.
Purpura, Lia
    Autopsy Report
        Iowa Review v33 no3 p85-91 Wint 2003/2004
Purring. Ferriss, L.
Pursuit. Hoffman, W.
Push comes to shove. Walpow, N.
Pushkin, Aleksandr Sergeevich
    The blackamoor of Peter the Great
        Pushkin, A. S. The collected stories; translated from the Russian by Paul Debreczeny; with an introduction by John Bayley; verse passages translated by Walter Arndt
    The blizzard
        Pushkin, A. S. The collected stories; translated from the Russian by Paul Debreczeny; with an introduction by John Bayley; verse passages translated by Walter Arndt
    The captain's daughter
        Pushkin, A. S. The collected stories; translated from the Russian by Paul Debreczeny; with an introduction by John Bayley; verse passages translated by Walter Arndt
    Dubrovskii
        Pushkin, A. S. The collected stories; translated from the Russian by Paul Debreczeny; with an introduction by John Bayley; verse passages translated by Walter Arndt
    Egyptian nights
        Pushkin, A. S. The collected stories; translated from the Russian by Paul Debreczeny; with an introduction by John Bayley; verse passages translated by Walter Arndt
    The guests were arriving at the dacha
        Pushkin, A. S. The collected stories; translated from the Russian by Paul Debreczeny; with an introduction by John Bayley; verse passages translated by Walter Arndt
    A history of the village of Goriukhino
        Pushkin, A. S. The collected stories; translated from the Russian by Paul Debreczeny; with an introduction by John Bayley; verse passages translated by Walter Arndt
    In the corner of a small square
        Pushkin, A. S. The collected stories; translated from the Russian by Paul Debreczeny; with an introduction by John Bayley; verse passages translated by Walter Arndt
    Kirdzhali
        Pushkin, A. S. The collected stories; translated from the Russian by Paul Debreczeny; with an introduction by John Bayley; verse passages translated by Walter Arndt
    Maria Schoning
        Pushkin, A. S. The collected stories; translated from the Russian by Paul Debreczeny; with an introduction by John Bayley; verse passages translated by Walter Arndt

A novel in letters
    Pushkin, A. S. The collected stories; translated from the Russian by Paul Debreczeny; with an introduction by John Bayley; verse passages translated by Walter Arndt
The queen of spades
    Pushkin, A. S. The collected stories; translated from the Russian by Paul Debreczeny; with an introduction by John Bayley; verse passages translated by Walter Arndt
Roslavlev
    Pushkin, A. S. The collected stories; translated from the Russian by Paul Debreczeny; with an introduction by John Bayley; verse passages translated by Walter Arndt
The shot
    Pushkin, A. S. The collected stories; translated from the Russian by Paul Debreczeny; with an introduction by John Bayley; verse passages translated by Walter Arndt
The squire's daughter
    Pushkin, A. S. The collected stories; translated from the Russian by Paul Debreczeny; with an introduction by John Bayley; verse passages translated by Walter Arndt
The stationmaster
    Pushkin, A. S. The collected stories; translated from the Russian by Paul Debreczeny; with an introduction by John Bayley; verse passages translated by Walter Arndt
A tale of Roman life
    Pushkin, A. S. The collected stories; translated from the Russian by Paul Debreczeny; with an introduction by John Bayley; verse passages translated by Walter Arndt
The undertaker
    Pushkin, A. S. The collected stories; translated from the Russian by Paul Debreczeny; with an introduction by John Bayley; verse passages translated by Walter Arndt
We were spending the evening at Princess D.'s dacha
    Pushkin, A. S. The collected stories; translated from the Russian by Paul Debreczeny; with an introduction by John Bayley; verse passages translated by Walter Arndt
PUSHKIN, ALEKSANDR SERGEEVICH, 1799-1837
About
Shrayer-Petrov, D. The Lanskoy road
Pussy Galore. Evans, L.
Put Not Thy Trust in Chariots. Tel, J.
Put yourself in my shoes. Carver, R.
Putting the Lizard to Sleep. Sanders, T.
Putting the pieces back. Pronzini, B.
Putting up signs. Cohen, R.
Puttkammer, Emil von *See* Ludwig, Otto, 1802-1875
The **puzzle** of Priipiirii. Tenn, W.
P´yetsukh, V.
    Killer Miller
        The Paris Review v44 no161 p76-81 Spr 2002
P´yetsukh, Vyacheskav
    Me and the sea
        The Virginia Quarterly Review v75 no1 p164-73 Wint 1999
Pygmalion with a Bad S. Tyennick, J.

Pyle, Howard
   The merry adventures of Robin Hood [excerpt]
      Swords and sorcerers; stories from the world
      of fantasy and adventure; edited by Clint
      Willis
Pynchon, Thomas
   Entropy
      The Best of The Kenyon review; edited by
      David Lynn; introduction by Joyce Carol
      Oates
The **pyramid**. Anderson, R.
The **Pyramid** of Amirah. Kelly, J. P.
Pyroclastic flow. Weldon, F.
PYTHAGORAS
                        About
   Rucker, R. v. B. The square root of Pythagoras
Python. Paschal, D.

Q

Q: Questing. Weaver, G.
Q Roo. Chiappone, R.
QUADROONS *See* Mulattoes
Quail. Adam, C.
The **Quaker**. Babel´, I.
QUAKERS *See* Society of Friends
Quality fuel for electric living. Nesbitt, M.
The **quality** of being a Ruby. Sucher, C. P.
Quality time. Banks, R.
Quality time. Ford, R.
Quality time. Provenzano, J.
Quan, Andy
   Hair
      Circa 2000; gay fiction at the millennium; ed-
      ited by Robert Drake & Terry Wolverton
The **quantity** of mercy. Berry, M. S.
The **quantum** rose. Asaro, C.
Quare name for a boy. Keegan, C.
The **Quarrel**. Vervaecke, K.
QUARRELING
   Smith, A. The start of things
   Spencer, E. The adult holiday
   Wolff, T. Hunters in the snow
The **quarry**. Wallace, R.
Quartermain. Malzberg, B. N.
QUAYLE, DAN
                        About
   Beckman, J. Babylon revisited redux
Que Quieres. Dybek, S.
QUÉBEC (PROVINCE) *See* Canada—Québec
   (Province)
QUÉBEC (QUÉBEC) *See* Canada—Québec
   (Québec)
La **quedada**. Lida, D.
Queen, Ellery
   The adventure of the Dauphin doll
      A Century of great suspense stories; edited by
      Jeffery Deaver
   The adventure of the one-penny black
      Murder most postal; homicidal tales that de-
      liver a message; edited by Martin H.
      Greenberg
   The adventure of the President's half disme
      The Best American mystery stories of the
      century; Tony Hillerman, editor; with an
      introduction by Tony Hillerman

Man bites dog
   Sports best short stories; edited by Paul D.
   Staudohar
A matter of seconds
   Boxing's best short stories; edited by Paul D.
   Staudohar
The **queen**. Pacheco, J. E.
Queen for a day. Banks, R.
The **queen** in yellow. Baker, K.
Queen Margaret. Alas, L.
The **queen** of air and darkness. Anderson, P.
The **Queen** of Fruit Cocktail. Cobb, W. J.
Queen of mean. Cody, L.
Queen of shadows. Ruiz, B.
Queen of soulmates.
The **queen** of spades. Pushkin, A. S.
The **queen** of Sparta. Bondurant, M.
The **queen** of worldly graces. Frank, J.
Queenie. Munro, A.
QUEENS
         See also Courts and courtiers names of
         queens
   Kushner, E. The unicorn masque
   Lindskold, J. M. Queen's gambit
   Whitty, J. A tortoise for the Queen of Tonga
QUEENS (NEW YORK, N.Y.) *See* New York
   (N.Y.)—Queens
Queen's gambit. Lindskold, J. M.
Quénum, Olympe Bhêly- *See* Bhêly-Quénum,
   Olympe
Quest. Anderson, P.
The **quest** for Saint Aquin. Boucher, A.
The **question**. Muller, R.
Question mark. Gomes, M. T.
A **question** of faith. Hogan, R.
Questionnaire. Felthousen, R. A.
Questions. Oates, J. C.
Questions of Home. Baingana, D.
Quick and the cat. Easton, R. O.
Quick bright things. Wallace, R.
Quicker than the eye. Pronzini, B. and Kurland,
   M.
Quid pro quo. Bradbury, R.
The **quiet** at the bottom of the pool. Louis, L. G.
Quiet game. Clark, W. L.
Quiet night. Highsmith, P.
Quiet people. Maguire, J.
A **quiet** revolution for death. Dann, J.
A **quiet** room with a view. Davidson, A.
The **Quijote** robot. Sheckley, R.
Quill, Monica
   Death takes the veil
      Quill, M. Death takes the veil and other sto-
      ries; with an introduction by Ralph
      McInerny
   Intent to kill
      Quill, M. Death takes the veil and other sto-
      ries; with an introduction by Ralph
      McInerny
   Miss Butterfingers
      Murder most divine; ecclesiastical tales of un-
      holy crimes; edited by Ralph McInerny and
      Martin H. Greenberg
      Quill, M. Death takes the veil and other sto-
      ries; with an introduction by Ralph
      McInerny

Quill, Monica—*Continued*
The other urn
Quill, M. Death takes the veil and other stories; with an introduction by Ralph McInerny
A rose is a rose is a rose
Quill, M. Death takes the veil and other stories; with an introduction by Ralph McInerny
A sound investment
Quill, M. Death takes the veil and other stories; with an introduction by Ralph McInerny
The visitor
Quill, M. Death takes the veil and other stories; with an introduction by Ralph McInerny
Quill, Monica, 1929-
For works written by this author under other names see McInerny, Ralph M., 1929-
Quill. Earley, T.
Quilting on the rebound. McMillan, T.
Quin-Harkin, Janet, 1941-
See also Bowen, Rhys, 1941-
Quinn, Seabury
The phantom farmhouse
The Literary werewolf; an anthology; edited by Charlotte F. Otten
The thing in the fog
The Literary werewolf; an anthology; edited by Charlotte F. Otten
Quinn's way. Bailey, D.
Quint and the braceros. Bishop, P.
Quintessence. Alvarez, A.
QUIROGA, JUAN FACUNDO, 1790-1835
About
Borges, J. L. A dialog between dead men
Quit screaming. Gores, J.
Quite contrary. Vukcevich, R.
Quitters, inc. King, S.
Quitting. Burton, M.
Quitting smoking. McKnight, R.
Quixotic. Leslie, N.
QUOTATIONS
Pronzini, B. and Malzberg, B. N. "Do I dare to eat a peach?"
Quotidian. Anderson, D.

R

Raab, Esther
Rose Jam
Sleepwalkers and other stories; the Arab in Hebrew fiction; edited by Ehud Ben-Ezer
Rabasa, George
For the Solitary Soul
South Carolina Review v33 no2 p76-81 Spr 2001
Rabb, Margo
How to tell a story
New stories from the South: the year's best, 2000; edited by Shannon Ravenel; with a preface by Ellen Douglas
Museum
New England Review v22 no4 p146-55 Fall 2001

My mother's first lover
Best new American voices 2000; guest editor Tobias Wolff; series editors John Kulka and Natalie Danford
Seduce me
Seventeen v60 no12 p174-83 D 2001
The **rabbi**. Babel´, I.
RABBIS
Asplund, Russell William. The Rabbi and the sorcerer
Bezmozgis, D. An animal to the memory
Dann, J. Jumping the road
Davenport, G. The chair
Englander, N. Reb Kringle
Goldstein, N. Barbary apes
Kellerman, F. Holy water
Kurlansky, M. The unclean
Leegant, J. The tenth
Michaels, L. Murderers
Ozick, C. The pagan rabbi
Papernick, J. The art of correcting
Sher, S. Tsuris
Singer, I. B. Androgynous
Singer, I. B. A boy knows the truth
Singer, I. B. A cage for Satan
Singer, I. B. Errors
Singer, I. B. Guests on a winter night
Singer, I. B. I place my reliance on no man
Singer, I. B. Joy
Singer, I. B. The last demon
Singer, I. B. A piece of advice
Singer, I. B. The plagiarist
Singer, I. B. The recluse
Singer, I. B. Something is there
Sloan, B. The good rabbi
Thurm, M. Moonlight
Weiss, Bernice F. Where does a golem go?
The **rabbi's** son. Babel´, I.
Rabbit. Lao She
The **Rabbit** Hole as Likely Explanation. Beattie, A.
Rabbit remembered. Updike, J.
RABBITS
Boylan, C. Ears
Cortázar, J. Letter to a young lady in Paris
Marshall, P. Bunnymoon
Meyers, K. A strange brown fruit
Tinti, H. Slim's last ride
Updike, J. The day of the dying rabbit
Rabbit's foot. Fracis, S. H.
Rabbit's foot. Leary, J. E.
RABIES
Drew, E. Mad dogs
Rabinovitch, Sholem *See* Sholem Aleichem, 1859-1916
Rabinowitz, Sholem Yakov *See* Sholem Aleichem, 1859-1916
Rabinowitz, Solomon *See* Sholem Aleichem, 1859-1916
Rabin's dead. Keret, E.
Raboteau, Emily Ishem
Bernie and me
Callaloo v25 no2 p367-80 Spr 2002
Kavita through glass
The Best American short stories, 2003; selected from U.S. and Canadian magazines by Walter Mosley with Katrina Kenison; with an introduction by Walter Mosley
Raccoon. Chiappone, R.

Raccoon. Smart, A.
RACCOONS
Kim, Junse. Yangban
Raccoons. Adams, A.
The **race** for last place. Bonnie, F.
RACE PROBLEMS *See* Race relations
RACE RELATIONS
 See also African Americans; Antisemitism; Culture conflict; Interracial marriage; Miscegenation; Prejudices
Bradbury, R. And the rock cried out
Harrison, H. American dead
Irsfeld, J. H. Ambivalence Hardy Fire
Africa
 See Africa—Race relations
England
 See England—Race relations
South Africa
 See South Africa—Race relations
United States
 See United States—Race relations
RACEHORSES *See* Horses
The **racer**. Melchior, I.
Rachel. Davis, M. K.
Rachel in love. Murphy, P.
Rachel Marker and Her Book of Shadows. Roth, M.
The **Rachel** Weisz Experiment. Katz, D.
Rachmil, Bryks
Bread
 When night fell; an anthology of Holocaust short stories; edited by Linda Schermer Raphael and Marc Lee Raphael
Children of the Lodz, ghetto
 When night fell; an anthology of Holocaust short stories; edited by Linda Schermer Raphael and Marc Lee Raphael
The last journey
 When night fell; an anthology of Holocaust short stories; edited by Linda Schermer Raphael and Marc Lee Raphael
RACIAL INTERMARRIAGE *See* Interracial marriage
RACING
 See also Automobile races; Bicycle racing; Boat racing; Horse racing; Yacht racing
Di Filippo, P. Neutrino drag
RACISM *See* Antisemitism; Prejudices; Race relations
RACKETEERS *See* Crime and criminals; Gangsters; Mafia
RACKETS *See* Gambling
Rackstraw, Loree
A Day in Paradise
 The North American Review v289 no3/4 p61-7 My/Ag 2004
Radiant doors. Swanwick, M.
Radiant green star. Shepard, L.
RADIATION
De Camp, L. S. The isolinguals
Physiological effect
Merril, J. That only a mother
Schroeder, K. The dragon of Pripyat
Shonk, K. My mother's garden
Sturgeon, T. Thunder and roses
RADICALISM *See* Radicals and radicalism

RADICALS AND RADICALISM
 See also Anarchism and anarchists
Broughton, T. A. Living the revolution
Malzberg, B. N. Turpentine
RADIO
Arvin, N. Radio ads
Carter, E. Luminous dial
Carter, E. WLUV
Leslie, N. Marconi's dream
Marcus, B. The least you need to know about radio
Mathews, H. The broadcast
Trevanian. Mrs. McGivney's nickel
Waugh, E. The sympathetic passenger
Radio ads. Arvin, N.
Radio baby. Chivers, D.
RADIO BROADCASTING
Campbell, R. No strings
Chacón, D. Aztlán, Oregon
Lochte, D. Mad Dog
Winegardner, M. Halftime
Radio disturbance. Treat, J.
RADIO PROGRAMS
Harris, M. The iron fist of oligarchy
Lessing, D. M. One off the short list
Lutz, J. S.O.S.
Oliver, C. The boy next door
Weinreb, M. Radio radio
Radio room. Hunnicutt, E.
RADIOACTIVITY
Clarke, A. C. Critical mass
Ra*e. Campbell, R.
Rafi. Kirchheimer, G. D.
The **raft**. Orner, P.
The **raft**. Ziegler, I.
Raft in water, floating. Homes, A. M.
A **rafter** in Miami Beach. Valeri, L.
RAFTING (SPORTS)
Carlson, R. Down the Green River
Houston, P. Cataract
Rosenfeld, S. Exactly the size of life
La **Ragazza**. Lee, A.
Ragazzi. Silber, J.
A **rage** forever. Shade, E.
The **raggle** taggle gypsy-o. Swanwick, M.
The **raiders**. Phillips, G.
RAILROAD ACCIDENTS
Ford, R. Optimists
Railroad incident, August 1995. Means, D.
RAILROADS
 See also Subways
Drake, R. Connections
Construction
Loomis, N. M. Tough hombre
Employees
Bukoski, A. Time between trains
Chekhov, A. P. Champagne
McPherson, J. A. A solo song: for Doc
Stations
Browder, C. The missing day
Chekhov, A. P. The complaints book
Chekhov, A. P. Fat and thin
Gonzalez, R. Train station
Ponte, A. J. Station H
Smith, A. Being quick
Trains
Allen, S. Passage
Allen, S. A place between stations
Coleman, J. C. Sandhill cranes

RAILROADS—Trains—*Continued*
Frym, G. Columbus Day
Grimsley, J. Jesus is sending you this message
Jones, G. These eyes
Kalman, J. Channel crossing
McElroy, C. J. A brief spell by the river
McHugh, M. F. The Lincoln train
Means, D. The grip
Padilla, I. Rhodesia Express
Schmatz, P. Tokyo trains
Smolens, J. Night train to Chicago
Vapnyar, L. Ovrashki's trains

Travel
The shape of things
Bradbury, R. On the Orient, North
Capote, T. A tree of night
Chekhov, A. P. The cattle-dealers
Dinh, L. Two who forgot
Duffy, S. Running dogs
Gilman, C. P. The girl in the pink hat
Harrar, G. The 5:22
Mazelis, J. Flock
Ponte, A. J. This life
Schoemperlen, D. How deep is the river?
Vivante, A. Train ride of a faun
Wharton, E. A journey

Rain. Engberg, S.
Rain. Kalman, J.
Rain. Tomaso, C.
RAIN AND RAINFALL
Bradbury, R. All summer in a day
Dumas, H. Rain God
Fleming, J. H. Wind and rain
The **rain** barrel. Nichols, J.
Rain dance. Leslie, N.
Rain itself. Winegardner, M.
Rainbow mama. Klass, P.
Rainbow rider. Overholser, W. D.
Raindrops. Kawabata, Y.
Raine, Norman Reilly
Tugboat Annie and the Cheapskate
The Saturday Evening Post v273 no3 p50-1,
76-84 My/Je 2001
The **rainmaker**. Rosenblum, M. H.
RAINMAKERS
Rosenblum, M. H. The rainmaker
Rainwater, Ana
Night rose
A Hot and sultry night for crime; edited by
Jeffery Deaver
Raise Children Here. Singleton, G.
Raisin eyes. Tawada, Y.
RALEIGH (N.C.) *See* North Carolina—Raleigh
The **Raleigh** Man. Gansworth, E. L.
Ralphie's Clarinet. McKean, R.
Ramadan. Pittalwala, I.
Ramaya, Shona
Destiny
Ramaya, S. Operation monsoon; stories
Gopal's kitchen
Ramaya, S. Operation monsoon; stories
The matchmakers
Ramaya, S. Operation monsoon; stories
Operation monsoon
Ramaya, S. Operation monsoon; stories
Re:mohit
Ramaya, S. Operation monsoon; stories
Ramírez, Sergio *See* Ramírez Mercado, Sergio,
1942-

Ramírez Mercado, Sergio
The centerfielder
The Vintage book of Latin American stories;
edited by Carlos Fuentes and Julio Ortega
Ramone. Troy, J.
Ramos, Luis Arturo
Othón, the Waiter Who Lost his Memory
Callaloo v26 no4 p954-61 Fall 2003
Ramos, Michael
The crab with the green mango belly
Prairie Schooner v73 no1 p119-20 Spr 1999
How the crow became black and the culeta lost
his crown of feathers
Prairie Schooner v73 no1 p121-22 Spr 1999
Rampling, Anne *See* Rice, Anne, 1941-
Ranch girl. Meloy, M.
RANCH LIFE
See also Cowboys
Aadland, D. East breeze
Adam, C. Moose
Adam, C. Red pony
Bass, R. Ogallala
Blakely, M. Laureano's wall
Borges, J. L. The Gospel according to Mark
Bower, B. M. The lamb of the Flying U
Bowles, P. At Paso Jojo
DeMarinis, R. Romance: a prose villanelle
Easton, R. O. Bonaparte's dreams
Easton, R. O. Death in October
Easton, R. O. Dynamite's day off
Easton, R. O. Jim Magee's sand
Easton, R. O. Nobody danced
Easton, R. O. To find a place
Easton, R. O. The wind of Pelican Island
Easton, R. O. Women and Dynamite
Everett, P. L. Wolf at the door
Flynn, T. T. Half interest in hell
Flynn, T. T. Ride to glory
Giles, J. H. The gift
Greene, A. C. The girl at Cabe ranch
Henry, W. Wolf-Eye
Kelton, E. North of the big river
Le May, A. Gray rider
Meloy, M. Ranch girl
Newton, D. B. Breakheart Valley
Newton, D. B. Reach high, top hand!
Pritchett, L. Dry roots
Pritchett, L. An easy birth
Pritchett, L. A fine white dust
Pritchett, L. Grayblue day
Pritchett, L. Hell's bottom
Pritchett, L. Jailbird gone songbird
Pritchett, L. A new name each day
Pritchett, L. Rattlesnake fire
Pritchett, L. The record keeper
Pritchett, L. Summer flood
Proulx, A. Brokeback Mountain
Proulx, A. The bunchgrass edge of the world
Proulx, A. The governors of Wyoming
Proulx, A. The half-skinned steer
Proulx, A. Pair a spurs
Proulx, A. People in hell just want a drink of
water
Roorbach, B. Anthropology
Sneve, V. D. H. Grandpa was a cowboy and an
Indian
Steinbeck, J. The murder
Swan, G. The chasm
Tilghman, C. Room for mistakes

Randisi, Robert J.
Black and white memories
   The World's finest mystery and crime stories, second annual collection; edited by Ed Gorman
Green legs and glam
   Murder most Celtic; tall tales of Irish mayhem; edited by Martin H. Greenberg
Initimate obsession
   Flesh and blood; erotic tales of crime and passion; edited by Max Allan Collins and Jeff Gelb
The Knights of Liberty
   The Blue and the gray undercover; edited by Ed Gorman
The nickel Derby
   A Century of noir; thirty-two classic crime stories; edited by Mickey Spillane and Max Allan Collins
(jt. auth) See Pelegrimas, Marthayn and Randisi, Robert J.
Randisi, Robert J. and Matthews, Christine
A night at the love nest resort
   Love and death; edited by Carolyn Hart
Randolph, Ladette
The girls
   Best new American voices 2000; guest editor Tobias Wolff; series editors John Kulka and Natalie Danford
Random access. Clark, J.
Random beatings and you. Reid, E.
Randy. Woods, E. R.
The **ranger** way. Cunningham, E.
Ranieri, Roman
The bandit who caught a killer
   Felonious felines; edited by Carol and Ed Gorman
Rankin, Ian
Adventures in babysitting
   Master's choice v2; mystery stories by today's top writers and the masters who inspired them; edited by Lawrence Block
The confession
   The World's finest mystery and crime stories, second annual collection; edited by Ed Gorman
A deep hole
   The Vintage book of contemporary Scottish fiction; edited and with an introduction by Peter Kravitz
The hanged man
   The World's finest mystery and crime stories, first annual collection; edited by Ed Gorman
Saint Nicked
   The best British mysteries; edited by Maxim Jakubowski
The serpent's back
   Crème de la crime; edited by Janet Hutchings
Tell me who to kill
   Edwards, M. Mysterious pleasures; a celebration of the Crime Writers' Association's 50th anniversary; edited by Martin Edwards
Ransom, Elmer
Fishing's just luck
   Fishing's best short stories; edited by Paul D. Staudohar
Ransom. Buck, P. S.
Ransom. Evans, E.

A **ransom** for Tedek. Wegner, H.
The **ransom** of Retta Chiefman. Cohen, S.
Rao, Hilary
Every day a little death
   Ploughshares v25 no2/3 p150-59 Fall 1999
Rao, Kutumba
The job
   Partisan Review v69 no2 p218-29 Spr 2002
RAPE
Addonizio, K. Inside out
Babel´, I. Makhno's boys
Bishop, P. Pattern of behavior
Bowles, P. Under the sky
Bradbury, R. The transformation
Browder, C. Center zone
Chabon, M. Son of the wolfman
Crider, B. An evening out with Carl
Ellin, S. You can't be a little girl all your life
Everett, P. L. Cry about a nickel
Ferriss, L. Stampede
Freudenberger, N. The orphan
Fromm, P. Willowy-wisps
Glave, T. Whose song?
Gorman, E. Aftermath
Herling, G. Beata, Santa
Johnson-Davies, D. Oleanders pink and white
Kalu, Anthonia C. Camwood
Keegan, C. The scent of winter
Le Clézio, J.-M. G. Ariadne
Lida, D. A beach day
Lida, D. Free trade
Maron, M. No, I'm not Jane Marple, but since you ask
McBain, E. The victim
McElroy, C. J. A brief spell by the river
Michaels, L. Manikin
Oates, J. C. Do with me what you will
Oates, J. C. The girl with the blackened eye
Packer, Z. Speaking in tongues
Potvin, E. A. To rise above
Rendell, R. The wink
Ritchie, E. A lovely day for tennis
Sánchez, R. Barrio chronicle
Seidman, L. Over my shoulder
Silber, J. Without Ellie
Singer, I. B. One day of happiness
Spencer, E. The girl who loved horses
Thomas, J. The flaying season
Vachss, A. H. Good for the soul
Walker, A. Advancing Luna—and Ida B. Wells
Wellen, E. Inside evidence
Wellen, E. Waswolf
The **rape** of reason. Jacobs, M.
Raphael, Frederic
All his sons
   Raphael, F. All his sons; a novella and nine stories
Bread, money, and liberty
   Raphael, F. All his sons; a novella and nine stories
Emile
   Raphael, F. All his sons; a novella and nine stories
God and mammon
   Raphael, F. All his sons; a novella and nine stories
L.S.D.
   Raphael, F. All his sons; a novella and nine stories

Raphael, Frederic—*Continued*

An older woman

  Raphael, F. All his sons; a novella and nine stories

Shared credit

  Raphael, F. All his sons; a novella and nine stories

The siren's song

  Raphael, F. All his sons; a novella and nine stories

Son of Enoch

  Raphael, F. All his sons; a novella and nine stories

Who whom?

  Raphael, F. All his sons; a novella and nine stories

Rapid-fire love in Automonster. Herko, M.

Rappaccini's daughter. Hawthorne, N.

Rappin' dog. Lochte, D.

Rappoport, Solomon *See* Ansky, S., 1863-1920

Raptor. Gores, J.

Rapture. Chekhov, A. P.

Rapture in space. Rucker, R. v. B.

The **raptures** of the deep. Love, R.

Rapunzel. Lee, T.

Rapunzel. Rollins, H.

Rara avis. Boyle, T. C.

Rare and ever rarer in this world of empirical facts. . . Roth, J.

RARE BOOKS

  Borges, J. L. The book of sand

Rare is a cold red center. Slavin, J.

RAS TAFARI MOVEMENT *See* Rastafari movement

Rascal. Reifler, N.

Rascals in the cane. Mosley, W.

Rash, Ron

Last rite

  This is where we live; short stories by 25 contemporary North Carolina writers; edited by Michael McFee

Speckle Trout

  The Kenyon Review v25 no2 p77-92 Spr 2003

Speckled trout

  Stories from the Blue Moon Cafe II; edited by Sonny Brewer

Tbe Corpse Bird

  South Carolina Review v35 no2 p28-35 Spr 2003

Raspberry Sherbet. Bache, E.

RASPUTIN, GRIGORIĬ EFIMOVICH, 1871-1916

About

Van Belkom, E. The debauched one

Rasputin, Valentin Grigor´evich

In a Siberian town

  Michigan Quarterly Review v38 no3 p363-77 Summ 1999

RASTAFARI MOVEMENT

  Buckell, T. S. Spurn Babylon

Rastrow's Island. Boyle, T. C.

Rat. Bingham, S.

Rat. Brady, C.

Rat. Brandt, W.

The **Rat**. Gombrowicz, W.

Rat. Kelly, J. P.

Rat boy. Buchanan, E.

Rat medicine. Davis, L.

Rat roulette. Matiella, A. C.

The **Rat** Spoon. Ponder, D. U.

The **ratchet**. Morgan, R.

The **Rate** Collector. Gray, J. and Gallagher, T.

Rath, Tina and Rath, Tony

Who killed fair Rosamund?

  Royal whodunnits; edited by Mike Ashley

Rath, Tony

(jt. auth) See Rath, Tina and Rath, Tony

The **rather** unlikely courtship of Edwin Anderson and Roz Rosenzweig. Nissen, T.

Rationing. Waters, M. Y.

RATS

Bishop, M. O happy day

Brandt, W. Rat

George, E. Good fences aren't always enough

Hodgson, W. H. The mystery of the derelict

Jenkins, G. The big cheese

Matiella, A. C. Rat roulette

Reifler, N. Personal foundations of self-forming through auto-identification with otherness

Rats eat cats. Richter, S.

Rattlesnake fire. Pritchett, L.

RATTLESNAKES

Troncoso, S. The snake

Ravel, Joseph Maurice *See* Ravel, Maurice, 1875-1937

RAVEL, MAURICE, 1875-1937

About

Bell, M. S. The pagodas of Ciboure

Ravelstein. Bellow, S.

Raven. Bunin, I. A.

Raven dream. Reed, R.

Ravendale loop. Shepard, J.

The **raven's** quest. Patton, F.

Raven's Wing. Oates, J. C.

Ravera, Lidia

You drive

  In the forbidden city; an anthology of erotic fiction by Italian women; edited by Maria Rosa Cutrufelli; translated by Vincent J. Bertolini

Raw daddy. LaValle, V. D.

Raw material. Byatt, A. S.

The **raw** material of ash. Fromm, P.

Rawley, Donald

At the Four Seasons Hotel

  Rawley, D. Tina in the back seat; stories

Baby Liz

  Rawley, D. Tina in the back seat; stories

The bible of insects

  Rawley, D. Tina in the back seat; stories

The closest thing to God

  Rawley, D. Tina in the back seat; stories

Iguana boy

  Rawley, D. Tina in the back seat; stories

Mother of pearl

  Rawley, D. Tina in the back seat; stories

A rumor of prayer

  Rawley, D. Tina in the back seat; stories

Saigon

  Rawley, D. Tina in the back seat; stories

The spells of an ordinary twilight

  LA shorts; edited by Steven Gilbar

  Rawley, D. Tina in the back seat; stories

The tiger's tooth

  Rawley, D. Tina in the back seat; stories

Tim

  Rawley, D. Tina in the back seat; stories

Rawley, Donald—*Continued*
  Tina in the back seat
    Rawley, D. Tina in the back seat; stories
  Vandeville
    Rawley, D. Tina in the back seat; stories
Rawlings, Ellen
  Poison
    Mystery midrash; an anthology of Jewish
      mystery & detective fiction; [edited by]
      Lawrence W. Raphael
Rawlins, Paul
  Monroe Service
    Western Humanities Review v58 no1 p24-35
      Spr 2004
Rawson, Eric
  Paris
    Iowa Review v34 no1 p97-102 Spr 2004
Rawson, JoAnna
  Eleven ways to live in the city
    Murphy, N. Twelve branches; stories from St.
      Paul; [by] Nora Murphy ... {et al.}
  The interview
    Murphy, N. Twelve branches; stories from St.
      Paul; [by] Nora Murphy ... {et al.}
  A working history of the alley
    Murphy, N. Twelve branches; stories from St.
      Paul; [by] Nora Murphy ... {et al.}
Ray, David
  The Short Version
    Southwest Review v88 no2/3 p380-91 2003
Ray, Sandra King *See* King, Cassandra, 1944-
Rayford, Paulette Rabia
  In the family
    African American Review v35 no1 p41-59 Spr
      2001
Raymer, Robert
  On Fridays
    The Literary Review (Madison, N.J.) v47 no1
      p121-5 Fall 2003
Raymond, Ilene
  The other woman
    Good Housekeeping v228 no5 p197-98+ My
      1999
Raymond, Midge
  Most Likely to Be Remembered
    The North American Review v289 no3/4 p15-
      19 My/Ag 2004
Raymond's run. Bambara, T. C.
Ray's shoes. White, M. C.
Re-deem the time. Lake, D. J.
Re-inventing the archives. Ritchie, E.
Reach, Alice Scanlan
  In the confessional
    Murder most divine; ecclesiastical tales of un-
      holy crimes; edited by Ralph McInerny and
      Martin H. Greenberg
Reach high, top hand!. Newton, D. B.
The **reach** of wonder. Coley, D.
Reaching back. Vachss, A. H.
Reaching for Sunlight. Moulton, M.
The **reaction**. Means, D.
The **reader**. Hay, E.
The **reading**. Engel, H.
Reading in His Wake. Painter, P.
Reading Sontag. Addonizio, K.
Reading the bones. Finch, S.
Reading the water. Burton, M.
Ready position. Boswell, M.
Reaffirmation. McManus, J.

REAGAN, NANCY, 1923-
  About
    Homes, A. M. The former First Lady and the
      football hero
REAGAN, RONALD, 1911-2004
  About
    Homes, A. M. The former First Lady and the
      football hero
A **real** durwan. Lahiri, J.
The **Real** Eleanor Rigby. Fulton, A.
REAL ESTATE
  Alvarez, A. Property values
  Bart, P. The founder
  Bart, P. The neighbors II
  Bart, P. Power play
  Canin, E. Where we are now
  Pronzini, B. Caught in the act
  Singer, I. B. The litigants
  Updike, J. Personal archaeology
Real estate. Moore, L.
REAL ESTATE BUSINESS
  Beattie, A. Janus
  Blair, J. Happy puppy
  Chabon, M. House hunting
  Hribal, C. J. Consent
  Phillips, D. R. What it cost travelers
  Singleton, G. Remember why we're here
  Smith, C. W. The Bundlelays
  Vonnegut, K. Any reasonable offer
Real family. Strandquist, R.
A **real** girl. Lewitt, S.
Real Indians. Earling, D. M.
Real life. Parra, E. A.
Real men. Love, R.
A **real** place. Glave, T.
REAL PROPERTY *See* Real estate
The **real** shape of the coast. Lutz, J.
The **real** story. Painter, P.
The **real** story. Reynolds, A.
The **real** thing. Gilman, C.
The **real** thing. Greer, R. O.
The **real** thing. Vachss, A. H.
Real time. Chaudhuri, A.
The **real** world. Utley, S.
The **real** world. Vachss, A. H.
The **Real** World School of Law. Gilman, J.
The **reality** of angels. Jenkins, G.
A **really** good jazz piano. Yates, R.
A **really** happy man. Gifford, B.
A **really** weird thing happened recently. Ingenito-
  DeSio, L.
Rear View. Nelson, A.
Rear window. Woolrich, C.
Reaser, Rick
  (jt. auth) *See* Scarborough, Elizabeth Ann and
    Reaser, Rick
The **reason** for angels. Padilla, M.
A **reason** to be. Kalman, J.
The **Reason** Was Us. Clarke, B.
The **reason** why. Gorman, E.
Reasoner, James
  Dead Man's Hollow
    Westward; a fictional history of the American
      West : 28 original stories celebrating the
      50th anniversary of the Western Writers of
      America; edited by Dale L. Walker
Reasons. Crownfield, D.
Reasons unknown. Ellin, S.
Reassurance. Gurganus, A.

Reave the Just. Donaldson, S. R.
Reaves, Michael
  The adventure of the Arab's manuscript
    Shadows over Baker Street; edited by Michael
      Reaves and John Pelan
Reb Kringle. Englander, N.
REBELLIONS *See* Revolutions
Rebirth [Cain and Abel]. Agustí, M.
Recall of the wild. Lord, N.
Receding horizon. Lethem, J. and Scholz, C.
The **receivers**. Lane, J.
Recipe for a happy marriage. Tyre, N.
The **recital**. Meredith, D.
Recitatif. Morrison, T.
A **recitation** of nomads. Azadeh, C.
A **reckless** moon. Warren, D.
The **reckoning**. Baida, P.
The **reckoning**. Wharton, E.
Reckonings. Davis, J. S.
The **reclining** woman. Archer, J.
RECLUSES
      See also Hermits
  Davidson, A. The cobblestones of Saratoga
    Street
  Doerr, A. The caretaker
  Gautreaux, T. The piano tuner
  Greer, R. O. Isolation
  Rhys, J. Pioneers, oh, pioneers
  Singer, I. B. The Key
RECONCILIATION
  Alcott, L. M. Little sunbeam
  Bausch, R. Consolation
  Fuchs, D. Man in the middle of the ocean
  Valeri, L. Turn these stones into bread
Reconciliation. Arruda, M. J.
RECONSTRUCTION
      See also United States—1865-1898
Reconstruction. Perabo, S.
The **record** keeper. Pritchett, L.
The **recovery**. Chopin, K.
The **recovery**. Wharton, E.
The **recruiting** officer. Lida, D.
RECTORS *See* Anglican and Episcopal clergy;
    Catholic priests
Recuperation. Doyle, R.
Recycle. Muller, M.
Red. Meloy, M.
Red. Rollins, H.
Red ant house. Cummins, A.
RED ARMY (SOVIET UNION) *See* Russia—
    Army
Red Army tales. Babel´, I.
Red Arrow. Barthelme, F.
Red as jade. Somtow, S. P.
Red azalea [excerpt] Min, A.
The **red** bathrobe. Dell'Oro, E.
The **red** boots. Cutter, L.
The **Red** Bow. Saunders, G.
Red butte showdown. L'Amour, L.
The **Red** Carpet. Sankaran, L.
Red clay. Malone, M.
The **red** convertible. Erdrich, L.
The **red** coral bracelet. Hermann, J.
Red dirt don't wash. Mais, R.
Red dress. Canty, K.
Red dresses. Foster, K.
Red Feather's daughter. Lee, W. W.
Red flag. Viganò, R.
Red from Green. Meloy, M.

Red hair. Nakagami, K.
The **red-haired** girl. Fitzgerald, P.
The **red** hat. Callaghan, M.
The **red** herring. Hodgson, W. H.
The **red** horse. Dubnov, E.
Red hot peppers. Chamoiseau, P.
Red lights like laughter. Davis, A.
The **red** lucky. Abbey, L.
Red meat. Viets, E.
The **red** monk. McGuire, I.
Red-nickel rhythms. Greer, R. O.
Red pony. Adam, C.
Red roses and cognac. Jenkins, G.
The **red** shoes. Buchanan, E.
The **red** suitcase. Earle, S.
Red wind. Chandler, R.
Reddi, Rishi P.
  Karma
    Prairie Schooner v76 no3 p99-117 Fall 2002
REDDING, OTIS, 1941-1967
      About
  Bischoff, D. Sittin' on the dock
Redel, Victoria
  He's back
    On the rocks; the KGB Bar fiction anthology;
      edited by Rebecca Donner ; foreword by
      Denis Woychuk
REDEMPTION *See* Atonement
Redemption. Spencer, J.
Redemption. Vernon, O. F.
Redgunk, Texas. Eakin, W.
Redman, Ben Ray
  The perfect crime
    The Best American mystery stories of the
      century; Tony Hillerman, editor; with an
      introduction by Tony Hillerman
Redneck. Estleman, L. D.
REDUCING
  Barker, N. Symbiosis: class cestoda
  Brownrigg, S. The lady in the desert
  Krouse, E. The fast
  McCorkle, J. Crash diet
  McGraw, E. Ax of the Apostles
  Rusch, K. K. Spinning
  Solwitz, S. Ballerina
  Van Loan, C. E. One-thirty-three—ringside
Redwood, James D.
  Numbers
    The Virginia Quarterly Review v75 no2 p385-
      96 Spr 1999
Reed, Ishmael
  Future Christmas
    Dark matter; a century of speculative fiction
      from the African diaspora; edited by Sheree
      R. Thomas
Reed, Kit
  Captive kong
    Redshift; extreme visions of speculative fic-
      tion; edited by Al Sarrantonio
  Missing Sam
    The Yale Review v90 no4 p124-43 O 2002
Reed, Lillian Craig *See* Reed, Kit, 1932-
Reed, Mary and Mayer, Eric
  Even kings die
    Royal whodunnits; edited by Mike Ashley
Reed, Myra Maybelle Shirley *See* Starr, Belle,
    1848-1889

Reed, Rick R.
Moving toward the light
The Crow; shattered lives & broken dreams;
edited by J. O'Barr and Ed Kramer
On line
The Darkest thirst; a vampire anthology
Reed, Robert
Aeon's child
Reed, R. The dragons of Springplace; stories
Chrysalis
Reed, R. The dragons of Springplace; stories
Coelacanths
The Year's best science fiction; twentieth an-
nual collection; edited by Gardner Dozois
The cuckoo's boys
The Year's best science fiction, sixteenth an-
nual collection; edited by Gardner Dozois
Decency
Reed, R. The dragons of Springplace; stories
The dragons of Springplace
Reed, R. The dragons of Springplace; stories
First Tuesday
The Best from fantasy & science fiction: the
fiftieth anniversary anthology; edited by
Edward L. Ferman and Gordon Van Gelder
Guest of honor
The Good new stuff; adventure SF in the
grand tradition; edited by Gardner Dozois
Reed, R. The dragons of Springplace; stories
Night of time
The year's best science fiction: twenty-first
annual collection; edited by Gardner Dozois
A place with shade
Worldmakers; SF adventures in terraforming;
edited by Gardner Dozois
Raven dream
The Year's best science fiction, nineteenth an-
nual collection; edited by Gardner Dozois
The remoras
Reed, R. The dragons of Springplace; stories
The shape of everything
Reed, R. The dragons of Springplace; stories
Stride
Reed, R. The dragons of Springplace; stories
To church with Mr. Multhiford
Reed, R. The dragons of Springplace; stories
The utility man
Reed, R. The dragons of Springplace; stories
Waging good
Reed, R. The dragons of Springplace; stories
Winemaster
The Year's best science fiction, seventeenth
annual collection; edited by Gardner Dozois
Reed, Sylvia
Fugue
South Carolina Review v33 no2 p103-8 Spr
2001
Reef. McAuley, P. J.
Reef Line. Jackson, T.
Reene, David
The Other Side
The Literary Review (Madison, N.J.) v46 no3
p443-7 Spr 2003
Rees, Richard
Headlong
The Sewanee Review v107 no4 p482-98 Fall
1999

Rees, David
I am a CBU-87/B combined effects munition
(CEM)
Politically inspired; edited by Stephen Elliott;
assistant editor, Gabriel Kram; associate ed-
itors, Elizabeth Brooks [et al.]
Reeve, Arthur Benjamin
The poisoned pen
Murder most postal; homicidal tales that de-
liver a message; edited by Martin H.
Greenberg
REEVES, KEANU
About
Yuknavitch, L. Male lead
Referee. Blake, J. C.
References available upon request. Henkin, J.
Refiner's fire. Nelson, R. F.
A **reflection**. Chopin, K.
The **reflection**. Tawada, Y.
Reflections. Čapek, K.
Reflections of a wild kid. Michaels, L.
Reflections of spring. Duong, T. H.
REFORMATORIES
Howard, C. The last one to cry
Refuge. Cohen, R.
Refuge. Honig, L.
Refuge. Kane, J. F.
Refuge [excerpt] Michael, S.
Refugee. Clarke, A. C.
Refugee. Karampur, F.
REFUGEES
See also Exiles
Barnes, S. The woman in the wall
Bellow, S. The Bellarosa connection
Karampur, F. Refugee
Vega, A. L. Cloud cover Caribbean
REFUGEES, CUBAN *See* Cuban refugees
REFUGEES, GERMAN *See* German refugees
REFUGEES, HAITIAN *See* Haitian refugees
REFUGEES, JEWISH *See* Jewish refugees
REFUGEES, POLISH *See* Polish refugees
REFUGEES, RUSSIAN *See* Russian refugees
REFUGEES, VIETNAMESE *See* Vietnamese
refugees
Refugees. Casey, K.
REFUSE AND REFUSE DISPOSAL
Avrich, J. Trash traders
Carlson, R. The governor's ball
Johnson-Davies, D. Garbage girl
Singleton, G. How I met my second wife
Regards at home. Yates, R.
Regen-Tuero, Karen
Wonderful, horrid, divine
The North American Review v287 no2 p12-17
Mr/Ap 2002
REGENCY ENGLAND *See* England—19th
century
REGENERATION
Evenson, B. Body
Moore, C. L. No woman born
Rucker, R. v. B. The fifty-seventh Franz Kafka
Regime. Ebershoff, D.
Régio, José
A brief comedy
Régio, J. The flame-coloured dress and other
stories; translated from the Portuguese by
Margaret Jull Costa

Régio, José—*Continued*
The flame-coloured dress
　Régio, J. The flame-coloured dress and other stories; translated from the Portuguese by Margaret Jull Costa
Maria do Ahu
　Régio, J. The flame-coloured dress and other stories; translated from the Portuguese by Margaret Jull Costa
Miss Olimpia and her maid Belarmina
　Régio, J. The flame-coloured dress and other stories; translated from the Portuguese by Margaret Jull Costa
A sad smile
　Régio, J. The flame-coloured dress and other stories; translated from the Portuguese by Margaret Jull Costa
The story of Rosa Brava
　Régio, J. The flame-coloured dress and other stories; translated from the Portuguese by Margaret Jull Costa
They used to go for long walks on Sundays
　. . .
　Régio, J. The flame-coloured dress and other stories; translated from the Portuguese by Margaret Jull Costa
Register: I'm not an Arab woman. Sammān, G.
Regret. Chopin, K.
Regrets. Lida, D.
Regrets, reveries the color of time. Proust, M.
Regular. Burroway, J.
Regular Flattop. Hayes, J. G.
A **regular** pair of minstrels. Straub, P.
The **rehearsal**. Dixon, S.
Rehearsals. Monteleone, T. F.
Reichert, Mickey Zucker
Home is where the hate is
　Thieve's world: turning points; edited by Lynn Abbey
The Ulfjarl's stone
　Magical beginnings; edited by Steven H. Silver and Martin H. Greenberg
Reid, Alastair
　(jt. auth) See Padilla, Ignacio
Reid, Annie
Spooks
　American short fiction, vol. 8, no 29-32
Reid, Elwood
All that good stuff
　Reid, E. What salmon know; stories
Buffalo
　Ploughshares v25 no2/3 p160-73 Fall 1999
　Reid, E. What salmon know; stories
Deck ape
　Gentlemen's Quarterly v71 no11 p282-92 N 2001
Dryfall
　Reid, E. What salmon know; stories
Happy Jack
　Reid, E. What salmon know; stories
Laura Borealis
　Reid, E. What salmon know; stories
Lime
　Reid, E. What salmon know; stories
No strings attached
　Reid, E. What salmon know; stories
Overtime
　Reid, E. What salmon know; stories

Random beatings and you
　Reid, E. What salmon know; stories
What salmon know
　Reid, E. What salmon know; stories
Reid, Nicole Louise
Honeydew
　The Southern Review (Baton Rouge, La.) v39 no3 p596-616 Summ 2003
Moving
　Calyx v21 no1 p94-106 Wint 2003
Reifler, Nelly
Auditor
　Reifler, N. See through; stories
Baby
　Reifler, N. See through; stories
Julian
　Lost tribe; jewish fiction from the edge
　Reifler, N. See through; stories
Memoir
　Reifler, N. See through; stories
Personal foundations of self-forming through auto-identification with otherness
　Reifler, N. See through; stories
Rascal
　Reifler, N. See through; stories
The river and Una
　Reifler, N. See through; stories
See through
　Reifler, N. See through; stories
The splinter
　Reifler, N. See through; stories
Sugar
　Reifler, N. See through; stories
Summer job
　Reifler, N. See through; stories
Teeny
　Reifler, N. See through; stories
Upstream
　Reifler, N. See through; stories
Reiken, Frederick
The Ocean
　The New Yorker v78 no26 p140-7 S 9 2002
Reilly, Gerald
Nixon under the bodhi tree
　Nixon under the bodhi tree and other works of Buddhist fiction; edited by Kate Wheeler ; foreword by Charles Johnson
　Prize stories, 1999; The O. Henry awards; edited and with an introduction by Larry Dark
Reilly, Lawrence
1984
　His 3: brilliant new fiction by gay writers; edited by Robert Drake and Terry Wolverton
Rein. Polansky, S.
REINCARNATION
　Atwood, M. My life as a bat
　Bradbury, R. The Laurel and Hardy love affair
　Cherryh, C. J. The general
　Cherryh, C. J. The only death in the city
　Collins, B. Aunt Emma's defense
　Eakin, W. How Boy Howdy saved the world
　Gordimer, N. Karma
　Singer, I. B. The warehouse
The **reincarnation** of Donaldo Fuertes. Gabriel, D.
Reiner, Carl
As easy as ABC
　Reiner, C. How Paul Robeson saved my life and other mostly happy stories

Reiner, Carl—*Continued*
Aunt Delia and her twins
  Reiner, C. How Paul Robeson saved my life
    and other mostly happy stories
Caz
  Reiner, C. How Paul Robeson saved my life
    and other mostly happy stories
Creation
  Reiner, C. How Paul Robeson saved my life
    and other mostly happy stories
Dear John
  Reiner, C. How Paul Robeson saved my life
    and other mostly happy stories
Deibenquist sounds famous
  Reiner, C. How Paul Robeson saved my life
    and other mostly happy stories
Dial 411 for legal smut
  Reiner, C. How Paul Robeson saved my life
    and other mostly happy stories
G. G. Giggler
  Reiner, C. How Paul Robeson saved my life
    and other mostly happy stories
Geoff and Kurt
  Reiner, C. How Paul Robeson saved my life
    and other mostly happy stories
Hampa Ham
  Reiner, C. How Paul Robeson saved my life
    and other mostly happy stories
The Heidi and Albert correspondence
  Reiner, C. How Paul Robeson saved my life
    and other mostly happy stories
Heshie and Joey
  Reiner, C. How Paul Robeson saved my life
    and other mostly happy stories
How could this happen?
  Reiner, C. How Paul Robeson saved my life
    and other mostly happy stories
How Paul Robeson saved my life
  Reiner, C. How Paul Robeson saved my life
    and other mostly happy stories
Lance and Gwendolyn
  Reiner, C. How Paul Robeson saved my life
    and other mostly happy stories
Mr. Gutman and Dr. Magic
  Reiner, C. How Paul Robeson saved my life
    and other mostly happy stories
The people versus De Marco
  Reiner, C. How Paul Robeson saved my life
    and other mostly happy stories
Sissy Sue and the Reverend Reverend
  Reiner, C. How Paul Robeson saved my life
    and other mostly happy stories
Sorry Solomon and Guey Jew
  Reiner, C. How Paul Robeson saved my life
    and other mostly happy stories
That SOB bastard Eddie
  Reiner, C. How Paul Robeson saved my life
    and other mostly happy stories
Too damned handsome
  Reiner, C. How Paul Robeson saved my life
    and other mostly happy stories
Warren Waits and the spaghetti-strap girl
  Reiner, C. How Paul Robeson saved my life
    and other mostly happy stories
Xavier
  Reiner, C. How Paul Robeson saved my life
    and other mostly happy stories

Yehudah Benjamin Aronowitz
  Reiner, C. How Paul Robeson saved my life
    and other mostly happy stories
Reinhorn, Holiday
Get Away from Me, David
  Ploughshares v30 no2/3 p116-34 Fall 2004
Reisman, Nancy
Common light
  Reisman, N. House fires
Confessions
  Reisman, N. House fires
Dreaming of the snail life
  The Kenyon Review ns21 no3-4 p152-65
    Summ/Fall 1999
  Reisman, N. House fires
Edie in winter
  Reisman, N. House fires
Girl on a couch
  Reisman, N. House fires
The good life
  Reisman, N. House fires
Heart of hearts
  Reisman, N. House fires
House fires
  Reisman, N. House fires
Illumination
  The Best American short stories 2001; select-
    ed from U.S. and Canadian magazines by
    Barbara Kingsolver with Katrina Kenison;
    with an introduction by Barbara Kingsolver
Many-splendored things
  New England Review v20 no3 p35-45 Summ
    1999
Rubies
  Reisman, N. House fires
Sharks
  Reisman, N. House fires
Strays
  Reisman, N. House fires
Tea
  Michigan Quarterly Review v42 no1 p214-29
    Wint 2003
Reitci, John George *See* Ritchie, Jack, 1922-1983
The **rejected** one. Callaghan, M.
Rejoice. Vukcevich, R.
Rejtman, Martin
Alplax
  Iowa Review v31 no2 p89-94 Fall 2001
REJUVENATION
  Bradbury, R. Death and the maiden
  Hawthorne, N. Dr. Heidegger's experiment
  Varley, J. Goodbye, Robinson Crusoe
Rekulak, Jason
Pinball
  Pieces; a collection of new voices; edited by
    Stephen Chbosky
RELATIVES *See* Family life
RELATIVITY (PHYSICS)
      See also Gravitation; Space and time
  Landis, G. A. Impact parameter
  Tevis, W. S. Rent control
Release. Stolar, D.
Release from Russia. Fioretos, A.
The **relentless** approximation of feeling. Lipsyte,
    S.
Relics. Rusch, K. K.
RELIEF, PUBLIC *See* Public welfare
Relief. Casey, M.

RELIGION
See also Biblical stories; Buddhism; Catholic faith; Christianity; Clergy; Conversion; Faith; God; Jehovah's Witnesses; Judaism; Mormons and Mormonism; Paganism

Agee, J. Earl

Bear, G. The visitation

Bergeron, A. The eighth register

Bishop, M. Among the handlers; or, The Mark 16 Hands-on Assembly of Jesus Risen, formerly Snake-o-rama

Bishop, M. The procedure

Blair, J. Julia loving the face of God

Butler, R. O. Heavy metal

Cadle, D. Anthem of the locusts

Chiang, T. Hell is the absence of God

Clark, B. C. By way of the forked stick

Clarke, A. C. The star

Dedman, S. From whom all blessings flow

Donaldson, S. R. Penance

Dowling, T. He tried to catch the light

Engel, M. P. Dis aliter visum

Engel, M. P. Philosophy of education

Engel, M. P. You got to learn how to read things right

Evenson, B. The prophets

Gilchrist, E. Witness to the crucifixion

Gilliland, G. Berkeley

Grimsley, J. Jesus is sending you this message

Gwyn, A. Against the pricks

Gwyn, A. The backsliders

Gwyn, A. Courtship

Gwyn, A. Dog on the cross

Gwyn, A. The offering

Gwyn, A. Truck

Hill, I. The ballad of Rappy Valcour

Karnezis, P. Wilt thou be made whole?

Malouf, D. Closer

Malzberg, B. N. Quartermain

Martin, G. R. R. The way of cross and dragon

McDonald, I. The Catharine wheel

Nash, S. Amen

Norris, H. Tutankhamen Calhoun

Oates, J. C. Mark of satan

Packer, Z. Speaking in tongues

Prather, P. The faithful

Singer, I. B. The accuser and the accused

Thomas, J. C. Young Reverend Zelma Lee Moses

Tolstoy, L., graf. A coffeehouse in the city of Surat

Touré. A hot time at the Church of Kentucky Fried Souls and the spectacular final Sunday sermon of the Right Revren Daddy Love

Updike, J. Pigeon feathers

Vasilenko, S. Little fool

Wilson, R. C. The inner inner city

Yolen, J. Creationism: an illustrated lecture in two parts

RELIGION, PRIMITIVE *See* Religion

Religion: Goy. Gold, H.

RELIGIOUS LIBERTY
Hawthorne, N. Endicott and the Red Cross

RELIGIOUS LIFE *See* Convent life; Monasticism and religious orders

RELIGIOUS PERSECUTION *See* Persecution

Rellas, Dorothy
Midnight
A Deadly dozen; tales of murder from members of Sisters in Crime/Los Angeles; edited by Susan B. Casmier, Aljean Harmetz and Cynthia Lawrence

The **reluctant** orchid. Clarke, A. C.

Remainders. Foster, K.

Remaining in favor. Bossert, J.

Remains. Brkic, C. A.

Remains of the Ray family. Naiyer Masud

Remaking the world. Lord, N.

A **remarkable** chemical phenomenon. Škvorecký, J.

A **remarkably** pretty girl. Bingham, S.

Remarks of the scholar graduate. Mathews, H.

REMARRIAGE
Chaudhuri, A. The second marriage
DeLancey, K. Jules Jr Michael Jules Jr
DeLancey, K. The mystery of George Jones
Ferré, R. A poisoned tale
Godwin, G. False lights
Singer, I. B. The power of darkness
Singer, I. B. Strangers

The **Rembrandt**. Wharton, E.

Rembrandt's bones. Moore, P.

Rembrandt's hat. Malamud, B.

Remedy. Homes, A. M.

The **remedy** man. Shepard, S.

Remember, I'll always love you. George, E.

Remember the Maine? Dams, J. M.

Remember why we're here. Singleton, G.

Remember Young Cecil. Kelman, J.

Remembered names. Wilson, R., Jr.

Remembering Nasser. Alameddine, R.

Remembering orchards. Lopez, B. H.

Remembering possibilities. Troncoso, S.

Remembering the Rain. Alger, D.

Remembrance. Hart, C. G.

A **remembrance** of ink past. Kalfus, K.

Reminders of Bouselham. Bowles, P.

Remnants of Earl. Brenner, W.

Re:mohit. Ramaya, S.

The **remoras**. Reed, R.

Remorse. Gilchrist, E.

Remorse. Smith, M.

Renado, Trevor
Get a lifestyle
Circa 2000; gay fiction at the millennium; edited by Robert Drake & Terry Wolverton

RENAISSANCE
See also Italy—15th century

Renaissance man. Oltion, J.

Rendall, Steven
Monsieur Marty: a Tale of Southwestern France
Southern Humanities Review v37 no1 p64-8 Wint 2003

Rendell, Ruth
The astronomical scarf
Rendell, R. Piranha to Scurfy and other stories
The beach butler
Rendell, R. Piranha to Scurfy and other stories
Burning end
A Century of great suspense stories; edited by Jeffery Deaver
The carer
Crème de la crime; edited by Janet Hutchings

Rendell, Ruth—Continued
The case of the shaggy caps
Murder most delectable; savory tales of culinary crimes; edited by Martin H. Greenberg
Catamount
Rendell, R. Piranha to Scurfy and other stories
Fair exchange
Rendell, R. Piranha to Scurfy and other stories
High mysterious union
Rendell, R. Piranha to Scurfy and other stories
The irony of hate
A moment on the edge; 100 years of crime stories by women; edited by Elizabeth George
Piranha to Scurfy
Rendell, R. Piranha to Scurfy and other stories
The professional
Rendell, R. Piranha to Scurfy and other stories
Walter's leg
Rendell, R. Piranha to Scurfy and other stories
When the wedding was over
Edwards, M. Mysterious pleasures; a celebration of the Crime Writers' Association's 50th anniversary; edited by Martin Edwards
The wink
Rendell, R. Piranha to Scurfy and other stories
The World's finest mystery and crime stories, third annual collection; edited by Ed Gorman and Martin H. Greenberg
Rending dark. Bull, E.
Renee: a war story. Bly, C.
Renfield; or, Dining at the bughouse. Zaget, B.
Rent control. Tevis, W. S.
Rentals. Singleton, G.
Renwick, Joyce
The dolphin story
Fishing's best short stories; edited by Paul D. Staudohar
The **repairman**. Harrison, H.
Repeater. Aylett, S.
"Repent, Harlequin!" said the Ticktockman. Ellison, H.
REPENTANCE
See also Sin
Chekhov, A. P. Rothschild's fiddle
Tolstoy, L., graf. The repentant sinner
The **repentant** sinner. Tolstoy, L., graf
Report from Junction. Vice, B.
A **report** from St. Domingue. Johnson, C. R.
REPORTERS See Journalists
REPRODUCTION, ASEXUAL See Asexual reproduction
A **reproduction**. Boylan, C.
The **repulsion**. Lebbon, T.
Repulsion. Leong, S.
The **requiem**. Chekhov, A. P.
Requiem for Rosebud. Hodgson, K.
The **requirements** of love. Tolstoy, L., graf
Rescue. Wilbur, E.
The **rescue** mission. Busch, F.
Rescue operation. Harrison, H.
Rescue party. Clarke, A. C.

RESCUES
Billman, J. Albatross
Browder, C. The missing day
Clarke, A. C. Maelstrom II
Clarke, A. C. Summertime on Icarus
DeAndrea, W. L. Prince Charming
Deason, L. Lady Emerdirael's rescue
Glover, D. H. Dog attempts to drown man in Saskatoon
Greenwood, K. Jetsam
Hagy, A. C. Semper paratus
Henry, W. The legend of Trooper Hennepin
Paine, T. Will you say something, Monsieur Eliot?
Sneve, V. D. H. Fool soldiers
Steinbeck, T. The night guide
Vivante, A. Crosscurrents
RESEARCH
Stollman, A. L. The dialogues of time and entropy
Waters, M. Y. Mirror studies
The **resemblance** between a violin case and a coffin. Williams, T.
Resenter. Aylett, S.
The **reserve** cavalry commander. Babel´, I.
Reset. Barthelme, F.
Resident priest. Hassler, J.
Residents and transients. Mason, B. A.
Resistance. Gautreaux, T.
RESISTANCE MOVEMENTS (WORLD WAR, 1939-1945) See World War, 1939-1945—Underground movements
Resnick, Laura
Wallgate
Tetrick, B. In the shadow of the wall; an anthology of Vietnam stories that might have been; edited by Byron R. Tetrick
Resnick, Mike
The elephants on Neptune
Nebula Awards showcase 2003; edited by Nancy Kress
Even butterflies can sting
Death dines at 8:30; edited by Claudia Bishop and Nick DiChario
Hothouse flowers
The Year's best science fiction, seventeenth annual collection; edited by Gardner Dozois
Resnick, Mike and Bell, M. Shayne
Flower children of Mars
Mars probes; edited by Peter Crowther
Resnick, Mike and Burstein, Michael A.
Reflections in black granite
Tetrick, B. In the shadow of the wall; an anthology of Vietnam stories that might have been; edited by Byron R. Tetrick
Resnick, Rachel
Day 'n nite
LA shorts; edited by Steven Gilbar
The **resolution** of nothing. Coshnear, D.
RESORTS See Hotels, taverns, etc.; Summer resorts
A **respectable** woman. Chopin, K.
Respiration. Steele, C.
Rest area. Chapman, C. M.
The **rest** of her life. Yarbrough, S.
The **rest** of your life. Barth, J.
The **rest** of your life. Hoffman, A.
Rest Stop. Davis, F. P.
Rest stop. Joseph, S.

Rest Stop. King, S.
RESTAURANTS, LUNCHROOMS, ETC.
Anderson, D. Barrie Hooper's dead
Banks, R. Lobster night
Bemelmans, L. Mespoulets of the Splendide
Block, L. How far it could go
Bowles, P. The successor
Boyle, T. C. A women's restaurant
Brennan, M. A snowy night on West Forty-
    ninth Street
Busch, F. Are we pleasing you tonight?
Cabrera Infante, G. Guilty of dancing the
    chachachá
Cabrera Infante, G. A woman saved from
    drowning
Cavell, B. Highway
Connor, J. The parrot man
Curtis, Rebecca. Hungry self
Davies, Tristan. Snapdragon
Davis, A. Spice
Dinh, L. California fine view
Dozois, G. R. Afternoon at Schraffts
Evans, E. Ransom
Fromm, P. Black tie and blue jeans
Gilchrist, E. Lunch at the best restaurant in the
    world
Greer, A. S. The future of the Flynns
Grooms, A. Food that pleases, food to take
    home
Gunn, K. Jesus, I know that guy
Harfenist, J. Salad girls
Harris, M. La Lumiére
Hart, C. G. Secrets
Hart, C. G. Spooked
Hayes, D. Sweet nothings
Hemingway, E. The killers
Holleran, A. Petunias
Jen, G. In the American society
Johnson, D. Markers
Kees, W. Mrs. Lutz
Krouse, E. Mercy
Lovesey, P. The usual table
Mason, B. A. Rolling into Atlanta
Mayo, W. Day cook
McBrearty, R. G. The dishwasher
McBrearty, R. G. The pearl diver
Moody, R. The double zero
Mosley, W. The thief
Nelson, A. Goodfellows
O'Nan, S. 20 burgers
Ortiz, S. J. Loose
Papernick, J. The King of the King of Falafel
Pearlman, E. The story
Pelecanos, G. P. The dead their eyes implore us
Phillips, L. In the house of simple sentences
Piazza, T. Brownsville
Roeske, P. Four characters, three small stories
Rosenfeld, S. How I went (recipe for lime curd)
Silber, J. Bobby Jackson
Simpson, H. Café society
Sojourner, M. Huevos
Stableford, B. M. The last supper
Steele, A. M. Her own private sitcom
Stolar, D. Crossing over
Touré. The playground of the ecstatically blasé
Troy, M. The Alibi Café
Weaver, G. Viewed from Lanta & Wally's
Restitution. Cannon, T.
Restoration. Padilla, M.

Restoration. Smith, P. V.
RESTORATION ENGLAND *See* England—17th
    century
Restrepo, Laura
    The scent of invisible roses
        Colchie, T. A whistler in the nightworld;
        short fiction from the Latin Americas; ed-
        ited by Thomas Colchie
RESURRECTION
Blish, J. A work of art
Bradbury, R. The wish
Singer, I. B. The man who came back
Resurrection. Lumley, B.
Resurrection. Morrell, D.
Resurrection of a life. Saroyan, W.
The **retiree.** Hensley, J. L.
RETIREMENT
        See also Old age
Bukoski, A. The moon of the grass fires
Davidson, A. Mr. Folsom feels fine
Theroux, P. Disheveled nymphs
Retirement. Perabo, S.
RETIREMENT COMMUNITIES
Bly, C. A committee of the whole
Breen, J. L. Longevity has its place
Connor, J. Florida
DeMarinis, R. Borrowed hearts
Leonard, E. Hanging out at the Buena Vista
Retreat. Barthelme, F.
Retreat from earth. Clarke, A. C.
Retribution. Fulton, J.
A **retrieved** reformation. Henry, O.
Retrograde summer. Varley, J.
RETROSPECTIVE STORIES
Bellow, S. Him with his foot in his mouth
Bunin, I. A. Rusya
King, S. The man in the black suit
A **return.** Barnes, H. L.
The **return.** MacLeod, A.
Return. Matheson, R.
The **return** of Alcibiade. Chopin, K.
The **return** of eros to academe. Bukiet, M. J.
The **return** of the Arapaho Kid. DeRosso, H. A.
The **Return** of the Dark Children. Coover, R.
The **return** of the Deep Ones. Lumley, B.
Return of the hippie shirt. Locklin, G.
The **return** of the kangaroo rex. Kagan, J.
Return of the king. West, M.
Return of the spirit. Guerrero, L.
A **return** to Jacmel. Dépestre, R.
Return to Kansas City. Shaw, I.
Return to the seed. See Carpentier, A. Journey
    back to the source See Carpentier, A. Jour-
    ney to the seed
Return to Waterloo. Davies, R.
Return trips. Adams, A.
The **returnees.** Highsmith, P.
Returning to Haifa. Kanafāni, G.
The **reunion.** Earle, S.
Reunion. Engberg, S.
Reunion. Englander, N.
Reunion. Ford, R.
Reunion. Haslett, A.
Reunion. Ptacek, K.
Reunion queen. Collins, B.
REUNIONS
Chenoweth, A. Going back
Collins, B. Reunion queen
Fairey, W. W. Grace

REUNIONS—Continued
Hall, D. The first woman
Lee, M. The secrets of Cooperstown
McCorkle, J. Hominids
Patterson, K. Manitoba Avenue
Restrepo, L. The scent of invisible roses
Singleton, G. Bank of America
Singleton, G. This itches, y'all
Stolar, D. Jack Landers is my friend
Traver, R. The intruder
Updike, J. Lunch hour
Weaver, G. Elder's revenge
Reunions. Chenoweth, A.
Rêve Canadien. April, J. P.
The **Revenant**. Bottomy, H.
The **revenant**. Falco, E.
REVENGE
Amanthis, J. Down there undercover
Arnott, Marion. Marbles
Attanasio, A. A. Hellbent
Baker, K. Son observe the time
Baum, L. F. The enchanted buffalo
Biguenet, J. It is raining in Bejucal
Bisson, T. Macs
Blake, J. C. Referee
Blake, J. C. Runaway horses
Block, L. Like a bone in the throat
Blumlein, M. Revenge
Borges, J. L. Death and the compass
Borges, J. L. Emma Zunz
Borges, J. L. The end
Borges, J. L. The man on the threshold
Bosley, D. Beware the gentle wife
Bowles, P. The delicate prey
Bradbury, R. The city
Bradbury, R. Exorcism
Bradbury, R. Sixty-six
Bradbury, R. The transformation
Bryant, E. Styx and bones
Burger, W. Countdown
Campbell, R. Twice by fire
Chesnutt, C. W. The doll
Clark, M. H. The funniest thing has been happening lately
Clarke, A. C. Hate
Clarke, A. C. The light of darkness
Cody, L. Queen of mean
Cohen, S. The battered mailbox
Cole, M. Enough was enough
Collins, B. Reunion queen
Collins, N. A. Variations on a theme
Connelly, M. Two-bagger
Cook, T. H. Fatherhood
Coward, M. You can jump
Craig, A. The French Boy
Cross, A. The perfect revenge
D'Amato, B. Of course you know that chocolate is a vegetable
Dann, J. Spirit dog
Davidson, A. The deed of the deft-footed dragon
Davis, C. A. Not long now
De Lint, C. The witching hour
Deane, J. F. The coffin master
Deaver, J. Eye to eye
Dedman, S. The wind shall blow for ever mair
DeRosso, H. A. The ways of vengeance
Devine, T. The pleasure game
DiChario, N. Where the wildflowers bloom

Dinh, L. A cultured boy
Douglas, C. N. Dirty dancing
Douglass, S. The mistress of Marwood Hagg
Dowling, T. The bone ship
DuBois, B. Dancing the night away
DuBois, B. The dark snow
DuBois, B. Her last gift
Dyson, J. A slate roof in the rain
Dyson, J. We who walk through walls
Ellin, S. The last bottle in the world
Elrod, P. N. The tea room beasts
Fleming, R. Speak no evil
Forsyth, F. The art of the matter
Forsyth, F. The veteran
Foster, A. D. Procrastinator
Gaiman, N. Murder mysteries
Gartner, Z. The nature of pure evil
Gerrold, D. The spell
Gilchrist, E. Traceleen, she's still talking
Gold, G. D. The tears of squonk, and what happened thereafter
Golden, C. Lament for the gunwitch
Gores, J. Faulty register
Gussoff, C. Unpretty
Hautman, P. Showdown at the Terminal Oasis
Hensley, J. L. A lot of sense
Hess, J. All's well that ends
Hess, J. Make yourselves at home
Hoch, E. D. The detective's wife
Hoggard, J. The scapegoat
Holdstock, P. Sitting pretty
Hornsby, W. New moon and rattlesnakes
Howard, C. The California contact
Howard, C. The color of death
Howard, C. Hanging it on a limb
Jacobs, M. The liberation of little heaven
James, H. Adina
Johnson, G. C. The obedient child
Kaminsky, S. M. Scorpion's kiss
Karnezis, P. A funeral of stones
Karnezis, P. On the first day of Lent
Karnezis, P. Sins of a harvest god
Kelman, J. Just desserts
Kelton, E. The burial of Letty Strayhorn
Kiernan, C. R. The king of birds
Kilpatrick, N. An eye for an eye
King, L. R. Paleta man
Kipling, R. Mary Postgate
Kittredge, W. We are not in this together
Knight, P. Set in stone
Kohler, S. Death in Rome
Lake, M. D. Tea for two
L'Amour, L. That man from the bitter sands
LaPierre, J. Da capo
Lawson, C. Unborn again
Le May, A. The braver thing
Lee, E. ICU
Link, K. Catskin
Lochte, D. Low Tide
Lovesey, P. Under the knife
Malouf, D. Blacksoil country
Marías, J. What the butler said
Masterton, G. The Ballyhooly boy
Matera, L. Counsel for the defense
Matera, L. Easy go
Matthews, C. Belated revenge
McCrumb, S. Foggy Mountain breakdown
McEwan, I. Pornography
McManus, J. The feed zone

REVENGE—*Continued*
McManus, J. Sleep on stones
Meyers, A. and Meyers, M. The Daffodil
Miller, R. Spike team
Miller, R. Walking to Paris
Niles, C. Revenge is the best revenge
Oates, J. C. Lover
O'Barr, J. Spooky, Codeine, and the dead man
Peters, E. Guide to doom
Pickard, N. Valentine's night
Poe, E. A. The cask of Amontillado
Pronzini, B. Fear
Pronzini, B. Putting the pieces back
Pushkin, A. S. Dubrovskii
Randisi, R. J. Intimate obsession
Reed, M. and Mayer, E. Even kings die
Reed, R. R. Moving toward the light
Rinehart, S. Burning luv
Rusch, K. K. Spinning
Saki. Sredni Vashtar
Sammān, G. The brain's closed castle
Sammān, G. Visitors of a dying person
Satterthwait, W. The cassoulet
Saunders, G. A sudden new city
Schlink, B. The other man
Schnitzler, A. Death of a bachelor
Schumacher, A. Along for the ride
Shade, E. Blood
Shaw, I. Sailor off the Bremen
Shields, C. Larry's words, 1983
Shirley, J. Wings burnt black
Slesar, H. The day of the 31st
Smith, J. Fresh paint
Spillane, M. The girl behind the hedge
Springer, N. Juggernaut
Straub, P. The ghost village
Straub, P. Mr. Clubb and Mr. Cuff
Sumner, P. For your eyes only
Taylor, L. Unspeakable
Tenn, W. Time in advance
Tinti, H. How to revitalize the snake in your life
Toole, F. X. The monkey look
Updike, J. Bech noir
Vachss, A. H. The concrete puppy
Vachss, A. H. The real thing
VanderMeer, J. The compass of his bones
Weiner, S. Eating Vic
Wellen, E. From parts unknown
Wellen, E. Rubout
Wellen, E. State of the art
Wellen, E. The taste of revenge
What, L. The cost of doing business
Williams, T. The vengeance of Nitocris
Williamson, C. The blood-red sea
Wolfe, G. The friendship light
Wolfe, G. The night chough
Wuori, G. K. Revenge
Wurts, J. Triad
Yolen, J. and Harris, R. J. Carrion crows
Young, T. Kraut
Revenge. Blumlein, M.
Revenge. Chekhov, A. P.
Revenge. Clark, J.
Revenge. Gilchrist, E.
Revenge. Millhauser, S.
Revenge. Wuori, G. K.
Revenge is the best revenge. Niles, C.
Revision. Greer, R. O.
Revival Road. Erdrich, L.

REVIVALS
Gwyn, A. Dog on the cross
REVOLUTION, AMERICAN, 1775-1783 *See*
United States—Revolution, 1775-1783
REVOLUTIONARIES *See* Revolutionists
REVOLUTIONARY WAR, 1775-1783 *See* United States—Revolution, 1775-1783
REVOLUTIONISTS
Banks, R. With Ché in New Hampshire
Borges, J. L. The shape of the sword
Clark, G. M. The Leopard Gang
Gores, J. Watch for it
Howard, C. When the black shadows die
Jacobs, M. Solidarity in green
Kelly, J. P. Undone
Krysl, M. The thing around them
Le Guin, U. K. The day before the revolution
Singer, I. B. The egotist
Singer, I. B. Grandfather and grandson
Taylor, L. The wedding at Esperanza
Wharton, E. The letters
Williams, M. Coley's war
REVOLUTIONS
See also Coups d'état; Revolutionists
Arenas, R. The parade ends
Babel', I. Gedali
Carey, P. The fat man in history
Dozois, G. R. Dinner party
Farren, M. Again the last plane out?
McTair, R. Just a lark; or, The crypt of Matthew Ashdown
Tenn, W. The masculinist revolt
Watson, I. Caucus winter
Waugh, E. Antony, who sought things that were lost
Reyes, Stephanie R.
Bad debts and vindictive women
Fantasmas; supernatural stories by Mexican American writers; edited by Rob Johnson; introduction by Kathleen J. Alcalá
Reyna, Ramiro
Snakes
Hanging Loose no84 p130 2004
Reynolds, Alastair
Galactic north
The Year's best science fiction, seventeenth annual collection; edited by Gardner Dozois
Glacial
The Year's best science fiction, nineteenth annual collection; edited by Gardner Dozois
Great walls of Mars
The Year's best science fiction, eighteenth annual collection; edited by Gardner Dozois
The real story
Mars probes; edited by Peter Crowther
Reynolds, April
Alcestis
The Bluelight corner; black women writing on passion, sex, and romantic love; edited by Rosemarie Robotham
Reynolds, Clay
A train to catch
Graham, D. Lone Star literature; from the Red River to the Rio Grande; edited by Don Graham
Reynolds, Rem
Tommy
The Literary Review (Madison, N.J.) v47 no3 p47-64 Spr 2004

Reyzen, Avrom
The Jew who destroyed the temple
 Neugroschel, J. No star too beautiful; Yiddish
  stories from 1382 to the present; compiled
  and translated by Joachim Neugroschel
RG. Casares, O.
Rheinheimer, Kurt
Neighborhood
 New stories from the South: the year's best,
  1999; edited by Shannon Ravenel; with a
  preface by Tony Earley
Shoes
 New stories from the South: the year's best,
  2001; edited by Shannon Ravenel; with a
  preface by Lee Smith
The Stop
 South Carolina Review v35 no1 p53-64 Fall
  2002
Rhett, Kathryn
The travelers
 The Massachusetts Review v42 no2 p177-95
  Summ 2001
Rhido wars. Barrett, N., Jr.
Rhine Ablaze. Toes, J.
RHINE RIVER
Toes, J. Rhine Ablaze
RHINOCEROS
Franklin, T. Dinosaurs
RHODE ISLAND
Reisman, N. Dreaming of the snail life
     Newport
James, H. Osborne's revenge
Wharton, E. The twilight of the God
     Providence
Cobb, T. Newswatch
Kaplan, H. Cuckle me
Rhodes, Eugene Manlove
The trouble man
 A Century of great Western stories; edited by
  John Jakes
Rhodes, Jewell Parker
Long distances
 The African American West; a century of
  short stories; edited by Bruce A. Glasrud
  and Laurie Champion
RHODESIA, NORTHERN *See* Zambia
RHODESIA, SOUTHERN *See* Zimbabwe
Rhonda and her children. Miner, C.
Rhyme game. Campbell, B. J.
Rhymes with useless. Young, T.
Rhys, Jean
Pioneers, oh, pioneers
 The Oxford book of Caribbean short stories;
  edited by Stewart Brown and John
  Wickham
A spiritualist
 Nightshade: 20th century ghost stories; edited
  by Robert Phillips
The **rhythm** of disintegration. Swick, M. A.
Rhythm travel. Baraka, I. A.
Riahi, Marjan
War letters
 A Feast in the mirror; stories by contempo-
  rary Iranian women; translated and edited
  by Mohammad Mehdi Khorrami, Shouleh
  Vatanabadi

Ribeiro, Edgard Telles
The turn in the river
 Colchie, T. A whistler in the nightworld;
  short fiction from the Latin Americas; ed-
  ited by Thomas Colchie
Ribeyro, Julio Ramón
The Wardrobe, Forefathers, and Death
 The Antioch Review v61 no3 p572-6 Summ
  2003
The wardrobe, the old man and death
 The Vintage book of Latin American stories;
  edited by Carlos Fuentes and Julio Ortega
Ricardo's virus. Tenn, W.
Rice, Anne
The mummy; or, Ramses the damned
 Into the mummy's tomb; edited by John
  Richard Stephens
Rice, Ben
Look at Me, I'm Beautiful!
 Granta no81 p237-46 Spr 2003
The specks in the sky
 The New Yorker v77 no41 p98-102, 104-17 D
  24-31 2001
Rice, David
The devil in the valley
 Fantasmas; supernatural stories by Mexican
  American writers; edited by Rob Johnson;
  introduction by Kathleen J. Alcalá
Rice, Jackson *See* Lish, Gordon
Rice, Robert
Counting Sheep
 New Letters v70 no1 p159-70 2003
Rice. Steiner, H.
The **rice** artist. Vaz, K.
A **Rich** Man. Jones, E. P.
The **rich** man's house. Thompson, J.
Rich men tend to be strange. Klíma, I.
RICH PEOPLE *See* Wealth
Rich people. Corin, L.
RICHARD I, KING OF ENGLAND, 1157-1199
     About
Devil's bargain
George, E. I, Richard
Holliday, L. Provenance
RICHARD II, KING OF ENGLAND, 1367-1400
     About
Baldry, C. The friar's tale
**RICHARD III, KING OF ENGLAND, 1452-
1485**
     About
Haskell, J. Good world
Myers, A. Happy the man . . .
Richard, the Lion Heart *See* Richard I, King of
 England, 1157-1199
Richard, Mark
All the Trimmings
 Harper's v305 p71-3 D 2002
Strays
 The Scribner anthology of contemporary short
  fiction; fifty North American stories since
  1970; Lex Williford and Michael Martone,
  editors
Walk on
 Gentlemen's Quarterly v71 no9 p271-2 S
  2001

Richard, Nancy
The order of things
The Pushcart prize XXIII: best of the small presses; an annual small press reader; edited by Bill Henderson with the Pushcart prize editors
What You Do Next
The Hudson Review v56 no3 p459-74 Aut 2003
Richard and poorer. Jenkins, G.
Richard Petty accepts national book ward. Singleton, G.
Richard said that. Burton, M.
Richards, Judith
How this song ends
Stories from the Blue Moon Café; edited by Sonny Brewer
Richards, Tony
The lords of zero
Gathering the bones; original stories from the world's masters of horror; edited by Dennis Etchison, Ramsey Campbell and Jack Dann
Riches. Bausch, R.
Richie by the sea. Bear, G.
Richmond, Michelle
Big bang
Richmond, M. The girl in the fall-away dress; stories
Choose your travel partner wisely
Stories from the Blue Moon Cafe II; edited by Sonny Brewer
Curvature
Richmond, M. The girl in the fall-away dress; stories
Does anyone know you are going this way
Richmond, M. The girl in the fall-away dress; stories
Down the shore everything's all right
Richmond, M. The girl in the fall-away dress; stories
Fifth grade: a criminal history
Richmond, M. The girl in the fall-away dress; stories
Virgin fiction 2
The girl in the fall-away dress
Richmond, M. The girl in the fall-away dress; stories
Intermittent waves of unusual size and force
Richmond, M. The girl in the fall-away dress; stories
The last bad thing
Richmond, M. The girl in the fall-away dress; stories
Mathematics and acrobatics
Richmond, M. The girl in the fall-away dress; stories
Monkey stew
Richmond, M. The girl in the fall-away dress; stories
Propaganda
Richmond, M. The girl in the fall-away dress; stories
Satellite
Richmond, M. The girl in the fall-away dress; stories
The world's greatest pants
Richmond, M. The girl in the fall-away dress; stories

Richter, Hans Peter
The teacher
When night fell; an anthology of Holocaust short stories; edited by Linda Schermer Raphael and Marc Lee Raphael
Richter, Joan
The dance of the Apsara
Death dance; suspenseful stories of the dance macabre; Trevanian, editor
The ones left behind
Living on the edge; fiction by Peace Corps writers; edited by John Coyne
Richter, Stacey
The beauty treatment
Richter, S. My date with Satan; stories
The cavemen in the hedges
Death dines at 8:30; edited by Claudia Bishop and Nick DiChario
Francis Ford Coppola's Zoetrope all-story 2; edited by Adrienne Brodeur and Samantha Schnee; with an introduction by Francis Ford Coppola
The Pushcart prize XXVI; best of the small presses, an annual small press reader; edited by Bill Henderson and the Pushcart prize editors
The first men
The Pushcart prize XXIV: best of the small presses; an annual small press reader; edited by Bill Henderson with the Pushcart prize editors
Richter, S. My date with Satan; stories
Goal 666
Granta no66 p147-61 Summ 1999
Richter, S. My date with Satan; stories
Goodnight
Richter, S. My date with Satan; stories
A groupie, a rock star
Richter, S. My date with Satan; stories
An Island of boyfriends
Richter, S. My date with Satan; stories
Seventeen v58 no8 p198-200+ Ag 1999
My date with Satan
Richter, S. My date with Satan; stories
The ocean
Richter, S. My date with Satan; stories
The prodigy of longing
Gentlemen's Quarterly v69 no6 p141-42+ Je 1999
Richter, S. My date with Satan; stories
Prom night
Richter, S. My date with Satan; stories
Rats eat cats
Richter, S. My date with Satan; stories
Rules for being human
Richter, S. My date with Satan; stories
Sally's story
Richter, S. My date with Satan; stories
Rick, Michelle
Next time
Pieces; a collection of new voices; edited by Stephen Chbosky
RICKSHAW MEN
Lao She. Also a triangle
Rushdie, S. The free radio
Rickstad, Eric
Out there, in the desert
The North American Review v284 no1 p10-16 Ja/F 1999

A **riddle**. Tabucchi, A.
The **riddle** of the golden monkeys. Estleman, L. D.
The **riddle** of the young protestor. Mallory, M.
The **ride**. Greer, R. O.
The **ride**. Nailah, A.
Ride. Robinson, L.
Ride if you dare. Keegan, C.
Ride the lightning. Lutz, J.
Ride to glory. Flynn, T. T.
Riders of the shadowlands. DeRosso, H. A.
Ridgway, Keith
 Fruit
  Circa 2000; gay fiction at the millennium; edited by Robert Drake & Terry Wolverton
Ridin' the moon in Texas. Shange, N.
Riding the black horse. Engstrom, E.
Riding the red. Hopkinson, N.
Rifaat, Alifa
 My world of the unknown
  The Vintage book of international lesbian fiction; edited and with an introduction by Naomi Holoch and Joan Nestle
Rifkin, Alan
 After the divorce
  Rifkin, A. Signal Hill; stories
 The honor system
  Rifkin, A. Signal Hill; stories
 The idols of sickness
  Rifkin, A. Signal Hill; stories
 Signal Hill
  Rifkin, A. Signal Hill; stories
 Sonority
  Rifkin, A. Signal Hill; stories
The **Rift**. McAuley, P. J.
The **right-hand** man. Coshnear, D.
The **right** kind of person. Yarbrough, S.
The **Right** Men. Smith, M. M.
The **Right** of Return. Gessen, K.
The **Right** Place For A Widow. Furman, L.
The **right** thing to do. Lee, W. W.
The **right** to life? Johnston, P. D.
The **right** to sing the blues. Lutz, J.
Rinehart, Steven
 American Arms
  Rinehart, S. Kick in the head; stories
 Another pyramid scheme
  Rinehart, S. Kick in the head; stories
 The blue Norton
  Rinehart, S. Kick in the head; stories
 Burning luv
  Rinehart, S. Kick in the head; stories
 Funny cars
  Rinehart, S. Kick in the head; stories
 Guns went off
  Rinehart, S. Kick in the head; stories
 Kick in the head
  Rinehart, S. Kick in the head; stories
 LeSabre
  Rinehart, S. Kick in the head; stories
 Make me
  Rinehart, S. Kick in the head; stories
 Mr. Big Stuff
  Rinehart, S. Kick in the head; stories
 The order of the arrow
  Rinehart, S. Kick in the head; stories
 Outstanding in my field
  Rinehart, S. Kick in the head; stories
The **ring**. Matiella, A. C.

The **ring**. Schulze, I.
Ring of love. Berberova, N.
Ring of sea and fire. Bailey, R. W.
The **ringdove** sign. Davenport, G.
Ringo Bingo. Nelson, K.
RINGS
 Barth, J. The ring
 Beattie, A. In Amalfi
 Edghill, R. The fairy ring
 Matiella, A. C. The ring
RIO DE JANEIRO (BRAZIL) *See* Brazil—Rio de Janeiro
Rio Grande gothic. Morrell, D.
RIOTS
 Arenas, R. The parade begins
 Vaswani, N. Where the long grass bends
Rip Van Winkle. Irving, W.
Ripe figs. Chopin, K.
Ripp, Victor
 My fabulous Baku fortune
  The Antioch Review v60 no2 p312-30 Spr 2002
Rippen, Chris
 Under my skin
  Death cruise; crime stories on the open seas; edited by Lawrence Block
The **rise** and fall of Mortimer Scrivens. Milne, A. A.
The **rise** of the middle class. Banks, R.
The **rising** of the South and Flonnie Rogers. Malone, M.
Rising with Surtsey. Lumley, B.
The **risk** profession. Westlake, D. E.
Risking it all. Johnson, S.
Rispondimi. Tamaro, S.
Ritchie, Elisavietta
 The Banana Pep Gal
  Ritchie, E. In haste I write you this note; stories and half-stories
 The Bardalees of Bordley Point
  Ritchie, E. In haste I write you this note; stories and half-stories
 Beatrice places a call
  Ritchie, E. In haste I write you this note; stories and half-stories
 The big sixtieth
  Ritchie, E. In haste I write you this note; stories and half-stories
 An evening of Eliot
  Ritchie, E. In haste I write you this note; stories and half-stories
 Hand-to-mouth
  Ritchie, E. In haste I write you this note; stories and half-stories
 Harvesttime
  Ritchie, E. In haste I write you this note; stories and half-stories
 "In haste I write you this note—"
  Ritchie, E. In haste I write you this note; stories and half-stories
 Inventories
  Ritchie, E. In haste I write you this note; stories and half-stories
 A letter from paradise
  Ritchie, E. In haste I write you this note; stories and half-stories
 A lovely day for tennis
  Ritchie, E. In haste I write you this note; stories and half-stories

Ritchie, Elisavietta—*Continued*
Lunch time
  Ritchie, E. In haste I write you this note; stories and half-stories
Marching as to war
  Ritchie, E. In haste I write you this note; stories and half-stories
Re-inventing the archives
  Ritchie, E. In haste I write you this note; stories and half-stories
Shopping expedition
  100% pure Florida fiction; an anthology; edited by Susan Hubbard and Robley Wilson
Telling Mr. M.
  Ritchie, E. In haste I write you this note; stories and half-stories
Territorial imperatives
  Ritchie, E. In haste I write you this note; stories and half-stories
The view from seven
  Ritchie, E. In haste I write you this note; stories and half-stories
Visitations
  Ritchie, E. In haste I write you this note; stories and half-stories
Wednesday afternoon, mid-October
  Ritchie, E. In haste I write you this note; stories and half-stories
Wild garlic: the journal of Maria X.
  Ritchie, E. In haste I write you this note; stories and half-stories
The woman who gave juice to the roofers
  Ritchie, E. In haste I write you this note; stories and half-stories
Ritchie, Jack
The absence of Emily
  The Best American mystery stories of the century; Tony Hillerman, editor; with an introduction by Tony Hillerman
  Master's choice v2; mystery stories by today's top writers and the masters who inspired them; edited by Lawrence Block
The little green book
  Death by espionage; intriguing stories of deception and betrayal; edited by Martin Cruz Smith
Rite Anthropologique. Svoboda, T.
RITES AND CEREMONIES
Chekhov, A. P. Art
Clark, J. Jungle wedding
Melville, P. English table wuk
Singer, I. B. Two
Ritual evolution. Rosen, S.
Rituals. Krawiec, R.
Rituals of departure. Deane, J. F.
The **rival** painters: a tale of Rome. Alcott, L. M.
The **rival** prima donnas. Alcott, L. M.
Rivas, Humberto
He wouldn't give up his turn
  Points of departure; new stories from Mexico; edited by Mónica Lavín; translated by Gustavo Segade
The **river**. Meloy, M.
River ambush. Farrell, C.
The **river** and Una. Reifler, N.
The **river** god. Pertwee, R.
The **river** in winter. Bass, R.
The **river** mouth. Matera, L.
River mouth. Wood, A.

River of decision. Henry, W.
The **River** Pig. Shayla, H.
River run. Doerr, A.
The **river** suite. Cheng, C.-W.
River watch. Van Pelt, L.
Rivera, Tomás
The portrait
  Graham, D. Lone Star literature; from the Red River to the Rio Grande; edited by Don Graham
The salamanders
  Fishing for chickens; short stories about rural youth; edited, with an introduction by Jim Heynen
Rivera Valdés, Sonia
Little poisons
  Dream with no name; contemporary fiction from Cuba; edited by Juana Ponce de León and Esteban Ríos Rivera
RIVERBOATS *See* Steamboats
Riverfest. Blackwood, S.
RIVERS
  See also Danube River; Mississippi River; Rhine River
Dunmore, H. The clear and rolling water
McCann, C. Everything in this country must
Riverworld roulette. Weinberg, R.
Ro Erg. Weinberg, R.
The **road**. Babel´, I.
Road detours. Sánchez, R.
Road kill. Haldeman, J. W.
The **road** not taken. Turtledove, H.
The **road** of no return. Korn, R. H.
The **road** out of Acorn Lake. Harfenist, J.
The **road** sweeper. Jurík, L.
The **road** to Brody. Babel´, I.
The **road** to Rankin's Point. MacLeod, A.
The **road** to reality. Jennings, P. C.
The **road** to Santiago de Compostela. Alexis, A.
The **road** to Stony Creek. Lindskold, J. M.
The **road** to the sea. Clarke, A. C.
The **road** to the year 3000. Harrison, H.
Road trip. Koja, K.
The **Road** Virus heads north. King, S.
Roadkill Fred. Eakin, W.
The **roadrunner**. Jones, T.
ROADS
Cady, J. The ghost of Dive Bomber Hill
Heinlein, R. A. The roads must roll
The **roads** must roll. Heinlein, R. A.
Roam. Hughes, K. B.
Roast suckling pig. Hall, D.
ROBBER BARONS *See* Capitalists and financiers
ROBBERIES
Collins, M. Harness bull
ROBBERS *See* Brigands and robbers; Robbery
The **robbers** of Karnataka. Spencer, J.
ROBBERY
  See also Bank robbers; Theft
Alessio, Carolyn. Casualidades
Alexie, S. South by Southwest
Barnard, R. Old dogs, new tricks
Blake, J. C. Aliens in the garden
Cioffari, P. Dangerously the summer burns
Davidson, A. Summon the watch!
DeLancey, K. It's dark
Delaney, E. J. Notes toward my absolution
Doyle, Sir A. C. The Jew's breastplate
Evans, E. English as a second language

ROBBERY—*Continued*
Frym, G. Sleepy
Gilchrist, E. The famous poll at Jody's Bar
Gorman, E. One of those days, one of those
   nights
Howard, C. New Orleans getaway
Lida, D. Taxi
McElroy, C. J. A brief spell by the river
Nesset, K. Mr. Agreeable
Robinson, L. Ride
Sánchez, R. Dallas
Schwartz, L. S. Intrusions
Smith, A. Paradise
Troncoso, S. Remembering possibilities
Wuori, G. K. Revenge
Robbins, James
Pictures of Darlene
   American short fiction, vol. 8, no 29-32
Roberge, Rob
Do not concern yourself with things Lee Nading
   has left out
   The Literary Review (Madison, N.J.) v43 no1
   p89-99 Fall 1999
ROBERT I, KING OF SCOTLAND, 1274-1329
About
Davidson, J. A stone of destiny
Robert the Bruce *See* Robert I, King of Scotland,
   1274-1329
Roberto narrates. Esterházy, P.
Roberts, Adam
Swiftly
   The Year's best fantasy & horror: sixteenth
   annual collection; edited by Ellen Datlow
   & Terri Windling
Roberts, Gillian
Clear sailing
   Mom, apple pie, and murder; edited by Nancy
   Pickard
Heart break
   Irreconcilable differences; Lia Matera, editor
Roberts, Les
The gathering of the klan
   The World's finest mystery and crime stories,
   second annual collection; edited by Ed
   Gorman
Roberts, Marlene
The Square Root of Reason
   Gettysburg Review v17 no2 p309-19 Summ
   2004
Roberts, Nathan
An Incomplete Map of the Northern Polarity
   Atlantic Monthly (1993) v293 no1 p205-14
   Ja/F 2004
This is not skin
   Best new American voices 2004; guest editor
   John Casey; series editors John Kulka and
   Natalie Danford
Roberts, Ralph
Second chance
   Tetrick, B. In the shadow of the wall; an an-
   thology of Vietnam stories that might have
   been; edited by Byron R. Tetrick
Roberts, Sarah
The Cougar Ladies
   Calyx v21 no3 p12-25 Wint 2004
Roberts, Teresa Noelle
Demon bone
   Such a pretty face; edited by Lee Martindale
Robert's bride. Mayo, W.

Robertson, Deborah
Proudflesh
   Grand Street no67 p220-32 Wint 1999
Robertson, Linda
Mrs. Hudson reminisces
   My Sherlock Holmes; untold stories of the
   great detective; edited by Michael Kurland
Robertson, R. Garcia y *See* Garcia y Robertson,
   R.
Robertson, Stanley
A monk's tail
   The Vintage book of contemporary Scottish
   fiction; edited and with an introduction by
   Peter Kravitz
ROBIN HOOD (LEGENDARY CHARACTER)
Pyle, H. The merry adventures of Robin Hood
   [excerpt]
Robins, Madeleine E.
La vie en ronde
   Starlight 3; edited by Patrick Nielsen Hayden
ROBINSON, JACKIE, 1919-1972
About
Parker, R. B. Harlem nocturne
Robinson, John
Centipedes on skates
   Ploughshares v25 no4 p74-83 Wint
   1999/2000
Robinson, Kim Stanley
The lucky strike
   The Best alternate history stories of the 20th
   century; edited by Harry Turtledove with
   Martin H. Greenberg
A Martian romance
   Worldmakers; SF adventures in terraforming;
   edited by Gardner Dozois
   The Year's best science fiction, seventeenth
   annual collection; edited by Gardner Dozois
Robinson, Lewis
Cuxabexis, Cuxabexis
   Robinson, L. Officer Friendly and other sto-
   ries
The diver
   Robinson, L. Officer Friendly and other sto-
   ries
The edge of the forest and the edge of the ocean
   Robinson, L. Officer Friendly and other sto-
   ries
Eiders
   Robinson, L. Officer Friendly and other sto-
   ries
Fighting at night
   Robinson, L. Officer Friendly and other sto-
   ries
Finches
   Robinson, L. Officer Friendly and other sto-
   ries
Officer Friendly
   Robinson, L. Officer Friendly and other sto-
   ries
Puckheads
   Robinson, L. Officer Friendly and other sto-
   ries
Ride
   Robinson, L. Officer Friendly and other sto-
   ries
Seeing the world
   Robinson, L. Officer Friendly and other sto-
   ries

Robinson, Lewis—*Continued*
  The toast
    Robinson, L. Officer Friendly and other stories
Robinson, Marilynne
  Kansas
    The New Yorker v80 no26 p72-83 S 13 2004
Robinson, Peter
  April in Paris
    Love and death; edited by Carolyn Hart
  The Duke's wife
    The best British mysteries; edited by Maxim Jakubowski
  In Flanders Fields
    The Best American mystery stories, 1999; edited and with an introduction by Ed McBain
  Missing in action
    The Best American mystery stories, 2001; edited and with an Introduction by Lawrence Block
    The World's finest mystery and crime stories, second annual collection; edited by Ed Gorman
  The wrong hands
    Crème de la crime; edited by Janet Hutchings
Robinson, Roxana
  Assistance
    Atlantic Monthly v284 no6 p97-100+ D 1999
  At the beach
    Good Housekeeping v236 no5 p229-30, 232, 234-6, 239 My 2003
  Blind Man
    Daedalus v133 no3 p105-15 Summ 2004
  The face-lift
    The Best American mystery stories, 2001; edited and with an Introduction by Lawrence Block
  Intersection
    Ms. v14 no3 p80-2 Fall 2004
  The Treatment
    Atlantic Monthly (1993) v290 no2 p117-20, 122, 124 S 2002
Robison, Mary
  An amateur's guide to the night
    Robison, M. Tell me: 30 stories
  Apostasy
    Robison, M. Tell me: 30 stories
  Care
    Robison, M. Tell me: 30 stories
  Coach
    Robison, M. Tell me: 30 stories
  Daughters
    Robison, M. Tell me: 30 stories
  Doctor's sons
    Robison, M. Tell me: 30 stories
  Father, grandfather
    Robison, M. Tell me: 30 stories
  For real
    Robison, M. Tell me: 30 stories
  Happy boy, Allen
    Robison, M. Tell me: 30 stories
  The help
    Robison, M. Tell me: 30 stories
  I am twenty-one
    Robison, M. Tell me: 30 stories
  I get by
    Robison, M. Tell me: 30 stories

  In Jewel
    Robison, M. Tell me: 30 stories
  In the woods
    Robison, M. Tell me: 30 stories
  Independence day
    Robison, M. Tell me: 30 stories
  Kite and paint
    Robison, M. Tell me: 30 stories
  Likely Lake
    The Paris Review v44 no162 p61-73 Summ 2002
    Robison, M. Tell me: 30 stories
  May Queen
    Robison, M. Tell me: 30 stories
  Mirror
    Robison, M. Tell me: 30 stories
  Pretty ice
    Robison, M. Tell me: 30 stories
  Seizing control
    Robison, M. Tell me: 30 stories
  Sisters
    Robison, M. Tell me: 30 stories
  Smart
    Robison, M. Tell me: 30 stories
  Smoke
    Robison, M. Tell me: 30 stories
  Trying
    Robison, M. Tell me: 30 stories
  The Wellman twins
    Robison, M. Tell me: 30 stories
  What I hear
    Robison, M. Tell me: 30 stories
  While home
    Robison, M. Tell me: 30 stories
  Your errant mom
    Robison, M. Tell me: 30 stories
  Yours
    Robison, M. Tell me: 30 stories
Robot dreams. Asimov, I.
The **robot** who wanted to know. Harrison, H.
Robotham, Rosemarie
  The cry
    The Bluelight corner; black women writing on passion, sex, and romantic love; edited by Rosemarie Robotham
ROBOTS
  Aldiss, B. W. Supertoys in other seasons
  Aldiss, B. W. Supertoys last all summer long
  Aldiss, B. W. Supertoys when winter comes
  Aldiss, B. W. Who can replace a man?
  Anderson, P. Epilogue
  Asimov, I. Robot dreams
  Barton, W. Off on a starship
  Bates, H. Farewell to the master
  Bester, A. Fondly Fahrenheit
  Boucher, A. The quest for Saint Aquin
  Bradbury, R. April 2026: The long years
  Bradbury, R. A blade of grass
  Bradbury, R. Changeling
  Bradbury, R. Downwind from Gettysburg
  Bradbury, R. G.B.S.- Mark V
  Cherryh, C. J. Companions
  Clarke, A. C. Encounter in the dawn
  Del Rey, L. Helen O'Loy
  Fleming, R. The blasphemer
  Gamelli, R. A hero, plain and simple
  Harrison, H. Arm of the law
  Harrison, H. From fanaticism; or, For reward
  Harrison, H. How the old world died

ROBOTS—*Continued*
Harrison, H. I have my vigil
Harrison, H. The robot who wanted to know
Harrison, H. The velvet glove
Harty, R. Why the sky turns red when the sun goes down
Lafferty, R. A. Eurema's dam
Leiber, F. A bad day for sales
Matheson, R. Brother to the machine
Matheson, R. Steel
Moore, C. L. No woman born
Padgett, L. The twonky
Pohl, F. The tunnel under the world
Pronzini, B. and Malzberg, B. N. Out of quarantine
Sheckley, R. The Quijote robot
Smith, C. Scanners live in vain
Steele, A. M. Agape among the robots
Steele, A. M. Jake and the enemy
Tenn, W. Child's play
Tiptree, J. The girl who was plugged in
Vinge, V. Long shot
Williamson, J. Jamboree
Williamson, J. With folded hands

Robyn, K. L.
They've got my (wrong) number
Hers 3: brilliant new fiction by lesbian writers; edited by Terry Wolverton with Robert Drake

Roche, Suzzy
Love
Carved in rock; short stories by musicians; edited by Greg Kihn

Roche, Thomas S.
Bank job
Flesh and blood: guilty as sin; erotic tales of crime and passion; edited by Max Allan Collins and Jeff Gelb
Dirty pool
Flesh and blood; erotic tales of crime and passion; edited by Max Allan Collins and Jeff Gelb
Hell on wheels
Speaking of lust; stories of forbidden desire; edited by Lawrence Block

Rochel Eisips. Porzecanski, T.

Rock, Peter
Balancing genius
Politically inspired; edited by Stephen Elliott; assistant editor, Gabriel Kram; associate editors, Elizabeth Brooks [et al.]
Wilderness
American short fiction, vol. 8, no 29-32

A **rock** and a hard place. Pickard, N.

Rock-and-roll fantasy. Davies, R.

Rock diver. Harrison, H.

ROCK MUSIC
Addonizio, K. 'Til there was you
Barrett, L. Meet the impersonators! (1986)
Benioff, D. When the nines roll over
Bruns, Don. Sing for your supper
Burdon, E. The Bukowski brothers
Coward, M. You can jump
Davies, R. Art lover
Davies, R. The deal
Davies, R. Dreams
Davies, R. The forty-eight-bar bridge
Davies, R. Home
Davies, R. Misfits

Davies, R. No more looking back
Davies, R. Rock-and-roll fantasy
Davies, R. The shirt
Davies, R. Still searching
Davies, R. Waterloo sunset
Davies, R. Where are they now?
Denton, B. We love Lydia love
Dinh, L. Boo hoo hoo
Dyer, S. N. Sins of the mothers
Harty, R. Crossroads
Hauptman, W. Good rockin' tonight
Hersh, K. The snowballing of Alt.Rock
Hitchcock, R. Narcissus
Howe, M. J. Killing the sixties
Jett, J. and Kihn, G. Bad reputation
Kieser, C. Completely overloaded
Kilpatrick, N. Creature comforts
Lipsyte, S. My life, for promotional use only
Magnuson, A. Mom comes home
McManus, J. Die like a lobster
McNally, J. The grand illusion
Mesler, C. The growth and death of Buddy Gardner
Moffett, M. Dead rock singer
Moody, R. Wilkie Fahnstock, the boxed set
Nichols, I. The last dance
Parker, G. Me and the Stones
Parker, G. Tinseltown, Morocco
Richter, S. Goal 666
Roche, S. Love
Roorbach, B. Blues machine
Rucker, R. v. B. Buzz
Ryman, G. Fan
Steele, A. M. Graceland
Sykes, J. Symptoms of loss
Wynn, S. Looked a lot like Che Guevara

ROCK MUSICIANS *See* Rock music

Rock Springs. Ford, R.

Rock star. Bean, B.

A **rock** trying to be a stone. Troncoso, S.

Rocket Day. Carlson, R.

Rocket science. White-Ring, W.

Rockets round the moon. Homes, A. M.

The **rocks** over Kyburz. Perabo, S.

The **rocky** hills of Trancas. Harrison, W.

ROCKY MOUNTAINS
DeMarinis, R. Wilderness
Rendell, R. Catamount

Rodburg, Maxine
Concessions
Rodburg, M. The law of return; short stories
Days of awe
Rodburg, M. The law of return; short stories
Keer Avenue, July 1967
Rodburg, M. The law of return; short stories
The law of return
Rodburg, M. The law of return; short stories
March of Dimes
Rodburg, M. The law of return; short stories
The orphan
Rodburg, M. The law of return; short stories
Pochantas in Camelot
Rodburg, M. The law of return; short stories
The widower Visarrion
Rodburg, M. The law of return; short stories

The **rodent**. Baida, P.

Rodeo. Coleman, J. C.

Rodeo inferno. Chapman, C. M.

Rodeo parole. Gautreaux, T.

Rodeo patrol. Gautreaux, T.
RODEOS
  Bowen, G. Barrel racers: El Charro
  Brownrigg, S. Hussy from the west
  Chapman, C. M. Rodeo inferno
  Coleman, J. C. Rodeo
  Gautreaux, T. Rodeo parole
  Gautreaux, T. Rodeo patrol
  Kennedy, A. L. Elsewhere
  L'Amour, L. Waltz him around again, Shadow
  Loomis, N. M. The coming home
  Proulx, A. The mud below
  Shange, N. Ridin' the moon in Texas
Roderick, David
  Box
    Michigan Quarterly Review v43 no3 p444-53
    Summ 2004
  Grass
    TriQuarterly no113 p41-52 Summ 2002
Rodgers, Dianna
  Star Woman's child
    Dead on demand; the best of ghost story
    weekend; edited by Elizabeth Engstrom
Rodgers, Susan Jackson
  Beautiful things
    Rodgers, S. J. The trouble with you is and
    other stories
  Bones and flowers
    Rodgers, S. J. The trouble with you is and
    other stories
  Bust
    Rodgers, S. J. The trouble with you is and
    other stories
  Chicken Man
    The North American Review v288 no5 p30-4
    S/O 2003
  Delivery
    Rodgers, S. J. The trouble with you is and
    other stories
  Fits and starts
    Rodgers, S. J. The trouble with you is and
    other stories
  Green beans
    Rodgers, S. J. The trouble with you is and
    other stories
  How I spent my summer vacation
    Rodgers, S. J. The trouble with you is and
    other stories
  Lost spirits
    Rodgers, S. J. The trouble with you is and
    other stories
  Luck
    Rodgers, S. J. The trouble with you is and
    other stories
  Remembering Tom Blake
    Rodgers, S. J. The trouble with you is and
    other stories
  The rice in question
    Rodgers, S. J. The trouble with you is and
    other stories
  Still life
    Rodgers, S. J. The trouble with you is and
    other stories
  The Trouble with You Is
    Prairie Schooner v77 no2 p184-92 Summ
    2003
    Rodgers, S. J. The trouble with you is and
    other stories

The two husbands
  Rodgers, S. J. The trouble with you is and
  other stories
Women of will
  Rodgers, S. J. The trouble with you is and
  other stories
Rodwell, Ian and Duffy, Steve
  The penny drops
    Death dines at 8:30; edited by Claudia Bishop
    and Nick DiChario
Roemer, Astrid
  The face of the Mesquaki woman
    Callaloo v24 no4 p1175-85 Fall 2001
  The inheritance of my father: a story for listen-
  ing
    The Oxford book of Caribbean short stories;
    edited by Stewart Brown and John
    Wickham
Roensch, Rob
  Hush
    South Carolina Review v35 no1 p88-93 Fall
    2002
Roeske, Paulette
  The ecstasy of Magda Brummel
    Roeske, P. Bridge of sighs; a novella and sto-
    ries
  Four characters, three small stories
    Roeske, P. Bridge of sighs; a novella and sto-
    ries
  From this distance
    Roeske, P. Bridge of sighs; a novella and sto-
    ries
  The hard fact
    Roeske, P. Bridge of sighs; a novella and sto-
    ries
  A history of swimming
    Roeske, P. Bridge of sighs; a novella and sto-
    ries
  Open arms
    Roeske, P. Bridge of sighs; a novella and sto-
    ries
  Smaller than life
    Roeske, P. Bridge of sighs; a novella and sto-
    ries
Roffé, Reina
  Transforming the desert
    English translations of short stories by con-
    temporary Argentine women writers; edited
    by Eliana Cazaubon Hermann ; translated
    by Sally Webb Thornton
Roffiel, Rosa María
  Forever lasts only a full moon
    The Vintage book of international lesbian fic-
    tion; edited and with an introduction by
    Naomi Holoch and Joan Nestle
Rog & Venus become an item. Alvarez, A.
Roger and Me. Weingarten, G.
Roger Malvin's burial. Hawthorne, N.
Rogers, Bruce Holland
  Cloud stalking mice
    Cat crimes through time; edited by Ed
    Gorman, Martin H. Greenberg, and Larry
    Segriff
  The dead boy at your window
    Best new horror 10; edited and with an intro-
    duction by Stephen Jones

Rogers, Bruce Holland—*Continued*

The Pushcart prize XXIV: best of the small presses; an annual small press reader; edited by Bill Henderson with the Pushcart prize editors

King Corpus

Mardi Gras madness; tales of terror and mayhem in New Orleans; edited by Martin H. Greenberg and Russell Davis

Lifeboat on a burning sea

The Best from fantasy & science fiction: the fiftieth anniversary anthology; edited by Edward L. Ferman and Gordon Van Gelder

Sleeping Beauty

Once upon a galaxy; edited by Will [sic] McCarthy, Martin H. Greenberg, and John Helfers

Spotted dolphin

The North American Review v284 no5 p23 S/O 1999

Thirteen ways to water

Nebula awards showcase 2000; the year's best SF and fantasy chosen by the science fiction and fantasy writers of america; edited by Gregory Benford

Rogers, Ethan M.

The eighth sacrament

The Literary Review (Madison, N.J.) v42 no3 p364-69 Spr 1999

Roger's new life. McNally, J.

Röggla, Kathrin

That's really no way to make money

Chicago Review v48 no2/3 p242-7 Summ 2002

Rogoff, Robert E.

The princess and the accountant

Once upon a galaxy; edited by Will [sic] McCarthy, Martin H. Greenberg, and John Helfers

Rogue. Mosley, W.

ROGUES AND VAGABONDS

Boylan, C. Affairs in order

Chopin, K. Vagabonds

Rohmer, Sax

The death-ring of Sneferu

Into the mummy's tomb; edited by John Richard Stephens

Rojo, Antonio Benítez- *See* Benítez-Rojo, Antonio, 1931-

Rojo, Pepe

Gray noise

Cosmos latinos: an anthology of science fiction from Latin America and Spain; translated, edited, & with an introduction & notes by Andrea L. Bell & Yolanda Molina-Gavilán

Roland Fogg. Bonnie, F.

Role model. Offutt, A. J.

Roley, Brian Ascalon

Training

The Georgia Review v55 no1 p45-63 Spr 2001

Roll call. Hoffman, W.

Rollerblading at Midnight. Tracey, C.

Rolling into Atlanta. Mason, B. A.

ROLLING STONES

Parker, G. Me and the Stones

Rollins, Hillary

Beauty and the beast

Rollins, H. The empress's new lingerie and other erotic fairy tales; bedtime stories for grown-ups

Cinderella

Rollins, H. The empress's new lingerie and other erotic fairy tales; bedtime stories for grown-ups

The empress's new lingerie

Rollins, H. The empress's new lingerie and other erotic fairy tales; bedtime stories for grown-ups

Goldie and the three bare bachelors

Rollins, H. The empress's new lingerie and other erotic fairy tales; bedtime stories for grown-ups

Hansel and Gretel

Rollins, H. The empress's new lingerie and other erotic fairy tales; bedtime stories for grown-ups

Jackie and the beanstalk

Rollins, H. The empress's new lingerie and other erotic fairy tales; bedtime stories for grown-ups

The miller's daughter (Rumpelstiltskin)

Rollins, H. The empress's new lingerie and other erotic fairy tales; bedtime stories for grown-ups

Rapunzel

Rollins, H. The empress's new lingerie and other erotic fairy tales; bedtime stories for grown-ups

Red

Rollins, H. The empress's new lingerie and other erotic fairy tales; bedtime stories for grown-ups

The sleeping beauty

Rollins, H. The empress's new lingerie and other erotic fairy tales; bedtime stories for grown-ups

Snow White and the seven dwarves

Rollins, H. The empress's new lingerie and other erotic fairy tales; bedtime stories for grown-ups

The three little pigs

Rollins, H. The empress's new lingerie and other erotic fairy tales; bedtime stories for grown-ups

Román, Ernesto Silva *See* Silva Román, Ernesto

Roman Berman, Massage Therapist. Bezmozgis, D.

ROMAN CATHOLIC CHURCH *See* Catholic faith

ROMAN CATHOLIC RELIGION *See* Catholic faith

ROMAN EMPIRE *See* Rome

Roman fever. Wharton, E.

Roman Honeymoon. Belfar, E.

A **Roman** of no importance. Foxwell, E.

Romance. Stern, S.

Romance: a prose villanelle. DeMarinis, R.

Romance in G minor. Aldrich, B. S.

The **romance** of a nose. Berners, G. H. T.-W., Baron

The **romance** of certain old clothes. James, H.

Romance with double-bass. Chekhov, A. P.

ROMANCES (LOVE STORIES) *See* Love affairs; Love stories

Romancing the yohrzeit light. Rosenbaum, T.
ROMANIA
  Fischer, T. Ice tonight in the hearts of young visitors
  Müller, H. About German mustaches and hair parts
  Müller, H. The intervillage bus
  Müller, H. Village chronicle
  Sheckley, R. A trick worth two of that
    Communism
    See Communism—Romania
A **romantic** interlude. DeMarinis, R.
Romantica. Gifford, B.
The **romantics.** Lutz, J.
ROME
  Lupoff, R. A. Jubilee
  Saylor, S. Poppy and the poisoned cake
  Silverberg, R. A hero of the empire
    30 B.C.-476 A.D.
  Pushkin, A. S. A tale of Roman life
ROME (ITALY) *See* Italy—Rome
Romero's shirt. Gilb, D.
Romo-Carmona, Mariana
  Death of the Rabbits
    The Literary Review (Madison, N.J.) v47 no3 p115-29 Spr 2004
Ronald, D_____!. Straub, P.
Ronan, Frank
  The last innocence of Simeon
    Circa 2000; gay fiction at the millennium; edited by Robert Drake & Terry Wolverton
Ronk, Martha
  Cones
    Chicago Review v45 no3/4 p61-71 1999
The **rooftop** dwellers. Desai, A.
Roofwalker. Power, S.
Rooke, Leon
  How to write a successful short story
    The Antioch Review v60 no3 p367-76 Summ 2002
  J. D.
    The Antioch Review v61 no1 p44-8 Wint 2003
  Magi Dogs
    World Literature Today v78 no2 p60-2 My/Ag 2004
  The Winds of Change, the Winds of Hope, the Winds of Disaster
    Daedalus v131 no4 p112-19 Fall 2002
Room 584, the Starr Hotel. Gifford, B.
Room for mistakes. Tilghman, C.
Room for two. Sade, marquis de
Room full of Cosmos. Hornosty, C. C.
ROOMING HOUSES *See* Boarding houses
ROOMMATES
  Davis, A. True story
  Dyson, J. Love in the time of Molyneux
  Gilliland, G. Berkeley
  Harrison, H. Roommates
  Hodgen, C. Take them in, please
  Jackson, S. Egg
  Kusel, L. Single white female
  Nissen, T. 819 Walnut
  Patterson, K. Gabriella: parts one and two
  Reisman, N. Girl on a couch
  Roeske, P. Open arms
  Sojourner, M. Monsters
  Winter, E. Contra dance
Roommates. Harrison, H.

Roorbach, Bill
  Anthropology
    Roorbach, B. Big Bend; stories
  Big bend
    Atlantic Monthly v287 no3 p60-7 Mr 2001
    New stories from the South: the year's best, 2002; edited by Shannon Ravenel; with a preface by Larry Brown
    Roorbach, B. Big Bend; stories
  Blues machine
    Roorbach, B. Big Bend; stories
  Fog
    Roorbach, B. Big Bend; stories
  Fredonia
    Roorbach, B. Big Bend; stories
  A job at Little Henry's
    Roorbach, B. Big Bend; stories
  Loneliness
    Roorbach, B. Big Bend; stories
  Taughannock Falls
    Roorbach, B. Big Bend; stories
  Thanksgiving
    Roorbach, B. Big Bend; stories
ROOSEVELT, THEODORE, 1858-1919
    About
  Compadres
  Pack, J. The Secret Staff
ROOSEVELT'S ROUGH RIDERS *See* United States. Army. Volunteer Cavalry, 1st
ROOSTERS
  Alas, L. "Socrates' rooster"
  Nordan, L. Sugar among the chickens
  Tinti, H. Gallus, gallus
Root cause. Campbell, R.
The **root** of the free radical is heart. Kempker, B.
Rope. Harmon, J.
Rope burns. Toole, F. X.
Roper, Martin
  Our house
    The New Yorker v77 no37 p100-11 N 26 2001
The **ropes.** Cavell, B.
The **ropy** thing. Sarrantonio, A.
Roquelaure, A. N. *See* Rice, Anne, 1941-
Rorvik's war. Landis, G. A.
Rosa, João Guimarães
  The third bank of the river
    The Vintage book of Latin American stories; edited by Carlos Fuentes and Julio Ortega
Rosa. Penn, W. S.
Rosa Blanca. Gifford, B.
Rosamojo. Salaam, K. I.
Rosaria 1988. Cantor, R.
ROSAS, JUAN MANUEL JOSÉ DOMINGO ORTIZ DE, 1793-1877
    About
  Borges, J. L. A dialog between dead men
Rosca, Ninotchka
  Sugar and Salt
    Ms. v12 no3 p90-4 Summ 2002
Roscoe, Patrick
  Gift
    The Canadian Forum v78 no881 p28-32 S 1999
Rose, Alexander
  Christmas story
    The North American Review v284 no6 p6-7 N/D 1999

ROSE, BILLY, 1899-1966
About
Bellow, S. The Bellarosa connection
Rose, Charles
Chairs
Southern Humanities Review v36 no2 p162-7
Spr 2002
Rose, Dilys
All the little loved ones
The Vintage book of contemporary Scottish
fiction; edited and with an introduction by
Peter Kravitz
A beautiful restoration
The Times Literary Supplement no5047 p11-
12 D 24 1999
Rose, Penny Susan
Dust
Calyx v22 no1 p6-16 Summ 2004
Rose. Biguenet, J.
Rose. Fulton, J.
Rose-Agathe. James, H.
The **Rose** City. Ebershoff, D.
A **rose** for Ecclesiastes. Zelazny, R.
The **rose** garden. Brennan, M.
A **rose** in the heart of New York. O'Brien, E.
The **rose** in twelve petals. Goss, T.
Rose into cauliflower. Matison, M.
A **rose** is a rose is a rose. Quill, M.
Rose Jam. Raab, E.
The **rose** of Paracelsus. Borges, J. L.
Rose red. Hoffman, A.
A **rose** with all its thorns. Carl, L. S.
Roselily. Walker, A.
Rosen, Norma Gangel
The orphan lover
The Antioch Review v59 no4 p690-9 Fall
2001
Rosen, Selina
Nuclear winter
Such a pretty face; edited by Lee Martindale
Ritual evolution
Thieve's world: turning points; edited by
Lynn Abbey
Rosena on the mountain. Dépestre, R.
Rosenbaum, Thane
Romancing the yohrzeit light
Neurotica: Jewish writers on sex; edited by
Melvin Jules Bukiet
Rosenberg, Yudel
The Golem; or, The miraculous deeds of Rabbi
Liva [excerpt]
Neugroschel, J. No star too beautiful; Yiddish
stories from 1382 to the present; compiled
and translated by Joachim Neugroschel
Rosenblatt, Benjamin
Zelig
The Best American short stories of the
century; John Updike, editor, Katrina
Kenison, coeditor; with an introduction by
John Updike
Rosenblatt, Roger
My Bear
The Kenyon Review v25 no2 p1-2 Spr 2003
Rosenblum, Mary Helene
Entrada
Reload: rethinking women + cyberculture; ed-
ited by Mary Flanagan and Austin Booth

The eye of God
The Good new stuff; adventure SF in the
grand tradition; edited by Gardner Dozois
The rainmaker
The Year's best fantasy & horror, twelfth an-
nual collection; edited by Ellen Datlow &
Terry Windling
Rosenfarb, Chava
Bociany
Neugroschel, J. No star too beautiful; Yiddish
stories from 1382 to the present; compiled
and translated by Joachim Neugroschel
Rosenfeld, Stephanie
Bing-bing and bong-bong
Rosenfeld, S. What about the love part?; sto-
ries
Cliff dweller
Rosenfeld, S. What about the love part?; sto-
ries
Exactly the size of life
Rosenfeld, S. What about the love part?; sto-
ries
Five dreams of falling
Rosenfeld, S. What about the love part?; sto-
ries
Good for the frog
Rosenfeld, S. What about the love part?; sto-
ries
Grasp special comb
Rosenfeld, S. What about the love part?; sto-
ries
How I went (recipe for lime curd)
Rosenfeld, S. What about the love part?; sto-
ries
Insects in amber
Rosenfeld, S. What about the love part?; sto-
ries
Inversion
Rosenfeld, S. What about the love part?; sto-
ries
The last known thing
Rosenfeld, S. What about the love part?; sto-
ries
Massachusetts, California, Timbuktoo
The Massachusetts Review v40 no2 p207-26
Summ 1999
To Sarah, wherever you are
Rosenfeld, S. What about the love part?; sto-
ries
Rosenfeld, Yoyne
Miss Bertha
Neugroschel, J. No star too beautiful; Yiddish
stories from 1382 to the present; compiled
and translated by Joachim Neugroschel
Rosenstock, David Yair
Simple Facts
Ploughshares v30 no2/3 p135-43 Fall 2004
Rosenthal, Kairol
What the water gave me
Tikkun v17 no1 p65-8 Ja/F 2002
Rosenthal unbound. Shapiro, G.
Rosero Diago, Evelio
Brides by night
Michigan Quarterly Review v38 no2 p279-80
Spr 1999
Roses, rhododendron. Adams, A.
Rosie since Vietnam. Frym, G.
Rosie's dance. Hardesty, E.
Roslavlev. Pushkin, A. S.

Rosovsky, Michael
Jen
The Virginia Quarterly Review v75 no3 p473-87 Summ 1999
Ross, J. Maclaren- *See* Maclaren-Ross, J., 1912-1964
Ross, Jenny
The immortals
Typical girls; new stories by smart women; edited by Susan Corrigan
Ross, Leone
Tasting songs
Dark matter; a century of speculative fiction from the African diaspora; edited by Sheree R. Thomas
Death dines at 8:30; edited by Claudia Bishop and Nick DiChario
Ross, Stuart
The president's cold legs
The Canadian Forum v78 no883 p28-29 N 1999
Ross Willow's new and used cars. Iribarne, M.
ROSSETTI, DANTE GABRIEL, 1828-1882
About
Davidson, A. Buchanan's head
Rossi, Alejandro
Orion's glow
The Vintage book of Latin American stories; edited by Carlos Fuentes and Julio Ortega
Rossi, Caila
Seeing a specialist
Gettysburg Review v12 no2 p241-48 Summ 1999
Rossi, Cristina Peri
White Beak, Blue Wings
The Antioch Review v62 no3 p566-76 Summ 2004 *See* Peri Rossi, Cristina, 1941-
Rosy's journey. Alcott, L. M.
Roth, Henry
A diving rock on the Hudson [excerpt]
Neurotica: Jewish writers on sex; edited by Melvin Jules Bukiet
Roth, Joseph
April: the story of a love affair
Roth, J. The collected stories of Joseph Roth; translated with an introduction by Michael Hofmann
Barbara
Roth, J. The collected stories of Joseph Roth; translated with an introduction by Michael Hofmann
The blind mirror
Roth, J. The collected stories of Joseph Roth; translated with an introduction by Michael Hofmann
The bust of the emperor
Roth, J. The collected stories of Joseph Roth; translated with an introduction by Michael Hofmann
Career
Roth, J. The collected stories of Joseph Roth; translated with an introduction by Michael Hofmann
The cartel
Roth, J. The collected stories of Joseph Roth; translated with an introduction by Michael Hofmann

The grand house opposite
Roth, J. The collected stories of Joseph Roth; translated with an introduction by Michael Hofmann
The honors student
Roth, J. The collected stories of Joseph Roth; translated with an introduction by Michael Hofmann
The leviathan
Roth, J. The collected stories of Joseph Roth; translated with an introduction by Michael Hofmann
The place I want to tell you about. . .
Roth, J. The collected stories of Joseph Roth; translated with an introduction by Michael Hofmann
Rare and ever rarer in this world of empirical facts. . .
Roth, J. The collected stories of Joseph Roth; translated with an introduction by Michael Hofmann
Sick people
Roth, J. The collected stories of Joseph Roth; translated with an introduction by Michael Hofmann
Stationmaster Fallmerayer
New England Review v23 no1 p136-50 Wint 2002
Roth, J. The collected stories of Joseph Roth; translated with an introduction by Michael Hofmann
Strawberries
Roth, J. The collected stories of Joseph Roth; translated with an introduction by Michael Hofmann
This morning, a letter arrived. . .
Roth, J. The collected stories of Joseph Roth; translated with an introduction by Michael Hofmann
The triumph of beauty
Roth, J. The collected stories of Joseph Roth; translated with an introduction by Michael Hofmann
Youth
Roth, J. The collected stories of Joseph Roth; translated with an introduction by Michael Hofmann
Roth, Moira
Rachel Marker and Her Book of Shadows
Art Journal v62 no3 p66-73 Fall 2003
Roth, Philip
The counterlife [excerpt]
Neurotica: Jewish writers on sex; edited by Melvin Jules Bukiet
Defender of the faith
The Best American short stories of the century; John Updike, editor, Katrina Kenison, coeditor; with an introduction by John Updike
Smart money
Wonderful town; New York stories from The New Yorker; edited by David Remnick with Susan Choi
Roth, William M.
La tempesta
The Literary Review (Madison, N.J.) v42 no3 p373-82 Spr 1999

Rothbart, Davy

First snow

Pieces; a collection of new voices; edited by Stephen Chbosky

Rothmayerová, Gabriela

In a danger zone

In search of homo sapiens; twenty-five contemporary Slovak short stories; editor, Pavol Hudík ; [translated by Heather Trebatická; American English editor, Lucy Bednár]

Rothschild, Victoria

How I came to love books

Critical Quarterly v41 no1 p32-45 Spr 1999

Rothschild's fiddle. Chekhov, A. P.

The **rotifer**. Gavell, M. L.

Rotten pears. Müller, H.

Rotten to the core. Healy, J. F.

Rough music. Tristram, C.

ROUGH RIDERS *See* United States. Army. Volunteer Cavalry, 1st

Rough Riders of Arizona. Henry, W.

The **round**. Le Clézio, J.-M. G.

Round Mountain. Freeman, C.

Round on Both Ends and High in the Middle. Gates, D.

The **rounds** don't matter. L'Amour, L.

Roundup in Texas. L'Amour, L.

The **roussalka**. Boroson, R.

Roustabout. Parrish, T.

Route 80. Leavitt, D.

Routley, B. J. *See* Routley, Jane

Routley, Jane

To avalon

Dreaming down-under; edited by Jack Dann and Janeen Webb

Row, Jess

Heaven lake

The Best American short stories, 2003; selected from U.S. and Canadian magazines by Walter Mosley with Katrina Kenison; with an introduction by Walter Mosley

Harvard Review (1992) no22 p156-66 Spr 2002

The secrets of bats

The Best American short stories 2001; selected from U.S. and Canadian magazines by Barbara Kingsolver with Katrina Kenison; with an introduction by Barbara Kingsolver

The Pushcart prize XXVI; best of the small presses, an annual small press reader; edited by Bill Henderson and the Pushcart prize editors

A **row** of trees. Kawabata, Y.

Rowan, Quentin

Bethune Street

The Paris Review v44 no161 p199-220 Spr 2002

Excellence

Bomb no85 p105-9 Fall 2003

Innocents abroad

The Paris Review v41 no152 p161-78 Fall 1999

Rowell, Carolyn

Fireweed

Dalhousie Review v81 no1 p67-93 Spr 2001

Rowell, John

Delegates

Rowell, J. The music of your life; stories; John Rowell

The mother-of-the-groom and I

Rowell, J. The music of your life; stories; John Rowell

The music of your life

Rowell, J. The music of your life; stories; John Rowell

Saviors

Rowell, J. The music of your life; stories; John Rowell

Spectators in love

Rowell, J. The music of your life; stories; John Rowell

Who lives you?

Rowell, J. The music of your life; stories; John Rowell

Wildlife of Coastal Carolina

Rowell, J. The music of your life; stories; John Rowell

Rowing to Eden. Bloom, A.

Rowing to Leiden. Taber, S. M.

Rowlands, Sioned Puw

A fantasy in memory of the Anglesey bone doctors

The Literary Review (Madison, N.J.) v44 no2 p352-6 Wint 2001

Roy. Somers, E.

The **royal** game. Zweig, S.

Royal Pain. Buckley, C.

The **royals** of Hegn. Le Guin, U. K.

Royalty. Desai, A.

Royle, Nicholas

Empty stations

Best new horror 12; edited and with an introduction by Stephen Jones

Hide and seek

The Year's best fantasy & horror: sixteenth annual collection; edited by Ellen Datlow & Terri Windling

The Inland Waterways Association

The best British mysteries; edited by Maxim Jakubowski

Standard gauge

The Mammoth book of best new horror 14; edited with an introduction by Stephen Jones

The Year's best fantasy & horror: sixteenth annual collection; edited by Ellen Datlow & Terri Windling

Rozan, S. J.

Childhood

The World's finest mystery and crime stories, second annual collection; edited by Ed Gorman

Double-crossing Delancey

The World's finest mystery and crime stories, third annual collection; edited by Ed Gorman and Martin H. Greenberg

Hoops

Crème de la crime; edited by Janet Hutchings

Rozanski, Joette M.

The search for a sipping house

Such a pretty face; edited by Lee Martindale

Rub me up, rub me down. Channer, C.

RUBBER INDUSTRY

Chesnutt, C. W. The averted strike

Rubber time. Watanabe McFerrin, L.

Ruben and Norma. Casares, O.

Ruben Mendoza Vega, Suzuki professor of early Caribbean history, University of Florida at Gainesville, offers a history of the United States based on personal experience. Lopez, B. H.

RUBIES
Sherman, D. The Parwat Ruby

Rubies. Reisman, N.

Rubin, Billie
Living next door to malice
The World's finest mystery and crime stories, third annual collection; edited by Ed Gorman and Martin H. Greenberg

Rubin, Jay
(jt. auth) See Murakami, Haruki

Rubin, Louis D. (Louis Decimus)
The man at the beach
The Cry of an occasion; fiction from the Fellowship of Southern Writers; edited by Richard Bausch; with a foreword by George Garrett

Rubina, Dina
Apples from Shlitzbutter's garden
With signs and wonders; an international anthology of Jewish fabulist fiction; edited by Daniel M. Jaffe

Rubout. Wellen, E.

Ruby, Wanda and Me, Late at Night, in the County Jail. Hurley, V.

Ruby's cape. Coleman, J. C.

Rucker, Lynda E.
No more a-roving
The Mammoth book of best horror 13; edited by Stephen Jones

Rucker, Rudy von Bitter
The Andy Warhol sandcandle
Rucker, R. v. B. Gnarl!; stories
As above, so below
Rucker, R. v. B. Gnarl!; stories
Big Jelly
Rucker, R. v. B. Gnarl!; stories
Bringing in the sheaves
Rucker, R. v. B. Gnarl!; stories
Buzz
Rucker, R. v. B. Gnarl!; stories
Chaos surfari
Rucker, R. v. B. Gnarl!; stories
Easy as pie
Rucker, R. v. B. Gnarl!; stories
Enlightenment Rabies
Rucker, R. v. B. Gnarl!; stories
The facts of life
Rucker, R. v. B. Gnarl!; stories
Faraway eyes
Rucker, R. v. B. Gnarl!; stories
The fifty-seventh Franz Kafka
Rucker, R. v. B. Gnarl!; stories
In frozen time
Rucker, R. v. B. Gnarl!; stories
The Indian rope trick explained
Rucker, R. v. B. Gnarl!; stories
Inertia
Rucker, R. v. B. Gnarl!; stories
Inside out
Rucker, R. v. B. Gnarl!; stories
Instability
Rucker, R. v. B. Gnarl!; stories

The Jack Kerouac disembodied school of poetics
Rucker, R. v. B. Gnarl!; stories
Jumpin' Jack Flash
Rucker, R. v. B. Gnarl!; stories
The last Einstein-Rosen bridge
Rucker, R. v. B. Gnarl!; stories
The man who ate himself
Rucker, R. v. B. Gnarl!; stories
The man who was a cosmic string
Rucker, R. v. B. Gnarl!; stories
Message found in a copy of Flatland
Rucker, R. v. B. Gnarl!; stories
Monument to the Third International
Rucker, R. v. B. Gnarl!; stories
A new experiment with time
Rucker, R. v. B. Gnarl!; stories
A new golden age
Rucker, R. v. B. Gnarl!; stories
Pac-Man
Rucker, R. v. B. Gnarl!; stories
Pi in the sky
Rucker, R. v. B. Gnarl!; stories
Plastic letters
Rucker, R. v. B. Gnarl!; stories
Probability pipeline
Rucker, R. v. B. Gnarl!; stories
Rapture in space
Rucker, R. v. B. Gnarl!; stories
Schrödinger's cat
Rucker, R. v. B. Gnarl!; stories
Soft Death
Rucker, R. v. B. Gnarl!; stories
The square root of Pythagoras
Rucker, R. v. B. Gnarl!; stories
Storming the cosmos
Rucker, R. v. B. Gnarl!; stories
Tales of Houdini
Rucker, R. v. B. Gnarl!; stories
Wishloop
Rucker, R. v. B. Gnarl!; stories

Rucker, Rudy von Bitter and Shirley, John
Pockets
Redshift; extreme visions of speculative fiction; edited by Al Sarrantonio

Rudd, Kelly
Fat Tuesday
Dead on demand; the best of ghost story weekend; edited by Elizabeth Engstrom

A **rude** awakening. Chopin, K.

Rudy's two wives. Louis, L. G.

Rue Guynemer. Tuck, L.

Ruffian's wife. Hammett, D.

The **rug**. Mullins, M.

Rug weaver. Moss, B. K.

RUGBY FOOTBALL
Kelman, J. Joe laughed
Perry, A. The end of innocence

RUGS
Moss, B. K. Rug weaver
Mullins, M. The rug

Ruins. Delany, S. R.

Ruins. Hewett, G.

The **ruins** of Contracoeur. Oates, J. C.

Ruiz, Bernardo
Queen of shadows
Points of departure; new stories from Mexico; edited by Mónica Lavín; translated by Gustavo Segade

Rule, Rebecca
 Walking the trapline
  Fishing for chickens; short stories about rural
   youth; edited, with an introduction by Jim
   Heynen
Rules for being human. Richter, S.
Rules of the lake. Ziegler, I.
Rules to live. Casey, M.
Rulfo, Juan
 Luvina
  The Vintage book of Latin American stories;
   edited by Carlos Fuentes and Julio Ortega
Ruling. Williams, D.
The **rull**. Van Vogt, A. E.
RUMANIA *See* Romania
Rumi and the Fish. Vigderman, P.
Rumor and a ladder. Bowles, P.
A **rumor** of prayer. Rawley, D.
RUMPELSTILTSKIN
 Brockmeier, K. A day in the life of half of
  Rumpelstiltskin
Rumpelstiltskin. Brady, C.
Rumpelstiltskin. Ferriss, L.
Rumpole and the absence of body. Mortimer, J.
 C.
Rumpole and the actor laddie. Mortimer, J. C.
Rumpole and the asylum seekers. Mortimer, J. C.
Rumpole and the Camberwell. Mortimer, J. C.
Rumpole and the old familiar faces. Mortimer, J.
 C.
Rumpole and the remembrance of things past.
 Mortimer, J. C.
Rumpole and the teenage werewolf. Mortimer, J.
 C.
Rumpole at sea. Mortimer, J. C.
Rumpole rests his case. Mortimer, J. C.
Run away, my pale love. Almond, S.
Run ragged. Davies, L.
A **run** through the jungle. Jones, T.
The **runaway**. Chekhov, A. P.
Runaway. Munro, A.
Runaway horses. Blake, J. C.
The **runaway** judge. Aldrich, B. S.
The **runaway** skyscraper. Jenkins, W. F.
RUNAWAYS (CHILDREN)
 Bowles, P. Here to learn
 Boylan, C. The picture house
 Packer, Z. Speaking in tongues
RUNAWAYS (YOUTH)
 Barrett, N., Jr. Perpetuity blues
 Blair, J. Running away
 Chekhov, A. P. Boys
 Erian, A. When animals attack
 Fromm, P. How all this started
 Guerrero, L. Blanca Rosa
 Packer, Z. Speaking in tongues
 Thien, M. Alchemy
 Thompson, S. Ernest
 Vonnegut, K. Runaways
 Winter, E. House in the woods
Runaways. Leong, R.
The **runaways**. Spencer, E.
Runaways. Vonnegut, K.
The **Rundown**. Andoe, J.
The **runner**. Le Clézio, J.-M. G.
RUNNING
 Bambara, T. C. Raymond's run
 Bonnie, F. The race for last place
 Cobb, W. J. Marathon

 Meredith, D. Wanamaker
 Neri, K. Sentence imposed
 Peri Rossi, C. Breaking the speed record
Running. Campbell, B. J.
Running away with the hairdresser. Mazelis, J.
Running dogs. Duffy, S.
Running from Legs. McBain, E.
Running in place. Foster, K.
Running out of dog. Lehane, D.
Running Rapids. Oates, N.
Running wolf. Blackwood, A.
Runyon, Alfred Damon *See* Runyon, Damon,
 1884-1946
Runyon, Damon
 Bred for battle
  Boxing's best short stories; edited by Paul D.
   Staudohar
 Sense of humor
  The Best American mystery stories of the
   century; Tony Hillerman, editor; with an
   introduction by Tony Hillerman
The **ruptures** and limits of absence. Singleton, G.
Rural legend. Kilpatrick, N.
RURAL LIFE *See* Country life
Rusch, Kristine Kathryn
 Blood trail
  Past imperfect; edited by Martin H. Green-
   berg and Larry Segriff
 Burial detail
  Rusch, K. K. Stories for an enchanted after-
   noon; with a foreword by Kevin J. Ander-
   son
 Coolhunting
  Rusch, K. K. Stories for an enchanted after-
   noon; with a foreword by Kevin J. Ander-
   son
 The dead line
  The Blue and the gray undercover; edited by
   Ed Gorman
 Details
  Crème de la crime; edited by Janet Hutchings
 Echea
  Rusch, K. K. Stories for an enchanted after-
   noon; with a foreword by Kevin J. Ander-
   son
 The gallery of his dreams
  Rusch, K. K. Stories for an enchanted after-
   noon; with a foreword by Kevin J. Ander-
   son
 Going native
  Rusch, K. K. Stories for an enchanted after-
   noon; with a foreword by Kevin J. Ander-
   son
 Harvest
  Rusch, K. K. Stories for an enchanted after-
   noon; with a foreword by Kevin J. Ander-
   son
 Judgment
  Greenberg, M. H. Faerie tales
 June Sixteenth at Anna's
  The year's best science fiction: twenty-first
   annual collection; edited by Gardner Dozois
 The light in Whale Cove
  Lighthouse hauntings; 12 original tales of the
   supernatural; edited by Charles G. Waugh
   & Martin H. Greenberg

Rusch, Kristine Kathryn—*Continued*

Millennium babies

Rusch, K. K. Stories for an enchanted afternoon; with a foreword by Kevin J. Anderson

Monuments to the dead

Rusch, K. K. Stories for an enchanted afternoon; with a foreword by Kevin J. Anderson

The perfect man

The World's finest mystery and crime stories, third annual collection; edited by Ed Gorman and Martin H. Greenberg

Relics

Past lives, present tense; edited by Elizabeth Ann Scarborough

The silence

The World's finest mystery and crime stories, second annual collection; edited by Ed Gorman

Sing

Magical beginnings; edited by Steven H. Silver and Martin H. Greenberg

Skin deep

Rusch, K. K. Stories for an enchanted afternoon; with a foreword by Kevin J. Anderson

Spinning

The World's finest mystery and crime stories, second annual collection; edited by Ed Gorman

Spirit guides

Rusch, K. K. Stories for an enchanted afternoon; with a foreword by Kevin J. Anderson

Strange creatures

Rusch, K. K. Stories for an enchanted afternoon; with a foreword by Kevin J. Anderson

The young shall see visions, and the old dream dreams

A moment on the edge; 100 years of crime stories by women; edited by Elizabeth George

Rush, Norman

Alone in Africa

Living on the edge; fiction by Peace Corps writers; edited by John Coyne

Rush. House, T.

Rushdie, Salman

The free radio

The Art of the story; an international anthology of contemporary short stories; edited by Daniel Halpern

Summer of Solanka

The New Yorker v77 no19 p66-75 Jl 16 2001

Vina Divina

The New Yorker v75 no6 p68-79 Ap 5 1999

Russ, Joanna

Souls

Brown, C. N. and Strahan, J. The Locus awards; thirty years of the best in science fiction and fantasy; edited by Charles N. Brown and Jonathan Strahan

RUSSELL, CHARLES M. (CHARLES MARION), 1864-1926

About

Mehor, E. L. Noah

Russell, Craig

Crab

Dalhousie Review v81 no3 p421-7 Aut 2001

Russell, Jacob

A Theology of Anorexia

Salmagundi no137/138 p169-78 Wint/Spr 2003

Russell, Jay

Hides

The Mammoth book of best new horror 14; edited with an introduction by Stephen Jones

The Year's best fantasy & horror: sixteenth annual collection; edited by Ellen Datlow & Terri Windling

Russell, John

The knife

Master's choice v2; mystery stories by today's top writers and the masters who inspired them; edited by Lawrence Block

Russell, Michael

Simple machines

New England Review v22 no3 p44-63 Summ 2001

The speed of sound

New England Review v20 no4 p149-58 Fall 1999

Russell, Ray

Evil star

Other people's mail; an anthology of letter stories; edited with an introduction by Gail Pool

RUSSIA

See also Lithuania; Siberia (Russia); Ukraine

Gabrielyan, N. The house in Metekhi Lane

Hobson, C. The bottle: a provincial tale

Kalfus, K. Salt

Newman, K. Amerikanski dead at the Moscow morgue

Rucker, R. v. B. Storming the cosmos

Shonk, K. The death of Olga Vasilievna

Shonk, K. My mother's garden

Shonk, K. Our American

Shonk, K. The wooden village of Kizhi

Shonk, K. The young people of Moscow

Shteyngart, G. Shylock on the Neva

Tawada, Y. Where Europe begins

Vapnyar, L. Ovrashki's trains

Vapnyar, L. There are Jews in my house

18th century

Pushkin, A. S. The captain's daughter

19th century

Chekhov, A. P. Anyuta

Chekhov, A. P. Ariadne

Chekhov, A. P. At a country house

Chekhov, A. P. Betrothed

Chekhov, A. P. The bishop

Chekhov, A. P. Boys

Chekhov, A. P. Choristers

Chekhov, A. P. The complaints book

Chekhov, A. P. The cook's wedding

Chekhov, A. P. A doctor's visit

Chekhov, A. P. From the diary of an assistant book-keeper

Chekhov, A. P. The grasshopper

Chekhov, A. P. Home

Chekhov, A. P. In trouble

Chekhov, A. P. Kashtanka

RUSSIA—19th century—*Continued*

Chekhov, A. P. The lady with the dog
Chekhov, A. P. The new villa
Chekhov, A. P. Shrove Tuesday
Chekhov, A. P. The steppe
Chekhov, A. P. A story without an end
Pushkin, A. S. A novel in letters
Pushkin, A. S. The queen of spades
Pushkin, A. S. Roslavlev
Pushkin, A. S. The stationmaster
Pushkin, A. S. The undertaker
Tolstoy, L., graf. Divine and human
Tolstoy, L., graf. Why did it happen?

1900-1917

Bunin, I. A. Styopa
Chekhov, A. P. "Anna on the neck"
Chekhov, A. P. At home
Chekhov, A. P. A gentleman friend
Chekhov, A. P. Kashtanka
Chekhov, A. P. The two Volodyas
Zinovyeva-Annibal, L. D. The bear cubs
Zinovyeva-Annibal, L. D. Wolves

20th century

Bunin, I. A. Antigone
Bunin, I. A. Caucasus
Bunin, I. A. Muza
Bunin, I. A. On one familiar street
Bunin, I. A. Raven
Bunin, I. A. Rusya

1917-1945

Babel´, I. The church in Novograd
Babel´, I. Doudou
Babel´, I. A hardworking woman
Babel´, I. Sulak
Englander, N. The twenty-seventh man
Jones, G. Modernity
Kalfus, K. Birobidzhan

1945-

Duncan, A. The chief designer
Erofeev, V. The parakeet
Kalfus, K. Anzhelika, 13
Kalfus, K. Orbit
Kalfus, K. Peredelkino
Kalfus, K. Pu-239
Renwick, J. The dolphin story
Rubina, D. Apples from Shlitzbutter's garden

Aristocracy

See Aristocracy—Russia

Army

Babel´, I. Beresteczko
Babel´, I. Evening
Babel´, I. The kiss
Babel´, I. The reserve cavalry commander
Babel´, I. The road to Brody
Babel´, I. Squadron Commander Trunov
Pushkin, A. S. The captain's daughter

Officers

Babel´, I. The widow
Chekhov, A. P. The kiss
Pushkin, A. S. The shot

Communism

See Communism—Russia

Courts and courtiers

See Courts and courtiers—Russia

Peasant life

See Peasant life—Russia

Revolution of 1917

See Russia—1917-1945

Rural life

Babel´, I. Shabos-Nakhamu
Bocock, M. The baker's daughter
Bunin, I. A. Ballad
Bunin, I. A. Sunstroke
Bunin, I. A. Zoyka and Valeriya
Chekhov, A. P. About love
Chekhov, A. P. Agafya
Chekhov, A. P. An artist's story
Chekhov, A. P. A chameleon
Chekhov, A. P. Champagne
Chekhov, A. P. The darling
Chekhov, A. P. Difficult people
Chekhov, A. P. Encased
Chekhov, A. P. Enemies
Chekhov, A. P. Gooseberries
Chekhov, A. P. The horse-stealers
Chekhov, A. P. The huntsman
Chekhov, A. P. Ionitch
Chekhov, A. P. Lights
Chekhov, A. P. The man in a case
Chekhov, A. P. Minds in ferment
Chekhov, A. P. Misery
Chekhov, A. P. Neighbours
Chekhov, A. P. Notes from the memoirs of a man of ideals
Chekhov, A. P. On official duty
Chekhov, A. P. Peasant wives
Chekhov, A. P. Peasants
Chekhov, A. P. The Petchenyeg
Chekhov, A. P. The privy councillor
Chekhov, A. P. The requiem
Chekhov, A. P. Rothschild's fiddle
Chekhov, A. P. The siren
Chekhov, A. P. The student
Chekhov, A. P. The Swedish match
Chekhov, A. P. The teacher of literature
Chekhov, A. P. Terror
Chekhov, A. P. The witch
Kalfus, K. Budyonnovsk
Pushkin, A. S. The blizzard
Pushkin, A. S. Dubrovskii
Pushkin, A. S. A history of the village of Goriukhino
Pushkin, A. S. The squire's daughter
Shonk, K. My mother's garden
Tolstoy, L., graf. The berries
Vasilenko, S. The gopher
Vasilenko, S. Little fool
Vasilenko, S. Piggy
Vasilenko, S. Poplar, poplar's daughter
Vasilenko, S. Shamara
Zinovyeva-Annibal, L. D. Will

Leningrad

See Russia—St. Petersburg

Moscow

Chekhov, A. P. A dreadful night
Chekhov, A. P. Oysters
Cherryh, C. J. Ice
Shonk, K. Kitchen friends
Shrayer-Petrov, D. Apple cider vinegar
Shrayer-Petrov, D. Rusty
Shrayer-Petrov, D. Tsukerman and his children
Vapnyar, L. Lydia's Grove
Zinik, Z. Mind the doors

St. Petersburg

Babel´, I. Chink
Babel´, I. An evening with the Empress
Babel´, I. Nine

RUSSIA—St. Petersburg—*Continued*
Babel´, I. The public library
Chekhov, A. P. An anonymous story
Pushkin, A. S. Egyptian nights
Pushkin, A. S. The guests were arriving at the dacha
Pushkin, A. S. In the corner of a small square
Pushkin, A. S. We were spending the evening at Princess D.'s dacha
RUSSIAN AMERICANS
Shonk, K. The wooden village of Kizhi
Russian master. *See* Chekhov, A. P. The teacher of literature
RUSSIAN REFUGEES
Nabokov, V. V. "That in Aleppo once . . . "
RUSSIAN REVOLUTION, 1905 *See* Russia—1900-1917
RUSSIAN REVOLUTION, 1917-1921 *See* Russia—1917-1945
RUSSIAN SOLDIERS *See* Soldiers—Russia
Russian vine. Ings, S.
The **Russian** Violinist. Visson, E.
RUSSIANS
England
Zinik, Z. Double act in Soho
Zinik, Z. A pickled nose
France
Berberova, N. About the hooks
Berberova, N. The Argentine
Berberova, N. Billancourt fiesta
Berberova, N. The Billancourt manuscript
Berberova, N. A gypsy romance
Berberova, N. An incident with music
Berberova, N. Kolka and Liusenka
Berberova, N. The little stranger
Berberova, N. The phantom of Billancourt
Berberova, N. Photogenique
Berberova, N. Ring of love
Berberova, N. Versts and sleeping cars
Berberova, N. The violin of Billancourt
Bunin, I. A. In Paris
Giono, J. Ivan Ivanovitch Kossiakoff
Germany
Zinovyeva-Annibal, L. D. The devil
Italy
Chekhov, A. P. Ariadne
Viganò, R. Peter
Netherlands
Carson, J. Captives
Poland
Babel´, I. At Saint Valentine's
Babel´, I. Konkin
Babel´, I. A letter
Babel´, I. Zamosc
United States
Bellow, S. Zetland: by a character witness
DuBois, B. Old soldiers
George, E. Good fences aren't always enough
Hill, I. The more they stay the same
Karbo, K. The palace of marriage
Kuryla, M. Mis-sayings
Leegant, J. Mezivosky
Padilla, M. Carrying Sergei
Penn, W. S. Neither
Shrayer-Petrov, D. Hände hoch!
Shrayer-Petrov, D. Hurricane Bob
Shrayer-Petrov, D. Old writer Foreman
Shteyngart, G. Several anecdotes about my wife
Singer, I. B. The egotist

Vapnyar, L. Mistress
Russo, Albert
Venetian thresholds
The Literary Review (Madison, N.J.) v42 no3 p385-89 Spr 1999
Russo, Richard
Buoyancy
Russo, R. The whore's child, and other stories
The dowry
Best of Prairie schooner; fiction and poetry; edited by Hilda Raz
The farther you go
Russo, R. The whore's child, and other stories
Joy ride
Russo, R. The whore's child, and other stories
Monhegan light
Esquire v136 no2 p122-9, 132 Ag 2001
Russo, R. The whore's child, and other stories
The mysteries of Linwood Hart
Russo, R. The whore's child, and other stories
Poison
Russo, R. The whore's child, and other stories
The whore's child
Russo, R. The whore's child, and other stories
The Student body; short stories about college students and professors; edited by John McNally
Rust. Boyle, T. C.
RUSTLERS, CATTLE *See* Cattle thieves
Rusya. Bunin, I. A.
RUTH, BABE, 1895-1948
About
Malzberg, B. N. Allegro marcato
Schofield, S. Stepping up to the plate
Ruth, George Herman *See* Ruth, Babe, 1895-1948
Rutherglen, Susannah
Farewell, Angelina
Seventeen v58 no3 p156-58+ Mr 1999
Ruthig, Ingrid
Snow Blind
Dalhousie Review v81 no3 p419-20 Aut 2001
Ruth's secret. Alcott, L. M.
Rutkowski, Ed
The Magisterium
Prairie Schooner v77 no1 p103-14 Spr 2003
Ruy Sánchez, Alberto
Voices of the water
The Vintage book of Latin American stories; edited by Carlos Fuentes and Julio Ortega
Ryan, Jean
Paradise
The Massachusetts Review v42 no3 p415-29 Aut 2001
Ryan, Mary
Murder in Kilcurry
Murder most Celtic; tall tales of Irish mayhem; edited by Martin H. Greenberg
Ryan, Patrick
Before Las Blancas
Best new American voices 2001; guest editor Charles Baxter; series editors John Kulka and Natalie Danford
Getting Heavy with Fate
The Yale Review v92 no4 p109-27 O 2004
Ground Control
Iowa Review v34 no1 p122-44 Spr 2004

Ryan, Patrick—*Continued*
Second island
  Men on men 2000; best new gay fiction for the millennium; edited and with an introduction by David Bergman and Karl Woelz
Ryan, Paula Langguth
Life is a highway
  Hers 3: brilliant new fiction by lesbian writers; edited by Terry Wolverton with Robert Drake
Rybicki, John
Into the Standing Corn
  The North American Review v289 no2 p32-3 Mr/Ap 2004
Ryder, Pamela
Solstice
  Prairie Schooner v73 no1 p72-77 Spr 1999
Rykena, Stephan
Conscience
  The World's finest mystery and crime stories, third annual collection; edited by Ed Gorman and Martin H. Greenberg
Ryman, Geoff
Birth days
  The year's best science fiction: twenty-first annual collection; edited by Gardner Dozois
Everywhere
  The Year's best science fiction, seventeenth annual collection; edited by Gardner Dozois
Fan
  Northern suns; edited by David G. Hartwell & Glenn Grant
Have not have
  The Year's best science fiction, nineteenth annual collection; edited by Gardner Dozois
V.A.O.
  The Year's best science fiction; twentieth annual collection; edited by Gardner Dozois

S

S & M: a brief history. Shields, D.
S.O.S.. Lutz, J.
Saavedra, Miguel de Cervantes *See* Cervantes Saavedra, Miguel de, 1547-1616
sab.o.tage. Anderson, D.
Sabbatai Sevi *See* Shabbethai Tzevi, 1626-1676
SABBATH
Babel´, I. Gedali
Saberhagen, Fred
Box number fifty
  Dracula in London; edited by P. N. Elrod
Sabo. Shacochis, B.
SABOTAGE
Harrison, H. Brave newer world
Kennett, S. A warm nest
Siodmak, C. FP 1 does not reply
Saboteur. Ha Jin
SABOTEURS *See* Sabotage
Sack, Daniel Ulanovsky
Home cooking
  With signs and wonders; an international anthology of Jewish fabulist fiction; edited by Daniel M. Jaffe
The **sacking** of Miss Plimsoll. Trevanian
Sacrament in the wind and the storm. Allegra, D.
SACRAMENTO (CALIF.) *See* California—Sacramento

The **sacred** mound. Foote, S.
The **sacred** society. What, L.
Sacred Statues. Trevor, W.
The **Sacred** Tree: Hawaiian. Loebel-Fried, C.
The **sacred** well. Wallace, R.
SACRIFICE
Karnezis, P. Sacrifice
SACRIFICE, HUMAN *See* Human sacrifice
Sacrifice. Karnezis, P.
Sacrifice. Lindskold, J. M.
Sacrifice. Thrasher, L. L.
Sad-eyed blonde. Lochte, D.
A **sad** smile. Régio, J.
Sada, Daniel
The basilisk
  Points of departure; new stories from Mexico; edited by Mónica Lavín; translated by Gustavo Segade
Saddlepoint: roughneck. Baxter, S.
Sade, marquis de
Augustine de Villeblanche; or, Love's strategy
  Sade, marquis de. The mystified magistrate and other tales; translated and with an introduction by Richard Seaver
Emilie de Tourville; or, Fraternal cruelty
  Sade, marquis de. The mystified magistrate and other tales; translated and with an introduction by Richard Seaver
An eye for an eye
  Sade, marquis de. The mystified magistrate and other tales; translated and with an introduction by Richard Seaver
The fortunate ruse
  Sade, marquis de. The mystified magistrate and other tales; translated and with an introduction by Richard Seaver
The Gascon wit
  Sade, marquis de. The mystified magistrate and other tales; translated and with an introduction by Richard Seaver
The husband who turned priest: a tale of Provence
  Sade, marquis de. The mystified magistrate and other tales; translated and with an introduction by Richard Seaver
The mystified magistrate
  Sade, marquis de. The mystified magistrate and other tales; translated and with an introduction by Richard Seaver
The properly punished pimp
  Sade, marquis de. The mystified magistrate and other tales; translated and with an introduction by Richard Seaver
Room for two
  Sade, marquis de. The mystified magistrate and other tales; translated and with an introduction by Richard Seaver
The teacher philosopher
  Sade, marquis de. The mystified magistrate and other tales; translated and with an introduction by Richard Seaver
Thieves and swindlers
  Sade, marquis de. The mystified magistrate and other tales; translated and with an introduction by Richard Seaver
The windbags of Provence
  Sade, marquis de. The mystified magistrate and other tales; translated and with an introduction by Richard Seaver

Sade, marquis de—*Continued*
Your wish is my command; or, As you like it
Sade, marquis de. The mystified magistrate
and other tales; translated and with an in-
troduction by Richard Seaver
Sade's mistress. Yuknavitch, L.
SADISM
See also Cruelty
Lawrence, D. H. The Prussian officer
Malouf, D. Night training
Sadler, Mark, 1924-
For works written by this author under oth-
er names see Collins, Michael, 1924-
The **sadness** of Doctor Mendoza. Herbert, J.
Sadness of the body. Brown, J.
Sadoff, Ira
In the house of the child
New England Review v22 no1 p115-28 Wint
2001
Stalky the clown
TriQuarterly no105 p73-85 Spr/Summ 1999
Saenz, Benjamin Alire
Exile
Graham, D. Lone Star literature; from the
Red River to the Rio Grande; edited by
Don Graham
Saer, Juan José
Community property
Iowa Review v31 no1 p117-20 Summ 2001
The investigation
Américas v51 no6 p64 N/D 1999
The non-cultural man
Iowa Review v31 no1 p121-4 Summ 2001
Safe. Braunbeck, G. A.
Safe forever. DeMarinis, R.
Safe love. Block, F. L.
Safe sex. Frisch, W.
Safe sex. Vachss, A. H.
Safe-T-Man. Ferriss, L.
The **safest** little town in Texas. Healy, J. F.
Safety. Brownstein, G.
Safety first. Talley, M.
Safety Man. Chaon, D.
Safety off, not a shot fired. Harfenist, J.
Safety Procedures. Gordimer, N.
Safeway. Bauman, B. A.
The **saga** of Pecos Bill. O'Reilly, E.
The **sages** of Cassiopeia. MacKay, S.
Sagstetter, Karen
The thing with Willie
New stories from the South: the year's best,
2000; edited by Shannon Ravenel; with a
preface by Ellen Douglas
SAHARA
Bowles, P. Istikhara, Anaya, Medagan and the
Medaganat
Saidi, William
The garden of evil
The Anchor book of modern African stories;
edited by Nadežda Obradovic ; with a fore-
word by Chinua Achebe
SAIGON (VIETNAM) *See* Vietnam—Ho Chi
Minh City
Saigon. Rawley, D.
Saigon Pull. Dinh, L.
Sail 25. Vance, J.
Sailing the painted ocean. Lee, D.
Sailing to Atlantis. Gorman, E.

SAILING VESSELS
Brown, J. Afternoon of the Sassanoa
Hodgson, W. H. The call in the dawn
Vivante, A. Crosscurrents
Sailor off the Bremen. Shaw, I.
SAILORS *See* Seamen
Sailors at their mourning: a memory. Deck, J.
Saint Anne. O'Connell, M.
Saint Augustine Was a Player Once. Almond, S.
Saint Bobby. Allyn, D.
Saint Catherine Laboure. O'Connell, M.
Saint Dymphna. O'Connell, M.
Saint Francis in Flint. Trevor, D.
SAINT JOHN (VIRGIN ISLANDS OF THE
U.S.)
Paine, T. The mayor of St. John
Saint Junior. Alexie, S.
SAINT LOUIS (MO.) *See* Missouri—Saint Louis
Saint-Malo, 1939. Hall, R.
Saint Marie. Erdrich, L.
Saint Martha. O'Connell, M.
Saint monster. Gurganus, A.
The **saint** of broken objects. Fennelly, B. A. and
Franklin, T.
SAINT PATRICK'S DAY
Hoch, E. D. Great day for the Irish
SAINT PETERSBURG (FLA.) *See* Florida—
Saint Petersburg
SAINT PETERSBURG (RUSSIA) *See* Russia—
St. Petersburg
Saint Therese of Lisieux. O'Connell, M.
SAINT THOMAS (VIRGIN ISLANDS OF THE
U.S.)
Buckell, T. S. Spurn Babylon
Saint Ursula and her maidens. O'Connell, M.
SAINT VALENTINE'S DAY *See* Valentine's
Day
SAINTS
Bowles, P. An inopportune visit
Lopez, B. H. The letters of heaven
Newman, S. Divine guidance
Saints. Mukherjee, B.
Sakaguchi, Joy Monica T.
A fortune
Pieces; a collection of new voices; edited by
Stephen Chbosky
Saki
Gabriel-Ernest
The Literary werewolf; an anthology; edited
by Charlotte F. Otten
The occasional garden
Of leaf and flower; stories and poems for gar-
deners; edited by Charles Dean and Clyde
Wachsberger; illustrations by Clyde
Wachsberger
The she-wolf
The Literary werewolf; an anthology; edited
by Charlotte F. Otten
Sredni Vashtar
Master's choice v2; mystery stories by to-
day's top writers and the masters who in-
spired them; edited by Lawrence Block
Saknussemm, Kris
Captain Galaxy comes back to earth
New Letters v68 no2 p77-87 2002
Faith and lightning
The Antioch Review v60 no3 p490-9 Summ
2002

Salaam, Kalamu ya *See* Kalamu ya Salaam, 1947-

Salaam, Kiini Ibura
  At life's limits
    Dark matter; a century of speculative fiction from the African diaspora; edited by Sheree R. Thomas
  Rosamojo
    Mojo: conjure stories; edited by Nalo Hopkinson

Salad days. Lee, W. W.

The **salad** diet. Johnson, S.

Salad girls. Harfenist, J.

Salak, Kira
  Beheadings
    Best new American voices 2001; guest editor Charles Baxter; series editors John Kulka and Natalie Danford
    Nixon under the bodhi tree and other works of Buddhist fiction; edited by Kate Wheeler ; foreword by Charles Johnson
    Prairie Schooner v75 no3 p160-85 Fall 2001

The **salamanders**. Rivera, T.

Saldaña, René
  El Bronco y La Lechuza
    Fantasmas; supernatural stories by Mexican American writers; edited by Rob Johnson; introduction by Kathleen J. Alcalá

The **Salem** Mass. See Hawthorne, N. Young Goodman Brown

Sales. Davies, P. H.

SALES PERSONNEL AND SELLING
  Anderson, P. The master key
  Barrett, L. To go
  Biguenet, J. The open curtain
  Cavell, B. Balls, balls, balls
  Cook, K. L. Costa Rica
  Davidson, R. What we leave behind
  Davies, P. H. Sales
  Deaver, J. Ninety-eight point six
  Dozois, G. R. Golden apples of the sun
  Edwards, M. 24 hours from Tulsa
  Eldridge, Courtney. Thieves
  Gansworth, E. L. The Raleigh Man
  Gurganus, A. Blessed assurance: a moral tale
  Gurganus, A. Saint monster
  Iribarne, M. Ross Willow's new and used cars
  Jen, G. Birthmates
  Kees, W. So cold outside
  Knight, M. Keeper of secrets, teller of lies
  Loomis, N. M. The St. Louis salesman
  Sánchez, R. Don Salomón
  Schaffert, T. Sound from the courtyard
  Singleton, G. The half-mammals of Dixie
  Singleton, G. Impurities
  Singleton, G. One man's indelible marks
  Tenn, W. Bernie the Faust
  Waugh, E. Too much tolerance

SALESMEN AND SALESMANSHIP *See* Sales personnel and selling

Ṣāliḥ, al-Ṭayyib
  A handful of dates
    The Anchor book of modern African stories; edited by Nadežda Obradović ; with a foreword by Chinua Achebe

Salih, Tayeb *See* Ṣāliḥ, al-Ṭayyib, 1929-

Salinas, Kim
  The Importance of Cardboard Boxes
    The Literary Review (Madison, N.J.) v46 no1 p8-11 Fall 2002

Salinger, J. D. (Jerome David)
  Slight rebellion off Madison
    Wonderful town; New York stories from The New Yorker; edited by David Remnick with Susan Choi

Salinger, Jerome David *See* Salinger, J. D. (Jerome David), 1919-

Salisbury, Ralph
  Hoopa, the white deer dance
    The Year's best fantasy & horror, twelfth annual collection; edited by Ellen Datlow & Terry Windling

Salkey, Andrew
  A proper Anno Domini feeling
    The Oxford book of Caribbean short stories; edited by Stewart Brown and John Wickham

Sallie C. Barrett, N., Jr.

Sallis, James
  Dear floods of her hair
    The Year's best fantasy & horror, thirteenth annual collection; edited by Ellen Datlow and Terri Windling

Sally the Slut. Beller, T.

Sally's story. Malouf, D.

Sally's story. Richter, S.

SALMON FISHING
  Dauenhauer, N. Egg boat
  Reid, E. What salmon know

Salt. Babel´, I.

Salt. Kalfus, K.

Salt Lake. Wieland, L.

Salt Women. Heller, Y. B.-Z.

Salter, James
  Bangkok
    The Paris Review v45 p202-9 Summ 2003
  Last Night
    The New Yorker v78 no35 p82-6 N 18 2002

Salter, John
  Barley
    The Massachusetts Review v40 no3 p368-74 Aut 1999
  Big ranch
    The Best American mystery stories, 2001; edited and with an Introduction by Lawrence Block

The **saltimbanques**. Dowling, T.

Salvage. Yolen, J.

SALVATION
  See also Atonement
  Swarthout, G. F. O captain, my captain

Salvatore, Diane
  A World Apart
    Good Housekeeping v235 no5 p213-18 N 2002

Salvatori, Claudia
  The flight of the elephant
    In the forbidden city; an anthology of erotic fiction by Italian women; edited by Maria Rosa Cutrufelli; translated by Vincent J. Bertolini

Salve Regina. Leroy, J. T.

Salve regina. Pritchard, M.

Salzer, Susan K.

Miss Libbie tells all

Westward; a fictional history of the American West : 28 original stories celebrating the 50th anniversary of the Western Writers of America; edited by Dale L. Walker

Sam Hall. Anderson, P.

The **samaritan**. Bishop, P.

Samba de los agentes. Codrescu, A.

The **Sambomorphosis**. Touré

The **same** in any language. Campbell, R.

Same old big magic. Henley, P.

Same place, same things. Gautreaux, T.

The **same** sea as every summer [excerpt] Tusquets, E.

Sammān, Ghādah

An air-conditioned egg

Sammān, G. The square moon; supernatural tales; translated from the Arabic by Issa J. Boullata

Beheading the cat

Sammān, G. The square moon; supernatural tales; translated from the Arabic by Issa J. Boullata

The brain's closed castle

Sammān, G. The square moon; supernatural tales; translated from the Arabic by Issa J. Boullata

The metallic crocodile

Sammān, G. The square moon; supernatural tales; translated from the Arabic by Issa J. Boullata

The other side of the door

Sammān, G. The square moon; supernatural tales; translated from the Arabic by Issa J. Boullata

The plot against Badi'

Sammān, G. The square moon; supernatural tales; translated from the Arabic by Issa J. Boullata

Register: I'm not an Arab woman

Sammān, G. The square moon; supernatural tales; translated from the Arabic by Issa J. Boullata

The swan genie

Sammān, G. The square moon; supernatural tales; translated from the Arabic by Issa J. Boullata

Thirty years of bees

Sammān, G. The square moon; supernatural tales; translated from the Arabic by Issa J. Boullata

Visitors of a dying person

Sammān, G. The square moon; supernatural tales; translated from the Arabic by Issa J. Boullata

Sampler. Aylett, S.

Samsara. Leong, R.

Samuel Beckett's Middlemarch. Berry, R. M.

SAMURAI

Yoshikawa, E. Musashi [excerpt]

SAN ANTONIO (TEX.) *See* Texas—San Antonio

SAN FRANCISCO (CALIF.) *See* California—San Francisco

The **San** Francisco Indians. Ortiz, S. J.

SAN MARTÍN, JOSÉ DE, 1778?-1850

About

Borges, J. L. Guayaquil

Sana, sana, colita de rana. Matiella, A. C.

Sanabria Santaliz, Edgardo

After the hurricane

The Oxford book of Caribbean short stories; edited by Stewart Brown and John Wickham

SANATORIUMS *See* Hospitals and sanatoriums

Sánchez, Alberto Ruy *See* Ruy Sánchez, Alberto, 1951-

Sánchez, Luis Rafael

Getting even

The Vintage book of Latin American stories; edited by Carlos Fuentes and Julio Ortega

Sánchez, Rosaura

Barrio chronicle

Sánchez, R. He walked in and sat down and other stories; English translation by Beatrice Pita

The brand new suit

Sánchez, R. He walked in and sat down and other stories; English translation by Beatrice Pita

Dallas

Sánchez, R. He walked in and sat down and other stories; English translation by Beatrice Pita

The ditch

Sánchez, R. He walked in and sat down and other stories; English translation by Beatrice Pita

Don Salomón

Sánchez, R. He walked in and sat down and other stories; English translation by Beatrice Pita

The fields

Sánchez, R. He walked in and sat down and other stories; English translation by Beatrice Pita

He rolled up his sleeves

Sánchez, R. He walked in and sat down and other stories; English translation by Beatrice Pita

He walked in and sat down

Sánchez, R. He walked in and sat down and other stories; English translation by Beatrice Pita

Like I was telling you . . .

Sánchez, R. He walked in and sat down and other stories; English translation by Beatrice Pita

Lucho

Sánchez, R. He walked in and sat down and other stories; English translation by Beatrice Pita

One morning: 1952

Sánchez, R. He walked in and sat down and other stories; English translation by Beatrice Pita

One night

Sánchez, R. He walked in and sat down and other stories; English translation by Beatrice Pita

Road detours

Sánchez, R. He walked in and sat down and other stories; English translation by Beatrice Pita

El tejón

Sánchez, R. He walked in and sat down and other stories; English translation by Beatrice Pita

Sánchez, Rosaura—*Continued*
  Three generations
    Sánchez, R. He walked in and sat down and
      other stories; English translation by Be-
      atrice Pita
Sanchez, Sonia
  Wounded in the house of a friend
    The Bluelight corner; black women writing on
      passion, sex, and romantic love; edited by
      Rosemarie Robotham
Sanctuary. Bissoondath, N.
Sanctuary. Novotny, R.
Sanctuary. Tenn, W.
Sanctuary. Wharton, E.
Sand and other grit. Smyth, C.
SAND CREEK MASSACRE, COLO., 1864
  Black, M. The hundred day men
Sand trap. L'Amour, L.
The **sandbox.** Skillings, R. D.
Sanders, Gregory
  The Pantomine [i.e. Pantomime] Horse
    South Carolina Review v33 no2 p93-100 Spr
      2001
Sanders, Ted
  Putting the Lizard to Sleep
    The Georgia Review v57 no4 p777-96 Wint
      2003
Sanders, William
  The scuttling; or, Down by the sea with Marvin
    and Pamela
    Witpunk; edited by Claude Lalumière and
      Marty Halpern
  The undiscovered
    The Best alternate history stories of the 20th
      century; edited by Harry Turtledove with
      Martin H. Greenberg
  When this world is all on fire
    The Year's best science fiction, nineteenth an-
      nual collection; edited by Gardner Dozois
Sanderson, Jim
  Commerce Street
    Graham, D. Lone Star literature; from the
      Red River to the Rio Grande; edited by
      Don Graham
  Ladies' man
    Texas bound. Book III; 22 Texas stories; ed-
      ited by Kay Cattarulla; foreword by Robert
      Flynn
Sandford, Rick
  Manifest white
    His 3: brilliant new fiction by gay writers; ed-
      ited by Robert Drake and Terry Wolverton
Sandhill cranes. Coleman, J. C.
Sandifer, Linda
  Betrayal
    Westward; a fictional history of the American
      West : 28 original stories celebrating the
      50th anniversary of the Western Writers of
      America; edited by Dale L. Walker
Sandkings. Martin, G. R. R.
Sandlin, Lisa
  Another exciting day in Santa Fe
    Sandlin, L. In the river province; stories
  Beautiful
    Sandlin, L. In the river province; stories
  Everything moves
    Sandlin, L. In the river province; stories
  I loved you then, I love you still
    Sandlin, L. In the river province; stories

Night class
    Sandlin, L. In the river province; stories
'Orita on the road to Chimayó
    A different plain; contemporary Nebraska fic-
      tion writers; edited by Ladette Randolph ;
      introduction by Mary Pipher
    Sandlin, L. In the river province; stories
The saint of bilocation
    Sandlin, L. In the river province; stories
Sandor, Marjorie
  Annunciation
    Sandor, M. Portrait of my mother, who posed
      nude in wartime; stories
  Capacity
    Sandor, M. Portrait of my mother, who posed
      nude in wartime; stories
    The Southern Review (Baton Rouge, La.) v37
      no3 p559-71 Summ 2001
  Elegy for Miss Beagle
    Sandor, M. Portrait of my mother, who posed
      nude in wartime; stories
  God's spies
    Sandor, M. Portrait of my mother, who posed
      nude in wartime; stories
  Gravity
    Sandor, M. Portrait of my mother, who posed
      nude in wartime; stories
  The handcuff king
    Sandor, M. Portrait of my mother, who posed
      nude in wartime; stories
  Legend
    Sandor, M. Portrait of my mother, who posed
      nude in wartime; stories
  Malingerer
    The Georgia Review v56 no4 p918-32 Wint
      2002
    Sandor, M. Portrait of my mother, who posed
      nude in wartime; stories
  Portrait of my mother, who posed nude in war-
    time
    Sandor, M. Portrait of my mother, who posed
      nude in wartime; stories
SANDSTORMS *See* Storms
Sandstrom, Eve K.
  The people's way
    Love and death; edited by Carolyn Hart
Sanford, Annette
  Bear the dead away
    Sanford, A. Crossing Shattuck Bridge; stories
  Crossing Shattuck Bridge
    Sanford, A. Crossing Shattuck Bridge; stories
  Fo Nut X
    Sanford, A. Crossing Shattuck Bridge; stories
  Goose girl
    Sanford, A. Crossing Shattuck Bridge; stories
  Helens and Roses
    Sanford, A. Crossing Shattuck Bridge; stories
  Housekeeping
    Sanford, A. Crossing Shattuck Bridge; stories
  In the Little Hunky River
    Sanford, A. Crossing Shattuck Bridge; stories
  Mr. Moore's old car
    Sanford, A. Crossing Shattuck Bridge; stories
    Texas bound. Book III; 22 Texas stories; ed-
      ited by Kay Cattarulla; foreword by Robert
      Flynn

Sanford, Annette—*Continued*
Nobody listens when I talk
The Best American short stories 2001; select-
ed from U.S. and Canadian magazines by
Barbara Kingsolver with Katrina Kenison;
with an introduction by Barbara Kingsolver
The oil of gladness
Sanford, A. Crossing Shattuck Bridge; stories
One summer
New stories from the South; the year's best,
2004; edited by Shannon Ravenel; preface
by Tim Gautreaux
Spring '41
Prairie Schooner v77 no4 p42-53 Wint 2003
Strangers and pilgrims
Sanford, A. Crossing Shattuck Bridge; stories
The **sanguine** blood of men. Gilchrist, E.

SANITATION
Blish, J. A dusk of idols
Bradbury, R. The garbage collector
The **Sanitorium** Syndrome. Duras, M.
Sanity. Leiber, F.
Sanity clause. Wellen, E.

Sankaran, Lavanya
The Red Carpet
Atlantic Monthly (1993) v292 no5 p163-8,
170-8 D 2003
Sans paroles. Karp-Gendre, J.
SANTA BARBARA (CALIF.) *See* California—
Santa Barbara
SANTA CLAUS
Baum, L. F. A kidnapped Santa Claus
Ellison, H. Santa Claus vs. S.P.I.D.E.R.
Englander, N. Reb Kringle
Gaiman, N. Nicholas was. . .
Gibson, W. Cyber-Claus
Matheson, R. C. Holiday
McCaffrey, A. A proper Santa Claus
Paul, B. Ho ho ho
Powell, J. The plot against Santa Claus
Thomsen, B. It's a wonderful miracle on 34th
Street's Christmas carol
Vonnegut, K. A present for Big Saint Nick
Vukcevich, R. Ceremony
Williamson, C. O come little children. . .
The **Santa** Claus caper. Crider, B.
Santa Claus vs. S.P.I.D.E.R. Ellison, H.
SANTA CRUZ (CALIF.) *See* California—Santa
Cruz
SANTA FE (N.M.) *See* New Mexico—Santa Fe
SANTA FE TRAIL
Henry, W. Comanche passport
Henry, W. The skinning of Black Coyote
Santa Monica. Carlson, R.
Santaliz, Edgardo Sanabria *See* Sanabria
Santaliz, Edgardo, 1951-
SANTAYANA, GEORGE, 1863-1952
About
Davenport, G. Dinner at the Bank of England
Santayana speaks through me. Singleton, G.
Santiesteban Prats, Angel
13th parallel south
Dream with no name; contemporary fiction
from Cuba; edited by Juana Ponce de León
and Esteban Ríos Rivera
**SANTO DOMINGO (DOMINICAN REPUB-
LIC)** *See* Dominican Republic—Santo Do-
mingo

Santos-Febres, Mayra
Flight
Colchie, T. A whistler in the nightworld;
short fiction from the Latin Americas; ed-
ited by Thomas Colchie
Sap rising. Lincoln, C.
SAPPHO
About
Yourcenar, M. Sappho; or, Suicide
Sappho; or, Suicide. Yourcenar, M.
Sarah, Robyn
Drift
The Hudson Review v57 no1 p57-66 Spr 2004
Sarah. Orner, P.
Sarah Canary [excerpt] Fowler, K. J.
Sarah Cole: a type of love story. Banks, R.
Sarah's story. Vromen, G.
SARAJEVO (BOSNIA AND HERCEGOVINA)
See Bosnia and Hercegovina—Sarajevo
Saramago, José
The tale of the unknown island
The Paris Review v41 no151 p16-32 Summ
1999
Sarath, Patrice E.
The djinn game
Such a pretty face; edited by Lee Martindale
Sarduy, Severo
Curriculum cubense
Dream with no name; contemporary fiction
from Cuba; edited by Juana Ponce de León
and Esteban Ríos Rivera
SARGENT, JOHN SINGER, 1856-1925
About
Gurganus, A. The practical heart
Sargent, Pamela
Dream of Venus
Worldmakers; SF adventures in terraforming;
edited by Gardner Dozois
Sari, Fereshteh
The absent soldier
A Feast in the mirror; stories by contempo-
rary Iranian women; translated and edited
by Mohammad Mehdi Khorrami, Shouleh
Vatanabadi
Sariol, José Prats
Grilled Shrimp Pasta
Boundary 2 v29 no3 p235-46 Fall 2002
Saro-Wiwa, Ken
Africa kills her sun
The Anchor book of modern African stories;
edited by Nadežda Obradovic ; with a fore-
word by Chinua Achebe
The Art of the story; an international antholo-
gy of contemporary short stories; edited by
Daniel Halpern
Saroyan, Aram
Bicoastal
Saroyan, A. Artists in trouble; new stories
Chloe
Saroyan, A. Artists in trouble; new stories
The dead
Saroyan, A. Artists in trouble; new stories
Double fries
Saroyan, A. Artists in trouble; new stories
The genius
Saroyan, A. Artists in trouble; new stories
Grand Street
Saroyan, A. Artists in trouble; new stories

Saroyan, Aram—*Continued*

Hollywood lessons
　Saroyan, A. Artists in trouble; new stories
Jobs
　Saroyan, A. Artists in trouble; new stories
Love scenes
　Saroyan, A. Artists in trouble; new stories
M
　Saroyan, A. Artists in trouble; new stories
The musician
　Saroyan, A. Artists in trouble; new stories
My literary life
　Saroyan, A. Artists in trouble; new stories
The shape of jazz to come
　Saroyan, A. Artists in trouble; new stories
Traffic school
　Saroyan, A. Artists in trouble; new stories
The war
　Saroyan, A. Artists in trouble; new stories

Saroyan, William

The pomegranate trees
　Of leaf and flower; stories and poems for gardeners; edited by Charles Dean and Clyde Wachsberger; illustrations by Clyde Wachsberger
Resurrection of a life
　The Best American short stories of the century; John Updike, editor, Katrina Kenison, coeditor; with an introduction by John Updike

Sarrantonio, Al

Billy the fetus
　Redshift; extreme visions of speculative fiction; edited by Al Sarrantonio
Pumpkin head
　The Ultimate Halloween; edited by Marvin Kaye
The ropy thing
　999: new stories of horror and suspense; edited by Al Sarrantonio
Wish
　Children of the night; stories of ghosts, vampires, werewolves, and "lost children"; edited by Martin H. Greenberg

Sarrushka and her daughter. Jaffe, D. M.

SARTRE, JEAN PAUL, 1905-1980

About

Brandt, W. The Jean-Paul Sartre experience

SASKATCHEWAN *See* Canada—Saskatchewan

Saskia. De Lint, C.

SATANISM

　See also Demoniac possession

Satellite. Richmond, M.

Satellites or airplanes. Grodstein, L.

SATIRE

　See also Humor; Irony; Parodies

Alexie, S. South by Southwest
Amis, M. Career move
Amis, M. The coincidence of the arts
Amis, M. Straight fiction
Arreola, J. J. Baby H. P.
Barthelme, D. Game
Barthelme, D. I bought a little city
Bennett, A. The laying on of hands
Berners, G. H. T.-W., Baron. Count Omega
Berners, G. H. T.-W., Baron. Far from the madding war
Berney, L. Stupid girl
Bester, A. The men who murdered Mohammed

Biguenet, J. My slave
Borges, J. L. The disinterested killer Bill Harrigan
Borges, J. L. Hakim, the masked dyer of Merv
Borges, J. L. Monk Eastman, purveyor of iniquities
Borges, J. L. Pierre Menard, author of the Quixote
Borges, J. L. A survey of the works of Herbert Quain
Boyle, T. C. Rara avis
Bradbury, R. The dragon danced at midnight
Bradbury, R. The John Wilkes Booth/Warner Brothers/MGM/NBC funeral train
Bradbury, R. Olé Orozco! Siqueiros, sí!
Bradbury, R. The watchful poker chip of H. Matisse
Budnitz, J. Average Joe
Budnitz, J. Got spirit
Budnitz, J. Yellville
Bukiet, M. J. Paper hero
Carlson, R. The Tablecloth of Turnin
Chan, M. At the premier's literary awards
Chekhov, A. P. A chameleon
Chekhov, A. P. Fat and thin
Chekhov, A. P. Hush!
Chekhov, A. P. No comment
Chekhov, A. P. The orator
Chekhov, A. P. Sergeant Prishibeyev
Chesnutt, C. W. Cartwright's mistake
Clarke, A. C. On golden seas
Clarke, B. The Lolita School
Codrescu, A. The herald
Cohen, S. How much justice can you afford?
DeMarco, T. Nahigian's Day in court
Derby, M. An appeal
Derby, M. Behavior pilot
Derby, M. The boyish mulatto
Derby, M. Crutches used as weapon
Derby, M. The end of men
Derby, M. The father helmet
Derby, M. First
Derby, M. Gantry's last
Derby, M. Home recordings
Derby, M. Instructions
Derby, M. Joy of eating
Derby, M. The life jacket
Derby, M. Meat tower
Derby, M. Night watchmen
Derby, M. Sky harvest
Derby, M. The sound gun
Derby, M. Stupid animals
Desplechin, M. Joy
Devereaux, R. Li'l Miss Ultrasound
Di Filippo, P. Weeping walls
Dilts, Tyler. Thug: signification and the (de) constuction of self
Disch, T. M. The first annual performance art festival at the Slaughter Rock Battlefield
Doctorow, C. Power punctuation!
Doctorow, C. To market, to market: the rebranding of Billy Bailey
Douglas, E. I just love Carrie Lee
Evenson, B. Moran's Mexico: a refutation by C. Stelzmann
Fitzgerald, F. S. Dalyrimple goes wrong
Fowler, K. J. The travails
Geng, V. Partners
Ha Jin. A tiger-fighter is hard to find

SATIRE—*Continued*

Hamburger, A. This ground you are standing on

Harris, M. From the desk of the troublesome editor

Hawthorne, N. Mrs. Bullfrog

Heller, J. Catch-23: Yossarian lives

Heller, J. Chief White Halfoat

Himes, C. Lunching at the Ritzmore

Hobson, C. The bottle: a provincial tale

Homes, A. M. The Chinese lesson

Jenkins, G. Spin

Johnson, A. Teen sniper

Keret, E. Goodman

Keret, E. The mysterious disappearance of Alon Shemesh

Keret, E. A souvenir of Hell

Keret, E. The story about a bus driver who wanted to be God

Knight, P. Set in stone

Kurlansky, M. Naked

Lafferty, R. A. Eurema's dam

Landis, G. A. What we really do here at NASA

Lao She. No distance too far, no sacrifice too great

Le Guin, U. K. Great joy

Mann, A. Taking care of Frank

Michaels, L. Some laughed

Morrow, J. Auspicious eggs

Newman, K. The intervention

Nuñez, M. E. A. The girl typist who worked for a provincial ministry of culture

Paine, T. Unapproved minutes of the Carthage, Vermont, Zoning Board of Adjustment

Paley, G. Wants

Parker, G. Scenes from new Europe

Pearlman, D. D. Over the H.I.L.L.

Pelevin, V. The life and adventures of shed number XII

Pronzini, B. A craving for originality

Pronzini, B. and Malzberg, B. N. Shakespeare MCMLXXXV

Reed, I. Future Christmas

Sade, marquis de. The windbags of Provence

Saki. The occasional garden

Saunders, G. Pastoralia

Saunders, G. The 400-pound CEO

Singleton, G. Richard Petty accepts national book ward

Skeet, Michael. I love Paree

Smith, J. Grief counselor

Sorrentino, G. The dignity of labor

Steele, A. M. Green acres

Steele, A. M. Tom Swift and his humongous mechanical dude

Stevenson, J. Crossing the water

Sturgeon, T. Microcosmic god

Tenn, W. On Venus, have we got a rabbi

Tenn, W. Time in advance

Touré. Afrolexicology today's biannual list of the top fifty words in African-American

Touré. The Sambomorphosis

Updike, J. During the Jurassic

Updike, J. How to love America and leave it at the same time

Updike, J. Minutes of the last meeting

Vaswani, N. An outline of no direction

Vega, A. L. Cloud cover Caribbean

Vinge, V. Win a Nobel Prize!

Wallace, D. F. Another pioneer

Wallace, D. F. Mister Squishy

Wallace, D. F. The Suffering Channel

Waugh, E. Basil Seal rides again

Waugh, E. An Englishman's home

Waugh, E. Love among the ruins

Waugh, E. On guard

Waugh, E. Winner takes all

Weaver, G. Gilded Quill: the story of Jones

Weaver, G. Solidarity forever!

Weldon, F. The ghost of potlatch past

Weldon, F. What the papers say

Wharton, E. Xingu

Whitty, J. Senti's last elephant

Worth, V. Geoffrey Sonnabend's obliscence: theories of forgetting and the problem of matter—an encapsulation

Yolen, J. Creationism: an illustrated lecture in two parts

Satire. Shields, D.

Satterthwait, Walter

The cassoulet

Murder most delectable; savory tales of culinary crimes; edited by Martin H. Greenberg

A mishap at the manor

Malice domestic 9

Saturday. Sell, S.

Saturday afternoon at the zoo with dad. Epstein, J.

Saturday Afternoon in the Holocaust Museum. Morgan, E. S.

Saturday belongs to the palomía. Garza, D. L.

The **Saturday** Morning Car Wash Club. Thomas, J. E.

Saturday Night Function. Lyon, A.

SATURN (PLANET)

Clarke, A. C. Saturn rising

Saturn. Gates, D.

The **Saturn** game. Anderson, P.

Saturn rising. Clarke, A. C.

Sauce for the goose. Brewer, G.

A **saucer** of loneliness. Sturgeon, T.

Saulnier, Beth

High maintenance

The Mysterious Press anniversary anthology; celebrating 25 years; by the editors of Mysterious Press

Sault Ste. Marie. Means, D.

Saum, Steven Boyd

Good night, Mr. Khrushchev

The Kenyon Review ns23 no3/4 p144-65 Summ/Fall 2001

Saumont, Annie

Dou you spik Frrench?

The Antioch Review v59 no4 p724-32 Fall 2001

Saunders, Charles R.

Gimmile's songs

Dark matter; a century of speculative fiction from the African diaspora; edited by Sheree R. Thomas

Saunders, George

Adams

The New Yorker v80 no22 p86-8 Ag 9-16 2004

The barber's unhappiness

The New Yorker v75 no39 p74-84 D 20 1999

Bohemians

The New Yorker v79 no43 p74-9 Ja 19 2004

Saunders, George—*Continued*
  I can speak!™
    The New Yorker v75 no16 p85+ Je 21-28 1999
  Jon
    The New Yorker v78 no44 p70-83 Ja 27 2003
  My flamboyant grandson
    The New Yorker v77 no45 p78-81 Ja 28 2002
  Pastoralia
    Prize stories, 2001; The O. Henry awards; edited and with an introduction by Larry Dark
  The Red Bow
    Esquire v140 no3 p192-5 S 2003
  Sea Oak
    Prize stories, 1999; The O. Henry awards; edited and with an introduction by Larry Dark
  The 400-pound CEO
    What are you looking at?; the first fat fiction anthology; edited by Donna Jarrell and Ira Sukrungruang

Saunders, Gerda
  The epistemology
    Saunders, G. Blessings on the sheep dog; stories
  My brother can tell
    Saunders, G. Blessings on the sheep dog; stories
  No money for stamps
    Saunders, G. Blessings on the sheep dog; stories
  A sudden new city
    Saunders, G. Blessings on the sheep dog; stories
  Walking legs
    Saunders, G. Blessings on the sheep dog; stories
  We'll get to now later
    Saunders, G. Blessings on the sheep dog; stories

Sausages. Hoover, M.
Sautéing the platygast. Paschal, D.

Savage, Les, Jr.
  The hangman's segundo
    Savage, L., Jr. The sting of Señorita Scorpion; a western trio
  His personal prisoner
    The First Five Star western corral; western stories; edited by Jon Tuska and Vicki Piekarski
  King of the buckskin breed
    A Century of great Western stories; edited by John Jakes
  The Lone Star camel corps
    Savage, L., Jr. The sting of Señorita Scorpion; a western trio
  The sting of Señorita Scorpion
    Savage, L., Jr. The sting of Señorita Scorpion; a western trio

Savage, Ron
  King of Handcuffs
    Film Comment v40 no4 p66, 68-71 Jl/Ag 2004

Savage, Tom
  One of us
    Blood on their hands; edited by Lawrence Block
The **savage**. Collins, M.

SAVANNAH (GA.) *See* Georgia—Savannah
Savant. Hensley, J. L.
Savasana. Moody, R.
Save the reaper. Munro, A.
Save yourself. Wexler, M.
Saved. Brite, P. Z. and Faust, C.

Savić, Milisav
  Stifling
    Grand Street no68 p215-22 Spr 1999

SAVING AND THRIFT
  Drake, R. Shrouds with pockets in them
Saving Saul. Krawiec, R.
Savior. Kress, N.
Saviors. Rowell, J.
The **saviors**. Vollmann, W. T.
Savoir faire. Barone, D.
Saw marks. Patterson, K.
Saw you see me. Harms, J.

Sawyer, Robert J.
  Black reflection
    Tetrick, B. In the shadow of the wall; an anthology of Vietnam stories that might have been; edited by Byron R. Tetrick
Sax and the single cat. Carole Nelson Douglas
Sax and the single cat. Douglas, C. N.

Saxon, Malachi
  (jt. auth) See Perry, Anne and Saxon, Malachi
Say goodbye to Middletown. Mann, W. J.
Say something to Miss Kathleen Lacey. Goran, L.
Say When. Townley, R.

Sayers, Dorothy L. (Dorothy Leigh)
  The man who knew how
    A moment on the edge; 100 years of crime stories by women; edited by Elizabeth George

Sayers, Valerie
  An Education in the Faith
    Prairie Schooner v77 no3 p33-54 Fall 2003
Saying goodbye to Sally. Yates, R.
Saying hello. Dobyns, S.

Saylor, Steven
  Poppy and the poisoned cake
    Crème de la crime; edited by Janet Hutchings
Sayonara. Hay, E.
Scaling ice. Anderson, D.
Scandal. Edghill, R.
The **scanner**. Frank, J.
Scanners live in vain. Smith, C.
Scar Vegas. Paine, T.

Scarborough, Dorothy
  From the wind [excerpt]
    Graham, D. Lone Star literature; from the Red River to the Rio Grande; edited by Don Graham

Scarborough, Elizabeth Ann
  The filial fiddler
    Greenberg, M. H. Faerie tales
  The invisible woman's clever disguise
    Mardi Gras madness; tales of terror and mayhem in New Orleans; edited by Martin H. Greenberg and Russell Davis
  Soulmates
    Past lives, present tense; edited by Elizabeth Ann Scarborough
  Tinkler Tam and the body snatchers
    Cat crimes through time; edited by Ed Gorman, Martin H. Greenberg, and Larry Segriff

Scarborough, Elizabeth Ann—*Continued*
Worse than the curse
Such a pretty face; edited by Lee Martindale
Scarborough, Elizabeth Ann and Reaser, Rick
Long time coming home
Tetrick, B. In the shadow of the wall; an anthology of Vietnam stories that might have been; edited by Byron R. Tetrick
Scarecrow. Canty, K.
Scarecrow. Davis, L.
Scarecrow. House, T.
Scarecrowed. Ockert, J.
SCARECROWS
Hawthorne, N. Feathertop
Hawthorne, N. Feathertop: a moralized legend
Lansdale, J. R. and others. The companion
The **scarf**. Oates, J. C.
Scaring the baddest animal. Spain, C.
The **scarlet** letters. Auchincloss, L.
The **scarred** man. Benford, G.
Scat. Paul, B.
Scattered thorns. Tremayne, P.
Scattershot. Bear, G.
Scavenger hunt. Stuckey-French, E.
The **scavenger's** eye. Leslie, N.
Scenes from the fall fashion catalog. Budnitz, J.
Scenes from the fifties. Updike, J.
The **scent** of winter. Keegan, C.
Schaefer, Jack Warner
Sergeant Houck
A Century of great Western stories; edited by John Jakes
Schaefer, William D.
Father's Day
The Virginia Quarterly Review v78 no4 p689-705 Aut 2002
Schaeffer, Susan Fromberg
The old farmhouse and the dog-wife
Best of Prairie schooner; fiction and poetry; edited by Hilda Raz
Schafer, Mark
(jt. auth) See Bolaño, Roberto
Schaffert, Timothy
Parts and labor
Prairie Schooner v75 no1 p52-61 Spr 2001
Sound from the courtyard
A different plain; contemporary Nebraska fiction writers; edited by Ladette Randolph ; introduction by Mary Pipher
Schaffler, Federico *See* Schaffler González, Federico, 1959-
Schaffler González, Federico
A miscalculation
Cosmos latinos: an anthology of science fiction from Latin America and Spain; translated, edited, & with an introduction & notes by Andrea L. Bell & Yolanda Molina-Gavilán
Schaller, Eric
The assistant to Dr. Jacob
The Year's best fantasy & horror: sixteenth annual collection; edited by Ellen Datlow & Terri Windling
Schandorsky's mother. Joseph, D.
Schaum, Melita
Triptych
The Literary Review (Madison, N.J.) v47 no2 p106-18 Wint 2004
Scheherazade. Tomlinson, N. C.

Scheheresade. Beltran, R.
Scheid, Susan
Daguerreotypy
Prairie Schooner v76 no3 p131-46 Fall 2002
Schein, Gina
Minnie gets married
The Vintage book of international lesbian fiction; edited and with an introduction by Naomi Holoch and Joan Nestle
Schering PC4—a love story. Knight, J.
Scherzo with tyrannosaur. Swanwick, M.
Schickler, David
Anna's way
Seventeen v60 no8 p238-42 Ag 2001
Jamaica
The New Yorker v77 no42 p64-70 Ja 7 2002
The smoker
Prize stories, 2001; The O. Henry awards; edited and with an introduction by Larry Dark
Wes Amerigo's Giant Fear
The New Yorker v79 no4 p130-9 Mr 17 2003
Schiff, Susan
Useful Fictions
The Massachusetts Review v43 no4 p660-7 Wint 2002/2003
Schiffman, Carl
A child's voice
New England Review v20 no2 p89-96 Spr 1999
Curly Hamson Learns How to Eat
The Antioch Review v61 no2 p345-59 Spr 2003
Seeing in the dark
Prairie Schooner v73 no1 p152-64 Spr 1999
Toys R Us
The Southern Review (Baton Rouge, La.) v37 no3 p572-87 Summ 2001
Schirmer, Robert
Burning
Prize stories, 1999; The O. Henry awards; edited and with an introduction by Larry Dark
Schism. Anderson, R.
SCHIZOPHRENIA
See also Dual personality; Personality disorders
Blish, J. Testament of Andros
Di Blasi, D. The season's condition
Sammān, G. The plot against Badi'
Weinberg, R. Ro Erg
Schlaks, Maximilian
The new maid
The Massachusetts Review v43 no1 p159-80 Spr 2002
Schlein, Katie
Advenar
The North American Review v288 no6 p29-31 N/D 2003
Schlink, Bernhard
The circumcision
Schlink, B. Flights of love; stories; translated from the German by John E. Woods
Girl with lizard
The New Yorker v77 no22 p64-77 Ag 6 2001
Schlink, B. Flights of love; stories; translated from the German by John E. Woods

Schlink, Bernhard—*Continued*
A little fling
  Schlink, B. Flights of love; stories; translated from the German by John E. Woods
The other man
  Schlink, B. Flights of love; stories; translated from the German by John E. Woods
The son
  Schlink, B. Flights of love; stories; translated from the German by John E. Woods
Sugar peas
  Schlink, B. Flights of love; stories; translated from the German by John E. Woods
The woman at the gas station
  Schlink, B. Flights of love; stories; translated from the German by John E. Woods
Schmand, Timothy
Come fly with me
  Ghost writing; haunted tales by contemporary writers; edited by Roger Weingarten
Schmatz, Pat
Tokyo trains
  Hers 3: brilliant new fiction by lesbian writers; edited by Terry Wolverton with Robert Drake
Schmid, Werner Art
Alone
  Prairie Schooner v73 no3 p109-10 Fall 1999
Schmidt, Heidi Jon
Blood poison
  Schmidt, H. J. Darling?
Darling?
  Schmidt, H. J. Darling?
An early death
  Schmidt, H. J. Darling?
Fishman's fascination
  Schmidt, H. J. Darling?
The funeral party
  Schmidt, H. J. Darling?
A girl like you
  Schmidt, H. J. Darling?
Out of Purmort
  Schmidt, H. J. Darling?
Six figures in search of an author
  Schmidt, H. J. Darling?
Songbirds
  Schmidt, H. J. Darling?
Wild rice
  Schmidt, H. J. Darling?
Schmidt, Stanley
The emperor's revenge
  Once upon a galaxy; edited by Will [sic] McCarthy, Martin H. Greenberg, and John Helfers
Schmitt, Richard
Leaving Venice, Florida
  New stories from the South: the year's best, 1999; edited by Shannon Ravenel; with a preface by Tony Earley
Schmitz, James H.
The second night of summer
  The Good old stuff; adventure SF in the grand tradition; edited by Gardner Dozois
Schneider, Peter
Burros gone bad
  Redshift; extreme visions of speculative fiction; edited by Al Sarrantonio

Des saucisses, sans doute
  999: new stories of horror and suspense; edited by Al Sarrantonio
Schnitzler, Arthur
Baron von Leisenbohg's destiny
  Schnitzler, A. Night gamesand other stories and novellas; and other stories and novellas; translated from the German by Margret Schaefer; with a foreword by John Simon
Blind Geronimo and his brother
  Schnitzler, A. Night gamesand other stories and novellas; and other stories and novellas; translated from the German by Margret Schaefer; with a foreword by John Simon
The dead are silent
  Schnitzler, A. Night gamesand other stories and novellas; and other stories and novellas; translated from the German by Margret Schaefer; with a foreword by John Simon
Death of a bachelor
  Schnitzler, A. Night gamesand other stories and novellas; and other stories and novellas; translated from the German by Margret Schaefer; with a foreword by John Simon
Dream story
  Schnitzler, A. Night gamesand other stories and novellas; and other stories and novellas; translated from the German by Margret Schaefer; with a foreword by John Simon
Dying
  Schnitzler, A. Desire and delusion; three novellas; selected and translated from the German by Margret Schaefer
A farewell
  Schnitzler, A. Night gamesand other stories and novellas; and other stories and novellas; translated from the German by Margret Schaefer; with a foreword by John Simon
Flight into darkness
  Schnitzler, A. Desire and delusion; three novellas; selected and translated from the German by Margret Schaefer
Fräulein Else
  Schnitzler, A. Desire and delusion; three novellas; selected and translated from the German by Margret Schaefer
Night games
  Schnitzler, A. Night gamesand other stories and novellas; and other stories and novellas; translated from the German by Margret Schaefer; with a foreword by John Simon
The second
  Schnitzler, A. Night gamesand other stories and novellas; and other stories and novellas; translated from the German by Margret Schaefer; with a foreword by John Simon
The widower
  Schnitzler, A. Night gamesand other stories and novellas; and other stories and novellas; translated from the German by Margret Schaefer; with a foreword by John Simon
Schoech, Samantha
This Is Living
  Gettysburg Review v15 no2 p241-9 Summ 2002
Schoemperlen, Diane
The antonyms of fiction
  Schoemperlen, D. Red plaid shirt; stories

Schoemperlen, Diane—*Continued*

A change is as good as a rest
  Schoemperlen, D. Red plaid shirt; stories
Clues
  Schoemperlen, D. Red plaid shirt; stories
Five small rooms (A murder mystery)
  Schoemperlen, D. Red plaid shirt; stories
Forms of devotion
  Schoemperlen, D. Red plaid shirt; stories
Frogs
  Schoemperlen, D. Red plaid shirt; stories
Hockey night in Canada
  Schoemperlen, D. Red plaid shirt; stories
How deep is the river?
  Schoemperlen, D. Red plaid shirt; stories
In a dark season
  Schoemperlen, D. Red plaid shirt; stories
The look of the lightning, the sound of the birds
  Schoemperlen, D. Red plaid shirt; stories
Losing ground
  Schoemperlen, D. Red plaid shirt; stories
The man of my dreams
  Schoemperlen, D. Red plaid shirt; stories
Mastering effective English (A linguistic fable)
  Schoemperlen, D. Red plaid shirt; stories
Nothing happens
  Schoemperlen, D. Red plaid shirt; stories
Railroading; or, Twelve small stories with the
    word train in the title
  Schoemperlen, D. Red plaid shirt; stories
Red plaid shirt
  Schoemperlen, D. Red plaid shirt; stories
A simple story
  Schoemperlen, D. Red plaid shirt; stories
Stranger than fiction
  Schoemperlen, D. Red plaid shirt; stories
This town
  Schoemperlen, D. Red plaid shirt; stories
Tickets to Spain
  Schoemperlen, D. Red plaid shirt; stories
Weights and measures
  Schoemperlen, D. Red plaid shirt; stories
Schoenewaldt, Pamela
Threads on the Mountain
  New Letters v69 no4 p7-19 2003
Schofield, Sandy
Stepping up to the plate
  Past lives, present tense; edited by Elizabeth
    Ann Scarborough
SCHOLARS
  See also Intellectuals
Alas, L. Two scholars
Borges, J. L. The bribe
Bowles, P. The circular valley
Bowles, P. A distant episode
Broughton, T. A. The classicist
Byatt, A. S. The pink ribbon
Epstein, J. Felix emeritus
George, E. I, Richard
Herling, G. A madrigal of mourning
Jones, G. Dark times
Leavitt, D. The list
Lee, V. Amour dure
Mathews, H. Remarks of the scholar graduate
McGarry, J. Among the Philistines
Meredith, D. The closer
Singer, I. B. Pigeons
Singer, I. B. Yentl the yeshiva boy
Singer, I. B. Zeidlus the Pope

Spencer, E. The visit
Yates, R. Liars in love
Scholars and lovers. Greenberg, A.
Scholz, Carter
Altamira
  Scholz, C. The amount to carry; stories
The amount to carry
  Lethem, J. and Scholz, C. Kafka Americana;
    [by] Jonathan Lethem [and] Carter Scholz
  Scholz, C. The amount to carry; stories
At the shore
  Scholz, C. The amount to carry; stories
Blumfeld, an elderly bachelor
  Lethem, J. and Scholz, C. Kafka Americana;
    [by] Jonathan Lethem [and] Carter Scholz
  Scholz, C. The amount to carry; stories
A catastrophe machine
  Scholz, C. The amount to carry; stories
A draft of Canto CI
  Scholz, C. The amount to carry; stories
The eve of the last Apollo
  Scholz, C. The amount to carry; stories
Invisible ink
  Scholz, C. The amount to carry; stories
The menageries of Babel
  Scholz, C. The amount to carry; stories
Mengele's Jew
  Scholz, C. The amount to carry; stories
The nine billion names of God
  Scholz, C. The amount to carry; stories
Travels
  Scholz, C. The amount to carry; stories
(jt. auth) See Lethem, Jonathan and Scholz, Car-
    ter
Schone, Robin
A man and a woman
  Fascinated; [by] Bertrice Small, Susan John-
    son, Thea Devine and Robin Schone
The **school**. Barthelme, D.
The **school** bus. Dixon, S.
The **school** bus. Gavell, M. L.
SCHOOL LIFE
Bausch, R. What feels like the world
Gray, A. Sinkings
Kohler, S. Cracks
Kohler, S. Underworld
                    Canada
Bezmozgis, D. An animal to the memory
Kalman, J. Eichmann's monogram
Potvin, E. A. Invert and multiply
Taylor, T. L. The resurrection plant
                    China
Ha Jin. Emperor
Wang Anyi. Between themselves
Wang Cengqi. Big Chan
                    Czechoslovakia
Škvorecký, J. Why I lernt how to reed
                    England
Alameddine, R. The changing room
Byatt, A. S. Jael
Crowther, P. Cat on an old school roof
Piccirilli, T. Of Persephone, Poe, and the Whis-
    perer
Waugh, E. Charles Ryder's schooldays
Waugh, E. Fragment of a novel
Waugh, E. Scott-King's modern Europe
                    Germany
Zinovyeva-Annibal, L. D. The devil

SCHOOL LIFE—*Continued*
India
Chaudhuri, A. Four days before the Saturday night social
Israel
Goldstein, N. The Roberto touch
Keret, E. The mysterious disappearance of Alon Shemesh
Keret, E. Siren
Japan
Massey, S. Junior high samurai
Nigeria
Kalu, Anthonia C. Independence
Scotland
O'Hagan, A. Glass cheques
United States
Adams, A. Truth or consequences
Aldrich, B. S. Juno's swans
Barthelme, D. The school
Baxter, C. Gryphon
Blaise, C. How I became a Jew
Boswell, M. New Wave
Broughton, T. A. The wars I missed
Broyard, B. The trouble with Mr. Leopold
Budnitz, J. Lessons
Butler, R. O. Hiram the desperado
Carlson, R. Keith
Castillo, R. The battle of the Alamo
Chacón, D. Mexican table
Cohen, R. Good with girls
Cohen, R. What makes you you
Di Blasi, D. An obscure geography
Eisenberg, D. The girl who left her sock on the floor
Gilchrist, E. Victory over Japan
Gonzalez, R. Spanish
Greer, A. S. Cannibal kings
Grodstein, L. Gazelles
Huffman, B., Jr. Some due process
Johnson, D. Melvin in the sixth grade
Jones, E. P. The first day
Jones, T. Tarantula
Lloyd, D. T. As always, Jason
Lloyd, D. T. Stain
Lloyd, D. T. Touch
McKnight, R. The kind of light that shines on Texas
Rabb, M. My mother's first lover
Rinehart, S. Make me
Robinson, L. Puckheads
Rodburg, M. March of Dimes
Sandlin, L. Beautiful
Smolens, J. Snow
Touré. They're playing my song
Updike, J. The alligators
Updike, J. A sense of shelter
Updike, J. Tomorrow and tomorrow and so forth
Vonnegut, K. Ambitious sophomore
Vonnegut, K. The boy who hated girls
Wilking, Joan. Proper dress
Yañez, R. Desert Vista
Yates, R. Doctor Jack-o'-Lantern
Yates, R. Fun with a stranger
SCHOOL SUPERINTENDENTS AND PRINCI-PALS
Auchincloss, L. The Devil and Guy Lansing
Chekhov, A. P. A man of ideas
Pritchard, M. Salve Regina

SCHOOL TEACHERS *See* Teachers
The **schoolmistress**. Chekhov, A. P.
SCHOOLS *See* School life
Schorer, Mark
(jt. auth) *See* Derleth, August William and Schorer, Mark
Schorn, Susan
Bobby Lee Carter and the hand of God
U.S. Catholic v66 no1 p34-6 Ja 2001
Schottenfeld, Stephen
Miss Ellen Jameson Is Not Deceased
TriQuarterly no117 p129-58 Fall 2003
Obituaries
Iowa Review v29 no3 p121-31 Wint 1999
Schow, David J.
The absolute last of the ultra-spooky, super-scary Hallowe'en horror nights
The Mammoth book of best new horror 14; edited with an introduction by Stephen Jones
Blessed event
Vanishing acts; a science fiction anthology; edited by Ellen Datlow
Unhasped
Best new horror 11; edited and with an introduction by Stephen Jones
Schrank, Ben
Consent
Lost tribe; jewish fiction from the edge
Schraufnagel, Joe
Like whiskey for Christmas
The Student body; short stories about college students and professors; edited by John McNally
Schreiber, Norman
Call me Wiggins
My Sherlock Holmes; untold stories of the great detective; edited by Michael Kurland
Schrekx and son. Porter, J. A.
Schrödinger's cat. Rucker, R. v. B.
Schrödinger's plague. Bear, G.
Schroeder, Karl
The dragon of Pripyat
The Year's best science fiction, seventeenth annual collection; edited by Gardner Dozois
Halo
Northern suns; edited by David G. Hartwell & Glenn Grant
Schtok, Fradel
At the mill
Beautiful as the moon, radiant as the stars; Jewish women in Yiddish stories : an anthology; edited by Sandra Bark; introduction by Francine Prose
Winter berries
Beautiful as the moon, radiant as the stars; Jewish women in Yiddish stories : an anthology; edited by Sandra Bark; introduction by Francine Prose
Schuemmer, Silke Andrea
The form of a fish is its knowledge of the water
Prairie Schooner v73 no3 p102-06 Fall 1999
Schulman, Helen
P.S.
Neurotica: Jewish writers on sex; edited by Melvin Jules Bukiet
Schulze, Ingo
Blinking baby
Grand Street no69 p116-23 Summ 1999

Schulze, Ingo—*Continued*
Cell phone
   Chicago Review v48 no2/3 p264-72 Summ 2002
Fish
   Grand Street no69 p124-30 Summ 1999
Letter from—Dresden
   The Times Literary Supplement no5036 p17 O 8 1999
The ring
   The Art of the story; an international anthology of contemporary short stories; edited by Daniel Halpern
Schumacher, Aileen
Along for the ride
   Blood on their hands; edited by Lawrence Block
Worth a thousand words
   The Blue and the gray undercover; edited by Ed Gorman
Schumacher, Julie
Passengers
   Atlantic Monthly v284 no5 p92-94+ N 1999
Schutz, Benjamin M.
Lost and found
   A Century of noir; thirty-two classic crime stories; edited by Mickey Spillane and Max Allan Collins
   Death cruise; crime stories on the open seas; edited by Lawrence Block
Not enough monkeys
   Crème de la crime; edited by Janet Hutchings
Schuyler, George Samuel
Black no more [excerpt]
   Dark matter; a century of speculative fiction from the African diaspora; edited by Sheree R. Thomas
Schwartz, Howard
The First Wedding
   Parabola v29 no1 p24-6 Spr 2004
Schwartz, John Burnham
Alpha Romeo
   Gentlemen's Quarterly v73 no5 p195, 216 My 2003
Schwartz, Lynne Sharon
By a dimming light
   Schwartz, L. S. Referred pain; and other stories
Deadly nightshade
   Schwartz, L. S. Referred pain; and other stories
Francesca
   Schwartz, L. S. Referred pain; and other stories
Heat
   Schwartz, L. S. Referred pain; and other stories
Hostages to fortune
   Schwartz, L. S. Referred pain; and other stories
Intrusions
   Schwartz, L. S. Referred pain; and other stories
Referred pain
   Schwartz, L. S. Referred pain; and other stories
Sightings of Loretta
   Schwartz, L. S. Referred pain; and other stories

The stone master
   Schwartz, L. S. Referred pain; and other stories
The trip to Halawa Valley
   Schwartz, L. S. Referred pain; and other stories
Twisted tales
   Schwartz, L. S. Referred pain; and other stories
What I did for love
   Best of Prairie schooner; fiction and poetry; edited by Hilda Raz
The word
   Schwartz, L. S. Referred pain; and other stories
Schwartz, Ronald
(jt. auth) See Tashi, Phuntshog
Schwartz, Sheila
Afterbirth
   Prize stories, 1999; The O. Henry awards; edited and with an introduction by Larry Dark
Schwartz, Steven
Stranger
   The North American Review v287 no5 p13-19 S/O 2002
Schwarz, Mauricio-José
Glimmerings on blue glass
   Cosmos latinos: an anthology of science fiction from Latin America and Spain; translated, edited, & with an introduction & notes by Andrea L. Bell & Yolanda Molina-Gavilán
Schwarzschild, Edward L.
Distance man
   Southwest Review v84 no3 p404-16 1999
Proposals and advice
   The Virginia Quarterly Review v75 no4 p723-38 Aut 1999
Schweighofer, Peter
The Cairo cat caper
   Felonious felines; edited by Carol and Ed Gorman
Schweikert, Ruth
Peanuts
   Chicago Review v48 no2/3 p273-80 Summ 2002
Schweitzer, Darrell
Tom O'bedlam's night out
   The Ultimate Halloween; edited by Marvin Kaye
Scibona, Salvatore
The plateform
   Best new American voices 2004; guest editor John Casey; series editors John Kulka and Natalie Danford
Science and the arts. Harrison, M. J.
The **Science** Fair. Vinge, V.
SCIENCE FICTION
   See also End of the world; Extrasensory perception; Fantasies; Future; Interplanetary visitors; Interplanetary voyages; Interplanetary wars; Life on other planets; Robots; Space colonies; Space flight; Space ships; Time travel
Abraham, D. Chimera 8
Aldiss, B. W. Apogee again
Aldiss, B. W. Cognitive ability and the light bulb

SCIENCE FICTION—*Continued*

Aldiss, B. W. Dark society
Aldiss, B. W. Galaxy Zee
Aldiss, B. W. III
Aldiss, B. W. Judas danced
Aldiss, B. W. A kind of artistry
Aldiss, B. W. Marvells of Utopia
Aldiss, B. W. A matter of mathematics
Aldiss, B. W. Near earth object
Aldiss, B. W. The old mythology
Aldiss, B. W. The pause button
Aldiss, B. W. Steppenpferd
Aldiss, B. W. Three types of solitude
Aldiss, B. W. Who can replace a man?
Aldrich, B. S. The outsider
Allen, C. Last Chance Gravity Fill Station
Amis, M. Denton's death
Anderson, P. Eutopia
Anderson, P. The horn of time the hunter
Anderson, P. Journeys end
Anderson, P. The problem of pain
Anderson, P. Quest
Anderson, P. Sam Hall
April, J. P. Rêve Canadien
Arnason, E. The potter of bones
Arnason, E. Stellar harvest
Arreola, J. J. Baby H. P.
Asaro, C. Ave de paso
Asaro, C. The quantum rose
Asimov, I. Nightfall
Atkins, P. King of outer space
Atwood, M. Freeforall
Aylett, S. Angel dust
Aylett, S. Dread honor
Aylett, S. Gigantic
Aylett, S. Maryland
Aylett, S. The met are all for this
Aylett, S. Repeater
Aylett, S. Resenter
Aylett, S. Shifa
Aylett, S. The Siri gun
Aylett, S. Tail
Aylett, S. Tug of war
Aylett, S. Tusk
Aylett, S. The waffle code
Bacigalupi, Paolo. The fluted girl
Ball, M. Shell game
Barrett, N., Jr. Cush
Barrett, N., Jr. "A day at the fair"
Barrett, N., Jr. Rhido wars
Barrett, N., Jr. Trading post
Barrett, N., Jr. Under old New York
Barth, J. The rest of your life
Barton, W. Down in the dark
Barton, W. Off on a starship
Baxter, S. Cilia-of-gold
Baxter, S. In the un-black
Baxter, S. Martian autumn
Baxter, S. On the Orion line
Baxter, S. Saddlepoint: roughneck
Baxter, S. Sun-Cloud
Baxter, S. The Xeelee flower
Bear, G. Blood music
Bear, G. Darwin's radio [excerpt]
Bear, G. The fall of the house of Escher
Bear, G. Hardfought
Bear, G. Heads
Bear, G. Judgment engine
Bear, G. Plague of conscience

Bear, G. Scattershot
Bear, G. The visitation
Bear, G. The way of all ghosts
Bear, G. The wind from a burning woman
Beckett, C. To become a warrior
Bell, M. S. Anomalous structures of my dreams
Bell, M. S. The thing about Benny
Benedict, P. Zog-19: a scientific romance
Benford, G. Anomalies
Benford, G. As big as the Ritz
Benford, G. A calculus of desperation
Benford, G. The clear blue seas of Luna
Benford, G. A dance to strange musics
Benford, G. The goldilocks problem
Benford, G. High abyss
Benford, G. A hunger for the infinite
Benford, G. Kollapse
Benford, G. Manassas, again
Benford, G. The scarred man
Benford, G. Shall we take a little walk?
Benford, G. The voice
Benford, G. World vast, world various
Benford, G. A worm in the well
Benford, G. Zoomers
Bergeron, A. The eighth register
Berliner, J. Eye of the day
Bester, A. Hobson's choice
Bischoff, D. Sittin' on the dock
Bishop, M. Cri de coeur
Bishop, M. Of crystalline labyrinths and the new creation
Bishop, M. The procedure
Bishop, M. Sequel on Skorpios
Bishop, M. and Page, G. W. Murder on Lupozny Station
Bisson, T. 10:07:24
Bisson, T. Bears discover fire
Bisson, T. Dead Man's Curve
Bisson, T. First fire
Bisson, T. Incident at Oak Ridge
Bisson, T. The Joe Show
Bisson, T. Not this Virginia
Bisson, T. The player
Bisson, T. Smoother
Blackford, R. The soldier in the machine
Blish, J. Citadel of thought
Blish, J. How beautiful with banners
Blish, J. Nor iron bars
Blish, J. The oath
Blish, J. Testament of Andros
Blumlein, M. Know how, can do
Bova, B. The café coup
Bova, B. Mount Olympus
Boyczuk, R. Doing time
Brackett, L. The last days of Shandakor
Bradbury, R. Dark they were, and golden-eyed
Bradbury, R. Icarus Montgolfier Wright
Bradbury, R. The Laurel and Hardy Alpha Centauri farewell tour
Bradbury, R. A little journey
Bradbury, R. The lonely ones
Bradbury, R. The love affair
Bradbury, R. The man
Bradbury, R. The million-year picnic
Bradbury, R. The square pegs
Bradbury, R. Time in hy flight
Bradbury, R. The veldt
Bradbury, R. Zero hour
Braunbeck, G. A. Who am a passer by

SCIENCE FICTION—*Continued*

Brennert, A. Her pilgrim soul
Brin, D. Temptation
Broderick, D. The Magi
Brown, E. Myths of the Martian future
Bujold, L. M. Barter
Burstein, M. A. Teleabsence
Byrne, Eugene. Bagged 'n' tagged
Cadigan, P. Mother's milt
Cady, J. Science fiction, utopia, and the spirit
Campbell, J. W. Who goes there?
Card, O. S. Investment counselor
Carey, P. The chance
Carl, L. S. A rose with all its thorns
Carneiro, A. Brain transplant
Cassutt, M. More adventures on other planets
Castro, A.-T. The funeral march of the Marionettes
Castro, A.-T. Sunday night yams at Minnie and Earl's
Castro, A.-T. The tangled strings of the Marionettes
Castro, A.-T. Unseen demons
Castro, Pablo A. Exerion
Chabon, M. The Martian agent, a planetary romance
Chalker, J. L. Dance band on the Titanic
Chandler, A. B. The mountain movers
Cherryh, C. J. Companions
Cherryh, C. J. A gift of prophecy
Cherryh, C. J. Homecoming
Cherryh, C. J. Pots
Cherryh, C. J. Poys
Cherryh, C. J. The Sandman, the Tinman, and Betty B.
Cherryh, C. J. The scapegoat
Chiang, T. The evolution of human science
Chiang, T. Liking what you see: a documentary
Chiang, T. Seventy-two letters
Chiang, T. Tower of Babylon
Chiang, T. Understand
Chilson, R. This side of independence
Choi, E. Divisions
Clarke, A. C. All the time in the world
Clarke, A. C. The awakening
Clarke, A. C. Before Eden
Clarke, A. C. Big game hunt
Clarke, A. C. Castaway
Clarke, A. C. Cosmic Casanova
Clarke, A. C. Critical mass
Clarke, A. C. The deep range
Clarke, A. C. Dial F for Frankenstein
Clarke, A. C. Dog Star
Clarke, A. C. Earthlight
Clarke, A. C. The food of the gods
Clarke, A. C. The forgotten enemy
Clarke, A. C. The hammer of God
Clarke, A. C. Holiday on the Moon
Clarke, A. C. I remember Babylon
Clarke, A. C. Into the comet
Clarke, A. C. Let there be light
Clarke, A. C. The lion of Comarre
Clarke, A. C. Love that Universe
Clarke, A. C. Nightfall
Clarke, A. C. No morning after
Clarke, A. C. The other tiger
Clarke, A. C. Out of the cradle, endlessly orbiting
Clarke, A. C. Out of the sun

Clarke, A. C. The parasite
Clarke, A. C. Playback
Clarke, A. C. Publicity campaign
Clarke, A. C. Refugee
Clarke, A. C. Retreat from earth
Clarke, A. C. The road to the sea
Clarke, A. C. Second dawn
Clarke, A. C. Security check
Clarke, A. C. A slight case of sunstroke
Clarke, A. C. The songs of distant earth
Clarke, A. C. The star
Clarke, A. C. Summertime on Icarus
Clarke, A. C. Superiority
Clarke, A. C. Transience
Clarke, A. C. Travel by wire!
Clarke, A. C. Trouble with the natives
Clarke, A. C. Trouble with time
Clarke, A. C. The ultimate melody
Clarke, A. C. The wall of darkness
Clarke, A. C. What goes up
Clarke, A. C. The wire continuum
Clayton, J. J. Let's not talk politics, please
Clement, H. Exchange rate
Clement, H. Proof
Clough, B. W. May be some time
Cody, L. Solar zits
Colebatch, H. G. P. The colonel's tiger
Collins, P. Wired dreaming
Compton, D. G. In which Avu Giddy tries to stop dancing
Cowdrey, A. E. Crux
Crowley, J. In blue
Daniel, T. Grist
Dann, J. Jumping the road
Dann, J. Voices
De Camp, L. S. A gun for dinosaur
De Camp, L. S. The isolinguals
Dedman, S. From whom all blessings flow
Del Rey, L. Helen O'Loy
Delany, S. R. Among the blobs
Delany, S. R. Aye, and Gomorrah. . .
Denton, B. The territory
Derby, M. An appeal
Derby, M. Behavior pilot
Derby, M. The boyish mulatto
Derby, M. Crutches used as weapon
Derby, M. The end of men
Derby, M. The father helmet
Derby, M. First
Derby, M. Gantry's last
Derby, M. Home recordings
Derby, M. Instructions
Derby, M. Joy of eating
Derby, M. The life jacket
Derby, M. Meat tower
Derby, M. Night watchmen
Derby, M. Sky harvest
Derby, M. The sound gun
Derby, M. Stupid animals
Di Filippo, P. Ailoura
Di Filippo, P. Have gun, will edit
Di Filippo, P. A Martian theodicy
Di Filippo, P. Neutrino drag
DiChario, N. Dragonhead
DiChario, N. The winterberry
Dick, P. K. I hope I shall arrive soon
Dickson, G. R. The man in the mailbag
DiFilippo, P. Science fiction
Dix, S. Matters of consequence

SCIENCE FICTION—*Continued*

Doctorow, C. All day sucker
Doctorow, C. Home again, home again
Doctorow, C. Shadow of mothaship
Doctorow, C. The Super Man and the bugout
Doctorow, C. To market, to market: the re-branding of Billy Bailey
Donaldson, S. R. What makes us human
Dorsey, C. J. (Learning about) machine sex
Douglas, C. N. Night owl
Dowling, T. He tried to catch the light
Dowling, T. Privateer's moon
Dozois, G. R. The gods of Mars
Dozois, G. R. Solace
Dozois, G. R. Strangers
Dozois, G. R. The visible man
Drake, D. Coming up against it
Drake, D. Facing the enemy
Drake, D. Failure mode
Drake, D. The tradesmen
Due, T. Patient zero
Dumas, H. The distributors
Duncan, A. The chief designer
Dyer, S. N. The July Ward
Edelman, S. Eros and agape among the asteroids
Edelman, S. Mom, the Martians, and me
Effinger, G. A. One
Egan, G. Oceanic
Egan, G. Oracle
Egan, G. Wang's carpets
Ellison, H. Killing Bernstein
Emshwiller, C. Creature
Encinosa Fú, M. Like the roses had to die
Evans, L. The stray
Evenson, B. Body
Fabra, N. M. On the planet Mars
Finch, S. Reading the bones
Finney, J. The coin collector
Fleming, P. L. Polyformus perfectus
Fowler, K. J. Face value
Frahm, L. Borderline
Friesen, R. E. Dancing in the ashes
Gaiman, N. The Monarch of the Glen
Garcia y Robertson, R. Forever free
Garcia y Robertson, R. Gone to glory
Garfinkle, R. The last invasion of Ireland
Goligorsky, E. The last refuge
Gores, J. The Andrech samples
Gores, J. Faulty register
Gorodischer, A. The violet's embryos
Green, R. J. Deck load strike
Green, Dominic. Send me a mentagram
Grimsley, J. Free in Asveroth
Grimsley, J. Into Greenwood
Haempffert, W. The diminishing draft
Haldeman, J. W. For White Hill
Haldeman, J. W. Forever peace [excerpt]
Haldeman, J. W. A separate war
Hamilton, P. F. Escape route
Hand, E. Cleopatra Brimstone
Hansen, J. Eater
Harrison, H. Captain Bedlam
Harrison, H. A civil service servant
Harrison, H. Dawn of the endless night
Harrison, H. Down to earth
Harrison, H. The ever-branching tree
Harrison, H. The gods themselves throw incense
Harrison, H. The greening of the green
Harrison, H. An honest day's work

Harrison, H. I see you
Harrison, H. If
Harrison, H. The k-factor
Harrison, H. Mute Milton
Harrison, H. The pliable animal
Harrison, H. The robot who wanted to know
Harrison, H. Rock diver
Harrison, H. Simulated trainer
Harrison, H. Space rats of the CCC
Harrison, H. Toy shop
Harrison, H. You men of violence
Harty, R. Why the sky turns red when the sun goes down
Heinlein, R. A. "—And he built a crooked house"
Heinlein, R. A. Jerry was a man
Heinlein, R. A. "They—"
Heinlein, R. A. Waldo
Heinlein, R. A. The year of the jackpot
Hejazi, K. Cling to life with your whole body
Herbert, W. Twilight of the real
Hjortsberg, W. The clone who ran for congress
Hjortsberg, W. Gray matters
Hjortsberg, W. Homecoming
Hjortsberg, W. Symbiography
Hoffman, N. K. Between disappearances
Hoffman, N. K. Voyage of discovery
Hood, R. Tamed
Hopkinson, N. Ganger (ball lightning)
Hopkinson, N. A habit of waste
Huff, T. Nanite, star bright
Huttner, H. Dr. Cyclops
Irvine, A. The sea wind offers little relief
Irvine, A. Agent provocateur
Jenkins, W. F. Exploration team
Jensen, J. L. Domestic slash and thrust
Jensen, J. L. The secret history of the ornithopter
Jones, R. F. The alien machine
Joseph, A. The African origins of UFOs [excerpt]
Kelly, J. P. Candy art
Kelly, J. P. Chemistry
Kelly, J. P. Feel the zaz
Kelly, J. P. Fruitcake theory
Kelly, J. P. Itsy bitsy spider
Kelly, J. P. The propagation of light in a vacuum
Kelly, J. P. The Pyramid of Amirah
Kelly, J. P. Undone
Knight, D. F. Masks
Knowles, T. W. Luck of the draw
Kress, N. Computer virus
Kress, N. Sleeping dogs
Lafferty, R. A. Narrow Valley
Lake, D. J. The truth about Weena
Landis, G. A. Across the darkness
Landis, G. A. Approaching Perimelasma
Landis, G. A. Beneath the stars of winter
Landis, G. A. Ecopoiesis
Landis, G. A. Ouroboros
Landis, G. A. Outsider's chance
Landis, G. A. Rorvik's war
Landis, G. A. The secret egg of the clouds
Landis, G. A. Snow
Landis, G. A. Winter fire
Lavín, G. Reaching the shore
Lawson, C. Unborn again
Lawson, C. Written in blood

SCIENCE FICTION—*Continued*

Le Guin, U. K. The birthday of the world
Le Guin, U. K. The building
Le Guin, U. K. The Island of the Immortals
Le Guin, U. K. Old Music and the slave women
Le Guin, U. K. A woman's liberation
Lee, T. Jedella ghost
Lee, T. The sky-green blues
Leiber, F. Sanity
Lessing, D. M. The reason for it
Lethem, J. Five fucks
Lethem, J. and Scholz, C. Receding horizon
Lindholm, M. Cut
Lindquist, R. C. Prelude to a nocturne
Lindskold, J. M. Queen's gambit
Long, A. R. The thought-monster
Love, R. The Total Devotion Machine
Love, R. Two recipes for magic beans
Lovegrove, J. Out of the blue, into the red
Lumley, B. Big "C"
Lupoff, R. A. 31.12.99
Lupoff, R. A. The adventures of Mr. Tindle
Lupoff, R. A. At Vega's taqueria
Lupoff, R. A. The child's story
Lupoff, R. A. Discovery of the Ghooric Zone
Lupoff, R. A. Green ice
Lupoff, R. A. The Heyworth Fragment
Lupoff, R. A. Jubilee
Lupoff, R. A. The monster and Mr. Greene
Lupoff, R. A. Mr. Greene and the monster
Lupoff, R. A. Stream of consciousness
MacKay, S. The sages of Cassiopeia
MacLean, K. Games
MacLeod, I. R. The summer isles
MacLeod, K. The human front
Malzberg, B. N. Amos
Malzberg, B. N. The only thing you learn
Malzberg, B. N. The prince of the steppes
Malzberg, B. N. Quartermain
Malzberg, B. N. Ship full of Jews
Malzberg, B. N. We're coming through the window
Martin, G. R. R. The hero
Matheson, R. Born of man and woman
Matheson, R. Brother to the machine
Matheson, R. Death ship
Matheson, R. Fm
Matheson, R. Lover when you're near me
Matheson, R. Return
Matheson, R. Shipshape home
Matheson, R. SRL ad
Matheson, R. Third from the sun
Mayhar, A. Fungi
McAllister, Laurent. Kapuzine and the wolf: a hortatory tale
McAuley, P. J. All tomorrow's parties
McAuley, P. J. The passenger
McAuley, P. J. Reef
McAuley, P. J. The Rift
McAuley, P. J. Sea change, with monsters
McAuley, P. J. Under Mars
McBain, E. But you know us
McCaffrey, A. Beyond between
McCaffrey, A. The ship that returned
McCaffrey, A. The ship who mourned
McCaffrey, A. The ship who sang
McCarthy, W. He died that day, in thirty years
McDevitt, J. The Emerson effect
McDonald, I. The days of Solomon Gursky

McDonald, I. The old cosmonaut and the construction worker dream of Mars
McGarry, M. J. The mercy gate
McHugh, M. F. The missionary's child
McHugh, M. F. Presence
McMullen, S. The dominant style
Meaney, J. The whisper of disks
Melko, Paul. Singletons in love
Menen Desleal, A. A cord made of nylon and gold
Merril, J. That only a mother
Metzger, T. Transorbital love probe
Mixon, L. J. At tide's turning
Moffett, J. The bear's baby
Monteiro, J. The crystal goblet
Moon, E. Silver lining
Moorcock, M. Lost sorceress of the silent citadel
Moore, C. L. No woman born
Morlan, A. R. Fast glaciers
Morrow, J. The war of the worldviews
Mosley, W. Little brother
Murphy, P. Wild girls
Newman, S. Divine guidance
Nickle, D. The dummy ward
Niven, L. All the myriad ways
Niven, L. Destiny's road [excerpt]
Niven, L. Procrustes
Niven, L. Smut talk
Niven, L. Ssoroghod's people
Niven, L. The woman in Del Rey crater
Niven, L. and Barnes, S. Saturn's race
Niven, L. and Cooper, B. Ice and mirrors
Nordley, G. D. Poles apart
Norton, A. All cats are gray
O'Leary, P. The me after the rock
Oliver, C. Any more at home like you?
Oliver, C. Artifact
Oliver, C. Between the thunder and the sun
Oliver, C. Didn't he ramble?
Oliver, C. Far from this earth
Oliver, C. Ghost town
Oliver, C. The gift
Oliver, C. If now you grieve a little
Oliver, C. Just like a man
Oliver, C. The land of lost content
Oliver, C. Let me live in a house
Oliver, C. Meanwhile, back on the reservation
Oliver, C. The mother of necessity
Oliver, C. Night
Oliver, C. North wind
Oliver, C. Of course
Oliver, C. Pilgrimage
Oliver, C. RIte of passage
Oliver, C. A star above it
Oliver, C. Stardust
Oliver, C. A stick for Harry Eddington
Oliver, C. Technical advisor
Oliver, C. The wind blows free
Oltion, J. Abandon in place
Oltion, J. Renaissance man
Palmer, T. Dream science [excerpt]
Palwick, S. Going after Bobo
Park, S. The cure for everything
Patton, F. The control device
Paul, B. Play nice
Pohl, F. The boy who would live forever
Pohl, F. Hatching the Phoenix
Pohl, F. Let the ants try

SCIENCE FICTION—*Continued*

Popkes, S. The ice
Popkes, S. Winters are hard
Pronzini, B. The REC field
Pronzini, B. and Malzberg, B. N. The Lyran case
Pronzini, B. and Malzberg, B. N. Out of quarantine
Pronzini, B. and Malzberg, B. N. Reading day
Pronzini, B. and Malzberg, B. N. Vanishing point
Pronzini, B. and Malzberg, B. N. Whither thou, ghost
Reed, K. Captive kong
Reed, R. Aeon's child
Reed, R. The cuckoo's boys
Reed, R. Decency
Reed, R. The dragons of Springplace
Reed, R. First Tuesday
Reed, R. Guest of honor
Reed, R. Night of time
Reed, R. A place with shade
Reed, R. The remoras
Reed, R. The shape of everything
Reed, R. Stride
Reed, R. Waging good
Reed, R. Winemaster
Resnick, M. and Bell, M. S. Flower children of Mars
Reynolds, A. Glacial
Reynolds, A. Great walls of Mars
Reynolds, A. The real story
Robinson, K. S. The lucky strike
Rogers, B. H. Lifeboat on a burning sea
Rogers, B. H. Sleeping Beauty
Rogoff, R. E. The princess and the accountant
Rosenblum, M. H. The eye of God
Ross, J. The immortals
Rucker, R. v. B. As above, so below
Rucker, R. v. B. Big Jelly
Rucker, R. v. B. Buzz
Rucker, R. v. B. Easy as pie
Rucker, R. v. B. Enlightenment Rabies
Rucker, R. v. B. The facts of life
Rucker, R. v. B. The fifty-seventh Franz Kafka
Rucker, R. v. B. The Indian rope trick explained
Rucker, R. v. B. Inertia
Rucker, R. v. B. Jumpin' Jack Flash
Rucker, R. v. B. The last Einstein-Rosen bridge
Rucker, R. v. B. The man who ate himself
Rucker, R. v. B. The man who was a cosmic string
Rucker, R. v. B. Message found in a copy of Flatland
Rucker, R. v. B. A new golden age
Rucker, R. v. B. Pi in the sky
Rucker, R. v. B. Plastic letters
Rucker, R. v. B. Probability pipeline
Rucker, R. v. B. Schrödinger's cat
Rucker, R. v. B. Soft Death
Rucker, R. v. B. Storming the cosmos
Rucker, R. v. B. and Shirley, J. Pockets
Rusch, K. K. Coolhunting
Rusch, K. K. Echea
Rusch, K. K. The gallery of his dreams
Rusch, K. K. Going native
Rusch, K. K. June Sixteenth at Anna's
Rusch, K. K. Relics
Rusch, K. K. Strange creatures

Ryman, G. V.A.O.
Salaam, K. I. At life's limits
Sanders, W. The scuttling; or, Down by the sea with Marvin and Pamela
Sargent, P. Dream of Venus
Scarborough, E. A. Soulmates
Schaffler González, F. A miscalculation
Schmidt, S. The emperor's revenge
Schmitz, J. H. The second night of summer
Schofield, S. Stepping up to the plate
Scholz, C. At the shore
Scholz, C. A catastrophe machine
Scholz, C. Mengele's Jew
Scholz, C. The nine billion names of God
Schow, D. J. Blessed event
Schroeder, K. Halo
Schwarz, M.-J. Glimmerings on blue glass
Seagren, R. Of wood and stone
Sheckley, R. The day the aliens came
Sheckley, R. Deep Blue Sleep
Sheckley, R. Mirror games
Sheffield, C. Phallicide
Shwartz, S. Suppose they gave a peace
Silva Román, E. The death star
Silverberg, R. The book of changes
Silverberg, R. A hero of the empire
Simak, C. D. Desertion
Simak, C. D. Founding father
Simmons, D. The end of gravity
Simmons, D. Looking for Kelly Dahl
Simmons, D. The ninth of av
Simmons, D. Orphans of the Helix
Siodmak, C. FP 1 does not reply
Skeet, M. Near enough to home
Skillingstead, Jack. Dead worlds
Spencer, W. B. The lights of Armageddon
Stableford, B. M. The age of innocence
Stableford, B. M. The invisible worm
Stableford, B. M. The pipes of Pan
Stableford, B. M. Snowball in hell
Stableford, B. M. Tenebrio
Steele, A. M. The death of Captain Future
Steele, A. M. The fine art of watching
Steele, A. M. Graceland
Steele, A. M. Missing time
Steele, A. M. The teb hunter
Steele, A. M. Tom Swift and his humongous mechanical dude
Steele, A. M. A walk across Mars
Steele, A. M. Warning warning
Sterling, B. Taklamakan
Strasser, D. The doppelganger effect
Stross, C. Antibodies
Stross, C. A colder war
Stross, C. Halo
Stross, C. Lobsters
Sturgeon, T. Microcosmic god
Sturgeon, T. Mr. Costello, hero
Sturgeon, T. A saucer of loneliness
Sturgeon, T. The sex opposite
Sturgeon, T. The skills of Xanadu
Sturgeon, T. The [widget], the [wadget], and boff
Swanwick, M. The dead
Swanwick, M. King dragon
Swanwick, M. Radiant doors
Swanwick, M. Scherzo with tyrannosaur
Swanwick, M. The very pulse of the machine
Talbot, N. The latest dream I ever dreamed

SCIENCE FICTION—*Continued*

Tenn, W. Bernie the Faust
Tenn, W. Child's play
Tenn, W. Confusion cargo
Tenn, W. Consulate
Tenn, W. The dark star
Tenn, W. The deserter
Tenn, W. The discovery of Morniel Mathaway
Tenn, W. Down among the dead men
Tenn, W. Dud
Tenn, W. Errand boy
Tenn, W. The flat-eyed monster
Tenn, W. Flirleflip
Tenn, W. Generation of Noah
Tenn, W. The ghost standard
Tenn, W. The girl with some kind of past. And George.
Tenn, W. Hallock's madness
Tenn, W. The house dutiful
Tenn, W. The Ionian cycle
Tenn, W. It ends with a flicker
Tenn, W. A lamp for Medusa
Tenn, W. The last bounce
Tenn, W. Lisbon cubed
Tenn, W. A matter of frequency
Tenn, W. Me, myself, and I
Tenn, W. Party of the two parts
Tenn, W. Project Hush
Tenn, W. The puzzle of Priipiirii
Tenn, W. Ricardo's virus
Tenn, W. Sanctuary
Tenn, W. The tenants
Tenn, W. There were people on Bikini, there were people on Attu
Tenn, W. Time in advance
Tenn, W. Wednesday's child
Tenn, W. Winthrop was stubborn
Tiedemann, M. W. Links
Tiptree, J. Mother in the sky with diamonds
Turner, G. Flowering mandrake
Turtledove, H. Islands in the sea
Turtledove, H. The road not taken
Unamuno, M. d. Mechanopolis
Van Vogt, A. E. Dear pen pal
Van Vogt, A. E. Vault of the beast
Vanasco, A. Post-boomboom
Vance, J. The new prime
VanderMeer, J. Balzac's war
VanderMeer, J. Detectives and cadavers
VanderMeer, J. A heart for Lucretia
VanderMeer, J. The sea, Mendeho, and moon-light
Vardeman, R. E. Feedback
Vinge, V. The accomplice
Vinge, V. Apartness
Vinge, V. The barbarian princess
Vinge, V. The Blabber
Vinge, V. The cookie monster
Vinge, V. Fast times at Fairmont High
Vinge, V. Just peace
Vinge, V. The Science Fair
Vinge, V. The ungoverned
Vinge, V. The whirligig of time
Vinge, V. Win a Nobel Prize!
Vonnegut, K. The package
Vukcevich, R. Beastly heat
Vukcevich, R. A holiday junket
Vukcevich, R. Mom's little friends
Vukcevich, R. No comet

Vukcevich, R. White guys in space
Wadholm, R. At the money
Wadholm, R. Green tea
Waldrop, H. Calling your name
Waldrop, H. One horse town
Waldrop, H. Sun's up!
Waldrop, H. Us
Waldrop, H. A voice and bitter weeping
Waldrop, H. and Kennedy, L. One-horse town
Walker, S. Hunting mother
Watson, I. The amber room
Watson, I. Ferryman
Watson, I. The shape of murder
Watson, I. When thought-mail failed
Weber, D. Changer of worlds
Weber, D. From the highlands
Weber, D. The hard way home
Weber, D. Ms. Midshipwoman Harrington
Weber, D. Nightfall
Weber, D. What price dreams?
Weinbaum, S. G. The adaptive ultimate
Wellen, E. Sanity clause
Wells, C. 'Bassador
West, M. The nightingale
What, L. The cost of doing business
Wilde, Dana. The green moon
Wilder, C. Looking forward to the harvest
Wilhelm, K. Forget luck
Williams, S. Evermore
Williams, S. A map of the mines of Barnath
Williams, W. J. Daddy's world
Williams, W. J. Lethe
Williams, W. J. The millennium party
Williamson, J. The ultimate earth
Willis, C. Even the queen
Willis, C. Inn
Willis, C. Newsletter
Wilson, R. C. Divided by infinity
Wilson, R. C. The great goodbye
Wilson, R. C. The observer
Wilson, R. C. Protocols of consumption
Wolfe, G. The death of Doctor Island
Wolfe, G. Shields of Mars
Wolfe, G. Viewpoint
Wylde, T. Spinning kingdoms, two
Yolen, J. Salvage
Yolen, J. The traveler and the tale
Science fiction, utopia, and the spirit. Cady, J.

SCIENTIFIC EXPEDITIONS
Anderson, P. The Saturn game
Clarke, A. C. Big game hunt
Clarke, A. C. Transit of earth
Delany, S. R. High weir
Howard, C. The ice shelf
McAuley, P. J. The Rift
Steinbeck, T. The dark watcher

SCIENTIFIC EXPERIMENTS
Barker, C. The age of desire
Bear, G. Blood music
Bear, G. Schrödinger's plague
Carey, P. The fat man in history
Haempffert, W. The diminishing draft
Hawthorne, N. The birthmark
Lugones, L. Yzur
Pohl, F. The gold at the starbow's end
Rucker, R. v. B. Faraway eyes
Stableford, B. M. The facts of life
Sterling, B. Swarm

SCIENTIFIC RESEARCH *See* Research

SCIENTISTS

See also Anthropologists; Archeologists; Astronomers; Biologists; Inventors; Paleontologists; Physicists; Women scientists

Barrett, A. The forest
Barrett, A. The mysteries of ubiquitin
Bisson, T. First fire
Bloch, R. Life in our time
Brennert, A. Her pilgrim soul
Bukiet, M. J. The swap
Clarke, A. C. The cruel sky
Clarke, A. C. Superiority
Gardner, J. A. Three hearings on the existence of snakes in the human bloodstream
Gilchrist, E. Light can be both wave and particle
Gores, J. Speak of the Devil
Hawthorne, N. The birthmark
Huttner, H. Dr. Cyclops
Iagnemma, K. Children of hunger
Landis, G. A. Beneath the stars of winter
MacLean, K. Games
MacLeod, I. New light on the Drake equation
Rucker, R. v. B. Big Jelly
Rucker, R. v. B. Faraway eyes
Scholz, C. At the shore
Sheffield, C. Out of copyright
Slesar, H. Letter from a very worried man
Temple, W. F. The 4-sided triangle
Vinge, V. The Science Fair
Waters, M. Y. Mirror studies
Wharton, E. The debt
Wharton, E. The descent of man

Scintilla. McManus, J.
The **scissors.** Benítez-Rojo, A.
Scissors kick. Huss, S.
The **scissors** lady and the green man. Edwards, M.

Scliar, Moacyr

The prophets of Benjamin Bok
With signs and wonders; an international anthology of Jewish fabulist fiction; edited by Daniel M. Jaffe
Van Gogh's ear
The Vintage book of Latin American stories; edited by Carlos Fuentes and Julio Ortega

Scollins-Mantha, Brandi

Holding pattern
The Literary Review (Madison, N.J.) v44 no4 p630-4 Summ 2001

Scorched Earth. Gosling, P.
Scores. Addonizio, K.
Scoring. Clifford, W.
The **scorpion.** Bowles, P.
The **scorpion** eater. Gonzalez, R.
Scorpion's kiss. Kaminsky, S. M.

SCOTLAND

Crowley, J. An earthly mother sits and sings
Gray, A. Wellbeing
Lee, A. Winter barley
Smith, A. Paradise
Williamson, D. Mary and the seal

To 1603

Allyn, D. St. Margaret's kitten
Barnett, P. Two dead men
Davidson, J. A stone of destiny
Marston, E. Perfect shadows
Tremayne, P. Night's black agents
Vink, R. A frail young life

19th century

Edghill, R. The fairy ring

20th century

Banks, I. The bridge [excerpt]
Boyle, T. C. Swept away
Douglas, B. My childhood
Fleming, M. St. Andrew's day
Galloway, J. The trick is to keep breathing [excerpt]
Jamieson, R. A. The last black hoose
Kennedy, A. L. Looking for the possible dance [excerpt]
Kuppner, F. A very quiet street [excerpt]
Legge, G. Life on a Scottish council estate vol. 1
Massie, A. In the bare lands
McCabe, B. Not about the kids
Spence, A. Brilliant

Farm life

See Farm life—Scotland

Rural life

Dunn, D. The political piano
Elphinstone, M. A sparrow's flight [excerpt]
McLean, D. Hours of darkness

Edinburgh

Atkinson, K. Temporal anomaly
Lingard, J. After Colette [excerpt]
Rankin, I. The serpent's back
Scarborough, E. A. Tinkler Tam and the body snatchers
Welsh, I. Trainspotting [excerpt]

Glasgow

Gray, A. Lanark [excerpt]
Kelman, J. The busconductor Hines [excerpt]
Kelman, J. Remember Young Cecil
MacDougall, C. The lights below [excerpt]
Mills, J. Watch out, the world's behind you
Turnbull, P. Weasal and the fish

SCOTS

France

Lingard, J. After Colette [excerpt]

Scott, Jenn

The Art of Romance
Gettysburg Review v17 no1 p53-62 Spr 2004

Scott, Joanna

Happy birthday, Gabriella
The Southern Review (Baton Rouge, La.) v35 no1 p114-27 Wint 1999
That Place
Daedalus v132 no4 p73-83 Fall 2003

Scott, Johnie

The coming of the Hoodlum
The African American West; a century of short stories; edited by Bruce A. Glasrud and Laurie Champion

Scott, Justin

Cat in love
Murder in the family; [by] the Adams Round Table

Scott, Lawrence

Ash on Guavas
Bomb no82 p98-100 Wint 2002/2003
Ballad for the new world
The Oxford book of Caribbean short stories; edited by Stewart Brown and John Wickham

Scott, Melissa
Trouble and her friends [excerpt]
Reload: rethinking women + cyberculture; edited by Mary Flanagan and Austin Booth
Scott, Timothy
Things of That Nature
The Massachusetts Review v43 no4 p618-32 Wint 2002/2003
Scott-King's modern Europe. Waugh, E.
SCOTTISH DIALECT *See* Dialect stories—Scottish
The **Scottish** wife. Berkman, P. R.
Scottoline, Lisa
Carrying concealed
A Century of great suspense stories; edited by Jeffery Deaver
Scouting for Boys. Theroux, P.
SCOUTS AND SCOUTING
Forsyth, F. Whispering wind
Scoville, Shelagh
Clara and Ben
Scoville, S. Ulu's dog and other stories
The dividing strand
Scoville, S. Ulu's dog and other stories
The gift of a car
Scoville, S. Ulu's dog and other stories
The pin collectors
Scoville, S. Ulu's dog and other stories
Pu'u Pu'iwa
Scoville, S. Ulu's dog and other stories
Ulu's dog
Scoville, S. Ulu's dog and other stories
Waiting for Zilly Finkbine
Scoville, S. Ulu's dog and other stories
Scratches on the back. Blatnik, A.
The **scream**. Davis, D. S.
A **scream** from the sepulcher. Tremayne, P.
Screenwriter. D'Ambrosio, C.
Screwdriver. Bonnie, F.
Scripted. Yuknavitch, L.
SCRIPTWRITERS *See* Authors
The **scruff** of the neck. Leavitt, D.
Scrupulous Amédée. Porter, J. A.
The **sculptor** of sands. Nair, M.
SCULPTORS
See also Women sculptors
Bell, M. S. The naked lady
Koja, K. Velocity
Malamud, B. Rembrandt's hat
Mazelis, J. Tongue
McClanahan, E. The little-known bird of the inner eye
Nair, M. The sculptor of sands
Richter, S. Rats eat cats
Vivante, A. The foundling
Wallace, D. F. The Suffering Channel
SCULPTURE
See also Soap sculpture; Statues; Wood carving
Archer, J. The reclining woman
Clarke, A. C. Trouble with time
Meyers, K. Making the news
'Scuse me, while I kiss this guy. Shepard, J.
Scutt, Cecily
Descent
Dreaming down-under; edited by Jack Dann and Janeen Webb
SEA *See* Ocean
SEA CAPTAINS *See* Seamen; Shipmasters

The **sea** cave. Lawrence, M. C.
Sea change. Grau, S. A.
Sea change, with monsters. McAuley, P. J.
The **sea** horse and the almond. Broks, P.
SEA MONSTERS
See also Loch Ness monster
Benét, S. V. Daniel Webster and the sea serpent
Sea Oak. Saunders, G.
The **sea** shore. O'Hagan, A.
SEA STORIES
See also Seamen names of wars with the subdivision Naval operations
Biguenet, J. And never come up
Buchan, J. The far islands
Davenport, S. Abba's mark
Hodgson, W. H. The bells of the "Laughing Sally"
Hodgson, W. H. The boats of the "Glen Carrrig"
Hodgson, W. H. The finding of the Graiken
Hodgson, W. H. The German spy
Renwick, J. The dolphin story
Shepard, J. Tedford and the megalodon
Steinbeck, T. Blind luck
Vega, A. L. Cloud cover Caribbean
Wetherell, W. D. Hyannis boat
Wolfe, G. The sailor who sailed after the sun
The **sea** wind offers little relief. Irvine, A.
Seagren, Ronnie
Of wood and stone
Once upon a galaxy; edited by Will [sic] McCarthy, Martin H. Greenberg, and John Helfers
Seal Territory. Allaback, S.
SEALS (ANIMALS)
Crowley, J. An earthly mother sits and sings
Rusch, K. K. Strange creatures
Scoville, S. Waiting for Zilly Finkbine
SEAMEN
See also Sea stories; Shipmasters; Vikings
Armstrong, K. Inside passage
Armstrong, K. Night watch
Auerbach, J. Episodes in autobiography
Auerbach, J. Escape
Auerbach, J. Transformations
Babel´, I. You missed the boat, Captain!
Bowles, P. The fourth day out from Santa Cruz
Boylan, C. Villa Marta
Hodgson, W. H. The adventure of the headland
Hodgson, W. H. The adventure with the claim jumpers
Hodgson, W. H. The boats of the "Glen Carrrig"
Hodgson, W. H. The drum of saccharine
Hodgson, W. H. From information received
Hodgson, W. H. The plans of the reefing biplane
Hodgson, W. H. The problem of the pearls
Hodgson, W. H. The thing in the weeds
Jackson, V. F. Victoria and Albert I: Running away to sea
Klíma, I. Long-distance conversations
L'Amour, L. The cross and the candle
L'Amour, L. It's your move
Melville, P. Don't give me your sad stories
Raphael, F. The siren's song
Steinbeck, T. Blighted cargo
Steinbeck, T. Blind luck

SEAMEN—*Continued*
Toes, J. Rhine Ablaze
SEAMSTRESSES *See* Dressmakers
SEANCES *See* Spiritualism
Search and rescue. Stuckey-French, E.
Search bay. Hagy, A. C.
The **search** engine. Alexie, S.
The **search** for a sipping house. Rozanski, J. M.
The **search** for Anna Boubouli. Milletti, C.
Searcher. Vachss, A. H.
Searching for Arthur's Stone. Prum, D.
Searching for Mahesh. Cloutier, N.
Searching for survivors. Banks, R.
Searle, Elizabeth
101
Searle, E. Celebrities in disgrace; a novella and stories
Celebration
Searle, E. Celebrities in disgrace; a novella and stories
Celebrities in disgrace
Searle, E. Celebrities in disgrace; a novella and stories
Memoir of a soon-to-be star
Searle, E. Celebrities in disgrace; a novella and stories
What it's worth
Searle, E. Celebrities in disgrace; a novella and stories
The young and the rest of us
Searle, E. Celebrities in disgrace; a novella and stories
SEASHORE
Boyle, T. C. Death of the cool
Bradbury, R. The sea shell
Brennan, M. In and out of never-never land
Brennan, M. A large bee
Kelman, J. My eldest
Sanabria Santaliz, E. After the hurricane
Updike, J. Nakedness
Williams, C. The machine
SEASIDE RESORTS
Adams, A. At the beach
Adams, A. By the sea
Adams, A. Flights
Adams, A. The haunted beach
Adams, A. La Señora
Joyce, G. Xenos Beach
Pronzini, B. A killing in Xanadu
Season finale. Vukcevich, R.
The **season** of divorce. Cheever, J.
The **season** of the dead. Gascar, P.
Seasons. Landwehr, A.
The **season's** condition. Di Blasi, D.
Seasons of the Ansarac. Le Guin, U. K.
A **seat** for the coming savior. Bottoms, G.
The **seat** of higher consciousness. Stollman, A. L.
Seaton's aunt. De la Mare, W.
SEATTLE (WASH.) *See* Washington (State)—Seattle
Seaworthy. Casey, M.
Sebald, Winfried Georg
Austerlitz
The New Yorker v77 no25 p50-8, 60-71 S 3 2001
Secession, XX. Wells, K.
The **second**. Schnitzler, A.
Second chances. De Lint, C.
The **second** cigarette. Highsmith, P.

The **second** coming. Gores, J.
The **second** coming [excerpt] Percy, W.
The **second** commandment. Armstrong, C.
Second dawn. Clarke, A. C.
The **second** drug. Lupoff, R. A.
The **Second** Floor. Burgin, R.
Second Hand. Offutt, C.
Second-hand man. Dove, R.
Second helping. Chapman, C. M.
Second honeymoon. Michaels, L.
Second island. Ryan, P.
The **second** marriage. Chaudhuri, A.
Second nature. Connor, J.
The **second** night of a one night stand. Painter, P.
The **second** night of summer. Schmitz, J. H.
The **second-oldest** profession. Grant, L.
Second person, secret self. Blegvad, P.
The **second** shepherd. Norris, H.
SECOND SIGHT *See* Clairvoyance; Extrasensory perception
Second skin. Ochsner, G.
Second son. Stolar, D.
Second spring. MacLeod, A.
Second story. Berry, R. M.
The **second-story** angel. Hammett, D.
The **Second** Sunday in October. Dubnov, E.
The **second** tree from the corner. White, E. B.
Second wife. Tuck, L.
The **second** wish. Lumley, B.
Secondhand Rose. Hay, E.
The **secret**. Clarke, A. C.
The **secret** [excerpt] Drought, J.
SECRET AGENTS *See* Secret service; Spies
The **secret** diary of Mrs Rochester. Boylan, C.
The **secret** egg of the clouds. Landis, G. A.
The **secret** garden. Hoffman, W.
The **Secret** Goldfish. Means, D.
Secret history of home cinema. Bottoms, G.
The **secret** miracle. Borges, J. L.
A **secret** murder. Franks, R.
The **secret** of cartwheels. Henley, P.
The **secret** of his sleep. McGarry, J.
Secret of Silver Springs. L'Amour, L.
The **secret** of the mummy's brain. Eakin, W.
SECRET SERVICE
See also International intrigue; World War, 1939-1945—Secret service
Jakes, J. Cloak and digger
Jakes, J. Dr. Sweetkill
Latour, J. Golam
Secret, silent. Oates, J. C.
The **Secret** Staff. Pack, J.
SECRETARIES
Bowles, P. At the Krungthep Plaza
Cheever, J. The five-forty-eight
Grillo, A. What my boss is thinking
Stevenson, J. The island of the day before yesterday
Trevanian. The sacking of Miss Plimsoll
Wharton, E. Full circle
Secrets. Cheng, C.-W.
Secrets. Hart, C. G.
The **secrets** of bats. Row, J.
The **secrets** of Cooperstown. Lee, M.
The **secrets** of Miss Plimsoll, private secretary. See Trevanian. The sacking of Miss Plimsoll
Secrets: three short stories. Browder, C.
The **Sect** of the Thirty. Borges, J. L.

SECTS
Borges, J. L. The Sect of the Thirty

Securitas. Herbert, Z.

Security check. Clarke, A. C.

The **seder**. Porzecanski, T.

Seduce me. Rabb, M.

SEDUCTION
Addonizio, K. Have you seen me?

Berkman, P. R. Men have more upper-body strength

Bukiet, M. J. The return of eros to academe

Bunin, I. A. Styopa

Capote, T. The walls are cold

Carlson, R. Keith

Carlson, R. Nightcap

Chekhov, A. P. A misfortune

DeLancey, K. The seven pearls

DeLancey, K. The Welsh engineer

Deming, R. Honeymoon cruise

Dyson, J. Love in the time of Molyneux

Erian, A. Standing up to the superpowers

Gay, W. Bonedaddy, Quincy Nell, and the fifteen thousand BTU electric chair

George, E. I, Richard

Gilb, D. About Tere who was in Palomas

Gilb, D. Mayela one day in 1989

Glover, D. H. Bad news of the heart

Guerrero, L. Blanca Rosa

Hamburger, A. Jerusalem

Iagnemma, K. The phrenologist's dream

Lida, D. Shuttered

Louis, L. G. The quiet at the bottom of the pool

Meredith, D. The closer

Oates, J. C. Where are you going, where have you been?

Schmidt, H. J. Darling?

Small, B. Mastering Lady Lucinda

Strauss, A. Recovering Larry

Weldon, F. Inspector remorse

Whitty, J. Stealing from the dead

Winegardner, M. The visiting poet

Yates, R. Evening on the Côte d'Azur

Zweig, S. The burning secret

The **seduction** of my sister. Bail, M.

The **seductress**. Campbell, R.

See How Small. Blackwood, S.

See how they run. Campbell, R.

See the pyramids. Beattie, A.

See through. Reifler, N.

See what the boys in the locked room will have. Crider, B.

Seed. Waters, M. Y.

The **seed** of the faith. Wharton, E.

Seeing a specialist. Rossi, C.

Seeing in the dark. Schiffman, C.

Seeing red. Collins, B.

Seeing the world. Robinson, L.

Seeing Things. Chang, D.

Seeker of the Sphinx. See Clarke, A. C. The road to the sea

Seepaul, Lionel
Pan for Pockot
The Oxford book of Caribbean short stories; edited by Stewart Brown and John Wickham

Sefarim, Mendele Mokher
The little man; or, The life story of Yitsik-Avrom the power broker
Neugroschel, J. No star too beautiful; Yiddish stories from 1382 to the present; compiled and translated by Joachim Neugroschel

Shem and Japeth on a train
Neugroschel, J. No star too beautiful; Yiddish stories from 1382 to the present; compiled and translated by Joachim Neugroschel

SEGREGATION *See* Race relations

Segriff, Larry
Specters in the moonlight
Children of the night; stories of ghosts, vampires, werewolves, and "lost children"; edited by Martin H. Greenberg

Seidman, Lisa
Over my shoulder
A Deadly dozen; tales of murder from members of Sisters in Crime/Los Angeles; edited by Susan B. Casmier, Aljean Harmetz and Cynthia Lawrence

Seiffert, Rachel
Architect
Seiffert, R. Field study

Blue
Seiffert, R. Field study

The crossing
Seiffert, R. Field study

Dimitroff
Seiffert, R. Field study

Dog-leg lane
Seiffert, R. Field study

Field Study
Granta no81 p73-88 Spr 2003
Seiffert, R. Field study

Francis John Jones, 1924-
Seiffert, R. Field study

The last spring
Seiffert, R. Field study

Reach
Seiffert, R. Field study

Second best
Seiffert, R. Field study

Tentsmuir sands
Seiffert, R. Field study

Seize the day. DeMarinis, R.

Seizing control. Robison, M.

Sekaran, Shanthi
Stalin
Best new American voices 2004; guest editor John Casey; series editors John Kulka and Natalie Danford

Selected lives in brief. Cole, C. B.

Self, Will
My idea of fun [excerpt]
Dark: stories of madness, murder, and the supernatural; edited by Clint Willis

SELF-DEFENSE *See* Martial arts

Self-defense. Norris, L.

Self knowledge. Bausch, R.

Self-love. Serna, E.

The **self-made** brain surgeon. Harris, M.

SELF-MADE MEN
See also Success

Self Portrait(s). Tomasula, S.

SELF-SERVICE LAUNDRIES
Carter, E. Clean clothes

SELFISHNESS
  Brennan, M. The rose garden
  Lao She. No distance too far, no sacrifice too
    great
Selgin, Peter
  Swimming
    The Literary Review (Madison, N.J.) v46 no4
      p698-713 Summ 2003
Seliki. McQuillin, C.
Sell, Scott
  Saturday
    Bomb no89 p94-7 Fall 2004
Sellers, Heather
  Fla. boys
    New stories from the South: the year's best,
      1999; edited by Shannon Ravenel; with a
      preface by Tony Earley
    Sellers, H. Georgia under water; stories
  Florida law
    Sellers, H. Georgia under water; stories
  The Gulf of Mexico
    Sellers, H. Georgia under water; stories
  In the drink
    Sellers, H. Georgia under water; stories
  It's water, it's not going to kill you
    Sellers, H. Georgia under water; stories
  Myself as a delicious peach
    Sellers, H. Georgia under water; stories
  Sinking
    Sellers, H. Georgia under water; stories
  Sleep creep leap
    Sellers, H. Georgia under water; stories
  Spurt
    Sellers, H. Georgia under water; stories
Selling delphinium. Bonnie, F.
Selling the house. Smith, S. J.
Seltz, Eugene
  Compelle intrare
    With signs and wonders; an international an-
      thology of Jewish fabulist fiction; edited by
      Daniel M. Jaffe
Selvon, Samuel
  The cricket match
    The Oxford book of Caribbean short stories;
      edited by Stewart Brown and John
      Wickham
SEMINARIANS
  Chekhov, A. P. The student
  Hegi, U. Hotel of the saints
  Updike, J. Lifeguard
Semley's necklace. Le Guin, U. K.
Semper paratus. Hagy, A. C.
Sempiterno's fears. Maleti, G.
SENATE (U.S.) *See* United States. Congress. Sen-
  ate
Senator Bilbo. Duncan, A.
SENATORS *See* United States. Congress. Senate
Send no money. Dozois, G. R.
Senior, Olive
  Do angels wear brassieres?
    The Oxford book of Caribbean short stories;
      edited by Stewart Brown and John
      Wickham
  Mad Fish
    Whispers from the cotton tree root; Caribbean
      fabulist fiction; edited by Nalo Hopkinson
Señor Alvaro. Francis, H. E.
Señor Ong and Señor Ha. Bowles, P.
La Señora. Adams, A.

A **Sense** of Colour. Humfrey, M.
Sense of humor. Runyon, D.
A **sense** of humour. Dorcey, M.
Sensible city. Ellison, H.
Sensitive things. Davis, L.
Senstad, Susan Schwartz
  And Who Shall Provide the Lamb?
    The Literary Review (Madison, N.J.) v47 no1
      p69-78 Fall 2003
The **sentence.** Berry, R. M.
Sentence imposed. Neri, K.
The **sentimental** education. Holleran, A.
Sentimental, heartbroken rednecks. Bottoms, G.
A **sentimental** journey. Taylor, P. H.
A **sentimental** soul. Chopin, K.
The **sentinel.** Clarke, A. C.
Sentinels. Pipik, J. and Vargo, J.
Senti's last elephant. Whitty, J.
Separate vacations. Trollope, J.
A **separate** war. Haldeman, J. W.
Separating. Updike, J.
Separation anxiety. Shockley, E.
SEPHARDIM
  Kirchheimer, G. D. Arbitration
  Kirchheimer, G. D. A case of dementia
  Kirchheimer, G. D. Changelings
  Kirchheimer, G. D. Feast of Lights
  Kirchheimer, G. D. Food of love
  Kirchheimer, G. D. Goodbye, evil eye
  Kirchheimer, G. D. Rafi
  Kirchheimer, G. D. Silver screen
  Kirchheimer, G. D. A skirmish in the desert
  Kirchheimer, G. D. Traffic manager
  Kirchheimer, G. D. The voyager
Sepia sun. Morgan, D.
SEPTEMBER 11 TERRORIST ATTACKS,
  2001
  Gray, A. Job's skin game
  Oates, J. C. The mutants
Sequel on Skorpios. Bishop, M.
The **Seraph** and the Zambesi. Spark, M.
SERBIANS
                United States
  Small, K. The b-zone open
Serdatzky, Yente
  Rosh Hashanah
    Beautiful as the moon, radiant as the stars;
      Jewish women in Yiddish stories : an an-
      thology; edited by Sandra Bark; introduc-
      tion by Francine Prose
  Two heads
    Beautiful as the moon, radiant as the stars;
      Jewish women in Yiddish stories : an an-
      thology; edited by Sandra Bark; introduc-
      tion by Francine Prose
The **sergeant.** Garcia, L. G.
Sergeant Houck. Schaefer, J. W.
Sergeant Prishibeyev. Chekhov, A. P.
SERGEANTS *See* Soldiers
The **sergeant's** cat. Van de Wetering, J.
Series. Pratt, D.
Sermon. Powell, P.
Serna, Enrique
  Self-love
    Points of departure; new stories from Mexico;
      edited by Mónica Lavín; translated by Gus-
      tavo Segade
The **serpent's** back. Rankin, I.
The **serpent's** gift [excerpt] Lee, H. E.

Serpent's tooth. Norton, A.
The **servant** problem. Tenn, W.
SERVANTS
>*See also* African American servants types of household employees
Alas, L. Torso
Alcott, L. M. Ruth's secret
Brennan, M. The servants' dance
Bunin, I. A. Little fool
Chang, L. S. Pipa's story
Chekhov, A. P. An anonymous story
Cheng Naishan. Hong Taitai
Gilman, C. P. Turned
Hunter, F. Laban and Murugi
Kohler, S. Africans
Lopes, H. The advance
Louie, D. W. Displacement
Marías, J. Unfinished figures
Melville, P. English table wuk
Richter, J. The ones left behind
Saidi, W. The garden of evil
Singer, I. B. Yanda
Spark, M. Another pair of hands
Tabatabai, N. The lark
Servants. Kavaler, R.
The **servants'** dance. Brennan, M.
Servants of the map. Barrett, A.
Service. Lovisi, G.
SERVICE STATIONS *See* Automobiles—Service stations
Set in stone. Knight, P.
Setting. Mazelis, J.
Settled. Slezak, E.
Setton, Ruth Knafo
>The cat garden
>>With signs and wonders; an international anthology of Jewish fabulist fiction; edited by Daniel M. Jaffe
Ševčovič, Peter
>Near to eternity
>>In search of homo sapiens; twenty-five contemporary Slovak short stories; editor, Pavol Hudík ; [translated by Heather Trebatická; American English editor, Lucy Bednár]
Seven. Danticat, E.
Seven drops of blood. Weinberg, R.
Seven fishes. Barolini, H.
Seven for a secret. De Lint, C.
Seven magpies. McWilliam, C.
The **seven** pearls. DeLancey, K.
Seven pictures not taken. Donoghue, E.
Seven swans. Chan, D. M.
Seven thousand flowers. Mazelis, J.
Seven types of ambiguity. Chaon, D.
Seven variations on the theme of untied shoelaces. Grushin, O.
Seven wild sisters. De Lint, C.
Seventeen syllables. Yamamoto, H.
The **seventh** year. Leegant, J.
Seventy-two letters. Chiang, T.
Several anecdotes about my wife. Shteyngart, G.
Several answers. Mandelbaum, P.
Several losses. Hay, E.
Severance: Three Fictions. Butler, R. O.
Severed hand. Jaffe, H.
Sevi, Sabbatai *See* Shabbethai Tzevi, 1626-1676
Sewer fauna. Hernández, C.

SEX
Adam, C. Porcupine
Addonizio, K. Angels
Addonizio, K. Bedtime story
Addonizio, K. Emergency room
Addonizio, K. The fall of Saigon
Addonizio, K. Gaps
Addonizio, K. The gift
Addonizio, K. In the box called pleasure
Addonizio, K. Inside out
Addonizio, K. Reading Sontag
Addonizio, K. Testimony
Agee, J. Was
Aniebo, I. N. C. Four dimensions
Armstrong, K. Night watch
Avalli, I. Simena
Avrich, J. Life in dearth
Baca, J. S. Mother's ashes
Banbury, J. Take, for example, meatpie
Barker, N. Dual balls
Barker, N. Skin
Barrett, N., Jr. Ginny Sweethips' Flying Circus
Bart, P. Dangerous company
Bausch, R. 1-900
Bausch, R. The voices from the other room
Berkman, P. R. Gold glitter
Berkman, P. R. Men have more upper-body strength
Bezmozgis, D. Natasha
Bilick, A. The psychologist (who doesn't love me)
Bingham, S. The big bed
Blair, J. Ghost river
Blaise, C. A North American education
Blatnik, A. Damp walls
Block, L. Speaking of lust
Block, L. Sweet little hands
Bobes, M. Ten years later
Boyczuk, R. Doing time
Boylan, C. Bad-natured dog
Bracken, M. Feel the pain
Bradbury, R. Junior
Brite, P. Z. and Faust, C. Saved
Brownrigg, S. Hussy from the west
Broyard, B. Snowed in
Budnitz, J. Skin care
Byers, M. The beautiful days
Campbell, R. The body in the window
Campbell, R. Dolls
Campbell, R. Loveman's comeback
Campbell, R. The other woman
Campbell, R. The seductress
Campbell, R. Stages
Campo, R. Like a banana
Carter, E. A
Casey, M. Drastic
Codrescu, A. Three simple hearts
Cody, L. Queen of mean
Cohen, R. Between hammers
Cole, M. Enough was enough
Collins, B. Dalliance at Sunnydale
Collins, M. and Lynds, G. A delicate mission
Coover, R. Visitation
Craig, A. The French Boy
Daniels, J. Middle of the mitten
Daniels, J. Sugar water
Davenport, G. The bicycle rider
Davenport, G. The ringdove sign
Davenport, G. Wo es war, soll ich werden

SEX—*Continued*

Davis, J. S. Pojo's and the buttery slope
De Lint, C. In this soul of a woman
De Noux, O. The Iberville mistress
Devereaux, R. Li'l Miss Ultrasound
Devine, T. The pleasure game
Di Blasi, D. Drowning hard
Di Blasi, D. Our perversions
Di Blasi, D. Pavlov's smile
Di Blasi, D. Where all things converge
Dinh, L. A cultured boy
Doenges, J. The money stays, the people go
Dorsey, C. J. (Learning about) machine sex
Duffy, S. Martha Grace
Dybek, S. We didn't
Dyson, J. All in the telling
Dyson, J. Love in the time of Molyneux
Eldridge, Courtney. The former world record
     holder settles down
Englander, N. Peep show
Erian, A. Alcatraz
Erian, A. On the occasion of my ruination
Erian, A. You
Esquivel, L. Blessed reality
Estep, M. Animals
Estep, M. Horses
Estep, M. Monkeys
Estep, M. The patient
Estep, M. Teeth
Estep, M. Tools
Farnham, B. Midnight trash
Fell, A. There's tradition for you
Fischer, T. I like being killed
Fleming, R. Havoc after dark
Fleming, R. Speak no evil
Freudenberger, N. The tutor
Fulton, J. First sex
Fulton, J. Iceland
Garrett, C. Circuits
Garrett, M. Candie-gram
Garrett, M. Sex crimes
Gates, D. The intruder
Gelb, J. Trophy wife
Gifford, B. The big love of Cherry Lane
Gifford, B. The brief confession of an unrepen-
     tant erotic
Gilb, D. Bottoms
Girardi, R. Sunday evenings at Contessa
     Pasquali's
Glassco, B. Taking loup
Goran, L. Keeping count
Gordimer, N. The diamond mine
Gorman, E. Such a good girl
Greenwood, K. Jetsam
Griffith, M. Bibliophilia
Grodstein, L. Gazelles
Hand, E. Cleopatra Brimstone
Harfenist, J. Body count
Harfenist, J. Pixie dust
Hayes, D. Shakedown
Hayes, D. What I wanted most of all
Hejazi, B. The pool
Hendricks, V. Stormy, mon amour
Hopkinson, N. Fisherman
Hopkinson, N. Ganger (ball lightning)
Hunter, F. A newsman scratches an itch
Iribarne, M. Sudden mysteries
Jesús, P. d. Images, questions re: beautiful dead
     woman

Jewell, L. Labia Lobelia
Johnson, A. The eighth sea
Johnson, S. Risking it all
Jong, E. En route to the congress of dreams; or,
     The zipless fuck
Joseph, D. Windows and words
Joyce, G. First, catch your demon
Kachtick, K. Hungry ghost
Keegan, C. Antarctica
Kelly, J. A Dick and Jane story
Kimber, J. Having myself a time
Koja, K. Bondage
Koja, K. and Malzberg, B. N. What we did that
     summer
Kosinski, J. N. Steps [excerpt]
Kuryla, M. Mis-sayings
La Spina, S. The night of crossed destinies
LaValle, V. D. Class trip
LaValle, V. D. Raw daddy
Le Guin, U. K. The royals of Hegn
Leong, R. A yin and her man
Lethem, J. Five fucks
Limsky, D. Hating yourself in the morning
Litzky, Tsaurah. End-of-the-world sex
Lochte, D. In the city of angels
Longstreet, K. A. The judgement of Paris
Lumley, B. The luststone
Maraini, D. The zipper
Marber, P. Peter Shelley
Marsten, R. Every morning
Massey, S. The convenience boy
McDermid, V. Metamorphosis
McEwan, I. Pornography
Means, D. Coitus
Means, D. The widow predicament
Mellick, C. Porno in August
Meyers, A. and Meyers, M. The Daffodil
Michaels, L. City boy
Millar, M. Dreams of sex and stage diving [ex-
     cerpt]
Miller, R. Walking to Paris
Mistress Morgana. All in a day's work
Moline, K. No parachutes
Mrabet, M. The canebrake
Mueller, D. P. M. R. C.
Munger, K. The man
Nair, M. Video
Nakagami, K. Red hair
Nesbitt, M. The ones who may kill you in the
     morning
Niles, C. Revenge is the best revenge
Nissen, T. Way back when in the now before
     now
Oates, J. C. Upholstery
Oates, J. C. Where are you going, where have
     you been?
O'Neill, S. Broken stone
O'Neill, S. The perils of Pappy
Painter, P. Inside her, in heaven
Paschal, D. By the light of the jukebox
Paschal, D. L'Annonciation
Paschal, D. Python
Pasquali, M. d. Envy
Paz, S. Don't tell her you love her
Pelegrimas, M. and Randisi, R. J. Money-back
     guarantee
Perabo, S. The rocks over Kyburz
Petrignani, S. Body
Phillips, G. The raiders

SEX—*Continued*

Phillips, S. Sockdolager
Piñón, N. House of passion
Polansky, S. Coda
Pomerantz, S. Ghost knife
Proulx, A. Pair a spurs
Randisi, R. J. Initimate obsession
Ravera, L. You drive
Rawley, D. A rumor of prayer
Reiner, C. Caz
Reiner, C. Dial 411 for legal smut
Rekulak, J. Pinball
Richter, S. My date with Satan
Richter, S. The ocean
Rinehart, S. The blue Norton
Roche, T. S. Bank job
Roche, T. S. Dirty pool
Rollins, H. Beauty and the beast
Rollins, H. Cinderella
Rollins, H. The empress's new lingerie
Rollins, H. Goldie and the three bare bachelors
Rollins, H. Hansel and Gretel
Rollins, H. Jackie and the beanstalk
Rollins, H. The miller's daughter (Rumpelstiltskin)
Rollins, H. Rapunzel
Rollins, H. Red
Rollins, H. The sleeping beauty
Rollins, H. Snow White and the seven dwarves
Rollins, H. The three little pigs
Rucker, R. v. B. Buzz
Rucker, R. v. B. Inside out
Rucker, R. v. B. Rapture in space
Ryan, P. L. Life is a highway
Sade, marquis de. Emilie de Tourville; or, Fraternal cruelty
Sade, marquis de. The husband who turned priest: a tale of Provence
Sade, marquis de. Room for two
Sade, marquis de. The teacher philosopher
Sade, marquis de. Your wish is my command; or, As you like it
Salvatori, C. The flight of the elephant
Sanchez, S. Wounded in the house of a friend
Schnitzler, A. Dream story
Schone, R. A man and a woman
Schulman, H. P.S.
Schulze, I. The ring
Shapiro, G. Worst-case scenarios
Sheffield, C. Phallicide
Sherman, C. W. Touch [excerpt]
Simonds, M. The blue of the Madrugada
Singer, I. B. The interview
Slavin, J. Painting house
Small, B. Mastering Lady Lucinda
Smith, M. M. Two shot
Sojourner, M. My tree
Sorrentino, G. Lost in the stars
Sorrentino, G. The moon in its flight
Sorrentino, G. Things that have stopped moving
Sosin, D. There are no green butterflies
Spatz, G. Anyone's Venus
Stamell, R. B. Love for a fat man
Stern, D. In the country of the young
Stern, S. The sin of Elijah
Sumner, M. Good-hearted woman
Swain, H. Sushi
Tani, C. The punishment
Taylor, L. Unspeakable

Tester, W. Where the dark ended
Theroux, P. A Judas memoir
Tillman, L. Pleasure isn't a pretty picture
Touré. A guest!
Touré. A hot time at the Church of Kentucky Fried Souls and the spectacular final Sunday sermon of the Right Revren Daddy Love
Troncoso, S. Angie Luna
Updike, J. The morning
Updike, J. Transaction
Updike, J. Wife-wooing
Vachss, A. H. Safe sex
Vapnyar, L. Love lessons — Mondays, 9 A.M.
Vardeman, R. E. Feedback
Vigano, V. Giraglia
Wallace, D. F. Adult world [I]
Wallace, D. F. Adult world [II]
Wallace, D. F. Brief interviews with hideous men [I]
Wallace, D. F. Brief interviews with hideous men [II]
Wallace, D. F. Brief interviews with hideous men [III]
Wallace, D. F. Brief interviews with hideous men [IV]
Watanabe McFerrin, L. Rubber time
Wells, K. A. wonderland
Welsh, I. Trainspotting [excerpt]
Wexler, M. What Marcia wanted
White, E. Forgetting Elena [excerpt]
Williams, D. Very, very, red
Wilson, M. Youthful offenders
Wilson, Jeff. Buddherotica
Wisenberg, S. L. Big Ruthie imagines sex without pain
Wisenberg, S. L. Big Ruthie imagines sex without pain
Wolverton, T. Sex less
Yuknavitch, L. Against interpretation
Yuknavitch, L. Sade's mistress
Yuknavitch, L. Signification
Sex and violence. Pickard, N.
Sex crimes. Garrett, M.
Sex less. Wolverton, T.
Sex, lies, and apple pie. LaPierre, J.
The **sex** opposite. Sturgeon, T.

SEX PROBLEMS

> *See also* Hermaphroditism; Incest; Marriage problems; Promiscuity; Sexual perversion; Transsexuals; Transvestism; Voyeurs

Brodkey, H. Innocence
Lessing, D. M. One off the short list

SEX ROLE

Armstrong, K. Hunga Pass
Atwood, M. Freeforall
Gilman, C. P. The cottagette
Gilman, C. P. Herland
Gilman, C. P. If I were a man
Gilman, C. P. What Diantha did
Gilman, C. P. With her in Ourland
Naranjo, C. Symbiotic encounter
Skillings, R. D. The sandbox
Winter, E. Pretty please

SEXUAL HARASSMENT

Bausch, R. Unjust
Klass, P. The province of the bearded fathers
Mosley, W. Pet fly
Winegardner, M. The visiting poet

SEXUAL INSTINCT
Boswell, M. Born again
Bush, M. Love
Carlson, R. Evil eye Allen
Chapman, C. M. Johnny pumpkinseed
Clarke, B. The Lolita School
Cutrufelli, M. R. Happiness
Davis, C. A. Brand new boyfriend
DeMarco, T. A boy's will is the winds's will
DeMarinis, R. Experience
DeMarinis, R. Hormone X
Dybek, S. Blue boy
Edgerton, C. Debra's flap and snap
Guerra, L. The virgin's passion
Gwyn, A. Against the pricks
Händler, E.-W. Language game
Henley, P. Picking time
Keegan, C. The Ginger Rogers sermon
LaValle, V. D. Who we did worship
Nair, M. The lodger in room 726
Naiyer Masud. Sheesha ghat
Orner, P. Sitting Theodore
Orringer, J. The smoothest way is full of stones
Paschal, D. Moriya
Reifler, N. Julian
Singer, I. B. A boy knows the truth
Slezak, E. Last year's Jesus (or Passion play)
Tester, W. Cousins
Williams, M. There aren't any foxes in that cave
Williams, M. Truth and goodness
Yates, R. A compassionate leave
Yi, T.-H. The blazing sun

SEXUAL PERVERSION
Campbell, R. Lilith's
Campbell, R. The limits of fantasy
Lansdale, J. R. Billie Sue
Theroux, P. The stranger at the Palazzo d'Oro

SEXUALLY TRANSMITTED DISEASES
Gilman, C. P. The crux
Knight, J. Schering PC4—a love story
MacLaverty, B. Between two shores
McHugh, M. F. Interview: on any given day
Sexy. Lahiri, J.

Seydel, Mimi
Admirable qualities
The Virginia Quarterly Review v75 no4 p698-715 Aut 1999

Seymour. Orner, P.
Seymour Rising. Orner, P.

SHABBETHAI TZEVI, 1626-1676
About
Muñiz-Huberman, A. The tower of Gallipoli
Shabos-Nakhamu. Babel´, I.

Shabtai, Yaakov
Uncle Peretz takes flight
Six Israeli novellas; [by] Ruth Almog [et al.]; edited and with an introduction by Gershon Shaked; translated from the Hebrew by Dalya Bilu, Philip Simpson, and Marganit Weinberger-Rotman

Shabthai Tsebi *See* Shabbethai Tzevi, 1626-1676

Shackelford, Richard T.
From Tucson to Tucumcari, from Tehachapi to Tonopah
Stories from the Blue Moon Café; edited by Sonny Brewer

Shacochis, Bob
Easy in the islands
Living on the edge; fiction by Peace Corps writers; edited by John Coyne
Mundo's sign
The Workshop; seven decades of the Iowa Writers' Workshop: 42 stories, recollections & essays on Iowa's place in 20th-century American literature; edited by Tom Grimes
Sabo
Harper's v302 no1813 p76-83 Je 2001
Squirrelly's grouper
Fishing's best short stories; edited by Paul D. Staudohar

Shade, Eric
Blood
Shade, E. Eyesores; stories
Eyesores
Shade, E. Eyesores; stories
A final reunion
Shade, E. Eyesores; stories
The heart hankers
Shade, E. Eyesores; stories
Hoops and wires and plugs
Shade, E. Eyesores; stories
Kaahumanu
Shade, E. Eyesores; stories
The last night of the county fair
Shade, E. Eyesores; stories
A rage forever
Shade, E. Eyesores; stories
Souvenirs
Shade, E. Eyesores; stories
Stability
Shade, E. Eyesores; stories
Superfly
Shade, E. Eyesores; stories

Shade work. Pronzini, B.
Shadow boxing. Yuknavitch, L.
The **shadow** over Innsmouth. Lovecraft, H. P.
The **shadow,** the darkness. Ligotti, T.
Shadowboxing. Allen, J. R.
Shadowboxing. Learst, A.
Shadows. Iorillo, J. and Pipik, J.
Shadows. Maraini, D.
Shadows. Short, B.
Shadows. Walker, D.
Shadows move in the Britannia Bar. Khan, I.
The **shadowy** third. Glasgow, E.
Shaft. Enright, A.

Shah, Sejal
Mary, Staring at Me
Meridians v2 no2 p36-40 2002

Shainberg, Lawrence
Memories of amnesia [excerpt]
The Vintage book of amnesia; an anthology; edited by Jonathan Lethem

The **Shaker** bridal. Hawthorne, N.

SHAKERS
Hawthorne, N. The Canterbury pilgrims
Hawthorne, N. The Shaker bridal

Shakespeare, Anne Hathaway *See* Hathaway, Anne, 1556?-1623

SHAKESPEARE, WILLIAM, 1564-1616
About
Baker, K. The dust enclosed here
Benford, G. In the dark backward
Berkman, P. R. Diamonds at her fingertips
Berkman, P. R. Gold

SHAKESPEARE, WILLIAM, 1564-1616—
About—*Continued*
  Berkman, P. R. In the bed
  Berkman, P. R. Jennet
  Berkman, P. R. Mary Mountjoy's dowry
  Berkman, P. R. No cause
  Borges, J. L. Shakespeare's memory
  Fitzgerald, F. S. Tarquin of cheapside
  Lane, A. The gaze of the falcon
  Pronzini, B. and Malzberg, B. N. Shakespeare
    MCMLXXXV
  Sanders, W. The undiscovered
  Updike, J. Tomorrow and tomorrow and so
    forth
              Characters
              Caliban
  Aldiss, B. W. Nothing in life is ever enough
            Lady Macbeth
  Berkman, P. R. The Scottish wife
  Henderson, L. Tragic heroines tell all
              Ophelia
  Berkman, P. R. Dark blue
              Titania
  Berkman, P. R. Magic wand
       Parodies, imitations, etc.
  Anderson, P. A midsummer tempest
  Avrich, J. Lady Macbeth, prickly pear queen
          Romeo and Juliet
  Berkman, P. R. Duty
Shakespeare's memory. Borges, J. L.
Shall we dance? Bingham, S.
Shall we take a little walk? Benford, G.
Shamara. Vasilenko, S.
Shambles. Monroe, D.
Shame the devil. Murray, M.
A **shameful** affair. Chopin, K.
Shamengwa. Erdrich, L.
The **shaming** of broken horn. Gulick, B.
Shange, Ntozake
  Every time my lil' world seems blue
    The Bluelight corner; black women writing on
      passion, sex, and romantic love; edited by
      Rosemarie Robotham
  Ridin' the moon in Texas
    The African American West; a century of
      short stories; edited by Bruce A. Glasrud
      and Laurie Champion
SHANGHAI (CHINA) *See* China—Shanghai
Shankman, Sarah
  If you can't take the heat
    Mom, apple pie, and murder; edited by Nancy
      Pickard
  Love thy neighbor
    Irreconcilable differences; Lia Matera, editor
Shannahan, Marilyn
  A Map of Stars
    Prairie Schooner v76 no4 p94-104 Wint 2002
Shannon, Ray *See* Haywood, Gar Anthony
Shannon made of sunlight and bones. Goran, L.
Shapcott, Tom
  The geography of the body
    The Literary Review (Madison, N.J.) v45 no1
      p195-8 Fall 2001
The **shape** of everything. Reed, R.
The **shape** of jazz to come. Saroyan, A.
A **shape** of light. Goyen, W.
The **shape** of murder. Watson, I.
The **shape** of the sword. Borges, J. L.
The **shape** of things. Steiber, E.

The **Shape-Up**. Hill, A. J.
Shapiro, Dani
  Plane crash theory
    On the rocks; the KGB Bar fiction anthology;
      edited by Rebecca Donner ; foreword by
      Denis Woychuk
    Ploughshares v27 no1 p162-76 Spr 2001
Shapiro, Gerald
  At the great divide
    Shapiro, G. Bad Jews and other stories
  Bad Jews
    A different plain; contemporary Nebraska fic-
      tion writers; edited by Ladette Randolph ;
      introduction by Mary Pipher
    Shapiro, G. Bad Jews and other stories
  The Feigenbaum Foundation
    Shapiro, G. Bad Jews and other stories
  Rosenthal unbound
    Shapiro, G. Bad Jews and other stories
  Shifman in paradise
    Shapiro, G. Bad Jews and other stories
  Suskind, the impresario
    Shapiro, G. Bad Jews and other stories
  The tutor
    Shapiro, G. Bad Jews and other stories
  The twelve plagues
    Shapiro, G. Bad Jews and other stories
  Worst-case scenarios
    Neurotica: Jewish writers on sex; edited by
      Melvin Jules Bukiet
    Shapiro, G. Bad Jews and other stories
Shapiro, Jane
  Mousetrap
    Snapshots: 20th century mother-daughter fic-
      tion; edited by Joyce Carol Oates and Janet
      Berliner
Shapiro, Janice
  Predation
    The North American Review v284 no5 p44-48
      S/O 1999
Shapiro, Joshua
  Getting Mario
    The Literary Review (Madison, N.J.) v44 no3
      p434-46 Spr 2001
Shapiro, Lamed
  The cross
    Neugroschel, J. No star too beautiful; Yiddish
      stories from 1382 to the present; compiled
      and translated by Joachim Neugroschel
Shapiro, Levi Joshua *See* Shapiro, Lamed, 1878-
    1948
Shared and stolen. Joseph, D.
Shared credit. Raphael, F.
The **sharers**. McBain, E.
Sharifzadeh, Mansureh
  Butterflies
    A Feast in the mirror; stories by contempo-
      rary Iranian women; translated and edited
      by Mohammad Mehdi Khorrami, Shouleh
      Vatanabadi
Sharing Hale-Bopp. Watmough, D.
Sharking. Hagy, A. C.
SHARKS
  Clarke, A. C. The deep range
  Lumley, B. No sharks in the Med
Sharks. Reisman, N.

Sharma, Akhil
Surrounded by sleep
The Best American short stories, 2002; selected from U.S. and Canadian magazines by Sue Miller with Katrina Kenison, with an introduction by Sue Miller
The New Yorker v77 no39 p90-7 D 10 2001
Sharon. Spencer, E.
The **sharp** light of trespassers. Davis, W.
Sharratt, Mary
The anatomy of a mermaid
The Year's best fantasy & horror, thirteenth annual collection; edited by Ellen Datlow and Terri Windling
Shaska Christ. Babel´, I.
Shatsi. Crowther, P.
Shattuck, Jessica
Bodies
The New Yorker v78 no29 p112-14, 116, 118, 120-2, 124-5 S 30 2002
SHAW, BERNARD, 1856-1950
About
Bradbury, R. G.B.S.- Mark V
Shaw, Christopher
Winds of Tehuantepec
New England Review v20 no1 p83-96 Wint 1999
Shaw, Dave
Any myth you can imagine
Shaw, D. Here comes the roar
A cure for gravity
Shaw, D. Here comes the roar
Diving with the devil
Shaw, D. Here comes the roar
Holding pattern at D.C. National
Shaw, D. Here comes the roar
Shaw, George Bernard *See* Shaw, Bernard, 1856-1950
Shaw, Irwin
The eighty-yard run
Gentlemen's Quarterly v69 no9 p292+ S 1999
Return to Kansas City
Boxing's best short stories; edited by Paul D. Staudohar
Sailor off the Bremen
Wonderful town; New York stories from The New Yorker; edited by David Remnick with Susan Choi
Whispers in bedlam
Sports best short stories; edited by Paul D. Staudohar
Shaw, Lau *See* Lao She, 1899-1966
Shawl, Nisi
At the huts of Ajala
Dark matter; a century of speculative fiction from the African diaspora; edited by Sheree R. Thomas
The tawny bitch
Mojo: conjure stories; edited by Nalo Hopkinson
The **shawl**. Erdrich, L.
The **shawl**. Ozick, C.
Shaykh, Hanan al- *See* Al-Shaykh, Hanan
Shayla, Heidi
The River Pig
Prairie Schooner v78 no1 p133-44 Spr 2004
Shayna Kupp. Felsenfeld, J.

Shayne, Alan
The minstrel tree
Good Housekeeping v233 no6 p97-108 D 2001
She. Brown, J.
She had mastered the art. Blitz, R.
She knows, I know, and heaven knows. Pak, W.-S.
She only goes out at night . . . Tenn, W.
She rote. Harvey, J.
She wasn't soft. Boyle, T. C.
She who caught buses. Brownrigg, S.
The **she-wolf**. Saki
She wore a yellow ribbon. Olsen, P.
Shea, Suzanne Strempek
The sweater
Yankee v63 no11 p64-9+ N 1999
Shearing, Joseph, 1886-1952
For works written by this author under other names see Bowen, Marjorie, 1886-1952
Shechter, Yakov
Midday
With signs and wonders; an international anthology of Jewish fabulist fiction; edited by Daniel M. Jaffe
Sheckley, Robert
Agamemnon's run
Sheckley, R. Uncanny tales
The city of the dead
Sheckley, R. Uncanny tales
The day the aliens came
Sheckley, R. Uncanny tales
Deep Blue Sleep
Sheckley, R. Uncanny tales
The dream of misunderstanding
Sheckley, R. Uncanny tales
Dukakis and the aliens
Sheckley, R. Uncanny tales
Emissary from a green and yellow world
Sheckley, R. Uncanny tales
Magic, maples, and Maryanne
Sheckley, R. Uncanny tales
Mind-slaves of Manotori
Sheckley, R. Uncanny tales
Mirror games
Sheckley, R. Uncanny tales
The new Horla
Sheckley, R. Uncanny tales
Pandora's box—open with care
Sheckley, R. Uncanny tales
The Quijote robot
Sheckley, R. Uncanny tales
Sightseeing, 2179
Sheckley, R. Uncanny tales
A trick worth two of that
Sheckley, R. Uncanny tales
The Universal Karmic Clearing House
Sheckley, R. Uncanny tales
Warm
The Vintage book of amnesia; an anthology; edited by Jonathan Lethem
She'd make a dead man crawl. Houarner, G.
Sheehan, Ronan
Telescope
The Anchor book of new Irish writing; the new Gaelach ficsean; edited and with an introduction by John Somer and John J. Daly

SHEEP
  Rhodes, E. M. The trouble man
The **sheep**. Giono, J.
Sheep. McNeely, T. H.
SHEEP FARMING *See* Sheep
Sheesha ghat. Naiyer Masud
A **sheet,** a clothesline, a bed. Learst, A.
Sheffield, Charles
  The devil of Malkirk
    Sheffield, C. The amazing Dr. Darwin
  The heart of Ahura Mazda
    Sheffield, C. The amazing Dr. Darwin
  The Lambeth immortal
    Sheffield, C. The amazing Dr. Darwin
  Out of copyright
    Worldmakers; SF adventures in terraforming;
      edited by Gardner Dozois
  Phallicide
    The Year's best science fiction, seventeenth
      annual collection; edited by Gardner Dozois
  The phantom of Dunwell Cove
    Sheffield, C. The amazing Dr. Darwin
  The Solborne vampire
    Sheffield, C. The amazing Dr. Darwin
  The treasure of Odirex
    Sheffield, C. The amazing Dr. Darwin
Shekhter, Íàakov *See* Shechter, Yakov
The **sheld-duck** of the Basingstoke Canal. Parker,
  G.
Sheldon, Alice Hastings Bradley *See* Tiptree,
  James, 1916-1987
Sheldon, Raccoona, 1916-1987
    See also Tiptree, James, 1916-1987
The **shell** collector. Doerr, A.
Shell game. Ball, M.
Shell Island. Bache, E.
**SHELLEY, MARY WOLLSTONECRAFT,
  1797-1851**
             About
  Bishop, M. The unexpected visit of a reanimat-
    ed Englishwoman
SHELLS
  Bradbury, R. The sea shell
Shelter. Dorbin, S.
Shen Garden. Mo Yan
Shepard, Jesse
  Already gone
    Shepard, J. Jubilee King; stories
  Blinkers
    Shepard, J. Jubilee King; stories
  First day she'd never see
    Shepard, J. Jubilee King; stories
  Flaw in the shelter
    Shepard, J. Jubilee King; stories
  In the open
    Shepard, J. Jubilee King; stories
  Jubilee King
    Shepard, J. Jubilee King; stories
  Night shot
    Shepard, J. Jubilee King; stories
  Nurturer by nature
    Shepard, J. Jubilee King; stories
  Ravendale loop
    Shepard, J. Jubilee King; stories
  Thirty head of killers
    Shepard, J. Jubilee King; stories
  Wax
    Shepard, J. Jubilee King; stories

  We'll talk later
    Shepard, J. Jubilee King; stories
Shepard, Jim
  Ajax Is All about Attack
    Harper's v306 p73-80 Ap 2003
  Climb aboard the mighty flea
    The Paris Review v44 no161 p14-32 Spr
      2002
  Dade County, November 2000
    Politically inspired; edited by Stephen Elliott;
      assistant editor, Gabriel Kram; associate ed-
      itors, Elizabeth Brooks [et al.]
  Glut your soul on my accursed ugliness
    Doubletake v7 no3 p92-5 Summ 2001
  Love and hydrogen
    The Best American short stories, 2002; select-
      ed from U.S. and Canadian magazines by
      Sue Miller with Katrina Kenison, with an
      introduction by Sue Miller
    Harper's v303 no1819 p63-8 D 2001
  'Scuse me, while I kiss this guy
    Writers harvest 3; edited and with an intro-
      duction by Tobias Wolff
  Tedford and the megalodon
    McSweeney's mammoth treasury of thrilling
      tales; edited by Michael Chabon
Shepard, Karen
  Incognito with My Brother
    Bomb no85 p82-5 Fall 2003
  Popular girls
    Atlantic Monthly v288 no3 p97-100 O 2001
Shepard, Lucius
  Limbo
    Datlow, E. The dark; new ghost stories; ed-
      ited by Ellen Datlow
  Radiant green star
    The Year's best science fiction, eighteenth an-
      nual collection; edited by Gardner Dozois
  The scalehunter's beautiful daughter
    Brown, C. N. and Strahan, J. The Locus
      awards; thirty years of the best in science
      fiction and fantasy; edited by Charles N.
      Brown and Jonathan Strahan
Shepard, Sam
  Berlin Wall piece
    Shepard, S. Great dream of heaven; stories
  Betty's cats
    Shepard, S. Great dream of heaven; stories
  Blinking eye
    Shepard, S. Great dream of heaven; stories
  Coalinga 1/2 way
    Shepard, S. Great dream of heaven; stories
  The company's interest
    Shepard, S. Great dream of heaven; stories
  Concepción
    Shepard, S. Great dream of heaven; stories
  Convulsion
    Shepard, S. Great dream of heaven; stories
  The door to women
    Shepard, S. Great dream of heaven; stories
  Foreigners
    Shepard, S. Great dream of heaven; stories
  A frightening seizure
    Shepard, S. Great dream of heaven; stories
  Great dream of heaven
    Shepard, S. Great dream of heaven; stories
  It wasn't Proust
    Shepard, S. Great dream of heaven; stories

Shepard, Sam—*Continued*
  Lajitas and the NFL
    Texas bound. Book III; 22 Texas stories; edited by Kay Cattarulla; foreword by Robert Flynn
  Living the sign
    Shepard, S. Great dream of heaven; stories
  The remedy man
    Shepard, S. Great dream of heaven; stories
  The stout of heart
    Shepard, S. Great dream of heaven; stories
  Tinnitus
    Shepard, S. Great dream of heaven; stories
  An unfair question
    The New Yorker v78 no3 p76-81 Mr 11 2002
    Shepard, S. Great dream of heaven; stories
Shephard, Jim
  The gun lobby
    Atlantic Monthly v287 no4 p82-5 Ap 2001
Shepherd, Paul
  Hungry everywhere
    U.S. Catholic v68 no6 p38-41 Je 2003
Shepherd, Reginald
  The black narcissus
    His 3: brilliant new fiction by gay writers; edited by Robert Drake and Terry Wolverton
SHEPHERDS
  Chekhov, A. P. Happiness
  Giono, J. The sheep
  Gloss, M. Lambing season
  Papernick, J. The ascent of Eli Israel
  Vivante, A. Train ride of a faun
Shepherd's Bush. Binchy, M.
Shepley, John
  A golem in Prague
    With signs and wonders; an international anthology of Jewish fabulist fiction; edited by Daniel M. Jaffe
  Mystery Play
    Southern Humanities Review v36 no4 p353-9 Fall 2002
Sher, Ira
  The half
    Gettysburg Review v12 no3 p525-31 Aut 1999
Sher, Steven
  Tsuris
    With signs and wonders; an international anthology of Jewish fabulist fiction; edited by Daniel M. Jaffe
SHERIDAN, FRANCES CHAMBERLAINE, 1724-1766
              About
  Donoghue, E. How a lady dies
The **sheriff** goes to church. Coover, R.
SHERIFFS
  Carlson, R. Phenomena
  Chesnutt, C. W. The sheriff's children
  Cunningham, J. M. The tin star
  Dawson, P. Night ride
  Deaver, J. Wrong time, wrong place
  DeLancey, K. Dinger and Blacker
  DeRosso, H. A. Killer
  Garfield, B. Peace officer
  Hensley, J. L. Killer scent
  Kittredge, W. The soap bear
  L'Amour, L. Marshal of Canyon Gap
  Le May, A. Lawman's debt
  Le May, A. The loan of a gun

  Le May, A. Star on his heart
  MacDonald, J. D. Nor iron bars
  McNeely, T. H. Sheep
  Newton, D. B. Born to the brand
  Overholser, W. D. The fence
  Savage, L., Jr. The sting of Señorita Scorpion
The **sheriff's** children. Chesnutt, C. W.
Sherlock, Patti
  Mother George, midwife
    American West; twenty new stories from the Western Writers of America; edited with an introduction by Loren D. Estleman
Sherman, Charlotte Watson
  Emerald City: Third & Pike
    The African American West; a century of short stories; edited by Bruce A. Glasrud and Laurie Champion
  Touch [excerpt]
    The Bluelight corner; black women writing on passion, sex, and romantic love; edited by Rosemarie Robotham
Sherman, Delia
  The faerie cony-catcher
    The Year's best fantasy & horror, twelfth annual collection; edited by Ellen Datlow & Terry Windling
  The Parwat Ruby
    The Year's best fantasy & horror, thirteenth annual collection; edited by Ellen Datlow and Terri Windling
Sherman, Jory
  The snows of August
    American West; twenty new stories from the Western Writers of America; edited with an introduction by Loren D. Estleman
Sherman, Joseph
  (jt. auth) See Singer, Isaac Bashevis
Sherman, Josepha
  Koschei the deathless
    Parabola v26 no4 p83-4 N 2001
  The magic-stealer
    Children of the night; stories of ghosts, vampires, werewolves, and "lost children"; edited by Martin H. Greenberg
  The Man and the Muskrat: African (from Botswana)
    Parabola v29 no2 p75-6 Summ 2004
Sherman, Suzan
  First Hair
    Bomb no84 p104-6, 108-9 Summ 2003
Sherman and the swan. Wells, K.
Sherwood, Frances
  Basil the dog
    Atlantic Monthly v284 no3 p84-90 S 1999
    The Best American short stories, 2000; selected from U.S. and Canadian magazines by E. L. Doctorow with Katrina Kenison; with an introduction by E. L. Doctorow
  Family
    New Letters v69 no1 p11-24 2002
  History
    Crossing the color line; readings in Black and white; edited by Suzanne W. Jones
She's anonymous. Valeri, L.
Shi Tiesheng
  Fate
    The Vintage book of contemporary Chinese fiction; edited by Carolyn Choa and David Su Li-qun

Shibusa. Waters, M. Y.
Shields, Carol
  Dressing down
    Saturday Night v114 no6 p60-66 Jl/Ag 1999
  Larry's words, 1983
    Valentine's Day: women against men; stories
      of revenge; introduction by Alice Thomas
  The next best kiss
    Atlantic Monthly v283 no1 p79-82+ Ja 1999
Shields, David
  Doubt
    Western Humanities Review v55 no1 p21-3
      Spr 2001
  Ice
    Ploughshares v27 no1 p177-9 Spr 2001
  Properties of language
    The Yale Review v89 no3 p128-34 Jl 2001
  S & M: a brief history
    Western Humanities Review v55 no1 p17-20
      Spr 2001
  Satire
    Western Humanities Review v55 no1 p24-6
      Spr 2001
Shields, Jody
  The Fig Eater [excerpt]
    A different plain; contemporary Nebraska fic-
      tion writers; edited by Ladette Randolph ;
      introduction by Mary Pipher
Shields of Mars. Wolfe, G.
Shifa. Aylett, S.
Shifman in paradise. Shapiro, G.
Shifra, Shin
  The night of the kid [excerpt]
    Sleepwalkers and other stories; the Arab in
      Hebrew fiction; edited by Ehud Ben-Ezer
Shifra. Baron, D.
Shift, shift, shift. Mosley, W.
Shifting gears. Campbell, B. J.
Shifu, you'll do anything for a laugh. Mo Yan
Shin, Kyoung-Sook
  The Blind Calf
    Harvard Review (1992) no23 p45-57 Fall
      2002
Shiner, Lewis
  (jt. auth) See Sterling, Bruce and Shiner, Lewis
The **shining** [excerpt] King, S.
Shining city. Johnson, G.
The **shining** mountains. Farrell, C.
Shining nowhere but in the dark. De Lint, C.
The **shining** ones. Clarke, A. C.
The **shining** red apple. Callaghan, M.
Shining through 24/7. Major, D.
SHIP CAPTAINS *See* Shipmasters
Ship full of Jews. Malzberg, B. N.
Ship island: the story of a mermaid. Spencer, E.
Ship, sea, mountain, sky. Grant, G. J. and Link,
  K.
The **ship** that returned. McCaffrey, A.
The **ship** who mourned. McCaffrey, A.
The **ship** who sang. McCaffrey, A.
SHIPBUILDING
  Knight, M. Gerald's monkey
Shipbuilding. Middleton, N.
SHIPMASTERS
  Alarcón, P. A. d. Captain Poison
  Bradbury, R. And the sailor, home from the sea
  Correa, A. The merry ghosts of the Grampus
  Harrison, H. Captain Honario Harpplayer, R.N.
  Heller, J. Macadam's log

  Helprin, M. Letters from the Samantha
  Hodgson, W. H. The adventure of the garter
  Hodgson, W. H. Contraband of war
  Hodgson, W. H. The diamond spy
  Hodgson, W. H. The drum of saccharine
  Hodgson, W. H. From information received
  Hodgson, W. H. The German spy
  Hodgson, W. H. My lady's jewels
  Hodgson, W. H. The painted lady
  Hodgson, W. H. The plans of the reefing bi-
    plane
  Hodgson, W. H. The problem of the pearls
  Hodgson, W. H. Trading with the enemy
  James, H. A landscape painter
  Steinbeck, T. Blighted cargo
Shippen, Jane R.
  Buenos Aires Side to Side
    The Virginia Quarterly Review v79 no2 p335-
      42 Spr 2003
  I am not like Nuñez
    New stories from the South: the year's best,
      2001; edited by Shannon Ravenel; with a
      preface by Lee Smith
SHIPPING
    See also Shipbuilding
The **Shiprock** Fair. Cummins, A.
SHIPS
    See also Sailing vessels; Steamboats;
    Submarines Titanic (Steamship) and names
    of ships; e.g. Amistad (Schooner)
  Carlson, R. On the U.S.S. Fortitude
  Chekhov, A. P. Gusev
  Dann, J. Going under
  Lee, D. Sailing the painted ocean
  Lopez, B. H. The construction of the Rachel
  Raphael, F. The siren's song
  Toes, J. Rhine Ablaze
    Officers
    See Shipmasters
Shipshape home. Matheson, R.
Shipwreck beach. Hirshberg, G.
SHIPWRECKS AND CASTAWAYS
    See also Survival (after airplane acci-
    dents, shipwrecks, etc.)
  García Márquez, G. The last voyage of the
    ghost ship
  Gregory, S. The White Ship murders
  Harrison, H. After the storm
  Hodgson, W. H. The bells of the "Laughing Sal-
    ly"
  Hodgson, W. H. The boats of the "Glen
    Carrrig"
  Hodgson, W. H. From the tideless sea, part one
  Hodgson, W. H. From the tideless sea, part two:
    further news of the Homebird
  Hodgson, W. H. The mystery of the derelict
  Paine, T. Will you say something, Monsieur El-
    iot?
  Russell, J. The knife
Shir-Jacob, Anita
  Maartiens, glory and me
    Dalhousie Review v81 no2 p257-81 Summ
      2001
Shirazi, Said
  The infiltrator
    The Paris Review v41 no150 p258-65 Spr
      1999

Shirazi, Said—*Continued*
Mandelstam in Exile
New England Review v24 no3 p199-213
Summ 2003
Shirley, John
Wings burnt black
The Crow; shattered lives & broken dreams;
edited by J. O'Barr and Ed Kramer
(jt. auth) See Laidlaw, Marc and Shirley, John
(jt. auth) See Rucker, Rudy von Bitter and Shir-
ley, John
Shirley Wants Her Nickel Back. Treadway, J.
The **shirt**. Davies, R.
The **shirts**. Čapek, K.
Shishin, Alex
The Eggplant Legacy
Prairie Schooner v77 no1 p69-84 Spr 2003
Mr. Eggplant goes home
The Student body; short stories about college
students and professors; edited by John
McNally
Shite hawks. Gray, M.
Shivani, Anis
They Stand and Serve Too
Dalhousie Review v84 no2 p243-9 Summ
2004
Shmuelian, Avi
Moonstruck sunflowers
With signs and wonders; an international an-
thology of Jewish fabulist fiction; edited by
Daniel M. Jaffe
The **shoals**. Hester, K. L.
Shockley, Evie
Separation anxiety
Dark matter; a century of speculative fiction
from the African diaspora; edited by Sheree
R. Thomas
Shoe and marriage. Link, K.
Shoe story. Orner, P.
Shoeless Joe Jackson comes to Iowa. Kinsella, W.
P.
Shoemaker, Karen Gettert
Playing horses
Prairie Schooner v75 no2 p154-65 Summ
2001
The **shoemaker** and the devil. Chekhov, A. P.
Shoemaker, Karen
Playing horses
A different plain; contemporary Nebraska fic-
tion writers; edited by Ladette Randolph ;
introduction by Mary Pipher
SHOEMAKERS
Chekhov, A. P. A day in the country
Chekhov, A. P. The shoemaker and the devil
Singer, I. B. The little shoemakers
Shoes. Keret, E.
Shoes. Rheinheimer, K.
Shoes for the rest of my life. Dueñas, G.
Shoggoth's old peculiar. Gaiman, N.
Shohei, Ooka
The Nervous Person
The Literary Review (Madison, N.J.) v46 no1
p89-102 Fall 2002
Sholem Aleichem
Hodel
Beautiful as the moon, radiant as the stars;
Jewish women in Yiddish stories : an an-
thology; edited by Sandra Bark; introduc-
tion by Francine Prose

Seventy-five thousand (a pack of tsoris)
Neugroschel, J. No star too beautiful; Yiddish
stories from 1382 to the present; compiled
and translated by Joachim Neugroschel
Sholom Aleichem *See* Sholem Aleichem, 1859-
1916
Shomer, Enid
Chosen
The Virginia Quarterly Review v79 no1 p143-
60 Wint 2003
The problem with Yosi
Neurotica: Jewish writers on sex; edited by
Melvin Jules Bukiet
Taking names
100% pure Florida fiction; an anthology; ed-
ited by Susan Hubbard and Robley Wilson
Shon, Frank
The farmer's wife
The Vintage book of contemporary Scottish
fiction; edited and with an introduction by
Peter Kravitz
Shonk, Katherine
The conversion
Shonk, K. The red passport
The death of Olga Vasilievna
American short fiction, vol. 8, no 29-32
Shonk, K. The red passport
Honey month
Shonk, K. The red passport
Kitchen friends
Shonk, K. The red passport
My mother's garden
The Best American short stories 2001; select-
ed from U.S. and Canadian magazines by
Barbara Kingsolver with Katrina Kenison;
with an introduction by Barbara Kingsolver
Shonk, K. The red passport
Our American
Shonk, K. The red passport
The Wooden Village of Kizhi
The Georgia Review v57 no3 p517-38 Fall
2003
Shonk, K. The red passport
The young people of Moscow
Shonk, K. The red passport
SHOOTING
See also Archery
Bausch, R. Two altercations
Blair, J. Julia loving the face of God
Deaver, J. Wrong time, wrong place
DeMarinis, R. A romantic interlude
Evenson, B. Calling the hour
Hardwick, E. Shot: a New York story
Hudson, S. The fall of the Nixon administration
Jones, T. My heroic mythic journey
López, L. To control a rabid rodent
Nelson, K. Tides
Offutt, C. Target practice
Padilla, I. Ballistics: some notes
Richmond, M. Fifth grade: a criminal history
Rinehart, S. Guns went off
Shooting. Yuknavitch, L.
A **shooting** star. Cooper, J. C.
Shopgirls. Barthelme, F.
SHOPKEEPERS *See* Merchants
SHOPLIFTING
Barker, N. Inside information
Barker, N. Skin
Harfenist, J. Voluntary breathers

SHOPLIFTING—*Continued*
James, S. Not singing exactly
Wilson, M. Petty theft
Shopper, Evan
If I Have to Hit One of You, I'll Hit You Both
The Massachusetts Review v44 no3 p510-26
Fall 2003
SHOPPING
Atkinson, K. Charlene and Trudi go shopping
Byatt, A. S. Baglady
Mazelis, J. Snakeskin becomes her
Simpson, H. Wirstigkeit
Strauss, A. Shrinking away
SHOPPING BAG LADIES *See* Homeless persons
Shopping expedition. Ritchie, E.
Shopping Trip. James, K. C.
The **Shore**. Ford, R.
The **shorefront** manor. Skloot, F.
Shores of light. Barolini, H.
Short, Brendan
Shadows
The Literary Review (Madison, N.J.) v47 no3
p104-12 Spr 2004
Short, Luke
Top hand
A Century of great Western stories; edited by
John Jakes
A **short** history of Indians in Canada. King, T.
A **short** horse. Drake, R.
The **Short** Version. Ray, D.
A **short** weekend. Johnson-Davies, D.
The **shortest** distance. Coward, M.
The **shortlist** season. Smith, A.
Shot. Oates, J. C.
The **shot**. Pushkin, A. S.
Shot: a New York story. Hardwick, E.
Shotgun Wedding. Almond, S.
Shotgun wedding. Campbell, B. J.
Shouse, Deborah
A portrait of angels
With signs and wonders; an international anthology of Jewish fabulist fiction; edited by
Daniel M. Jaffe
Shout. Gilb, D.
Show-and-tell. Singleton, G.
Show me the bones. Wheat, C.
Showdown at the Terminal Oasis. Hautman, P.
The **Showman**. Bojanowski, M.
Shraer-Petrov, David *See* Shrayer-Petrov, David, 1936-
Shrake, Bud *See* Shrake, Edwin, 1931-
Shrake, Edwin
Strange peaches [excerpt]
Graham, D. Lone Star literature; from the
Red River to the Rio Grande; edited by
Don Graham
Shrapnel. Yi, T.-H.
Shrayer, Maxim D.
The afterlove
The Kenyon Review ns23 no3/4 p176-94
Summ/Fall 2001
Baggage
The Massachusetts Review v44 no3 p546-61
Fall 2003
(jt. auth) *See* Aizman, David

Shrayer-Petrov, David
Apple cider vinegar
Shrayer-Petrov, D. and Shrayer, M. Jonah and
Sarah; Jewish stories of Russia and America; edited by Maxim D. Shrayer
David and Goliath
Shrayer-Petrov, D. and Shrayer, M. Jonah and
Sarah; Jewish stories of Russia and America; edited by Maxim D. Shrayer
Dismemberers
Shrayer-Petrov, D. and Shrayer, M. Jonah and
Sarah; Jewish stories of Russia and America; edited by Maxim D. Shrayer
Hände hoch!
Shrayer-Petrov, D. and Shrayer, M. Jonah and
Sarah; Jewish stories of Russia and America; edited by Maxim D. Shrayer
He, she and the others
Shrayer-Petrov, D. and Shrayer, M. Jonah and
Sarah; Jewish stories of Russia and America; edited by Maxim D. Shrayer
Hurricane Bob
Shrayer-Petrov, D. and Shrayer, M. Jonah and
Sarah; Jewish stories of Russia and America; edited by Maxim D. Shrayer
In the Reeds
The Massachusetts Review v40 no2 p175-83
Summ 1999
Shrayer-Petrov, D. and Shrayer, M. Jonah and
Sarah; Jewish stories of Russia and America; edited by Maxim D. Shrayer
Jonah and Sarah
Shrayer-Petrov, D. and Shrayer, M. Jonah and
Sarah; Jewish stories of Russia and America; edited by Maxim D. Shrayer
The Lanskoy road
Shrayer-Petrov, D. and Shrayer, M. Jonah and
Sarah; Jewish stories of Russia and America; edited by Maxim D. Shrayer
Old writer Foreman
Shrayer-Petrov, D. and Shrayer, M. Jonah and
Sarah; Jewish stories of Russia and America; edited by Maxim D. Shrayer
Rusty
Shrayer-Petrov, D. and Shrayer, M. Jonah and
Sarah; Jewish stories of Russia and America; edited by Maxim D. Shrayer
Tsukerman and his children
Shrayer-Petrov, D. and Shrayer, M. Jonah and
Sarah; Jewish stories of Russia and America; edited by Maxim D. Shrayer
Young Jews and two gymnasium girls
Shrayer-Petrov, D. and Shrayer, M. Jonah and
Sarah; Jewish stories of Russia and America; edited by Maxim D. Shrayer
The **shrine** for lost children. Anderson, P.
SHRINES
Bowles, P. The waters of Izli
Shrink. Olsen, S. S.
Shrinking. Almog, R.
Shroff, Murzban F.
Third Eye Rising
Confrontation no86/87 p142-63 Spr/Summ
2004
Shrouds with pockets in them. Drake, R.
Shrove Tuesday. Chekhov, A. P.

Shteyngart, Gary
  Love's Triangle Lost
    Gentlemen's Quarterly v73 no5 p193 My
    2003
  Several anecdotes about my wife
    Granta no78 p203-33 Summ 2002
    Lost tribe; jewish fiction from the edge
  Shylock on the Neva
    Fishman, B. Wild East; stories from the last
    frontier; edited with an introduction by Bo-
    ris Fishman
    The New Yorker v78 no25 p130-6, 138 S 2
    2002
Shtok, Fradel
  The archbishop
    Neugroschel, J. No star too beautiful; Yiddish
    stories from 1382 to the present; compiled
    and translated by Joachim Neugroschel
Shu, Ch'ing-ch'un *See* Lao She, 1899-1966
Shu Yang *See* Su Shuyang, 1938-
Shua, Ana María
  The white Guanaco in the middle of France
    English translations of short stories by con-
    temporary Argentine women writers; edited
    by Eliana Cazaubon Hermann ; translated
    by Sally Webb Thornton
Shubuta. Franklin, T.
Shunn, William
  Dance of the yellow-breasted Luddites
    Vanishing acts; a science fiction anthology;
    edited by Ellen Datlow
  Strong medicine
    The year's best science fiction: twenty-first
    annual collection; edited by Gardner Dozois
Shut the final door. Hensley, J. L.
Shut the last door. See Hensley, J. L. Shut the fi-
  nal door
Shuttered. Lida, D.
Shwartz, Susan
  The fires of her vengeance
    Magical beginnings; edited by Steven H. Sil-
    ver and Martin H. Greenberg
  Suppose they gave a peace
    The Best alternate history stories of the 20th
    century; edited by Harry Turtledove with
    Martin H. Greenberg
Shylock on the Neva. Shteyngart, G.
SIAMESE CATS *See* Cats
SIAMESE TWINS
  Dowling, T. Jenny come to play
  Leegant, J. The tenth
  Wells, K. Secession, XX
Siasoco, Ricco Villanueva
  Deaf mute
    The North American Review v286 no1 p16-19
    Ja/F 2001
SIBERIA (RUSSIA)
  Chekhov, A. P. In exile
  L'Amour, L. Coast patrol
  L'Amour, L. Flight to the north
  Oren, Y. The Cat Man
            Prisoners and prisons
    See Prisoners and prisons—Siberia (Rus-
    sia)
Siberia. Erpenbeck, J.
Siberia: still life of a moving image. Yuknavitch,
  L.
SIBYLS *See* Oracles

SICILY
  Holliday, L. Provenance
  Theroux, P. The stranger at the Palazzo d'Oro
Sicily. Lee, A.
Sick baby. Chiappone, R.
Sick child. Joseph, D.
SICK CHILDREN
  Aidoo, A. A. A gift from somewhere
  Alcott, L. M. Mrs. Gay's hint, and how it was
    taken
  Alexie, S. Do not go gentle
  Banks, R. The child screams and looks back at
    you
  Chiappone, R. Sick baby
  Chopin, K. A matter of prejudice
  DeLancey, K. Washed
  Delaney, E. J. What I have noticed
  Gordimer, N. Message in a bottle
  Joseph, D. Sick child
  Klass, P. Rainbow mama
  McIntyre, V. N. Of mist, and grass, and sand
  Taraqqi, G. The Shemiran bus
  Wieland, L. Gray's anatomy
Sick in public. Patterson, K.
Sick people. Roth, J.
The **sickness**. Tenn, W.
Side Angle Side. Gates, D.
Side job. Chiappone, R.
A **side** of the sea. Campbell, R.
Sides, Danna Layton
  Look Into Their Own Dark Places
    Prairie Schooner v77 no2 p114-25 Summ
    2003
Sideshow champion. L'Amour, L.
The **siege** of London. James, H.
Siegel, Benjamin *See* Siegel, Bugsy, 1906-1947
SIEGEL, BUGSY, 1906-1947
            About
  Spencer, D. Caution: men in trees
SIENA (ITALY) *See* Italy—Siena
SIERRA LEONE
  Houghteling, M. K. Ma Kamanda's latrine
**SIERRA NEVADA MOUNTAINS (CALIF.
  AND NEV.)**
  Travis, T. V. Down here in the garden
Sight unseen. Gussoff, C.
The **sighting**. Coberly, L. M.
The **sights** of Cork. Honig, L.
Sightseeing, 2179. Sheckley, R.
Sign. Forbes, C.
The **sign**. Kees, W.
Sign here. De Lint, C.
Sign language. Bonnie, F.
Sign of the times. Pickard, N.
SIGN PAINTING
  Updike, J. The kid's whistling
Signal Hill. Rifkin, A.
Significant moments in the life of my mother.
  Atwood, M.
Signification. Yuknavitch, L.
Signifying nothing. Wallace, D. F.
Signs. Wheeler, G. R.
SIGNS AND SIGNBOARDS
  Perry, D. Love is gnats today
  Shepard, S. Living the sign
Signs of Life. Warner, S. O.

Sigsgaard, Palle
Three Strangers
The Literary Review (Madison, N.J.) v47 no3
p33-4 Spr 2004
SIKHS
Mukherjee, B. The management of grief
Šikula, Vincent
Grannie
In search of homo sapiens; twenty-five con-
temporary Slovak short stories; editor,
Pavol Hudík ; [translated by Heather
Trebatická; American English editor, Lucy
Bednár]
Silber, Joan
Ashes of love
Silber, J. Ideas of heaven; a ring of stories;
Joan Silber
Bobby Jackson
Silber, J. In my other life
Comforts
Silber, J. In my other life
Commendable
Ploughshares v25 no2/3 p174-89 Fall 1999
Silber, J. In my other life
Covered
Silber, J. In my other life
The dollar in Italy
Silber, J. In my other life
First marriage
Silber, J. In my other life
Gaspara Stampa
Silber, J. Ideas of heaven; a ring of stories;
Joan Silber
The high road
The O. Henry Prize stories, 2003; edited and
with an introduction by Laura Furman;
jurers David Gutterson, Diane Johnson,
Jennifer Egan
Ploughshares v28 no2/3 p178-97 Fall 2002
Silber, J. Ideas of heaven; a ring of stories;
Joan Silber
Ideas of heaven
Silber, J. Ideas of heaven; a ring of stories;
Joan Silber
Lake Natasink
Silber, J. In my other life
My shape
Silber, J. Ideas of heaven; a ring of stories;
Joan Silber
Ordinary
Silber, J. In my other life
Partners
Silber, J. In my other life
Ragazzi
Silber, J. In my other life
The same ground
Silber, J. Ideas of heaven; a ring of stories;
Joan Silber
What lasts
Silber, J. In my other life
Without Ellie
Silber, J. In my other life
The silence. Barnes, J.
Silence. Dubois, J.
Silence. Kawabata, Y.
Silence. Munro, A.
The silence. Rusch, K. K.
Silence and slow time. Lundquist, R.
The silence of the Asonu. Le Guin, U. K.

The **Silence** of the lambs. Abouzeid, C.
Silence please. Clarke, A. C.
Silences. Lee, H. E.
Silent cruise. Taylor, T. L.
The **silent** majority. Weinberg, R.
Silent night: non-verbal sex at the Galactic Cafe.
Johnston, P. D.
Silent partner. Collins, M.
Silent protest. McWhorter, C. T.
Siler, Jenny
Africa
Tart noir; edited by Stella Duffy & Lauren
Henderson
SILESIA
Wegner, H. On the road to Szkaradowo
Wegner, H. The pilots of the rose trellis
Wegner, H. The stone girl
Silk stockings. Callaghan, M.
Silk strands. Smith, J.
Silko, Leslie
Lullaby
Still wild; short fiction of the American West,
1950 to the present; edited by Larry
McMurtry
Silman, Roberta
Her Father's Voice
The Virginia Quarterly Review v79 no2 p287-
300 Spr 2003
Winter dark
The Virginia Quarterly Review v77 no3 p514-
28 Summ 2001
Silva, David B.
Dry whiskey
The Best American mystery stories, 1999; ed-
ited and with an introduction by Ed
McBain
The World's finest mystery and crime stories,
third annual collection; edited by Ed
Gorman and Martin H. Greenberg
Silva Román, Ernesto
The death star
Cosmos latinos: an anthology of science fic-
tion from Latin America and Spain; trans-
lated, edited, & with an introduction &
notes by Andrea L. Bell & Yolanda Moli-
na-Gavilán
SILVER, GEORGE, FL. 1599
About
Moon, E. Silver lining
Silver, Marisa
Gunsmoke
The New Yorker v77 no14 p74-81 Je 4 2001
What I saw from where I stood
The Best American short stories 2001; select-
ed from U.S. and Canadian magazines by
Barbara Kingsolver with Katrina Kenison;
with an introduction by Barbara Kingsolver
The **Silver** Coffer. Herling, G.
A **silver** dish. Bellow, S.
Silver lining. Moon, E.
Silver lining. Mosley, W.
Silver maple. Browder, C.
SILVER MINES AND MINING
L'Amour, L. Riches beyond dream
Silver screen. Kirchheimer, G. D.
Silver Spectre. Breen, J. L.
Silver water. Bloom, A.

Silvera, Makeda
Caribbean chameleon
  The Oxford book of Caribbean short stories; edited by Stewart Brown and John Wickham
  The Vintage book of international lesbian fiction; edited and with an introduction by Naomi Holoch and Joan Nestle

Silverberg, Robert
Amanda and the alien
  Witpunk; edited by Claude Lalumière and Marty Halpern
The book of changes
  Silverberg, R. Legends II; new short novels by the masters of modern fantasy; edited by Robert Silverberg
Getting to know the dragon
  Far horizons; all new tales from the greatest worlds of science fiction; edited by Robert Silverberg
A hero of the empire
  One lamp; alternate history stories from The magazine of Fantasy & Science Fiction; edited by Gordon van Gelder
  The Year's best science fiction, seventeenth annual collection; edited by Gardner Dozois
Passengers
  Masterpieces: the best science fiction of the century; edited by Orson Scott Card

Silverstein, Shel
The guilty party
  The Best American mystery stories, 2000; edited and with an introduction by Donald E. Westlake
  Murder and obsession; edited by Otto Penzler

Sim, Al
The Freedom Pig
  The Literary Review (Madison, N.J.) v46 no1 p162-79 Fall 2002

Sim Denny. Jones, M.

Simak, Clifford D.
Desertion
  The SFWA grand masters v1; edited by Frederik Pohl
Founding father
  The SFWA grand masters v1; edited by Frederik Pohl
Grotto of the dancing deer
  The SFWA grand masters v1; edited by Frederik Pohl
Huddling place
  The Science fiction hall of fame: volume one, 1929-1964; the greatest science fiction stories of all time chosen by the members of the Science Fiction Writers of America; edited by Robert Silverberg

Simena. Avalli, I.

Simenon, Georges
The little house at Croix-Rousse
  A Century of great suspense stories; edited by Jeffery Deaver

Simeon Dimsby's workshop. Lupoff, R. A.

Simmons, Dan
The end of gravity
  Simmons, D. Worlds enough & time; five tales of speculative fiction
Looking for Kelly Dahl
  Simmons, D. Worlds enough & time; five tales of speculative fiction

The ninth of av
  Simmons, D. Worlds enough & time; five tales of speculative fiction
On K2 with Kanakaredes
  Redshift; extreme visions of speculative fiction; edited by Al Sarrantonio
  Simmons, D. Worlds enough & time; five tales of speculative fiction
  The Year's best science fiction, nineteenth annual collection; edited by Gardner Dozois
Orphans of the Helix
  Far horizons; all new tales from the greatest worlds of science fiction; edited by Robert Silverberg
  Simmons, D. Worlds enough & time; five tales of speculative fiction

Simms, Renee
The Art of Heroine Worship
  The North American Review v288 no6 p20-3 N/D 2003

Simon, Beth
Bialy Café
  Gettysburg Review v16 no4 p567-77 Wint 2003

Simonds, Merilyn
The blue of the Madrugada
  Simonds, M. The lion in the room next door
The day of the dead
  Simonds, M. The lion in the room next door
The distance to Delphi
  Simonds, M. The lion in the room next door
In the city of the split sky
  Simonds, M. The lion in the room next door
King of the Cowboys, Queen of the West
  Simonds, M. The lion in the room next door
The lion in the room next door
  Simonds, M. The lion in the room next door
Navigating the Kattegat
  Simonds, M. The lion in the room next door
Nossa Senhora dos Remédios
  Simonds, M. The lion in the room next door
Song of the Japanese white-eye
  Simonds, M. The lion in the room next door
The still point
  Simonds, M. The lion in the room next door
Taken for delirium
  Simonds, M. The lion in the room next door

Simonetta, Rita
The Boxer
  Dalhousie Review v84 no2 p277-83 Summ 2004

Simple arithmetic. Moriconi, V.
A **simple** elegy. Wilson, R., Jr.
Simple Facts. Rosenstock, D. Y.
A **simple** idea. Tillman, L.
Simple machines. Russell, M.
The **simple** presence of geese. See Earley, T. Aliceville
A **simple** question. Deaver, J.
Simple recipes. Thien, M.
Simply indispensable. Bishop, M.

Simpson, Helen
Burns and the bankers
  Simpson, H. Getting a life; stories
Café society
  Simpson, H. Getting a life; stories
Cheers
  Simpson, H. Getting a life; stories

Simpson, Helen—*Continued*
Costume drama
The New Yorker v75 no34 p88-94 N 15 1999
Getting a life
Simpson, H. Getting a life; stories
Golden apples
Simpson, H. Getting a life; stories
Hurrah for the hols
Simpson, H. Getting a life; stories
Millennium blues
Simpson, H. Getting a life; stories
Opera
Simpson, H. Getting a life; stories
Wirstigkeit
Simpson, H. Getting a life; stories
With a bang
Granta no65 p179-91 Spr 1999
Simpson, Mona
Admissions
Harper's v303 no1816 p87-95 S 2001
Approximations
Breaking into print; early stories and insights into getting published; a Ploughshares anthology; edited by DeWitt Henry
Coins
The Best American short stories, 2003; selected from U.S. and Canadian magazines by Walter Mosley with Katrina Kenison; with an introduction by Walter Mosley
Harper's v305 p79-83 Ag 2002
Dependents
Atlantic Monthly (1993) v293 no2 p129-32, 134-7 Mr 2004
Simulated trainer. Harrison, H.
SIN
See also Repentance
Hawthorne, N. Ethan Brand
Mayo, W. Mortal sins
Sin: Early Impressions. Updike, J.
The **sin** eaters. Alexie, S.
The **sin** of Elijah. Stern, S.
The **sin** of Jesus. Babel´, I.
SINAI (EGYPT)
Grossman, D. Yani on the mountain
Since my house burned down. Waters, M. Y.
Sinclair, Bertha Muzzy *See* Bower, B. M., 1871-1940
Sinclair, Iain
The keeper of the Rothenstein tomb
Best new horror 12; edited and with an introduction by Stephen Jones
Lu **Sing**. Alcott, L. M.
Sing. Rusch, K. K.
Sing Fat and the Imperial Duchess of Woo. Steinbeck, T.
Sing, you Sacher tortes. Allen, W.
SINGAPORE
Mendes, B. Tooth marks
Singer, Isaac Bashevis
The accuser and the accused
Singer, I. B. Collected stories; One night in Brazil to The death of Methuselah
The admirer
Singer, I. B. Collected stories: A friend of Kafka to Passions
The adventure
Singer, I. B. Collected stories: A friend of Kafka to Passions

Advice
Singer, I. B. Collected stories; One night in Brazil to The death of Methuselah
Alone
Singer, I. B. Collected stories; Gimpel the fool to the Letter writer; Isaac Bashevis Singer
Altele
Singer, I. B. Collected stories: A friend of Kafka to Passions
Androgynous
Beautiful as the moon, radiant as the stars; Jewish women in Yiddish stories : an anthology; edited by Sandra Bark; introduction by Francine Prose
The New Yorker v79 no28 p94-100 S 29 2003
The angry man
Singer, I. B. Collected stories; One night in Brazil to The death of Methuselah
The beard
Singer, I. B. Collected stories: A friend of Kafka to Passions
The beggar said no
Singer, I. B. Collected stories; Gimpel the fool to the Letter writer; Isaac Bashevis Singer
The betrayer of Israel
Singer, I. B. Collected stories; One night in Brazil to The death of Methuselah
Between shadows
Singer, I. B. Collected stories; One night in Brazil to The death of Methuselah
Big and little
Singer, I. B. Collected stories; Gimpel the fool to the Letter writer; Isaac Bashevis Singer
The bird
Singer, I. B. Collected stories; One night in Brazil to The death of Methuselah
The bishop's robe
Singer, I. B. Collected stories: A friend of Kafka to Passions
The bitter truth
Singer, I. B. Collected stories; One night in Brazil to The death of Methuselah
The black wedding
Singer, I. B. Collected stories; Gimpel the fool to the Letter writer; Isaac Bashevis Singer
The blasphemer
Singer, I. B. Collected stories: A friend of Kafka to Passions
The blizzard
Singer, I. B. Collected stories: A friend of Kafka to Passions
Blood
Singer, I. B. Collected stories; Gimpel the fool to the Letter writer; Isaac Bashevis Singer
The bond
Singer, I. B. Collected stories; One night in Brazil to The death of Methuselah
A boy knows the truth
Singer, I. B. Collected stories; One night in Brazil to The death of Methuselah
The briefcase
Singer, I. B. Collected stories: A friend of Kafka to Passions

Singer, Isaac Bashevis—*Continued*

The brooch
  Singer, I. B. Collected stories; Gimpel the
    fool to the Letter writer; Isaac Bashevis
    Singer
Brother Beetle
  Singer, I. B. Collected stories; One night in
    Brazil to The death of Methuselah
The building project
  Singer, I. B. Collected stories; One night in
    Brazil to The death of Methuselah
Burial at sea
  Singer, I. B. Collected stories; One night in
    Brazil to The death of Methuselah
The bus
  Singer, I. B. Collected stories; One night in
    Brazil to The death of Methuselah
By the light of memorial candles
  Singer, I. B. Collected stories; Gimpel the
    fool to the Letter writer; Isaac Bashevis
    Singer
The cabalist of East Broadway
  Singer, I. B. Collected stories: A friend of
    Kafka to Passions
The cafeteria
  Dark: stories of madness, murder, and the su-
    pernatural; edited by Clint Willis
  Singer, I. B. Collected stories: A friend of
    Kafka to Passions
  Wonderful town; New York stories from The
    New Yorker; edited by David Remnick
    with Susan Choi
A cage for Satan
  Singer, I. B. Collected stories; One night in
    Brazil to The death of Methuselah
The captive
  Singer, I. B. Collected stories: A friend of
    Kafka to Passions
Caricature
  Singer, I. B. Collected stories; Gimpel the
    fool to the Letter writer; Isaac Bashevis
    Singer
The chimney sweep
  Singer, I. B. Collected stories: A friend of
    Kafka to Passions
Cockadoodledoo
  Singer, I. B. Collected stories; Gimpel the
    fool to the Letter writer; Isaac Bashevis
    Singer
The conference
  Singer, I. B. Collected stories; One night in
    Brazil to The death of Methuselah
Confused
  Singer, I. B. Collected stories; One night in
    Brazil to The death of Methuselah
A crown of feathers
  Singer, I. B. Collected stories: A friend of
    Kafka to Passions
Cunegunde
  Singer, I. B. Collected stories; Gimpel the
    fool to the Letter writer; Isaac Bashevis
    Singer
The dance
  Singer, I. B. Collected stories: A friend of
    Kafka to Passions
A dance and a hop
  Singer, I. B. Collected stories: A friend of
    Kafka to Passions

A day in Coney Island
  Singer, I. B. Collected stories: A friend of
    Kafka to Passions
Dazzled
  Singer, I. B. Collected stories; One night in
    Brazil to The death of Methuselah
The dead fiddler
  Singer, I. B. Collected stories; Gimpel the
    fool to the Letter writer; Isaac Bashevis
    Singer
The death of Methuselah
  Singer, I. B. Collected stories; One night in
    Brazil to The death of Methuselah
The destruction of Kreshev
  Singer, I. B. Collected stories; Gimpel the
    fool to the Letter writer; Isaac Bashevis
    Singer
Disguised
  Singer, I. B. Collected stories; One night in
    Brazil to The death of Methuselah
The divorce
  Singer, I. B. Collected stories; One night in
    Brazil to The death of Methuselah
Dr. Beeber
  Singer, I. B. Collected stories: A friend of
    Kafka to Passions
The egotist
  Singer, I. B. Collected stories: A friend of
    Kafka to Passions
Elka and Meier
  Singer, I. B. Collected stories; One night in
    Brazil to The death of Methuselah
The enemy
  Singer, I. B. Collected stories; One night in
    Brazil to The death of Methuselah
Errors
  Singer, I. B. Collected stories: A friend of
    Kafka to Passions
Escape from civilization
  Singer, I. B. Collected stories; One night in
    Brazil to The death of Methuselah
Esther Kreindel the second
  Singer, I. B. Collected stories; Gimpel the
    fool to the Letter writer; Isaac Bashevis
    Singer
Eulogy to a shoelace
  Singer, I. B. Collected stories; One night in
    Brazil to The death of Methuselah
Exes
  Singer, I. B. Collected stories; One night in
    Brazil to The death of Methuselah
The fast
  Singer, I. B. Collected stories; Gimpel the
    fool to the Letter writer; Isaac Bashevis
    Singer
The fatalist
  Singer, I. B. Collected stories: A friend of
    Kafka to Passions
Fate
  Singer, I. B. Collected stories: A friend of
    Kafka to Passions
Fire
  Singer, I. B. Collected stories; Gimpel the
    fool to the Letter writer; Isaac Bashevis
    Singer
A friend of Kafka
  Singer, I. B. Collected stories: A friend of
    Kafka to Passions

Singer, Isaac Bashevis—*Continued*

From the diary of one not born
  Singer, I. B. Collected stories; Gimpel the fool to the Letter writer; Isaac Bashevis Singer
The gentleman from Crakow
  Singer, I. B. Collected stories; Gimpel the fool to the Letter writer; Isaac Bashevis Singer
Getzel the monkey
  Singer, I. B. Collected stories; Gimpel the fool to the Letter writer; Isaac Bashevis Singer
Gifts
  Singer, I. B. Collected stories; One night in Brazil to The death of Methuselah
Gimpel the fool
  Singer, I. B. Collected stories; Gimpel the fool to the Letter writer; Isaac Bashevis Singer
Grandfather and grandson
  Singer, I. B. Collected stories: A friend of Kafka to Passions
The gravedigger
  Singer, I. B. Collected stories: A friend of Kafka to Passions
Guests on a winter night
  Singer, I. B. Collected stories: A friend of Kafka to Passions
Hanka
  Singer, I. B. Collected stories: A friend of Kafka to Passions
Henne fire
  Singer, I. B. Collected stories; Gimpel the fool to the Letter writer; Isaac Bashevis Singer
Her son
  Singer, I. B. Collected stories: A friend of Kafka to Passions
Hershele and Hanele' or, The power of a dream
  Singer, I. B. Collected stories; One night in Brazil to The death of Methuselah
The hotel
  Singer, I. B. Collected stories; One night in Brazil to The death of Methuselah
The house friend
  Singer, I. B. Collected stories; One night in Brazil to The death of Methuselah
I place my reliance on no man
  Singer, I. B. Collected stories; Gimpel the fool to the Letter writer; Isaac Bashevis Singer
The image
  Singer, I. B. Collected stories; One night in Brazil to The death of Methuselah
The impresario
  Singer, I. B. Collected stories; One night in Brazil to The death of Methuselah
In the poorhouse
  Singer, I. B. Collected stories; Gimpel the fool to the Letter writer; Isaac Bashevis Singer
The interview
  Singer, I. B. Collected stories; One night in Brazil to The death of Methuselah
Jachid and Jechidah
  Singer, I. B. Collected stories; Gimpel the fool to the Letter writer; Isaac Bashevis Singer

The jew from Babylon
  Singer, I. B. Collected stories; One night in Brazil to The death of Methuselah
The joke
  Singer, I. B. Collected stories: A friend of Kafka to Passions
Joy
  Singer, I. B. Collected stories; Gimpel the fool to the Letter writer; Isaac Bashevis Singer
The key
  The Best American short stories of the century; John Updike, editor, Katrina Kenison, coeditor; with an introduction by John Updike
  Singer, I. B. Collected stories: A friend of Kafka to Passions
The lantuch
  Singer, I. B. Collected stories: A friend of Kafka to Passions
The last demon
  Singer, I. B. Collected stories; Gimpel the fool to the Letter writer; Isaac Bashevis Singer
The last gaze
  Singer, I. B. Collected stories; One night in Brazil to The death of Methuselah
The lecture
  Singer, I. B. Collected stories; Gimpel the fool to the Letter writer; Isaac Bashevis Singer
The letter writer
  Singer, I. B. Collected stories; Gimpel the fool to the Letter writer; Isaac Bashevis Singer
The litigants
  Singer, I. B. Collected stories; One night in Brazil to The death of Methuselah
The little shoemakers
  Singer, I. B. Collected stories; Gimpel the fool to the Letter writer; Isaac Bashevis Singer
Logorihims
  Singer, I. B. Collected stories; One night in Brazil to The death of Methuselah
Loshikl
  Singer, I. B. Collected stories; One night in Brazil to The death of Methuselah
Lost
  Singer, I. B. Collected stories: A friend of Kafka to Passions
The magazine
  Singer, I. B. Collected stories: A friend of Kafka to Passions
The man who came back
  Singer, I. B. Collected stories; Gimpel the fool to the Letter writer; Isaac Bashevis Singer
The manuscript
  Singer, I. B. Collected stories; One night in Brazil to The death of Methuselah
The mathematician
  Singer, I. B. Collected stories; One night in Brazil to The death of Methuselah
The mentor
  Singer, I. B. Collected stories: A friend of Kafka to Passions

Singer, Isaac Bashevis—*Continued*

Miracles

Singer, I. B. Collected stories; One night in Brazil to The death of Methuselah

The mirror

Neugroschel, J. No star too beautiful; Yiddish stories from 1382 to the present; compiled and translated by Joachim Neugroschel

Singer, I. B. Collected stories; Gimpel the fool to the Letter writer; Isaac Bashevis Singer

The missing line

Singer, I. B. Collected stories; One night in Brazil to The death of Methuselah

The mistake

Singer, I. B. Collected stories; One night in Brazil to The death of Methuselah

Moishele

Singer, I. B. Collected stories: A friend of Kafka to Passions

Moon and madness

Singer, I. B. Collected stories; One night in Brazil to The death of Methuselah

Morris and Timna

Singer, I. B. Collected stories; One night in Brazil to The death of Methuselah

My adventures 25 as an idealist

Singer, I. B. Collected stories; One night in Brazil to The death of Methuselah

The needle

Singer, I. B. Collected stories; Gimpel the fool to the Letter writer; Isaac Bashevis Singer

Neighbors

Singer, I. B. Collected stories: A friend of Kafka to Passions

A nest egg for paradise

Singer, I. B. Collected stories; One night in Brazil to The death of Methuselah

The New Year party

Singer, I. B. Collected stories: A friend of Kafka to Passions

A night in the poorhouse

Singer, I. B. Collected stories; One night in Brazil to The death of Methuselah

Not for the Sabbath

Singer, I. B. Collected stories; One night in Brazil to The death of Methuselah

Old love

Singer, I. B. Collected stories: A friend of Kafka to Passions

The old man

Singer, I. B. Collected stories; Gimpel the fool to the Letter writer; Isaac Bashevis Singer

On a wagon

Singer, I. B. Collected stories: A friend of Kafka to Passions

On the way to the poorhouse

Singer, I. B. Collected stories; One night in Brazil to The death of Methuselah

One day of happiness

Singer, I. B. Collected stories; One night in Brazil to The death of Methuselah

One night in Brazil

Singer, I. B. Collected stories; One night in Brazil to The death of Methuselah

The painting

Singer, I. B. Collected stories; One night in Brazil to The death of Methuselah

A pair

Singer, I. B. Collected stories: A friend of Kafka to Passions

The parrot

Singer, I. B. Collected stories; Gimpel the fool to the Letter writer; Isaac Bashevis Singer

A party in Miami Beach

Singer, I. B. Collected stories; One night in Brazil to The death of Methuselah

Passions

Singer, I. B. Collected stories: A friend of Kafka to Passions

A peephole in the gate

Singer, I. B. Collected stories; One night in Brazil to The death of Methuselah

A piece of advice

Singer, I. B. Collected stories; Gimpel the fool to the Letter writer; Isaac Bashevis Singer

Pigeons

Singer, I. B. Collected stories: A friend of Kafka to Passions

Pity

Singer, I. B. Collected stories; One night in Brazil to The death of Methuselah

The plagiarist

Singer, I. B. Collected stories; Gimpel the fool to the Letter writer; Isaac Bashevis Singer

The pocket remembered

Singer, I. B. Collected stories; One night in Brazil to The death of Methuselah

The power of darkness

Singer, I. B. Collected stories; One night in Brazil to The death of Methuselah

Powers

Singer, I. B. Collected stories: A friend of Kafka to Passions

The primper

Singer, I. B. Collected stories: A friend of Kafka to Passions

The prodigy

Singer, I. B. Collected stories: A friend of Kafka to Passions

Property

Singer, I. B. Collected stories: A friend of Kafka to Passions

The psychic journey

Singer, I. B. Collected stories; One night in Brazil to The death of Methuselah

A quotation from Klopstock

Singer, I. B. Collected stories: A friend of Kafka to Passions

The recluse

Singer, I. B. Collected stories; One night in Brazil to The death of Methuselah

Singer, I. B. Collected stories: A friend of Kafka to Passions

The reencounter

Singer, I. B. Collected stories; One night in Brazil to The death of Methuselah

Remnants

Singer, I. B. Collected stories; One night in Brazil to The death of Methuselah

Singer, Isaac Bashevis—*Continued*

The riddle
  Singer, I. B. Collected stories: A friend of Kafka to Passions
Runners to nowhere
  Singer, I. B. Collected stories; One night in Brazil to The death of Methuselah
Sabbath in Gehanna
  Singer, I. B. Collected stories; One night in Brazil to The death of Methuselah
Sabbath in Portugal
  Singer, I. B. Collected stories: A friend of Kafka to Passions
The safe deposit
  Singer, I. B. Collected stories; One night in Brazil to The death of Methuselah
Sam Palka and David Vishkover
  Singer, I. B. Collected stories: A friend of Kafka to Passions
Schloimele
  Singer, I. B. Collected stories: A friend of Kafka to Passions
The seance
  Singer, I. B. Collected stories; Gimpel the fool to the Letter writer; Isaac Bashevis Singer
The secret
  Singer, I. B. Collected stories; One night in Brazil to The death of Methuselah
The shadow of a crib
  Singer, I. B. Collected stories; Gimpel the fool to the Letter writer; Isaac Bashevis Singer
Shiddah and Kuziba
  Singer, I. B. Collected stories; Gimpel the fool to the Letter writer; Isaac Bashevis Singer
Short Friday
  Singer, I. B. Collected stories; Gimpel the fool to the Letter writer; Isaac Bashevis Singer
The slaughterer
  Singer, I. B. Collected stories; Gimpel the fool to the Letter writer; Isaac Bashevis Singer
The smuggler
  Singer, I. B. Collected stories; One night in Brazil to The death of Methuselah
Something is there
  Singer, I. B. Collected stories: A friend of Kafka to Passions
The son
  Singer, I. B. Collected stories: A friend of Kafka to Passions
The son from America
  Singer, I. B. Collected stories: A friend of Kafka to Passions
The sorcerer
  Singer, I. B. Collected stories: A friend of Kafka to Passions
The Spinoza of Market Street
  Singer, I. B. Collected stories; Gimpel the fool to the Letter writer; Isaac Bashevis Singer
Stories from behind the stove
  Singer, I. B. Collected stories: A friend of Kafka to Passions

Strangers
  Singer, I. B. Collected stories; One night in Brazil to The death of Methuselah
Strong as death is love
  Singer, I. B. Collected stories; One night in Brazil to The death of Methuselah
Taibele and her demon
  Neurotica: Jewish writers on sex; edited by Melvin Jules Bukiet
  Singer, I. B. Collected stories; Gimpel the fool to the Letter writer; Isaac Bashevis Singer
A tale of two liars
  Singer, I. B. Collected stories; Gimpel the fool to the Letter writer; Isaac Bashevis Singer
A tale of two sisters
  Singer, I. B. Collected stories: A friend of Kafka to Passions
Tanhum
  Singer, I. B. Collected stories; One night in Brazil to The death of Methuselah
A telephone call on Yom Kippur
  Singer, I. B. Collected stories; One night in Brazil to The death of Methuselah
There are no coincidences
  Singer, I. B. Collected stories; One night in Brazil to The death of Methuselah
The third one
  Singer, I. B. Collected stories: A friend of Kafka to Passions
Three encounters
  Singer, I. B. Collected stories: A friend of Kafka to Passions
Three tales
  Singer, I. B. Collected stories; Gimpel the fool to the Letter writer; Isaac Bashevis Singer
The trap
  Singer, I. B. Collected stories; One night in Brazil to The death of Methuselah
A tutor in the village
  Singer, I. B. Collected stories: A friend of Kafka to Passions
Two
  Singer, I. B. Collected stories; One night in Brazil to The death of Methuselah
Two corpses go dancing
  Singer, I. B. Collected stories; Gimpel the fool to the Letter writer; Isaac Bashevis Singer
Two markets
  Singer, I. B. Collected stories: A friend of Kafka to Passions
Two weddings and one divorce
  Singer, I. B. Collected stories; One night in Brazil to The death of Methuselah
Under the knife
  Singer, I. B. Collected stories; Gimpel the fool to the Letter writer; Isaac Bashevis Singer
The unseen
  Singer, I. B. Collected stories; Gimpel the fool to the Letter writer; Isaac Bashevis Singer
Vanvild Kava
  Singer, I. B. Collected stories; One night in Brazil to The death of Methuselah

Singer, Isaac Bashevis—*Continued*
The wager
  Singer, I. B. Collected stories: A friend of
  Kafka to Passions
The warehouse
  Singer, I. B. Collected stories; Gimpel the
  fool to the Letter writer; Isaac Bashevis
  Singer
A wedding in Brownsville
  Singer, I. B. Collected stories; Gimpel the
  fool to the Letter writer; Isaac Bashevis
  Singer
Why Heisherik was born
  Singer, I. B. Collected stories; One night in
  Brazil to The death of Methuselah
The wife killer
  Singer, I. B. Collected stories; Gimpel the
  fool to the Letter writer; Isaac Bashevis
  Singer
The witch
  Singer, I. B. Collected stories: A friend of
  Kafka to Passions
Yanda
  Singer, I. B. Collected stories; Gimpel the
  fool to the Letter writer; Isaac Bashevis
  Singer
The yearning heifer
  Singer, I. B. Collected stories: A friend of
  Kafka to Passions
Yentl the yeshiva boy
  Beautiful as the moon, radiant as the stars;
  Jewish women in Yiddish stories : an an-
  thology; edited by Sandra Bark; introduc-
  tion by Francine Prose
  Singer, I. B. Collected stories; Gimpel the
  fool to the Letter writer; Isaac Bashevis
  Singer
Yochna and Schmelke
  Singer, I. B. Collected stories; One night in
  Brazil to The death of Methuselah
Zeidlus the Pope
  Singer, I. B. Collected stories; Gimpel the
  fool to the Letter writer; Isaac Bashevis
  Singer
Zeitl and Rickel
  Singer, I. B. Collected stories; Gimpel the
  fool to the Letter writer; Isaac Bashevis
  Singer
Singer, Israel Joshua
Magda
  Neugroschel, J. No star too beautiful; Yiddish
  stories from 1382 to the present; compiled
  and translated by Joachim Neugroschel
Singer, Shelley
Lost polars
  Mystery midrash; an anthology of Jewish
  mystery & detective fiction; [edited by]
  Lawrence W. Raphael
The **singer** and the song. Yolen, J.
Singer, Julia Klatt
Chicken
  Murphy, N. Twelve branches; stories from St.
  Paul; [by] Nora Murphy ... {et al.}
From one window
  Murphy, N. Twelve branches; stories from St.
  Paul; [by] Nora Murphy ... {et al.}
Translations
  Murphy, N. Twelve branches; stories from St.
  Paul; [by] Nora Murphy ... {et al.}

SINGERS
  Alas, L. Queen Margaret
  Alcott, L. M. The rival prima donnas
  Becker, G. Black Elvis
  Boylan, C. Gods and slaves
  Carlson, R. Dr. Slime
  Cather, W. Double birthday
  Channer, C. I'm still waiting
  Chekhov, A. P. Mari d'elle
  DeLancey, K. Swingtime
  Denton, B. We love Lydia love
  Dumas, H. The voice
  Duncan, A. Daddy Mention and the Monday
    skull
  Dybek, S. Song
  Gomez, J. Chicago 1927
  Kurlansky, M. Packets and paperscraps
  Lee, V. A wicked voice
  Lumley, B. Vanessa's voice
  Mathews, H. Letters from Yerevan
  McCrumb, S. Among my souvenirs
  Murguía, A. This war called love
  Paul, B. Scat
  Ross, L. Tasting songs
  Schnitzler, A. Baron von Leisenbohg's destiny
  Spencer, E. The eclipse
  Stollman, A. L. Enfleurage
  Tem, M. Piano bar blues
  Walker, A. Nineteen fifty-five
SINGING AND VOICE CULTURE
  Bradbury, R. I get the blues when it rains (A re-
    membrance)
  Chaudhuri, A. White lies
  Jenkins, G. Gotta sing
The **singing** boy. Gambone, P.
The **singing** cashier. Keegan, C.
Singing in the desert. Peri Rossi, C.
SINGLE MEN
    See also Widowers
  Adams, A. Flights
  Archer, J. A weekend to remember
  Banks, R. Comfort
  Barthelme, F. Pool lights
  Barthelme, F. Shopgirls
  Barthelme, F. Violet
  Berberova, N. The Argentine
  Bingham, S. Stanley
  Boswell, M. Karma wheel
  Boswell, M. Venus/Mars
  Bowen, E. Summer night
  Boyle, T. C. Termination dust
  Budnitz, J. Average Joe
  Bunin, I. A. Antigone
  Callaghan, M. Silk stockings
  Chekhov, A. P. At the bath-house
  Coleman, A. S. The little grey house
  Daniels, J. Sugar water
  Epstein, J. Don Juan Zimmerman
  Gunn, K. Jesus, I know that guy
  Harrar, G. The 5:22
  Hawkins, T. Wedding night
  Hayes, D. Twenty-six hours, twenty-five min-
    utes
  Hermann, J. Hunter Johnson music
  Highsmith, P. Man's best friend
  James, H. Benvolio
  James, H. The diary of a man of fifty
  Kafka, F. Blumfeld, an elderly bachelor
  Lord, N. The man who went through everything

SINGLE MEN—*Continued*

McGarry, J. The thin man
Mencken, S. H. The last of the beaux
Penn, W. S. Talking turkey, not goose
Perillo, L. M. Bad boy number seventeen
Rifkin, A. The honor system
Roorbach, B. Loneliness
Scholz, C. Blumfeld, an elderly bachelor
Singer, I. B. The letter writer
Škvorecký, J. Three bachelors in a fiery furnace
Tammuz, B. My brother
Trevor, W. The hill bachelors
Trevor, W. Three people
Updike, J. I am dying, Egypt, dying
Weaver, G. On watch for Big Red
Weinreb, M. All I know about it
Weinreb, M. Bear claws the size of her head
Weinreb, M. The fox hunters
Weinreb, M. L.A., baby
Weinreb, M. Old men on spring break
Weinreb, M. Pictures of my family
Weinreb, M. Radio radio
Weinreb, M. Satisfaction
Weinreb, M. What I would tell her
Wharton, E. After Holbein
Wuori, G. K. Angles

SINGLE-PARENT FAMILY

Cooper, J. C. The eagle flies
Le Clézio, J.-M. G. Moloch
McCorkle, J. Dogs
Singleton, G. Page-a-day
Stuckey-French, E. Plywood rabbit
Tenorio, L. A. Superassassin
Williams, J. The last generation
Single woman for long walks on the beach. Carlson, R.

SINGLE WOMEN

See also Unmarried mothers; Widows

Adams, A. Berkeley house
Adams, A. Great sex
Adams, A. Raccoons
Adams, A. Tide pools
Adams, A. An unscheduled stop
Adams, A. A very nice dog
Agee, J. Cupid
Agee, J. I can't stop loving you
Agee, J. My last try
Aldrich, B. S. The woman who was forgotten
Almog, R. Shrinking
Almond, S. The evil B. B. Chow
Atkinson, K. Transparent fiction
Avrich, J. La belle dame sans merci
Avrich, J. Waiting rooms
Bank, M. The girls' guide to hunting and fishing
Banks, R. The guinea pig lady
Barker, N. Bendy-Linda
Barker, N. Parker Swells
Barker, N. Skin
Barrett, L. Meet the impersonators! (1986)
Barthelme, F. Shopgirls
Bass, R. Wild horses
Bear, G. Webster
Bennett, A. Miss Fozzard finds her feet
Berberova, N. The little stranger
Berney, L. Stupid girl
Bidisha. Talking in bed
Bingham, S. Apricots
Blatnik, A. The taste of blood

Boylan, C. A particular calling
Bradbury, R. Death and the maiden
Bradbury, R. Triangle
Bradbury, R. The whole town's sleeping
Brenner, W. Remnants of Earl
Broughton, T. A. The classicist
Brownrigg, S. The girl in the red chair
Budnitz, J. Hook, line and sinker
Butler, R. O. Fair warning
Butler, R. O. The grotto
Capote, T. Among the paths to Eden
Carter, E. All the men are called McCabe
Carter, E. Glory goes and gets some
Casey, M. Drastic
Casey, M. Relief
Casey, M. Talk show lady
Cherry, K. Lunachick
Chopin, K. Elizabeth Stock's one story
Chopin, K. Fedora
Chopin, K. The impossible Miss Meadows
Chopin, K. Ma'ame Pélagie
Chopin, K. Polly
Chopin, K. Regret
Connolly, C. Bare
Connor, J. I wouldn't do that if I were you
Cummins, A. Where I work
Daum, M. Alternative lifestyle alert
Davidson, A. Summon the watch!
Davis, J. S. Tammy, imagined
Day, C. Jennie Dixiana
Desai, A. The rooftop dwellers
Desplechin, M. Haiku
Di Blasi, D. Blind
Divakaruni, C. B. The blooming season for cacti
Dodd, S. M. Lady Chatterley's root canal
Dozois, G. R. Send no money
Drake, R. Auntee and the two nieces
Dunmore, H. The icon room
Dunmore, H. Living out
Edwards, K. The way it felt to be falling
Eugenides, J. Baster
Foster, K. Crush
Gabrielyan, N. The studio apartment
Galloway, J. Test
Gartner, Z. City of my dreams
Gartner, Z. How to survive in the bush
Gartner, Z. Measuring death in column inches (a nine-week manual for girl rim pigs)
Gautreaux, T. The piano tuner
Gilchrist, E. Jade Buddhas, red bridges, fruits of love
Gilliland, G. Freedom
Gilliland, G. Kindnesses
Glover, D. H. La Corriveau
Goldner, B. Taxi dancer
Goran, L. Jenny and the Episcopalian
Grodstein, L. Hey, beautiful
Grodstein, L. Lonely planet
Grodstein, L. Yellow morning
Guerra, L. The virgin's passion
Guerrero, L. Hotel Arco Iris
Gurganus, A. The practical heart
Gussoff, C. Djinni
Haake, K. All this land
Harfenist, J. Fully bonded by the state of Minnesota
Hayes, D. Hope
Heath, R. A. K. The master tailor and the teacher's skirt

SINGLE WOMEN—*Continued*

Hegi, U. Doves
Hegi, U. Lower Crossing
Hendel, Y. Fata morgana across the street
Henley, P. Lessons in joy
Hermann, J. Camera obscura
Hermann, J. Sonja
Highsmith, P. Doorbell for Louisa
Highsmith, P. Nothing that meets the eye
Highsmith, P. Where the door is always open
    and the welcome mat is out
Hodgen, C. Take them in, please
Hoffman, W. Landings
Honig, L. The truly needy
Houston, P. The best girlfriend you never had
Iagnemma, K. Kingdom, order, species
Jackson, S. The bus
Jackson, S. Nightmare
Jackson, S. The possibility of evil
Jackson, V. F. Living alone
Jacobs, M. The egg queen rises
James, H. The Aspern papers
James, S. Billy Mason from Gloucester
Jarrell, D. The displaced overweight homemak-
    er's guide to finding a man
Kane, J. F. How to become a publicist
Karnezis, P. Stella the spinster's afternoon
    dreams
Kimber, J. Having myself a time
Kohler, S. Ambush
Krouse, E. My weddings
Krouse, E. Other people's mothers
Krouse, E. Too big to float
Krouse, E. What I wore
Kusel, L. Bars
Kusel, L. Craps
Kusel, L. Juvenile hall
Kusel, L. Other fish in the sea
Kusel, L. Prairie dogs
Kusel, L. Single white female
Kusel, L. SWM
Lahiri, J. The treatment of Bibi Haldar
LaPierre, J. Da capo
Lee, D. The Lone Night Cantina
Lida, D. La quedada
Lieu, J. Safety
Link, K. Most of my friends are two-thirds wa-
    ter
Louis, L. G. Fur
Mason, B. A. Rolling into Atlanta
Mason, N. The bad seed: a guide
Mastretta, A. Aunt Cristina
Mastretta, A. Aunt Fátima
McCann, C. As Kingfishers catch fire
McCorkle, J. Dogs
Meissner, J. Placedo junction
Mencken, S. H. Clinging vine
Mencken, S. H. Ladies and lovers
Mencken, S. H. Miss Rebecca
Metzgar, L. Cat and mouse
Munro, A. Hateship, friendship, courtship,
    loveship, marriage
Munro, A. Meneseteung
Nelson, A. The lonely doll
Ng'ugĩ wa Thiong'o. Minutes of glory
Nixon, C. Lunch at the Blacksmith
Oates, J. C. Gunlove
Oates, J. C. Subway
Oates, J. C. Ugly

Oz, A. Nomad and viper
Pearlman, E. Skin deep
Penn, W. S. Toothpaste
Potvin, E. A. The traveller's hat
Pritchard, M. Funktionlust
Régio, J. Miss Olimpia and her maid Belarmina
Régio, J. They used to go for long walks on
    Sundays . . .
Reisman, N. Edie in winter
Reisman, N. Strays
Rendell, R. The carer
Richmond, M. The last bad thing
Richter, S. An Island of boyfriends
Rodgers, S. J. The trouble with you is
Rosenfeld, S. Good for the frog
Sanford, A. Housekeeping
Santos-Febres, M. Flight
Schoemperlen, D. A change is as good as a rest
Schoemperlen, D. Frogs
Schoemperlen, D. The look of the lightning, the
    sound of the birds
Schoemperlen, D. Red plaid shirt
Searle, E. What it's worth
Serdatzky, Yente. Two heads
Silber, J. Commendable
Simonds, M. The blue of the Madrugada
Singer, I. B. A dance and a hop
Singer, I. B. One day of happiness
Singer, I. B. The primper
Singer, I. B. The Spinoza of Market Street
Sojourner, M. Armageddon coffee
Sojourner, M. Huevos
Sojourner, M. Monsters
Sojourner, M. What they write in other coun-
    tries
Sosin, D. Mother Superior
Strauss, A. The way you left
Sumner, M. The guide
Swan, M. By the sea, by the sea
Thompson, J. Who do you love
Tippens, E. Make a wish
Tomioka, T. Time table
Treat, J. Honda
Trevor, W. Against the odds
Trevor, W. Three people
Waugh, E. On guard
Weldon, F. GUP—or, Falling in love in Helsin-
    ki
Wilson, R., Jr. Remembered names
Winter, E. The boys
Winter, E. Spin cycle
Winter, E. Spring
Yasrebi, C. Love and scream
Zabytko, I. John Mars, all-American
Zhang Jie. Love must not be forgotten
Singles' club. Henkel, V.

Singleton, George
  Answers
    Singleton, G. The half-mammals of Dixie;
      stories
  Bank of America
    Singleton, G. The half-mammals of Dixie;
      stories
  Caulk
    New stories from the South: the year's best,
      1999; edited by Shannon Ravenel; with a
      preface by Tony Earley
    Singleton, G. These people are us; short sto-
      ries

Singleton, George—*Continued*

Cleft for me
Singleton, G. These people are us; short stories

Crawl space
Singleton, G. These people are us; short stories

Deer gone
Singleton, G. The half-mammals of Dixie; stories

Dialectic, abrasions, the backs of heads again
Singleton, G. These people are us; short stories

Directions for seeing, directions for singing
Singleton, G. These people are us; short stories

Duke power
Singleton, G. The half-mammals of Dixie; stories

Fossils
Singleton, G. The half-mammals of Dixie; stories

The half-mammals of Dixie
Harper's v302 no1809 p82-7 F 2001
Singleton, G. The half-mammals of Dixie; stories

How I met my second wife
Singleton, G. These people are us; short stories

How to collect fishing lures
Singleton, G. The half-mammals of Dixie; stories

I could've told you if you hadn't asked
Singleton, G. These people are us; short stories

Impurities
Singleton, G. The half-mammals of Dixie; stories

Jesus of Nazareth
New England Review v20 no1 p147-56 Wint 1999

The Morton's Salt Boy
New England Review v24 no2 p182-90 Spr 2003

My last essay
New England Review v22 no1 p133-42 Wint 2001

Normal
Singleton, G. These people are us; short stories

One man's indelible marks
Stories from the Blue Moon Cafe II; edited by Sonny Brewer

Outlaw head and tail
Singleton, G. These people are us; short stories

Page-a-day
Singleton, G. The half-mammals of Dixie; stories

Public relations
New stories from the South: the year's best, 2001; edited by Shannon Ravenel; with a preface by Lee Smith
Singleton, G. The half-mammals of Dixie; stories

Raise Children Here
The Georgia Review v57 no1 p84-95 Spr 2003

New stories from the South; the year's best, 2004; edited by Shannon Ravenel; preface by Tim Gautreaux

Remember why we're here
Singleton, G. These people are us; short stories

Rentals
Singleton, G. These people are us; short stories

Richard Petty accepts national book ward
Singleton, G. The half-mammals of Dixie; stories

The ruptures and limits of absence
Singleton, G. These people are us; short stories
The Southern Review (Baton Rouge, La.) v35 no2 p295-314 Spr 1999

Santayana speaks through me
Singleton, G. These people are us; short stories

Show-and-tell
Atlantic Monthly v288 no1 p123-9 Jl/Ag 2001
New stories from the South: the year's best, 2002; edited by Shannon Ravenel; with a preface by Larry Brown
Singleton, G. The half-mammals of Dixie; stories

These people are us
Singleton, G. These people are us; short stories

This itches, y'all
Singleton, G. The half-mammals of Dixie; stories

Vietnam
Stories from the Blue Moon Café; edited by Sonny Brewer

What slide rules can't measure
Singleton, G. The half-mammals of Dixie; stories

When children count
Singleton, G. The half-mammals of Dixie; stories
The Southern Review (Baton Rouge, La.) v35 no1 p128-44 Wint 1999

Singleton. Egan, G.

The **singular** habits of wasps. Landis, G. A.

The **singular** incident of the dog on the beach. Davidson, A.

A **singular** indiscretion. O'Bannion, S.

The **singular** we. DeMarinis, R.

Sinking. Sellers, H.

Sinner or saint. Westlake, D. E.

Sinor, Bradley H.
Eleven to seven
Such a pretty face; edited by Lee Martindale
"Places for act two!"
Dracula in London; edited by P. N. Elrod

Sins of a harvest god. Karnezis, P.

The **sins** of Jesus. Vasseur, T. J.

The **sins** of the fathers. Deane, J. F.

Sins of the mothers. Dyer, S. N.

Sintra. Adams, A.

Siodmak, Curt
FP 1 does not reply
Science-fiction classics; the stories that morphed into movies; compiled by Forrest J. Ackerman

SIOUX INDIANS *See* Dakota Indians

Sir Edmund Orme. James, H.

Sir Gervais in the enchanted forest. Trevanian
Sir Karl LaFong or current resident. Hodgen, C.
Siren. Adam, C.
The **siren**. Chekhov, A. P.
Siren. Keret, E.
The **siren** and the shill. Jakes, J.
Siren Song. Frame, R.
The **siren's** song. Raphael, F.
The **Siri** gun. Aylett, S.
Siriol, she-devil of naked madness. Mazelis, J.
Sis' Becky's pickaninny. Chesnutt, C. W.
Sissman loses his way. Stern, S.
Sissy Sue and the Reverend Reverend. Reiner, C.
Sister. Abu, J. D.
Sister. Baron, D.
Sister. Tozzi, F.
Sister Attanasia's chickens. Maraini, D.
Sister death. Yolen, J.
Sister Emily's lightship. Yolen, J.
Sister Godzilla. Erdrich, L.
Sister Josepha. Dunbar-Nelson, A. M.
Sister Lilith. Jeffers, H. F.
SISTERS
> *See also* Brothers and sisters; Half-sisters; Stepsisters; Twins

Agee, J. Dead space
Agee, J. The October horse
Alcott, L. M. The sisters' trial
Allen, S. Marisol's things
Allison, D. Compassion
Atwood, M. Wilderness tips
Bauman, B. A. Wildlife of America
Bausch, R. Equity
Beattie, A. Perfect recall
Bergelson, D. In the boardinghouse
Bikis, G. Cleo's back
Blair, J. Memorial day
Bloom, A. Silver water
Bowles, P. Doña Faustina
Bowles, P. You are not I
Boylan, C. The picture house
Boyle, T. C. The black and white sisters
Bradbury, R. Triangle
Brady, C. Don't run
Brady, C. Driving
Brady, C. Home movies
Budnitz, J. Flush
Budnitz, J. Skin care
Bukoski, A. The absolution of Hedda Borski
Burleson, D. R. The watcher at the window
Butler, R. O. Twins
Casey, M. The arrangement of the night office in summer
Chang, L. S. The eve of the spirit festival
Chekhov, A. P. An artist's story
Chopin, K. Ma'ame Pélagie
Coates, G. S. Le Bonnet Rouge
Cobb, W. J. Motel ice
Connolly, C. Granville Hill
Davies, R. The sisters
Davis, A. Prints
De Lint, C. Seven wild sisters
Di Blasi, D. The season's condition
Doerr, A. For a long time this was Griselda's story
Dunmore, H. Emily's ring
Furman, L. Buddy
Furman, L. What would Buddha do?
Gates, D. The crazy thought

Gilchrist, E. The brown cape
Gilman, C. P. Unpunished
Goldner, B. Farm wife
Goldner, B. Wake
Greer, R. O. Prime
Grodstein, L. Such a pretty face
Gussoff, C. Unpretty
Hegi, U. Lower Crossing
Heker, L. Berkley; or, Mariana of the universe
Henderson, L. Dark mirror
Henley, P. Worship of the common heart
Henry, O. The higher pragmatism
Hood, A. Joelle's mother
Hribal, C. J. War babies
Iwaszkiewicz, J. The Wilko girls
Jackson, V. F. A small independence
James, H. A London life
James, H. The romance of certain old clothes
James, S. John Hedward
Johnson, D. Three ladies sipping tea in a Persian garden
Jones, C. Irregularities
Jones, G. Babies
Jones, T. Daddy's girl
Kalman, J. Rain
Kavaler, R. Sisters
Keegan, C. The singing cashier
Keegan, C. Sisters
Kees, W. Every year they came out
Kelly, R. En famille
Kingsbury, K. A nice cup of tea
Kohler, S. The adulterous woman
Kohler, S. Africans
Kohler, S. Correspondence I
Kohler, S. Correspondence II
Lamsley, T. Climbing down from heaven
Lavin, M. A gentle soul
Le Clézio, J.-M. G. The great life
Leegant, J. Henny's wedding
Leegant, J. The lament of the rabbi's daughters
Light, D. Three days. a month. more.
Lindquist, R. C. Prelude to a nocturne
Matthews, C. Dear Lottie
Moody, R. Demonology
Moore, L. You're ugly, too
Munro, A. Queenie
Navarro, Y. A beacon shall I shine
Nawrocki, S. Locusts
Nelson, A. The other daughter
Nikas, E. Fatal tears
Orphée, E. The journey of Amatista and the dirty prince
Ortiz, S. J. 3 women
Padilla, M. The reason for angels
Perillo, L. M. Bad boy number seventeen
Prose, F. Talking dog
Régio, J. The story of Rosa Brava
Reifler, N. Memoir
Reifler, N. The river and Una
Reisman, N. Heart of hearts
Richmond, M. Curvature
Richmond, M. The world's greatest pants
Robison, M. Sisters
Rusch, K. K. Coolhunting
Sanford, A. Bear the dead away
Saroyan, A. The musician
Schmidt, H. J. Songbirds
Shepard, S. Blinking eye
Silber, J. What lasts

SISTERS—*Continued*

Simonds, M. The blue of the Madrugada
Singer, I. B. A dance and a hop
Singer, I. B. The power of darkness
Singer, I. B. A tale of two sisters
Skillings, R. D. Outcomes
Slezak, E. If you treat things right
Slezak, E. Settled
Smith, A. Paradise
Spatz, G. Wonderful tricks
Stanton, M. My sister's novel
Swan, M. Down by the lake
Thomas, D. The Steckley girls
Tomioka, T. Happy birthday
Van Winckel, N. The expectation of abundance
Vivante, A. Fall and rise
Walker, A. Blaze
Walker, A. Kindred spirits
Walker, A. Uncle Loaf and Auntie Putt-Putt
Weldon, F. Pyroclastic flow
Wharton, E. Bunner Sisters
Wildgen, M. Healer
Yolen, J. Blood sister
Yuknavitch, L. Shadow boxing
Ziegler, I. Blue Springs
Ziegler, I. Cliffs notes
Ziegler, I. Feud of the maids
Ziegler, I. Hooked

Sisters. Bear, G.
Sisters. Kavaler, R.
Sisters. Keegan, C.
Sisters. Robison, M.
Sisters. Tolstoy, L., graf
SISTERS AND BROTHERS *See* Brothers and sisters
SISTERS-IN-LAW

Barthelme, F. Margaret & Bud
Canty, K. Little palaces
Drake, R. A short horse
Pryor, J. Wrong numbers
Ritchie, J. The absence of Emily
Warren, D. Hawk's landing

The **sisters'** trial. Alcott, L. M.
Sita Dulip's Method. Le Guin, U. K.
Sitcom Mom. Haven, C.
A **site** for contingencies. Bachmann, I.
Sittin' on the dock. Bischoff, D.
Sitting pretty. Holdstock, P.
Sitting shivah with cousin Benny. Blaise, C.
Sitting Theodore. Orner, P.
Sitting with the dead. Trevor, W.
Six Chinese Cooks Rose into the Air. Poore, M.
Six eagles and a child. Kanafāni, G.
Six figures in search of an author. Schmidt, H. J.
Six-four, four-three, deuce, a ghost story of sorts. Cohen, S.
Six horses. Galloway, J.
Six short pieces. Bai Xiao-Yi
Six this, six that. Van de Wetering, J.
Sixteen days in December. Nair, M.
Sixteen Jackies. Olsen, L.
Size does matter. Matiella, A. C.
Sjoholm, Barbara *See* Wilson, Barbara, 1950-
Skármeta, Antonio

The cyclist of San Cristóbal Hill
    The Vintage book of Latin American stories; edited by Carlos Fuentes and Julio Ortega

SKATEBOARDING

Huff, T. He said, sidhe said

The **skater**. Spencer, E.
Skeeks. Westlake, D. E.
Skeet, Michael

Near enough to home
    Northern suns; edited by David G. Hartwell & Glenn Grant
Skeet, Michael

I love Paree
    Witpunk; edited by Claude Lalumière and Marty Halpern
Skeleton krewe. Holder, N.
SKELETONS

Bhêly-Quénum, O. A child in the bush of ghosts
Skelton's party. McGuane, T.
Skibell, Joseph

Kindertotenlieder or, Daycare among the Paste-eaters
    Tikkun v18 no3 p60-5 My/Je 2003
Skiff, Micheal

Blood brothers
    His 3: brilliant new fiction by gay writers; edited by Robert Drake and Terry Wolverton
A **skill** you'll develop. Lisick, B.
Skillings, R. D. (Roger D.)

Ashes
    Skillings, R. D. Where the time goes
At least
    Skillings, R. D. Where the time goes
Constant concupiscence
    Skillings, R. D. Where the time goes
Coughlan Dice at his closet window
    Skillings, R. D. Where the time goes
Czezarley Zoo gets out
    Skillings, R. D. Where the time goes
Doggy
    Skillings, R. D. Where the time goes
Easter at the old homestead
    Skillings, R. D. Where the time goes
God knows
    Skillings, R. D. Where the time goes
Here I am
    Skillings, R. D. Where the time goes
Job ops
    Skillings, R. D. Where the time goes
The line
    Skillings, R. D. Where the time goes
The news
    Skillings, R. D. Where the time goes
No escape for yours truly
    Skillings, R. D. Where the time goes
Noon, afternoon, night
    Skillings, R. D. Where the time goes
Outcomes
    Skillings, R. D. Where the time goes
Paint
    Skillings, R. D. Where the time goes
The present
    Skillings, R. D. Where the time goes
The sandbox
    Skillings, R. D. Where the time goes
The spiritus step
    Skillings, R. D. Where the time goes
Tabletalk
    Skillings, R. D. Where the time goes
Theatre of the real
    Skillings, R. D. Where the time goes
The throes
    Skillings, R. D. Where the time goes

Skillings, Roger D. *See* Skillings, R. D. (Roger D.), 1937-
Skillingstead, Jack
  Dead worlds
    The year's best science fiction: twenty-first annual collection; edited by Gardner Dozois
The **skills** of Xanadu. Sturgeon, T.
SKIN
                    Diseases
  Gray, A. Job's skin game
Skin. Barker, N.
Skin care. Budnitz, J.
Skin deep. Benítez-Rojo, A.
Skin deep. Pearlman, E.
Skin deep. Rusch, K. K.
SKIN DIVING
  Lopez, B. H. Light action in the Caribbean
  Shaw, D. Diving with the devil
Skin so green and fine. Wheeler, W.
SKINHEADS
  Leonard, E. Fire in the hole
The **Skinned**. Tangh, J.
Skinner, José
  Age of copper
    Skinner, J. Flight and other stories
  Archangela's place
    Skinner, J. Flight and other stories
  Careful
    Skinner, J. Flight and other stories
  Cosas, Inc.
    Skinner, J. Flight and other stories
  Desiring desire
    Skinner, J. Flight and other stories
  Dogs
    Skinner, J. Flight and other stories
  Eloy
    Skinner, J. Flight and other stories
  Every head's a world
    Skinner, J. Flight and other stories
  Flight
    Skinner, J. Flight and other stories
  Pickup
    Skinner, J. Flight and other stories
  Spring
    Skinner, J. Flight and other stories
  Tongue
    Skinner, J. Flight and other stories
  Trial day
    Skinner, J. Flight and other stories
  Weeds
    Skinner, J. Flight and other stories
The **skinning** of Black Coyote. Henry, W.
A **skirmish** in the desert. Kirchheimer, G. D.
SKIS AND SKIING
  Adams, A. Snow
  Clyde, M. Jumping
  Cohen, S. I'm sorry, Mr. Griggs
  Fulton, J. Liars
  Updike, J. Man and daughter in the cold
  Updike, J. The rescue
Skiv. Lee, W. W.
Skloot, Floyd
  Cream of kohlrabi
    Tikkun v16 no4 p65-9 Jl/Ag 2001
  The shorefront manor
    The North American Review v284 no3-4 p58-59 My/Ag 1999

The tour
    The North American Review v286 no6 p29-33 N/D 2001
The **skull**. Oates, J. C.
Skunk. Wuori, G. K.
SKUNKS
  Wuori, G. K. Skunk
Škvorecký, Josef
  According to Poe
    Škvorecký, J. When Eve was naked; stories of a life's journey
  The cuckoo
    Škvorecký, J. When Eve was naked; stories of a life's journey
  Dr. Strass
    Škvorecký, J. When Eve was naked; stories of a life's journey
  The end of Bull Macha
    Škvorecký, J. When Eve was naked; stories of a life's journey
  Eve was naked
    Škvorecký, J. When Eve was naked; stories of a life's journey
  Feminine mystique
    Škvorecký, J. When Eve was naked; stories of a life's journey
  Filthy cruel world
    Škvorecký, J. When Eve was naked; stories of a life's journey
  Fragments about Rebecca
    Škvorecký, J. When Eve was naked; stories of a life's journey
  How my literary career began
    Škvorecký, J. When Eve was naked; stories of a life's journey
  An insoluble problem of genetics
    Škvorecký, J. When Eve was naked; stories of a life's journey
  Jezebel from Forest Hill (A love story)
    Škvorecký, J. When Eve was naked; stories of a life's journey
  Laws of the jungle
    Škvorecký, J. When Eve was naked; stories of a life's journey
  A magic mountain and a willowy wench
    Škvorecký, J. When Eve was naked; stories of a life's journey
  My teacher, Mr. Katz
    Škvorecký, J. When Eve was naked; stories of a life's journey
  My Uncle Kohn
    Škvorecký, J. When Eve was naked; stories of a life's journey
  The mysterious events at night
    Škvorecký, J. When Eve was naked; stories of a life's journey
  Pink champagne
    Škvorecký, J. When Eve was naked; stories of a life's journey
  A remarkable chemical phenomenon
    Škvorecký, J. When Eve was naked; stories of a life's journey
  Song of forgotten years
    Škvorecký, J. When Eve was naked; stories of a life's journey
  Spectator on a February night
    Škvorecký, J. When Eve was naked; stories of a life's journey

Škvorecký, Josef—*Continued*

Three bachelors in a fiery furnace

Škvorecký, J. When Eve was naked; stories of a life's journey

Wayne's hero (An English story)

Škvorecký, J. When Eve was naked; stories of a life's journey

Why do people have soft noses?

Škvorecký, J. When Eve was naked; stories of a life's journey

Why I lernt how to reed

Škvorecký, J. When Eve was naked; stories of a life's journey

Skwar, Henryk

The five seasons of a writer

The Ohio Review no59 p133-40 1999

The **sky-blue** ball. Oates, J. C.

A **sky** full of migrating birds. Farkašová, E.

The **sky-green** blues. Lee, T.

Sky harvest. Derby, M.

The **Sky** People. Anderson, P.

Slager, Daniel

(jt. auth) See Mora, Terézia

Slash (1976). Perillo, L.

A **slate** roof in the rain. Dyson, J.

Slater, Judy

The glass house

A different plain; contemporary Nebraska fiction writers; edited by Ladette Randolph ; introduction by Mary Pipher

Slaughter, Karin

Necessary women

Tart noir; edited by Stella Duffy & Lauren Henderson

The **Slaughterhouse**. Brown, P.

SLAUGHTERING AND SLAUGHTER-HOUSES

Jews

Singer, I. B. Blood

Singer, I. B. The slaughterer

The **slave**. Doyle, R.

Slave. LaValle, V. D.

Slave for a Day. Cantor, R.

SLAVE TRADE

Chamoiseau, P. The old man slave and the mastiff

Davidson, A. The necessity of his condition

SLAVERY

See also African Americans; Fugitive slaves; Slave trade

Anderson, P. The master key

Biguenet, J. My slave

Borges, J. L. The cruel redeemer Lazarus Morell

Cable, G. W. The story of Bras-Coupé

Chesnutt, C. W. The passing of Grandison

Dunbar, P. L. The ingrate

Finlay, C. C. We come not to praise Washington

Fleming, R. Bordering on the divine

Frost, G. The prowl

Hambly, B. The horsemen and the morning star

Harrison, H. Survival planet

Hayden, G. M. The maids

Johnson, C. R. Confession

Johnson, C. R. A lion at Pendleton

Johnson, C. R. Martha's dilemma

Johnson, C. R. The mayor's tale

Johnson, C. R. Murderous thoughts

Johnson, C. R. A soldier for the crown

Johnson, C. R. The transmission

Le Guin, U. K. Old Music and the slave women

Lincoln, C. A hook will sometimes keep you

McHugh, M. F. The Lincoln train

Page, T. N. Unc' Edinburg's drowndin'

Thomas, S. R. How Sukie cross de big wata

Wier, A. Tehano [excerpt]

SLAVES *See* Slavery

Slavin, Julia

Babyproofing

Slavin, J. The woman who cut off her leg at the Maidstone Club and other stories

Beauty and Rudy

Slavin, J. The woman who cut off her leg at the Maidstone Club and other stories

Blighted

Slavin, J. The woman who cut off her leg at the Maidstone Club and other stories

Covered

Slavin, J. The woman who cut off her leg at the Maidstone Club and other stories

Dentaphilia

Slavin, J. The woman who cut off her leg at the Maidstone Club and other stories

He came apart

Slavin, J. The woman who cut off her leg at the Maidstone Club and other stories

Lives of the invertebrates

Slavin, J. The woman who cut off her leg at the Maidstone Club and other stories

Painting house

Slavin, J. The woman who cut off her leg at the Maidstone Club and other stories

Pudding

Slavin, J. The woman who cut off her leg at the Maidstone Club and other stories

Rare is a cold red center

Gentlemen's Quarterly v69 no5 p120+ My 1999

Slavin, J. The woman who cut off her leg at the Maidstone Club and other stories

Swallowed whole

Slavin, J. The woman who cut off her leg at the Maidstone Club and other stories

The woman who cut off her leg at the Maidstone Club

Slavin, J. The woman who cut off her leg at the Maidstone Club and other stories

SLED DOG RACING

Billman, J. Calcutta

SLEEP

Hawthorne, N. David Swan

Jackson, S. Sleep

Padilla, I. Time regained

Sheckley, R. Deep Blue Sleep

Wallace, D. F. Oblivion

Winterson, J. Disappearance I

Winterson, J. Disappearance II

Yoshimoto, B. Asleep

Sleep. Dixon, S.

Sleep. Pourciau, G.

Sleep creep leap. Sellers, H.

The **sleep** of trees. Yolen, J.

Sleep on stones. McManus, J.

Sleep the big sleep. Gores, J.

The **sleeper**. Collins, M.

Sleepers holding hands. Canty, K.

Sleeping Bear lament. Means, D.

Sleeping beauty. Clarke, A. C.

Sleeping Beauty. Rogers, B. H.
The **sleeping** beauty. Rollins, H.
The **sleeping** detective. Phillips, G.
Sleeping dogs. Kress, N.
Sleeping Mask. LaSalle, P.
The **sleeping** Picasso. Morris, I.
Sleeping sickness. Campbell, B. J.
Sleeping with my dog. Knight, M.
Sleepside story. Bear, G.
Sleepwalkers. Buchan, J.
Sleepy. Chekhov, A. P.
Sleepy. Frym, G.
Sleepy Gap. Morgan, R.
Sleepyhead. See Chekhov, A. P. Sleepy
SLEIGHS AND SLEDGES
    Chekhov, A. P. Misery
Sleights. Polansky, S.
Slesar, Henry
    Change partners
        Death dance; suspenseful stories of the dance
            macabre; Trevanian, editor
    The day of the 31st
        Blood on their hands; edited by Lawrence
            Block
    The day of the execution
        The Best American mystery stories of the
            century; Tony Hillerman, editor; with an
            introduction by Tony Hillerman
    Letter from a very worried man
        Murder most postal; homicidal tales that de-
            liver a message; edited by Martin H.
            Greenberg
Slezak, Ellen
    By heart
        Slezak, E. Last year's Jesus; a novella and
            nine stories
    The geese at Mayville
        Slezak, E. Last year's Jesus; a novella and
            nine stories
    Head, heart, legs or arms
        Slezak, E. Last year's Jesus; a novella and
            nine stories
    Here in car city
        Slezak, E. Last year's Jesus; a novella and
            nine stories
    If you treat things right
        Slezak, E. Last year's Jesus; a novella and
            nine stories
    Last year's Jesus (or Passion play)
        Slezak, E. Last year's Jesus; a novella and
            nine stories
    Lucky
        Slezak, E. Last year's Jesus; a novella and
            nine stories
    Patch
        Slezak, E. Last year's Jesus; a novella and
            nine stories
    Settled
        Slezak, E. Last year's Jesus; a novella and
            nine stories
    Tomato watch
        Slezak, E. Last year's Jesus; a novella and
            nine stories
Slice. Hildt, R.
Slice of the cake. Johnson-Davies, D.
A **slight** case of sunstroke. Clarke, A. C.
Slight rebellion off Madison. Salinger, J. D.
Slight return. Anderson, R.
Slightly guilty. Hershman, M.

The **slim** butte ghost. Sneve, V. D. H.
Slinkers. Henley, P.
Slippered feet. Wallace, D.
Slither. Jakober, M.
Sloan, Bob
    The good rabbi
        Mystery midrash; an anthology of Jewish
            mystery & detective fiction; [edited by]
            Lawrence W. Raphael
Sloan, Lynn L.
    A Paris Story
        The Literary Review (Madison, N.J.) v46 no1
            p147-57 Fall 2002
Sloan's daughter. Swan, G.
The **slope**. Kanafāni, G.
Slow and good. Chacón, D.
Slow burn. Harvey, J.
Slow burn. Lustbader, E. V.
Slow cold chick. Hopkinson, N.
Slow life. Swanwick, M.
The **slow** mirror. Zimler, R.
Slow monkeys. Nichols, J.
Slow motion. Vachss, A. H.
Slow poison. Nfah-Abbenyi, J. M.
A **slow** Saturday night at the Surrealist Sporting
    Club. Moorcock, M.
Slow sculpture. Sturgeon, T.
Slow waltz. Barton, M.
Slowik, Mary
    Lessons in fire
        Iowa Review v29 no1 p154-67 Spr 1999
The **Slugger** comes into his own. McNulty, J.
Slumber party, 1975. Pietrzyk, L.
Small, Bertrice
    Mastering Lady Lucinda
        Fascinated; [by] Bertrice Small, Susan John-
            son, Thea Devine and Robin Schone
Small, Kate
    The b-zone open
        Best new American voices 2000; guest editor
            Tobias Wolff; series editors John Kulka
            and Natalie Danford
    Maximum sunlight
        New stories from the South: the year's best,
            2002; edited by Shannon Ravenel; with a
            preface by Larry Brown
A **small** and private war. Gorman, E.
Small arms fire. Abrams, T.
Small Bright Thing. Levy, E. J.
Small change. Hendel, Y.
Small creatures. Olivares Baró, C.
Small degrees. Brockmeier, K.
A **small** independence. Jackson, V. F.
A **small** indulgence. Alvarez, A.
A **small** madness. Hannah, B.
A **small** measure of safety. Haake, K.
The **small** revelation. Blitz, R.
Small song. Braunbeck, G. A.
A **small** thing that mattered greatly. Abrams, T.
SMALL TOWN LIFE
    Adams, A. Roses, rhododendron
    Agee, J. What the Fall brings
    Aldrich, B. S. Alma, meaning "To cherish"
    Aldrich, B. S. The man who caught the weather
    Aldrich, B. S. Trust the Irish for that
    Aldrich, B. S. The victory of Connie Lee
    Aldrich, B. S. The weakling
    Avrich, J. Life in dearth
    Barrett, N., Jr. Diner

SMALL TOWN LIFE—*Continued*

Barrett, N., Jr. Perpetuity blues
Barthelme, D. A city of churches
Berry, M. S. Armistice
Berry, M. S. Exit Miss Tish
Berry, M. S. Final payment
Berry, M. S. The four hundred ninety-first time
Berry, M. S. The hawk
Berry, M. S. The long dark hall
Berry, M. S. The long view
Berry, M. S. Next-door neighbors
Berry, M. S. The passing night
Berry, M. S. Philip's room
Berry, M. S. The quantity of mercy
Berry, W. A consent
Berry, W. The discovery of Kentucky
Berry, W. Thicker than liquor
Berry, W. Watch with me
Berry, W. The wild birds
Blaise, C. Notes beyond history
Bly, C. Chuck's money
Bly, C. The dignity of life
Bly, C. The last of the gold star mothers
Bonnie, F. The cookie trick
Bradbury, R. Colonel Stonesteel's genuine home-made truly Egyptian mummy
Bradbury, R. Colonel Stonesteel's genuine homemade truly Egyptian mummy
Budnitz, J. Yellville
Cady, J. Halloween 1942
Capote, T. Children on their birthdays
Capote, T. Jug of silver
Carlson, R. Phenomena
Clark, B. C. The Apache pest control
Clark, B. C. Between girls and gamecocks
Clark, B. C. By way of the forked stick
Clark, B. C. The last picture show
Coates, G. S. The truth
Coberly, L. M. Early transparent
Coberly, L. M. The evidence of things not seen
Coberly, L. M. The fellowsip at Wysong's Clearing
Coberly, L. M. The handywoman
Coberly, L. M. The sighting
Connor, J. Second nature
Daum, M. Alternative lifestyle alert
Davidson, A. The cost of Kent Castwell
Davies, Tristan. Snowflake
Day, C. Boss man
Day, C. Circus People
Day, C. The King and His Court
Deaver, J. Eye to eye
DeLancey, K. Carley's knees
DeLancey, K. Dinger and Blacker
DeLancey, K. It's dark
DeLancey, K. The mystery of George Jones
DeMarco, T. The rose festival boxed lunch
Doran, M. M. Showdown
Doran, M. M. Wedding at the Gormay Cafe
Drake, R. Connections
Drake, R. The convertible
Drake, R. How come you reckon he did that?
Drake, R. The pickup truck
DuBois, B. The dark snow
Earle, S. The red suitcase
Earley, T. The prophet from Jupiter
Ebershoff, D. The bank president
Franklin, T. Shubuta
Fromm, P. Wind

Garcia, L. G. The day they took my uncle
Gavell, M. L. Las Altas
Gay, W. Bonedaddy, Quincy Nell, and the fifteen thousand BTU electric chair
Gay, W. The lightpainter
Gifford, B. The lonely and the lost
Gilman, C. P. The unnatural mother
Grau, S. A. The lovely April
Gurganus, A. He's one, too
Hart, C. G. Secrets
Hassler, J. Chase
Hassler, J. Good news in Culver Bend
Hassler, J. Yesterday's garbage
Highsmith, P. The mightiest mornings
Hodgen, C. Going out of business forever
Hoffman, W. Stones
Holladay, C. C. Merry-go-sorry
Jackson, S. The possibility of evil
Joseph, D. Expatriates
Knight, M. Birdland
Lee, M. Another wonder of the world
Leslie, N. Dancing with Lawrence of Arabia
Leslie, N. Marconi's dream
Leslie, N. Prayer wheel
Leslie, N. The scavenger's eye
Lundquist, R. A stone house of many rooms
Lundquist, R. The visitation
Malone, M. A deer on the lawn
Malone, M. Fast love
Malone, M. Maniac loose
Malone, M. Miss Mona's bank
Malone, M. Red clay
Mason, B. A. Charger
Mason, B. A. Night flight
Matthews, B. Everything must go
McCorkle, J. Billy goats
McMurtry, L. The last picture show [excerpt]
Meyers, K. Abiding by law
Meyers, K. The smell of the deer
Meyers, K. Two-speed
Morgan, R. Murals
Mueller, D. How animals mate
Muñoz, M. Loco
Norris, H. Judgment day
Paine, T. Unapproved minutes of the Carthage, Vermont, Zoning Board of Adjustment
Patterson, K. Boatbuilding
Patterson, K. Country of cold
Patterson, K. Les is more
Patterson, K. Manitoba Avenue
Patterson, K. Saw marks
Patterson, K. Structure is constant
Porter, J. A. Yours
Robison, M. In Jewel
Shade, E. Eyesores
Shade, E. A final reunion
Shade, E. Hoops and wires and plugs
Shade, E. Souvenirs
Singleton, G. Duke power
Smith, L. Between the lines
Sosin, D. Mother Superior
Spence, J. Missing women
Spencer, E. The business venture
Spencer, E. A Christian education
Spencer, E. First dark
Swan, G. Gate of ivory, gate of horn
Tilghman, C. The way people run
Treat, J. Honda
Troy, M. We're still Keeneys

SMALL TOWN LIFE—*Continued*
Updike, J. The corner
Updike, J. The Indian
Updike, J. the Indian
Updike, J. When everyone was pregnant
Updike, J. The women who got away
Vivante, A. Escapes
Vonnegut, K. Lovers Anonymous
Vonnegut, K. Poor little rich town
Weaver, G. The white elephant
Wharton, E. The day of the funeral
Wharton, E. The pretext
Winterson, J. Newton
Wuori, G. K. Angles
Wuori, G. K. Condoms
Wuori, G. K. Crime
Wuori, G. K. Fire
Wuori, G. K. Glory
Wuori, G. K. Illusions
Wuori, G. K. Laughter
Wuori, G. K. Murder
Wuori, G. K. Nose
Wuori, G. K. Nude
Wuori, G. K. Revenge
Small world. Davies, P. H.
Smaller than life. Roeske, P.
The **smallest** man in the world. Campbell, B. J.
The **smallest** people alive. Banner, K.
Smart, Ariel
The bridge players
    Smart, A. The Green Lantern & other stories
Emily
    Smart, A. The Green Lantern & other stories
The Green Lantern
    Smart, A. The Green Lantern & other stories
Hunter
    Smart, A. The Green Lantern & other stories
Jersey Joe versus the Rock
    Smart, A. The Green Lantern & other stories
Mud and strawberries
    Smart, A. The Green Lantern & other stories
Posing
    Smart, A. The Green Lantern & other stories
Raccoon
    Smart, A. The Green Lantern & other stories
The turtle
    Smart, A. The Green Lantern & other stories
Vincent
    Smart, A. The Green Lantern & other stories
The wedding Dress
    Smart, A. The Green Lantern & other stories
Smart. Robison, M.
Smart Alec. Baker, K.
Smart guys don't snore. Gores, J.
Smart money. Roth, P.
Smee, Bill
The old ones cast
    Dead on demand; the best of ghost story weekend; edited by Elizabeth Engstrom
Smee. Burrage, A. M.
The **smell** of a car. Parrish, T.
The **smell** of life. White, M. C.
The **smell** of the deer. Meyers, K.
Smelling of earth, dreaming of sky. What, L.
Smilansky, Moshe
Latifa
    Sleepwalkers and other stories; the Arab in Hebrew fiction; edited by Ehud Ben-Ezer
Smilansky, Yizhar *See* Yizhar, S., 1916-

Smile!. Kheradmand, F.
A **smile** from the past. Johnson-Davies, D.
The **smile** of a turtle. DeMarinis, R.
The **smilers**. Fitzgerald, F. S.
Smiley, Jane
Long distance
    The Workshop; seven decades of the Iowa Writers' Workshop: 42 stories, recollections & essays on Iowa's place in 20th-century American literature; edited by Tom Grimes
The **smilies** meet the brooders. Coshnear, D.
Smith, Ali
Being quick
    Smith, A. The whole story and other stories
Believe me
    Smith, A. The whole story and other stories
The book club
    Smith, A. The whole story and other stories
Erosive
    Smith, A. The whole story and other stories
Gothic
    Smith, A. The whole story and other stories
The hanging girl
    Grand Street no67 p183-97 Wint 1999
The heat of the story
    Smith, A. The whole story and other stories
May
    Smith, A. The whole story and other stories
Paradise
    Smith, A. The whole story and other stories
The shortlist season
    The Times Literary Supplement no5037 p16-17 O 15 1999
The start of things
    Smith, A. The whole story and other stories
The universal story
    Smith, A. The whole story and other stories
The unthinkable happens to people every day
    The Vintage book of contemporary Scottish fiction; edited and with an introduction by Peter Kravitz
Smith, Barbara Burnett
Death of a damn moose
    Death dance; suspenseful stories of the dance macabre; Trevanian, editor
Smith, C. W. (Charles William)
The Bundlelays
    Texas bound. Book III; 22 Texas stories; edited by Kay Cattarulla; foreword by Robert Flynn
Smith, Charles William *See* Smith, C. W. (Charles William), 1940-
Smith, Cordwainer
Mother Hitton's littul kittons
    The Good old stuff; adventure SF in the grand tradition; edited by Gardner Dozois
Scanners live in vain
    The Science fiction hall of fame: volume one, 1929-1964; the greatest science fiction stories of all time chosen by the members of the Science Fiction Writers of America; edited by Robert Silverberg
When the people fell
    Worldmakers; SF adventures in terraforming; edited by Gardner Dozois

Smith, Cotton
Thirty rangers
Westward; a fictional history of the American West : 28 original stories celebrating the 50th anniversary of the Western Writers of America; edited by Dale L. Walker
Smith, Curtis
Insomnia
Ghost writing; haunted tales by contemporary writers; edited by Roger Weingarten
Smith, Darryl A.
The pretended
Dark matter; a century of speculative fiction from the African diaspora; edited by Sheree R. Thomas
Smith, Dean Wesley
The gift of a dream
Past imperfect; edited by Martin H. Greenberg and Larry Segriff
Smith, Douglas
By her hand, she draws you down
The Mammoth book of best horror 13; edited by Stephen Jones
Smith, E. A. Wyke- *See* Wyke-Smith, E. A. (Edward Augustine), 1871-1935
Smith, Giles
Last requests
Speaking with the angel; original stories; edited by Nick Hornby
Smith, Harmon
The War Years
The North American Review v288 no3/4 p54-9 My/Ag 2003
Smith, Iain Crichton
In the middle of the wood [excerpt]
The Vintage book of contemporary Scottish fiction; edited and with an introduction by Peter Kravitz
SMITH, JEDEDIAH STRONG, 1798-1831
About
Blevins, W. Melodies the song dogs sing
Smith, Julie
Always Othello
Smith, J. Mean rooms
Blood types
Smith, J. Mean rooms
Crime wave in Pinhole
Smith, J. Mean rooms
Cul-de-sac
Smith, J. Mean rooms
The end of the earth
Smith, J. Mean rooms
Fresh paint
Irreconcilable differences; Lia Matera, editor
Smith, J. Mean rooms
Grief counselor
Smith, J. Mean rooms
Montezuma's other revenge
Smith, J. Mean rooms
Project Mushroom
Smith, J. Mean rooms
Silk strands
Smith, J. Mean rooms
Strangers on a plane
Smith, J. Mean rooms
Too mean to die
Smith, J. Mean rooms
Where the boys are
Smith, J. Mean rooms

Smith, Lee
Between the lines
The Cry of an occasion; fiction from the Fellowship of Southern Writers; edited by Richard Bausch; with a foreword by George Garrett
Intensive care
The Scribner anthology of contemporary short fiction; fifty North American stories since 1970; Lex Williford and Michael Martone, editors
Smith, Michael
Remorse
American short fiction, vol. 8, no 29-32
Smith, Michael Marshall
The book of irrational numbers
999: new stories of horror and suspense; edited by Al Sarrantonio
Everybody goes
Best new horror 10; edited and with an introduction by Stephen Jones
The handover
Best new horror 12; edited and with an introduction by Stephen Jones
A place to stay
The Year's best fantasy & horror, twelfth annual collection; edited by Ellen Datlow & Terry Windling
The Right Men
Gathering the bones; original stories from the world's masters of horror; edited by Dennis Etchison, Ramsey Campbell and Jack Dann
Two shot
Redshift; extreme visions of speculative fiction; edited by Al Sarrantonio
Welcome
Best new horror 11; edited and with an introduction by Stephen Jones
The Year's best fantasy & horror, thirteenth annual collection; edited by Ellen Datlow and Terri Windling
What you make it
The Year's best fantasy & horror, thirteenth annual collection; edited by Ellen Datlow and Terri Windling
Smith, Nora Archibald
(jt. auth) See Wiggin, Kate Douglas Smith and Smith, Nora Archibald
Smith, Paula V.
Restoration
The North American Review v288 no2 p15-18 Mr/Ap 2003
Smith, Penny
See also Sumner, Penny
Smith, Peter Moore
Forgetting the girl
The Best American mystery stories, 2000; edited and with an introduction by Donald E. Westlake
Oblivion, Nebraska
The Pushcart prize XXIV: best of the small presses; an annual small press reader; edited by Bill Henderson with the Pushcart prize editors
Smith, R. T.
Blaze
The Southern Review (Baton Rouge, La.) v38 no3 p587-9 Summ 2002

Smith, R. T.—*Continued*
Docent
New stories from the South; the year's best, 2004; edited by Shannon Ravenel; preface by Tim Gautreaux
I have lost my right
New stories from the South: the year's best, 2002; edited by Shannon Ravenel; with a preface by Larry Brown
Jesus Wept
The Southern Review (Baton Rouge, La.) v40 no2 p343-51 Spr 2004
Plinking
The Southern Review (Baton Rouge, La.) v37 no1 p141-6 Wint 2001
Stop the Rocket
Prairie Schooner v77 no4 p71-9 Wint 2003
Tube Rose
The Virginia Quarterly Review v80 no1 p208-11 Wint 2004
Uke Rivers Delivers
The Southern Review (Baton Rouge, La.) v39 no3 p547-55 Summ 2003
Smith, Rosamond, 1938-
See also Oates, Joyce Carol, 1938-
Smith, Sarah Jane
Black bean soup
Smith, S. J. No thanks and other stories
Gar fishing
Smith, S. J. No thanks and other stories
Healing the mare
Smith, S. J. No thanks and other stories
Jack in Chicago
Smith, S. J. No thanks and other stories
Looping
Smith, S. J. No thanks and other stories
Metamorphose, oboe
Smith, S. J. No thanks and other stories
My father weeping
Smith, S. J. No thanks and other stories
No thanks
Smith, S. J. No thanks and other stories
Oboe camp
Smith, S. J. No thanks and other stories
Selling the house
Smith, S. J. No thanks and other stories
Turtle hunting with black
Smith, S. J. No thanks and other stories
Valerie rakes the leaves
Smith, S. J. No thanks and other stories
The woman in chains [excerpt]
Neugroschel, J. No star too beautiful; Yiddish stories from 1382 to the present; compiled and translated by Joachim Neugroschel
Smith, Sybil
Communion
U.S. Catholic v64 no3 p35-38 Mr 1999
Poppies
U.S. Catholic v64 no11 p38-41 N 1999
Smith, Troy D.
The big die-up
Westward; a fictional history of the American West : 28 original stories celebrating the 50th anniversary of the Western Writers of America; edited by Dale L. Walker
The purification of Jim Barnes
American West; twenty new stories from the Western Writers of America; edited with an introduction by Loren D. Estleman

Smith, Zadie
I'm the only one
Speaking with the angel; original stories; edited by Nick Hornby
Martha, Martha
Granta no81 p323-39 Spr 2003
Stuart
The New Yorker v75 no40 p60+ D 27 1999-Ja 3 2000
The Trials of Finch
The New Yorker v78 no40 p116-23 D 23-30 2002
The wrestling match
The New Yorker v78 no16 p116-19, 121-5, 127-9 Je 17-24 2002
Smith and the pharaohs. Haggard, H. R.
SMITHSONIAN INSTITUTION
Bates, H. Farewell to the master
Smoke. McNally, J.
Smoke. Mosley, W.
Smoke. Robison, M.
Smoke and ash. Davis, L.
Smoke City. Blackford, R.
Smoke, ice. McIlvoy, K.
The **smoker.** Schickler, D.
SMOKING
Chopin, K. An Egyptian ciagarette
Dunmore, H. The fag
Huffman, B., Jr. Bench trial
Kelman, J. It happened to me once
King, S. Quitters, inc.
Lipsyte, S. Less tar
Locklin, G. The bummer
McCorkle, J. Life prerecorded
Smolazh, Yoysef
The open grave
Neugroschel, J. No star too beautiful; Yiddish stories from 1382 to the present; compiled and translated by Joachim Neugroschel
Smolens, John
Absolution
Smolens, J. My one and only bomb shelter; stories
Cold
Smolens, J. My one and only bomb shelter; stories
Disciple pigeons
Smolens, J. My one and only bomb shelter; stories
The errand
Smolens, J. My one and only bomb shelter; stories
The Meetinghouse
Smolens, J. My one and only bomb shelter; stories
My one and only bomb shelter
Smolens, J. My one and only bomb shelter; stories
Night train to Chicago
Smolens, J. My one and only bomb shelter; stories
Snow
Smolens, J. My one and only bomb shelter; stories
The you is understood
Smolens, J. My one and only bomb shelter; stories
Smoother. Bisson, T.
The **smoothest** way is full of stones. Orringer, J.

SMUGGLERS *See* Smuggling
Smuggler's island. Pronzini, B.
SMUGGLING
  Borges, J. L. The dead man
  Fish, R. L. The wager
  Forsyth, F. The citizen
  Hodgson, W. H. The adventure of the garter
  Hodgson, W. H. Contraband of war
  Hodgson, W. H. From information received
  Hodgson, W. H. My lady's jewels
  Hodgson, W. H. The red herring
  Hodgson, W. H. Trading with the enemy
  Mastretta, A. Aunt Elena
  Steinbeck, T. Blighted cargo
  Winter, E. Dragon box
Smyth, Cherry
  Near the bone
    The Anchor book of new Irish writing; the
    new Gaelach ficsean; edited and with an
    introduction by John Somer and John J.
    Daly
  Sand and other grit
    Hers 3: brilliant new fiction by lesbian writ-
    ers; edited by Terry Wolverton with Robert
    Drake
Snake. Hopkinson, N.
The **snake**. Troncoso, S.
The **snake** hunters. Hagy, A. C.
SNAKES
  Adam, C. ASP
  Benedict, P. The Sutton Pie Safe
  Bishop, M. Among the handlers; or, The Mark
    16 Hands-on Assembly of Jesus Risen, for-
    merly Snake-o-rama
  Bowles, P. Allal
  Byatt, A. S. A lamia in the Cévennes
  Doerr, A. The shell collector
  Honwana, L. B. Papa, snake & I
  Johnston, B. A. Anything that floats
  McIntyre, V. N. Of mist, and grass, and sand
  Paschal, D. Python
  Tinti, H. How to revitalize the snake in your life
  Ts'an-hsüeh. The child who raised poisonous
    snakes
  Vice, B. Chickensnake
  Wellen, E. The plan of the snake
Snakes. Berkman, P. R.
Snakes. McCorkle, J.
Snakes. Reyna, R.
The **Snakeshooter**. Hall, M. L.
Snakeskin becomes her. Mazelis, J.
Snap beans and petits fours. Coberly, L. M.
Snapshots. Kalotay, D. E.
Snare. Burke, S.
Snarker's son. Lumley, B.
Snatch off your cap, kid!. Trevanian
Snatched. Allegra, D.
Snatcher. Koontz, D. R.
Sneed, Christine
  Immortal
    The Massachusetts Review v43 no4 p548-66
    Wint 2002/2003
  This Parrot Is Hilarious
    New England Review v23 no4 p104-16 Fall
    2002
The **sneering**. Campbell, R.
SNEEZE
  Chekhov, A. P. The death of a government clerk

Sneider, Vern
  A long way from home
    Retrieving bones; stories and poems of the
    Korean War; edited and with an introduc-
    tion by W. D. Ehrhart and Philip K. Jason
Sneve, Virginia Driving Hawk
  All the time in the world
    Sneve, V. D. H. Grandpa was a cowboy & an
    Indian and other stories
  Badlands bones
    Sneve, V. D. H. Grandpa was a cowboy & an
    Indian and other stories
  Clean hands
    Sneve, V. D. H. Grandpa was a cowboy & an
    Indian and other stories
  The first Christmas
    Sneve, V. D. H. Grandpa was a cowboy & an
    Indian and other stories
  The flower nation
    Sneve, V. D. H. Grandpa was a cowboy & an
    Indian and other stories
  Fool soldiers
    Sneve, V. D. H. Grandpa was a cowboy & an
    Indian and other stories
  Grandpa was a cowboy and an Indian
    Sneve, V. D. H. Grandpa was a cowboy & an
    Indian and other stories
  Jimmy Yellow Hawk
    Sneve, V. D. H. Grandpa was a cowboy & an
    Indian and other stories
  The medicine bag
    Sneve, V. D. H. Grandpa was a cowboy & an
    Indian and other stories
  The slim butte ghost
    Sneve, V. D. H. Grandpa was a cowboy & an
    Indian and other stories
  The speck in the sky
    Sneve, V. D. H. Grandpa was a cowboy & an
    Indian and other stories
  Sun gazer
    Sneve, V. D. H. Grandpa was a cowboy & an
    Indian and other stories
  Takoza said "goo"
    Sneve, V. D. H. Grandpa was a cowboy & an
    Indian and other stories
  The tribe of the burnt thigh
    Sneve, V. D. H. Grandpa was a cowboy & an
    Indian and other stories
  The twelve moons
    Sneve, V. D. H. Grandpa was a cowboy & an
    Indian and other stories
  The white buffalo calf woman
    Sneve, V. D. H. Grandpa was a cowboy & an
    Indian and other stories
Sniff. Westlake, D. E.
Snipe. McCorkle, J.
The **snipe** hunt. See McCorkle, J. Snipe
The **snob**. Callaghan, M.
SNOBS AND SNOBBISHNESS
  Aldrich, B. S. The great wide world of men
  Callaghan, M. The snob
  Fitzgerald, F. S. The four fists
  Gilliland, G. Permanence
  Hoffman, W. Doors
  Waugh, E. An Englishman's home
SNOW
  Brennan, M. The children are there, trying not
    to laugh

SNOW—*Continued*

Brennan, M. A snowy night on West Forty-ninth Street

Kawabata, Y. First snow on Fuji

Smolens, J. Night train to Chicago

Snow. Adams, A.

Snow. Chinodya, S.

Snow. Crowley, J.

Snow. Gilb, D.

Snow. Kaminsky, S. M.

Snow. Landis, G. A.

Snow. Lloyd, D. T.

Snow. Smolens, J.

Snow and rooks. Chudoba, A.

Snow angel. Kilpatrick, N.

Snow, ashes. Hagy, A.

Snow Blind. Ruthig, I.

Snow dreams. Bailey, T.

Snow, Houston, 1974. McNeely, T. H.

The **snow** image: a childish miracle. Hawthorne, N.

Snow in summer. Yolen, J.

Snow job. Dozois, G. R.

Snow-job. Tillman, L.

Snow man. Coyne, J.

SNOW STORMS *See* Storms

Snow White and the seven dwarves. Rollins, H.

Snowball in hell. Stableford, B. M.

The **snowballing** of Alt.Rock. Hersh, K.

Snowbound. Tomlinson, N. C.

Snowbound. Ward, L.

Snowed in. Broyard, B.

Snowing in Greenwich Village. Updike, J.

The **snows** of August. Sherman, J.

The **snows** of Saint Stephen. Owen, M. G.

The **snowstorm.** See Pushkin, A. S. The blizzard

SNOWSTORMS *See* Storms

A **snowy** night on West Forty-ninth Street. Brennan, M.

Snug Harbor. LaSalle, P.

Snyder, William, Jr.

The Ferdinand Magellan

100% pure Florida fiction; an anthology; edited by Susan Hubbard and Robley Wilson

So cold outside. Kees, W.

So far you can't imagine. Dodd, S. M.

So I've Got That Going for Me. Alsup, B.

So many chances. Doerr, A.

So much water, underground. Penn, W. S.

So, Sweetie, what's your Wilhelm been up to? Keller, C.

So to speak. Dubnov, E.

So where've you buried the missus then, Paddy? Coward, M.

So wild, so free. Flynn, T. T.

So You Can Stay. Bucknell, L.

So young, so fair, so dead. Lutz, J.

Soap opera. Mathews, H.

SOAP SCULPTURE

Kittredge, W. The soap bear

Soaring. Mo Yan

Sobeloff, Judy

Triangles

American short fiction, vol. 8, no 29-32

Sober, exper., work guar. Gavell, M. L.

A **sober** reading of Dr. Sigmund Freud. Locklin, G.

Sobott-Mogwe, Gaele

Smile of fortune

The Anchor book of modern African stories; edited by Nadežda Obradovic ; with a foreword by Chinua Achebe

SOCCER

Davenport, G. Boys smell like oranges

Lipsyte, S. Beautiful game

Marías, J. In uncertain time

Wetherell, W. D. Watching girls play

Social ambitions and musical tastes of Bouvard and Pécuchet. Proust, M.

SOCIAL CLASSES

See also Class distinction

Cheng, C.-W. Betel nut town

Cheng Naishan. Hong Taitai

Chesnutt, C. W. The wife of his youth

James, H. Crawford's consistency

James, H. Daisy Miller: a study

James, H. A London life

Lavin, M. A cup of tea

SOCIAL CONDITIONS *See* Social problems

The **social** contract. Frym, G.

Social dreaming of the Frin. Le Guin, U. K.

SOCIAL GROUPS

Updike, J. Minutes of the last meeting

SOCIAL ISOLATION

Pesetsky, B. Offspring of the first generation

SOCIAL PROBLEMS

See also Child labor; Crime and criminals; Divorce; Drug abuse; Drug addiction; Homeless persons; Juvenile delinquency; Poverty; Prejudices; Prostitution; Race relations; Suicide; Technology and civilization; Unemployed; Violence

Evans, E. Ransom

SOCIAL SATIRE *See* Satire

SOCIAL STATUS

Chekhov, A. P. A chameleon

Chekhov, A. P. Fat and thin

Frym, G. Tagging

Waugh, E. Winner takes all

Wharton, E. Autres temps . . .

Wharton, E. The introducers

SOCIAL WORKERS

Browder, C. Amnesty

Browder, C. Animal heaven

Carter, E. Glory B. and the baby Jesus

Engel, M. P. M to F

Johnson, B. Michiganders, 1979

Nesbitt, M. The children's book of victims

Silber, J. Lake Natasink

Strike, Johnny. Crazy Carl's thing

Svoboda, T. A mama

Thompson, J. Who do you love

SOCIETY OF FRIENDS

Babel', I. The Quaker

Davidson, A. The man who saw the elephant

Hawthorne, N. The gentle boy

The **society** of friends. Cherry, K.

SOCRATES

About

Alas, L. "Socrates' rooster"

"**Socrates'** rooster". Alas, L.

Soft clocks. Aramaki, Y.

Soft Core. Oates, J. C.

Soft day. Lee, W. W.

Soft Death. Rucker, R. v. B.

Soft song of the sometimes sane. McBrearty, R. G.

Soft Targets. Abel, R. H.

SOFTBALL

Hochman, A. Diamonds are a girl's best friend

Reid, E. All that good stuff

Sogged. Kudritzki, J.

Soho revisited. Paolucci, A.

Sojourner, Mary

Absolute proof of the cosmos in life

Sojourner, M. Delicate; stories; Mary Sojourner

Armageddon coffee

Sojourner, M. Delicate; stories; Mary Sojourner

Bear house

Sojourner, M. Delicate; stories; Mary Sojourner

Betabank

Sojourner, M. Delicate; stories; Mary Sojourner

Binky

Sojourner, M. Delicate; stories; Mary Sojourner

Delicate

Sojourner, M. Delicate; stories; Mary Sojourner

Estrella Ranchos: where the real west begins

Sojourner, M. Delicate; stories; Mary Sojourner

Hag

Sojourner, M. Delicate; stories; Mary Sojourner

Huevos

Sojourner, M. Delicate; stories; Mary Sojourner

Luzianne

Sojourner, M. Delicate; stories; Mary Sojourner

Messin' with the kid

Sojourner, M. Delicate; stories; Mary Sojourner

Monsters

Sojourner, M. Delicate; stories; Mary Sojourner

The most amazing thing

Sojourner, M. Delicate; stories; Mary Sojourner

My tree

Sojourner, M. Delicate; stories; Mary Sojourner

Officer Magdalena, White Shell Woman, and me

Sojourner, M. Delicate; stories; Mary Sojourner

Riv

Sojourner, M. Delicate; stories; Mary Sojourner

Squirrel

Sojourner, M. Delicate; stories; Mary Sojourner

What they write in other countries

Sojourner, M. Delicate; stories; Mary Sojourner

Solace. Dozois, G. R.

SOLAR ENERGY

Asimov, I. The last question

Clarke, A. C. The wind from the sun

Solari, Maria Teresa

Death and transfiguration of a teacher

Short stories by Latin American women; the magic and the real; edited by Celia Correas de Zapata; foreword by Isabel Allende

The **Solborne** vampire. Sheffield, C.

Soldán, Edmundo Paz See Paz Soldán, Edmundo, 1967-

A **soldier** for the crown. Johnson, C. R.

The **soldier** in the machine. Blackford, R.

SOLDIERS

See also Women soldiers

Baxter, S. On the Orion line

Bowles, P. The wind at Beni Midar

Bradbury, R. By the numbers!

Burdick, E. Cold day, cold fear

Burke, J. L. We Build Churches, Inc.

Cacek, P. D. Belief

Carlson, R. What we wanted to do

Chamberlain, W. The trapped battalion

Deck, J. Sailors at their mourning: a memory

Drought, J. The secret [excerpt]

Fresan, R. National sovereignty

Gordimer, N. The diamond mine

Hinojosa, R. Hoengsong

Malzberg, B. N. Final war

Ponte, A. J. This life

Power, M. Graves

Schnitzler, A. Night games

Singer, I. B. Why Heisherik was born

Sneider, V. A long way from home

Whitmore, S. Lost soldier

Africa

Enekwe, O. O. The last battle

Maja-Pearce, A. Civil War I-VII

Australia

Bail, M. Camouflage

Malouf, D. Night training

Murray, S. Walkabout

Canada

Patterson, K. Starlight, starbright

China

Cherryh, C. J. The general

Lao She. Also a triangle

Mo Yan. Abandoned child

Cuba

Santiesteban Prats, A. 13th parallel south

France

Babel', I. The deserter

Babel', I. On the field of honor

Babel', I. Papa Marescot's family

Giono, J. Ivan Ivanovitch Kossiakoff

Sade, marquis de. The Gascon wit

Germany

Lawrence, D. H. The Prussian officer

Lawrence, D. H. The thorn in the flesh

Pearlman, D. D. The colonel's jeep

Trotter, W. R. The bleeding of Hauptmann Gehlen

Great Britain

Christie, A. The case of the discontented soldier

Honduras

Jacobs, M. The ballad of Tony Nail

India

Murray, S. Order of precedence

Iran

Riahi, M. War letters

Israel

Grossman, D. Yani on the mountain

SOLDIERS—Israel—*Continued*
Keret, E. Cocked and locked
Seltz, E. Compelle intrare
Yizhar, S. The prisoner

Japan
Hensley, J. L. Paint doctor
Murray, S. Colossus
Murray, S. Guinea

Nigeria
Aiyejina, F. The one-handed hero

Paraguay
Jacobs, M. Two dead Indians

Russia
See also Cossacks
Babel´, I. After the battle
Babel´, I. The commander of the second brigade
Babel´, I. Crossing the River Zbrucz
Babel´, I. Czesniki
Babel´, I. Dolgushov's death
Babel´, I. Italian sun
Babel´, I. Ivan and Ivan
Babel´, I. Konkin
Babel´, I. A letter
Babel´, I. The life story of Matvey Rodionovich
    Pavlichenko
Babel´, I. My first goose
Babel´, I. The rabbi
Babel´, I. The rabbi's son
Babel´, I. Salt
Babel´, I. Shaska Christ
Babel´, I. The tachanka theory
Babel´, I. Treason
Babel´, I. Zamosc
Benioff, D. The affairs of each beast
Bunin, I. A. Cold fall
Bunin, I. A. Sunstroke
Pushkin, A. S. The queen of spades
Pushkin, A. S. The stationmaster
Shonk, K. Our American

United States
See also African American soldiers The
    shape of things
Abrams, T. The biggest rat in the world
Abrams, T. I will hide in God
Abrams, T. Small arms fire
Abrams, T. Top
Barnes, H. L. Stonehands and the tigress
Barnes, H. L. Tunnel rat
Block, L. Speaking of lust
Bowen, K. The thief of Tay Ninh
Carr, P. M. Diary of a union soldier
Casey, J. A more complete cross-section
Coberly, L. M. Growing up in the Navy
Davidson, A. Dragon skin drum
Doogan, M. War can be murder
Dozois, G. R. Dinner party
Frierson, E. P. An adventure in the Big Horn
    Mountains; or, The trials and tribulations of
    a recruit
Goran, L. A day at the lake
Gurganus, A. Reassurance
Hannah, B. Midnight and I'm not famous yet
Harty, R. Crossroads
Harty, R. What can I tell you about my brother?
Heller, J. Catch-23: Yossarian lives
Heller, J. Yossarian survives
Henry, W. River of decision
Irsfeld, J. H. Ambivalence Hardy Fire
Irsfeld, J. H. Death of a soldier

Irsfeld, J. H. It's fun to say yes, but sometimes
    you just got to say no
Irsfeld, J. H. Puerto Rico ´61
Jones, T. The roadrunner
Kingrea, Eric. A waltz in the snow
Kingsbury, Suzanne. Panama
Knight, M. Killing Stonewall Jackson
Kuttner, H. We are the dead
Landis, G. A. Rorvik's war
Malouf, D. At Schindler's
Martin, P. P. Amor de madre—Mother's love
Meloy, M. Red
Murray, S. Colossus
Murray, S. Guinea
O'Brien, T. Going after Cacciato
O'Brien, T. The things they carried
O'Neill, S. Butch
O'Neill, S. Commendation
O'Neill, S. Don't mean nothing
O'Neill, S. Drugs
O'Neill, S. The perils of Pappy
O'Neill, S. This rough magic
O'Neill, S. Three minor love stories
O'Neill, S. What dreams may come
Ortiz, S. J. A story of Rios and Juan Jesus
Paine, T. The battle of Khafji
Pak, W.-S. Encounter at the airport
Ritchie, E. Marching as to war
Roth, P. Defender of the faith
Stanton, M. Ping-pong
Swarthout, G. F. The attack on the mountain
Wisenberg, S. L. Liberator
Yates, R. Bells in the morning
Yates, R. A compassionate leave
Yates, R. Jody rolled the bones

Vietnam
Dinh, L. Brother News from Home
SOLDIERS, BLACK *See* African American sol-
diers
SOLDIERS OF FORTUNE
Drake, D. Choosing sides
Drake, D. Neck or nothing
Drake, D. The political process
SOLICITORS *See* Law and lawyers
Solidarity forever!. Weaver, G.
Solidarity in green. Jacobs, M.
SOLITAIRE (GAME)
Updike, J. Solitaire
Solitaire. Mencken, S. H.
SOLITUDE
Chekhov, A. P. The bet
Disch, T. M. The squirrel cage
Vance, J. Ullward's retreat
Solitude. Le Guin, U. K.
The **solitude** of compassion. Giono, J.
A **solo** song: for Doc. McPherson, J. A.
Solomon, Robert
The Great Wall of California
    The Antioch Review v61 no1 p168-78 Wint
    2003
Solomon and his wives. Wexler, M.
SOLOMON ISLANDS
Marshall, T. American model
Solomon's big day. Touré
Solotaroff, Virginia
Lolly
    New England Review v22 no3 p133-43 Summ
    2001
Solstice. Ryder, P.

The **solution**. James, H.

Solved. Doenges, J.

Solwitz, Sharon

  Ballerina

    What are you looking at?; the first fat fiction anthology; edited by Donna Jarrell and Ira Sukrungruang

  The universal daughter

    TriQuarterly no110/111 p444-68 Fall 2001

Soma. Hernandez-Ramdwar, C.

SOMALIA

  Farah, N. My father, the Englishman, and I

Some blue hills at sundown. Gilchrist, E.

Some breed of magic. Foster, C.

Some due process. Huffman, B., Jr.

Some kind of wonderful. Blegvad, P.

Some laughed. Michaels, L.

Some nights when nothing happens are the best nights in this place. McNulty, J.

Some of our work with monsters. Carlson, R.

Some Other, Better Otto. Eisenberg, D.

Some other me. Hodge, B.

Some people are meant to live alone. Collymore, F.

Some retired ladies on a tour. Boylan, C.

Some say the world. Perabo, S.

Some things collide. Davis, J. S.

Some thoughts that morning. Kelman, J.

Some time I shall sleep out. Maclaren-Ross, J.

Some words with a mummy. Poe, E. A.

Somebody cares. Powell, T.

Someone Else's Mouth. Cotter, J.

Someone had to. Galloway, J.

Someone is crying in the chateau de Berne. Holleran, A.

Someone to contact. Lisick, B.

Someone to watch over me. Bausch, R.

Someone who understands me. Costello, M. J.

Somers, Evelyn

  Roy

    The Georgia Review v53 no4 p693-711 Wint 1999

Somers, Jane *See* Lessing, Doris May, 1919-

Something for nothing. Archer, J.

Something for Nothing. Gautreaux, T.

Something for the sweeper. Davis, N.

Something from the seventies. Malzberg, B. N.

Something important. Tilghman, C.

Something is happening on the top floor. Arenas, R.

Something like friends. Pratt, L.

Something simple. Kantner, R.

Something temporary. Paddock, J.

Something to cling to. Jenkins, G.

Something to hitch meat to. Hopkinson, N.

Something to remember me by. Bellow, S.

Something to remember me by. Johnson, D.

Something's going on. Ortiz, S. J.

Sometimes he borrowed a horse. Van Winckel, N.

Sometimes night never ends. Young, T.

Sometimes something goes wrong. Kaminsky, S. M.

Sometimes they bite. Block, L.

Somewhere South of Melrose. O'Callaghan, M.

SOMNAMBULISM

  Bester, A. The four-hour fugue

Somtow, S. P.

  Bird catcher

    The Museum of horrors; edited by Dennis Etchison

  Red as jade

    The Crow; shattered lives & broken dreams; edited by J. O'Barr and Ed Kramer

The **son**. Schlink, B.

Son in the afternoon. Williams, J. A.

Son observe the time. Baker, K.

The **son** of a thief. Tolstoy, L., graf

Son of Enoch. Raphael, F.

Son of man. Hodson, E.

Son of Mogar. Keene, J.

The **son** of the Head of the Mossad. Keret, E.

Son of the wolfman. Chabon, M.

Sonata for harp and bicycle. Aiken, J.

Sonata form. Galloway, J.

Sonde, Susan

  Who loves you, Baby?

    The Ohio Review no64/65 p312-17 2001

The **song**. Babel´, I.

Song. Dybek, S.

Song. Steinke, D.

Song-and-dance man. Dodd, S. M.

Song for a certain girl. Winegardner, M.

The **song** my sister sang. Laws, S.

Song of ascent. Goliger, G.

Song of forgotten years. Škvorecký, J.

Song of the blind. Gorky, M.

Song of the Chile bird. Bumas, E. S.

Song of the Japanese white-eye. Simonds, M.

The **Song** Reader. Tucker, L.

Songbirds. Schmidt, H. J.

SONGS

  Babel´, I. The song

  Delany, S. R. Corona

  Wellman, M. W. O ugly bird!

SONGS, POPULAR *See* Popular music

Songs and Sorrows. Brooks, B.

The **songs** of distant earth. Clarke, A. C.

Songs of leaving. Crowther, P.

Songs Without Words. Holmes, C.

SONGWRITERS *See* Composers

Sonja. Hermann, J.

Sonnenberg, Brittani

  Tierney's Gourmet

    Ploughshares v29 no4 p146-64 Wint 2003/2004

Sonny Liston was a friend of mine. Jones, T.

Sonority. Rifkin, A.

SONS *See* Fathers and sons; Mothers and sons; Stepsons

Sons. Leong, R.

The **son's** burden. Caponegro, M.

SONS-IN-LAW

  Bonnie, F. Squatter's rights

  Oates, J. C. Au sable

  Orner, P. Birth of a son-in-law

  Yarbrough, S. The right kind of person

Sons of God. Wilson, J.

The **Son's** Point of View. Clarke, B.

Sontag, Susan

  The way we live now

    The Best American short stories of the century; John Updike, editor, Katrina Kenison, coeditor; with an introduction by John Updike

Sontag, Susan—*Continued*

The Scribner anthology of contemporary short fiction; fifty North American stories since 1970; Lex Williford and Michael Martone, editors

Wonderful town; New York stories from The New Yorker; edited by David Remnick with Susan Choi

Soon. Durban, P.

Soon. Munro, A.

Sophia. López, L.

Sophie and the angel. Alonso, D.

Soppe, Rebecca

The Pantyhose Man

Ploughshares v29 no4 p165-77 Wint 2003/2004

The **sorcerer's** apprentice. Johnson, C.

SORCERY *See* Witchcraft

The **Sorge** spy ring. Hemon, A.

Sorokin, Vladimir

Hiroshima

Fishman, B. Wild East; stories from the last frontier; edited with an introduction by Boris Fishman

Grand Street no71 p48-55 Spr 2003

Sorrentino, Gilbert

Allegory of innocence

Sorrentino, G. The moon in its flight

A beehive arranged on humane principles

Sorrentino, G. The moon in its flight

Decades

Sorrentino, G. The moon in its flight

The dignity of labor

Sorrentino, G. The moon in its flight

Facts and their manifestations

Sorrentino, G. The moon in its flight

Gorgias

Sorrentino, G. The moon in its flight

In loveland

Sorrentino, G. The moon in its flight

It's time to call it a day

Sorrentino, G. The moon in its flight

Land of cotton

Sorrentino, G. The moon in its flight

Life and letters

Sorrentino, G. The moon in its flight

Lost in the stars

Sorrentino, G. The moon in its flight

The moon in its flight

Neurotica: Jewish writers on sex; edited by Melvin Jules Bukiet

Sorrentino, G. The moon in its flight

Pastilles

Sorrentino, G. The moon in its flight

Perdído

Bomb no87 p82-4, 86 Spr 2004

Sorrentino, G. The moon in its flight

Psychopathology of everyday life

Sorrentino, G. The moon in its flight

Sample writing sample

Sorrentino, G. The moon in its flight

The sea, caught in roses

Sorrentino, G. The moon in its flight

Subway

Sorrentino, G. The moon in its flight

Things that have stopped moving

Sorrentino, G. The moon in its flight

Times without number

Sorrentino, G. The moon in its flight

Sorrow. Chekhov, A. P.

Sorrow. Kamov, J. P.

A **sorrowful** woman. Godwin, G.

Sorrow's end. Haessig, J. J.

Sorry. Thurm, M.

Sorry blood. Gautreaux, T.

Sorry, Frank. O'Callaghan, M.

Sorry Solomon and Guey Jew. Reiner, C.

Sosin, Danielle

Garden primitives

Sosin, D. Garden primitives; stories

Ice age

Sosin, D. Garden primitives; stories

Internal medicine

Sosin, D. Garden primitives; stories

Mother Superior

Sosin, D. Garden primitives; stories

The only course

Sosin, D. Garden primitives; stories

Planted

Sosin, D. Garden primitives; stories

Still life

Sosin, D. Garden primitives; stories

Submersion

Sosin, D. Garden primitives; stories

There are no green butterflies

Sosin, D. Garden primitives; stories

This third year of returning

Sosin, D. Garden primitives; stories

What Mark couldn't see

Sosin, D. Garden primitives; stories

You're so simple

Sosin, D. Garden primitives; stories

SOTO, HERNANDO DE, CA. 1500-1542
About

Morgan, R. The tracks of Chief de Soto

Soukup, Martha

Up above Diamond City

Snapshots: 20th century mother-daughter fiction; edited by Joyce Carol Oates and Janet Berliner

SOUL

See also Transmigration

Brennert, A. Her pilgrim soul

Singer, I. B. Jachid and Jechidah

West, M. Winter

Soul City Gazette profile: Crash Jinkin, last of the chronic crashees. Touré

The **Soul** Is Not a Smithy. Wallace, D. F.

The **soul** molecule. Almond, S.

Soul walker. Fawcett, B.

The **soulcatcher**. Johnson, C. R.

Soulmates. Scarborough, E. A.

Souls belated. Wharton, E.

Souls burning. Pronzini, B.

Sound Advice. Compton, V.

The **sound** gun. Derby, M.

A **sound** investment. Quill, M.

The **sound** is so shallow here. Mathes, T. S.

The **sound** of asthma. Heller, J.

The **sound** of the horn. Colvin, C.

Sounds like. O'Driscoll, M.

The **sounds** that arrive in the present. Frank, J.

Sour cherry pits. Pirzad, Z.

SOUTH (U.S.) *See* Southern States

The **south**. Borges, J. L.

SOUTH AFRICA

See also Africa

Hunter, F. A newsman scratches an itch

SOUTH AFRICA—*Continued*
Karodia, F. The woman in green
Kohler, S. Africans
Kohler, S. Poor cousins
Lessing, D. M. A letter from home
Magona, S. It was Easter Sunday the day I went to Netreg
Ndebele, N. S. The prophetess
Saunders, G. Walking legs
Sobott-Mogwe, G. Smile of fortune
Spark, M. The Seraph and the Zambesi
Native peoples
Wicomb, Z. You can't get lost in Cape Town
Race relations
Archer, J. A change of heart
Bishop, M. Apartheid, superstrings, and Mordecai Thubana
Gordimer, N. Country lovers
Gordimer, N. Karma
Saunders, G. A sudden new city
Theroux, P. An African story
Williams, K. They came at dawn
Johannesburg
Gunthorp, D. Gypsophila
Modisane, B. The dignity of begging
SOUTH AFRICANS
See also Afrikaners
Italy
Gordimer, N. L. U. C. I. E.
Madagascar
Hunter, F. Madagascar
United States
Saunders, G. No money for stamps
Saunders, G. We'll get to now later
SOUTH AMERICA
See also Amazon River Valley
Kurlansky, M. Desaparecidos
South Beach, 1992. Glave, T.
South by Southwest. Alexie, S.
SOUTH CAROLINA
Lehane, D. Running out of dog
Morgan, R. A brightness new & welcoming
Morgan, R. Poinsett's Bridge
Searle, E. Memoir of a soon-to-be star
Singleton, G. How I met my second wife
Singleton, G. One man's indelible marks
Singleton, G. The ruptures and limits of absence
Charleston
Nelson, K. Tides
SOUTH DAKOTA
McNeal, T. Watermelon Days
South for the winter. Bradford, A.
South Georgia crossing. Estleman, L. D.
SOUTH SEA ISLANDS *See* Islands of the Pacific
SOUTHEAST ASIA
VanderMeer, J. The bone carver's tale
SOUTHEAST ASIANS
Israel
Pearlman, E. Allog
A **southern** landscape. Spencer, E.
SOUTHERN RHODESIA *See* Zimbabwe
SOUTHERN STATES
See also Confederate States of America names of individual states
Adams, A. New best friends
Adams, A. Truth or consequences
Berry, M. S. Armistice
Berry, M. S. Exit Miss Tish

Berry, M. S. Final payment
Berry, M. S. The four hundred ninety-first time
Berry, M. S. The hawk
Berry, M. S. The long dark hall
Berry, M. S. The long view
Berry, M. S. Next-door neighbors
Berry, M. S. The passing night
Berry, M. S. Philip's room
Berry, M. S. The quantity of mercy
Blaise, C. South
Bocock, M. The funeral
Durban, P. Soon
Fitzgerald, F. S. The ice palace
Gautreaux, T. The piano tuner
Koger, L. Bypass
Mencken, S. H. Absolutely perfect
Mencken, S. H. Birthday
Mencken, S. H. Clinging vine
Mencken, S. H. Each in her own day
Mencken, S. H. Grown-up
Mencken, S. H. Ladies and lovers
Mencken, S. H. The last of the beaux
Mencken, S. H. Little lady
Mencken, S. H. Little white girl
Mencken, S. H. Namesake
Mencken, S. H. Solitaire
Mencken, S. H. Southern town
Mencken, S. H. Twilight of chivalry
Norris, H. Tutankhamen Calhoun
O'Connor, F. The life you save may be your own
Offutt, C. Out of the woods
Southern strategy
Spencer, E. The fishing lake
Spencer, E. The girl who loved horses
Farm life
See Farm life—Southern States
Mountain life
See Mountain life—Southern States
Race relations
Singleton, G. Fossils
SOUTHERN STATES DIALECT *See* Dialect stories—Southern States
Southern strategy Turtledove, H. Alternate generals II; ed. by Harry Turtledove
Southern town. Mencken, S. H.
Southgate, Martha
The kick inside
The Bluelight corner; black women writing on passion, sex, and romantic love; edited by Rosemarie Robotham
SOUTHWEST, NEW *See* Southwestern States
The **Southwest** Experimental Fast Oxide Reactor. Gilchrist, E.
SOUTHWESTERN STATES
See also Santa Fe Trail
Bausch, R. Old west
Burleson, D. R. Pump Jack
Coleman, J. C. Marvel Bird
DeMarinis, R. Paraiso: an elegy
Evans, M. Candles in the bottom of the pool
Gonzalez, R. Mountain
Gonzalez, R. The scorpion eater
Southwick, Scott
The Mercenary Goes to Church
Gettysburg Review v15 no2 p313-20 Summ 2002
Souvenir. Allen, S.
Souvenir. Vonnegut, K.

A **souvenir** of Hell. Keret, E.
Souvenirs. Shade, E.
The **Soviet** circus comes to Havana. Suarez, V.
SOVIET UNION *See* Russia
Soy la Avon lady. López, L.
Space. Brockmeier, K.
SPACE AND TIME
  See also Relativity (Physics); Time travel
 Bear, G. The way of all ghosts
 Bisson, T. The edge of the universe
 Bisson, T. Get me to the church on time
 Blish, J. Common time
 Cherryh, C. J. The Threads of time
 Ellison, H. Jeffty is five
 Meaney, J. The whisper of disks
 Reed, R. The shape of everything
 Rucker, R. v. B. In frozen time
 Rucker, R. v. B. The last Einstein-Rosen bridge
 Simmons, D. Looking for Kelly Dahl
 Steele, A. M. The days between
SPACE COLONIES
 Anderson, P. The big rain
 Benford, G. Shall we take a little walk?
 Blish, J. Surface tension
 Garcia y Robertson, R. Gone to glory
 Harrison, H. The man from P.I.G.
 Jennings, P. C. The road to reality
 Keith, W. H. Fossils
 Kessel, J. The juniper tree
 Kessel, J. Stories for men
 Kress, N. Ej-es
 Landis, G. A. Ecopoiesis
 McAuley, P. J. How we lost the moon, a true
  story by Frank W. Allen
 McDonald, I. The Catharine wheel
 McKenna, R. Hunter, come home
 Oliver, C. Field expedient
 Oliver, C. The gift
 Oliver, C. Second nature
 Pronzini, B. Epitaph
 Reynolds, A. Glacial
 Robinson, K. S. A Martian romance
 Rusch, K. K. Skin deep
 Wilder, C. The Dancing Floor
SPACE FLIGHT
  See also Astronauts; Interplanetary voyages; Science fiction
 Bishop, M. Cri de coeur
 Blish, J. Common time
 Blish, J. Nor iron bars
 Clarke, A. C. The star
 Davidson, A. Now let us sleep
 Delany, S. R. The star pit
 Duncan, A. The chief designer
 Effinger, G. A. One
 Egan, G. Wang's carpets
 Harrison, H. The repairman
 Haskell, J. Good world
 Kelly, J. P. Glass cloud
 Lumley, B. Big "C"
 Oliver, C. Blood's a rover
 Scholz, C. At the shore
 Schroeder, K. Halo
 Simmons, D. The end of gravity
 Strasser, D. The doppelganger effect
 Vonnegut, K. Thanasphere
SPACE FLIGHT TO JUPITER
 Clarke, A. C. A meeting with Medusa

SPACE FLIGHT TO MARS
 Bradbury, R. The exiles
 Clarke, A. C. How we went to Mars
SPACE FLIGHT TO THE MOON
 Clarke, A. C. The sentinel
 Clarke, A. C. Venture to the Moon
 Johnson, A. The Canadanaut
 Oliver, C. Technical advisor
 Oltion, J. Abandon in place
 Ortiz, S. J. Men on the moon
Space rats of the CCC. Harrison, H.
SPACE SHIPS
 Anderson, P. Kyrie
 Asimov, I. The Martian way
 Bear, G. Perihesperon
 Bear, G. Scattershot
 Blish, J. Surface tension
 Bradbury, R. The machineries of joy
 Bradbury, R. The rocket
 Cherryh, C. J. Homecoming
 Clarke, A. C. Hide-and-seek
 Clarke, A. C. Inheritance
 Clarke, A. C. Jupiter five
 Clarke, A. C. Maelstrom II
 Clarke, A. C. Out of the cradle, endlessly orbiting
 Clarke, A. C. Refugee
 Clarke, A. C. Summertime on Icarus
 Clement, H. Proof
 Finlay, C. C. The political officer
 Godwin, T. The cold equations
 Harrison, H. Pressure
 Jenkins, W. F. First contact
 Kelly, J. P. Undone
 Landis, G. A. Across the darkness
 Le Guin, U. K. Solitude
 Matheson, R. Shipshape home
 McAuley, P. J. The passenger
 McCaffrey, A. The ship that returned
 McCaffrey, A. The ship who mourned
 McCaffrey, A. The ship who sang
 Oliver, C. Stardust
 Oliver, C. The wind blows free
 Reed, R. Aeon's child
 Reed, R. Chrysalis
 Rucker, R. v. B. Storming the cosmos
 Simmons, D. Orphans of the Helix
 Steele, A. M. The days between
 Steele, A. M. The death of Captain Future
 Van Pelt, J. The long way home
 Vance, J. Sail 25
 Waldrop, H. Sun's up!
 Williams, S. Evermore
 Zettel, S. Fool's errand
SPACE STATIONS
 Clarke, A. C. The other side of the sky
 Jenkins, W. F. Exploration team
 Mixon, L. J. At tide's turning
 Nordley, G. D. Dawn Venus
 Sargent, P. Dream of Venus
The **space** traders. Bell, D. A.
SPACE TRAVEL *See* Space flight
Spaceship. Gonzalez, R.
Spain, Chris
 Scaring the baddest animal
  Coppola, F. F. Francis Ford Coppola's
  Zoetrope: all story; edited by Adrienne
  Brodeur and Samantha Schnee; introduction
  by Francis Ford Coppola

SPAIN
Casa Pérez, R. d. l. The day we went through the transition
Frost, P. S. Clamour
Singer, I. B. The bus
  17th century
Sandlin, L. The saint of bilocation
  19th century
Alarcón, P. A. d. Captain Poison
Alarcón, P. A. d. Moors and Christians
Alarcón, P. A. d. The nun
Alas, L. The burial of the sardine
Alas, L. Change of light
Alas, L. A day laborer
Alas, L. Doña Berta
Alas, L. The lord
Alas, L. Torso
Alas, L. The two boxes
Alas, L. Two scholars
  Rural life
Brown, C. Miniature man
  Andalusia
Melville, P. The duende
  Barcelona
Adams, A. Barcelona
Anderson, R. The pyramid
  Granada
Alarcón, P. A. d. The nun
  Grenada
Lee, V. The Virgin of the Seven Daggers
  Madrid
Abrams, T. The book of thieves
  Majorca
 See Majorca (Spain)
SPANIARDS
  Egypt
Posadas, Carmen. The Nubian lover
Spanish. Gonzalez, R.
SPANISH AMERICANS
Austin, M. H. Old Spanish gardens
Spanish grammar. Swan, M.
Spanish omens. Boswell, M.
Spanish Prelude to a Second Marriage. Updike, J.
Spare the rod. Wylie, P.
Spared. Kennedy, A. L.
Spariosu, Mihai and Benedek, Dezsö
The bitang
 The Literary werewolf; an anthology; edited by Charlotte F. Otten
Spark, Debra
Chocolate mice
 New England Review v20 no4 p123-44 Fall 1999
Lady of the Wild Beasts
 Ploughshares v30 no2/3 p144-67 Fall 2004
Spark, Muriel
Another pair of hands
 Spark, M. The ghost stories of Muriel Spark
The executor
 Spark, M. The ghost stories of Muriel Spark
The hanging judge
 Spark, M. The ghost stories of Muriel Spark
The house of the famous poet
 Spark, M. The ghost stories of Muriel Spark
The leaf-sweeper
 Nightshade: 20th century ghost stories; edited by Robert Phillips
 Spark, M. The ghost stories of Muriel Spark

The Portobello Road
 Spark, M. The ghost stories of Muriel Spark
The Seraph and the Zambesi
 Spark, M. The ghost stories of Muriel Spark
Spark. Gussoff, C.
The **sparkling** bitch. Melville, P.
Sparks, Nicholas
A bend in the road
 Good Housekeeping v234 no3 p191-214 Mr 2002
Sparks. Leonard, E.
A **sparrow's** flight [excerpt] Elphinstone, M.
Spatz, Gregory
Anyone's Venus
 Spatz, G. Wonderful tricks; stories
Body
 Spatz, G. Wonderful tricks; stories
A holier temple
 Iowa Review v31 no3 p26-36 Wint 2001/2002
Inversion
 Spatz, G. Wonderful tricks; stories
Lisa picking cockles
 Spatz, G. Wonderful tricks; stories
Paradise was this
 Spatz, G. Wonderful tricks; stories
Plenty of pools in Texas
 Spatz, G. Wonderful tricks; stories
Stone fish
 Spatz, G. Wonderful tricks; stories
Walking in my sleep
 Spatz, G. Wonderful tricks; stories
Wonderful tricks
 Spatz, G. Wonderful tricks; stories
Zigzag cabinet
 Spatz, G. Wonderful tricks; stories
Spaziani, Maria Luisa
The Story of Lalò
 Southern Humanities Review v37 no4 p334-45 Fall 2003
Speak no evil. Pickard, N.
Speak of the Devil. Gores, J.
Speaking in tongues. Packer, Z.
Speaking of greed. Block, L.
Speaking of lust. Block, L.
Speaking to the wind. Yolen, J.
Spear blood. Marías, J.
The **specialist's** hat. Link, K.
The **speck** in the sky. Sneve, V. D. H.
Speckle Trout. Rash, R.
The **specks** in the sky. Rice, B.
Spectacles. Osborne, K. L.
Spectator on a February night. Škvorecký, J.
Spectators in love. Rowell, J.
Specters in the moonlight. Segriff, L.
Spector, Mordkhe
The Jewish muzhik [excerpt]
 Neugroschel, J. No star too beautiful; Yiddish stories from 1382 to the present; compiled and translated by Joachim Neugroschel
Spedding, Sally
Strangers waiting
 The best British mysteries; edited by Maxim Jakubowski
Speece, Merry
Fire sermon
 Nixon under the bodhi tree and other works of Buddhist fiction; edited by Kate Wheeler ; foreword by Charles Johnson

SPEECH DISORDERS
See also Stuttering
Speech sounds. Butler, O. E.
SPEECHES, ADDRESSES, ETC.
See also Lectures and lecturing
Pronzini, B. and Malzberg, B. N. Inaugural
Speed bump. Dixon, S.
The **speed** of sound. Russell, M.
Speed of the cheetah, roar of the lion. Harrison, H.
The **speedboat**. Brownstein, G.
The **spell**. Gerrold, D.
Spellchecked. Pearlman, D. D.
The **spells** of an ordinary twilight. Rawley, D.
Spence, Alan
Brilliant
The Vintage book of contemporary Scottish fiction; edited and with an introduction by Peter Kravitz
Spence, June
Missing women
This is where we live; short stories by 25 contemporary North Carolina writers; edited by Michael McFee
Spencer, Brent
This is the last of the nice
A different plain; contemporary Nebraska fiction writers; edited by Ladette Randolph ; introduction by Mary Pipher
Spencer, Darrell
The 12-inch dog
Spencer, D. Caution, men in trees; stories
Blood work
Spencer, D. Caution, men in trees; stories
Caution: men in trees
Spencer, D. Caution, men in trees; stories
It's a lot scarier if you take Jesus out
Spencer, D. Caution, men in trees; stories
Late-night TV
Spencer, D. Caution, men in trees; stories
Park host
Spencer, D. Caution, men in trees; stories
Please to forgive sloppiness
Spencer, D. Caution, men in trees; stories
Pronto bucks
Spencer, D. Caution, men in trees; stories
There's too much news
Spencer, D. Caution, men in trees; stories
Spencer, Elizabeth
The adult holiday
Spencer, E. The southern woman; new and selected fiction
The Boy in the Tree
The Southern Review (Baton Rouge, La.) v40 no3 p488-99 Summ 2004
The Bufords
Spencer, E. The southern woman; new and selected fiction
The business venture
Crossing the color line; readings in Black and white; edited by Suzanne W. Jones
Spencer, E. The southern woman; new and selected fiction
A Christian education
Spencer, E. The southern woman; new and selected fiction
The cousins
Spencer, E. The southern woman; new and selected fiction

The eclipse
Spencer, E. The southern woman; new and selected fiction
The everlasting light
The Cry of an occasion; fiction from the Fellowship of Southern Writers; edited by Richard Bausch; with a foreword by George Garrett
The finder
Spencer, E. The southern woman; new and selected fiction
First child
Spencer, E. The southern woman; new and selected fiction
First dark
Spencer, E. The southern woman; new and selected fiction
The fishing lake
Spencer, E. The southern woman; new and selected fiction
The girl who loved horses
Spencer, E. The southern woman; new and selected fiction
I, Maureen
Spencer, E. The southern woman; new and selected fiction
Indian summer
Spencer, E. The southern woman; new and selected fiction
Jack of diamonds
Spencer, E. The southern woman; new and selected fiction
The legacy
Spencer, E. The southern woman; new and selected fiction
The light in the piazza
Spencer, E. The southern woman; new and selected fiction
The little brown girl
Spencer, E. The southern woman; new and selected fiction
The master of Shongalo
Spencer, E. The southern woman; new and selected fiction
Owl
Nightshade: 20th century ghost stories; edited by Robert Phillips
Spencer, E. The southern woman; new and selected fiction
The runaways
Spencer, E. The southern woman; new and selected fiction
Sharon
Spencer, E. The southern woman; new and selected fiction
Ship island: the story of a mermaid
Spencer, E. The southern woman; new and selected fiction
The skater
Spencer, E. The southern woman; new and selected fiction
A southern landscape
Spencer, E. The southern woman; new and selected fiction
The visit
Spencer, E. The southern woman; new and selected fiction

Spencer, Elizabeth—*Continued*
The weekend travelers
Spencer, E. The southern woman; new and selected fiction
The white azalea
Spencer, E. The southern woman; new and selected fiction
Spencer, James
Redemption
The Virginia Quarterly Review v75 no1 p95-108 Wint 1999
The robbers of Karnataka
The Best American short stories, 1999; selected from U.S. and Canadian magazines by Amy Tan with Katrina Kenison, with an introduction by Amy Tan
Spencer, Lady Diana *See* Diana, Princess of Wales, 1961-1997
Spencer, Wen
Wyvern
Greenberg, M. H. Faerie tales
Spencer, William Browning
The halfway house at the heart of darkness
The Year's best science fiction, sixteenth annual collection; edited by Gardner Dozois
The lights of Armageddon
Witpunk; edited by Claude Lalumière and Marty Halpern
SPENDTHRIFTS
Davies, R. The Fashion Plate
Speonk. Leavitt, D.
Sperm. Jackson, S.
Sperm-and-egg tango. Tuller, D.
SPHINXES (MYTHOLOGY)
Connor, J. Writing the war novel
Spice. Davis, A.
Spider Boy. Oates, J. C.
The **spider** of Bumba. Gasco, E.
SPIDERS
Bradbury, R. The Finnegan
Wallace, D. F. Philosophy and the mirror of nature
Spiderweb trail. Cunningham, E.
Spiegel, Isaiah
A ghetto dog
When night fell; an anthology of Holocaust short stories; edited by Linda Schermer Raphael and Marc Lee Raphael
Spielberg, Peter
Apocrypha
Spielberg, P. The noctambulists & other fictions
Cry wolf
Spielberg, P. The noctambulists & other fictions
A happening
Spielberg, P. The noctambulists & other fictions
The noctambulists
Spielberg, P. The noctambulists & other fictions
Trading down
Spielberg, P. The noctambulists & other fictions
Vanishing
Spielberg, P. The noctambulists & other fictions

Withholding
Spielberg, P. The noctambulists & other fictions
SPIES
See also International intrigue; Secret service
Aldrich, B. S. The outsider
Allyn, D. The turncoat
Berliner, J. Other.........1
Bierce, A. The story of a conscience
Borges, J. L. The garden of forking paths
Bowen, R. Doppelganger
Clarke, A. C. Hide-and-seek
Cobb, J. H. Monica Van Telflin and the proper application of pressure
Collins, M. A. and Clemens, M. V. Lie beside me
Collins, M. The sleeper
Collins, M. Success of a mission
Collins, M. and Lynds, G. A delicate mission
Correa, A. Spy's fate
Crider, B. Belle Boyd, the rebel spy
Doyle, Sir A. C. The adventure of the Bruce-Partington plans
DuBois, B. The invisible spy
DuBois, B. Old soldiers
Ehlers, J. "Wangeroog, de schone . . ."
Engel, H. The ant trap
Estleman, L. D. South Georgia crossing
Foxwell, E. Alice and the agent of the Hun
Gorman, E. A small and private war
Haddam, J. Port Tobacco
Harrison, H. The greening of the green
Harrison, P. Zero-G dogfight
Hemon, A. The Sorge spy ring
Hoch, E. D. The counterfeit copperhead
Hoch, E. D. Enemy territory
Hodgson, W. H. The adventure of the garter
Hodgson, W. H. The diamond spy
Hodgson, W. H. The German spy
Hodgson, W. H. The plans of the reefing bi-plane
Iarrera, C. A telephone call too many
Jakes, J. Cloak and digger
Jakober, M. Slither
Kaminsky, S. M. What you don't know
L'Amour, L. Wings over Khabarovsk
Lindskold, J. M. The road to Stony Creek
Lutz, J. Hobson's choice
Lutz, J. Winds of change
Mendes, B. Tooth marks
Nagle, P. G. The courtship of Captain Swenk
Nevins, F. M., Jr. The other man in the pin-stripe
Oppel, J.-H. A demon in my head
Phillips, G. The measure
Randisi, R. J. The Knights of Liberty
Rusch, K. K. The dead line
Schumacher, A. Worth a thousand words
Sterling, B. Taklamakan
Twain, M. A curious experience
Vukcevich, R. The swan
Spike song. Miller, B.
Spike team. Miller, R.
Spikes. Chabon, M.
Spillage. Hsueh, M.

Spillane, Mickey
The girl behind the hedge
A Century of great suspense stories; edited by Jeffery Deaver
Tomorrow I die
A Century of noir; thirty-two classic crime stories; edited by Mickey Spillane and Max Allan Collins
SPILLANE, MICKEY, 1918-
Parodies, imitations, etc.
DeAndrea, W. L. The adventure of the cripple parade
Spilman, Richard
Agent of the Revolution
The Literary Review (Madison, N.J.) v47 no2 p123-35 Wint 2004
Spin. Jenkins, G.
Spin cycle. Winter, E.
Spin-off. Clark, J.
Spinnen, Burkhard
The tower
Prairie Schooner v73 no3 p18-31 Fall 1999
Spinning. Rusch, K. K.
Spinning kingdoms, two. Wylde, T.
SPINSTERS *See* Single women
The **spiral**. Kaplan, H.
Spirit dog. Dann, J.
Spirit guides. Rusch, K. K.
The **spirit** of the tree. Boylan, C.
Spirits fly south. Weldon, F.
SPIRITUALISM
Chekhov, A. P. A dreadful night
Leslie, N. Give me a sign
Rodgers, S. J. Lost spirits
Singer, I. B. The prodigy
Singer, I. B. The seance
Weaver, G. Ed Stein, Ed Stein, speak to me!
Weaver, G. Psychic friends
Wells, K. My guardian, Claire
Wharton, E. The looking-glass
A **spiritualist**. Rhys, J.
The **spiritus** step. Skillings, R. D.
Spivack, Kathleen
The empty rocker
The North American Review v284 no1 p17-21 Ja/F 1999
Spleen. Novakovich, J.
The **Splinter**. Bingham, S.
The **splinter**. Reifler, N.
Splinters. Bukiet, M. J.
SPLIT PERSONALITY *See* Dual personality
SPOKANE INDIANS
Alexie, S. Class
Alexie, S. Dear John Wayne
Alexie, S. One good man
Alexie, S. Saint Junior
Alexie, S. The toughest Indian in the world
Spooked. Hart, C. G.
Spooks. Reid, A.
Spooky, Codeine, and the dead man. O'Barr, J.
The **spoon**. Blegvad, P.
Spoon. Greer, R. O.
The **spoon** children. Paine, T.
Spoonfed. Chapman, C. M.
Spores. Tawada, Y.
SPORTS
See also Athletes; Coaching (Athletics); Games; Swimming; Track (Athletics)
Cavell, B. Balls, balls, balls

Škvorecký, J. A remarkable chemical phenomenon
Spot of Trouble. Parotti, P.
Spots. Barthelme, F.
Spotted dolphin. Rogers, B. H.
Spraker, Suzy
If My Mother's Soul Can Hear
The Southern Review (Baton Rouge, La.) v39 no2 p355-67 Spr 2003
SPRING
Fitzgerald, F. S. May Day
Zinovyeva-Annibal, L. D. The midge
Spring. Skinner, J.
Spring. Tippens, E.
Spring. Winter, E.
Spring 1933. Stein, D. B.
Spring '41. Sanford, A.
Spring beauties. Coates, G. S.
Spring break. Chacón, D.
Spring is now. Williams, J.
Spring rain. Cheng, C.-W.
Spring rite. Berdine, T.
Springer, Nancy
Juggernaut
The World's finest mystery and crime stories, third annual collection; edited by Ed Gorman and Martin H. Greenberg
SPRINGSTEEN, BRUCE
About
Richmond, M. Down the shore everything's all right
Spruill, Steven G.
Hemophage
999: new stories of horror and suspense; edited by Al Sarrantonio
Spur the nightmare. Wellen, E.
Spurn Babylon. Buckell, T. S.
Spurt. Sellers, H.
Spy's fate. Correa, A.
Squabble. Holman, J.
Squadron Commander Trunov. Babel´, I.
The **square** reporter. Wheeler, R. S.
The **square** root of Pythagoras. Rucker, R. v. B.
The **Square** Root of Reason. Roberts, M.
Squash flowers. Stanton, M.
Squatter's rights. Bonnie, F.
Squeak in the sycamore. Lish, G.
Squeak, memory. Bukiet, M. J.
Squeeze play. Bishop, P.
SQUIDS
Clarke, A. C. Big game hunt
Clarke, A. C. The shining ones
Squire, Elizabeth Daniels
Down the garden path
Malice domestic 10; an anthology of original traditional mystery stories
A passion for the cook
Death dines at 8:30; edited by Claudia Bishop and Nick DiChario
The **squire's** daughter. Pushkin, A. S.
The **squirrel** cage. Disch, T. M.
Squirrelly's grouper. Shacochis, B.
SQUIRRELS
Brenner, W. Four squirrels
Holtzer, S. The golden rounds
Reifler, N. Personal foundations of self-forming through auto-identification with otherness
Sredni Vashtar. Saki

SRI LANKA
Bowles, P. In the red room
Davies, L. Mr. Roopratna's chocolate
Srinivasan, A. A.
Tusk
TriQuarterly no105 p46-57 Spr/Summ 1999
SRL ad. Matheson, R.
Ssoroghod's people. Niven, L.
St. Andrew's day. Fleming, M.
St. Guilhem-le-Désert. Tuck, L.
The **St.** Louis salesman. Loomis, N. M.
St. Margaret's kitten. Allyn, D.
St. Mawr. Lawrence, D. H.
ST. PATRICK'S DAY *See* Saint Patrick's Day
ST. PAUL (MINN.) *See* Minnesota—St. Paul
ST. PETERSBURG (RUSSIA) *See* Russia—St. Petersburg
ST. VALENTINE'S DAY *See* Valentine's Day
Stability. Shade, E.
Stableford, Brian M.
The age of innocence
Stableford, B. M. Designer genes; tales of the biotech revolution
Another branch of the family tree
Stableford, B. M. Designer genes; tales of the biotech revolution
Art in the blood
Shadows over Baker Street; edited by Michael Reaves and John Pelan
Chanterelle
Black heart, ivory bones; [edited by] Ellen Datlow & Terri Windling
The facts of life
Stableford, B. M. Designer genes; tales of the biotech revolution
Hot blood
Stableford, B. M. Designer genes; tales of the biotech revolution
The house of mourning
Stableford, B. M. Designer genes; tales of the biotech revolution
The invisible worm
Stableford, B. M. Designer genes; tales of the biotech revolution
The last supper
Stableford, B. M. Designer genes; tales of the biotech revolution
The milk of human kindness
Stableford, B. M. Designer genes; tales of the biotech revolution
The pipes of Pan
Stableford, B. M. Designer genes; tales of the biotech revolution
Snowball in hell
Stableford, B. M. Designer genes; tales of the biotech revolution
The Year's best science fiction, eighteenth annual collection; edited by Gardner Dozois
Tenebrio
Vanishing acts; a science fiction anthology; edited by Ellen Datlow
The werewolves of London
The Literary werewolf; an anthology; edited by Charlotte F. Otten
What can Chloe want?
Stableford, B. M. Designer genes; tales of the biotech revolution

Stack, Frank
State briefly why you want to be a waiter at Pizza Place
The North American Review v284 no6 p25 N/D 1999
Stacked deck. Pronzini, B.
Staffel, Megan
Lessons in another language
Ploughshares v25 no1 p68-107 Spr 1999
Stafford, Jean
Children are bored on Sunday
Wonderful town; New York stories from The New Yorker; edited by David Remnick with Susan Choi
The interior castle
The Best American short stories of the century; John Updike, editor, Katrina Kenison, coeditor; with an introduction by John Updike
STAGE LIFE *See* Theater life
Stage to Lordsburg. Haycox, E.
STAGECOACH LINES
Haycox, E. Stage to Lordsburg
Hogan, R. A question of faith
L'Amour, L. Alkali Basin
L'Amour, L. Stage to Willowspring
Stages. Campbell, R.
Stahl, Anna Kazumi
Natural disasters
Colchie, T. A whistler in the nightworld; short fiction from the Latin Americas; edited by Thomas Colchie
Stairs. Barrett, N., Jr.
Stakeout. Pronzini, B.
A **stakes** horse. Meloy, M.
STALIN, JOSEPH, 1879-1953
About
Kalfus, K. Anzhelika, 13
Stalingrad. Ely, S.
Stalker. Morrison, J.
The **stalker.** Oates, J. C.
STALKING
Cavin, R. The Mechanique affair
Deaver, J. Beautiful
Louis, L. G. Thirty yards
Rusch, K. K. The perfect man
Stalky the clown. Sadoff, I.
A **stalwart** girl. Frank, J.
STAMBOLIAN, GEORGE
About
Agabian, N. Ghosts and bags
Stamell, Rhoda B.
Also Known as Alonzo Jones
The Kenyon Review v25 no3/4 p100-10 Summ/Fall 2003
Love for a fat man
What are you looking at?; the first fat fiction anthology; edited by Donna Jarrell and Ira Sukrungruang
The **Stamp.** Novakovich, J.
STAMPA, GASPARA, CA. 1523-CA. 1554
About
Silber, J. Gaspara Stampa
Stampede. Ferriss, L.
The **stand.** Braun, M.
Standard gauge. Royle, N.
Standards & practices. Malzberg, B. N.

Standiford, Les
Succubus
Stories from the Blue Moon Cafe II; edited by Sonny Brewer
Standing, Sue
Fast Sunday
Ploughshares v29 no2/3 p173-86 Fall 2003
Standing by peaceful waters. Gay, W.
Standing Ground. Le Guin, U. K.
Standing up to the superpowers. Erian, A.
Standish, Burt L.
Seeking the secret of the double shot
Dead balls and double curves; an anthology of early baseball fiction; edited and with an introduction by Trey Strecker ; with a foreword by Arnold Hano
Stanley, Ferdinando *See* Derby, Ferdinando Stanley, 5th Earl of, 1559?-1594
Stanley, M. Adam
Blackout
Prairie Schooner v73 no2 p131-32 Summ 1999
Stanley. Bingham, S.
Stanton, Mary, 1947-
See also Bishop, Claudia, 1947-
Stanton, Maura
The cat and the clown
Stanton, M. Do not forsake me, oh my darling
The cliffs of the moon
Stanton, M. Do not forsake me, oh my darling
Glass house
Ploughshares v27 no2/3 p198-210 Fall 2001
How to converse in Italian
Stanton, M. Do not forsake me, oh my darling
Marie Antoinette's harp
Stanton, M. Do not forsake me, oh my darling
My death
Stanton, M. Do not forsake me, oh my darling
My sister's novel
Stanton, M. Do not forsake me, oh my darling
Ping-pong
Stanton, M. Do not forsake me, oh my darling
Squash flowers
Stanton, M. Do not forsake me, oh my darling
The ugly virgin
Stanton, M. Do not forsake me, oh my darling
Stanton, Schuyler *See* Baum, L. Frank (Lyman Frank), 1856-1919
The **star**. Clarke, A. C.
Star baby. Gates, D.
Star-dogged moon. Wells, K.
The **star** in the valley. Craddock, C. E.
Star Lake, long ago. Penn, W. S.
Star on his heart. Le May, A.
The **star** pit. Delany, S. R.
Star seed. Nawrocki, S.
Star struck. Lovesey, P.
The **Star** Tavern. Streckfuss, A.
The **star** thief. DuBois, B.
The **star** train. Abrams, T.

STAR TREK (TELEVISION PROGRAM)
DeMarinis, R. Aliens
Star Woman's child. Rodgers, D.
Starburst. Cummins, A.
Stardust. Drake, R.
Stark, Richard
For works written by this author under other names see Westlake, Donald E.
The **Starlight** Express. Gilchrist, E.
Starlight, starbright. Patterson, K.
Starlings. McCorkle, J.
STARR, BELLE, 1848-1889
About
Sandifer, L. Betrayal
Starr, Georgina
Tuberama: a musical on the Northern Line (or how to be in touch with your emotions)
Typical girls; new stories by smart women; edited by Susan Corrigan
Starr, Myra Maybelle Shirley *See* Starr, Belle, 1848-1889
Starring Nohj Anyew. Faust, I.
STARS
Asimov, I. The last question
Asimov, I. Nightfall
Clarke, A. C. The star
Delany, S. R. The star pit
Stars at elbow and foot. Bloom, A.
Stars of Motown shining bright. Orringer, J.
The **start** of something. Mueller, D.
Starting with Sneakers. Melnyczuk, A.
STARVATION
Chekhov, A. P. Oysters
Kalu, Anthonia C. Relief duty
Loomis, N. M. When the children cry for meat
Lustig, A. The lemon
Murray, S. Order of precedence
West, M. Hunger
Stashower, Daniel
The adventure of the agitated actress
The Best American mystery stories, 2003; edited by Michael Connelly and Otto Penzler
Murder, my dear Watson; new tales of Sherlock Holmes; edited by Martin H. Greenberg, Jon Lellenberg, Daniel Stashower
Stasi. Weldon, F.
State briefly why you want to be a waiter at Pizza Place. Stack, F.
State of England. Amis, M.
State of grace. Estleman, L. D.
State of the art. Wellen, E.
State of the nation. Glover, D. H.
The **state** of union. Foley, S.
State v. Stucky. Johnston, T.
The **statement** of Henry Worthy. Lumley, B.
States, Bert O.
The painting
Michigan Quarterly Review v38 no2 p225-37 Spr 1999
Station H. Ponte, A. J.
The **station** of the cow. Dib, M.
The **stationmaster**. Pushkin, A. S.
Stationmaster Fallmerayer. Roth, J.
Stations of the cross. Orringer, J.
STATISTICIANS
Chekhov, A. P. Verotchka
Heinlein, R. A. The year of the jackpot
A **statue** of Aphrodite. Gilchrist, E.

STATUES

Alcott, L. M. Victoria: a woman's statue
Biguenet, J. The work of art
Boylan, C. Ears
Coates, G. S. Plaster of Paris
Davidson, A. Buchanan's head
Davidson, A. The ikon of Elijah
James, H. The last of the Valerii
James, H. Rose-Agathe
Lee, V. The Virgin of the Seven Daggers
Trevor, W. Sacred statues
Wharton, E. The duchess at prayer

Statuesque. Steinbach, M.
STATUETTES *See* Art objects; Statues
The **status** quo. Carlson, R.

Stavans, Ilan

Blimunda
    The Year's best fantasy & horror, twelfth annual collection; edited by Ellen Datlow & Terry Windling

Stay up Late. Lewis, J.
Stay with me. Steinberg, S.
Staying. Dillon, M.
Steak tartare. D'Amato, B.
The **stealer** of dreams. Lumley, B.
Stealing. Fulton, J.
Stealing from the dead. Whitty, J.
Stealing purses. Gussoff, C.
Stealing the dark. Adams, J.
Stealing the llama farm. Zafris, N.
The **steam-powered** word processor. Clarke, A. C.

STEAMBOATS

Dumas, H. Ark of bones
Farrell, C. Fire in their stacks
King, G. The little convent girl

A **Steamer** Trunk. Dybek, S.

Steavenson, Wendell

Gika
    Fishman, B. Wild East; stories from the last frontier; edited with an introduction by Boris Fishman

Steckevicz, Edwin M.

Making the weight
    The Kenyon Review ns24 no2 p7-23 Spr 2002

Steel. Matheson, R.

Steele, Allen M.

Agape among the robots
    Steele, A. M. American beauty; stories
The days between
    The Year's best science fiction, nineteenth annual collection; edited by Gardner Dozois
The death of Captain Future
    The Best alternate history stories of the 20th century; edited by Harry Turtledove with Martin H. Greenberg
The fine art of watching
    Steele, A. M. American beauty; stories
Graceland
    Steele, A. M. American beauty; stories
Green acres
    Steele, A. M. American beauty; stories
Her own private sitcom
    Steele, A. M. American beauty; stories
Jake and the enemy
    Steele, A. M. American beauty; stories
Missing time
    Steele, A. M. American beauty; stories

The teb hunter
    Witpunk; edited by Claude Lalumière and Marty Halpern
Tom Swift and his humongous mechanical dude
    Steele, A. M. American beauty; stories
A walk across Mars
    Mars probes; edited by Peter Crowther
    Steele, A. M. American beauty; stories
Warning warning
    Steele, A. M. American beauty; stories

Steele, Chandra

Respiration
    Pieces; a collection of new voices; edited by Stephen Chbosky

Steele, Max

The unripe heart
    New stories from the South: the year's best, 2002; edited by Shannon Ravenel; with a preface by Larry Brown

Steele, Wilbur Daniel

Blue Murder
    The Best American mystery stories of the century; Tony Hillerman, editor; with an introduction by Tony Hillerman

STEEPLECHASING *See* Horse racing

Steeves, Rafael Franco

The couple and the stranger
    Colchie, T. A whistler in the nightworld; short fiction from the Latin Americas; edited by Thomas Colchie

Stefaniak, Mary Helen

Arlo on the fence
    The Antioch Review v59 no4 p653-65 Fall 2001
Believing Marina
    A different plain; contemporary Nebraska fiction writers; edited by Ladette Randolph ; introduction by Mary Pipher
A note to biographers regarding famous author Flannery O'Connor
    New stories from the South: the year's best, 2000; edited by Shannon Ravenel; with a preface by Ellen Douglas

Stegner, Lynn

Hired man
    Stegner, L. Pipers at the gates of dawn; a triptych
Indian summer
    Stegner, L. Pipers at the gates of dawn; a triptych
Pipers at the gates of dawn
    Stegner, L. Pipers at the gates of dawn; a triptych

Stegner, Wallace Earle

Buglesong
    Still wild; short fiction of the American West, 1950 to the present; edited by Larry McMurtry
Chip off the old block
    The Workshop; seven decades of the Iowa Writers' Workshop: 42 stories, recollections & essays on Iowa's place in 20th-century American literature; edited by Tom Grimes
The colt
    Fishing for chickens; short stories about rural youth; edited, with an introduction by Jim Heynen

Steiber, Ellen
The cats of San Martino
　　Black heart, ivory bones; [edited by] Ellen
　　　Datlow & Terri Windling
The shape of things
　　Death dines at 8:30; edited by Claudia Bishop
　　　and Nick DiChario
Stein, Donna Baier
Coming Clean
　　The Literary Review (Madison, N.J.) v46 no4
　　　p648-54 Summ 2003
Spring 1933
　　The Virginia Quarterly Review v79 no1 p85-
　　　96 Wint 2003
STEIN, GERTRUDE, 1874-1946
About
McGarry, J. The last time
Stanton, M. Ping-pong
Steinbach, Meredith
Statuesque
　　TriQuarterly no117 p218-62 Fall 2003
Tripped Oasis
　　Ploughshares v28 no4 p159-76 Wint
　　　2002/2003
Steinbeck, John
Morgan le Fay
　　Swords and sorcerers; stories from the world
　　　of fantasy and adventure; edited by Clint
　　　Willis
The murder
　　The Best American mystery stories of the
　　　century; Tony Hillerman, editor; with an
　　　introduction by Tony Hillerman
Steinbeck, Thomas
Blighted cargo
　　Steinbeck, T. Down to a soundless sea
Blind luck
　　Steinbeck, T. Down to a soundless sea
The dark watcher
　　Steinbeck, T. Down to a soundless sea
The night guide
　　Steinbeck, T. Down to a soundless sea
Sing Fat and the Imperial Duchess of Woo
　　Steinbeck, T. Down to a soundless sea
An unbecoming grace
　　Steinbeck, T. Down to a soundless sea
The wool gatherer
　　Steinbeck, T. Down to a soundless sea
Steinberg, Janice
Wailing reed
　　Mystery midrash; an anthology of Jewish
　　　mystery & detective fiction; [edited by]
　　　Lawrence W. Raphael
Steinberg, Susan
Away!
　　Steinberg, S. The end of free love
The end of free love
　　Steinberg, S. The end of free love
Far
　　Steinberg, S. The end of free love
Forward
　　Steinberg, S. The end of free love
Isla
　　Steinberg, S. The end of free love
Life
　　Steinberg, S. The end of free love
Nothing
　　Steinberg, S. The end of free love

Opening
　　Steinberg, S. The end of free love
Saturday
　　Steinberg, S. The end of free love
Standstill
　　Steinberg, S. The end of free love
Start
　　Steinberg, S. The end of free love
Stay with me
　　The Massachusetts Review v42 no1 p125-32
　　　Spr 2001
　　Steinberg, S. The end of free love
Testing,
　　New Letters v67 no2 p33-8 2001
　　Steinberg, S. The end of free love
There's a window
　　Steinberg, S. The end of free love
Trees
　　Steinberg, S. The end of free love
Vulgar
　　Steinberg, S. The end of free love
What makes you think
　　Steinberg, S. The end of free love
Winner
　　Steinberg, S. The end of free love
Steiner, George
At five in the afternoon
　　The Kenyon Review ns24 no1 p81-113 Wint
　　　2002
Steiner, Henry
Rice
　　Retrieving bones; stories and poems of the
　　　Korean War; edited and with an introduc-
　　　tion by W. D. Ehrhart and Philip K. Jason
Steinfeld, J. J.
Would you hide me?
　　Dalhousie Review v81 no2 p251-6 Summ
　　　2001
Steinke, Darcey
Song
　　The Literary Review (Madison, N.J.) v47 no2
　　　p15-18 Wint 2004
Steinkoler, Manya
The Body Retriever
　　Literature and Psychology v48 no1/2 p102-14
　　　2002
Steinwachs, Mark
Swimming out to Holly
　　Virgin fiction 2
Stella the spinster's afternoon dreams. Karnezis, P.
Stemple, Adam
A piece of flesh
　　Greenberg, M. H. Faerie tales
Stemple, Jane H. Yolen *See* Yolen, Jane
Step men. Nevai, L.
A **step** off from fathering. Chapman, C. M.
STEPBROTHERS
　　See also Half-brothers
Hardesty, E. Rosie's dance
James, H. Guest's confession
James, H. The impressions of a cousin
Kittredge, W. Thirty-four seasons of winter
Maleti, G. Acedia
Slavin, J. Painting house
STEPCHILDREN
　　See also Stepdaughters; Stepsons
STEPDAUGHTERS
Barnes, S. The woman in the wall
Barthelme, F. From Mars

STEPDAUGHTERS—*Continued*
Blackwood, S. Alias
Knight, M. Mitchell's girls
Stuckey-French, E. Leufredus
STEPFATHERS
Beattie, A. The women of this world
Broughton, T. A. L'americana
Burke, J. Mea culpa
Chapman, C. M. A step off from fathering
Cook, K. L. Marty
DeMarinis, R. Experience
Fairey, W. W. Family pets
Gilchrist, E. The stucco house
Keegan, C. Close to the water's edge
Lopez, B. H. Remembering orchards
Maleti, G. The visit
McCorkle, J. Toads
Robison, M. Smoke
Shade, E. The last night of the county fair
Simpson, M. Approximations
Tester, W. Wet
Stephanie's book [excerpt] Best, M.
STEPHANOPOULOS, GEORGE
About
Beattie, A. The big-breasted pilgrim
Stephen and Anne. Lustig, A.
Stephens, Mariflo
Stone swans
The Virginia Quarterly Review v77 no1 p139-
48 Wint 2001
Stephens, Meic
Damage
The Literary Review (Madison, N.J.) v44 no2
p357-69 Wint 2001
STEPMOTHERS
Barnard, R. Everybody's girl
Bishop, E. The farmer's children
Bloom, A. Light into dark
Bloom, A. Night vision
Cannell, D. The high cost of living
Ferré, R. A poisoned tale
Keegan, C. Burns
Reisman, N. Sharks
Richter, S. A prodigy of longing
Slezak, E. By heart
Sosin, D. You're so simple
White, E. Cinnamon skin
Yolen, J. Snow in summer
The **steppe**. Chekhov, A. P.
Steppenpferd. Aldiss, B. W.
Stepping stone. Vachss, A. H.
Stepping up to the plate. Schofield, S.
Steps [excerpt] Kosinski, J. N.
STEPSISTERS
See also Half-sisters
Hood, A. Joelle's mother
Klass, P. Love and modern medicine
Mazelis, J. The diving girls
Silber, J. Without Ellie
STEPSONS
Asaro, C. Dance in blue
Jones, T. A midnight clear
Joseph, D. If I close them
Leslie, N. A little wild
Stepto, Robert B.
Mendez
Callaloo v24 no4 p1186-93 Fall 2001
STERILITY
Singer, I. B. Altele

Sterling, Bruce
Maneki Neko
The Best from fantasy & science fiction: the
fiftieth anniversary anthology; edited by
Edward L. Ferman and Gordon Van Gelder
Brown, C. N. and Strahan, J. The Locus
awards; thirty years of the best in science
fiction and fantasy; edited by Charles N.
Brown and Jonathan Strahan
Sunken gardens
Worldmakers; SF adventures in terraforming;
edited by Gardner Dozois
Swarm
The Good new stuff; adventure SF in the
grand tradition; edited by Gardner Dozois
Taklamakan
The Year's best science fiction, sixteenth an-
nual collection; edited by Gardner Dozois
Sterling, Bruce and Shiner, Lewis
Mozart in mirrorshades
The Best alternate history stories of the 20th
century; edited by Harry Turtledove with
Martin H. Greenberg
Stern, Daniel
The #63 bus from the Gare de Lyon
Stern, D. In the country of the young; stories
Apraxia
Stern, D. In the country of the young; stories
Chaos
Stern, D. In the country of the young; stories
Comfort
Stern, D. In the country of the young; stories
The exchange
Stern, D. In the country of the young; stories
The fellowship
Prairie Schooner v75 no2 p29-52 Summ 2001
Foxx hunting
Stern, D. In the country of the young; stories
Imperato placeless
Stern, D. In the country of the young; stories
In the country of the young
Stern, D. In the country of the young; stories
Lunch with Gottlieb
Stern, D. In the country of the young; stories
Messenger
Stern, D. In the country of the young; stories
Time will tell
Stern, D. In the country of the young; stories
Stern, Richard G.
Downsized
The Antioch Review v59 no2 p347-70 Spr
2001
Grandpa
Southwest Review v84 no3 p423-39 1999
The illegibility of this world
The Workshop; seven decades of the Iowa
Writers' Workshop: 42 stories, recollections
& essays on Iowa's place in 20th-century
American literature; edited by Tom Grimes
Stern, Steve
Bruno's metamorphosis
Stern, S. The wedding jester
Romance
Stern, S. The wedding jester
The sin of Elijah
Neurotica: Jewish writers on sex; edited by
Melvin Jules Bukiet
Stern, S. The wedding jester

Stern, Steve—*Continued*
Sissman loses his way
Stern, S. The wedding jester
A string around the moon: a children's story
Stern, S. The wedding jester
Swan song
Stern, S. The wedding jester
The tale of a kite
Stern, S. The wedding jester
With signs and wonders; an international anthology of Jewish fabulist fiction; edited by Daniel M. Jaffe
The wedding jester
The Pushcart prize XXIV: best of the small presses; an annual small press reader; edited by Bill Henderson with the Pushcart prize editors
Stern, S. The wedding jester
Yiddish twilight
Stern, S. The wedding jester
Sterne, Melvin
Thanksgiving
South Carolina Review v36 no2 p137-53 Spr 2004
Sterns, Aaron
The third rail
Dreaming down-under; edited by Jack Dann and Janeen Webb
Watchmen
Gathering the bones; original stories from the world's masters of horror; edited by Dennis Etchison, Ramsey Campbell and Jack Dann
Stet. Paul, B.
Stevens, David
What we sell in the room today
Harper's v304 no1821 p25-6 F 2002
Stevens, Francis
The elf trap
Tales before Tolkien; the roots of modern fantasy; edited by Douglas A. Anderson
Stevens, J. David
Hunger
The Paris Review v43 no159 p165-81 Fall 2001
Stevens, R. L. *See* Hoch, Edward D., 1930-
STEVENS, WALLACE, 1879-1955
About
Scholz, C. The amount to carry
STEVENSON, ADLAI, 1930-
About
Southern strategy
Stevenson, James
Notes from a bottle
Wonderful town; New York stories from The New Yorker; edited by David Remnick with Susan Choi
Stevenson, Jane
The Colonel and Judy O'Grady
Stevenson, J. Several deceptions
Crossing the water
Stevenson, J. Several deceptions
The island of the day before yesterday
Stevenson, J. Several deceptions
Law and order
Stevenson, J. Several deceptions
Stevenson, M. M.
The adjustment
The North American Review v284 no2 p39 Mr/Ap 1999

Stevenson, Robert Louis
The bottle imp
The 13 best horror stories of all time; edited by Leslie Pockell
Markheim
Master's choice v2; mystery stories by today's top writers and the masters who inspired them; edited by Lawrence Block
STEVENSON, ROBERT LOUIS, 1850-1894
About
Baker, K. The literary agent
Russell, J. Hides
Stevie. Feliu-Pettet, R.
The **Steviewondermobile**. Touré
Stew. Bauman, B. A.
Steward, D. E.
Gener
The Massachusetts Review v42 no3 p391-6 Aut 2001
Stewart, Barbara A.
Thieves
The North American Review v286 no5 p30-4 S/O 2001
Stewart, Isobel
Can I forget you?
Good Housekeeping v228 no4 p189-90+ Ap 1999
Change of heart
Good Housekeeping v228 no2 p163-66 F 1999
Don't say sorry
Good Housekeeping v233 no2 p185-92 Ag 2001
The homecoming
Good Housekeeping v233 no1 p195-207 Jl 2001
Good Housekeeping v229 no6 p95-96+ D 1999
My sister Alice
Good Housekeeping v236 no5 p241-2, 246-8 My 2003
Stewart, John
The old men used to dance
The Oxford book of Caribbean short stories; edited by Stewart Brown and John Wickham
Stewart, Trenton Lee
In the valley of the shadow
The Georgia Review v53 no1 p107-09 Spr 1999
Moriah
New England Review v24 no2 p52-63 Spr 2003
The **stick**. Frym, G.
The **stick** and the bearded lady. Loomis, N. M.
Stick man. Coover, R.
Sticking Pins in the Chancellor. Trudell, D.
Sticks and stones. Davis, A.
Sticky kisses. Johnson, G.
A **Stiffer** Breeze. Everett, P.
Stifling. Savić, M.
STIGMATIZATION
Biguenet, J. The vulgar soul
Still, James
The nest
Home and beyond; an anthology of Kentucky short stories; edited by Morris Allen Grubbs; with an introduction by Wade Hall and an afterword by Charles E. May

Still among the living. Hoffman, A.
Still life. Malamud, B.
Still life. Mathews, H.
Still life. Sosin, D.
Still Life with Dog. Bain, T.
Still-life with particle board. Buck, C.
Still life with plaster. Erian, A.
The still point. Simonds, M.
The still point of the turning world. Highsmith, P.
Still searching. Davies, R.
Still the same old story. Busch, F.
Stillness. Brkic, C. A.

Stillwell, Christy
  Telly's Body Shop
    The Massachusetts Review v44 no3 p474-93
      Fall 2003

Stine, Peter
  Boxcars, 1974
    Iowa Review v32 no3 p94-8 Wint 2002/2003
  Meat Squad, 1982
    Iowa Review v32 no3 p102-10 Wint 2002/2003
  Out-of-Work Line, 1980
    Iowa Review v32 no3 p99-101 Wint 2002/2003

The sting of Señorita Scorpion. Savage, L., Jr.
Stir crazy. Boswell, M.
Stitch. Dowling, T.
Stitch and bitch. Wright, J. B.
Stitches. Nelson, A.
Stitches in time. Louise, D. D.

STOCK EXCHANGE
  DeMarco, T. Dancing bare
  Harrison, C. The commuter
  Paine, T. A predictable nightmare on the eve of the stock market first breaking 6,000

Stockton, Frank
  The Griffin and the minor canon
    The American fantasy tradition; edited by Brian M. Thomsen
    Tales before Tolkien; the roots of modern fantasy; edited by Douglas A. Anderson

Stoker, Bram
  Dracula's guest
    The 13 best horror stories of all time; edited by Leslie Pockell
  The Jewel of Seven Stars
    Into the mummy's tomb; edited by John Richard Stephens

STOKER, BRAM, 1847-1912
  Parodies, imitations, etc.
  Barrett, J. A most electrifying evening
  Bennett, N. and Elrod, P. N. Wolf and hound
  Bergstrom, E. The three boxes
  Bogen, K. B. Good help
  Braunbeck, G. A. Curtain call
  Conrad, R. L. The dark downstairs
  DeWeese, G. An essay on containment
  Gruss, A. L. and Kingsgrave-Ernstein, C. Beast
  Huff, T. To each his own kind
  Kilpatrick, N. Berserker
  Nye, J. L. Everything to order
  Proctor, J. Dear Mr. Bernard Shaw
  Saberhagen, F. Box number fifty
  Sinor, B. H. "Places for act two!"
  Yarbro, C. Q. Long-term investment
  Zaget, B. Renfield; or, Dining at the bughouse

Stolar, Daniel
  Crossing over
    Stolar, D. The middle of the night
  Fundamentals
    Stolar, D. The middle of the night
  Home in New Hampshire
    Stolar, D. The middle of the night
  Jack Landers is my friend
    Stolar, D. The middle of the night
  Marriage lessons
    Stolar, D. The middle of the night
  The Middle of the Night
    Bomb no83 p104-6, 108-11 Spr 2003
  Mourning
    Ramaya, S. Operation monsoon; stories
  Release
    The Virginia Quarterly Review v80 no3 p180-98 Summ 2004
  Second son
    Stolar, D. The middle of the night
  The trip home
    Stolar, D. The middle of the night

The stolen child. Boylan, C.
Stolen chocolates. Hegi, U.
Stolen Hearts. Zipes, D. and Zipes, J.
Stolen horses. Lopez, B. H.
Stolen Kisses. Hooper, C.
Stolen Photo. Haines, L.
The Stolen Wife. Yolen, J.

Stollman, Aryeh Lev
  The adornment of days
    Stollman, A. L. The dialogues of time and entropy
  The creation of Anat
    Stollman, A. L. The dialogues of time and entropy
  The dialogues of time and entropy
    Stollman, A. L. The dialogues of time and entropy
  Enfleurage
    Stollman, A. L. The dialogues of time and entropy
  Die grosse Liebe
    Lost tribe; jewish fiction from the edge
    Stollman, A. L. The dialogues of time and entropy
  If I have found favor in your eyes
    Stollman, A. L. The dialogues of time and entropy
  The little poet
    Stollman, A. L. The dialogues of time and entropy
  Mr. Mitochondria
    Stollman, A. L. The dialogues of time and entropy
  New memories
    Stollman, A. L. The dialogues of time and entropy
  The seat of higher consciousness
    Stollman, A. L. The dialogues of time and entropy

Stone, Robert
  Dominion
    The New Yorker v75 no40 p76-82+ D 27 1999-Ja 3 2000
  Fun with Problems
    The New Yorker v78 no19 p68-77 Jl 15 2002

STONE, SHARON
About
Brandt, W. The Jean-Paul Sartre experience
Stone, Weldon
The big buffalo bass
Fishing's best short stories; edited by Paul D. Staudohar
STONE CARVING
Bear, G. Petra
Vivante, A. Stones aplenty
Stone fish. Spatz, G.
The **stone** girl. Wegner, H.
The **stone** hot-water bottle. Brennan, M.
A **stone** house of many rooms. Lundquist, R.
A **stone** of destiny. Davidson, J.
Stone or Water. Thompson, J. L.
Stone swans. Stephens, M.
A **Stone** Woman. Byatt, A. S.
STONECUTTERS
Hawthorne, N. Ethan Brand
Stonehands and the tigress. Barnes, H. L.
Stones. Gilliland, G.
Stones. Hoffman, W.
Stoop ladies. Krasnoff, B.
The **Stop**. Rheinheimer, K.
Stop breakin down. McManus, J.
Stop breaking down. McManus, J.
Stop frame. Philip, M. N.
Stop the fight!. Katkov, N.
Stop the Rocket. Smith, R. T.
Stop, thief!. Groves, J. W.
The **store**. Chitwood, M.
The **storekeeper**. Haschemeyer, O.
STORES
Daniels, J. Bonus
Engel, M. P. Dis aliter visum
Frym, G. Sleepy
Lao She. An old and established name
Tippens, E. Make a wish
Storey, Donna George
Courtesan with a Lover
Gettysburg Review v17 no1 p5-16 Spr 2004
Hot Spring
Prairie Schooner v76 no4 p115-24 Wint 2002
STORIES ABOUT DIARIES *See* Diaries (Stories about)
STORIES ABOUT LETTERS *See* Letters (Stories about)
Stories for men. Kessel, J.
STORIES IN DIARY FORM *See* Diaries (Stories in diary form)
STORIES OF THE FUTURE *See* Future
Stories of the hunt. Mindt, A.
Stories that could not be true. Cooley, N.
The **stork-men**. Goytisolo, J.
The **storm**. Chopin, K.
The **storm**. Dozois, G. R.
Storm-tossed. Joyce, M.
Storm warnings. Pickard, N.
Storm watch. Penn, W. S.
Storming the cosmos. Rucker, R. v. B.
STORMS
See also Hurricanes; Tornadoes
Brennan, M. A snowy night on West Forty-ninth Street
Brown, J. Afternoon of the Sassanoa
Chekhov, A. P. On official duty
Davies, R. I will keep her company
Davis, A. Red lights like laughter

DeMarinis, R. Under the wheat
Dozois, G. R. The storm
Dufresne, J. Johnny too bad
Gass, W. H. The Pedersen kid
Hall, D. Christmas snow
Heynen, J. What happened during the ice storm
Jones, E. P. A dark night
L'Amour, L. Meeting at Falmouth
Mason, B. A. Thunder snow
Mathews, H. Their words, for you
Meloy, M. Garrison Junction
Oliver, C. A lake of summer
Proulx, A. The half-skinned steer
Pushkin, A. S. The blizzard
Singer, I. B. The blizzard
Singer, I. B. There are no coincidences
Steinbeck, T. The night guide
Thompson, J. Ice angels
Updike, J. Unstuck
Storms. Keegan, C.
Stormy, mon amour. Hendricks, V.
Stormy Weather: Yin Tian. Chi, S. Y.
The **story**. Bloom, A.
Story. Montemarano, N.
The **story**. Pearlman, E.
The **story** about a bus driver who wanted to be God. Keret, E.
A **story** about someone else. Foster, K.
The **story** from Rosendo Juárez. Borges, J. L.
A **story** from the eighties. Händler, E.-W.
The **story** of a cat. Porzecanski, T.
The **story** of a conscience. Bierce, A.
The **story** of a horse. Babel', I.
The **story** of a masterpiece. James, H.
Story of a parrot. Menendez, A.
Story of a Teacher's Wife. Orner, P.
The **story** of a year. James, H.
The **story** of Ali Baba and the forty thieves. Wiggin, K. D. S. and Smith, N. A.
The **story** of an hour. Chopin, K.
The **story** of Bras-Coupé. Cable, G. W.
The **story** of Hu. Painter, P.
The **story** of Lahcen and Idir. Bowles, P.
The **Story** of Lalò. Spaziani, M. L.
The **story** of my dovecote. Babel', I.
The **story** of my life. Edwards, K.
The **story** of my travels. O'Connor, M. B.
A **story** of Rios and Juan Jesus. Ortiz, S. J.
The **story** of Rosa Brava. Régio, J.
The **story** of rough niall of the speckled rock. Jacobs, J.
The **Story** of the Crooked Woman. Hahn, B.
The **story** of the deep dark. Whitty, J.
The **story** of the door. Huddle, D.
The **story** of the German parachutist who landed forty-two years late. Mathews, A.
The **story** of the lizard who had the habit of dining on his wives. Galeano, E. H.
Story of the warrior and the captive maiden. Borges, J. L.
Story of your life. Chiang, T.
The **story** story. Locklin, G.
The **story** that won't go away. Keyes, J.
A **story** with a pattern. Lavin, M.
A **story** with no address. Hendel, Y.
STORY WITHIN A STORY
Alarcón, P. A. d. The tall woman
Alcott, L. M. Mabel's May day

STORY WITHIN A STORY—*Continued*

Alcott, L. M. The monk's island: a legend of the Rhine
Anderson, P. The problem of pain
Bass, R. The hermit's story
Berberova, N. About the hooks
Berberova, N. The Billancourt manuscript
Biguenet, J. And never come up
Borges, J. L. The shape of the sword
Boroson, R. The roussalka
Boyle, T. C. Going down
Breen, J. L. Immortality
Bunin, I. A. Ida
Caudwell, S. The triumph of Eve
Chekhov, A. P. About love
Chekhov, A. P. Gooseberries
Chekhov, A. P. The head-gardener's story
Chekhov, A. P. The man in a case
Chekhov, A. P. Zinotchka
Cherry, K. Love in the Middle Ages
Chesnutt, C. W. The conjurer's revenge
Chesnutt, C. W. Dave's neckliss
Chesnutt, C. W. A deep sleeper
Chesnutt, C. W. The dumb witness
Chesnutt, C. W. The gray wolf's ha'nt
Chesnutt, C. W. Hot-foot Hannibal
Chesnutt, C. W. Lonesome Ben
Chesnutt, C. W. Mars Jeems's nightmare
Chesnutt, C. W. Po' Sandy
Chesnutt, C. W. Sis' Becky's pickaninny
Clarke, A. C. Hide-and-seek
Clarke, A. C. The pacifist
Clarke, A. C. Patent pending
Collymore, F. Some people are meant to live alone
Fish, R. L. The wager
Friesner, E. M. Auntie Elspeth's Halloween story; or, The gourd, the bad, and the ugly
Hall, D. Argument and persuasion
Hermann, J. The red coral bracelet
Hodgson, W. H. From the tideless sea, part one
Hodgson, W. H. From the tideless sea, part two: further news of the Homebird
Jaffe, D. M. Sarrushka and her daughter
James, H. The sweetheart of M. Briseux
Lavin, M. A story with a pattern
Lawrence, D. H. A fragment of stained glass
Lincoln, C. A hook will sometimes keep you
Lincoln, C. Last will
Lundquist, R. A stone house of many rooms
Marías, J. What the butler said
Meloy, M. Last of the white slaves
Menendez, A. Hurricane stories
Nevins, F. M., Jr. Fair game
Oates, J. C. The high school sweetheart
Oren, Y. The Cat Man
Ortiz, S. J. Pennstuwehniyaahtse: Quuti's story
Paine, T. The hotel on Monkey Forest Road
Pickard, N. Dr. Couch saves a cat
Rendell, R. Fair exchange
Rodwell, I. and Duffy, S. The penny drops
Rossi, A. Orion's glow
Russo, R. The whore's child
Sarrantonio, A. Pumpkin head
Singer, I. B. The blizzard
Singer, I. B. The enemy
Singer, I. B. The gravedigger
Singer, I. B. Loshikl
Singer, I. B. The manuscript

Singer, I. B. Moon and madness
Singer, I. B. A night in the poorhouse
Singer, I. B. Not for the Sabbath
Singer, I. B. The parrot
Singer, I. B. Passions
Singer, I. B. Runners to nowhere
Singer, I. B. The secret
Singer, I. B. The sorcerer
Singer, I. B. A tale of two sisters
Singer, I. B. Two weddings and one divorce
Singer, I. B. The wager
Stevenson, J. The Colonel and Judy O'Grady
Straub, P. Perdido: a fragment from a work in progress
Wellen, E. The perfect rotter
Yarbrough, S. Veneer
Zweig, S. Amok

A **story** without a title. Chekhov, A. P.
A **story** without an end. Chekhov, A. P.
Story without words. Čapek, K.
The **storyteller**. Cardoso, O. J.
Storytellers without souls. Tawada, Y.

STORYTELLING

Antoni, R. My grandmother's tale of the buried treasure and how she defeated the King of Chacachacari and the entire American Army with her venus-flytraps
Bear, G. The white horse child
Berry, W. Turn back the bed
Cardoso, O. J. The storyteller
Chesnutt, C. W. Dave's neckliss
De Lint, C. Forest of stone
Dyson, J. All in the telling
Esterházy, P. Roberto narrates
Firth, C. The Department of Nothing
Forsyth, F. The miracle
Fowler, C. Learning to let go
Gaiman, N. October in the chair
House, R. Gabe and the doctor
Kingrea, Eric. A waltz in the snow
Leslie, N. Bigger than life
Painter, P. Island tales
Ponte, A. J. The summer in a barbershop
Tawada, Y. Storytellers without souls
Tillman, L. To find words
Tuma, H. The Waldiba story
Updike, J. Should wizard hit mommy?
Vega, A. L. Eye-openers
Yolen, J. The traveler and the tale
Zinik, Z. A pickled nose

Storytelling. Gordon, M.

Stösser, Achim
Magnifying glass
Prairie Schooner v73 no3 p68-69 Fall 1999

Stout, Rex
Fourth of July picnic
A Century of great suspense stories; edited by Jeffery Deaver
Poison à la carte
Murder most delectable; savory tales of culinary crimes; edited by Martin H. Greenberg

The **stout** of heart. Shepard, S.

Straight, Susan
Back
Breaking into print; early stories and insights into getting published; a Ploughshares anthology; edited by DeWitt Henry

Straight, Susan—*Continued*

Mines

The Best American short stories, 2003; selected from U.S. and Canadian magazines by
Walter Mosley with Katrina Kenison; with
an introduction by Walter Mosley

Straight fiction. Amis, M.

Strand, Ginger

Lucky

Gettysburg Review v14 no3 p464-7 Aut 2001

Third arm

Gettysburg Review v14 no3 p459-63 Aut
2001

The **stranded** man. Dixon, S.

Strandquist, Robert

The car

Strandquist, R. The inanimate world; stories

Clean room

Strandquist, R. The inanimate world; stories

Collecting shadows

Strandquist, R. The inanimate world; stories

Deeper than the world

Strandquist, R. The inanimate world; stories

Frank's friends

Strandquist, R. The inanimate world; stories

Groman Creek

Strandquist, R. The inanimate world; stories

The inanimate world

Strandquist, R. The inanimate world; stories

Real family

Strandquist, R. The inanimate world; stories

Thrill kill

Strandquist, R. The inanimate world; stories

Turn me on, dead man

Strandquist, R. The inanimate world; stories

Strange attractors. Jenkins, G.

Strange bedfellows. Kahn, M. A.

A **strange** brown fruit. Meyers, K.

Strange creatures. Rusch, K. K.

Strange matter. Mora, T.

Strange new homeland. Freidson, M.

A **Strange** Place. Cole, I.F.

The **stranger**. Pritchard Jones, H.

Stranger. Schwartz, S.

The **stranger**. Ziegler, I.

A **Stranger** in America. Kim, C.

Strangers. Dozois, G. R.

Strangers and pilgrims. Sanford, A.

Strangers on a plane. Smith, J.

Strangers when we meet. Kureishi, H.

The **strangest** feeling in Bernard's bathroom.
Mathews, A.

Stransky, Oonagh

(jt. auth) See Spaziani, Maria Luisa

Strasser, Dirk

The doppelganger effect

Dreaming down-under; edited by Jack Dann
and Janeen Webb

Straub, Peter

Ashputtle

Straub, P. Magic terror; seven tales

Bunny is good bread

Straub, P. Magic terror; seven tales

The ghost village

Straub, P. Magic terror; seven tales

Hunger, an introduction

Ghost writing; haunted tales by contemporary
writers; edited by Roger Weingarten

Straub, P. Magic terror; seven tales

Isn't it romantic?

Straub, P. Magic terror; seven tales

Mr. Clubb and Mr. Cuff

Best new horror 10; edited and with an introduction by Stephen Jones

Straub, P. Magic terror; seven tales

The Year's best fantasy & horror, twelfth annual collection; edited by Ellen Datlow &
Terry Windling

Perdido: a fragment from a work in progress

The Museum of horrors; edited by Dennis
Etchison

Pork pie hat

Best new horror 11; edited and with an introduction by Stephen Jones

Straub, P. Magic terror; seven tales

A regular pair of minstrels

Esquire v135 no1 p84-5 Ja 2001

Ronald, D_____!

Murder in the family; [by] the Adams Round
Table

Strauch, Thomas J.

The Alberscine's vigil

The Darkest thirst; a vampire anthology

Straus, Dorothea

What is this thing called love?

Raritan v21 no1 p148-53 Summ 2001

Strauss, Alix

Addressing the dead

Strauss, A. The joy of funerals; a novel in
stories

The joy of funerals

Strauss, A. The joy of funerals; a novel in
stories

Post-dated

Strauss, A. The joy of funerals; a novel in
stories

Recovering Larry

Strauss, A. The joy of funerals; a novel in
stories

Shrinking away

Strauss, A. The joy of funerals; a novel in
stories

Still life

Strauss, A. The joy of funerals; a novel in
stories

Swimming without Annette

Strauss, A. The joy of funerals; a novel in
stories

Versions of you

Strauss, A. The joy of funerals; a novel in
stories

The way you left

Strauss, A. The joy of funerals; a novel in
stories

STRAUSS, RICHARD, 1864-1949

About

Blish, J. A work of art

Strawberries. Roth, J.

Strawberry cream. James, S.

Strawberry spring. King, S.

The **stray**. Evans, L.

Stray. Fracis, S. H.

Stray cats. Van Daele, R.

Stray dogs. Norris, L.

Strayed, Cheryl
Good
  Kulka, J. and Danford, N. The New American voices 2003; guest editor Joyce Carol Oates; series editors John Kulka and Natalie Danford
Strays. Chinodya, S.
Strays. Davis, L.
Strays. Hardy, M.
Strays. Reisman, N.
Strays. Richard, M.
STREAM OF CONSCIOUSNESS
Arenas, R. The parade ends
Barthelme, D. The school
Bowles, P. Massachusetts 1932
Bowles, P. New York 1965
Bowles, P. Tangier 1975
Bunin, I. A. Late hour
Disch, T. M. The squirrel cage
Händler, E.-W. Max
Lao She. Ding
Mathews, H. The network
Michaels, L. In the fifties
Saroyan, W. Resurrection of a life
Schnitzler, A. Fräulein Else
Sorrentino, G. A beehive arranged on humane principles
Sorrentino, G. Decades
Updike, J. Leaves
Updike, J. The music school
Stream of consciousness. Lupoff, R. A.
Streckfuss, Adolf
The Star Tavern
  Early German and Austrian detective fiction; an anthology; translated and edited by Mary W. Tannert and Henry Kratz
A **street** was chosen. Campbell, R.
The **streets** of Ashkelon. Harrison, H.
The **Streets** of Laredo. Henry, W.
Strength. Kelman, J.
Strickland, Lee
Animal sounds
  Gettysburg Review v12 no3 p497-507 Aut 1999
A goldfish, a plant, a bowl of fresh fruit
  Gettysburg Review v14 no4 p609-22 Wint 2001
Paper trail
  Gettysburg Review v14 no1 p89-101 Spr 2001
Stride. Reed, R.
Strieber, Whitley
Hole in the head
  Murder in the family; [by] the Adams Round Table
Strike, Johnny
Crazy Carl's thing
  Carved in rock; short stories by musicians; edited by Greg Kihn
Strike-pay. Lawrence, D. H.
Strikebreaker. Asimov, I.
STRIKES AND LOCKOUTS
Asimov, I. Strikebreaker
Heinlein, R. A. The roads must roll
Lawrence, D. H. Strike-pay
McPherson, J. A. A loaf of bread
A **string** around the moon: a children's story. Stern, S.

Stringer, Sandra
The Girl in Snow
  Confrontation no86/87 p221-8 Spr/Summ 2004
Strip Battleship. Brown, A. K.
The **stripper**. Boucher, A.
STRIPTEASERS
Boswell, M. Stir crazy
Gelb, J. Perfection
Johnson, D. Break any woman down
Lovisi, G. Service
Matthews, C. I'm a dirty girl
Reifler, N. See through
Troy, M. Mercy the midget
Strober, Robin
Poker face
  Hers 2: brilliant new fiction by lesbian writers; edited by Terry Wolverton with Robert Drake
STROKE *See* Cerebrovascular disease
The **stroke** of midnight. Balza, J.
Strom, Dao
Chickens
  Still wild; short fiction of the American West, 1950 to the present; edited by Larry McMurtry
Strong at the broken places. Westmoreland, T. A.
Stross, Charles
Antibodies
  The Year's best science fiction, eighteenth annual collection; edited by Gardner Dozois
A colder war
  The Year's best science fiction, eighteenth annual collection; edited by Gardner Dozois
Halo
  The Year's best science fiction; twentieth annual collection; edited by Gardner Dozois
Lobsters
  Nebula awards showcase 2004; edited by Vonda McIntyre
  The Year's best science fiction, nineteenth annual collection; edited by Gardner Dozois
Rogue farm
  The year's best science fiction: twenty-first annual collection; edited by Gardner Dozois
Strout, Elizabeth
Winter concert
  Ms. v9 no6 p74-80 O/N 1999
Structure. Kohler, S.
Structure is constant. Patterson, K.
Struloeff, Cynthia
The Sugar Shell
  Iowa Review v34 no2 p1-18 Fall 2004
Struloeff, John
It comes back
  The Literary Review (Madison, N.J.) v44 no4 p755-63 Summ 2001
Struthers, Ann
Election
  The North American Review v286 no6 p37-43 N/D 2001
Struwwelpeter. Hirshberg, G.
Stuart, Dabney
Bed and breakfast
  Stuart, D. No visible means of support; stories
The egg lady
  Stuart, D. No visible means of support; stories

Stuart, Dabney—*Continued*
Loose ends
  Stuart, D. No visible means of support; stories
No visible means of support
  Stuart, D. No visible means of support; stories
One good turn
  Stuart, D. No visible means of support; stories
Stuart, J. E. B. *See* Stuart, Jeb, 1833-1864
Stuart, James Ewell Brown *See* Stuart, Jeb, 1833-1864
Stuart, Jane
The affair with Rachel Ware
  Home and beyond; an anthology of Kentucky short stories; edited by Morris Allen Grubbs; with an introduction by Wade Hall and an afterword by Charles E. May
STUART, JEB, 1833-1864
    About
Garcia y Robertson, R. Forever free
Stuart, Jesse
Lost land of youth
  Home and beyond; an anthology of Kentucky short stories; edited by Morris Allen Grubbs; with an introduction by Wade Hall and an afterword by Charles E. May
Stuart. Smith, Z.
Stubbs, Harry Clement *See* Clement, Hal, 1922-2003
The **stucco** house. Gilchrist, E.
Stuckey-French, Elizabeth
Blessing
  Stuckey-French, E. The first paper girl in Red Oak, Iowa and other stories
Doodlebug
  Stuckey-French, E. The first paper girl in Red Oak, Iowa and other stories
Electric wizard
  Stuckey-French, E. The first paper girl in Red Oak, Iowa and other stories
Famous poets
  Stuckey-French, E. The first paper girl in Red Oak, Iowa and other stories
The first paper girl in Red Oak, Iowa
  Stuckey-French, E. The first paper girl in Red Oak, Iowa and other stories
Junior
  Stuckey-French, E. The first paper girl in Red Oak, Iowa and other stories
Leufredus
  Stuckey-French, E. The first paper girl in Red Oak, Iowa and other stories
Mudlavia
  Atlantic Monthly (1993) v292 no2 p121-4, 126-8, 130-2, 134 S 2003
Plywood rabbit
  Stuckey-French, E. The first paper girl in Red Oak, Iowa and other stories
Professor claims he found formula for ancient steel
  Stuckey-French, E. The first paper girl in Red Oak, Iowa and other stories
Scavenger hunt
  Stuckey-French, E. The first paper girl in Red Oak, Iowa and other stories

Search and rescue
  Stuckey-French, E. The first paper girl in Red Oak, Iowa and other stories
The visible man
  Stuckey-French, E. The first paper girl in Red Oak, Iowa and other stories
Stuckrad-Barre, Benjamin von
Laundromat
  Chicago Review v48 no2/3 p300-2 Summ 2002
The **student**. Chekhov, A. P.
STUDENTS
    See also College life; College students; School life; Seminarians; Youth
Aboulela, L. The museum
Adams, A. Winter rain
Araújo, H. Asthmatic
Berkman, P. R. Veronica
Bunin, I. A. Zoyka and Valeriya
Carlson, R. Hartwell
Chekhov, A. P. Anyuta
Chekhov, A. P. Volodya
Coates, G. S. A pine tree
Erian, A. You
James, H. The pupil
Johnson-Davies, D. Mr. Pritchard
Joseph, D. Windows and words
Lee, R. Fialta
Michaels, L. Manikin
Ponte, A. J. Tears in the Congri
Richmond, M. Fifth grade: a criminal history
Robison, M. An amateur's guide to the night
Robison, M. Trying
Schickler, D. The smoker
Solari, M. T. Death and transfiguration of a teacher
Spencer, E. The Bufords
Vivante, A. The Italian class
Vivante, A. Osage orange
Vivante, A. The sugar maples
Williams, J. Spring is now
Studio dick drowns near Malibu. Baker, K.
A **study** in emerald. Gaiman, N.
A **study** in orange. Tremayne, P.
The **stuff** of heroes. Friesner, E. M.
The **stump-grubber**. Lindgren, T.
STUNT MEN
Leonard, E. Tenkiller
The **stunted** house. Lamsley, T.
Stuntman. Vachss, A. H.
Stupendous. Harvey, J.
Stupid animals. Derby, M.
Stupid girl. Berney, L.
A **stupid** story. Bottoms, G.
The **Sturbridge** tale. Gilliland, G.
Sturgeon, Theodore
Bianca's hands
  Sturgeon, T. Selected stories
Bright segment
  Sturgeon, T. Selected stories
The golden helix
  Sturgeon, T. Selected stories
It
  Sturgeon, T. Selected stories
Killdozer!
  Sturgeon, T. Selected stories
The man who lost the sea
  Sturgeon, T. Selected stories

Sturgeon, Theodore—*Continued*

Microcosmic god

    The Science fiction hall of fame: volume one, 1929-1964; the greatest science fiction stories of all time chosen by the members of the Science Fiction Writers of America; edited by Robert Silverberg

Mr. Costello, hero

    Sturgeon, T. Selected stories

A saucer of loneliness

    Masterpieces: the best science fiction of the century; edited by Orson Scott Card

The sex opposite

    Sturgeon, T. Selected stories

The skills of Xanadu

    Sturgeon, T. Selected stories

Slow sculpture

    The American fantasy tradition; edited by Brian M. Thomsen

    Sturgeon, T. Selected stories

Thunder and roses

    Sturgeon, T. Selected stories

A way of thinking

    Sturgeon, T. Selected stories

The [widget], the [wadget], and boff

    Sturgeon, T. Selected stories

Stutter step. Lutz, J.

STUTTERING

Lutz, J. Stutter step

Orringer, J. Note to sixth-grade self

Styopa. Bunin, I. A.

Stypes, Aaron

Magnolia stellata

    The North American Review v288 no3/4 p47-52 My/Ag 2003

Styx and bones. Bryant, E.

Su, David Li-qun

Beijing opera [excerpt]

    The Vintage book of contemporary Chinese fiction; edited by Carolyn Choa and David Su Li-qun

Su, Shu-yang *See* Su Shuyang, 1938-

Su, T'ung *See* Su Tong, 1963-

Su Liqun *See* Su, David Li-qun, 1945-

Su Shuyang

Between life and death

    The Vintage book of contemporary Chinese fiction; edited by Carolyn Choa and David Su Li-qun

Su Tong

Cherry

    The Vintage book of contemporary Chinese fiction; edited by Carolyn Choa and David Su Li-qun

Young Muo

    The Vintage book of contemporary Chinese fiction; edited by Carolyn Choa and David Su Li-qun

Suárez, Patricia

An Encounter on a Train

    The Literary Review (Madison, N.J.) v47 no2 p19-26 Wint 2004

Suarez, Virgil

The Soviet circus comes to Havana

    Western Humanities Review v56 no1 p84-92 Spr 2002

Submarine races. Olsen, S. S.

The **submariners**. Brown, J.

SUBMARINES

Clark, S. Fenian ram

Clarke, A. C. Cold war

Clarke, A. C. Hate

Submersion. Sosin, D.

Substitutes. Eggers, P.

Subterranean river. Arredondo, I.

Suburban blight. Lamsley, T.

SUBURBAN LIFE

    See also Commuters

Bail, M. Life of the party

Barthelme, F. Domestic

Boyle, T. C. Rara avis

Bukiet, M. J. The suburbiad

Carlson, R. Towel season

Cheever, J. The country husband

Cheever, J. The swimmer

Cobb, W. J. For all you dorks, blah blah blah

Deane, J. F. Nighthawk

Ellin, S. Reasons unknown

Greer, A. S. How it was for me

Homes, A. M. The Chinese lesson

Homes, A. M. Rockets round the moon

Knight, M. Dogfight

Mueller, D. Torturing creatures at night

Swan, M. Max-1970

Symons, J. The tigers of Subtopia

Thompson, J. Fire dreams

The **suburbiad**. Bukiet, M. J.

SUBURBS *See* Suburban life

SUBVERSIVE ACTIVITIES

    See also Terrorism

SUBWAYS

Budnitz, J. Train

Colgan, J. The wrong train

Dyson, J. City deep

Grodstein, L. John on the train: a fable for our cynical friends

Honig, L. No friends, all strangers

Kelman, J. Some thoughts that morning

Kilpatrick, N. The middle of nowhere

Oates, J. C. Subway

Sorrentino, G. Subway

Starr, G. Tuberama: a musical on the Northern Line (or how to be in touch with your emotions)

Zinik, Z. Mind the doors

SUCCESS

    See also Ambition

DeMarco, T. Lieutenant America and Miss Apple Pie

Engel, M. P. Unnatural acts

Gifford, B. A really happy man

Hawley, L. The good life

Roth, P. Smart money

Success of a mission. Collins, M.

Success story. Banks, R.

SUCCESSION *See* Inheritance and succession

The **successor**. Bowles, P.

Succor. Allen, D., Jr.

Such a good girl. Gorman, E.

Such a pretty face. Grodstein, L.

Such dedication. Watson, I.

Sucher, Cheryl Pearl

Murmuring

    Southwest Review v86 no1 p72-80 Wint 2001

The quality of being a Ruby

    Neurotica: Jewish writers on sex; edited by Melvin Jules Bukiet

Suckers. Naipaul, V. S.
Sucking stones. Kureishi, H.
SUDAN
 Johnson-Davies, D. The garden of Sheikh Osman
SUDDEN INFANT DEATH SYNDROME
 Klass, P. Love and modern medicine
 Louis, L. G. Her slow and steady
 Watanabe McFerrin, L. Los mariachis del muerto
Sudden mysteries. Iribarne, M.
A **sudden** new city. Saunders, G.
The **sudden** physical development of Debra Dupuis. Campbell, B. J.
SUFFERING
 See also Good and evil; Pain
 Schwartz, L. S. Referred pain
SUFFOLK (ENGLAND) *See* England—Suffolk
SUFFRAGE
 Butler, R. O. The ironworkers' hayride
Sugar. Reifler, N.
Sugar among the chickens. Nordan, L.
Sugar and Salt. Rosca, N.
Sugar City. Billman, J.
Sugar Creek. Bean, B.
Sugar, Magic, Grace. Vandiver, E. B.
Sugar peas. Schlink, B.
The **Sugar** Shell. Struloeff, C.
The **sugar-tit**. Cooke, C.
Sugarbaby. Gay, W.
Sui Sin Far
 Away Down in Jamaica
 Legacy v21 no1 p90-5 2004
SUICIDE
 Abrams, T. The good doctor
 Agee, J. The suicide who came to visit
 Aquin, H. Back on April eleventh
 Arenas, R. End of a story
 Arenas, R. Something is happening on the top floor
 Banner, K. The smallest people alive
 Baumer, J. R. The party over there
 Bausch, R. Rare & endangered species
 Berners, G. H. T.-W., Baron. Percy Wallingford
 Bernhard, T. Amras
 Bernhard, T. Playing Watten
 Bhattacharyya, R. Loss
 Blair, J. A small church in the country
 Blake, J. C. Texas woman blues
 Block, L. A moment of wrong thinking
 Bloom, A. Silver water
 Bly, C. Chuck's money
 Bly, C. The tomcat's wife
 Bowles, P. Julian Vreden
 Brewer, G. The gesture
 Bunin, I. A. Caucasus
 Burford, M. David and Kitty
 Calisher, H. In Greenwich, there are many gravelled walks
 Carson, J. Brilliant company
 Carter, E. Cute in camouflage
 Carver, R. Bright red apples
 Carver, R. The third thing that killed my father off
 Cather, W. Paul's case
 Chalker, J. L. Dance band on the Titanic
 Chaon, D. Burn with me
 Chapman, C. M. Honey well hung
 Chekhov, A. P. Volodya

 Coleman, J. C. Ruby's cape
 Cooke, J. P. After you've gone
 Cortázar, J. Letter to a young lady in Paris
 D'Ambrosio, C., Jr. Open house
 Daniels, J. Bonus
 Daniels, J. Karaoke moon
 Davies, R. The Fashion Plate
 Davis, A. Circling the drain
 Deane, J. F. Poste restante
 DeMarinis, R. Disneyland
 Dokey, R. The suicide
 Doran, M. M. Golden anniversary
 Eggers, P. The year five
 Estep, M. The patient
 Estep, M. Tools
 Evans, E. Suicide's girlfriend
 Furman, L. That boy
 Gay, W. Come home, come home, it's suppertime
 Gay, W. Crossroads blues
 Gay, W. I hate to see that evening sun go down
 Gilchrist, E. Among the mourners
 Giles, M. Two words
 Glover, D. H. Iglaf and Swan
 Glover, D. H. Why I decide to kill myself and other jokes
 Goodis, D. The plunge
 Greer, R. O. Grief
 Harrison, H. Portrait of the artist
 Haskell, J. Capucine
 Hegi, U. Freitod
 Hensley, J. L. Decision
 Herling, G. The height of summer: a Roman story
 Hill, K. The anointed
 Hodgen, C. The tender of unmarked graves
 Jackson, V. F. A small independence
 James, H. Osborne's revenge
 Kavan, A. The zebra-struck
 Keegan, C. The Ginger Rogers sermon
 Keret, E. Kneller's happy campers
 Klass, P. The province of the bearded fathers
 Lipsyte, S. Admiral of the Swiss Navy
 Marsten, R. Every morning
 Matthews, C. Belated revenge
 Means, D. The woodcutter
 Michaels, L. Manikin
 Millar, M. The couple next door
 Mueller, D. Ice breaking
 Munro, A. Comfort
 Nissen, T. When the rain washes you clean you'll know
 Niven, L. All the myriad ways
 Nolan, W. F. An act of violence
 Nordan, L. Tombstone
 Oates, J. C. Aiding and abetting
 Oates, J. C. Au sable
 Oates, J. C. A Manhattan romance
 O'Callaghan, M. Wolf winter
 O'Connell, M. The patron saint of travelers
 Ozick, C. The pagan rabbi
 Paddock, J. And when I should feel something
 Pickard, N. Afraid all the time
 Pittalwala, I. Trivedi Park
 Rheinheimer, K. Shoes
 Richter, S. Goodnight
 Robinson, P. April in Paris
 Robison, M. Pretty ice
 Rucker, R. v. B. In frozen time

SUICIDE—*Continued*
  Sandor, M. Elegy for Miss Beagle
  Schmidt, H. J. The funeral party
  Schnitzler, A. Night games
  Scoville, S. Clara and Ben
  Shabtai, Y. Uncle Peretz takes flight
  Singer, I. B. The bishop's robe
  Singer, I. B. One day of happiness
  Singer, I. B. Zeitl and Rickel
  Skillings, R. D. Theatre of the real
  Smith, J. Cul-de-sac
  Spencer, D. It's a lot scarier if you take Jesus
    out
  Spencer, D. Park host
  Spencer, E. I, Maureen
  Spillane, M. The girl behind the hedge
  Stuckey-French, E. Electric wizard
  Tawada, Y. The bath
  Taylor, T. L. Doves of Townsend
  Van Pelt, L. River watch
  Vonnegut, K. Hal Irwin's magic lamp
  Wallace, D. F. Good old neon
  Weinberg, R. Ro Erg
  Westlake, D. E. This is death
  Wharton, E. The day of the funeral
  Wharton, E. Joy in the house
  Wharton, E. The young gentlemen
  Wilmot, J. Dirt angel
  Wilson, R., Jr. Hard times
  Wuori, G. K. Angles
  Yi, T.-H. Dark valley
  Zivkovic, Z. The violin-maker
Suicide. Ford, E.
Suicide as a sort of present. Wallace, D. F.
Suicide coast. Harrison, M. J.
Suicide's girlfriend. Evans, E.
A **suitable** good-bye. Tilghman, C.
Sukrungruang, Ira
  The golden mix
    Nixon under the bodhi tree and other works
      of Buddhist fiction; edited by Kate Wheeler
      ; foreword by Charles Johnson
Sulak. Babel´, I.
Suleyman and Salieri. Kaminer, W.
Suliman's friend learns many things in one night.
    Kanafāni, G.
Sullivan, Michelle
  A night to remember
    'Teen v43 no3 p108-09 Mr 1999
Sullivan, Walter
  Bare Ruined Choirs
    The Sewanee Review v111 no4 p495-511 Fall
      2003
  Losses
    The Cry of an occasion; fiction from the Fel-
      lowship of Southern Writers; edited by
      Richard Bausch; with a foreword by
      George Garrett
  Love's mysteries
    The Sewanee Review v109 no4 p493-510 Fall
      2001
  Only the dance
    The Sewanee Review v107 no2 p170-86 Spr
      1999
Summa mathematica. Doolittle, S.
SUMMER
  Bradbury, R. With smiles as wide as summer
  Steele, M. The unripe heart
Summer. Nair, M.

Summer, an elegy. Gilchrist, E.
SUMMER CAMPS
  Atwell, M. S. Blue night, Clover Lake
  Atwood, M. Death by landscape
  Boswell, M. Born again
  Davis, A. The very moment they're about
  Harris, M. Titwillow
  Lipsyte, S. Admiral of the Swiss Navy
  Packer, Z. Brownies
  Umansky, E. M. How to make it to the prom-
    ised land
Summer flood. Pritchett, L.
Summer fog. Gores, J.
Summer girl. Vachss, A. H.
Summer girls. Bensko, J.
Summer girls. Connor, J.
SUMMER HOMES
  Broyard, B. At the bottom of the lake
  Chimera, B. July
  Gunn, K. The meatyard
A **summer** house, later. Hermann, J.
The **summer** in a barbershop. Ponte, A. J.
The **summer** isles. MacLeod, I. R.
Summer job. Reifler, N.
Summer Masquerades. Van Dyke, H.
Summer night. Bowen, E.
Summer of Solanka. Rushdie, S.
Summer of the Hot Tubs. Proulx, A.
The **summer** of vintage clothing. Carlson, R.
The **summer** of Zubeyde. Treat, J.
Summer party. Lear, P.
The **summer** people. DuBois, B.
Summer People. Henkin, J.
SUMMER RESORTS
  Adams, A. The haunted beach
  Chopin, K. The awakening
  Cody, L. Where's Stacey?
  Flynt, C. Dancing with father
  Gilman, C. P. The cottagette
  Jackson, S. The summer people
  Marías, J. Flesh Sunday
  Rendell, R. The beach butler
  Shrayer-Petrov, D. In the Reeds
Summer shore. Grau, S. A.
Summer solstice. Paolucci, A.
Summer sweat. Oates, J. C.
SUMMER VACATIONS *See* Vacations
The **summer** visitor. See Trevor, W. Le visiteur
Summerhouse, later. Hermann, J.
Summers, Hollis Spurgeon
  The vireo's nest
    Home and beyond; an anthology of Kentucky
      short stories; edited by Morris Allen
      Grubbs; with an introduction by Wade Hall
      and an afterword by Charles E. May
Summer's Lease. Wallenstein, J.
Summertime on Icarus. Clarke, A. C.
Summon the watch!. Davidson, A.
Sumner, Melanie
  Good-hearted woman
    New stories from the South: the year's best,
      2000; edited by Shannon Ravenel; with a
      preface by Ellen Douglas
  The guide
    Living on the edge; fiction by Peace Corps
      writers; edited by John Coyne

Sumner, Penny
For your eyes only
Brought to book; murderous stories from the literary world; Penny Sumner, editor
SUN
Clarke, A. C. Out of the sun
Clarke, A. C. Summertime on Icarus
Clement, H. Proof
Niven, L. Inconstant moon
Sun/flight. Yolen, J.
Sun. Coskran, K.
Sun-Cloud. Baxter, S.
Sun damage. Henley, P.
Sun gazer. Sneve, V. D. H.
The **sun** in the sky. Iribarne, M.
The **sun,** the moon, the stars. Díaz, J.
The **sun,** the sea, and the silent scream. Lumley, B.
SUNDAY
Updike, J. Sunday teasing
Sunday cricket. Breeze, J. B.
Sunday evenings at Contessa Pasquali's. Girardi, R.
Sunday in the Park With Boy. Herring, J.
Sunday morning: Key West. Holleran, A.
Sunday night yams at Minnie and Earl's. Castro, A.-T.
Sunday visit. Nailah, A.
Sundays. Knight, M.
Sundown Corral. Le May, A.
Sundress. Svoboda, T.
Sunflowers. McDowell, I.
Sunken gardens. Sterling, B.
Sunny. Furman, L.
Sunny Billy Day. Carlson, R.
Sunrise. West, M.
Sun's up!. Waldrop, H.
Sunset. Babel′, I.
Sunset in heaven. Gautreaux, T.
Sunstroke. Bunin, I. A.
Sunstroke. Hadley, T.
Suor Strega. Herling, G.
Super-Frog save Tokyo. Murakami, H.
Super-Frog saves Tokyo. Murakami, H.
Super Goat Man. Lethem, J.
Superassassin. Tenorio, L. A.
Superfly. Shade, E.
Superiority. Clarke, A. C.
Superman. Daugherty, T.
Supernatural. Galaviz-Budziszewski, A.
SUPERNATURAL PHENOMENA
See also Demoniac possession; Ghost stories; Horror stories Miriam
Adams, J. Stealing the dark
Alarcón, P. A. d. The tall woman
Aminoff, J. Fate
Baumer, J. R. The party over there
Benítez-Rojo, A. The scissors
Bishop, M. Apartheid, superstrings, and Mordecai Thubana
Blackwood, A. The willows
Borges, J. L. The circular ruins
Bowles, P. Things gone and things still here
Bradbury, R. Banshee
Bradbury, R. The poems
Bradbury, R. The wind
Byatt, A. S. The thing in the forest
Chopin, K. Her letters
Crowley, J. Antiquities

Cummins, A. Blue fly
Davidson, A. Twenty-three
Davies, L. Run ragged
Davis, L. The Golden Benefactors of Brewster McMahon
De Lint, C. Masking Indian
Dowling, T. The saltimbanques
Duncan, A. Daddy Mention and the Monday skull
Dyson, J. A slate roof in the rain
Dyson, J. We who walk through walls
Estleman, L. D. Hell on the draw
Fintushel, E. White man's trick
Fleming, R. Life after bas
Fleming, R. A lizard's kiss
Fleming, R. Speak no evil
Fleming, R. The ultimate bad luck
Gabaldon, D. Lord John and the succubus
Gaiman, N. American gods [excerpt]
García Márquez, G. The last voyage of the ghost ship
Gorman, E. A girl like you
Hambly, B. The horsemen and the morning star
Hawthorne, N. The hollow of the three hills
Hawthorne, N. The snow image: a childish miracle
Hensley, J. L. Savant
Hodgson, W. H. The boats of the "Glen Carrrig"
Hopkinson, N. Precious
Hopkinson, N. Snake
Houarner, G. She'd make a dead man crawl
James, H. De Grey: a romance
Jance, J. A. Death of a snowbird
Kilpatrick, N. Brina
Koja, K. At Eventide
Lamsley, T. Climbing down from heaven
Lee, V. The legend of Madame Krasinska
Lee, V. Prince Alberic and the snake lady
Lee, V. The Virgin of the Seven Daggers
Lee, V. A wedding chest
Ligotti, T. Our temporary supervisor
Lugones, L. An inexplicable phenomenon
Lumley, B. Inception
Lumley, B. Rising with Surtsey
MacLeod, I. The chop girl
Major, D. Shining through 24/7
Matthews, C. The dirt eaters
McDowell, I. Sunflowers
McTair, R. Just a lark; or, The crypt of Matthew Ashdown
Navarro, Y. A beacon shall I shine
Paschal, D. By the light of the jukebox
Paulsen, S. Ma rung
Phillips, G. '53 Buick
Power, S. A hole in the sheets
Pronzini, B. Toy
Rhys, J. A spiritualist
Rifaat, A. My world of the unknown
Rucker, R. v. B. The Jack Kerouac disembodied school of poetics
Sammān, G. An air-conditioned egg
Sammān, G. The brain's closed castle
Sammān, G. The swan genie
Sammān, G. Visitors of a dying person
Scliar, M. The prophets of Benjamin Bok
Sheckley, R. A trick worth two of that
Shouse, D. A portrait of angels
Singer, I. B. A crown of feathers

SUPERNATURAL PHENOMENA—See also—
Continued
Singer, I. B. The enemy
Singer, I. B. The missing line
Singer, I. B. Powers
Singer, I. B. The psychic journey
Singer, I. B. Stories from behind the stove
Singer, I. B. A telephone call on Yom Kippur
Singer, I. B. Three tales
Steiber, E. The shape of things
Stern, S. The wedding jester
Stern, S. Yiddish twilight
Swarthout, G. F. Gersham and the saber
Tangh, J. The Skinned
Thomas, S. R. How Sukie cross de big wata
Valdés, Javier. People like us
Vanderhaeghe, G. The Jimi Hendrix experience
Wells, K. My guardian, Claire
Wharton, E. Kerfol
Whiteford, W. Night of the wandjina
Wilson, R. C. Plato's mirror
Wolfe, G. The walking sticks

SUPERSTITION
      See also Occultism; Vampires; Voodoo-
      ism; Werewolves
Anderson, P. Eutopia
Bowles, P. The empty amulet
Bowles, P. An inopportune visit
Cabrera Infante, G. The great ekbó
Carl, L. S. The eye of the beholder
Chesnutt, C. W. Sis' Becky's pickaninny
Dumas, H. Ark of bones
Dumas, H. Devil bird
Dumas, H. Echo tree
Dumas, H. Rain God
Harrison, H. Rescue operation
Malamud, B. Still life
Melville, P. The conversion of Millicent Vernon
Senior, O. Mad Fish
Watanabe McFerrin, L. Los mariachis del
      muerto

Supertoys in other seasons. Aldiss, B. W.
Supertoys last all summer long. Aldiss, B. W.
Supertoys when winter comes. Aldiss, B. W.
The **supper** at Elsinore. Dinesen, I.
Support your local Griffin. Cady, J.
Support your local police. Bullins, E.
Suppose they gave a peace. Shwartz, S.
Sure, blue, and dead, too. Van de Wetering, J.
Surface calm. Martin, V.
Surface reading. Gussoff, C.
Surface tension. Blish, J.

SURFERS
Lee, D. The possible husband
Surfiction. Wideman, J. E.

SURGEONS
      See also Physicians; Women physicians
Clyde, M. Howard Johnson's house
Glasgow, E. The shadowy third
Herling, G. Don Ildebrando
Murray, J. A few short notes on tropical butter-
      flies
Simak, C. D. Huddling place

SURGERY
      See also Amputation; Plastic surgery;
      Transplantation of organs, tissues, etc.
Anderson, D. Luck
Gwyn, A. The offering
Lewis, T. The marijuana tree

Ross, L. Tasting songs
Stafford, J. The interior castle
Surgery. Chekhov, A. P.
Surplus value books: catalogue number 13.
      Moody, R.

SURPRISE ENDINGS
Chopin, K. The locket
Dokey, R. Never trust the weatherman
Fish, R. L. The wager
Gores, J. You're putting me on, aren't you?
Harrison, H. Speed of the cheetah, roar of the
      lion
Ritchie, J. The absence of Emily
Waugh, E. Mr. Loveday's little outing
Weaver, G. A dialogue
Surprise endings. Kennedy, T. E.
The **surprise** of his life. George, E.

SURREALISM
Agnon, S. Y. The night
Alvarez, A. Rog & Venus become an item
Anderson, R. The pyramid
Barker, N. Inside information
Berners, G. H. T.-W., Baron. The camel
Bocock, M. And silently steal away
Brandt, W. The Jean-Paul Sartre experience
Budnitz, J. Directions
Budnitz, J. Dog days
Budnitz, J. Hershel
Budnitz, J. Hundred-pound baby
Budnitz, J. Train
Codrescu, A. Monsieur Teste in America
Codrescu, A. Perfume: a tale of felicity
Cooper, B. Hunters and gatherers
Cortázar, J. Summer
Dann, J. A quiet revolution for death
Dyson, J. A last look at the sea
Dyson, J. A visit from Val Koran
Edugyan, E. The woman who tasted of rose oil
Gao Xingjian. In an instant
Gilb, D. Mayela one day in 1989
Grand, D. Louse [excerpt]
Hendel, Y. Small change
Jackson, S. Blood
Jackson, S. Cancer
Jackson, S. Egg
Jackson, S. Foetus
Jackson, S. Nerve
Jackson, S. Sperm
Koskinen, M. Dies Irae
Kureishi, H. The penis
Kurlansky, M. Desaparecidos
Legge, G. Life on a Scottish council estate vol.
      1
Maleti, G. Argia
Mathews, A. The story of the German parachut-
      ist who landed forty-two years late
McBrearty, R. G. Back in town
McCann, C. Cathal's lake
Menendez, A. Miami relatives
Murakami, H. Super-Frog saves Tokyo
Murakami, H. UFO in Kushiro
Orphée, E. The journey of Amatista and the
      dirty prince
Ozick, C. The shawl
Parrish, T. After the river
Ponte Landa, M. Blind madness
Reifler, N. Baby
Schwartz, L. S. The stone master
Seltz, E. Compelle intrare

SURREALISM—*Continued*
Slavin, J. Swallowed whole
Smith, A. Erosive
Smith, A. May
Tawada, Y. A guest
Tawada, Y. Raisin eyes
Tawada, Y. Spores
Tawada, Y. Tongue dance
Tillman, L. Thrilled to death
Valenzuela, L. Panther eyes
VanderMeer, J. The city
VanderMeer, J. Secret life
Vukcevich, R. The barber's theme
Vukcevich, R. Beatniks with banjos
Vukcevich, R. By the time we get to Uranus
Vukcevich, R. Fancy pants
Vukcevich, R. Finally fruit
Vukcevich, R. A holiday junket
Vukcevich, R. Home remedy
Vukcevich, R. Message in a fish
Vukcevich, R. Poop
Vukcevich, R. Rejoice
Vukcevich, R. There is danger
Webb, Don. Metamorphosis no. 5
Wharton, T. The paper-thin garden
Winterson, J. Adventure of a lifetime
Winterson, J. Disappearance I
Winterson, J. Disappearance II
Winterson, J. A green square
Yuknavitch, L. The garden of earthly delights
The **Surrogate**. Hadley, T.
SURROGATE MOTHERS
Goran, L. The chorus girl
McAllister, B. The girl who loved animals
Surrogates. Hall, R.
Surrounded by sleep. Sharma, A.
Surveillance. Brkic, C. A.
A **survey** of the works of Herbert Quain. Borges, J. L.
SURVEYORS
Chekhov, A. P. Overdoing it
SURVIVAL (AFTER AIRPLANE ACCIDENTS, SHIPWRECKS, ETC.)
See also Shipwrecks and castaways
Bass, R. The hermit's story
Bocock, M. La humanidad
Boyle, T. C. After the plague
Butler, O. E. Speech sounds
Dann, J. Going under
Grau, S. A. Hunter
Greenberg, A. Found
L'Amour, L. Crash landing
Landis, G. A. A walk in the sun
Sturgeon, T. The golden helix
Tran, V. The coral reef
Survival. Hansen, J.
Survival instinct. O'Callaghan, M.
The **survival** of the fittest. Gilchrist, E.
Survival planet. Harrison, H.
Survival rates. Clyde, M.
SURVIVORS, HOLOCAUST *See* Holocaust survivors
Survivors. Dixon, S.
Survivor's ball; or, The Donner party. Link, K.
Sushi. Swain, H.
Suskind, the impresario. Shapiro, G.
The **suspect** genome. Hamilton, P. F.

SUSPENSE NOVELS
See also Adventure; Conspiracies; Horror stories; International intrigue; Kidnapping; Murder stories; Mystery and detective stories; Secret service; Spies; Terrorism
Suspension. Brkic, C. A.
Sussex, Lucy
Matilda told such dreadful lies
Dreaming down-under; edited by Jack Dann and Janeen Webb
My lady tongue
Centaurus: the best of Australian science fiction; edited by David G. Hartwell and Damien Broderick
Sustenance sustenance. Kelman, J.
Sutton, Barbara
The brotherhood of healing
The Antioch Review v60 no3 p409-24 Summ 2002
Maybe, Maybe Not
Harvard Review (1992) no26 p147-57 2004
The **Sutton** Pie Safe. Benedict, P.
Suzette. Chopin, K.
Švenková, Viera
Pharaoh's smile
In search of homo sapiens; twenty-five contemporary Slovak short stories; editor, Pavol Hudík ; [translated by Heather Trebatická; American English editor, Lucy Bednár]
Svikiro. Nangle, P.
Svirsky, Gila
Meeting Natalia
The Vintage book of international lesbian fiction; edited and with an introduction by Naomi Holoch and Joan Nestle
Svoboda, Terese
Arcane high
A different plain; contemporary Nebraska fiction writers; edited by Ladette Randolph ; introduction by Mary Pipher
Car frogs
Svoboda, T. Trailer girl and other stories
Cave life
Svoboda, T. Trailer girl and other stories
Devil Dogs
The Literary Review (Madison, N.J.) v46 no4 p621-4 Summ 2003
Doll
Svoboda, T. Trailer girl and other stories
Electricity
Svoboda, T. Trailer girl and other stories
The Haight
The Literary Review (Madison, N.J.) v45 no3 p603-5 Spr 2002
I dreamt he fell three floors and lived
Svoboda, T. Trailer girl and other stories
In Black and White
The Yale Review v91 no4 p129-32 O 2003
Leadership
Svoboda, T. Trailer girl and other stories
Lost the baby
Svoboda, T. Trailer girl and other stories
A mama
Svoboda, T. Trailer girl and other stories
Morning glory Harley
Iowa Review v32 no1 p46-9 Spr 2002
Party girl
Svoboda, T. Trailer girl and other stories

Svoboda, Terese—_Continued_
Petrified woman
  The Antioch Review v57 no1 p99-101 Wint
    1999
  Svoboda, T. Trailer girl and other stories
Polio
  Svoboda, T. Trailer girl and other stories
Psychic
  Svoboda, T. Trailer girl and other stories
Rite Anthropologique
  Iowa Review v34 no2 p65-9 Fall 2004
Sundress
  Svoboda, T. Trailer girl and other stories
Trailer girl
  Svoboda, T. Trailer girl and other stories
Venice
  The Ohio Review no59 p158-61 1999
Water
  Svoboda, T. Trailer girl and other stories
What did you bring me?
  Svoboda, T. Trailer girl and other stories
White
  Svoboda, T. Trailer girl and other stories
Swain, Dwight V.
Gamblin' man
  A Century of great Western stories; edited by
    John Jakes
Swain, Heather
Sushi
  Virgin fiction 2
Swallowed whole. Slavin, J.
Swallowing angels whole. Wells, K.
Swamp Boy. Bass, R.
SWAMPS
  Blaise, C. Relief
  Gores, J. Quit screaming
  Zinovyeva-Annibal, L. D. The monster
Swan, Gladys
Backtracking
  Swan, G. News from the volcano; stories
Carnevale: the first night
  The Literary Review (Madison, N.J.) v42 no3
    p433-46 Spr 1999
The chasm
  Swan, G. News from the volcano; stories
A Garden Amid Fires
  The Sewanee Review v111 no1 p32-49 Wint
    2003
Gate of ivory, gate of horn
  Swan, G. News from the volcano; stories
Lucinda
  The Ohio Review no64/65 p397-408 2001
News from the volcano
  Swan, G. News from the volcano; stories
The orange bird
  The Sewanee Review v107 no3 p319-32
    Summ 1999
Sloan's daughter
  Swan, G. News from the volcano; stories
Swan, Mary
1917
  Harper's v305 p31-4 D 2002
  Swan, M. The deep and other stories
At the river
  Swan, M. The deep and other stories
By the sea, by the sea
  Swan, M. The deep and other stories

The deep
  Prize stories, 2001; The O. Henry awards; ed-
    ited and with an introduction by Larry
    Dark
  Swan, M. The deep and other stories
Down by the lake
  Swan, M. The deep and other stories
Emma's hands
  Swan, M. The deep and other stories
Hour of lead
  Swan, M. The deep and other stories
In the story that won't be written
  Swan, M. The deep and other stories
The manual of remote sensing
  Swan, M. The deep and other stories
Max-1970
  Swan, M. The deep and other stories
The new wife
  Swan, M. The deep and other stories
On the border
  Swan, M. The deep and other stories
Peach
  Swan, M. The deep and other stories
Spanish grammar
  Swan, M. The deep and other stories
The **swan**. Vukcevich, R.
The **swan** genie. Sammān, G.
Swan song. Stern, S.
Swann, Maxine
Flower children
  The Pushcart prize XXIII: best of the small
    presses; an annual small press reader; ed-
    ited by Bill Henderson with the Pushcart
    prize editors
The **Swannanoa** review. Isaacs, N. D.
SWANS
  McCann, C. Cathal's lake
  Wells, K. Sherman and the swan
Swan's Song. Wieland, M.
Swanwick, Michael
The blind minotaur
  The Good new stuff; adventure SF in the
    grand tradition; edited by Gardner Dozois
The dead
  Nebula awards 33; the year's best SF and
    fantasy chosen by the science-fiction and
    fantasy writers of America; edited by
    Connie Willis
Dirty little war
  Tetrick, B. In the shadow of the wall; an an-
    thology of Vietnam stories that might have
    been; edited by Byron R. Tetrick
The dog said bow-wow
  Nebula awards showcase 2004; edited by
    Vonda McIntyre
  The Year's best science fiction, nineteenth an-
    nual collection; edited by Gardner Dozois
King dragon
  The year's best science fiction: twenty-first
    annual collection; edited by Gardner Dozois
Radiant doors
  Nebula awards showcase 2001; the year's best
    SF and fantasy chosen by the science fic-
    tion and fantasy writers of America; edited
    by Robert Silverberg
The raggle taggle gypsy-o
  The Year's best science fiction, eighteenth an-
    nual collection; edited by Gardner Dozois

Swanwick, Michael—*Continued*
Scherzo with tyrannosaur
The Year's best science fiction, seventeenth annual collection; edited by Gardner Dozois
Slow life
The Year's best science fiction; twentieth annual collection; edited by Gardner Dozois
The very pulse of the machine
The Year's best science fiction, sixteenth annual collection; edited by Gardner Dozois
(jt. auth) See Gibson, William and Swanwick, Michael
The **swap**. Bukiet, M. J.
Swarm. Sterling, B.
Swarthout, Glendon Fred
The attack on the mountain
A Century of great Western stories; edited by John Jakes
Swarthout, G. F. Easterns and westerns; short stories; edited by Miles Hood Swarthout
The ball really carries in the Cactus League because the air is dry
Swarthout, G. F. Easterns and westerns; short stories; edited by Miles Hood Swarthout
Death to everybody over thirty
Swarthout, G. F. Easterns and westerns; short stories; edited by Miles Hood Swarthout
Four older men
Swarthout, G. F. Easterns and westerns; short stories; edited by Miles Hood Swarthout
Gersham and the saber
Swarthout, G. F. Easterns and westerns; short stories; edited by Miles Hood Swarthout
A glass of blessings
Swarthout, G. F. Easterns and westerns; short stories; edited by Miles Hood Swarthout
Going to see George
Swarthout, G. F. Easterns and westerns; short stories; edited by Miles Hood Swarthout
A horse for Mrs. Custer
Swarthout, G. F. Easterns and westerns; short stories; edited by Miles Hood Swarthout
Ixion
Swarthout, G. F. Easterns and westerns; short stories; edited by Miles Hood Swarthout
Mulligans
Swarthout, G. F. Easterns and westerns; short stories; edited by Miles Hood Swarthout
O captain, my captain
Swarthout, G. F. Easterns and westerns; short stories; edited by Miles Hood Swarthout
Pancho Villa's one-man war
Swarthout, G. F. Easterns and westerns; short stories; edited by Miles Hood Swarthout
Poteet caught up in lust and history
Swarthout, G. F. Easterns and westerns; short stories; edited by Miles Hood Swarthout
What every man knows
Swarthout, G. F. Easterns and westerns; short stories; edited by Miles Hood Swarthout
The **swastika** on our door. Adams, A.
SWAT. Frym, G.
The **sweater**. Shea, S. S.
The **sweater**. Vukcevich, R.
The **sweating** statue. Hoch, E. D.
SWEDEN

Rural life
Lindgren, T. The stump-grubber
Lindgren, T. Water

SWEDES
See also Vikings
Swedish Bricks and Minerals. Angrist, M.
The **Swedish** match. Chekhov, A. P.
Sweeney, Eamonn
Lord McDonald
The Anchor book of new Irish writing; the new Gaelach ficsean; edited and with an introduction by John Somer and John J. Daly
Sweeney, J. Erin
The monsoon season
New Letters v67 no3 p85-95 2001
The **sweeper**. Ely, S.
Sweet. Falco, E.
The **sweet** and sour tongue. What, L.
Sweet cactus wine. Muller, M.
Sweet little hands. Block, L.
The **sweet** old lady who sits in the park. O'Callaghan, M.
The **sweet** science. Dwyer, M.
Sweet Seconds. Tenorio, G. A.
Sweet shrub. Coberly, L. M.
Sweet thunderous twilight. Mandelbaum, P.
The **sweetest** man in the world. Westlake, D. E.
The **sweetheart** of M. Briseux. James, H.
Sweetness. Warner, S. O.
Swenson, Laura
Crazy
The Kenyon Review ns23 no1 p24-8 Wint 2001
Swept away. Boyle, T. C.
Swick, Marly A.
Crete
A different plain; contemporary Nebraska fiction writers; edited by Ladette Randolph ; introduction by Mary Pipher
The rhythm of disintegration
The Student body; short stories about college students and professors; edited by John McNally
The zealous mourner
The Workshop; seven decades of the Iowa Writers' Workshop: 42 stories, recollections & essays on Iowa's place in 20th-century American literature; edited by Tom Grimes
Swift, Graham
Learning to swim
The Art of the story; an international anthology of contemporary short stories; edited by Daniel Halpern
SWIFT, JONATHAN, 1667-1745
Parodies, imitations, etc.
Fowler, K. J. The travails
Roberts, A. Swiftly
Swiftly. Roberts, A.
The **swimmer**. Cheever, J.
Swimmer. Gordon, P.
Swimmers. Norris, L.
SWIMMING
Adams, A. A public pool
Cheever, J. The swimmer
Dunmore, H. Swimming into the millennium
Dybek, S. Undertow
Gunn, K. The swimming pool
Jones, T. Fields of purple forever
Maugham, W. S. A friend in need
Mazelis, J. The diving girls
Roeske, P. A history of swimming

SWIMMING—*Continued*
Swift, G. Learning to swim
Tuck, L. Horses
Vivante, A. Crosscurrents
Wallace, D. F. Forever overhead
Watanabe McFerrin, L. Amphibians
Weldon, F. Leda and the swan
Ziegler, I. The raft
Swimming. Selgin, P.
The **swimming** contest. *See* Tammuz, B. The swimming race
Swimming in Moonlight. Nelson, K.
Swimming out. Brkic, C. A.
Swimming out to Holly. Steinwachs, M.
The **swimming** pool. Gunn, K.
The **swimming** race. Tammuz, B.
Swimming upstream. Deutchman, J.
Swimming with Chairman Mao. Dabydeen, C.
SWINDLERS AND SWINDLING
    See also Business—Unscrupulous methods
Armstrong, K. The cane field
Casares, O. Jerry Fuentes
Greer, R. O. Prime
Hamburger, A. Control
James, H. Four meetings
Nevins, F. M., Jr. Bagworms
Phillips, D. R. What it cost travelers
Sade, marquis de. Thieves and swindlers
Singer, I. B. The man who came back
Singer, I. B. A tale of two liars
Updike, J. A gift from the city
Weldon, F. Percentage trust
Swing. Dybek, S.
The **swing**. Gavell, M. L.
Swing shift. Locklin, G.
Swinging in the Breeze. Williams, S. P.
Swingtime. DeLancey, K.
Swire, Benjamin
Walter Cronkite with Hospital Corners
South Carolina Review v36 no1 p98-103 Fall 2003
SWISS ALPS *See* Alps
Switzer, Robert
Death of a prize fighter
Boxing's best short stories; edited by Paul D. Staudohar
SWITZERLAND
Vevey
James, H. Daisy Miller: a study
Swofford, Anthony
Freedom Oil
Politically inspired; edited by Stephen Elliott; assistant editor, Gabriel Kram; associate editors, Elizabeth Brooks [et al.]
The **Sword** of the North. Edghill, R.
SWORDS
Edghill, R. Scandal
Edghill, R. The Sword of the North
Holliday, L. Provenance
Sykes, Jerry
Seduced
The best British mysteries; edited by Maxim Jakubowski
Symptoms of loss
The World's finest mystery and crime stories, first annual collection; edited by Ed Gorman

Sylvester, Harry A.
A boxer: old
Boxing's best short stories; edited by Paul D. Staudohar
I won't do no dive
Sports best short stories; edited by Paul D. Staudohar
Sylvie. Giono, J.
Symbiosis: class cestoda. Barker, N.
Symbiotic encounter. Naranjo, C.
SYMBOLISM
    See also Allegories; Parables
Alcott, L. M. The little seed
Arvin, N. Electric fence
Jordan, N. The dream of a beast
Kafka, F. Blumfeld, an elderly bachelor
Lawrence, D. H. The man who died
Lawrence, D. H. St. Mawr
Mahmudi, S. The Fin Garden of Kashan
Oz, A. Nomad and viper
Rosa, J. G. The third bank of the river
Yehoshua, A. B. Facing the forests
Symbols and signs. Nabokov, V. V.
Symons, Julian
A theme for Hyacinth
Speaking of lust; stories of forbidden desire; edited by Lawrence Block
The tigers of Subtopia
Edwards, M. Mysterious pleasures; a celebration of the Crime Writers' Association's 50th anniversary; edited by Martin Edwards
The **sympathetic** passenger. Waugh, E.
SYMPATHY
Lopez, B. H. The deaf girl
Norman, G. Maxine
Singer, I. B. Moon and madness
Sympathy. Furman, L.
Sympathy. Painter, P.
Symptoms of loss. Sykes, J.
SYNAGOGUES
What, L. You gotta believe
Synthesis of the community standard. Huffman, B., Jr.
SYRIANS
United States
Sammān, G. An air-conditioned egg
A **system** of wheels. Williams, T.
Szántó, Gábor
The Funeral
Iowa Review v34 no2 p144-9 Fall 2004
Szmura's Room. Hemon, A.

T

Tabatabai, Nahid
The lark
A Feast in the mirror; stories by contemporary Iranian women; translated and edited by Mohammad Mehdi Khorrami, Shouleh Vatanabadi
Tabby won't tell. Grape, J.
Taber, Sara Mansfield
Rowing to Leiden
Southwest Review v87 no2/3 p396-405 2002
Table Fifteen. Dobbs, K.
The **Tablecloth** of Turnin. Carlson, R.
Tabletalk. Skillings, R. D.
TABOO *See* Superstition

Tabucchi, Antonio
Books Never Written, Journeys Never Made
Grand Street no72 p9-20 Fall 2003
A riddle
The Art of the story; an international anthology of contemporary short stories; edited by Daniel Halpern
The **tachanka** theory. Babel', I.
Tachick, Christine
The next greatest thing
Seventeen v58 no4 p156-58+ Ap 1999
Taco Bell. Denton, E.
Tactical exercise. Waugh, E.
Tademy, Lalita
Cane river
Good Housekeeping v232 no6 p187-200 Je 2001
Tafolla, Carmen
Tia
Fantasmas; supernatural stories by Mexican American writers; edited by Rob Johnson; introduction by Kathleen J. Alcalá
Tag. Vachss, A. H.
Tag Sale. Luxenberg, H.
Tagging. Frym, G.
Tagore, Sir Rabindranath and Noble, Margaret Elizabeth
The Kabuliwallah (The Fruitseller from Kabul)
International Journal of Humanities and Peace v18 no1 p72-4 2002
TAHOE, LAKE (CALIF. AND NEV.) *See* Lake Tahoe (Calif. and Nev.)
Tahorah. Means, D.
Taibele and her demon. Singer, I. B.
Tail. Aylett, S.
Tailgunner. Morgan, R.
The **tailor** of Yuma. Matthews, C.
TAILORS
Grimm, J. and Grimm, W. The gallant tailor
Heath, R. A. K. The master tailor and the teacher's skirt
Lipenga, K. Wainting for a turn
Painter, P. Murder one
Singer, I. B. The power of darkness
Trevor, W. Mrs. Acland's ghosts
Trueba, A. d. "The adventures of a tailor"
Tails. Dixon, S.
Taing, Vanara
Bloodlines: Conversations with my Mother
Meridians v4 no2 p80-6 2004
Tait, John
Canton, NY
Prairie Schooner v76 no2 p107-20 Summ 2002
TAIWAN
Cheng, C.-W. Autumn night
Cheng, C.-W. Betel nut town
Cheng, C.-W. The coconut palms on campus
Cheng, C.-W. A fisherman's family
Cheng, C.-W. God of thunder's gonna getcha
Cheng, C.-W. Hair
Cheng, C.-W. The last of the gentlemen
Cheng, C.-W. The mosquito
Cheng, C.-W. The river suite
Cheng, C.-W. Secrets
Cheng, C.-W. Spring rain
Cheng, C.-W. The three-legged horse
Farm life
See Farm life—Taiwan

Take, for example, meatpie. Banbury, J.
Take it away. Westlake, D. E.
Take them in, please. Hodgen, C.
Take your child to work. Arvin, N.
Taken for delirium. Simonds, M.
Takeout. Christmas, J.
Taking a stitch in a dead man's arm. Vaz, K.
Taking care. Williams, J.
Taking care of Frank. Mann, A.
Taking care of the O'Learys. Campbell, B. J.
Taking loup. Glassco, B.
Taking names. Shomer, E.
Taklamakan. Sterling, B.
Takoza said "goo". Sneve, V. D. H.
Talbot, Norman
The latest dream I ever dreamed
Dreaming down-under; edited by Jack Dann and Janeen Webb
A **tale** about a woman. Babel', I.
The **tale** of a kite. Stern, S.
The **Tale** of Many Jersualems. Freund, C. P.
A **tale** of Roman life. Pushkin, A. S.
The **tale** of the unknown island. Saramago, J.
The **tale** of the velvet pillows. Traba, M.
A **tale** of two losers. Abrams, T.
A **tale** without a title. See Chekhov, A. P. A story without a title
Tales of Houdini. Rucker, R. v. B.
The **talisman.** Tawada, Y.
Talk show lady. Casey, M.
Talk, talk, talk. Vasseur, T. J.
Talking. Wallace, R.
The **talking** cure. Busch, F.
Talking dog. Prose, F.
Talking in bed. Bidisha
Talking in the dark. Louis, L. G.
The **talking** kimono. Kalpakian, L.
Talking turkey, not goose. Penn, W. S.
Tall man, large cat. Coward, M.
TALL STORIES *See* Improbable stories
Tall tales from the Mekong Delta. Braverman, K.
The **tall** woman. Alarcón, P. A. d.
The **tall** woman and her short husband. Feng Jicai
Tallent, Elizabeth
Eight hundred pages
Politically inspired; edited by Stephen Elliott; assistant editor, Gabriel Kram; associate editors, Elizabeth Brooks [et al.]
The **tallest** Indian in Toltepec. Henry, W.
Talley, Marcia
Conventional wisdom
Malice domestic 9
Safety first
Blood on their hands; edited by Lawrence Block
Tamarind stew. Gonsalves, G.
Tamaro, Susanna
The burning forest
Tamaro, S. Rispondimi; translated from the Italian by John Cullen
Hell does not exist
Tamaro, S. Rispondimi; translated from the Italian by John Cullen
Rispondimi
Tamaro, S. Rispondimi; translated from the Italian by John Cullen
Tamed. Hood, R.
The **taming** of Johnny Peters. Newton, D. B.

Tammuz, Benjamin
My brother
  Six Israeli novellas; [by] Ruth Almog [et al.];
    edited and with an introduction by Gershon
    Shaked; translated from the Hebrew by
    Dalya Bilu, Philip Simpson, and Marganit
    Weinberger-Rotman
The swimming race
  Sleepwalkers and other stories; the Arab in
    Hebrew fiction; edited by Ehud Ben-Ezer
Tammy, imagined. Davis, J. S.
TAMPA (FLA.) *See* Florida—Tampa
Tan, Amy
Two kinds
  The Scribner anthology of contemporary short
    fiction; fifty North American stories since
    1970; Lex Williford and Michael Martone,
    editors
Tan-Tan and Dry Bone. Hopkinson, N.
Tanaka, Shimon
Video ame
  Best new American voices 2000; guest editor
    Tobias Wolff; series editors John Kulka
    and Natalie Danford
Taneytown. Earle, S.
Tangents. Bear, G.
Tangerine. Bradbury, R.
Tangh, Jarla
The Skinned
  Mojo: conjure stories; edited by Nalo Hopkin-
    son
TANGIER (MOROCCO) *See* Morocco—Tangier
Tangier 1975. Bowles, P.
A **tangle** by the rapid river. Doerr, A.
The **tangled** strings of the Marionettes. Castro,
  A.-T.
Tango in Amsterdam. Lock, N.
Tango is my life. Friedman, M.
Tango was her life. Lutz, J.
Tani, Cinzia
The punishment
  In the forbidden city; an anthology of erotic
    fiction by Italian women; edited by Maria
    Rosa Cutrufelli; translated by Vincent J.
    Bertolini
Tanner, Mika
Bullies
  The Virginia Quarterly Review v80 no3 p200-
    13 Summ 2004
Tanner, Ron
The day his wife's face froze
  The Massachusetts Review v42 no3 p319-22
    Aut 2001
Tante Cat'rinette. Chopin, K.
Tanuki. Hodgman, J.
TANZANIANS
                    United States
Doerr, A. Mkondo
TAPE AND WIRE RECORDERS *See* Tape
  recordings
A **tape** for Bronko. Paolucci, A.
TAPE RECORDINGS
Bradbury, R. Tête-à-tête
Brennan, M. The servants' dance
Brenner, W. The human side of instrumental
  transcommunication
Tapestry. Delany, S. R.
A **tapestry** of little murders. Bishop, M.
TAPEWORMS *See* Cestoda

Tapiama. Bowles, P.
Tapka. Bezmozgis, D.
Tappan's burro. Grey, Z.
Taraghi, Goli *See* Taraqqī, Gulī
Tarantula. Jones, T.
Tarantulas. Penn, W. S.
Taraqqi, Goli *See* Taraqqī, Gulī
Taraqqī, Gulī
The bizarre comportment of Mr. Alpha in exile
  Taraqqī, G. A mansion in the sky; and other
    short stories
Father
  Taraqqī, G. A mansion in the sky; and other
    short stories
Grandma's house
  Taraqqī, G. A mansion in the sky; and other
    short stories
The maid
  Taraqqī, G. A mansion in the sky; and other
    short stories
A mansion in the sky
  Taraqqī, G. A mansion in the sky; and other
    short stories
My little friend
  Taraqqī, G. A mansion in the sky; and other
    short stories
The Shemiran bus
  Taraqqī, G. A mansion in the sky; and other
    short stories
Targan, Barry
Avalon
  Prairie Schooner v76 no4 p142-53 Wint 2002
Derrida's sandwich
  The North American Review v284 no3-4 p48-
    49 My/Ag 1999
Target practice. Offutt, C.
Tarnished glory; Custer and the Waffen SS Tur-
  tledove, H. Alternate generals II; ed. by
  Harry Turtledove
Tarnished halo. Tremayne, P.
The **tarnished** star. Breen, J. L.
TAROT
West, M. Turn of the card
Tarquin of cheapside. Fitzgerald, F. S.
Tarrera, Carmen
Dance with death
  Death dance; suspenseful stories of the dance
    macabre; Trevanian, editor
Tarses, Mallory
Details
  Confrontation no86/87 p113-30 Spr/Summ
    2004
Leaving Reseda
  The North American Review v284 no5 p34-42
    S/O 1999
World Series, 1979
  Ploughshares v28 no4 p177-9 Wint
    2002/2003
Tart of Darkness. Hiaasen, C.
TARTARS *See* Tatars
Tashi, Phuntshog
Guests of the Or Tog Bar
  World Literature Today v78 no1 p57-61
    Ja/Ap 2004
The **taste** of blood. Blatnik, A.
The **taste** of ironwater. Miller, J. W.
A **taste** of paradise. Pronzini, B.
The **Taste** of Penny. Parker, J.
The **taste** of revenge. Fiorani, S.

The **taste** of revenge. Wellen, E.
A **taste** of song. Wentworth, K. D.
Tasting songs. Ross, L.
Tat. Berkman, P. R.
TATARS
 Chekhov, A. P. In exile
Tatiana, Mon Amour. Danticat, E.
The **tattered** man. Hall, D.
A **tatting** man. López, L.
TATTOOING
 Berkman, P. R. Tat
 Bradbury, R. The illustrated man
 Cobb, W. J. The white tatto
 Connolly, C. Bare
 Dann, J. Tattoos
 Hand, E. The least trumps
 Jaime-Becerra, M. Gina and Max
 Karnezis, P. Cassandra is gone
 Mazelis, J. Siriol, she-devil of naked madness
 McQuain, K. Erasing Sonny
 Phillips, G. Branded
Tattoos. Dann, J.
Tatum, Robert
 On the Russian River
  American short fiction, vol. 8, no 29-32
Taughannock Falls. Roorbach, B.
Tavares, Braulio
 Stuntmind
  Cosmos latinos: an anthology of science fic-
  tion from Latin America and Spain; trans-
  lated, edited, & with an introduction &
  notes by Andrea L. Bell & Yolanda Moli-
  na-Gavilán
The **tavern**. Tozzi, F.
TAVERNS *See* Hotels, taverns, etc.
Tawada, Yoko
 The bath
  Selden, Y. and Tawada, Y. Where Europe be-
  gins; translated from the German by Susan
  Bernofsky; from the Japanese by Yumi Sel-
  den; with a preface by Wim Wenders
 Canned foreign
  Selden, Y. and Tawada, Y. Where Europe be-
  gins; translated from the German by Susan
  Bernofsky; from the Japanese by Yumi Sel-
  den; with a preface by Wim Wenders
 A guest
  Selden, Y. and Tawada, Y. Where Europe be-
  gins; translated from the German by Susan
  Bernofsky; from the Japanese by Yumi Sel-
  den; with a preface by Wim Wenders
 Notes recorded on the Lofoten Islands
  Chicago Review v48 no2/3 p303-4 Summ
  2002
 Raisin eyes
  Selden, Y. and Tawada, Y. Where Europe be-
  gins; translated from the German by Susan
  Bernofsky; from the Japanese by Yumi Sel-
  den; with a preface by Wim Wenders
 The reflection
  Selden, Y. and Tawada, Y. Where Europe be-
  gins; translated from the German by Susan
  Bernofsky; from the Japanese by Yumi Sel-
  den; with a preface by Wim Wenders
 Spores
  Selden, Y. and Tawada, Y. Where Europe be-
  gins; translated from the German by Susan
  Bernofsky; from the Japanese by Yumi Sel-
  den; with a preface by Wim Wenders

Storytellers without souls
  Selden, Y. and Tawada, Y. Where Europe be-
  gins; translated from the German by Susan
  Bernofsky; from the Japanese by Yumi Sel-
  den; with a preface by Wim Wenders
The talisman
  Selden, Y. and Tawada, Y. Where Europe be-
  gins; translated from the German by Susan
  Bernofsky; from the Japanese by Yumi Sel-
  den; with a preface by Wim Wenders
Tongue dance
  Selden, Y. and Tawada, Y. Where Europe be-
  gins; translated from the German by Susan
  Bernofsky; from the Japanese by Yumi Sel-
  den; with a preface by Wim Wenders
Where Europe begins
  Selden, Y. and Tawada, Y. Where Europe be-
  gins; translated from the German by Susan
  Bernofsky; from the Japanese by Yumi Sel-
  den; with a preface by Wim Wenders
The **tawny** bitch. Shawl, N.
TAXATION
 Reifler, N. Auditor
Taxi. Lida, D.
Taxi dancer. Goldner, B.
Taxi driver, minus Robert De Niro. Ampuero, F.
A **taxi** to himself. Johnson-Davies, D.
TAXICABS
 Ampuero, F. Taxi driver, minus Robert De Niro
 Johnson-Davies, D. A taxi to himself
 Malzberg, B. N. The prince of the steppes
 McNulty, J. A man like Grady, you got to know
  him first
 Smith, A. The book club
The **taxidermist**. Mathews, H.
The **Taxidermist** (The Father). Lazo, N.
TAXIDERMY
 Collins, B. Cat got your tongue
A **taxpayer** & a citizen. Morgan, R.
Taylor, Art
 Visions and Revisions
  The North American Review v289 no3/4 p25-
  31 My/Ag 2004
Taylor, Benjamin
 Walnuts, when the husks are green
  Neurotica: Jewish writers on sex; edited by
  Melvin Jules Bukiet
TAYLOR, ELIZABETH, 1932-
                  About
 Rawley, D. Baby Liz
Taylor, Julie
 Gifts & grace
  'Teen v45 no12 p94-7 D 2001/Ja 2002
Taylor, Linnet
 The wedding at Esperanza
  The Year's best fantasy & horror, thirteenth
  annual collection; edited by Ellen Datlow
  and Terri Windling
Taylor, Lucy
 Unspeakable
  The Year's best fantasy & horror: sixteenth
  annual collection; edited by Ellen Datlow
  & Terri Windling
Taylor, Pat Ellis
 Leaping Leo
  Graham, D. Lone Star literature; from the
  Red River to the Rio Grande; edited by
  Don Graham

Taylor, Peter Hillsman
A sentimental journey
Wonderful town; New York stories from The
New Yorker; edited by David Remnick
with Susan Choi
Venus, cupid, folly and time
The Best of The Kenyon review; edited by
David Lynn; introduction by Joyce Carol
Oates
Taylor, Robert Love
The angel of the airwaves
The Southern Review (Baton Rouge, La.) v38
no3 p590-605 Summ 2002
Colorado
The Ohio Review no64/65 p422-36 2001
Pink Miracle in East Tennessee
New stories from the South: the year's best,
2001; edited by Shannon Ravenel; with a
preface by Lee Smith
Taylor, Timothy L.
The Boar's Head Easter
Taylor, T. L. Silent cruise & other stories;
[by] Timothy Taylor
Doves of Townsend
Taylor, T. L. Silent cruise & other stories;
[by] Timothy Taylor
Francisco's watch
Taylor, T. L. Silent cruise & other stories;
[by] Timothy Taylor
Newstart 2.0 TM
Taylor, T. L. Silent cruise & other stories;
[by] Timothy Taylor
Pope's own
Taylor, T. L. Silent cruise & other stories;
[by] Timothy Taylor
Prayers to Buxtehude
Taylor, T. L. Silent cruise & other stories;
[by] Timothy Taylor
The resurrection plant
Taylor, T. L. Silent cruise & other stories;
[by] Timothy Taylor
Silent cruise
Taylor, T. L. Silent cruise & other stories;
[by] Timothy Taylor
Smoke's fortune
Taylor, T. L. Silent cruise & other stories;
[by] Timothy Taylor
Taylor-Hall, Mary Ann
Winter facts
Home and beyond; an anthology of Kentucky
short stories; edited by Morris Allen
Grubbs; with an introduction by Wade Hall
and an afterword by Charles E. May
Taylor, Nick
The smell of despair
Politically inspired; edited by Stephen Elliott;
assistant editor, Gabriel Kram; associate ed-
itors, Elizabeth Brooks [et al.]
Ťažký, Ladislav
A parting gift
In search of homo sapiens; twenty-five con-
temporary Slovak short stories; editor,
Pavol Hudík ; [translated by Heather
Trebatická; American English editor, Lucy
Bednár]
Tbe Corpse Bird. Rash, R.
TCHAIKOVSKY, PETER ILICH, 1840-1893
About
Malzberg, B. N. Andante lugubre

Te Awekotuku, Ngahuia
Paretipua
The Vintage book of international lesbian fic-
tion; edited and with an introduction by
Naomi Holoch and Joan Nestle
Tea, Michelle
9/11 L.A. bookstore
Politically inspired; edited by Stephen Elliott;
assistant editor, Gabriel Kram; associate ed-
itors, Elizabeth Brooks [et al.]
Tea. Dann, J.
Tea. Louis, L. G.
Tea. Reisman, N.
Tea and comfortable advice. Connor, J.
Tea at the house. Wolitzer, M.
Tea for two. Lake, M. D.
Tea for two. Pickard, N.
Tea on the mountain. Bowles, P.
The **tea** room beasts. Elrod, P. N.
The **teacher**. Richter, H. P.
The **teacher** of literature. Chekhov, A. P.
The **teacher** philosopher. Sade, marquis de
TEACHERS
See also Students; Tutors
Adam, C. Zoo
Adams, A. Ocracoke Island
Adams, A. To see you again
Addonizio, K. Have you seen me?
Alas, L. The burial of the sardine
Aldrich, B. S. The man who dreaded to go
home
Aldrich, B. S. Pie
Aldrich, B. S. The victory of Connie Lee
Aldrich, B. S. Welcome home, Hal!
Aldrich, B. S. The woman who was forgotten
Almog, R. Shrinking
Alvarez, A. Flatware
Anderson, D. Barrie Hooper's dead
Azadeh, C. Bronagh
Bagley, J. E. Children of chance
Barker, N. Dual balls
Barrett, A. Two rivers
Barth, J. And then there's the one
Barthelme, D. The school
Barthelme, F. Instructor
Barthelme, F. Pupil
Barthelme, F. Red Arrow
Barthelme, F. Retreat
Bausch, R. Self knowledge
Bausch, R. Spirits
Baxter, C. Gryphon
Bean, B. Honey
Bean, B. Sugar Creek
Berry, W. A consent
Biguenet, J. Do me
Billman, J. Kerr's fault
Bowles, P. The time of friendship
Bradbury, R. Let's play poison
Brand, D. Madame Alaird's breasts
Braunbeck, G. A. Safe
Brockmeier, K. Apples
Broughton, T. A. The burden of light
Broughton, T. A. The wars I missed
Broyard, B. The trouble with Mr. Leopold
Budnitz, J. Lessons
Bukiet, M. J. The return of eros to academe
Bukoski, A. Time between trains
Busch, F. A handbook for spies
Butler, R. O. Hiram the desperado

TEACHERS—*Continued*

Byatt, A. S. Raw material
Carlson, R. Hartwell
Carr, P. M. An El Paso Idyll
Cassill, R. V. And in my heart
Chacón, D. The biggest city in the world
Chacón, D. Mexican table
Chaon, D. Late for the wedding
Chaudhuri, A. Portrait of an artist
Chaudhuri, A. White lies
Chekhov, A. P. An artist's story
Chekhov, A. P. A dreary story
Chekhov, A. P. Encased
Chekhov, A. P. The man in a case
Chekhov, A. P. The schoolmistress
Chekhov, A. P. The teacher of literature
Cheng, C.-W. The coconut palms on campus
Cherry, K. Chapters from *A dog's life*
Chesnutt, C. W. The bouquet
Chesnutt, C. W. Cicely's dream
Chesnutt, C. W. The march of progress
Chesnutt, C. W. White weeds
Chopin, K. Aunt Lympy's interference
Clair, M. October Brown
Cobb, T. I'll never get out of this world alive
Cobb, W. J. There's nothing the matter with
    Gwen
Coberly, L. M. Miss Carrollene tells a story
Coberly, L. M. Over Sulphur Mountain
Coberly, L. M. The sighting
Cohen, R. The varieties of romantic experience:
    an introduction
Connor, J. Tea and comfortable advice
Coyne, J. Snow man
Crowley, J. Lost and abandoned
Cullin, M. The cosmology of Bing [excerpt]
Davidson, R. Field observations
Davies, P. H. What you know
DeMarco, T. P-413: Psycho-Sociology
Di Blasi, D. An obscure geography
Dixon, S. Hand
Dodd, S. M. So far you can't imagine
Drake, R. Alone
DuBois, B. Richard's children
Erdrich, L. Revival Road
Erian, A. Almonds and cherries
Erian, A. Standing up to the superpowers
Erian, A. You
Evans, E. Beautiful land
Evans, E. English as a second language
Farrell, C. The lady was a dude
Ferriss, L. Leaving the neighborhood
Galef, D. The art of the interview
Galef, D. Metafiction
Galef, D. Triptych
Gartner, Z. Boys growing
Gautreaux, T. Dancing with the one-armed gal
Gavell, M. L. His beautiful handwriting
George, E. I, Richard
Gerard, P. Death by reputation
Goldstein, N. The verse in the margins
Goliger, G. Maedele
Goran, L. Hello, good-bye
Gray, A. Aiblins
Greenberg, A. Found
Greenberg, A. Immersion
Greenberg, A. Scholars and lovers
Griffith, M. Hooper gets a perm
Guerrero, L. Butterfly

Guerrero, L. Hotel Arco Iris
Ha Jin. An official reply
Haake, K. This is geology to us
Hall, D. Argument and persuasion
Hamburger, A. Garage sale
Hamburger, A. Jerusalem
Hamburger, A. Sympathetic conversationalist
Harris, M. Flattery
Harrison, H. The ever-branching tree
Harty, R. Don't call it Christmas
Harty, R. Ongchoma
Haslett, A. War's end
Hayes, D. Prayers
Hazel, R. White Anglo-Saxon Protestant
Highsmith, P. Miss Juste and the green rompers
Hirshberg, G. Mr. Dark's carnival
Hodgen, C. The great Americans
Hodgen, C. The tender of unmarked graves
Hoffman, W. Place
Honig, L. After
Horgan, P. The peach stone
Howard, M. Children with matches
Hunter, F. Elizabeth who disappeared
Iribarne, M. Sudden mysteries
Jenkins, G. Strange attractors
Johnson-Davies, D. The dream
Kalman, J. A property of childhood
Kalu, Anthonia C. Independence
Kees, W. The life of the mind
Kendall, G. In loco parentis
Klass, P. Intimacy
Knight, M. Sundays
Kohler, S. Underworld
Krauss, N. Future emergencies
LaFarge, P. Lamentation over the destruction of
    Ur
Lahiri, J. When Mr. Pirzada came to dine
Lao She. Attachment
Le Guin, U. K. April in Paris
Lee, M. Paradise dance
Lee, M. Wives, lovers, Maximilian
Lee, R. The banks of the Vistula
Lloyd, D. T. Touch
Locklin, G. Circuitry
Locklin, G. The English girl
Locklin, G. Not to worry
López, L. A tatting man
Lovecraft, H. P. The call of cthulhu
Luntta, K. A virgin twice
Maleti, G. The word
Maraini, D. Walls of darkness
Matiella, A. C. The braid
McBrearty, R. G. Soft song of the sometimes
    sane
McGraw, E. Ax of the Apostles
McNally, J. The politics of correctness
Michaels, L. Reflections of a wild kid
Michaels, L. Some laughed
Moore, L. Beautiful grade
Moses, J. Girls like you
Munro, A. Comfort
Murphy, W. Motherly love
Nissen, T. Fundamentals of communication
Norris, L. Self-defense
Oates, J. C. The doll
Oates, J. C. The instructor
Oates, J. C. Mrs. Halifax and Rickie Swann: a
    ballad
Oates, J. C. Questions

TEACHERS—*Continued*

Offill, J. The deer
O'Hagan, A. Glass cheques
Olsen, S. S. Free writing
Otis, M. Aida South, flower
Packer, Z. Our Lady of Peace
Painter, P. The last word
Pearlman, D. D. Death in the des(s)ert
Pearlman, D. D. Spellchecked
Pitt, M. The mean
Pittalwala, I. Mango season
Polansky, S. Pantalone
Potvin, E. A. Sister Marguerite
Raphael, F. All his sons
Reid, E. Happy Jack
Richmond, M. Fifth grade: a criminal history
Richter, H. P. The teacher
Richter, S. The first men
Rinehart, S. Make me
Robinson, P. April in Paris
Robison, M. In Jewel
Row, J. Heaven lake
Row, J. The secrets of bats
Russo, R. Buoyancy
Russo, R. The farther you go
Russo, R. The whore's child
Sánchez, R. He rolled up his sleeves
Sánchez, R. He walked in and sat down
Sandlin, L. Night class
Schickler, D. The smoker
Schmidt, H. J. Wild rice
Schraufnagel, J. Like whiskey for Christmas
Searle, E. 101
Shishin, A. Mr. Eggplant goes home
Simmons, D. Looking for Kelly Dahl
Simonds, M. Nossa Senhora dos Remédios
Singer, I. B. The briefcase
Singer, I. B. The safe deposit
Singer, I. B. The witch
Škvorecký, J. According to Poe
Škvorecký, J. Jezebel from Forest Hill (A love story)
Škvorecký, J. Laws of the jungle
Škvorecký, J. My teacher, Mr. Katz
Smart, A. Vincent
Sojourner, M. What they write in other countries
Solari, M. T. Death and transfiguration of a teacher
Spencer, E. The Bufords
Spencer, E. The eclipse
Spencer, E. The master of Shongalo
Steinbeck, T. The dark watcher
Stevenson, J. The island of the day before yesterday
Stuckey-French, E. Electric wizard
Swain, H. Sushi
Swick, M. A. Crete
Taraqqi, G. The bizarre comportment of Mr. Alpha in exile
Theroux, P. White lies
Thurm, M. Marquise
Treat, J. The summer of Zubeyde
Trevor, W. Death of a professor
Turchi, P. The night sky
Tusquets, E. The same sea as every summer [excerpt]
Updike, J. My father on the verge of disgrace

Updike, J. Tomorrow and tomorrow and so forth
Vapnyar, L. Love lessons — Mondays, 9 A.M.
Vaswani, N. Sita and Ms. Durber
Vivante, A. The cricket
Vivante, A. The Italian class
Vivante, A. Osage orange
Vivante, A. Stones aplenty
Vivante, A. The sugar maples
Wallace, D. F. The soul is not a smithy
Wallace, R. Quick bright things
Wang Cengqi. Big Chan
Waugh, E. Scott-King's modern Europe
Weaver, G. Q. Questing
Weihe, E. Girl in the coat
Wexler, M. Helen of Alexandria
Whalen, T. Professors
Wickham, J. The light on the sea
Winegardner, M. Keegan's load
Winegardner, M. The untenured lecturer
Winsloe, C. The child Manuela [excerpt]
Wuori, G. K. Family
Wuori, G. K. Madness
Yates, R. Doctor Jack-o'-Lantern
Yates, R. Fun with a stranger
Young, T. Too busy swimming
Ziegler, I. Cliffs notes

Tear out my heart. Olson, T.
Tear sheet. Mathews, H.
Tears for Ersulie Freda: men without shadow. Prevost, C.-M.
Tears in the Congri. Ponte, A. J.
Tears need shedding. Coberly, L. M.
The **Tears** of Cortés. Montoya, M. J. R.
The **tears** of the solitaire. Agénor, M.
Technical difficulties and the plague. Boylan, C.
Technical error. Clarke, A. C.

TECHNOLOGY AND CIVILIZATION

Clayton, J. J. Let's not talk politics, please
Derby, M. An appeal
Derby, M. Behavior pilot
Derby, M. The boyish mulatto
Derby, M. Crutches used as weapon
Derby, M. The end of men
Derby, M. The father helmet
Derby, M. First
Derby, M. Gantry's last
Derby, M. Home recordings
Derby, M. Instructions
Derby, M. Joy of eating
Derby, M. The life jacket
Derby, M. Meat tower
Derby, M. Night watchmen
Derby, M. Sky harvest
Derby, M. The sound gun
Derby, M. Stupid animals
Doctorow, C. OwnzOred
Händler, E.-W. Max
Ryman, G. Have not have
Unamuno, M. d. Mechanopolis
Yánez Cossío, A. The IWM 1000

Ted. Catalano, M.

TEDDY BEARS

Harrison, H. I always do what Teddy says
Steele, A. M. The teb hunter

Tedious story. See Chekhov, A. P. A dreary story
Teen angel. Gingher, M.
Teen sniper. Johnson, A.

TEENAGERS *See* Adolescence; Youth

Teeny. Reifler, N.
TEETH
  Chekhov, A. P. Surgery
  Evenson, B. Müller
  Lansdale, J. R. Chompers
  Slavin, J. Dentaphilia
              Diseases
  Chekhov, A. P. A horsy name
  Melville, P. The conversion of Millicent Vernon
Teeth. Estep, M.
Tehano [excerpt] Wier, A.
Teigeler, Piet
  The wind & Mary
    Death cruise; crime stories on the open seas;
      edited by Lawrence Block
El **tejón**. Sánchez, R.
Tel, Jonathan
  Put Not Thy Trust in Chariots
    Granta v85 p205-27 Spr 2004
  Zaghrouda
    Granta no78 p155-65 Summ 2002
TEL AVIV (ISRAEL) *See* Israel—Tel Aviv
Teleabsence. Burstein, M. A.
TELECOMMUNICATION
        See also Telephone; Television
  Clarke, A. C. Dial F for Frankenstein
The **Telemachus** box. Jacobs, M.
TELEPATHY
  Anderson, P. Call me Joe
  Anderson, P. Journeys end
  Anderson, P. Kyrie
  Anderson, P. The martyr
  Bradbury, R. The veldt
  Delany, S. R. Corona
  Malzberg, B. N. The prince of the steppes
  Matheson, R. Lover when you're near me
  Shaw, I. Whispers in bedlam
  Smith, C. Mother Hitton's littul kittons
  Vance, J. The miracle workers
  Weber, D. The hard way home
TELEPHONE
  Bausch, R. 1-900
  Bisson, T. He loved Lucy
  Bradbury, R. Beasts
  Brenner, W. Awareness
  Chekhov, A. P. On the telephone
  Cummins, A. Dr. War is a voice on the phone
  Eldridge, Courtney. Becky
  Klíma, I. Long-distance conversations
  Pittalwala, I. Mango season
  Porter, J. A. Touch wood
  Pryor, J. Wrong numbers
  Reiner, C. Dial 411 for legal smut
  Weinberg, R. Dial your dreams
  Zeman, A. Hello?
A **telephone** call too many. Iarrera, C.
The **telephone** game. Trevor, W.
TELESCOPE
  Arvin, N. Telescope
Telescope. Arvin, N.
Telescope. Sheehan, R.
TELEVISION
  Arvin, N. Two thousand Germans in
    Frankenmuth
  Bishop, M. Simply indispensable
  Bradbury, R. Almost the end of the world
  Clarke, A. C. I remember Babylon
  Etchison, D. Inside the cackle factory
  Mueller, D. Torturing creatures at night

  Ortiz, S. J. Men on the moon
  Richmond, M. Satellite
  Steele, A. M. Her own private sitcom
  Touré. The commercial channel: a unique business opportunity
  Updike, J. Commercial
  Waters, M. Y. Kami
TELEVISION ANNOUNCERS *See* Television announcing
TELEVISION ANNOUNCING
  Delaney, E. J. The anchor and me
TELEVISION BROADCASTING *See* Television announcing
The **television** helps, but not very much. McNulty, J.
TELEVISION PRODUCERS AND DIRECTORS
  Bender, K. E. Anything for money
  Dunn, D. The political piano
  Wallace, D. F. Tri-stan: I sold sissee nar to Ecko
TELEVISION PROGRAMS
  Brenner, W. The Cantankerous Judge
  Casey, M. Talk show lady
  Clark, J. Spin-off
  Davis, L. Something spooky on Geophys
  Hayter, S. The diary of Sue Peaner, Marooned! contestant
  Henderson, L. Tragic heroines tell all
  Leavitt, D. Speonk
  McBrearty, R. G. Improvising
  Searle, E. The young and the rest of us
  Stuckey-French, E. Scavenger hunt
  Vukcevich, R. Season finale
Tell Borges If You See Him. LaSalle, P.
Tell her. Cherry, K.
Tell him what happen, Joe, see will he believe you. McNulty, J.
Tell me everything. Michaels, L.
Tell me Moore. Leon, A. d.
Tell me the reason, do. Purdy, K. W.
Tell me you forgive me? Oates, J. C.
The **tell-tale** heart. Poe, E. A.
The **tell-tale** tattoo. Beck, K. K.
Tell the truth. Hoffman, A.
Tell them they are all full of shit and they should fuck off. Bisson, T.
The **tellers**. Dixon, S.
Telling. Conlon, E.
Telling George. Cannell, D.
Telling Mr. M. Ritchie, E.
Telling stories. Jackson, V. F.
Tells. Bátorová, M.
Telly's Body Shop. Stillwell, C.
Tem, Melanie
  Gardens
    Gathering the bones; original stories from the world's masters of horror; edited by Dennis Etchison, Ramsey Campbell and Jack Dann
  Piano bar blues
    The Museum of horrors; edited by Dennis Etchison
Tem, Steve Rasnic
  Halloween Street
    Best new horror 11; edited and with an introduction by Stephen Jones
    The Year's best fantasy & horror, thirteenth annual collection; edited by Ellen Datlow and Terri Windling

Tem, Steve Rasnic—*Continued*
Heat
The Year's best fantasy & horror, thirteenth
annual collection; edited by Ellen Datlow
and Terri Windling
Out late in the park
Gathering the bones; original stories from the
world's masters of horror; edited by Dennis
Etchison, Ramsey Campbell and Jack Dann
Pareidolia
Best new horror 12; edited and with an intro-
duction by Stephen Jones
Tricks & treats one night on Halloween Street
Best new horror 11; edited and with an intro-
duction by Stephen Jones
What slips away
Best new horror 10; edited and with an intro-
duction by Stephen Jones
TEMPERANCE
Collins, B. Carry's cat
TEMPERATURES, LOW *See* Low temperatures
La **tempesta**. Roth, W. M.
Temping. Halpern, N.
Temple, William F.
The 4-sided triangle
Science-fiction classics; the stories that
morphed into movies; compiled by Forrest
J. Ackerman
The **Temple**. Gao Xingjian
The **Temple** of Amun. Meier, E.
TEMPLES, BUDDHIST *See* Buddhist temples
Temporary light. Braverman, K.
A **temporary** matter. Lahiri, J.
Temporary residence. Blatnik, A.
Temptation. Brin, D.
Temptation. Čapek, K.
Ten for the devil. De Lint, C.
The **ten** lives of Talbert. Collins, B.
Ten secrets of beauty. Coleman, J.
Ten years later. Bobes, M.
Tenant. Hoffman, W.
Tenant. Knight, M.
Tenanting. Ahuja, A.
Tenants. Halloff, P.
The **tenants**. Tenn, W.
Tendeléo's story. McDonald, I.
The **tender** of unmarked graves. Hodgen, C.
The **tender** organizations. Bly, C.
Tenderhead. Mullen, H. R.
Tenderness. Codrescu, A.
Tenebrio. Stableford, B. M.
Tenenboim, Yoysef
Hear, O Israel
Neugroschel, J. No star too beautiful; Yiddish
stories from 1382 to the present; compiled
and translated by Joachim Neugroschel
Teng, Yu-mei *See* Deng Youmei, 1931-
Tenkiller. Leonard, E.
Tenn, William
Alexander the bait
Tenn, W. Immodest proposals; introduction
by Connie Willis; edited by James A.
Mann and Mary C. Tabasko
Bernie the Faust
Tenn, W. Here comes civilization; introduc-
tion by Robert Silverberg; afterword by
George Zebrowski; edited by James A.
Mann and Mary C. Tabasko

Betelgeuse Bridge
Tenn, W. Here comes civilization; introduc-
tion by Robert Silverberg; afterword by
George Zebrowski; edited by James A.
Mann and Mary C. Tabasko
Brooklyn project
Tenn, W. Immodest proposals; introduction
by Connie Willis; edited by James A.
Mann and Mary C. Tabasko
Child's play
Tenn, W. Immodest proposals; introduction
by Connie Willis; edited by James A.
Mann and Mary C. Tabasko
Confusion cargo
Tenn, W. Here comes civilization; introduc-
tion by Robert Silverberg; afterword by
George Zebrowski; edited by James A.
Mann and Mary C. Tabasko
Consulate
Tenn, W. Immodest proposals; introduction
by Connie Willis; edited by James A.
Mann and Mary C. Tabasko
The dark star
Tenn, W. Immodest proposals; introduction
by Connie Willis; edited by James A.
Mann and Mary C. Tabasko
The deserter
Tenn, W. Immodest proposals; introduction
by Connie Willis; edited by James A.
Mann and Mary C. Tabasko
The discovery of Morniel Mathaway
Tenn, W. Here comes civilization; introduc-
tion by Robert Silverberg; afterword by
George Zebrowski; edited by James A.
Mann and Mary C. Tabasko
Down among the dead men
Tenn, W. Immodest proposals; introduction
by Connie Willis; edited by James A.
Mann and Mary C. Tabasko
Dud
Tenn, W. Here comes civilization; introduc-
tion by Robert Silverberg; afterword by
George Zebrowski; edited by James A.
Mann and Mary C. Tabasko
Eastward ho!
Tenn, W. Immodest proposals; introduction
by Connie Willis; edited by James A.
Mann and Mary C. Tabasko
Errand boy
Tenn, W. Here comes civilization; introduc-
tion by Robert Silverberg; afterword by
George Zebrowski; edited by James A.
Mann and Mary C. Tabasko
Everybody loves Irving Bommer
Tenn, W. Here comes civilization; introduc-
tion by Robert Silverberg; afterword by
George Zebrowski; edited by James A.
Mann and Mary C. Tabasko
Firewater
Tenn, W. Immodest proposals; introduction
by Connie Willis; edited by James A.
Mann and Mary C. Tabasko
The flat-eyed monster
Tenn, W. Immodest proposals; introduction
by Connie Willis; edited by James A.
Mann and Mary C. Tabasko

Tenn, William—*Continued*

Flirleflip

Tenn, W. Here comes civilization; introduction by Robert Silverberg; afterword by George Zebrowski; edited by James A. Mann and Mary C. Tabasko

Generation of Noah

Tenn, W. Immodest proposals; introduction by Connie Willis; edited by James A. Mann and Mary C. Tabasko

The ghost standard

Tenn, W. Immodest proposals; introduction by Connie Willis; edited by James A. Mann and Mary C. Tabasko

The girl with some kind of past. And George.

Tenn, W. Here comes civilization; introduction by Robert Silverberg; afterword by George Zebrowski; edited by James A. Mann and Mary C. Tabasko

Hallock's madness

Tenn, W. Here comes civilization; introduction by Robert Silverberg; afterword by George Zebrowski; edited by James A. Mann and Mary C. Tabasko

The house dutiful

Tenn, W. Here comes civilization; introduction by Robert Silverberg; afterword by George Zebrowski; edited by James A. Mann and Mary C. Tabasko

The human angle

Tenn, W. Here comes civilization; introduction by Robert Silverberg; afterword by George Zebrowski; edited by James A. Mann and Mary C. Tabasko

The Ionian cycle

Tenn, W. Here comes civilization; introduction by Robert Silverberg; afterword by George Zebrowski; edited by James A. Mann and Mary C. Tabasko

It ends with a flicker

Tenn, W. Here comes civilization; introduction by Robert Silverberg; afterword by George Zebrowski; edited by James A. Mann and Mary C. Tabasko

The jester

Tenn, W. Immodest proposals; introduction by Connie Willis; edited by James A. Mann and Mary C. Tabasko

A lamp for Medusa

Tenn, W. Here comes civilization; introduction by Robert Silverberg; afterword by George Zebrowski; edited by James A. Mann and Mary C. Tabasko

The last bounce

Tenn, W. Immodest proposals; introduction by Connie Willis; edited by James A. Mann and Mary C. Tabasko

The lemon-green spaghetti-loud dynamite-dribble day

Tenn, W. Immodest proposals; introduction by Connie Willis; edited by James A. Mann and Mary C. Tabasko

The liberation of earth

Tenn, W. Immodest proposals; introduction by Connie Willis; edited by James A. Mann and Mary C. Tabasko

Lisbon cubed

Tenn, W. Immodest proposals; introduction by Connie Willis; edited by James A. Mann and Mary C. Tabasko

The malted milk monsters

Tenn, W. Here comes civilization; introduction by Robert Silverberg; afterword by George Zebrowski; edited by James A. Mann and Mary C. Tabasko

A man of family

Tenn, W. Immodest proposals; introduction by Connie Willis; edited by James A. Mann and Mary C. Tabasko

The masculinist revolt

Tenn, W. Immodest proposals; introduction by Connie Willis; edited by James A. Mann and Mary C. Tabasko

A matter of frequency

Tenn, W. Here comes civilization; introduction by Robert Silverberg; afterword by George Zebrowski; edited by James A. Mann and Mary C. Tabasko

Me, myself, and I

Tenn, W. Here comes civilization; introduction by Robert Silverberg; afterword by George Zebrowski; edited by James A. Mann and Mary C. Tabasko

Mistress Sary

Tenn, W. Here comes civilization; introduction by Robert Silverberg; afterword by George Zebrowski; edited by James A. Mann and Mary C. Tabasko

My mother was a witch

Tenn, W. Immodest proposals; introduction by Connie Willis; edited by James A. Mann and Mary C. Tabasko

Null-P

Tenn, W. Immodest proposals; introduction by Connie Willis; edited by James A. Mann and Mary C. Tabasko

On Venus, have we got a rabbi

Tenn, W. Immodest proposals; introduction by Connie Willis; edited by James A. Mann and Mary C. Tabasko

Party of the two parts

Tenn, W. Immodest proposals; introduction by Connie Willis; edited by James A. Mann and Mary C. Tabasko

Project Hush

Tenn, W. Immodest proposals; introduction by Connie Willis; edited by James A. Mann and Mary C. Tabasko

The puzzle of Priipiirii

Tenn, W. Here comes civilization; introduction by Robert Silverberg; afterword by George Zebrowski; edited by James A. Mann and Mary C. Tabasko

Ricardo's virus

Tenn, W. Here comes civilization; introduction by Robert Silverberg; afterword by George Zebrowski; edited by James A. Mann and Mary C. Tabasko

Sanctuary

Tenn, W. Here comes civilization; introduction by Robert Silverberg; afterword by George Zebrowski; edited by James A. Mann and Mary C. Tabasko

Tenn, William—*Continued*

The servant problem
  Tenn, W. Immodest proposals; introduction by Connie Willis; edited by James A. Mann and Mary C. Tabasko

She only goes out at night . . .
  Tenn, W. Here comes civilization; introduction by Robert Silverberg; afterword by George Zebrowski; edited by James A. Mann and Mary C. Tabasko

The sickness
  Tenn, W. Immodest proposals; introduction by Connie Willis; edited by James A. Mann and Mary C. Tabasko

The tenants
  Tenn, W. Immodest proposals; introduction by Connie Willis; edited by James A. Mann and Mary C. Tabasko

There were people on Bikini, there were people on Attu
  Tenn, W. Here comes civilization; introduction by Robert Silverberg; afterword by George Zebrowski; edited by James A. Mann and Mary C. Tabasko

Time in advance
  Tenn, W. Immodest proposals; introduction by Connie Willis; edited by James A. Mann and Mary C. Tabasko

Venus and the seven sexes
  Tenn, W. Immodest proposals; introduction by Connie Willis; edited by James A. Mann and Mary C. Tabasko

Venus is a man's world
  Tenn, W. Immodest proposals; introduction by Connie Willis; edited by James A. Mann and Mary C. Tabasko

Wednesday's child
  Tenn, W. Immodest proposals; introduction by Connie Willis; edited by James A. Mann and Mary C. Tabasko

"Will you walk a little faster"
  Tenn, W. Here comes civilization; introduction by Robert Silverberg; afterword by George Zebrowski; edited by James A. Mann and Mary C. Tabasko

Winthrop was stubborn
  Tenn, W. Immodest proposals; introduction by Connie Willis; edited by James A. Mann and Mary C. Tabasko

TENNESSEE

Chenoweth, A. Powerman
Drake, R. Connections
Drake, R. Every Friday afternoon
Drake, R. How come you reckon he did that?
Drake, R. Let there be light
Norris, H. The flying hawk

Farm life
See Farm life—Tennessee

Knoxville
Richmond, M. Propaganda
Wagner, K. E. Where the summer ends

Memphis
Drake, R. The Peabody ducks and all the rest
Mesler, C. The growth and death of Buddy Gardner

Tennessee. Linney, R.

TENNIS
Gilchrist, E. In the land of dreamy dreams
Louis, L. G. Thirty yards

Touré. It's life and death at the Slush Puppie Open
Verghese, A. Tension
Wilson, M. Youthful offenders

Tenorio, Georgie A.
Cigarette Love
  Hanging Loose no84 p132-3 2004
Sweet Seconds
  Hanging Loose no84 p131 2004

Tenorio, Lesley A.
Superassassin
  Best new American voices 2001; guest editor Charles Baxter; series editors John Kulka and Natalie Danford

Tenorio, Lysley
Monstress
  Atlantic Monthly (1993) v291 no5 p77-84 Je 2003

Tension. Verghese, A.
The **tenth**. Leegant, J.
Tepoztlan tomorrow. Desai, A.
Teratophobia. Munson, P.
The **term** paper artist. Leavitt, D.
TERMINAL ILLNESS
Adams, A. Elizabeth
Allyn, D. Puppyland
Berry, W. Fidelity
Bloom, A. Hold tight
Brown, J. Animal stories
Brown, L. A roadside resurrection
Burford, M. Aloha, Les
Carlson, R. Oxygen
Carson, J. Dog Star
Caspers, N. Vegetative states
Cobb, T. Oncology
Connolly, C. Granville Hill
Franklin, T. Blue horses
Goldner, B. Deep down to the bottom of this
Highsmith, P. The trouble with Mrs. Blynn, the trouble with the world
Jance, J. A. A flash of chrysanthemum
Kaplan, H. Live life king-sized
MacLeod, A. The road to Rankin's Point
Nevai, L. Faith healer
Robison, M. Yours
Smith, L. Intensive care
Steele, C. Respiration
Strayed, C. Good
Turzillo, M. A. Mars is no place for children
Updike, J. The dark
Westmoreland, T. A. Strong at the broken places
Winter, E. Dragon box
Wood, M. Ernie's ark
Terminal misunderstanding. McBain, E.
Termination dust. Boyle, T. C.
Termite colonies. Griffith, D.
TERMITES
Clarke, A. C. The next tenants
Murray, J. The carpenter who looked like a boxer
The **terrace** of the leper king. West, K.
The **terrapin**. Highsmith, P.
The **terrible-tempered** rube. O'Rourke, F.
Territorial imperatives. Ritchie, E.
Territorial rights. Lee, M.
Territory. Leavitt, D.
Terror. Chekhov, A. P.
Terror by night. Weinberg, R.

TERRORISM
 See also Violence
Alexie, S. Can I get a witness?
Aylett, S. The passenger
Bishop, M. Last night out
Broughton, T. A. The terrorist
DeAndrea, W. L. Snowy reception
Gilchrist, E. Götterdämmerung, in which Nora
    Jane and Freddy Harwood confront evil in
    a world they never made
Gordimer, N. Karma
Huang, M. J. Martyr
Lempel, Blume. Scenes on a bare canvas
Mukherjee, B. The management of grief
Ramaya, S. Operation monsoon
Shonk, K. Kitchen friends
Sorrentino, G. Lost in the stars
Taylor, Nick. The smell of despair
Vinge, V. Conquest by default
Ward, A. E. Should I be scared ?
TERRORISTS *See* Terrorism
TESLA, NIKOLA, 1856-1943
                    About
Landis, G. A. The eyes of America
Tessier, Thomas
 Lulu
    Best new horror 11; edited and with an intro-
        duction by Stephen Jones
 Moments of change
    Gathering the bones; original stories from the
        world's masters of horror; edited by Dennis
        Etchison, Ramsey Campbell and Jack Dann
Test. Galloway, J.
The **test**. Matheson, R.
TEST PILOTS *See* Air pilots
Testament of Andros. Blish, J.
Tester, William
 Bad day
    Tester, W. Head; stories
 Cousins
    Tester, W. Head; stories
 Floridita
    Tester, W. Head; stories
 Immaculate
    Tester, W. Head; stories
 The living and the dead
    Tester, W. Head; stories
 Wet
    Tester, W. Head; stories
 Where the dark ended
    Tester, W. Head; stories
 Whisperers
    Tester, W. Head; stories
 Who's your daddy now?
    Tester, W. Head; stories
Testimony. Addonizio, K.
Testimony. Davis, A.
Testing,. Steinberg, S.
Tête-à-tête. Bradbury, R.
Tetrick, Byron
 The angel of the wall
    Tetrick, B. In the shadow of the wall; an an-
        thology of Vietnam stories that might have
        been; edited by Byron R. Tetrick

Tevis, Walter S.
 The hustler
    The Workshop; seven decades of the Iowa
        Writers' Workshop: 42 stories, recollections
        & essays on Iowa's place in 20th-century
        American literature; edited by Tom Grimes
 Rent control
    Home and beyond; an anthology of Kentucky
        short stories; edited by Morris Allen
        Grubbs; with an introduction by Wade Hall
        and an afterword by Charles E. May
Tex. Jakes, J.
TEXAS
             See also Alamo (San Antonio, Tex.)
Adam, C. Hen
Anderson, R. Death and the maid
Barrett, N., Jr. Trading post
Barthelme, F. Export
Bass, R. Swamp Boy
Berry, Betsy. Family and flood
Blake, J. C. Runaway horses
Blake, J. C. Texas woman blues
Blake, J. C. La vida loca
Blakely, M. Laureano's wall
Casares, O. Big Jesse, Little Jesse
Casares, O. Chango
Casares, O. Charro
Casares, O. Domingo
Casares, O. Jerry Fuentes
Casares, O. Mr. Z
Casares, O. Mrs. Perez
Casares, O. RG
Casares, O. Yolanda
Castillo, R. The battle of the Alamo
Cook, K. L. Breaking glass
Cook, K. L. Easter weekend
Cook, K. L. Gone
Cook, K. L. Knock down, drag out
Cook, K. L. Marty
Cook, K. L. Nature's way
Cook, K. L. Thrumming
Crumley, J. Whores
Cutter, L. The red boots
DeMarinis, R. Novias
Doctorow, E. L. Child, dead, in the rose garden
Dunn, K. The allies
Earle, S. Wheeler County
Flynn, R. Truth and beauty
Froh, R. The two trail ride tricksters
Fromm, P. How all this started
Furman, L. The woods
Garcia, L. G. Alone
Garcia, L. G. Always verbena
Garcia, L. G. Delivering meat
Garcia, L. G. Eladio comes home
Garcia, L. G. The emergency room
Garcia, L. G. Girl
Garcia, L. G. Mammogram
Garcia, L. G. Mister Tyrone
Garcia, L. G. Nano returns
Garcia, L. G. Parents
Garcia, L. G. The sergeant
Garcia, L. G. Uncle Willy
Garcia, L. G. West Texas cowboys
Gavell, M. L. The blessing
Gavell, M. L. The last daughter-in-law
Gonzalez, R. Invisible country
Graves, J. The last running
Greene, A. C. The girl at Cabe ranch

TEXAS—*Continued*

Healy, J. F. The safest little town in Texas

Hearon, S. A prince of a fellow [excerpt]

Henry, O. Art and the bronco

Henry, W. Home place

Hickey, D. The closed season

Hickey, D. I'm bound to follow the longhorn cows

Hinojosa, R. The Gulf Oil -Can Santa Claus

Johnston, B. A. Corpus

Johnston, B. A. Two liars

Kelton, E. North of the big river

LaSalle, P. A guide to some small border airports

Loomis, N. M. The St. Louis salesman

Mazor, J. The lone star kid

McMurtry, L. The last picture show [excerpt]

Meissner, J. Placedo junction

Osborn, C. My brother is a cowboy

Peery, J. Huevos

Phillips, D. R. What it cost travelers

Pickens, W. Jim Crow in Texas

Poirier, M. J. Worms

Reynolds, C. A train to catch

Roorbach, B. Big bend

Sanford, A. Strangers and pilgrims

Scarborough, D. From the wind [excerpt]

Smith, C. W. The Bundlelays

Troy, J. Ramone

Webb, Don. Metamorphosis no. 5

Farm life

See Farm life—Texas

Politics

See Politics—Texas

Alamo

See Alamo (San Antonio, Tex.)

Austin

Cobb, W. When we were cool

Isle, R. Wild turkey

Corpus Christi

Johnston, B. A. Anything that floats

Johnston, B. A. Birds of Paradise

Johnston, B. A. Buy for me the rain

Johnston, B. A. Corpus Christi

Johnston, B. A. In the tall grass

Johnston, B. A. Waterwalkers

Dallas

Barthelme, F. Bag boy

Shrake, E. Strange peaches [excerpt]

Taylor, P. E. Leaping Leo

El Paso

Carr, P. M. An El Paso Idyll

Gilb, D. Mayela one day in 1989

Gilb, D. The pillows

Gilb, D. Romero's shirt

Gonzalez, R. Away

Gonzalez, R. The black pig

Gonzalez, R. Train station

Saenz, B. A. Exile

Troncoso, S. The abuelita

Troncoso, S. Angie Luna

Troncoso, S. Espiritu Santo

Troncoso, S. The last tortilla

Troncoso, S. Punching chickens

Troncoso, S. A rock trying to be a stone

Troncoso, S. The snake

Troncoso, S. Time magician

Yañez, R. Rio Grande

Galveston

Barthelme, F. Galveston

Grape, J. Cat o'nine lives

Houston

Viswanathan, L. Cool wedding

Wisenberg, S. L. Liberator

San Antonio

Rivera, T. The portrait

Sanderson, J. Commerce Street

Waco

Butler, R. O. Heavy metal

Du Bois, W. E. B. Jesus Christ in Texas

The **Texas** Ranger. Gilliland, G.

TEXAS RANGERS

Cunningham, E. Beginner's luck

Cunningham, E. Blotting the triangle

Cunningham, E. The hammer thumb

Cunningham, E. The hermit of Tigerhead Butte

Cunningham, E. The ranger way

Cunningham, E. Spiderweb trail

Cunningham, E. The trail of a fool

Cunningham, E. Wanted—?

Cunningham, E. Ware calls it a day

Smith, C. Thirty rangers

Texas Wherever You Look. Duff, G.

Texas woman blues. Blake, J. C.

TGE. Bird, D.

THAILAND

Bowles, P. At the Krungthep Plaza

Bowles, P. You have left your lotus pods on the bus

Bangkok

Freudenberger, N. The orphan

Somtow, S. P. Bird catcher

Thailand. Murakami, H.

Thanasphere. Vonnegut, K.

Thanksgiving. Roorbach, B.

Thanksgiving. Sterne, M.

THANKSGIVING DAY

Bloom, A. Light into dark

Capote, T. The Thanksgiving visitor

Collins, B. To grandmother's house we go

Davies, P. H. Cakes of baby

Denton, B. Timmy and Tommy's Thanksgiving secret

Fallis, G. Comes the revolution

Gifford, B. For this we give thanks

Locklin, G. Turkey Day

Orringer, J. Pilgrims

Roorbach, B. Thanksgiving

Taylor, P. H. A sentimental journey

That Awning on Third West. Bang, N.

That bad woman. Boylan, C.

That boy. Furman, L.

That damn cat. Collins, B.

That day. Ahmadi Khorasani, N.

That day at Eagle's Point. Gorman, E.

That distant land. Berry, W.

That easy kind of life. Valeri, L.

That evening sun. See Faulkner, W. That evening sun go down

That evening sun go down. Faulkner, W.

That feeling, you can only say what it is in French. King, S.

That Fox-of-a-Beñat. Trevanian

"**That** in Aleppo once . . . ". Nabokov, V. V.

"**That** Little Boy": An English Translation of Jyotirmoyee Devi's Bengali Short Story "Shei Chheleta". Devi, J.

That only a mother. Merril, J.
That Place. Scott, J.
That share of glory. Kornbluth, C. M.
That smell. Mosley, W.
That SOB bastard Eddie. Reiner, C.
That the heart no longer moves. Henry, G.
That was me. Chabon, M.
That was then. Kureishi, H.
That winter. Leebron, F. G.
The **Thatch** weave. Fromm, P.
Thatcher's Britain. Boylan, C.
That's how straight boys dance. Cole, C. B.
That's really no way to make money. Röggla, K.
That's true of everybody. Winegardner, M.
Thaw. Ludington, M.
The: Dancer's Hand. Kunz, D.
The **theater**. Little, B.
THEATER LIFE
> *See also* Actors; Actresses names of actors and actresses

Babel', I. Di Grasso
Clark, J. K2
Doble, J. After six weeks in New York
Dodd, S. M. Song-and-dance man
Matthews, C. Death of a glamour cat
Scoville, S. Waiting for Zilly Finkbine
Theatre of the real. Skillings, R. D.
Théâtre Optique. Maso, C.
THEATRICAL TROUPES *See* Theater life
THEFT
> *See also* Embezzlement; Robbery; Thieves

Archer, J. The reclining woman
Arvin, N. The prototype
Bishop, P. The framing game
Bishop, P. The thief of Christmas
Bowles, P. The husband
Callaghan, M. All the years of her life
Cannell, D. The purloined purple pearl
Chaudhuri, A. The man from Khurda district
Chekhov, A. P. An upheaval
Cheng, C.-W. Hair
Cohen, S. Neville
Cohen, S. Those who appreciate money hate to touch the principal
Connor, J. Tea and comfortable advice
Crider, B. Tinseltown Follies of 1948
Crowther, P. Cat on an old school roof
Davidson, A. The ikon of Elijah
DeLancey, K. I loved the squire
Dunlap, S. People who sit in glass houses
Gilb, D. Maria de Covina
Gorman, C. The Death Cat of Hester Street
Greer, R. O. Backup
Holtzer, S. The golden rounds
Iagnemma, K. The phrenologist's dream
Krich, R. M. "You win some . . . "
Lee, W. W. Letting the cat out of the bag
Louise, D. D. Stitches in time
Maron, M. Till 3:45
Morgan, R. The balm of Gilead tree
O'Callaghan, M. An insignificant crime
Perry, A. Daisy and the Christmas goose
Roorbach, B. A job at Little Henry's
Scoville, S. The pin collectors
A **theft**. Bellow, S.
Theft. Porter, K. A.
The **theft** of the bingo card. Hoch, E. D.
The **theft** of the Halloween pumpkin. Hoch, E. D.

The **theft** of the sandwich board. Hoch, E. D.
Their mother's purse. Callaghan, M.
Their story. Glave, T.
Their words, for you. Mathews, H.
Thelwell, Ekwueme Michael *See* Thelwell, Michael, 1939-
Thelwell, Michael
Community of victims
> Crossing the color line; readings in Black and white; edited by Suzanne W. Jones

Direct action
> The African American West; a century of short stories; edited by Bruce A. Glasrud and Laurie Champion

Them!. Marshall, W. L.
A **theme** for Hyacinth. Symons, J.
Theme from a summer place. Cohen, R.
The **theme** of the traitor and the hero. Borges, J. L.
Then later. Kelman, J.
Then they say you're drunk. Fischer, T.
The **theologians**. Borges, J. L.
A **Theology** of Anorexia. Russell, J.
Theories of rain. Barrett, A.
The **theory** of everything. Czuchlewski, D.
A **theory** of fiction. Berry, R. M.
Theory of flight. Banks, R.
A **Theory** of Probability. McCormack, J.
Theory of relativity. Nye, J. L.
Theory of the Leisure Class. Levy, E. J.
The **theory** of the tachanka. See Babel', I. The tachanka theory
There are blows in life so hard—. Naranjo, A. G.
There are more things. Borges, J. L.
There are no dead. Bisson, T.
There are no green butterflies. Sosin, D.
There aren't any foxes in that cave. Williams, M.
There goes Ravelaar. Van de Wetering, J.
There is danger. Vukcevich, R.
There was a river. Walker, A.
There were people on Bikini, there were people on Attu. Tenn, W.
There will come soft rains. Bradbury, R.
There'll never be another you. Bean, B.
There's a Garden of Eden. Gilchrist, E.
There's no such thing. De Lint, C.
There's Nothing. Henry, J.
There's nothing the matter with Gwen. Cobb, W. J.
There's too much news. Spencer, D.
There's tradition for you. Fell, A.
Theroux, Paul
An African story
> Theroux, P. The stranger at the Palazzo d'Oro and other stories

Disheveled nymphs
> Theroux, P. The stranger at the Palazzo d'Oro and other stories

A Judas memoir
> Theroux, P. The stranger at the Palazzo d'Oro and other stories

Scouting for Boys
> *Granta* v80 p185-225 Wint 2002

The stranger at the Palazzo d'Oro
> Theroux, P. The stranger at the Palazzo d'Oro and other stories

White lies
> Living on the edge; fiction by Peace Corps writers; edited by John Coyne

These eyes. Jones, G.
These hands. Brockmeier, K.
These people are us. Singleton, G.
"**They—**". Heinlein, R. A.
They. Kipling, R.
They better don't stop the carnival. Anthony, M.
They came at dawn. Williams, K.
They don't seem to be talking to Grogan. McNulty, J.
They have numbered all my bones. Westmoreland, T. A.
They only hang you once. Hammett, D.
They Stand and Serve Too. Shivani, A.
They used to go for long walks on Sundays . . . Régio, J.
They'd have taken him if he was only a torso. McNulty, J.
They're playing my song. Touré
They've got my (wrong) number. Robyn, K. L.
Thick as thieves. Perabo, S.
Thicker than water. Gallico, P.
Thief. Brown, J.
The **thief**. Mosley, W.
The **thief** of Christmas. Bishop, P.
The **thief** of flowers. Connor, J.
The **thief** of Tay Ninh. Bowen, K.
O **thief,** what is the life you lead? Le Clézio, J.-M. G.

Thien, Madeleine
Alchemy
　Thien, M. Simple recipes; stories
Bullet train
　Thien, M. Simple recipes; stories
Dispatch
　Thien, M. Simple recipes; stories
Four days from Oregon
　Thien, M. Simple recipes; stories
House
　Thien, M. Simple recipes; stories
A map of the city
　Thien, M. Simple recipes; stories
Simple recipes
　Thien, M. Simple recipes; stories

THIEVES
　　　See also Cattle thieves; Horse thieves; Kleptomania; Theft
Anderson, F. I. Blind man's buff
Anderson, K. Burglary in progress
Avrich, J. The braid
Banks, R. The burden
Bellow, S. A silver dish
Borges, J. L. Ibn-Hakam al-Bokhari, murdered in his labyrinth
Carew, J. Tilson Ezekiel alias Ti-Zek
Carey, P. The fat man in history
Cherryh, C. J. A thief in Korianth
Clarke, A. C. Trouble with time
Cobb, W. J. For all you dorks, blah blah blah
Cohen, S. I'm sorry, Mr. Turini
Collins, M. The choice
Collins, M. Clay pigeon
Collins, M. Occupational hazard
Collins, M. Silent partner
Connolly, C. Paradise Drive
Cook, C. The pickpocket
Crider, B. How I found a cat, lost true love, and broke the bank at Monte Carlo
Davidson, A. Captain Pasharooney
Davis, D. S. Christopher and Maggie

Deane, J. F. The experience of what is beautiful
DeMarinis, R. Billy Ducks among the pharaohs
Dexter, P. The jeweler
Doerr, A. The caretaker
Ford, R. Rock Springs
Franklin, T. Christmas 1893
Gallagher, S. Jailbird for Jesus
Gautreaux, T. Easy pickings
Gifford, B. A fair price
Greer, R. O. Revision
Gussoff, C. Stealing purses
Hammett, D. The second-story angel
Henry, O. A retrieved reformation
Highsmith, P. A dangerous hobby
Kaminsky, S. M. Sometimes something goes wrong
Koontz, D. R. Snatcher
Kramer, W. East Side story
Le Clézio, J.-M. G. O thief, what is the life you lead?
Lee, W. W. Miami
Mendes, B. Noble causes
Myers, T. The stay-at-home thief
Painter, P. Grief
Pickard, N. Storm warnings
Sade, marquis de. Thieves and swindlers
Sakaguchi, J. M. T. A fortune
Santos-Febres, M. Flight
Singer, I. B. The brooch
Singer, I. B. In the poorhouse
Singer, I. B. Not for the Sabbath
Škvorecký, J. Pink champagne
Smith, C. Mother Hitton's littul kittons
Smith, J. Montezuma's other revenge
Smith, J. Where the boys are
Tilghman, C. The late night news
Tolstoy, L., graf. The son of a thief
Tyre, N. A nice place to stay
Vachss, A. H. Just the ticket
Vachss, A. H. Stepping stone
Waugh, E. Multa Pecunia
Wellen, E. The perfect rotter
Westlake, D. E. The burglar and the whatsit
Westlake, D. E. Devilishly
Westlake, D. E. Last-minute shopping
Yorke, M. Mugs
Thieves. Burnett, E.
Thieves. Evans, E.
Thieves. Stewart, B. A.
Thieves. Yates, R.
Thieves and swindlers. Sade, marquis de
Thin end of the wedge. Lychack, W.
The **thin** man. McGarry, J.
Thin walls. Viganò, R.
Thing. Kharms, D.
The **thing** about Benny. Bell, M. S.
A **thing** about cars!. Lumley, B.
The **thing** around them. Krysl, M.
The **thing** in the fog. Quinn, S.
The **thing** in the forest. Byatt, A. S.
The **thing** in the weeds. Hodgson, W. H.
The **thing** with Willie. Sagstetter, K.
Things. Carnahan, P.
Things come to mind. Chiappone, R.
Things fall apart. Maddern, P. C.
Things gone and things still here. Bowles, P.
Things had gone badly. Highsmith, P.
Things He Gave Her. Thompson, B.
The **things** he told her. Gunn, K.

Things I didn't know my father knew. Crowther, P.

The **things** I don't know about. McBrearty, R. G.

Things invisible to see. Kinsella, W. P.

Things left undone. Tilghman, C.

Things of That Nature. Scott, T.

Things that fall from the sky. Brockmeier, K.

Things that make your heart beat faster. Anderson, J.

The **things** they carried. O'Brien, T.

Things you can make something out of. Foster, K.

Things You Should Know. Holmes, A. M.

Things you should know. Homes, A. M.

Think about if you want. Nissen, T.

Think of England. Davies, P. H.

Thinking. Wallace, M.

Thinning the herd. Lefcourt, P.

Thiong'o, Ng'ugĩ wa *See* Ng'ugĩ wa Thiong'o, 1938-

The **third** and final continent. Lahiri, J.

Third arm. Strand, G.

Third Avenue medicine. McNulty, J.

The **third** bank of the river. Rosa, J. G.

Third Eye Rising. Shroff, M. F.

Third from the sun. Matheson, R.

The **third** Manny. Faherty, T.

The **third** Mrs. Kessler. Epstein, J.

The **third** nation. Hoffman, L.

The **third** person. Gasco, E.

The **third** person. Groff, D.

The **third** policeman [excerpt] O'Brien, F.

The **third** rail. Sterns, A.

The **third** sacred well of the temple. Davidson, A.

The **third** terrace. Alexis, A.

The **third** thing that killed my father off. Carver, R.

Third time lucky. Huff, T.

Thirlwell, Adam

  The Cyrillic Alphabet

    Granta no81 p341-50 Spr 2003

Thirsty deer. Jacobs, M.

Thirteen & a half. Meloy, M.

Thirteen coils. Estleman, L. D.

Thirteen lies about hummingbirds. Bishop, M.

Thirteen ways to water. Rogers, B. H.

Thirteen windows. Chaon, D.

The **thirteenth** fey. Yolen, J.

Thirty-four seasons of winter. Kittredge, W.

Thirty head of killers. Shepard, J.

Thirty rangers. Smith, C.

The **thirty-sixth** chicken of Master Wu. Fischerová, D.

Thirty yards. Louis, L. G.

Thirty-year-old. Winegardner, M.

Thirty years of bees. Sammān, G.

This bitter earth. Dwyer, M.

This blessed house. Lahiri, J.

This country, that country. Kawabata, Y.

This imaginary me. Pritchett, L.

This is death. Westlake, D. E.

"**This** Is Earl Sandt". Butler, R. O.

This is geology to us. Haake, K.

This is how it happened. Walker, A.

This Is Living. Schoech, S.

This is not it. Tillman, L.

This is the world. Penn, W. S.

This is what it means to say Phoenix, Arizona. Alexie, S.

This Is What You Owe Me. Bain, T.

This Island Queens. Ochoa, G.

This itches, y'all. Singleton, G.

This lady was a Bostonian they call them. McNulty, J.

This life. Ponte, A. J.

This morning, a letter arrived. . . Roth, J.

This Parrot Is Hilarious. Sneed, C.

This picnic you're having. Blitz, R.

This place you return to is home. Gunn, K.

This rough magic. O'Neill, S.

This side of independence. Chilson, R.

This side of the legend. Mungan, M.

This side of the Oder. Hermann, J.

This son of mine. Vonnegut, K.

This third year of returning. Sosin, D.

This time. Campbell, R.

Thomas, Dorothy

  The car

    Thomas, D. and Pappas, C. The getaway and other stories; edited and with an introduction by Christine Pappas

  The Christmas whopper

    Thomas, D. and Pappas, C. The getaway and other stories; edited and with an introduction by Christine Pappas

  Flowers appear on the earth

    Thomas, D. and Pappas, C. The getaway and other stories; edited and with an introduction by Christine Pappas

  Frost in the morning

    Thomas, D. and Pappas, C. The getaway and other stories; edited and with an introduction by Christine Pappas

  The getaway

    Thomas, D. and Pappas, C. The getaway and other stories; edited and with an introduction by Christine Pappas

  The girl from follow

    Thomas, D. and Pappas, C. The getaway and other stories; edited and with an introduction by Christine Pappas

  Grandma and the sentimental travler

    Thomas, D. and Pappas, C. The getaway and other stories; edited and with an introduction by Christine Pappas

  Grandma Hotel Adams

    Thomas, D. and Pappas, C. The getaway and other stories; edited and with an introduction by Christine Pappas

  The joybell

    Thomas, D. and Pappas, C. The getaway and other stories; edited and with an introduction by Christine Pappas

  My pigeon pair

    Thomas, D. and Pappas, C. The getaway and other stories; edited and with an introduction by Christine Pappas

  The Steckley girls

    Thomas, D. and Pappas, C. The getaway and other stories; edited and with an introduction by Christine Pappas

  Up in the hills

    Thomas, D. and Pappas, C. The getaway and other stories; edited and with an introduction by Christine Pappas

Thomas, H. Nigel

  The village cock

    Whispers from the cotton tree root; Caribbean fabulist fiction; edited by Nalo Hopkinson

Thomas, James Ellis
The Saturday Morning Car Wash Club
New stories from the South: the year's best, 2001; edited by Shannon Ravenel; with a preface by Lee Smith
Thomas, Jeffrey
The flaying season
Death dines at 8:30; edited by Claudia Bishop and Nick DiChario
Thomas, Joyce Carol
Young Reverend Zelma Lee Moses
The African American West; a century of short stories; edited by Bruce A. Glasrud and Laurie Champion
Thomas, Michael W.
Delfigo Street
The Antioch Review v60 no2 p292-300 Spr 2002
Thomas, Randolph
The Lives of Pioneers
Southwest Review v87 no2/3 p327-37 2002
Thomas, Sheree Renée
How Sukie Come Free
Meridians v2 no2 p185-7 2002
How Sukie cross de big wata
Mojo: conjure stories; edited by Nalo Hopkinson
Thomas, Stephen P.
Petroglyphs
The North American Review v288 no1 p14-21 Ja/F 2003
Thomas, Sue
Correspondence [excerpt]
Reload: rethinking women + cyberculture; edited by Mary Flanagan and Austin Booth
Thomas, Victoria
See also DeWeese, Gene, 1934-
Thomas Lowdermilk's generosity. Lopez, B. H.
Thompson, Alice
Pandora
The Literary Review (Madison, N.J.) v45 no2 p377-95 Wint 2002
Thompson, Barbara
Things He Gave Her
Parnassus: Poetry in Review v27 no1/2 p181-6 2003
Thompson, Clifford
Judgment
Crossing the color line; readings in Black and white; edited by Suzanne W. Jones
Thompson, Janet L.
Stone or Water
New Letters v69 no2/3 p173-87 2003
Thompson, Jean
All shall love me and despair
Thompson, J. Who do you love; stories
The Amish
Thompson, J. Who do you love; stories
Antarctica
Thompson, J. Who do you love; stories
Fire dreams
Thompson, J. Who do you love; stories
Forever
Thompson, J. Who do you love; stories
Heart of gold
Thompson, J. Who do you love; stories
Ice angels
Thompson, J. Who do you love; stories

The little heart
Thompson, J. Who do you love; stories
The lost child
Thompson, J. Who do you love; stories
Mercy
Thompson, J. Who do you love; stories
Mother nature
Thompson, J. Who do you love; stories
Poor Helen
Thompson, J. Who do you love; stories
The rich man's house
Thompson, J. Who do you love; stories
Who do you love
Thompson, J. Who do you love; stories
The widower
Thompson, J. Who do you love; stories
Thompson, Monroe
Jesus, beans, and butter rum lifesavers
Stories from the Blue Moon Café; edited by Sonny Brewer
Thompson, Sidney
Arnold's number
Stories from the Blue Moon Café; edited by Sonny Brewer
Ernest
Stories from the Blue Moon Cafe II; edited by Sonny Brewer
Floating
The Southern Review (Baton Rouge, La.) v38 no1 p176-87 Wint 2002
Thompson, Thomas
Gun job
A Century of great Western stories; edited by John Jakes
Thomsen, Brian
It's a wonderful miracle on 34th Street's Christmas carol
A yuletide universe; sixteen fantastical tales; edited by Brian M. Thomsen
Thomson, Amy
Virtual girl [excerpt]
Reload: rethinking women + cyberculture; edited by Mary Flanagan and Austin Booth
Thon, Melanie Rae
First, body
The Scribner anthology of contemporary short fiction; fifty North American stories since 1970; Lex Williford and Michael Martone, editors
Heavenly Creatures: For Wandering Children and Their Delinquent Mother
The Paris Review v46 p222-47 Spr 2004
Little white sister
Breaking into print; early stories and insights into getting published; a Ploughshares anthology; edited by DeWitt Henry
Thorazine Johnny Felsun loves me (from his permanent cage of lifelong confinement). Jones, T.
THOREAU, HENRY DAVID, 1817-1862
                    About
Davenport, G. The Concord sonata
The **thorn** in the flesh. Lawrence, D. H.
Thorns for Johnny Spring. Farrell, C.

Thornton, Kate
  Ai witness
    A Deadly dozen; tales of murder from members of Sisters in Crime/Los Angeles; edited by Susan B. Casmier, Aljean Harmetz and Cynthia Lawrence
Thornton, W. J.
  The Widow in Her Weeds
    The Literary Review (Madison, N.J.) v47 no2 p145-55 Wint 2004
Those Deep Elm Brown's Ferry Blues. Gay, W.
Those kooks. Cohen, R.
Those little foreign beauties. Chiappone, R.
Those Tender Mayfly Childhood Sweetheart Games. Doherty, M.
Those that trespass. Tremayne, P.
Those vanished I recognize. Piccirilli, T.
Those who appreciate money hate to touch the principal. Cohen, S.
Those who know. What, L.
Thou still unravished bride. Davidson, A.
The **thought-monster**. Long, A. R.
THOUGHT TRANSFERENCE *See* Telepathy
A **thousand** days for Mokhtar. Bowles, P.
Thrasher, L. L.
  Sacrifice
    The Best American mystery stories, 1999; edited and with an introduction by Ed McBain
Threads on the Mountain. Schoenewaldt, P.
THREATENED SPECIES *See* Endangered species
Three. Čapek, K.
Three. Grau, S. A.
Three Annas. See Chekhov, A. P. "Anna on the neck"
Three bachelors in a fiery furnace. Škvorecký, J.
The **three** boxes. Bergstrom, E.
The **three** button trick. Barker, N.
Three Chronicles. Atwood, M.
Three days. a month. more. Light, D.
Three days in that autumn. Pak, W.-S.
Three-Dot Po. Paretsky, S.
Three feet of water. Cobb, W. J.
Three Figures Out of Schools. Winner, A.
The **three** friends. Winterson, J.
Three generations. Sánchez, R.
Three German fantasies. Murakami, H.
Three ghosts. Betts, D.
Three Girls. Oates, J. C.
Three hearings on the existence of snakes in the human bloodstream. Gardner, J. A.
Three hearts and three lions. Anderson, P.
Three ladies sipping tea in a Persian garden. Johnson, D.
Three-legged dog. Watson, I.
The **three-legged** horse. Cheng, C.-W.
Three Letters. King, L. L.
The **three** little pigs. Rollins, H.
Three men in a flying saucer. See Clarke, A. C. Trouble with the natives
Three minor love stories. O'Neill, S.
The **three** musketeers [excerpt] Dumas, A.
Three nil. Coward, M.
Three parting shots and a forecast. Hodgen, C.
Three people. Trevor, W.
Three pigs in five days [excerpt] Prose, F.
Three ravens on a red ground. Girardi, R.
Three simple hearts. Codrescu, A.

Three Sisters. Justice, J. R.
Three sketches. Zhao Danian
Three steps back. Weinberg, R.
Three Strangers. Sigsgaard, P.
Three strikes people. Wilson, I. R.
Three studies for figures on beds after Francis Bacon and Antonin Artaud. Yuknavitch, L.
Three tales of the Revolution. Blake, J. C.
Three types of solitude. Aldiss, B. W.
Three versions of Judas. Borges, J. L.
Three whacks a buck. White, M. C.
Three-wheeler. Mason, B. A.
Three Women by the River—At One Time or Another. Hines, V.
Thrill kill. Strandquist, R.
The **thrill** of a good ride. Johnson, S.
Thrilled to death. Tillman, L.
The **throes**. Skillings, R. D.
Through road, no whither. Bear, G.
Through steel and stone. Brand, M.
Through the walls. Campbell, R.
A **throw** of the book of changes. Ponte, A. J.
Thumbs. Orner, P.
Thunder and roses. Sturgeon, T.
The **thunder** of guilt. Lutz, J.
Thunder snow. Mason, B. A.
Thurber, James
  The catbird seat
    The Best American mystery stories of the century; Tony Hillerman, editor; with an introduction by Tony Hillerman
    Wonderful town; New York stories from The New Yorker; edited by David Remnick with Susan Choi
Thurm, Marian
  Ancient history
    Thurm, M. What's come over you?; stories
  Cold
    Thurm, M. What's come over you?; stories
  Earthbound
    Thurm, M. What's come over you?; stories
  Housecleaning
    Thurm, M. What's come over you?; stories
  Jumping ship
    Thurm, M. What's come over you?; stories
  Like something in this world
    Thurm, M. What's come over you?; stories
  Marquise
    Thurm, M. What's come over you?; stories
  Miss Grace at her best
    Thurm, M. What's come over you?; stories
  Moonlight
    Thurm, M. What's come over you?; stories
  Mourners
    Thurm, M. What's come over you?; stories
  Passenger
    Thurm, M. What's come over you?; stories
  Personal correspondence
    Thurm, M. What's come over you?; stories
  Pleasure palace
    Thurm, M. What's come over you?; stories
Thurmond, Jane
  Beauty of blood
    Hers 3: brilliant new fiction by lesbian writers; edited by Terry Wolverton with Robert Drake
Thursday night at the Gopher Hole, April 1992. Orner, P.
Thursday the sixteenth. Nesbitt, M.

Thus ended my days of watching over the house. Pak, W.-S.

Ti Démon. Chopin, K.

Ti Frère. Chopin, K.

Tia. Tafolla, C.

TIBET (CHINA) *See* China—Tibet

Tichborne, Roger Charles Doughty- *See* Doughty-Tichborne, Roger Charles, 1829-1854

Ticket to freedom. Posey, J. R.

Ticket to Minto. Fracis, S. H.

Ticket to Ride. Luddy, K. G.

Ticket to ride [excerpt] Potter, D.

Tickle torture. McNeely, T. H.

Tide pools. Adams, A.

Tides. Nelson, K.

Tieck, Ludwig

The elves

Tales before Tolkien; the roots of modern fantasy; edited by Douglas A. Anderson

Tiedemann, Mark W.

Links

Vanishing acts; a science fiction anthology; edited by Ellen Datlow

Psyché

The Year's best fantasy & horror, twelfth annual collection; edited by Ellen Datlow & Terry Windling

Tierney's Gourmet. Sonnenberg, B.

A **tiger-fighter** is hard to find. Ha Jin

Tiger moth. Joyce, G.

Tiger! tiger!. Bear, E.

TIGERS

Barnes, H. L. Stonehands and the tigress

Borges, J. L. Blue tigers

Cain, J. M. The baby in the icebox

Ha Jin. A tiger-fighter is hard to find

Jakes, J. The siren and the shill

Spain, C. Scaring the baddest animal

The **tigers** of hystria feed only on themselves. Bishop, M.

The **tiger's** tooth. Rawley, D.

Tijuana, mon amour. Ellroy, J.

Tijuana, mon amour 2. Ellroy, J.

'Til there was you. Addonizio, K.

Tilghman, Christopher

A gracious rain

Nightshade: 20th century ghost stories; edited by Robert Phillips

The late night news

Tilghman, C. The way people run; stories

Mary in the mountains

Breaking into print; early stories and insights into getting published; a Ploughshares anthology; edited by DeWitt Henry

Room for mistakes

Tilghman, C. The way people run; stories

Something important

Tilghman, C. The way people run; stories

A suitable good-bye

Tilghman, C. The way people run; stories

Things left undone

Tilghman, C. The way people run; stories

The way people run

Tilghman, C. The way people run; stories

Till 3:45. Maron, M.

Till death do us part. Davis, D. S.

Tillinghast, David

Calico Rock Cave

South Carolina Review v35 no1 p169-78 Fall 2002

Tillman, Lynne

Come and go

Tillman, L. This is not it; stories

Dead sleep

Tillman, L. This is not it; stories

Flowers

Tillman, L. This is not it; stories

Hold me

Tillman, L. This is not it; stories

Living with contradictions

Tillman, L. This is not it; stories

The lost city of words

Tillman, L. This is not it; stories

Lust for love

Tillman, L. This is not it; stories

Madame Realism

Tillman, L. This is not it; stories

Madame Realism: a fairy tale

Tillman, L. This is not it; stories

Madame Realism lies here

Tillman, L. This is not it; stories

Madame Realism looks for relief

Tillman, L. This is not it; stories

Madame Realism's torch song

Tillman, L. This is not it; stories

Ode to Le Petomane

Tillman, L. This is not it; stories

Phantoms

Tillman, L. This is not it; stories

A picture of time

Tillman, L. This is not it; stories

Pleasure isn't a pretty picture

Tillman, L. This is not it; stories

A simple idea

The Literary Review (Madison, N.J.) v45 no3 p453-6 Spr 2002

Snow-job

Tillman, L. This is not it; stories

This is not it

Tillman, L. This is not it; stories

Thrilled to death

Tillman, L. This is not it; stories

To find words

Tillman, L. This is not it; stories

TV tales

Tillman, L. This is not it; stories

The undiagnosed

Tillman, L. This is not it; stories

Wild life

Tillman, L. This is not it; stories

Tillmans, Andrea

Why poets shouldn't be trusted

Prairie Schooner v73 no3 p65-67 Fall 1999

Tilson Ezekiel alias Ti-Zek. Carew, J.

Tim. Rawley, D.

Timberline. Busch, F.

Timberline. Wister, O.

TIME

See also Clocks and watches

Bisson, T. 10:07:24

Borges, J. L. The garden of forking paths

Borges, J. L. The secret miracle

Bradbury, R. Season of disbelief

Bradbury, R. Time intervening

Brennert, A. Her pilgrim soul

TIME—*Continued*

Clarke, A. C. All the time in the world
Clarke, A. C. Trouble with time
Dybek, S. Paper lantern
Ellison, H. "Repent, Harlequin!" said the Ticktockman
Tevis, W. S. Rent control
Tillman, L. A picture of time
Waldrop, H. One horse town
Waldrop, H. and Kennedy, L. One-horse town

TIME, TRAVELS IN *See* Time travel

TIME AND SPACE *See* Space and time

Time between trains. Bukoski, A.

Time considered as a helix of semi-precious stones. Delany, S. R.

Time exposure. Lutz, J.

The **time** I died. Carlson, R.

Time in advance. Tenn, W.

Time intervening. Bradbury, R.

Time is Strange. Mulekwa, C.

TIME MACHINES

Bester, A. The men who murdered Mohammed
Bradbury, R. Forever and the Earth
Bradbury, R. The Kilimanjaro device
Bradbury, R. The Toynbee convection
Clarke, A. C. Time's arrow
Knight, D. F. I see you
Malzberg, B. N. We're coming through the window
Padgett, L. Mimsy were the borogoves
Rucker, R. v. B. Schrödinger's cat

Time magician. Troncoso, S.

The **time** of friendship. Bowles, P.

The **time** of his life. Wheat, C.

Time of terror. L'Amour, L.

Time-share. Ferriss, L.

Time share. Laurence, J.

Time share. Vachss, A. H.

Time stands still. Čapek, K.

Time table. Tomioka, T.

The **time** that time forgot. Cady, J.

TIME TRAVEL

Anderson, P. Death and the knight
Anderson, P. Delenda est
Aylett, S. Dread honor
Bailey, R. W. Doing time
Baker, K. The dust enclosed here
Baker, K. Facts relating to the arrest of Dr. Kalugin
Baker, K. Hanuman
Baker, K. The hotel at Harlan's Landing
Baker, K. Lemuria will rise!
Baker, K. The likely lad
Baker, K. The literary agent
Baker, K. Monster story
Baker, K. Noble mold
Baker, K. Old flat top
Baker, K. The queen in yellow
Baker, K. Smart Alec
Baker, K. Son observe the time
Baker, K. Studio dick drowns near Malibu
Baker, K. Welcome to Olympus, Mr. Hearst
Baker, K. The wreck of the Gladstone
Bear, G. Through road, no whither
Benford, G. In the dark backward
Bester, A. Hobson's choice
Bisson, T. Dear Abbey
Bradbury, R. The F. Scott/Tolstoy/Ahab accumulator

Bradbury, R. Last rites
Bradbury, R. The Mafioso cement-mixing machine
Bradbury, R. Quid pro quo
Bradbury, R. Sixty-six
Bradbury, R. Sometime before dawn
Bradbury, R. Time in hy flight
Braunbeck, G. A. Palimpsest day
Campbell, J. W. Twilight
Casa Pérez, R. d. l. The day we went through the transition
Crowley, J. Great work of time
Crowther, P. Things I didn't know my father knew
De Camp, L. S. A gun for dinosaur
Doctorow, C. A place so foreign
Dozois, G. R. A knight of ghosts and shadows
Dozois, G. R. Snow job
Duane, D. In the company of heroes
Edghill, R. May Eve
Heinlein, R. A. "All you zombies—"
Hoffman, N. K. Mint condition
Hogan, J. P. Convolution
Jenkins, W. F. The runaway skyscraper
Keith, W. H. Iterations
Kelly, J. P. 1016 to 1
Kelly, J. P. Proof of the existence of God
Kelly, J. P. Undone
Kessel, J. It's all true
Kornbluth, C. M. The little black bag
Lake, D. J. Re-deem the time
Lake, D. J. The truth about Weena
Le Guin, U. K. April in Paris
Lindskold, J. M. Jeff's best joke
Link, K. Lull
Louise, D. D. Stitches in time
Malzberg, B. N. The only thing you learn
Massie-Ferch, K. M. A touch through time
Moore, W. Bring the jubilee
Moujan Otaño, M. Gu ta gutarrak (we and our own)
Nye, J. L. Theory of relativity
Offutt, C. Chuck's bucket
Oliver, C. If now you grieve a little
Oliver, C. Rewrite man
Oliver, C. A star above it
Oliver, C. Transfusion
Piper, H. B. Gunpowder god
Pronzini, B. and Malzberg, B. N. On the nature of time
Rucker, R. v. B. The Andy Warhol sandcandle
Rucker, R. v. B. The facts of life
Rucker, R. v. B. A new experiment with time
Rusch, K. K. Blood trail
Scholz, C. Altamira
Smith, D. W. The gift of a dream
Tenn, W. Brooklyn project
Tenn, W. Winthrop was stubborn
Utley, S. The real world
Van Vogt, A. E. Far centaurus
Watson, I. Nanunculus
Waugh, E. Out of depth
Williams, W. J. The Green Leopard Plague
Wolfe, G. The lost pilgrim
Yolen, J. The traveler and the tale

Time waits for Winthrop. See Tenn, W. Winthrop was stubborn

Time will tell. Stern, D.

Time's arrow. Clarke, A. C.

Times fifty. Clough, B. W.
Times Square Romance. Lavalle, V.
Timeshare. Eugenides, J.
Timing the strike. Burton, M.
Timothy Harshaw's flute. Callaghan, M.
The **tin** star. Cunningham, J. M.
Tina in the back seat. Rawley, D.
The **tinder** box. Walters, M.
Ting-a-ling. Dann, J.
Tinhorn trouble. Newton, D. B.
Tinkering with What's Left. Lorenz, E.
TINKERS
  Inyama, N. Hot days, long nights
Tinkler Tam and the body snatchers. Scarborough,
  E. A.
Tinnitus. Shepard, S.
Tinsel bright. Gunn, K.
Tinseltown Follies of 1948. Crider, B.
Tinseltown, Morocco. Parker, G.
Tinsley, Molly Best
  Love lottery
    Prairie Schooner v75 no4 p3-19 Wint 2001
  White
    New England Review v20 no4 p109-19 Fall
    1999
Tinti, Hannah
  Animal crackers
    Tinti, H. Animal crackers; Hannah Tinti
  Bloodworks
    Tinti, H. Animal crackers; Hannah Tinti
  Gallus, gallus
    Tinti, H. Animal crackers; Hannah Tinti
  Hit man of the year
    Tinti, H. Animal crackers; Hannah Tinti
  Home sweet home
    The Best American mystery stories, 2003; ed-
    ited by Michael Connelly and Otto Penzler
    Tinti, H. Animal crackers; Hannah Tinti
  How to revitalize the snake in your life
    Tinti, H. Animal crackers; Hannah Tinti
  Miss Waldron's red colobus
    Tinti, H. Animal crackers; Hannah Tinti
  Preservation
    Tinti, H. Animal crackers; Hannah Tinti
  Reasonable terms
    Tinti, H. Animal crackers; Hannah Tinti
  Slim's last ride
    Tinti, H. Animal crackers; Hannah Tinti
  Talk turkey
    Tinti, H. Animal crackers; Hannah Tinti
Tiny ape. Barthelme, F.
A **tiny** history. Franklin, T.
TINY TIM, D. 1996
                    About
  Connor, J. The butterfly effect
Tippens, Elizabeth
  Make a wish
    New stories from the South: the year's best,
    2001; edited by Shannon Ravenel; with a
    preface by Lee Smith
    On the rocks; the KGB Bar fiction anthology;
    edited by Rebecca Donner ; foreword by
    Denis Woychuk
  Spring
    Ploughshares v25 no2/3 p190-209 Fall 1999
Tiptree, James
  The girl who was plugged in
    Reload: rethinking women + cyberculture; ed-
    ited by Mary Flanagan and Austin Booth

Mother in the sky with diamonds
    The Good old stuff; adventure SF in the
    grand tradition; edited by Gardner Dozois
The only neat thing to do
    Brown, C. N. and Strahan, J. The Locus
    awards; thirty years of the best in science
    fiction and fantasy; edited by Charles N.
    Brown and Jonathan Strahan
Tired old man. Ellison, H.
Tiresome story. See Chekhov, A. P. A dreary sto-
  ry
TITANIC (STEAMSHIP)
  Eberts, M. Lost lives
  Jones, G. The house of breathing
Tithes of mint and rue. Bishop, M.
Titipu. Greer, A. S.
Titwillow. Harris, M.
Tlön, Uqbar, Orbis Tertius. Borges, J. L.
To avalon. Routley, J.
To become a warrior. Beckett, C.
To change life in a good way. Ortiz, S. J.
To church with Mr. Multhiford. Reed, R.
To control a rabid rodent. López, L.
To Da-duh, in memoriam. Marshall, P.
To dance again. Blackwell, K.
To dream of death. Tozzi, F.
To each his own kind. Huff, T.
To every thing there is a season. MacLeod, A.
To feed the night. Hensher, P.
To find a place. Easton, R. O.
To find words. Tillman, L.
To forget Mary Ellen. Davis, D. S.
To go. Barrett, L.
To Go. West, P.
To grandmother's house we go. Collins, B.
To kill a cat. Collins, B.
To laugh in the morning. Heller, J.
To make a rabbit sing. Matthews, C.
To my former mother, Mrs. Callahan. House, T.
To my young husband. Walker, A.
To Philosophise with a Hammer. Nath, M.
To remember is to relive. Fiorani, S.
To Sarah, wherever you are. Rosenfeld, S.
"**To** see her in sunlight was to see Marxism die".
  Frym, G.
To see you again. Adams, A.
To seize the earth. Plá, J.
To speak with angels. West, M.
To tempt a woman. Boylan, C.
To the mountains. Horgan, P.
To the shores of San Clemente. Locklin, G.
To Tom. Dixon, S.
To whom the victory? Pulver, M. M.
Toad. McKillip, P. A.
Toads. McCorkle, J.
Toads and diamonds. Perrault, C.
The **toast**. Robinson, L.
Toasting the Bride. Koehler, J.
TOBACCO HABIT *See* Smoking
TOBOGGANING
  Chekhov, A. P. A joke
Tobrah. Mason, B. A.
Toccata and feud. Peel, J.
Der **Tod** in Venedig. Weathers, W.
Today is Sunday. Davies, P. H.
Today is today is today. Maraini, D.
Today never happened before. Johnston, P. D.

Todd, Charles
The man who never was
Malice domestic 9
Todd, René L.
Vinegar
Best new American voices 2004; guest editor
John Casey; series editors John Kulka and
Natalie Danford
Toes, Jac.
Known unto God
The World's finest mystery and crime stories,
third annual collection; edited by Ed
Gorman and Martin H. Greenberg
Rhine Ablaze
Death cruise; crime stories on the open seas;
edited by Lawrence Block
Toft, Mark
Tourist trap
Virgin fiction 2
Togneri, Elaine
Guardian angel
Blood on their hands; edited by Lawrence
Block
Tohill, Sylvia Mullen
The Unfaithful Wife
The North American Review v288 no1 p34-5
Ja/F 2003
Tóibín, Colm
The heather blazing [excerpt]
Circa 2000; gay fiction at the millennium; ed-
ited by Robert Drake & Terry Wolverton
Toilet training. Allen, J. R.
TOKLAS, ALICE B.
About
McGarry, J. The last time
TOKYO (JAPAN) *See* Japan—Tokyo
Tokyo, my love. Canty, K.
Tokyo trains. Schmatz, P.
**TOLKIEN, J. R. R. (JOHN RONALD REUEL),
1892-1973**
Parodies, imitations, etc.
Duncan, A. Senator Bilbo
Tolkien, John Ronald Reuel *See* Tolkien, J. R. R.
(John Ronald Reuel), 1892-1973
Tolkin, Michael
Treatments
Film Comment v38 no1 p20-1 Ja/F 2002
TolstaιSaS, Tat´iana
On the golden porch
The Art of the story; an international antholo-
gy of contemporary short stories; edited by
Daniel Halpern
Tolstaya, Tatyana *See* TolstaιSaS, Tat´iana, 1951-
Tolstoy, Leo, graf
After the Ball
New England Review v24 no1 p104-11 Wint
2003
The berries
Tolstoy, L., graf. Divine and human and other
stories; new translations by Peter Sekirin
A coffeehouse in the city of Surat
Tolstoy, L., graf. Divine and human and other
stories; new translations by Peter Sekirin
Divine and human
Tolstoy, L., graf. Divine and human and other
stories; new translations by Peter Sekirin
Esarhaddon, King of Assyria
Parabola v27 no4 p37-40 N 2002

A grain of rye the size of a chicken egg
Tolstoy, L., graf. Divine and human and other
stories; new translations by Peter Sekirin
Kornei Vasiliev
Tolstoy, L., graf. Divine and human and other
stories; new translations by Peter Sekirin
The poor people
Tolstoy, L., graf. Divine and human and other
stories; new translations by Peter Sekirin
The power of childhood
Tolstoy, L., graf. Divine and human and other
stories; new translations by Peter Sekirin
The prayer
Tolstoy, L., graf. Divine and human and other
stories; new translations by Peter Sekirin
The repentant sinner
Tolstoy, L., graf. Divine and human and other
stories; new translations by Peter Sekirin
The requirements of love
Tolstoy, L., graf. Divine and human and other
stories; new translations by Peter Sekirin
Sisters
Tolstoy, L., graf. Divine and human and other
stories; new translations by Peter Sekirin
The son of a thief
Tolstoy, L., graf. Divine and human and other
stories; new translations by Peter Sekirin
Why did it happen?
Tolstoy, L., graf. Divine and human and other
stories; new translations by Peter Sekirin
Tom. Lavin, M.
Tom Brightwind; or, How the fairy bridge was
built at Thoresby. Clarke, S.
Tom, Dick, or Harry. Hammett, D.
Tom O'bedlam's night out. Schweitzer, D.
Tom Swift and his humongous mechanical dude.
Steele, A. M.
Tomaso, Carla
Rain
Hers 2: brilliant new fiction by lesbian writ-
ers; edited by Terry Wolverton with Robert
Drake
Tomasula, Steve
Self Portrait(s)
Iowa Review v33 no1 p33-52 Spr 2003
Tomato watch. Slezak, E.
Tomboy. Mencken, S. H.
Tombstone. Nordan, L.
TOMBSTONES
Kawabata, Y. Chrysanthemum in the rock
Tombstone's daughter. Le May, A.
The **tomcat's** wife. Bly, C.
Tome. Meloy, M.
Tomioka, Taeko
Days of dear death
Tomioka, T. The funeral of a giraffe; seven
stories; translated by Kyoko Selden and
Mizuta Noriko
A dog's eye view
Tomioka, T. The funeral of a giraffe; seven
stories; translated by Kyoko Selden and
Mizuta Noriko
The funeral of a giraffe
Tomioka, T. The funeral of a giraffe; seven
stories; translated by Kyoko Selden and
Mizuta Noriko

Tomioka, Taeko—*Continued*

Happy birthday

Tomioka, T. The funeral of a giraffe; seven stories; translated by Kyoko Selden and Mizuta Noriko

Time table

Tomioka, T. The funeral of a giraffe; seven stories; translated by Kyoko Selden and Mizuta Noriko

Yesterday's girl

Tomioka, T. The funeral of a giraffe; seven stories; translated by Kyoko Selden and Mizuta Noriko

Yesteryear

Tomioka, T. The funeral of a giraffe; seven stories; translated by Kyoko Selden and Mizuta Noriko

Tomlinson, Norma Crawford

Aki

Tomlinson, N. C. The day of the dance; stories

The day of the dance

Tomlinson, N. C. The day of the dance; stories

The majesty

Tomlinson, N. C. The day of the dance; stories

The nurses' house

Tomlinson, N. C. The day of the dance; stories

The picture

Tomlinson, N. C. The day of the dance; stories

Playing Holi

Tomlinson, N. C. The day of the dance; stories

The pretty surprise

Tomlinson, N. C. The day of the dance; stories

Scheherazade

Tomlinson, N. C. The day of the dance; stories

Snowbound

Tomlinson, N. C. The day of the dance; stories

Venus de Milo

Tomlinson, N. C. The day of the dance; stories

Tomlinson, Tim

Blasphemy

Gettysburg Review v12 no1 p147-49 Spr 1999

Tommy. Reynolds, R.

Tomorrow I die. Spillane, M.

Tomorrow's bird. Frazier, I.

Tom's homecoming. Jones, H.

TONGA

Whitty, J. A tortoise for the Queen of Tonga

Tongue. Mazelis, J.

Tongue. Skinner, J.

Tongue dance. Tawada, Y.

Tongue of the Jews. Bukiet, M. J.

TONTINES *See* Trust funds

The **Tonto** woman. Leonard, E.

Tony Takitani. Murakami, H.

Tony's wife. Dunbar-Nelson, A. M.

Too big to float. Krouse, E.

Too busy swimming. Young, T.

Too damned handsome. Reiner, C.

Too far from home. Bowles, P.

Too many coincidences. Archer, J.

Too many crooks. Westlake, D. E.

Too many have lived. Hammett, D.

Too many tomcats. Collins, B.

Too mean to die. Smith, J.

Too much tolerance. Waugh, E.

Too perfect. Mazelis, J.

Too skinny. O'Brien, T.

Too tough to kill. L'Amour, L.

Too white. Chacón, D.

Toole, F. X.

Black Jew

Toole, F. X. Rope burns; stories from the corner

Fightin in Philly

Toole, F. X. Rope burns; stories from the corner

Frozen water

Toole, F. X. Rope burns; stories from the corner

Midnight emissions

The Best American mystery stories, 2002; edited and with an introduction by James Ellroy; Otto Penzler, series editor

Million $$$ baby

Toole, F. X. Rope burns; stories from the corner

The monkey look

Toole, F. X. Rope burns; stories from the corner

Rope burns

Toole, F. X. Rope burns; stories from the corner

Tools. Estep, M.

The **tools** of ignorance. Bukoski, A.

Toomer, Jean

Blood-burning moon

The Best American short stories of the century; John Updike, editor, Katrina Kenison, coeditor; with an introduction by John Updike

Tooth and Claw. Boyle, T. C.

Tooth marks. Mendes, B.

Toothpaste. Penn, W. S.

The **Tootsie** Roll factor. Lupoff, R. A.

Top. Abrams, T.

Top hand. Short, L.

TOPAZ

James, H. Adina

Topless in Tucson. Wallace, R.

TORNADOES

Blair, J. Running away

Torockio, Christopher

High crimes

Iowa Review v31 no1 p132-52 Summ 2001

TORONTO (ONT.) *See* Canada—Toronto

Torquemada. Lipsyte, S.

Torrington, Jeff

The fade

The Vintage book of contemporary Scottish fiction; edited and with an introduction by Peter Kravitz

Torso. Alas, L.

A **tortoise** for the Queen of Tonga. Whitty, J.

La **Tortuga**. Lord, C.

TORTURE

Biguenet, J. The torturer's apprentice

Bishop, M. With a little help from her friends

Glave, T. A real place

TORTURE—*Continued*
Yuknavitch, L. Chair
Torture!. Berry, R. M.
Torture. McNally, J.
Torture fantasy. Chacón, D.
The **torturer's** apprentice. Biguenet, J.
Torturing creatures at night. Mueller, D.
Toscana, David
The big brush
    Points of departure; new stories from Mexico; edited by Mónica Lavín; translated by Gustavo Segade
The new guy
    Iowa Review v31 no1 p16-24 Summ 2001
TOSCANINI, ARTURO, 1867-1957
About
Malzberg, B. N. Allegro marcato
The **Total** Devotion Machine. Love, R.
TOTALITARIANISM
        See also Communism; Dictators; National socialism
Andahazi, F. The sleep of the just
Arenas, R. Traitor
Cabrera Infante, G. Guilty of dancing the chachachá
Castro, Pablo A. Exerion
Emshwiller, C. The general
Feeley, G. The crab lice
Glave, T. The pit
Goligorsky, E. The last refuge
Jacobs, M. How birds communicate
Krysl, M. The thing around them
Monteiro, J. The crystal goblet
Pak, W.-S. My very last possession
Pak, W.-S. Thus ended my days of watching over the house
VanderMeer, J. Flight is for those who have not yet crossed over
Weldon, F. Stasi
Williams, M. Coley's war
Yuknavitch, L. Blood opus
Touch [excerpt] Sherman, C. W.
Touch of a vanish'd hand. Mann, P.
Touch positive. Kennedy, A. L.
A **touch** through time. Massie-Ferch, K. M.
Touch wood. Porter, J. A.
Touched. Kureishi, H.
Touching Idamae Low. Harris, M.
Touching Tiananmen. Jones, G.
The **touchstone**. Wharton, E.
A **tough** case to figure. Lochte, D.
Tough hombre. Loomis, N. M.
Tough people. Offutt, C.
The **toughest** Indian in the world. Alexie, S.
The **tour**. Skloot, F.
La **Tour** dreams of the wolf girl. Huddle, D.
Touré
The African-American aesthetics hall of fame; or, 101 elements of blackness (things that'll make you say: yes! that there's some really black
    Touré. The portable promised land; stories
Afrolexicology today's biannual list of the top fifty words in African-American
    Touré. The portable promised land; stories
Attack of the love dogma
    Touré. The portable promised land; stories
Blackmanwalkin
    Touré. The portable promised land; stories

The breakup ceremony
    Touré. The portable promised land; stories
The commercial channel: a unique business opportunity
    Touré. The portable promised land; stories
Falcon Malone can fly no mo
    Touré. The portable promised land; stories
A guest!
    Touré. The portable promised land; stories
A hot time at the Church of Kentucky Fried Souls and the spectacular final Sunday sermon of the Right Revren Daddy Love
    Francis Ford Coppola's Zoetrope all-story 2; edited by Adrienne Brodeur and Samantha Schnee; with an introduction by Francis Ford Coppola
    Touré. The portable promised land; stories
How Babe Ruth saved my life
    Touré. The portable promised land; stories
It's life and death at the Slush Puppie Open
    Touré. The portable promised land; stories
My history
    Touré. The portable promised land; stories
Once an oreo, always an oreo
    Touré. The portable promised land; stories
The playground of the ecstatically blasé
    Touré. The portable promised land; stories
The sad, sweet story of Sugar Lips Shinehot, the man with the portable promised land
    Touré. The portable promised land; stories
The Sambomorphosis
    Touré. The portable promised land; stories
Solomon's big day
    Touré. The portable promised land; stories
Soul City Gazette profile: Crash Jinkin, last of the chronic crashees
    Touré. The portable promised land; stories
The Steviewondermobile
    Touré. The portable promised land; stories
They're playing my song
    Touré. The portable promised land; stories
We words
    Touré. The portable promised land; stories
You are who you kill
    Touré. The portable promised land; stories
Young, black, and unstoppable; or, Death of a zeitgeist jockey
    Touré. The portable promised land; stories
Touring. Dozois, G. R.
TOURIST COURTS *See* Motels
TOURIST TRADE
Aickman, R. The cicerones
Ardizzone, T. Larabi's ox
Broughton, T. A. A tour of the islands
Davidson, A. The third sacred well of the temple
Goldstein, L. Tourists
Lahiri, J. Interpreter of maladies
Singer, I. B. The bus
Singleton, G. Raise children here
Tourist trap. Toft, M.
The **tourist** who wasn't there. DuBois, B.
TOURISTS *See* Tourist trade
Tourists. Goldstein, L.
Tourists from the south arrive in the independent state. Galloway, J.
Tov, Sharona Ben- *See* Ben-Tov, Sharona
Towel season. Carlson, R.

Tower, Wells

The brown coast
The Paris Review v44 no161 p161-79 Spr 2002

Down through the valley
The Paris Review v43 no159 p78-96 Fall 2001

The **tower**. Spinnen, B.

Tower of Babylon. Chiang, T.

The **tower** of Gallipoli. Muñiz-Huberman, A.

The **tower** pig. Antworth, S.

Tower, Wells

Everything ravaged, everything burned
Pushcart prize XXVII; best of the small presses; edited by Bill Henderson with the Pushcart prize editors

TOWERS

Chiang, T. Tower of Babylon

A **town** like ours. Hegi, U.

Townley, Roderick

Say When
New Letters v69 no1 p89-92 2002

Townshend, Pete

The plate from horse's neck
Carved in rock; short stories by musicians; edited by Greg Kihn

Toxic round-up. Coshnear, D.

Toy guns. Norris, L.

Toy shop. Harrison, H.

Toyboxed. LeRoy, J. T.

TOYS

See also Teddy bears

Chwedyk, Richard. Bronte's egg

Ellison, H. Killing Bernstein

Fesler, P. J. Coin of the realm

Padgett, L. Mimsy were the borogoves

Pronzini, B. Toy

Tenn, W. Child's play

Willis, C. In Coppelius's Toyshop

Toys R Us. Schiffman, C.

Tozzi, Federigo

Assunta
Tozzi, F. Love in vain; selected stories of Federigo Tozzi; translated, with an introduction, by Minna Proctor

The boardinghouse
Tozzi, F. Love in vain; selected stories of Federigo Tozzi; translated, with an introduction, by Minna Proctor

The clocks
Tozzi, F. Love in vain; selected stories of Federigo Tozzi; translated, with an introduction, by Minna Proctor

The crucifix
Tozzi, F. Love in vain; selected stories of Federigo Tozzi; translated, with an introduction, by Minna Proctor

Dead man in the oven
Tozzi, F. Love in vain; selected stories of Federigo Tozzi; translated, with an introduction, by Minna Proctor

First love
Tozzi, F. Love in vain; selected stories of Federigo Tozzi; translated, with an introduction, by Minna Proctor

House for sale
Tozzi, F. Love in vain; selected stories of Federigo Tozzi; translated, with an introduction, by Minna Proctor

The idiot
Tozzi, F. Love in vain; selected stories of Federigo Tozzi; translated, with an introduction, by Minna Proctor

L'Amore
Tozzi, F. Love in vain; selected stories of Federigo Tozzi; translated, with an introduction, by Minna Proctor

Life
Tozzi, F. Love in vain; selected stories of Federigo Tozzi; translated, with an introduction, by Minna Proctor

Love in vain
Tozzi, F. Love in vain; selected stories of Federigo Tozzi; translated, with an introduction, by Minna Proctor

The lovers
Tozzi, F. Love in vain; selected stories of Federigo Tozzi; translated, with an introduction, by Minna Proctor

Mad for music
Tozzi, F. Love in vain; selected stories of Federigo Tozzi; translated, with an introduction, by Minna Proctor

The miracle
Tozzi, F. Love in vain; selected stories of Federigo Tozzi; translated, with an introduction, by Minna Proctor

One evening, on the banks of the Tiber
Tozzi, F. Love in vain; selected stories of Federigo Tozzi; translated, with an introduction, by Minna Proctor

Poverty
Tozzi, F. Love in vain; selected stories of Federigo Tozzi; translated, with an introduction, by Minna Proctor

Sister
Tozzi, F. Love in vain; selected stories of Federigo Tozzi; translated, with an introduction, by Minna Proctor

The tavern
Chicago Review v47 no1 p53-62 Spr 2001
Tozzi, F. Love in vain; selected stories of Federigo Tozzi; translated, with an introduction, by Minna Proctor

To dream of death
The Literary Review (Madison, N.J.) v44 no3 p468-71 Spr 2001
Tozzi, F. Love in vain; selected stories of Federigo Tozzi; translated, with an introduction, by Minna Proctor

Vile creatures
Tozzi, F. Love in vain; selected stories of Federigo Tozzi; translated, with an introduction, by Minna Proctor

Traba, Marta

The tale of the velvet pillows
Short stories by Latin American women; the magic and the real; edited by Celia Correas de Zapata; foreword by Isabel Allende

Traceleen at dawn. Gilchrist, E.

Traceleen, she's still talking. Gilchrist, E.

Traceleen turns east. Gilchrist, E.

Tracey, Caitlin

Rollerblading at Midnight
The North American Review v288 no6 p36-42 N/D 2003

TRACK (ATHLETICS)

Gilchrist, E. Revenge

The **tracks** of Chief de Soto. Morgan, R.
Trade wars. DuBois, B.
TRADERS
  Haggard, H. R. Black heart and white heart: a
    Zulu idyl
  Harrison, H. The streets of Ashkelon
Trading down. Spielberg, P.
Trading hearts at the Half Kaffe Cafe. De Lint, C.
Trading post. Barrett, N., Jr.
Trading with the enemy. Hodgson, W. H.
Tradition and the individual talent:the "Bratislava
  spiccato". Mathews, H.
Trafalgar. Hagenston, B.
Traffic. Mendoza, R.
TRAFFIC ACCIDENTS
    See also Hit-and-run drivers
  Atkinson, K. Temporal anomaly
  Banks, I. The bridge [excerpt]
  Barthelme, F. Harmonic
  Bausch, R. Valor
  Baxter, C. Innocent
  Blaise, C. The salesman's son grows older
  Bonnie, F. Fifty winters
  Brown, J. Head on
  Brownstein, G. Safety
  Broyard, B. Ugliest faces
  Burford, M. Pesce volante
  Chaon, D. Among the missing
  Chaon, D. Fraternity
  Clark, J. Beltway Dostoyevsky
  Clarke, A. C. Critical mass
  Cobb, T. A cold, cotton shirt
  Cooper, R. R. Johnny Hamburger
  Di Blasi, D. Chairman of the board
  Earley, T. Just married
  Evans, E. Blood and gore
  Evans, E. A new life
  Fleming, R. The inhuman condition
  Gao Xingjian. The accident
  Gilman, C. P. Unpunished
  Glave, T. Accidents
  Goran, L. Keeping count
  Heller, J. Lot's wife
  Hood, A. Lost parts
  Iribarne, M. Make them laugh
  Iribarne, M. Sudden mysteries
  Johnston, T. Irish girl
  Kaplan, H. Dysaesthesia
  Koja, K. Road trip
  Lumley, B. Beneath the moors
  Martin, V. Messengers
  McKee, J. Under the influence
  Morgan, R. The ratchet
  Nelson, A. One dog is people
  Nesbitt, M. What good is you anyway?
  Nfah-Abbenyi, J. M. Accidents are a sideshow
  Nissen, T. Jono, an elegy
  Norris, L. Black ice
  Oates, J. C. Death cup
  Oates, J. C. I was in love
  O'Callaghan, M. Sorry, Frank
  O'Connor, F. A good man is hard to find
  Orringer, J. The Isabel fish
  Pronzini, B. and Malzberg, B. N. Night rider
  Richmond, M. Does anyone know you are going
    this way
  Richmond, M. Mathematics and acrobatics
  Rinehart, S. Funny cars
  Rinehart, S. LeSabre

  Ryan, P. L. Life is a highway
  Shade, E. Stability
  Shi Tiesheng. Fate
  Stolar, D. Home in New Hampshire
  Touré. Soul City Gazette profile: Crash Jinkin,
    last of the chronic crashees
  Troncoso, S. Day of the dead
  Updike, J. The corner
  Updike, J. The taste of metal
  Weihe, E. The morning room
  Wellen, E. Devil's pass
  Westmoreland, T. A. They have numbered all
    my bones
  Williams, J. The farm
  Wuori, G. K. Nude
Traffic manager. Kirchheimer, G. D.
Traffic school. Saroyan, A.
A **tragedy** of error. James, H.
The **tragedy** of premature death among geniuses.
  Gartner, Z.
Trager-Mendel, Liz
  Mixed Emotions
    The North American Review v289 no3/4
    p32-8 My/Ag 2004
Tragic heroines tell all. Henderson, L.
Trail driver's luck. Le May, A.
The **trail** of a fool. Cunningham, E.
A **trail** of mirrors. Knight, T.
Trailer girl. Svoboda, T.
TRAILER PARKS
  Banks, R. Black man and white woman in dark
    green rowboat
  Banks, R. Comfort
  Banks, R. Dis bwoy, him gwan
  Banks, R. The fisherman
  Banks, R. The guinea pig lady
  McCorkle, J. Migration of the love bugs
  Svoboda, T. Trailer girl
Trailer people. Norris, L.
Trailer trash. Goudsward, S. T.
TRAILERPARKS *See* Trailer parks
The **trailing** spouse. Kane, J. F.
Train. Budnitz, J.
Train dreams. Johnson, D.
Train line. Carter, E.
Train station. Gonzalez, R.
The **train,** the lake, the bridge. Lott, B.
Train to Chinko. Harshbarger, K.
TRAIN TRAVEL *See* Railroads—Travel
Training. Roley, B. A.
TRAINS *See* Railroads—Trains
Trainspotting [excerpt] Welsh, I.
Traitor. Arenas, R.
TRAITORS *See* Treason
Trampoline lessons. Black, C.
TRAMPS *See* Homeless persons
Tran, Henri
  Little murmurs
    His 3: brilliant new fiction by gay writers; ed-
    ited by Robert Drake and Terry Wolverton
Tran, Vu
  The back streets of Hoi An
    Tran, V. The dragon hunt; five stories; trans-
    lated from the Vietnamese by Nina
    McPherson and Phan Huy Duong
  The coral reef
    Tran, V. The dragon hunt; five stories; trans-
    lated from the Vietnamese by Nina
    McPherson and Phan Huy Duong

Tran, Vu—*Continued*

The dragon hunt

Tran, V. The dragon hunt; five stories; translated from the Vietnamese by Nina McPherson and Phan Huy Duong

Gunboat on the Yangtze

Tran, V. The dragon hunt; five stories; translated from the Vietnamese by Nina McPherson and Phan Huy Duong

Nha Nam

Tran, V. The dragon hunt; five stories; translated from the Vietnamese by Nina McPherson and Phan Huy Duong

Transactional paralysis. Coshnear, D.

TRANSCENDENTALISM

See also Idealism

TRANSEXUALITY

Varley, J. Retrograde summer

The **transformation**. Momaday, N. S.

Transformations. Auerbach, J.

Transience. Clarke, A. C.

Transit of earth. Clarke, A. C.

TRANSLATORS

Foer, J. S. The very rigid search

Klein, Anne Carolyn. The mantra and the typist: a story of east and west

Mathews, H. The dialect of the tribe

Paul, B. French asparagus

Rendell, R. High mysterious union

Singer, I. B. My adventures 25 as an idealist

Tawada, Y. The bath

Treat, J. Nicaraguan birds

Vonnegut, K. Der Arme Dolmetscher

Wilson, B. Wie bitte?

Zinik, Z. No cause for alarm

The **Translator's** Husband. Gordon, M.

TRANSMIGRATION

See also Reincarnation

Bowles, P. You are not I

The **transmission**. Johnson, C. R.

Transorbital love probe. Metzger, T.

Transparency. Hwang, F.

TRANSPLANTATION OF ORGANS, TISSUES, ETC.

Archer, J. A change of heart

Brown, J. Driving the heart

Budnitz, J. Guilt

Davis, C. A. Not long now

Hegi, U. Moonwalkers

Ramaya, S. Gopal's kitchen

Stableford, B. M. What can Chloe want?

Vachss, A. H. Harvest time

Transposing. Martin, V.

TRANSSEXUALS

Bloom, A. A blind man can see how much I love you

Engel, M. P. M to F

Händler, E.-W. Trigger

TRANSVESTISM

Anderson, B. Lark till dawn, princess

Boyle, T. C. A women's restaurant

Evenson, B. Promisekeepers

Gorodischer, A. The violet's embryos

Holleran, A. The penthouse

Kay, J. Trumpet [excerpt]

Kurlansky, M. Beautiful Mayagüez women

Matthews, C. I'm not that kind of girl

Morrow, B. "Ciccone youths 1990"

Padilla, I. Ever wrest: log of the journey

Paine, T. General Markman's last stand

Pelegrimas, M. I'm not that kind of girl

Weldon, F. A great antipodean scandal

Trap shoot. Viganò, R.

Trapeze. Cummins, A.

The **trapped** battalion. Chamberlain, W.

TRAPPERS AND TRAPPING

Rule, R. Walking the trapline

Sneve, V. D. H. Jimmy Yellow Hawk

Stegner, W. E. Buglesong

TRAPPING *See* Trappers and trapping

Trash traders. Avrich, J.

TrashTraders. Avrich, J.

Trastevere. Lavin, M.

Tratnik, Suzana

Under the ironwood trees

The Vintage book of international lesbian fiction; edited and with an introduction by Naomi Holoch and Joan Nestle

Trauma plate. Johnson, A.

Trauma plate. Johnson, A. M.

The **travails**. Fowler, K. J.

TRAVEL

Bingham, S. Loving

Chekhov, A. P. The steppe

Hodgen, C. The hero of loneliness

James, H. Four meetings

Klíma, I. Uranus in the house of death

Le Guin, U. K. Sita Dulip's Method

Lee, A. Brothers and sisters around the world

Mazelis, J. The game

Potvin, E. A. The traveller's hat

Roeske, P. The ecstasy of Magda Brummel

Roeske, P. From this distance

Silber, J. Ashes of love

Spencer, E. The white azalea

Swarthout, G. F. A glass of blessings

Troy, M. A little zip

Tumasonis, D. The prospect cards

Updike, J. I am dying, Egypt, dying

Vaswani, N. An outline of no direction

Vivante, A. Reflection

Winterson, J. The world and other places

Yuknavitch, L. How to lose an eye

Travel & leisure. Barthelme, F.

Travel by wire!. Clarke, A. C.

The **traveler** and the tale. Yolen, J.

TRAVELERS

See also Foreign visitors

Campbell, R. All for sale

Davidson, A. Great is Diana

Mathews, H. Journeys to six lands

Porter, J. A. Yours

Smith, A. Paradise

Tawada, Y. Storytellers without souls

Tawada, Y. Where Europe begins

Thomas, D. Grandma and the sentimental travler

Tillman, L. Lust for love

Warren, D. A reckless moon

Wolfe, G. A traveler in desert lands

The **travelers**. Rhett, K.

Travelers advisory. Winegardner, M.

Traveling companions. Drake, R.

Traveling princess. Carroll, L.

Traveller from an antique land. Davidson, A.

Travelling companions. James, H.

TRAVELS IN TIME *See* Time travel

Travels with Mr. Slush. Delaney, E. J.

Travels with the Snow Queen. Link, K.

Traver, Robert
The big brown trout
Fishing's best short stories; edited by Paul D. Staudohar
The intruder
Fishing's best short stories; edited by Paul D. Staudohar
Travis, Tia V.
Down here in the garden
Death dines at 8:30; edited by Claudia Bishop and Nick DiChario
The kiss
The Year's best fantasy & horror, thirteenth annual collection; edited by Ellen Datlow and Terri Windling
TRAVIS, WILLIAM BARRET, 1809-1836
About
Breen, J. V. A man alone
Travis, B. Meloy, M.
Traylor, James L.
Dicks are blind
Flesh and blood: guilty as sin; erotic tales of crime and passion; edited by Max Allan Collins and Jeff Gelb
The **treacherous** age. Auchincloss, L.
Treadway, Jessica
Shirley Wants Her Nickel Back
Ploughshares v30 no2/3 p168-204 Fall 2004
TREASON
See also Defectors; Spies
Borges, J. L. The theme of the traitor and the hero
Cheng, C.-W. The three-legged horse
MacDonald, J. D. Betrayed
Treason. Babel', I.
Treasure hunt. Faulkner, J.
The **treasure** hunter's daughter. Ziegler, I.
The **treasure** of Odirex. Sheffield, C.
TREASURE-TROVE *See* Buried treasure
Leslie, N. The scavenger's eye
Treat, Jessica
Ants
Treat, J. Not a chance
Dead end
Treat, J. Not a chance
His sweater
Treat, J. Not a chance
Honda
Treat, J. Not a chance
Nicaraguan birds
Treat, J. Not a chance
Not a chance
Treat, J. Not a chance
Radio disturbance
Treat, J. Not a chance
The summer of Zubeyde
Treat, J. Not a chance
Walking
Treat, J. Not a chance
Treat me nice. Van Winckel, N.
The **treatment.** Menaker, D.
The **Treatment.** Robinson, R.
The **treatment** of Bibi Haldar. Lahiri, J.
Treatments. Tolkin, M.
The **trebuchet** murder. Gregory, S.
The **tree.** Bocock, M.
The **tree.** Bombal, M. L.
The **tree** baby. Cleage, P.
The **tree** is my hat. Wolfe, G.

A **tree** to be desired. Gilchrist, E.
TREES
See also Apple trees; Christmas trees
Agee, J. A pleasant story
Arenas, R. In the shade of the almond tree
Blackwood, A. The willows
Browder, C. Silver maple
Coates, G. S. Black cherries
Coates, G. S. Trees of heaven
Deane, J. F. Nighthawk
Hopkinson, N. Whose upward flight I love
Kawabata, Y. A row of trees
Slavin, J. Blighted
Smith, A. May
Stableford, B. M. Another branch of the family tree
Vaswani, N. Twang (Release)
Vivante, A. The sugar maples
Waggoner, T. The September people
Williamson, J. The firefly tree
Trees of heaven. Coates, G. S.
Tremain, Rose
John-Jin
The Art of the story; an international anthology of contemporary short stories; edited by Daniel Halpern
Tremayne, Peter
Abbey sinister
Tremayne, P. Hemlock at Vespers; fifteen Sister Fidelma mysteries
At the tent of Holofernes
Tremayne, P. Hemlock at Vespers; fifteen Sister Fidelma mysteries
A canticle for Wulfstan
Tremayne, P. Hemlock at Vespers; fifteen Sister Fidelma mysteries
Hemlock at Vespers
Tremayne, P. Hemlock at Vespers; fifteen Sister Fidelma mysteries
The High King's sword
Tremayne, P. Hemlock at Vespers; fifteen Sister Fidelma mysteries
Holy blood
Tremayne, P. Hemlock at Vespers; fifteen Sister Fidelma mysteries
The horse that died for shame
Tremayne, P. Hemlock at Vespers; fifteen Sister Fidelma mysteries
Invitation to a poisoning
Tremayne, P. Hemlock at Vespers; fifteen Sister Fidelma mysteries
Murder by miracle
Tremayne, P. Hemlock at Vespers; fifteen Sister Fidelma mysteries
Murder in repose
Tremayne, P. Hemlock at Vespers; fifteen Sister Fidelma mysteries
Night's black agents
Royal whodunnits; edited by Mike Ashley
Our lady of death
Tremayne, P. Hemlock at Vespers; fifteen Sister Fidelma mysteries
The poisoned chalice
Tremayne, P. Hemlock at Vespers; fifteen Sister Fidelma mysteries
Scattered thorns
Murder most Celtic; tall tales of Irish mayhem; edited by Martin H. Greenberg

Tremayne, Peter—*Continued*

A scream from the sepulcher
Tremayne, P. Hemlock at Vespers; fifteen Sister Fidelma mysteries

A study in orange
My Sherlock Holmes; untold stories of the great detective; edited by Michael Kurland

Tarnished halo
Tremayne, P. Hemlock at Vespers; fifteen Sister Fidelma mysteries

Those that trespass
Tremayne, P. Hemlock at Vespers; fifteen Sister Fidelma mysteries
The World's finest mystery and crime stories, first annual collection; edited by Ed Gorman

Tremors. Greenberg, A.

Trespass. Barnes, J.

Trespass. Ebershoff, D.

Trespass. Matheson, R.

Trespass. Wilson, R., Jr.

The **trespasser**. Whitaker, A.

Trespassing. Casey, M.

Trevanian

After hours at Rick's
Trevanian. Hot night in the city

The apple tree
The Best American short stories 2001; selected from U.S. and Canadian magazines by Barbara Kingsolver with Katrina Kenison; with an introduction by Barbara Kingsolver
Trevanian. Hot night in the city

Easter story
Trevanian. Hot night in the city

The engine of fate
Trevanian. Hot night in the city

Hot night in the city
Trevanian. Hot night in the city

Hot night in the city II
Trevanian. Hot night in the city

How the animals got their voices
Trevanian. Hot night in the city

Minutes of a village meeting
Trevanian. Hot night in the city

Mrs. McGivney's nickel
Trevanian. Hot night in the city

The sacking of Miss Plimsoll
Trevanian. Hot night in the city

Sir Gervais in the enchanted forest
Trevanian. Hot night in the city

Snatch off your cap, kid!
Trevanian. Hot night in the city

That Fox-of-a-Beñat
Trevanian. Hot night in the city

Waking to the Spirit Clock
The Antioch Review v61 no3 p409-41 Summ 2003

Trevor, Doug

Central Square
New England Review v23 no3 p31-43 Summ 2002

Saint Francis in Flint
The Paris Review v43 no158 p231-51 Spr/Summ 2001

Trevor, William

Against the odds
Harper's v298 no1784 p73-81 Ja 1999
Trevor, W. The hill bachelors

A bit on the side
The New Yorker v77 no33 p70-5 O 29 2001

Death of a professor
Trevor, W. The hill bachelors

A friend in the trade
The New Yorker v74 no45 p66-71 F 8 1999
Trevor, W. The hill bachelors

Good news
Trevor, W. The hill bachelors

The hill bachelors
The New Yorker v75 no33 p80-87 N 8 1999
Trevor, W. The hill bachelors

Justina's priest
The New Yorker v77 no43 p74-9 Ja 14 2002

Low Sunday, 1950
Trevor, W. The hill bachelors

The mourning
Trevor, W. The hill bachelors

Mrs. Acland's ghosts
Nightshade: 20th century ghost stories; edited by Robert Phillips

Of the cloth
Trevor, W. The hill bachelors

On the Streets
The New Yorker v79 no5 p72-7 Mr 24 2003

Sacred Statues
The New Yorker v78 no20 p64-71 Jl 22 2002
The O. Henry Prize stories, 2003; edited and with an introduction by Laura Furman; jurers David Gutterson, Diane Johnson, Jennifer Egan

Sitting with the dead
The New Yorker v77 no21 p70-4 Jl 30 2001

The telephone game
Trevor, W. The hill bachelors

Three people
Trevor, W. The hill bachelors

The Virgin's gift
Trevor, W. The hill bachelors

Le visiteur
Trevor, W. The hill bachelors

Tri-stan: I sold sissee nar to Ecko. Wallace, D. F.

Triad. Wurts, J.

The **trial**. Babel´, I.

Trial. Hensley, J. L.

Trial day. Due, T.

Trial day. Skinner, J.

TRIALS

See also Witnesses

Archer, J. Crime pays
Archer, J. The expert witness
Benét, S. V. The Devil and Daniel Webster
Breen, J. L. Four views of justice
Chekhov, A. P. In the court
Chekhov, A. P. An incident at law
Chekhov, A. P. Sergeant Prishibeyev
Chesnutt, C. W. The web of circumstance
Clarke, A. C. Moving spirit
DeMarco, T. Nahigian's Day in court
Dokey, R. The monster
Due, T. Trial day
Galef, D. The jury
Girardi, R. The defenestration of Aba Sid
Hare, C. Name of Smith
Hensley, J. L. Trial
Hensley, J. L. Whistler
Hribal, C. J. The clouds in Memphis
Huffman, B., Jr. Fair and impartial

TRIALS—*Continued*

Huffman, B., Jr. Synthesis of the community standard

Jakes, J. Celebrity and justice for all

Ludwig, O. The dead man of St. Anne's Chapel

Mortimer, J. C. Rumpole and the actor laddie

Mortimer, J. C. Rumpole and the asylum seekers

Mortimer, J. C. Rumpole and the Camberwell

Mortimer, J. C. Rumpole and the old familiar faces

Mortimer, J. C. Rumpole and the remembrance of things past

Mortimer, J. C. Rumpole and the teenage werewolf

Mortimer, J. C. Rumpole rests his case

Oates, J. C. The vampire

Schmidt, H. J. Out of Purmort

Scottoline, L. Carrying concealed

Shomer, E. Taking names

Tolstoy, L., graf. The son of a thief

The **Trials** of Finch. Smith, Z.

Triangle. Deaver, J.

Triangles. Sobeloff, J.

Triathlon. Franklin, T.

The **tribe** of the burnt thigh. Sneve, V. D. H.

TRIBES

Borges, J. L. Brodie's report

Sandstrom, E. K. The people's way

The **tribunal**. Čapek, K.

Tribute. Hoffman, W.

The **trick** is to keep breathing [excerpt] Galloway, J.

A **trick** of memory. Wallace, R.

Trick or treat. Garner, J.

Trick or treat with Jesus. Brahen, M. M.

A **trick** worth two of that. Sheckley, R.

The **Trickle-Down** Effect. Proulx, A.

Tricks & treats one night on Halloween Street. Tem, S. R.

A **trifle** from life. Chekhov, A. P.

A **trifle** from real life. See Chekhov, A. P. A trifle from life

Trifling occurrence. See Chekhov, A. P. A trifle from life

Trigger. Händler, E.-W.

Trimming Hedge. Bernard, K.

Trinidad. LaValle, V. D.

TRINIDAD AND TOBAGO

Anthony, M. They better don't stop the carnival

Antoni, R. A world of canes

James, C. L. R. Triumph

LaValle, V. D. Trinidad

Mendes, A. H. Pablo's fandango

Seepaul, L. Pan for Pockot

Sherwood, F. Basil the dog

Stewart, J. The old men used to dance

Politics

See Politics—Trinidad and Tobago

Port of Spain

Khan, I. Shadows move in the Britannia Bar

TRINIDADIANS

Canada

Alexis, A. The night piece

A **Trio** for Inferno. Firan, C.

The **trip** back from Whidbey. Lewis, W. H.

The **trip** home. Stolar, D.

Trip report (confidential). Lord, N.

Triple X. Youngblood, S.

Tripped Oasis. Steinbach, M.

Triptych. D'Aguiar, F.

Triptych. Galef, D.

Triptych. Schaum, M.

TRISTAN (LEGENDARY CHARACTER)

Updike, J. Four sides of one story

Tristram, Claire

Pray for the dead

The Massachusetts Review v43 no1 p59-72 Spr 2002

Rough music

The Massachusetts Review v40 no1 p100-08 Spr 1999

Triumph. James, C. L. R.

The **triumph** of beauty. Roth, J.

The **triumph** of Eve. Caudwell, S.

The **triumph** of night. Wharton, E.

Trivedi Park. Pittalwala, I.

Trobaugh, Augusta

A very unusual gift

Good Housekeeping v237 no5 p215-16, 218-24, 226, 228, 231, 235 N 2003

Trocheck, Kathy Hogan

See also Andrews, Mary Kay, 1954-

TROJAN WAR

Church, A. The Iliad for boys and girls [excerpt]

Dedman, S. A walk-on part in the war

A **troll** story: lesson in what matters, No. 1. Griffith, N.

TROLLEYS

Bradbury, R. The trolley

Trollope, Joanna

Finding my faith

Good Housekeeping v233 no6 p221-4 D 2001

Separate vacations

Good Housekeeping v232 no5 p199-206 My 2001

TROLLS *See* Fairies

TROMBONISTS

Berners, G. H. T.-W., Baron. Count Omega

Troncoso, Sergio

The abuelita

Troncoso, S. The last tortilla & other stories

Angie Luna

Troncoso, S. The last tortilla & other stories

Day of the dead

Troncoso, S. The last tortilla & other stories

Espiritu Santo

Troncoso, S. The last tortilla & other stories

The gardener

Troncoso, S. The last tortilla & other stories

The last tortilla

Troncoso, S. The last tortilla & other stories

My life in the city

Troncoso, S. The last tortilla & other stories

Punching chickens

Troncoso, S. The last tortilla & other stories

Remembering possibilities

Troncoso, S. The last tortilla & other stories

A rock trying to be a stone

Troncoso, S. The last tortilla & other stories

The snake

Troncoso, S. The last tortilla & other stories

Time magician

Troncoso, S. The last tortilla & other stories

Trophy Bill. O'Dell, C. D.

Trophy wife. Gelb, J.

Tropical Fish. Baingana, D.

The **tropics**. Mejides, M.

Trotter, William R.
The bleeding of Hauptmann Gehlen
The Darkest thirst; a vampire anthology

Trotters. Chen, W.

Trouble a-bruin. Friesner, E. M.

Trouble and her friends [excerpt] Scott, M.

Trouble light. Wellen, E.

The **trouble** man. Rhodes, E. M.

The **trouble** with Harry. Matteson, S.

The **trouble** with money. Cooke, C.

The **trouble** with Mr. Leopold. Broyard, B.

The **trouble** with Mrs. Blynn, the trouble with the world. Highsmith, P.

The **trouble** with Sophie. Klass, P.

Trouble with the natives. Clarke, A. C.

The **trouble** with the truth. Agee, J.

Trouble with time. Clarke, A. C.

The **Trouble** with You Is. Rodgers, S. J.

The **troubled** dog. Fulton, J.

Troubles on Morning Glory Road. Krawiec, R.

Troy, Judy
Ramone
Texas bound. Book III; 22 Texas stories; edited by Kay Cattarulla; foreword by Robert Flynn

Troy, Mary
The Alibi Café
Troy, M. The Alibi Café and other stories
Bird of pardise
Troy, M. The Alibi Café and other stories
Dinosaur
Troy, M. The Alibi Café and other stories
Do you believe in the chicken hanger?
Troy, M. The Alibi Café and other stories
A little zip
Troy, M. The Alibi Café and other stories
Mercy the midget
Troy, M. The Alibi Café and other stories
The Most Beautiful Girl in the World
River Styx no67 p68-83 2004
Tulipville
Troy, M. The Alibi Café and other stories
Turning colder
Troy, M. The Alibi Café and other stories
We're still Keeneys
Troy, M. The Alibi Café and other stories

TROY (ANCIENT CITY)
See also Trojan War
Dedman, S. A walk-on part in the war
Waldrop, H. One horse town
Waldrop, H. and Kennedy, L. One-horse town

TRUCK DRIVERS
Delaney, E. J. Travels with Mr. Slush
DeMarinis, R. Horizontal snow
Dinh, L. For gristles
Jaime-Becerra, M. Lopez Trucking Incorporated
Morgan, R. The ratchet
Offutt, C. High water everywhere
Roorbach, B. Fredonia
Ryan, P. L. Life is a highway
Shackelford, R. T. From Tucson to Tucumcari, from Tehachapi to Tonopah
Wellen, E. Devil's pass

Truck stop. Frangello, G.

TRUCKS

Accidents
See Traffic accidents

Trudeau, Smoky
Good-bye, Emily Dickinson
Calyx v21 no2 p27-32 Summ 2003

Trudell, Dennis
& other stories
The Ohio Review no59 p149-55 1999
Sticking Pins in the Chancellor
The North American Review v289 no1 p8-14 Ja/F 2004

Trudy. Nailah, A.

True. Bauman, B. A.

True blue. McCaffety, M.

True colors. Herber, P. J.

True colors. Vachss, A. H.

True confession. Hoffman, A.

The **true** facts about the death of Wes Hardin. Crider, B.

The **true** friends. Henry, W.

True north. Bessette, A.

True romance. Hansen, R.

True story. Davis, A.

A **true** story, repeated word for word as I heard it. Twain, M.

True Thomas. Hill, R.

True to form. Berg, E.

Trueba, Antonio de
"The adventures of a tailor"
Fedorchek, R. M. Stories of enchantment from nineteenth-century Spain; translated from the Spanish by Robert M. Fredorchek; introduction by Alan E. Smith
"The king's son-in-law"
Fedorchek, R. M. Stories of enchantment from nineteenth-century Spain; translated from the Spanish by Robert M. Fredorchek; introduction by Alan E. Smith

Truly great people. Pendleton, J.

The **truly** needy. Honig, L.

Truly yours, John R. Jacks. Hensley, J. L.

TRUMAN, HARRY S., 1884-1972
About
Kaminsky, S. M. The buck stops here
Pickard, N. Dr. Couch saves a president

Trumpet [excerpt] Kay, J.

TRUMPET PLAYERS
Jaime-Becerra, M. La fiesta brava
Kay, J. Trumpet [excerpt]

Trunk, Y. Y.
A Roman philosopher writes a letter
Neugroschel, J. No star too beautiful; Yiddish stories from 1382 to the present; compiled and translated by Joachim Neugroschel

Trust. Kohler, S.

TRUST FUNDS
James, H. The impressions of a cousin

Trust the Irish for that. Aldrich, B. S.

The **truth**. Coates, G. S.

Truth. Kilpatrick, N.

The **truth** about Alicia. Matiella, A. C.

The **truth** about Weena. Lake, D. J.

Truth and beauty. Flynn, R.

Truth and goodness. Williams, M.

Truth or consequences. Adams, A.

Truth or consequences. Ferrell, C.

TRUTHFULNESS AND FALSEHOOD
Alexie, S. Dear John Wayne
Banks, R. My mother's memoirs, my father's lie, and other true stories
Chekhov, A. P. A trifle from life

TRUTHFULNESS AND FALSEHOOD—*Continued*

Freudenberger, N. Letter from the last bastion
Goran, L. Why he never left his wife
James, H. The marriages
Knight, M. Keeper of secrets, teller of lies
Lao She. A man who doesn't lie
Moulessehoul, M. The wicked tongue
Powers, S. The baker's wife
Singer, I. B. The bitter truth
Try love. Bergman, S.
Trying. Robison, M.
Trying out for the race. Yates, R.
Trying to Say. Brown, R.
Ts'ai, Ts'e-hai *See* Cai Cehai, 1954-
Ts'an-hsüeh
The child who raised poisonous snakes
The Art of the story; an international anthology of contemporary short stories; edited by Daniel Halpern
Tsebi, Shabthai *See* Shabbethai Tzevi, 1626-1676
Tsunami. Cabiles, N.
Tsuris. Sher, S.
TUAMOTU ISLANDS *See* Islands of the Pacific
Tube Rose. Smith, R. T.
Tuberama: a musical on the Northern Line (or how to be in touch with your emotions). Starr, G.
TUBERCULOSIS
Barrett, A. The cure
Butler, R. O. Carl and I
Yates, R. No pain whatsoever
Yates, R. Out with the old
Tucci, Niccolò
The evolution of knowledge
Wonderful town; New York stories from The New Yorker; edited by David Remnick with Susan Choi
Tuck, Lily
Dream house
Tuck, L. Limbo, and other places I have lived; stories
Fortitude
Tuck, L. Limbo, and other places I have lived; stories
Gold leaf
The Antioch Review v59 no2 p238-46 Spr 2001
Tuck, L. Limbo, and other places I have lived; stories
Horses
Tuck, L. Limbo, and other places I have lived; stories
Hotter
Tuck, L. Limbo, and other places I have lived; stories
L'Esprit de L'Escalier
Tuck, L. Limbo, and other places I have lived; stories
Limbo
Tuck, L. Limbo, and other places I have lived; stories
La Mayonette
Tuck, L. Limbo, and other places I have lived; stories
Next of kin
Tuck, L. Limbo, and other places I have lived; stories

Ouarzazate
Tuck, L. Limbo, and other places I have lived; stories
Rue Guynemer
Tuck, L. Limbo, and other places I have lived; stories
Second wife
Tuck, L. Limbo, and other places I have lived; stories
St. Guilhem-le-Désert
Ploughshares v28 no2/3 p198-207 Fall 2002
Verdi
Tuck, L. Limbo, and other places I have lived; stories
The view from Madama Butterfly's house
Tuck, L. Limbo, and other places I have lived; stories
Tucker, S. Brady
Falling in Love During Wartime
The North American Review v288 no3/4 p38-9 My/Ag 2003
TUDOR ENGLAND *See* England—16th century
Tug of war. Aylett, S.
Tugboat Annie and the Cheapskate. Raine, N. R.
TUGBOATS
Armstrong, K. Inside passage
Tulips from Amsterdam. Watson, I.
Tulipville. Troy, M.
Tuller, David
Sperm-and-egg tango
Men on men 2000; best new gay fiction for the millennium; edited and with an introduction by David Bergman and Karl Woelz
Tully, Cameron
Vitacare
Dalhousie Review v81 no3 p409-18 Aut 2001
Tuma, Hama
The Waldiba story
The Anchor book of modern African stories; edited by Nadežda Obradović ; with a foreword by Chinua Achebe
Tumasonis, Don
The prospect cards
The Mammoth book of best new horror 14; edited with an introduction by Stephen Jones
The Year's best fantasy & horror: sixteenth annual collection; edited by Ellen Datlow & Terri Windling
The wretched thicket of thorn
The Mammoth book of best new horror 14; edited with an introduction by Stephen Jones
The **tumblers**. Englander, N.
Tunesmith. Biggle, L.
Tunica. Mason, B. A.
The **tuning** of perfection. MacLeod, A.
The **Tunisian** notebook. Gifford, B.
The **tunnel**. Lake, M. D.
Tunnel rat. Barnes, H. L.
The **tunnel** under the world. Pohl, F.
TUNNELS
Kiernan, C. R. In the water works (Birmingham, Alabama 1888)
Turchi, Peter
Everybody's Alien
Western Humanities Review v57 no2 p70-83 Fall 2003

Turchi, Peter—*Continued*
The night sky
    This is where we live; short stories by 25 contemporary North Carolina writers; edited by Michael McFee
Night, truck, two lights burning
    Ploughshares v28 no2/3 p208-17 Fall 2002
TURIN (ITALY) *See* Italy—Turin
TURKEY
Meredith, D. Ferry from Kabatas
        Ankara
Gabriel, D. The kapici's wife
        Istanbul
Fitzgerald, P. The prescription
Turkey Day. Locklin, G.
A **turkey** hunt. Chopin, K.
Turn me on, dead man. Strandquist, R.
Turn of the card. West, M.
Turn of the world. Winterson, J.
Turn these stones into bread. Valeri, L.
Turnaround. Hart, C. G.
Turnbull, Peter
Weasal and the fish
    The best British mysteries; edited by Maxim Jakubowski
The **turncoat**. Allyn, D.
TURNCOATS *See* Defectors
Turned. Gilman, C. P.
Turner, George
And now doth time waste me
    Dreaming down-under; edited by Jack Dann and Janeen Webb
Flowering mandrake
    Centaurus: the best of Australian science fiction; edited by David G. Hartwell and Damien Broderick
    The Good new stuff; adventure SF in the grand tradition; edited by Gardner Dozois
Turner, Guinevere
Cookie and me
    Typical girls; new stories by smart women; edited by Susan Corrigan
Turner, Robert
Eleven o'clock bulletin
    Master's choice v2; mystery stories by today's top writers and the masters who inspired them; edited by Lawrence Block
Turning colder. Troy, M.
Turpentine. Malzberg, B. N.
The **turret**. Lupoff, R. A.
Turtle. Adam, C.
Turtle. Allan, M. C.
The **turtle**. Smart, A.
Turtle hunting with black. Smith, S. J.
The **Turtle** That Had Elevated Thoughts. Neumann, A. W.
Turtledove, Harry
Black tulip
    Redshift; extreme visions of speculative fiction; edited by Al Sarrantonio
Islands in the sea
    The Best alternate history stories of the 20th century; edited by Harry Turtledove with Martin H. Greenberg
Joe Steele
    The year's best science fiction: twenty-first annual collection; edited by Gardner Dozois

The last article
    One lamp; alternate history stories from The magazine of Fantasy & Science Fiction; edited by Gordon van Gelder
The road not taken
    Masterpieces: the best science fiction of the century; edited by Orson Scott Card
TURTLES
Adam, C. Turtle
Barker, N. Bendy-Linda
Highsmith, P. The terrapin
Lord, C. La Tortuga
Sosin, D. Submersion
Waldrop, H. Willow Beeman
Whitty, J. A tortoise for the Queen of Tonga
Turtles. McCorkle, J.
Turzillo, Mary A.
Mars is no place for children
    Nebula awards showcase 2001; the year's best SF and fantasy chosen by the science fiction and fantasy writers of America; edited by Robert Silverberg
Tuscaloosa. Weesner, T.
TUSCANY (ITALY) *See* Italy—Tuscany
Tushinski, Jim
Home
    His 3: brilliant new fiction by gay writers; edited by Robert Drake and Terry Wolverton
Tushnet, Leonard
The ban
    When night fell; an anthology of Holocaust short stories; edited by Linda Schermer Raphael and Marc Lee Raphael
Tusk. Aylett, S.
Tusk. Oates, J. C.
Tusk. Srinivasan, A. A.
Tusquets, Esther
The same sea as every summer [excerpt]
    The Vintage book of international lesbian fiction; edited and with an introduction by Naomi Holoch and Joan Nestle
Tussing, Justin
The artificial cloud
    Death dines at 8:30; edited by Claudia Bishop and Nick DiChario
Tutankhamen Calhoun. Norris, H.
The **Tutor**. Freudenberger, N.
The **tutor**. Shapiro, G.
TUTORS
Freudenberger, N. The tutor
Greer, A. S. Cannibal kings
Helms, B. American wives
James, H. Gabrielle de Bergerac
James, H. The pupil
Johnson-Davies, D. Mr. Pritchard
Leavitt, D. Crossing St. Gotthard
Malamud, B. The German refugee
Poirier, M. J. Gators
Sade, marquis de. The teacher philosopher
Singer, I. B. A tutor in the village
Waugh, E. A house of gentlefolks
Tuttle, Lisa
"The mezzotint"
    Gathering the bones; original stories from the world's masters of horror; edited by Dennis Etchison, Ramsey Campbell and Jack Dann
Tuxedo. Warren, D.

Tužinský, Ján
  A murmur
    In search of homo sapiens; twenty-five con-
      temporary Slovak short stories; editor,
      Pavol Hudík ; [translated by Heather
      Trebatická; American English editor, Lucy
      Bednár]
TV tales. Tillman, L.
Twa Corbies. Cooke, C.
Twa Corbies. De Lint, C.
Twain, Mark
  A Connecticut Yankee at King Arthur's court
    [excerpt]
    Swords and sorcerers; stories from the world
      of fantasy and adventure; edited by Clint
      Willis
  A curious experience
    Death by espionage; intriguing stories of de-
      ception and betrayal; edited by Martin Cruz
      Smith
  A ghost story
    The American fantasy tradition; edited by Bri-
      an M. Thomsen
  A murder, a mystery, and a marriage
    Atlantic Monthly v288 no1 p54-64 Jl/Ag 2001
  This experiment was baseball
    Dead balls and double curves; an anthology
      of early baseball fiction; edited and with an
      introduction by Trey Strecker ; with a fore-
      word by Arnold Hano
  A true story, repeated word for word as I heard
    it
    Southern local color; stories of region, race,
      and gender; edited by Barbara C. Ewell and
      Pamela Glenn Menke; with notes by An-
      drea Humphrey
TWAIN, MARK, 1835-1910
                About
  Denton, B. The territory
          Parodies, imitations, etc.
  Pendarvis, Jack. Escape by Zebra
Tweedsmuir, John Buchan, Baron See Buchan,
  John, 1875-1940
Twelve legions of angels Turtledove, H. Alternate
  generals II; ed. by Harry Turtledove
The twelve moons. Sneve, V. D. H.
Twelve of the little buggers. Coward, M.
The twelve plagues. Shapiro, G.
Twentieth century design. Barrett, L.
Twenty-five bucks. Farrell, J. T.
The twenty-seventh man. Englander, N.
Twenty-three. Davidson, A.
Twenty-three. Deane, J. F.
Twenty ways to look at fire. Anderson, D.
Twice, at once, separated. Addison, L.
Twice by fire. Campbell, R.
Twice-cooked Yorky. Matiella, A. C.
Twilight. Campbell, J. W.
Twilight. Freed, L.
Twilight. Johnson, R.
Twilight of chivalry. Mencken, S. H.
The twilight of the God. Wharton, E.
Twilight of the real. Herbert, W.
TWINS
          See also Siamese twins
  Addison, L. Twice, at once, separated
  Agustí, M. Rebirth [Cain and Abel]

Bukoski, A. The month that brings winter; or,
  How Mr. Truzynski carried Vietnam home
  with him
Butler, R. O. Twins
Davis, L. Strays
Grodstein, L. Such a pretty face
Hegi, U. A town like ours
Karnezis, P. A funeral of stones
Kiernan, C. R. Postcards from the King of Tides
Lowenthal, M. Into a mirror
Lumley, B. Aunt Hester
Oates, J. C. Death cup
Patterson, K. Sick in public
Poirier, M. J. Buttons
Robison, M. The Wellman twins
Spatz, G. Wonderful tricks
Stevenson, J. Law and order
Swan, M. The deep
Updike, J. The invention of the horse collar
Twins. Butler, R. O.
Two altercations. Bausch, R.
Two-bagger. Connelly, M.
Two Betsy Hamilton Letters. Moore, I. M.
Two border stories. Gifford, B.
The two boxes. Alas, L.
Two bums here would spend freely except for
  poverty. McNulty, J.
Two dead Indians. Jacobs, M.
Two dead men. Barnett, P.
The two dicks One lamp; alternate history stories
  from The magazine of Fantasy & Science
  Fiction; edited by Gordon van Gelder
The two Dicks. McAuley, P. J.
Two disagreeable pigeons. Highsmith, P.
Two-eleven all around. Offutt, C.
Two fathers. Čapek, K.
Two fishers. Maupassant, G. d.
Two for a cent. Fitzgerald, F. S.
Two for One. Mullen, J.
The Two Franzes. Bukiet, M. J.
Two kinds. Tan, A.
The Two Lands. Bondurant, M.
Two lives. Bell, M. S.
The Two of Them. Dillard, A.
Two Poes. Orner, P.
Two portraits. Chopin, K.
Two recipes for magic beans. Love, R.
Two revolts in one family. Fischerová, D.
Two rivers. Barrett, A.
Two rules. Boilard, J.
The two Sams. Hirshberg, G.
Two scholars. Alas, L.
Two sharp knives. Hammett, D.
Two shot. Smith, M. M.
Two-speed. Meyers, K.
Two strippers. DeLancey, K.
Two summers and two souls. Chopin, K.
Two thousand Germans in Frankenmuth. Arvin, N.
Two thousand years of torture. Carson, J.
The two trail ride tricksters. Froh, R.
The two Volodyas. Chekhov, A. P.
Two-way radio. Vachss, A. H.
Two Ways of Telling. Paley, G.
Two who forgot. Dinh, L.
Two windows. Foster, K.
Two women. Blitz, R.
Two words. Giles, M.
Two worlds. Johnson-Davies, D.
The twonky. Padgett, L.

Tyau, Kathleen
  Pick up your pine
    Fishing for chickens; short stories about rural
      youth; edited, with an introduction by Jim
      Heynen
TYCOONS *See* Millionaires
Tyennick, Joe
  Life without Valentino
    The Literary Review (Madison, N.J.) v44 no4
      p764-87 Summ 2001
  Pygmalion with a Bad S
    The Literary Review (Madison, N.J.) v47 no3
      p84-103 Spr 2004
  An Un-hip Hip Incident
    The Literary Review (Madison, N.J.) v46 no4
      p714-30 Summ 2003
Tying St. Anthony's feet. Matiella, A. C.
TYPEWRITERS
  Shrayer-Petrov, D. Dismemberers
TYPHOID FEVER
  Chekhov, A. P. The bishop
Typhus. Chekhov, A. P.
TYPHUS FEVER
  Chekhov, A. P. Typhus
TYPISTS
  Depew, D. R. Indigenous girls
  Gilchrist, E. Hearts of Dixie
  Klein, Anne Carolyn. The mantra and the typist:
    a story of east and west
  Nuñez, M. E. A. The girl typist who worked for
    a provincial ministry of culture
Typographical error. Lutz, J.
Tyre, Nedra
  A nice place to stay
    A moment on the edge; 100 years of crime
      stories by women; edited by Elizabeth
      George
  Recipe for a happy marriage
    Murder most delectable; savory tales of culi-
      nary crimes; edited by Martin H. Greenberg
Tyrwhitt-Wilson, Gerald Hugh *See* Berners, Ger-
    ald Hugh Tyrwhitt-Wilson, Baron, 1883-
    1950
Tzevi, Shabbethai *See* Shabbethai Tzevi, 1626-
    1676

U

U-BOATS *See* Submarines
U.F.O. in Kushiro. Murakami, H.
U.F.O.'S *See* Flying saucers
Udall, Brady
  Buckeye the elder
    The Workshop; seven decades of the Iowa
      Writers' Workshop: 42 stories, recollections
      & essays on Iowa's place in 20th-century
      American literature; edited by Tom Grimes
  Funny Valentine
    Gentlemen's Quarterly v73 no5 p192 My
      2003
UFO in Kushiro. Murakami, H.
Ugliest faces. Broyard, B.
The **ugliest** girl. Dinh, L.
The **ugliest** house in the world. Davies, P. H.
UGLINESS
  De Lint, C. Freak
  Oates, J. C. Ugly
Ugly. Oates, J. C.

O **ugly** bird!. Wellman, M. W.
Ugly girl. See Oates, J. C. Ugly
The **ugly** virgin. Stanton, M.
Ugolone da Todi: obituary of a philosopher.
    Herling, G.
Uke Rivers Delivers. Smith, R. T.
UKRAINE
Odessa
  Babel', I. The aroma of Odessa
  Babel', I. The end of the almshouse
  Babel', I. The father
  Babel', I. Di Grasso
  Babel', I. How things were done in Odessa
  Babel', I. In the basement
  Babel', I. Justice in parentheses
  Babel', I. Lyubka the Cossack
  Babel', I. Odessa
  Babel', I. Sunset
UKRAINIAN AMERICANS
  Hemon, A. Fatherland
  Zabytko, I. The celebrity
  Zabytko, I. John Mars, all-American
  Zabytko, I. The last boat
  Zabytko, I. Lavender soap
  Zabytko, I. My black Valiant
  Zabytko, I. Obligation
  Zabytko, I. Pani Ryhotska in love
  Zabytko, I. The prodigal son enters heaven
  Zabytko, I. Saint Sonya
  Zabytko, I. Steve's bar
UKRAINIANS
United States
  Browder, C. Pizza man
The **Ulfjarl's** stone. Reichert, M. Z.
Ullward's retreat. Vance, J.
Ulrikke. Borges, J. L.
The **ultimate** earth. Williamson, J.
The **Ultimate** Film Writing Exercise. Morris, M.
The **ultimate** melody. Clarke, A. C.
Ulysses sees the moon in the bedroom window.
    Wilson, R. C.
Umansky, Ellen M.
  How to make it to the promised land
    Lost tribe; jewish fiction from the edge
Umbrella. Dessen, S.
The **umbrella**. Kureishi, H.
An **Un-hip** Hip Incident. Tyennick, J.
Unacademic exercise: a nature story. Waugh, E.
Unamuno, Miguel de
  Mechanopolis
    Cosmos latinos: an anthology of science fic-
      tion from Latin America and Spain; trans-
      lated, edited, & with an introduction &
      notes by Andrea L. Bell & Yolanda Moli-
      na-Gavilán
Unapproved minutes of the Carthage, Vermont,
    Zoning Board of Adjustment. Paine, T.
An **unbecoming** grace. Steinbeck, T.
Unborn again. Lawson, C.
UNBORN CHILD *See* Fetus
Unc' Edinburg's drowndin'. Page, T. N.
Unc foils show foe. Jakes, J.
Unc probes pickle plot. Jakes, J.
Uncertain treasure. Highsmith, P.
Unchained melody. Allyn, D.
The **uncharted** heart. Hardy, M.
The **uncivil** teacher of court etiquette Kôtsuké no
    Suké. Borges, J. L.

Uncle Alf Turtledove, H. Alternate generals II; ed. by Harry Turtledove
Uncle Aron. Grynberg, H.
Uncle Evil Eye. Buggé, C.
Uncle Gerard. McKendry, J.
Uncle Gorby and the baggage ghost. What, L.
Uncle Jack. Epstein, J.
Uncle Joe's Old-Time Communist Nostalgia Bar. Jacobs, M.
Uncle Loaf and Auntie Putt-Putt. Walker, A.
Uncle Obadiah and the alien. Philp, G.
Uncle Peretz takes flight. Shabtai, Y.
Uncle Remus. Harris, J. C.
Uncle Remus initiates the little boy. Harris, J. C.
Uncle Tom's cabin. Dinh, L.
Uncle Wellington's wives. Chesnutt, C. W.
Uncle Willy. Garcia, L. G.
Uncle Wolfie. Cohen, R.
The **unclean**. Kurlansky, M.

UNCLES
See also Nephews
Alameddine, R. The perv
Alcott, L. M. Uncles Smiley's boys
Arvin, N. Radio ads
Bates, H. E. The lily
Berberova, N. The Argentine
Berry, W. Thicker than liquor
Bhêly-Quénum, O. A child in the bush of ghosts
Chaon, D. Burn with me
Chekhov, A. P. The privy councillor
Chopin, K. Polly
Cohen, R. Delicate destinies
Cohen, R. Uncle Wolfie
Collymore, F. Some people are meant to live alone
Daniels, J. Bonus
Desaulniers, J. After Rosa Parks
Drake, R. All under one roof
Dybek, S. A minor mood
Dybek, S. Song
Fairey, W. W. Family album
Fleming, P. The kill
Flythe, S. A family of breast feeders
Frym, G. Homologue
Garcia, L. G. The day they took my uncle
Garrett, G. P. Feeling good, feeling fine
Gonzalez, R. The garden of Padre Anselmo
Heller, J. Castle of snow
Hemon, A. Exchange of pleasant words
Leslie, N. Prayer wheel
McCabe, P. The hands of Dingo Deery
Melton, F. Counting
Michaels, L. Viva la Tropicana
Offutt, C. Inside out
Reisman, N. The good life
Richard, M. Strays
Robison, M. Sisters
Saroyan, W. The pomegranate trees
Shade, E. Blood
Škvorecký, J. My Uncle Kohn
Spencer, E. The fishing lake
Spencer, E. Indian summer
Spencer, E. Sharon
Stegner, L. Indian summer
TolstaıSaS, T. On the golden porch
Updike, J. The lucid eye in silver town
Yi, T.-H. Shrapnel
Zabytko, I. The last boat
Uncles Smiley's boys. Alcott, L. M.

Uncommon sense. Clement, H.
The **uncorking** of Uncle Finn. Yolen, J.
The **undeniable** likeness of twins. Hudec, I.
Under glass. Hopkinson, N.
Under hoof. Marks, J.
Under Mars. McAuley, P. J.
Under my skin. Rippen, C.
Under Number Nine. Liberty, H. J.
Under old New York. Barrett, N., Jr.
Under suspicion. Howard, C.
Under the bright and hollow sky. Wilson, A. J.
Under the hanging wall. L'Amour, L.
Under the hill. Yolen, J.
Under the Influence. McKee, J.
Under the ironwood trees. Tratnik, S.
Under the knife. Lovesey, P.
Under the pyramids. Lovecraft, H. P.
Under the radar. Ford, R.
Under the sierra. Blake, J. C.
Under the skin. Pronzini, B.
Under the skin. West, M.
Under the sky. Bowles, P.
Under the tree. Agnon, S. Y.
Under the wheat. DeMarinis, R.
Underfoot. O'Grady, T.
Underground. Desai, A.
The **underground** gardens. Boyle, T. C.
UNDERGROUND MOVEMENTS (WORLD WAR, 1939-1945) See World War, 1939-1945—Underground movements
Underneath. Hochman, A.
Understand. Chiang, T.
Understanding entropy. Malzberg, B. N.
The **undertaker**. Pushkin, A. S.
UNDERTAKERS AND UNDERTAKING
Bly, C. The dignity of life
Bradbury, R. The handler
Brown, C. The house on Belle Isle
Lynch, T. Blood sport
Mason, B. A. The funeral side
Offutt, C. Inside out
Pushkin, A. S. The undertaker
Watson, B. The dead girl
UNDERWATER COLONIES
Blish, J. Surface tension
Underwood, Laura J.
The wife of Ben-y-ghloe
Such a pretty face; edited by Lee Martindale
UNDERWORLD
See also Crime and criminals; Gangsters; Mafia
Greenberg, A. A couple of dead men
The **undiagnosed**. Tillman, L.
The **undiscovered**. Sanders, W.
UNDOCUMENTED ALIENS
Blake, J. C. Aliens in the garden
Blake, J. C. The house of Esperanza
Delaney, E. J. The drowning
Guerrero, L. Even in heaven
Le Clézio, J.-M. G. The runner
Murguía, A. Rose-colored dreams
Sánchez, R. The fields
Yañez, R. Rio Grande
Undone. Kelly, J. P.
"**Undr**". Borges, J. L.
Undue haste. Heron, L.
UNEMPLOYED
Bausch, R. The person I have mostly become
Blair, J. American standard

UNEMPLOYED—*Continued*

Blair, J. Happy puppy

Casares, O. Chango

Clair, M. Water seeks its own level

Davis, J. S. What kind of man

DeLancey, K. It's dark

Delaney, E. J. Notes toward my absolution

Fitzgerald, P. The axe

Foster, K. The kind I'm likely to get

Frym, G. SWAT

Gautreaux, T. Dancing with the one-armed gal

Holman, J. Squabble

Jackson, V. F. Victoria and Albert II: Day-trippers

Jones, T. Mouses

Lawrence, D. H. England, my England

Le Clézio, J.-M. G. O thief, what is the life you lead?

Leonard, E. Chickasaw Charlie Hoke

MacDougall, C. The lights below [excerpt]

Mayo, W. Who made you

McNally, J. Limbs

Mo Yan. Shifu, you'll do anything for a laugh

Morgan, R. The bullnoser

Packer, Z. Geese

Perry, D. Love is gnats today

Rivera, T. The salamanders

Saroyan, A. Jobs

Tilghman, C. The way people run

Troy, M. Dinosaur

Upadhyay, S. The good shopkeeper

Updike, J. Ace in the hole

Valenzuela, L. Who, me a bum?

Waters, M. Y. Egg-face

Wood, M. Ernie's ark

UNESCO

Greenberg, P. The subjunctive mood

The **unexpected**. Chopin, K.

The **unexpected** corpse. L'Amour, L.

An **unexpected** interlude between two characters. Herranz Brooks, J.

The **unexpected** visit of a reanimated English-woman. Bishop, M.

An **unfair** question. Shepard, S.

The **Unfaithful** Wife. Tohill, S. M.

Unferth, Deb Olin

The container

The Literary Review (Madison, N.J.) v44 no3 p472-4 Spr 2001

Mr. Simmons Takes a Prisoner

Harper's v307 p86-8, 90 Ag 2003

Unfinished business. Warren, L.

Unfinished business. Weinberg, R.

Unfinished figures. Marías, J.

UNFINISHED STORIES

Kafka, F. Blumfeld, an elderly bachelor

Pushkin, A. S. The blackamoor of Peter the Great

Pushkin, A. S. Egyptian nights

Pushkin, A. S. The guests were arriving at the dacha

Pushkin, A. S. A history of the village of Goriukhino

Pushkin, A. S. In the corner of a small square

Pushkin, A. S. Maria Schoning

Pushkin, A. S. A novel in letters

Pushkin, A. S. Roslavlev

Pushkin, A. S. A tale of Roman life

Pushkin, A. S. We were spending the evening at Princess D.'s dacha

Unfinished Symphony. Poliner, E.

Unfinished symphony. Yasgur, B. S. and Malzberg, B. N.

The **unfolding**. McBrearty, R. G.

Unforeseen Circumstances. Kalpakian, L.

The **unfortunated** city. Chenoweth, A.

Unger, Douglas

Leslie and Sam

Southwest Review v86 no2/3 p272-83 Spr/Summ 2001

Looking for War

TriQuarterly no115 p25-58 Spr 2003

Ungerer, Klaus

Black out

Prairie Schooner v73 no3 p11-17 Fall 1999

The **ungoverned**. Vinge, V.

Unhasped. Schow, D. J.

Unheard Music. Meinke, P.

The **unicorn** masque. Kushner, E.

Unicorn stew. Eakin, W.

UNICORNS

Dann, J. The black horn

De Lint, C. Seven for a secret

Eakin, W. Unicorn stew

Unicycle. Norman, H.

UNIDENTIFIED FLYING SAUCERS *See* Flying saucers

The **unified** front. Nelson, A.

The **unimportant** Lila Parr. Muñoz, M.

The **uninsured**. Gilchrist, E.

Unique visitors. Kelly, J. P.

UNITED NATIONS EDUCATIONAL, SCIENTIFIC AND CULTURAL ORGANIZATION *See* Unesco

UNITED STATES

See also Middle Western States; Southern States; Southwestern States; Western States names of individual states

18th century

Finlay, C. C. We come not to praise Washington

Revolution, 1775-1783

Johnson, C. R. A soldier for the crown

Louise, D. D. Stitches in time

19th century

James, H. The point of view

Civil War, 1861-1865

Alcott, L. M. Milly's messenger

Allyn, D. The turncoat

Auchincloss, L. The veterans

Barton, M. Final spring

Berliner, J. Other.........1

Bierce, A. The story of a conscience

Black, M. The hundred day men

Bradbury, R. The drummer boy of Shiloh

Carr, P. M. Diary of a union soldier

Chopin, K. The locket

Cobb, J. H. Monica Van Telflin and the proper application of pressure

Crider, B. Belle Boyd, the rebel spy

Dann, J. Spirit dog

Denton, B. The territory

DuBois, B. The invisible spy

Estleman, L. D. South Georgia crossing

Garcia y Robertson, R. Forever free

Gorman, E. A small and private war

Gurganus, A. Reassurance

UNITED STATES—Civil War, 1861-1865—*Continued*

Haddam, J. Port Tobacco
Hoch, E. D. The counterfeit copperhead
Jakober, M. Slither
Knight, M. Killing Stonewall Jackson
Lindskold, J. M. The road to Stony Creek
Lutz, J. Hobson's choice
Moore, W. Bring the jubilee
Nagle, P. G. The courtship of Captain Swenk
Phillips, G. The measure
Ponder, D. U. The rat spoon
Randisi, R. J. The Knights of Liberty
Reasoner, J. Dead Man's Hollow
Rusch, K. K. Burial detail
Rusch, K. K. The dead line
Rusch, K. K. The gallery of his dreams
Schumacher, A. Worth a thousand words
Skeet, M. Near enough to home
Smith, R. T. I have lost my right
Twain, M. A curious experience
Vukcevich, R. The swan
Wellman, M. W. The valley was still
Wolfe, T. O lost

Casualties
James, H. The story of a year

1865-1898
McHugh, M. F. The Lincoln train

20th century
Michaels, L. In the fifties
Updike, J. How to love America and leave it at the same time

Armed forces
DeMarinis, R. An airman's goodbye

College life
See College life—United States

Communism
See Communism—United States

Defenses
Vinge, V. "Bookworm, run!"

Politics
See Politics—United States

Presidents
See Presidents—United States

Prisoners and prisons
See Prisoners and prisons—United States

Race relations
Bocock, M. Heaven lies about
Bocock, M. Play me "Stormy weather," please
Bottoms, G. The metaphor
Bradbury, R. Chrysalis
Bradbury, R. The transformation
Chesnutt, C. W. A matter of principle
Chesnutt, C. W. The sheriff's children
Chesnutt, C. W. The web of circumstance
Chesnutt, C. W. White weeds
Chopin, K. Désirée's baby
Davis, M. M. A bamboula
Du Bois, W. E. B. The comet
Dumas, H. Fon
Dumas, H. Goodbye, sweetwater
Dumas, H. Rope of wind
Dumas, H. Thrust counter thrust
Engel, M. P. What Addie wants
Folayan, A. Breakfast at Woolworth's, 1956
Frym, G. No clubs allowed
Glave, T. —and love them?
Gurganus, A. Blessed assurance: a moral tale
Harris, J. C. Where's Duncan?

Harrison, H. Mute Milton
Himes, C. Lunching at the Ritzmore
Hoffman, W. Stones
Lee, A. The golden chariot
Lee, A. The pulpit
Mazor, J. The lone star kid
McBain, E. The sharers
McCorkle, J. Starlings
McKnight, R. The kind of light that shines on Texas
McNally, J. The politics of correctness
Means, D. McGregor's day on
Mencken, S. H. Little white girl
Morrison, T. Recitatif
Nailah, A. Bucket
Nailah, A. The ride
Nailah, A. Trudy
Packer, Z. Brownies
Packer, Z. Doris is coming
Pak, T. The court interpreter
Pickens, W. Jim Crow in Texas
Posey, J. R. Ticket to freedom
Price, R. The fare to the moon
Schuyler, G. S. Black no more [excerpt]
Spencer, E. The business venture
Stolar, D. Crossing over
Thelwell, M. Community of victims
Thelwell, M. Direct action
Thompson, C. Judgment
Toomer, J. Blood-burning moon
Touré. Once an oreo, always an oreo
Touré. The sad, sweet story of Sugar Lips Shinehot, the man with the portable promised land
Touré. You are who you kill
Touré. Young, black, and unstoppable; or, Death of a zeitgeist jockey
Vega Yunqué, E. Eight morenos
Wald, M. Keys to the city
Williams, J. Spring is now
Wright, R. Bright and morning star

UNITED STATES. AIR FORCE
Clark, J. Wild blue
Shaw, D. A cure for gravity

UNITED STATES. ARMY
Gilliland, G. News of the world
Harford, D. K. A death on the Ho Chi Minh Trail
Reiner, C. How Paul Robeson saved my life
Roth, P. Defender of the faith

Officers
Bierce, A. The story of a conscience
Casey, J. A more complete cross-section
James, H. A most extraordinary case
O'Brien, T. The things they carried
Vaughn, S. Able, Baker, Charlie, Dog

UNITED STATES. ARMY. 1ST CAVALRY (VOLUNTEER) *See* United States. Army. Volunteer Cavalry, 1st

UNITED STATES. ARMY. CALVARY
Carney, O. How I happened to put on the blue

UNITED STATES. ARMY. CAVALRY
Farrell, C. Thorns for Johnny Spring
Frierson, E. P. An adventure in the Big Horn Mountains; or, The trials and tribulations of a recruit

UNITED STATES. ARMY. VOLUNTEER CAVALRY, 1ST
Henry, W. Rough Riders of Arizona

UNITED STATES. CENTRAL INTELLIGENCE AGENCY
Lida, D. The recruiting officer
Oppel, J.-H. A demon in my head
Phillips, A. Wenceslas Square

UNITED STATES. CIVILIAN CONSERVATION CORPS See Civilian Conservation Corps (U.S.)

UNITED STATES. COAST GUARD
Hagy, A. C. Semper paratus

UNITED STATES. CONGRESS
Cavell, B. The art of the possible

UNITED STATES. CONGRESS. HOUSE
Phillips, G. The raiders

UNITED STATES. CONGRESS. SENATE
Clarke, A. C. Death and the senator

UNITED STATES. DEPT. OF JUSTICE. FEDERAL BUREAU OF INVESTIGATION
See United States. Federal Bureau of Investigation

UNITED STATES. FEDERAL BUREAU OF INVESTIGATION
DuBois, B. Old soldiers
Lee, W. W. Miles deep
Malzberg, B. N. The intransigents
Westlake, D. E. Take it away

UNITED STATES. FEDERAL BUREAU OF INVESTIGATION {BPI RECORD; WILSON SIC}
Doctorow, E. L. Child, dead, in the rose garden

UNITED STATES. MARINE CORPS
Bukoski, A. The bird that sings in the bamboo
Bukoski, A. A geography of snow
Bukoski, A. The value of numbers
Dubus, A. Corporal Lewis
Jones, T. The roadrunner

UNITED STATES. NATIONAL AERONAUTICS AND SPACE ADMINISTRATION
Landis, G. A. What we really do here at NASA
Oltion, J. Abandon in place

UNITED STATES. NAVY
Capote, T. The walls are cold
Haschemeyer, O. The designated marksman
Yates, R. Evening on the Côte d'Azur

UNITED STATES. PEACE CORPS See Peace Corps (U.S.)
The **universal** daughter. Solwitz, S.
The **Universal** Karmic Clearing House. Sheckley, R.

UNIVERSE
Barth, J. The big shrink
Bisson, T. The edge of the universe
Bisson, T. Get me to the church on time
The **universe**, concealed. McCann, R.
UNIVERSITY LIFE See College life
UNIVERSITY STUDENTS See College life
Unknown donor. Mitchell, J. C.
The **unknown** errors of our lives. Divakaruni, C. B.

UNMARRIED COUPLES
Agee, J. Billy Kitchen
Atkinson, K. Transparent fiction
Barker, N. Symbiosis: class cestoda
Bingham, S. The hunt
Bingham, S. The pump
Bingham, S. Rat
Boswell, R. Glissando
Boyle, T. C. Captured by the Indians
Broyard, B. Loose talk

Budnitz, J. Vacation
Cooke, C. Bob darling
Davies, Tristan. Grouper Schmidt
Davies, Tristan. The thing itself
DeLancey, K. Fast coming and then going
DeMarinis, R. Feet
Di Blasi, D. Drowning hard
Di Blasi, D. Prayers of an accidental nature
Ford, R. Rock Springs
Galloway, J. Sonata form
Gilman, C. P. An honest woman
Henley, P. Lessons in joy
Jaime-Becerra, M. Gina and Max
Janowitz, T. Physics
Klass, P. Intimacy
Krauss, N. Future emergencies
Krawiec, R. Listening to the gay boys fight
Krouse, E. Momentum
Kuryla, M. Mis-sayings
Lieu, J. This world
Lord, N. Why owls die with wings outspread
Matera, L. The river mouth
Mazor, J. The munster final
McKnight, R. Quitting smoking
Meloy, M. Garrison Junction
Offutt, C. Second hand
Offutt, C. Tough people
Perry, D. Love is gnats today
Power, S. Watermelon seeds
Saunders, G. Walking legs
Schnitzler, A. Dying
Schoemperlen, D. Tickets to Spain
Spencer, E. First child
Stern, D. Chaos
Stern, D. Comfort
Valeri, L. Hugo, Arthur, and Bobby Joe
Valeri, L. That easy kind of life
Warren, D. Moving pictures
Wesley, V. W. Afraid of the dark
Wieland, L. Purgatory

UNMARRIED MOTHERS
Adams, A. Great sex
Blackwood, S. One of us is hidden away
Bloom, A. A blind man can see how much I love you
Brady, C. Chatter
Canty, K. Flipper
Ferrell, C. Truth or consequences
Gilman, C. P. Turned
Keegan, C. Quare name for a boy
Klass, P. For women everywhere
Lincoln, C. Like dove wings
Moses, J. Girls like you
O'Connell, M. I fly unto you
Robison, M. Smart
The **unnamable**. Lovecraft, H. P.
The **unnatural** mother. Gilman, C. P.
Unpaid consultant. Vonnegut, K.
The **unpleasant** profession of Jonathan Hoag. Heinlein, R. A.
Unpretty. Gussoff, C.
Unpunished. Gilman, C. P.
Unreasonable doubt. Collins, M. A.
The **unripe** heart. Steele, M.
An **unscheduled** stop. Adams, A.
Unseen demons. Castro, A.-T.
Unspeakable. Taylor, L.
The **unspoken** (Il nondetto). Gifford, B.
An **unsuspected** condition of the heart. Burke, J.

The **untenured** lecturer. Winegardner, M.
The **unthinkable** happens to people every day.
    Smith, A.
Until Gwen. Lehane, D.
Until the butterflies. Berliner, J.
Untitled prose sketch. Faulkner, J.
The **unuseable** talent. Blitz, R.
UNWED MOTHERS *See* Unmarried mothers
An **unwelcome** guest. Papernick, J.
Unworthy. Borges, J. L.
Uom and Tak. Kelin, D. A.
Up above Diamond City. Soukup, M.
Up among the eagles. Valenzuela, L.
Up at the Riverside. Muller, M.
Up close. Alvarez, A.
Up in the air. Kirn, W.
Upadhyay, Samrat
    The good shopkeeper
        The Best American short stories, 1999; select-
            ed from U.S. and Canadian magazines by
            Amy Tan with Katrina Kenison, with an in-
            troduction by Amy Tan
Updike, John
    A & P
        Updike, J. The early stories, 1953-1975
    Ace in the hole
        Updike, J. The early stories, 1953-1975
    The alligators
        Updike, J. The early stories, 1953-1975
    Archangel
        Updike, J. The early stories, 1953-1975
    The astronomer
        Updike, J. The early stories, 1953-1975
    At a bar in Charlotte Amalie
        Updike, J. The early stories, 1953-1975
    Augustine's concubine
        Updike, J. The early stories, 1953-1975
    Avec la bébé-sitter
        Updike, J. The early stories, 1953-1975
    The baluchitherium
        Updike, J. The early stories, 1953-1975
    Bech noir
        The Best American mystery stories, 1999; ed-
            ited and with an introduction by Ed
            McBain
    Believers
        Updike, J. The early stories, 1953-1975
    The blessed man of Boston, my grandmother's
        thimble, and Fanning Island
        Updike, J. The early stories, 1953-1975
    The Bulgarian poetess
        Updike, J. The early stories, 1953-1975
    The carol sing
        Updike, J. The early stories, 1953-1975
    The cats
        Updike, J. Licks of love; short stories and a
            sequel
    The Christian roommates
        Updike, J. The early stories, 1953-1975
    Commercial
        Updike, J. The early stories, 1953-1975
    A constellation of events
        Updike, J. The early stories, 1953-1975
    The corner
        Updike, J. The early stories, 1953-1975
    The crow in the woods
        Updike, J. The early stories, 1953-1975
    The dark
        Updike, J. The early stories, 1953-1975

Daughter, Last glimpses of
    Updike, J. The early stories, 1953-1975
The day of the dying rabbit
    Updike, J. The early stories, 1953-1975
The deacon
    Updike, J. The early stories, 1953-1975
Dear Alexandros
    Updike, J. The early stories, 1953-1975
Delicate Wives
    The New Yorker v79 no45 p76-9 F 2 2004
Dentistry and doubt
    Updike, J. The early stories, 1953-1975
The doctor's wife
    Updike, J. The early stories, 1953-1975
During the Jurassic
    Updike, J. The early stories, 1953-1975
Eclipse
    Updike, J. The early stories, 1953-1975
Eros rampant
    Updike, J. The early stories, 1953-1975
Ethiopia
    Updike, J. The early stories, 1953-1975
The family meadow
    Updike, J. The early stories, 1953-1975
Flight
    Updike, J. The early stories, 1953-1975
Four sides of one story
    Updike, J. The early stories, 1953-1975
Free
    The New Yorker v76 no41 p74-7 Ja 8 2001
Friends from Philadelphia
    Updike, J. The early stories, 1953-1975
Gesturing
    The Best American short stories of the
        century; John Updike, editor, Katrina
        Kenison, coeditor; with an introduction by
        John Updike
    Updike, J. The early stories, 1953-1975
A gift from the city
    Updike, J. The early stories, 1953-1975
Giving blood
    Updike, J. The early stories, 1953-1975
The guardians
    The New Yorker v77 no5 p82-5 Mr 26 2001
The gun shop
    Updike, J. The early stories, 1953-1975
The happiest I've been
    Updike, J. The early stories, 1953-1975
Harv is plowing now
    Updike, J. The early stories, 1953-1975
The hermit
    Updike, J. The early stories, 1953-1975
The hillies
    Updike, J. The early stories, 1953-1975
His finest hour
    Updike, J. The early stories, 1953-1975
His oeuvre
    The New Yorker v74 no43 p74-81 Ja 25 1999
    Updike, J. Licks of love; short stories and a
        sequel
Home
    Updike, J. The early stories, 1953-1975
How to love America and leave it at the same
    time
    Updike, J. The early stories, 1953-1975
How was it, really?
    The New Yorker v75 no11 p78-83 My 17
    1999

Updike, John—*Continued*

Updike, J. Licks of love; short stories and a sequel

I am dying, Egypt, dying

Updike, J. The early stories, 1953-1975

I will not let thee go, except thou bless me

Updike, J. The early stories, 1953-1975

In football season

Updike, J. The early stories, 1953-1975

Incest

Updike, J. The early stories, 1953-1975

The Indian

Ghost writing; haunted tales by contemporary writers; edited by Roger Weingarten

The invention of the horse collar

Updike, J. The early stories, 1953-1975

Jesus on Honshu

Updike, J. The early stories, 1953-1975

The kid's whistling

Updike, J. The early stories, 1953-1975

Killing

Updike, J. The early stories, 1953-1975

The laughter of the gods

The New Yorker v77 no47 p76-81 F 11 2002

Leaves

Of leaf and flower; stories and poems for gardeners; edited by Charles Dean and Clyde Wachsberger; illustrations by Clyde Wachsberger

Updike, J. The early stories, 1953-1975

Licks of love in the heart of the Cold War

Updike, J. Licks of love; short stories and a sequel

Lifeguard

Updike, J. The early stories, 1953-1975

Love song, for a moog synthesizer

Updike, J. The early stories, 1953-1975

The lucid eye in silver town

Updike, J. The early stories, 1953-1975

Lunch hour

Updike, J. Licks of love; short stories and a sequel

A madman

Updike, J. The early stories, 1953-1975

Man and daughter in the cold

Updike, J. The early stories, 1953-1975

The man who loved extinct mammals

Updike, J. The early stories, 1953-1975

Marching through Boston

Updike, J. The early stories, 1953-1975

Metamorphosis

The New Yorker v75 no22 p66-70 Ag 9 1999

Updike, J. Licks of love; short stories and a sequel

Minutes of the last meeting

Updike, J. The early stories, 1953-1975

The morning

Updike, J. The early stories, 1953-1975

Museums and women

Updike, J. The early stories, 1953-1975

The music school

Updike, J. The early stories, 1953-1975

My father on the verge of disgrace

Updike, J. Licks of love; short stories and a sequel

My lover has dirty fingernails

Updike, J. The early stories, 1953-1975

Nakedness

Updike, J. The early stories, 1953-1975

Natural color

Updike, J. Licks of love; short stories and a sequel

Nevada

Updike, J. The early stories, 1953-1975

New York Girl

Updike, J. Licks of love; short stories and a sequel

Oliver's evolution

Updike, J. Licks of love; short stories and a sequel

The orphaned swimming pool

Updike, J. The early stories, 1953-1975

Packed dirt, churchgoing, a dying cat, a traded car

Updike, J. The early stories, 1953-1975

The persistence of desire

Updike, J. The early stories, 1953-1975

Personal archaeology

The Best American short stories 2001; selected from U.S. and Canadian magazines by Barbara Kingsolver with Katrina Kenison; with an introduction by Barbara Kingsolver

Pigeon feathers

Updike, J. The early stories, 1953-1975

Plumbing

Updike, J. The early stories, 1953-1975

Problems

Updike, J. The early stories, 1953-1975

Rabbit remembered

Updike, J. Licks of love; short stories and a sequel

The rescue

Updike, J. The early stories, 1953-1975

Scenes from the fifties

Updike, J. Licks of love; short stories and a sequel

The sea's green sameness

Updike, J. The early stories, 1953-1975

A sense of shelter

Updike, J. The early stories, 1953-1975

Separating

Fault lines; stories of divorce; collected and edited by Caitlin Shetterly

Updike, J. The early stories, 1953-1975

Should wizard hit mommy?

Updike, J. The early stories, 1953-1975

Sin: Early Impressions

The New Yorker v78 no38 p110-13, 116, 118-20 D 9 2002

The slump

Updike, J. The early stories, 1953-1975

Snowing in Greenwich Village

Updike, J. The early stories, 1953-1975

Wonderful town; New York stories from The New Yorker; edited by David Remnick with Susan Choi

Solitaire

Updike, J. The early stories, 1953-1975

Son

Updike, J. The early stories, 1953-1975

Spanish Prelude to a Second Marriage

Harper's v305 p71-5 O 2002

The stare

Updike, J. The early stories, 1953-1975

Still life

Updike, J. The early stories, 1953-1975

Sublimating

Updike, J. The early stories, 1953-1975

Updike, John—*Continued*
Sunday teasing
  Updike, J. The early stories, 1953-1975
The tarbox police
  Updike, J. The early stories, 1953-1975
The taste of metal
  Updike, J. The early stories, 1953-1975
the Indian
  Updike, J. The early stories, 1953-1975
Tomorrow and tomorrow and so forth
  Updike, J. The early stories, 1953-1975
Toward evening
  Updike, J. The early stories, 1953-1975
Transaction
  Updike, J. The early stories, 1953-1975
A trillion feet of gas
  Updike, J. The early stories, 1953-1975
Twin beds in Rome
  Updike, J. The early stories, 1953-1975
Unstuck
  Updike, J. The early stories, 1953-1975
Varieties of Religious Experience
  Atlantic Monthly (1993) v290 no4 p93-6, 98-100, 102-4 N 2002
The Walk with Elizanne
  The New Yorker v79 no18 p66-71 Jl 7 2003
Walter Briggs
  Updike, J. The early stories, 1953-1975
When everyone was pregnant
  Updike, J. The early stories, 1953-1975
Who made yellow roses yellow?
  Updike, J. The early stories, 1953-1975
Wife-wooing
  Updike, J. The early stories, 1953-1975
The women who got away
  Updike, J. Licks of love; short stories and a sequel
You'll never know, dear, how much I love you
  Updike, J. The early stories, 1953-1975
Your lover just called
  Updike, J. The early stories, 1953-1975
An **upheaval**. Chekhov, A. P.
Upholstery. Oates, J. C.
The **upper** berth. Crawford, F. M.
Upper Captiva. Ford, J.
Upson, William Hazlett
Botts at sea
  The Saturday Evening Post v273 no4 p42-3, 77-87 Jl/Ag 2001
Botts Puts the Show on the Road
  The Saturday Evening Post v276 no3 p70, 72-4, 76-8, 80-2, 84 My/Je 2004
Upstaging murder. Hart, C. G.
Upstairs. Watt-Evans, L.
Upstream. Reifler, N.
Upton, Jesse
China Flats
  Gettysburg Review v15 no3 p477-91 Aut 2002
URANUS (PLANET)
Landis, G. A. Into the blue abyss
Uranus in the house of death. Klíma, I.
The **Urban** Forest. Otto, L.
Uribe, Alvaro
The hostage
  Points of departure; new stories from Mexico; edited by Mónica Lavín; translated by Gustavo Segade

Urrea, Luis Alberto
Mr. Mendoza's paintbrush
  The Year's best fantasy & horror: sixteenth annual collection; edited by Ellen Datlow & Terri Windling
Ursa major in Vermont. Connor, J.
Ursu, Anne
The president's new clothes
  Politically inspired; edited by Stephen Elliott; assistant editor, Gabriel Kram; associate editors, Elizabeth Brooks [et al.]
Ursus horribilis. Adam, C.
URUGUAY
Borges, J. L. The dead man
Montevideo
Borges, J. L. Avelino Arredondo
Us. Waldrop, H.
USAF *See* United States. Air Force
The **used**. Estleman, L. D.
Used to dream. Cole, C. B.
Useful Fictions. Schiff, S.
The **Usual** Human Disabilities. Montemarano, N.
The **usual** table. Lovesey, P.
The **usual** trickery!. Kajane, J.
UTAH
Carlson, R. Dr. Slime
McManus, J. Deseret
Spencer, D. Blood work
Spencer, D. It's a lot scarier if you take Jesus out
Spencer, D. Park host
Uterus. Keret, E.
The **utility** man. Reed, R.
Utley, Steven
The real world
  The Year's best science fiction, eighteenth annual collection; edited by Gardner Dozois
UTOPIAS
Adorno, J. N. The distant future
Anderson, P. Eutopia
Britto García, L. Future
Gilman, C. P. Herland
Gilman, C. P. Moving the mountain
Gilman, C. P. With her in Ourland
Le Guin, U. K. The ones who walk away from Omelas
Ryman, G. Everywhere

V

V-2. Hoch, E. D.
V.A.O.. Ryman, G.
Vaca, Alvar Nuñez Cabeza de *See* Nuñez Cabeza de Vaca, Alvar, 16th cent.
Vacation. Budnitz, J.
A **vacation** and a voice. Chopin, K.
VACATIONS
Bowles, P. In the red room
Boylan, C. Some retired ladies on a tour
Boylan, C. Villa Marta
Chopin, K. Ozème's holiday
Fischer, T. We ate the chef
Foley, S. Off Grenada
Grodstein, L. Family vacation
Hess, J. Make yourselves at home
Lee, A. The golden chariot
McBain, E. The couple next door
McMillan, T. Quilting on the rebound

VACATIONS—*Continued*
  Mercader, Mercer. The postponed journey
  Miller, A. L. Off-season travel
  Richmond, M. Choose your travel partner wisely
  Škvorecký, J. Eve was naked
  Tuck, L. La Mayonette
  Varley, J. Goodbye, Robinson Crusoe
  Wilson, R., Jr. Florida
Vachss, Andrew H.
  Big sister
    Crème de la crime; edited by Janet Hutchings
    Vachss, A. H. Everybody pays; stories
  Charmed life
    Vachss, A. H. Everybody pays; stories
  The concrete puppy
    Vachss, A. H. Everybody pays; stories
  Curtains
    Vachss, A. H. Everybody pays; stories
  Dope fiend
    Vachss, A. H. Everybody pays; stories
  Dress-up day
    Vachss, A. H. Everybody pays; stories
  Escort service
    Vachss, A. H. Everybody pays; stories
  Everybody pays
    Vachss, A. H. Everybody pays; stories
  Fireman
    Vachss, A. H. Everybody pays; stories
  Gamblers
    Vachss, A. H. Everybody pays; stories
  Goin' down slow
    Esquire v131 no6 p148 Je 1999
    Vachss, A. H. Everybody pays; stories
  Going home
    Vachss, A. H. Everybody pays; stories
  Good for the soul
    Vachss, A. H. Everybody pays; stories
  Harvest time
    Vachss, A. H. Everybody pays; stories
  Hit man
    Vachss, A. H. Everybody pays; stories
  Homeless
    Vachss, A. H. Everybody pays; stories
  Just the ticket
    Vachss, A. H. Everybody pays; stories
  Last date
    Vachss, A. H. Everybody pays; stories
  Mission
    Vachss, A. H. Everybody pays; stories
  Perp walk
    Vachss, A. H. Everybody pays; stories
  Piecework
    Vachss, A. H. Everybody pays; stories
  Pigeon drop
    Vachss, A. H. Everybody pays; stories
  Proving it
    Vachss, A. H. Everybody pays; stories
  Reaching back
    Vachss, A. H. Everybody pays; stories
  The real thing
    The Crow; shattered lives & broken dreams;
      edited by J. O'Barr and Ed Kramer
    Vachss, A. H. Everybody pays; stories
  The real world
    Vachss, A. H. Everybody pays; stories
  Safe sex
    Vachss, A. H. Everybody pays; stories
  Searcher
    Vachss, A. H. Everybody pays; stories

  Slow motion
    Vachss, A. H. Everybody pays; stories
  Stepping stone
    Vachss, A. H. Everybody pays; stories
  Stuntman
    Vachss, A. H. Everybody pays; stories
  Summer girl
    Vachss, A. H. Everybody pays; stories
  Tag
    Vachss, A. H. Everybody pays; stories
  Time share
    Vachss, A. H. Everybody pays; stories
  True colors
    Vachss, A. H. Everybody pays; stories
  Two-way radio
    Vachss, A. H. Everybody pays; stories
  Word play
    Vachss, A. H. Everybody pays; stories
  The writing on the wall
    Vachss, A. H. Everybody pays; stories
Vadija. Lundoff, C.
Vafi, Fariba
  My mother, behind the glass
    A Feast in the mirror; stories by contempo-
      rary Iranian women; translated and edited
      by Mohammad Mehdi Khorrami, Shouleh
      Vatanabadi
VAGABONDS *See* Rogues and vagabonds
Vagabonds. Chopin, K.
VAGRANTS *See* Homeless persons
Vain Empires. Woodward, S. T.
Val. Dinh, L.
Valdés, Javier
  People like us
    Colchie, T. A whistler in the nightworld;
      short fiction from the Latin Americas; ed-
      ited by Thomas Colchie
The **vale** of the white horse. McCrumb, S.
Valentine. Galloway, J.
VALENTINE'S DAY
  Berkman, P. R. February 14
  Gaiman, N. Harlequin Valentine
  Galloway, J. Valentine
  Nair, M. Vishnukumar's Valentine's Day
Valentine's night. Pickard, N.
Valenzuela, Luisa
  Panther eyes
    The Vintage book of Latin American stories;
      edited by Carlos Fuentes and Julio Ortega
  Up among the eagles
    Short stories by Latin American women; the
      magic and the real; edited by Celia Correas
      de Zapata; foreword by Isabel Allende
  Who, me a bum?
    The Art of the story; an international antholo-
      gy of contemporary short stories; edited by
      Daniel Halpern
Valera, Juan
  "The green bird"
    Fedorchek, R. M. Stories of enchantment
      from nineteenth-century Spain; translated
      from the Spanish by Robert M. Fredorchek;
      introduction by Alan E. Smith
  "The wizard"
    Fedorchek, R. M. Stories of enchantment
      from nineteenth-century Spain; translated
      from the Spanish by Robert M. Fredorchek;
      introduction by Alan E. Smith

Valeri, Laura
  Hugo, Arthur, and Bobby Joe
    Valeri, L. The kind of things saints do
  The kind of things saints do
    Valeri, L. The kind of things saints do
  A rafter in Miami Beach
    Valeri, L. The kind of things saints do
  She's anonymous
    Valeri, L. The kind of things saints do
  That easy kind of life
    Valeri, L. The kind of things saints do
  Turn these stones into bread
    Valeri, L. The kind of things saints do
  Whatever he did, he did enough
    Valeri, L. The kind of things saints do
Valerie rakes the leaves. Smith, S. J.
Vallbona, Rima de
  Penelope's silver wedding anniversary
    Short stories by Latin American women; the
      magic and the real; edited by Celia Correas
      de Zapata; foreword by Isabel Allende
The **valley** of childish things, and other emblems.
    Wharton, E.
The **valley** was still. Wellman, M. W.
Valor. Bausch, R.
The **value** of numbers. Bukoski, A.
The **vampire**. Oates, J. C.
VAMPIRE BATS *See* Bats
Vampire dreams. Lochte, D.
VAMPIRES
  Alexis, A. The night piece
  Arruda, M. J. Reconciliation
  Barrett, J. A most electrifying evening
  Bennett, N. and Elrod, P. N. Wolf and hound
  Bergstrom, E. The three boxes
  Bogen, K. B. Good help
  Braunbeck, G. A. Curtain call
  Breen, J. L. Woollcott and the vamp
  Burke, S. Snare
  Carter, M. L. Mercy
  Collins, N. A. Variations on a theme
  Conrad, R. L. The dark downstairs
  Crider, B. King of the night
  Davenport, S. Abba's mark
  De Lint, C. In this soul of a woman
  De Lint, C. There's no such thing
  Devereaux, R. Nocturne a tre in b-double-sharp
    minor
  DeWeese, G. An essay on containment
  Donaldson, S. R. Penance
  Dozois, G. R. Down among the dead men
  Filipak, C. and Vargo, J. Vampire's kiss
  Fleming, R. Havoc after dark
  Goldberg, D. G. K. The boy next door
  Gomez, J. Chicago 1927
  Goudsward, S. T. Trailer trash
  Gruss, A. L. and Kingsgrave-Ernstein, C. Beast
  Haessig, J. J. Sorrow's end
  Hendee, B. Before a fall
  Hoffman, N. K. Food chain
  Hopkinson, N. Greedy choke puppy
  Huff, T. To each his own kind
  Iorillo, J. Vesper tolls
  Jett, J. and Kihn, G. Bad reputation
  Kilpatrick, N. Berserker
  Kilpatrick, N. What matters
  Lansdale, J. R. Bar talk
  Lochte, D. Vampire dreams
  Lumley, B. Dead Eddy

  Lumley, B. Dinosaur dreams
  Lumley, B. Resurrection
  Marffin, K. Waiting for the 400
  Markus, D. For the love of vampires
  McMahon, P. How Brando was made
  Newman, K. Castle in the desert
  Newman, K. The other side of midnight
  Nye, J. L. Everything to order
  Oliver, C. Anachronism
  Parks, J. A. The covenant of Il Vigneto
  Pipik, J. Nightwatcher
  Pipik, J. and Vargo, J. The Dark Tower
  Proctor, J. Dear Mr. Bernard Shaw
  Pronzini, B. and Malzberg, B. N. Opening a
    vein
  Reed, R. R. On line
  Rozanski, J. M. The search for a sipping house
  Saberhagen, F. Box number fifty
  Sinor, B. H. "Places for act two!"
  Smith, M. M. A place to stay
  Somtow, S. P. Red as jade
  Spruill, S. G. Hemophage
  Stableford, B. M. Hot blood
  Stoker, B. Dracula's guest
  Strauch, T. J. The Alberscine's vigil
  Tenn, W. The human angle
  Tenn, W. She only goes out at night . . .
  Trotter, W. R. The bleeding of Hauptmann
    Gehlen
  Van Belkom, E. The debauched one
  Watson, I. My vampire cake
  Wilder, C. Finishing school
  Wilson, F. P. Good Friday
  Yarbro, C. Q. Long-term investment
  Yolen, J. Sister death
  Zaget, B. Renfield; or, Dining at the bughouse
Vampire's kiss. Filipak, C. and Vargo, J.
The **van**. Waitt, A.
Van Belkom, Edo
  Catabolism
    Felonious felines; edited by Carol and Ed
      Gorman
  The debauched one
    The Darkest thirst; a vampire anthology
Van Daele, Rudy
  Joshua's holiday
    Cross Currents v51 no3 p394-5 Fall 2001
  Stray cats
    Cross Currents v51 no3 p395-8 Fall 2001
Van de Wetering, Janwillem
  The bongo bungler
    Van de Wetering, J. The Amsterdam cops;
      collected stories
  The deadly egg
    Murder most delectable; savory tales of culi-
      nary crimes; edited by Martin H. Greenberg
    Van de Wetering, J. The Amsterdam cops;
      collected stories
  Heron Island
    Van de Wetering, J. The Amsterdam cops;
      collected stories
  Holiday patrol
    Van de Wetering, J. The Amsterdam cops;
      collected stories
  Houseful of mussels
    Van de Wetering, J. The Amsterdam cops;
      collected stories

Van de Wetering, Janwillem—*Continued*
Hup three
    Van de Wetering, J. The Amsterdam cops; collected stories
Lady Hillary
    A Century of great suspense stories; edited by Jeffery Deaver
The letter in the peppermint jar
    Van de Wetering, J. The Amsterdam cops; collected stories
Letter present
    Van de Wetering, J. The Amsterdam cops; collected stories
The machine gun and the mannequin
    Van de Wetering, J. The Amsterdam cops; collected stories
Non-interference
    Death by espionage; intriguing stories of deception and betrayal; edited by Martin Cruz Smith
The sergeant's cat
    Van de Wetering, J. The Amsterdam cops; collected stories
Six this, six that
    Van de Wetering, J. The Amsterdam cops; collected stories
Sure, blue, and dead, too
    Van de Wetering, J. The Amsterdam cops; collected stories
There goes Ravelaar
    Van de Wetering, J. The Amsterdam cops; collected stories
Van der Meersch, Maxence *See* Meersch, Maxence van der, 1907-1951
Van Dyke, Henry
The fatal success
    Fishing's best short stories; edited by Paul D. Staudohar
Summer Masquerades
    The Antioch Review v60 no4 p588-602 Fall 2002
Van Dyne, Edith *See* Baum, L. Frank (Lyman Frank), 1856-1919
Van Eekhout, Greg
Wolves till the world goes down
    Starlight 3; edited by Patrick Nielsen Hayden
Van Gogh's ear. Scliar, M.
Van Loan, Charles E.
Mathewson, Incog.
    Dead balls and double curves; an anthology of early baseball fiction; edited and with an introduction by Trey Strecker ; with a foreword by Arnold Hano
One-thirty-three—ringside
    Boxing's best short stories; edited by Paul D. Staudohar
Van Pelt, James
The boy behind the gate
    The Mammoth book of best new horror 14; edited with an introduction by Stephen Jones
A flock of birds
    The Year's best science fiction; twentieth annual collection; edited by Gardner Dozois
The long way home
    The year's best science fiction: twenty-first annual collection; edited by Gardner Dozois

Van Pelt, Lori
River watch
    American West; twenty new stories from the Western Writers of America; edited with an introduction by Loren D. Estleman
Van Vogt, A. E. (Alfred Elton)
Black destroyer
    The SFWA grand masters; edited by Frederik Pohl
Dear pen pal
    The SFWA grand masters; edited by Frederik Pohl
Far centaurus
    The SFWA grand masters; edited by Frederik Pohl
The rull
    The Good old stuff; adventure SF in the grand tradition; edited by Gardner Dozois
Vault of the beast
    The SFWA grand masters; edited by Frederik Pohl
The weapon shop
    The Science fiction hall of fame: volume one, 1929-1964; the greatest science fiction stories of all time chosen by the members of the Science Fiction Writers of America; edited by Robert Silverberg
Van Vogt, Alfred Elton *See* Van Vogt, A. E. (Alfred Elton), 1912-2000
Van Winckel, Nance
Beside ourselves
    Van Winckel, N. Curtain Creek Farm; stories
The expectation of abundance
    Van Winckel, N. Curtain Creek Farm; stories
Funeral of the Virgin
    The Georgia Review v57 no3 p465-75 Fall 2003
Immunity
    American short fiction, vol. 8, no 29-32
    Van Winckel, N. Curtain Creek Farm; stories
The land of anarchy
    Van Winckel, N. Curtain Creek Farm; stories
The lap of luxury
    Van Winckel, N. Curtain Creek Farm; stories
Making headway
    Van Winckel, N. Curtain Creek Farm; stories
Sometimes he borrowed a horse
    Van Winckel, N. Curtain Creek Farm; stories
Treat me nice
    Van Winckel, N. Curtain Creek Farm; stories
Vanasco, Alberto
Post-boomboom
    Cosmos latinos: an anthology of science fiction from Latin America and Spain; translated, edited, & with an introduction & notes by Andrea L. Bell & Yolanda Molina-Gavilán
Vance, Jack
The miracle workers
    The SFWA grand masters; edited by Frederik Pohl
The new prime
    The Good old stuff; adventure SF in the grand tradition; edited by Gardner Dozois
Sail 25
    The SFWA grand masters; edited by Frederik Pohl

Vance, Jack—*Continued*
Ullward's retreat
The SFWA grand masters; edited by Frederik Pohl
Vance, John Holbrook *See* Vance, Jack, 1916-
VANCOUVER (B.C.) *See* Canada—Vancouver
VANCOUVER ISLAND (B.C.)
Munro, A. The children stay
VANDALISM
Cohen, S. The battered mailbox
Davidson, R. The Hillside Slasher
Johnson, D. Work
Pronzini, B. A craving for originality
Vandals. Carver, R.
Vanderbes, Jennifer
The hatbox
Best new American voices 2000; guest editor Tobias Wolff; series editors John Kulka and Natalie Danford
Vanderhaeghe, Guy
The Jimi Hendrix experience
Ghost writing; haunted tales by contemporary writers; edited by Roger Weingarten
VanderMeer, Jeff
Balzac's war
VanderMeer, J. Secret life; with an introduction by Jeffrey Ford
Black Duke blues
VanderMeer, J. Secret life; with an introduction by Jeffrey Ford
The bone carver's tale
VanderMeer, J. Secret life; with an introduction by Jeffrey Ford
The cage
The Mammoth book of best new horror 14; edited with an introduction by Stephen Jones
The city
VanderMeer, J. Secret life; with an introduction by Jeffrey Ford
The compass of his bones
VanderMeer, J. Secret life; with an introduction by Jeffrey Ford
Corpse mouth and spore nose
VanderMeer, J. Secret life; with an introduction by Jeffrey Ford
Detectives and cadavers
VanderMeer, J. Secret life; with an introduction by Jeffrey Ford
The Emperor's reply
VanderMeer, J. Secret life; with an introduction by Jeffrey Ford
Exhibit H: torn pages discovered in the vest pocket of an unidentified tourist
VanderMeer, J. Secret life; with an introduction by Jeffrey Ford
Experiment #25 from the book of winter; the croc and you
VanderMeer, J. Secret life; with an introduction by Jeffrey Ford
The Festival of the Freshwater Squid
VanderMeer, J. Secret life; with an introduction by Jeffrey Ford
Flight is for those who have not yet crossed over
VanderMeer, J. Secret life; with an introduction by Jeffrey Ford

The General who is dead
VanderMeer, J. Secret life; with an introduction by Jeffrey Ford
Ghost dancing with Manco Tupac
VanderMeer, J. Secret life; with an introduction by Jeffrey Ford
Greensleeves
VanderMeer, J. Secret life; with an introduction by Jeffrey Ford
A heart for Lucretia
VanderMeer, J. Secret life; with an introduction by Jeffrey Ford
Learning to leave the flesh
VanderMeer, J. Secret life; with an introduction by Jeffrey Ford
London burning
VanderMeer, J. Secret life; with an introduction by Jeffrey Ford
The machine
VanderMeer, J. Secret life; with an introduction by Jeffrey Ford
Mahout
VanderMeer, J. Secret life; with an introduction by Jeffrey Ford
The mansions of the moon (A cautionary tale)
VanderMeer, J. Secret life; with an introduction by Jeffrey Ford
The sea, Mendeho, and moonlight
VanderMeer, J. Secret life; with an introduction by Jeffrey Ford
Secret life
VanderMeer, J. Secret life; with an introduction by Jeffrey Ford
Vanderslice, John
Blind Date
South Carolina Review v33 no2 p31-8 Spr 2001
Vandeville. Rawley, D.
Vandiver, E. B.
Sugar, Magic, Grace
Calyx v22 no1 p75-83 Summ 2004
Vanessa's voice. Lumley, B.
The **vanished** blonde. L'Amour, L.
Vanishing. Spielberg, P.
Vanishing act. Link, K.
Vanishing act. Pronzini, B. and Kurland, M.
VANISHING SPECIES *See* Endangered species
VANITY *See* Egoism
Vanka. Chekhov, A. P.
Vapnyar, Lara
Broccoli
The New Yorker v79 no41 p76-81 Ja 5 2004
Love Lessons Mondays, 9 A.M.
The New Yorker v79 no16 p133-4, 136, 138-40, 143-4, 146, 155 Je 16-23 2003
Vapnyar, Laura
Love lessons — Mondays, 9 A.M.
Vapnyar, L. There are Jews in my house
Lydia's Grove
Vapnyar, L. There are Jews in my house
Mistress
Vapnyar, L. There are Jews in my house
Ovrashki's trains
Vapnyar, L. There are Jews in my house
A question for Vera
Vapnyar, L. There are Jews in my house
There are Jews in my house
Vapnyar, L. There are Jews in my house

Vardeman, Robert E.
Feedback
Redshift; extreme visions of speculative fiction; edited by Al Sarrantonio
Vargo, Joseph
Lilith
Tales from The Dark Tower; illustrated by Joseph Vargo; edited by Joseph Vargo and Christine Filipak
Watcher at the gate
Tales from The Dark Tower; illustrated by Joseph Vargo; edited by Joseph Vargo and Christine Filipak
(jt. auth) See Filipak, Christine and Vargo, Joseph
(jt. auth) See Pipik, James and Vargo, Joseph
VARIATION (BIOLOGY) *See* Mutation (Biology)
Variations on a game. Highsmith, P.
Variations on a theme. Collins, N. A.
Varieties of Religious Experience. Updike, J.
The **varieties** of romantic experience: an introduction. Cohen, R.
Varley, John
Goodbye, Robinson Crusoe
The Good new stuff; adventure SF in the grand tradition; edited by Gardner Dozois
The persistence of vision
Brown, C. N. and Strahan, J. The Locus awards; thirty years of the best in science fiction and fantasy; edited by Charles N. Brown and Jonathan Strahan
Retrograde summer
Worldmakers; SF adventures in terraforming; edited by Gardner Dozois
Varley, John
The Bellman
The year's best science fiction: twenty-first annual collection; edited by Gardner Dozois
Varon, Policarpo
The feast
The Vintage book of Latin American stories; edited by Carlos Fuentes and Julio Ortega
VASECTOMY
Rushdie, S. The free radio
Vasilenko, Svetlana
Going after goat antelopes
Vasilenko, S. and Goscilo, H. Shamara and other stories; translated from the Russian; edited and with an introduction and notes by Helena Goscilo
The gopher
Vasilenko, S. and Goscilo, H. Shamara and other stories; translated from the Russian; edited and with an introduction and notes by Helena Goscilo
Little fool
Vasilenko, S. and Goscilo, H. Shamara and other stories; translated from the Russian; edited and with an introduction and notes by Helena Goscilo
Piggy
Vasilenko, S. and Goscilo, H. Shamara and other stories; translated from the Russian; edited and with an introduction and notes by Helena Goscilo

Poplar, poplar's daughter
Vasilenko, S. and Goscilo, H. Shamara and other stories; translated from the Russian; edited and with an introduction and notes by Helena Goscilo
Shamara
Vasilenko, S. and Goscilo, H. Shamara and other stories; translated from the Russian; edited and with an introduction and notes by Helena Goscilo
Vasseur, Thomas Jeffrey
The angels
Vasseur, T. J. Discovering the world; thirteen stories
The enduring nights of Sidney Wingcloud
Vasseur, T. J. Discovering the world; thirteen stories
First love
Vasseur, T. J. Discovering the world; thirteen stories
Flood
Vasseur, T. J. Discovering the world; thirteen stories
The life and death of stars
Vasseur, T. J. Discovering the world; thirteen stories
Malololailai; or, Discovering the world
Vasseur, T. J. Discovering the world; thirteen stories
The most beautiful day of your life
Vasseur, T. J. Discovering the world; thirteen stories
Noonan
Vasseur, T. J. Discovering the world; thirteen stories
Pig summer
Vasseur, T. J. Discovering the world; thirteen stories
The sins of Jesus
Vasseur, T. J. Discovering the world; thirteen stories
Talk, talk, talk
Vasseur, T. J. Discovering the world; thirteen stories
The windmill of happiness
Vasseur, T. J. Discovering the world; thirteen stories
The woman who sugared strawberries
Vasseur, T. J. Discovering the world; thirteen stories
The **vastness** of the dark. MacLeod, A.
Vaswani, Neela
Bing-Chen
Vaswani, N. Where the long grass bends; stories; Neela Vaswani
Blue, without sorrow
Vaswani, N. Where the long grass bends; stories; Neela Vaswani
Bolero
Vaswani, N. Where the long grass bends; stories; Neela Vaswani
Domestication of an imaginary goat
Vaswani, N. Where the long grass bends; stories; Neela Vaswani
The excrement man
Vaswani, N. Where the long grass bends; stories; Neela Vaswani

Vaswani, Neela—*Continued*

Five objects in Queens

 Vaswani, N. Where the long grass bends; stories; Neela Vaswani

An outline of no direction

 Vaswani, N. Where the long grass bends; stories; Neela Vaswani

The pelvis series

 Vaswani, N. Where the long grass bends; stories; Neela Vaswani

Possession at the tomb of Sayyed Pir Hazrat Baba Bahadur Saheed Rah Aleh

 Vaswani, N. Where the long grass bends; stories; Neela Vaswani

The rigors of dance lessons

 Vaswani, N. Where the long grass bends; stories; Neela Vaswani

Sita and Ms. Durber

 Vaswani, N. Where the long grass bends; stories; Neela Vaswani

Twang (Release)

 Vaswani, N. Where the long grass bends; stories; Neela Vaswani

Where the Long Grass Bends

 Prairie Schooner v76 no4 p42-50 Wint 2002

 Vaswani, N. Where the long grass bends; stories; Neela Vaswani

VATICAN

Pearlman, D. D. The Vatican's secret cabinet

The **Vatican's** secret cabinet. Pearlman, D. D.

Vaughn, Evelyn

Winter solstice

 Witches' brew; edited by Yvonne Jocks

Vaughn, Stephanie

Able, Baker, Charlie, Dog

 The Scribner anthology of contemporary short fiction; fifty North American stories since 1970; Lex Williford and Michael Martone, editors

The **vault** break-in. Groller, B.

Vault of the beast. Van Vogt, A. E.

Vaysenberg, I. M.

A father and his sons

 Neugroschel, J. No star too beautiful; Yiddish stories from 1382 to the present; compiled and translated by Joachim Neugroschel

Vaz, Katherine

East Bay Grease

 The Antioch Review v62 no3 p416-29 Summ 2004

My family, posing for Rodin

 The Antioch Review v59 no3 p536-49 Summ 2001

The rice artist

 Iowa Review v33 no2 p145-6 Fall 2003

Taking a stitch in a dead man's arm

 Bomb no77 p98-102 Fall 2001

Vázquez, Diego, Jr.

The fat-brush painter

 Murphy, N. Twelve branches; stories from St. Paul; [by] Nora Murphy ... {et al.}

The first time I saw St. Paul

 Murphy, N. Twelve branches; stories from St. Paul; [by] Nora Murphy ... {et al.}

My friend Cintia

 Murphy, N. Twelve branches; stories from St. Paul; [by] Nora Murphy ... {et al.}

Vazquez, Maria Esther

Returning by train with Borges

 English translations of short stories by contemporary Argentine women writers; edited by Eliana Cazaubon Hermann ; translated by Sally Webb Thornton

Vega, Ana Lydia

Cloud cover Caribbean

 Short stories by Latin American women; the magic and the real; edited by Celia Correas de Zapata; foreword by Isabel Allende

Eye-openers

 The Oxford book of Caribbean short stories; edited by Stewart Brown and John Wickham

Liliane's Sunday

 Callaloo v24 no2 p582-8 Spr 2001

Vega Yunqué, Edgardo

Eight morenos

 Colchie, T. A whistler in the nightworld; short fiction from the Latin Americas; edited by Thomas Colchie

Vegetative states. Caspers, N.

The **Veil** of Things. Kerr, J. B.

Velasco, Magali

You are Here

 Callaloo v26 no4 p972-4 Fall 2003

The **veldt**. Bradbury, R.

Velvet ear-pads. Wharton, E.

The **velvet** glove. Harrison, H.

VENDETTA *See* Revenge

Vendetta. Gifford, B.

VENEREAL DISEASES *See* Sexually transmitted diseases

Venetian thresholds. Russo, A.

VENEZUELA

Melville, P. The parrot and Descartes

VENGEANCE *See* Revenge

The **vengeance** of Nitocris. Williams, T.

The **venging**. Bear, G.

VENICE (CALIF.) *See* California—Venice

VENICE (FLA.) *See* Florida—Venice

VENICE (ITALY) *See* Italy—Venice

Venice. Svoboda, T.

A **Venice** story. White, E.

Venice unbound. Nilon, J.

Venice via hell & Belgrade. Gibbons, R.

VENTRILOQUISTS

Chapman, C. M. Chatterbox

Venture to the Moon. Clarke, A. C.

Venus/Mars. Boswell, M.

VENUS (PLANET)

Anderson, P. The big rain

Bradbury, R. All summer in a day

Clarke, A. C. Before Eden

Nordley, G. D. Dawn Venus

Pronzini, B. And then we went to Venus

Sargent, P. Dream of Venus

Smith, C. When the people fell

Tenn, W. On Venus, have we got a rabbi

Zelazny, R. The doors of his face, the lamps of his mouth

Venus and the seven sexes. Tenn, W.

Venus de Milo. Tomlinson, N. C.

Venus is a man's world. Tenn, W.

Venus rising. Barr, N.

Veranda. Miner, V.

Verdi. Tuck, L.

Verghese, Abraham

Lilacs

The Workshop; seven decades of the Iowa Writers' Workshop: 42 stories, recollections & essays on Iowa's place in 20th-century American literature; edited by Tom Grimes

Tension

100% pure Florida fiction; an anthology; edited by Susan Hubbard and Robley Wilson

Verlie I say unto you. Adams, A.

Vermeulen, John

Canon

The World's finest mystery and crime stories, third annual collection; edited by Ed Gorman and Martin H. Greenberg

Vermiculture. Kilpatrick, N.

VERMONT

Connor, J. And I, Isolde

Connor, J. The day the world declined to end

Connor, J. Second nature

Connor, J. Ursa major in Vermont

Dodd, S. M. What I remember now

Gates, D. The crazy thought

Paine, T. Unapproved minutes of the Carthage, Vermont, Zoning Board of Adjustment

Singleton, G. Remember why we're here

Stegner, L. Hired man

Stegner, L. Indian summer

Stegner, L. Pipers at the gates of dawn

Farm life

See Farm life—Vermont

VERMOUTH *See* Wine and wine making

Verne, Jules

Five weeks in a balloon

On glorious wings; the best flying stories of the century; edited and introduced by Stephen Coonts

Vernissage. Howard, M.

Vernon, David

Arrival

Men on men 2000; best new gay fiction for the millennium; edited and with an introduction by David Bergman and Karl Woelz

Couple kills

Circa 2000; gay fiction at the millennium; edited by Robert Drake & Terry Wolverton

Vernon, Olympia F.

Redemption

African American Review v36 no1 p101-5 Spr 2002

Verolin, Irma

The stairway in the gray patio

English translations of short stories by contemporary Argentine women writers; edited by Eliana Cazaubon Hermann ; translated by Sally Webb Thornton

Verona: a young woman speaks. Brodkey, H.

The **Veronese** Circle. Goldfaden, J.

Veronica. Berkman, P. R.

Veronica. Jones, G.

Veronica's veil. O'Connell, M.

Verotchka. Chekhov, A. P.

VERSAILLES (FRANCE) *See* France—Versailles

Versts and sleeping cars. Berberova, N.

Vertical administration. Kurlansky, M.

Vervaecke, Kris

The Quarrel

Ploughshares v29 no4 p178-91 Wint 2003/2004

A **very** close conspiracy. Lincoln, C.

A **very** fine fiddle. Chopin, K.

A **very** Merry Christmass. McBain, E.

The **very** moment they're about. Davis, A.

A **very** nice dog. Adams, A.

The **very** pulse of the machine. Swanwick, M.

A **very** quiet street [excerpt] Kuppner, F.

The **very** rigid search. Foer, J. S.

The **very** strange house next door. Jackson, S.

The **Very** Thought of You. Haslem, S.

A **very** unusual gift. Trobaugh, A.

Very, very, red. Williams, D.

Vesper tolls. Iorillo, J.

Vespers. Busch, F.

Vestibule. Williams, V.

The **veteran**. Forsyth, F.

VETERANS

Brady, C. Rumpelstiltskin

Bukoski, A. The world at war

Daniel, T. A dry, quiet war

Davidson, R. Inventory

Howard, C. Old soldiers

Pertwee, R. The river god

Yates, R. A clinical romance

Yates, R. Thieves

VETERANS (AMERICAN CIVIL WAR, 1861-1865)

Lutz, J. Veterans

Mencken, S. H. Twilight of chivalry

Morgan, R. A brightness new & welcoming

VETERANS (KOREAN WAR, 1950-1953)

Bowen, R. O. A matter of price

Collins, M. Homecoming

Foley, S. Cave fish

Ortiz, S. J. Where o where

Traver, R. The big brown trout

Vonnegut, K. The cruise of *The Jolly Roger*

Whisnant, L. Across from the Motoheads

VETERANS (PERSIAN GULF WAR, 1991)

Huddle, D. The story of the door

Mason, B. A. Thunder snow

Mueller, D. The start of something

Paine, T. The battle of Khafji

VETERANS (VIETNAMESE WAR, 1961-1975)

Addonizio, K. The fall of Saigon

Barnes, H. L. Gunning for Ho

Barnes, H. L. Plateau lands

Beattie, A. Mermaids

Braverman, K. Tall tales from the Mekong Delta

Brown, J. Sadness of the body

Bukoski, A. The bird that sings in the bamboo

Bukoski, A. The month that brings winter; or, How Mr. Truzynski carried Vietnam home with him

Bukoski, A. Private Tomaszewski

Cohen, S. I'm sorry, Mr. Griggs

Corcoran, T. The octopus alibi

Daniels, J. Renegade

Desaulniers, J. After Rosa Parks

Dinh, L. In the vein

Doenges, J. Occidental

Earle, S. The reunion

Engel, M. P. Rat

Evans, M. The heart of the matter

VETERANS (VIETNAMESE WAR, 1961-1975)—*Continued*
Falco, E. The revenant
Freudenberger, N. Letter from the last bastion
Gilliland, G. Purple Heart
Goldner, B. Cardiff-by-the-Sea
Greer, R. O. Revision
Harrington, J. A letter to Amy
Hoffman, W. Landings
Howard, C. The color of death
Howard, C. Hanging it on a limb
Jones, T. Fields of purple forever
Jones, T. My heroic mythic journey
Lee, M. Koza nights
Lee, M. The secrets of Cooperstown
Leonard, E. Fire in the hole
Lundquist, R. When the blood came faster than the water
Means, D. The woodcutter
Nichols, J. Jade
Nichols, J. Mackerel
Norris, H. The bower-bird
O'Brien, T. What went wrong
Rawley, D. Saigon
Rogers, B. H. Thirteen ways to water
Salisbury, R. Hoopa, the white deer dance
Smith, T. D. The purification of Jim Barnes
Sojourner, M. Luzianne
Thompson, J. The Amish
Vachss, A. H. Fireman
Vachss, A. H. Mission
Vachss, A. H. The real world
Vasseur, T. J. Malololailai; or, Discovering the world
Vasseur, T. J. The most beautiful day of your life
Weaver, G. Learst's last stand
Weaver, G. On watch for Big Red
White, M. C. Marked men
VETERANS (WORLD WAR, 1914-1918)
Bradbury, R. Lafayette, farewell
Fitzgerald, F. S. Dalyrimple goes wrong
Iwaszkiewicz, J. The Wilko girls
Jones, R. Meredith Evans' kiss
VETERANS (WORLD WAR, 1939-1945)
Berry, W. Making it home
Goran, L. Say something to Miss Kathleen Lacey
Griffin, W. E. B. Going back to the bridge in Berlin
Kerslake, L. Lookin' 'n' jivin'
Lennon, J. R. The fool's proxy
Lessing, D. M. A love child
McBain, E. Happy New Year, Herbie
Morgan, R. Tailgunner
Morgan, R. The welcome
Murray, S. Walkabout
Rusch, K. K. Details
Seiffert, R. Francis John Jones, 1924-
Vonnegut, K. Souvenir
White, M. C. Marked men
Yates, R. The B.A.R. man
Yates, R. The canal
Yates, R. Regards at home
The **veterans**. Auchincloss, L.
Veterans. Lutz, J.
VETERINARIANS
Allyn, D. Puppyland
Brenner, W. Four squirrels

Busch, F. The talking cure
Collins, B. Too many tomcats
Doran, M. M. The giver
Knight, M. Now you see her
Knight, T. A trail of mirrors
Pickard, N. Dr. Couch saves a president
Rinehart, S. Kick in the head
VEVEY (SWITZERLAND) *See* Switzerland—Vevey
The **viaduct**. Viganò, R.
Vibini and the virgin tongue. Wiebe, D. E.
Vice, Brad
Chickensnake
    Kulka, J. and Danford, N. The New American voices 2003; guest editor Joyce Carol Oates; series editors John Kulka and Natalie Danford
Report from Junction
    Atlantic Monthly (1993) v290 no1 p139-46 Jl/Ag 2002
    New stories from the South: the year's best, 2003; edited by Shannon Ravenel; with a preface by Roy Blount Jr.
Vicious Circle. McGuane, T.
The **victim**. McBain, E.
Victim by consent. DeLoach, N.
Victor *See* Wild Boy of Aveyron, d. 1828
Victor and St. Valentine. Binchy, M.
Victor the Bear. Alderete, P.
VICTORIA, QUEEN OF GREAT BRITAIN, 1819-1901
About
Baxter, S. The modern Cyrano
VICTORIA (B.C.) *See* Canada—Victoria (B.C.)
Victoria: a woman's statue. Alcott, L. M.
Victoria and Albert I: Running away to sea. Jackson, V. F.
Victoria and Albert II: Day-trippers. Jackson, V. F.
VICTORIAN ENGLAND *See* England—19th century
A **Victorian** ghost story. Newman, K.
Victor's funeral urn. Clyde, M.
Victory. Henley, P.
Victory and the blight. Lovelace, E.
The **victory** of Connie Lee. Aldrich, B. S.
Victory over Japan. Gilchrist, E.
La **vida** loca. Blake, J. C.
Video. Nair, M.
Video ame. Tanaka, S.
VIDEO ART
Clark, J. Jungle wedding
VIDEO GAMES
Rucker, R. v. B. Pac-Man
Vidor and Mummy. Maleti, G.
La **vie** en ronde. Robins, M. E.
VIENNA (AUSTRIA) *See* Austria—Vienna
Vienna, City of My Dreams. Johnson, W.
VIETNAM
Dinh, L. California fine view
Dinh, L. The cave
Dinh, L. Chopped Steak Mountain
Dinh, L. Dead on arrival
Dinh, L. For gristles
Dinh, L. Hope and standards
Dinh, L. Two who forgot
Dinh, L. Western music
Duong, T. H. Reflections of spring
Nguyen, D. T. Peace

VIETNAM—_Continued_
Richter, J. The dance of the Apsara
Shepard, L. Radiant green star
Tran, V. The back streets of Hoi An
Tran, V. Nha Nam

Hanoi
Dinh, L. Saigon Pull

Ho Chi Minh City
Dinh, L. The hippie chick

Saigon
See Vietnam—Ho Chi Minh City
Vietnam. Singleton, G.

VIETNAM VETERANS MEMORIAL (WASH-INGTON, D.C.)
Allen, Paul. While the band played
Belfiore, Michael P. What's in a name
Blair, J. Memorial day
Brotherton, Michael. Blood bone tendon stone
Card, O. S. 50 WPM
Cutter, Leah R. Obsessions
DiChario, N. The one-half boy
Haldeman, J. W. Names in marble
Malzberg, B. N. Getting there
Modesitt, L. E., Jr. The pilots
Resnick, L. Wallgate
Resnick, M. and Burstein, Michael A. Reflec-tions in black granite
Roberts, R. Second chance
Sawyer, R. J. Black reflection
Scarborough, E. A. and Reaser, Rick. Long time coming home
Small, K. Maximum sunlight
Swanwick, M. Dirty little war
Tetrick, B. The angel of the wall

VIETNAMESE

France
Tran, V. The dragon hunt

United States
Butler, R. O. A good scent from a strange mountain
Butler, R. O. Mr. Green
Dinh, L. 555
Leong, R. Bodhi leaves
Leong, R. Geography one
Strom, D. Chickens

VIETNAMESE AMERICANS

Vietnamese Americans
Small, K. Maximum sunlight

VIETNAMESE REFUGEES
Eggers, P. How the water feels
Eggers, P. The year five
Tran, V. The coral reef

VIETNAMESE SOLDIERS _See_ Soldiers—Viet-nam

VIETNAMESE WAR, 1961-1975
Abrams, T. The biggest rat in the world
Abrams, T. I will hide in God
Abrams, T. Small arms fire
Abrams, T. Top
Allen, D., Jr. Deferment
Allen, Paul. While the band played
Barnes, H. L. A lovely day in the A Shau Val-ley
Barnes, H. L. A return
Barnes, H. L. Stonehands and the tigress
Barnes, H. L. Tunnel rat
Belfiore, Michael P. What's in a name
Berent, M. Raid on Thud Ridge

Bishop, M. The tigers of hystria feed only on themselves
Bowen, K. The thief of Tay Ninh
Brotherton, Michael. Blood bone tendon stone
Card, O. S. 50 WPM
Coonts, S. Corey Ford buys the farm
Cutter, Leah R. Obsessions
DiChario, N. The one-half boy
Doble, J. Two letters from the doctor
Grau, S. A. Homecoming
Haldeman, J. W. Names in marble
Hannah, B. Midnight and I'm not famous yet
Harford, D. K. A death on the Ho Chi Minh Trail
Harrison, M. LZ ambush
Iribarne, M. Ross Willow's new and used cars
Irsfeld, J. H. Death of a soldier
Jones, T. A run through the jungle
Little, B. Connie
Lupoff, R. A. A freeway for Draculas
Malzberg, B. N. Getting there
Modesitt, L. E., Jr. The pilots
O'Brien, T. Going after Cacciato
O'Brien, T. The things they carried
O'Neill, S. The boy from Montana
O'Neill, S. Butch
O'Neill, S. Commendation
O'Neill, S. Don't mean nothing
O'Neill, S. Drugs
O'Neill, S. The exorcism
O'Neill, S. Hope is the thing with a golf club
O'Neill, S. Medcap
O'Neill, S. Monkey on our backs
O'Neill, S. One positive thing
O'Neill, S. The perils of Pappy
O'Neill, S. Perquisites
O'Neill, S. Prometheus burned
O'Neill, S. Psychic hand
O'Neill, S. This rough magic
O'Neill, S. Three minor love stories
O'Neill, S. What dreams may come
Paulsen, S. Ma rung
Resnick, L. Wallgate
Resnick, M. and Burstein, Michael A. Reflec-tions in black granite
Roberts, R. Second chance
Sawyer, R. J. Black reflection
Scarborough, E. A. and Reaser, Rick. Long time coming home
Shwartz, S. Suppose they gave a peace
Straub, P. The ghost village
Swanwick, M. Dirty little war
Swarthout, G. F. Death to everybody over thirty
Tetrick, B. The angel of the wall

Prisoners and prisons
Barnes, H. L. The cat in the cage

Viets, Elaine
Red meat
Blood on their hands; edited by Lawrence Block

The **view.** Wesolowska, M.
View From a Headlock. Lethem, J.
The **view** from Madama Butterfly's house. Tuck, L.
The **view** from seven. Ritchie, E.
The **view** from the kitchen. Brennan, M.
Viewed from Lanta & Wally's. Weaver, G.
Viewpoint. Wolfe, G.

Vieyra, Myriam Warner- *See* Warner-Vieyra, Myriam

Viganò, Renata

Acquitted

Viganò, R. Partisan wedding; stories; translated with an introduction by Suzanne Branciforte

Argelide

Viganò, R. Partisan wedding; stories; translated with an introduction by Suzanne Branciforte

The big opportunity

Viganò, R. Partisan wedding; stories; translated with an introduction by Suzanne Branciforte

Campalbo

Viganò, R. Partisan wedding; stories; translated with an introduction by Suzanne Branciforte

The commander

Viganò, R. Partisan wedding; stories; translated with an introduction by Suzanne Branciforte

Death of a mother

Viganò, R. Partisan wedding; stories; translated with an introduction by Suzanne Branciforte

He knew German

Viganò, R. Partisan wedding; stories; translated with an introduction by Suzanne Branciforte

The house on the ice

Viganò, R. Partisan wedding; stories; translated with an introduction by Suzanne Branciforte

The last action

Viganò, R. Partisan wedding; stories; translated with an introduction by Suzanne Branciforte

November 1943

Viganò, R. Partisan wedding; stories; translated with an introduction by Suzanne Branciforte

Partisan wedding

Viganò, R. Partisan wedding; stories; translated with an introduction by Suzanne Branciforte

Peter

Viganò, R. Partisan wedding; stories; translated with an introduction by Suzanne Branciforte

The portrait of Garibaldi

Viganò, R. Partisan wedding; stories; translated with an introduction by Suzanne Branciforte

Red flag

Viganò, R. Partisan wedding; stories; translated with an introduction by Suzanne Branciforte

Thin walls

Viganò, R. Partisan wedding; stories; translated with an introduction by Suzanne Branciforte

Trap shoot

Viganò, R. Partisan wedding; stories; translated with an introduction by Suzanne Branciforte

The viaduct

Viganò, R. Partisan wedding; stories; translated with an introduction by Suzanne Branciforte

Wool socks

Viganò, R. Partisan wedding; stories; translated with an introduction by Suzanne Branciforte

Vigano, Valeria

Giraglia

In the forbidden city; an anthology of erotic fiction by Italian women; edited by Maria Rosa Cutrufelli; translated by Vincent J. Bertolini

Vigderman, Patricia

Rumi and the Fish

The Kenyon Review v25 no2 p97-8 Spr 2003

Vigil. Gates, D.

The **vigil**. Oates, J. C.

VIGILANCE COMMITTEES

Gorman, E. Out there in the darkness

Symons, J. The tigers of Subtopia

VIKINGS

Russ, J. Souls

Tower, Wells. Everything ravaged, everything burned

Vikings. Dorst, D.

Vila-Matas, Enrique

The Boy on the Swing (Barcelona, 1981)

Grand Street no70 p108-45 Spr/Summ 2002

Vile creatures. Tozzi, F.

VILLA, PANCHO, 1878-1923

About

Coleman, J. C. Borderlands

Swarthout, G. F. Pancho Villa's one-man war

Villa Aurora. Le Clézio, J.-M. G.

Villa Marta. Boylan, C.

Villa of the veiled lady. Milletti, C.

A **village** after dark. Ishiguro, K.

Village chronicle. Müller, H.

The **village** cock. Thomas, H. N.

Villalobos, José Pablo

(jt. auth) See Antúnez, Rafael

(jt. auth) See Ramos, Luis Arturo

(jt. auth) See Velasco, Magali

Villane, Michael

The color of rain

Men on men 2000; best new gay fiction for the millennium; edited and with an introduction by David Bergman and Karl Woelz

Villani, Luisa

Language of the self

The Literary Review (Madison, N.J.) v42 no4 p526-30 Summ 1999

Villanueva, Alma

Golden glass

Fishing for chickens; short stories about rural youth; edited, with an introduction by Jim Heynen

Villatoro, Marcos

American Overhaul

Prairie Schooner v77 no2 p107-13 Summ 2003

Villoro, Juan

Coyote

Points of departure; new stories from Mexico; edited by Mónica Lavín; translated by Gustavo Segade

Villoro, Juan—*Continued*

The Vintage book of Latin American stories; edited by Carlos Fuentes and Julio Ortega

VILNA (LITHUANIA) *See* Lithuania—Vilnius

VILNIUS (LITHUANIA) *See* Lithuania—Vilnius

El **Vilvoy** de las islas. Davidson, A.

Vina Divina. Rushdie, S.

Vincent. Smart, A.

Vinci, Leonardo da *See* Leonardo, da Vinci, 1452-1519

Vine, Barbara, 1930-

See also Rendell, Ruth, 1930-

VINEYARDS *See* Wine and wine making

Vinge, Vernor

The accomplice

Vinge, V. The collected stories of Vernor Vinge

Apartness

Vinge, V. The collected stories of Vernor Vinge

The barbarian princess

Vinge, V. The collected stories of Vernor Vinge

The Blabber

The Good new stuff; adventure SF in the grand tradition; edited by Gardner Dozois

Vinge, V. The collected stories of Vernor Vinge

Bomb scare

Vinge, V. The collected stories of Vernor Vinge

"Bookworm, run!"

Vinge, V. The collected stories of Vernor Vinge

Conquest by default

Vinge, V. The collected stories of Vernor Vinge

The cookie monster

The year's best science fiction: twenty-first annual collection; edited by Gardner Dozois

Fast times at Fairmont High

Vinge, V. The collected stories of Vernor Vinge

Gemstone

Vinge, V. The collected stories of Vernor Vinge

Just peace

Vinge, V. The collected stories of Vernor Vinge

Long shot

Vinge, V. The collected stories of Vernor Vinge

Original sin

Vinge, V. The collected stories of Vernor Vinge

The peddler's apprentice

Vinge, V. The collected stories of Vernor Vinge

The Science Fair

Vinge, V. The collected stories of Vernor Vinge

The ungoverned

Vinge, V. The collected stories of Vernor Vinge

The whirligig of time

Vinge, V. The collected stories of Vernor Vinge

Win a Nobel Prize!

Vinge, V. The collected stories of Vernor Vinge

Vink, Renée

A frail young life

Royal whodunnits; edited by Mike Ashley

Vins fins. Canin, E.

Vins fins (I). Canin, E.

Vinson, in Passing homage à Don. Cobb, T.

Vint. Chekhov, A. P.

Vinten, Robyn

Character witness

Brought to book; murderous stories from the literary world; Penny Sumner, editor

Viola acherontia. Lugones, L.

Violante or high society. Proust, M.

The **violated** dream. Levinson, L. M.

VIOLENCE

See also Child abuse; Riots; Terrorism; Wife abuse

Aldiss, B. W. Headless

Aylett, S. Angel dust

Aylett, S. Repeater

Aylett, S. Shifa

Aylett, S. The waffle code

Barker, N. Layla's nose job

Barnard, R. Going through a phase

Beattie, A. The women of this world

Bell, M. S. Mrs. Lincoln's china

Berry, W. The hurt man

Blackwood, S. Riverfest

Blake, J. C. La vida loca

Borges, J. L. Man on pink corner

Borges, J. L. The story from Rosendo Juárez

Boyle, T. C. Captured by the Indians

Boyle, T. C. Killing babies

Buchanan, E. Miami heat

Cavell, B. Balls, balls, balls

Cobb, W. J. For all you dorks, blah blah blah

Cody, L. Love in vain

Davis, L. Drop in any time

Deane, J. F. The experience of what is beautiful

DeLancey, K. Carley's knees

DeLancey, K. Jules Jr Michael Jules Jr

Ellison, H. The whimper of whipped dogs

Engel, M. P. What Addie wants

Evenson, B. Barcode Jesus

Fischer, T. Ice tonight in the hearts of young visitors

Franklin, T. The ballad of Duane Juarez

Gartner, Z. Odds that, all things considered, she'd someday be happy

Gay, W. Bonedaddy, Quincy Nell, and the fifteen thousand BTU electric chair

Gay, W. Charting the territories of the red

Gay, W. The lightpainter

Gay, W. Sugarbaby

Glave, T. The pit

Gorman, E. Eye of the beholder

Gorriti, J. M. The dead man's fiancée

Gorriti, J. M. Gubi Amaya

Gorriti, J. M. The mazorquero's daughter

Hall, D. The fifth box

Händler, E.-W. Trigger

Harris, J. C. Where's Duncan?

Harty, R. What can I tell you about my brother?

Hazel, R. White Anglo-Saxon Protestant

Hirshberg, G. Struwwelpeter

Irsfeld, J. H. Puerto Rico '61

VIOLENCE—*Continued*
  Johnson, A. Trauma plate
  Johnston, B. A. In the tall grass
  Kilpatrick, N. Generation why
  Kohler, S. Baboons
  Lankford, T. Detour Drive
  LaValle, V. D. Ancient history
  LaValle, V. D. Chuckie
  LaValle, V. D. Ghost story
  Le Guin, U. K. Woeful tales from Mahigul
  Leslie, N. Projectiles
  Leslie, N. The scavenger's eye
  Malouf, D. Dream stuff
  Matthews, C. The moving statue of Ballinspittle
  McCann, C. Cathal's lake
  McNally, J. The vomitorium
  Means, D. Railroad incident, August 1995
  Moody, R. On the carousel
  Nakagami, K. The cape
  Nesbitt, M. The ones who may kill you in the morning
  Oates, J. C. In Copland
  Oates, J. C. Secret, silent
  Oates, J. C. The stalker
  Oates, J. C. Tusk
  Pak, T. The court interpreter
  Papernick, J. The King of the King of Falafel
  Parker, G. Aub
  Reid, E. Dryfall
  Rinehart, S. Mr. Big Stuff
  Robinson, L. The diver
  Robinson, R. The face-lift
  Salter, J. Big ranch
  Sánchez, R. Barrio chronicle
  Sánchez, R. The fields
  Singleton, G. Bank of America
  Spencer, D. There's too much news
  Sterns, A. Watchmen
  Swick, M. A. Crete
  Tamaro, S. Hell does not exist
  Vasseur, T. J. The sins of Jesus
  Winter, E. Call me Ruby
  Winter, E. Spin cycle
Violence. Kohler, S.
Violet. Barthelme, F.
The **violin-maker**. Zivkovic, Z.
VIOLIN MAKERS
  Zivkovic, Z. The violin-maker
The **violin** of Billancourt. Berberova, N.
VIOLINISTS
  Alas, L. The two boxes
  Bly, C. An apprentice
  Campbell, R. No strings
  Chopin, K. With the violin
  De Lint, C. The big sky
  Deane, J. F. A migrant bird
  Erdrich, L. Shamengwa
  Mathews, H. Tradition and the individual talent:the "Bratislava spiccato"
  McGarry, J. Body and soul
  Singer, I. B. The dead fiddler
  Sweeney, E. Lord McDonald
  Taylor, R. L. Pink Miracle in East Tennessee
  Vivante, A. Musico
  Williams, T. The resemblance between a violin case and a coffin
Viollca, the child from Albania. Maraini, D.
The **vireo's** nest. Summers, H. S.
The **virgin**. Carson, J.

The **virgin**. Lichtenstein, A.
VIRGIN ISLANDS OF THE UNITED STATES
    See also Saint Thomas (Virgin Islands of the U.S.)
  Updike, J. At a bar in Charlotte Amalie
Virgin Mary *See* Mary, Blessed Virgin, Saint
A **virgin** twice. Luntta, K.
VIRGINIA
    See also Chesapeake Bay (Md. and Va.)
  Bell, M. S. Two lives
  Bocock, M. Heaven lies about
  Bocock, M. Play me "Stormy weather," please
  Brown, C. Father Judge Run
  Hoffman, W. Blood
  Hoffman, W. Doors
  Hoffman, W. Place
  Hoffman, W. Prodigal
  Hoffman, W. Roll call
  Hoffman, W. Tenant
  Hoffman, W. Winter wheat
  Mazor, J. The lost cause
  Mazor, J. The modern age
  Morgan, E. S. Saturday afternoon in the Holocaust Museum
  Mueller, D. The start of something
  Page, T. N. Unc' Edinburg's drowndin'
            Williamsburg
  Davies, Tristan. In the woodlands
The **Virginia** redbird. Auchincloss, L.
VIRGINITY
  Dinh, L. A cultured boy
  Erian, A. On the occasion of my ruination
  Weinreb, M. The last American virgin
Virgins and Buddhas. Leong, R.
The **Virgin's** gift. Trevor, W.
The **virgin's** passion. Guerra, L.
Virtual. Evenson, B.
Virtual girl [excerpt] Thomson, A.
Virtual Maiden. Grimsley, J.
VIRTUAL REALITY
  Asaro, C. Dance in blue
  Aylett, S. The idler
  Barth, J. Click
  Benford, G. Zoomers
  Bisson, T. In the upper room
  Bisson, T. An office romance
  Blackford, R. Smoke City
  Borges, J. L. The other death
  Esquivel, L. Blessed reality
  Kelly, J. P. Feel the zaz
  Landis, G. A. Rorvik's war
  Lewitt, S. A real girl
  Rosenblum, M. H. Entrada
  Rucker, R. v. B. Enlightenment Rabies
  Scott, M. Trouble and her friends [excerpt]
  Spencer, W. B. The halfway house at the heart of darkness
  Thomson, A. Virtual girl [excerpt]
  Watson, I. When thought-mail failed
Virtuoso. Daniels, L.
Virtuoso Mio. Palmer, K.
VIRUSES
  Boyle, T. C. After the plague
Vis, Jacob
  The mermaid
    Death cruise; crime stories on the open seas; edited by Lawrence Block
Vishnukumar's Valentine's Day. Nair, M.
The **visible** man. Dozois, G. R.

The **visible** man. Stuckey-French, E.
VISION
    See also Eye
Vision. MacLeod, A.
The **Vision** of Mr. Brand. Fayer, S.
VISIONS
    See also Dreams; Hallucinations and illusions
  Anderson, R. Ice age
  Boyle, T. C. The miracle at Ballinspittle
  Bradbury, R. The Messiah
  Cherryh, C. J. Cassandra
  Gonzalez, R. The apparition
  Jacobs, M. Mud Man
Visions. Fulton, J.
Visions and Revisions. Taylor, A.
The **visit**. Adams, A.
The **visit**. Banks, R.
The **visit**. Boyers, R.
The **visit**. Chenoweth, A.
The **visit**. Davis, A.
The **visit**. Lee, A.
The **visit**. Maleti, G.
The **visit**. Spencer, E.
A **visit** from the king. Blegvad, P.
A **visit** from Val Koran. Dyson, J.
A **visit** to Avoyelles. Chopin, K.
A **visit** to my uncle. Delaney, E. J.
The **visitation**. Bear, G.
Visitation. Coover, R.
The **visitation**. Coyne, S.
The **visitation**. Lundquist, R.
Visitations. Ritchie, E.
Le **visiteur**. Trevor, W.
VISITING
  Desai, A. Royalty
  Gunn, K. Visitor
  Leavitt, D. Territory
  Singer, I. B. The admirer
  Spencer, E. The visit
  Trevor, W. Le visiteur
Visiting George. Gordimer, N.
Visiting hours. Budnitz, J.
The **visiting** poet. Winegardner, M.
Visitor. Gunn, K.
The **visitor**. Quill, M.
VISITORS, FOREIGN *See* Foreign visitors
VISITORS FROM OUTER SPACE *See* Interplanetary visitors
A **visitor's** guide to Berlin. Apelman, M.
Visitors of a dying person. Sammān, G.
Visson, Ellen
  The Russian Violinist
    The Literary Review (Madison, N.J.) v47 no1 p111-17 Fall 2003
Viswanathan, Latha
  Cool wedding
    New stories from the South: the year's best, 2003; edited by Shannon Ravenel; with a preface by Roy Blount Jr.
Vitacare. Tully, C.
Vital signs. Miner, V.
VITICULTURE *See* Wine and wine making
Viva la Tropicana. Michaels, L.
Viva Las Vegas. LeRoy, J. T.
Vivante, Arturo
  Can-can
    Vivante, A. Solitude, and other stories

Company
  Vivante, A. Solitude, and other stories
The cove
  Vivante, A. Solitude, and other stories
The cricket
  Vivante, A. Solitude, and other stories
Crosscurrents
  Vivante, A. Solitude, and other stories
Dante
  Vivante, A. Solitude, and other stories
Doves
  Vivante, A. Solitude, and other stories
Escapes
  Vivante, A. Solitude, and other stories
Fall and rise
  Vivante, A. Solitude, and other stories
Fisherman's terrace
  Of leaf and flower; stories and poems for gardeners; edited by Charles Dean and Clyde Wachsberger; illustrations by Clyde Wachsberger
The foghorn
  Vivante, A. Solitude, and other stories
The foundling
  Vivante, A. Solitude, and other stories
The homing pigeon
  Vivante, A. Solitude, and other stories
Honeymoon
  Vivante, A. Solitude, and other stories
The Italian class
  Vivante, A. Solitude, and other stories
Musico
  Vivante, A. Solitude, and other stories
Osage orange
  Vivante, A. Solitude, and other stories
The park
  Vivante, A. Solitude, and other stories
Reflection
  Vivante, A. Solitude, and other stories
Shelter
  Vivante, A. Solitude, and other stories
Solitude
  Vivante, A. Solitude, and other stories
Stones aplenty
  Vivante, A. Solitude, and other stories
The sugar maples
  Vivante, A. Solitude, and other stories
To mock the years
  Vivante, A. Solitude, and other stories
Train ride of a faun
  Vivante, A. Solitude, and other stories
Vivian, Robert
  The Fog Sleepers
    The Massachusetts Review v44 no3 p453-7 Fall 2003
VIVISECTION *See* Medicine—Research
Vlad the nefarious. McManus, J.
Voelker, John Donaldson *See* Traver, Robert, 1903-1991
Vogan, Sara
  When the earth moves
    Prairie Schooner v75 no1 p126-38 Spr 2001
The **voice**. Benford, G.
A **voice** and bitter weeping. Waldrop, H.
Voice crisis. Lê, L.
A **voice** from the other world. Maḥfūẓ, N.
The **voice** of a child. Kaminsky, S. M.
The **Voice** of America. DeMarinis, R.
Voices. Dann, J.

Voices. Mosley, W.

Voices. White, M. C.

The **voices** from the other room. Bausch, R.

Voices in the dark. Davies, R.

Voices of the water. Ruy Sánchez, A.

Voir dire. Healy, J. F.

Voir dire. Lee, D.

Voivodoi. Williams, L.

VOLCANOES

Scoville, S. Ulu's dog

Volkmer, Jon

The elevator man

Fishing for chickens; short stories about rural youth; edited, with an introduction by Jim Heynen

Vollmann, William T.

Breakout

Grand Street no72 p176-214 Fall 2003

The Last Field Marshal

The Paris Review v45 p129-72 Spr 2003

The saviors

The New Yorker v75 no16 p128+ Je 21-28 1999

War movies

Film Comment v38 no2 p20-1, 76 Mr/Ap 2002

Vollmer, Matthew

The Gospel of Mark Schneider

The Virginia Quarterly Review v79 no2 p349-61 Spr 2003

Oh land of national paradise, how glorious are thy bounties

The Paris Review v43 no158 p176-86 Spr/Summ 2001

Watchman, tell us of the night

New Letters v67 no2 p67-83 2001

Volodya. Chekhov, A. P.

Volpi, Jorge

Ars poetica

Colchie, T. A whistler in the nightworld; short fiction from the Latin Americas; edited by Thomas Colchie

Voluntary breathers. Harfenist, J.

The **volunteer**. Haslett, A.

The **volunteers**. Lee, C.-R.

The **vomitorium**. McNally, J.

VON NEUMANN, JOHN, 1903-1957

About

Rucker, R. v. B. Instability

Von Puttkammer, Emil *See* Ludwig, Otto, 1802-1875

Vonnegut, Kurt

2BRO2B

Vonnegut, K. Bagombo snuff box; uncollected short fiction

Ambitious sophomore

Vonnegut, K. Bagombo snuff box; uncollected short fiction

Any reasonable offer

Vonnegut, K. Bagombo snuff box; uncollected short fiction

Der Arme Dolmetscher

Vonnegut, K. Bagombo snuff box; uncollected short fiction

Bagombo snuff box

Vonnegut, K. Bagombo snuff box; uncollected short fiction

The Boy Who Hated Girls

The Saturday Evening Post v276 no5 p74-6, 78, 80-2, 84 S/O 2004

Vonnegut, K. Bagombo snuff box; uncollected short fiction

The cruise of *The Jolly Roger*

Vonnegut, K. Bagombo snuff box; uncollected short fiction

Custom-made bride

Vonnegut, K. Bagombo snuff box; uncollected short fiction

Find me a dream

Vonnegut, K. Bagombo snuff box; uncollected short fiction

Hal Irwin's magic lamp

Vonnegut, K. Bagombo snuff box; uncollected short fiction

Lovers Anonymous

Vonnegut, K. Bagombo snuff box; uncollected short fiction

Mnemonics

Vonnegut, K. Bagombo snuff box; uncollected short fiction

A night for love

Vonnegut, K. Bagombo snuff box; uncollected short fiction

The no-talent kid

Vonnegut, K. Bagombo snuff box; uncollected short fiction

The package

Vonnegut, K. Bagombo snuff box; uncollected short fiction

Poor little rich town

Vonnegut, K. Bagombo snuff box; uncollected short fiction

The powder-blue dragon

Vonnegut, K. Bagombo snuff box; uncollected short fiction

A present for Big Saint Nick

Vonnegut, K. Bagombo snuff box; uncollected short fiction

Runaways

Vonnegut, K. Bagombo snuff box; uncollected short fiction

Souvenir

Vonnegut, K. Bagombo snuff box; uncollected short fiction

Thanasphere

Vonnegut, K. Bagombo snuff box; uncollected short fiction

This son of mine

Vonnegut, K. Bagombo snuff box; uncollected short fiction

Unpaid consultant

Vonnegut, K. Bagombo snuff box; uncollected short fiction

Voodoo girls on ice. Evans, E.

VOODOOISM

See also Zombies

Brite, P. Z. O death, where is thy spatula?

Carroll, J. Curtis's charm

Cohen, S. Neville

Collins, B. Obeah, my love

Fleming, R. The tenderness of Monsieur Blanc

Khan, I. Shadows move in the Britannia Bar

Prevost, C.-M. Tears for Ersulie Freda: men without shadow

Sturgeon, T. A way of thinking

Tenn, W. Mistress Sary

The **vortex**. Ferriss, L.
Vourlis, John P.
  A case of insomnia
    Shadows over Baker Street; edited by Michael
    Reaves and John Pelan
The **Vow**. Diwakar, S.
Voyage of discovery. Hoffman, N. K.
The **voyage** out. Callaghan, M.
The **voyager**. Kirchheimer, G. D.
VOYAGES AND TRAVELS
      See also Adventure; Air travel; Rail-
      roads—Travel; Sea stories; Tourist trade;
      Travelers
  Dumas, H. The university of man
  MacLeod, A. Vision
  Ortiz, S. J. Pennstuwehniyaahtse: Quuti's story
  Tilghman, C. A suitable good-bye
VOYEURS
  Boyle, T. C. Peep Hall
  Brownstein, G. Wakefield, 7E
  Campbell, R. The limits of fantasy
  Campbell, R. Stages
  Devereaux, R. Li'l Miss Ultrasound
  Hall, J. Crack
  Knight, M. Now you see her
  Kurlansky, M. Naked
  McCabe, P. The hands of Dingo Deery
  Michaels, L. Murderers
  Molyneux, J. Desire lines
  Mueller, D. How animals mate
  Smith, M. M. Two shot
  Tester, W. Immaculate
  Tester, W. Whisperers
  Woolrich, C. Rear window
Vreeland, Susan
  A Flower for Ginette
    Ploughshares v29 no2/3 p187-93 Fall 2003
Vromen, Galina
  Sarah's story
    With signs and wonders; an international an-
    thology of Jewish fabulist fiction; edited by
    Daniel M. Jaffe
Las **Vueltas**. Henderson, G. E.
Vukcevich, Ray
  The barber's theme
    Vukcevich, R. Meet me in the moon room;
    stories
  Beastly heat
    Vukcevich, R. Meet me in the moon room;
    stories
  Beatniks with banjos
    Vukcevich, R. Meet me in the moon room;
    stories
  A breath holding contest
    Vukcevich, R. Meet me in the moon room;
    stories
  By the time we get to Uranus
    Vukcevich, R. Meet me in the moon room;
    stories
    The Year's best fantasy & horror, twelfth an-
    nual collection; edited by Ellen Datlow &
    Terry Windling
  Catch
    Vukcevich, R. Meet me in the moon room;
    stories
  Ceremony
    Vukcevich, R. Meet me in the moon room;
    stories

Doing time
  Vukcevich, R. Meet me in the moon room;
  stories
Fancy pants
  Vukcevich, R. Meet me in the moon room;
  stories
Finally fruit
  Vukcevich, R. Meet me in the moon room;
  stories
The finger
  The Best from fantasy & science fiction: the
  fiftieth anniversary anthology; edited by
  Edward L. Ferman and Gordon Van Gelder
  Vukcevich, R. Meet me in the moon room;
  stories
Giant step
  Vukcevich, R. Meet me in the moon room;
  stories
A holiday junket
  Vukcevich, R. Meet me in the moon room;
  stories
Home remedy
  Vukcevich, R. Meet me in the moon room;
  stories
In the refrigerator
  Vukcevich, R. Meet me in the moon room;
  stories
Jumping
  Witpunk; edited by Claude Lalumière and
  Marty Halpern
Meet me in the moon room
  Vukcevich, R. Meet me in the moon room;
  stories
Message in a fish
  Vukcevich, R. Meet me in the moon room;
  stories
Mom's little friends
  Vukcevich, R. Meet me in the moon room;
  stories
My mustache
  Vukcevich, R. Meet me in the moon room;
  stories
The next best thing
  Vukcevich, R. Meet me in the moon room;
  stories
No comet
  Vukcevich, R. Meet me in the moon room;
  stories
The perfect gift
  Vukcevich, R. Meet me in the moon room;
  stories
Pink smoke
  Vukcevich, R. Meet me in the moon room;
  stories
Poop
  Vukcevich, R. Meet me in the moon room;
  stories
Pretending
  Vukcevich, R. Meet me in the moon room;
  stories
Quite contrary
  Vukcevich, R. Meet me in the moon room;
  stories
Rejoice
  Vukcevich, R. Meet me in the moon room;
  stories
Season finale
  Vukcevich, R. Meet me in the moon room;
  stories

Vukcevich, Ray—*Continued*

The swan

The Blue and the gray undercover; edited by
Ed Gorman

The sweater

Vukcevich, R. Meet me in the moon room;
stories

There is danger

Vukcevich, R. Meet me in the moon room;
stories

We kill a bicycle

Vukcevich, R. Meet me in the moon room;
stories

Whisper

Vukcevich, R. Meet me in the moon room;
stories

White guys in space

Vukcevich, R. Meet me in the moon room;
stories

The **vulgar** soul. Biguenet, J.

Vulture. Adam, C.

W

W.S.. Hartley, L. P.

Wa Thiong'o, James *See* Ng'ugĩ wa Thiong'o,
1938-

Waberi, Abdourahman A.

August 1966

Grand Street no70 p172-7 Spr/Summ 2002

Wachtel, Chuck

The Annunciation

Daedalus v133 no1 p79-90 Wint 2004

Wadholm, Richard

At the money

The Year's best science fiction; twentieth annual collection; edited by Gardner Dozois

Green tea

The Year's best science fiction, seventeenth
annual collection; edited by Gardner Dozois

Wadsworth, Sarah

If there be any praise

The Hudson Review v54 no4 p543-56 Wint
2002

The **waffle** code. Aylett, S.

The **waffle** maker. Blaise, C.

The **wager**. Fish, R. L.

WAGERS

Ellin, S. The moment of decision

Fish, R. L. The wager

Jenkins, G. The bet

Singer, I. B. The wager

Waugh, E. Unacademic exercise: a nature story

Waggoner, Tim

Picking up Courtney

Gathering the bones; original stories from the
world's masters of horror; edited by Dennis
Etchison, Ramsey Campbell and Jack Dann

The September people

Greenberg, M. H. Faerie tales

Waging good. Reed, R.

Wagner, Bruce

Man overboard

Film Comment v37 no6 p12-13, 77 N/D 2001

Wagner, Karl Edward

Where the summer ends

The American fantasy tradition; edited by Brian M. Thomsen

Wägner, Wilhelm

The Hegeling legend [excerpt]

Swords and sorcerers; stories from the world
of fantasy and adventure; edited by Clint
Willis

The legend of Beowulf

Swords and sorcerers; stories from the world
of fantasy and adventure; edited by Clint
Willis

WAGON TRAINS

Coleman, J. C. Fiddle case

Farrell, C. Five aces west

Farrell, C. I'm going to California

Gulick, B. The shaming of broken horn

Wahl, Sharon

The Calculus of Felicity

Iowa Review v33 no2 p10-20 Fall 2003

Zeno and the distance between us

Iowa Review v29 no2 p28-33 Fall 1999

Wailing reed. Steinberg, J.

The **wait**. Borges, J. L.

WAITERS

Bemelmans, L. Mespoulets of the Splendide

Mason, B. A. Rolling into Atlanta

McPherson, J. A. A solo song: for Doc

Michaels, L. Honeymoon

Michaels, L. Second honeymoon

Singer, I. B. The enemy

Waiting for Marilyn. Galloway, J.

Waiting for Stella. Adams, A.

Waiting for the 400. Marffin, K.

Waiting for the Mwami. Hunter, F.

The **waiting** list. Ziegler, I.

The **waiting** room. Arango, A.

The **waiting** room. Čapek, K.

The **waiting** room. Ellis, Z.

The **waiting** room. Frank, J.

The **waiting** room. Joseph, S.

Waiting rooms. Avrich, J.

Waiting to discover electricity. Wexler, M.

Waiting to see. Yuknavitch, L.

WAITRESSES

Adams, A. By the sea

Agee, J. Over the point of cohesion

Bell, M. S. Customs of the country

Carver, R. Fat

Coleman, W. The Friday night shift at the Taco
House blues (wah-wah)

Curtis, Rebecca. Hungry self

Gunn, K. Visitor

Hart, C. G. Secrets

Kees, W. Mrs. Lutz

McCrumb, S. Among my souvenirs

Ng'ugĩ wa Thiong'o. Minutes of glory

Nichols, J. Magic

Oates, J. C. Ugly

Randisi, R. J. Black and white memories

Shade, E. Stability

Shepard, S. Great dream of heaven

Slavin, J. Rare is a cold red center

Slezak, E. Here in car city

Steele, A. M. Her own private sitcom

Swan, G. News from the volcano

Tilghman, C. The way people run

Waitt, Albert

The van

The Literary Review (Madison, N.J.) v44 no3
p523-37 Spr 2001

Wake. Goldner, B.

Wake Island. Le Guin, U. K.
Wakefield. Hawthorne, N.
Wakefield, 7E. Brownstein, G.
Waking to the Spirit Clock. Trevanian
Waking up the dead. Lawrence, M. F.
WAL-MART STORES, INC.
Evenson, B. Barcode Jesus
Walbert, Kate
The gardens of Kyoto
Prize stories, 2000; The O. Henry awards; edited and with an introduction by Larry Dark
The Pushcart prize XXIV: best of the small presses; an annual small press reader; edited by Bill Henderson with the Pushcart prize editors
The intervention
The Paris Review v41 no151 p114-25 Summ 1999
Walcott-Hackshaw, Elizabeth
Pine Hill
Callaloo v25 no2 p426-36 Spr 2002
Wald, Ann Himmelberger
What the Heart Wants
The North American Review v287 no5 p27-33 S/O 2002
Wald, Malvin
Keys to the city
The African American West; a century of short stories; edited by Bruce A. Glasrud and Laurie Champion
Walden, Sally
Caboose
The North American Review v286 no3/4 p13-18 My/Ag 2001
Waldo. Heinlein, R. A.
Waldrop, Howard
Black as the pit, from pole to pole
Waldrop, H. Custer's last jump and other collaborations; [by] Howard Waldrop and Leigh Kennedy [et al.]
Calling your name
The year's best science fiction: twenty-first annual collection; edited by Gardner Dozois
Custer's last jump!
Waldrop, H. Custer's last jump and other collaborations; [by] Howard Waldrop and Leigh Kennedy [et al.]
Household words; or, the powers-that-be
A yuletide universe; sixteen fantastical tales; edited by Brian M. Thomsen
The latter days of the law
Waldrop, H. Custer's last jump and other collaborations; [by] Howard Waldrop and Leigh Kennedy [et al.]
Lunchbox
Wondrous beginnings; edited by Steven H. Silver and Martin H. Greenberg
Men of Greywater Station
Waldrop, H. Custer's last jump and other collaborations; [by] Howard Waldrop and Leigh Kennedy [et al.]
One horse town
Waldrop, H. Custer's last jump and other collaborations; [by] Howard Waldrop and Leigh Kennedy [et al.]
Our mortal span
Black heart, ivory bones; [edited by] Ellen Datlow & Terri Windling

Sun's up!
Waldrop, H. Custer's last jump and other collaborations; [by] Howard Waldrop and Leigh Kennedy [et al.]
Us
The Year's best science fiction, sixteenth annual collection; edited by Gardner Dozois
A voice and bitter weeping
Waldrop, H. Custer's last jump and other collaborations; [by] Howard Waldrop and Leigh Kennedy [et al.]
Willow Beeman
Waldrop, H. Custer's last jump and other collaborations; [by] Howard Waldrop and Leigh Kennedy [et al.]
Waldrop, Howard and Kennedy, Leigh
One-horse town
The Year's best science fiction, nineteenth annual collection; edited by Gardner Dozois
WALES
Davies, R. The sisters
Granelli, R. Disturbing the peace
James, S. A house of one's own
Rural life
Davies, R. The dilemma of Catherine Fuchsias
Davies, R. The Fashion Plate
Jones, R. Meredith Evans' kiss
Cardiff
James, S. Happy as Saturday night
The **walk**. Collins, M.
A **walk** across Mars. Steele, A. M.
A **walk** in the dark. Clarke, A. C.
A **walk** in the park. Berman, M.
A **walk** in the sun. Landis, G. A.
Walk on. Richard, M.
A **walk-on** part in the war. Dedman, S.
A **walk** outside. Guista, M.
The **Walk** with Elizanne. Updike, J.
Walkabout. Murray, S.
Walker, Alice
Advancing Luna—and Ida B. Wells
Crossing the color line; readings in Black and white; edited by Suzanne W. Jones
Blaze
Walker, A. The way forward is with a broken heart
The brotherhood of the saved
Walker, A. The way forward is with a broken heart
Charms
Walker, A. The way forward is with a broken heart
Conscious birth
Walker, A. The way forward is with a broken heart
Cuddling
Walker, A. The way forward is with a broken heart
Everyday use
Snapshots: 20th century mother-daughter fiction; edited by Joyce Carol Oates and Janet Berliner
The flowers
Fishing for chickens; short stories about rural youth; edited, with an introduction by Jim Heynen
Growing out
Walker, A. The way forward is with a broken heart

Walker, Alice—*Continued*
"How did I get away with killing one of the biggest lawyers in the state? It was easy."
Ms. v12 no3 p36-8 Summ 2002
Kindred spirits
Walker, A. The way forward is with a broken heart
Nineteen fifty-five
The Scribner anthology of contemporary short fiction; fifty North American stories since 1970; Lex Williford and Michael Martone, editors
Olive oil
Walker, A. The way forward is with a broken heart
Roselily
The Bluelight corner; black women writing on passion, sex, and romantic love; edited by Rosemarie Robotham
There was a river
Walker, A. The way forward is with a broken heart
This is how it happened
Walker, A. The way forward is with a broken heart
To my young husband
Walker, A. The way forward is with a broken heart
Uncle Loaf and Auntie Putt-Putt
Walker, A. The way forward is with a broken heart

Walker, Brenda
Mrs. Holland
The Kenyon Review ns24 no1 p51-7 Wint 2002
Mt Fuji
The Literary Review (Madison, N.J.) v45 no1 p184-7 Fall 2001

Walker, Dale L.
York's story
Westward; a fictional history of the American West : 28 original stories celebrating the 50th anniversary of the Western Writers of America; edited by Dale L. Walker

Walker, Daly
Shadows
The Sewanee Review v111 no1 p50-72 Wint 2003

Walker, Sage
Hunting mother
The Year's best science fiction, seventeenth annual collection; edited by Gardner Dozois
The **walker**. Greer, A. S.
Walkin' the dog. Mosley, W.
WALKING
Bowen, E. The happy autumn fields
Bradbury, R. The pedestrian
Walking. Bernhard, T.
Walking. Treat, J.
Walking circles. López, L.
Walking in my sleep. Spatz, G.
Walking into the wind. O'Farrell, J.
Walking legs. Saunders, G.
Walking on Water. Mantel, T.
Walking strawberry. Cobb, W.
Walking the trapline. Rule, R.
Walking to Carcassonne. Ely, S.
Walking to Paris. Miller, R.
The **wall**. Williams, M.

The **wall** of darkness. Clarke, A. C.
WALL STREET (NEW YORK, N.Y.)
See also Stock exchange
A **wall** too high. Hoch, E. D.
Wallace, Daniel
Slippered feet
This is where we live; short stories by 25 contemporary North Carolina writers; edited by Michael McFee
Wallace, David Foster
Adult world [I]
Wallace, D. F. Brief interviews with hideous men
Adult world [II]
Wallace, D. F. Brief interviews with hideous men
Another pioneer
Wallace, D. F. Oblivion; stories
Asset
The New Yorker v75 no16 p93-94 Je 21-28 1999
Brief interviews with hideous men [I]
Wallace, D. F. Brief interviews with hideous men
Brief interviews with hideous men [II]
Wallace, D. F. Brief interviews with hideous men
Brief interviews with hideous men [III]
Wallace, D. F. Brief interviews with hideous men
Brief interviews with hideous men [IV]
Wallace, D. F. Brief interviews with hideous men
Church not made with hands
Wallace, D. F. Brief interviews with hideous men
Datum centurio
Wallace, D. F. Brief interviews with hideous men
Death is not the end
Wallace, D. F. Brief interviews with hideous men
The depressed person
Prize stories, 1999; The O. Henry awards; edited and with an introduction by Larry Dark
Wallace, D. F. Brief interviews with hideous men
The devil is a busy man
Wallace, D. F. Brief interviews with hideous men
Forever overhead
Wallace, D. F. Brief interviews with hideous men
Good old neon
Wallace, D. F. Oblivion; stories
Incarnations of burned children
Wallace, D. F. Oblivion; stories
Mister Squishy
Wallace, D. F. Oblivion; stories
Oblivion
Wallace, D. F. Oblivion; stories
Octet
Wallace, D. F. Brief interviews with hideous men

Wallace, David Foster—*Continued*
On his deathbed, holding your hand, the acclaimed new young off-Broadway playwright's father begs a boon
Wallace, D. F. Brief interviews with hideous men
Philosophy and the mirror of nature
Wallace, D. F. Oblivion; stories
Signifying nothing
Wallace, D. F. Brief interviews with hideous men
The Soul Is Not a Smithy
Agni no57 p22-61 2003
Wallace, D. F. Oblivion; stories
The Suffering Channel
Wallace, D. F. Oblivion; stories
Suicide as a sort of present
Wallace, D. F. Brief interviews with hideous men
Tri-stan: I sold sissee nar to Ecko
Wallace, D. F. Brief interviews with hideous men
Wallace, Jamie
Driven to kill
A Deadly dozen; tales of murder from members of Sisters in Crime/Los Angeles; edited by Susan B. Casmier, Aljean Harmetz and Cynthia Lawrence
Wallace, Marilyn
The collaboration
Love and death; edited by Carolyn Hart
Splitting
A Hot and sultry night for crime; edited by Jeffery Deaver
Thinking
Mom, apple pie, and murder; edited by Nancy Pickard
Wallace, Ronald
Animal rights
Wallace, R. Quick bright things; stories
Cross country
Wallace, R. Quick bright things; stories
The little woman
Wallace, R. Quick bright things; stories
Logjam
Wallace, R. Quick bright things; stories
The new sidewalks
Wallace, R. Quick bright things; stories
The night nurse
Wallace, R. Quick bright things; stories
The Penguin Parade
TriQuarterly no115 p160-4 Spr 2003
The quarry
Wallace, R. Quick bright things; stories
Quick bright things
Wallace, R. Quick bright things; stories
The sacred well
Wallace, R. Quick bright things; stories
Talking
Wallace, R. Quick bright things; stories
Topless in Tucson
Wallace, R. Quick bright things; stories
A trick of memory
Wallace, R. Quick bright things; stories
Wordplay
Wallace, R. Quick bright things; stories
Wallace Porter sees the elephant. Day, C.

Wallenstein, James
Concerning love
The Hudson Review v54 no2 p269-78 Summ 2001
A fan despite himself
The Antioch Review v59 no4 p666-89 Fall 2001
Summer's Lease
The Hudson Review v56 no2 p275-92 Summ 2003
Waller, Easton
The war against the lawns
Nixon under the bodhi tree and other works of Buddhist fiction; edited by Kate Wheeler ; foreword by Charles Johnson
Wallington, Aury
Day of the dead
Pieces; a collection of new voices; edited by Stephen Chbosky
WALLPAPER
Gilman, C. P. The yellow wallpaper
Walls of darkness. Maraini, D.
Walnuts, when the husks are green. Taylor, B.
Walpole, Peter
Island of Three Pines
Iowa Review v32 no2 p85-91 Fall 2002
Walpow, Nathan
Push comes to shove
The Best American mystery stories, 2001; edited and with an Introduction by Lawrence Block
A Deadly dozen; tales of murder from members of Sisters in Crime/Los Angeles; edited by Susan B. Casmier, Aljean Harmetz and Cynthia Lawrence
Walrond, Eric
Drought
The Oxford book of Caribbean short stories; edited by Stewart Brown and John Wickham
Walser, Alissa
The lesser half of the world
Chicago Review v48 no2/3 p311-19 Summ 2002
Walser, Martin
Assemblies
New England Review v22 no2 p142-5 Spr 2001
Walt Kaplan reads Hiroshima, March 1947. Orner, P.
Walter, Charmed. Harding, P.
Walter Cronkite with Hospital Corners. Swire, B.
Walter John Harmon. Doctorow, E. L.
Walter Kaplan reads John Hersey's Hiroshima, March 1947. Orner, P.
Walters, Mark
Piggies
Iowa Review v34 no2 p159-69, 171 Fall 2004
Walters, Minette
English autumn-American fall
A moment on the edge; 100 years of crime stories by women; edited by Elizabeth George
The tinder box
The World's finest mystery and crime stories, first annual collection; edited by Ed Gorman
Walter's leg. Rendell, R.

Walton, Anthony
Divorce education
Fault lines; stories of divorce; collected and edited by Caitlin Shetterly
Walton, Isaac *See* Walton, Izaak, 1593-1683
WALTON, IZAAK, 1593-1683
About
Boylan, C. The complete angler
Waltz him around again, Shadow. L'Amour, L.
Walz, Thomas
The littlest guest uninvited
Iowa Review v29 no3 p88-93 Wint 1999
Wanamaker. Meredith, D.
Wandrei, Howard
George is all right
Death dines at 8:30; edited by Claudia Bishop and Nick DiChario
Wang, An-i *See* Wang Anyi, 1954-
Wang, Ceng-qi *See* Wang Cengqi, 1920-1997
Wang Anyi
Between themselves
The Vintage book of contemporary Chinese fiction; edited by Carolyn Choa and David Su Li-qun
Life in a small courtyard
The Vintage book of contemporary Chinese fiction; edited by Carolyn Choa and David Su Li-qun
Wang Cengqi
Big Chan
The Vintage book of contemporary Chinese fiction; edited by Carolyn Choa and David Su Li-qun
Wang Meng
The lovesick crow and other fables
The Vintage book of contemporary Chinese fiction; edited by Carolyn Choa and David Su Li-qun
"Wangeroog, de schone . . .". Ehlers, J.
Wang's carpets. Egan, G.
Wanted—?. Cunningham, E.
Wanted—dead and alive. Marlowe, S.
Wants. Paley, G.
WAR
See also Imaginary wars and battles; Interplanetary wars; Nuclear warfare names of individual wars
American mandate
Anderson, D. Baby teeth
Benford, G. High abyss
Benford, G. Manassas, again
Cacek, P. D. Belief
Carlson, R. What we wanted to do
Cherryh, C. J. Cassandra
Cherryh, C. J. The general
Donaldson, S. R. Penance
Drake, D. Coming up against it
Drake, D. Facing the enemy
Drake, D. Failure mode
Drake, D. The tradesmen
Drake, D. With the sword he must be slain
Feist, R. E. The messenger
Haldeman, J. W. For White Hill
Haldeman, J. W. Forever peace [excerpt]
Haldeman, J. W. A separate war
Harrison, H. American dead
Hemon, A. A coin
Karampur, F. Refugee

LaFarge, P. Lamentation over the destruction of Ur
Landis, G. A. Rorvik's war
Landis, G. A. Winter fire
Lansdale, J. R. In the cold, dark time
Lee, M. Memo to our journalists
Lopez, B. H. In the Garden of the Lords of War
Malzberg, B. N. Final war
Roberts, A. Swiftly
Sari, F. The absent soldier
Seiffert, R. The crossing
Sneve, V. D. H. Fool soldiers
Stross, C. A colder war
Swofford, A. Freedom Oil
Tolstoy, L., graf. Why did it happen?
Vinge, V. The ungoverned
Vinge, V. The whirligig of time
Waldrop, H. One horse war
Waldrop, H. A voice and bitter weeping
Waldrop, H. and Kennedy, L. One-horse town
What, L. A dark fire, burning from within
Casualties
Babel´, I. Doudou
Swarthout, G. F. Death to everybody over thirty
The **war.** Saroyan, A.
WAR AND CHILDREN
Card, O. S. Ender's game
Okri, B. In the shadow of war
War babies. Hribal, C. J.
WAR CORRESPONDENTS *See* Journalists
WAR CRIMINALS
Baida, P. A doctor's story
Dann, J. Tea
WAR GAMES
Card, O. S. Ender's game
War letters. Riahi, M.
The **war** lovers. Bukiet, M. J.
War movies. Vollmann, W. T.
WAR OF THE ROSES *See* England—15th century
War of the roses. Edghill, R.
The **war** of the worldviews. Morrow, J.
War with Japan. Barthelme, F.
The **War** Years. Smith, H.
Warburton, Geoffrey
Merry Roderick
Best new horror 12; edited and with an introduction by Stephen Jones
Ward, Amanda Eyre
Should I be scared ?
Politically inspired; edited by Stephen Elliott; assistant editor, Gabriel Kram; associate editors, Elizabeth Brooks [et al.]
Ward, Arthur Sarsfield *See* Rohmer, Sax
Ward, Caryl
Wolf Man
Mr. Roopratna's chocolate; the winning stories from the 1999 Rhys Davies competition
Ward, Liza
Dancing Lessons
Atlantic Monthly (1993) v290 no3 p128-32, 134-6 O 2002
Best new American voices 2004; guest editor John Casey; series editors John Kulka and Natalie Danford
Outside Valentine
The Antioch Review v61 no1 p49-67 Wint 2003

Ward, Liza—*Continued*
Snowbound
  The Georgia Review v57 no3 p567-84 Fall
  2003
Ward no. 6. Chekhov, A. P.
The **Wardrobe,** Forefathers, and Death. Ribeyro,
  J. R.
The **wardrobe,** the old man and death. Ribeyro, J.
  R.
Ware calls it a day. Cunningham, E.
WARHOL, ANDY, 1928?-1987
            About
  Rucker, R. v. B. The Andy Warhol sandcandle
WARLOCKS *See* Witchcraft
Warm. Sheckley, R.
A **warm** nest. Kennett, S.
A **warm** welcome to the President, insh'allah!.
  Nair, M.
Warner, Alan
The man who walks
  The Vintage book of contemporary Scottish
  fiction; edited and with an introduction by
  Peter Kravitz
WARNER, JACK L., 1892-1978
            About
  Jenkins, G. A portrait of the artist at Warner
  Bros.
Warner, Marina
Cancellanda
  Raritan v23 no2 p24-42 Fall 2003
Warner, Sharon Oard
Signs of Life
  Prairie Schooner v77 no1 p6-20 Spr 2003
Sweetness
  Prairie Schooner v78 no2 p46-63 Summ 2004
Warner-Vieyra, Myriam
Passport to paradise
  The Oxford book of Caribbean short stories;
  edited by Stewart Brown and John
  Wickham
Warning warning. Steele, A. M.
Warnings. Parkison, A.
The **warp** and the weft. Delaney, E. J.
Warren, Dianne
Bone garden
  Warren, D. A reckless moon and other stories
Hawk's landing
  Warren, D. A reckless moon and other stories
Long gone and Mister Lonely
  Warren, D. A reckless moon and other stories
Michelangelo
  Warren, D. A reckless moon and other stories
Moving pictures
  Warren, D. A reckless moon and other stories
A reckless moon
  Warren, D. A reckless moon and other stories
Tuxedo
  Warren, D. A reckless moon and other stories
Warren, Larkin
Unfinished business
  Good Housekeeping v234 no1 p171-8 Ja 2002
Warren, Robert Penn
Blackberry winter
  Home and beyond; an anthology of Kentucky
  short stories; edited by Morris Allen
  Grubbs; with an introduction by Wade Hall
  and an afterword by Charles E. May

Christmas gift
  The Best American short stories of the
  century; John Updike, editor, Katrina
  Kenison, coeditor; with an introduction by
  John Updike
Warren, Lee Gay
Vials of life
  Stories from the Blue Moon Cafe II; edited
  by Sonny Brewer
Warren Waits and the spaghetti-strap girl. Reiner,
  C.
War's end. Haslett, A.
WARSAW (POLAND) *See* Poland—Warsaw
Was Me Mudda. Kempadoo, O.
Wash, rinse, spin. Bauman, B. A.
Washed. DeLancey, K.
Washerbaum the crestfallen. Mizelle, T.
WASHERWOMEN *See* Laundresses
The **washing** machine. Klíma, I.
Washington, Alex *See* Harris, Mark, 1922-
WASHINGTON, GEORGE, 1732-1799
            About
  Queen, E. The adventure of the President's half
  disme
WASHINGTON, MARTHA, 1731-1802
            About
  Hoch, E. D. Martha's parrot
  Johnson, C. R. Martha's dilemma
WASHINGTON (D.C.)
  Barrett, L. Macy is the other woman
  Bates, H. Farewell to the master
  Bean, B. There'll never be another you
  Chenoweth, A. Wingtips
  Jones, E. P. A rich man
  Mazor, J. Friend of mankind
  Mazor, J. Skylark
  Pelecanos, G. P. The dead their eyes implore us
  Pynchon, T. Entropy
  Swarthout, G. F. Poteet caught up in lust and
  history
            20th century
  Everett, P. L. The fix
WASHINGTON (STATE)
  Berdine, T. Spring rite
  Lewis, W. H. The trip back from Whidbey
            Seattle
  Alexie, S. Do you know where I am?
  Canty, K. Aquarium
  Girardi, R. Three ravens on a red ground
  Greer, A. S. Blame it on my youth
  Gussoff, C. Bruce Lee
  Gussoff, C. The wave: a novella
  Weihe, E. Love spots
WASHINGTON AND LEE UNIVERSITY
  Smith, R. T. Docent
WASINGTON (D.C.)
            Wasington (D.C.)
  Mazor, J. On experience
The **wasp** factory [excerpt] Banks, I.
WASPS
  Connor, J. Let us now praise dead white men
Waswolf. Wellen, E.
Watanabe McFerrin, Linda
Amphibians
  Watanabe McFerrin, L. The hand of Buddha;
  stories
Childproofing
  Watanabe McFerrin, L. The hand of Buddha;
  stories

Watanabe McFerrin, Linda—*Continued*
Coyote comes calling
Watanabe McFerrin, L. The hand of Buddha; stories
God and all the angels
Watanabe McFerrin, L. The hand of Buddha; stories
The hand of Buddha
Watanabe McFerrin, L. The hand of Buddha; stories
How to fall in love
Watanabe McFerrin, L. The hand of Buddha; stories
Khalida's dog
Watanabe McFerrin, L. The hand of Buddha; stories
A little variety
Watanabe McFerrin, L. The hand of Buddha; stories
Los mariachis del muerto
Watanabe McFerrin, L. The hand of Buddha; stories
Masai heart
Watanabe McFerrin, L. The hand of Buddha; stories
Pickled eggs
Watanabe McFerrin, L. The hand of Buddha; stories
Rubber time
Watanabe McFerrin, L. The hand of Buddha; stories
Watch dog. Adam, C.
Watch for it. Gores, J.
Watch out, the world's behind you. Mills, J.
Watch the animals. Dark, A. E.
Watched and listened: stories about the boys. Heynen, J.
Watcher. Hensley, J. L.
Watcher at the gate. Vargo, J.
The **watcher** at the window. Burleson, D. R.
Watching from the Wings. Bache, E.
Watching girls play. Wetherell, W. D.
Watchman, tell us of the night. Vollmer, M.
WATCHMEN
Chekhov, A. P. A bad business
Kees, W. The evening of the Fourth of July
Naipaul, V. S. The night watchman's occurrence book
Watchmen. Sterns, A.
Watchtower. Chan, D. M.
WATER
See also Wells
Water. Lindgren, T.
Water. Svoboda, T.
Water Baby. Kohler, S.
Water dog god. Watson, B.
The **water** faucet vision. Jen, G.
The **water-girl**. Packer, G.
Water marks. Barker, N.
Water of an undetermined depth. Chiappone, R.
Water off a black dog's back. Link, K.
Water seeks its own level. Clair, M.
Water thieves. McNamer, D.
The **waterfall**. Chinodya, S.
WATERFALLS
Harrison, H. By the falls
Waterline. Brown, J. L.
Waterloo sunset. Davies, R.

Waterman, Daniel
A lepidopterist's tale
The Best American mystery stories, 2002; edited and with an introduction by James Ellroy; Otto Penzler, series editor
Bomb no77 p105-12 Fall 2001
Watermelon days. McNeal, T.
Watermelon seeds. Power, S.
Waters, Jesse
A Man Identifies A Body
Iowa Review v33 no3 p97-103 Wint 2003/2004
Waters, Mary Yukari
Aftermath
The Best American short stories, 2002; selected from U.S. and Canadian magazines by Sue Miller with Katrina Kenison, with an introduction by Sue Miller
Waters, M. Y. The laws of evening; stories
Circling the hondo
Waters, M. Y. The laws of evening; stories
Egg-face
Francis Ford Coppola's Zoetrope all-story 2; edited by Adrienne Brodeur and Samantha Schnee; with an introduction by Francis Ford Coppola
Waters, M. Y. The laws of evening; stories
Kami
Waters, M. Y. The laws of evening; stories
The laws of evening
Waters, M. Y. The laws of evening; stories
Mirror studies
Waters, M. Y. The laws of evening; stories
Rationing
The Best American short stories, 2003; selected from U.S. and Canadian magazines by Walter Mosley with Katrina Kenison; with an introduction by Walter Mosley
Waters, M. Y. The laws of evening; stories
Seed
The Pushcart prize XXIV: best of the small presses; an annual small press reader; edited by Bill Henderson with the Pushcart prize editors
Waters, M. Y. The laws of evening; stories
Shibusa
TriQuarterly no105 p38-45 Spr/Summ 1999
Waters, M. Y. The laws of evening; stories
Since my house burned down
Waters, M. Y. The laws of evening; stories
The way love works
Waters, M. Y. The laws of evening; stories
Waters. Obejas, A.
The **waters**. Orner, P.
The **waters** of Izli. Bowles, P.
Watkins, Steve
Critterworld
100% pure Florida fiction; an anthology; edited by Susan Hubbard and Robley Wilson
Watmough, David
Sharing Hale-Bopp
His 3: brilliant new fiction by gay writers; edited by Robert Drake and Terry Wolverton
Watson, Brad
The dead girl
Stories from the Blue Moon Café; edited by Sonny Brewer

Watson, Brad—*Continued*
  Last days of the dog-men
    Stories from the Blue Moon Cafe II; edited
      by Sonny Brewer
  Water dog god
    The Best American mystery stories, 2000; ed-
      ited and with an introduction by Donald E.
      Westlake
Watson, Ian
  Ahead!
    Watson, I. The great escape
  The amber room
    Watson, I. The great escape
  The boy who lost an hour, the girl who lost her
    life
    Watson, I. The great escape
  Caucus winter
    Watson, I. The great escape
  The China cottage
    Watson, I. The great escape
  A day without Dad
    Watson, I. The great escape
  The descent
    Watson, I. The great escape
  Early, in the evening
    Watson, I. The great escape
  Ferryman
    Watson, I. The great escape
  The great escape
    Watson, I. The great escape
  The last beast out of the box
    Watson, I. The great escape
  My vampire cake
    Watson, I. The great escape
  Nanunculus
    Watson, I. The great escape
  The shape of murder
    Watson, I. The great escape
  Such dedication
    Watson, I. The great escape
  Three-legged dog
    Watson, I. The great escape
  Tulips from Amsterdam
    Watson, I. The great escape
  What actually happened in Docklands
    Watson, I. The great escape
  When thought-mail failed
    Watson, I. The great escape
Watson-Aifah, Jené
  Escrava Anastácia Speaks
    Meridians v4 no1 p228-31 2003
Watson and the shark. Murray, J.
Watt-Evans, Lawrence
  Upstairs
    Best new horror 10; edited and with an intro-
      duction by Stephen Jones
Watterson, Kathryn
  He Did It for Morgan
    TriQuarterly no113 p148-55 Summ 2002
Watts, Leander
    See also Metzger, Th.
Waugh, Evelyn
  Antony, who sought things that were lost
    Waugh, E. The complete stories of Evelyn
      Waugh
  The balance
    Waugh, E. The complete stories of Evelyn
      Waugh

  Basil Seal rides again
    Waugh, E. The complete stories of Evelyn
      Waugh
  Bella Fleace gave a party
    Waugh, E. The complete stories of Evelyn
      Waugh
  By special request
    Waugh, E. The complete stories of Evelyn
      Waugh
  Charles Ryder's schooldays
    Waugh, E. The complete stories of Evelyn
      Waugh
  Compassion
    Waugh, E. The complete stories of Evelyn
      Waugh
  Conspiracy to murder
    Waugh, E. The complete stories of Evelyn
      Waugh
  Cruise
    Waugh, E. The complete stories of Evelyn
      Waugh
  The curse of the horse race
    Waugh, E. The complete stories of Evelyn
      Waugh
  Edward of unique achievement
    Waugh, E. The complete stories of Evelyn
      Waugh
  An Englishman's home
    Waugh, E. The complete stories of Evelyn
      Waugh
  Essay
    Waugh, E. The complete stories of Evelyn
      Waugh
  Excursion in reality
    Waugh, E. The complete stories of Evelyn
      Waugh
  Fidon's confetion
    Waugh, E. The complete stories of Evelyn
      Waugh
  Fragment of a novel
    Waugh, E. The complete stories of Evelyn
      Waugh
  Fragments: they dine with the past
    Waugh, E. The complete stories of Evelyn
      Waugh
  The house: an anti-climax
    Waugh, E. The complete stories of Evelyn
      Waugh
  A house of gentlefolks
    Waugh, E. The complete stories of Evelyn
      Waugh
  Incident in Azania
    Waugh, E. The complete stories of Evelyn
      Waugh
  Love among the ruins
    Waugh, E. The complete stories of Evelyn
      Waugh
  Love in the slump
    Waugh, E. The complete stories of Evelyn
      Waugh
  Lucy Simmonds
    Waugh, E. The complete stories of Evelyn
      Waugh
  The man who liked Dickens
    Waugh, E. The complete stories of Evelyn
      Waugh
  The manager of "The Kremlin"
    Waugh, E. The complete stories of Evelyn
      Waugh

Waugh, Evelyn—*Continued*

Mr. Loveday's little outing
  Waugh, E. The complete stories of Evelyn Waugh

Multa Pecunia
  Waugh, E. The complete stories of Evelyn Waugh

My father's house
  Waugh, E. The complete stories of Evelyn Waugh

The national game
  Waugh, E. The complete stories of Evelyn Waugh

On guard
  Waugh, E. The complete stories of Evelyn Waugh

Out of depth
  Waugh, E. The complete stories of Evelyn Waugh

Period piece
  Waugh, E. The complete stories of Evelyn Waugh

Portrait of young man with career
  Waugh, E. The complete stories of Evelyn Waugh

Scott-King's modern Europe
  Waugh, E. The complete stories of Evelyn Waugh

The sympathetic passenger
  Waugh, E. The complete stories of Evelyn Waugh

Tactical exercise
  Waugh, E. The complete stories of Evelyn Waugh

Too much tolerance
  Waugh, E. The complete stories of Evelyn Waugh

Unacademic exercise: a nature story
  Waugh, E. The complete stories of Evelyn Waugh

Winner takes all
  Waugh, E. The complete stories of Evelyn Waugh

Wave. Holman, J.

The **wave**: a novella. Gussoff, C.

Wax. Shepard, J.

Waxing. Goldner, B.

The **Way** a World Can Change. Gloeggler, T.

Way back when in the now before now. Nissen, T.

The **way** he knew it. Zind, Rick

The **way** home. Mathews, H.

The **way** it felt to be falling. Edwards, K.

The **way** it used to be. Gorman, E.

The **way** love works. Waters, M. Y.

The **way** of all ghosts. Bear, G.

The **way** of cross and dragon. Martin, G. R. R.

The **way** of the transgressor. Coates, G. S.

A **way** of thinking. Sturgeon, T.

The **way** people run. Tilghman, C.

The **way** we live now. Sontag, S.

The **way** you do it. Cusk, R.

The **way** you see horses. Ortiz, S. J.

Wayfaring at Waverly in Silver Lake. McCourt, J.

Wayman, Tom
  The freelance demolitionist
    The Hudson Review v53 no4 p554-76 Wint 2001

WAYNE, JOHN, 1907-1979
About

Alexie, S. Dear John Wayne

Wayne's hero (An English story). Škvorecký, J.

Ways of the World. Howard, R.

The **ways** of vengeance. DeRosso, H. A.

We are cartographers. Daniel, S.

We are the dead. Kuttner, H.

We ate the chef. Fischer, T.

We Build Churches, Inc. Burke, J. L.

We call it blog. Lisick, B.

"**We** Got Married". Liksom, R.

We Have a Pope!. Buckley, C.

We have met the enemy. Edghill, R.

We huv tae fight tae perty. Welsh, I.

We, in some strange power's employ, move on a rigorous line. Delany, S. R.

We kill a bicycle. Vukcevich, R.

We love Lydia love. Denton, B.

We often think of Lenin at the clothespin factory. Davenport, G.

We were spending the evening at Princess D.'s dacha. Pushkin, A. S.

We were worried about you. Oates, J. C.

We who live apart. Connor, J.

We who walk through walls. Dyson, J.

We will sleep in one nest. Brkic, C. A.

We words. Touré

The **Weak** Sister. Osborn, C.

The **weakling**. Aldrich, B. S.

WEALTH
    See also Capitalists and financiers; Millionaires

  Archer, J. Too many coincidences
  Auchincloss, L. The heiress
  Bart, P. Power play
  Bausch, R. Riches
  Bowles, P. In absentia
  Byatt, A. S. Baglady
  Chekhov, A. P. A doctor's visit
  Chopin, K. Miss McEnders
  Corin, L. Rich people
  Dann, J. The diamond pit
  Fitzgerald, F. S. The cut-glass bowl
  Fitzgerald, F. S. The diamond as big as the Ritz
  Gay, W. Homecoming
  Hoffman, W. Humility
  Iwaszkiewicz, J. The mill on the River Utrata
  Johnson, D. Clay's thinking
  Kees, W. The Purcells
  Lessing, D. M. Victoria and the Staveneys
  Miller, R. Nancy
  Nesbitt, M. The ones who may kill you in the morning
  Oliver, C. King of the hill
  Pak, W.-S. She knows, I know, and heaven knows
  Rawley, D. The bible of insects
  Robison, M. Smoke
  Singer, I. B. The building project
  Singer, I. B. A party in Miami Beach
  Vonnegut, K. Custom-made bride
  Vonnegut, K. Hal Irwin's magic lamp
  Vonnegut, K. The package
  Westlake, D. E. Love in the lean years
  Wharton, E. The twilight of the God

The **weapon** shop. Van Vogt, A. E.

WEAPONS See Arms and armor; Nuclear weapons

The **wearing** of the green. DuBois, B.

A **weary** man's utopia. Borges, J. L.

WEATHER

    See also Storms

    Aldrich, B. S. The man who caught the weather

    Bradbury, R. The cold wind and the warm

    Connor, J. The year of no weather

Weather. Anderson, D.

The **weather** outside is sunny and bright. Homes, A. M.

Weathers, Steve

    Following Leuda

        American short fiction, vol. 8, no 29-32

Weathers, Winston

    Der Tod in Venedig

        The Literary Review (Madison, N.J.) v42 no3 p451-53 Spr 1999

Weaver, Gordon

    And what should I do in Illyria?

        Weaver, G. Last stands; stories; by Gordon Weaver

    A dialogue

        Weaver, G. Last stands; stories; by Gordon Weaver

    Dirt

        Weaver, G. Last stands; stories; by Gordon Weaver

    The divorced men's mall walkers club

        Weaver, G. Long odds; stories

    Ed Stein, Ed Stein, speak to me!

        Weaver, G. Long odds; stories

    Elder's revenge

        Weaver, G. Last stands; stories; by Gordon Weaver

    The emancipation of hoytie rademacher

        Weaver, G. Last stands; stories; by Gordon Weaver

    Gilded Quill: the story of Jones

        Weaver, G. Long odds; stories

    Imagining the structure of free space on Pioneer Road

        Weaver, G. Long odds; stories

    Learst's last stand

        Weaver, G. Last stands; stories; by Gordon Weaver

    Long odds

        Weaver, G. Long odds; stories

    Looking for the lost Eden

        Weaver, G. Last stands; stories; by Gordon Weaver

    Mannequin

        Weaver, G. Long odds; stories

    On watch for Big Red

        Weaver, G. Long odds; stories

    Psychic friends

        Weaver, G. Last stands; stories; by Gordon Weaver

    Q: Questing

        The Student body; short stories about college students and professors; edited by John McNally

        Weaver, G. Long odds; stories

    Solidarity forever!

        Weaver, G. Long odds; stories

    Viewed from Lanta & Wally's

        Weaver, G. Long odds; stories

    The white elephant

        Weaver, G. Last stands; stories; by Gordon Weaver

Without spot or wrinkle

    Weaver, G. Long odds; stories

The **web** of circumstance. Chesnutt, C. W.

The **web** of Möbius. Galef, D.

Webb, Don

    Diary from an empty studio

        Witpunk; edited by Claude Lalumière and Marty Halpern

Webb, Janeen

    Blake's angel

        Gathering the bones; original stories from the world's masters of horror; edited by Dennis Etchison, Ramsey Campbell and Jack Dann

Webb, Don

    Metamorphosis no. 5

        Graham, D. Lone Star literature; from the Red River to the Rio Grande; edited by Don Graham

Weber, David

    Changer of worlds

        Weber, D. Changer of worlds

    From the highlands

        Weber, D. Changer of worlds

    The hard way home

        Worlds of Honor

    Ms. Midshipwoman Harrington

        Weber, D. Changer of worlds

    Nightfall

        Weber, D. Changer of worlds

    What price dreams?

        Worlds of Honor

Weber, Katharine

    Mr. Antler's princess dust

        Southwest Review v87 no1 p126-32 2002

Webster, Barry

    A piano shudders

        Dalhousie Review v79 no2 p245-55 Summ 1999

WEBSTER, DANIEL, 1782-1852

    About

    Benét, S. V. The Devil and Daniel Webster

Webster. Bear, G.

The **wedding**. Chaudhuri, A.

The **wedding**. Garcia, L. G.

The **wedding** album. Marusek, D.

WEDDING ANNIVERSARIES

    Aldrich, B. S. Will the romance be the same?

    Vallbona, R. d. Penelope's silver wedding anniversary

The **wedding** at Esperanza. Taylor, L.

The **wedding** cake in the middle of the road. Cherry, K.

Wedding dance. Iribarne, M.

The **wedding** Dress. Smart, A.

A **wedding** gift. Foote, J. T.

The **wedding** gig. King, S.

The **Wedding** Gowns. McGarry, J.

The **wedding** jester. Stern, S.

The **wedding** knell. Hawthorne, N.

Wedding night. Hawkins, T.

Wedding night. Igloria, L. A.

The **wedding** present. Gaiman, N.

Wedding symphony. Jackson, G.

WEDDINGS

    Alcott, L. M. A golden wedding: and what came of it

    Babel´, I. The King

    Barker, N. Water marks

WEDDINGS—*Continued*

Breen, J. L. It's hard to dance with the devil on your back (with Rita A. Breen)
Canty, K. Honeymoon
Caponegro, M. The father's blessing
Carlson, R. A kind of flying
Chekhov, A. P. The cook's wedding
Doran, M. M. Wedding at the Gormay Cafe
Garcia, L. G. The wedding
Geng, V. Partners
Gilchrist, E. Revenge
Guerrero, L. Return of the spirit
Hawthorne, N. The wedding knell
Iribarne, M. Wedding dance
Jackson, G. Wedding symphony
Jaime-Becerra, M. Lopez Trucking Incorporated
Julavits, H. Marry the one who gets there first
Krouse, E. My weddings
Leegant, J. Henny's wedding
Lieu, J. Troubles
Means, D. The interruption
Moody, R. The Mansion on the Hill
Orner, P. The Moraine on the lake
Rowell, J. The mother-of-the-groom and I
Shepard, J. Blinkers
Singer, I. B. A wedding in Brownsville
Singer, I. B. Yochna and Schmelke
Stern, S. The wedding jester
Thurm, M. Ancient history
Trevor, W. The telephone game
Viswanathan, L. Cool wedding
Walker, A. Roselily
Weinstein, L. The Llipkin -Wexler affair
Wharton, E. The last asset
Whittenberg, A. Bloom of Zenobia
Wilson, R., Jr. A day of splendid omens
Zhou Libo. The family on the other side of the mountain

Wedler, Rainer
Fragment
  Prairie Schooner v73 no3 p72-76 Fall 1999
Wednesday afternoon, mid-October. Ritchie, E.
Wednesday night, Thursday morning. Mead, H.
Wednesday's child. Tenn, W.
Weeds. DeMarinis, R.
Weeds. Skinner, J.
A **weekend** to remember. Archer, J.
The **weekend** travelers. Spencer, E.
The **weekender**. Deaver, J.
Weems, Richard K.
Anything He Wants
  Gettysburg Review v16 no1 p89-96 Spr 2003
The **weeping** masks. Lowder, J.
Weeping walls. Di Filippo, P.
Weesner, Ted, Jr.
Tuscaloosa
  Ploughshares v29 no4 p192-205 Wint 2003/2004
Wegner, Hart
The blue line
  Wegner, H. Off Paradise; stories
Cockshut light
  Wegner, H. Off Paradise; stories
Dogs of autumn
  Wegner, H. Off Paradise; stories
Following the nun
  Wegner, H. Off Paradise; stories
Off Paradise
  Wegner, H. Off Paradise; stories

On the road to Szkaradowo
  Wegner, H. Off Paradise; stories
The pilots of the rose trellis
  Wegner, H. Off Paradise; stories
A ransom for Tedek
  Wegner, H. Off Paradise; stories
The stone girl
  Wegner, H. Off Paradise; stories
Wei, Jonathan
Mind of Winter
  The North American Review v288 no3/4 p41-5 My/Ag 2003
Weidman, Jerome
Good man, bad man
  The Best American mystery stories of the century; Tony Hillerman, editor; with an introduction by Tony Hillerman
Weighing of the heart. Fleming, J. H.
The **weight**. Bausch, R.
Weight. Wideman, J. E.
WEIGHT LIFTING
Bezmozgis, D. The second strongest man
Jenkins, G. Private places
Johnson, A. The eighth sea
The **weight** of obligation. Beach, R.
WEIGHTLESSNESS
Heinlein, R. A. Waldo
Weihe, Edwin
All clear
  Weihe, E. Another life & other stories
Another life
  Weihe, E. Another life & other stories
Girl in the coat
  Weihe, E. Another life & other stories
Green Lake
  Weihe, E. Another life & other stories
Her birthday suit
  Weihe, E. Another life & other stories
Love spots
  Weihe, E. Another life & other stories
The morning room
  Weihe, E. Another life & other stories
Off season
  Weihe, E. Another life & other stories
Weinbaum, Stanley G.
The adaptive ultimate
  Science-fiction classics; the stories that morphed into movies; compiled by Forrest J. Ackerman
A Martian odyssey
  The Science fiction hall of fame: volume one, 1929-1964; the greatest science fiction stories of all time chosen by the members of the Science Fiction Writers of America; edited by Robert Silverberg
Weinberg, Robert
The apocalypse quatrain
  Weinberg, R. Dial your dreams & other nightmares
Chant
  Weinberg, R. Dial your dreams & other nightmares
Dial your dreams
  Weinberg, R. Dial your dreams & other nightmares
Elevator girls
  Weinberg, R. Dial your dreams & other nightmares

Weinberg, Robert—*Continued*
Endure the night
  Weinberg, R. Dial your dreams & other
    nightmares
The midnight el
  Weinberg, R. Dial your dreams & other
    nightmares
Riverworld roulette
  Weinberg, R. Dial your dreams & other
    nightmares
Ro Erg
  Speaking of lust; stories of forbidden desire;
    edited by Lawrence Block
  Weinberg, R. Dial your dreams & other
    nightmares
Seven drops of blood
  Weinberg, R. Dial your dreams & other
    nightmares
The silent majority
  Weinberg, R. Dial your dreams & other
    nightmares
Terror by night
  Weinberg, R. Dial your dreams & other
    nightmares
Three steps back
  Weinberg, R. Dial your dreams & other
    nightmares
Unfinished business
  Weinberg, R. Dial your dreams & other
    nightmares
Wolf watch
  Weinberg, R. Dial your dreams & other
    nightmares
Weiner, Cynthia
Boyfriends
  Ploughshares v30 no1 p158-74 Spr 2004
Weiner, Shelley
Eating Vic
  Valentine's Day: women against men; stories
    of revenge; introduction by Alice Thomas
Weingarten, Gene
Roger and Me
  New Letters v68 no3/4 p223-5 Spr/Summ
    2002
Weingarten, Roger
Aura, cry, fall, and fit
  Ghost writing; haunted tales by contemporary
    writers; edited by Roger Weingarten
Weinreb, Michael
All I know about it
  Weinreb, M. Girl boy etc.
Bear claws the size of her head
  Weinreb, M. Girl boy etc.
The fox hunters
  Weinreb, M. Girl boy etc.
Girl boy etc.
  Weinreb, M. Girl boy etc.
L.A., baby
  Weinreb, M. Girl boy etc.
The last American virgin
  Weinreb, M. Girl boy etc.
Old men on spring break
  Weinreb, M. Girl boy etc.
Pictures of my family
  Weinreb, M. Girl boy etc.
Radio radio
  Weinreb, M. Girl boy etc.
Satisfaction
  Weinreb, M. Girl boy etc.

What I would tell her
  Weinreb, M. Girl boy etc.
Weinstein, Louis
The Llipkin -Wexler affair
  Browning, A. Murder is no mitzvah; edited
    by Abigail Browning
Weinstein, Rafael
Night Train to Napa
  South Carolina Review v35 no2 p91-8 Spr
    2003
Weird row. Cady, J.
The **weird** wines of Naxas Niss. Lumley, B.
Weisberg, Joseph
10th grade
  Doubletake v7 no4 p54-7 Fall 2001
Weiss, Erich *See* Houdini, Harry, 1874-1926
Weiss, Ernst
Heart Suture
  Parnassus: Poetry in Review v27 no1/2 p54-
    66 2003
Weiss, Bernice F.
Where does a golem go?
  Browning, A. Murder is no mitzvah; edited
    by Abigail Browning
Weissman, Benjamin
Of two minds
  Bomb no79 p88-9 Spr 2002
Welch, Nancy
Mental
  Prairie Schooner v73 no2 p148-61 Summ
    1999
The **welcome**. Morgan, R.
Welcome. Smith, M. M.
Welcome home, Hal!. Aldrich, B. S.
Welcomeland. Campbell, R.
Welcoming committee. Harrison, H.
Welcoming Moon. Wuori, G. K.
Welding with children. Gautreaux, T.
Weldon, Fay
Come on, everyone!
  Weldon, F. A hard time to be a father
The ghost of potlatch past
  Weldon, F. A hard time to be a father
A great antipodean scandal
  Weldon, F. A hard time to be a father
GUP—or, Falling in love in Helsinki
  Weldon, F. A hard time to be a father
A hard time to be a father
  Weldon, F. A hard time to be a father
Inside the whale; or, I don't know but I've been
    told
  Weldon, F. A hard time to be a father
Inspector remorse
  Weldon, F. A hard time to be a father
Leda and the swan
  Valentine's Day: women against men; stories
    of revenge; introduction by Alice Thomas
A libation of blood
  Weldon, F. A hard time to be a father
Move out: move on
  Weldon, F. A hard time to be a father
My mother said
  Weldon, F. A hard time to be a father
New Year's Day
  Weldon, F. A hard time to be a father
Noisy into the night
  Weldon, F. A hard time to be a father
Once in love in Oslo
  Weldon, F. A hard time to be a father

Weldon, Fay—*Continued*
  Percentage trust
    Weldon, F. A hard time to be a father
  Pyroclastic flow
    Weldon, F. A hard time to be a father
  Spirits fly south
    Weldon, F. A hard time to be a father
  Stasi
    Weldon, F. A hard time to be a father
  What the papers say
    Weldon, F. A hard time to be a father
WELK, LAWRENCE, 1903-1992
        About
  Rowell, J. The music of your life
The **well**. Kinsella, J.
We'll get to now later. Saunders, G.
A **well-imagined** life. Gasco, E.
A **well-respected** man. Coel, M.
We'll talk later. Shepard, J.
A **well-tempered** heart. Earle, S.
Well well well. Parker, G.
Well, what do you have to say for yourself? Brad-
    bury, R.
Wellen, Edward
  The adventure of the blind alley
    Wellen, E. Perps; a short story collection
  Born victims
    Wellen, E. Perps; a short story collection
  Death and taxes
    Wellen, E. Perps; a short story collection
  Devil's pass
    Wellen, E. Perps; a short story collection
  Experiment
    Wellen, E. Perps; a short story collection
  Fair exchange
    Wellen, E. Perps; a short story collection
  Final acquittal
    Wellen, E. Perps; a short story collection
  From parts unknown
    Wellen, E. Perps; a short story collection
  Hangover
    Wellen, E. Perps; a short story collection
  Inside evidence
    Wellen, E. Perps; a short story collection
  It ain't hay
    Wellen, E. Perps; a short story collection
  The last mile
    Wellen, E. Perps; a short story collection
  Mrs. Grady's swan song
    Wellen, E. Perps; a short story collection
  The perfect rotter
    Wellen, E. Perps; a short story collection
  The plan of the snake
    Wellen, E. Perps; a short story collection
  Play death
    Wellen, E. Perps; a short story collection
  The postmaster & the slave
    Wellen, E. Perps; a short story collection
  Rubout
    Wellen, E. Perps; a short story collection
  Sanity clause
    Wellen, E. Perps; a short story collection
  Spur the nightmare
    Wellen, E. Perps; a short story collection
  State of the art
    Wellen, E. Perps; a short story collection
  The taste of revenge
    Wellen, E. Perps; a short story collection

  Trouble light
    Wellen, E. Perps; a short story collection
  Waswolf
    Wellen, E. Perps; a short story collection
  The whisper of gold
    Wellen, E. Perps; a short story collection
  A wreath for justice
    Wellen, E. Perps; a short story collection
WELLES, ORSON, 1915-1985
        About
  Haskell, J. Crimes at midnight
  Kessel, J. It's all true
Wellman, Manly Wade
  O ugly bird!
    The American fantasy tradition; edited by Bri-
      an M. Thomsen
  The valley was still
    The American fantasy tradition; edited by Bri-
      an M. Thomsen
The **Wellman** twins. Robison, M.
Wells, Catherine
  'Bassador
    Redshift; extreme visions of speculative fic-
      tion; edited by Al Sarrantonio
Wells, H. G. (Herbert George)
  The country of the blind
    The 13 best horror stories of all time; edited
      by Leslie Pockell
WELLS, H. G. (HERBERT GEORGE), 1866-
  1946
        About
  Kessel, J. Buffalo
Wells, Herbert George *See* Wells, H. G. (Herbert
    George), 1866-1946
Wells, Kellie
  A. wonderland
    Wells, K. Compression scars; stories
  Blue skin
    Wells, K. Compression scars; stories
  Cassandra mouth
    Wells, K. Compression scars; stories
  Compression scars
    Wells, K. Compression scars; stories
  Godlight
    Wells, K. Compression scars; stories
  Hallie out of this world
    Prairie Schooner v73 no3 p119-32 Fall 1999
    Wells, K. Compression scars; stories
  My guardian, Claire
    Wells, K. Compression scars; stories
  Secession, XX
    The Kenyon Review ns24 no2 p45-64 Spr
      2002
    Wells, K. Compression scars; stories
  Sherman and the swan
    Wells, K. Compression scars; stories
  Star-dogged moon
    Gettysburg Review v15 no1 p61-74 Spr 2002
    Wells, K. Compression scars; stories
  Swallowing angels whole
    Wells, K. Compression scars; stories
WELLS
  Parker, G. Well well well
Welsch, Gabriel
  Nguyen Van Thieu Is Dead at 78
    The Georgia Review v57 no4 p826-38 Wint
      2003

Welsh, Irvine
Catholic guilt (you know you love it)
    Speaking with the angel; original stories; edited by Nick Hornby
Trainspotting [excerpt]
    The Vintage book of contemporary Scottish fiction; edited and with an introduction by Peter Kravitz
We huv tae fight tae perty
    Harper's v302 no1813 p29-32 Je 2001
WELSH
United States
DeLancey, K. The Welsh engineer
The **Welsh** engineer. DeLancey, K.
Welshons, Robert
Mr. Connaughton (From the Song by Ralph McTell)
    The North American Review v288 no6 p43-9 N/D 2003
Welty, Eudora
The doll
    The Georgia Review v53 no1 p25-30 Spr 1999
The hitch-hikers
    The Best American short stories of the century; John Updike, editor, Katrina Kenison, coeditor; with an introduction by John Updike
WENCESLAUS, DUKE OF BOHEMIA, 907?-935?
About
Owen, M. G. The snows of Saint Stephen
The **wench** is dead. Brown, F.
Wendling, Linda
Inappropriate babies
    New stories from the South: the year's best, 2001; edited by Shannon Ravenel; with a preface by Lee Smith
Wentworth, K. D.
A taste of song
    Such a pretty face; edited by Lee Martindale
The **wer-trout**. Proulx, A.
We're all chicken here. Kuhr, J.
"**We're** all in this alone". Bishop, M. and DiFilippo, P.
We're coming through the window. Malzberg, B. N.
We're still Keeneys. Troy, M.
The **were-wolf**. Housman, C.
Were-wrath. Norton, A.
The **werewolf**. Field, E.
WEREWOLVES
Banister, M. M. Eena
Biss, G. The door of the unreal
Blackwood, A. Running wolf
Crider, B. It happened at grandmother's house
Crider, B. The nighttime is the right time
De Lint, C. Trading hearts at the Half Kaffe Cafe
Derleth, A. W. and Schorer, M. The woman at Loon Point
Elliott, B. Wolves don't cry
Field, E. The werewolf
Fleming, P. The kill
Fleming, R. Life after bas
Housman, C. The were-wolf
King, S. February, cycle of the werewolf
Kipling, R. The mark of the beast
Leiber, F. The hound

Marie. The lay of the were-wolf
Maupassant, G. d. The wolf
Mayo, W. What rough beasts
Ovid. Lycaon's punishment
Palwick, S. Gestella
Quinn, S. The phantom farmhouse
Quinn, S. The thing in the fog
Saki. Gabriel-Ernest
Saki. The she-wolf
Spariosu, M. and Benedek, D. The bitang
Stableford, B. M. The werewolves of London
Stoker, B. Dracula's guest
Weinberg, R. Wolf watch
Wellen, E. Waswolf
Yolen, J. Green messiah
Werewolves in their youth. Chabon, M.
The **werewolves** of London. Stableford, B. M.
Werner, Irving
Elsa
    The Massachusetts Review v45 no1 p130-42 Spr 2004
Werner, Jürgen
The Hunter's Freedom
    Southern Humanities Review v36 no3 p261-74 Summ 2002
Werve, Scott
If I were lemon pie
    Virgin fiction 2
WERWOLVES *See* Werewolves
Wes Amerigo's Giant Fear. Schickler, D.
Wesley, Valerie Wilson
Afraid of the dark
    The Bluelight corner; black women writing on passion, sex, and romantic love; edited by Rosemarie Robotham
Wesolowska, Monica
The view
    Best new American voices 2000; guest editor Tobias Wolff; series editors John Kulka and Natalie Danford
West, Dorothy
My baby . . .
    The Best American short stories 2001; selected from U.S. and Canadian magazines by Barbara Kingsolver with Katrina Kenison; with an introduction by Barbara Kingsolver
West, Kathleene
Angkor Wat
    Prairie Schooner v73 no1 p165-66 Spr 1999
Identity crisis
    Prairie Schooner v73 no1 p167 Spr 1999
The terrace of the leper king
    Prairie Schooner v73 no1 p168 Spr 1999
West, Michelle
Birthnight
    Magical beginnings; edited by Steven H. Silver and Martin H. Greenberg
Diamonds
    West, M. Speaking with angels; stories
Elegy
    West, M. Speaking with angels; stories
Faces made of clay
    Mardi Gras madness; tales of terror and mayhem in New Orleans; edited by Martin H. Greenberg and Russell Davis
Four attempts at a letter
    West, M. Speaking with angels; stories
Ghostwood
    West, M. Speaking with angels; stories

West, Michelle—*Continued*
  Gifted
    West, M. Speaking with angels; stories
  Hunger
    West, M. Speaking with angels; stories
  The law of man
    West, M. Speaking with angels; stories
  The nightingale
    Once upon a galaxy; edited by Will [sic]
      McCarthy, Martin H. Greenberg, and John
      Helfers
  Return of the king
    West, M. Speaking with angels; stories
  The stolen child
    Greenberg, M. H. Faerie tales
  Sunrise
    West, M. Speaking with angels; stories
  To speak with angels
    West, M. Speaking with angels; stories
  Turn of the card
    West, M. Speaking with angels; stories
  Under the skin
    West, M. Speaking with angels; stories
  Winter
    West, M. Speaking with angels; stories
West, Owen. *See* Koontz, Dean R. (Dean Ray),
    1945-
West, Paul
  To Go
    Agni no57 p206-21 2003
WEST (U.S.) *See* Western States
WEST AFRICA
  Drew, E. Mad dogs
  Ekstrom, L. S. On Sunday there might be Amer-
    icans
  Hunter, F. The barking dog
  Sumner, M. The guide
WEST INDIAN DIALECT *See* Dialect stories—
    West Indian
WEST INDIANS
                    Canada
  Hopkinson, N. And the lillies-them a-blow
                    England
  Melville, P. Mrs. Da Silva's carnival
  Selvon, S. The cricket match
                  United States
  Greer, R. O. Choosing sides
  Kincaid, J. Poor Visitor
WEST INDIES
    See also Trinidad and Tobago
  Chen, W. Trotters
  Kurlansky, M. The unclean
  Salkey, A. A proper Anno Domini feeling
  Updike, J. The doctor's wife
WEST INDIES REGION *See* Caribbean region
West Texas cowboys. Garcia, L. G.
WEST VIRGINIA
  Bailey, D. Quinn's way
  Coberly, L. M. The evidence of things not seen
  Oates, J. C. The vampire
West Wind. Lewis, T.
WESTCHESTER COUNTY (N.Y.) *See* New
    York (State)—Westchester County
The **western** film scam. See Nevins, F. M., Jr.
    Bagworms
Western music. Dinh, L.
The **western** paradise of Eddie Bin. Leong, R.
WESTERN STATES
  Adam, C. Porcupine

  Bausch, R. The man who knew Belle Starr
  Bellow, S. Leaving the yellow house
  Billman, J. Custer complex
  Billman, J. Indians
  Billman, J. Sugar City
  DeMarinis, R. Under the wheat
  Kittredge, W. Be careful what you want
  Ossana, D. White line fever
  Shepard, S. Great dream of heaven
  Winter, E. The planting
                    Farm life
    See Farm life—Western States
          Frontier and pioneer life
    See Frontier and pioneer life—Western
      States
WESTERN STORIES
    See also Adventure; Cowboys; Frontier
    and pioneer life—Western States; Ranch
    life; Western States
  Barrett, N., Jr. Winter on the Belle Fourche
  Bausch, R. The man who knew Belle Starr
  Blevins, W. Melodies the song dogs sing
  Boggs, J. D. A piano at Dead Man's Crossing
  Bonham, F. Burn him out
  Bower, B. M. The lamb of the Flying U
  Bradbury, R. The beautiful shave
  Brand, M. The bright face of danger
  Brand, M. Eagles over Crooked Creek
  Brand, M. The Golden Horus
  Brand, M. Through steel and stone
  Brand, M. Wine on the desert
  Braun, M. The stand
  Breen, J. L. The tarnished star
  Carroll, L. Traveling princess
  Castro, A.-T. The magic bullet theory
  Champlin, T. For the good of the service
  Cleary, R. Horse tradin'
  Coleman, J. C. Borderlands
  Coleman, J. C. Fiddle case
  Coleman, J. C. A pair to draw to
  Coleman, J. C. Sandhill cranes
  Coleman, J. C. Wild flower
  Coover, R. The sheriff goes to church
  Crider, B. The true facts about the death of Wes
    Hardin
  Crumley, J. Coming around the mountain
  Cunningham, E. Beginner's luck
  Cunningham, E. Blotting the triangle
  Cunningham, E. The hammer thumb
  Cunningham, E. The hermit of Tigerhead Butte
  Cunningham, E. The ranger way
  Cunningham, E. Spiderweb trail
  Cunningham, E. The trail of a fool
  Cunningham, E. Wanted—?
  Cunningham, E. Ware calls it a day
  Cunningham, J. M. The tin star
  Curry, P. S. Geranium house
  Cushman, D. Killers' country!
  Dawson, P. Night ride
  DeRosso, H. A. Bad blood
  DeRosso, H. A. Dark purpose
  DeRosso, H. A. Fear in the saddle
  DeRosso, H. A. The happy death
  DeRosso, H. A. Killer
  DeRosso, H. A. The return of the Arapaho Kid
  DeRosso, H. A. Riders of the shadowlands
  DeRosso, H. A. The ways of vengeance
  DeRosso, H. A. Witch
  Easton, R. O. First dawning

WESTERN STORIES—_Continued_

Easton, R. O. The happy man
Easton, R. O. The legend of Shorm
Easton, R. O. Quick and the cat
Easton, R. O. Wild challenge
Eckhardt, C. F. The fevers
Eickhoff, R. L. Dove's song
Estleman, L. D. Big Tim Magoon and the wild west
Estleman, L. D. Hell on the draw
Estleman, L. D. Thirteen coils
Farrell, C. Day of the dedication
Farrell, C. The day the outlaws came
Farrell, C. Desperate journey
Farrell, C. Five aces west
Farrell, C. He knew all about women
Farrell, C. Hung up at Parley's store
Farrell, C. The lady was a dude
Farrell, C. The pay-back race
Farrell, C. Picture bride
Farrell, C. Thorns for Johnny Spring
Flynn, T. T. Ghost guns for gold
Flynn, T. T. The gun wolf
Flynn, T. T. Half interest in hell
Flynn, T. T. Ride to glory
Flynn, T. T. So wild, so free
Forsyth, F. Whispering wind
Foster, A. D. Jackalope
Froh, R. I killed King Fisher
Froh, R. The two trail ride tricksters
Garfield, B. Peace officer
Giles, J. H. The gift
Gorman, E. Wolf moon
Graebner, J. E. The living land
Graebner, J. E. The whispering
Grey, Z. Tappan's burro
Grove, F. The Mystery Dogs
Gulick, B. The shaming of broken horn
Hamilton, D. The guns of William Longley
Hammett, D. The man who killed Dan Odams
Harte, B. How Santa Claus came to Simpson's Bar
Haseloff, C. H. Favorite son
Haycox, E. Stage to Lordsburg
Henry, W. Blizzard at Bald Rock
Henry, W. Comanche passport
Henry, W. ". . . Fired by the hand of Robert Ford"
Henry, W. Ghost wolf of Thunder Mountain
Henry, W. The great Northfield raid
Henry, W. Home place
Henry, W. The legend of Trooper Hennepin
Henry, W. Not wanted dead or alive
Henry, W. River of decision
Henry, W. Rough Riders of Arizona
Henry, W. The skinning of Black Coyote
Henry, W. The Streets of Laredo
Henry, W. The true friends
Henry, W. Wolf-Eye
Hodgson, K. Requiem for Rosebud
Hogan, R. A question of faith
House, R. Gabe and the doctor
Hunter, E. The killing at Triple Tree
Jakes, J. Manitow and Ironhand
Kelton, E. The burial of Letty Strayhorn
Kelton, E. Hewey and the wagon cook
Kittredge, W. The stone corral
Knight, A. W. Do the dark dance
L'Amour, L. Alkali Basin

L'Amour, L. Beyond the chaparral
L'Amour, L. Booty for a badman
L'Amour, L. The Cactus Kid
L'Amour, L. Caprock rancher
L'Amour, L. The courting of Griselda
L'Amour, L. The defense of Sentinel
L'Amour, L. Desperate men
L'Amour, L. Duffy's man
L'Amour, L. Dutchman's Flat
L'Amour, L. Elisha comes to Red Horse
L'Amour, L. End of the drive
L'Amour, L. From the listening hills
L'Amour, L. Get out of town
L'Amour, L. The gift of Cochise
L'Amour, L. Home is the hunter
L'Amour, L. A huband for Janey
L'Amour, L. Ironwood Station
L'Amour, L. Let the cards decide
L'Amour, L. Marshal of Canyon Gap
L'Amour, L. A mule for Santa Fe
L'Amour, L. Murphy plays his hand
L'Amour, L. A night at wagon camp
L'Amour, L. The one for the Mohave Kid
L'Amour, L. One for the pot
L'Amour, L. One night stand
L'Amour, L. Red butte showdown
L'Amour, L. Roundup in Texas
L'Amour, L. Rustler roundup
L'Amour, L. Secret of Silver Springs
L'Amour, L. The skull and the arrow
L'Amour, L. Stage to Willowspring
L'Amour, L. That man from the bitter sands
L'Amour, L. To make a stand
L'Amour, L. Trap of gold
L'Amour, L. War party
Le May, A. The battle of Gunsmoke Lode
Le May, A. The bells of San Juan
Le May, A. The braver thing
Le May, A. Eyes of doom
Le May, A. Gray rider
Le May, A. Lawman's debt
Le May, A. The little kid
Le May, A. The loan of a gun
Le May, A. Star on his heart
Le May, A. Sundown Corral
Le May, A. Tombstone's daughter
Le May, A. Trail driver's luck
Leonard, E. Hurrah for Capt. Early
Leonard, E. The Tonto woman
Long, E. Letters to the stove
Loomis, N. M. The coming home
Loomis, N. M. The man who had no thumbs
Loomis, N. M. Maverick factory
Loomis, N. M. The stick and the bearded lady
Mehor, E. L. Noah
Miller, R. The darkness of the deep
Morgan, D. Sepia sun
Muller, M. Sweet cactus wine
Newton, D. B. Black Dunstan's skull
Newton, D. B. Born to the brand
Newton, D. B. Breakheart Valley
Newton, D. B. Reach high, top hand!
Newton, D. B. The taming of Johnny Peters
Newton, D. B. Tinhorn trouble
Overholser, S. The last ride of Gunplay Maxwell
Overholser, W. D. The fence
Overholser, W. D. The leather slapper
Overholser, W. D. Rainbow rider

WESTERN STORIES—*Continued*

Pronzini, B. Fear
Pronzini, B. "Give-a-Damn" Jones
Rhodes, E. M. The trouble man
Sandifer, L. Betrayal
Savage, L., Jr. The hangman's segundo
Savage, L., Jr. His personal prisoner
Savage, L., Jr. King of the buckskin breed
Savage, L., Jr. The Lone Star camel corps
Savage, L., Jr. The sting of Señorita Scorpion
Schaefer, J. W. Sergeant Houck
Sherman, J. The snows of August
Short, L. Top hand
Smith, C. Thirty rangers
Smith, T. D. The big die-up
Swain, D. V. Gamblin' man
Swarthout, G. F. The attack on the mountain
Thompson, T. Gun job
Van Pelt, L. River watch
Wellen, E. The whisper of gold
Wheeler, R. S. The last days of Dominic Prince
Wheeler, R. S. The square reporter
Wister, O. Timberline
Zanjani, S. S. Dead game man

Westlake, Donald E.

Art & craft
  The World's finest mystery and crime stories, second annual collection; edited by Ed Gorman
Art and craft
  Westlake, D. E. Thieves' dozen
Ask a silly question
  Westlake, D. E. Thieves' dozen
Breathe deep
  Westlake, D. E. A good story and other stories
The burglar and the whatsit
  Westlake, D. E. A good story and other stories
Come again?
  The Mysterious Press anniversary anthology; celebrating 25 years; by the editors of Mysterious Press
  The World's finest mystery and crime stories, third annual collection; edited by Ed Gorman and Martin H. Greenberg
The curious facts preceding my execution
  Westlake, D. E. A good story and other stories
Devilishly
  Westlake, D. E. A good story and other stories
The Dortmunder workout
  Westlake, D. E. Thieves' dozen
Fugue for felons
  Westlake, D. E. Thieves' dozen
The girl of my dreams
  Flesh and blood; erotic tales of crime and passion; edited by Max Allan Collins and Jeff Gelb
Give till it hurts
  Westlake, D. E. Thieves' dozen
Good night, good night
  Westlake, D. E. A good story and other stories
A good story
  Westlake, D. E. A good story and other stories

Horse laugh
  Westlake, D. E. Thieves' dozen
Jumble sale
  Westlake, D. E. Thieves' dozen
Last-minute shopping
  Westlake, D. E. A good story and other stories
Love in the lean years
  Westlake, D. E. A good story and other stories
A midsummer daydream
  Westlake, D. E. Thieves' dozen
The mother of invention is worth a pound of cure
  Westlake, D. E. A good story and other stories
Nackles
  A yuletide universe; sixteen fantastical tales; edited by Brian M. Thomsen
Never shake a family tree
  A Century of noir; thirty-two classic crime stories; edited by Mickey Spillane and Max Allan Collins
  Westlake, D. E. A good story and other stories
Now what?
  Westlake, D. E. Thieves' dozen
  The World's finest mystery and crime stories, first annual collection; edited by Ed Gorman
One on a desert island
  Westlake, D. E. A good story and other stories
Party animal
  Westlake, D. E. Thieves' dozen
The risk profession
  Westlake, D. E. A good story and other stories
Sinner or saint
  Westlake, D. E. A good story and other stories
Skeeks
  Westlake, D. E. A good story and other stories
Sniff
  Westlake, D. E. A good story and other stories
The sweetest man in the world
  Westlake, D. E. A good story and other stories
Take it away
  Westlake, D. E. A good story and other stories
This is death
  A Century of great suspense stories; edited by Jeffery Deaver
Too many crooks
  The Best American mystery stories of the century; Tony Hillerman, editor; with an introduction by Tony Hillerman
  Master's choice [v1]; mystery stories by today's top writers and the masters who inspired them; edited by Lawrence Block
  Westlake, D. E. Thieves' dozen
You put on some weight
  Westlake, D. E. A good story and other stories

Westmacott, Mary, 1890-1976

See also Christie, Agatha, 1890-1976

Westmoreland, Timothy A.
Blood knot
  Westmoreland, T. A. Good as any; stories
The buried boy
  Westmoreland, T. A. Good as any; stories
Darkening of the world
  Best new American voices 2001; guest editor
    Charles Baxter; series editors John Kulka
    and Natalie Danford
  Westmoreland, T. A. Good as any; stories
Good as any
  Westmoreland, T. A. Good as any; stories
Near to gone
  Westmoreland, T. A. Good as any; stories
Strong at the broken places
  Westmoreland, T. A. Good as any; stories
They have numbered all my bones
  Westmoreland, T. A. Good as any; stories
Winter Island
  Westmoreland, T. A. Good as any; stories
Westward ho. Harrison, J.
Wet. Tester, W.
Wetering, Janwillem van de *See* Van de
  Wetering, Janwillem, 1931-
Wetherell, W. D.
Hills like white hills
  The Virginia Quarterly Review v75 no2 p248-
    66 Spr 1999
Hyannis boat
  Ghost writing; haunted tales by contemporary
    writers; edited by Roger Weingarten
Watching girls play
  Prize stories, 1999; The O. Henry awards; ed-
    ited and with an introduction by Larry
    Dark
Wexelblatt, Robert
Citizenship
  Michigan Quarterly Review v40 no2 p295-
    311 Spr 2001
Wexler, Merin
The closet
  Wexler, M. The porno girl and other stories
Don Giovanni in the tub
  Wexler, M. The porno girl and other stories
Helen of Alexandria
  Wexler, M. The porno girl and other stories
The Maginot Line
  Wexler, M. The porno girl and other stories
The nanny trap
  Wexler, M. The porno girl and other stories
Pink is for punks
  Wexler, M. The porno girl and other stories
The porno girl
  Wexler, M. The porno girl and other stories
Save yourself
  Wexler, M. The porno girl and other stories
Solomon and his wives
  Wexler, M. The porno girl and other stories
Waiting to discover electricity
  Wexler, M. The porno girl and other stories
What Marcia wanted
  Wexler, M. The porno girl and other stories
The **wey** it can turn. Kelman, J.
Whale on the beach. Karnezis, P.
Whalen, Tom
Professors
  The Student body; short stories about college
    students and professors; edited by John
    McNally

WHALES
Connor, J. The deposition of the prince of
  whales
Whan, Edgar
The women of Gustav Klimt
  The Ohio Review no64/65 p472-6 2001
Wharton, Edith
After Holbein
  Wharton, E. Collected stories, 1911-1937
Afterward
  Wharton, E. Collected stories, 1891-1910
All Souls'
  The Ultimate Halloween; edited by Marvin
    Kaye
  Wharton, E. Collected stories, 1911-1937
The angel at the grave
  Wharton, E. Collected stories, 1891-1910
Atrophy
  Wharton, E. Collected stories, 1911-1937
Autres temps . . .
  Wharton, E. Collected stories, 1911-1937
The best man
  Wharton, E. Collected stories, 1891-1910
Bewitched
  Wharton, E. Collected stories, 1911-1937
A bottle of Perrier
  Wharton, E. Collected stories, 1911-1937
Bunner Sisters
  Wharton, E. Collected stories, 1911-1937
Charm incorporated
  Wharton, E. Collected stories, 1911-1937
Coming home
  Wharton, E. Collected stories, 1911-1937
Confession
  Wharton, E. Collected stories, 1911-1937
A cup of cold water
  Wharton, E. Collected stories, 1891-1910
The daunt Diana
  Wharton, E. Collected stories, 1891-1910
The day of the funeral
  Wharton, E. Collected stories, 1911-1937
The debt
  Wharton, E. Collected stories, 1891-1910
The descent of man
  Wharton, E. Collected stories, 1891-1910
The duchess at prayer
  Wharton, E. Collected stories, 1891-1910
Duration
  Wharton, E. Collected stories, 1911-1937
Expiation
  Wharton, E. Collected stories, 1891-1910
The eyes
  Wharton, E. Collected stories, 1891-1910
Full circle
  Wharton, E. Collected stories, 1891-1910
The fulness of life
  Wharton, E. Collected stories, 1891-1910
A glimpse
  Wharton, E. Collected stories, 1911-1937
Her son
  Wharton, E. Collected stories, 1911-1937
The hermit and the wild woman
  Wharton, E. Collected stories, 1891-1910
His father's son
  Wharton, E. Collected stories, 1891-1910
The House of the Dead Hand
  Wharton, E. Collected stories, 1891-1910
The introducers
  Wharton, E. Collected stories, 1891-1910

Wharton, Edith—*Continued*
A journey
  Wharton, E. Collected stories, 1891-1910
Joy in the house
  Wharton, E. Collected stories, 1911-1937
Kerfol
  Wharton, E. Collected stories, 1911-1937
The lady's maid's bell
  Wharton, E. Collected stories, 1891-1910
The lamp of Psyche
  Wharton, E. Collected stories, 1891-1910
The last asset
  Wharton, E. Collected stories, 1891-1910
The legend
  Wharton, E. Collected stories, 1891-1910
The letters
  Wharton, E. Collected stories, 1891-1910
The long run
  Wharton, E. Collected stories, 1911-1937
The looking-glass
  Wharton, E. Collected stories, 1911-1937
The Marne
  Wharton, E. Collected stories, 1911-1937
Miss Mary Pask
  Wharton, E. Collected stories, 1911-1937
The mission of Jane
  Wharton, E. Collected stories, 1891-1910
The moving finger
  The American fantasy tradition; edited by Brian M. Thomsen
  Wharton, E. Collected stories, 1891-1910
Mr. Jones
  Wharton, E. Collected stories, 1911-1937
Mrs. Manstey's view
  Wharton, E. Collected stories, 1891-1910
The muse's tragedy
  Wharton, E. Collected stories, 1891-1910
The other two
  Wharton, E. Collected stories, 1891-1910
The pelican
  Wharton, E. Collected stories, 1891-1910
Pomegranate seed
  Nightshade: 20th century ghost stories; edited by Robert Phillips
  Wharton, E. Collected stories, 1911-1937
The pot-boiler
  Wharton, E. Collected stories, 1891-1910
The pretext
  Wharton, E. Collected stories, 1891-1910
The reckoning
  Wharton, E. Collected stories, 1891-1910
The recovery
  Wharton, E. Collected stories, 1891-1910
The Rembrandt
  Wharton, E. Collected stories, 1891-1910
Roman fever
  Wharton, E. Collected stories, 1911-1937
Sanctuary
  Wharton, E. Collected stories, 1891-1910
The seed of the faith
  Wharton, E. Collected stories, 1911-1937
Souls belated
  Wharton, E. Collected stories, 1891-1910
The touchstone
  Wharton, E. Collected stories, 1891-1910
The triumph of night
  Wharton, E. Collected stories, 1911-1937
The twilight of the God
  Wharton, E. Collected stories, 1891-1910

The valley of childish things, and other emblems
  Wharton, E. Collected stories, 1891-1910
Velvet ear-pads
  Wharton, E. Collected stories, 1911-1937
Writing a war story
  Wharton, E. Collected stories, 1911-1937
Xingu
  Wharton, E. Collected stories, 1911-1937
The young gentlemen
  Wharton, E. Collected stories, 1911-1937
Wharton, Thomas
The paper-thin garden
  The Year's best fantasy & horror, thirteenth annual collection; edited by Ellen Datlow and Terri Windling
What, Leslie
Clinging to a thread
  What, L. The sweet and sour tongue
The cost of doing business
  Nebula awards showcase 2001; the year's best SF and fantasy chosen by the science fiction and fantasy writers of America; edited by Robert Silverberg
A dark fire, burning from within
  What, L. The sweet and sour tongue
The emperor's new (and improved) clothes
  What, L. The sweet and sour tongue
How to feed your inner troll
  What, L. The sweet and sour tongue
Is that hard science; or, Are you just happy to see me
  Witpunk; edited by Claude Lalumière and Marty Halpern
The leap
  What, L. The sweet and sour tongue
The man I loved was an elf
  What, L. The sweet and sour tongue
Nothing without a name
  What, L. The sweet and sour tongue
The sacred society
  What, L. The sweet and sour tongue
Smelling of earth, dreaming of sky
  What, L. The sweet and sour tongue
The sweet and sour tongue
  What, L. The sweet and sour tongue
Those who know
  What, L. The sweet and sour tongue
Uncle Gorby and the baggage ghost
  What, L. The sweet and sour tongue
You are who you eat
  What, L. The sweet and sour tongue
You gotta believe
  What, L. The sweet and sour tongue
What About the Gun? Wickersham, J.
What actually happened in Docklands. Watson, I.
What are cicadas? Enright, A.
What Diantha did. Gilman, C. P.
What did you bring me? Svoboda, T.
What dreams may come. O'Neill, S.
What ever happened to Frank Snake Church? Alexie, S.
What every man knows. Swarthout, G. F.
What Flows Through Me That You Call Time. Mulligan, S.
What gives us voice. Looney, G.
What God hath joined. Aldrich, B. S.
What goes up. Clarke, A. C.
What good is you anyway? Nesbitt, M.

What happened. Budnitz, J.

What happened. Gibbons, R.

What happened during the ice storm. Heynen, J.

What happened to me on my holiday. Amis, M.

What he needed. Lippman, L.

What Home Can Mean. Winegardner, M.

What I cannot say to you. Jackson, V. F.

What I did for love. Schwartz, L. S.

What I did on my summer vacation. Nieson, M. S.

What I didn't see. Fowler, K. J.

What I eat. Morgan, C.

What I have noticed. Delaney, E. J.

What I hear. Robison, M.

What I hope for. Means, D.

What I Know Now. Ma, K.

What I learned from Clara. Kobin, J.

What I remember about the cold war. McManus, J.

What I remember now. Dodd, S. M.

What I saw from where I stood. Silver, M.

What I should have said. Haigh, J.

What I was thinking. Dulac, B.

What I wore. Krouse, E.

What if I had married you? Bordiuk, A.

What I'm doing in Missouri. Agee, J.

What Indians do. Ortiz, S. J.

What is remembered. Munro, A.

What is this thing called love? Straus, D.

What Is Visible. Elkins, K.

What it cost travelers. Phillips, D. R.

What It Is. Connor, J.

What it was like, seeing Chris. Eisenberg, D.

What It's Like to Be a Man. Almond, S.

What it's worth. Searle, E.

What kind of day did you have? Bellow, S.

What Kind of Furniture Would Jesus Pick? Proulx, A.

What kind of man. Davis, J. S.

What lasts. Silber, J.

What makes us human. Donaldson, S. R.

What makes you you. Cohen, R.

What Marcia wanted. Wexler, M.

What Mark couldn't see. Sosin, D.

What matters. Kilpatrick, N.

What Men Don't Say. Bingham, S.

What men love for. Phillips, D. R.

What more is there to see? See Davidson, A. The man who saw the elephant

What Mr. McGregor saw. Cannell, D.

What my boss is thinking. Grillo, A.

What price dreams? Weber, D.

What Remains. Bell, K.

What remains. Joseph, D.

What rough beasts. Mayo, W.

What safety is. Nissen, T.

What salmon know. Reid, E.

What she left me. Doenges, J.

What she was doing. Beeman, R.

What slide rules can't measure. Singleton, G.

What slips away. Tem, S. R.

What strange stars and skies. Davidson, A.

What the body knows. Divakaruni, C. B.

What the butler said. Marías, J.

What the cat dragged in. Dawson, J.

What the Heart Wants. Wald, A. H.

What the hell. DeLancey, K.

What the papers say. Weldon, F.

What the periwinkle remember. Douglas, M.

What the rabbi said to the priest. Hodgen, C.

What the sky delivers. MonPere, C.

What the sky sees. McGregor, J.

What the Thunder Said. Liddle, R.

What the water gave me. Rosenthal, K.

What then, my life? Oates, J. C.

What they did. Means, D.

What They Lost. Barnes, J.

What they teach you in engineering school. Arvin, N.

What to bring to an American picnic. Kalpakian, L.

What to name the baby. Cooper, B.

What to say when you talk to yourself. Coshnear, D.

What Was Meant to Be. Kettler, G.

What was washing around out there. Lord, N.

What we are up against. Phillips, D. R.

What We Cannot Speak about We Must Pass Over in Silence. Wideman, J. E.

What we did that summer. Koja, K. and Malzberg, B. N.

What We Do To Ourselves (1994). Pasulka, B. K.

What we forgot to tell Tina about boys. Hawley, E.

What we leave behind. Davidson, R.

What we really do here at NASA. Landis, G. A.

What we save. Orringer, J.

What we sell in the room today. Stevens, D.

What we wanted to do. Carlson, R.

What went wrong. Kleinman, L.

What went wrong. O'Brien, T.

What winter brings. Frank, J.

What would Buddha do? Furman, L.

What would you do? Mosley, W.

What would you like to see? Carver, R.

What You Do Next. Richard, N.

What you don't know. Kaminsky, S. M.

What you don't know can hurt you. Lutz, J.

What You Eat. Ehrenreich, B.

What you know. Davies, P. H.

What you left in the ditch. Bender, A.

What you make it. Smith, M. M.

What you owe me. Campbell, B. M.

What You Pawn I Will Redeem. Alexie, S.

What you usually find in novels. Chekhov, A. P.

What you're worth. Lisick, B.

Whatever happened to Nick Neptune? Lupoff, R. A.

Whatever he did, he did enough. Valeri, L.

What's in a name? Kalman, J.

What's in a name? Maron, M.

What's it take? Agee, J.

What's more. Hochman, A.

What's up there. Lisick, B.

Wheat, Carolyn

The adventure of the rara avis

Murder, my dear Watson; new tales of Sherlock Holmes; edited by Martin H. Greenberg, Jon Lellenberg, Daniel Stashower

A bus called pity

Mom, apple pie, and murder; edited by Nancy Pickard

Cousin Cora

Master's choice v2; mystery stories by today's top writers and the masters who inspired them; edited by Lawrence Block

Wheat, Carolyn—*Continued*
　Ghost Station
　　A moment on the edge; 100 years of crime stories by women; edited by Elizabeth George
　Oh, to be in England!
　　Malice domestic 9
　The only good judge
　　Women before the bench; edited by Carolyn Wheat; introduction by Linda Fairstein
　　The World's finest mystery and crime stories, third annual collection; edited by Ed Gorman and Martin H. Greenberg
　The princess and the pickle
　　White House pet detectives; tales of crime and mystery at the White House from a pet's-eye view; edited by Carole Nelson Douglas
　Show me the bones
　　The World's finest mystery and crime stories, first annual collection; edited by Ed Gorman
　The time of his life
　　Death cruise; crime stories on the open seas; edited by Lawrence Block
　What the dormouse said
　　A Hot and sultry night for crime; edited by Jeffery Deaver

WHEATLEY, PHILLIS, 1753-1784
About
Johnson, C. R. Poetry and politics
Wheeler, Gerald R.
　Signs
　　The North American Review v288 no1 p36-42 Ja/F 2003
Wheeler, Richard S.
　The last days of Dominic Prince
　　American West; twenty new stories from the Western Writers of America; edited with an introduction by Loren D. Estleman
　The square reporter
　　Westward; a fictional history of the American West : 28 original stories celebrating the 50th anniversary of the Western Writers of America; edited by Dale L. Walker
Wheeler, Wendy
　Skin so green and fine
　　The Year's best fantasy & horror, thirteenth annual collection; edited by Ellen Datlow and Terri Windling
Wheeler County. Earle, S.
The **wheels** on the bus go. Chapman, C. M.
When Amelia smiled. Gilliland, G.
When animals attack. Erian, A.
When, Before and After She Learned About Trudy. Lake, R.
When children count. Singleton, G.
When I was a witch. Gilman, C. P.
When I was mortal. Marías, J.
When I Woke Up This Morning, Everything I Had Was Gone. Boyle, T. C.
When lilacs last. Leslie, N.
When Love dies, Where Is It Buried? Gold, H.
When love gets worn. Phillips, D. R.
When Luz sings her solo. Browder, C.
When Mr. Pirzada came to dine. Lahiri, J.
When shadows come back. Kilpatrick, N.
When Shankland comes. Owens, A.
When she is old and I am famous. Orringer, J.

When Skeptics Die: A Story. Goldstein, Y.
When the Aliens Came. Goranson, A.
When the black shadows die. Howard, C.
When the blood came faster than the water. Lundquist, R.
When the children cry for meat. Loomis, N. M.
When the earth moves. Vogan, S.
When the nines roll over. Benioff, D.
When the people fell. Smith, C.
When the rain washes you clean you'll know. Nissen, T.
When the universe was young. Frank, J.
When the waker sleeps. Matheson, R.
When the women come out to dance. Leonard, E.
When this world is all on fire. Sanders, W.
When thought-mail failed. Watson, I.
When we were cool. Cobb, W.
When we were Wolves. Billman, J.
When women love men. Ferré, R.
When you see. Davis, J. S.
When your breath freezes. Dougherty, K.
Where all is emptiness there is room to move. Bradbury, R.
Where all things converge. Di Blasi, D.
Where all things perish. Lee, T.
Where are they now? Davies, R.
Where are you going, where have you been? Oates, J. C.
Where Beautiful Ladies Dance for You. Finn, P. M.
Where do people live who never die? Leong, R.
Where Europe begins. Tawada, Y.
Where I come from. Barbarese, J. T.
Where I work. Cummins, A.
Where I'm calling from. Carver, R.
Where is Harry Beal? Lutz, J.
Where it comes from, where it goes. Gaston, B.
Where It Is That Things Go. Keyes, J.
Where none is the number. Brkic, C. A.
Where o where. Ortiz, S. J.
Where she stays. Frym, G.
Where the boys are. Smith, J.
Where the dark ended. Tester, W.
Where the door is always open and the welcome mat is out. Highsmith, P.
Where the f stops. Enders, A.
Where the jackals howl. Oz, A.
Where the Long Grass Bends. Vaswani, N.
Where the summer ends. Wagner, K. E.
Where the water's deepest. Keegan, C.
Where they lived. Campbell, R.
Where we are now. Canin, E.
Where Were We. Eggers, D.
Where what gets into people comes from. Crone, M.
Where you find it. Galloway, J.
Where's Duncan? Harris, J. C.
Where's Fran Haynes? Coshnear, D.
Whetstone, Diane McKinney- *See* McKinney-Whetstone, Diane
While home. Robison, M.
While Pilar Tobillo sleeps. Luz Montes, A. M. d. l.
Whileaway. Bertles, J.
The **whimper** of whipped dogs. Ellison, H.
The **whimsied** world. Mason, N.
A **whirl** of witches. Kriseová, E.
The **whirligig** of time. Vinge, V.

WHISKEY
Berry, W. A half-pint of Old Darling
Stegner, W. E. Chip off the old block
Whisnant, Luke
Across from the Motoheads
This is where we live; short stories by 25 contemporary North Carolina writers; edited by Michael McFee
Whisper. Vukcevich, R.
The **whisper** of disks. Meaney, J.
The **whisper** of gold. Wellen, E.
The **whisperer**. Lumley, B.
Whisperers. Tester, W.
The **whispering**. Graebner, J. E.
Whispering wind. Forsyth, F.
Whispers in bedlam. Shaw, I.
Whispers in the dark. Mosley, W.
Whistler. Hensley, J. L.
Whitaker, Alexandra
The trespasser
Death dance; suspenseful stories of the dance macabre; Trevanian, editor
Whitaker, Rodney See Trevanian
White, E. B. (Elwyn Brooks)
The second tree from the corner
The Best American short stories of the century; John Updike, editor, Katrina Kenison, coeditor; with an introduction by John Updike
Wonderful town; New York stories from The New Yorker; edited by David Remnick with Susan Choi
White, Edmund
Cinnamon skin
The Art of the story; an international anthology of contemporary short stories; edited by Daniel Halpern
Fault lines; stories of divorce; collected and edited by Caitlin Shetterly
Forgetting Elena [excerpt]
The Vintage book of amnesia; an anthology; edited by Jonathan Lethem
Give it up for Billy
Granta no78 p185-202 Summ 2002
A Venice story
Men on men 2000; best new gay fiction for the millennium; edited and with an introduction by David Bergman and Karl Woelz
White, Elwyn Brooks See White, E. B. (Elwyn Brooks), 1899-1985
White, Jacob
Gulf Breeze
Southern Humanities Review v37 no3 p261-72 Summ 2003
You Will Miss Me When I Burn
New Letters v70 no2 p7-19 2004
White, Michael C.
Burn patterns
White, M. C. Marked men; stories
The cardiologist's house
White, M. C. Marked men; stories
Crossing
White, M. C. Marked men; stories
Disturbances
White, M. C. Marked men; stories
Fugitives
White, M. C. Marked men; stories
Heights
White, M. C. Marked men; stories

Instincts
White, M. C. Marked men; stories
Marked men
White, M. C. Marked men; stories
Ray's shoes
White, M. C. Marked men; stories
The smell of life
White, M. C. Marked men; stories
Three whacks a buck
White, M. C. Marked men; stories
Voices
White, M. C. Marked men; stories
White, Patrick
The age of a wart
The Kenyon Review ns23 no2 p50-71 Spr 2001
White, William Anthony Parker See Boucher, Anthony, 1911-1968
White. Lebbon, T.
White. Svoboda, T.
White. Tinsley, M. B.
White angel. Cunningham, M.
White Anglo-Saxon Protestant. Hazel, R.
The **white** azalea. Spencer, E.
White Beak, Blue Wings. Rossi, C. P.
White bird. Lord, N.
The **White** Bows. Frazier, K.
The **white** buffalo calf woman. Sneve, V. D. H.
The **white** carousel horse. Dillingham, D. G.
White cloud. Jacobs, M.
The **white** eagle. Chopin, K.
White fang. Foreman, W.
White flour. Murray, J.
White guys in space. Vukcevich, R.
The **white** horse child. Bear, G.
The **white** house. Klíma, I.
White house at night. Kennedy, A. L.
White lies. Chaudhuri, A.
White lies. Theroux, P.
White line fever. Ossana, D.
The **white** man in the tree. Kurlansky, M.
White man's trick. Fintushel, E.
White moths. Joyce, M.
WHITE MOUNTAINS (N.H. AND ME.)
Hawthorne, N. The ambitious guest
Hawthorne, N. The great stone face
White Out. Clark, J.
The **white** pony. Callaghan, M.
White rat. Jones, G.
White-Ring, Wendy
Rocket science
The North American Review v284 no3-4 p34 My/Ag 1999
White sandals. Jackson, V. F.
The **White** Ship murders. Gregory, S.
White sugar and red clay. Marshall, B.
WHITE SUPREMACY MOVEMENTS See Skinheads
The **white** tatto. Cobb, W. J.
White trash noir. Malone, M.
White veil. Coshnear, D.
A **white** veil for tomorrow. Edwards, S.
White Vitrock China. Bourke, R. W.
White weeds. Chesnutt, C. W.
Whitebrow. Chekhov, A. P.
Whiteford, Wynne
Night of the wandjina
Dreaming down-under; edited by Jack Dann and Janeen Webb

Whitelight. Kilpatrick, N.
A **whiter** Mars. Aldiss, B. W.
Whitey. Diamond, P.
WHITMAN, WALT
About
Leslie, N. When lilacs last
WHITMAN, WALT, 1819-1892
About
Gurganus, A. Reassurance
Whitmore, Stanford
Lost soldier
Retrieving bones; stories and poems of the
Korean War; edited and with an introduc-
tion by W. D. Ehrhart and Philip K. Jason
Whiton, Tanya
Getaway
Western Humanities Review v57 no2 p103-9
Fall 2003
Whittenberg, Allison
Bloom of Zenobia
Virgin fiction 2
WHITTLING *See* Wood carving
Whitton, David
The Lee Marvins
Dalhousie Review v82 no2 p273-80 Summ
2002
Whitton, Laura
Froggies
Redshift; extreme visions of speculative fic-
tion; edited by Al Sarrantonio
Whitty, Julia
The daguerrotype
Whitty, J. A tortoise for the Queen of Tonga
Darwin in heaven
Whitty, J. A tortoise for the Queen of Tonga
The dreams of dogs
Whitty, J. A tortoise for the Queen of Tonga
Falling umbrella
Whitty, J. A tortoise for the Queen of Tonga
Jimmy under water
Whitty, J. A tortoise for the Queen of Tonga
Lucifer's alligator
Whitty, J. A tortoise for the Queen of Tonga
Senti's last elephant
Whitty, J. A tortoise for the Queen of Tonga
Stealing from the dead
Whitty, J. A tortoise for the Queen of Tonga
The story of the deep dark
Whitty, J. A tortoise for the Queen of Tonga
A tortoise for the Queen of Tonga
Prize stories, 1999; The O. Henry awards; ed-
ited and with an introduction by Larry
Dark
Whitty, J. A tortoise for the Queen of Tonga
The **whiz** kids. Homes, A. M.
Who am a passer by. Braunbeck, G. A.
Who buried the baby. Corin, L.
Who can replace a man? Aldiss, B. W.
Who do you love. Thompson, J.
Who goes there? Campbell, J. W.
Who had good ears. Heynen, J.
Who I was supposed to be. Perabo, S.
Who in the modern world can keep up with Julia
Juárez? Padilla, M.
Who is Beatrice? Boggs, B.
Who killed Bob Teal? Hammett, D.
Who killed fair Rosamund? Rath, T. and Rath, T.
Who lives you? Rowell, J.
Who loves you, Baby? Sonde, S.

Who made you. Mayo, W.
Who, me a bum? Valenzuela, L.
Who we did worship. LaValle, V. D.
Who whom? Raphael, F.
Who you are. Goliger, G.
WHODUNITS *See* Mystery and detective stories
A **whole** new man. McGraw, E.
The **whole** numbers of families. Doenges, J.
The **Whole** Story. Mirosevich, T.
The **whole** truth and nothing but. Hochman, A.
Whore. Alameddine, R.
The **whore** of Mensa. Allen, W.
The **whore's** child. Russo, R.
Who's Irish? Jen, G.
Who's your authority? Fracis, S. H.
Who's Your Daddy? Bledsoe, B.
Who's your daddy now? Tester, W.
Whose ghosts are these. Grant, C. L.
Whose ghosts these are. Grant, C. L.
Whose song? Glave, T.
Whose upward flight I love. Hopkinson, N.
Why. Hunt, S.
Why come back? Lavín, M.
Why crabs are boiled alive. Hearn, L.
Why did it happen? Tolstoy, L., graf
Why do people have soft noses? Škvorecký, J.
Why fly fishing ain't my cup a tea. Burton, M.
Why Gran'mammy didn't like pound-cake. Mac-
Dowell, K. S. B.
Why he never left his wife. Goran, L.
Why I decide to kill myself and other jokes. Glov-
er, D. H.
Why I lernt how to reed. Škvorecký, J.
Why I Married My Wife. Harvey, M.
Why I returned. Bontemps, A. W.
Why I'm talking. Phillips, D. R.
Why It Remains Unfinished. Harris, W.
Why owls die with wings outspread. Lord, N.
Why poets shouldn't be trusted. Tillmans, A.
Why the sky turns red when the sun goes down.
Harty, R.
Why the Tears, Miss Earhart? DeMarinis, R.
Why we left. Menendez, A.
Why you? Cobb, W. J.
Wicked girl. Allende, I.
Wickersham, Joan
Munich
The Hudson Review v54 no4 p557-68 Wint
2002
What About the Gun?
Agni no59 p25-7 2004
Wickham, John
The light on the sea
The Oxford book of Caribbean short stories;
edited by Stewart Brown and John
Wickham
Wicks, Vicky
I have the serpent brought
Fishing for chickens; short stories about rural
youth; edited, with an introduction by Jim
Heynen
Wicomb, Zoë
You can't get lost in Cape Town
The Art of the story; an international antholo-
gy of contemporary short stories; edited by
Daniel Halpern
The **wide** sea. Earley, T.

Wideman, John Edgar

Ascent by balloon from the yard of Walnut Street Jail
Callaloo v24 no2 p589-93 Spr 2001

Doc's story
The Art of the story; an international anthology of contemporary short stories; edited by Daniel Halpern

Fever
The Scribner anthology of contemporary short fiction; fifty North American stories since 1970; Lex Williford and Michael Martone, editors

More
Callaloo v24 no4 p1198-1209 Fall 2001

Surfiction
The African American West; a century of short stories; edited by Bruce A. Glasrud and Laurie Champion

Weight
Prize stories, 2000; The O. Henry awards; edited and with an introduction by Larry Dark

What We Cannot Speak about We Must Pass Over in Silence
Harper's v307 p65-73 D 2003

Widening the road. Bonnie, F.

The **[widget],** the [wadget], and boff. Sturgeon, T.

The **widow**. Babel´, I.

Widow. Hensley, J. L.

The **Widow**. Johnston, B. A.

The **widow**. Linney, R.

The **widow** Ching—pirate. Borges, J. L.

The **Widow** in Her Weeds. Thornton, W. J.

The **widow** predicament. Means, D.

The **widower**. Schnitzler, A.

The **widower**. Thompson, J.

The **widower** Visarrion. Rodburg, M.

WIDOWERS

Adam, C. Bat

Adams, A. The last lovely city

Archer, J. The endgame

Baca, J. S. Matilda's garden

Berberova, N. The phantom of Billancourt

Biguenet, J. Rose

Bowles, P. Rumor and a ladder

Boylan, C. Concerning virgins

Boyle, T. C. Mexico

Broughton, T. A. The burden of light

Broughton, T. A. Leaving home

Bukoski, A. Bird of passage

Busch, F. Laying the ghost

Busch, F. Malvasia

Canty, K. Little palaces

Capote, T. Among the paths to Eden

Cheng, C.-W. Hair

Cheng, C.-W. Spring rain

Chiappone, R. A girl, the jungle, monkeys

Cushman, S. Me and Dr. Bob

Day, C. Wallace Porter

Deane, J. F. Rituals of departure

DiChario, N. Carp man

Dixon, S. Sleep

Dokey, R. The shopper

Duggin, Richard. Why won't you talk to me?

Edugyan, E. The woman who tasted of rose oil

Epstein, J. Dubinsky on the loose

Gerard, P. Death by reputation

Gilliland, G. All their secrets

Greer, A. S. The walker

Hall, D. Widowers' woods

Hoffman, N. K. Gone

Iribarne, M. A dream, not alone

Iwaszkiewicz, J. The birch grove

Johnson, D. Train dreams

Jones, E. P. A rich man

Kaplan, H. Goodwill

Karnezis, P. A funeral of stones

Lavin, M. In the middle of the fields

Lee, D. Widowers

Lord, N. The attainable border of the birds

Lorfing, Jake. Old horse

Louis, L. G. Fur

Mason, B. A. The funeral side

McNulty, J. The television helps, but not very much

Means, D. Railroad incident, August 1995

Meredith, D. French letters

Meyers, K. Glacierland

Morrow, B. Lush

Painter, P. Grief

Pearlman, E. Skin deep

Randisi, R. J. Black and white memories

Reiner, C. Sorry Solomon and Guey Jew

Roorbach, B. Big Bend

Russo, R. Monhegan light

Schaffert, T. Sound from the courtyard

Schlink, B. The other man

Schnitzler, A. The widower

Schwartz, L. S. Sightings of Loretta

Singer, I. B. Androgynous

Singer, I. B. The power of darkness

Spencer, E. The runaways

Stern, D. Foxx hunting

Stolar, D. The trip home

Swan, M. On the border

Thompson, J. The widower

Thurm, M. Like something in this world

Trevor, W. Against the odds

White, M. C. Ray's shoes

Whitty, J. Falling umbrella

Yañez, R. Amoroza Tires

Young, T. Maintenance

Widowers. Lee, D.

The **Widower's** House. McGill, R.

Widower's walk. Hansen, J.

Widowers' woods. Hall, D.

WIDOWS Miriam

Abrams, T. The drinking of spirits

Adams, A. The islands

Adams, A. Lost luggage

Aldrich, B. S. The heirs

Aldrich, B. S. It's never too late to live

Allen, S. Passage

Anderson, R. The name of the dead

Bausch, R. Consolation

Bean, B. Sugar Creek

Bloom, A. Light into dark

Bloom, A. Night vision

Bloom, A. The story

Bly, C. After the baptism

Bly, C. My Lord Bag of Rice

Boylan, C. Life on Mars

Boyle, T. C. My widow

Bradbury, R. Leftovers

Broughton, T. A. Bill's women

Brown, C. Wings

Brownrigg, S. The lady in the desert

WIDOWS—*Continued*

Budnitz, J. Permanent wave
Byatt, A. S. Crocodile tears
Chaon, D. Safety Man
Chapman, C. M. Correspondence of corpses
Chekhov, A. P. The darling
Chekhov, A. P. The marshal's widow
Chesnutt, C. W. White weeds
Chopin, K. The godmother
Chopin, K. Madame Martel's Christmas Eve
Chopin, K. The story of an hour
Cooper, B. Graphology
Dann, J. Tea
Davis, J. S. Pojo's and the buttery slope
Davis, J. S. When you see
Davis, L. Calendar waltz
Divakaruni, C. B. Mrs. Dutta writes a letter
DuBois, B. Her last gift
Engel, M. P. Strangers and sojourners
Epstein, J. A loss for words
Erdrich, L. Lulu's boys
Frym, G. The dean's widow
Fulton, J. Rose
George, E. Remember, I'll always love you
Gilchrist, E. 1944
Gilchrist, E. The young man
Gilman, C. P. The widow's might
Goldner, B. Farm wife
Goran, L. Shannon made of sunlight and bones
Grau, S. A. Housekeeper
Grau, S. A. Three
Grau, S. A. Widow's walk
Hendel, Y. Apples in honey
Hendel, Y. The leter that came in time
Hoffman, W. Doors
Hood, A. Lost parts
Jackson, V. F. The outing
Johnston, B. A. The widow
Lavin, M. In a café
Lavin, M. In the middle of the fields
Lavin, M. Trastevere
Lavin, M. The widow's son
Le Guin, U. K. The day before the revolution
Leavitt, D. Crossing St. Gotthard
Levy, J. A woman 49er
Lloyd, D. T. Snow
Lovett, S. Buried treasure
Malone, M. A deer on the lawn
Malone, M. Maniac loose
Martin, P. P. Amor e ilusion—Love and illusion
Martin, P. P. Amor inolvidable—Unforgettable love
Matthews, B. Everything must go
Mazor, J. The lost cause
McCorkle, J. Monkeys
Means, D. The widow predicament
Melville, P. The duende
Melville, P. Mrs. Da Silva's carnival
Meyers, K. The smell of the deer
Muller, M. Sweet cactus wine
Muñoz, M. The unimportant Lila Parr
Munro, A. Comfort
Nelson, A. One dog is people
Orner, P. Atlantic City
Orner, P. Early November
Ortiz, S. J. Home country
Ozick, C. The pagan rabbi
Padilla, M. Flora in shadows
Pak, W.-S. Butterfly of illusion

Pak, W.-S. She knows, I know, and heaven knows
Perabo, S. The greater grace of Carlisle
Petter, S. Widow's peak
Pickard, N. Lucky devil
Pittalwala, I. The change
Potvin, E. A. The death of a husband
Régio, J. A brief comedy
Rinehart, S. Guns went off
Robison, M. I get by
Rossi, A. Orion's glow
Schone, R. A man and a woman
Schwartz, L. S. What I did for love
Shouse, D. A portrait of angels
Singer, I. B. The bus
Singer, I. B. The painting
Skillings, R. D. The present
Slezak, E. Patch
Stollman, A. L. Die grosse Liebe
Strauss, A. Recovering Larry
Stuckey-French, E. The visible man
Swarthout, G. F. Mulligans
Tamaro, S. Hell does not exist
Thomas, D. The joybell
Thurm, M. Pleasure palace
Tilghman, C. A gracious rain
Trevanian. Mrs. McGivney's nickel
Waters, M. Y. Aftermath
Waters, M. Y. Kami
Waters, M. Y. Since my house burned down
West, M. Faces made of clay
Westlake, D. E. Never shake a family tree
Wharton, E. Roman fever
White, M. C. Crossing
Whitty, J. The dreams of dogs
Wieland, L. Irradiation
Winter, E. Blue-sky day
Young, T. The new world
Zabytko, I. The celebrity
The **Widow's** Daughter. Freed, L.
The **widow's** might. Gilman, C. P.
Widow's peak. Petter, S.
The **widow's** son. Lavin, M.
Widows' walk. Adisa, O. P.
Widow's walk. Grau, S. A.
The **widow's** widow. Moss, R.
Wie bitte? Wilson, B.
Wiebe, Dallas E.
Vibini and the virgin tongue
The North American Review v284 no5 p24-32 S/O 1999
Wieland, Liza
Cirque du Soleil
Wieland, L. You can sleep while I drive; stories
Gray's anatomy
The Southern Review (Baton Rouge, La.) v35 no3 p544-66 Summ 1999
Wieland, L. You can sleep while I drive; stories
Halloween
Wieland, L. You can sleep while I drive; stories
Irradiation
Wieland, L. You can sleep while I drive; stories
Laramie
Wieland, L. You can sleep while I drive; stories

Wieland, Liza—_Continued_

The loop, the snow, their daughters, the rain

    The Pushcart prize XXIV: best of the small presses; an annual small press reader; edited by Bill Henderson with the Pushcart prize editors

    Wieland, L. You can sleep while I drive; stories

Méthode champenoise

    The Georgia Review v53 no2 p249-63 Summ 1999

Purgatory

    Wieland, L. You can sleep while I drive; stories

Salt Lake

    Wieland, L. You can sleep while I drive; stories

You can sleep while I drive

    Wieland, L. You can sleep while I drive; stories

Wieland, Mitch

Beware the pale horse comes riding

    The Sewanee Review v109 no1 p1-20 Wint 2001

The King of Infinite Space

    The Sewanee Review v111 no4 p512-29 Fall 2003

The Mistress of the Horse God

    The Southern Review (Baton Rouge, La.) v39 no4 p782-93 Aut 2003

Swan's Song

    The Kenyon Review v25 no2 p15-32 Spr 2003

Wier, Allen

Tehano [excerpt]

    The Cry of an occasion; fiction from the Fellowship of Southern Writers; edited by Richard Bausch; with a foreword by George Garrett

The **wife**. Jordan, J.

WIFE ABUSE

Baida, P. Family ties

Baumer, J. R. The party over there

Bausch, R. Fatality

Brady, C. Wild, wild horses

Chopin, K. In Sabine

Cisneros, S. Woman Hollering Creek

Collins, B. World's greatest mother

Davis, D. S. To forget Mary Ellen

Davis, L. Rat medicine

DeLancey, K. Jules Jr Michael Jules Jr

DeMarinis, R. The Voice of America

Dorcey, M. A sense of humour

Gorman, E. That day at Eagle's Point

Hopkinson, N. Precious

Kennedy, A. L. A bad son

King, L. R. Paleta man

Krouse, E. Mercy

Lao She. Neighbors

Maraini, D. Macaque

Miller, R. Delia

Nakagami, K. House on fire

Ní Dhuibhne-Almqvist, É. The Garden of Eden

Parrish, T. Complicity

Rodgers, S. J. Beautiful things

Schaffert, T. Sound from the courtyard

Smolens, J. Absolution

Steinbeck, T. An unbecoming grace

Walters, M. English autumn-American fall

Winter, E. Have a prayer

Wuori, G. K. Justice

Yi, T.-H. Dark valley

WIFE AND HUSBAND _See_ Husband and wife

WIFE BEATING _See_ Wife abuse

The **wife** in the story. Kinder, C.

The **wife** of Ben-y-ghloe. Underwood, L. J.

The **wife** of his youth. Chesnutt, C. W.

The **wife** of the Indian. Perillo, L. M.

WIFE SWAPPING _See_ Marriage problems

Wifely duties. Newman, C.

The **wig**. Englander, N.

Wiggen, Henry W. _See_ Harris, Mark, 1922-

Wiggin, Kate Douglas Smith and Smith, Nora Archibald

The story of Ali Baba and the forty thieves

    Swords and sorcerers; stories from the world of fantasy and adventure; edited by Clint Willis

Wilbur, Ellen

The Doctor

    The Yale Review v92 no3 p129-39 Jl 2004

Rescue

    The Georgia Review v55 no2 p330-7 Summ 2001

Wilbur, Richard

A game of catch

    Sports best short stories; edited by Paul D. Staudohar

The **wild**. Powers, S.

Wild blue. Clark, J.

WILD BOY OF AVEYRON, D. 1828

            About

Connor, J. Victor learns to speak

Wild California. Nelson, V.

Wild challenge. Easton, R. O.

WILD CHILDREN

Connor, J. Victor learns to speak

Wild flower. Coleman, J. C.

Wild garlic: the journal of Maria X. Ritchie, E.

Wild horses. Bass, R.

Wild horses. De Lint, C.

Wild life. Tillman, L.

Wild plums. Coates, G. S.

Wild rice. Schmidt, H. J.

Wild things. Howard, C.

Wild turkey. Isle, R.

Wild, wild horses. Brady, C.

Wilde, Lady

The horned women

    Witches' brew; edited by Yvonne Jocks

Wilde, Francesca Speranza _See_ Wilde, Lady, 1826-1896

Wilde, Jane Francesca Elgee _See_ Wilde, Lady, 1826-1896

Wilde, Dana

The green moon

    One lamp; alternate history stories from The magazine of Fantasy & Science Fiction; edited by Gordon van Gelder

Wilder, Cherry

The Dancing Floor

    Dreaming down-under; edited by Jack Dann and Janeen Webb

    The Year's best science fiction, sixteenth annual collection; edited by Gardner Dozois

Finishing school

    Gathering the bones; original stories from the world's masters of horror; edited by Dennis Etchison, Ramsey Campbell and Jack Dann

Wilder, Cherry—*Continued*
Looking forward to the harvest
  Centaurus: the best of Australian science fic-
    tion; edited by David G. Hartwell and Da-
    mien Broderick
Wilderness. DeMarinis, R.
Wilderness. Rock, P.
A **wilderness** station. Munro, A.
Wilderness tips. Atwood, M.
Wildgen, Michelle
Act Like a Man
  TriQuarterly no115 p174-92 Spr 2003
Healer
  Best new American voices 2004; guest editor
    John Casey; series editors John Kulka and
    Natalie Danford
Wilding, Michael
Literary lunch
  Critical Survey v11 no3 p147-54 1999
Wildlife of America. Bauman, B. A.
Wildlife of Coastal Carolina. Rowell, J.
Wilhelm, Kate
Forget luck
  The Best from fantasy & science fiction: the
    fiftieth anniversary anthology; edited by
    Edward L. Ferman and Gordon Van Gelder
Wilhelm, Vinnie
Body, Numinous, Words
  The Southern Review (Baton Rouge, La.) v40
    no3 p555-67 Summ 2004
Wilkie Fahnstock, the boxed set. Moody, R.
Wilking, Joan
Proper dress
  Politically inspired; edited by Stephen Elliott;
    assistant editor, Gabriel Kram; associate ed-
    itors, Elizabeth Brooks [et al.]
Wilkins, Connie
Meluse's counsel
  Such a pretty face; edited by Lee Martindale
Wilkins, Mary Eleanor, 1852-1930 *See* Freeman,
    Mary Eleanor Wilkins, 1852-1930
Wilkinson, Crystal E.
Humming back yesterday
  Home and beyond; an anthology of Kentucky
    short stories; edited by Morris Allen
    Grubbs; with an introduction by Wade Hall
    and an afterword by Charles E. May
Wilkinson, Margaret
A man's book
  Brought to book; murderous stories from the
    literary world; Penny Sumner, editor
The **Wilko** girls. Iwaszkiewicz, J.
The **will**. Lavin, M.
Will. Zinovyeva-Annibal, L. D.
Will the romance be the same? Aldrich, B. S.
Will you say something, Monsieur Eliot? Paine, T.
"**Will** you walk a little faster". Tenn, W.
WILLARD, JESS
                        About
Duncan, A. The Pottawatomie Giant
Willi. Doctorow, E. L.
**WILLIAM I, THE CONQUEROR, KING OF
    ENGLAND, 1027 OR 8-1087**
                        About
Reed, M. and Mayer, E. Even kings die
**WILLIAM II, KING OF ENGLAND, 1056?-
    1100**
                        About
Holt, T. Accidental death

WILLIAM, 1103-1120
                        About
Gregory, S. The White Ship murders
William and Antonio, Giotto and Mae. Ander, Z.
Williams, Ann Joslin
Before this day there were many days
  Ploughshares v27 no2/3 p223-30 Fall 2001
Williams, Conrad
City in aspic
  The Mammoth book of best horror 13; edited
    by Stephen Jones
Imbroglio
  The Museum of horrors; edited by Dennis
    Etchison
The machine
  The Year's best fantasy & horror: sixteenth
    annual collection; edited by Ellen Datlow
    & Terri Windling
Williams, David
Bobby Angel
  TriQuarterly no113 p213-17 Summ 2002
A nose for murder
  The best British mysteries; edited by Maxim
    Jakubowski
Williams, Diane
A dull, orderly job
  The Ohio Review no64/65 p479 2001
Her hair is red
  The Ohio Review no64/65 p477 2001
Ruling
  The Ohio Review no64/65 p478 2001
Very, very, red
  The Pushcart prize XXIV: best of the small
    presses; an annual small press reader; ed-
    ited by Bill Henderson with the Pushcart
    prize editors
WILLIAMS, ESTHER
                        s
Ziegler, I. Feud of the maids
Williams, Joan
Spring is now
  Crossing the color line; readings in Black and
    white; edited by Suzanne W. Jones
Williams, John Alfred
Son in the afternoon
  The African American West; a century of
    short stories; edited by Bruce A. Glasrud
    and Laurie Champion
  Crossing the color line; readings in Black and
    white; edited by Suzanne W. Jones
Williams, Joy
The blue men
  100% pure Florida fiction; an anthology; ed-
    ited by Susan Hubbard and Robley Wilson
The farm
  The Art of the story; an international antholo-
    gy of contemporary short stories; edited by
    Daniel Halpern
Hawk
  Granta no67 p87-102 Aut 1999
The last generation
  The Workshop; seven decades of the Iowa
    Writers' Workshop: 42 stories, recollections
    & essays on Iowa's place in 20th-century
    American literature; edited by Tom Grimes

Williams, Joy—*Continued*
Taking care
The Scribner anthology of contemporary short fiction; fifty North American stories since 1970; Lex Williford and Michael Martone, editors
Williams, Karen
They came at dawn
The Vintage book of international lesbian fiction; edited and with an introduction by Naomi Holoch and Joan Nestle
Williams, Kat
Chasing the moonlight
The Literary Review (Madison, N.J.) v42 no3 p401-10 Spr 1999
Williams, Linda Verlee *See* Grant, Linda
Williams, Liz
Voivodoi
The Year's best science fiction, sixteenth annual collection; edited by Gardner Dozois
Williams, Lynna
Comparative religion
Atlantic Monthly v284 no2 p69-78 Ag 1999
Williams, Margaret
Grazing in good pastures
The African American West; a century of short stories; edited by Bruce A. Glasrud and Laurie Champion
Williams, Miller
Cantaloupes
Williams, M. The lives of Kelvin Fletcher; stories mostly short
Coley's war
Williams, M. The lives of Kelvin Fletcher; stories mostly short
The journal
Williams, M. The lives of Kelvin Fletcher; stories mostly short
One Saturday afternoon
Williams, M. The lives of Kelvin Fletcher; stories mostly short
There aren't any foxes in that cave
Williams, M. The lives of Kelvin Fletcher; stories mostly short
Truth and goodness
Williams, M. The lives of Kelvin Fletcher; stories mostly short
The wall
Williams, M. The lives of Kelvin Fletcher; stories mostly short
The year Ward West took away the raccoon and Mr. Hanson's garage burneddown
Williams, M. The lives of Kelvin Fletcher; stories mostly short
WILLIAMS, ROGER, 1604?-1683
About
Hawthorne, N. Endicott and the Red Cross
Williams, Sean
Entre les beaux morts en vie (Among the beautiful living dead)
Dreaming down-under; edited by Jack Dann and Janeen Webb
Evermore
The Year's best science fiction, seventeenth annual collection; edited by Gardner Dozois
A map of the mines of Barnath
Centaurus: the best of Australian science fiction; edited by David G. Hartwell and Damien Broderick

Williams, Stephen P.
Fig
Bomb no84 p92 Summ 2003
Fortune
Bomb no84 p93 Summ 2003
Swinging in the Breeze
Bomb no84 p92-3 Summ 2003
Williams, Tad
The happiest dead boy in the world
Silverberg, R. Legends II; new short novels by the masters of modern fantasy; edited by Robert Silverberg
WILLIAMS, TED, 1918-2002
About
Lee, M. The Albright Kid
Williams, Tennessee
In Spain There Was Revolution
The Hudson Review v56 no1 p50-6 Spr 2003
The resemblance between a violin case and a coffin
The Best American short stories of the century; John Updike, editor, Katrina Kenison, coeditor; with an introduction by John Updike
A system of wheels
Michigan Quarterly Review v38 no4 p504-11 Fall 1999
The vengeance of Nitocris
Into the mummy's tomb; edited by John Richard Stephens
Williams, Tess
The body politic
Dreaming down-under; edited by Jack Dann and Janeen Webb
Williams, Thomas
The fisherman who got away
The Workshop; seven decades of the Iowa Writers' Workshop: 42 stories, recollections & essays on Iowa's place in 20th-century American literature; edited by Tom Grimes
Williams, Thomas Lanier *See* Williams, Tennessee, 1911-1983
Williams, Walter Jon
Daddy's world
Nebula awards showcase 2002; edited by Kim Stanley Robinson
The Year's best science fiction, seventeenth annual collection; edited by Gardner Dozois
The Green Leopard Plague
The year's best science fiction: twenty-first annual collection; edited by Gardner Dozois
Lethe
Nebula awards showcase 2000; the year's best SF and fantasy chosen by the science fiction and fantasy writers of america; edited by Gregory Benford
The millennium party
The Year's best science fiction; twentieth annual collection; edited by Gardner Dozois
Prayers on the wind
The Good new stuff; adventure SF in the grand tradition; edited by Gardner Dozois
WILLIAMSBURG (VA.) *See* Virginia—Williamsburg
Williamson, Chet
The blood-red sea
The Crow; shattered lives & broken dreams; edited by J. O'Barr and Ed Kramer

Williamson, Chet—*Continued*
O come little children. . .
　A yuletide universe; sixteen fantastical tales;
　　edited by Brian M. Thomsen
Excerpts from the Records of the New Zodiac
　and the diaries of Henry Watson Fairfax
　999: new stories of horror and suspense; ed-
　　ited by Al Sarrantonio
Williamson, Duncan
Mary and the seal
　The Vintage book of contemporary Scottish
　　fiction; edited and with an introduction by
　　Peter Kravitz
Williamson, Graeme
Memoirs of an amnesiac
　Dalhousie Review v79 no2 p221-6 Summ
　　1999
Williamson, Jack
The firefly tree
　The SFWA grand masters v1; edited by
　　Frederik Pohl
Jamboree
　The SFWA grand masters v1; edited by
　　Frederik Pohl
The ultimate earth
　Nebula Awards showcase 2003; edited by
　　Nancy Kress
With folded hands
　The SFWA grand masters v1; edited by
　　Frederik Pohl
Williford, Lex
My Mother's Wedding Dress
　Prairie Schooner v77 no2 p21-6 Summ 2003
Willing. Moore, L.
The **Willing** Suspension of Disbelief. Sumner, M.
Willis, Connie
Adaptation
　Willis, C. Miracle and other Christmas stories
Cat's paw
　Willis, C. Miracle and other Christmas stories
Epiphany
　Willis, C. Miracle and other Christmas stories
Even the queen
　Brown, C. N. and Strahan, J. The Locus
　　awards; thirty years of the best in science
　　fiction and fantasy; edited by Charles N.
　　Brown and Jonathan Strahan
　A Woman's liberation; a choice of futures by
　　and about women; edited by Connie Willis
　　and Sheila Williams
In Coppelius's Toyshop
　Willis, C. Miracle and other Christmas stories
Inn
　Willis, C. Miracle and other Christmas stories
Miracle
　Willis, C. Miracle and other Christmas stories
　A yuletide universe; sixteen fantastical tales;
　　edited by Brian M. Thomsen
Newsletter
　Willis, C. Miracle and other Christmas stories
The pony
　Willis, C. Miracle and other Christmas stories
Willis, Meredith Sue
Another perversion
　Willis, M. S. Dwight's house and other sto-
　　ries
Attack
　Willis, M. S. Dwight's house and other sto-
　　ries

Dwight's house
　Willis, M. S. Dwight's house and other sto-
　　ries
Tales of the abstract expressionists
　Willis, M. S. Dwight's house and other sto-
　　ries
Tiny gorillas
　Willis, M. S. Dwight's house and other sto-
　　ries
Willoughby, Jennifer
I Forbid You This Recurring Dream
　Prairie Schooner v77 no2 p194-5 Summ 2003
It Is Not Entirely My Fault
　Prairie Schooner v77 no2 p193 Summ 2003
Minneapolis & The Flattening of the Vault of
　Heaven
　Prairie Schooner v77 no2 p195-6 Summ 2003
Willow Beeman. Waldrop, H.
The **willows**. Blackwood, A.
Willowy-wisps. Fromm, P.
WILLS
Bellow, S. Leaving the yellow house
Bradbury, R. One for his lordship, and one for
　the road
Lavin, M. The will
Smith, J. Blood types
Spark, M. The executor
Spencer, E. The skater
Will's Valentine. Coberly, L. M.
Willy Mae goes north. Coberly, L. M.
Wilmot, Jeanne
Dirt angel
　The Art of the story; an international antholo-
　　gy of contemporary short stories; edited by
　　Daniel Halpern
Wilson, Andrew J.
Under the bright and hollow sky
　Gathering the bones; original stories from the
　　world's masters of horror; edited by Dennis
　　Etchison, Ramsey Campbell and Jack Dann
Wilson, Antoine
Home, James, and don't spare the horses
　Best new American voices 2001; guest editor
　　Charles Baxter; series editors John Kulka
　　and Natalie Danford
Wilson, Barbara
Archeology
　Hers 3: brilliant new fiction by lesbian writ-
　　ers; edited by Terry Wolverton with Robert
　　Drake
Wie bitte?
　Brought to book; murderous stories from the
　　literary world; Penny Sumner, editor
**Wilson, David Niall and Macomber, Patricia
　Lee**
Death did not become him
　Shadows over Baker Street; edited by Michael
　　Reaves and John Pelan
Wilson, Derek A.
The curse of the unborn dead
　Royal whodunnits; edited by Mike Ashley
Wilson, F. Paul (Francis Paul)
Aftershock
　Best new horror 11; edited and with an intro-
　　duction by Stephen Jones
Good Friday
　999: new stories of horror and suspense; ed-
　　ited by Al Sarrantonio

Wilson, Francis Paul *See* Wilson, F. Paul (Francis Paul)

Wilson, Gahan

The big green grin

Gathering the bones; original stories from the world's masters of horror; edited by Dennis Etchison, Ramsey Campbell and Jack Dann

The dead ghost

Datlow, E. The dark; new ghost stories; edited by Ellen Datlow

Wilson, Ian Randall

Three strikes people

The North American Review v284 no6 p26-30 N/D 1999

Wilson, Jonathan

An Inspector in Palestine

New England Review v24 no2 p78-82 Spr 2003

Sons of God

Ploughshares v28 no2/3 p218-25 Fall 2002

Wilson, Kevin

Blowing Up on the Spot

Ploughshares v29 no4 p206-19 Wint 2003/2004

Wilson, Martin

Petty theft

Pieces; a collection of new voices; edited by Stephen Chbosky

Youthful offenders

Virgin fiction 2

Wilson, Robert Charles

Divided by infinity

Wilson, R. C. The Perseids and other stories

The Year's best science fiction, sixteenth annual collection; edited by Gardner Dozois

The fields of Abraham

Wilson, R. C. The Perseids and other stories

The great goodbye

The Year's best science fiction, eighteenth annual collection; edited by Gardner Dozois

The inner inner city

Wilson, R. C. The Perseids and other stories

The observer

Wilson, R. C. The Perseids and other stories

Pearl baby

Wilson, R. C. The Perseids and other stories

The Perseids

Wilson, R. C. The Perseids and other stories

Plato's mirror

Wilson, R. C. The Perseids and other stories

Protocols of consumption

Wilson, R. C. The Perseids and other stories

Ulysses sees the moon in the bedroom window

Wilson, R. C. The Perseids and other stories

Wilson, Robley, Jr.

Barber

Wilson, R., Jr. The book of lost fathers; stories

California

Wilson, R., Jr. The book of lost fathers; stories

A day of splendid omens

Wilson, R., Jr. The book of lost fathers; stories

Dorothy and her friends

Wilson, R., Jr. The book of lost fathers; stories

Florida

Wilson, R., Jr. The book of lost fathers; stories

Grief

Wilson, R., Jr. The book of lost fathers; stories

Hard times

Wilson, R., Jr. The book of lost fathers; stories

Parts runner

Wilson, R., Jr. The book of lost fathers; stories

Remembered names

Wilson, R., Jr. The book of lost fathers; stories

A simple elegy

Wilson, R., Jr. The book of lost fathers; stories

Trespass

Wilson, R., Jr. The book of lost fathers; stories

WILSON, WOODROW, 1856-1924

About

Swarthout, G. F. Pancho Villa's one-man war

Wilson, Jeff

Buddherotica

Nixon under the bodhi tree and other works of Buddhist fiction; edited by Kate Wheeler ; foreword by Charles Johnson

Wilt thou be made whole? Karnezis, P.

Win a Nobel Prize!. Vinge, V.

Winch, Terence

Ordinary Mortals

Hanging Loose no83 p106-8 2003

Wind. Fromm, P.

The **wind** & Mary. Teigeler, P.

Wind across the breaks. Norris, L.

Wind and rain. Fleming, J. H.

The **wind** at Beni Midar. Bowles, P.

The **wind** from a burning woman. Bear, G.

The **wind** from the sun. Clarke, A. C.

The **wind** of Pelican Island. Easton, R. O.

Wind rower. Meyers, K.

The **wind** shall blow for ever mair. Dedman, S.

The **wind** shifting west. Grau, S. A.

The **windbags** of Provence. Sade, marquis de

Windigo. Lay, C.

Windmill. Anderson, P.

The **windmill** of happiness. Vasseur, T. J.

The **window**. Lane, J.

The **window**. Mo Shen

The **window**. Müller, H.

Window lights. Mason, B. A.

WINDOWS

Brockmeier, K. The light through the window

Windows and words. Joseph, D.

WINDS

Yolen, J. Speaking to the wind

Winds of change. Lutz, J.

The **Winds** of Change, the Winds of Hope, the Winds of Disaster. Rooke, L.

Winds of Tehuantepec. Shaw, C.

WINDSOR, EDWARD, DUKE OF, 1894-1972

About

Lupoff, R. A. News from New Providence

The **Windsor** ballet. Morgan, D.

WINE AND WINE MAKING

Bradbury, R. One for his lordship, and one for the road

WINE AND WINE MAKING—*Continued*

Chesnutt, C. W. The goophered grapevine

Ellin, S. The last bottle in the world

Poe, E. A. The cask of Amontillado

Pronzini, B. Connoisseur

Wine on the desert. Brand, M.

Winegardner, Mark

Ace of hearts

  Winegardner, M. That's true of everybody; stories

Halftime

  Winegardner, M. That's true of everybody; stories

How we came to Indiana

  Winegardner, M. That's true of everybody; stories

Janda's sister

  Winegardner, M. That's true of everybody; stories

Keegan's load

  New stories from the South: the year's best, 2003; edited by Shannon Ravenel; with a preface by Roy Blount Jr.

  Winegardner, M. That's true of everybody; stories

Last love song at the Valentine

  Winegardner, M. That's true of everybody; stories

Obvious questions

  Winegardner, M. That's true of everybody; stories

Rain itself

  Winegardner, M. That's true of everybody; stories

Song for a certain girl

  Winegardner, M. That's true of everybody; stories

That's true of everybody

  TriQuarterly no110/111 p469-83 Fall 2001

Thirty-year-old

  Winegardner, M. That's true of everybody; stories

Travelers advisory

  Winegardner, M. That's true of everybody; stories

The untenured lecturer

  Winegardner, M. That's true of everybody; stories

The visiting poet

  Winegardner, M. That's true of everybody; stories

What Home Can Mean

  New Letters v68 no3/4 p152-75 Spr/Summ 2002

Winemaster. Reed, R.

Wing, Betsy

Art history

  The Southern Review (Baton Rouge, La.) v35 no2 p315-24 Spr 1999

Wing walking. Meredith, D.

Wingless angels. De Lint, C.

Wings, Mary

Empty arms

  Brought to book; murderous stories from the literary world; Penny Sumner, editor

Wings. Brown, C.

Wings. Greenland, C.

Wings burnt black. Shirley, J.

Wings over Brazil. L'Amour, L.

Wingtips. Chenoweth, A.

The **wink**. Rendell, R.

Winn, Tracy

Missing

  Western Humanities Review v55 no1 p93-6 Spr 2001

Winner, Anthony

Three Figures Out of Schools

  The Kenyon Review v25 no2 p125-41 Spr 2003

Winner, David

The Pang of Queer

  Confrontation no86/87 p202-11 Spr/Summ 2004

The **winner**. Gifford, B.

The **winner**. Lichtenstein, A.

Winner takes all. Waugh, E.

Winners and losers. Malone, M.

Winsloe, Christa

The child Manuela [excerpt]

  The Vintage book of international lesbian fiction; edited and with an introduction by Naomi Holoch and Joan Nestle

Winston, Diana

Mi Mi May

  Nixon under the bodhi tree and other works of Buddhist fiction; edited by Kate Wheeler ; foreword by Charles Johnson

Winston's wife. Lee, W. W.

Winter, Ellen

Blue-sky day

  Winter, E. The price you pay; stories

The boys

  Winter, E. The price you pay; stories

Call me Ruby

  Winter, E. The price you pay; stories

Camp

  The Antioch Review v61 no1 p95-108 Wint 2003

A color of sky

  Winter, E. The price you pay; stories

Contra dance

  Winter, E. The price you pay; stories

Dragon box

  Winter, E. The price you pay; stories

Fox Hill

  Winter, E. The price you pay; stories

Full moon howl

  Winter, E. The price you pay; stories

Have a prayer

  Winter, E. The price you pay; stories

House in the woods

  Winter, E. The price you pay; stories

Love in the desert

  Winter, E. The price you pay; stories

The planting

  Winter, E. The price you pay; stories

Pretty please

  Winter, E. The price you pay; stories

The price you pay

  Winter, E. The price you pay; stories

Spin cycle

  Winter, E. The price you pay; stories

Spring

  Winter, E. The price you pay; stories

WINTER

Kilpatrick, N. Cold comfort

Smith, T. D. The big die-up

Winter. Miller, A. L.

Winter. West, M.

Winter barley. Lee, A.

Winter chores. Heynen, J.

Winter concert. Strout, E.

Winter dark. Silman, R.

Winter dog. MacLeod, A.

Winter dreams. Fitzgerald, F. S.

Winter facts. Taylor-Hall, M. A.

Winter fat. Billman, J.

The **winter** father. Dubus, A.

Winter fire. Landis, G. A.

Winter fish. Chiappone, R.

Winter in Los Angeles. McNeal, T.

Winter Island. Westmoreland, T. A.

Winter on the Belle Fourche. Barrett, N., Jr.

Winter rain. Adams, A.

Winter solstice. Vaughn, E.

Winter weeds. Bukoski, A.

Winter wheat. Hoffman, W.

The **winter** without milk. Avrich, J.

The **winterberry**. DiChario, N.

Winters are hard. Popkes, S.

Winter's wheat. Lincoln, C.

Winterscape. Desai, A.

Winterson, Jeanette

The 24-hour dog

Winterson, J. The world and other places

Adventure of a lifetime

Esquire v131 no3 p98+ Mr 1999

Winterson, J. The world and other places

Atlantic crossing

Winterson, J. The world and other places

Disappearance I

Winterson, J. The world and other places

Disappearance II

Winterson, J. The world and other places

The green man

The Art of the story; an international anthology of contemporary short stories; edited by
Daniel Halpern

Winterson, J. The world and other places

A green square

Winterson, J. The world and other places

Holy matrimony

Winterson, J. The world and other places

Lives of saints

Winterson, J. The world and other places

Newton

Winterson, J. The world and other places

O'Brien's first Christmas

Winterson, J. The world and other places

Orion

Winterson, J. The world and other places

The poetics of sex

Winterson, J. The world and other places

Psalms

Winterson, J. The world and other places

The three friends

Winterson, J. The world and other places

Turn of the world

Winterson, J. The world and other places

The world and other places

Winterson, J. The world and other places

Winthrop was stubborn. Tenn, W.

Winton, Tim

Commission

Harper's v309 p71-2, 74-7 S 2004

The **wire** continuum. Clarke, A. C.

Wired dreaming. Collins, P.

Wirstigkeit. Simpson, H.

WISCONSIN

Bukoski, A. A concert of minor pieces

Bukoski, A. Dry spell

Bukoski, A. Immigration and naturalization

Bukoski, A. The wood of such trees

Marffin, K. Waiting for the 400

Farm life

See Farm life—Wisconsin

Madison

Cherry, K. Block party

Cherry, K. The prowler

Cherry, K. Tell her

Cherry, K. Your chances of getting married

WISDOM

Singer, I. B. Logorihims

Wisenberg, S. L.

Big Ruthie imagines sex without pain

Neurotica: Jewish writers on sex; edited by
Melvin Jules Bukiet

Liberator

When night fell; an anthology of Holocaust
short stories; edited by Linda Schermer Raphael and Marc Lee Raphael

My mother's war

When night fell; an anthology of Holocaust
short stories; edited by Linda Schermer Raphael and Marc Lee Raphael

Wisenberg, S. L.

Big Ruthie imagines sex without pain

What are you looking at?; the first fat fiction
anthology; edited by Donna Jarrell and Ira
Sukrungruang

Wiser than a god. Chopin, K.

Wish. Mason, B. A.

Wish. Sarrantonio, A.

WISHES

Berners, G. H. T.-W., Baron. The camel

Bradbury, R. Heart transplant

Caballero, F. "The wishes"

Gilman, C. P. When I was a witch

Jacobs, W. W. The monkey's paw

Sarrantonio, A. Wish

Stevenson, R. L. The bottle imp

"The **wishes**". Caballero, F.

The **wishes**. Cobb, W. J.

Wishes. Lincoln, C.

Wishful thinking. Pronzini, B.

Wishloop. Rucker, R. v. B.

Wishnia, Kenneth

(jt. auth) See Gordin, Jacob

Wisniewski, Mark

Addenda

The Yale Review v87 no4 p77-85 O 1999

Behind the Suits I Wear to Work

The Yale Review v92 no2 p103-17 Ap 2004

Descending

The Pushcart prize XXIII: best of the small
presses; an annual small press reader; edited by Bill Henderson with the Pushcart
prize editors

A Good, Cheap Thrill

South Carolina Review v36 no1 p66-70 Fall
2003

Hollowbrook

River Styx no67 p84-92 2004

Pariahs

TriQuarterly no110/111 p107-22 Fall 2001

Wisniewski, Mark—*Continued*
Precious Blood
   The Georgia Review v58 no1 p147-59 Spr
   2004
Wister, Owen
Timberline
   A Century of great Western stories; edited by
   John Jakes
WIT *See* Humor
Witch. Berkman, P. R.
The **witch**. Chekhov, A. P.
Witch. DeRosso, H. A.
The **witch**. Prose, F.
The **witch** of Greenwich. Dôle, G.
The **Witch** of Truro. Hoffman, A.
The **witch** who hated Halloween. Kaye, T.
WITCHCRAFT
      See also Demoniac possession; Exor-
   cism; Voodooism
   Berkman, P. R. Witch
   Betancourt, J. G. The devil's own
   Blavatsky, H. P. Can the double murder?
   Bowles, P. Doña Faustina
   Bowles, P. The eye
   Bradbury, R. The exiles
   Bradbury, R. Exorcism
   Bradbury, R. The witch doctor
   Campbell, R. Dolls
   Campbell, R. The seductress
   Chekhov, A. P. The witch
   Dann, J. Bad medicine
   Douglass, S. The mistress of Marwood Hagg
   Doyle, Sir A. C. Lot no. 249
   Edghill, R. The Christmas witch
   Ellison, H. The goddess in the ice
   Erdrich, L. Fleur
   Freeman, M. E. W. The witch's daughter
   Hawthorne, N. Feathertop
   Hawthorne, N. Feathertop: a moralized legend
   Hawthorne, N. Young Goodman Brown
   Heinlein, R. A. Magic, inc.
   Hughes, D. B. The Granny Woman
   Jackson, S. The very strange house next door
   Jakes, J. The man who wanted to be in the
      movies
   Kaminsky, S. M. In thunder, lightning or in rain
   Kaye, T. The witch who hated Halloween
   Kilpatrick, N. Heartbeat
   Lackey, M. Nightside
   Lida, D. Bewitched
   Lindskold, J. M. Sacrifice
   Link, K. Catskin
   Little, B. Maya's mother
   Lovecraft, H. P. Witches' Hollow
   Okorafor, N. Asuquo; or, The winds of Harmat-
      tan
   Perrault, C. Toads and diamonds
   Ptacek, K. Reunion
   Singer, I. B. Cunegunde
   Singer, I. B. The jew from Babylon
   Singer, I. B. The sorcerer
   Tenn, W. Mistress Sary
   Tenn, W. My mother was a witch
   Trueba, A. d. "The adventures of a tailor"
   Turner, G. And now doth time waste me
   Vaughn, E. Winter solstice
   Vinge, V. The peddler's apprentice
   Wilde, Lady. The horned women
WITCHES *See* Witchcraft

Witches. Gilliland, G.
Witches' Hollow. Lovecraft, H. P.
The **witching** hour. De Lint, C.
The **witch's** daughter. Freeman, M. E. W.
The **witch's** tale. Frazer, M.
With a bang. Simpson, H.
With a little help from her friends. Bishop, M.
With Ché in New Hampshire. Banks, R.
With clouds at our feet. Brown, S.
With folded hands. Williamson, J.
With her. McGarry, J.
With her in Ourland. Gilman, C. P.
With jazz. Mason, B. A.
With my eyes closed. Arenas, R.
With myth and fire. Masiki, T.
With old man Makhno. See Babel', I. Makhno's
   boys
With Ray & Judy. Barthelme, F.
With smiles as wide as summer. Bradbury, R.
With thanks to Agatha Christie. Mason, S. J.
With the violin. Chopin, K.
Withholding. Spielberg, P.
Without Blood. Baricco, A.
Without Ellie. Silber, J.
Without spot or wrinkle. Weaver, G.
The **witness**. Earle, S.
Witness. Martin, T.
Witness Protection. Jacobs, M.
Witness to breath. Hyde, C. R.
Witness to the crucifixion. Gilchrist, E.
Witness to the league of blond hip hop dancers.
   Allegra, D.
WITNESSES
   Dokey, R. Monkey
   Ellison, H. The whimper of whipped dogs
   Estleman, L. D. The used
   L'Amour, L. Too tough to kill
   Parrish, T. The smell of a car
   Paul, B. The favor
Witwer, H. C. (Harry Charles)
   The Chickasha Bone Crusher
      Boxing's best short stories; edited by Paul D.
      Staudohar
   The leather pushers
      Sports best short stories; edited by Paul D.
      Staudohar
Wives, lovers, Maximilian. Lee, M.
Wiwa, Ken Saro- *See* Saro-Wiwa, Ken
"The **wizard**". Valera, J.
A **wizard** from Gettysburg. Chopin, K.
WIZARD OF OZ (MOTION PICTURE)
   Nagy, S. The Hanged Man of Oz
WIZARDS *See* Magicians
WLUV. Carter, E.
Wo es war, soll ich werden. Davenport, G.
Wodehouse, P. G. (Pelham Grenville)
   The debut of Battling Billson
      Boxing's best short stories; edited by Paul D.
      Staudohar
   The heart of a goof
      Sports best short stories; edited by Paul D.
      Staudohar
Wodehouse, Pelham Grenville *See* Wodehouse,
   P. G. (Pelham Grenville), 1881-1975
Woeful tales from Mahigul. Le Guin, U. K.
The **wolf**. Maupassant, G. d.
Wolf and hound. Bennett, N. and Elrod, P. N.
Wolf at the door. Everett, P. L.
Wolf-Eye. Henry, W.

A **Wolf** in Virginia. Dunlap, M.
Wolf Man. Ward, C.
Wolf moon. Gorman, E.
Wolf watch. Weinberg, R.
Wolf winter. O'Callaghan, M.
Wolfe, Gene
  Bed & breakfast
    The American fantasy tradition; edited by Brian M. Thomsen
  Copperhead
    Wolfe, G. Innocents aboard; new fantasy stories
  The dead man
    Wondrous beginnings; edited by Steven H. Silver and Martin H. Greenberg
  The death of Doctor Island
    Brown, C. N. and Strahan, J. The Locus awards; thirty years of the best in science fiction and fantasy; edited by Charles N. Brown and Jonathan Strahan
  The eleventh city
    Wolfe, G. Innocents aboard; new fantasy stories
  The fat magician
    Such a pretty face; edited by Lee Martindale
  A fish story
    Best new horror 11; edited and with an introduction by Stephen Jones
    Wolfe, G. Innocents aboard; new fantasy stories
  The friendship light
    Wolfe, G. Innocents aboard; new fantasy stories
  Houston, 1943
    Wolfe, G. Innocents aboard; new fantasy stories
  How the bishop sailed to Inniskeen
    Wolfe, G. Innocents aboard; new fantasy stories
  The legend of Xi Cygnus
    Wolfe, G. Innocents aboard; new fantasy stories
  The lost pilgrim
    Wolfe, G. Innocents aboard; new fantasy stories
  The Monday man
    Wolfe, G. Innocents aboard; new fantasy stories
  The night chough
    The Crow; shattered lives & broken dreams; edited by J. O'Barr and Ed Kramer
    Wolfe, G. Innocents aboard; new fantasy stories
  No planets strike
    The Best from fantasy & science fiction: the fiftieth anniversary anthology; edited by Edward L. Ferman and Gordon Van Gelder
  The old woman whose rolling pin is the sun
    Wolfe, G. Innocents aboard; new fantasy stories
  Pocketful of diamonds
    Wolfe, G. Innocents aboard; new fantasy stories
  Queen
    Wolfe, G. Innocents aboard; new fantasy stories
  The sailor who sailed after the sun
    Wolfe, G. Innocents aboard; new fantasy stories

Shields of Mars
  Mars probes; edited by Peter Crowther
Slow children at play
  Wolfe, G. Innocents aboard; new fantasy stories
A traveler in desert lands
  Wolfe, G. Innocents aboard; new fantasy stories
The tree is my hat
  999: new stories of horror and suspense; edited by Al Sarrantonio
  Wolfe, G. Innocents aboard; new fantasy stories
  The Year's best fantasy & horror, thirteenth annual collection; edited by Ellen Datlow and Terri Windling
Under hill
  Wolfe, G. Innocents aboard; new fantasy stories
Viewpoint
  Redshift; extreme visions of speculative fiction; edited by Al Sarrantonio
The waif
  Wolfe, G. Innocents aboard; new fantasy stories
The walking sticks
  Wolfe, G. Innocents aboard; new fantasy stories
Wolfer
  Wolfe, G. Innocents aboard; new fantasy stories
The wrapper
  Wolfe, G. Innocents aboard; new fantasy stories
Wolfe, Sarah
  My mother's heart
    The Ohio Review no60 p122-32 1999
Wolfe, Thomas
  O lost
    The Pushcart prize XXVI; best of the small presses, an annual small press reader; edited by Bill Henderson and the Pushcart prize editors
WOLFE, THOMAS, 1900-1938
        About
  Bradbury, R. Forever and the Earth
Wolff, Tobias
  The Benefit of the Doubt
    The New Yorker v79 no19 p76-83 Jl 14-21 2003
  Class Picture
    The New Yorker v78 no41 p70-9 Ja 6 2003
  Hunters in the snow
    What are you looking at?; the first fat fiction anthology; edited by Donna Jarrell and Ira Sukrungruang
  Kiss
    The New Yorker v75 no5 p88-92+ Mr 29 1999
  The night in question
    The Art of the story; an international anthology of contemporary short stories; edited by Daniel Halpern
Wolfie. Phillips, R. S.

Wolitzer, Meg
 Tea at the house
  The Pushcart prize XXIII: best of the small
  presses; an annual small press reader; ed-
  ited by Bill Henderson with the Pushcart
  prize editors
WOLLSTONECRAFT, MARY, 1759-1797
                About
 Jones, G. On the piteous death of Mary Woll-
  stonecraft
Wolven, Scott
 Controlled burn
  The Best American mystery stories, 2003; ed-
  ited by Michael Connelly and Otto Penzler
 The copper kings
  The Best American mystery stories, 2002; ed-
  ited and with an introduction by James
  Ellroy; Otto Penzler, series editor
Wolverine grudge. Lord, N.
Wolverton, Terry
 Sex less
  Hers 2: brilliant new fiction by lesbian writ-
  ers; edited by Terry Wolverton with Robert
  Drake
WOLVES
 Chekhov, A. P. Whitebrow
 Cherryh, C. J. Ice
 Chesnutt, C. W. The gray wolf's ha'nt
 Gorman, E. Wolf moon
 Henry, W. Ghost wolf of Thunder Mountain
 Hopkinson, N. Riding the red
 Lord, N. Recall of the wild
 O'Callaghan, M. Wolf winter
 Popkes, S. Winters are hard
 Zinovyeva-Annibal, L. D. Wolves
Wolves. Zinovyeva-Annibal, L. D.
Wolves don't cry. Elliott, B.
Wolves till the world goes down. Van Eekhout, G.
Wolzien, Valerie
 Just one bite won't kill you
  Death dines at 8:30; edited by Claudia Bishop
  and Nick DiChario
A **woman** 49er. Levy, J.
The **woman** at Loon Point. Derleth, A. W. and
  Schorer, M.
The **woman** at the gas station. Schlink, B.
The **woman** from New York. Ha Jin
Woman Hollering Creek. Cisneros, S.
Woman in a wheelchair. Llywelyn, M.
The **woman** in the front seat. Hart, R.
The **woman** in the wall. Barnes, S.
The **woman** in the water. Haake, K.
A **woman** saved from drowning. Cabrera Infante,
  G.
Woman singing. Ortiz, S. J.
The **woman** who cut off her leg at the Maidstone
  Club. Slavin, J.
The **woman** who gave juice to the roofers. Ritch-
  ie, E.
The **woman** who loved pigs. Donaldson, S. R.
The **woman** who rode away. Lawrence, D. H.
The **woman** who said no. Ferriss, L.
The **woman** who sugared strawberries. Vasseur, T.
  J.
The **woman** who tasted of rose oil. Edugyan, E.
The **Woman** Who Tortured and Nurtured Turge-
  nev. Hochstein, R.
The **woman** who was forgotten. Aldrich, B. S.
The **woman** who would marry a bear. Lord, N.

Woman without arms. Mayo, W.
A **woman** without prejudices. Chekhov, A. P.
A **woman's** liberation. Le Guin, U. K.
A **woman's** perfume. Hegi, U.
The **womb**. Broderick, D.
WOMEN
        See also African American women; Jew-
    ish women; Muslim women; Single women
 Adams, A. Elizabeth
 Adams, A. The end of the world
 Adams, A. Mexican dust
 Adams, A. Molly's dog
 Adams, A. A public pool
 Adams, A. Return trips
 Adams, A. Sintra
 Adams, A. Waiting for Stella
 Adams, A. Your doctor loves you
 Agee, J. What I'm doing in Missouri
 Alcott, L. M. The rival prima donnas
 Aldrich, B. S. What God hath joined
 Aniebo, I. N. C. Four dimensions
 Auchincloss, L. The Virginia redbird
 Beattie, A. The women of this world
 Bellow, S. A theft
 Berners, G. H. T.-W., Baron. Far from the mad-
  ding war
 Bly, C. The last of the gold star mothers
 Borges, J. L. Story of the warrior and the cap-
  tive maiden
 Boylan, C. Some retired ladies on a tour
 Brownrigg, S. Amazon
 Brownrigg, S. Hussy from the west
 Budnitz, J. Scenes from the fall fashion catalog
 Butler, R. O. Christmas 1910
 Byatt, A. S. A stone woman
 Cabrera Infante, G. The doors open at three
 Carter, E. East on Houston
 Casares, O. Mrs. Perez
 Cobb, W. J. Three feet of water
 Codrescu, A. Julie
 Davies, Tristan. Talent show
 Day, C. The circus house
 Desplechin, M. At sea
 Doctorow, E. L. Jolene: a life
 Douglas, M. What the periwinkle remember
 Drummond, L. L. Absolutes
 Drummond, L. L. Cleaning your gun
 Drummond, L. L. Finding a place
 Drummond, L. L. Katherine's elegy
 Drummond, L. L. Keeping the dead alive
 Drummond, L. L. Lemme tell you something
 Drummond, L. L. Something about a scar
 Drummond, L. L. Taste, touch, sight, sound,
  smell
 Drummond, L. L. Under control
 Drummond, L. L. Where I come from
 Ellis, Z. The waiting room
 Endrezze, A. The humming of stars and bees
  and waves
 Estep, M. Teeth
 Fitzgerald, F. S. Bernice bobs her hair
 Gilchrist, E. The famous poll at Jody's Bar
 Gilchrist, E. There's a Garden of Eden
 Homes, A. M. The weather outside is sunny and
  bright
 Hudson, Suzanne. The seamstress
 Kennedy, A. L. Awaiting an adverse reaction
 Lawrence, D. H. St. Mawr
 Lee, A. About fog and cappuccino

WOMEN—*Continued*

Lee, A. Brothers and sisters around the world
Lee, A. Dancing with Josefina
Lee, A. Interesting women
Lilly, J. M. Going home money
Maleti, G. Mirta
Marías, J. The Italian legacy
Mason, B. A. Tunica
Mastretta, A. Aunt Chila
Mastretta, A. Aunt Fernanda
Mastretta, A. Big-eyed women [excerpt]
Mayhall, J. The men
Mejides, M. The tropics
Moody, R. Ineluctable modality of the vaginal
Morgan, R. A taxpayer & a citizen
Nfah-Abbenyi, J. M. Bayam-sellam
O'Connell, M. Saint Ursula and her maidens
Painter, P. Going wild
Peri Rossi, C. Singing in the desert
Peterson, P. W. Africa
Peterson, P. W. Alfie and Grace
Piñón, N. House of passion
Proulx, A. A lonely coast
Rhys, J. A spiritualist
Robinson, R. The face-lift
Robison, M. Mirror
Rodgers, S. J. Delivery
Rodgers, S. J. Green beans
Rodgers, S. J. Women of will
Sammān, G. Register: I'm not an Arab woman
Sammān, G. Visitors of a dying person
Sanford, A. Crossing Shattuck Bridge
Schmidt, H. J. Darling?
Schmidt, H. J. Fishman's fascination
Schoemperlen, D. Weights and measures
Scott, M. Trouble and her friends [excerpt]
Sherman, C. W. Emerald City: Third & Pike
Silber, J. Comforts
Silber, J. Covered
Slavin, J. Blighted
Taylor-Hall, M. A. Winter facts
Weldon, F. Inside the whale; or, I don't know
  but I've been told
Whitty, J. The story of the deep dark
Wilkinson, C. E. Humming back yesterday
Yuknavitch, L. Beauty

Employment

Harris, M. Touching Idamae Low

Psychology

Adam, C. Siren
Adams, A. Home is where
Adams, A. The islands
Adams, A. Old love affairs
Addonizio, K. In the box called pleasure
Agee, J. This is for Chet
Agee, J. The tire man
Alavi, T. Disappearance of an ordinary woman
Anderson, R. Echo
Arastuyi, S. I came to have tea with my daughter
Arvin, N. Electric fence
Auchincloss, L. The interlude
Azadeh, C. Bronagh
Banks, R. Theory of flight
Barker, N. The three button trick
Barrett, L. The former Star Carlson
Bauman, B. A. Safeway
Bausch, R. Rare & endangered species
Beagan, G. The great master of ecstasy

Bender, A. Dearth
Berry, W. A jonquil for Mary Penn
Bertles, J. Whileaway
Bocock, M. A citizen of the world at large
Boylan, C. The Little Madonna
Brady, C. Pilgrimage
Braverman, K. Tall tales from the Mekong Delta
Braverman, K. Temporary light
Broughton, T. A. L'americana
Brownrigg, S. The lady in the desert
Brownrigg, S. She who caught buses
Broyard, B. Loose talk
Budnitz, J. Flush
Byatt, A. S. The thing in the forest
Carlson, R. Gary Garrison's wedding vows
Carter, E. The bride
Carter, E. My big red heart
Casey, M. Dirt
Chaon, D. Prosthesis
Cheng, C.-W. The coconut palms on campus
Cherry, K. Block party
Clark, J. Frazzle
Clark, J. Revenge
Clyde, M. Farming butterflies
Clyde, M. Jumping
Connor, J. Tea and comfortable advice
Connor, J. We who live apart
Connor, J. Women's problems
De Varennes, Monique. Cabeza
Deane, J. F. Twenty-three
DeMarco, T. Dancing bare
DeMarinis, R. The singular we
Dinh, L. The ugliest girl
Divakaruni, C. B. What the body knows
Dorcey, M. A sense of humour
Erian, A. Bikini
Foley, S. A history of sex
Foley, S. Life in the air ocean
Foley, S. The state of union
Foster, K. Remainders
Fowler, K. J. The Elizabeth complex
Friesner, E. M. A birthday
Gabrielyan, N. Happiness
Galloway, J. The trick is to keep breathing [excerpt]
Garro, E. Blame the Tlaxcaltecs
Gartner, Z. The nature of pure evil
Gartner, Z. Pest control for dummies
Gasco, E. Can you wave bye bye, baby?
Gasco, E. The third person
Gasco, E. A well-imagined life
Gasco, E. You have the body
Glover, D. H. Why I decide to kill myself and
  other jokes
Goldner, B. Plan B
Goliger, G. Edith Teilheimer's war
Graver, E. The mourning door
Greenberg, A. Crimes against humanity
Haake, K. Arrow math
Haake, K. The land of sculpture
Haake, K. The woman in the water
Hall, J. B. If you can't win
Harrison, K. Planting
Hayes, D. Hope
Hearon, S. Order
Henley, P. Sun damage
Highsmith, P. The still point of the turning world

WOMEN—Psychology—*Continued*

Hochman, A. What's more
Homes, A. M. Georgica
Honig, L. Refuge
Hood, A. After Zane
Howard, M. Children with matches
Iribarne, M. The sun in the sky
Jacobs, M. Dove of the back streets
Johnston, B. A. Anything that floats
Jordan, J. The wife
Joseph, D. Naming stories
Kaplan, H. Dysaesthesia
Keegan, C. Antarctica
Keegan, C. Love in the tall grass
Kees, W. Gents 50/Ladies 25
Kheradmand, F. Smile!
Kincaid, J. The autobiography of my mother [excerpt]
Kittredge, W. Balancing water
Klíma, I. The washing machine
Kohler, S. All the days of my life
Kohler, S. Paris by night
Kohler, S. Rain check
Krouse, E. The fast
Krouse, E. The husbands
Krouse, E. No universe
Lawrence, D. H. The border line
Lewis, T. The marijuana tree
Louis, L. G. Divining the waters
Louis, L. G. Talking in the dark
Martin, V. The mechanics of it
Martin, V. Surface calm
Mason, B. A. With jazz
McGarry, J. Lavare
McNeal, T. Winter in Los Angeles
Meredith, D. Comic Valentine
Miller, R. Bryna
Miller, R. Paula
Moore, L. Real estate
Munro, A. Floating bridge
Munro, A. Nettles
Munro, A. Post and beam
Munro, A. Queenie
Munro, A. What is remembered
Nawrocki, S. Farmer boy
Nelson, A. Incognito
Ní Dhuibhne-Almqvist, É. The Garden of Eden
Norris, L. Interior country
Norris, L. Toy guns
Oates, J. C. The dark prince
Oates, J. C. Faithless
Oates, J. C. Fire
Oates, J. C. The instructor
Oates, J. C. Tell me you forgive me?
Oates, J. C. Upholstery
Oates, J. C. You, little match-girl
O'Connell, M. Saint Anne
O'Connell, M. Veronica's veil
Olsen, S. S. Free writing
Ossana, D. White line fever
Painter, P. The second night of a one night stand
Pak, W.-S. Three days in that autumn
Pesetsky, B. Offspring of the first generation
Pittalwala, I. Great Guruji
Potvin, E. A. Deflection
Potvin, E. A. Ghost
Potvin, E. A. Open skies
Potvin, E. A. To rise above

Potvin, E. A. The way home
Power, S. A hole in the sheets
Powers, S. The wild
Rawley, D. A rumor of prayer
Reisman, N. Dreaming of the snail life
Richmond, M. The girl in the fall-away dress
Richmond, M. Propaganda
Rick, M. Next time
Rivera Valdés, S. Little poisons
Rodgers, S. J. Bust
Rosenfeld, S. Cliff dweller
Ryman, G. Fan
Sammān, G. An air-conditioned egg
Schnitzler, A. Fräulein Else
Schoemperlen, D. In a dark season
Schoemperlen, D. The man of my dreams
Schwartz, L. S. Intrusions
Schwartz, S. Afterbirth
Shon, F. The farmer's wife
Simpson, H. Getting a life
Simpson, H. Millennium blues
Simpson, H. Opera
Simpson, H. Wirstigkeit
Slavin, J. Pudding
Slavin, J. Swallowed whole
Smith, L. Between the lines
Sojourner, M. Squirrel
Solwitz, S. Ballerina
Sosin, D. Planted
Spatz, G. Inversion
Spatz, G. Wonderful tricks
Spencer, E. I, Maureen
Starr, G. Tuberama: a musical on the Northern Line (or how to be in touch with your emotions)
Strauss, A. The joy of funerals
Strauss, A. Shrinking away
Strauss, A. Still life
Strauss, A. Versions of you
Stuckey-French, E. Scavenger hunt
Swan, M. By the sea, by the sea
Swan, M. Hour of lead
Swick, M. A. Crete
Swick, M. A. The zealous mourner
Thompson, J. Heart of gold
Thompson, J. Ice angels
Thompson, J. The rich man's house
Tilghman, C. Mary in the mountains
Tillman, L. Thrilled to death
Tinti, H. Miss Waldron's red colobus
Tinti, H. Preservation
Treat, J. His sweater
Treat, J. Radio disturbance
Treat, J. The summer of Zubeyde
Tuck, L. Dream house
Tuck, L. La Mayonette
Tuck, L. Rue Guynemer
Tuck, L. Verdi
Wallace, D. F. The depressed person
Wallace, M. Thinking
Watanabe McFerrin, L. Childproofing
Watanabe McFerrin, L. Coyote comes calling
Watanabe McFerrin, L. Masai heart
Watanabe McFerrin, L. Pickled eggs
Weldon, F. Move out: move on
Wells, K. Hallie out of this world
White, M. C. Heights
Wieland, L. Irradiation
Wieland, L. Purgatory

WOMEN—Psychology—*Continued*
Winter, E. Call me Ruby
Yoshimoto, B. Asleep
Relation to other women
Bell, M. S. Customs of the country
Best, M. Stephanie's book [excerpt]
Blackwood, S. One flesh, one blood
Brownrigg, S. A gal of ambition
Brownrigg, S. Mars needs women!
Capote, T. The bargain
Casey, M. Indulgence
Casey, M. Rules to live
Coberly, L. M. The death of Alma Ruth
Craig, A. The French Boy
Davis, J. S. Some things collide
Desplechin, M. The kiwi-seller
Divakaruni, C. B. The blooming season for cacti
Divakaruni, C. B. The lives of strangers
Dunmore, H. You stayed awake with me
Epstein, J. Love and The Guinness book of records
Fairey, W. W. The bad hand
Ferré, R. When women love men
Fleming, R. A lizard's kiss
Frym, G. Rosie since Vietnam
Gilchrist, E. The big cleanup
Gilchrist, E. In the land of dreamy dreams
Glaspell, S. A jury of her peers
Gussoff, C. The wave: a novella
Hay, E. Cézanne in a soft hat
Hay, E. A clear record
Hay, E. Cowgirl
Hay, E. Earrings
Hay, E. The fight
Hay, E. The fire
Hay, E. The friend
Hay, E. Hand games
Hay, E. January through March
Hay, E. Johnny's smile
Hay, E. The kiss
Hay, E. Makeup
Hay, E. Overnight visitor
Hay, E. The parents
Hay, E. A personal letter
Hay, E. Purge me with hyssop
Hay, E. The reader
Hay, E. Sayonara
Hay, E. Secondhand Rose
Hay, E. Several losses
Helms, B. Oysters
Henley, P. Friday night at Silver Star
Highsmith, P. Quiet night
Hoffman, A. Local girls
Hood, A. The rightness of things
James, S. Love, lust, life
Johnson, D. Mouthful of sorrow
Johnson, D. Three ladies sipping tea in a Persian garden
Klass, P. Freedom fighter
Kohler, S. Death in Rome
Kohler, S. Structure
Krasnoff, B. Stoop ladies
Krawiec, R. Rituals
Kusel, L. Bones
Kusel, L. The other side
Lee, A. Un petit d'un petit
Lee, A. The visit
Lessing, D. M. The grandmothers
Link, K. Louise's ghost

Mastretta, A. Aunt Marcela and Aunt Jacinta
Mastretta, A. Aunt Pilar and Aunt Marta
Matiella, A. C. Size does matter
Melville, P. Lucifer's shank
Moose, R. Friends and oranges
Nissen, T. 819 Walnut
Nixon, C. Lunch at the Blacksmith
Norris, L. Black ice
Orner, P. Melba Kuperchmid returns
Orner, P. Melba Kuperschmid returns
Padilla, M. Flora in shadows
Padilla, M. Who in the modern world can keep up with Julia Juárez?
Reisman, N. Girl on a couch
Rosenfeld, S. To Sarah, wherever you are
Schoemperlen, D. Clues
Schoemperlen, D. Hockey night in Canada
Schoemperlen, D. The look of the lightning, the sound of the birds
Searle, E. What it's worth
Simonds, M. The still point
Simpson, H. Café society
Simpson, H. Cheers
Smart, A. Raccoon
Sojourner, M. Bear house
Sojourner, M. Hag
Stanton, M. The cat and the clown
Stanton, M. Marie Antoinette's harp
Stanton, M. The ugly virgin
Stuckey-French, E. Search and rescue
Swan, M. Peach
Tomioka, T. Yesterday's girl
Updike, J. The rescue
Warren, D. Tuxedo
Watanabe McFerrin, L. Khalida's dog
Weldon, F. Come on, everyone!
Winter, E. Have a prayer
Wright, J. B. Stitch and bitch
Yoshimoto, B. Love songs
Social conditions
See also Feminism
Ahmadi Khorasani, N. That day
Aqai, F. One woman, one love
Blake, J. C. Texas woman blues
Bukiet, M. J. But, Microsoft! what byte through yonder windows breaks?
Castellanos, R. Culinary lesson
Chekhov, A. P. Anyuta
Chekhov, A. P. Betrothed
Chekhov, A. P. The chorus girl
Chekhov, A. P. A gentleman friend
Elliott, S. B. The heart of it
Fadavi, P. The bitter life of Shirin
Gilman, C. P. An honest woman
Gilman, C. P. Making a change
Gilman, C. P. Turned
Hajizadeh, F. Contrary to democracy
Karampur, F. Refugee
Lao She. Also a triangle
Lawrence, D. H. The woman who rode away
Le Guin, U. K. A woman's liberation
Mencken, S. H. Ladies and lovers
Mencken, S. H. Solitaire
Roth, J. The cartel
Sánchez, R. Barrio chronicle
Sharifzadeh, M. Butterflies
Tabatabai, N. The lark
Vafi, F. My mother, behind the glass
Vonnegut, K. Lovers Anonymous

WOMEN, BLACK *See* African American women
WOMEN, JEWISH *See* Jewish women
WOMEN, MUSLIM *See* Muslim women
Women and Dynamite. Easton, R. O.
WOMEN ARTISTS
  Adams, A. Berkeley house
  Borges, J. L. The duel
  Byatt, A. S. Body art
  Cisneros, S. Never marry a Mexican
  Divakaruni, C. B. The unknown errors of our lives
  Gabrielyan, N. Bee heaven
  Gabrielyan, N. Master of the grass
  Lord, N. Candace counts coup
  Mastretta, A. Aunt Natalia
  Miller, R. Louisa
  Shange, N. Every time my lil' world seems blue
  Silber, J. First marriage
  Skillings, R. D. The line
  Skillings, R. D. Outcomes
  Smith, J. Fresh paint
  Warren, D. Tuxedo
  Whitty, J. Stealing from the dead
  Wisenberg, S. L. My mother's war
WOMEN ASTRONAUTS
  Landis, G. A. A walk in the sun
WOMEN ATHLETES
  Boyle, T. C. She wasn't soft
WOMEN AUTHORS
  Auchincloss, L. The facts of fiction
  Belle, J. Book of Nick
  Berliner, J. Until the butterflies
  Bloom, A. The story
  Bowles, P. Tea on the mountain
  Byatt, A. S. Raw material
  Chekhov, A. P. A drama
  Duffy, S. Could be better
  Dunlap, S. Bad review
  Edghill, R. The intersection of Anastasia Yeoman and light
  Frame, R. La Plume de ma tante
  Gilchrist, E. Anna, Part I
  Gilchrist, E. The sanguine blood of men
  Gilchrist, E. A statue of Aphrodite
  Gilman, C. P. The yellow wallpaper
  Howe, M. J. Acting tips
  Kane, J. F. Exposure
  Lake, M. D. Tea for two
  Lee, C. Luisa
  Link, K. Most of my friends are two-thirds water
  Linzner, G. Author, author
  Maraini, D. Letters to Marina [excerpt]
  Moorhead, F. Four characters, four lunches
  Munro, A. Family furnishings
  Prose, F. Three pigs in five days [excerpt]
  Rubina, D. Apples from Shlitzbutter's garden
  Rusch, K. K. The perfect man
  Sojourner, M. Bear house
  Stanton, M. The cliffs of the moon
  Stanton, M. My sister's novel
  Tillman, L. To find words
  Vinten, R. Character witness
  Watanabe McFerrin, L. Rubber time
  Wharton, E. Expiation
  Wharton, E. Writing a war story
  Wilkinson, M. A man's book
  Wings, M. Empty arms

WOMEN BOXERS
  Toole, F. X. Million $$$ baby
WOMEN CLERGY
  Thomas, J. C. Young Reverend Zelma Lee Moses
WOMEN DRAMATISTS
  Goran, L. O'Casey and the career
WOMEN EDITORS
  Gunthorp, D. Pikeman and the Bagwoman
  Miller, R. Greta
  Paul, B. Stet
WOMEN IN BUSINESS *See* Businesswomen
WOMEN IN POLITICS
  Singer, I. B. The conference
WOMEN JOURNALISTS
  Bianchini, A. Years later
  Carson, J. Invaders
  Daum, M. Alternative lifestyle alert
  Lee, A. Anthropology
  Lida, D. Bewitched
  Menendez, A. Her mother's house
  Munro, A. Family furnishings
  Nair, M. Sixteen days in December
  Oates, J. C. In Copland
  Pickard, N. Afraid of the dark
  Poirier, M. J. Worms
  Saulnier, B. High maintenance
  Sturgeon, T. The sex opposite
  Yates, R. Trying out for the race
WOMEN LAWYERS
  Cannon, T. Restitution
  Caudwell, S. The triumph of Eve
  DeLoach, N. Victim by consent
  Devane, T. Decoys
  Huffman, B., Jr. Judicial economy
  Jacobs, J. Built upon the sand
  Jones, G. The word 'Ruby'
  Kahn, M. A. Strange bedfellows
  Krich, R. M. "You win some . . . "
  Matera, L. Counsel for the defense
  Matera, L. Dead drunk
  Matera, L. Dream lawyer
  Matera, L. Easy go
  Meloy, M. Tome
  Oates, J. C. Murder-two
  O'Shaughnessy, P. Juggernaut
  Ravera, L. You drive
  Rawley, D. Vandeville
  Simpson, H. Burns and the bankers
  Wheat, C. The only good judge
  Youmans, C. Mortmain
The **women** of Gustav Klimt. Whan, E.
The **women** of this world. Beattie, A.
WOMEN PAINTERS
  Alameddine, R. Whore
WOMEN PHOTOGRAPHERS
  Morgan, D. Sepia sun
  Searle, E. 101
  Smith, C. Insomnia
WOMEN PHYSICIANS
  Gilman, C. P. The crux
  Gilman, C. P. Mr. Peebles heart
  Goliger, G. Maladies of the inner ear
  Klass, P. Freedom fighter
  Klass, P. Love and modern medicine
  Klass, P. Necessary risks
  Murakami, H. Thailand
  Ohlin, A. Transcription
  Pak, W.-S. Three days in that autumn

WOMEN PHYSICIANS—*Continued*
Stollman, A. L. The creation of Anat
Updike, J. Metamorphosis
WOMEN POETS
De Lint, C. Saskia
Gilchrist, E. The cabal
Lee, D. The price of eggs in China
Mayo, W. Woman without arms
Mueller, D. Birds
Oates, J. C. In hiding
Singer, I. B. The interview
Smith, J. Silk strands
Solari, M. T. Death and transfiguration of a teacher
Updike, J. The Bulgarian poetess
WOMEN PSYCHIATRISTS
Allyn, D. Saint Bobby
WOMEN SCIENTISTS
Klass, P. The province of the bearded fathers
Murray, J. The hill station
Norris, L. Swimmers
Vaswani, N. The pelvis series
WOMEN SCULPTORS
Adams, A. Legends
Yates, R. Oh, Joseph, I'm so tired
WOMEN SOLDIERS
Min, A. Red azalea [excerpt]
The **women** who got away. Updike, J.
WOMEN'S CLUBS *See* Clubs
WOMEN'S LIBERATION MOVEMENT *See* Feminism
Women's problems. Connor, J.
A **women's** restaurant. Boyle, T. C.
Wonder bread. Anderson, D.
The **wonder** spot. Bank, M.
Wonderful gesture. Furman, L.
Wonderful, horrid, divine. Regen-Tuero, K.
The **wonderful** Tar-Baby story. Harris, J. C.
Wonderful teen. Ferrell, C.
Wonderful tricks. Spatz, G.
The **wonders** of the invisible world. Gates, D.
Wong, David T. K.
The Cocktail Party
The Literary Review (Madison, N.J.) v47 no4 p111-17 Summ 2004
Wood, Arlo
River mouth
The Antioch Review v57 no4 p471-81 Fall 1999
Wood, David
Feathers on the solar wind
Best new American voices 2000; guest editor Tobias Wolff; series editors John Kulka and Natalie Danford
Wood, Monica
Disappearing
What are you looking at?; the first fat fiction anthology; edited by Donna Jarrell and Ira Sukrungruang
Ernie's ark
The Pushcart prize XXIII: best of the small presses; an annual small press reader; edited by Bill Henderson with the Pushcart prize editors
That one autumn
The Best American mystery stories, 2003; edited by Michael Connelly and Otto Penzler
Wood. McCann, C.

WOOD CARVING
Armstrong, K. Drowning in air
Hawthorne, N. Drowne's wooden image
Trevor, W. Sacred statues
The **wood-choopers**. Chopin, K.
The **wood** of such trees. Bukoski, A.
The **woodcutter**. Means, D.
The **Wooden** Village of Kizhi. Shonk, K.
Woodrell, Daniel
The Amnesty Barracks
New Letters v69 no2/3 p79-92 2003
Woodrow, Marnie
Perdita's wrapper
The Canadian Forum v78 no875 [i.e. no876] p29-33 Ap 1999
Woods, Elizabeth Rhett
Randy
Dalhousie Review v83 no3 p405-13 Aut 2003
The **woods**. Furman, L.
The **woods** at the back of our houses. Phillips, D. R.
Woodward, Solon Timothy
Plants and ghosts
African American Review v36 no1 p55-64 Spr 2002
Vain Empires
Gettysburg Review v15 no2 p327-41 Summ 2002
Woodworker. Kilpatrick, N.
The **wool** gatherer. Steinbeck, T.
Wool socks. Viganò, R.
Woolf, Virginia
The lady in the looking-glass: a reflection
Harper's v299 no1794 p89-91 N 1999
WOOLF, VIRGINIA, 1882-1941
About
Crowley, J. The reason for the visit
WOOLLCOTT, ALEXANDER, 1887-1943
About
Breen, J. L. Woollcott and the vamp
Woollcott and the vamp. Breen, J. L.
Woolrich, Cornell
The black curtain [excerpt]
The Vintage book of amnesia; an anthology; edited by Jonathan Lethem
Rear window
The Best American mystery stories of the century; Tony Hillerman, editor; with an introduction by Tony Hillerman
Woolson, Constance Fenimore
Felipa
Southern local color; stories of region, race, and gender; edited by Barbara C. Ewell and Pamela Glenn Menke; with notes by Andrea Humphrey
The **word**. Maleti, G.
Word play. Vachss, A. H.
The **word** 'Ruby'. Jones, G.
Wordplay. Wallace, R.
The **words** of Guru. Kornbluth, C. M.
Words of power. Yolen, J.
Words, silences. Chaudhuri, A.
The **words** that remain. De Lint, C.
WORDSWORTH, DOROTHY, 1771-1855
About
Davidson, A. One morning with Samuel, Dorothy, and William

WORDSWORTH, WILLIAM, 1770-1850
About
Davidson, A. One morning with Samuel, Dorothy, and William
Work. Harvey, J.
Work. Johnson, D.
The **work** of art. Biguenet, J.
A **work** of art. Blish, J.
A **work** of art. Chekhov, A. P.
The **work** of art in the age of mechanical reproduction. Galef, D.
A **Working** Man's Apocrypha. Luvaas, W.
Working without a Net. Hildt, R.
Works cited. Ayers, M. A.
The **world** and other places. Winterson, J.
A **World** Apart. Salvatore, D.
The **world** at war. Bukoski, A.
The **world** below. Miller, S.
The **World** Famous Tightrope Walker. Dworkin, S.
World full of great cities. Heller, J.
The **world** is mine; or, Deeds that make heaven weep. Carlson, P. M.
A **world** of canes. Antoni, R.
The **world** of things. Zadoorian, M.
The **world** of weather. Mori, K.
World Series, 1979. Tarses, M.
World vast, world various. Benford, G.

WORLD WAR, 1914-1918
Lawson, C. and Brown, S. No Man's Land
Pastor, B. Achilles' grave
Aerial operations
The white feather ace
Faulkner, W. All the dead pilots
Hunter, J. D. For want of a Fokker
Kipling, R. Mary Postgate
Yeates, V. M. Learning to fly
Casualties
Barnes, J. Evermore
England
Perry, A. The end of innocence
France
Babel', I. On the field of honor
Foxwell, E. No man's land
Perry, A. Heroes
Swan, M. 1917
Swan, M. The deep
Wharton, E. Coming home
Wharton, E. The Marne
Wales
James, S. Billy Mason from Gloucester

WORLD WAR, 1939-1945
Auerbach, J. Escape
Auerbach, J. Transformations
Bradbury, R. Bang! You're dead!
Bradbury, R. The enemy in the wheat
Coberly, L. M. Growing up in the Navy
Ehlers, J. "Wangeroog, de schone . . ."
Gordimer, N. The diamond mine
Hoch, E. D. Enemy territory
Kornbluth, C. M. Two dooms
L'Amour, L. Flight to the north
L'Amour, L. Wings over Brazil
Tarnished glory
Trotter, W. R. The bleeding of Hauptmann Gehlen
Vonnegut, K. Der Arme Dolmetscher
Waters, M. Y. Aftermath
Yates, R. A compassionate leave

Aerial operations
Deighton, L. Hell over Germany
Gann, E. K. An hour to San Francisco
Heller, J. Chief White Halfoat
Hersey, J. The raid
Michener, J. A. The milk run
Robinson, K. S. The lucky strike
Atrocities
See also Holocaust, Jewish (1933-1945)
Jews
See also Holocaust, Jewish (1933-1945)
Pearlman, D. D. The colonel's jeep
Singer, I. B. The manuscript
Prisoners and prisons
See also Concentration camps
Hayden, G. M. War crimes
Murray, S. Guinea
Murray, S. Walkabout
Waters, M. Y. Seed
Secret service
Collins, M. A part of history
Underground movements
Škvorecký, J. Feminine mystique
Viganò, R. Acquitted
Viganò, R. Argelide
Viganò, R. The big opportunity
Viganò, R. Campalbo
Viganò, R. The commander
Viganò, R. He knew German
Viganò, R. The house on the ice
Viganò, R. The last action
Viganò, R. November 1943
Viganò, R. Partisan wedding
Viganò, R. Red flag
Viganò, R. Thin walls
Viganò, R. Trap shoot
Viganò, R. The viaduct
Viganò, R. Wool socks
Australia
Malouf, D. At Schindler's
Malouf, D. Sally's story
Belgium
Kingrea, Eric. A waltz in the snow
Czechoslovakia
Škvorecký, J. The cuckoo
England
Bowen, E. The happy autumn fields
Byatt, A. S. The thing in the forest
Jakes, J. Dr. Sweetkill
Joyce, G. The Coventry boy
MacLeod, I. The chop girl
Meloy, M. Red
Spark, M. The house of the famous poet
VanderMeer, J. London burning
France
Butler, R. O. Mother in the trenches
Germany
Rusch, K. K. Judgment
Yates, R. Bells in the morning
Indonesia
Murray, S. Folly
Italy
Forsyth, F. The miracle
Viganò, R. Acquitted
Viganò, R. Argelide
Viganò, R. The big opportunity
Viganò, R. Campalbo
Viganò, R. The commander
Viganò, R. Death of a mother

WORLD WAR, 1939-1945—Italy—*Continued*
Viganò, R. He knew German
Viganò, R. The house on the ice
Viganò, R. The last action
Viganò, R. November 1943
Viganò, R. Partisan wedding
Viganò, R. Peter
Viganò, R. The portrait of Garibaldi
Viganò, R. Red flag
Viganò, R. Thin walls
Viganò, R. Trap shoot
Viganò, R. The viaduct
Viganò, R. Wool socks
Japan
Waters, M. Y. Aftermath
Waters, M. Y. Shibusa
Netherlands
Carson, J. Captives
New Guinea
Murray, S. Guinea
Pacific Ocean
Hensley, J. L. Paint doctor
L'Amour, L. Down Paagumene way
Philippines
Murray, S. The caprices
Murray, S. Colossus
Murray, S. Intramuros
Murray, S. Position
Russia
Gordimer, N. Karma
Singapore
Murray, S. Order of precedence
United States
Cady, J. Halloween 1942
Coberly, L. M. Early transparent
Coberly, L. M. Night-blooming cereus
Doogan, M. War can be murder
Gilchrist, E. Victory over Japan
Hart, C. G. Spooked
Kennett, S. A warm nest
Morgan, R. Murals
Price, R. The fare to the moon
Roth, P. Defender of the faith
Wetherell, W. D. Hyannis boat
Wilson, R., Jr. Hard times
Wales
Davies, P. H. Think of England
Yugoslavia
Waugh, E. Compassion
World without end. Ordoña, R.
World's greatest mother. Collins, B.
The **world's** greatest pants. Richmond, M.
The **world's** one breathing. Madden, D.
A **worm** in the well. Benford, G.
A **worm** in the winesap. Dunlap, S.
WORMS
Adam, C. Nightcrawler
Blumlein, M. Know how, can do
Worms. Poirier, M. J.
Worry. Blackwood, S.
Worse than bones. Campbell, R.
Worse than the curse. Scarborough, E. A.
Worship of the common heart. Henley, P.
Worst-case scenarios. Shapiro, G.
The **worst** degree of unforgivable. Montemarano, N.

Worth, Valentine
Geoffrey Sonnabend's obliscence: theories of forgetting and the problem of matter—an encapsulation
The Vintage book of amnesia; an anthology; edited by Jonathan Lethem
Worth a thousand words. Schumacher, A.
Wortman-Wunder, Emily
Home Improvements
The North American Review v289 no3/4 p9-14 My/Ag 2004
The **would-be** widower. Page, K. H.
Would you feel better? Anderson, D.
Would you hide me? Steinfeld, J. J.
Would you know it wasn't love? Kaplan, H.
The **Wounded** Angel. Olsen, L.
Wounded in the house of a friend. Sanchez, S.
WOUNDS AND INJURIES
Agee, J. The luck of Junior Strong
Billman, J. Albatross
Dixon, S. Hand
Polansky, S. Leg
Richter, S. The beauty treatment
Ziegler, I. Blue Springs
Ziegler, I. The treasure hunter's daughter
Woven, sir. Berger, J.
Wrap it up. Gifford, B.
Wrap your troubles in dreams. Dwyer, M.
A **wreath** for justice. Wellen, E.
The **wreck** of the Gladstone. Baker, K.
Wreckers. Kane, J. F.
Wrench. Harrison, W.
A **wrestler** with sharks. Yates, R.
WRESTLING
Carlson, R. Dr. Slime
Chan, D. M. Brilliant disguise
Goliger, G. In this corner
Lloyd, D. T. Spider
Rinehart, S. Outstanding in my field
Walpow, N. Push comes to shove
Wrestling Al Gore. Pierce, T. J.
Wrestling jailbait. Nissen, T.
The **wrestling** match. Smith, Z.
Wright, Andrew
In the cage
The Sewanee Review v110 no2 p183-93 Spr 2002
Wright, Austin Tappan
The story of Alwina
Tales before Tolkien; the roots of modern fantasy; edited by Douglas A. Anderson
Wright, David
Dialogue of men and boys
Stories from the Blue Moon Cafe II; edited by Sonny Brewer
Wright, Jack R. *See* Harris, Mark, 1922-
Wright, James Arlington
The lambs on the boulder
The Ohio Review no64/65 p494-6 2001
Wright, Jane Barker
Stitch and bitch
Valentine's Day: women against men; stories of revenge; introduction by Alice Thomas
Wright, John C.
Awake in the night
The year's best science fiction: twenty-first annual collection; edited by Gardner Dozois

Wright, Richard
Bright and morning star
  The Best American short stories of the century; John Updike, editor, Katrina Kenison, coeditor; with an introduction by John Updike
Wright, William *See* De Quille, Dan, 1829-1898
WRITERS *See* Authors
WRITING
Barker, N. Parker Swells
Chekhov, A. P. The exclamation mark
Writing a war story. Wharton, E.
The **writing** of the god. Borges, J. L.
The **writing** on the wall. Vachss, A. H.
Writing the body. Ander, Z.
Written in blood. Lawson, C.
The **wrong** arm. Lipsyte, S.
The **wrong** hands. Robinson, P.
The **wrong** Mexico. Adams, A.
Wrong numbers. Pryor, J.
The **wrong** shape. Chesterton, G. K.
A **wrong** thing. Kennedy, A. L.
Wrong time, wrong place. Deaver, J.
The **wrong** train. Colgan, J.
A **wronged** husband. Gates, D.
The **wronged** wife. Boylan, C.
Wu, Carson H.
Dueling grandmothers
  The North American Review v287 no1 p36-42 Ja/F 2002
Wu, Ch'êng-ên
Monkey [excerpt]
  Swords and sorcerers; stories from the world of fantasy and adventure; edited by Clint Willis
Wunder, Wendy
Inertia
  Gettysburg Review v15 no4 p665-71 Wint 2002
Wuori, G. K.
Angles
  Wuori, G. K. Nude in tub; stories of Quillifarkeag, Maine
Condoms
  Wuori, G. K. Nude in tub; stories of Quillifarkeag, Maine
Crime
  Wuori, G. K. Nude in tub; stories of Quillifarkeag, Maine
Family
  Wuori, G. K. Nude in tub; stories of Quillifarkeag, Maine
Fire
  Wuori, G. K. Nude in tub; stories of Quillifarkeag, Maine
Glory
  Wuori, G. K. Nude in tub; stories of Quillifarkeag, Maine
Golden
  Wuori, G. K. Nude in tub; stories of Quillifarkeag, Maine
Illusions
  Wuori, G. K. Nude in tub; stories of Quillifarkeag, Maine
Justice
  Wuori, G. K. Nude in tub; stories of Quillifarkeag, Maine

Laughter
  Wuori, G. K. Nude in tub; stories of Quillifarkeag, Maine
Madness
  Wuori, G. K. Nude in tub; stories of Quillifarkeag, Maine
Mothers
  Wuori, G. K. Nude in tub; stories of Quillifarkeag, Maine
Murder
  Wuori, G. K. Nude in tub; stories of Quillifarkeag, Maine
Nose
  Wuori, G. K. Nude in tub; stories of Quillifarkeag, Maine
Nude
  Wuori, G. K. Nude in tub; stories of Quillifarkeag, Maine
Parents
  Wuori, G. K. Nude in tub; stories of Quillifarkeag, Maine
Revenge
  Wuori, G. K. Nude in tub; stories of Quillifarkeag, Maine
Skunk
  Wuori, G. K. Nude in tub; stories of Quillifarkeag, Maine
Welcoming Moon
  Gettysburg Review v16 no2 p235-42 Summ 2003
Wurts, Janny
Triad
  The Crow; shattered lives & broken dreams; edited by J. O'Barr and Ed Kramer
Wyatt, Charles
John Gardner's Ghost
  Hanging Loose no82 p68-81 2003
Listening
  Hanging Loose no84 p85-96 2004
Wyatt, Jiri
Now That They Are Dead
  Partisan Review v70 no1 p61-2 Wint 2003
Wyke-Smith, E. A. (Edward Augustine)
Golithos the ogre
  Tales before Tolkien; the roots of modern fantasy; edited by Douglas A. Anderson
Wyke-Smith, Edward Augustine *See* Wyke-Smith, E. A. (Edward Augustine), 1871-1935
Wylde, Thomas
Spinning kingdoms, two
  Once upon a galaxy; edited by Will [sic] McCarthy, Martin H. Greenberg, and John Helfers
Wylie, Philip
Light tackle
  Fishing's best short stories; edited by Paul D. Staudohar
Spare the rod
  Fishing's best short stories; edited by Paul D. Staudohar
Wynn, Steve
Looked a lot like Che Guevara
  Carved in rock; short stories by musicians; edited by Greg Kihn
WYOMING
Billman, J. Albatross
Billman, J. Ash
Billman, J. Atomic Bar

WYOMING—*Continued*
Billman, J. Calcutta
Billman, J. Honeyville
Billman, J. Kerr's fault
Billman, J. When we were Wolves
Billman, J. Winter fat
Gilchrist, E. A Christmas in Wyoming
Offutt, C. Two-eleven all around
Proulx, A. Brokeback Mountain
Proulx, A. The bunchgrass edge of the world
Proulx, A. The governors of Wyoming
Proulx, A. The half-skinned steer
Proulx, A. Job history
Proulx, A. A lonely coast
Proulx, A. Pair a spurs
Proulx, A. People in hell just want a drink of
    water
Wieland, L. Laramie
    Frontier and pioneer life
    See Frontier and pioneer life—Wyoming

X

X. Cooper, B.
X and O. Mogan, J.
X: the unknown quantity. Adam, C.
Xavier. Reiner, C.
The **Xeelee** flower. Baxter, S.
Xelipe. Mujica, B.
Xenos Beach. Joyce, G.
Xi Xi
A Girl Like Me
    The Literary Review (Madison, N.J.) v47 no4
    p43-58 Summ 2004
Xingu. Wharton, E.
Xmas. Banks, R.
Xu Xi
The Art of Love
    The Literary Review (Madison, N.J.) v47 no4
    p92-100 Summ 2004

Y

YACHT RACING
Clarke, A. C. The wind from the sun
YACHTS AND YACHTING
Amdrup, E. Chess on board
Deming, R. Honeymoon cruise
Yaffe, James
Mom remembers
    Browning, A. Murder is no mitzvah; edited
    by Abigail Browning
    Mystery midrash; an anthology of Jewish
    mystery & detective fiction; [edited by]
    Lawrence W. Raphael
Yamamoto, Hisaye
Seventeen syllables
    Fishing for chickens; short stories about rural
    youth; edited, with an introduction by Jim
    Heynen
Yamashita's gold. Murray, S.
Yañez, Richard
Amoroza Tires
    Yañez, R. El Paso del Norte; stories on the
    border
Desert Vista
    Yañez, R. El Paso del Norte; stories on the
    border
Good time
    Yañez, R. El Paso del Norte; stories on the
    border
I&M Plumbing
    Yañez, R. El Paso del Norte; stories on the
    border
Lucero's Mkt.
    Yañez, R. El Paso del Norte; stories on the
    border
Rio Bravo
    Yañez, R. El Paso del Norte; stories on the
    border
Rio Grande
    Yañez, R. El Paso del Norte; stories on the
    border
Sacred Heart
    Yañez, R. El Paso del Norte; stories on the
    border
Yánez Cossío, Alicia
The IWM 1000
    Short stories by Latin American women; the
    magic and the real; edited by Celia Correas
    de Zapata; foreword by Isabel Allende
Yani on the mountain. Grossman, D.
Yankee Doodle dandy. Fitch, B.
Yankee traders. Gavell, M. L.
Yao's Chick. Apple, M.
Yarbro, Chelsea Quinn
Long-term investment
    Dracula in London; edited by P. N. Elrod
Yarbrough, Steve
The rest of her life
    The Best American short stories, 1999; select-
    ed from U.S. and Canadian magazines by
    Amy Tan with Katrina Kenison, with an in-
    troduction by Amy Tan
The right kind of person
    Stories from the Blue Moon Café; edited by
    Sonny Brewer
Veneer
    Stories from the Blue Moon Cafe II; edited
    by Sonny Brewer
Yardumian, Rob
The Doorman
    The Antioch Review v61 no2 p335-44 Spr
    2003
Yasgur, Batya Swift
Kaddish
    Browning, A. Murder is no mitzvah; edited
    by Abigail Browning
    Mystery midrash; an anthology of Jewish
    mystery & detective fiction; [edited by]
    Lawrence W. Raphael
Yasgur, Batya Swift and Malzberg, Barry N.
Unfinished symphony
    The Georgia Review v53 no2 p299-304
    Summ 1999
Yasrebi, Chista
Love and scream
    A Feast in the mirror; stories by contempo-
    rary Iranian women; translated and edited
    by Mohammad Mehdi Khorrami, Shouleh
    Vatanabadi
Yates, Donald A.
(jt. auth) See Brau, Edgar

Yates, Richard
The B.A.R. man
  Yates, R. The collected stories of Richard
    Yates; introduction by Richard Russo
Bells in the morning
  Harper's v302 no1809 p31-2 F 2001
  Yates, R. The collected stories of Richard
    Yates; introduction by Richard Russo
The best of everything
  Yates, R. The collected stories of Richard
    Yates; introduction by Richard Russo
Builders
  Yates, R. The collected stories of Richard
    Yates; introduction by Richard Russo
The canal
  The New Yorker v76 no42 p76-81 Ja 15 2001
  Yates, R. The collected stories of Richard
    Yates; introduction by Richard Russo
A clinical romance
  Yates, R. The collected stories of Richard
    Yates; introduction by Richard Russo
A compassionate leave
  Yates, R. The collected stories of Richard
    Yates; introduction by Richard Russo
The comptroller and the wild wind
  Yates, R. The collected stories of Richard
    Yates; introduction by Richard Russo
A convalescent ego
  Yates, R. The collected stories of Richard
    Yates; introduction by Richard Russo
Doctor Jack-o'-Lantern
  Yates, R. The collected stories of Richard
    Yates; introduction by Richard Russo
Evening on the Côte d'Azur
  Yates, R. The collected stories of Richard
    Yates; introduction by Richard Russo
Fun with a stranger
  Yates, R. The collected stories of Richard
    Yates; introduction by Richard Russo
A glutton for punishment
  Yates, R. The collected stories of Richard
    Yates; introduction by Richard Russo
Jody rolled the bones
  Yates, R. The collected stories of Richard
    Yates; introduction by Richard Russo
A last fling, like
  Yates, R. The collected stories of Richard
    Yates; introduction by Richard Russo
Liars in love
  Yates, R. The collected stories of Richard
    Yates; introduction by Richard Russo
A natural girl
  Yates, R. The collected stories of Richard
    Yates; introduction by Richard Russo
No pain whatsoever
  Yates, R. The collected stories of Richard
    Yates; introduction by Richard Russo
Oh, Joseph, I'm so tired
  Yates, R. The collected stories of Richard
    Yates; introduction by Richard Russo
Out with the old
  Yates, R. The collected stories of Richard
    Yates; introduction by Richard Russo
A private possession
  Yates, R. The collected stories of Richard
    Yates; introduction by Richard Russo
A really good jazz piano
  Yates, R. The collected stories of Richard
    Yates; introduction by Richard Russo

Regards at home
  Yates, R. The collected stories of Richard
    Yates; introduction by Richard Russo
Saying goodbye to Sally
  Yates, R. The collected stories of Richard
    Yates; introduction by Richard Russo
Thieves
  Yates, R. The collected stories of Richard
    Yates; introduction by Richard Russo
Trying out for the race
  Yates, R. The collected stories of Richard
    Yates; introduction by Richard Russo
A wrestler with sharks
  Yates, R. The collected stories of Richard
    Yates; introduction by Richard Russo
The **Yattering** and Jack. Barker, C.
Yeager, Laura
Dumpster diving
  The North American Review v286 no3/4
    p34-9 My/Ag 2001
The **year** draws in the day. Horton, H.
The **year** five. Eggers, P.
The **year** of getting to know us. Canin, E.
The **Year** of Mad Weather. Benni, S.
The **year** of the jackpot. Heinlein, R. A.
The **year** the world turned. Bosworth, B.
The **year** Ward West took away the raccoon and
    Mr. Hanson's garage burneddown. Wil-
    liams, M.
Yearbook. Allen, S.
The **yearbook**. Nyren, R.
Yearn. Gautier, A.
Years ago and in a different place. Kurland, M.
Years later. Bianchini, A.
Yeates, V. M. (Victor M.)
Learning to fly
  On glorious wings; the best flying stories of
    the century; edited and introduced by Ste-
    phen Coonts
Yeates, Victor M. *See* Yeates, V. M. (Victor M.)
**YEATS, W. B. (WILLIAM BUTLER), 1865-
1939**
About
In the prison of his days
Yeats, William Butler *See* Yeats, W. B. (William
    Butler), 1865-1939
Yeh, these stages. Kelman, J.
Yehoshua, Abraham B.
Facing the forests
  Sleepwalkers and other stories; the Arab in
    Hebrew fiction; edited by Ehud Ben-Ezer
Yehudah Benjamin Aronowitz. Reiner, C.
Yellow. Lee, D.
Yellow and red. Lee, T.
The **yellow** house. McBrearty, R. G.
Yellow jacket. Adam, C.
Yellow morning. Grodstein, L.
The **yellow** palace. Gifford, B.
The **yellow** sign. Chambers, R. W.
The **yellow** sweater. Little, B.
The **yellow** wallpaper. Gilman, C. P.
Yellow with black horns. Young, T.
YELLOWSTONE NATIONAL PARK
Sojourner, M. Squirrel
Yellville. Budnitz, J.

Yerby, Frank
  Health card
    The African American West; a century of
      short stories; edited by Bruce A. Glasrud
      and Laurie Champion
Yesterday's garbage. Hassler, J.
Yesterday's girl. Tomioka, T.
Yesteryear. Tomioka, T.
Yi, Tong-Ha
  At the door
    Yi, T.-H. Shrapnel and other stories; [by]
      Dong-ha Lee; edited and translated by
      Hyun-Jae Yee Sallee
  The blazing sun
    Yi, T.-H. Shrapnel and other stories; [by]
      Dong-ha Lee; edited and translated by
      Hyun-Jae Yee Sallee
  Dark valley
    Yi, T.-H. Shrapnel and other stories; [by]
      Dong-ha Lee; edited and translated by
      Hyun-Jae Yee Sallee
  Perspiration
    Yi, T.-H. Shrapnel and other stories; [by]
      Dong-ha Lee; edited and translated by
      Hyun-Jae Yee Sallee
  Shrapnel
    Yi, T.-H. Shrapnel and other stories; [by]
      Dong-ha Lee; edited and translated by
      Hyun-Jae Yee Sallee
Yiddish twilight. Stern, S.
Yielding to science. Huffman, B., Jr.
A **yin** and her man. Leong, R.
Yizhar, S.
  The prisoner
    Sleepwalkers and other stories; the Arab in
      Hebrew fiction; edited by Ehud Ben-Ezer
YMCA
  McBrearty, R. G. A night at the Y
Yoda. Doyle, B.
Yoder, Edwin M., Jr.
  Blackmail
    The Sewanee Review v110 no4 p555-91 Fall
      2002
YOGA
  Louis, L. G. Tea
Yolanda. Casares, O.
Yolen, Jane
  Allerleirauh
    Yolen, J. Sister Emily's lightship and other
      stories
  The barbarian and the queen: thirteen interviews
    Starlight 3; edited by Patrick Nielsen Hayden
  Become a warrior
    The Year's best fantasy & horror, twelfth an-
      nual collection; edited by Ellen Datlow &
      Terry Windling
    Yolen, J. Sister Emily's lightship and other
      stories
  Belle bloody merciless dame
    Yolen, J. Sister Emily's lightship and other
      stories
  Blood sister
    Yolen, J. Sister Emily's lightship and other
      stories
  Creationism: an illustrated lecture in two parts
    Yolen, J. Sister Emily's lightship and other
      stories

Dick W. and his Pussy; or, Tess and her Ade-
    quate Dick
    Yolen, J. Sister Emily's lightship and other
      stories
Dusty loves
    Yolen, J. Sister Emily's lightship and other
      stories
A ghost of an affair
    Yolen, J. Sister Emily's lightship and other
      stories
The gift of the magicians, with apologies to you
    know who
    Yolen, J. Sister Emily's lightship and other
      stories
Godmother death
    Yolen, J. Sister Emily's lightship and other
      stories
Granny rumple
    Yolen, J. Sister Emily's lightship and other
      stories
Great gray
    Yolen, J. Sister Emily's lightship and other
      stories
Green messiah
    The Literary werewolf; an anthology; edited
      by Charlotte F. Otten
Journey into the dark
    Yolen, J. Sister Emily's lightship and other
      stories
Lost girls
    Nebula awards showcase 2000; the year's best
      SF and fantasy chosen by the science fic-
      tion and fantasy writers of america; edited
      by Gregory Benford
    Yolen, J. Sister Emily's lightship and other
      stories
Memoirs of a bottle djinn
    Yolen, J. Sister Emily's lightship and other
      stories
The Old Lady in the Cave
    Parabola v28 no4 p65 Wint 2003
Salvage
    Yolen, J. Sister Emily's lightship and other
      stories
The singer and the song
    Yolen, J. Sister Emily's lightship and other
      stories
Sister death
    Yolen, J. Sister Emily's lightship and other
      stories
Sister Emily's lightship
    Nebula awards 33; the year's best SF and
      fantasy chosen by the science-fiction and
      fantasy writers of America; edited by
      Connie Willis
    Yolen, J. Sister Emily's lightship and other
      stories
The sleep of trees
    Yolen, J. Sister Emily's lightship and other
      stories
Snow in summer
    Black heart, ivory bones; [edited by] Ellen
      Datlow & Terri Windling
    Yolen, J. Sister Emily's lightship and other
      stories
Speaking to the wind
    Yolen, J. Sister Emily's lightship and other
      stories

Yolen, Jane—*Continued*
The Stolen Wife
  Parabola v29 no1 p80-2 Spr 2004
Sun/flight
  Yolen, J. Sister Emily's lightship and other
    stories
The thirteenth fey
  Yolen, J. Sister Emily's lightship and other
    stories
The traveler and the tale
  Yolen, J. Sister Emily's lightship and other
    stories
The uncorking of Uncle Finn
  Yolen, J. Sister Emily's lightship and other
    stories
Under the hill
  Yolen, J. Sister Emily's lightship and other
    stories
Words of power
  Yolen, J. Sister Emily's lightship and other
    stories
Yolen, Jane and Harris, Robert J.
Carrion crows
  The Crow; shattered lives & broken dreams;
    edited by J. O'Barr and Ed Kramer
YOM KIPPUR
Singer, I. B. The riddle
Yorke, Margaret
Mugs
  Edwards, M. Mysterious pleasures; a celebra-
    tion of the Crime Writers' Association's
    50th anniversary; edited by Martin Edwards
York's story. Walker, D. L.
Yoshikawa, Eiji
Musashi [excerpt]
  Swords and sorcerers; stories from the world
    of fantasy and adventure; edited by Clint
    Willis
Yoshimoto, Banana
Asleep
  Yoshimoto, B. Asleep; translated from the
    Japanese by Michael Emmerich
Helix
  The Art of the story; an international antholo-
    gy of contemporary short stories; edited by
    Daniel Halpern
Love songs
  Yoshimoto, B. Asleep; translated from the
    Japanese by Michael Emmerich
Night and night's travelers
  Yoshimoto, B. Asleep; translated from the
    Japanese by Michael Emmerich
Yoshimura, Akira
Glorious Days
  Grand Street no71 p230-43 Spr 2003
Yossarian survives. Heller, J.
You. Erian, A.
You. Galef, D.
You are here. Lowenthal, M.
You are Here. Velasco, M.
You are not I. Bowles, P.
You are not your characters. Kinder, C.
You are who you eat. What, L.
You are who you kill. Touré
You can jump. Coward, M.
You can sleep while I drive. Wieland, L.
You can't be a little girl all your life. Ellin, S.
You can't be too careful. Keegan, C.
You can't get lost in Cape Town. Wicomb, Z.

You can't tell how you'll get clobbered. McNulty,
  J.
You cheated, you lied. Jones, T.
You don't have to be mad . . . Newman, K.
You don't know me. Meyers, A.
You don't know me, Charlie. Lupoff, R. A.
You don't know you're alive. Boylan, C.
You drive. Ravera, L.
You Go When You Can No Longer Stay. Kay, J.
You gotta believe. What, L.
You have left your lotus pods on the bus. Bowles,
  P.
You Have Never Heard Their Voices. Keyes, J.
You have the body. Gasco, E.
You have to say something. Davidson, R.
The **you** is understood. Smolens, J.
You know I am lying. Agee, J.
You, little match-girl. Oates, J. C.
You men of violence. Harrison, H.
You missed the boat, Captain!. Babel´, I.
You must change your life. Gilchrist, E.
You put on some weight. Westlake, D. E.
You Were a Better Liar in Paris. Antúnez, R.
You Were My Favorite Scarecrow. Nissen, T.
You were real, the white radical said to me. Ortiz,
  S. J.
You Will Miss Me When I Burn. White, J.
"You win some . . . ". Krich, R. M.
Youmans, Claire
Mortmain
  Women before the bench; edited by Carolyn
    Wheat; introduction by Linda Fairstein
Youmans, Marly
A girl in summer
  This is where we live; short stories by 25
    contemporary North Carolina writers; ed-
    ited by Michael McFee
Young, Terence
The Berlin Wall
  Young, T. Rhymes with useless; stories
The day the lake went down
  Young, T. Rhymes with useless; stories
Dead
  Young, T. Rhymes with useless; stories
Fast
  Young, T. Rhymes with useless; stories
In bed
  Young, T. Rhymes with useless; stories
Kraut
  Young, T. Rhymes with useless; stories
Maintenance
  Young, T. Rhymes with useless; stories
The new world
  Young, T. Rhymes with useless; stories
Pig on a spit
  Young, T. Rhymes with useless; stories
Rhymes with useless
  Young, T. Rhymes with useless; stories
Sometimes night never ends
  Young, T. Rhymes with useless; stories
Too busy swimming
  Young, T. Rhymes with useless; stories
Yellow with black horns
  Young, T. Rhymes with useless; stories
The **young** and the rest of us. Searle, E.
Young, black, and unstoppable; or, Death of a
  zeitgeist jockey. Touré
Young Collectors' Day. Dahlie, M.
The **young** gentlemen. Wharton, E.

A **young** girl's confession. Proust, M.
Young Goodman Brown. Hawthorne, N.
Young Hemingways. Cole, C. B.
Young love. Lee, N.
The **young** man. Gilchrist, E.
A **young** man's game. MacDonald, J. D.
YOUNG MEN'S CHRISTIAN ASSOCIATIONS
    See YMCA
Young Muo. Su Tong
Young Reverend Zelma Lee Moses. Thomas, J. C.
Youngblood, Shay
    Triple X
        The Bluelight corner; black women writing on
        passion, sex, and romantic love; edited by
        Rosemarie Robotham
Younger brother. Callaghan, M.
Your borders, your rivers, your tiny villages.
    Bloom, A.
Your burden is lifted, love returns. DeMarinis, R.
Your chances of getting married. Cherry, K.
Your doctor loves you. Adams, A.
Your errant mom. Robison, M.
Your madness, not mine. Nfah-Abbenyi, J. M.
Your own backyard. Johnson, A.
Your story. DeMarinis, R.
Your wish is my command; or, As you like it.
    Sade, marquis de
Yourcenar, Marguerite
    Sappho; or, Suicide
        The Vintage book of international lesbian fic-
        tion; edited and with an introduction by
        Naomi Holoch and Joan Nestle
You're putting me on, aren't you? Gores, J.
You're so simple. Sosin, D.
You're ugly, too. Moore, L.
Yours. Porter, J. A.
Yours. Robison, M.
Yours truly. Davis, L.
YOUTH
            See also Adolescence; Boys; Girls; Stu-
        dents
    Alameddine, R. Grace
    Alcott, L. M. The cross on the church tower
    Allen, D., Jr. Deferment
    Allen, S. Yearbook
    Bass, R. Pagans
    Bellow, S. Something to remember me by
    Berkman, P. R. Playing crucifixion
    Boylan, C. Appearances
    Boyle, T. C. Death of the cool
    Bradbury, R. Hopscotch
    Broyard, B. Snowed in
    Calisher, H. In Greenwich, there are many grav-
        elled walks
    Chacón, D. Slow and good
    Coates, G. S. A pine tree
    Cooke, C. Girl of their dreams
    Daniels, J. Cross country
    Davis, A. The very moment they're about
    DeLancey, K. Dinger and Blacker
    DeLancey, K. The seven pearls
    Doenges, J. Crooks
    Dumas, H. Double nigger
    Dumas, H. Six days you shall labor
    Dybek, S. Orchids
    Evans, E. A new life
    Ferrell, C. Proper library
    Fitzgerald, F. S. Babes in the woods
    Fitzgerald, F. S. The camel's back

Fitzgerald, F. S. The jelly-bean
Fleming, M. St. Andrew's day
Gilchrist, E. The Southwest Experimental Fast
    Oxide Reactor
Gilchrist, E. Witness to the crucifixion
Glasgow, G. Home at last
Granelli, R. Disturbing the peace
Gray, A. Big pockets with buttoned flaps
Gussoff, C. Astronaut
Händler, E.-W. Morgenthau
Henley, P. Picking time
Hodgen, C. A jeweler's eye for flaw
Irsfeld, J. H. The horse fountain
LaValle, V. D. Trinidad
MacLeod, A. The golden gift of grey
Malouf, D. Jacko's reach
McHugh, M. F. Interview: on any given day
McManus, J. Vlad the nefarious
Mencken, S. H. Absolutely perfect
Nelson, A. Goodfellows
Papernick, J. Lucky eighteen
Parker, G. Aub
Prete, D. After we left Yonkers and before we
    came back
Prete, D. Self-respecting Neapolitans
Richter, S. Goodnight
Robinson, L. Officer Friendly
Shade, E. Eyesores
Silber, J. Comforts
Silber, J. Ragazzi
Škvorecký, J. The end of Bull Macha
Škvorecký, J. Three bachelors in a fiery furnace
Smolens, J. My one and only bomb shelter
Spain, C. Scaring the baddest animal
Spencer, E. Ship island: the story of a mermaid
Straight, S. Mines
Swarthout, G. F. Four older men
Swarthout, G. F. A glass of blessings
Tenorio, L. A. Superassassin
Updike, J. A & P
Updike, J. Friends from Philadelphia
Updike, J. The happiest I've been
Updike, J. The hillies
Valeri, L. The kind of things saints do
Vivante, A. The cove
Warren, D. Bone garden
Waugh, E. The balance
Welsh, I. Trainspotting [excerpt]
Yañez, R. Good time
Young, T. Dead
Youth. Roth, J.
Youth not wasted. Kilpatrick, N.
Youthful offenders. Wilson, M.
You've Really Learned How. Magruder, J.
YoYo. Chuculate, E. D.
Y's story. Foley, S.
Ysrael. Díaz, J.
Yu, Charles
    The Man Who Became Himself
        Gettysburg Review v17 no2 p173-83 Summ
        2004
    Problems for Self-Study
        Harvard Review (1992) no23 p16-22 Fall
        2002
Yu, Young-Nan
    (jt. auth) See Shin, Kyoung-Sook

Yu, F. S.
The shield
  Politically inspired; edited by Stephen Elliott;
    assistant editor, Gabriel Kram; associate ed-
    itors, Elizabeth Brooks [et al.]
Yu Pingfu *See* Su Shuyang, 1938-
YUGOSLAV WAR, 1991-1995
Brkic, C. A. Adiyo, kerido
Brkic, C. A. The angled city
Brkic, C. A. The daughter
Brkic, C. A. In the jasmine shade
Brkic, C. A. Passage
Brkic, C. A. The peacebroker
Brkic, C. A. Remains
Brkic, C. A. Stillness
Brkic, C. A. Suspension
Brkic, C. A. Swimming out
Brkic, C. A. We will sleep in one nest
Brkic, C. A. Where none is the number
Jergović, M. The Condor
YUGOSLAVIA
    See also Bosnia and Hercegovina
Harrison, H. Rescue operation
Hemon, A. Imitation of life
Hemon, A. The Sorge spy ring
Sarajevo
    See Bosnia and Hercegovina—Sarajevo
YUGOSLAVS
United States
Collins, M. Freedom fighter
Yuknavitch, Lidia
Against interpretation
  Yuknavitch, L. Liberty's excess; fictions
An American couple
  Yuknavitch, L. Liberty's excess; fictions
Beatings
  Yuknavitch, L. Real to reel
Beauty
  Yuknavitch, L. Liberty's excess; fictions
Blood opus
  Yuknavitch, L. Liberty's excess; fictions
Blue movie
  Yuknavitch, L. Real to reel
Bravo America
  Yuknavitch, L. Liberty's excess; fictions
Burning the commodity
  Yuknavitch, L. Liberty's excess; fictions
Chair
  Yuknavitch, L. Real to reel
Citations of a heretic
  Yuknavitch, L. Liberty's excess; fictions
Cusp
  Yuknavitch, L. Liberty's excess; fictions
From the boy stories
  Yuknavitch, L. Liberty's excess; fictions
The garden of earthly delights
  Yuknavitch, L. Liberty's excess; fictions
How to lose an eye
  Yuknavitch, L. Real to reel
Male lead
  Yuknavitch, L. Real to reel
Outtakes
  Yuknavitch, L. Real to reel
Sade's mistress
  Yuknavitch, L. Liberty's excess; fictions
Scripted
  Yuknavitch, L. Real to reel
Shadow boxing
  Yuknavitch, L. Liberty's excess; fictions

Shooting
  Yuknavitch, L. Real to reel
Siberia: still life of a moving image
  Yuknavitch, L. Real to reel
Signification
  Yuknavitch, L. Real to reel
Three studies for figures on beds after Francis
    Bacon and Antonin Artaud
  Yuknavitch, L. Liberty's excess; fictions
Waiting to see
  Yuknavitch, L. Liberty's excess; fictions
YUKON TERRITORY *See* Canada—Yukon Ter-
    ritory
Yumiura. Kawabata, Y.
Yunqué, Edgardo Vega *See* Vega Yunqué,
    Edgardo
Yurokon. Harris, W.
Yzur. Lugones, L.

Z

Zabytko, Irene
The celebrity
  Zabytko, I. When Luba leaves home; stories
John Mars, all-American
  Zabytko, I. When Luba leaves home; stories
The last boat
  Zabytko, I. When Luba leaves home; stories
Lavender soap
  Zabytko, I. When Luba leaves home; stories
My black Valiant
  Zabytko, I. When Luba leaves home; stories
Obligation
  Zabytko, I. When Luba leaves home; stories
Pani Ryhotska in love
  Zabytko, I. When Luba leaves home; stories
The prodigal son enters heaven
  Zabytko, I. When Luba leaves home; stories
Saint Sonya
  Zabytko, I. When Luba leaves home; stories
Steve's bar
  Zabytko, I. When Luba leaves home; stories
Zacharias, Lee
At Random
  The Southern Review (Baton Rouge, La.) v39
    no2 p368-86 Spr 2003
Zadoorian, Michael
Investigations of a tourist by Mrs. Wendell A.
    Prescott
  The North American Review v284 no2 p38
    Mr/Ap 1999
The world of things
  The Literary Review (Madison, N.J.) v42 no2
    p306-17 Wint 1999
Zafris, Nancy
Digging the hole
  New England Review v22 no3 p112-30 Summ
    2001
Stealing the llama farm
  The Kenyon Review ns21 no2 p55-61 Spr
    1999
Zaget, Bill
Renfield; or, Dining at the bughouse
  Dracula in London; edited by P. N. Elrod
Zaghrouda. Tel, J.
The **Zahir**. Borges, J. L.

Zaiman, Elana
Porcelain
  Dalhousie Review v81 no2 p283-90 Summ
    2001
Zaimoglu, Feridun
The father's story
  Chicago Review v48 no2/3 p331-4 Summ
    2002
ZAIRE
Hunter, F. Card players
Hunter, F. Equateur
Hunter, F. Lenoir
Hunter, F. Waiting for the Mwami
Zak, Avrom
A wounded man [excerpt]
  Neugroschel, J. No star too beautiful; Yiddish
    stories from 1382 to the present; compiled
    and translated by Joachim Neugroschel
ZAMBIA
Saidi, W. The garden of evil
Zamosc. Babel', I.
Zanduce at second. Carlson, R.
Zane, David
James's story
  Michigan Quarterly Review v41 no3 p413-21
    Summ 2002
Zanjani, Sally Springmeyer
Dead game man
  American West; twenty new stories from the
    Western Writers of America; edited with an
    introduction by Loren D. Estleman
ZANZIBAR
Avrich, J. Zanzibar
Zanzibar. Avrich, J.
ZAPOTEC INDIANS
Lincoln, C. Last will
Zavala, Hernan Lara
Mirror images
  The Vintage book of Latin American stories;
    edited by Carlos Fuentes and Julio Ortega
Zawieyski, Jerzy
Conrad in the ghetto
  When night fell; an anthology of Holocaust
    short stories; edited by Linda Schermer Ra-
    phael and Marc Lee Raphael
The **zealous** mourner. Swick, M. A.
Zealous representation. Huffman, B., Jr.
The **zebra-struck.** Kavan, A.
Zelazny, Roger
The doors of his face, the lamps of his mouth
  The Good old stuff; adventure SF in the
    grand tradition; edited by Gardner Dozois
The keys to December
  Worldmakers; SF adventures in terraforming;
    edited by Gardner Dozois
A rose for Ecclesiastes
  The Science fiction hall of fame: volume one,
    1929-1964; the greatest science fiction sto-
    ries of all time chosen by the members of
    the Science Fiction Writers of America; ed-
    ited by Robert Silverberg
Zelda, Zelda. Johnson, G.
Zelig. Rosenblatt, B.

Zelinka, Milan
The blue carp
  In search of homo sapiens; twenty-five con-
    temporary Slovak short stories; editor,
    Pavol Hudík ; [translated by Heather
    Trebatická; American English editor, Lucy
    Bednár]
Zelinová, Hana
The order of wolves
  In search of homo sapiens; twenty-five con-
    temporary Slovak short stories; editor,
    Pavol Hudík ; [translated by Heather
    Trebatická; American English editor, Lucy
    Bednár]
Zelitch, Simone
Ten plagues
  Lost tribe; jewish fiction from the edge
Zeman, Angela
Green heat
  A Hot and sultry night for crime; edited by
    Jeffery Deaver
Hello?
  Mom, apple pie, and murder; edited by Nancy
    Pickard
Zemecki's cat. Carter, E.
ZENO, OF ELEA, B. CA. 490 B.C.
                About
Pearlman, D. D. Zeno evil
Zeno and the distance between us. Wahl, S.
Zeno evil. Pearlman, D. D.
ZEPPELINS *See* Airships
Zero. Mueller, D.
Zetland: by a character witness. Bellow, S.
Zettel, Sarah
Fool's errand
  A Woman's liberation; a choice of futures by
    and about women; edited by Connie Willis
    and Sheila Williams
Zhang Jie
Love must not be forgotten
  The Vintage book of contemporary Chinese
    fiction; edited by Carolyn Choa and David
    Su Li-qun
Zhao Danian
Three sketches
  The Vintage book of contemporary Chinese
    fiction; edited by Carolyn Choa and David
    Su Li-qun
Zhou Libo
The family on the other side of the mountain
  The Vintage book of contemporary Chinese
    fiction; edited by Carolyn Choa and David
    Su Li-qun
Zhu Zhiyu
(jt. auth) See Xi Xi
Zhurya. Zinovyeva-Annibal, L. D.
Ziegler, Irene
Blind spot
  Ziegler, I. Rules of the lake; stories
Blue Springs
  Ziegler, I. Rules of the lake; stories
Cliffs notes
  Ziegler, I. Rules of the lake; stories
Feud of the maids
  Ziegler, I. Rules of the lake; stories
Hooked
  Ziegler, I. Rules of the lake; stories
How to breathe underwater
  Ziegler, I. Rules of the lake; stories

Ziegler, Irene—*Continued*
  My last deer
    Ziegler, I. Rules of the lake; stories
  Nobody home: an epilogue
    Ziegler, I. Rules of the lake; stories
  The raft
    Ziegler, I. Rules of the lake; stories
  Rules of the lake
    Ziegler, I. Rules of the lake; stories
  The stranger
    Ziegler, I. Rules of the lake; stories
  The treasure hunter's daughter
    Ziegler, I. Rules of the lake; stories
  The waiting list
    Ziegler, I. Rules of the lake; stories
Zigzag cabinet. Spatz, G.
Zigzags of treachery. Hammett, D.
Zilkowski's theorem. Iagnemma, K.
ZIMBABWE
  Chinodya, S. Among the dead
  Chinodya, S. Bramson
  Chinodya, S. Brothers and sisters
  Chinodya, S. Can we talk
  Chinodya, S. Going to see Mr. B. V.
  Chinodya, S. Hoffman Street
  Chinodya, S. The man who hanged himself
  Chinodya, S. Play your cards
  Chinodya, S. Snow
  Chinodya, S. Strays
  Chinodya, S. The waterfall
  Clark, G. M. The Leopard Gang
  Marechera, D. Thought tracks in the snow
                    Politics
        See Politics—Zimbabwe
Zimler, Richard
  The slow mirror
    Tikkun v14 no4 p48-50+ Jl/Ag 1999
Zind, Rick
  The way he knew it
    Ghost writing; haunted tales by contemporary
    writers; edited by Roger Weingarten
Zinik, Zinoviĭ
  Double act in Soho
    Zinik, Z. Mind the doors; long short stories
  Mind the doors
    Zinik, Z. Mind the doors; long short stories
  No cause for alarm
    Zinik, Z. Mind the doors; long short stories
  The notification
    Zinik, Z. Mind the doors; long short stories
  A pickled nose
    Zinik, Z. Mind the doors; long short stories
Zinotchka. Chekhov, A. P.
Zinovyeva-Annibal, Lidiya Dmitrievna
  The bear cubs
    Zinovyeva-Annibal, L. D. The tragic menag-
    erie; translated from the Russian and with
    an introduction by Jane Costlow
  The centaur-princess
    Zinovyeva-Annibal, L. D. The tragic menag-
    erie; translated from the Russian and with
    an introduction by Jane Costlow
  Deaf Dasha
    Zinovyeva-Annibal, L. D. The tragic menag-
    erie; translated from the Russian and with
    an introduction by Jane Costlow
  The devil
    Zinovyeva-Annibal, L. D. The tragic menag-
    erie; translated from the Russian and with
    an introduction by Jane Costlow
  The midge
    Zinovyeva-Annibal, L. D. The tragic menag-
    erie; translated from the Russian and with
    an introduction by Jane Costlow
  The monster
    Zinovyeva-Annibal, L. D. The tragic menag-
    erie; translated from the Russian and with
    an introduction by Jane Costlow
  Will
    Zinovyeva-Annibal, L. D. The tragic menag-
    erie; translated from the Russian and with
    an introduction by Jane Costlow
  Wolves
    Zinovyeva-Annibal, L. D. The tragic menag-
    erie; translated from the Russian and with
    an introduction by Jane Costlow
  Zhurya
    Zinovyeva-Annibal, L. D. The tragic menag-
    erie; translated from the Russian and with
    an introduction by Jane Costlow
The **zipper**. Maraini, D.
Ziva. Baron, D.
Zivkovic, Zoran
  The violin-maker
    The Year's best fantasy & horror: sixteenth
    annual collection; edited by Ellen Datlow
    & Terri Windling
Zoellner's definition. Bail, M.
Zog-19: a scientific romance. Benedict, P.
ZOMBIES
  Barnes, S. Heartspace
  Brown, S. With clouds at our feet
  Gaiman, N. Bitter grounds
  Garris, M. Forever Gramma
  Link, K. The hortlak
  Lumley, B. The disapproval of Jeremy Cleave
  Swanwick, M. The dead
  Wandrei, H. George is all right
Zoo. Adam, C.
ZOOLOGICAL GARDENS *See* Zoos
ZOOLOGISTS
  Carlson, R. Plan B for the middle class
Zoomers. Benford, G.
ZOOS
  Adam, C. Emu and elephant
  Adam, C. Zoo
  Gies, M. Zoo animal keeper 1, REC-SVC-ZK
  Johnson, A. Your own backyard
  Nesbitt, M. Gigantic
  Padilla, I. A bestiary
  Sosin, D. Garden primitives
  Tinti, H. Reasonable terms
  Watkins, S. Critterworld
  White, M. C. Instincts
  Whitty, J. Lucifer's alligator
Zoyka and Valeriya. Bunin, I. A.
Zugzwang. Draitser, E.
Zugzwang. Griffith, M.
ZULUS (AFRICAN PEOPLE)
  Haggard, H. R. Black heart and white heart: a
    Zulu idyl
  Kohler, S. Africans
  Saunders, G. We'll get to now later

Zweig, Stefan
Amok
Zweig, S. The royal game & other stories; with an introduction by Jeffrey B. Berlin; translated from the German by Jill Sutcliffe
The burning secret
Zweig, S. The royal game & other stories; with an introduction by Jeffrey B. Berlin; translated from the German by Jill Sutcliffe
Fear
Zweig, S. The royal game & other stories;
with an introduction by Jeffrey B. Berlin; translated from the German by Jill Sutcliffe
Letter from an unknown woman
Zweig, S. The royal game & other stories; with an introduction by Jeffrey B. Berlin; translated from the German by Jill Sutcliffe
The royal game
Zweig, S. The royal game & other stories; with an introduction by Jeffrey B. Berlin; translated from the German by Jill Sutcliffe

PART II

List of Collections Indexed

The **3** button trick and other stories. Barker, N.

50 in 50. Harrison, H.

100% pure Florida fiction; an anthology; edited by Susan Hubbard and Robley Wilson. University Press of Fla. 2000 203p ISBN 0-8130-1752-1 LC 99-39571

The **13** best horror stories of all time; edited by Leslie Pockell. Warner Bks. 2002 388p ISBN 0-446-67950-X LC 2002-16843

999: new stories of horror and suspense; edited by Al Sarrantonio. Avon Bks. 1999 666p ISBN 0-380-97740-0 LC 99-20895

A

Abbey, Lynn

(ed) Thieve's world: turning points. *See* Thieve's world: turning points

Abrams, Tom

The drinking of spirits; stories. Livingston Press (Livingston) 2000 170p ISBN 0-942979-69-9

Ackerman, Forrest J.

(comp) Science-fiction classics. *See* Science-fiction classics

Acts of contrition. Cobb, T.

Acts of love on Indigo Road. Agee, J.

Adam, Christina, d. 2003

Any small thing can save you; a bestiary. BlueHen Bks. 2001 226p ISBN 0-399-14913-9 LC 2001-35464

Adams, Alice, 1926-1999

The last lovely city; stories. Knopf 1999 191p ISBN 0-679-45441-1 LC 98-14585

The stories of Alice Adams. Knopf 2002 621p ISBN 0-375-41285-9 LC 2002-70940

Addonizio, Kim, 1954-

In the box called pleasure; stories. FC2 1999 150p ISBN 1-57366-081-7 LC 99-45089

Africa, Africa! Hunter, F.

The **African** American West; a century of short stories; edited by Bruce A. Glasrud and Laurie Champion. University Press of Colo. 2000 463p ISBN 0-87081-559-8 LC 99-58822

After the earthquake. Murakami, H.

After the plague. Boyle, T. C.

Agee, Jonis

Acts of love on Indigo Road; new & selected stories. Coffee House Press 2003 319p ISBN 1-56689-138-8 LC 2003-41246

Taking the wall; stories. Coffee House Press 1999 180p ISBN 1-56689-088-8 LC 99-35463

Alameddine, Rabih

The perv; stories. Picador 1999 193p ISBN 0-312-20041-2 LC 99-25993

Alarcón, Pedro Antonio de, 1833-1891

The nun and other stories; translated from the Spanish by Robert M. Fedorchek; introduction by Stephen Miller. Bucknell Univ. Press 1999 180p ISBN 0-8387-5415-5 LC 98-39220

Alas, Leopoldo, 1852-1901

Ten tales; translated from the Spanish by Robert M. Fedorchek; introduction by John W. Kronik. Bucknell Univ. Press 2000 206p ISBN 0-8387-5436-8 LC 99-36769

Albert, Susan Wittig

An unthymely death and other garden mysteries. Berkley Books 2003 254p ISBN 0-425-19002-1 LC 2002-43933

Alcott, Louisa May, 1832-1888
The early stories of Louisa May Alcott, 1852-1860; with an introduction by Monika Elbert. Ironweed Press 2000 367p (Ironweed American classics) ISBN 0-9655309-6-5 LC 99-53595

The uncollected works of Louisa May Alcott; v1 Short stories; with an introduction by Monika Elbert. Ironweed Press 2001 295p (Ironweed American classics) ISBN 0-9655309-9-X LC 2001-24531

Aldiss, Brian Wilson, 1925-
Supertoys last all summer long; and other stories of future time. St. Martin's Griffin 2001 232p ISBN 0-312-28061-0 LC 2001-31837

Aldrich, Bess Streeter, 1881-1954
The collected short works, 1920-1954; edited and introduced by Carol Miles Petersen. University of Neb. Press 1999 321p ISBN 0-8032-1052-3 LC 98-19283

Alexie, Sherman, 1966-
Ten little Indians; stories. Grove Press 2003 243p ISBN 0-8021-1744-9 LC 2003-44832

The toughest Indian in the world. Atlantic Monthly Press 2000 238p ISBN 0-87113-801-8 LC 99-86360

Alexis, André
Despair and other stories. Holt & Co. 1999 212p ISBN 0-8050-5979-2 LC 98-41602

The **Alibi** Café and other stories. Troy, M.

All his sons. Raphael, F.

All the anxious girls on earth. Gartner, Z.

Allegra, Donna, 1953-
Witness to the league of blond hip hop dancers; a novella and short stories. Alyson Bks. 2000 306p ISBN 1-55583-550-3

Allen, Stephanie, 1962-
A place between stations; stories. University of Miss. 2003 167p ISBN 0-8262-1444-4 LC 2002-14508

Alpha male. Brandt, W.

Alternate generals II; ed. by Harry Turtledove. Baen, Distributed by Simon & Schuster 2002 339p ISBN 0-7434-3528-1 LC 2002-18604

Alvarez, Aldo
Interesting monsters; fictions. Graywolf Press 2001 186p ISBN 1-55597-356-6 LC 2001-88673

The **amazing** Dr. Darwin. Sheffield, C.

American beauty. Steele, A. M.

American Falls. Gifford, B.

The **American** fantasy tradition; edited by Brian M. Thomsen. TOR Bks. 2002 604p ISBN 0-7653-0152-0 LC 2002-68565

American short fiction, vol. 8, no 29-32. University of Tex. Press 1998 4v ISSN 1051-4813

American standard. Blair, J.

American West; twenty new stories from the Western Writers of America; edited with an introduction by Loren D. Estleman. Forge 2001 367p ISBN 0-312-87317-4 LC 00-48446

American wives. Helms, B.

Amis, Martin
Heavy water and other stories. Harmony Bks. 1999 208p ISBN 0-609-60129-6 LC 98-21779

Among the missing. Chaon, D.

Amor eterno. Martin, P. P.

The **amount** to carry. Scholz, C.

The **Amsterdam** cops. Van de Wetering, J.

Anatomies. Hochman, A.

The **Anchor** book of modern African stories; edited by Nadežda Obradovic ; with a foreword by Chinua Achebe. Anchor Books 2002 xxiv, 375p ISBN 0-385-72240-0 LC 2002-74441

The **Anchor** book of new Irish writing; the new Gaelach ficsean; edited and with an introduction by John Somer and John J. Daly. Anchor Bks. (NY) 2000 366p ISBN 0-385-49889-6 LC 99-89822

And fools of God. Krawiec, R.

Anderson, Donald, 1946-
Fire road. University of Iowa Press 2001 196p (John Simmons short fiction award) ISBN 0-87745-778-6 LC 2001-33589

Anderson, Poul, 1926-2001
Going for infinity; a literary journey. TOR Bks. 2002 416p ISBN 0-7653-0359-0 LC 2001-58351

Anderson, Robert, 1964-
Ice age; stories. University of Ga. Press 2000 182p ISBN 0-8203-2243-1 LC 00-29901

The **angel** on the roof. Banks, R.

Animal crackers. Tinti, H.

The **anniversary** and other stories. Auchincloss, L.

Another life & other stories. Weihe, E.

Antarctica. Keegan, C.

Antipodes. Padilla, I. and Reid, A.

Anton Chekhov: early short stories, 1883-1888. Chekhov, A. P.

Anton Chekhov: later short stories, 1888-1903. Chekhov, A. P.

Any small thing can save you. Adam, C.

Anything you say can and will be used against you. Drummond, L. L.

Apukhtin, A. N., 1841-1893
Three tales; English translations, notes and a foreword by Philip Taylor. Fairleigh Dickinson Univ. Press 2002 152p ISBN 0-8386-3945-3 LC 2001-54531

Archer, Jeffrey, 1940-
To cut a long story short. HarperCollins Pubs. 2000 272p ISBN 0-06-018552-X LC 00-63169

Arenas, Reinaldo, 1943-1990
Mona and other tales; selected and translated from the Spanish by Dolores M. Koch. Vintage Bks. 2001 190p ISBN 0-375-72730-2 LC 2001-26552

Armstrong, Kevin, 1973-
Night watch. Harcourt 2003 179p ISBN 0-15-601349-5 LC 2003-7708

The **Art** of the story; an international anthology of contemporary short stories; edited by Daniel Halpern. Viking 1999 667p ISBN 0-670-88761-7 LC 99-13816

Artists in trouble. Saroyan, A.

Arvin, Nick
In the electric Eden; stories. Penguin Bks. 2003 207p ISBN 0-14-200256-9 LC 2002-32267

The **ascent** of Eli Israel and other stories. Papernick, J.

Ashley, Mike, 1948-
(ed) Royal whodunnits. *See* Royal whodunnits

Asimov, Isaac, 1920-1992
The return of the black widowers. 2003 335p ISBN 0-7867-1248-1

Asleep. Yoshimoto, B.

Assorted fire events. Means, D.

Astronauts & other stories. Iribarne, M.

At the Jim Bridger. Carlson, R.

Atkinson, Kate
Not the end of the world; stories. Little, Brown 2002 244p il ISBN 0-316-61430-0 LC 2003-40117

Auchincloss, Louis
The anniversary and other stories. Houghton Mifflin 1999 192p ISBN 0-395-97074-1 LC 99-18697

Manhattan monologues. Houghton Mifflin 2002 226p ISBN 0-618-15289-X LC 2001-51618

Auerbach, John, 1922-2002
Tales of Grabowski; Transformations, Escape & other stories. Toby Press 2003 307p ISBN 1-902881-80-X

The **avenging** chance. Berkeley, A.

Avrich, Jane
The winter without milk; stories. Houghton Mifflin 2003 211p ISBN 0-618-25142-1 LC 2002-192180

Aye, and Gomorrah. Delany, S. R.

Aylett, Steve, 1967-
Toxicology; stories. Four Walls Eight Windows 1999 140p ISBN 1-56858-131-9 LC 99-33899

Azadeh, Carol, 1964-
The marriage at Antibes; fiction. Carroll & Graf Pubs. 1999 214p ISBN 0-7867-0708-9

B

B. Horror and other stories. Mayo, W.

Babel´, I. (Isaac), 1894-1940

The complete works of Isaac Babel; edited by Nathalie Babel; translated with notes by Peter Constantine; introduction by Cynthia Ozick. Norton 2002 1072p il, maps ISBN 0-393-04846-2 LC 2001-44036

Baca, Jimmy Santiago, 1952-

The importance of a piece of paper. Grove Press 2004 225p ISBN 0-8021-1765-1 LC 2003-57089

Bad Jews and other stories. Shapiro, G.

Bad news of the heart. Glover, D. H.

Bagombo snuff box. Vonnegut, K.

Baida, Peter

A nurse's story and others. University Press of Miss. 2001 238p ISBN 1-57806-318-3 LC 00-49525

Bail, Murray, 1941-

Camouflage; stories. Farrar, Straus & Giroux 2002 195p ISBN 0-374-11827-2 LC 2001-53254

Baker, Kage

Black projects, white knights; the Company dossiers. Golden Gryphon Press 2002 288p ISBN 1-930846-11-8 LC 2002-2503

The **balm** of Gilead tree. Morgan, R.

Banks, Russell, 1940-

The angel on the roof; the stories of Russell Banks. HarperCollins Pubs. 2000 506p ISBN 0-06-017396-3 LC 99-57738

A **bar** in Brooklyn. Codrescu, A.

Bark, Sandra

(ed) Beautiful as the moon, radiant as the stars. *See* Beautiful as the moon, radiant as the stars

Barker, Nicola, 1966-

The 3 button trick and other stories. Ecco Press 1999 216p ISBN 0-88001-677-9 LC 98-50624

Barnes, H. Lee, 1944-

Gunning for Ho; Vietnam stories; afterword by John Clark Pratt. University of Nev. Press 2000 156p (Western literature series) ISBN 0-87417-346-9 LC 99-37249

Barolini, Helen, 1925-

More Italian hours and other stories. Bordighera 2001 175p (VIA folios, 28) ISBN 1-88441-948-8 LC 2001-35466

Baron, Devorah, 1887-1956

"The first day" and other stories; translated by Naomi Seidman with Chana Kronfeld; edited by Chana Kronfeld and Naomi Seidman. University of Calif. Press 2001 236p ISBN 0-520-08536-1 LC 00-55162

Barr, Nevada

(comp) Malice domestic 10. *See* Malice domestic 10

Barrett, Andrea

Servants of the map; stories. Norton 2002 270p map ISBN 0-393-04348-7 LC 2001-44209

Barrett, Lynne

The secret names of women; stories. Carnegie-Mellon Univ. Press 1999 152p ISBN 0-88748-287-2

Barrett, Neal, Jr.

Perpetuity blues and other stories. Golden Gryphon Press 2000 247p ISBN 0-9655901-4-3 LC 99-76110

Bart, Peter

Dangerous company; dark tales from Tinseltown. Miramax 2003 208p ISBN 1-4013-5190-5

Barth, John

The book of ten nights and a night; eleven stories. Houghton Mifflin 2004 295p il ISBN 0-618-40566-6 LC 2003-67532

Barthelme, Frederick

The law of averages; new & selected stories. Counterpoint 2000 364p ISBN 1-58243-115-9 LC 00-55516

Bauman, Beth Ann, 1964-

Beautiful girls; stories. MacAdam/Cage 2002 186p ISBN 1-931561-35-4 LC 2002-153548

Bausch, Richard, 1945-

(ed) The Cry of an occasion. *See* The Cry of an occasion

Someone to watch over me; stories. HarperFlamingo 1999 214p ISBN 0-06-017333-5 LC 98-50193

The stories of Richard Bausch. HarperCollins Pubs. 2003 651p ISBN 0-06-019649-1 LC 2003-42318

Wives and lovers; three short novels; Richard Bausch. 1st ed. Perennial 2004 p. cmp ISBN 0-06-057183-7 LC 2003-63245

Baxter, Charles

(ed) Best new American voices 2001. *See* Best new American voices 2001

Bean, Barbara, 1939-

Dream house; stories. Center for Literary Pub. 2001 178p (Series in contemporary fiction) ISBN 0-87081-617-9 LC 00-64382

Bear, Greg, 1951-

The collected stories of Greg Bear. TOR Bks. 2002 653p ISBN 0-7653-0160-1 LC 2002-20466

The **beast** God forgot to invent. Harrison, J.

Beattie, Ann

Perfect recall; new stories. Scribner 2001 347p ISBN 0-7432-1169-3 LC 00-50465

Beautiful as the moon, radiant as the stars; Jewish women in Yiddish stories : an anthology; edited by Sandra Bark; introduction by Francine Prose. Warner Books 2003 336p ISBN 0-446-69136-4 LC 2003-52599

Beautiful girls. Bauman, B. A.

Before Gatsby. Fitzgerald, F. S.

Bell, Andrea L., 1960-

(ed) Cosmos latinos: an anthology of science fiction from Latin America and Spain. *See* Cosmos latinos: an anthology of science fiction from Latin America and Spain

Bellow, Saul

Collected stories; preface by Janis Bellow; introduction by James Wood. Viking 2001 xx, 442p ISBN 0-670-89486-9 LC 2001-17595

The **bells** of San Juan. Le May, A.

Ben-'Ezer, Ehud, 1936-

(ed) Sleepwalkers and other stories. *See* Sleepwalkers and other stories

Bending heaven. Kane, J. F.

Beneath the moors and darker places. Lumley, B.

Benford, Gregory, 1941-

(ed) Nebula awards showcase 2000. *See* Nebula awards showcase 2000

Worlds vast and various; stories. Avon Eos 2000 312p ISBN 0-380-79054-8 LC 00-31789

Bennett, Alan, 1934-

The laying on of hands; stories. Picador 2002 198p ISBN 0-312-29051-9 LC 2001-59050

Berberova, Nina

Billancourt tales; translated from the Russian with an introduction by Marian Schwartz. New Directions 2001 175p ISBN 0-8112-1481-8 LC 2001-42583

Bergman, David, 1950-

(ed) Men on men 2000. *See* Men on men 2000

Berkeley, Anthony

The avenging chance. 2004 ISBN 1-932009-14-0

Berkman, Pamela

The falling nun and other stories; illustrations by Karen Roze. Simon & Schuster 2003 162p ISBN 0-7432-3019-1 LC 2002-29210

Berkman, Pamela Rafael

Her infinite variety; stories of Shakespeare and the women he loved. Scribner Paperback Fiction 2001 173p ISBN 0-7432-1255-X LC 00-68790

Berliner, Janet

(ed) Snapshots: 20th century mother-daughter fiction. *See* Snapshots: 20th century mother-daughter fiction

Berners, Gerald Hugh Tyrwhitt-Wilson, Baron, 1883-1950

Collected tales and fantasies of Lord Berners. Helen Marx Bks. 1999 434p ISBN 1-885983-38-7

Bernhard, Thomas, 1931-1989
  Three novellas; translated by Peter Jansen and Kenneth J. Northcott; with a foreword by Brian Evenson. University of Chicago Press 2003 174p ISBN 0-226-04432-7 LC 2002-45580
Berry, Minta Sue, 1931-
  Who is my neighbor? University of Tenn. Press 2001 186p ISBN 1-57233-115-1 LC 00-10298
Berry, R. M.
  Dictionary of modern anguish; fictions. FC2 2000 200p ISBN 1-57366-085-X LC 00-25819
Berry, Wendell, 1934-
  That distant land; the collected stories of Wendell Berry. Shoemaker & Hoard, Distributed by Publishers Group West 2004 440p ISBN 1-593-76027-2 LC 2003-25213
The **Best** alternate history stories of the 20th century; edited by Harry Turtledove with Martin H. Greenberg. Ballantine Bks. 2001 415p ISBN 0-345-43990-2 LC 2001-93752
The **Best** American mystery stories, 1999; edited and with an introduction by Ed McBain. Houghton Mifflin 1999 457p ISSN 1094-8384
The **Best** American mystery stories, 2000; edited and with an introduction by Donald E. Westlake. Houghton Mifflin 2000 489p ISSN 1094-8384
The **Best** American mystery stories, 2001; edited and with an Introduction by Lawrence Block. Houghton Mifflin 2001 349p ISSN 1094-8384
The **Best** American mystery stories, 2002; edited and with an introduction by James Ellroy; Otto Penzler, series editor. Houghton Mifflin 2002 405p ISBN 0-618-12494-2; 0-618-12493-4
The **Best** American mystery stories, 2003; edited by Michael Connelly and Otto Penzler. Houghton 2003 352p ISBN 0-618-32966-8; 0-618-32965-X (pa)
The **Best** American mystery stories of the century; Tony Hillerman, editor; with an introduction by Tony Hillerman. Houghton Mifflin 2000 813p ISBN 0-618-01267-2
The **Best** American short stories, 1999; selected from U.S. and Canadian magazines by Amy Tan with Katrina Kenison, with an introduction by Amy Tan. Houghton Mifflin 1999 410p ISSN 0067-6233
The **Best** American short stories, 2000; selected from U.S. and Canadian magazines by E. L. Doctorow with Katrina Kenison; with an introduction by E. L. Doctorow. Houghton Mifflin 2000 381p ISSN 0067-6233
The **Best** American short stories 2001; selected from U.S. and Canadian magazines by Barbara Kingsolver with Katrina Kenison; with an introduction by Barbara Kingsolver. Houghton Mifflin 2001 378p ISSN 0067-6233
The **Best** American short stories, 2002; selected from U.S. and Canadian magazines by Sue Miller with Katrina Kenison, with an introduction by Sue Miller. Houghton Mifflin 2002 375p ISBN 0-618-11749-0; 0-618-13173-6
The **Best** American short stories, 2003; selected from U.S. and Canadian magazines by Walter Mosley with Katrina Kenison; with an introduction by Walter Mosley. Houghton Mifflin 2003 360p ISBN 0-618-19732-X; 0-618-19733-8
The **Best** American short stories of the century; John Updike, editor, Katrina Kenison, coeditor; with an introduction by John Updike. Houghton Mifflin 1999 xxiv, 775p ISBN 0-395-84368-5
The **best** British mysteries; edited by Maxim Jakubowski. Allison & Busby 2003 345p ISBN 0-7490-0696-X
The **Best** from fantasy & science fiction: the fiftieth anniversary anthology; edited by Edward L. Ferman and Gordon Van Gelder. Doherty Assocs. 1999 381p ISBN 0-312-86973-8 LC 99-40560
The **best-known** man in the world and other misfits. Pearlman, D. D.
Best new American voices 2000; guest editor Tobias Wolff; series editors John Kulka and Natalie Danford. Harcourt 2000 434p ISBN 0-15-601322-3 LC 00-35045
Best new American voices 2001; guest editor Charles Baxter; series editors John Kulka and Natalie Danford. Harcourt 2001 310p ISBN 0-15-601065-8

Best new American voices 2004; guest editor John Casey; series editors John Kulka and Natalie Danford. Harcourt 2003 306p ISBN 0-15600722-3

Best new horror 10; edited and with an introduction by Stephen Jones. Carroll & Graf Pubs. 1999 489p ISBN 0-7867-0690-2

Best new horror 11; edited and with an introduction by Stephen Jones. Carroll & Graf Pubs. 2000 572p ISBN 0-7867-0792-5

Best new horror 12; edited and with an introduction by Stephen Jones. Carroll & Graf Pubs. 2001 494p ISBN 0-7867-0919-7

The **best** of animals. Grodstein, L.

Best of Prairie schooner; fiction and poetry; edited by Hilda Raz. University of Neb. Press 2001 xxi, 319p ISBN 0-8032-8972-3 LC 00-59970

The **Best** of The Kenyon review; edited by David Lynn; introduction by Joyce Carol Oates. Sourcebooks 2003 441p ISBN 1-4022-0035-8 (alk. paper) LC 2003-4791

The **best** short stories of William Kittredge. Kittredge, W.

Between man and woman keys. Brackenbury, R.

Beyond the Great Snow Mountains. L'Amour, L.

Bezmozgis, David, 1973-
Natasha and other stories. Farrar, Straus and Giroux 2004 147p ISBN 0-374-28141-6 LC 2003-21582

Bibliophilia. Griffith, M.

Big as life. Howard, M.

Big Bend. Roorbach, B.

Biguenet, John
The torturer's apprentice; stories. Ecco Press 2001 176p ISBN 0-06-019835-4 LC 00-55145

Billancourt tales. Berberova, N.

Billman, Jon
When we were wolves; stories. Random House 1999 239p ISBN 0-375-50258-0 LC 99-14952

Bingham, Sallie
Transgressions; stories. Sarabande Bks. 2002 180p ISBN 1-88933-077-9 LC 2002-1259

The **birch** grove and other stories. Iwaszkiewicz, J.

Bishop, Claudia, 1947-
(ed) Death dines at 8:30. *See* Death dines at 8:30

Bishop, Michael, 1945-
Blue Kansas sky; four short novels of memory, magic, surmise & estrangement; with an introduction by James Morrow. Golden Gryphon Press 2000 263p ISBN 0-9655901-0-0 LC 00-37147

Brighten to incandescence; 17 stories. Golden Gryphon Press 2003 295p ISBN 1-930846-16-9 LC 2002-151200

Bishop, Paul
Pattern of behavior; a short story collection. Five Star 2000 285p (Five Star standard print mystery series) ISBN 0-7862-2670-6 LC 00-30841

Bisson, Terry
In the upper room and other likely stories. Doherty Assocs. 2000 284p ISBN 0-312-87404-9 LC 00-25138

Bitter asylum. Maleti, G.

Black cherries. Coates, G. S.

Black heart, ivory bones; [edited by] Ellen Datlow & Terri Windling. Avon Bks. 2000 368p ISBN 0-380-78623-0 LC 99-50293

Black projects, white knights. Baker, K.

Blackwood, Scott
In the shadow of our house; stories. Southern Methodist Univ. Press 2001 159p ISBN 0-87074-464-X LC 2001-31353

Blades of grass. Lao She

Blair, John
American standard. University of Pittsburgh Press 2002 181p ISBN 0-8229-4192-9 LC 2004-268260

Blaise, Clark
Southern stories; with an introduction by Fenton Johnson. Porcupine's Quill 2000 190p ISBN 0-88984-219-1 (pa) LC 2001-334286

Blake, James Carlos
Borderlands; short fictions. Avon Bks. 1999 241p ISBN 0-380-79485-3

Blatnik, Andrej, 1963-
Skinswaps; translated from the Slovenian by Tamara Soban. Northwestern Univ. Press 1998 109p (Writings from an unbound Europe) ISBN 0-8101-1656-1 LC 98-34133

Blessings on the sheep dog. Saunders, G.

A **blind** man can see how much I love you. Bloom, A.

Blish, James, 1921-1975
In this world, or another; stories. Five Star 2003 416p ISBN 0-7862-5349-5 LC 2003-52849

Blitz, Renee, 1931-
In Berkeley's green and pleasant land; stories. Regent Press 2002 270p ISBN 1-58790-001-4 LC 2001-19833

Block, Lawrence, 1938-
(ed) The Best American mystery stories, 2001. *See* The Best American mystery stories, 2001
(ed) Blood on their hands. *See* Blood on their hands
(ed) Death cruise. *See* Death cruise
(ed) Master's choice [v1] *See* Master's choice [v1]
(ed) Master's choice v2. *See* Master's choice v2
(ed) Speaking of lust. *See* Speaking of lust

Blood on their hands; edited by Lawrence Block. Berkley Prime Crime 2003 340p ISBN 0-425-19035-8 LC 2003-41927

Bloom, Amy
A blind man can see how much I love you; stories. Random House 2000 163p ISBN 0-375-50268-8 LC 99-55153

The **Blue** and the gray undercover; edited by Ed Gorman. Forge 2001 318p ISBN 0-312-87487-1 LC 2001-40486

Blue Kansas sky. Bishop, M.

The **Bluelight** corner; black women writing on passion, sex, and romantic love; edited by Rosemarie Robotham. Three Rivers Press (NY) 1999 352p ISBN 0-609-80354-9 LC 98-28877

Bly, Carol
My Lord Bag of Rice; new and selected stories. Milkweed Eds. 2000 361p ISBN 1-57131-031-2 LC 99-47930

The **boats** of the "Glen Carrig" and other nautical adventures. Hodgson, W. H.

Bocock, Maclin, 1920-
A citizen of the world; short fiction. Zoland Bks. 1999 246p ISBN 1-58195-000-4 LC 98-54309

Bonnie, Fred
Widening the road; stories. Livingston Press (Livingston) 2000 166p ISBN 0-942979-66-4

The **book** of lost fathers. Wilson, R., Jr.

The **book** of ten nights and a night. Barth, J.

Booth, Austin
(ed) Reload: rethinking women + cyberculture. *See* Reload: rethinking women + cyberculture

Borderlands. Blake, J. C.

Borderlands. Coleman, J. C.

Borges, Jorge Luis, 1899-1986
Collected fictions; translated by Andrew Hurley. Viking 1998 565p ISBN 0-670-84970-7 LC 98-21217

Born to the brand. Newton, D. B.

Borrowed hearts. DeMarinis, R.

The **Bostons**. Cooke, C.

Boswell, Marshall, 1965-
Trouble with girls. Algonquin Bks. of Chapel Hill 2003 306p ISBN 1-565-12344-1 LC 2002-38611

Bottoms, Greg
Sentimental, heartbroken rednecks; stories. Context Bks. 2001 215p ISBN 1-893956-15-6 LC 2001-2863

Bowles, Paul, 1910-1999
The stories of Paul Bowles; introduction by Robert Stone. Ecco Press 2001 657p ISBN 0-06-621273-1 LC 2001-51231

Boxing's best short stories; edited by Paul D. Staudohar. Chicago Review Press 1999 330p ISBN 1-55652-364-5 LC 99-14335

Boylan, Clare
The collected stories. Counterpoint 2002 396p ISBN 1-582-43261-9 LC 2002-22752

Boyle, T. Coraghessan
   After the plague; stories. Viking 2001 303p ISBN 0-670-03005-8
      LC 2001-26585
Boys. Lloyd, D. T.
Boys keep being born. Frank, J.
Brackenbury, Rosalind
   Between man and woman keys; stories. John Daniel 2002 191p ISBN
      1-880284-52-9 LC 2001-6807
Bradbury, Ray, 1920-
   Bradbury stories; 100 of his most celebrated tales. Morrow 2003 893p
      ISBN 0-06-054242-X LC 2003-42189
   The cat's pajamas; stories. Morrow 2004 234p ISBN 0-06-058565-X
      LC 2004-42617
   One more for the road; a new short story collection. Morrow 2002
      289p ISBN 0-06-621106-9 LC 2001-26384
Bradbury stories. Bradbury, R.
Brady, Catherine, 1955-
   The end of the class war. Calyx Bks. 1999 241p ISBN 0-934971-67-6
      LC 99-19880
Brand, Max, 1892-1944
   The bright face of danger; a James Geraldi trio. Five Star 2000 287p
      (Five Star first edition western series) ISBN 0-7862-2123-2
      LC 00-44281
Brandt, William
   Alpha male. Victoria Univ. Press 1999 191p ISBN 0-86473-378-X
Break any woman down. Johnson, D.
Breaking into print; early stories and insights into getting published; a
      Ploughshares anthology; edited by DeWitt Henry. Beacon Press
      2000 284p ISBN 0-8070-6235-9 LC 99-57070
Breen, Jon L., 1943-
   The drowning icecube and other stories. Five Star 1999 276p (Five
      Star standard print mystery series) ISBN 0-7862-2250-6
   Kill the umpire; the calls of Ed Gorgon. Crippen & Landru Publishers
      2003 181p ISBN 1-932009-19-1
Brennan, Maeve, 1917-1993
   The rose garden; short stories. Counterpoint 2000 307p ISBN
      1-58243-050-0 LC 99-45921
Brenner, Wendy
   Phone calls from the dead; stories. Algonquin Bks. 2001 226p ISBN
      1-56512-245-3 LC 2001-35537
Brewer, Sonny
   (ed) Stories from the Blue Moon Café. *See* Stories from the Blue
      Moon Café
   (ed) Stories from the Blue Moon Cafe II. *See* Stories from the Blue
      Moon Cafe II
The **bridegroom**. Ha Jin
Bridge of sighs. Roeske, P.
A **brief** history of the flood. Harfenist, J.
Brief interviews with hideous men. Wallace, D. F.
Briefly told lives. Cole, C. B.
The **bright** face of danger. Brand, M.
Brighten to incandescence. Bishop, M.
Bring me your saddest Arizona. Harty, R.
Brkic, Courtney Angela, 1972-
   Stillness and other stories. Farrar, Straus and Giroux 2003 205p ISBN
      0-374-26999-8 LC 2002-29777
Brockmeier, Kevin
   Things that fall from the sky. Pantheon Bks. 2002 217p ISBN
      0-375-42134-3 LC 2001-36222
Broderick, Damien
   (ed) Centaurus: the best of Australian science fiction. *See* Centaurus:
      the best of Australian science fiction
Brodeur, Adrienne
   (ed) Francis Ford Coppola's Zoetrope: all story. *See* Francis Ford
      Coppola's Zoetrope: all story
   (ed) Francis Ford Coppola's Zoetrope all-story 2. *See* Francis Ford
      Coppola's Zoetrope all-story 2
Broken lives and other stories. Kalu, Anthonia C.

Brought to book; murderous stories from the literary world; Penny Sumner, editor. Women's Press 1998 227p ISBN 0-7043-4578-1

Broughton, T. Alan (Thomas Alan), 1936-
Suicidal tendencies; stories. Center for Literary Publishing & University Press of Colorado 2003 311p (The series in contemporary fiction) ISBN 1-88563-505-2 LC 2002-155447

Browder, Catherine
Secret lives; stories. Southern Methodist Univ. Press 2003 223p ISBN 0-87074-480-1 LC 2003-42720

Brown, Carrie, 1959-
The house on Belle Isle and other stories. Algonquin Bks. 2002 248p ISBN 1-56512-300-X LC 2001-55234

Brown, Jason
Driving the heart and other stories. Norton 1999 224p ISBN 0-393-04721-0 LC 98-37725

Brown, Stewart, 1951-
(ed) The Oxford book of Caribbean short stories. *See* The Oxford book of Caribbean short stories

Brownrigg, Sylvia
Ten women who shook the world. Farrar, Straus & Giroux 2000 125p ISBN 0-374-27289-1

Brownstein, Gabriel
The curious case of Benjamin Button, Apt. 3W. Norton 2002 223p ISBN 0-393-05151-X LC 2002-23556

Brownsville. Casares, O.

Broyard, Bliss
My father, dancing; stories. Knopf 1999 189p ISBN 0-375-40060-5 LC 99-31090

The **brutal** language of love. Erian, A.

Budnitz, Judy
Flying leap; stories. Picador 1998 244p ISBN 0-312-18097-7 LC 97-36088

Bukiet, Melvin Jules
A faker's dozen; stories. Norton 2003 268p ISBN 0-393-05816-6 LC 2003-53956

(ed) Neurotica: Jewish writers on sex. *See* Neurotica: Jewish writers on sex

Bukoski, Anthony
Polonaise; stories. Southern Methodist Univ. Press 1998 180p ISBN 0-87074-434-8 LC 98-26101

Time between trains; stories. Southern Methodist Univ. Press 2003 188p ISBN 0-87074-479-8 LC 2003-42719

Bumper crop / Joe R. Lansdale. Lansdale, J. R.

Bunin, Ivan Alekseevich, 1870-1953
Sunstroke; selected stories; translated from the Russian and with an introduction by Graham Hettlinger. Dee, I.R. 2002 190p ISBN 1-56663-426-1

Burford, Miles, 1919-
Flying lessons and other stories. Fithian Press 2001 131p ISBN 1-56474-370-5 LC 00-12306

Burton, Mallory, 1952-
Green River virgins and other passionate anglers; stories. Lyons Press 2000 208p ISBN 1-58574-142-6 LC 00-62161

The **bus** driver who wanted to be God and other stories. Keret, E.

Busch, Frederick, 1941-
Don't tell anyone. Norton 2000 309p ISBN 0-393-04973-6 LC 00-34871

Butler, Robert Olen
Had a good time; stories from American postcards. Grove Press 2004 267p il ISBN 0-8021-1777-5 LC 2003-67771

Buying a fishing rod for my grandfather. Gao, X. and Lee, M.

By the light of the jukebox. Paschal, D.

By way of the forked stick. Clark, B. C.

Byatt, A. S. (Antonia Susan), 1936-
Elementals; stories of fire and ice. Random House 1999 229p ISBN 0-375-50250-5 LC 99-10627

Little black book of stories; A.S. Byatt. 1st American ed. Knopf, Distributed by Random House 2004 240p ISBN 1-400-04177-5 (alk. paper) LC 2003-65940

C

The **cabal** and other stories. Gilchrist, E.

Cabrera Infante, G. (Guillermo), 1929-
Guilty of dancing the chachachá; translated from Spanish by the author. Welcome Rain 2001 109p ISBN 1-56649-187-8 LC 2001-26248

Cady, Jack, 1932-2004
Ghosts of yesterday. Night Shade Bks. 2003 239p ISBN 1-892389-48-7 (pa); 1-892389-28-2

Cake. Davies, Tristan

Call if you need me. Carver, R.

Callaghan, Morley
The New Yorker stories. Exile Eds. 2001 143p ISBN 1-55096-628-6

Camouflage. Bail, M.

Campbell, Bonnie Jo, 1962-
Women & other animals; stories. University of Mass. Press 1999 198p ISBN 1-558-49219-4 LC 99-15159

Campbell, Ramsey, 1946-
(ed) Gathering the bones. *See* Gathering the bones
Ghosts and grisly things. Doherty Assocs. 2000 300p ISBN 0-312-86758-1
Scared stiff; tales of sex and death. TOR Bks. 2002 239p ISBN 0-7653-0004-4 LC 2002-68474

Camping with strangers. Nawrocki, S.

Can we talk and other stories. Chinodya, S.

Can you wave bye bye, baby? Gasco, E.

Candy bars. Locklin, G.

Cannell, Dorothy
The family jewels and other stories. Five Star 2001 237p (Five Star first edition mystery series) ISBN 0-7862-3144-0 LC 2001-33055

Canty, Kevin
Honeymoon and other stories. Talese 2001 161p ISBN 0-385-49161-1 LC 00-47979

The **cape** and other stories from the Japanese ghetto. Nakagami, K.

Čapek, Karel, 1890-1938
Cross roads; translated from the Czech and with an introduction by Norma Comrada; illustrated by Paul Hoffman. Catbird Press 2002 256p ISBN 0-945774-55-9 LC 2002-1282

Caponegro, Mary, 1956-
The complexities of intimacy; stories. Coffee House Press 2001 233p ISBN 1-566-89120-5 LC 2001-32482

Capote, Truman, 1924-1984, and Price, Reynolds, 1933-
The complete stories of Truman Capote; introduction by Reynolds Price. Random House 2004 300p ISBN 0-679-64310-9 LC 2004-46876

The **caprices**. Murray, S.

Card, Orson Scott
(ed) Masterpieces: the best science fiction of the century. *See* Masterpieces: the best science fiction of the century

Carlson, Ron, 1947-
At the Jim Bridger; stories. Picador 2002 194p ISBN 0-312-28605-8
A kind of flying; selected stories; with an introduction by the author. Norton 2003 464p ISBN 0-393-32479-6 LC 2003-17889

Carp fishing on valium and other tales of the stranger road traveled. Parker, G.

Carson, Josephine, 1919-
Dog Star and other stories. Santa Barbara Review Publs. 1998 159p ISBN 0-9655497-2-0 LC 98-60131

Carter, Emily, 1960-
Glory goes and gets some; stories. Coffee House Press 2000 239p ISBN 1-56689-101-9 LC 00-43022

Carved in rock; short stories by musicians; edited by Greg Kihn. Thunder's Mouth Press, Distributed by Publishers Group West 2003 330p ISBN 1-560-25453-X LC 2003-541781

Carver, Raymond
Call if you need me; the uncollected fiction and other prose; edited by William L. Stull; foreword by Tess Gallagher. Vintage Bks. 2001 300p il ISBN 0-375-72628-4 LC 00-43834

Casares, Oscar, 1964-
    Brownsville; stories. Back Bay Bks. 2003 192p ISBN 0-316-14680-3
        LC 2002-26293
Casey, John, 1939-
    (ed) Best new American voices 2004. *See* Best new American voices
        2004
Casey, Maud
    Drastic; stories. Morrow 2002 207p ISBN 0-688-17696-8
        LC 2002-66030
Casmier, Susan B.
    (ed) A Deadly dozen. *See* A Deadly dozen
Castro, Adam-Troy
    Tangled strings. Five Star 2003 365p (Five Star first edition
        speculative fiction series) ISBN 0-7862-5342-8 LC 2003-52919
Cat crimes through time; edited by Ed Gorman, Martin H. Greenberg,
    and Larry Segriff. Carroll & Graf Pubs. 1999 335p ISBN
    0-7867-0555-8
Catch as catch can. Heller, J.
The **cat's** pajamas. Bradbury, R.
Cattarulla, Kay
    (ed) Texas bound. Book III. *See* Texas bound. Book III
Caution, men in trees. Spencer, D.
Cavell, Benjamin
    Rumble, young man, rumble. Knopf 2003 191p ISBN 0-375-41464-9
        LC 2002-27525
Celebrities in disgrace. Searle, E.
Centaurus: the best of Australian science fiction; edited by David G.
        Hartwell and Damien Broderick. Doherty Assocs. 1999 525p ISBN
        0-312-86556-2 LC 99-21936
A **Century** of great suspense stories; edited by Jeffery Deaver. Berkley
        Prime Crime 2001 590p ISBN 0-425-18192-8 LC 2001-25881
A **Century** of great Western stories; edited by John Jakes. Forge 2000
        525p ISBN 0-312-86986-X LC 99-462096
A **Century** of noir; thirty-two classic crime stories; edited by Mickey
        Spillane and Max Allan Collins. New Am. Lib. 2002 521p ISBN
        0-451-20596-0 LC 2001-58708
Chabon, Michael
    (ed) McSweeney's mammoth treasury of thrilling tales. *See*
        McSweeney's mammoth treasury of thrilling tales
    Werewolves in their youth; stories. Random House 1999 212p ISBN
        0-679-41587-4 LC 98-18980
Chacón, Daniel
    Chicano chicanery; short stories. Arte Público Press 2000 152p ISBN
        1-55885-280-8 LC 00-20792
Champion, Laurie
    (ed) The African American West. *See* The African American West
Chan, David Marshall, 1970-
    Goblin fruit; stories. Context Bks. 2003 214p ISBN 1-89395-632-6
        LC 2002-10110
Changer of worlds. Weber, D.
Changing planes. Le Guin, U. K.
Chaon, Dan
    Among the missing. Ballantine Bks. 2001 258p ISBN 0-345-44162-1
        LC 00-66695
Chapman, Clay McLeod
    Rest area; stories. Hyperion 2002 178p ISBN 0-7868-6737-X
        LC 2001-16659
The **Charlotte** Perkins Gilman reader. Gilman, C. P.
Chasing shadows. Guerrero, L.
Chaudhuri, Amit, 1962-
    Real time; stories and a reminiscence. Farrar, Straus & Giroux 2002
        184p ISBN 0-374-28169-6
Chbosky, Steve
    (ed) Pieces. *See* Pieces
Check up and other stories. Lee, W. W.
Chekhov, Anton Pavlovich, 1860-1904
    Anton Chekhov: early short stories, 1883-1888; edited by Shelby
        Foote; translated by Constance Garnett. Modern Lib. 1999 642p
        ISBN 0-679-60317-4 LC 98-20049

Chekhov, Anton Pavlovich, 1860-1904—*Continued*
Anton Chekhov: later short stories, 1888-1903; edited by Shelby Foote; translated by Constance Garnett. Modern Lib. 1999 628p ISBN 0-679-60316-6 LC 98-20048

The comic stories; translated from the Russian and with an introduction by Harvey Pitcher. Dee, I.R. 1999 217p ISBN 1-56663-241-2 LC 98-49198

The essential tales of Chekhov; edited and with an introduction by Richard Ford; translated by Constance Garnett. Ecco Press 1998 337p ISBN 0-88001-607-8 LC 98-8436

Cheng, Ch'ing-wen
Three-legged horse; edited by Pang-yuan Chi. Columbia Univ. Press 1999 225p (Modern Chinese literature from Taiwan) ISBN 0-231-11386-2 LC 98-22603

Chenoweth, Avery
Wingtips; stories. Johns Hopkins Univ. Press 1999 154p ISBN 0-8018-6023-7 LC 98-19492

Cherry, Kelly
The society of friends; stories. University of Mo. Press 1999 192p ISBN 0-8262-1243-3 LC 99-15516

Cherryh, C. J., 1942-
The collected short fiction of C.J. Cherryh. 2004 642p ISBN 0-7564-0217-4

Chesnutt, Charles Waddell, 1858-1932
Stories, novels & essays; [by] Charles W. Chesnutt. Library of America 2002 939p ISBN 1-931082-06-5 LC 2001-38120

Chesnutt, Charles Waddell, 1858-1932, and Duncan, Charles, 1962-
The northern stories of Charles W. Chesnutt; edited by Charles Duncan. Ohio University Press 2004 xxvii, 262p ISBN 0-8214-1542-5; 0-8214-1543-3 (pa) LC 2004-2173

Chiang, Ted
Stories of your life and others. TOR Bks. 2002 333p ISBN 0-765-30418-X LC 2001-59658

Chiappone, Richard
Water of an undetermined depth. Stackpole Bks. 2002 131p ISBN 0-8117-0033-X LC 2002-8078

Chicano chicanery. Chacón, D.

Children of the night; stories of ghosts, vampires, werewolves, and "lost children"; edited by Martin H. Greenberg. Cumberland House 1999 224p (Children of the night series) ISBN 1-58182-037-2 LC 99-51818

Chinodya, Shimmer
Can we talk and other stories. Heinemann Educ. Pubs. 2001 154p (African writers series) ISBN 0-435-91205-4 LC 2001-278265

Choa, Carolyn
(ed) The Vintage book of contemporary Chinese fiction. *See* The Vintage book of contemporary Chinese fiction

Choi, Susan, 1969-
(ed) Wonderful town. *See* Wonderful town

Chopin, Kate, 1851-1904
Complete novels and stories. Library of America 2002 1071p ISBN 1-931082-21-9 LC 2002-19450

Circa 2000; gay fiction at the millennium; edited by Robert Drake & Terry Wolverton. Alyson Bks. 2000 434p ISBN 1-55583-517-1 LC 00-32773

Circling the drain. Davis, A.

The **circus** in winter. Day, C.

A **citizen** of the world. Bocock, M.

City with houses. Händler, E.-W.

Claremont tales. Lupoff, R. A.

Claremont tales II. Lupoff, R. A.

Clark, Billy C., 1928-
By way of the forked stick. University of Tenn. Press 2000 149p ISBN 1-57233-094-5 LC 00-8431

Clark, Joseph
Jungle wedding; stories. Norton 1999 271p ISBN 0-393-04526-9 LC 98-17126

Clarke, Arthur C., 1917-
> The collected stories of Arthur C. Clarke. Doherty Assocs. 2000 966p ISBN 0-312-87821-4

Close range. Proulx, A.

The **clouds** in Memphis. Hribal, C. J.

Clyde, Mary
> Survival rates; stories. University of Ga. Press 1999 161p ISBN 0-8203-2049-8 LC 98-19074

Coal miner's holiday. DeLancey, K.

Coates, Grace Stone, 1881-1976
> Black cherries; introduction to the Bison Books edition by Mary Clearman Blew. University of Neb. Press 2003 99p ISBN 0-8032-6429-1 LC 2002-28527

Cobb, Thomas
> Acts of contrition. Texas Review Press 2003 154p ISBN 1-88151-559-1 LC 2003-8909

Cobb, William J., 1957-
> The white tattoo; a collection of short stories. Ohio St. Univ. Press 2002 228p ISBN 0-8142-0901-7; 0-8142-5096-3 (pa) LC 2001-6643

Coberly, Lenore M.
> The handywoman stories. Swallow Press/Ohio University Press 2002 155p ISBN 0-8040-1044-7; 0-8040-1041-2 (pa) LC 2001-55126

Codrescu, Andrei, 1946-
> A bar in Brooklyn; novellas & stories, 1970-1978. Black Sparrow Press 1999 237p ISBN 1-57423-098-0 LC 99-22178

Cody, Liza
> Lucky dip and other stories. Crippen & Landru Publishers 2003 182p ISBN 1-932009-08-6

The **coffin** master and other stories. Deane, J. F.

Cohen, Richard, 1952-
> Pronoun music; stories. Pleasure Boat Studio 2000 245p ISBN 0-929355-03-3

Cohen, Robert, 1957-
> The varieties of romantic experience; stories. Scribner 2002 217p ISBN 0-7432-2962-2 LC 2001-57756

Cohen, Stanley, 1928-
> A night in the Manchester store and other stories. Five Star 2002 300p (Five Star first edition mystery series) ISBN 0-7862-3935-2 LC 2001-59219

Colchie, Thomas
> A whistler in the nightworld. *See* A whistler in the nightworld

Cold comfort. Kilpatrick, N.

Cole, C. Bard
> Briefly told lives. St. Martin's Press 2000 205p il ISBN 0-312-25351-6 LC 00-29119

Coleman, Jane Candia
> Borderlands; western stories. Five Star 2000 228p (Five Star first edition western series) ISBN 0-7862-2122-4 LC 00-44282

Collected fictions. Borges, J. L.

The **collected** short fiction of C.J. Cherryh. Cherryh, C. J.

The **collected** short stories of Louis L'Amour. L'Amour, L.

The **collected** short works, 1920-1954. Aldrich, B. S.

Collected stories. Bellow, S.

The **collected** stories. Boylan, C.

Collected stories. Gilchrist, E.

The **collected** stories. Pushkin, A. S.

Collected stories. Singer, I. B.

Collected stories, 1891-1910. Wharton, E.

Collected stories, 1911-1937. Wharton, E.

Collected stories: A friend of Kafka to Passions. Singer, I. B.

The **collected** stories of Arthur C. Clarke. Clarke, A. C.

The **collected** stories of Greg Bear. Bear, G.

The **collected** stories of Joseph Roth. Roth, J.

The **collected** stories of Richard Yates. Yates, R.

The **collected** stories of Vernor Vinge. Vinge, V.

Collected tales and fantasies of Lord Berners. Berners, G. H. T.-W., Baron

Collins, Barbara, 1948-

Too many tomcats and other feline tales of suspense; edited and introduced by Max Allan Collins. Five Star 2000 211p (Five Star first edition mystery series) ISBN 0-7862-2899-7 LC 00-61726

Collins, Barbara, 1948-, and Collins, Max Allan

Murder—his and hers; short stories; [by] Barbara Collins & Max Allan Collins. Five Star 2001 174p (Five Star first edition mystery series) ISBN 0-7862-3145-9 LC 2001-18150

Collins, Max Allan

(ed) A Century of noir. *See* A Century of noir

(ed) Flesh and blood. *See* Flesh and blood

(ed) Flesh and blood: guilty as sin. *See* Flesh and blood: guilty as sin

Murder—his and hers. See Collins, Barbara, 1948-, and Collins, Max Allan

Collins, Michael, 1924-

Spies and thieves, cops and killers, etc. Five Star 2002 273p (Five Star first edition mystery series) ISBN 0-7862-3932-8 LC 2001-59221

Come up and see me sometime. Krouse, E.

The **comic** stories. Chekhov, A. P.

Complete novels and stories. Chopin, K.

The **complete** short stories of Marcel Proust. Proust, M.

Complete stories, 1864-1874. James, H.

Complete stories, 1874-1884. James, H.

Complete stories, 1884-1891. James, H.

The **complete** stories of Evelyn Waugh. Waugh, E.

The **complete** stories of Truman Capote. Capote, T. and Price, R.

The **complete** works of Isaac Babel. Babel´, I.

The **complexities** of intimacy. Caponegro, M.

Compression scars. Wells, K.

Connolly, Cressida, 1960-

The happiest days. Picador 2000 185p ISBN 0-312-26171-3 LC 00-47864

Connor, Joan

History lessons; stories. University of Massachusetts Press 2003 192p ISBN 1-558-49418-9 LC 2003-9137

We who live apart; stories. University of Mo. Press 2000 138p ISBN 0-8262-1293-X LC 00-41794

Cook, K. L.

Last call. University of Nebraska Press 2004 252p (Prairie schooner prize in fiction) ISBN 0-8032-1540-1 LC 2004-3458

Cooke, Carolyn

The Bostons. Houghton Mifflin 2001 180p ISBN 0-618-01768-2 LC 00-46541

Coonts, Stephen, 1946-

(ed) On glorious wings. *See* On glorious wings

Cooper, Bernard, 1951-

Guess again. Simon & Schuster 2000 208p ISBN 0-684-86586-6 LC 00-41293

Cooper, J. California

The future has a past; stories. Doubleday 2000 265p ISBN 0-385-49680-X LC 00-34602

Corpus Christi. Johnston, B. A.

Correas de Zapata, Celia

(ed) Short stories by Latin American women. *See* Short stories by Latin American women

Corrigan, Susan, 1968-

(ed) Typical girls. *See* Typical girls

Coshnear, Daniel, 1961-

Jobs & other preoccupations; stories; with an introduction by Rosellen Brown. Helicon Nine Eds. 2001 213p ISBN 1-884235-34-4 LC 2001-31543

Cosmos latinos: an anthology of science fiction from Latin America and Spain; translated, edited, & with an introduction & notes by Andrea L. Bell & Yolanda Molina-Gavilán. Wesleyan Univ. Press 2003 352p (Wesleyan early classics of science fiction series) ISBN 0-8195-6633-0; 0-8195-6634-9 (pa) LC 2003-41182

Counsel for the defense and other stories. Matera, L.

Country of cold. Patterson, K.

The **county** of birches. Kalman, J.
Coyne, John, 1940-
(ed) Living on the edge. *See* Living on the edge
Creatures of habit. McCorkle, J.
Crème de la crime; edited by Janet Hutchings. Carroll & Graf Pubs.
2000 406p ISBN 0-7867-0738-0
Crider, Bill, 1941-
The nighttime is the right time; a collection of stories. Five Star 2001
231p (Five Star first edition mystery series) ISBN 0-7862-3045-2
LC 00-50310
Crime from the mind of a woman. *See* A moment on the edge
Crime on her mind. Hart, C. G.
Crime time: mystery and suspense stories. Jakes, J.
Cross roads. Čapek, K.
Crossing Shattuck Bridge. Sanford, A.
Crossing the color line; readings in Black and white; edited by Suzanne
W. Jones. University of S.C. Press 2000 290p ISBN 1-57003-376-5
LC 00-9501
The **Crow**; shattered lives & broken dreams; edited by J. O'Barr and Ed
Kramer. Ballantine Pub. Group 1998 368p il ISBN 0-345-41711-9
LC 98-43345
Crowded lives and other stories of desperation and danger. Howard, C.
Crowley, John, 1942-
Novelties and souvenirs; collected short fiction; John Crowley. 1st ed.
Perennial 2004 p. cmp ISBN 0-380-73106-1 (trade pbk.)
LC 2003-66350
Crowther, Peter
(ed) Mars probes. *See* Mars probes
The **Cry** of an occasion; fiction from the Fellowship of Southern
Writers; edited by Richard Bausch; with a foreword by George
Garrett. Louisiana State Univ. Press 2001 210p ISBN
0-8071-2635-7 LC 00-63288
Cummins, Ann
Red ant house; stories. Houghton Mifflin 2003 179p ISBN
0-618-26925-8 LC 2002-192153
Cunningham, Eugene, 1896-1957
Trails west; western stories. Five Star 2000 232p (Five Star standard
print western series) ISBN 0-7862-1899-1 LC 99-55132
The **curious** case of Benjamin Button, Apt. 3W. Brownstein, G.
Curtain Creek Farm. Van Winckel, N.
Custer's last jump and other collaborations. Waldrop, H.
Cutrufelli, Maria Rosa
(ed) In the forbidden city. *See* In the forbidden city

D

Daly, John J.
(ed) The Anchor book of new Irish writing. *See* The Anchor book of
new Irish writing
Dangerous company. Bart, P.
Daniels, Jim
Detroit tales; [by] Jim Ray Daniels. Michigan State University Press
2003 184p ISBN 0-87013-662-3 LC 2002-153205
Dann, Jack
(ed) Dreaming down-under. *See* Dreaming down-under
(ed) Gathering the bones. *See* Gathering the bones
Jubilee. TOR Bks. 2003 c2001 441p ISBN 0-7653-0676-X
LC 2002-73275
Dark, Larry
(ed) Prize stories, 1999. *See* Prize stories, 1999
(ed) Prize stories, 2000. *See* Prize stories, 2000
(ed) Prize stories, 2001. *See* Prize stories, 2001
The **dark**; new ghost stories; edited by Ellen Datlow. 1st ed. Tor 2003
378p ISBN 0-7653-0444-9 (acid-free paper) LC 2003-54336
Dark matter; a century of speculative fiction from the African diaspora;
edited by Sheree R. Thomas. Warner Bks. 2000 427p ISBN
0-446-52583-9 LC 00-22288

Dark: stories of madness, murder, and the supernatural; edited by Clint Willis. Thunder's Mouth Press 2000 381p ISBN 1-56025-277-4 LC 00-44294

The **Darkest** thirst; a vampire anthology. Design Image Group 1998 247p ISBN 1-891946-00-5 LC 98-70435

Darkness. Maraini, D.

Darling?. Schmidt, H. J.

Dating Miss Universe. Polansky, S.

Datlow, Ellen
  (ed) Black heart, ivory bones. *See* Black heart, ivory bones
  (ed) Vanishing acts. *See* Vanishing acts
  (ed) The Year's best fantasy & horror: sixteenth annual collection. *See* The Year's best fantasy & horror: sixteenth annual collection
  (ed) The Year's best fantasy & horror, thirteenth annual collection. *See* The Year's best fantasy & horror, thirteenth annual collection
  (ed) The Year's best fantasy & horror, twelfth annual collection. *See* The Year's best fantasy & horror, twelfth annual collection

Davenport, Guy, 1927-
  The death of Picasso; new and selected writing. Shoemaker & Hoard 2003 379p ISBN 1-59376-002-7 LC 2003-13385

Davidson, Avram, 1923-1993
  The investigations of Avram Davidson; edited by Grania Davis and Richard A. Lupoff. St. Martin's Press 1999 246p ISBN 0-312-19931-7 LC 98-44012
  The other nineteenth century; a story collection; edited by Grania Davis and Henry Wessells. TOR Bks. 2001 327p ISBN 0-312-84874-9 LC 2001-54537

Davidson, Rob
  Field observations; stories. University of Mo. Press 2001 193p ISBN 0-8262-1334-0 LC 2001-23364

Davies, Peter Ho, 1966-
  Equal love; stories. Houghton Mifflin 2000 178p ISBN 0-618-00699-0

Davies, Ray, 1944-
  Waterloo sunset. Hyperion 2000 277p ISBN 0-7868-6535-0 LC 99-18688

Davies, Rhys, 1903-1978
  A human condition. Parthian Books 2002 2001 128p ISBN 1-902638-18-2 LC 2002-437396

Davies, Tristan
  Cake; stories. Johns Hopkins University Press 2003 154p (Johns Hopkins, poetry and fiction) ISBN 0-8018-7414-9 (pa) LC 2002-154021

Davis, Amanda
  Circling the drain; stories. Morrow 1999 191p ISBN 0-688-16780-2 LC 99-10760

Davis, Dorothy Salisbury, 1916-
  In the still of the night; tales to lock your doors by. Five Star 2001 214p (Five Star first edition mystery series) ISBN 0-7862-3007-X LC 00-51067

Davis, Jennifer S., 1973-
  Her kind of want. University of Iowa Press 2002 138p (The Iowa short fiction award) ISBN 0-87745-818-9 LC 2002-18061

Davis, Lauren, 1955-
  Rat medicine & other unlikely curatives. Mosaic Press (Oakville) 2000 193p ISBN 0-88962-690-1 LC 00-455024

Davis, Russell, 1970-
  (ed) Mardi Gras madness. *See* Mardi Gras madness

Day, Cathy
  The circus in winter. Harcourt 2004 274p ISBN 0-15-101048-X LC 2003-25033

The **day** of the dance. Tomlinson, N. C.

The **day** they took my uncle and other stories. Garcia, L. G.

De Lint, Charles, 1951-
  Moonlight and vines; a Newford collection. Doherty Assocs. 1999 384p ISBN 0-312-86518-X LC 98-44610
  Tapping the dream tree. TOR Bks. 2002 540p ISBN 0-312-87401-4 LC 2002-75449

Dead balls and double curves; an anthology of early baseball fiction; edited and with an introduction by Trey Strecker ; with a foreword by Arnold Hano. Southern Illinois University Press 2004 xxiii, 332p (Writing baseball) ISBN 0-8093-2561-6; 0-8093-2562-4 (pa) LC 2003-18728

Dead on demand; the best of ghost story weekend; edited by Elizabeth Engstrom. Triple Tree Pub. 2001 245p ISBN 0-9666272-5-3 LC 00-110128

A **Deadly** dozen; tales of murder from members of Sisters in Crime/Los Angeles; edited by Susan B. Casmier, Aljean Harmetz and Cynthia Lawrence. UglyTown Productions 2000 219p ISBN 0-9663473-2-3

Deadly hunger and other tales. Hensley, J. L.

Deal with the Devil and other stories. O'Callaghan, M.

Dean, Charles Randall
(ed) Of leaf and flower. See Of leaf and flower

DeAndrea, William L.
Murder-all kinds; introduction by Jane Haddam. Crippen & Landru Publishers 2003 208p ISBN 1-932009-12-4; 1-932009-13-2 (pa)

Deane, John F.
The coffin master and other stories. Blackstaff Press 2000 187p ISBN 0-85640-664-3

Dear Paramount Pictures. Pittalwala, I.

Death by espionage; intriguing stories of deception and betrayal; edited by Martin Cruz Smith. Cumberland House 1999 415p ISBN 1-58182-040-2 LC 99-26711

Death cruise; crime stories on the open seas; edited by Lawrence Block. Cumberland House 1999 408p ISBN 1-58182-007-0 LC 99-20020

Death dance; suspenseful stories of the dance macabre; Trevanian, editor. Cumberland House 2002 223p ISBN 1-581-82250-2 LC 2001-52983

Death dines at 8:30; edited by Claudia Bishop and Nick DiChario. Berkley Prime Crime 2001 286p ISBN 0-425-17470-0 LC 00-46847

Death dines in; edited by Claudia Bishop and Dean James. 1st ed. Berkley Prime Crime 2004 xiv, 317p ISBN 0-425-19262-8 LC 2003-63629

The **death** of Picasso. Davenport, G.

Death takes the veil and other stories. Quill, M.

Deaver, Jeff
(ed) A Century of great suspense stories. See A Century of great suspense stories
(ed) A Hot and sultry night for crime. See A Hot and sultry night for crime

The **deep** and other stories. Swan, M.

DeLancey, Kiki, 1959-
Coal miner's holiday; stories. Sarabande Bks. 2002 220p ISBN 1-88933-070-1 LC 2001-42945

Delaney, Edward J.
The drowning and other stories. Carnegie-Mellon Univ. Press 1999 155p ISBN 0-88748-314-3 LC 98-74659

Delany, Samuel R.
Aye, and Gomorrah; stories. Vintage Bks. 2003 383p ISBN 0-375-70671-2 LC 2002-35854

Delicate. Sojourner, M.

DeMarco, Tom
Lieutenant America and Miss Apple Pie; stories; Tom DeMarco. Down East Books 2003 219p ISBN 0-89272-586-9 LC 2002-106461

DeMarinis, Rick, 1934-
Borrowed hearts; new and selected stories. Seven Stories Press 1999 322p ISBN 1-888363-98-3 LC 98-55233

The **demon** of longing. Gilliland, G.

Demonology. Moody, R.

Derby, Matthew, 1973-
Super flat times; stories. Little, Brown 2003 196p ISBN 0-316-73857-3 LC 2002-34131

DeRosso, H. A. (Henry Andrew), 1917-1960
Riders of the shadowlands; western stories; edited by Bill Pronzini. Five Star 1999 229p (Five Star standard print western series) ISBN 0-7862-1329-9 LC 98-42377

Desai, Anita, 1937-
Diamond dust; stories. Houghton Mifflin 2000 207p ISBN 0-618-04213-X LC 00-35082

Designer genes. Stableford, B. M.

Desire and delusion. Schnitzler, A.

Despair and other stories. Alexis, A.

Desperate journey. Farrell, C.

Desplechin, Marie, 1959-
Taking it to heart; translated from the French by Will Hobson. Granta 2001 170p ISBN 1-86207-407-0

Detroit tales. Daniels, J.

Di Blasi, Debra, 1957-
Prayers of an accidental nature; stories. Coffee House Press 1998 188p ISBN 1-56889-083-7 LC 98-56287

Dial your dreams & other nightmares. Weinberg, R.

The **dialogues** of time and entropy. Stollman, A. L.

Diamond dust. Desai, A.

DiChario, Nick
(ed) Death dines at 8:30. *See* Death dines at 8:30

Dictionary of modern anguish. Berry, R. M.

A **different** plain; contemporary Nebraska fiction writers; edited by Ladette Randolph ; introduction by Mary Pipher. University of Nebraska Press 2004 398p ISBN 0-8032-3958-0; 0-8032-9002-0 (pa) LC 2004-603

Dinh, Linh, 1963-
Fake House; stories. Seven Stories Press 2000 207p ISBN 1-58322-039-9 LC 00-30802

Discovering the world. Vasseur, T. J.

Distance no object. Frym, G.

Divakaruni, Chitra Banerjee, 1956-
The unknown errors of our lives; stories. Doubleday 2001 267p ISBN 0-385-49727-X LC 00-47509

Divine and human and other stories. Tolstoy, L., graf

Diving girls. Mazelis, J.

Dixon, Stephen, 1936-
Sleep; stories. Coffee House Press 1999 283p ISBN 1-56689-081-0 LC 98-56280

Do me a favor and other short stories. Paolucci, A.

Do not forsake me, oh my darling. Stanton, M.

Doctorow, Cory
A place so foreign and eight more stories; introduction by Bruce Sterling. Four Walls Eight Windows 2003 243p ISBN 1-56858-286-2 LC 2003-54890

Doctorow, E. L., 1931-
(ed) The Best American short stories, 2000. *See* The Best American short stories, 2000
Sweet land stories. Random House 2004 147p ISBN 1-400-06204-7 LC 2003-58780

Dodd, Susan M., 1946-
O careless love; stories and a novella. Morrow 1999 274p ISBN 0-688-16999-6 LC 99-11468

Doenges, Judy, 1959-
What she left me; stories and a novella. University Press of New England 1999 173p ISBN 0-87451-937-3 LC 99-30945

Doerr, Anthony, 1973-
The shell collector; stories. Scribner 2002 219p ISBN 0-7432-1274-6 LC 2001-40031

Dog on the cross. Gwyn, A.

Dog Star and other stories. Carson, J.

Dogfight and other stories. Knight, M.

Doghouse roses. Earle, S.

Dokey, Richard
Pale morning dun; stories. University of Missouri Press 2004 164p ISBN 0-8262-1511-4 LC 2003-22909

Donaldson, Stephen R.
Reave the Just and other tales; stories. Bantam Bks. 1999 370p ISBN 0-553-11034-9 LC 98-24075

Donner, Rebecca, 1971-
(ed) On the rocks. *See* On the rocks

Don't mean nothing. O'Neill, S.

Don't tell anyone. Busch, F.

Doors. Hoffman, W.

Doran, Maggie Morgan

Gentle hearts, guilty sins. TripleTree Publishing 2003 187p ISBN 0-9716638-3-1 LC 2002109712

Douglas, Carole Nelson

(ed) White House pet detectives. *See* White House pet detectives

Down to a soundless sea. Steinbeck, T.

Dozois, Gardner R.

(ed) The Good new stuff. *See* The Good new stuff

(ed) The Good old stuff. *See* The Good old stuff

(ed) Worldmakers. *See* Worldmakers

(ed) The Year's best science fiction. *See* The Year's best science fiction

(ed) The Year's best science fiction, eighteenth annual collection. *See* The Year's best science fiction, eighteenth annual collection

(ed) The Year's best science fiction, nineteenth annual collection. *See* The Year's best science fiction, nineteenth annual collection

(ed) The Year's best science fiction, seventeenth annual collection. *See* The Year's best science fiction, seventeenth annual collection

(ed) The Year's best science fiction, sixteenth annual collection. *See* The Year's best science fiction, sixteenth annual collection

(ed) The year's best science fiction: twenty-first annual collection. *See* The year's best science fiction: twenty-first annual collection

Dracula in London; edited by P. N. Elrod. Ace Bks. 2001 263p ISBN 0-441-00858-5 LC 00-67858

The **dragon** hunt. Tran, V.

The **dragons** of Springplace. Reed, R.

Drake, David, 1945-

Grimmer than hell. Baen Bks. 2003 373p ISBN 0-7434-3590-7 LC 2002-34194

Paying the piper. Baen Bks. 2002 358p ISBN 0-7434-3547-8 LC 2002-18522

Drake, Robert

(ed) Circa 2000. *See* Circa 2000

(ed) Hers 2: brilliant new fiction by lesbian writers. *See* Hers 2: brilliant new fiction by lesbian writers

(ed) Hers 3: brilliant new fiction by lesbian writers. *See* Hers 3: brilliant new fiction by lesbian writers

(ed) His 3: brilliant new fiction by gay writers. *See* His 3: brilliant new fiction by gay writers

Drake, Robert, 1930-2001

The picture frame and other stories. Mercer Univ. Press 2000 176p ISBN 0-86554-689-4

Drastic. Casey, M.

Dream date. McGarry, J.

Dream house. Bean, B.

Dream stuff. Malouf, D.

Dream with no name; contemporary fiction from Cuba; edited by Juana Ponce de León and Esteban Ríos Rivera. Seven Stories Press 1999 303p ISBN 1-888363-72-X

Dreaming down-under; edited by Jack Dann and Janeen Webb. TOR Bks. 2001 550p ISBN 0-312-87811-7

Dreams and realities. Gorriti, J. M. and Waisman, S. G. and Masiello, F.

Drinking coffee elsewhere. Packer, Z.

The **drinking** of spirits. Abrams, T.

Drinking with the cook. Furman, L.

Driving the heart and other stories. Brown, J.

The **drowning** and other stories. Delaney, E. J.

The **drowning** icecube and other stories. Breen, J. L.

Drummond, Laurie Lynn, 1956-

Anything you say can and will be used against you; Laurie Lynn Drummond. 1st ed. HarperCollinsPublishers 2004 xii, 250p ISBN 0-06-056162-9 (acid-free paper); 0-06-056163-7 (pbk. : acid-free paper) LC 2003-51133

Duel. Matheson, R.

Duffy, Stella
(ed) Tart noir. *See* Tart noir

Dumas, Henry, 1934-1968, and Redmond, Eugene B.
Echo tree; the collected short fiction of Henry Dumas; edited and with a foreword by Eugene B. Redmond ; critical introduction by John S. Wright. Coffee House Press 2003 l, 381p (The Coffee House Press black arts movement series) ISBN 1-56689-149-3 (alk. paper) LC 2003-55120

Duncan, Charles, 1962-
The northern stories of Charles W. Chesnutt. See Chesnutt, Charles Waddell, 1858-1932, and Duncan, Charles, 1962-

Dunmore, Helen, 1952-
Ice cream. Grove Press 2000 217p ISBN 0-8021-1733-3 LC 2002-29727

Dwight's house and other stories. Willis, M. S.

Dwyer, Maggie
Misplaced love; short stories. Turnstone Press (Winnipeg) 2001 136p ISBN 0-88801-257-8 LC 2001-347272

Dybek, Stuart, 1942-
I sailed with Magellan. Farrar, Straus and Giroux 2003 307p ISBN 0-374-17407-5 LC 2003-49052

Dyson, Jeremy
Never trust a rabbit. Duckworth 2000 231p ISBN 0-7156-3015-6

E

Eakin, William
Redgunk tales; apocalypse and kudzu from Redgunk, Mississippi. Invisible Cities Press 2001 278p ISBN 0-9679683-4-8 LC 2001-16614

Earle, Steve
Doghouse roses; stories. Houghton Mifflin 2001 207p ISBN 0-618-04026-9 LC 00-68247

Early German and Austrian detective fiction; an anthology; translated and edited by Mary W. Tannert and Henry Kratz. McFarland & Co. 1999 242p ISBN 0-7864-0659-3 LC 98-54255

The **early** stories, 1953-1975. Updike, J.

The **early** stories of Louisa May Alcott, 1852-1860. Alcott, L. M.

Easterns and westerns. Swarthout, G. F.

Easton, Robert Olney
To find a place; western stories. Five Star 1999 188p (Five Star standard print western series) ISBN 0-7862-1894-0 LC 99-35273

Ebershoff, David
The Rose City; stories. Viking 2001 220p ISBN 0-670-89483-4 LC 00-52756

Echo tree. Dumas, H. and Redmond, E. B.

The **edge** of marriage. Kaplan, H.

Edghill, Rosemary
Paying the piper at the gates of dawn. Five Star 2003 333p (Five Star first edition speculative fiction series) ISBN 0-7862-5345-2 LC 2003-49153

Edwards, Sonia
A white veil for tomorrow. Parthian Bks. 2001 83p ISBN 1-902638-17-4

Eggers, Paul
How the water feels; stories. Southern Methodist Univ. Press 2002 183p ISBN 0-87074-473-9 LC 2002-75820

Ehrhart, W. D. (William Daniel), 1948-
(ed) Retrieving bones. *See* Retrieving bones

Eldridge, Courtney
Unkempt. Harcourt 2004 262p ISBN 0-15-101084-6 LC 2003-23234

Elementals. Byatt, A. S.

Ellroy, James
(ed) The Best American mystery stories, 2002. *See* The Best American mystery stories, 2002

Elrod, P. N.
(ed) Dracula in London. *See* Dracula in London

Emporium. Johnson, A.

The **empress's** new lingerie and other erotic fairy tales. Rollins, H.

The **end** of free love. Steinberg, S.

The **end** of the class war. Brady, C.

The **Ends** of Our Tethers. Gray, A.

Engel, Mary Potter

Strangers and sojourners; stories from the lowcountry. Counterpoint 2004 222p ISBN 1-582-43264-3 LC 2003-20892

Englander, Nathan

For the relief of unbearable urges. Knopf 1999 205p ISBN 0-375-40492-9 LC 98-41727

English translations of short stories by contemporary Argentine women writers; edited by Eliana Cazaubon Hermann ; translated by Sally Webb Thornton. Edwin Mellen Press 2002 187p ISBN 0-7734-6920-6 LC 2002-33688

Engstrom, Elizabeth, 1951-

(ed) Dead on demand. *See* Dead on demand

Epstein, Joseph, 1937-

Fabulous small Jews. Houghton Mifflin 2003 340p ISBN 0-395-94402-3 LC 2002-27621

Equal love. Davies, P. H.

Erian, Alicia

The brutal language of love; stories. Villard Bks. 2001 209p ISBN 0-375-50478-8 LC 00-43460

Erotic stories. Gomes, M. T.

Erratics. Hart, R.

Essence of camphor. Naiyer Masud

The **essential** tales of Chekhov. Chekhov, A. P.

Estep, Maggie

Soft maniacs; stories. Simon & Schuster 1999 220p ISBN 0-684-86333-2 LC 99-26941

Esther stories. Orner, P.

Estleman, Loren D.

(ed) American West. *See* American West

Etchison, Dennis, 1943-

(ed) Gathering the bones. *See* Gathering the bones

(ed) The Museum of horrors. *See* The Museum of horrors

Evans, Elizabeth, 1951-

Suicide's girlfriend; a novella and short stories. HarperCollins Pubs. 2002 180p ISBN 0-06-095467-1

Evenson, Brian, 1966-

The wavering knife; stories. FC2 2004 210p ISBN 1-573-66113-9 LC 2003-20424

Every night is ladies' night. Jaime-Becerra, M.

Everybody pays. Vachss, A. H.

Ewell, Barbara C.

(ed) Southern local color. *See* Southern local color

Eyesores. Shade, E.

F

Fabulous small Jews. Epstein, J.

Faerie tales. 2004 ISBN 0-7564-0182-8

Fairey, Wendy W.

Full house; stories. Southern Methodist Univ. Press 2003 241p ISBN 0-87074-483-6 LC 2003-57336

Faithless: tales of transgression. Oates, J. C.

Fake House. Dinh, L.

A **faker's** dozen. Bukiet, M. J.

The **falling** nun and other stories. Berkman, P.

The **family** jewels and other stories. Cannell, D.

The **fantasies** of Robert A. Heinlein. Heinlein, R. A.

Fantasmas; supernatural stories by Mexican American writers; edited by Rob Johnson; introduction by Kathleen J. Alcalá. Bilingual Press/Editorial Bilingüe 2001 185p ISBN 1-931010-02-1 LC 2001-25282

Far from this earth and other stories. Oliver, C.

Far horizons; all new tales from the greatest worlds of science fiction; edited by Robert Silverberg. Avon Eos 1999 482p ISBN 0-380-97630-7 LC 98-46853

Farrell, Cliff
Desperate journey; edited by R.E. Briney. Five Star 1999 261p (Five Star standard print western series) ISBN 0-7862-1332-9 LC 98-52068

Fascinated; [by] Bertrice Small, Susan Johnson, Thea Devine and Robin Schone. Kensington Bks. 2000 378p ISBN 1-57566-606-5

Fate of a prisoner and other stories. Johnson-Davies, D.

Fault lines; stories of divorce; collected and edited by Caitlin Shetterly. Berkley Bks. 2001 357p ISBN 0-425-18161-8 LC 2001-35972

A **Feast** in the mirror; stories by contemporary Iranian women; translated and edited by Mohammad Mehdi Khorrami, Shouleh Vatanabadi. Lynne Rienner Pubs. 2000 235p ISBN 0-89410-889-1 LC 00-32855

Fedorchek, Robert M., 1938-
Stories of enchantment from nineteenth-century Spain. *See* Stories of enchantment from nineteenth-century Spain

Felonious felines; edited by Carol and Ed Gorman. Five Star 2000 175p (Five Star first edition mystery series) ISBN 0-7862-2689-7 LC 00-34754

Female trouble. Nelson, A.

Ferman, Edward L.
(ed) The Best from fantasy & science fiction: the fiftieth anniversary anthology. *See* The Best from fantasy & science fiction: the fiftieth anniversary anthology

Ferriss, Lucy, 1954-
Leaving the neighborhood and other stories. Mid-List Press 2001 163p ISBN 0-922811-50-4 LC 2001-30173

A **few** short notes on tropical butterflies. Murray, J.

Field observations. Davidson, R.

Field study. Seiffert, R.

Filipak, Christine
(ed) Tales from The Dark Tower. *See* Tales from The Dark Tower

Fingers pointing somewhere else. Fischerová, D.

Fire road. Anderson, D.

"The **first** day" and other stories. Baron, D.

The **First** Five Star western corral; western stories; edited by Jon Tuska and Vicki Piekarski. Five Star 2000 235p (Five Star standard print western series) ISBN 0-7862-1848-7 LC 99-55130

The **first** paper girl in Red Oak, Iowa and other stories. Stuckey-French, E.

First snow on Fuji. Kawabata, Y.

Fischer, Tibor, 1959-
I like being killed; stories. Metropolitan Bks. 2000 261p ISBN 0-8050-6601-2 LC 00-29576

Fischerová, Daniela, 1948-
Fingers pointing somewhere else; stories; translated from the Czech by Neil Bermel. Catbird Press 2000 174p ISBN 0-945774-44-3 LC 99-16409

Fishing for chickens; short stories about rural youth; edited, with an introduction by Jim Heynen. Persea Bks. 2001 177p ISBN 0-89255-264-6 LC 2001-021494

Fishing's best short stories; edited by Paul D. Staudohar. Chicago Review Press 2000 365p ISBN 1-55652-403-X LC 00-25135

Fitzgerald, F. Scott (Francis Scott), 1896-1940
Before Gatsby; the first twenty-six stories; edited by Matthew J. Bruccoli with the assistance of Judith S. Baughman. University of S.C. Press 2001 xxxiv, 550p il ISBN 1-570-03371-4 LC 00-12600

Fitzgerald, Penelope
The means of escape. Houghton Mifflin 2000 117p ISBN 0-618-07994-7 LC 00-38914

The **flame-coloured** dress and other stories. Régio, J.

Flanagan, Mary, 1969-
(ed) Reload: rethinking women + cyberculture. *See* Reload: rethinking women + cyberculture

Fleming, Robert
   Havoc after dark; tales of terror; foreword by Tananarive Due. Dafina; Turnaround 2004 241p ISBN 0-7582-0575-9
Flesh and blood; erotic tales of crime and passion; edited by Max Allan Collins and Jeff Gelb. Mysterious Press 2001 351p ISBN 0-446-67777-9 LC 00-47743
Flesh and blood: guilty as sin; erotic tales of crime and passion; edited by Max Allan Collins and Jeff Gelb. Mysterious Press 2003 366p ISBN 0-446-69039-2 LC 2002-32160
Flight and other stories. Skinner, J.
Flights of love. Schlink, B.
Flying leap. Budnitz, J.
Flying lessons and other stories. Burford, M.
Flynn, T. T.
   Ride to glory; a Western quartet. Five Star 2000 255p (Five Star first edition western series) ISBN 0-7862-2108-9 LC 00-37128
Foley, Sylvia
   Life in the air ocean; stories. Knopf 1999 161p ISBN 0-375-40063-X LC 98-14212
For the relief of unbearable urges. Englander, N.
Ford, Richard, 1944-
   A multitude of sins; stories. Knopf 2002 286p ISBN 0-375-41212-3 LC 2001-38402
Forsyth, Frederick, 1938-
   The veteran; five heart-stopping stories. Thomas Dunne Bks. 2001 367p ISBN 0-312-28691-0
Foster, Ken
   The kind I'm likely to get; a collection. Quill 1999 193p ISBN 0-688-16980-5 LC 99-11175
Fracis, Sohrab Homi, 1958-
   Ticket to Minto; stories of India and America. University of Iowa Press 2001 210p (Iowa short fiction award) ISBN 0-87745-779-4 LC 2001-33590
Francis Ford Coppola's Zoetrope: all story; edited by Adrienne Brodeur and Samantha Schnee; introduction by Francis Ford Coppola. Harcourt 2000 356p ISBN 0-15-601110-7 LC 99-57273
Francis Ford Coppola's Zoetrope all-story 2; edited by Adrienne Brodeur and Samantha Schnee; with an introduction by Francis Ford Coppola. Harcourt 2003 402p ISBN 0-15-601368-1 LC 2003-3940
Frank, Joan
   Boys keep being born; stories. University of Mo. Press 2001 161p il ISBN 0-8262-1355-3 LC 2001-45080
Franklin, Tom
   Poachers; stories. Morrow 1999 192p ISBN 0-688-16740-3 LC 98-51982
Free and other stories. Nailah, A.
Freudenberger, Nell
   Lucky girls; stories. Ecco Press 2003 225p ISBN 0-06-008879-6 LC 2003-44875
Friend of mankind and other stories. Mazor, J.
Frigid tales. Jesús, P. d.
From the listening hills. L'Amour, L.
Fromm, Pete, 1958-
   Night swimming; stories. Picador 1999 182p ISBN 0-312-20936-3 LC 99-22213
Frym, Gloria
   Distance no object; stories. City Lights Bks. 1999 168p ISBN 0-87286-358-1 LC 99-34686
Fuentes, Carlos, 1928-
   (ed) The Vintage book of Latin American stories. *See* The Vintage book of Latin American stories
Full house. Fairey, W. W.
Fulton, John
   Retribution. Picador 2001 194p ISBN 0-312-27680-X LC 2001-21931
The **funeral** of a giraffe. Tomioka, T.
Furman, Laura
   Drinking with the cook. Winedale Pub. 2001 262p ISBN 0-9701525-2-3 LC 00-69318

Furman, Laura—*Continued*
(ed) The O. Henry Prize stories, 2003. *See* The O. Henry Prize stories, 2003

The **future** has a past. Cooper, J. C.

Futureland. Mosley, W.

G

Gabriel, David
Making peace with the Muslims; stories. Welcome Rain 2003 207p ISBN 1-566-49265-3 LC 2002-41175

Gabrielyan, Nina
Master of the grass; translated by Kathleen Cook, Joanne Turnbull, Jean MacKenzie, and Sofi Cook. GLAS Pubs 2004 208p ISBN 5-7172-0066-8

Galef, David
Laugh track. University Press of Miss. 2002 222p ISBN 1-578-06422-8 LC 2001-26903

Galloway, Janice
Where you find it; stories. Simon & Schuster 2002 235p ISBN 0-684-84450-8 LC 2001-49668

Gao, Xingjian, and Lee, Mabel
Buying a fishing rod for my grandfather; stories; Gao Xingjian ; translated from the Chinese by Mabel Lee. 1st ed. HarperCollinsPublishers 2004 127p ISBN 0-06-057555-7 (acid-free paper) LC 2003-51138

Garcia, Lionel G.
The day they took my uncle and other stories. Texas Christian Univ. Press 2001 234p ISBN 0-87565-235-2 LC 00-57716

Garden primitives. Sosin, D.

Gartner, Zsuzsi
All the anxious girls on earth. Anchor Bks. (NY) 2000 198p ISBN 0-385-49911-6 LC 00-701538

Gasco, Elyse
Can you wave bye bye, baby?; stories. Picador 1999 238p ISBN 0-312-20631-3 LC 99-27174

Gates, David, 1947-
The wonders of the invisible world; stories. Knopf 1999 257p ISBN 0-679-43668-5 LC 99-18497

Gathering the bones; original stories from the world's masters of horror; edited by Dennis Etchison, Ramsey Campbell and Jack Dann. TOR Bks. 2003 447p ISBN 0-765-30179-2 LC 2003-42617

Gautreaux, Tim
Welding with children. Picador 1999 209p ISBN 0-312-20308-X LC 99-36020

Gavell, Mary Ladd, 1919-1967
I cannot tell a lie, exactly and other stories. Random House 2001 220p ISBN 0-375-50612-8 LC 2001-19105

Gay, William
I hate to see that evening sun go down; collected stories. Free Press 2002 303p ISBN 0-7432-4088-X LC 2002-73945

Gelb, Jeff
(ed) Flesh and blood: guilty as sin. *See* Flesh and blood: guilty as sin

Gelb, Jeff
(ed) Flesh and blood. *See* Flesh and blood

Gentle hearts, guilty sins. Doran, M. M.

Gentle insanities and other states of mind. Matthews, C.

George, Elizabeth
I, Richard; stories of suspense. Bantam Bks. 2002 244p ISBN 0-553-80258-5 LC 2001-56697

(ed) A moment on the edge. *See* A moment on the edge

Georgia under water. Sellers, H.

The **getaway** and other stories. Thomas, D. and Pappas, C.

Getting a life. Simpson, H.

The **ghost** of John Wayne and other stories. Gonzalez, R.

The **ghost** stories of Muriel Spark. Spark, M.

Ghost wolf of Thunder Mountain. Henry, W.

Ghost writing; haunted tales by contemporary writers; edited by Roger Weingarten. Invisible City/Red Hill Press 2000 316p ISBN 0-9679683-0-5 LC 00-57242

Ghosts and grisly things. Campbell, R.

Ghosts of yesterday. Cady, J.

Gifford, Barry, 1946-
American Falls; the collected short stories. Seven Stories Press 2002 251p ISBN 1-583-22470-X LC 2002-1130

Gigantic. Nesbitt, M.

Gilb, Dagoberto, 1950-
Woodcuts of women. Grove Press 2001 167p il ISBN 0-8021-1679-5 LC 00-60060

Gilbar, Steven, 1941-
(ed) LA shorts. *See* LA shorts

Gilchrist, Ellen, 1935-
The cabal and other stories. Little, Brown 2000 272p ISBN 0-316-31491-9 LC 99-36893
Collected stories. Little, Brown 2000 563p ISBN 0-316-29948-0 LC 00-35667
I, Rhoda Manning, go hunting with my daddy, & other stories. Little, Brown 2002 291p ISBN 0-316-17358-4 LC 2001-37678

Gilliland, Gail
The demon of longing; short stories. Carnegie-Mellon Univ. Press 2001 263p ISBN 0-88748-362-3 LC 2001-91296

Gilman, Charlotte Perkins, 1860-1935
The Charlotte Perkins Gilman reader; edited and introduced by Ann J. Lane. University Press of Va. 1999 xlviii, 208p ISBN 0-8139-1876-6 LC 98-53475

Giono, Jean, 1895-1970
The solitude of compassion; translated by Edward Ford. Seven Stories Press 2002 171p ISBN 1-583-22524-2 LC 2002-10009

Girardi, Robert
A vaudeville of devils; 7 moral tales. Delacorte Press 1999 421p ISBN 0-385-33397-8 LC 99-17795

Girl boy etc. Weinreb, M.

The **girl** in the fall-away dress. Richmond, M.

A **girl** with a monkey. Michaels, L.

Glasrud, Bruce A.
(ed) The African American West. *See* The African American West

Glave, Thomas
Whose song? and other stories. City Lights Bks. 2000 249p ISBN 0-87286-375-1 LC 00-34641

Glory goes and gets some. Carter, E.

Glover, Douglas H.
Bad news of the heart. Dalkey Archive Press 2003 212p ISBN 1-564-78286-7 LC 2002-41510

Gnarl!. Rucker, R. v. B.

Goblin fruit. Chan, D. M.

Going for infinity. Anderson, P.

Goldner, Beth
Wake; stories. Counterpoint 2003 219p ISBN 1-582-43269-4 LC 2003-6392

Goldstein, Naama, 1969-
The place will comfort you; stories. Scribner 2004 211p ISBN 0-7432-5135-0 LC 2003-68609

Goliger, Gabriella
Song of ascent; stories. Raincoast Bks. 2000 177p ISBN 1-55192-374-2

Gomes, Manuel Teixeira, 1862-1941
Erotic stories; translated by Alison Aiken. Carcanet Press 1999 110p ISBN 1-85754-389-0

Gonzalez, Ray
The ghost of John Wayne and other stories. University of Ariz. Press 2001 168p (Camino del sol) ISBN 0-8165-2065-8 LC 01-1465

Good as any. Westmoreland, T. A.

The **Good** new stuff; adventure SF in the grand tradition; edited by Gardner Dozois. St. Martin's Griffin 1999 450p ISBN 0-312-19890-6 LC 98-42824

The **Good** old stuff; adventure SF in the grand tradition; edited by Gardner Dozois. St. Martin's Griffin 1998 xxv, 434p ISBN 0-312-19275-4 LC 98-23489

A **good** story and other stories. Westlake, D. E.

The **good** times. Kelman, J.

Goodbye, evil eye. Kirchheimer, G. D.

Goodnight, nobody. Knight, M.

Goran, Lester
Outlaws of the Purple Cow and other stories. Kent State Univ. Press 1999 358p ISBN 0-87338-639-6 LC 99-13044

Gordimer, Nadine, 1923-
Loot and other stories. Farrar, Straus & Giroux 2003 240p ISBN 0-374-19090-9 LC 2002-42601

Gores, Joe
Speak of the Devil; 14 tales of crimes and their punishments. Five Star 1999 220p (Five Star standard print mystery series) ISBN 0-7862-2035-X LC 99-27150

Gorman, Carol
(ed) Felonious felines. *See* Felonious felines

Gorman, Edward
(ed) The Blue and the gray undercover. *See* The Blue and the gray undercover
(ed) Cat crimes through time. *See* Cat crimes through time
(ed) Felonious felines. *See* Felonious felines
Such a good girl and other crime stories; with an introduction by Richard Laymon. Five Star 2001 243p (Five Star first edition mystery series) ISBN 0-7862-2998-5 LC 00-51069
(ed) The World's finest mystery and crime stories, first annual collection. *See* The World's finest mystery and crime stories, first annual collection
(ed) The World's finest mystery and crime stories, second annual collection. *See* The World's finest mystery and crime stories, second annual collection
(ed) The World's finest mystery and crime stories, third annual collection. *See* The World's finest mystery and crime stories, third annual collection

Gorriti, Juana Manuela, 1818-1892, and Waisman, Sergio Gabriel, 1967-, and Masiello, Francine, 1948-
Dreams and realities; selected fiction of Juana Manuela Gorriti; translated from the Spanish by Sergio Waisman ; edited, with an introduction and notes by Francine Masiello. Oxford University Press 2003 lxiii, 270p (Library of Latin America) ISBN 0-19-511737-9; 0-19-511738-7 (pa) LC 2002-31175

Goscilo, Helena
Shamara and other stories. See Vasilenko, Svetlana, 1956-, and Goscilo, Helena

Got to be real; four original love stories; [by] E. Lynn Harris [et al.] New Am. Lib. 2000 384p ISBN 0-451-20223-6

The **grandmothers**. Lessing, D. M.

Grandpa was a cowboy & an Indian and other stories. Sneve, V. D. H.

Grant, Glenn
(ed) Northern suns. *See* Northern suns

Grau, Shirley Ann, 1929-
Selected stories; with a foreword by Robert Phillips. Louisiana State Univ. Press 2003 274p ISBN 0-8071-2883-X LC 2003-40141

Graveyard of the Atlantic. Hagy, A. C.

Gray, Alasdair
The Ends of Our Tethers; thirteen sorry stories. Canongate 2003 181p il ISBN 1-84195-440-3

Great dream of heaven. Shepard, S.

The **great** escape. Watson, I.

The **Green** Lantern & other stories. Smart, A.

Green River virgins and other passionate anglers. Burton, M.

Greenberg, Alvin
How the dead live; stories. Graywolf Press 1998 229p ISBN 1-55597-281-0 LC 98-84457

Greenberg, Martin Harry
(ed) The Best alternate history stories of the 20th century. *See* The Best alternate history stories of the 20th century

Greenberg, Martin Harry—*Continued*

(ed) Cat crimes through time. *See* Cat crimes through time

(ed) Children of the night. *See* Children of the night

(ed) Lighthouse hauntings. *See* Lighthouse hauntings

(ed) Mardi Gras madness. *See* Mardi Gras madness

(ed) Murder most Celtic. *See* Murder most Celtic

(ed) Murder most delectable. *See* Murder most delectable

(ed) Murder most divine. *See* Murder most divine

(ed) Murder most postal. *See* Murder most postal

(ed) Murder, my dear Watson. *See* Murder, my dear Watson

(ed) Once upon a galaxy. *See* Once upon a galaxy

(ed) Past imperfect. *See* Past imperfect

(ed) The World's finest mystery and crime stories, third annual collection. *See* The World's finest mystery and crime stories, third annual collection

Greer, Andrew Sean

How it was for me. Picador 2000 211p ISBN 0-312-24105-4 LC 99-56643

Greer, Robert O., 1944-

Isolation, and other stories. Davies Group 2001 195p ISBN 1-88857-047-4 LC 2001-28684

Griffith, Michael

Bibliophilia; a novella and stories. Arcade Pub. 2003 223p ISBN 1-559-70676-7 (pa) LC 2003-45323

Grimes, Tom, 1954-

(ed) The Workshop. *See* The Workshop

Grimmer than hell. Drake, D.

Grodstein, Lauren

The best of animals; stories. Persea Bks. 2002 182p ISBN 0-89255-281-6

Grubbs, Morris Allen, 1963-

(ed) Home and beyond. *See* Home and beyond

Guerrero, Lucrecia

Chasing shadows; stories. Chronicle Bks. 2000 175p il ISBN 0-8118-2794-1 LC 99-55166

Guess again. Cooper, B.

Guilty of dancing the chachachá. Cabrera Infante, G.

Gunn, Kirsty

This place you return to is home. Atlantic Monthly Press 1999 200p ISBN 0-87113-741-0 LC 98-39767

Gunning for Ho. Barnes, H. L.

Gurganus, Allan

The practical heart; four novellas. Knopf 2001 322p ISBN 0-679-43763-0 LC 2001-32665

Gussoff, Caren

The wave; a novella and other stories. Serpent's Tail Pub. 2003 181p LC 2002-115464

Gwyn, Aaron

Dog on the cross; stories; by Aaron Gwyn. 1st ed. Algonquin Books of Chapel Hill 2004 217p ISBN 1-565-12412-X LC 2003-66445

H

Ha Jin, 1956-

The bridegroom; stories. Pantheon Bks. 2000 225p ISBN 0-375-42067-3 LC 00-28405

Haake, Katharine

The height and depth of everything; stories. University of Nev. Press 2001 175p (Western literature series) ISBN 0-87417-488-0 LC 2001-1407

Had a good time. Butler, R. O.

Hagy, Alyson Carol

Graveyard of the Atlantic; short stories. Graywolf Press 2000 186p ISBN 1-55597-301-9 LC 99-67242

Half in love. Meloy, M.

The **half-mammals** of Dixie. Singleton, G.

Hall, Donald, 1928-
Willow Temple; new and selected stories. Houghton Mifflin 2003 210p ISBN 0-618-32981-1 LC 2002-27585
Halpern, Daniel, 1945-
(ed) The Art of the story. *See* The Art of the story
Halpern, Marty
(ed) Witpunk. *See* Witpunk
Hamburger, Aaron
The view from Stalin's Head; stories. Random House Trade Paperbacks 2004 255p ISBN 0-8129-7093-4 (pa) LC 2003-47063
Hammett, Dashiell, 1894-1961
Nightmare town; stories; edited by Kirby McCauley, Martin H. Greenberg, and Ed Gorman. Knopf 1999 396p ISBN 0-375-40111-3 LC 99-37237
The **hand** of Buddha. Watanabe McFerrin, L.
Händler, Ernst-Wilhelm, 1953-
City with houses; translated from the German and with an afterword by Martin Klebes. Northwestern Univ. Press 2002 228p ISBN 0-8101-1818-1; 0-8101-1912-9 (pa) LC 2001-4687
The **handywoman** stories. Coberly, L. M.
The **happiest** days. Connolly, C.
Happy or otherwise. Joseph, D.
Hard language. Padilla, M.
A **hard** time to be a father. Weldon, F.
Harfenist, Jean
A brief history of the flood; stories. Knopf 2002 212p ISBN 0-375-41393-6 LC 2002-19068
Harmetz, Aljean
(ed) A Deadly dozen. *See* A Deadly dozen
Harris, Mark, 1922-
The self-made brain surgeon and other stories; with an introduction by Jon Surgal. University of Neb. Press 1999 208p ISBN 0-8032-7319-3 LC 98-42925
Harrison, Harry, 1925-
50 in 50; a collection of short stories, one for each of fifty years. TOR Bks. 2001 623p il ISBN 0-312-87789-7 LC 2001-21947
Harrison, Jim, 1937-
The beast God forgot to invent. Atlantic Monthly Press 2000 274p ISBN 0-87113-821-2 LC 00-38620
Harry Keogh. Lumley, B.
Hart, Carolyn G.
Crime on her mind; a collection of short stories. Five Star 1999 268p (Five Star standard print mystery series) ISBN 0-7862-1735-9 LC 99-176041
(ed) Love and death. *See* Love and death
Hart, Roger, 1948-
Erratics. Texas Review Press 2001 131p ISBN 1-881515-37-0 LC 2001-40657
Hartwell, David G.
(ed) Centaurus: the best of Australian science fiction. *See* Centaurus: the best of Australian science fiction
(ed) Northern suns. *See* Northern suns
Harty, Ryan, 1965-
Bring me your saddest Arizona. University of Iowa City 2003 158p (The John Simmons short fiction award) ISBN 0-87745-869-3 LC 2003-42643
Harvey, John, 1938-
Now's the time. Slow Dancer Press 1999 299p ISBN 1-871033-58-6
Haskell, John, 1958-
I am not Jackson Pollock. Farrar, Straus & Giroux 2003 180p il ISBN 0-374-17399-0 LC 2002-33889
Haslett, Adam
You are not a stranger here. Talese 2002 240p ISBN 0-385-50952-9
Hassler, Jon
Keepsakes & other stories; wood engravings by Gaylord Schanilec. Afton Hist. Soc. Press 1999 118p ISBN 1-890434-17-5 LC 99-33888
Hateship, friendship, courtship, loveship, marriage. Munro, A.
Havoc after dark. Fleming, R.

Hawthorne, Nathaniel, 1804-1864

The Hawthorne treasury. Modern Lib. 1999 1409p ISBN 0-679-60322-0 LC 98-47424

The **Hawthorne** treasury. Hawthorne, N.

Hay, Elizabeth

Small change. Counterpoint 2001 244p ISBN 1-58243-167-1 LC 2001-28857

Hayes, Daniel, 1952-

Kissing you; stories. Graywolf Press 2003 190p ISBN 1-55597-379-5 LC 2002-111716

He walked in and sat down and other stories. Sánchez, R.

Head. Tester, W.

Heading west. Loomis, N. M.

The **heart** is deceitful above all things. LeRoy, J. T.

The **heavenly** World Series. O'Rourke, F.

Heavy water and other stories. Amis, M.

Hegi, Ursula

Hotel of the saints; stories. Simon & Schuster 2001 170p ISBN 0-684-84310-2 LC 2001-42944

The **height** and depth of everything. Haake, K.

Heinlein, Robert A. (Robert Anson), 1907-1988

The fantasies of Robert A. Heinlein. Doherty Assocs. 1999 352p ISBN 0-312-87245-3 LC 99-38362

Helfers, John

(ed) Once upon a galaxy. *See* Once upon a galaxy

Heller, Joseph

Catch as catch can; the collected stories and other writings; edited by Matthew J. Bruccoli and Park Bucker. Simon & Schuster 2003 333p ISBN 0-7432-4374-9 LC 2002-42875

Hell's bottom, Colorado. Pritchett, L.

Helms, Beth, 1965-

American wives. University of Iowa Press 2003 150p ISBN 0-87745-868-5

Hemlock at Vespers. Tremayne, P.

Hemon, Aleksandar, 1964-

The question of Bruno. Talese 2000 230p il ISBN 0-385-49923-X LC 99-57519

Hendel, Yehudit, 1926-

Small change; a collection of stories. Brandeis Univ. Press 2003 142p ISBN 1-58465-279-9

Henderson, Bill, 1941-

(ed) The Pushcart prize XXIII: best of the small presses. *See* The Pushcart prize XXIII: best of the small presses

(ed) The Pushcart prize XXIV: best of the small presses. *See* The Pushcart prize XXIV: best of the small presses

(ed) Pushcart prize XXVII. *See* Pushcart prize XXVII

Henderson, Lauren, 1966-

(ed) Tart noir. *See* Tart noir

Henley, Patricia, 1947-

Worship of the common heart; new and selected stories. MacMurray & Beck 2000 357p ISBN 1-87844-802-1 LC 00-41817

Henry, DeWitt

(ed) Breaking into print. *See* Breaking into print

Henry, Will, 1912-1991

Ghost wolf of Thunder Mountain; frontier stories. Five Star 2000 223p (Five Star first edition western series) ISBN 0-7862-2119-4 LC 00-44272

Tumbleweeds; frontier stories. Five Star 1999 251p (Five Star standard print western series) ISBN 0-7862-1327-2 LC 98-42376

Hensley, Joe L., 1926-

Deadly hunger and other tales. Five Star 2001 220p (Five Star first edition mystery series) ISBN 0-7862-3141-6 LC 2001-16000

Her infinite variety. Berkman, P. R.

Her kind of want. Davis, J. S.

Here comes civilization. Tenn, W.

Here comes the roar. Shaw, D.

Herling, Gustaw, 1919-2000

The Noonday Cemetery and other stories; translated from the Polish by Bill Johnston. New Directions 2003 281p ISBN 0-8112-1529-6 LC 2003-358

Hermann, Eliana Cazaubon, 1930-

(ed) English translations of short stories by contemporary Argentine women writers. *See* English translations of short stories by contemporary Argentine women writers

Hermann, Judith, 1970-

Summerhouse, later; stories; translated from the German by Margot Bettauer Dembo. Ecco Press 2002 205p ISBN 0-06-000686-2 LC 2001-40886

Hers 2: brilliant new fiction by lesbian writers; edited by Terry Wolverton with Robert Drake. Faber & Faber 1997 255p ISBN 0-571-19909-7 LC 96-37877

Hers 3: brilliant new fiction by lesbian writers; edited by Terry Wolverton with Robert Drake. Faber & Faber 1999 270p ISBN 0-571-19962-3 LC 98-33106

Hess, Joan

(comp) Malice domestic 9. *See* Malice domestic 9

Heynen, Jim, 1940-

(ed) Fishing for chickens. *See* Fishing for chickens

Hidden and other stories. Kaminsky, S. M.

Highsmith, Patricia, 1921-1995

Nothing that meets the eye; the uncollected stories of Patricia Highsmith. Norton 2002 455p ISBN 0-393-05187-0 LC 2002-70121

The **hill** bachelors. Trevor, W.

Hillerman, Tony

(ed) The Best American mystery stories of the century. *See* The Best American mystery stories of the century

Hirshberg, Glen, 1966-

The two Sams; ghost stories. Carroll & Graf Pubs. 2003 210p ISBN 0-7867-1255-4

His 3: brilliant new fiction by gay writers; edited by Robert Drake and Terry Wolverton. Faber & Faber 1999 280p ISBN 0-571-19963-1 LC 98-33107

History lessons. Connor, J.

Hjortsberg, William

Odd corners. 2004 ISBN 1-59376-021-3

Hochman, Anndee

Anatomies; a novella and stories. Picador 2000 226p ISBN 0-312-24118-6

Hodgen, Christie, 1974-

A jeweler's eye for flaw; stories. University of Mass. Press 2002 167p ISBN 1-55849-574-3 LC 2002-7577

Hodgson, William Hope, 1877-1918

The boats of the "Glen Carrig" and other nautical adventures; being the first volume of The collected fiction of William Hope Hodgson; edited by Jeremy Lessen. Night Shade Bks. 2003 513p ISBN 1-892389-39-8

Hoffman, Alice

Local girls. Putnam 1999 197p ISBN 0-399-14507-9 LC 98-50632

Hoffman, William, 1925-

Doors; stories. University of Mo. Press 1999 187p ISBN 0-8262-1238-7 LC 98-56143

Holleran, Andrew

In September, the light changes; the stories of Andrew Holleran. Hyperion 1999 306p ISBN 0-7868-6461-3 LC 98-43997

Holoch, Naomi

(ed) The Vintage book of international lesbian fiction. *See* The Vintage book of international lesbian fiction

Home and beyond; an anthology of Kentucky short stories; edited by Morris Allen Grubbs; with an introduction by Wade Hall and an afterword by Charles E. May. University Press of Ky. 2001 xxiv, 400p ISBN 0-8131-2192-2 LC 00-12275

Homes, A. M.

Things you should know; a collection of stories. HarperCollins Pubs. 2002 213p ISBN 0-688-16712-8 LC 2002-23286

Honeymoon and other stories. Canty, K.

Honig, Lucy, 1948-
   The truly needy and other stories. University of Pittsburgh Press 1999
      205p ISBN 0-8229-4107-4 LC 99-6563
Hood, Ann, 1956-
   An ornithologist's guide to life; Ann Hood. 1st ed. W.W. Norton 2004
      237p ISBN 0-393-05900-6 LC 2004-6112
Hopkinson, Nalo
   (ed) Mojo: conjure stories. *See* Mojo: conjure stories
   Skin folk. Warner Bks. 2001 255p ISBN 0-446-67803-1
      LC 2001-26416
   (ed) Whispers from the cotton tree root. *See* Whispers from the cotton
      tree root
Hornby, Nick
   (ed) Speaking with the angel. *See* Speaking with the angel
A **Hot** and sultry night for crime; edited by Jeffery Deaver. Berkley
      Prime Crime 2003 385p ISBN 0-425-18839-6 LC 2002-33240
Hot night in the city. Trevanian
Hotel of the saints. Hegi, U.
An **hour** in paradise. Leegant, J.
House fires. Reisman, N.
The **house** of breathing. Jones, G.
The **house** on Belle Isle and other stories. Brown, C.
How animals mate. Mueller, D.
How it was for me. Greer, A. S.
How Paul Robeson saved my life and other mostly happy stories.
      Reiner, C.
How the dead live. Greenberg, A.
How the water feels. Eggers, P.
How to breathe underwater. Orringer, J.
Howard, Clark
   Crowded lives and other stories of desperation and danger. Five Star
      2000 220p (Five Star standard print mystery series) ISBN
      0-7862-2366-9 LC 99-54226
Howard, Maureen, 1930-
   Big as life; three tales for spring. Viking 2001 225p il ISBN
      0-670-89978-X LC 2001-17904
Hribal, C. J.
   The clouds in Memphis; stories and novellas. University of Mass.
      Press 2000 212p ISBN 1-55849-266-6 LC 00-30278
Hubbard, Susan, 1951-
   (ed) 100% pure Florida fiction. *See* 100% pure Florida fiction
Hudík, Pavol
   (ed) In search of homo sapiens. *See* In search of homo sapiens
Huffman, Bob, Jr.
   Legal fiction. Creative Arts 1999 114p ISBN 0-88739-205-9
      LC 97-78450
A **human** condition. Davies, R.
The **human** country. Mathews, H.
Hunter, Frederic
   Africa, Africa!; fifteen stories. Cune 2000 263p ISBN 1-885942-17-6
Hutchings, Janet
   (ed) Crème de la crime. *See* Crème de la crime

I

I am no one you know. Oates, J. C.
I am not Jackson Pollock. Haskell, J.
I cannot tell a lie, exactly and other stories. Gavell, M. L.
I hate to see that evening sun go down. Gay, W.
I like being killed. Fischer, T.
I, Rhoda Manning, go hunting with my daddy, & other stories. Gilchrist,
      E.
I, Richard. George, E.
I sailed with Magellan. Dybek, S.
Iagnemma, Karl
   On the nature of human romantic interaction. Dial Press 2003 212p
      ISBN 0-385-33593-8 LC 2003-40953
Ice age. Anderson, R.

Ice cream. Dunmore, H.

Ideas of heaven. Silber, J.

Immodest proposals. Tenn, W.

Impact parameter and other quantum realities. Landis, G. A.

The **importance** of a piece of paper. Baca, J. S.

In a café. Lavin, M.

In Berkeley's green and pleasant land. Blitz, R.

In Cuba I was a German shepherd. Menendez, A.

In haste I write you this note. Ritchie, E.

In my other life. Silber, J.

In our nature: stories of wildness; selected and introduced by Donna Seaman. Dorling Kindersley 2000 258p ISBN 0-7894-2642-0 LC 00-29475

In search of homo sapiens; twenty-five contemporary Slovak short stories; editor, Pavol Hudík ; [translated by Heather Trebatická; American English editor, Lucy Bednár] Bolchazy-Carducci/Publishing House of the Slovak Writers Society 2002 264p il ISBN 0-86516-532-7 (pa) LC 2002-22872

In September, the light changes. Holleran, A.

In the box called pleasure. Addonizio, K.

In the cold of the Malecón & other stories. Ponte, A. J.

In the country of the young. Stern, D.

In the electric Eden. Arvin, N.

In the forbidden city; an anthology of erotic fiction by Italian women; edited by Maria Rosa Cutrufelli; translated by Vincent J. Bertolini. University of Chicago Press 2000 185p ISBN 0-226-13223-4 LC 00-24265

In the river province. Sandlin, L.

In the shadow of our house. Blackwood, S.

In the shadow of the wall; an anthology of Vietnam stories that might have been; edited by Byron R. Tetrick. Cumberland House 2002 270p ISBN 1-58182-252-9 LC 2002-5773

In the still of the night. Davis, D. S.

In the stone house. Malzberg, B. N.

In the upper room and other likely stories. Bisson, T.

In this world, or another. Blish, J.

The **inanimate** world. Strandquist, R.

Indelible acts. Kennedy, A. L.

Innocents aboard. Wolfe, G.

Interesting monsters. Alvarez, A.

Interesting women. Lee, A.

Interpreter of maladies. Lahiri, J.

Intimacy. Kureishi, H.

Into the mummy's tomb; edited by John Richard Stephens. Berkley Bks. 2001 352p ISBN 0-425-17664-9 LC 00-65128

The **investigations** of Avram Davidson. Davidson, A.

Iribarne, Matthew
    Astronauts & other stories. Simon & Schuster 2001 318p ISBN 0-7432-0380-1 LC 2001-20545

Irreconcilable differences; Lia Matera, editor. HarperCollins Pubs. 1999 354p ISBN 0-06-019225-9 LC 99-10691

Irsfeld, John H., 1937-
    Radio Elvis and other stories. TCU Press 2002 197p ISBN 0-87565-265-4 LC 2002-1242

Island. MacLeod, A.

Isolation, and other stories. Greer, R. O.

Iwaszkiewicz, Jarosław, 1894-1980
    The birch grove and other stories; translated by Antonia Lloyd-Jones ; with an introduction by Leszek Kołakowski. Central European Univ. Press 2002 268p (Central European classics (Budapest, Hungary)) ISBN 963-924145--8 LC 2002-3353

J

Jack be quick and other crime stories. Paul, B.

Jackson, Shelley
    The melancholy of anatomy; stories. Anchor Bks. (NY) 2002 179p ISBN 0-385-72120-X LC 2001-55329

Jackson, Vanessa Furse
What I cannot say to you; stories. University of Mo. Press 2003 173p ISBN 0-8262-1463-0 LC 2002-153274

Jacobs, Mark
The liberation of little heaven and other stories. Soho Press 1999 231p ISBN 1-56947-135-5 LC 98-39432

Jaffe, Daniel M.
(ed) With signs and wonders. *See* With signs and wonders

Jaime-Becerra, M. (Michael)
Every night is ladies' night; stories; Michael Jaime-Beccerra. 1st ed. Rayo/HarperCollins Publishers 2004 x, 288p ISBN 0-06-055962-4 (acid-free paper) LC 2003-54814

Jakes, John, 1932-
(ed) A Century of great Western stories. *See* A Century of great Western stories
Crime time: mystery and suspense stories. Five Star 2001 235p (Five Star first edition mystery series) ISBN 0-7862-3157-2 LC 2001-33054

Jakubowski, Maxim
(ed) The best British mysteries. *See* The best British mysteries

James, Henry, 1843-1916
Complete stories, 1864-1874. Library of Am. 1999 972p ISBN 1-883011-70-1 LC 98-53919
Complete stories, 1874-1884. Library of Am. 1999 941p ISBN 1-883011-63-9 LC 98-19252
Complete stories, 1884-1891. Library of Am. 1999 904p ISBN 1-883011-64-7 LC 98-19250

James, Siân
Outside paradise. Parthian Bks. 2002 c2001 128p ISBN 1-902638-19-0

Jarrell, Donna
(ed) What are you looking at? *See* What are you looking at?

Jason, Philip K., 1941-
(ed) Retrieving bones. *See* Retrieving bones

Jen, Gish
Who's Irish?; stories. Knopf 1999 207p ISBN 0-375-40621-2 LC 98-42801

Jenkins, Greg, 1952-
Night game; stories. Creative Arts 1999 193p ISBN 0-88739-183-4

Jesús, Pedro de
Frigid tales; translated from the Spanish by Dick Cluster. City Lights Bks. 2002 105p ISBN 0-87286-399-9 LC 2002-24180

A **jeweler's** eye for flaw. Hodgen, C.

Jobs & other preoccupations. Coshnear, D.

Jocks, Yvonne
(ed) Witches' brew. *See* Witches' brew

Johnson, Adam
Emporium; stories. Viking 2002 246p ISBN 0-670-03072-4 LC 2001-26804

Johnson, Charles Richard, 1948-
Soulcatcher and other stories. Harcourt 2001 110p ISBN 0-15-601112-3 LC 00-53950

Johnson, Dana, 1967-
Break any woman down; stories. University of Ga. Press 2001 157p ISBN 0-8203-2315-2 LC 2001-27723

Johnson, Rob, 1961-
(ed) Fantasmas. *See* Fantasmas

Johnson-Davies, Denys
Fate of a prisoner and other stories. Quartet Bks. 1999 222p ISBN 0-7043-8118-4

Johnston, Bret Anthony
Corpus Christi; stories; Bret Anthony Johnston. 1st ed. Random House 2004 viii, 255p ISBN 1-400-06211-X LC 2003-69315

Jonah and Sarah. Shrayer-Petrov, D. and Shrayer, M.

Jones, Gail, 1955-
The house of breathing; stories. Braziller 2000 159p ISBN 0-8076-1455-6 LC 99-21328

Jones, Stephen, 1953-
(ed) Best new horror 10. *See* Best new horror 10
(ed) Best new horror 11. *See* Best new horror 11

Jones, Stephen, 1953-—*Continued*
(ed) Best new horror 12. *See* Best new horror 12
(ed) The Mammoth book of best horror 13. *See* The Mammoth book of best horror 13
(ed) The Mammoth book of best new horror 14. *See* The Mammoth book of best new horror 14
Jones, Suzanne Whitmore
(ed) Crossing the color line. *See* Crossing the color line
Jones, Thom
Sonny Liston was a friend of mine; stories. Little, Brown 1999 312p ISBN 0-316-47223-9 LC 98-37999
Joseph, Diana
Happy or otherwise. Carnegie-Mellon Univ. Press 2003 201p ISBN 0-08748-396-8 LC 2002-115405
The **joy** of funerals. Strauss, A.
Jubilee. Dann, J.
Jubilee King. Shepard, J.
Jungle wedding. Clark, J.

K

Kafka Americana. Lethem, J. and Scholz, C.
Kalfus, Ken
Pu-239 and other Russian fantasies. Milkweed Eds. 1999 289p ISBN 1-57131-029-0 LC 99-18183
Kalman, Judith
The county of birches; stories. St. Martin's Press 1998 183p ISBN 0-312-20886-3
Kalu, Anthonia C.
Broken lives and other stories; foreword by Emmanuel N. Obiechina. Ohio University Press 2003 xxii, 183p (Research in international studies, Africa series, no. 79) ISBN 0-89680-229-9 LC 2003-43362
Kaminsky, Stuart M.
Hidden and other stories. Five Star 1999 278p (Five Star standard print mystery series) ISBN 0-7862-2034-1 LC 99-27153
Kanafāni, Ghassān
Palestine's children; returning to Haifa & other stories; translated by Barbara Harlow & Karen E. Riley, with an introduction and a biographical essay on Ghassan Kanafani. Lynne Rienner Pubs. 2000 199p ISBN 0-89410-865-4 LC 00-24783
Kane, Jessica Francis, 1971-
Bending heaven; stories. Counterpoint 2002 196p ISBN 1-582-43206-6 LC 2001-7345
Kaplan, Hester
The edge of marriage. University of Ga. Press 1999 176p ISBN 0-8203-2148-6 LC 99-19713
Karnezis, Panos, 1967-
Little infamies; stories. Farrar, Straus & Giroux 2003 280p ISBN 0-374-18937-4 LC 2002-112478
Kavaler, Rebecca
A little more than kin; a collection of short stories. Hamilton Stone Eds. 2001 181p ISBN 0-9654043-8-2 LC 2001-24532
Kawabata, Yasunari, 1899-1972
First snow on Fuji; translated by Michael Emmerich. Counterpoint 1999 227p ISBN 1-58243-022-5 LC 99-35103
Kaye, Marvin
(ed) The Ultimate Halloween. *See* The Ultimate Halloween
Keegan, Claire
Antarctica. Atlantic Monthly Press 2001 207p ISBN 0-87113-779-8 LC 00-49604
Keepsakes & other stories. Hassler, J.
Kees, Weldon
Selected short stories of Weldon Kees; edited and with an introduction by Dana Gioia. University of Neb. Press 2002 170p ISBN 0-8032-7806-3 LC 2002-71455

Kelly, James Patrick

Strange but not a stranger; with an introduction by Connie Willis. Golden Gryphon Press 2002 297p ISBN 1-930846-12-6 LC 2002-2464

Kelman, James

The good times; stories. Anchor Bks. (NY) 1999 246p ISBN 0-385-49580-3 LC 99-22448

Kenison, Katrina

(ed) The Best American short stories, 1999. *See* The Best American short stories, 1999

(ed) The Best American short stories, 2000. *See* The Best American short stories, 2000

(ed) The Best American short stories 2001. *See* The Best American short stories 2001

(ed) The Best American short stories, 2002. *See* The Best American short stories, 2002

(ed) The Best American short stories, 2003. *See* The Best American short stories, 2003

(ed) The Best American short stories of the century. *See* The Best American short stories of the century

Kennedy, A. L., 1965-

Indelible acts; stories. Knopf 2003 191p ISBN 1-400-04055-8 LC 2002-30179

Keret, Etgar, 1967-

The bus driver who wanted to be God and other stories. Thomas Dunne Bks. 2001 182p ISBN 0-312-26188-8 LC 2001-41942

Khorrami, Mohammad Mehdi, 1960-

(ed) A Feast in the mirror. *See* A Feast in the mirror

Kick in the head. Rinehart, S.

Kihn, Greg, 1952-

(ed) Carved in rock. *See* Carved in rock

Kill the umpire. Breen, J. L.

Kilpatrick, Nancy

Cold comfort. Darktales Pubs. 2001 183p ISBN 1-930997-09-4

The **kind** I'm likely to get. Foster, K.

A **kind** of flying. Carlson, R.

The **kind** of things saints do. Valeri, L.

Kingsolver, Barbara

(ed) The Best American short stories 2001. *See* The Best American short stories 2001

Kirchheimer, Gloria DeVidas

Goodbye, evil eye; stories. Holmes & Meier 2000 150p ISBN 0-8419-1404-4 LC 00-20443

Kissing you. Hayes, D.

Kittredge, William

The best short stories of William Kittredge. Graywolf 2003 220p ISBN 1-55597-384-1

Klass, Perri, 1958-

Love and modern medicine; stories. Houghton Mifflin 2001 182p ISBN 0-618-10960-9 LC 00-66978

Klíma, Ivan

Lovers for a day; translated from the Czech by Gerald Turner. Grove Press 1999 229p ISBN 0-8021-1651-5 LC 99-27586

Knight, Michael, 1969-

Dogfight and other stories. Plume Bks. 1998 161p ISBN 0-452-27894-5 LC 98-15709

Goodnight, nobody. Atlantic Monthly Press 2003 160p ISBN 0-87113-867-0 LC 2002-27944

Kohler, Sheila

One girl; a novel in stories. Helicon Nine Eds. 1999 157p ISBN 1-884235-29-8 LC 99-37346

Stories from another world. Ontario Review Press 2003 152p ISBN 0-86538-110-0 LC 2003-46288

Kramer, Edward E.

(ed) The Crow. *See* The Crow

Kratz, Henry

(ed) Early German and Austrian detective fiction. *See* Early German and Austrian detective fiction

Kravitz, Peter
(ed) The Vintage book of contemporary Scottish fiction. *See* The Vintage book of contemporary Scottish fiction
Krawiec, Richard
And fools of God; stories. Avisson Press 2000 143p ISBN 1-888105-42-9
Kress, Nancy, 1948-
(ed) Nebula Awards showcase 2003. *See* Nebula Awards showcase 2003
Krouse, Erika
Come up and see me sometime. Scribner 2001 202p ISBN 0-7432-0244-9 LC 00-66077
Kureishi, Hanif
Intimacy; a novel; and, Midnight all day: stories. Scribner Paperback Fiction 2001 333p ISBN 0-7432-1714-4 LC 2001-41168
Kurland, Michael, 1938-
(ed) My Sherlock Holmes. *See* My Sherlock Holmes
Kurlansky, Mark
The white man in the tree and other stories. Washington Sq. Press 2000 301p ISBN 0-671-03605-X
Kusel, Lisa, 1960-
Other fish in the sea. Hyperion 2003 290p ISBN 0-7868-8802-4 LC 2002-32941

L

LA shorts; edited by Steven Gilbar. Heyday Bks. 2000 278p ISBN 1-890771-29-5 LC 00-8216
Lahiri, Jhumpa
Interpreter of maladies; stories. Houghton Mifflin 1999 198p ISBN 0-395-92720-X LC 98-50895
Lalumière, Claude
(ed) Witpunk. *See* Witpunk
L'Amour, Louis, 1908-1988
Beyond the Great Snow Mountains. Bantam Bks. 1999 282p ISBN 0-553-10963-4 LC 99-11757
The collected short stories of Louis L'Amour; The frontier stories: volume 1. Random House 2004 424p ISBN 0-553-80357-3
From the listening hills. Bantam Bks. 2003 231p ISBN 0-553-80328-X LC 2003-271028
May there be a road. Bantam Bks. 2001 276p ISBN 0-553-80213-5 LC 2001-18127
Off the Mangrove Coast. Bantam Bks. 2000 277p ISBN 0-553-80160-0 LC 99-86061
Landis, Geoffrey A.
Impact parameter and other quantum realities; with a foreword by Joe Haldeman. Golden Gryphon Press 2001 340p ISBN 1-930846-06-1 LC 2001-33977
Lansdale, Joe R., 1951-
Bumper crop / Joe R. Lansdale. 1st ed. Golden Gryphon Press 2004 xi, 199p ISBN 1-930846-24-X (hardcover : alk. paper) LC 2003-19750
Lao She, 1899-1966
Blades of grass; the stories of Lao She; translated from the Chinese by William A. Lyell and Sarah Wei-ming Chen; general editor, Howard Goldblatt. University of Hawaii Press 1999 310p ISBN 0-8248-1803-2 LC 99-11832
Last call. Cook, K. L.
The **last** lovely city. Adams, A.
Last stands. Weaver, G.
The **last** tortilla & other stories. Troncoso, S.
Last year's Jesus. Slezak, E.
Laugh track. Galef, D.
LaValle, Victor D., 1972-
Slapboxing with Jesus; stories. Vintage Bks. 1999 213p ISBN 0-375-70590-2 LC 99-26222

Lavin, Mary, 1912-1996
In a café; selected stories; edited by Elizabeth Walsh Peavoy; foreword by Thomas Kilroy. Penguin Bks. 1999 312p ISBN 0-14-118040-4

Lavín, Mónica, 1955-
(ed) Points of departure. *See* Points of departure

The **law** of averages. Barthelme, F.

The **law** of return. Rodburg, M.

Lawrence, Cynthia
(ed) A Deadly dozen. *See* A Deadly dozen

Lawrence, D. H. (David Herbert), 1885-1930
Selected short stories of D. H. Lawrence; edited, with an introduction by James Wood. Modern Lib. 1999 xxvi, 487p ISBN 0-679-60327-1 LC 99-17368

The **laws** of evening. Waters, M. Y.

The **laying** on of hands. Bennett, A.

Le Clézio, J.-M. G. (Jean-Marie Gustave), 1940-
The round & other cold hard facts; translated by C. Dickson. University of Neb. Press 2002 214p ISBN 0-8032-1946-1; 0-8032-8007-6 (pa) LC 2002-18085

Le Guin, Ursula K., 1929-
Changing planes; illustrated by Eric Beddows. Harcourt 2003 246p il ISBN 0-15-100971-6 LC 2002-14919

Le May, Alan, 1899-1964
The bells of San Juan; western stories. Five Star 2001 196p (Five Star first edition western series) ISBN 0-7862-2766-4 LC 00-50309

Leap day and other stories. Nevins, F. M., Jr.

Leaving the neighborhood and other stories. Ferriss, L.

Leavitt, David, 1961-
The marble quilt; stories. Houghton Mifflin 2001 241p ISBN 0-395-90244-4 LC 2001-24522

Lee, Andrea, 1953-
Interesting women; stories. Random House 2002 222p ISBN 0-375-50586-5 LC 2001-48228

Lee, Don, 1959-
Yellow; stories. Norton 2001 255p ISBN 0-393-02562-4 LC 00-50047

Lee, Mabel
Buying a fishing rod for my grandfather. See Gao, Xingjian, and Lee, Mabel

Lee, Michael, 1946-
Paradise dance; stories; with an introduction by James Carroll. Leapfrog Press 2002 213p ISBN 0-9679520-6-9 LC 2002-3294

Lee, Vernon, 1856-1935
Supernatural tales; excursions into fantasy; with an introduction by I. Cooper Willis. Peter Owen 2003 222p ISBN 0-7206-1194-6

Lee, W. W. (Wendi W.), 1956-
Check up and other stories. Five Star 2001 240p (Five Star first edition mystery series) ISBN 0-7862-3552-7 LC 2001-51237

Leegant, Joan
An hour in paradise; stories. Norton 2003 224p ISBN 0-393-05439-X LC 2003-5445

Legal fiction. Huffman, B., Jr.

Legends II; new short novels by the masters of modern fantasy; edited by Robert Silverberg. 1st ed. Del Rey\Ballantine Books 2004 ISBN 0-345-45644-0 LC 2003-62516

Lellenberg, Jon L.
(ed) Murder, my dear Watson. *See* Murder, my dear Watson

Leonard, Elmore, 1925-
When the women come out to dance; stories. Morrow 2002 228p ISBN 0-06-008397-2; 0-06-008398-0 (pa) LC 2002-26426

Leong, Russell, 1950-
Phoenix eyes and other stories. University of Wash. Press 2000 172p ISBN 0-295-97944-5

LeRoy, J. T., 1980-
The heart is deceitful above all things. Bloomsbury Pub. 2001 247p ISBN 1-58234-142-7 LC 2001-25112

Leslie, Naton
Marconi's dream. Texas Review Press 2002 153p ISBN 1-88151-551-6 LC 2002-14493

Lessing, Doris May, 1919-
The grandmothers; [by] Doris Lessing. Flamingo 2003 311p ISBN 0-00-715279-5
Lethem, Jonathan
(ed) The Vintage book of amnesia. *See* The Vintage book of amnesia
Lethem, Jonathan, and Scholz, Carter
Kafka Americana; [by] Jonathan Lethem [and] Carter Scholz. Norton 2001 100p ISBN 0-393-32253-X
The **liberation** of little heaven and other stories. Jacobs, M.
Liberty's excess. Yuknavitch, L.
Licks of love. Updike, J.
Lida, David
Travel advisory; stories of Mexico. Morrow 2000 208p ISBN 0-688-17406-X LC 99-23557
Lieu, Jocelyn
Potential weapons. 2004 194p ISBN 1-55597-397-3
Lieutenant America and Miss Apple Pie. DeMarco, T.
Life in the air ocean. Foley, S.
Light action in the Caribbean. Lopez, B. H.
Light in the crossing. Meyers, K.
Lighthouse hauntings; 12 original tales of the supernatural; edited by Charles G. Waugh & Martin H. Greenberg. Down East Bks. 2002 252p ISBN 0-89272-519-2 LC 2002-110437
Limbo, and other places I have lived. Tuck, L.
Lincoln, Christine
Sap rising. Pantheon Bks. 2001 164p ISBN 0-375-42140-8 LC 2001-21959
Link, Kelly
Stranger things happen. Small Beer Press 2001 266p ISBN 1-931520-00-3
The **lion** in the room next door. Simonds, M.
Lipsyte, Sam
Venus drive; stories. Open City Bks. 2000 160p ISBN 1-890447-25-0
Lisick, Beth, 1968-
This too can be yours. Manic D Press 2001 141p ISBN 0-916397-73-4 LC 2001-5507
The **Literary** werewolf; an anthology; edited by Charlotte F. Otten. Syracuse Univ. Press 2002 xxxii, 295p ISBN 0-8156-2965-6; 0-8156-0753-9 (pa) LC 2002-9335
Little black book of stories. Byatt, A. S.
Little infamies. Karnezis, P.
A **little** more than kin. Kavaler, R.
The **lives** of Kelvin Fletcher. Williams, M.
Living on the edge; fiction by Peace Corps writers; edited by John Coyne. Curbstone Press 1999 317p ISBN 1-880684-57-8 LC 98-17464
Living with saints. O'Connell, M.
Lloyd, David T., 1954-
Boys; stories and a novella; [by] David Lloyd. Syracuse University Press 2004 178p ISBN 0-8156-0797-0 LC 2003-23083
Local girls. Hoffman, A.
Lochte, Dick
Lucky dog and other tales of murder. Five Star 2000 207p (Five Star first edition mystery series) ISBN 0-7862-2688-9 LC 00-34753
Locklin, Gerald
Candy bars; selected stories. Water Row Press 2000 267p ISBN 0-934953-69-4 LC 00-20772
The **Locus** awards; thirty years of the best in science fiction and fantasy; edited by Charles N. Brown and Jonathan Strahan. 1st ed. Eos 2004 xiii, 512p ISBN 0-06-059426-8 (acid-free paper) LC 2004-42054
Lone Star literature; from the Red River to the Rio Grande; edited by Don Graham. 1st ed. W. W. Norton & Co 2003 733p ISBN 0-393-05043-2 LC 2003-16321
The **long** and short of it. Painter, P.
Long odds. Weaver, G.
Loomis, Noel M., 1905-
Heading west; western stories; edited by Bill Pronzini. Five Star 1999 216p (Five Star standard print western series) ISBN 0-7862-1844-4 LC 99-41706

Loot and other stories. Gordimer, N.

Lopez, Barry Holstun, 1945-
   Light action in the Caribbean; stories. Knopf 2000 162p ISBN
     0-679-43455-0 LC 00-20310

López, Lorraine, 1956-
   Soy la Avon lady and other stories. Curbstone Press 2002 238p ISBN
     1-88068-486-1 LC 2001-7704

Lord, Nancy
   The man who swam with beavers; stories. Coffee House Press 2001
     251p ISBN 1-56689-110-8 LC 00-65895

Lost tribe; jewish fiction from the edge. Perennial 2003 512p ISBN
   0-06-053346-3 (pa)

Louis, Laura Glen
   Talking in the dark; stories. Harcourt 2001 210p ISBN 0-15-100522-2
     LC 00-46144

Love. Martin, V.

Love and death; edited by Carolyn Hart. Berkley Prime Crime 2001
   275p ISBN 0-425-18316-5

Love and modern medicine. Klass, P.

Love in vain. Tozzi, F.

Lovers for a day. Klíma, I.

Lucky dip and other stories. Cody, L.

Lucky dog and other tales of murder. Lochte, D.

Lucky girls. Freudenberger, N.

Lugones, Leopoldo, 1874-1938
   Strange forces; translated by Gilbert Alter-Gilbert. Latin Am. Literary
     Review Press 2001 126p ISBN 1-891270-0502

Lumley, Brian
   Beneath the moors and darker places. Doherty Assocs. 2002 384p
     ISBN 0-312-87694-7 LC 2001-54061
   Harry Keogh; necroscope and other weird heroes! TOR Bks. 2003
     319p ISBN 0-7653-0847-9 LC 2003-42619
   The whisperer and other voices. Doherty Assocs. 2001 333p ISBN
     0-312-87695-5 LC 00-49624

Lundquist, Richard, 1957-
   What we come in for; stories. University of Mo. Press 2000 159p
     ISBN 0-8262-1270-0 LC 00-20453

Lupoff, Richard A., 1935-
   Claremont tales. Golden Gryphon Press 2001 290p il ISBN
     1-930846-00-2 LC 00-53553
   Claremont tales II. Golden Gryphon Press 2002 298p il ISBN
     1-930846-07-X LC 2001-55523

Lutz, John, 1939-
   The Nudger dilemmas; a short story collection. Five Star 2001 312p
     (Five Star first edition mystery series) ISBN 0-7862-3147-5
     LC 2001-23901

Lynn, David
   (ed) The Best of The Kenyon review. *See* The Best of The Kenyon
     review

M

MacLeod, Alistair
   Island; the complete stories. Norton 2001 434p ISBN 0-393-05035-1
     LC 00-51524

Magic terror. Straub, P.

Magical beginnings; edited by Steven H. Silver and Martin H.
   Greenberg. DAW Bks. 2003 343p ISBN 0-7564-0121-6

Making peace with the Muslims. Gabriel, D.

Maleti, Gabriella, 1942-
   Bitter asylum; translated by Sharon Wood. Carcanet Press 1999 159p
     (Carcanet fiction) ISBN 1-85754-436-6 LC 00-273243

Malice domestic 10; an anthology of original traditional mystery stories.
   Avon Bks. 2001 212p ISBN 0-380-80484-0

Malice domestic 8. Avon Bks. 1999 242p ISBN 0-380-79407-1

Malice domestic 9. Avon Bks. 2000 214p ISBN 0-380-80483-2

Malone, Michael

Red clay, blue Cadillac; stories of twelve Southern women. Sourcebooks 2002 294p ISBN 1-57071-824-5 LC 2001-54287

Malouf, David, 1934-

Dream stuff; stories. Pantheon Bks. 2000 185p ISBN 0-375-42053-3 LC 99-88859

Malzberg, Barry N.

In the stone house. Arkham House Pubs. 2000 247p ISBN 0-87054-178-1 LC 00-58270

On account of darkness and other SF stories. See Pronzini, Bill, and Malzberg, Barry N.

The **Mammoth** book of best horror 13; edited by Stephen Jones. Carroll & Graf Pubs. 2002 582p ISBN 0-7867-1063-2

The **Mammoth** book of best new horror 14; edited with an introduction by Stephen Jones. Carroll & Graf Pubs. 2003 590p ISBN 0-7867-1237-6

The **man** who swam with beavers. Lord, N.

Manhattan monologues. Auchincloss, L.

A **mansion** in the sky. Taraqqi, G.

Maraini, Dacia

Darkness; fiction; translated by Martha King. Steerforth Press 2002 162p ISBN 1-586-42048-8 LC 2002-7049

The **marble** quilt. Leavitt, D.

Marconi's dream. Leslie, N.

Mardi Gras madness; tales of terror and mayhem in New Orleans; edited by Martin H. Greenberg and Russell Davis. Cumberland House 2000 239p ISBN 1-58182-077-1 LC 99-58601

Marías, Javier, 1951-

When I was mortal; translated by Margaret Jull Costa. New Directions 2000 162p ISBN 0-8112-1431-1 LC 99-89177

Marked men. White, M. C.

Maron, Margaret

(comp) Malice domestic 8. See Malice domestic 8

Suitable for hanging. 2004 208p ISBN 1-932009-10-8

The **marriage** at Antibes. Azadeh, C.

Mars probes; edited by Peter Crowther. DAW Bks. 2002 315p ISBN 0-7564-0088-0

Martin, Patricia Preciado

Amor eterno; eleven lessons in love. University of Ariz. Press 2000 105p ISBN 0-8165-1994-3 LC 99-6918

Martin, Valerie

Love; short stories. Lost Horse Press 1999 79p ISBN 0-9668612-3-X

Martindale, Lee, 1949-

(ed) Such a pretty face. See Such a pretty face

Martone, Michael

(ed) The Scribner anthology of contemporary short fiction. See The Scribner anthology of contemporary short fiction

Masiello, Francine, 1948-

Dreams and realities. See Gorriti, Juana Manuela, 1818-1892, and Waisman, Sergio Gabriel, 1967-, and Masiello, Francine, 1948-

Mason, Bobbie Ann

Zigzagging down a wild trail; stories. Random House 2001 209p ISBN 0-679-44924-8 LC 00-66480

Master of the grass. Gabrielyan, N.

Masterpieces: the best science fiction of the century; edited by Orson Scott Card. Ace Bks. 2001 422p ISBN 0-441-00864-X LC 2001-45074

Master's choice [v1]; mystery stories by today's top writers and the masters who inspired them; edited by Lawrence Block. Berkley Prime Crime 1999 244p ISBN 0-425-17031-4 LC 99-30270

Master's choice v2; mystery stories by today's top writers and the masters who inspired them; edited by Lawrence Block. Berkley Prime Crime 2000 369p ISBN 0-425-17676-2 LC 99-30270

Mastretta, Angeles, 1949-

Women with big eyes; {translated by Amy Schildhouse Greenberg}. Riverhead Books 2003 372p ISBN 1-57322-346-8 LC 2003-46818

Matera, Lia

Counsel for the defense and other stories. Five Star 2000 176p (Five Star first edition mystery series) ISBN 0-7862-2537-8 LC 00-24237

Matera, Lia—*Continued*

(ed) Irreconcilable differences. *See* Irreconcilable differences

Matheson, Richard, 1926-

Duel; terror stories. TOR Bks. 2003 394p ISBN 0-7653-0695-6; 0-312-87826-5 (pa) LC 2002-73276

Mathews, Harry

The human country; new and collected stories. Dalkey Archive Press 2002 186p il ISBN 1-564-78321-9 LC 2002-73509

Matiella, Ana Consuelo

The truth about Alicia and other stories. University of Ariz. Press 2002 141p ((Camino del Sol)) ISBN 0-8165-2161-1; 0-8165-2163-8 (pa) LC 2001-3544

Matthews, Christine

Gentle insanities and other states of mind. Five Star 2001 267p (Five Star first edition mystery series) ISBN 0-7862-3555-1 LC 2001-42854

May there be a road. L'Amour, L.

Mayo, Wendell

B. Horror and other stories. Livingston Press (Livingston) 1999 128p ISBN 0-942979-62-1

Mazelis, Jo

Diving girls. Parthian Bks. 2003 c2002 137p ISBN 1-902638-23-9

Mazor, Julian, 1929-

Friend of mankind and other stories; by Julian Mazor. 1st Paul Dry Books ed. Paul Dry Books 2004 p. cmp ISBN 1-589-88016-1 (hardcover : alk. paper) LC 2003-26634

McBain, Ed, 1926-

(ed) The Best American mystery stories, 1999. *See* The Best American mystery stories, 1999

Running from Legs and other stories; [by] Ed McBain a.k.a. Evan Hunter. Five Star 2000 202p (Five Star first edition mystery series) ISBN 0-7862-2671-4 LC 00-34747

McBrearty, Robert Garner

A night at the Y; a collection of short stories. Daniel, J. 1999 126p ISBN 1-880284-36-7 LC 99-12912

McCarthy, Wil

(ed) Once upon a galaxy. *See* Once upon a galaxy

McCorkle, Jill, 1958-

Creatures of habit; stories. Algonquin Bks. 2001 240p ISBN 1-56512-256-9 LC 2001-34835

McCourt, James, 1941-

Wayfaring at Waverly in Silver Lake; stories. Knopf 2002 322p ISBN 0-394-52362-8 LC 2001-38265

McFee, Michael, 1954-

(ed) This is where we live. *See* This is where we live

McGarry, Jean

Dream date; stories. Johns Hopkins University Press 2002 235p (Johns Hopkins, poetry and fiction) ISBN 0-8018-6937-4 LC 2001-7188

McInerny, Ralph M., 1929-

(ed) Murder most divine. *See* Murder most divine

McIntyre, Vonda N.

(ed) Nebula awards showcase 2004. *See* Nebula awards showcase 2004

McManus, John, 1977-

Stop breakin down; stories. Picador 2000 263p ISBN 0-312-26278-7 LC 00-27723

McMurtry, Larry

(ed) Still wild. *See* Still wild

McNally, John, 1965-

(ed) The Student body. *See* The Student body

Troublemakers. University of Iowa Press 2000 208p (John Simmons short fiction award) ISBN 0-87745-727-1 LC 00-39247

McNulty, John, d. 1956

This place on Third Avenue; the New York stories of John McNulty; memoir by Faith McNulty; photographs by Morris Engel. Counterpoint 2001 xxxix, 187p ISBN 1-58243-117-5 LC 00-65863

McSweeney's mammoth treasury of thrilling tales; edited by Michael Chabon. Vintage Books 2003 479p ISBN 1-4000-3339-X LC 2002-192265

Mean rooms. Smith, J.
Means, David
   Assorted fire events; stories. Context Bks. 2000 165p ISBN
   1-893956-05-9
The **means** of escape. Fitzgerald, P.
Meet me in the moon room. Vukcevich, R.
The **melancholy** of anatomy. Jackson, S.
Meloy, Maile
   Half in love; stories. Scribner 2002 172p ISBN 0-7432-1647-4
   LC 2001-54217
Melville, Pauline
   The migration of ghosts. Bloomsbury Pub. 1998 209p ISBN
   0-58234-020-X LC 98-215800
Men on men 2000; best new gay fiction for the millennium; edited and
   with an introduction by David Bergman and Karl Woelz. Penguin
   Bks. 2000 323p ISBN 0-452-28082-6 LC 99-45321
Men on the moon. Ortiz, S. J.
Mencken, Sara Haardt, 1898-1935
   Southern souvenirs; selected stories and essays; edited with an
   introduction by Ann Henley. University of Ala. Press 1999 317p
   ISBN 0-8173-0977-2 LC 98-58124
Menendez, Ana
   In Cuba I was a German shepherd. Grove Press 2001 229p ISBN
   0-8021-1688-4 LC 00-67187
Menke, Pamela Glenn, 1940-
   (ed) Southern local color. *See* Southern local color
Meredith, Don, 1938-
   Wing walking. Texas Review Press 2000 143p ISBN 1-881515-32-X
   LC 00-45140
Meyers, Kent
   Light in the crossing; stories. St. Martin's Press 1999 226p ISBN
   0-312-20337-3 LC 99-22069
Michaels, Leonard, 1933-2003
   A girl with a monkey; new and selected stories. Mercury House 2000
   238p ISBN 1-56279-120-6 LC 99-86600
The **middle** of the night. Stolar, D.
The **migration** of ghosts. Melville, P.
Miller, Rebecca
   Personal velocity. Grove Press 2001 179p ISBN 0-8021-1699-X
   LC 2001-35093
Miller, Sue
   (ed) The Best American short stories, 2002. *See* The Best American
   short stories, 2002
Mind the doors. Zinik, Z.
Miracle and other Christmas stories. Willis, C.
Misplaced love. Dwyer, M.
Mo Yan, 1956-
   Shifu, you'll do anything for a laugh; translated from the Chinese by
   Howard Goldblatt. Arcade Pub. 2001 189p ISBN 1-55970-565-5
   LC 2001-22673
Mojo: conjure stories; edited by Nalo Hopkinson. Warner Bks. 2003
   340p ISBN 0-446-67929-1 LC 2002-34922
Molina-Gavilán, Yolanda, 1963-
   (ed) Cosmos latinos: an anthology of science fiction from Latin
   America and Spain. *See* Cosmos latinos: an anthology of science
   fiction from Latin America and Spain
Mom, apple pie, and murder; edited by Nancy Pickard. Berkley Prime
   Crime 1999 311p ISBN 0-425-16890-5
A **moment** on the edge; 100 years of crime stories by women; edited
   by Elizabeth George. HarperCollins 2004 540p ISBN 0-06-058821-7
   LC 2003-67608
Mona and other tales. Arenas, R.
Moody, Rick
   Demonology; stories. Little, Brown 2000 306p ISBN 0-316-58874-1
   LC 00-34811
The **moon** in its flight. Sorrentino, G.
Moonlight and vines. De Lint, C.
More Italian hours and other stories. Barolini, H.
More oddments. Pronzini, B.

Morgan, Robert, 1944-
The balm of Gilead tree; new and selected stories. Gnomon Press 1999 344p ISBN 0-917788-73-7
Mortimer, John Clifford, 1923-
Rumpole rests his case; [by] John Mortimer. Viking 2002 211p ISBN 0-670-03139-9 LC 2002-19046
Mosley, Walter
(ed) The Best American short stories, 2003. *See* The Best American short stories, 2003
Futureland. Warner Bks. 2001 356p ISBN 0-446-52954-0 LC 2001-93241
Six Easy pieces; Easy Rawlins stories. Atria Bks. 2003 278p ISBN 0-7434-4252-0
Walkin' the dog. Little, Brown 1999 260p ISBN 0-316-96620-7 LC 99-16407
Mr. Roopratna's chocolate; the winning stories from the 1999 Rhys Davies competition. Seren Bks. 2000 119p ISBN 1-85411-267-8
Mueller, Daniel
How animals mate; stories. Overlook Press 1999 191p (Sewanee writers' series) ISBN 0-87951-925-8 LC 98-31823
Müller, Herta, 1953-
Nadirs; (Niederungen); translated and with an afterword by Sieglinde Lug. University of Neb. Press 1999 122p (European women writers series) ISBN 0-8032-8254-0 LC 98-48347
A **multitude** of sins. Ford, R.
Muñoz, Manuel
Zigzagger. Northwestern University Press 2003 185p (Latino voices) ISBN 0-8101-2098-4; 0-8101-2099-2 (pa) LC 2003-10038
Munro, Alice
Hateship, friendship, courtship, loveship, marriage; stories. Knopf 2001 323p ISBN 0-375-41300-6 LC 2001-29870
Murakami, Haruki, 1949-
After the earthquake; stories; translated from the Japanese by Jay Rubin. Knopf 2002 181p ISBN 0-375-41390-1; 0-375-71327-1 (pa) LC 2001-38829
Murder-all kinds. DeAndrea, W. L.
Murder and obsession; edited by Otto Penzler. Delacorte Press 1999 406p ISBN 0-385-31800-6 LC 98-41039
Murder—his and hers. Collins, B. and Collins, M. A.
Murder in the family; [by] the Adams Round Table. Berkley Prime Crime 2002 337p ISBN 0-425-18335-1 LC 2002-71658
Murder is no mitzvah; edited by Abigail Browning. 1st ed. Thomas Dunne Books/St. Martin's Minotaur 2004 285p ISBN 0-312-32506-1 LC 2003-62544
Murder most Celtic; tall tales of Irish mayhem; edited by Martin H. Greenberg. Cumberland House 2001 291p ISBN 1-581-82161-1 LC 2001-17264
Murder most delectable; savory tales of culinary crimes; edited by Martin H. Greenberg. Cumberland House 2000 340p ISBN 1-58182-119-0 LC 00-31800
Murder most divine; ecclesiastical tales of unholy crimes; edited by Ralph McInerny and Martin H. Greenberg. Cumberland House 2000 348p ISBN 1-581-82121-2 LC 00-64421
Murder most postal; homicidal tales that deliver a message; edited by Martin H. Greenberg. Cumberland House 2001 307p ISBN 1-58182-162-X LC 2001-17244
Murder, my dear Watson; new tales of Sherlock Holmes; edited by Martin H. Greenberg, Jon Lellenberg, Daniel Stashower. Carroll & Graf Pubs. 2002 227p ISBN 0-7867-1081-0
Murguía, Alejandro, 1949-
This war called love; nine stories. City Lights 2002 155p ISBN 0-87286-394-8 LC 2002-20888
Murphy, Nora
Twelve branches. *See* Twelve branches
Murray, John, 1962-
A few short notes on tropical butterflies; stories. HarperCollins Pubs. 2003 274p ISBN 0-06-050928-7 LC 2002-68883

Murray, Sabina
    The caprices. Houghton Mifflin 2002 210p ISBN 0-618-09525-X
       LC 2001-24527
The **Museum** of horrors; edited by Dennis Etchison. Leisure Bks. 2001
    374p ISBN 0-8439-4928-7
The **music** of your life. Rowell, J.
My date with Satan. Richter, S.
My father, dancing. Broyard, B.
My Lord Bag of Rice. Bly, C.
My one and only bomb shelter. Smolens, J.
My people's waltz. Phillips, D. R.
My Sherlock Holmes; untold stories of the great detective; edited by
    Michael Kurland. St. Martin's Minotaur 2003 370p ISBN
    0-312-28093-9 LC 2002-35664
My very last possession and other stories. Pak, W.-S.
Mysterious pleasures; a celebration of the Crime Writers' Association's
    50th anniversary; edited by Martin Edwards. Little, Brown 2003 x,
    370p ISBN 0-316-72563-3
The **Mysterious** Press anniversary anthology; celebrating 25 years; by
    the editors of Mysterious Press. Mysterious Press 2001 xx, 357p
    ISBN 0-89296-739-0 LC 00-68667
Mystery midrash; an anthology of Jewish mystery & detective fiction;
    [edited by] Lawrence W. Raphael. Jewish Lights Pub. 1999 299p
    ISBN 1-58023-055-5 LC 99-30222
The **mystified** magistrate and other tales. Sade, marquis de

N

Nadirs. Müller, H.
Nailah, Anika
    Free and other stories. Doubleday 2002 207p ISBN 0-385-50293-1
       LC 2001-47572
Nair, Meera, 1963-
    Video; stories. Pantheon Bks. 2002 191p ISBN 0-375-42111-4
       LC 2001-36951
Naiyer Masud
    Essence of camphor; translated from the Urdu by Muhammad Umar
    Memon and others. New Press (NY) 1999 187p ISBN
    1-56584-583-8
Nakagami, Kenji, 1946-1992
    The cape and other stories from the Japanese ghetto; translated, with
    a preface and afterword by Eve Zimmerman. Stone Bridge Press
    1999 191p ISBN 1-88065-639-6 LC 99-12378
Natasha and other stories. Bezmozgis, D.
Nawrocki, Sarah
    Camping with strangers; stories. Publishers Group West 1999 150p
    ISBN 0-9651879-9-3 LC 99-17582
Nebula awards 33; the year's best SF and fantasy chosen by the
    science-fiction and fantasy writers of America; edited by Connie
    Willis. Harcourt 1999 272p ISBN 0-15-100372-6
Nebula awards showcase 2000; the year's best SF and fantasy chosen
    by the science fiction and fantasy writers of america; edited by
    Gregory Benford. Harcourt 2000 xxiii, 288p il ISBN 0-15-100479-X
Nebula awards showcase 2001; the year's best SF and fantasy chosen
    by the science fiction and fantasy writers of America; edited by
    Robert Silverberg. Harcourt 2001 252p ISBN 0-15-100581-8
Nebula awards showcase 2002; edited by Kim Stanley Robinson. Roc
    2002 304p ISBN 0-451-45878-8
Nebula Awards showcase 2003; edited by Nancy Kress. ROC 2003
    230p ISBN 0-451-45909-1
Nebula awards showcase 2004; edited by Vonda McIntyre. Roc 2004
    272p ISBN 0-451-45957-1
Nelson, Antonya
    Female trouble; a collection of short stories. Scribner 2002 249p ISBN
    0-7432-1871-X LC 2001-49669
Nesbitt, Marc
    Gigantic; stories. Grove Press 2002 178p ISBN 0-8021-1709-0
    LC 2001-40707

Nestle, Joan, 1940-
  (ed) The Vintage book of international lesbian fiction. *See* The Vintage book of international lesbian fiction
Neurotica: Jewish writers on sex; edited by Melvin Jules Bukiet. Norton 1999 360p ISBN 0-393-04808-X LC 99-27452
Never trust a rabbit. Dyson, J.
Nevins, Francis M., Jr.
  Leap day and other stories. Five Star 2003 211p ISBN 0-7862-4321-X LC 2003-43422
The **New** American voices 2003; guest editor Joyce Carol Oates; series editors John Kulka and Natalie Danford. Harcourt 2002 305p ISBN 0-15-600716-9
New stories from the South; the year's best, 2004; edited by Shannon Ravenel; preface by Tim Gautreaux. Algonquin Books 2004 334p ISBN 1-56512-432-4 (pa)
New stories from the South: the year's best, 1999; edited by Shannon Ravenel; with a preface by Tony Earley. Algonquin Bks. 1999 306p ISBN 1-56512-247-X
New stories from the South: the year's best, 2000; edited by Shannon Ravenel; with a preface by Ellen Douglas. Algonquin Bks. 2000 299p ISBN 1-56512-295-X
New stories from the South: the year's best, 2001; edited by Shannon Ravenel; with a preface by Lee Smith. Algonquin Bks. 2001 346p ISBN 1-56512-311-5
New stories from the South: the year's best, 2002; edited by Shannon Ravenel; with a preface by Larry Brown. Algonquin Bks. 2002 328p ISBN 1-56512-375-1
New stories from the South: the year's best, 2003; edited by Shannon Ravenel; with a preface by Roy Blount Jr. Algonquin Bks. of Chapel Hill 2003 368p ISBN 1-56512-395-0
The **New** Yorker stories. Callaghan, M.
News from the volcano. Swan, G.
Newton, D. B. (Dwight Bennett), 1916-
  Born to the brand; western stories. Five Star 2001 246p (Five Star first edition western series) ISBN 0-7862-2729-X LC 00-54253
Nfah-Abbenyi, Juliana Makuchi, 1958-
  Your madness, not mine: stories of Cameroon; with an introduction by Eloise A. Brière. Ohio Univ. Center for Int. Studies 1999 xxiv, 157p (Monographs in international studies. Africa series, no.70) ISBN 0-89680-206-X LC 98-48353
Nichols, Jim
  Slow monkeys and other stories. Carnegie-Mellon Univ. Press 2002 164p ISBN 0-88748-379-8
Nielsen Hayden, Patrick
  (ed) Starlight 3. *See* Starlight 3
A **night** at the Y. McBrearty, R. G.
Night game. Jenkins, G.
Night gamesand other stories and novellas. Schnitzler, A.
A **night** in the Manchester store and other stories. Cohen, S.
Night swimming. Fromm, P.
Night watch. Armstrong, K.
Nightmare town. Hammett, D.
Nightshade: 20th century ghost stories; edited by Robert Phillips. Carroll & Graf Pubs. 1999 470p ISBN 0-7867-0614-7
The **nighttime** is the right time. Crider, B.
Nissen, Thisbe, 1972-
  Out of the girls' room and into the night. University of Iowa Press 1999 244p (John Simmons short fiction award) ISBN 0-87745-691-7 LC 99-16672
Niven, Larry
  Scatterbrain; Larry Niven. 1st ed. Tor 2003 317p ISBN 0-7653-0137-7 (acid-free paper) LC 2003-42685
Nixon under the bodhi tree and other works of Buddhist fiction; edited by Kate Wheeler ; foreword by Charles Johnson. Wisdom Publications 2004 260p ISBN 0-86171-354-0 LC 2003-27339
No star too beautiful; Yiddish stories from 1382 to the present; compiled and translated by Joachim Neugroschel. Norton 2002 p. cmp ISBN 0-393-05190-0 LC 2002-69222
No thanks and other stories. Smith, S. J.

No visible means of support. Stuart, D.

The **noctambulists** & other fictions. Spielberg, P.

The **Noonday** Cemetery and other stories. Herling, G.

Norris, Helen, 1916-
One day in the life of a born again loser and other stories. University of Ala. Press 2000 197p (Deep South books) ISBN 0-8173-1029-0 LC 99-6957

Norris, Lisa, 1958-
Toy guns; stories. Helicon Nine Eds. 2000 145p ISBN 1-884235-31-X LC 00-57565

The **northern** stories of Charles W. Chesnutt. Chesnutt, C. W. and Duncan, C.

Northern suns; edited by David G. Hartwell & Glenn Grant. Doherty Assocs. 1999 382p ISBN 0-312-86461-2 LC 99-12846

Not a chance. Treat, J.

Not the end of the world. Atkinson, K.

Nothing that meets the eye. Highsmith, P.

Novelties and souvenirs. Crowley, J.

Now's the time. Harvey, J.

Nude in tub. Wuori, G. K.

The **Nudger** dilemmas. Lutz, J.

The **nun** and other stories. Alarcón, P. A. d.

A **nurse's** story and others. Baida, P.

O

The **O.** Henry Prize stories, 2003; edited and with an introduction by Laura Furman; jurers David Gutterson, Diane Johnson, Jennifer Egan. Anchor Bks. 2003 366p ISBN 1-4000-3131-1

O **careless** love. Dodd, S. M.

Oates, Joyce Carol, 1938-
Faithless: tales of transgression. Ecco Press 2001 386p ISBN 0-06-018525-2 LC 00-60007

I am no one you know; stories. Ecco 2004 290p ISBN 0-06-059288-5 LC 2003-61283

(ed) The New American voices 2003. *See* The New American voices 2003

(ed) Snapshots: 20th century mother-daughter fiction. *See* Snapshots: 20th century mother-daughter fiction

O'Barr, J. (James)
(ed) The Crow. *See* The Crow

Oblivion. Wallace, D. F.

Obradovi´c, Nadežda
(ed) The Anchor book of modern African stories. *See* The Anchor book of modern African stories

O'Callaghan, Maxine
Deal with the Devil and other stories. Five Star 2001 158p (Five Star first edition mystery series) ISBN 0-7862-3142-4 LC 2001-18147

O'Connell, Mary, 1966-
Living with saints. Atlantic Monthly Press 2001 228p ISBN 0-87113-826-3 LC 2001-22912

Odd corners. Hjortsberg, W.

Oddments. Pronzini, B.

Of leaf and flower; stories and poems for gardeners; edited by Charles Dean and Clyde Wachsberger; illustrations by Clyde Wachsberger. Persea Bks. 2001 182p ISBN 0-89255-269-7 LC 2001-34645

Off Paradise. Wegner, H.

Off the Mangrove Coast. L'Amour, L.

Officer Friendly and other stories. Robinson, L.

Offutt, Chris
Out of the woods; stories. Simon & Schuster 1999 172p ISBN 0-684-82556-2 LC 98-43041

Oliver, Chad, 1928-1993
Far from this earth and other stories; volume 2 of selected stories. NESFA 2003 480p ISBN 1-886778-48-5

A star above it and other stories; volume 1 of selected stories. NESFA 2003 480p ISBN 1-886778-45-0

On account of darkness and other SF stories. Pronzini, B. and Malzberg, B. N.

On glorious wings; the best flying stories of the century; edited and introduced by Stephen Coonts. Forge 2003 464p ISBN 0-312-87724-2 LC 2003-46853

On the nature of human romantic interaction. Iagnemma, K.

On the rocks; the KGB Bar fiction anthology; edited by Rebecca Donner ; foreword by Denis Woychuk. St. Martin's Griffin 2002 282p ISBN 0-312-30152-9 (pa) LC 2002-5134

Once upon a galaxy; edited by Will [sic] McCarthy, Martin H. Greenberg, and John Helfers. DAW Bks. 2002 318p ISBN 0-7564-0091-0

One day in the life of a born again loser and other stories. Norris, H.

One girl. Kohler, S.

One lamp; alternate history stories from The magazine of Fantasy & Science Fiction; edited by Gordon van Gelder. Four Walls Eight Windows 2003 433p ISBN 1-56858-276-5

One more for the road. Bradbury, R.

O'Neill, Susan

Don't mean nothing; short stories of Vietnam. Ballantine Bks. 2001 252p ISBN 0-345-44608-9 LC 2001-43878

Operation monsoon. Ramaya, S.

Orner, Peter

Esther stories. Houghton Mifflin 2001 227p ISBN 0-618-12873-5 LC 2001-24991

An **ornithologist's** guide to life. Hood, A.

O'Rourke, Frank, 1916-1989

The heavenly World Series; timeless baseball fiction; edited by Edith Carlson; introduction by Darryl Brock. Carroll & Graf Pubs. 2002 xx, 325p ISBN 0-7867-0950-2

Orringer, Julie

How to breathe underwater; stories. Knopf 2003 226p ISBN 1-400-04111-2 LC 2002-43436

Ortega, Julio

(ed) The Vintage book of Latin American stories. *See* The Vintage book of Latin American stories

Ortiz, Simon J., 1941-

Men on the moon; collected short stories. University of Ariz. Press 1999 203p (Sun tracks, v37) ISBN 0-8165-1929-3 LC 98-58145

Other fish in the sea. Kusel, L.

The **other** nineteenth century. Davidson, A.

Other people's mail; an anthology of letter stories; edited with an introduction by Gail Pool. University of Mo. Press 2000 275p ISBN 0-8262-1246-8 LC 99-49609

Otten, Charlote F.

(ed) The Literary werewolf. *See* The Literary werewolf

Out of the girls' room and into the night. Nissen, T.

Out of the woods. Offutt, C.

Outlaws of the Purple Cow and other stories. Goran, L.

Outside paradise. James, S.

Overholser, Wayne D., 1906-

Rainbow rider; a western trio. Five Star 2001 236p (Five Star first edition western series) ISBN 0-7862-2738-9 LC 2001-40523

The **Oxford** book of Caribbean short stories; edited by Stewart Brown and John Wickham. Oxford Univ. Press 1999 xxxiii, 476p ISBN 0-19-283241-7 LC 98-29731

P

Packer, ZZ, 1973-

Drinking coffee elsewhere. Riverhead Bks. 2003 238p ISBN 1-57322-234-8 LC 2002-73971

Padilla, Ignacio, 1968-, and Reid, Alastair, 1926-

Antipodes; Ignacio Padilla ; translated by Alastair Reid. 1st American ed. Farrar, Straus, and Giroux 2004 p. cmp ISBN 0-374-10533-2 (alk. paper) LC 2003-16432

Padilla, Mike
Hard language. Arte Público Press 2000 164p ISBN 1-55885-298-0 LC 00-41632

Paine, Tom
Scar Vegas and other stories. Harcourt 2000 215p ISBN 0-15-100489-7 LC 99-16416

Painter, Pamela
The long and short of it; short stories. Carnegie-Mellon Univ. Press 1999 202p ISBN 0-88748-286-4 LC 98-071950

Pak, Wan-So
My very last possession and other stories; translated by Chun Kyung-Ja et al. Sharpe, M.E. 1999 220p ISBN 0-7656-0428-0 LC 99-10681

Pale morning dun. Dokey, R.

Palestine's children. Kanafāni, G.

Paolucci, Anne
Do me a favor and other short stories. Griffon House 2001 147p ISBN 0-918680-92-1 LC 00-54862

Papernick, Jon
The ascent of Eli Israel and other stories. Arcade Pub. 2002 182p ISBN 1-559-70619-8 LC 2002-105002

Pappas, Christine
The getaway and other stories. See Thomas, Dorothy, and Pappas, Christine

Paradise dance. Lee, M.

Parker, Graham
Carp fishing on valium and other tales of the stranger road traveled. St. Martin's Press 2000 227p ISBN 0-312-26485-2 LC 00-27855

Parrish, Tim
Red stick men; stories. University Press of Miss. 2000 227p ISBN 1-57806-263-2 LC 99-87871

Partisan wedding. Viganò, R.

Paschal, Dean
By the light of the jukebox. Ontario Review Press 2002 146p ISBN 0-86538-105-4 LC 2001-58097

El **Paso** del Norte. Yañez, R.

Past imperfect; edited by Martin H. Greenberg and Larry Segriff. DAW Bks. 2001 314p ISBN 0-7564-0012-0

Past lives, present tense; edited by Elizabeth Ann Scarborough. Ace Bks. 1999 342p ISBN 0-441-00649-3

Pattern of behavior. Bishop, P.

Patterson, Kevin, 1964-
Country of cold; stories of sex and death. Talese 2003 254p ISBN 0-385-50627-9 LC 2002-28987

Paul, Barbara, 1931-
Jack be quick and other crime stories. Five Star 1999 219p (Five Star standard print mystery series) ISBN 0-7862-1919-X LC 99-22369

Paying the piper. Drake, D.

Paying the piper at the gates of dawn. Edghill, R.

Pearlman, Daniel D., 1935-
The best-known man in the world and other misfits. Aardwolf Press 2001 256p ISBN 0-9706225-0-3 LC 00-112238

Pelan, John
(ed) Shadows over Baker Street. *See* Shadows over Baker Street

Penn, W. S. (William S.), 1949-
This is the world. Michigan State Univ. Press 2000 212p ISBN 0-87013-561-9 LC 00-8702

Penzler, Otto, 1942-
(ed) Murder and obsession. *See* Murder and obsession

Perabo, Susan
Who I was supposed to be; short stories. Simon & Schuster 1999 191p ISBN 0-684-86233-6 LC 99-12256

Perfect recall. Beattie, A.

Perpetuity blues and other stories. Barrett, N., Jr.

Perps. Wellen, E.

The **Perseids** and other stories. Wilson, R. C.

Personal velocity. Miller, R.

The **perv**. Alameddine, R.

Peterson, Paula W.
Women in the grove; Paula W. Peterson. Beacon Press 2004 205p ISBN 0-8070-8352-6 (cloth : alk. paper) LC 2003-14314

Phillips, Dale Ray
My people's waltz. Norton 1999 190p ISBN 0-393-04715-6 LC 98-37090

Phillips, Robert S.
(ed) Nightshade: 20th century ghost stories. *See* Nightshade: 20th century ghost stories

Phoenix eyes and other stories. Leong, R.

Phone calls from the dead. Brenner, W.

Pickard, Nancy
(ed) Mom, apple pie, and murder. *See* Mom, apple pie, and murder
Storm warnings. Five Star 1999 183p (Five Star standard print mystery series) ISBN 0-7862-1811-8 LC 98-56117

The **picture** frame and other stories. Drake, R.

Pieces; a collection of new voices; edited by Stephen Chbosky. Pocket Bks. 2000 159p ISBN 0-671-00195-7 LC 00-60656

Piekarski, Vicki
(ed) The First Five Star western corral. *See* The First Five Star western corral

Pipers at the gates of dawn. Stegner, L.

Piranha to Scurfy and other stories. Rendell, R.

Pittalwala, Iqbal, 1962-
Dear Paramount Pictures; stories. Southern Methodist Univ. Press 2002 172p ISBN 0-87074-475-5 LC 2002-75822

A **place** between stations. Allen, S.

A **place** so foreign and eight more stories. Doctorow, C.

The **place** will comfort you. Goldstein, N.

Poachers. Franklin, T.

Pockell, Leslie
(ed) The 13 best horror stories of all time. *See* The 13 best horror stories of all time

Pohl, Frederik, 1919-
(ed) The SFWA grand masters. *See* The SFWA grand masters
(ed) The SFWA grand masters v1. *See* The SFWA grand masters v1
(ed) The SFWA grand masters v2. *See* The SFWA grand masters v2

Points of departure; new stories from Mexico; edited by Mónica Lavín; translated by Gustavo Segade. City Lights Bks. 2001 159p ISBN 0-87286-381-6 LC 00-65636

Poirier, Mark Jude
Unsung heroes of American industry; stories. Hyperion 2001 169p ISBN 0-7868-6827-9

Polansky, Steven
Dating Miss Universe; nine stories. Ohio State Univ. Press 1999 185p ISBN 0-8142-0818-5 LC 98-47410

Politically inspired; edited by Stephen Elliott; assistant editor, Gabriel Kram; associate editors, Elizabeth Brooks [et al.] MacAdam/Cage Pub. 2003 276p ISBN 1-931561-58-3; 1-931561-45-1 (pa) LC 2003-17623

Polonaise. Bukoski, A.

Ponce de León, Juana
(ed) Dream with no name. *See* Dream with no name

Ponte, Antonio José, 1964-
In the cold of the Malecón & other stories; translated from the Spanish by Cola Franzen and Dick Cluster. City Lights Bks. 2000 127p ISBN 0-87286-374-3 LC 00-34640
Tales from the Cuban empire; translated from the Spanish by Cola Franzen. City Lights Bks. 2002 90p ISBN 0-87286-407-3 LC 2002-73891

Pool, Gail
(ed) Other people's mail. *See* Other people's mail

The **porno** girl and other stories. Wexler, M.

The **portable** promised land. Touré

Porter, Joseph Ashby, 1942-
Touch wood; short stories. Turtle Point Press 2002 192p ISBN 1-88558-664-7 LC 2002-103859

Portrait of my mother, who posed nude in wartime. Sandor, M.

Potential weapons. Lieu, J.

Potvin, Elizabeth Ann, 1958-
The traveller's hat; [by] Liza Potvin. Raincoast Books 2003 270p ISBN 1-55192-594-X LC 2003-447202
The **practical** heart. Gurganus, A.
Prayers of an accidental nature. Di Blasi, D.
Prete, David
Say that to my face; fiction. Norton 2003 187p ISBN 0-393-05798-4 LC 2003-8690
Price, Reynolds, 1933-
The complete stories of Truman Capote. See Capote, Truman, 1924-1984, and Price, Reynolds, 1933-
The **price** you pay. Winter, E.
Pritchett, Laura, 1971-
Hell's bottom, Colorado. Milkweed Eds. 2001 142p ISBN 1-57131-036-3 LC 2001-30966
Prize stories, 1999; The O. Henry awards; edited and with an introduction by Larry Dark. Anchor Bks. (NY) 1999 443p ISBN 0-385-49358-4
Prize stories, 2000; The O. Henry awards; edited and with an introduction by Larry Dark. Anchor Bks. (NY) 2000 404p ISBN 0-385-49877-2
Prize stories, 2001; The O. Henry awards; edited and with an introduction by Larry Dark. Anchor Bks. (NY) 2001 xx, 442p ISBN 0-385-49878-0
Pronoun music. Cohen, R.
Pronzini, Bill
More oddments. Five Star 2001 228p (Five Star first edition mystery series) ISBN 0-7862-3557-8 LC 2001-50162
Oddments; a short story collection. Five Star 2000 198p (Five Star first edition mystery series) ISBN 0-7862-2894-6 LC 00-61029
Sleuths. Five Star 1999 278p (Five Star standard print mystery series) ISBN 0-7862-1702-2 LC 98-44598
Pronzini, Bill, and Malzberg, Barry N.
On account of darkness and other SF stories; [by] Bill Pronzini and Barry N. Malzberg. Five Star 2004 272p ISBN 1-59414-038-3 LC 2003-64229
Proulx, Annie
Close range; Wyoming stories. Scribner 1999 283p ISBN 0-684-85221-7 LC 98-56066
Proust, Marcel, 1871-1922
The complete short stories of Marcel Proust; compiled and translated by Joachim Neugroschel; foreword by Roger Shattuck. Cooper Sq. Pubs. 2001 201p ISBN 0-8154-1136-7 LC 00-65739
Pu-239 and other Russian fantasies. Kalfus, K.
The **Pushcart** prize XXIII: best of the small presses; an annual small press reader; edited by Bill Henderson with the Pushcart prize editors. Pushcart Press 1999 606p ISBN 1-888889-09-8 LC 76-58675
The **Pushcart** prize XXIV: best of the small presses; an annual small press reader; edited by Bill Henderson with the Pushcart prize editors. Pushcart Press 2000 585p ISBN 1-888889-19-5 LC 76-58675
The **Pushcart** prize XXVI; best of the small presses, an annual small press reader; edited by Bill Henderson and the Pushcart prize editors. Pushcart Press 2002 619p ISBN 1-888889-30-6; 1-888889-31-4
Pushcart prize XXVII; best of the small presses; edited by Bill Henderson with the Pushcart prize editors. Pushcart Press 2003 632p ISBN 1-888889-33-0; 1-888889-35-7 (pa)
Pushkin, Aleksandr Sergeevich, 1799-1837
The collected stories; translated from the Russian by Paul Debreczeny; with an introduction by John Bayley; verse passages translated by Walter Arndt. rev expanded ed. Knopf 1999 548p (Everyman's library, 251) ISBN 0-375-40549-6

Q

The **question** of Bruno. Hemon, A.

Quick bright things. Wallace, R.
Quill, Monica, 1929-
  Death takes the veil and other stories; with an introduction by Ralph McInerny. Five Star 2001 216p (Five Star first edition mystery series) ISBN 0-7862-3143-2 LC 2001-33052

R

Radio Elvis and other stories. Irsfeld, J. H.
Rainbow rider. Overholser, W. D.
Ramaya, Shona
  Operation monsoon; stories. Graywolf Press 2003 254p ISBN 1-55597-387-6 LC 2003-101169
Randolph, Ladette
  (ed) A different plain. *See* A different plain
Raphael, Frederic, 1931-
  All his sons; a novella and nine stories. Catbird Press 2001 187p ISBN 0-945774-49-4 LC 00-69407
Raphael, Lawrence, 1946?-
  (ed) Mystery midrash. *See* Mystery midrash
Raphael, Linda Schermer, 1943-
  (ed) When night fell. *See* When night fell
Raphael, Marc Lee
  (ed) When night fell. *See* When night fell
Rat medicine & other unlikely curatives. Davis, L.
Ravenel, Shannon
  (ed) New stories from the South. *See* New stories from the South
  (ed) New stories from the South: the year's best, 1999. *See* New stories from the South: the year's best, 1999
  (ed) New stories from the South: the year's best, 2000. *See* New stories from the South: the year's best, 2000
  (ed) New stories from the South: the year's best, 2001. *See* New stories from the South: the year's best, 2001
  (ed) New stories from the South: the year's best, 2002. *See* New stories from the South: the year's best, 2002
  (ed) New stories from the South: the year's best, 2003. *See* New stories from the South: the year's best, 2003
Rawley, Donald, 1957-
  Tina in the back seat; stories. Bard 1999 149p ISBN 0-380-80723-8 LC 99-27618
Raz, Hilda
  (ed) Best of Prairie schooner. *See* Best of Prairie schooner
Real time. Chaudhuri, A.
Real to reel. Yuknavitch, L.
Reave the Just and other tales. Donaldson, S. R.
Reaves, Michael
  (ed) Shadows over Baker Street. *See* Shadows over Baker Street
A **reckless** moon and other stories. Warren, D.
Red ant house. Cummins, A.
Red clay, blue Cadillac. Malone, M.
The **red** passport. Shonk, K.
Red plaid shirt. Schoemperlen, D.
Red stick men. Parrish, T.
Redgunk tales. Eakin, W.
Redmond, Eugene B.
  Echo tree. See Dumas, Henry, 1934-1968, and Redmond, Eugene B.
Redshift; extreme visions of speculative fiction; edited by Al Sarrantonio. ROC 2001 544p ISBN 0-451-45859-1 LC 2001-41639
Reed, Robert
  The dragons of Springplace; stories. Golden Gryphon Press 1999 312p ISBN 0-9655901-6-X LC 98-37689
Referred pain. Schwartz, L. S.
Régio, José, 1901-1969
  The flame-coloured dress and other stories; translated from the Portuguese by Margaret Jull Costa. Carcanet Press 1999 207p ISBN 1-85754-386-6
Reid, Alastair, 1926-
  Antipodes. See Padilla, Ignacio, 1968-, and Reid, Alastair, 1926-

Reid, Elwood

What salmon know; stories. Doubleday 1999 226p ISBN 0-385-49121-2 LC 98-55516

Reifler, Nelly

See through; stories. Simon & Schuster 2003 148p ISBN 0-7432-3608-4 LC 2003-50379

Reiner, Carl, 1922-

How Paul Robeson saved my life and other mostly happy stories. Cliff St. Bks. 1999 159p ISBN 0-06-019451-0 LC 99-31107

Reisman, Nancy, 1961-

House fires. University of Iowa Press 1999 207p il (Iowa short fiction award) ISBN 0-87745-692-5 LC 99-29218

Reload: rethinking women + cyberculture; edited by Mary Flanagan and Austin Booth. MIT Press 2002 581p il ISBN 0-262-06227-5 LC 2001-56235

Remnick, David

(ed) Wonderful town. *See* Wonderful town

Rendell, Ruth, 1930-

Piranha to Scurfy and other stories. Crown 2001 c2000 218p ISBN 0-609-60853-3 LC 00-43135

Rest area. Chapman, C. M.

Retribution. Fulton, J.

Retrieving bones; stories and poems of the Korean War; edited and with an introduction by W. D. Ehrhart and Philip K. Jason. Rutgers Univ. Press 1999 xlii, 225p ISBN 0-8135-2638-8 LC 98-52668

The **return** of the black widowers. Asimov, I.

Rhymes with useless. Young, T.

Richmond, Michelle, 1970-

The girl in the fall-away dress; stories. University of Mass. Press 2001 169p ISBN 1-55849-315-8 LC 01-2724

Richter, Stacey, 1965-

My date with Satan; stories. Scribner 1999 223p ISBN 0-684-85701-4 LC 99-13146

Ride to glory. Flynn, T. T.

Riders of the shadowlands. DeRosso, H. A.

Rifkin, Alan

Signal Hill; stories. City LightsBks. 2003 128p ISBN 0-87286-424-3 LC 2003-14658

Rinehart, Steven

Kick in the head; stories. Doubleday 2000 224p ISBN 0-385-49853-5 LC 99-55774

Ríos Rivera, Esteban

(ed) Dream with no name. *See* Dream with no name

Rispondimi. Tamaro, S.

Ritchie, Elisavietta

In haste I write you this note; stories and half-stories. Washington Writers' Pub. House 2000 171p ISBN 0-931846-58-7 LC 00-97437

Robinson, Kim Stanley

(ed) Nebula awards showcase 2002. *See* Nebula awards showcase 2002

Robinson, Lewis

Officer Friendly and other stories. HarperCollins Pubs. 2003 228p ISBN 0-06-051368-3 LC 2002-68816

Robison, Mary

Tell me: 30 stories. Counterpoint 2002 277p ISBN 1-58243-258-9 LC 2002-8499

Robotham, Rosemarie, 1957-

(ed) The Bluelight corner. *See* The Bluelight corner

Rodburg, Maxine

The law of return; short stories. Carnegie-Mellon Univ. Press 1999 179p ISBN 0-88748-313-5 LC 98-74658

Rodgers, Susan Jackson, 1960-

The trouble with you is and other stories. Mid-List Press 2004 158p (First series--short fiction) ISBN 0-922811-60-1 LC 2004-960

Roeske, Paulette

Bridge of sighs; a novella and stories. Story Line Press 2002 134p ISBN 1-58654-019-X LC 2002-7752

Rollins, Hillary

The empress's new lingerie and other erotic fairy tales; bedtime stories for grown-ups. Harmony Bks. 2001 156p ISBN 0-609-60705-7 LC 2001-24769

Roorbach, Bill, 1953-

Big Bend; stories. University of Ga. Press 2001 174p ISBN 0-8203-2283-0 LC 00-44729

Rope burns. Toole, F. X.

The **Rose** City. Ebershoff, D.

The **rose** garden. Brennan, M.

Rosenfeld, Stephanie, 1968-

What about the love part?; stories. Ballantine Bks. 2002 211p ISBN 0-345-44823-5 LC 2002-19746

Roth, Joseph, 1894-1939

The collected stories of Joseph Roth; translated with an introduction by Michael Hofmann. Norton 2002 281p ISBN 0-393-04320-7 LC 2001-44747

The **round** & other cold hard facts. Le Clézio, J.-M. G.

Rowell, John, 1964-

The music of your life; stories; John Rowell. Simon & Schuster 2003 258p ISBN 0-7432-3695-5 LC 2002-45272

The **royal** game & other stories. Zweig, S.

Royal whodunnits; edited by Mike Ashley. Carroll & Graf Pubs. 1999 434p ISBN 0-7867-0634-1

Rucker, Rudy von Bitter, 1946-

Gnarl!; stories. Four Walls Eight Windows 1999 566p ISBN 1-56858-159-9 LC 99-86601

Rules of the lake. Ziegler, I.

Rumble, young man, rumble. Cavell, B.

Rumpole rests his case. Mortimer, J. C.

Running from Legs and other stories. McBain, E.

Rusch, Kristine Kathryn

Stories for an enchanted afternoon; with a foreword by Kevin J. Anderson. Golden Gryphon Press 2001 284p ISBN 1-930846-02-9 LC 00-53574

Russo, Richard, 1949-

The whore's child, and other stories. Knopf 2002 225p ISBN 0-375-41168-2 LC 2002-19023

S

Sade, marquis de, 1740-1814

The mystified magistrate and other tales; translated and with an introduction by Richard Seaver. Arcade Pub. 2000 211p ISBN 1-55970-432-2

Sammān, Ghādah

The square moon; supernatural tales; translated from the Arabic by Issa J. Boullata. University of Ark. Press 1998 203p ISBN 1-55728-534-9 LC 98-30084

Sánchez, Rosaura

He walked in and sat down and other stories; English translation by Beatrice Pita. University of N.M. Press 2000 246p ISBN 0-8263-2213-1 LC 99-50426

Sandlin, Lisa

In the river province; stories. Southern Methodist University Press 2004 165p ISBN 0-87074-488-7 LC 2003-67384

Sandor, Marjorie

Portrait of my mother, who posed nude in wartime; stories. Sarabande Books 2003 213p ISBN 1-88933-083-3; 1-88933-082-5 (pa) LC 2002-9887

Sanford, Annette

Crossing Shattuck Bridge; stories. Southern Methodist Univ. Press 1999 200p ISBN 0-87074-442-9 LC 99-23578

Sap rising. Lincoln, C.

Saroyan, Aram

Artists in trouble; new stories. Black Sparrow Press 2001 234p ISBN 1-57423-172-3 LC 2001-43736

Sarrantonio, Al

(ed) 999: new stories of horror and suspense. *See* 999: new stories of horror and suspense

(ed) Redshift. *See* Redshift

Saunders, Gerda

Blessings on the sheep dog; stories. Southern Methodist Univ. Press 2002 244p ISBN 0-87074-468-2 LC 2002-19373

Savage, Les, Jr.

The sting of Señorita Scorpion; a western trio. Five Star 2000 188p ISBN 0-7862-2398-7 LC 00-57802

Say that to my face. Prete, D.

Scar Vegas and other stories. Paine, T.

Scarborough, Elizabeth Ann

(ed) Past lives, present tense. *See* Past lives, present tense

Scared stiff. Campbell, R.

Scatterbrain. Niven, L.

Schlink, Bernhard

Flights of love; stories; translated from the German by John E. Woods. Pantheon Bks. 2001 308p ISBN 0-375-42090-8 LC 2001-31399

Schmidt, Heidi Jon

Darling? Picador 2001 245p ISBN 0-312-28178-1 LC 2001-31952

Schnee, Samantha

(ed) Francis Ford Coppola's Zoetrope: all story. *See* Francis Ford Coppola's Zoetrope: all story

(ed) Francis Ford Coppola's Zoetrope all-story 2. *See* Francis Ford Coppola's Zoetrope all-story 2

Schnitzler, Arthur, 1862-1931

Desire and delusion; three novellas; selected and translated from the German by Margret Schaefer. Dee, I. R. 2003 264p ISBN 1-566-63542-X LC 2003-53165

Night gamesand other stories and novellas; and other stories and novellas; translated from the German by Margret Schaefer; with a foreword by John Simon. Dee, I.R. 2002 272p ISBN 1-566-63386-9 LC 2001-28196

Schoemperlen, Diane, 1954-

Red plaid shirt; stories. Penguin Books 2003 310p ISBN 0-14-200320-4 LC 2002-192496

Scholz, Carter

The amount to carry; stories. Picador 2003 208p ISBN 0-312-26901-3 LC 2002-192667

Kafka Americana. See Lethem, Jonathan, and Scholz, Carter

Schwartz, Lynne Sharon

Referred pain; and other stories. Counterpoint 2003 271p ISBN 1-582-43301-1 LC 2003-15678

Science-fiction classics; the stories that morphed into movies; compiled by Forrest J. Ackerman. TV Bks. 1999 446p ISBN 1-57500-040-7

The **Science** fiction hall of fame: volume one, 1929-1964; the greatest science fiction stories of all time chosen by the members of the Science Fiction Writers of America; edited by Robert Silverberg. TOR Bks. 2003 c1998 560p ISBN 0-765-30536-4

Scoville, Shelagh, 1928-

Ulu's dog and other stories. Fithian Press 2003 301p ISBN 1-56474-415-9 LC 2002-156646

The **Scribner** anthology of contemporary short fiction; fifty North American stories since 1970; Lex Williford and Michael Martone, editors. Scribner Paperback Fiction 1999 671p ISBN 0-684-85796-0 LC 99-39518

Seaman, Donna

(ed) In our nature: stories of wildness. *See* In our nature: stories of wildness

Searle, Elizabeth, 1962-

Celebrities in disgrace; a novella and stories. Graywolf Press 2001 183p ISBN 1-55597-324-8 LC 00-105091

Secret life. VanderMeer, J.

Secret lives. Browder, C.

The **secret** names of women. Barrett, L.

See through. Reifler, N.

Segriff, Larry
  (ed) Cat crimes through time. *See* Cat crimes through time
  (ed) Past imperfect. *See* Past imperfect
Seiffert, Rachel
  Field study. Pantheon Books 2004 215p ISBN 0-375-42259-5
    LC 2003-66364
Selden, Yumi, and Tawada, Yoko, 1960-
  Where Europe begins; translated from the German by Susan
    Bernofsky; from the Japanese by Yumi Selden; with a preface by
    Wim Wenders. New Directions 2002 208p ISBN 0-8112-1515-6
    LC 2002-5196
Selected short stories of D. H. Lawrence. Lawrence, D. H.
Selected short stories of Weldon Kees. Kees, W.
Selected stories. Grau, S. A.
Selected stories. Sturgeon, T.
The **self-made** brain surgeon and other stories. Harris, M.
Sellers, Heather, 1964-
  Georgia under water; stories. Sarabande Bks. 2001 217p ISBN
    1-889330-56-6 LC 00-58799
Sentimental, heartbroken rednecks. Bottoms, G.
Servants of the map. Barrett, A.
Several deceptions. Stevenson, J.
The **SFWA** grand masters; edited by Frederik Pohl. TOR Bks. 2001
    477p ISBN 0-312-86877-4 LC 99-21933
The **SFWA** grand masters v1; edited by Frederik Pohl. Doherty Assocs.
    1999 383p ISBN 0-312-86881-2 LC 99-21933
The **SFWA** grand masters v2; edited by Frederik Pohl. Doherty Assocs.
    2000 ISBN 0-312-86879-0 LC 99-21933
Shade, Eric, 1970-
  Eyesores; stories. University of Ga. Press 2003 205p ISBN
    0-8203-2432-9 LC 2002-7151
Shadows over Baker Street; edited by Michael Reaves and John Pelan.
    Ballantine Bks. 2003 446p ISBN 0-345-45528-2
Shaked, Gershon
  (ed) Six Israeli novellas. *See* Six Israeli novellas
Shamara and other stories. Vasilenko, S. and Goscilo, H.
Shapiro, Gerald, 1950-
  Bad Jews and other stories. Zoland Bks. 1999 325p ISBN
    1-58195-012-8 LC 99-31835
Shaw, Dave, 1966-
  Here comes the roar. University of North Texas Press 2003 135p
    ISBN 1-574-41170-5 LC 2003-12961
Sheckley, Robert, 1928-
  Uncanny tales. Five Star 2003 252p ISBN 0-7862-5341-X
    LC 2003-52850
Sheffield, Charles
  The amazing Dr. Darwin. Baen Bks. 2002 328p ISBN 0-7434-3529-X
    LC 2002-22328
The **shell** collector. Doerr, A.
Shepard, Jesse
  Jubilee King; stories. Bloomsbury Press 2003 183p ISBN
    1-58234-340-3
Shepard, Sam, 1943-
  Great dream of heaven; stories. Knopf 2002 142p ISBN
    0-375-40505-4 LC 2002-70054
Shetterly, Caitlin
  (ed) Fault lines. *See* Fault lines
Shifu, you'll do anything for a laugh. Mo Yan
Shonk, Katherine, 1968-
  The red passport. Farrar, Straus & Giroux 2003 209p ISBN
    0-374-24847-8 LC 2003-7680
Short stories by Latin American women; the magic and the real; edited
    by Celia Correas de Zapata; foreword by Isabel Allende. Modern
    Lib. 2003 246p ISBN 0-8129-6707-0 LC 2002-26424
Shrapnel and other stories. Yi, T.-H.
Shrayer, Maxim, 1967-
  Jonah and Sarah. See Shrayer-Petrov, David, 1936-, and Shrayer,
    Maxim, 1967-

Shrayer-Petrov, David, 1936-, and Shrayer, Maxim, 1967-
Jonah and Sarah; Jewish stories of Russia and America; edited by Maxim D. Shrayer. Syracuse Univ. Press 2003 184p (The library of modern Jewish literature) ISBN 0-8156-0764-4 LC 2003-9848

Signal Hill. Rifkin, A.

Silber, Joan
Ideas of heaven; a ring of stories; Joan Silber. W.W. Norton 2004 250p ISBN 0-393-05908-1 (hardcover) LC 2003-24324
In my other life. Sarabande Bks. 2000 223p ISBN 1-889330-43-4 LC 99-37966

Silent cruise & other stories. Taylor, T. L.

Silverberg, Robert
(ed) Far horizons. *See* Far horizons
(ed) Nebula awards showcase 2001. *See* Nebula awards showcase 2001
(ed) The Science fiction hall of fame: volume one, 1929-1964. *See* The Science fiction hall of fame: volume one, 1929-1964

Simmons, Dan
Worlds enough & time; five tales of speculative fiction. HarperCollins Pubs. 2002 262p ISBN 0-06-050604-0 LC 2002-69224

Simonds, Merilyn, 1949-
The lion in the room next door. Putnam 2000 255p ISBN 0-399-14591-5 LC 99-37416

Simple recipes. Thien, M.

Simpson, Helen
Getting a life; stories. Knopf 2001 196p ISBN 0-375-41109-7 LC 2001-90388

Singer, Isaac Bashevis, 1904-1991
Collected stories; Gimpel the fool to the Letter writer; Isaac Bashevis Singer. Library of America 2004 789p (Library of America) ISBN 1-931082-61-8 LC 2003-66055
Collected stories; One night in Brazil to The death of Methuselah. Library of America 2004 899p (Library of America) ISBN 1-931082-63-4 LC 2003-66081
Collected stories: A friend of Kafka to Passions. Library of America 2004 856p (Library of America) ISBN 1-931082-62-6 LC 2003-66057

Singleton, George, 1958-
The half-mammals of Dixie; stories. Algonquin Bks.of Chapel Hill 2002 287p ISBN 1-565-12354-9 LC 2002-23205
These people are us; short stories. Black Belt Press 2000 232p ISBN 1-880216-94-9 LC 00-11228

Sister Emily's lightship and other stories. Yolen, J.

Six Easy pieces. Mosley, W.

Six Israeli novellas; [by] Ruth Almog [et al.]; edited and with an introduction by Gershon Shaked; translated from the Hebrew by Dalya Bilu, Philip Simpson, and Marganit Weinberger-Rotman. Godine 1999 338p (Verba Mundi) ISBN 1-56792-091-8 LC 98-34323

Skillings, R. D. (Roger D.), 1937-
Where the time goes. University Press of New England 1999 168p (Hardscrabble books) ISBN 0-87451-939-X LC 99-19856

Skin folk. Hopkinson, N.

Skinner, José, 1956-
Flight and other stories. University of Nev. Press 2001 186p (Western literature series) ISBN 0-87417-359-0 LC 00-11122

Skinswaps. Blatnik, A.

Škvorecký, Josef
When Eve was naked; stories of a life's journey. Farrar, Straus & Giroux 2002 2000 352p ISBN 0-374-14975-5 LC 2002-20652

Slapboxing with Jesus. LaValle, V. D.

Slavin, Julia
The woman who cut off her leg at the Maidstone Club and other stories. Holt & Co. 1999 194p ISBN 0-8050-6085-5 LC 98-50765

Sleep. Dixon, S.

Sleepwalkers and other stories; the Arab in Hebrew fiction; edited by Ehud Ben-Ezer. Lynne Rienner Pubs. 1999 183p ISBN 0-89410-852-2 LC 98-25852

Sleuths. Pronzini, B.

Slezak, Ellen
  Last year's Jesus; a novella and nine stories. Hyperion 2002 237p
    ISBN 0-7868-6741-8 LC 2001-57391
Slow monkeys and other stories. Nichols, J.
Small change. Hay, E.
Small change. Hendel, Y.
Smart, Ariel, 1941-
  The Green Lantern & other stories. Fithian Press 1999 110p ISBN
    1-56474-271-7 LC 98-19963
Smith, Ali, 1962-
  The whole story and other stories. Anchor Books 2004 177p ISBN
    1-400-07567-X LC 2003-63020
Smith, Julie, 1944-
  Mean rooms. Five Star 2000 196p (Five Star standard print mystery
    series) ISBN 0-7862-2364-2 LC 99-56408
Smith, Martin Cruz
  (ed) Death by espionage. *See* Death by espionage
Smith, Sarah Jane
  No thanks and other stories. New Issues 2001 201p (New Issues
    poetry & prose) ISBN 1-930974-10-8 LC 2001-278550
Smolens, John
  My one and only bomb shelter; stories. Carnegie-Mellon Univ. Press
    2000 178p ISBN 0-88748-329-1 LC 99-74434
Snapshots: 20th century mother-daughter fiction; edited by Joyce Carol
    Oates and Janet Berliner. Godine 2000 241p ISBN 1-56792-114-0
    LC 00-57669
Sneve, Virginia Driving Hawk
  Grandpa was a cowboy & an Indian and other stories. University of
    Neb. Press 2000 116p ISBN 0-8032-4274-3 LC 00-23483
The **society** of friends. Cherry, K.
Soft maniacs. Estep, M.
Sojourner, Mary
  Delicate; stories; Mary Sojourner. 1st Scribner trade pa. ed. Scribner
    2004 258p ISBN 0-7432-2970-3 (pbk.) LC 2003-66300
Solitude, and other stories. Vivante, A.
The **solitude** of compassion. Giono, J.
Someone to watch over me. Bausch, R.
Somer, John, 1936-
  (ed) The Anchor book of new Irish writing. *See* The Anchor book of
    new Irish writing
Song of ascent. Goliger, G.
Sonny Liston was a friend of mine. Jones, T.
Sorrentino, Gilbert, 1929-
  The moon in its flight. 2004 266p ISBN 1-56689-152-3 LC 2004-665
Sosin, Danielle, 1959-
  Garden primitives; stories. Coffee House Press 2000 204p ISBN
    1-56689-100-0 LC 99-86398
Soulcatcher and other stories. Johnson, C. R.
Southern local color; stories of region, race, and gender; edited by
    Barbara C. Ewell and Pamela Glenn Menke; with notes by Andrea
    Humphrey. University of Ga. Press 2002 lxvi, 323p ISBN
    0-8203-2316-0 LC 2001-27722
Southern souvenirs. Mencken, S. H.
Southern stories. Blaise, C.
The **southern** woman. Spencer, E.
Soy la Avon lady and other stories. López, L.
Spark, Muriel
  The ghost stories of Muriel Spark. New Directions 2003 135p ISBN
    0-8112-1549-0 LC 2003-14485
Spatz, Gregory, 1964-
  Wonderful tricks; stories. Mid-List Press 2002 246p ((First series:
    short stories)) ISBN 0-922811-55-5 LC 2002-10874
Speak of the Devil. Gores, J.
Speaking of lust; stories of forbidden desire; edited by Lawrence Block.
    Cumberland House 2001 368p (Seven deadly sins series) ISBN
    1-58182-153-0 LC 2001-17266
Speaking with angels. West, M.
Speaking with the angel; original stories; edited by Nick Hornby.
    Riverhead Bks. 2001 233p ISBN 1-57322-858-3 LC 00-51761

Spencer, Darrell, 1947-
Caution, men in trees; stories. University of Ga. Press 2000 193p ISBN 0-8203-2182-6 LC 99-35587

Spencer, Elizabeth
The southern woman; new and selected fiction. 2001 Modern Library ed. Modern Lib. 2001 462p ISBN 0-679-64218-8 LC 00-54612

Spielberg, Peter
The noctambulists & other fictions. Fiction Collective Two 2001 166p ISBN 1-57366-097-3 LC 2001-1413

Spies and thieves, cops and killers, etc. Collins, M.

Spillane, Mickey, 1918-
(ed) A Century of noir. *See* A Century of noir

Sports best short stories; edited by Paul D. Staudohar. Chicago Review Press 2001 433p ISBN 1-556-52429-3 LC 2001-42133

The **square** moon. Sammān, G.

Stableford, Brian M.
Designer genes; tales of the biotech revolution. Five Star 2004 287p ISBN 1-59414-033-2 LC 2003-64703

Stanton, Maura
Do not forsake me, oh my darling. University of Notre Dame Press 2002 163p (The Richard Sullivan prize in short fiction) ISBN 0-268-02555-X; 0-268-02556-8 (pa) LC 2001-3522

A **star** above it and other stories. Oliver, C.

Starlight 3; edited by Patrick Nielsen Hayden. TOR Bks. 2001 350p ISBN 0-312-86780-8 LC 2001-27118

Stashower, Daniel
(ed) Murder, my dear Watson. *See* Murder, my dear Watson

Staudohar, Paul D.
(ed) Boxing's best short stories. *See* Boxing's best short stories
(ed) Fishing's best short stories. *See* Fishing's best short stories
(ed) Sports best short stories. *See* Sports best short stories

Stavans, Ilan
Collected stories: A friend of Kafka to Passions. See Singer, Isaac Bashevis, 1904-1991

Steele, Allen M.
American beauty; stories. Five Star 2003 261p ISBN 0-7862-5339-8 LC 2003-49154

Stegner, Lynn
Pipers at the gates of dawn; a triptych. University Press of New England 2000 270p (Hardscrabble books) ISBN 1-58465-063-X LC 00-9138

Steinbeck, Thomas
Down to a soundless sea. Ballantine Bks. 2002 283p ISBN 0-345-45576-2 LC 2003-266413

Steinberg, Susan
The end of free love. FC2 2003 230p ISBN 1-573-66106-6 LC 2002-9562

Stephens, John Richard
(ed) Into the mummy's tomb. *See* Into the mummy's tomb

Stern, Daniel, 1928-
In the country of the young; stories. Southern Methodist Univ. Press 2001 211p ISBN 0-87074-457-7 LC 00-45025

Stern, Steve, 1947-
The wedding jester. Graywolf Press 1999 223p ISBN 1-55597-290-X LC 98-88488

Stevenson, Jane, 1959-
Several deceptions. Houghton Mifflin 2000 c1999 263p ISBN 0-618-04933-9 LC 00-61319

Still wild; short fiction of the American West, 1950 to the present; edited by Larry McMurtry. Simon & Schuster 2000 414p ISBN 0-684-86882-2 LC 99-52848

Stillness and other stories. Brkic, C. A.

The **sting** of Señorita Scorpion. Savage, L., Jr.

Stolar, Daniel
The middle of the night. Picador 2003 242p ISBN 0-312-30409-9 LC 2003-43390

Stollman, Aryeh Lev
The dialogues of time and entropy. Riverhead Bks. 2003 226p il ISBN 1-573-22235-6 LC 2002-68269

Stop breakin down. McManus, J.

Stories for an enchanted afternoon. Rusch, K. K.

Stories from another world. Kohler, S.

Stories from the Blue Moon Café; edited by Sonny Brewer. MacAdam/Cage 2002 351p ISBN 1-931561-09-5 LC 2002-9685

Stories from the Blue Moon Cafe II; edited by Sonny Brewer. MacAdam\Cage Pub 2003 361p ISBN 1-931561-43-5 LC 2003-13976

Stories, novels & essays. Chesnutt, C. W.

The **stories** of Alice Adams. Adams, A.

Stories of enchantment from nineteenth-century Spain; translated from the Spanish by Robert M. Fredorchek; introduction by Alan E. Smith. Bucknell Univ. Press 2002 288p ISBN 0-8387-5533-X LC 2002-21541

The **stories** of Paul Bowles. Bowles, P.

The **stories** of Richard Bausch. Bausch, R.

Stories of your life and others. Chiang, T.

Storm warnings. Pickard, N.

Strandquist, Robert, 1952-
  The inanimate world; stories. Anvil Press (Vancouver) 2001 179p ISBN 1-895636-33-7 LC 2001-431195

Strange but not a stranger. Kelly, J. P.

Strange days; fabulous journeys with Gardner Dozois; edited by Tim Szczesuil and Ann Broomhead. NESFA Press 2001 544p ISBN 1-886778-26-4

Strange forces. Lugones, L.

The **stranger** at the Palazzo d'Oro and other stories. Theroux, P.

Stranger things happen. Link, K.

Strangers and sojourners. Engel, M. P.

Straub, Peter
  Magic terror; seven tales. Random House 2000 335p ISBN 0-375-50393-5 LC 99-53216

Strauss, Alix
  The joy of funerals; a novel in stories. St. Martin's Press 2003 259p ISBN 0-312-30917-1 LC 2003-41357

Strecker, Trey, 1966-
  (ed) Dead balls and double curves. *See* Dead balls and double curves

Stuart, Dabney, 1937-
  No visible means of support; stories. University of Mo. Press 2001 200p ISBN 0-8262-1320-0 LC 00-52742

Stuckey-French, Elizabeth
  The first paper girl in Red Oak, Iowa and other stories. Doubleday 2000 203p ISBN 0-385-49893-4 LC 99-86606

The **Student** body; short stories about college students and professors; edited by John McNally. University of Wis. Press 2001 280p ISBN 0-299-17404-2 LC 2001-1947

Sturgeon, Theodore, 1918-1985
  Selected stories. Vintage Bks. 2000 439p ISBN 0-375-70375-6

Su, David Li-qun, 1945-
  (ed) The Vintage book of contemporary Chinese fiction. *See* The Vintage book of contemporary Chinese fiction

Such a good girl and other crime stories. Gorman, E.

Such a pretty face; edited by Lee Martindale. Meisha Merlin Pub. 2000 304p ISBN 0-892065-28-2 LC 00-8903

Suicidal tendencies. Broughton, T. A.

Suicide's girlfriend. Evans, E.

Suitable for hanging. Maron, M.

Sukrungruang, Ira
  (ed) What are you looking at? *See* What are you looking at?

Summerhouse, later. Hermann, J.

Sumner, Penny
  (ed) Brought to book. *See* Brought to book

Sunstroke. Bunin, I. A.

Super flat times. Derby, M.

Supernatural tales. Lee, V.

Supertoys last all summer long. Aldiss, B. W.

Survival rates. Clyde, M.

Svoboda, Terese
Trailer girl and other stories. Counterpoint 2001 230p ISBN 1-582-43085-3 LC 00-64447
Swan, Gladys, 1934-
News from the volcano; stories. University of Mo. Press 2000 191p ISBN 0-8262-1296-4 LC 00-36409
Swan, Mary
The deep and other stories. Random House 2003 219p ISBN 0-375-50851-1 LC 2002-68099
Swarthout, Glendon Fred
Easterns and westerns; short stories; edited by Miles Hood Swarthout. Michigan State Univ. Press 2001 220p ISBN 0-87013-572-4 LC 2001-310
The **sweet** and sour tongue. What, L.
Sweet land stories. Doctorow, E. L.
Swords and sorcerers; stories from the world of fantasy and adventure; edited by Clint Willis. Thunder's Mouth Press 2003 338p ISBN 1-560-25415-7 LC 2002-75692

T

Taking it to heart. Desplechin, M.
Taking the wall. Agee, J.
Tales before Tolkien; the roots of modern fantasy; edited by Douglas A. Anderson. Ballantine Bks. 2003 p. cmp ISBN 0-345-45854-0; 0-345-45855-9 (pbk.) LC 2003-43846
Tales from the Cuban empire. Ponte, A. J.
Tales from The Dark Tower; illustrated by Joseph Vargo; edited by Joseph Vargo and Christine Filipak. Monolith Graphics 2000 284p il ISBN 0-9675756-1-3 LC 99-75958
Tales of Grabowski. Auerbach, J.
Talking in the dark. Louis, L. G.
Tamaro, Susanna, 1957-
Rispondimi; translated from the Italian by John Cullen. Talese 2002 215p ISBN 0-385-50351-2 LC 2001-44290
Tan, Amy
(ed) The Best American short stories, 1999. *See* The Best American short stories, 1999
Tangled strings. Castro, A.-T.
Tannert, Mary W., 1957-
(ed) Early German and Austrian detective fiction. *See* Early German and Austrian detective fiction
Tapping the dream tree. De Lint, C.
Taraqqı, Guli
A mansion in the sky; and other short stories. University of Texas Press; Combined Academic 2003 160p ISBN 0-292-70226-4
Tart noir; edited by Stella Duffy & Lauren Henderson. Berkley Prime Crime 2002 309p ISBN 0-425-18643-1 LC 2002-74621
Tawada, Yoko, 1960-
Where Europe begins. See Selden, Yumi, and Tawada, Yoko, 1960-
Taylor, Timothy L., 1963-
Silent cruise & other stories; [by] Timothy Taylor. Counterpoint 2002 p. cmp ISBN 1-58243-216-3 LC 2002-22796
Tell me: 30 stories. Robison, M.
Ten little Indians. Alexie, S.
Ten tales. Alas, L.
Ten women who shook the world. Brownrigg, S.
Tenn, William, 1920-
Here comes civilization; introduction by Robert Silverberg; afterword by George Zebrowski; edited by James A. Mann and Mary C. Tabasko. NESFA Press 2001 562p (Complete science fiction of William Tenn, v2) ISBN 1-886778-28-0
Immodest proposals; introduction by Connie Willis; edited by James A. Mann and Mary C. Tabasko. NESFA Press 2001 618p (Complete science fiction of William Tenn, v1) ISBN 1-886778-19-1

Tester, William
  Head; stories. Sarabande Bks. 2000 197p ISBN 1-889330-48-5
    LC 99-59918
Tetrick, Byron
  In the shadow of the wall. *See* In the shadow of the wall
Texas bound. Book III; 22 Texas stories; edited by Kay Cattarulla;
    foreword by Robert Flynn. Southern Methodist Univ. Press 2001
    286p (Southwest life and letters) ISBN 0-87074-459-3
    LC 2001-20272
That distant land. Berry, W.
That's true of everybody. Winegardner, M.
There are Jews in my house. Vapnyar, L.
Theroux, Paul
  The stranger at the Palazzo d'Oro and other stories. Houghton Mifflin
    2004 296p ISBN 0-618-26515-5 LC 2003-50893
These people are us. Singleton, G.
Thien, Madeleine, 1974-
  Simple recipes; stories. Little, Brown and Company 2001 227p ISBN
    0-316-83316-9 LC 2001-50475
Thieves' dozen. Westlake, D. E.
Thieve's world: turning points; edited by Lynn Abbey. TOR Bks. 2002
    317p ISBN 0-312-87517-7 LC 2002-20463
Things that fall from the sky. Brockmeier, K.
Things you should know. Homes, A. M.
This is not it. Tillman, L.
This is the world. Penn, W. S.
This is where we live; short stories by 25 contemporary North Carolina
    writers; edited by Michael McFee. University of N.C. Press 2000
    278p ISBN 0-8078-2583-2 LC 00-29929
This place on Third Avenue. McNulty, J.
This place you return to is home. Gunn, K.
This too can be yours. Lisick, B.
This war called love. Murguía, A.
Thomas, Dorothy, and Pappas, Christine
  The getaway and other stories; edited and with an introduction by
    Christine Pappas. University of Nebraska Press 2002 120p ISBN
    0-8032-9448-4 LC 2001-53193
Thomas, Sheree R.
  (ed) Dark matter. *See* Dark matter
Thompson, Jean, 1950-
  Who do you love; stories. Harcourt 1999 306p ISBN 0-15-100416-1
    LC 98-44378
Thomsen, Brian
  (ed) The American fantasy tradition. *See* The American fantasy
    tradition
  (ed) A yuletide universe. *See* A yuletide universe
Three-legged horse. Cheng, C.-W.
Three novellas. Bernhard, T.
Three tales. Apukhtin, A. N.
Thurm, Marian
  What's come over you?; stories. Delphinium Bks. 2001 225p ISBN
    1-88328-521-6 LC 00-65966
Ticket to Minto. Fracis, S. H.
Tilghman, Christopher
  The way people run; stories. Random House 1999 209p ISBN
    0-679-44971-X LC 98-33888
Tillman, Lynne
  This is not it; stories. Distributed Art Pubs. 2002 287p il ISBN
    1-89102-446-9 LC 2002-7136
Time between trains. Bukoski, A.
Tina in the back seat. Rawley, D.
Tinti, Hannah
  Animal crackers; Hannah Tinti. Dial Press 2004 vii, 197p ISBN
    0-385-33743-4 LC 2003-70125
To cut a long story short. Archer, J.
To find a place. Easton, R. O.
Tolstoy, Leo, graf, 1828-1910
  Divine and human and other stories; new translations by Peter Sekirin.
    Zondervan Bks. 2000 211p ISBN 0-310-22367-9 LC 00-20791

Tomioka, Taeko, 1935-
The funeral of a giraffe; seven stories; translated by Kyoko Selden and Mizuta Noriko. Sharpe, M.E. 2000 181p (Japanese women writing) ISBN 0-7656-0441-8 LC 98-55994

Tomlinson, Norma Crawford, 1924-
The day of the dance; stories. Fithian Press 2001 156p ISBN 1-56474-376-4 LC 2001-233

Too many tomcats and other feline tales of suspense. Collins, B.

Toole, F. X., 1930-2002
Rope burns; stories from the corner. Ecco Press 2000 237p ISBN 0-06-019820-6 LC 00-37568

A **tortoise** for the Queen of Tonga. Whitty, J.

The **torturer's** apprentice. Biguenet, J.

Touch wood. Porter, J. A.

The **toughest** Indian in the world. Alexie, S.

Touré
The portable promised land; stories. Little, Brown 2002 256p ISBN 0-316-66643-2 LC 2002-102896

Toxicology. Aylett, S.

Toy guns. Norris, L.

Tozzi, Federigo, 1883-1920
Love in vain; selected stories of Federigo Tozzi; translated, with an introduction, by Minna Proctor. New Directions 2001 xxvi, 164p ISBN 0-8112-1471-0 LC 00-52719

The **tragic** menagerie. Zinovyeva-Annibal, L. D.

Trailer girl and other stories. Svoboda, T.

Trails west. Cunningham, E.

Tran, Vu
The dragon hunt; five stories; translated from the Vietnamese by Nina McPherson and Phan Huy Duong. Hyperion 1999 146p ISBN 0-7868-6418-4 LC 98-19994

Transgressions. Bingham, S.

Travel advisory. Lida, D.

The **traveller's** hat. Potvin, E. A.

Treat, Jessica, 1958-
Not a chance. FC2 2000 169p ISBN 1-57366-089-2 LC 00-9717

Tremayne, Peter
Hemlock at Vespers; fifteen Sister Fidelma mysteries. St. Martin's Minotaur 2000 398p ISBN 0-312-25288-9 LC 99-87936

Trevanian
(ed) Death dance. *See* Death dance
Hot night in the city. St. Martin's Press 2000 277p il ISBN 0-312-24202-6 LC 00-29679

Trevor, William, 1928-
The hill bachelors. Viking 2000 244p ISBN 0-670-89373-0 LC 00-32485

Troncoso, Sergio, 1961-
The last tortilla & other stories. University of Ariz. Press 1999 220p (Camino del sol) ISBN 0-8165-1960-9 LC 98-58155

Trouble with girls. Boswell, M.

The **trouble** with you is and other stories. Rodgers, S. J.

Troublemakers. McNally, J.

Troy, Mary, 1948-
The Alibi Café and other stories. BkMk Press 2003 139p ISBN 1886157413 LC 2002-13249

The **truly** needy and other stories. Honig, L.

The **truth** about Alicia and other stories. Matiella, A. C.

Tuck, Lily, 1938-
Limbo, and other places I have lived; stories. HarperCollins Pubs. 2002 170p ISBN 0-06-620942-0 LC 2001-39216

Tumbleweeds. Henry, W.

Turtledove, Harry
Alternate generals II. *See* Alternate generals II
(ed) The Best alternate history stories of the 20th century. *See* The Best alternate history stories of the 20th century

Tuska, Jon, 1942-
(ed) The First Five Star western corral. *See* The First Five Star western corral

Twelve branches; stories from St. Paul; [by] Nora Murphy ... {et al.}.
   Coffee House Press 2003 191p ISBN 1-566-89140-X
   LC 2003-41221
The **two** Sams. Hirshberg, G.
Typical girls; new stories by smart women; edited by Susan Corrigan.
   St. Martin's Griffin 1999 199p ISBN 0-312-20679-8 LC 99-12777

U

The **Ultimate** Halloween; edited by Marvin Kaye. Simon & Schuster
   2001 326p ISBN 0-7437-2396-8
Ulu's dog and other stories. Scoville, S.
Uncanny tales. Sheckley, R.
The **uncollected** works of Louisa May Alcott. Alcott, L. M.
Unkempt. Eldridge, Courtney
The **unknown** errors of our lives. Divakaruni, C. B.
Unsung heroes of American industry. Poirier, M. J.
An **unthymely** death and other garden mysteries. Albert, S. W.
Updike, John
   (ed) The Best American short stories of the century. *See* The Best
      American short stories of the century
   The early stories, 1953-1975. Knopf 2003 838p ISBN 1-4000-4072-8
      LC 2002-44824
   Licks of love; short stories and a sequel. Knopf 2000 359p ISBN
      0-375-41113-5 LC 00-34906

V

Vachss, Andrew H.
   Everybody pays; stories. Vintage Bks. 1999 368p (Vintage crime/black
      Lizard) ISBN 0-375-70743-3 LC 99-28773
Valentine's Day: women against men; stories of revenge; introduction
   by Alice Thomas. Duckworth 2000 224p ISBN 0-7156-3006-7
Valeri, Laura
   The kind of things saints do. University of Iowa Press 2002 149p (The
      John Simmons short fiction award) ISBN 0-87745-819-7
      LC 2002-18058
Van de Wetering, Janwillem, 1931-
   The Amsterdam cops; collected stories. Soho Press 1999 254p ISBN
      1-569-47171-1 LC 99-23243
Van Gelder, Gordon
   (ed) The Best from fantasy & science fiction: the fiftieth anniversary
      anthology. *See* The Best from fantasy & science fiction: the fiftieth
      anniversary anthology
   (ed) One lamp. *See* One lamp
Van Winckel, Nance
   Curtain Creek Farm; stories. Persea Bks. 2000 186p ISBN
      0-89255-250-6 LC 00-23712
VanderMeer, Jeff
   Secret life; with an introduction by Jeffrey Ford. Golden Gryphon
      Press 2004 305p ISBN 1-930846-27-4 LC 2003-27519
Vanishing acts; a science fiction anthology; edited by Ellen Datlow.
   TOR Bks. 2000 380p ISBN 0-312-86962-2 LC 00-26512
Vapnyar, Laura, 1971-
   There are Jews in my house. Pantheon Books 2003 160p ISBN
      0-375-42250-1 LC 2003-42975
Vargo, Joseph
   (ed) Tales from The Dark Tower. *See* Tales from The Dark Tower
The **varieties** of romantic experience. Cohen, R.
Vasilenko, Svetlana, 1956-, and Goscilo, Helena
   Shamara and other stories; translated from the Russian; edited and
      with an introduction and notes by Helena Goscilo. Northwestern
      Univ. Press 2000 xxii, 245p (Writings from an unbound Europe)
      ISBN 0-8101-1721-5 LC 99-56625
Vasseur, Thomas Jeffrey
   Discovering the world; thirteen stories. Mercer Univ. Press 2001 352p
      ISBN 0-86554-718-1 LC 2001-18293

Vaswani, Neela, 1974-
Where the long grass bends; stories; Neela Vaswani. 1st ed. Sarabande Books 2004 275p ISBN 1-88933-096-5 (pbk. : alk. paper) LC 2003-3869
Vatanabadi, Shouleh, 1955-
(ed) A Feast in the mirror. *See* A Feast in the mirror
A **vaudeville** of devils. Girardi, R.
Venus drive. Lipsyte, S.
The **veteran**. Forsyth, F.
Video. Nair, M.
The **view** from Stalin's Head. Hamburger, A.
Viganò, Renata, 1900-1976
Partisan wedding; stories; translated with an introduction by Suzanne Branciforte. University of Mo. Press 1999 233p ISBN 0-8262-1228-X LC 99-37940
Vinge, Vernor
The collected stories of Vernor Vinge. TOR Bks. 2001 464p ISBN 0-312-87373-5 LC 2001-53966
The **Vintage** book of amnesia; an anthology; edited by Jonathan Lethem. Vintage Bks. 2000 414p ISBN 0-375-70661-5 LC 00-20649
The **Vintage** book of contemporary Chinese fiction; edited by Carolyn Choa and David Su Li-qun. Vintage Bks. 2001 308p ISBN 0-375-70093-5 LC 2001-25832
The **Vintage** book of contemporary Scottish fiction; edited and with an introduction by Peter Kravitz. Vintage Bks. 1999 555p ISBN 0-679-77550-1 LC 99-21327
The **Vintage** book of international lesbian fiction; edited and with an introduction by Naomi Holoch and Joan Nestle. Vintage Bks. 1999 349p ISBN 0-679-75952-2 LC 98-32138
The **Vintage** book of Latin American stories; edited by Carlos Fuentes and Julio Ortega. Vintage Bks. 2000 380p ISBN 0-679-77551-X LC 00-712739
Virgin fiction 2. Weisbach Bks. 1999 419p ISBN 0-688-17014-5 LC 99-24081
Vivante, Arturo
Solitude, and other stories. University of Notre Dame Press 2004 199p (The Richard Sullivan prize in short fiction) ISBN 0-268-04365-5 (alk. paper); 0-268-04366-3 LC 2004-743
Vonnegut, Kurt, 1922-
Bagombo snuff box; uncollected short fiction. Putnam 1999 295p ISBN 0-399-14505-2 LC 99-13665
Vukcevich, Ray
Meet me in the moon room; stories. Small Beer Press 2001 253p ISBN 1-931520-01-1 LC 2001087878

W

Wachsberger, Clyde
(ed) Of leaf and flower. *See* Of leaf and flower
Waisman, Sergio Gabriel, 1967-
Dreams and realities. See Gorriti, Juana Manuela, 1818-1892, and Waisman, Sergio Gabriel, 1967-, and Masiello, Francine, 1948-
Wake. Goldner, B.
Waldrop, Howard
Custer's last jump and other collaborations; [by] Howard Waldrop and Leigh Kennedy [et al.] Golden Gryphon Press 2003 254p ISBN 1-930846-13-4 LC 2002-151194
Walker, Alice, 1944-
The way forward is with a broken heart. Random House 2000 200p ISBN 0-679-45587-6 LC 00-27172
Walker, Dale L.
(ed) Westward. *See* Westward
Walkin' the dog. Mosley, W.
Wallace, David Foster
Brief interviews with hideous men. Little, Brown 1999 273p ISBN 0-316-92541-1 LC 98-50944
Oblivion; stories. Little, Brown 2004 ISBN 0-316-91981-0

Wallace, Ronald, 1945-
Quick bright things; stories. Mid-List Press 2000 172p ISBN 0-922811-44-X LC 99-88117

Warren, Dianne
A reckless moon and other stories. Raincoast Bks. Publishers Group West 2002 237p ISBN 1-551-92455-2 LC 2002-391830

Watanabe McFerrin, Linda, 1953-
The hand of Buddha; stories. Coffee House Press 2000 206p ISBN 1-56689-104-3 LC 00-43099

Water of an undetermined depth. Chiappone, R.

Waterloo sunset. Davies, R.

Waters, Mary Yukari
The laws of evening; stories. Scribner 2003 177p ISBN 0-7432-4332-3 LC 2002-29429

Watson, Ian, 1943-
The great escape. Golden Gryphon Press 2002 283p ISBN 1-930846-09-6 LC 2002-1581

Waugh, Charles G. (Charles Gordon), 1943-
(ed) Lighthouse hauntings. *See* Lighthouse hauntings

Waugh, Evelyn, 1903-1966
The complete stories of Evelyn Waugh. Little, Brown 1999 c1998 535p ISBN 0-316-92546-2 LC 99-20837

The **wave**. Gussoff, C.

The **wavering** knife. Evenson, B.

The **way** forward is with a broken heart. Walker, A.

The **way** people run. Tilghman, C.

Wayfaring at Waverly in Silver Lake. McCourt, J.

We who live apart. Connor, J.

Weaver, Gordon, 1937-
Last stands; stories; by Gordon Weaver. University of Missouri Press 2004 ISBN 0-8262-1521-1 (alk. paper) LC 2003-24711
Long odds; stories. University of Mo. Press 2000 194p il ISBN 0-8262-1291-3 LC 00-24574

Webb, Janeen
(ed) Dreaming down-under. *See* Dreaming down-under

Weber, David, 1952-
Changer of worlds. Baen Bks. 2001 374p (Worlds of honor, #3) ISBN 0-671-31975-2 LC 00-51939

The **wedding** jester. Stern, S.

Wegner, Hart
Off Paradise; stories. University of Nev. Press 2001 212p (Western literature series) ISBN 0-87417-486-4 LC 2001-1405

Weihe, Edwin
Another life & other stories. Pleasure Boat Studio 2000 208p ISBN 1-929355-01-7

Weinberg, Robert
Dial your dreams & other nightmares. DarkTales Pub. 2001 199p ISBN 1-93099711-6

Weingarten, Roger
(ed) Ghost writing. *See* Ghost writing

Weinreb, Michael
Girl boy etc. Red Dress Ink 2004 234p ISBN 0-373-25056-8

Welding with children. Gautreaux, T.

Weldon, Fay
A hard time to be a father. St. Martin's Press 1999 242p ISBN 1-58234-011-0

Wellen, Edward
Perps; a short story collection. Five Star 2001 252p (Five Star first edition mystery series) ISBN 0-7862-2997-7 LC 2001-18145

Wells, Kellie, 1962-
Compression scars; stories. University of Ga. Press 2002 192p ISBN 0-8203-2431-0 LC 2002-5542

Werewolves in their youth. Chabon, M.

West, Michelle, 1963-
Speaking with angels; stories. Five Star 2003 341p ISBN 0-7862-5343-6 LC 2003-45645

Westlake, Donald E.
(ed) The Best American mystery stories, 2000. *See* The Best American mystery stories, 2000

Westlake, Donald E.—*Continued*

A good story and other stories. Five Star 1999 259p (Five Star standard print mystery series) ISBN 0-7862-1943-2 LC 99-25259

Thieves' dozen. Mysterious Press 2004 183p ISBN 0-446-69302-2 LC 2003-70612

Westmoreland, Timothy A.

Good as any; stories. Harcourt 2002 275p ISBN 0-15-100852-3 LC 2001-24955

Westward; a fictional history of the American West : 28 original stories celebrating the 50th anniversary of the Western Writers of America; edited by Dale L. Walker. Forge 2003 432p ISBN 0-7653-0451-1 LC 2002-45481

Wexler, Merin

The porno girl and other stories. St. Martin's Press 2003 225p ISBN 0-312-31057-9 LC 2003-41587

Wharton, Edith, 1862-1937

Collected stories, 1891-1910. Library of Am. 2001 928p ISBN 1-88301-193-0 LC 00-57596

Collected stories, 1911-1937. Library of Am. 2001 848p ISBN 1-88301-194-9 LC 00-57595

What, Leslie

The sweet and sour tongue. Wildside Press 2000 146p ISBN 1-58715-158-8

What about the love part? Rosenfeld, S.

What are you looking at?; the first fat fiction anthology; edited by Donna Jarrell and Ira Sukrungruang. Harcourt 2003 274p ISBN 0-15-602907-3 LC 2003-40633

What I cannot say to you. Jackson, V. F.

What salmon know. Reid, E.

What she left me. Doenges, J.

What we come in for. Lundquist, R.

What's come over you? Thurm, M.

Wheat, Carolyn

(ed) Women before the bench. *See* Women before the bench

Wheeler, Kate, 1955-

(ed) Nixon under the bodhi tree and other works of Buddhist fiction. *See* Nixon under the bodhi tree and other works of Buddhist fiction

When Eve was naked. Škvorecký, J.

When I was mortal. Marías, J.

When Luba leaves home. Zabytko, I.

When night fell; an anthology of Holocaust short stories; edited by Linda Schermer Raphael and Marc Lee Raphael. Rutgers Univ. Press 1999 300p ISBN 0-8135-2662-0 LC 98-52808

When the women come out to dance. Leonard, E.

When we were wolves. Billman, J.

Where Europe begins. Selden, Y. and Tawada, Y.

Where the long grass bends. Vaswani, N.

Where the time goes. Skillings, R. D.

Where you find it. Galloway, J.

The **whisperer** and other voices. Lumley, B.

Whispers from the cotton tree root; Caribbean fabulist fiction; edited by Nalo Hopkinson. Invisible Cities Press 2000 318p ISBN 0-9679683-1-3 LC 00-57250

A **whistler** in the nightworld; short fiction from the Latin Americas; edited by Thomas Colchie. Plume 2002 410p ISBN 0-452-28358-2 LC 2002-22450

White, Michael C.

Marked men; stories. University of Mo. Press 2000 199p ISBN 0-8262-1294-8 LC 00-32557

White House pet detectives; tales of crime and mystery at the White House from a pet's-eye view; edited by Carole Nelson Douglas. Cumberland House 2002 243p ISBN 1-58182-243-X LC 2002-7585

The **white** man in the tree and other stories. Kurlansky, M.

The **white** tattoo. Cobb, W. J.

A **white** veil for tomorrow. Edwards, S.

Whitty, Julia

A tortoise for the Queen of Tonga. Houghton Mifflin 2002 183p ISBN 0-618-11980-9 LC 2001-51607

Who do you love. Thompson, J.

Who I was supposed to be. Perabo, S.

Who is my neighbor? Berry, M. S.

The **whole** story and other stories. Smith, A.

The **whore's** child, and other stories. Russo, R.

Who's Irish? Jen, G.

Whose song? and other stories. Glave, T.

Wickham, John

(ed) The Oxford book of Caribbean short stories. *See* The Oxford book of Caribbean short stories

Widening the road. Bonnie, F.

Wieland, Liza

You can sleep while I drive; stories. Southern Methodist Univ. Press 1999 254p ISBN 0-87074-441-0 LC 99-18493

Wild East; stories from the last frontier; edited with an introduction by Boris Fishman. 1st ed. Justin, Charles & Co, Distributed by National Book Network 2003 ISBN 1-932112-15-4 LC 2003-60444

Williams, Miller

The lives of Kelvin Fletcher; stories mostly short. University of Ga. Press 2002 167p ISBN 0-8203-2439-6 LC 2002-1550

Williams, Sheila

(ed) A Woman's liberation. *See* A Woman's liberation

Williford, Lex, 1954-

(ed) The Scribner anthology of contemporary short fiction. *See* The Scribner anthology of contemporary short fiction

Willis, Clint

(ed) Dark: stories of madness, murder, and the supernatural. *See* Dark: stories of madness, murder, and the supernatural

(ed) Swords and sorcerers. *See* Swords and sorcerers

Willis, Connie

Miracle and other Christmas stories. Bantam Bks. 1999 328p ISBN 0-553-11111-6 LC 99-15686

(ed) Nebula awards 33. *See* Nebula awards 33

(ed) A Woman's liberation. *See* A Woman's liberation

Willis, Meredith Sue

Dwight's house and other stories. Hamilton Stone Editions 2004 189p ISBN 0-9714873-2-4 LC 2003-56696

Willow Temple. Hall, D.

Wilson, Robert Charles, 1953-

The Perseids and other stories. TOR Bks. 2000 224p ISBN 0-312-87374-3 LC 00-26704

Wilson, Robley, Jr.

(ed) 100% pure Florida fiction. *See* 100% pure Florida fiction

The book of lost fathers; stories. Johns Hopkins Univ. Press 2001 226p (Johns Hopkins, poetry and fiction) ISBN 0-8018-6717-7 LC 00-12113

Windling, Terri

(ed) Black heart, ivory bones. *See* Black heart, ivory bones

(ed) The Year's best fantasy & horror: sixteenth annual collection. *See* The Year's best fantasy & horror: sixteenth annual collection

(ed) The Year's best fantasy & horror, thirteenth annual collection. *See* The Year's best fantasy & horror, thirteenth annual collection

(ed) The Year's best fantasy & horror, twelfth annual collection. *See* The Year's best fantasy & horror, twelfth annual collection

Winegardner, Mark, 1961-

That's true of everybody; stories. Harcourt 2002 212p ISBN 0-15-100864-7 LC 2002-6199

Wing walking. Meredith, D.

Wingtips. Chenoweth, A.

Winter, Ellen, 1962-

The price you pay; stories. Southern Methodist Univ. Press 2000 222p ISBN 0-87074-456-9 LC 00-58771

The **winter** without milk. Avrich, J.

Winterson, Jeanette, 1959-

The world and other places. Knopf 1998 227p ISBN 0-375-40240-3 LC 98-28257

Witches' brew; edited by Yvonne Jocks. Berkley Bks 2002 326p ISBN 0-425-18609-1 LC 2002-71279

With signs and wonders; an international anthology of Jewish fabulist fiction; edited by Daniel M. Jaffe. Invisible Cities Press 2001 333p ISBN 0-9679683-5-6 LC 2001-16615

Witness to the league of blond hip hop dancers. Allegra, D.

Witpunk; edited by Claude Lalumière and Marty Halpern. Four Walls Eight Windows 2003 346p ISBN 1-568-58256-0 LC 2002-192768

Wives and lovers. Bausch, R.

Woelz, Karl

(ed) Men on men 2000. *See* Men on men 2000

Wolfe, Gene, 1931-

Innocents aboard; new fantasy stories. Tor Books 2004 304p ISBN 0-7653-0790-1 LC 2003-71143

Wolff, Tobias, 1945-

(ed) Best new American voices 2000. *See* Best new American voices 2000

(ed) Writers harvest 3. *See* Writers harvest 3

Wolverton, Terry

(ed) Circa 2000. *See* Circa 2000

(ed) Hers 2: brilliant new fiction by lesbian writers. *See* Hers 2: brilliant new fiction by lesbian writers

(ed) Hers 3: brilliant new fiction by lesbian writers. *See* Hers 3: brilliant new fiction by lesbian writers

(ed) His 3: brilliant new fiction by gay writers. *See* His 3: brilliant new fiction by gay writers

The **woman** who cut off her leg at the Maidstone Club and other stories. Slavin, J.

A **Woman's** liberation; a choice of futures by and about women; edited by Connie Willis and Sheila Williams. Warner Bks. 2001 302p ISBN 0-446-67742-6 LC 2001-17794

Women & other animals. Campbell, B. J.

Women before the bench; edited by Carolyn Wheat; introduction by Linda Fairstein. Berkley Prime Crime 2001 287p ISBN 0-425-17231-7 LC 00-68899

Women in the grove. Peterson, P. W.

Women with big eyes. Mastretta, A.

Wonderful town; New York stories from The New Yorker; edited by David Remnick with Susan Choi. Random House 2000 480p ISBN 0-375-50356-0 LC 99-48838

Wonderful tricks. Spatz, G.

The **wonders** of the invisible world. Gates, D.

Wondrous beginnings; edited by Steven H. Silver and Martin H. Greenberg. DAW Bks. 2003 316p ISBN 0-7564-0098-8

Woodcuts of women. Gilb, D.

The **Workshop**; seven decades of the Iowa Writers' Workshop: 42 stories, recollections & essays on Iowa's place in 20th-century American literature; edited by Tom Grimes. Hyperion 1999 766p ISBN 0-7868-6503-2 LC 99-24268

The **world** and other places. Winterson, J.

Worldmakers; SF adventures in terraforming; edited by Gardner Dozois. St. Martin's Griffin 2001 446p ISBN 0-312-27570-6 LC 2001-41957

Worlds enough & time. Simmons, D.

The **World's** finest mystery and crime stories, first annual collection; edited by Ed Gorman. Doherty Assocs. 2000 638p ISBN 0-312-87480-4

The **World's** finest mystery and crime stories, second annual collection; edited by Ed Gorman. Doherty Assocs. 2001 684p ISBN 0-765-30029X

The **World's** finest mystery and crime stories, third annual collection; edited by Ed Gorman and Martin H. Greenberg. Forge 2002 640p ISBN 0-7653-0234-9; 0-7653-0235-7 (pa) LC 2002-25034

Worlds of Honor. Baen Bks. 1999 343p ISBN 0-671-57786-7 LC 98-47810

Worlds vast and various. Benford, G.

Worship of the common heart. Henley, P.

Writers harvest 3; edited and with an introduction by Tobias Wolff. Dell 2000 258p ISBN 0-385-33377-3 LC 99-33278

Wuori, G. K.
  Nude in tub; stories of Quillifarkeag, Maine. Algonquin Bks. 1999
    273p ISBN 1-56512-223-2 LC 98-41977

Y

Yañez, Richard, 1967-
  El Paso del Norte; stories on the border. University of Nevada Press
    2003 138p (Western literature series) ISBN 0-87417-533-X
    LC 2002-11993
Yates, Richard, 1926-1992
  The collected stories of Richard Yates; introduction by Richard Russo.
    Holt & Co. 2001 xx, 472p ISBN 0-8050-6693-4 LC 00-61400
The **Year's** best fantasy & horror: sixteenth annual collection; edited by
    Ellen Datlow & Terri Windling. St. Martin's Griffin 2003 564p
    ISBN 0-312-31424-8; 0-312-31425-6 (pa)
The **Year's** best fantasy & horror, thirteenth annual collection; edited by
    Ellen Datlow and Terri Windling. St. Martin's Press 2000 cxxvi,
    514p ISBN 0-312-26274-4 LC 91-659320
The **Year's** best fantasy & horror, twelfth annual collection; edited by
    Ellen Datlow & Terry Windling. St. Martin's Press 1999 cx, 496p
    ISBN 0-312-20962-2
The **Year's** best science fiction; twentieth annual collection; edited by
    Gardner Dozois. St. Martin's Griffin 2003 648p ISBN
    0-312-30859-0; 0-312-30860-4 (pa)
The **Year's** best science fiction, eighteenth annual collection; edited by
    Gardner Dozois. St. Martin's Griffin 2001 xlvii, 617p ISBN
    0-312-27465-3
The **Year's** best science fiction, nineteenth annual collection; edited by
    Gardner Dozois. St. Martin's Griffin 2002 xliv, 637p ISBN
    0-312-28878-6
The **Year's** best science fiction, seventeenth annual collection; edited by
    Gardner Dozois. St. Martin's Press 2000 liii, 625p ISBN
    0-312-26275-2
The **Year's** best science fiction, sixteenth annual collection; edited by
    Gardner Dozois. St. Martin's Press 1999 lix, 609p ISBN
    0-312-20963-0
The **year's** best science fiction: twenty-first annual collection; edited by
    Gardner Dozois. St. Martin's Griffin 2004 672p ISBN 0-12-95006-8
Yellow. Lee, D.
Yi, Tong-Ha, 1942-
  Shrapnel and other stories; [by] Dong-ha Lee; edited and translated by
    Hyun-Jae Yee Sallee. White Pine Press 2002 176p ISBN
    1-893996-53-0 LC 2002-107446
Yolen, Jane
  Sister Emily's lightship and other stories. TOR Bks. 2000 300p ISBN
    0-312-87378-6 LC 00-29908
Yoshimoto, Banana, 1964-
  Asleep; translated from the Japanese by Michael Emmerich. Grove
    Press 2000 177p ISBN 0-8021-1669-8 LC 99-88699
You are not a stranger here. Haslett, A.
You can sleep while I drive. Wieland, L.
Young, Terence, 1953-
  Rhymes with useless; stories. Raincoast Bks. 2000 197p ISBN
    1-55192-354-8 LC 00-421874
Your madness, not mine: stories of Cameroon. Nfah-Abbenyi, J. M.
Yuknavitch, Lidia
  Liberty's excess; fictions. FC2 2000 177p ISBN 1-573-66084-1
    LC 00-27715
  Real to reel. FC2 2003 175p ISBN 1-573-66107-4 LC 2002-12646
A **yuletide** universe; sixteen fantastical tales; edited by Brian M.
    Thomsen. Warner Bks. 2003 257p ISBN 0-446-69187-9
    LC 2003-45069

Z

Zabytko, Irene
When Luba leaves home; stories. Algonquin Bks. 2003 230p ISBN 1-56512-332-8 LC 2002-38525
Ziegler, Irene
Rules of the lake; stories. Southern Methodist Univ. Press 1999 192p ISBN 0-87074-447-X
Zigzagger. Muñoz, M.
Zigzagging down a wild trail. Mason, B. A.
Zinik, Zinoviĭ
Mind the doors; long short stories. Context Bks. 2001 184p ISBN 1-89395-604-0 LC 2001-767
Zinovyeva-Annibal, Lidiya Dmitrievna, 1866-1907
The tragic menagerie; translated from the Russian and with an introduction by Jane Costlow. Northwestern Univ. Press 1999 xxii, 185p (European classics) ISBN 0-8101-1483-6 LC 98-48373
Zweig, Stefan, 1881-1942
The royal game & other stories; with an introduction by Jeffrey B. Berlin; translated from the German by Jill Sutcliffe. Holmes & Meier 2000 211p ISBN 0-8419-1405-2 LC 99-88166

PART III

Directory of Periodicals

African American Review. q ISSN (1062-4783) African American Review, Arts & Sciences Administration, Saint Louis University, Ritter Hall 125, 220 N. Grand Blvd., St. Louis, MO 63103-2007

Amerasia Journal. 3 times a yr ISSN (0044-7471) University of California, Los Angeles, Asian American Studies Center, 3230 Campbell Hall, Los Angeles, CA 90024-1546

The American Poetry Review. bi-m ISSN (0360-3709) The American Poetry Review, 1721 Walnut St., Philadelphia, PA 19103

Américas. 6 times a yr ISSN (0379-0940) Américas, P.O. Box 3000, Denville, NJ 07834-3000

The Antioch Review. q ISSN (0003-5769) Antioch Review, Subscriptions, P.O. Box 148, Yellow Springs, OH 45387

Arizona Highways. m ISSN (0004-1521) Arizona Highways, 2039 W. Lewis Ave., Phoenix, AZ 85009

Atlantic Monthly (1993). m (bi-m Ja/F and Jl/Ag) ISSN (1072-7825) Atlantic Subscription Processing Center, Box 52661, Boulder, CO 80322

Bomb. q ISSN (0743-3204) New Art Publications, Subscriptions Dept., P.O. Box 3000, Denville, NJ 07834

Book (Summit, N.J.). bi-m ISSN (1520-3204) West Egg Communications, 18 Bank St., Summit, NJ 07901
    Publication suspended with no. 31 (November-December, 2003)

Callaloo. q ISSN (0161-2492) Johns Hopkins University Press, Journals Publishing Div., 2715 North Charles St., Baltimore, MD 21218-4363

Canadian Literature. q ISSN (0008-4360) Canadian Literature, Buchanan E158, 1866 Main Mall, Vancouver, B.C. V6T 1Z1, Canada

Chicago Review. q ISSN (0009-3696) Chicago Review, 5801 S. Kenwood, Chicago, IL 60637

The Christian Century. bi-w ISSN (0009-5281) Christian Century Subscription Service, 407 S. Dearborn St., Chicago, IL 60605-1150

Christianity Today. m (semi-m Ap, O) ISSN (0009-5753) Christianity Today Subscription Services, P.O. Box 37059, Boone, IA 50037-0059

Cincinnati Magazine. m ISSN (0746-8210) Emmis Broadcasting Corp., 705 Central Ave., Ste. 370, Cincinnati, OH 45202

Commentary. m ISSN (0010-2601) American Jewish Committee, 165 E. 56th St., New York, NY 10022

Critical Quarterly. q ISSN (0011-1562) Blackwell Publishers, Subscriber Services Coordinator, 238 Main St., Cambridge, MA 02142

Critical Survey. 3 times a yr ISSN (0011-1570) Oxford University Press, Journals Subscriptions Dept., Walton St., Oxford OX2 6DP, England

Cross Currents. q ISSN (0011-1953) Cross Currents, College of New Rochelle, New Rochelle, NY 10805-2308

Daedalus. q ISSN (0011-5266) MIT Press Journals, 5 Cambridge Center, Cambridge, MA 02142

Dalhousie Review. 3 times a yr ISSN (0011-5827) Dalhousie Review, Business Manager, Dalhousie University, Halifax, N.S. B3H 3J5, Canada

Doubletake. q ISSN (1080-7241) Doubletake Community Service Corp., 55 Davis Square, Somerville, MA 02144-2908
    Temporarily suspended after v. 8, no. 4 (Spring 2003)

Esquire. m ISSN (0194-9535) Esquire Subscriptions, P.O. Box 7146, Red Oak, IA 51591

Essence. m ISSN (0014-0880) Essence, P.O. Box 53400, Boulder, CO 80322-3400

Etc. q ISSN (0014-164X) International Society for General Semantics, Box 728, Concord, CA 94522

Film Comment. bi-m ISSN (0015-119X) Film Comment, P.O. Box 3000, Denville, NJ 07834-9925

Gentlemen's Quarterly. m ISSN (0016-6979) Gentlemen's Quarterly, Box 53816, Boulder, CO 80322

The Georgia Review. q ISSN (0016-8386) University of Georgia, Athens, GA 30602

Gettysburg Review. q ISSN (0898-4557) Gettysburg Review, Gettysburg College, Gettysburg, PA 17325-1491

Good Housekeeping. m ISSN (0017-209X) Good Housekeeping, P.O. Box 7186, Red Oak, IA 51591-0186

GQ. See Gentlemen's Quarterly

Grand Street. semi-ann ISSN (0734-5496) Grand Street Press, 214 Sullivan St., Ste. 63, New York, NY 10012
    Suspended publication with no. 69 (Summ. 1999); Resumed publication with no. 70 (Spr. 2002)

Granta. q ISSN (0017-3231) Granta USA Ltd., 1755 Broadway, 5th fl., New York, NY 10019-3780

Harper's. m ISSN (0017-789X) Harper's Magazine, P.O. Box 7511, Red Oak, IA 51591-0511

The Hudson Review. q ISSN (0018-702X) The Hudson Review, 684 Park Ave., New York, NY 10021

Iowa Review. 3 times a yr ISSN (0021-065X) University of Iowa, 308EPB, Iowa City, IA 52242-1492

The Kenyon Review. q ISSN (0163-075X) The Kenyon Review, Kenyon College, Gambier, OH 43022

Ladies' Home Journal. m ISSN (0023-7124) Ladies' Home Journal, P.O. Box 53940, Boulder, CO 80322-3940

The Literary Review (Madison, N.J.). q ISSN (0024-4589) Fairleigh Dickinson University, 285 Madison Ave., Madison, NJ 07940

The Massachusetts Review. q ISSN (0025-4878) University of Massachusetts, Memorial Hall, Amherst, MA 01002

Michigan Quarterly Review. q ISSN (0026-2420) University of Michigan, 3032 Rackham Bldg., Ann Arbor, MI 48109

The Mississippi Quarterly. q ISSN (0026-637X) Mississippi State University, College of Arts and Sciences, Box 5272, Mississippi State, MS 39762

Model Railroader. m ISSN (0026-7341) Kalmbach Publishing Company, 2107 Crossroads Circle, Waukesha, WI 53186-4055

Modern Age. q ISSN (0026-7457) Intercollegiate Studies Institute, Inc., PO Box 4431, Wilmington, DE 19807-0431

Ms. q ISSN (0047-8318) Ms. Magazine, P.O. Box 5299, Harlan, IA 51593

New England Review. q ISSN (1053-1297) New England Review, Univ. Press of New England, 23 S. Main St., Hanover, NH 03755-2048

New Letters. q ISSN (0146-4930) University of Missouri-Kansas City, 5100 Rockhill Rd., Kansas City, MO 64110

The New Yorker. w (except 6 combined issues) ISSN (0028-792X) The New Yorker, Box 56447, Boulder, CO 80328-6447

The North American Review. q ISSN (0029-2397) University of Northern Iowa, 1222 W. 27th St., Cedar Falls, IA 50614

Parabola. q ISSN (0362-1596) Parabola, 656 Broadway, New York, NY 10012-2317

The Paris Review. q ISSN (0031-2037) The Paris Review, 45-39 171 Place, Flushing, NY 11358

Parnassus: Poetry in Review. semi-ann ISSN (0048-3028) Parnassus: Poetry in Review, 205 W. 89th St., #8F, New York, NY 10024

Partisan Review. q ISSN (0031-2525) Boston University, 236 Bay State Rd., Boston, MA 02215
Ceased publication with v. 70, no. 2 (Spr. 2003)

Ploughshares. 3 times a yr ISSN (0048-4474) Ploughshares, Inc., Emerson College, 120 Boylston St., Boston, MA 02116-4624

PMLA. 6 times a yr ISSN (0030-8129) Modern Language Association of America, Member and Customer Services Office, 10 Astor Place, New York, NY 10003-6981

Poets & Writers. 6 times a yr ISSN (0891-6136) Poets & Writers, Inc., 72 Spring St., New York, NY 10012

Prairie Schooner. q ISSN (0032-6682) University of Nebraska, 201 Andrews Hall, Lincoln, NE 68588

Publications of the Modern Language Association of America. See PMLA

Raritan. q ISSN (0275-1607) Rutgers University, 31 Mine St., New Brunswick, NJ 08903

The Review of Contemporary Fiction. 3 times a yr ISSN (0276-0045) Review of Contemporary Fiction, Fairchild Hall, Illinois State Univ., Normal, IL 61761

Salmagundi. q ISSN (0036-3529) Skidmore College, Saratoga Springs, NY 12866

The Saturday Evening Post. bi-m ISSN (0048-9239) Saturday Evening Post Subscription Offices, P.O. Box 420235, Palm Coast, FL 32142-1235

Seventeen. m ISSN (0037-301X) Seventeen Subscription Dept., Box 55195, Boulder, CO 80322-5195

The Sewanee Review. q ISSN (0037-3052) Sewanee Review, Sewanee, TN 37383-1000

Southern Humanities Review. q ISSN (0038-4186) Auburn University, 9088 Haley Center, Auburn, AL 36849

The Southern Review (Baton Rouge, La.). q ISSN (0038-4534) Southern Review, 43 Allen Hall, LSU, Baton Rouge, LA 70803-5005

Southwest Review. q ISSN (0038-4712) Southwest Review, 6410 Airline Rd., SMU, Dallas, TX 75275

'Teen. m ISSN (0040-2001) Petersen Publishing Co., 6420 Wilshire Blvd., Los Angeles, CA 90048-5515
Ceased publication with v. 46, no. 4 (May 2002).

Tikkun. bi-m ISSN (0887-9982) Tikkun, Tikkun Subscription Service, P.O. Box 460926, Escondido, CA 92046

The Times Literary Supplement. w ISSN (0307-661X) TLS Subscriptions, P.O. Box 3000, Denville, NJ 07834

TLS. See The Times Literary Supplement

TriQuarterly. 3 times a yr ISSN (0041-3097) TriQuarterly, Northwestern Univ., 2020 Ridge Ave., Evanston, IL 60208

TV Guide. w ISSN (0039-8543) TV Guide, Box 400, Radnor, PA 19088

U.S. Catholic. m ISSN (0041-7548) U.S. Catholic, 205 W. Monroe St., Chicago, IL 60606

Utopian Studies. 2 times a yr ISSN (1045-991X) Lyman Tower Sargent, Society for Utopian Studies, Dept. of Political Science, University of Missouri-St. Louis, St. Louis, MO 63121-4499

The Virginia Quarterly Review. q ISSN (0042-675X) The University of Virginia, One West Range, Charlottesville, VA 22903

VQR. See The Virginia Quarterly Review

Washingtonian. m ISSN (0043-0897) Washingtonian Subscription Service, P.O. Box 58897, Boulder, CO 80322-8897

Western Humanities Review. semi-ann ISSN (0043-3845) Western Humanities Review, University of Utah, English Dept., 255 South Central Campus Dr., Rm. 3500, Salt Lake City, UT 84112-0494

Women's Studies. 8 times a yr ISSN (0049-7878) Taylor & Francis, Inc., 325 Chestnut St., Philadelphia, PA 19106

The Yale Review. q ISSN (0044-0124) Blackwell Publishers, Yale Review, Subscriber Services Coordinator, 238 Main St., Cambridge, MA 02142

Yankee. m ISSN (0044-0191) Yankee, P.O. Box
37017, Boone, IA 50037-0017